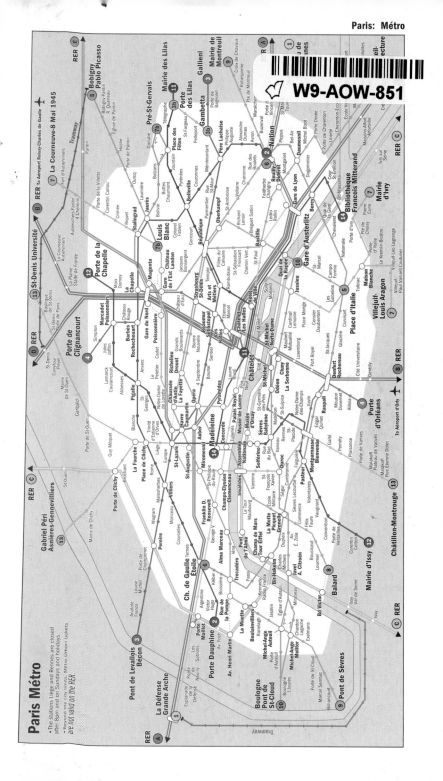

Paris Métro

Paris: Métro

- The stations Liège and Rennes are closed after 8pm and on Sundays and holidays.
- Beyond the city limits, Métro urban tickets are **not valid on the RER**.

W9-AOW-851

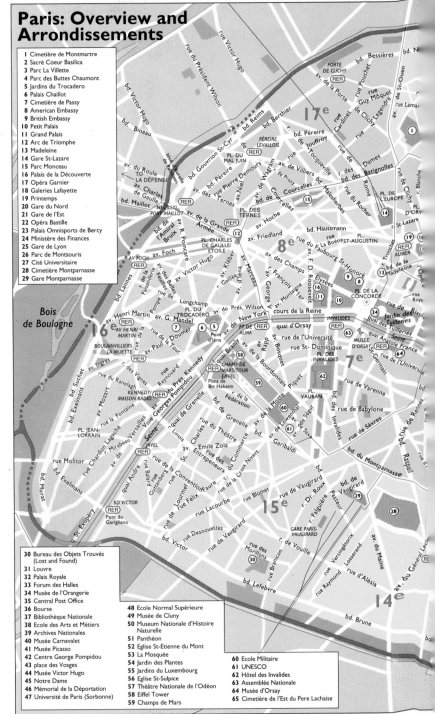

Paris: 1er and 2e

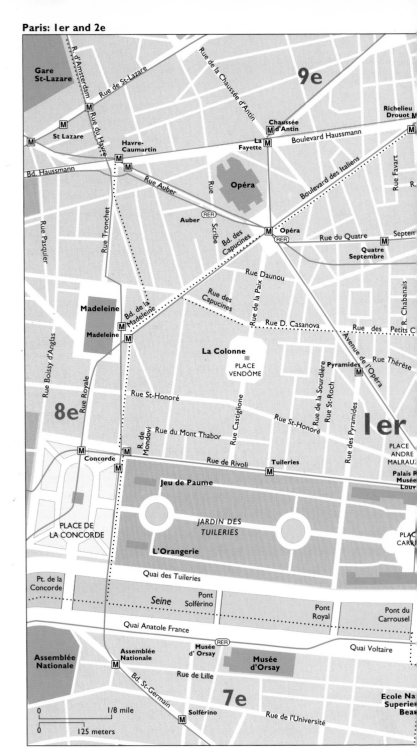

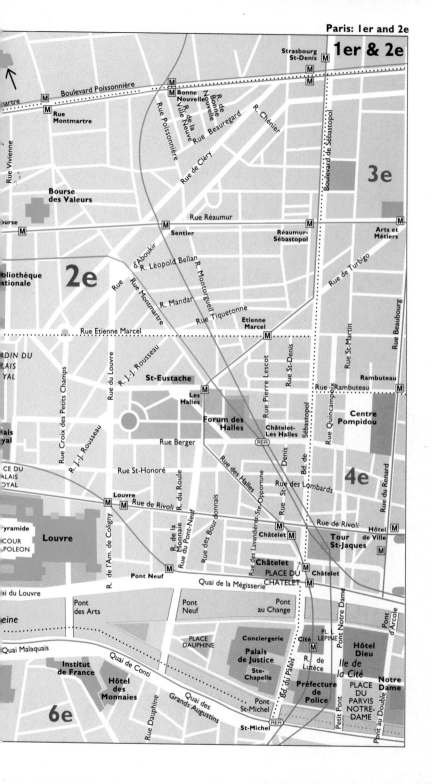

Paris: 5e and 6e

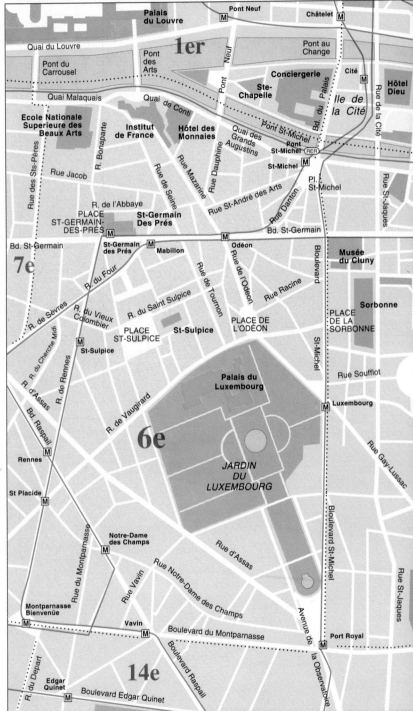

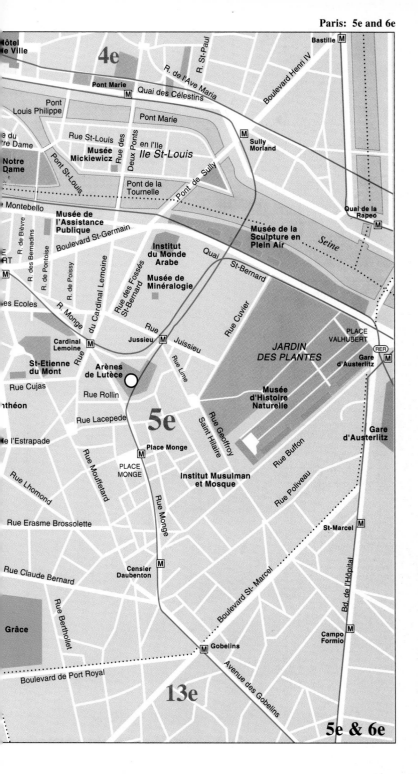

5e & 6e

Paris: RER

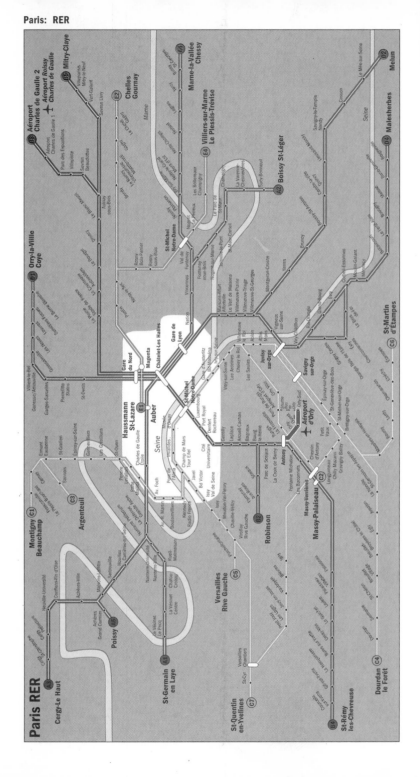

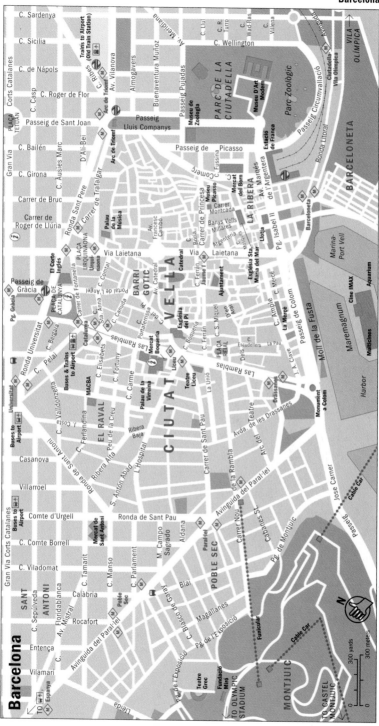

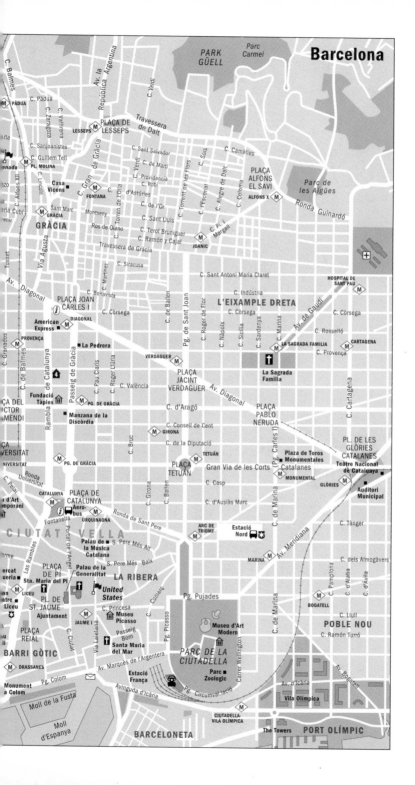

Barcelona Metro

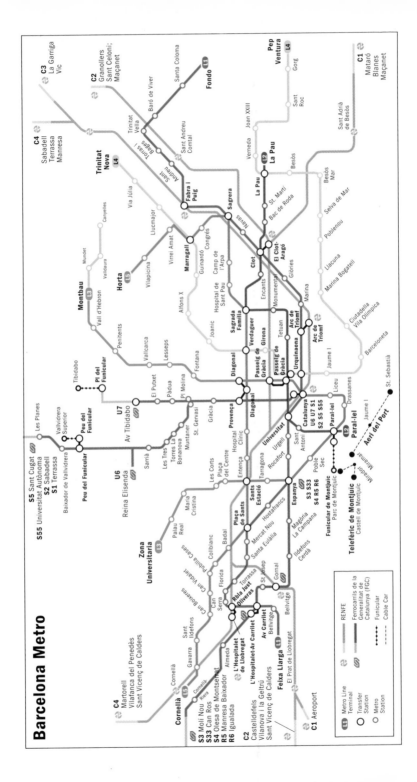

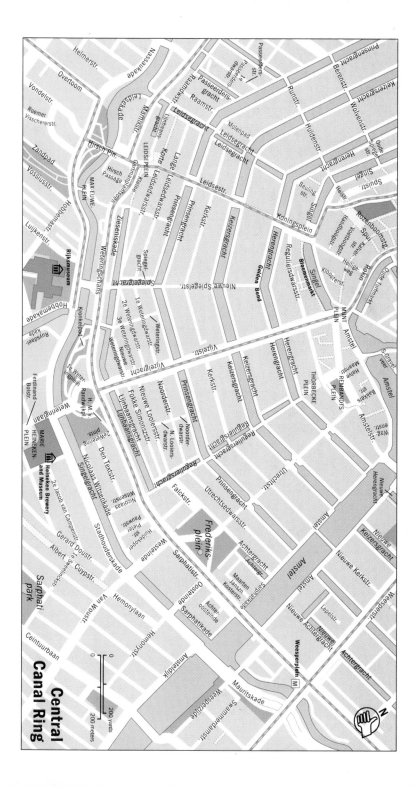

Central Canal Ring

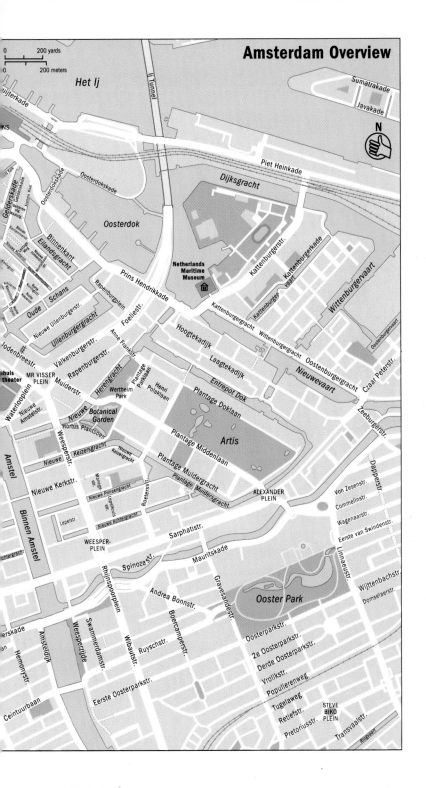

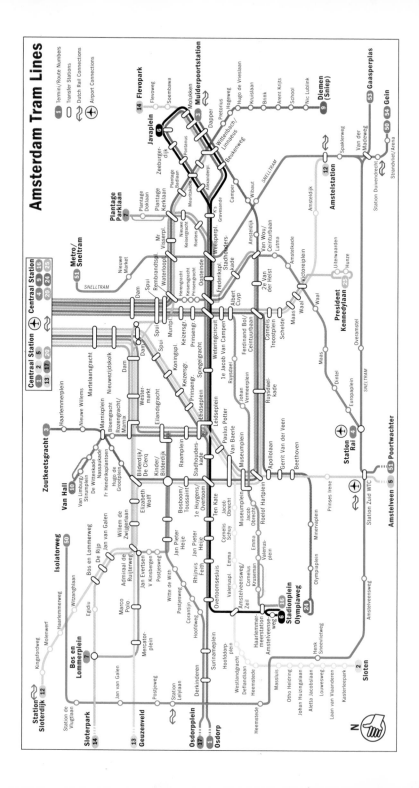

Amsterdam Tram Lines

Berlin Transit

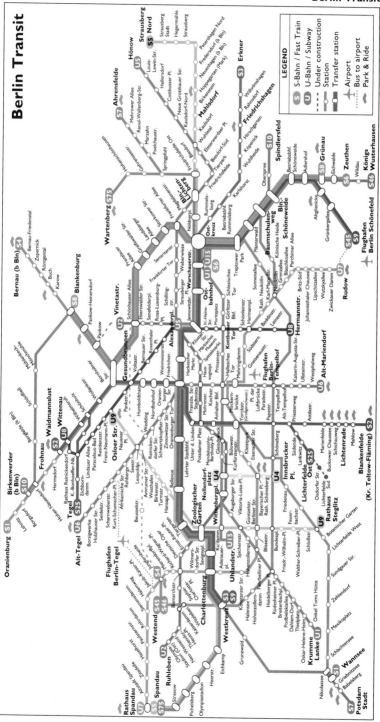

Munich Transit

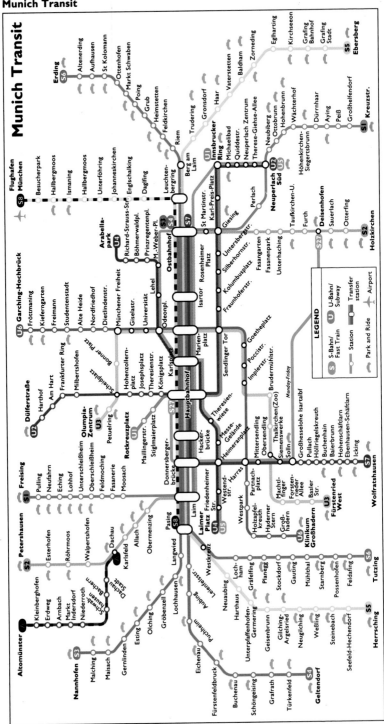

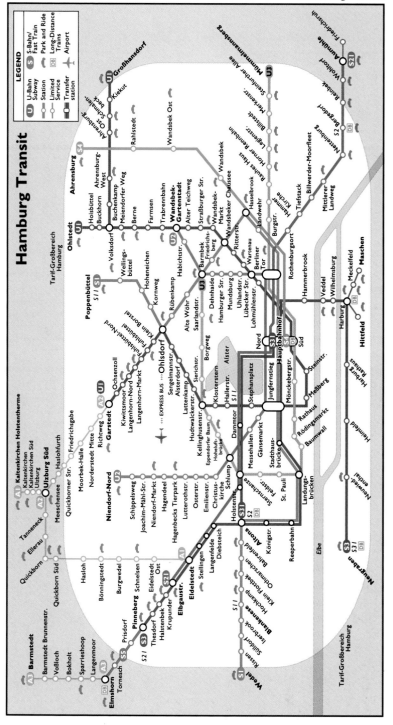

Frankfurt Transit

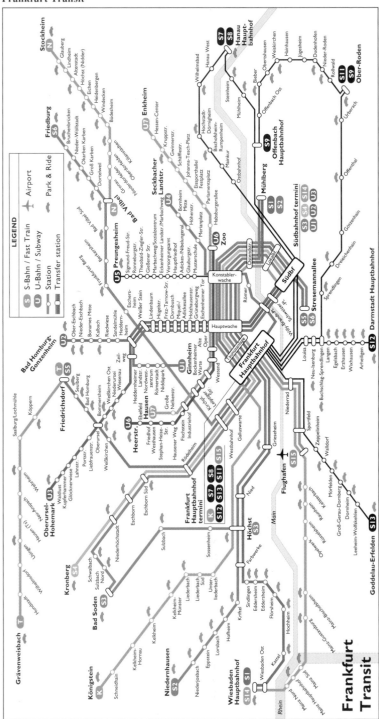

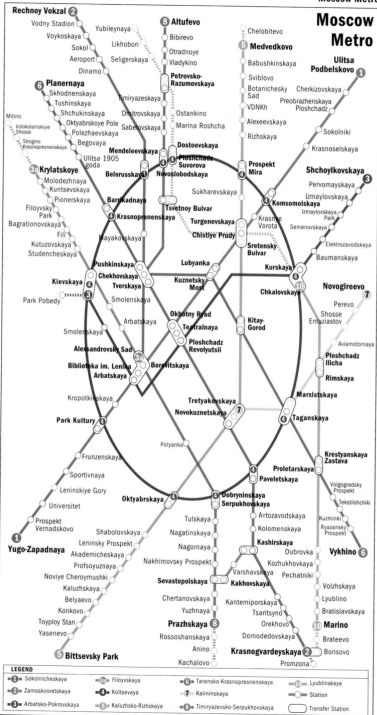

Moscow

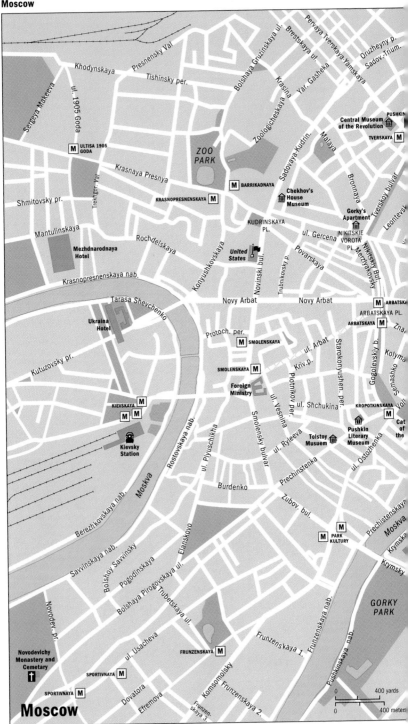

Khodynskaya

Presnensky Val

ul. 1905 Goda

Sergeya Makeeva

Tishinsky per.

Bolshaya Gruzinskaya ul.

Brestskaya ul.

Krasina

Pervaya Tverskaya-Yamskaya

Yar. Gasheka

Oruzheyny p.

Sadov.-Trium.

Central Museum of the Revolution 🏛 PUSHKIN

M ULTISA 1905 GODA

Zoologicheskaya

Sadovaya-Kudrin.

Malaia

TVERSKAYA **M**

Krasnaya Presnya

ZOO PARK

M BARRIKADNAYA

Chekhov's House Museum 🏛

Bronnaya

Tverskoy bulvar

Leontevsk

Shmitovsky pr.

Trekhgor. Val

KRASNOPRESNENSKAYA **M**

KUDRINSKAYA PL.

Gorky's Apartment 🏛

NIKITSKIE VOROTA PL.

Nikitsky Bul.

Merzlyakovsky

Mantulinskaya

Rochdelskaya

Konyushkivskaya

United States 🚩

ul. Gercena

Povarskaya

Trubnikovsky p.

Mezhdnarodnaya Hotel

Krasnopresnenskaya nab.

Novinski bul.

Tarasa Shevchenko

Novy Arbat

Novy Arbat

M ARBATSKA

ARBATSKAYA PL.

Ukraina Hotel

Protoch. per.

M SMOLENSKAYA

ARBATSKAYA **M**

Zna

ul. Arbat

Starokonyushen. per.

Gogolevskiy b.

Kolyma

Kutuzovsky pr.

SMOLENSKAYA **M**

Foreign Ministry

Kriv. p.

Plotnikov per.

ul. Shchukina

Semashko

KIEVSKAYA **M**

M **M**

Rostovskaya nab.

ul. Plyuschikha

ul. Veshna

ul. Ryleeva

ul. Shchukina

KROPOTKINSKAYA **M**

M Cat of the

🗿 **Kievsky Station**

Smolensky bulvar

Tolstoy Musuem 🏛

Pushkin Literary Museum 🏛

ul. Ostozhenka

Berezhkovskaya nab.

Moskva

Burdenko

Prechinstenka

Prechistenka

Savvinskaya nab.

Bolshoy Savvinsky

Pogodinskaya

Elanskovo

Zubov. bul.

M PARK KULTURY

Prechistenskaya

Moskva

Krymska

Novodev. pr.

Bolshaya Pirogovskaya

Trubetskaya ul.

Frunzenskaya nab.

Krymsky

GORKY PARK

Novodevichy Monastery and Cemetary ✝

ul. Usacheva

FRUNZENSKAYA **M**

Frunzenskaya 1.

Pushkinskaya nab.

SPORTIVNAYA **M**

Dovatora

Komsomolsky

Frunzenskaya 2.

SPORTIVNAYA **M**

Efremova

Frunzenskaya 3.

0   400 yards

0   400 meters

Moscow

Moscow

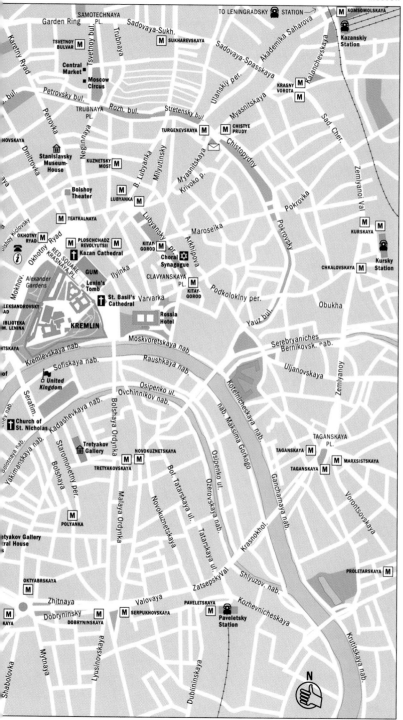

Московское Метро

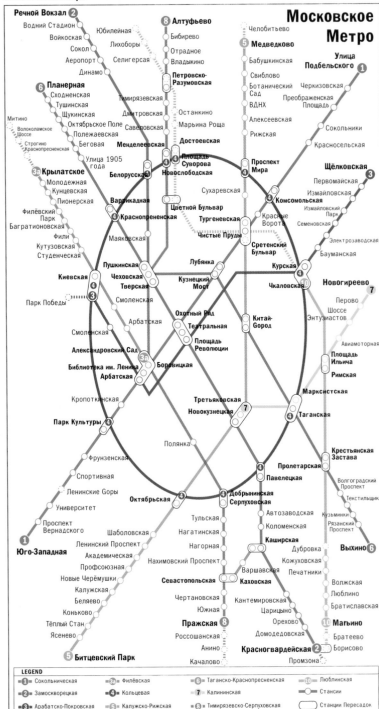

Московское Метро

Речной Вокзал ② · Водный Стадион · Войкоская · Сокол · Аэропорт · Динамо · Юбилейная · Лихоборы · Селигерсая · Алтуфьево ⑧ · Бибирево · Отрадное · Владыкино · Петровско-Разумовская · Челобитьево · Медведково ⑤ · Бабушкинская · Свиблово · Ботанический Сад · ВДНХ · Алексеевская · Рижская · Улица Подбельского ① · Черкизовская · Преображенская Площадь · Сокольники · Красносельская

Планерная ⑥ · Сходненская · Тушинская · Щукинская · Октябрьское Поле · Полежаевская · Беговая · Митино · Волоколамское Шоссе · Строгино · Красноспресненская · Крылатское ③а · Молодежная · Кунцевская · Пионерская · Филёвский Парк · Багратионовская · Фили · Кутузовская · Студенческая · Тимирязевская · Дмитровская · Савёловская · Менделеевская · Останкино · Марьина Роща · Достоевская · Площадь Суворова ④ · Новослободская · Проспект Мира · Щёлковская ③ · Первомайская · Измайловская · Измайловский Парк · Семеновская · Электрозаводская · Бауманская

Улица 1905 года · Белорусская ④ · Баррикадная ⑤ · Краснопресненская · Сухаревская · Цветной Бульвар · Тургеневская · Чистые Пруды · Комсомольская ⑤ · Красные Ворота · Сретенский Бульвар · Курская ④ · Чкаловская · Новогиреево ⑦ · Перово · Шоссе Энтузиастов · Авиамоторная

Маяковская · Пушкинская · Чеховская · Тверская · Лубянка · Кузнецкий Мост · Киевская ④ · Парк Победы · Смоленская · Арбатская · Охотный Ряд · Театральная · Площадь Революции · Китай-Город · Площадь Ильича · Римская

Смоленская · Александровский Сад · Библиотека им. Ленина · Арбатская · Боровицкая ③а · Кропоткинская · Третьяковская · Новокузнецкая ⑦ · Марксистская · Таганская ④ · Крестьянская Застава · Волгоградский Проспект · Текстильщики

Парк Культуры ④ · Фрунзенская · Спортивная · Ленинские Горы · Университет · Проспект Вернадского · Юго-Западная ① · Шаболовская · Октябрьская ④ · Полянка · Павелецкая ④ · Пролетарская · Добрынинская · Серпуховская · Автозаводская · Коломенская · Каширская · Кузьминки · Рязанский Проспект · Выхино ⑥ · Дубровка · Кожуховская · Печатники · Волжская · Люблино · Братиславская · Марьино ⑩

Ленинский Проспект · Академическая · Профсоюзная · Новые Черёмушки · Калужская · Беляево · Коньково · Тёплый Стан · Ясенево · Битцевский Парк ⑤ · Тульская · Нагатинская · Нагорная · Нахимовский Проспект · Севастопольская · Чертановская · Южная · Пражская ⑧ · Россошанская · Анино · Качалово · Варшавская · Каховская · Кантемировская · Царицыно · Орехово · Домодедовская · Красногвардейская ② · Промзона · Братеево · Борисово

LEGEND

① Сокольническая	④ Филёвская	⑥ Таганско-Краснопресненская	⑩ Люблинская
② Замоскворецкая	④ Кольцевая	⑦ Калининская	○ Станции
③ Арбатско-Покровская	⑤ Калужско-Рижская	⑧ Тимирязевско-Серпуховская	⬭ Станции Пересадок

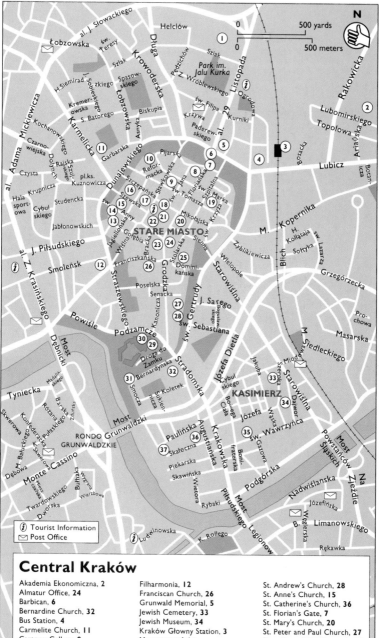

Prague

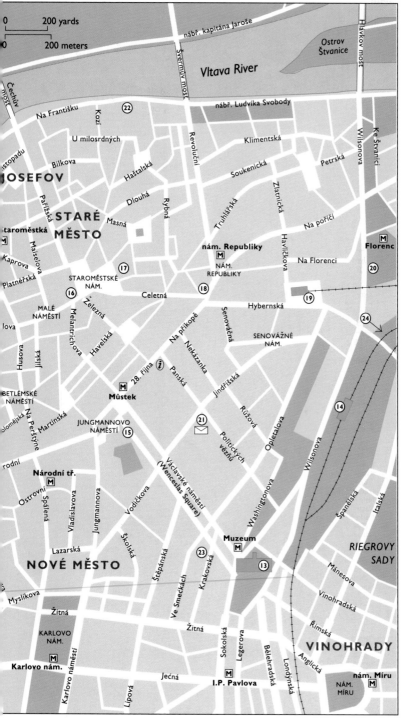

Prague

0   200 yards

0   200 meters

nábř. kapitána Jaroše

Vltava River

Ostrov
Štvanice

Havkov most

Švermův most

Čechův most

Na Františku

Kozí

(22)

nábř. Ludvíka Svobody

U milosrdných

Klimentská

Wilsonova

Ke Švanici

JOSEFOV

Bílkova

Haštalská

Soukenická

Petrská

Pařížská

Dlouhá

Rybná

Truhlářská

Zlatnická

Na poříčí

STARÉ
MĚSTO

Masná

taroměstská
M

nám. Republiky
M
NÁM.
REPUBLIKY

Florenc
M

Maiselova

Kaprova

(17)

Havlíčkova

Na Florenci

(20)

Platnéřská

STAROMĚSTSKÉ
NÁM.

(16)

Železná

Celetná

(18)

Hybernská

(19)

(24)

MALÉ
NÁMĚSTÍ

Melantrichova

Na příkopě

Senovážná

SENOVÁŽNÉ
NÁM.

Iova

Havelská

Nekázanka

Jindřišská

Husova

Martinská

Panská

Růžová

Opletalova

(14)

BETLÉMSKÉ
NÁMĚSTÍ

28. října

Můstek
M

(i)

Wilsonova

JUNGMANNOVO
NÁMĚSTÍ
(15)

(21)

Politických
vězňů

rodní

Národní tř.
M

Václavské náměstí
(Wenceslas Square)

Washingtonova

Špánělská

Italská

Ostrovní

Spálená

Vladislavova

Jungmannova

Vodičkova

Školská

Muzeum
M

RIEGROVY
SADY

Lazarská

NOVÉ MĚSTO

Štěpánská

Krakovská

(23)

(13)

Mánesova

Vinohradská

Myslíkova

Žitná

Ve Smečkách

Žitná

Sokolská

Legerova

Římská

VINOHRADY

KARLOVO
NÁM.

Belehradská

Londýnská

Anglická

nám. Míru

Karlovo nám.
M

Karlovo náměstí

Lipová

Ječná

I.P. Pavlova
M

NÁM.
MÍRU
M

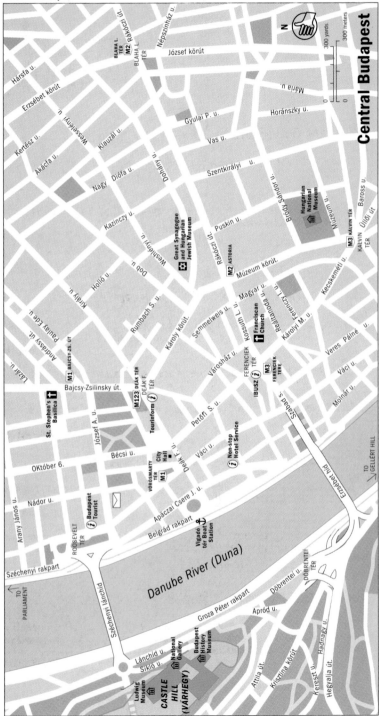

Central Budapest

🖊 Let's Go writers travel on your budget.

"Guides that penetrate the veneer of the holiday brochures and mine the grit of real life."

—*The Economist*

"The writers seem to have experienced every rooster-packed bus and lunar-surfaced mattress about which they write."

—*The New York Times*

"All the dirt, dirt cheap."

—*People*

🖊 Great for independent travelers.

"The guides are aimed not only at young budget travelers but at the independent traveler; a sort of streetwise cookbook for traveling alone."

—*The New York Times*

"A guide should tell you what to expect from a destination. Here *Let's Go* shines."

—*The Chicago Tribune*

"An indispensible resource, *Let's Go*'s practical information can be used by every traveler."

—*The Chattanooga Free Press*

🖊 Let's Go is completely revised each year.

"A publishing phenomenon...the only major guidebook series updated annually. *Let's Go* is the big kahuna."

—*The Boston Globe*

"Unbeatable: good sight-seeing advice; up-to-date info on restaurants, hotels, and inns; a commitment to money-saving travel; and a wry style that brightens nearly every page."

—*The Washington Post*

🖊 All the important information you need.

"*Let's Go* authors provide a comedic element while still providing concise information and thorough coverage of the country. Anything you need to know about budget traveling is detailed in this book."

—*The Chicago Sun-Times*

"*Let's Go* guidebooks take night life seriously."

—*The Chicago Tribune*

Let's Go Publications

Let's Go: Alaska & the Pacific Northwest 2002
Let's Go: Amsterdam 2002 **New Title!**
Let's Go: Australia 2002
Let's Go: Austria & Switzerland 2002
Let's Go: Barcelona 2002 **New Title!**
Let's Go: Boston 2002
Let's Go: Britain & Ireland 2002
Let's Go: California 2002
Let's Go: Central America 2002
Let's Go: China 2002
Let's Go: Eastern Europe 2002
Let's Go: Egypt 2002 **New Title!**
Let's Go: Europe 2002
Let's Go: France 2002
Let's Go: Germany 2002
Let's Go: Greece 2002
Let's Go: India & Nepal 2002
Let's Go: Ireland 2002
Let's Go: Israel 2002
Let's Go: Italy 2002
Let's Go: London 2002
Let's Go: Mexico 2002
Let's Go: Middle East 2002
Let's Go: New York City 2002
Let's Go: New Zealand 2002
Let's Go: Paris 2002
Let's Go: Peru, Ecuador & Bolivia 2002
Let's Go: Rome 2002
Let's Go: San Francisco 2002
Let's Go: South Africa with Southern Africa 2002
Let's Go: Southeast Asia 2002
Let's Go: Southwest USA 2002 **New Title!**
Let's Go: Spain & Portugal 2002
Let's Go: Turkey 2002
Let's Go: USA 2002
Let's Go: Washington, D.C. 2002
Let's Go: Western Europe 2002

Let's Go Map Guides

Amsterdam	New Orleans
Berlin	New York City
Boston	Paris
Chicago	Prague
Dublin	Rome
Florence	San Francisco
Hong Kong	Seattle
London	Sydney
Los Angeles	Venice
Madrid	Washington, D.C.

Let's Go

EUROPE
2002

Amy Cain editor
Anna Byrne associate editor
James Crawford associate editor
Harriet Green associate editor
Jasha Hoffman associate editor

researcher-writers
Cara Delzer
Justin Skinner

Naz F. Firoz managing editor
David Fisher map editor

St. Martin's Press ≋ New York

Maps by David Lindroth copyright © 2002, 2001, 2000, 1999, 1998, 1997, 1996, 1995, 1994, 1993, 1992, 1991, 1990, 1989, 1988 by St. Martin's Press.

Distributed outside the USA and Canada by Macmillan.

ISBN: 0-312-27045-3

First edition
10 9 8 7 6 5 4 3 2 1

Let's Go: Europe is written by Let's Go Publications, 67 Mount Auburn Street, Cambridge, MA 02138, USA.

HOW TO USE THIS BOOK

Welcome to *Let's Go: Europe 2002*. Whether your upcoming European adventure is like that thrilling first date, dinner with an old flame, or a golden anniversary, we can help you plan the perfect outing. We'll arm you with places to go, suave conversation topics, and all the practical details to make sure your excursion is as smooth as you are. Unsure where to dine? Forget your wallet? Need a room? Fear not—*Let's Go* in hand, you'll dive straight into a love affair with Europe.

ORGANIZATION OF THIS BOOK

INTRODUCTORY MATERIAL. The first chapter, **Discover Europe**, provides you with an overview of what there is to see and do in Europe—including **Suggested Itineraries** that tell you what you shouldn't miss in each region and how long it should take you to do. The **Story of Europe** chapter provides you with a general introduction to the history of Europe, as well as its artistic and cultural movements. The **Essentials** section outlines important practical information, while the **Transportation** chapter will help you get to and around Europe.

COUNTRY CHAPTERS. We've organized your potential destinations alphabetically by country. The **black tabs** in the margins will help you to navigate easily between chapters. In each chapter, you'll find a **Discover** section with the highlights of the country, as well as an **Essentials** section with practical information. Capitals are covered first, and larger cities are broken down into manageable bite-size sections: transportation, practical information, accommodations, food, sights, entertainment, and nightlife. We've also included **daytrips** from major destinations.

LANGUAGE BASICS. We've included a **glossary** of useful foreign words, and a **phrasebook** of handy phrases in 27 languages.

LET'S GO FORMAT

RANKING ESTABLISHMENTS. In each section (accommodations, food, etc.), we list establishments in order from best to worst. Our absolute favorites are so denoted by the highest honor given out by Let's Go, the Let's Go thumbs-up (◙).

PHONE CODES AND NUMBERS. The **phone code** for each region, city, or town appears opposite the name of that region, city, or town, and is denoted by the ☎ icon. **Phone numbers** in text are also preceded by the ☎ icon.

GRAYBOXES AND WHITEBOXES. Grayboxes at times provide wonderful cultural insight, at times simply crude humor. In any case, they're usually amusing, so enjoy. **Whiteboxes,** on the other hand, provide important practical information, such as warnings (▮), further resources (▧), and border crossings (▩).

CONTENTS

ACKNOWLEDGMENTS

TEAM EUROPE LOVES: Scandinavian superstars Cara and Justin, and the Europe researcher-writers who put the meat in this book. All the country and city editors for their guidance and friendship. Naz for advising us through the end. Caleb, Jen, Melissa, and Vanessa for computer/design skills. Dan, Fish, and Mapland. EEUR and Fine-people for good times in the Europod. Princes of Europe, single and otherwise, for spicing up the summer. And bike-tour Mike for his professionalism.

AMY THANKS: Mare, for bonding through red bandana interviews, Danish translations, and G-diddy episodes. My AEs: Anna, for keeping it giddy, raunchy, and occasionally violent; James, for putting flavor into the book and making it *so yummy*; Harriett, for being my dance-boyband-style pop partner; Jascha, for taking on Eastern Europe with a uniquely *jaschers* flair; and index-queen Celeste, for chart love and candy. Frederik, *jeg er ugift.* Avi, George, Mazza, and Blaz for office fun. Roomies, Tony, and Adam for channels 9 and 76. Roe, Gita, Melissa, and B-town girls for summer frolicking. And Jimps, Haechun, Franzous, and Toby for the love.

ANNA THANKS: Amy, the best editor ever; Harriett, for her sensitivity towards Bourbon Chicken; Celeste, for her infinite computer wisdom and swedish fish; James, for his love of America, especially Texas; and Jascha, for his humor. To the SPAM folks–George, Sophia and Sarah, for their infinite knowledge of, well, SPAM. Justin, for being a great, enthusiastic RW. And who could forget the fam, Mom, Dad, Em, Rach, Matt for being so interesting and loving, Melissa, Meggie, Cait, Megha, Ryan, Paul, the Big Green Egg, the Wrap, Ginger, my SA skanks, and high UV indexes.

JAMES THANKS: SuperAmyMare, the editing juggernaut for editing heroics and continual guidance; Anna for tolerating my motherland; Jascha for outlandish absurdity; Celeste for sweet, sweet candy; and Harriett for being the Martin to my Lewis. To the roomies: Dave for being the Lewis to my Martin; Steeeeev for learning me; Owen for toleration; and Ben for tennis and hip-hop. To Eliot, Avi and Mazza and the cow for making me laugh until my sides hurt; to Gautam and Sharmelita for receptive ears; to the Dad, Mum, Si, Nikki, Netties and Sonja, again, Gros Bisous.

HARRIETT THANKS: Amy for our dance teenybopper-pop adventures; Mare for staying strong in the face of Haakon's abandonment; Anna for helping me fight the Bourbon Chicken; James for the Frank Sinatra serenades; Celeste for the talks and abundance of energy food; and Jascha for Animal Farm and Dead Prez. Helen, Wei, and Kathy for being awesome summer roommates; Grandma and Grandpa Green, Grandma and Grandpa Howell, Mom, Dad, Heather, Hillary, and Harrison for your love, support, and encouragement in everything I do; and God for blessing me with this opportunity.

JASCHA THANKS: Amy for that *name*; Anna for country; Celeste for tiny chicken; Harriett for rap; James for emphasis; Mare for that dance. Avi for icy deadpan; Eliot for phone calls; Katie for tracksuit; Martha for composure. Ben & Allie for the Boss. Matt & Naz. Emi, Owen, Sarah for Moscow. Paul for *meia lua*. Leila, Will, Marian, Toure, Badou and the kids of Yoff, Senegal for fables **(www.cresp.sn/ecoyoff)**. C&A for squats. Bach for vinyl. Aud, Steph, Aron for Canada. Marjo & Mando for *stroop*; Rafe & Loren for *eupsch*. Paulinha. Dot, Bernie, Rhoda. Jared, Brad, Zoe, Eli and Emma. Mom & Dad for love and support. And Mike for flow, and other intros.

CELESTE THANKS: The whole ◼(W)EUR team: Amy, for the chocolate-covered strawberries; Mare for being a loveable Swiss miss; James for being on my wavelength (most of the time); Harriet for all the lunchtime chats; Jascha for keeping it funky; and Anna for all the loooooove. Avi for the egg man and baseball talk; Emily, Andrea, David, Abby, and all the GER/A&S folks for all their hard work. Annie for making me laugh for more than a decade (even ☎ long distance); Mom, Dad, & Sis for raising me, teaching me, loving me, and humoring me. And Matt, for keeping me sane, understanding me, and loving me.

RESEARCHER-WRITERS

Cara Delzer   *Finland, Sweden*
Just as modest as the Swedes and Finns, Cara faithfully sent back her copy with an optimistic energy that was uniquely hers. She dutifully sifted through seas of denim-jacketed blondes, green-faced street performers, and dysfunctional phones to find the true gems of Sweden and Finland. This fashionable South Dakota black-belt handled it all with style and grace, discipline and determination, and—above all—a huge smile on her face. Thank you, and happy birthday, Cara.

Justin Skinner   *Iceland, Norway*
Traversing two entire countries was easy for Justin, a veteran researcher for *Let's Go: Central America 1998*, who was used to chopping through Guatemalan jungles with a machete and a machine gun. Outgoing and athletic, Justin befriended Icelandic Elisabeth Shue look-alikes and explored Norway's fjords up-close by kayak. In between it all, this Vermont boy found time to entertain us with his stories, hone his mad Ultimate frisbee skills, and produce virtually flawless copy.

REGIONAL EDITORS AND RESEARCHER-WRITERS

LET'S GO: AMSTERDAM 2002
Karen Kiang   *Editor*
Monica Noelle Sullivan   *Associate Editor*
David Fagundes *Amsterdam, Wadden Is., Leiden, The Hague, Haarlem, Arnhem, Zandvoort-an-Zee, Scheveningen*
Rebecca Shapiro *Amsterdam, Hoorn, Utrecht, Groningen, Hoge Veluwe, Maastricht, Apeldoorn*
Meredith Schweig *Amsterdam, Edam, Delft, Rotterdam*

LET'S GO: AUSTRIA AND SWITZERLAND 2002
David Huyssen   *Editor*
Abigail Burger   *Associate Editor*
Matthew R. Cordell *Jungfrau, Graubünden, Ticino, and Swiss National Park*
Mattias Frey *Vienna, Upper Austria, Lower Austria*
Kalen Ingram *Northwestern Switzerland, Zurich, Bern, Neuchâtel, Lac Léman*
Chris Townsend *Salzburg, Hohe Tauern, Tyrol, Liechtenstein*
Eugénie Suter *Styria, Salzburger Land, Upper Austria*

LET'S GO: BARCELONA 2002
Sarah Thérèse Kenney   *Editor*
Monica Noelle Sullivan   *Associate Editor*
Emily Gann   *Barcelona*
Tom Malone   *Barcelona*
Meredith Petrin   *Barcelona*

LET'S GO: BRITAIN 2002
Matthew B. Sussman   *Editor*
Kate D. Nesin   *Associate Editor*
Matthew D. Firestone *Northeast and Northwest England, Southern and Central Scotland*
Nathaniel D. Myers *Wales, Midlands, Northwest England*
Jennifer O'Brien *South and Northeast England, Heart of England, East Anglia, Midlands*
A. Morgan Rodman *Southwest and Northern England, Heart of England, Midlands*
Robert Willison *Glasgow, Central Scotland, Highlands and Islands*

LET'S GO: EASTERN EUROPE 2002
Katharine M. Holt   *Editor*
Martha Deery, Eliot I. Hodges, Avi Steinberg   *Associate Editors*
Eli Bard Richlin   *Czech Republic*
Ben Wasserstein   *Hungary*
Teddy Andrews   *Estonia, Latvia, Lithuania*
Eugene Chislenko   *Moscow, St. Petersburg*
Brett Egan   *Crimea, Moscow Nightlife*

Joshua Gardner	Romania
Karolina Maciag	Poland
Amy McGoldrick	Belarus, Eastern Poland, Ukraine
Asen Parachkevov	Bulgaria, Romanian Black Sea Coast
Eli Bard Richlin	Czech Republic
Jack Pettibone Riccobono	Bosni a, Croatia
Natalia Truszkowska	Slovakia, Slovenia
Ben Wasserstein	Hungary

LET'S GO: FRANCE 2002

Emily Jane Griffin	Editor
Sarah E. Eno, Sarah Y. Resnick	Associate Editors
Rebecca Bienstock	Côte d'Azur, Corsica, the Alps
Tamar Katz	Berry-Limousin, Périgord, Poitou-Charentes, the Loire Valley
Catherine Koss	Brittany and Western Normandy
Annalise Nelson	Champagne, Alsace-Lorraine, Franche-Comté, Flanders, Eastern Normandy
Angela Peluse	Lyon, Burgundy, Provence
Nathaniel L. Schwartz	Aquitaine, Gascony, and Pays Basque, Languedoc-Roussillon, Périgord

LET'S GO: GERMANY 2002

Emily Harrison	Editor
Andrea Deeker	Associate Editor
Jesse Andrews	Berlin, Brandenburg, Saxony-Anhalt
Caryn Davies	Bavaria
Daniel C. Fehder	Hesse, North Rhine-Westphalia, Lower Saxony, Bremen
E. Rebecca Gantt	Saxony, Thuringia, Hesse
Aaron Parsons	Saxony-Anhalt, Lower Saxony, Baden-Württemburg, Rhineland-Palatinate
Marah Stith	Hamburg, Schleswig-Holstein, Mecklenburg-Western Pomerania
Eugénie E. Suter	Baden-Württemburg

LET'S GO: GREECE 2002

Erzulie D. Coquillon	Editor
John Mazza	Associate Editor
Alaina Aguanno	Athens and the Cyclades
Helen Dimos	The Dodecanese
Kate Greer	Peloponnese and Ionian Islands
Andrew Kleimeyer	Central and Northern Greece
Helen Stevens	Crete and the Cyclades
Jonathan Wood	Central Greece, the Sporades, Saronic Gulf, Northeastern Aegean Islands

LET'S GO: IRELAND 2002

Daniel L. Wagner	Editor
Sonja Nikkila	Associate Editor
Sheila A. Baynes	Southwest
Melissa Johnson	Dublin, Midlands, East, Southeast
Michael Liam O'Byrne	Connemara, Co. Antrim, Derry, Donegal
Jacob Rubin	Westport, Co. Clare, Galway, Sligo

LET'S GO: ITALY 2002

Shannon F. Ringvelski	Editor
David James Bright, Sarah Y. Resnick	Associate Editors
Jeffrey Barnes	Tuscany and Umbria
Eric Graves Brown	The Veneto, Friuli-Venezia Giulia, Trentino-Alto Adige, Valle d'Aosta
Dennis Feehan	Liguria and Sardinia
Celeste Fine	Apulia, Campania
David Justin Hodge	Lombardy, the Piedmont, Emiglia-Romagna
Megan E. Low	Sicily

LET'S GO: LONDON 2002

| D. Jonathan Dawid | Editor and London |

LET'S GO: PARIS 2002

| Anne Jump | Editor |
| Valérie de Charette | Paris |

Europe

N

0   400 miles
0   400 kilometers

ICELAND
Reykjavik

Faroe Islands

Shetland Islands

Orkney Islands

North Sea

SCOTLAND
Glasgow
Edinburgh

NORTHERN IRELAND
Belfast

IRELAND
Dublin

GREAT BRITAIN

WALES
Cardiff

ENGLAND

London

ATLANTIC OCEAN

THE NETHERLANDS
Amsterda

Brussels
BELGIUM

Paris

LUXEMBO

LIECHTENSTEIN
Zurich
SWITZERLAND
Bern

Nantes

Bay of Biscay

Bordeaux

Lyon
Milan

FRANCE

Marseille
Nice
Flore

MONACO

Santiago de Campostela

PORTUGAL

ANDORRA

Madrid

Barcelona

Corsica (Fr.)

Lisbon

SPAIN

Valencia

Sevilla
Granada

Balearic Islands (Sp.)

Sardinia (It.)

Tangier
GIBRALTAR

Mediterranean Se

Rabat
Fez
MOROCCO

ALGERIA
Algiers

Tunis
TU

Be

DE

Hamb

GE

XIV

DISCOVER EUROPE

Never one to be upstaged, Europe has always hogged the limelight. While she's petite in stature (the svelte second-smallest continent), she's never shy about taking center stage in world culture and politics. She stole the opening scenes and launched her career as the Greeks, Romans, Franks, and Vikings conquered the countryside. Like any starlet, she suffered identity crises as crusades and rebellions pitted religious and ethnic factions against each other. She struggled in the early 20th century as her World War series (parts I and II) flopped big-time. But after popes and Puritans, reformers and revolutionaries, and colonies and communists had all played their parts, Europe pulled together for a triumphant comeback. Today, she stars as a flashy dancing queen in the nightclubs of Berlin and as a material girl in the ritzy boutiques of Paris. She plays the reserved, sophisticated matron in Vienna just as well as the fun-loving teenager in Ibiza. Want to meet her up-close and personal? Grab a camera, a backpack, and a fresh copy of *Let's Go: Europe 2002*—your backstage pass—and go get her autograph for yourself.

FACTS AND FIGURES

POPULATION: 728,887,000 (2000).

LANGUAGES: Over 60 native tongues in three major language families: Romance, Germanic, and Slavic.

RELIGIONS: Catholic (36.97%), Eastern Orthodox (23.59%), Protestant (10.93%), Jewish (0.33%).

LAND MASS: 4 million sq. mi.

MOUNTAIN RANGES: Alps, Apennines, Balkans, Carpathians, Dolomites, Pyrenees, and Urals.

MAJOR RIVERS: Danube, Dnieper, Don, Elbe, Loire, Oder, Rhine, Rhône, Seine, Thames, Volga, Vistula.

WHEN TO GO

Summer is the high-season for travel in Europe. Throngs of tourists fill hostels and crowd museums, particularly during the months of July and August; you may find June or September a better time to travel. Additionally, climate can serve as a very good guide for the best time to travel in certain areas.

Average Temperature and Precipitation	January			April			July			October		
	°C	°F	in	°C	°F	in	°C	°F	in	°C	°F	in
Amsterdam	3.3	38.0	3.1	8.3	47.0	1.5	16.7	62.0	2.9	10.6	51.0	4.1
Athens	10.0	50.0	1.9	15.0	59.0	0.9	27.2	81.0	0.2	19.4	67.0	2.1
Berlin	-0.6	31.0	1.6	7.8	46.0	1.6	18.3	65.0	2.0	9.4	49.0	1.0
Budapest	0.2	32.4	1.2	11.2	52.2	1.5	20.9	69.3	2.3	10.8	51.4	1.4
Copenhagen	0.6	33.0	1.7	6.1	43.0	1.6	16.7	62.0	2.6	9.4	49.0	2.1
Dublin	5.6	42.0	2.5	8.3	47.0	1.9	15.6	60.0	2.6	10.6	51.0	2.9
İstanbul	5.4	41.7	3.6	11.5	52.7	1.7	23.4	74.1	1.0	16.0	60.8	2.6

Average Temperature and Precipitation	January			April			July			October		
	°C	°F	in	°C	°F	in	°C	°F	in	°C	°F	in
Kraków	-3.7	25.3	1.3	7.9	46.2	1.9	18.4	65.1	3.5	8.6	47.5	1.7
London	3.9	39.0	3.1	7.8	46.0	2.1	16.7	62.0	1.8	11.0	51.0	2.9
Madrid	5.6	42.0	1.8	11.7	53.0	1.8	24.4	76.0	0.4	14.4	58.0	1.8
Moscow	-10.3	13.5	1.4	4.4	39.9	1.5	18.5	65.3	3.2	4.2	39.6	2.0
Paris	3.9	39	0.2	10.0	50.0	0.2	19.4	67.0	0.2	11.7	53.0	0.2
Prague	-1.7	29.0	0.8	7.2	45.0	1.4	17.2	63.0	2.6	8.3	47.0	1.2
Rome	8.3	47.0	3.2	12.8	55.0	2.6	75.0	75.0	0.6	17.8	64.0	4.5
Stockholm	-4.1	24.6	1.2	4.4	39.9	1.1	17.1	62.8	2.5	7.3	45.1	2.0
Vienna	0.0	32.0	1.5	9.4	49.0	2.0	20.0	68.0	2.9	10.6	51.0	1.9

WHAT TO DO

Museum hoppers, architecture lovers, sporty outdoorsmen, wild clubbers, and sun-worshipers, check out the **themed highlights** that follow. Peruse our **Let's Go Picks** for quirky gems, and design your own route around Europe using our **Suggested Itineraries**. For more country-specific attractions, see the **Discover** sections at the beginning of each chapter, and for advice on when to go, consult the **Essentials** section. But don't let us cramp your style—mix and match, and choose your own adventure.

MUSEUM MANIA

Museum hoppers, look no further—these cultural wonders are the best Europe has to offer. **London** (p. 141) is one of Europe's finest museum cities: ogle the Rosetta Stone and other imperialist booty at the **British Museum;** saunter through the histories of art, design, and style at the **Victoria and Albert Museum;** and don't miss the spectacular art in the **Tate Modern Gallery,** a converted power plant. On the other side of the Chunnel, **Paris** (p. 318) is just as impressive—the *Venus de Milo* and *Mona Lisa* at the **Louvre** will stop you in your tracks; the **Musée d'Orsay** will impress with all that is Impressionist; and the pipes and modern art of the **Centre National d'Art et de Culture Georges-Pompidou** will wriggle their way into your heart. Drop down to Spain for the striking **Museo Guggenheim** in **Bilbao** (p. 887) and the **Dalí Museum** in **Figueres** (p. 880). **Madrid** (p. 830) abounds with stunning museums: the **Prado** shelters the world's largest collection of paintings; the **Museo Thyssen-Bornemizsa** contains all the major artistic trends in painting; and the **Museo Nacional Centro de Arte Reina Sofía** harbors Picasso's *Guernica*. Delight in **Barcelona's** fanciful *Modernista* buildings and its museums devoted to Picasso and Miró (p. 867).

In **Italy,** first stop at **Venice** (p. 592), whose winding waterways embrace the offerings of the **Accademia** and the modern art of the **Collezione Guggenheim.** Next up: **Florence** (p. 620), home of the Renaissance. The **Uffizi** is crammed with world-class art, and the **Accademia** holds Michelangelo's *David*, the image of human perfection. When in **Rome** (p. 572), the **Sistine Chapel** in the **Vatican Museums** will leave you in awe. In Central Europe, **Vienna** (p. 87) hosts the renowned **Kunsthistoriches Museum** and the **Austrian Gallery.** Across the German border, wander through the technological **Deutsches Museum** in **Munich** and twin **Pinakotheks** (p. 458), then take in superb modern art at the **Staatsgalerie Stuttgart** (p. 449). For the established *meisters*, zip over to the **Kunstmuseum Bonn** (p. 437), then get racy at Hamburg's **Erotic Art Museum** (p. 431). Celebrate Germany's reunification at the **East Side Gallery** in **Berlin** (p. 413), a huge open-air gallery that's the longest remaining stretch of the Wall. Believe it or not, the biggest sin you could commit in **Amsterdam** (p. 680) would be to miss the **Rijksmuseum;** note also the **van Gogh Museum** and the **Hash Marijuana Hemp Museum.**

In Russia, **Moscow's Kremlin** once contained the secrets to an empire; it still holds the legendary Fabergé eggs (p. 795). The **Hermitage,** in **St. Petersburg,** holds the world's largest art collection (p. 804). Budapest's **Museum of Fine Arts** houses little-seen but nonetheless spectacular works by Raphael, Rembrandt, and the rest of the usual suspects (p. 516). Finally, the **Occupation Museum** in **Rīga** (p. 648), which depicts the Soviet occupation, may be the finest museum in the Baltics.

RUINS AND RELICS

For those who prefer their history in the wild instead of a museum case, Europe's castles, churches, and ruins are a dream come true. In **London** (p. 156), royals do the waving thing around **Buckingham Palace** and **St. James's Palace,** while choirboys croon at **Westminster Abbey** and **St. Paul's Cathedral.** Venture away from the city to ponder the mysteries of **Stonehenge** (p. 177) and scale the towers of magnificent **Warwick Castle** (p. 185). Across the water, don't miss Paris's breathtaking **Cathédrale de Notre-Dame** (p. 333). Elsewhere in France, the *châteaux* of the **Loire Valley** (p. 353) and Normandy's fortified abbey of **Mont-St-Michel** (p. 349) are must-sees, as is the fortress of **Carcassonne** (p. 363). To the south, Spain houses the largest Gothic cathedral in the world, in **Sevilla** (p. 852), as well as the amazingly luxurious **Palacio Real** in **Madrid** (p. 838). Muslim-infused southern Spain also awaits, offering the mosque in **Córdoba** (p. 847) and the **Alhambra** in **Granada** (p. 860). In Italy, **Rome** (p. 572) almost invented architecture as we know it; can we say **Pantheon, Colosseum,** and **Forum?** Oh yeah, and Michelangelo's *Pietà* in **St. Peter's Basilica.** Dive off the heel of the boot into Greece, where the crumbling **Acropolis,** the very foundation of Western civilization, still towers above **Athens** (p. 472). After visiting one of the fore-most collections of classical art at Athens' **National Archaeological Museum,** journey to the navel of the ancient world to learn your fate from the oracle at **Delphi** (p. 479) or visit the **temple of Apollo** on **Delos** (p. 494). Across the Aegean in Turkey, discover the Byzantine **Hagia Sophia** and Ottoman **Blue Mosque,** well as the nerve center of the Ottoman Empire, **Topkapi Palace,** in **İstanbul** (p. 944). Don't neglect the Classical finds at **Ephesus** (p. 958).

In Switzerland, Lord Byron once scratched his name into a pillar in the chilling **Château de Chillon** at **Montreux** (p. 925). Cross into Germany to marvel at the **Cathedral at Cologne** (p. 436) and the breathtaking **Schloß Sans Souci** at **Potsdam** (p. 418), including the pure gold tea house. Go a little crazy in **Mad King Ludwig's castles** in the **Bavarian Alps** (p. 464), then head north to Denmark's **Kvaerndrup** (p. 281) and marvel at the optical illusion that makes **Egeskov Slot** appear to float on water. The kaleido-scopic onion domes of **St. Basil's Cathedral** are the emblem of **Moscow** (p. 795), and **Prague Castle** has been the seat of the Bohemian government for 1000 years (p. 257).

THE GREAT OUTDOORS

Enough urban warrior—you're ready to escape from civilization and heed the call of the wild. Britain brims with national parks; our favorite is the **Lake District National Park** (p. 193). For more dramatic scenery, head north to the **Scottish Highlands;** the **Isle of Skye** (p. 214) and the **Outer Hebrides** (p. 214) are particularly breathtaking. Ireland's **Ring of Kerry** (p. 554) provides wee Irish towns, while **Killarney National Park** (p. 553) features spectacular mountains. In the French Alps, **Chamonix** (p. 381) tempts skiers with some of the world's steepest slopes, while **Grenoble** (p. 380) brims with hiking opportunities. In Spain, the **Parque Nacional de Ordesa** (p. 882) is set among the breath-taking Pyrenees. Across the Mediterranean, the **Aeolian Islands** (p. 642) north of Sicily boast pristine beaches, dramatic volcanoes, and bubbling thermal springs. Drop down to Greece and hike up **Mt. Olympus** (p. 485), where the gods used to sip ambrosia; a two-day hike will bring you to the summit. In **Crete,** get in touch with your inner mountain goat with a trek down the **Samaria Gorge** (p. 499). Turkey's **Butterfly Valley** (p. 963), near **Fethiye,** will enchant and astound. The dramatic **Tatra** mountain range stretches across Eastern Europe; lace up your hiking boots in Slovakia's **Starý Smokovec** (p. 816) or Poland's **Zakopane**

(p. 747). Austria's **Kitzbühel** (p. 110) and **Innsbruck** (p. 107) quench every hiking and skiing desire. For fresh Swiss Alpine air, make the pilgrimage to the **Matterhorn** (p. 937), or dive into the adventure sports of **Interlaken** (p. 936). From there, soak up the scenery of Germany's **Saxon Switzerland** (p. 423), then hike through the **Black Forest** (p. 450)—but leave a trail of crumbs so you can find your way out to tackle the **fjords** and **glaciers** of western Norway (p. 714).

LET'S GO HEDONISM

So you've seen all the sights and climbed all the mountains—now indulge in sunny beaches and wild nightlife. Check out the crazy scene in **London** (p. 141) and **Edinburgh** (p. 202), which has the highest concentration of pubs in Europe. When it's not raining, even England hosts a tempting beach culture. The old artists' enclave of **St. Ives** (p. 179) offers sparkling beaches and blue water, while **Newquay** (p. 180) is a surfing capital. **Malin Head** (p. 561), at Ireland's northernmost point on the **Inishowen Peninsula**, offers a beach covered with semi-precious stones. The hearty pub scene in **Dublin** (p. 540) knocks back a few at **Temple Bar, Grafton Street,** and the **Guinness Brewery.** France's **St-Malo** (p. 350) combines the beauty and history of Normandy. Skip down to Portugal, where you can party all night and sun all day along the **Algarve**, particularly at **Lagos** (p. 766). Along Spain's **Costa del Sol**, hip clubs line the beaches of **Marbella** (p. 859), while **Tossa de Mar** (p. 880) along the **Costa Blanca** boasts beaches, red cliffs, small bays, and medieval alleys. Spain's **Balearic Islands** are a must for party kids; **Ibiza** (p. 889) is manic by night. Dance your way through the mad nightlife of **Madrid** (p. 830), **Barcelona** (p. 867), **Lisbon** (p. 756), and the **French Riviera** (p. 368) before recovering in the serene fishing villages of Italy's **Cinque Terre** (p. 616). Farther north in Italy, Europe's deepest lake, **Lake Como**, is peaceful perfection (p. 604), and the night scene in **Milan** (p. 606) is chic and dynamic. Most visitors to Italy don't venture south of Rome—a huge mistake, given the breathtaking, almost unspeakable, beauty of the **Amalfi Coast** (p. 639) where the bikini was invented. The **Blue Grotto** glows nearby on the island of **Capri** (p. 640). Bop down to the Greek islands: **Corfu** harbors the beautiful beach of **Agios Gordios** (p. 490); as the sun sets over volcanic beaches in **Santorini** (p. 497), the bars salute Helios with classical music. **Ios** (p. 496), a frat party run amok, has more places to get drunk than anywhere else in Greece. Drag your tanned and tired self to Turkey's **Blue Lagoon** of **Ölüdeniz**, near **Fethiye** (p. 963). Discover your inner beer connoisseur in the brewhouses of **Munich** (p. 453), then head to **Berlin** (p. 400) or **Dresden** (p. 419) for the best club scenes in east Germany. Farther east, **Prague** (p. 247) and **Moscow** (p. 790) are the hottest spots after sunset.

⬛ LET'S GO PICKS

LEAST EXCLUSIVE PARTY: Every Liechtensteiner (all 31,000) is invited to the prince's palace for the annual national celebration in Vaduz (p. 650).

WORST PLACE TO TELL A SECRET: London's Whispering Gallery (p. 156), where whatever you slip can be heard at the room's other end.

BEST SEAT IN THE HOUSE: The lip-shaped sofa in Dalí's house (p. 881), in Cadaqués, Spain.

EDEN ON EARTH: Lokrum (p. 239), off-shore of Dubrovnik, where nude beaches and botanical gardens go hand in hand.

BEST BOY BAND: The Vienna Boys' Choir wows fans every Sunday at the Hofburg (p. 87).

WEIRDEST RELIGIOUS RELIC: The light-up right hand of St. Stephen in Budapest (p. 515).

WETTEST T-SHIRT CONTEST: The Sant Joan festival in Alicante, Spain (p. 864), when the whole city is doused with fire-hoses.

BEST BOOTY: The imperialist goods, especially the Rosetta Stone and the Elgin Marbles, at London's British Museum (p. 163).

FÊTES! FESTAS! FESTIVALS!

COUNTRIES	APR. – JUNE	JULY – AUG.	SEPT. – MAR.
AUSTRIA & SWITZERLAND	**Vienna Festival** (mid-May to mid-June)	**Salzburger Festspiele** (late July to late Aug.) **Open-Air St. Gallen** (late June)	**Fasnacht** (Basel; Mar.) **Escalade** (Geneva; early Dec.)
BRITAIN & IRELAND	**Bloomsday** (Dublin; June 16)	**Edinburgh Int'l Festival** (Aug. 11-31) **Fringe Festival** (Aug. 4-26) **Mardi Gras** (Manchester; late Aug.)	**St. Patrick's Day** (Mar. 17) **Cork Guiness Jazz Festival** (Oct.)
CROATIA	**World Festival of Animated Film** (Zagreb; May)	**Int'l Folklore Festival** (July) **Zagreb Summer Festival** (July-Aug.)	**Int'l Puppet Festival** (Sept.) **Zagreb Fest** (Nov.)
CZECH REPUBLIC	**Prague Spring Festival** (mid-May to early July)	**Karlovy Vary Int'l Film Festival** (July) **Cesky Krumlov Int'l Music Fest** (Aug.)	**Int'l Organ Fest** (Olomouc; Sept.)
FRANCE	**Cannes Film Festival** (May)	**Festival d'Avignon** (July-Aug.) **Bastille Day** (July 14) **Tour de France** (July)	**Carnevale** (Nice, Nantes; Feb. 7-17) **Vineyard Festival** (Nice; Sept.)
GERMANY	**May Day** (Berlin; May 1) **Christopher St. Day** (late June) **G-Move** (early June)	**Love Parade** (early July) **Rhine in Flames Festival** (Rhine Valley; mid-Aug.)	**Fasching** (Munich; Jan. 7-Feb. 12) **Oktoberfest** (Munich; Sept. 21-Oct. 16) **Karneval** (Feb. 7-17)
HUNGARY	**Golden Shell Folklore** (Siófor; June)	**Sziget Rock Fest** (Budapest; July) **Baroque Festival** (Eger; July)	**Eger Vintage Days** (Sept.) **Festival of Winge Songs** (Pécs; Sept.)
ITALY	**Maggio Musicale** (Florence; May) **Scoppio del Carro** (Florence; Easter Su)	**Il Palio** (Siena; July 2, Aug. 16) **Umbria Jazz Festival** (July and Aug.)	**Carnevale** (Feb. 7-17) **Festa di San Gennaro** (Naples; Dec. 16, Sept. 19, 1st Sa in May) **Dante Festival** (Ravenna; mid-Sept.)
THE NETHERLANDS	**Queen's Day** (Apr. 30) **Holland Festival** (June)	**Gay Pride Parade** (Aug.)	**Flower Parade** (Aalsmeer; Sept.) **Cannabis Cup** (Nov.)
POLAND	**Int'l Short Film** (Kraków; May) **Festival of Jewish Culture** (Kraków; June)	**Street Theater** (Kraków; July) **Highlander Folklore** (Zakopane; Aug.)	**Kraków Jazz Fest** (Oct.) **Nat'l Blues Music** (Toruń; Nov.)
PORTUGAL	**Burning of the Ribbons** (Coimbra; early May)	**Feira Internacional de Lisboa** (June) **Feira Popular** (mid-July)	**Carnival** (mid-Mar.) **Semana Santa** (Mar. 24-31)
SCANDINAVIA	**Midsummer** (June 21-23) **Bergen Festival** (May) **Norwegian Wood** (Oslo; early June)	**Quart Music Festival** (Kristiansand; early July) **Savonlinna Opera Fest.** (early July to early Aug.)	**Helsinki Festival** (Aug. 23-Sept.8)
SPAIN	**Feria de Abril** (Sevilla; late Apr.)	**San Fermines** (Pamplona; July 6-14)	**Semana Santa** (Mar. 24-31) **Las Fallas** (Valencia; mid-Mar.) **Carnival** (Feb. 7-17)

SUGGESTED ITINERARIES

THE BASIC TOUR (1 OR 2 MONTHS)

THE BEST OF EUROPE IN 32 DAYS

THE BEST OF EUROPE IN 9 WEEKS

THE BEST OF EUROPE IN 1 MONTH

Start in **London** (3 days; p. 141), spinning from theater to museum to club, then chunnel to the sights and shops of **Paris** (3 days; p. 318). Sample the cuisine and nightlife of **Lyon** (1 day; p. 383) en route to glittering **Barcelona** (2 days; p. 867). Hit the French Riviera in **Nice** (1 day; p. 371), then dive into Renaissance art in **Florence** (2 days; p. 620). Allow **Rome** to awe you (3 days; p. 572) before gliding through **Venice** (2 days; p. 592). Break out the clubbing clothes in **Milan** (1 day; p. 606), then don your banker's suit in **Geneva** (1 day; p. 920). Grab a frothy pint in **Munich** (2 days; p. 453) and a cup of coffee in **Vienna** (2 days; p. 87). Follow the crowd to enrapturing **Prague** (2 days; p. 247), then head to hip **Kraków** (2 days; p. 742). Overwhelm yourself in sprawling **Berlin** (2 days; p. 400). Indulge in the goods in **Amsterdam** (2 days; p. 680), then finish off with a day in **Brussels** (p. 117).

THE BEST OF EUROPE IN 2 MONTHS

From **London** (4 days; p. 141), catch a cheap flight to energetic **Dublin** (2 days, p. 540). Get studious for a day in **Oxford** (1 day; p. 180), then take in the natural beauty of the **Cotswolds** en route to elegant **Bath** (2 days; p. 172). Then chunnel from London to the museums and cafes of **Paris** (4 days; p. 318), and explore the gorgeous châteaux of the **Loire Valley** (1 day; p. 355). Venture south to the all-night party in **Madrid** (2 days; p. 830), and marvel at the architectural gems of **Barcelona** (3 days; p. 867). Soak in the Riviera's rays at **Nice** (1 day; p. 371) and relax in Italy's **Cinque Terre** (1 day; p. 616). Continue on to the orange roofs of **Florence** (2 days; p. 620), and stop at stunning **Siena** (1 day; p. 630) en route to **Rome** (3 days; p. 572). Wind through **Venice** (2 days; p. 592) on your way to posh **Milan** (1 day; p. 606). Drop by **Lyon** (1 day; p. 383) before heading to **Geneva** (1 day; p. 920). Scale the Swiss Alps around **Zermatt** (1 day; p. 937) and **Interlaken** (1 day; p. 936). Do high culture in **Zürich** (1 day; p. 928) before indulging your passion for Mozart in **Salzburg** (1 day; p. 99). After an opera in **Vienna** (2 days; p. 87), soak in the baths of **Budapest** (2 days; p. 508). Check out the castle and churches in **Kraków** (2 days; p. 742), then head to **Prague** (3 days; p. 247) and gorgeous **Český Krumlov** (1 day; p. 263). Love your beer in **Munich** (2 days; p. 453), then take a sobering daytrip to **Dachau** (1 day; p. 461). Traverse the **Romantic Road** (2 days; p. 462) on your way to **Berlin** (3 days; p. 400). Head north to cosmopolitan **Copenhagen** (2 days; p. 271) and drop down to restless **Hamburg** (2 days; p. 427). Continue to **Amsterdam** (3 days; p. 680), and top off your trip in both **Brussels** (p. 117) or **Bruges** (p. 123).

REGIONAL ROUTES (20-40 DAYS)

THE BEST OF THE MEDITERRANEAN

THE MEDITERRANEAN (39 DAYS)

From **Madrid** take the high-speed train to flower-filled **Sevilla** (2 days; p. 852) before partying in the Costa del Sol resort town of **Marbella** (1 day; p. 859). Skip inland to **Granada** (2 days; p. 860) and wind your way through the Albacín to the Alhambra. From **Valencia** (2 days; p. 865) island hop in the **Balearic Islands** between the foam parties at **Ibiza** and **Formentera** (3 days; p. 889). Ferry to vibrant **Barcelona** (3 days; p. 867) before hitting the **Costa Brava** and the Dalí museum in **Figueres** (2 days; p. 880). Head to France and follow van Gogh's traces in **Arles** (1 day; p. 365). More glory awaits in **Avignon** (1 day; p. 364) before reveling in **Aix-en-Provence** (1 day; p. 366). Bask in spicy **Marseille** (1 day; p. 366) and move on to the glittery Côte d'Azur. Watch movie stars in flashy **Cannes** (1 day; p. 369) and keep up the action in the Riviera's capital, **Nice** (2 days; p. 371). If you have any money left, hit the world-famous casino at **Monte-Carlo** (1 day; p. 376). Vacation from your vacation in Italy's **Finale Ligure** (2 days; p. 615) and snap photos in **Pisa** (1 day; p. 631) before David-hopping in the magnificent art collection at **Florence** (3 days; p. 620). Check out the two-tone *duomo* of **Siena** (2 days; p. 630) and find a forum for all things ancient in **Rome** (4 days; p. 572). From **Naples** (2 days; p. 634), home to pizza and pickpockets, finish off your trip in captivating **Capri** (2 days; p. 640). Or, continue your journey using the **Greece** and **Turkey** itinerary.

BRITAIN AND IRELAND (28 DAYS)

After visiting **London** (4 days; p. 141), get studious in **Cambridge** (1 day; p. 185) and **Oxford** (1 day; p. 180). Explore the **Cotswolds** (1 day; p. 183) and **Bath** (1 day; p. 172). Check out Shakespeare's hometown, **Stratford-upon-Avon** (1 day; p. 184), also near Warwick Castle. Hit up the arts and nightlife in industrial **Manchester** (1 day; p. 188) before worshipping the Beatles in **Liverpool** (1 day; p. 190); or, check out the castles in **Conwy** and **Caernarfon** (1 day; p. 200). Depending on which route you choose, cross the Irish Sea from either Liverpool or Holyhead (near Conwy and Caernarfon; p. 200) to **Dublin** (3 days; p. 540), home to James Joyce and Guinness. Answer the call of rural Ireland in the heather-covered **Wicklow Mountains** (1 day; p. 549) and the **Ring of Kerry** (2½ days; p. 554). **Galway** (1½ days; p. 557), a center of Irish culture, is also close to the limestone land-

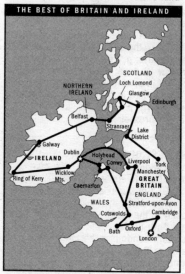

THE BEST OF BRITAIN AND IRELAND

scape of the Aran Islands. Then on to politically divided and exciting **Belfast** (2 days; p. 561). From there it's back across the Irish Sea to **Stranraer,** then on a train to energetic **Glasgow** (1 day; p. 207) and nearby **Loch Lomond.** Explore historic **Edinburgh** (3 days; p. 202) and the sublime **Lake District** (2 days; p. 193); **York** (1 day; p. 191) completes the southbound journey. Return to London to kick back with a West End play and a Guinness.

SPAIN AND PORTUGAL (25 DAYS)

Hop off the Paris-Madrid train at gorgeous **San Sebastián** (2 days; p. 884), then check out the new Guggenheim in **Bilbao** (1 day; p. 887) before having some urban fun in **Madrid** (3 days; p. 830). Take a daytrip to the winding streets of **Toledo** (1 day; p. 842), then head to serenely beautiful **Trujillo** (1 day; p. 847). Cross the border into Portugal to marvel at the painted tiles in **Lisbon** (2½ days; p. 756). Bake in the sun along the Algarve in **Lagos** (2½ days; p. 766) before heading to **Algeciras** to catch a ferry into Morocco. Head to **Fez** via **Tangier** (2 days; p. 673) before returning to Spain for the flower-filled plazas of **Sevilla** (2½ days; p. 852). Don't forget to see **Córdoba**'s stunning mosque (1 day; p. 847). Tan some more in **Marbella** (1½ day; p. 859), then love the Alhambra in **Granada** (2 days; p. 860). In northeastern Spain, hit the sunny **Costa Brava** (2 days; p. 880) and the Dalí Museum in **Figueres** (1 day; p. 880). Then meet up with the two-month itinerary at **Barcelona** (p. 867).

CENTRAL EUROPE (22-25 DAYS)

For the long route, link up from **Berlin** to **Gdańsk** (1 day; p. 749) stopping off in **Toruń** (1 day; p. 749), the home of Copernicus on the way to sprawling **Warsaw** (3 days; p. 733); then head to trendy **Kraków** (3 days; p. 742). Or, skip straight from **Prague** to **Kraków**. From there, take a hike in the Tatra Mountains surrounding **Zakopane** (2 days; p. 747) and **Starý Smokovec** (1 day; p. 748). Next stop is vibrant **Budapest** (3 days; p. 508), then the shallow waters of **Lake Balaton** (2 days; p. 522). In Croatia, get down in **Zagreb** (2 days; p. 233), and sample the Dalmatian Coast in **Dubrovnik** (3 days; p. 238) and **Split** (2 days; p. 236). Then pass through lovely **Ljubljana** (2 days; p. 821) before linking up with the basic route in **Venice** (p. 592) or **Vienna** (p. 87).

BEST OF GREECE AND TURKEY

THE BEST OF THE BLACK SEA

GREECE AND TURKEY (28 DAYS)

Hop off the boot from **Brindisi** or **Bari,** where overnight ferries go to Greece (1 day). Get off at **Corfu** (1 day; p. 490), beloved by literary luminaries and partyers alike, then continue on to **Patras** (1 day; p. 480). Discover the "mysteries of love" in the ruins of **Corinth** (1 day; p. 484). On to chaotic **Athens,** a jumble of things ancient and modern (2 days; p. 472), then the Cyclades. Party all night long on **Mykonos** (p. 494), then daytrip to sacred **Delos** (p. 494) before continuing on to the earthly paradise of **Santorini** (total 4 days; p. 497). Catch the ferry to **Crete,** where chic **Iraklion** and **Knossos,** home to the Minotaur, await (2 days; p. 497). Base yourself in **Rethymno** or **Hania** and hike the spectacular **Samaria Gorge** (2 days; p. 499). Backtrack to Iraklion to catch the ferry to the Dodecanese, hitting historical **Rhodes** (2 days; p. 501) and partying in **Kos** (1 day; p. 502). Cross over to **Bodrum,** Turkey, the "Bedroom of the Mediterranean" (2 days; p. 961). From there, two routes diverge; they both meet up in **Cappadocia.** If you've come to see **ruins,** head up to **Kuşadasi** to check out the crumbling magnificence at **Ephesus** (1½ days; p. 960). Move on to the thermal springs of **Pamukkale** and **Aphrodisias** (2½ days; p. 960); then on to Cappadocia. Or, if you're into **beaches,** head from Bodrum to **Fethiye** and serene **Ölüdeniz** (1 day; p. 963) and the eternal flame of **Olimpos** (2 days; p. 964); then experience the surreal world of **Göreme** (2 days; p. 966) in Cappadocia. Take an overnight bus to **İstanbul** and go a little crazy (3 days; p. 944) before heading home or linking up with the **Black Sea** itinerary.

THE BLACK SEA (19 DAYS)

From **İstanbul,** discover the lovely beach town of **Sozopol** (2 days; p. 229) on the Bulgarian Black Sea coast. Zip through **Sofia** (1 day; p. 222) to **Bucharest** (3 days; p. 777), once the gem of Romania. Detour to **Braşov,** in the heart of Transylvania (2 days; p. 781). Head up to **Odessa** (3 days; p. 978), the former USSR's party town, then head via **Simferopol** to beachy **Yalta** (3 days; p. 978). Catch the night train to ancient **Kiev** (3 days; p. 973), then pass through **Lviv** (2 days; p. 976) to link up with the two-month or Central Europe itinerary in **Kraków** (p. 742).

THE BALTIC SEA (22 DAYS)

Take the ferry from Helsinki or the train from Central or Eastern Europe to reach the charming medieval streets of **Tallinn** (2 days; p. 290), then relax on the tranquil and secluded **Estonian Islands** (4 days; p. 293). Move on to lively **Tartu,** the oldest city in the Baltics (2 days; p. 293), before immersing yourself in the Soviet-ness of **Rīga** (2 days; p. 646). Swing over to **Klaipėda** in Lithuania and relax on the dreamy beach at **Nida** (2 day; p. 659). Continue to up-and-coming **Vilnius** (3 days; p. 654), one of the many "New Pragues," then get some shut-eye on the night train to **Moscow,** where you can survey Red Square and see history in action (4 days; p. 790). Cap it off spending some time in **St. Petersburg,** home of the ornate delights of the Hermitage (3 days; p. 800).

THE BEST OF BALTIC EUROPE

DISCOVER

THE BEST OF SCANDINAVIA

SCANDINAVIA (20 DAYS)

From modern **Copenhagen** (4 days; p. 271), daytrip to the glorious Elsinore castle in **Helsingør** (1 day; p. 278). Head to Sweden through **Malmo** (1 day; p. 908) to reach luxurious **Gothenburg** (2 days; p. 909). Zip to Norway's bustling capital, **Oslo** (2 days; p. 707) and take the Oslo-Bergen railway to reach lovely **Bergen** (2 days; p. 714) before diving into the fjords. Marvel at the natural wonders that are **Sognefjord** (1 day; p. 720) and **Geirangerfjord** (1 day; p. 722), and head back to Oslo. Sleep your way on the night train to Sweden's **Stockholm** (2 days; p. 898), the jewel of Scandinavia. Take a daytrip to **Uppsala** (1 day; p. 906), home of Sweden's oldest university. Hop on the ferry to Finland's **Helsinki** (2 days; p. 299), where east meets west, and daytrip to **Porvoo** (1 day; p. 304). Ferry to Estonia's **Tallinn** (p. 290) to link with the **Baltic Sea** itinerary.

THE STORY OF EUROPE

(AN ABRIDGED VERSION)

Europe has enough history and culture to keep you busy for a lifetime. Here it is short and sweet. Our quick primer—split into historical time periods as well as cultural movements—will get you up to speed before you see Europe for yourself.

CLASSICAL GREECE AND ROME

The Golden Age of ancient Greece, particularly the two powerful city-states **Athens** and **Sparta**, witnessed the birth of many modern concepts: the world's first democracy, historical documentation, and philosophy. But the glory of Greece came to a halt with the **Peloponnesian War** between Athens and Sparta, which left Greece politically unstable in the hands of the victorious Spartans. Nearby Macedonia took advantage of Sparta's poor leadership and conquered Greece, uniting the country in a fight against Persia. **Alexander** took charge of Greece, gaining a huge empire of more than one million square miles as well as the nickname "The Great".

This period also saw the rise of **Rome,** which soon conquered Greece, spreading Greek culture and ideas across the massive empire it established. Despite all its glory, the Roman Empire split into two halves: a western empire whose capital was Rome, and an eastern empire whose capital was Constantinople. The western crumbled soon after the invading Germanic **Visigoths** captured Rome. The eastern half of the empire survived, flourishing as the **Byzantine Empire.**

500-200 BC
Classical and Hellenistic Greece

431-404
Peloponnesian War

27 BC-AD 293
Imperial Rome

476
Fall of Rome

THE MIDDLE AGES

In the West, great cities fell apart and the orderly rule of Roman law ended during the following **Middle Ages.** The fallen western empire sank into **feudalism,** a system of allegiance and service in exchange for protection. During the **Dark Ages,** a period of political and cultural stagnation, the **Christian Church** became increasingly powerful, becoming one of the few bastions of knowledge and civilization in the West. **Charlemagne,** king of the Franks, united Europe under his control. But at his death, his sons divided his empire, leading to Europe's political and cultural breakup. Europe became somewhat unified by the bloody **Crusades,** an expedition in which Christians from all over Europe traveled to Jerusalem to fight Muslims. The Crusades brought Europe into contact with new lands and new ideas, stimulating European creativity.

800
Charlemagne crowned Holy Roman Emperor

1095-1291
Holy Wars: the seven Crusades

1347-52
Black Plague kills one-third of Europe

THE RENAISSANCE

Universities sprang up all over Europe, with Paris becoming the primary center of learning. At Italian universities, scholars took

1450
Gutenberg invents printing press

1490s
Beginning of the Age of Exploration

1517
Luther posts his *95 Theses*

1618-48
Thirty Years' War

1643
Louis XIV becomes the King of France

1682-1725
Peter the Great campaigns to reform Russia

1700-1800
The Industrial Revolution kicks off in Northern England

1751-1770s
Diderot's *Encyclopedia* is published

1756-63
Seven Years' War

new interest in the Greek and Roman world, sparking the "rebirth" of learning known as the **Renaissance.** The driving force behind the Renaissance was **humanism,** the idea that the arts deserved praise in their own rights and not just as a means of religious expression. **Realism** characterized the artwork of the period, with the use of perspective and the focus on accurate human anatomy. The revival of ancient Greek and Roman values corresponded with a gradual decline in the cultural power of the Church.

THE REFORMATION

As more people read the Bible, many decided that the Church's teachings had moved away from the Bible's original meaning. Church leaders seemed extravagant, selling **indulgences** to reduce time spent in purgatory. A German monk named **Martin Luther** nailed a list of criticisms of the Church called the *95 Theses* to the door of **Wittenberg Cathedral** (p. 426). His ideas quickly spread across Europe, sparking the **Reformation.** His supporters, who opposed the Catholics, became known as the **Protestants.** The tensions between the two groups exploded into a century of religious wars.

ABSOLUTISM

After the Reformation, the Church was no longer the dominant governing power. That role was soon filled by a series of "absolute" monarchs. **Louis XIV** of France reputedly declared, "L'état, c'est moi" ("I am the state"), indicating that all power was consolidated in the hands of the king. States that had been fragmented were now being reassembled into huge conglomerate empires. **Leopold I** established control over Austria, added Hungary, and combined the two under the powerful **Habsburg Empire.** In Germany, **Frederick I** unified the various German regions into Brandenburg-Prussia, and literally crowned himself its king. In the east, **Ivan IV** declared himself czar of Russia; the rapid expansion of his empire across almost the entire continent earned him the title "the Awe-inspiring," although it's usually translated as "the Terrible."

THE ENLIGHTENMENT

Toward the end of the era came a renewed interest in nature, sparking scientific experimentation and inquiry. In *On the Revolution of Heavenly Bodies*, **Copernicus** declared that the earth orbited the sun; **Kepler** and **Galileo** built on his theories. When Galileo refined the telescope, he helped begin the **Age of Exploration;** ships could now reach new lands in North America, Asia, and Africa. The newfound spirit of intellectualism gave rise to the **Enlightenment,** a time of tremendous faith in human reason. In England, **Isaac Newton** laid the groundwork for the field of physics and **Francis Bacon** declared that science could explain everything, while in France **Denis Diderot** attempted to compile all human knowledge in his *Encyclopedia.* "Enlightened" rulers saw themselves as servants of the state and began to institute reforms: **Joseph II** of Austria granted freedom of the press and limited freedom of religion, while **Catherine the Great** instituted legal reform in Russia.

THE FRENCH REVOLUTION

The Enlightenment had generated the idea that all men were created equal, but reality hadn't caught up to philosophy. In France, the excesses of Louis XVI's court combined with widespread hunger to bring these tensions to the breaking point. Inspired by the recent American Revolution, the French staged their own revolt, storming the **Bastille** (p. 335) and drafting a new constitution. However, the revolution soon deteriorated into the **Reign of Terror,** a time when enemies (including the royal family) were executed at the **Place de la Concorde** (p. 335). Taking advantage of this crisis, **Napoleon Bonaparte** seized power in 1799 and declared himself emperor. He conquered much of Europe, but his attempt to invade Russia failed miserably, and after a brief period of exile and escape, Napoleon was defeated for good at **Waterloo** (p. 122).

1789
French Revolution begins

1793
Louis XIV is tried and hanged; the "Reign of Terror" begins

THE INDUSTRIAL REVOLUTION

The reason and science of the Enlightenment produced another type of revolution: the **Industrial Revolution.** A series of inventions such as the spinning jenny, the flying shuttle, and the steam engine paved the way for mass production and increased mechanization in the 19th century. Urban areas expanded rapidly, and most of the lower classes worked over 18 hours in factories or mines. Increasing domestic products and competition for colonies overseas provoked strong feelings of **nationalism—** the idea that people gain their identity from their nationality. In **1848** over 50 revolutions erupted across Europe as fractured regions like France, Italy, Austria, and Germany tried to form themselves into cohesive nations. Toward the end of the century, **Metternich** consolidated Austria and **Bismarck** unified Germany into a powerful empire. However, the new nations were unstable, putting Europe on shaky ground.

1799-1814
Napoleon comes to power but falls at Waterloo

1800-50
Industrial Revolution spreads throughout Western Europe

1867
Dual monarchy of Austria-Hungary created

1880-1914
Age of Imperialism; scramble for Africa and Asia

WORLD WAR I

At the turn of the 20th century, Europe split into two power alignments: the **Triple Alliance** and the **Triple Entente.** Tensions exploded when Archduke Ferdinand, heir to the Austro-Hungarian throne, was assassinated during his visit to **Sarajevo,** sparking **World War I.** After over four years of trench warfare and heavy artillery, Germany and its allies could no longer continue to fight. The **Treaty of Versailles** placed such an economic burden on Germany that international tensions lingered for decades. Meanwhile, popular frustration with Tsarist government and Russia's crippled wartime economy erupted in the **Russian Revolution.** The **Bolsheviks** came to power in 1917, establishing Russia's first communist government, led by **Vladimir Lenin.** The old Russian empire crumbled, leading to the birth of many newly independent Eastern European nations in the 1920s, such as Czechoslovakia and Yugoslavia.

1914
World War I begins

1918
World War I ends with Allied victory

1918-21
Civil war in Russia between the Bolsheviks and Mensheviks

WORLD WAR II

The 1930s saw economic stagnation and the proliferation of dictatorships across Europe. When **Adolf Hitler** invaded Poland, Britain and France declared war, beginning **World War II.** Russia joined the war in 1941, and the United States joined in 1942, ultimately defeating Germany. Warsaw, Budapest, and Bel-

1920
Adolf Hitler creates the Nazi Party

1939-45
World War II

1941-45
Six million Jews die
in the Holocaust

1945
United Nations
formed at Yalta

1949
NATO founded

1953
Stalin dies

1956
Suez Canal crisis

1961
Construction of
Berlin Wall

1962
Cuban Missile
Crisis almost
brings nuclear war

1986
Chernobyl disaster
spreads radioac-
tive gases

1989
Fall of Berlin Wall
and Iron Curtain

1992
EEA founded

1995
Civil War between
Croats, Muslims,
and Serbs

1998-99
War in Kosovo
between Alba-
nians and Serbs

grade were ruined; Berlin and London were also heavily damaged. Hitler's **"final solution"** nearly eliminated Jewish communities in Eastern Europe.

THE LAST FIFTY YEARS

THE COLD WAR. By the end of World War II, differences between the USSR and the Western nations had grown into barely concealed hostility. Fifteen Western nations joined together to form the **North Atlantic Treaty Organization (NATO)** in order to "keep the Americans in, the Russians out, and the Germans down", starting the 40-year period known as the **Cold War.** Tensions peaked in the 1960s and 1970s as powerful nuclear weapons were developed. In 1985, however, Soviet leader **Mikhail Gorbachev** instituted two new polices—*perestroika* (restructuring) and *glasnost* (openness)—and the Eastern bloc began to break down. The Berlin Wall fell, and the Soviet Union collapsed soon after when **Boris Yeltsin** ousted Gorbachev. Recent years have seen democratic elections and increased personal freedom in the former Soviet republics, although some areas have been devastated by ethnic conflict.

GLOBALIZATION. World War II showed that an international organization was necessary to prevent a third global war. In 1945, the **United Nations (UN)** was intended as a forum for resolving international disputes. Economically, Europe has become increasingly unified. The formation of the **European Economic Community** eliminated tariffs between members, and the **European Economic Area** eliminated national barriers for the movement of goods, services, workers, and capital. In July 2002, all countries in the **European Union (EU)** will replace their currencies with the **Euro** (p. 21).

SOCIAL MOVEMENTS. The postwar era also saw the rise of the **welfare state.** Sweden and other Scandinavian nations began allocating funds for public housing, education, and the unemployed; Britain and other nations soon followed their example. As the state took responsibility for the public's well-being, it replaced the church's traditional charity role, leading to increased **secularization.** Women also benefited in the postwar era. *The Second Sex* by **Simone de Beauvoir** advocated equality for women, prompting France to grant women equal access to civil service jobs and to guarantee **equal pay for equal work.** Other nations followed suit, and the percentage of working women in France, Britain, and Germany nearly doubled.

In the postwar era, the number of cars in Europe increased **air pollution** and **acid rain.** Some nations passed new environmental protection laws, while others tried to find alternative sources of energy such as **nuclear power.**

EUROPEAN CULTURE
FROM CLASSICISM TO COMMERCIALISM

Parthenon. Athens, Greece (**p. 476**). The Parthenon captures the grace, balance, and perfection of Greek architecture. Its blend of the simple Doric and elegant Ionian styles was the ideal of Classical architecture.

Troy, Turkey (p. 957). The city of Troy was the inspiration for Homer's epic poems about the Trojan War, the *Iliad* and the *Odyssey*. Homer's works influenced authors of the Western world for centuries, laying the foundation for the European Classical tradition.

Colosseum. Rome, Italy (**p. 584**). The Colosseum, which once drew huge crowds to its bloody gladiator fights, exemplifies Roman architecture with its refined arches. Like Rome's culture, Roman buildings drew on Greek traditions.

Pio-Clementine Museum. Rome, Italy (p. 588). The collection of antique sculpture exemplifies expressive Roman art, particularly the Laocoön sculpture of sea serpents attacking a Trojan priest and his sons. Virgil told the story of the Laocoön family in his famed *Aeneid*.

Ancient Greece and Rome lay the foundations for European art. Greek sculptures captured movement and expression, while Greek architecture featured flawless buildings based on simple shapes. Roman art incorporated these Greek features to a larger scale. Both Greek and Roman culture had a lasting influence, becoming reincarnated in later movements like the Renaissance and Neoclassicism.

MEDIEVAL AND BYZANTINE

In the **Dark Ages,** the arts came to a halt everywhere but the Church. In the eastern world of the **Byzantine Empire,** however, the arts continued to flourish as they had in Greek and Roman times. In the east art was also rooted in the Church, and basilicas were adorned with colorful mosaics and golden icons portraying religious scenes.

Santiago de Compostella, Spain (p. 891). In medieval times when the Church dominated everyday life, worshippers flocked to this town—considered the end of a pilgrimage that was thought to reduce time in purgatory.

Salisbury Cathedral. Salisbury, England (p. 177). Britain's largest medieval cathedral, the Salisbury Cathedral was built to capture God's glory in stone and glass.

Cathédrale de Notre-Dame de Paris. Paris, France (p. 333). A well-known example of medieval architecture, the Gothic cathedral has pointed steeples and huge stained-glass windows. Its façade depicts religious scenes and figures that would have educated the poor about the bible.

Basilica di San Vitale. Ravenna, Italy (**p. 619**). The mosaics in San Vitale feature the formal poses and holy figures characteristic of religious Byzantine art.

"Our Lady of Vladimir". Moscow, Russia; Tretyakov Gallery (p. 798). Unlike earlier Byzantine art, "Our Lady of Vladimir" goes beyond religious expression. The mother's interaction with the child is more human and tender—representative of the developing humanism that would fuel the Renaissance.

RENAISSANCE

In Italy, a renewed interest in Classical Greek and Roman civilization sparked the rebirth of the arts and sciences throughout Europe known as the **Renaissance.** Wealthy patrons eager to display their power supported the arts, which began moving away from the Church; **humanism,** or art for art's sake, was the Renaissance mentality. The development of perspective and a scientific interest in human anatomy brought artistic perfection to the works of masters like Leonardo da Vinci, Michelangelo, and Raphael.

"School of Athens". Rome, Italy; The Vatican (p. 588). Raphael's painting pays tribute to ancient Greek thinkers like Plato and Aristotle. Many of the Greek figures bear resemblance to artistic masters of the Renaissance, revealing the movement's link to the Classical past.

Shakespeare's Globe Theatre. London, England (p. 159). As Europe emerged from the Dark Ages, the arts flourished. A renewed interest in theater led playwrights like William Shakespeare to write experimental works that combined elements of tragedy and comedy.

Chambord Palace. Loire Valley, France (p. 354). The most imaginative of the Loire Valley châteaux, the Chambord Palace features the geometric shapes characteristic of renaissance architecture as well as graceful details.

Cattedrale di Santa Maria del Fiore. Florence, Italy (p. 626). Brunelleschi, one of the most famed renaissance architects, designed the dome. The cathedral's design is based on the simple shapes of ancient Greek and Roman architecture.

"Mona Lisa". Paris, France; Musée du Louvre (p. 337). Leonardo da Vinci's masterpiece is a renowned example of renaissance portraiture. Although somewhat overrepresented today, it represents a fresh style of painting.

BAROQUE AND ROCOCO

"Ecstasy of Saint Theresa". Rome, Italy; Church of Santa Maria della Vittoria (p. 587). Giovanni Lorenzo Bernini was one of the quintessential Baroque artists. This statue represents the style with its billowing robes and intense drama.

Palace at Versailles. Versailles, France (p. 344). The monumental size, dramatic layout, and ornate decorations symbolized the power, grandeur, and luxury of the era's absolute monarchs.

Johann-Sebastian-Bach-Museum. Leipzig, Germany (p. 424). The museum depicts the life of one of the greatest Baroque composers, whose music utilized the exaggerated movements typical of the style.

Gemaldgalerie der Neuen Meister. Dresden, Germany (p. 422). The gallery contains several works by Jean-Antoine Watteau, one of the most prominent Rococo painters. *Plaisirs d'Amour* (Pleasures of Love) probably exemplifies the style best.

Baroque art was a reaction against the straight lines and regularly ordered layouts of Renaissance art and architecture. The word "baroque" still refers to something that is irregular, illogical, or unexpectedly eccentric. As the Enlightenment sapped the power of the aristocracy, Baroque mellowed into **Rococo,** which, like the declining aristocracy, was primarily nonfunctional and mostly decorative.

ENLIGHTENMENT AND NEOCLASSICISM

The Panthéon. Paris, France (p. 334). Buried in the crypt are two of the greatest Enlightenment thinkers: Voltaire, author of *Candide;* and Rousseau, a proto-anarchist. The building itself is an excellent example of Neoclassical architecture. Its façade imitates the Roman Pantheon.

Saint Paul's Cathedral. London, England (p. 157). Designed by Sir Christopher Wren, the church features graceful columns and a beautiful Neoclassical dome.

Musée du Louvre. Paris, France (p. 337). Houses several works by Jacques-Louis David, one of the main Neoclassical painters. His *Oath of the Horatii* uses Classical elements while retaining the drama of the previous Baroque era. Delacroix's *Napoleon Crossing the Alps* glorifies the French leader.

Mozarts Wohnhaus and Geburtshaus. Salzburg, Austria (p. 103). Neoclassical music flourished in the German-speaking areas of Europe. Composers like Mozart rejected romantic expressiveness, and created music that was polished and melodic. For the first time, instrumental music became more important than vocal music.

The increased faith in man's intellect gave rise to a myriad of new writers, philosophers, and ideas that formed the **Enlightenment.** Artists and architects also began to see the previous Baroque and Rococo styles of art as too frivolous. The discovery of the Roman cities of Herculaneum and Pompeii (p. 638) in the early 18th century prompted these artists to create works rooted in Classical Greek and Roman tradition— hence, **Neoclassicism.**

ROMANTICISM AND IMPRESSIONISM

The **Romantic** movement grew in reaction to the intellectualism of the Enlightenment. Romantic artists valued emotion over reason, looked for authentic experience in themselves and in nature, and tried to break free of religious and social convention. The **Impressionist** movement arose as a reaction against industrialization, focusing on the perceptions of the individual artist.

Goethehaus and **Goethe-Nationalmuseum.** Weimar, Germany (p. 424). A prominent romantic, Johann Wolfgang van Goethe once wrote, "Feeling is everything."

Keats-Shelley Memorial Museum. Rome, Italy (p. 586). The house where the young poet John Keats succumbed to consumption 1821.

Houses of Parliament. London, England (p. 160). The Gothic Revival style gives the building a medieval feel; its turrets, towers and pointed spires reflect the soul's yearning to reach God. The romantic resurgence of faith may explain the renewed interest in Gothic.

Musée d'Orsay. Paris, France (p. 337). *The* place for Impressionist art, featuring works by Edgar Degas, Pierre-Auguste Renoir, Edouard Manet, and Camille Pissaro.

Karl-Marx-Haus. Trier, Germany (p. 445). So Karl Marx isn't an Impressionist, but he has similar concerns about the dehumanizing effects of industrialization in works such as the *Communist Manifesto* and *Das Kapital*.

MODERNISM

The ills of industrialization and the horror of the world wars drove many to make art that broke with previous norms. Diverse artistic movements such as **Abstract Expressionism, Existentialism, Dadaism, Surrealism,** and **Cubism** flourished. Writers like Franz Kafka wrote tales of alienation and despair, while artists across Europe turned to the fractured and the bizarre to express a growing feeling of disorientation.

Eiffel Tower. Paris, France (p. 334). It may be clichéd now, but when it was built the Eiffel Tower was a showcase of the newest materials and construction techniques of the Industrial Era.

Bertolt-Brecht-Haus. Berlin, Germany (p. 412). Visit the house of Bertolt Brecht, whose plays *The Three-Penny Opera* defied convention and satirized war.

James Joyce Cultural Center. Dublin, Ireland (p. 546). Honors the author that changed modern fiction with his English-bending prose. His novel *Ulysses*, which tells the story of one day in one man's life, is reenacted all over Dublin on Bloomsday (June 16).

Collezione Peggy Guggenheim. Venice, Italy (p. 599). Houses a superb collection of surrealist paintings, including works by Salvador Dalí, Max Ernst, and René Magritte.

Museo Reina Sofia. Madrid, Spain (p. 839). See Pablo Picasso's masterwork *Guernica*, which depicts the bombing of a Basque town during the Spanish Civil War in a fractured cubist style.

Teatre-Museu Dalí. Figueres, Spain (p. 880). Displays the work of Salvador Dalí, whose erotic and nightmarish dreamscapes defined surrealism.

POST-WAR MOVEMENTS

Centre Pompidou. Paris, France (p. 337). The building features a funky inside-out design with brightly colored exterior piping. It holds a museum of modern art as well as contemporary exhibit halls.

Bauhaus Museum. Weimar, Germany (p. 424). Founded to fulfill Walter Gropius' dictum "form follows function", the Bauhaus sought to unify art and technology.

Moderna Museet. Stockholm, Sweden (p. 903). The museum displays an impressive array of pop art, a movement whose creators (including Andy Warhol and Roy Lichtenstein) drew inspiration from commercial printing techniques.

Kunst Haus Wien. Vienna, Austria (p. 97). Artist-activist Friedrich Hundertwasser designed this building without any straight lines (which he called "the devil's work").

Karlovy Vary International Film Festival. Czech Republic (p. 261). Founded in 1936, this festival acted as a communist propaganda tool for decades. Recently, it's attracted some of the best films in Europe.

Since World War II, art has taken a turn for the extreme, the massive, and above all, the commercial. Nabokov's *Lolita* and Beckett's *Waiting for Godot* pushed the limits of literature, while architecture rose to new heights in modern metropolises. Art and technology merged as commercial production techniques were adopted in the art world. Film, radio and television rose to prominence, with mass media dominating culture.

ESSENTIALS

ENTRANCE REQUIREMENTS.
Passport (p. 19): Required for all citizens visiting any European country.
Visa (p. 20): Western European countries require visas for citizens of South Africa, but not for citizens of Australia, Canada, Ireland, New Zealand, the UK, or the US (for stays shorter than 3 months). Eastern European countries are more likely to require visas. Belarus, Russia, and Ukraine require invitations.
Immunizations (p. 30): Travelers to Europe should be up to date on vaccines for measles, mumps, rubella, diptheria, tetanus, pertussis, polio, haemophilus influenza B, hepatitis B, and hepatitis A.
Work Permit (p. 21): Required for all foreigners planning to work in Europe, except for citizens of EU member countries.
Driving Permit (p. 76): An International Driving Permit is required for those planning to drive.

DOCUMENTS AND FORMALITIES

PASSPORTS

REQUIREMENTS. Citizens of Australia, Canada, Ireland, New Zealand, South Africa, the UK, and the US need valid passports to enter European countries and to reenter their own countries. Most countries do not allow entrance if the holder's passport expires in under six months. Returning home with an expired passport is illegal, and may result in a fine.

PHOTOCOPIES. Be sure to photocopy the page of your passport with your photo, passport number, and other identifying information, as well as any visas, travel insurance policies, plane tickets, or traveler's check serial numbers. Carry one set of copies in a safe place, apart from the originals, and leave another set at home. Consulates also recommend that you carry an expired passport or an official copy of your birth certificate in a part of your baggage separate from other documents.

LOST PASSPORTS. If you lose your passport, immediately notify the local police and the nearest embassy or consulate of your home government. To expedite its replacement, you will need to know all information previously recorded and show ID and proof of citizenship. In some cases, a replacement may take weeks to process, and it may be valid only for a limited time. Any visas stamped in your old passport will be irretrievably lost. In an emergency, ask for immediate temporary traveling papers that will permit you to reenter your home country. Your passport is a public document belonging to your nation's government. You may have to surrender it to a foreign government official, but if you don't get it back in a reasonable amount of time, inform the nearest mission of your home country.

NEW PASSPORTS. Citizens of Australia, Canada, Ireland, New Zealand, the UK, and the US can apply for a passport at the nearest post office, passport office, or court of law. Citizens of South Africa can apply for a passport at the nearest office of Foreign Affairs. Any new passport or renewal applications must be filed well in advance of the departure date, although most passport offices offer rush services for a steep fee. Citizens living abroad who need a passport or renewal services should contact the nearest consular service of their home country.

Australia: ☎ 13 12 32; passports.australia@dfat.gov.au; www.passports.gov.au. Apply at a post office, passport office, or an overseas embassy or diplomatic mission. Passports AUS$132 (32-page) or AUS$198 (64-page); valid for 10 years. Under 18 AUS$66 (32-page) or AUS$99 (64-page); valid for 5 years.

Canada: Passport Office, Department of Foreign Affairs and International Trade, Ottawa, ON K1A 0G3 (☎ 800-567-6868 or 613-994-3500; www.dfait-maeci.gc.ca/passport). Applications available at passport offices, Canadian missions, and post offices. Passports CDN$60; valid for 5 years.

Ireland: Pick up an application at a Garda station or post office, or request one from a passport office. Then apply by mail to the Department of Foreign Affairs, Passport Office, Molesworth St., Dublin 2 (☎(01) 671 1633; fax 671 1092; www.irlgov.ie/iveagh), or the Passport Office, Irish Life Building, 1A South Mall, Cork (☎(021) 27 25 25 or (021) 27 69 64). Passports IR£45 (32-page) or IR£55 (48-page); valid for 10 years. Under 16 or over 65 IR£10; valid for 3 years.

New Zealand: Send applications to the Passport Office, Department of International Affairs, P.O. Box 10526, Wellington (☎(0800) 225 050 or (04) 474 8100; fax (04) 474 8010; www.passports.govt.nz; passports@dia.govt.nz). Standard processing time is 10 working days. Passports NZ$80; valid for 10 years. Children NZ$40; valid for 5 years. 3 day "urgent service" NZ$160; children NZ $120.

South Africa: Department of Home Affairs (usaembassy.southafrica.net/visaforms/passport/passport2000.html). Passports are issued only in Pretoria, but all applications must still be submitted or forwarded to the nearest South African consulate. Processing time is 3 months or more. Passports SAR192; valid for 10 years. Children SAR136; valid for 5 years.

UK: ☎(0870) 521 0410; www.open.gov.uk/ukpass/ukpass.htm. Get an application from a passport office, main post office, travel agent, or online (UK residents only) at www.ukpa.gov.uk/forms/f_app_pack.htm. Apply by mail, in person at a passport office, or through a High Street Partner (UK£4 extra). The process takes about 4 weeks; faster service is an additional £12 at the passport office. Passports UK£28; valid for 10 years. Under 15 UK£14.80; valid for 5 years.

US: For passport services and information: visit www.travel.state.gov/passport_services.html; or call ☎ 1-900-225-5674 (US$0.35 per min.) or 1-888-362-8668 (US$4.95 per call). Apply at any US Passport Agency, authorized post office, or federal or state courthouse; see the US Government/State Department section of the telephone book or a post office for addresses. Processing takes 3-4 weeks. Passports may be renewed by mail or in person for US$40. Add US$35 for 3-day expedited service. New passports US$60; valid for 10 years. Under 16 US$40; valid for 5 years.

VISAS, INVITATIONS, & WORK PERMITS

VISAS. Some countries require a visa—a stamp, sticker, or insert in your passport specifying the purpose of your travel and the permitted duration of your stay—in addition to a valid passport for entrance. Most standard visas cost US$10-70, are valid for one to three months, and must be validated within six months to one year from the date of issue. Many countries are willing to grant double-entry visas for a premium. The **Center for International Business and Travel** (**CIBT;** US ☎ 800-925-2428) secures visas for travel to almost any country for a variable service charge.

The requirements in the chart below only apply to tourist stays shorter than three months. If you plan to stay longer than 90 days, or if you plan to work or study abroad, your requirements will differ. In any case, check with the nearest embassy or consulate of your desired destination for up-to-date information. US citizens can also consult www.travel.state.gov/foreignentryreqs.html.

Note that the following countries are not listed in this chart: **Austria, Belgium, Croatia, Denmark, Finland, France, Germany, Greece, Iceland, Italy, Luxembourg, the Netherlands, Norway, Portugal, Slovenia, Spain,** and **Sweden.** These require visas of South Africans, but not nationals of Australia, Canada, Ireland, New Zealand, the UK, or the US (for stays shorter than three months). Also not listed are the

> **ONE EUROPE.** The idea of European unity has come a long way since 1958, when the European Economic Community (EEC) was created in order to promote solidarity and cooperation between its six founding states. Since then, the EEC has become the European Union (EU), with political, legal, and economic institutions spanning 15 member states: Austria, Belgium, Denmark, Finland, France, Germany, Greece, Ireland, Italy, Luxembourg, the Netherlands, Portugal, Spain, Sweden, and the UK.
>
> What does this have to do with the average non-EU tourist? Well, the Schengen Treaty, fully implemented since 1995, has resulted in **freedom of movement** across 14 European countries—the entire EU minus Denmark, Ireland, and the UK, but plus Iceland and Norway. This means that border controls between participating countries have been abolished, and visa policies harmonized. While you're still required to carry a passport (or government-issued ID card for EU citizens) when crossing an internal border, once you've been admitted into one country, you're free to travel to all participating states. Britain and Ireland have also formed a **common travel area,** abolishing passport controls between the UK and the Republic of Ireland, meaning that the only times you'll see a border guard within the EU are traveling between the British Isles and the Continent—and of course, in and out of Denmark.
>
> For more important consequences of the EU for travelers, see **The Euro** (p. 24) and **European Customs** (p. 23).

ESSENTIALS

UK, Ireland, Malta, and **Switzerland,** which do not require visas for any of the seven nationalities listed above (including South Africans) for stays shorter than 90 days. Travelers to **Andorra** should contact a French or Spanish embassy with any inquiries, while those going to **Liechtenstein** should contact a Swiss embassy.

INVITATIONS AND WORK PERMITS. In addition to a visa, **Belarus, Russia,** and **Ukraine** currently also require that visitors from Australia, Canada, Ireland, New Zealand, the UK, and the US obtain an invitation from a sponsoring individual or organization. Requirements change rapidly, so double-check. See individual chapters to learn how to acquire invitations. Visitors to any European country, with the exception of EU citizens in EU countries, who want to work will need a work permit (see Alternatives to Tourism, p. 49).

IDENTIFICATION

When you travel, always carry two or more forms of identification on your person, including at least one form of photo ID; a passport and a driver's license or birth certificate is usually adequate. Many establishments, especially banks, may require several forms of ID to cash traveler's checks. Never carry all your ID together in case of theft or loss, and bring photocopies of your passport. Also bring passport-size photos to affix to any IDs or passes you may acquire along the way.

The **International Student Travel Confederation** (ISTC; ☎+31 20 421 2800; fax 421 2810; istcinfo@istc.org; www.istc.org) offers three forms of identification.

STUDENT IDENTIFICATION. The **International Student Identity Card (ISIC),** the most widely accepted form of student ID, provides discounts on sights, accommodations, food, and transport. The ISIC is preferable to an institution-specific card (such as a university ID) because it is more likely to be recognized (and honored) abroad. All cardholders have access to a 24hr. emergency helpline for medical, legal, and financial emergencies (in North America call ☎877-370-ISIC, elsewhere call US collect ☎+1 715-345-0505), and US cardholders are also eligible for insurance benefits (see Insurance, p. 34). The card is valid from September of one year to December of the following year and costs US$22.

ESSENTIALS

DO I NEED A VISA? FOR STAYS OF 3 MONTHS OR LESS IN:		AUS	CAN	IRE	NZ	SA	UK	US
	BELARUS	Y^I	Y^I	Y^I	Y^I	Y^I	Y^I	Y^I
	BOSNIA	Y	N	N^30	Y	Y	N	N^30
	BULGARIA	N^30	N^30	N^30	N^30	Y	N^30	N^30
	CROATIA	N	N	N	N	Y	N	N
	CZECH REP.	Y	Y	N	N	Y	N	N^1
	ESTONIA	N	Y	N	N	Y	N	N
	HUNGARY	Y	N	N	N	N^30	N	N
	LATVIA	N^10	Y	N	Y	Y	N	N
	LITHUANIA	N	N	N	N	Y	N	N
	MACEDONIA	Y	Y	N	N	Y	N	N
	POLAND	Y	Y	N	Y	Y	N	N
	ROMANIA	Y	Y	N^30	Y	Y	N^30	N^30
	RUSSIA	Y^I	Y^I	Y^I	Y^I	Y^I	Y^I	Y^I
	SLOVAKIA	Y	N	N	Y	N^30	N	N^30
	UKRAINE	Y^I	Y^I	Y^I	Y^I	Y^I	Y^I	Y^I
	TURKEY	Y^B	Y^B	Y^B	N	N^30	Y^B	Y^B

KEY: Y tourist visa required; **N** tourist visa not required; **N^30** tourists can stay up to 30 days without visa; **N^10** tourists can stay up to 10 days without visa; **Y^I** invitation required; **Y^B** tourist visa available on arrival/at border

Applicants must be degree-seeking students of a secondary or post-secondary school and must be of at least 12 years of age. Because of the proliferation of fake ISICs, some services (particularly airlines) require additional proof of student identity, such as a school ID or a letter attesting to your student status, signed by your registrar and stamped with your school seal. Many student travel agencies issue ISICs, including STA Travel in Australia and New Zealand; Travel CUTS in Canada; usit in the Republic of Ireland and Northern Ireland; SASTS in South Africa; Campus Travel and STA Travel in the UK; Council Travel (www.counciltravel.com/idcards/default.asp) and STA Travel in the US (p. 54).

YOUTH IDENTIFICATION. The International Student Travel Confederation also issues a discount card to non-student travelers 25 and under. This one-year **International Youth Travel Card** (**IYTC;** formerly the **GO 25** Card) offers many of the same benefits as the ISIC. Most organizations that sell the ISIC also sell the IYTC (US$22).

TEACHER IDENTIFICATION. The **International Teacher Identity Card (ITIC)** offers the same insurance coverage as the ISIC, as well as similar but limited discounts. The fee is AUS$13, UK£5, or US$22.

CUSTOMS

Upon entering a country, you must declare certain items from abroad and pay a duty on the value of those articles. Note that goods and gifts purchased at **duty-free** shops are not exempt from duty or sales tax upon return and must be declared; "duty-free" just means tax-free in the country of purchase. Duty-free allowances were abolished for travel between EU member states on July 1, 1999, but still exist for those arriving from outside the EU. Upon returning home, you must declare all articles acquired abroad and pay duty on their value. In order to expedite your return, make a list of any valuables brought from home and register them with customs before traveling abroad. Also be sure to keep receipts for all goods acquired abroad.

TAXES. The European Union imposes a **value-added tax (VAT)** on goods and services purchased within the EU (usually included in the sticker price). Non-EU citizens may obtain a **refund** for taxes paid on retail goods, but not for taxes paid on services. As the VAT in Europe is 15-25%, it might be worth it to file for a refund. You must first obtain Tax-free Shopping Cheques, available from shops sporting the blue, white, and silver Europe Tax-free Shopping logo, and then save the receipts from all of the purchases for which you want to be refunded. Upon leaving the last EU country on your itinerary, present your (unused) goods, invoices, and passport to Customs and have them stamp your Cheques. Then go to an ETS cash refund office or file for a refund once back home. Keep in mind that goods must be taken out of the country within three months of the end of the month of purchase, and that some stores require minimum purchase amounts to become eligible for refund. For more information on tax-free shopping, visit www.globalrefund.com.

CUSTOMS IN THE EU. As well as freedom of movement of people within the EU, travelers in the countries that are members of the EU (Austria, Belgium, Denmark, Finland, France, Germany, Greece, Ireland, Italy, Luxembourg, the Netherlands, Portugal, Spain, Sweden, and the UK) can also take advantage of the freedom of movement of goods. This means that there are no customs controls at internal EU borders (i.e., you can take the blue customs channel at the airport), and travelers are free to transport whatever legal substances they like as long as it is for their own personal (non-commercial) use—up to 800 cigarettes, 10L of spirits, 90L of wine (60L of sparkling wine), and 110L of beer. You should also be aware that duty-free has been abolished for travel between EU member states; however, travelers between the EU and the rest of the world still get a duty-free allowance when passing through customs.

FURTHER RESOURCES

Australia: Customs National Information Line (in Australia ☎+1 (300) 363 263, from elsewhere call ☎+61 (2) 6275 6666; information@customs.gov.au; www.customs.gov.au).

Canada: Customs, 2265 St. Laurent Blvd., Ottawa, ON K1G 4K3 (24hr. ☎800-461-9999 or 506-636-5064 outside Canada; www.revcan.ca).

Ireland: Customs Information Office, Irish Life Centre, Lower Abbey St., Dublin 1 (☎(01) 878 8811; fax 878 0836; taxes@revenue.iol.ie; www.revenue.ie.)

New Zealand: Customhouse, 17-21 Whitmore St., Box 2218, Wellington (☎(04) 473 6099; fax 473 7370; www.customs.govt.nz).

South Africa: Commissioner for Customs and Excise, Privat Bag X47, Pretoria 0001 (☎(012) 314 9911; fax 328 6478; www.gov.za).

UK: Her Majesty's Customs and Excise, Dorset House, Stamford Street, London SE1 9PY (☎0845 010 9000; fax 8910 3933; www.hmce.gov.uk).

US: US Customs Service, 1300 Pennsylvania Ave. NW, Washington, D.C. 20229 (☎202-354-1000; fax 354-1010; www.customs.gov).

MONEY

CURRENCY AND EXCHANGE

As a general rule, it's cheaper to convert money in Europe than at home. However, you should bring enough foreign currency for the first 24 to 72 hours of a trip to avoid being if you arrive after bank hours or on a holiday. Travelers from the US can call **International Currency Express** (☎888-278-6628) which delivers foreign currency or traveler's checks 2nd-day (US$12) at competitive exchange rates.

When changing money abroad, try to go only to banks or change bureaus that have at most a 5% margin between their buy and sell prices. Since you lose money with every transaction, convert large sums, but no more than you'll need.

If you use traveler's checks or bills, carry some in small denominations (the equivalent of US$50 or less) in case you must exchange money at disadvantageous rates, but bring a range of denominations since charges may be levied per check cashed. Store your money in a variety of forms; carry cash, traveler's checks, and an ATM and/or credit card. All travelers should also consider carrying about $50 worth of US dollars, which are often preferred by local tellers.

ESSENTIALS

> **THE EURO.** Since January 2001, the official currency of 12 members of the European Union (EU)—Austria, Belgium, Finland, France, Germany, Greece, Ireland, Italy, Luxembourg, the Netherlands, Portugal, and Spain—has been the Euro. The old national currencies remain legal tender through July 1, 2002, after which it's all Euros all the time. *Let's Go: Europe 2002* lists prices in both Euros (€) and local currencies.
>
> The Euro has some important—and positive—consequences for travelers hitting more than one Euro-zone country. Money-changers across the Euro-zone are obliged to exchange money at the official, fixed rate (see below), and at no commission (though they may still charge a small service fee). So now you can change your *guilders* into *escudos* and your *escudos* into *lire* without losing fistfuls of money on every transaction. Euro-denominated travelers cheques also allow you to pay for goods and services across the Euro-zone, again at the official rate and commission-free.
>
> The exchange rate between Euro-zone currencies was permanently fixed on January 1, 1999. See www.europa.eu.int for more information.

For **currency exchange information** please see the opening page of each country chapter. Check a large newspaper or the web (e.g. finance.yahoo.com or www.xe.com) for the latest exchange rates.

1 EURO =	
13.7603 Austrian schillings	340.750 Greek drachmas
40.3399 Belgian francs	40.3399 Luxembourg francs
2.20371 Dutch guilders	0.787564 Irish pounds
6.55957 French francs	1936.27 Italian lire
5.94573 Finnish markka	200.482 Portuguese escudos
1.95583 German marks	166.386 Spanish pesetas

TRAVELER'S CHECKS

Traveler's checks are a safe and easy way to carry funds. Several agencies and banks sell them for a small commission. Each agency provides refunds if checks are lost or stolen, and many offer additional services, such as toll-free refund hotlines abroad, emergency message services, and stolen credit card assistance.

While traveling, keep check receipts and a record of which checks you've cashed separate from the checks themselves. Also leave a list of check numbers with someone at home. Never countersign checks until you're ready to cash them, and always bring your passport with you to cash them. If your checks are lost or stolen, immediately contact a refund center (of the company that issued your checks) to be reimbursed; they may require a police report verifying the loss or theft. Less-touristed countries may not have refund centers at all, in which case you might have to wait to be reimbursed. Ask about toll-free refund hotlines and the location of refund centers when purchasing checks, and always carry emergency cash. **American Express** and **Visa** are the most widely recognized.

American Express: In Australia ☎(800) 25 1902; in New Zealand ☎(0800) 44 1068; in the UK ☎(0800) 521 313; in the US and Canada ☎800-221-7282. Elsewhere call US collect ☎+1 801-964-6665; www.aexp.com. Traveler's checks are available in 10 currencies at 1-4% commission at AmEx offices and banks, commission-free at AAA offices. *Cheques for Two* can be signed by either of 2 people traveling together.

Citicorp: In the US and Canada call ☎800-645-6556; elsewhere call US collect ☎+1 813-623-1709. Traveler's checks (available only in US dollars, British pounds, and German marks) at 1-2% commission. Call 24hr.

Thomas Cook MasterCard: In the US and Canada ☎800-223-7373; in the UK ☎(0800) 622 101; elsewhere call UK collect ☎+44 (1733) 318 950. Checks available in 13 currencies at 2% commission. Thomas Cook offices cash checks commission-free.

Visa: In the US call ☎800-227-6811; in the UK ☎(0800) 895 078; elsewhere call UK collect ☎+44 (20) 7937 8091; www.visa.com. Call to find the nearest office.

CREDIT CARDS

Where they are accepted, credit cards often offer superior exchange rates—up to 5% better than the retail rate used by banks and other currency exchange establishments. Credit cards may also offer services such as insurance or emergency help, and are sometimes required to reserve hotel rooms or rental cars. **MasterCard** (a.k.a. EuroCard or Access in Europe) and **Visa** (a.k.a. Carte Bleue or Barclaycard) are the most welcomed; **American Express** cards work at some ATMs and at AmEx offices and major airports. However, budget travelers will probably find that few of the establishments they frequent accept credit cards; aside from the occasional splurge, you will probably reserve use of your credit card for financial emergencies.

Credit cards are also useful for **cash advances,** which allow you instantly to withdraw local currency from associated banks and ATMs throughout Europe. However, transaction fees for all credit card advances (up to US$10 per advance, plus 2-3% extra on foreign transactions after conversion) tend to make credit cards more costly than using ATMs or traveler's checks. In an emergency, however, the transaction fee may prove worth the cost. To be eligible for an advance, you'll need to get a **Personal Identification Number (PIN)** from your credit card company (see Cash (ATM) Cards, below). Be sure to check with your credit card company before you leave home, though; some have started to charge foreign transaction fees.

CREDIT CARD COMPANIES. Visa (US ☎800-336-8472) and **MasterCard** (US ☎800-307-7309) are issued in cooperation with banks and other organizations. **American Express** (US ☎800-843-2273) has an annual fee of up to US$55. AmEx cardholders may cash personal checks at AmEx offices abroad, access 24hr. emergency medical and legal assistance (in North America, ☎800-554-2639; elsewhere call US collect ☎+1 715-343-7977), and enjoy AmEx Travel Service benefits (including plane, hotel, and car rental reservation changes; baggage loss and flight insurance; mailgram and international cable services; and held mail).

CASH (ATM) CARDS

Cash cards—popularly called ATM cards—are widespread in Europe. Depending on the system that your home bank uses, you can most likely access your personal bank account from abroad. ATMs get the same wholesale exchange rate as credit cards, but there is often a limit on the amount of money you can withdraw per day (around US$500), and unfortunately computer networks sometimes fail. There is typically a surcharge of US$1-5 per withdrawal. Be sure to memorize your PIN code in numeric form since machines elsewhere may not have letters on their keys. Also, if your PIN is longer than four digits, ask your bank whether you need a new number. The two major international money networks are **Cirrus** (US ☎800-424-7787) and **PLUS** (US ☎800-843-7587). Call these numbers for ATM locations, or consult www.visa.com/pd/atm or www.mastercard.com/atm.

GETTING MONEY FROM HOME

AMERICAN EXPRESS. Cardholders can withdraw cash from their checking accounts at any of AmEx's major offices and many representative offices (up to US$1000 every 21 days; no service charge, no interest). AmEx "Express Cash" withdrawals from any AmEx ATM in Europe are automatically debited from the cardholder's checking account or line of credit. Green card holders may withdraw up to US$1000 in any seven-day period (2% transaction fee; minimum US$2.50, maximum

Money From Home In Minutes.

If you're stuck for cash on your travels, don't panic. Millions of people trust Western Union to transfer money in minutes to over 185 countries and over 95,000 locations worldwide. Our record of safety and reliability is second to none. You can even send money by phone without leaving home by using a credit card. For more information, call Western Union: USA 1-800-325-6000, Canada 1-800-235-0000.

www.westernunion.com

WESTERN UNION | MONEY TRANSFER

The fastest way to send money worldwide.

US$20). To enroll in Express Cash, cardmembers may call ☎ 800-227-4669 in the US; elsewhere call the US collect ☎ +1 336-668-5041.

WESTERN UNION. Travelers from Canada, the UK, and the US can wire money abroad through Western Union's money transfer services. In Canada, call ☎ 800-235-0000; in the UK, ☎ (0800) 833 833; in the US, ☎ 800-325-6000. The rates for sending cash are generally US$10-11 cheaper than with a credit card, and the money is usually available within an hour. Western Union maintains offices throughout Europe; to find the nearest location, consult www.westernunion.com.

FEDERAL EXPRESS. Some people choose to send money abroad in cash via FedEx to avoid transmission fees and taxes. While FedEx is reasonably reliable, this method is illegal. In the US and Canada, FedEx can be reached by calling ☎ 800-463-3339; in the UK, ☎ (0800) 123800; in Ireland, ☎ (800) 535 800; in Australia, ☎ 132 610; in New Zealand, ☎ (0800) 733 339; and in South Africa, ☎ 011 923 8000.

US STATE DEPARTMENT (US CITIZENS ONLY). In dire emergencies only, the US State Department will forward money within hours to the nearest consular office, which will then disburse it according to instructions for a US$15 fee. Contact the Overseas Citizens Service, American Citizens Services, Consular Affairs, Room 4811, US Department of State, Washington, D.C. 20520 (☎ 202-647-5225; nights, Sundays, and holidays ☎ 202-647-4000; http://travel.state.gov).

COSTS

The cost of a trip varies considerably depending on where you go, how you travel, and where you stay. Your single biggest expense will probably be your return (round-trip) **airfare** to Europe (p. 54); a **railpass** would be another major pre-departure expense (p. 65). Before you go, spend some time calculating a reasonable per-day **budget** that will meet your needs. To give you a general idea, a bare-bones day in Western Europe (camping or sleeping in hostels, buying food at supermarkets) would cost about US$25-35, excluding the cost of a plane ticket and railpass; a slightly more comfortable day (sleeping in hostels and the occasional budget hotel, eating one meal a day at a restaurant, going out at night) would run US$35-60; and for a luxurious day, the sky's the limit. Countries such as Britain, Italy, and Switzerland tend to be more costly for tourists, while Spain and Greece are relatively inexpensive alternatives. You can expect to spend US$5-10 less per day in parts of Eastern Europe and Turkey; similarly, if you will be traveling in Scandinavia, add on US$10-15 per day. If you're camping or traveling by campervan, knock off US$5-10, more if you plan to take advantage of free camping.

For example, the typical first-time, under-26 traveler planning to spend most of his or her time in Western Europe and then tack on a quick jaunt into Eastern Europe, sleeping in hostels and traveling on a two-month unlimited Eurail pass, can probably expect to spend about US$2000, plus cost of plane fare (US$300-800), railpass (US$882), and backpack (US$150-400). Also, don't forget emergency reserve funds (at least US$200).

TIPS FOR STAYING ON A BUDGET. Since saving just a few dollars a day over the course of your trip might pay for days or weeks of additional travel, pinching pennies is worth it. Learn to take advantage of freebies: for example, museums are usually free once a week or once a month, and cities often host free open-air concerts and/or cultural events (especially in the summer). Bring a sleepsack (p. 35) to save on sheet charges in European hostels, and do your **laundry** in the sink (unless you're explicitly prohibited from doing so). You can split **accommodations** costs (in hotels and some hostels) with trustworthy fellow travelers; multi-bed rooms almost always work out cheaper per person than singles. To cut down on the cost of **meals,** buy food in supermarkets instead of eating out; you'd be surprised how tasty a simple meal of bread, cheese, and fruit can be.

SAFETY AND SECURITY

While tourists may be more vulnerable than the average individual, a few simple precautions will help you avoid problems.

PERSONAL SAFETY

EXPLORING. See if you can blend in a little. Dress more conservatively. Get familiar with your surroundings before setting out, and look confident; if you must check a map on the street, duck into a shop. If you are traveling alone, don't admit it, and be sure someone at home knows your itinerary. When walking at night, stick to busy, well-lighted streets, and do not cross through parks or parking lots. Look for children playing, women walking in the open, and other signs of an active community. If you feel uncomfortable, leave. But don't live in fear: persistent exploration will build confidence and make your stay even more rewarding.

SELF-DEFENSE. There is no sure-fire way to avoid threatening situations when you travel, but a **self-defense course** will give you concrete ways to react to unwanted advances. **Impact, Prepare,** and **Model Mugging** can refer you to courses in the US (☎800-345-5425) and Vancouver (☎604-878-3838). Workshops (2-3hr.) start at US$50; full courses US$350-500. Both women and men are welcome.

TRANSPORTATION. Look out for pickpockets in any **subway** system. **Intercity trains** are safe throughout most of Europe, and second-class travel is more than comfortable. **Overnight trains** are the most risky, as your vigilance is limited while you sleep. If you are using a **car**, learn local driving signals and wear a seatbelt. Study route maps before you hit the road, and if your car breaks down, wait for the police to assist you. For long drives, invest in a cellular phone and a roadside assistance program (p. 76). Be sure to park your vehicle in a garage or well traveled area, and use a steering wheel locking device in larger cities. **Sleeping in your car** is one of the most dangerous (and often illegal) ways to get your rest. *Let's Go* does not recommend **hitchhiking** under any circumstances, particularly for women.

CIVIL UNREST. Risks of civil unrest tend to be localized and rarely directed toward tourists. Keep an eye on the news, heed travel warnings, steer clear of big crowds and demonstrations. Still, moments of unrest occasionally arise. Though the peace process in Northern Ireland is progressing, tension and violence tend to surround the July "marching season"; Corsica in Italy and the Basque region in Spain have well-known separatist movements; the November 17 group in Greece is known for anti-Western acts, though they do not target tourists; and while guerilla conflict has subsided in Southeast Turkey, recently Chechen sympathizers have targeted Western travelers. For now, it is safest to avoid conflict-ridden Macedonia, Serbia, Montenegro, and Bosnia-Herzegovina. The box below will help you get to an up-to-date list of your government's travel advisories.

TRAVEL ADVISORIES. The following government offices provide travel information and advisories by telephone, by fax, or via the web:

Australian Department of Foreign Affairs and Trade: ☎(2) 6261 1111; www.dfat.gov.au.

Canadian Department of Foreign Affairs and International Trade (DFAIT): In Canada, ☎800-267-8316; elsewhere ☎+1 613-944-4000; voyage.dfait-maeci.gc.ca. Call for free booklet, *Bon Voyage...But.*

New Zealand Ministry of Foreign Affairs: ☎(04) 494 85 00; fax 494 85 06; www.mft.govt.nz/trav.html.

UK Foreign and Commonwealth Office: ☎(020) 7008 0232; fax 7008 0155; www.fco.gov.uk.

US Department of State: ☎202-647-5225, automatic faxback 202-647-3000; http://travel.state.gov. For *A Safe Trip Abroad*, call ☎202-512-1800.

> **! TROUBLE WITH THE LAW.** Travelers who run into trouble with the law, both accidentally and knowingly, do not retain the rights of their home country; instead, they have the same rights a citizen of the country they are visiting. The law mandates that police notify the embassy of a traveler's home country if he or she is arrested. In custody, a traveler is entitled to a visit from a Consular officer. US citizens should check the Department of State's website (www.state.gov) for more information.

FINANCIAL SECURITY

PROTECTING YOUR VALUABLES. There are a few steps you can take to minimize the financial risk associated with traveling. First, **bring as little with you as possible.** Leave expensive watches, jewelry, cameras, and electronic equipment at home; chances are you'd break them, lose them, or get sick of lugging them around. Second, buy a few combination **padlocks** to secure your belongings either in your pack—which you should **never leave unattended**—or in a hostel or train station locker. Third, **carry as little cash as possible;** instead carry traveler's checks and ATM/credit cards, keeping them in a **money belt**—not a "fanny pack"—along with your passport and ID cards. Fourth, **keep a small cash reserve separate from your primary stash.** This should entail about US$50 sewn into or stored in the depths of your pack, along with your traveler's check numbers and important photocopies.

CON ARTISTS AND PICKPOCKETS. In large cities, **scams** can be a pain. Con-artists often work in groups, and children are among the most effective. Beware of certain classic ruses: sob stories that require money, rolls of bills "found" on the street, mustard spilled onto your shoulder to distract you while they snatch your bag. Don't ever give your passport to someone whose authority you question (ask to accompany them to a police station if they insist), and don't ever let your passport or your bag out of your sight. Never trust a "station-porter" who insists on carrying your bag or stowing it in the baggage compartment or a "new friend" who offers to guard your bag while you buy a train ticket or use the restroom. Be alert and cautious with your calling card number in public telephone booths. Beware of **pickpockets** in city crowds, especially on public transportation. Cities such as Rome, Paris, London and Moscow have higher rates of petty crime.

ACCOMMODATIONS AND TRANSPORTATION. Never leave your belongings unattended in even the safest hostel or hotel. Bring your own **padlock** for hostel lockers, and don't ever store valuables in any locker.

Be particularly careful on **buses** and **trains;** horror stories abound about determined thieves who wait for travelers to fall asleep, and the Warsaw-Moscow line is especially notorious. Carry your backpack in front of you where you can see it. When traveling with others, sleep in alternate shifts. Use good judgement in selecting a train compartment: never stay in an empty one, and lock your pack to the luggage rack. Try to sleep on top bunks with your luggage stored above you (if not in bed with you), and keep documents and other valuables on your person.

If traveling by **car,** don't leave valuables (such as radios or luggage) in it while you are away. If your tape deck or radio is removable, hide it in the trunk or take it with you. If it isn't, at least conceal it. Similarly, hide baggage in the trunk.

DRUGS AND ALCOHOL

Drug and alcohol laws vary widely throughout Europe: whereas in the Netherlands you can buy soft drugs on the open market, in Turkey and much of Eastern Europe drug possession may lead to a prison sentence. You're subject to the laws of the country in which you travel when you're abroad, so familiarize yourself with those laws before leaving. If you carry **prescription drugs,** it is vital to have both a copy of the prescriptions themselves and a note from a doctor, especially at border crossings. **Avoid public drunkenness;** it is culturally unacceptable and against the law in many countries, and can also jeopardize your safety.

ESSENTIALS

HEALTH AND INSURANCE

Travelers complain most often about their feet and their gut, so take precautionary measures. Drink fluids to prevent dehydration and constipation. Wear sturdy, broken-in shoes and clean socks, and use talcum powder to keep your feet dry.

BEFORE YOU GO

Preparation can help minimize the likelihood of contracting a disease and maximize the chances of receiving effective health care in the event of an emergency. For tips on packing a basic **first-aid kit** and other health essentials, see p. 35.

In your **passport,** write the names of any people you wish to be contacted in case of a medical emergency, and also list any allergies or medical conditions of which you would want doctors to be aware. Matching a prescription to a foreign equivalent is not always easy, safe, or possible. Carry up-to-date, legible prescriptions or a statement from your doctor stating the medication's trade name, manufacturer, chemical name, and dosage. While traveling, be sure to keep all medication with you in your carry-on luggage. Most prescription and over-the-counter **drugs** available elsewhere are available throughout Europe, though often under different names. See www.rxlist.com to figure out what to ask for at the pharmacy counter.

IMMUNIZATIONS AND PRECAUTIONS

Travelers over two years old should be sure that the following vaccines are up to date: MMR (for measles, mumps, and rubella); DTaP or Td (for diptheria, tetanus, and pertussis), OPV (for polio), HbCV (for haemophilus influenza B), and HBV (for hepatitis B). For travelers going to Eastern or Southern Europe, Hepatitis A vaccine and/or immune globulin (IG), as well as typhoid vaccine, are recommended. While yellow fever is only endemic to parts of South America and sub-Saharan Africa, some countries may deny entrance to travelers arriving from these zones without a certificate of vaccination. For more **region-specific information** on vaccination requirements, as well as recommendations on immunizations and prophylaxis, consult the CDC (see below) in the US or the equivalent in your home country.

USEFUL ORGANIZATIONS AND PUBLICATIONS

The US **Centers for Disease Control and Prevention (CDC;** US ☎877-394-8747; www.cdc.gov/travel) maintains an international fax information service and an international travelers hotline (☎404-332-4559). The CDC's comprehensive booklet *Health Information for International Travel*, an annual rundown of disease, immunization, and general health advice, is free online or US$25 via the Public Health Foundation (US ☎877-252-1200). Consult the appropriate government agency of your home country for consular information sheets on health, entry requirements, and other issues for various countries (see the listings in the box on **Travel Advisories,** p. 28). For quick information on health and other travel warnings, call the **Overseas Citizens Services** (US ☎202-647-5225; after-hours ☎202-647-4000), contact a passport agency or an embassy or consulate abroad. US citizens can send a self-addressed, stamped envelope to the Overseas Citizens Services, Bureau of Consular Affairs, #4811, US Department of State, Washington, D.C. 20520. For information on medical evacuation services and travel insurance firms, see the **US State Department** website at travel.state.gov/medical.html, or the **British Foreign and Commonwealth Office** website at www.fco.gov.uk.

For detailed information on travel health, including a country-by-country overview of diseases, try the **International Travel Health Guide,** Stuart Rose, MD (Travel Medicine, US$24.95; www.travmed.com). For general health information, contact the **American Red Cross** (US ☎800-564-1234).

AVAILABLE MEDICAL ASSISTANCE

While health care systems in Western Europe tend to be quite accessible and of high quality, medical care varies greatly across Eastern and Southern Europe.

Within the EU, all EU travelers can receive free first-aid and emergency services by presenting an **E11 form.** Major cities such as Prague and Budapest will have English-speaking medical centers or hospitals for foreigners, whereas in relatively untouristed countries like Belarus or Latvia, English-speaking facilities are nearly nonexistent (tourist offices may have names of local doctors who speak English). In general, medical service in these regions is not up to Western standards; though basic supplies are always there, specialized treatment is not. If available, private hospitals tend to have better facilities than state-operated ones. Make sure to have good health insurance when traveling abroad.

If you are concerned about being able to access medical support while traveling, contact one of these two services: *MedPass* from **GlobalCare, Inc.** (US ☎ 800-860-1111; fax 770-475-0058; www.globalems.com), provides 24hr. international medical assistance, support, and medical evacuation resources. The **International Association for Medical Assistance to Travelers** (**IAMAT;** US ☎ 716-754-4883, Canada ☎ 416-652-0137, New Zealand ☎ (03) 352 2053; www.sentex.net/~iamat) has free membership, lists English-speaking doctors worldwide, and offers detailed information on immunization requirements and sanitation. If your regular insurance policy does not cover travel abroad, you may wish to purchase additional coverage (p. 34).

Those with medical conditions (diabetes, allergies to antibiotics, epilepsy, heart conditions) may want to get a stainless-steel **Medic Alert** ID tag (first year US$35, US$20 thereafter), which identifies the condition and gives a 24hr. collect-call number. Contact the Medic Alert Foundation (US ☎ 888-633-4298; www.medicalert.org). The **American Diabetes Association** (US ☎ 800-232-3472; www.diabetes.org) offers copies of "Travel and Diabetes" and a multilingual diabetic ID card.

ONCE IN EUROPE

ENVIRONMENTAL HAZARDS

Heat exhaustion and dehydration: Characterized by fatigue, headaches, or wooziness, heat exhaustion can be prevented by drinking plenty of fluids, eating salty foods, and avoiding dehydrating beverages (e.g. alcohol, coffee, tea, and caffeinated soda). Continuous heat stress can lead to heatstroke; symptoms include a rising temperature, severe headache, and cessation of sweating. Victims should be cooled off with wet towels and taken to a doctor.

Sunburn: Bring sunscreen and apply it liberally to avoid burns and skin cancer. You can get burned through clouds, especially if you're near the water or in the snow. If you get burned, drink more fluids than usual and apply Calamine or an aloe-based lotion.

Hypothermia and frostbite: Keep dry, wear layers, and stay out of the wind. In the mountains, temperatures can fall to freezing even in the summer months. Symptoms include a rapid drop in core body temperature, shivering, exhaustion, poor coordination or slurred speech, hallucinations, or amnesia. Do not let hypothermia victims fall asleep. When the temperature is below freezing, watch out for frostbite. If your skin turns white, waxy, and cold, do not rub the area. Drink warm beverages, get dry, and slowly warm the area with dry fabric or steady body contact until a doctor can be found.

High altitude: Allow your body a couple of days to adjust to less oxygen before exerting yourself. Note that alcohol is more potent and UV rays are stronger at high elevations.

INSECT-BORNE DISEASES

Be aware of insects—particularly mosquitoes, fleas, ticks, and lice—especially when hiking and camping in wet or forested areas. **Mosquitoes** are most active from dusk to dawn. Wear pants and long sleeves, tuck pants into socks, and sleep in a mosquito net. If you don't mind chemicals, use insect repellents, such as DEET, or spray gear with permethrin (licensed in the US for use on clothing). Consider natural repellents like vitamin B-12 or garlic pills. To stop the itch after being bitten, try Calamine lotion or topical cortisones (like Cortaid), or take a bath with a half-cup of baking soda or oatmeal. Ticks can give you **Lyme disease.**

When walking in wooded areas, pause periodically to brush off ticks. If you find a tick attached to your skin, grasp the head with tweezers as close to the skin as possible and pull slowly and steadily. Don't use chemicals. Removing a tick within 24hr. greatly reduces the risk of infection, which is marked by a 2in.-wide bull's-eye, and symptoms that include fever, headache, fatigue, and aches and pains. Left untreated, Lyme disease can cause serious problems in joints, the heart, and the nervous system. Antibiotics are effective if administered early. Ticks can also give you **encephalitis,** a viral infection. Symptoms can range from headaches and flu-like symptoms to swelling of the brain. While a vaccine is available, the immunization schedule is impractical, and the risk of contracting the disease is relatively low, especially if precautions are taken against tick bites.

FOOD- AND WATER-BORNE DISEASES

Unpeeled fruit and vegetables and tap water should be safe throughout most of Europe, particularly Western Europe, but may not be in parts of Turkey, Southern Europe, and Eastern Europe. Remember to be cautious of ice cubes and anything washed in tap water, like salad. Other culprits are raw shellfish, unpasteurized milk, and sauces containing raw eggs. Buy bottled water, or purify your own water by bringing it to a rolling boil or treating it with **iodine tablets.** Food and waterborne diseases are a common cause of illness in Morocco and parts of Turkey, and the CDC recommends that travelers drink only bottled or boiled water. Wherever you are, wash your hands before eating or bring a quick-drying liquid hand cleaner.

Traveler's diarrhea: Results from drinking untreated water or eating uncooked foods; a temporary (and fairly common) reaction to the bacteria in new food ingredients. Symptoms include nausea, bloating, urgency, and malaise. Try quick-energy, non-sugary foods with protein and carbohydrates to keep your strength up. Over-the-counter anti-diarrheals (e.g. Imodium) may counteract the problems, but can complicate serious infections. The most dangerous side effect is dehydration; drink 8oz. water with ½tsp. of sugar or honey and a pinch of salt, try uncaffeinated soft drinks, or munch on salted crackers. Consult a doctor if a fever develops, symptoms remain after 4-5 days, or for the treatment of diarrhea in children.

Cholera: An intestinal disease caused by a bacteria found in contaminated food. A danger in the Russian Federation and the Ukraine. Symptoms include watery diarrhea, dehydration, vomiting, and muscle cramps. See a doctor immediately; if left untreated, it may be fatal. Antibiotics are available, but rehydration is most important. Consider getting a vaccine (50% effective) if you have stomach problems or will be living where the water is not reliable.

Hepatitis A: A viral liver infection acquired primarily through contaminated water, but also through sexual contact. An intermediate risk in Eastern Europe. Symptoms include fatigue, fever, loss of appetite, nausea, dark urine, jaundice, vomiting, aches and pains, and light stools. Risk is highest in rural areas. Get the **vaccine** (Havrix or Vaqta) or an injection of immune globulin (IG; formerly called gamma globulin) before leaving.

Parasites: Microbes, tapeworms, etc. that hide in unsafe water and food. **Giardiasis,** for example, is acquired by drinking untreated water from streams or lakes all over the world (including Europe). Symptoms include swollen glands or lymph nodes, fever, rashes or itchiness, digestive problems, eye problems, and anemia. Boil water, wear shoes, avoid bugs, and eat only cooked food.

Mad Cow Disease: The human variant is called Cruetzfeldt-Jakob disease (nvCJD), and involves invariably fatal brain diseases. Incidents have been tentatively linked to consuming infected beef, but the risk is calculated to be around 1 per 10 billion servings of meat. Information on nvCJD is not conclusive, but it is believed that milk and milk products do not pose a risk.

Foot and Mouth Disease (FMD): FMD experienced one of its worst outbreaks in 2001, largely in the United Kingdom and other Western European countries. FMD does not pose a real health threat to humans but is devastating to animals. It can be transmitted by human as well as animal contact. Western European countries have not, as of publication, restricted travel to infested countries, but do limit excursions to farms and other rural areas. FMD is believed to be killed by heat, making cooked meats apparently safe for consumption. Fish, poultry, fruits, and vegetables pose no FMD risk.

OTHER INFECTIOUS DISEASES

Rabies: Transmitted through the saliva of infected animals; fatal if untreated. By the time symptoms appear (thirst and muscle spasms), the disease is in its terminal stage. If you are bitten, wash the wound thoroughly, seek immediate medical care, and try to have the animal located. A rabies vaccine, which consists of 3 shots given over a 21-day period, is available but is only semi-effective.

Hepatitis B: A viral infection of the liver transmitted via bodily fluids or needle-sharing. Symptoms may not surface until years after infection. Vaccinations are recommended for health-care workers, sexually active travelers, and anyone planning to seek medical treatment abroad. The 3-shot vaccination series must begin 6mos. before traveling.

Hepatitis C: Like Hep B, but the mode of transmission differs. IV drug users, those with occupational exposure to blood, hemodialysis patients, and recipients of blood transfusions are at the highest risk, but the disease can also be spread through sexual contact or sharing items like razors and toothbrushes that may have traces of blood on them.

AIDS and HIV: The virus that leads to Acquired Immune Deficiency Syndrome (AIDS) is most commonly transmitted by sexual intercourse. Take along a supply of latex condoms, which can be difficult to find on the road. Never share intravenous drug, tattooing, or other needles, and take precautions to avoid any blood transfusions or injections while abroad (if you do need medical care, ask to receive screened blood and sterilized equipment). Some countries like Belarus, Bulgaria, Luxembourg, Russia and Ukraine screen incoming travelers for HIV, primarily those planning extended visits for work or study, and deny entrance to those who test HIV-positive. For detailed information on AIDS in Europe, call the **US Centers for Disease Control** 24hr. hotline at ☎800-342-2437, or contact the **Joint United Nations Programme on HIV/AIDS (UNAIDS),** 20, av. Appia, CH-1211 Geneva 27, Switzerland (☎+41 (22) 791 36 66; fax 791 41 87). Council's brochure, *Travel Safe: AIDS and International Travel,* is available at all Council Travel offices and on their website (www.ciee.org/Isp/safety/travelsafe.htm).

Sexually transmitted diseases (STDS): STDS such as **gonorrhea, chlamydia, genital warts, syphilis,** and **herpes** are easier to catch than HIV and can be just as deadly. Hepatitis B and C are also serious STDs (see above). Though condoms may protect you from some STDs, oral or even tactile contact can lead to transmission. Warning signs include swelling, sores, bumps, or blisters on sex organs, the rectum, or the mouth; burning and pain during urination and bowel movements; itching around sex organs; swelling or redness of the throat; and flu-like symptoms. If these symptoms develop, see a doctor immediately.

WOMEN'S HEALTH

Women traveling in unsanitary conditions are vulnerable to **urinary tract** and **bladder infections,** common and very uncomfortable bacterial conditions that cause a burning sensation and painful (sometimes frequent) urination. To try to avoid these infections, drink plenty of clean water and juice rich in vitamin C, and urinate frequently, especially right after intercourse. Untreated, these infections can lead to kidney infections, sterility, and even death. If symptoms persist, see a doctor.

Vaginal yeast infections may flare up in hot and humid climates. Wearing loosely fitting trousers or a skirt and cotton underwear will help, as will over-the-counter remedies like Monostat or Gynelotrimin. Bring supplies from home if you are prone to infection, as they may be difficult to find on the road. Since **tampons, pads,** and reliable **contraceptive devices** are sometimes hard to find when traveling and your preferred brand will rarely be available, bring supplies with you.

If you need an abortion while abroad, contact **Marie Stopes International** in the UK, (☎(0171) 574 7400, fax 574 7417; services@stopes.org.uk; www.mari-estopes.org.uk). Outside the UK, see www.ippf.org/regions/europe for country profiles and organizations. In some countries, especially in eastern and southern Europe, it may be necessary to leave the country to find safe abortion services.

INSURANCE

Travel insurance generally covers four basic areas: medical/health problems, property loss, trip cancellation/interruption, and emergency evacuation. Although your regular insurance policies may well extend to travel-related accidents, you may consider purchasing travel insurance if the cost of potential trip cancellation/interruption or emergency medical evacuation is greater than you can absorb. Prices for travel insurance purchased separately generally run about US$50 per week for full coverage, while trip cancellation/interruption may be purchased separately at a rate of about US$5.50 per US$100 of coverage.

Medical insurance (especially university policies) often covers costs incurred abroad; check with your provider. **US Medicare** does not cover foreign travel. **Canadians** are protected by their home province's health insurance plan for up to 90 days after leaving the country; check with the provincial Ministry of Health or Health Plan Headquarters for details. **Australians** traveling in New Zealand, the UK, the Netherlands, Sweden, Finland, or Italy are entitled to many services they would receive at home as part of the Reciprocal Health Care Agreement. **Homeowners' insurance** (or your family's coverage) often covers theft during travel and loss of travel documents (such as passport, plane ticket, or railpass) up to US$500.

ISIC and **ITIC** (p. 21) provide basic insurance benefits, including US$100 per day of in-hospital sickness for up to 60 days, US$3000 of accident-related medical reimbursement, and US$25,000 for emergency medical transport. Cardholders have access to a toll-free 24hr. helpline (run by the insurance provider TravelGuard) for medical, legal, and financial emergencies overseas (US and Canada ☎877-370-4742, elsewhere call US collect +1 715-345-0505). **American Express** (US ☎800-528-4800) grants most cardholders automatic car rental insurance (collision and theft, but not liability) and ground travel accident coverage of US$100,000 on flight purchases made with the card.

INSURANCE PROVIDERS. Council and **STA** (p. 54) offer a range of plans that can supplement your basic coverage. Other private insurance providers in the US and Canada include: **Access America** (☎800-284-8300); **Berkely Group/Carefree Travel Insurance** (☎800-323-3149; www.berkely.com); **Globalcare Travel Insurance** (☎800-821-2488; www.globalcare-cocco.com); and **Travel Assistance International** (☎800-821-2828; www.worldwide-assistance.com). Providers in the **UK** include **Campus Travel** (☎(01865) 258000) and **Columbus Travel Insurance** (☎(020) 7375 0011). In **Australia**, try **CIC Insurance** (☎9202 8000).

PACKING

PACK LIGHT. Lay out only what you absolutely need, then take half the clothes and twice the money. The less you have, the less you have to lose (or store, or carry on your back). Any extra space left will be useful for any souvenirs or items you might pick up along the way. If you plan to do a lot of hiking, also see the section on Camping and the Outdoors, p. 40.

LUGGAGE. If you plan to cover most of your itinerary by foot, a sturdy **frame backpack** is unbeatable. (For the basics on buying a pack, see p. 40.) Toting a **suitcase** or **trunk** is fine if you plan to live in one or two cities and explore from there, but a very bad idea if you're going to be moving around. In addition to your main piece of luggage, a **daypack** (a small backpack or courier bag) is a must.

CLOTHING. No matter when you're traveling, it's always a good idea to bring a **warm jacket** or wool sweater, a **rain jacket** (Gore-Tex® is both waterproof and breathable), sturdy shoes or **hiking boots,** and **thick socks. Flip-flops** or waterproof sandals are must-haves for grubby hostel showers. You may also want to add one outfit beyond the jeans and t-shirt uniform, and maybe a nicer pair of shoes if you have the room. If you plan to visit any religious or cultural sites, remember that you'll need something besides tank tops and shorts to be respectful.

SLEEPSACK. Some hostels require that you either provide your own linen or rent sheets from them. Save cash by making your own sleepsack: fold a full-size sheet in half the long way, then sew it closed along the long side and one of the short sides.

CONVERTERS AND ADAPTERS. In Europe, electricity is 220/240 volts AC, enough to fry any 110V North American appliance. **Americans** and **Canadians** should buy an **adapter** (which changes the shape of the plug; around US$7) and a **converter** (which changes the voltage; US$20). If your appliance is **dual voltage,** you can switch it to 220V and just use an adapter. **New Zealanders, South Africans,** and **Australians** won't need a converter, but will need a set of adapters to use anything electrical. You can purchase converters and adapters at most electronics and travel stores.

TOILETRIES. Toothbrushes, towels, cold-water soap, talcum powder (to keep feet dry), deodorant, razors, tampons, and condoms are often available, but may be difficult to find, so bring extras. **Contact lenses,** on the other hand, may be expensive and difficult to find, so bring enough extra pairs and solution for your entire trip. Also bring your glasses and a copy of your prescription in case you need emergency replacements. If you use heat-disinfection, either switch temporarily to a chemical disinfection system (check first to make sure it's safe with your brand of lenses), or buy a converter to 220/240V.

FIRST-AID KIT. For a basic first-aid kit, pack: bandages, pain reliever, antibiotic cream, a thermometer, a Swiss Army knife, tweezers, moleskin, decongestant, motion-sickness remedy, diarrhea or upset-stomach medication (Pepto Bismol or Imodium), an antihistamine, sunscreen, insect repellent, burn ointment, and a syringe for emergencies (get an explanatory letter from your doctor).

FILM. Film and developing in Europe can be expensive, so consider bringing along enough film for your entire trip and developing it at home. Less serious photographers may want to bring **disposable cameras** rather than an expensive permanent one. Despite disclaimers, airport security X-rays *can* fog film, so buy a lead-lined pouch at a camera store or ask security to hand-inspect it. Always pack film in your carry-on luggage, since higher-intensity X-rays are used on checked luggage.

OTHER ITEMS. For safety purposes, you should bring a **money belt** and small **padlock.** Basic **outdoors equipment** (plastic water bottle, compass, waterproof matches, pocketknife, sunglasses, sunscreen, hat) may also prove useful. **Quick repairs** of torn garments can be done on the road with a needle and thread; also consider bringing electrical tape for patching tears. Doing your **laundry** by hand (where allowed) is both cheaper and more convenient than doing it at a laundromat—bring detergent, a small rubber ball to stop up the sink, and string for a makeshift clothes line. **Other things** you're liable to forget: an umbrella; sealable **plastic bags** (for damp clothes, soap, food, shampoo, and other spillables); an **alarm clock;** safety pins; rubber bands; a flashlight; earplugs; garbage bags; and a small **calculator.**

IMPORTANT DOCUMENTS. Don't forget your **passport, traveler's checks, ATM and/ or credit cards,** and adequate **ID.** Also check that you have any of the following that might apply to you: a **hosteling membership card** (p. 37); **driver's license; travel insurance forms**; and/or **rail or bus pass.** It's a good idea to make photocopies to leave at home with family or friends.

ACCOMMODATIONS

HOSTELS

Europe in the summer is overrun by young budget travelers. Hostels are the hub of this subculture, allowing young people from around the world to meet, find travel partners, and learn about places to visit. Hostels are generally laid out dorm-style, often with large single-sex rooms and bunk beds, with a common bathroom and a

ESSENTIALS

Travel better.

Hostelling International goes far beyond hostels and affordable travel. For almost 70 years, we have helped people of all ages explore distant lands and cultures; and learned a few things along the way.

Go online and tap into our collective road wisdom. Check the schedule of upcoming travel workshops throughout the USA.

Go online and join Hostelling International today.

Your journey begins with a simple click.
Visit our web site at: **www.hiayh.org**

lounge down the hall. Some offer private rooms for families and couples. They sometimes offer kitchens and utensils, bike or moped rentals, storage areas, and laundry facilities. There can be drawbacks: some hostels close during certain daytime "lockout" hours, have a curfew, don't accept reservations, impose a maximum stay, or, less frequently, require that you do chores. A bed in a hostel will average around US$10-25 in Western Europe and US$5-10 in Eastern Europe.

 A HOSTELER'S BILL OF RIGHTS. Unless we state otherwise, you can assume that every hostel we list has certain standard features: no lockout, no curfew, free hot showers, secure luggage storage, and no key deposit.

HOSTELLING INTERNATIONAL

Joining the youth hostel association in your own country automatically grants you membership privileges in **Hostelling International (HI),** a federation of national hosteling associations. HI hostels are scattered throughout Europe and are typically less expensive than private hostels. Many accept reservations via the **International Booking Network** (Australia ☎(02) 9261 1111; Canada ☎800-663-5777; England and Wales ☎(1629) 58 14 18; Northern Ireland ☎(1232) 324 733; Republic of Ireland ☎(01) 830 1766; New Zealand ☎(03) 379 9808; Scotland ☎(8701) 553 255; US ☎800-909-4776; www.hostelbooking.com). HI's web page (www.iyhf.org), which lists the web addresses and phone numbers of all national associations, can be a great place to begin researching hostelling in a specific region. Other comprehensive hostelling websites include www.hostels.com and www.hostelplanet.com.

Most HI hostels also honor **guest memberships**—you get a blank card with space for six validation stamps. Each night you pay a nonmember supplement (one-sixth the membership fee) and earn one guest stamp; with six stamps, and you're a member. This system works well in most of Western Europe, but in some countries you may need to remind the hostel reception. Most student travel agencies (p. 54) sell HI cards, as do all of the national hosteling organizations listed below. All prices listed below are valid for **one-year memberships** unless otherwise noted.

Australian Youth Hostels Association (AYHA), Level 3, 10 Mallett St., Camperdown NSW 2050 (☎(02) 9565 1699; fax 9565 1325; www.yha.org.au). AUS$52, under 18 AUS$16.

Hostelling International-Canada (HI-C), 400-205 Catherine St., Ottawa, ON K2P 1C3 (☎800-663-5777 or 613-237-7884; fax 237-7868; info@hostellingintl.ca; www.hostellingintl.ca). CDN$35, under 18 free.

An Óige (Irish Youth Hostel Association), 61 Mountjoy St., Dublin 7 (☎(01) 830 4555; fax 830 5808; anoige@iol.ie; www.irelandyha.org). IR£10, under 18 IR£4.

Youth Hostels Association of New Zealand (YHANZ), P.O. Box 436, 193 Cashel St., 3rd Floor Union House, Christchurch 1 (☎(03) 379 9970; fax 365 4476; info@yha.org.nz; www.yha.org.nz). NZ$40, under 17 free.

Hostels Association of South Africa, 3rd fl. 73 St. George's St. Mall, P.O. Box 4402, Cape Town 8000 (☎(021) 424 2511; fax 424 4119; info@hisa.org.za; www.hisa.org.za). SAR45.

Scottish Youth Hostels Association (SYHA), 7 Glebe Crescent, Stirling FK8 2JA (☎(01786) 891400; fax 891333; www.syha.org.uk). UK£6.

Youth Hostels Association (England and Wales) Ltd., Trevelyan House, 8 St. Stephen's Hill, St. Albans, Hertfordshire AL1 2DY, UK (☎(0870) 870 8808; fax (01727) 844126; www.yha.org.uk). UK£12.50, under 18 UK£6.25, families UK£25.

Hostelling International Northern Ireland (HINI), 22-32 Donegall Rd., Belfast BT12 5JN, Northern Ireland (☎(02890) 315 435; fax 439 699; info@hini.org.uk; www.hini.org.uk). UK£10, under 18 UK£6.

Hostelling International-American Youth Hostels (HI-AYH), 733 15th St. NW, #840, Washington, D.C. 20005 (☎202-783-6161; fax 783-6171; hiayhserv@hiayh.org; www.hiayh.org). US$25, under 18 free.

ESSENTIALS

ESSENTIALS

OTHER TYPES OF ACCOMMODATIONS

YMCAS AND YWCAS

Young Men's Christian Association (YMCA) lodgings are usually cheaper than a hotel but more expensive than a hostel. Not all YMCA locations offer lodging; those that do are often located in urban downtowns. Many YMCAs accept women and families; some will not lodge those under 18 without parental permission.

Y's Way International, 224 E. 47th St., New York, NY 10017 (☎212-308-2899; fax 308-3161). For a small fee ($3 in North America, $5 elsewhere), this "booking service" makes reservations for the YMCAs throughout Europe.

World Alliance of YMCAs, 12 Clos Belmont, 1208 Geneva, Switzerland (☎(22) 849 5100, fax 849 5110; office@ymca.int; www.ymca.int).

HOTELS, GUESTHOUSES, AND PENSIONS

In Britain, Switzerland, Austria, and northern Europe, hotels cost about US$25 per person. Elsewhere, couples and larger groups can get by fairly well. You'll typically share a hall bathroom; a private bathroom will cost extra, as may hot showers. Some hotels offer "full pension" (all meals) and "half pension" (no lunch). Smaller guesthouses and pensions are often cheaper than hotels. If you make reservations in writing, indicate your night of arrival and the number of nights you plan to stay. The hotel will send you a confirmation and may request payment for the first night. Not all hotels take reservations, and few accept checks in foreign currency. Enclosing two International Reply Coupons will ensure a prompt reply (each US$1.05; available at any post office).

BED AND BREAKFASTS (B&BS)

For a cozy alternative to impersonal hotel rooms, B&Bs (private homes with rooms available to travelers) range from the acceptable to the sublime. Hosts will sometimes go out of their way to be accommodating by accepting travelers with pets, giving personalized tours, or offering home-cooked meals. On the other hand, many B&Bs do not provide phones, TVs, or private bathrooms. B&Bs are particularly popular in Britain and Ireland. For more information on B&Bs, see **InnFinder** (www.inncrawler.com), or **InnSite** (www.innsite.com).

UNIVERSITY DORMS

Many **colleges and universities** open their residence halls to travelers when school is not in session; some do so even during term-time. These dorms are often close to student areas—good sources for information on things to do—and are usually very clean. Getting a room may take a couple of phone calls and require advanced planning, but rates tend to be low, and many offer free local calls.

HOME EXCHANGES AND HOME RENTALS

Home exchange offers the traveler various types of homes (houses, apartments, condominiums, villas, even castles in some cases), plus the opportunity to live like a native and to cut down on accommodation fees. For more information, contact **HomeExchange.Com** (☎805-898-9660; www.homeexchange.com), **Intervac International Home Exchange** (www.intervac.com), or **The Invented City: International Home Exchange** (US ☎800-788-CITY, elsewhere ☎415-252-1141; www.invented-city.com). **Home rentals** are more expensive than exchanges, but they can be cheaper than comparably serviced hotels. Both home exchanges and rentals are ideal for families with children, or travelers with special dietary needs; you often get your own kitchen, maid service, TV, and telephones.

ESSENTIALS

CAMPING AND THE OUTDOORS

Organized campgrounds exist just outside most European cities. Showers, bathrooms, and a small restaurant or store are common; some have more elaborate facilities. Prices are low, at US$5-15 per person with additional charges for tents and/or cars. While camping is a cheaper option than hostelling, the cost of transportation to the campsites can add up. **Free camping** allows you to camp in parks or public land (in some cases, such as Sweden, even on private land) for free.

USEFUL PUBLICATIONS AND RESOURCES

A variety of publishing companies offer hiking guidebooks to meet the educational needs of novice or expert. Campers heading to Europe should consider buying an **International Camping Carnet**. Similar to a hostel membership card, it's required at a few campgrounds and provides discounts at others. It is available in North America from the Family Campers and RVers Association and in the UK from The Caravan Club (see below). For information about camping, hiking, and biking, write or call the publishers listed below to receive a **free catalog**. An excellent resource for travelers planning on camping or spending time in the outdoors is the **Great Outdoor Recreation Pages** (www.gorp.com).

Automobile Association, A.A. Publishing. Orders and enquiries to TBS Frating Distribution Centre, Colchester, Essex, CO7 7DW, UK (☎ (01206) 255678; www.theaa.co.uk). Publishes *Camping and Caravanning: Europe and Britain & Ireland* (UK£8-9) as well as *Big Road Atlases* for Europe, France, Spain, Germany, and Italy.

The Caravan Club, East Grinstead House, East Grinstead, West Sussex, RH19 1UA (UK ☎ (01342) 326944; www.caravanclub.co.uk). For UK£27.50, members receive equipment discounts, a 700-page directory and handbook, and a monthly magazine.

The European Federation of Campingsite Organisations, EFCO Secretariat, 6 Pullman Court, Great Western Road, Gloucester, GL 1 3 ND (UK ☎ (1452) 526911; efco@bhhpa.org.uk; www.campingeurope.com). The website has a comprehensive list of links to campsites in most European countries.

Sierra Club Books, 85 Second St., 2nd fl., San Francisco, CA 94105, USA (☎ 415-977-5500; www.sierraclub.org/books). Publishes general resource books on hiking, camping, and women traveling in the outdoors.

The Mountaineers Books, 1001 SW Klickitat Way, #201, Seattle, WA 98134, USA (☎ 800-553-4453 or 206-223-6303; www.mountaineersbooks.org). Over 400 titles on hiking, biking, mountaineering, natural history, and conservation.

CAMPING AND HIKING EQUIPMENT

WHAT TO BUY...

Good camping equipment is both sturdy and light. Camping equipment is generally more expensive in Australia, New Zealand, and the UK than in North America.

Sleeping Bag: Most sleeping bags are rated by season ("summer" means 30-40°F at night; "four-season" or "winter" often means below 0°F). They are made either of **down** (warmer and lighter, but more expensive, and miserable when wet) or of **synthetic** material (heavier, more durable, and warmer when wet). Prices range US$80-210 for a summer synthetic to US$250-300 for a good down winter bag. **Sleeping bag pads** include foam pads (US$10-20), air mattresses (US$15-50), and Therm-A-Rest self-inflating pads (US$45-80). Bring a **stuff sack** to store your bag and keep it dry.

Tent: The best tents are free-standing (with their own frames and suspension systems), set up quickly, and only require staking in high winds. Low-profile dome tents are the best all-around. Good 2-person tents start at US$90, 4-person at US$300. Seal the seams of your tent with waterproofer, and make sure it has a rain fly. Other tent accessories include a **battery-operated lantern**, a **plastic groundcloth**, and a **nylon tarp.**

Backpack: Internal-frame packs mold better to your back, keep a lower center of gravity, and flex adequately to allow you to hike difficult trails. **External-frame packs** are more comfortable for long hikes over even terrain, as they keep weight higher and distribute it more evenly. Make sure your pack has a strong, padded hip-belt to transfer weight to your legs. Any serious backpacking requires a pack of at least 4000 cubic inches, plus 500 cubic inches for sleeping bags in internal-frame packs. Sturdy backpacks cost anywhere from US$125-420. This is one area in which it doesn't pay to economize. Fill up any pack with something heavy and walk around the store with it to get a sense of how it distributes weight before buying it. Either buy a **waterproof backpack cover,** or store all of your belongings in plastic bags inside your pack.

Boots: Be sure to wear hiking boots with good **ankle support.** They should fit snugly and comfortably over 1-2 pairs of wool socks and thin liner socks. Break in boots over several weeks first in order to spare yourself painful and debilitating blisters.

Other Necessities: Synthetic layers, like those made of polypropylene, and a **pile jacket** will keep you warm even when wet. A **"space blanket"** will help you to retain your body heat and doubles as a groundcloth (US$5-15). Plastic **water bottles** are virtually shatter- and leak-proof. Bring **water-purification tablets** for when you can't boil water. Although most campgrounds provide campfire sites, you may want to bring a small **metal grate** or **grill** of your own. For those places that forbid fires or the gathering of firewood (this includes virtually every organized campground in Europe), you'll need a **camp stove** (the classic Coleman starts at US$40) and a propane-filled **fuel bottle** to operate it. Also don't forget a **first-aid kit, pocketknife, insect repellent, calamine lotion,** and **waterproof matches** or a **lighter.**

...AND WHERE TO BUY IT

The mail-order/online companies listed below offer lower prices than many retail stores, but a visit to a local camping or outdoors store will give you a good sense of the look and weight of certain items.

Campmor, 28 Parkway, P.O. Box 700, Upper Saddle River, NJ 07458 (US ☎888-226-7667; elsewhere US ☎201-825-8300; www.campmor.com).

Discount Camping, 880 Main North Rd., Pooraka, South Australia 5095, Australia (☎(08) 8262 3399; www.discountcamping.com.au).

Eastern Mountain Sports (EMS), 327 Jaffrey Rd., Peterborough, NH 03458, USA (☎888-463-6367 or 603-924-7231; www.shopems.com).

L.L. Bean, Freeport, ME 04033 (US and Canada ☎800-441-5713; UK ☎(0800) 891297; elsewhere, call US ☎207-552-3028; www.llbean.com).

Mountain Designs, P.O. Box 1472, Fortitude Valley, Queensland 4006, Australia (☎(07) 3252 8894; www.mountaindesign.com.au).

Recreational Equipment, Inc. (REI), Sumner, WA 98352, USA (☎800-426-4840 or 253-891-2500; www.rei.com).

YHA Adventure Shop, 14 Southampton St., London, WC2E 7HA, UK (☎(020) 7836 8541). The main branch of one of Britain's largest outdoor equipment suppliers.

CAMPERS AND RVS

Renting an RV will always be more expensive than tenting or hosteling, but it's cheaper than staying in hotels and renting a car (see Rental Cars, p. 74), and the convenience of bringing along your own bedroom, bathroom, and kitchen makes it an attractive option, especially for older travelers and families with children. Rates vary widely by region, season (July and August are the most expensive months), and type of RV. It always pays to contact several different companies to compare vehicles and prices.

Auto Europe (US ☎800-223-5555; UK ☎(0800) 899893; www.autoeurope.com) rents RVs in New Zealand, Australia, Florence, London, Paris, Lyon, Marseille, Nice, Hamburg, Frankfurt, Munich, and Berlin.

ORGANIZED ADVENTURE TRIPS

Organized adventure tours offer another way of exploring the wild. Activities include hiking, biking, skiing, canoeing, kayaking, rafting, climbing, photo safaris, and archaeological digs. Tourism bureaus can often suggest parks, trails, and outfitters;

other good sources for information are stores and organizations that specialize in camping and outdoor equipment like REI and EMS (see above).

Specialty Travel Index, 305 San Anselmo Ave., #313, San Anselmo, CA 94960, USA (☎800-442-4922 or 415-459-4900; www.specialtytravel.com). Tours worldwide.

ENVIRONMENTALLY RESPONSIBLE TOURISM. The idea behind responsible tourism is to leave no trace of human presence behind. A campstove is the safer (and more efficient) way to cook than using vegetation, but if you must make a fire, keep it small and use only dead branches or brush rather than cutting vegetation. Make sure your campsite is at least 150ft. (50m) from water supplies or bodies of water. If there are no toilet facilities, bury human waste (but not paper) at least 4in. (10cm) deep and above the high-water line, and 150ft. or more from any water supplies and campsites. Always pack your trash in a plastic bag and carry it with you until you reach the next trash receptacle. For more information on these issues, contact one of the organizations listed below.

Earthwatch, 3 Clock Tower Place #100, Box 75, Maynard, MA 01754, USA (☎800-776-0188 or 978-461-0081; info@earthwatch.org; www.earthwatch.org).

Ecotourism Society, P.O. Box 668, Burlington, VT 05402, USA (☎802-651-9818; ecomail@ecotourism.org; www.ecotourism.org).

National Audobon Society, Nature Odysseys, 700 Broadway, New York, NY 10003 (☎212-979-3066; travel@audobon.org; www.audobon.org).

Tourism Concern, Stapleton House, 277-281 Holloway Rd., London N7 8HN, UK (☎(020) 7753 3330; www.tourismconcern.org.uk).

COMMUNICATION

BY MAIL

SENDING MAIL HOME FROM EUROPE

Airmail is the best way to send mail home from Europe. From Western Europe to North America, airmail averages seven days; from Central or Eastern Europe, allow anywhere from seven days to three weeks (in Russia, Ukraine, and Belarus, your mail may never leave the post office). **Aerogrammes**, printed sheets that fold into envelopes and travel via airmail, are available at post offices. Write "par avion" (or *por avion, mit Luftpost, via aerea*, etc.) on the front. Most post offices will charge exorbitant fees or simply refuse to send aerogrammes with enclosures. **Surface mail** is by far the cheapest and slowest way to send mail. It takes one to three months to cross the Atlantic and two to four to cross the Pacific—good for items you won't need to see for a while, such as souvenirs or other articles you've acquired along the way that are weighing down your pack.

SENDING MAIL TO EUROPE

Mark envelopes "par avion" or "airmail" in the language of your country; otherwise, your letter or postcard will not arrive. In addition to the standard postage system, **Federal Express** (Australia ☎13 26 10; US and Canada ☎800-247-4747; New Zealand ☎(0800) 733339; UK ☎(0800) 123800; www.fedex.com) handles express mail services from most home countries to Europe.

Australia: Allow 5-7 days for regular **airmail** to Europe. Postcards and letters up to 20g cost AUS$1; packages up to 0.5kg AUS$13, up to 2kg AUS$46. **EMS** can get a letter there in 2-3 days for AUS$32. www.auspost.com.au/pac.

Canada: Allow 4-7 days for regular **airmail** to Europe. Postcards and letters up to 20g cost CDN$1.05; packages up to 0.5kg CDN$10.20, up to 2kg CDN$34.00. www.canadapost.ca/CPC2/common/rates/ratesgen.html#international.

Ireland: Allow 2-3 days for regular airmail to the UK and Western Europe. Postcards and letters up to 25g cost IR£0.30 to the UK, IR£0.32 to the continent. International Swiftpost zips letters to some major European countries for an additional IR£260 on top of priority postage. www.letterpost.ie.

New Zealand: Allow 6-12 days for regular airmail to Europe. Postcards NZ$1.50. Letters up to 200g cost NZ$2-5; small parcels up to 0.5kg NZ$16.50, up to 2kg NZ$52.61. www.nzpost.net.nz/nzpost/control/ratefinder.

UK: Allow 2-3 days for airmail to Europe. Letters up to 20g cost UK£0.36; packages up to 0.5kg UK£2.67, up to 2kg UK£9.42. UK Swiftair delivers letters a day faster for an extra UK£2.85. www.royalmail.com/International/calculator.

US: Allow 4-7 days for regular **airmail** to Europe. Postcards/aerogrammes cost US$0.70; letters under 1oz. US$0.80; packages under 1lb. US$14; larger packages up to 5lb. $22.75). **Global Express Mail** takes 2-3 days; 0.5lb. costs US$20, 1lb. US$24.75. **US Global Priority Mail** delivers flat-rate envelopes to Europe in 3-5 days for US$5-9. http://ircalc.usps.gov.

RECEIVING MAIL IN EUROPE

There are several ways to arrange pick-up of letters sent to you by friends and relatives while you are abroad. Mail can be sent via **Poste Restante** (General Delivery; *Lista de Correos, Fermo Posta, Postlagernde Briefe*, etc.) to almost any city or town in Europe with a post office. See individual country chapters to see how to address *Poste Restante* letters. The mail will go to a special desk in the central post office, unless you specify a post office by street address or postal code. It's best to use the largest post office, since mail may be sent there regardless. It is usually safer and quicker, though more expensive, to send mail express or registered. Bring your passport (or other photo ID) for pick-up; there may be a small fee. If the clerks insist that there is nothing for you, check under your first name as well. *Let's Go* lists post offices in the **Practical Information** section for each city and most towns.

American Express travel offices offer a free **Client Letter Service** (mail held up to 30 days and forwarded upon request) for cardholders who contact them in advance. Address the letter as you would for Poste Restante. Some offices offer these services to non-cardholders (especially AmEx Travelers Cheque holders), but call ahead. *Let's Go* lists AmEx office locations for most large cities in **Practical Information** sections; for a complete, free list, call US ☎800-528-4800.

BY TELEPHONE

TIME DIFFERENCES

All of Europe falls within three hours of **Greenwich Mean Time (GMT)**. Consult the **time zone map** on the inside back cover. GMT is five hours ahead of New York time, eight hours ahead of Vancouver and San Francisco time, two hours behind Johannesburg time, 10 hours behind Sydney time, and 12 hours behind Auckland time. Some countries ignore **daylight savings time;** fall and spring switchover times vary.

CALLING HOME FROM EUROPE

A **calling card** is probably cheapest. Calls are billed collect or to your account. You can frequently call collect without even possessing a company's calling card just by calling their access number and following the instructions. **To obtain a calling card** from your national telecommunications service before leaving home, contact the appropriate company listed below:

AT&T (US): ☎800-225-5288.
British Telecom: ☎(800) 345144.
Canada Direct: ☎800-668-6878.
Ireland Direct: ☎(800) 400 000.
MCI (US): ☎800-444-3333.
Telecom New Zealand: ☎(0800) 000 000.

Sprint (US): ☎800-877-4646.
Telkom South Africa: ☎10 219.
Telstra Australia ☎132 200.

To **call home with a calling card,** contact the operator for your service provider in the country of your travel by dialing the appropriate toll-free access number (listed in the Essentials section of each country under Communications). Keep in mind that phone cards can be problematic in Russia, Ukraine, Belarus, and Slovenia—double-check with your provider before setting out. You can usually make **direct international calls** from pay phones, but if you aren't using a calling card, you may need to drop your coins as quickly as your words. Where available, prepaid phone cards and occasionally major credit cards can be used for direct international calls, but they are still less cost-efficient. (See the box on **Placing International Calls** (p. 44) for directions on how to place a direct international call.) Placing a **collect call** through an international operator is a more expensive alternative. You can typically place collect calls through the service providers listed above, even if you don't possess one of their phone cards.

CALLING WITHIN EUROPE

The simplest way to call within the country is to use a coin-operated phone. However, much of Europe has switched to a **prepaid phone card** system, and in some countries you may have a hard time finding any coin-operated phones at all. Prepaid phone cards (available at newspaper kiosks and tobacco stores), which carry a certain amount of phone time depending on the card's denomination, usually save time and money in the long run. The computerized phone will tell you how much time, in units, you have left on your card. Another kind of prepaid telephone card comes with a Personal Identification Number (PIN) and a toll-free access number. Instead of inserting the card into the phone, you call the access number and follow the directions on the card. These cards can be used to make international as well as domestic calls. Phone rates typically tend to be highest in the morning, lower in the evening, and lowest on Sunday and late at night.

PLACING INTERNATIONAL CALLS. To call Europe from home or to call home from Europe, dial:

1. The **international dialing prefix.** To dial out of **Australia,** dial 0011; **Canada** or the **US,** 011; the **Republic of Ireland, New Zealand,** or the **UK,** 00; **South Africa,** 09.
2. The **country code** of the country you want to call. To call **Australia,** dial 61; **Canada** or the **US,** 1; the **Republic of Ireland,** 353; **New Zealand,** 64; **South Africa,** 27; the **UK,** 44.
3. The **city/area code.** *Let's Go* lists the city/area codes for cities and towns opposite the city or town name within each country's chapter, next to a ☎. If the first digit is a zero (e.g., 020 for London), omit the zero when calling from abroad (e.g., dial 20 from Canada to reach London).
4. The **local number.**

BY EMAIL AND INTERNET

Email is a popular and easily accessible in most of Europe. Take advantage of free **web-based email accounts** (e.g., www.hotmail.com and www.yahoo.com); while it's sometimes possible to forge a remote link with your home server, in most cases this is a much slower and more expensive option. Travelers with laptops can call an Internet service provider via a **modem.** Long-distance phone cards specifically intended for such calls can defray normally high phone charges; check with your long-distance phone provider to see if it offers this option. **Internet cafes** and the occasional free Internet terminal at a public library or university are listed in the **Practical Information** sections of major cities. For lists of additional cybercafes in Europe, check out cybercaptive.com or netcafeguide.com.

SPECIFIC CONCERNS

WOMEN TRAVELERS

Women exploring on their own inevitably face some additional safety concerns, but you can still be adventurous without taking undue risks. If you are concerned, consider staying in hostels with single rooms that lock from the inside or in religious organizations with rooms for women only. Communal showers in some hostels are safer than others; check them before settling in. Stick to centrally located accommodations and avoid solitary late-night treks or metro rides. Always carry extra money for a phone call, bus, or taxi. **Hitchhiking** is never safe for women, or even for two women traveling together. Choose train compartments occupied by women or couples; ask the conductor to put together a women-only compartment if he or she doesn't offer to do so first. Look as if you know where you're going and approach older women or couples for directions if you're lost or uncomfortable.

In general, the less you look like a tourist, the better off you'll be. Try to dress conservatively, especially in rural areas. Wearing a conspicuous **wedding band** may help prevent unwanted overtures; some travelers report that carrying pictures of a "husband" or "children" is extremely useful to help document marriage status. Even a mention of a husband waiting back at the hotel may be enough in some places to discount your potentially vulnerable, unattached appearance. Solo women travelers are a phenomenon in Eastern Europe, as Eastern European women never eat out by themselves, so you might get a few surprised stares. Consider wearing skirts rather than shorts to blend in; avoid baggy jeans, T-shirts, and sneakers, since they may make it obvious that you're a foreigner.

FURTHER READING: WOMEN TRAVELERS.
Active Women Vacation Guide, Evelyn Kaye. Blue Panda Publications (US$18).
A Foxy Old Woman's Guide to Traveling Alone: Around Town and Around the World, Jay Ben-Lesser. Crossing Press (US$11).
A Journey of One's Own: Uncommon Advice for the Independent Woman Traveler, Thalia Zepatos. Eighth Mountain Press (US$17).
Safety and Security for Women Who Travel, Sheila Swan. Travelers' Tales Guides, Inc. (US$13).

Your best answer to verbal harassment is no answer at all; feigning deafness, sitting motionless, and staring straight ahead will do a world of good that reactions usually don't achieve. The extremely persistent can often be dissuaded by a firm, loud, and very public "Go away!" in the appropriate language (see Language Basics). Don't hesitate to seek out a police officer or passersby if you are being harassed. Memorize the emergency numbers in places you visit, and consider carrying a whistle or airhorn on your keychain. A **self-defense course** will not only prepare you for a potential attack, but will also raise your level of awareness of your surroundings and your confidence (p. 28). Also be aware of the health concerns that women face when traveling (p. 33). *Journeywoman* (www.journeywoman.com) posts an online newsletter and other resources providing female-specific travel tips. *Women Traveling Together* (www.women-traveling.com) places women in small groups to explore the world.

SOLO TRAVELERS

There are many benefits to traveling alone, among them greater independence and more opportunities to interact with the residents of the region you're visiting. On the other hand, a solo traveler is more vulnerable to harassment and street theft. Lone travelers need to be well-organized and look confident at all times. Try not to stand out as a tourist, and be especially careful in deserted or very crowded areas. If questioned, never admit that you are traveling alone. Maintain regular contact with someone at home who knows your itinerary. The **Travel Companion Exchange,** P.O. Box 833, Amityville, NY 11701 (US ☎631-454-0880 or 800-392-1256; www.whytravelalone.com) links solo travelers with companions who have similar travel habits; subscribe to their bi-monthly newsletter for more information (US$48). The books and organizations listed below provide information and services for the lone wanderer.

> **FURTHER RESOURCES: SOLO TRAVELERS.**
> **American International Homestays,** P.O. Box 1754, Nederland, CO 80466 (US ☎303-258-3234; www.aihtravel.com). Arranges lodgings with host families across the world.
> **Connecting: Solo Travel Network,** 689 Park Road, Unit 6, Gibsons, BC V0N 1V7 (☎604-886-9099; www.cstn.org; membership US$28), offers solo travel tips, host information, and individuals looking for travel companions.
> *Traveling Solo,* Eleanor Berman. Globe Pequot Press (US$17).
> *Travel Alone & Love It: A Flight Attendant's Guide to Solo Travel,* Sharon B. Wingler. Chicago Spectrum Press (US$15).

OLDER TRAVELERS

Senior citizens are eligible for discounts on transportation, museums, movies, theaters, concerts, restaurants, and accommodations. If you don't see a senior citizen price listed, ask, and you might be surprised. However, keep in mind that some hostels, particularly in Germany, do not allow guests over age 26; call ahead to check. The books *No Problem! Worldwise Tips for Mature Adventurers,* by Janice Kenyon (Orca Book Publishers; US$16) and *Unbelievably Good Deals and Great Adventures That You Absolutely Can't Get Unless You're Over 50,* by Joan Rattner Heilman (NTC/Contemporary Publishing; US$13) are both excellent resources. For more information, contact one of the following organizations:

ElderTreks, 597 Markham St., Toronto, ON M6G 2L7 (Canada ☎800-741-7956; www.eldertreks.com). Adventure travel programs for ages 50+ in Finland and Iceland.

Elderhostel, 11 Ave. de Lafayette, Boston, MA 02111 (US ☎877-426-8056; www.elderhostel.org). Organizes one- to four-week "educational adventures" throughout Europe on varied subjects for those 55+.

The Mature Traveler, P.O. Box 15791, Sacramento, CA 95852 (US ☎800-460-6676). Deals, discounts, and travel packages for the 50+ traveler. Subscription US$30.

Walking the World, P.O. Box 1186, Fort Collins, CO 80522, (US ☎800-340-9255; www.walkingtheworld.com). Organizes trips for 50+ travelers to Britain, the Czech Republic, France, Ireland, Italy, Norway, Portugal, Scotland, Slovakia, and Switzerland.

BISEXUAL, GAY, & LESBIAN TRAVELERS

Attitudes toward bisexual, gay, and lesbian travelers are particular to each region in Europe. Acceptance is generally highest in large cities and The Netherlands, and generally lower in eastern nations, particularly Turkey. Listed below are contact organizations, mail-order bookstores, and publishers that offer materials addressing some specific concerns. **Out and About** (www.planetout.com) offers a biweekly newsletter addressing travel concerns as well as a comprehensive site.

Gay's the Word, 66 Marchmont St., London WC1N 1AB (UK ☎(020) 7278 7654, international +44 (20) 7278 7654; www.gaystheword.co.uk). The largest gay and lesbian bookshop in the UK, with both fiction and non-fiction titles. Mail-order service available.

Giovanni's Room, 1145 Pine St., Philadelphia, PA 19107 (US ☎215-923-2960; www.queerbooks.com). An international lesbian/feminist and gay bookstore with mail-order service (carries many of the publications listed below).

International Gay and Lesbian Travel Association, International Lesbian and Gay Association (ILGA), 81 rue Marché-au-Charbon, B-1000 Brussels, Belgium (☎+32 (2) 502 2471; www.ilga.org). Provides political info, like homosexuality laws of countries.

> **FURTHER READING: BISEXUAL, GAY, AND LESBIAN.**
> *Damron Men's Travel Guide, Damron Women's Traveller, Damron's Accommodations,* and *Damron Amsterdam Guide.* Damron Travel Guides (US$10-19). For more info, call ☎800-462-6654 or visit www.damron.com.
> *Ferrari Guides' Gay Travel A to Z, Ferrari Guides' Men's Travel in Your Pocket,* and *Ferrari Guides' Inn Places.* Ferrari Publications (US$16-20). Purchase the guides online at www.ferrariguides.com.
> *The Gay Vacation Guide: The Best Trips and How to Plan Them,* Mark Chesnut. Citadel Press (US$15).
> *Odysseus International Gay Travel Planner,* Eli Angelo and Joseph Bain. Odysseus Enterprises Ltd. (US$31).
> *Spartacus International Gay Guide 2001-2002,* Bruno Gmunder Verlag (US$33).

TRAVELERS WITH DISABILITIES

Countries vary in accessibility to travelers with disabilities. Some national and regional tourist boards provide directories on the accessibility of various accommodations and transportation services. If these services are not available, contact institutions of interest directly. Those with disabilities should inform airlines and hotels of their disabilities when making reservations; some time may be needed to prepare special accommodations. Call ahead to restaurants, museums, and other facilities to find out about the existence of ramps, the widths of doors, or the dimensions of elevators. **Guide dog owners** should inquire as to the quarantine policies of each destination country. At the very least, they will need to provide a certificate of immunization against rabies.

Rail is probably the most convenient form of travel for disabled travelers in Europe: many stations have ramps, and some trains have wheelchair lifts, special seating areas, and specially equipped toilets. Large stations in Britain are equipped with wheelchair facilities, and the French national railroad offers wheelchair compartments on all TGV (high speed) and Conrail trains. All Eurostar, some InterCity (IC) and some EuroCity (EC) trains are wheelchair-accessible and CityNightLine trains, French TGV (high speed) and Conrail trains feature special compartments. In general, the countries with the most **wheelchair-accessible rail networks** are: Denmark (IC and Lyn trains), France (TGVs and other long-distance trains), Germany (ICE, EC, IC, and IR trains), Italy (all Pendolino and many EC and IC trains), the Netherlands (most trains), the Republic of Ireland (most major trains), Sweden (X2000s, most IC and IR trains), and Switzerland (all IC, most EC, and some regional trains). Austria, Poland, and Great Britain offer accessibility on selected routes. Greece and Spain's rail systems have limited resources for wheelchair accessibility. For those who wish to rent cars, some major **car rental** agencies (Hertz, Avis, and National) offer hand-controlled vehicles.

USEFUL ORGANIZATIONS

Mobility International USA (MIUSA), P.O. Box 10767, Eugene, OR 97440 (US ☎541-343-1284, voice and TDD; www.miusa.org). Sells *A World of Options: A Guide to International Educational Exchange, Community Service, and Travel for Persons with Disabilities* (US$35).

Moss Rehab ResourceNet, (www.mossresourcenet.org). An Internet information resource center on international travel accessibility and other travel-related concerns for those with disabilities.

Society for the Advancement of Travel for the Handicapped (SATH), 347 Fifth Ave., #610, New York, NY 10016 (US ☎212-447-7284; www.sath.org). An advocacy group that publishes free online travel information and the travel magazine *OPEN WORLD* (US$18, free for members). Annual membership US$45, students and seniors US$30.

TOUR AGENCIES

Directions Unlimited, 123 Green Ln., Bedford Hills, NY 10507 (US ☎800-533-5343 or 914-241-1700; www.travel-cruises.com). Specializes in arranging individual and group vacations, tours, and cruises for the physically disabled.

The Guided Tour Inc., 7900 Old York Rd., #114B, Elkins Park, PA 19027 (☎800-783-5841 or 215-782-1370; www.guidedtour.com). Organizes travel programs for persons with developmental and physical challenges around Ireland, London, and Rome.

>
> **FURTHER READING: DISABILITIES.**
> *Access in London,* Gordon Couch. Cimino Publishing Group (US$12).
> *Around the World Resource Guide,* Patricia Smither. Access for Disabled American Publishing (US$15).
> *Resource Directory for the Disabled,* Richard Neil Shrout. Facts on file (US$45).
> *Wheelchair Around the World,* Patrick D. Simpson. Pentland Press, Inc. (US$25).
> *Wheelchair Through Europe,* Annie Mackin. Graphic Language Press (US$13).

MINORITY TRAVELERS

In general, minority travelers will find a high level of tolerance in large cities; the small towns and the countryside are more unpredictable. *Romany* (Gypsies) encounter the most hostility throughout Eastern Europe, and travelers with darker skin of any nationality might be mistaken for *Romany* and face unpleasant consequences. Other minority travelers, especially those of African or Asian descent, will usually meet with more curiosity than hostility; travelers of Arab ethnicity may also be treated more suspiciously. Skinheads are on the rise in Europe, and minority travelers, especially Jews and blacks, should regard them with caution. Anti-Semitism is still a problem in many countries; sad to say, it is generally best to be discreet about your religion. Still, attitudes will vary from country to country and town to town; travelers should use common sense—consult **Safety and Security** (p. 28) for tips on how to avoid unwanted attention.

TRAVELERS WITH CHILDREN

Family vacations often require that you slow your pace, and always require that you plan ahead. When deciding where to stay, remember the special needs of young children; if you pick a B&B or a small hotel, call ahead and make sure it's child-friendly. If you rent a car, make sure the rental company provides a car seat for younger children. **Be sure that your child carries some sort of ID** in case of an emergency or in case he or she gets lost.

Museums, tourist attractions, accommodations, and restaurants often offer discounts for children. Children under two generally fly for 10% of the adult airfare on international flights (this does not necessarily include a seat). International fares are usually discounted 25% for children from two to 11.

> **FURTHER READING: TRAVELERS WITH CHILDREN.**
> *Backpacking with Babies and Small Children,* Goldie Silverman. Wilderness Press (US$10).
> *Take Your Kids to Europe,* Cynthia W. Harriman. Globe Pequot Press (US$18).
> *How to take Great Trips with Your Kids,* Sanford and Jane Portnoy. Harvard Common Press (US $10).
> *Have Kid, Will Travel: 101 Survival Strategies for Vacationing With Babies and Young Children,* Claire and Lucille Tristram. Andrews McMeel Publishing (US$9).
> *Adventuring with Children: An Inspirational Guide to World Travel and the Outdoors,* Nan Jeffrey. Menasha Ridge Press (US$15).
> *Trouble Free Travel with Children,* Vicki Lansky. Book Peddlers (US$9).

DIETARY CONCERNS

Vegetarians should have no problem finding suitable cuisine in most of Western Europe. Particularly in city listings, *Let's Go* notes many restaurants that cater to vegetarians or that offer good vegetarian selections. The North American Vegetarian Society, P.O. Box 72, Dolgeville, NY 13329 (US ☎518-568-7970; www.navs-online.org), publishes information about vegetarian travel, including *Transformative Adventures, a Guide to Vacations and Retreats* (US$15).

> **FURTHER RESOURCES: DIETARY CONCERNS.**
> **North American Vegetarian Society,** P.O. Box 72, Dolgeville, NY 13329 (US ☎518-568-7970, fax 568-7979; navs@telenet.com; www.navs-online.org).
> **The Vegetarian Society of the UK (VSUK),** Parkdale, Dunham Rd, Altringham, Cheshire WA14 4QG (☎(0161) 925 2000; fax 926 9182; www.vegsoc.org).
> *The Vegan Travel Guide: UK and Southern Ireland.* Book Publishing Co. (US$15).
> *Europe on 10 Salads a Day,* by Greg and Mary Jane Edwards. Mustang Publishing; (US$10).
> *The Vegetarian Traveler: Where to Stay if You're Vegetarian, Vegan, Environmentally Sensitive,* Jed and Susan Civic. Larson Publications (US$16).

Travelers who keep **kosher** should contact synagogues in larger cities for information on food options. Your own synagogue or college Hillel should have access to lists of Jewish institutions across the nation. If you are strict in your observance, you may have to prepare your own food on the road. A good resource is the *Jewish Travel Guide*, by Michael Zaidner (Vallentine-Mitchell; US$17). *A Travel Guide to Jewish Europe*, by Ben G. Frank (Pelican Publishing; US$23), lists local Jewish neighborhoods, synagogues, and kosher restaurants in 18 countries.

ALTERNATIVES TO TOURISM

For an extensive listing of "off-the-beaten-track" and specialty travel opportunities, try the **Specialty Travel Index,** 305 San Anselmo Ave., #313, San Anselmo, CA 94960, USA (☎800-442-4922 or 415-459-4900; www.specialtytravel.com; US$10). **Transitions Abroad** (www.transabroad.com) publishes a bimonthly on-line newsletter for work, study, and specialized travel abroad.

STUDYING ABROAD

The opportunities for studying in Europe are plenty: whether you seek a college semester abroad, a summer of foreign-language immersion, or a top-notch cooking school, you are almost sure to find a program tailored to your needs. Most American undergraduates enroll in programs sponsored by US universities. Those with adequate language skills may find it cheaper to enroll directly in a European university (though getting credit may be more difficult). Direct enrollment usually involves passing a language-proficiency test.

Studying abroad in Europe, particularly enrolling as a full-time student, generally requires applying for a special **study visa,** issued for a duration longer than a tourist visa. Applying for such a visa usually requires proof of admission to an appropriate university or program. In some countries, student status will affect your right to work. Information on visa and other requirements should be available from foreign embassies at home. For further information, including links to many study abroad organizations, visit the on-line directory at We Study Abroad (www.westudyabroad.com).

UNIVERSITY PROGRAMS

American Institute for Foreign Study, College Division, River Plaza, 9 West Broad St., Stamford, CT 06902, USA (☎800-727-2437, ext. 5163; www.aifsabroad.com). Organizes programs for high school and college study in universities in Austria, Czech Republic, England, France, the Netherlands, Ireland, Italy, and Spain.

Arcadia University for Education Abroad, 450 S. Easton Rd., Glenside, PA 19038, USA (☎866-927-2234; www.arcadia.edu/cea). Operates programs in Britain, Greece, Ireland, Italy, Scotland, Spain, and Wales. $2400 (summer) to $20,000 (full-year).

Central College Abroad, Office of International Education, 812 University, Pella, IA 50219, USA (☎800-831-3629 or 641-628-5284; studyabroad.com/central). Offers semester- and year-long programs in Austria, Britain, France, the Netherlands, and Spain. US$25 application fee.

Council on International Educational Exchange (CIEE), 633 3rd Ave. 20th floor, New York, NY 10017-6706 USA (☎888-268-6245; www.ciee.org/isp) sponsors work, volunteer, academic, and internship programs throughout Western Europe.

International Association for the Exchange of Students for Technical Experience (IAESTE), 10400 Little Patuxent Pkwy. #250, Columbia, MD 21044, USA (☎410-997-2200; www.aipt.org). 8- to 12-week programs in Western European countries for college students who have completed 2 years of technical study. US$25 application fee.

School for International Training, College Semester Abroad, Admissions, Kipling Rd., P.O. Box 676, Brattleboro, VT 05302, USA (☎800-336-1616 or 802-258-3267; www.sit.edu). Semester- and year-long programs throughout Western Europe run US$10,600-13,700. Also runs the **Experiment in International Living** (☎800-345-2929; fax 802-258-3428; eil@worldlearning.org), 3- to 5-week summer programs that offer high-school students cross-cultural homestays, community service, ecological adventure, and language training in Britain, France, Ireland, Italy, Spain and Switzerland, and cost US$1900-5000.

LANGUAGE SCHOOLS

Eurocentres, 101 N. Union St. #300, Alexandria, VA 22314, USA (☎703-684-1494; fax 684-1495; www.eurocentres.com) or in Europe, Head Office, Seestr. 247, CH-8038 Zurich, Switzerland (☎+41 1 485 50 40; fax 481 61 24; info@eurocentres.com). Language programs for beginning to advanced students with homestays in Britain, France, Germany, Italy, and Spain.

Language Immersion Institute, 75 South Manheim Blvd., SUNY-New Paltz, New Paltz, NY 12561, USA (☎914-257-3500; www.newpaltz.edu/lii). 2-week summer language courses and overseas courses in France, Italy, and Spain. Program fees US$295 per weekend or US$750 per 2 weeks.

FURTHER RESOURCES: STUDYING ABROAD.
StudyAbroad.Com Program Search (www.studyabroad.com)
Academic Year Abroad 2001-2002. Institute of International Education Books (US$47).
Peterson's Study Abroad 2001. Peterson's (US$30).
Peterson's Summer Study Abroad 2001. Peterson's (US$30).
Short Term Study Abroad 2000-2001. Institute of International Education Books (US$43).

LanguagesPLUS, 317 Adelaide St. W., Suite 900, Toronto, Ontario M5V 1P9 (US ☎888-526-4758; international 416-925-7117; www.languagesplus.com), runs 2-36 week programs in France, Spain, Italy, and Germany from US$595-3000 that include tuition, accommodations with host families or apartments, and activities. Must be 18+.

World Exchange, Ltd., White Birch Rd., Putnam Valley, NY 10579 (US ☎800-444-3924; 845-526-2505; fax 845-528-9187; www.worldexchange.org), offers 1- to 4-week language-based homestay programs offered in France and Spain.

WORKING AND VOLUNTEERING

There's no better way to submerge yourself in a foreign culture than to become part of its economy. **European Union citizens** can work in any EU country, and if your parents were born in an EU country, you may be able to claim the right to a work permit. Friends and family in Europe can often help expedite work permits or arrange work-for-accommodations swaps. In general, **non-EU citizens** can officially hold a job in Europe only with a **work permit,** obtained by your employer, usually demonstrating that you have skills that locals lack. Reportedly, many permit-less agricultural workers go untroubled. Contact the consulate or embassy of your destination country for more information.

For US college students, recent graduates, and young adults, the simplest way to get legal work permission to work abroad is through **Council on International Educational Exchange** (205 East 42nd Street, New York, NY 10017; US ☎888-268-6245; www.ciee.org). Fees are from US$300-425. Council can help you obtain a three to six month work permit/visa and also provides assistance finding jobs and housing.

FURTHER READING: WORKING ABROAD.
Directory of Jobs and Careers Abroad. Vacation Work Publications (US$17).
How to Get a Job in Europe, Robert Sanborn and Cheryl Matherly. Surrey Books (US$22).
International Jobs: Where they Are, How to Get Them, Eric Kocher and Nina Segal. Perseus Books (US$17).
International Directory of Voluntary Work. Vacation Work (US$16).
Overseas Summer Jobs 2001, David Woodworth. Vacation Work (US$17).
Teaching English Abroad, Susan Griffith and Victoria Pybus. Vacation Work (US$18).
Work Abroad: The Complete Guide to Finding a Job Overseas, Clayton Hubbs. Transitions Abroad (US$16).
Work Your Way Around the World, Susan Griffith. Vacation Work ($18).

AU PAIR ORGANIZATIONS

Accord Cultural Exchange, 750 La Playa, San Francisco, CA 94121, USA (☎415-386-6203; www.cognitext.com/accord). US$40 program fee.

Childcare International, Ltd., Trafalgar House, Grenville Pl., London NW7 3SA (☎+44 (020) 8906 3116; fax 8906 3461; www.childint.co.uk). UK£100 application fee.

InterExchange, 161 Sixth Ave., New York, NY 10013 USA (☎212-924-0446; fax 924-0575; info@interexchange.org;, www.interexchange.org).

TEACHING ENGLISH

International Schools Services, Educational Staffing Program, P.O. Box 5910, Princeton, NJ 08543, USA (☎609-452-0990; www.iss.edu). Recruits teachers and administrators for American and English schools in Western Europe. US$150 program fee.

Office of Overseas Schools, US Department of State, Room H328, SA-1, Washington, D.C. 20522, USA (☎202-261-8200; fax 261-8224; www.state.gov/www/about_state/schools/). Keeps a comprehensive list of schools abroad and agencies that arrange placement for Americans to teach abroad.

ARCHAEOLOGICAL DIGS

Archaeological Institute of America, 656 Beacon St., Boston, MA 02215, USA (☎617-353-9361; www.archaeological.org). The *Archaeological Fieldwork Opportunities Bulletin* (US$20 for non-members) lists field sites throughout Europe. Purchase the bulletin from Kendall/Hunt Publishing, 4050 Westmark Dr., Dubuque, Iowa 52002, USA (☎800-228-0810).

VOLUNTEERING

Volunteer jobs are readily available, and many provide room and board in exchange for labor. You can sometimes avoid high application fees by contacting the individual workcamps directly.

Earthwatch, 3 Clocktower Pl., P.O. Box 75, Maynard, MA 01754 (☎800-776-0188 or 978-461-0081; www.earthwatch.org). Arranges 1- to 3-week programs all over Europe to promote conservation of natural resources. Programs average US$1600.

Habitat for Humanity International, 121 Habitat St., Americus, GA 31709, USA (☎800-422-4828; www.habitat.org). Offers opportunities in Germany, Britain, the Netherlands, and Portugal, to live with and build houses in a host community. Costs US$1200-3500.

Service Civil International Voluntary Service (SCI-IVS), 814 NE 40th St., Seattle, WA 98105, USA (☎/fax 206-545-6585; www.sci-ivs.org). Arranges placement in workcamps in Denmark, Belgium, and the Netherlands for those 18+. Registration fee US$65-150.

Volunteers for Peace, 1034 Tiffany Rd., Belmont, VT 05730, USA (☎802-259-2759; www.vfp.org). Arranges placement in workcamps in Europe. Annual *International Workcamp Directory* US$20. Registration fee US$200. Free newsletter.

OTHER RESOURCES

Let's Go tries to cover all aspects of budget travel, but we can't include *everything*. Listed below are books, organizations, and websites for your own research.

TRAVEL PUBLISHERS AND BOOKSTORES

Adventurous Traveler Bookstore, 245 S. Champlain St., Burlington, VT 05401, USA (☎800-282-3963 or 802-860-6776; www.adventuroustraveler.com), offers information and gear for outdoor and adventure travel.

Bon Voyage!, 2069 W. Bullard Ave., Fresno, CA 93711, USA (☎800-995-9716, elsewhere call US ☎559-447-8441; fax 447-8456; www.bon-voyage-travel.com), specializes in Europe and sells videos, travel gear, books, maps, and railpasses. Free newsletter.

Hippocrene Books, Inc., 171 Madison Ave., New York, NY 10016 USA (☎212-685-4371; orders 718-454-2366; www.hippocrenebooks.com). Publishes travel guides, as well as foreign language dictionaries and learning guides. Free catalog.

Hunter Publishing, 130 Campus Dr., Edison, NJ 08818, USA (☎800-255-0343; www.hunterpublishing.com). Has an extensive catalog of travel guides and diving and adventure travel books.

Rand McNally, 8255 N. Central Park Ave., Skokie, IL 60076, USA (☎800-275-7263; international (847) 329 6656; fax 329 6659; www.randmcnally.com), publishes a number of comprehensive road atlases (from US$10).

Travel Books & Language Center, Inc., 4437 Wisconsin Ave. NW, Washington, D.C. 20016, USA (☎800-220-2665 or 202-237-1322; www.bookweb.org/bookstore/travelbks). Sells travel aids, language cassettes, dictionaries, travel books, atlases, and maps. No web orders, but ships worldwide.

THE WORLD WIDE WEB

Almost every aspect of budget travel is accessible via the web. Within 10min. at the keyboard, you can make a reservation at a hostel, get advice on travel hotspots from other travelers who have just returned from Europe, or find out exactly how much a train from Paris to Munich costs.

Listed here are some budget travel sites to start off your surfing; other relevant web sites are listed throughout the book. Because web-site turnover is high, use search engines (such as www.google.com) to strike out on your own.

LEARNING THE ART OF BUDGET TRAVEL

Backpacker's Ultimate Guide: www.bugeurope.com. Tips on packing, transportation, and where to go. Also tons of country-specific travel information.

Backpack Europe: www.backpackeurope.com. Helpful tips, a bulletin board, and links.

How to See the World: www.artoftravel.com. A compendium of great travel tips, from cheap flights to self defense to interacting with local culture.

Rec. Travel Library: www.travel-library.com. A fantastic set of links for general information and personal travelogues.

TripSpot: www.tripspot.com/europefeature.htm. An outline of links to help plan trips, transportation, sleeping accommodations, and packing.

COUNTRY-SPECIFIC INFORMATION

CIA World Factbook: www.odci.gov/cia/publications/factbook/index.html. Tons of vital statistics on European geography, governments, economies, and politics.

Foreign Language for Travelers: www.travlang.com. Provides free online translating dictionaries and lists of phrases in European languages from Albanian to Yiddish.

DESTINATION GUIDES

Atevo Travel: www.atevo.com/guides/destinations. Detailed introductions, transportation tips, and suggested itineraries. Free travel newsletter.

CNN: europe.cnn.com/TRAVEL. Detailed information about services, sites, shopping, dining, nightlife, and recreation in the major cities of Europe.

Columbus Travel Guides: www.travel-guides.com/navigate/region/eur.asp. Well-organized site with practical information on geography, government, communication, health precautions, economy, and useful addresses.

Geographia: www.geographia.com. Describes highlights and attractions of the various European countries.

In Your Pocket: www.inyourpocket.com. Extensive virtual guides to select Baltic and Eastern European cities

MyTravelGuide: www.mytravelguide.com. Country overviews, with everything from history to transportation to local newspapers and weather.

LINKS TO EUROPEAN TOURISM PAGES

TravelPage: www.travelpage.com. Links to official tourist office sites throughout Europe.

Lycos: cityguide.lycos.com/europe. General introductions to cities and regions throughout Europe, accompanied by links to applicable histories, news, and local tourism sites.

PlanetRider: www.planetrider.com/travel-guide.cfm/Destinations/Europe.htm. A subjective list of links to the "best" websites covering the culture and tourist attractions of major European cities.

AND OUR PERSONAL FAVORITE...

Let's Go: www.letsgo.com. Our website features photos and streaming video, information about our books, a travel forum buzzing with stories and tips, and helpful links.

FURTHER READING: SURFING THE WEB.
Internet Travel Planner (US$19), by Michael Shapiro. Globe Pequot Press (US$19).
Travel Planning Online for Dummies, by Noah Vadnai. IDG Books (US$25).
Ten Minute Guide to Travel Planning on the Net, by Thomas Pack. QUE. (US$15).
300 Incredible Things for Travelers on the Internet, by Ken Leebow. 300Incredible.com. (US$9).

TRANSPORTATION

GETTING TO EUROPE

BY PLANE

When it comes to airfare, a little effort can save you a bundle. If your plans are flexible enough to deal with the restrictions, courier fares are the cheapest. Tickets bought from consolidators and standby seating are also good deals, but last-minute specials, airfare wars, and charter flights often beat these fares. The key is to hunt around, to be flexible, and to ask persistently about discounts. Students, seniors, and those under 26 should never pay full price for a ticket.

AIRFARES

Airfares to Europe peak between mid-June and early September; holidays are also expensive. The cheapest times to travel are November to mid-December and early January to March. Midweek (M-Th morning) return flights run US$40-50 cheaper than weekend flights, but they are generally more crowded and less likely to permit frequent-flier upgrades. Traveling with an "open return" ticket can be pricier than fixing a return date when buying the ticket. Return flights are by far the cheapest; "open-jaw" tickets (arriving in and departing from different cities, e.g. London-Paris and Rome-London) tend to be pricier. Patching one-way flights together is the most expensive way to travel. Flights between Europe's capitals or regional hubs—London, Paris, Amsterdam and Frankfurt—tend to be cheaper.

If Europe is only one stop on a more extensive globe-hop, consider a round-the-world (RTW) ticket. Tickets usually include at least five stops and are valid for about a year; prices range US$1200-5000. Try **Northwest Airlines/KLM** (US ☎ 800-447-4747; www.nwa.com) or **Star Alliance,** a consortium of 22 airlines including United Airlines (US ☎ 800-241-6522; www.star-alliance.com).

BUDGET AND STUDENT TRAVEL AGENCIES

While knowledgeable agents specializing in flights to Europe can make your life easier and help you save, they may not spend the time to find you the lowest possible fare—they get paid on commission. Travelers holding **ISIC and IYTC cards** (p. 21) qualify for big discounts from student travel agencies. Most flights from budget agencies are on major airlines, but in peak season some may sell seats on less reliable chartered aircraft.

Council Travel (www.counciltravel.com). Countless US offices, including branches in Atlanta, Boston, Chicago, L.A., New York, San Francisco, Seattle, and Washington, D.C. Check the web site or call ☎ 800-226-8624 for the nearest office. Also located at 28A Poland St. (Oxford Circus), **London** W1V 3DB (☎ (0207) 437 7767).

CTS Travel, 44 Goodge St., **London** W1T 2AD (☎ (0207) 636 0031; fax 637 5328; ctsinfo@ctstravel.co.uk).

STA Travel, 7890 S. Hardy Dr., Ste. 110, Tempe, AZ 85284 (24hr. reservations and information US ☎ 800-777-0112; fax 480-592-0876; www.statravel.com). A student and youth travel organization with over 250 offices worldwide (check their web site for a listing of all their offices), including US offices in Boston, Chicago, L.A., New York, San Francisco, Seattle, and Washington, D.C. Ticket booking, travel insurance, railpasses, and more. In the UK, walk-in office 11 Goodge St., **London** W1T 2PF or call ☎ (0870) 160 6070. In New Zealand, 10 High St., **Auckland** (☎ (09) 309 0458). In Australia, 366 Lygon St., **Melbourne** Vic 3053 (☎ (03) 9349 4344).

Travel CUTS (Canadian Universities Travel Services Limited), 187 College St., **Toronto,** ON M5T 1P7 (☎416-979-2406; fax 979-8167; www.travelcuts.com). 60 offices across Canada. In UK, 295-A Regent St., **London** W1R 7YA (☎(0207) 255 1944).

usit world (www.usitworld.com). Over 50 **usit campus** branches in the UK (www.usitcampus.co.uk), including 52 Grosvenor Gardens, **London** SW1W 0AG (☎(0870) 240 1010); **Manchester** (☎(0161) 273 1880); and **Edinburgh** (☎(0131) 668 3303). Nearly 20 **usit NOW** offices in Ireland, including 19-21 Aston Quay, O'Connell Bridge, **Dublin** 2 (☎(01) 602 1600; www.usitnow.ie), and **Belfast** (☎(02) 890 327 111; www.usitnow.com). Offices in Athens, Auckland, Brussels, Frankfurt, Johannesburg, Lisbon, Luxembourg, Madrid, Paris, Sofia, and Warsaw.

Wasteels, Skoubogade 6, 1158 **Copenhagen** (☎(45) 3314 4633; fax 3314 0865; www.wasteels.dk/uk). A huge chain with 165 locations across Europe. BIJ tickets discounted 30-45%. 2nd-class international point-to-point train tickets with unlimited stopovers for those under 26 (sold only in Europe).

✈ **FLIGHT PLANNING ON THE INTERNET.** The Internet is one of the best places to look for travel bargains—it's fast and convenient, and you can spend as long as you like exploring options without driving your travel agent insane.

Many airline sites offer special last-minute deals on-line. Yet, many require email addresses, so be wary of each site's privacy policy before you submit. Airlines like Continental (www.continental.com/cool), TWA (www.twa.com/dcspecials), United (www.united.com, click on "Special Deals") require membership logins or email subscriptions before allowing access to special prices. Other sites do the legwork and compile the deals for you—try www.bestfares.com, www.onetravel.com, www.lowestfare.com, and www.travelzoo.com.

STA (www.sta-travel.com), **Council** (www.counciltravel.com), and ▨ **Student Universe** (www.studentuniverse.com) provide quotes on student tickets, while **Expedia** (msn.expedia.com) and **Travelocity** (www.travelocity.com) offer full travel services. **Priceline** (www.priceline.com) allows you to specify a price, and obligates you to buy any ticket that meets or beats it; be prepared for antisocial hours and odd routes. **Skyauction** (www.skyauction.com) allows you to bid on both last-minute and advance-purchase tickets.

Just one last note—to protect yourself, make sure that the site you use has a secure server before handing over any credit card details.

COMMERCIAL AIRLINES

The commercial airlines' lowest regular offer is the **APEX** (Advance Purchase Excursion) fare, which provides confirmed reservations and allows "open-jaw" tickets. Generally, reservations must be made 7 to 21 days ahead of departure, with 7- to 14-day minimum-stay and up to 90-day maximum-stay restrictions. These fares carry hefty cancellation and change penalties (fees rise in summer). Book peak-season APEX fares early; by May you will have a hard time getting your desired departure date. Use **Microsoft Expedia** (msn.expedia.com) or **Travelocity** (www.travelocity.com) to get an idea of the lowest published fares, then use the resources outlined here to try and beat those fares. Low-season fares should be appreciably cheaper than the high-season (mid-June to August) ones listed here.

TRAVELING FROM NORTH AMERICA

Basic return fares to Europe are roughly US$200-800: to Frankfurt, US$300-750; London, US$200-600; Paris, US$250-800. Standard commercial carriers like American (☎800-433-7300; www.aa.com) and United (☎800-241-6522; www.ual.com) will probably offer the most convenient flights, but they may not be the cheapest, unless you grab a special promotion ticket. You might find flying one of the following airlines a better deal, if any of their limited departure points is convenient for you.

TRANSPORTATION

Icelandair: ☎800-223-5500; www.icelandair.com. Stopovers in Iceland for no extra cost on most transatlantic flights. New York to Frankfurt May-Sept. US$500-730; Oct.-May US$390-$450.

Finnair: ☎800-950-5000; www.us.finnair.com. Cheap return fares from San Francisco, New York, and Toronto to Helsinki. Connections throughout Europe.

Martinair: ☎800-627-8462; www.martinairusa.com. Fly from California or Florida to Amsterdam mid-June to mid-Aug. US$880; mid-Aug. to mid-June US$730.

TRAVELING FROM THE UK AND IRELAND

Because many carriers fly from the British Isles to the continent, we only include discount airlines or those with cheap specials here. The **Air Travel Advisory Bureau** in London (☎(020) 7636 5000; www.atab.co.uk) provides referrals to travel agencies and consolidators that offer discounted airfares out of the UK.

Aer Lingus: Ireland ☎(01) 886 8888; www.flyaerlingus.com. Return tickets from Belfast, Dublin, Cork, Galway, Kerry, and Shannon to Amsterdam, Brussels, Düsseldorf, Frankfurt, Madrid, Milan, Munich, Paris, Rome, Stockholm, and Zürich (IR£102-244).

British Midland Airways: UK ☎(0870) 607 0555; www.britishmidland.com. Departures from throughout the UK. London to Brussels (UK£83), Madrid (UK£194), Milan (£108), and Paris (UK£87).

buzz: UK ☎(0870) 240 7070; www.buzzaway.com. A subsidiary of KLM. From London to Berlin, Frankfurt, Helsinki, Milan, Montpellier, Paris, and Vienna (UK£30-70). Tickets cannot be changed or refunded.

easyJet: UK ☎(0870) 600 0000; www.easyjet.com. London to Amsterdam, Athens, Barcelona, Geneva, Madrid, Nice, and Zürich (UK£47-136). On-line tickets.

Go-Fly Limited: UK ☎(0845) 605 4321, elsewhere call UK 1279 666 388; www.go-fly.com. A subsidiary of British Airways. From London to Barcelona, Copenhagen, Edinburgh, Naples, Prague, Rome, and Venice (return UK£53-180).

KLM: UK ☎(0870) 507 4074; www.klmuk.com. Cheap return tickets from London and elsewhere direct to Amsterdam, Brussels, Frankfurt, and Zürich; via Amsterdam Schiphol Airport to Düsseldorf, Milan, Paris, Rome, and elsewhere.

Ryanair: Ireland ☎(01) 812 1212, UK ☎(0870) 156 9569; www.ryanair.ie. From Dublin, London, and Glasgow to destinations in France, Germany, Ireland, Italy, Scandinavia, and elsewhere. Deals from as low as UK£9 on limited weekend specials.

TRAVELING FROM AUSTRALIA AND NEW ZEALAND

Air New Zealand: New Zealand ☎(0800) 352 266; www.airnz.co.nz. Auckland to London and Frankfurt.

Qantas Air: Australia ☎13 13 13; New Zealand ☎(0800) 808 767; www.qantas.com.au. Flights from Australia and New Zealand to London AUS$2400-3000.

Singapore Air: Australia ☎13 10 11; New Zealand ☎(0800) 808 909; www.singaporeair.com. Flies from Auckland, Sydney, Melbourne, and Perth to Amsterdam, Brussels, Frankfurt, London, Manila, and more.

Thai Airways: Australia ☎(1300) 651 960; New Zealand ☎(09) 377 3886; www.thaiair.com. Auckland, Sydney, and Melbourne to Amsterdam, Frankfurt, and London.

TRAVELING FROM SOUTH AFRICA

Air France: ☎(01) 18 80 80 40; www.airfrance.com. Johannesburg to Paris; connections throughout Europe.

British Airways: ☎(0860) 011 747; www.british-airways.com/regional/sa. Johannesburg to London direct, and connections to the rest of Western Europe from SAR3400.

Lufthansa: ☎(011) 484 4711; www.lufthansa.co.za. From Cape Town and Johannesburg to Germany with connections throughout Western Europe.

Virgin Atlantic: ☎(011) 340 3400; www.virgin-atlantic.co.za. Flies to London from both Cape Town and Johannesburg.

AIR COURIER FLIGHTS

Those who travel light should consider courier flights. Couriers help transport cargo on international flights by using their checked luggage space for freight. Generally, couriers must travel with carry-ons only and must deal with complex flight restrictions. Most flights are return with short fixed-length stays (usually one week) and a limit of one ticket per issue. Most flights also operate only out of gateway cities, mostly in North America. Generally, you must be over 21 (in some cases 18). In summer, popular destinations usually require advance reservation of about two weeks (you can usually book up to two months ahead). Super-discounted fares are common for "last-minute" flights (three to 14 days ahead).

TRAVELING FROM NORTH AMERICA. Return courier fares from the US to Europe run about US$200-500. Most flights leave from New York, Los Angeles, San Francisco, or Miami in the US; and from Montreal, Toronto, or Vancouver in Canada. The first four organizations below provide their members with lists of opportunities and courier brokers worldwide for an annual fee (typically US$50-60). Alternatively, you can contact a courier broker (such as the last listing) directly; most charge registration fees, but a few don't. Prices quoted below are return.

Air Courier Association, 15000 W. 6th Ave. #203, Golden, CO 80401 (☎800-282-1202; elsewhere call US ☎303-215-9000; www.aircourier.org). Ten departure cities throughout the US and Canada to London, Madrid, Paris, Rome, and throughout Western Europe (high-season US$150-360). One-year US$64.

International Association of Air Travel Couriers (IAATC), 220 South Dixie Highway #3, P.O. Box 1349, Lake Worth, FL 33460 (☎561-582-8320; fax 582-1581; www.courier.org). From 9 North American cities to Western European cities, including London, Madrid, Paris, and Rome. One-year US$45-50.

Global Courier Travel, P.O. Box 3051, Nederland, CO 80466 (www.globalcouriertravel.com). Searchable on-line database. 6 departure points in the US and Canada to Amsterdam, Athens, Brussels, Copenhagen, Frankfurt, London, Madrid, Milan, Paris, and Rome. One-year US$40, 2 people US$55.

NOW Voyager, 74 Varick St. #307, New York, NY 10013 (☎212-431-1616; fax 219-1753; www.nowvoyagertravel.com). To Amsterdam, Brussels, Copenhagen, Dublin, London, Madrid, Milan, Paris, and Rome (US$499-699). Usually one-week max. stay. One-year US$50. Non-courier discount fares available.

Worldwide Courier Association (☎800-780-4359, ext. 441; www.massiveweb.com). From New York, San Francisco, Los Angeles, and Chicago to Western Europe, including London, Milan, Paris, and Rome (US$259-299). One-year US$58.

FROM THE UK, IRELAND, AUSTRALIA, AND NEW ZEALAND. Although the courier industry is most developed from North America, limited courier flights exist in other areas. The minimum age for couriers from the **UK** is usually 18. **Brave New World Enterprises,** P.O. Box 22212, London SE5 8WB (guideinfo@nry.co.uk; www.nry.co.uk/bnw) publishes a directory of all the companies offering courier flights in the UK (UK£10, in electronic form UK£8). The **International Association of Air Travel Couriers** (see above) often offers courier flights from London to Budapest. **Global Courier Travel** (see above) also offer flights from London and Dublin to continental Europe. **British Airways Travel Shop** (☎(0870) 606 1133; www.british-airways.com/travelqa) will arrange some flights from London to destinations in continental Europe (specials may be as low as UK£60; no registration fee). From **Australia** and **New Zealand, Global Courier Travel** (see above) often has listings from Sydney and Auckland to London and occasionally Frankfurt.

STANDBY FLIGHTS

Traveling standby requires considerable flexibility in arrival and departure dates and cities. Companies dealing in standby flights sell vouchers rather than tickets, along with the promise to get to your destination (or near your destination) within a certain window of time (typically 1-5 days). You call in before your specific window of time to hear your flight options and the probability that you will be able to board each flight. You can then decide which flights you want to try to make, show up at the appropriate airport at the appropriate time, present your voucher, and board if space is available. Vouchers can usually be bought for both one-way and return travel. You may receive a monetary refund only if every available flight within your date range is full; if you opt not to take an available (but perhaps less convenient) flight, you can only get credit toward future travel. Carefully read agreements with any company offering standby flights, as tricky fine print can leave you in a lurch. To check on a company's service record in the US, call the Better Business Bureau (☎212-533-6200). It is difficult to receive refunds, and clients' vouchers will not be honored when an airline fails to receive payment in time. One established standby company in the US is **Whole Earth Travel Inc.,** 325 W. 38th St., New York, NY 10018 (☎800-326-2009; fax 212-864-5489; www.4standby.com) and 13470 Washington Blvd, Suite 205, Marina Del Rey, CA 90292 (☎800-397-1098), which offers one-way flights to groups of European cities from the Northeast (US$169), West Coast (US$249), and the Midwest (US$219).

TICKET CONSOLIDATORS

Ticket consolidators, or **"bucket shops,"** buy unsold tickets in bulk from commercial airlines and sell them at discounted rates. The best place to look is in the Sunday travel section of any major newspaper (such as the *New York Times*), where many bucket shops place tiny ads. Call quickly, as availability is typically extremely limited. Not all bucket shops are reliable, so insist on a receipt that gives full details of restrictions, refunds, and tickets, and pay by credit card (in spite of the 2-5% fee) so you can stop payment if you never receive your tickets. For more information, see www.travel-library.com/air-travel/consolidators.html.

TRAVELING FROM NORTH AMERICA. Travel Avenue (☎800-333-3335; www.travelavenue.com) searches for best available published fares and then uses several consolidators to attempt to beat that fare. **NOW Voyager,** 74 Varick St., Ste. 307, New York, NY 10013 (☎212-431-1616; fax 219-1793; www.nowvoyagertravel.com) arranges discounted flights, mostly from New York, to Barcelona, London, Madrid, Milan, Paris, and Rome. Other consolidators worth trying are **Interworld** (☎305-443-4929; fax 305-443-0351); **Pennsylvania Travel** (☎800-331-0947); **Rebel** (☎800-227-3235; travel@rebeltours.com; www.rebeltours.com); **Cheap Tickets** (☎800-377-1000; www.cheaptickets.com); and **Travac** (☎800-872-8800; fax 212-714-9063; www.travac.com). Yet more consolidators on the web include the **Internet Travel Network** (www.itn.com); **Travel Information Services** (www.tiss.com); **TravelHUB** (www.travelhub.com); and **The Travel Site** (www.thetravelsite.com). Keep in mind that these are just suggestions to get you started in your research; *Let's Go* does not endorse any of these agencies. As always, be cautious, and research companies before you hand over your credit card number.

TRAVELING FROM THE UK, AUSTRALIA, AND NEW ZEALAND. In London, the **Air Travel Advisory Bureau** (☎(0207) 636 5000; www.atab.co.uk) can provide names of reliable consolidators and discount flight specialists. From Australia and New Zealand, look for consolidator ads in the travel section of the *Sydney Morning Herald* and other papers.

CHARTER FLIGHTS

Charters are flights a tour operator contracts with an airline to fly extra loads of passengers during peak season. Charter flights fly less frequently than major airlines, make refunds particularly difficult, and are almost always fully booked. Schedules and itineraries may also change or be cancelled at the last moment (as late as 48 hours before the trip, and without a full refund), and check-in, boarding, and baggage claim are often much slower. However, they can also be cheaper.

Discount clubs and fare brokers offer members savings on last-minute charter and tour deals. Study contracts closely; you don't want to end up with an unwanted overnight layover. **Travelers Advantage,** Trumbull, CT, USA (☎203-365-2000; www.travelersadvantage.com; US$60 annual fee includes discounts and cheap flight directories) specializes in European travel and tour packages.

BY CHUNNEL FROM THE UK

Traversing 27 mi. under the sea, the Chunnel is undoubtedly the fastest, most convenient, and least scenic route from England to France.

BY TRAIN. Eurostar, Eurostar House, Waterloo Station, London SE1 8SE runs a frequent train service between London and the continent. Ten to twenty-eight trains per day run to Paris (3hr., US$75-159, 2nd class), Brussels (4hr., US$75-159, 2nd class), and Eurodisney. Routes include stops at Ashford in England, and Calais and Lille in France. Book at major rail stations in the UK, at the office above, by phone, or on the web. (UK ☎(0990) 186 186; US ☎800-387-6782; elsewhere call UK ☎(1233) 617 575; www.eurostar.com; www.raileurope.com.)

BY BUS. Eurolines provides bus-ferry combinations (p. 72).

BY CAR. If you're traveling by car, **Eurotunnel** (UK ☎(0800) 969 992; www.eurotunnel.co.uk) shuttles cars and passengers between Kent and Nord-Pas-de-Calais. Return fares for vehicle and all passengers range from UK£219-299 with car and UK£259-598 with campervan. Same-day return costs UK£110-150, five-day return UK£139-195. Book on-line or via phone. Travelers with cars can also look into sea crossings by ferry (see below).

BY FERRY FROM THE UK AND IRELAND

The following fares listed are **one-way** for **adult foot passengers** unless otherwise noted. Though standard return fares are in most cases simply twice the one-way fare, **fixed-period returns** (usually within five days) are almost invariably cheaper. Ferries run **year-round** unless otherwise noted. **Bikes** are usually free, although you may have to pay up to UK£10 in high-season. For a **camper/trailer** supplement, you will have to add anywhere from UK£20-140 to the "with car" fare. If more than one price is quoted, the quote in UK£ is valid for departures from the UK, etc. A directory of ferries in this region can be found at www.seaview.co.uk/ferries.html.

Brittany Ferries: UK ☎(0870) 901 2400; France ☎(08) 25 82 88 28; www.brittany-ferries.com. **Plymouth** to **Roscoff, France** (6hr., in summer 1-3 per day, off-season 1 per week, UK£20-58 or 140-300F) and **Santander, Spain** (24-30hr., 1-2 per week, return UK£80-145). **Portsmouth** to **Caen** (6hr., 1-3 per day, 140-290F), France and **St-Malo** (8¾hr., 1-2 per day, 150-320F). **Poole** to **Cherbourg** (4¼hr., 1-2 per day, 140-290F). **Cork** to **Roscoff** (13½hr., Apr.-Sept. 1 per week, 340-650F).

DFDS Seaways: UK ☎(08705) 333 000; www.scansea.com. **Harwich** to **Hamburg** (20hr.) and **Esbjerg, Denmark** (19hr.). **Newcastle** to **Amsterdam** (14hr.); **Kristiansand, Norway** (19hr.); and **Gothenburg, Sweden** (22hr.).

Fjord Line: www.fjordline.no. Norway ☎(55) 54 88 00; UK ☎(0191) 296 1313. **Newcastle, England** to **Stavanger** (19hr.) and **Bergen** (26hr.), Norway. Also between **Bergen** and **Egersund**, Norway, and **Hanstholm**, Denmark.

Hoverspeed: UK ☎(08702) 40 80 70; France ☎(03) 21 46 14 54; www.hoverspeed.co.uk. **Dover** to **Calais** (35-55min., every hr., UK£24) and **Ostend, Belgium** (2hr., 5-7 per day, UK£28). **Folkestone** to **Boulogne, France** (55min., 3-4 per day, UK£24). **Newhaven** to **Dieppe, France** (2¼-4¼hr., 1-3 per day, UK£28).

Irish Ferries: France ☎(01) 44 94 20 40; Ireland ☎(1890) 31 31 31; UK ☎(08705) 17 17 17; www.irishferries.ie. **Rosslare** to **Cherbourg** (18hr., IR£57-82); **Roscoff** (17hr., Apr.-Sept. 1-9 per week, 470-680F); and **Pembroke, England** (3¾hr.). **Holyhead, England** to **Dublin** (2-3hr., return IR£20-60).

P&O North Sea Ferries: UK ☎(0870) 129 6002; www.ponsf.com. Daily ferries from **Hull** to **Rotterdam, Netherlands** (13½hr.) and **Zeebrugge, Belgium** (14hr.). Both UK£38-48, students UK£24-31, cars UK£63-78. on-line bookings.

P&O Stena Line: UK ☎(08706) 000 611; from Europe 13 04 86 40 03; www.posl.com. **Dover** to **Calais** (1¼hr., every 30min.-1hr. 30 per day, UK£24).

SeaFrance: UK ☎(08705) 71 17 11; France ☎(03) 21 46 80 00; www.seafrance.co.uk. **Dover** to **Calais** (1½hr., 15 per day, UK£15).

Stena Line: UK ☎(01233) 64 68 26; www.stenaline.co.uk. **Harwich, England** to **Hook of Holland** (5hr., UK£25). **Fishguard** to **Rosslare** (1-3½hr., UK£22-30). **Holyhead** to **Dublin** (4hr., UK£18-20) and **Dún Laoghaire** (1-3½hr., £20-28). **Stranraer** to **Belfast** (1¾-3¼hr., UK£18-24; Mar.-Jan.).

GETTING AROUND EUROPE

Fares on all modes of transportation are either **single** (one-way) or **return** (round-trip). "Period returns" require that you to return within a specific number of days. "Day returns" require you to return on the same day. Unless stated otherwise, *Let's Go* always lists single fares. Return fares on trains and buses in Europe are simply double the one-way fare.

BY PLANE

Although flying is almost invariably more expensive than traveling by train, if you are short on time (or flush with cash) you might consider it. Student travel agencies sell cheap tickets, and budget fares are frequently available in the spring and summer on high-volume routes between northern Europe and resort areas in Greece, Italy, and Spain; consult budget travel agents and local newspapers. For information on cheap flights from Britain to the continent, see **Traveling from the UK,** p. 58. In addition, a number of European airlines offer coupon packets that considerably discount the cost of each flight leg. Most are only available as tack-ons to their transatlantic passengers, but some are available as stand-alone offers. Most must be purchased before departure, so research in advance.

Alitalia: US ☎800-223-5730; www.alitaliausa.com. "Europlus" allows you to tack 3 or more flights to 30 airports in Europe and North Africa. Must be purchased in conjunction with an Alitalia transatlantic flight; the first ticket must be booked to a specific city, but the remaining trips can be determined as you go. US$299 for 3; each additional ticket US$100.

Austrian Airlines: US ☎800-843-0002; www.austrianair.com/greatdeals/europe_airpass.html. "European Airpass," good to cities served by AA and partner airlines, is available in the US to Austrian Airlines transatlantic passengers (3 cities min., 10 max.). Price based on mileage between destinations.

Europe by Air: US ☎888-321-4737; www.europebyair.com. Coupons good on 30 partner airlines to 150 European cities in 30 countries. Must be purchased prior to arrival in Europe. US$99 each, excluding airport tax. Also offers 15- and 21-day unlimited passes; US$699-$899.

Iberia: US ☎800-772-4642; http://194.224.55.25/ibusa/ofertas/index.html. "Euro-Pass" allows Iberia passengers flying from the US to Spain to tack on a minimum of 2 additional destinations in Europe. Most US$125 each; some US $155 each.

KLM/Northwest: US ☎800-800-1504. "Passport to Europe," available to US transatlantic passengers on either airline, connects 90 European cities, mostly Western European, but including a few Eastern European and North African destinations (3 cities min., 12 max.). US$100 each.

Lufthansa: US ☎800-399-5838; www.lufthansa.com. "Discover Europe" available to US travelers on a transatlantic Lufthansa flights (3 cities min., 9 max.). US$119 each.

Scandinavian Airlines: US ☎800-221-2350; www.scandinavian.net. One-way coupons for travel within Scandinavia, the Baltics, or all of Europe. US$65-225, 8 coupons max.

Most are available only to transatlantic SAS passengers, but some United and Lufthansa passengers also qualify.

BY TRAIN

Trains in Europe are generally comfortable, convenient, and reasonably swift. Second-class travel is pleasant, and compartments, which seat two to six, are great places to meet fellow travelers. For long trips make sure you are on the correct car, as trains sometimes split at crossroads. Towns listed in parentheses on European train schedules require a train switch at the town listed immediately before the parenthesis.

You can either buy a **railpass** (see below) which allows you unlimited travel within a particular region for a given period of time, or buy individual **point-to-point** tickets as you go. Almost all countries give students or youths (usually defined as anyone under 26) direct discounts on regular domestic rail tickets, and many also sell a student or youth card that provides 20-50% off all fares for up to a year.

RESERVATIONS AND SUPPLEMENTS. While seat reservations are required only for selected trains (usually on major lines), you are not guaranteed a seat without one (usually US$3-10). Reservations are available on major trains as much as two months in advance, and Europeans often reserve far ahead of time; you should strongly consider reserving during peak holiday and tourist seasons (at the very latest a few hours ahead). You will need to purchase a **supplement** (US$10-50) or special fare for high-speed or -quality trains such as the Cisalpino, Spain's AVE, Finland's Pendolino S220, Italy's ETR500 and Pendolino, Germany's ICE, and certain French TGVs. InterRail holders must also purchase supplements (US$10-25) for trains like EuroCity, InterCity, Sweden's X2000, and many French TGVs; these supplements are unnecessary for Eurailpass and Europass holders.

OVERNIGHT TRAINS. Night trains have their advantages: you won't waste valuable daylight hours traveling, and you will be able to forego the hassle and considerable expense of securing a night's accommodation. However, night travel has its drawbacks: discomfort and sleepless nights are the most obvious, and the scenery probably won't look as enticing in pitch black. **Sleeping accommodations** on trains differ from country to country, but typically you can either sleep upright in your seat (for free) or pay for a separate space. **Couchettes** (berths) typically have four to six seats per compartment (about US$20 per person); **sleepers** (beds) in private sleeping cars offer more privacy and comfort, but are considerably more expensive (US$40-150). If you are using a railpass valid only for a restricted number of days, inspect train schedules to maximize the use of your pass: an overnight train or boat journey uses up only one of your travel days if it departs after 7pm (you need write in only the next day's date on your pass).

MULTINATIONAL RAILPASSES

EURAILPASS. Eurail is valid in most of Western Europe: Austria, Belgium, Denmark, Finland, France, Germany, Greece, Hungary, Italy, Luxembourg, the Netherlands, Norway, Portugal, the Republic of Ireland, Spain, Sweden, and Switzerland. It is not valid in the UK. Standard **Eurailpasses,** valid for a given number of consecutive days, are most suitable for those planning on spending extensive time on trains every few days. **Flexipasses,** valid for any 10 or 15 (not necessarily consecutive) days in a two-month period, are more cost-effective for those traveling longer distances less frequently. **Saverpasses** provide first-class travel for travelers in groups of two to five (prices are per person). **Youthpasses** and **Youth Flexipasses** provide parallel second-class perks for those under 26.

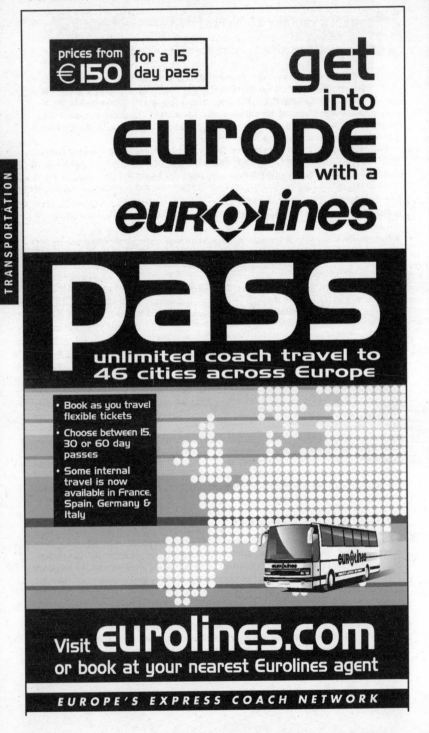

SHOULD YOU BUY A RAILPASS? In theory, railpasses allow you to jump on any train in Europe, go wherever you want whenever you want, and change your plans at will. In practice, it's not so simple. You must stand in line to validate your pass, pay for supplements, and fork over cash for seat and couchette reservations. More importantly, railpasses don't always pay off. Consult our railplanner (at the front of this book) to estimate the point-to-point cost of each leg of your journey; add them up and compare the total with the cost of a railpass. If you are planning on hopping between big cities, a railpass will probably be worth it. But in many cases, especially if you are under 26, point-to-point tickets may prove a cheaper option.

You may find it tough to make your railpass pay for itself in Belgium, Greece, Ireland, Italy, Luxembourg, the Netherlands, Portugal, Spain, Eastern Europe, or the Balkans, where train fares are reasonable, distances short, or buses preferable. If, however, the total cost of your trip nears the price of the pass, the convenience of avoiding ticket lines may be worth the difference.

EURAILPASSES	15 DAYS	21 DAYS	1 MONTH	2 MONTHS	3 MONTHS
1st class Eurailpass	US$554	US$718	US$890	US$1260	US$1558
Eurail Saverpass	US$470	US$610	US$756	US$1072	US$1324
Eurail Youthpass	US$388	US$499	US$623	US$882	US$1089

EURAIL FLEXIPASSES	10 DAYS IN 2 MONTHS	15 DAYS IN 2 MONTHS
1st class Eurail Flexipass	US$654	US$862
Eurail Saver Flexipass	US$556	US$732
Eurail Youth Flexipass	US$458	US$599

Passholders receive a timetable for major routes and a map with details on possible ferry, steamer, bus, car rental, hotel, and Eurostar discounts. Passholders often also receive reduced fares or free passage on many bus and boat lines. **Eurail freebies** (excepting surcharges such as reservation fees and port taxes) include: ferries between Ireland (Rosslare/Cork) and France (Cherbourg/Le Havre); sightseeing cruises on the Rhine (Cologne-Mainz) and Mosel (Koblenz-Cochem), as well as Europabus rides down the Romantic Road (Frankfurt-Füssen; 75% off) and Castle Road (Mannheim-Heidelberg-Nuremberg), in Germany; ferries between Italy and Sardinia (Civitavecchia-Golfo Aranci), Sicily (Villa S. Giovanni-Messina), and Greece (Brindisi-Patras); and boat trips between Sweden and Denmark (Helsingborg-Helsingør), Germany (Trelleborg-Sassnitz), and Finland (Ümea/Sundsvall-Vaasa).

EUROPASS. The Europass is a slimmed-down version of the Eurailpass: it allows five to 15 days of unlimited travel in any two-month period within France, Germany, Italy, Spain, and Switzerland. **First-Class Europasses** (for individuals) and **Saverpasses** (for people traveling in groups of 2-5) range from US$348/296 per person (5 days) to US$688/586 (15 days). **Second-Class Youthpasses** for those ages 12-25 cost US$244-482. For a fee, you can add **additional zones** (Austria/Hungary; Belgium/Luxembourg/Netherlands; Greece Plus, including the ADN/HML ferry between Italy and Greece; and/or Portugal): $60 for one associated zone, $100 for two. You are entitled to the same **freebies** afforded by the Eurailpass (see above), but only when they are within or between countries that you have purchased. Plan your itinerary before buying a Europass: it will save you money if your travels are confined to three to five adjacent Western European countries, or if you only want to go to large cities, but would be a waste if you plan to make lots of side-trips. If you're tempted to add many rail days and associate countries, consider a Eurailpass.

SHOPPING AROUND FOR A EURAIL- OR EUROPASS.

Eurailpasses and Europasses are designed by the EU itself, and are purchasable only by non-Europeans, almost exclusively from non-European distributors. These passes must be sold at uniform prices determined by the EU. However, some travel agents tack on a US$10 handling fee, and others offer certain bonuses with purchase, so shop around. Also, keep in mind that pass prices usually go up each year, so if you're planning to travel early in the year, you can save cash by purchasing before January 1 (you have 3 months from the purchase date to validate your pass in Europe). It is best to buy your Eurail- or Europass before leaving; only a few places in major European cities sell them, and at a marked-up price. Once in Europe, you'd probably have to use a credit card to buy over the phone from a railpass agent in a non-EU country (one on the North American East Coast would be closest) who could send the pass to you by express mail. Eurailpasses are non-refundable once validated; if your pass is completely unused and invalidated and you have the original purchase documents, you can get an 85% refund from the place of purchase. You can get a replacement for a lost pass only if you have purchased insurance on it under the Pass Protection Plan (US$10). Eurailpasses are available through travel agents, student travel agencies like STA and Council (p. 54), and **Rail Europe,** 500 Mamaroneck Ave., Harrison, NY 10528 (US☎888-382-7245, fax 800-432-1329; Canada ☎800-361-7245, fax 905-602-4198; UK ☎(08705) 848 848; www.raileurope.com) or **DER Travel Services,** 9501 W. Devon Ave. #301, Rosemont, IL 60018 (US☎888-337-7350; fax 800-282-7474; www.dertravel.com).

INTERRAIL PASS. If you have lived for at least six months in one of the European countries where InterRail Passes are valid, they prove an economical option. There are eight InterRail **zones:** A (Great Britain, Northern Ireland, Republic of Ireland), B (Norway, Sweden, and Finland), C (Germany, Austria, Denmark, and Switzerland), D (Croatia, Czech Republic, Hungary, Poland, and Slovakia), E (France, Belgium, Netherlands, and Luxembourg), F (Spain, Portugal, and Morocco), G (Greece, Italy, Slovenia, and Turkey, including a Greece-Italy ferry), and H (Bulgaria, Romania, Yugoslavia, and Macedonia). The **Under 26 InterRail Card** allows either 22 days or one month of unlimited travel within one, two, three or all of the eight zones; the cost is determined by the number of zones the pass covers (UK₤129-229). If you buy a ticket including the zone in which you have claimed residence, you must still pay 50% fare for tickets inside your own country. The **Over 26 InterRail Card** provides the same services as the Under 26 InterRail Card, but at higher prices: UK₤185-319.

Passholders receive **discounts** on rail travel, Eurostar journeys, and most ferries to Ireland, Scandinavia, and the rest of Europe. Most exclude **supplements** for high-speed trains. For information and ticket sales in Europe contact **Student Travel Center,** 24 Rupert St., 1st fl., London W1V 7FN (☎(020) 7437 8101; fax 7734 3836; www.student-travel-centre.com). Tickets are also available from travel agents or main train stations throughout Europe.

OTHER MULTINATIONAL PASSES. If your travels will be limited to one area, regional passes are often good values. The **ScanRail Pass,** which gives unlimited rail travel in Denmark, Finland, Norway, and Sweden, is available both in the UK and the US (standard/under 26 passes for 5 out of 15 days of 2nd-class travel US$204/153; 10 days out of 2 months US$310/233; 21 consecutive days US$360/270). The **Benelux Tourrail Pass** for Belgium, the Netherlands, and Luxembourg is available in the UK, in the US (5 days in 1 month 2nd-class US$155, under 26 US$104; 50% discount for companion traveler), and at train stations in Belgium and Luxembourg (but not the Netherlands). The **Balkan Flexipass,** which is valid for travel in Bulgaria, Greece, Macedonia, Montenegro, Romania, Serbia, and Turkey (5 days in 1 month US$152, under 26 US$90). The **European East Pass** covers Austria, the Czech Republic, Hungary, Poland, and Slovakia (5 days in 1 month US$210).

Take advantage of the specialty and high-speed trains of Europe!

FREE Thomas Cook timetable with railpass orders over $1,000   We offer most European railpasses

TRANSPORTATION

DOMESTIC RAILPASSES

If you are planning to spend a significant amount of time within one country or region, a national pass—valid on all rail lines of a country's rail company—will probably be more cost-effective than a multinational pass. Several national and regional passes offer companion fares, allowing two adults traveling together to save about 50% on the price of one pass. But consider the cons as well: many national passes are limited and don't provide the free or discounted travel on many private railways and ferries that Eurail does. Some of these passes can be bought only in Europe, some only outside of Europe; check with a railpass agent or with national tourist offices.

NATIONAL RAILPASSES. The domestic analogs of the Eurailpass, national rail-passes are valid either for a given number of consecutive days or for a specific number of days within a given time period. Usually, they must be purchased before you leave. Though they will usually save frequent travelers some money, in some cases (particularly in Eastern Europe) you may find that they are actually a more expensive alternative to point-to-point tickets. Examples include: Britrail Pass, BritIreland Flexipass, Freedom of Scotland Travelpass, Irish Explorer, Ireland's Emerald Isle Card and Irish Rover, France Flexipass, German Flexipass, Austrian Flexipass, Greek Flexipass, Italian Railpass and Flexipass, Swiss Railpass and Flexipass, Holland Flexipass, Norway Flexipass, Sweden Railpass, Finnrail Flexipass, Iberic Flexipass, Spain Flexipass, Portuguese Flexipass, Bulgarian Flexipass, Polrail Pass, Czech Flexipass, Hungarian Flexipass, and Romanian Flexipass. For more information, contact Rail Europe (p. 68).

EURO DOMINO. Like the InterRail Pass, the Euro Domino pass is available to anyone who has lived in Europe for at least six months; however, it is only valid in one country (which you designate upon buying the pass). It is available for 29 European countries including Morocco. The Euro Domino pass is available for first- and second-class travel (with a special rate for those under 26), for three to eight days of unlimited travel within a one-month period. It is not valid on Eurostar or Thalys trains. **Supplements** for many high-speed (e.g., French TGV, German ICE, and Swedish X2000) trains are included (Spanish AVE is not), though you must still pay for **reservations** where they are compulsory (e.g., about 20F on the TGV). The pass must be bought within your country of residence (except for the Euro Domino Plus pass for the Netherlands, which also includes all bus, tram, and metro rides and can be bought in the Netherlands); each country has its own price for the pass. Inquire with your national rail company for more information.

REGIONAL PASSES

Another type of regional pass covers a specific area within a country or a return trip from any border to a particular destination and back; these are useful as add-ons when your main pass isn't valid. The **Prague Excursion Pass** is a common purchase for Eurailers, whose passes are not valid in the Czech Republic; it covers travel from any Czech border to Prague and back out of the country (return trip must be completed within 7 days; 2nd-class US$35, under 26 US$30). **The Copenhagen Pass** is valid for Europass or German railpass holders from any German or Danish border to Copenhagen and back, while the **BritRail Southeast Pass** permits unlimited travel in southeast England (3 out of 8 days US$73).

RAIL-AND-DRIVE PASSES

In addition to simple railpasses, many countries (as well as Europass and Eurail) offer rail-and-drive passes, which combine car rental with rail travel—a good option for travelers who wish both to visit cities accessible by rail and to make side trips into the surrounding areas.

TRANSPORTATION

DISCOUNTED RAIL TICKETS

For travelers under 26, **BIJ** tickets (Billets Internationals de Jeunesse; a.k.a. **Wasteels, Eurotrain,** and **Route 26**) are a great alternative to railpasses. Available for international trips within Europe, travel within France, and most ferry services, they knock 20-40% off regular second-class fares. Issued for a specific international route between two points, they must be used in the direction and order of the designated route and must be bought in Europe. However, tickets are good for 60 days after purchase and allow a number of stopovers along the normal direct route of the train journey. The equivalent for those over 26, **BIGT** tickets provide a 20-30% discount on 1st- and 2nd-class international tickets for business travelers, temporary residents of Europe, and their families. Both types of tickets are available from European travel agents, at Wasteels or Eurotrain offices (usually in or near train stations), or directly at the ticket counter in some nations. For more information, contact **Wasteels,** Victoria Station, London SW1V 1JT (☎ (0171) 630 7627).

> ↰ **FURTHER RESOURCES ON TRAIN TRAVEL.**
> **Point-to-point fares and schedules:** www.raileurope.com/us/rail/ fares_schedules/index.htm. Allows you to calculate whether buying a railpass would save you money. For a more convenient resource, see our **railplanner** at the end of this chapter.
> **European Railway Servers:** mercurio.iet.unipi.it/home.html. Links to rail servers throughout Europe.
> **Info on rail travel and railpasses:** www.eurorail.com; www.raileuro.com.
> *Thomas Cook European Timetable,* updated monthly, covers all major and most minor train routes in Europe. In the US, order it from Forsyth Travel Library (US$28; ☎ 800-367-7984; www.forsyth.com). In Europe, find it at any Thomas Cook Money Exchange Center. Alternatively, buy directly from Thomas Cook (www.thomascook.com).
> *Guide to European Railpasses,* Rick Steves. Available on-line or by mail. US ☎ 425-771-8303; fax 425-671-0833; www.ricksteves.com). Free; delivery $8.
> *On the Rails Around Europe: A Comprehensive Guide to Travel by Train,* Melissa Shales. Thomas Cook Ltd. (US$18.95).
> *Eurail and Train Travel Guide to Europe.* Houghton Mifflin (US$15).
> *Europe By Eurail 2000,* Laverne Ferguson-Kosinski. Globe Pequot Press (US$16.95).

BY BUS

Though European trains and railpasses are extremely popular, buses may prove a better option. In Spain, Hungary, and the Baltics, the bus and train systems are on par; in Britain, Greece, Ireland, Portugal, and Turkey, bus networks are more extensive, efficient, and often more comfortable; and in Iceland and parts of northern Scandinavia, bus service is the only ground transportation available. In the rest of Europe, bus travel is more of a crapshoot; scattered offerings from private companies are often cheap but sometimes unreliable. Amsterdam, Athens, İstanbul, London, Munich, and Oslo are centers for lines that offer long-distance rides across Europe. Often cheaper than railpasses, **international bus passes** typically allow unlimited travel on a hop-on, hop-off basis between major European cities. In general these services tend to be more popular among non-American backpackers. Note that **Eurobus,** a former UK-based bus service, is no longer in operation.

> **Eurolines,** 52 Grosvenor Gardens, London SW1 (☎ (1582) 400 694; www.eurolines.co.uk or www.eurolines.com). The largest operator of Europe-wide coach services. Unlimited 30-day (UK£229, under 26 and over 60 UK£199) or 60-day (UK£279/249) travel between 30 major European cities in 16 countries.

PRICES (US$)AND TRAVEL TIMES

	Amster-	Barce-	Berlin	Brussels	Budap-	Copen-	Florence	Frankfurt	London	Madrid	Milan	Munich	Paris	Prague	Rome	Venice	Vienna	Warsaw	Zürich
Amster-		16¼hr.[1]	7hr.	2½hr.	17½hr.[1]	14hr.	18½hr.[1]	5hr.	9hr.	17½hr.[1]	14½hr.	9½hr.	4¼hr.	12½hr.[1]	20hr.[1]	17hr.[1]	13hr.[1]	13hr.[1]	9hr.
Barce-	$21		27¼hr.[1]	14hr.[1]	26½hr.[1]	34¾hr.[1]	19hr.[1]	21hr.[1]	18hr.[1]	7hr.	13hr.	16¾hr.[1]	12¼hr.	27¼hr.[1]	21¼hr.[1]	22hr.[1]	23hr.[1]	34¼hr.[1]	13hr.
Berlin	$10	$310		11hr.	13hr.	7½hr.	19½hr.	4¼hr.	13½hr.[1]	25¼hr.[1]	17¼hr.[1]	10hr.	12hr.	5½hr.	21¼hr.[1]	17hr.	10hr.	6hr.	8hr.[1]
Brussels	$43	$191	$129		16½hr.[1]	12hr.	16hr.[1]	5½hr.	4hr.	15hr.[1]	12hr.	8½hr.	1¾hr.	13½hr.[1]	18¾hr.[1]	15¼hr.[1]	15hr.[1]	17¼hr.[1]	8hr.
Budap-	$20	$315	$157	$193		20½hr.[1]	14½hr.[1]	12½hr.	19hr.[1]	31¼hr.[1]	15¾hr.[1]	8hr.	18hr.	7¾hr.	25hr.[1]	13hr.	3hr.	11¼hr.[1]	13½hr.
Copen-	$17	$341	$89	$173	$246		19½hr.[1]	9hr.	14½hr.[1]	27¾hr.[1]	22hr.	10½hr.[1]	15¼hr.	12¼hr.	25hr.[1]	22hr.[1]	17½hr.[1]	13½hr.[1]	15hr.[1]
Florence	$21	$114	$198	$155	$118	$262		13hr.[1]	17hr.[1]	25hr.[1]	3½hr.	9hr.	12½hr.	15hr.[1]	1¾hr.	27½hr.[1]	11½hr.	19¾hr.[1]	8hr.
Frankfurt	$80	$215	$103	$84	$137	$173	$154		6½hr.[1]	26½hr.[1]	9hr.	3½hr.	6½hr.	7½hr.	14hr.	11hr.[1]	9hr.[1]	10¼hr.[1]	4hr.
London	$20	$278	$288	$159	$352	$332	$314	$243		17¾hr.[1]	12hr.[1]	13hr.[1]	4¼hr.	16hr.[1]	19hr.[1]	17hr.[1]	19½hr.[1]	19¾hr.[1]	12¾hr.[1]
Madrid	$23	$49	$327	$206	$330	$266	$163	$230	$293		25¼hr.[1]	24hr.	13¼hr.	28¼hr.[1]	30½hr.[1]	30½hr.[1]	28¼hr.[1]	36½hr.[1]	21¼hr.[1]
Milan	$18	$155	$220	$132	$111	$290	$28	$131	$290	$204		7½hr.	2½hr.	13½hr.[1]	4½hr.	3hr.	12¾hr.	21hr.[1]	3¾hr.
Munich	$13	$235	$132	$146	$83	$213	$66	$80	$287	$250	$38		8½hr.	6hr.	10¼hr.	7hr.	5hr.	16½hr.[1]	4¼hr.
Paris	$96	$119	$193	$72	$196	$222	$159	$96	$159	$134	$131	$116		15hr.	14¼hr.	12½hr.	15hr.	19hr.[1]	8¼hr.
Prague	$18	$337	$52	$184	$54	$141	$132	$103	$343	$352	$129	$66	$218		16¼hr.[1]	13½hr.	5hr.	10½hr.	11½hr.
Rome	$22	$127	$217	$168	$129	$298	$28	$167	$315	$176	$45	$85	$176	$151		4¾hr.	13hr.	24hr.[1]	8¼hr.
Venice	$19	$180	$195	$157	$86	$276	$25	$151	$316	$229	$25	$63	$156	$129	$43		9hr.	17¼hr.[1]	8hr.
Vienna	$17	$291	$132	$179	$33	$221	$85	$104	$342	$306	$88	$59	$172	$44	$103	$67		8¼hr.	9¼hr.
Warsaw	$13	$341	$31	$173	$58	$120	$229	$134	$332	$358	$251	$163	$224	$45	$150	$114	$47		20¼hr.[1]
Zürich	$14	$77	$178	$90	$109	$248	$75	$89	$249	$241	$54	$62	$107	$128	$91	$71	$88	$206	

1 These routes do not require a change of trains. Travel times do not include layover.

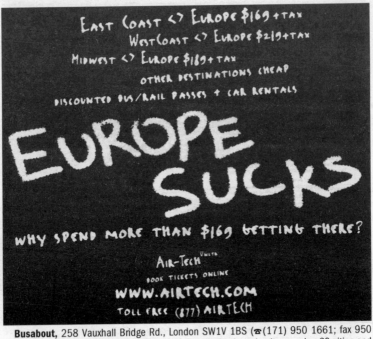
Busabout, 258 Vauxhall Bridge Rd., London SW1V 1BS (☎(171) 950 1661; fax 950 1662; www.busabout.com). Offers 5 interconnecting bus circuits covering 60 cities and towns in Europe. Consecutive Day Passes and Flexi Passes both available. Consecutive Day Standard/student passes are valid for 15 days (US$229/207), 21 days (US$324/295), 1 month (US$428/384), 2 months (US$666/592), 3 months (US$740/894), or for the season (US$977/873).

BY CAR

Cars offer speed, freedom, access to the countryside, and an escape from the town-to-town mentality of trains. They also insulate you from the *esprit de corps* of rail travel. Weigh the independence of being able to arrange your own schedule against the financial and cultural costs when deciding to road-trip it.

RENTING

While a single traveler won't save cash by renting a car, four typically will. Rail Europe and other railpass vendors offer **rail-and-drive packages** both for individual countries and all of Europe. **Fly-and-drive packages** are often available from travel agents or airline/rental agency partnerships. Cheaper cars tend to be less reliable and harder to handle on difficult terrain. Less expensive 4WD vehicles in particular tend to be more top heavy and are more dangerous when navigating particularly bumpy roads. Keep in mind that almost all European cars are manual transmission and assess your stick-shift skills before deciding to rent.

RENTAL AGENCIES. It is usually less expensive to reserve a car from the US in advance than when already in Europe, so make reservations before you leave by calling a US-based firm with European offices (Avis, Budget, or Hertz), a European-based company with local representatives (Europcar), or a tour operator (Auto Europe or Europe By Car) that will arrange a rental for you from a European company at its own rates. Multinationals offer greater flexibility, but tour operators often strike better deals. Occasionally the price and availability information they give doesn't jive with what local offices in your country will tell you. Try checking with both numbers to make sure you get accurate information and the best price. Local desk numbers are included in town listings; for home-country numbers, call your toll-free directory. Also, be sure to consider your location carefully; for example, it's usually cheaper to rent a car in Belgium or the Netherlands than in Paris.

Minimum age to rent a car varies from country to country but is usually 21-25; some companies charge those aged 21-24 an additional insurance fee. Policies and prices vary from agency to agency; be sure to ask about the insurance coverage and deductible, and always check the fine print. Rental agencies in Europe include:

Auto Europe, 39 Commercial St, P.O. Box 7006, Portland, ME 04112 (US☎888-223-5555; fax 207-842-2222; www.autoeurope.com).

Avis, US ☎800-230-4898; Canada ☎800-272-5871; UK ☎0870 606 0100; Australia ☎136 333; www.avis.com.

Budget, 4225 Naperville Rd., Lisle, IL 60532 (US ☎800-527-0700; international (630) 955 1900; www.budget.com).

Europe by Car (US ☎800-223-1516 or 212-581-3040; www.europebycar.com)

Europcar, 3 avenue du Centre, 78 881 Saint Quentin en Yvelines Cedex, France (☎(03) 31 30 44 90 00); US ☎678 461-9880; www.europcar.com).

Hertz, 225 Brae Boulevard, Park Ridge, NJ 07656 (US ☎800-654-3131; Canada ☎800-263-0600; UK ☎(0870) 844 8844; Australia ☎(613) 9698 2555; www.hertz.com)

Kemwel Holiday Autos (US ☎800-576-1590 or ☎(914) 825 3000; www.kemwel.com).

COSTS AND INSURANCE. Rates vary widely by country; expect to pay anywhere from US$200-400 per week, plus 5-25% tax. Reserve ahead and pay in advance if possible. Expect to pay more for larger cars and for 4WD. Cars with **automatic transmission** are far more expensive (sometimes $300 more per week) than standard manuals (stick shift), and in most of Europe automatic transmission is hard to find. It is virtually impossible to find an automatic 4WD.

Many rental packages offer unlimited kilometers, while others offer 200km per day with a surcharge of around $0.15 per kilometer after that. Return the car with a full tank of petrol to avoid high fuel charges at the end. Remember that if you are driving a conventional vehicle on an **unpaved road** in a rental car, you are almost never covered by insurance; ask about this before leaving the rental agency. Always check if prices quoted include tax and **insurance** against theft and collision; some credit card companies cover the deductible on collision insurance, allowing their customers to decline the collision damage waiver. Be aware that cars rented on **American Express** or **Visa/Mastercard Gold or Platinum** credit cards in Europe might *not* carry the automatic insurance that they would in some other countries; check with your credit card company. Ask about discounts and check the terms of insurance, particularly the size of the deductible.

ON THE ROAD

Before setting off, know the laws of the countries in which you'll be driving (e.g., headlights and seatbelts must be on at all times in Sweden, and vehicles drive on the left in Ireland and the UK). For an informal primer on European road signs, driving conventions, and driving guidelines, check out www.travlang.com/signs. **Petrol (gasoline)** prices are generally most expensive in Scandinavia; in any country, petrol is usually cheaper in large cities than outlying areas.

DANGERS. Roads in Western Europe are generally excellent, but keep in mind that each area has its own hazards. While you'll need to watch for moose and elk in Scandinavia (particularly in low light), cars driving 150kph will probably pose more of a threat on the Autobahn. Even in areas with official speed limits, Europeans drive *fast*, and roads are often curvy, particularly in mountainous areas. Road conditions fluctuate with the seasons; for instance, winter weather will make driving difficult in some countries, while warm weather causes flooding due to melted ice in others. Be aware that as you travel eastward, roads may become a bit rougher. The **Association for Safe International Road Travel (ASIRT),** 11769 Gainsborough Rd.,

Potomac, MD, 20854 (US ☎301-983-5252; fax 983-3663; www.asirt.org; email asirt@erols.com) can provide specific information about road conditions. ASIRT considers road travel to be relatively safe in most of western Europe and slightly less safe in developing nations due to poorly maintained roads and inadequately enforced traffic laws. Carry emergency equipment with you (see Driving Precautions, below) and know what to do in case of a breakdown.

CAR ASSISTANCE. Each country has its own national automobile organization; consult the introduction to a specific country for the location and phone number of its group.

> **❗ DRIVING PRECAUTIONS.** When traveling in the summer or in the desert, bring substantial amounts of water (5L of water per person per day) for drinking and for the radiator. For long drives to unpopulated areas, register with police before beginning your trek, and again upon arrival at the destination. Check with the local automobile club for details. When traveling for long distances, make sure tires are in good repair and have enough air, and get good maps. A compass and a car manual can also be very useful. You should always carry a spare tire and jack, jumper cables, extra oil, flares, a torch (flashlight), and heavy blankets (in case your car breaks down at night or in the winter). If you don't know how to change a tire, learn before heading out, especially if you are planning on traveling in deserted areas. Blowouts on dirt roads are exceedingly common. If you do have a breakdown, stay with your car; if you wander off, there's less likelihood that trackers will find you.

DRIVING PERMITS AND CAR INSURANCE

INTERNATIONAL DRIVING PERMIT (IDP). If you plan to drive a car while in Europe, you must be over 18 and have an International Driving Permit (IDP), although certain countries (such as the UK) allow travelers to drive with a valid American or Canadian license for a limited number of months. It may be a good idea to get one anyway, in case you're in an accident or stranded in a smaller town where the police do not know English; information on the IDP is printed in 10 languages, including French, Spanish, Russian, German, Arabic, Italian, Scandinavian, and Portuguese.

Your IDP, valid for one year, must be issued in your own country before you depart. You must be at least 18 years old and have a valid driver's license. An application for an IDP usually requires one or two passport photos, a current local license, and a fee (generally about US$10). To apply, contact the national or local branch of your home country's Automobile Association.

CAR INSURANCE. If you rent, lease, or borrow a car, you will need a **green card,** or **International Insurance Certificate,** to certify that you have liability insurance and that it applies abroad. Green cards can be obtained at car rental agencies, car dealers (for those leasing cars), some travel agents, and some border crossings. Rental agencies may require you to purchase theft insurance in countries that they consider to have a high risk of auto theft.

BY FERRY

Most European ferries are slow but inexpensive and quite comfortable; the cheapest ticket typically still includes a reclining chair or couchette. However, ferries often dock in remote parts of the country, forcing you to arrange connections to larger cities at additional cost. Plan ahead and reserve tickets in advance, or you may spend days waiting in port for the next sailing. Fares jump sharply in July and August; ask for **discounts** (ISIC holders can often get student fares, and Eurailpass holders get many reductions and free trips. You'll occasionally have to pay a port tax (under US$10). For more information, consult the

Official Steamship Guide International (available at travel agents), or www.youra.com/ferry.

ENGLISH CHANNEL AND IRISH SEA FERRIES. Ferries are frequent and dependable. The main route across the **English Channel,** from England to France, is Dover-Calais. The main ferry port on the southern coast of England is Portsmouth, with connections to France and Spain. Ferries also cross the **Irish Sea,** connecting Northern Ireland with Scotland and England, and the Republic of Ireland with Wales. For more information on sailing (or hovering) in this region, see **By Ferry from the UK and Ireland,** p. 62, or www.ferrybooker.com.

NORTH AND BALTIC SEA FERRIES. Ferries in the **North Sea** are reliable and cheap. For information on ferries heading across the North Sea to and from the UK, see p. 62. **Baltic Sea** ferries service routes between Poland and Scandinavia.

Polferries: Sweden ☎(40) 97 61 80; www.polferries.se. Ystad, Sweden to Swinoujscie (7hr.), Poland and Oxelösund-Stockholm to Gdansk (17hr.).

Color Line: Norway ☎(22) 94 44 00; www.colorline.com. Offers ferries between Norway and Denmark, Sweden and Germany.

Silja Line: US sales ☎800-323-7436, Finland ☎+358 (09) 18041; www.silja.com. Helsinki to Stockholm (16hr., June-Dec.); Tallinn, Estonia (3hr., June to mid-Sept.); and Rostock, Germany (23-25hr., June to mid-Sept.). Also Turku to Stockholm (12hr.).

Scandinavian Seaways: US ☎800-533-3755; www.seaeurope.com. Copenhagen to Oslo (16hr.), Gothenburg to Kristiansand (4hr.).

MEDITERRANEAN AND AEGEAN FERRIES. Mediterranean ferries may be the most glamorous, but they can also be the most rocky. Ferries run from Spain to Morocco, from Italy to Tunisia, and from France to Morocco and Tunisia. Reservations are recommended, especially in July and August. Ferries run on erratic schedules, with similar routes and varying prices; shop around, and beware of dinky, unreliable companies that don't take reservations. Bring toilet paper.

Ferries also run across the **Aegean,** from Ancona, Italy to Patras, Greece (19hr.), and from Bari, Italy to Igoumenitsa (9hr.) and Patras (15hr.), Greece. **Eurail** is valid on certain ferries between Brindisi, Italy and Corfu (8hr.), Igoumenitsa, and Patras, Greece. Countless ferry companies operate these routes simultaneously; see specific country chapters for more information.

BY BICYCLE

Biking is one of the key elements of the classic budget Eurovoyage. With a mountain bike, you can also do some serious natural sightseeing. Many airlines will count your bike as your second free piece of luggage; a few charge extra (US$60-110 one-way). Bikes must be packed in a cardboard box with the pedals and front wheel detached; airlines often sell bike boxes at the airport (US$10). Most ferries let you take your bike for free or for a nominal fee, and you can always ship your bike on trains. Renting a bike beats bringing your own if your touring will be confined to one or two regions. Some youth hostels rent bicycles for low prices. In Switzerland, train stations rent bikes and often allow you to drop them off elsewhere; check train stations throughout Europe for similar deals.

EQUIPMENT. In addition to **panniers** to hold your luggage, you'll need a good **helmet** (from US$25) and a U-shaped **Citadel or Kryptonite lock** (from US$20). For equipment, **Bike Nashbar,** 6103 State Rte. 446, Canfield, OH 44406 (US ☎800-627-4227; www.nashbar.com), beats all competitors' offers and ships anywhere in the US or Canada. For more information, purchase *Europe by Bike,* by Karen and Terry Whitehill (US$15), from Mountaineers Books, 1001 S.W. Klickitat Way #201, Seattle, WA 98134 (US ☎800-553-4453 or 206-223-6303; www.mountaineersbooks.org).

BIKE TOURS. If you are nervous about striking out on your own, **Blue Marble Travel** (Canada ☎519-624-2494; France ☎01 42 36 02 34; US ☎973-326-9533; www.blue-marble.org) offers bike tours for small groups for ages 20 to 50 through the Alps,

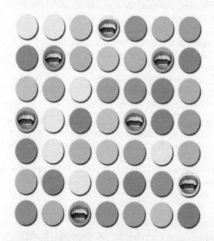

Austria, France, Germany, Italy, Portugal, Scandinavia, and Spain. **CBT Tours,** 2506 N. Clark St., #150, Chicago, IL 60614 (US ☎800-736-2453; www.cbttours.com), offers full-package 7- to 12-day biking, mountain biking, and hiking tours (around US$100 per day) to Belgium, the Czech Republic, England, France, Germany, the Netherlands, Italy, Ireland, Scotland, and Switzerland.

BY MOPED AND MOTORCYCLE

Motorized bikes (mopeds) don't use much gas, can be put on trains and ferries, and are a good compromise between the high cost of car travel and the limited range of bicycles. However, they're uncomfortable for long distances, dangerous in the rain, and unpredictable on rough roads and gravel. Always wear a helmet and never ride with a backpack. If you've never been on a moped before, a twisting Alpine road is not the place to start. Expect to pay about US$20-35 per day; try auto repair shops, and remember to bargain. Motorcycles can be much more expensive and normally require a license, but are better for long distances. Before renting, ask if the quoted price includes tax and insurance, or you may be hit with an unexpected additional fee. Avoid handing your passport over as a deposit; if you have an accident or mechanical failure you may not get it back until you cover all repairs. Pay ahead of time instead. For more information, try *Motorcycle Journeys through the Alps and Corsica*, by John Hermann (Whitehorse Press, US$20) or *Motorcycle Touring and Travel*, by Bill Stermer (Whitehorse Press, US$20).

BY FOOT

Europe's grandest scenery can often be seen only by foot. *Let's Go* describes many daytrips for those who want to hoof it, but native inhabitants (Europeans are fervent hikers), hostel proprietors, and fellow travelers are the best source for tips. Many European countries have hiking and mountaineering organizations; alpine clubs in Germany, Austria, Switzerland, and Italy, as well as tourist organizations in Scandinavia, provide accommodations in splendid settings.

BY THUMB

! *Let's Go* strongly urges you to consider the risks before you choose to hitch. We do not recommend hitching as a safe means of transportation, and none of the information presented here is intended to do so.

No one should hitch without careful consideration of the risks involved. Hitching means entrusting your life to a random person that happens to stop beside you on the road and risking theft, assault, sexual harassment, and unsafe driving. In spite of this, there are advantages to hitching when it is safe: it allows you to meet local people and get where you're going, especially in northern Europe and Ireland, where public transportation is sketchy. The choice, however, remains yours.

BY REGION. Britain and Ireland are probably the easiest places in Western Europe to get a lift. Hitching in Scandinavia is slow but steady. Long-distance hitching in the developed countries of northwestern Europe demands close attention to expressway junctions, rest stop locations, and often a destination sign. Hitching in southern Europe is generally mediocre; France is the worst. In some Central and Eastern European countries, the line between hitching and taking a taxi is quite thin; drivers may expect to be paid the cost of a bus ticket to your destination.

SAFETY TIPS. Safety-minded hitchers avoid getting in the back of a two-door car (or any car they wouldn't be able to get out of in a hurry) and never let go of their backpacks. If they ever feel threatened, they insist on being let off immediately. Acting as if they are going to open the car door or vomit on the upholstery will usually get a driver to stop. Hitchhiking at night can be particularly dangerous; experienced hitchers stand in well-lit places and expect drivers to be leery of nocturnal thumbers.

SUCCESSFUL HITCHING. For women traveling alone, hitching is just too dangerous. A man and a woman are a safer combination, two men will have a harder time, and three will go nowhere. Where one stands is vital. Experienced hitchers pick a spot outside of built-up areas, where drivers can stop, return to the road without causing an accident, and have time to look over potential passengers as they approach. Hitching (or even standing) on super-highways is usually illegal: one may only thumb at rest stops or at the entrance ramps to highways. In the **Practical Information** section of many cities, *Let's Go* lists the tram or bus lines that take travelers to strategic hitching points. Success depends on appearance. Successful hitchers travel light and stack their belongings in a compact but visible cluster. Most Europeans signal with an open hand rather than a thumb; many write their destination on a sign in large, bold letters and draw a smiley-face under it. Drivers prefer hitchers who are neat and wholesome. No one stops for anyone wearing sunglasses.

RIDE SERVICES. Most Western European countries offer a ride service (listed in the **Practical Information** for major cities), a cross between hitchhiking and the ride boards common at many universities, which pairs drivers with riders; the fee varies according to destination. **Eurostop International** (**Verband der Deutschen Mitfahrzentralen** in Germany and **Allostop** in France) is one of the largest in Europe. Riders and drivers can enter their names on the Internet through the **Taxistop** website (www.taxistop.be).

TRANSPORTATION

ANDORRA

Welcome to Andorra (pop. 65,000; 464 sq. km), the forgotten country sandwiched between France and Spain. The serenity of this Pyrenean nation's stunning landscapes vies for attention with its neon-lit streets. Catalán is the official **language,** but French and Spanish are widely spoken. With no **currency,** all establishments must accept both Spanish and French currencies, although *pesetas* are more prevalent. Because of Andorra's diminutive size, one day can include sniffing aisles of duty-free perfume, hiking through a pine-scented valley, and relaxing in a luxury spa.

TRANSPORTATION. The only way to get to Andorra is by **car** or **bus.** Forget about airports or train stations. Traffic from France must enter through **Pas de la Casa;** the Spanish gateway town is **La Seu d'Urgell. Andor-Inter/Samar buses** (Madrid ☎ (914) 68 41 90; Toulouse ☎ (561) 58 14 53; Andorra ☎ 82 62 89) connect Andorra la Vella to **Madrid** (9hr.; Tu, F, Sa and Su 11am; W, Th, and Su 10pm; 5200ptas/€31.20), while **Alsina Graells** (Andorra ☎ 82 65 67) and **Eurolines** run to **Barcelona** (3-4hr., 4 per day, 2855-2975ptas/€17-18). To go anywhere else in Spain, take a **La Hispano-Andorra bus** (☎ 82 13 72) from Andorra la Vella to La Seu d'Urgell (30min.; 6-8 per day M-Sa 7:45am-8pm, Su 8:45am-8pm; 400ptas/€2.40) and change there for an Alsina Graells bus. Intercity buses (100-300ptas/€0.60-1.80) connect the villages; Andorra la Vella buses make all stops, so look at the direction sign in the front window of the bus.

PRACTICAL INFORMATION. Andorra la Vella (pop. 20,000), the capital, is little more than a cluttered road flanked by duty-free shops. All buses go to the **Estació d'Autobusos,** on C. Bonaventura Riberaygua. To get to the **tourist office** on Av. Dr. Villanova from the bus stop on Av. Princep Benlloch, continue east (away from Spain) just past the *plaça* on your left and take Av. Dr. Villanova down to the right. (Open July-Aug. daily 9am-9pm, Sept.-June M-Sa 9am-1pm and Su 9am-1pm.) **Phones** require an STA *teletarjeta* (telecard) available at the tourist office, post office, or kiosk (500ptas/€3). You cannot make collect calls, and AT&T does not have an international access code. **Directory assistance:** ☎ 111. **Country code:** ☎ 376. Send **email** from **@Centre** C. Maria Pla, 8. (☎ 86 09 30. 500ptas/€3 per hr., 125ptas/€0.75 min. Open M-Sa 7am-3am. Closed Sundays.) Dream of duty-free cheese at **Hotel Viena,** C. de la Vall, 3. (Singles 4000ptas/€24; doubles 5000ptas/€30.) Drool at the chocolate bars at the supermarket in Grans Magatzems Pyrénées, Av. Meritxell, 11. (Open Sept.-July M-F 9:30am-8pm, Sa 9:30am-9pm, Su 9:30am-7pm; Aug. M-Sa 9:30am-9pm and Su 9:30am-7pm.)

SIGHTS. "Spend your time in Andorra exploring the countryside. The **Caldea-Spa,** in nearby **Escaldes-Engordany,** is the largest in Europe, with luxurious treatments and prices to match. (☎ 80 09 95. Open daily 10am-11pm. 3000ptas/€18 per 3hr., includes baths and relaxing light treatment.) **Ordino** (pop. 2219), 5km northeast of La Massana, is convenient for hiking and skiing adventures. It's also home of the **Microminiature Exam,** Edifici Coma, a modern wonder by all accounts. (☎ 83 83 38. Open Tu-Sa 9;30am-1:30pm and 3:30-7pm, Su 9:30am-1:30pm. 300ptas/€1.80.)

The masses also flock to Andorra's four outstanding **ski resorts,** all of which rent equipment. The tiny town of **Canillo,** in the center of the country, is a convenient location from which to access the resorts. Free shuttles pick up skiers from their hotels and take them to **Soldeu-El Tarter,** (☎ 89 05 00) which occupies 840 hectares of skiable area between Andorra la Vella and Pas de la Casa, France. Contact **SKI Andorra** (☎ 86 43 89; www.skiandorra.ad) or pick up the tourist office's winter edition of *Andorra* for more information.

An extensive system of **hiking trails** traverse the tiny country; most are easy enough for even the least-seasoned outdoor enthusiasts. Pick up the free *Sports Activities* brochure at the tourist office for itineraries and potential routes.

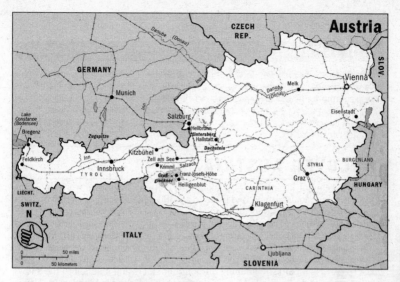

AUSTRIA
(ÖSTERREICH)

US$1 = 16.15AS	10AS = US$0.62
CDN$1 = 10.58AS	10AS = CDN$0.95
UK£1 = 22.71AS	10AS = UK£0.44
IR£1 = 17.47AS	10AS = IR£0.57
AUS$1 = 8.14AS	10AS = AUS$1.23
NZ$1 = 6.53AS	10AS = NZ$1.53
ZAR1 = 1.95AS	10AS = ZAR5.13
EUR€1 = 13.76AS	10AS = EUR€0.73

PHONE CODES	**Country code: 43. International dialing prefix:** 00 (from Vienna, **900**). From outside Austria, dial int'l dialing prefix (see inside back cover) + 43 + city code + local number. To call **Vienna** from outside Austria, dial int'l dialing prefix + 43 + 1 + local number.

The mighty Austro-Hungarian Empire may have crumbled after World War I, but Austria remains a complex, multi-ethnic country. Drawing on centuries of Habsburg political maneuvering, Austria has become a skillful mediator between Eastern and Western Europe, connecting Germany, Switzerland, and Italy with Slovenia, Hungary, Slovakia, and the Czech Republic. Renowned for its brilliant artists, writers, and musicians—from Gustav Klimt's *Jugendstil* paintings to Arthur Schnitzler's dark insights into imperial decadence to Beethoven's thundering symphonies—Austria has had an indelible impact on Western art and literature. Today, Austria owes its much of its glory to the overpowering Alpine landscape that hovers over the remnants of its tumultuous past. A mention of Austria evokes images of onion-domed churches set against snow-capped peaks, lush meadows, dark forests, and mighty castles.

For extensive and entertaining information on Austria's attractions, pick up a copy of *Let's Go: Austria & Switzerland 2002.*

FACTS AND FIGURES

Official Name: Republic of Austria.
Capital: Vienna.
Major Cities: Salzburg, Innsbruck, Graz.
Population: 8.2 million.
Land Area: 83,858 sq. km.

Climate: Cool summers; cold winters with rain in the lowlands and snow in the mountains.
Languages: German.
Religions: Roman Catholic (80%), Protestant (5%).

DISCOVER AUSTRIA

In Austria's capital, **Vienna** (p. 87), soak up cafe culture, stare down works by Klimt and other Secessionist artists, and listen to a world-famous opera or orchestra for a mere pittance. An easy stopover between Vienna and Munich, **Salzburg** (p. 99) was home to both the von Trapp family and Mozart—some travelers find the overabundance of kitsch a tad overwhelming. Hike around historic **Hallstatt** (p. 105) in the nearby **Salzkammergut** region, or explore the natural pleasures of the **Hohe Tauern National Park** (p. 106), including the Krimml Waterfalls (p. 107). Farther west, **Innsbruck** (p. 107) is a fantastic jumping off point for skiers and hikers into the snow-capped peaks of the Tyrolean Alps. For superior skiing, head to **Kitzbühel** (p. 110).

ESSENTIALS

WHEN TO GO

November to March is peak ski season, so prices in western Austria double and travelers need reservations months in advance. The situation reverses in the summer, when the flatter, eastern half fills with vacationers. Sights and accommodations are cheaper and less crowded in the shoulder season (May-June, Sept.-Oct.). But some Alpine resorts close in May and June—call ahead. The Vienna State Opera, the Vienna Boy's Choir, and many major theaters throughout Austria don't have any performances during July and August.

DOCUMENTS AND FORMALITIES

VISAS. Citizens of Australia, Canada, New Zealand, South Africa, and the US need valid passports to enter Austria and can stay three months without a visa.

EMBASSIES. All foreign embassies in Austria are in Vienna (p. 89). Austrian embassies at home: **Australia,** 12 Talbot St., Forrest, Canberra ACT 2603 (☎ (02) 62 95 15 33; fax 62 39 67 51); **Canada,** 445 Wilbrod St., Ottawa, ON KIN 6M7 (☎ 613-789-1444; fax 789-3431); **Ireland,** 15 Ailesbury Court Apts., 93 Ailesbury Rd., Dublin 4 (☎ (01) 269 45 77; fax 283 08 60); **New Zealand,** Level 2, Willbank House, 57 Willis St., Wellington (☎ (04) 499 63 93; fax 499 63 92); **South Africa,** 1109 Duncan St., Momentum Office Park, Brooklyn, Pretoria 0011 (☎ (012) 46 33 61; fax 46 11 51); **UK,** 118 Belgrave Mews West, London SW1 X 8HU (☎ (020) 72 35 37 31; fax 344 02 92); **US,** 33524 International Ct. NW, Washington, D.C. 20008-3035 (☎ 202-895-6700; fax 895-6750).

TRANSPORTATION

BY PLANE. The only major international airport is Vienna's Schwechat Flughafen. European flights also land in Salzburg, Graz, and Innsbruck. From the UK, **buzz** flies to Vienna (☎ (0870) 240 70 70; www.buzzaway.com.)

BY TRAIN. The **Österreichische Bundesbahn (ÖBB),** Austria's federal railroad, operates an efficient 5760km of tracks accommodating frequent, fast, and comfortable trains.

The ÖBB publishes the yearly *Fahrpläne Kursbuch Bahn-Inland*, a compilation of all transportation schedules in Austria. **Eurail, InterRail,** and **Europe East** passes are valid in Austria. The **Austrian Railpass** allows three days of travel within any 15-day period on all rail lines; it also entitles holders to 40% off on bike rental at train stations (2nd-class US$107, each additional day US$15).

BY BUS AND CAR. The efficient Austrian bus system consists mainly of orange **BundesBuses,** which cover areas inaccessible by train. They usually cost about as much as trains, and railpasses are not valid. You can buy discounted tickets, valid for one week, for any particular route. A **Mehrfahrtenkarte** gives you six tickets for the price of five. For bus information, dial (0222) 711 01 within Austria from 7am-8pm. Driving is a convenient way to see more isolated parts of Austria, but many small towns prohibit cars. The roads are generally very good and well-marked, and Austrian drivers are quite careful. Renting a car is usually cheaper in Germany.

BY BIKE AND BY THUMB. Bikes are a great way to get around Austria; roads are generally level and safe. Many train stations rent bikes and allow you to return them to any participating station. Consult local tourist offices for bike routes and maps. *Let's Go* does not recommend hitchhiking. A safer option are the **Mitfahrzentrale** (ride-sharing services) in larger cities, which pair drivers with riders for a small fee. Riders then negotiate fares with the drivers.

TOURIST SERVICES AND MONEY

EMERGENCY	Police: ☎ 133. Ambulance: ☎ 144. Fire: ☎ 122.

TOURIST OFFICES. Virtually every town has a tourist office marked by a green "i" sign. Most brochures are available in English. Visit www.experienceaustria.com or www.austria-tourism.at for more Austrian tourist information.

MONEY. The unit of currency in Austria is the **Schilling**, abbreviated as **AS, ÖS,** or, within Austria, simply **S**. Each *Schilling* is subdivided into 100 *Groschen* (g). Coins come in 2, 5, 10, and 50g, and 1, 5, 10, and 20AS denominations. Bills come in 20, 50, 100, 500, 1000, and 5000AS amounts. Austria has accepted the **Euro (€)** as legal tender, and Schillings will be phased out by July 1, 2002. For more information, see p. 21. If you stay in hostels and prepare most of your own food, expect to spend anywhere from 400-850AS/€29-€62, or US$30-65, per person per day. Accommodations start at about 150AS/€10.90, or US$10, while a basic sit-down meal usually costs around 170AS/€13, or US$12. In Austria, menus will say whether service is included (*Preise inclusive* or *Bedienung inclusiv*); if it is, you don't have to tip. If it's not, leave a tip up to 10%. Austrian restaurants expect you to seat yourself, and servers will not bring the bill until you ask them to do so. Say *Zahlen bitte* (TSAHL-en BIT-uh) to settle your accounts, and don't leave tips on the table. Be aware that some restaurants charge for each piece of bread that you eat during your meal. Don't expect to bargain in shops or markets in Austria, except at flea markets and the Naschmarkt in Vienna. Austria has a 20-34% value-added tax (VAT), which is applied to items such as books, clothing, souvenir items, art items, jewelry, perfume, alcohol, and cigarettes. You can get it refunded if the total is at least 1000AS (US$95) at one store.

COMMUNICATION

MAIL. Letters take 1-2 days within Austria. Airmail to North America takes 5-7 days, but up to two weeks to Australia and New Zealand. Mark all letters and packages "mit Flugpost" or "par avion." Aerogrammes are the cheapest option. Address mail to be held: First name SURNAME, Postlagernde Briefe, A-1010 Vienna, Austria.

TELEPHONES. You can usually make international calls from a pay phone, but a better option is to buy phone cards *(Wertkarten)* at post offices, train stations, and *Tabak/Trafik* (50 or 100AS). Direct dial access numbers include: **AT&T,** ☎ (0800) 20 02 88; **British Telecom,** ☎ (0800) 20 02 09; **Canada Direct,** ☎ (0800) 20 02 17;

HIKING AND SKIING. Nearly every town has **hiking** trails in its vicinity; consult the local tourist office. Trails are usually marked with either a red-white-red marker (only sturdy boots and hiking poles necessary) or a blue-white-blue marker (mountaineering equipment needed). Most mountain hiking trails and mountain huts are only open from late June to early September because of snow in the higher passes. Western Austria is one of the world's best **skiing** regions; the areas around Innsbruck and Kitzbühel are saturated with lifts and runs. High season normally runs from mid-December to mid-January and from February to March. Tourist offices provide information on regional skiing and can suggest budget travel agencies that offer ski packages.

Ireland Direct, ☎ (0229) 030 353; **MCI, ☎** (0800) 20 02 35; **Sprint, ☎** (0800) 20 02 36; **Telecom New Zealand, ☎** (0800) 20 02 22; **Telkom South Africa, ☎** (0800) 20 02 30.

INTERNET ACCESS. Most towns in Austria have Internet cafes. Rates are usually about 50-100AS/€3.65-7.30 per hr.

LANGUAGE. German is the official language. English is the most common second language, but outside of cities and among older residents, English is less common. *Grüss Gott* is the typical greeting. For basic German phrases, see p. 984.

ACCOMMODATIONS AND CAMPING

Always ask if your lodging provides a **guest card** (*Gästekarte*), which grants discounts on activities, museums, and public transportation. In Austria, the 10AS/€0.75 tax that most accommodations add to your bill funds these discounts—take advantage of them to get your money's worth. In Austria, the *Österreicher Jugendherbergsverband-Hauptverband* (OJH) runs the over 80 **hostels** in the country. Because of the rigorous standards of the national organizations, hostels are usually as clean as any hotel. Most hostels charge 179-300AS/€13-22 per night for dorms; non-HI members are usually charged a surcharge. **Hotels** are expensive (singles 200-350AS/€15-26; doubles 400-800AS/€30-59). The cheapest have Gasthof, Gästehaus, or Pension-Garni in the name. Renting a **Privatzimmer** (room in a family home) is an inexpensive and friendly way to house yourself. Rooms range from 250 to 400AS a night. Contact the local tourist office for a list of private rooms. Slightly more expensive, **Pensionen** (pensions) are similar to American and British bed-and-breakfasts. **Camping** in Austria is less about getting out into nature and more about having a cheap place to sleep; most sites are large plots with many vans and cars and are open in summer only. Prices run 50-70AS/€3.65-5 per person and 25-60AS /€1.85-€4.50 per tent (plus 8-9.50AS /€0.60-0.70 tax if over age 15).

FOOD AND DRINK

Loaded with fat, salt, and cholesterol, traditional Austrian cuisine is a cardiologist's nightmare but a delight to the palate. Staple foods include pork, veal, sausage, eggs, cheese, bread, and potatoes. Austria's best known dish, *Wienerschnitzel*, is a breaded meat cutlet (usually veal or pork) fried in butter. Vegetarians should look for *Spätzle* (noodles), *Eierschwammerl* (yellow mushrooms), or anything with the word "Vegi" in it. The best supermarkets are Billa and Hofer, where you can buy cheap rolls, fruits, and veggies. Natives nurse their sweet tooths with *Kaffee und Kuchen* (coffee and cake). Try *Sacher Torte*, a rich chocolate cake layered with marmalade; *Linzer Torte*, a light yellow cake with currant jam; *Apfelstrudel*; or just about any pastry. Austrian beers are outstanding—try *Stiegl Bier*, a Salzburg brew; *Zipfer Bier* from upper Austria; and *Gösser Bier* from Styria.

HOLIDAYS AND FESTIVALS

Holidays: New Year's Day (Jan. 1-2); Epiphany (Jan. 6); Good Friday (Mar. 29); Easter Monday (Apr. 1); Labor Day (May 1); Ascension (May 9); Whitmonday (May 20); Corpus

Christi (May 30); Assumption Day (Aug. 15); Austrian National Day (Oct. 26); All Saints' Day (Nov. 1); Immaculate Conception (Dec. 8); Christmas (Dec. 25-26).

Festivals: Just about everything closes down on public holidays, so plan accordingly. Austrians celebrate **Fasching** (Carneval) during the first 2 weeks of February. Austria's most famous summer music festivals are the **Wiener Festwochen** (mid-May to mid-June) and the **Salzburger Festspiele** (late July to late Aug.).

VIENNA (WIEN)   ☎ 0222

From its humble origins as a Roman camp along the Danube, Vienna became the cultural heart of Europe for centuries, the setting for fledgling musicians, writers, artists, philosophers, and politicians to achieve greatness—or infamy. At the height of its artistic ferment at the turn of the century, during the smoky days of its great cafe culture, the Viennese self-mockingly referred to their city as the "merry apocalypse": its smooth veneer of waltzes and *Gemütlichkeit* (good nature) concealed a darker side expressed in Freud's theories, Kafka's dark fantasies, and Mahler's deathly beautiful music. Vienna has a reputation for living absent-mindedly in this grand past, but as the last fringes of the Iron Curtain have been drawn back, Vienna has tried to reestablish itself as the gateway to Eastern Europe and as a place where experimentalism thrives.

✈ INTERCITY TRANSPORTATION

Flights: The **Wien-Schwechat Flughafen** (☎ 700 72 22 31, departure info 700 72 21 84) is home to **Austrian Airlines** (☎ 517 89; www.aua.com; open M-F 7am-10pm, Sa-Su 8am-8pm). Daily flights to and from **New York,** and frequent flights to **Berlin, London, Rome,** and other major cities are available. The **airport** is far from the city center (18km); the cheapest way to reach the city is S7 "Flughafen/Wolfsthal," which stops at Wien Mitte (30min., every 30min. 5am-9:30pm, 38AS/€2.76; Eurail not valid). The heart of the city, Stephanspl., is a short metro ride from Wien Mitte on the U3 line. It's more convenient (but also more expensive) to take the **Vienna Airport Lines Shuttle Bus,** which runs between the airport and the City Air Terminal, at the Hilton opposite Wien Mitte (every 20min. 6:30am-11:10pm; every 30min. midnight-6am; 70AS/€5.09). **Buses** connect the airport to the Südbahnhof and Westbahnhof (see below; every 30min. 8:55am-7:25pm; every hr. 8:20pm-8:25am).

Trains: Vienna has two main train stations with international connections. For general train information, dial ☎ 17 17 (24hr.) or check www.bahn.at.

Westbahnhof, XV, Mariahilferstr. 132. Most trains head west, but a few go east and north. To: **Amsterdam** (14½hr., 7:17pm, 2280AS/€165.70); **Berlin Zoo** (11hr., 9:19pm, 1682AS/€122.24); **Bregenz** (8hr., 5 per day 5am-10:15pm, 790AS/€57.41); **Budapest** (3-4hr., 6 per day 8:25am-6pm, 428AS/€31.10); **Hamburg** (9½hr., 10:17am and 7:45pm, 2410AS/€175.15); **Innsbruck** (5-6hr., every 2hr. 5am-11:25pm, 660AS/€47.97); **Munich** (4½hr., 5 per day 5:45am-3:45pm, 824AS/€59.88); **Paris** (14hr., 8:47am and 8:21pm, 2140AS/€155.52); **Salzburg** (3½hr., every hr. 460AS/€33.43); **Zurich** (9¼hr., 3 per day 7:15am-9:15pm, 1104AS/€80.23). **Info counter** open daily 7:30am-8:40pm.

Südbahnhof, X, Wiedner Gürtel 1a, on the D tram. To get to the city take the tram (dir. Nußdorf) to Opera/Karlspl. Trains leave for destinations south and east. To: **Berlin Ostbahnhof** (9¼hr., 10:55am, 1160AS/€84.30); **Graz** (2¾hr., every hr. 6am-10:30pm, 310AS/€22.53); **Krakow** (7-8hr., 9:25am and 9:25pm, 496AS/€36.05); **Prague** (4½hr., 3 per day 6:55am-2:55pm, 524AS/€38.08); **Rome** (14hr., 7:34am and 7:36pm, 1352AS/€98.26); **Venice** (9-10hr., 3 per day 7:30am-10:30pm, 880AS/€63.95). **Info counter** open daily 6:30am-9:20pm.

Buses: Buses in Austria are seldom cheaper than trains; compare prices before buying a ticket. **City bus terminals** at Wien Mitte/Landstr., Hütteldorf, Heiligenstadt, Floridsdorf, Kagran, Erdberg, and Reumannpl. **BundesBuses** run from these stations. **Ticket counter** open M-F 6am-5:50pm, Sa-Su 6am-3:50pm. Many international bus lines also have agencies in the stations. For info, call BundesBus (☎ 711 01; 7am-7pm).

Hitchhiking: *Let's Go* does not recommend hitching. **Hitchhikers** headed for Salzburg take U4: Hütteldorf. The highway is 10km farther. Hitchers traveling south often ride tram #67 to the last stop and wait at the rotary near Laaerberg. A safer alternative is ride sharing; **Mitfahrzentrale Wien,** VIII, Daung. 1a (☎ 408 22 10), off Laudong., pairs drivers and riders. Call to see what's available, then take tram #43 to Skodag. to meet your ride. Open M-F 8am-noon and 2-7pm, Sa-Su 1-3pm. A ride to **Salzburg** costs 210AS/€15.26, to **Prague** 450AS/€32.70. Reserve 2 days in advance.

✴ ORIENTATION

Vienna is divided into 23 **districts** *(Bezirke)*. The first is the *Innenstadt* (city center), defined by the **Ringstraße** on three sides and the Danube Canal on the fourth. The Ringstraße (or "Ring") consists of many different segments, each with its own name, such as Opernring, Kärntner Ring, or Dr.-Karl-Lueger-Ring. Many of Vienna's major attractions are in District I and immediately around the Ringstraße. Districts II-IX spread out from the city center following the clockwise, one-way traffic of the Ring. The remaining districts expand from yet another ring, the **Gürtel** ("belt"). Like the Ring, this major two-way thoroughfare has numerous segments, including Margaretengürtel, Währinger Gürtel, and Neubaugürtel. Street signs indicate the district number in Roman or Arabic numerals *before* the street and number. **Let's Go includes district numbers for establishments in Roman numerals before the street address.**

▐ LOCAL TRANSPORTATION

Public transportation in Vienna is extensive and dependable; call 580 00 for general information. The **subway** (U-Bahn), **tram** (Straßenbahn), **elevated train** (S-Bahn), and **bus** systems operate under one ticket system. A **single fare** (22AS/€1.60 on bus, 19AS/€1.38 in advance from a ticket machine, ticket office, or tobacco shop), lets you travel to any single destination in the city and switch from bus to U-Bahn to tram to S-Bahn, as long as your travel is uninterrupted. To **validate a ticket,** punch it in the machine immediately upon entering the first vehicle, but don't stamp it again when you switch trains. Otherwise, plainclothes inspectors may fine you 560AS/€40.70. Other ticket options (available at the same places as pre-purchased single tickets) are a **24hr. pass** (60AS/€4.36), a **3-day "rover" ticket** (150AS/€10.90), a **7-day pass** (155AS/€11.26; valid M 9am to M 9am), or an **8-day pass** (300AS/€21.80; valid any 8 days, not necessarily consecutive; valid also for several people traveling together). The **Vienna Card** (210AS/€15.26) offers free travel for 72hr. as well as discounts at museums, sights, and events.

Regular trams and subway cars stop running between 12:30-5am. **Nightbuses** run every 30min. along most routes; "N" signs with yellow eyes designate night bus stops. (15AS/€1.09; 45AS/€3.27 for 4; day transport passes not valid.) A complete night bus schedule is available at bus information counters in U-Bahn stations. **Information stands** in many stations help with tickets and have an indispensable free pocket map of the U- and S-Bahn systems. Stands in the U-Bahn at Karlspl., Stephanspl., and the Westbahnhof are the most likely to have information in English. (Open M-F 6:30am-6:30pm, Sa-Su and holidays 8:30am-4pm.)

Taxis: (☎ 313 00, 401 00, 601 60, or 814 00). Stands at Westbahnhof, Südbahnhof, Karlspl. in the city center, and by the Bermuda Dreiecke for late-night revelers. Accredited taxis have yellow and black signs on the roof. Rates generally run 27AS/€1.96, plus 14AS/€1.02 per km. 27AS/€1.96 extra Su, holidays, and 11pm-6am.

Car Rental: Avis, I, Opernring 3-5 (☎ 587 62 41). Open M-F 7am-8pm, Sa 8am-2pm, Su 8am-1pm. **Hertz** (☎ 70 07 26 61), at the airport. Open M-F 7:15am-11pm, Sa 8am-8pm, Su 8am-11pm.

Bike Rental: At Wien Nord and Westbahnhof. 150AS/€10.90 per day, 90AS/€6.54 with train ticket from day of arrival. **Pedal Power,** II, Ausstellungsstr. 3 (☎ 729 72 34), rents bikes (60AS/€4.36 per hr., 395AS/€28.71 for 24hr. with delivery) and offers bike tours (180-280AS/€13.08-20.35). Student and Vienna Card discounts. Open May-Sept. daily 8am-8pm. *Vienna By Bike,* at the tourist office, has biking information.

LITTLE PIECES OF REVOLUTION Travelers may be perplexed by the little paper strips taped around columns in train stations, subway stops, and crowded streets. The slips, known as *Pflücktexte* (from *pflücken*, to pluck), contain short poems with vaguely anti-establishment messages and are meant to be "plucked" from the columns, whereupon they are mysteriously replaced. *Let's Go* sleuths have determined that the poems are composed by one Helmut Seethaler, Wasnerg. 43/8, 1200 Wien, who offers more insurgent poems via mail "for a small bill."

CRIME IN THE CITY Vienna is a metropolis with crime like any other; use common sense, especially after dark. Karlspl. is home to many pushers and junkies. Avoid areas in districts V, X and XIV, as well as Landstraßer Hauptstr. and Prater Park, after dark. Vienna's Red Light District covers sections of the Gürtel.

ℤ PRACTICAL INFORMATION

TOURIST AND FINANCIAL SERVICES

Main Tourist Office: I, Albertinpl. (www.info.wien.at). Follow Operng. up 1 block from the Opera House. The staff gives a free map of the city and the pamphlet *Youth Scene*, and books rooms for a 40AS/€2.95 fee plus 1-night deposit. Open daily 9am-7pm.

Embassies and Consulates: Australia, IV, Mattiellistr. 2 (☎512 85 80). **Canada,** I, Laurenzerberg 2 (☎531 38 30 00; fax 531 38 33 21). **Ireland,** I, Rotenturmstr. 16-18 5th fl. (☎71 54 24 60). **New Zealand,** contact the embassy in Germany, Friedrichstr. 60, 10117 Berlin (☎(030) 20 62 10; fax 20 62 11 14). Consulate, XIX, Springsiedelg. 28 (☎318 85 05). **South Africa,** XIX, Sandg. 33 (☎320 64 93; fax 320 64 93 51). **UK,** III, Jauresg. 12 (☎716 13 51 51; fax 716 1359 00). **US,** IX, Boltzmanng. 16 (☎313 39; fax 406 52 60).

Currency Exchange: ATMs are your best bet. The 24hr. exchange at the **main post office** has excellent rates and an 80AS/€5.85 fee for US$1100 in travelers' checks.

American Express: I, Kärntnerstr. 21-23, P.O. Box 28, A-1015 (☎515 40), down the street from Stephanspl. Cashes AmEx and Thomas Cook (3% commission) checks, sells theater tickets, and holds mail for 4 weeks. Open M-F 9am-5:30pm, Sa 9am-noon.

LOCAL SERVICES

Gay and Lesbian Organizations: The bisexual, gay, and lesbian community in Vienna is more integrated than in other Austrian cities. Pick up either the monthly magazine (in German) called *Extra Connect;* the free monthly publication *Bussi* at any gay bar, cafe, or club; or consult the straight *Falter* newspaper, which lists gay events under a special heading. **Rosa Lila Villa,** VI, Linke Wienzeile 102 (☎586 81 50), is a favored resource and social center for homosexual Viennese and visitors alike. Friendly staff speaks English and provides information, a library, and nightclub listings. Open M-F 5-8pm.

Laundromat: Schnell und Sauber, VII, Westbahnhofstr. 60. U6: Burgg. Stadthalle. Wash 60AS/€4.40; dry 10AS/€0.75 per 15min. Soap included. Open 24hr.

EMERGENCY AND COMMUNICATION

Police: ☎33. **Ambulance:** ☎144. **Fire:** ☎122.

Crisis Hotlines: All have English speakers. **Rape Crisis Hotline:** ☎523 22 22. M 10am-6pm, Tu 2-6pm, W 10am-2pm, Th 5-9pm. **24hr. immediate help:** ☎717 19.

Medical Assistance: Allgemeines Krankenhaus (hospital), IX, Währinger Gürtel 18-20 (☎404 00 19 64). **Emergency care:** ☎141. **24hr. pharmacy:** ☎15 50. Consulates have lists of English-speaking doctors, or call **Fachärzte Zugeck** (☎512 18 18; 24hr.).

Internet Access: bigNET.internet.cafe, I, Karntnerstr. 61 (☎503 98 44) or I, Hoher markt 8-9 (☎533 29 39). 50AS/€3.65 per 30min. and hip English-speaking crew.

Libro, XXII, Donauzentrum (☎202 52 55), provides free access at 6 terminals. Open M-F 7am-7pm, Sa 9am-5pm. **Jugend-Info des Bundesministeriums,** I, Franz-Josefs-Kai 51 (☎533 70 30), has free access at 2 PCs. Open M-F 11am-6pm.

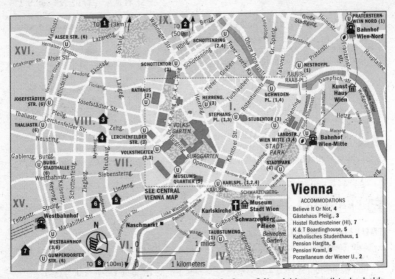

Vienna

ACCOMMODATIONS

Believe It Or Not, **4**
Gästehaus Pfeilg., **3**
Hostel Ruthensteiner (HI), **7**
K & T Boardinghouse, **5**
Katholisches Studenthaus, **1**
Pension Hargita, **6**
Pension Kraml, **8**
Porzellaneum der Wiener U., **2**

Post Offices: Hauptpostamt, I, Fleischmarkt 19. Open 24hr. Address mail to be held: SURNAME, First Name; Postlagernde Briefe; Hauptpostamt; Fleischmarkt 19; A-1010 Wien. Branches throughout the city and at the train stations; look for the yellow signs with the trumpet logo. **Postal Codes:** A-1XX0, where XX is the number of the district in Arabic numerals (ex.: District I: A-1010, District II: A-1020, District XVII: A-1170.)

ACCOMMODATIONS AND CAMPING

One of the few unpleasant aspects of visiting Vienna is the hunt for cheap rooms during peak tourist season (June-Sept.). Write or call for reservations at least five days in advance. The summer crunch for budget rooms is slightly alleviated in July, when university dorms convert into makeshift hostels. If you're staying for a longer period of time, try **Odyssee Reisen und Mitwohnzentrale,** VIII, Laudong. 7, which arranges for you to house-sit or sublet apartments. Bring your passport to register. (☎402 60 61. Open M-F 10am-2pm and 3-6pm.)

HOSTELS AND HOTELS

▨ **Wombats City Hostel,** XIV, Grang. 6 (☎897 23 36). Exit Westbahnhof at the main exit, turn right onto Mariahilferstr., right onto Rosinang., and continue until Grang. While near train tracks and a number of auto-body shops, this superb modern hostel compensates with a pub and various perks. Breakfast 35AS/€2.54. Shower included. Laundry 50AS/€3.65. Internet 1AS/€0.07 per min. Bike or inline skate rental 100AS/€7.30 per day. 2-, 4-, and 6-bed dorms 190-245AS/€13.85-17.85 per person.

▨ **Hostel Ruthensteiner (HI),** XV, Robert-Hamerlingg. 24 (☎893 42 02). Exit Westbahnhof at the main entrance, turn right, head to Mariahilferstr., turn right onto Mariahilferstr., and continue until Haidmannsg. Turn left, then take the 1st right on Robert-Hammer-lingg. A top-notch hostel with a knowledgeable, English-speaking staff, spotless rooms, and a snack bar. Breakfast 29AS/€2.11. Showers and sheets (except for 10-bed rooms) included. Lockers and kitchen available. Internet 20AS/€1.45. 4-night max. stay. Reception 24hr. Reservations recommended. "The Outback" summer dorm 135AS/€9.85; 4- to 10-bed dorms 135-159AS/€9.85-11.60; 3- to 5-bed dorms 169-179AS/€12.30-13; doubles 470-518AS/€34.20-37.65. AmEx/MC/V.

Believe It Or Not, VII, Myrtheng. 10, Apt. #14 (☎526 46 58). From Westbahnhof, take U6 (dir. Heiligenstadt) to Burgg./Stadthalle, then bus #48A (dir. Ring) to Neubaug. Walk back on Burgg. 1 block and take the 1st right on Myrtheng. Ring the bell. A converted apartment, with kitchen and 2 co-ed bedrooms. Reception 8am until early afternoon. Lockout 10:30am-12:30pm. 160AS/€11.65; Nov.-Easter 110AS/€8.

Hostel Panda, VII, Kaiserstr. 77, 3rd fl. (☎522 53 53). From Westbahnhof, take tram #5 to Burgg. From Sudbahnhof, take tram #18 to Westbahnhof, then tram #5 to Burgg. Housed in an old-fashioned Austrian apartment building, this fun and eclectic hostel has 2 co-ed dorms. Kitchen and TV. Bring lock for lockers. Dorms 160AS/€11.65; Nov.-Easter 110AS/€8. 1-night stays add 50AS/€3.65.

Kolpinghaus Wien-Meidling, XIII, Bendlg. 10-12 (☎813 54 87). U6: Niederhofstr. Head right on Niederhofstr., and take the 4th right onto Bendlg. Breakfast 50AS/€3.65. Sheets included. Showers in all rooms. Reception 24hr. Check-out 9am. 8- and 10-bed dorms 170AS/€12.35; 4- and 6- bed dorms 180-195AS/€13-14.20. MC/V.

Jugendgästehaus Wien Brigittenau (HI), XX, Friedrich-Engels-Pl. 24 (☎332 82 94 or 330 05 98). U1 or U4: Schwedenpl., then Tram N to Floridsdorferbrücke/Friedrich-Engels-Pl. and follow the signs. This roomy hostel has excellent facilities for the disabled, but it's 25min. from the city center. Breakfast, lockers, and sheets included. Internet access. 5-night max. stay. Reception 24hr. Lockout 9am-1pm. 24-bed dorms 145AS/€10.55; 4-bed dorms 180AS/€13.10; 2-bed dorms with bath 210AS/€15.30 per person. Nonmembers add 40AS/€2.95.

PENSIONS

Pension Kraml, VI, Brauerg. 5 (☎587 85 88). U3: Zierierg. Exit onto Otto-Bauerg., take 1st left, then 1st right. From Südbahnhof, take bus #13A to Esterhazyg. and walk up Brauerg. Near the *Innenstadt* with large rooms, a lounge, cable TV, and a kind staff. Breakfast buffet 40AS/€2.95. Singles 310AS/€22.55; doubles 560AS/€40.70, with shower 640AS/€46.55, with bath 760AS/€55.25; triples 720AS/€52.35, with shower 930AS/€67.60. MC/V.

Pension Hargita, VII, Andreasg. (☎526 19 28). U3: Zieglerg. Use the Andreasg. exit. Amicable service and a prime location. Breakfast 40AS/€2.95. Reception 8am-10pm. Singles 400AS/€29.10, with shower 450AS/€32.70; doubles 600AS/€43.60, with shower 700AS/€50.90, with bath 800-900AS/€53-66.

K & T Boardinghouse, VII, Mariahilferstr. 72, 3rd fl. (☎523 29 89; fax 522 03 45; kaled@chello.at). U3: Neubaug. Big, sunny rooms above a sex shop. Free Internet access. Laundry 120AS. 2-night min. stay. Reserve ahead. Singles 600AS/€43.60; doubles with bath 800AS/€58.15; triples 1050AS/€76.35.

UNIVERSITY DORMITORIES

From July through September, many university dorms become hotels with singles, doubles, and a few triples and quads. The rooms don't have much character, but showers and sheets are standard, and their cleanliness and relatively low cost suffice for most budget travelers, particularly for longer stays.

Porzellaneum der Wiener Universität, IX, Porzellang. 30 (☎31 77 28 20). From Südbahnhof, take tram D (dir. Nußdorf) to Fürsteng. From Westbahnhof, take tram #5 to Franz-Josefs Bahnhof, then tram D (dir. Südbahnhof) to Fürsteng. Great location in the student district. Sheets included. Reception 24hr. Call ahead. Singles 210AS/€15.30; doubles 420AS/€30.55; quads 840AS/€61.

Katholisches Studentenhaus, XIX, Peter-Jordanstr. 29 (☎34 74 73 12). From Westbahnhof, U6: Nußdorferstr., then bus #35A or tram #38 to Hardtg. and turn left. From Südbahnhof, take tram D to Schottentor, then tram #38 to Hardtg. Reception until 10pm. Call ahead. Singles 250AS/€18.17; doubles 400AS/€29.07.

Gästehaus Pfeilgasse, VIII, Pfeilg. 6 (☎401 74). U2: Lerchenfelderstr. Go right, turn right on Langeg., and left onto Zeltg., which becomes Pfeilg. Breakfast included. Reception 24hr. Call ahead. Singles 270AS/€19.65; doubles 480AS/€34.90; triples 600AS/€43.60.

CAMPING

Wien-West, Hüttelbergstr. 80 (☎914 23 14). U4: Hütteldorf, then bus #14B or 152 (dir. Campingpl.) to Wien West. This convenient campground is crowded but grassy and pleasant. Laundry, grocery stores, wheelchair access, and cooking facilities.

AUSTRIA

Reception 7:30am-9:30pm. Closed Feb. July-Aug. 75AS/€5.45 per person, Sept.-June 68AS/€4.95; 45AS/€3.30 per tent. Electricity 40AS/€2.91.

Campingplatz Schloß Laxenburg (☎(02236) 713 33), at Münchendorfer Str., Laxenburg, 15km from Vienna. Restaurant, boat rental, heated pool, and supermarket. Open Apr.-Oct. In July-Aug. 82AS/€6 per person, 45AS/€3.30 per tent; Sept.-Oct. and Apr.-June 75AS/€5.45 per person, 40AS/€2.91 per tent. Electricity 40AS/€3.

◻ FOOD

Vienna's restaurants are as varied as its cuisine. The restaurants near Kärntnerstr. are generally expensive—a better bet is the neighborhood north of the university and near the *Votivkirche* (U2 to "Schottentor"), where Universitätsstr. and Währingerstr. meet. Cafes with cheap meals also line **Burggasse** in District VI. The area radiating from the Rechte and Linke Wienzeile near Naschmarkt (U4 to "Kettenbrückeg.") houses cheap restaurants, and the **Naschmarkt** itself contains stands where you can purchase bread and a variety of ethnic foods. Almost all year long, **Rathausplatz** hosts food stands tied into the current festival. The open-air **Brunnenmarkt** (U6: Josefstädterstr.; walk up Veronikag. one block and turn right) is cheap and cheerful. Supermarkets chains include **Billa, Hofer,** and **Spar.** Kosher groceries are available at the **Kosher Supermarket,** II, Hollandstr. 10 (☎216 96 75).

INSIDE THE RING

Margaritaville, I, Bartensteing. 3. U2: Lerchenfelderstr. Exit onto Museumstr. and cut across the triangular green to Bartensteing. Offers authentic Tex-Mex food among Spanish-speakers. Open M-F 4pm-midnight, Sa-Su 11am-midnight. MC/V.

Bizi Pizza, I, Rotenturmstr. 4. 1 block up Rotenturmstr. from Stephanspl. Bizi will whip up fresh food cafeteria-style for a pittance. Open daily 11am-11:30pm.

Inigo, I, Bäckerstr. 18. This popular dining spot, founded by a Jesuit priest as part of a socio-economic reintegration program, provides transit employment, training, and social work for the unemployed. Menu includes international dishes, many whole wheat and vegetarian options, and a salad bar. Entrees 69-128AS/€5-€9.30. Open M-Su 8:30am-11:30pm; July-Aug. closed Sa-Su. MC/V.

Zimolo, I, Ballg. 5, near Stephanspl. off Weihburgg. A charming cafe with candlelit tables, opera, and Italian dishes. Open M-Sa 11:30am-2:30pm and 6:30pm-midnight.

Levante, I, Wallnerstr. 2. Walk down Graben away from the Stephansdom, turn left on Kohlmarkt, and right onto Wallnerstr. Greek-Turkish fare, including vegetarian dishes. Entrees 90-160AS/€6.55-11.65. Open daily 11:30am-11:30pm.

OUTSIDE THE RING

🕱 **OH Pot, OH Pot,** IX, Währingerstr. 22. U2: Schottentor. This adorable joint serves filling "pots" (stew-like veggie or meat concoctions; 88-125AS/€6.40-€9.10). Open M-F 7:30am-11:00pm, Sa-Su 6pm-late.

Hunger Künstler, VI, Gumpendorferstr. 48. U3: Neubaug. A quiet, candlelit restaurant with outstanding food (around 110AS/€8). Open Su-Sa 11am-2am.

Tunnel, VIII, Florianig. 39. U2: Rathaus. With your back to the *Rathaus*, head right on Landesgerichtstr. and left on Florianig. Pronounced "Too-nehl," this is a popular student paradise with live nightly music, daily lunch *Menüs* (55AS/€4), and Italian, Austrian, and Middle Eastern dishes (many vegetarian). Open daily 9am-2am.

Centimeter, IX, Liechtensteinstr. 42. Tram D: Bauernfeldpl. This chain offers huge portions of greasy Austrian fare and an unbelievable selection of beers. Open M-F 10am-2am, Sa 11am-2am, Su 11am-midnight.

Café Willendorf, VI, Linke Wienzeile 102. U4: Pilgramg. Look for the big pink building which also houses the Rosa Lila Villa, Vienna's gay and lesbian center. This cafe, bar, and restaurant with a leafy outdoor terrace serves creative vegetarian fare for under 100AS/€7.30; meat dishes 100-125AS/€7.30-€9.10. Open daily 6pm-2am.

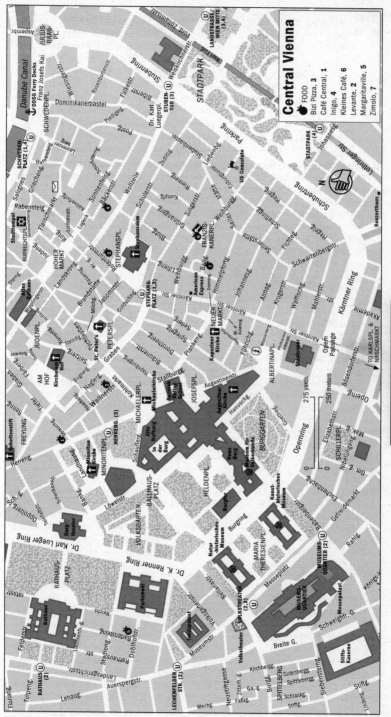

AUSTRIA

Central Vienna

🍴 FOOD
Bizi Pizza, 3
Café Central, 1
Iñigo, 4
Kleines Café, 6
Levante, 2
Margaritaville, 5
Zimolo, 7

VIENNA COFFEE CULTURE. The 19th-century coffeehouse was a haven for artists, writers, and thinkers, who stayed long into the night composing operettas, writing books, and cutting into each other's work. The bourgeoisie followed suit, and the coffeehouse became the living room of the city. The original literary cafes were Café Griensteidl, Café Central, and Café Herrenhof. Cafes still exist under all these names, but only Café Central looks like it used to. Most cafes also serve hot food, but don't order anything but pastries with your coffee unless you want to be really gauche. The most serious dictate of coffeehouse etiquette is that you linger; the waiter (*Herr Ober*) will serve you when you sit down, then leave you to sip, read, and brood. When you're ready to leave, just ask to pay: *"Zahlen bitte!"* Vienna has many coffeehouses; the best are listed below.

■ **Kleines Café,** I, Franziskanerpl. 3. Turn off Kärtnerstr. onto Weihburg. and follow it to the *Franziskanerkirche*. This tiny, cozy cafe features courtyard tables and salads that are minor works of art. Open M-Sa 10am-2am, Su 1pm-2am.

■ **Café Sperl,** VI, Gumpendorferstr. 11. U2: Museumsquartier. Exit to Mariahilferstr., walk along Getreidemarkt, and turn right on Gumpendorferstr. One of Vienna's oldest, most beautiful cafes. Open M-Sa 7am-11pm, Su 3-11pm; July-Aug. closed Su.

Café Central, I, at the corner of Herreng. and Strauchg. inside Palais Fers. Café Central has become touristy because of its fame, but this mecca of the cafe world is still worth a visit. Open M-Sa 8am-8pm, Su 10am-6pm.

Hotel Sacher, I, Philharmonikerstr. 4, behind the opera house. This historic sight has served world-famous *Sacher Torte* (50AS) in red velvet opulence for years. Cafe open daily 11am-11:30pm. Bakery open daily 9am-11:30pm. AmEx/MC/V.

Vegetasia, III, Ungarg. 57. Tram O: Neulingg. A cozy Taiwanese vegetarian restaurant with tofu, *seitan*, and soy delights artfully disguised as beef, chicken, and fish. Open-daily 11:30am-3pm and 5:30-11:00pm; closed Tu evenings.

University Mensa, IX, Universitätsstr. 7, on the 7th fl. of the university building, between U2 stops Rathaus and Schottentor. Ride the old-fashioned *Pater Noster* elevator (no doors and never stops, so jump in and out and say your prayers) to the 6th fl. and take the stairs up. Not much atmosphere, but the food is cheap. Typical cafeteria meals 40-60AS/€3-4.40. Open M-F 11am-2pm; closed July-Aug. but snack bar open 8am-3pm.

◎ SIGHTS

Vienna's streets are by turns startling, cozy, scuzzy, and grandiose; expect contrasts around every corner. To wander on your own, grab the brochure *Vienna from A to Z* (with Vienna Card discount 50AS; available at the tourist office). The range of available **tours** is overwhelming—there are 42 themed walking tours alone, detailed in the brochure *Walks in Vienna* from the tourist office. Contact **Vienna-Bike,** IX, Wasag. (☎319 12 58), for bike rental (60AS/€4.40) or a 2-3hr. cycling tour (280AS/€20.35). Bus tours are given by **Vienna Sight-seeing Tours,** III, Stelzhamerg. 4/11 (☎712 46 83) and **Cityrama,** I, Börgeg. 1 (☎534 13). Tours start at 400AS/€30. The sights below are arranged for a do-it-yourself walking tour.

INSIDE THE RING

District I is Vienna's social and geographical epicenter as well as a gallery of the history of aesthetics, from Romanesque to *Jugendstil* (Art Nouveau).

STEPHANSPLATZ, GRABEN, AND PETERSPLATZ. *(U1 or U3: Stephanspl.)* Right at the heart of Vienna, this square is home to the massive **Stephansdom** (St. Stephen's Cathedral), Vienna's most treasured symbol. The elevator in the North Tower (50AS) leads to a view of the city; the 343 steps of the South Tower climb to a 360° view. *(Open daily 9am-5:30pm. 35AS/€2.55.)* Downstairs in the **catacombs,** the skeletons of thousands of plague victims line the walls. The **Gruft** (vault) stores all of the Habsburg innards. *(Cathedral tours M-Sa 10:30am and 3pm, Su and holidays 3pm; in English at 3:45pm; 45AS/€3.30.)* From Stephanspl., follow **Graben** for a landscape of

Jugendstil architecture, including the **Ankerhaus** (#10), the red-marble **Grabenhof** by Otto Wagner, and the underground public toilet complex, designed by Adolf Loos. Graben leads to **Petersplatz** and the 1663 **Pestsäule** (Plague Column), which was built to commemorate the passing of the Black Death.

HOHER MARKT AND STADTTEMPEL. *(Take Milchg. out of Peterspl., turn right, and go 3 blocks on Tuchlauben; Hoher Markt is on the right.)* Once both market and execution site, **Hoher Markt** was the heart of the Roman encampment, Vindobona. Roman ruins lie beneath the shopping arcade on its south side. *(Open Tu-Su 9am-12:15pm and 1pm-4:40pm. 25AS/€1.85, students 10AS/€0.75.)* The biggest draw is the 1914 *Jugendstil* **Ankeruhr** (clock), whose 3m historical figures—from Marcus Aurelius to Maria Theresia—rotate past the old Viennese coat of arms accompanied by music of their time period. *(1 figure per hr. At noon all figures appear.)* Follow Judeng. from Hoher Markt to Ruprechtspl. Hidden at Seitenstetteng. 2-4 is the **Stadttempel** (City Temple), the only synagogue in Vienna to escape Nazi destruction during *Kristallnacht* because it was concealed from the street. *(Bring passport. Open Su-F. Free.)*

ALTES RATHAUS, AM HOF, AND FREYUNG. *(Backtrack to Hoher Markt and follow Wipplingerstr.)* The **Altes Rathaus** (Old Town Hall), Wipplingerstr. 8, was occupied from 1316 to 1885. It's also home to the **Austrian Resistance Museum,** chronicling anti-Nazi activity during World War II and temporary exhibits. *(Open M and W-Th 9am-5pm. Free.)* Follow Drahtg. to Am Hof, a grand courtyard which was once a medieval jousting square and now houses the **Kirche am Hof** (Church of the Nine Choirs of Angels). Just west of Am Hof, **Freyung** is an uneven square with the **Austriabrunnen** (Austria fountain) in the center. Freyung ("sanctuary") got its name from the **Schottenstift** (Monastery of the Scots) just behind the fountain, where fugitives could claim asylum in medieval times. It was once used for public executions, but the annual **Christkindl markt** held here blots out such unpleasant memories.

HOFBURG. *(From Freyung, follow Herreng. to Michaelerpl. and head through the half-moon-shaped Michaelertor.)* The sprawling **Hofburg** was the winter residence of the Hapsburg emperors. Construction began in 1279, and hodge-podge additions and renovations continued until the end of the family's reign in 1918. When you come through the Michaelertor, you'll first enter the courtyard called **In der Burg** ("within the fortress"). On your left is the red-and-black-striped **Schweizertor** (Swiss Gate), erected in 1552. On your right is the entrance to the **Kaiserappartements** (Imperial Apartments), which were once the private quarters of Emperor Franz Josef and Empress Elisabeth. The **Hofsilber und Tafelkammer** (Court Silver and Porcelain Collection), on the ground floor opposite the ticket office, displays examples of the outrageously ornate Imperial cutlery. *(Both open daily 9am-4:30pm. Combined admission 95AS/€7, students 75AS/€5.50.)* Head through the Schweizertor to the **Schweizerhof,** the inner courtyard of the **Alte Burg** (Old Fortress). The stairs to the right of the Schweiztor lead to the Gothic **Burgkapelle** (chapel), where the members of the **Wiener Sängerknaben** (Vienna Boys' Choir) raise their heavenly voices every Sunday. Beneath the stairs is the entrance to the **Weltliche und Geistliche Schatzkammer** ("Worldy and Spiritual Treasury"), containing Habsburg jewels, the "horn of a unicorn" (really a narwhale's horn) and a tooth allegedly from the mouth of John the Baptist. *(Open W-M 10am-6pm. 100AS/€7.30, students 70AS€5.10. Free audio guide available in English.)* Attached to the northeast side of the Alte Burg is the **Stallburg,** the home of the Royal Lipizzaner stallions. The cheapest way to get a glimpse of the famous steeds is to watch them train. *(Mid-Feb. to June and late Aug. to early Nov. Tu-F 10am-noon. Tickets at the door at Josefspl., Gate 2, from about 8:30am. 160AS/€11.65.)* The **Neue Burg** is the youngest wing of the palace and houses the fantastic **Völkerkunde Museum** (see Museums, p. 97) and the **Österreichische Nationalbibliothek** (Austrian National Library), whose buff statues allegedly inspired the 11-year-old Arnold Schwarzenegger to pump up. *(Open Oct.-June M-F 9am-7pm, Sa 9am-12:45pm; July-Aug. and Sept. 22-30 M-F 9am-3:45pm, Sa 9am-12:45pm; closed Sept. 1-22.)* High masses are still held in the 14th-century **Augustinerkirche** (St. Augustine's Church), and the **Herzgrüftel** (Little Heart Crypt) contains the hearts of the Habsburgs. *(Open M-Sa 10am-6pm, Su 11am-6pm. Mass 11am. Free.)*

AUSTRIA

AUSTRIAN GRAFFITI Scratched into the stones near the entrance of the Stephansdom is the mysterious abbreviation "O5." It's not a sign of hoodlums up to no good, but rather a reminder of a different kind of subversive activity. During World War II, "O5" was the secret symbol of Austria's resistance movement against the Nazis. The capital letter "O" and the number "5," for the fifth letter of the alphabet, form the first two letters of "Oesterreich"—meaning Austria. Recently the monogram has received new life. Every time alleged Nazi collaborator and ex-president of Austria Kurt Waldheim attends mass, the symbol is highlighted in chalk. Throughout the city, "O5" has also been appearing on buildings and flyers in protest against the anti-immigrant policies of Jörg Haider and the Freedom Party.

OUTSIDE THE RING

As the city expands beyond the Ring in all directions, the distance between notable sights also expands. But what the area outside the Ring gives up in accessibility, it makes up for in its varied attractions.

KARLSPLATZ AND NASCHMARKT. *(U1, U2, or U4: Karlspl. Or, from the Hofburg, walk down Tegetthoffstr. to Neuer Markt and follow Kärntnerstr. to Karlspl.)* Karlspl. is home to Vienna's most beautiful Baroque church, the **Karlskirche,** an eclectic masterpiece with a Neoclassical portico, a Baroque dome and towers on either side. *(Open M-F 7:30am-7pm, Sa 8:30am-7pm, Su 9am-7pm. Free.)* West of Karlspl., along Linke Wienzeile, is the **Naschmarkt,** a colorful, multi-ethnic food bazaar. On Saturdays, the Naschmarkt becomes a massive flea market. (Open M-F 7am-6pm, Sa 7am-1pm.)

SCHLOß BELVEDERE. *(Take tram #71 or tram D one stop past Schwarzenbergpl. Or, from Karlspl., face the Künstlerhaus and turn right on Friedrichstr., follow it to Schwarzenbergpl., and head southeast, away from the city center.)* **Schloß Belvedere** (Belvedere Castle) was originally the summer residence of Prince Eugène of Savoy, Austria's greatest military hero. The grounds stretch from Schwarzenberg Palace to the Südbahnhof and contain three spectacular gardens and several excellent museums (p. 96).

SCHLOß SCHÖNBRUNN. *(U4 : Schönbrunn.)* From its humble beginnings as a hunting lodge, **Schönbrunn** ("beautiful brook") was Maria Theresia's favorite residence. Tours of some of the palace's 1500 rooms reveal the elaborate taste of her era. Both the Grand (44 rooms) and the Imperial (22 rooms) tours give you access to the **Great Gallery,** where the Congress of Vienna met, and the **Hall of Mirrors,** where 6-year-old Mozart played. *(Palace open daily Apr.-June and Sept.-Oct. 8:30am-5pm; Nov.-Mar. 8:30am-4:30pm; July-Aug. 8:30am-7pm. Imperial Tour 105AS/€7.65, students 95AS/€6.90. Grand Tour 135AS/€9.85, 110AS/€8. Audio-guides included. Guided tour 170AS/ €12.35, 145AS/€10.55.)* Even more impressive than the palace itself are the classical **gardens** behind it, which extend nearly four times the length of the palace and contain a hodgepodge of attractions, including the world's oldest menagerie and the **Schmetterlinghaus** (Butterfly House). *(Park open 6am-dusk. Free.)*

ZENTRALFRIEDHOF (CENTRAL CEMETERY). **Tor I** (Gate 1) leads to the **Jewish Cemetery,** which mirrors the fate of Vienna's Jewish population—many of the headstones are cracked, broken, or neglected because the families of most of the dead have left Austria. Behind **Tor II** (Gate 2) are Beethoven, Strauss, and an honorary monument to Mozart, whose true resting place is an unmarked paupers' grave in the **Cemetery of St. Mark,** III, Leberstr. 6-8. **Tor III** (Gate 3) leads to the Protestant section and the new Jewish cemetery. *(Main entrance at XI, Simmeringer Hauptstr. 234. Take tram #71 from Schwarzenbergpl., tram #72 from Schlachthaus, or S7 to Zentralfriedhof. Open May-Aug. 7am-7pm; Mar.-Apr. and Sept.-Oct. 7am-6pm; Nov.-Feb. 8am-5pm.)*

🏛 MUSEUMS

Vienna owes its vast selection of masterpieces to the acquisitive Habsburgs and to the city's own crop of art schools and world-class artists. An exhaustive list is impossible to include here, but the tourist office's free *Museums* brochure lists all opening hours and admission prices. All museums run by the city of Vienna are **free on Friday** before noon (except on public holidays). If you're going to be in town for a while, invest in the **Museum Card** (ask at any museum ticket window).

■ **Österreichische Galerie** (Austrian Gallery), III, Prinz-Eugen-Str. 27, in the Belvedere Palace behind Schwarzenbergpl. (p. 96). Walk up from the Südbahnhof, take tram D to Schloß Belvedere, or tram #71 to Unteres Belvedere. The **Upper Belvedere** houses European art of the 19th and 20th centuries, including Klimt's *The Kiss*. The **Lower Belvedere** contains an extensive collection of sculptures, David's portrait of Napoleon on horseback, and the **Museum of Medieval Austrian Art**. Both open Tu-Su 10am-6pm. Upper open Th until 9pm. 100AS/€7.30, students 70AS/€5.10.

■ **Kunsthistorisches Museum** (Museum of Fine Arts). U2: Museumsquartier, U2/U3: Volkstheater, or tram 1, 2, D, J. Across from the Burgring and Heldenpl. on Maria Theresia's right. The world's 4th-largest art collection, including Venetian and Flemish paintings, Classical art, and an Egyptian burial chamber. Open Tu-Su 10am-6pm. 120AS/€8.75, students 80AS/€5.85. In summer English guided tours (3pm 30AS/€2.20).

■ **Museum für Völkerkunde** (Ethnology Museum), I, in the Neue Burg on Heldenpl. (p. 95). U2, U3, trams 1, 2, D, or J: Volkstheater. Collected here are Benin bronzes, Chinese paper kites, West African Dan heads, and a Japanese Doll Festival. The focal point, however, is undoubtedly the crown of Montezuma, still drawing a crowd of protesters wishing its return to Mexico. Open Apr.-Dec. W-M 10am-6pm. 100AS/€7.30, students 70AS/€5.10, free May 16, Oct. 26, Dec. 10 and 24.

Museumsquartier. U2: Museumsquartier, or U2/U3, tram 1, 2, D, J: Volkstheater. A huge conglomeration of museums. Kunsthalle Wien features thematic exhibitions of international contemporary artists. Open F-W 10am-7pm, Th 10am-10pm. Hall 1 80AS/€5.85, students 60AS/€4.40; Hall 2 60AS/€4.40, 40AS/€3; both 100AS/€7.27, 80AS/€5.85. Museum Moderner Kunst (Museum of Modern Art) holds Central Europe's largest collection of modern art. Open Tu-Su 10am-6pm, Th until 9pm. 90AS/€6.50, students 70AS/€5.

Historisches Museum der Stadt Wien (Historical Museum of the City of Vienna), IV, Karlspl., to the left of the Karlskirche (p. 96). This amazing collection of historical artifacts and paintings documents Vienna's evolution from a Roman encampment, through the Turkish siege of Vienna to the subsequent 640 years of Habsburg rule. Open Tu-Su 9am-6pm. 50AS/€3.65, students 20AS/€1.45.

Sigmund Freud Haus, IX, Bergg. 19. U2: Schottentor. Walk up Währingerstr. to Bergg or take tram D to Schlickg. Sorry folks, the infamous couch is not here, but this former Freud home provides lots of photos and documents, including the young Freud's report cards and circumcision certificate. Open July-Sept. 9am-6pm; Oct.-June 9am-4pm. 70AS/€5.10, students 45AS/€3.30.

Kunst Haus Wien, III, Untere Weißgerberstr. 13. U1 or U4: Schwedenpl., then tram N to Radetzkypl. Artist and environmental activist Friedenreich Hundertwasser built this museum without straight lines—even the floor bends and swells. In addition to Hunderwasser's own work, it also hosts contemporary art from around the world. Open daily 10am-7pm. 95AS/€6.90, students 70AS/€5.10; M half-price.

🎵 ENTERTAINMENT

While Vienna offers all the standard entertainments in the way of theater, film, and festivals, the heart of the city beats to music. All but a few of classical music's marquee names lived, composed, and performed in Vienna. Mozart, Beethoven, and Haydn wrote their greatest masterpieces in Vienna, creating the First Viennese School; a century later, Schönberg, Webern, and Berg teamed up to form the Second Viennese School. Every Austrian child must learn to play an instrument during schooling, and the Vienna **Konservatorium** and **Hochschule** are world-renowned conservatories. All year, Vienna has performances ranging from the above average to the sublime, with many accessible to the budget traveler. Note that the venues below have **no performances in July and August.**

AUSTRIA

Vienna hosts an array of important annual festivals, mostly musical. The **Vienna Festival** (mid-May to mid-June) has a diverse program of exhibitions, plays, and concerts. (☎58 92 20; www.festwochen.or.at.) The Staatsoper and Volkstheater host the annual **Jazzfest Wien** during the first weeks of July, featuring many famous acts. (☎503 5647; www.viennajazz.org.) From mid-July to mid-August, the **Im-Puls Dance Festival** (☎523 55 58; www.impuls-tanz.com) attracts some of the world's great dance troupes and offers seminars to enthusiasts. In mid-October, the annual city-wide international film festival, the **Viennale,** kicks off.

Staatsoper, Opernring 2 (www.wiener-staatsoper.at), is Vienna's premier opera, performing nearly every night Sept.-June. **Standing-room tickets** are available right before the performance (1 per person, balcony 30AS/€2.18, orchestra 50AS/€3.63). The **Box office (Bundestheaterkasse),** I, Hanuschg. 3, around the corner from the opera, sells tickets in advance via fax, phone, or in person. (☎514 44 78 80; fax 514 44 29 69. Open M-F 8am-6pm, Sa-Su 9am-noon, 1st Sa of each month 9am-5pm.) You can also get tickets at www.bundestheater.at, but there's a 20% commission.

Wiener Philharmoniker (Vienna Philharmonic Orchestra) plays in the **Musikverein,** Austria's premier concert hall. Write or visit the box office of the Musikverein for tickets, including standing room tickets (Gesellschaft der Musikfreunde, Bösendorferstr. 12, A-1010 Wien) or stop by the Bundestheaterkasse (see Staatsoper, above). Tickets are available at www.wienerphilharmoniker.at; note that there's a hefty commission.

Wiener Sängerknaben (Viennese Boys' Choir). Their main showcase is mass mid-Sept. to late May, every Sunday at 9:15am in the **Hofburgkapelle** (U3: Herreng.). Contact hofmusikkapelle@asn-wien.ac.at for more info.

⚑ NIGHTLIFE

With one of the highest bar-to-cobblestone ratios in the world, Vienna is a great place to party, whether you're looking for a quiet evening with a glass of wine or a wild night in a disco full of black-clad Euro musclemen and drag queens. Take U1 or U4 to Schwedenplatz, which will drop you within blocks of the **Bermuda Dreiecke** (Triangle), an area packed with lively, crowded clubs. If your vision isn't foggy yet, head down Rotenturmstr. toward Stephansdom or walk around the areas bounded by the Jewish synagogue and Ruprechtskirche. Slightly outside the Ring, the streets off **Burggasse** and **Stiftgasse** in the 7th district and the **university quarter** (Districts XIII and IX) have tables in outdoor courtyards and loud, hip bars.

Viennese nightlife starts late, often after 11pm. For the scoop, pick up a copy of the indispensable *Falter* (28AS), which prints listings of everything from opera and theater to punk concerts and updates on the gay and lesbian scene.

▨ **Objektiv,** VII, Kirchbergg. 26. U2 or U3: Volkstheater. Follow Burgg. 2 blocks; turn right on Kirchbergg. One of the most eclectic bars in Vienna. Mellow atmosphere, lively local crowd, and cheap drinks. Happy Hour daily 11pm-1am. Open daily 6pm-2am.

▨ **U-4,** XII, Schönbrunnerstr. 222. U4: Meidling Hauptstr. In the late 80s, U-4 hosted Nirvana, Mudhoney, and Hole before they were famous. Check in advance to catch the theme night for you. Two dance areas, multiple bars. Th Heaven Gay Night. Cover 100AS/€7.27. Open daily 10pm-5am.

SOUTHERN AUSTRIA

GRAZ ☎ 0316

Wonderfully under-touristed, Graz's *Altstadt* rewards the traveler with an unhurried, Mediterranean feel and picturesque red-tiled roofs and Baroque domes. The second largest of Austria's cities, Graz offers a sweaty, energetic nightlife thanks to the 45,000 students at Karl-Franzens-Universität.

E **TRANSPORTATION.** Trains run from the **Hauptbahnhof,** Europapl. (☎05 17 17 12; open 7am-8:45pm), to: Innsbruck (6hr., 4 per day 8:20am-10pm, 570AS/€41.45); Munich (via Salzburg, 808AS/€58.75); Salzburg (4¼hr., 4 per day 6:30am-8:20pm, 460AS/€33.45); Vienna Südbahnhof (2½hr., 9 per day 5:30am-9:20pm, 340AS/€24.75); and Zurich (8½hr., 10pm, 1002AS/€80.10).

⑦ **PRACTICAL INFORMATION.** From the train station, go down Annenstr. and cross the bridge to reach **Hauptplatz,** the center of town. Nearby is **Jakominiplatz,** the hub of the public transportation system; **Herrengasse,** a pedestrian street lined with cafes and boutiques, connects the two. The **tourist office,** Herreng. 16, has free city maps and a walking site-guide of the city. The staff offers **tours** (2hr.; Tu-Su 4pm; Nov.-Mar. Sa 2:30pm; 75AS/€5.45) and makes room reservations. (☎807 50. Open M-F 9am-7pm, Sa 9am-6pm, Su 10am-4pm, holidays 10am-3pm; Oct.-May M-F 9am-6pm, Sa 9am-3pm, Su 10am-3pm.) **Postal code:** A-8010.

[icon] **ACCOMMODATIONS AND FOOD.** In Graz, most accommodations are pricey, and many are out in the boondocks. Luckily, the web of local transport provides a reliable and easy commute to and from the city center. To reach **Jugendgästehaus Graz (HI),** Idlhofg. 74, from the train station, cross the street, head right on Eggenberger Gürtel, turn left on Josef-Huber-G., then take the first right; the hostel is through the parking lot. Buses #31 and 32 run here from Jakominipl. All rooms have baths, and if the hostel is full, you can stay in the "Notlager" basement rooms with hall bathrooms. (☎71 48 76. Breakfast included. Internet 20AS/€1.50 per 20min. Reception 7am-10pm. From 10pm-2am, doors open every 30min. 4-bed dorms 230AS/€16.75; singles 325AS/€23.65; doubles 550AS/€40; basement 190AS/€13.80. 30AS/€2.20 surcharge stays less than 3 nights. MC/V.) For **Camping Central,** Martinhofstr. 3., take bus #32 from Jakomininpl. to Bad Straßgang and follow the signs. (☎(0676) 378 51 02. Shower included. Laundry 60AS/€4.40. Reception 7am-10pm. Open Apr.-Oct. 155AS/€11.30 per person, includes site and pool access; additional adults 80AS/€5.85.)

Concession stands on **Hauptpl.** sell sandwiches and *Wurst* (20-40AS/€1.45-2.95). There are also **markets** along Rösselmühlg., an extension of Josef-Huber-G., and on Jakoministr., directly off Jakominipl. Cheap student hangouts line **Zinzendorfg.** near the university, and a supermarket, **Sparmarkt,** is just a few blocks from the hostel on Prankerg. (Open M-Th 8am-7pm, F 7:30am-7:30pm, Sa 7:30am-5pm.)

[icon] **SIGHTS AND NIGHTLIFE.** The wooded **Schloßberg** ("Castle Mountain") rises 123m above Graz. It's named for the castle which stood there from 1125 until 1809, when it was destroyed by Napoleon's troops. Although the castle is mostly gone, the Schloßberg remains a beautiful city park. Climb the zigzagging stone steps of the **Schloßbergstiege,** built by Russian prisoners during world War I, for sweeping views of the vast plain. The **Landeszeughaus** (Provincial Arsenal), Herreng. 16, details the history of Ottoman attacks on the arsenal and has enough weapons to outfit 28,000 burly mercenaries. (☎01 798 10. Open March-Oct. Tu-Su 9am-5pm, Nov.-Dec. Tu-Su 10am-3pm. 20AS/€1.50.) At the solemn 17th-century Habsburg **Mausoleum,** the elaborate domed tomb holds the remains of Ferdinand II in an underground chamber. (Open M-Sa 11am-noon and 2-3pm. 10AS/€0.75, guide text 3AS/€0.25.) The hub of after-hours activity is the so-called **Bermuda Triangle,** an area of the old city behind Hauptpl. and bordered by Mehlpl., Färberg., and Prokopig. At **Kulturhauskeller,** Elisabethstr. 30, a young crowd demands ever louder and more throbbing dance music, but the partying doesn't get started until 11pm on weekends. (Weißbier 38AS/€2.80. No sports or military clothing. 19+. Obligatory coat check and security fee 25AS/€1.85. Open Tu-Sa from 10pm.)

SALZBURG ☎0662

From its position as the ecclesiastical center of Austria, Salzburg offers both spectacular sights and a rich musical culture. Whether it's enthusiastic tourists singing songs, street musicians playing medieval ballads, or a famed soprano bringing the house down, Salzburg's streets really do resonate with music. The city's passion for homegrown genius Wolfgang Amadeus Mozart and the arts reaches a dizzying climax every summer during the **Salzburger Festspiele** (p. 104), a five-week music festival featuring hundreds of operas, concerts, plays, and open-air performances.

⌐ TRANSPORTATION

Trains: Hauptbahnhof (☎05 17 17), in Südtirolerpl. To: **Graz** (4hr., every 2hr. 5:20am-5:10pm, 460AS/€33.45); **Innsbruck** (2hr., every 2hr. 12:35am-9:15pm, 380AS/€27.65); **Munich** (2hr., 27 per day 4am-11:30pm, 298AS/€21.70); **Vienna** (3½hr., 29 per day 2:15am-9:30pm, 460AS/€33.50); **Zurich** (6hr., 3 per day 12:35am-12:30pm, 884AS/€64.25). Reservations daily 7am-10pm (☎051717). Regular ticket office open 24hr.

Public Transportation: Lokalbahnhof (☎44 80 61 66), next to the train station. Single tickets (20AS/€1.45) available at automatic machines or from the bus drivers. Books of **five tickets** (90AS), **daypasses** (40AS/€2.91), and **week passes** (125AS/€9.10) available at *Tabak* shops (newsstand/tobacco shops) and at the ticket office. Punch your ticket when you board in order to validate it. Buses usually make their last run at 10:30-11:30pm, but **BusTaxi** fills in when the public buses stop. Get on at Hanuschpl. or Theaterg. and tell the driver where you need to go (every 30min. nightly 11:30pm-1:30am; 35AS/€2.55 for anywhere within the city limits).

✴ 🔊 ORIENTATION AND PRACTICAL INFORMATION

Just a few kilometers from the German border, Salzburg covers both banks of the **Salzach River.** Two hills loom up in the skyline: the **Mönchesberg** over the **Altstadt** (old city) on the south side and the **Kapuzinerberg** by the **Neustadt** (new city) on the north side. The *Hauptbahnhof* is on the northern side of town beyond the *Neustadt*; take bus #1, 5, 6, 51, or 55 to Mirabellpl. in the *Neustadt*. On foot, turn left out of the station onto Rainerstr. and follow it all the way to Mirabellpl.

Tourist Office, Mozartpl. 5 (☎88 98 73 30; www.salzburginfo.or.at), in the *Altstadt*. From the train station, take bus #5, 6, 51, or 55 to Mozartsteg, cross the river, then curve around the building into Mozartpl. The office gives free hotel maps (exactly the same as the 10AS city map), offers guided tours of the city (daily 12:15pm, 100AS/€7.27), and sells the **Salzburg Card,** which grants admission to all museums and sights as well as unlimited public transportation (24hr. card 230AS/€16.75, 48hr. 320AS/€23.25, 72hr. 410AS/€29.80). The staff will also reserve rooms for a 30AS/€2.18 fee. Open July-Aug. M-Sa 9am-7pm; Sept.-June 9am-6pm.

Currency Exchange: Rieger Bank, at Alter Markt 15, has extended currency exchange hours. Open July-Aug. M-F 9am-8pm, Sa 9am-6:30pm, Su 9:30am-5pm; Sept.-June M-F 9am-6pm, Sa 9am-3pm, Su 10am-5pm.

American Express: Mozartpl. 5 (☎80 80), near the tourist office. Provides all banking services; no commission on AmEx checks. Holds mail, books tours, and reserves *Festspiele* tickets. Open M-F 9am-5:30pm, Sa 9am-noon.

Luggage Storage: At the train station. 24hr. lockers 30-50AS/€2.18-3.63. Luggage check 30AS/€2.18 per piece per day. Open daily 6am-10pm.

Bi-Gay-Lesbian Organizations: Homosexual Initiative of Salzburg (HOSI), Müllner Hauptstr. 11 (☎435 927), hosts regular workshops and meetings, including a **cafe-bar** open F from 9pm and Sa from 8pm.

Laundromat: Norge Exquisit Textil Reinigung, Paris-Lodronstr. 16 (☎87 63 81). Self-serve wash and dry 125AS/€9.10. Open M-F 7:30am-4pm, Sa 8-10am. Full-serve 185AS/€13.50; next-day pickup. Open M-F 7:30am-6pm, Sa 8am-noon.

Emergencies: Police, ☎133. **Ambulance,** ☎144. **Fire,** ☎122.

Pharmacies: Elisabeth-Apotheke, Elisabethstr. 1a (☎87 14 84). Most pharmacies open M-F 8am-6pm, Sa 8am-noon. There are always 3 pharmacies open for emergencies; check the list on the door of any closed pharmacy.

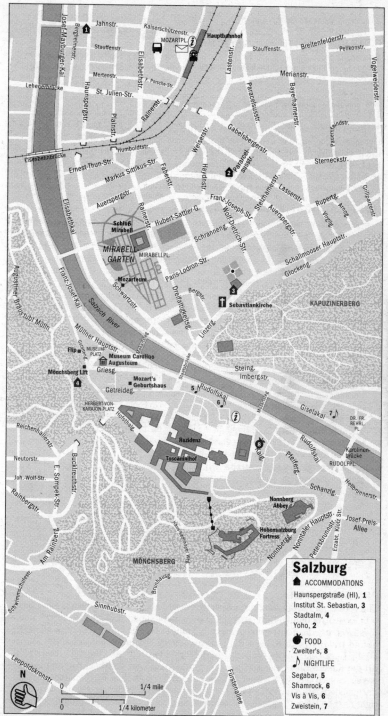

AUSTRIA

Salzburg

🏠 ACCOMMODATIONS

Haunspergstraße (HI), **1**
Institut St. Sebastian, **3**
Stadtalm, **4**
Yoho, **2**

🍎 FOOD

Zwelter's, **8**

♪ NIGHTLIFE

Segabar, **5**
Shamrock, **6**
Vis à Vis, **6**
Zweistein, **7**

Internet Access: Cybar, Gstätteng. 3 (☎84 48 23), and **Internet Café,** Mozartpl. 5 (☎84 48 22). Both 2AS/€0.15 per minute, minimum 20AS/€1.45. Both open Nov.- May daily 10am-11pm; June-Oct. 10am-midnight.

Post Office: At the Hauptbahnhof (☎88 30 30), with **currency exchange.** Address mail to be held: First name SURNAME, *Postlagernde Briefe*, Bahnhofspostamt, **A-5020** Salzburg, AUSTRIA. Open M-F 6:30am-9:30pm, Sa 8am-8pm, Su 1-6pm.

ACCOMMODATIONS AND CAMPING

Salzburg has no shortage of hostels—but then, it has no shortage of tourists either. Housing in Salzburg is expensive; most affordable options lie on the outskirts of town. Be wary of hotel hustlers at the station. Instead, ask for the tourist office's list of **private rooms** or the *Hotel Plan* (which has information on hostels). From mid-May to mid-September, hostels fill by mid-afternoon; call ahead, and be sure to make reservations during the *Festspiele* (p. 104).

HOSTELS, DORMS, AND CAMPING

Stadtalm, Mönchsberg 19c (☎84 17 29). Take bus #1 (dir. Maxglan) to Mönchsbergaufzug, then go down the street and through the stone arch on the left to the Mönchsberglift (Mönchsberg elevator) and ride up (9am-11pm, return 27AS/€1.96). At the top, turn right, climb the steps, and follow signs for Stadtalm. Breakfast included. Shower 10AS/€0.73 per 4min. Reception 9am-8pm. Curfew 1am. Reservations recommended. Open May-Sept. Dorms 170AS/€12.40. AmEx/D/MC/V.

Institut St. Sebastian, Linzerg. 41 (☎87 13 86). From the station, take bus #1, 5, 6, 51, or 55 to Mirabellpl. Continue in same direction as the bus, turn left onto Bergstr., and turn left onto Linzerg; the hostel is through the arch on the left. Rooftop and kitchen. Free lockers. Sheets 30AS/€2.18. Free laundry; sign up ahead of time. Reception 8am-noon and 4-9pm. No curfew. Dorms 190AS/€13.80; singles 360AS/€26.20, with shower 420AS/€30.55; doubles 530AS/€38.55, 720AS/€53.25; triples 675AS/€49, 930AS/€67.60; quads 956AS/€69.50, 1120AS/€81.40.

International Youth Hotel (YoHo), Paracelsusstr. 9 (☎87 96 49 or 834 60). Exit the train station to the left down Rainerstr., turn left onto Gabelsbergerstr. through the tunnel, and take the 2nd right onto Paracelsusstr. No room keys. Breakfast 35-50AS/ €2.50-3.65. Shower 10AS/€0.73 per 6min. 24hr. lockers 10AS/€0.73. Linen deposit 100AS/€7.27. Reception 24hr. Curfew 1am; ring the bell to get in at any time. 6-8 person dorms 170AS/€12.40; 4-person dorms 190/€13.80; 2-person dorms 220AS/ €16. All rooms 20AS/€1.45 cheaper after 1st night.

Jugendherberge Haunspergstraße (HI), Haunspergstr. 27 (☎87 50 30), near the train station. Walk straight out Kaiserschützenstr., which becomes Jahnstr., then take the 3rd left onto Haunspergstr. Breakfast, shower, and sheets included. Key deposit 100AS/ €7.27. Reception 7am-2pm and 5pm-midnight. Checkout 9am. No curfew. Open July-Aug. 3- or 4-person dorms 200AS/€14.55; singles 260AS/€18.90.

Panorama Camping Stadtblick, Rauchenbichlerstr. 21 (☎45 06 52). Take bus #51 to Itzling-Pflanzmann, walk back 50m, then turn right onto Rauchenbichlerstr., cross the footbridge, and continue along the gravel path. On-site store. Laundry 70AS/€5.10. Open Mar. 20-Oct. 31. 75AS/€5.45 per person; 20AS/€1.45 per tent; 100AS/€7.27 per bed in tent. With *Let's Go* 70AS/€5.10 per person.

PRIVATZIMMER

The rooms on **Kasern Berg** are officially out of Salzburg, which means the tourist office can't recommend them, but the personable hosts and bargain prices make these *Privatzimmer* (rooms in a family home) a terrific housing option. All northbound trains run to Kasern Berg (4min., every 30min. 6:15am-11:15pm, 20AS/ €1.45; Eurail valid). Get off at Salzburg-Maria Plain and take the only road uphill. All the Kasern Berg pensions are along this road. **Haus Christine,** Panoramaweg 3, has spacious rooms with a friendly family atmosphere. (☎45 67 73. Breakfast and laundry included. 180-200AS/€13-14.50 per person. MC/V.) **Haus Lindner,** Panoramaweg 5, is right next to Haus Christine and offers homey rooms, some with mountain views.

(☎45 66 81. Breakfast included. Call for pickup from the station. 170-200AS/€12.35-14.50 per person.) At **Germana Kapeller,** Kasern Bergstr. 64, hostess Germana speaks good English and maintains trim rooms. (☎45 66 71. Breakfast and showers included. 200AS/€14.50 per person.)

⬛ FOOD

Countless beer gardens and pastry-shop patios make Salzburg a great place to eat outdoors. Local specialties include *Salzburger Nockerl* (egg whites, sugar, and raspberry filling baked into three mounds that represent the three hills of Salzburg), *Knoblauchsuppe* (a rich cream soup loaded with croutons and pungent garlic), and the world-famous *Mozartkugeln* (hazelnut coated in marzipan, nougat, and chocolate). **Supermarkets** cluster on the Mirabellpl. side of the river, and **open-air markets** are held on Universitätpl. (Open M-F 6am-7pm, Sa 6am-1pm.) The cozy interior of **Zweitler's,** Kaig. 3, in the *Altstadt*, turns into a lively bar. (Open daily 4pm-1am, during the *Festspiele* 11am-1am.) **Café Tomaselli,** Alter Markt 9, has been a favorite with wealthier Salzburgers since 1705. (Open M-Sa 7am-9pm, Su 8am-9pm.) **Zum Fidelen Affen,** Priesterhausg. 8, serves hearty, honest Austrian food that keeps everyone coming back "To the Jolly Monkey." (Open M-Sa 5pm-11pm.)

⬛ SIGHTS

THE NEUSTADT

MIRABELL PALACE AND GARDENS. Mirabellpl. holds the marvelous **Schloß Mirabell,** which the supposedly celibate ArchbishopWolf Dietrich built for his mistress and their 10 children in 1606. Behind the palace, the delicately cultivated **Mirabellgarten** is a maze of seasonal flower beds and groomed shrubs. The Mirabellgarten contains a wooden, moss-covered shack called the **Zauberflötenhäuschen,** allegedly where Mozart composed *The Magic Flute* in just five months. It was transplanted from Vienna as a gift to the **Mozarteum,** Salzburg's music school.

MOZARTS WOHNHAUS. Just down the street from the Mozarteum stands the house in which the composer lived from 1773-1780. See some Mozart memorabilia, and hear lots of excerpts from his music, but be prepared to be frustrated by the museum's audio guides. *(Makartpl. 8. Open Sept.-June daily 9am-6pm; July-Aug. until 7pm. 65AS/€4.75, students 50AS/€3.65.)*

SEBASTIANSKIRCHE AND MAUSOLEUM. A little way down Linzerg. from the river stands the 18th-century **Sebastianskirche,** with an Italian-style graveyard containing the gaudy **mausoleum** of Prince Archbishop Wolf Dietrich. Ornate gravestones and frescoes line the walls. The tombs of Mozart's wife and father are along the main path. *(Linzerg. 41. Open Apr.-Oct. 9am-7pm; Nov.-Mar. 9am-4pm.)*

THE ALTSTADT

MOZARTS GEBURTSHAUS. Mozart's birthplace, on the 2nd floor of Getreideg. 9, holds an impressive collection of the child genius's belongings: his first viola and violin, a pair of keyboardish instruments, and a lock of hair. Come before 11am to avoid the crowd. *(Open July-Aug. 9am-6:30pm; Sept.-June 9am-5:30pm. 70AS/€5.10, students and seniors 55AS/€4.)*

TOSCANINIHOF, CATACOMBS, AND THE DOM. Steps lead from **Toscaninihof,** the courtyard of **St. Peter's Monastery,** up the Mönchesberg cliffs. Adjacent to Toscaninihof, **Stiftskirche St. Peter** features a marble portal from 1244. In the 18th century, the building was remodeled in Rococo style. *(Open daily 9am-12:15pm and 2:30-6:30pm.)* Near the far end of the cemetery against the Mönchsberg is the entrance to the **Catacombs.** In the lower room (St. Gertrude's Chapel), a fresco commemorates the martyrdom of Thomas á Beckett. *(Open May-Sept. Tu-Su 10:30am-5pm; Oct.-Apr. W-F 10:30am-4pm, Sa-Su 10:30am-4pm. 12AS/€0.90, students 8AS/€0.60.)* The exit at the other end of the cemetery leads to the immense Baroque **Dom** (cathedral), where Mozart was christened in 1756 and later worked as *Konzertmeister* and court organist. The square leading out of the cathedral, **Domplatz,** features a statue of the Virgin Mary and figures representing Wisdom, Faith, the Church, and the Devil. Be prepared to give a small donation.

RESIDENZ. Salzburg's ecclesiastical elite have resided in the magnificent Residenz for the last 700 years. Stunning Baroque **Prunkräume** (state rooms) house gigantic ceiling frescoes (including a three-dimensional one by Rottmayr), gilded furniture, Flemish tapestries from the 1600s, and ornate stucco work. A **gallery** exhibits 16th- to 19th-century art. *(Open daily 10am-5pm. 100AS/€7.30, students 76AS/€5.50.)*

FESTUNG HOHENSALZBURG. Built between 1077 and 1681, Festung Hohen-salzburg (Hohensalzburg Fortress), which looms over Salzburg from atop Mönchesberg, is the largest completely preserved castle in Europe—probably because it was never successfully attacked. *(Take the trail or the Festungsbahn funicular up to the fortress from the Festungsg. May-Sept. every 10min. 9am-9pm; Oct.-Apr. 9am-5pm. Ascent 76AS/€5.50, return 87AS/€6.35; includes entrance to fortress.)* The castle contains a "torture" chamber (which was never used), the fortress organ (nicknamed the "Bull of Salzburg" for its off-key snorting), and an watchtower that affords an unmatched view of the city and surrounding mountains. You'll also see the arch-bishop's medieval indoor toilet—a technological marvel of its day. The Burgmus-eum inside the fortress displays medieval instruments of torture and has side-by-side histories of Salzburg, the Festung, and the world. *(Grounds open mid-June to mid-Sept. 8:30am-8pm, mid-Sept. to mid-Mar. 9:30am-5pm, mid-Mar. to mid-June 9am-6pm. Interior open mid-June to mid-Sept. 9:30am-5:00pm, mid-Sept. to mid-Mar. 9am-5pm, mid-Mar. to mid-June 9:30am-5:30pm. If you walk up, entrance to fortress 49AS/€3.60; combo ticket including fortress, castle interiors, and museum 98AS/€7.15.)*

🎵 ENTERTAINMENT

Max Reinhardt, Richard Strauss, and Hugo von Hofmannsthal founded the renowned **Salzburger Festspiele** in 1920. Ever since, Salzburg has become a musical mecca from late July to the end of August. On the eve of the festival's opening, over 100 dancers don regional costumes and perform a *Fackeltanz* (torchdance) on Residenzpl. Operas, plays, films, concerts, and tourists overrun every available public space. Information and tickets for Festspiele events are available through the Festspiele Kartenbüro (ticket office) and Tageskasse (daily box office) in Kara-janpl., against the mountain and next to the tunnel. (Open M-F 9:30am-3pm; July 1-July 22 M-Sa until 5pm; July 23-end of festival daily until 6:30pm.)

Even when the *Festspiele* are not on, many other concerts and events occur around the city. The **Salzburg Academy of Music and Performing Arts** performs a number of concerts on a rotating schedule in the **Mozarteum,** and the **Dom** also has a concert program in July and August (Th-F 11:15am. 120AS/€8.75, students 100AS/€7.30). In addition, from May through August there are **outdoor performances,** including concerts, folk-singing, and dancing, around the Mirabellgarten. The tourist office has leaflets on scheduled events, but an evening stroll through the park might prove just as enlightening. **Mozartpl.** and **Kapitelpl.** are also popular stops for talented street musicians and touring school bands.

🎵 NIGHTLIFE

Munich may be known as the world's beer capital, but a lot of that liquid gold flows south to Austria's **Biergärten** (beer gardens). These lager oases cluster in the city center by the Salzach River. Altstadt nightclubs (especially along Gstätteng. and near Chiemseeg.) attract a younger crowd and tourists; the other side of the river has a less juvenile atmosphere. Settle into an armchair at **Vis à Vis,** Rudolfskai 24. (Open daily 8pm-4am.) **Shamrock,** Rudolfskai 24, has plenty of room and nightly live music. (Open daily 3pm-4am.) **Zweistein,** Giselakai 9, is *the* place to come for Salzburg's gay and lesbian scene. (Open Su-W 8pm-4am, Th-Sa 8pm-5am.) Sip cocktails (most 78AS/€5.70)

> **BOVINE BEFUDDLEMENT** During the **Peasant Wars,** peasants surrounded the fortress in an attempt to starve the archbishop out. When the stubborn archbishop had only one cow left, he painted it with different spots on both sides and paraded it back and forth along the castle wall in view of the peasants below. Since the peasants, as the saying goes, were simple-minded folk, they believed that the archbishop had a great reserve of food and decided to give up their assault.

under the sloping stone roof at **Flip,** Gstatteng. 17. (Open daily 8pm-4am.) **Segabar,** Rudolfskai 18, has a popular party scene. (Cover 40AS/€2.95. Open F-Sa 8pm-4am, Su-Th 8pm-2am.)

▓ DAYTRIPS FROM SALZBURG

LUSTSCHLOß HELLBRUNN AND UNTERSBERG PEAK. Just south of Salzburg lies the unforgettable **Lustschloß Hellbrunn,** a sprawling estate with a large palace, fish ponds, flower gardens, and the **Wasserspiele,** elaborate water-powered figurines and a booby-trapped table that could spout water on drunken guests. Pictures of you getting sprayed are available at the end of the tour. (Open July-Aug. 9am-10pm; May-June and Sept. 9am-5:30pm; Apr. and Oct. 9am-4:30pm. Mandatory castle tour 40AS/€2.95, students 30AS/€2.20. Wasserspiele tour 80AS/€5.85, students 60AS/€4.40. Combined tour 100AS/€7.30, students 80AS/€5.85.) Continue on bus #55 to St. Leonhard, where Charlemagne supposedly rests under luscious Untersberg Peak, prepared to return and reign over Europe when he is needed. A cable car glides over the rocky cliffs to the summit, and from there hikes lead off into the distance. On top is a memorial cross and some unbelievable mountain scenery. Don't leave your camera behind. (Open July-Sept. Su-Tu and Th-Sa 8:30am-5:30pm; Mar.-June and Oct. 9am-5pm; Dec.-Feb. 10am-4pm. Ascent 135AS/€9.85, descent 120AS/€8.75, both 225AS/€16.35; students 105AS/€7.65, 80AS/€5.85, 155AS/€11.30.) To reach Lustschloß Hellbrunn and the Wasserspiele, take **bus** #55 (dir. Anif) to Hellbrunn from the train station, Mirabellpl., or Mozartsteg.

HOHE TAUERN NATIONAL PARK. Conquer Europe's largest national park, boasting the **Krimml Waterfalls** and the spectacular **Großglocknerstraße** (p. 106).

WESTERN AUSTRIA

HALLSTATT   ☎ 06134

Tiny Hallstatt seems to defy gravity by clinging to the face of a stony slope at the southern tip of the Salzkammergut. It's easily the most beautiful lakeside village in the Salzkammergut, if not all of Austria. The 2500-year-old **Salzbergwerke** are the oldest saltworks in the world; zip down a wooden mining slide on a burlap sack to an eerie lake deep inside the mountain on a fascinating guided tour. (☎ (06132) 200 24 00. English and German tours 1hr. Open May-Sept. 9:30am-4:30pm; Oct. 9:30am-3pm. 140AS/€10.20; guest card holders, students, seniors 126AS/€9.20.) In the 19th century, Hallstatt was also the site of an immense, incredibly well-preserved Iron Age archaeological find. The **Prähistorisches Museum,** across from the tourist office, and the smaller **Heimatmuseum** around the corner exhibit some of the treasures. The museums are being combined, with the new complex slated to open May 2002, so hours and prices may change. (www.museum-hall-statt.at. Open daily Apr. 10am-4pm; May-Sept. 10am-6pm; Oct. 10am-4pm. 82.60AS/€6; English texts 25AS/€185.) The fascinating **charnel house** next to St. Michael's Chapel is a bizarre repository filled with the remains of over 610 villagers dating from the 16th century on; the latest were added in 1995. The dead were previously buried in the mountains, but villagers soon ran out of space and transferred older bones to the charnel house to make room for more corpses.

From the ferry dock, follow the signs marked "K.Kirche." (Open May-Oct. daily 10am-4pm. 10AS/€0.75, students 5AS/€0.40.)

Buses are the cheapest way to get to Hallstatt from Salzburg (130AS/€9.45) but require layovers in both Bad Ischl and Gosaumühle. The **train station** is on the other side of the lake, but there is no staffed office to help travelers. All trains come from Attnang-Puchheim in the north or Stainach-Irdning in the south. **Trains** run hourly to Bad Ischl (30min., 38AS/€2.75) and Salzburg via Attnang-Puchheim (210AS/€15.25). A **ferry** shuttles passengers between the town and the station (10min., 7am-6:40pm, 25AS/€1.85). The **tourist office,** Seestr. 169, finds rooms and offers help with the town's confusing system of street numbers. (☎82 08; www.tiscover.com/hallstatt. Open M-F 9am-5pm, Sa 10am-4pm, Su 10am-2pm; Sept.-June M-F 9am-noon and 2-5pm.) To reach **Gästehaus Zur Mühle,** Kirchenweg 36, from the tourist office, walk uphill, heading for a short tunnel at the upper right corner of the square; it's right at the end of the tunnel by the waterfall. (☎83 18. Breakfast 40AS/€2.95. Showers included. Sheets 40AS/€2.95. Reception 10am-2pm and 4-10pm. Closed Nov. Dorms 120AS/€8.75.) To get to **Camping Klausner-Höll,** Lahnstr. 201, turn right out of the tourist office and follow Seestr. for 10min. (☎832 24. Breakfast 70-110AS/€5.10-8. Showers included. Laundry service 100AS/€7.30. Gate closed daily noon-3pm and 10pm-7:30am. Open mid-Apr. to mid-Oct. 67AS/€4.86 per person; 45AS/€3.27 per ten. Electricity 35AS/€2.54. The cheapest eats are at the **Konsum** supermarket across from the bus stop; the butcher's counter prepares sandwiches on request. (Open M, Tu, Th, F 7:30am-12:30pm and 3-6pm, W 7:30am-12:30pm, Sa 7:30am-noon.) **Postal code:** A-4830.

◪ DAYTRIP FROM HALLSTATT: DACHSTEIN ICE CAVES. In nearby Obertraun, the magnificent **Dachstein Ice Caves** are proof of the region's geological hyperactivity. From Hallstatt, catch the bus to Obertraun (10min., every hr. 8:30am-4:45pm, 27AS/€2), stop at Dachstein, and ride up to Schönbergalm for the ice and mammoth caves (every 15min., 8:40am-5:30pm, 170AS/€12.40 return). The cave temperatures are near freezing, so wear good footwear and something warm. Tours are required and offered in English and German. (☎(06134) 84 00. Open May to mid-Oct. daily 9am-5pm. 100AS/€7.30; guest card, students, seniors, 90AS/€6.60.)

HOHE TAUERN NATIONAL PARK

The enormous **Hohe Tauern** range, part of the Austrian Central Alps, boasts 246 glaciers and 304 mountains over 3000m. One of the park's goals is preservation, so there are no large campgrounds or recreation areas; most of it is pristine. The best way to explore this rare preserve is to **hike** one of the park's numerous trails, ranging from pleasant ambles to difficult mountain ascents. *An Experience in Nature,* available at park offices and most area tourist offices, plots and briefly describes 84 different hikes. The center of the park is **Franz-Josefs-Höhe** and the **Pasterze glacier,** which sits right above the town of Heiligenblut. Aside from the skiing and hiking, the main tourist attractions are the **Krimml Waterfalls,** in the northwestern corner near Zell am See, and the **Großglocknerstraße,** a spectacular high mountain road that runs south from Zell am See through Franz-Josef-Höhe.

⬗ TRANSPORTATION. Trains arrive in **Zell am See** from: Innsbruck (1½-2hr., 2am-11:30pm, 270AS); Kitzbühel (45min., 12:45am-8:30pm, 112AS); and Salzburg (1½hr., 22 per day 3am-10pm, 150AS). From Zell am See, a **rail** line runs west along the northern border of the park, terminating in Krimml (1½hr., 19 per day 6am-10:55pm, 93AS); a **bus** also runs directly to the Höhe (2hr.; June 14-Sept. 30 daily 9:20am; July 7-Sept. 30 12:20pm; 107AS). The park itself is criss-crossed by **bus** lines that all stop at the Höhe but operate on incredibly complicated timetables; be sure to ask for specific connections at local tourist offices.

FRANZ-JOSEFS-HÖHE. This tourist center, stationed above the Pasterze glacier, has an amazing view of the Großglockner (3797m). The Höhe has its own park office and information center at the beginning of the parking area. (Open daily mid-May to mid-Oct. 10am-4pm; July and Aug. 9am-6pm.) The free elevator next to the information center leads to the **Swarovski Observation Center,** a crystal-shaped building with binoculars for viewing the surrounding terrain. (Open daily 10am-4pm. Free.) Some of the larger souvenir shops sell sandwiches (19-29AS).

HEILIGENBLUT. The most convenient base for exploring the Hohe Tauern region, Heiligenblut got its name ("holy blood") from a legend about a Byzantine general who perished nearby in a snowstorm while carrying a vial of Christ's blood, which is now housed in the town church. Heiligenblut can be reached by **bus** from Franz-Josefs-Höhe (30min., May-Oct. 9:30am-4:30pm, 40AS) and Zell am See (2½hr., 3 per day 9:20am-12:20pm, 147AS; connect in Franz-Josefs-Höhe). The **tourist office,** Hof 4, up the street from the bus stop, dispenses information about accommodations, hiking, and park transportation. (☎200 121; www.heiligen-blut.at. Open Sept.-June M-F 8:30am-noon and 2:30-6pm, Sa 9am-noon and 4-6pm; July-Aug. M-F 8:30am-6pm, Sa 9am-noon and 4-6pm.)

KRIMML. Over 400,000 visitors per year arrive here to see the extraordinary **Krimml Waterfalls,** a set of three cascades spanning 380m. (8am-6pm 20AS; free after 6pm.) These waterfalls are usually enjoyed as a daytrip from Zell am See; **buses** run from Zell am See (1½ hr., 11 per day 6:05am-8:55pm, 103AS) to Maustelle Ort, the start of the path to the falls. To reach the **tourist office,** Oberkrimml 37, follow the road from the Krimml Ort bus stop and turn right down the hill in front of the church. (☎72 39. Open M-F 8am-noon and 2:30-5:30pm, Sa 8:30-10:30am.)

INNSBRUCK ☎0512

The 1964 and 1976 winter Olympics were held in Innsbruck, bringing international recognition to this beautiful mountain city. The nearby Tyrolean Alps await skiers and hikers, and the tiny cobblestoned streets of the *Altstadt* are peppered with fancy façades and remnants of the Habsburg Empire.

▐▌ TRANSPORTATION AND PRACTICAL INFORMATION

Trains: Hauptbahnhof, Südtirolerpl. (☎05 17 17). To: **Munich** (2hr., 13 per day 4:30am-8:30pm, 416AS/€30.25); **Salzburg** (2-2½hr., 13 per day 2:35am-11:30pm, 380AS/€27.60); **Vienna Westbahnhof** (5½-7hr., 10 per day 2:30am-12:30am, 660AS/€48); **Zurich** (4hr., 4 per day 2:35am-12:40pm, 600AS/€43.60).

Public Transportation: For schedules and information on transportation in Innsbruck, head to the **IVB** Office, Stainerstr. 2 (☎530 17 99), near Maria-Theresien-Str. Open M-F 7:30am-6pm. The main bus station is in front of the main entrance to the train station. Buses stop running at 10:30 or 11:30pm; 3 *Nachtbus* lines run after hours.

Tourist Office: Innsbruck Tourist Office, Burggraben 3 (☎588 50), off the end of Museumstr., up 2 flights of stairs, sells maps (10AS/€0.75) and the **Innsbruck Card,** which provides free access to public transportation and many sights. (24hr. 260AS/€19, 48hr. 330AS/€24, 72hr. 400AS/€29). Open M-F 8am-6pm, Sa 8am-noon.

Police: ☎133. **Ambulance:**144 or 142. **Fire:** ☎122.

Internet Access: International Telephone Discount, Bruneckstr. 12 (☎59 42 72 61). Turn right from the train station; it's on the left just past the end of Südtirolerpl. 1.50AS/€0.10 per min. Open daily 9am-11pm.

Post Office: Maximilianstr. 2 (☎500 79 00). Open M-F 7am-11pm, Sa 7am-9pm, Su 8am-9pm. Address mail to be held: Postlagernde Briefe für First Name SURNAME, Hauptpostamt, Maximilianstr. 2, **A-6020** Innsbruck AUSTRIA.

▐▌ ACCOMMODATIONS AND FOOD

Inexpensive accommodations are scarce in June when only two hostels are open: **Jugendherberge Innsbruck** and **Jugendherberge St. Niklaus.** The opening of student dorms to backpackers in July and August somewhat alleviates the crush. Visitors should join

AUSTRIA

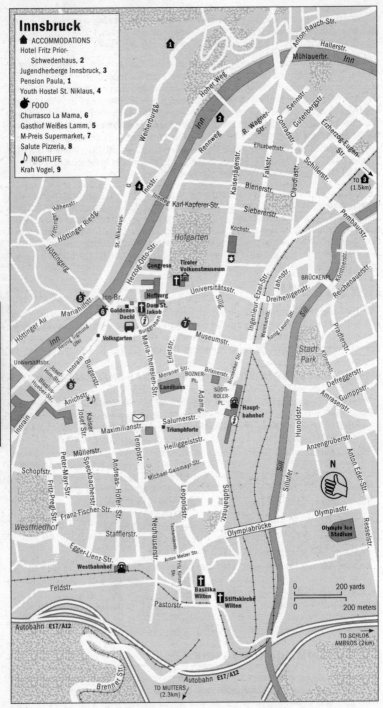

Innsbruck

ACCOMMODATIONS
Hotel Fritz Prior-
 Schwedenhaus, **2**
Jugendherberge Innsbruck, **3**
Pension Paula, **1**
Youth Hostel St. Niklaus, **4**

FOOD
Churrasco La Mama, **6**
Gasthof Weißes Lamm, **5**
M-Preis Supermarket, **7**
Salute Pizzeria, **8**

NIGHTLIFE
Krah Vogel, **9**

the free **Club Innsbruck** by registering at any Innsbruck accommodation. Membership gives discounts on skiing, bike tours, and the club's hiking program

From the Altstadt, cross the Inn river to Innstr. for ethnic restaurants and cheap pizzerias. There are **M-Preis Supermarkets** at Museumstr. 34 and across from the train station. (Open M-F 7:30am-6:30pm, Sa 7:30am-5pm.) **Salute Pizzeria,** Innrain 35, is a popular student hangout. (Open daily 11am-midnight.) **Gasthof Weißes Lamm,** Mariahilfstr. 12, on the 2nd floor, serves Austrian fare to a mostly local crowd. (Open F-W noon-2pm and 6pm-midnight.)

Haus Wolf, Dorfstr. 48 (☎54 86 73). Exit the train station through the main exit (under the neon clock). At the 3rd traffic island, take the Stubaitalbahn to Mutters, walk toward the church, and turn right on Dorfstr. 170-180AS/€12.35-13 per person.

Hostel Fritz Prior-Schwedenhaus (HI), Rennweg 17b (☎58 58 14). From the station, take bus A or tram 4 to Handelsakademie, continue to the end and straight across Rennweg to the river. Spacious, clean rooms with private shower and bathroom. No door locks, but closet keys available. Breakfast 7-8am, 45AS/€3.30. Sheets 20AS/€1.45. Laundry 75AS/€5.45. Reception daily 7-9:30am and 5-10:30pm. Lockout 9:30am-5pm. Curfew 10:30pm; keys with ID deposit. Open July-Aug. and Dec. 27-Jan. 5. Dorms 125AS/€9.10; doubles 370AS/€26.90; triples 495AS/€36.

Jugendherberge Innsbruck (HI), Reichenauer Str. 147 (☎34 61 79). From the train station, take tram 3 to Sillpark and bus O to Jugendherberge. Internet access. Breakfast, hall showers, and sheets included. Laundry until 10pm. 45AS/€3.30. Reception daily 5-10pm; July-Aug. also 3-5pm. Lockout 10am-5pm. Curfew 11pm; ask for key. Quiet time from 10pm. 6-bed dorms 155AS/€11.25, after 1st night 125AS/€9.10; 4-bed dorms 190AS/€13.85, 160AS/€11.65; singles with shower 360AS/€26.20; doubles with shower 260AS/€18.90. Nonmembers add 40AS/€2.90.

Pension Paula, Weiherburgg. 15 (☎29 22 62). Take bus D to Schmelzerg. and head uphill. Large, well-furnished rooms, many with balconies. Breakfast included. Reservations recommended in summer. Singles 350AS/€25.45, with shower 450AS/€32.70; doubles 580AS/€42.15, 700AS/€50.90; triples 770/€56, 930AS/€67.60.

Youth Hostel St. Niklaus (HI), Innstr. 95 (☎286 515). Take bus D to Schmelzerg. and cross the street. Breakfast and showers included. Internet 2AS/€0.20 per min. Reception 8am-2pm and 5-10pm. Lockout 10am-5pm. Curfew 11pm; key deposit 200AS/€14.55. 6-8 bed dorms 190AS/€13.80, after 1st night 180AS/€13.10; 4-bed dorms 205AS/€14.90; doubles 500AS/€36.35, with shower and toilet 600AS/€43.60.

👁 SIGHTS

Inside the **Goldenes Dachl** (Golden Roof) on Herzog-Friedrich-Str., the tiny **Maximilianeum** commemorates emperor Maximilian I. (Open May-Sept. 10am-6pm; Oct.-Apr. Tu-Su 10am-12:30pm and 2-5pm. 50AS/€3.65, students 20AS/€1.45.) A block behind the Goldenes Dachl rise the twin towers of the **Dom St. Jakob,** which displays *trompe l'oeil* ceiling murals. (Open daily Apr.-Sept. 8am-7:30pm; Oct.-Mar. 8am-6:30pm. Free.) The entrance to the grand **Hofburg** (Imperial Palace) is behind the *Dom* and to the right. (Open daily 9am-5pm. 70AS/€5.10, students 45AS/€3.30.) Across Rennweg sits the **Hofkirche** (Imperial Church), with larger-than-life bronze statues of saints and Roman emperors, some by Dürer. (Open daily 9am-5pm. 30AS/€2.20, students 20AS/€1.45.) The **Tiroler Volkskunstmuseum** (Tyrolean Folk Art Museum), in the same building, details the everyday life of the Tyrolean people. (Open M-Sa 9am-5pm, Su 9am-noon. 60AS/€4.40, students 35AS/€2.55.) Up Rennweg past the *Dom,* the **Hofgarten** (Imperial Garden) is a beautiful park complete with ponds, a concert pavilion, and an outdoor chess set with huge pieces.

🎿 🏂 HIKING AND SKIING

A **Club Innsbruck** membership (see Accommodations, above) grants access to a **hiking** program with guides, transportation, and equipment (including boots) at no additional cost. Participants meet in front of the Congress Center (June-Sept. daily 9am). To hike on your own, take the #6 tram to Igls (35min., every hr. 8am-7am, 22AS/€1.60), head out of the station toward town, and follow the signs to Patscherkofel Seilbahnen, a lift to moderate hikes (return 190AS/€13.85.) For Club-Innsbruck-led **ski excursions,** take the complimentary ski shuttle (schedules at the tourist office) to any cable car. The **Innsbruck Gletscher Ski Pass** (available at all cable cars and at Innsbruck-Information offices) is valid for all 59 lifts in the region (with Club Innsbruck card 3-day 1101AS/ €80, 6-day 1941AS/€141). The tourist office also rents **ski equipment** (160- 270AS/ €11.65-19.65 per day) and offers summer ski packages (640AS/€46.55 including bus, lift, and rental).

▶️ DAYTRIPS FROM INNSBRUCK

SCHLOß AMBRAS. In the late 16th century, Ferdinand II transformed a royal hunting lodge into one of Austria's most beautiful castles, **Schloß Ambras,** and filled it with vast collections of art, armor, weapons, and trinkets. Don't miss the famous **Spanischer Saal** (Spanish Hall) and the impressive **Portrait Gallery** (open in summer only). The **gardens** outside vary from manicured shrubs with modern sculptures to shady, forested hillsides. (Schloßstr. 20. Open Dec.-Mar. W-M 2-5pm; Apr.-Oct. daily 10am-5pm. Dec.-Mar. 60AS/€4.40, students 40AS/€2.90; Apr.-Oct 100AS/€7.30, students 70AS/€5.10.) The castle is accessible by tram #6 (dir. Igls) to Tummelplatz/ Schloß Ambras (20min., 22AS/€1.60); follow the signs from the stop.

KITZBÜHEL. Kitzbühel's ski area—known as the **Ski Circus**—is one of the best in the world. A one-day **ski pass** grants passage on 64 lifts and the shuttle buses connecting them. (Purchase passes at any lift. 400-450AS/€29.10-32.70.) For summer visitors, more than 70 **hiking trails** snake up the mountains; get a free map at the tourist office or take advantage of their guided mountain hikes. (June-Oct. M-F 8:45am from tourist office. Free with guest card, see below.) **Mountain bike trails** abound; rent bikes from **Stanger Radsport,** Josef-Pirchlstr. 42. (☎ (05356)625 49. Open M-F 8am-noon and 1:15-6pm, Sa 9am-noon. 250AS/€18.20 per day.) The **Kitzbüheler Hornbahn lift** ascends to the **Alpenblumengarten,** where more than 120 different types of flowers bloom. (Open daily late May to mid-Oct. 8:30am-5pm.) The **tourist office,** Hinterstadt 18, by the Rathaus in the Fußgängerzone, gives free **guest cards,** which offer discounts around town. (☎62 15 50; www.kitzbuehel.com. Open July-Aug. and Christmas to mid-Mar. M-F 8:30am-6:30pm, Sa 8:30am-noon and 4-6pm, Su 10am-noon and 4-6pm; Nov.-Christmas and mid-Mar. to June M-F 8:30am-12:30pm and 2:30-6pm, Sa 8:30am-noon.) **Trains** run from Innsbruck to Kitzbühel (1hr., every other hr., 184AS/€13.40).

BELARUS
(БЕЛАРУСЬ)

BELARUSSIAN RUBLE

US$1 = 1430BR	1000BR = US$0.70
CDN$1 = 910BR	1000BR = CDN$1.10
UK£1 = 2000BR	1000BR = UK£0.50
IR£1 = 1665BR	1000BR = IR£0.60
AUS$1 = 770BR	1000BR = AUS$1.30
NZ$1 = 625BR	1000BR = NZ$1.60
ZAR1 = 170BR	1000BR = ZAR5.80
DM1 = 665BR	1000BR = DM1.50
EUR€1 = 1250BR	1000BR = EUR€0.8

PHONE CODE

Country code: 375. **International dialing prefix:** 810. From outside Belarus, dial int'l dialing prefix (see inside back cover) + 375 + city code + local number.

Flattened by the Nazis from 1941 to 1945 and exploited by the Soviets from 1946 to 1990, Belarus seems to have lost its sense of self. A collection of sprawling urban landscapes surrounded by unspoiled forest villages, the country today has become the unwanted stepchild of Russia. For those willing to endure the difficulties inherent to traveling in Belarus, the country offers a fascinating look at a people in transition; others should look to countries better prepared for foreign tourists.

For more on Belarus, consult *Let's Go: Eastern Europe 2002*.

FACTS AND FIGURES

Official Name: Republic of Belarus.

Capital: Minsk.

Population: 10,366,719.

Land Area: 207,600 sq. km.

Climate: Continental and maritime.

Language: Belarussian, Russian.

Religions: Eastern Orthodox (80%), other (20%).

ESSENTIALS

DOCUMENTS AND FORMALITIES. To visit Belarus, you must secure a **visa,** an invitation, and medical insurance. If you have an acquaintance in Belarus who can provide you with an official invitation, you may obtain a 90-day single-entry (5-day service US$50; next-day US$100) or multiple-entry (5-day processing US$170; next-day US$340) visa at an embassy or consulate. Those without contacts can turn to **Russia House** (see Russia, p. 785), which will get you an invitation and visa in five business days (US$225; 3-day processing US$275; next-day US$325). **Host Families Association (HOFA)** provides invitations for its guests (see Russia, p. 785). You may also obtain an invitation through a **Belintourist** office. Transit visas (US$20-30), valid for 48 hours, are issued at a consulate and theoretically at the border, but avoid the latter option anywhere other than Brest. **Foreign embassies** are all in Minsk (see p. 112). At home, contact: **UK,** 6 Kensington Ct., London, W8 5DL (☎ (020) 7937 3288; fax 7361 0005); **US,** 1619 New Hampshire Ave. NW, Washington, DC 20009 (☎202-986-1606; fax 202-986-1805; www.belarusembassy.org). Belarus requires that all foreign nationals who enter the country purchase **medical insurance** at the port-of-entry, regardless of any other insurance one might already have. The price of the insurance varies according to length of stay—currently, it costs US$1 for one-day stay, US$15 for 60-day stay, and up to US$85 for a stay of one year.

TRANSPORTATION. You can fly into Minsk on **Belavia,** Belarus's national airline (if you trust the old planes) from many European capitals. **LOT** also flies from Warsaw, and **Lufthansa** has daily flights from Frankfurt. Leaving Belarus by air can be horrific, as customs officials may rip through your bags. Some international train tickets must be paid partly in US dollars and partly in Belarussian rubles. All immigration and customs are done on the trains. Tickets for same-day trains within Belarus are purchased at the station. **Eurail** is not valid. For **city buses,** buy tickets at a kiosk (or from the driver for a surcharge) and punch them on board.

TOURIST SERVICES AND MONEY. In an **emergency,** call ☎03, **fire,** ☎01 and **police,** ☎02. **Belintourist** (Белінтурiст) is all that's left of the once omnipotent Intourist. It does not cater to budget travelers. Hotel Belarus and Hotel Yubilyenaya in Minsk have private travel agencies. Be sure to carry plenty of hard cash; US dollars, Deutschmarks, and Russian rubles are preferred. There are few ATMs outside Minsk, and most bank clerks scratch their heads at the mention of "traveler's checks." Some hotels accept credit cards, mostly AmEx and Visa. Belarussian rubles are impossible to exchange abroad. Inflation is rampant, so we list many prices in US\$. Posted prices in Belarus often drop the final three zeros and *Let's Go* prices follow that convention. Bills printed in 2000 and later also omit the zeros, but the old bills remain in circulation and are difficult to distinguish from the new ones.

COMMUNICATION. Avoid the mail system at all costs. Local calls require tokens sold at kiosks or magnetic cards, available at the post office, train station, and some hotels (200-500BR). International calls must be placed at the telephone office and paid for in advance, in cash. Write down the number you're calling and say *"Ya ha-tchoo po-ZVAH-neet"* ("I'd like to call...") followed by the name of the country; pay with exact change. Calls to the US and Western Europe cost US\$1-3 per minute. International direct dial numbers include: **AT&T,** ☎8 800 101; **British Telecom,** ☎8 800 44; **Canada Direct,** ☎8 800 111; **MCI,** ☎8 800 103 from Grodna, Brest, Minsk, and Vitebsk, ☎10 800 103 from Gomel and Mogilev; **Sprint,** ☎8 800 102; **Telecom New Zealand,** ☎8 800 641 from Grodna, Brest, Minsk, and Vitebsk, ☎10 800 641 from Gomel and Mogilev; and **Telstra Australia,** ☎810.

ACCOMMODATIONS AND CAMPING. Keep all receipts from hotels; you may have to show them to the authorities to avoid fines when leaving Belarus. **Hotels** are very cheap for Belarussians, outrageous for foreigners, and in-between for CIS member countries. The desk clerks will ask where you are from and request your passport, making it impossible to pass as a native. Some **private hotels** don't accept foreigners at all, but those that do are usually much cheaper and friendlier than the Soviet dinosaurs. To find a **private room,** look around for postings at train stations, or ask taxi drivers, who may know of a lead. The *babushki* at train stations might quote high prices, but they'll be willing to feed and house you for US\$10 or less.

HEALTH AND SAFETY. Today, more than 10 years after the 1986 Chernobyl accident, it is possible to travel through the formerly contaminated areas. None of the cities *Let's Go* covers are in affected regions. It is important to be aware of a few safety considerations. Avoid inexpensive dairy products, which likely come from contaminated areas—opt instead for something German or Dutch—and stay away from mushrooms and berries, which tend to collect radioactivity. Drink only bottled water; tap water, especially in the southeast, may be contaminated.

HOLIDAYS. Orthodox Christmas (Jan. 7); International Women's Day (Mar. 8); Constitution Day (Mar. 15); Catholic Easter (Apr. 15-16); Victory Day and Mother's Day (May 9); Independence Day (July 3); Remembrance Day (Nov. 2); October Revolution Day (Nov. 7); and Catholic Christmas (Dec. 25).

MINSK (МIНСК) ☎(8)172

If you're looking for the supreme Soviet city, skip Moscow and head to Minsk (pop. 1.7 million), where the fall of Communism has led to a reluctant shuffle rather than a wanton gallop westward. With imaginary political reforms and concrete everywhere—not to mention the Minsk police on the prowl—everyone is asking whether Belarussian authorities are really giving Minsk a new face, or just a new façade.

▣ TRANSPORTATION AND PRACTICAL INFORMATION. Trains depart from **Tsentralny Vakzal** (Центральный Вакзал; ☎220 99 89 and 596 54 10), on Privakzalnaya pl., for: Berlin (1 per day, US$60); Kiev (14hr., 2 per day, US$16); Moscow (14hr., 13 per day, US$22); Prague (1 per day, US$60); St. Petersburg (3 per day, US$24); Vilnius (4½hr., 6 per day, US$10); and Warsaw (12hr., 3-5 per day, US$27). Buy tickets at Belintourist (see below). **Buses** go from **Avtovakzal Tsentralny** (Автовакзал Центральный), vul. Babruyskaya 6 (Бабруйская; ☎227 78 20), to the right of the train station, to Prague (6 per day, US$20) and Vilnius (4hr., 4 per day, US$6). From the train station, go up vul. Leningradskaya and left on Svyardlova (Свярдлова) to **pl. Nezalezhnastsi** (Незалежнасці; Independence Sq), connected by pr. F. Skoriny (Францішка Скарыны) to pl. Peramohi (Перамогі). **Belintourist** (Белінтурiст), pr. Masherava 19 (Машэрава), is next to Hotel Yubileynaya; pr. Masherava is perpendicular to pr. F. Skoriny. (☎226 90 56; belintourist@infonet.by. M-blue: Neyamiha. Open M-F 10am-5:30pm.) **Embassies: Russia,** vul. Staravilenskaya 48 (Старавіленская; ☎250 36 66); **UK,** vul. Karla Marxa 37 (Карла Маркса; ☎210 59 20); **Ukraine,** vul. Kirava 17 (283 19 58); **US,** vul. Staravilenskaya 46 (☎210 12 83; open M-F 8:30am-5:30pm). All **phone numbers** have seven digits and start with a "2," so for six-digit numbers, add an initial "2". Check the web at **Internet Klass** (Интернет класс), vul. Karla Marksa 10. (M-red: Ploshcha nezalazhnasti. US$1 per hr. Open daily 10am-10pm.)

ⴕ ACCOMMODATIONS. To get to hotel **Gastsinitsa Sputnik** (Спутник), vul. Brilevskaya 2 (Брилевская), from pl. Nezalezhnasti (directions from train station above), cross the street and take trolleybus #2 just past the bridge for 5min. (☎229 36 19. Basic rooms with bath, fridge, TV. Singles 38,500BR; doubles 46,000BR.) From M-red: Park Chelyuskintsev (Парк Челюскинцев), take a right on the street in front of you, which runs perpendicular to the main road, to reach **Gastsinitsa Druzhba** (Дружба), vul. Tolbukhina 3. (☎266 24 81. Reserve ahead. Dorms US$8.)

◩◪ SIGHTS AND ENTERTAINMENT. After most of Minsk's buildings were obliterated in World War II, the city was rebuilt in high Soviet style. A block north of the train stations, grand government buildings loom at **ploschad Nezalezhnastsi,** formerly pl. Lenina (M-red: pl. Nezalezhnastsi; пл. Незалежнасці), the symbol of Belarussian independence. A few pre-War jewels remain, mainly in the **Old Town** quarter on the other side of the Svisloch, as well as a few churches. The **Church of St. Simon,** Savetskaya 15, wards against dragons at pl. Nezalezhnastsi, while pl. Svobody is home to the dazzling 17th-century **Cathedral of the Holy Spirit,** vul. Mefodiya 3 (M-blue: Nyamiha; Няміга). The **Jewish memorial,** vul. Zaslavskaya, commemorates more than 5000 Jews who were shot and buried here by the Nazis in 1941 (M-blue: Nyamiha; Няміга). Lovely **parks** line the banks of the Svislac east of the Old Town. The **National Arts Museum** (Нацыянальны Мастацкі Музей Распублікі Беларусь; Natsyanalny Mastatski Muzey Raspubliki Belarus), pr. Lenina 20 (Леніна), brims with fantastic Russian and Belarussian art. (Open W-M 11am-7pm. 250BR.) The grim **Museum of the Great Patriotic War** (Музей Великой Отечественной Войны; Muzey Velikoy Otechestvennoy Voyny) is at pr. Skoriny 25a. (M-red: Kastrytchnitskaya. Open Tu-Su 10am-7pm. 250BR.) The monument of **Victory Square** disrupts vul. F. Skoriny before continuing to the **Opera and Ballet Theater,** vul. Paryzhskai Kamuny 1 (Парыжскай Камуны·, one of the best ballets in the former USSR. (M-blue: Nyamiha; Няміга. ☎234 06 66. Tickets under US$5.)

BELARUS

THE NYAMIHA TRAGEDY On May, 1999, thousands of people were attending an outdoor concert when all of a sudden the weather soured and many of the concert-goers rushed into the near-by Nyamiha Metro to take cover. A stampede ensued in which 53 people perished. A permanent memorial to the victims of this tragedy is just outside the north entrance of the Nyamiha Metro station. Fifty-three sculpted roses, one for each of the victims, are scattered on a small staircase. Another makeshift memorial lies just inside the entrance. Solemn passers-by can be seen pausing at the memorial as they enter and exit the station.

BELGIUM
(BELGIQUE, BELGIË)

BELGIAN FRANCS

US$1 = 44.03BF	10BF = US$0.23
CDN$1 = 28.55BF	10BF = CDN$0.35
UK£1 = 63.74BF	10BF = UK£0.16
IR£1 = 51.23BF	10BF = IR£0.20
AUS$1 = 23.60BF	10BF = AUS$0.42
NZ$1 = 19.36BF	10BF = NZ$0.52
ZAR1 = 5.32BF	10BF = ZAR1.88
EUR€1 = 40.34BF	10BF = EUR€0.25

PHONE CODE	**Country code:** 32. **International dialing prefix:** 00. From outside Belgium, dial int'l dialing prefix (see inside back cover) + 32 + city code + local number.

Situated between France and Germany, little Belgium (pop. 10.2 million; 30,510 sq. km) rubs shoulders with some of Western Europe's most powerful cultural and intellectual traditions. Travelers too often mistake Belgium's subtlety for dullness, but its cities offer some of Europe's finest art and architecture, and its castle-dotted countryside provides a beautiful escape for hikers and bikers. Brussels, the capital and home to NATO and the European Union, buzzes with international decision-makers. Regional tension persists within Belgium's borders between Flemish-speaking Flanders and French-speaking Wallonie. But some things transcend politics: from the deep caves of the Ardennes to the white sands of the North Sea coast, Belgium's diverse beauty is even richer than its chocolate.

FACTS AND FIGURES

Official Name: Kingdom of Belgium.

Capital: Brussels.

Major Cities: Antwerp, Ghent, Charleroi, Liège.

Population: 10,208,000.

Land Area: 30,528 sq. km.

Climate: Maritime climate; cool summers and damp winters.

Language: Dutch, French, German.

Religions: Roman Catholic (88%), Muslim, other Christian, Jewish, other (12%).

DISCOVER BELGIUM

Start out in the northern region of Flanders; take in the old city and diverse museums of **Brussels** (p. 122), then spend at least two days in the real Belgian gem of **Bruges** (p. 123), a majestic town with a Gothic beauty unparalleled elsewhere in Europe. Spend a day in bustling **Antwerp** (p. 127) and a day (and definitely a night) with the students in **Ghent** (p. 128), then head south to the Wallonie region for a day or two of biking and exploration in and around **Namur** and **Dinant** (p. 129).

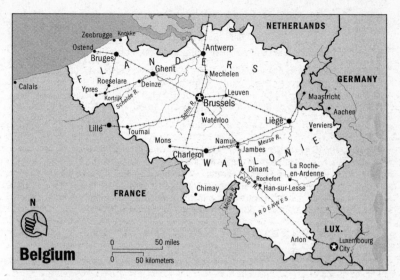

Belgium

ESSENTIALS

WHEN TO GO

Belgium, temperate and rainy, is best visited May to September, when temperatures average 13-21°C (54-72°F). Winter temperatures average 0-5°C (32-43°F). Bring a sweater and umbrella whenever you go.

DOCUMENTS AND FORMALITIES

VISAS. Visas are generally not required for tourist stays under three months; South African citizens are the exception.

EMBASSIES. All foreign embassies are in Brussels (p. 122). For Belgian embassies at home: **Australia,** 19 Arkana St., Yarralumla, Canberra, ACT 2600 (☎(02) 62 73 25 01; fax 62 73 33 92); **Canada,** 80 Elgin St., 4th fl., Ottawa, ON K1P 1B7 (☎613-236-7267; fax 613-236-7882; **Ireland,** 2 Shrewsbury Rd., Ballsbridge, Dublin 4 (☎(353) 269 20 82, fax 283 84 88); **New Zealand,** Axon House, Willeston St. 1-3, 12th fl., PB 3379, Wellington (☎(04) 472 95 58; fax 471 27 64); **South Africa,** 625 Leyds St., Muckleneuk, Pretoria 0002 (☎(2712) 44 32 01; fax 44 32 16); **UK,** 103-105 Eaton Sq., London SW1W 9AB (☎(020) 7470 3700; fax 7259 62 13; www.belgium-embassy.co.uk); **US,** 3330 Garfield St NW, Washington, D.C. 20008 (☎202-333-6900; fax 202-333-3079; www.diplobel.org/usa).

TRANSPORTATION

BY PLANE. Several major airlines fly into Brussels from Europe, North America, and Africa; many offer cheap deals. **Sabena** (Belgium ☎(02) 723 62 19; US ☎800-955-2000; www.sabena.com) serves many locations, including Australia, Ireland, North America, South Africa, and the United Kingdom.

BY TRAIN AND BUS. The extensive and reliable **Belgian Rail** (www.sncb.be) network traverses the country in 4hr. **Eurail** is valid in Belgium (US ☎1-877-456-RAIL, Canada 1-800-361-RAIL). The **Benelux Tourrail Pass** covers five days of travel in Belgium, The Netherlands, and Luxembourg in any one-month period (4680BF/€116, under 26 3510BF/€87). A good deal for travelers under 26 is the **Go Pass,**

which allows 10 trips over six months in Belgium and may be used by more than one person at a time (1550BF/€38.45). For travelers over 26, the **Rail Pass** allows 10 trips in Belgium after 9am (2280BF/€56.55). Because the train network is so extensive, **buses** are used primarily for municipal transport (40-50BF/€1-1.25).

BY FERRY. P&O European Ferries (UK ☎(01482) 795141; Belgium ☎(050) 54 34 30; www.ponsf.com) cross the Channel from Zeebrugge, north of Bruges, to Hull, England (14hr.; £38-48, under 26 £24-31; departures 6:15pm). **Ostend Lines** also crosses from Ostend to Ramsgate, England, 2hr. from London's Victoria Station (☎(059) 55 99 55; 6 per day; 1600BF/€39.70 return). For information on Ostend, Zeebrugge, and Knokke, see p. 127.

BY CAR, BY BIKE, AND BY THUMB. Belgium honors most foreign drivers' licenses, including those from Australia, Canada, the EU, and the US. Fuel costs about 40BF/€1 per liter. Biking is popular, and many roads have bike lanes (which you are required to use). Hitchhiking is not popular in Belgium and is not recommended as a safe means of transport, but hitchers still report a fair amount of success in some areas. *Let's Go* does not recommend hitchhiking.

TOURIST SERVICES AND MONEY

EMERGENCY	Police: ☎101. Ambulance: ☎105. Fire: ☎100.

TOURIST OFFICES. Bureaux de Tourisme, marked by green-and-white signs labeled "i," are supplemented by **Infor-Jeunes/Info-Jeugd,** a service that helps young people secure accommodations. For information, contact the main office of the **Belgian Tourist Board,** 63, r. de Marché aux Herbes, B-1000 Brussels. (☎(02) 504 03 90; fax 504 02 70; www.tourism-belgium.net. Open daily 9am-6pm.) The weekly English-language *Bulletin* (85BF/€2.15) lists everything from movies to job openings.

MONEY. The unit of currency is the **Belgian franc;** bills come in 100, 200, 500, 1000, 2000, 5000 and 10,000 denominations, coins in 1, 5, 20 and 50. There are 100 centimes in one franc. Belgium has accepted the **Euro (€)** as legal tender, and francs will be phased out by July 1, 2002. For more information, see p. 21. Expect to pay 800-1200BF/€19.85-29.75 for a room; 380-550BF/€9.45-13.65 for a hostel bed; 200-500BF/€5-12.40 for a cheap restaurant meal; and 250-500BF/€6.20-12.40 for a day's groceries. A bare-bones day in Belgium might cost US$15-30; a slightly more comfortable day might cost US$30-40. Service charges are usually included in the price in restaurants and taxis, but tip for exceptional service. Bathroom attendants usually receive 10-20BF/€0.25-0.50. Belgium's VAT (generally 21%) is always included in price; refunds (usually 17% of purchase price) are available for a minimum purchase of 5000BF/€123.95 per invoice.

BUSINESS HOURS. Banks are open Monday to Friday 9am to 3:30 or 4pm, sometimes with a lunch break. Stores are open Monday to Saturday 10am-6pm. Most sights open Sunday but close Monday except in Bruges and Tournai, where museums are closed Tuesday or Wednesday. Most stores close on holidays; museums stay open during all except for Christmas, New Year's, and Armistice Day.

COMMUNICATION

MAIL. A postcard or letter (up to 20g) sent to a destination within the European Union costs 21BF/€0.55, and to the rest of the world costs 34BF/€0.84. Most post offices open M-F 9am to 4 or 6pm (sometimes with a midday break) and sometimes Sa 9 or 10am to noon or 1pm.

TELEPHONES. Phones require a 200BF/€5 phone card, available at PTT offices and magazine stands. Coin-operated phones are more expensive and require either 5BF or 20BF coins. Calls are cheapest from 6:30pm to 8am and Sa-Su. For operator assistance within Benelux, dial ☎13 07; for international assistance,

☎13 04 (10BF/€0.25). International direct dial numbers include: **AT&T,** ☎0800 100 10; **British Telecom,** ☎0800 89 0032; **Canada Direct,** ☎0800 100 19 or 0800 700 19; **Ireland Direct,** ☎0800 110 353; **MCI,** ☎0800 100 12; **Telecom New Zealand,** ☎0800 104 23; **Sprint,** ☎0800 100 14; **Telkom South Africa,** ☎0800 100 27; and **Telstra Australia,** ☎0800 100 61.

INTERNET ACCESS. There are cybercafes in the larger towns and cities in Belgium. For access to the web, expect to pay 100-130BF/€2.50-3.25 per 30min.

LANGUAGE. Flemish (a variety of Dutch, spoken in Flanders), French (spoken in Wallonie), and German. Most people, especially in Flanders, speak English. In Brussels, both Flemish and French are used. For the basics, see p. 982.

ACCOMMODATIONS AND CAMPING

Hotels in Belgium are fairly expensive, with "trench-bottom" singles from 800BF/€19.85 and doubles at 1000-1100BF/€24.80-27.30. Belgium's 31 **HI youth hostels,** which charge about 405BF/€10.05 per night, are generally modern and many boast cheap bars, but **private hostels** often cost the same and are much nicer. Pick up a free copy of *Camping* at any tourist office for complete listings of hostels and campsites. **Campgrounds** charge about 130BF/€3.25 per night. An international camping card is not required in Belgium.

FOOD AND DRINK

An authentic Belgian meal may cost as much as a night in a decent hotel. *Moules* (steamed mussels), regarded as the national dish, are usually tasty and reasonably affordable (around 430BF/€10.70 per pot). Belgians claim that they invented *frites* (potato fries), which they drown in mayonnaise. Belgian beer is both a national pride and a national pastime; more varieties are produced here than in any other country. Regular or quirky blonde goes for as little as 40BF, and dark beers cost about 60-90BF/€1.50-2.25 per bottle. Leave room for *gaufres* (Belgian waffles)—soft, warm, glazed ones on the street (50BF/€1.25) and bigger, crispier ones piled high with toppings at cafes (80-200BF/€2-5)—and for the famous delectable Godiva chocolates.

HOLIDAYS AND FESTIVALS

Holidays: New Year's Day (Jan. 1); Easter (Mar. 31); Easter Monday (Apr. 1); Labor Day (May 1); Ascension Day (June 9); Whit Sunday (May 19); Whit Monday (May 20); Independence Day (July 21); Assumption Day (Aug. 15); All Saints Day (Nov. 1); Armistice Day (Nov. 11); Christmas (Dec. 25).

Festivals: Ghent hosts the **Gentse Feesten,** also know as 10 Days Off (July 20-29). Wallonie hosts a slew of quirky and creative carnival-like festivals, including the **Festival of Fairground Arts** (late May), **Les Jeux Nautiques** (early Aug.), and the **International French-language Film Festival** (early Sept.) in Namur, and the **International Bathtub Regatta** (mid-Aug.) in Dinant.

BRUSSELS (BRUXELLES, BRUSSEL) ☎02

Despite Brussels' association with NATO and the European Union, the diplomats in suits have always been outshone by the city's two boy heroes: Tintin and the Mannekin Pis. In the late 1920s, cartoonist Hergé created Tintin, who righted international wrongs long before Brussels became the capital of the EU. The cherubic Mannekin Pis perpetually pees three blocks from the Grand-Place, breaking the formality of international politics. The museums of Brussels are rich with collections of Flemish masters, modern art, and antique sculptures, but you don't need to go inside for a visual feast. Restaurants, lounges, and movie theaters that keep the town abuzz are built in the style of art nouveau architect Victor Horta.

TRANSPORTATION

Flights: Brussels International Airport (info ☎ 753 42 21 or 753 31 11; www.Brusselssairport.be). **Trains** run to the airport, 14km outside the city, from Gare du Midi (25min., every 20min., 90BF/€2.25); all stop at Gare Centrale and Gare du Nord.

Trains: Info ☎ 555 25 55. All international trains stop at **Gare du Midi/Zuid;** most also stop at **Gare Centrale** (near the Grand-Place) or **Gare du Nord** (near the Botanical Gardens). To: **Amsterdam** (2½hr.; 1310BF/€32.50, under 26 640BF/€15.90); **Antwerp** (30min., 200BF/€4.96); **Bruges** (45min., 390BF/€9.70); **Cologne** (2¾hr.; 1260BF/€31.25, under 26 900BF/€22.35); **Luxembourg City** (1¾hr., 930BF/€23.05); **Paris** (1½hr.; 2180BF/€54.05, under 26 1000BF/€24.80). **Eurostar** goes to **London** (2¾hr.; from 6200BF/€153.70, under 26 2100BF/€52.10).

Buses: Société des Transports Intercommunaux Bruxellois (STIB), Gare du Midi. Open M-F 7:30am-5pm, 1st and last Su each month 8am-2pm. **Branches** at Porte de Namur and Rogier Métro stops. Open M-F 8:30am-5:15pm. Schedule info ☎ 515 20 00.

Public Transportation: Runs daily 6am-midnight. 1hr. tickets (55BF/€1.40) valid on **buses,** the **Métro (M),** and **trams.** Day pass 145BF/€3.60, 5-trip pass 240BF/€5.95, 10-trip pass 360BF/€8.95.

Hitchhiking: *Let's Go* does not recommend hitchhiking. Hitchers headed to **Antwerp** and **Amsterdam** take tram #52 or 92 from Gare du Midi or Gare du Nord to Heysel; **Ghent** and **Bruges,** bus #85 from the Bourse to the stop before the terminus, then follow E40 signs; **Paris,** tram #52, 55, or 91 to r. de Stalle, then walk toward the E19.

ORIENTATION AND PRACTICAL INFORMATION

Most major attractions are clustered between the **Bourse** (Stock Market) to the west, the **Parc de Bruxelles** to the east, and the **Grand-Place.** Two **Métro** lines circle the city, and efficient trams run north to south. A **tourist passport** (*Carte d'un Jour;* 300BF/€7.45 at the TIB and bookshops) includes two days of public transit, a map, and reduced museum prices.

Tourist Offices: National, 63, r. du Marché aux Herbes (☎504 03 90; fax 504 02 70; tourism.brussels@tib.be), 1 block from the Grand-Place. Books rooms all over Belgium and gives out the free weekly *What's On.* Open M-F 9am-6pm, Su 10am-2pm. **TIB** (**Tourist Information Brussels;** ☎513 89 40; fax 513 83 20), on the Grand-Place, in the Town Hall, offers walking tours (3hr.; 800BF/€19.90, students 720BF/€17.90.) Open July-Aug. M-F 9am-6pm; May-June and Sept.-Oct. M-F 9am-6pm, Sa-Su 9am-1pm and 2-6pm; Nov.-Apr. Su only 10am-2pm.

Budget Travel: Infor-Jeunes, 9A, r. du St. Catherine (☎514 41 11; bruxelles@inforjeunes.be). Information for young travelers. Open M-F 10am-5pm.

Embassies: Australia, 6-8, r. Guimard, 1040 (☎231 05 00; fax 230 68 02). **Canada,** 2 av. Tervueren, 1040 (☎741 06 11; fax 448 00 00). **Ireland,** 89/93, r. Froissart, 1040 (☎230 53 37; fax 230 53 12). **New Zealand,** 47 bd. du Régent, 1000 (☎513 48 56). **South Africa,** 26, r. de la Loi (☎285 44 02), generally open M-F 9am-5pm. **UK,** 85, r. Arlon (☎287 62 11; fax 287 63 55). **US,** 27 bd. du Régent, 1000 (☎508 21 11; fax 511 96 52; www.usinfo.be), open M-F 9am-noon.

Currency Exchange: Many exchange booths near the Grand-Place stay open until 11pm. Most banks and booths charge 100-150BF/€2.50-3.75 commission to cash checks. **CBC-Automatic Change,** 7 Grand-Place (☎547 11 29). Open 24hr.

Gay and Lesbian Services: Call ☎733 10 24 for information on local events. Staffed Tu 8-10pm, W 8-11pm, F 8-11pm.

Laundromat: Salon Lavoir, 62, r. Blaes, around the corner from the Jeugdherberg Brueghel. M: Gare Centrale. Wash and dry 240BF/€5.95. Open daily 7am-10pm.

Emergencies: Ambulance or **first aid,** ☎100. **Police,** ☎101.

Pharmacies: Neos-Bourse Pharmacie (☎218 06 40), bd. Anspach at r. du Marché-aux-Polets. M: Bourse. Open M-F 8:30am-6:30pm, Sa 9am-6:30pm.

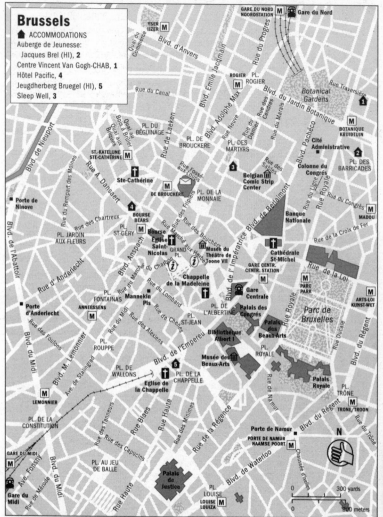

Medical Assistance: Free Clinic, 154a chaussée de Wavre (☎512 13 14). Misleading name—you'll have to pay. Open M-F 9am-6pm. **Medical Services,** 24hr. ☎479 18 18.

Internet Access: easyEverything, 9-13 de Brouckère. 50BF/€1.25 per 66min.

Post Office: Pl. de la Monnaie, Centre Monnaie, 2nd fl. (info ☎226 23 10 or 226 23 11). M: de Brouckère. Open M-F 8am-7pm, Sa 9:30am-3pm. Address mail to be held: First name SURNAME, Poste Restante, Pl. de la Monnaie, **1000** Bruxelles, BELGIUM.

ACCOMMODATIONS

Accommodations in Brussels can be difficult to find, especially on weekends in June and July. In general, hotels and hostels are well-kept and centrally located. Staffs will call each other if prospective guests arrive and they are booked.

Hôtel Pacific, 57, r. Antoine Dansaert (☎511 84 59). M: Bourse. Follow the street in front of the Bourse, which becomes Dansaert after the intersection; it's on the right.

Excellent location and basic rooms. Breakfast and showers included. Reception 7am-midnight. Curfew midnight. Singles 1200BF/€29.75; doubles 2000BF/€49.60.

Sleep Well, 23, r. du Damier (☎218 50 50; info@sleepwell.be), near Gare du Nord. M: Rogier. Exit onto r. Jardin Botanique, face the pyramid and go right; take the 1st right on r. des Cendres, then continue onto r. de Damier. Breakfast included. Internet. Curfew 3am. Lockout 10am-4pm. Dorms 490-655BF/€16.25; singles 950BF/€23.55; doubles 1450BF/€35.95.

Auberge de Jeunesse "Jacques Brel" (HI), 30, r. de la Sablonnière (☎218 01 87), on pl. des Barricades. M: Botanique. Walk down r. Royale with the botanical gardens to your right, and take the 1st right onto Sablonnière. Spacious rooms. Breakfast included. Dinner 295BF/€7.35. Sheets 130BF/€3.25. Reception 8am-1am. Dorms 430BF/€10.70; singles 820BF/€20.35; doubles 1200BF/€29.75; triples 1530BF/€37.95.

Centre Vincent Van Gogh-CHAB, 8, r. Traversière (☎217 01 58; chab@ping.be). M: Botanique. Exit on r. Royale, head right facing the botanical gardens, and turn right. Internet 50BF/€1.25 per 15min. Laundry 180BF/€4.50. Reception 7am-2am. Dorms 340-480BF/€8.45-11.90; singles 700BF/€17.35; doubles 1120-1160BF/€27.80-28.75.

Jeugdherberg Brueghel (HI), 2, r. de Saint Esprit (☎511 04 36; jeugdherberg.bruegel@ping.be). From the back exit of Gare Centrale, go right on bd. de l'Empereur past Palais de Congrès on your left, and take the 2nd left after Pl. de la Justice. Sheets 130BF. Reception 7am-1am. Lockout 10am-2pm. Curfew 1am. Dorms 430BF/€10.70; singles 820BF/€20.35; doubles 1200BF/€29.75; quads 2040BF/€50.60.

Generation Europe (HI), r. de l'Elephant (☎410 38 58; gener.europe@infonie.be; www.laj.be). M: Comte de Flandre. Take the Maison Communale exit and follow the yellow signs. Be careful walking there at night. Private bathrooms. Reception 7:30am-1am. Lockout 11am-3pm. Sheets and breakfast included. Laundry 200BF/€5. Dorms 505BF/€12.50; singles 908BF/€22.50; doubles 1412BF/€35.

⬛ FOOD

Cheap restaurants cluster around the **Grand-Place.** To the north, shellfish are piled on ice and speciality *paella* is served up on **rue des Bouchers.** The restaurants on **quai aux Briques,** in the Ste-Catherine area behind pl. St-Gery, serve cheaper seafood. South of the Grand-Place, **rue du Marché-aux-Fromages** is lined with Greek eateries. **Belgaufras** can be found everywhere and has hot waffles (50-80BF/€1.25-2).

Léon, r. des Bouchers 18. Seafood popular with locals and tourists alike. An order of mussels and chips (around 600F/€14.90) can serve two. Open daily noon-11pm.

Sole d'Italia, r. Grétry 67. Offers huge servings of spaghetti with bread for only 195BF/€4.85. Open daily noon-3pm and 6-11pm.

Zebra, St-Gèry 33-35. This chic cafe is centrally located and serves light, tasty sandwiches and pastas (around 250BF/€6.20). Open daily 10am-1am.

Hemispheres, r. de l'Ecuver 65. Libyan, Turkish, Chinese, and Indian cuisine convene at this summit of great Eastern platters. Vegetarian meals 280-400BF/€6.95-9.95. Open M-F noon-3pm and 6:30-10:30pm, Sa 6:30pm-midnight.

Ultième Hallutinatie, r. Royale 316. Bring your camera to this splendid stained glass art nouveau house and garden. Salads, pastas, and omelettes in the Tavern from 250BF/€6.20. Open M-F noon-2:30pm and 6pm-midnight, Sa until 1am, Su closed.

⬛ SIGHTS

GRAND-PLACE AND ENVIRONS. One look and you'll understand why Victor Hugo called the gold-trimmed **Grand-Place** "the most beautiful square in the world" after he lived at #26 Grand Place in 1852. Built in the 15th century and ravaged by French troops in 1695, the square was restored to its original splendor in five years. A daily flower market and feverish tourist activity add color. At night 800 multi-colored floodlights illuminate the **Town Hall** on the Grand Place, accompanied by loud classical music. *(Apr.-Aug. and Dec. daily around 10 or 11pm.)* Three blocks behind the Town

INTERNATIONAL MAN OF MYSTERY Tintin (pronounced "tan-tan") is the greatest comic-strip hero in the French-speaking world. The journalist remains perpetually young to fans who play the hardest of hardball at auctions for Tintin memorabilia. His creator, Georges Rémi (whose pen-name, "Hergé," is his initials pronounced backwards) sent him to the Kremlin, Shanghai, the Congo, outer space, and even the vast wilderness of... Chicago. Countless dissertations and novels have been written about Tintin's possible androgyny; many also say that Indiana Jones was Tintin made into a man. But Tintin is more than your average cartoon Joe: when former French president Charles de Gaulle was asked whom he feared the most, he replied, "Tintin is my only international competitor."

Hall on the corner of r. de l'Etuve and r. du Chêne is Brussels' most giggled-at sight, the **Mannekin Pis,** a statue of an impudent boy steadily urinating. Locals have created hundreds of outfits for him, competitively dressing him with the ritual coats of their organization or region, each with a little hole for his you-know-what. *(Free.)*

ART MUSEUMS. The ▧**Musées Royaux des Beaux Arts** houses a collection of Flemish masters, including Brueghel the Elder's *Landscape with the Fall of Icarus* and works by Rubens. The collection is divided into four color-coded wings. The **Musée d'Art Ancien** spans the blue (15th to 16th century) and brown (17th to 18th century) sections. Across the main entrance hall, the yellow (19th century) and green (20th century) sections make up the **Musée d'Art Moderne,** which contains David's *Death of Marat.* The panoramic view of Brussels' cityscape from the fourth floor of the 19th-century wing is worth the admission fee—you can see all the way to the Atomium and beyond. *(R. de la Régence 3. M: Parc or port de Namur, a block south of the Parc. Open Tu-Su 10am-5pm. 150BF/€3.75, students 100BF/€2.50. 1st W of each month free 1-5pm.)* The **Musée du Cinquantenaire (Musées Royaux d'Art et d'Histoire)** covers a wide variety of periods and parts—Roman torsos without heads, Syrian heads without torsos, and Egyptian caskets with feet. The "Salle au Tresor" is one the museum's main attractions. *(10 parc du Cinquantenaire. M: Mérode. From the station, walk through the arch, turn left, go past the doors that appear to be the entrance, and turn left again for the real entrance. Open Tu-Su 10am-5pm. 150BF/€3.75, students 100F/€2.50.)* Victor Horta's graceful home, today the **Musée Horta,** is an application of his Art Nouveau style. *(25, r. Américaine. M: Louise. Walk down Av. Louise, bear right on r. Charleroi, and turn left on r. Américaine (15-20min.). Open Tu-Su 2-5:30pm. 200BF/€5.)*

BELGIAN COMIC STRIP CENTRE. This museum in the "Comic Strip Capital of the World" pays homage to *les bandes dessineés.* The **museum library** features a reproduction of Tintin's rocket ship and works by over 700 artists. *(20, r. des Sables. M: Rogier. From the Gare Centrale, take bd. de l'Impératrice until it becomes bd. de Berlaimont, and turn left onto r. des Sables. Open Tu-Su 10am-6pm. 200BF/€5.)*

ATOMIUM AND BRUPARCK ENTERTAINMENT COMPLEX. The **Atomium,** a shining monument of aluminum and steel built for the 1958 World's Fair, represents a cubic iron crystal structure magnified 165 billion times to a height of 102m. It houses a **science museum** featuring fauna and minerals from around the world. The Atomium towers over the **Bruparck entertainment complex,** home of the **Kinepolis cinema** and **IMAX,** the largest movie theater in Europe, as well as **Mini-Europe,** a collection of European landmark miniatures, and the **Oceade** water park. *(Bd. du Centenaire. M: Huysel. ☎474 89 77; www.atomium.be. Atomium open daily Apr.-Aug. 9am-7:30pm; Sept.-Mar. 10am-5:30pm. 220BF/€5.45. Movies 250BF/€6.20. Mini-Europe open daily Mar.-June 9:30am-5pm; July-Aug. 9:30am-7pm. 380BF/€9.45. Oceade open Apr.-June Tu-F 10am-6pm, Sa-Su 10am-10pm; Sept.-Mar. W-F 10am-6pm, Sa-Su 10am-10pm. 490BF/€12.15)*

OTHER SIGHTS. Stroll through the **Galerie St. Hubert,** one block behind the Grand Place, to windowshop for everything from square umbrellas to marzipan frogs. Built over the course of six centuries, the Gothic **Saints Michel et Gudule Cathedral** mixes in a little Romanesque and modern architecture as well. *(Pl. St-Gudule, just north of Central Station. Open M-F 7am-7pm, Sa-Su 8:30am-7pm. Free.)* Wander the charming hills of **Sablon,**

home to antique markets, art galleries, and lazy cafes, or bargain at the morning flea market at **le Jeu de Balles.** The **European Parliament** has been called Caprice des Dieux—"Whim of the Gods"—perhaps because of its exorbitant cost. *(43, r. Wiertz. M: Schuman. Visits M-Th 10am and 5pm, F 10am. Apr. 14-Oct.13 also open Sa 10, 11:30am, 2:30pm.)* For a lazy afternoon, try the **Botanical Gardens** on r. Royale, next to a 12th-century château. *(Open in summer daily 10am-5:30pm; in winter 10am-4pm.)*

🎵 🎭 ENTERTAINMENT AND NIGHTLIFE

Snag a free copy of *What's On* from the tourist office. The flagship of Brussels' theater network is the **Théâtre Royal de la Monnaie,** on pl. de la Monnaie. (M: de Brouck-ère. Information ☎ (070) 233 939; www.lamonnaie.be. 300-3000BF/€7.45-74.40.) Renowned throughout the world for its opera and ballet, the theater had a performance of the opera *Muette de Portici* in August 1830 that inspired the audience to leave the theater early, take to the streets, and begin the revolt that led to Belgium's independence. Experience a distinctly Belgian art form at the **Theatre Toone,** 21, r. des Bouchers, a 170-year-old puppet theater that stages marionette performances. (☎ 513 54 86. Shows in French; in German, Flemish, or English upon request. Usually Tu-Sa 8:30pm. 400BF/€9.95, students 250BF/€6.20.) In summer, **concerts** are held on the **Grand-Place,** the **Place de la Monnaie,** and in the **Parc de Bruxelles.**

On summer nights, the **Grand-Place** and the **Bourse** come to life with street performers and live concerts. The nightlife in Brussels ranges from catching a drink on a cobble-stone street at the Grand-Place to dancing the night away at a raging disco near the Bourse. The 19th-century puppet theater **Poechenellekelder,** r. de Chêne 5, across from the Mannekin Pis, is today filled with lavishly costumed marionettes and Belgian beers. (Open daily noon-midnight, F-Sa until 1 or 2am. Beers from 50BF/€1.25.) **À La Bécasse,** r. de Tabora 11, two of Brussels' oldest and best-known cafes, specialize in the local wheat beer. (Beer 50-90BF/€1.25-2.25. Open daily 10am-midnight.) **L'Archiduc,** 6, r. Dan-saert, is a pricey but casual Art Deco 20's lounge-turned-jazz bar. (Open daily 4pm-late.) **Le Fuse,** 208, r. Blaes, one of Belgium's trendiest clubs, pays homage to the gods of techno and rave. (Open daily 10pm-late.) Gay men socialize in a mellow atmosphere at **L'Incognito,** 36, r. des Pierres, off r. de Midi. (☎ 513 37 88. Open daily 4pm-dawn.)

🔲 DAYTRIPS FROM BRUSSELS

WATERLOO. At Waterloo, site of the famous Napoleonic battle, war buffs and fans of the diminutive dictator shell out for a glimpse at the town's little slice of history. **The Lion's Mound,** 5km outside of town, is a huge hill overlooking the battlefield; nearby, the visitors center houses a panoramic painting of the battle and a brief movie about Waterloo. (Open daily Apr.-Sept. 9:30am-6:30pm; Oct. 9:30am-5:30pm; Nov.-Feb. 10:30am-4pm; Mar. 10:30am-5pm. Lion's Mound 40BF/€1; with movie and panorama 305BF/€7.60, students 250BF/€6.20.) In the center of Waterloo, **Musée Wellington,** Chaussée de Bruxelles 147, was British General Wellington's headquar-ters and has artifacts from the battle. (Open daily Apr.-Oct. 9:30am-6:30pm; Nov.-Mar. 10:30am-5pm. 100BF/€2.50, students 80BF/€2.) **Bus W** leaves pl. Rouppe near Brussels' Gare Midi (every 51min., 105BF/€2.60) and stops at: Waterloo Church, across the street from Musée Wellington; a gas station near Lion's Mound; and the train station in Braine L'Alleud. Belgian Railways offers a **B-excursion ticket,** which gives return transit between Brussels Midi (also available from Brussels Nord) and Braine L'Alleud, a bus pass from Braine L'Alleud to Waterloo, and entrance to all sights (710BF/€17.60, students 660BF/€16.40). The **tourist office** is next to the Musée Wellington, at Chaussée de Bruxelles 149. (☎ 354 99 10. Open daily Apr. to mid-Nov. 9:30am-6:30pm; mid-Nov. to Mar. 10:30am-5pm.) ☎ 02.

MECHELEN (MALINES). Historically the ecclesiastical capital of Belgium, Mechelen is best known today for its treasure-filled churches and its grim role in the Holocaust. The **Grote Markt** is lined with early Renaissance buildings, including the **Stadhuis** (city hall) and St. Rumbold's Cathedral. (Stadhuis open M-Sa 8:30am-5:30pm, Su 2-5:30pm.) The church is dominated by **St. Rumbold's Tower,** which rises 97m over Grote Markt, chimes out the town's daily rhythm. You can climb the tower with a guide. (M 2:15pm and 7:15pm. 100BF/€2.50.) The 15th-century **Church of St. John** boasts Rubens's magnificent triptych *The Adoration of the Magi* (1619). The ▧**Jewish Museum of Deportation and Resistance,** 153 Goswin de Stassartstr., is housed in the military barracks used during the Holocaust as a temporary camp for Belgian and Dutch Jews en route to Auschwitz-Birkenau. From the Grote Markt, follow Wollemarkt, which becomes Goswin de Stassartstr. (Open Su-Th 10am-5pm, F 10am-1pm. Free.) On your way back to the station, stop by the **botanical gardens** along the canal for a picnic. **Trains** arrive from Brussels and Antwerp (both 15min., 120BF/€3). The **tourist office** in the Stadhuis finds rooms for free. (☎29 76 55. Open Easter-Oct. M-F 8am-6pm, Sa-Su 9:30am-12:30pm and 1:30-5pm; June-Sept. M until 7pm; Nov.-Easter reduced hours.) ☎**015.**

FLANDERS (VLAANDEREN)

In Flanders, the Flemish-speaking part of Beligum, you can party in Antwerp, bask in Bruges, and sate your castle cravings with Ghent's Gravensteen. The three major cities offer a taste of Flanders' 16th-century Golden Age, when its commercial centers were among the largest in Europe and its innovative artists motivated the Northern Renaissance. The well-preserved cities are rich in art as well as friendly, multilingual people who pride their region more than their country.

BRUGES (BRUGGE)   ☎050

The capital of Flanders is one of the most beautiful cities in Europe, and tourists know it: famed for its lace, the home of Jan van Eyck has become the largest tourist attraction in the country. The entire city remains one of the best-preserved examples of Northern Renaissance architecture, with a beauty that belies the destruction it sustained in World War I. In 2002, Bruges will be honored as the "Cultural Capital of Europe," and will host a major celebration of the arts throughout the year (☎44 20 02; info@brugge2002.be; www.brugge2002.be).

▐ TRANSPORTATION

Trains: Depart from **Stationsplein** (☎38 23 82; open daily 7am-9pm), 15min. south of the city center. To: **Antwerp** (1hr., 395BF/€9.80); **Brussels** (1hr., 380BF/€9.45); **Ghent** (25min., 175BF/€4.35); **Ostend** (17min., 110BF/€2.75); **Zeebrugge** (10min., 80F/€2).

Bike Rental: At the train station (☎30 23 29); 325BF/€8.10 per day; 500BF/€12.40 deposit. **'t Koffieboontje,** Hallestr. 4 (☎33 80 27), off the Markt by the belfry. 325BF/€8.10 per day, 225BF/€5.60 per half day, student discount. Open daily 9am-10pm. Many hostels and hotels also rent bikes for about 300BF/€7.45 per day. Pick up *5x by bike around Bruges* (50BF/€1.25) at the tourist office for routes and tours.

Hitchhiking: Those hitching to Brussels reportedly take bus #7 to St. Michiels or pick up the highway behind the train station. *Let's Go* does not recommend hitchhiking.

✳ 🛈 ORIENTATION AND PRACTICAL INFORMATION

Bruges is enclosed by a circular canal, with the train station just beyond its southern extreme. Its historic district is entirely accessible on foot. The dizzying Belfort (belfry) towers high at the center of town, presiding over the handsome Markt.

Tourist Offices: Burg 11 (☎44 86 86; toerisme@brugge.be; www.brugge.be), in Burg Square. Head left from the station to 't Zand square, right on Zuidzandstr., and right on Breidelstr. through the Markt (15min.). Books rooms (400BF/€9.95 deposit) and sells maps (25BF/€0.65). Open Apr.-Sept. M-F 9:30am-6:30pm, Sa-Su 10am-noon and 2-6:30pm;

Oct.-Mar. M-F 9:30am-5pm, Sa-Su 9:30am-1pm and 2-5:30pm. **Branch** at the train station open 10:30am-1:15pm and 2-5:30pm.

Tours: Quasimodo Tours (☎37 04 70; www.quasimodo.be), leads excellent 30km countryside bike and bus tours to windmills, castles, and WWII bunkers. Bike tours depart mid-Mar. to Sept. daily from the tourist office at the Burg. 650BF/€16.15, under 26 550BF/€13.65. The Triple Treat trip on M, W, F visits medieval castles, with chocolate and beer stops along the way. 1500BF/€37.20, under 26 1200BF/€29.75.

Currency Exchange: Currency exchanges fill the streets around the Markt, but there is no place to change money at the train station.

Luggage Storage: At the train station. 55-130BF/€1.40-3.25. **Lockers** at the tourist office. 50BF/€1.25.

Laundromat: Belfort, Ezelstr. 51, next to Snuffel's Sleep-In (see below). Wash 100-140BF/€2.50-3.50, dry 200-300BF/€5-7.45. Open daily 7am-10pm.

Emergency: ☎100. **Police,** ☎101. Police station at Hauwerstr. 7 (☎44 88 44).

Internet Access: The Coffee Link, Mariastraat 38 (☎34 99 73), in the Oud Sint-Jon Historic Hospital. 50BF/€1.25 per 15min. Open M-Sa 10am-9:30pm, Su 10am-7:30pm.

Post Office: Hoedenmakerstr. 2. Open M-F 9am-5pm, Tu 9am-7pm. Address mail to be held: First name SURNAME, *Poste Restante,* Hoedenmakerstr. 2, Brugge **8000** BELGIUM.

ACCOMMODATIONS AND CAMPING

Reasonable accommodations are available just a few blocks away from the center, but can be hard to come by on weekends when tourists flock to Bruges.

The Passage, Dweersstr. 26 (☎34 02 32). From the station, cross the street in front and go left along the path. At the end of the path bear left onto 't Zand, take a right onto Zuidzanstr., then take the 1st left onto Dweersstr. The hostel is on the left (15min.). Breakfast 100BF/€2.50. Reception 8:30am-midnight. Closed mid-Jan. for renovations. Dorms 450BF/€11.20; singles 900BF/€22.35; doubles 1400BF/€37.70.

Hotel Lybeer, Korte Vuldersstr. 31 (☎33 43 55, hotel.lybeer@pandora.be, www.hotellybeer.com). Follow directions for The Passage up to Zuidzanstr., then take the 1st right onto Hoogste van Brugge, followed by a left. Old-fashioned charm with modern comforts. Internet free. Breakfast included. Reception 8am-10:30pm. Singles 900BF/€22.50; doubles 1600BF/€39.70; triples 2175BF/€53.95; quads 2800BF/€69.45.

't Keizershof, Oostmeers 126 (☎33 87 28; hotel.keizershof@12move.be; http://users.skynet.be/keizershof). From the station, walk to the traffic lights on the left, cross the street, follow signs pointing to the Memling Museum and Oud St. Jan. The hotel is 80m on your left. Pretty, comfortable rooms on a quiet street. Breakfast included. Laundry 300BF/€7.45. Singles 988BF/€24.5; doubles 1452/€36; triples 2178F/€54; quads 2602BF/€64.50.

Bauhaus International Youth Hotel, Langestr. 133-137 (☎34 10 93; bauhaus@bauhaus.be or info@bauhaus.be). Take bus #6 or 16 to Gerechtshof and go right about 50m; it's on your left. Cybercafe and popular bar. Nearby laundromat. Breakfast 80BF/€2. Belgian dinner from 275BF/€6.85. Reception 8am-2am. Dorms 380BF/€9.45; singles 550-900BF/€13.65-€22.35; doubles 1000-1400BF/€24.80-34.70; triples 1350-1950BF/€33.50-48.35.

Snuffel's Sleep-In, Ezelstr. 49 (☎33 31 33; snuffel@flanderscoast.be). From the Markt, follow St-Jakobstr., bearing right at Moerstr., and St-Jakobsrt. becomes Ezelstr. (10min.). Or take bus #3 or 13 from the station to Normaalschool. Internet access. Breakfast 80BF/€2. Sheets 80BF/€2. Reception 8am-6am. Snug dorms 350-390BF/€8.70-9.70; quads 1960BF/€48.60.

Europa International Youth Hostel (HI), Baron Ruzettelaan 143 (☎35 26 79; brugge@vjh.be). Quiet, away from the Markt and the nightlife. Turn right from the station and follow Buiten Katelijnevest to Baron Ruzettelaan (15min.). Or take bus #2 to Wantestraat. Breakfast included. Sheets 125BF/€3.10. Key deposit 100BF/€2.50. Reception 7:30-10am and 1-11pm. 430BF/€10.70; nonmembers 530BF/€13.15.

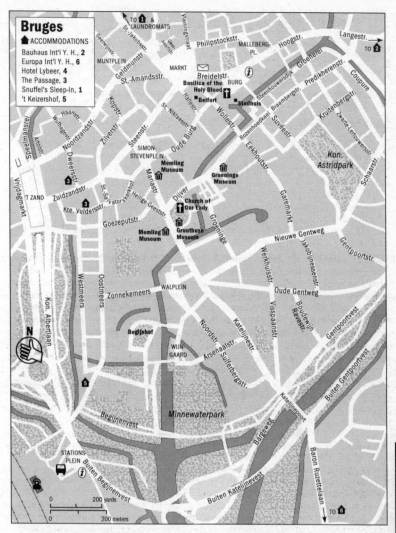

Bruges

🏠 ACCOMMODATIONS
Bauhaus Int'l Y. H., **2**
Europa Int'l Y. H., **6**
Hotel Lybeer, **4**
The Passage, **3**
Snuffel's Sleep-In, **1**
't Keizershof, **5**

Camping: St-Michiel, Tillegemstr. 55 (☎ 38 08 19). From the station take bus #7 to Jagerstr, take a left onto Jagerstr., bear left at the 1st intersection, and go around the rotary to Tillegemstr. (25min.). 115BF/€2.85 per person, 135BF/€3.35 per tent.

🛑 FOOD

Splurge on a pot of Belgium's *mosselen* (mussels), which at 450-500BF/€11.20-12.40 often includes appetizers and dessert, even in the Markt. To avoid high prices, look a block or two away from the city center. From the Burg, cross the river and turn left to buy fresh seafood at the **Vismarkt.** For cheaper fare, head to **Nopri Supermarket,** Noordzandstr. 4, just off 't Zand. (Open M-Sa 9:30am-6:30pm.) **Ganzespel,** Ganzestr. 37, serves up hearty portions of simple food. From the Burg, turn up Hoogstr. and take the second right after the river. (Meals 245-530BF/€6.10-13.15. Quiche 230BF/€5.70. Open W-F noon-2:30pm and 6-10pm, Su noon-10pm.)

👁 SIGHTS

Small enough to be thoroughly explored by short walks, and lined with gorgeous canals, Bruges is best seen on foot. The tourist office leads **walking tours** (July-Aug. daily 3pm; 150BF/€3.75). **Boat tours** also ply Bruges' canals (every 30min., 190BF/€4.70); ask at the tourist office or pick up tickets at the booth on the bridge between Wollestr. and Dijver. The **museum combination ticket** covers the Gruuthuse, the Groeninge Museum, the Arentshuis, and the Stadhuis (400BF/€9.95).

MARKT AND BURG. Over the **Markt** looms the 88m medieval bell tower of the **Belfort.** Climb its dizzying 366 steps during the day for a great view; return at night when the tower becomes the city's torch. (*Open daily 9:30am-5pm. Tickets sold until 4:15pm. Bell concerts M, W, Sa 9pm; Su 2:15pm. 100BF/€2.50, students 80BF/€2.*) Behind the Markt, the **Burg** square is dominated by the flamboyant Gothic façade of the medieval **Stadhuis** (City Hall), filled with paintings and wood carvings. Upstairs is a gilded hall where many Bruges residents still get married. (*Open daily 9:30am-5pm. 150BF/€3.75.*) Hidden in the corner of the Burg next to the Stadhuis, the **Basilica of the Holy Blood** houses a relic that allegedly holds the blood of Christ. (*Open daily Apr.-Sept. 9:30am-noon and 2-6pm; Oct.-Mar. 10am-noon and 2-4pm; closed W afternoon. Free. Worship of relic F 8:30-10am (ground floor), 10-11am and 3-4pm (upstairs). 40BF/€1.*)

MUSEUMS. From the Burg, follow Wollestr. left and head right on Dijver to reach the **Groeninge Museum** for a comprehensive collection of works by Bruges-based Jan Van Eyck, Bruges-born Hans Memling, and the master of medieval macabre himself, Hieronymous Bosch. (*Dijver 12. Open daily 9:30am-5pm; in winter closed Tu. 250BF/€6.20, students 200BF/€5. Last tickets sold 4:30pm.*) Next door, the **Gruuthuse Museum,** in the lavish 15th-century home of beer magnates, houses an amazing collection of weapons, tapestries, musical instruments, and coins that date back to the 6th century. (*Dijver 17. Open Apr.-Sept. daily 9:30am-5pm; Oct.-Mar. closed Tu. 130BF/€3.25, students 100BF/€2.50.*) Continue as Dijver becomes Gruuthusestr. and walk under the stone archway to enter the **Memling Museum,** housed in St. John's Hospital, one of the oldest surviving medieval hospitals in Europe. (*Mariastr. 38. Open Apr.-Sept. daily 9:30am-5pm; Oct.-Mar. Th-Tu 9:30am-12:30pm and 2-5pm. 80BF/€2, students 50BF/€1.25.*)

OTHER SIGHTS. The **Church of Our Lady,** at Mariastr. and Gruuthusestr. near the Groeninge Museum, contains Michelangelo's *Madonna and Child*, one of his few works to have left Italy, as well as a number of medieval frescoed tomb fragments and the 16th-century mausoleums of Mary of Burgundy and Charles the Bold. (*Open daily 10am-noon and 2-5pm. Church free; tomb fragment viewing 70BF/€1.75, students 35BF/€0.90.*) From the Church, turn left and stroll along the Mariastr., turn right onto Stoofstr., where you will come to Walplein. Cross the footbridge to enter the Beguinage, a grassy cove encircled by the picturesque residences of medieval cloistered women, inhabited today by Benedictine nuns. (*Open Mar.-Nov. 10am-noon and 1:45-5pm; open until 6pm during summer months. Gate closes at sunset. 60BF/€1.50.*) The 230-year-old windmill **Sint-Janshuismolen,** is still used to grind flour. From the Burg, follow Hoogstr., which becomes Langestr., and turn left at the end on Kruisvest. (*Open May-Sept. daily 9:30am-12:30pm and 1:30-5pm. 40BF/€1, students 20BF/€0.50.*)

🎵 NIGHTLIFE

The best nightlife consists of wandering through the city's romantic streets and over its cobblestoned bridges. But if that isn't enough, take your pick from the 300 varieties of beer at **'t Brugs Beertje,** Kemelstr. 5, off Steenstr. (Open M 4pm-1am, F-Sa 4pm-2am, Su 4pm-1am.) Next door, the **Dreipelhuisje** serves tantalizingly fruity *jenever*, a flavored Dutch gin. (Open M-F 6pm-midnight, Sa-Su 6pm-2am.) **Rica Rokk,** 't Zand 6, is popular with local twenty-somethings. (Beers from 50BF. No cover. Open daily 8am-5am.) Continue next door to **The Break,** 't Zand 9, where pulsing music and glammed up glances await. (Beer from 55BF. No cover. Open M-Sa 10am-late, Su 1pm-late.)

🔢 DAYTRIPS FROM BRUGES: ZEEBRUGGE AND OSTEND

Belgium's North Sea coast lure visitors with its beaches. **Zeebrugge** has an international port, a large fish market, and a promenade that extends far into the sea. **Ostend** (Oostende) has a popular beach lined with restaurants and bars. For information on **ferries** from Zeebrugge and Ostend to the UK, see p. 62. Get ferry tickets from travel agents, at ports, or in the Ostend train station. **Trains** run to Ostend (15min., 3 per hr., 110BF/€2.75) and Zeebrugge (15min., 3 per hr., 150BF/€3.75).

ANTWERP (ANTWERPEN, ANVERS)   ☎ 03

Home to the Golden Age master painter Rubens, Antwerp today is distinctly cosmopolitan. Its main street, the **Meir,** showcases trendy clothing, diamond jewelry, and delectable chocolate. At the end of the Meir, beer flows so cheaply that crowds pass another round in lieu of breakfast.

🖪🔢 TRANSPORTATION AND PRACTICAL INFORMATION. Trains go from Berchem Station to: Amsterdam (2hr., 970BF/€24); Brussels (45-53min., 200BF/€5); and Rotterdam (1½hr., 700BF/€17.35). To get from the station to the **tourist office,** Grote Markt 15, take tram #8 to Groenplaats. (☎232 01 03; fax 231 19 37. Open M-Sa 9am-6pm, Su 9am-5pm). **Postal code:** 2000.

🔢🔲 ACCOMMODATIONS AND FOOD. The **New International Youth Hotel,** Provinciestr. 256, is centrally located. To get there, take tram #2, 11, or 15 to Plantin, go under the bridge onto Baron Joostensstr., take a right onto Van Den Nestlei, head left onto Kruikstr., and take an immediate right onto Provinciestr. (☎230 05 22; niyh@pandora.be. Breakfast and sheets included. Reception 8am-11pm. No lockout. 8-bed dorms 3760BF/€93.25; singles 1020BF/€25.30; doubles 1560BF/€38.70; quads 2560BF/€63.50.) To reach the modern **Jeugdherberg Op-Sinjoorke (HI),** Eric Sasselaan 2, take tram #8 or 11 to Groenplaats, then take tram #2 (dir. Hoboken) to Bouwcentrum. From the tram stop, walk toward the fountain, take a left, and follow the yellow signs. (☎238 02 73. Breakfast included. Sheets 135BF/€3.35. Lockout 10am-4pm. Dorms 430BF/€10.70, nonmembers 530BF/€13.15; doubles 585BF.) Near the Jeugdherberg Op-Sinjoorke, there is **camping** at **Sted. Kamp Vogelzangan.** Follow the directions to the hotel; when you get off the tram and are facing the Bouwventrum, turn right and walk away from the fountain, cross the street to make your first left, and the campground will be on your left after the gates. (☎238 57 17. Open Apr.-Sept. 65BF/€1.65 per person, 35BF/€0.90 per car, 35BF/€0.90 per tent, 85BF/€2.15 per tent with electricity.) **Ultimatum,** on the Grote Markt at Suikerrui, has outdoor seating and "world kitchen" dishes from Norway, Russia, and Morocco. (Open daily 11am-late. Kitchen closes 11pm.)

🔲🖪 SIGHTS AND NIGHTLIFE. Many of Antwerp's best sights are free. Fanciful mansions built in the city's Golden Age line the **Cogels Osylei.** A stroll down the promenade by the Schelde River leads to the 13th-century **Steen Castle,** which houses the **National Maritime Museum.** (Open Tu-Su 10am-5pm. 150BF/€4.) The **Cathedral of our Lady,** Groenpl. 21, boasts a magnificent Gothic tower and Rubens' *Descent from the Cross.* (Open M-F 10am-5pm, Sa 10am-3pm, Su 1-4pm. 80BF/€2.) Nearby, the dignified **Stadhuis** (City Hall) stands in Grote Markt. (Information ☎203 95 33. 30BF/€30.75.) The **Mayer van den Bergh Museum,** Lange Gasthuisstr. 19, features a formerly private collection and showcases Bruegel's *Mad Meg.* (Open Tu-Su 10am-5pm. 150BF/€3. F free.) The **Rubens Huis,** Wapper 9-11, off Meir, was built by Antwerp's favorite son and is filled with his masterful art. (Open Tu-Su 10am-5pm. 200BF/€5; F free.) The **Royal Museum of Fine Arts,** Leopold De Waelpl. 1-9, has one of the world's finest collections of Old Flemish Master paintings. (Open Tu-Su 10am-5pm. 150BF/€3.75, students 120BF/€3; F free.)

Get *Play* at the tourist office for information on Antwerp's 300 bars and nightclubs. The streets behind the cathedral throb at night; **Bierland,** Korte Nieuwstr. 28, is a popular student hang-out. (Open Su-Th 9am-12pm, F-Sa 8am-2am.) Next to the cathedral, over 600 Flemish religious figurines collect along with curious drinkers at **Elfde Gebod,** Torfburg 10. (Beer 70-120BF/€1.75-3. Open daily noon-1am, Sa-Su until 2am.) Sample local *elixir d'Anvers* in the candle-lit, 15th-century **Pelgrom,** Pelgrimstr. 15. (Open daily noon-late.) Gay nightlife clusters on **Van Schoonhoven-straat,** just north of Centraal Station.

GHENT (GENT)   ☎ 09

Once the heart of the Flemish textile industry, Ghent lives and breathes industrial pride, with many of its grand buildings and monuments testifying to its former grandeur. During the **Gentse Feesten** ("10 Days Off" celebration; July 20-29, 2002; ☎ 269 09 45), which commemorates the first vacation granted to sweatshop workers in 1860, the streets come to life with performers, live music, and carnival rides.

◪ꔍ TRANSPORTATION AND PRACTICAL INFORMATION. Trains run from Sint-Pietersstation (take tram #1 or 12) to Brussels (40min., 245BF/€6.10) and Bruges (20min., 175BF/€4.35). The **tourist office** is in the belfry's crypt, Botermarkt 17a. (☎ 266 52 32. Open daily Apr.-Oct. 9:30am-6:30pm; Nov.-Mar. 9:30am-4:30pm.) **Postal Code:** 9000.

ꔍ◪ ACCOMMODATIONS AND FOOD. Modern **De Draeke (HI),** St-Widostr. 11, is in the shadow of a castle. From the station, take tram #1, 10, or 11 to Gravensteen (15min.). Facing the castle, head left, then head right on Gewad and right again on St-Widostr. (☎ 233 70 50; youthhostel.gent@skynet.be. Breakfast included. Sheets 125BF/€3.15. Reception daily 7:30am-11pm. Dorms 510BF/€12.65; singles 820BF/€20.40; doubles 1200BF/€29.75. Nonmembers add 100BF/€2.50.) **The Hotel Flandria,** Barrestr. 3, offers big breakfasts. (☎ 223 06 26; gent@flandria.centrum.be; www.flandria-centrum.be. Reception 7am-9pm. Singles 1600BF/€39.70; doubles 1800-1900BF/€44.70-47.10.) To get to **Camping Blaarmeersen,** Zuiderlaan 12, take bus #9 from Sint-Pietersstation and ask the driver to connect you to bus #38 to Blaarmeersen. When you get off, take the first street on your left to the end. (☎ 221 53 99; blaarmeersen@gent.be. Open Mar. to mid-Oct. 130BF/€3.25 per person, 140BF/€3.50 per tent.) Good meals run about 250BF/€6.20. Eat around **Korenmarkt,** in front of the post office; **Vrijdagmarkt,** a few blocks from the town hall; and **St-Piet-ersnieuwstraat,** near the university. Students meet up at **Magazyne,** Bredestraat 159, in the historic district. (Lunch served from noon-2pm, dinner from 6-10pm.)

◪ꔍ SIGHTS AND NIGHTLIFE. The **Leie canal** runs through the center of the city and wraps around the sprawling medieval fortress of **Gravensteen,** St-Veerle-plein 11, which holds a crypt, dungeon, and torture chamber. (Open daily Apr.-Aug. 9am-6pm.; Sept.-Mar. 9am-5pm. 200BF/€5, students 100BF/€2.50.) The castle is near the historic **Partershol** quarter, a network of well-preserved 16th- to 18th-century houses. Wind your way up the towering **Belfort** for some major vertigo. (Open mid-Mar. to mid-Nov. daily 10am-12:30pm and 2-5:30pm. 100BF/€2.50.) The **Stadhuis** (Town Hall) is a mix of Gothic and Renaissance architecture. A block away on Limburgstr., the 14th- to 16th-century **Saint Bavo's Cathedral** boasts van Eyck's *Adoration of the Mystic Lamb* and Rubens's *The entry of St. Bavo into the monastery.* (Cathedral open Apr.-Oct. daily 8:30am-6pm; Nov.-Mar. M-Sa 8:30am-5pm, Su 2-7pm. Free. Crypt and *Mystic Lamb* open M-Sa 9:30am-5pm, Su 1-5pm. 100BF/€2.50, audio tour included; children 50BF/€1.25, audio tour excluded.) Head to Citadel Park, near the center, to see the 14th- to 16th-century Flemish school collection at the **Museum voor Schone Kunsten.** (Open Tu-Su 9:30am-5pm. 100BF/€2.50, students 50BF/€1.25.) Also in Citadel Park is the contemporary art collection at the **Stedelijk Museum voor Actuele Kunst (SMAK).** (Open Tu-Su 10am-6pm. 200BF/€5, students 150BF/€3.75.)

From October to July 15, scholars cavort in the cafes and discos near the university restaurant on **Overpoortstraat.** The Art Deco bar **Vooruit,** on St-Pietersnieuwstr., was once the meeting place of the Socialist Party and was later occupied by Nazis. (Open daily 11:30am-10pm.) Beer lovers flock to **Dulle Grief,** on the Vrijdagmarkt, for the 1.2 liter "Max" for 350BF/€8.70 and the traditional exchange of a shoe. (Open noon-12:30am, Su noon-7:30pm, M 4:30pm-12:30am.)

WALLONIE

The towns in Wallonie's castle-dotted **Ardennes** offer a relaxing hideaway, with excellent hiking trails and cool caves. Gorgeous train lines sweep through peaceful farmland in Wallonie's southeast corner. Although nature lovers will want to spend a night in this part of the region, urban addicts can enjoy the scenery en route to Brussels, Paris, or Luxembourg City.

NAMUR
☎ 081

Namur, in the heart of Wallonie, is close to **hiking, biking, caving,** and **kayaking** options that make it the best base for exploring the Ardennes. The **citadel,** atop a rocky hill to the south, was built by the Spanish in the Middle Ages, expanded by the Dutch in the 19th century, witness to a bloody battle in World War I, and occupied until 1978. Hike, or take a **mini-bus** from the tourist office at Sq. Leopold and r. de Grognon (every hr., 40BF/€1); the bus will let you off at the Citadel, where you can pick up a **tour** of the fortress. (Open daily 11am-5pm. 210BF/€5.25.)

    Trains link Namur to Brussels (1hr., 245BF/€6.10). Two **tourist offices,** one a few blocks left of the train station at place de la Gare, and the other in the **Hôtel de Ville,** help plan excursions. (Train station ☎22 28 49, Hôtel de Ville ☎24 64 44; www.ville.namur.be. Both open daily 9:30am-6pm.) To reach the friendly **Auberge Félicien Rops (HI),** 8 av. Félicien Rops, take bus #3 directly to the door, or take bus #4 and ask the driver to let you off. (☎22 36 88; namur@laj.be. Bikes 500BF/€12.40 per day. Breakfast included. Sheets 110BF/€2.75. Laundry 260BF/€6.45. Reception 7:30am-1am. Lockout 11am-3pm. Dorms 440BF/€10.95; singles 820BF/€20.35; doubles 1210BF/€30. Nonmembers add 100BF/€2.50.) To **camp** at **Les Trieux,** 99, r. des Tris, 6km away in Malonne, take bus #6. (☎44 55 83. Open Apr.-Oct. 85BF/€2.15 per person or per tent.)

■ **DAYTRIP FROM NAMUR: DINANT.** Tiny Dinant is a good launching pad for climbing and kayaking excursions, with an imposing **citadel** rising over the town. Explore on your own, or ride the cable car up and follow a French or Dutch tour. (Citadel 19F/€0.50. Open daily 10am-6pm. Mandatory tours every 20min.) Bring a sweater to the tour of the chilly, cascade-filled caves of **La Grotte Merveilleuse,** route de Phillippeville 142. To reach the Grotte from the citadel, cross the bridge and take the second left onto rte. de Phillippeville. (Open daily Apr.-Oct. 10am-6pm; Mar. and Nov. 11am-5pm. 190BF/€4.75. Mandatory tours in French, Dutch, and English every hr., on the hr.) **Dakota Raid Adventure,** r. Saint Roch 17, leads rock-climbing daytrips in the area. (☎22 32 43. Open daily 10am-5pm.) Dinant is accessible by **train** from Brussels (1½hr., 360BF/€8.95) or by **bike** from Namur; on summer weekends, take a one-way river cruise from Namur (3½hr.) on the river. The **tourist office,** Quai Cadoux 8, helps plan outdoor activities and books rooms. (☎22 28 70; www.maison-du-tourisme.net.) With your back to the train station, turn right, take your first left, and your next left will land you there. ☎ **082.**

BOSNIA-HERZEGOVINA

BOSNIAN CONVERTIBLE MARKS

US$1 = 2.10KM	1KM = US$0.50
CDN$1 = 1.40KM	1KM = CDN$0.70
UK£1 = 3.10KM	1KM = UK£0.30
IR£1 = 2.50KM	1KM = IR£0.40
AUS$1 = 1.15KM	1KM = AUS$0.90
NZ$1 = 0.95KM	1KM = NZ$1.10
ZAR1 = 0.25KM	1KM = ZAR3.90
DM1 = 1KM	1KM = DM1
HRV KUNA1 = 3.90KM	1KM = HRV KUNA0.26
EUR€1 = 2KM	1KM = EUR€0.50

PHONE CODE	**Country code:** 387. **International dialing prefix:** 00. From outside Bosnia-Herzegovina, dial int'l dialing prefix (see inside back cover) + 387 + city code + local number.

In August 1999, the US State Department reiterated its **Travel Warning** against unnecessary travel to Bosnia, particularly the Republika Srpska. No warnings have been issued since. For updates, see travel.state.gov/travelwarnings.html.

The mountainous heart of the former Yugoslavia, Bosnia-Herzegovina has defied the odds to stand today as an independent nation. Bosnia's distinctiveness—and its troubles—spring from its role as a mixing ground for Muslims, Croats, and Serbs. In Sarajevo, that ideal is at least verbally maintained, but ethnic problems continue in the countryside. The country is marked by rolling hills and sparkling rivers, but its lush valleys are now punctuated with abandoned houses and gaping rooftops. The past decade has been brutal, with much of the population displaced, and a bloody war broadcast nightly to the world. Bosnia's future is uncertain, particularly with the withdrawal of NATO troops, but its citizens tend to be optimistic. In this period of post-Dayton peace, Bosnia is slowly rebuilding.

Learn more about Bosnia's past and present in *Let's Go: Eastern Europe 2002*.

FACTS AND FIGURES

Official Name: Bosnia and Herzegovina.

Capital: Sarajevo.

Major Cities: Mostar.

Population: 3,482,000 (40% Serbs, 38% Bosnian Muslims, 22% Croats).

Administrative Division: 51% Muslim/Croat Federation, 49% Serb-led Republika Srpska.

Land Area: 51,233 km.

Climate: Mild continental and rainy; cold winters, hot summers. Visit in summer.

Languages: Bosnian, Serbian, Croatian.

Religions: Muslim (40%), Orthodox (31%), Catholic (15%), Protestant (4%), other (10%).

ESSENTIALS

DOCUMENTS AND FORMALITIES

VISAS. Citizens of Canada, Ireland, the UK, and the US may visit Bosnia visa-free for up to one month; **visas** are required for citizens of Australia, New Zealand, and South Africa. There are occasional police checkpoints within Bosnia; register with your embassy upon arrival, and keep your papers with you at all times. Visitors are required to register with the police upon arrival—lodgings will usually do it for you.

Bosnia-Herzegovina

EMBASSIES. Foreign embassies in Bosnia-Herzogovina are all in **Sarajevo** (p. 133). For Bosnian embassies at home: **Australia,** 27 State Circle, Forest, Canberra ACT 2603 (☎(02) 6239 5955; fax 6239 5793); **UK,** Morley House, 7th fl. 320 Regent St., London W1R 3BF (☎(020) 7255 3758; fax 7255 3760; bosnia@embassy_london.ision.co.uk); **US,** 2109 E St. NW, Washington, D.C. 20037 (☎202-337-1500; fax 202-337-1502; consular ☎212-593-0264; info@bosnianembassy.org; www.bosnianembassy.org).

TRANSPORTATION

Buses are reliable, clean, and not very crowded, but brace yourself for Balkan driving. Buses run daily between Sarajevo and Dubrovnik, and Split and Zagreb. Commercial **plane** service into Sarajevo is limited and expensive: **Lufthansa** (US ☎800-645-3880; www.lufthansa.com); **Croatia Airlines** (☎+385 (1) 487 27 27; www.croatiaairlines.hr); and **Swiss Air** (US ☎800-221-4750; www.swissair.com) service Sarajevo. **Railways** are not functional and should not be considered an option. **Eurail** is not valid. Because of road hazards, you should avoid **driving. Biking** and **hitchhiking** are also uncommon and inadvisable.

TOURIST SERVICES AND MONEY

EMERGENCY	Police: ☎92. Fire: ☎93. Ambulance: ☎94.

The new Bosnian currency, the **convertible mark (KM),** was introduced in the summer of 1998. It is fixed to the *Deutschmark* at a 1:1 exchange rate. *Deutschmarks* can be changed directly into convertible marks for no commission at most Sarajevo banks. The Bosnian *dinar* is not a valid currency. The Croatian **kuna** was named an official Bosnian currency in the summer of 1997; while not legal tender in Sarajevo, it is accepted in the western (Croatian) area of divided Mostar. Change your money back to Deutschmarks when you leave; it is inconvertible outside Bosnia. Banks are the best places to exchange money. Traveler's checks can be cashed at some Sarajevo banks. There are no ATMs in Bosnia. Most restaurants accept credit cards; Visa is best for getting cash advances. If your itinerary lies outside of Sarajevo, bring Deutschmarks with you. Accommodations are fairly pricey, at US$15-30; food remains affordable at US$2-5 per meal. Tip waitstaff only for excellent service.

WATCH YOUR TONGUE Croat, Serb, and Bosnian refer to people of each ethnicity. Croatian, Serbian, and Bosnian indicate the country. Thus, a Bosnian Serb denotes a Serb living in Bosnia (most often in the Republika Srpska (RS), the Serb-dominated area in northeast Bosnia). Likewise, a Bosnian Croat is a Croat living in Bosnia. Bosnian Muslims usually go by the term "Bosniak." Bosnians often refer to their Bosnian Serb enemies as "Četnik," or "Chetnik," a revived World War II ethnic slur. In other words, a Serb is different from a Chetnik—do not make this mistake. Another reminder: the Bosnian Army is precisely that, *not* the "Muslim Army."

COMMUNICATION

Yellow-and-white "PTT" signs indicate post offices. Few towns outside the capital have mail service. Mail to Australia, Canada, New Zealand, the US, and South Africa, usually takes one to two weeks, somewhat less time to Ireland and the UK. Postcards cost 1KM to mail. Poste Restante is unavailable. Telephones are troublesome and expensive; the best option is to call collect from the Sarajevo post office. Calling the UK is roughly 3.50KM per minute, the US 5KM, but prices vary. International direct dialing numbers include **AT&T,** ☎ 00 800 0010.

ACCOMMODATIONS AND CAMPING

Housing prices are stabilizing in Bosnia and Herzegovian. A room in a **pension** costs as little as 30KM, and relatively cheap **private rooms** (30-50KM) are available all over. Discounts are usually available for longer stays. **Camping** is not an option.

HEALTH AND SAFETY

Outside Sarajevo, **do NOT set foot off the pavement** under any circumstances. Even in Sarajevo, stay on paved roads and hard-covered surfaces. Do not pick up any objects on the ground. Millions of **landmines** and unexploded ordinance (UXOs) cover the country, many on road shoulders and in abandoned houses. The **Mine Action Center (MAC),** Zmaja od Bosne 8 (☎ 66 73 10 and 20 12 99), has more information. In Sarajevo, finding medical help and supplies is not a problem; your embassy is your best resource. Peacekeeping operations have brought English-speaking doctors, but not insurance; **cash** is the only method of payment. All drugs are sold at pharmacies, while basic hygiene products are sold at many drugstores.

HOLIDAYS

Bosnia celebrates many Catholic, Orthodox, and Islamic religious holidays; *Let's Go* does not list them all, as most are days of observance, not public holidays.

Holidays: New Year's (Jan. 1); Orthodox Christmas (Jan.7); Republic Day (Jan. 9); Orthodox New Year's (Jan. 14); Independence Day (Mar. 1); Catholic Easter (Apr. 15); Orthodox Easter (Apr. 30); Labor Day (May 1); St. George's Day (May 6); Vidovdan (June 28); Petrovdan (July 12); Ilindan (Aug. 2); Velika gospa (Aug. 15); Assumption (Aug. 28); Ramadan (roughly Nov. 6-Dec. 5); Eid al-Fitr (Dec. 6); National Day (Nov. 25); Catholic Christmas (Dec. 25).

ALTERNATIVES TO TOURISM Many visitors to Bosnia are interested in helping the country to rebuild. These organizations gladly accept volunteers and donations. All numbers require the Sarajevo prefix, ☎ (0)33.

La Benevolencija, Hamdije Krešavljakovića 59, Sarajevo (☎ 66 34 72; la_bene@soros.org.ba). Organizes local public service with injured or orphaned children. Call at least one week in advance. Open M-F 9am-4pm.

OXFAM, Hiseta 2, Sarajevo (☎ 66 81 33).

UNICEF, Kolodvorska 6, Sarajevo (☎ 52 37 11; fax 64 29 70).

UNHCR, United Nations High Commission for Refugees. (☎ 66 61 60).

SARAJEVO ☎033

Although the city is being rebuilt, its people have suffered through a recent war, and the trauma will remain with Sarajevans, despite the optimism of the young. Most of Sarajevo's tourist features aren't functional, but the old Turkish Quarter market, burgeoning arts scene, and revived nightlife are inspiring. Visitors may rub shoulders with uniformed SFOR officers, camera-wielding journalists, and foreign aid workers, as well as a recent influx of refugees.

> **!** The following outlying areas of Sarajevo are at particular risk for **mines:** Grbavica, Lukavica, Illidža, and Dobrinja.

⚏ ▣ TRANSPORTATION AND PRACTICAL INFORMATION. Buses (☎53 28 74) run from Kranjćevića 9, behind the Holiday Inn at the corner with Halida Kajtaza, to: Dubrovnik (7hr., 2 per day, 40KM); Frankfurt (15hr., 1 per day, 196KM); Split (8hr., 4 per day, 36KM); Vienna (12hr., 1 per day, 81KM); Zagreb (9hr., 3 per day, 51KM). The city's main street is **Maršala Tita.** To reach the **tourist bureau,** Zelenih Beretki 22a, bear right on Maršala Tita past the eternal flame, continue until you see the Catholic church on your left, turn right down Strosmajerova, then left onto Zelenih Beretki. (☎22 07 24. Open M-F 8:30-11:30am and 2-4pm.) Most accommodations owners will register your passport number with the police, but visitors planning to stay longer than one month in Bosnia should register at their embassy.

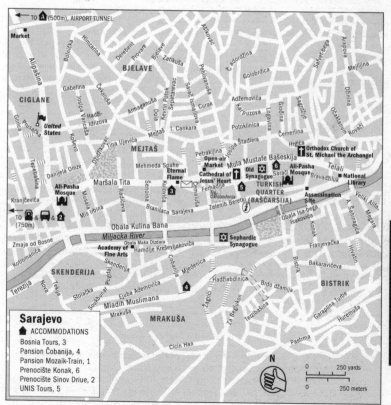

Sarajevo

▲ ACCOMMODATIONS
Bosnia Tours, 3
Pansion Čobanija, 4
Pansion Mozaik-Train, 1
Prenocište Konak, 6
Prenocište Sinov Driue, 2
UNIS Tours, 5

BOSNIA-HERZEGOVINA

SARAJEVO ROSES All along Sarajevo's main thoroughfare, Maršala Tita, the pavement is littered with splash-shaped indentations. These distinctive marks were created by exploding grenades during the city's Serbian siege. Those marks filled in with red concrete are called "Sarajevo Roses" and commemorate civilians killed on that spot by the grenade. The roses are avoided out of respect for the deceased. Even in the most normalized and seamless of Sarajevo's neighborhoods, they are a constant reminder of the war and the thousands of Bosnians lost.

Embassies: Australians should contact the embassy in Vienna (p. 89); **Canada,** Logavina 7 (☎44 79 00; open M-F 8:30am-noon and 1-5pm); citizens of **New Zealand** should contact the embassy in Rome (p. 573); **UK,** Tina Ujevića 8 (☎44 44 29; open M-F 8:30am-5pm); and **US,** Alipašina 43 (☎44 57 00; open M-F 9am-1pm). **Central Profit Bank,** Zelenih Beretki 24, changes money. (Open M-F 8:30am-7pm, Sa 9am-2pm.) Some of the few **ATMs** in Sarajevo are along Maršala Tita 48, a few blocks before the flame.

⌂❐ ACCOMMODATIONS AND FOOD. Relatively cheap **private rooms** (30-50KM) are all over; ask a taxi driver at the station if you arrive late. From Maršala Tita, go left at the eternal flame and walk two blocks past the market to get to **Prenoćište "Konak,"** Mula Mustafe Bašeskije 48, on the right. (☎53 35 06. Reception 24hr. Singles 40KM; doubles 60KM.) Scour the Turkish Quarter for **Čevabdžinića** shops; 3KM buys a *čevapčici* (nicknamed *čevaps*), lamb sausages sheathed in *somun*, Bosnia's elastic flat bread. **Postal code:** 71000.

◪ SIGHTS. The **eternal flame,** where Maršala Tita splits into Ferhadija and Mula Mustafe Bašeskije, has burned on and off since 1945 as a memorial to all Sarajevans who died in World War II; its homage to South Slav unity now seems painfully ironic. Steady reconstruction has hidden most signs of the recent four-year siege within the city center. The glaring **treeline** in the hills marks the front lines; Bosnians trapped in Sarajevo cut down all the available wood for winter heat. From Maršala Tita, walk toward the river to **Obala Kulina Bana** and turn left to find the **National Library,** at the tip of the Turkish Quarter. Once the most beautiful buildings in the city, its remains are now smothered in scaffolding. At the second bridge on Obala Kulina Bana, walking from the National Library toward the center, Serbian terrorist Gavrilo Princip shot the Austrian Archduke Franz Ferdinand on June 28, 1914, triggering the build-up to World War I.

Walk left at the flame on Ferhadija, which becomes Sarači, to find the 16th-century **Gazi Husrev-Bey mosque,** Sarači 12, perhaps Sarajevo's most famous building. The interior is closed for repairs, but prayer continues in the beautiful courtyard. Surrounding the mosque are the low, red-roofed buildingsthat make up Baščaršija, the **Turkish Quarter.** The main Orthodox church, **Saborna,** is also closed, but the old **Orthodox Church of St. Michael the Archangel,** on Mula Mustafe Bašeskije, remains open. (Open daily 7am-6pm.) The 1889 **Cathedral of Jesus' Heart** (Katedrala Srce Isusovo), on Ferhadija, designed by Josipa Vancasa, is the spiritual center for local Catholics. (English mass every Su noon.) The **National Museum** and the **History Museum** are at Zmaja od Bosne 3 and 5, respectively. The former is among the Balkans' most famous museums; the latter used to contain historical relics but now houses modern art, much pertaining to the civil war. (National Museum open Tu-Th and Su 10am-2pm. 5KM, students 1KM. History Museum open M-F 9am-2pm, Sa-Su 9am-1pm. Free.) The 1580 **old synagogue,** on Mula Mustafe Bašeskije, between the Eternal Flame and St. Michael's, houses the **Jewish Museum.**

⌨ ENTERTAINMENT. Every summer in July, the Turkish Quarter hosts the Baš‾aršija Noci (Turkish Nights) featuring open-air music, theater, and film. In late August, the **Sarajevo Film Festival** rolls into theaters throughout the city. (]/fax 66 45 47; www.sff.ba. Box office open in summer M-F 9am-6pm. 4-5KM per film.) Sarajevo also holds the annual **Sarajevska Zima** (Sarajevan Winter;]20 79 48) from

December to January, a celebration of art and culture that persisted even through the siege. **Futura 2002** in late July will feature techno and house. There are always underground events going on; the best way to find out about them is to befriend some young Sarajevans. Since an 11pm curfew was lifted in 1997, the cafes along **Ferhadija** and **Maršala Tita** are flourishing. At Mula Mustafe Bašeskije 5, next to the eternal flame, ▨ **Jazz Bar "Clou"** hosts local bands on F and Sa. (Beer 5km. Open nightly 8:30pm-5am.)

BRITAIN

BRITISH POUNDS

US$1 = UK£0.69	UK£1 = US$1.44
CDN$1 = UK£0.45	UK£1 = CDN$2.23
IR£1 = UK£0.80	UK£1 = IR£1.25
AUS$1 = UK£0.37	UK£1 = AUS$2.71
NZ$1 = UK£0.30	UK£1 = NZ$3.30
ZAR1 = UK£0.08	UK£1 = ZAR11.99
EUR€1 = UK£0.63	UK£1 = EUR€1.58

PHONE CODE	**Country code:** 44. **International dialing prefix:** 00. From outside Britain, dial int'l dialing prefix (see inside back cover) + 44 + city code + local number.

Take pity on "this earth of majesty, this seat of Mars/this other Eden, demi-paradise." After Britain founded modern democracy, led the Industrial Revolution, spread colonies across the globe, and helped stave off Nazi Europe in World War II, a former colony displaced it as the world's economic power, and her once proud offshoots of Ireland and Scotland gained fledgling autonomy. Travelers should be aware that names hold political force. "Great Britain" refers to England, Scotland, and Wales; it's neither accurate nor polite to call a Scot or Welshman "English." The political term "United Kingdom" refers to these nations as well as Northern Ireland; *Let's Go* uses the term "Britain" to refer to England, Scotland, and Wales because of legal and currency distinctions.

At first glance, Britain may not seem quite exotic enough for more than a cursory visit, but look beyond London and allow time for medieval castles, rugged coasts, sweeping greenery, eerie prehistoric monuments, and wild islands. From the rural to the more urbane, Britain's once vibrant, feudal empire belies a rich cultural fountainhead. The sonnets and poetic dramatics of Shakespeare; the economic theories of Adam Smith; the scientific laws of Isaac Newton; the philosophy of John Locke; the literature of Virginia Woolf, Charles Dickens, and George Orwell; even the lyrics of John Lennon and the blonde-obsessed, macabre cinema of Alfred Hitchcock demonstrate that Europe's civilization has been as much influenced by British minds as well as British might. The sun may have set on the Empire, but within her protracted dominion, her majesty and splendor still remain.

For more detailed, exhilarating coverage of Britain and London, pore over *Let's Go: Britain & Ireland 2002* or *Let's Go: London 2002*.

FACTS AND FIGURES

Official Name: United Kingdom of Great Britain and Northern Ireland.

Capital: London.

Major Cities: Manchester, Liverpool, Cardiff, Glasgow, Edinburgh.

Population: 59.5 million.

Land Area: 244,820 sq. km.

Climate: Temperate; summer 55-70°F (12-21°C); winter 36-41°F (2-7°C); often overcast.

Language: English, Welsh, Scottish Gaelic.

Religions: Anglican (45%), Roman Catholic (15%), other (40%).

DISCOVER BRITAIN

London (p. 141) is brimming with cultural wonders—wonders from other cultures, that is. The British and the Victoria and Albert Museums testify to the avarice of Empire. While in the capital, don't miss a trip to the Thames' South Bank, including the Globe Theater to revisit the London of Shakespeare's time. Southwest of London, **Winchester** (p. 176) offers a massive Norman cathedral and celebrates native daughter Jane Austen, while prehistoric **Stonehenge** (p. 177) and the massive cathedral at **Salisbury** (p. 177) are close by. Farther west in the Cornish Coast, **Newquay** (p. 180) is Britain's contribution to surfer culture. Back toward London, **Oxford** (p. 180) and **Cambridge** (p. 185) battle to see who's smarter, while **Stratford-Upon-Avon** (p. 184) is Shakespeare-crazy. Near Oxford, **Blenheim Palace** (p. 182) is almost oppressive in its opulence. Walk from pretty village to pretty village in the **Cotswolds** (p. 183), then hit **Bath** (p. 185), which once offered Roman-style healing baths to the rich and famous of Georgian England. In nearby Wales, cavort with the sheep and commune with nature in **Snowdonia National Park** (p. 199) and enjoy the theaters of **Cardiff** (p. 196). Back in England, **Liverpool** (p. 190) basks in Beatles mania. After exploring industrial **Manchester** (p. 188) and its raucous nightlife, you can escape to the dramatic **Lake District National Park** (p. 193), filled with rugged hills and windswept fells. To munch on haggis and live out your wildest *Braveheart* fantasies, head farther north to Scotland. Enjoy the cultural capitals of **Edinburgh** (p. 202) and **Glasgow** (p. 207), then take the low road to the bonnie, bonnie banks of **Loch Lomond** (p. 213) followed by a journey to the highlands of beautiful **Isle of Skye** (p. 214) and the famed **Loch Ness** (p. 215), where Nessie awaits.

ESSENTIALS

DOCUMENTS AND FORMALITIES

VISAS. EU citizens do not need a visa to enter Britain or Ireland. For visits of less than six months, citizens of Australia, Canada, New Zealand, South Africa, and the US do not need a visa to enter.

EMBASSIES. Foreign embassies for Britain are in **London** (p. 141). For British embassies and high commissions at home: **Australia,** British High Commission, Commonwealth Ave., Yarralumla, Canberra, ACT 2600 (☎ (02) 6270 6666; www.uk.emb.gov.au); **Canada,** British High Commission, 80 Elgin St., Ottawa, K1P 5K7 (☎ 613-237-1530; www.britain-in-canada.org); **Ireland,** British Embassy, 29 Merrion Rd., Ballsbridge, Dublin 4 (☎ (01) 205 3700; www.britishembassy.ie); **New Zealand,** British High Commission, 44 Hill St., Thorndon, Wellington 1 (☎ (04) 472 6049; www.britain.org.nz); **South Africa,** British High Commission, 91 Parliament St., Cape Town 8001 (☎ 021 461 7220); **US,** British Embassy, 3100 Massachusetts Ave. NW, Washington, D.C. 20008 (☎ 202-588-6500; www.britainusa.com).

TRANSPORTATION

BY PLANE. Most flights into Britain that originate outside Europe land at London's Heathrow and Gatwick airports. Flights from Europe also hit: Luton and Stansted, near London; Cardiff, Liverpool, Manchester, Edinburgh, and Glasgow.

BY TRAIN. There is no longer a single national rail company, although the various companies are often still referred to under the umbrella of "British Rail." Prices and schedules often change: find up-to-date information from **National Rail Inquiries** (☎ (08457) 484950), or online at **Railtrack** (www.railtrack.co.uk; no price information). Despite multiple providers, rail service in Britain is extensive (and expensive). The **BritRail Pass,** available to non-British travelers outside Britain, allows unlimited travel in England, Wales, and Scotland (8-day US$265, under 26 US$215; 22-day US$499, under 26 US$355), but must be **bought before traveling to Britain.** The one-year **Young Person's Railcard** (£18), which grants 33% off most fares in addition to discounts on some ferries, is available to those ages 16 to 25, and to full-time students at British universities over age 25, at major British Rail Travel Centres in the UK. **Eurail** is not valid in Britain.

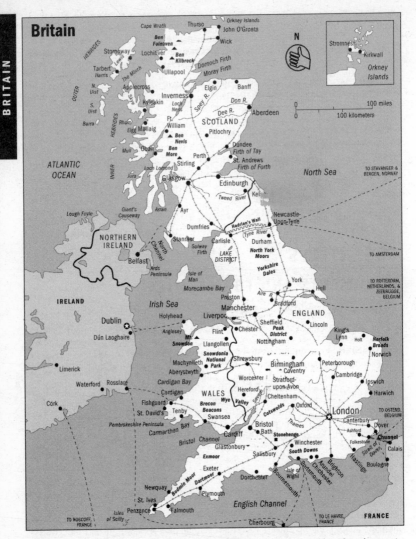

BY BUS. Long-distance coach travel in Britain is more extensive than in most European countries, and is the cheapest travel option. **National Express** (☎(08705) 808080; www.gobycoach.co.uk) is the principal long-distance coach service operator in Britain, although **Scottish Citylink** (☎(08705) 505050) has coverage in Scotland. **Discount Coachcards** are available for seniors over 50, students, and young persons ages 16-25 for £9 and reduce fares on National Express by about 30%. For those planning a lot of coach travel, the **Tourist Trail Pass** offers unlimited travel for a number of days within a given period (2 days out of 3 £49, students, seniors, and children £39; 5 out of 10 £85/£69; 7 out of 21 £120/£94; 14 out of 30 £187/£143).

BY FERRY. Several ferry lines ply the route across the English Channel; the most popular crossing is from Dover to Calais, France. Ask for discounts; ISIC holders can sometimes get student fares, and **Eurail pass-holders** can get reductions and free trips. Book ahead June through August. Other routes between the Continent and England include Bergen, Norway to Lerwick or Newcastle; Esbjerg, Denmark to Harwich; Göteborg, Sweden to Harwich or Newcastle; Hamburg to Harwich or Newcastle; Oostende, Belgium to Ramsgate; and Hook of Holland to Harwich. For information on boats from Wales to Dublin and Rosslare, Ireland, see p. 196; from Scotland to Belfast, see p. 200; from England to the Continent, see p. 170.

BY CAR. You must be 17 and have a license to drive in Britain. The country is covered by a high-speed system of **motorways** ("M-roads") that connect London with major cities around the country. Remember you may not be used to **driving on the left,** or driving a manual transmission (far more common than automatic transmissions in cheap rental cars); enter roundabouts from the left. Roads are generally well maintained, but parking in London is impossible and traffic is slow.

BY BIKE AND BY THUMB. Much of Britain's countryside is well suited for **biking.** Many cities and villages have bike rental shops and maps of local cycle routes; ask at the tourist office. Large-scale Ordnance Survey maps detail the extensive system of long-distance **hiking** paths. Tourist offices and National Park Information Centres can provide extra information about routes. *Let's Go* does not recommend hitch-hiking; it is illegal on M motorways and always risky.

TOURIST SERVICES AND MONEY

EMERGENCY	Police, Ambulance, and Fire: ☎ 199.

TOURIST OFFICES. The **British Tourist Authority** (BTA; www.visitbritain.com) is an umbrella organization coordinating the activities of the separate UK tourist boards outside the UK. **tourist offices** usually stock maps and information regarding sites and accommodations; they will book rooms for a 10% deposit and/or a £1-3 pound fee, which will be deducted from the cost of your stay.

MONEY. The **Pound Sterling** is the main unit of currency in the United Kingdom. It is divided into 100 *pence*, issued in standard denominations of 1p, 2p, 5p, 10p, 20p, 50p, and £1 in coins, and £5, £10, £20, and £50 in notes. Scotland uses a £1 note, and you may see the discontinued £2 coin. Scotland has its own bank notes, which can be used interchangeably with English currency, though you may have difficulty using Scottish £1 notes outside Scotland. Expect to spend anywhere from £15-30 per person per day, depending on where you choose to visit. Accommodations start at about £6 a night for a bed in a **hostel** in rural areas, or £12 per night in a **B&B,** while a basic sit-down meal at a pub costs about £5. London in particular is a budget-buster, with £25-35 a day being the bare minimum for accommodations, food, and transport. **Tips** in restaurants are usually included in the bill, sometimes as a "service charge." If gratuity is not included then you should tip 10-15%. Tipping the barman in pubs is not at all expected, though a waiter or waitress should be tipped. Taxi drivers should receive a 10% tip, and bellhops and chambermaids usually expect somewhere between £1 and £3. Aside from open-air markets, don't expect to barter anywhere else, including hostels, taxis, and tour guides. Britain has a 17.5% **Value Added Tax (VAT),** a sales tax applied to everything except food, books, medicine, and children's clothing. The tax is included within the price indicated—no extra expenses should be added at the register.

COMMUNICATION

MAIL. To send a **postcard** to another European country costs UK£0.36; to send one to any other international destination via airmail costs UK40p. To send a **letter** within Britain costs UK£0.27p. To send one via airmail to another European country (including the Republic of Ireland) costs UK£0.37 (up to 20g), and to a non-European international destination costs UK£0.45 for letters up to 10g, and UK£0.65 for letters weighing 10-20g. Address *Poste Restante* letters to the post office, highlighting the last name (First Name SURNAME, *Poste Restante*, New Bond St. Post Office, Bath BA1 1A5, United Kingdom).

TELEPHONES. Public pay phones in Britain are mostly run by **British Telecom (BT)**. The BT phonecard, available in denominations from £2-20, and are useful purchases, as BT phones are everywhere. Public phones charge a minimum of 10p, and don't accept 1p, 2p, or 5p coins. For directory inquiries, which are free from payphones, call ☎192 in Britain. International direct dial numbers include: **AT&T,** ☎(0800) 013 0011; **British Telecom (Ireland),** ☎(0800) 550144; **Canada Direct,** ☎(0800) 890016; **MCI,** ☎(0800) 890222; **Sprint,** ☎(0800) 890877; and **Telkom South Africa** ☎(0800) 890027.

INTERNET ACCESS. Britain is one of the world's most wired countries, and cybercafes can usually be found in larger cities. They cost £4-6 per hour, but often you can pay only for time used, not for the whole hour. On-line guides to cybercafes in Britain and Ireland that are updated daily include The **Cybercafe Search Engine** (http://cybercaptive.com) and **Cybercafes.com** (www.cybercafes.com).

LANGUAGE. The official languages are English and Welsh. Scottish Gaelic, though unofficial, is spoken in some parts of Scotland along with English.

ACCOMMODATIONS AND CAMPING

Youth hostels in Britain are run by the **Youth Hostels Association (YHA) of England and Wales** and the **Scottish Youth Hostels Association (SYHA)**. Unless noted as "self-catering," the YHA hostels listed in *Let's Go* (not including SYHA ones) offer cooked meals at standard rates—breakfast £3.20, small/standard packed lunch £2.80/£3.65, evening meal £4.15 (or £4.80 for a three-course meal in some hostels), and children's meals (breakfast £1.75, lunch or dinner £2.70). In Britain, a bed in a hostel will cost around £6 in rural areas, £12 in larger cities, and £13-20 in London. For a cozier alternative to impersonal hotel rooms, **B&Bs** and guest houses (often private homes with rooms available to travelers) range from the acceptable to the sublime. You can book B&Bs by calling directly, or by asking the local **tourist office** (TIC) to help you find accommodations; most can also book B&Bs in other towns. Tourist offices usually charge a 10% deposit on the first night's or the entire stay's price, deductible from the amount you pay the B&B proprietor. Often a flat fee of £1-3 is added on. **Campsites** tend to be privately owned, with basic ones costing £3 per person, and posh ones up to £10 per person. It is illegal to camp in national parks, since much of their land is privately owned.

FOOD AND DRINK

British cuisine's lackluster reputation redeems itself in many areas. Britain is largely a nation of carnivores; the best native dishes are roasts—beef, lamb, and Wiltshire hams. And meat isn't just for dinner; the British like their breakfasts meaty and cholesterol-filled. Before you leave the country, you must try a sweet, glorious British pudding. The "ploughman's lunch" consists of cheese, bread, relish, chutney, and tomato. Fish and chips are traditionally drowned in vinegar and salt. Caffs (full meals £5-6) are the British equivalent of US diners. To escape English food, try Chinese, Greek, or especially Indian cuisine. British **"tea"** refers both to a drink and a social ritual. Tea the drink is served strong and milky; if you want it any other way, say so in advance. Tea the social can be a meal unto itself. Afternoon high tea as served in rural Britain includes cooked meats, salad, sandwiches, and pastries. Cream tea, a specialty of Cornwall and Devon, includes toast, shortbread, crumpets, scones, jam, and clotted cream.

HOLIDAYS AND FESTIVALS

Holidays: New Year's Day (Jan. 1); Good Friday (Apr. 13); Easter Sunday and Monday (Apr. 15 and 16); May Day (May 6); Bank holiday (May 27); and Christmas (Dec. 25-26). Scotland also kicks back on Jan. 2 and Aug. 5 (both bank holidays).

FLAKES AND SMARTIES British food has character (of one sort or another), and the traditional menu is a mad hodgepodge of candy, crisps, yeasts, and squashes. Britain has a greater variety of **candy** for sale than most countries, including Flake by Cadbury, Crunchies (honeycombed magic), and the ever-popular Smarties. Watch out for the orange ones—they're made of orange chocolate. Potato chips, or **crisps** as they are known in England, come in a range of flavors including Prawn Cocktail, Beef, Chicken, and Fruit 'n' Spice. All this sugar and salt can be washed down with the pineapple-and-grapefruit-flavored soda Lilt or a can of Ribena, a red currant syrup which has to be diluted with water. Ribena belongs to a family of drinks known as **squash,** all of which are diluted before consumption. But the food that expatriate Britons miss most is **Marmite,** a yeast extract spread on bread or toast. If you weren't fed Marmite as a baby, you'll never appreciate it; most babies don't either.

Festivals: The largest festival in the world is the **Edinburgh International Festival** (Aug. 11-31 in 2002); also highly recommended is the **Fringe Festival** Aug. 4-26 in 2002. Manchester's Gay Village hosts **Mardi Gras** (late Aug.). Muddy fun abounds at the **Glastonbury Festival. Highland Games** have caber-tossing fun in Edinburgh (mid-July).

ENGLAND

In a land where the staid and stately once prevailed, where "public" school means "private," and where royalty have left their mark in almost every nook, England's 20th-century image as the aging seat of a dying empire has turned upside down in recent years. Conservatism has been given the boot in two successive landslide elections, a wild profusion of the avant-garde has emerged from hallowed academic halls, and—shock! horror! dismay!—even the Queen must pay taxes on her vast holdings. More than ever, England is embracing its sizable immigrant communities and allowing the class boat to be rocked. But traditionalists can rest easy; for all the moving and shaking in the large metropolis, around the corner there are handfuls of quaint countryside towns, dozens of picturesque castles, and scores of comforting cups of tea.

LONDON ☎ 020

The crown jewel of Britain's sceptered isle, London lives to a beat all its own, where all partake of the hybrid fruits of a thousand cultural cross-fertilizations. Here is where Jinnah and Gandhi studied; where the Mayflower set sail and Thomas Paine wrote *The Rights of Man;* where Voltaire and Marx sought refuge from persecution; where thousands arrive daily to seek a better future. The world's first industrial city, London turned postmodern when her rivals were still modernizing. To the visitor, London offers a dizzying array of choices: tea at the Ritz or chilling in the Fridge; Leonardo at the National or Damian at Tate Modern; Rossini at the Royal Opera or Les Mis at the Palace; Bond Street couture or Covent Garden cutting-edge.

Such a city deserves an entire book—*Let's Go: London 2002* is just the ticket.

✈ INTERCITY TRANSPORTATION

Flights: Heathrow (☎(0870) 000 0123) is London's main airport; **Underground** (Piccadilly Line) heads to central London (40-60min.; every 4-5min.; £3.50, under 16 £1.50); the **Heathrow Express** train shuttles to Paddington station (☎(0845) 600 1515; 15min., every 15min.; £12, return £22). From **Gatwick Airport** (☎(0870) 000 2468), the **Gatwick Express** heads to Victoria (☎(0870) 0002 468; 30-35min.; every 15min. before midnight, every hr. midnight-5am; £10.50, return £20.).

Trains: London has 8 major stations: **Charing Cross** (serves south England); **Euston** (the north and northwest); **King's Cross** (the north and northeast); **Liverpool St.** (East Anglia); **Paddington** (the west); **St. Pancras** (Midlands and northwest); **Victoria** (the south); and **Waterloo** (the south, southwest and the Continent). All stations are linked by the Underground. Get info at station ticket office or from **National Rail Inquiries Line** (☎(08457) 484950; www.britrail.com).

Buses: Long-distance buses (known as coaches in the UK) arrive in London at **Victoria Coach Station,** 164 Buckingham Palace Rd. (Tube: Victoria); some services stop at nearby **Eccleston Bridge,** behind Victoria train station.

✈ ORIENTATION

The heart of London is the vaguely defined **West End,** which stretches east from Park Lane to Kingsway and south from Oxford St. to the River Thames; within this area you'll find the shopping streets around **Oxford Circus,** aristocratic **Mayfair,** the bars and clubs of **Soho,** the street performers and boutiques of **Covent Garden,** and the grandeur of **Trafalgar Square.** East of the West End, you'll pass legalist **Holborn** before hitting the ancient **City of London** (a.k.a. "the City"), site of the original Roman settlement and home to St. Paul's Cathedral and the Tower of London. The City's eastern border jostles the ethnically diverse, working-class **East End.**

Westminster extends south of Trafalgar Sq. along the Thames; this is the heart of royal and political London, with the Houses of Parliament, Buckingham Palace, and Westminster Abbey; farther west lies artsy, prosperous **Chelsea.** Across the river from Westminster and the West End, the **South Bank** has an incredible variety of entertainment and museums, from Shakespeare's Globe to the Tate Modern. The enormous space of **Hyde Park** lies to the west of the West End; along its southern border crowd chi-chi **Knightsbridge,** home to Harrods and Harvey Nicks, and posh **Kensington.** North of Hyde Park are media-infested **Notting Hill** and B&B-filled **Bayswater.** Bayswater, Mayfair, and **Marylebone** meet at Marble Arch, on Hyde Park's northeast corner; from here, Marylebone stretches west to meet bookish **Bloomsbury,** north of Soho and Holborn. Further from the center, **Camden Town, Islington, Hampstead,** and **Highgate** lie some way to the north of Bloomsbury and the City.

A good street atlas is essential for efficient navigation; the best is *London A to Z,* available at all bookstores and many newsagents and souvenir stores.

▤ LOCAL TRANSPORTATION

Public Transportation: Run by Transport for London (TfL; 24hr. info and assistance ☎7222 1234; www.transportforlondon.gov.uk). Pick up free maps at Tube stations. Pick up free maps and guides at TfL **Information Centres** (look for the lower-case "i" logo on signs) at the following Tube stations: Euston, Victoria, King's Cross, Liverpool St., Oxford Circus, Picadilly St., James's Park, and Heathrow Terminals 1, 2, 3.

Underground: The Underground (a.k.a. Tube) networks is divided into 6 concentric zones; fares depend on the number of zones crossed. Buy your ticket before you board and pass it through automatic gates at both ends of your journey. A one-way trip in Zone 1 costs £1.50. The Tube runs approx. 5:30am-12:30am, depending on the line.

Buses: Divided into 4 zones; zones 1-3 are identical to the Tube zones. Single £0.70-1 depending on the zone. Regular buses run 6am-midnight or so, after which a limited network of **Night Buses** (prefixed by "N") takes over; fares for Night Buses are £1.50 for Zone 1, elsewhere £1.

Passes: The **Travelcard** is valid for travel on all TfL services; available in daily, weekend, weekly, monthly, and annual periods. 1-Day travelcard from £4 (Zones 1-2). All passes expire 4:30am the morning after their printed expiry date (so a 1-day pass works for a post-clubbing bus home).

Licensed Taxicabs: A lit "taxi" sign on the roof signals availability. Expensive, but drivers know their stuff. For pick-up, call **Computer Cabs** (☎7286 0286), £1.20 extra charge.

7 PRACTICAL INFORMATION

TOURIST, FINANCIAL, AND LOCAL SERVICES

Tourist Offices: Britain Visitor Centre (www.visitbritain.com), 1 Regent St. Tube: Oxford Circus. Ideal for travelers headed beyond London. Open M 9:30am-6:30pm, Tu-F 9am-6:30pm, Sa-Su 10am-4pm. **London Visitor Centres** (www.londontouristboard.com) are run by the London Tourist Board. Books accommodations for £5; call ☎ 7932 2020. Locations include: **Heathrow Terminals 1, 2, 3,** in the Tube station (Open Oct-Aug. daily 8am-6pm; Sept. M-Sa 9am-7pm and Su 8am-6pm); **Liverpool Street,** in the Tube station (Open June-Sept. M-Sa 8am-7pm, Su 8am-6pm; Oct.-May daily 8am-6pm); **Victoria Station** (Open Easter-Sept. M-Sa 8am-8pm, Su 8am-6pm; Oct.-Easter daily 8am-6pm); **Waterloo International,** Arrivals hall (Open daily 8:30am-10:30pm.)

Embassies: Australia, Australia House, Strand (☎ 7379 4334). Tube: Temple. Open 9:30am-3:30pm. **Canada,** MacDonald House, 1 Grosvenor Sq. (☎ 7258 6600). Tube: Bond St. Open 8:30am-5pm. **Ireland,** 17 Grosvenor Pl. (☎ 7235 2171). Tube: Hyde Park Corner. Open M-F 9:30am-4:30pm. **New Zealand,** New Zealand House, 80 Haymarket (☎ 7930 8422). Tube: Leicester Sq. Open M-F 10am-noon and 2-4pm. **South Africa,** South Africa House, Trafalgar Sq. (☎ 7451 7299). Tube: Charing Cross. Open M-F 8:45am-12:45pm. **US,** 24 Grosvenor Sq. (☎ 7499 9900). Tube: Bond St. Open M-F 8:30am-12:30pm and 2-5pm. Phones answered 24hr.

Currency Exchange: The best rates are found at banks, such as **Barclays, HSBC, Lloyd's and National Westminster** (NatWest). Most banks open M-F 9:30am-4:30pm.

American Express: Offices throughout London; call ☎ (0800) 521313 for locations.

Gay and Lesbian Services: London Lesbian and Gay Switchboard (☎ 7837 7324). 24hr. advice and support service.

EMERGENCY AND COMMUNICATIONS

Emergency: Medical, Police, and **Fire** ☎ 999. no coins required.

Hospitals: For non-life threatening injuries, you can be treated at no charge in the Accidents and Emergency (A&E) ward of a hospital. The following have 24hr. walk-in A&E (casualty) departments: **Royal London Hospital,** Whitechapel Rd. (☎ 7377 7000. Tube: Whitechapel); **Royal Free,** Pond St. (☎ 7794 0500. Tube: Belsize Park or Rail: Hampstead Heath); **St. Mary's,** Praed St. (☎ 7725 6666. Tube: Paddington); **St. Thomas's,** Lambeth Palace Rd. (☎ 7928 9292. Tube: Waterloo); and **University College Hospital,** Grafton Way (☎ 7387 9300; Tube: Warren St.).

Chemists (Pharmacies): Most chemists keep standard store hours (approx. M-Sa 9:30am-5:30pm). Late-night chemists are rare. **Zafash Pharmacy,** 233 Old Brompton Rd. (☎ 7373 2798. Tube: Earls Court), is open 24hr. **Bliss Chemists,** 5-6 Marble Arch (☎ 7723 6116. Tube: Marble Arch). Open daily 9am-midnight.

Police: London is covered by two police forces: the **City of London Police** (☎ 7601 2222) and the **Metropolitan Police** (☎ 7230 1212). The main central-London station is **West End Central,** 27 Savile Row (☎ 7437 1212). Tube: Oxford Circus. Open 24hr.

Internet Access: Cybercafes punctuate London. ▨ **easyEverything** (☎ 7907 7800; www.easyeverything.com) cybercafes open 24hr. From £1 per hr. Locations include 9-13 Wilson Rd, directly opposite Victoria Station.

Post Office: Post offices are everywhere; call ☎ (08457) 740740 for locations. When sending mail to London, be sure to include the full post code, since London has 7 King's Roads, 8 Queen's Roads, and 2 Mandela Streets. The largest office is the **Trafalgar Square Post Office,** 24-28 William IV St., WC2N 4DL (☎ 7484 9304; Tube: Charing Cross). All mail sent *Poste Restante* or general delivery to unspecified post offices ends up here. Open M-Th and Sa 8am-8pm, F 8:30am-8pm.

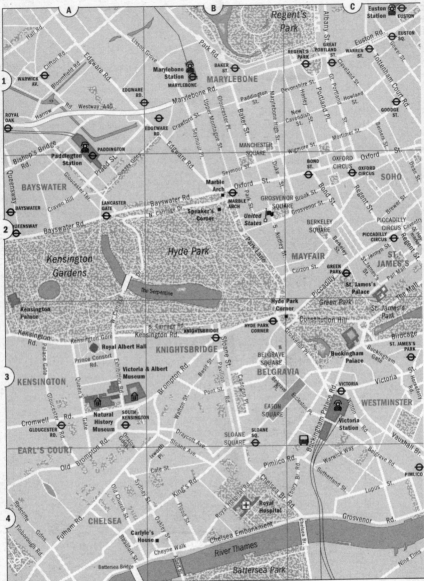

Central London: Major Street Finder

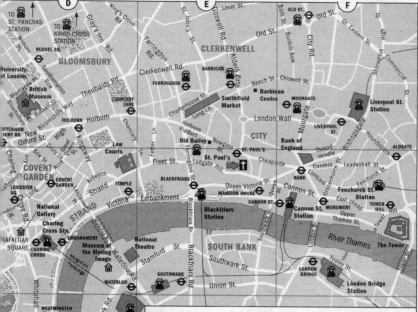

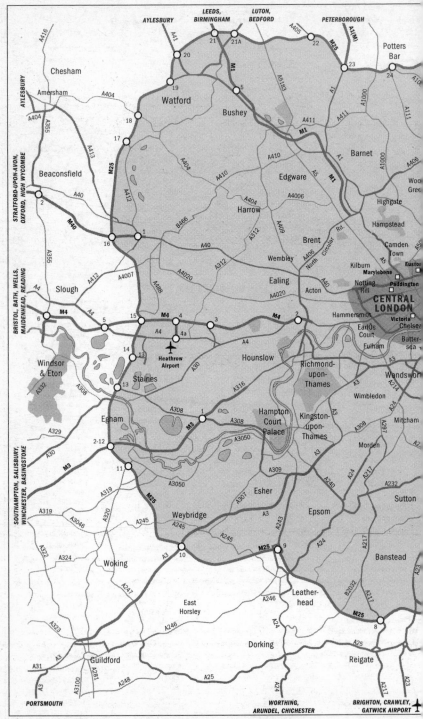

Greater London Area

○ 9 Motorway Interchanges

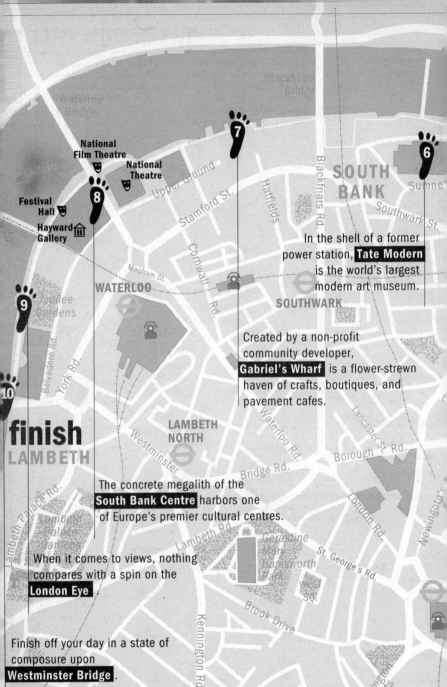

National Film Theatre

National Theatre

7

Upper Ground

SOUTH BANK

6

Sumne

Festival Hall

8

Hayward Gallery

Stamford St.

Hatfields

Blackfriars Rd.

Southwark St.

Cornwall Rd.

In the shell of a former power station, **Tate Modern** is the world's largest modern art museum.

9

Jubilee Gardens

Mapham St.

WATERLOO

SOUTHWARK

Belvedere Rd.

York Rd.

Created by a non-profit community developer, **Gabriel's Wharf** is a flower-strewn haven of crafts, boutiques, and pavement cafes.

Lancaster St. Rd.

10

LAMBETH NORTH

Borough Rd.

London Rd.

Newington

finish
LAMBETH

Westminster

Waterloo Rd.

Bridge Rd.

The concrete megalith of the **South Bank Centre** harbors one of Europe's premier cultural centres.

Lambeth Palace Rd.

Lambeth Palace Gardens

Lambeth Rd.

Geraldine Mary Harmsworth Park

St. George's Rd.

When it comes to views, nothing compares with a spin on the **London Eye**

Kennington Rd.

Brook Drive

Newington Butts

Finish off your day in a state of composure upon **Westminster Bridge**.

If you're not exhausted by now, continue over the river for Parliament, Big Ben, Westminster Abbey, and Buckingham Palace.

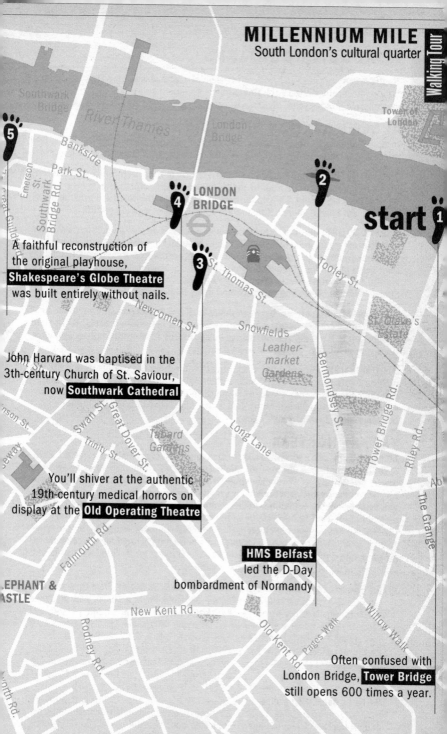

MILLENNIUM MILE
South London's cultural quarter

Walking Tour

Tower of London

River Thames

Southwark Bridge

Bankside

Park St.

Emerson St.

Southwark Bridge Rd.

Great Guildhall

5

London Bridge

4 LONDON BRIDGE

2

start **1**

Tooley St.

St. Olave's Estate

St. Thomas St.

3

Newcomen St.

A faithful reconstruction of the original playhouse, **Shakespeare's Globe Theatre** was built entirely without nails.

John Harvard was baptised in the 3th-century Church of St. Saviour, now **Southwark Cathedral**

Snowfields

Leather-market Gardens

Bermondsey St.

Tower Bridge Rd.

Riley St.

Swan St.

Great Dover St.

Trinity St.

Tabard Gardens

Long Lane

The Grange

Ab

nson St.

geway

You'll shiver at the authentic 19th-century medical horrors on display at the **Old Operating Theatre**

HMS Belfast led the D-Day bombardment of Normandy

Falmouth Rd.

:EPHANT & :ASTLE

New Kent Rd.

Rodney Rd.

Old Kent Rd.

Pages Walk

Willow Walk

orth Rd.

Often confused with London Bridge, **Tower Bridge** still opens 600 times a year.

ACCOMMODATIONS

No matter where you plan to stay, it is essential to **plan ahead,** especially in summer; London accommodations are almost always booked solid. Be sure to check the cancellation policy before handing over the deposit; some are non-refundable.

ACCOMMODATION DISTRICTS

Budget accommodations lie all over London, but most are concentrated in a few areas; if you land without a reservation, these are the best places to start hunting.

WESTMINSTER. Quiet **Pimlico,** south of Victoria station, is full of budget hotels; the highest concentration is along **Belgrave Road.** Places tend to be nicer the further you go from the station. Though fairly close to major sights such as Parliament and Buckingham Palace, there's little in the way of restaurants and nightlife.

EARL'S COURT. West of Kensington, this area feeds on the budget tourism; some streets seem populated solely by B&Bs and hostels. The area has a vibrant gay and lesbian population and is also tremendously popular with Aussie travelers cooling their heels in London (in the 1970s, it earned the nickname "Kangaroo Valley"). Be careful at night and be wary of guides trying to lead you from the station to a hostel. Some B&Bs conceal grimy rooms behind fancy lobbies; always ask to see a room.

BAYSWATER. The streets between **Queensway** and **Paddington** station house London's highest concentration of cheap sleeps, with countless hostels, B&Bs, and budget hotels. It's fairly central, with plenty of nearby restaurants, but accommodations vary in quality—be sure to see a room first.

BLOOMSBURY. Bloomsbury is the best-located accommodation district for nightlife, with dozens of B&Bs and student halls within striking distance of Soho and the British Museum. Plenty of cheap restaurants add to the allure of this quiet, academic neighborhood. Many B&Bs are on busy roads. The neighborhood becomes seedy toward King's Cross.

YHA/HI HOSTELS

London hostels are not always able to accommodate every written request for reservations, much less on-the-spot inquiries, but they frequently hold a few beds available—it's always worth checking. To secure a place, show up as early as possible, or call in advance and book with a credit card. In order to stay at YHA hostels, you usually must be a member (see Accommodations and Camping, p. 140). **Linens** are included at all London hostels, but **towels** are not; buy one from reception (£3.50). All hostels have well-equipped kitchens, laundry facilities, and luggage storage in addition to in-room **lockers** (padlock required); most have a **cafeteria** for cheap evening meals (£5). YHA hostels also sell discount tickets to theaters and major attractions. None have **lockouts** or **curfews.**

🛏 **YHA Hampstead Heath,** 4 Wellgarth Rd., NW11 (☎ 8458 9054). From Golders Green Tube (Zone 3), turn left onto North End Rd.; Wellgarth Rd. is a 10min. walk up on the left. **Internet,** currency exchange. Breakfast included. Reception 24hr. 4- to 6-bed dorms £19.90; doubles £46; family (at least one child under 18) £36; triples £67, £53; quads £82, £51; quints £101, £88; 6-person £121, £102. AmEx/MC/V.

YHA City of London, 36 Carter Ln., EC4 (☎ 7236 4965). Tube: St. Paul's. In the frescoed former buildings of St. Paul's Choir School, close to the cathedral. **Internet.** Secure luggage storage. English breakfast included. Reception 7am-11pm. Dorms £21.15-24.70, under 18 £18.90-21; private rooms £23.70-£138, families £41-123. MC/V.

YHA Earl's Court, 38 Bolton Gdns., SW5 (☎ 7373 7083). Tube: Earl's Court. Rambling Victorian townhouse, more casual than most YHAs. Ongoing refurbishment. Single-sex dorms. Reserve 1 month ahead. Prepacked continental breakfast £3.30. Dorms £18.50, under 18 £16.50; twins (breakfast included) £51. AmEx/MC/V.

YHA Holland House, Holland Walk, W8 (☎ 7937 0748). Tube: High St. Kensington or Holland Park. On the edge of Holland Park, accommodation is split between a 17th-century mansion and a 1970s unit; both with 12-20 bunk rooms. Book 1 month ahead in summer. Breakfast included. £20.50, under 18 £18.50. AmEx/MC/V.

PRIVATE HOSTELS

Private hostels don't require a YHA/HI membership, and are generally much cheaper. Alternately, standards vary widely; generally, private hostels are less well-maintained than YHA hostels, and sometimes don't have single-sex rooms.

■ **The Generator,** Compton Pl. WC1, off 37 Tavistock Pl. Tube: Russell Square. (☎ 7388 7666). Looks like it's straight out of *Blade Runner*. Basement dorms with lockers and military-style bathrooms. Late bar, cafeteria, Internet. No noise after 9pm. Reserve ahead for weekends. Dorms £15-22.50; singles £36.50-41; twins £46-53. MC/V.

■ **Hyde Park Hostel,** 2-6 Inverness Terr., W2 (☎ 7229 5101). Tube: Queensway. Women's and mixed dorms have little room, but smaller rooms are more spacious. Internet, bar, cafeteria, kitchen, laundry, lounge, luggage room. Continental breakfast included. Ages 16-35 only. Reserve 2 weeks ahead. Dorms £10-17.50; twins £40-45. MC/V.

■ **Indian YMCA,** 41 Fitzroy Sq., W1 (☎ 7387 0411). Tube: Warren St. Standard rooms, with desk, phone, and institutional shared bathrooms, but price includes continental breakfast and Indian dinner. Reservations essential. Dorms £20; singles £33; doubles £46, with bath £52. AmEx/MC/V.

Hyde Park Inn, 48-50 Inverness Terr., W2 (☎ 7229 0000). Very cheap and fairly cheerful. Tube: Bayswater. Internet, kitchen, laundry, lockers (£1 per day), luggage store (£1.50 per bag per day). Continental breakfast included. £10 key and linen deposit. Dorms £9-19; singles £29-32; double/twins £18-21. MC/V (2.5% surcharge).

STUDENT RESIDENCE HALLS

The best accommodation deals in town are in university residence halls, which often rent out rooms over the summer and Easter vacations for little more than the price of a hostel bed. Don't expect luxury, but rooms are generally clean and the halls often have extra facilities such as game rooms and sports facilities.

■ **High Holborn Residence,** 178 High Holborn, WC1 (☎ 7379 5589). Tube: Holborn. Comfortable modern student residence. Flats of 4-5 rooms, with phone, sharing kitchen and bathroom. Laundry. Continental breakfast included. Open mid-June to late Sept. Singles £28-35; twins £47-57, with bath £57-67; triples with bath £67-77. MC/V.

Carr-Saunders Hall, 18-24 Fitzroy St., W1 (☎ 7580 6338). Tube: Warren St. Rooms are larger than most student halls and have sink and phone. Breakfast on the panoramic roof terrace. Reserve 6-8 weeks ahead July-Aug. Open Easter and mid-June to mid-Sept. English breakfast included. Singles £23.50-27; twins £37-45, with bath £42-50. MC/V.

Commonwealth Hall, 1-11 Cartwright Gardens, WC1 (☎ 7685 3500). Tube: Russell Sq. Post-war block with 400 basic student singles; unbeatable value. Open Easter and mid-June to mid-Sept. Reserve 2 months ahead July-Aug.; no walk-ins. English breakfast included. Singles £22, with dinner £26; students £19 (dinner included). MC/V.

Wellington Hall, 71 Vincent Sq. SW1 (☎ 7834 4740). Tube: Victoria. Edwardian building overlooking Westminster School's playing fields. TV lounge, bar and laundry. Breakfast included. Open Easter and mid-June to mid-Sept. Singles £27.50; twins £42.

BED AND BREAKFASTS

WESTMINSTER

■ **Luna Simone Hotel,** 47/49 Belgrave Rd., SW1 (☎ 7834 5897). Tube: Victoria. Stuccoed Victorian façade conceals ultra-modern rooms with TV, phone, kettle, and hairdryer. English breakfast. Singles £35-40, with bath £35-45; doubles £50-65, £60-80; triples with bath £80-100. Discount for longer stays in the low season. MC/V.

▨ **Morgan House,** 120 Ebury St., SW1 (☎7730 2384). Tube: Victoria. 11 beautifully kept rooms, with TVs, kettles, phones, and some fireplaces. English breakfast. Singles £42, with bath £65; doubles £62, £80; quads with bath £120. MC/V.

Georgian House Hotel, 35 St. George's Drive, SW1 (☎7834 1438). Tube: Victoria. Rooms are large with TV, phone, hairdryer, kettle. English breakfast. Singles £36; doubles £42; triples £69; quads with bath £90; quints with bath £96. MC/V.

Surtees Hotel, 94 Warwick Way, SW1 (☎7834 7163). Tube: Victoria. Doubles and triples are on the small side but bright and nicely decorated. English breakfast. Singles £30, with bath £50; doubles £55, £65; triples £70, £80; quad £80, £90. MC/V.

KENSINGTON AND EARL'S COURT

▨ **Vicarage Private Hotel,** 10 Vicarage Gate, W8 (☎7229 4030). Tube: High St. Kensington. Beautifully kept house with ornate hallways, TV lounge, and superb rooms: cast-iron beds, solid wood furnishings, lovely drapes, kettle and hairdryer. English breakfast. Singles £45; doubles £74, with bath £98; triples £90; quads £98. No credit cards.

Abbey House Hotel, 11 Vicarage Gate, W8 (☎7727 2594). Tube: High St. Kensington. Spacious pastel rooms with TV, desk, and sink. Very helpful staff. English breakfast. Singles £45; doubles £74; triples £90; quads £100. No credit cards.

Beaver Hotel, 57-59 Philbeach Gdns., W14 (☎7373 4553). Tube: Earl's Court. Displays unusual attention to detail. Spotless bathrooms, many with bathtub. English breakfast. Singles £40, with bath £60; doubles with bath £85; triples with bath £99. AmEx/MC/V.

BAYSWATER

▨ **Admiral Hotel,** 143 Sussex Gdns., W2 (☎7723 7309). Tube: Paddington. Beautifully kept. 19 summery, non-smoking rooms with bathroom, TV, and kettle. Singles £40-48; doubles £55-70; triples £75-90; quads £88-100; quints £92-115. MC/V.

▨ **Hyde Park Rooms Hotel,** 137 Sussex Gdns., W2 (☎7723 0225). Tube: Paddington. White rooms with fluorescent-colored bedspreads all have sink and TV. Reserve 2 weeks ahead in summer. Singles £30, with bath £40; doubles £40-45, £50-55; triples £60, £72; quads £80, £96. AmEx/MC/V (5% surcharge).

Barry House Hotel, 12 Sussex Pl., W2 (☎7723 7340). Tube: Paddington. Very bright rooms, most with en suite bathrooms. Singles £32-38, with bath £48-50; doubles £78, £65; triples £92, £75; quads £114, £99. AmEx/MC/V (3% surcharge).

Garden Court Hotel, 30-31 Kensington Gdns. Sq., W2 (☎7229 2553). Tube: Bayswater. Reception feels like a Tuscan resort, but rooms are solidly English B&B. English breakfast. Singles £39, with bath £58; doubles £58, £88; triples £72, £99. MC/V.

BLOOMSBURY

▨ **Crescent Hotel,** 49-50 Cartwright Gdns., WC1 (☎7387 1515). Tube: Russell Sq. Real family-run atmosphere. All rooms have TV, kettle, and phone. Singles £43, with shower £48, with bath £70; doubles with bath £82; triples with bath £93; quads with bath £105. More for one night stays, cheaper for longer stays. MC/V.

▨ **Arosfa Hotel,** 83 Gower St., WC1 (☎7636 2115). Tube: Warren St. Lives up to its name, which means "place to rest". English breakfast. Singles £37; doubles £50, with bath £66; triples £68, £79; quad with bath £92. MC/V (2% surcharge).

George Hotel, 58-60 Cartwright Gdns., WC1 (☎7387 8777). Tube: Russell Sq. Meticulous rooms with TV, kettle, phone, and sink. Singles £50, with shower £65, and with WC £75; doubles £69.50, £77, £90; triples £83, £91.50, £105; quads £95. MC/V.

Hotel Ibis Euston, 3 Cardington St., NW1 (☎7304 7712). Tube: Euston. Spacious, modern rooms. Cable TV, phone, desk, and bathroom. Snack bar. Restaurant serves dinner 6-10:30pm. Breakfast £4.50. Doubles and twins £70. MC/V.

Langland Hotel, 29-31 Gower St., WC1 (☎7636 5801). Tube: Goodge St. Family atmosphere, with sparkling bathrooms. Rooms have TV, kettle, and fan. Singles £40, with bath £55; doubles £50, £75; triples £70, £90; quads £90, £110. AmEx/MC/V.

◘ FOOD AND PUBS

Forget stale stereotypes of food: in terms of quality and choice, London's restaurants offer a gastronomic experience as diverse, stylish, and satisfying as you'll find anywhere on the planet—until you see the bill. That said, it *is* possible to eat cheaply and well in London. The trick is knowing where and when to eat. Lunchtime and early-evening **special offers** make it possible to dine in style and stay on budget, while **pub grub** offers hearty food for lunch and occasionally dinner. Many of the best budget meals are found in the amazing variety of **ethnic restaurants.** For the best, head to the source: Whitechapel for Bengali *baltis*, Islington for Turkish *meze*, Marylebone for Lebanese *shwarma*, and Soho for Cantonese *dim sum*.

AFTERNOON TEA

Afternoon tea is perhaps the high point of English cuisine. A social ritual as much as a meal, at its best it involves a long afternoon of sandwiches, scones, pastries, tinkling china, and restrained conversation. The main attraction of afternoon tea today is the chance to lounge in sumptuous surroundings that at any other time would be beyond all but a Sultan's budget. Note that you'll often need to book in advance, especially for weekends, while many hotels have a strict dress code.

The Lanesborough, Hyde Park Corner (☎ 7259 5599). Tube: Hyde Park Corner. The Regency's interior out-ritzes The Ritz. Set tea £22.50; champagne tea £26.50. A la cart includes scones with jam and clotted cream (£6.50). Minimum £9.50 per person.

The Ritz, Piccadilly (☎ 7493 8181). Tube: Green Park. The world's most famous tea. Reserve at least 1 month ahead for the weekday sittings, 3 months for weekends; alternatively, skip lunch and arrive at noon for an early tea. No jeans or trainers; jacket and tie preferred for men. Sittings daily 3:30 and 5pm. Set tea £27.

RESTAURANTS AND PUBS

THE WEST END

▨ busaba eathai, 106-110 Wardour St. Tube: Tottenham Court Rd. Wildly popular Thai eatery. Get in line for great food (£5-8) at shared square tables in a cozy setting. Open M-Th noon-11pm, F-Sa noon-11:30pm, Su noon-10pm.

Bar Italia, 22 Frith St. Tube: Tottenham Court Rd. A fixture of the late-night Soho scene. You won't find anything stronger than an espresso here (£1.60), but it's still *the* place for a post-club panini (£3.50-5). Open 24hr., except M 3-7am.

Wong Kei, 41-43 Wardour St. Tube: Piccadilly Circus. Renovations have removed much of this Chinatown stalwart's kitschy charm, but little else has changed: the waiters remain as famously curt as ever, and prices are rock-bottom. Won-ton noodle soup £2.50; roast duck and rice £3.50. Open daily noon-11:30pm. Cash only.

HOLBORN AND CLERKENWELL

▨ Bleeding Heart Tavern, corner of Greville St. and Bleeding Heart Yard. Tube: Farringdon. Light, laid-back upstairs pub and cozy restaurant below, where thick tablecloths, fresh roses, and candles make a romantic backdrop to hearty English fare. Two courses for £10. 5-7:30pm. Tavern open M-F 11am-11pm.

▨ Ye Olde Cheshire Cheese, Wine Office Ct. Tube: Blackfriars. Dark labyrinth of oak-panelled rooms dating from 1667; one-time haunt of Johnson, Dickens, and Mark Twain. Multiple bars and restaurants with traditional English food. Open M-F 11:30am-11pm, Sa 11:30am-3pm and 5:30-11pm, Su noon-3pm. Food M-F noon-9:30pm, Sa noon-2:30pm and 6-9:30pm, Su noon-2:30pm. AmEx/MC/V.

Tinseltown 24-Hour Diner, 44-46 St. John St. Tube: Farringdon. Cavernous underground haven for pre- and post-clubbers. Food ranges from burgers (£5.50) to full-on shakes with added chocolate bar (£3.50). Open 24hr.

THE CITY OF LONDON

☒ **Futures,** 8 Botolph Alley, off Botolph Ln. Tube: Monument. Suits besiege this tiny take-away for a changing variety of vegetarian dishes (£2-4). Open M-F 7:30-10am and 11:30am-3pm. **Branch** in Exchange Sq. (behind Liverpool St).

The Place Below, St. Mary-le-Bow. Tube: St. Paul's. In the 11th-century crypt of St. Mary-le-Bow church, vegetarian dishes provide salvation for the weary traveler. Salads and hot dishes £6.50-7.50, sandwiches £5; take-away £1-2 less (plenty of benches in the churchyard). Open M-F 7:30am-4pm, lunch 11:30am-2:30pm.

Simpson's, Ball Court, off 38½ Cornhill. Tube: Bank. "Established 1757" says the sign on the alley leading to this pub. Different rooms divide the classes: drinkers populate the basement wine bar (sandwiches £2-4) and ground-floor bar, diners the ground-floor and upstairs restaurants (main dishes £6-7). Open M-F 11:30am-3pm.

SOUTH BANK

☒ **Tas,** 72 Borough High St. (Tube: London Bridge) and 33 The Cut (Tube: Waterloo). Stylish and affordable Turkish food. Main courses £6-8. Reservations essential. Open M-Sa 12:30-11:30pm, Su 12:30-10:30pm.

Gourmet Pizza Co., Gabriel's Wharf, 56 Upper Ground. Tube: Southwark. On the embankment, this adventurous pizzeria offers the best-value riverside dining in town. Pizza £6-9. Open M-Sa noon-11pm.

WESTMINSTER

☒ **Jenny Lo's Teahouse,** 14 Eccleston St. Tube: Victoria. Stripped-down Chinese fare at communal tables. Teas (from £0.85), blended in-house. Open M-F 11:30am-3pm and 6-10pm, Sa noon-3pm and 6-10pm. £5 minimum. Cash only.

Red Lion, 48 Parliament St. Tube: Westminster. The MPs' hangout. A "division bell" alerts MPs to drink up when a vote is about to be taken. Dishes £3-6. Open M-Sa 11am-11pm, Su noon-7pm; food served daily noon-3pm.

KNIGHTSBRIDGE, KENSINGTON, AND EARL'S COURT

☒ **Stockpot,** 6 Basil St. Tube: Knightsbridge. No-frills pinewood interior is the setting for bargains like beef stroganoff (£3.65) and grilled lamb cutlets (£4.30). 2-course set menu £3.90. Open M-Sa 7:30am-11pm, Su noon-10:30pm.

☒ **The Troubadour,** 265 Old Brompton Rd. Tube: Earl's Court. Cozy old-fashioned interior festooned with curious and a shady rear garden. Sandwich platters £4-5; hot specials £5-10. Poetry and folk-music nights. Open daily 9am-midnight.

Raison d'Être, 18 Bute St. Tube: South Kensington. Catering to the local French community with a bewildering range of filled *baguettes* (£2.20-5) and *salades* (£3.50-4.70). Open M-F 8am-6pm, Sa 9:30am-4pm. Cash only.

NOTTING HILL AND BAYSWATER

☒ **George's Portobello Fish Bar,** 329 Portobello Rd. Tube: Ladbroke Grove. Choose your piece from the recently fried fillets on display or ask them to rustle up a new one (£4-5), add a generous helping of chunky chips (£1), and wolf it down outside (no inside seating). Open Su-F 11am-midnight, Sa 11am-9pm. Cash only.

☒ **Royal China,** 13 Queensway Tube: Bayswater. London's best *dim sum* (£2-3 per dish), served M-Sa noon-5pm, Su 11am-5pm; arrive early or expect to wait up to 45min. Open M-Th noon-11pm, F-Sa noon-11:30pm, Su 11am-10pm.

Books for Cooks, 4 Blenheim Crescent. Tube: Ladbroke Grove. Eric and his crew of culinary pros "test" recipes from new titles. You can rely on the cakes (£2). Food served M-Sa 10am-2:30pm or so. Bookstore open M-Sa 10am-6pm.

MARYLEBONE AND BLOOMSBURY

☒ **Diwana Bhel Poori House,** 121-123 Drummond St. Tube: Warren St. No frills or frippery here—just great, cheap south Indian vegetarian food. Fill yourself for £5. Open daily noon-11:30pm.

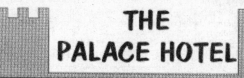

THE
PALACE HOTEL

A very central location close to Hyde Park and the vibrant Bayswater area. With easy access to all London's main attractions and easy access to all Airports and Main Line Railway stations. We have all types of rooms from Dorms to Twins at reasonable prices. Weekly rates also available.

48-49 PRINCES SQ (LEINSTER SQ) LONDON W2 4PX
TEL. 020 7221 5628 / 020 7792 5922 / 020 7792 2269. FAX 020 7221 5890
WEB. www.palacegroup.co.uk   E-MAIL info-palacehotel@quista.net

ECCo (Express Coffee Co.), 46 Goodge St. 11″ thin-crust pizzas, made to order, cost an incredible £3; sandwiches and baguettes from £1, rolls from 50p. Buy any hot drink before noon and get a fresh-baked croissant for free. Pizzas available noon onward. Open daily 7am-11pm. Cash only.

The Lamb, 94 Lamb's Conduit St. Tube: Russell Sq. This old-fashioned pub is as actors' hangout—Peter O'Toole is a regular. Open M-Sa 11am-11pm, Su noon-10:30pm. Food served daily noon-2:30pm and M-Sa 6-9pm.

◉ SIGHTS

ORGANIZED TOURS

The classic London **bus tour** is on an open-top double-decker—and in good weather, it's undoubtedly the best way to get a good overview of the city. Tickets for the **Big Bus Company,** 48 Buckingham Palace Rd. (☎7233 9533; www.bigbus.co.uk; Tube: Victoria) are valid for 24hr. on 3 hop-on, hop-off routes, with 1hr. walking tours and a short Thames cruise included. (£15, kids £7.) For a more in-depth account, you can't beat a **walking tour** led by a knowledgeable guide. **Original London Walks** (☎7624 9255) is the biggest walking-tour company, running 12 walks per day, from "Magical Mystery Tour" to nighttime "Jack the Ripper's Haunts" and guided visits to some museums. Most walks last 2hr., starting from a Tube station. (£5, students £4.)

THE WEST END

MAYFAIR AND ST. JAMES'S

Home to Prince Charles, the Ritz, and exclusive gentlemen's clubs, this is London's aristocratic quarter; on **Jermyn Sreet,** one block south of Piccadilly, stores cater to traditional English squires with hand-cut suits and hunting gear.

BURLINGTON HOUSE. The only one of Piccadilly's aristocratic mansions to survive, Burlington House was built in 1665. Today, it houses numerous regal societies, including the **Royal Academy,** heart of the British artistic establishment (p. 165).

ST. JAMES'S PALACE. Built in 1536, St. James's is London's only remaining purpose-built palace; Prince Charles lives here now. The only part of the Palace you're likely to get into is the **Chapel Royal,** open for Sunday services from October to Easter at 8:30 and 11am. From Easter to September, services are held in the **Queen's Chapel,** across from the Palace. *(Between the Mall and Pall Mall. Tube: Green Park.)*

SOHO

Soho has a history of welcoming all colors and creeds to its streets. Early settlers included French Huguenots fleeing religious persecution in the 17th century; today, **Old Compton Street** is the heart of gay London.

PICCADILLY CIRCUS. In the glow of its lurid neon signs, five of the West End's major arteries merge and swirl round the **statue of Eros,** dedicated to the Victorian philanthropist Lord Shaftesbury. Eros originally pointed down Shaftesbury Ave., but recent restoration work has put his aim significantly off. *(Tube: Piccadilly Circus.)*

LEICESTER SQUARE. Amusements at this entertainment nexus range from London's largest cinemas to the **Swiss Centre glockenspiel,** whose atonal renditions of Beethoven's *Moonlight Sonata* are enough to make even the tone-deaf weep. Be true to your inner tourist by having your name engraved on a grain of rice, getting a henna tattoo, and sitting for a caricature. *(Tube: Leicester Sq. or Piccadilly Circus.)*

CHINATOWN. Tourist-ridden **Gerrard Street,** with scroll-worked dragon gates and pagoda-capped phone booths, contrasts with gritty, more authentic **Lisle Street** in this little slice of Canton. Chinatown is most vibrant during the raucous Chinese New Year in February. *(Between Leicester Sq., Shaftesbury Ave., and Charing Cross Rd.)*

COVENT GARDEN

Covent Garden piazza is one of the few parts of London popular with both locals and tourists. On the spot where Samuel Pepys saw his first Punch and Judy show, street performers entertain those who flock here year round. *(Tube: Covent Garden.)*

THE ROYAL OPERA HOUSE. The Royal Opera House reopened in 2000 after a major expansion. After wandering the ornate lobby of the original 1858 theater, head up to the enormous **Floral Hall.** From here, take the escalator to the **terrace,** which has great views of London. *(Bow St. Open daily 10am-3:30pm. 75min. backstage tour M-Sa 10:30am, 12:30, 2:30pm; reservations essential. £7, students £6.)*

THEATRE ROYAL DRURY LANE. Founded in 1663, this is London's oldest surviving theater, where David Garrick ruled the roost in the 18th century. Pieces of Drury Ln. lore are brought to life in the actor-led backstage tours. *(Entrance on Catherine St. ☎7240 5357. Tours M-Tu, Th-F, Su 3 per day; W, Sa 2 per day. £7.50, children £5.50.)*

TRAFALGAR SQUARE AND THE STRAND

Trafalgar Square (coincidentally London's largest traffic roundabout) commemorates Nelson's victory over Napoleon's navy at the Battle of Trafalgar in 1805. Nelson stands atop his fluted pillar with four bronze lions regally nestled below. The reliefs at the column's base are cast from captured French and Spanish cannons. Every December, the square hosts a giant **Christmas Tree,** donated by Norway to thank the British for assistance against the Nazis. *(Tube: Charing Cross.)*

ST. MARTIN-IN-THE-FIELDS. James Gibbs's 1720s creation was the model for countless Georgian churches in Britain and America. Downstairs the **crypt** has a life of its own, home to a cafe, bookshop, art gallery, and the **London Brass Rubbing Centre.** *(St. Martin's Lane, in the northeast corner of Trafalgar Sq. Tube: Leicester Sq. Brass Rubbing Centre open M-Sa 10am-6pm, Su noon-6pm. Brass rubbing £5-8.)*

SOMERSET HOUSE. A magnificent Palladian structure completed in 1790, Somerset House was originally home to the Royal Academy and the Royal Society;

the building now harbors the magnificent ◪Courtauld Institute (p. 165). In winter, the central Fountain Courtyard is iced over to make an open-air rink. *(On the Strand. Tube: Charing Cross. Courtyard open daily 7:30am-11pm.)*

HOLBORN

Squeezed between the unfettered capitalism of the City and the rampant commercialism of the West End, Holborn is historically the London home of two of the world's least-loved professions—lawyers and journalists.

INNS OF COURT. These venerable institutions, mostly founded in the 13th century, provide apprenticeships for law students and house the chambers of practising barristers. *(Between Fleet St., Essex St., Victoria Embankment, and Temple Ave./Bouvier St. Tube: Temple.)* The 12th-century Temple Church is the finest surviving round church in England. *(Open W-Th 11am-4pm, Sa 9:30am-1:30pm, Su 12:45-4pm. Free.)*

FLEET STREET. Named for the river (now underground) that flows from Hampstead to the Thames, Fleet Street's association with publishing goes back to 1500, when Wyken de Worde relocated from Westminster to the precincts of St. Bride's church. Christopher Wren's odd steeple is the original inspiration for the tiered wedding cake. *(St. Bride's Ave., just off Fleet St. Tube: Temple. Open daily 8am-4:45pm. Free.)*

ROYAL COURTS OF JUSTICE. This elaborate neo-Gothic structure—easily mistaken for a cathedral—straddles the official division between the Westminster and the City of London; the courtrooms are open to the public during cases. *(Where the Strand becomes Fleet St. Tube: Temple. Open M-F 9am-6pm. Cases start 10am).*

THE CITY OF LONDON

Until the 18th century, the City *was* London, the rest being merely outlying villages. Its appearance belies a 2000-year history; what few buildings survived the Great Fire of 1666 and the World War II Blitz are now overshadowed by giant temples of commerce. Today, of the 300,000 people who work in the City, only 8000 call it home. The City of London Information Centre, St. Paul's Churchyard offers acres of leaflets and maps, sells tickets to sights and shows, and gives information on a host of traditional municipal events. *(☎7332 1456. Tube: St. Paul's. Open Apr.-Sept. daily 9:30am-5pm; Oct.-Mar. M-F 9:30am-5pm, Sa 9:30am-12:30pm.)*

ST. PAUL'S CATHEDRAL

St. Paul's Churchyard. Tube: St. Paul's. Audioguides £3.50, students £3. 1½hr. tours M-F 4 per day. £2.50, students £2. Open M-Sa 8:30am-4pm; open for worship daily 7:15am-6pm. £5, students £4; worshippers free.

Sir Christopher Wren's masterpiece is the fifth cathedral to occupy the site; the original was built in AD 604. Wren's succeeded "Old St. Paul's," begun in 1087 and with a steeple as third as high again as the current 111m dome. By 1666, when the Great Fire swept away it away, Old St. Paul's was ripe for replacement. After having three designs rejected by the bishops, Wren, with Charles II's support, just started building—sneakily, he had persuaded the king to let him make "necessary alterations" as work progressed, and the building that emerged from the scaffolding in 1708 bore little resemblance to the "Warrant Model" Charles had approved.

With space to seat 2500 worshippers, the nave is festooned with monuments to great Britons; the tombs, including those of Nelson, Wellington, and Florence Nightingale, are all downstairs, in the crypt. Surrounded by Blake, Turner, and Henry Moore, Christopher Wren lies beneath the epitaph *Lector, si monumentum requiris circumspice* ("Reader, if you seek his monument, look around"). For a different perspective of the second-tallest freestanding dome in Europe (after St. Peter's in the Vatican), climb the 259 steps to the Whispering Gallery on its inner surface. The gallery is a perfect resounding chamber: whisper into the wall, and your friend on the opposite side should be able to hear you. From here 119 more steps reach to Stone Gallery, on the outer base of the dome, and another 152 to the vertiginous Golden Gallery at the summit. Back inside, the marble **High Altar** is overlooked by the mosaic of *Christ Seated in Majesty*. The statue of **John Donne** in the south quire aisle is one of the few monuments to survive from Old St. Paul's.

THE TOWER OF LONDON

> *Tower Hill. Tube: Tower Hill. Audioguides £3. Tours M-Sa 9:30am-3:30pm, Su 10am-3:30pm; free. Open Mar.-Oct. M-Sa 9am-5:30pm, Su 10am-5:30pm; Nov.-Feb. closes 4:30pm. £11.30, students £8.50. Tickets also sold at Tube stations; buy them in advance since lines at the door are horrendous.*

The Tower of London, palace and prison of English monarchs for over 900 years, is steeped in blood and history. Conceived by William the Conqueror as protection for and from his new subjects, his wooden palisade of 1067 was replaced in 1078 by a stone structure that would grow into the White Tower. Colorfully dressed Yeomen Warders, or "Beefeaters"—a reference to their allowance of meat in former times—double as guards and tourist guides; each one is a distinguished armed-serviceman.

From **Middle Tower,** pass over the moat (now a garden) and enter the **Outer Ward** though **Byward Tower.** Just beyond Byward Tower, the **Bell Tower** dates from 1190; the curfew bell has been rung nightly for over 500 years. **Traitor's Gate** is associated with the prisoners who passed through it on their way to execution at **Tower Green.** Some of the victims are buried in the **Chapel Royal of St. Peter ad Vincula,** including Henry VIII's wives Catherine Howard and Anne Boleyn and Catholic martyr Sir Thomas More. The green abuts the **White Tower,** the castle's original fortification, now home to a fearsome display of arms and armor from the Royal Armory.

The Tower's most famous sights are the **Crown Jewels;** moving walkways ensure no awestruck gazers hold up the line. While the eye is naturally drawn to the **Imperial State Crown,** don't miss the **Sceptre with the Cross,** topped with First Star of Africa, the largest quality cut diamond in the world. Other famous gems include the **Koh-i-Noor,** set into the **Queen Mother's Crown;** legend claims the stone will only bring luck to women. A fascinating history of the jewels, including numerous retired crowns, is displayed in the **Martin Tower,** at the end of **Wall Walk.**

OTHER CITY OF LONDON SIGHTS

BANK OF ENGLAND AND AROUND. Government financial difficulties led to the founding of the "Old Lady of Threadneedle St." in 1694. More hallowed institutions stand on the streets nearby: the **Stock Exchange,** on Throgmorton St. and the 18th-century **Mansion House,** on Walbrook, the official residence of the Lord Mayor. The most famous modern structure in the City is **Lloyd's of London,** on Leadenhall, designed by Richard Rogers. With metal ducts, lifts, and chutes on the outside, it wears its heart (or at least its internal organs) on its sleeve. *(Tube: Bank.)*

MONUMENT. Raised in 1677, Christopher Wren's 60m column stands exactly that distance from the bakery on Pudding Lane where the Great Fire started in 1666. Bring stern resolution to climb its 311 steps. *(Monument St. Tube: Monument. Open daily 10am-6pm. £1.50; joint ticket with Tower Bridge Experience £6.75.)*

TOWER BRIDGE. This iconic symbol of London is often mistaken for its plain upriver sibling, London Bridge. The **Tower Bridge Experience** offers a cutesy introduction to the history and technology of the unique lifting mechanism, though the view isn't all it's cracked up to be. *(Tube: Tower Hill. Open Apr.-Oct. daily 10am-6:30pm; Nov.-Mar. daily 9:30am-6pm. £6.25, students £4.25.)*

WREN CHURCHES. Aside from St. Paul's Cathedral, the City's greatest architectural treasures are the 22 surviving churches designed by Christopher Wren to replace those lost in the Great Fire of 1666. The most famous is **St. Mary-le-Bow;** tradition places cockneys as those born within range of its bells. *(Cheapside, by Bow Ln. ☎ 7246 5139. Tube: St. Paul's. Open M-F 6:30am-6pm. Free.)*

SOUTH BANK

From the Middle Ages until Cromwell spoiled the party, the South Bank was London's entertainment quarter; banished from the strictly-regulated City, all manner of illicit attractions sprouted in "the Borough," at the southern end of London Bridge. Today, the South Bank is once again at the heart of London entertainment, with some of the city's top concert halls, theaters, cinemas, and galleries.

LONDON EYE. Also known as the Millennium Wheel, at 135m the London Eye is the world's biggest observational wheel. The ellipsoid glass "pods" give uninterrupted views at the top of each 30min. revolution. *(Jubilee Gardens. ☎(0870) 500 0600. Tube: Waterloo. Open daily late May to early Sept. 9:30am-10pm; Apr. to late May and late Sept. 10:30am-8pm; Jan.-Mar. and Oct.-Dec. 10:30am-7pm. Ticket office in the corner of County Hall; advance booking recommended. July-Sept. £9.50; Oct.-June £9.)*

THE SOUTH BANK CENTRE. Sprawling on either side of Waterloo Bridge along the Thames, this symphony of concrete is Britain's premier cultural center. Its nucleus is the **Royal Festival Hall;** close by, the **Purcell Room** and **Queen Elizabeth Hall** cater for smaller concerts, while the **Hayward Gallery** shelters excellent shows of modern art. Beneath Waterloo Bridge, the **National Film Theatre** offers London's most varied cinema. Past the bridge looms the **National Theatre** (p. 166), which also offers tours three times daily. *(Between Hungerford and Waterloo Bridges. Tours £5, students £4.25.)*

TATE MODERN AND THE MILLENNIUM BRIDGE. Opposite each other on Bankside are the biggest success and most abject failure of London's millennial celebrations. **Tate Modern** (p. 164) is as visually arresting as its contents are thought-provoking. Built to link the Tate to the City, the **Millennium Bridge** was completed far too late for Y2K festivities, and following a literally shaky debut, it promptly closed. With luck, it will reopen sometime in 2002. *(Queen's Walk. Tube: Southwark.)*

SHAKESPEARE'S GLOBE THEATRE. In the shadow of Tate Modern, the half-timbered Globe (opened 1997) rises just 200m from where the original burned down in 1613. Tours of the theater itself are given mornings only during the performance season. *(Bankside. ☎7902 1500. Tube: Southwark. Open daily May-Sept. 9am-noon and 1-4pm (exhibition only); Oct.-Apr. daily 10am-5pm. £7.50. students £6, See also p. 166.)* Nearby lie the ruins of the 1587 **Rose Theatre,** Bankside's first, where both Shakespeare and Marlowe performed; not much remains. *(56 Park St. ☎7593 0026. Open: daily 11am-5pm. £4, students £3; £1 less with Globe exhibition ticket.)*

WESTMINSTER

The City of Westminster, now a borough of London, has been the seat of English and British power for over a thousand years. William the Conqueror was crowned in Westminster Abbey on Christmas Day, 1066, and his successors built the Palace of Westminster that would one day house Parliament.

BUCKINGHAM PALACE

The Mall. Entrance to State Rooms on Buckingham Palace Rd. Tube: Victoria, Green Park, or St. James's Park. State Rooms open early Aug.-Sept. daily 9:30am-4:30pm. Tickets from ☎7321 2233 or the Ticket Office, Green Park from late July. £11.

Originally built for the Dukes of Buckingham, Buckingham House was converted into full-scale palace by George IV. The palace was found to be too small for Victoria's growing brood; a solution was found by closing off the three-sided courtyard, concealing the best architecture. During the summer opening of the **State Rooms,** visitors have access to the **Throne Room,** the **Galleries** (with pictures by Rubens, Rembrandt, and Van Dyck), and the **Music Room,** where Mendelssohn played for Queen Victoria, among others. In the opulent **White Room,** the large mirror fireplace conceals a door used by the Royal Family at formal dinners. Since 2001, Liz has also allowed visitors a brief excursion into the **gardens**—keep off the grass!

CHANGING OF THE GUARD. The Palace is protected by a detachment of Foot Guards in full dress uniform. Accompanied by a band, the "New Guard" starts marching down Birdcage Walk from Wellington Barracks around 10:30am, while the "Old Guard" leaves St. James's Palace around 11:10am. When they meet at the gates of the palace, the officers touch hands, symbolically exchanging keys, *et voilà*, the guard is changed. Show up well before 11:30am and stand directly in front of the palace. *(Apr.-Oct. daily; Nov.-Mar. every other day, provided the Queen is in residence, it's not raining too hard, and there are no pressing state functions. Free.)*

WESTMINSTER ABBEY

Parliament Sq. Access Old Monastery, Cloister, and Garden from Dean's Yard, behind the Abbey. Tube: Westminster. Abbey open M-F 9am-4:45pm, Sa 9am-2:45pm, Su open for services only. Pyx Chamber and Museum open daily 10:30am-4pm. Chapter House open daily Apr.-Oct. 10am-5:30pm; Nov.-Mar. 10am-4pm. Cloisters open daily 8am-6pm. Garden open Tu-Th Apr.-Sept. 10am-6pm; Oct.-Mar. 10am-4pm. Abbey £6, students £3; entry to services free. Old Monastery £2.50; joint entry with Abbey £1 extra on Abbey prices. Cloisters and Garden free.

On December 28, 1065, Edward the Confessor, last Saxon King of England, was buried in the church of the West Monastery; almost exactly a year later, the Abbey saw the coronation of William the Conqueror. Thus, even before it was completed, the Abbey's twin traditions as the figurative birthplace and literal resting place of royalty had been established. It was this royal connection that allowed Westminster, uniquely of the great monasteries of England, to escape wholesale destruction during Henry VIII's campaign against the Pope.

The **north transept** contains memorials to Victorian statesmen, including Prime Ministers Disraeli and Gladstone. Early English kings lie arrayed around the Confessor's tomb in the **Shrine of St. Edward,** behind which the **Coronation Chair** stands at the entry to the Tudor **Lady Chapel.** Henry VII and his wife Elizabeth lie at the end of the chapel. Queen Elizabeth I and the cousin she had beheaded, Mary Queen of Scots, are buried on opposite sides of the chapel. **Poet's Corner** begins with Geoffrey Chaucer, buried in 1400; plaques at his feet commemorate both poets and prose writers, as does the stained-glass window above. At the center of the Abbey, the **Sanctuary** holds the altar; this is where coronations and royal weddings are held. After a detour through the Cloisters, visitors re-enter the nave. At the western end is the **Tomb of the Unknown Warrior,** with an oration poured from molten bullets; just beyond is the simple grave of **Winston Churchill.** The north aisle holds **Scientists Corners,** with physicists and biologists arrayed around Isaac Newton and Charles Darwin respectively. The **Old Monastery** sights include the **Great Cloister,** festooned with monuments and plaques, from where passages lead to the **Chapter House,** the original meeting place of Parliament, the **Pyx Chamber,** formerly the Abbey treasury, and the **Abbey Museum,** with an array of royal funeral effigies. The pleasant **Gardens** are also reached from the cloisters; concerts are occasionally held here in summer.

THE HOUSES OF PARLIAMENT

Parliament Sq. Tube: Westminster. Debates open to all while Parliament is in session (Oct.-July). Advance tickets required for Prime Minister's Question Time (W 3-3:30pm). M-Th after 6pm and F are least busy. Lords usually sits M-W from 2:30pm, Th 3pm, occasionally F 11:30am; closing times vary. Commons sits M-W 2:30-10:30pm, Th 11:30am-7:30pm, F 9:30am-3pm. Free. Tours Aug.-Sept. M-Sa 9:15am-4:30pm; reserve at Ticketmaster (☎ 7344 9966); in person from mid-July. £3.50.

The Palace of Westminster, as the building in which Parliament sits is officially known, has been at the heart of English governance since the 11th century with Edward the Confessor. Under William the Conqueror, the palace was greatly extended. Westminster Hall aside, what little of the Norman palace to remain following was entirely destroyed in the massive conflagration of October 16, 1834.

OUTSIDE THE HOUSES. At the midpoint of the complex, a statue of Oliver Cromwell stands in front of **Westminster Hall,** the sole survivor of the fire. Unremarkable from the outside, the Hall's chief feature is a magnificent roof, constructed in 1394 and considered the finest timber roof ever made; the hall now sees use for public ceremonies and exhibitions. The **Clock Tower** is universally misknown as **Big Ben,** which refers only to the bell within—it's named after the portly Sir Benjamin Hall, who served as Commissioner of Works when the bell was cast in 1858

DEBATING CHAMBERS. Visitors to the debating chambers first pass through **St. Stephen's Hall,** formerly the king's private chapel, and one-time meeting place of the House of Commons. At the end of the hall, the **Central Lobby** marks the separation of the two houses, with the Commons to the north and the Lords to the south. The ostentatious **House of Lords** is dominated by the Throne of State under a gilt canopy. The Lord Chancellor presides over the Peers from the giant red **Woolsack.** In contrast is the restrained **House of Commons,** with simple green-backed benches under a plain wooden roof. The **Speaker** sits at the rear of the chamber, with government MPs to his right and the opposition to his left. With room for only 437 out of 635 MPs, things are hectic when all are present.

OTHER WESTMINSTER SIGHTS

WHITEHALL. Whitehall is a street synonymous with the British civil service. All that remains of the original royal palace is Inigo Jones's **Banqueting House,** with magnificent ceiling paintings by Rubens. *(Whitehall. Tube: Westminster. Open M-Sa 10am-5pm; last admission 4:30pm. £3.90, students £3.10, children £2.30.)* Opposite Banqueting house, tourists line up to be photographed with the burnished cuirassiers of the Household Cavalry at **Horseguards;** the guard is changed Monday through Friday 11am, Saturday 10am. Just off Whitehall, King James St. leads to the **Cabinet War Rooms,** where Churchill, his ministers, generals, and support staff lived and worked underground from 1939-1945. *(Clive Steps. Tube: Westminster. Open daily Apr.-Sept. 9:30am-6pm; Oct.-Mar. 10am-6pm. £5.40, students £3.90.)* Current Prime Minister Tony Blair lives on **Downing Street,** separated from Whitehall by steel gates. Traditionally the Prime Minister lives at No. 10, but Tony's family is too big, so he's swapped with the Chancellor, Gordon Brown, at No. 11.

WESTMINSTER CATHEDRAL. London's first Catholic cathedral since Henry VIII espoused Protestantism was started in 1887; in 1903, money ran out, leaving the interior partially completed. The blackened brick domes contrast dramatically with the swirling marble of the lower walls and the glorious side chapels. *(Cathedral Piazza, off Victoria St. Tube: Victoria. Cathedral open daily 7am-7pm. Free; suggested donation £2. Bell Tower open Apr.-Nov. daily 9am-5pm; Dec.-Mar Th-Su. £2, students £1.)*

KENSINGTON AND KNIGHTSBRIDGE

Nobody took much notice of **Kensington** before 1689, when William III and Mary II moved into Kensington Palace. Now home to London's most expensive stores, including Harrods and Harvey Nichols, it's hard to imagine that in the 18th century **Knightsbridge** was a racy district known for taverns and highwaymen.

KENSINGTON PALACE. Remodelled by Wren for William III and Mary II in 1689, parts are still in use as a royal residence—Princess Diana was the most famous recent inhabitant. Inside, the **Royal Ceremonial Dress Collection** displays 19th-century court costumes along with the Queen's demure evening gowns and some of Diana's racier numbers. *(Eastern edge of Kensington Gardens; enter through the park. Tube: High St. Kensington. Open daily Mar.-Oct. 10am-5pm; Nov.-Feb. 10am-4pm. £8.80.)*

HYDE PARK AND KENSINGTON GARDENS. Surrounded by London's wealthiest neighborhoods, giant Hyde Park has served as the model for city parks around the world, including Central Park in New York and Paris's Bois de Boulogne. The adjacent **Kensington Gardens** is to the west. Innumerable people pay to row and swim in the 16 hectare **Serpentine.** At the northeastern corner of the park, near Marble Arch, proselytizers, politicos, and flat-out crazies dispense knowledge at **Speaker's Corner** on Sundays. *(Tube: Queensway, Lancaster Gate, Marble Arch, Hyde Park Corner, or High St. Kensington. Hyde Park open daily 5am-midnight. Kensington Gardens. open dawn-dusk. Free.)*

MARYLEBONE AND BLOOMSBURY

Marylebone's most famous resident (and address) never existed; 221b Baker Street was the fictional lodging house of Sherlock Holmes. 221 Baker St. is actually the headquarters of the Abbey National bank (there was never a 221b).

A little farther down the street, the **Sherlock Holmes Museum** gives its address out as 221b, although a little sleuthing will reveal that it in fact stands at no. 239 (£6). East of Marylebone, Bloomsbury's intellectual reputation was bolstered in the early-20th century as Gordon Sq. resounded with the philosophizing and womanizing of the **Bloomsbury Group,** an early 20th-century coterie of intellectuals including Virginia Woolf, John Maynard Keynes, Lytton Strachey, and Bertrand Russell.

■ BRITISH LIBRARY. Since its 1998 opening, the new British Library has won plaudits from visitors and users alike. Underground, the shelving can hold up to 12 million books. The brick building is home to reading rooms, a dramatic glass cube containing the 65,000 volumes of George III's King's Library, and a stunning display of books, manuscripts, and artifacts, from the 2nd-century *Unknown Gospel* to Joyce's handwritten draft of *Finnegan's Wake*. *(96 Euston Rd. ☎ 7412 7332. Tube: King's Cross. Tours M, W, F 3pm; Sa 10:30am and 3pm. £5, students £3.50. Tours including reading rooms Tu 6:30pm, Su 11:30am and 3pm; £6, £4.50. Reservations recommended for all tours. Open M and W-F 9:30am-6pm, Tu 9:30am-8pm, Sa 9:30am-5pm, Su 11am-5pm. Free.)*

ACADEMIA. The strip of land along **Gower Street** and to its west is London's academic heartland. **University College London** was Britain's first to admit Catholics, Jews, and women. The embalmed body of its founder, **Jeremy Bentham,** occupies the South Cloister. *(Main entrance on Gower St. Tube: Warren St.)* The **Senate House** was the model for the Ministry of Truth in *1984*—George Orwell worked there as part of the World War II BBC propaganda unit. *(At the southern end of Malet St. Tube: Goodge St.)*

NORTH LONDON

CAMDEN TOWN. An island of good honest tawdriness in an increasingly affluent sea, Camden Town has effortlessly thrown off attempts at gentrification thanks to the ever-growing **Camden Market** (p. 168).

HAMPSTEAD HEATH. Hampstead Heath is one of the last remaining commons in England, open to all since at least 1312. **Parliament Hill** is the highest open space in London, with excellent views across the city. Farther north, ■**Kenwood** is a picture-perfect 18th-century country estate, designed by Robert Adams for the first Earl of Mansfield and home to the impressive **Iveagh Bequest** of Old Masters, including works by Rembrandt, Vermeer, Turner, and Botticelli. *(Tube: Hampstead or Rail: Hampstead Heath. Heath open 24hr.; Kenwood open daily Apr.-Sept. 8am-8pm; Oct.-Mar. 8am-4pm.)*

WEST LONDON

ROYAL BOTANICAL GARDENS, KEW. No ordinary park, Kew is a living collection of thousands of flowers, fruits, trees, and vegetables from across the globe. The three great **conservatories,** housing a staggering variety of plants ill-suited to the English climate, are the highlight of the gardens. *(Main entrance at Victoria Gate. Tube: Kew Gardens. Open Apr.-Aug. M-F 9:30am-6:30pm, Sa-Su 9:30-7:30pm; Sept.-Oct. daily 9:30am-6pm; Nov.-Mar. daily 9:30am-4:15pm. Glasshouses close Apr.-Oct. 5:30pm; Nov.-Mar. 3:45pm. £6.50, students £4.50, "late entry" (45min. before close) £4.50.)*

■ HAMPTON COURT PALACE. Although a monarch hasn't lived here for 250 years, Hampton Court still exudes regal charm. In addition to touring the sumptuous rooms of the palace, including **Henry VIII's State Apartments** and William's **King's Apartments,** be sure to leave time for the vast gardens, including the devilishly difficult hedgerow **maze.** *(Take the train from Waterloo (32min., every 30min., day return £4) or a boat from Westminster Pier (4hr.; 4 per day; £10, return £14); to leave time to see the palace, take the boat one way, and return by train. Open mid-Mar. to late Oct. M 10:15am-6pm, Tu-Su 9:30am-6pm; late Oct. to mid-Mar. closes 4:30pm. Palace and gardens £10.80, students £8.30. Maze only £2.90. Gardens (excluding south gardens) free.)*

EAST LONDON

Whitechapel, the oldest part of the East End, thronged in the 19th century with Jewish refugees from Eastern Europe; today it's the heart of London's Bangladeshi community, centered around the restaurants and markets of **Brick Lane.** The most recent wave of immigrants is made up of artists. *(Tube: Aldgate East).* Where it touches the river, the East End becomes **Docklands.** This man-made archipelago of docks and wharves was for centuries the commercial heart of the British Empire. In 1981, the Thatcher government decided to redevelop this vast area as a showpiece of unrestrained entrepreneurial development. The showpiece of the regeneration is **Canary Wharf,** with Britain's highest skyscraper, the 800ft., pyramid-topped **One Canada Square.** Under the tower, the vast **Canada Place** and **Cabot Square** malls suck in shoppers from all over London, while the dockside plaza is lined with pricey corporate drinking and eating haunts. *(Tube: Canary Wharf.)*

🏛 MUSEUMS

Centuries as the capital of an empire upon which the sun never set, together with a decidedly English penchant for collecting, have endowed London with spectacular museums. Art lovers, history buffs, and ethnologists will not know which way to turn. Even better, the government is shifting all major collections to free admission.

🖾 BRITISH MUSEUM

Great Russell St., Bloomsbury. Rear entrance on Montague St. Tube: Tottenham Court Rd. Audioguide £2.50. Highlights tour (1½hr.) M-Sa 10:30am and 1pm; Su 11am, 12:30, 1:30, 2:30, 4pm; £7, students £4. Great Court open M 9am-6pm, Tu-W and Su 9am-9pm, Th-Sa 9am-11pm. Galleries open Sa-W 10am-5:30pm, Th-F 10am-8:30pm. Free; £2 suggested donation. Temporary exhibitions around £7, students £3.50.

The funny thing about the British Museum is that there's almost nothing British in it; it was founded in 1753 as the personal collection of Sir Hans Sloane. The opening of the **Great Court** in December 2000—the largest covered square in Europe— finally restored to the museum its focal point. For the past 150 years used as the stacks of the British Library, the courtyard remains dominated by the enormous rotunda of the **Reading Room,** whose desk have shouldered the weight of research by Marx, Lenin, Trotsky, and almost every major British writer and intellectual.

The most famous items in the collection are found in the **Western Galleries;** here Room 4 harbors Egyptian sculpture, including the **Rosetta Stone,** and Room 18 is entirely devoted to the Athenian **Elgin Marbles.** Other highlights include giant **Assyrian** and **Babylonian** reliefs, the Roman **Portland Vase,** and bits and bobs from two Wonders of the Ancient World, the **Temple of Artemis** at Ephesus and the **Mausoleum of Halikarnassos.** Just when you thought you'd nailed antiquity, the **Northern Galleries** strike back with eight galleries of **mummies** and **sarcophagi** and nine of artifacts from the ancient Near East, including the **Oxus Treasure** from Iran. Also in the northern wing are the excellent **African** and **Islamic** galleries, the giant **Asian** collections, and the frankly pathetic **Americas** collection. The upper level of the **South** and **East Galleries** is dedicated to ancient and medieval Europe, some of which is actually British. Famous remains include the preserved body of **Lindow Man,** an Iron Age Celt apparently sacrificed in a gruesome ritual (Room 50) and treasures excavated from the **Sutton Hoo Burial Ship** (Room 41). Next door, Room 42 is home to the enigmatic **Lewis Chessmen,** an 800-year-old chess set mysteriously abandoned in Scotland.

🖾 NATIONAL GALLERY

Main entrance on north side of Trafalgar Sq. Tube: Charing Cross or Leicester Sq. Audioguides free; £4 suggested donation. 1hr. gallery tours daily 11:30am and 2:30pm, W also 6:30pm; free. Open Th-Tu 10am-6pm, W 10am-9pm. Sainsbury Wing exhibitions until 10pm. Free; some temporary exhibitions £6-7, students £3.

The National Gallery was founded by an Act of Parliament in 1824 in a townhouse; it grew so rapidly in size and popularity that a purpose-built gallery was constructed in 1838. The new **Sainsbury Wing** houses the oldest, most fragile paintings, including the 14th-century English *Wilton Diptych* and Botticelli's *Venus and Mars*. With paintings from 1510 to 1600, the **West Wing** is dominated by the Italian High Renaissance and early Flemish art. In room 8, the artists of Rome and Florence duke it out, with versions of the *Madonna and Child* by Raphael and Michelangelo. The **North Wing** spans the 17th century, with exceptional Flemish work. Room 23 boasts no fewer than 17 Rembrandts; the famous *Self Portrait at 63* gazes knowingly at his *Self Portrait at 34*. The **East Wing** is the most popular in the gallery, thanks to the Impressionists including Van Gogh's *Sunflowers* and Cézanne's *Bathers*, and two of Monet's *Waterlilies*. A reminder that there was art on this side of the channel too, Room 34 flies the flag with six luminescent Turners.

TATE BRITAIN

Millbank, near Vauxhall Bridge, in Westminster. Wheelchair access via Clore Wing. Tube: Pimlico. Audioguides £1. Highlights tour M-F 2:30 and 3:30pm, Sa 3pm; free. Open daily 10am-5pm. Free; special exhibitions £3-5.

The original Tate opened in 1897 as a showcase for modern British art. Before long, the remit had expanded to include contemporary art from all over the world, as well as British art from the Middle Ages on. Despite many expansions, it was clear that the dual role was too much for one building; the problem was resolved in 1999 with the relocation of almost all the contemporary art to the new Tate Modern at Bankside (see below). At the same time, the original Tate was rechristened and rededicated to British art. The **Clore Gallery** continues to display the Turner Bequest of 282 oils and 19,000 watercolors; other painters featuring heavily are William Blake, John Constable, Joshua Reynolds, Dante Gabriel Rossetti, Lucien Freud, and David Hockney. Despite the Tate Modern's popular explosion, the annual **Turner Prize** for contemporary art is still held here. The short-listed works go on show from early November to mid-January every year.

■ TATE MODERN

Bankside, the South Bank. Main entrance on Holland St. Tube: Blackfriar's. Audioguides £1. Tours meet on the gallery concourses; free. History/Memory/Society 10:30am, level 3; Nude/Body/Action 11:30am, level 3; Landscape/Matter/Environment 2:30pm, level 5; Still Life/Object/Real Life 3:30pm, level 5. Open Su-Th 10am-6pm, F-Sa 10am-10pm. Free; special exhibitions £5-7, students £4-6 off.

Since opening in May 2000, Tate Modern has been credited with single-handedly reversing the long-term decline in museum-going numbers in Britain. The largest modern art museum in the world, its most striking aspect is the building, formerly Bankside power station. A conversion by Swiss firm Herzog and de Meuron has added a seventh floor with wraparound views of north and south London, and turned the old **Turbine Hall** into an immense atrium that often overpowers the installations commissioned for it. For all its popularity, the Tate has been criticized for its controversial curatorial method, which groups works according to themes rather than period or artist: the four overarching divisions are **Still Life/Object/Real Life, Landscape/Matter/Environment, Nude/Action/Body,** and **History/Memory/Society.** Even skeptics admit that this arrangement throws up some interesting contrasts, such as the juxtaposition of Monet's *Waterlilies* with Richard Long's energetic *Waterfall Line*. The achievement of the thematic display is that it forces visitors into contact with an exceptionally wide range of art. It's now impossible to see the Tate's more famous pieces, which include Marcel Duchamp's *Large Glass* and Picasso's *Weeping Woman*, without also confronting challenging and invigorating works by little-known contemporary artists.

VICTORIA AND ALBERT

Main entrance on Cromwell Rd., in Kensington. Tube: South Kensington. Introductory tours daily 10:30, 11:30am, 1:30, 2:30pm; W also 4:30pm. Gallery talks daily 1pm; free. Talks, tours, and live music W from 6:30pm; last F of month fashion shows, debates, and DJs. Open Th-Tu 10am-5:45pm, W and last F of month 10am-10pm. Free; additional charge for some exhibitions.

Founded in 1852 to encourage excellence in art and design, the V&A is the largest museum of the decorative (and not so decorative) arts in the world. The subject of a £31 million refit, the vast **British Galleries** hold a series of recreated rooms from every period between 1500 and 1900, mirrored by the vast **Dress Collection,** a dazzling array of the finest *haute couture* through the ages. If you only see one thing in the museum, make it the **Raphael Gallery,** hung with paintings commissioned by Leo X in 1515. The **Sculpture Gallery,** home to Canova's *Three Graces* (1814-17), is not to be confused with the **Cast Courts,** a plaster-cast collection of the world's sculptural greatest hits, from Trajan's Column to Michelangelo's *David*. The V&A's **Asian** collections are particularly formidable with Indian carvings, Persian carpets, Chinese porcelain, and Japanese ceramics. In contrast to the geographically laid-out ground floor, the **upper levels** are mostly arranged in specialist galleries devoted to everything from jewelry to musical instruments to stained glass. An exception to the materially themed arrangements is the large **20th-century** collection, featuring design classics from Salvador Dalí's "Mae West" sofa lips to a pair of rubber hotpants. The **Frank Lloyd Wright** gallery contains a recreation of the office commissioned by Edgar J. Kauffmann for his 1935 Pittsburgh department store.

OTHER MUSEUMS AND GALLERIES

■ **Courtauld Institute,** Somerset House, Strand. Tube: Charing Cross. The small, outstanding collection holds 14th- to 20th-century abstractions, focusing on Impressionism. Open M-Sa 10am-6pm, Su noon-6pm. £4, free M 10am-2pm.

■ **Imperial War Museum,** Lambeth Rd. Tube: Lambeth North. The commendably un-jingoistic exhibits follow every aspect of war from 1914, covering conflicts large and small. Open daily 10am-6pm. £6.50, students £5.50; free after 4:30pm.

■ **Institute of Contemporary Arts (ICA),** Nash House, the Mall. Tube: Charing Cross. Down the road from Buckingham Palace, Britain's center for contemporary arts is nicely located for attacking the establishment. Open M noon-11pm, Tu-Sa noon-1am, Su noon-10:30pm; galleries close 7:30pm. M-F £1.50, Sa-Su £2.50.

■ **London's Transport Museum,** Covent Garden Piazza. Tube: Covent Garden or Charing Cross. Informative and fun, kids and adults will find themselves engrossed in the history of London's public transportation system. Open Sa-Th 10am-6pm, F 11am-6pm. £6, students £4, under 16 free with adult.

■ **Museum of London,** London Wall. Enter through the Barbican. Tube: Barbican. This engrossing collection traces the history of London from its foundations to the present day. Open M-Sa 10am-5:50pm, Su noon-5:50pm. £5, students £3.

■ **National Maritime Museum,** Trafalgar Rd., Greenwich Docklands Light Railway: Cutty Sark. Child-friendly displays cover almost every aspect of seafaring history. Open daily June to early Sept. 10am-6pm; early Sept. to May 10am-5pm. £7.50; students £6. Combined ticket with Queen's House and Royal Observatory £10.50, students £8.40.

■ **Natural History Museum,** Cromwell Rd. Tube: South Kensington. This cathedral-like building is home to an array of animals and minerals, though remarkably few vegetables. Open M-Sa 10am-5:50pm, Su 11am-5:50pm. Free.

■ **Royal Academy,** Burlington House, Piccadilly. Tube: Piccadilly Circus. Founded in 1768 as both an art school and meeting place for Britain's foremost artists, the Academy holds outstanding exhibitions on all manner of art. Open Sa-Th 10am-6pm, F 10am-10pm. Around £7, students £1-4 less.

■ **Sir John Soane's Museum,** 13 Lincoln's Inn Fields. Tube: Holborn. Architect John Soane let his imagination run free when designing this intriguing museum for his own collection of art. Open Tu-Sa 10am-5pm, first Tu of month also 6-9pm. Free; £1 donation.

■ **Wallace Collection,** Manchester Sq. Tube: Bond St. Palatial Hertford House holds a stunning array of porcelain, medieval armor, and the largest weaponry collection outside the Tower of London. Open M-Sa 10am-5pm, Su noon-5pm. Free.

Sherlock Holmes Museum, 239 Baker St. (marked 221bv). Tube: Baker St. It takes a master sleuth to deduce that this meticulously recreated home-from-Holmes is entirely fictional. Or was he? Open daily 9:30am-6:30pm. £6, ages 7-16 £4.

📑 ENTERTAINMENT

On any given day in London, you may choose from the widest possible range of entertainment. The West End is perhaps the world's theater capital, supplemented by a justly famous National Theatre, while new bands continually pop up. Dance, film, sports, and countless other events will leave you amazed at the variety. *Time Out* magazine's weekly listings are indispensable (£2.20, every Wednesday).

THEATER

The stage for a national dramatic tradition over 500 years old, London theaters maintain unrivaled breadth of choice. At a **West End** theater (a term referring to all the major stages, whether or not they're actually in the West End), you can expect a professional (if mainstream) production, top-quality performers, and (usually) comfortable seats. **Off-West End** theaters usually present more challenging work, while remaining as professional as their West End brethren. The **Fringe** is refers to the scores of smaller, less commercial theaters, often just a room in a pub basement with a few benches and a team of dedicated amateurs.

The **Leicester Square Half-Price Ticket Booth** is run by the theaters themselves and releases (genuine!) half-price tickets on the day of the show. The catch is that you have to buy them in person, in cash, with no choice in seating (most expensive tickets sold first) and no way of knowing in advance what shows will have tickets available that day. Come early and be prepared to wait, especially Sa. (South side of Leicester Sq.—look for the long lines. Tube: Leicester Sq. £2 booking fee per ticket. Max. 4 tickets per person. Open M-Sa 10am-7pm, Su noon-2:30pm.)

Barbican Theatre, Barbican (☎ 7638 8891). Main entrance on Silk St. Tube: Barbican. A futuristic auditorium seating 1166 in steeply raked, forward-leaning balconies. In May 2002, the **Royal Shakespeare Company** will give its last performances in residence at the Barbican. Tickets £6-30, cheapest M-F evening and Sa matinee. Student standbys from 9am day of performance. In the same complex, **The Pit** is an intimate 200-seater theater used primarily for new and experimental productions. Tickets £10-15.

National Theatre, just downriver of Waterloo bridge (info ☎ 7452 3400). Tube: Waterloo. Since its 1963 opening, the National has been at the forefront of British theater. The **Olivier** stage fans out 1160 seats, the **Lyttelton** is a proscenium theater with 890 seats; while the 300-seat **Cottesloe** offers flexible staging for experimental drama. Box office open M-Sa 10am-8pm. Horrendously complex pricing scheme; £10-30, day seats (from 10am) £10-13, standby (2hr. before curtain) £15; students £8-15.

Royal Court Theatre, Sloane Sq. (☎ 7565 5000). Called "the most important theater in Europe" by the *New York Times,* dedicated to challenging new writing and innovative interpretations of classics. Experimental work runs in the intimate Upstairs auditorium. Main stage £5-25; students £9 in advance, £5 that day; standing places 10p 1hr. before curtain. Upstairs £5-15, students £9. M all seats £5.

Shakespeare's Globe Theatre, 21 New Globe Walk (☎ 7401 9919). Tube: London Bridge. This may be a faithful reproduction of the Shakespeare's original 16th-century playhouse. Choose between the backless wooden benches or stand through a performance as a "groundling." For tours of the Globe, see p. 159. Performances mid-May to late Sept. Tu-Sa 7:30pm, Su 6:30pm; from June also Tu-Sa 2pm, Su 1pm. Box office open M-Sa 10am-6pm. Seats £11-27, students £9-23; yard (i.e. standing) £5.

CINEMA

London's film scene offers everything. The degenerate heart of the celluloid monster is **Leicester Square** (p. 156), where the latest releases premiere a day before hitting the chains. **The Empire** (☎ (0870) 010 2030) is the most famous first-run theater.

National Film Theatre (NFT), on the south bank, right underneath Waterloo Bridge (☎ 7928 3232). Tube: Waterloo, Embankment, or Temple. One of the world's leading cinemas, with a mind-boggling array of films. 6 different movies hit the 3 screens every evening, starting around 6pm. All films £6.85, students £5.25.

The Prince Charles, Leicester Pl. (☎ 7957 4009). Tube: Leicester Sq. Features *Sing-a-long-a-Sound-of-Music*, where Von Trappists dress as everything from nuns to "Ray, a drop of golden sun" (F 7:30pm; Su 2pm; £12.50), and the live-troupe accompanied *Rocky Horror Picture Show* (F 11:45pm; £6, students £3). Otherwise it screens second-run Hollywood and recent independent. £3.50, M-F before 5pm £1.75, M evenings £2.

MUSIC

ROCK AND POP

Birthplace of the Rolling Stones, the Sex Pistols, and the Chemical Brothers, home to Madonna and Paul McCartney, London is a town steeped in rock 'n' roll history.

Borderline, Orange Yard, off Manette St. (☎ 7734 2095). Tube: Tottenham Court Rd. Basement space still trading off its secret REM gig years ago, now used for lesser-known groups. Music M-Sa from 8pm. Box office open M-F 1-7:30pm. £5-10 in advance.

The Water Rats, 328 Grays Inn Rd. (☎ 7837 7269). Tube: King's Cross/St. Pancras. A pub-cafe by day, a stomping venue for top new talent by night. Open for coffee M-F 8am-noon, lunches (£4-6) M-F noon-2pm, and music M-Sa 8pm-midnight (cover £5).

CLASSICAL

Home to four orchestras, three major concert halls, two opera houses and ballet companies, this is ground zero for serious music. To hear the world's top choirs for free, try Westminster Abbey (p. 160) or St. Paul's Cathedral (p. 157) for Evensong.

Barbican Hall, details as for Barbican Theatre (p. 166). Tube: Barbican. One of Europe's leading concert halls. The resident **London Symphony Orchestra** plays throughout year; the hall also hosts international orchestras, jazz and world musicians. Tickets £6-35.

English National Opera, at the Coliseum, St. Martin's Lane (☎ 7632 8300). Tube: Charing Cross or Leicester Sq. All the classics, plus contemporary and avant-garde work, sung in English. £6-60, under 18 half-price with adult. Day seats for the dress-circle (£29) and balcony (£3) released M-F 10am (12:30pm by phone).

The Proms (www.bbc.co.uk/proms/), at the Royal Albert Hall, Kensington Gore. Tube: Knightsbridge. Summer season of classical music, with concerts every night from mid-July to mid-Sept. Lines often start mid-afternoon. Tickets go on sale in mid-May (£5-30); standing places sold from 1½hr. before the concert (£3).

Royal Opera House, Bow St. (☎ 7304 4000). Tube: Covent Garden. Also home to the **Royal Ballet.** Productions tend to be conservative but lavish, like the wealthy patrons. Standing room and restricted-view seating in the upper balconies is under £5. Standby 4hr. before curtain £12.50-15. Day seats £10-40 from 10am on performance day.

Royal Festival Hall, on the south bank of the Thames between Hungerford and Waterloo bridges (☎ 7960 4242). Tube: Waterloo or Embankment. 2500-seat concert hall with the best acoustics in London. The two resident orchestras, the **Philharmonia** and the **London Philharmonic,** predominate, but big-name jazz, latin, and world-music groups also visit. Classical concerts £6-30, others around £10-30.

JAZZ, FOLK, AND WORLD

London's **jazz** scene is small but serious; top clubs pull in big-name performers. **Folk** and **world** music keep a lower profile, mostly restricted to pubs.

Ronnie Scott's, 47 Frith St. (☎ 7439 0747). Tube: Tottenham Court Rd. London's oldest and most famous jazz club. Music starts M-Sa 9:30pm, Su 8:30pm. Reservations recommended—if it's sold out, come back for the midnight set. Cover £8-20.

Spitz, 109 Commercial St. (☎ 7392 9032). Tube: Shoreditch. Hosts an eclectic range of live music, from jazz and world music to indie pop and rap. All profits go to help Bosnian and Kosovar children. Music most Tu-Sa 8pm. Cover £5-8.

SPECTATOR SPORTS

FOOTBALL. During the season (late Aug. to May), over half a million people attend professional football matches every Saturday, dressed in team colors. The big three

London teams are ■**Arsenal,** Highbury Stadium, Avenell Rd. (☎7704 4000; Tube: Arsenal); **Chelsea,** Stamford Bridge, Fulham Rd. (☎7386 7799; Tube: Fulham Broadway); and **Tottenham Hotspur,** White Hart Lane (☎8365 5000; Rail: White Hart Lane).

CRICKET. London's two grounds stage both county and international contests. **Lord's,** St. John's Wood Rd. (☎7432 1033. Tube: St. John's Wood) and the **Oval,** Kennington (☎7582 7764; Tube: Oval). Every summer a touring nation plays England in a series of matches around the country, including a customary thrashing every four years at the hands of the ■**Australian Cricket Team.**

TENNIS. For two weeks in late June and early July, tennis buffs focus flock to **Wimbledon.** Reserve months ahead or arrive by 6am to secure Centre and no. 1 court tickets; otherwise, get a "grounds" tickets to the outer courts. (All England Lawn Tennis Club. ☎8971 2473. Tube: Southfields. Grounds £7-12; show courts £17-50.)

◪ SHOPPING

Built upon two millennia of commerce London has always been a trading city; the range of goods is unmatched anywhere. From Harrods's boast to supply "all things to all people," to African crafts in Brixton market, you could shop for lifetime.

DEPARTMENT STORES

Harrods, 87-135 Old Brompton Rd. Tube: Knightsbridge. The only thing bigger than the store itself is the price mark-up. No wonder only tourists and oil sheikhs actually shop here. Bewildering. Open M-Sa 10am-7pm. AmEx/MC/V/Your Soul.

Harvey Nichols, 109-125 Knightsbridge. Tube: Knightsbridge. Imagine Bond St., Rue St. Honore, and Fifth Avenue all rolled up and translated into 5 floors of fashion, from the biggest names to the hippest contemporary unknowns. Open M-Tu and Sa 10am-7pm, W-F 10am-8pm, Su noon-6pm. AmEx/MC/V.

Hamley's, 188 Regent St. Tube: Oxford Circus. Seven floors with every toy imaginable. Open M-F 10am-8pm, Sa 9:30am-8pm, Su noon-6pm. AmEx/MC/V.

CLOTHING AND FOOTWEAR

■ **Cyberdog/Cybercity,** Stables Market. Tube: Camden Town. Unbelievable club clothes for superior lifeforms. Alien goddesses will want to try on steel corsets with rubber breast hoses. Open M-F 11am-6pm, Sa-Su 10am-7pm. AmEx/MC/V.

Dr. Marten's Dept. Store, 1-4 King St. Tube: Covent Garden. Tourist-packed 5-tiered megastore, with baby docs, papa docs, and the classic yellow-stitched boots. Open M-W and F-Sa 10am-7pm, Th 10:30am-8pm, Su noon-6pm. AmEx/MC/V.

Dolly Diamond, 51 Pembridge Rd. Tube: Notting Hill Gate. Jackie Onassis or Audrey Hepburn? Choose your look from the great selection of classic 50s-70s clothes, along with some elegant 20s-40s evening gowns. Open M-F 10:30am-6:30pm, Sa 9:30am-6:30pm, Su 11am-5pm. "Cash preferred."

STREET MARKETS

Camden Markets, off Camden High St. and Chalk Farm Rd. Tube: Camden Town. Now London's 4th-biggest tourist attraction, on Sundays the market fills all available space with hordes on the lookout for the latest mainstream, vintage and offbeat fashions.

Brick Lane Market. Tube: Shoreditch or Aldgate East. Famous weekly market with a South Asian flair (food, rugs, spices, bolts of fabric, strains of sitar). Open Su 8am-2pm.

◪ NIGHTLIFE

The West End, and in particular **Soho,** is the scene of most of London's after-dark action, from the glitzy (and best avoided) Leicester Sq. tourist traps such as the Hippodrome and Equinox to semi-secret underground clubs. The other major axis of London nightlife is the East's **Shoreditch** and **Hoxton** (known as Shoho).

BARS

An explosion of club-bars has invaded the previously forgotten zone between pubs and clubs, with stylish surroundings, top-flight DJs, and plentiful lounging space. Usually, club-bars are open from noon or early evening to 1 or 2am; skip the cover charge by arriving early and staying put as the scene shifts around you. And remember—don't tip the barman!

☒ Soshomatch, 2 Tabernacle St. (☎ 7920 0701). Tube: Moorgate. A 2-floor bar/restaurant that converts into a stylish club Th-Sa; a DJ-driven atmosphere with acres of comfy leather couches. Open M-W 11am-midnight, Th-Sa 11am-2pm. F-Sa £5.

AKA, 18 West Central St. (☎ 7419 9199). Tube: Tottenham Ct. Rd. There's nowhere like the candlelit island lounge for people watching. Cocktails £6-7. It's "members only," but you can join at the door. Dress nicely! Open Su-F 6pm-3am, food to 1am. Free-£5.

Dogstar, 389 Coldharbour Ln. (☎ 7733 7515). Tube: Brixton. At 9pm, the tables are cleared from the dance floor and the projectors turned on. House, hip-hop, and dance music. Open Su-Th noon-2am, F-Sa noon-4am. Su-Th free; F £5, 10-11pm £4, before 10pm free; Sa £7, 10-11pm £5, before 10pm free.

Freud, 198 Shaftesbury Ave. (☎ 7240 9933). Invigorate your psyche in this offbeat underground hipster hangout. Sand-blasted walls occasionally echo to live music. Cheap cocktails (from £3.40) beat an hour on the couch. Light meals 11am-4:30pm (£3.50-6). Open M-Sa 11am-11pm, Su noon-10:30pm. No cover.

Shoreditch Electricity Showrooms, 39a Hoxton Sq. (☎ 7739 6934). Tube: Old St. If you wanted to know where the super-cool go, this is the answer. Bottled beer £2.70-3. Food (e.g. crispy squid, £5) served 1-3:45pm. Open Tu-W noon-11pm, Th noon-midnight, F-Sa noon-1am, Su noon-10:30pm. No cover.

Vibe Bar, 91-95 Brick Ln. (☎ 7247 3479). Tube: Aldgate East. Young, fun, clubby bar, with an interior straight out of a style mag. DJs from 7:30pm M-F and 6pm Sa-Su; in summer, the fun extends outside with a second DJ working the shady courtyard. Tends toward soul/jazz/funk. Open Su-Th noon-11pm, F-Sa noon-1am. Free-£2.

NIGHTCLUBS

Every major DJ in the world either lives in London or makes frequent visits to the city. Such is the fast-changing nature of London nightlife that even weekly publications have trouble keeping up; use the listings below as a guide, but check *Time Out* or call the club before heading out to prevent surprises; as always, earlier means cheaper cover charge.

☒ Fabric, 77a Charterhouse St. (☎ 7336 8898). Tube: Farringdon. Bigger than a B52 and 100 times as loud. When they powerup the underfoot subwoofer, lights dim across London. Three dance floors, chill-out beds, multiple bars, and unisex toilets crammed with up to 2500 dance-crazed Londoners. Various monthlies F 9:30pm-5am, Sa mega dance fest *Fabric Live* 9:30pm-7am. Cover £10-15.

☒ Scala, 275 Pentonville Rd. (☎ 7833 2022, tickets 7771 2000). Tube: Kings Cross. Huge main floor embraces its cinematic past: DJs spin from the projectionist's box, balconies provide multiple levels, and a giant screen pulsates with visuals. F gay/mixed eclectica 10pm-5am; Sa house-dominated; every other Su *Latin 8* has 6hr. of salsa 8pm-2am; free dance workshop 8:30-9:30pm. Dress up. Cover £8-10.

93 Feet East, 150 Brick Lane (☎ 7247 3293). Tube: Aldgate East. One of the hottest new clubs in East London. Barn-like main dance floor and sofa-strewn upstairs room. W salsa with a live Latin band 7-11pm; Th world-dance mixes 9pm-3am; F techno and house 9pm-3am; Sa anything from house to ska 9pm-2am. Cover £3-10.

The Fridge, Town Hall Parade, Brixton Hill (☎ 7326 5100). Tube: Brixton. Turn left from the station and bear right at the fork. Giant split-level dance floor. F total trance glo-stick madness 10pm-6am; Sa usually gay nights 10am-6pm. Cover £9-13. After parties start Sa-Su mornings 5:30am at the neighboring Fridge Bar (£6).

Ministry of Sound, 103 Gaunt St. (☎ 7378 6528). Tube: Elephant and Castle. The granddaddy of all serious clubbing—arrive early or wait all night. Dress code generally

casual, but err on the side of smartness (*no* sports shoes!). F garage and R&B
10:30pm-6am; Sa US and vocal house midnight-9am. Cover £12-15.

Sound, 10 Wardour St. (☎7287 1010). Tube: Leicester Sq. A real labyrinth, with rooms
secreted over 4 floors. Th R&B, soul, and UK garage 10pm-3am; F R&B 10pm-4am; Sa
■ *Carwash* 70s retro fest—funky dress a must 10pm-4:30am. Cover £5-12.

GAY AND LESBIAN NIGHTLIFE

London has a very visible gay scene, from flamboyant to mainstream. Gay newspapers include *Capital Gay*, *Pink Paper*, and *Shebang* (for women). *Boyz* magazine and the *Ginger Beer* website (www.gingerbeer.co.uk) track gay and lesbian
nightlife scenes. Soho (especially **Old Compton Street**) is the heart of gay London.

The Box, 32-34 Monmouth St. (☎7240 5828). Spacious gay/mixed bar-brasserie is
popular with a stylish media/fashion crowd. Daily changing food specials (main
courses around £9). Unisex toilets. Open M-Sa 11am-11pm, Su 7-10:30pm.

Candy Bar, 23-24 Bateman St. (☎7437 1977). Tube: Tottenham Ct. Rd. The UK's first
full-time lesbian den. Groovy bar and basement dance floor. DJs W-Su. Open M-Tu 5pm-
1am, W-F 5pm-3am, Sa 3pm-3am, Su 5-11pm. F-Sa £5 after 9pm.

Comptons of Soho, 53 Old Compton St. (☎7479 7461). Tube: Leicester Sq. Soho's
"official" gay pub is always busy. Horseshoe bar, while upstairs (open 6pm) offers a
more mellow scene with pool table. Open M-Sa 11am-11pm, Su noon-10:30pm. MC/V.

G-A-Y (☎(0906) 100 0160). M and Th at the Mean Fiddler, 165 Charing Cross Rd. F-Sa
at the London Astoria, 157 Charing Cross Rd. Tube: Tottenham Court Rd. London's biggest gay and lesbian nights, 4 nights a week. Sa is *G-A-Y*'s big night out, rocking the
capacity crowd with commercial-dance DJs, and live pop performances. Open M, Th, F
until 4am, Sa until 5am. Cover free-£10.

⚡ DAYTRIPS FROM LONDON

OXBRIDGE. Don your academic regalia for a day in the intellectual meccas of
Oxford (p. 180) and **Cambridge** (p. 185), both an hour from London by train.

BRIGHTON. Just over an hour from London by train, indulge in a "dirty weekend"
in **Brighton** (p. 174).

SALISBURY AND CANTERBURY. Make like a pilgrim and head to **Canterbury** (p.
174) or ponder the beyond at **Salisbury Cathedral** and **Stonehenge** (p. 177), all under
two hours from London by train.

SOUTHERN ENGLAND

Sprawling toward the continent, the landscape of southern England simultaneously
asserts Britain's island heritage and belies a continental link deeper than the Chunnel. Early Britons settled the counties of Kent, Sussex, and Hampshire from across
the English Channel, and William the Conqueror left his mark upon the downsland
in the form of staggering cathedrals. Geoffrey Chaucer, Jane Austen, Charles Dickens, E.M. Forster, and Virginia Woolf also all drew inspiration from these lands. To
the west, the counties of Somerset, Avon, and Wiltshire boast Salisbury's medieval
cathedral, the Roman Baths at Bath, and the forever mysterious Stonehenge.

✈ FERRIES AND TRAINS TO FRANCE, SPAIN, AND BELGIUM

Ferries chug from **Portsmouth** (p. 175) to **St. Malo** (p. 350) and **Caen, France** (p. 347);
from **Folkestone** to **Boulogne, France** and from **Newhaven** to **Dieppe, France.** Travelers
with cars can head through the **Chunnel** (from Dover to Calais) on **Le Shuttle.**

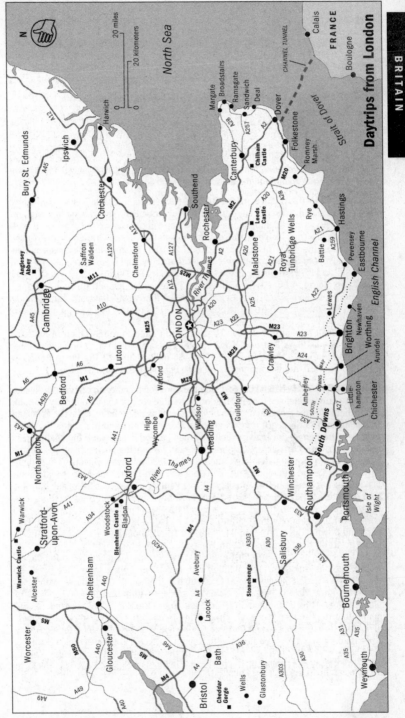

BRITAIN

Daytrips from London

N

North Sea

20 miles
20 kilometers

FRANCE
Calais
Boulogne

CHANNEL TUNNEL

Strait of Dover

English Channel

Harwich
Ipswich
Bury St. Edmunds
Colchester
Southend
Rochester
Margate
Broadstairs
Ramsgate
Sandwich
Deal
Dover
Folkestone
Romney Marsh
Canterbury
Chilham Castle
A28
A257
A2
M20
Maidstone
Leeds Castle
A20
A21
Royal Tunbridge Wells
Hastings
Battle
A259
Pevensey
Eastbourne
Rye
A22
Lewes
Newhaven
Brighton
Worthing
Arundel
Littlehampton
Chichester
South Downs
SOUTH DOWNS WAY
A27
A32
Amberley
A24
A23
Crawley
M23
A22
A25
M25
A20
Southampton
Winchester
Portsmouth
Isle of Wight
A3
A33
A36
Salisbury
Bournemouth
A31
A35
Weymouth
A30
A303
Glastonbury
Wells
Cheddar Gorge
Bristol
Bath
Lacock
Avebury
A4
A420
Oxford
Woodstock
Bladon
Blenheim Castle
A34
A40
Cheltenham
Gloucester
Worcester
Alcester
Warwick
Warwick Castle
Stratford-upon-Avon
M5
M50
A49
A46
A36
A303
A4
M4
High Wycombe
Reading
Windsor
River Thames
Guildford
M3
Watford
M25
M1
Luton
Bedford
A6
A5
A41
Northampton
A43
A428
Cambridge
Anglesey Abbey
Saffron Walden
A10
A45
M11
Chelmsford
A12
A120
A127
LONDON
River Thames
M25
A10
A1
A6
A40
A49
A38
A33
A35
M4
A4
A30
A303
A36
A46
A420

BATH
☎ 01225

A visit to the elegant Georgian city of Bath (pop. 83,000) remains *de rigueur*, even though today it's more of a museum (or a museum gift shop) than a resort. But expensive trinkets can't conceal the fact that Bath, immortalized by Austen and Dickens, once stood second only to London as the social capital of England.

🖅 🔁 TRANSPORTATION AND PRACTICAL INFORMATION. Trains head frequently to: Bristol (15min., 3 per hr., £4.60); Exeter (1¼hr., every hr., £21.50); and London's Paddington Station (1½hr., 2 per hr., £34). National Express **buses** (☎(08705) 808080) run to London's Victoria Station (3hr., 9 per day, £11.50) and Oxford (2hr., 6 per day, £12). Both arrive near the south end of Manvers St.; walk up to the Terrace Walk roundabout and turn left on York St. to reach the **tourist office**, in Abbey Chambers. (☎477101. Open May-Sept. M-Sa 9:30am-6pm, Su 10am-4pm; Oct.-Apr. M-Sa 9:30am-5pm, Su 10am-4pm.) **Postal code:** BA1 1A5.

🖬 🛏 ACCOMMODATIONS AND FOOD. B&Bs (from £18) cluster on Pulteney Rd., Pulteney and Crescent Gardens, and Widcombe Hill. The **YHA youth hostel**, on Bathwick Hill, is in a secluded mansion 20 steep minutes above the city; catch Badgerline bus #18 (dir. University) from the bus station or the Orange Grove rotary. (☎465674. Laundry. Dorms £11, under 18 £7.75.) The **International Backpackers Hostel**, 13 Pierrepont St., is up the street from the stations and is just three blocks from the baths. (☎446787. Internet. Breakfast £1. Laundry £3. Dorms £12.) To get to **Toad Hall Guest House**, 6 Lime Grove, go across Pulteney Bridge and through Pulteney Gardens. (☎423254. £20-26 per person.) To reach **Newton Mill Camping**, 4km west on Newton Rd., take bus #5 from the bus station (£1.60 return) to Twerton and ask to be let off at the campsite. (☎333909. Reserve ahead. £11.95 for 2 people, tent, and car.) **Guildhall Market** is between High St. and Grand Parade. (Open M-Sa 8am-5:30pm.) Try **⛫Tilleys Bistro**, 3 North Parade Passage, for French or English fare. (Open M-Sa noon-2:30pm and 6:30-11pm, Su 6:30-10:30pm.) **The Pump Room**, in Abbey Courtyard, holds a monopoly on Bath Spa mineral water (£0.50).

🎦 🔁 SIGHTS AND NIGHTLIFE. Once the spot for naughty sightings, the **Roman Baths** are now a must-see for all. Most of the visible complex is not actually Roman, but rather reflects Georgian dreams of what Romans might have built. The **⛫Roman Baths Museum** underneath reveals genuine Roman Baths and highlights the complexity of Roman engineering, which included central heating and internal plumbing. Its recovered artifacts, scale models, and hot springs bring back to life the Roman spa city Aquae Salis—first unearthed in 1880 by sewer diggers. (Open daily Apr.-July and Sept. 9am-6pm; Aug. 9am-6pm and 8pm-10pm; Oct.-Mar. 9:30am-5pm; last admission 30min. before closing. £6.70.) Penny-pinchers can view one bath for free by entering through the **Pump Room** in Abbey Churchyard. Next to the baths, the towering and tombstoned 15th-century **Bath Abbey** has a whimsical west façade with several angels climbing ladders up to heaven—and, curiously enough, two climbing down. (Open M-Sa 9am-4:30pm, Su 1pm-2:30pm and 4:30-5:30pm. £1.50.) Head north up Stall St., turn left on Westgate St., and turn right on Saw Close to reach Queen Sq., where Jane Austen lived at #13. Continue on Gay St. to **The Circus**, where Thomas Gainsborough, William Pitt, and David Livingstone once lived. To the left down Brock St. is the **Royal Crescent**, a half-moon of Gregorian townhouses bordering **Royal Victoria Park**. The **botanical gardens** within nurture 5000 species of plants. (Open M-Sa 9am-dusk, Su 10am-dusk. Free.) Backtrack down Brock St. and bear left at the Circus (or take a right at The Circus from Gay St.) to reach Bennett St. and the dazzling **Museum of Costume**, which will satisfy any fashion fetish. (Open daily 10am-5pm. £3.90; joint ticket with Roman Baths £7.50.) **The Garrick's Head**, St. John's Pl. (☎448819), is a scoping ground for the stage door of the Theatre Royal., while the **The Pig and Fiddle** pub, on the corner of Saracen St. and Broad St., packs in a rowdy, and enthusiastic young crowd.

It's not where you are going...
it's how you get there that counts.

Eurail: A European Tradition

Get your Eurail pass at
LetsGo.com

CANTERBURY
☎01227

Six hundred years ago, in his famed *Canterbury Tales*, Chaucer captured the irony of tourists visiting England's most famous execution site. His sometimes lewd, sometimes reverent tales speak of the pilgrims of the Middle Ages who flocked from London to the **Canterbury Cathedral.** Archbishop Thomas à Becket was beheaded there in 1170 after an irate Henry II asked, "Will no one rid me of this troublesome priest?" (Cathedral open Easter-Sept. M-Sa 9am-6:30pm, Su 12:30-2:30pm and 4:30-5:30pm; Oct.-Easter M-Sa 9am-5pm, Su 12:30-2:30pm and 4:30-5:30pm. Evensong services M-F 5:30pm, Sa 3:15pm, Su 6:30pm. £3.50, students £2.50. Audio tour £2.50.) **The Canterbury Tales,** on St. Margaret's St., is a museum that simulates the journey of Chaucer's pilgrims; the gap-toothed Wife of Bath and her waxen companions will entertain you with an abbreviated, Modern English version of the Tales. (Open July-Aug. daily 9am-5.30pm; Mar.-June and Sept.-Oct. daily 9:30am-5:30pm; Nov.-Feb. Su-F 10am-4:30pm, Sa 9:30am-5:30pm. £5.90, students £4.90.) On Stour St., the **Canterbury Heritage Museum** tells the history of Canterbury from medieval times to World War II. (☎452747. Open June-Oct. M-Sa 10:30am-5pm, Su 1:30-5pm; Nov.-May M-Sa 10:30am-5pm. £1.90, students and children £1.20.) To see two of South England's most storied castles, head 20km southeast to **Deal.** Here you'll find **Deal Castle,** which was designed by Henry VIII as a coastal fortification, as well as **Walmer Castle,** which has been converted from a military bastion to an elegant country estate. **Trains** leave regularly from Canterbury (£3).

For those who can't make the pilgrimage from Canterbury on horseback, **trains** from London's Victoria Station arrive at Canterbury's **East Station** (1½ hr., every 30min., £15.70), while trains from London's Charing Cross and Waterloo Stations arrive at **West Station** (1½hr., every hr., £15.70). **National Express buses** (☎(08705) 808080) leave from St. George's Ln. for **London** (2hr., 1 per hr., £6-8). The **tourist office,** 34 St. Margaret's St., stocks free mini-guides to Canterbury. (☎780063. Open M-Sa 9:30am-5:30pm, Su 10am-4pm.) Check email at **I2M Internet Cafe,** corner of St. Dunstan's St. and Station Rd. West. (www.i2m.co.uk. Open M-Sa 10am-6pm, Su noon-5pm £3 per hr.) **B&Bs** cluster near both train stations; mainly around the intersections of London Rd. and Whitstable Rd., and High St. and New Dover Rd. **The Tudor House,** 6 Best Ln., is off High St. in the town center. Eat breakfast in front of a Tudor fireplace in this flowery 16th-century house. Try to get a front room for a gorgeous view of the cathedral. (☎765650 Singles £18; doubles £36, with bath, £44.) The **Hampton House,** 40 New Dover Rd. (☎464912), offers quiet, luxurious rooms (£20-25), and the wonderfully named **Let's Stay,** 26 New Dover Rd has vegetarian breakfast (☎463628; £11 per person). The **Camping and Caravaning Club Site** on Bekesbourne Ln. has good facilities. (☎463216. £5.30 per person; £4.75 pitch fee.) **High Street** is crowded with pubs, and restaurants. For **groceries,** head to **Safeway supermarket,** on St. George's Pl. (Open M-F 8am-8pm, Su 10am-4pm.) **Marlowe's,** 55 St. Peter's St., prides itself on an eclectic mix of vegetarian and beefy English, American, and Mexican styles. (☎462194. Open daily 11:30am-10:30pm.) **C'est la Vie,** 17b Burgate, attracts locals and students who take away inventive sandwiches on freshly baked bread. (☎457525 Open daily 9am-6pm.) **Postal code:** CT1 2BA.

BRIGHTON
☎01273

According to legend, the future King George IV scuttled into Brighton (pop. 250,000) for some decidedly un-regal hanky-panky around 1784. Today, Brighton is still the unrivaled home of the "dirty weekend"—it sparkles with a tawdry luster all its own. Before indulging, check out England's long-time obsession with the Far East at the excessively ornate **Royal Pavilion,** on Pavilion Parade, next to Old Steine. (Open June-Sept. daily 10am-6pm, Oct.-May 10am-5pm; £5.20, students £3.75. Guided tours at 11:30am and 2:30pm, £1.25. Audio tour £1.) Around the corner on Church St. stands the **Brighton Museum and Art Gallery,** with paintings, English pottery, and a wild collection of Art Deco and Art Nouveau pieces—leer at Salvador Dalí's sexy red sofa, *Mae West's Lips.* (Open M-Tu and Th-Sa 10am-5pm, Su 2-5pm. Limited wheelchair access. Free.) Before heading

A CASTLE FIT FOR A HORSE George IV loved his horses, but not as much as he loved himself. Before the Royal Pavilion was rebuilt, the grounds housed a building for George's fleet of horses and army of attendants. Accommodations for all these beasts and their servants required an enormous structure (designed in the style of Indian architecture), and Brighton's citizens jokingly whispered that the horses lived better than the Prince. Bridled by such remarks and spurred to action, George nagged his architects to design an even more impressive home in the same Eastern style; he would not be outflanked by his own stallions. Several years and a modern equivalent of £20 million later, the Royal Pavilion took shape, allowing George to jockey for the respect he desired and reclaim his title as the stud of Brighton.

out to the rocky **beach,** stroll the **Lanes,** a jumble of 17th-century streets forming the heart of Old Brighton. Brighton brims with nightlife options; pick up *The Punter* or *What's On* at music stores, news agents, and pubs for tips.

Take a drink to the beach and watch the sunset at **Fortune of War,** 157 King's Rd. Arches (open M-Sa 10:30am-11pm, Su 11am-10:30pm), or sup at the former parish house, now a rock n' roll shrine, **The Font and Firkin,** 7 Union St., The Lanes (Open M-Sa noon-11pm, Su noon-10:30pm). **Paradox** and **Event II,** on West St., are the most popular clubs. **The Beach,** 171-181 King's Rd. Arches, produces some of the beachfront's fattest beats, while **Casablanca,** on Middle St., plays live jazz to a mostly student crowd. The converted World War II tunnels of **Zap Club,** on King's Rd., provide space for dirty dancing. (Most clubs in Brighton are open M-Sa 10pm-2am.) Brighton is also *the* gay nightlife spot in Britain outside London; pick up *Gay Times* (£2.75) or *Capital Gay* (free). **Queen's Arms,** at 8 George St (☎696873), packs an enthusiastic gay and lesbian crowd into its Saturday night cabaret.

Trains (☎(0345) 484950) roll to London (1¼hr., 6 per hr., £10.50) and Portsmouth (1½hr., every hr., return £12.30). National Express **buses** (☎383744) head to London (2hr., 15 per day, return £8). The **tourist office** is at 10 Bartholomew Sq. (☎(09067) 112255. Open Mar.-Oct. M-Tu and Th-F 9am-5pm, W Sa 10am-5pm, and Su 10am-4pm. Closed Nov.-Feb. Su) The rowdy **Brighton Backpackers Hostel,** 75-76 Middle St., is the best place for meeting other backpackers. (☎777717. Internet £1.50 per 30min. Dorms £10-11; doubles £25.) **Baggies Backpackers,** 33 Oriental Pl., has mellow vibes, exquisite murals, and a mosaic floor. Head west of West Pier along King's Rd., and Oriental Pl. is on the right. (☎733740. Dorms £10; doubles £27.) To get to the **YHA youth hostel,** on Patcham Pl., 6½km away, take Patcham Bus #5 or 5A from Old Steine in front of the Royal Pavilion to the Black Lion Hotel. (☎556196. Curfew 11pm. Dorms £11, under 18 £7.) For cheap eats, try the fish 'n' chip shops along the beach and north of the Lanes, or head to **Safeway Supermarket,** 6 St. James's St. (Open M-Sa 8am-9pm, Su 11am-5pm). **Postal code:** BN1 1BA.

GLASTONBURY

☎01458

The reputed birthplace of Christianity in England and the seat of Arthurian myth, Glastonbury (pop. 6900) has evolved into an intersection of mysticism and religion. Present-day pagan pilgrimage site **Glastonbury Tor** is supposedly the site of the mystical Isle of Avalon, where the Messiah is slated to return. To make the trek up to the Tor, turn right at the top of High St., continue up to Chilkwell St., turn left onto Wellhouse Ln., and take the first right up the hill (buses in summer £0.50). On your way down, visit the **Chalice Well,** on the corner of Welhouse Ln., the supposed resting place of the Holy Grail. (Open daily Easter-Oct. 10am-6pm; Nov.-Feb. 1-4pm. £1.50.) In town, the ruins of **Glastonbury Abbey,** England's oldest Christian foundation, stands behind the archway on Magdalene St. (Open daily June-Aug. 9am-6pm; Sept.-May 9:30am-6pm. £3, students £2.50.) No trains serve Glastonbury, but Baker's Dolphin **buses** (☎(01934) 616000) run from London (3¼hr., 1 per day, return £5); Badgerline buses (☎(01225) 464446) come from Bath (£4; change at Wells). From the bus stop, turn right on High St. to reach the **tourist office,** The Tribunal, 9 High St.

(☎832954. Open Apr.-Sept. Su-Th 10am-5pm, F-Sa 10am-5:30pm; Oct.-Mar. S-Th 10am-4pm, F-Sa 10am-4:30pm.) ▒**Glastonbury Backpackers,** in the Crown Hotel on Market Pl., contributes its own splashes of color to the city's tie-dye. (☎833353. Internet. Dorms £10; doubles £26-30.) Sleep in comfort at **Blake House,** 3 Bove Town. (☎831680. £19 per person.) **Postal code:** BA6 9HG.

PORTSMOUTH
☎023

Set Victorian prudery against prostitutes, drunkards, and a lot of bloody cursing sailors, and there you have a basic 900-year history of Portsmouth (pop. 190,500). On the **seafront,** visitors relive D-Day, explore warships, and learn of the days when Britannia truly ruled the waves. War buffs and historians will want to plunge head first into the unparalleled **Naval Heritage Centre,** in the Naval Base, which houses a virtual armada of Britain's most storied ships. The center includes England's first attempt at a warship, Henry VIII's Mary Rose. Although Henry was particularly fond of her, she—like many women with whom Henry associated—passed on before her time, sinking soon after setting sail from Portsmouth in July, 1545. Resurrect the past with these floating monuments to Britain's former majesty of the seas—even the staunchest Army man can't help but be awed by the history within the galleries of the **Royal Naval Museum.** Entrance is next to the tourist office on The Hard—follow the signs to Portsmouth Historic Ships. (Ships open Mar.-Oct. daily 10am-5:30pm; Nov.-Feb. 10am-5pm. Individual site tickets £6. All-inclusive passport ticket £17.50, seniors £15.50, children £12.50.)

For information on **ferries** to France, see p. 62. **Trains** (☎(0345) 484950) run to Southsea Station, on Commercial Rd., from: Chichester (40min., 2 per hr., £5); London's Waterloo Station (1½hr., 3 per hr., £19); and Salisbury (2hr., every hr., £8.25). National Express **buses** (☎(08705) 808080) rumble from London (2½hr., 1 per hr., £10.50) and Salisbury (2hr., 1 per day, £8.25). The **tourist office** is on The Hard; there's a branch next to the train station. (☎9282 6722. Open daily 9:30am-5:45pm.) Moderately priced **B&Bs** (around £20) clutter **Southsea,** 2.5km east of The Hard along the coast. Take any Southsea bus and get off at The Strand to reach the energetic and lively ▒**Portsmouth and Southsea Backpackers Lodge,** 4 Florence Rd. (☎9283 2495. Internet £2.50 per 30min. Dorms £10; doubles £22.) **Birchwood Guest House,** 44 Waverly Rd., offers bright, spacious ensuite rooms and an ample breakfast. (☎9281 1337. Singles £18, doubles £36.) Take any bus to Cosham (including #1, 3, and 40) to the police station and follow the signs to get to the **YHA Portsmouth** at Wymering Manor, on Old Wymering Ln., Medina Rd. (☎9237 5661. Lockout 10am-5pm. Curfew 11pm. Open Feb.-Aug. daily; Sept.-Nov. F-Sa. Dorms £9.15, under 18 £6.20.) The **Tesco supermarket,** on Craswell St., is just off the town center. (☎839222. Open 24hr. M 7am through Sa 10pm, Su 10am-4pm.) **Pubs** near The Hard provide weary sailors with galley fare and jars of gin. **Postal code:** PO1 1AA.

WINCHESTER
☎01962

The glory of Winchester (pop. 32,000) stretches back to Roman times. William the Conqueror deemed it the center of his kingdom, and years later, Jane Austen and John Keats both lived and wrote in town. Duck under the archway, pass through the square, and behold the 900-year-old **Winchester Cathedral,** 5 The Close. Famed for the small stone figure in its nave, the 169m-long cathedral is the longest medieval building in Europe; the interior holds magnificent tiles and Jane Austen's tomb. The **Norman crypt,** supposedly the oldest in England, can only be viewed in the summer by guided tour. The 12th-century Winchester Bible resides in the library. (Open daily 7:15am-5:30pm; East End closes 5pm. Tours 10am-3pm; free. Donation £3.50, students £2.30.) About 25km north of Winchester is the meek village of **Chawton,** where Jane Austen lived. It was in her **cottage** that she penned *Pride and Prejudice, Emma, Northanger Abbey,* and *Persuasion,* among others—some of her manuscripts are on display. Take Hampshire **bus** #X64 (M-Sa 11 per day, return £4.50), or the London and Country bus #65 Su, from the bus station; ask to be let off at the Chawton roundabout and follow the brown signs. (☎(01420) 83262. Open Mar.-Dec. daily 11am-4:30pm; Jan.-Feb. Sa-Su 11am-4:30pm. £3.50.) **Royal Oak,** on

Royal Oak Passage, next to the Godbegot House off High St., is yet another pub that claims to be the kingdom's oldest. (Open daily 11am-11pm.)

Trains (☎(0345) 484950) arrive at Winchester's Station Hill, at City Rd. and Sussex St., from London's Waterloo Station (1hr., 2 per hr., £16.60) and Portsmouth (1hr., every hr., £7). National Express **buses** (☎(08705) 808080) go to London (1½hr., 7 per day, £12); Hampshire Stagecoach (☎(01256) 464501) goes to Salisbury (#68; 45min., 7 per day, return £4.45) and Portsmouth (#69; 1½hr., 12 per day, return £4.45). The **tourist information center,** at The Guildhall, Broadway, is by the statue of Alfred the Great. (☎840500; fax 850348. Open June-Sept. M-Sa 10am-6pm, Su 11am-2pm; Oct.-May M-Sa 10am-5pm.) The lovely home of **Mrs. P. Patton,** 12 Christchurch Rd., between St. James Ln. and Beaufort Rd., is 5min. from the cathedral. (☎854272. Singles £25-28; doubles £33-40.) Go past the Alfred statue, across the bridge, and left before Cricketers Pub to reach the **YHA youth hostel,** 1 Water Ln. (☎853723. Lockout 10am-5pm. Curfew 11pm. Open July-Aug. daily; mid-Feb. to June and Sept.-Oct. M-Sa. £9.25.) Get **groceries** at **Sainsbury,** on Middle Brook St., off High St. (Open M-Th 8am-6:30pm, F 8am-9pm, Sa 7:30am-6pm.) **Postal code:** SO23 8WA.

SALISBURY

☎01722

Salisbury (pop. 36,890) revolves around ◼**Salisbury Cathedral,** and its spire that rises an astounding 404 feet. The bases of the pillars literally bend inward under the strain of 6400 tons of limestone; if a pillar rings when you knock on it, you should probably move away. (Open June-Aug. M-Sa 7:15am-8:15pm, Su 7:15am-6:15pm; Sept.-May daily 7:15am-6:15pm. **Free tours** May-Oct. M-Sa 9:30am-4:45pm; Nov.-Feb. M-Sa 10am-4pm; May-Sept. Su 4-6:15pm. **Roof and tower tours,** 1½hr.; May-Sept. M-Sa 11am, 2, 3pm, Su 4:30pm; June-Aug. M-Sa also 6:30pm; winter hours vary; £3, students £2. Call ahead. **Evensong** M-Sa 5:30pm, Su 3pm. Donation £3.50, students and seniors £2.50.) One of four surviving copies of the **Magna Carta** rests in the **Chapter House.** (Open June-Aug. M-Sa 9:30am-7:45pm, Su 9:30am-5:30pm; Sept.-May daily 9:30am-5:30pm, Su 1-3:15pm. Free.)

Trains arrive on South Western Rd from London (1½hr., every hr., £22-30) and Winchester (1½hr., every hr., £10.60). National Express **buses** (☎(08705) 808080) pull into 8 Endless St. from London's Victoria Station (2¾hr., 4 per day, £11.50); Wilts & Dorset buses (☎336855) arrive from Bath (#X4; 2hr., 6 per day, £3). The **tourist information center** is on Fish Row in the Guildhall, in Market Sq.; turn left on South Western Rd., bear right on Fisherton St., continue on Bridge St., cross the bridge onto High St., and walk straight on Silver St., which becomes Butcher Row and Fish Row (10-15min.). From the bus station, head left on Endless St., which (shockingly) ends and becomes Queen St., and turn right at the first old building to the right to enter Fish Row. (☎334956; fax 422059. Open June-Sept. M-Sa 9:30am-6pm, Su 10:30am-4:30pm; Oct.-Apr. M-Sa 9:30am-5pm; May M-Sa 9:30am-5pm, Su 10:30am-4:30pm.) From the tourist office, head left on Fish Row, right on Queen St., left on Milford St., and straight under the overpass to find the **YHA youth hostel,** in Milford Hill House, on Milford Hill. (☎327572. Lockout 10am-1pm. Curfew 11:30pm. Dorms £11. **Camping** £7 per person.) **Matt and Tiggy's,** 51 Salt Ln., in a welcoming 450-year-old house with warped floors and ceiling beams, is just up from the bus station. (☎327443. Dorms £11-12.) At ◼**Harper's "Upstairs Restaurant",** 6/7 Ox Rd., inventive international and English dishes (£6-10) make hearty meals, and the "8B48" (2 generous courses for £8 before 8pm) buys a heap of food. (☎333118. Open M-F noon-2pm and 6-9:30pm, Sa noon-2pm and 6-10pm, Su 6-9pm.) **Sainsbury's supermarket** is at The Maltings. (Open M-Th 8am-8pm, F 8am-9pm, Sa 7:30am-7pm, Su 10am-4pm.) **Postal code:** SP1 1AB.

◼ **DAYTRIP FROM SALISBURY: STONEHENGE.** A submerged colossus amid swaying grass and indifferent sheep, Stonehenge stands unperturbed by whipping winds and the legions of people who have been by its side for over 5000 years. The monument's present shape—once a complete circle of 7m high stones weighing up to 45 tons—dates from about 1500 BC. The most famous Stonehenge legend holds that the circle was built of Irish stones magically transported by Merlin.

BRITAIN

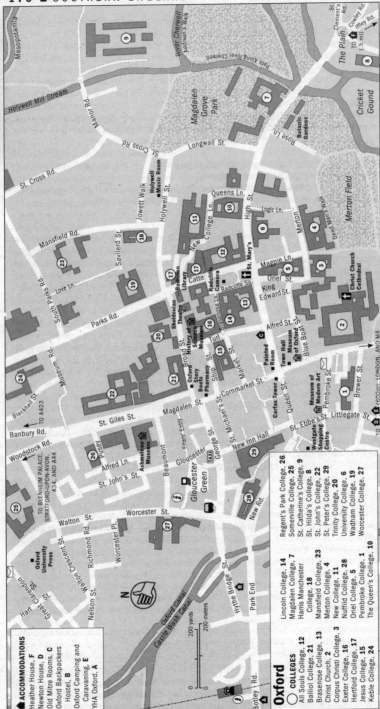

ACCOMMODATIONS

Heather House, **F**
Newton House, **D**
Old Mitre Rooms, **C**
Oxford Backpackers
Hostel, **B**
Oxford Camping and
Caravaning, **E**
YHA Oxford, **A**

Oxford

○ COLLEGES

All Souls College, **12**
Balliol College, **21**
Brasenose College, **13**
Christ Church, **2**
Corpus Christi College, **3**
Exeter College, **16**
Hertford College, **17**
Jesus College, **15**
Keble College, **24**

Lincoln College, **14**
Magdalen College, **7**
Harris Manchester
College, **18**
Mansfield College, **23**
Merton College, **4**
New College, **11**
Nuffield College, **28**
Oriel College, **5**
Pembroke College, **1**
The Queen's College, **10**

Regent's Park College, **26**
Somerville College, **25**
St. Catherine's College, **9**
St. Hilda's College, **8**
St. John's College, **22**
St. Peter's College, **29**
Trinity College, **20**
University College, **6**
Wadham College, **19**
Worcester College, **27**

Other stories alternately attribute the monument to giants, Phoenicians, Mycenaean Greeks, Druids, Smurfs, Romans, Danes, and aliens; regardless, the builders methods continue to confound archaeologists. For centuries, religious devotees have come for its mystical karmic energies, building temples and leaving us to marvel at the awe-inspiring site. Pagans use the stone circle to celebrate the Summer Solstice. You can admire Stonehenge for free from nearby **Amesbury Hill,** 2½km up A303, or pay admission at the site. (☎ (01980) 624715. Open daily June-Aug. 9am-7pm; mid-Mar. to May and Sept. to mid-Oct. 9:30am-6pm; mid-Oct. to mid-Mar. 9:30am-4pm. £4.20, students £3.20.) Wilts & Dorset **buses** (☎336855) connect from Salisbury's center and train station (40min., return £5.25).

EXETER
☎01392

Besieged by William the Conqueror in 1068 and flattened by German bombs in 1942, Exeter (pop. 110,000), has undergone frantic rebuilding, resulting in an odd mixture of the venerable and the banal: ruins punctuate parking lots and department store cash registers ring atop medieval catacombs. **Exeter Cathedral** was heavily damaged in World War II but still retains exquisite detail. The cathedral library's **Exeter Book** is the richest treasury of early Anglo-Saxon poetry in the world. (Cathedral open daily 7am-6:30pm. Library open M-F 2-5pm. Evensong M-F 5:30pm, Sa-Su 3pm. Free tours Apr.-Oct. M-F 11:30am and 2:30pm, Sa 11am. Donation £2.50.) Six-hundred-year-old **underground passages** are accessible from the Romangate Passage next to Boots on High St. (Open July-Sept. M-Sa 10am-5:30pm; Oct.-June Tu-F 2-5pm, Sa 10am-5pm. Tours £3.75, students £2.75. Book tickets by noon during July and Aug.)

Trains arrive in Exeter from Bristol (1½hr., every hr., £13.60) and London's Paddington Station (2½hr., 2 per hr., £39). National Express **buses** (☎(08705) 808080) pull into Paris St., off High St. outside the city walls, from London's Victoria Coach Station (4hr., every 1½hr., return £16) and Bath (2¾hr., 3 per day, £13); walk through the arcade to Sidwell St. and turn left to reach High St. The **tourist office,** at the Civic Centre, in the City Council Building on Paris St., is opposite the rear of the bus station. (☎265700. Open M-Sa 9am-5pm; in summer also Su 10am-4pm.) To reach the **YHA youth hostel,** 47 Countess Wear Rd., 3km from the city center off Topsham Rd, take minibus K or T from High St. to the Countess Wear Post Office (£1), and follow Exe Vale Rd. to the end and turn left. (☎873329. Reception 8-10am and 5-10pm. Dorms £11, under 18 £7.75. **Camping** half-price.) Pack a picnic at **Sainsbury's supermarket,** in the Guildhall Shopping Centre, off High St. (Open M-W and F 8am-6:30pm, Th 8am-7pm, Sa 7:30am-6pm, Su 10:30am-4:30pm.). **Postal code:** EX1 1AA.

THE CORNISH COAST

PENZANCE. Penzance is the very model of an ancient English pirate town: waterlogged, stealthy, and unabashed. A Benedictine monastery was built on the spot where St. Michael dropped by in AD 495, and today **St. Michael's Mount** sits offshore. The interior is unspectacular, but the grounds are more textured, and the 30-story views are captivating. (Open Apr.-Oct. M-F 10:30am-5:30pm, in summer also most weekends; Nov.-Mar. in good weather. £4.40.) A causeway links the mount to the island; or take ferry bus #2 or 2A to Marazion (M-Sa 3 per hr., return £0.80) and catch a ferry during high tide (return £1). **Trains** (☎(08457) 484950) go to: Exeter (3hr., every hr., £18.60); London (5½hr., every hr., £54); and Plymouth (2hr., every hr., £10). National Express (☎(08705) 808080) **buses** run to: London (8hr., 8 per day, £27) and Plymouth (3hr., 2 per hr., £6). Between the two stations is the **tourist office,** on Station Rd. (☎(01736) 362207. Open in summer M-F 9am-5pm, Sa 9am-4pm, Su 10am-1pm; in winter M-F 9am-5pm, Sa 10am-1pm.) **Penzance Backpackers,** Blue Dolphin, Alexandra Rd., is a relaxed, eclectic place to take a load off. (☎(01736) 363836. Dorms £8-9; doubles £18-22.) **The Turk's Head** pub, 49 Chapel St., was built in the 13th century, and sacked by Spanish pirates in 1595. ☎01736.

ST. IVES. St. Ives perches 15km north of Penzance, on a spit of land lined by pastel beaches and azure waters. Virginia Woolf was bewitched by the energy of the Atlantic at St. Ives: her masterpiece *To the Lighthouse* is thought to refer to the Godrevy

Lighthouse in the distance. Whether seeking the perfect subject or the perfect strip of sand, St. Ives has it, if hidden beneath a veneer of postcards and ice cream cones. Some **trains** (☎ (08457) 484950) go directly to Penzance (3-6 per day), but most connect via St. Erth (10min., 2 per hr., £3). Western National **buses** go to Penzance (3 per hr., off-season M-Sa only, £2.50) and Newquay (#57). National Express (☎(08705) 808080) stops in St. Ives between Plymouth and Penzance (6 per day). The **tourist office** is in the Guildhall on Street-an-Pol. From the stations, walk down to the foot of Tregenna Hill and turn right. (☎796297. Open M-Sa 9:30am-6pm, Su 10am-1pm; in winter closed Sa-Su.) **St. Ives International Backpackers,** The Stenmack, fills a renovated 19th-century Methodist church. (☎799444. Dorms £8-12.) Places to camp abound in nearby **Hayle;** try **Trevalgan Camping Park** (☎796433). **Fore St.** is packed with small bakeries; many places also sell Cornish cream teas (tea with scones, jam, and clotted cream). ☎**01736.**

NEWQUAY. An outpost of surfer subculture, Newquay lures the bald, the bleached-blond, and even the blue-haired to its surf and pubs. Winds descend on **Fistral Beach** with a vengeance, creating what some consider the best surfing conditions in all of Europe, and the enticing **Lusty Glaze Beach** beckons from the bay side. The party beast stirs around 9pm and reigns into the wee hours. Drink up at **The Red Lion,** on North Quay Hill, at Tower Rd., then ride the wave down Fore St. to **Sailors.** (Cover £4-10.) Go on and shake what your momma gave you at **Bertie's,** on East St. (Open daily until 1am.) From the train station, off Cliff Rd., **trains** go to Penzance (2hr., every hr., £10.30) and Plymouth (2hr., every hr., £8.10). From the **bus station,** 1 East St., Western National runs to St. Ives (2hr., June-Sept. 1 per day, £5). National Express (☎(08705) 808080) runs to London (5¾hr., 3 per day, £26.50). Facing the street from the train station, go four blocks left to reach the **tourist office,** on Marcus Hill. (☎854022. Open M-Sa 9am-6pm, Su 9am-4pm; low season reduced hours.) **Newquay Backpackers International,** 69-73 Tower Rd., offers free shuttle service to its sister hostel in St. Ives. (☎879366. Dorms £10.) ☎**01637.**

EAST ANGLIA AND THE MIDLANDS

The plush farmlands of **East Anglia** stretch northeast from London, cloaking the counties of Cambridgeshire, Norfolk, and Suffolk. While the area is still characterized by its rustic beauty, the **Midlands** to the west are known for the mills that sprang up in the Industrial Revolution.

OXFORD   ☎01865

Almost a millennium of scholarship lies behind Oxford—22 British Prime Ministers were educated here, as well as numerous other world leaders. Amid the modern mess of rumbling trucks, screeching brakes, and hurried pedestrians, the academic pilgrim can still find places to pay homage: whether delving in the basement room of Blackwell's Bookstore, exploring the enthralling galleries of the Ashmolean Museum, or strolling through the perfectly maintained quadrangles of Oxford's 39 colleges, travelers can discover Oxford's irrepressible grandeur.

▐▊ TRANSPORTATION AND PRACTICAL INFORMATION

Trains (☎794422) run from Botley Rd., down Park End, west of Carfax, to London's Paddington Station (1hr., 2-4 per hr., return £14.80). **Buses** depart from Gloucester Green. **Oxford CityLink** (☎785400) connects from London's Victoria Station (1¾hr., 1-4 per hr., return £7.50, students £6.50), Gatwick, and Heathrow. **National Express** (☎(08705) 808080) offers domestic routes. Most local service buses board on the streets around Carfax and have fares around 70p. The **tourist office,** The Old School, Gloucester Green, books rooms for a £2.50 fee, It sells accommodation lists (£0.60 and maps (£1). (☎726871. 2hr. walking tours £5. Open M-Sa 9:30am-5pm, Su 10am-

3:30pm.) You can access the **Internet** at **Pickwick Papers,** 90 Gloucester Green, near the bus station. (£1 per 15min. Open daily 4:30am-6:30pm.) **Postal code:** OX1.

ACCOMMODATIONS AND CAMPING

In summer, book at least one week ahead. **B&Bs** line the main roads out of town; take Cityline **buses** or walk 15-45 minutes. More B&Bs are located in the 300s on **Banbury Rd.** (take bus #2A, 2C, or 2D); cheaper ones lie in the 200s and 300s on **Iffley Rd.** (bus #4), between 250 and 350 on **Cowley Rd.** (bus #51 or 52), and on **Abingdon Rd.** in South Oxford (bus #16). Expect to pay £20-25. ▨**Oxford Backpacker's Hotel,** 9a Hythe Bridge St., has a lively backpacker atmosphere. (☎721761. Internet £1.50 per 15min. Guests must show passport. £11-12.) The **YHA Oxford,** 2a Botley Rd., is an immediate right from the train station; a superb location with bright surroundings. Most rooms have 4-6 bunks. (☎762997. Breakfast included. Dorms £18, under 18 £13.50, £1 off for students.) Lincoln College dorms with shaggy green carpets are available at **Old Mitre Rooms,** 4b Turl St. (☎279821; fax 279 963. Open July to early Sept. Singles £32; doubles £48.50, with bath £53; triples £63.50.) Walk 20 minutes or take the "Rose Hill" bus from the bus station, train station, or Carfax Tower to reach **Heather House,** 192 Iffley Rd. (☎249757. Singles £27; doubles with bath £58; cheaper for longer stays.) Take any Abingdon bus across Folly Bridge to reach **Newton House,** 82-84 Abingdon Rd., 800m from the town center. (☎240561. Singles £48; doubles £54-64, with bath £58.) **Oxford Camping and Caravaning,** 426 Abingdon Rd., behind the Touchwoods camping store, has 84 sites. (☎244088. Toilet and laundry facilities. 2-night max. stay for non-members. £4.90-6.25 per tent. Showers free.)

FOOD

Oxford students fed up with cafeteria grub keep cheap restaurants in business. After hours, **kebab vans** roam around Broad St., High St., Queen St., and St. Aldate's St. Across Magdalen Bridge, try restaurants along the first four blocks of **Cowley Rd. Café CoCo,** 23 Cowley Rd., has a great Mediterranean menu. Entrees £5.95-8.50. (Open daily 10am-11pm.) **The Nosebag,** 6-8 St. Michael's St., has a gourmet-grade menu served cafeteria-style. (Lunch under £6.50; dinner under £8. Open M 9:30am-5:30pm, Tu-Th 9:30am-10pm, F-Sa 9:30am-10:30pm, Su until 9pm.) **Chiang Mai,** 130a High St., tucked down an alley, is a popular Thai restaurant with plenty of veggie options. Try the jungle curry with wild rabbit for £7. Reserve in advance or go for lunch to beat the crowds. (Open M-Sa noon-2:30pm and 6-11pm, Su noon-3pm and 6-10pm.) Near Magdalen College, **Harvey's of Oxford,** 58 High St., has great takeout. Try the cherry-apple flapjacks for 85p or large sandwiches for £1.60-3. (Open M-F 8am-7pm, Sa 8am-6pm, Su 8:30am-6pm.) **Heroes,** 8 Ship St., is filled with students feeding on sandwiches and freshly baked breads. (☎723459. Open M-F 8am-7pm, Sa 8:30am-5pm, Su 10am-5pm.) **Covered Market,** between Market St. and Carfax, sells produce, deli goods, and breads. (Open M-Sa 8am-5:30pm.)

SIGHTS

King Henry II founded Britain's first university in 1167; today, Oxford's alumni register reads like a who's who of British history, literature, and philosophy—including Lewis Carroll, C.S. Lewis, and J.R.R. Tolkien. The tourist office's *Welcome to Oxford* guide (£2) lists the colleges' public visiting hours. Start by hiking up the 99 steps of **Carfax Tower** for a great view of the city. (Open daily Apr.-Oct. 10am-5:30pm; Nov.-Mar. 10am-3:30pm. £1.20.) Just down St. Aldate's St. from Carfax, **Christ Church College** has Oxford's grandest quad and its most socially distinguished students. The **Christ Church Chapel** is also Oxford's cathedral. The Reverend Charles Dodgson (a.k.a. Lewis Carroll) was friendly with Dean Liddell of Christ Church—and friendlier with his daughter, Alice. (☎276492. Open M-Sa 9:30am-5:30pm, Su 11:30am-5:30pm. Services Su 8, 10, 11:15am, 6pm; weekdays 7:30am, 6pm. £2.50, students £1.50.) The **Botanic Garden** on High St. cultivates a sumptuous array of plants that have flourished for three centuries. The path connecting the Botanic Garden to the Christ Church Meadow provides a beautiful view of the Thames. From Carfax, head down High St.; the garden is on the right. (Open daily Apr.-Sept. 9am-5pm; Oct.-Mar. 9am-4:30pm. Late June to early Sept. £2, children free. Free rest of the year.) North of Carfax, the imposing ▨**Ashmolean Museum,** Beaumont St., houses works by Leonardo, Monet, Manet, van Gogh, Michelangelo, Rodin, and Matisse. The **Cast Gallery,** behind the museum, exhibits over 250 casts of Greek sculptures—the finest classical collection outside London. From Carfax, head up Cornmarket St., which becomes Magdalen St.; Beaumont St. is on the left. (Open Tu-Sa 10am-5pm, Su 2-5pm. Free.) **Bodleian Library,** Catte St., is Oxford's principal reading and research library with over five million books; no one has ever been permitted to check one out. Take High St. and turn left on Catte. (Open M-F 9am-6pm, Sa 9am-1pm. £3.50.) Next to the Bodleian, the **Sheldonian Theatre** is a Roman-style jewel of an auditorium, where graduation ceremonies are conducted in Latin. The cupola affords an inspiring view of Oxford's spires. (Open M-Sa 10am-12:30pm and 2-4:30pm. £1.50, children £1.) You could browse for days at **Blackwell's Bookstore,** on Broad St., which according to Guinness is the world's largest room devoted to bookselling. (☎ 792792. Open M and W-Sa 9am-6pm, Tu 9:30am-6pm, Su 11am-5pm.) Oscar Wilde attended **Magdalen** (MAUD-lin) **College,** considered by many to be Oxford's most handsome college. (☎ 276000. Open July-Sept. M-F noon-6pm, Sa-Su 2-6pm; Oct.-June daily 2-5pm. Apr.-Sept. £2, students £1; Oct.-Mar. free.)

♫▣ ENTERTAINMENT AND NIGHTLIFE

Punting on the river Thames (known in Oxford as the Isis) or on the River Cherwell (CHAR-wul) is a traditional Oxford past-time. Punters receive a tall pole, a small oar, and an advisory against falling into the water. Don't be surprised if you suddenly come across **Parson's Pleasure,** a small riverside area where men sometimes sunbathe nude. **Magdalen Bridge Boat Co.,** Magdalen Bridge, east of Carfax along High St., rents boats from March to November. (☎ 202643. M-F £9 per hr., Sa-Su £10 per hr.; deposit £20 plus ID. Open daily 10am-9pm.) Music and drama at Oxford are cherished arts. Attend a concert or Evensong service at one of the colleges—the **New College Choir** is one of the best boy choirs around—or a performance at the **Holywell Music Rooms,** the oldest in the country. The **Oxford Playhouse,** 11-12 Beaumont St., is a venue for bands, dance troupes, and the Oxford Stage Company. (☎ 798600. Tickets from £6, standby tickets available for seniors and students.) College **theater groups** also stage productions in local gardens and cloisters. The **City of Oxford Orchestra,** the city's professional orchestra, gives monthly concerts in the Sheldonian Theatre. (☎ 744457. Tickets £10-15; 25% student discount.)

  Pubs far outnumber colleges in Oxford. Sprawling underneath the city, the 13th-century ▨**Turf Tavern** on Bath Pl., off Holywell St., is popular student bar. (Open M-Sa 11am-11pm, Su noon-10:30pm. Kitchen open noon-8pm.) **The Eagle and Child,** 49 St. Giles St., moistened the tongues of C.S. Lewis and J.R.R. Tolkien for 25 years; *The Chronicles of Narnia* and *The Hobbit* were first read aloud here. (Open M-Sa 11am-11pm, Su 11am-10:30pm.) **The King's Arms,** Holywell St, is Oxford's unofficial student union. (Open M-Sa 10:30am-11pm, Su 10:30am-10:30pm.) Although pubs in Oxford tend to close down by 11pm, nightlife can last until 3am; grab *This Month in Oxford* at the tourist office. **Park End,** Park End St., is a flashy favorite of students and locals. (Cover £2-5. Open M-Sa 5pm-1am.) **Walton Street** and **Cowley Road** host late-night clubs, as well as a fascinating jumble of ethnic restaurants, used bookstores, and offbeat shops.

▣ DAYTRIP FROM OXFORD: BLENHEIM PALACE

The largest private home in England and one of the loveliest, **Blenheim** (BLEN-em) **Palace** features sprawling grounds, a lake, and a fantastic garden. While attending a party here, Winston Churchill's mother gave birth to the future Prime Minister in a closet; his grave rests nearby in the village churchyard of **Bladon.** The palace rent is a single French franc, payable each year to the Crown—not a bad deal for a palace with 187 furnished rooms. Blenheim's full glory is on display in Kenneth Branagh's film version of *Hamlet.* (☎ (01993) 811091. Open daily mid-Mar. to Oct. 10:30am-5:30pm; grounds open year-round 9am-9pm. £9, students £7.) Blenheim sprawls in **Woodstock,** 13km north of Oxford on the A44. Stagecoach Express **buses** (☎ (01865) 772250) run to Blenheim Palace (20min., return £3.50) from Gloucester Green station in Oxford; the same route also goes to Stratford and Birmingham.

THE COTSWOLDS

Stretching across western England—bounded by Banbury in the northeast, Bradford-upon-Avon in the southwest, Cheltenham in the north, and Malmesbury in the south—the Cotswolds' verdant, vivid hills enfold tiny towns barely touched by modern life. These old Roman settlements and Saxon villages, hewn from the famed Cotswold stone, demand a place on any itinerary, although their relative inaccessibility via public transportation means extra effort to get there.

E TRANSPORTATION. Useful gateway cities are Cheltenham, Oxford, and Bath. **Trains** (☎ (08457) 484950) to Cheltenham arrive from: Bath (1½hr., every hr., £11.10); Exeter (2hr., every 2hr., £28.50); and London (2½hr., every hr., £31.50). National Express **buses** (☎ (08705) 808080) also roll in from: Exeter (3½hr., every 2hr., £18); London (3hr., every hr., £10.50); and Stratford-Upon-Avon (2¼hr., 2 per day, £7.50).

From Oxford, **trains** zip to: Moreton-in-Marsh (30min., Every hr., £7.50) and Charlbury (20min., every hr., £3.80)—the only villages in the Cotswolds with train stations. Several **bus** companies cover the Cotswolds, but most routes are very infrequent (1-2 per week). Two unusually regular services run from Cheltenham; **Pulham's Coaches** (☎ (01451) 820369) run to Moreton via Bourton-on-the-Water and Stow-on-the-Wold (50min., M-Sa 7 per day, £1.50). **Castleway's Coaches** (☎ (01242) 602949) depart for Broadway via Winchcombe (50min., M-Sa 4 per day, £1.80). Snag the *Connection* timetable from any bus station or tourist office, and the Cheltenham tourist office's *Getting There from Cheltenham.* Local roads are perfect for biking; the closely spaced villages make ideal watering holes. **Country Lanes Cycle Center** rents bikes at the Moreton-on-the-Marsh train station. (☎ (01608) 650065. £14 per day. Call ahead. Open daily 9:30am-5:30pm.)

COTSWOLD WAY. Experience the Cotswolds as the English have for centuries by treading well-worn footpaths from village to village. **Cotswold Way,** spanning 160km from Bath to Chipping Camden, gives hikers glorious vistas of hills and dales. The *Cotswold Way Handbook* (£2) lists **B&Bs** along the Cotswold Way. There are **hostels** in Slimbridge and Stow-on-the-Wold, with dorms averaging £10. Most **campsites** are close to Cheltenham; Bourton-on-the-Water, Stow-on-the-Wold, and Moreton-on-the-Marsh also have places to put your Tent-on-the-Ground. The *Gloucestershire Caravan and Camping Guide* is free at local tourist centers.

CHELTENHAM. The spa town of Cheltenham (pop. 107,000) is a pleasant break from heavily touristed Bath and Stratford and a useful launching pad into the rest of the Cotswolds. Enjoy the diuretic and laxative effects of the waters at the **Town Hall.** Sip, don't gulp. (Open M-F 9:30am-5:30pm. Water tasting free.) Sunbathe at the exquisite **Imperial Gardens. Trains** run into town at the station on Queen's Rd. The **tourist office,** 77 The Promenade, one block east of the bus station, posts vacancies after-hours. (☎ (01242) 522878. Open M-Sa 9:30am-5:15pm.) The well-situated **YMCA,** on Vittoria Walk, accepts both men and women. At Town Hall, turn left off Promenade and walk three blocks—Vittoria Walk is on the right. (☎ 524024. Breakfast included. Reception 24hr. Singles £15.) **Cross Ways,** 57 Bath Rd., features home-sewn bedding and curtains, and a tasty breakfast with veggie options. (☎ 527683. £20-22 per person.) **Benton's Guest House,** 71 Bath Rd., has an exuberant garden and breakfasts that barely fit on the plates. (☎ 517412. £25-35.) Fruit stands and bakeries dot **High Street.** ☎ **01637.**

STOW-ON-THE-WOLD, WINCHCOMBE, AND CIRENCESTER. Stow-on-the-Wold is a sleepy town with fine views, cold winds, and authentic stocks. The **tourist office** is in Hollis House on The Square. (☎ (01451) 831082. Open Easter-Oct. M-Sa 9:30am-5:30pm, Su 10:30am-4pm; Nov.-Easter M-Sa 9:30am-4:30pm.) The **YHA youth hostel** stands just a few yards from the stocks. (☎ (01451) 830497. Open Apr.-Oct. daily. ₤10.85, students ₤9.85.)

West of Stow-on-the-Wold and 10km north of Cheltenham on A46, **Sudeley Castle,** once the manor of King Ethelred the Unready, enserfs the town of **Winchcombe.** (Open Apr.-Oct. daily 10:30am-5pm. ₤6.20.) Just 2½km southwest of Sudeley Castle lies **Belas Knap,** a 4000-year-old burial mound, evidence that the area was inhabited in prehistoric times. The **tourist office** is in Town Hall, near Cheltenham. (☎ (01242) 602925. Open Apr.-Oct. M-Sa 10am-1pm and 2-5pm, Su 10am-1:30pm and 2-5pm.)

Sometimes regarded as the capital of the region, **Cirencester** is the site of **Corinium,** a Roman town founded in AD 49, second in importance only to Londinium. Its **Corinium Museum,** on Park St., houses a formidable collection of Roman paraphernalia. (Open Apr.-Oct. M-Sa 10am-5pm, Su 2-5pm; Nov.-Mar. Tu-Sa 10am-5pm, Su 2-5pm. ₤2.50, students ₤1.) The **Cirencester Parish Church** is Gloucestershire's largest parish church. The money to build it was endowed by wealthy local wool merchants. (Open daily 10am-5pm.) On Fridays, the town turns into a mad antique marketplace. The **tourist office** is in Corn Hall, on Market Pl. (☎ (01285) 654180. Open Apr.-Oct. M 9:45am-5:30pm, Tu-Sa 9:30am-5:30pm; Nov.-Mar. daily 9:30am-5pm.) Cirencester and the ruins are best seen in a daytrip from Cheltenham.

STRATFORD-UPON-AVON ☎ 01789

Former native William Shakespeare is now the area's industry; you'll find the even the most vague of connections to the Bard exploited here to their full potential. Of course, all the perfumes of Arabia will not sweeten the exhaust from tour buses, but beyond the "Will Power" t-shirts, the essence of Shakespeare does lurk in Stratford: in the groves of the once-Forest of Arden and in the pin-drop silence before a soliloquy in the Royal Shakespeare Theatre.

☰ JOURNEY'S END. Thames **trains** roll in from: Birmingham (1hr., ₤3.60); London's Paddington Station (2¼hr., 7-10 per day, return ₤22.50); and Warwick (25min., ₤2.60). National Express runs **buses** from London's Victoria Station (3hr., 4 per day, return ₤4); Stagecoach buses from Oxford (return ₤5.25).

⁊ HERE CEASE MORE QUESTIONS. The **tourist office,** Bridgefoot, across Warwick Rd. at Bridge St. toward the waterside park, sells maps and has a free accommodations guide. (☎ 293127. Open Apr.-Oct. M-Sa 9am-6pm, Su 11am-5pm; Nov.-Mar. M-Sa 9am-5pm.) Romeo and Juliet would have lived happily ever after if they had email; surf the **Internet** at **Java Café,** 28 Greenhill St. (₤3 per 30min., ₤5 per hr.; students ₤2.50, ₤4.) **Postal code:** CV37 6PU.

┏ TO SLEEP, PERCHANCE TO DREAM. To B&B or not to B&B? This hamlet has tons of them (₤15-26), but 'tis nobler in summer to make advance reservations. The nearest hostel is more than 3km away, and the cost is comparable to many B&Bs after adding in return bus fare. Keep an eye out for B&Bs on **Grove Road, Evesham Place,** and **Evesham Road. Bradbourne Guest House,** 44 Shipston Rd., is a recently redecorated Tudor-style home; an 8min. walk from the town center. (☎ 204178. Singles ₤25-30; doubles ₤44-48.) Warm and attentive proprietors consider **The Hollies,** 16 Evesham Pl., their labor of love. (☎ 266857. Doubles ₤35, with bath ₤45.) The **Stratford Backpackers Hotel,** 33 Greenhill St., is conveniently located just across the bridge from the train station and has clean rooms, a common room, and kitchen. (☎ 263838. Dorms ₤12.) The **YHA youth hostel,** Hemmingford House, on Wellesbourne Rd., Alveston, has large, attractive grounds; take bus #X18 from Bridge St. which runs every hour for ₤1.70. (☎ 297093. Breakfast included. Reception 7am-midnight. Dorms ₤15.50, under 18 ₤11.55.) **Riverside Caravan Park,** Tiddington Rd., 1½km east of Stratford on B4086, provides beautiful, but sometimes crowded, sunset views on the Avon. (☎292312. Open Easter-Oct. Tent and 2 people £7, each additional person £1.) Await what dreams may come.

▐ FOOD OF LOVE. Hussain's Indian Cuisine, 6a Chapel St., has fantastic chicken *tikka masala;* keep an eye out for regular Ben Kingsley. (Lunch £6, main dishes from £6.50. Open Th-Su 12:30-2:30pm and daily 5pm-midnight.) Drink deep ere you depart at the ▓**Dirty Duck Pub,** on Waterside, a destination of the theater crowd and the actors themselves. (Traditional pub lunch £3-9; dinner £6-18. Open M-Sa 11am-11pm, Su noon-10:30pm.) To get to the **Safeway supermarket** on Alcester Rd., take the Avon shuttle from the town center, or just cross the bridge past the rail station. (Open M-Th and Sa 8am-9pm, F 8am-10pm, Su 10am-4pm.)

◪ THE GILDED MONUMENTS. Bardolatry peaks around 2pm, so try to hit any Will-centered sights before 11am or after 4pm. Die-hard fans can buy the **combination ticket** (£12, students £11) for admission to five official Shakespeare properties: Shakespeare's Birthplace, Anne Hathaway's cottage (1½km away), Mary Arden's House and Countryside Museum (6½km away), New Place and Nash's House, and Hall's Croft. For a little less of the Bard, buy a **Shakespeare's Town Heritage Trail ticket** (£8.50, students £7.50), which covers only the sights in town—the Birthplace, Hall's Croft, and New Place. **Shakespeare's Birthplace,** Henley St., is equal parts period re-creation and Shakespeare's life-and-works exhibition. (Open Mar. 20-Oct. 19 M-Sa 9am-5pm, Su 9:30am-5pm; Oct. 20-Mar. 19 M-Sa 9:30am-4pm, Su 10am-4pm. £6, students £5.50.) **New Place,** on High St., was Stratford's hippest address when Shakespeare bought it in 1597. Only the foundation remains—it can be viewed from **Nash's House,** which belonged to the first husband of Shakespeare's granddaughter, Elizabeth. **Hall's Croft** and **Mary Arden's House** bank on their tenuous connections to Shakespeare's extended family, but provide exhibits of what life was like in Shakespeare's time. For dramatic cohesiveness, pay homage to Shakespeare's grave—his little, little grave—in the **Holy Trinity Church,** on Trinity St. (£0.60, students £0.40.)

▐ THE PLAY'S THE THING. Get thee to a performance at the world-famous **Royal Shakespeare Company;** recent sons include Kenneth Branagh and Ralph Fiennes. Tickets (£5-40) for all three theaters—the Royal Shakespeare Theatre, the Swan Theatre, and The Other Place—are sold through the box office in the foyer of the Royal Shakespeare Theatre, on Waterside. (Reservations from 9am ☎403403, 24hr. recording ☎403404. Open M-Sa 9am-8pm; arrive at least 20min. before opening for same-day sales. Student and senior standbys for £8-12 exist in principle.)

▐ DAYTRIP FROM STRATFORD: WARWICK CASTLE. Many medievalists, architects, and fire-breathing dragons regard Warwick Castle as one of England's finest; it makes an excellent daytrip from Stratford. Climb the 530 steps up the towers of Warwick and see the countryside unfold like a fairy tale kingdom of hobbits and elves. The dungeons are filled with life-size wax figures of people readying for battle, while "knights" and "craftsmen" talk about their trades. (Open Apr.-Oct. daily 10am-6pm; Nov.-Mar. 10am-5pm. Mid-May to early Sept. £11.50, students £8.60. Mar. to early May and early Sept. to mid-Feb. £10.25, students £7.80). **Trains** arrive from Stratford (20min., return £4) and Birmingham (40min., return £4.70).

CAMBRIDGE   ☎01223

Cambridge (pop. 105,000) is steadfastly determined to remain a city under its academic robes—the tourist office "manages," rather than encourages, visitors. Most colleges close to visitors during official quiet periods in May and early June, but when exams end, cobblestoned Cambridge explodes in gin-soaked glee. May Week (in mid-June, naturally) hosts a dizzying schedule of cocktail parties.

▐▐ TRANSPORTATION AND PRACTICAL INFORMATION. Trains (☎(0345) 484950) run from Station Rd. to London's King Cross and London's Liverpool St. (1¼hr., 2 per hr., £14.90.) **Buses** run from Drummer St.; **National Express** (☎(01604)

620077) goes to London's Victoria Station (2hr., 17 per day, from £8), and **Stage-coach Express** runs to Oxford (2¾hr., 10-12 per day, £7). The **tourist office,** on Wheeler St., is just south of the marketplace and books rooms for a £3 fee plus a 10% deposit. (☎322640; fax 457588; www.tourismcambridge.com. Walking tour £7. Open Apr.-Oct. and Nov.-Mar. M-F 10am-5:30pm, Sa 10am-5pm.) Access the **Internet** at **CBI,** 32 Mill Rd., near the hostel. (5p per min. Open M-Sa 10am-8pm, Su 11am-7pm. Also at 5-7 Norfolk St. Open daily 8am-11pm.)

█▐ ACCOMMODATIONS AND FOOD. Many of the **B&Bs** around **Portugal Street** and **Tenison Road** are open only in July and August. Check the list at the tourist office or pick up their guide to accommodations (50p). Two blocks from the train station, **Tenison Towers Guest House,** 148 Tenison Rd., is impeccable. (☎566511. Singles £22; doubles £42.) **Warkworth Guest House,** Warkworth Terr., near the bus station, offers sunny rooms and packed lunches on request. (☎363682. Singles £30-35;

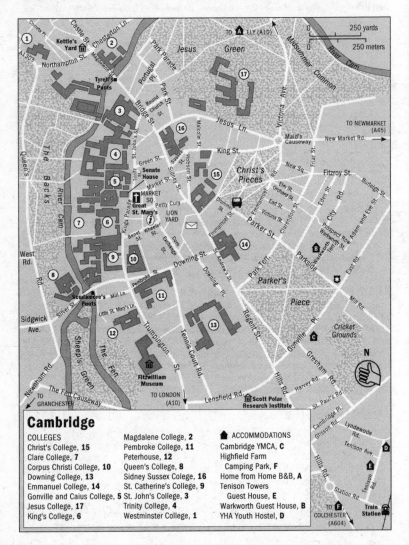

Cambridge

COLLEGES
Christ's College, **15**
Clare College, **7**
Corpus Christi College, **10**
Downing College, **13**
Emmanuel College, **14**
Gonville and Caius College, **5**
Jesus College, **17**
King's College, **6**

Magdalene College, **2**
Pembroke College, **11**
Peterhouse, **12**
Queen's College, **8**
Sidney Sussex Colege, **16**
St. Catherine's College, **9**
St. John's College, **3**
Trinity College, **4**
Westminster College, **1**

▲ ACCOMMODATIONS
Cambridge YMCA, **C**
Highfield Farm
  Camping Park, **F**
Home from Home B&B, **A**
Tenison Towers
  Guest House, **E**
Warkworth Guest House, **B**
YHA Youth Hostel, **D**

doubles £55.) Twenty minutes from the center, **Home from Home B&B**, 39 Milton Rd., has sparkling rooms and a welcoming hostess. (☎323555. Breakfast included. Call ahead with credit card for reservations. Singles £35; doubles from £48.) The **YHA Youth Hostel**, 97 Tenison Rd., has a welcoming atmosphere. (☎354601. Kitchen. Laundry. TV lounge. 3 to 4-bed dorms. £15.10; under 18 £11.40.) **Cambridge YMCA**, Gonville Pl., between the train station and town center, has clean rooms. (☎356998. Breakfast included. Singles £23; doubles £37.) Take Cambus #118 from the Drummer St. bus station to reach **Highfield Farm Camping Park**, Long Rd., Comberton. (☎262308. Showers. Laundry. £7 per tent; £8.75 with car.)

Cantabrigians are too busy learning Latin to flavor their food, so try the fruit and vegetables at **Market Square** (Open M-Sa 9:30am-4:30pm.) **Groceries** are available at **Sainsbury's**, 44 Sidney St. (Open M-F 8am-9pm, Sa 7:30am-9pm, Su 11am-5pm.) **The Little Tea Room**, 1 All Saints' Passage, off Trinity St., serves a "post-tutorial tea." (Open M-Sa 10am-5:30pm, Su 1-5:30pm.) Beautiful people meet for cappuccino and quiche at **Clown's**, 54 King St. (Open daily 7:30am-midnight.) **Postal code:** CB2 3AA.

◙Ṗ SIGHTS AND ENTERTAINMENT. Cambridge is an architect's dream—it packs some of the most breathtaking examples of English architecture into less than 3 sq. km. It's most exciting during the university's three eight-week terms: Michaelmas (Oct.-Dec.), Lent (Jan.-Mar.), and Easter (Apr.-June). **Trinity College** houses the stunning **Wren Library**, Trinity St., which keeps such notable treasures as A.A. Milne's handwritten manuscript of *Winnie the Pooh*. (Chapel and courtyard open daily 10am-5pm; library open M-F noon-2pm, Sa 10:30am-12:30pm; both closed during exams. £1.75.) **King's College**, south of Trinity on King's Parade, is E.M. Forster's alma mater. Rubens's magnificent *Adoration of the Magi* hangs behind the altar of the college's spectacular Gothic chapel. (College open M-F 9:30am-4:30pm, Su 9:30am-2:30pm. Tours arranged through the tourist office. £3.50, students £2.50.) A welcome break from the academia of the colleges, the **Fitzwilliam Museum**, Trumpington St., 10min. from King's College, boasts a hoard of Egyptian, Greek, and Asian treasures that only the Brits could have assembled. (Open Tu-Sa 10am-5pm, Su 2:15-5pm. Guided tours Sa 2:30pm. £3 donation requested. Tours £3.) Today you can sip tea at **The Orchard**, on Mill Way, where luminaries once discussed the ways of the world. Start the delightful walk there by crossing the Silver St. Bridge in Cambridge and following Newnham Rd. until it turns into Grantchester St.; at the dead end, take a right onto Grantchester Meadows and follow it to the footpath. Pick up *The Orchard* from the tourist office for inspiration.

The best source of information on student activities is the student newspaper *Varsity;* the tourist office's free *Cambridge Nightlife Guide* is also helpful. **Punts** (gondola-like boats) are a favorite form of entertainment in Cambridge. Beware that punt-bombing—jumping from bridges into the river alongside a punt, thereby tipping its occupants into the Cam—has evolved into an art form. **Tyrell's**, at Magdalene Bridge, rents boats for £8 per hour plus a £40 deposit. Even more traditional is **pub-crawling**. Cambridge hangouts are great year-round, although they lose some of their character (and their best customers) in summer. **The Eagle**, Benet St., is the oldest pub in Cambridge. (Open daily 11am-11pm, Su noon-10:30pm.)

NORTHERN ENGLAND

Cradled between the Pennines and the North Sea, the Northeast attracts with its calm coast and rich national parkland, including some f the most beautifully desolate areas in England. Extensive paths lace the gray and purple moors that captured the imagination of the Brontës and the emerald dales that figure so prominently in the stories of James Herriot.

PEAK DISTRICT NATIONAL PARK

Britain's first national park sprawls across 1400 sq. km of rolling hills and windswept moors, offering a playground for its 22 million urban neighbors. In the

BRITAIN

northern Dark Peak area, deep *groughs* (gullies) gouge the hard peat moorland against a backdrop of gloomy cliffs, and well-marked footpaths lead over mildly rocky hillsides to village clusters. Abandoned milestones, derelict lead mines, and country homes are scattered throughout the southern White Peak.

Contact **Peak District National Park Office**, Aldern House, Barlow Rd., Bakewell DE4 5AE (☎(01629) 816200), for more information. The **National Park Information Centres** at Bakewell (see below), Castleton (☎(01433) 620679), and Edale (☎(01433) 670207) have walking guides; also ask questions at **tourist offices** in Buxton (☎(01298) 25106) and Matlock Bath (☎(01629) 55082). **YHA youth hostels** in the park cost from £7.50 to £13.75 and are in: Bakewell, Castleton; Edale; Buxton (☎(01298) 22287), and Matlock (☎(01629) 582983). There are 13 **YHA Camping Barns** (£3.60 per night) throughout the park; book ahead at the **Camping Barns Reservation Office,** 6 King St., Clitheroe, Lancashire (☎(01200) 420102) The park authority operates six **Cycle Hire Centres** (£10 per day); call Ashbourne (☎(01335) 343156) or Hayfield (☎(01663) 746222) for information.

◨ TRANSPORTATION. The invaluable *Peak District Timetable* (£0.60; available in all Peak tourist offices) has transport routes and a map. Two **rail** lines originate in **Manchester** and enter the park from the west: one stops at **Buxton** near the park's edge (1hr., every hr., £5.30), and the other crosses the park via **Edale, Hope** (near Castleton), and **Hathersage** (1½hr.; 9-17 per day; Manchester to Sheffield £10.40, Manchester to Edale £6.30) on its way to **Sheffield.** From the south, a train heads from **Nottingham** to **Matlock,** on the park's southeastern edge. Trent **bus** TP (Transpeak; ☎(01298) 230 98) serves the southern half of the park, stopping at **Buxton, Bakewell, Matlock,** and **Derby** between Manchester and Nottingham. A one-day **Wayfarer** pass (£7) covers unlimited train and bus travel within Greater Manchester, including most of the Peak District.

BAKEWELL, EDALE, AND CASTLETON. The Southern Peak is better served by public transportation than its northern counterpart, and is consequently more trampled. Thirty miles southeast of Manchester, **Bakewell** is the best spot for exploration. Near several scenic walks through the White Peaks, the town is known for its Bakewell pudding, created when a flustered cook inadvertently erred while making a tart. Bakewell's **National Park Information Center** (☎(01629) 813227), is in Old Market Halland Bridge St. The small and cozy **YHA youth hostel,** Fly Hill, is 5min. from the town center. (☎(01629) 812313. Open mid-July to Aug. daily; Sept.-Oct. and Easter to mid-July F-Sa. Dorms £8.50.) **Postal code:** DE45 1EF.

The northern Dark Peak area contains some of the wildest and most rugged hill country in England. **Edale** offers little in the way of civilization other than a church, cafe, pub, school, and nearby **YHA youth hostel.** (☎(01433) 67 03 02. Dorms £11.) Its environs, however, are arguably the most spectacular in northern England. The National Park Authority's *8 Walks Around Edale* (£1.20) details nearby **hiking** trails. Stay at the hostel (see above) or **camp** at **Fieldhead,** behind the tourist office. (☎670386. £3.40 per person, £1.20 per car. Showers £0.50.) From Edale, the 5½km hike to **Castleton** affords a breathtaking view of the dark gritstone Edale Valley (Dark Peak) and the lighter limestone Hope Valley (White Peak) to the south. Castleton's river-carved limestone engulfs several famous caverns; **Treak Cliff Cavern** holds breathtaking stalactite chambers and massive seams of the unique Blue John Stone. (Mandatory tour 40min., every 15-30min.; £5.50, students and YHA members £4.50, children £3.) Stay at the excellent **YHA youth hostel** (☎(01433) 620235; open Feb. to late Dec.; dorms £13.75) or **Cryer House,** across from the tourist office (☎(01433) 620244; doubles with bath £44).

MANCHESTER ☎0161

The Industrial Revolution transformed the once unremarkable village of Manchester into a northern hub, now Britain's second-largest urban conglomeration. With few attractive areas and fewer budget accommodations in the city center, Manchester proves that you don't have to be pretty to be popular, attracting thousands with its pulsing nightlife and vibrant arts scene.

TRANSPORTATION. Trains leave **Piccadilly Station,** on London Rd., and **Victoria Station,** on Victoria St., for: London Euston (2½hr., 1 per hr., £84.50); Birmingham (1¾hr., 2 per hr., £14.20); Chester (1hr., 1 per hr., £8.50); Edinburgh (4hr., 12 per day, £41.60-51.50); Liverpool (50min., 2 per hr., £6.95); and York (40min., 2 per hr., £15.80). **Piccadilly Gardens** is home to about 50 bus stops; pick up a route map at the tourist office. National Express **buses** (☎(08705) 808080) go from Chorlton St. to London (4-5hr.; 7 per day; £15) and Liverpool (1hr.; 1 per hr.; £4).

PRACTICAL INFORMATION. The **Manchester Visitor Centre,** in the Town Hall Extension on Lloyd St., has helpful maps and books accommodations for £2.50. (☎234 31 57; information (0891) 715533. Open M-Sa 10am-5:30pm, Su 11am-4pm.) Check **email** at **interc@fe,** Piccadilly Square on the 1st floor of Debenhams. (☎832 86 66. £1.50 per 30min. Open M, W-F 9:30am-5:30pm, Tu 10am-5:30pm, Sa 9am-5:30pm, Su 11am-4:30pm.) **Postal code:** M2 2AA.

ACCOMMODATIONS AND FOOD. Take bus #33 from Piccadilly Gardens toward Wigan to reach the swanky **YHA Manchester,** Potato Wharf, Castlefield. (☎839 9960; manchester@yha.org.uk. Lockers £1-2. Laundry £1.50. Reception 7am-11:30pm. **Internet.** Dorms £18, under 18 £13.10.) To get to the friendly **Woodies Backpackers Hostel,** 19 Blossom St., Ancoats, walk 5min. up Newton St. from Piccadilly Gardens and cross Great Ancoats St., just past the Duke of Edinburgh pub. (☎228 3456; backpackers@woodiesuk.freeserve.co.uk. Dorms £12, £60 per week.) **Cornerhouse Café,** 70 Oxford St., is part of the trendy Cornerhouse Arts Center. (Main dishes from £3.50. Open daily 11am-8:30pm; kitchen open noon-2:30pm and 5-7pm; bar open M-Sa noon-11pm, Su noon-10:30pm.) **On the 8th Day,** 107-111 Oxford Rd., serves up vegetarian and vegan fare for under £4. (Open M-F 9am-7pm, Sa 10am-4:30pm.) **Tesco supermarket** is on Market St. (Open M-Sa 8am-8pm, Su 11am-5pm.)

SIGHTS AND ENTERTAINMENT. The exception to Manchester's unspectacular buildings is the neo-Gothic **Manchester Town Hall,** in St. Peter's Sq. behind the tourist office. Nearby, the domed **Central Library** stands as one of the largest municipal libraries in Europe. (Open M-Th 10am-8pm, F-Sa 10am-5pm.) In the **Museum of Science and Industry,** on Liverpool Rd. in Castlefield, working steam engines provide a dramatic vision of Britain's industrialization. (Open daily 10am-5pm. £6.50, students £3.50.) At the **Manchester United Museum and Tour Centre,** on Sir Matt Busby Way at the Old Trafford football stadium, learn all about the football team Manchester United. Follow the signs up Warwick Rd. from the Old Trafford Metrolink stop. (Open daily 9am-5pm. Tours run every 10min. 9:40am-4:30pm. Museum £5.50, seniors and children £3.75. Tour £3, seniors and children £2.) One of Manchester's biggest draws is its artistic community, most notably its theater and music scenes; the **Royal Exchange Theatre,** on St. Ann's Sq., regularly puts on Shakespeare and original works. (☎833 9833. Box office open M-Sa 9:30am-7:30pm. M-Th and Sa tickets £7-23. Student discounts.) Come nightfall, try the lively pub ▨**The Lass O'Gowrie,** 36 Charles St., for good food at even better prices. (Food served 9am-7pm. Open M-Sa 11am-11pm, Su 11:30am-10:30pm.) **Infinity,** Peter St., a sleek player in Manchester's trendsetting club scene, plays a hypnotizing mix of garage, house, and trance. (Dress smart. Cover M-Th £2-4, F-Sa £6-8. Open M-W 9am-2pm, Th-Sa 9pm-3am.) Northeast of Princess St., the **Gay Village** rings merrily at night; drink at bars lining **Canal Street,** the center of the village. Enthusiastic crowds pack **Cruz 101,** 101 Princess St., the champion of Manchester's nightlife. (Cover £2-5, M free. Open M-F 10:30pm-2:30am.)

LIVERPOOL ☎ 0151

On the banks of the Mersey, Liverpool's history is rooted in its docks. Today, Liverpool (pop. 520,000) boasts two huge cathedrals, a dynamic arts scene, wild nightlife, and—oh yeah—the Beatles.

▐▀ TICKET TO RIDE. Trains (☎ (08457) 484950) leave Liverpool's Lime St. Station for: Birmingham (1¾hr., 2-5 per day, £18.50); Edinburgh (4hr., every 2hr., £41.60); Glasgow (4½hr., every hr., £38.90); London Euston (3hr., every hr., £48.40); and Manchester (1½hr., 2 per hr., £7.20). National Express **buses** (☎ (08705) 808080) go from Norton St. Coach Station to: Birmingham (2½hr., 5 per day, £7.50); London (4½hr., 5 per day, £16.50); and Manchester (1hr., 1-2 per hr., £4.50). The Isle of Man Steam Packet Company (☎ (08705) 523523) runs **ferries** to Dublin.

▐ HELP! The main **tourist office,** in the Queen Square Centre in Queen Sq., sells the handy *Visitor Guide to Liverpool and Merseyside* (£1.50) and books beds for a 10% deposit. (☎ (0906) 680 6886. £0.25 per min. Open M and W-Sa 9am-5:30pm, Tu 10am-5:30pm, Su 10:30am-4:30pm.) **Phil Hughes** runs an excellent Beatles tour in an eight-seat bus. (☎ 236 9091. £11.50.) Check email at the **Central Library**, William Brown St. (Free. Open M-Sa 9am-5pm, Su noon-5pm.) **Postal code:** L1 1AA.

▐▀ HARD DAY'S NIGHT. Budget hotels are mostly on **Lord Nelson Street,** next to the train station, and **Mt. Pleasant,** one block from Brownlow Hill. ▓**Embassie Youth Hostel,** 1 Falkner Sq., 15-20min. from the bus or train station at the end of Canning St., feels like a laid-back student's flat, with laundry, TV, pool table, kitchen, and all the toast and jam you can eat. (☎ 707 1089. Dorms £13.50.) The **YHA Liverpool,** 24 Tabley St., The Wapping, is in an ideal location. From the train station, follow the signs to Albert Dock, turn left on Strand St., and it's on the left. (☎ 709 8888. Breakfast included. Dorms £18.) **Selal Housing Group,** 1 Rodney St., off Mt. Pleasant, is a former YWCA that accepts both men and women. (☎ 709 7791. £12.)

▐ STRAWBERRY FIELDS FOREVER. Trendy vegetarian cafes and reasonably priced Indian restaurants line **Bold Street,** while cheap takeout clusters on **Hardnon Street** and **Berry Street.** Self-caterers should try **St. John's Market,** sprawled across the top of St. John's shopping mall, for fresh produce and local color. The booklined walls of **The Beehive** pub, 7 Paradise St. give an escape from shoppers. (Open M-Sa 11am-11pm, Su noon-10:30pm. Food served M-Sa 11am-11pm, Su noon-3pm.)

▐ MAGICAL MYSTERY TOUR. At Albert Dock, **The Beatles Story** pays tribute to the group's work with a recreation of the Cavern Club, and, of course, a yellow submarine. (Open daily Apr.-Oct. 10am-6pm; Nov.-Mar. 10am-5pm. £7, students £5.) The tourist office's **Beatles Map** (£2.50) leads through Beatles-themed sights, including Strawberry Fields and Penny Lane. **Albert Dock,** at the western end of Hanover St., is a row of Victorian warehouses transformed into restaurants and museums; don't miss the impressive, modern art collection at a branch of London's **Tate Gallery.** (Open Tu-Su 10am-6pm. Free; some special exhibits £3.) Begun in 1904, the Anglican **Liverpool Cathedral** on Upper Duke St. boasts the highest Gothic arches ever built, and the highest and heaviest bells in the world. Climb to the top of the 100m tower for a view stretching to North Wales. (Cathedral open daily 9am-6pm. Suggested donation £2.50.) In contrast, the **Metropolitan Cathedral of Christ the King,** Mt. Pleasant, with gorgeous neon-blue stained glass, looks more like an inverted rocket launcher. (Open M-F 8am-6pm, Sa-Su 8:30am-6pm; in winter M-F 8am-6pm, Sa 8:30am-5pm, Su 8:30am-5:30pm. Free.) If not here for the Beatles, tourists usually arrive for the football. **Liverpool** and **Everton football clubs**—intense rivals—both offer tours of their grounds. (Bus #26 from the city center travels to both stadiums. Everton tour £5.50. Liverpool tour £8.50. Book in advance.)

▐▐ PLEASE PLEASE ME. Almost every street teems with pubs; **Slater St.** in particular brims with £1 pints. John Lennon once said that the worst thing about fame was "not being able to get a quiet pint at the Phil." The rest of us can sip in solitude at **The Philharmonic,** 36 Hope St. (Draughts £1.70 and up. Open M-Sa noon-11pm, Su noon-10:30pm.) **The Jacaranda,** Slater St., site of the Beatles' first paid gig, has live bands and a dance floor. (Open M-Sa noon-2am, Su noon-10:30pm.) Try *Ink*, at the tourist office, for up-to-date arts and nightlife information. ⬛**Cream,** in Wolstonholme Sq. off Parr St., is Liverpool's world-renowned super-club. (Cover £11. Open Sa and the last F of every month.) **The Cavern Club,** 10 Mathew St., is on the site where the Fab Four gained prominence; today it plays regular club music (M and F-Sa 9pm-2am; free before 10pm) and showcases live music (Sa 2-6pm). At the end of August, a **Beatles Convention** draws fans from around the world.

YORK
☎01904

More organized than the Roman with his long spear, more ruthless than the Viking with his broad sword, more thorough than the Norman with his strong bow, the Tourist vanquishes all with her zoom camera. Unlike those before her, she invades neither for wealth nor power. She comes for history: medieval thoroughfares, Georgian townhouses, and the largest Gothic cathedral in Britain.

⬛⬛ **TRANSPORTATION AND PRACTICAL INFORMATION. Trains** run from Station Rd. to: Edinburgh (2-3hr., 2 per hr., £49); London King's Cross (2hr., 2 per hr., £61); Manchester Piccadilly (1½hr., 2 per hr., £16.10); and Newcastle (1hr., 2 per hr., £14.60). National Express **buses** (☎(08705) 808080) depart from Rougier St. for: Edinburgh (5hr., 2 per day, £22); London (4½hr., 6 per day, £17); and Manchester (3hr., 6 per day, £8). To reach the **tourist information centre,** in De Grey Rooms, Exhibition Sq., follow Station Rd., which turns into Museum St., go over the bridge, and turn left on St. Leonards Pl. (Open June-Oct. daily 9am-6pm; Nov.-May 9am-5pm.) Check your **email** at the **Cafe of the Evil Eye,** 42 Stonegate (£1 per hr.).

⬛⬛ **ACCOMMODATIONS AND FOOD.** Competition for inexpensive **B&Bs** (from £18) is fierce in summer; try side streets along Bootham/Clifton or The Mount area (past the train station and down Blossom St.) The ⬛**Avenue Guest House,** 6 The Avenue, 1km down Bootham/Clifton, is immaculate. From the train station, take the river footpath to the bottom of The Avenue. (☎620575. Singles £15-17; doubles £28-40.) ⬛**York Backpackers Hostel,** 88-90 Micklegate radiates a fun atmosphere in a stately, 18th-century urban mansion and has a "Dungeon Bar" open three nights per week, long after the pubs close. (☎627720. Dorms £9-12; doubles £30.) To reach **YHA York,** Water End, Clifton from Exhibition Sq., walk about 1km on Bootham and take a left at Water End. Reception 7am-10:30pm. Open mid-Jan. to mid-Dec. (☎653147. Dorms £16, under 18 £12; singles £18.50; doubles £37). Expensive tea rooms, medium-range bistros, and cheap eateries rub elbows in York. **Oscar's Wine Bar and Bistro,** 8 Little Stonegate, stuffs patrons with massive portions of hearty pub grub for £6-8. (Open daily 11am-11pm.) Grocers peddle at **Newgate market** between Parliament St. and Shambles. (Open M-Sa 9am-5pm; Apr.-Dec. also Su 9am-4:30pm.) **Postal code:** YO1 2DA.

⬛⬛ **SIGHTS AND NIGHTLIFE.** The best introduction to the city is a 4km walk along its medieval walls; sign up for a **walking tour** at the tourist office. The **Association of Voluntary Guides** runs a good architecture tour (2hr.); meet in front of the York City Art Gallery opposite the tourist office (June-Aug. daily 10:15am, 2:15, and 7pm; Apr.-May and Sept.-Oct. daily 10:15am and 2:15pm; Nov.-Mar. 10:15am. Free.) The tourist stampede abates in the early morning and toward dusk, but everyone and everything converges at the enormous ⬛**York Minster,** built between 1220 and 1470. Half of all the medieval stained glass in England glitters here; the **Great East Window** depicts the beginning and end of the world in over a hundred scenes. Climb 275 steps to the top of the **Central Tower** for a view of York's red roofs. (Cathedral open in summer daily 7am-8:30pm; in winter 7am-6pm. Tours 9:30am-3:30pm. Tower open June-Sept. daily 9:30am-6:30pm; Mar.

and Nov. 10am-4:30pm; Apr. and Oct. 10am-5:30pm; May 10am-6pm. £3.) The ⬛**York Castle Museum,** in Minster Yard, by the river, is Britain's premier showcase devoted to everyday life. (Open Apr.-Oct. daily 9:30am-5pm; Nov.-Mar. daily 9:30am-4:30pm. £5.75, students £3.50.) In the gardens off Museum St., peacocks strut among the haunting ruins of **St. Mary's Abbey,** once northern England's most influential Benedictine monastery. There are more **pubs** in the center of York than gargoyles on the east wall of the Minster; for entertainment options, pick up *What's On* or *Evening Entertainment* from the TIC.

⬛ DAYTRIPS FROM YORK: CASTLE HOWARD AND DURHAM CITY. The breathtaking ⬛**Castle Howard** presides over 4 sq. km of stunning gardens, fountains, and lakes. (☎(01653) 648333. Open mid-Mar. to Nov. daily 11am-4:30pm; gardens mid-Mar. to Nov. daily 10am-6:30pm. £7.50; gardens only £4.50.) Yorkshire Coast-liner bus #842 runs excursions to the castle (5 per day, return £4.50).

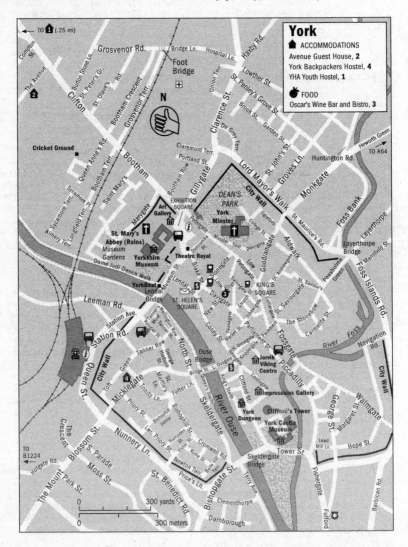

Nearby **Durham City** holds England's greatest Norman edifice, the **Durham Cathedral.** The view from the **tower** is well worth the 325-step climb. (Cathedral open daily May-Sept. 7:30am-8pm; Oct.-Apr. 7:30am-6pm. Tower open mid-Apr. to Sept. 9:30am-4pm; Oct. to mid-Apr. M-Sa 10am-3pm. £2.50 suggested donation.) Across the cathedral green, **Durham Castle** was once a stalwart defensive fortress, but now houses students. **Trains** (☎(08457) 484950) run from York (1hr., 2 per hr., £20).

NEWCASTLE-UPON-TYNE ☎0191

Hardworking Newcastle is legendary for its pub and club scene. While you can still see straight, explore the masterful **Tyne Bridge,** neighboring **Castle Keep,** the elegant **Cathedral Church of St. Nicholas,** the interactive **International Centre for Life,** and the avant-garde ▨**Laing Art Gallery.** (**Castle** open Apr.-Sept. Tu-Su 9:30am-5:30pm; Oct.-Mar. daily 9:30am-4:30pm. £1.50, students £0.50. Church open M-F 7am-6pm, Sa 8am-4pm, Su 7am-noon and 4-7pm. Free. **Center** open daily 10am-6pm. £6.95, seniors and students £5.50, children £4.50, families £19.95. **Gallery** open M-Sa 10am-5pm, Su 2-5pm. Free.) To partake in the true pub experience, try flashy **Chase,** 10-15 Sandhill, or beachy **Offshore 44,** 40 Sandhill. (Both open M-Sa 11am-11pm and Su 12pm-6pm). Revelers sway even before they've imbibed at **The Tuxedo Princess,** a boat/dance club under the Tyne Bridge. (Open M, W-Sa 7:30pm-2am.) Gays and lesbians flock to Waterloo St. to drink and dance at **Rockshots 2** (Open M-Sa 7pm-2am) and **The Powerhouse** (Open M and Th 10pm-2am, Tu-W 11pm-1am, F-Sa 10pm-3am).

Trains (☎(08457) 484950) leave for London (3hr., every hr., £75) and Edinburgh (1½hr., M-Sa 23 per day, Su 9 per day; £33). National Express **buses** (☎08705 808080) leave Percy St. for London (6hr., 6 per day, return £32) and Edinburgh (3hr., 3 per day, return £21). The **tourist office,** 132 Granger St., facing Grey's Monument, has essential maps. (☎277 8000. Open M-W and F-Sa 9:30am-5:30pm, Th 9:30am-7:30pm; June-Sept. also Su 10am-4pm.) To get to the **YHA youth hostel,** 107 Jesmond Rd., take the metro to "Jesmond," turn left on Jesmond Rd., and walk past the traffic lights. (☎281 2570. Lockout 10am-5pm. Curfew 11pm, or ask for the code. Open Feb.-Dec. Dorms £10.85, students £9.75, under 18 £7.15.) The **University of Northumbria,** Coach Ln., offers dorm rooms in a central location. (☎227 4024. Breakfast included. Open late Mar. to mid-Apr. and June to mid-Sept. Singles £18.75; doubles £35.) **Don Vito's,** 82 Pilgrim St., stands out among the many Italian eateries. (Open M-F 11:45am-2pm and 5-10pm, Sa 11:45am-10:30pm.) **Postal code:** NE1 7AB

LAKE DISTRICT NATIONAL PARK

In the Lake District, quite possibly the most beautiful place in England, mountainsides plummet down to shores gently embraced by lapping waves, and water winds its way in every direction. The area's jagged peaks and windswept fells stand in desolate splendor, except in July and August, when outdoor enthusiasts outnumber water molecules. Use **Windermere, Ambleside, Grasmere,** and **Keswick** as bases from which to ascend into the hills—the farther west you go from the **A591** connecting these towns, the more countryside you'll have to yourself.

The **National Park Visitor Centre** is in **Brockhole,** halfway between Windermere and Ambleside. (☎(015394) 466 01. Open Easter-Oct. daily 10am-5pm; Oct.-Easter Sa-Su 10am-5pm.) **National Park Information Centres** book accommodations and dispense information on the camping-barn network. While **B&Bs** line every street in every town (£15-20) and the region has the highest concentration of youth hostels in the world, lodgings do fill up in July and August; book ahead.

◤**TRANSPORTATION.** Two rail lines (☎(08457) 484950) flank the park: the south-north **Preston-Lancaster-Carlisle** line skirts the park's eastern edge, while the **Barrow-Carlisle** line serves the western coast. **Oxenholme,** on the **P-L-C,** on the southeastern edge of the Lake District, and **Penrith,** to the northeast, are accessible from: **Manchester's** Piccadilly Station (2hr., 5-7 per day, £12.70); **Edinburgh** (2½-3hr., 6 per day, £30.80); and **London's** Euston Station (4-5hr., 11-16 per day, £59.60). From Oxenholme, a short branch line covers the 16km to **Windermere** (20min., every hr.,

£3.50). **National Express buses** (☎(08705) 808080) go directly to Windermere from London (7½hr., 1 per day, £26), and continue north through **Ambleside** and **Grasmere** to **Keswick. Stagecoach Cumberland buses** (☎(01946) 63222) serve over 25 towns and villages within the district; pick up the essential *Lakeland Explorer* at any tourist office. An **Explorer** ticket offers unlimited all-day travel on all area Stagecoach buses (£6.50) or the highly recommended unlimited 4-day travel ticket (£15). The Amble-

---

BEFORE THERE WERE POWERBARS About the only thing more common in Lakeland than tourists and outdoor shops is the hiking essential known by locals as mint cake. Although there are multiple varieties for sale, the original recipe dates back to 1913 when James Wilson of Kendal boiled down sugar, peppermint oil and a touch of salt in an open copper pan to create a delicious and nourishing energy food. Since then, Kendal Mint Cakes have accompanied back-packers to the top of Mount Everest and deep into the Sahara Desert. Before setting out on your expedition to the nearby fells, be sure to bring along a few mint cakes (for an extra energy boost, try the chocolate covered variety). Beware: at 95 grams of sugar per serving, you'd better save room in your rucksack for a toothbrush.

---

side YHA Youth Hostel offers a convenient **minibus service** (☎(015394) 32304; £2.50) between hostels as well as free service from the Windermere train station to the Windermere and Ambleside hostels. Potential cyclists can get **bike rental** information at tourist offices; *Ordnance Survey Cycle Tours* (£10) has route maps.

WINDERMERE AND BOWNESS. Windermere and sidekick **Bowness-on-Windermere** fill to the gills with vacationers in summer, when sailboats and waterskiers swarm over Lake Windermere. **Windermere Lake Cruises** runs the **Lake Information Centre** (☎433 60), at the north end of Bowness Pier, which provides maps, rents rowboats and motorboats, and books lake cruises. From Easter to October, boats sail north to Waterhead Pier in Ambleside (30min., 2 per hr., return £5.70) and south to Lakeside (40min., every hr., return £6). The **train station** sends Lakeland Experience **buses** to Bowness (#599; 3 per hr., £1). The **tourist information centre** is next door. (☎46499. Open daily July-Aug. 9am-7:30pm; Easter-June and Sept.-Oct. 9am-6pm; Nov.-Easter 9am-5pm.) The local **National Park Information Centre,** on Glebe Rd., is beside Bowness Pier. (☎42895. Open July-Aug. daily 9:30am-6pm; Apr.-June and Sept.-Oct. daily 9am-5:30pm; Nov.-Mar. F-Su 10am-4pm.) To get to the spacious **YHA youth hostel,** on High Cross, Bridge Ln., Troutbeck, 1½km north of Windermere off A591, take the Ambleside bus to Troutbeck Bridge and walk 1.25km uphill, or catch the YHA shuttle from the train station. (☎43543; windermere@yha.org.uk. Bike rental. Open mid-Feb. to Oct. £11.) To reach the social **Lake District Backpackers Hostel,** on High St., look for the sign on the right as you descend the hill from the train station. (☎46374. Reception 9am-1pm and 5-9pm. £11) **Camp** at **Limefitt Park,** 7.25km north of the pier on A592, below the Kirkstone path. (☎32300. £3 per person; 2 people with tent and car £12.) ☎**015394**

AMBLESIDE. About a mile north of Lake Windermere, Ambleside has adapted to the tourist influx without selling its soul. You can't go wrong **hiking** in any direction near Ambleside; however, hidden trail markings, steep slopes, and weather-sensitive visibility all necessitate a good map and compass. Excellent guided **walks** leave from National Park and tourist offices. The top of **Loughrigg,** 4km from Ambleside (5½km circuit descent), provides a view of higher surrounding fells. For gentler, shorter hikes, *Ambleside Walks in the Countryside* (£0.30) lists three easy walks from the town center. Lakeslink **bus** #555 (☎32231; every hr.) rolls into Kelsick Rd. from Windermere, Grasmere, and Keswick. The **tourist office** is located at Central Buildings, Market Place (☎31576. Open daily 9am-5:30pm.) To reach the **National Park Information Centre,** Waterside, walk south on Lake or Borrans Rd. from town to the pier. (☎32729. Open daily Easter-Oct. 9:30am-6pm.) Bus #555 also stops in front of the superb ◪**Ambleside YHA Youth Hostel,** 1½km south of Ambleside and 5km north of Windermere, on the north shore of Windermere Lake. (☎323 04. Bike rental. Nov.-Feb. midnight curfew. £11.15.) ☎**015394**

GRASMERE. The peace that Wordsworth enjoyed in the village of Grasmere is still apparent on quiet mornings. The 17th-century ◘**Dove Cottage**, 10 minutes from the center of town, was Wordsworth's home from 1799 to 1808, and remains almost exactly as he left it; next door is the outstanding **Wordsworth Museum.** (Both open daily mid-Feb. to mid-Jan. 9:30am-5pm. £5, students £4.20.) The **Wordsworth Walk** (9½km) circumnavigates the two lakes of the Rothay River, passing the poet's grave, Dove Cottage, and ◘**Rydal Mount,** where the poet lived until his death. (Open daily Mar.-Oct. 9:30am-5pm; Nov.-Feb. W-M 10am-4pm. £3.75, students £3.25.) **Bus** #555 stops in Grasmere every hour on its way south to Ambleside or north to Keswick; bus #599 stops every 20 minutes. The combined **tourist office** and **National Park Information Centre** lies on Redbank Rd. (☎35245. Open daily Easter-Oct. 9:30am-5:30pm; Nov.-Easter F-Su 10am-4pm.) **Grasmere YHA** (☎35316; fax 35798; grasmerebh@yha.org.uk) is split into two buildings: Butterlip and Thorney How. To reach **Butterlip How,** on Easedale Rd., follow the road to Easedale for 140km and turn right down the sign-posted drive. (Open Apr.-Oct. daily; Nov.-Jan. F-Sa; Feb.-Mar Tu-Sa. £12.50.) To reach **Thorney How,** follow Easedale Rd. 800m out of town, turn right at the fork, and look for it 400m down on the left. (Open Apr.-Sept. daily; mid-Feb. to Mar. and Oct.-Dec. Th-M. £10.) Sarah Nelson's famed Grasmere Gingerbread, a staple since 1854, is a steal at £0.22 in **Church Cottage,** outside St. Oswald's Church. (Open Easter-Nov. M-Sa 9:15am-5:30pm, Su 12:30-5:30pm; Dec.-Easter M-Sa 9:15am-5pm, Su 12:30-5pm.) ☎**015394**.

KESWICK. Between towering Skiddaw peak and the north edge of Lake Derwentwater, Keswick (KEZ-ick) rivals Windermere as the Lake District's tourist capital but surpasses it in charm. A popular day hike that starts from the town centre visits the lake shore and two popular viewpoints nearby. Leave Keswick Market Place by Borrowdale Rd. and turn right into Lake Road, which passes the boathouses and jetties by the lakeshore. A footpath continues on from the road that leads to **Friar's Crag** (praised by Ruskin, Wordsworth, and *Let's Go*), a rocky and wooded promontory with views down Derwentwater to the **Jaws of Borrowdale.** There, the valley narrows between steep, tooth-like hills. After conquering the fells, retrace the path back to the boat landings, and take the path on the right just before the public toilets into **Cockshott Wood.** Continue on this path into **Castlehead Wood,** and then follow the rocky trail up to the top of **Castle Head.** To return to Keswick, continue through the woods and then follow the path to Springs Road. Follow the road to the end, and turn left onto Ambleside road, which returns you to the market place. The **National Park Information Centre,** in Moot Hall, is behind the clock tower in Market Sq. (☎72645. Open daily Aug. 9:30am-6pm; Sept.-July 9:30am-5:30pm.) From the tourist office, bear left down Station Rd. and follow the signs to the stellar **Keswick YHA Youth Hostel.** (☎72484; keswick@yha.org.uk. Kitchen. Curfew 11:30pm. Open mid-Feb. to late Dec. £11.) It's worth the 3km ride south on B5289 (bus #79; every hr.) to Seatoller to stay at the ◘**Derwentwater YHA Youth Hostel,** in Barrow House, Borrowdale, where you can relax by its waterfall. (☎77246. Open Jan.-Oct. £11.) **Camp** at **Castlerigg Hall,** southeast of Keswick on A591. (☎724 37. Open Apr.-Nov. £2.70-3.20 per person; £1 per car. Showers £0.50.) ☎**017687**

WALES

Wales borders England, but if many of the 2.9 million Welsh people had their way, it would be floating miles away. Wales clings steadfastly to its Celtic heritage, continuing a centuries-old struggle for independence. Travelers come for the miles of sandy beaches, grassy cliffs, and dramatic mountains that typify the rich landscape of this corner of Britain, or to scan the numerous castles that dot the towns, remnants of centuries of warfare with England.

⚓ FERRIES TO IRELAND

Irish Ferries (☎ (1890) 313131; www.irishferries.ie) run to **Dublin, Ireland** from **Holyhead** (2hr., return £28-60); and **Rosslare** from **Pembroke** (4hr., return £28-35). Stena Line ☎ (08705) 707070; www.stenaline.co.uk), runs from **Holyhead** to **Dublin** (4hr., £18-20) and **Dún Laoghaire** (1-3½hr., UK£20-28). **Swansea Cork Ferries** ☎ (01792) 456116 run from King's Dock, **Swansea** to **Cork,** Ireland (10hr., £24-34).

CARDIFF (CAERDYDD)   ☎029

Once a sleepy little town, Cardiff (pop. 340,000), burst onto the scene in the late 19th century as the main shipping center of Welsh coal; at its height, it was the world's busiest port. Today, the buzzing capital of Wales brims with theaters and clubs as well as remnants of its past. The flamboyant **Cardiff Castle** was restored in mock-medieval style, with a different theme for each room; climb the steps of the Norman keep for a sweeping view of town. (Open Mar.-Oct. daily 9:30am-6pm; Nov.-Feb. 9:30am-4:30pm. £5.25, children £4.20, family £14.75.) The **National Museum and Gallery of Wales** has a collection of Western European art and an audiovisual exhibit on "The Evolution of Wales." (Open Tu-Su 10am-5pm. Free.)

   Trains (☎ (08457) 484950) stop in Cardiff from Bath (1-1½hr., 3 per hr., £11.90); Edinburgh (7hr., 7 per day, £100.80); and London's Paddington Station (2hr., 1 per hr., £37). National Express **buses** (☎ (0990) 808080) roll to Cardiff from London's Victoria Station (3½hr., 12 per day, £14) and Manchester (6hr., 11 per day, £25). The **tourist office**, at 16 Wood St. across from the bus station, books B&Bs and stocks maps. (☎ 2022 7281. Open July.-Aug. M-Sa 9am-6pm, Su 10am-4pm; Sept.-June M-Sa 9am-5pm, Su 10am-4pm.) **Internet Exchange** is at 8 Church St, by St. John's Church. (Open M-Sa 9am-9pm, Su 10am-7pm. £2 per hr., 1hr. minimum.)

   The best B&Bs are off Cathedral Rd. (take bus #32 or walk 15min. from the castle). To get to the colorful **Cardiff International Backpacker,** 98 Neville St., from the train station, go down Wood St., cross the river, turn right on Fitzham Embankment, and turn left at the end of the road onto Despenser St. (☎ 2034 5577; fax 2023 0404. Toast and tea included. Dorms £14; doubles £36; triples £42.) The Victorian **Central Market** is in the arcade between St. Mary St. and Trinity St. (Open M-Sa 9am-5pm.) **The Prince of Wales,** at the corner of St. Mary's St. and Wood St., offers great food and atmosphere (Open M-Sa 11am-11pm, Su noon-10:30pm.) Cardiff's specialty, **Brains S.A.** (Special Ale), known by locals as "Brains Skull Attack," is proudly served in many local pubs. Head to the **Clwb Ifor Bach** (the Welsh Club), 11 Womanby St., for dancing and the local music scene. (Cover £2-8. Open M-Th until 2am, F-Sa until 3am.) **Postal code:** CF10 2SJ.

WYE VALLEY

Wordsworth once came to the Wye Valley (Afon Gwy) to escape the "fever of the world"; the region's tranquility has since been disturbed by a feverish tourist trade. Nonetheless, much of this region remains unsullied. Below Monmouth, moving past Wordsworth's steep cliffs, orchard tufts, and pastoral farms, the Wye brings green to the door of even the larger towns.

◪ TRANSPORTATION. The valley is best entered from the south, at Chepstow. **Trains** chug to Chepstow from Cardiff and Newport (40min.; M-Sa 8 per day, Su 7 per day; £5.20) and Hereford (1hr., every hr., £11.70), the nearest station to Hay-on-Wye. National Express **buses** (☎ (08705) 808080) also ride from Cardiff (50min., 5 per day, £3.25) and London (2¼hr., 10 per day, £16.50). Bus service in the region is rare on Sundays. Pick up *Discover the Wye Valley on Foot and by Bus* in area tourist offices for schedules. Stagecoach Red and White local bus #69 loops between Chepstow, Tintern, and Monmouth (4-8 per day). One-day **Network Rider passes** ($4.50) will save money if you take the bus frequently.

Hikers enjoy walks of all difficulties and lengths. The **Wye Valley Walk** heads north from Chepstow and passes the abbey at Tintern, the cathedral at Hereford, and the breathtaking vista at Symonds Yat en route to Hay-on-Wye and Prestatyn. Across the river, the **Offa's Dyke Path** runs the entire length of the England-Wales border, providing 285km of hiking trails.

CHEPSTOW. Chepstow's strategic position at the mouth of the river and the base of the English border made it an important fortification and commerce center in Norman times. **Chepstow Castle,** built by a comrade of William the Conqueror, is Britain's oldest stone castle and offers awesome views of the Wye River. (Open Apr.-May daily 9:30am-4pm; Jun.-Sept. 9:30am-6pm; Oct.-Mar. M-Sa 9:30am-4pm, Su 11am-4pm. $3; students, seniors, and children $2; families $18.) **Trains** arrive at Station Rd.; **buses** stop above the town gate in front of the Somerfield supermarket. Ask about bus tickets at **The Travel House,** 9 Moor St. (☎623031. Open M-Sa 9am-5:30pm.) The **tourist office** is in the castle parking lot. (☎623772. Open Apr.-Sept. daily 10am-5:35pm; Oct.-Mar. 10am-4:30pm.) Take bus #69 to the hostel near Tintern (see below) or stay in Chepstow at **Lower Hardwick House,** 350m up Mt. Pleasant from the bus station. (☎(01291) 622162. Singles $18; doubles $30-36. **Camping** $5 per tent.) Postal code: NP6 5DA.☎**01291.**

TINTERN. Five miles north of Chepstow on the A466, the haunting arches of ▓**Tintern Abbey** shade crowds of tourists in the summer and, according to Wordsworth's famous poem written just a few miles north, "connect the landscape with the quiet of the sky." (☎689251. Open June-Sept. daily 9:30am-6pm; Apr.-May and Oct. daily 9:30am-5pm; Nov.-Mar. M-Sa 9:30am-4pm, Su 11am-4pm. $2.50; students, seniors, and children $2; families $7.) Near the iron footbridge, footpaths lead to **Offa's Dyke** (45min.) and the **Devil's Pulpit** (1½hr.). A mile north of the abbey, the **Old Station** houses the **tourist office.** (☎/fax 689566. Open Apr.-Oct. daily 10:30am-5:30pm.) The **YHA youth hostel,** 6½km northeast of Tintern, in England, occupies a 13th-century castle complete with dungeon. (☎(01594) 530272. Dorms $10.85, under 18 $7.40.) Postal code: NP6 6SB. ☎**01291.**

HEREFORD AND HAY-ON-WYE. Ideal for excursions into Wales, **Hereford** (pop. 60,000) also draws its own visitors with its 11th-century **cathedral** and the 13th-century **Mappa Mundi** within—a map of the world drawn on animal skin c.1290. (Cathedral open Th-Tu until evensong at 6pm, W 24hr. Mappa Mundi shown May-Sept. M-Sa 10am-4:15pm, Su 11am-3:15pm; Oct.-Apr. M-Sa 11am-3:15pm. $4, students $3.50.) The **tourist office,** 1 King St., in front of the cathedral, books beds for a 10% deposit. (☎268430. Open May-Sept. M-Sa 9am-5pm, Su 10am-4pm; Oct.-Apr. M-Sa 9am-5pm.) The T-junction at the end of **Bodenham Road** hosts many of the cheaper B&Bs (around $26). Otherwise, try **Bourvrie House,** 26 Victoria St., a mere 5min. from downtown. (☎266265. TV. Singles $20; doubles $18.50 per person; family room $23 per person.) **Postal code:** HR4 9HQ. ☎**01432.**

Bookseller Richard Booth transformed **Hay-on-Wye** into the world-renowned "Town of Books." Forty secondhand and antiquarian book shops attract browsers, and a 10-day **literary festival** in summer brings luminaries like Toni Morrison and P.D. James to give readings. The **tourist information center,** on Oxford Rd., books beds for a $2 fee. (☎820144. Open Apr.-Oct. daily 10am-1pm and 2-5pm; Nov.-Mar. 11am-1pm and 2-4pm.) **The Bear,** Bear St., has traditional rooms and warm hospitality. (☎821302; fax 820506. Singles $24 and up.) **Postal code:** HR3 5AE. ☎**01497.**

BRECON BEACONS NATIONAL PARK

Brecon Beacons National Park encompasses dramatic 1340 sq. km divided into four regions. The fringe towns of Brecon and Abergavenny facilitate access to the park. **Trains** (☎(08457) 484950) run from London Paddington Station to Abergavenny at the park's southeastern corner, as well as to Merthyr Tydfil on the southern edge. **National Express** (☎(08705) 808080) bus #509 runs once a day to Brecon, on the north side of the park, from London and Cardiff. **Stagecoach Red and White** (☎(01633) 266336) crosses the park to Brecon from: Cardiff via Merthyr Tydfil (#43, changing to X4; 1½hr.; M-Sa 5 per day; £5-7); Swansea (#63; 1½hr., M-Sa 3 per day; Su 4 per day, £3.70); and Hereford via Hay-on-Wye (#39, M-Sa 5 per day). **Yeomans** (☎(01432) 356201) bus #40 runs the same route (Su 2 per day; £2.80-4.10).

Just north of the mountains, **Brecon** is the best hiking base. Buses arrive at **The Bulwark**, the central square. The **tourist office** is in the parking lot; pass through Bethel Sq. off Lion St. (☎(01497) 623156. Open daily in summer 10am-6pm, in winter 9:30am-5:30pm.) Only three minutes from town, **The Watton** is ripe with **B&Bs** (£17-20). **Camp** at **Brynich Caravan Park,** 2½km east of town on the A40, signposted from the A40-A470 roundabout. (☎(01874) 623325. Showers and laundry. Open Mar.-Oct. £6.50-7.50 per person, £4 per walk-in.)

At the park's center, the **Brecon Beacons** lure hikers with pastoral slopes and barren peaks. Since many paths are unmarked, Landranger *Ordnance Survey maps 12 and 13* (£6.50 each) are essential to navigate the park. From the Mountain Center, a 1hr. stroll among daredevil sheep and panoramic views ends at the scant remains of an **Iron Age fort.** The most convenient route to the top of **Pen-y-Fan** (pen-uh-van; 886m) begins at **Storey Arms,** a large parking lot and bus stop 8km south of Libanus on A470. A more pleasant hiking route starts in **Llanfaes,** a western suburb of Brecon, and passes **Llyn Cwm Llwch** (HLIN-koom-hlooch), a 600m deep glacial pool. Follow Ffrwdgrech Rd. in Llanfaesm until you reach a fork; take the middle branch after the first bridge, where the trail begins.

In the **Waterfall District,** forest rivers tumble through rapids, gorges, and spectacular falls near **Ystradfellte** (uh-strahd-FELTH-tuh), 11km southwest of the Beacons. The **YHA Ystradfellte** is the best base. (☎(01639) 720301. Open Apr. to mid-July and Sept.-Oct. F-Tu; mid-July to Aug. daily. Dorms £8.10, under 18 £5.65.) Follow marked paths from Gwann Hepste and stand on the cliff face behind the **Sgwdyr Elra** waterfall. To the west near **Abercave,** the **Dan-yr-Ogof Showcaves** impress with enormous stalagmites. (☎(01639) 730284; 24hr. ☎730801. Open Apr.-Oct. 10:30am-3pm, later in summer. Tours every 20min; £7.50.) **Stagecoach Red and White** bus #63 stops at the hostel, caves, and country park en route from Brecon.

In the easternmost section of the park, the **Black Mountains** are a group of lofty ridges that offer 130 sq. km of solitude linked by ridge walks. The Ordnance Survey Outdoor Leisure **map 13** costs £6.50. Begin forays from **Crickhowell** or travel the eastern boundary along **Offa's Dyke Path,** which is dotted with a handful of impressive ruins. There is almost no public transportation along valley routes, but **Stagecoach Red and White** bus #39 descends the north side of the Black Mountains.

ABERYSTWYTH ☎01970

Halfway down the sweeping Cardigan Bay coastline, the university town of Aberystwyth (Abber-RIST-with) offers plenty of raucous pubs as you wait for your connection to Wales and points elsewhere. The **National Library of Wales,** off Penglais Rd., houses the earliest surviving manuscript of *The Canterbury Tales* and almost every written book in Welsh pertaining to Wales. (Open M-F 9:30am-6pm, Sa 9:30am-5pm. Free.) Aberystwyth's beachfront and promenade remain as they were in Victorian times. If you have a spare half-day, don't miss the steam engine ride on the **Vale of Rheidol Railway** through mountains and the waterfalls and gorges of **Jacob's Ladder.** (☎625819. Call for schedule. Rides £11, accompanied child £2.) The **train station,** on Alexandria Rd., is at the receiving end of the main rail line from England into central Wales. For destinations on the scenic Cambrian Coast to the north, change at **Machynlleth** (4-7 per day, 30min., £4.60). **Arriva Cymru** (☎(08706) 082608) covers buses in the region; call for schedules. The **tourist office,** in Lisburne House on Terrace Rd., has information on **B&Bs.** (☎612125. Open July-Aug. daily 9am-6pm; Sept.-June M-Sa 10am-5pm.) **Mrs. E. V. Williams,** 28 Bridge St. offers large rooms with staggeringly comfortable beds. (☎612550 £15 per person.) Eat and drink at **The Academy,** St. James Sq., a chapel converted into a lively student pub. (Open M-Sa 11am-11pm, Su 11am-10:30pm.)

SNOWDONIA NATIONAL PARK

Stretching from forested Machynlleth in the south to sand-strewn Conwy in the north, the 2175 sheep-dotted sq. km of Snowdonia National Park accommodate droves of visitors with untrammeled corners and quiet hikes. Known in Welsh as *Eryri* (Place of Eagles), Snowdonia's upper reaches are as barren and lonesome as the name suggests; the park also embraces dark pine forests, deep glacial lakes, sun-pierced coves, and shimmering estuaries. **Mount Snowden** (1085m) is the highest peak in England and Wales and the most popular destination in the park.

The **Snowdonia National Park Information Headquarters**, Penrhyndeudraeth, Gwynedd, Wales (☎(01766) 770274), stocks walk leaflets and Ordnance Survey Maps (£5.25-6.50), and can best direct you to the nearest of the eight quality **YHAs** in the park as well as the region's other **tourist offices (TICs)**. Check out www.gwynedd.gov.uk for the region's tourist information.

⊏TRANSPORTATION. Trains (☎(08457) 484950) stop at several large towns on the park's outskirts, including **Bangor** (p. 200) and **Conwy** (p. 200). The **Conwy Valley Line** runs through the park from **Llandudno** through **Betws-y-Coed** to **Blaenau Ffestiniog** (1hr., 2-7 per day, return £14.20). Buses run to the interior from these towns as well as others near the edge of the park, such as **Caernarfon** (p. 200). At Blaneau Ffestiniog the Conwy Valley Line connects with the narrow-gauge **Ffestiniog Railway** (☎(01766) 516000), which runs through the mountains to Porthmadog, meeting the Cambrian Coaster Service to **Llanberis** and **Aberystwyth**. Consult the indispensable *Gwynedd Public Transport Maps and Timetables*, available in all regional TICs.

HARLECH. On the Cambrian coast, south of the Llŷn Peninsula and the foothills of Snowdonia, tiny Harlech clings to a steep hillside. ◧**Harlech Castle,** a World Heritage Site, crowns a 60m rock with sweeping views of Snowdonia and the bay. (☎780552. Open Apr.-May and Oct. daily 9:30am-5pm; June-Sept. daily 9:30am-6pm; Nov.-Mar. M-Sa 9:30am-4pm, Su 11am-4pm. £3, students £2.) The tourist office, in Gwyddfor House, Stryd Fawr, doubles as the **Snowdonia National Park Information Centre.** (☎/fax 780658. Open daily Easter-June and Sept.-Oct. 10am-1pm and 2-6pm; July-Aug. 10am-6pm.) Revel in spacious rooms and what may be the best view in Harlech at ◧**Arundel,** Stryd Fawr. Walk past the tourist office on Stryd Fawr and take a right before the Yr Ogof Bistro. ☎**01766.**

LLYN PENINSULA   ☎01766

The Llŷn has been a hotbed of tourism since the Middle Ages, when crowds of religious pilgrims tramped through on their way to Bardsey Island, off the peninsula's western tip. Now eager apostles to sun-cult make the pilgrimage to the endless beaches that line the southern coast, putting their faith in the region's unusually good weather. **Porthmadog,** on the southeastern part of the peninsula, is the main gateway. This travel hub's principal attraction is the jolly puffing **Ffestiniog Railway** (☎516000), which runs from Harbour Station on High St. into the hills of Snowdonia (1hr., mid-Feb. to Nov. 2-10 per day, £13.80). **Portmeirion,** 3¼km east of Porthmadog, proves an eccentric landmark of Italy-fixation, with Mediterranean courtyards, pastel houses, palm trees, and exotic statues constituting an otherworldly diversion from the standard Welsh castles and cottages. (Open daily 9:30am. Shops close 5:30pm, but it's possible to stay later. £5, students £4; Nov.-Mar. discount.) **Bus** #98 runs from Porthmadog to **Minffordd,** a scenic 2½km from Portmeirion. Minffordd is also a stop on the Cambrian Coaster train line (M-Sa 6-7 per day), while other trains arrive through the adjacent Snowdonia National Park. The **tourist office** is at the opposite end of High St., by the harbor. (☎512981. Open Easter-Oct. daily 10am-6pm; Nov.-Easter 9:30am-5pm.) Sleep comfortably in Lawrence of Arabia's first home at **Snowdon Backpackers,** 10min. from the train station. (☎515354. Apr.-Oct. £12.50 per person; Nov.-Mar. £11.50.)

NORTHERN COAST

CAERNARFON. Perched on the edge of the Menai Strait, Caernarfon (car-NAR-von) lures visitors with North Wales's grandest medieval castle. Built by Edward I beginning in 1283, the ◨**Caernarfon Castle** was left unfinished when Edward ran out of money and was distracted by rebelling Scots. (Open June-Sept. daily 9:30am-6pm; Apr.-May and Oct. daily 9:30am-5pm; Nov.-Mar. M-Sa 9:30am-4pm, Su 11am-4pm. £4.20, students £3.20). **Buses** arrive on Penllyn; Arriva Cymru (☎(08706) 082608) runs from Bangor (#5, 5A, 5B, and 5X; £1.55) and Conwy (£2.85). The **tourist office,** on Castle St., is opposite the castle gate. (☎672232. Open Apr.-Oct. daily 10am-6pm; Nov.-Mar. Th-Tu 9:30am-4:30pm.) Stay in comfy bunks at ◨**Totter's Hostel,** 2 High St., at the end of the street. (☎672963. Dorms £11.) Watch the sunset, pint in hand, from **Anglesey Arms,** on the Promenade just below the castle. (Open M-Sa 11am-11pm, Su noon-10:30pm.) ☎**01286.**

CONWY. The central attraction of this modern tourist mecca is the 13th-century **Conwy castle,** built as another link in Edward I's rings of fortresses. (Open June-Sept. daily 9:30am-6pm; Apr.-May and Oct. daily 9:30am-5pm; Nov.-Mar. M-Sa 9:30am-4pm, Su 11am-4pm. £3.60, students £2.60. Tours £1.) Arriva Cymru **buses** #5 and 5X from Caernarfon and Bangor stop along the main streets in Conwy. National Express rolls in from: Liverpool (2¾hr., 1 per day); Manchester (4hr., 1 per day, £10.75); and Newcastle (10hr., 1 per day). The **tourist office** is at the entrance to the castle. (☎592248. Open Easter-Oct. daily 9:30am-6pm; Nov.-Mar. Th-Sa 10am-4pm.) **Swan Cottage,** 18 Berry St., is one of the few B&Bs within the city walls, featuring cozy rooms with timber ceilings and TVs. The loft room charms with a view of the estuary. (☎596840. £16 per person.) ☎**01492.**

ISLE OF ANGLESEY   ☎01248

The isle attracts visitors with its prehistoric ruins and eerie Celtic burial mounds set in its flat landscape. Less ancient is ◨**Beaumaris Castle,** the last of Edward I's Welsh fortresses and today a World Heritage site. (Open June-Sept. daily 9:30am-6pm; Apr.-May and Oct. daily 9:30am-5pm; Nov.-Mar. M-Sa 9:30am-4pm, Su 11am-4pm. £2.50, students £2.) **Bangor,** on the mainland, is probably *the* hub to explore the island. For information on **ferries** to Dublin and Dún Laoghaire, Ireland from **Holyhead,** see p. 540. Get to Holyhead via hourly **trains** (☎(08457) 484950) from Bangor (30min., £5.05); Chester (1½hr., £16.15); and London (4½-6hr., £57.30).

SCOTLAND

At its best, Scotland is a world apart, a defiantly distinct nation within the United Kingdom with a culture and world view all its own. Exuberant Glasgow boasts a mind-bending nightlife, and Edinburgh is the festive epicenter of Scottish culture. A little over half the land size of England but with a tenth of its population, Scotland possesses open spaces and natural splendor its southern neighbor cannot rival. The heather-covered mountains and glassy lochs of the west coast and luminescent mists of the Hebrides demand worship; the farmlands to the south and the rolling river valleys of the east coast display a gentler beauty; and the frayed northwestern coast remains one of the last stretches of true wilderness in Europe.

TRANSPORTATION

National Express buses (☎(08705) 808080) connecting England with **Glasgow** and **Edinburgh** (10hr., 5 per day, £28) are much cheaper than **ScotRail trains** (☎(0141) 332 9811 or (08547) 484950; 5hr., return £80-90). **British Airways** (☎(08457) 773 3377) sells a limited number of APEX return tickets from £70. **British Midland** (☎(08706) 070555) offers a Saver fare from **London** to **Glasgow** (from £70 return). Reserve as far

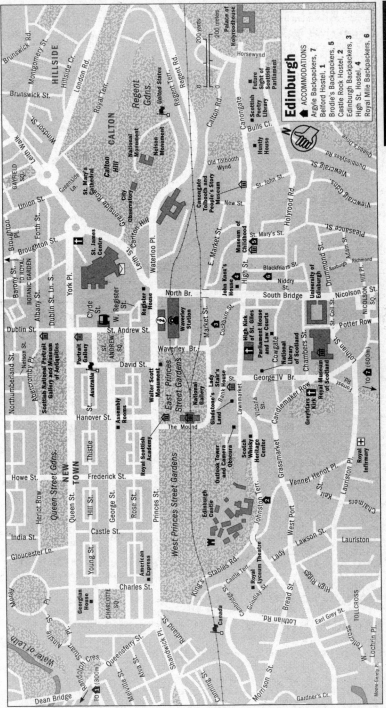

Edinburgh

ACCOMMODATIONS
Argyle Backpackers, **7**
Belford Hostel, **1**
Brodie's Backpackers, **5**
Castle Rock Hostel, **2**
Edinburgh Backpackers, **3**
High St. Hostel, **4**
Royal Mile Backpackers, **6**

ahead as possible (at least two weeks) for the cheapest fare. Scotland is also linked by **ferry** to **Northern Ireland.** From **Stranraer, Stena Line** (☎ (1233) 646826) ferries skim the water to **Belfast** (1¾hr.-3¼hr., 10 per day, £29-31).

Frequent trains and buses run throughout the **Lowlands** (south of Stirling and north of the Borders). In the **Highlands,** trains snake slowly on a few restricted routes, bypassing almost the entire Northwest region. Bus service is reduced in the Northwest Highlands and grinds to a standstill on Sundays. **Buses** are more frequent, extensive, and affordable than trains. **Citylink** (☎ (08705) 505050) operates most intercity service buses. The **Freedom of Scotland Travelpass** (any 4 in 8 days £79, any 8 in 15 days £109) allows unlimited train travel and transportation on certain ferry lines. Purchase the pass at almost any train station or order through Rail Europe (p. 68). **Hop-on, hop-off bus tours** are often a good way to reach more inaccessible areas: try **Haggis,** 60 High St., Edinburgh EH1 1NB (☎ (0131) 557 9393; www.radicaltravel.com; day tour £19, 3-day £79, 6-day £139; Flexitour from £69); or **MacBackpackers,** 105 High St., Edinburgh EH1 1SG (☎ (0131) 558 9900; www.macbackpackers.com; 3-day £55, 5-day £89, 7-day £129).

EDINBURGH   ☎ 0131

Framed by rolling hills and the blue Firth of Forth, Edinburgh (ED-din-bur-ra; pop. 500,000) is the jewel of Scotland. The country's capital since the 12th century; seeds of the Reformation were sown here in the 16th century when John Knox became minister of the High Kirk of St. Giles. An outpouring of talent later made the city a capital of the Enlightenment; the philosopher David Hume presided over a republic of letters that fostered both Adam Smith's invisible hand and the literary wanderings of Sir Walter Scott. Today, Edinburgh Castle stands watch over a litany of literary ghosts, exuberant festivals, and the ever-present pint of dark ale.

▐◗ TRANSPORTATION

Flights: Edinburgh International Airport, 11km west of the city center (☎ 333 1000). **LRT's Airlink 100** (☎ 555 6363; £3.30) and the **Edinburgh Airbus Express** (☎ 556 2244; £3.60) shuttle to the airport (25min.); both depart from Waverley Bridge.

Trains: Waverley Station (☎ (0345) 484950), near the center of town between North and Waverley Bridges. To: **Glasgow** (1hr., 2 per hr., £7.30); **Aberdeen** (2½hr., every hr., £28); and **London's** King's Cross (5hr., every 30min., £80-90).

Buses: The **south side of St. Andrew Sq.** (☎ (08705) 505950) 3 blocks from the east end of Princes St., serves as the temporary **St. Andrew Sq. Bus Station** until early 2002. **Scottish Citylink** buses (☎ (0990) 505050) serve: **Aberdeen** (every hr., £14.50); **Glasgow** (4 per hr., £3); and **Inverness** (every hr., £14). **National Express** goes to **London** (2 per day £28).

Public Transportation: Although it's easy to walk around Edinburgh, the city also has a comprehensive bus system. **Lothian Regional Transport (LRT)** (☎ 555 6363), with a fleet of maroon double-deckers, provides the best service. Be sure to carry coins; drivers do not carry much change for the 80p-£1 fares. You can buy a one-day **Day-Saver Ticket** (£2.40, children £1.50) and longer-term passes from any driver or from the main office, 1-4 Shrub Pl., on the Old Town side of Waverley Bridge.

Bike Rental: Edinburgh Rent-a-Bike, 29 Blackfriars St. (☎ 556 5560), off High St. Bikes £5-15 per day. City tours and Highland safaris also available. Open July-Sept. daily 9am-9pm; Oct.-June daily 10am-6pm.

Hitchhiking: *Let's Go* does not recommend hitching. Those who choose to hitch to Newcastle, York, or Durham often take bus #15, 26, or 43 to get to the Musselburgh and the A1; to other points south, bus #4 or 15 to Fairmilehead and A702 to Biggar. To points north, hitchers take bus #18 or 40 to Barnton and the Forth Rd. Bridge.

■✴? ORIENTATION AND PRACTICAL INFORMATION

Princes St. is the main thoroughfare in **New Town,** the northern section of Edinburgh. **The Royal Mile** (Lawnmarket, High St., and Canongate), the major road in the Old Town—the south half of the city—connects **Edinburgh Castle** and **Holyrood Palace. North Bridge, Waverley Bridge,** and **The Mound** connect the Old and New Towns.

Tourist Office: Edinburgh and Scotland Information Centre, Waverley Market, 3 Princes St. (☎473 3800), next to Waverley Station. Books rooms for a £3 fee with a 10% deposit. Sells bus, tour, and theater tickets. Open July-Aug. M-Sa 9am-8pm, Su 10am-8pm; May-June and Sept. closes 7pm; Oct.-Apr. closes at 6pm.

Budget Travel Services: Radical Travel Center, 60 High St. (☎557 9393), is geared toward backpackers and can help get you the best rates on car rentals and other travel-related services. Open daily 8am-7pm. **Edinburgh Travel Centre,** in Potterow Union, Bristo Sq. (☎668 2221.) Also at 92 South Clerk St. (☎667 9488.) Both open M-W and F 9am-5:30pm, Th 10am-5:30pm, Sa 10am-1pm.

American Express: 139 Princes St. (☎718 2503), 5 long blocks west of Waverley Station. Mail held. Open M-F 9am-5:30pm, Sa 9am-4pm.

Gay and Lesbian Services: Gay and Lesbian Switchboard (☎556 4049). Pick up *Gay Information* at the tourist office or *Gay Scotland* at bookstores.

Emergency: Dial 999; no coins required. **Police,** 5 Fettes Ave. (☎311 3131).

Crisis Lines: Rape Crisis Center (☎556 9437). Staffed M-W and F 7-9pm, Th 1-3pm, Sa 9:30-11am.

Hospital: Royal Infirmary of Edinburgh, 1 Lauriston Pl. (☎536 1000; emergency ☎536 4040). From The Mound, take bus #23 or 27.

Internet Access: easyEverything, 58 Rose St. (☎220 3577), is the undisputed champion of cheap internet access. Rates fluctuate, but £1 can often get you as many as 3hr. of email. Open 24hr.

Post Office: Main office at 8-10 St. James Centre (☎556 9546). Address mail to be held: First name SURNAME, *Poste Restante,* GPO, 8-10 St. James Centre, Edinburgh **EH1 3SR,** Scotland, UK. Open M 9am-5:30pm, Tu-F 8:30am-5:30pm, Sa 8:30am-6pm.

⌂ ACCOMMODATIONS

Edinburgh is packed with backpacker hostels, but in Festival season (late July-early Sept.), there are few available rooms. Book ahead. The tourist office has free hostel lists and finds rooms (£3 with 10% deposit). Most of Edinburgh's countless **B&Bs** are clustered in three areas: **Bruntsfield** in the southwest, **Newington** in the southeast, and **Leith** in the northeast.

▨ **Brodies Backpackers,** 12 High St. (☎/fax 556 6770), at St. Mark's St. Friendly, relaxed and delightfully cozy. Book ahead. Reception 7am-midnight. Dorms M-Th £11.90, F-Su £13.50. Rates higher Aug.

Edinburgh Backpackers, 65 Cockburn St. (☎220 1717, reservations ☎221 0022.) From North Bridge, turn right onto High St. and right again onto Cockburn St. "Legendary" guided pub crawls Tu in summer. Pool table, ping-pong, TV, and **Internet access.** Reception 24hr. Check-out 10am. Dorms £12, £15 during Festival season.

Castle Rock Hostel, 15 Johnston Terr. (☎225 9666). Walking toward the castle on the Royal Mile, turn left onto Johnston Terr. Regal views of the castle. Laundry service. **Internet access.** Breakfast £1.60. Book ahead (months ahead for Aug.). Dorms £10.50-13

Royal Mile Backpackers, 105 High St. (☎557 6120). Walk down High St. from Cockburn St.; the hostel is directly opposite the red Telecom Centre. Fosters a great communal feeling. Laundry £2.50. Dorms £10.50-13.

High St. Hostel, 8 Blackfriars St. (☎557 3984). Spacious accommodations and youthful energy. Pool table, TV, movies. Continental breakfast £1.60. Dorms £10.50-13

Argyle Backpackers, 14 Argyle Pl. (☎667 9991; fax 662 0002; argylr@aol.co.uk), south of the Meadows and the Royal Mile. Take bus #40 or 41 from The Mound to Melville Dr. Two cozy, renovated townhouses with a relaxing back patio. Some rooms with TV. Check-out 10:30am. Dorms £10; doubles and twins £15 per person. £5 more Aug.

Camping: Edinburgh Caravans, Marine Dr. (☎312 6874), by the Forth. Take bus #28A from Frederick St. off Princes St. (90p). Toilets, electricity, showers, hot water, and laundry machines. Arrive before 8pm. Open Apr.-Oct. £4 per person, £1.50 per car, £3 per tent.

HAGGIS: WHAT'S IN THERE?
Although restaurants throughout Scotland produce steamin' plates o' haggis for eager tourists, we at *Let's Go* believe you should know what's inside that strange-looking bundle before taking the plunge. An age-old recipe calls for the following ingredients: the large stomach bag of a sheep, the small (knight's hood) bag, the pluck (including lungs, liver, and heart), beef, suet, oatmeal, onions, pepper, and salt. Today's haggis is available conveniently canned and includes: lamb, lamb offal, oatmeal, wheat flour, beef, suet, onions, salt, spices, stock, and liquor (1%). Restaurants will probably serve it to you in non-traditional forms as well: unbagged, vegetarian, and deep-fried in batter.

◨ FOOD

You can get cheap haggis in many pubs. **South Clerk Street** and **Lothian Road** have plenty of shops offering reasonably priced Chinese or Indian takeout. For groceries, try **Sainsbury's Central** on South Saint David St., just north of the Scott monument. (Open M-Sa 7am-9pm, Su 9am-8pm.)

▨ **The Basement,** 10a-12a Broughton St. The menu changes daily, with plenty of vegetarian options and Thai and Mexican specialties. A lively mix of students and musicians in its candle-lit, cavernous environment. Kitchen open daily noon-10pm.

The Black Medicine Coffee Co., 2 Nicolson St. Sophisticated students pack the Native American interior. Many sandwiches and smoothies (£1-3). Live music (mainly acoustic guitar) Th and Su afternoons. Open daily 8am-8pm.

The Last Drop, 72-74 Grassmarket. "Haggis, tatties, and neeps" (haggis, potatoes, and turnips) in omnivorous and veggie versions. The whole menu (save the steak) is £3 for students and hostelers until 7:30 pm. A packed pub at night. Open daily 10am-2am.

Ndebele, 57 Home St. Named after a southern African tribe, it serves copious amounts of exotic food for under £5. Daily African specials and a huge array of African and South American coffees and juices. Open daily 10am-10pm.

Kebab Mahal, 7 Nicolson Sq. Chicken *tikka masala* (£5.25) is the specialty, but try the kebabs (£2.25-4.50). Open Su-Th noon-midnight, F-Sa noon-2am.

The City Cafe, 19 Blair St. Right off the Royal Mile behind the Tron Kirk, this Edinburgh institution serves venison burgers (£4-6) and incredible shakes, immortalized in the film *Trainspotting*. Dance club downstairs. Food served until 10pm. Open daily 11am-1am.

◎ SIGHTS

With museums, gardens and castles in abundance, Edinburgh is a marvel of sights. Experience the heritage of this Scottish capital city from the traditional to the contemporary on a tour from Edinburgh Castle to the new Scottish Parliament, with stops at the Royal Museum and Holyrood Park between.

THE OLD TOWN AND THE ROYAL MILE

The Royal Mile (Lawnmarket, High St., Canongate) defines the length of the Old Town. Defended by Edinburgh Castle at the top of the hill and the Palace of Holyroodhouse at the bottom, the Old Town once packed thousands of inhabitants into a few square miles—still visible in the narrow shop fronts and 13-story slum buildings—but today the street is more the domain of tourists than slum lords.

■ **EDINBURGH CASTLE.** Crowning the top of the Royal Mile, the castle contains structures that were rebuilt in recent centuries. Inside, **St. Margaret's Chapel,** a 12th-century Norman church, is believed to be the oldest structure in Edinburgh. The castle displays the 15th-century Scottish Crown Jewels and the legendary **Stone of Scone.** *(At top of the Royal Mile. Open Apr.-Sept. daily 9:30am-6pm; Oct.-Mar. 9:30am-5pm. £7.)*

ALONG THE ROYAL MILE. Near the castle, through Milne's Close, the new **Scottish Parliament** convenes in the temporary **Debating Chamber.** Watch the MPs debate. *(Sept.-June, W 2:30-5:30pm, Th 9:30am-12:30pm and 2:30-5:30pm. Free.)* You can also get reserved tickets (bookings ☎ 348 5411) in the nearby Visitor Centre, at the corner of the Royal Mile and the George IV Bridge. *(☎ 348 5000. Open Sept.-June M and F 10am-5pm, Tu-Th 9am-5pm; July-Aug. M-F 10am-5pm, Sa same hours for Aug. and early Sept. Free.)* Nearby, **Lady Stair's House,** a 17th-century townhouse, contains the **Writer's Museum,** with memorabilia and manuscripts belonging to three of Scotland's greatest literary figures: Robert Burns, Sir Walter Scott, and Robert Louis Stevenson. *(Through the passage at 477 Lawnmarket St. Open M-Sa 10am-5pm; during Festival also Su 2-5pm. Free.)* The **High Kirk of St. Giles** (St. Giles Cathedral), Scotland's principal church, once stood at the center of the country's turbulent religious history. Here, John Knox delivered the fiery Presbyterian sermons that drove Mary, Queen of Scots, into exile. Now it offers free concerts year-round. *(Where Lawnmarket becomes High St., opposite Parliament. Open Easter to mid-Sept. M-F 9am-7pm, Sa 9am-5pm, Su 1-5pm; mid-Sept. to Easter M-Sa 9am-5pm, Su 1-5pm. £1.)* The 17th-century chapel **Canongate Kirk** is the resting place of Adam Smith; royals also worship here when in residence. Canongate, the steep hill at the end of the Mile, has **two museums** and an excellent **Scottish Poetry Library,** all free. *(Museums open M-Sa 10am-5pm; during Festival also Su 2-5pm. Library open M-F noon-6pm, Sa noon-4pm.)*

PALACE OF HOLYROODHOUSE. Once the home of Mary, Queen of Scots, this spectacular Stewart palace, which dates from the 16th and 17th centuries, is now Queen Elizabeth II's official residence in Scotland. Behind the palace lies the 12th-century abbey ransacked during the Reformation. *(At the eastern end of the Royal Mile. Open Apr.-Oct. daily 9:30am-5:15pm; Nov.-Mar. M-Sa 9:30am-3:45pm; closed during official residences in late May and late June to early July. £6.)*

OTHER SIGHTS IN THE OLD TOWN. On Chambers St., just south of the George IV Bridge, the new **Museum of Scotland** and the connected **Royal Museum** are not to be missed. The former houses a definitive collection of Scottish artifacts in a stunning contemporary building; the latter contains a varied mix of art and natural history, plus the new **Millennium Clock,** which chimes every hour. *(Open M and W-Sa 10am-5pm, Tu 10am-8pm, Su noon-5pm. Admission includes both museums; £3, students £1.50. Free Tu 4:30-8pm.)* Just across the street stands the statue of the loyal pooch, Greyfriars' Bobby, marking the entrance to **Greyfriars Kirk,** built in 1620 in a beautiful and supposedly haunted churchyard. *(Gaelic services Su 12:30pm, English 11am. Kirk visiting hours Easter-Oct. M-F 10:30am-4:30pm, Sa until 2:30pm. Free.)* Be sure to explore the nearby streets: **Candlemaker's Row, Victoria St.,** and the **Grassmarket,** where Edinburgh's criminals once hung from the gallows.

THE NEW TOWN

Edinburgh's New Town is a masterpiece of Georgian planning. James Craig, a 23-year-old architect, won the city planning contest in 1767 with the design you see today: the three main parallel streets (Queen, George, and Princes) form a rectangular, symmetrical gridiron linking two large squares (Charlotte and St. Andrew). The design was chosen to reflect the Scottish Enlightenment's belief in order. Another stop in your stroll through the New Town is the elegant **Georgian House,** a restored townhouse. *(7 Charlotte Sq. From Princes St., turn right on Charlotte St. and take your 2nd left. Open Apr.-Oct. M-Sa 10am-5pm, Su 2-5pm. £5, students £3.50.)* The **Walter Scott Monument** is a grotesque Gothic "steeple without a church" containing statues of Scott and his dog. Climb the winding 287-step staircase for an eagle's-eye view of Princes St. Gardens, the castle, and Old Town's Market St. *(On Princes St., between The Mound and Waverley Bridge. Open Apr.-Sept. M-Sa 9am-6pm; Oct.-Mar. M-Sa 9am-3pm. £2.50.)*

THE NATIONAL GALLERIES. Today, you can enlighten yourself by viewing the premier works of art in the elegant New Town buildings of the **National Galleries of Scotland.** There are four galleries, and all are free (sometimes a charge for special exhibits), top-rate, and a free shuttle bus runs between them every hour. *(All open M-Sa 10am-5pm, Su noon-5pm.)* The flagship of these four is the **National Gallery of Scotland,** on The Mound, which houses a superb collection of works by Renaissance, Romantic, and Impressionist masters and a fine spread of Scottish art. *(This gallery also open during Festival M-Sa 10am-6pm, Su 11am-6pm.)* The **Scottish National Portrait Gallery,** 1 Queen St., north of St. Andrew Sq, mounts the mugs of famous Scots. West of town, across the street from each other, are the **Scottish National Gallery of Modern Art,** 75 Belford Rd., and the new **Dean Gallery,** 73 Belford Rd., specializing in Surrealist and Dada art. You can also take bus #13 from Princes St. or walk 15min. down Queensferry Rd. and then Belford Rd. For information on Edinburgh's other (mostly free) museums, pick up the *Edinburgh Gallery Guide* at the tourist office.

GARDENS AND PARKS. You're depriving yourself if you don't at least try to climb **Arthur's Seat,** the extinct volcano at the east end of the city and Edinburgh's sample of the Highlands. Along with the **Salisbury Crags,** it rises from the vast **Holyrood Park,** at the east end of the Royal Mile; a relatively easy 45min. walk up the mountain culminates with a stunning view of the city. For more great views, try the even easier **Calton Hill,** just past the east end of Princes St., which also boasts the towering **Nelson Monument** and an ersatz Parthenon. A little more manicured are the lovely **Royal Botanic Gardens,** north of the city center. Walk north along Hanover St. from Princes St. or take buses #23 or 27. *(☎ 552 71 71. Open Apr.-Aug. daily 9:30am-7pm; Mar. and Sept. until 6pm; Feb. and Oct. until 5pm; Nov.-Jan. until 4pm. Free.)*

🎵🎭 ENTERTAINMENT AND NIGHTLIFE

The summer season overflows with music in the gardens and a multitude of theater and film events around town. For details on pubs and clubs, pick up *The List* (£1.95). Perhaps the most omnipresent form of tourist entertainment are the countless **walking tours** available around the city. The most worthwhile is the McEwan's Edinburgh Literary Pub Tour, a 2hr. alcohol-friendly crash course in Scottish literature, led by professional actors. (☎ 226 6665. £7, children and students £5.)

HIKING. If you have limited time in Scotland, there is a thriving industry of backpacker tour companies eager to whisk you away into the Highlands. The two main companies are **MacBackpackers,** 105 High St. (☎ 558 9900; www.macbackpackers.com. Day trips £15, 3-7 day tours £39-129, Jump on-Jump off £55), and **HAGGIS,** 60 High St. (☎ 557 9393; www.radicaltravel.com. Day trips £19, 3-6 day tours £79-139, Flexitour from £85); both offer tours of the Highlands departing from Edinburgh. Hop-on, hop-off tours let you travel Scotland at your own pace with the convenience of their transportation and company.

THEATER, MUSIC AND FILM. The **Festival Theatre,** 13-29 Nicholson St., stages ballet and opera, while the affiliated **King's Theatre,** 2 Leven St., promotes serious and comedic fare, musicals, and opera. Same-day seats (£5.50) for the Festival Theatre go on sale daily at 10am. (☎ 529 6000. Box office open daily 11am-6pm.) Scottish bands and country dancing abound at the **Ross Open-Air Theatre.** (☎ 228 8616. From 7pm). The **Filmhouse,** 88 Lothian Rd., offers quality cinema—European, Arthouse, and Hollywood. (☎ 228 2688. Tickets £1.20-5.20.)

FESTIVALS. For a few weeks in August, Edinburgh hosts the spectacular **🎭Edinburgh International Festival** (Aug 11-31, 2002), featuring a kaleidoscopic program of music, drama, dance, and art. Tickets (£5-50) are sold beginning in April, but you can usually get tickets at the door; look for half-price tickets after 1pm on performance days. For tickets and a schedule, contact **The HUB,** Edinburgh's Festival Centre, Castlehill, Edinburgh EH1 2NE. It's the church-like structure just downhill from the Castle. (Information ☎473 2001, bookings 473 2000.) Around the festival has grown a more spontaneous **Festival Fringe** (Aug. 4-26 in 2002), which now includes over 500 amateur and professional companies presenting theater, comedy, children's shows, folk and classical music, poetry, dance, and opera events. Tickets up to £5). Contact the **Fringe Festival Office,** 180 High St., Edinburgh EH1 1QS. (☎226 5257, bookings 226 5138. Box office open July M-F 10am-6pm; daily in Aug.) Another August festival is the **Military Tattoo**—a spectacle of military bands, bagpipes, and drums—considered by some to be the highlight of the month. For tickets (£9-21), contact the **Tattoo Ticket Office,** 33-34 Market St. (☎225 1188. Open M-F 10am-4:30pm or until the show. Shows M-Sa night.) Don't forget the **International Jazz and Blues Festival** (Late July to early Aug.; ☎467 5200, tickets go on sale in May £5-30).

NIGHTLIFE. If you can't find a pub in Edinburgh, you're not looking hard enough. Edinburgh claims to have the highest density of pubs anywhere in Europe, and we don't doubt it. Pubs directly on the **Royal Mile** usually attract an older crowd, while students tend to loiter in the **Old Town** pubs clustered around the university. ◪**The Tron,** 9 Hunter Sq., off the High St. is smashingly popular with smashingly drunk youths, who benefit from its many student/hosteler deals. There's frequent live music on its three hopping floors. (☎226 09 31. Open daily 11:30am-1am.) ◪**The Globe,** 3a Merchant Street, across from Greyfriar's Cemetery, deservedly bills itself as Edinburgh's true backpacker destination. If you're feeling particularly adventurous, absinthe shots direct from the Czech Republic are only £4. (Open daily 10:00am until 1am.) The new **Espionage Bar and Club Complex,** Victoria St., has five floors of trendy partying in exotic settings. (No cover. Open daily 5pm-3am, until 4am on weekends.) At **Subway** on Cowgate, drinks Su-Th are only a quid. Open 7pm-3am. The Broughton St. area of the New Town (better known as the **Broughton Triangle**) is the center of the lesbian, gay, and bisexual community of Edinburgh. **C.C. Bloom's,** 23-24 Greenside Pl. on Leith St., is a super-friendly, super-fun gay club, with no cover. (Open daily 6pm-3am; during the Festival until 5am.)

▶ DAYTRIPS FROM EDINBURGH

GLASGOW. Less than an hour from Edinburgh by train, Glasgow exudes trendy creativity and energy without attracting too many tourists (p. 207).

STIRLING. ◪**Stirling Castle** and the **Wallace Monument Tower** (in honor of William Wallace of *Braveheart* fame) await only 50 minutes from Edinburgh (p. 211).

ST. ANDREWS. After a two-hour train ride, tee off at St. Andrews (p. 211).

GLASGOW ☎ 0141

Although it has traditionally suffered a reputation for industrial lackluster, Scotland's largest city, Glasgow (pop. 675,000), thrives with a renewed energy. Today's Glasgow is an architectural wonder, from the stately Victorian beauty of the City Chambers in George Square to the dazzling curves of its brand new £100 million Science Centre. The millions of pounds the city has poured into the arts are reflected in its free museums, extensive galleries, and first-rate theaters; the West End oozes with trendy, vibrant creativity. While it rivals Edinburgh, its sister to the east, in cultural attractions, Glasgow also remains much less touristy, infused with a flourishing economy, a passion for football, and the energy of spirited locals.

▗ TRANSPORTATION

Flights: Glasgow Airport (☎887 1111), 15km west in Abbotsinch. Citylink buses connect to **Buchanan Station** (20min., 2 per hr., £3).

Trains: Two main stations. **Central Station,** on Gordon St. U: St. Enoch. To **London-King's Cross** (5-6hr., 5-20 per day, £50) and **Stranraer** (2½hr., 3-8 per day, £15.30). **Queen St. Station,** on George Sq. U: Buchanan St. To: **Aberdeen** (2½hr., 11-24 per day, £36.40); **Edinburgh** (50min., 2 per hr., £7.30); and **Inverness** (3¼hr., 5 per day, £29.90). Bus #398 runs between the 2 stations (4 per hr., £0.50).

Buses: Buchanan Station (☎(0870) 608 2608), on North Hanover St., 2 blocks north of the Queen St. Station. **Scottish Citylink** (☎(08705) 505050) to: **Aberdeen** (4hr., 1 per hr., £14.50); **Edinburgh** (1hr., 2-4 per hr., £3); **Inverness** (3½-4½hr., 1 per hr., £12.80); and **Oban** (3hr., 2-3 per day, £10.70). **National Express** (☎(08705) 80 80 80) buses arrive daily from **London** (8hr.; 1 per hr.; £22, return £31).

Public Transportation: The circular **Underground (U)** subway line, a.k.a. the "Clockwork Orange" runs M-Sa 6:30am-10:45pm, Su 11am-6pm. Single-fare £0.80. Wave to stop **buses** and carry exact change. Single-fare £0.45-0.95.

✴ ? ORIENTATION AND PRACTICAL INFORMATION

George Square is the physical center of town. Sections of Sauchiehall St., Argyle St., and Buchanan St. are pedestrian areas. **Charing Cross,** in the northwest, where Bath St. crosses M8, is used as a reference landmark. The vibrant **West End** revolves around **Byres Road** and **Glasgow University,** 1½km northwest of the city center. To reach the **tourist office** from Central Station, exit on Union St., turn left, walk two blocks, turn right on St. Vincent St., and it's 3½ blocks up on your right. From Queen St. Station, exit onto George St., and cross George Sq. From the Buchanan Bus Station, exit on North Hanover St. and follow it right to George Sq.

Tourist Office: 11 George Sq. (☎204 4400). U: Buchanan St. Books rooms for £2 fee plus 10% deposit. **Walking tours** depart M-Sa 6pm, Su 10:30am (1½hr.; £5, students £4). Open July-Aug. M-Sa 9am-8pm, Su 10am-6pm; June and Sept. M-Sa 9am-7pm, Su 10am-6pm; Oct.-May M-Sa 9am-6pm.

American Express: 115 Hope St. (☎(08706) 001060). Open July-Aug. M-F 8:30am-5:30pm, Sa 9am-5pm; Sept.-June M-F 8:30am-5:30pm, Sa 9am-noon.

Laundromat: Coin-Op Laundromat, 39/41 Bank St. (☎339 8953). U: Kelvin Bridge. Open M-F 9am-7:30pm, Sa-Su 9am-5pm.

Emergency: ☎999; no coins required. **Police:** (☎532 3000), on Stewart St.

Hospital: Glasgow Royal Infirmary, 84-106 Castle St. (☎211 4000).

Internet Access: The Best deal in town is **easyEverything Internet Cafe,** 57-61 St. Vincent Street (☎222 2365). £1 buys 40-75 min. depending on time of day. Open 24hr., 7 days a week. Also, **The Internet Café,** 569 Sauchiehall St. (☎564 1052), serves the West End. £3 per 30min., students £2.50. Open M-Th 9am-11pm, F-Su 9am-7pm.

Post Office: 47 St. Vincent St. Address mail: First name SURNAME, *Poste Restante,* 47 St. Vincent St., **G2 5QX** Glasgow, UK. Open M-F 8:30am-5:45pm, Sa 9am-5:30pm.

▐ ACCOMMODATIONS

Reserve B&Bs and hostels in advance, especially in August. Last-minute planners may consider calling **SYHA Loch Lomond** (p. 213). Most B&Bs cluster on **Great Western Road,** in the university area, or near **Westercraigs Road,** east of the Necropolis.

Bunkum Backpackers, 26 Hillhead St. (☎581 4481). Though located away from the city center, Bunkum is minutes away from the vibrant West End. Spacious dorms with comfy beds. Lockers. Laundry (£1.50 wash). Dorms £9 per day, £45 per week.

Glasgow Backpackers Hostel, 17 Park Terr. (☎332 9099). U: St. George's Cross. Clean, friendly, and social hostel close to the West End party scene. Internet. Laundry £2.50 for wash, dry, and fold. Open July-Sept. Dorms £10.50; twins £24.

SYHA Glasgow, 7-8 Park Terr. (☎332 3004). U: St. George's Cross. From Central Station, take bus #44 from Hope St., ask for the first stop on Woodlands Rd. then follow the signs. This hostel maintains an air of luxury. All rooms with bath. TV and game

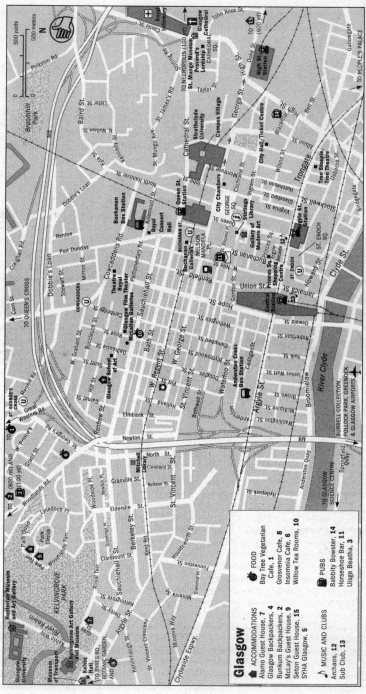

500 yards
500 meters

N

TO NECROPOLIS (100 yd)
St. Mungo Museum
Provand's Lordship
GLASGOW CATHEDRAL
Glasgow Cathedral

TO (600 yd)

John Knox St.
Castle St.
Royal Infirmary
John Knox St.

High St. Station

TO PEOPLE'S PALACE
Gallowgate

Strathclyde University
Campus Village

City Hall/Ticket Centre
City Chambers
GEORGE SQ.
Stirlings Library
Gallery of Modern Art

Tron Steeple, Tron Theatre
Trongate

Queen St. Station
Buchanan Bus Station
Royal Concert Hall

Buchanan Galleries
NELSON MANDELA PL.

Argyle St. Station
ST. ENOCH SQ.
St. Enoch Shopping Centre

Theatre Royal
Glasgow Film Theatre
McLellan Galleries

Central Station

Glasgow School of Art

Anderston Cross Bus Station

Mitchell Library

TO GLASGOW SCIENCE CENTRE

TO ST. GEORGE'S CROSS

TO QUEEN'S CROSS

BURRELL COLLECTION, POLLOCK PARK, GREENOCK & GLASGOW AIRPORTS

Hunterian Museum and Art Gallery
Kelvingrove Art Gallery and Museum
KELVINGROVE PARK
Glasgow University
Museum of Transport
Kelvin Hall

TO BYRES RD., BOTANIC GARDEN, AND

River Clyde
River Kelvin
Clydeside Expwy.

Glasgow

ACCOMMODATIONS
Alamo Guest House, 7
Glasgow Backpackers, 4
Bunkum Backpackers, 2
McLay's Guest House, 9
Seton Guest House, 15
SYHA Glasgow, 5

MUSIC AND CLUBS
Archaos, 12
Sub Club, 13

FOOD
Bay Tree Vegetarian Cafe, 1
Grosvenor Cafe, 8
Insomnia Cafe, 6
Willow Tea Rooms, 10

PUBS
Babbity Bowster, 14
Horseshoe Bar, 11
Uisge Beatha, 3

rooms. Breakfast included. Laundry. Dorms July-Aug. £11.50, under 18 £9.50; Sept-Oct. £11, £9.50; Nov.-Feb. £10, 8.50; Apr.-June £11, £9.50.

McLay's Guest House, 268 Renfrew St. (☎332 4796; fax 353 0422). Excellent central location near the Glasgow School of Art and Sauchiehall St. With satellite TV and phones in each of the 62 rooms and 3 dining rooms, it looks and feels more like a hotel than a B&B. Singles £22, with bath £27; doubles £38, £46.

Alamo Guest House, 46 Gray St. (☎339 23 95), opposite the Kelvingrove Museum. Gracious proprietors and spacious, quiet rooms. Singles £20-22; doubles from £34.

Seton Guest House, 6 Seton Terr. (☎556 76 54), 20min. east of George Sq. Hop on bus #6, 6A, or 41A. Kindly hosts keep large immaculate rooms with ornate chandeliers. Out of the way, but all the quieter for it. Singles £17; doubles £32.

▐ FOOD

The area bordered by Otago St. in the west, St. George's Rd. in the east, and along Great Western Rd., Woodlands Rd., and Eldon St. brims with cheap kebab 'n' curry joints. **Byres Road** and **Ashton Lane,** a tiny cobblestoned alley parallel to Byres Rd., thrive with cheap, trendy cafes. **Woodlands Grocers,** 110 Woodlands Rd., is open 24hr. There's also a **Safeway** at 373 Byres Rd. (Open M-Sa 8am-8pm, Su 9am-7pm).

Grosvenor Café, 31-35 Ashton Ln. Stuff yourself silly from the endless menu, but beware of the long lines. Desserts and stuffed rolls 95p-£1.20, bigger dishes £3-4; A more elaborate dinner menu (main courses £5.25-8.45) is available Tu-Sa 7-11pm. Open M 9am-7pm, Tu-Sa 9am-11pm, Su 10:30am-5:30pm.

Insomnia Café, 38/40 Woodlands Rd., near the hostels, is the hip place to gorge, day or night. Cafe and adjoining deli open 24hr.

Bay Tree Vegetarian Café, 403 Great Western Rd., at Park Rd., also near the hostels (cut through Kelvingrove Park); pitas with hummus and salad £3.50-4.50. Open M-Sa 9am-9pm, Su 9am-8pm.

The Willow Tea Room, 217 Sauchiehall St. Upstairs from Henderson the Jewellers. A Glasgow landmark. Sip one of 28 kinds of tea. £1.20-1.45 per pot. High tea £7.75. Open M-Sa 9:30am-4:30pm, Su noon-4:15pm.

◉ SIGHTS

The red-paved **George Square** marks the busiest part of the city. The **City Chambers,** on the east side of the square, conceal an ornate marble interior in the Italian Renaissance style. (Tours M-F 10:30am and 2:30pm.) Follow George St. from the square and take a left on High St., which turns into Castle St., to reach the Gothic **Glasgow Cathedral,** the only full-scale cathedral spared the fury of the 16th-century Scottish Reformation. (Open Apr.-Sept. M-Sa 9:30am-6pm, Su 2-5pm; Oct.-Mar. M-Sa 9:30am-4pm, Su 2-4pm. Free.) On the same street is the **St. Mungo Museum of Religious Life and Art,** 2 Castle St., which surveys every religion from Hindu to Yoruba. (Open M-Sa 10am-5pm, Su 11am-5pm. Free.) Behind the cathedral is the spectacular **Necropolis,** a terrifying hilltop cemetery filled with broken tombstones. (Open 24hr. Free.) In the West End, the large, wooded **Kelvingrove Park** lies on the banks of the River Kelvin. In the southwest corner of the park, at Argyle and Sauchiehall St., sits the magnificent, spired **Kelvingrove Art Gallery and Museum,** which shelters works by van Gogh, Monet, and Rembrandt. (U: Kelvin Hall. Open M-Th and Sa 10am-5pm, F and Su 11am-5pm. Free.) Farther west rises the Gothic edifices of the **University of Glasgow.** The main building is on University Ave., which runs into Byres Rd. While walking through campus, which has churned out 57 Nobel laureates, stop by the **Hunterian Museum** or the **Hunterian Art Gallery,** across the street. (U: Hillhead. Open M-Sa 9:30am-5pm. Free.) Several buildings designed by Charles Rennie Mackintosh, Scotland's most famous architect, are open to the public; the **Glasgow School of Art,** 167 Renfrew St., south of the river, reflects a uniquely Glaswegian Modernist style. (Tours M-F 11am and 2pm, Sa 10:30am. £5, students £3.) Tired of all that culture? Shop at **Princes Sq.**, 48 Buchanan St., a gorgeous high-end mall. If your wallet has any life left, hit **Sauchiehall St.**, which hosts shops and art galleries as well.

ENTERTAINMENT AND NIGHTLIFE

Glaswegians have a reputation for partying hard. *The List* (£1.95 from newsagents) lets you know which club is best each night. The infamous **Byers Road** pub crawl slithers past the Glasgow University area, starting at Tennant's Bar and heads toward the River Clyde. **Uisge Beatha**, 232 Woodlands Rd., serves over 100 kinds of malt whiskey. (£1.85-35 for each. Open M-Th 11am-11pm, F-Sa 11am-midnight, Su 12:30-11pm.) Go to **Babbity Bowster**, 16-18 Blackfriar St., for good drink and football talk. When you step into the bar, you become a Glasgow Celtic fan. (Open daily 8am-midnight, 8am-midnight.) **Russell Bar-Café**, 77 Byres Rd., is a log cabin with live DJs and meal deals. (Open Su-Th 11am-11pm, F-Sa 11am-midnight.) Fifteen bartenders staff the largest continuous bar in the UK at **Horseshoe Bar**, 17-21 Drury St. (Open M-Sa 8am-midnight.) Look for skeletons hanging outside the second-floor windows of club **Archaos**, 25 Queen St. (Cover £3-9. Open Th-Su until 3am, Sa until 3:30am.) All types grind at sweating **Sub Club**, 22 Jamaica St. (Cover £3-6; Sa £8. Open Th-F and Su 11pm-3am, Sa 11pm-3:30am.)

STIRLING ☎ 01786

The third point of a strategic triangle with Glasgow and Edinburgh, Stirling has historically presided over the region's north-south movement; it was once said that whoever controlled Stirling controlled Scotland. At the 1297 Battle of Stirling Bridge, **William Wallace** (of *Braveheart* fame) overpowered the English army, enabling Robert the Bruce to finally overthrow the English in 1314 at **Bannockburn**, 3.25km south of town, and lead Scotland to 400 years of independence. The **Stirling Castle** possesses prim gardens and superb views of the Forth Valley that belie its militant and murderous past. (Open daily Apr.-Oct. 9:30am-6pm; Nov.-Mar. 9:30am-5pm. £6. Tours free.) The castle also contains the fascinating **Regimental Museum of the Argyll and Sutherland Highlanders.** (Open Easter-Sept. M-Sa 10am-5:45pm, Su 11am-4:45pm; Oct.-Easter daily 10am-4:15pm. Free.) The 19th-century **Wallace Monument Tower**, on Hillfouts Rd., 2½km from town, offers incredible views atop a set of wind-whipped stairs. Check out Wallace's 5½ ft. sword on display. (Open daily July-Aug. 9:30am-6:30pm; June and Sept. 10am-6pm; Mar.-May and Oct. 10am-5pm; Nov.-Feb. 10am-4pm. £3.30, students £3.05.)

Trains run from Goosecroft Rd. (☎ (08457) 484950) for: Aberdeen (2hr., every hr., £28); Edinburgh (50min., 2 per hr., £5.10); Glasgow (30min., 1-3 per hr., £4.30); and Inverness (3hr., 4 per day, £32). National Express **buses** leave from Goosecroft Rd. to Inverness (every hr., £11.40) and Glasgow (2-3 per hr., £3.60). The **Stirling Visitor Centre** is next to the castle. (☎ 462517. Open daily July-Aug. 9am-6:30pm; Apr.-June and Sept.-Oct. 9:30am-6pm; Nov.-Mar. 9:30am-5pm.) The **Willy Wallace Hostel**, 77 Murray Pl., holds clean rooms in a social environment near the bus and train stations. (☎ 446773. Dorms £10; doubles £26.) **Postal code:** FK8 2BP.

ST. ANDREWS ☎ 01334

The "tyrannising game" golf overruns the small city of St. Andrews; the rules of the sport were even formally established here. The **Old Course**, a frequent site of the British Open, is a golf pilgrim's Canterbury. (☎ 466666; fax 477036. Reserve ahead to play or enter the on-the-spot lottery for starting times. £80 per round.) The **Balgove Course** is a much cheaper alternative offering 9 holes for £7. If you're more interested in watching than playing, the **British Golf Museum**, next to the Old Course, details the ancient origins of golf. (Open Easter-Oct. daily 9:30am-5:30pm; Nov.-Easter Th-M 11am-3pm. £3.75, students £2.75.) Despite the onslaught of pastel and polyester, one need not worship the wedge to love this city; its medieval streets and castle ruins transcend even golf. Though today it's only a shell, in the Middle Ages pilgrims journeyed to **St. Andrews Cathedral** to pray at the Saint's Shrine. Nearby, **St. Andrews Castle** maintains secret tunnels, bottle-shaped dungeons, and high stone walls to keep rebellious heretics in or out. (Cathedral and castle open Apr.-Sept. daily 9:30am-6:30pm; Oct.-Mar. 9:30am-4:30pm. Joint ticket £3.75.) Scotland's oldest university, **St. Andrews,** founded in the 15th century, lies just west of the castle, between North St. and The Scores; ▧Prince William is a current student.

Stagecoach Express Fife **buses** (☎474238) pull in from Edinburgh (bus #X59 or X60; 2hr., 2 per hr. until 6:45pm; fewer Su; £5.70, students £3.60) and Glasgow (#X24, change at Glenrothes to X59; 2½hr.; M-Sa 1 per hr., fewer Su; £5.50). **Trains** (☎(0345) 550033) arrive at Edstop 8km away in Leuchars (1hr., every hr., £8.10), where **buses** #93, 94, 95, and 96 (£1.45) depart for St. Andrews. To get to the **tourist office,** 70 Market St., from the bus station, turn right on City Rd. and take the first left. (☎472021. Open July-Aug. M-Sa 9:30am-7pm, Su 11am-6pm; May-June and Sept. M-Sa 9:30am-6pm, Su 11am-5pm; Apr. closes daily at 5pm; Oct.-Mar. M-Sa 9:30am-5pm.) Just across the street, hop on the **Internet** at **Costa Coffee,** 83 Market St. (£1.50 per 15min., students 75p. Open M-Sa 8am-8pm, Su 10am-8pm.) The tourist office has **B&B** lists (many B&Bs line Murray Pl. and Murray Park near the bus station). **Brownlees,** 7 Murray Pl., offers elegant housing a few blocks from the Old Course. (☎473868. £18-25 per person.)

FORT WILLIAM AND BEN NEVIS   ☎01397

With a slew of beautiful lakes and valleys, **Fort William** makes an excellent base for mountain excursions to **Ben Nevis** (1342m), the highest peak in Britain. To ascend the well-beaten trail from Fort William to the summit, go 800m north on the A82 and follow signs (5-6hr. return). **Trains** arrive in Fort William from Glasgow's Queen St. Station (3¾hr., 2-4 per day, £18) and London's Euston Station (12hr., 3 per day, £70-96.50). Scottish Citylink (☎(08705) 505050) goes to: Edinburgh (6hr., 2 per day, £15.20); Glasgow (3hr., 4 per day, £11.90); and Inverness (2hr., 5-6 per day, £7.20). Buses and trains leave from the northern end of High St.; nearby, the **tourist office** provides information on the West Highlands. (☎703781. Open mid-June to mid-July M-Sa 9am-7pm, Su 10am-6pm; mid-July to Aug. M-Sa 9am-8:30pm, Su 9am-6pm; Sept.-Oct. M-Sa 9am-6pm, Su 10am-5:30pm; Nov.-Mar. M-Sa 9am-5pm, Su 10am-4pm; Mar.-June M-Sa 9am-6pm, Su 10am-4pm.) By far the best place to stay within striking distance of Ben Nevis is the comfy ▧**Farr Cottage Accommodation and Activity Center** in Corpach. (☎772315. £11.) The owner puts on his kilt almost every night and gives Scottish history lessons and whisky talks (and samples). To get there, take the train two stops north of Fort William or take the bus from High St. (10min., 1-3 per hr., 80p). The **Fort William Backpackers Guesthouse,** on Alma Rd., is 5min. from the Fort William train station. (☎700711. Curfew 2am. £10-11.) The **Glen Nevis Caravan & Camping Park,** on Glen Nevis Rd., is 5½km east of town. (☎702191. Showers included. Open mid-Mar. to Oct. £8.70 per 2 people and tent.)

INVERNESS AND LOCH NESS   ☎01463

The charms of Inverness, like the Loch Ness monster herself, are somewhat elusive but still satisfying. Disillusionment awaits those who remember Inverness as the home of Shakespeare's *Macbeth.* Nothing of the "Auld Castlehill" remains; the present reconstructed **castle** looks like it was made out of pink Legos this very morning. (Tours Easter-Nov. M-Sa 10:30am-5:30pm. £3, students and seniors £2.70.) The **Tourist Trail Day Rover bus** (summer only; £6, students £4) allows unlimited travel to most sights near Inverness. The Jacobite cause died in 1746 on **Culloden Battlefield,** east of Inverness; take **Highland county bus** #12 from the post office at Queensgate (£2 return). Just 2½km south of Culloden, the stone circles and chambered *cairns* (mounds of rough stones) of the **Cairns of Clava** recall civilizations of the Bronze Age. Bus #12 also travels to the impressive maze at **Cawdor Castle,** the home of the Cawdors since the 15th century. (Open May-Sept. daily 10am-5:30pm. £5.50, students and seniors £4.50, children £2.80.) Of course, no trip to Inverness would be complete without taking in the deep and mysterious **Loch Ness,** which guards its secrets 7½km south of Inverness. In AD 565, St. Columba repelled a savage sea beast as it attacked a monk; whether a prehistoric leftover, giant seasnake, or cosmic wanderer, the monster has captivated the world's imagination ever since. Tour agencies are the most convenient way to see the loch; **Kenny's Tours** skirt around the entire loch and back to Inverness on a minibus. (☎252411. Tours 10:30am-2:20pm or 2:30pm-5pm. £12.50, students £9.50.) Even if you don't see the real monster, vendors are happy to sell you a cute stuffed one.

Trains (☎(08457) 484950) run from Academy St., in Station Sq., to: Aberdeen, (2¼hr., 7-10 per day, £18.20); Edinburgh (3½-4hr., 1-2 per hr., £30.60); Glasgow (3½hr., 5-7 per day, £30.60); and London (8hr., 1 per day, £27-98). Scottish Citylink **buses** (☎(08705) 505050) run from Farraline Park, off Academy St., to Edinburgh (4½hr., 8-10 per day, £14) and Glasgow (4½hr., 10-12 per day, £14). To reach the **tourist office,** Castle Wynd, from the stations, turn left on Academy St., and right on Union St. (Open roughly mid-June to Aug. M-Sa 9am-7pm, Su 9:30am-5pm; Sept. to mid-June M-Sa 9am-5pm, Su 10am-4pm.) ■**Mr. and Mrs. Lyall,** 20 Argyll St., with its friendly atmosphere and ample living space, probably is the best value B&B in the Highlands. (☎710267. Continental breakfast included. £10.) To reach the **Inverness Student Hotel,** 8 Culduthel Rd., face the tourist office, go left on Bridge St. and turn right on Castle St., to Culduthel Rd. (☎236556. Reception 6:30am-2:30am. Check-out 10:30am. Dorms July-Sept. £11. Oct.-June £10.)

LOCH LOMOND AND THE TROSSACHS

LOCH LOMOND. With Britain's largest inland freshwater body as its base, the landscape of Loch Lomond is filled with lush bays, thickly wooded islands, and bare hills. Hikers on the northeastern edge of Loch Lomond are rewarded with stunning views, quiet splendor, and small beaches. The **West Highland Way** snakes along the entire eastern side of the Loch, stretching 155km from Milngavie north to Fort William. **Balloch,** at the southern tip of Loch Lomond, is the major town in the area. Across the River Leven, the **Balloch Castle Country Park** provides 200 acres of gorgeous grounds, as well as a 19th-century castle housing a **Visitor's Centre.** Look for the pixies in **Fairy Glen.** (Park open daily dawn-dusk. Visitor's Centre open Easter-Oct. daily 10am-6pm. Free.) **Sweeney's Cruises** (☎752376) boat tours depart from the tourist office side of the River Leven (1hr., every hr., £4.80).

Trains arrive on Balloch Rd., opposite the tourist office, from Glasgow's Queen St. Station (45min., 2 per hr., £3.20). Citylink (☎(08705) 808080) **buses** #926, 975, and 976 arrive from Glasgow (3-5 per day); First Midland (☎(01324) 613777) travels from Stirling (1½hr., 3 per day). Buses arrive a few minutes down Balloch Rd., across the bridge to the left of the **tourist office,** in Old Station Building. (☎753533. Open daily July-Sept. 9:30am-7pm; June 9:30am-6pm; Apr.-May and Oct. 10am-5pm.) **B&Bs** congregate on **Balloch Road.** ■**SYHA Loch Lomond,** in a 19th-century castle-like building 3¼km north of town, is one of Scotland's largest hostels. (☎850226. Open early Mar. to Oct. £12.25-13.25.) To reach the **SYHA Rowardennan,** the first hostel along the West Highland Way, take the Inverberg ferry (☎(01301) 702356; May-Sept. 3 per day, £4) across the Loch to Rowardennan. (☎(01360) 870259. Curfew 11:30pm. Open Mar.-Oct. £9.25.) The **Tullichewan Caravan and Camping Site,** on Old Luss Rd., is up Balloch Rd. from the tourist office. (☎759475. Reception 8:30am-10pm. £6.50-9 2 people and tent; £8.50-12.50 with car.) ☎**01389.**

TROSSACHS. The gentle mountains and lakes of the Trossachs form the northern boundary of central Scotland. A road for walkers and cyclists traces the Loch's shoreline; tourists drop like flies after half a mile, leaving the Loch's joys to more hardy travelers. The **Steamship Sir Walter Scott** (☎376316) steams between Loch Katrine's Trossachs Pier and Stronachlachar. (Apr.-Oct. 2-3 per day, £4.60-6.) Only a few buses each day go to the area's two main towns, **Aberfoyle** and **Callander.** Citylink **bus** #974 runs through Edinburgh and Stirling to Fort William, stopping in Callander (2hr., 2 per day, £7). The Trossachs Trundler is a 1950s-style bus that creaks to Callander, Aberfoyle, and Trossachs Pier in time for the sailing of the *Sir Walter Scott* (July-Sept. Su-F 4 per day, £8). Bus #59 from Stirling connects with the Trundler in Callander. Call the **Stirling Council Public Transport Helpline** (☎(01786) 442707) for info. **Trossachs Cycle Hire,** on the pier, rents bikes. (☎382614. £12 per day. Open Apr.-Oct. daily 8:30am-5:30pm.) ☎**01877.**

THE INNER HEBRIDES

ISLE OF SKYE

Often described as the jewel in the Hebridean crown, Skye radiates splendor from the serrated peaks of the Cuillin Hills to the rugged northern tip of the Trotternish Peninsula. Touring Skye takes effort; pick up the *Public Transport Guide to Skye and the Western Isles* (£1) at a tourist office. **Buses** on the island are infrequent; **biking** and **hiking** are better options. **MacBackpackers** in Kyleakin (☎(01599) 534510) offers **mini-bus day tours** (£15) and the ✦**Skye Trekker Tour,** an outdoor experience with all camping equipment provided (2 days, £45).

KYLE OF LOCHALSH AND KYLEAKIN. The **Skye Bridge** links **Kyle of Lochalsh,** the last stop on the mainland before the Isle, with Kyleakin (Kyle-ACK-in), on Skye's southeastern tail fin. On the mainland side perches the made-for-postcard **Eilean Donan Castle,** which struck a pose for the movie *Highlander.* Take a Scottish Citylink bus and get off at Dornie. (Open daily Apr.-Oct. 10am-5:30pm; Mar. and Nov. 10am-3pm. £3.95, students £3.20.) **Skye-Ways** (☎(01599) 534328), in conjunction with **Scottish Citylink,** runs **buses** through Kyle of Lochalsh on their way to Kyleakin from: Fort William (2hr., 3 per day, £11); Glasgow (5½hr., 3 per day, £18); and Inverness (2½hr., 2 per day, £10). **Trains** (☎(08457) 484950) arrive in Kyle from Inverness (2½hr., 2-4 per day, £15). The train station (☎(01599) 534205) is near the pier and the **tourist office** (TIC) is on the hill right above. The staff books beds on either side of the channel for £3. (☎(01599) 534276. Open Apr.-Oct. M-Sa 9am-5:30pm; July-Sept. Su 10am-4pm.) **Cúchulainn's Backpackers Hostel,** in Kyle of Lochalsh, has especially cozy beds. (☎(01599) 534492.

When you're ready to skip the mainland and dive into Skye, traverse the 2½km footpath or take the **shuttle bus** (2 per hr., £0.70) across the Skye Bridge. Across the water, quiet **Kyleakin** harbor is resplendent at sunset. A slippery scramble leads to the small ruins of **Castle Moil;** cross the bridge behind the SYHA hostel, turn left, follow the road to the pier, and take the gravel path. Lodgings cluster alongside the park a few hundred yards from the pier. The best place to stay is the fun and comfortable ✦**Dun Caan Hostel.** (☎(01599) 534087. Book ahead. Dorms £10.)

SLIGACHAN. West of Kyleakin, the smooth, conical Red Cuillin and the rough, craggy Black Cuillin Hills meet in **Sligachan,** where paths wind their way up the mountains. If you plan to scale some peaks, stay at the **SYHA Glenbrittle** in Glenbrittle near the southwest coast, where expert mountaineers can give you advice on exploring the area. (☎(01478) 640278. Dorms £8.50.) For camping, head to the excellent **Glenbrittle Campsite.** (☎(01478) 640404. Open Mar.-Oct. £3.50 per person.) Take bus #360 from Portree and Sligachan to Glenbrittle (M-Sa 2 per day).

PORTREE. In northern Skye is the island's capital, **Portree** (pop. 2500), with busy shops and an attractive harbor. Buses run from Portree to **Dunvegan Castle,** the seat of the clan MacLeod. The castle holds the **Fairy Flag,** made of silk dated from the 4th through 7th centuries AD and swathed in clan legend. (Open late Mar. to Oct. daily 10am-5:30pm; Nov.-Mar. daily 11am-4pm. £5.50.) **Buses** stop at Somerled Sq. The busy **tourist office** is on Bayfield Rd., near the harbor. (☎(01478) 612137. Open July-Aug. M-Sa 9am-8pm, Su 10am-6pm; Sept.-Oct. and Apr.-June M-F 9am-5:30pm, Su 10am-5pm; Nov.-Apr. M-F 9am-5pm, Sa 10am-4pm.) The **Portree Independent Hostel** is off Somerled Sq. (☎(01478) 613737. Dorms £9.50; doubles £21.)

THE OUTER HEBRIDES

The magical Outer Hebridean archipelago is not just extraordinarily sublime, but also astoundingly ancient. Much of its exposed rock has existed for about three billion years, and inhabitants of the island in the distant past have left behind a rich sediment of tombs, standing stones, and Neolithic remains. The vehemently Calvinist islands of Lewis and Harris observe the Sabbath strictly: all shops, restaurants and public transportation **close on Sundays.** Television and tourism are diluting some local customs, but the islands are remote enough to retain much of their charm, and Gaelic is still heard on the streets.

⌐ **TRANSPORTATION.** Three major Caledonian MacBrayne **ferries** (☎(01475) 650100) serve the Western Isles—from **Oban** to **Barra** and **South Uist,** from **Skye** to **Harris,** and from **Ullapool** to **Lewis.** Ferries and infrequent **buses** connect the islands, and **hitchers** and **cyclists** enjoy success except during frequent rain storms. *Let's Go* does not recommend hitchhiking. Except in bilingual Stornoway and Benbecula, all road signs are in Gaelic. Tourist offices often carry translation keys, and *Let's Go* lists the Gaelic place names after the English ones where necessary. For up-to-date transport information, consult the *Skye and Western Isles Public Transport Travel Guide* (£1 at tourist offices).

LEWIS AND HARRIS. The island of Lewis (Leodhas) is famous for its atmosphere: drifting mists off the Atlantic Ocean shroud the untouched miles of moorland and small lakes in quiet luminescence. The unearthly setting is ideal for exploring the island's many archaeological sites, most notably the **Callanish Stones,** an extraordinary Bronze Age circle. **Buses** on the W2 route from Stornoway run past the stones at Calanais (M-Sa 5 per day). Caledonian MacBrayne **ferries** from Ullapool on the mainland serve **Stornoway** (Steornobhaigh), the largest town in northwestern Scotland (M-Sa 2-3 per day, £13; 5-day return £22.35). To get from the ferry terminal to the **tourist office,** 26 Cromwell St., turn right from the ferry terminal, then hang a left on Cromwell St. (☎703088. Open Apr.-Sept. M-Sa 9am-6pm and to meet the late ferries; Oct.-Mar. 9am-5pm.) Lay your head at the new ⊠**Fair Haven Hostel,** at the intersection of Francis and Keith St., over the surf shop. (☎705862. Dorms £10, with cooked breakfast £12.50, with full board £20.) ☎**01851.**

Although **Harris** (Na Hearadh) is technically part of the same island as Lewis, it is an entirely different world. Lewis is mainly flat and watery, while Harris, is more rugged and spectacular, with steel-gray mountains. Toward the west coast, the barricade of the **Forest of Harris** (ironically, a treeless mountain range) descends to brilliant crescents of yellow beaches bordered by indigo waters and *machair*—sea meadows of green grass and summer flowers. **Ferries** serve **Tarbert** (An Tairbeart), the biggest town on Harris, from Uig on Skye (M-Sa 1-2 per day; £8.50, return £14.55). Pick up essential Ordnance Survey hiking maps at the **tourist office,** on Pier Rd. (☎502011. Open early Apr. to mid-Oct. M-Sa 9am-5pm and for late ferry arrivals.) Walk up the hill and turn left at the grocery store to reach the comfy **Rockview Bunkhouse,** Main St. (☎502211. Dorms £9.) ☎**01859.**

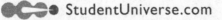

Check out our new
City Guides

Barcelona 2002

photos

walking tours

service directory

amusing anecdotes

detailed map coverage

Amsterdam 2002

&

you know you love

our special Let's Go Thumbpicks

BULGARIA

(БЪЛГАРИЯ)

BULGARIAN LEVA

US$1 = 2.10LV	1LV = US$0.47	
CDN$1 = 1.40LV	1LV = CDN$0.73	
UK£1 = 3.00LV	1LV = UK£0.33	
IR£1 = 2.50LV	1LV = IR£0.40	
AUS$1 = 1.40LV	1LV = AUS$0.89	
NZ$1 = 0.90LV	1LV = NZ$1.10	
ZAR1 = 0.30LV	1LV = ZAR3.90	
DM1 = 1.00LV	1LV = DM1.00	
EUR€1 = 1.90LV	1LV = EUR€0.51	

PHONE CODE	**Country code:** 359. **International dialing prefix:** 00. From outside Bulgaria, dial int'l dialing prefix (see inside back cover) + 359 + city code + local number.

Bulgaria is blessed with a lush countryside, rich in natural resources and ancient tradition. The history of the Bulgarian people, however, is centered around oppression and struggle. Once the most powerful state in the Balkans and the progenitor of the Cyrillic alphabet, Bulgaria spent 500 years under Ottoman rule. These years yielded minarets, underground monasteries, and, finally, the National Revival of the 19th century, when much of the majestic, very European architecture now gracing its cities was built. Today, Bulgaria struggles with a flagging economy and a lack of western attention, though it remains one of the most stable countries in the region. Though often passed by, Bulgaria offers coastline, hikes, and lovely monasteries to the budget traveler.

For more detailed coverage of Bulgaria, get *Let's Go: Eastern Europe 2002*.

FACTS AND FIGURES

Official Name: Republic of Bulgaria.

Capital: Sofia.

Major Cities: Varna, Burgas, Ruse.

Population: 8.2 million.

Land Area: 110,550 sq. km.

Climate: Temperate; cold, damp winters; hot, dry summers.

Language: Bulgarian.

Religions: Bulgarian Orthodox (85%), Muslim (13%), other (2%).

DISCOVER BULGARIA

Bulgaria is a great stopover between Western Europe and Greece or Turkey. Start in **Sofia** (p. 222), where more than 1500 years of Orthodox Churches and cobblestone alleyways hide among the city's vast boulevards. Nestled in the highest mountains on the Balkan Peninsula, **Rila Monastery** (p. 226) is the masterpiece of Bulgarian religious art. **Plovdiv** (p. 227) shelters Roman ruins and art museums, and is only 30min. from the splendid **Bachkovo Monastery** (p. 227). Whether you're into drunken discos or deserted beaches, no visit to Bulgaria is complete without a trip to the **Black Sea Coast** (p. 228). On your way to the coast from western Bulgaria, be sure to stop in **Veliko Turnovo** (p. 228), the most beautiful town in the country.

ESSENTIALS

WHEN TO GO

The best time to visit the Black Sea Coast is summer. For everywhere else, spring and fall weather is ideal. Year-round it's milder than other Balkan countries due to the proximity of the Mediterranean and Black Sea coasts; winter can be quite cold.

DOCUMENTS AND FORMALITIES

VISAS. Citizens of Australia, Canada, the EU, New Zealand, and the US may visit Bulgaria without visas for up to 30 days. Citizens of South Africa and anyone planning to stay more than 30 days must obtain a 90-day visa from their local embassy or consulate.

EMBASSIES. Foreign embassies in Bulgaria are all in Sofia (p. 196). For Bulgarian embassies at home: **Australia (consular),** 14 Carlotta Rd., Double Bay, Sydney, NSW 2028; P.O. Box 1000, Double Bay, NSW 1360 (☎ (02) 9327 7592; fax 9327 8067; bulcg-syd@bigpond.com); **Canada,** 325 Stewart St., Ottawa, ON K1N 6K5 (☎ 613-789-3215; fax 613-789-3524); **Ireland,** 22 Bulington Rd. Dublin 4 (☎ (01) 660 3293; fax 660 3915); **South Africa,** 1071 Church St., Hatfield, Pretoria 0083; P.O. Box 32569, Arcadia (☎ (012) 342 37 20; fax 342 37 21; embulgsa@iafrica.com); **UK,** 186-188 Queensgate, London SW7 5HL (☎ (020) 7584 9400; fax 7584 4948); **US,** 1621 22nd St. NW, Washington, D.C. 20008 (☎ 202-387-0174 or 202-387-7969; fax 212-234-7973; consulate@bulgaria-embassy.org; www.bulgaria-embassy.org).

TRANSPORTATION

BY PLANE. Balkan Bulgarian Airlines (☎ (0)2 98 44 89; www.balkan.com) flies to several large cities worldwide. Its domestic fares are fairly cheap (Sofia-Varna: US$41, return US$71).

BY TRAIN. Bulgarian trains run to Hungary, Romania, and Turkey and are better for transportation in the north and sometimes in the south; **Rila** is the main international train company. The train system is comprehensive but slow, crowded, and old. There are three types of trains: *ekspres* (express; експрес); *burz* (fast; бърз); and *putnicheski* (slow; пътнически). Avoid *putnicheski* like the plague—they stop at anything that looks inhabited, even if only by goats. *Purva klasa* (first-class seating; първа клаcа) is very similar to *vtora klasa* (second-class; втора клаcа), and not worth the extra money. Some useful words: *vlak* (train; влак); *avtobus* (bus; автобус); *gara* (station; гара); *peron* (platform; перон); *kolovoz* (track; коловоз); *bilet* (ticket; билет); *zami-navashti* (departure; заминаващи); *pristigashti* (arrival; пристигащи); and *ne/pushachi* (non-/smoking; не/пушачи).

BY BUS. Buses head north from Ruse, and to Istanbul from anywhere on the Black Sea Coast and are better for travel in eastern and western Bulgaria. Bus trips are more comfortable, quicker, and only slightly more expensive than trains. For long distances, **Group Travel** and **Etap** offer modern buses at prices 50% higher than trains. Buy a seat from the agency office or pay when boarding. Grueling local buses stop everywhere. Due to the political situation in the former Yugoslavia, *Let's Go* does not recommend that travelers take direct buses from Bulgaria to Central and Western Europe; go up to Bucharest and begin your journey westward from there.

BY CAR AND BY TAXI. Major car rental companies such as **Hertz** and **EuroDollar** are in most large cities. The cheapest cars average US$70-80 per day. In Sofia, Odysseia rents reliable cars for US$15 per day. Be prepared for poor driving and unfamiliar signs. Yellow taxis are everywhere. Refuse to pay in dollars and insist on a metered ride *("sus apparata");* ask the distance and price per kilometer to do your own calculations. Some Black Sea towns can only be reached by taxi.

BY BIKE AND BY THUMB. Biking is uncommon as it is nearly impossible to rent a bicycle. Hitchhiking can be risky, but some claim it yields a refreshing taste of *gostelyubivnost* (hospitality) to those who are polite, patient, and cautious. *Let's Go* does not recommend hitchhiking.

TOURIST SERVICES AND MONEY

EMERGENCY   Police: ☎ 166. Ambulance: ☎ 150. Fire: ☎ 160.

TOURIST OFFICES. Tourist offices are fairly common, as are local travel agencies. Staff is helpful but generally does not speak English. In big hotels you can often find an English-speaking receptionist and maps to purchase.

MONEY. The **lev** (lv; plural *leva*) is the standard monetary unit. It's illegal to exchange money on the street. Private banks and exchange bureaus are best for exchanging money. The latter tend to have extended hours and better rates, but may not change anything other than dollars. Traveler's checks can usually only be cashed at banks. Banks also give Visa cash advances. Credit cards are rarely accepted except in larger hotels and expensive resorts. ATMs are usually inconspicuous, but major banks have them either inside or nearby, as do many post offices; ATMs accept Cirrus, MC, and Visa. It is illegal to exchange currency on the street. Bulgaria has recently tied its currency to the Deutschmark; 1 *leva* always equals 1 DM. Staying in campgrounds and shopping at grocery stores in Bulgaria will run you about US$10; a comfortable day (staying in hostels/hotels and eating out) won't cost more than US$20. Food from restaurants average 6lv per meal. Tipping is not obligatory, as most people just round up to the nearest leva, but 10% doesn't hurt, especially in Sofia. A 7-10% service charge will occasionally be added for you; always check the bill or the menu. Tipping taxi drivers usually means rounding up to the nearest half-leva. Bargaining for fares is not done, but make sure there is a meter or agree on a price.

RUN FOR YOUR LIFE You may notice that Bulgarian pedestrians faithfully obey crosswalk signs, and that when they do cross the road they run like they're being chased by wild dogs. Cars, not pedestrians, have the right of way here, and drivers aren't about to let anyone forget it.

BUSINESS HOURS. Businesses open at 8 or 9am and take a one-hour lunch break between 11am and 2pm. Train and bus cashiers and post office attendants take occasional 15min. coffee breaks—be patient. Banks are usually open 8:30am to 4pm, but some close at 2pm. *Vseki den* (every day; всеки ден) usually means Monday through Friday, and "non-stop" doesn't guarantee a place will be open 24hr.

COMMUNICATION

MAIL. Sending a letter abroad costs 0.60lv for any European destination, 0.80lv for the US, and 0.80-1.00lv for Australia, New Zealand, or South Africa; note that a Bulgarian return address is required to do so. Mail can be received in Bulgaria general delivery through *Poste Restante*, though it is unreliable at best.

TELEPHONES. Making international telephone calls from Bulgaria can be a challenge. Payphones are ludicrously expensive; opt for the phones in a telephone office. If you must make an international call from a pay phone with a card, purchase the 400 unit card. Units run out quickly. To call collect, dial ☎01 23 for an international operator. The Bulgarian phrase for collect call is *za tyahna smetka* (за тяхна сметка). For local calls, it's best to buy a phone card. There are two brands: Bulfon (orange) and Mobika (blue), which work only at telephones of the same brand sold at kiosks, restaurants, shops, and post offices. (400 units=20lv; 200 units=12lv; 100 units=7.50lv; 50 units=4.90lv.) In Sofia or Varna, calls to the US average US$2 per minute, but expect to pay as much as US$4 per minute at hotels. International direct dial numbers include: **AT&T,** ☎00 800 0010; **British Telecom,** ☎00 800 99 44; **Canada Direct,** ☎00 800 1359; **MCI,** ☎00 800 001; and **Sprint,** ☎00 800 1010. **Email** is widespread and cheap, around 1-2lv per hour.

LANGUAGES. Bulgarian is a South Slavic language similar to Russian. English is mostly spoken by young people and in tourist areas. German is understood in many places. It's advisable to learn the Cyrillic alphabet. For useful phrases, see p. 982.

> ◤ **YES AND NO.** Bulgarians shake their heads to indicate "yes" and "no" in the opposite directions from Brits and Yanks. For the uncoordinated, it's easier to just hold your head still and say *dah* or *neh*.

HEALTH AND SAFETY

Public bathrooms (Ж for women, M for men) are often holes in the ground; pack a small bar of soap and toilet paper, and expect to pay 0.05-0.20lv. The sign "Аптека" (apteka) denotes a pharmacy. There is always a night-duty pharmacy in larger towns; its address is posted on the doors of the others. Emergency care is far better in Sofia than in the rest of the country; services at the Pirogov State Hospital are free, some doctors speak English, and the tourist office will send someone along to interpret for you. Locals generally don't trust the police. Exercise caution around strangers, and don't volunteer where you're staying to them. Don't buy bottles of alcohol from street vendors, and watch out for homemade liquor—there have been cases of poisoning and contamination. While incidents of hate crimes are rare, persons of a foreign ethnicity might receive stares and suspicious looks. The Bulgarian government recently recognized homosexuality, but acceptance is slow in coming.

> # BATHROOM ETIQUETTE
> Bathtubs are a rarity in Bulgaria; more often you'll find an inconspicuous shower nozzle sticking out of the wall. Just put the toilet seat down, set the trash can outside, and let the water flow. Also, most public bathrooms do not have toilet paper ("pay toilets," 0.20-0.30lv, generously issue about 4 meager squares).

ACCOMMODATIONS AND CAMPING

Upon crossing the border, citizens of South Africa may receive a statistical card to document where they sleep. If you don't get a card at all, don't worry. Ask hotels or private room bureaus to stamp your passport or a receipt-like paper that you can show upon border re-crossing, otherwise you stand to pay a fine. If you are staying with friends, you'll have to register with the Bulgarian Registration Office. See the consular section of your embassy for details.

Solo travelers should look for **"private rooms"** signs (частни квартири; tschastnee kvartiri). They can be arranged through Balkantourist or other tourist offices for US$5-15 per night (be sure to ask for a central location), or from individuals in train and bus stations. Be careful if alone, and don't hand over any money until you've checked the place out. *Babushki* are the best; try to bargain them down. Bulgarian **hotels** are classed on a star system and licensed by the Government Committee on Tourism; rooms in one-star hotels are almost identical to those in two- and three-star hotels, but have no private bathrooms. Expect to pay US$15-50 per night, although foreigners are always charged higher prices. The majority of Bulgarian **youth hostels** are in the countryside. Outside major towns, most **campgrounds** provide spartan bungalows and tent space.

FOOD AND DRINK

Kiosks sell *kebabcheta* (sausage burgers; кебабчета), sandwiches, pizzas, and *banitsa sus sirene* (cheese-filled pastries; баница със сирене). Fruit and vegetables are sold in a *plod-zelenchuk* (fruit store; плод-зеленчук), *pazar* (market; пазар), or on the street. Try *shopska salata* (шопска салата), a mix of tomatoes, peppers, and cucumbers with feta cheese. *Tarator* (таратор), a cold soup made with yogurt, cucumber, garlic, and sometimes walnuts, is also tasty. Vegetarian options with eggs (omelettes; омлети) and cheese are ubiquitous. Bulgarians are known for cheese and yogurt. Baklava and *sladoled* (ice cream; сладолед) are sold in *sladkarnitsy* (сладкарници). In restaurants, seat yourself and directly ask for the bill.

HOLIDAYS

New Year's (Jan. 1); Orthodox Christmas (Jan. 7); 1878 Liberation Day (Mar. 3); Orthodox Good Friday (Apr. 13); Orthodox Easter (Apr. 15); Labor Day (May 1); Cyrillic Alphabet Day, St. George's Day, and Bulgarian Army Day (May 24); Day of Union (Sept. 6); Independence Day (Sept. 22); Bulgarian Culture Celebration (Nov. 1); Catholic Christmas (Dec. 24-25).

SOFIA (СОФИЯ)   ☎ 02

Sofia is full of Bulgarian culture—you just have to dig a little to find it. That might mean sifting through pairs of fake Nikes to locate the handmade lace at a bazaar, or dodging trams and cars on the way to the theater, but it's well worth the effort. There are still plenty of places to find traditional Bulgarian food, folk music, and handmade souvenirs. Fifteen hundred years of majestic churches are not quite dwarfed by Soviet-era concrete blocks, and 19th-century elegance is gracefully weathering the fast food invasion.

▐ TRANSPORTATION

Flights: Airport Sofia (☎ 79 80 35). The adventurous can take bus #84 to the city center (0.40lv, to the left as you exit international arrivals). Everyone else should take a taxi (see below), which shouldn't cost more than 5lv.

Trains: Tsentralna Gara (Централна Гара; Central Train Station), north of the city center on Knyaginya Maria Luiza St. (Мария Луиза). Trams #1 and 7 go to pl. Sv. Nedelya (Пл. Св. Неделя); trams #9 and 12 down Hristo Botev (Христо Ботев); buses #85, 213, 305, and 31 go back to the station. **Ticket office** (☎843 42 80) is open M-F 7am-7pm, Sa 7am-2pm. To: **Burgas** (7 per day, 8.20-15.30lv); **Plovdiv** (15 per day,

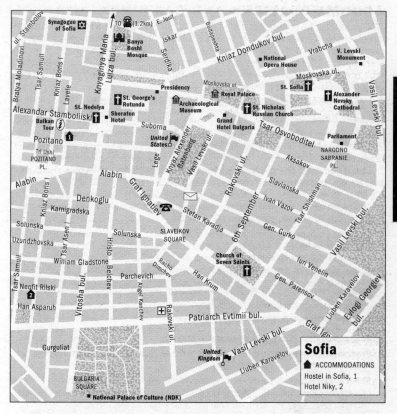

Sofia

⬆ ACCOMMODATIONS
Hostel in Sofia, 1
Hotel Niky, 2

3.80lv). To left of main entrance, **Rila Travel Bureau** (Рила) sells tickets to: **Athens** (1 per day, 80lv); **Budapest** via Bucharest (1 per day, 130lv); and **İstanbul** (1 per day, 100-110lv).

Buses: Private buses, which leave from the parking lot across from the train station, are cheap and fast, and more reliable than government buses. **Group Travel** (☎ 32 01 22) has a kiosk in the parking lot that sends buses to: **Burgas** (2 per day, 15lv); **Varna** (5 per day, 18lv); **Veliko Tarnovo** (4 per day, 8.50lv). Arrive 30-45 min. early to get a seat.

Local Transportation: Trams, trolleybuses, and **buses** cost 0.40lv per ride. Day-pass 2lv; 5-day pass 9lv. Buy tickets at kiosks with signs saying "билети" (tickets; *bileti*) or from the driver. Punch them in the machines between the bus windows to avoid a 10lv fine. If you put your backpack on a seat, you might be required to buy a second ticket. Officially runs 5am-1am, but rides are scarce after 9pm.

Taxis: Taxi S-Express (☎ 12 80), **OK Taxi** (☎973 21 21), and **INEX** (☎919 19) are reliable. Fares are 0.32-0.40lv per km (and rising with gas prices), and upwards of 0.35lv per km after 10pm. It's wise to take a cab at night. Rather than bargain, make sure the meter is on.

🔆🛈 ORIENTATION AND PRACTICAL INFORMATION

The city center, **pl. Sveta Nedelya** (пл. Света Неделя), is a triangle formed by Tsurkva Sv. Nedelya, the Sheraton Hotel, and Tsentralen Universalen Magazin (TSUM). **Bul. Knyaginya Maria Luiza** (Княгиня Мария Луиза) connects pl. Sveta Nedelya to the train station. Trams #1 and 7 run from the train station through pl. Sveta Nedelya and up **bul. Vitosha** (Витоша), a main shopping and nightlife thoroughfare. Vitosha links pl. Sveta Nedelya to pl. Bulgaria and the huge, concrete **National Palace of Culture** (Национален Дворец Култура; NDK; Natsionalen Dvorets Kultura). Historical bul. Tsar Osvoboditel (бул. Цар Освободител; Tsar the Liberator) heads to the university and the hottest spots for dancing and drinking in Sofia. Maps and the monthly English-language *Sofia City Guide* (2.4lv) can be found in the lobby of the Sheraton Hotel and in bookstores, such as Slaveikov Square (пл. Славйков) on Graf Ignatiev (Граф Игнатиев).

TOURIST, FINANCIAL, AND LOCAL SERVICES

Tourist Office: Odysseia-In, Stambolysky bul. 20-V (Страмболийски; ☎989 05 38; odysseia@omega.bg; www.newtravel.com). From pl. Sv. Nedelya, head down Stambolysky and take the 2nd right on Lavele; Odysseia is halfway down on the left, 2 floors up. A great resource. Open M-Sa 9am-6:30pm. Consultation 5lv per 30min.

Embassies: Australians, Canadians, New Zealanders and **South Africans** should contact the **UK embassy,** bul. (*not* ul.) Vasil Levski 38 (☎980 12 20 and 980 12 21). Open M-Th 8:30am-12:30pm and 1:30-5pm, F 8:30am-1pm. **US,** ul. Suborna 1a (Съборна; ☎937 51 004). Consular section at Kapitan Andreev 1 (Капитан Андреев; ☎963 00 89), behind NDK. Open M-F 9am-5pm.

Currency Exchange: Bulbank (Булбанк; ☎984 11 11), pl. Sv. Nedelya 7, cashes traveler's checks for 1.4% commission and gives Visa cash advances for 4% commission. Open M-F 8:30am-4pm. ATMs everywhere.

American Express: Ul. Vasil Levski 21 (☎980 88 89). Open M-F 9am-6pm.

Luggage Storage: Downstairs at the Central Train Station. 0.80lv per piece; hand luggage only. Open daily 5;30am-midnight.

EMERGENCY AND COMMUNICATIONS

Emergency: Police: ☎166. **Ambulance:** ☎150. **Fire:** ☎160.

Pharmacy: All over town; just look for the word Аптека *(Apteka).* Apteka #7 (pl. Sv. Nedelya 5; ☎986 54 53) open 24hr.

Medical Assistance: State-owned hospitals offer foreigners free emergency aid. **Pirogov Emergency Hospital,** Gen. Totleben bul. 21 (Ген. Тотлебен; ☎515 31), opposite Hotel Rodina. Take trolleybus #5 or 19 from city center. Open 24hr.

Telephones: Ul. Gurko 4. After taking a left from the post office, it's the large white building one block down. Phone, fax, email, and Internet access. Open 24hr.

Internet Access: Club Cyberia, Stephan Karadzha 18B (☎988 73 50; www.cyberianet.net). 1.50lv per hr; 9pm-noon 1lv per hr. Open 24 hr. **ICN** (☎65 81 21; www.inagency.com), in NDK. 4lv per hr. Open daily 9am-10:30pm.

Post Office: Gen. Gurko 6 (Гурко). Send international mail at window #7 in the second hall; receive at window #12. Open M-F 7am-8:30pm. Address mail to be held: First name SURNAME, *Poste Restante*, Gen. Gurko 6, Sofia **1000**, BULGARIA.

ACCOMMODATIONS AND FOOD

Big hotels are rarely worth the exorbitant price—if the hostel is full, **private rooms** are the best option. Camping is another inexpensive choice. A friendly staff awaits at **Hostel in Sofia** (a.k.a. Naska's Home for Weary Travelers), Pozitano 16 (Позитано). From pl. St. Nedelya, walk down Vitosha, and go right on Pozitano. (☎/fax 989 85 82. Breakfast included. Communal showers and toilet. Kitchen. Reception 5pm-noon. Check-out noon. US$10.) To get to **Hotel Stivan-Iskar,** ul. Iskar 11B (☎986 67 50; fax 980 43 45; hoteliskar@dir.bg), walk up bul. Maria Luiza to ul. Ekzah Iosif (Екзарх Йосиф), turn right one block and then left, then follow sign. Breakfast $2. Check-out noon. Doubles US$25-35. Apartment with fridge, microwave, and hot tub $50. Group discounts. **Hotel Niky** is on Neofit Rilski 16, off Vitosha (Витоша). (☎51 19 15. Communal showers and toilet. Singles US$22; doubles US$40. Students 10% discount.)

From fast food to Bulgarian specialties, cheap meals are easy to find. In general, meals at restaurants run from 6-10lv, but vendors will fill you up for 2lv. **Vitosha** abounds with 24-hour supermarkets. In summer, an **outdoor market** lines the sides of Graf Ignatiev (Граф Игнатиев), past Slaveikov Square (Пл. Славейков), near the Church of Seven Saints. The first floor of TZUM (at pl. Sv. Nedelya) has a large international **grocery store**. ■**Bai Gencho**, bul. Dundukov (Дундуков), down bul. Maria Luiza towards the mosque, then right on bul. Dundukov for three blocks, serves delicious Bulgarian meals (2-10lv) with an incredible wine selection. (☎986 65 50. Open M-Su 11:30am-11pm.) **Murphy's Irish Pub,** Karnigradska 6 (Кърниградска), is a real Irish pub that attracts an international crowd. (☎980 28 70. Main dishes 6-10vl. Murphy's pint 4lv. Open daily 11:30am-1am.) **Trops House** (Тропс Къща), Saborna 11, is a convenient and quick restaurant with surprisingly good cafeteria-style food. (Entrees 1-2lv. Open daily 8am-9:30pm.) For the best ice cream in town, visit **Jimmy's,** Angel Kunchev 11 (Ангел Кънчев), 0.50lv per scoop).

◉ SIGHTS

PL. ALEXANDER NEVSKY. In the city center stands Sofia's pride and joy, the gold-domed **Cathedral of St. Alexander Nevsky** (Sv. Aleksandr Nevsky; Св. Александр Невски), which was erected in memory of the 200,000 Russians who died in the 1877-1878 Russo-Turkish War. Through a separate entrance left of the main church, the **crypt** houses a spectacular array of painted icons and religious artifacts, the richest collection of its kind in Bulgaria. *(Cathedral open daily 7:30am-7pm; free. Crypt open W-M 10:30am-6:30pm. 3lv, students 1.5lv.)* At the **markets** surrounding the square, Soviet paraphernalia, World War II relics and handmade crafts are sold.

AROUND PL. SVETA NEDELYA. The focal point of Sofia is the **Cathedral of St. Nedelya** (Katedralen Hram Sv. Nedelya; Катедрален Храм Св. Неделя), filled with soot-blackened frescoes. The church is a reconstruction of a 14th-century original destroyed by a bomb in an attempt on Tsar Boris III's life in 1925; the tsar escaped, but the cupola buried 190 generals and politicians. Sunday liturgy shows off the church's great acoustics. *(Open daily 7am-6:30pm.)* In the courtyard behind the Sheraton Hotel stands the 4th-century **St. George's Rotunda** (Sv. Georgi; Св. Георги). Accompanied by a former Roman bath and the remains of the ancient town of Serdica, the church has three layers of frescoes dating back as far as the 10th century. *(Open daily 8am-6pm.)* In the underpass between pl. Sv. Nedelya and TSUM, the tiny, 14th-century **Church of St. Petya of Samardzhiyska** (Tsurkva Hram Sv. Petya Samardzhiyska; Църква Храм Св. Петя Самарджийска) is rumored to have originally held the bones of Vasil Levsky, Bulgaria's national hero. *(Open M-Sa 8am-7pm, Su 9am-noon; Nov.-Apr. M-Sa 9:30am-6pm, Su 9am-noon. 5lv; tours 10lv.)* Walk up bul. Maria Luiza and take a left on Tsar Simeon to reach the **Synagogue of Sofia** (Sofiaski Synagoga; Софийска Синагора), a beautifully renovated synagogue, where a museum upstairs outlines the history of Jews in Bulgaria. *(Open Su-F 9am-5pm, Sa 10am-6:30pm. Weekly service Sa 6:30pm. Donations welcome.)*

ALONG BUL. TSAR OSVOBODITEL. Historical bul. Tsar Osvoboditel is weighted down on the ends by the **House of Parliament** and the **Royal Palace.** Midway sits the 1913 Russian **Church of St. Nicholas** (Sv. Nikolai; Св. Николай), with five Russian Orthodox-style onion domes. *(Open daily 8am-6pm.)*

MUSEUMS. From St. Nedelya, head down Suborna and take your first left on Lege to reach the **National Archaeological Museum** (Arheologicheski Muzey; Археологически Музей), which houses armor, tombstones and steles. *(Open Tu-Su 10am-6pm.)* The Royal Palace houses the **National Museum of Ethnography** (Natsionalen Etnografski Muzey; Национален Етнографски), which gives a detailed photographic history of the *karacachans*, a Bulgarian nomadic people. *(Open Tu-Su 10am-5pm. 3lv, students 1.50lv.)* It also houses the **National Art Gallery** (Natsionalna Hudozhestvena Galeriya; Национална Художествена Галерийа). *(Open Tu-Su 10am-6:30pm. 3lv, students 1.50lv.)*

ENTERTAINMENT

The main **opera** and **theater** seasons run from September to June; good theater seats are sometimes less than US$1. (☎987 70 11, 987 14 66, and 981 14 67. Box office open daily 9am-7pm. No performances M.) You can get tickets for the **Ivan Vazov National Theater** at Rakovski 98 (☎07 23 03). Cinemas often show subtitled Hollywood movies—try Vitosha 62 and pl. Vasil Levski 1.

By night, smartly dressed Sofians roam the main streets, filling the outdoor bars along **bul. Vitosha** and the cafes around the **NDK.** Most nightlife centers around bul. Vitosha or, for the younger set, the **University of Sofia** at the intersection of Vasil Levski and Tsar Osvoboditel. When out on the town, don't draw too much attention to yourself, and you should be fine. Enter **Bibloteka** (Библиотека), in St. Cyril and Methodius Library, from Obhorishte. (Cover 3lv. Open W-Sa 11pm-5am.) **Spartakus** (Спартакус), in the underpass past the pl. Narodno Subranie, leading toward Vasil Levski, keeps its somewhat exclusive gay and straight clientele happy with pounding techno and strobe lights. (Cover 3lv. Open daily 11pm-late.) **Dali,** behind the University on Krakra, is the best Latin club in Sofia. Get your Bulgarian friend to make a reservation. (☎46 51 29. Men 31zl; women free. Open daily until 6am.)

DAYTRIPS FROM SOFIA

RILA MONASTERY. Holy Ivan of Rila built the 10th-century Rila Monastery (Rilski Manastir; Рилски Манастир), Bulgaria's largest and most famous monastery, as a refuge from the worldly temptation. Moved to its current location in the 14th century, the monastery sheltered the arts of icon painting and manuscript copying during the Byzantine and Ottoman occupations, and remained an oasis of Bulgarian culture for five centuries. Today's monastery was built between 1834 and 1837; little remains from the earlier structure. Examine the 1200 brilliantly colored **frescoes** (on the central chapel), or check out the **museum.** (Open daily 8:30am-4:30pm. 5lv, students 3lv. English tours 15lv.) The quickest way to get to Rila Town is to take a **bus** from Novotel Europa in Sofia to Blagoevgrad (2hr., 4lv), then from Blagoevgrad to Rila Town (45min., every hr., 1.20lv). From Rila Town, catch the bus up to the monastery (45min., 3 per day, 1.10lv). ◙**Hotel Tsarev Vrukh** (Царев Врьх) is a new hotel with luxury facilities. (☎/fax 22 80. Breakfast US$2. US$15.) The hotel is 50m down the path that follows the river from behind the monastery. Inquire at room #170 in the monastery about staying in a spartan, but heated, monastic cell. (☎22 08. Curfew midnight. US$10 per person.) Behind the monastery is a cluster of restaurants, cafes, snack bars, and a small mini-market. ☎07054.

KOPRIVSHTITSA. Todor Kableshkov's movement for rebellion against Ottoman rule started in this little town, tucked away in the Sredna Gora mountains. Today, the town is a historical center, where the National Revival period of 125 years ago is still well-preserved in its buildings. If you miss the folk festivals, beginning in May and continuing through mid-August, the preserved **National Revival houses** are the thing to see. Many homes of the leaders of the 1876 Uprising have become museums, for which you can get tickets and maps at the tourist office. The most notable is the 1845 **Todor Kableshkov Museum-House** (Kushtamuzey Todor Kableshkov; Къща-музей Тодор Каблешков), which has an impressive facade, carved ceilings, and weapons upstairs. (Open Tu-Su 9:30am-noon and 1:30-5:30pm.) **Trains** come from Sofia (2hr., 6 per day, 2.70lv) and Plovdiv via Karlovo (3½hr., 3 per day, 2.30lv). Take a bus (1lv) from the train station into town, and get off at the **bus station** (a wooden building), which posts bus and train schedules. To reach the **main square,** backtrack along the river bisecting town. The **tourist office,** in the main square (☎21 91; koprivshitza@hotmail.com; open daily 10:30am-6pm), has an invaluable map (2lv) with a guide to museums, monuments, and places to stay and eat. ☎07184.

LET'S DO THE CHALGA It's everywhere—on buses, in pubs, even in the clubs: chalga (Чалга), Bulgaria's most popular music genre for the past several years. The trend grew out of traditional Bulgarian folk music mixed with techno rhythms. Today, chalga appeals to adult and teenagers alike. You might hear the same song in a refined restaurant or rocking in a night club. Here's how to dance the dance: spread your arms, bend your head, and slowly move your chest back and forth.

PLOVDIV (ПЛОВДИВ)   ☎032

While Plovdiv is smaller than Sofia, it is widely hailed as the cultural capital of Bulgaria. In the convoluted Old Town, National Revival houses protrude from the cobblestones below, windows stare into alleys at impossible angles, and churches and mosques hide in secluded corners. Most of Plovdiv's historic and cultural treasures are concentrated in the three hills (the **Trimondium**) of the Old Town. Take a right off Knyaz Aleksandr (Княз Александр) to Stanislav Dospevski (Станислав Доспевски), turn right at the end of the street, and take the stairs to the left to reach the 2nd-century Roman **amphitheater** (Античен Театр; Antichen Teatr), a marble masterpiece from the early Roman occupation of the Balkans. (Open daily 9am-dusk. 2lv.) It currently serves as a popular venue for concerts and shows, hosting the **Festival of the Arts** in the summer and early fall, and the **Opera Festival** in June. Return to Knyaz Aleksandr and follow it to the end to pl. Dzhumaya (Джумая), home to the **Dzhumaya Mosque** (Джамия; Dzhumaya Dzhamiya; services daily 6pm) and the ancient **Philipoplis Stadium.** The gladiator's entrance is still intact and a restaurant-cafe serves traditional Bulgarian food on the stadium's tiers. (Barbecue 0.80-2lv. Open daily 11am-midnight.) At the end of Suborna (Съборна), the ▓**Museum of Ethnography** (Етнографски Музей; Etnografski Muzey) has some *kukerski maski* (masks used to scare away evil spirits) and other Bulgarian artifacts. (Open Tu-Su 9am-noon and 2-6pm. 3lv.) At night, head to the fountainside cafe in **Tsentralni Park** (Централни Парк), by pl. Tsentralen (пл. Централен).

Trains arrive from: Sofia (2½hr., 15 per day, 3.80lv); Burgas (5hr., 7 per day, 6lv); and Varna (5½hr., 3 per day, 7.80lv). Buy tickets at **Rila**, bul. Hristo Botev 31a. (☎63 19 48. Open daily 8am-6pm.) **Buses** arrive from Sofia (2hr., every hr., 7lv) at Yug (Юг) station, Hristo Botev 47 (Христо Ботев), diagonally across from the train station. **Traffic Express** (Трафик Экспрес; ☎26 57 90), in the station, services the Black Sea coast. **Puldin Tours** (Пълдин), bul. Bulgaria 106 (България), finds rooms, arranges tours, and changes money. From the train station, ride trolley #2 or 102 (0.20lv) nine stops to bul. Bulgaria and backtrack a block. (☎95 51 42. Open May-Sept. M-F 9am-6:30pm.) An up-to-date map is essential—street vendors sell good Cyrillic ones for 3lv. Check **email** at **VooDoo Net,** Stan Knyaz Aleksander 3, near the mosque, up two flights. (1lv per hr. Open 24hr.) It is important to make reservations for rooms in Plovdiv in the summer. **Hostel Touristicheski Dom** (Туристически Дом), P.R. Slaveykov 5 (П.Р. Славейков), is in the Old Town (Стари Град; Stari Grad). From Knyaz Aleksandr (Княз Александр), take Patriarch Evtimii (Патриарх Евтимий) into town, passing under Tsar Boris, and hang a left on Slaveykov. (☎63 32 11. Curfew 11pm. 22lv.) From Rodopi bus station, head away from the train track on Dimitar Talev (Димитър Талив), and take the second right after Nikola Vapstarov (Никола Вапцаров) to **Hotel Feniks** (Феникс), Silivria 18A (Силиврия); it's a 20min. walk. (☎77 48 51. Singles US$9-10; doubles US$18-20.) **Postal code:** 4000.

▓ **DAYTRIP FROM PLOVDIV: BACHKOVO MONASTERY.** About 28km south of Plovdiv, in the plush green Rodopi mountain slopes, is Bulgaria's second-largest monastery, **Bachkovo Monastery** (Бачковски Манастир; Bachkovski Manastir), built in the 11th century. The main church is home to the **icon of the Virgin Mary and Child** (икона Света Богородица; ikona Sveta Bogoroditsa), which is said to have miraculous healing power. (Open daily 8am-dusk.) **Buses** run from Plovdiv's Yug station to Asenovgrad (25min., 21 per day, 0.70lv), as do **trains** (25min., every hr., 0.80lv). From Asenovgrad's bus station, catch a bus to the monastery (2nd stop, 20min., every 30min., 0.60lv).

VELIKO TARNOVO (ВЕЛИКО ТЪРНОВО) ☎062

Veliko Tarnovo has been watching over Bulgaria for 5000 years—for centuries the city has been the center of of Bulgarian politics: its residents led the national uprising against Byzantine rule in 1185, and revolutionaries wrote the country's first constitution here in 1879. The remains of the ◧**Tsarevets** (Царевец), a fortress that once housed a cathedral and the king's castle during the Second Bulgarian Kingdom, stretch across a hilltop above the city. (Open daily 8am-7pm; Oct. 8am-6pm; Nov.-Mar. 9am-5pm. 4lv, students 2lv.) At the top of the hill is the **Church of the Ascension** (Tsurkva Vuzneseniegospodne; Църква Възнесениегосподне), restored in 1981 on the 13th centennial of the Bulgarian state. From pl. Maika Bulgaria, go down Nezavisimost, which turns into Nikola Pikolo, and turn right at ul. Ivan Vazov. The **National Revival Museum** (Muzey na Vuzrazhdaneto; Музей на Възраждането) documents Bulgaria's 19th-century cultural and religious revival. (Open M and W-Su 8am-noon and 1-5:30pm. 4lv, students 2lv. Guided tours 8lv.) On summer evenings, there is often a **sound and light show** above Tsarvets Hill.

All **trains** stop at nearby **Gorna Oryahovitsa** (Горна Ораховица; 30min., 0.80lv), where they then leave for Burgas (5½hr., 6 per day, 8lv) and Sofia (5hr., 10 per day, 7.50lv). City buses #7 and 10 go from the station to the town center. Bookstores along **Rakovski** (Раковски), the small street two minutes from Hotel Trapezitsa on the way to Hotel Comfort, have good maps for 3lv. **Rila Travel Bureau** is down Hristo Botev on the left. (Open M-F 9am-6pm.) Check **email** up the stairs and to the right of **La Scalla, Pizzeria Italian.** (1lv per hr. Open 24hr.) ◧**Hostel Trapezitsa (HI)** (Хотел Трапезица), Stefan Stambolov 79, is an excellent hostel with clean rooms. From the town center, walk down Nevvisimost toward the post office and follow the street right. (☎220 61. Singles 25lv; triples 15lv per person.) **Hotel Comfort** (Комфорт), Panayot Tipografov 5 (Панайот Типографов), has an amazing view of Tsarvets. From Stambolov, walk left on Rakovski (Раковски), turn left on the small square, and look for the street sign. (☎287 28. US$10 per person.) **Postal code:** 5000.

BLACK SEA COAST

The Black Sea, the most popular vacation spot in Bulgaria for foreigners and natives alike, has tiny fishing villages with secluded bays, vibrant seaside towns, and pricey resorts. In between, you'll find sandy beaches in the south, and a rockier white-cliffed coast to the north. You're bound to run into more English speakers than in any other part of Bulgaria, along with higher (but still reasonable) prices.

VARNA (ВАРНА) ☎52

Varna's appeal is its many **beaches** and Mediterranean-like climate, and its summer arts and music festival. The beaches stretch north from the train station and are separated from bul. Primorsky by seaside gardens. The well-preserved **Roman Thermal Baths** (Римски Терми; Rimski Termi) stand on San Stefano in the city's old quarter, **Grutska Makhala.** (Гръцка Махала. Open Tu-Su 10am-5pm. 2lv.) In the park behind Maria Luiza, the ◧**Archaeological Museum** (Археологически Музей; Arkheologicheski Muzey) traces the country's history from the Early Stone Age, and contains the world's oldest gold treasure. (Open Tu-Sa 10am-5pm. 2lv.) Both the **National Revival Museum,** which sits just off pl. Ekzarkh Yossif (Екзарх Йосиф; open Tu-Su 10am-5pm; 1.50lv), and the **Ethnographic Museum** (Етнографски Музей; Etnografski Muzey), at Sofronii Vrachanski 22 (Софроний Врачански; open Tu-Sa 10am-5pm; 2lv), maintain displays of 19th-century folk crafts in well-preserved buildings from Bulgaria's historic National Revival Period. Varna is home to many arts events; for schedules, tickets, and information, check the **Festivalen Complex,** on bul. Primorsky (Приморски), which also has cafes and a movie theater.

Trains, near the commercial port, go to: Gorna Oryahovitza (3hr., 5 per day, 5.40lv); Plovdiv (5½hr., 3 per day, 7.80lv); and Sofia (7hr., 7 per day, 10.20lv). **Buses,** at Ul. Vladislav Varenchik (Владислав Варенчик), go to Burgas (3hr., 3 per day, 7lv) and Sofia (6hr., 16 per day, 18lv). The **Megatours** in the Hotel Cherno More, Slivnitsa 33, has fine tourist information. (Open M-Sa 9am-7pm; Oct.-May M-F 9am-6pm.)

Astra Tour, near track #4 at the train station, finds rooms for US$6-10 per person. (☎60 58 61; astratour@mail.vega.bg. Open in summer daily 6am-10pm.) **Hotel Trite Delfina** (Трите Делфина; Three Dolphins), at ul. Gabrovo 27, is close to the train station. Go up Simeon from the station and take a right on Gabrovo. (☎60 09 11. Singles US$20-25; doubles US$25-30. Call ahead.)

BURGAS. Burgas (Бургас) is a transport hub for the Southern Black Sea Coast. The bus and train stations are near the port at Garov pl. (Гаров). **Trains** go to Sofia via Plovdiv (7hr., 7 per day, 9.70lv); **buses** serve the Black Sea Coast (to Varna: 4½hr., 5 per day, 4.80lv), while cheaper **minibuses** run to the coastal resorts from the side of the bus station facing away from the train station. Many smaller resorts don't have places to change money. **Bulbank,** across the street from Hotel Bulgaria on Aleksandrovska, cashes traveler's checks and has an **ATM.** (Open M-F 8:30am-4pm.) If you stay the night here, secure a room at **Febtours Bourgas** (Фебтурс), 20 Lermnotov (Лермонтов). (☎84 20 30; febtours@abv.bg. Open M-F 9am-5pm. Singles 10lv; doubles 18lv.) Or, go to **Hotel Mirage** (Мираж), Lermontov 18; from the station, go up Aleksandrovska, take a right on Bogoridi, pass the Hotel Bulgaria, and take the first left on Lermontov. (☎92 10 19. Doubles US$20; triples US$30.) ☎**056.**

NESEBUR. Nesebur (Несебър), a museum town atop the peninsula at the south end of Sunny Beach, has preserved its charm. A walk through its ancient **Stari Grad** begins with the 3rd-century stone **fortress walls.** The Byzantine gate and port date from the 5th century. The **Archaeological Museum** (Археологически Музей; Arheologicheski Muzey), to the right of the town gate, exhibits ancient ceramics and icons. (Open May-Oct. daily 9am-1:30pm and 2-7:30pm; Nov.-Apr. M-F 9am-9pm. 2.10lv, children 0.85lv. English tour 4lv.) The 11th-century **New Metropolitan Church of St. Stephen** (Църквата Свети Стефан; Tsurkvata Sveti Stefan) is plastered with 16th-century frescoes. From the town center, continue down Mesembria and take a right on Ribarska. (Open June-Sept. 7am-7:30pm. 1.70lv, students 0.85lv.) Along the harbor, steet kiosks sell fruit and nuts or small meals. Get to Nesebur by **bus** from Burgas (40min., every 40min., 2lv). ☎**0554.**

SOZOPOL. Sozopol (Созопол), settled in 610 BC, is Bulgaria's oldest Black Sea town. Once the resort of choice for Bulgaria's artistic community, it still caters to a creative set and is quieter and cheaper than its neighbors. Take a **boat cruise** (15lv per boat) from the seaport behind the bus station and get a closer look at the two nearby islands, **St. Peter** and **St. Ivan.** The best time to go is around sunset. To explore some of Sozopol's less-crowded **beaches,** rent a motorbike near the bus station and cruise along the shoreline (10lv per hr). **Buses** arrive from Burgas (45min., every 30min., 1.90lv). Turn left on Apolonia (Аполония) to reach **Stari Grad** (Old Town). To get to **Novi Grad** (New Town), go right through the park and turn left on Republikanska (Републиканска). The tourist bureau **Lotos,** at the bus station, arranges private rooms. (☎22 82. US$7 per person. Open daily 8am-8pm.) ☎**05514.**

CROATIA
(HRVATSKA)

CROATIAN KUNA

US$1 = 8.30KN	10KN = US$1.20
CDN$1 = 5.40KN	10KN = CDN$1.90
UK£1 = 12KN	10KN = UK£0.80
IR£1 = 9.60KN	10KN = IR£1
AUS$1 = 4.50KN	10KN = AUS$2.30
NZ$1 = 3.60KN	10KN = NZ$2.80
ZAR1 = 1KN	10KN = ZAR10
DM1 = 2.60KN	10KN = DM2.60
EUR€1 = 8KN	10KN = EUR€1.30

PHONE CODE	**Country code: 385. International dialing prefix:** 00. From outside Croatia, dial int'l dialing prefix (see inside back cover) + 385 + city code + local number.

Croatia is a land of unearthly beauty. Blessed with thick forests, wispy plains, underground streams, and translucent sea, it has served for centuries as a summer playground. Positioned at the convergence of the Mediterranean, the Alps, and the Pannonian plain, Croatia has also been situated on dangerous divides—between the Frankish and Byzantine empires in the 9th century, the Catholic and Orthodox churches since the 11th century, Christian Europe and Islamic Turkey from the 15th to the 19th centuries, and split between its own fractious ethnic groups in the past decade. Dancing in the nightclubs of Dubrovnik or lounging on the beaches of Pula, it's easy to forget the tensions that have played out here. Independent for the first time in 800 years, Croatians are finally free to enjoy the extraordinary landscape in peace.

For more glistening coverage of Croatia, get *Let's Go: Eastern Europe 2002.*

FACTS AND FIGURES

Official Name: Republic of Croatia.

Capital: Zagreb.

Major Cities: Split, Dubrovnik.

Population: 4.7 million (78% Croat, 12% Serb, 1% Bosniak, 9% other).

Land Area: 56,538 sq. km.

Climate: Inland, hot summers and cold winters; along the coast, dry summers and mild winters.

Languages: Croatian.

Religions: Catholic (77%), Orthodox (11%), Muslim (1%), other (11%).

DISCOVER CROATIA

With Mediterranean beaches, Roman ruins, and lively cities, Croatia is certainly worth the trip. The capital, **Zagreb** (p. 233), is a mix of Habsburg splendor, Mediterranean relaxation, and the hippest cafe scene in the Balkans. Croatia's most impressive ruins are in **Pula** (p. 235), the 2000-year-old heart of Istria. The true highlight of Croatia, however, is the fabled **Dalmatian Coast** (p. 236), one of the Mediterranean's most dazzling natural spectacles, where pristine beaches and azure waters mingle; bask in **Split** (p. 236) on the central coast. George Bernard Shaw called **Dubrovnik** (p. 238) "paradise on earth" for its stunning seascapes and walled city center.

Croatia

ESSENTIALS

WHEN TO GO

Croatia's mild Mediterranean climate means that there is no wrong time to visit. The high season (July to Aug.) may bring crowds to the coast; going in June or September will reward visitors with lower prices and more breathing room.

DOCUMENTS AND FORMALITIES

VISAS. Citizens of Australia, Canada, Ireland, New Zealand, the UK, and the US do not need visas for stays of up to 90 days. Visas are required of South African citizens. All visitors must **register with the police** within two days of arrival, regardless of their length of stay. Hotels, campsites, and accommodations agencies should automatically register you, but those staying with friends or in private rooms must do so themselves to avoid fines or expulsion. Police may check passports anywhere. There is no entry fee at the border.

EMBASSIES. Foreign embassies in Croatia are all in **Zagreb** (p. 233). For Croatian embassies at home: **Australia,** 14 Jindalee Crescent, O'Malley, Canberra ACT 2606 (☎(06) 286 69 88; croemb@dynamite.com.au); **Canada,** 229 Chapel Street, Ottawa, ON K1N 7Y6 (☎613-562-7820; fax 613-562-7821; info@croatiaemb.net; www.croatiaemb.net); **New Zealand Consulate,** 131 Lincoln Rd., Henderson, P.O. Box 83200, Edmonton, Auckland (☎(09) 836 5581; fax 836-5481); **South Africa,**

1160 Church St., Colbyn, Pretoria; P.O. Box 11335, Hatfield 0028 (☎(012) 342 1206; fax 342 1819); **UK**, 21 Conway St., London W1P 5HL (☎(020) 7387 2022; fax 7387 0936); **US**, 2343 Massachusetts Ave. NW, Washington, D.C. 20008 (☎202-588-5899; fax 202-588-8936; www.croatiaemb.org).

TRANSPORTATION

BY PLANE. Zagreb is Croatia's main entry point; **Croatia Airlines** often continues to Dubrovnik and Split. Rijeka, Zadar, and Pula also have international airports.

BY TRAIN, BY BUS, AND BY CAR. Trains are *very* slow, and nonexistent south of Split. *Odlazak* means departures, *dolazak* arrivals. **Eurail** is not valid. For domestic travel, **buses** work best. Tickets are cheaper if you buy them on board. You can **rent a car** in larger cities, but parking and gas can be expensive, rural roads are in poor condition, and in the Krajina region and other conflict areas, drivers should be wary of off-road land mines. Speed limits are 50kph in cities, 130kph on highways.

BY FERRY. If you're on the coast, take one of the ferries run by **Jadrolinija**. Boats sail the Rijeka-Split-Dubrovnik route with islands stops. Ferries also float from Split (p. 236) to Ancona, Italy (p. 634), and from Dubrovnik (p. 238) to Bari, Italy.

BY THUMB. Hitchhiking in Croatia is highly discouraged.

TOURIST SERVICES AND MONEY

EMERGENCY	Police: ☎92. Ambulance: ☎94. Fire: ☎93.

TOURIST OFFICES. Even the smallest towns have a branch of the excellent, English-speaking **state-run tourist board** (*turistička zajednica;* www.htz.hr). Private accommodations are handled by private tourist agencies (*turistička/ putnička agencija),* the largest of which is the ubiquitous Atlas with branches in every major city. Most banks, tourist offices, hotels, and transportation stations exchange currency and traveler's checks. Banks usually have the best rates. Croatia's monetary unit is the **kuna (kn),** which is divided into 100 lipa and is virtually impossible to exchange abroad, except in Hungary and Slovenia. Neither South African rand nor Irish pounds are exchangeable in Croatia. ATMs *(bankomat)* are common. Most banks give MC/Visa cash advances, and credit cards are widely accepted. A basic day in Croatia runs about US$25. Tipping is not expected, but you may round up to the nearest whole kuna; in some cases, the establishment will do it for you—check your change. Always try bargaining. Shops and banks are usually open between Monday and Friday 8am and 8pm, and on Saturday mornings. Most stores close for a long lunch.

COMMUNICATION

Mail from the US arrives in seven days or less; if addressed to *Poste Restante*, it will be held for 90 days at the main (not always the most central) post office. *Avionski* and *zrakoplovom* both mean "airmail" in Croatian. Post offices usually have **public phones;** pay after you talk. All phones on the street require phone cards *(telekarta),* sold at all newsstands and post offices. Fifty "impulses" cost 23kn (1 impulse = 3min. domestic, 36sec. international; 50% discount 10pm-7am, Su, and holidays). Calls to the US are expensive (20kn per min.). International direct dial numbers include: **AT&T,** (☎0800 22 01 11); **British Telecom,** (☎0800 22 00 44); **Canada Direct,** (☎0800 22 01 01); **MCI,** (☎0800 22 01 12); and **Sprint,** (☎0800 22 01 13). Technically, this operator assistance is free, but some phones demand a *telekarta* card. Croats speak **Croatian** and write in Roman characters. Street designations on maps often differ from those on signs by "-va" or "-a" because of grammatical declensions. In Zagreb and most tourist offices, some people know English, but the most common language on the coast is Italian.

ACCOMMODATIONS AND CAMPING

Two words: **private rooms.** Apart from the country's five **youth hostels** (in Zagreb, Pula, Zadar, Dubrovnik, and Punat) and **camping** (bring your own tent), they are the only affordable option. Look for *sobe* signs, especially near transportation stations. Agencies generally charge 30-50% more if you stay less than three nights. All accommodations are subject to a tourist tax of 5-10kn. If you opt for a hotel, call a few days in advance, especially during the summer. For information on HI hostels around Croatia, contact the **Croatian Youth Hostel Association** in Zagreb (☎482 92 94; fax 482 92 96; hfhs@alf.tel.hr). Wherever you stay, hot water is fleeting at best.

HEALTH AND SAFETY

Although Croatia is no longer at war, travel to the Slavonia and Krajina regions remains dangerous due to **unexploded mines.** Crime is rare. Pharmacies are generally well stocked with Western products. Croatians are friendly toward foreigners and sometimes a little too friendly to female travelers; going out in public with a companion will help ward off unwanted displays of machismo. Croatians are just beginning to accept homosexuality; discretion may be wise.

FOOD AND DRINK

Cuisine *à la* Hrvatska is defined by the country's geography; in continental Croatia around and east of Zagreb, typically heavy Slavic meals predominate, while on the coast, seafood blends with Italian pasta dishes. *Purica s mlincima* (turkey with pasta) is the regional dish near Zagreb, and spicy *Slavonian kulen* is considered one of the world's best sausages by the panel of fat German men who decide such things. Along the coast, try *lignje* (squid) or *Dalmatinski pršut* (Dalmatian smoked ham). The oysters from Ston Bay have received a number of awards; *slane sardele* (salted sardines) are a tasty (and cheaper) substitute. *Grešak varivo* (green bean stew), *tikvice va lešo* (steamed zucchini in olive oil), and *grah salata* (beans and onion salad) are meatless favorites. Croatia also offers excellent wines; price is usually the best indicator of quality. Mix red wine with tap water to get the popular *bevanda*, and white with carbonated water to get *gemišt*. *Karlovačko* and *Ožujsko* are the most popular beers, especially with fishermen.

HOLIDAYS AND FESTIVALS

Holidays: New Year's Day (Jan. 1); Holy Trinity (Jan. 6); Catholic Easter (Apr. 23-24); Labor Day (May 1); Independence Day (May 30); Croatian National Uprising Day (June 22); Homeland Gratitude Day (Aug. 5); Feast of the Assumption (Aug. 15); All Saints' Day (Nov. 1); Catholic Christmas (Dec. 25-26).

Festivals: Zagreb hosts many festivals: the **International Folklore Festival** in July, is the premier gathering of European folk dancers and singing groups. The **Zagreb Summer Festival** (July-Aug.) hosts open-air concerts and theatrical performances. On Korčula, the **Festival of Sword Dances** (Festival Viteških Igara) takes place each July. During both the **Split** and **Dubrovnik Summer Festivals** (July-Aug.), the cities feature theater, ballet, opera, classical music, and jazz.

ZAGREB   ☎01

Despite wide boulevards, sprawling public parks, and hulking buildings, this 900-year-old capital has the charm of a small town. In Zagreb, Mediterranean breezes blow past churches and lively outdoor cafes. The scars of the recent civil wars have all but vanished from the city streets, and rapid renovations continue.

▐ **TRANSPORTATION.** Trains leave the **Glavni Kolodvor station,** Trg kralja Tomislava 12 (☎(660) 33 34 44), for: Budapest (7hr., 4 per day, 140kn); Ljubljana (2½hr., 4 per day, 81kn); Venice (7hr., 2 per day, 260kn); Vienna (6½hr., 2 per day, 320kn); and Zurich (8hr., 1 per day, 625kn). To reach the main square, **Trg bana Josipa Jelačića,** with your back to the train station, walk across the street, staying along the left side of the park until it ends, and follow Praška. **Buses** (☎ (060) 31 33 33) head from **Autobusni Kolodvor,** Držićeva, to: Ljubljana (2hr., 2per day, 115kn); Sarajevo (9hr., 3 per day, 500kn); and Vienna (8hr., 2 per day, 200kn). Exit on Držićeva, turn left toward the bridge, and the main square will be on the left.

⚐ PRACTICAL INFORMATION. The **tourist office** is at Trg b. Jelačića 11. (☎481 40 51; info@zagreb-touristinfo.hr; www.zagreb-touristinfo.hr. Open M-F 8:30am-9pm and Sa 8:30am-3pm.) All foreigners staying in private accommodations must register at their point of arrival within two days. In Zagreb, register at the **Department for Foreign Visitors** in room 103 at the central police station, Petrinjska 30. Use Form 14. (☎456 36 23. Open M-F 8am-4pm.) Hotels and hostels register guests automatically, bypassing this frustrating process. Find **Internet** access at **Aquariusnet,** Drzislavova 4. (☎461 88 73. Open M-Sa 9am-4am, Su noon-2am. 40 lipa per min.; 20hr. card 100kn.) **Postal code:** 10000.

⌂ ACCOMMODATIONS AND FOOD. Rooms in Zagreb are not cheap. **Omladinski Turistićki Centar (HI),** Petrinjska 77, is well-located; from the train station, walk right on Branimirova, and Petrinjska is on the left. (☎484 12 61; fax 484 12 69. Reception 24hr. Dorms 67kn, non-members 72kn; singles 149kn, 202kn with bath; doubles 204kn/274kn. Cash only.) **Hotel Astoria,** Petrinjska 71, is just a few steps past Omladinski. (☎484 12 22; fax 484 12 12. Breakfast included. Singles 330kn; doubles 500kn; triples 600kn.) For a traditional Croatian feast, save up for ⊠**Baltazar,** Nova Ves 4. (Main dishes 35-80kn. Cover 5kn. Open daily noon-midnight.) **Groceries** are available throughout the city. Try **Konzum,** Britanski Trg 12, at the corner of Prevadovica and Hebranger. (Open M-F 7am-8pm, Sa 7am-3pm.)

⬛ SIGHTS. Start exploring Zagreb by riding the funicular (*uspinjača;* 2kn), which allows easy access to many sights in Gornji Grad. After a short walk down Ilica from Trg b. Jelačica, turn right on Tomiceva. Once at the top, **Lotrščak Tower,** on the left, provides a spectacular view of the city. **St. Catherine's Church** is in the square to the right of the tower; follow ul. Cirilometodska to Markov Trg. The colorful tiles of Gothic **St. Mark's Church** (*Crkva sv. Marka)* depict the coats of arms of Croatia, Dalmatia, and Slavonia on the left and of Zagreb on the right. The church also contains works by Ivan Meštrovic, Croatia's most famous sculptor. Follow ul. Kamenita to the **Stone Gate** (*Kamenita Vrata)*, the only gate left from the original Gradec city walls. **Kaptol Hill** is dominated by the 11th-century **Cathedral of the Assumption of the Virgin Mary** and its striking neo-Gothic bell towers. (Open M-Sa 10am-5pm, Su and holy days 1-5pm. Free.) Take an 8min. bus ride from Kaptol to Mirogoj 1, the country's largest and most stunning cemetery, in front of the Cathedral where Croatia's first President, Franjo Tudjman, is buried. (Open M-F 6am-8pm, Su 7:30am-6pm. Free.) Zagreb's museums house Croatia's best artwork: the **Gallery of Modern Art,** Herbranga 1, displays 20th-century paintings. (Open Tu-Sa 10am-6pm, Su 10am-1pm. 20kn, students 10kn.) The nearby **Strossmayer Gallery,** Zrinjskog Trg 11, shows Renaissance and Baroque works. (Open Tu-Su 10am-1pm. 10kn, students 5kn.) The **Ivan Meštrovic Foundation,** Mletačka 8, shows off the work of the master sculptor. (Open Tu-F 9am-2pm, Sa 10am-6pm. 10kn, students 5kn.)

◫▣ FESTIVALS AND NIGHTLIFE. Festival season opens with the **World Festival of Animated Film** in May. **Cest is d'Best,** in the second week of June, brings all kinds of street performers to Zagreb. The **International Folklore Festival,** July 17-21, is the premier gathering of European folk dancers and singing groups. **Zagreb Summer Festival** hosts open-air concerts and theatrical performances during July and August; some of the best concerts take place in the Muzejski Prostor Atrium, Jezuitski Trg 4 (☎27 89 57). The annual **International Puppet Festival** at the beginning of September is lots of fun, and **Zagreb Fest,** a pop festival in November, attracts rock bands from all over Europe. For up-to-date information on these and many other festivals, contact the **Zagreb Convetion Bureau.** (☎481 43 43; fax 481 49 49; see events calendar at www.zagreb-convention.hr; zagreb.convention@ccb.hr).

LET'S GET NAKED Part of the coastline from Poreč south to Rovinj holds the title of the world's longest stretch of nude beaches, many of which are privately owned by naturist camps. Anyone interesting in getting naked should take off his or her clothes. Go ahead, take your shirt off. However, anyone interested in getting naked *at the beach* should apply for a membership card at any of the naturist camps, since you can't get in without one. No special attributes are necessary to obtain the card, although men are not allowed into the camps alone, even with membership.

Dance and swim at the lakeside club ◪**Aquarius,** on Lake Jarun (☎364 02 31). To get there, take tram #17 and get off at Srednjaci at the third unmarked stop (15min.). Turn around, cross the street, follow any one of the dirt paths to the lake, and walk left along the boardwalk. Aquarius is the last building. (Cover 30kn. Club open W-Su 10pm-4am. Cafe open daily 9am-9pm.) Or mix with locals and their beer at **Bulldog,** Bogoviceva 6. (Open M-Th and Su 9pm-1am, F-Sa 9pm-2am.)

NORTHERN COAST

As you head from Zagreb toward the coast, you'll approach the islands of the **Gulf of Kvarner,** including Pag and Rab, which are blessed by long summers and gentle coastal breezes. Farther north along the coast lies **Croatian Istria,** home to Pula, where the Mediterranean laps at the foot of the Alps. Today, the region seems almost more Italian than Croatian in language, tradition, and culture.

PULA ☎052

If you only get to visit one city in Istria, it should be Pula—not only for its cool, clear water, but for its winding medieval corridors, outdoor cafes, and breathtaking Roman ◪**amphitheater,** the 2nd-largest in the world. (Open daily 8am-9pm. 16kn, students 8kn.) To get there from the bus station, take a left on Istarska. Follow Istarska in the opposite direction from the station to the **Arch of the Sergians** (Slavoluk obitelji Sergii), which dates from 29 BC; go through the gates and down bustling **ul. Sergijevaca** to the **Forum,** which holds the **Temple of Augustus** (Augustov hram.), built between 2 BC and AD 14. Buy a bus ticket from any newsstand (8kn) and take bus #1 to the Stója campground or bus #2 toward the hostel to reach Pula's **beaches.** Catch a **train** (☎54 17 33; tickets ☎54 19 82) at Kolodvorska 5 for Ljubljana (7½hr., 3 per day, 120kn) and Zagreb (7hr., 4 per day, 97-120kn). **Buses** (☎21 89 28) run from the station at Matta Balotta 6 to Trieste, Italy (3¾hr., 4 per day, 98kn) and Zagreb (5-6hr., 15 per day, 137kn). The **tourist office,** Forum 3, near the forum, can help find **private rooms** (☎21 29 87; www.gradpula.com; open daily 9am-8pm), as can travel agencies, such as **Arenaturist,** Giardini 4. (☎21 86 96; arenaturist1@pu.tel.hr.) To get to the **Omladinski Hostel (HI),** Zaljev Valsaline 4, walk right from the bus station on Istarska, take bus #2 (dir. Veruda) from the small park on Giardini to the last stop, and follow the signs. (☎39 11 33; hfhspuls@pu.tel.hr. 63-97kn.) **Postal code:** 52100.

⚑ DAYTRIP FROM PULA: BRIJUNI ARCHIPELAGO. To anyone interested in Yugoslav history, a visit to scenic Brijuni is essential. The largest island in the archipelago, **Veli Brijun** has been the site of a Roman resort, a Venetian colony, the discovery of a cure for malaria, and the residence of former Yugoslav president Josip Brož Tito. To see the island, you should get a guided tour. The **Brijuni Agency,** Brijunska 10, in Fazana, has the lowest rates (☎52 58 83; np-brijuni@pu.tel.hr. Round-trip ferry and a 4hr. tour 160kn. Tours daily 11:30am; call the day before to reserve a spot. Open daily 8am-7pm.)

RAB ☎051

An extraordinarily beautiful town whose narrow streets and whitewashed stone houses seem to rise out of the sea, Rab will seduce you with its beaches and buildings. A stroll along Gornja ul. runs from the remains of **St. John's Church**

(Crkva sv. Jvana), an outstanding Roman basilica, to **St. Justine's Church** (Crkva sv. Justine), which houses a museum of Christian art. (Open daily 9am-noon and 7:30-10pm. 7kn.) Sunsets from the top of **St. Mary's Bell Tower** are truly stupendous. (Open daily 9am-noon and 7:30-10pm.) The 12th-century **Virgin Mary Cathedral** (Katedrala Djevice Marije) and nearby 14th-century **St. Anthony's Monastery** (Samostan sv. Antuna) lie farther down Gornja ul. Rab's greatest assets are its **beaches**, scattered all over the island; ask at the tourist office for transport information. **Buses** arrive from Zagreb (5½hr., 3 per day, 127kn). The **tourist office** is on the other side of the bus station. (☎77 11 11. Open daily 8am-10pm.) **Katurbo,** M. de Dominisa, between the bus station and the town center, arranges private rooms. (☎/fax 72 44 95; katurbo-tourist-agency@ri.tel.hr. Open daily 8am-1pm and 4-9pm. Singles 60-90kn; 2-person studio 260-360kn. 30% surcharge on stays less than 3 nights. Tourist tax 7kn.) Walk along the bay to reach **Camping Padova,** 2km east of the bus station. (☎72 43 55. 22kn per person, 20kn per tent. Daily tax 7kn. Registration 4kn.) There's a **supermarket** in the basement of **Merkur,** Palit 71, across from the tourist office. (Open daily 7am-9pm.) **Postal code:** 51280.

PAG ISLAND ☎023

The island of Pag has a lush coast and a barren interior. **Pag Town,** often overlooked by foreign tourists, is in the middle of harsh terrain, but is quite beautiful, especially at dusk. Pag's famous lace *(paška čipka)* is sold out of private homes and from the **Lace Gallery** near the main square, Kralja Zvonimira 1. (Open daily 7:30-11pm.) The last weekend in July, see traditional dance at the **summer carnival** in the main square. **Zrće beach,** close to the nearby resort-town of Novalja, has paddle boats, kayaks, and the **Blato,** a natural mineral spa. Buses run from Pag Town to Novalja (40min., 5 per day, 15kn); minivans run July-Aug. from Novalja to Zrće. (15min, 7kn).

To get to Pag, take a **bus** from Zadar (1hr., 1 per day, 24kn) or Zagreb (6hr., 4 per day, 120kn). If you're heading south along the coast, have the driver drop you off at Prizna, walk 2km down to the water and catch a **ferry** to Zigljen on Pag Island. Buses to Pag Town meet the ferries. To get to the center from the bus stop, face the sea and walk left along the water. Turn left onto Vela Ulica to reach the small main square. The **tourist office,** Katine bb, is on the waterfront. (☎/fax 61 13 01. Open daily 7am-9pm.) **Meridijan 15 Travel Agency,** A. Starčevića 1, next to the bus stop in the same building complex as Hotel Pagus, books rooms. (☎61 21 62; meridijan-15@zd.tel.hr. Open May-Oct. daily 8am-9pm. Singles 60-80kn; doubles 100-200kn. Tourist tax 5.50-7kn.) If you have a tent, camp on the beach at **Autocamp Šimuni.** (☎69 82 08. July-Aug. 96kn per person; May-June and Sept. 56kn. Tourist tax 4kn.) To get there from town, grab a Zagreb-bound bus; get let off at Šimuni (20min., 5 per day) then follow signs downhill. There is an **open-air market** in front of Tamaris. (Open daily 6am-10pm.) **Postal code:** 23250.

DALMATIAN COAST

Stretching from the Rijeka harbor to Dubrovnik in the south, Croatia's coast is stunningly beautiful. With more than 1100 islands (only 66 of which are inhabited), Dalmatia boasts the Mediterranean's largest archipelago and cleanest waters, as well as bronze beaches and Roman ruins.

SPLIT ☎021

The aesthetic appeal of Split's female population is rivaled only by the geography and architecture of this palace-city by the sea. The **Stari Grad** (Old Town), wedged between a high mountain range and palm-lined waterfront, sprawls around a luxurious **palace** where Roman Emperor Diocletian, known for his violent persecution of Christians, used to spend his summers. The **cellars** of the city are near the entrance to the palace, under a flag past the taxis on the waterfront; turn in either direction to wander around this labyrinth. (Open daily 10am-7pm. 6kn, students 3kn.) Through the cellars and up the stairs is the open-air **peristyle,** a colonnaded square, and the open-domed **vestibule,** which serves as the backstage for the **summer festival**. The **cathedral** on the right side of the peristyle was originally the mausoleum of Diocletian. (Open daily 8:30am-9:30pm.) A 25min. walk away along the waterfront, the **Meštrović Gallery**, Setaliste Ivana Meštrovica 46, features a collection of Croatia's most famous modern sculptor. (Open June-Aug. Tu-Sa 10am-6pm, Su 10am-3pm; Sept.-May Tu-Sa 10am-4pm, Su 10am-2pm. 15kn, students 10kn.)

Trains (☎ 33 85 35) go from Obala kneza Domagoja 10 to: Budapest (16hr., 1 per night, 320kn); Ljubljana (12hr., 2 per week, 200kn); and Zagreb (7½hr., 4 per day, 124kn). **Buses** (☎ 33 84 83) go to: Dubrovnik (4½hr., 15 per day, 110kn); Ljubljana (11hr., 1 per day, 233kn); Sarajevo (7½hr., 6 per day, 171kn); and Zagreb (8hr., every 30min., 163-194kn). **Ferries** (☎ 33 83 33) head from the terminal across from the train and bus stations to Dubrovnik (8hr., 5 per week, 72kn) and Ancona, Italy (10hr., 4 per week, 256kn). From the train or bus station, follow Obala kneza Domagoja to the waterside mouthful **Obala hrvatskog narodnog preporoda,** which runs roughly east-west. The **tourist office** is at Obala hrv. narodnog preporoda 12. (☎/fax 34 21 42. Open M-F 7:30am-8:30pm, Sa 8am-2pm.) The **Daluma Travel Agency**, Obala kneza domagoja 1, helps find private rooms. (☎ 33 84 84; daluma-st@st.tel.hr. May-Oct. singles 100kn, doubles 200kn; Nov.-Apr. 80/160kn. Open M-F 8am-8pm, Sa 8am-12:30pm.) To get from the stations to a bed at **Prenoćište Slavija**, Buvinova 2, follow Obala hrv., turn right on Trg Braće Radića, go right on Mihovilova širina, and go up the stairs in the left-hand corner. (☎ 34 70 53; fax 59 15 58. Breakfast included. Singles 180kn, with shower 220kn; doubles 210/260kn; triples 250/300kn; quads 280/360kn.) There is a **supermarket** at Svačićeva 4. (Open daily 7am-10pm.) Facing the water on Obala hrv., walk right along the waterfront for 10min., following the curves onto Branimirova Obala, to **Jugo Restoran,** Uvala Baluni bb. (Main dishes 26-65kn. Open daily 9am-midnight.) The closest beach to downtown Split is sandy **Bačvice,** a nighttime favorite for local skinny dippers and the starting point of a great strip of bars along the waterfront. **Postal code:** 21000.

KORČULA
☎ 020

The central Dalmatian island of Korčula, whose sacred monuments and churches date from the time of the Apostles, stretches parallel to the nearby mainland. The **Festival of Sword Dances** clangs into town July-Aug. (40kn; tickets available at tourist office). Korčula can be reached via **buses,** which board a short ferry to the mainland and head to: Dubrovnik (3½hr., 1 per day, 62kn); Sarajevo (6½hr., 4 per week, 145kn); and Zagreb (11-13hr., 1 per day, 190kn). **Ferries** run to Dubrovnik (3½hr., 5 per week, 64kn). To get to the **tourist office,** face the water and walk left around the peninsula to Hotel Korčula; the office is next door. (☎ 71 57 01. Open M-Sa 8am-3pm and 4-9pm, Su 9am-1pm.) Private rooms are the only budget lodgings available; **Marko Polo,** Biline 5, can arrange one for you, though it makes sense to shop around. (☎ 71 54 00; marko-polo-tours@du.tel.hr. Singles 76-160kn; doubles 100-212kn; triples 140-272kn. Tourist tax 4.50-7kn. Open daily 8am-10pm.) **Postal code:** 20260.

BRAČ ISLAND AND BOL
☎ 021

Central Dalmatia's largest island, Brač is a tourist's paradise. Most visitors come here for **Zlatni rat,** a peninsula just a short walk from the town center of Bol with a white pebble beach and pine forests. The 1475 **Dominican Monastery** and adjacent **museum,** on the eastern tip of Bol, display collection of prehistoric artifacts, ecclesiastic robes, and the town's old archives. (Open daily 10am-noon and 5-7pm. 10kn.) The **ferry** from Split docks at **Supetar** (45min., 7-13 per day, 15kn). From there, take a **bus** to Bol (1hr., 6 per day, 12kn). The last bus back to the ferry leaves at 5:50pm. Facing the sea from the bus station, walk left for 5min. to reach the **tourist office,** Porad bolskich pomorca bb. (☎ 63 56 38; tzo-bol@st.tel.hr.) **Adria Tours**, Obala Vladimira Nazora 28, to the right facing the sea from the bus station, rents bikes (45kn), mopeds (150kn), and cars (400kn including mileage), and also books rooms. (☎ 63 59 66; adria-tours-bol@st.tel.hr; www.tel.hr/adria-tours-bol. Open daily 8am-9pm. Rooms 50-108kn per person. Tax 5.50kn.) There are five **campsites** around Bol; the largest is **Kito**, Bračka cesta bb, on the road into town. (☎63 54 24. Open May 1-Sept. 30. 38kn per person; tent included.) **Postal code:** 21420.

DUBROVNIK ☎020

George Bernard Shaw once wrote: "Those who seek Paradise on earth should come to Dubrovnik." He wasn't far off the mark—nearly scarless despite recent wars, the city continues to draw visitors with azure waters and copper sunsets over 14th-century city walls. If you make it as far south as Dubrovnik, you might never leave.

■■ **TRANSPORTATION AND PRACTICAL INFORMATION.** Jadrolinija **ferries** (☎41 80 00) leave from opposite Obala S. Radica 40 for Bari, Italy (9hr., 2 per week, 257kn) and Split (8hr., 1 per day, 72kn). **Buses** (☎35 70 88) go to: Sarajevo (6hr., 2 per day, 156kn); Split (4½hr., 15 per day, 103kn); Trieste (15hr., 1 per day, 210kn); and Zagreb (11hr., 8 per day, 190kn). To reach Stari Grad, face the bus station, walk around the building, turn left on ul. Ante Starčević, and follow it uphill to the Old Town's western gate (30min.). Or, to reach the ferry terminal, head left (with your back to the bus station) and then bear right. All local buses except #5, 7, and 8 go to Stari Grad's Pile Gate. (Tickets 7kn at kiosks, 10kn from driver.) From the bus stop at Pile Gate, walk up Ante Starčeviča away from Stari Grad; the **Tourist Board,** A. Starčeviča 7, is on the left. (☎416 999. Open M-Sa 8am-7pm.) **Postal code:** 20000.

■■ **ACCOMMODATIONS AND FOOD.** For two people a **private room** is cheapest; arrange one through the Tourist Board (☎416 999; 80-120kn) or **Atlas**, Lučrica 1; next to the Church of St. Blasius. (☎44 25 28; www.atlas-croatia.com. Open M-Sa 8am-9pm, Su 9am-1pm; off-season M-Sa 8am-7pm. Singles 100-150kn; doubles 120-180kn.) For cheaper rooms, try your luck with the women around the ferry and bus terminals. The ■**HI youth hostel**, at b. Josipa Jelačića 15/17 is one of the best in Croatia. From the bus station, walk up ul. Ante Starčević, turn right at the lights (10min.), turn right on b. Josipa Jelačića, and look for the hidden HI sign on your left just before #17. (☎42 32 41. Breakfast included. Check-out 10am. Open May-Dec. 65-87kn.) Call ahead to the cozy **Begović Boarding House,** Primorska 17, for a ride from the station. Or, from the bus station, take bus #6 toward Dubrava and tell the driver to let you off at Post Office Lapud; facing the pedestrian walkway, turn right at the intersection, bear left, turn right onto Primorska, and continue to the top of the hill. (☎43 51 91. Reserve ahead. 75-90kn.) ■**Marco Polo,** Lučarica 6, is a local favorite that serves meat dishes for 45-76kn. (Open daily 10am-midnight.) Behind the Church of St. Blasius, on Gunduliceva Poljana, you'll find an **open-air market.** Supermarket **Mediator,** Od puča 4, faces the market. (Open M-Sa 6:30am-9pm, Su 7am-9pm.)

■ **SIGHTS.** The entrance to the staggering city walls *(gradske zidine)* lies just inside the **Pile Gate,** on the left. Make sure you have an hour for the 2km walk along the top. (Open daily 9am-7:30pm. 15kn, children 5kn.) The **Franciscan Monastery** (Franjevački samostan), next to the city wall entrance on Placa, houses the oldest working pharmacy in Croatia and a pharmaceutical museum. (Open daily 9am-6pm. 5kn.) The Renaissance **Sponza Palace** and its bell tower mark the end of Placa

---

PRICE ISN'T EVERYTHING When you get off the ferry or bus in Dubrovnik, you will hear chants of *sobe!, rooms!,* and *zimmer!* from the throngs of ladies done up in their Sunday best. While the prospect of a soft bed may be tempting, keep the following in mind. If Dubrovnik is your first stop in Croatia, you must **register with the police** (p. 231). If the rooms you see are approved by the tourist bureau—that is, if a stamped and signed document with the price listed is posted in the room—then you're good to go. If there is no such paper posted, do not stay, as they cannot register you. If the police find you unregistered for any reason, you will be fined. So pick your woman wisely.

and house the city archives. (Open daily 10am-1pm and 7-11pm. 5kn.) Across from the Sponza Palace stands the **Church of St. Blasius** (Crkva sv. Vlaha), whose namesake can be seen in statues adorning the city walls. (Open daily 9am-noon and 6-9pm.) The **Dominican Monastery** (Dominikanski samostan), Sv. Dominikanska 4, between the city walls and the Old Port, is still home to monks. Inside, you'll find a museum comprising the cloister and sacristy, as well as most of Dubrovnik's religious art. (Open daily 9am-6pm. Museum 10kn.) Behind the Church of St. Blasius on Drzićeva Poljana stands the **Rector's Palace** (Knežev Dvor), which houses 16th- and 18th-century weapons, paintings, coins, and furniture. (Open M-Sa 9am-7pm. 10kn, students 5kn.) The **cathedral** (riznica) dominates Bunićeva Poljana. Its treasury holds saintly relics, including the "Diapers of Jesus," which date from year 0. (Treasury open daily 9am-7pm. 5kn. Cathedral open daily 6:30am-8pm.) The 4000 Bosnian Muslims in Dubrovnik come to pray at the tiny **Islamic Mosque,** Miha Pracata 3, on the eighth street off Placa from the Pile Gate. (Open daily 10am-1pm and 8-9pm.) Around the corner from the mosque is the 19th-century **Serbian Orthodox Church,** Od Puča 8, and its Museum of Icons (Muzej Ikona). (Open M-Sa 9am-1pm. 10kn.) The defunct **Sephardic Synagogue** (Sinagoga), Žudioska 5, is the second-oldest of its kind in Europe. (Open M and Th-F 10am-noon.)

■■ **ENTERTAINMENT AND NIGHTLIFE.** In summer, the Dubrovnik Summer Festival (Dubrovački Ijetni Festival; ☎42 88 64; mid-July to mid-Aug.) presents theater, ballet, opera, classical music, and jazz events. Head to the island of **Lokrum** for a **nude beach;** ferries run from the Old Port (15min., every hr. 9am-8pm, return 25kn). Once there, take a break from the sun to stroll through the **botanical garden** and look back on Dubrovnik from the fortress.

Dubrovnik is by far the liveliest Croatian city by night. There's a wide variety of music, you can almost always find a live band in summer, and many bars will stay open until 4 or 5am every night. Crowds gravitate to a few areas; often, they overflow from **Stari Grad** and the cafes on **Bunićeva Poljana.** Another great center of nightlife is outside the city walls on **B. Josipa Jelačica** by the youth hostel, otherwise known as Bourbon St. **▨Divinae Follie,** Put Vatroslava Lisinskog 56, Babin Kuk, has two bars, a techno tent, and lots of outdoor seating. (☎43 56 77. Beer 15kn. Cover 70kn. Open June-July and Sept. Sa 11pm-5am, nightly in Aug., but call ahead to make sure.) **Troubadour,** Bunićeva Poljana 2, is a huge cafe with nightly jazz. Draft *Tuborg* 30kn. Open daily 9am-late.

> **! WATCH YOUR STEP.** As tempting as it may be to stroll in the hills above Dubrovnik or to wander down unpaved paths on Lopud island, both may still be laced with **landmines.** Stick to the paved paths and beach.

■ **DAYTRIP FROM DUBROVNIK: LOPUD ISLAND.** Less than an hour from Dubrovnik, Lopud is an island of the Elafiti Archipelago. The tiny village, dotted with white buildings, chapels, and parks, stretches along the island's waterfront *(obala)*. Currently under renovation, **Dorđič Mayneri** remains among the most beautiful parks in Croatia. Signs from Kavana Dubrava on the waterfront point to the **museum,** the meeting place for tours of the church, museum, and monastery. (Tours Th 9am.) The island's highlight is its **beach,** Plaza Šunj. This cove has one thing that most of the Dalmatian Coast lacks: sand.

Ferries run from Dubrovnik to the Elafiti islands (50min., 1-2 per day, return 25kn). The beach is on the opposite side of the island from the village. On the road between the high wall and the palm park, look for the "Konoba Barbara" sign and turn off the road onto a large path. Ignore small paths branching off; when the path forks, keep right.

CYPRUS (Κυπρος)

CYPRUS POUNDS

US$1 = £0.63	£1 = US$1.58
CDN$1 = £0.41	£1 = CDN$2.44
UK£1 =£0.92	£1 = UK£1.08
IR£1 = £0.74	£1 = IR£1.35
AUS$1 = £0.34	£1 = AUS$2.95
NZ$1 = £0.28	£1 = NZ$3.59
ZAR1 = £0.08	£1 = ZAR13.23
GRD100 = £0.17	£1 = GRD585.32
EUR€1 = £0.58	£1 = EUR€1.72

PHONE CODES	**Country code:** 357. **International dialing prefix:** 080. From outside Cyprus, dial int'l dialing prefix (see inside back cover) + 357 + city code + local number.

Aphrodite blessed Cyprus with an abundance of natural beauty, from the sandy beaches of Agia Napa to the serene Troodos Mountains. After long-standing territorial disputes and a Turkish invasion, the island was left partitioned in 1974 among Greeks in the south and Turks in the north, divided by the UN-manned Green Line. Restrictions prohibit travel from north to south except for tourists making short daytrips across the Green Line in Nicosia. *Let's Go: Europe 2002* only includes coverage of southern Cyprus.

For more coverage of this lovely isle, check out *Let's Go: Greece 2002*. Journeys to northern Cyprus require careful planning and must begin in Turkey. For information on northern Cyprus, see *Let's Go: Turkey 2002*.

ESSENTIALS

DOCUMENTS AND FORMALITIES

VISAS. Citizens of Australia, Canada, Great Britain, Ireland, New Zealand, and the US do not need a visa to enter Cyprus for stays of up to 90 days; South Africans can stay without visas for up to 30 days.

EMBASSIES. Foreign embassies are in Nicosia. For Cypriot embassies at home: **Australia,** 30 Beale Cr., Deakin, Canberra, ACT 2600 (☎6281 0832); **Canada,** 365 Bloor St. E., Suite 1010, Box #43, Toronto, ON M4W 3L4 (☎416-944-0998); **Greece,** 16 Herodotou, Athens (☎72 32 727); **UK,** 93 Park St., London W1Y 4ET (☎(0171) 499 82 72); and **US,** 22211 R St. NW, Washington, D.C. 20008 (☎202-462-5772).

TRANSPORTATION

Cyprus is served by **Olympic Airlines** (US ☎800-223-1226; Cyprus ☎(04) 62 79 50; www.olympic-airways.gr), **Cyprus Airways** (US ☎212-714-2190; Cyprus ☎(02) 44 30 54; www.cyprusair.com.cy), and other major airlines. Return fares from Athens to Larnaka cost about US$145. The international airports are in Paphos and Larnaka. An island-wide **bus schedule** is available at tourist offices. **Service taxis** are the most reliable form of transportation on Cyprus and are quite affordable; each taxi seats 4-7 passengers. (Taxis generally run M-Sa every 30min. 6am-6pm, Su 7am-5pm £2.50-6.) After 7pm, transportation is limited to private taxis. By **ferry,** both Limassol and Larnaka are accessible from a number of points, including Rhodes, Crete, and Hafia, Israel. Schedules are available at the ports; expect to pay around £45 for a ferry to Cyprus, a few pounds more if your trip begins in Israel.

FROM
TOWER OF LONDON

TO
EIFFEL TOWER

VIA
A HIGH SPEED ATTRACTION

THE CENTRE OF **LONDON** TO THE CENTRE OF **PARIS** IN JUST 3 HOURS.

eurostar.com

enjoy your journey eurostar

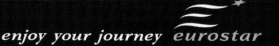

TOURIST SERVICES AND COMMUNICATION

EMERGENCY	Police, Ambulance, and Fire: ☎ 199.

Tourist offices in Cyprus (in Limassol, Nicosia, Larnaka, Paphos, Polis, and Platres) are extremely helpful and efficient. **Cyprus Tourism Organization (CTO;** ☎ (02) 337 715; cto@cyta.com.cy), provides free maps and information on buses, museums, and events. The useful *Cyprus Traveler's Handbook* (free) is available at tourist offices. Officials generally speak English, Greek, German, and French.

In Southern Cyprus, direct overseas calls can be made from all public phones. Direct overseas calls can be made from all public phones, but you need a **phone card** to activate them even if you plan to use your own service provider. Cards are available in denominations of £3, £5, and £10 and are sold at banks and kiosks. Private phones in hotels may have a 10% surcharge.

LARNAKA (Λαρνακα)   ☎ 04

Although many tourists come to Larnaka for its beaches, the wonders of its ancient history are more impressive. Segments of the ancient city walls and aqueducts, Bronze Age temples, and the Hala Sultan Tekke Mosque—which dates back to the first Arab invasion of Cyprus in AD 647—poke through into the present. **Leoforos Athinon** (a.k.a. the **Finikoudhes,** "Palm Tree Promenade," or simply **Athinon**) runs along the waterfront at the heart of the tourist district and hops with eateries and night spots. **Larnaka Fort** presides over the southern end of Athinon. Larnaka was built over the 13th-century BC city of **Kition** and retains monuments from its long history; the **temple** complex of Kition is the oldest spot in Larnaka. (Open M-Sa 9am-2:30pm, Th 3-5pm, Su 10am-1pm. £0.75.) Most recently rebuilt after a devastating fire in 1970, beautifully adorned 9th-century ⬛**Church of Agios Lazarus,** near the fortress, rests on the sepulcher of Lazarus, whom Jesus raised from the dead. (Museum open 8am-12:30pm and 3:30-6:30pm. £0.50. Services Su 6-9:30am. Dress modestly.) The **Pierides Foundation Museum,** 4 Zinonos Kitieos, showcases artifacts spanning 3000 years of Cypriot history. (Open M-F 9am-1pm and 3-6pm, Sa 9am-1pm, Su 10am-1pm. £1, under 18 free.) Two kilometers west of Larnaka Airport, the ⬛**Hala Sultan Tekke Mosque** houses the tomb of Umm Haram, Muhammad's maternal aunt. Take bus #19, bound for Kiti, from Pl. Ag. Lazarus (15min., 14 per day, £0.50). Ask the driver to be let off at Tekke. After you're dropped off, walk along the paved road for 1km. (Open in summer daily 7:30am-7:30pm. Free.) At night, check out the beachfront pubs and eateries on **Athinon.** If disappointed by Larnaka's dusty shores, daytrip to **Agia Napa** (Αγια Ναπα), a tourist resort with white, sandy beaches and raucous nightlife; hop on a **bus** (4-9 per day, £1) from Leforos Athinon on the waterfront opposite Four Lanterns hotel. **Petrou Bros. Holiday Apartments,** Armenikis Ekklisias 1, two blocks from the waterfront is immaculate. (☎650 600. Reception 24hr. Doubles £22; quads £30.) The **Youth Hostel (HI),** Nikolaou Rossou 27, in Pl. Ag. Lazarus, is in a former mosque. (☎621 188. Dorms £4.)

Most **flights** to Cyprus land at the Larnaka airport; take bus #19 (M-Sa in summer 6:20am-7pm; in winter 6:20am-5:45pm; £0.50) or a taxi (£3-5) to the town center. **Buses** leave from Athinon for Lefkosia (4-6 per day, £2) and Limassol (3-4 per day, £1.70). One **tourist office** is at the airport (☎643 000; open 24hr.); another is at Pl. Vasileos Pavlou. (☎654 322. Open M-Tu, Th-F 8:15am-2:15pm and 4-6:15pm; W and Sa 8:15am-2:15pm; off-season hours vary.) **Postal codes:** 6900, 6902.

LIMASSOL (Λεμεσος)   ☎ 05

Limassol is a transport hub and the point of arrival or departure by sea. **Poseidon Lines** (☎745 666; open M-F 8am-noon and 3-5pm, Sa 10am-2pm) and **Salamis Tours** (☎355 555) run ferries to: Haifa, Israel (11hr., 2 per week, £50); Rhodes, Greece (18hr., 2 per week, £44); and Piraeus via Rhodes (45hr., 2 per week, £47). **Buses** traverse the island (check times with the tourist office). **KEMEK** (☎747 532), 400m north of the castle at the corner of Irinis and Enosis, serves Lefkosia (M-F 5 per day,

Sa 3 per day; £1.50) and Paphos (6-10 per week, M-Sa 9am, £1.50). **Kallenos** (☎(04) 654 850) heads for Larnaka (M-Sa 3-4 per day, £1.70). **Service taxis** are a more personal but expensive option, running 6am-6:30pm to Larnaka (£3), Lefkosia (£3.45), and Paphos (£2.50). Contact **Makris** (☎365 550). **Postal code:** 3900.

TROODOS AND PLATRES (Τροοδος, Πλατρες)   ☎05

With crisp mountain air, authentic village life, and Byzantine churches tucked amongst its pine-covered mountains, the **Troodos Mountains** are the perfect escape for hikers who wish to avoid Cyprus' summer heat. In winter, **Mt. Olympus,** the highest point in Cyprus (1951m), is host to hundreds of skiers.

Platres is an inexpensive base for exploring the Troodos Mountains. The town of **Troodos** is 10km (and a £5 taxi ride) southwest of Platres. Four spectacular hikes originate near Troodos; maps are available at all tourist offices. From Troodos, **Artemis** begins 200m up the road to Prodromos. The circular trail wraps around Mt. Olympus for 7km (3½hr.), providing majestic views of Cyprus. From the Troodos post office, the **Atalante** trail mimics the Artemis trail at a lower altitude; a fresh mountain spring 3km into the hike sustains the photo-happy. The 3km **Persephone** trail leaves from the coffee shop in Pl. Troodos and gradually descends to a divine lookout point among huge limestone slabs. The **Kaledonia** trail, the shortest of the four, begins 2km from Troodos on the road to Platres, passes the **Kaledonia Falls,** and ends at the **Psilo Dentro** restaurant near Platres. Platres is fairly accessible by public transportation, although bus schedules change frequently and often run 30min. late. **Zingas Bus** (☎463 989) in **Lefkosia,** runs to Platres (M-Sa 12:15pm, £2) on a reservation basis; call ahead. The **tourist office,** in Pano Platres, is left of the parking lot in the *plateia* (square). (☎421 316. Open M-F 9am-3:30pm, Sa 9am-2:30pm.) From the post office, go down the hill and left to find the simple rooms at the **Kallithea Hotel.** (☎421 746. Breakfast included. Doubles £11.)

PAPHOS (Παφος)   ☎06

Travelers flock to Paphos, the favorite city of Aphrodite, for the celebrated blend of limestone remnants and crystal waters brushing the sandy shores. The upper section of town, **Ktima Paphos,** referred to simply as Paphos, centers around Pl. Kennedy, while the lower **Kato Paphos** hosts the city's nightlife. Kato Paphos features over 2000 sq. m of mosaic floors, depicting scenes from Greek mythology and daily life, in the 2nd-century **House of Dionysus,** the **House of Theseus,** and the **House of Aion.** (Open daily 7:30am-7:30pm. £1.) Ag. Pavlou holds the musty **Catacombs,** including a chapel with deteriorating Byzantine frescoes dedicated to St. Solomoni (Hannah). St. Paul was whipped for preaching Christianity at **St. Paul's Pillar.** The **Tomb of the Kings** is 2km up the road of the same name; take bus #15. Local aristocracy, not kings, were interred in the tombs. (Open daily 8am-7:30pm. £0.75.) Ktima Paphos boasts the **Paphos Archaeology Museum,** on Grivas Digenes (open M-F 7:30am-2:30pm and 3-5pm, Sa-Su 10am-1pm; £0.75), the **Ethnographic Museum,** Exo Vrysi 1 (open M-Sa 9am-6pm, Su 10am-1pm; £1), and the **Byzantine Museum,** Andreou Ioannou 5 (open M-F 9am-5pm, Sa 9:10am-1pm; £1).

Nea Amoroza Co. buses, Pallikaridi 79 (☎23 68 22), in Pl. Kennedy, go to Polis (M-F 10 per day, £1). Contact **Travel&Express** (☎233 181), on Eagorou, for service **taxis** to Limassol (every 30min; M-Sa 5:45am-6:30pm, Su 7am-5:30pm; £2.50). The **tourist office** is at Gladstone 3. (☎232 841. Open M-Tu and Th-F 8:15am-2:30pm and 3-5:15pm, W and Sa 8:15am-1:30pm.) ◪**Triaron Hotel Guest House** is at Makarios 99. (☎232 193. Singles £5; doubles £7.) To get to the **Youth Hostel (HI),** El. Venizelou 45, leave the *plateia* on Pallikaridi, walk until Venizelou, then turn right. (☎232 588. First night £5; additional nights £4.) Nightlife centers around **Agias Napas** and **Ag. Antoniou,** a couple blocks inland from the waterfront in Kato Paphos.

CZECH REPUBLIC
(ČESKÁ REPUBLIKA)

CZECH KORUNA

US$1 = 37KČ	10KČ = US$0.27
CDN$1 = 24KČ	10KČ = CDN$0.41
UK£1 = 54KČ	10KČ = UK£0.19
IR£1 = 43KČ	10KČ = IR£0.23
AUS$1 = 20KČ	10KČ = AUS$0.50
NZ$1 = 16KČ	10KČ = NZ$0.61
ZAR1 = 4.5KČ	10KČ = ZAR0.22
DM1 = 17KČ	10KČ = DM0.57
EUR€1 = 34KČ	10KČ = EUR€0.29

PHONE CODE	**Country code:** 420. **International dialing prefix:** 00. From outside the Czech Republic, dial int'l dialing prefix (see inside back cover) + 420 + city code + local number.

From the Holy Roman Empire through the Nazis and Soviets, foreigners have driven Czech internal affairs; even the 1968 Prague Spring was frozen by the iron rumble of Soviet tanks. In November 1989, following the demise of Communist governments in Hungary and Poland and the fall of the Berlin Wall, Czechs peacefully threw off the Communists and chose dissident playwright Václav Havel to lead them westward. Havel attempted to preserve the Czech-Slovak union, but on New Year's Day, 1993, after more than 75 years of relatively calm coexistence, the two nations split bloodlessly. The Czechs, unlike many of their neighbors, have rarely fought back as countries have marched through their borders, and a result, their towns and cities are among the best-preserved in Europe.

Check *Let's Go: Eastern Europe 2002* before you wreck yourself.

FACTS AND FIGURES

Official Name: Czech Republic.
Capital: Prague.
Major Cities: Brno, Ostrava.
Population: 10.3 million.
Land Area: 78,864 sq. km.

Climate: Temperate; cool summers, cold, cloudy, humid winters.
Languages: Czech.
Religions: Catholic (39%), Protestant (4%), other (56%).

DISCOVER THE CZECH REPUBLIC

Everything you've heard is true: from the medieval alleys of Staré Město and the fabulous Baroque and art nouveau architecture to the world's best beer value, **Prague** (p. 247) is the starlet of Central Europe. A freaky daytrip awaits in nearby **Kutná Hora** (p. 261), where femurs and crania hang from the ceilings and chandeliers. In Western Bohemia, international hipsters flock to **Karlovy Vary** (p. 261) every summer for its film festival and its *Becherovka*, a local herb liqueur with "curative powers" rivaled only by those of the many local hot springs. In Southern Bohemia, **Český Krumlov** (p. 263), everybody's favorite town, charms visitors with its 13th-century castle, a medieval summer festival, and the best nightlife this side of the Vltava.

ESSENTIALS

WHEN TO GO

Spring and fall are the best times to visit, although spring can be rainy. Summer is drier, but the country is mobbed. Winters are very cold, damp, and snowy.

DOCUMENTS AND FORMALITIES

VISAS. Americans may visit the Czech Republic without a visa for up to 30 days, Irish and New Zealand citizens for up to 90 days, and UK citizens for up to 180 days. Australians, Canadians and South Africans must obtain 30-day tourist visas. Visas are available at an embassy or consulate, but not at the border. Single-entry visas cost US$38 for Australians, and US$21 for citizens of most other countries. Travelers on a visa must register with the Czech Immigration Police within three days of arrival; guests in hotels are registered automatically.

EMBASSIES. All foreign embassies in Czech Republic are in **Prague** (p. 247). For Czech embassies at home: **Australia,** 8 Culgoa Circuit, O'Malley, Canberra, ACT 2606 (☎(02) 6290 1386; fax 6290 0006; canberra@embassy.mzv.cz); **Canada,** 541 Sussex Dr., Ottawa, ON K1N 6Z6 (☎613-562-3875; fax 613-562-3878; ottowa@embassy.mzv.cz); **Ireland,** 57 Northumberland Rd., Ballsbridge, Dublin 4 (☎(01) 668 1135; fax 668 1660; dublin@embassy.mzv.cz); **New Zealand Honorary Consul,** 48 Hair St., Wainuiomata, Wellington (☎/fax (04) 564 6001); **South Africa,** 936 Pretorius St., Arcadia 0083, Pretoria; P.O. Box 3326, Pretoria 0001 (☎(012) 342 3477; fax 430 2033; pretoria@embassy.mzv.cz; www.icon.co.za/czmzv); **UK,** 26 Kensington Palace Gardens, London W8 4QY (☎(020) 7243 1115; fax 7727 9654; london@embassy.mzv.cz); **US,** 3900 Spring of Freedom St. NW, Washington, D.C. 20008 (☎202-274-9121; fax 202-363-6308; www.mzv.cz/washington).

TRANSPORTATION

BY PLANE. Air France, British Airways, ČSA, Delta, KLM, Lufthansa, and Swissair are among the major carriers that fly into Prague.

BY TRAIN. The easiest and most economical way to enter and travel through the country is by train. **Eastrail** is accepted in the Czech Republic, but **Eurail** is valid only with a special supplement. The fastest trains are *EuroCity* and *InterCity* (*expresní*, marked in blue on schedules). *Rychlík* trains, also known as *zrychlený vlak*, are fast domestic trains, marked in red on schedules. Avoid slow *osobní* trains, marked in white. **ČSD**, the national transportation company, publishes the monster *Jízdní řád* train schedule (74Kč), which has a two-page English explanation. *Odjezdy* (departures) are printed in train stations on yellow posters, *příjezdy* (arrivals) are on white posters. Seat reservations (*místenka*; 10Kč) are recommended on express and international trains and for all first-class seating; snag them at the counter with a boxed "R."

BY BUS. Buses are the preferred means of domestic travel, but are inefficient for crossing borders. **ČSAD** runs national and international bus lines. Consult the timetables posted at stations or buy your own bus schedule (25Kč) from kiosks.

BY CAR, BY BIKE, AND BY THUMB. It is not necessary to have an International Driving Permit, but having one won't hurt. Speed limits in residential areas are 50kph, on expressways 130kph, and 90kph on all other roads. Always park in guarded lots, as there is a high incidence of car theft. The blood alcohol limit is zero. In an emergency, dial ☎1230 or ☎1240, or contact **Ustřední Automotoklub ČR (UAMK),** Na Strž i, 146 01, Praha 4 (☎(02) 61 10 41 11; www.uamk.cz). For help planning your trip, contact **Autoturist,** at the same address (☎(02) 61 10 43 33). Biking is common in Southern Bohemia; roads and bike trails are in good condition and motorists yield bikers the right of way. You can rent bikes from most hotels and hostels and through major tourist offices. Hitchhikers report success in the Czech Republic. Although it is a common way for young people to get around, *Let's Go* does not recommend hitchhiking.

TOURIST SERVICES AND MONEY

EMERGENCY	Police: ☎158. Ambulance: ☎155. Fire: ☎150.

TOURIST OFFICES. CKM, a junior affiliate of the communist dinosaur Čedok, is helpful for the budget and student traveler, serving as a clearinghouse for youth hostel beds and issuing ISICs and HI cards. Municipal tourist offices in major cities provide printed matter on sights and cultural events, as well as lists of hostels and hotels. If they're nice, they might even book you a room.

MONEY. The Czech unit of currency is the **koruna** (crown), plural *koruny* (Kč). Inflation is around 3.5%, meaning prices and exchange rates should be relatively stable. ATMs are everywhere—look for the red and black "Bankomat" signs—and offer the best exchange rates available. Traveler's checks can be exchanged almost everywhere, if at times for an obscene commission. **Komerční banka** and **Česká spořitelna** are common bank chains. Mastercard and Visa are accepted at most expensive places, but rarely at hostels.

A bare-bones day in the Czech Republic (sleeping in campgrounds, shopping at grocery stores) will run US$10; a more extravagant day (hostels/hotels, eating in restaurants) costs no more than US$25. To tip, add about 10% to the cost of your meal and tell the waiter the new amount; don't leave a few *koruny* on the table, as it is considered offensive. Visitors can apply for value-added tax (VAT) reimbursement when leaving the country. The minimum price of a single item to be refunded is 1000Kč. Refunds are available for of all purchases made within 30 days prior to their departure from the country. Foreigners must claim the reimbursement at the store where they bought the goods within three months after the day of purchase.

BUSINESS HOURS. Banks are usually open Monday to Friday 8am to 4pm. Shops are open Monday to Friday 9am-5pm and Saturday 9am-noon. Nearly all museums and galleries close on Mondays.

COMMUNICATION

MAIL. The Czech Republic's postal system is efficient; letters reach the US in less than 10 days. A postcard to the US costs 8Kč, to Australia 7Kč. When sending by air mail, stress that you want it to go on a *plane (letecky)*. Go to the customs office to send packages heavier than 2kg abroad. Mail can be received general delivery through *Poste Restante*. Address mail to be held: First name SURNAME, *Poste Restante*, Ceska Posta, Jindřišská 14, 110 00 Praha 1, Czech Republic.

TELEPHONES. To make a call, seek out the blue card phones (150Kč per 50 units). Calls run 31Kč per minute to the UK; 63Kč per minute to Australia, Canada, or the US; and 94Kč per minute to New Zealand. Making calls abroad through an operator doesn't require a card—just dial one of these toll-free numbers. The international operator is at ☎013 15; for lower rates, try: **AT&T,** ☎00 42 00 01 01; **British Telecom,** ☎00 42 00 44 01; **Canada Direct,** ☎00 42 00 01 51; **MCI,** ☎00 42 00 01 12; and **Sprint,** ☎00 42 08 71 87.

INTERNET. The web has reached most towns in the Czech Republic. Internet cafes are the best bet if you're just passing through; the computers are fast and cheap, with rates around 2Kč per minute. Most public libraries also have Internet access, but many require a membership card (100-500Kč).

LANGUAGES. Russian *was* every student's mandatory second language, but these days, English will earn you more friends. A few German phrases go further, but might make you some enemies. For some survival-level savvy in Czech, see p. 982.

ACCOMMODATIONS AND CAMPING

Hostels, particularly in **university dorms,** are the cheapest option in July and August; two- to four-bed rooms are 200-300Kč per person. CKM's **Junior Hotels** (year-round hostels giving discounts to ISIC and HI cardholders) are comfortable but often full. **Private hostels** have broken the CKM monopoly. **Pensions** are the next most affordable option; expect to pay 600Kč, including breakfast. Reserve at least one week ahead from June to September in Prague, Český Krumlov, and Brno. If you can't keep a reservation, call to cancel. **Private homes** are not nearly as popular (or as cheap) as in the rest of Eastern Europe; scan train stations for *Zimmer frei* signs. Outside Prague, local tourist offices and CKM/GTS book rooms, with private agencies around train and bus stations. **Campgrounds** are strewn throughout the countryside, most only open mid-May to September. *Ubytování v ČSR*, in decodable Czech, lists all the hotels, hostels, huts, and campgrounds in Bohemia and Moravia.

FOOD AND DRINK

Anyone in the mood for true Czech cuisine should start learning to pronounce *knedlíky* (KNED-lee-kee). These thick, pasty loaves of dough serve as staples of Czech meals. The Czech national meal is *vepřové* (roast pork), *knedlíky*, and *zelí* (known as *vepřo-knedlo-zelo*), but *guláš* (stew) runs a close second. The main food groups are *hovězí* (beef), *sekaná pečeně* (meatloaf), *klobása* (sausage), and *brambory* (potatoes). If you're in a hurry, get *párky* (frankfurters) at a *bufet*, or *samoobsluha* or *občerstvení* at food stands. **Vegetarian** restaurants serve *šopský salát* (salad with feta cheese) and other *bez masa* (meatless) dishes; at most restaurants, however, vegetarians will be limited to *smažený sýr* (fried cheese). Ask for *káva espresso* rather than *káva* to avoid the mud Czechs call coffee. The most beloved dessert is *koláč*—a tart with poppy-seed jam or sweet cheese. The most prominent beer is *Plzeňský Prazdroj* (Pilsner Urquell), although many Czechs are loyal to *Budvar* or *Krušovice*.

HOLIDAYS AND FESTIVALS

Holidays: New Year's Day (Jan. 1); Catholic Easter (Apr. 15); May Day (May 1); Liberation Day (May 8); Cyril and Methodius Day (July 5); Jan Hus Day (July 6); St. Wenceslas Day (Sept. 28); 1918 Republic Day (Oct. 28); Student Day (Day of Fight for Freedom and Democracy, Nov. 17); Catholic Christmas (Dec. 24-26).

UNPRONOUNCEABLE Not quite a Spanish "r" and simply not the Polish "rz," Czech's own linguistic blue note, the letter "ř," lies excruciatingly in between. Although many of Prague's ex-pats would sacrifice a month of Saturdays at Jo's Bar to utter the elusive sound just once, few manage more than a strangely trilled whistle. Most foreigners resign themselves to using the "ž" in its place, but what we consider a subtle difference often confuses Czechs. For all those linguistic daredevils in the audience, here's a sure-fire method of tackling the randy Mr. Ř: roll your tongue and quickly follow with a "ž", then repeat.

Festivals: The **Prague Spring Festival**, Prague, mid-May through early June, attracts international music lovers in hoards. Music also fills the streets in Český Krumlov for their **International Music Festival** in early August. Film lovers flock to the **Karlovy Vary International Film Festival** in July.

PRAGUE (PRAHA)   ☎02

According to legend, Countess Libuše stood above the Vltava and declared, "I see a city whose glory will touch the stars." Medieval kings, benefactors, and architects fulfilled the prophecy, building soaring cathedrals and lavish palaces that reflected Prague's status as capital of the Holy Roman Empire. Yet legends of demons, occult forces, and a maze of alleys lent this "city of dreams" a dark side that inspired Franz Kafka's tales of paranoia. Since the fall of the Iron Curtain, hordes of foreigners have flooded the city. In summer, tourists pack streets so tightly that crowd-surfing seems a viable way to travel. Yet walk a few blocks from any of the major sights and you'll be lost among cobblestone alleys and looming churches; head to an outlying metro stop and you'll find haggling *babičky* and supermodel-esque natives, without a backpack in sight.

PHONE MAYHEM. Prague continues to reform its phone system. Businesses often receive no more than three weeks' notice before their numbers change. The four- to eight-digit numbers provided in these listings probably won't change by the time you read this—but be aware that they do change fast.

⌸ TRANSPORTATION

Flights: Ruzyně Airport (☎20 11 33 21), 20km northwest of the city. Take bus #119 to Metro A: Dejvická (daily 5am-midnight; 12Kč; luggage 6Kč); buy tickets from kiosks or machines. Late at night, take night tram #51 to Divoká Šárka, then take a night bus #510 to the center. **Airport buses** (☎20 11 42 96) leave every 30min. from outside Metro stops at Nám. Republiky (90Kč) and Dejvická (60Kč). Taxis to the airport are extremely expensive (400-600Kč).

Trains: (☎24 22 42 00; international ☎24 61 52 49; www.cdrail.cz). Prague has 4 terminals. **Hlavní station** (☎24 22 42 00; Metro C: Hlavní nádraží) is the largest. **BIJ Wasteels** (☎24 22 18 72; fax 24 61 74 54; www.wasteels.cz), 2nd fl., to the right of the stairs, sells discount international tickets to those under 26, books *couchettes*, and sells bus tickets. Open in summer M-F 7:30am-8pm, Sa 8-11:30am, and 12:30-3pm; off season M-F 8:30am-6pm. Most international service runs from **Holešovice station:** (☎24 61 72 65; Metro C: Nádraží Holešovice). Buy BIJ Wasteels and regular train tickets from the **Czech Railways Travel Agency** (☎24 23 94 64; fax 24 22 36 00). Open M-F 9am-5pm, Sa-Su 8am-4pm. To: **Berlin** (5hr., 5 per day, 1400Kč); **Bratislava** (5½hr., 7 per day, 400Kč); **Budapest** (10hr., 5 per day, 1300Kč); **Kraków** (8½hr., 3 per day, 1000Kč); **Moscow** (30hr., 1 per day, 2500Kč); **Munich** (6hr., 3 per day, 1700Kč); **Vienna** (4½hr., 3 per day, 750Kč); **Warsaw** (9½hr., 3 per day, 870Kč). Catch domestic trains at **Masarykovo station** at the corner of Hybernská and Havlíčkova (☎24 61 72 60; Metro B: Nám. Republiky) and **Smíchov station** opposite Vyšehrad (☎24 61 72 55; Metro B: Smíchovské nádraží).

Buses: (Info ☎1034 daily 6am-9pm; www.vlakbus.com, www.jiznirday.cz). **ČSAD** has several bus stations. The biggest is **Florenc,** Křižíkova 4 (☎129 99; Metro B, C: Florenc). Little English spoken. Office open M-F 6am-9pm, Sa 6am-6pm, Su 8am-8pm. Buy tickets in advance. To: **Berlin** (8hr., 1 per day, 850Kč); **Sofia** (26hr., 4 per day, 1600Kč); **Vienna** (8½hr., 1 per day, 870Kč). Students may get 10% discount. The **Tourbus** office upstairs (☎24 21 02 21; www.eurolines.cz) sells tickets for Eurolines and airport buses. Open M-F 8am-8pm, Sa-Su 9am-8pm.

Public Transportation: Buy tickets for the **metro, tram,** or **bus** from newsstands and *tabák* kiosks, machines in stations, or **DP** (*Dopravní Podnik;* transport authority) kiosks. The basic 8Kč ticket is good for 15min. on a tram (or 4 stops on the metro); 12Kč is valid for 1hr. during the day, 1½hr. 8pm-5am and weekends, with unlimited connections between bus, tram and metro in any one direction. Large bags and bikes require extra 6Kč ticket. Validate ticket in machines above escalators or face a 400Kč fine; if fined, look for a badge and get a receipt. The 3 lines of the **metro** run daily 5am-midnight: A is green on maps, B is yellow, C is red. **Night trams** #51-58 and **buses** run all night after the last metro and can be picked up at the Charles Bridge; look for dark blue signs at bus stops. Tourist office in Old Town Hall sells **multi-day passes** valid for entire network (24hr. 70Kč, 3 days 200Kč, 1 week 250Kč). Student 30-day pass 210Kč.

Taxis: RadioTaxi (☎24 91 66 66) or **AAA** (☎10 80 or 312 21 12). Both open 24hr. Taxi drivers are notorious scam artists. Check that the meter is set to zero, and ask the driver to start it (*"Zapněte taximetr"*). Always ask for a receipt (*"Prosím, dejte mi paragon"*) with distance traveled and price paid. If the driver doesn't write the receipt or set the meter to zero, you aren't obligated to pay. Set rate 30Kč, plus 22Kč per km.

⚡ ORIENTATION

Straddling the river **Vltava,** Prague is a mess of labyrinthine medieval streets and suburbs. Fortunately, nearly everything of interest lies within the compact, walkable downtown. The river Vltava runs south-northeast through central Prague and separates the **Staré Město** (Old Town) and the **Nové Město** (New Town) from **Malá Strana** (Lesser Side). On the right bank of the river, the Old Town's **Staroměstské náměstí** (Old Town Square) is the focal point of the city. From the square, the elegant **Pařížská ulice** (Paris Street) leads north into **Josefov,** the old Jewish ghetto; unfortunately, all that remains are six synagogues and the Old Jewish Cemetery. In the opposite direction from Pařížská lies **Nové Město.** It houses **Václavské náměstí** (Wenceslas Square), the administrative and commercial heart of the city. West of Staroměstské nám., **Karlův most** (Charles Bridge) traverses the Vltava and connects the Old Town with **Malostranské náměstí** (Lesser Town Square). **Pražský Hrad** (Prague Castle) sits on the Hradčany hilltop above Malostranské nám.

Prague's main train station, **Hlavní nádraží,** and Florenc bus station sit in the northeastern corner of Václavské nám. All train and bus terminals are on or near the excellent metro system. To get to Staroměstské nám., take the Metro A line to Staroměstská and walk down Kaprova away from the river. *Tabák* stands and bookstores sell the *plán města* (map); this, along with the English-language weekly *The Prague Post,* is essential for visitors.

🔢 PRACTICAL INFORMATION

TOURIST AND FINANCIAL SERVICES

Tourist Offices: Green "i"s mark tourist information. **Pražská Informační Služba** (Prague Info Service) is in the Old Town Hall (☎24 48 25 62; English ☎54 44 44). **Branches** at Na příkopě 20, Hlavní nádraží, and in the tower on the Malá Strana side of the Charles Bridge. All open in summer M-F 9am-7pm, Sa-Su 9am-6pm; off-season M-F 9am-6pm, Sa-Su 9am-5pm.

Budget Travel: CKM, Manesova 77 (☎22 72 15 95; ckmprg@login.cz; www.ckm-praha.cz). Metro A, B: Jiriho z Podebrad. Budget air tickets for those under 26. Also books lodgings in Prague from 260Kč. Open M-Th 10am-6pm, F 10am-4pm.

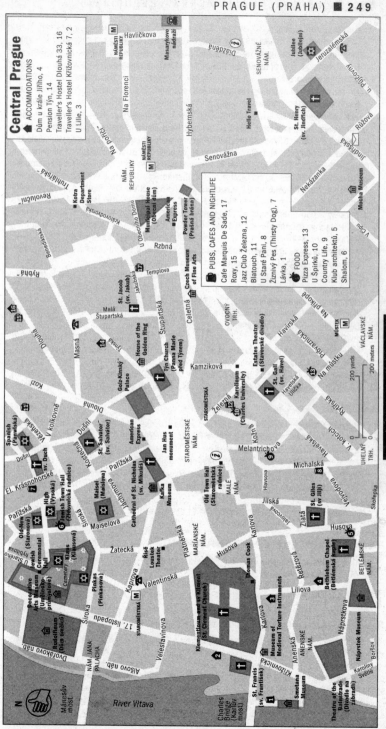

Central Prague

♦ ACCOMMODATIONS
Dům u krále Jiřího, 4
Pension Týn, 14
Traveller's Hostel Dlouhá 33, 16
Traveller's Hostel Křižovnická 7, 2
U Lilie, 3

🍺 PUBS, CAFES AND NIGHTLIFE
Cafe Marquis De Sade, 17
Roxy, 15
Jazz Club Železná, 12
Blatouch, 11
U Staré Paní, 8
Žíznivý Pes (Thirsty Dog), 7
Lávka, 1

🍴 FOOD
Pizza Express, 13
U Špirků, 10
Country Life, 9
Klub architektů, 5
Shalom, 6

CZECH REPUBLIC

KMC, Karoliny Světlé 30 (☎/fax 22 22 03 47; kmc@kmc.cz; www.kmc.cz). Metro B: Národní třída. Books hostels from 200Kč. Open M-Th 9am-noon and 2-4pm.

Passport Office: Foreigner police headquarters at Olšanská 2 (☎683 17 39). Metro A: Flora. From the Metro, turn right onto Jičínská with the cemetery on your right, and turn right again onto Olšanská. Or take tram #9 from Václavské nám. toward Spojovací and get off at Olšanská. For a **visa extension,** get a 90Kč stamp inside, line up in front of doors #2-12, and prepare to wait up to 2hr. Little English spoken. Open M-Tu and Th 7:30-11:30am and 12:30-2:30pm, W 7:30-11:30am and 12:30-5pm, F 7:30am-noon.

Embassies: Australia (☎24 31 00 71) and **New Zealand** (☎25 41 98) have consuls, but citizens should contact the UK embassy in an emergency. **Canada,** Mickiewiczova 6 (☎72 10 18 00). Metro A: Hradčanská. Open M-F 8:30am-12:30pm. **Hungary,** Badeniho 1 (☎33 32 44 54). Metro A: Hradčanská. Open M-W and F 9am-noon. **Ireland,** Tržiště 13 (☎57 53 00 61). Metro A: Malostranská. Open M-F 9:30am-12:30pm and 2:30-4:30pm. **Poland,** Valdštejnské nám. 8 (☎57 53 03 88). Metro A: Malostranská. Open M-F 9am-1pm. **Russia,** Pod Kaštany 1 (☎33 37 15 49). Metro A: Hradčanská. Open M-F 8am-5pm. **South Africa,** Ruská 65 (☎67 31 11 14). Metro A: Flora. Open M-F 9am-noon. **UK,** Thunovská 14 (☎57 53 02 78). Metro A: Malostranská. Open M-F 9am-noon. **US,** Tržiště 15 (☎57 53 06 63; emergency after-hours ☎53 12 00). Metro A: Malostranská. From Malostranské nám., head down Karmelitská and take a right onto Tržiště. Open M-F 9am-4pm.

Currency Exchange: Exchange counters are everywhere with wildly varying rates. **Chequepoints** may be the only ones open when you need cash, but usually charge a 3% commission. **Komerční banka,** Na příkopě 33 (☎24 43 21 11), buys notes and checks for 2% commission. Open M-F 8am-5pm. **ATMs** ("Bankomats") abound and offer the best rates, but sometimes charge large fees.

American Express: Václavské nám. 56 (☎22 80 02 37; fax 22 21 11 31). Metro A, C: Muzeum. The **ATM** outside takes AmEx cards. Grants MC/Visa **cash advances** for 3% commission. Open daily 9am-7pm. **Branches** on Mostecká 12 (☎57 31 36 38; open daily 9:30am-7:30pm), Celetná 17 (☎/fax 24 81 82 74; open daily 8:30am-7:15pm), and Staroměstské nám. 5 (☎24 81 83 88; open daily 9am-8:30pm).

LOCAL SERVICES

Luggage Storage: Lockers in all train and bus stations take two 5Kč coins. If these are full, or if you need to store your cargo longer than 24hr., use the luggage offices to the left in the basement of **Hlavní station** (15-30Kč per day; open 24hr.) and halfway up the stairs at **Florenc** (10-25Kč per day; open daily 5am-11pm).

English Bookstore: The Globe, Pštrossova 6 (☎24 91 62 64). Metro B: Národní třída. Exit left on Spálená, right on Ostrovní, left to Pštrossova. Open daily 10am-midnight.

Laundromat: Laundry Kings, Dejvická 16 (☎312 37 43), one block from Metro A: Hradčanská. Cross the tram and railroad tracks, and turn left. Wash 60Kč per 6kg; dry 15Kč per 8min. Soap 10-20Kč. Beer 15Kč. Open M-F 6am-10pm, Sa-Su 8am-10pm.

EMERGENCY AND COMMUNICATION

Medical Assistance: Na Homolce (Hospital for Foreigners), Roentgenova 2 (☎57 27 21 46; after-hours ☎57 77 20 25). Open M-F 8am-4pm. 24hr. emergency service. **American Medical Center,** Janovského 48 (☎807 756). Major foreign insurance accepted. On call 24hr. Appointments preferable M-F 9am-4pm. Average consultation 50-200Kč.

Pharmacy: "U Anděla," Štefánikova 6 (☎57 32 09 18). Metro B: Anděl. Open 24hr.

Internet Access: Prague is Internet Nirvana. **Bohemia Bagel,** Masna 2 (☎24 81 25 60; www.bohemiabagel.cz). 1½Kč per min. Open M-F 7am-midnight, Sa-Su 8am-midnight. **Cafe Electra,** Rašínovo nábřeží 62 (☎297 038). Metro B: Karlovo nám. Exit on the Palackého nám. side. 80Kč per hr. Open M-F 9am-midnight, Sa-Su 11am-midnight.

Telephones: Phone cards sell for 175Kč per 50 units at kiosks, post offices, and some exchange places; don't let kiosks rip you off.

Post Office: Jindřišská 14. Metro A, B: Můstek (☎21 13 11 11). Airmail to the US takes 7 days. Mail can be held *Poste Restante.* Open daily 7am-8pm.

ACCOMMODATIONS AND CAMPING

With hotel prices through the roof, the glutted hostel market has stabilized prices around 270-420Kč per night. Reservations are a must at hotels, which can be booked solid months in advance, and a good idea at the few hostels that accept them. Most accommodations have 24hr. reception and require check-out by 10am. A few hotels are cheap, and a growing number of Prague residents rent rooms.

ACCOMMODATIONS AGENCIES

Many of the room hawkers at the train station offer legitimate deals, but there are always some who just want to rip you off. The going rate for apartments hovers around 600-1200Kč, depending on proximity to the city center. Haggling is possible. If you don't want to bargain on the street, try a **private agency.** Ask where the nearest tram, bus, or metro stop is, and don't pay until you know what you're getting; ask for details in writing. You can often pay in US dollars or German marks, but prices are lower if you pay in Czech crowns. Some travel agencies book rooms as well (see Budget Travel, p. 248).

Ave., Hlavní nádraží (☎24 22 352 26; fax 24 23 07 83; ave@avetravel.cz), on the 2nd floor of the train station next to the left-most stairs. Books rooms starting at 800Kč per person; hostels from 290Kč. Open daily 6am-11pm.

Hello Travel Ltd., Senovážné nám. 3 (☎24 21 26 47; fax 24 21 28 24; hello@hello.cz). Metro B: Náměstí Republiky. In summer, 500-1500Kč per person; off season 400-1200Kč. Open M-F 8am-7pm.

HOSTELS

If you're schlepping a backpack in Hlavní nádraží or Holešovice, you *will* be bombarded by hostel runners trying to coerce you back to their hostels. Many are university dorms that free up from June to August, and often you'll be offered transport to the room—an easy option for those arriving in the middle of the night without a reservation. If you prefer more than just a place to sleep, smaller places are a better alternative. It's a good idea to call as soon as you know your plans, if only the night before you arrive or at 10am when they know who's checking out. Like everywhere else in Prague, the staff typically speaks English. Curfews are distant memories.

Hostel Boathouse, Lodnická (☎/fax 402 10 76), south of the city center. From Hlavní nádraží, Karlovo nám., Staré Město, or the Charles Bridge, take tram #3 south toward Sídliště and get off at "Černý Kůň" (20min.). From Holešovice, take tram #17. From the tram stop, follow the yellow signs down to the Vltava. As Věra the owner says, "This isn't a hostel, it's a crazy house." Summer camp vibe. Dorms 300-320Kč.

Penzion v podzámčí, V podzámčí 27 (☎/fax 41 44 46 09; evacib@yahoo.com), south of the city center. From Metro C: Budějovická, take bus #192 to the 3rd stop (Nad Rybníky). Homy, with kitchen and laundry. Dorms 280Kč; doubles 640Kč; triples 900Kč.

WINDOW OF INOPPORTUNITY
At decisive points in European history, unlucky men tend to fall from Prague's window ledges. The Hussite wars began in 1419 after Catholic councillors were thrown to the mob from the New Town Hall on Karlovo nám. The Thirty Years' War devastated Europe after Habsburg officials were tossed from the windows of Prague Castle into a heap of manure in 1618. Two more falls this century have continued the tradition. In 1948, liberal foreign minister Jan Masaryk fell to his death from the top floor of his ministry just two weeks after the Communist takeover; murder was always suspected, but never proven. In 1997, Bohumil Hrabal, popular author of *Closely-Observed Trains*, fell from the fifth floor of his hospital window and died in his pajamas. Nothing unusual here, except that two of his books describe people killing themselves—by jumping out of fifth-floor windows.

CZECH REPUBLIC

Domov Mládeže, Dykova 20 (☎/fax 22 51 17 77; jana.dyrsmidova@telecom.cz), in Vinohrady. Metro A: Jiřího z Poděbrad. Follow Nitranská and turn left on Dykova; it's 2 blocks down on the right. So quiet you might forget you're in Prague. Breakfast included. Dorms 350Kč; doubles 400Kč. Sister hostels: **Amadeus,** Slavojova 108/8. Metro C: Vyšehrad; go down the bridge to Čiklova and turn left. **Máchova,** Máchova 11. Metro A: Nám. Míru; walk down Ruská and turn right on Máchova. **Košická,** Košická 12. Metro A: Nám. Míru. All hostels have the same phone number and prices.

Hostel U Melounu, Ke Karlovu 7 (☎/fax 24 91 83 22; pus.praha@worldline.cz; www.hostelumelonu.cz), in Nové Město. Metro C: I.P. Pavlova; follow Sokolská to Na Bojišti and turn left at the street's end onto Ke Karlovu. A historic building with great facilities. Breakfast included. Reservations accepted. Dorms 380Kč; singles 450Kč; doubles 840Kč. 100Kč ISIC discount.

Traveller's Hostels, in Staré Město (☎24 82 66 62; fax 24 82 66 65; hostel@travellers.cz; www.travellers.cz). These summertime big-dorm specialists round up travelers at bus and train stations and herd them into one of their central hostels for lots of beds and beer. Breakfast included. Internet 27Kč per 15min.

> **Dlouhá 33** (☎24 82 66 62; fax 24 82 66 65). Metro B: Nám Republiky. Follow Revoluční toward the river, turn left on Dlouhá. Unbeatable location; in the same building as the Roxy, but soundproof. Open year-round. Dorms 370-400Kč; doubles 580Kč; triples 450Kč.
>
> **Husova 3** (☎22 22 00 78). Metro B: Národní třída; turn right on Spálená (which becomes Na Perštýně after Národní), and again on Husova. Open July-Aug. Dorms 400Kč.
>
> **Křížovnická 7** (☎232 09 87). Metro A: Staroměstská. Open July-Aug. Dorms 250Kč.
>
> **Střelecký ostrov** (☎24 91 01 88), on an island off Most Legií. Metro B: Národní třída. Open mid-June to mid-Sept. Dorms 300Kč.
>
> **Růžový 5** (☎24 21 67 71). Metro C: Hlavní nádraží. Open mid-June to mid-Sept. Dorms 270Kč.

Pension Týn, Týnská 19 (☎/fax 24 80 83 33; backpacker@razdva.cz), near the Staré Město. Metro A: Staroměstská. From Old Town Square, head down Dlouhá, then bear right at Masná and right onto Týnská. A quiet getaway located right in the center of Staré Město. Immaculate facilities. Dorms 400Kč; doubles 1100Kč. 30Kč ISIC discount.

Welcome Hostel at Strahov Complex, Vaníčkova 5 (☎33 35 92 75). Take bus #217 or 143 from Metro A: Dejvická to Koleje Strahov. Known as a "hostel ghetto," Strahov is 10 concrete blocks of high-rise dorms next to the stadium. A little far, but there's always space, and free beer at check-in. Singles 300Kč; doubles 240Kč. ISIC 10% discount.

Hostel Sokol, Nosticova 2 (☎57 00 73 97; fax 57 00 73 40) in Mala Strana. Metro A: Malostranská. From the Metro, take tram #12 or 22 down to Hellichova; take a left onto Hellichova and the last left onto Nosticova where the road ends, then look for signs. Clean dorms and a nice rooftop terrace. Kitchen. Reception 24hr. 270Kč.

HOTELS AND PENSIONS

With so much tourist traffic in Prague, budget hotels are now scarce. Many of the cheaper places require reservations up to a month in advance, though some don't accept them. You may want to call several months ahead if you plan to visit during the summer (call first, then confirm by fax with a credit card). If you can't book one, try an agency or a hostel (above). Make sure the hotel doesn't bill you for a more expensive room than the one you stayed in.

> **Pension Unitas/Cloister Inn,** Bartolomějská 9 (☎232 77 00; fax 232 77 09; cloister@cloister-inn.cz), in Staré Město. Metro B: Národní třída. Cross Národní, head up Na Perštýně away from Tesco, and turn left on Bartolomějská. Renovated rooms in the cells of a former prison where Václav Havel was incarcerated. Breakfast included. Singles 1020Kč; doubles 1200Kč; triples 1650Kč.
>
> **Dům U krále Jiřího,** Liliová 10 (☎22 22 09 25; fax 22 22 17 07; kinggeorge@kinggeorge.cz; www.kinggeorge.cz), in Staré Město. Metro A: Staroměstská. Exit onto Nám. Jana Palacha, walk down Křížovnická toward the Charles Bridge, turn left onto Karlova, and Liliová is the first right. Gorgeous rooms with private baths. Buffet breakfast included. Singles 1500-1790Kč; doubles 2700-3050Kč.
>
> **U Lilie,** Liliová 15 (☎22 22 04 32; fax 22 22 06 41; pensionulilie@centrum.cz), in Staré Město. Metro A: Staroměstská. Follow directions to U krále Jiřího (above). TV. Breakfast included. Singles with shower 1800Kč; doubles 2000-2850Kč.

Hotel Kafka, Cimburkova 24 (☎/fax 22 78 13 13), in Žižkov near the TV tower. From Metro C: Hlavní nádraží, take tram #5 toward Harfa, #9 toward Spojovací, or #26 toward Nádraží Hostivař; get off at Husinecká. Head uphill along Seifertova 3 blocks and go left on Cimburkova. As the tram schedule changes, call first for directions. Brand-new hotel amid 19th-century buildings, close to plenty of beerhalls. Apr.-Oct. singles 1710Kč; doubles 2120Kč; triples 2530Kč; quads 2740Kč. Nov.-Mar. singles 1160Kč; doubles 1520Kč; triples 1780Kč; quads 1940Kč.

B&B U Oty (Ota's House), Radlická 188 (☎/fax 57 21 53 23; mb@bbuoty.cz; www.bbuoty.cz), west of the center. Metro B: Radlická. Exit the Metro up the stairs to the left and go right 400m up the road. Charming, English-speaking Ota will make your stay a pleasure. Kitchen. Laundry. Singles 700Kč; doubles 770Kč; triples 990Kč; quads 1250Kč. One-night surcharge 100Kč.

Hotel Legie, Sokolská 33 (☎24 26 62 31; reservations 24 26 62 40; fax 24 26 62 34; hotel@legie.cz; www.legie.cz), in Nové Město. Metro C: I. P. Pavlova. Turn left onto Ječná; the hotel is across the street on the corner. A real hotel: private showers, TV, and views of Prague Castle. Breakfast included. Doubles 2800Kč; triples 3700Kč. Off-season doubles 2300Kč; triples 3100Kč.

CAMPING

Campsites can be found in both the outskirts and the centrally located Vltava islands. Bungalows must be reserved in advance, but tent space is generally available without prior notice. Tourist offices sell a guide to sites near the city (15Kč).

Císařská louka, on a peninsula on the Vltava. Metro B: Smíchovské nádraží. Take any bus numbered in the 300s to Lihovar, go toward the river, and take a the left on the path. Or, take the ferry one street over from Smíchovské nádraží. **Caravan Park** (☎57 31 86 81) is near the ferry. 90-140Kč per tent, plus 95Kč per person. 2-bed bungalows 480Kč, 4-bed 720Kč.

Caravan Camping, Císařská louka 162 (☎54 56 82; campcsk@mox.vol.cz) is near the tram. 95Kč per person, 90-120Kč per tent.

Sokol Troja, Trojská 171 (☎/fax 83 85 04 86), north of the center in the Troja district. Metro C: Nádraží Holešovice. Take bus #112 to Kazanka. Similar places line the road. 90-180Kč per tent, 130Kč per person. Dorms 270Kč; bungalow 230Kč per person.

Na Vlachovce, Zenklova 217 (☎/fax 688 02 14). Take bus #102 or 175 from Nádraží Holešovice toward Okrouhlická, get off, and continue in the same direction up the hill. Reserve a week ahead. Romantic 2-person "barrels" 400Kč. Doubles with bath 975Kč.

FOOD

The nearer you are to **Staroměstské náměstí,** the **Karlův most** (Charles Bridge), and **Václavské náměstí,** the more you'll pay. Away from the center, you can get pork, cabbage, dumplings, and a half-liter of beer for 50Kč. Check your bill carefully; you'll pay for everything the waiter brings to the table. Most restaurants accept only cash. Outlying Metro stops become markets in the summer. **Tesco,** Národní třída 26, has **groceries** right next to Metro B: Národní třída. (Open M-F 7am-8pm, Sa 8am-7pm, Su 9am-7pm.) Look for the **daily market** where Havelská and Melantrichova meet in Staré Město. After a night out, grab a *párek v rohlíku* (hot dog) or a *smažený sýr* (fried cheese sandwich) from a Václavské nám. vendor, or a gyro from a stand on Spálená or Vodíčkova.

RESTAURANTS

🗺 **U Špirků,** Kožná ulička 12, in Staré Město. Metro A: Staroměstská. With your back to the astronomical clock on Staroměstské nám., go through the arch down Melantrichova and take the first left onto Kožná. Some of the city's best and cheapest food in a spacious pub. Main dishes about 100Kč. Open daily 11am-midnight.

🗺 **Velryba** (The Whale), Opatovická 24, in Nové Město. Metro B: Národní třída. Exit to the left, turn right onto Ostrovní, and left onto Opatovická. Relaxed cafe-restaurant with a gallery in back. International and Czech dishes (38-155Kč), and veggie platters. Open M-Th and Sa-Su 11am-midnight, F 11am-2am.

▨ **Bar bar,** Všehrdova 17, in Malá Strana. Metro A: Malostranská. Follow the tram tracks down Letenská Malostranské nám.; turn left on Všehrdova after the museum. Good vibe, good music, and 40 varieties of whiskey (from 55Kč). Open daily noon-midnight.

Universal, V jirchářích 6 (☎24 91 81 82), in Nové Město. Metro B: Národní třída; turn left onto Spálená and right on Myslíkova, then right on Křemencova. A transplanted California-style eatery with huge, fresh salads (115-165Kč). Open daily 11:30am-1am.

Klub architektů, Betlémské nám. 52, in Staré Město. Metro B: Národní třída. Exit station to the right, keep walking, and take a left. A 12th-century cellar thrust into the 20th century. Veggie options 80-90Kč; meat dishes 120-150Kč. Open daily 11:30am-11pm.

Lotos, Platnéřská 13, in Staré Město. Metro A: Staroměstská; go left down Valentinská and turn right on Platnélská. Vegetarian Czech restaurant with organic menu (68-152Kč). half-liter of wheat-yeast Pilsner 30Kč. Open daily 11am-10pm.

U Sádlů, Klimentskà 2 (☎24 81 38 74). Metro B: Nám Republiky. From the square, walk down Revoluční toward the river, then go right on Klimentskà. Theme restaurant with bountiful portions; call ahead. Czech only menu lists traditional meals (115-230Kč). Open daily 11am-11:30pm.

Shalom, Maiselova 18. Metro A: Staroměstská. Walk down Kaprova away from the river and go left on Maiselov. Fine kosher lunches in the old Jewish Quarter. Buy tickets for lunch at Legacy Tours, the travel agent across the road. (☎232 19 51. Open M-F and Su 9am-6pm.) Open for lunch M-Sa 11:30am-2pm. 220-520Kč.

Malostranská Restaurace, Karmelitská 25, in Malá Strana. Metro A: Malostranská. Go down Klárov, right on Letenská, then bear left through Malostranské nám. and continue on Karmelitská. Czech main dishes 70-80Kč. Open daily 10am-midnight.

Radost FX, Bělehradská 120, is a both a club and a late-night veggie cafe. Metro C: I.P. Pavlova. Entrees 150Kč. Open Su-Th 11am-late, F-Sa 11am-later.

CAFES AND TEAHOUSES

When Prague journalists are bored, they churn out yet another "Whatever happened to cafe life?" feature. The answer: it turned into *čajovna* (teahouse) culture.

▨ **U malého Glena,** Karmelitská 23. Metro A: Malostranská. Take tram #12 to Malostranské nám. Their motto is: "Eat, Drink, Drink Some More." Killer margaritas 80Kč. Nightly jazz or blues 9pm. Cover 60-120Kč. Open daily 10am-2am, Su brunch 10am-3pm.

Kavarná Imperial, Na Poříčí 15. Metro B: Nám. Republiky. Pillars and mosaic tiles make this place feel refined. Live jazz F-Sa 9pm. Open Su-Th 9am-12pm, F-Sa 9am-1am.

Propaganda, Pštrossova 29. Metro B: Národní třída. See directions to Globe Bookstore (p. 250). Comfy low slung chairs and sunny yellow interior with a cheap Budvar (25Kč) and espresso (19Kč). Open daily 3pm-2am.

Dobrá Čajovna U Čajovníka (Good Tearoom), Boršov 2. Metro A: Staroměstská; follow Křížovnická past the Charles Bridge and bear left onto Karoliny Světlé; Boršov is a tiny street on the left. 90 teas (12-150Kč). Open M-Sa 10am-midnight, Su noon-midnight.

Jazz Café 14, Opatovická 14. Metro B: Národní třída. Around the corner from Velryba on Opatovická. Usually filled with smoke and 20-somethings. Coffee (14Kč) and snacks (30Kč). Open daily noon-11pm.

The Globe Coffeehouse, Pštrossova 6. Metro B: Narodni Trida. At the Globe Bookstore (p. 250). Tasty, strong black coffee (20Kč), gazpacho (35Kč), and English speakers trying to make a love connection (priceless). Open daily 10am-midnight.

Kavárna Medúza, Belgická 17. Metro A: Nám. Míru. Walk down Rumunská and turn left at Belgická. Cafe masquerading as an antique shop. Fluffed-up Victorian seats and lots of coffee (19-30Kč). Open M-F 11am-1am, Sa-Su noon-late.

◉ SIGHTS

The only Central European city left unscathed by either natural disaster or World War II, Prague at its center is a blend of maze-like alleys and Baroque architecture.

VÁCLAV COCKTAIL During the Cold War era, **Václav Havel** (VAA-tslav HA-vel) outraged party functionaries with his plays and essays, which openly opposed the communist establishment. In 1977, he became a leader of Charter 77, a political-intellectual protest against the violation of human rights in Czechoslovakia. Even repeated incarceration did not silence Havel; after leading the Velvet Revolution in 1989, he was elected President. But his years as an *enfant terrible* were not yet over. During eleven years of presidency, he exhibited few of the characteristics of a well-behaved statesman. Today politicians, the media, and the public alike indulge in criticizing him for anything he says or does. A marriage to younger actress Dagmar Veškrnová, less than a year after his first wife's death, outraged the public. Likewise, Havel's New Year's speech of 1998, in which he expressed disgust with the political and moral climate of the country, earned him an all-time low in popularity polls. Yet Havel does nothing but maintain the qualities that made him famous: saying what others don't want to hear, and doing what others don't dare to.

You can easily escape the packs by venturing away from **Staroměstské náměstí**, the **Charles Bridge**, and **Václavské náměstí**. Compact central Prague is best explored on foot. Don't leave without wandering the back alleys of **Josefov**, exploring the hills of **Vyšehrad**, and getting lost in the maze of the streets of **Malá Strana**.

NOVÉ MĚSTO

Established in 1348 by Charles IV, Nové Město has aged well. Today it forms the commercial center of Prague, complete with American chain stores.

FRANCISCAN GARDENS AND VELVET REVOLUTION MEMORIAL. No one is sure how the monks manage to preserve the immaculate **rose garden** (Františkánská zahrada) in the heart of Prague's bustling commercial district. *(Metro A, B: Můstek; Metro B: Národní tří da. Enter through the arch to the left of Jungmannova and Národní, behind the statue. Open daily mid-Apr. to mid-Sept. 7am-10pm; mid-Sept. to mid-Oct. 8am-8pm; mid-Oct. to mid-Apr. 8am-7pm. Free.)* A plaque under the arcades halfway down Národní třída memorializes the hundreds of citizens beaten by police on November 17, 1989, when a wave of mass protests led to the total collapse of communism in Czechoslovakia during the **Velvet Revolution.**

WENCESLAS SQUARE (VÁCLAVSKÉ NÁMĚSTÍ). Not so much a square as a broad boulevard running through the center of Nové Město, Wenceslas Square owes its name to the Czech ruler and saint **Wenceslas** (Václav), whose statue sits in front of the **National Museum** (Národní muzeum). Wenceslas has presided over a century of turmoil and triumph, witnessing no fewer than five revolutions from his pedestal: the declaration of the new Czechoslovak state in 1918, the invasion of Hitler's troops, the arrival of Soviet tanks in 1968, Jan Palach setting himself on fire to protest the Soviet invasion, and the 1989 Velvet Revolution. The square sweeps down from the statue past department stores, discos, posh hotels, sausage stands, and trashy casinos. The glass **Radio Prague Building**, behind the National Museum, was the scene of a tense battle during the Prague Spring, as citizens tried to protect the radio studios from Soviet tanks with a human barricade. *(Metro A, C: Muzeum.)*

THE DANCING HOUSE. Built by American architect Frank Gehry of Guggenheim-Bilbao fame (see p. 887), the undulating building at the corner of Resslova and Rašínovo nábřeží is referred to as the "Dancing House" (Taneční dům) by Czechs. It opened in 1996, next to President Havel's former apartment building; he moved out when construction began. *(Metro B: Karlovo nám. As you walk down Resslova toward the river, the building is on the left.)*

STARÉ MĚSTO (OLD TOWN)

The narrow roads and Old World alleys of the Staré Město make it easy to get lost. But that's the best way to appreciate this 1000-year-old neighborhood's charm.

CHARLES BRIDGE (KARLŮV MOST). Thronged with tourists and the hawkers who feed on them, this bridge is Prague's most recognizable landmark. Five years ago, the bridge's vendors peddled Red Army gear and black market currency deals; today, they sell watercolors and other junk. The statue of St. Jan Nepomucký marks the spot where the saint was tossed over the side of the bridge for guarding the queen's extramarital secrets from a suspicious King Wenceslas IV.

OLD TOWN SQUARE (STAROMĚSTSKÉ NÁMĚSTÍ). The heart of Staré Město is Old Town Square, surrounded by no fewer than eight magnificent towers. Next to the grassy knoll, **Old Town Hall** (Staroměstská radnice) is the multi-facaded building with a bit blown off the front. The building was partially demolished by the Nazis in the final week of World War II, receiving Prague's only visible damage from the war. Crowds mob on the hour to watch the wonderful **astronomical clock** chime with its procession of apostles, and a skeleton representing Death. *(Metro A: Staroměstská; Metro A, B: Mrštek. Museum open in summer daily 9am-5:30pm. 30Kč, students 20Kč. Clock animated until 9pm. Clock tower open daily 10am-6pm.)* The Czech Republic's most famous martyred theologian, **Jan Hus**, hovers over Old Town Square in bronze effigy. Opposite the Old Town Hall, the spires of **Týn Church** (Matka Boží před Týnem) rise above a mass of medieval homes. The famous astronomer Tycho de Brahe is buried inside—he overindulged at one of Emperor Rudolf's lavish dinner parties, where it was unacceptable to leave the table unless the Emperor himself did so. When poor Tycho de Brahe needed to go (you know, *go*), he was forced to stay seated, and his bladder burst. In front of the Jan Hus statue lies the Rococo **Goltz-Kinský Palace**, from whose balcony Klement Gottwald declared communism victorious on February 21, 1948. *(Open Tu-Su 10am-6pm; closes early in summer for daily concerts.)*

POWDER TOWER AND MUNICIPAL HOUSE (PRAŠNÁ BRÁNA, OBECNÍDŮM). One of the original eight city gates, the Gothic **Powder Tower** (Prašná brána) looms at the edge of Nám. Republiky as the entrance to Staré Město. A small history exhibit is inside, but skip it for a climb to the top. On the sight of a former royal court next door, the Municipal House captures the opulence of Prague's 19th-century cafe culture. The Czechoslovak state declared independence here on October 28, 1918. Today it showcases music and art. *(Nám. Republiky 5. Metro B: Nám. Republiky. Tower open Apr.-Sept. 10am-6pm. House open daily 10am-6pm. Guided tours 150Kč.)*

JOSEFOV

Metro A: Staroměstská. ☎ 231 71 91. Synagogues and museum open Su-F 9am-6pm. Closed for Jewish holidays. All sights except New Synagogue 490Kč, students 340Kč. New Synagogue 200Kč, students 140Kč. Museum only 290Kč, students 200Kč.

Prague's historic Jewish neighborhood and the oldest Jewish settlement in Europe, Josefov lies north of Staromětstské nám., along Maiselova and several sidestreets. In 1180, Prague's citizens built a 12ft. wall around the area. The closed city bred legends, many focusing on **Rabbi Loew ben Bezalel** (1512-1609) and his legendary *golem*—a mud creature that supposedly came to life to protect Prague's Jews. For the next 500 years, the city's Jews were exiled to this ghetto, which was vacated in World War II when the residents were deported to death camps. Though it's only a fraction of its former size, a Jewish community still exists in Prague today.

THE SYNAGOGUES. The **Maisel Synagogue** (Maiselova synagoga) has artifacts from the extensive collections of the Jewish Museum. *(On Maiselova, between Široká and Jáchymova.)* Turn left down Široká to reach the 16th-century **Pinkas Synagogue** (Pinkasova synagoga), converted in 1958 into a sobering memorial to the 80,000 Czech Jews killed in the Holocaust. Upstairs is an exhibit of drawings made by children in the Terezin camp, most of whom died in Auschwitz. Backtrack up Široká and go left on Maiselova to see the oldest operating synagogue in Europe, the 700-year-old **Old-New Synagogue** (Staronová synagoga). Further up Široká on Dušní is the ornate Moorish interior of the **Spanish Synagogue** (Španělská synagoga).

OLD JEWISH CEMETERY. The Old Jewish Cemetery (Starý židovský hřbitov) remains Josefov's most popular attraction. Between the 14th and 18th centuries,

20,000 graves were laid in 12 layers. The striking clusters of tombstones result from a process in which the older stones were lifted from underneath. Rabbi Loew is buried by the wall directly opposite the entrance. *(At the corner of Široká and Žatecká.)*

MALÁ STRANA

The seedy hangout for criminals and counter-revolutionaries for nearly a century, the cobblestone streets of Malá Strana have become the most prized real estate on either side of the Vltava. The Malá Strana is centered around **Malostranské náměstí** and its centerpiece, the Baroque **St. Nicholas' Cathedral** (Chrám sv. Mikuláš), whose towering dome is one of Prague's most notable landmarks. *(Metro A: Malostranská; then follow Letenská to Malostranské nám. Open daily 9am-4pm. 45Kč, students 20Kč.)* Along Letenská, a wooden gate opens through a 10m wall into the beautiful **Wallenstein Garden** (Valdštejnská zahrada), one of Prague's best-kept secrets. *(Letenská 10. Metro A: Malostranská. Open daily 10am-6pm.)* Hidden on Velkoprerovske nam., just off Kampa Island, is a 1990s version of the infamous **John Lennon Wall.** *(Metro A: Malostranská. Walk down U Lužického semináře to the Charles Bridge, descend the stairs leading to Na Kampě, take the 1st right onto Hroznová, and bear right close to the wall over the bridge onto Velkopřerovské nám.)* **Church of Our Lady Victorious** (Kostel Panna Marie Vítězná) is notable not for its exterior but for the famous wax statue of the **Infant Jesus of Prague** inside, said to bestow miracles on the faithful. *(Metro A: Malostranská. Follow Letenská through Malostranské nám. and continue onto Karmelitská. Open M-F 9:45am-5:30pm, Sa 9:45am-8pm, Su open for mass. Free.)*

PRAGUE CASTLE (PRAŽSKÝ HRAD)

Metro A: Hradčanská. Open Apr.-Oct. daily 9am-5pm; Nov.-Mar. 9am-4pm. Buy tickets opposite St. Vitus' Cathedral, inside the castle walls. 3-day ticket valid at Royal Crypt, Cathedral and Powder Towers, Old Royal Palace, and Basilica of St. George. 120Kč, students 60Kč.

Prague Castle has been the seat of the Bohemian government since its founding 1000 years ago. From the metro, cross the tram tracks and turn left onto Tychonova, which leads to the newly renovated **Royal Summer Palace** (Královský letohrádek). The main castle entrance is at the other end of the **Royal Garden** (Královská zahrada), across the **Powder Bridge** (Prašný most). Before exploring, pass the main gate to see the **Šternberský Palace.**

ST. VITUS' CATHEDRAL (KATEDRÁLA SV. VÍTA). Inside the castle walls stands Prague Castle's centerpiece, the colossal St. Vitus' Cathedral, which may look Gothic but in fact was only finished in 1929—600 years after construction began. To the right of the high altar stands the **tomb of St. Jan Nepomucký,** 3m of solid, glistening silver weighing 1800kg. In the main church, the walls of **St. Wenceslas Chapel** (Svatováclavská kaple) are lined with precious stones and a painting cycle depicting the legend of this saint. Climb the 287 steps of the **Cathedral Tower** for the best view of the city, or step downstairs to see the tomb of Charles IV.

OLD ROYAL PALACE (STARÝ KRÁLOVSKÝ PALÁC). The Old Royal Palace, to the right of the cathedral behind the Old Provost's House and the statue of St. George, houses the lengthy expanse of the **Vladislav Hall,** which once hosted jousting competitions. Upstairs is the **Chancellery of Bohemia,** where on May 23, 1618, angry Protestants flung two Habsburg officials (and their secretary) out the window, triggering the bloody Thirty Years' War.

ST. GEORGE'S BASILICA AND AROUND. Behind the cathedral and across the courtyard from the Old Royal Palace stand St. George's Basilica (Bazilika sv. Jiří) and its adjacent convent. The convent houses the **National Gallery of Bohemian Art,** with art ranging from Gothic to Baroque. *(Open Tu-Su 10am-6pm. 50Kč, students 20Kč.)* The Old Royal Palace street, **Jiřská,** begins to the right of the basilica. Halfway down, the tiny **Golden Lane** (Zlatá ulička) heads off to the right; alchemists once worked here, and Kafka later lived at #22. Back on Jiřská, after passing out of the Prague Castle between the two armed sentries, peer over the battlements on the right for a fine cityscape.

OUTER PRAGUE

The city's outskirts are packed with greenery, churches, and panoramic vistas, all peacefully tucked away from the tourist hordes. **Petřín Gardens** (Petřínské sady), the largest in Prague, provide some of the most spectacular views of the city. A cable car from just above the intersection of Vítězná and Újezd goes to the top. *(8Kč; look for lanová dráha signs. Open daily 11am-6pm and 7-11pm.)* At the summit is a small Eiffel tower and a wacky labyrinth of mirrors at **Bludiště.** *(Open Tu-Su 10am-7pm. 30Kč, students 20Kč.)* **Vyšehrad** is the former haunt of Prague's 19th-century Romantics; quiet walkways wind between crumbling stone walls to one of the Czech Republic's most celebrated sites, **Vyšehrad Cemetery,** home to the remains of (de)composer Antonin Dvořák. For an old-time Eastern European market, check out **Prague Market** (Pražskátrznice) has acres of stalls selling all kinds of wares. *(Take tram #5 from Nám Republiky toward Vozovna Kobylisy and get off at Pražskátrznice.)*

🏛 MUSEUMS

Prague's magnificence isn't best reflected in its museums, which often have striking façades but mediocre collections. But the city is victim to many rainy days, and it has a few public museums that shelter interesting and quirky collections.

🏛HOUSE OF THE GOLDEN RING (DŮM U ZLATÉHO PRSTENU). Behind Týn Church, at Týnská 6, this museum houses an astounding collection of 20th-century Czech art. *(Metro A: Staroměstská. Open Tu-Su 10am-6pm. 60Kč, students 30Kč for top 3 floors; 140Kč, students 70Kč for whole museum; 1st Tu of each month free.)*

NATIONAL GALLERY (NÁRODNÍ GALERIE). The massive National Gallery collection is spread around nine different locations; the notable **Šternberský palác** and **Klášter St. Jiří** are in the Prague Castle (see p. 257). **St. Agnes' Cloister** (Klášter sv. Anežky) is the other major branch of the National Gallery, with a collection of 19th-century Czech art, but it's undergoing renovation, and its collection has been moved to the **Trade Fair Palace and the Gallery of Modern Art** (Veletržní palác a Galerie moderního umění), which also exhibits 20th-century Czech art. *(Dukelských hrdinř 47. Metro C: Vltavská. Both open Tu-Su 10am-6pm. 150Kč, students 70Kč.)*

THE CZECH MUSEUM OF FINE ARTS (ČESKÉ MUZEUM VÝTVARNÝCH UMĚNÍ). At Celetná 34, itself one of Prague's best examples of Cubist architecture, the Museum of Fine Arts contains a complementary collection of Czech Cubism. *(Metro A: Nám. Republiky. Open Tu-Su 10am-6pm. 35Kč, students 15Kč.)*

🎭 ENTERTAINMENT

For concerts and performances, consult *The Prague Post*, *Threshold*, or *Do města-Downtown* (the latter two are free at many cafes and restaurants). Most performances start at 7pm and offer unsold tickets 30min. before show time. From mid-May to early June, the **Prague Spring Festival** draws musicians from around the world. For tickets, try **Bohemia Ticket International,** Malé nám. 13, next to Čedok. (☎24 22 78 32; www.ticketsbti.cz. Open M-F 9am-5pm, Sa 9am-2pm.) The **National Theater** (Národní divadlo), Národní třída 2/4, features drama, opera, and ballet. (☎24 92 15 28. Metro B: Národní třída. Box office open M-F 10am-6pm, Sa-Su 10am-12:30pm and 3-6pm, and 30min. before performances.) **Estates Theater** (Stavovské divadlo), Ovocný trh 1, is to the left of the pedestrian Na Příkopě (Metro A, B: Můstek) *Don Giovanni* premiered here; shows today are mostly classic theater. Use the National Theater box office, or show up 30min. before showtime.

🍺 NIGHTLIFE

The best way to experience Prague at night is in an alcoholic fog. With some of the best beers in the world on tap, it's no surprise that pubs and beer halls are the most popular nighttime hangouts. These days, however, authentic pub experiences are restricted to the suburbs and outlying metro stops; nearly everything in central Prague has been overrun by tourists. Prague is not a clubbing city, although there are enough dance clubs pumping out ABBA and techno to satisfy any Eurotrash cravings; more popular are the city's many excellent jazz and rock clubs. Otherwise, you can always retreat to the Charles Bridge to sing along with aspiring Brit-pop guitarists into the wee hours.

BARS

■ **U Fleků,** Křemencova 11. Metro B: Národní třída. Turn right on Spálená away from Národní, right on Myslíkova, and head right on Křemencova. The oldest brewhouse in Prague. A steep 49Kč per 0.4L of home-brewed beer. Open daily 9am-11pm.

■ **Kozička** (The Little Goat), Kozí 1. Metro A: Staroměstské. Take Dlouhá from the northeast corner of the square, then left onto Kozí, and look for the iron goat. This giant cellar bar is always packed; you'll know why after your first 0.5L of *Krušovice* (25Kč). Czech twenty-somethings stay all night. Open M-F noon-4am, Sa-Su 6pm-4am.

Vinárna U Sude, Vodičkova 10. Metro A, B: Můstek. Cross Václavské nám. to Vodičkova, follow the curve left, and it's on your left. Infinite labyrinth of cavernous cellars. Red wine 110Kč per 1L. Open M-F 11am-midnight, Sa-Su 2pm-midnight.

Le Châpeau Rouge, Jakubská 2. Metro B: Náměstí Republiky. Walk through the Powder Tower to Celetná, turn right on Templová, and look for the corner of Templová and Jakubská. The Châpeau recharges the tired souls of travelers by fulfilling all of their earthly needs. Open M-Th noon-3am, F noon-4am, Sa 4pm-4am, Su 4am-2am.

Újezd, Újezd 18. Metro B: Národní třída. Exit onto Národní, turn left toward the river, cross the Legií bridge, continue straight on Vítězná, and turn right on Újezd. Mellow DJ or live acid jazz 3 times a week. Beer just 22Kč. Open daily 11am-4am.

Cafe Marquis de Sade, Templová 8. Metro B: Nám Republiky. Go by the Powder Tower to Celetná; turn right on Templová. Live music Th. Beer 35Kč. Open daily 11am-2am.

Molly Malone's, U obecního dvora 4. Metro A: Staroměstská. Turn right on Křižonvická away from the Charles Bridge, turn right after Nám. Jana Palacha on Široká, which veers left and becomes Vězeňská, and turn left at the end. Beer 30Kč; Guinness 75Kč (cheaper than in Ireland). Open Su-Th 11am-1am, F-Sa 11am-2am.

Zanzibar, Saská 6 (☎0602 75 24 74). Metro A: Malostranská; head down Nostecká toward the Charles Bridge, turn right on Lázeňská, and left on Saská. The classiest place to see and be seen. Cocktails 75-150Kč. Reserve weekends. Open daily 5pm-3am.

Jo's Bar and Garáž, Malostranské nám. 7. Metro A: Malostranská. All-Anglophone with foosball, darts, cards and a DJ. Beer 12Kc during daily happy hour (6pm-10pm). Open daily 11am-2am.

CLUBS AND DISCOS

■ **Roxy,** Dlouhá 33. Metro B: Nám. Republiky. Walk up Revoluční toward the river and turn left on Dlouhá. People come here for experimental DJs, theme nights, and endless dancing. Cover 100-350Kč. Open July-Aug. daily 9pm-late; Sept.-June Tu-Su 9pm-late.

■ **U staré paní,** Michalská 9. Metro A, B: Můstek. Walk down Na můstku at the end of Václavské nám., continue on Melantrichova, turn left on Havelská, then right on Michalská. Some of Prague's finest jazz vocalists in a dark and classy venue. Shows nightly 9pm-midnight. Cover 160Kč, includes one drink. Open for shows 7pm-1am.

> **ABSINTHE-MINDED** Shrouded in Bohemian mystique, this translucent turquoise fire-water is a force to be reckoned with. Although absinthe has been banned in all but three countries this century due to allegations of opium-lacing and fatal hallucinations, Czechs have had a long love affair with the liquor. It has been the mainstay spirit of the Prague intelligentsia since Kafka's days, and during World War II every Czech adult was rationed a half-liter per month. Today's backpackers (who apparently will drink anything) have discovered the liquor, which at its strongest can be 160 proof. The bravest and most seasoned ex-pats sip it on the rocks, but you can douse a spoonful of sugar in the alcohol, torch it with a match until the sugar caramelizes and the alcohol burns off, and dump the residue into your glass. So bottoms up.

U malého Glena II, Karmelitská 23 (☎535 81 15). This small bar hosts bouncy jazz, blues, and funk nightly at 9pm. Beer 25Kč. Cover 100-150Kč. On weekends, call ahead to reserve a table. Open daily 8pm-2am.

Jazz Club Železná, Železná 16. Metro A, B: Staroměstská. From the Old Town Square, go down Železná, opposite the clock. Overflowing dark cellar bar showcases live jazz nightly. Beer 30Kč. Cover 80-150Kč. Shows 9-11:30pm. Open daily 3pm-12:30am.

Radost FX, Bělehradská 120 (www.radostfx.cz). Metro C: I.P. Pavlova. Techno, jungle, and house. Creative drinks. Cover 80-150Kč. Open M-Sa 10pm-late.

Palác Akropolis, Kubelíkova 27 (www.palacakropolis.cz). Metro A: Jiřího z Poděbrad. Head down Slavíkova and turn right onto Kubelíkova. Live bands several times a week. Top Czech act *Psí vojáci* are occasional visitors. Open daily 10pm-5am.

Karlovy Lázně, Novotného lávka 1. Four floors of serious partying under the Charles bridge. Cover 100Kč, 50Kč before 10pm. Open nightly 9pm-late.

GAY NIGHTLIFE

At any of the places below, you can pick up a copy of *Amigo* (39Kč), the most thorough guide to gay life in the Czech Republic and Slovakia, with a lot in English, or *Gayčko* (59Kč), a glossier piece of work, mostly in Czech.

☒ U střelce, Karolíny Světlé 12. Metro B: Národní třída. Under the archway on the right, this gay club draws a diverse crowd for its F and Sa night cabarets. Cover 80Kč. Open Tu and Th 9pm-midnight; W, F, Sa 9:30pm-5am with shows after midnight.

A Club, Milíčova 25. Metro C: Hlavní nádraží. Take tram #3, 5, 9, 26, or 55 uphill and get off at Lipsanká. A lesbian nightspot, but men are free to enter, although they might get a few side glances. Beer 20Kč. Open nightly 7pm-dawn.

Pinocchio, Seifertova 3. See directions to A Club above; exit tram at Husinecka and walk back downhill. Not just a nightclub, but an all-male complex, including poker machines, live strip shows, and video arcades. Beer 25Kč. Men only. Open daily 3pm-late.

◤ DAYTRIPS FROM PRAGUE

TEREZÍN (THERESIENSTADT). In 1941, when Terezín became a concentration camp, Nazi propaganda films touted the area as a spa resort where Jews would live a normal life. In reality, 35,000 died here, some of starvation and disease, others at the hands of brutal guards. Another 85,000 Jews were transported to death camps further east, such as Auschwitz. The **Ghetto Museum,** on Komenského in town, sets Terezín in the wider Nazi context. (Open daily Apr.-Sept. 9am-6pm; Oct.-Mar. 9am-5:30pm. Tickets to museum, barracks, and small fortress 150Kč, students 110Kč.) You can explore the **Small Fortress** (Malá Peunost) east of town across the river. (Open daily Apr.-Sept. 8am-6pm; Oct.-Mar. 8am-4:30pm.) The furnaces and autopsy lab at the **Jewish cemetery** and **crematorium** are as they were 50 years ago, with the addition of tributes left by the victims' ancestors. Men should cover their heads. (Open Mar.-Nov. Su-F 10am-5pm.) Life goes on in present-day Terezin, with families living in former barracks, and supermarkets in Nazi offices. The **bus** from Prague's Florenc station (1hr., 7 per day, 66Kč) stops by the central square, where the **tourist office** sells a 25Kč map. (Open Tu-Su 9am-4pm.) ☎0416.

KARLŠTEJN. A gem of the Bohemian countryside, Karlštejn is a turreted fortress built by Charles IV to house his crown jewels and holy relics. (Open July-Aug. Tu-Su 9am-6pm; May-June and Sept. 9am-5pm; Apr. and Oct. 9am-4pm; Nov.-Mar. 9am-3pm. English tours 50min.; 7-8 per day; 200Kč, students 100Kč.) The **Chapel of the Holy Cross** is inlaid with precious stones and 128 apocalyptic paintings by medieval Master Theodorik. (Open July-Aug. Tu-Su 9am-5pm. Mandatory tours 200Kč, in English 600Kč. By reservation only; ☎(02) 740 081 546 or reservace@spusc.cz.) Karlštejn can be reached by **train** from Hlavní nádraží or Praha-Smíchov (45min., every hr., 44Kč round-trip). Turn right out of the station, go left over the modern bridge, and walk through the village toward the castle. ☎0311.

MĚLNÍK. In one relaxing daytrip, you can sample the castle's homemade wines, tour the stately Renaissance chateau, savor your favorite vintage over lunch in the old schoolhouse overlooking the Říp Valley, and visit a crypt if you want. The town is known for its wine-making, which was perfected about 1000 years ago, when St. Wenceslas, the patron saint of Bohemian wine-makers, is said to have been initiated in the vineyards of Mělník. Wine tasting (110Kč) is available with a reservation. (☎62 21 21; www.lobkowicz-melnik.cz. Open daily 10am-6pm. Tours 40Kč, students 30Kč.) Directly across from the chateau is the 15th-century **St. Peter and Paul Cathedral,** whose crypt houses the bones of 10,000 medieval plague victims. (Open Tu-Su 10am-4pm. 15-20Kč.) **Buses** run from Holesovice (45min., approx. every 30min, 32Kč). From the station, make a right onto Bezručova and head up the left fork onto Kpt. Jaroše, to the town center. Once you enter the Old Town Square *(Nàm Míru)*, the castle is down Svatovaclvska to your left. ☎0206.

KUTNÁ HORA. East of Prague, the former mining town of Kutná Hora (Mining Mountain) has a history as morbid as the **bone church** that has made the city famous. In the 13th century, the town's 100,000 silver-crazed diggers were hit by the black plague. After monks sprinkled soil from a biblical cemetery on Kutná Hora's own cemetery, everybody wanted to be buried there. It got crowded. Neighbors started to complain about the stench by the 15th century, when the Cistercian order built a chapel and started cramming in bodies. Who knows why the monk in charge began designing floral shapes out of pelvises and crania; he never finished, but the artist František Rint eventually completed the project in 1870 with the bones of over 400,000 people, including flying butt-bones, femur crosses, and a chandelier made from every bone in the human body. (Open Apr.-Oct. daily 8am-6pm; Nov.-Mar. 9am-noon and 1-4pm. 30Kč, students 15Kč.) Take a **bus** (1½hr., 6 per day, 46Kč) from Prague's Florenc station, then walk or take a local bus to Sedlec Tabák (2km) and follow the signs for the chapel.

ČESKÝ RÁJ NATIONAL PRESERVE. The narrow pillars and deep gorges of the **Prachov rocks** (Prachovské skály) make for climbing and hikes with stunning views. The rocks also boast the ruins of the 14th-century rock castle **Pařez** and rock pond **Pelíšek.** (Open Apr.-Oct. daily 8am-5pm; swimming May-Aug. 25Kč, students 10Kč.) The 588 acres of the park are interwoven by a dense network of **trails;** green signs mark the roundabout route, yellow the most challenging trails, and red the extremely long "Golden Trail," which connects Prachovské skály to **Hrubá Skála,** a rock town surrounding a hilltop castle where hikers enjoy the best view of the sandstone rocks. From the Hrubá Skála castle, the red trail leads up to what remains of **Valdštejn** (Wallenstein) castle. **Buses** run from Prague's Florenc station to **Jičín** (1½hr., 7 per day, 53Kč), where other buses go to Prachovské skály and Český Ráj (15min., every hr., 9Kč). ☎0433.

WEST AND SOUTH BOHEMIA

Bursting with curative springs, West Bohemia is the Czech bath belt. Over the centuries, emperors and intellectuals alike have soaked in the waters of Karlovy Vary *(Carlsbad* in German). South Bohemia is more rustic, with brooks, virgin forests, scattered villages, and castle ruins. Its low hills are great for wildlife-watching, castle-traipsing, and *Budvar*-guzzling.

KARLOVY VARY (CARLSBAD)   ☎017

A stroll through Karlovy Vary's spa district or up into its hills reveals why this lovely town developed into one of the great "salons" of Europe, frequented by Johann Sebastian Bach, Peter the Great, Sigmund Freud, and Karl Marx. These days, older Germans seeking the therapeutic powers of the springs are the main vacationers. In early July, however, the International Film Festival draws students from around the country and film stars from around the world.

CZECH REPUBLIC

▢▢ TRANSPORTATION AND PRACTICAL INFORMATION. Trains go from **Horní nádraží,** northwest of town, to Prague (4½hr. with 1-2hr. layover in Chomutov, 4-5 per day, 152Kč). To reach the town center from the train station, take bus #11 or 13 (8Kč) to the end. Faster **buses** zoom from **Dolní nádraží,** on Západní, to Prague (2½hr., 25 per day, 89-130Kč). Buy tickets at the **ČSAD office,** Dr. Engla 6. (Open M 6am-6pm, Tu-F 8am-6pm, Sa 8am-noon, Su 12:30-6pm.) To get to the town center from the bus station, turn left on Západní, continue past the Becher building, and bear right on T. G. Masaryka, which runs parallel to Bechera, the other main thoroughfare. Call ☎ 322 29 98 for a Centrum **taxi.** In Sprudel Colonnade, **Kur-info** (☎ 322 40 97) sells maps (25-45Kč), theater tickets (60-400Kč), and books accommodations, from 400Kč. *Promenada,* a part-English monthly booklet with information and event schedules, is available here and at kiosks throughout town. (Open Jan.-Oct. M-F 7am-5pm, Sa-Su 10am-4pm; Nov.-Dec. M-F 7am-5pm.) **Post Office:** Masaryka 1. Open M-F 7:30am-7pm, Sa-Su 8am-noon. **Postal code:** 36001.

▢▢ ACCOMMODATIONS AND FOOD. City Info, Masaryka 9, speaks English and offers pension singles from 600Kč and hotel doubles from 860Kč. (☎ 322 33 51. Open daily 9am-6pm.) Follow the directions from the bus and train stations to T.G. Masaryka and bear right at the post office to find **Hotel Kosmos,** Zahradní 39, in the center of the spa district. (☎ 322 54 76. Singles 540-820Kč; doubles 860-1450Kč.) From the main stop on Západní, take bus #6 toward Stará Kysibelská and get off at the fourth stop, Blahoslavova, to get to **Pension Hestia,** Stará Kysibelská 45. Spacious rooms are worth the trip. (☎ 322 59 85; hestiakv@volny.cz. Reception 24hr. Singles 320Kč; doubles 640Kč.) For meals, try the mostly **Vegetarian Restaurant,** I.P. Pavlova 25 (open daily 11am-9pm), or the **supermarket,** Horova 1, in the large building with the "Městská tržnice" sign over the local bus station (open M-F 6am-7pm, Sa 7am-5pm, Su 9am-5pm). Karlovy Vary is known for its sweet *oplatky* (spa wafers); try them at a street vendor (5Kč).

▢▢ SIGHTS AND ENTERTAINMENT. The spa district (with its springs, baths, and colonnades), officially begins with the Victorian **Bath 5** (Lázně 5), Smetanovy Sady 1, across the street from the post office, marked by flowers displaying the date. (Thermal baths 330Kč. Underwater massages 460Kč. Open M-F 7am-9pm, Sa-Su 10am-6pm.) The pedestrian **Mlýnské nábř.** meanders alongside the Teplá beneath shady trees to **Bath 3,** which is to the right, just before **Freedom Spring** (Pramen svobody). Next door, the imposing **Mill Colonnade** (Mlýnská kolonáda) shelters five different springs. The **Zawojski House,** Trižiště 9, now the Živnostenská Banka, is a cream-and-gold Art Nouveau building. The **Strudel Spring** (Vřídlo pramen), Karlovy Vary's hottest and highest-shooting spring, inside the **Sprudel Colonnade** (Vřídelní kolonáda), spouts 30L of 72°C (162°F) water each second. (Open daily 6am-6:30pm.) Follow Stará Louka until signs point you to the funicular, which leads to the 555m **Diana Observatory** (Rozhledna) and a magnificent panorama of the city. (Funicular runs every 15min. 9am-7pm. 25Kč, return 40Kč. Tower open daily 9am-7pm. 10Kč.) *Promenáda* lists the month's concerts and performances, including the ▩ **International Film Festival,** which screens independent films from all over the globe in the first two of weeks of July. Tickets sell out quickly. (www.iffkv.cz. Student 3-day 200Kč, full-festival 500Kč.) **Propaganda,** Jaltská 5, off Bechera, attracts a hip, young crowd with live music and a trendy blue-steel interior. (Mixed drinks 40-100Kč. Open daily 5pm-late.)

ČESKÉ BUDĚJOVICE   ☎ 038

No amount of beer will ever help you correctly pronounce České Budějovice (CHESS-kay BOOD-yeh-yoh-vee-tsay). The town was known as Budweis in the 19th century, when it inspired the name of the popular but pale North American Budweiser, bears little relation to the malty local *Budvar*. Surrounded by Renaissance and Baroque buildings, cobblestone **Nám. Otakara II** is the largest square in the country. The 72m **Black Tower** (Černá věž) in one corner looms over the town. Beware: the treacherous stairs are difficult even for the sober. (Open July-Aug.

THIS BUD'S FOR EU Until recently many Yankees, having tasted the malty goodness of a *Budvar* brew, returned home to find it conspicuously unavailable. What's up? The answer lies in a tale of trademarks and town names. České Budějovice (Budweis in German) had been brewing its own style of lager for centuries when the Anheuser-Busch brewery in St. Louis came out with its Budweiser-style beer in 1876. Not until the 1890s, however, did the Budějovice Pivovar (Brewery) begin producing a beer labeled "Budweiser." International trademark conflicts ensued, and in 1911 the companies signed a non-competition agreement: *Budvar* got markets in Europe and Anheuser-Busch took North America. When Anheuser-Busch attempted to buy a controlling interest in the makers of *Budvar*, the Czech government summarily replied: "nyeh" and *Budvar* lobbied to make the "Budweiser" a designation as exclusive as that of "Champagne"—meaning that any brand sold in the EU under that name would have to come from the Budweiser region. But now, at long last, *Budvar* has assumed its rightful place among the better beers available on American shelves.

daily 10am-6pm; Sept.-Oct. and Apr.-June Tu-Su 10am-6pm. 15Kč.) The **Budvar Brewery**, Karoliny Světlé 4, can be reached from the center by buses #2 and 4. (English tours 118Kč per person, in Czech and for students 68Kč; includes beer tasting.)

Trains travel to Nádražní 12 from Brno (4½hr., 2 per day, 152Kč) and Prague (2½hr., 11 per day, 114Kč). The TIC **tourist office**, Nám. Otakara II 2, books central private rooms from 320Kč. (☎/fax 635 94 80; infocb@c-budejovice.cz. Open M-F 8:30am-6pm, Sa 8:30am-5pm, Su 10am-4pm; Oct.-Apr. M-F 8am-6pm, Sa 8am-4:30pm.) To get to the center of town from the train station, walk right on Nádražní, turn left at the first crosswalk, and follow the pedestrian street, Lannova třída, as it becomes Kanovnická and pours into the square. **Postal code:** 37001.

To get to the friendly **Penzion U Výstavište**, U Výstavište 17, from the bus station, opposite and to the left of the train station, take bus #1 five stops to "U parku" and continue 150m along the side street that branches off to the right. (☎724 01 48. First night 250Kč, 200Kč thereafter.) The University of South Bohemia **dorms**, Studentská 15, are open to tourists July to mid-September. Take tram #1 from the bus station five stops to U parku; backtrack down Husova, then take the second right on Studentská. (☎777 44 00. Doubles 300Kč. ISIC 20% discount.) **Večerka grocery** is at Palachého 10; enter on Hroznova. (Open M-F 7am-8pm, Sa 7am-1pm, Su 8am-8pm.) Try Czech food at **Restaurant Rio**, Hradební 14, right off ul. Černé věže. (Dishes 70-130Kč. Open M-Th 11am-11pm, F 11am-midnight, Sa 6pm-midnight.)

⚡ DAYTRIP ČESKÉ BUDĚJOVICE: HLUBOKÁ NAD VLTAVOU. Hluboká's extraordinary castle owes its appearance to Eleonora Schwarzenberg, who turned the castle into a Windsor-style fairy-tale stronghold in the mid-19th century. (Castle open Apr. and Sept.-Oct. Tu-Su 9am-4:30pm; May-June Tu-Su 9am-5pm; July-Aug. daily 9am-5pm. Approx. 3 English tours per day. 150Kč, students 80Kč. Frequent Czech tours 80/40Kč.) **Buses** run to Hluboká from Ceske Budejovice (25min., 12Kč) frequently during the week, less so on the weekends. Get off at Pod Kostolem, head right, then take the first right and follow signs up to the castle. ☎038.

ČESKÝ KRUMLOV ☎0337

What can be said about everyone's new favorite Czech destination? The worst part is having to leave. Weaving medieval streets, cobblestone promenades, and Bohemia's second-largest castle make this UNESCO-protected town one of the most popular spots in Eastern Europe. Come for a day, but you might stay for weeks.

📧⚡ TRANSPORTATION AND PRACTICAL INFORMATION. Frequent **buses** arrive from České Budějovice (30-45min., every 30min., 26Kč). To get to Nám. Svornosti, take the uphill path from the back of the terminal, near stops #20-25. Turn right at Kaplická, then cross the highway and head straight onto Horní, which leads into the square. The **tourist office,** Nám Svornosti 1, books pension rooms (from 600Kč) as well as cheaper private rooms. (☎70 46 21; infocentrum@ckrf.ckrumlov.cz; www.ckrumlov.cz/infocentrum. Open daily July-Aug. 9am-8pm; May-June and Sept. 9am-7pm; Oct.-Aug. 9am-6pm.) **Postal code:** 38101.

▓▓ ACCOMMODATIONS AND FOOD. To get to ▓**U vodníka,** Po vodě 55, or ▓**Krumlov House,** Rooseveltova 68, both run by an American expat couple, follow the directions above from the station and turn left onto Rooseveltova after the light, just before the bridge. From there, follow the signs to U vodníka or continue down the street to Krumlov House. (☎71 19 35; vodnik@ck.bohem-net.cz; www.krumlovhostels.com. Laundry. Bike rental. Dorms 250Kč; doubles 300Kč.) To get to the wilder **Ryba Hostel,** Rybářská 5, start across from the tourist office, drift left onto Kájovská, head over the bridge and then right on Rybářská; you'll see it from the bridge. (☎71 18 01. Dorms 200-250Kč. 7th night free.) **Hostel U Šneka,** Panská 19, is 50m straight down Panská from Nám. Svornosti. If the receptionist is out, go to **Hotel u Maléko Vítka** on Radniční 27, around the corner. It's fairly quiet despite the rock club below. (☎71 19 25; www.krumlos.cz. 10-bed dorm 250Kč; doubles 250Kč.) From the square, go down Na louži opposite the tourist office and turn right on Kájovská to get to **Na louži,** Kájovská 66, which serves generous portions of Czech dishes. (85-118Kč. Open daily 10am-10pm.) **Šatlavská,** Horní 157, on the corner of Šatlavská and Masná just off the square, features big chunks of meat on the old "open grill." (95-200Kč. Open daily 11am-midnight.) Get groceries at **SPAR,** Linecká 49. (Open M-Sa 7am-6pm, Su 9am-6pm.)

▓▓ SIGHTS AND NIGHTLIFE. If you get off a bus at the small **Špičák** stop on the northern outskirts of town, it's an easy walk downhill to the medieval center. Take the overpass to cross the highway, continue through **Budějovice gate** and follow **Latrán** past the castle and over the **Vltava** river. The stone courtyards of the **castle,** perched high above the town, are free to the public. Two tours cover different parts of the lavish interior, including a frescoed ballroom, a splendid Baroque theater, and Renaissance-style rooms. The eerie **galleries of the crypts** showcase local artists' sculptures and ceramics. Climb the 162 steps of the **tower** for a fabulous view. (Castle open Tu-Su June-Aug. 9am-6pm; May and Sept. 9am-5pm; Apr. and Oct. 9am-4pm. 1hr. tours in English 150Kč, students 75Kč. Crypts open May-Oct. Tu-Su 10am-5pm; July-Aug. daily 10am-5pm. 30Kč, students 20Kč. Tower open daily May-Sept. 9am-6pm; Apr. and Oct. 11am-3pm. 30Kč, students 20Kč.) The castle gardens also contain the **Revolving Theater,** an outdoor venue which holds operas and musicals in Czech during the summer. (Open June to early-Sept. Shows at 9:30pm. Tickets in castle courtyard.) The Austrian painter Egon Schiele (1890-1918) lived in Český Krumlov—until the citizens ran him out for painting burghers' daughters in the nude. Decades later, the ▓**Egon Schiele International Cultural Center,** Široká 70-72, displays his work, along with paintings by other 20th-century Central European artists. (Open daily 10am-6pm. 120Kč, students 60Kč.)

Rent a **raft** or kayak from Maleček, Roosevltova 28, and navigate the Vltava, or hike into the hills to go **horseback riding** at Jezdecký klub Slupenec, Slupenec 1; from the town center, follow Horní to the highway, take the second left on Křížová, and follow the red trail up to Slupenec. (☎71 10 53. Open Tu-Sa 9am-6pm. 220Kč per hr. Call ahead.) Rent a **bike** (300Kč per day) from **Vltava,** Kájovská 62, to cruise the Bohemian countryside, or pedal to **Zlatá Koruna,** a monastery built in 1263.

Rybářska hosts a number of swinging bars: **U Hada** (Snake Bar), Rybářská 37 (open daily 7pm-3am) and **Babylon,** Rybářská 6 (open daily noon-late).

MORAVIA

Wine-making Moravia makes up the eastern third of the Czech Republic. Home of the country's finest folk-singing tradition and two of its leading universities, it's also the birthplace of Tomáš G. Masaryk, Czechoslovakia's founder and first president, and psychoanalyst Sigmund Freud. Another famous Moravian, Gregor Mendel, founded modern genetics in his pea garden in a Brno monastery.

BRNO ☎ 05

The Czech Republic's second-largest city, Brno has been an international market-place since the 13th century. Today, global corporations compete with family-owned produce stands, and historic churches soften the glare of the erotic clubs that line some of its streets. Brno allows travelers to experience a living Czech city.

TRANSPORTATION AND PRACTICAL INFORMATION. Trains (☎42 21 48 03) go to: Bratislava (2hr., 9 per day, 115Kč); Budapest (4½hr., 2 per day, 872Kč); Prague (3hr., 16 per day, 164-224Kč); and Vienna (2hr., 1 per day, 525Kč). From the main exit, cross the three tram lines on Nádražní to Masarykova to reach **Nám. Svobody,** the main square. **Buses** (☎43 21 77 33) leave from Zvonařka, down Plotní from the train station, for Prague (3hr., 112-116Kč) and Vienna (2½hr., 3 per day, 250Kč). To get from the bus to the train station, follow Plotní as it becomes Dornych, and turn left onto Nádražni. The **tourist office** (Kulturní a informační centrum města Brna), Radnická 8, inside the town hall, books rooms (from 400Kč) and hostels (200Kč). From Nám. Svobody, head down Masarykova and turn right onto Pruchodni. (☎42 21 10 90; fax 42 21 07 58. Open M-F 8am-6pm, Sa-Su 9am-5pm.) **Internet Center Cafe,** Masarykova 2/24, is right in the center of town. (40Kč per hr. Open daily 8am-midnight.) **Postal code:** 60200.

ACCOMMODATIONS AND FOOD. From the train station, head up Masarykova and turn right on Josefská, which leads to Novobranská and the new **Hotel Astorka,** at #3. (☎42 51 03 70; fax 42 51 01 06; astorka@jamu.cz. Open July-Aug. Doubles 840Kč, students 420Kč; triples 94/472.50Kč.) To get to **Ubytovani Tkalovska,** Tkalcovska 5, take tram #2, 4, 7 or 9 from the train station to the Tkalcovska stop. Then head back on Ceji and take the first left onto Tkalcovska. (☎45 16 22 50. Call ahead in summer. Singles 190Kč.) A **Tesco** supermarket is behind the train station. (Open M-F 7am-8pm, Sa 7am-7pm, Su 8am-6pm.)

SIGHTS AND NIGHTLIFE. If you like morbidity, try the **Capuchin Monastery Crypt** (Hrobka Kapucínského kláštera), just left of Masarykova from the train station, where the dry bones of monks lie on the floors. (Open M-Sa 9am-noon and 2-4:30pm, Sa 11-noon and 2-4:30pm. 40Kč, students 20Kč.) On Petrov Hill, just south of Zelný trh and across the square from the town hall, the bells of **Peter and Paul Cathedral** (Biskupská katedrála sv. Petra a Pavla). Brno was allegedly saved from a Swedish siege in 1645 when the besieging general told his army he would withdraw if they hadn't captured the town by noon. The folks of Brno rang the bells early, and the Swedes slunk away; ever since, the bells have been striking noon at 11am. (Cathedral open M-Sa 6:15am-6:15pm, Su 7am-6pm. Free.) The **Mendelianum,** Mendlovo nám. 1a, documents the life and work of Johann Gregor Mendel, father of modern genetics. (Open daily July-Aug. 9am-6pm; Sept.-June 8am-5pm. 8Kč, students 4Kč.) Take tram #3 or 11 from Česká to Tábor, and continue down to **Mersey,** Minská 15, a nice dance club. (Beer 19Kč. Open M-Sa 7pm-late.)

DAYTRIPS FROM BRNO: TELČ AND OLOMOUC. The Italian aura of **Telč** is a result of a trip the town's ruler took to Genoa in 1546, and the squad of Italian artists and craftsmen he brought back with him. As you step over the cobblestone footbridge to the main square—flanked by long arcades of peach gables and time-worn terra-cotta roofs—it's easy to see why UNESCO designated the gingerbread town a World Heritage Monument. Watch children from neighboring towns sing folk songs and dance in traditional Czech attire every Sunday, and definitely don't miss a tour of the **castles.** *Trasa A* leads you through Renaissance hallways, through the old chapel, and under extravagant ceilings; *trasa B* leads through rooms decorated in later styles. (Open Tu-Su 9-noon and 1-5pm. Tours 60Kč, students 30Kč.) You can rent a **rowboat** from **Půjčovná lodí,** on the shore, to view the castle and town from the swan-filled lake. (Open June 20-Aug. daily 10am-8pm. 20Kč per 30min.) In winter, look out for midnight ice hockey. **Buses** running between Brno and České Budějovice stop at Telč (2hr., 8 per day, 70-80Kč). From the station, follow the walkway and turn right on Tyršova, then left on Masarykovo, and pass under the archway on the right to reach the square, **Nám. Zachariáše z Hradce.** The **tourist office,** Nám. Zachariáše z Hradce 10, books private rooms. (☎724 31 45; info@telc-etc.cz; www.telc-etc.cz. Open M-F 8am-6pm, Sa-Su 9am-6pm.)

The historic capital of North Moravia, **Olomouc** (OH-lo-mohts) is a university city that embodies the best of the Czech Republic. The masterfully rebuilt town center offers a charming network of cobblestone paths, triangular squares, and Baroque architecture with a dose of modern sleekness. In the middle of **Horní náměstí** in the center of town, the massive 1378 **town hall** towers above cafes and restaurants. From the square, follow 28 října to the **Church of St. Maurice,** whose blockish tower and ramparts seem more suited to a castle. From the church, turn right on Pekařská, follow it as it turns into Denisova and 1. máje, and turn left on Dómská to reach **Václavské nám.** The square houses the **St. Wenceslas Cathedral,** a church that both Mother Theresa and the Pope have visited on account of its beauty, and the **Přemysl Palace,** one of the few buildings in the country with obvious remains of Romanesque architecture. **Hostel Betánie,** Wurmova 5, has cheap beds and clean rooms 5min. from the square. Take tram #2 or 4 for three stops to U Domu on 1. máje; Wurmova is on the left. (☎523 38 60. Doubles 200Kč per person.) At night Olomouc's student hordes converge on **Depo No. 9,** Nam. Republiky 1, which hosts live bands every few nights. **Buses** (90min., 10 per day, 82Kč) and **trains** (90min., 7-8 per day, 66Kč) run to Olomouc from Brno. From the train station, take any tram five stops to the town center.

DENMARK
(DANMARK)

DANISH KRONER

US$1 = 8.31KR	10KR = US$1.20
CDN$1 = 5.45KR	10KR = CDN$1.84
UK£1 = 11.85KR	10KR = UK£0.84
IR£1 = 9.46KR	10KR = IR£1.06
AUS$1 = 4.30KR	10KR = AUS$2.33
NZ$1 = 3.56KR	10KR = NZ$2.81
ZAR1 = 0.99KR	10KR = ZAR10.07
EUR€1 = 7.45KR	10KR = EUR€1.34

PHONE CODE	**Country code:** 45. **International dialing prefix:** 00. Denmark has no city codes. From outside Denmark, dial int'l dialing prefix (see inside back cover) + 45 + local number.

Like Thumbelina, the heroine of native son Hans Christian Andersen's fairy tales, Denmark (pop. 5.3 million; 43,094 sq. km) has a tremendous personality crammed into a tiny body. Danes delight in their eccentric traditions, such as burning witches in effigy on Midsummer's Eve and eating pickled herring on New Year's Day. Although the Danes are justifiably proud of their fertile farmlands and pristine beaches, their sense of self-criticism is reflected in the Danish literary canon: the more famous voices are Andersen, Søren Kierkegaard, and Isak Dinesen. Wedged between Sweden and Germany, the country is the geographic and cultural bridge between Scandinavia and continental Europe. With its Viking past behind it, Denmark now has one of the most comprehensive social welfare structures in the world, and liberal immigration policies have diversified the erstwhile homogeneous population. Today, Denmark has a progressive youth culture that beckons travelers to the hip pub scene in Copenhagen.

FACTS AND FIGURES

Official Name: Kingdom of Denmark.
Capital: Copenhagen.
Major Cities: Aalborg, Århus, Odense.
Population: 5,360,000.
Land Area: 43,075 sq. km.

Climate: Temperate, overcast with humidity; mild winters and cool summers.
Languages: Danish, Faroese, Greenlandic.
Religions: Evangelical Lutheran (91%), other Protestant/Roman Catholic (2%).

DISCOVER DENMARK

Begin in chic, progressive **Copenhagen** (p. 271), where you can cruise the canals, party until dawn, and ponder Kierkegaard. Daytrip north to the fabulous **Louisiana** museum and **Elsinore** (p. 278), Hamlet's castle, or shoot south to **Roskilde** (p. 278) and the fascinating Viking Ship Museum (p. 278). If you time it right, you'll hit the massive Roskilde Festival, when rock takes over the city. For the best beaches in Denmark, ferry to the island of **Bornholm** (p. 279). Move west over the Storebæltsbro bridge to Funen and **Odense** (p. 280), the hometown of Hans Christian Andersen, then head south to the stunning 16th-century castle **Egeskov Slot** (p. 281). From the southern end of Funen, hop on a ferry to the idyllic island of **Ærø** (p. 281), a throwback to the Denmark of several centuries ago. Cross the Lillebælt to Jutland,

DENMARK

where laid-back **Århus** (p. 282) delights with students and culture, then play with blocks at nearby **Legoland** (p. 284). On your way back down south, stop in historic **Ribe** (p. 285).

ESSENTIALS

DOCUMENTS AND FORMALITIES

VISAS. Visas are generally not required for tourist stays under three months; South African citizens are the exception.

EMBASSIES. Foreign embassies are in **Copenhagen** (p. 271). For Danish embassies at home: **Australia,** 15 Hunter St., Yarralumla, ACT 2600 (☎(02) 62 73 21 95; fax 62 73 38 64); **Canada,** 47 Clarence St., Suite 450, Ottawa, ON K1N 9K1 (☎613-562-1811; fax 613-562-1812; www.tradecomm.com/danish); **Ireland,** 121 St. Stephen's Green, Dublin 2 (☎(01) 475 64 04; fax 478 45 36; www.denmark.ie); **New Zealand,** (consulate), Level 7, 45 Johnston St., Wellington, P. O. Box 10-874 (☎(04) 471 05 20; fax 471 05 21); **South Africa,** 8th fl., Sanlam Centre, corner of Pretorius and Andries St., P.O. Box 2942, Pretoria 0001 (☎(012) 322 05 95; fax 322 05 96); **UK,** 55 Sloane St., London SW1X 9SR (☎(020) 73 33 02 00 or 72 35 12 55; fax 73 33 02 70; www.denmark.org.uk); **US,** 3200 Whitehaven St. NW, Washington, D.C. 20008-3683 (☎202-234-4300; fax 202-328-1470; www.denmarkemb.org).

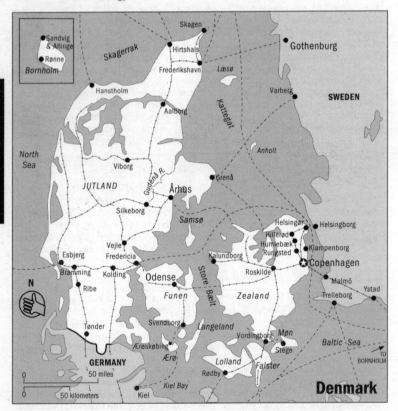

TRANSPORTATION

BY PLANE. The airport in Copenhagen (p. 271) handles international flights from cities around the world, mostly by **SAS, Delta, United, British Airways, Air France, KLM, Lufthansa,** and **Swissair.** Billund Airport (☎ 76 50 50 50; www.billund-airport.dk) in Jutland handles flights to other European cities. SAS (Scandinavian Airlines; US ☎ 800-437-5804; www.scandinavian.net), the national airline company, offers youth, spouse, and senior discounts to some destinations.

BY TRAIN AND BY BUS. **Eurail** is valid on all state-run **DSB** routes. The *buy-in-Scandinavia* **Scanrail Pass** allows five days within 15 (1540kr, under 26 1155kr) or 21 consecutive days (2390kr/1795kr) of unlimited rail travel through Denmark, Norway, Sweden, and Finland, as well as many 25-50% discounted ferry and bus rides. This differs from the *buy-outside-Scandinavia* **Scanrail Pass,** which allows five days within two months (US$204, under 26 US$153), 10 days within two months (US$310/$233), or 21 consecutive days (US$360/$270). For contact information, check out www.scanrail.com. Remote towns are typically served by **buses** from the nearest train station. The national **bus** network is also very reliable and fairly cheap. You can take buses or trains over the new Østersund bridge from Copenhagen to Malmö, Sweden.

BY FERRY. **Railpasses** earn discounts or free rides on many Scandinavian ferries. The free *Vi Rejser* newspaper, at tourist offices, can help you sort out the dozens of smaller ferries that serve Denmark's outlying islands. For information on ferries from Copenhagen to Norway, Sweden, and Poland, see p. 271. For more on connections from Jutland to England, Sweden, and Norway, see p. 282; from Bornholm to Sweden and Germany, see p. 279.

BY CAR. Roads are toll-free, except for the **Storebæltsbro** (Great Belt Bridge; 210kr) and the **Øresund bridge** (around 300kr). Car rental is generally around US$75 per day, plus insurance and a per-kilometer fee; to rent a car, you must be at least 20 years old (in some cases even 25). Speed limits are 50km per hr. (30mph) in urban areas, 80km per hr. (50mph) on highways, and 110km per hr. (68mph) on motorways. Service centers for motorists, called **Info-terias,** are spaced along Danish highways. Gas averages 6.50kr per liter. Watch out for bikes, which have the right-of-way. For more information on driving in Denmark, contact the **Forenede Danske Motorejere (FDM),** Firskovvej 32, Box 500, DK-2800 Lyngby (☎ 70 13 30 40; fax 45 27 09 33; www.fdm.dk).

BY BIKE AND BY THUMB. Flat terrain, well-marked bike routes, bike paths in the countryside, and bike lanes in towns and cities make Denmark a cyclist's dream. You can rent bikes (40-55kr per day) from some tourist offices, rental shops, and a few train stations. The **Dansk Cyklist Førbund** (Danish Cycle Federation), Rømersg. 7, 1362 Copenhagen K (☎ 33 32 31 21; fax 33 32 76 83; www.dcf.dk), can hook you up with longer-term rentals. For information on bringing your bike on a train (which costs 50kr or less), pick up *Bikes and Trains* at any train station. Hitchhiking is legal in Denmark, but *Let's Go* does not recommend hitchhiking.

TOURIST SERVICES AND MONEY

EMERGENCY Police, Ambulance, and Fire: ☎ 112.

TOURIST OFFICES. Contact the main tourist board in Denmark at Vesterbrog. 6D, 1620 Copenhagen V (☎ 33 11 14 15; fax 33 93 14 16; dt@dt.dk; www.visitdenmark.dt.dk).

MONEY. The Danish unit of currency is the **kroner** (kr), divided into 100 *øre*. The easiest way to get cash is from ATMs: Cirrus and PLUS cash cards are widely accepted, and many machines give advances on credit cards. Denmark has a high cost of living; expect to spend from US$30 (hostels and supermarkets) to US$60

DENMARK

(cheap hotels and restaurants) per day. There are no hard and fast rules, but it's always polite to round up to the nearest 10kr in restaurants and for taxis. In general, service at restaurants is included in the bill. Tipping up to 15% is becoming common in Copenhagen. Denmark has one of the highest VATs in Europe, a flat 25% on just about everything except food. You can get a VAT refund upon leaving the country if you have spent at least US$95 in one store.

BUSINESS HOURS. Shop hours are normally Monday to Thursday from about 9 or 10am to 6pm, and Friday until 7 or 8pm; they are also usually open Saturday mornings (Copenhagen shops stay open all day Saturday). Regular banking hours are Monday to Wednesday and Friday 9:30am-4pm, Thursday 9:30am-6pm.

COMMUNICATION

MAIL. Mailing a postcard/letter to Australia, Canada, New Zealand, the US, or South Africa costs 5.50kr; to elsewhere in Europe, 4.50kr. Domestic mail costs 4kr.

TELEPHONES. There are no city codes; include all digits for local *and* international calls. Buy phone cards at post offices or kiosks (30 units 30kr; 53 units 50kr; 110 units 100kr). For domestic directory information, call ☎118; international information, ☎113; collect calls, ☎141. International direct dial numbers include: **AT&T,** ☎80 01 00 10; **British Telecom** ☎0800 89 00 45; **Canada Direct,** ☎80 01 00 11; **Ireland Direct,** ☎80 01 03 53; **MCI,** ☎80 01 00 22; **Sprint,** ☎80 01 08 77; **Telecom New Zealand,** ☎80 01 00 64; **Telkom South Africa,** ☎80 01 00 27; and **Telstra Australia,** ☎80 01 00 61.

LANGUAGE. Danish. The Danish add *æ* (like the "e" in "egg"), ø (like the "i" in "first"), and å (sometimes written as *aa;* like the "o" in "lord") to the end of the alphabet; thus Århus would follow Viborg in an alphabetical listing of cities. Knowing *ikke* ("not") will help you figure out such signs as "No smoking" *(ikke-ryger); aben/lukket* (O-ben/loock-eh) means open/closed. Nearly all Danes speak flawless English, but a few Danish words might help break the ice: try *skal* (skoal), or "cheers." Danish has a distinctive glottal stop known as a *stød.* For useful Danish words, see p. 982.

ACCOMMODATIONS AND CAMPING

Denmark's 101 **HI youth hostels** *(vandrerhjem)* are cheap (less than 100kr per night; nonmembers add 25kr), well-run, and have no age limit. The one- to five-star rating system doesn't take lovely settings, friendly owners, or serendipitous encounters into account, but higher-rated hostels may have in-room bathrooms and longer opening hours. Sheets cost about 45-50kr more. Breakfast buffets usually run 45kr. Reception desks normally take a break from noon to 4pm and close for the day between 9 and 11pm. Reservations are required in winter and highly recommended in summer, especially near beaches. For more information, contact the **Danish Youth Hostel Association** (☎31 31 36 12; fax 31 31 36 26; ldv@danhostel.dk; www.danhostel.dk), or grab a *Danhostel* booklet. Denmark's **hotels** are generally expensive (300-850kr per night). Many tourist offices book rooms in private homes (125-175kr), which are often in the suburbs. Denmark's 525 official **campgrounds** (about 60kr per person) rank from one-star (toilets and drinking water) to three-star (showers and laundry) to five-star (swimming, restaurants, and stoves). You'll either need a **Camping Card Scandinavia,** available at all campgrounds and valid for one year (75kr), or a **Camping Card International.** If you only plan to camp for a night, you can buy a 24hr. pass for 20kr. The **Danish Camping Council** *(Campingradet;* ☎39 27 80 44) sells the campground handbook, *Camping Denmark,* and passes. Sleeping in train stations, in parks, and on public property is illegal.

FOOD AND DRINK

A "Danish" in Denmark is a *wienerbrød* ("Viennese bread"), found in bakeries alongside other flaky treats. For more substantial fare, Danes favor open-faced sandwiches called *smørrebrød.* For cheap eats, look for *dagens ret* (lunch specials) and *spis alt du kan* or *tag selv buffet* (all-you-can-eat buffets).

National beers are Carlsberg and Tuborg; bottled brew tends to be cheaper. A popular alcohol alternative is *snaps* or *aquavit*, a clear distilled liquor flavored with fiery spices, usually served chilled and unmixed. Many *vegetarret* (vegetarian) options are the result of Indian and Mediterranean influences, but *grøntsaker* (salads and veggies) can be found on most menus. For more on being veggie in Denmark, contact Dansk Vegetarforening, Borups Allé 131, 2000 Frederiksberg (☎38 34 24 48).

HOLIDAYS AND FESTIVALS

Holidays: Easter (Mar. 31); Common Prayer Day (Apr. 26); Ascension Day (May 9); Whit Sunday and Monday (May 19-20); Constitution Day (June 5); Christmas (Dec. 24-26); New Year's Eve (Dec. 31).

Festivals: Danes celebrate **Fastelavn** (Carneval) in Feb. and Mar. In May, the **Copenhagen Jazz Festival** does a week of concerts, many free. The **Roskilde Festival** is an immense open-air music festival held in Roskilde in June.

COPENHAGEN (KØBENHAVN)

Despite the swan ponds and cobblestone clichés that Hans Christian Andersen's fairy-tale imagery brings to mind, Denmark's capital is a fast-paced modern city that offers cafes, nightlife, and style to rival those of the great European cities. But if you still crave Andersen's Copenhagen, the *Lille Havfrue* (Little Mermaid), Tivoli, and Nyhavn's Hanseatic gingerbread houses are also yours to discover.

▐ TRANSPORTATION

Flights: Kastrup Airport (☎32 47 47 47). S-trains connect the airport to Central Station (12min., every 20min., 18kr).

Trains: Trains stop at **Hovedbanegården** (Central Station). Domestic travel ☎70 13 14 15; international ☎70 13 14 16. To: **Berlin** (9hr.; 1 per day; 895kr, under 26 580kr); **Hamburg** (4½hr.; 5 per day; 485kr, under 26 320kr); **Oslo** (9hr.; 3 per day; 740kr/530kr); **Stockholm** (5½hr.; 4-5 per day; 700kr/540kr). **Reservations mandatory** (20kr). For cheaper travel to **Gothenburg, Stockholm, Oslo,** and **Östersund,** buy a **Scanrabat** ticket a week ahead; you must reserve.

Ferries: Scandinavian Seaways (☎33 42 33 42) departs daily at 5pm for **Oslo** (16hr.; 480-735kr; under 26 315-570kr; 50% Eurail and Scanrail discount). Trains to **Sweden** cross over on the **Helsingør-Helsingborg** ferry at no extra charge. Hourly **hydrofoils** (☎33 12 80 88) to **Malmö** go from Havnegade, at the end of Nyhavn (40min., 19-49kr). Both **Flyvebådene** and **Pilen** run hourly hydrofoils to Malmö from 9am-11pm (45min., 50kr). **Polferries** (☎33 11 46 45) set out Su, M, and W 8am, and Th and F 7:30pm from Nordre Toldbod, 12A (off Esplanaden) to **Świnoujście, Poland** (10hr., 340kr; ISIC 285kr).

Public Transportation: Bus info ☎36 13 14 15 (daily 7am-9:30pm); **train** info ☎33 14 17 01 (daily 7am-9pm). **Buses** and **S-trains** (subways and suburban trains; M-Sa 5am-12:30am, Su 6am-12:30am) operate on a zone system; 2-zone **tickets** run 13kr; add 6kr per additional zone. The cheaper **rabatkort** (rebate card), available from kiosks and bus drivers, gets you 10 "clips," each good for 1 journey within a specified number of zones. The blue 2-zone *rabatkort* (80kr) can be clipped more than once for longer trips. Tickets and clips allow 1hr. of transfers. The **24hr. pass** grants unlimited bus and train transport in greater Copenhagen (70kr); buy at the Tivoli tourist office or any train station. **Railpasses,** including **Eurail,** are good on S-trains but not buses. **Night buses** run on more limited routes during the remaining hours and charge double fare. The **Copenhagen Card,** sold in hotels, tourist offices, and train stations, grants unlimited travel in North Zealand, discounts on ferries to Sweden, and admission to most sights (175kr per 24hr., 295kr per 48hr., 395kr per 72hr.; children ages 10-15 half-price), but isn't always worth it unless you plan to ride the bus frequently and see several museums in one day.

Copenhagen is set to open a newly renovated **metro** system in 2002, so metropolitan transportation should become even more efficient.

Taxis: ☎35 35 35 35, 38 77 77 77, or 38 10 10 10. Base fare 22kr; add 8kr per km 7am-4pm, 10kr per km 4pm-7am. From Hovedbanegården to airport costs 150kr.

Bike Rental: City Bike lends bikes for free. Deposit 20kr at any of 150 bike racks city-wide and retrieve the coin upon return at any rack. **Københavns Cykler,** Reventlows-gade 11, in Hovedbanegården (☎33 33 86 13), rents for 50kr per day, 90kr per 2 days, 125kr per 3 days; 300kr deposit. Open July-Aug. M-F 8am-5:30pm, Sa 9am-1pm; Su 10am-1pm; Sept.-June closed Su.

Hitchhiking: Use It has ride boards (see Tourist Office, below). *Let's Go* does not recommend hitchhiking.

■ ORIENTATION

Copenhagen lies on the east coast of the island of **Zealand** (Sjælland), across the sound (Øresund) from Malmö, Sweden. The 17-mile **Øresund bridge and tunnel,** opened July 1, 2000, established the first "fixed link" between the two countries. Copenhagen's **Hovedbanegården** (Central Station) lies near the city's heart. North of the station, **Vesterbrogade** passes **Tivoli** and **Rådhuspladsen** (the central square and terminus of most bus lines), then cuts through the city center as **Strøget** (STROY-yet), the world's longest pedestrian thoroughfare. The main pedestrian areas are **Orstedsparken, Botanisk Have,** and **Rosenborg Have.**

■ PRACTICAL INFORMATION

TOURIST, FINANCIAL, AND LOCAL SERVICES

Tourist Office: Use It, Rådhusstr. 13 (☎33 73 06 20; www.useit.dk). From the station, follow Vesterbrog., cross Rådhuspladsen onto Frederiksbergg., and turn right on Rådhusstr. Indispensable and geared toward budget travelers. Pick up a copy of *Play Time.* Finds lodgings and holds mail. Open mid-June to mid-Sept. daily 9am-7pm; mid-Sept. to mid-June M-W 11am-4pm, Th 11am-6pm, F 11am-2pm.

Budget Travel: Wasteels Rejser, Skoubog. 6 (☎33 14 46 33). Open M-F 9am-7pm, Sa 10am-3pm. **Kilroy Travels,** Skinderg. 28 (☎33 11 00 44). Open M-F 10am-5:30pm, Sa 10am-2pm.

Embassies: Australia (consulate), Strand Boulevarden 122, 5th fl. (☎39 29 20 77; fax 39 29 60 77). **Canada,** Kristen Bernikowsg. 1 (☎33 48 32 00; fax 33 48 32 21). **Ireland,** Østerbaneg. 21 (☎35 42 32 33; fax 35 43 18 58). New Zealanders should contact the **New Zealand** embassy in Brussels (p. 118). **South Africa,** Gammel Vartovvej 8 (☎39 18 01 55; fax 39 18 40 06). **UK,** Kastelsvej 36-40 (☎35 44 52 00; fax 35 44 52 93). **US,** Dag Hammarskjölds Allé 24 (☎35 55 31 44; fax 35 43 02 23).

Currency Exchange: Forex, in Hovedbanegården. 25kr commission on cash, 15kr per traveler's check. Open daily 8am-9pm.

Luggage Storage: Free at **Use It** tourist office and most hostels. At **Hovedbanegården,** 25-35kr per 24hr. Open M-Sa 5:30am-1am and Su 6am-1am.

Laundromats: Look for **Vascomat** and **Møntvask** chains. At Borgerg. 2, Nansensg. 39, and Istedg. 45. Wash and dry 40-50kr. Most open daily 7am-9pm.

Gay and Lesbian Services: National Association for Gay Men and Women, Teglgårdsstr. 13 (☎33 13 19 48). Open M-F 5-7pm. The monthly *Gay and Lesbian Guide to Copenhagen* lists clubs, cafes, and organizations, and is available at several gay clubs (p. 277). Also check out www.copenhagen-gay-life.dk, www.gayonline.dk., or www.panbladet.dk.

EMERGENCY AND COMMUNICATIONS

Emergency: ☎112. **Police** headquarters are at Polititorvet (☎33 14 14 48).

Pharmacy: Steno Apotek, Vesterbrog. 6c (☎33 14 82 66). Open 24hr.; ring the bell.

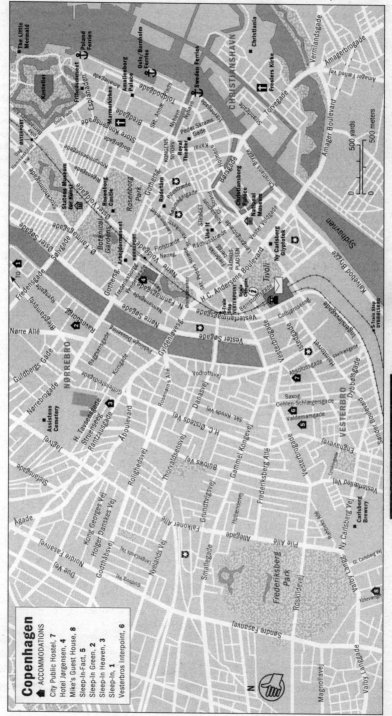

Copenhagen

▲ ACCOMMODATIONS
City Public Hostel, 7
Hotel Jørgensen, 4
Mike's Guest House, 8
Sleep-In-Fact, 5
Sleep-In Green, 2
Sleep-In Heaven, 3
Sleep-In, 1
Vesterbros Interpoint, 6

DENMARK

Medical Assistance: Doctors on Call (☎33 93 63 00). Open M-F 8am-4pm; after hours, call ☎38 88 60 41. Visits 120-350kr. **Emergency rooms** at **Sundby Hospital,** Kastrup 63 (☎32 34 32 34), and **Bispebjerg Hospital,** Bispebjerg Bakke 23 (☎35 31 35 31).

Internet Access: Free at **Use It** and at **Copenhagen Hovedbibliotek** (Central Library), Krystalg. 15 (☎33 73 60 60). Open M-F 10am-7pm, Sa 10am-2pm.

Post Office: In Hovedbanegården. Address mail to be held: First name SURNAME, Post Denmark, Hovedbangardens Posthus, Hovedbanegarden, **1570** Kobenhavn V. Mail also held at **Use It.** Address mail to be held: First name SURNAME, *Poste Restante,* Use It, 13 Rådhusstræde, **1466** Copenhagen K.

▌ ACCOMMODATIONS AND CAMPING

Comfortable and inexpensive accommodations can be hard to find in the city center, where most hostels are like enormous warehouses packed with 50 or more beds. On the upside, many hostels feature a lively social scene. For better accommodations try the Danhostels outside the city center or stay at the five-star hostel in nearby Ishoj. During holidays (such as the national vacation in early August) and the largest festivals—especially Karneval (mid-May), Roskilde (late June), and Copenhagen Jazz (late July)—reserve rooms well in advance.

▨ **Sleep-In-Fact,** Valdemarsg. 14 (☎33 79 67 79; info@sleep-in-fact.dk). Go out the back exit of Hovedbanegården, turn left onto Vesterbrogade, and left onto Valdemarstr. Clean, comfortable rooms in a new factory-turned-hostel. Free lockers. Breakfast 30kr. Sheets 30kr. Reception 24hr. Lockout 10am-4pm. Open June 11-Sept. Dorms 110kr.

Hotel Jørgensen, Rømersg. 11 (☎33 13 81 86), 25min. from Hovedbanegården and 5min. from Strøget. S-train: Nørreport. Go right along Vendersgade; it's on the 2nd corner on the left. Breakfast included. Sheets 30kr. Reception 24hr. Lockout 11am-3pm. No dorm reservations. Dorms 120kr; singles 400kr; doubles from 500kr; quads 640kr.

Vesterbros Interpoint, Vesterbros KFUM (YMCA), Valdemarsg. 15 (☎33 31 15 74). From Central Station, walk west on Vesterbrog. and turn left. Friendly staff and atmosphere. Kitchen. Breakfast 25kr. Sheets 15kr. Reception 8:30-11:30am, 3:30-5:30pm, and 8pm-12:30am. Curfew 12:30am. Open late June to early Aug. Dorms 85kr.

City Public Hostel, Absalonsg. 8 (☎33 31 20 70), in the Vesterbro Youth Center. From the station, walk away from the Rådhuspladsen on Vesterbrog. and turn left on Absalonsg. Prime location. Happening lounge and BBQ. Kitchen. Breakfast 20kr. Sheets 30kr. Reception 24hr. Open early May to late Aug. Dorms 120kr.

Sleep-In Heaven, Struenseeg. 7 (☎35 35 46 48; sleepinheaven@get2net.dk), in Nørrebro. Take bus #8 (dir. Tingbjerg) 5 stops to Rantzausg.; continue in the same direction as the bus, turn right on Kapelvej, left on Tavsensg., and left on (poorly marked) Struenseeg. Lively social atmosphere close to hip Skt. Hans Torv nightlife. Internet 20kr per 30min. Reception 24hr. Dorms 100kr; doubles 400kr.

Sleep-In, Blegdamsvej 132 (☎35 26 50 59). Bus #1, 6, or 14: Trianglen. S-train: Østerport. Facing the station, go left, walk 10min. up Hammerskjölds (across the square from the 7-11). Near the city center and Østerbro nightlife. Quantity over privacy at this popular and noisy warehouse of a hostel. Kitchen. Internet. Sheets 30kr. Reception 24hr. Lockout noon-4pm. Open July 28-Aug. 31. No reservations. Dorms 90kr.

Sleep-In Green, Ravnsborgg. 18, Baghuset (☎35 37 77 77). Take bus #16 from the station to Nørrebrog, and then walk down Ravnsborgg. Cozy, eco-friendly dorms outside the city center. Organic breakfast 30kr. Sheets 30kr. Reception 24hr. Check-out noon. Lockout noon-4pm. Open mid-May to mid-Oct. Dorms 95kr.

Mike's Guest House, Kirkevænget 13 (☎36 45 65 40), 10min. by bus or train from Hovedbanegården. Call ahead. Clean, spacious rooms—some with private balconies—in his own home. Quiet neighborhood. Singles 200kr; doubles 290kr; triples 400kr.

Ajax, Bavnehøj Allé 30 (☎33 21 24 56). S-train A: Sydhavn. Walk north on Enghavevej (with the Netto to your left and the train tracks to your right), turn left on Bavnehøj Allé, and look for signs on the right. Or, take bus #10 (dir. Vigerslev) and walk up Bavnehoj Allé.

Kitchen. Breakfast 20kr. Sheets 20kr. Reception 8am-midnight. Open July-Aug. Dorms 60kr; doubles 200kr; triples 225kr. Camping 50-55kr.

København Vandrerhjem Bellahøj (HI), Herbergvejen 8 (☎38 28 97 15; bellahoj@danhostel.dk), in Bellahøj. Take bus #11 (dir. Bellahoj/Bronshoj Torv) from the station to Primulavej. Large, modern hostel far from the city center. Breakfast included. Sheets 35kr. Wash 25kr, dry 10kr. Reception 24hr. Open Mar. to mid-Jan. Dorms 95kr; doubles 250kr.

Bellahøj Camping, Hvidkildevej 66 (☎38 10 11 50), 5km from the city center. Take bus #11 to Bellahøj" Shower included. Kitchen. Cafe and market. Reception 24hr. Open June-Aug. 57kr per person; tents available for extra charge.

🍴 FOOD

The Vikings once slobbered down mutton and salted fish in Copenhagen; today, you can seek out more refined offerings. Around **Kongens Nytorv**, elegant cafes serve sandwiches *(smørrebrød)* for around 35kr. All-you-can-eat buffets (40-70kr) are popular, especially at Turkish, Indian, and Italian restaurants. **Fakta** and **Netto super-markets** are budget fantasies; there are several around the Norreport area (S-Train: Norreport.) **Open-air markets** provide fresh fruits and veggies; try the one at **Israels Plads** near Nørreport Station. (Open M-Th 9am-5:30pm, F 9am-6:30pm, Sa 9am-3pm.) **Fruit stalls** line Strøget and the side streets to the north.

Nyhavns Færgekro, Nyhavn 5. Upscale fisherman's cottage atmosphere along the canal. Lunch on 10 varieties of all-you-can-eat herring (89kr). Open daily 9:30am-11:30pm.

Café Norden, Østerg. 61, on Strøget and Nicolaj Plads, in sight of the fountain. A French-style cafe with the best vantage point on Strøget. Crepes 59-62kr; sandwiches 59-64kr; pastries 15-40kr. Open daily 9am-midnight.

Café Europa, Amagertorv 1, on Nicolaj Plads opposite Café Norden. If Norden is the place to see, trendy Europa is the place to be seen. Sandwiches 23-44kr. Beer 45kr per pint. Great coffee. Open M-W 9am-midnight, F-Sa 9am-1am, and Su 10am-7pm.

Kafe Kys, Læderstr. 7, on a quiet street running south of and parallel to Strøget. Sand-wiches and salads 48-75kr. Beer 35kr. Open M-Th 11am-1am, F-Sa 11am-2am (kitchen closes 10pm), Su noon-10pm.

Den Grønne Kælder, Pilestr. 48. Popular, classy vegetarian and vegan dining. Hummus 35-45kr. Veggie burgers 35kr. Meals 35-80kr. Open M-Sa 11am-10pm.

👁 SIGHTS

Compact Copenhagen is best seen by foot or bike; pick up a free **city bike** (p. 271) to survey its stunning architecture. Various **tours** are detailed in Use It's *Play Time* and tourist office brochures. The squares along the lively pedestrian **Strøget**, which divides the city center, are **Nytorv, Nicolaj Plads**, and **Kungens Nytorv**. Opposite Kungens Nytorv is **Nyhavn**, the "new port" where Hans Christian Andersen wrote his first fairy tale, lined with Hanseatic houses and sailing boats. There are several canal tours, but **Netto boats** offers the best value (late Apr. to mid-Sept. every 20min. 10am-5pm; 20kr). **Bus #6** travels through Vesterbro, Rådhuspladsen, alongside Strøget, and on to Østerbro, acting as a sight-seeing guide to the city

CITY CENTER. The first sight you'll see as you exit the train station is **Tivoli**, the famed 19th-century amusement park, which delights with botanical gardens, marching toy soldiers, and rides. Wednesday and weekend nights culminate with music and fireworks. An increasingly popular Christmas market is open at Tivoli mid-Nov. to mid-Dec. *(Vesterbrog. 3. Open late Apr. to mid-Sept. Su-Th 11am-midnight, F-Sa 11am-1am. Children's rides open noon, others 11:30am. 50kr; ride tickets 10kr, 1-5 tickets per ride. Tour day pass 180kr.)* From Hovedbanegården, turn right on Bernstorffsg. and left on Tietgensg. to partake of the ancient and Impressionist art and sculpture at the beautiful ◼**Ny Carlsberg Glyptoket**. *(Dantes Plads 7. Open Tu-Su 10am-4pm. 30kr; free W and Su or with ISIC.)* Continue along Tietgensg., which becomes Stormg., to dive into Denmark's Viking treasures and other tidbits of its cultural history at the

National Museum. *(Ny Vestergade 10. Open Tu-Su 10am-5pm. 40kr, students 30kr; W free.)*
Christiansborg Castle, Prins Jørgens Gård, features subterranean ruins, royal reception rooms, and the *Folketing* (Parliament) chambers. To get there, continue down Tietgensg. from the city center until you cross the canal. *(Tours May-Sept. daily 11am and 3pm; June-Aug. daily 11am, 1 and 3pm; Oct.-Apr. Tu-Th and Sa-Su 11am and 3pm. 40kr. Ruins 20kr, students 15kr. Ask about free Parliament tours.)*

CHRISTIANSHAVN. In the southern section of Christianshavn, the "free city" of **Christiania,** founded in 1971 by youthful squatters in abandoned military barracks, is inhabited by a thriving group of artists and alterna-thinkers promoting 70's activism and free love. During Christmas, there is a fabulous market with goods from all over the world. Exercise caution in the **Pusher Street** area, aptly named as the site of many hash and marijuana sales. Always ask before taking pictures, **never** take pictures on Pusher St. itself, and exercise caution in the area at night. Climb the golden spire of **Vor Frelsers Kirke** (Our Savior's Church) for a great view. *(Sankt Annæg. 29. Turn left off Prinsesseg. Church open daily Mar.-Nov. 9am-4:30pm, Dec.-Feb. 10am-2pm. Free. Tower open Mar.-Nov. 9am-4:30pm. 20kr.)* The area is accessible from Hovedbanegården by bus #8; it stops right at the church.

FREDERIKSTADEN. Edvard Eriksen's **den Lille Havfrue** (The Little Mermaid), a tiny but touristed statue at the opening of the harbor, honors favorite son Hans Christian Andersen. *(S-train: Østerport. Turn left out of the station, left on Folke Bernadottes Allé, go right and follow the path bordering the canal, go left up the stairs and then right along the street. Open daily 6am-dusk.)* Retrace your steps and turn left to cross the moat to **Kastellet,** a 17th-century fortress-turned-park. Cross through Kastellet to the fascinating **Frihedsmuseet** (Museum of Danish Resistance), which chronicles the Nazi occupation from 1940 to 1945. *(At Churchillparken. Open May to mid-Sept. Tu-Sa 10am-4pm, Su 10am-5pm; mid-Sept. to Apr. Tu-Sa 11am-3pm, Su 11am-4pm. 30kr, under 16 free; W free.)* From the museum, walk south down Amalieng. to reach the lovely ■ **Amalienborg Palace,** residence of Queen Margarethe II and the royal family; most of the interior is closed to the public, but you can see the apartments of Christian VII. The changing of the palace guard takes place at noon on the brick plaza. *(Open June-Aug. daily 10am-4pm; May-Oct. daily 10am-4pm; Nov.-Apr. Tu-Su 11am-4pm. 40kr, students 25kr.)* The 19th-century **Marmokirken** (Marble Church), opposite the palace, features Europe's third-largest dome. *(Church open M-Tu and Th-Sa 10:30am-4:30pm, W 10:30am-6:30pm, Su noon-4:30pm; free. Dome 20kr.)* A few blocks north, **Statens Museum for Kunst** (State Museum of Fine Arts) displays an eclectic collection in a beautifully designed building. From the church, head away from Amalienborg, go left on Store Kongensg., turn right on Dronningens Tværg., and take an immediate right and then left onto Sølvg. *(Sølvg. 48-50. ☎ 33 15 32 86. S-train: Norreport. Walk up Ostervolgade. Open Tu and Th-Su 10am-5pm, W until 8pm. 40kr. W Free.)* Opposite the museum, **Rosenborg Slot** (Rosenborg Palace and Gardens) hoards royal treasures, including the ■**crown jewels.** *(Øster Volg. 4A. S-train: Norreport. Walk up Ostervolgade; it's on the left past the intersection. Open May-Sept. daily 10am-4pm; Oct. daily 11am-3pm; Nov.-Apr. Tu-Su 11am-2pm. 50kr, students 30kr.)*

OTHER SIGHTS. A trip to the **Carlsberg Brewery** will reward you with a wealth of ale-related knowledge and, more importantly, free samples. *(Ny Carlsbergvej 140. Take bus #6 west from Rådhuspladsen to Valby Langg. Open Tu-Su 10am-4pm. Free.)* If the breweries haven't confused your senses enough, play with science at the hands-on **Experimentarium** (Danish Science Center). *(Tuborg Havnevej 7. in Hellerup. Take bus #6 north from Rådhuspladsen. Open late June to mid-Aug. daily 10am-5pm; late Aug. to early June M and W-F 9am-5pm, Tu 9am-9pm, Sa-Su 11am-5pm. 85kr, children 60kr.)*

🎵 ENTERTAINMENT

For events, consult *Copenhagen This Week* (free at hostels and tourist offices), or pick up *Use It News* from Use It. The **Royal Theater** is home to the world-famous Royal Danish Ballet; the box office is at Tordenskjoldsgade 7. (Open M-Sa 10am-6pm.) For same-day half-price tickets, head to the **Tivoli ticket office,** Vesterbrog. 3. (☎33 15 10 12. Open mid-Apr. to mid-Sept. daily 9am-9pm;

mid-Sept. to mid-Apr. 9am-7pm. Royal theater tickets available at 4 or 5pm, others at noon.) Call **Arte**, Hvidkildevej 64 (☎38 88 22 22), to ask about student discounts. The relaxed **Kul-Kaféen**, Teglgårdsstr. 5, is a great place to see live performers and get information on music, dance, and theater. (Open M-Sa 11am-midnight.) During the world-class **Copenhagen Jazz Festival** (mid-July; ☎33 93 20 13; www.cjf.dk), the city teems with free outdoor concerts complementing the more refined venues. In anticipation of the summer blowout, the **Swingin' Copenhagen** festival sets the city grooving to traditional jazz (www.swingincopenhagen.dk), and **Copenhagen Autumn Jazz** in early November keeps the city bopping long after summer is gone.

☕ NIGHTLIFE

Copenhagen's weekends often begin on Wednesday, and nights rock until 5am; "morning pubs" that open when the clubs close let you party around the clock. On Thursday, most bars and clubs have reduced covers and cheap drinks. The central pedestrian district reverberates with crowded bars and discos; **Kongens Nytorv** has fancier joints. Many buy beer at a supermarket and head to the boats and cafes of **Nyhavn** for its salty charisma. The **Scala** complex, opposite Tivoli, has many bars and restaurants; students enliven the cheaper bars in the **Nørrebro** area. Copenhagen's gay and lesbian scene is one of Europe's best.

Park, Østerbrog. 79, in Østerbro. Lose your inhibitions and your friends in this enormous club with 2 packed dance floors, live music hall, and rooftop patio. Pints 40kr. Cover F-Sa 50kr. Open Su-W 10am-2am, Th 10am-4am, F-Sa 10am-5am.

Rust, Guldbergsg. 8, in the Nørrebro. Twenty-somethings pack this disco with an underground feel. Long lines by 1am. Cover 50kr; free before 11pm. Open Tu-Su 10pm-5am.

Café Pavillionen, Borgmester Jensens Allé 45, in Fælleaparken. This summer-only outdoor cafe has local bands 8-10pm, plus a disco W-Sa 10pm-5am. On Mondays, enjoy a concert 2:30-5pm, then tango lessons and dancing until midnight.

Enzo, Nørreg. 41. Doll yourself up and dance with a young stylish crowd. Dress code. 21+. Cover 60kr. Open F-Sa 9pm-5:30am.

IN Bar, Nørreg. 1. Drink cheap and dance on speakers. F-Sa cover 150kr, includes open bar. Th-Sa 20+. Open Su-Th 10pm-5am, F-Sa 10pm-10am.

JazzHouse, Niels Hemmingsens G. 10 (www.jazzhouse.dk). Turn left off Strøget from Gammeltorv (closer to Råhuspladsen) and Nytorv. Copenhagen's premier jazz venue makes for a sophisticated and potentially expensive evening. Check the calendar for prices. Concerts Su-Th 8:30pm, F-Sa 9:30pm. Club open midnight-5am.

PAN Club and Café, Knabrostr. 3. Gay cafe, bar, and disco. Homoguide available. Cover W 30kr, F-Sa 50kr; Th no cover. Cafe opens daily 8pm, disco 11pm. Both open late.

Sebastian Bar and Disco, Hyskenstr. 10, off Strøget. The city's best-known gay and lesbian bar. Homoguide available. Happy Hour 5-9pm. Open daily noon-2am.

☕ DAYTRIPS FROM COPENHAGEN

Stunning castles, white sand beaches, and a world-class museum hide in North, Central, and South Zealand, all within easy reach of Copenhagen by train. A northern train route (every 20min.) offers easy access to many attractive daytrips that lie within an hour of Copenhagen in North Zealand.

RUNGSTED AND HUMLEBÆK. In North Zealand, the quiet harbor town of **Rungsted** (30min., 40kr or 4 clips on the blue *rabatkort*), where Karen Blixen (pseudonym Isak Dinesen) wrote *Out of Africa*, houses the author's abode, personal effects, and grave at the **Karen Blixen Museum**, Rungsted Strandvej 111. From the station, turn left on Stationsvej, right on Rungstedsvej, and left on Rungsted Strandvej. (Open May-Sept. daily 10am-5pm; Oct.-Apr. W-F 1-4pm, Sa-Su 11am-4pm. 35kr.) **Humlebæk** (45min., 38.50kr or 4 clips), farther up the coast, distinguishes itself with the spectacular **Louisiana Museum of Modern Art**, named for the three wives (all named Louisa) of the estate's original owner. The museum contains works by Picasso, Warhol, Lichtenstein, Calder, and other 20th-century masters; the building and its sculpture-studded grounds overlooking the sea are themselves worth the trip. Follow signs 1½km north from the Humlebæk station or snag bus #388. (Open Th-Tu 10am-5pm, W 10am-10pm. 60kr, students 52kr.)

HELSINGØR AND HORNBÆK. At the end of the northern line lies **Helsingør** (1hr.), evidence of the Danish monarchy's fondness for lavish architecture. In a region famous for castles, the most famous is the 15th-century **Kronborg Slot** in Helsingør, also known as **Elsinore,** the setting for Shakespeare's *Hamlet* (although neither the historical "Amled" nor the Bard ever visited Kronborg). Viking chief Holger Danske is buried in the castle's spooky dungeon; legend has it that he still rises to face any threat to Denmark's safety. The castle also houses the **Danish Maritime Museum,** which contains the world's oldest sea biscuit, from 1853. From the train station, turn left and follow the signs on the waterfront to the castle. (Open May-Sept. daily 10:30am-5pm; Apr. and Oct. Tu-Su 11am-4pm; Nov.-Mar. Tu-Su 11am-3pm. 60kr.) The **tourist office,** Havnepladsen 3, is housed inside **Kulturhuset;** the entrance is around the corner. (☎49 21 13 33. Open mid-June to Aug. M-Th 9am-5pm, F-Sa 10am-6pm, Su 10am-3pm; Sept. to mid-June M-F 9am-4pm, Sa 10am-1pm.) **Hornbæk** offers beautiful beaches where you can see Danes at their aesthetic best. There's a wild **harbor festival** on the fourth weekend in July. **Bus** #340 and the **train** outside the station run from Helsingør to Hornbæk (20min., 20kr).

HILLERØD AND FREDENSBORG. Another northern route brings you to **Hillerød** (at the end of S-train lines A and E via Lyngby; 40min., 42kr), home of the moated **Frederiksborg Slot,** arguably the most impressive of North Zealand's castles, with exquisite gardens and brick ramparts. Free concerts are given Thursdays at 1:30pm on the famous 1610 **Esaias Compenius organ** in the chapel. To get there from the station, cross the street onto Vibekeg. and follow the signs. (Open daily Apr.-Oct. 10am-3pm; Nov.-Mar. 11am-3pm. 40kr, students 10kr.) A final stop on the northern castle tour is **Fredensborg Castle,** on the "Lille Nord" rail line connecting Hillerød and Helsingør, at the Fredensborg stop. Built in 1722, the castle still serves as the spring and fall royal residence. (Palace and gardens open July 7-Aug. 5. Mandatory tours every 15-30min. 1-4:30pm; 30kr. Gardens free.) Sleep near the royals and enjoy a fantastic palace garden view at **Fredensborg Youth Hostel (HI),** Østrupvej 3, 1km from the train station. (☎48 48 03 15. Sheets 45kr. Reception 7am-9pm. Dorms 95kr; singles 185-210kr; doubles 260-325kr; triples 335-400kr.)

ROSKILDE. In Central Zealand, Roskilde (25-30min., 38.50kr or 4 clips) served as Denmark's first capital when King Harald Bluetooth built the country's first Christian church here in 980. Several Danish monarchs repose in the ornate sarcophagi of **Roskilde Domkirke.** (Open Apr.-Sept. M-F 9am-4:45pm, Sa 9am-noon, Su 12:30-4:45pm; Oct.-Mar. M-F 10am-3:45pm, Sa 11:30-3:45pm, Su 12:30-3:45pm. Concerts June-Aug. Th 8pm. 15kr, students 10kr.) The **Viking Ship Museum,** on Strandengen along the harbor, houses remnants of five trade ships and warships sunk circa 1060 and salvaged in the late 1960s. In summer, book a ride on a Viking longboat, but be prepared to take an oar. From the tourist office, walk to the cathedral and downhill through the park. (Open daily May-Sept. 9am-5pm; Oct.-Apr. 10am-4pm. May-Sept. 54kr; Oct.-Apr. 50kr. Boat trip 40kr; book ahead.) Roskilde hosts one of Europe's largest **music festivals,** drawing over 90,000 fans with bands such as REM, U2, Radiohead, Smashing Pumpkins, and Metallica. (June 27-30, 2002; ☎46 36 66 13; www.roskilde-festival.dk.) The **tourist office,** Gullandsstr. 15, sells festival tickets and books rooms for a 25kr fee. From the train station, turn left on Jernbaneg., right on Allehelgansg., and left again on Barchog. (☎46 35 27 00. Open Apr.-June M-F 9am-5pm, Sa 10am-1pm; July-Aug. M-F 9am-6pm, Sa 10am-2pm; Sept.-Mar. M-Th 9am-5pm, F 9am-4pm, Sa 10am-1pm.) The **HI youth hostel,** Vineboder 7, on the harbor next to the Viking museum shipyard, is always booked during the festival. (☎46 35 21 84. Reception 9am-noon and 4-8pm. Open Feb.-Dec. 90kr, nonmembers 115kr.)

To camp by the beach at **Roskilde Camping,** Baunehøjvej 7, 4km north of town, take bus #603 toward Veddelev. (☎46 75 79 96. Reception 8am-10pm. Open Apr. to mid-Sept. 60kr per person.)

KLAMPENBORG AND CHARLOTTENLUND. Klampenborg and Charlottenlund, on the coastal line (and at the end of S-train line C), feature **topless beaches.** Although less ornate than Tivoli, **Bakken** in Dyrehaven, Klampenborg, the world's oldest amusement park, delivers more thrills. From the Klampenborg train station, turn left, cross the overpass, and head through the park. (Open June to early Sept. daily noon-midnight; mid-Sept. to Apr. M-F 2pm-midnight, Sa 1pm-midnight, Su noon-midnight. Rides start at 2pm; 30-35kr each.) Bakken borders the **Jægersborg Deer Park,** the royal family's former hunting grounds, still home to their **Eremitage** summer château, miles of wooded paths, and more than 2000 red deer.

MØN. To see what Andersen called one of the most beautiful spots in Denmark, head south of Copenhagen (2hr.) to the isle of Møn's white cliffs. Locals travel to Møn to spend quiet days shopping in the villages and exploring the gorgeous chalk cliffs and the cottage-strewn pastoral landscape. Take the **train** from Copenhagen to Vordingborg, then **bus** #62 or 64 to Stege (2 per hr., 20kr). Once on the island, you can take bus #632 to **Liselund Slot,** the world's only thatched castle. The **Møns Turist-bureau,** Storeg. 2, is at the bus stop in Stege. (☎55 81 44 11. Open mid-June to Aug. M-F 10am-5pm, Sa 9am-6pm, Su 11am-1pm; Sept. to mid-June M-F 10am-5pm, Sa 9am-noon.) Stay lakeside at the **youth hostel (HI),** Langebjergve 1. (☎55 81 20 30. Breakfast 45kr. Sheets 30-45kr. Reception 8am-noon and 4-8pm. Dorms 95kr; singles 200kr; doubles 260kr.)

BORNHOLM

Ideal for avid bikers and nature-lovers, Bornholm's red-roofed cliffside villas may seem southern European, but the flowers and half-timbered houses are undeniably Danish. The unique **round churches** were both places of worship and fortresses for waiting out pirate attacks. The sandiest and longest **beaches** are at Dueodde, on the island's southern tip. For more information, check out www.bornholminfo.dk.

E TRANSPORTATION. Trains from Copenhagen to **Ystad, Sweden** are timed to meet the ferry to **Rønne,** Bornholm's capital (train ☎70 13 14 15; 1¾hr., 5-6 per day; ferry 1½hr.; total trip 190kr.) **Bornholmstrafikken** (Rønne ☎56 95 18 66, M-F 9am-5pm; Copenhagen ☎33 13 18 66; Ystad ☎+46 (411) 558 700; www.bornholmferries.dk) offers this combo train/ferry route, and also operates ferries from **Fährhafen Sassnitz** in **Germany** (☎+49 38392 35226; 3½hr., 1-2 per day, 80-110kr). Bornholm has an efficient local BAT **bus** service. (☎56 95 21 21; 35kr to Gudhjem or Sandvig-Allinge, 40kr to Svaneke; 100kr 24hr. pass). There are numerous cycling paths between all the major towns; pick up a guide at the tourist office in Rønne. Reserve rooms well in advance.

RØNNE. Amid cafes and cobblestoned streets, tiny but charming Rønne, on the southwest coast, is Bornholm's principal port of entry. The town serves mainly as an outpost to biking trips through surrounding fields, forests, and beaches. Rent a **bike** from **Bornholms Cykeludlejning,** Ndr. Kystvej 5. (65kr per day. Open May-Sept. daily 7am-4pm and 8:30-9pm.) The **tourist office** (Bornholms Velkomst-center), Nordre Kystvej 3, behind the gas station by the Bornholmstrafikken terminal, books private rooms for 140kr. (☎70 23 20 76. Open mid-June to mid-Aug. M-Sa 10am-6pm, Su 10am-4pm; mid-Aug. to mid-June M-F 9am-4pm, Sa 10am-1pm.) To reach the **HI youth hostel,** Arsenalvej 12, take the bus directly from the ferry terminal or walk 15min. along Munch Petersens Vej; when the road forks go left up the hill, then turn left onto Zahrtmannsvej, right at the roundabout onto Søndre Allé, right onto Arsenalvej, and follow the signs. (☎56 95 13 40. Reception Su-F 9am-8pm, Sa 8am-8pm. Dorms 100kr.) **Galløkken Camping** is centrally located at Strandvejen 4. (☎56 95 23 20. Open mid-May to Aug. 52kr per person.)

Get **groceries** at **Kvickly,** in the Snellemark Centret. (Open mid-June to late Aug. daily 9am-8pm; Sept. to early June M-F 9am-8pm, Sa 8am-5pm, Su 10am-4pm.) **Postal code:** 3700.

SANDVIG AND ALLINGE. On the tip of the spectacular northern coast, the white-sand beaches in these little towns attract bikers and bathers. A few kilometers from central Allinge down Hammershusvej, **Hammershus** is northern Europe's largest castle ruin. The **Nordbornholms Turistbureau,** Kirkeg. 4, is in Allinge. (☎56 48 00 01; fax 56 48 02 26. Open June-Aug. M-F 10am-5pm, Sa 10am-3pm; Sept.-May closes Sa noon.) Just outside Sandvig is the **Sandvig Vandrerhjem (HI),** Hammershusvej 94. (☎56 48 03 62. Breakfast 45kr. Sheets 60kr. Reception 9-11am and 4-6pm. Members only; sells HI cards. Open Apr.-Oct. Dorms 100kr; singles 250kr; doubles 350kr.) **Sandvig Familie Camping,** Sandlinien 5, has sites on the sea. (☎56 48 04 47. Rents bikes. Reception 8am-noon and 2-9pm. Open Apr.-Oct. 50kr per person, 15kr per tent.) Near Sandvig, take bus #3 or 9 to **Østerlars** to see the popular **Rundkirke.** (Round church. Open Apr.-Aug. M-Th 9am-5:30pm, F until 6pm, Su until noon. 5kr.)

FUNEN (FYN)

Between Zealand to the east and the Jutland Peninsula to the west, the island of Funen is Denmark's garden. This remote breadbasket is no longer isolated from the rest of Denmark—a bridge and tunnel now connect it to Zealand. Pick up maps (75kr) of the **bike paths** covering the island at Funen tourist offices.

ODENSE

Odense (OH-n-sa), the hometown of Hans Christian Andersen and Denmark's third-largest city, warrants only a short visit. At **H.C. Andersens Hus,** Hans Jensens Stræde 37-45, you can learn about the author's eccentricities and see free performances of his work. From the tourist office, walk right on Vesterg. to Torveg., turn left, and turn right on Hans Jensens Str. (Performances June 19-July 30 11am, 1, 3pm. Museum open mid-June to Aug. daily 9am-7pm; Sept. to mid-June Tu-Su 10am-4pm. 30kr.) A few scraps of Andersen's own ugly-duckling childhood are on display at **H.C. Andersens Barndomshjem** (Childhood Home), Munkemøllestr. 3-5. (Open mid-June to Aug. daily 10am-4pm; Sept. to mid-June Tu-Su 11am-3pm. 10kr.) Next to the main H. C. Andersens Hus, don headphones and listen to the work of another Great Dane at the **Carl Nielsen Museum,** Claus Bergs G. 11. (Open July-Aug. Tu-Su noon-4pm; Sept-May Th-Su noon-4pm. 15kr.) Walk back to the tourist office and all the way down Vesterg., the main pedestrian drag, to the outstanding ◪**Brandts Klæde-fabrik,** Brandts Passage 37 and 43. This former factory houses a modern art gallery, the **Museum of Photographic Art,** and the **Danish Press/Graphic Arts Museum.** (All open July-Aug. daily 10am-5pm; Sept.-June closed M. 25-30kr, joint ticket 50kr.) The **Fyns Kunstmuseum** (Funen Art Gallery), Jernbaneg. 13, features Danish art. (Open Tu-Su 10am-4pm. 25kr.) **Ringe,** 30km away, hosts the rock-and-folk-music **Midtfyns Festival** (early July), which has featured the Eurythmics, Macy Gray, Moby, and Counting Crows (☎62 62 58 24; www.mf.dk).

    Trains arrive from Copenhagen via Fredericia (2¼hr.) and from Svendborg via Kværndrup (1¼hr.). **Buses** depart behind the train station (13kr). The **tourist office,** on Rådhuspladsen, books rooms (125-175kr per person) for a 25kr fee and sells the **Odense Adventure Pass,** good for museum admission, discounts on plays, and unlimited public transport (85kr per 24hr.; 125kr per 48hr.). From the train station, take Nørreg., which becomes Asylg., turn left at the end on Vesterg., and it'll be on your right. (☎66 12 75 20. Open mid-June to Aug. M-Sa 9am-7pm, Su 10am-5pm; Sept. to mid-June M-F 9:30am-4:30pm, Sa 10am-1pm.) The brand-new **Danhostel Odense City (HI)** is attached to the station. (☎63 11 04 25. Reception 8am-noon and 4-8pm. Call ahead. Dorms 145kr; singles 335kr; doubles 410kr; triples 495kr.) To camp next to the Fruens Boge park at **DCU Camping,** Odensevej 102, take bus #41 or 81. (☎66 11 47 02. Swimming pool. Reception 7am-10pm. Open late Mar. to Sept. 50kr per person.) Get **groceries** at **Aktiv Super,** at Nørreg.

and Skulkenborgg. (Open M-F 9am-7pm, Sa 8:30am-4pm, Su noon-4pm.) **Postal code:** 5000.

☒ DAYTRIP FROM ODENSE: KVÆRNDUP. About 30min. south of Odense on the Svendborg rail line is the town of Kværndup and its ◼**Egeskov Slot,** a stunning 16th-century castle that appears to float on the surrounding lake (it's actually supported by 12,000 oak piles). Spend at least two hours in the magnificently preserved Renaissance interior and the equally splendid grounds, which include a large bamboo labyrinth. On summer Sundays at 5pm, classical concerts resound in the **Knight Hall.** (Open daily May-June and Aug.-Sept. 10am-5pm; July 10am-6pm. 55kr. Grounds open daily May and Sept. 10am-5pm; June and Aug. 10am-6pm; July 10am-8pm. 60kr. Ticket window closes 1hr. before castle closing time.) To get to Egeskov, exit the Svendborg-bound train at Kværndrup; go right from the station until you reach Bøjdenvej, the main road. Wait for bus #920 (every hr., 13kr), or turn right and walk 2km through wheat fields to the castle.

SVENDBORG

On Funen's south coast, an hour from Odense by train, **Svendborg** is a beautiful harbor town and a departure point for ferries to the south Funen islands. Near Svendborg on an adjacent island, Tåsinge, the regal 17th-century estate of **Valdemars Slot,** built by Christian IV for his son, holds a new **yachting museum** and a **beach.** (Open daily 10am-5pm. Castle 50kr, museum 25kr; joint ticket 65kr.) Cruise there on the antique passenger steamer **M/S Helge,** which leaves from Jensens Mole, behind the train station (45min., 4 per day, return 55kr).

Ferries to Ærø (see below) leave behind the train station. The **tourist office,** on the Centrum Pladsen, books ferries and accommodations. From the train station, go left on Jernbaneg. and then right onto Brogade, which turns into Gerritsg., and again right onto Kyseborgstr. The office is on the right in the plaza. (☎ 62 21 09 80. Open late June-Aug. M-F 9am-6pm, Sa 9am-3pm; Sept. to mid-June M-F 9:30am-5:30pm, Sa 9:30am-1pm.) To get from the station to the five-star **HI youth hostel,** Vesterg. 45, turn left on Jernbaneg. and walk with the coast to your left, then go right onto Valdemarsg. which becomes Vesterg. (☎ 62 21 66 99; dk@danhostel-svenborg.dk. Bikes 50kr per day. Breakfast, sheets, and laundry 45kr each. Reception M-F 8am-6pm, Su 8am-noon and 4-6pm. Check-out 9:30am. Dorms 100kr; overflow mattresses on the floor 50kr.) To get to **Carlsberg Camping,** Sundbrovej 19, across the sound on Tåsinge, take bus #800, 801, or 910 from the ferry terminal to Bregninge Tåsinge and walk up the street. (☎ 62 22 53 84. Reception 8am-10pm. Open May-Oct. 51kr.) **Jette's Diner,** at Kullingg. 1 between the train station and the docks, puts a Danish spin on diner fare. (Open daily noon-9:30pm.) **Postal code:** 5700.

ÆRØ

The wheat fields, harbors, and cobblestone hamlets of Ærø (EH-ruh), a small island off the south coast of Funen, quietly preserve an earlier era in Danish history. Rather than real estate developers, cows lay claim to the beautiful land here.

⊟ TRANSPORTATION. Several **trains** from Odense to **Svendborg** are timed to meet the **ferry** (☎ 62 52 40 00) from Svendborg to **Ærøskøbing** (1¼hr.; 6 per day; 75kr, round-trip 125kr; buy tickets on board). From **Mommark,** on Jutland, **Ærø-Als** (☎ 62 58 17 17) sails to **Søby** (☎ 62 58 17 17; 1hr.; Apr.-Sept. 2-5 per day, Oct.-Mar. Sa-Su only; 60kr), on Ærø's northwestern shore. **Bus** #990 travels between Ærøskøbing, Marstal, and Søby (16kr), but Ærø is best seen by **bike.**

ÆRØSKØBING. Thanks to economic stagnation followed by conservation efforts, the town of Ærøskøbing appears today almost as it did 200 years ago. Rosebushes and half-timbered houses attract tourist yachts from Sweden and Germany as well as vacationing Danes, but you don't have to get too far out of town to find your own serene spot. The **tourist office,** Vestergade 1, opposite the ferry landing, arranges rooms (170kr) in private homes. (☎ 62 52 13 00. Open

June-Aug. M-F 9am-5pm, Sa 9am-2pm, Su 10am-noon; Sept.-May M-F 9am-4pm, Sa 8:45-11:45am.) To get from the landing to the **HI youth hostel,** Smedevejen 15, walk left on Smedeg., which becomes Nørreg., Østerg., and finally Smedevejen. (☎62 52 10 44. Breakfast 40kr. Sheets 35kr. Reception 8am-noon and 4-8pm. Check-in by 5pm or call ahead. Reserve far in advance. Open Apr. to mid-Oct. Dorms 90kr; nonmembers 115kr.) **Ærøskøbing Camping,** Sygehusvejen 40b, is 10min. to the right along Sygehusvejen, of Vestre Alle as you leave the ferry. (☎62 52 18 54. Reception 8am-1pm and 3-9pm. Open May-Sept. 50kr per person, 20kr per tent.) **Emerko supermarket** is at Statene 3; walking uphill from the ferry on Vesterg., turn right on Sluttergyden, which becomes Statene. (Open M-Th 9am-5pm, F 9am-6pm, Sa 9am-4pm, Su 10am-4pm.) Rent a **bike** at the hostel or campground (40-50kr per day) to explore the towns of **Marstal** and **Søby,** on the more remote shores of the island.

JUTLAND (JYLLAND)

Homeland of the Jutes who joined the Anglos and Saxons in the conquest of England, the Jutland peninsula is Denmark's largest landmass. Beaches and campgrounds mark the peninsula as prime summer vacation territory, while rolling hills, marshland, and sparse forests add color and variety. Jutland may be a bit out of the way, but you can take a weekend beach fling there without denting your budget.

✈ FERRIES TO ENGLAND, NORWAY, AND SWEDEN

From **Esbjerg,** on Jutland's west coast, **DFDF** sails to Harwich, England (18hr., 3-4 per week). From **Frederikshavn** (p. 284), on the northern tip of Jutland, **Stena Line** ferries (☎96 20 02 00; www.stenaline.com) leave for Gothenburg, Sweden (2-3¼hr., 155kr; 50% Scanrail discount) and Oslo (8½hr., 180kr; 50% Scanrail discount). **SeaCat** (☎96 20 32 00; www.silja.com), a subsidiary of Silja Line offers cheaper service to Gothenburg (2hr., 3 per day, 110-130kr). **Color Line** (☎99 56 20 00; www.colorline.dk) sails to Larvik, Norway (6¼hr., 160-340kr; 50% student and senior discount). Color Line boats also go from Hirtshals, on the northern tip of Jutland, to Oslo (8-8½hr., 160-350kr) and Kristiansand, Norway (2½-4½hr., 160-350kr).

ÅRHUS

Århus (ORE-hoos), Denmark's second-largest city and a Danish favorite, bills itself as "the world's smallest big city." Studded with impressive museums and architectural gems from prehistoric times through the 21st century, the city is a visual treat. Many travelers to this manageably sized and laid-back student and cultural center find themselves agreeing that size doesn't matter.

☎◪ TRANSPORTATION AND PRACTICAL INFORMATION. You can reach Århus by **train** from Aalborg (1¾hr.), Copenhagen (3hr.), Fredericia (2hr.), and Frederikshavn (2½hr.). Most public buses leave from the train station or outside the tourist office. The **tourist office,** in the town hall, books private rooms (125-175kr) for free and sells the **Århus Passport,** which includes unlimited public transit and admission to most museums and sights (1-day 88kr, 2-day 110kr). If you're only interested in one or two museums, consider the **Tourist Punch Ticket** (45kr), which provides unlimited bus transportation. To find the office, go left across Banegardspladsen as you exit the train station, and take the first right on Park Alle. (☎89 40 67 00; www.aarhus-tourist.dk. Open late June to early Sept. M-F 9:30am-6pm, Sa 9:30am-5pm, Su 9:30am-1pm; early Sept. to Apr. M-F 9:30am-4:30pm, Sa 10am-1pm; May to mid-June M-F 9:30am-5pm, Sa 10am-1pm.) **Postal Code:** 8100.

☎◪ ACCOMMODATIONS AND FOOD. Hip **Århus City Sleep-In,** Havneg. 20, 10min. from the train station, is in the middle of the city's nightlife. Walk out of the train station and follow Ryesg. (off of Banegardspladsen), which becomes Sønderg., all the way to the canal. Before crossing the canal, take the steps or elevator down to Aboulevarden, cross the canal and go right, walk to the end of the canal, go left on Mindebrogade, crossing Skolegade, then left again on Havneg. (☎86 19 20 55; sleep-in@citysleep-in.dk. Kitchen. Internet. Bikes 50kr per day; deposit 200kr. Breakfast 35kr. Sheets 35kr; deposit 30kr. Laundry 25kr. Key deposit 50kr. Reception 24hr. Check-out noon. Dorms 95kr; doubles 240-280kr.) **Pavillonen (HI),** Marienlundsvej 10, is in the Risskov forest, 3km from the city center and 5min. from the beach. Take bus #1, 6, 9, 16, or 56 to Marienlund, then walk 300m into the park. (☎86 16 72 98; danhostel.aarhus@get2net.dk. Breakfast 45kr. Sheets 30kr. Laundry. Reception 7:30-10am and 4-11pm. Dorms 90kr, nonmembers 110kr; singles, doubles, and triples 270-400kr.) **Blommehavenn Camping,** Ørneredevej 35, in the Marselisborg forest, is by a beach and the royal family's summer residence. In summer, take bus #19 from the station to the grounds; in winter, take bus #6 to Hørhavevej. (☎86 27 02 07; info@blommehaven.dk. Reception Apr.-July 7:30am-10pm; Aug.-Mar. 8am-9pm. In summer 55kr per person.) **Den Grønne Hjørne,** Frederiksg. 60, has an all-you-can-eat Danish buffet (noon-10pm, 99kr). From the tourist office, turn left on Radhuspl., and then take an immediate right. (☎86 13 52 47. Open daily 11am-10pm.) Get **groceries** at **Fakta,** Østerg. 8-12. (Open M-F 9am-7pm, Sa 9am-4pm.)

◘ SIGHTS. In the town center, the 13th-century **Århus Domkirke** (cathedral) dominates Bispetorv and the pedestrian streets that fan out around its Gothic walls. (Open May-Sept. M-Sa 9:30am-4pm; Oct.-Apr. 10am-3pm. Free.) Next door, reclaim herstory at the **Women's Museum,** Domkirkeplads 5, where provocative exhibits chronicle women throughout time. (Open June-Aug. daily 10am-5pm; Sept.-May Tu-Su 10am-4pm. 25kr.) Just west of the town center lies **Den Gamle By,** Viborgvej 2, an open-air museum displaying a collection of Danish buildings from the Renaissance through the 20th century. From the center, take bus #3, 14, 15, 25, or 51. (Open June-Aug. 9am-6pm; Apr.-May and Sept.-Oct. 10am-5pm; Nov.-Dec. 10am-4pm; Feb.-Mar. 10am-4pm. Jan. 11am-3pm. 60kr; Jan-Mar. 45kr. Grounds free after-hours.) The **Århus Kunstmuseum,** on Vennelystparken, has a fine collection of Danish Golden Age paintings. (Open Tu-Su 10am-5pm, W to 8pm. 40kr.) Just outside town lies the spectacular **Moesgård Museum of Prehistory,** Moesgard Alle 20, which chronicles Århus's history from 4000 BC through the Viking age. Two millennia ago, the casualties of infighting were entombed in a nearby bog and mummified by its antiseptic acidity. Today you can visit the ◙**Grauballe Man,** the only perfectly preserved bog person. Take bus #6 from the train station to the end. (Open Apr.-Sept. daily 10am-5pm; Oct.-Mar. Tu-Su 10am-4pm. 35kr, students 25kr.) Save time for the **Prehistoric Trail,** which leads from behind the museum to a sandy **beach** (3km). In summer, bus #19 (last bus 10:18pm) returns from the beach to the Århus station. The exquisite rose garden of **Marselisborg Slot,** Kongevejen 100, is open to the public. From the train station, take bus #1, 18, or 19. (Palace closed July and whenever the Queen is in residence. Changing of the guard takes place daily at noon.)

▣▣ ENTERTAINMENT AND NIGHTLIFE. Åboulevarden, lined with trendy cafes, is the heart of the town, and makes a perfect stop for beer and sunshine. Århus hosts an acclaimed jazz festival in late July (☎89 31 82 10; www.jazzfest.dk). The **Århus Festuge** (☎89 31 82 70; www.aarhusfestuge.dk) celebrates theater, dance, and music. You can visit a smaller version of Tivoli, the **Tivoli Friheden,** Skovbrynet 1. Take bus #1, 4, 6, 8, 18, or 19. (Open June 19-Aug. 8 daily 2-11pm; Apr. 19-June 18 and Aug. 9-15 2-10pm. 35kr.) At night, chill at the jazz club **Bent J,** Nørre Allé 66, which jams Monday nights. **Valdemar,** Store Torv 4, is a popular disco in the city center. (No cover. 23+. Open Th 11pm-5am, F-Sa 10pm-5am.) **Aboulevarden** rocks at night, too; many bars offer live music and drink specials.

DENMARK

DAYTRIP FROM ÅRHUS: BILLUND. Billund is renowned as the home of **Legoland,** an amusement park built of 40 million Lego pieces. Don't skip the impressive indoor exhibitions. Unfortunately, private buses make Legoland a bit expensive. To get there, take the train from Århus to **Vejle** (45min., every hr.), then bus #912 or 44 (dir. Grindsted). A joint ticket for the bus and park (including rides) costs 150kr. (☎ 75 33 13 33; www.legoland.dk. Open daily July 10am-9pm; Mar.-June and Sept.-Oct. 10am-6pm; rides close 2hr. earlier.)

AALBORG

The site of the earliest known Viking settlement, Aalborg (OLE-borg) is Denmark's fourth-largest city. Aalborg's spotless streets and white church garnered the title of "Europe's Tidiest City" in 1990. Check out Aalborg's rowdy precursors at **Lindholm Høje,** Vendilavej 11, which has 700 graves and a museum of Viking life. To reach the site, take bus #6 or 25 (13kr) from outside the tourist office. (Site open daily dawn-dusk. Museum open Apr. to mid-Oct. daily 10am-5pm; late Oct. to mid-Mar. Tu and Su 10am-4pm. 20kr.) The frescoed 15th-century **Monastery of the Holy Ghost,** on C.W. Obelsplads, is Denmark's oldest social institution. From the tourist office, cross the street and head down Adelg. (English tours late June to mid-Aug. Tu and Th-F at 1:30pm. 40kr.) The **Budolfi Church,** on Algade, has a brilliantly colored interior. From the tourist office, turn left onto Østerågade and right on Algade. (Open May-Sept. M-F 9am-4pm, Sa 9am-2pm, Oct-Apr. M-F 9am-3pm, Sa 9am-noon. Carillon plays every hr. on the hr. from 9am-10pm.) At the corner of Algade and Mollegad, in front of the Sallig department store, an elevator goes down to the medieval ruins of the **Franciscan Friary.** (Open Tu-Su 10am-5pm. 20kr; buy your ticket from the machine.) For serious rollercoasters, visit **Tivoliland,** on Karolinelundsvej. From the tourist office, turn left on Østerågade, turn right on Nytorv, and follow it until you see the rides. (Open Apr.-Sept. daily noon-8pm. 40kr; full-day 160kr.)

Trains arrive from Århus (1¾hr.) and Copenhagen. From the station, cross J.F.K. Plads, then turn left on Boulevarden, which becomes Østerågade, to find the **tourist office,** Østerågade 8. (☎ 98 12 60 22; www.aalborg.dk. Open mid-June to mid-Aug. M-F 9am-6pm, Sa 10am-5pm; mid-Aug. to mid-June M-F 9am-4:30pm, Sa 9am-1pm.) **Aalborg Vandrerhjem and Camping (HI),** Skydebanevej 50, has cabins with modern facilities next to a beautiful fjord. Take bus #2, 8, or 9 (dir. Fjordparken) to the end. (☎ 45 98 11 60 44; fax 45 98 12 47 11; aalborg@danhostel.dk. Laundry. Reception late June to mid-Aug. 7:30am-11pm; late Jan. to mid-June and early Aug. to mid-Dec. 8am-noon and 4-9pm. Dorms 85-100kr; singles 250-398kr; doubles 325-398kr. Camping 49kr.) Bars and restaurants line **Jomfru Ane Gade;** from the tourist office, turn right on Østerågade and left onto Bispensg. **Postal code:** 9000.

FREDERIKSHAVN

Despite efforts to showcase its endearing streets and hospitality, Frederikshavn is primarily used for its **ferry** links (p. 282). The **tourist office,** Skandia Torv, 1, inside the Stena Line terminal south of the rail station, reserves rooms for a 25kr fee. (☎ 98 42 32 66; fax 98 42 12 99; www.frederikshavn.dk. Open mid-June to mid-Aug. M-Sa 8:15am-7pm, Su 11am-7pm; mid-Aug. to mid-June M-Sa 9am-4pm.) From the tourist office, walk left 10min. to reach the bus and train stations. To get from the train and bus station to the **HI youth hostel,** Buhlsvej 6, walk right on Skippergade for 10min., then turn left onto Norregade; follow the signs. (☎ 98 42 14 75. Reception in summer 8am-noon and 4-9pm. Call ahead. Open Feb.-Dec. Dorms 53kr; singles 150-200kr; doubles 210-270kr.) **Nordstrand Camping** is at Apholmenvej 40. (☎ 98 42 93 50. Open Apr. to mid-Sept. 52kr per person, 30kr per tent.) **Postal code:** 9900.

SKAGEN

Perched on Denmark's northernmost tip, sunny Skagen (SKAY-en) is a beautiful summer retreat amid long stretches of sea and white-sand dunes. The powerful currents of the North and Baltic Seas collide at **Grenen.** Don't try to swim in these dangerous waters; every year some hapless soul is carried out to sea. To get to Grenen, take bus #99 or 79 from the Skagen station to **Gammel** (11kr) or walk 3km down Fyrvej; turn left out of the train station and bear left when the road forks. In summer, you can climb the lighthouse tower for an amazing view of the rough seas at Grenen (5kr). The spectacular **Råberg Mile** sand dunes, formed by a 16th-century storm, migrate 15m east each year. From here, you can swim along 60km of **beaches**, where the endless summer light attracted Denmark's most famous late 19th-century painters. Their works are displayed in the wonderful **Skagen Museum**, Brøndumsvej 4. (Open June-Aug. daily 10am-6pm; Nov.-Mar. W-F 1-4pm, Sa 11am-4pm, Su 11am-3pm; Apr. and Oct. Tu-Su 11am-4pm; May and Sept. 10am-5pm. 50kr.) You can also tour the artists' homes at **Michael og Anna Archers Hus**, Markvej 2-4, and **Holger Drachmanns Hus**, Hans Baghsvej 21. Skagen has a large annual **Dixieland music festival** in late June (up to 150kr); contact the tourist office.

Nordjyllands Trafikselskab (☎ 98 44 21 33) runs **buses** and **trains** from Frederikshavn to Skagen (1hr., 36kr; 50% Scanrail discount). Rent **bikes** at **Skagen CykelUdlejning**, Banegardspladsen, right next to the bus station. The **tourist office** is in the train station. (☎ 98 44 13 77; fax 98 45 02 94; www.skagen.dk. Open June-Aug. M-Sa 9am-7pm, Su 10am-2pm; Sept.-May reduced hrs.) The **Skagen Ny Vandrerhjem**, Rolighedsvej. 2, is wildly popular among vacationing Danish families. From the station, turn right on Chr. X's Vej, which turns into Frederikshshavnvej, and left on Rolighedsvej (☎ 98 44 22 00. Reception 9am-noon and 4-6pm. Open Mar.-Nov. Dorms 100kr; singles 250-400kr; doubles 300-500kr.) **Campgrounds** abound in the area; most are open early May to early Sept. (55kr per person). Bus #79 passes by several sites. Try **Grenen**, Fyrvej 16 (☎ 98 44 25 46) or **Øster Klit**, Flagbakkevej 53 (☎ 98 44 31 23), both near the city center.

RIBE

Well aware of their town's historic value, the town government of Ribe forged preservation laws forcing residents to maintain the character of their houses and to live in them year-round. The result is a magnificently preserved medieval town, situated beautifully on the salt plains near Jutland's west coast. Ribe is particularly proud of the arrival of migratory storks who always roost on the roof of the town hall. For a great view of the birds and the surrounding landscape, climb the 248 steps through the clockwork and huge bells of the 12th-century **cathedral** tower. (Open Apr.-Oct. M-Sa 10am-6pm, Su noon-6pm; May and Sept. M-Sa 10am-5pm, Su noon-6pm; Apr. and Oct. daily 11am-4pm; Nov.-Mar. M-Su 11am-3pm. 12kr.) Next to the **Det Gamle Rådhus** (Old Town Hall), Von Støckens Plads, a nameless former debtor's prison houses a small museum on medieval torture. (Open June-Aug. daily 1-3pm; May and Sept. M-F 1-3pm. 15kr.) Follow the **night watchman** on his rounds for an English or Danish 35min. tour of town beginning in Torvet, the main square. (June-Aug. 8 and 10pm; May and Sept. 10pm. Free.) Across from the train station, **Museet Ribes Vikinger**, Odin Plads 1, houses artifacts recovered from an excavation of the town, once an important Viking trading post. (Open Apr.-June and Sept.-Oct. daily 10am-4pm; July-Aug. 10am-6pm, W until 9pm; Nov.-Mar. Tu-Su 10am-4pm. 50kr.) South of town, the open-air **Ribe Vikingcenter**, Lustrupvej 4, re-creates a Viking town, complete with farm and marketplace. (Open July-Aug. daily 11am-4:30pm; May-June and Sept. M-F 11am-4pm. 50kr.) The **Vadehavscentret** (Wadden Sea Center), Okholmvej 5 in Vestervedsted, does tours of the local marshes. Take the Mandobus (☎ 75 44 51 07; 50kr) from the station. (Open Apr.-Oct. daily 10am-5pm; Feb.-Mar. and Nov. 10am-4pm. 45kr. Combo bus and center 80kr.)

Trains to Ribe run from nearby Bramming (25min., 4-5 per day, 28kr) and Esbjerg (40min., every hr., 46kr). The **tourist office**, Torvet 3, has free maps and arranges accommodations for a 20kr fee. From the train station, walk down Dagmarsg., to the left of the Viking museum, and it'll be on your right in the main square. (☎ 75 42 15 030; www.ribe.dk. Open July-Aug. M-F 9:30am-5:30pm, Sa 10am-5pm; Apr.-June and Sept.-Oct. M-F 9am-5pm, Sa 10am-1pm; Nov.-Mar. M-F 9am-4:30pm, Sa 10am-1pm.) The central **Ribe Vandrerhjem (HI)**, Sct. Pedersg. 16,

DENMARK

offers bike rental (50kr per day) and a gorgeous view of the flatlands. From the station, cross the Viking Museum parking lot, bear right, walk down Sct. Nicolaj G. to the end, turn right on Saltg., and immediately left on Sct. Peters G. (☎ 75 42 06 20. Breakfast 45kr. Sheets 38kr. Reception 8am-noon and 4-8pm; longer hours May-Sept. Open Feb.-Nov. Dorms 80-100kr; singles 250kr; doubles 295kr.) **Ribe Camping**, Farupvej 2, is 1½km from the town center. From the station, turn to face the Vikings Museum and go right on Rosen Alle until it becomes Norre-marksvej. After the traffic light, go left along the bike path (Gronnestien) and cross onto Farupvej; it's on the second street on the right. Or grab bus #715 (every 1½hr.) from the station to Gredstedbro. (☎ 75 41 07 77. 50kr per person; 175kr per 2-person cabin.) **Supermarkets** are around the town center and near the hostel. (Most open M-F 10am-6pm, Sa 10am-4pm).

ESTONIA (EESTI)

ESTONIAN KROON

1 US$ = 17.12 EEK	10 EEK = 0.58 US$
1 CDN = 11.08 EEK	10 EEK = 0.90 CDN
1 UK£ = 24.74 EEK	10 EEK = 0.40 UK£1
1 IR£ = 19.88 EEK	10 EEK = 0.50 IR£
1 AUS$ = 9.13 EEK	10 EEK = 1.10 AUS$
1 NZ$ = 7.51 EEK	10 EEK = 0.13 NZ$
1 ZAR = 2.06 EEK	10 EEK = 4.85 ZAR
1 DM = 8.00 EEK	10 EEK = 0.12 DM
1 EUR€ = 15.65 EEK	10 EEK = 0.64 EUR€

PHONE CODE	**Country code:** 372. **International dialing prefix:** 800. From outside Estonia, dial int'l dialing prefix (see inside back cover) + 372 + city code + local number.

Happy to discard its Soviet past, Estonia has been quick to revive its ties to its Nordic neighbors, as Finnish wealth revitalizes the nation. Material trappings mask the declining living standards common outside big cities, but having overcome successive centuries of domination by Danes, Swedes, and Russians, Estonians are now ready to take their place in modern Europe.

Get Estonian with *Let's Go: Eastern Europe 2002.*

FACTS AND FIGURES

Official Name: Republic of Estonia.
Capital: Tallinn.
Major Cities: Tartu, Pärnu.
Land Area: 45,226 sq. km.
Climate: Maritime; wet, moderate to severe winters, cool summers.

Population: 1,440,000 (65% Estonia, 28% Russian, 7% other).
Language: Estonian (official), Russian, Ukrainian, English, Finnish.
Religions: Evangelical Lutheran, Russian Orthodox, Estonian Orthodox.

ESSENTIALS

WHEN TO GO

The best time to visit is May-September. Though it's quite far north, Estonia's climate is relatively mild due to its proximity to water. Winters can be very severe.

DOCUMENTS AND FORMALITIES

VISAS. Citizens of Australia, Ireland, New Zealand, and the US do not need a visa for up to 90 days in a six-month period, UK citizens for 180 days in a year. Canadians and South Africans must obtain a visa at the nearest consulate, and may also use a Latvian or Lithuanian visa to enter the country. Single-entry visas (valid for 30 days) are US$11, multiple-entry (maximum continuous stay 90 days) US$55. Visa extensions are not granted, and visas cannot be purchased at the border. For visa information, consult the Estonian Ministry of Foreign Affairs (www.vm.ee).

EMBASSIES. Foreign embassies are all in **Tallinn** (p. 290). For Estonian embassies at home: **Australia,** 86 Louisa Rd., Birchgrove NSW, 2041 (☎(02) 9810 7468); **Canada** (Consulate), 958 Broadview Ave., Toronto, ON M4K 2R6 (☎416-461-0764); **South Africa** (Consulate), 16 Hofmeyer St., Welgemoed, 7530 (☎(021) 913 38 50);

UK, 16 Hyde Park Gate, London SW7 5DG (](020) 7589 3428; www.estonia.gov.uk); and **US,** 2131 Massachusetts Ave. NW, Washington, D.C. 20008 (☎202-588-0101; www.estemb.org).

TRANSPORTATION

BY PLANE, TRAIN, BUS, AND FERRY. Estonian Air, Finnair, Lufthansa, and **SAS** have flights to Tallinn. If you're coming from Russia or a Baltic state, **trains** may be cheaper than ferries, but expect more red tape during border crossings. Domestic **buses** are cheaper and more efficient than trains. During the school year (Sept.-June 25), student bus tickets are half-price. Several **ferry lines** connect to Tallinn's harbor (☎631 85 50); see Tallinn: Ferries, p. 290. It is easiest and cheapest to enter Estonia by ferry from Finland or Sweden (200-300EEK).

BY CAR. Driving conditions are passable. Expressways are in good condition; other roads are plagued by potholes and gravel. Americans need International Driving Permits; European licenses are sufficient. Drivers can be quite aggressive. Speed limits are 50kph in cities and 70 to 100kph on expressways. Park in guarded lots; Estonia has high rates of auto theft. Car rentals are 350-900EEK.

BY BIKE AND BY THUMB. On the islands, bike rentals (100EEK per day) are an excellent means of exploration. *Let's Go* does not recommend hitchhiking. Those who choose to do so should stretch out an open hand. Or, call the agency **Vismutar** (☎(8290) 010 50) and leave your name, number, destination, and time of departure; they will match you with a driver going in your direction 24hr. before you leave.

TOURIST SERVICES AND MONEY

EMERGENCY	Police: ☎112. Ambulance: ☎112. Fire: ☎112. In Tallinn, add (0).

TOURIST OFFICES. Unlike most of the former Soviet Union, Estonia is grasping the importance of tourist services; most towns have well-equipped tourist offices with literature and English-speaking staff. Smaller information booths, marked with a green "i," sell maps and give away brochures.

MONEY. The unit of currency is the **kroon** (EEK), divided into 100 *senti*. Inflation is around 3%, so prices and exchange rates should be relatively stable. Hansapank and Eesti Ühispank, the biggest and most stable banks, cash traveler's checks. Many establishments take Visa and MasterCard. ATMs are common. When purchasing items in a shop, cash is not passed between hands, but placed in a small tray on counter tops. Tipping is uncommon in Estonia, although a service charge might be included in the bill.

BUSINESS HOURS. Most businesses are open Monday to Friday 9 or 10am to 6 or 7pm and Saturday 10am to 2 or 3pm. Some food shops stay open until 10pm or later and are also open on Sunday. Businesses take hour-long breaks at noon, 1, or 2pm. Banks are open Monday to Friday 9am-4pm.

COMMUNICATION

MAIL. An airmail letter costs 6.50EEK to Europe and the CIS, and 7.50EEK to the rest of the world. Postcards are 6EEK to Europe and the CIS or 8EEK everywhere else. Mail can be received through *Poste Restante*. Address envelope as follows: First name SURNAME, *Poste Restante*, Narva mnt. 1, Tallinn 0001, ESTONIA.

TELEPHONES. Telephone calls are paid for with digital cards, available at any bank or newspaper kiosk. Cards come in denominations of 30, 50, and 100EEK. International calls can be made at post offices. Calls to the Baltic states cost 5EEK per min., to Russia 10EEK. Phoning the US costs US$1-4 per min. The phone system in Estonia is a little chaotic. Tallinn numbers all begin with the number 6 and have 7 digits.

Estonia

Gulf of Finland

Baltic Sea

RUSSIA

Numbers in smaller towns, however, often have only 5 digits. Tallinn, unlike other Estonian cities, has no city code The 0 listed in parentheses before each city code need only be dialed when placing calls within Estonia. Eesti Telefon's information number is ☎07. For help, call the English-speaking **Ekspress Hotline** (☎0 11 88). International direct dial numbers include: **AT&T** ☎800 800 10 01; **British Telecom** ☎800 800 10441; **Canada Direct** ☎0 800 800 1011; and **MCI** ☎0 800 800 1122.

LANGUAGES. Estonian is a Finno-Ugric language, with 14 cases and all sorts of letters. Estonians speak the best English in the Baltic states; most young people also know Finnish or Swedish, but German is more common among the older set. Russian used to be mandatory, but Estonians usually don't like to use it. Try English first, making it clear you're not Russian, then switch to Russian if needed. The exception to this is along the eastern border, where many prefer Russian. For Estonian basics, see p. 983.

ACCOMMODATIONS AND CAMPING

Tourist offices have accommodations listings and can often arrange beds. There is little distinction between hotels, hostels, and guesthouses. Some **hostels** are part of larger hotels, so ask for the cheaper rooms. For information on HI hostels, contact the **Estonian Youth Hostel Association,** Tatari (☎646 14 57; eyha.jg.ee). Some upscale **hotels** have hall toilets and showers, and many provide laundry services for a fee. **Homestays** are common and cheap, but the cheapest hostels can be a better deal. The word *võõrastemaja* (guest house) in a place's name often implies that it is less expensive. There are **campgrounds** throughout Estonia.

FOOD AND DRINK

While *schnitel* (a breaded, fried pork fillet) still appears on nearly every menu, salads, pasta, pizza, curries and more innovative meat preparation can now be found. Estonian specialties include the Baltic *seljanka* meat stew and *pelmenid* dumplings, plus smoked salmon and trout. Pancakes with cheese curd and berries are a delicious dessert. If you visit the islands, try picking up some *Hiumaa leib*; a loaf of this black bread easily weighs a kilo. Beer (*õlu*) is the national drink for good reason—it's cheap, savory, and plentiful, and above all, delicious. The national brand *Saku* is excellent, as is the darker *Saku Tume*.

HOLIDAYS AND FESTIVALS

Holidays: New Year's Day (Jan. 1); Independence Day (1918; Feb. 24); Good Friday (Mar. 29); Easter (Mar. 15); Spring Day (May 1); Whit Sunday (May 19); Victory Day (Battle of Võnnu, 1919; June 23); Jaanipäev (St. John's Day, Midsummer; June 24); Restoration of Independence (Aug. 20); Christmas (Dec. 25-26).

Festivals: Old Town Days (late May to early June), in Tallinn, host open-air concerts throughout Vanalinn. **Beersummer,** the 1st week of July, gives one more excuse to loose the taps in Tallinn bars, as if it were necessary.

TALLINN   ☎(0)

Talinn is quickly regaining the status it once enjoyed in the 14th and 15th centuries. The outskirts are a bit drab, but the center is fresh with new life: cosmopolitan shops downtown contrast with the medieval serenity of the Old Town, whose German spires, Danish towers, and Russian domes rise above the sea.

⌐ TRANSPORTATION

Trains: Toompuiestee 35 (☎615 68 51; www.evrekspress.ee). Trams #1 and 5 connect the station to Hotel Viru. English-speaking information desk. To **Moscow** (17½hr., 1 per day, 638EEK) and **St. Petersburg** (10hr., 1 per day, 168EEK).

Buses: Lastekodu 46 (☎601 03 86), 1½km southeast of Vanalinn. Take trams #2 or 4 or bus #2 to the city center. Buy tickets at the station or from the driver. Buses—frequent and cheap—are the best way to travel domestically and internationally. **Eurolines** (☎601 17 00; www.eurolines.ee) sends buses to: **Berlin** (27hr., 1 per day, 1360EEK); **Rīga** (6hr., 1 per day, 200EEK); **St. Petersburg** (9-10hr., 5 per day, 200EEK); and **Vilnius** (10hr., 2 per day, 300EEK); **Warsaw** (6½hr., 4 per week, 640EEK).

Ferries: (☎631 85 50). At the end of Sadama, 15min. from the city center. These companies sail or hydrofoil to **Helsinki: Nordic Jet Line,** Terminal C (☎613 70 00; www.njl.ee; 1½hr., 6 per day, 465EEK); **Tallinn Express,** Terminal D (☎640 98 90; 1½hr., 3 per day, 260-400EEK); **Eckerö Line,** Terminal B (☎631 86 06; www.eckeroline.ee; 3½hr.; 1 per day; 200EEK, students 150EEK); **Silja Line,** Terminal D (611 66 61; www.silja.ee; 3hr., 1 per day, 325EEK).

Public Transportation: Buses, trams, and **trolleybuses** cover the entire metropolitan area 6am-midnight. Buy tickets (*talong*; 10EEK) from kiosks around town and validate them in the metal boxes on board (at least 500EEK fine for riding without a valid ticket).

Taxis: (☎612 00 00, 655 60 00, 644 24 42, or 627 55 55). Check the cab for a meter and expect to pay 5-10EEK per km.

⊞🛈 ORIENTATION AND PRACTICAL INFORMATION

The ring around Tallinn's egg-shaped **Vanalinn** (Old Town) is made up of Rannamäe tee, Mere pst., Pärnu mnt., Kaarli pst., and Toompuiestee. The old town has two sections: **All-linn,** or Lower Town, which is larger and busier, and **Toompea,** a fortified rocky hill. Enter Vanalinn through the 15th-century **Viru värarad,** the main gates in the city wall, 500m from **Hotel Viru,** Tallinn's central landmark. To get to Vanalinn from the ferry terminal, walk 15min. along Sadama, which turns into Põhja pst., and turn left on Pikk through **Fat Margaret** (Paks Margareeta) gate. From the train station, cross under Toompuiestee and continue straight on **Nunne;** turn left on Pikk and right on Kinga to get to **Town Hall Square** (Raekoja plats), the center of All-linn.

Tourist Office: Raekoja pl. 10 (☎645 77 77; turismiinfo@talinnlv.ee; www.tallinn.ee). Indispensable *Tallinn in Your Pocket* 19EEK. Open M-F 9am-6pm, Sa-Su 10am-4pm. The **Tallinn Card** covers a city tour, transportation, and entry to most museums (1-day 205EEK, 2-day 275EEK, 3-day 325EEK).

Embassies: For a complete directory, see foreign ministry's site (www.vm.ee) or *Tallinn This Week.* **Australia,** Kopli 25 (☎650 93 08; fax 654 13 33; mati@standard.ee).

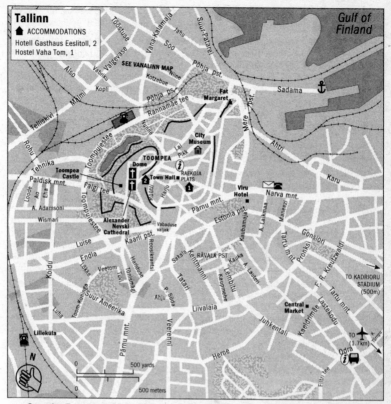

Tallinn

▲ ACCOMMODATIONS
Hotell Gasthaus Eeslitoll, 2
Hostel Vaha Tom, 1

Gulf of Finland

Canada, Toomkooli 13 (☎627 33 11; fax 627 33 12; canembt@zzz.ee). Open M, W, F 9am-noon. **Russia,** Pikk 19 (☎646 41 75; visa ☎646 41 69; fax 646 41 78). Open M-F 9am-noon. **UK,** Wismari 6 (☎667 47 00; fax 667 47 23; www.britishembassy.ee). Open Tu-Th 2:30-4:30pm. **US,** Kentmanni 20 (☎668 81 00; fax 668 81 34; talinn@usemb.ee; www.usemb.ee). Open M-F 9am-noon and 2-5pm.

Currency Exchange: Throughout the city. **ATMs** are on nearly every street in Vanalinn.

American Express: Suur-Karja 15, 10140 (☎626 62 62; fax 626 62 12; sales@estravel.ee). Books hotels and tours. Sells airline, ferry, and rail tickets. Arranges visas. Open M-F 9am-6pm, Sa 10am-5pm; off season M-F 9am-6pm only.

Emergencies: Ambulance, Fire, Police: ☎0112.

Pharmacy: Raeapteek, 2 doors from Tourist Office. Open M-F 9am-7pm, Sa 9am-5pm, Su 9am-4pm.

Internet Access: Everywhere. Try **Cafe ENTER,** Gonsiori 4 (☎626 73 67). 60EEK per hr. Open daily 10am-10pm.

Post Office: Narva mnt. 1, 2nd fl. (☎625 72 00), opposite Hotel Viru. Open M-F 7:30am-8pm, Sa 8am-6pm. Address mail to be held: First name SURNAME, Narva mnt. 1, Tallinn **0001,** Estonia.

🏠🍴 ACCOMMODATIONS AND FOOD

Hostels fill fast, so book ahead. **Rasastra,** Mere 4 (☎641 22 91), finds rooms in private homes from 260EEK.

🛏 **Hostel Vana Tom,** Väike-Karja 1, 2nd fl. (☎631 32 52; vana.tom@hostel.ee; www.hostel.ee), in Vanalinn. Dorms 195EEK; doubles 550EEK. HI members 15EEK discount.

Hotell Gasthaus Eeslitall, Dunkri 4, 2nd fl. (☎631 32 52; www.eeslitall.ee), just off Raekoja pl. Colorful, clean rooms. Breakfast 36EEK. Singles 450EEK; doubles 585EEK.

Try the pubs and cafes around the Old Town Square for a wide selection. **Puffet,** Suur-karja 18, downstairs from **Coffile,** serves affordable and filling meals for 50EEK. (Open daily 11am-7pm.) **Lübeck,** Pikk 43, has large portions and a medieval theme. (Meals 60EEK. Open daily 11am-11pm.) Groceries can be found at **Kaubahall** on Aia and Inseneri, left off Viru walking out of Vanalinn. **Open-air markets** set up most days near Lastekodu 10.

🔘 SIGHTS

VANALINN (OLD TOWN)

ALL-LINN. Enter the Old Town through the Viru gate; up Viru lies Europe's oldest town hall in **Town Hall Square** (Raekoja pl.), where beer flows in outdoor cafes and local troupes perform in summer. **Old Thomas** (Vana Toomas), the 16th-century cast-iron weathervane figurine of Tallinn's legendary defender, tops the 14th-century *raekoja. (Open June-Aug. daily 11am-6pm. Tours 30EEK.)* Head up Mündi on the street next to Molly Malone's and turn right on Pühavaimu to reach the 14th-century **church of the Holy Ghost** (Pühavaimu kirik), which has an intricate 17th-century wooden clock. *(Open M-Sa 10am-2pm. Free concerts M 6pm.)* Continue down Pühavaimu and turn left on Vene to reach the **Dominican Cloister** (Dominiiklaste Klooster), the oldest building in Vanalinn. *(Vene 16. Open daily 9:30am-6pm. 25EEK.)* Continue up Vene, turn left on Olevimägi, and turn right on Pikk for a view of the medieval city's north towers. At the end of Pikk, in the squat tower known as **Fat Margaret** (Paks Margareeta), the **Maritime Museum** (Meremuuseum) examines Tallinn's port history. *(Pikk 70. Open W-Su 10am-6pm. 15EEK, students 7EEK.)* Head to the other end of Pikk and turn left on Rataskaevu to see **St. Nicholas Church** (Niguliste kirik) and its mighty spire. *(Open W-Su 10am-5pm. 15EEK.)*

TOOMPEA. From Raekoja pl., head down Kullassepa, right on Niguliste, and uphill on Lühike jalg to reach Toompea's **Castle Square** (Lossi pl.), dominated by the Russian onion domes of golden **Aleksander Nevsky Cathedral.** *(Open daily 8am-7pm. Services 9am and 6pm.)* Directly behind **Toompea Castle,** the current seat of the Estonian Parliament (closed to the public), an Estonian flag tops **Tall Hermann** (Pikk Hermann), Tallinn's tallest tower and most impressive medieval fortification.

ROCCA-AL-MARE

On the peninsula of Rocca-al-Mare, 10km west of the city center, the **Estonian Open-Air Museum** is full of 18th- to 20th-century wooden mills and homesteads, collected from all over Estonia and rebuilt in the park. Estonian folk troupes perform here regularly. *(Vabaõhumuuseumi 12. From Tallinn's train station, take bus #21 or 21a (25min.). Open May-Oct. daily 10am-8pm; winter 10am-6pm. 25EEK, students and seniors 9EEK.)*

🎵🔘 ENTERTAINMENT AND NIGHTLIFE

Pick up *Tallinn This Week* (free) at the tourist office. **Estonia Theater,** Estonia pst. 4, offers opera, ballet, musicals, and chamber music. (☎626 02 15; www.opera.ee. Ticket office open daily noon-7pm.) **Eesti Kontsert,** Estonia pst. 4, features classical music nearly every night. (☎614 77 60; fax 614 77 69; www.concert.ee. Box office open M-F noon-7pm, Sa-Su noon-5pm. Students 30EEK.) During **Old Town Days** (usually the last week of May to the first week of June), the city fills with open-air concerts. The first week of July brings **Beersummer,** a celebration of all that foams. On summer Sundays, Tallinn converges on the **beach** of **Pirita,** a few kilometers from the city center (bus #1, 1a, 8, 34, or 38). Vanalinn is packed with bars that offer a great night out. One relaxed and classy joint is **Nimeta Baar** (No Name Bar), Suur Karja 6. (Beer 32EEK. Open Su-Th 11am-2am, F-Sa 11am-4am.) Or, for a submarine decor, try **Cafe V.S.** (Võitlev Sõna), Parnu mnt. 28. (Beer 30EEK. Open M-Th 10am-1am, F-Sa 10am-3am, Su 1pm-1am.)

STONE COLD LOVE Estonian folklore has an interesting take on the origins of Toompea. As the story goes, young *Kalevipoeg* was out hunting with his brothers when a Finnish sorcerer, pounced on *Kalevipoeg*'s mother Linda and dragged her off to his northern fortress to make his solitude a little less solitary. Linda's cries for help went unheeded until the magician had lugged her nearly to the shores of the Baltic, when the forces of nature—never sympathetic in Estonia—intervened. A bolt of lightning stunned the villain, but also turned his ill-gotten mistress into the rocky mound where the Estonian Parliament now stands.

TARTU
☎(0)7

Tartu may be the oldest city in the Baltics, but its young population and nightlife keep it lively. From the 1775 **Town Hall Square** (Raekoja plats), follow Ülikooli from behind the town hall to **Tartu University** (Tartu Ülikool). Farther up Ülikooli (which becomes Jaani), **St. John's Church** (Jaani-kirik), Lutsu 16/24, holds hundreds of figures of saints and martyrs. On **Cathedral Hill** (Toomemägi), marvel at the ruins of the 15th-century **Cathedral of St. Peter and Paul** (Toomkirik). At night, try ▨**Wilde Bar,** Vallikraavi 4, where the crowd chugs Irish beer. (Beer 25EEK. Live music F and Sa. Open Su-Tu noon-midnight, W-Th noon-1am, F-Sa noon-2am.)

 Buses (☎47 72 27) leave from Turu 2, at Riia and Turu, 300m southeast of Raekoja pl. along Vabaduse, to: **Rīga** (5hr., 1 per day, 150EEK); St. Petersburg (10hr., 2 per day, 160EEK); and Tallinn (2-5hr., 44 per day, 85-90EEK). Buses #5 and 6 run from the train station to the city center and then to the bus station. **Trains,** generally less reliable than buses, go from Vaksali 6 (☎37 32 20), at Kuperjanovi and Vaksali, 1½km from the city center, to Tallinn (3½hr., 3 per day, 70EEK). From the bus station, follow Riia mnt. and turn right on Ülikoali to Raekoja pl. to reach the **tourist office,** Raekoja pl. 14. (☎/fax 43 21 41; tartu@visitestonia.com. Open M-F 10am-6pm, Sa 10am-3pm.) **Hostel Tartu (HI),** Soola 3a, is in the center of town, opposite the bus station. (☎43 20 91; fax 43 30 41. Check-out noon. Singles 200EEK, nonmembers 410EEK; doubles 720/900EEK.) The **Tartu Kaubamaja supermarket** is at Riia 2. (Open M-F 10am-8pm, Sa 10am-6pm, Su 11am-5pm.) **Postal code:** 51003.

ESTONIAN ISLANDS

Worried about providing an easy escape route to the West, the Soviets once cordoned these islands off from foreigners and Estonians; they now remain a preserve for all that is distinctive about Estonia.

SAAREMAA. Kuressaare, the largest city of the island of Saaremaa, is making a comeback with summer influxes of young Estonians. Head south from Raekoja pl. along Lossi, through the park, and across the moat to reach the **Bishopric Castle** (Piiskopilinnus). Inside, the **Saaremaa Regional Museum** chronicles the islands' history. (Open May-Aug. daily 11am-7pm; Sept.-Apr. W-Su 11am-7pm. 30EEK, students 15EEK.) Rent a **bike** at **Oü Bivarix,** Tallinna 26, near the bus station (120EEK per day), and pedal to the **beaches** in southwest Saaremaa (8-12km from Kuressaare) or to the **Kaarma Church** in east Saaremaa. Direct **buses** (☎316 61) leave from Pihtla tee 2, at the corner of Tallinna, for **Tallinn** (4hr., 7 per day, 150EEK) and **Pärnu** (3½hr., 4 per day, 115EEK). The **tourist office,** Tallinna 2, in the town hall, has maps and arranges homestays for free. (☎/fax 331 20; kuressaare@visitestonia.com; www.visitestonia.com. Open May to mid-Sept. M-F 9am-7pm, Sa 9am-5pm, Su 10am-3pm; mid-Sept. to Apr. M-F 9am-5pm.) If you'd rather stay in a hotel, try **Hotell Pärna,** Pärna 3. (☎/fax 575 21. Doubles 400EEK, with bath 550EEK.) ☎(0)245.

ESTONIA

COPS VS. PUNKS In Kuressaare, someone had the bright idea to put these epic rivals together on the pitch to let out their aggressions. Since that day, very June, the blue uniforms and the rainbow mohawks have had at each other with slide tackles and flurries of obscenities. The quality of the football is usually poor, and the keg of beer on the sideline doesn't help. But the game is a town spectacle that draws crowds of fans. Almost everyone who attends sides with the underdogs.

HIIUMAA. By restricting access to Hiiumaa (HEE-you-ma) for 50 years, the Soviets unwittingly preserved the island's rare plant and animal species. **Kärdla,** the island's biggest city, contains as many creeks and trees as houses. You can **hike** or **camp** in the **West-Estonian Islands Biosphere Reserve,** which hosts more than two-thirds of all Estonia's plant species. Other interesting sights lie along the coast; rent a **bike** (100EEK) from **Kerttu Sport,** Vabrikuväljak 1, just across the bridge from the bus station. (☎963 73. Open M-F 10am-6pm, Sa 10am-3pm.) Don't miss the tiny island of **Kassari,** attached to Hiiumaa by a land bridge. **Ferries** run between north Saaremaa's Triigi port and south Hiiumaa's Sõru port (1hr., 2 per day, 20EEK). Direct **buses** run from Sadama 13 (☎320 77), north of Kärdla's main square, Keskväljak, to Tallinn (4hr., 3 per day, 115EEK). **Postal code:** 92411. ☎(0)246.

FINLAND (SUOMI)

FINNISH MARKKA

US$1 = 7.10MK	1MK = US$0.14
CDN$1 = 4.60MK	1MK = CDN$0.21
UK£1 = 9.90MK	1MK = UK£0.10
IR£1 = 7.55MK	1MK = IR£0.132
AUS$1 = 3.40MK	1MK = AUS$0.26
NZ$1 = 2.95MK	1MK = NZ$0.34
ZAR1 = 0.90MK	1MK = ZAR1.03
EUR€1 = 5.95MK	1MK = EUR€0.168

PHONE CODES	**Country code:** 358. **International dialing prefix:** 00. From outside Finland, dial the int'l dialing prefix (see inside back cover) + 358 + city code + local number.

Although neutral in character, Finland is a country with shocking natural extremes. Endlessly lit summer nights contrast with dark winter days, and provincial seaside towns stand against bustling, modern Helsinki. Even Finnish culture varies with its Swedish influence in the west and Russian characteristics in the east. Apart from its striking architecture and design, the way of life in Finland is one of understated simplicity. After seven centuries in the crossfire of warring Sweden and Russia, Finland gained autonomy in 1917 and never looked back. Hearty nationalism is expressed in typical Finnish fashion—with a heavy dose of modesty and prudence. Now, as a member of the European Community, Finland mixes its turbulent past with its longstanding Nordic neutrality.

FACTS AND FIGURES

Official Name: Republic of Finland.
Capital: Helsinki.
Major Cities: Tampere, Turku, Oulu.
Population: 5,160,000.
Land Area: 305,000 sq. km.

Climate: Temperate but cold; in some places subarctic.
Languages: Finnish, Swedish.
Religions: Evangelical Lutheran (85%), Greek Orthodox (1%), none (14%).

DISCOVER FINLAND

Perched on the edge of Scandinavia and Russia, **Helsinki** (p. 299) mixes Orthodox cathedrals and Lutheran churches, sleek 20th-century architecture, and grand 19th-century avenues. Daytrip to oft-photographed **Porvoo** (p. 304) and seaside **Hanko** (p. 304) before heading westward to **Turku** (p. 309), Finland's oldest city. Check out Moomin World in nearby **Naantali** (p. 310) before ferrying to the lovely **Åland Islands** (p. 305). The Lake District's **Savonlinna** (p. 308) was once a tsarist resort. Stop in **Tampere** (p. 307) before heading into **Lapland** (p. 310), where you can sit in Santa's lap and frolic with reindeer.

ESSENTIALS

WHEN TO GO

The long days of Finnish summers make for a tourist's dream; even night owls get out in the light of the midnight sun. After coming out of the two-month *kaamos* (polar night) without any sunlight, winter fanatics start hitting the slopes in early February; the skiing continues into March and April.

DOCUMENTS AND FORMALITIES

VISAS. South Africans need a visa to enter as short-stay tourists; citizens of Australia, Canada, Ireland, New Zealand, the UK, and the US can visit Scandinavia for up to 90 days without a visa. For more than 90 days in Finland, Iceland, Norway, and/or Sweden, you will need a visa.

EMBASSIES. Foreign embassies are in Helsinki (p. 229). For Finnish embassies at home: **Australia,** 10 Darwin Ave., Yarralumla, ACT 2600 (☎(02) 62 73 38 00; fax 62 73 36 03); **Canada,** 55 Metcalfe St., Suite 850, Ottawa ON, K1P 6L5 (☎613-236-2389; fax 613-238-1474; finembott@synapse.net); **Ireland,** Russell House, Stokes Pl., St. Stephen's Green, Dublin 2 (☎(01) 478 13 44; fax 478 37 27); **South Africa,** P.O. Box 443, Pretoria 0001 (☎(012) 343 02 75; fax 343 30 95); **UK,** 38 Chesham Pl., London SW1X 8HW (☎(020) 78 38 62 00; fax 72 35 36 80); **US,** 3301 Massachusetts Ave., NW, Washington, D.C. 20008 (☎202-298-5800; fax 202-298-6030; www.finland.org).

TRANSPORTATION

BY PLANE. Finnair (toll-free in Finland ☎02 03 140 160; English 24hr. info ☎818 83 83; fax (09) 818 87 35; www.finnair.com) flies from 50 international cities and covers the domestic market. Contact them in **Australia,** Avion House, 249-251 Pulteney St., Adelaide SA 5000 (☎(08) 83 06 84 11; fax 83 06 84 39); in **New Zealand,** Trust Bank Building, 229 Queen St., 6th fl., Auckland (☎(09) 308 33 65; fax 308 33 88); or in the **US,** 20 Park Plaza, Suite 912, Boston, MA 02116 (☎617-482-4952 or 800-950-5000; fax 617-482-5932). Finnair gives a domestic discount of up to 50% for ages 17-24, and has summer and snow rates that reduce fares by up to 60%.

BY TRAIN. Eurailpass is valid in Finland. The national rail company is **VR Ltd., Finnish Railways,** P.O.Box 488, 00101 Helsinki (☎30 72 09 00; www.vr.fi). Efficient trains run at typical Nordic prices (Turku to Helsinki 106-136mk/€17.80-22.85, Helsinki to Rovaniemi 360mk/€60.45); seat reservations (20-30mk/€3.40-5.05) are not required except on **InterCity** trains. The *buy-in-Scandinavia* **Scanrail Pass** allows unlimited rail travel through Denmark, Norway, Sweden, Finland, and many free or 20-50% discounted ferry rides. (5 days within 15 days 1606mk/€269.60; 21 consecutive days 2486mk/€417.35.) This differs from the *buy-outside-Scandinavia* **Scanrail Pass** (p. 68). A **Finnrail Pass** gives one month of unlimited rail travel. (3 days 650mk/€109.15, 5 days 870mk/€146.05, 10 days 1180mk/€198.10.)

BY BUS. Buses cost the same as or more than trains, and often take longer. But they are the only way to reach some smaller towns and travel in northern Finland. **Onni Vilkas Ltd** (www.onnivilkas.planet.fi/pietarie.ht) runs a daily bus between Helsinki and St. Petersburg, as well as domestic service. **Expressbus** covers a lot of Finland (www.expressbus.com). For bus information, call ☎ 02 00 40 00 (6.34mk/€1.10 per min.). ISIC cardholders can buy a **student card** (32mk/€5.40 plus passport-sized photo) that discounts tickets by 50%, from bus stations. With student ID, drivers will give the student discount. **Railpasses** are valid on VR Ltd. buses when trains are not in service.

BY FERRY. Viking Line (Helsinki ☎ (09) 123 51; fax 123 52 92; Stockholm ☎ (08) 452 40 00, fax 452 40 75) runs from Stockholm to: **Helsinki** (15hr.; 240mk/€40.30, students 220mk/€36.96; off season 250mk/€42, 200mk/€33.60); **Mariehamn** on **Åland** (6½hr.; 70mk/€11.75, students 55mk/€9.25); and **Turku** (12hr.; 160mk/€26.90, students 130mk/€21.85; off season 110mk/€18.50, 95mk/€15.95). Scanrail holders get 50% off on Viking; Eurailers ride free. **Silja Line** (Helsinki ☎ (09) 180 41; fax 180 4402; Stockholm ☎ (08) 452 50 00; fax 452 40 30; Turku ☎ (02) 335 6244; www.silja.com/english) sails from Stockholm to: **Helsinki** (15hr., 200-245mk/€33.60-41.15); **Mariehamn** (5½hr.; 125mk/€21, students 115mk/€19.35); and **Turku** (11hr.; 2 per day; from 110mk/€18.50, students from 95mk/€15.95). For Eurailers, Stockholm to Helsinki is 145mk/€24.35 and to Turku at night is 100mk/€16.80. **Birka Lines** (Mariehamn ☎ (018) 270 27; Stockholm ☎ (08) 702 72 30; info@birkacruises.com) launches *Princess* daily from Stockholm to Mariehamn (24hr., 125mk/€21).

BY CAR. Driving conditions are good, but be wary of snow and ice in winter, and reindeer crossings. Drive on the right side of the road. Drinking and driving laws result in fines and/or imprisonment for violators. For car rentals, contact **Europcar** (☎ (0800) 121 54; fax 75 15 54 54; www.europcar.com) or **Hertz** (☎ (0800) 11 22 33 or (020) 555 24 00; www.hertz.com); both charge about 2400mk/€402.90 per week.

BY BIKE AND BY THUMB. Finland has 10,000km of cycling paths. Some campgrounds, hostels, and tourist offices rent bikes. Rates average 30-80mk/€5.05-13.45 per day or 200mk/€33.60 per week. Hitchhikers find more rides in Finland than elsewhere in Scandinavia; truck drivers may be likely to stop. *Let's Go* does not recommend hitchhiking.

TOURIST SERVICES AND MONEY

EMERGENCY	Police: ☎ 122. Ambulance: ☎ 123. Fire: ☎ 124.

TOURIST OFFICES. The helpful **Finnish tourist boards** offer a comprehensive website (www.mek.fi). Contact the tourist office of the region you plan to visit.

MONEY. Finland's currency unit is the **markka** (also known as the Finnish mark or Finmark). Finland has accepted the **Euro (€)** as legal tender, and *markka* will be phased out by July 1, 2002. For more information, see p. 24. Banks exchange currency and accept ATM cards. ATMs offer the best exchange rates. Orange "Otto" bank machines accept Cirrus, MC, Visa, and ATM cards. Food costs run 60-100mk/€10.10-16.80 per day. Meals generally cost at least 30mk/€5.05. Restaurants include a 14-15% gratuity in the meal price. Round the fare up for cab drivers. A normal tip for bellhops, train porters, and sauna and cloakroom attendants is 5mk/€0.85. The Value Added Tax (VAT) is 22%, 17% on food, and 8% on select services. For VAT refund or general information, contact Global Refund Finland Oy, Salamonkatu 17A, 00101 Helsinki (☎ 020 355 432; www.globalrefund.com).

BUSINESS HOURS. Most shops are open Monday to Friday until 5 or 6pm (10pm in Helsinki), and Saturday until 2 or 3pm. Urban supermarkets may stay open until 9pm, Saturday 6pm. Shops may also be open June to August. on Sunday. Kiosks sell basic food, snacks, and toiletries until 9 or 10pm. Banks are typically open Monday to Friday 9:15am-4:15pm.

COMMUNICATION

MAIL. Mail service is fast and efficient. Post offices are open Monday to Friday from 9am until 5 or 6pm. First-class and priority postal rates for postcards and letters

FINLAND

under 20g is 3.20mk/€0.55 to other EU countries; 2.70mk/€0.50 to non-EU European countries; 6.30mk/€1.10 for letters and 3.40mk/€0.60 for postcards going outside Europe. Domestic letters and postcards under 50g cost 3mk/€0.55. *Poste Restante* can be sent to any town's main post office.

TELEPHONES. To make a long-distance call within Finland, dial 0 and the number. Local and long-distance calls within Finland usually cost 3mk/€0.55; many pay phones take 1-, 5-, and 10mk/€1.70 coins. Phone cards are available from R-kiosks and post offices in 30-, 50-, 70-, and 100mk/€16.80 denominations. "Sonera" or "Nonstop" cards work nationwide; other cards only work in one city. There are two types of phone cards: those inserted vertically and those inserted horizontally. Check the pay phone you plan to use before purchasing a card. Also, some pay phones block toll-free calls. Some card telephones take credit cards. Cell phones are the main mode of Finnish conversation, and international cell cards are widely available. For domestic information, call ☎118. For international information, call ☎020 208. International direct dial numbers include: **AT&T,** ☎0800 100 10; **British Telecom,** ☎0800 11 04 40; **Canada Direct,** ☎0800 11 00 11; **Ireland Direct,** ☎0800 11 03 53; **MCI,** ☎08001 102 80; **Sprint,** ☎0800 11 02 84; **Telkom South Africa,** ☎0800 11 02 70; and **Telstra Australia,** ☎0800 11 00 610.

LANGUAGES. Finnish, a Finno-Ugric language, is spoken by most of the population. In Helsinki, about 90% of the city speaks English, and Swedish is officially spoken as well. In smaller towns like Lahti, there are fewer English speakers, but the language barrier won't pose a problem. Sami (Lappish) is the tongue of about 1700 people. Some town names modify form on train and bus schedules due to a lack of prepositions in Finland. For example, "To Helsinki" is "Helsinkiin"; "From Helsinki" is "Helsingistä." For useful phrases, see p. 983.

ACCOMMODATIONS AND CAMPING

Finland has more than 120 **youth hostels** (*retkeilymaja*; RET-kay-loo-MAH-yah); 70 are open all year. Prices average 60-160mk/€10.10-26.90; non-HI-members add 15mk/€2.55. Most have laundry and a kitchen; some have saunas and rent bicycles, boats, and ski equipment. The **Finnish Youth Hostel Association** (Suomen Retkeily-maja-järjestö-SRM; ☎(09) 565 71 50; information ☎060 092 484, 2.85mk/€0.50 per min.; fax 565 715 10; info@srm.inet.fi; www.srmnet.org) is at Yrjönkatu 38B, 00100 Helsinki. **Hotels** are often exorbitant (over 300mk/€50.40); *kesähotelli* (summer hotels) operate June-Aug. and cost 40-110mk/€6.75-18.50. The **Finland Tourism Board** (www.mek.fi) keeps a database of booking agencies for year-round and summer hotels. **Private room** rental is not particularly common, but local tourist offices may help you find the cheapest accommodations. Without permission it is illegal to **camp** outside campsites. About 360 campgrounds dapple the country; 200 to the Finnish Travel Association's national network (tent sites 30-100mk/€5.05-16.80 per night; *mökit* (small cottages) from 150mk/€25.20). Seventy are open year-round. Finnish or International Camping Cards (FICC) earn discounts at most campgrounds. Buy a membership card from camping sites (25mk/€4.20 per family). For a campground guide, contact the **Finnish Travel Association/Camping Department,** Atomitie 5C, 00370 Helsinki (☎(09) 622 62 80; fax 654 3 58).

FOOD AND DRINK

A *kahvila* serves food, coffee, and beer; a *grilli* is a fast-food stand. A *ravintola* (restaurant) covers the spectrum from cafeterias to pubs. The best budget dining is at common all-you-can-eat lunch buffets (40-60mk/€6.75-10.10), often found at otherwise pricier restaurants. Kebab and pizza joints are cheap, although quality varies (small pizza or kebab plate from 25mk/€4.20). The **Golden Rax Pizza Buffet** chain offers cheap pizza and salads. The cheapest supermarkets are **Alepa, Euromarket, Valintalo,** and any type of **K market.** The Finns are proud of their fish, including *kir-jolohi* (rainbow trout), *silakka* (Baltic herring), and *lohi* (salmon) cured, pickled, smoked, poached, or baked. Finnish dietary staples include rye bread, potatoes, sour milk, Karelian pastries, and *viili* (yogurt). Reindeer meat, roasted or in a stew, is on some menus. In summer, blueberries, cranberries, lingonberries, and, in the far north, Arctic cloudberries are picked for desserts, wines, vodka, and other liquors. You must be 18 to purchase beer and wine, and 20 for hard liquor; the age limit in bars and pubs is usually 18 but can be as high as 25. Outside bars and restaurants, all alcohol stronger than *Olut* III must be purchased at state-run Alko liquor stores. For "cheers," Finns say *"hi," "kippis,"* or the Scandinavian *"skal."*

HOLIDAYS AND FESTIVALS

Holidays: Epiphany (Jan. 6); Good Friday (Mar. 29), May Day (May 1); Ascension Day (May 26); Midsummer (June 21-23); All Saints' Day (Nov. 2); Independence Day (Dec. 6); Christmas Day (Dec. 25); Boxing Day (Dec. 26). Many stores and museums, as well as all banks and post offices, are closed for Easter (Mar. 31), Christmas (Dec. 24-26), and New Year's Day. During Midsummer, when Finns party all night to the light of *kokko* (bonfires) and the midnight sun, virtually the entire country shuts down.

Festivals: The **Helsinki Festival** (Aug. 23-Sept. 8 in 2002; p. 299) has concerts, dance, theater, and opera. Savonlinna's **Opera Festival** (early July to early Aug.; p. 308), is in Olavinlinna Castle. **Naantali** has a Chamber Music Festival (June; p. 310).

HELSINKI (HELSINGFORS) ☎ 09

With all the appeal and none of the grime of a big city, Helsinki's broad avenues, grand architecture, and green parks make it a model of 19th-century city planning. The city also distinguishes itself with a decidedly multicultural flair: Lutheran and Russian Orthodox cathedrals stand almost face-to-face, and youthful energy mingles with old world charm. Baltic Sea produce fills the marketplaces and restaurants, while St. Petersburg and Tallinn are only a short cruise away.

▐▀ TRANSPORTATION

Flights: Helsinki-Vantaa Airport (☎96 00 81 00; 3.40mk/€0.60 per min.) **Buses** #615 (more direct) and 616 run frequently between the airport and the train station square (15mk/€2.55). A **Finnair bus** shuttles between the airport and the Finnair building at Asemaaukio 3, next to the train station (35min., every 15min. 5am-midnight, 27mk/€4.55).

Trains: (☎0307 20 900 or 03 02 72 09 00.) To: **Moscow** (15hr., daily 5:34pm, 495mk/€83.10; reservations needed); **Rovaniemi** (7-10hr., 5-8 per day, 388mk/€65.15); **Tampere** (2hr., 6am-10pm, 124mk/€21); **Turku** (2hr., 12 per day, 124mk/€21); **St. Petersburg** (7hr., 2 per day, 294mk/€49.40).

Buses: (☎02 00 40 90; for Espoo and Vantaa buses ☎010 01 11.) The station is between Salomonkatu and Simonkatu; from the Mannerheimintie side of the train station, head down Postikatu past the statue of Mannerheim. Cross Mannerheimintie onto Salomonkatu and the station will be to your left. To: **Lahti** (1½hr., 2 per hr., 114mk/€19.35); **Tampere** (2½hr., every hr., 105mk/€17.65); **Turku** (2½hr., 2 per hr., 124mk/€21).

Ferries: For route options, see p. 297. **Silja Line,** Mannerheimintie 2 (☎980 07 45 52 or 091 80 41). Take tram #3B or 3T from the city center to the Olympic terminal. **Viking Line,** Mannerheimintie 14 (☎12 35 77). **Tallink,** Erottajankatu 19 (☎22 82 12 77). Viking Line and **Finnjet** (contact Silja Line) depart from Katajanokka Island, east of Kauppatori (take tram #2 or 4). Silja Line sails from South Harbor, south of Kauppatori (take tram #3T).

Local Transportation: (☎010 01 11; 2mk/€0.35 per call). The metro, trams, and buses run roughly 5:30am-11pm. (Major tram and bus lines, including tram #3T, continue until 1:30am.) There is only 1 metro line, which runs approximately east to west, 10 tram lines, and many more bus lines. Night buses, marked with an N, run after 1:30am. You can buy single-fare tickets on buses and trams or from machines at the metro station (15mk/€2.55); 10-trip tickets (120mk/€20.15) are available at R-kiosks and at the **City Transport** office in the Rautatientori metro station (open M-Th

FINLAND

7:30am-6pm, F 7:30am-4pm; in winter open 1hr. later). Tickets are valid for 1hr. (transfers free); punch your ticket on board. The **Tourist Ticket,** a convenient bargain for a 5-day stay, is available at City Transport and tourist offices and provides unlimited bus, tram, metro, and local train transit (1-day 25mk/€4.20, 3-day 50mk/€8.40, 5-day 75mk/€12.60; half-price for children).

■ 🛈 ORIENTATION AND PRACTICAL INFORMATION

Sea surrounds Helsinki on the east and west, and the city center is bisected by two lakes. Water shapes everything in the Finnish capital, from relaxing city beaches to gorgeous parks around the lakes. Helsinki's main street, **Mannerhei-mintie,** passes between the bus and train stations on its way to the city center, eventually crossing **Esplanadi.** This tree-lined promenade leads east to **Kauppatori** (Market Square) and the beautiful South Harbor. Both Finnish and Swedish are used on all street signs and maps. *Let's Go* uses the Finnish names in all listings and maps.

TOURIST, FINANCIAL, AND LOCAL SERVICES

Tourist Offices: City Tourist Office, Pohjoisesplanadi 19 (☎169 37 57; fax 169 38 39; www.hel.fi). From the train station, walk 2 blocks down Keskuskatu and turn left on Pohjoisesplanadi. Open May-Sept. M-F 9am-8pm, Sa-Su 9am-6pm; Oct.-Apr. M-F 9am-5pm, Sa 9am-3pm. The **Finnish Tourist Board,** Eteläesplanadi 4 (☎41 76 93 00; fax 41 76 93 01; www.mek.fi), has information on all of Finland. Open June-Aug. M-F 9am-5pm, Sa 10am-2pm; Sept.-May M-F 9am-5pm. **Hotellikeskus** (Hotel Booking Center; ☎22 88 14 00; fax 22 88 14 99), in the train station, books rooms for a fee of 30mk/€5.05 in person, but free by phone or email. Open June-Aug. M-F 9am-7pm, Sa-Su 10am-6pm; Sept.-May M-F 9am-5pm. The **Helsinki Card,** sold at the tourist office, Hotellikeskus, central R-kiosks, and most hotels, provides museum discounts and unlimited local transportation (1-day 130mk/€21.85, 3-day 190mk/€31.90).

Embassies: Canada, Pohjoisesplanadi 25B (☎17 11 41). Open M-F 8:30am-noon and 1-4:30pm. **Estonia,** Itäinen Puistotie 10 (☎622 02 88). **Ireland,** Erottajankatu 7A (☎64 60 06). **Latvia,** Armfeltintie 10 (☎476 47 20). **Lithuania,** Rauhankatu 13A (☎60 82 10). **Poland,** Armas Lindgrenintie 21 (☎684 80 77). **Russia,** Tehtaankatu 1B (☎66 18 76). **South Africa,** Rahapajankatu 1A 5 (☎68 60 31 00). **UK,** Itäinen Puistotie 17 (☎22 86 51 00). Also handles diplomatic matters for **Australians** and **New Zealanders.** Open M-F 8:30am-5pm. **US,** Itäinen Puistotie 14A (☎17 19 31). Open M-F 8:30am-5pm, 9am-noon for consulate. By appointment only.

Currency Exchange: Exchange, Kaivokatu 6, across from the train station. No fee for cash exchange, but 30mk/€5.05 fee for up to 6 traveler's checks. Open M-F 8am-8pm, Sa 10am-4pm. The 5 Helsinki **Forex** offices are a good choice. Hours vary but the Rautatieasema/Jvgstn location in the train station is open 7am-9pm.

Luggage Storage: Train station lockers 10mk/€1.70 per day.

Laundromat: Easywash, Runeberginkatu 47 (☎40 69 82). Open M-Th 10am-9pm, F 10am-6pm, Sa 10am-4pm.

EMERGENCY AND COMMUNICATIONS

Emergency: ☎112. **Police:** ☎100 22.

Pharmacy: Yliopiston Apteekki, Mannerheimintie 96 (☎41 78 03 00). Open 24hr.

Medical Assistance: Aleksin lääkäriasema, Mannerheimintie 8 (☎77 50 84 00).

Internet Access: Cable Book Library, Mannerheimintie 22-24, in the Lasipalatsi mall directly across from the bus station. Open M-Th 10am-8pm, Su noon-6pm.

Post Office: Mannerheiminaukio 1A (☎020 451 44 00). Open M-F 9am-6pm. Address mail to be held: First name SURNAME, *Poste Restante,* Mannerheiminaukio 1A, **00100** Helsinki, Finland. Open M-F 7am-9pm, Sa 9am-6pm, Su 11am-9pm.

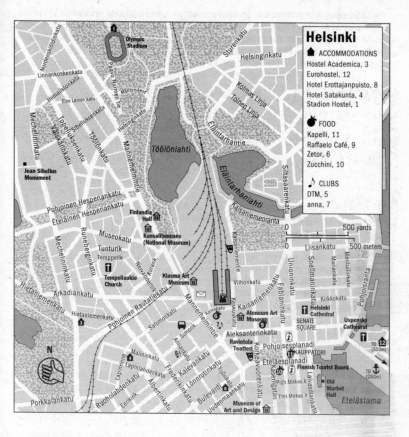

Helsinki

📍 ACCOMMODATIONS
Hostel Academica, 3
Eurohostel, 12
Hotel Erottajanpuisto, 8
Hotel Satakunta, 4
Stadion Hostel, 1

🍴 FOOD
Kapelli, 11
Raffaelo Café, 9
Zetor, 6
Zucchini, 10

🎵 CLUBS
DTM, 5
anna, 7

ACCOMMODATIONS AND CAMPING

Helsinki hotels tend to be expensive, but budget hostels are often quite nice. In June and July, it's wise to make reservations a few weeks in advance.

Eurohostel (HI), Linnankatu 9, Katajanokka (☎ 622 04 70; fax 65 50 44; www.eurohostel.fi). 200m from Viking Line/Finnjet ferry terminal. From the train station, head right to Mannerheimintie, and take tram #2 to Mastokatu; or tram #4 to Munkkiniemi (both dir. Katajanokka). From Uspensky Cathedral, head down Kanavankatu, turn left on Pikku Satamankatu, and bear right on Linnankatu. The largest hostel in Finland, with bright rooms, non-smoking floors, and sauna. Kitchen and cafe. Linens included. Reception 24hr. Dorms 110mk/€18.50; singles 190mk/€31.90; doubles 210mk/€35.30; triples 315mk/€52.90. Nonmembers add 15mk/€2.55. Student discounts in winter.

Hostel Erottanjanpuisto (HI), Uudenmaankatu 9 (☎ 64 21 69; fax 680 27 57). Turn right from the train station, left onto Mannerheimintie, and bear right onto Erottajankatu; Uudenmaankatu is on the right. Central locations and well-kept rooms make this hostel popular; call ahead. Kitchen. Breakfast 25-35mk/€4.20-5.90. Lockers 12mk/€2.05. Laundry 40mk/€6.75. Reception 24hr. Check-out 10pm. In summer, dorms 150mk/€25.20; singles 260mk/€43.65; doubles 340mk/€57.10. Off season 10-35mk/€1.70-5.90 less. Nonmembers add 15mk/€2.55.

Hotel Satakunta (HI), Lapinrinne 1A (☎ 695 85 231; fax 68 54 245; ravintola.satakunta@sodexho.fi). Take the metro to Kampi and walk downhill, or take bus #55 or 55a and tell the driver your destination. Spacious, well-equipped rooms with balconies. Breakfast and linens 30mk/€5.05 each; included in non-dorm prices. Reception 24hr. Check-in 2pm. Check-out noon. Open June-Aug. Dorms 65mk/€10.95; singles 225mk/€37.80; doubles 325mk/€54.60. Nonmembers add 15mk/€2.55.

Stadion Hostel (HI), Pohj. Stadiontie 3B (☎49 60 71; fax 49 64 66). Take tram #7A or 3 to the Auroran Sairaala stop. Walk to the right of the stop about 250m, following the signs; it's inside the fence. The hostel, on the far side of the Stadium, is converted athletic space with sports memorabilia popular with school groups. Kitchen. Breakfast 25mk/€4.20. Sheets 15-25mk/€2.55-4.20. Laundry 15mk/€2.55. Reception June to early Sept. 7am-3am; mid-Sept. to May 8-10am and 4pm-2am. Lockout noon-4pm. Dorms 70mk/€11.75; singles 115mk/€19.35; doubles 220mk/€36.95. Nonmembers add 15mk/€2.55.

Hostel Academica, Hietaniemenkatu 14A (☎1311 43 34; fax 441 201; hostel.academica@hyy.fi). Take tram #3T to Kauppakorkeakoulu, go left to the end of Lapuankatu and turn right on Hietaniemenkatu. Open in summer only. Reception 24hr. Check-in 2pm. Check-out noon. Breakfast 30mk/€5.05, linens 20mk/€3.40; both included in non-dorm prices. Dorms 95mk/€15.95; singles 225mk/€37.80; doubles 325mk/€54.60; triples 340mk/€57.10. Nonmembers add 15mk/€2.55.

Rastila Camping (☎31 65 51; fax 344 15 78), 12km east of the city center. Take the metro east to Rastila (a Vuosaari, not Mellunmäki train); the campsite is 100m away to the right. Toilets, showers, and washing and cooking facilities. Reception mid-May to mid-Sept. 24hr; mid-Sept. to mid-May 8am-10pm. Beach access. Camping 50mk-80/€8.40-13.45 per person; 2-person cabins 220mk/€36.95, 4-person cabins 360mk/€60.45. Summer hostel: dorms 95mk/€15.95; singles 150mk/€25.20; doubles 260mk/€43.65; triples 360mk/€60.45.

▶ FOOD

Escape pricey restaurants at **Alepa supermarket,** under the train station. (Open M-F 7:30am-10pm, Sa 9am-10pm, Su 10am-10pm.) **Open-air markets** line **Kauppatori,** by the port. (Open June-Aug. M-Sa 6:30am-2pm and 4-8pm; Sept.-May M-F 7am-2pm.) **Vanha Kauppahalli** (Old Market Hall) is nearby. (Open M-F 8am-8pm, Sa 8am-3pm.)

Golden Rax Pizza Buffet, in Forum, opposite the post office. All-you-can-eat pasta and pizza bargain extravaganza 39-43mk/€6.55-7.25. Open M-Th 10:30am-9pm, F-Sa 10:30am-10pm, Su 11:30am-9pm.

Zetor, Kaivokatu 10, in Kaivopiha, the mall directly opposite the train station. The name translates to tractor, which explains the farm decor. For a truly Finnish experience, partake in traditional dancing (Th-Sa) and homemade beer (26mk/€4.40). Entrees 40-115mk/€6.75-19.35. Open Su-M 3pm-1am, Tu-Th 3pm-3am, F-Sa 3pm-4am.

Raffaelo Cafe, Alexandrankatu 46, near Senate Square. Daily lunch specials 44mk/€7.30. Bar and menu entrees 58-132mk/€10.10-21.85. Open M-W 11am-1am, Th-Sa 11am-2am, Su 1pm-1am.

Kappeli, Eteläesplanadi 1, at the Unionkatu end of Esplanadi park. The distinctive yellow building has catered to trendies since 1837. A great spot for people-watching. Entrees 70-130mk/€11.75-21.85. Open Su-Th 9am-1:30am, F-Sa 9am-3:30am.

Zucchini, Fabianinkatu 4, near the tourist office. A casual *kasvisravintola* (vegetarian restaurant) that serves a daily lunch special with salad and bread (42mk/€7.20). Open M-F 11am-4pm; closed July.

▣ SIGHTS

Home to a bold new designs and polished Neoclassical works, Helsinki proves famed Finnish architect Alvar Aalto's statement, "Architecture is our form of expression because our language is so impossible." Much of the layout and architecture of the old center, however, is the brainchild of a German. After Helsinki became the capital of the Grand Duchy of Finland in 1812, Carl Engel designed a grand city modeled after St. Petersburg. **Tram #3T** circles past the major attractions in an hour, offering the cheapest city tour (16mk/€2.60). Better yet, walk—most sights are packed within 2km of the train station. Pick up *See Helsinki on Foot* from the Helsinki tourist office. Helsinki's beautiful parks are must-sees, especially the promenade along **Töölönlahti,** which blooms with lilacs in the summer, and **Tahtitorninvuori** (Observatory Park), overlooking Uspensky Cathedral.

SENAATIN TORI (SENATE SQUARE). The square and its gleaming white **Tuomiokirkko** (Dome Church) showcase Engel's work and exemplify the splendor of Finland's Russian period. *(On the corner of Aleksanterinkatu and Unioninkatu in the city center. Open June-Aug. M-Sa 9am-6pm, Su noon-8pm; Sept.-May Su-F 10am-4pm, Sa 10am-6pm.)*

USPENSKINKATEDRAADI (USPENSKY ORTHODOX CATHEDRAL). Mainly known for its red and gold cupolas and great spires, which jut prominently out of the city skyline, the Cathedral also has an ornate interior. *(Follow Esplanadi down to Kauppatori. Interior open M and W-F 9:30am-4pm, Tu 9:30am-6pm, Sa 9am-4pm, Su noon-3pm.)*

SUOMEN KANSALLISMUSEO (NATIONAL MUSEUM OF FINLAND). The museum displays intriguing bits of Finnish culture, from Gypsy and Sami costumes to *ryijyt* (rugs), as well as a magnificent roof mural by Akseli Gallen-Kallela. *(Up the street from the Finnish Parliament House. Open Tu-W 11am-8pm and Th-Su 11am-6pm. 25mk/€4.20. Call ☎ 94 05 01 or consult the board outside the museum.)*

MUSEUM OF ART AND DESIGN. Even the museum's stairs, a showcase of Finnish and international design, are a mesh masterpiece. *(Korkeavuorenkatu 23. Open in summer M-Su 11am-6pm; in winter Tu and Th-Su 11am-6pm, W 11am-8pm. 40mk/€6.75, students 30mk/€5.05)*

OTHER MUSEUMS. Ateneum Taidemuseo, Finland's largest art museum, features a comprehensive look at Finnish art from the 1700s to the 1960s. *(Kaivokatu 2, opposite the train station. Open Tu and F 9am-6pm, W-Th 9am-8pm, Sa-Su 11am-5pm. 25mk/€4.20, students 20mk/€3.40; special exhibits 40-45mk/€6.75-7.60.)* **Kiasma** picks up where Ateneum leaves off with great modern art in a funky silver building. *(Mannerheiminaukio 2. Open Tu 9am-5pm, W-Su 10am-10pm. 45mk/€7.60, students 40mk/€6.75.)*

FINLANDIA TALO. The magnificent white marble concert hall stands testament to the skill of the Finnish architect Alvar Aalto, who also designed the interior and furnishings. *(Mannerheimintie 13E. Open M-F 9am-4pm; in summer also Sa-Su noon-4pm.)*

TEMPPELIAUKIO KIRKKO. Designed in 1969 by Tuomo and Timo Suomalainen, this inspiring church is built into a hill of rock, with only the roof visible from the outside. Inside, its huge domed ceiling appears to be supported by rays of sunshine. *(Lutherinkatu 3. Walk away from the main post office near the train station on Paasikivenaudio, which becomes Arkadiagatan, then turn right on Fredrikinatu. Open M-F 10am-8pm, Sa 10am-6pm, Su noon-1:45pm and 3:15pm-5:45pm. Services in English Su 2pm.)*

JEAN SIBELIUS MONUMENT. Dedicated in 1967 by sculptor Eila Hiltunen to one of the 20th-century's greatest composers, the Sibelius monument looks like a cloud of organ pipes ascending to heaven. A well-touristed spot in a scenic area, the monument and its surrounding park makes a great place for an afternoon picnic. *(On Mechelininkatu in Sibelius Park. Catch bus #24, dir. Seurasaari, from Mannerheimintie; get off at Rasjasaarentie and the monument will be behind you and to the left.)*

SUOMENLINNA. This 18th-century Swedish military fortification consists of five interconnected islands used by the Swedes to repel attacks on Helsinki. The old fortress's dark passageways are exciting to explore, and the island's museums are worth a visit; check out the model ship collection of the Ehrensvärd and the submarine Vesikko. *(Most museums open in summer 10am-5pm; Mar.-May Sa-Su 11am-4pm. 20mk/€3.40, students 10mk/€1.70; some museums have additional admission. Ferries depart from Market Square every hr. 8am-11pm; return 16mk/€2.70.)*

SEURASAARI. A quick walk across the beautiful white bridge from the mainland brings you to the many paths of the island of Seurasaari, lined by old churches and farmsteads transplanted from all over the country. An open-air museum allows entrance into many of the island's historical buildings. Visit during Midsummer to witness the *kokko* (bonfires) and Finnish revelry in its full splendor. *(Take bus #24 from Erottaja, outside the Swedish Theater, to the last stop. The island is always open for hiking. Museum open M-F 9am-3pm, Sa-Su 11am-5pm. 20mk/€3.40, children free.)*

🎵 🎭 ENTERTAINMENT AND NIGHTLIFE

Sway to afternoon music in **Esplanadi** (the park between Pohjoiesplanadi and Eteläesplanadi) or party with a younger crowd at **Kaivopuisto park** (on the corner of Puistokatu and Ehrenstromintie in the southern part of town) or **Hietaniemi beach.** (From Mannerheimintie, head down Hesperiankatu to the western shore.) The free English-language papers *Helsinki This Week, Helsinki Happens,* and *City* list popular cafes, bars, nightclubs, and events. You must be at least 22-years-old to enter many clubs. Bouncers and cover charges usually relax on weeknights; speaking English may help. With the exception of licensed restaurants and bars, the state-run liquor store **Alko** has a monopoly on sales of alcohol more potent than light beer. (Branch at Mannerheimintie 1, in Kaivopiha across from the train station. Open M-F 9am-8pm, Sa 9am-6pm.) **DTM** (Don't Tell Mama), Annankatu 32, has a gay and mixed crowd. (Cover F-Sa 25mk/€4.20. 20+. Open daily 9pm-4am.) Sip 80-proof on the terrace at **Vanha** (Old Students' House), Mannerheimintie 3. The wide selection includes 130 beers. (Beer from 25mk/€4.20. Cover 30-40mk/€5.05-6.75 for live bands. Open M-Th 11am-2am, F-Sa 11am-4am, Su noon-midnight.) **Unity,** a moving club with Finland's best DJ, is a roving hotspot. Check www.clubunity.org for location and ticket information.

🏞 DAYTRIPS FROM HELSINKI

PORVOO. Porvoo's picturesque cobblestone roads wind around historic wooden houses along the River Porvoo. The nation's most photographed town (pop. 44,000), Porvoo is on Old King Rd., which continues from Helsinki to Russia. In 1809, Tsar Alexander I granted Finland autonomy at the Porvoo **cathedral** in the old town. (Open May-Sept. M-F 10am-6pm, Sa 10am-2pm, Su 2pm-5pm; Oct.-Apr. Tu-F 10am-2pm, Su-M 2-4pm. Free.) The former home of **Johan Ludvig Runeberg,** Aleksanterinkatu 3, is now a museum memorializing the beloved Finnish poet who lived in Porvoo in the mid-19th century. Admission includes a sculpture exhibition at Aleksanterinkatu 5. (House open May-Aug. M-Sa 10am-4pm, Su 11am-5pm; Sept.-Apr. W-Sa 10am-4pm, Su 11am-5pm. 20mk/€3.40, students 10mk/€1.70. Exhibition open same hours in summer; in winter W-Su 11am-3pm.) The **Tea and Coffee Shop Helmi,** Välikatu 7, captures Porvoo's 19th-century appeal. (Open M-Sa 10am-5pm, Su 11am-6pm.) **Buses** roll into Porvoo from Helsinki (1hr., every 15min., 40mk/€6.75). The helpful **tourist office,** Rihkamakatu 4, has free maps. (☎ 58 01 45; www.porvoo.fi. Open in summer M-F 10am-6pm, Sa-Su 10am-4pm; in winter M-F 10am-4:30pm, Sa 10am-2pm.) ☎**019.**

HANKO. The seaside resort of Hanko juts out into a beautiful archipelago. Great villas lining Hanko's miles of coastland reflect the decadence of the now-vanished Russian nobility. Choose from over 30km of **beaches;** those along Appelgrenintie are the most popular. **Trains** arrive from Helsinki (2hr., 6 per day, 80mk/€13.45), as do **buses** (2¼hr., 5 per day, 80mk/€13.45). The **tourist office,** Raatihuoneentori 5, helps find rooms. (☎220 34 11; fax 248 58 21; www.hanko.fi. Open in summer M-F 9am-5pm, Sa 10am-2pm; in winter M-F 8am-4pm.) Many **guesthouses** are in former villas along Appelgrenintie; try **Villa Doris** at #23 for ocean views. (☎248 12 28. 80-200mk/€33.60.) The cafe at **Neljän Tuulen Tupa** (The House of the Four Winds) was once owned by a Finnish war hero and is a peaceful place to watch the ocean. (Sandwiches 16mk/€2.70, cakes from 15mk/€2.55.) Follow Appelgrenintie until the sign for the house leads down a dirt path called Långsanda (15min.). ☎**019.**

LAHTI. World-class winter sports facilities make Lahti a pleasant afternoon away from fast-paced Helsinki. The **Ski Museum** has ski-jump and biathalon simulators.

(Open M-F 10am-5pm, Sa-Su 11am-5pm. 20mk/€3.40, students 15mk/€2.55.) Cross-country **ski trails** (100km) also begin here. Lahti also serves as a transportation hub, with **buses** to Jyväskylä (3hr., 96mk/€16.15) and Savonlinna (4hr., 121mk/€20.30). **Trains** go to: Helsinki (1½hr., 70-100mk/€11.75-16.80); Savonlinna (3½hr., 198-210mk/€33.25-35.30); St. Petersburg, Russia (5hr., 224mk/€37.65); and Tampere (2hr., 100-130mk/€21.85). The **tourist office** is at Aleksanterinkatu 16. (☎814 45 66; fax 814 45 64; www.lahtitravel.fi. Open in summer M-F 9am-6pm, Sa 10am-2pm; in winter M-F 9am-5pm.) To reach **Lahden Kansanopisto Hotel (HI)**, Harjukatu 46, from the train station, walk opposite of the station on Vesijärvenkatu one block and then turn right on Harjukatu. (☎878 11 81; fax 878 12 34. Reception M-F 8am-9pm, Sa-Su 8am-noon and 4-9pm. Open June-Aug. Dorms 90mk/€15.15; singles 145mk/€24.35. Nonmembers add 15mk/€2.55.) ☎03.

ÅLAND ISLANDS (AHVENANMAA)　☎018

Åland is a series of 6500 tiny islands that were part of Sweden until 1809, and then part of Finland until it became autonomous in 1921. Now the islands have their own flag, parliament, and postal system—but they retain strong ties to both countries. The Åland Islands' miles of beaches and flower-covered bike trails offer at least 6500 reasons to explore and experience the blend of Swedish and Finnish cultures.

⎕ TRANSPORTATION. For information on traveling to Mariehamn on the **Viking Line** or **Silja Line**, see **By Ferry**, p. 76. **Birka Lines** launches its *Princess* daily from Stockholm to Mariehamn. (Mariehamn ☎270 27; Stockholm ☎(08) 702 72 30; info@birkacruises.com. 8hr., 150mk/€25.20.) **Inter-island ferries** are free for foot passengers and cyclists; passengers with cars pay (30-40mk/€5.05-6.75; 200mk/€33.60 if landing on Åland, Uårdö, or the mainland). **Ferry** and **bus** schedules are at the Mariehamn tourist office. The main island, Åland, with extensive paths and wide roads, is best explored by bike. **RoNo Rent,** facing the ferry terminal in Mariehamn in the Eastern harbor, rents **bikes** for 40mk/€6.75, mopeds for 200mk/€33.60, and boats from 220mk/€36.95. (☎128 21. Open June-Aug. daily 9am-6pm; May and Sept. call for hours.) The other islands are accessible from Mariehamn by a combo of ferries, buses, and bikes.

MARIEHAMN. On the south coast of the main island, Mariehamn (pop. 10,500) is the only actual town in Åland. Stock up on groceries, as most of the island consists of small campgrounds, beaches, and a few cafes. Although the outdoors are spectacular, the town itself also has some interesting sights. The **Åland Art Museum** and **Åland Museum,** at Stadshusparken off Storagatan, display Åland's historical and cultural richness. (Open W-M 10am-4pm, Tu 10am-8pm. 15mk/€2.55, students 10mk/€1.70.) Visible from the ferry terminal, the moored ship **Pommern** recreates the high seas experience. (Open Oct.-June and Aug. 9am-5pm; July 9am-7pm. Free tours in English. 25mk/€4.20.)

For maps and information, head to the **tourist office,** Storagatan 8. From the ferry terminal, go left up Hamngatan and turn right on Storagatan. (☎240 00; fax 242 65; www.goaland.net. Open June-Aug. daily 9am-6pm; Sept. and May M-F 9am-4pm, Sa 10am-4pm; closed Oct. and Feb. Call for off-season hours.) **Ålandsresor,** Torggatan 2, books rooms and cottages (from 120mk/€20.15) for all the islands for a 35mk/€5.90 fee. (☎280 40; fax 283 80; www.alandsresor.fi. Open M-F 8:30am-5pm. Book ahead.) Docked at the Eastern harbor, the botel **Alida** offers small rooms close to town. (☎137 55. Reception 8am-10pm. Open May-Sept. Singles 150mk/€25.20; doubles 200mk/€33.60.) **Gröna Uddens Camping** is 10min. from the town center. (☎211 21. Shower included. Laundry. Open mid-May to Aug. 90mk/€15.15.) Inflated restaurant prices make **supermarkets** alluring; try **Fokus** at Torggatan 14 (open M-F 9am-6pm, Sa 9am-4pm), or **Mathis Hallen,** on the corner of Norragaten and Ålandsvagen (open M-F 9am-7pm, Sa 9am-4pm, Su 11am-4pm). Cafes and pizza joints are the only real bargains. The Finnish chain **Koti Pizza** has lunch specials for 34-42mk/€5.75-7.05. (Open M-Sa 11am-9pm, Su noon-

9pm.) **Café Julius,** Torggatan 10, serves the island's specialty, *Alands Pannkaka* (a custardy thin cake with berry sauce and whipped cream), for 13mk/€2.20. (Open daily 7am-8pm.) Island nights heat up at **Alva's,** Ålandsvagen 42, a bar that becomes a club on the weekends. (Cover 40mk/€6.75. Open daily 8pm-4am.)

SUND. Northeast of Mariehamn lies the province of Sund. **Bike** along the cycling route to Godby or take **bus #4** (30min., 8 per day, 19mk/€3.20) to Kastelholm and see the 13th-century **Kastelholms Slott,** with the prison room where mad King Erik XIV was kept during his bout with lead poisoning. (Open May-Sept. daily 10am-5pm; in winter by appointment. 30mk/€5.05, students 25mk/€4.20. Includes guided tour; English tours usually available.) Up the hill, the **Vita Björn** museum features prison cells through the centuries, up to 1975. (Open May-Sept. same hours as castle. 10mk/€1.70, students 7mk/€1.20.) An open-air homestead museum, **Jan Karls-gården,** boasts authentic wooden buildings from Åland on a gorgeous plot of land. (Open May-Sept. daily 10am-5pm. Free.) Ten kilometers down the road in **Bomar-sund** is a tsarist Russian fortress destroyed by British and French forces during the Crimean War. (Bus #4. 27mk/€4.55 from Mariehamn, 13mk/€2.20 from Kastelholm.) **Puttes Camping** (☎440 16; fax 440 47), at Bomarsund, has a kitchen, laundry, and bike and boat rental. 15mk/€2.55 per tent; cabins from 160mk/€26.90.) From the Prästö bridge, the campground is 100m to the right.

RAUMA
☎02

Farther up the Baltic Coast lies the culturally bustling town of Rauma, known for its distinct lace and dialect. Old Rauma, an old Nordic wooden town located in the town center, is a UNESCO World Heritage site. The town also has great **beaches** less than 2km away and a **Rock Festival** featuring Finnish bands during Midsummer (www.raumanmerenjuhannus.com). The **Old Town Hall Museum,** Kauppakatu 13, is full of Rauma's maritime history. In the summer, you can also see the home of a shipowner, a seaman, and a pottery workshop. (Open in summer daily 10am-5pm; in winter Tu-Su 11am-5pm.)

   Buses arrive every hour from Pori (1hr., 53mk/€8.90) and Turku (2hr., 74-87mk/€14.65). The **tourist office,** Valtakatu 2, has extensive information. From the bus terminal, walk down Nortamonkatu and turn right. (☎834 4551; www.rauma.fi. Open in summer M-F 8am-6pm, Sa 10am-3pm, Su 11am-2pm; in winter M-F 8am-4pm.) **Kesahotelli Rauma,** Satamakatu 20, is a summer hotel and hostel. (☎82 40 130. Breakfast and linens 15mk/€2.55 each; included for singles and doubles. Reception 6am-10pm. Dorms 55mk/€9.25; singles 195mk/€32.75; doubles 290mk/€48.70.)

PORI
☎02

Each July the coastal town of Pori overflows with tourists attending the **Pori Jazz Festival,** which attracts varied acts from Big Bad Voodoo Daddy to Kool and the Gang. (July 13-21 in 2002. Information ☎626 22 00; tickets ☎626 22 15; www.pori-jazz.fi. Tickets 100-300mk/€16.80-50.40.) Head to the **Pori Art Museum,** on the corner of Etelärantakatu and Raatihuonekatu behind the tourist office, for Finnish and international modern art. (Open Tu-Su 11am-6pm, W 11am-8pm. 20-30mk/€3.40-5.05, students 6-15mk/€1.05-2.55.) Walk by the river to view beautiful architecture and spectacular greenery or get out to **Yteri** beach and **Repossaari,** the fishing village, on bus #2. **Trains** run from Helsinki (4hr, 6 per day, 158-176mk/€26.55-29.55) and Tampere (1½hr., 6 per day, 98-110mk/€16.45-18.50). **Buses** roll in from Tampere (2hr., 4 per day, 81mk/€13.60) and Turku (2hr., 6-7 per day, 114mk/€19.20). The **tourist office,** Hallituskatu 9A, is attractively designed by Carl Engel. (☎621 12 73; fax 621 12 75; www.pori.fi. Open in summer M-F 8am-6pm, Sa 10am-3pm; in winter M-F 8am-4pm.) A student dorm in winter, the **Youth Hostel Tekunkorpi** is far from town. Take bus #2, 30 or 40 (15min., 11mk/€1.90) to the corner of Professorintie and Korpraalintie and follow the signs 750m up Teknikantie. (☎634 84 00. Singles with breakfast 165mk/€27.70; doubles with breakfast 185mk/€31.10. Extra bed 100mk/€16.80. Nonmembers add 15mk/€2.55.)

NAKED NORTHERNERS True to the stories, the sauna is an integral part of almost every Finn's life. More than simply a place to cleanse oneself thoroughly after a shower, saunas have developed a certain mystique and are immortalized in *Kalevala*, the Finnish national epic. Associated with cleanliness, strength, and endurance, there are over 1½ million saunas in Finland, or one for every three people. Modern saunas are found in every hotel, most hostels, and many campgrounds. These wooden rooms reach temperatures around 88°C, so hot that no metal parts may be exposed, lest the bathers be burned. Water thrown on heated stones brings humidity as high as 100%. Finland's electricity use skyrockets on Friday and Saturday evenings, when hundreds of thousands of saunas are heated.

TAMPERE ☎03

Once the country's industrial leader, Tampere is still an important Finnish city. Quirky museums, expansive beaches, energetic nightlife, and frequent cultural festivals make the compact city a great stop.

🖃🔁 TRANSPORTATION AND PRACTICAL INFORMATION. Trains head to: Helsinki (2hr., 12 per day, 106-136mk/€17.80-22.85); Oulu (5hr., 8 per day, 278-290mk/€46.70-48.70); and Turku (2hr., 10 per day, 98-126mk/€16.50-21.20). **Boats** (☎212 48 04) cruise to Ruovesi (4½hr.; Tu, Th, Sa; 167mk/€28.05) and beyond to Virrat (7½hr., 226mk/€37.95) or to Hämeenlinna (8hr., 1 per day, 202mk/€37.95). The ◪**tourist office,** Verkatehtaankatu 2, and its army zipping around town on green scooters, offers incredible service and free Internet. From the train station, walk up Hämeenkatu, turn left before the bridge, and look for the sign. (☎31 46 68 00; fax 31 46 64 63; touristbureau@tampere.fi; www.tampere.fi. Open June-Aug. M-F 8:30am-8pm, Sa-Su 10am-5pm; Sept.-May M-F 8:30am-5pm.)

🏠🍴 ACCOMMODATIONS AND FOOD. Tampeeren NNKY (HI), Tuomiokirkonkatu 12 (☎254 40 20; fax 254 40 22), offers rooms with balconies facing the cathedral. From the train station, walk down Hämeenkatu and make a right onto Tumoiokirkoukatu. (Breakfast 30mk/€5.05. Sheets 25mk/€4.20. Reception 4-11pm. Dorms 60-70mk/€10.10-11.75; singles 155mk/€26.05; doubles 210mk/€35.30. Nonmembers add 15mk/€2.55.) Overlooking Lake Pyhäjärvi, **Camping Härmälä** is accessible by bus #1 for 12mk/€2.05. (☎265 13 55. Open late May to late Aug. 75-95mk/€12.60-15.95 per person and tent; cabins 150-340mk/€25.20-57.10.) Sample *mustamakkara*, sausage made with flour and cow's blood, at the ever-popular **Market Hall** (Kauppahalli), Hämeenkatu 19. (Open M-Th 8am-5pm, Sa 8am-3pm.) Chow at Tampere's oldest pizzeria, **Napoli**, Aleksanterinkatu 31. (Lunch specials 37-40mk/€6.25-6.75. Open M-Th 11am-10pm, F 11am-11pm, Sa noon-11pm, Su noon-11pm.)

◪ SIGHTS. Tampere has some of the wackiest museums in Europe. The **Spy Museum,** Hatanpäänvaltatie 42, exhibits a variety of sneaky devices. (Open M-F noon-6pm, Sa-Su 10am-4pm; Sept.-Apr. M-F 4pm-7pm, Sa-Su 10am-4pm. 35mk/€5.90, students 25mk/€4.20.) A defiant proletarian spirit burns at the last existing **Lenin Museum,** Hämeenpuisto 28, third floor. The museum and its founders, the **Finnish-Soviet Friendship Society,** share the building where the first conference of Lenin's revolutionary party was held and where Lenin and Stalin first met. (Open M-F 9am-6pm, Sa-Su 11am-4pm. 20mk/€3.40, students 10mk/€1.70.) The **Amuri Museum,** Makasiininkatu 12, presents the cramped living quarters of 25 workers and their families between 1882 and 1973. (Open mid-May to mid-Sept. Tu-Su 10am-6pm. 20mk/€3.40, students 5mk/€0.85.) The **Moominvalley Museum,** Hämeenpuisto 20 in the City Library, pays homage to the classic children's series with tiny Moomins on display in doll houses. (Open Tu-F 9am-5pm, Sa-Su 10am-6pm. 20mk/€3.40, students and children 5mk/€0.85.) Bus #27 goes to **Pyynikki beach;** or, for a more Finnish beach experience—which involves jumping from a hot sauna into chilly water—take bus #2 to **Rauhaniemi beach.** Bus #27 will also take you to **Pyynikki forest park,**

which offers walking trails and great views of the Näsijärvi and Pyhäjärvi lakes. Take the stairs or ride an elevator to the top of the observation tower for a panoramic view. (Bus #27. Open daily 9am-8pm. 5mk/€0.85.) For an even more spectacular sight, take the elevator up the 124m **Näsinuela** in the **Särkänniemi** amusement complex. (Open daily 11am-midnight. 20mk/€3.40.) Other Särkänniemi attractions include an amusement park, a dolphinarium, a children's zoo, and a planetarium. (Open May-Aug. daily noon-8pm. 20mk/€3.40.) Tampere also has two cathedrals: the **Orthodox cathedral,** Tummiokirkonkatu 27, evocative of St. Basil's in Russia with its onion domes (open May M-Sa 10am-4pm; June-Aug. M-Sa 11am-5pm, Su noon-4pm) and the **Lutheran cathedral,** featuring once-controversial interior murals by Hugo Simberg and Magnus Ecknell. (Open daily May-Aug. 9am-6pm; Sept.-Apr. 11am-3pm.)

🎵🎭 **ENTERTAINMENT AND NIGHTLIFE.** The quirky **Short Film Festival** (☎213 00 34; Mar. 6-10 in 2002) features works from 30 countries. August brings the **International Theater Festival** (Aug. 6-11 in 2002), transforming parks and streets into stages. (☎223 10 66; tampere.fi/festival/theatre.) Tampere's nights are energetic along **Hämeenkatu,** its main drag. **Cafe Europa,** Aleksanterinkatu 29, offers beer for 23mk/€3.90, meals for 30-60mk/€5.05-10.10, and free dancing upstairs Th-Sa. (20+ after 6pm. Open Su-Th noon-2am, F-Sa noon-3am.) For a traditional club scene, head to **Nightlife,** in the Hotel Cumulus Koskikatu, on Kyttalankatu. (24+. Cover 30mk/€5.05. Open Su-Th 10pm-4am, F-Sa 9pm-4am.)

SAVONLINNA ☎015

Savonlinna perches atop a chain of islands connected by bridges. The tsarist aristocracy was the first to discover Savonlinna's potential as a vacation spot, and soon turned it into a fashionable spa town. The elegant **Olavinlinna Castle,** built to reinforce the Swedish-Finnish border with Russia in 1475, impresses with its towering spires and high-vaulted ceilings. From the Market Square, follow the docks along the water and hug Linnankatu as it winds between old wooden houses until you reach the castle. (Open daily June to mid-Aug. 10am-5pm; mid-Aug. to May 10am-3pm. 30mk/€5.05, students 20mk/€3.40. Free tours every hr.) Performers and spectators alike flock to Savonlinna's **International Opera Festival.** (☎47 67 50; www.operafestival.fi. July 5-Aug. 4 in 2002.) The **Sulosaari beaches** are a welcome retreat from the hordes of tourists in town for the festival. Cross the footbridge behind Market Square, walk past the baths, and cross the footbridge for a stunning view.

Trains run to Savonlinna from Helsinki (5hr., 4 per day, 220mk/€36.95); hop off at Savonlinna-Kauppatori in the center of town rather than at the distant Savonlinna stop. The **tourist office,** Puistokatu 1, across the bridge from the market, books rooms. (☎51 75 10; fax 517 51 23; www.travel.fi/fin/savonlinna. Open daily June-Aug. 8am-8pm; Sept.-May M-F 9am-5pm.) **Vuorilinna Hostel (HI),** on Kylpylaitoksentie, Kasinosaari, is next to the spa and casino area. (☎739 50; fax 27 25 24. Kitchen. Reception 7am-11pm. Open June-Aug. Dorms 105mk/€17.65; singles 230-440mk/€38.65-73.90; doubles 350-440mk/€58.80-73.90. Nonmembers add 15mk/€2.55.) **Malakias Hostel (HI),** Pihlajavedenkuja 6, is 2km from the city center. Go right on Olavinkatu from the tourist office, and bear left on Tulliportinkatu. (☎53 32 83. Reception 7am-11pm. Open June-Aug. Dorms 105mk/€17.65; singles 385mk/€64.65; doubles 355mk/€59.60. Nonmembers add 15mk/€2.55.)

🔎 **DAYTRIPS FROM SAVONLINNA: KERIMÄKI AND THE RETRETTI.** The largest wooden church in the world, seating 3000, was constructed in the late 1800s in **Kerimäki,** after the town decided that a church for only 1500 would not do. (Open June 1-11 10am-5pm; June 12-Aug. 15 10am-6pm; Aug. 16-31 10am-4pm. Free.) Take the **bus** to Kerimäki from Savonlinna (35min., 25-30mk/€4.20-5.05); the church will be visible from there. About 30min. from Savonlinna by rail, the **Retretti Art Center** has impressive exhibition space inside huge caves. (Open daily May-June and Aug. 10am-5pm; July 10am-6pm; exhibitions open 1hr. later. 75mk/€12.60, students and seniors 60mk/€10.10, children 30mk/€5.05.) The Retretti is near the fabulous **Punkaharju Ridge,** a narrow 7km stretch of gorgeous scenery surrounded by water. Hop off at the Punkaharju station and check out the information stand.

TURKU (ÅBO)   ☎02

Turku (pop. 163,000), Finland's oldest city, became capital in 1809 when Tsar Alexander I snatched Finland from Sweden and granted it autonomy. After the capital moved to Helsinki in 1812, the worst fire in Scandinavian history devoured Turku's wooden buildings. Despite this, Turku flourishes as a cultural and academic center.

▣▨ TRANSPORTATION AND PRACTICAL INFORMATION. Trains arrive from Helsinki (1½hr., 14 per day, 124-148mk/€20.85-24.85) and Tampere (2hr., 8 per day, 126-140mk/€21.20-23.50). Viking and Silja Line **ferries** depart for Åland and Stockholm (see **By Ferry,** p. 297); to get to the terminal at the southwestern end of Linnankatu, hop the train (3 per day) to the *satama* (harbor) or catch bus #1 from Market Square (10mk/€1.70). The **tourist office,** Aurakatu 2, has accommodations information. (☎262 74 44; fax 262 76 79; www.turkutouring.fi. Open in summer M-F 8:30am-6pm, Sa-Su 9am-4pm; in winter M-F 8:30am-6pm, Sa 10am-3pm.) Check **email** at the **library,** Linnankatu 2, 2nd fl. (Open M-Th 10am-7pm, F 10am-4pm. Free.)

▨◨ ACCOMMODATIONS AND FOOD. The **Hostel Turku (HI),** Linnankatu 39, is on the river between the ferry terminals and the train station. From the station, walk west four blocks on Ratapihankatu, take a left on Puistokatu to the river, and make a right on Linnankatu. From the ferry, walk 20min. up Linnankatu. (☎262 76 80; fax 262 76 75. Breakfast 23mk/€3.90. Sheets 25mk/€4.20. Laundry 5mk/€0.85. Reception closed 10am-3pm. Dorms 60mk/€10.10; doubles 180mk/€30.25; quads 250mk/€42. Nonmembers add 15mk/€2.55.) For immaculate rooms and immaculate reception, try nun-run **Bridgettine Sisters' Guesthouse,** Ursininkatu 15A, near the corner of Puutarhakatu. (☎250 19 10; fax 250 30 78; birgitta.turku@kolubus.fi. Reception 8am-9pm. Singles with bath 210mk/€35.30; doubles with bath 320mk/€53.75.) **Ruissalo Camping,** on Ruissalo Island, is open in summer. Hop on bus #8 from Eerinkinkatu. (☎262 76 81. 85mk/€14.30 per tent.) Produce fills **Kauppatori** (open M-Sa 7am-2pm) and **Kauppahalli,** on Eerikinkatu, Market Hall (open M-Th 8am-5pm, F 8am-2pm, Sa 8am-2pm). Or head to **Valintalo supermarket,** Eerikinkatu 19. (Open M-F 9am-9pm, Sa 9am-6pm.)

◪▣ SIGHTS AND NIGHTLIFE. Turku surrounds the river Aura, and most of the sights are within meters of its banks. The **Turku Cathedral** towers above Tuomiokirkkotori (Cathedral Square). (Open daily mid-Apr. to mid-Sept. 9am-8pm; mid-Sept. to mid-Apr. 9am-7pm.) The 700-year-old **Turun Linna** (Turku Castle), about 3km from the town center, contains a **historical museum** with dark passageways, medieval artifacts, and Iron Age dioramas. Catch the #1 bus (10mk/€1.70) from Market Square. (Open mid-Apr. to mid-Sept. daily 10am-6pm; mid-Sept. to mid-Apr. Tu-Su 10am-3pm. 30mk/€5.05, students 20mk/€3.40.) **Luostarinmäki,** the only neighborhood to survive the 1827 fire, now houses an open-air **handicrafts museum** with over 30 workshops. (Open mid-Apr. to mid-Sept. daily 10am-6pm; mid-Sept. to mid-Apr. Tu-Su 10am-3pm. 20mk/€3.40, students 15mk/€2.55.) The collections of the **Turun Taidemuseo** (Art Museum), including vibrant *Kalevala* paintings by Akseli Gallen-Kallela, are temporarily being housed on Vartiovuorenmaki in a building designed by Carl Engel. (Open Tu-Su 10am-4pm, Th 10am-7pm. 40mk/€6.75, students 30mk/€5.05.) **Aboa Vetus Ars Nova** combines two museums in the Rettig palace, a 1928 building refurbished and filled with modern and international art. (Open May-Aug. daily 11am-7pm; Sept.-Apr. Th-Su 11am-7pm. 55mk/€9.25, students 40mk/€6.75.) Posh **Prima,** Aurakatu 16, is decked out in red decor and features a club and bar above its restaurant. (International dishes 45-89mk/€7.60-14.95; restaurant open daily 11am-11pm. Club F 22+, Sa 24+. Open F-Su 10pm-4am.) Turku proper hosts **Down by the Laituri,** a music and city cultural festival that lasts several days in mid-June. (☎250 44 20; www.dbtl.fi.) Ruissalo Island in Turku hosts **Ruisrock** in mid-July, attracting names like Björk, the Beastie Boys, David Bowie, and Sting for Finland's largest rock festival. (☎(06) 001 04 95; www.ruisrock.fi.)

▶ DAYTRIP FROM TURKU: NAANTALI (NADENDAL). Naantali, an enclave of old wooden houses 15km west of Turku, is awakened each summer by vacationing Finns. Mannerheiminkatu leads to the **Old Town,** where buildings date to the late 18th century. Across the harbor is the Finnish president's fortress-like summer home, **Kultaranta;** if the flag's up, keep an eye out for her. The tourist office offers daily tours of the park around the home from late June to mid-Aug. (☎435 98 00.) A bus leaves from the tourist office daily at 10am (45mk/€7.60, children 25mk/€4.20) or from the park's main gate at 2pm and 3pm (30mk/€5.05, children 15mk/€2.55). The main attraction is **Moomin World,** a harborside fantasy theme park. (☎511 11 11. Open June to mid-Aug. daily 10am-7pm. 80mk/€13.45, children 60mk/€10.10.) The **Naantali Music Festival** (☎434 53 63; www.naantalimusic.com) brings classical music and opera in early June. The most traditional Naantali summer event is **Sleepyhead Day** (July 27), when the residents of Naantali get up at 6am, wake anyone still sleeping, and, dressed in carnival costumes, proceed to crown the year's Sleepyhead and throw him or her into the harbor. **Buses** #10, 11, and 110 run to Naantali from the marketplace in Turku (30-45min., 20mk/€3.40). The **tourist office,** Kaivotori 2, helps find accommodations. From the bus station, walk southwest on Tullikatu to Kaivokatu and go right 300m; it will be on the left. (☎435 08 50; fax 435 08 52; www.naantalinmatkailu.fi. Open June to mid-Aug. M-F 9am-6pm, Sa-Su 10am-4pm; mid-Aug. to May M-F 9am-4:30pm.) ☎02.

ROVANIEMI   ☎016

Just south of the Arctic Circle and home to the world's favorite jolly fat man, the modern capital of Finnish Lapland is a popular spot for tourists during the summer and December. Fulfill childhood fantasies any time of year at **Santa Claus's Village** to meet jolly St. Nick himself. When he's in his office, you can shop, view reindeer or huskies, and stand on the Arctic Circle. Take bus #8 from the train station (16mk/€2.70, return 28mk/€4.75) to the Arctic Circle Center. (Open daily Jan.-June 10am-5pm; June to mid-Aug. 9am-8pm; mid-Aug. to Sept. 9am-6pm; Oct.-Nov. 10am-5pm; Dec. 9am-7pm.) Santa's **theme park** (120mk/€20.15) is 2km away; take the bus (12mk/€2.05) to the park from the village. The **Arktikum** center, Pohjoisranta 4, houses the **Arctic Science Center** and the **Provincial Museum of Lapland,** a wonderland of information on Arctic peoples, culture, landscapes, and wildlife. (Open June-Aug. daily 9am-7pm; Sept.-Nov. and Jan.-Apr. Tu-Su 10am-6pm; Dec. daily 10am-6pm. 60mk/€10.10, students 50mk/€8.40.) The **Ranua Wildlife Park,** 60km south of Rovaniemi, has 3km of paths through areas of fenced-in Arctic elk, bears, and wolves. Doe-eyed reindeer lovers should skip the gift shop, which sells Rudolph's fur, skin, and ribs. (Open daily May and mid-Aug. to Sept. 10am-6pm; June to mid-Aug. 9am-8pm; Oct.-Apr. 10am-4pm. 60mk/€10.10, children 50mk/€8.40.)

Four **trains** per day roll into Rovaniemi from Helsinki (388mk/€65.15) via Oulu (148mk/€24.85). **Buses** run to destinations throughout northern Finland, with connections to Nordkapp, Norway, and Murmansk, Russia. The staff of the **tourist office,** Koskikatu 1, combs the town on yellow mopeds. If you don't spot them at the train station, head right on Ratakatu, pass the post office, go under the bridge onto Hallituskatu, turn left on Korkalonkatu, and continue right on Koskikatu to the river. (☎34 62 70; www.rovaniemi.fi. Open June-Aug. M-F 8am-6pm, Sa-Su 10am-4pm; Sept.-May M-F 8am-4pm.) **Lapland Safaris,** Koskikatu 1 (☎331 12 00), offers cruises (2hr., 210mk/€35.30), rafting (3hr., 430mk/€72.20), and Husky and snowmobile safaris (3-6hr., 350-780mk/€58.80-130.95). To get to the austere **HI youth hostel,** Hallituskatu 16, follow the directions to Hallituskatu. (☎34 46 44. Reception, showers, and kitchen 6-10am and 5-10pm. Breakfast 30mk/€5.05. Linens 20mk/€3.40. Dorms 75mk/€12.60, nonmembers 95mk/€15.95.) **Ounaskoski Camping** is across the river, next to a rocky beach.

(☎34 53 04. Open June-Aug. 95-105mk/€15.95-17.65 per person.) **Monte Rose,** Pekankatu 9, in City Hotel, serves a Lapland treat—sauteed reindeer and lingonberry sauce over mashed potatoes—for 97mk/€16.30. (Open M-Tu 10am-11pm, W-Th 10am-midnight, F 10am-1am, Sa noon-1am, Su 1-11pm.) Cold Rovaniemi nights heat up on **Koskikatu.** Test your seductive powers at **Flirt,** Koskiatu 23. (Cover 20mk/€3.40. Open W-Su 10pm-3:30am.)

OULU
☎08

Flower-lined avenues and warm winds give Oulu a southern feel. On the Gulf of Bothnia, the crystal-clear waters of **Nallikari** tempt everyone to take a dip. Take **bus #5** from Otto Karhin Park or Nallikari (12mk/€2.05). The adjacent **Nallikari Camping** has colorful bungalows. (☎55 86 13 50; fax 55 86 17 13. 50mk/€8.40 per person; 4-person cabins 130-300mk/€21.85-50.40.) Closer to the city center, the azure sea at **Pikisaari,** an island lined with multi-colored cottages, is ideal for picnics; take the footbridge at the end of Kaarlenväylä. Across from Pikisaari is the boisterous **marketplace,** lined with worn warehouses housing cafes and gift stores (corner of Rantakatu and Kaarlenväylä), and outdoor concerts in the summer. A 15min. ride away on bus #19 (12mk/€2.05), 5m cactuses, gigantic banana plants, and other exotic flora flourish in the glass pyramids of the University of Oulu's **Botanical Gardens,** Kaitoväylä 5. (Pyramids open June-Aug. Tu-F 8am-4pm, Sa-Su 10am-4pm; Sept.-May Tu-F 8am-3pm, Sa-Su noon-3pm. 10mk/€1.70. Open-air gardens open daily in summer 8am-9pm; off season 7am-5pm, snow willing. Free.) The **Tietomaa,** Nahkatehtaankatu 6, has interactive science exhibits, a huge IMAX theater, and pants made for the world's heaviest man. (Open July daily 10am-8pm; Sept.-June M-F 10am-6pm. 60mk/€10.10, students 50mk/€8.40.)

All **trains** between northern and southern Finland pass through Oulu, heading to Helsinki (8hr., 5 per day, 336-348mk/€56.45-58.45) and Rovaniemi (2½ hr., 8-10 per day, 148mk/€24.85). The **tourist office,** Torikatu 10, provides information on the entire Ostrobothnia region. Take Hallituskatu, the broad avenue perpendicular to the train station, up to the second left after passing through the park. (☎55 84 13 30; fax 55 84 17 11; www.oulutourism.fi. Open M-F 9am-4pm.) **Oppimestari Summer Hostel,** Nahkatehtaankatu 3, has bright student dorms for rent in the summer. From the train station, cross Rautatienkatu straight onto Asemakatu for four blocks. Turn right on Isokatu, which becomes Kasarmintie, and turn right onto Nahkatehtaankatu. (☎88 48 527; fax 88 48 772; www.merikoski.fi/hotel. Breakfast and linens included. Internet free. Singles 120mk/€20.15; doubles 270mk/€45.35.) Nightlife revolves around the pavilion on **Kirkkokatu,** the terraces lining **Otto Karhin Park** on Hallituskatu, and the club-lined **Asemakatu.**

KUOPIO
☎017

Eastern Finland's largest and most important city, Kuopio (pop. 86,000) is a center of religion and culture. The archbishop of the Finnish Orthodox Church resides here, and the city holds the magnificent **Orthodox Church Museum,** Karjalankatu 1. (Open May-Aug. Tu-Su 10am-4pm; Sept.-Apr. M-F noon-3pm, Sa-Su noon-5pm. 30mk/€5.05, students 15mk/€2.55.) For a heavenly view of the forest- and lake-covered region, take bus #18 from Kauppatori to reach **Puijo Tower.** (Open May-Aug. 9am-10pm. 15mk/€2.55.) Inquire about **cruises** at the guest harbor; Kuopio Roll Cruises (☎266 24 66) and Koski Laiva Oy (☎262 19 55) set sail every hour to view nearby islands. (1½-3hr., 50-60mk/€8.40-10.10). The world's largest sauna, **Jatkankamppa,** is open on Tuesday and Friday nights; traditional Finnish food, music, and dancing complete the sauna experience. (90mk/€15.15. 50mk/€8.40 for sauna only. See Rauhalahti Hostel, below.)

Trains chug to Kuopio from Helsinki (5½hr., 5 per day, 258-270mk/€43.35-45.35) and Oulu (4½hr., 4 per day, 215-228mk/€36.10-38.30). The **tourist office,** Haapaniemenkatu 17, has a stand at the train station to help you with accommodations. To get to their office from the station, go right on Asemakatu, turn left on Haapaniemenkatu, and walk for three blocks. (☎18 25 84; fax 18 25 85; www.kuopioinfo.fi.

FINLAND

Open M-F in summer 9am-6pm, Sa-Su 9am-2pm; in winter 9am-4pm.) Close to the train station, **Retkeilymaja Virkkula,** Asemakatu 3, is a schoolhouse-turned-hostel. (☎263 18 39. Linens 30mk/€5.05. Open in summer. Dorms 75mk/€12.60.) **Rauhalahti Hostel (HI),** Katiskaniementie 8, offers its guests use of its nightclub, spa, and the Jatkankamppa sauna (see above). Fresh produce and fish are available at **Kauppa-tori,** the market square in the center of town. (Open daily 7am-3pm.) Kick up your heels in late June at the **Kuopio Dance Festival** (www.kuopiodancefestival.fi), and toast to early July's **Wine Festival,** a week-long celebration of a chosen country known for its wine.

FRANCE

FRENCH FRANCS

US$1 = 7.15F	1F = US$0.14
CDN$1 = 4.64F	1F = CDN$0.22
UK£1 = 10.35F	1F = UK£0.10
IR£1 = 8.33F	1F = IR£0.12
AUS$1 = 3.83F	1F = AUS$0.26
NZ$1 = 3.15F	1F = NZ$0.32
ZAR1= 0.86F	1F = ZAR1.15
EUR€1 = 6.56F	1F = EUR€0.15

PHONE CODE	Country code: 33. International dialing prefix: 00. France has no city codes. From outside France, dial int'l dialing prefix (see inside back cover) + 33 + local number.

The French have long celebrated the senses like no one else: the vineyards of Bordeaux, the savory dishes of Dijon, the sandy expanses of the Riviera, and the crisp air of the Alps combine for an exhilarating experience. France welcomes over 70 million visitors to its cities, châteaux, mountains, and beaches each year, making it the most popular tourist destination in the world. Yet to the French, it is only natural that outsiders should flock to their beloved homeland, so steeped in history, rich in art and architecture, and magnificently endowed with beautiful, diverse landscapes. The fruits of France include the rationalism of Voltaire, Sartre, and Derrida; the rich literature of Hugo, Proust, and Camus; and the visionary art of Rodin, Monet, and Degas. From the ambition of Napoleon to the birth of existentialism and postmodernism, the French for many centuries occupied the driver's seat of history. While France no longer controls the course of world events, it has nonetheless secured a spot as one of the most influential forces in Western history.

If you too are smitten by France, pick up a copy of *Let's Go: France 2002* or *Let's Go: Paris 2002* for more fact- and flavor-filled coverage.

FACTS AND FIGURES

Official Name: French Republic.
Capital: Paris.
Major Cities: Lyon, Nice, Marseilles.
Population: 59,329,691.

Land Area: 547,030 sq. km.
Climate: Mild summers and cool winters.
Language: French.
Religions: Roman Catholic (90%).

DISCOVER FRANCE

Paris—ah, Paris. Aside from the requisite croissant-munching, tower-climbing activities, don't miss the less heralded sights. A stroll down the **Champs-Elysées** (p. 335), through the youthful **Latin Quarter** (p. 334), or into medieval **Montmartre** (p. 336) will reveal the unique facets of the city. When you've had your fill, be sure to squeeze in daytrips to ornate **Versailles** (p. 344) and the Gothic cathedral in **Chartres** (p. 345). Northwest of Paris lies **Rouen** (p. 346), home to a cathedral that caught Claude Monet in its spell of light. The story of William the Conqueror is depicted in the tapestry at nearby **Bayeux** (p. 347), which serves as a good base for exploring the **D-Day beaches** (p. 348) of Normandy. The majestic abbey of **Mont-St-Michel** (p. 349) rises from the sea above shifting sands between Normandy and Brittany, while the château-studded **Loire Valley** (p. 354) brings visitors back to the days of royal intrigue and opulence. Sweep down to wine-filled **Bordeaux** (p. 358) before exploring the *vieille ville* of **Carcassonne** (p. 363)with its spectacular medieval ramparts. To see Provence's **Camargue** (p. 365), an untamed flatland of bulls, wild horses, and flamingoes, stay in **Arles** (p. 365), whose picturesque streets once enchanted van Gogh. Arles also has the largest Roman amphitheater in France, but its sister in **Nimes** (p. 364) is even more well preserved. Seven popes who called nearby **Avignon** (p. 364) home in the 15th century left behind an impressive palace. **Marseilles** (p. 366) and its wild nightlife are the gateway to the famously decadent **French Riviera** (p. 368). **Nice** (p. 371), with its excellent museums and nightlife, is the first stop on most itineraries, but its rocky beaches will send you to better sand strips in more secluded towns. The star-studded beach enclaves of **Cannes** (p. 369) and **St-Tropez** (p. 368) are also worth a look. In the shadow of Mont Blanc lies **Chamonix** (p. 381), which features fantastic skiing and mountain climbing. Then stop over in the bustling metropolis of **Lyon** (p. 383) before exploring the mix of French and German culture in **Strasbourg** (p. 388), home to an amazing Gothic cathedral and the beginning of **La Route du Vin** (p. 389).

ESSENTIALS

WHEN TO GO

In July, Paris starts to shrink, and by August it is devoid of Parisians, animated only by tourists and the pickpockets who love them. On the other hand, the rest of France fills with Frenchmen during these months, especially along the Atlantic coast. The Côte d'Azur is filled with Anglophones from June to September. Early summer and autumn are the best times to visit Paris—the city has warmed up, but not completely emptied out. The north and west of France have cool winters and mild summers, while the less crowded center and east of the country have a more continental climate. From December to February, the Alps provide some of the best skiing in the world, while the Pyrenees offer a calmer, if less climatically dependable, alternative.

DOCUMENTS AND FORMALITIES

VISAS. For stays shorter than 90 days, only citizens of South Africa need a short-stay visa (30-day visas ZAR174.50; 90-day ZAR209.35-244.25). For stays longer than 90 days, all non-EU citizens require long-stay visas (650F/€99.10).

EMBASSIES. Foreign embassies in France are in Paris (p. 321). For **French embassies** at home: **Australia,** Consulate General, Level 26, St. Martins Tower, 31 Market St., Sydney NSW 2000 (☎(02) 92 61 57 79; fax 92 83 12 10; www.france.net.au/consulat/index.htm); **Canada,** Consulate General, 1 pl. Ville Marie, 26th fl., Montréal, QC H3B 4SE (☎514-878-4385; fax 514-878-3981; www.consulfrance-montreal.org); **Ireland,** Consulate Section, 36 Ailesbury Rd., Ballsbridge, Dublin 4 (☎(01) 260 16 66; www.ambafrance.ie); **New Zealand,** 34-42 Manners St., P.O. Box 11-343, Wellington (☎(04) 384 25 55; fax 384 25 77; www.ambafrance.net.nz); **South Africa,** Consulate General at Johannesburg, 191 Smuts Ave., Rosebank; mailing address P.O. Box 1027, Parklands 2121 (☎(011) 778 5600; visas 778 56005; fax 778 5601; www.france.co.za); **UK,** Consulate General, 21 Cromwell Rd., London SW7 2EN (☎(020) 7838 2000; fax 7838 2001; www.ambafrance.org.uk); **US,** Consulate General, 4101 Reservoir Rd., NW, Washington, D.C. 20007 (☎202-944-6000; fax 202-994-6148; www.consulfrance-washington.org).

TRANSPORTATION

BY PLANE. The two major international airports in Paris are **Roissy-Charles de Gaulle** (to the north) and **Orly** (to the south). For information on cheap flights from the UK, see p. 58.

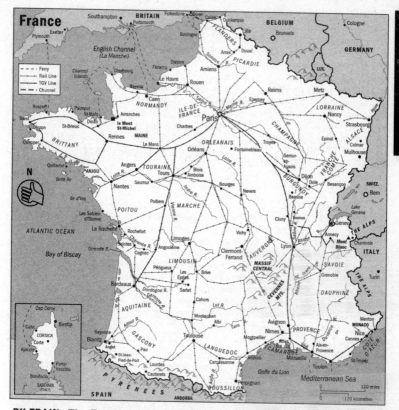

France

- – – – Ferry
- ——— Rail Line
- ——— TGV Line
- – – – Chunnel

BY TRAIN. The French national railway company, **SNCF** (☎ 08 36 35 35 35; www.sncf.fr), manages one of Europe's most efficient rail networks. **TGV** (*train à grande vitesse*, or high-speed) trains, the fastest in the world, run from Paris to major cities in France, as well as to Geneva and Lausanne, Switzerland. **Rapide** trains are slower, and local **Express** trains are, oddly, the slowest option. The **Eurostar** provides rapid connections to London and Brussels (p. 62). SNCF offers a wide range of discounted return tickets called *tarifs Découvertes*. Get a calendar from a train station detailing *période bleue* (blue period), *période blanche* (white period), and *période rouge* (red period) times and days; blue gets the most discounts, while red gets none. Those under age 25 have two great options: the **Découverte 12-25** (270F/€41.20) gives a 25% discount for any blue-period travel; and the **Carte 12-25** (270F/€41.20), valid for a year, is good for 25-50% off all TGV trains, 50% off all other trips that started during a blue period, and 25% off those starting in a white period. Tickets must be validated in the orange machine at the entrance to the platforms at the *gare* (train station) and revalidated at any connections in your trip. Seat reservations, recommended for international trips, are mandatory on EuroCity (EC), InterCity (IC), and TGV trains. All three require a ticket supplement (travelers under 26 with ID are entitled to a discount) and reservation fee.

   Eurail is valid in France. The SNCF's **France Railpass** grants three days of unlimited rail travel in France in any 30-day period (US$175; companion travelers US$141 each; up to 6 extra days US$30 each); the parallel **Youthpass** provides those under 26 with four days of unlimited travel within a two-month period (US$130; up to 6 extra days US$20 each). The **France Rail 'n' Drive pass** combines three days of rail travel with two days of car rental (US$240; companion travelers US$170 each; extra rail days US$30 each, extra car days US$49).

BY BUS. Within France, long-distance buses are a secondary transportation choice; service is infrequent compared to that in most other European countries. However, in some regions buses can be indispensable for reaching out-of-the-way towns. Bus services operated by the SNCF accept railpasses. *Gare routière* is French for "bus station."

BY FERRY. Ferries across the English Channel *(La Manche)* link France to England and Ireland. The shortest and most popular route is between **Dover** (p. 62) and **Calais,** and is run by **P&O Stena Line, SeaFrance,** and **Hoverspeed** (p. 62). Hoverspeed also travels from **Dieppe** to **Newhaven, England. Brittany Ferries** (☎ 08 03 82 88 28; www.brittanyferries.co.uk) travels from **Cherbourg** (p. 349) to **Poole,** from **Caen** (p. 347) to **Portsmouth,** and from **St-Malo** (p. 350) to **Portsmouth. Irish Ferries** (☎ 01 44 94 20 40; www.irishferries.ie) has overnight ferries from **Cherbourg** and **Roscoff** to **Rosslare, Ireland** (p. 549). **Eurail** is valid on boats to Ireland (excluding 30F/€4.60 port tax). Students usually receive a 10% discount. For schedules and prices on English Channel ferries, see p. 62. For information on ferries from **Nice** and **Marseilles** to **Corsica,** see p. 377.

BY CHUNNEL. Traversing 43½km under the sea, the Chunnel is undoubtedly the fastest, most convenient, least scenic route from England to France. There are two types of passenger service. **Eurostar** runs a frequent train service from London to Paris and Brussels, with stops at Ashford in England and Calais and Lille in France. Book reservations in UK, by phone, or over the web (UK ☎ 0990 18 61 86; US ☎ 800-387-6782; elsewhere ☎ 1233 61 75 75; www.eurostar.com, www.raileurope.com.) Eurostar tickets can also be bought at most major travel agents. **Eurotunnel** shuttles cars and passengers between Kent and Nord-Pas-de-Calais. (UK ☎ 0800 096 99 92; France ☎ 03 21 00 61 00; www.eurotunnel.co.uk.)

BY CAR. Unless you are traveling in a group of three or more, you won't save money traveling long distance by car rather than train, thanks to highway tolls, high gasoline cost, and rental charges. If you can't decide between train and car travel, get a **Rail 'n Drive pass** from railpass vendors (see above). The French drive on the right-hand side of the road; France maintains its roads well, but the landscape itself often makes the roads a menace, especially in twisting Corsica.

BY BIKE AND BY THUMB. Of all Europeans, the French may be alone in loving cycling more than football. French drivers usually accommodate bikers on the wide country roads, and many cities banish cars from select streets each Sunday. Renting a bike beats bringing your own if your touring will be confined to one or two regions (50-120F/€7.65-18.30 per day). Many consider France the hardest country in Europe to get a lift. *Let's Go* does not recommend hitchhiking. In major cities there are ride-sharing organizations that pair drivers and riders. Contact **Eurostop International** (**Allostop** in France; www.ecritel.fr/allostop/). Not all organizations screen drivers and riders.

TOURIST SERVICES AND MONEY

EMERGENCY	Police: ☎ 122. Ambulance: ☎ 123. Fire: ☎ 124.

TOURIST OFFICES. The extensive French tourism support network revolves around **syndicats d'initiative** and **offices de tourisme** (in the smallest towns, the **Mairie,** the mayor's office, deals with tourist concerns), all of which *Let's Go* labels "tourist office." All three distribute maps and pamphlets, help you find accommodations, and suggest excursions to the countryside. For up-to-date events and regional information, try www.francetourism.com.

MONEY. The national currency of France is the **franc français** or French Franc (abbreviated to FF or F). Each franc is divided into 100 *centimes*. The franc is available in brightly colored 20, 50, 100, 200, and 500F notes, smart two-tone 10 and 20F coins, silvery 1, 2, and 5F coins, and pale copper 5, 10, 20, and 50 *centime* pieces.

France has accepted the **Euro (€)** as legal tender, and francs will be phased out by July 1, 2002. For more information, see p. 24. If you stay in hostels and prepare your own food, expect to spend about 100-140F/€15.25-21.35 per person per day. Accommodations start at about 130F/€19.85 for double room, and a decent sit-down meal with wine starts at about 65F/€9.95. By law, service must be included at all restaurants, bars, and cafes in France. It is not unheard of to leave extra *monnaie* (change) at a cafe or bar, maybe a franc or two per drink; exceptionally good service may be rewarded with a 5-10% tip. Otherwise, **tipping** is only expected for taxis and hairdressers; 10-15% is the norm. **Bargaining** is appropriate at flea markets *(marchés aux puces)*. Most purchases in France include a 20.6% **value-added tax** (VAT; TVA is the French acronym). Non-EU residents (including EU citizens who reside outside the EU) who are in France for less than six months can reclaim 17.1% of the purchase price on goods over 1200F/€182.95 bought in one store. Only certain stores participate in this *vente en détaxe* refund process; ask before you buy.

ACCOMMODATIONS AND CAMPING

Hostels generally offer dormitory accommodations in large single-sex rooms with 4-10 beds, though some have as many as 60. At the other end of the scale, many offer private singles and doubles. In France, a bed in a hostel averages around 50-100F/€7.65-15.25. The French **Hostelling International (HI)** (p. 37) affiliate is the **Fédération Unie des Auberges de Jeunesse (FUAJ)** and it operates 178 hostels within France. Some hostels accept reservations through the **International Booking Network** (p. 37). Two or more people traveling together will often save money by staying in cheap **hotels** rather than hostels. The French government employs a four star hotel ratings system. Most hotels listed by *Let's Go* have zero stars or one, with a smattering of two stars. **Gîtes d'étapes** are rural accommodations for cyclists, hikers, and other ramblers, and are in less-populated areas. Expect *gîtes* to provide beds, a kitchen facility, and a resident caretaker. After three thousand years of settled history, true wilderness in France is hard to find. It's **illegal to camp** in most public spaces, including and especially national parks. Instead, look forward to organized *campings* (campsites), where you'll share your splendid isolation with vacationing families and all manner of programmed fun. Most campsites have toilets, showers, and electrical outlets, though you may have to pay extra for such luxuries (10-40F/€1.55-6.10); you'll often need to pay a supplement for your car, too (20-50F/€3.05-7.65). Otherwise, expect to pay 50-90F/€7.65-13.75 per site.

FOOD AND DRINK

French chefs cook for one of the most finicky clienteles in the world. The largest meal of the day is *le déjeuner* (lunch). A complete French meal includes an *apértif* (drink), an *entrée* (appetizer), a *plat* (main course), salad, cheese, dessert, fruit, coffee, and a *digestif* (after-dinner drink). The French drink wine with virtually every meal; *boisson comprise* entitles you to a free drink (usually wine) with your meal. Most restaurants offer a *menu à prix fixe* (fixed-price meal) that costs less than ordering *à la carte*. The *formule* is a cheaper, two-course version for the hurried luncher. Odd-hour cravings between lunch and dinner can be satisfied at *brasseries*, the middle ground between the casual cafe and structured restaurant. *Service compris* means the tip is included in *l'addition* (check). It's easy to get satisfying dinner for under 60F/€9.15 with staples such as cheese, pâtés, wine, bread, and chocolate; for a picnic, get fresh produce at a *marché* (outdoor market) and then hop between specialty shops. Start with a *boulangerie* (bakery) for bread, proceed to a *charcuterie* (butcher) for meats, and then *pâtisseries* and *confiseries* (pastry and candy shops) will satiate the sweetest tooth. When choosing a cafe, remember that you pay for its location—those on a major boulevard are more expensive than smaller places a few steps down a side street. Prices are cheaper at the *comptoir* (counter) than in the *salle* (seating area). For supermarket shopping, look for the chains Carrefour, Casino, Monoprix, and Prisunic.

COMMUNICATION

MAIL. Airmail letters under 1oz. between the US and France take four to seven days and cost US$1. Letters from Canada cost CDN$0.95 for 20g. Allow at least five working days from Australia (postage AUS$1 for up to 20g) and three days from Britain (postage UK£0.30 for up to 20g). Envelopes should be marked *"par avion"* (airmail) to avoid having letters sent by sea. Mail can be held for pick-up through *Poste Restante* (General Delivery) to almost any city or town with a post office. Address letters to: SURNAME, First name; *Poste Restante: Recette Principale;* [5-digit postal code] TOWN; FRANCE. Mark the envelope HOLD.

TELEPHONES. When calling from abroad, drop the leading zero of the local number. French payphones only accept stylish phonecards called *Télécartes*, available in 50-unit (49F/€7.50) and 120-unit (98F/€14.95) denominations at train stations, post offices, and *tabacs*. *Décrochez* means pick up; you'll then be asked to *patientez* (wait) to insert your card; at *numérotez* or *composez* you can dial. Use only public France Télécom payphones as privately owned ones charge more. An expensive alternative is to call collect *(faire un appel en PCV);* an English-speaking operator can be reached by dialing the appropriate service provider listed below. The information number is ☎12; international operator, ☎00 33 11. International direct dial numbers include: **AT&T,** ☎0 800 99 00 11; **British Telecom,** ☎0 800 99 02 44; **Canada Direct,** ☎0 800 99 00 16 or 99 02 16; **Ireland Direct,** ☎0 800 99 03 53; **MCI,** ☎0 800 99 00 19; **Sprint,** ☎0 800 99 00 87; **Telecom New Zealand,** ☎0 800 99 00 64; **Telkom South Africa,** ☎0 800 99 00 27; **Telstra Australia,** ☎0 800 99 00 61.

INTERNET ACCESS. Most large towns in France have a cybercafe. Rates and speed of connection vary widely; occasionally there are free terminals in technologically-oriented museums or exhibition spaces. **Cybercafé Guide** (www.cyberia-cafe.net/cyberia/guide/ccafe.htm#working_france) lists cybercafes in France.

LANGUAGE. Contrary to popular opinion, even flailing efforts to speak French will be appreciated, especially in the countryside. Be lavish with your *Monsieurs*, *Madames*, and *Mademoiselles*, and greet people with a friendly *bonjour* (*bonsoir* in the evening). For basic French vocabulary and pronunciation, see p. 984.

HOLIDAYS AND FESTIVALS

Holidays: Le Jour de l'an St-Sébastian (New Year; Jan. 1); Le lundi de Pâques (Easter Monday; Apr. 5); La Fête du Travail (Labor Day; May 1); L'Anniversaire de la Liberation (celebrates the Liberation in 1944; May 8); L'Ascension (Ascension Day; June 1); Le lundi de Pentecôte (Whitmonday; June 12); La Fête Nationale (Bastille Day; July 14); L'Assomption (Feast of the Assumption; Aug. 15); La Toussaint (All Saints' Day; Nov. 1); L'Armistice 1918 (Armistice Day; Nov. 11); and Le Noël (Christmas; Dec. 25).

Festivals: Most festivals, like **fête du cinema** and **fête de la musique** (late June, when musicians rule the streets), are in summer. The **Cannes Film Festival** (May; www.festi-val-cannes.com) is mostly for directors and stars, but provides good people watching. The **Festival d'Avignon** (July-Aug.; www.festival-avignon.com/gbindex3.html) is famous for its theater. **Bastille Day** (July 14) is marked by military parades and fireworks nationwide. Although you may not be competing in the **Tour de France** (3rd or 4th Su in July; www.letour.fr), you'll enjoy all the hype. A **Vineyard Festival** (Sept., in Nice; www.nice-coteazur.org/americain/tourisme/vigne/index.html) celebrates the grape harvest with music, parades, and wine tastings. Nice and Nantes celebrate **Carnaval** in the last week or two before Ash Wednesday (culminating with Mardi Gras celebrations).

PARIS

City of light, of majestic panoramas and romantic cafes, of stunning art and savory cuisine—Paris manages to be it all. From the world's best bistros to the hottest of *haute couture*, from the medieval stone of Notre Dame to the sleek corporate

NO PRÉSERVATIFS ADDED Having invented the French kiss and the French tickler, the speakers of the language of love have long had *savoir faire* in all things sexual—safety included. French pharmacies provide 24hr. condom (*préservatif* or *capote*) dispensers. In wonderful French style, they unabashedly adorn the sides of buildings on public streets and vending machines in the Métro. When dining out, don't ask for foods without *préservatifs* or mistake your raspberry compote for a *capote*. Funny looks will greet you, as the French have not yet caught on to the international craze for condom-eating, and will think you a bit odd.

atmosphere of La Défense, Paris establishes itself as a guardian of tradition and a leader of the cutting edge. You can't conquer Paris, but you can certainly get acquainted with the *grande dame* of world capitals. For dazzling coverage of Paris and its environs, check out *Let's Go: Paris 2002.*

✈ INTERCITY TRANSPORTATION

Flights: Aéroport Roissy-Charles de Gaulle, 23km northeast of Paris, services most transatlantic flights. For flight info, call the 24hr. English-speaking information center (☎01 48 62 22 80; www.parisairports.com). **Aéroport d'Orly** (English recording ☎01 49 75 15 15), 18km south of Paris, is used by charters and many continental flights. The cheapest and fastest ways to get into the city are by **RER** or **bus.**

Trains: There are 6 train stations in Paris.

Gare du Nord: M: Gare du Nord. Serves Belgium, Britain, northern France, northern Germany, The Netherlands, and Scandinavia. To **Amsterdam** (4-5hr., 503F/€76.70) and **Brussels** (2hr., 324F/€49.40). The **Eurostar** departs from here for **London** (2hr., up to 1700F/€259.20).

Gare de l'Est: M: Gare de l'Est. To Austria, eastern France, southern Germany, Luxembourg, and northern Switzerland. To: **Munich** (8-10hr., 683F/€104.15); **Vienna** (14hr., 1052F/€160.40); **Zürich** (6-7hr., 432F/€65.90).

Gare de Lyon: M: Gare de Lyon. To southeastern France, Greece, Italy, and parts of Switzerland. To: **Geneva** (3½-4hr., 420F/€64.05) and **Rome** (13hr., 828F/€126.25).

Gare d'Austerlitz: M: Gare d'Austerlitz. Serves southwestern France, the Loire Valley, Portugal, and Spain. To **Barcelona** (9hr., 558F/€85.10) and **Madrid** (12-13hr., 713F/€108.70).

Gare St-Lazare: M: Gare St-Lazare. Serves Normandy. To **Rouen** (1-2hr., 105F/€16).

Gare de Montparnasse: M: Montparnasse-Bienvenüe. Serves Brittany; also the departure point for **TGVs** to southwestern France.

Buses: Gare Routière Internationale du Paris-Gallieni, 28, av. du Général de Gaulle (☎08 36 69 52 52; www.eurolines.fr), just outside Paris in Bagnolet. M: Gallieni.

✦ ORIENTATION

The **Ile de la Cité** and **Ile St-Louis** sit at the geographical center of the city, while the **Seine,** flowing east to west, splits Paris into two large expanses: the **Rive Gauche** (Left Bank) to the south and the **Rive Droite** (Right Bank) to the north. The Left Bank, with its older architecture and narrow streets, has traditionally been considered bohemian and intellectual, while the Right Bank, with its grand avenues and designer shops, is more chic. Administratively, Paris is divided into 20 **arrondissements** (districts) that spiral clockwise around the Louvre. Areas of interest are compact and central, and sketchier neighborhoods tend to lie on the outskirts of town. Refer also to the **color maps** of Paris at the front of this book.

RIVE GAUCHE (LEFT BANK). The **Latin Quarter,** encompassing the 5*ème* and parts of the 6*ème* around the **Sorbonne** and the **Ecole des Beaux-Arts,** has been home to students for centuries; the animated **boulevard St-Michel** is the boundary between the two *arrondissements*. The area around east-west **boulevard St-Germain,** which crosses bd. St-Michel just south of pl. St-Michel in the 6*ème*, is known as **St-Germain des Prés.** To the west, the gold-domed **Les Invalides** and the stern Neoclassical **Ecole Militaire,** which faces the **Eiffel Tower** across the **Champ-de-Mars,**

recall the military past of the 7ème and northern 15ème, now full of traveling businesspeople. South of the Latin Quarter, **Montparnasse,** in the 14ème, eastern 15ème, and southwestern 6ème, lolls in the shadow of its tower. The glamorous **boulevard du Montparnasse** belies the more residential districts around it. The eastern Left Bank, comprising the 13ème, is the city's newest hotspot, centered on the **place d'Italie.**

RIVE DROITE (RIGHT BANK). The **Louvre** and **rue de Rivoli** occupy the sight- and tourist-packed 1er and the more business-oriented 2ème. The crooked streets of **Marais,** in the 3ème and 4ème, escaped Baron Haussmann's redesign of ancient Paris and now support many diverse communities. From **place de la Concorde,** at the western end of the 1er, the **Avenue des Champs-Elysées** bisects the 8ème as it sweeps up toward the **Arc de Triomphe** at **Charles de Gaulle-Etoile.** South of the Etoile, old and new money fills up the exclusive 16ème, bordered to the west by the **Bois de Boulogne** park and to the east by the Seine and the **Trocadéro,** which faces the Eiffel Tower across the river. Back toward central Paris, the 9ème, just north of the 2ème, is defined by the sumptuous **Opéra.** East of the 9ème, the 10ème hosts cheap lodgings and the **Gares du Nord** and **de l'Est.** The 10ème, 3ème, and the happening 11ème (which peaks with the nightlife of **Bastille**) meet at **place de la République.** South of the Bastille, the 12ème surrounds the **Gare de Lyon,** petering out at the **Bois de Vincennes.** East of Bastille, the party atmosphere gives way to the quieter, more residential 20ème and 19ème, while the 18ème is home to **Montmartre,** capped by the **Sacré-Cœur.** To the east, the 17ème starts in the red-light district of **Pigalle** and bd. de Clichy, growing more elegant toward the Etoile, the **Opéra Garnier,** and the 16ème. Continuing west along the *grande axe* defined by the Champs-Elysées, the skyscrapers of **La Défense,** Paris's newest quarter, are across the Seine from the Bois de Boulogne.

⊡ LOCAL TRANSPORTATION

Public Transportation: The efficient **Métropolitain,** or **Métro (M),** runs 5:30am-12:30am. Lines are generally referred to by their number and final destinations; connections are called *correspondances*. **Single-fare tickets** within the city cost 8.50F/€1.30; **carnet** (packet) of 10 61F/€9.30. Buy extras for when ticket booths are closed (after 10pm) and keep your ticket until you exit. The **RER** (*Réseau Express Régional*), the commuter train to the suburbs, serves as an express subway within central Paris; changing to and getting off the RER requires sticking your validated ticket into a turnstile. Watch the signboards next to the RER tracks and check that your stop is lit up before riding. **Buses** use the same 8.50F/€1.30 tickets (bought on the bus; validate in the machine by the driver), but transfers require a new ticket. Buses run 6:30am-8:30pm, *Autobus du Soir* until 1am, and *Noctambus* (3-4 tickets) every hr. 1:30-5:30am at stops marked with the bug-eyed moon between the Châtelet stop and the *portes* (city exits). The **Mobilis** pass covers the Métro, RER, and buses only (1-day 33F/€5.05). To qualify for a weekly pass (*hebdomadaire*), valid from M (87F/€13.30), bring a photo ID to the ticket counter to get the necessary **Carte Orange.** Refer to the **color maps** of Paris's transit network at the front of this book.

Taxis: Taxis Bleus (☎01 49 36 10 10) or **Taxis G7** (☎01 47 39 47 39). Cabs are expensive and only take 3 passengers. The meter starts running when you phone. Cab stands are near train stations and major bus stops.

Car Rental: Autorent, 98, r. de la Convention, 15ème (☎01 45 54 22 45). M: Boucicaut. Also at 36, r. Fabert, 7ème (☎01 45 55 12 54). M: Invalides. Open M-F 8:30am-7pm, Sa 8am-noon. AmEx/MC/V.

Bike Rental: Paris-Vélo, 2, r. de Fer-à-Moulin, 5ème (☎01 43 37 59 22). M: Censier Daubenton. Bike rental 90F/€13.73 per day with 2000F/€305 deposit includes accident insurance. Open M-Sa 10am-12:30pm and 2-7pm.

Hitchhiking: *Let's Go* does not recommend hitchhiking. Don't waste time at the *portes* of the city, as traffic there is too heavy for cars to stop.

7 PRACTICAL INFORMATION

TOURIST AND FINANCIAL SERVICES

Tourist Offices: Bureau d'Accueil Central, 127, av. des Champs-Elysées, 8ème (☎08 36 68 31 12; www.paris-touristoffice.com). M: Georges V. English speaking and mobbed. Open daily 9am-8pm; low season Su 11am-6pm. **Branches** at Gare de Lyon (open M-Sa 8am-8pm) and the Eiffel Tower (open May-Sept. daily 11am-6pm).

Budget Travel: Council Exchange, 1, pl. Odéon, 6ème (☎01 44 41 89 80; www.councilexchange.org). M: Odéon. Sells ISICs, plane tickets, and train tickets (including BIJ/ Eurotrain). Open M-F 9:30am-6:30pm, Sa 10am-5pm.

Embassies: Australia, 4, r. Jean-Rey, 15ème (☎01 40 59 33 00; www.austgov.fr). M: Bir-Hakeim. Open M-F 9:15am-noon and 2-4:30pm. **Canada,** 35, av. Montaigne, 8ème (☎01 44 43 29 00). M: Franklin-Roosevelt or Alma-Marceau. Open M-F 9am-noon and 2-5pm. **Ireland,** 12, av. Foch, 16ème (☎01 44 17 67 48). M: Argentine. Open M-F 9:30am-noon. **New Zealand,** 7ter, r. Léonard de Vinci, 16ème (☎01 45 00 24 11). M: Victor-Hugo. Open M-F 9am-1pm and 2-5:30pm. **South Africa,** 59, quai d'Orsay, 7ème (☎01 53 59 23 23). M: Invalides. Open M-F 8:30am-12:30pm and 1:30-5:15pm. **UK,** 35, r. du Faubourg-St-Honoré, 8ème (☎01 44 51 31 00). M: Concorde. Open M-F 9:30am-12:30pm and 2:30-5pm. **US,** 2, av. Gabriel, 8ème (☎01 43 12 22 22). M: Concorde. Open M-F 9am-6pm.

Currency Exchange: Hotels, train stations, and airports offer poor rates but have extended hours; Gare de Lyon, Gare du Nord, and both airports have booths open 6:30am-10:30pm. Most **ATMs** accept **Visa** ("CB/VISA") and **MasterCard** ("EC"). Crédit Lyonnais ATMs take **AmEx;** Crédit Mutuel and Crédit Agricole ATMs are on the **Cirrus** network; and most Visa ATMs accept **PLUS**-network cards.

American Express: 11, r. Scribe, 9ème (☎01 47 14 50 00), opposite rear of the Opéra. M: Opéra or Auber. Mail held for cardholders and AmEx traveler's checks holders. Open M-F 9am-6:30pm, Sa 10am-5:30pm. Exchange counters open Su 10am-5pm.

LOCAL SERVICES

Bookstore: Gibert Jeune, 5, pl. St-Michel, 5ème. M: St-Michel. The best bookstore in town, with several departments along bd. St-Michel. Books in all languages for all tastes. Open M-Sa 9:30am-7:30pm.

Gay and Lesbian Services: Centre Gai et Lesbien, 3, r. Keller, 11ème (☎01 43 57 21 47). M: Ledru Rollin. Info hub of all gay services and associations in Paris. English spoken. Open M-Sa 2-8pm, Su 2-7pm. **Les Mots à la Bouche,** 6, r. Ste-Croix de la Bretonnerie. Serves as an unofficial information center for queer life (☎01 42 78 88 30; www.motalabouche.com.) M: Hôtel-de-Ville. Open M-Sa 11am-11pm and Su 2-8pm.

Laundromats: Laundromats are everywhere, especially in the 5ème and 6ème.

EMERGENCY AND COMMUNICATIONS

Ambulance: ☎15. **Fire:** ☎18. **Police:** ☎17. For non-emergencies, head to the local *gendarmerie* (police force) in each *arrondissement.*

Crisis Lines: Rape, SOS Viol (☎0 800 05 95 95). Call free anywhere in France for counseling (medical and legal). Open M-F 10am-7pm. **SOS Help!** (☎01 47 23 80 80). Anonymous, confidential English crisis hotline. Open daily 3-11pm.

Pharmacies: Every *arrondissement* should have a **pharmacie de garde** which will be open 24hr. in case of emergencies; the name of the nearest one is posted on each pharmacy's door. **British & American Pharmacy,** 1, r. Auber, 9ème (☎01 42 65 88 29). M: Auber or Opéra. Open M-F 8:30am-8pm, Sa 10am-8pm.

Medical Assistance: Hôpital Américain de Paris, 84, bd. Saussaye, Neuilly (☎01 46 41 25 25). M: Port Maillot, then bus #82 to the end of the line. A private hospital. **Hôpital Bichat,** 46, r. Henri Buchard, 18ème (☎01 40 25 80 80). M: Port St-Ouen. Emergency services.

Telephones: To use the phones, you'll need to buy a **phone card** (*télécarte*), available at post offices, Métro stations, and *tabacs*. For **directory info,** call ☎12.

Internet Access: ■ **Easy Everything,** 37, bd. Sébastopol, 1*er.* M: Châtelet-les-Halles. Purchase a User ID (min. 20F/€3.05) and recharge with 10F/€1.53 or more. Number of minutes depends on how busy the store is. Open 24hr. **WebBar,** 32, r. de Picardie, 3è*me.* M: République. 20F/€3.05 per hr. Open daily 8:30am-2am. **Luxembourg Micro,** 83, bd. St-Michel, 5è*me.* M: St-Michel. RER: Luxembourg. 40F/€6.10 per hr. Membership 100-275F/€15.25-41.95. Open daily 10am-10pm.

Post Office: Poste du Louvre, 52, r. du Louvre, 1*er* (info ☎01 40 28 20 40). M: Louvre. Open 24hr. Address mail to be held: SURNAME, First name *Poste Restante,* 52, r. du Louvre, 75001 Paris, France. **Postal Code:** 750xx, where "xx" is the *arrondissement* (e.g., 75003 for any address in the 3è*me*).

■ ACCOMMODATIONS

High season in Paris falls around Easter and from May to October, peaking in July and August. Paris's hostels skip many standard restrictions—sleep sheets, curfews, and the like—but they do tend to have flexible maximum stays. The city's six HI hostels are for members only. The rest of Paris's dorm-style beds are either private hostels or quieter and more private *foyers* (student dorms). Hotels may be the most practical accommodations for the majority of travelers. Groups of two to four may also find hotels more economical than hostels. Expect to pay at least 150F/€22.90 for a single or 200-400F/€30.50-61 for a double *if* you're lucky. In cheaper hotels, few rooms have private baths; hall showers can cost 15-25F/€2.30-3.85 per use. Rooms fill quickly after morning check-out (usually 10am-noon), so arrive early or reserve ahead. Most hotels accept reservations with a one-night credit card deposit. Most hostels and *foyers* include the **taxe de séjour** (1-5F/€0.15-0.80 per person per day) in listed prices, but some do not. If you haven't made a reservation in advance, tourist offices and some organizations, listed below, can find and book rooms.

ACCOMMODATION SERVICES

La Centrale de Réservations (FUAJ-HI), 60, r. Vitruve, 20è*me* (☎01 55 25 35 20). M: Port de Bagnolet or Maraichers. Open M-F 8:30am-5:30pm.

OTU-Voyage (Office du Tourisme Universitaire), 119, r. St-Martin, 4è*me* (☎08 20 817 817). 10F/€1.55 service fee. Full price due with reservation. English spoken. Open M-F 9:30am-7pm, Sa 10am-noon and 1:30pm-5pm. Also at 2, r. Malus, 5è*me* (☎01 44 41 74 74). M: Pl. Monge. Open M-Sa 9-6pm.

ILE DE LA CITÉ

■ **Henri IV,** 25, pl. Dauphine (☎01 43 54 44 53). M: Pont Neuf. One of Paris's best-located and least expensive hotels. Reserve at least one month in advance, even earlier in the summer. Singles 140F/€21.35; doubles 165-215F/€25.20-32.80, with shower and toilet 350F/€53.40; triples 255F/€38.90, 305F/€46.50; quads 300F/€45.75.

1ER AND 2ÈME: LOUVRE-PALAIS ROYAL

Central to the **Louvre,** the **Tuileries,** the **Seine,** and the ritzy **pl. Vendôme,** this area still has a few budget hotels. Avoid r. St-Denis.

■ **Centre International de Paris (BVJ)/Paris Louvre,** 20, r. J.-J. Rousseau (☎01 53 00 90 90; fax 01 53 00 90 91). M: Louvre or Palais-Royal. Bright, dorm-style rooms with 2-10 beds per room. Reception 24hr. Reserve by phone 1 week in advance. Rooms held only 10min. after expected check-in time; call if late. 145F/€22.15 per person.

■ **Hôtel du Palais,** 2, quai de la Mégisserie (☎01 42 36 98 25; fax 01 42 21 41 67). M: Châtelet-Les-Halles. Most rooms have views of the Seine and Left Bank. Reserve ahead. Singles 293F/€44.70, with bath 363F/€55.35; doubles 336F/€51.25, 366-396F/€55.80-60.40; triples 462F/€70.45; quads 562F/€85.70; quints 662F/€100.95; 6-person 772F/€117.70. Extra bed 70F/€10.70. AmEx/MC/V.

Hôtel Vivenne, 40, r. Vivienne (☎01 42 33 13 26; fax 01 40 41 98 19), off bd. Montmartre. M: Grands Boulevards. Singles 310F/€47.30, with toilet 480F/€73.20; doubles 400F/€61, 480F/€73.20. MC/V.

Hôtel St-Honoré, 85, r. St-Honoré (☎01 42 36 20 38 or 01 42 21 46 96; fax 01 42 21 44 08). M: Louvre, Châtelet, or Les Halles. All rooms with full bath. Breakfast 29F/€4.45. Reserve ahead and confirm the night before. Singles 320F/€48.80; doubles 440-490F/€67.10-74.75; triples and quads 540F/€82.35. AmEx/MC/V.

Maisons des Jeunes de Rufz de Lavison, 18, r. J.-J. Rousseau (☎01 45 08 02 10; fax 01 40 28 11 43), next door to BVJ Louvre. M: Louvre or Palais-Royal. In winter, an all-male dorm; in summer, co-ed. 5-night min. stay. Reception 9am-7pm. Reservations require 1-night's payment. Singles 165F/€25.20; doubles 290F/€44.25.

Timhotel Le Louvre, 4, r. Croix des Petits-Champs (☎01 42 60 34 86; fax 01 42 60 10 39). M: Palais-Royal. Expensive, but has the only wheelchair-accessible rooms at reasonable prices in the 1er. Great location next to the Louvre. Singles 905F/€138; doubles 905F/€138; 1 triple 1102F/€168.05. AmEx/MC/V.

3ÈME AND 4ÈME: THE MARAIS

The Marais's 17th-century mansions now house budget hotels close to the **Centre Pompidou** and the **Ile St-Louis**; the area is also convenient for sampling nightlife, as Paris's night buses converge in the 4ème at M: Châtelet.

▨ **Hôtel des Jeunes (MIJE)** (☎01 42 74 23 45; fax 01 40 27 81 64; www.mije.com). Books beds in Le Fourcy, Le Fauconnier, and Maubuisson (see below), 3 small hostels in old Marais residences. No smoking. English spoken. Breakfast, shower, and sheets included. Ages 18-30 only. 7-day max. stay. Reception 7am-1am. Curfew 1am. Check-in before noon (call ahead if late). Reserve 1 month in advance. 4- to 6-bed dorms 145F/€22.15; singles 240F/€36.60; doubles 175F/€26.70; triples 155F/€23.65.

Le Fourcy, 6, r. de Fourcy. M: St-Paul. Walk opposite the traffic down r. François-Miron and turn left on r. de Fourcy. Hostel surrounds a social courtyard.

Le Fauconnier, 11, r. du Fauconnier. M: St-Paul. Take r. du Prevôt, turn left on r. Charlemagne, and turn right on r. du Fauconnier. Steps away from the Seine and Ile St-Louis.

Maubuisson, 12, r. des Barres. M: Pont Marie. Walk opposite traffic on r. de l'Hôtel de Ville and turn right on r. des Barres, a silent street by the St-Gervais monastery. Elevator.

▨ **Grand Hôtel Jeanne d'Arc,** 3, r. de Jarente (☎01 48 87 62 11; fax 01 48 87 37 31; www.hoteljeannedarc.com). M: St-Paul. Nicely renovated rooms. 2 wheelchair-accessible rooms. Reserve 2 months in advance. Singles 347F/€53; doubles 420-479F/€64-73; triples 702F/€107; quads 800F/€122. Extra bed 75F/€11.45. MC/V.

▨ **Hôtel de la Place des Vosges,** 12, r. de Birague (☎01 42 72 60 46; fax 01 42 72 02 64), by pl. des Vosges. M: Bastille. Baths in all rooms. Reserve by fax 2 months ahead with 1 night's deposit. Singles 495F/€75.50; doubles 600F/€91.50, with twin beds 690F/€105.25; quads 900F/€137.25. AmEx/MC/V.

Hôtel de Nice, 42bis, r. de Rivoli (☎01 42 78 55 29; fax 01 42 78 36 07). M: Hôtel-de-Ville. Wonderful, bright rooms. Breakfast 40F/€6.10. Check-in 2pm, but leave your bags earlier. Check-out 11:30am. Reserve by fax or phone with 1 night's deposit 1 month ahead for summer. Singles 380F/€57.95; doubles 580F/€88.45; triples 710F/€108.60; quads 810F/€123.55. Extra bed 130F/€19.85. MC/V.

Hôtel Practic, 9, r. d'Ormesson (☎01 48 87 80 47; fax 01 48 87 40 04). M: St-Paul. A clean hotel in the heart of the Marais. Modest and bright rooms. English spoken. Reserve by fax 1 month ahead. Singles 290F/€44.25, with bath 420-520F/€64.05-79.30; doubles 409F/€62.40, 460-560F/€70.15-85.40; triples 635F/€96.85. Extra bed 80F/€12.20. Tax 3F/€0.50. MC/V.

Hôtel du 7ème Art, 20, r. St-Paul (☎01 44 54 85 00; fax 01 42 77 69 10). All rooms have cable TV, phones, and safes. Breakfast 46F/€7.02. Singles 328F/€50.05; rooms for 1 or 2 people with bath 460-789F/€70.15-120.35; rooms with twin beds and full baths 525-789F/€80.10-120.35. Extra bed 132F/€20.15. MC/V.

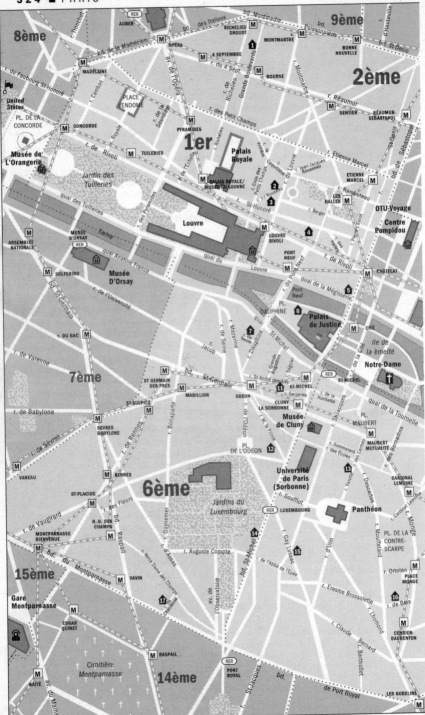

Central Paris

▲ ACCOMMODATIONS

Centre International de Paris/Maison des Jeunes de Rufz de Lavision, **3**

Centre International de Paris (BVJ)/Paris Louvre, **2**

Foyer International des Etudiantes, **14**

Grand Hôtel Jeanne d'Arc, **8**

Henri IV, **6**

Hôtel de Chevreuse, **17**

Hôtel de Neslé, **7**

Hôtel de la Place des Vosges, **10**

Hôtel des Jeunes, **9**

Hôtel du Lys, **11**

Hôtel du Palais, **5**

Hôtel Gay Lussac, **15**

Hôtel Saint-Honoré, **4**

Hôtel Stella, **12**

Hôtel St-Jacques, **13**

Hôtel Vivenne, **1**

Young + Happy Hostel, **16**

Start collecting culture at the small but valuable **Musée Picasso.** So valuable, in fact, that it paid off Picasso's federal taxes after his death. (p. 133)

Walk across the oldest bridge in Paris, **the Pont Neuf** (p. 60), to reach the oldest part of Paris, the *Île de la Cité.*

Rest your feet and mind at **Le Rouge et Blanc** while you fill your belly with traditional southern French cooking. (p. 158)

Housed in the Abbot of Cluny's beautiful 14th-century monastery, which was itself built over 1st-century Roman ruins, the **Musée de Cluny** houses one of the best medieval art collections in the world. (p. 134)

Shed your bohemian scarf for the expensive threads of **bd. St-Germain.** (p. 214)

finish

The best way to see this thoroughfare is from the outside tables of **Les Deux Magots** and **Café de Flore.** Watch the passing throngs, have wine with a light dinner, and appreciate the fact that the walls around you have seen more history than many American states. (p. 167)

Drink your *digestif* (and much more) at **Le Bar Dix,** where existentialism fills the air and even postmodernism is *passé.* (p. 195)

Take an early-evening stroll through the **Jardin du Luxembourg** to contemplate the excesses of the French royalty at the Italianate Palais, the notoriety of the Médicis, and the physics behind the game of *boules* played here. (p. 80)

Improve yourself at the **Collège de France,** perhaps not as world-famous as the Sorbonne, but much more accessible. Check the schedule outside; you may be able to catch a free lecture by the likes of Milan Kundera. (p. 76)

If you've ever wanted to come face to face with your idol (be it Rousseau for you *philosophes*, Marie Curie for you pre-meds, or even Ste-Geneviève for you theologists), they lie in the **Panthéon.** (p. 76)

Find the trashy and philosophical, the art and anti-art at the *bouquinistes* along the **quai du Louvre.** These booths are here to browse in, their owners to bargain with. (p. 123)

The most recently-recognized form of art? Fashion. It's been around for a long time on **rue de Rivoli,** keeping les Parisiennes chic and *haute couture*-d (p. 73).

Move on to the **Place des Vosg** *the* cultural center of Paris du the 17th century. Salons, sipp sarcasm, and sex went on in th beautiful *hôtels particuliers*. Sto at the **Maison de Victor H** to see a different side of intellectual–his paintings. (p.

The postcard-darling of Paris, **the Cathedral of Notre Dame** held Joan of Arc's heresy trial and saw the coronation of Napoleon. Abused throughout the last two centuries, however, it was only after the printing of Hugo's wildly popular *Hunchback of Notre Dame* that the government thought to restore it to its gothic glory. (p. 56)

Cross the Seine and enter the *Quartier Latin,* the academic center of Paris. First stop: **Shakespear** Sylvia Beach no longer hosts Hemingway and Joyce, and Allen Ginsburg no longer rings up your pu but the selection is wonderful and you're sure to meet the latest crowds of ex-pats at Sunday tea.

This *arrondissement* is for walking. Visit the small galleries that hide in every alley, buy your very own vintage accessory at Antiquités New-Puces at no. 45 (p. 216), or grab a crêpe like a real starving student along **rue Mouffetard,** the neighborhood's main drag.

For students, poets bohemians and *artiste.*

Hôtel du Marais, 16, r. de Beauce (☎01 42 72 30 26). M: Temple or Filles-de-Calvaire. This bargain of a hotel has character. Curfew 2-2:30am. 3rd-fl. showers 15F/€2.30. Singles 130F/€19.85; doubles 180F/€27.45.

Hôtel Paris France, 72, r. de Turbigo (☎01 42 78 00 04; reservations 01 42 78 64 92; fax 01 42 71 99 43). M: République or Temple. On a noisy street. Singles 400F/€61; doubles 560F/€85.40; triples 700F/€106.75. AmEx/MC/V.

5ÈME AND 6ÈME: THE LATIN QUARTER AND ST-GERMAIN-DES-PRÉS

The lively *quartier latin* and St-Germain-des-Prés offer proximity to the **Notre-Dame,** the **Panthéon,** the **Jardin du Luxembourg,** and the bustling student cafe culture.

☒ **Young and Happy (Y&H) Hostel,** 80, r. Mouffetard (☎01 45 35 09 53; fax 01 47 07 22 24). M: Monge. Clean rooms and commission-free currency exchange. Breakfast included. Dorms 137-157F/€20.90-23.95. Jan.-Mar. 10F/€1.55 lower per night.

☒ **Hôtel St-Jacques,** 35, r. des Ecoles (☎01 44 07 45 45; fax 01 43 25 65 50). M: Maubert-Mutualité. Singles 270F/€41.20, with bath 415F/€63.30; doubles 470F/€71.70, 630F/€96.05; triples 700F/€106.75. Daily tax 5F/€0.80. AmEx/MC/V.

Hôtel du Lys, 23, r. Serpente (☎01 43 26 97 57; fax 01 44 07 34 90), off r. Danton. M: Odéon or St-Michel. French country feel. Reserve 1 month ahead. Singles 430-580F/€65.60-88.45; doubles 630F/€96.10; triples 680F/€103.70. MC/V.

Hôtel des Argonauts, 12, r. de la Huchette (☎01 43 54 09 82; fax 01 44 07 18 84). M: St-Michel. Breakfast 25F/€3.85. Reserve 3-4 weeks ahead. Singles 285F/€43.45, with bath 405F/€61.75; doubles 320F/€48.80, 460F/€70.15; triples 465F/€70.90 (request in advance). AmEx/MC/V.

Hôtel d'Esmeralda, 4, r. St-Julien-le-Pauvre (☎01 43 54 19 20; fax 01 40 51 00 68). M: St-Michel. Views of the Seine. Singles 180F/€27.45, with bath 380F/€57.95; doubles 450-490F/€68.65-74.75; triples 580F/€88.45; quads 650F/€99.10.

Hôtel Stella, 41, r. Monsieur-le-Prince (☎01 40 51 00 25 or 06 07 03 19 71; fax 01 43 54 97 28). M: Odéon. Reserve ahead with deposit. Singles 262F/€40; doubles 328F/€50; triples 450F/€70; quads 525F/€80. No credit cards.

Hôtel Gay-Lussac, 29, r. Gay-Lussac (☎01 43 54 23 96; fax 01 40 51 79 49). M: Luxembourg. Stately old rooms. Reserve by fax 1 month ahead. Singles 200F/€30.50, with bath 310-390F/€47.30-59.50; doubles 340F/€51.85, 420F/€64.05; triples 350F/€53.40, 370-480F/€56.45-73.20; quads 620F/€94.55.

Hôtel de Chevreuse, 3, r. de Chevreuse (☎01 43 20 93 16; fax 01 43 21 43 72). M: Vavin. Small, clean, quiet rooms. Reserve 1 month ahead; confirm by fax. Singles 235F/€35.85, with bath 385-415F/€58.75-63.30; doubles 295F/€45, 385-415F/€58.75-63.30; triples 535F/€81.60. Daily tax 3F/€0.50. MC/V.

Centre International de Paris (BVJ): Paris Quartier Latin, 44, r. des Bernardins (☎01 43 29 34 80; fax 01 53 00 90 91). M: Maubert-Mutualité. Lively, slightly worn hostel. Breakfast included. Showers in rooms. Reception 24hr. Reserve well in advance and confirm, or arrive 9am to check for room. 138 beds. 5- and 6-bed dorms 145F/€22.15; singles 175F/€26.70; doubles and triples 155F/€23.60 per person.

Foyer International des Etudiantes, 93, bd. St-Michel (☎01 43 54 49 63). RER: Luxembourg. Everything elegant. Breakfast included. July-Sept. co-ed, open 24hr.; Oct.-June women only. Reserve in writing 2 months in advance, and as early as Jan. for co-ed summer months. 200F/€30.50 deposit. Check-out 10am. Call ahead or arrive by 10am for no-shows. 2-bed dorms 122F/€18.65; singles 172F/€26.25.

7ÈME: THE EIFFEL TOWER AND LES INVALIDES

☒ **Hôtel du Champs de Mars,** 7, r. du Champ de Mars (☎01 45 51 52 30; fax 01 45 51 64 36). M: Ecole-Militaire. Reserve 1 month ahead and confirm by fax with a credit card number. Singles 400F/€61; doubles 440F/€67.10; triples 560F/€85.40. MC/V.

☒ **Hôtel Montebello,** 18, r. Pierre Leroux (☎01 47 34 41 18; fax 01 47 34 46 71). M: Vaneau. Clean, cheery rooms with full baths. Reserve at least 2 weeks in advance. Breakfast 22F/€3.40. Singles 240F/€36.60; doubles 260F/€39.65.

Grand Hôtel Lévêque, 29, r. Cler (☎01 47 05 49 15; fax 01 45 50 49 36; www.hotel-leveque.com). M: Ecole-Militaire. Clean rooms with many amenities. English spoken. Reserve 1 month ahead. Singles 300F/€45.75; doubles 400-450F/€61-68.60, with twin beds 450-500F/€68.60-76.25; triples 600F/€91.47. AmEx/MC/V.

Hôtel de France, 102, bd. de la Tour Maubourg (☎01 47 05 40 49; fax 01 45 56 96 78). M: Ecole Militaire. Staff offers advice on Paris. Newly renovated rooms with full baths. Breakfast 45F/€6.90. Singles 420F/€64.05; doubles 530F/€80.85; 2 wheelchair accessible rooms 500F/€76.25. AmEx/MC/V.

8ÈME: CHAMPS-ELYSÉES

Hôtel d'Artois, 94, r. La Boétie (☎01 43 59 84 12 or 42 25 76 65; fax 01 43 59 50 70), near the Champs-Elysées. M: St-Philippe de Roule. Spacious bathrooms and bedrooms. Breakfast 35F/€5.35. Reserve 2 weeks in advance Mar.-June. Singles 300F/€45.75, with bath 445F/€67.90; doubles 340F/€51.85, 490F/€74.75. MC/V.

Foyer de Chaillot, 28, av. George V, 3rd fl. (☎01 47 23 35 32; fax 01 47 23 77 16; www.ufjt.org), in the Centre Chaillot Galliera. M: George V. Well-equipped, modern rooms in an upscale dorm-like environment for women ages 18-25 only. 1-month min. stay. Doubles 3150F/€480.30 per month; after a stay of 2 months, you can request a single for 3600F/€548.90 per month.

9ÈME AND 10ÈME: OPÉRA AND GARE DE NORD

The northern part of the *9ème* mixes pumping nightlife with a red-light district; avoid M: Pigalle, M: Barbès-Rochechouart, bd. de Clichy, the Gare de Nord, r. Faubourg St-Denis, bd. de Magenta, and near M: Barbés.

■ **Hôtel Beauharnais,** 51, r. de la Victoire (☎01 48 74 71 13; fax 01 44 53 98 80). M: Le Peletier. Reserve 2 weeks in advance. With *Let's Go:* doubles 320F/€48.80; triples 600F/€91.50; quads 800F/€122; quints 1000F/€152.50. No credit cards.

Woodstock Hostel, 48, r. Rodier (☎01 48 78 87 76; fax 01 48 78 01 63; www.woodstock.fr). M: Anvers or Gare du Nord. Safe deposit box, Internet, and fax. Sheets 20F/€3.05. Call ahead to reserve. 2-week max. stay. Singles 147F/€22.45; doubles 127F/€19.40; 3-4 person dorms 117F/€17.85; extra mattress 107F/€16.35.

Cambrai Hôtel, 129bis, bd. de Magenta (☎01 48 78 32 13; fax 01 48 78 43 55; www.hotel-cambrai.com). M: Gare du Nord. Singles 200F/€30.50, with bath 240-300F/€36.60-45.75; doubles 270F/€41.18, 300-380F/€45.75-57.95; triples 500F/€76.25; wheelchair accessible suite 550F/€83.90. MC/V.

11ÈME AND 12ÈME: BASTILLE AND RÉPUBLIQUE

Convenient to hopping nightlife, but take caution in the area at night.

Centre International du Séjour de Paris: CISP "Ravel," 6, av. Maurice Ravel (☎01 44 75 60 00; fax 01 43 44 45 30). M: Porte de Vincennes. Walk east on cours de Vincennes, take the 1st right on bd. Soult, turn left on r. Jules Lemaître, and turn right on av. Maurice Ravel. Large, clean rooms. Breakfast included. Reception 6:30am-1:30am. Reserve ahead by phone. 4-bed dorms 126F/€19.25; singles 196F/€29.90; doubles 156F/€23.80. AmEx/MC/V.

Hôtel Rhetia, 3, r. du Général Blaise (☎01 47 00 47 18; fax 01 48 06 01 73). M: Voltaire. Calm and clean. Breakfast 15F/€2.30. Reception 7:30am-10pm. Reserve ahead. Singles 180F/€27.45, with shower 223F/€34.05; doubles 206F/€31.45, 246F/€37.55; triples 309F/€47.15; quads 359F/€54.75.

Plessis Hôtel, 25, r. du Grand Prieuré (☎01 47 00 13 38; fax 01 43 57 97 87). M: Oberkampf. 5 floors of clean, bright rooms. Breakfast 38F/€5.80. Closed Aug. Singles 232F/€35.50, with bath 328-348F/€50-53; doubles 233-394F/€35.50-60; twin beds with shower 413F/€63. AmEx/MC/V.

Auberge de Jeunesse "Jules Ferry" (HI), 8, bd. Jules Ferry (☎01 43 57 55 60; fax 01 43 14 82 09). M: République. Clean rooms with 100 bunk beds and sinks. Party atmosphere. Breakfast and showers included. Lockers 10F/€1.55. Sheets included. Laundry

FRANCE

30F/€4.60. 7-night max. stay. Internet 1F/€0.15 per min. Reception 24hr. Lockout 10am-2pm. No reservations; arrive by 8am. Dorms 118-120F/€18-18.30. MC/V.

Hôtel de Reims, 26, r. Hector Malot (☎01 43 07 46 18; fax 01 43 07 56 62), off av. Daumesnil near Opéra Bastille and the Gare de Lyon. M: Gare de Lyon. 27 clean rooms. Breakfast 30F/€4.60. Reserve by phone 1 week in advance and confirm in writing or by fax. Singles 180F/€27.45, with shower 250F/€38.52; doubles 220F/€33.55, 260-280F/€39.65-42.70; triples 300F/€45.75. MC/V.

Maison Internationale des Jeunes pour la Culture et pour la Paix, 4, r. Titon (☎01 43 71 99 21; fax 01 43 71 78 58), off r. de Montreuil. M: Faidherbe Chaligny. A bit out of the way, but has simple, clean rooms. Breakfast included. Sheets 15F/€2.30. Ages 18-30 only. Reception 6am-2pm. 5-night max. stay. Reserve ahead. 125F/€19 per night.

13ÈME TO 15ÈME: MONTPARNASSE

Just south of the Latin Quarter, Montparnasse mixes intellectual charm with thriving commercial centers and cafes.

🏨 **Hôtel Printemps**, 31, r. du Commerce (☎01 45 79 83 36; fax 01 45 79 84 88). M: La Motte-Picquet-Grenelle. Pleasant and clean. Reserve 3-4 weeks ahead. Singles and doubles 176F/€26.85, with bath 216-256F/€32.95-39.05. MC/V.

🏨 **La Maison Hostel**, 67bis, r. Dutot (☎01 42 73 10 10). M: Volontaires. In a quiet neighborhood. Breakfast included. Sheets 15F/€2.30; included with doubles. Reception 8am-2am. Reserve 1 month ahead. June-Aug. 2- and 3-bed dorms 137F/€20.90; doubles 157F/€23.95; Nov.-Mar. dorms 117F/€17.85; doubles 137F/€20.90.

Three Ducks Hostel, 6, pl. Etienne Pernet (☎01 48 42 04 05; fax 01 48 42 99 99; www.3ducks.fr). M: Félix Faure. Aimed at Anglo fun-seekers. Breakfast included. Reception 8am-2am. 1-week max. stay. Reserve ahead with credit card. 2- to 8-bed dorms 137F/€20.90; doubles 157F/€23.95. Nov.-Mar. 10F/€1.55 less. MC/V.

🍴 FOOD

For most Parisians, life is about eating. Establishments range from the famous repositories of *haute cuisine* to corner *brasseries*. Inexpensive bistros and *crêperies* offer the breads, cheeses, wines, pâtés, *pôtages*, and pastries central to French cuisine. *Gauche* or gourmet, French or foreign, you'll find it in Paris. **CROUS (Centre Regional des Oeuvres Universitaires et Scolaires)**, 39, av. Georges Bernanos, *5ème*, has information on university restaurants. (M: Port-Royal. Open M-F 9am-5pm.) To assemble a picnic, visit the specialty shops of the **Marché Montorgueil**, *2ème*, **rue Mouffetard**, *5ème*, or the **Marché Bastille** on bd. Richard-Lenoir. (M: Bastille. Open Th and Su 7am-1:30pm.)

1ER AND 2ÈME: LOUVRE-PALAIS ROYAL

Cheap options surround **Les Halles**, 1*er* and 2*ème*. Near the **Louvre**, the small streets of the 2*ème* teem with traditional bistros.

🍴 **Jules**, 62, r. Jean-Jacques Rousseau. M: Les Halles. Blend of new and traditional French cooking. 4-course *menu* 130F/€19.85. Open M-F noon-2:30pm and 7-10:30pm.

🍴 **Les Noces de Jeannette**, 14, r. Favart, and 9, r. d'Amboise. M: Richelieu Drouot. *Menu du Bistro* 172F/€26.25. Reserve ahead. Open daily noon-1:30pm and 7-9:30pm.

🍴 **Le Fumoir**, 6, r. de l'Amiral Coligny. M: Louvre. Serves the best brunch in Paris (120F/€18.30). Coffee 15F/€2.30. Open daily 11am-2am.

Lamen Kintar, 24, r. St-Augustin. M: Quatre Septembre. In the heart of Paris's Japanese quarter. Noodle bowls 50F/€7.65; lunch *menu* with entree, sushi, sashimi, and soup 90-135F/€13.75-20.60. Open M-Sa 11:30am-10pm.

La Victoire Suprême du Coeur, 41, r. des Bourdonnais. M: Châtelet. Run by the devotees of guru Sri Chinmoy. All vegetarian and very tasty. All-day 3-course *menu* 95F/€14.50. Open M-F noon-3:30pm and 6-10pm, Sa noon-10pm.

3ÈME AND 4ÈME: THE MARAIS

The Marais offers chic bistros, kosher delis, and couple-friendly cafes.

■ **Chez Omar,** 47, r. de Bretagne. M: Arts et Métiers. One of the better Middle Eastern places in town. Couscous 70F/€10.70; meats 90-140F/€13.73-21.35. Open M-Sa noon-2:30pm and 7:30pm-midnight, Su 7:30pm-midnight.

■ **Au Petit Fer à Cheval,** 30, r. Vieille-du-Temple. M: St-Paul. An oasis of *chèvre, kir,* and *Gauloises.* Open daily 10am-2am; food served noon-1:15am. If full, try the neighboring **Les Philosophes** or **La Chaise au Plafond.**

L'As du Falafel, 34, r. des Rosiers. M: St-Paul. Lenny Kravitz loves this kosher falafel stand and restaurant. Falafel special 25F/€3.85. Open Su-Th 11:30am-11:30pm.

Le Réconfort, 37, r. de Poitou. M: St-Sébastien-Froissart. Swank French, Indian, and Middle Eastern cuisine. Lunch *menu* 72-92F/€11-14.05. Open M-F noon-2pm and 8-11pm, Sa 8-11pm.

En Attendant Pablo, 78, r. Vieille-du-Temple. M: Hôtel-de-Ville. This *pâtisserie*/lunch cafe serves huge salads (58F/€8.80). Juice 26-28F/€4-4.30. Open W-Su noon-6pm.

L'Apparement Café, 18, r. des Coutures St-Gervais, next to the Picasso Museum. M: St-Paul. Coffee 12F/€1.85; make-your-own salads 45F/€6.90; Su brunch 95F/€14.50 or 125F/€19.05. Open M-Sa noon-2am, Su 11:30am-midnight.

Les Enfants Gâtés, 43, r. des Francs-Bourgeois. M: St-Paul. "Spoiled children" is a sexy spot to brood and linger. Coffee 15F/€2.30. Brunch 95-135F/€14.50-20.60. Food served until 4:30pm. Open daily 11am-8pm.

Café Beaubourg, 43, r. St-Merri, facing Centre Pompidou. M: Hôtel-de-Ville. This is *the* spot to see and be seen during the day. Coffee 17F/€2.60. Breakfast 80F/€12.20; brunch 130F/€19.85. Open M-Th and Su 8am-1am, F-Sa 8am-2am.

5ÈME AND 6ÈME: THE LATIN QUARTER AND ST-GERMAIN-DES-PRÉS

Tiny low-priced restaurants pack the quadrangle bounded by **boulevard St-Germain, boulevard St-Michel, rue de Seine,** and the **Seine. Rue de Buci** harbors Greek restaurants and a street market, while **rue Gregoire de Tours** has cheap, greasy restaurants.

■ **Le Bistro d'Henri,** 16, r. Princesse. M: Mabillon. Classic Left Bank bistro. Dinner *menu* 160F/€24.40. Open daily noon-2:30pm and 7-11:30pm. Around the corner is **Le Machon d'Henri,** 8, r. Guisarde, serving the same *menus* in a smaller setting.

■ **Aux Portes de l'Orient,** 39, r. Geoffrey St-Hilaire, in the Mosquée de Paris. M: Censier Daubenton. An exquisitely soothing Islamic cafe. Persian mint tea 10F/€1.55. Tea room open daily 9am-11:30pm. Restaurant open daily noon-3pm and 7:30-10:30pm.

Café de Flore, 172, bd. St-Germain. M: St-Germain-des-Prés. Sartre composed *Being and Nothingness* here; Apollinaire, Picasso, Breton, and Thurber sipped brew. Espresso 25F/€3.85; pastries 38-65F/€5.80-9.95. Open daily 7am-1:30am.

Au Jardin des Pâtés, 4, r. Lacépède. M: Jussieu. Organic gourmet pastas, including *pâtés de seigle* (ham, white wine, and sharp comté cheese; 58F/€8.85). Main dishes 47-77F/€7.20-11.75. Open daily noon-2:30pm and 7-11pm.

Le Sélect, 99, bd. du Montparnasse, across the street from La Coupole. M: Vavin. Trotsky, Satie, Breton, Cocteau, and Picasso all frequented this huge art deco cafe. Coffee 7-12F/€1.10-1.85. Open daily 7am-3am.

7ÈME: THE EIFFEL TOWER AND LES INVALIDES

■ **Au Pied de Fouet,** 45, r. de Babylone. M: Vaneau. Straightforward French home-cooking at bargain prices. Appetizers 13-20F/€2-3.05, main dishes 45-70F/€6.90-10.70. Open M-F noon-2:30pm and 7-9:30pm, Sa noon-2pm.

■ **Café du Marché,** 38, r. Cler. M: Ecole Militaire. Good American-style food like a Caesar salad (50F/€7.65). Open M-Sa 7am-1am, Su 7am-3pm; M-Sa food served until 11pm.

8ÈME: CHAMPS-ELYSÉES

The 8*ème* is as glamorous and expensive as it gets. If you're not interested in such extravagance, there are some affordable restaurants around **rue La Boétie.**

🔲 **Antoine's: Les Sandwiches des 5 Continents,** 31, r. de Ponthieu. M: Franklin D. Roosevelt. Bright, modern sandwich shop. Full meal 40F/€6.10. Open M-F 8am-6pm.

Restaurant La Maline, 40, r. de Ponthieu. M: Franklin D. Roosevelt. A simple, candle-lit restaurant. 2-course *menu* 150F/€22.90. Open M-F noon-2:30pm and 7-11:30pm.

9ÈME: OPÉRA

Meals close to the Opéra cater to the after-theater and movie crowd and can be quite expensive. **Rue Faubourg-Montmartre** is packed with cheap eateries.

🔲 **Haynes Restaurant Américain,** 3, r. Clauzel. M: St-Georges. A former hangout of Louis Armstrong, James Baldwin, and Richard Wright. Generous portions under 100F/ €15.25. Open Tu-Sa 7pm-12:30am.

Paris-Dakar, 95, r. du Faubourg St-Martin. M: Gare de l'Est. Senegalese cuisine. Lunch *menu* 59F/€9; dinner *menu* 149F/€22.75; African *menu* 199F/€30.35. Open Tu-Th and Sa-Su noon-3pm and 7pm-2am, F 7pm-2am.

11ÈME: LA BASTILLE

La Bastille swells with fast-food joints. Reasonably priced African, Asian, and French spots lie on **rue Charonne, rue Keller, rue de Lappe,** and **rue Oberkampf.**

🔲 **Chez Paul,** 13, r. de Charonne (☎04 47 00 34 57). M: Bastille. Worn exterior hides a kicking bistro. Peppercorn steak 78F/€11.90. Reservations a must. Open daily noon-2:30pm and 7pm-2am; food served until 12:30am; closed for lunch Aug.1-15.

Café de l'Industrie, 16, r. St-Sabin. M: Breguet-Sabin. Huge and happening cafe pays tribute to the lighter side of Colonialism. Coffee 10F/€1.55; salads 45-58F/€6.90-8.85. After 10pm, add 4F/€0.65. Open Su-F 10-2am; lunch served noon-1pm.

13ÈME THROUGH 16ÈME: MONTPARNASSE

Scores of Asian restaurants pack Paris's **Chinatown,** south of pl. d'Italie on av. de Choisy. The 14*ème* is bordered at the top by the busy **boulevard du Montparnasse,** which is lined with a diverse array of restaurants. R. du Montparnasse, which intersects with the boulevard, teems with reasonably priced *crêperies.* **Rue Daguerre** is lined with vegetarian-friendly restaurants. Inexpensive restaurants cluster on **rue Didot, rue du Commerce, rue de Vaugirard,** and **boulevard de Grenelle.**

🔲 **Phinéas,** 99, r. de l'Ouest. M: Pernety. The restaurant also doubles as a comic book shrine. Open Tu-Sa 9am-noon for takeout, noon-11:30pm for dine-in.

Aux Artistes, 63, r. Falguière. M: Pasteur. One of the coolest spots in the 15*ème.* Lunch *menu* 58F/€8.85, dinner *menu* 80F/€12.20. Open M-F noon-12:30am, Sa noon-2pm.

Restaurant GR5, 19, r. Gustave Courbet. M: Rue de la Pompe. *Fondue savoyarde* for 2 (210F/€32.05) on checkered table cloths. Main dishes 70-90F/€10.70-13.75; *menu* 125F/€19.10. Open M-Sa 11am-11pm.

18ÈME: MONTMARTRE

Bistros cluster in **place du Tertre** and **place St-Pierre.** Be cautious in the area, particularly at night. Charming bistros and cafes lie near **rue des Abbesses** and **rue Lepic.**

🔲 **Refuge des Fondues,** 17, r. des Trois Frères. M: Abbesses. Only 2 main dishes: *fondue bourguignonne* (meat fondue) and *fondue savoyarde* (cheese fondue). The wine is served in baby bottles; leave your Freudian hang-ups at home. *Menu* 92F/€14.05. Reserve or show up early. Open W-M 5pm-2am; closed part of July-Aug.

🔲 **Le Sancerre,** 35, r. des Abbesses. M: Abbesses. Classic Montmartre cafe with an edgy bohemian crowd and throbbing techno music. Beer 17-24F/€2.60-3.70; wines 17-30F/€2.60-4.60. Brunch Sa-Su 65F/€9.95. Open daily 7am-2am.

◎ SIGHTS

In a few hours, you can walk from the heart of the Marais in the east to the Eiffel Tower in the west, passing most major monuments along the way. Try to reserve a day for wandering; you don't have a true sense of Paris until you know how close medieval Notre-Dame is to the modern Centre Pompidou, or the *Quartier Latin* to the Louvre. After dark, spotlights illuminate everything from the Panthéon to the Eiffel Tower, Notre Dame to the Obélisque.

ILE DE LA CITÉ AND ILE ST-LOUIS

CATHÉDRALE DE NOTRE-DAME DE PARIS

M: St-Michel-Notre-Dame; exit on the island side. From the Left Bank, cross Pont au Double and turn right. Open M-F 8am-6:45pm, Sa-Su 8am-7:45pm. Towers open daily 9:30am-6pm; 35F/€15.35, under 25 23F/€3.55. Treasury open M-Sa 9:30-11:30am and 1-6pm; 15F/ €2.30, students 10F/€1.55. Crypt open daily 10am-6pm; 22F/€3.55, under 27 and over 60 free. Tours in English leave from the right of the entrance; W and Th noon, Sa 2:30pm; free.

This 12th- to 14th-century cathedral, begun under Bishop Maurice Sully, is one of the most famous and beautiful examples of medieval architecture. After the Revolution, the building fell into disrepair and was even used to shelter livestock until Victor Hugo's 1831 novel *Notre-Dame-de-Paris* (a.k.a. *The Hunchback of Notre Dame*) inspired citizens to lobby for restoration. Architect Eugène Viollet-le-Duc made subsequent modifications, including the addition of the spire and the gargoyles. The intricately carved, apocalyptic façade and soaring, apparently weightless walls, produced by brilliant Gothic engineering and optical illusions, are inspiring even for the most church weary. The cathedral's biggest draws are its enormous stained-glass **rose windows** that dominate the north and south ends of the transept. A staircase inside the towers leads to a spectacular perch from which weather-worn gargoyles survey the city.

OTHER SIGHTS

ILE DE LA CITÉ. If any place could be called the heart of Paris, it is this island in the river. In the 3rd century BC, when it was inhabited by the *Parisii*, a Gallic tribe of hunters, sailors, and fishermen, the Ile de la Cité was all there was to Paris. Although the city has expanded in all directions, all distance-points in France are measured from *kilomètre zéro*, a sundial on the ground in front of Notre-Dame.

▨ STE-CHAPELLE AND CONCIERGERIE. Within the courtyard of the **Palais de Justice**, which has harbored Paris's district courts since the 13th century, the opulent, Gothic **Ste-Chapelle** was built by Saint Louis (Louis IX) to house his most precious possession, Christ's crown of thorns (now in Notre Dame). In the **Upper Chapel,** twin walls of stained glass glow and frescoes of saints and martyrs shine. *(4, bd. du Palais, within the Palais de la Cité. M: Cité. Open daily Apr.-Sept. 9:30am-6:30pm; Oct.-Mar. 10am-5pm. 36F/€5.50; joint ticket with Conciergerie 50F/€7.65, seniors and ages 18-25 23F/ €3.55, under 18 free.)* The **Conciergerie,** around the corner from Ste-Chapelle, was one of Paris's most famous prisons; Marie-Antoinette and Robespierre were imprisoned here during the Revolution. *(1, quai de l'Horloge. M: Cité. Open daily Apr.-Sept. 9:30am-6:30pm; Oct.-Mar. 10am-5pm. 36F/€5.50, students 23F/€3.55. Includes tour in French 11am and 3pm. For tours in English, call in advance.)*

ILE ST-LOUIS. The Ile St-Louis is home to some of Paris's most privileged elite, such as the Rothschilds and Pompidou's widow, and former home to other superfamous folks, including Voltaire, Baudelaire, and Marie Curie. At night, the island glows in the light of cast-iron lamps and candlelit bistros. Look for Paris's best ice cream at Ile St-Louis' **Berthillon,** 31, r. St-Louis-en-Ile. *(Across the Pont St-Louis from Notre-Dame; also across the Pont Marie from M: Pont Marie. Berthillon open Sept. to mid-July; take-out W-Su 10am-8pm; eat-in W-F 1-8pm, Sa-Su 2-8pm. Closed 2 weeks in both Feb. and Apr.)*

THE LATIN QUARTER AND ST-GERMAIN-DES-PRÉS

The autumn influx of Parisian students is the prime cultural preservative of the *quartier latin*, so named because prestigious *lycées* and universities taught in Latin until 1798. Since the violent student riots in protest of the outmoded university system in May 1968, many artists and intellectuals have migrated to the less expensive outer *arrondissements*, and the *haute bourgeoisie* has moved in. The 5*ème* still presents the most diverse array of bookstores, cinemas, bars, and jazz clubs in the city. Designer shops and fascinating galleries line **St-Germain-des-Prés.**

CAFES. Cafes along bd. St-Germain-des-Prés have long been gathering places for literary and artistic notables such as Hemingway and Mallarmé. **Aux Deux Magots,** 6, pl. St-Germain-des-Prés, named for two porcelain figures that adorned a store selling Chinese silk and imports on the same spot in the 19th century, quickly became a favorite hangout of Verlaine and Rimbaud, later attracting Breton, Artaud, and Picasso. **Café de Flore,** 172, bd. St-Germain, established in 1890, was made famous in the 1940s and '50s by literati Sartre and Camus, who favored its wood-burning stoves over their cold apartments. *(M: St-Germain-des-Prés.)*

BOULEVARD ST-MICHEL AND ENVIRONS. At the center of the Latin Quarter, bd. St-Michel, which divides the 5*ème* and 6*ème*, is filled with cafes, restaurants, bookstores, and clothing boutiques. **Place St-Michel,** at its northern tip, is filled with students, often engaged in typically Parisian protests, and lots of tourists. *(M: St-Michel.)*

JARDIN DU LUXEMBOURG. South along bd. St-Michel, the formal French gardens of the Jardin du Luxembourg are fabulous for strolling, reading, and watching the famous *guignol* puppet theater. *(RER: Luxembourg; exit onto bd. St-Michel. The main entrance is on bd. St-Michel. Open daily Apr.-Oct. 7:30am-9:30pm; Nov.-Mar. 8:15am-5pm.)*

PANTHÉON. The **crypt** of the Panthéon, which occupies the highest point on the Left Bank, houses the tombs of Voltaire, Rousseau, Victor Hugo, Emile Zola, Jean Jaurès, and Louis Braille; you can spy each tomb from behind locked gates. The **dome** features uninspiring Neoclassical frescoes. *(On pl. du Panthéon, east of the Jardin du Luxembourg. M: Cardinal Lemoine; follow r. du Cardinal Lemoine uphill and turn right on r. Clovis. Or, from RER: Luxembourg, head north on bd. St-Michel and turn right on r. Soufflot. Open daily in summer 9:30am-6:30pm; in winter 10am-6:15pm. 42F/€6.40, students 26F/€4.)*

EGLISE ST-GERMAIN-DES-PRÉS. Scarred by centuries of weather, revolution, and war, the Eglise St-Germain-des-Prés, which dates from 1163, is the oldest standing church in Paris. *(3, pl. St-Germain-des-Prés. M: St-Germain-des-Prés. Open daily 8am-7:45pm.)*

JARDIN DES PLANTES. Opened in 1640 to grow medicinal plants for King Louis XIII, the garden now features natural science museums and a **zoo,** which Parisians raided for food during the Prussian siege of 1871. *(On pl. Valhubert. M: Jussieu; follow r. Jussieu southeast along the university building.)*

MOSQUÉE DE PARIS. The cool courtyards and ornate archways of this mosque provide a soothing setting for prayer, mint tea, or an afternoon in the *hammam*. *(Pl. du Puits de l'Ermite. M: Jussieu. From r. Linné, turn right on r. Lacépède, and left on r. de Quatrefages. Open June-Aug. Sa-Th 9am-noon and 2-6pm. Tours 15F/€2.29, students 10F/€1.55.)*

THE EIFFEL TOWER AND LES INVALIDES

EIFFEL TOWER. Built in 1889 as the centerpiece of the World's Fair, the Tour Eiffel has come to symbolize the city. Despite criticism, tacky souvenirs, and Gustave Eiffel's own sentiment that "France is the only country in the world with a 300m flagpole," the tower is unfailingly elegant and commands an excellent view of the city. At night, it will impress even the most jaded tourist. *(M: Bir Hakeim. Follow bd. de Grenelle to the Seine and turn right on quai Branly. Or, from RER: Champ de Mars-Tour Eiffel, follow quai Branly. Open daily June-Aug. 9am-midnight; Sept.-June. 9:30am-11pm. Lift to 1st fl. 24F/€3.70, 2nd fl. 45F/€6.90, 3rd fl. 65F/€9.95. Stairs to 1st and 2nd fl. 20F/€3.05.)*

THE GHOSTS OF PARIS PAST The Quai Voltaire, in the 7ème, generally known for its lovely views of Seine bridges, boasts an artistic heritage more distinguished than any other block in the city. Voltaire spent his last days at no. 27. No. 19 housed cultural powerhouses: Baudelaire in 1856-58 while he wrote *Les Fleurs du Mal (Flowers of Evil)*, Richard Wagner as he composed *Die Meistersinger* in 1861-62, and Oscar Wilde while he was in exile. Eugène Delacroix lived at no. 13 from 1829-1836, and the landscape painter Jean-Baptiste-Camille Corot also resided at no. 13. At no. 11, Jean-Auguste-Dominique Ingres died in 1867. The famous Russian ballet dancer Rudolf Nureyev lived at no. 23 from 1981 until his death in 1993.

LES INVALIDES. The tree-lined **Esplanade des Invalides** runs from the impressive **Pont Alexandre III** to the gold leaf domed **Hôtel des Invalides.** The Hôtel, built for veterans under Louis XIV, now houses the **Musée de l'Armée** and **Napoleon's Tomb.** The **Musée Rodin** (p. 337) is nearby, on r. Varenne. *(M: Invalides, Latour Maubourg, or Varenne.)*

THE LOUVRE, OPÉRA, MARAIS, AND LA BASTILLE

■**MARAIS.** This area, made up of the 3ème and 4ème *arrondissements*, became the most chic place to live with Henri IV's construction of the elegant **place des Vosges** at the beginning of the 17th century; several remaining mansions now house museums. Today, the streets of the Marais house the city's Jewish and gay communities as well as fun, hip restaurants and shops. At the confluence of the 1er, 2ème, 3ème, and 4ème, the **Centre Pompidou** (p. 337) looms like a colorful factory over the vast *place*, where artists, musicians, and pickpockets gather. Linger during the day, but be cautious at night. *(M: Rambuteau; take r. Rambuteau to pl. Georges Pompidou. Or, from M: Chatelet-Les Halles, take r. Rambuteau or r. Aubry le Boucher.)*

AROUND THE LOUVRE. World-famous art museum and former residence of kings, the **Louvre** (p. 337) occupies about one-seventh of the 1er *arrondissement.* **Le Jardin des Tuileries,** at the western foot of the Louvre, was commissioned by Catherine de Médicis in 1564 and improved by André Le Nôtre (designer of the gardens at Versailles) in 1649. *(M: Tuileries. Open daily Apr.-Sept. 7am-9pm; Oct.-Mar. 7:30am-7:30pm. Free tours in English from the Arc de Triomphe du Carrousel.)* Three blocks north along r. de Castiglione, **Place Vendôme** hides 20th-century offices and luxury shops behind 17th-century façades. Look out for Napoleon on top of the column in the center of the *place*—he's the one in the toga. *(M: Tuileries or Concorde.)* The **Palais-Royal** was commissioned in 1632 by Cardinal Richelieu, who gave it to Louis XIII. In 1784, the elegant buildings enclosing the palace's formal garden became *galeries,* the prototype of a shopping mall. The revolutions of 1789, 1830, and 1848 all began with angry crowds in the same garden. *(M: Palais-Royal/Musée du Louvre or Louvre-Rivoli.)*

OPÉRA. North of the Louvre, the grandiose **Opéra** was built under Napoleon III in the eclectic style of the Second Empire. Gobelin tapestries, a 1964 Marc Chagall ceiling, and a six-ton chandelier adorn the magnificent interior. *(M: Opéra. Open daily in summer 10am-6pm; off-season 10am-5pm. 30F/€4.60, students 20F/€3.05. Tours in English in summer daily at noon; off-season varies; 60F/€9.15, students 45F/€6.90.)*

LA BASTILLE. Charles V built the Bastille to guard the eastern entrance to his capital. When Louis XIII made it a state prison, it housed religious heretics and political undesirables. On July 14, 1789, revolutionaries stormed the Bastille, looking for gunpowder and political prisoners. By 1792, nothing was left but its outline on the *place*. On July 14, 1989, François Mitterrand inaugurated the glittering **Opéra Bastille** to celebrate the destruction of Charles's fortress. *(130, r. de Lyon. M: Bastille. Daily tours usually 1 or 5pm. 60F/€9.15, students 45F/€6.90.)*

CHAMPS-ELYSÉES AND LA DÉFENSE

PLACE DE LA CONCORDE. Paris's most famous public square lies at the eastern terminus of the Champs-Elysées. Constructed between 1757 and 1777 to hold a monument to Louis XV, the area soon became the *place de la Révolution*, site of a guillotine that severed 1343 necks. After the Reign of Terror, the square was optimistically renamed (*concorde* means "peace"). The huge, rose-granite, 13th-century BC **Obélisque de Luxor** depicts the deeds of Egyptian pharaoh Ramses II. Given to Charles X by the Viceroy of Egypt, it is Paris's oldest monument. (*M: Concorde.*)

ARC DE TRIOMPHE. Napoleon commissioned the **Arc de Triomphe,** at the western terminus of the Champs-Elysées, in 1806 in honor of his Grande Armée. In 1940, Parisians were brought to tears as Nazis goose-stepped through the Arc; on August 26, 1944, British, American, and French troops liberating the city from Nazi occupation marched through to the roaring cheers of thousands. The terrace at the top has a fabulous view. (*On pl. Charles de Gaulle. M: Charles-de-Gaulle-Etoile. Open daily Apr.-Sept. 9:30am-11pm; Oct.-Mar. 10am-10:30pm. 42F/€6.45, under 26 26F/€4.*) The **Tomb of the Unknown Soldier** has been under the Arc since November 11, 1920. It bears the inscription, "Here lies a French soldier who died for his country, 1914-1918," but represents the 1½ million men who died during World War I.

BOIS DE BOULOGNE. Avenue Foch, one of Haussmann's finest creations, runs from the Arc de Triomphe to the Bois de Boulogne. Though popular by day for picnics, the park is a risky choice at night—until recently it was home to many drug dealers and prostitutes. (*16ème. M: Porte Maillot, Sablons, Pont de Neuilly, or Porte Dauphine.*)

LA DÉFENSE. Outside the city limits, the skyscrapers and modern architecture of La Défense make up Paris's newest (unofficial) *arrondissement*, home to the headquarters of 14 of France's top 20 corporations. The **Grande Arche,** inaugurated in 1989, completes the *axe historique* running through the Louvre, pl. de la Concorde, and the Arc de Triomphe. There's yet another stunning view from the top. Trees, shops, and sculptures by Miró and Calder line the esplanade. (*M: La Défense, zone 2; RER, zone 3. Open daily 10am-8pm. 46F/€7.05, students 35F/€5.35.*)

MONTMARTRE AND PÈRE-LACHAISE

BASILIQUE DU SACRÉ-COEUR. The Basilique du Sacré-Coeur crowns the **butte Montmartre** like an enormous white meringue. Its onion dome is visible from almost anywhere in the city, and its 112m bell tower is the highest point in Paris, offering a view that stretches up to 50km. (*35, r. du Chevalier de la Barre, 18ème. M: Château-Rouge, Abbesses, or Anvers. From Anvers, take r. de Steinkerque off bd. de Rochechouart and climb the steps. Open daily 7am-11pm; free. Dome and crypt open daily 9am-6pm; each 15F/€2.30, students 8F/€1.25.*) Nearby, **place du Tertre** features outdoor cafes and sketch artists.

CIMETIÈRE PÈRE LACHAISE. The Cimetière Père Lachaise holds the remains of Balzac, Sarah Bernhardt, Colette, Danton, David, Delacroix, La Fontaine, Haussmann, Molière, Proust, and Seurat within its peaceful, winding paths and elaborate sarcophagi. Foreigners buried here include Amadeo Modigliani, Gertrude Stein, and Oscar Wilde, but the most visited grave is that of Jim Morrison. French Leftists make ceremonious pilgrimage to the **Mur des Fédérés** (Wall of the Federals), where 147 revolutionary *Communards* were executed and buried. (*16, r. du Repos, 20ème. M: Père-Lachaise. Open Mar.-Oct. M-F 8am-6pm, Sa 8:30am-6pm, Su 9am-6pm; Nov.-Feb. M-F 8am-5:30pm, Sa 8:30am-5:30pm, Su 9am-5:30pm. Free.*)

🏛 MUSEUMS

For updated information, check *Paris Museums and Monuments*, available at the Champs-Elysées tourist office. *Pariscope* (3F/€0.50) and *L'Officiel des Spectacles* (2F/€0.35) list museum hours and temporary exhibits. The **Carte Musées et Monuments** grants entry to 70 Paris museums; it's available at major museums and Métro stations (1-day 85F/€13, 3-day 170F/€25.95, 5-day 255F/€38.90).

■ MUSÉE DU LOUVRE

M: Palais-Royal/Musée du Louvre. Open M and W 9am-9:45pm, Th-Su 9am-6pm. Last entry 45min. before closing. 46F/€7.05 M and W-Sa 9am-3pm; 30F/€4.60 M and W-Sa 3pm-close, Su; 1st Su of the month free. Tours in English M and W-Sa; 17F/€2.60.

A short list of its masterpieces includes the *Code of Hammurabi*, Jacques-Louis David's *The Oath of Horatii*, Vermeer's *Lacemaker*, and Delacroix's *Liberty Leading the People*. Oh, yeah, and there's that lady with the mysterious smile, too—the *Mona Lisa*. Enter through I.M. Pei's controversial glass **Pyramid** in the Cour Napoléon, or skip lines by entering directly from the Métro. When visiting the Louvre, strategy is everything. Think like a four-star general: the goal is to come and see without being conquered. The Louvre is organized into three different wings: Sully, Richelieu, and Denon. Each is divided into different sections according to the artwork's date, national origin, and medium. The color-coding and room numbers on the free maps correspond to the colors and numbers on the plaques at the entrances to every room within the wing.

The Italian Renaissance collection, on the 1st floor of the Denon wing, is rivaled only by that of the Uffizi museum in Florence. Look for Raphael's *Portrait of Balthazar Castiglione* and Titian's *Man with a Glove*. Titian's *Fête Champêtre* inspired Manet's *Déjeuner sur l'Herbe* (see Musée d'Orsay, below). Bought by François I during the artist's visit to Paris, Leonardo da Vinci's *Mona Lisa* (or *La Joconde*, the Smiling One), smiles mysteriously at millions each year. Don't overlook her remarkable neighbors—da Vinci's *Virgin of the Rocks* displays his famous *sfumato* (smoky) technique. *Venus de Milo* and the *Winged Victory of Samothrace* are the tip of the Greek, Etruscan, and Roman antiquities iceberg.

MUSÉE D'ORSAY

62, r. de Lille, 7ème. RER: Musée d'Orsay. Open June 20-Sept. 20 Tu-W and F-Su 9am-6pm, Th 9am-9:30pm; Sept. 21-June 19 open Tu-W and F-Su 10am-5:45pm, Th 10am-9:45pm. 45F/€6.90, under 26 and Su 33F/€5.05.

While it's considered the premier Impressionist museum, the museum is dedicated to presenting all major artistic movements between 1848 and World War I. On the ground floor, works from Classicism and Proto-Impressionism are on display, and include Manet's *Olympia*, a painting that caused a scandal when it was unveiled in 1865. The 1st room of the upper level features Manet's *Déjeuner sur l'Herbe (Luncheon in the Grass)*. Other highlights include: Monet's *La Gare St-Lazare (St-Lazare Train Station)* and *Cathédrale de Rouen (Rouen Cathedral)* series, Renoir's *Le bal du Moulin de la Galette (The dance at the Moulin de la Galette)*, Edgar Dégas's *La classe de danse (The Dance Class)*, Whistler's *Portrait of the Artist's Mother*, and paintings by Sisley, Pissaro, and Morisot. Over a dozen diverse works by Van Gogh follow, including his tormented *Portrait de l'Artiste (Portrait of an Artist)*. Cézanne's works experiment with the soft colors and geometric planes that would open the door to Cubism.

OTHER MUSEUMS

■ **CENTRE NATIONAL D'ART ET DE CULTURE GEORGES-POMPIDOU.** This odd inside-out building has inspired debate since its inauguration in 1977. The exterior is a sight, with chaotic colored piping and ventilation ducts (blue for air, green for water, yellow for electricity, red for heating). Yet the wacky outside is an appropriate shell for the collection of Fauves, Cubists, and Pop and Conceptual artists. Its exhibit halls, library, and superb museum collections (including the **Musée d'Art Moderne**) are excellent. *(Palais Beaubourg, 4ème. M: Rambuteau. Open W-M 11am-9pm, last ticket sales 8pm. Permanent collection 30F/€4.60, students and over 60 20F/€3.05, under 13 and 1st Su each month free.)*

■ **MUSÉE RODIN.** The 18th-century Hôtel Biron holds hundreds of sculptures by Auguste Rodin (and his student and lover, Camille Claudel), including the *Gates of Hell*, *The Thinker*, *Burghers of Calais*, and *The Kiss*. *(77, r. de Varenne, 7ème, off bd. des Invalides. M: Varenne. Open Tu-Su Apr.-Sept. 9:30am-5:45pm; Oct.-Mar. 9:30am-4:45pm. 28F/€4.30, students and Su 18F/€2.75. Sculpture park 5F/€0.80.)*

■ **MUSÉE PICASSO.** This museum catalogs Picasso's career—from his early work in Barcelona and his Cubist and Surrealist years in Paris to his Neoclassical work on the Riviera. *(5, r. de Thorigny, 3ème. M: Chemin-Vert. From bd. Beaumarchais, take r. St-Gilles, which becomes r. du Parc Royal, and bear right at pl. de Thorigny. Open W-M Apr.-Sept. 9:30am-6pm; Oct.-Mar. 9:30am-5:30pm. 30F/€4.60, under 26 and Su 20F/€3.05.)*

■ **MUSÉE DE CLUNY.** One of the world's finest collections of medieval art, the Musée de Cluny is housed in a medieval monastery built on top of Roman baths. Works include *La Dame et La Licorne (The Lady and the Unicorn)*, one of the most beautiful extant medieval tapestry series. *(6, pl. Paul-Painlevé, 5ème. M: Cluny-Sorbonne. Follow bd. St-Michel away from the Seine and turn left on r. P. Sarrazin. Open W-M 9:15am-5:45pm. 36F/€5.50, under 18 25F/€3.85.)*

MUSÉE MARMOTTAN MONET. Owing to generous donations by the families of Monet and others, this hunting-lodge-turned-mansion features an eclectic collection of Empire furniture, Impressionist Monet and Renoir canvases, and medieval illuminations. *(2, r. Louis-Boilly, 16ème. M: La Muette. Follow Chaussée de la Muette (av. du Ranelagh) through the Jardin du Ranelagh, turn right on av. Raphaël, and then turn left on r. L. Boilly. Open Tu-Su 10am-5:30pm. 40F/€6.10, students 20F/€3.05.)*

LA VILLETTE. This vast urban renewal project encloses a landscaped park, a huge science museum (open M-Sa 10am-6pm, Su 10am-7pm; 50F/€7.65), a planetarium, a conservatory, a jazz club, a concert/theater space, and a high-tech music museum *(19ème. M: Porte de la Villette or Porte de Pantin. Open Tu-Th and Sa noon-6pm, F noon-9:30pm, Su 10am-6pm. 40F/€6.10, under 18 15F/€2.30.)*

THE INVALIDES MUSEUM. The resting place of Napoleon also hosts the Musée de l'Armée, which celebrates French military history, and the Musée de l'Ordre de la Libération (entrance on bd. de Latour-Maubourg), which tells about those who fought for the liberation of France. *(Esplanade des Invalides, 7ème. M: Invalides. Open daily Apr.-Sept. 10am-6pm; Oct.-Mar. 10am-5pm. 40F/€6.10, students under 26 30F/€4.60.)*

MUSÉE D'ART MODERNE DE LA VILLE DE PARIS. Paris's second best collection of 20th-century art (after the Pompidou) contains works by Matisse and Picasso; its temporary exhibits vary. *(11, av. du Président Wilson, 16ème, in the Palais de Tokyo. M: Iéna. From pl. d'Iéna, take av. du Président Wilson to pl. de Tokyo. ☎01 53 67 40 00. Open Tu-F 10am-5:30pm, Sa-Su 10am-6:45pm. 30-45F/€4.60-6.90, students 20-35F/€3.05-5.35.)*

INSTITUT DU MONDE ARABE. Featuring art from the Maghreb and the Near and Middle East, the riverside façade is shaped like a boat, representing the migration of Arabs to France. The opposite side has camera-lens windows with Arabic motifs that open and close to control the amount of sunlight in the museum. *(1, r. des Fossés St-Jacques, 5ème. M: Jussieu. Take r. Jussieu away from r. Linné, and turn right on r. des Fossés St-Bernard. Open Tu-Su 10am-7pm. 25F/€3.85, ages 12-18 20F/€3.05.)*

MUSÉE DE L'ORANGERIE. L'Orangerie houses Renoirs, Cézannes, Rousseaus, Matisses, and Picassos, but is most famous for Monet's eight gigantic *Water Lilies*. *(1er. M: Concorde. Closed until December 2003.)*

MUSÉE CARNAVALET. In a 16th-century *hôtel particulier*, Carnavalet traces Paris's history from its very origins and guards Voltaire and Rousseau's writing supplies. *(23, r. de Sévigné, 3ème. M: Chemin-Vert. Take r. St-Gilles, which becomes r. du Parc Royal, to r. de Sévigné. Open Tu-Su 10am-5:40pm. 35F/€5.35.)*

♫ ENTERTAINMENT

Paris's cabarets, cinemas, theaters, and concert halls can satisfy all tastes and desires. The bibles of Paris entertainment, the weekly *Pariscope* (3F/€0.50) and the *Officiel des Spectacles* (2F/€0.35), on sale at any kiosk or *tabac*, have every conceivable listing. *Pariscope* includes an English-language pull-out section. When going out, remember that some popular nightlife areas, such as Pigalle, Gare St-Lazare, and Beaubourg, are not always safe. To avoid expensive late-night taxis, keep an eye on the time and hop on the Métro before it closes at 12:30am.

OPERA AND THEATER

Opéra Garnier, pl. de l'Opéra, 9ème. M: Opéra. Hosts the Ballet de l'Opéra de Paris, operas, symphonies, and chamber music. Tickets available 2 weeks before shows. Box office open M-Sa 11am-6pm. Ballet tickets 33-420F/€5.05-64.05; opera tickets up to 690F/€105.25. Last-minute discount tickets available 1hr. before showtime.

La Comédie Française, 2, r. de Richelieu, 1er. M: Palais-Royal. Founded by Molière, the granddaddy of French theater. Expect wildly gesticulated slapstick farce; you don't need to speak French to understand the jokes. Performances take place in the 892-seat Salle Richelieu. Box office open daily 11am-6pm. Tickets 30-190F/€4.60-29, under 27 30-50F/€4.60-7.65. Student rush tickets (66F/€10) available 1hr. before showtime.

JAZZ AND CABARET

Au Duc des Lombards, 42, r. des Lombards, 1er. M: Châtelet. From r. des Halles, walk down r. de la Ferronnerie, turn right on r. St-Denis and another right on r. des Lombards. Still the best in French jazz, with occasional American soloists, and hot items in world music. Cover 80-120F/€12.20-18.30, music students 50-90F/€7.65-13.75. Beer 28-48F/€4.30-7.35; cocktails 55F/€8.40. Open daily 9:30pm-2am; in winter 9pm-2am; on weekends until 3am.

Au Lapin Agile, 22, r. des Saules, 18ème. M: Lamarck-Coulaincourt. Picasso, Verlaine, Renoir, and Apollinaire hung out here in the heyday of Montmartre. Shows Tu-Su 9pm-2am. Cover 130F/€19.85 includes 1st drink, students 90F/€13.75. Subsequent drinks 35F/€5.35.

CINEMA

Musée du Louvre, 1er (www.louvre.fr). M: Louvre. Art films, films on art, and silent movies. Open Sept.-June. Free.

Les Trois Luxembourg, 67, r. Monsieur-le-Prince, 6ème. M: Cluny. High-quality independent, classic, and foreign films in original language. Tickets 40F/€6.10, students and seniors 30F/€4.60.

▢ SHOPPING

1ER AND 2ÈME: ETIENNE-MARCEL AND LES HALLES

Fabrics here are a little cheaper, and the style younger. At the **agnès b.** empire on r. du Jour, you'll find classy, casual fashion. The stores on r. Etienne Marcel and r. Tiquetonne are best for outrageous club wear. **Forum Les Halles,** a subterranean shopping mall south of the Etienne-Marcel area, and the surrounding streets contain a large range for a full urban warrior aesthetic. (M: Etienne-Marcel.)

4ÈME AND THE LOWER 3ÈME: THE MARAIS

The Marais has a line-up of affordable, trendy boutiques, mostly mid-priced clothing chains, independent designer shops, and vintage stores that line **rue Vieille-du-Temple, rue de Sévigné, rue Roi de Sicile,** and **rue des Rosiers.** Lifestyle shops line **rue de Bourg-Tibourg** and **rue des Francs-Bourgeois.** The best selection of affordable menswear in Paris is found along **rue Ste-Croix-de-la-Bretonnerie.** (M: St-Paul or Hôtel de Ville.)

6ÈME TO 8ÈME: ST-GERMAIN-DES-PRÉS AND CHAMPS-ELYSÉES

St-Germain-des-Prés, particularly the triangle bordered by **boulevard St-Germain, rue St-Sulpice,** and **rue des Sts-Pères,** is saturated with high-budget names. **Rue du Four** (M: St-Germain-des-Prés) boasts fun and affordable designers such as **Paul and Joe** (no. 40; open daily 11am-7:30pm) and **Sinéquanone** (no. 16; open M-Sa 10am-7:30pm). The sleek **Nauninani** on r. St-Sulpice sells distinctive handbags and outfits. (M: Mabillon.) Near Luxembourg, calm r. de Fleurus hosts **A.P.C.** as well as **t***** at no. 7 (M: St-Placide). In the 7ème, visit r. de Pré-aux-Clercs and r. de Grenelle; though generally expensive, there are some impressive little boutiques around the Bon Marché department store on r. de Sèvres, and r. du Cherche Midi. *(M: Vaneau, Duroc, Sèvres-Babylone, R. du Bac.)* Anchored by the Arc de Triomphe on the west and the place de Concorde to the east, the **Avenue des Champs-Elysées** is lined with luxury shops, *haute couture* boutiques, cafes, and cinemas.

NIGHTLIFE

The primary leisure pastimes of Parisians would seem to be fomenting revolution and burning buildings, but their nighttime pleasures tend more toward drinking, relaxing, and people watching. Those looking for live music, especially jazz, are in heaven. Dancing kings and queens may be frustrated by Paris's rather exclusive club scene, but *Let's Go* tries to list places that are tolerant of non-models. If you'd rather just watch the world go by, Parisian bars won't disappoint. In the 18ème, tourists, especially women, should avoid the areas around M: Pigalle, M: Anvers and M: Barbès-Rochechouart at night. Bisexual, lesbian, and gay entertainment centers around the Marais in the 4th *arrondissement*, with most establishments near r. du Temple, r. Ste-Croix de la Bretonnerie, r. des Archives, and r. Vieille du Temple.

3ÈME, 4ÈME, 11ÈME: MARAIS AND RÉPUBLIQUE

L'Apparement Café, 18, r. des Coutures St-Gervais. M: St-Paul. Beautiful wood-and-red lounge complete with games and a calm, young crowd. Late-night meals 68-82F/€10.35-12.55, served until closing.

Chez Richard, 37, r. Vieille-du-Temple. M: Hôtel-de-Ville. Inside a courtyard off r. Vieille-du-Temple, and reminiscent of Casablanca. Beer 23-36F/€3.55-5.50; cocktails 52-60F/€7.95-9.15. Open daily 6pm-2am.

Lizard Lounge, 18, r. du Bourg-Tibourg. M: Hôtel-de-Ville. A happening space for Anglo/Franco twenty-somethings. Happy Hour upstairs 6-8pm (cocktails 30F/€4.60), everywhere 8-10pm (cocktails 28F/€4.30). Pint of lager 33F/€5.05. Open daily noon-2am.

Café Charbon, 109, r. Oberkampf. M: Parmentier or Ménilmontant. A spacious bar that manages to pack in a crowd of young locals and artists. Beer 15-20F/€2.30-3.05. Happy Hour 5-9pm. Open daily 9am-2am.

Le Bar Sans Nom, 49, r. de Lappe, facing the Mix Café. M: Bastille. Dim, jazzy lounge famous for its inventive cocktails (60F/€9.15). Open M-Sa 7pm-2am.

Les Bains, 7, r. du Bourg l'Abbé. M: Etienne-Marcel or Réaumur-Sébastopol. Ultra-selective, crowded, and expensive. Funky house and garage grunge, W is hip-hop. Cover Su-Th 100F/€15.25 includes 1st drink; F-Sa 120F/€18.30. Clubbing daily 11pm-6am.

Amnésia Café, 42, r. Vieille-du-Temple. M: Hôtel-de-Ville. Attracts a largely gay crowd; one of the top hot spots in the Marais. Espresso 12F/€1.85. Open daily noon-2am.

Cox, 15, r. des Archives. M: Hôtel-de-Ville. Buns-to-the-wall crowded men's bar with bulging and beautiful boys. Very cruisy; not the place for a quiet cocktail. Happy Hour (beer half-off) daily 6-9pm. Beer 19F/€2.90. Open daily noon-2am.

Les Scandaleuses, 8, r. des Ecouffes. M: St-Paul. Hip lesbian bar set to techno beats. Beer 23F/€3.55. Happy Hour 6-8pm. Open daily 6pm-2am.

Le Café du Trésor, 5, r. du Trésor. M: St-Paul. All the Paris cool kids lounge about while DJs spin house, deep house, and funk. Beer 25-40F/€3.85-6.10. Open daily 9am-2am; food served M-F 12:30-3pm and 7:30-10:30pm, Sa-Su 12:30-10:30pm.

Le Dépôt, 10, r. aux Ours. M: Etienne Marcel. A pleasure complex for gay men. Women welcome after 11pm; lesbian night W. Cover M-Th 45F/€6.90, F-Su 55-60F/€8.40-9.15 includes 1 drink; W 10F/€1.55 without drink for ladies. Open daily 2pm-8am.

Boteco, 131, r. Oberkampf. M: Parmentier. Popular, techno-generation Brazilian bar/restaurant with trendy wait staff, grafitti art, and flip-up benches transforms into a dance space. Beer 20-24F/€3.05-3.70. Open daily 9am-2am.

Boobs Bourg, 26, r. de Montmorency (☎ 01 42 74 04 82). M: Rambuteau. Well-spiked, stylishly punk girls go here to find one another. Beer 22F/€3.40; mixed drinks 35F/€5.35. Open Tu-Su 4pm-2am.

Sanz Sans, 49, r. du Faubourg St-Antoine. M: Bastille. Popular, upbeat bar with bouncer control. A large screen projects black and white scenes from the bar. Outdoor seating. Beer from 15F/€2.30. Open daily 9:30pm-1am.

La Belle Hortense, 31, r. Vieille-du-Temple. M: St-Paul. A breath of fresh air for those worn out by the hyper-chic scene along the rest of the *rue*. Wine from 25F/€3.85 per glass, 125F/€19.10 per bottle. Coffee 7F/€1.10. Open daily 7pm-2am.

5ÈME, 6ÈME, 7ÈME, 13ÈME: LATIN QUARTER

🖾 **Le Reflet,** 6, r. Champollion. M: Cluny-La Sorbonne. Crowded with youth. Beer 11-16F/ €1.70-2.45; cocktails 12-32F/€1.85-4.90. Open M-Sa 10am-2am, Su noon-2am.

🖾 **Le Caveau des Oubliettes,** 52, r. Galande. Attracts a set of mellow folk. Jazz concerts nightly 50F/€7.65. Beers 25-45F/€3.85-6.90; rum 25F/€3.85. Happy Hour 5-9pm. Open daily 5pm-2am.

Le Piano Vache, 8, r. Laplace. M: Cardinal Lemoine or Maubert-Mutualité. A dark bar behind the Panthéon. 2nd drink free with *Let's Go*. Happy Hour 6-9pm. Open July-Aug. M-F 6pm-2am, Sa-Su 9pm-2am; Sept.-June M-F noon-2am, Sa-Su 9pm-2am.

Le Bar Dix, 10, r. de l'Odéon. M: Odéon. A classic student hangout. Sangria 19F/€2.90. Open daily 5:30pm-2am.

Chez Georges, 11, r. des Cannettes. M: Mabillon. Upstairs is a wine bar; downstairs is a candle-lit cellar packed with students. Beer 23-30F/€3.55-4.60; wine 10-22F/€1.55-3.40. Open Tu-Sa noon-2am (upstairs); cellar 10pm-2am. Closed Aug.

Le Club des Poètes, 30, r. de Bourgogne. M: Varenne. A restaurant by day, but at 10pm, a troupe of readers transform the place into a poetry salon. Drinks 60F/€9.15, students 45F/€6.90. Open M-Sa noon-2:30pm and 8pm-1am.

Le Saint, 7, r. St-Séverin. M: St-Michel. Reggae to techno to R&B. The club slowly evolves from an intimate bar to a tiny, flashy dance floor. Cover Tu-Th 70F/€10.70, F 90F/€13.75, Sa 100F/€15.25. Drinks 15-50F/€2.30-7.65. Open daily 11pm-6am.

1ER, 2ÈME, 8ÈME: CHAMPS-ELYSÉES

🖾 **Le Petit Opportun,** 15, r. des Lavandières-Ste-Opportune. M: Châtelet. Some of the best modern jazz around, including Americans. Cover 80-100F/€12.20-15.25. Drinks 30-60F/€4.60-9.15. Open Sept.-July Tu-Sa 9pm-5am; music begins 9:30-10:30pm.

🖾 **Le Baiser Salé,** 58, r. des Lombards. M: Châtelet. Cuban, African, and Antillean music are featured together with modern jazz and funk. Cover 40-100F/€6.10-15.25. Beer 26F/€4; cocktails 46F/€7.05. Bar and club open daily 4pm-dawn.

🖾 **buddha-bar,** 8, r. Boissy d'Anglas. M: Madeleine or Concorde. Step off the private jet and slip on stilettos. Mixed drinks and martinis 69F/€10.55. Open daily 6pm-2am.

Banana Café, 13-15, r. de la Ferronnerie. M: Châtelet. The most popular gay bar in the 1er. Legendary theme nights. Drinks (except cocktails) 2-for-1 4-10pm. Beer 34F/ €5.20 weekdays, 44F/€6.75 weekends. Open daily 4pm-dawn.

Le Champmeslé, 4, r. Chabanais. M: Pyramides or Quatre Septembre. This comfy lesbian bar is Paris's oldest and most famous. Mixed crowd in front, women-only in back. Drinks 30-45F/€4.60-6.90. Open M-Th 2pm-2am, F-Sa 2pm-5am.

Chesterfield Café, 124, r. La Boétie. M: Franklin D. Roosevelt. Friendly and happening American bar with live music and good ol' yankee fare. Cocktails 49F/€7.50; beer 23-48F/€3.55-7.35. No cover Su-Th. Open daily 10am-5am.

Latina Café, 114, av. des Champs-Elysées. M: George V. Draws one of the largest nightclub crowds on the glitzy Champs-Elysées. Drinks 56F/€8.55. Cover 100F/€15.25. Open daily 7:30pm-2am; club open daily 11:30am-6:30am.

Café Oz, 18, r. St-Denis. M: Châtelet. Friendly Australian bar with big tables and cheerful bartenders. Happy Hour daily 6-8pm with cocktails 30F/€4.60. Open Su-Th 3pm-2am, F 3pm-3am, Sa 12pm-3am.

Le Queen, 102, av. des Champs-Elysées. M: George V. Come taste the fiercest funk in town pumping from a 10,000 gig watt sound system; one of the cheapest yet most fashionable clubs in Paris. Mostly male crowd; not easy for women to enter. Cover Su-Th 50F/€7.65, F-Sa 100F/€15.25. Drinks 50F/€7.65. Open daily midnight to dawn.

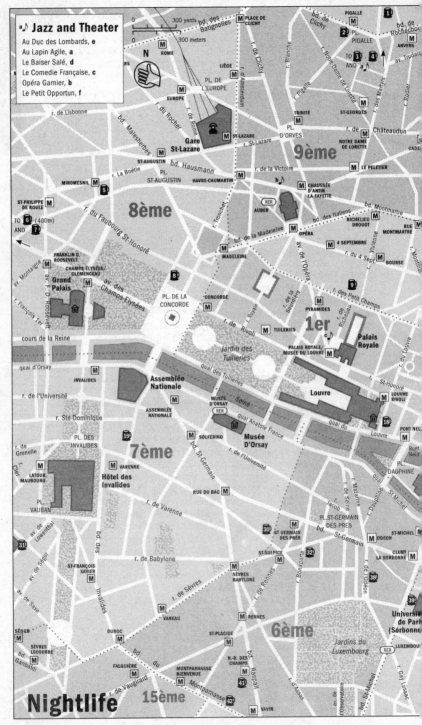

♪ Jazz and Theater

Au Duc des Lombards, **e**
Au Lapin Agile, **a**
Le Baiser Salé, **d**
Le Comedie Française, **c**
Opéra Garnier, **b**
Le Petit Opportun, **f**

Nightlife

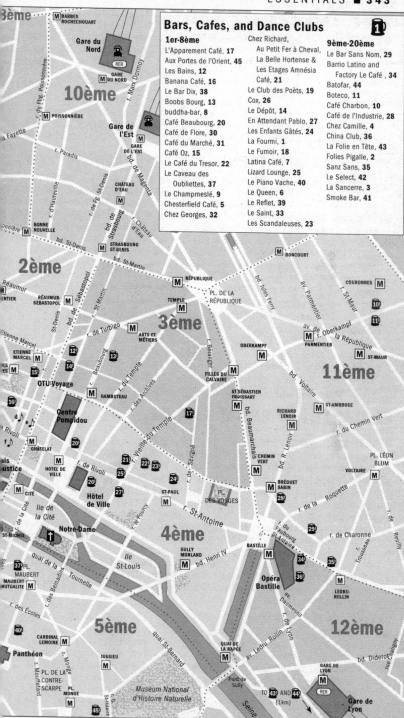

Bars, Cafes, and Dance Clubs

1er–8ème
L'Apparement Café, **17**
Aux Portes de l'Orient, **45**
Les Bains, **12**
Banana Café, **16**
Le Bar Dix, **38**
Boobs Bourg, **13**
buddha-bar, **8**
Café Beaubourg, **20**
Café de Flore, **30**
Café du Marché, **31**
Café Oz, **15**
Le Café du Tresor, **22**
Le Caveau des
  Oubliettes, **37**
Le Champmeslé, **9**
Chesterfield Café, **5**
Chez Georges, **32**

Chez Richard,
  Au Petit Fer à Cheval,
  La Belle Hortense &
  Les Etages Amnésia
  Café, **21**
Le Club des Poètes, **19**
Cox, **26**
Le Dépôt, **14**
En Attendant Pablo, **27**
Les Enfants Gâtés, **24**
La Fourmi, **1**
Le Fumoir, **18**
Latina Café, **7**
Lizard Lounge, **25**
Le Piano Vache, **40**
Le Queen, **6**
Le Reflet, **39**
Le Saint, **33**
Les Scandaleuses, **23**

9ème–20ème
Le Bar Sans Nom, **29**
Barrio Latino and
  Factory Le Café , **34**
Batofar, **44**
Boteco, **11**
Café Charbon, **10**
Café de l'Industrie, **28**
Chez Camille, **4**
China Club, **36**
La Folie en Tête, **43**
Folies Pigalle, **2**
Sanz Sans, **35**
Le Select, **42**
La Sancerre, **3**
Smoke Bar, **41**

9ÈME, 18ÈME: PLACE PIGALLE

▨ **Chez Camille,** 8, r. Ravignan. M: Abbesses. Small, trendy bar. Coffee 6-8F/€0.95-1.25; tea 14F/€2.15; beer 15-20F/€2.30-3.05; wine from 15F/€2.30; cocktails 30-50F/€4.60-7.65. Open Tu-Sa 9am-2am, Su 9am-8pm.

La Fourmi, 74, r. des Martyrs. M: Pigalle. A hip, energetic, and scrappy young crowd. Beer 15-21F/€2.30-3.20; wine 16-19F/€2.45-2.90; cocktails 45-60F/€6.90-9.15. Open M-Th 8:30am-2am, F-Sa 8:30am-4am, Su 10:30am-2am.

Folies Pigalle, 11, pl. Pigalle. M: Pigalle. The largest and wildest club of the sleazy Pigalle. Su gay and transsexual night. Very crowded. Cover 100F/€15.25 includes 1st drink. Drinks 50F/€7.65. Open Tu-Th 11pm-6am, F-Sa 11pm-noon, Su 5pm-6am.

12ÈME, 13ÈME, 14ÈME: MONTPARNASSE

▨ **La Folie en Tête,** 33, r. de la Butte-aux-Cailles. M: Corvisart. The artsy axis mundi of the 13ème. Beer 10F/€1.55 before 8pm, 15F/€2.30 after; cocktails 35-40F/€5.35-6.10. Open M-Sa 6pm-2am; in winter 5pm-2am.

▨ **China Club,** 50, r. de Charenton, on the corner of r. Ledru-Rollin. M: Ledru-Rollin or Bastille. Swank Hong Kong club. Cocktails 49-75F/€7.50-11.45. Happy Hour 7-9pm; all drinks 35F/€5.35. Closed 3 weeks in Aug. Open M-Th 7pm-2am, F-Sa 7pm-3am.

▨ **Barrio Latino,** 46/48, r. du Faubourg St-Antoine. M: Bastille. No wallflowers on this hot latin dance floor. No attitude at the door as long as you look respectable. Strawberry margarita 56F/€8.55. Open noon-2am.

Batofar, facing 11, quai François-Mauriac. M: Quai de la Gare. This barge/bar/club is popular with the electronic music crowd. Friendly, industrial environment. Cover up to 60F/€9.15; usually includes 1st drink. Open Su-Th 9pm-3am, F-Sa until 4am.

Factory Café, 20, r. du Faubourg St-Antoine. M: Bastille. Hip hopping every night, and a cinch to get into. Cover 50F/€7.65 includes 1st drink, ladies free; F-Sa 80F/€12.20. Subsequent drinks 50F/€7.65. Open Su-Th 11pm-4am, F-Sa 10pm-6am.

Smoke Bar, 29, r. Delambre. M: Vavin. The perfect place to pose with your cigarette, bask in the dim lighting, and feel treacherously beautiful. Cocktails 32-45F/€4.90-6.90; beer 14-17F/€2.30-2.60. Open M-Sa 5pm-2am.

🖪 DAYTRIPS FROM PARIS

VERSAILLES. Louis XIV, the Sun King, built and held court at Versailles' extraordinary palace, 12km west of Paris. The incredibly lavish château embodies the extravagance of the Old Regime, especially in the **Hall of Mirrors** and fountain-filled **gardens.** (Château open Tu-Su May-Sept. 9am-6:30pm; Oct.-Apr. 9am-5:30pm. 49F/€7.50, after 3:30pm and under 25 35F/€5.35 (entrance A). Audio (1hr., 26F/€4) and guided tours (1-2hr., 26-50F/€4-7.65) available at entrances C and D, respectively. Gardens open daily sunrise-sundown. Free.) A **shuttle** (return 33F/€5.05) runs behind the palace to the **Grand** and **Petit Trianons,** and to Marie Antoinette's peasant fantasy, the **Hameau.** (Both Trianons open Tu-Sa Nov.-Mar. noon-5:30pm; Apr.-Oct. noon-6pm; 30F/€4.60.)

Take any **RER C5 train** beginning with a "V" from M: Invalides to the Versailles Rive Gauche station (30-40min., every 15min., return 31F/€4.75). Buy your RER ticket before getting to the platform; a Métro ticket will not get you through the RER turnstiles at Versailles.

CHÂTEAU DE FONTAINEBLEAU. The Château de Fontainebleau achieves the grandeur of Versailles with a unique charm. François I and Napoleon stand out among the parade of post-Renaissance kings who lived here; the former was responsible for the dazzling ballrooms lined with work from Michelangelo's school, the latter restored the post-Revolution dilapidation to a home befitting an emperor. In the long **Galerie de François I,** the most famous room at Fontainebleau, muscular figures by Il Rosso illustrate mythological tales of heroism. Since the 17th century, every queen and empress of France has slept in the gold and green **Queen's Bed**

Chamber. The **Musée Napoléon** features a collection of the Emperor's personal toothbrush, his tiny shoes, his field tent, and state gifts.

From the Gare de Lyon in Paris, **trains** run to Fontainebleau (45min., every hr., return 96F/€14.65). The castle is a 30min. walk or a 10min. bus ride away. (Castle open W-M June-Sept. 9:30am-6pm; Oct.-May 9:30am-5pm. 36F/€5.50; students, seniors, and Su 26F/€4.)

CHARTRES. Chartres' stunning **Cathédrale Notre-Dame** is one of the most beautiful surviving creations of the Middle Ages. Arguably the finest example of early Gothic architecture in Europe, the cathedral retains several of its original 12th-century stained-glass windows; the rest of the windows and the magnificent sculptures on the main portals date from the 13th century, as does the carved floor in the rear of the nave. You can only enter the 9th-century **crypt** from La Crypte, opposite the cathedral's south entrance. (Cathedral open daily 8am-8pm. Tower open May-Aug. M-Sa 9am-6pm, Su 2-6pm; Sept.-Oct. and Mar-Apr. M-Sa 9:30-11:30am and 2-5pm, Su 2-5pm; Nov.-Feb M-Sa 10-11:30am and 2-4pm, Su 2-4pm. 1¼hr. tours in English Easter to early Nov. M-Sa noon and 2:45pm. 52F/€8, students 33F/€5.)

Trains run from Paris's Gare Montparnasse (1hr.; every hr.; return 148F/€22.60, under 26 112F/€14.10). From the station, walk straight, turn left into the pl. de Châtelet, turn right on r. Ste-Même, then turn left on r. Jean Moulin.

DISNEYLAND PARIS. It's a small, small world, and Disney is hell-bent on making it even smaller. When Euro Disney opened in 1992, it was met by jeers of French intellectuals and the popular press. However, resistance subsided once it was renamed Disneyland Paris and started serving wine. Everything in Disneyland Paris is in English and French. (www.disneylandparis.com. Open daily 9am-11pm; in winter hours vary. Buy *passeports* (tickets) on Disneyland Hotel's ground floor, at the Paris tourist office, or at any major station on RER line A. Apr.-Sept. and Dec. 23-Jan. 7 220F/€33.55; low-season 170F/€25.95.)

From Paris, take the **RER A4** Marne-la-Vallée to the last stop, Marne-la-Vallée/Chessy (45min., every 30min., return 78F/€11.90); the last train back leaves at 12:22am, but arrives after the Métro closes. Eurailers can take the **TGV** from Roissy/Charles de Gaulle Airport to the park in 15min.

GIVERNY. Today, Monet's house and gardens in Giverny are maintained by the **Fondation Claude Monet.** From April to July, Giverny overflows with roses, hollyhocks, poppies, and the heady scent of honeysuckle. The water lilies, the Japanese bridge, and the weeping willows seem to be plucked straight from Monet's paintings. Monet's thatched-roof house holds his collection of 18th- and 19th-century Japanese prints. (Open Apr.-Oct. Tu-Su 10am-6pm. 35F/€5.35, students and ages 12-18 25F/€3.85. Gardens 25F/€3.85.)

Trains (☎ 08 36 35 35 35) run infrequently from Paris-St-Lazare to Vernon, the station nearest Giverny (return 136F/20.75). When you purchase your ticket from St-Lazare, check the timetables or ask for the **bus** schedules for travel from Vernon to Giverny. (Buses ☎ 02 32 71 06 39. 10min.; 4-6 per day; 12F/€1.85, return 20F/€3.05.) Taxis in front of the train station are another option.

ROUEN. Enchanting **Rouen** is home to the cathedral that captivated Monet over and over again, just 1½ hr. from Paris by train. (p. 346).

LYON. Sample the cuisine and nightlife of France's second-largest city, a 2hr. train ride away (p. 383).

BAYEUX. Bayeux is a convenient base for exploring the D-Day beaches and also contains a stunning tapestry, 2½ hr. from Paris by train (p. 347).

NORMANDY (NORMANDIE)

Fertile Normandy is a land of fields, fishing villages, and cathedrals. Vikings seized the region in the 9th century, and invasions have twice secured Normandy's place in military history: in 1066, William of Normandy conquered England; on D-Day, June 6, 1944, Allied armies began the liberation of France on Normandy's beaches.

ROUEN

Despite Emma Bovary's experiences, Rouen (pop. 108,000) is no provincial town. The city enjoyed prosperity and status from the 10th to 12th centuries as the capital of the Norman empire, and Monet's multiple renditions of the cathedral made it a fixture in museums worldwide. The most famous of Rouen's "hundred spires" are those of the **Cathédrale de Notre-Dame,** in pl. de la Cathédrale, with the tallest spire in France (151m). The façade incorporates nearly every style of Gothic architecture; don't miss the stained glass in the **Chapelle St-Jean de la Nef.** (Open M-Sa 8am-7pm, Su 8am-6pm.) Behind the cathedral, the flamboyant **Eglise St-Maclou,** in pl. Barthélémy, features an elaborately carved pipe organ. (Open M-Sa 10am-noon and 2-5:30pm, Su 3-5:30pm.) Beyond the church to the left, at the poorly marked 186, r. de Martainville, is the **Aître St-Maclou,** which served as the church's charnel house and cemetery through the later Middle Ages. Suspended behind a glass panel is the cadaver of a cat entombed alive to exorcise spirits. (Open daily 8am-8pm. Free.) Joan of Arc died on **place du Vieux Marché,** to the left as you exit the station on r. du Donjon. A 6½m cross marks the spot, near the unsightly **Eglise Ste-Jeanne d'Arc,** designed to resemble an overturned Viking boat. Follow r. de Crosne from pl. de Vieux Marché for the **Musée Flaubert et d'Histoire de la Médecine,** 51, r. de Lecat, which showcases a gruesome array of medical instruments—including gallstone crushers and a battlefield amputation kit—and writer Gustave Flaubert's possessions. (Open Tu 10am-6pm, W-Sa 10am-noon and 2-6pm. 12F/€1.85, students free.) A block up r. Jeanne d'Arc, the **Musée des Beaux-Arts,** on pl. Verdrel, houses an excellent collection of European masters from the 16th to 20th centuries, including Monet and Renoir. (Open W-M 10am-6pm. 20F/€3.05, ages 18-25 13F/€2.)

Trains leave r. Jeanne d'Arc for Lille (3hr., 5 per day, 163F/€24.85) and Paris (1½hr., every hr., 106F/€16.20). From the station, walk down r. Jeanne d'Arc and turn left on r. du Gros Horloge to reach pl. de la Cathédrale and the **tourist office,** 25, pl. de la Cathédrale. (☎ 02 32 08 32 40; fax 02 32 08 32 44. Open May-Sept. M-Sa 9am-7pm, Su 9:30am-12:30pm and 2-6pm; Oct.-Mar. M-Sa 9am-6pm, Su 10am-1pm.) Check **email** at **Place Net,** 37, r. de la République, near the Eglise St-Maclou. (40F/€6.10 per hr. Open M-Sa 11am-midnight, Su 2-10pm.) **Hôtel des Arcades,** 52, r. de Carmes, is bright and clean. (☎ 02 35 70 10 30; fax 02 35 70 08 91; www.hotel-des-arcades.fr. Reception M-F 7am-8pm, Sa-Su 7:30am-8pm. Singles and doubles 157F/€24, with shower 223-262F/€34-40. AmEx/MC/V.) **Hôtel du Palais,** 12, r. Tambour, off r. du Gros Horloge, is in a prime location. (Breakfast 25F/€3.85. Showers 15F/€2.30. Reception 24hr. Singles 120F/€18.30; doubles 140F/€21.35, with bath 160-240F/€24.40-36.60. AmEx/MC/V.) Cheap eateries crowd **place du Vieux-Marché** and the **Gros Horloge** area. **Al Dente,** 24, r. Cauchoise, off pl. du Vieux-Marché, serves pizzas from 48F/€7.35. (Open Tu-Su noon-2:30pm and 7-10:30pm.) **Monoprix supermarket** is at 73-83, r. du Gros Horloge. (Open M-Sa 8:30am-9pm.) **Postal code:** 76000.

NORMANDY COAST

The coast of Normandy has long been a hotspot for invasion, from the Vikings to the Allied forces during World War II. Numerous plaques and monuments commemorate the area's liberation from German forces in 1944. Soaring cliffs and beautiful beaches also provide a respite from Normandy's larger cities.

LE HAVRE. An elegy to concrete, Le Havre (pop. 200,000) can brag of being France's largest transatlantic port and little else. For information on **ferries** to Portsmouth, see p. 62. **Trains** leave from cours de la République for: Fécamp (1hr., 9 per day, 44F/€6.75) via Etretat; Paris (2hr., 8 per day, 154F/€23.50); and Rouen (50min., 13 per day, 74F/€11.30). If you must stay in town, the spacious **Hôtel Le Monaco,** 16, r. de Paris, is near the ferry terminal. (☎ 02 35 42 21 01. Reception daily 6:30am-11pm. Singles 150F/€22.90, with bath 185-220F/€28.25-33.55; doubles 175F/€26.70, with bath 230-270F/€35.10-41.20. AmEx/MC/V.) Get food for the ferry ride at **Super U,** bd. François 1er, near the tourist office. (Open M-Sa 8:30am-8:30pm.)

CAEN

Although Allied bombing leveled three-quarters of its buildings in World War II, Caen has since skillfully rebuilt itself. Its biggest draw is the powerful ◪**Mémorial de Caen,** the best of Normandy's World War II museums, which includes footage of the war, displays on pre-war Europe and the Battle of Normandy, and a haunting testament to the victims of the Holocaust. Take bus #17 to Mémorial. (Open daily mid-July to Aug. 9am-8pm; Feb. to mid-July and Sept.-Oct. 9am-7pm; mid-Jan. to Feb. and Nov.-Dec. 9am-6pm. 76F/€11.60, students 66F/€10.10.) The twin abbeys **Abbaye-aux-Hommes,** off r. Guillaume le Conquérant, and **Abbaye-aux-Dames,** off r. des Chanoines, hold the tombs of William the Conqueror and his wife. (Abbaye-aux-Hommes open 9:15am-noon and 2-6pm. 10F/€1.55, students 5F/€0.80. Abbaye-aux-Dames open M-Sa 8am-5:30pm, Su 9:30am-12:30pm. Free.) Between the abbeys sprawl the ruins of William's **château.** Inside, the **Musée des Beaux-Arts** contains a collection of 16th- and 17th-century Flemish works and 19th-century Impressionist paintings. (Château open daily May-Sept. 6am-1am; Oct.-Apr. 6am-7:30pm. Museum open W-M 9:30am-6pm. 25F/€3.85, students 15F/€2.30, W free.) Walk around the château walls on r. de Geôle and turn left on r. Bosnières for the romantic **Jardin des Plantes,** on pl. Blot. (Open daily June-Aug. 8am-dusk; Sept.-May 8am-5:30pm.)

Trains (☎08 36 35 35 35) run to: Paris (2½hr., 12 per day, 170F/€25.95); Rennes (3hr., 3 per day, 166F/€25.35); Rouen (2hr., 5 per day, 118F/€18); and Tours (3½hr., 2 per day, 172F/€26.25). To the left of the station, **Bus Verts** (☎08 01 21 42 14) covers the region. The **tourist office,** pl. St-Pierre, offers free maps. (☎02 31 27 14 14; fax 02 31 27 14 18; www.ville-caen.fr. Open July-Aug. M-Sa 9:30am-7pm, Su 10am-1pm and 2-5pm; Sept.-June M-Sa 10am-1pm and 2-6pm, Su 10am-1pm.) The social **Auberge de Jeunesse (HI),** 68bis, r. Eustache-Restout, is at Foyer Robert Reme. Take a right from the train station, take your second right on r. de Vaucelles, walk one block, and catch bus #5 or 17 (dir. Fleury or Grâce de Dieu) from the stop on your left to Lycée Fresnel. (☎02 31 52 19 96; fax 02 31 84 29 49. Breakfast 10F/€1.55. Sheets 15F/€2.30. Reception 5-10pm. Dorms 62F/€9.45.) **Hôtel du Château,** 5, av. du 6 juin, has large bright rooms. (☎02 31 86 15 37; fax 02 31 86 58. Reception 24hr. Singles 240F/€36.60; doubles 170-260F/€25.95-39.65; triples 310F/€47.30; quads 360F/€54.90. Prices 20F/€3.05 lower Oct.-Easter. MC/V.) ◪**Terrain Municipal,** rte. de Louvigny, has gorgeous riverside **campsites.** Take bus #13 (dir. Louvigny) to Camping. (☎02 31 73 60 92. Reception 8am-1pm and 5-9pm. Open June-Sept. 18F/€2.75 per person, 10.50F/€1.60 per tent, 10.50F/€1.60 per car.) Ethnic restaurants, *crêperies,* and *brasseries* line the **quartier Vaugueux** near the château as well as the streets between **Eglise St-Pierre** and **Eglise St-Jean.** Get your groceries at **Monoprix supermarket,** 45, bd. du Maréchal Leclerc. (Open M-Sa 8am-8:30pm.) Caen's old streets pulsate by moonlight, especially around **rue de Bras, rue des Croisiers,** and **rue St-Pierre. Postal code:** 14000 (specify "Gambetta" for *Poste Restante*).

BAYEUX

Beautiful Bayeux (pop. 15,000) is an ideal base for exploring the nearby D-Day beaches. However, visitors should not overlook its 900-year-old ◪**Tapisserie de Bayeux,** 70m of embroidery that relates the tale of William the Bastard's invasion of England and his earning of a more acceptable name—"the Conqueror." The tapestry is displayed in the **Centre Guillaume le Conquérant,** on r. de Nesmond. (Open daily May-Aug. 9am-7pm; mid-Mar. to Apr. and Sept. to mid-Oct. 9am-6:30pm; mid-Oct. to mid-Mar. 9:30am-12:30pm and 2-6pm. 41F/€6.25, students 16F/€2.45.) Nearby is the original home of the tapestry, the extraordinary **Cathédrale Notre-Dame.** (Open July-Aug. M-Sa 8am-7pm, Su 9am-7pm; Sept.-June M-Sa 8:30am-noon and 2:30-7pm, Su 9am-12:15pm and 2:30-7pm. Free.) The amazing **Musée de la Bataille de Normandie,** bd. Fabian Ware, recounts the D-Day landing and 76-day battle. (Open May to mid-Sept. 9:30am-6:30pm; mid-Sept. to Apr. 10am-12:30pm and 2-6pm; closed early Jan.

34F/€5.20, students 16F/€2.45) Across the street, the **British Cemetery** is a strikingly simple and far more moving wartime record.

Trains (☎02 31 92 80 50) arrive at pl. de la Gare from: Caen (20min., 15 per day, 32F/€4.90); Cherbourg (1hr., 12 per day, 82F/€12.50); and Paris (2½hr., 12 per day, 174F/€26.55). To reach the **tourist office,** pont St-Jean, turn left on the highway (bd. Sadi-Carnot), bear right, follow the signs to the *centre ville,* and follow r. Larcher to r. St-Martin. (☎02 31 51 28 28; fax 02 31 51 28 29. Open mid-June to mid-Sept. M-Sa 9am-7pm, Su 9:30am-12:30pm and 2:30-6:30pm; mid-Sept. to mid-June M-Sa 9am-noon and 2-6pm.) From the tourist office, turn right onto r. St-Martin, continue down through several name changes, and turn left onto r. General de Dais to reach the **Family Home/Auberge de Jeunesse (HI),** 39, r. General de Dais. (☎02 31 92 15 22; fax 02 31 92 55 72. Breakfast included. Dorms 100F/€15.25, nonmembers 110F/€16.80.) Follow r. Genas Duhomme to the right and continue straight on av. de la Vallée des Prés for **Camping Municipal,** on bd. d'Eindhoven. (☎02 31 92 08 43. Open May-Sept. 18.30F/€27.95 per person, 22.60F/€3.45 per tent, 22.60F/€3.45 per car.) Get **groceries** at **Champion,** on bd. d'Eindhoven. **Postal code:** 14400.

D-DAY BEACHES

On June 6, 1944, over one million Allied soldiers invaded the beaches of Normandy—code-named Utah and Omaha (American), Gold and Sword (British), and Juno (Canadian). Today, reminders of the battle can be clearly seen in sobering gravestones, remnants of German bunkers, and the pockmarked landscape.

▐ **TRANSPORTATION.** Most of the beaches and museums can reached from Caen and Bayeux with **Bus Verts** (☎08 10 21 42 14); ask about the special "D-Day" line. You may want to buy a day pass (100F/€15.25; three-day pass 150F/€22.90) if you plan to make many stops. **Utah Beach** is accessible only by car or by foot from **Ste-Mère-Eglise.** Take a **train** from Bayeux to Caretan (30min., 10 per day, 43F/€6.60) and then a **bus** from Caretan to Ste-Mère-Eglise (15min., 1 per day 12:50pm, return 6:35pm; 18.20F/€2.80). **Victory Tours** leads four- and eight-hour tours in English that leave from behind the Bayeux tourist office. (☎02 31 51 98 14; fax 02 31 51 07 01; www.victory-tours.com. 4hr. tour 12:30pm, 175F/€26.70; 8hr. tour 9:15am, 300F/€45.75. Reservations required.)

BEACHES NEAR BAYEUX. At **Utah Beach,** near Ste-Marie du Mont, the Americans headed the western flank of the invasion. The **Musée du Débarquement** here shows how 836,000 troops, 220,000 vehicles, and 725,000 tons of equipment came ashore. (☎02 33 71 53 35. Open June-Sept. daily 9:30am-6:30pm; Oct.-May reduced hours. 30F/€4.60.) The most difficult landing was that of the First US Infantry Division at **Pointe du Hoc.** The Pointe is considered a military cemetery because many who perished are still there, crushed beneath collapsed concrete bunkers. **Omaha Beach,** next to Colleville-sur-Mer and east of the Pointe du Hoc, is perhaps the most famous beach and is often referred to as "bloody Omaha." Overlooking the beach, 9387 American graves stretch over the **American Cemetery.** (Open daily mid-Apr. to Sept. 8am-6pm; Oct. to mid-Apr. 9am-5pm.) Ten kilometers north of Bayeux and just east of Omaha is **Arromanches,** a small town at the center of **Gold Beach,** where the British built the artificial **Port Winston** in a single day to provide shelter while the Allies unloaded their supplies. The **Musée du Débarquement** uses detailed models to show how the port was put together under fire. (Open daily May-Aug. 9am-7pm; Sept. 9am-6pm; Oct.-Apr. reduced hours; closed Jan. 35F/€5.35, students 22F/€3.) The **Arromanches 360° Cinéma** combines images of modern Normandy with those of D-Day. Turn left on r. de la Batterie from the museum and climb the steps. (Open daily June-Aug. 9:40am-6:40pm; Sept.-May reduced hours; closed Jan. 24F/€3.70.)

BEACHES NEAR CAEN. East of Arromanches lies **Juno Beach,** the landing site of the Canadian forces. The **Canadian Cemetery** is at **Bény-sur-Mer-Reviers.** In **Ouistreham,** the **No. 4 Commando Museum,** on pl. Alfred Thomas, tells the story of French troops who participated in the attack on **Sword Beach.** (Open mid-Mar. to Oct. 10:30am-6pm. 25F/€3.85, students 15F/€2.30.)

CHERBOURG

On the northern tip of the Cotentin peninsula, Cherbourg (pop. 28,000) was the "Gateway to France," serving as the major supply port following the D-Day offensive of 1944. Today, the town's many ferry lines shuttle tourists from France to England and Ireland. **Ferries,** which leave from bd. Maritime, northeast of the *centre ville,* connect to Rosslare, Portsmouth, and Poole (p. 62). Make sure to **reserve ahead** and check the most up-to-date schedules. To get to the train station, go left at the roundabout onto av. A. Briand and follow it as it becomes av. Carnot; it's at the end of the canal right off av. Carnot on av. Millet (25min.). **Trains** go to: Bayeux (1hr., 8 per day, 82F/€12.50); Caen (1½hr., 10 per day, 100F/15.25); Paris (3hr., 7 per day, 222F/€33.85); and Rouen (4½hr., 4 per day, 186F/€28.40). A **shuttle bus** connects the ferry and train station. To reach the **tourist office,** 2, quai Alexandre III, turn right from the ferry terminal onto bd. Felix Amiot, go straight at the roundabout, turn right to cross the canal, and it will be on your left. (☎ 02 33 93 52 02; fax 02 33 53 66 97; www.ot-cherbourg-cotentin.fr. Open June-Aug. M-Sa 9am-6:30pm, Su 10am-12:30pm; Sept.-May M-Sa 9am-12:30pm and 2-6pm.) **Postal Code:** 50100.

MONT-ST-MICHEL

The fortified island of Mont-St-Michel is a dazzling 8th-century labyrinth of stone arches, spires, and stairways that climb up to the **abbey,** balanced precariously on the jutting rock. To reach the abbey entrance (the departure point for free tours), walk along the ramparts and the twisting **Grande Rue,** the town's major thoroughfare. **La Merveille,** the 13th-century Gothic monastery adjacent to the ornate abbey **church,** encloses a seemingly endless web of passageways and chambers. The descent to the frigid **crypts** beneath the church leads to its dark, chilly foundations, where walls are up to 2m thick. (Open daily mid-July to Aug. 9am-7pm; May to mid-July and Sept. 9am-5:30pm; Oct.-Apr. 9:30am-4:30pm. 42F/€6.40, ages 18-25 26F/€4. Audio tour 30F/€4.60. Free 1hr. tour.) The Mont is most stunning at night, but there is no late-night public transport off the island. Mont-St-Michel is best visited as a daytrip via the Courriers Bretons **bus** (☎ 02 33 60 11 43) from Rennes (1½hr., 3-6 per day, 65F/€9.95) or St-Malo (1½hr., 3-4 per day, 57F/€8.70).

BRITTANY (BRETAGNE)

Lined with spectacular beaches and cliffs gnawed by the sea into long crags and inlets, stubbornly maintains its Celtic traditions despite Paris's ceaseless efforts to fully assimilate the province. Britons fled to this beautiful peninsula during the 5th to 7th centuries to escape Anglo-Saxon invaders, and maintained their independence until they united with France in 1532. Breton traditions linger in the pristine islands off the Atlantic coast and lilting *Brezhoneg* (Breton) can still be heard at pubs and ports in the western part of the province.

RENNES

The administrative center of Brittany and an academic center with two major universities, Rennes (pop. 210,000) balances Parisian sophistication with traditional Breton spirit. Its *vieille ville* of half-timbered medieval houses teems with hip cafes and bars, where by nightfall, this youthful city succumbs to the frenzy of its sizzling nightlife. A popular stopover between Paris and Mont-St-Michel, Rennes merits a weekend excursion on its own.

▐ **TRANSPORTATION. Trains** (☎ 02 99 29 11 92) leave from the pl. de la Gare for: Brest (2-2½hr., every hr., 175F/€26.70); Caen (3hr., 8 per day, 167F/€25.50); Nantes (1¼-2hr., 7 per day, 114F/€17.40); Paris (2hr., every hr., 289-349F/€44.10-53.20); and St-Malo (1hr., 15 per day, 70F/€10.70). **Anjou buses** (☎ 02 99 30 87 80) leave from 16, pl. de la Gare, left of the train station, for Angers (2½-3hr., 3-4 per day, 98F/€14.95, express 122F/€18.60) and Mont-St-Michel (2½hr., 1-2 per day, 64F/€9.80.)

⚑ PRACTICAL INFORMATION. To get from the train station to the **tourist office**, 11, r. St-Yves, take av. Jean Janvier to quai Chateaubriand, turn left and walk along the river until you reach r. George Dottin, turn right, and then right again on r. St-Yves. (☎02 99 67 11 11; fax 02 99 67 11 10. Open Apr.-Sept. M-Sa 9am-7pm, Su 11am-6pm; Oct.-Mar. M-Sa 9am-6pm, Su 11am-6pm.) Surf the **internet** at **Cyberspirit**, 22, r. de la Visitation. (30F/€4.60 per hr. Open July-Aug. Tu-Su 2-10pm; Sept-June M 2-9pm, Tu noon-9pm, W-F noon-10pm, Sa 2-10pm.) **Postal code:** 35032.

⚑🛏 ACCOMMODATIONS AND FOOD. To get from the train station to the **Auberge de Jeunesse (HI)**, 10-12, canal St-Martin, take av. Jean Janvier straight to the canal where it becomes r. Gambetta. After five blocks, turn left on r. des Fossés, take r. de la Visitation to pl. Ste-Anne, follow r. de St.-Malo down the hill, cross the canal, and the hostel is on the left. (☎02 99 33 22 33; fax 02 99 59 06 21. Breakfast included. Reception daily 7am-11pm. 2- to 4-bed dorms 74F/€11.30; singles 129F/€19.70. MC/V.) The central **Hôtel Maréchal Joffre**, 6, r. Maréchal Joffre, offers a variety of rooms. (☎02 99 79 37 74; fax 02 99 78 38 51. Breakfast 30F/€4.60. Reception 24hr. Closed last week in July, 1st week in Aug., and Dec. 25-Jan. 1. Singles 120F/€18.30, with bath 175F/€26.70; doubles 130F/€19.85, 220F/€33.60; Twin beds 200-220F/€30.5-33.55; triples 220F/€33.55, 260F/€39.65. MC/V.) **Camping Municipal des Gayeulles**, in Parc les Gayeulles, is packed with activities. Take bus #3 (dir. Gayeulles/St-Laurent) from pl. de la Mairie to Piscine/Gayeulles, the 3rd stop after reaching the park. Then follow the paths and signs to the campgrounds. (☎02 99 36 91 22; fax 02 23 20 06 23. Reception mid-June to mid-Sept. 7:30am-1pm and 2-8pm; mid-Sept. to mid-June 9am-12:30pm and 4:30-8pm. Gates close 10pm. 20F/€3.05 per adult, 10F/€1.55 per child, 10F/€1.55 per car. Electricity 17F/€2.60. MC/V.) Rennes is a *gourmand*'s dream—seek out your fancy on **rue St-Malo, place St-Michel** or at the huge ■**market** every Saturday in pl. des Lices. As you walk from r. de l'Hotel Dieu to the hostel, a **Marché Plus supermarket** is on the left. (Open M-Sa 9am-8pm.)

◑🎭 SIGHTS AND ENTERTAINMENT. In the *vieille ville*, the **Cathédrale St-Pierre** boasts a magnificent gilded ceiling. (Open daily 9:30am-noon and 3-6pm.) Across the street from the cathedral stands the **Porte Mordelaise**, the last remnants of the city's medieval walls. The **Musée des Beaux-Arts**, 20, quai Emile Zola, houses an eclectic collection ranging from Egyptian pottery to Picasso. (Open W-M 10am-noon and 2-6pm. Adults 26F/€4, students 13F/€2, under 18 free.) Sculptures and fountains grace the labyrinthine **Jardin du Thabor**, reputedly one of the most beautiful gardens in France. (Open daily June-Sept. 7am-9:30pm.) In early July, the **Tombées de la Nuit** festival (☎02 99 67 11 11; www.ville-rennes.fr) brings nine days of nonstop music, theater, and dance. *Rennais* nightlife heats up **place Ste-Anne, place St-Michel**, and the radiating streets. **Le Papagayo**, 10, r. Marechal Joffre, transforms from an unassuming tapas bar by day to a wild party at night. (Open until 1am.)

ST-MALO

St-Malo (pop. 52,000) is the ultimate oceanside getaway. Tourists converge on its miles of warm, sandy beaches and crystalline blue waters, as well as its historic *centre ville*. Enter the walled city through the Porte St-Vincent and follow the stairs up on the right to get the best view of St-Malo from its ramparts. **Trains** run from pl. de l'Hermine to: Dinan (1hr., 5 per day, 48F/€7.35); Paris (5hr., 3 per day, 321F/€48.95); and Rennes (1hr., 8-12 per day, 69F/€10.55). As you exit the station, cross bd. de la République and follow esplanade St-Vincent straight to the **tourist office**. (☎02 99 56 64 48; fax 02 99 56 67 00; www.saint-malo-tourisme.com. Open July-Aug. M-Sa 8:30am-8pm, Su 10am-7pm; Sept.-June reduced hrs.) **Auberge de Jeunesse (HI)**, 37, av. du Révérend Père Umbricht, is three blocks from the beach.

Follow bd. de la République right from the station, after two blocks turn right on av. Ernest Renan, turn left on r. Guen (which becomes av. de Moka), turn right on av. Pasteur, which becomes av. du Révérend Père Umbricht, and keep right. Or, take bus #5 (dir. Paramé or Davier) or 1 (dir. Rothéneuf) from the train station to Auberge Jeunesse. (☎ 02 99 40 29 80; fax 02 99 40 29 02. Reception 24hr. Dorms 72-89F/€11-13.60.) **Hôtel le Neptune,** 21, r. de l'Industrie, is 5min. from the beach, station, and *vieille ville*. From the station, turn right onto bd. de la République, bear left when it ends, and r. de l'Industrie will be on the left. (☎ 02 99 56 82 15. Breakfast 30F/€4.60. Reception 8am-midnight. Singles and doubles 130-180F/€19.85-27.45; quads 210-230F/€32.05-35.10; quints 260F/€39.65. MC/V.) **Champion supermarket,** on av. Pasteur, is near the hostel. (Open M-F 8:30am-1pm and 3-7:30pm, Sa 8:30am-7:30pm, Su 9:30am-noon. Longer hours July-Aug.) **Postal code:** 35400.

DINAN

Tranquil Dinan (pop. 10,000) may be the best-preserved medieval town in Brittany; 15th-century houses inhabited by traditional artisans line the cobblestone streets of the *vieille ville*. The 13th-century **Porte du Guichet** is the entrance to the **Château de Dinan.** Climb the steps to the terrace to look out over the town, or inspect the galleries of the **Tour de Coëtquen,** which include a spooky subterranean room full of funerary ornaments. (Open June-Sept. daily 10am-6:30pm; Oct. to mid-Nov. and mid-Mar. to May W-M 10am-noon and 2-6pm; mid-Nov. to Dec. and Feb. 7 to mid-Mar. W-M 1:30-5:30pm. 25F/€3.85.) On the other side of the ramparts from the château is the entrance to the **Jardin du Val Cocherel,** a creative park with a larger-than-life checkerboard and small zoo. (Open daily 8am-7:30pm.) From port St-Louis, turn right onto r. du Général de Gaulle and go down the Promenade de la Duchesse Anne to reach the Romanesque **Basilica St-Saveur.**

Trains run from pl. 11 novembre to Paris (3hr., 8 per day, 323F/€49.25) and Rennes (1hr., 8 per day, 72F/€11). To get from the station to the **tourist office,** r. de Château, bear left across pl. 11 novembre to r. Carnot, turn right on r. Thiers, turn left into the old city, bear right onto r. du Marchix, which becomes r. de la Ferronerie. Pass the large parking lots and it's on your right. (☎ 02 96 87 69 76; fax 02 96 87 69 77; www.dinantourisme.com. Open mid-June to mid-Sept. M-Sa 9am-7pm, Su 10am-12:30pm and 2:30-6pm; mid-Sept to mid-June M-Sa 9am-12:30pm and 2-6:15pm. Tours daily Apr.-Sept.; 25F/€3.85.) To walk to the wonderful **Auberge de Jeunesse (HI) Moulin du Méen,** in Vallée de la Fontaine-des-Eaux, turn left as you exit the station, head left across the tracks, turn right, follow the tracks and signs downhill, and turn right after 1½km onto a wooded lane. (☎ 02 96 39 10 83; fax 02 96 39 10 62. Breakfast 19F/€2.90. Sheets 17F/€2.60. Reception daily 8am-noon and 5-8pm. Curfew 11pm. Dorms 54F/€8.25.) **Hôtel de l'Océan,** pl. du 11 novembre 1918, is near the station. (☎ 02 96 39 21 51; fax 02 96 87 05 27. Reception daily 6:30am-10pm. Breakfast 28F/€4.30. Singles and doubles 115-190F/€17.55-29; triples 190F/€29; quads 250F/€38.15. MC/V.) Get **groceries** at **Monoprix,** on r. de la Ferronerie. (Open M-Sa 9am-7:30pm.) Cheap *brasseries* line **rue de la Ferronerie. Postal code:** 22100.

CÔTE D'EMERAUDE AND CÔTE DE GRANITE ROSE

ST-BRIEUC. A commercial center situated between the Côte d'Emeraude and the Côte de Granite Rose, St-Brieuc is a perfect base for daytrips to the scenic countryside. **Trains** leave bd. Charner for Dinan (1hr., 2-3 per day, 84F/€12.85) and Rennes (1hr., 15 per day, 132F/€20.15). From the train station, walk down r. de la Gare and bear right at the fork to reach pl. de la Résistance and the **tourist office,** 7, r. St-Gouéno. (☎ 02 96 33 32 50; www.mairie-saint-brieuc.fr. Open July-Aug. M-Sa 9am-12:30pm and 2-7pm, Su 10am-1pm; Sept.-June M-Sa 9am-12:30pm and 2-6pm.) For the **Auberge de Jeunesse (HI),** in a 15th-century house outside of town, take bus #2 (dir. Centre Commercial les Villages). From the stop, turn right on bd. de l'Atlantique, take the second left onto r. du Vau Meno, turn right on r. de la Ville Guyomard, and it's on the left. (☎ 02 96 78 70 70. Dorms 75F/€11.45. MC/V.)

CAP FRÉHEL. Northeast of St-Brieuc, the rust-hued cliffs of Cap Fréhel, a landscape artist's dream, mark this northern point of the Côte d'Emeraude. Catch a CAT **bus** from St-Brieuc (1½hr., July-Aug. 5 per day, 45F/€6.90) and follow the red-and-white-striped markers along the well-marked **GR34 trail** on the edge of the peninsula. The 13th-century **Fort La Latte** boasts drawbridges and a hair-raising view of the Cap (1½hr.). To reach the **Auberge de Jeunesse Cap Fréhel (HI),** in La Ville Hadrieux, in Kerivet, get off the bus one stop after Cap Fréhel at Auberge de Jeunesse, take the only road that cuts away from the stop, and follow the fir-tree hostel signs. The hostel **rents bikes** (48F/€7.35 per half-day) and has maps of the GR34. (☎02 96 41 48 98; mid- Sept. to Apr. ☎02 98 78 70 70. Breakfast 19F/€2.90. Sheets 17F/€2.60. Lockout noon-5:30pm. Open May-Sept. Dorms 45F/€6.90.)

PAIMPOL. On the border of the Côte de Granite Rose and Côte de Goëlo, Paimpol offers easy access to nearby islands, beaches, and hiking. **Buses** run to the dramatic pink granite **Pointe de l'Arcouest,** 6km north of Paimpol (15min., 5-7 per day, 11F/€1.70). **Trains** (1hr., 4-5 per day, 70F/€10.70) and CAT **buses** (1¼hr.; 8 per day; 45F/€6.90, students 36F/€5.50) leave from av. Général de Gaulle for St-Brieuc. From the train station, go straight on r. du 18 Juin and turn right on r. de l'Oise, which becomes r. St-Vincent, to reach the **tourist office,** on pl. de la République. (☎02 96 20 83 16. Open July-Aug. M-Sa 9am-7:30pm, Su 10am-1pm; Sept.-June Tu-Sa 10am-12:30pm and 2:30-6pm.) To get to the **Auberge de Jeunesse (HI)** from the bus and train stations, turn left onto av. Général de Gaulle, turn right onto r. du Marne, turn left onto r. Bécot, bear right on r. de Pen Ar Run, and turn left at the end. (☎02 96 20 83 60. Breakfast 19F/€2.90. Dorms 48F/€7.35. **Camping** 27F/€4.15.)

BREST

Brest (pop. 156,217) combines the prosperity of a major port with the liveliness of a university town. Brest's **château** was the only building in town to survive World War II and is now the world's oldest active military institution. You can only enter the château through the **Musée de la Marine,** a museum on local maritime history. (Open Apr.-Sept. W-M 10am-6:30pm, Tu 2-6:30pm; Oct.-Mar. Tu-Su 10am-noon and 2-6pm. 29F/€4.60, students 20F/€3.05.) The amazing **Océanopolis Brest,** port de Plaisance, has computer-based and hands-on exhibits on marine life, biodiversity, and conservation. Take bus #7 (dir. Port de Plaisance; M-Sa, every 30min. until 7:30pm, 6.50F/€1) from the Liberty terminal to Océanopolis. (Open daily Apr. to mid-Sept. 9am-7pm; mid-Sept. to May 9am-6pm. 90F/€13.75.)

Trains (☎02 98 31 51 72) depart pl. du 19ème Régiment d'Infanterie for: Nantes (4hr., 6 per day, 244F/€37.20) and Rennes (1½hr., 15 per day, 170F/€25.95). From the station, av. Georges Clemenceau leads to the intersection of r. de Siam and Jean Jaurès and the **tourist office,** at the pl. de la Liberté. (☎02 98 44 24 96. Open mid-June to mid-Sept. M-Sa 9:30am-12:30pm and 2-6:30pm, Su 2-4pm; mid-Sept. to mid-June M-Sa 10am-12:30pm and 2-6pm.) Surf the **Internet** at **@cces.cibles,** 31, av. Clemenceau. (20F/€3.05 per hr. Open M-Sa 11am-1am, Su 2-11pm.) To get to the **Auberge de Jeunesse (HI),** 5, r. de Kerbriant, 4km away, take bus #7, diagonally opposite the station, to the final stop at Port de Plaisance (M-Sa until 7:30pm, Su until 6pm; 6.50F/€1); then facing the port, turn left toward the beach, take another quick left and follow the signs. (☎02 98 41 90 41. Breakfast included. Reception M-F 7-9am and 6-8pm, Sa-Su 7-10am and 5-8pm. Lockout 10am-5pm. Curfew July-Aug. midnight; Sept.-June 11pm; ask for key. Dorms 74F/€11.30.) To reach **Camping du Goulet,** 7km from Brest, take bus #14 (dir. Plouzane) to Le Cosquer. (☎02 98 45 86 84. Laundry 18F/2.75. 22F/€3.35 per person, 25F/€3.85 per tent. Electricity 11-16F/€1.70-2.45. Shower included.) For **groceries,** try the **Monoprix,** on r. de Siam. (Open M-Sa 8:30am-7:30pm.) **Postal code:** 29200 (29279 for *Poste Restante*).

CROZON PENINSULA

With spectacular scenery, rugged terrain, and few inhabitants, the Crozon Peninsula *(Presqu'île de Crozon)* is an outdoorsman's paradise. Its rugged interior contains a dense web of trails lined with *gîte d'étapes* (rural accommodations), providing excellent opportunities for hiking and cycling, while the rocky coastline offers snorkeling and kayaking. **Hikers** can take the 14km trail from Morgat Port to **Cap de la Chèvre** for a spectacular tour of the peninsula. The **Centre de Plongee ISA**, at the port of Plaisance, in Morgat, offers scuba diving, snorkeling lessons, and tours. (☎ 02 98 27 05 00. Daily excursions 115-230F/€17.55-35.10. Open daily 9am-noon and 2:30-6pm.) Two of the peninsula's major towns are **Crozon** and **Morgat**. Only 2½km apart, Corzon and Morgat are often considered to be one town.

From Brest, the **Vedettes Armoricaines ferry** (☎ 02 98 44 44 04) sails to Le Fret on the peninsula (4km from Crozon), and shuttles passengers to the three towns (45min., Apr.-Oct. 3 per day, 57F/€8.70). Buses stop at the Crozon **tourist office**. (☎ 02 98 27 07 92. Open July-Aug. M-Sa 9:30am-7pm, Su 10am-12:30pm; Sept.-June M-Sa 9:15am-noon and 2-6pm.) From Crozon, you can walk or bike the 2½km to Morgat. From the Crozon tourist office, turn left onto r. St-Yves, right on r. Louis Pasteur, right on r. Alsace Lorraine, and the 2nd left on bd. de la France Libre. The **tourist office** is straight ahead. (☎ 02 98 27 29 49. Open July-Aug. M-Sa 10am-7pm; Sept-June 10am-noon and 3-6pm.) **Hôtel du Clos St-Yves,** 61, r. Alsace Lorraine, in Crozon, has decent rooms. From the bus stop, with the tourist office on your right, go left on r. St-Yves and right on r. Alsace Lorraine. (☎ 02 98 27 00 10. Breakfast 35F/€5.35. Doubles 150-250F/€22.90-38.10; triples 330F/€20.35. MC/V.) A few kilometers south of Morgat, down r. de la Cap de la Chèvre, is the plush 20-bed **Gite St-Hernot.** (☎ 02 98 27 15 00. Breakfast 27F/€4.10. Doubles 55F/€8.40.) For groceries, try the large and central **Shoppi.** (Open July-Aug. M-Sa 8:30am-8pm, Su 9am-1pm; Sept.-June M-Sa 8:30am-12:30pm and 2:30-7:30pm, Su 9am-12:30pm.)

LOIRE VALLEY (VAL DE LOIRE)

Between Paris and Brittany lies the fertile valley of the Loire, France's longest and most celebrated river. Famed for its fertile vineyards and majestic châteaux, the Loire Valley also produced some of the brightest stars of French thought, including Rabelais, Descartes, and Balzac. **Tours** is the region's rail hub, although the châteaux Sully-sur-Loire, Chambord, and Cheverny aren't accessible by train. Infrequent public transit from larger cities can strand travelers. Train stations distribute the invaluable *Châteaux pour Train et Vélo* with train schedules and bike and car rental info, which are the best ways to explore the region.

ORLÉANS

Often considered a suburb of the capital, charming Orléans (pop. 200,000) clings to its history of Joan of Arc, and is a gateway to the nearby châteaux. The stained-glass windows of the stunning **Cathédrale Ste-Croix**, in pl. Ste-Croix, depict Joan's dramatic story. (Open daily July-Aug. 9:15am-noon and 2:15-7pm; Sept.-June reduced hrs. Free.) The **Musée des Beaux-Arts**, 1, r. Ferdinand Rabier, has a fine collection of Italian, Flemish, Dutch, and French works spanning the last five centuries. (Open Th-Sa 10am-6pm, Tu and Su 11am-6pm, W 10am-8pm. 20F/€3.05, students 10F/€1.55.) The **Maison de Jeanne d'Arc**, 3, pl. de Gaulle, off pl. du Martroi, celebrates Orléans's favorite liberator. (Open May-Oct. Tu-Su 10am-noon and 2-6pm; Nov.-Apr. 2-6pm. 13F/€2, students 6.50F/€1.) A daytrip down the Loire lies the imposing and historically rich 14th-century fortress **Sully-sur-Loire,** accessible by bus from the bus station, 2, r. Marcel Proust (1hr., 3 per day, 57F/€8.70).

Trains arrive at Gare d'Orléans, on pl. Albert 1*er*, from: Blois (30min., 12 per day, 54F/€8.25); Paris (1¼hr., 3 per hr., 94F/€14.35); and Tours (1hr., 12 per day, 91F/€13.90). To get from the station to the **tourist office,** 6, pl. Albert 1*er*, go left under the tunnel to pl. Jeanne d'Arc, and it's across the street on the right. (☎ 02 38 24 05 05; fax 02 38 54 49 84; www.tourismloiret.com. Open July-Aug. M-Sa 9am-7pm, Su 9:30am-12:30pm and 3-6:30pm; Apr.-June and Sept. M-Sa 9am-7pm, Su 10am-noon; Oct.-Mar. M-Sa 9am-6:30pm, Su 10am-noon.) The **Auberge de Jeunesse (HI),** 1, bd. de la Motte, is in a beautiful old mansion between the highway and river. Take bus RS (dir. Rosette) or SY (dir. Concyr/La Bolière) from pl. d'Arc to Pont Bourgogne;

follow bd. de la Motteand and it's up on the right. (☎02 38 53 60 06. Reception 9am-noon and 5-10pm. Dorms 61F/€9.30; singles 100F/€15.25.) **Carrefour,** in the back of the mall at pl. d'Arc, has **groceries.** (Open M-Sa 8:30am-9pm.) **Postal code:** 45000.

BLOIS

Blois (pop. 60,000) relishes its position as a gateway to the Loire Valley and welcomes visitors with pastoral charm. Home to monarchs Louis XII and François I, Blois's **château** was the Versailles of the late 15th and early 16th centuries; today it houses museums. (Open daily July-Aug. 9am-7:30pm; Apr.-June and Sept. 9am-6pm; Jan.-Mar. and Oct.-Dec. 9am-12:30pm and 2-5:30pm. 38F/€5.80, students 20F/€3.05.) Although Blois has plenty of sights, taking a stroll through its *vieille ville*, with hilly streets and ancient staircases, is enjoyable and memorable.

Trains run to: Orléans (30min., 14 per day, 54F/€8.25); Paris (1¾hr., 8 per day, 125F/€19.05) via Orléans; and Tours (1hr., 10 per day, 57F/€8.70). Transports Loir-et-Cher (TLC) (☎02 54 58 55 44), sends **buses** from the station and pl. Victor Hugo to nearby châteaux (1¼hr., 4 per day, 35F/€5.35). Or rent a **bike** from **Cycles Leblond,** 44, levée des Tuileries, to take the hour-long ride to the valley. (80F/€12.20 per day. Open daily 9am-9pm.) The **tourist office,** 3, av. Jean Laigret, can point the way. (☎02 54 90 41 41; fax 02 54 90 41 49; www.loiredeschâteaux.com. Open mid-Apr. to mid-Oct. Tu-Sa 9am-7pm; Su-M and holidays 10am-7pm; low season reduced hrs.) The rustic **Auberge de Jeunesse Verte (HI),** levée de la Loire, off D951, 11km away in Montlivault, is convenient for Chambord visitors. Take TLC bus #1 (dir. Beaugency) and ask to be dropped off by the Auberge de Jeunesse in Montlivault. (☎/fax 02 54 78 27 21. Open July-Aug. Dorms 45F/€6.90. **Camping** 27F/€4.15.) **Hôtel du Bellay,** 12, r. des Minimes, at the top of porte Chartraine, is next to the *centre ville.* (☎02 54 78 23 62; fax 02 54 78 52 04. Breakfast 25F/€3.85. Singles and doubles 135-185F/€20.60-28.20; triples 240F/€36.60; quads 280F/€42.70.) *Pâtisseries* entice pedestrians along **rue Denis Papin.** Restaurants line **rue St-Lubin, rue Drussy,** and **place Ploids du Roi,** near the cathedral. **Postal code:** 41000.

■ **DAYTRIPS FROM BLOIS: CHAMBORD AND CHEVERNY.** Built to satisfy François I's egomania, **Chambord** is the largest and most extravagant of the Loire châteaux. Seven hundred of François I's trademark stone salamanders are stamped throughout this "hunting lodge," whose 365 fireplaces kept him and his hounds warm in the 440 rooms. A double-helix staircase dominates the castle's center. (Open daily July-Aug. 9am-6:45pm; Sept. and Apr.-June 9am-6:15pm; Oct.-Mar. 9am-5:15pm. 42F/€6.40, ages 18-25 26F/€4.) Take **TLC bus #2** from Blois (45min., 20F/€3.05); hop on the TLC **Chambord-Cheverny bus circuit** (65F/€9.95, students 50F/€7.65, 25% discount on châteaux with bus ticket); or, **bike** from Blois (1hr.; take the D956 south 2-3km, and then go left on the D33).

Behind its impeccable grounds, **Cheverny** features magnificent furnishings, including delicate Delft vases and elegant tapestries. (Open daily Apr. to mid-Sept. 9:15am-6:15pm; July-Aug. 9:15am-6:45pm; Oct. and Mar. 9:30am-noon and 2:15-5:30pm; Nov.-Feb. 9:30am-noon and 2:15-5pm. 38F/€5.80, students 25F/€3.85.) Take the **bus** (see above) or **bike** from Blois (take D956 south for 45min.).

AMBOISE

The battlements of the 15th-century château at **Amboise** stretch out protectively across the hill above the town. Charles VIII, Louis XI, Louis XII, and the bacchanalian François I were among the six French kings who ruled France from this château. The jewel of the grounds is the 15th-century **Chapelle St-Hubert,** the final resting place of Leonardo da Vinci. (Open daily Apr.-June 9am-6:30pm; July-Aug. 9am-8pm; Sept.-Nov. 9am-6pm; Dec.-Jan. 9am-noon and 2-5pm; Feb.-Mar. 9am-noon and 2-5:30pm. 41F/€6.25, students 34F/€5.20.) After being invited to France by François I, da Vinci spent his last four years at **Clos Lucé** manor. Its main attraction is a collection of 40 unrealized inventions, built with the materials that would have been available during da Vinci's time.

(Open daily July-Aug. 9am-8pm; Sept.-June reduced hrs. 40F/€6.10, students 32F/€4.90.)

Trains run from bd. Gambetta to: Blois (20min., 15 per day, 35F/€5.35); Paris (2¼hr., 5 per day, 147F/€22.45); and Tours (20min., 14 per day, 28F/€4.30). The **tourist office**, on quai du Général de Gaulle, is 30m to the right of the bridge. (Open July-Aug. M-Sa 9am-8pm, Su 10am-6pm; Sept.-June M-Sa 9am-12:30pm and 2-6:30pm, Su 10am-noon.) The **Centre International de Séjour Charles Péguy (HI)**, on Ile d'Or, sits on an island in the middle of the Loire. (☎ 02 47 30 60 90; fax 02 47 30 60 91. Sheets 19F/€2.90. Reception M-F 3-7pm. Dorms 54F/€8.25.) **Postal code:** 35400.

TOURS

While Tours (pop. 250,000) boasts fabulous nightlife and a good collection of sights, it works best as a base for nearby Loire châteaux. The **Cathédrale St-Gatien,** on r. Jules Simon, has dazzling stained glass. (Open daily 9am-7pm. Free.) At the **Musée du Gemmail,** 7, r. du Murier, works of *gemmail* (a fusion of shards of brightly colored glass with enamel) by Picasso and Braque glow in rooms of dark velvet. (Open Apr. to mid-Nov. Tu-Su 10am-noon and 2-6:30pm; mid-Nov. to Mar. W-Su 10am-noon and 2-6:30pm. 30F/€4.60, students 20F/€3.05.)

Trains leave 3, r. Édouard Vaillant, for: Bordeaux (2½hr., 6 per day, 229F/€34.95) and Paris (2¼hr., 7 per day, 160F/€24.40). The **tourist office**, 78/82, r. Bernard Palissy, has free maps and books rooms. (☎ 02 47 70 37 37; fax 02 47 61 14 22; www.ligeris.com. Open mid-Apr. to mid-Oct. M-Sa 8:30am-7pm, Su 10am-12:30pm and 2:30-5pm; mid-Oct. to mid-Apr. M-Sa 9am-12:30pm and 1:30-6pm, Su 10am-1pm.) ▨**Foyer des Jeunes Travailleurs,** 24, r. Bernard Palissy, is centrally located. (☎ 02 47 60 51 51. Singles 100F/€15.25; doubles 160F/€24.40.) **Auberge de Jeunesse (HI),** av. d'Arsonval, in Parc de Grandmont, is too far from town to walk. Buses #3, 6, or 11 leave from pl. da Vinci outside the station for Auberge de Jeunesse. (☎ 02 47 25 14 45; fax 02 47 48 26 59. Breakfast included. Reception 7-11am and 4-10pm. Dorms 70F/€10.70; singles 109F/€16.65. MC/V.) Try **place Plumereau** for great restaurants, cafes, and bars. ▨**La Souris Gourmande,** 100, r. Colbert, is a friendly restaurant specializing in regional cheese dishes and fondues. (Open Tu-Sa noon-2pm and 7-10:30pm.) **Postal code:** 37000.

LOIRE CHÂTEAUX

Biking along the Loire between châteaux is enchanting; for the more efficient **bus tours,** contact Saint-Eloi Excursions (☎ 02 47 37 08 04; www.saint-eloi.com); Touraine Evasion (☎ 06 07 39 13 31); and Sillione Val (☎ 02 47 59 13 14). Expect to shell out 100-300F/€15.25-45.75, which normally includes admission. **ADA,** 49, bd. Thiers (☎ 02 47 64 94 94), rents **cars** from 99F/€15.10 per day. **Amster Cycles,** 5, r. du Rempart (☎ 02 47 61 22 23), rents bikes (85F/€12.95 1st day, 40F/€6.10 thereafter).

CHENONCEAU. A series of women designers created the exquisite beauty of Chenonceau, the site of many a wild Renaissance party. The bridge over the river Cher that connects two sections of the château also marked the border between annexed and Vichy France during World War II. Chenonceau's beautiful setting makes it the most popular of the châteaux. (Open mid-Mar. to mid-Sept. daily 9am-7pm; call for off-season hours. 50F/€7.65, students 40F/€6.10.) **Trains** from Tours arrive at the station 2km away (45min., 3 per day, 36F/€5.50). Fil Vert **buses** leave for Chenonceau from Tours (25min., 2 per day, 13F/€2).

VILLANDRY. Villandry's restored French **gardens** with waterfalls, vine-covered walkways, and over 120,000 plants, are considered the most beautiful in the Loire Valley. (Gardens open daily July-Aug. 9am-7:30pm; Sept.-June 9am-7pm. Château open daily July-Aug. 9am-6:30pm; Sept. to mid-Nov. and mid-Feb. to June 9am-6pm. Gardens 33F/€5.05, students 22F/€3.35; with château 46F/€7.05, 32F/€4.90.) Villandry is hard to reach by public transport; take the **train** from Tours to **Savonnières** (10min., 2 per day, 19F/€2.90) and walk or bike 4km along the Loire. From Tours, **cyclists** should follow the D16, while **drivers** take the D7.

FRANCE

LOCHES. The walled medieval town of Loches surrounds its grand château, which has two distinct structures at opposite ends of a hill. To the north, the 11th-century keep and watchtowers went from keeping enemies out to keeping them in when Louis XI turned it into a state prison, complete with suspended cages. The **Logis Royal** pays tribute to the famous ladies who held court here. (Open daily Apr.-Sept. 9am-7pm; Oct.-Mar. 9:30am-12:30pm and 2-5pm. Logis Royal or keep 24F/€3.65, students 17F/€2.60; combined 32F/€4.90, students 22F/€3.35.) **Buses** run from the Tours train station to Loches (50min.; 4 per day; 49F/€7.50, pay on board). Nine **trains** also make the trip (1hr., 49F/€7.50).

AZAY-LE-RIDEAU. Azay-le-Rideau gazes peacefully at its reflection from an island in the Indre. Intended to rival Chambord in beauty, Azay succeeded so well that François I seized the château before its third wing was completed. Azay's flamboyant style is apparent in the ornate Italian second-floor staircase. (Open daily July-Aug. 9:30am-7pm; Apr.-June and Sept.-Oct. 9:30am-6pm; Nov.-Mar. 9:30am-12:30pm and 2-5:30pm. 36F/€5.50, ages 18-25 23F/€3.50.) **Trains** run from Tours to the town of **Azay-le-Rideau**, 2km from the château (30min., 3 per day, 28F/€4.30). **Buses** run from Tours' train station to the tourist office, pl. de l'Europe (45min.; 1-3 per day; one-way 30F/€4.60, pay on board).

ANGERS

Angers (pop. 220,000) offers shops and inexpensive restaurants in a youthful atmosphere, while preserving its medieval traditions. Behind the massive stone walls of the 13th-century **Château d'Angers**, on pl. Kennedy, the Dukes of Anjou ruled the surrounding countryside and a certain island across the Channel. Inside the château, the 14th-century **Tapisserie de l'Apocalypse**, the world's largest tapestry, depicts the Book of Revelations. (Open daily June to mid-Sept. 9:30am-7pm; mid-Sept. to Oct. and mid-Mar. to May 10am-6pm; Nov. to mid-Mar. 10am-5pm. 36F/€5.50, students 23F/€3.55.) Angers's second woven masterpiece, the **Chant du Monde** ("Song of the World"), in the **Musée Jean Lurçat**, 4, bd. Arago, illustrates a symbolic journey through human destiny. (Open daily mid-June to mid-Sept. 9am-6:30pm; mid-Sept. to mid-June Tu-Su 10am-noon and 2-6pm. 20F/€3.05.) A 28F/€4.30 **ticket**, sold at the tourist office and museums, gives admission to five museums and the 50F/€7.65 *billet jumelé* includes château admission.

Trains roll from r. de la Gare to: Orléans (3-4hr., 6 per day, 150F/€22.90); Paris (2-4hr., 3 per day, 254-320F/€38.75-48.80); and Tours (1hr., 7 per day, 86F/€13.15). **Buses** go from pl. de la République to Rennes (3hr., 2 per day, 97F/€14.80). To get from the station to the **tourist office**, on pl. Kennedy, exit straight onto r. de la Gare, turn right on pl. de la Visitation onto r. Talot, turn left on bd. du Roi-René, and it's across from the château. (☎02 41 23 50 00; fax 02 41 23 50 09. Open June-Sept. M-Sa 9am-7pm, Su 10am-6pm; Oct.-May M-Sa 9am-6pm.) To get to the **Centre d'Accueil du Lac de Maine (HI),** 49, av. du Maine, take bus #6 or 16 to Accueil Lac de Maine, turn around and cross the street, and follow signs on the right-hand side. (☎02 41 22 32 10; fax 02 41 22 32 11. Breakfast included. HI members only. Singles 177F/€27; doubles 120F/€18.30; quads 85F/€13.) **Hotel des Lices,** 25, r. des Lices, near the château, has 13 plain, clean rooms. (☎02 41 87 44 10. Reception M-F 7am-9pm, Sa-Su 4:30pm-9pm. Singles and doubles 130F/€19.85, with bath 180F/€27.45; triples 190-240F/€29-36.60.) Take bus #6 to Camping Lac de Maine to reach the four-star **Camping du Lac de Maine,** av. du Lac de Maine. (☎02 41 73 05 03; fax 02 41 73 02 20. Open Mar. 25-Oct. 10. 86-89F/€13.15-13.60 for 2 people, tent, and car. Electricity 18.50F/€2.85.) Cheap international food is available along **rue St-Laud.** Fresh produce and baked goods are sold at the **covered market** in the basement of **Les Halles**, on r. Plantagenêt, behind the cathedral. (Open Tu-Sa 7am-8pm, Su 7am-1:30pm.) **Postal code:** 49052 (specify "Angers-Ralliement" for *Poste Restante*).

PÉRIGORD AND AQUITAINE

The images of Périgord and Aquitaine are seductive: green countryside splashed with yellow sunflowers, white chalk cliffs, golden wine, and plates of black truffles. First settled 150,000 years ago, the area around Les Eyzies-de-Tayac has turned up more stone-age artifacts than any other place on earth.

PÉRIGUEUX

Encircled by the river Isle, Périgueux (pop. 37,700) preserves significant architecture in both the medieval and Roman halves of the town. The city is also a good base for visiting the caves of Périgord. The *vieille ville* features medieval-Renaissance architecture while the multi-domed **Cathédrale St-Front** combines styles of several eras. (Open daily 8am-7:30pm.) The remarkable ruin **Tour de Vésone** was once a *cella*, the holiest place and center of worship of a Roman temple. (Open daily Apr.-Sept. 7:30am-9pm; Oct.-Mar. 7:30am-6:30pm.)

Trains leave r. Denis Papin for: Bordeaux (1½hr., 7 per day, 99F/€15.10); Paris (4-6hr., 12 per day, 277F/€42.25); and Toulouse (4hr., 8 per day, 183F/€27.90). The **tourist office**, 26, pl. Francheville, has free maps. From the station, turn right on r. Denis Papin, bear left on r. des Mobiles-de-Coulmiers, which becomes r. du Président Wilson, take the next right after passing r. Guillier, and it's on the left. (☎ 05 53 53 10 63; fax 05 53 09 02 70. Open July-Aug. M-Sa 9am-7pm, Su 10am-6pm; Sept.-June M-Sa 9am-6pm.) **Les Charentes**, 16, r. Denis Papin, is across from the train station. (☎ 05 53 53 37 13. 145-205F/€22.10-31.25 per person; add 30F/€4.60 per extra person. AmEx/MC/V.) **Monoprix supermarket** is on pl. de la République. (Open M-Sa 8:30am-8pm.) **Postal code:** 24070 (24017 for *Poste Restante*).

SARLAT

The golden medieval *vieille ville* of Sarlat (pop. 10,700) has been the focus of tourist and movie cameras—Gérard Depardieu's *Cyrano de Bergerac* was filmed here. Today, its narrow 14th- and 15th-century streets fill with flea markets, dancing violinists, and purveyors of *gâteaux aux noix* (cakes with nuts) and golden Monbazillac wines. **Trains** go to Bordeaux (2½hr., 4 per day, 119F/€18.15) and Périgueux (3hr., 1 per day, 75F/€11.45). Stop by the **tourist office**, on r. Tourny in the Ancien Eveche. (☎ 05 53 31 45 45. Open May-Sept. M-Sa 9am-7pm, Su 10am-noon and 2-6pm; Oct.-Apr. M-Sa 9am-noon and 2-6pm.) Rent **bikes** at **Peugeot Cycles**, 36, av. Thiers. (☎ 05 53 28 51 87. 70F/€10.70 for 24hr. Open Tu-Sa 9:30am-7pm. MC/V.) Sarlat's **Auberge de Jeunesse**, 77, av. de Selves, is 40min. from the train station but only 10min. from the *vieille ville*. From the *vieille ville*, go straight on r. de la République, which becomes av. Gambetta, bear left at the fork onto av. de Selves. (☎ 05 53 59 47 59 or 05 53 30 21 27. Reception 6-8:30pm. Open mid-Mar. to Nov. Reserve ahead. Dorms 50-60F/€7.60-9.15. **Camping** 35F/€5.35.) **Champion supermarket** is near the hostel on rte. de Montignac; continue following av. de Selves away from the *centre ville*. (Open M-Sa 9am-7:30pm, Su 9am-noon.) **Postal code:** 24200.

⚑ DAYTRIP FROM SARLAT: THE DORDOGNE VALLEY. Steep, craggy cliffs overlook the Dordogne River, 15km south of Sarlat. The numerous châteaux fortresses now keep watch over tourists, but by avoiding the major towns, it's still possible to find solitude. The town of **Castelnaud-La Chapelle** snoozes 10km south of Sarlat in the shadow of its crumbling, pale-yellow-stone château, a fortress of the 12th to 15th centuries, and now the most visited castle in Aquitaine. **Domme,** the best defended of the Dordogne Valley's villages, was built by King Philippe III (Philippe the Bold) in 1280 on a high dome of solid rock. Domme is also a great place to rent a canoe and paddle down the Dordogne for a view of the châteaux perched on their hills. **Cenac Canoes** rents canoes. (☎ 05 53 28 22 01. Half day 150F/€22.90, whole day 240F/€36.60.) To travel around the valley, you'll need to rent a car or be prepared for a good bike workout—the hills are steep but manageable. A **Hertz** car rental office is located right in front of the train station in Perigueux. Ask at any tourist office for lists of *chambres d'hôtes*, which rent out cheap rooms.

⚡ DAYTRIPS FROM SARLAT AND PÉRIGUEUX: CAVE PAINTINGS. The most spectacular cave paintings yet discovered hide in the **caves of Lascaux,** near the town of **Montignac,** 25km north of Sarlat. Discovered in 1940 by a couple of teenagers, the caves were closed in 1963 after it was discovered that the humidity from oohs and ahhs of the millions of tourists had fostered algae and micro-stalactites, ravaging the paintings. **Lascaux II** duplicates every inch of the original cave, in the same pigments used 17,000 years ago. Although the reproduction may lack ancient awe and mystery, the new caves—filled with paintings of 5m tall bulls, horses, and bison—nevertheless manage to inspire a wonder all their own. The **ticket office** shares a building with the Montignac **tourist office,** on pl. Bertram-de-Born. (Ticket office M-F ☎05 53 35 50 10, Sa-Su 05 53 51 95 03. Open daily 9am until tickets sell out.) One **bus** for Montignac leaves Périgueux each night (1½hr., 40F/€6.10) and three CFTA buses leave Sarlat each day from the pl. de 14 Juillet (30min., 30F/€4.60) and return in early evening. Get the schedule at the tourist office in Sarlat.

At the **Grotte de Font-de-Gaume,** a 10min. walk from **Les Eyzies-de-Tayac,** 1km down D47, 15,000-year-old horses, bison, and woolly mammoths line the cave walls. (☎05 53 06 86 00. Open daily Apr.-Sept. 9am-noon and 2-6pm; Mar. and Oct. 9:30am-noon and 2-5:30pm; Nov.-Feb. 10am-noon and 2-5pm. 36F/€5.50, ages 18-25 23F/€3.50.)

BORDEAUX

Enveloped by emerald vineyards, Bordeaux (pop. 714,000) toasts the violet wine that made it famous. Not just a temple to wine connoisseurs, the city also has spirited nightclubs, a stunning opera house, and some of France's best food.

🚆 TRANSPORTATION AND PRACTICAL INFORMATION. Trains leave Gare St-Jean, r. Charles Domercq (☎05 56 33 11 83), for: Nice (9-10hr., 5 per day, 436F/€66.50); Paris (TGV: 3-4hr., 15-25 per day, 359F/€54.75); and Toulouse (2-3hr., 11 per day, 179F/€27.30). From the train station, take bus #7 or 8 (dir. Grand Théâtre) to pl. Gambetta and walk toward the Monument des Girondins for the **tourist office,** 12, cours du 30 juillet, which arranges winery tours. (☎05 56 00 66 00; fax 05 56 00 66 01; www.bordeaux-tourisme.com. Open May-Oct. M-Sa 9am-7pm, Su 9:30am-6:30pm; Nov.-Apr. M-Sa 9am-6:30pm, Su 9:45am-4:30pm.) **American Express** is at 14, cours de l'Intendance. (Open M-F 8:45am-noon and 1:30-5:30pm.) Walk away from the river up r. Judaique for **internet** access at **France Telecom,** 2, r. Château d'Eau, near pl. Gambetta. (Open M-F noon-7pm. 30F/€4.60 per hr., students 20F/€3.05.) **Postal code:** 33065.

🍴 ACCOMMODATIONS AND FOOD. The newly renovated **Auberge de Jeunesse (HI),** 22, cours Barbey, still has a smaller branch at 208, cours de l'Argonne (☎05 56 94 51 66; fax 05 56 94 51 66), a ten-minute walk from pl. de la Victoire. The main *auberge* is in a seedy area near the train station and 30 minutes from the *centre ville.* (☎05 56 33 00 70; fax ☎05 56 33 00 71. Breakfast 15F/€2.30. HI members 80F/€12.20; nonmembers extra 10F/€1.55 to stay 1 night.) To reach ⚡**Hôtel Studio,** 26, r. Huguerie, walk one block down r. Georges Clemenceau from the pl. Gambetta, and half a block to the left on the r. Huguerie. (☎05 56 48 00 14; fax 05 56 81 25 71. Singles 98-135F/€15.20-20.60; doubles 120-160F/€18.30-24.40; triples 180F/€27.45; quads and quints 200-250F/€30.50-38.15.) Across from the train station is the clean **Hôtel Regina,** 34, r. Charles Domercq. (☎05 56 91 66 07. Reception 24hr. Singles 145F/€22.15, with bath 185-205F/€28.25-31.25; doubles 185F/€28.25, 205-225F/€31.25-34.30.)

As center of the *région de bien manger et de bien vivre* (region of fine eating and living), Bordeaux takes its food as seriously as its wine. Hunt around **rue St-Remi** and **place St-Pierre** for splendid regional specialties, including oysters, *foie gras,* and beef braised in wine sauce. The English-speaking staff at the elegant and romantic **La Casuccia,** 49, r. St-Rémi, serve French and Italian delicacies from 65F/€9.95. (Open daily lunch 11:30am, dinner 7pm-midnight.) Stock up at **Auchan supermarket,** at the Centre Meriadeck on r. Claude Bonnier. (Open M-Sa 8:30am-10pm.) Locals buy wine at **Vinothèque,** 8, cours du 30 Juillet. (Open M-Sa 9:15am-7:30pm.)

🎭🎵 **SIGHTS AND ENTERTAINMENT.** Near the tourist office, on pl. de Quinconces, the elaborate fountains of the **Monument aux Girondins** commemorate revolutionary leaders from towns bordering the Gironde river. Retrace your steps to the breathtaking **Grand Théâtre**, on pl. de la Comédie, to see a performance or take a tour. (Tours 30F/€4.60, students 20F/€3.05.) Follow r. Ste-Catherine from the pl. de la Comédie, facing the theater, to reach the Gothic **Cathédrale St-André**, in pl. Pey-Berland. (Open daily Apr.-Oct. 7:30-11:30am and 2-6:30pm; Nov.-Mar. M-F 7:30-11:30am and 2-6:30pm. 25F/€3.85, under 25 and seniors 15F/€2.30.) Walking toward the river along cours d'Alsace, turn left onto quai Richelieu for the **place de la Bourse,** with pillars and fountains reflecting Bordeaux's grandeur. On the left is the surprisingly interesting **Musée National des Douanes.** (Open daily Apr.-Sept. 10am-noon and 1-6pm; Oct.-Mar. M-Sa 10am-noon and 1-5pm. 20F/€3.05, students and seniors 10F/€1.55.) Near the river, just off quai des Chartrons, **Vinorama de Bordeaux,** 12, cours du Médoc, features elaborate dioramas and wine samples. (Open June-Sept. Tu-Sa 10:30am-12:30pm and 2:30-6:30pm, Su 2-6:30pm; Oct.-May Tu-F 2-6:30pm, Sa 10:30am-12:30pm and 2:30-6:30pm. 35F/€5.35, 15F/€2.30.)

For an overview of Bordeaux nightlife, pick up a free copy of *Clubs and Concerts* at the tourist office, or purchase the magazine *Bordeaux Plus* (2F/€0.30). **Place de la Victoire** and **place Gambetta** are year-round hotspots. **La Plana,** 22, pl. de la Victoire, is packed nightly with locals and foreigners. (Open daily 7pm-2am.)

🍷 **WINERIES.** Make a trip to the **Maison du Vin/CIVB,** 1, cours du 30 Juillet, where there's a wine bar and information on local châteaux and vineyards. Their two-hour "Initiation to Wine Tasting" course, available in English, teaches the art of oenophilia (wine tasting) through comparative tasting. (Open M-Th 8:30am-6pm, F 8:30am-5:30pm. 100F/€15.25.) Just 35km from Bordeaux are the **St-Emilion** vineyards, whose viticulters have been refining their techniques since Roman times. The **Maison du Vin de St-Emilion,** pl. Pierre Meyrat, offers a one-hour wine course on local wines. (Open Mar.-July and Sept.-Nov. M-Sa 10am-12:30pm and 2-6:30pm, Su 10am-12:30pm and 2:30-6:30pm; Aug. daily 10am-7pm; Dec.-Feb. daily 10am-12:30pm and 2:30-6pm. Wine course offered mid-July to mid-Sept. 11am; 110F/€16.80.) **Trains** run from Bordeaux to St-Emilion (30min., 2 per day, 66F/€10.10).

THE PAYS BASQUE AND GASCONY

On the border of Spain and the Pyrénées, the forests recede and the mountains of Gascony begin, shielded from the Atlantic by the Basque Country. Both Gascons and Basques are descended from the *Vascone* people. Long renowned as fierce fighters, the Basque people continue their struggle today, striving to win independence for their long-suffering homeland. Meanwhile, Gascons have long considered themselves French. Today, people come to Gascony to be healed; millions of believers descend on Lourdes hoping for miracle cures while thousands of others undergo scarcely more scientific treatments in the many *thermes* of the Pyrénées.

BAYONNE

Bayonne (pop. 43,000) is a grand port with small town appeal. The twin steeples of the 13th-century **Cathédrale Ste-Marie** needle the sky. (Open M-Sa 7am-noon and 3-7pm, Su 3:30-10pm.) Highlights of the **Musée Bonnat,** 5, r. Jacques Laffitte, in Petit-Bayonne, include works by Rubens, El Greco, and Goya. (Open W-M 10am-12:30pm and 2-6pm. 35F/€5.35, students 20F/€3.05.)

Trains (☎05 59 55 50 50) depart from the station, pl. de la République, to: Bordeaux (1½hr., 9 per day, 130-138F/€19.85-21.05); Toulouse (4hr., 5 per day, 200F/€30.50); and San Sebastián, Spain (1½hr.; change at Hendalye). Trains run between Bayonne and Biarritz (10min., 10-22 per day, 12F/€1.85), but the local **bus** network provides more comprehensive and cheaper regional transit. Local **STAB buses** depart from the Hôtel de Ville, running to Anglet and Biarritz (every 30-40min.; last bus M-Sa 8pm, Su 7pm; 7.50F/€1.15, packets of 10 62F/€9.45).

The **tourist office,** on pl. des Basques, offers maps and finds rooms. From the train station, take the middle fork onto pl. de la République, veer right over pont St-Esprit, pass through pl. Réduit, cross pont Mayou, turn right on r. Bernède, which becomes av. Bonnat, and turn left on pl. des Basques. (☎05 59 46 01 46; fax 05 59 59 37 55. Open July-Aug. M-Sa 9am-7pm, Su 10am-1pm; Sept.-June M-F 9am-6:30pm, Sa 10am-6pm.) Decent lodgings are near the train station and pl. Paul Bert. The ◼Hôtel Paris-Madrid, on pl. de la Gare, has cozy rooms and English-speaking owners. (☎05 59 55 13 98; fax 05 59 55 07 22. Breakfast 25F/ €3.85. Reception daily 6am-12:30am. Singles and doubles 95-180F/€14.50-27.45, triples and quads 235-250F/€35.85-38.10.) For **Camping de la Chêneraie,** take bus #1 from the station to Navarre stop; it's a 1½km walk along a busy highway. (☎05 59 59 08 02. Reception July-Aug. 8am-10pm; Easter-June and Sept. 8:30am-noon and 5-7:30pm. 26F/€3.90 per person, 58F/€8.85 per tent and car.) Get groceries at **Monoprix supermarket,** 8, r. Orbe. (Open M-Sa 8:30am-7:30pm.)

◼ **DAYTRIP FROM BAYONNE: ST-JEAN-DE-PORT.** The village of St-Jean-Pied-de-Port, historically an important crossroads for religious travelers, still hosts a continual procession of pilgrims on their way to Spain. Its cobblestone streets wind through the *haute ville* to a dilapidated fortress, offering views of rolling green hills and red-tiled roofs. **Trains** arrive from Bayonne (1hr., 5 per day, 47F/€5.20). Rent **bikes** at **Garazi Cycles,** 1, pl. St-Laurent. (☎05 59 37 21 79. 120F/€18.30 per day, 150F/€22.90 per weekend. Passport deposit. Open M-Sa 8:30am-noon and 3-6pm.) From the station, turn right on av. Renaud, follow it up the slope until av. de Gaulle, and turn right to reach the **tourist office,** 14, av. de Gaulle. (☎05 59 37 03 57; fax 05 59 37 34 91. Open July-Aug. M-Sa 9am-12:30pm and 2-7pm, Su 10:30am-12:30pm and 3-6pm; Sept.-June M-F 9am-noon and 2-7pm, Sa 9am-noon and 2-6pm.)

BIARRITZ

Biarritz (pop. 29,000) is not a budget dream, but its free **beaches** make a daytrip *de luxe*—you too can sunbathe where Napoleon III, Bismarck, and Queen Victoria summered. At the **Grande Plage,** you'll find a wealth of surfers and bathers, and just to the north at the less-crowded **plage Miramar,** bathers repose *au naturel.* A short **hike** to **Pointe St-Martin** affords a priceless view. **BASC Subaquatique,** near Plateau de l'Atalaye (☎05 59 24 80 40), organizes **scuba** excursions in summer for 155F/€23.65. **Trains** roll into **Biarritz-la-Négresse,** 3km out of town. Hop on bus #2 (dir. Bayonne via Biarritz) or green bus #9 (dir. Biarritz HDV) to get to the *centre ville.* Or, get off the train in Bayonne and hop on STAB **buses** #1 or 2 to the central Hôtel de Ville (30min.). The **tourist office,** 1, sq. d'Ixelles, helps find accommodations. (☎05 59 22 37 10; fax 05 59 24 14 19. Open daily July-Aug. 8am-8pm; Sept.-June 9am-6pm.) The **Auberge de Jeunesse (HI),** 8, r. de Chiquito de Cambo, has a friendly staff and lakefront location. To walk from the *centre ville,* take av. Marèchal Foch, continue as it becomes av. du President J. F. Kennedy, turn right on r. Ph. Veyrin, and it's at the bottom of the hill. (☎05 59 41 76 00; fax 05 59 41 76 07. Breakfast included. Sheets 17F/€2.60. **HI members only.** 78F/€11.90 per person.) ◼Hôtel Barnetche, 5bis, r. Charles-Floquet, is the best deal in town. (☎05 59 24 22 25; fax 05 59 24 98 71; www.hotel-barnetche.fr. Breakfast included; in Aug., obligatory half-pension 100F/ €15.25. Reception 7:30am-10:30pm. Open May-Sept. 12-bed dorm 110F/€16.80; doubles 380F/€57.95; triples and quads 160F/€24.40 per person.) **Shopi,** 2, r. du Centre, off r. Gambetta, has **groceries.** (Open M-Sa 8:45am-12:25pm and 3-7:10pm.)

◼ **DAYTRIP FROM BIARRITZ: ST-JEAN-DE-LUZ.** The vibrant seaport of St-Jean-de-Luz lures visitors with the **Maison Louis XIV,** pl. Louis XIV, which temporarily housed the Sun King. (Obligatory tours every 30min. Open July-Aug. M-Sa 10:30am-noon and 2:30-6:30pm, Su 2:30-6:30pm; Sept.-June closes 5:30pm.) The village's earlier days of piracy funded its unique buildings, exemplified in the **Eglise St-Jean-Baptiste,** r. Gambetta, built to resemble a fishing boat. **Trains** roll in to bd. du Cdt. Passicot from Biarritz (15min., 10 per day, 16F/€2.45) and Bayonne (30min., 7 per day, 25F/€3.85). ATCRB **buses** (☎05 59 08 00 33), across from the train station, also run to Biarritz (7-13 per day, 18F/€2.75) and Bayonne (7-13 per day, 23F/€3.55). The **tourist office** is at pl. Foch. (☎ 05 59 26 03 16. Open July-Aug. M-Sa 9am-8pm, Su 10:30am-1pm and 3-7pm; Sept.-June M-Sa 9am-12:30pm and 2-7pm.)

LOURDES

In 1858, 14-year-old Bernadette Soubirous saw the first of 18 visions of the Virgin Mary in the Massabielle grotto in Lourdes (pop. 16,300). Bernadette may have gotten more than she bargained for—today five million rosary-toting faithful make pilgrimages annually. To get from the tourist office to the **Grotte de Massabielle (La Grotte)** and the two **basilicas** looming above it, follow av. de la Gare, turn left on bd. de la Grotte, and follow it across the river. (10min.) **Processions** depart daily from the grotto at 5pm and 8:45pm from the grotto. (Dress modestly. Grotto open daily 5am-midnight. Basilicas open daily Easter-Oct. 6am-7pm; Nov.-Easter 8am-6pm.)

    Trains leave 33, av. de la Gare for: Bayonne (2hr., 5 per day, 108F/€16.50); Bordeaux (3hr., 7 per day, 176F/€26.85); and Toulouse (2½hr., 8 per day, 127F/€19.40). To get from the train station to the **tourist office**, on pl. Peyramale, turn right on av. de la Gare, bear left on av. Marasin, cross the bridge above bd. du Papacca, walk uphill, and look to the right. (☎ 05 62 42 77 40; fax 05 62 94 60 95. Open May to mid-Oct. M-Sa 9am-7pm; Nov. 1-15 M-Sa 9am-noon and 2-7pm; Nov. 16 to mid-Mar. M-Sa 9am-noon and 2-6pm; mid-Mar. to Apr. M-Sa 9am-noon and 2-7pm.) For **Hôtel Arbizon**, 37, r. des Petits Fossés, follow av. Herlios away from the train station as it curves down the hill. Bear right and go under the bridge on bd. du Lapacca. Turn left onto r. Basse, and then take your first left. (☎/fax 05 62 94 29 36. Breakfast 25F/€3.85. Reception 7am-midnight. Open Feb. 9-Nov. 11. Singles 90F/€13.75; doubles 120F/€18.30; triples 150F/€22.90.) **Camping de la Poste**, 26, r. de Langelle, is just a few minutes from the center of town. (☎ 05 62 94 40 35. Open Easter to mid-Oct. 15F/€2.30 per person, 23F/€3.55 per site. Electricity 16F/€2.45. Shower 8F/€1.25.) Save money by heading to **Prisunic supermarket**, 9, pl. du Champ-Commun. (Open M-Sa 8:30am-12:30pm and 2-7:30pm, Su 8am-noon.) **Postal code:** 65100.

CAUTERETS

Nestled 930m up in a breathtaking valley among towering peaks is tiny Cauterets. Renowned for centuries for its hot water *thermes*, most visitors today come to take advantage of the hiking and skiing. For easy access to the mountains, the **Téléphérique du Lys** cable car leaves every 30min. from the center of town. Head to the **tourist office**, on pl. Foch, for information on sights in town. (☎ 05 62 92 50 27; fax 05 62 92 59 12. Open daily July-Aug. 9am-7pm; Sept.-June 9am-12:30pm and 2-6:30pm.) For hiking information and maps, head to Parc National Office (see below). **Skilys**, rte. de Pierrefitte, pl. de la Gare, rents **bikes** and **skates**. (☎ 05 62 92 52 10. Bikes with guide 250-350F/€38.10-53.40 per day, without guide 100F/€15.25 per day; deposit 1500-2500F/€228.70-381.15. Open daily 9am-7pm; in winter 8am-7:30pm.) SNCF **buses** run from Lourdes to Cauterets (1hr.; 6 per day; 39F/€5.95, students 30F/€4.60). The rustic ◪**Gîte d'Etape UCJG**, av. du Docteur Domer, is near the town center. From the Parc National Office, cross the parking lot and street, and turn left up the hill; the *gîte* is just beyond the tennis courts. (☎ 05 62 92 52 95. Shower and sheets included. Open mid-June to mid-Sept. Beds 40-55F/€6.10-8.40. **Camping** 20F/€3.05.) The covered **Halles market**, on av. du Général Leclerc, has fresh produce. (Open daily 8:30am-12:30pm and 2:30-7:30pm.) **Postal code:** 65110.

◪ DAYTRIP FROM CAUTERETS: THE PYRENEES. The striking **Parc National des Pyrénées** shelters thousands of endangered animals in its snow-capped mountains and lush valleys. Touch base with the friendly and helpful **Parc National Office**, Maison du Parc, pl. de la Gare, before braving the wilderness. They have tons of information on the park and the 15 different trails beginning and ending in Cauterets. The trails in the park are designed for a range of aptitudes, from rugged outdoorsmen to novice hikers. From Cauterets, the **GR10** winds through **Luz-St-Saveur**, over the mountain, and then on to **Gavarnie**, another day's hike up the valley; this is also known as the **"circuit de Gavarnie."** One of the most spectacular trails follows the GR10 to the turquoise **Lac de Gaube,** and then to the end of the glacial valley (2hr. past the lake) where you can spend the night at the **Refuges Des Oulettes,** the first shelter past the lake. (☎05 62 92 62 97. Open June-Sept. 80F/€12.20.) Dipping into the Vallée Lutour, the **Refuge Estom** rests near Lac d'Estom. (Summer ☎05 62 92 72 93, off-season 05 62 92 75 07. 60-70F/€9.15-1.70 per night.)

LANGUEDOC-ROUSSILLON

An immense region called Occitania once stretched from the Rhône Valley to the foothills of the Pyrenees. The region was eventually integrated into the French kingdom, and the Cathar religion, popular among Occitanians, was severely persecuted by the Crown and Church. Their *langue d'oc* dialect of French faded, and in 1539, the *langue d'oïl* spoken in the north became official. Latent nationalism lingers, however, in vibrant cities like Toulouse and Pérpignan. Many speak Catalán, a relative of *langue d'oc*, and look to Barcelona, rather than Paris, for inspiration.

TOULOUSE

When all of France starts to look alike, rose-tinted Toulouse, or *la ville en rose* (the city in pink) provides a breath of fresh air with its stately architecture and vibrant youthful population. Toulouse (pop. 350,000) has always retained an element of independence. A rebellious city during the Middle Ages, today Toulouse pushes the frontiers of knowledge as a university town and the prosperous capital of the French aerospace industry.

TRANSPORTATION AND PRACTICAL INFORMATION. Trains leave **Gare Matabiau,** 64, bd. Pierre Sémard, for: Bordeaux (2-3hr., 14 per day, 169F/€25.80); Lyon (6½hr., 3-4 per day, 310F/€47.30); Marseilles (4½hr., 8 per day, 246F/€37.55); Paris (8-9hr., 4 per day, 450F/€68.65). To get from the station to the **tourist office,** r. Lafayette, in sq. Charles de Gaulle, turn left along the canal, turn right on allée Jean Jaurès, bear right around pl. Wilson, turn right on r. Lafayette, and it's in a park near r. d'Alsace-Lorraine. (☎05 61 11 02 22; fax 05 61 22 03 63; www.mairie-toulouse.fr. Open May-Sept. M-Sa 9am-7pm, Su 10am-1pm and 2-6:30pm; Oct.-Apr. M-F 9am-6pm, Sa 9am-12:30pm and 2-6pm, Su 10am-12:30pm and 2-5pm.) Surf the **Internet** at **Espace Wilson Multimedia,** 7, allées du Président Roosevelt, at pl. Wilson. (20F/€3.05 per hr. Open M-F 10am-7pm, Sa 10am-6pm.) **Postal code:** 31000.

ACCOMMODATIONS AND FOOD. Antoine de St-Exupéry stayed in room #32 at the **Hôtel du Grand Balcon,** 8, r. Romiguières, the official hotel of the French airborne postal service. (☎05 61 21 48 08; fax 05 61 21 59 98. Breakfast 25F/€3.85. Singles and doubles 180F/€27.45, with bath 230-240F/€35.10-36.60; triples 270F/€41.20; quads without bath 210F/€32.05.) **Hôtel Anatole France,** 46, pl. Anatole France, is in a calm *place* near the student quarter. (☎05 61 23 19 96; fax 05 61 21 47 66. Singles and doubles 125F/€19.10, with bath 145-190F/€22.15-29.) Take bus #64 (dir. Colomiers) and ask for St-Martin-du-Touch to **camp** at **La Bouriette,** 201, chemin de Tournefeuille. (☎05 61 49 64 46. 25F/€3.85 per person, 18-26F/€2.75-4 per site.) **Markets** line **place des Carmes, place Victor Hugo,** and **boulevard de Strasbourg** (open Tu-Su 6am-1pm). Cheap eateries line **rue du Taur** and **place Wilson.**

SIGHTS AND ENTERTAINMENT. The brick palace next door to the tourist office is the city's most prominent monument, the **Capitole.** (Open M-F 8:30am-noon and 1:30-7pm, Sa-Su 10am-noon and 2-6pm. Free.) Just up r. du Taur from pl. du Capitole is the **Eglise Notre-Dame-du-Taur,** originally named St-Sernin-du-Taur after the priest Saturninus, who died in AD 250 after being tied to the tail of a wild bull by pagans. (Open daily July-Sept. 9am-6:30pm; Oct.-June 8am-noon and 2-6pm.) Continuing on r. du Taur leads to the **Basilique St-Sernin,** the longest Romanesque structure in the world; its **crypt** houses ecclesiastical relics gathered from Charlemagne's time. (Church open July-Sept. M-Sa 9am-6:30pm, Su 9am-7:30pm; Oct.-June reduced hours. Free. Crypt open July-Sept. M-Sa 10am-6pm, Su 12:30-6pm; Oct.-June M-Sa reduced hours. 10F/€1.55.) Backtrack to the pl. du Capitole, take a right on r. Romiguières, and turn left on r. Lakanal to get to the 13th-century **Les Jacobins**, built in the Southern Gothic style. The ashes of Saint Thomas Aquinas take center stage in elevated under lit tomb. (Open daily 9am-7pm. Cloister 14F/€2.75.) Retracing your steps back r. de Metz, takes you to the restored **Hôtel d'Assézat**, at pl. d'Assézat on r. de Metz, which houses the **Fondation Bemberg**, with an impressive collection of Bonnards, Dufys, Pisarros, and Gauguins. (Open Tu and F-Su 10am-6pm, Th 10am-9pm. 20F/€3.05.) Toulouse has something to please almost any nocturnal whim, although nightlife is liveliest when students are in town. Numerous cafes flank **place St-Georges** and **place du Capitole**, and late-night bars line **rues St-Rome** and **des Filatiers**. The best dancing is at **Bodega-Bodega**, 1, r. Gabriel Péri, just off bd. Lazare Carnot. (Open Sa 7pm-6am, Su-Fri 7pm-2am.)

CARCASSONNE

Round towers capped by red tile roofs guard the entrance to the fairy-tale city of Carcassonne (pop. 45,000), with ramparts that now echo with the exclamations of tourist hordes instead of the clash of knights' armor. Constructed as a palace in the 12th century, the **Château Comtal**, 1, r. Viollet-le-Duc, was transformed into a citadel following submission to royal control in 1226. (Open daily June-Sept. 9am-7:30pm; Apr.-May and Oct. 9am-7pm; Nov.-Mar. 9:30am-5pm. 36F/€5.50, ages 18-25 23F/€3.55.) In the lower town, **Cathédrale St-Michel**, r. Voltaire, has 14th-century fortifications. (Open M-Sa 7am-noon and 2-7pm, Su 9:30am-noon.) Although nightlife is limited, several bars and cafes along **rue Omer Sarraut** and **place Verdun** offer some excitement. For two weeks in early August, Carcassonne returns to the Middle Ages for the **Spectacles Médiévaux** (☎ 04 68 71 35 35; www.terredhistoire.com).

Trains (☎ 04 68 71 79 14) arrive behind Jardin St-Chenier from: Lyon (5½hr., 2 per day, 271F/€41.35); Marseilles (3hr., every 2hr., 205F/€31.30); Nîmes (2½hr., 12 per day, 142F/€21.70; and Toulouse (50min., 24 per day, 75F/€11.45). Shops, hotels, and the train station are located in the **bastide St-Louis**, once called the *basse ville*. Walk 30min. uphill or catch the *navette* in front of the station (every 30min.) to reach the *cité*. To get from the train station to the **tourist office**, 15, bd. Camille Pelletan, in pl. Gambetta, walk down av. de Maréchal Joffre, which becomes r. Clemenceau, and after pl. Carnot, turn left on r. Verdun and walk into pl. Gambetta. (☎ 04 68 10 24 30; fax 04 68 10 24 38. Open daily July-Aug. 9am-7pm; Sept.-June 9am-12:15pm and 1:45-6:30pm.) The ▨**Auberge de Jeunesse (HI)**, r. de Vicomte Trencavel, is in the middle of the *cité*. (☎ 04 68 25 23 16; fax 04 68 71 14 84. Breakfast included. Sheets 17F/€2.60. Reception 24hr. HI members only. Dorms 76F/€11.60.) **Hôtel Le Cathare**, 53, r. Jean Bringer, has cozy, bright rooms. (☎ 04 68 25 65 92; fax 04 68 47 15 02. Breakfast 27F/€4.15. Singles and doubles 115F/€17.55, with shower 160-170F/€24.40-25.95; triples 200F/€30.50. MC/V.) Carcassonne's speciality is *cassoulet* (a stew of white beans, herbs, and meat). Inexpensive restaurants line **rue du Plo** and **boulevard Omer Sarraut** in the lower city; try a dessert at one of the many outdoor *crêperies* in **place Marcou**. **Postal code:** 11000 (11012 for *Poste Restante*).

PROVENCE

Since Roman times, writers and artists have rhapsodized about Provence's fragrant and varied landscape—from majestic mountains to the east to flat marshlands in the Camargue. Marseilles is the second most populous city in France and links Provence to the flash of the Riviera. With their Roman remnants and cobblestone grace, Orange and Arles meet the Rhône as it flows to the Mediterranean. Briefly home to the medieval papacy, Avignon still holds the formidable Palais des Papes. Provence is known for its festivals; in the summer, even the smallest hamlets whirl with music, dance, theater, and antique markets.

NÎMES

Southern France flocks to Nîmes (pop. 135,000) for the *férias*, celebrations featuring bullfights, flamenco dancing, and all manner of hot-blooded fanfare. Yet Nîmes' star power comes from its incredible Roman structures. The magnificent Roman amphitheater **Les Arènes**, built in the first century AD, is the city's pride and joy. The best way to experience it is to attend a bullfight or concert. (Open daily 9am-6:30pm; in winter 9am-5:30pm. 28F/€4.30, students 20F/€3.05.) The exquisitely sculpted **Maison Carré** is a rectangular temple built in dedication to the grandson and adopted son of Augustus. (Open daily 9am-noon and 2:30-7pm; in winter 9am-12:30pm and 2-6pm. Free.) Walk from the Maison down pl. Foch to the left along the canals to relax by the beautiful fountains of the **Jardins de la Fontaine,** which also house the Roman ruins of the **Temple de Diane** and the **Tour Magne.** (Gardens and temple open daily Apr. to mid-Sept. 7:30am-10pm; mid-Sept. to Oct. 7:30am-6:30pm; Nov.-Mar. 8am-7pm. Free. *Tour* open daily July-Aug. 9am-7pm; Sept.-June 9am-5pm. 15F/€2.30, students 12F/€1.85.) Thirty minutes from Nîmes by bus is the amazing Roman **Pont du Gard,** The aqueduct carried water 50km from the Eure springs near Uzès to Nîmes. **STDG buses** run to the Pont du Gard from Avignon (45min., 7 per day, 33F/€5.05) and Nîmes (30min., 2-5 per day, 31F/€4.75).

Trains chug from bd. Talabot to: Arles (30min., 10 per day, 48F/€7.35); Marseilles (1¼hr., 6 per day, 98F/€14.95); and Toulouse (3hr., 10 per day, 187F/€28.55). **Buses** (☎04 66 29 52 00) leave r. Ste-Félicité, behind the train station for Avignon (1½hr., 2-8 per day, 44F/€6.75). To get from the stations to the **tourist office,** 6, r. Auguste, head straight on bd. Victor Hugo for five blocks and it's opposite Maison Carré. (☎04 66 67 29 11; fax 04 66 21 81 04. Open July-Aug. M-F 8am-8pm, Sa 9am-7pm, Su 10am-6pm; Sept.-May M-F 8am-7pm, Sa 9am-7pm, Su 10am-6pm.) The relaxed **Auberge de Jeunesse (HI),** 257, chemin de l'Auberge de la Jeunesse, off chemin de la Cigale 4½km from quai de la Fontaine, is far but newly renovated. Take bus #2 (dir. Alès or Villeverte) to Stade, Route d'Alès and follow the signs uphill; after the buses stop running, call for pick-up. (☎04 66 68 03 20; fax 04 66 68 03 21. Breakfast €3.20. 4- to 6-bed dorms 53F/€8.65.) **Camp** at **Domaine de la Bastide,** on rte. de Générac. (☎/fax 04 66 38 09 21. 48F/€7.35 per person, 76F/€11.60 per 2 people. Caravan with electricity 68F/€10.40 per person, 96F/€14.65.) Stock up at **Marché U supermarket,** 19, r. d'Alès, downhill from the hostel. (Open M-Sa 8am-12:45pm and 3:30-8pm.) **Postal codes:** 30000 and 30900.

AVIGNON

The city of Avignon (pop. 100,000) has danced with cultural and artistic brilliance ever since it temporarily snatched the papacy away from Rome some 700 years ago. Film festivals, street musicians, and Europe's most prestigious theatrical gathering keep this university town shining. The massive 14th-century **Palais des Papes** is the largest Gothic palace in Europe, and hosts an annual art exhibition from May through September. (Open daily July-Sept. 9am-8pm; Apr.-June and Oct. 9am-7pm; Nov. to mid-Mar. 9:30am-5:45pm; mid-Mar. to late Mar. 9:30am-6:30pm. 46F/€7.05.) At the **Festival d'Avignon,** a theater festival also known as the **IN,** from early July to early Aug., Gregorian chanters rub shoulders with *Odyssey*-readers and African dancers. (☎04 90 14 14 14. Tickets free-200F/€30.50. Reservations accepted from mid-June. Tickets also available 45min. before shows; 50% student discount.)

Trains run from porte de la République to Marseilles (1¼hr. 6 per day, 94F/€14.35) and Nîmes (30min., 14 per day, 47F/€7.20). From the train station, walk through porte de la République onto cours Jean Jaurès to reach the **tourist office,** 41, cours Jean Jaurès. (☎04 32 74 32 74; fax 04 90 82 95 03. Open July M-Sa 10am-8pm, Su 10am-5pm; Apr.-June and Aug.-Sept. M-Sa 9am-6pm; Oct.-Mar. M-F 9am-6pm, Sa 9am-1pm and 2-5pm, Su 10am-noon.) Access the **Internet** at **Cyberdrome,** 68, r. Guillaume Puy. (30F/€4.60 per hr. Open daily 8am-1am.) To reach the **Foyer Bagatelle,** Ile de la Barthelasse, from the station, turn left and follow the city wall, cross pont Daladier, the second bridge, and Bagatelle is on the right (10min.). Or, take bus #10 or #11 to La Barthelasse. (☎04 90 86 30 39 or 04 90 85 78 45; fax 04 90 27 16 23.

Reception daily 11am-10pm. Reserve ahead. Dorms 65F/€9.95; doubles 140F/€21.35. **Camping** reception 8am-10pm. 44F/€6.75 per person and tent, 71F/€10.85 per 2 people and tent. MC/V.) The central **Innova Hôtel**, 100, r. Joseph Vernet, has spare but clean rooms. (☎ 04 90 82 54 10; fax 04 90 82 52 39. Singles 150F/€22.90; doubles 230F/€35.10, with bath 250F/€38.15. MC/V.) A **Petit Casino** supermarket is at 3, r. Corps Saints. (Open M-Sa 8am-noon and 2:30-6:30pm.) **Postal code:** 84000.

ARLES

The beauty and ancient history of Arles (pop. 35,000) has made it a Provence favorite. The streets of Arles all seem to lead to and from the great Roman arena, **Les Arènes**, which is still used for bullfights. (20F/€3.05, students 15F/€2.30.) The city's Roman past comes back to life in the excellent **Musée d'Arles Antique**, on av. de la 1er D.F.L. (Open daily Mar.-Oct. 9am-7pm; Nov.-Feb. 9am-5pm. 35F/€5.35, students 25F/€3.85, children 5F/€0.80.) The **Fondation Van Gogh**, 26, Rond-Point des Arènes, doesn't have any van Goghs, but houses tributes to the master by artists, poets, and composers. (Open daily Apr. to mid-Oct. 10am-7pm; mid-Oct. to Mar. Tu-Su 9:30am-noon and 2-5:30pm. 30F/€4.60, students and children 20F/€3.05.) The contemporary **Musée Réattu**, r. du Grand Prieuré, houses 57 drawings with which Picasso honored Arles in 1971. (Open daily Apr.-Sept. 10am-noon and 2-6:30pm; Oct.-Mar. reduced hours. 30F/€4.60, students 25F/€3.85.) The city celebrates **Fête d'Arles** in costume the last weekend in June and the first in July.

Trains leave av. P. Talabot for: Avignon (30min., 15-19 per day, 36F/€5.50); Marseilles (1hr., 8 per day, 76F/€11.60); Montpellier (1hr., 6-7 per day, 76F/€11.60); and Nîmes (30min., 7-15 per day, 42F/€6.40). **Buses** (☎ 04 90 49 38 01) depart from next to the station for Avignon (45min., M-Sa 5 per day, 46F/€7.05) and Nîmes (50min., M-Sa 5 per day, 34F/€5.20). To get to the **tourist office**, esplanade Charles de Gaulle, on bd. des Lices, turn left from the station, walk to pl. Lamartine, turn left and follow bd. Emile Courbes to the big intersection, and then turn right on bd. des Lices. (☎ 04 90 18 41 20; fax 04 90 18 41 29. Open daily Apr.-Sept. 9am-6:45pm; Oct.-Mar. M-Sa 9am-5:45pm, Su 10am-2:30pm.) To get from the tourist office to the **Auberge de Jeunesse (HI)**, on av. Maréchal Foch, cross bd. des Lices, walk down av. des Alyscamps, and follow the signs. (☎ 04 90 96 18 25; fax 04 90 96 31 26. Breakfast included. Reception 7-10am and 5-11pm. Lockout 10am-5pm. Curfew midnight; in winter 11pm. Reserve ahead Apr.-June. Bunks 82F/€12.50, 70F/€11 subsequent nights.) The friendly **Hôtel Mirador**, 3, r. Voltaire, is centrally located. (☎ 04 90 96 28 05; fax 04 90 96 59 89. Breakfast 28F/€4.30. Reception 7am-10pm. Singles and doubles 190F/€29, with bath 245F/€37.35. AmEx/MC/V.) Take the Starlette bus to Clemencau and then take bus #2 (dir. Pont de Crau) to Hermite for **Camping-City**, 67, rte. de Crau. (☎ 04 90 93 08 86. Reception 8am-8pm. Open Apr.-Sept. 25F/€3.85 per person, 25F/€3.85 per site, 18F/€2.75 per car.) **Monoprix supermarket** is on pl. Lamartine near the station. (Open M-Th and Sa 8:30am-7:30pm, F 8:30am-8pm.) Try the hip cafes in **place du Forum** or **place Voltaire**. **Postal code:** 13200.

◪ DAYTRIP FROM ARLES: THE CAMARGUE. Between Arles and the Mediterranean coast stretches the Camargue. Pink flamingos, black bulls, and the famous white Camargue horses roam freely across this flat expanse of protected wild marshland. Stop at the **Centre d'Information de Ginès**, along D570, for more information. (☎ 04 90 97 86 32. Open daily Apr.-Sept. 10am-5:30pm; Oct.-Mar. Sa-Th 9:30am-5pm.) Next door, the **Parc Ornithologique de Pont de Gau** offers views of birds and grazing bulls. (Open daily Apr.-Sept. 9am-dusk; Oct.-Mar. 10am-dusk. 36F/€5.50, children 18F/€2.75.) The best way to see the Camargue is on horseback; call the **Association Camarguaise de Tourisme Equestre** (☎ 04 90 97 86 32) for more information. Other options include jeep safaris (☎ 04 66 70 09 65; 2hr. trips 200F/€30.50, 4hr. trips 220F/€33.55) and boat trips (☎ 04 90 97 84 72; 1½hr., 3-4 per day 60F/€9.15). Biking is another way to see the area. Informative trail maps are available from the Stes-Maries-de-la-Mer **tourist office**, 5, av. Van Gogh. (☎ 04 90 97 82 55. Open daily July-Aug. 9am-8pm; Apr.-June reduced hours.) **Buses** run from Arles to **Stes-Maries-de-la-Mer** (1hr., 4-6 per day, 39F/€5.95), the Camargue's largest town.

AIX-EN-PROVENCE

The city of Paul Cézanne, Victor Vasarely, and Émile Zola, the golden façades and dusty cafes of Aix (pop. 150,000) all have had a brush with greatness. Today a large student population keeps the city on the cultural cutting edge. The **Chemin de Cézanne**, at 9, av. Paul Cézanne, features a self-guided walking tour devoted to the artist, including a visit to his studio. (Open daily July-Aug. 10am-6:30pm; Apr.-May and Sept. 10am-noon and 2:30-6pm; Oct.-Mar. 10am-noon and 2-5pm. 35F/€5.35; in winter 25F/€3.85; students 10F/€1.55.) The **Fondation Vasarely**, on av. Marcel-Pagnol, Jas de Bouffan, designed by artist Victor Vasarely, is a must-see for modern art fans. (Open daily July-Sept. 10am-7pm; Oct.-May 10am-1pm and 2-6pm. 40F/€6.10, students 25F/€3.85.) **Cathédrale St-Sauveur**, on r. Gaston de Saporta, is a dramatic mix of Romanesque, Gothic, and Baroque carvings and reliefs. (Open daily 8am-noon and 2-6pm.) Aix's **International Music Festival**, June to July, features operas and concerts. (☎04 42 17 34 34; www.aix-en-provence.com/festartlyrique. Tickets 100-350F/€15.25-53.40.) Aix also hosts a two-week **Jazz Festival** at the beginning of July (tickets 30-120F/€4.60-18.30) followed by a two-week **Dance Festival** (☎04 42 23 41 24; tickets 90-250F/€13.75-38.15, students 50-160F/€3.85-24.40). The **Office des Fêtes et de la Culture**, 1, pl. John Rewald, on Espace Forbin, has festival information. (☎04 42 96 27 79; fax 04 42 21 24 14.) Partying is a year-round pastime in Aix. Bars line the **Forum des Cardeurs**, behind the Hôtel de Ville. House and club music prevail at the underground **Le Richelm**, 24, r. de la Verrerie. (Cover Tu-Th 60F/€9.15, includes 1 drink, women free; F 80F/€12.20; Sa 100F/€15.25. Open Tu-Sa 11:30pm-dawn.) Techno, R&B, house, and bodies surge at **Le Mistral**, 3, r. F. Mistral. (Tu ladies night, women free with 1 drink, men cover 100F/€15.25; W-F 70F/€10.70; Sa 100F/€15.25. No casual dress. Open Tu-Sa 11:30pm-5am.)

 Trains, at the end of av. Victor Hugo, run almost exclusively to Marseilles (35min., 21 per day, 38F/€5.80). **Buses**, av. de l'Europe (☎04 42 91 26 80), run to Avignon (2hr., M-Sa 5 per day, 86F/€13.15) and Marseilles (30min., every 10min., 26F/€4). From the train station, follow av. Victor Hugo, bearing left at the fork, until it feeds into La Rotonde. On the left is the **tourist office**, 2, pl. du Général de Gaulle, which books rooms for free and offers the free guides *Le Mois à Aix* and *Bienvenue*. (☎04 42 16 11 61; fax 04 42 16 11 62. Open daily July-Aug. 8:30am-10pm; Sept.-June M-Sa 8:30am-10pm, Su 10am-6pm.) You can surf the **Internet** at **Virtu@us**, 40, r. Cordeliers. (15F/€2.30 per 30min., 25F/€3.85 per hr. Open M-Sa 10am-1am, Su 2pm-1am.) To get to the sparse **Auberge de Jeunesse (HI)**, 3, av. Marcel Pagnol, in quartier du Jas de Bouffan, follow av. de Belges from La Rotonde, turn right on av. de l'Europe, bear left at the first roundabout after the overpass, climb the hill, and it's on the left (35min.). Or, take bus #4 (dir. La Mayanelle; every 15-30min. until 9:45pm, 7F/€1.10) from La Rotonde to Vasarely. (☎04 42 20 15 99; fax 04 42 59 36 12. Breakfast included. Reception closed noon-5pm and after 11pm. Strict curfew midnight. 82F/€12.50 per person first night, 69F/€10.55 person afterward.) **Hôtel des Arts**, 69, bd. Carnot, has compact, modern rooms. (☎04 42 38 11 77; fax 04 42 26 77 31. Breakfast 28F/€4.30. Singles and doubles 149-205F/€22.75-31.25. MC/V.) To **camp** at **Arc-en-Ciel**, on rte. de Nice, take bus #3 from La Rotonde to Trois Sautets and Val St-André. (☎04 42 26 14 28. 36F/€5.50 per person, 32F/€4.90 per tent.) Explore **rue Verrerie** and the roads north of **cours Mirabeau** for restaurants. Stock up at **Monoprix**, 25, cours Mirabeau. (Open M-Sa 8:30am-8pm.) **Postal code:** 13100.

MARSEILLES (MARSEILLE)

France's third-largest city, Marseilles (pop. 900,000) is like the *bouillabaisse* soup for which it is famous: steaming hot and pungently spiced, with a little bit of everything mixed in. Even without the glamour of the Riviera or the pastoral charm of Provence, the city that Alexandre Dumas called "the meeting place of the entire world" remains strangely alluring, a jumble of color and commotion.

 ☰ TRANSPORTATION. Trains leave Gare St-Charles, pl. Victor Hugo, for: Lyon (3½hr., 3 per day, 213F/€32.50); Nice (2¾hr., 13 per day, 152F/€23.20); and Paris

(4¾hr., 17 TGVs per day, 406-496F/€61.90-75.62). **Buses** leave Gare des Autocars, pl. Victor Hugo (☎04 91 08 16 40) for: Aix-en-Provence (every 20min., 26F/€4); Arles (2-3hr., 5 per day, 88F/€13.45); Avignon (2hr., 4 per day, 92F/€14.05); Cannes (2¼-3hr., 4 per day, 100F/€15.25); and Nice (2¾hr., 4 per day, 140F/€21.35). **SNCM**, 61, bd. des Dames (☎08 91 70 18 01), runs **ferries** to Corsica (640-720F/€97.60-109.80 return, 12% student discount) and Sardinia (750-850F/€11.335-129.60). **RTM**, 6-8, r. des Fabres (☎04 91 91 92 10) sells **bus** and **metro** tickets at bus and metro stations (day pass 25F/€3.85; 7-14 day **Carte Liberté** 50-100F/€7.65-15.25). The **metro** runs M-Th 5am-9pm and F-Su 5am-12:30am.

🛈 PRACTICAL INFORMATION. La Canebière separates the city into north and south, funneling into the *vieux port* to the west and becoming bland urban sprawl to the east. North of the *vieux port* and west of bd. République, working-class residents of varied ethnicities pack the hilltop neighborhood of **Le Panier,** where the original Greek city stood. East of Le Panier, between cours Belsunce and bd. Athènes, the dilapidated buildings of the **Belsunce Quarter** house the city's Arab and African communities; this area is not safe at night. East of the *vieux port*, **rues de Rome, St-Ferreol,** and **Paradis** contain large stores and fashion boutiques. Past r. de Rome near La Canebière, narrow streets teem with colorful African markets. Farther southeast, **cours Julien** has distinct counterculture feel. The **tourist office,** 4, La Canebière, offers free maps and accommodation services. (☎04 91 13 89 00; fax 04 91 13 89 20. Open July-Aug. M-Sa 9am-8pm, Su 10am-6pm; Oct.-June M-Sa 9am-7pm, Su and holidays 10am-5pm.) An annex is at the train station. (☎04 91 50 59 18. Open daily 10am-6pm; closed weekends 3-4pm.) Access the **Internet** at **InfoCafe,** 1, quai Rive Neuve. (25F/€3.85 per hr. Open M-Sa 9am-10pm, Su 2:30-7:30pm.) Also try **Bug's Cafe,** 80, cours Julien. (30F/€4.60 per hr. Open M-Sa 10am-11pm, Su 2-7pm.)

🛏🍴 ACCOMMODATIONS AND FOOD. To reach the **Auberge de Jeunesse Bonneveine (HI),** impasse Bonfils, off av. J. Vidal, from the station, take metro line #2 to Rond-Point du Prado, and transfer to bus #44 to pl. Bonnefon. From there, walk back toward the traffic circle and turn left at J. Vidal. After #47, turn onto impasse Bonfils and it's on the left. Swimming and sunbathing are just 200m away. (☎04 91 17 63 30; fax 04 91 73 97 23. Breakfast included. 6-night max. stay. Reception daily 7am-1am. Curfew 1am. Reserve ahead. HI members only. Closed Dec. 22-Feb. Apr.-Aug. dorms 72-83F/€11-12.65; doubles 93-103F/€14.20-15.70; Sept.-Dec. and Feb.-Mar. dorms 67-78F/€10.25-11.90; doubles 93-98F/€14.20-14.95. MC/V.) The comfortable **Hôtel Beaulieu Glaris,** 1, pl. des Marseillaises, is near the train station. (☎04 91 90 70 59; fax 04 91 56 14 04. Breakfast 25F/€3.85. Reception 7am-midnight. Singles 130-160F/€24.40; doubles 200-250F/€30.50-38.15; triples 250-320F/€38.15-48.80. MC/V.) The safe and clean **Hôtel Le Provençal,** 32, r. Paradis, is two minutes from the *vieux port.* (☎04 91 33 11 15; fax 04 91 33 47 08. Breakfast 25F/€3.85. Reception 24hr. Singles 145F/€22.10; doubles 165F/€25.15, with shower 195F/€29.75; triples 220F/€33.55, with shower 250F/€38.15. AmEx/MC/V.) For the city's famed seafood and North African fare, explore the *vieux port,* especially **place Thiers** and **cours d'Estienne d'Orves,** where you can eat for as little as 60F/€9.15. For cheaper fare, head up to **cours Julien,** northeast of the harbor. **Hippopotamus,** 33, quai des Belges, serves enormous portions of meats and other savory fare. (*Menus* from 76F/€11.60. Open daily 8am-midnight.) Pick up groceries at **Monoprix,** on La Canebière, across from the AmEx office. (Open M-Sa 8:30am-8pm.) **Postal code:** 13001.

◑♫ SIGHTS AND ENTERTAINMENT. To truly experience Marseilles, wander through its diverse collection of neighborhoods. From the tourist office, walk up r. Breteuil, turn left on r. Grignon, and turn right again on r. Fort du Sanctuaire to reach the majestic 19th-century **Basilique de Notre-Dame de la Garde.** The battle-scarred church offers a beautiful view of the city and holds a golden statue of the Madonna known as "the good mother." (Open daily 7am-8pm; off-season 7am-7pm. Free.) The imposing **Abbaye St-Victor,** on r. Sainte, at the end of quai de Rive Neuve, holds eerie catacombs as well as pagan and Christian relics. (Open daily 8:30am-

6:30pm. Crypts 10F/€1.55.) **Musée Cantini**, 19, r. Grignan, exhibits memorable art from Fauvism to the present day. (Open Tu-Su 11am-6pm. 16F/€4.45, students 8F/€1.25, children and seniors free.) Bus #83 (dir. Rond Pont du Prado) takes you from the *vieux port* to Marseilles's **beaches;** get off just after the statue of David (25min.). Nightlife centers in **cours Julien** and **place Thiers. Trolleybus,** 24, quai de Rive Neuve, is a mega-club with a discotheque built around two boule-courts. (Cover Sa 60F/€9.15, includes 1 drink. Open W-Sa 11pm-7am; in winter Th-Sa 11pm-7am.)

FRENCH RIVIERA (CÔTE D'AZUR)

Between Marseilles and the Italian border, the sun-drenched beaches and warm waters of the Mediterranean form the backdrop for this fabled playground of the rich and famous—F. Scott Fitzgerald, Cole Porter, Picasso, Renoir, and Matisse are among those who flocked to the coast in its heyday. Despite the Riviera's glorious past, today this choice stretch of sun and sand is a curious combination of high-handed millionaires and low-budget tourists. High society steps out yearly for the Cannes Film Festival and the Monte-Carlo Grand Prix, both in May. Less exclusive are Nice's raucous *Carnaval* in February and various summer jazz festivals.

> ❗ Every woman who has traveled on the Riviera has a story to tell about men in the big beach towns. Unsolicited pick-up techniques range from subtle invitations to more, uh, bare displays of interest. Brush them off with a biting *"laissez-moi tranquille!"* ("leave me alone") or stony indifference, but don't be shy about enlisting the help of passersby or the police to fend off Mediterranean Don Juans.

ST-TROPEZ

Nowhere does the glitz and glamour of the Riviera shine more than in St-Tropez. The "Jewel of the Riviera" unfailingly attracts Hollywood stars and curious backpackers with its exclusive clubs and nude beaches. The free **shuttle** *(navette municipale)* leaves pl. des Lices four times a day to **Les Salins,** a secluded sunspot, and **plage Tahiti** (Capon-Pinet stop), the first of the famous **plages des Pampelonne.** Take a break from the sun at **La Musée de l'Annonciade,** pl. Grammont, with its Fauvist and neo-Impressionist paintings. (Open June-Sept. W-M 10am-noon and 3-7pm; Oct.-May 10am-noon and 2-6pm. Closed Nov. 30F/€4.60, students 15F/€2.30.)

Les Bateaux de St-Raphaël **ferries** (☎ 04 94 95 17 46), at the old port, sail to St-Tropez from St-Raphaël (1hr.; 2-5 per day; 60F/€9.15, return 110F/€16.80). Sodetrav **buses** (☎ 04 94 97 88 51) leave av. Général Leclerc for St-Raphaël (2hr., 8-14 per day, 55F/€8.40.) The **tourist office,** on quai Jean Jaurès, has schedules of the shuttle transport and a *Manifestations* guide that lists local events. (☎ 04 94 97 45 21; fax 04 94 97 82 66; www.saint-tropez.st. Open daily July-Aug. 9:30am-1:30pm and 3:30-10pm; May-June and Sept. 9:30am-1pm and 2-7pm; Oct.-Apr. 9am-noon and 2-6pm.) Budget hotels do not exist in St-Tropez, and the closest youth hostel is in Fréjus (see below). **Camping** is the cheapest option—a ferry to **Les Prairies de la Mer,** Port Grimaud, (30F/€4.60, return 58F/€8.85) leaves for St-Tropez every hour. (☎ 04 94 79 09 09; prairies@campazur.com. Open Apr.-Oct. 82F/€12.50 per person and tent; 84F/€12.80 per couple; 115F/€17.55 per car.) The **vieux port** and the streets behind the waterfront are lined with charmingly expensive restaurants, so create your own meal at **Prisunic supermarket,** 7, av. du Général Leclerc. (Open M-Sa 9am-8pm, Su 9am-1pm.) The restaurant-bar **Bodega de Papagayo,** on the old port, and nightclub **Le Papagayo** are magnets for tanned youth. (Cover 130F/€19.85. Open daily June-Aug. 11:30pm-5am; Sept.-May F-Su 11:30pm-5am.)

ST-RAPHAËL AND FRÉJUS

The twin cities of St-Raphaël and Fréjus provide an excellent base for exploring the Riviera with cheap accommodations, convenient transport, and proximity to the sea. In **St-Raphaël,** the **boardwalk** turns into a carnival and golden **beaches** stretch along the coast. The first weekend in July brings the **Compétition Internationale de Jazz New Orleans** (☎04 98 11 89 00). In Fréjus, the **Roman Amphitheater,** on r. Henri Vadon, holds rock concerts and bullfights. (Open M and W-Sa Apr.-Oct. 10am-1pm and 2:30-6:30pm; Nov.-Mar. M and W-F 10am-noon and 1:30-5:30pm, Sa 9:30am-12:30pm and 1:30-5:30pm. Bullfights 140-400F/€21.35-61.) The **Musée Archeologique Municipal,** on pl. Calvini, houses Fréjus' city emblem, a stunning double-headed sculpture. (Open Apr.-Oct. M and W-Sa 10am-1pm and 2:30-6:30pm; Nov.-Mar. 10am-noon and 1:30-5:30pm. Free.)

St-Raphaël sends **trains** every 30 minutes to Cannes (25min., 34F/€5.20) and Nice (1hr., 57F/€8.70). **Buses** leave from behind the train station in St-Raphaël for Cannes (1¼hr., 8 per day, 34.50F/€5.30) and Nice (1¼hr., 1 per day, 55F/€8.40). The **tourist office,** on r. Waldeck Rousseau, is opposite the train station. (☎04 94 19 52 52; fax 04 94 83 85 40; www.saint-raphael.com. Open daily July-Aug. 9am-8pm; Sept.-June M-Sa 9am-12:30pm and 2-6:30pm.) Take bus #6 from St-Raphaël to pl. Paul Vernet to get to the **tourist office** in Fréjus, 325, r. Jean Jaurès. (☎04 94 19 52 52; fax 04 94 83 85 40; www.ville-frejus.fr. Open daily 9am-7pm; Sept.-June M-Sa 9am-noon and 2-6pm.) Take av. du 15ème Corps d'Armée from the tourist office and turn left on chemin de Councillier after the next roundabout to reach the **Auberge de Jeunesse de St-Raphaël-Fréjus (HI),** chemin du Counillier. (☎04 94 52 93 93 or 04 94 53 18 75; fax 04 94 53 25 86. Breakfast included. Sheets 18F/€2.75. Reception 8-10am and 6-8pm. Closed Dec.-Jan. Dorms 75F/€11.45. **Camping** 40F/€6.10 per person with tent.) To reach the rooms at **Le Touring,** in St-Raphaël at 1, quai Albert 1er, take your 3rd right after the train station. (☎04 94 95 01 72; fax 04 94 95 86 09. Closed mid-Nov. to mid-Dec. Singles and doubles 210F/€32.05, with bath 260-350F/€39.65-53.40; triples 450F/€68.65. AmEx/MC/V.) From St-Raphaël, a shuttle bus (8.50F/€1.30) leaves quai #7 of the bus station for the hostel. St-Raphaël's **Monoprix supermarket** is on 14, bd. de Félix Martin, off av. Alphonse Karr near the train station. (Open M-Sa 8:30am-8pm.) **Postal codes:** St-Raphaël 83700; Fréjus 83600.

CANNES

The name of Cannes (pop. 78,000) conjures up classic Riviera images of gorgeous film stars reclining by the poolside. Today, the red carpets roll out every May for the renowned **Festival International du Film,** which imports Hollywood's *crème de la crème.* None of the festival's 350 screenings are open to the public, but the sidewalk show is free. Yet for the other 11 months in the year, Cannes is the most accessible Riviera town—neither as rich as Monte Carlo nor as exclusive as St-Tropez, anyone can sport the famous Cannes style. Stroll along **rue d'Antibes** and **boulevard de la Croisette** for the best window-shopping on the Riviera. **L'Eglise de la Castre** and its courtyard provide an excellent view of the city, and the **Musée de la Castre** inside displays weapons, masks, and instruments from Africa. (Open July-Sept. W-M 10am-12:15pm and 3-7pm; Oct.-Mar. 10am-noon and 2-5pm; Apr.-June 10am-noon and 2-6pm. 10F/€1.55, students free.) The most accessible of Cannes's three casinos is **Le Casino Croisette,** 1, jetée Albert Eduoard, next to the Palais des Festivals, with slots, blackjack, and roulette. (Gambling daily 7:30pm-4am; open for slots at 10am. No shorts, jeans, or t-shirts. 18+.) See live blues and Irish folk music at **Morrison's,** 10, r. Teisseire, a rowdy Irish pub. (Beer from 18F/€2.75. Music starts at 10pm. Open 5pm-2:30am.) **Le Loft,** 13, r. du Dr. Monod, has no cover and a lively dance floor, and the Asian-French restaurant **Tantra** downstairs morphs into a hot club on weekends. (No cover. Open daily 10pm-2:30am.)

Coastal **trains** run from 1, r. Jean-Jaurès to: Antibes (15min., 14F/€2.15); Monaco (1hr., 46F/€7.05); Nice (35min., 32F/€4.90); and St-Raphaël (25min., 34F/€5.20). Hourly trains run to Marseilles (2hr., 6:30am-11:05pm, 100F/€15.25). **TGV** trains go to Paris via Marseilles (450-540F/€68.60-82.35). The **tourist office,** 1, bd. de la Croisette, has maps and guides. (☎04 93 39 24 53. Open daily July-Aug. 9am-8pm; Sept.-June M-F 9am-6:30pm, Sa 9am-6:30pm, Su 10am-6pm.) The town's **centrale de reservation** arranges hotel reservations. (☎04 97 06 53 07. Open daily 9am-7pm.) Access the **Internet** at **Cyber Café Institut Riviera Langue,** 26, r. de Mimont. (35F/€5.35 per hr. Open daily 9am-10pm.) Plan accommodations in advance; for

> **A NOSE FOR BUSINESS** What does it take to make it in the perfume world? A good Nose—at least, that's what the *haute couture* master perfumers are called. Noses train for 15 years before extracting an essence; by the time they're ready to mix a scent, which can take up to two years, the sniffing students have memorized around 2000 smells. With only a handful in the world, Noses are hot commodities and are required by contract to protect their precious snouts. Alcohol, smoking, and eating spicy foods—in France, the ultimate sacrifices—are strictly forbidden.

the film festival, you should book at least a year in advance and expect to pay triple the rate. **Centre International de Séjour de Cannes (HI)**, 35, av. de Vallauris, has 6-bunk dorms in a sunny mansion. To avoid the underground passageway, leave the station and turn left on bd. Jean-Jaurès, left on bd. de la République, and right on av. de Vallauris. (☎04 93 99 26 79; fax 04 93 99 26 79; www.perso.wanadoo.fr/hostelling-cannes. First breakfast free, then 10F/€1.55. Laundry 25F/€3.85. Reception daily 8am-12:30pm and 2:30-10:30pm. Curfew 2am. May-Aug. dorms 80F/€12.20; Sept.-Apr. 70F/€10.70.) As you exit the station, turn right on bd. Carnot, right on av. 11 November, and left onto av. Galliéni to reach **Auberge de Jeunesse—Le Chalit**, 27, av. Maréchal Galliéni. (☎/fax 04 93 99 22 11. Sheets 17F/€2.60. Reception daily June-Sept. 8:30am-1pm and 5-8pm; Oct.-May 9am-noon and 1-8pm. Lockout 10:30am-5pm. 4- to 8-bed dorms 90F/€13.75.) To reach **Hôtel Mimont**, 39, r. de Mimont, turn left on bd. de la République from the station, and turn left on r. de Mimont. Clean, spacious rooms with showers and TV. (☎04 93 39 51 64; fax 04 93 99 65 35. Breakfast 33F/€5.05. Reception daily 8am-11pm. Singles 170-190F/€25.95-29; doubles 230-260F/€35.10-39.65; triples 325F/€49.55. Extra person 65F/€9.95. AmEx/MC/V.) **Camp** at **Parc Bellevue**, 67, av. M. Chevalier in La Bocca. Take the #9 bus to the La Boissière stop (30min.) and walk for 100m; it's on the right. (☎04 93 47 28 97; fax 04 93 48 66 25. 60F/€9.15 for 1 person and tent, 80-90F/€12.20-13.75 for 2 people with tent, 10F/€1.55 per car.) Save money at **Champion supermarket**, 6, r. Meynadier. (Open M-Sa 9am-7:30pm.) Inexpensive restaurants lie near **rue Meynadier. Postal code:** 06400.

ANTIBES-JUAN-LES-PINS

Although joined as one in the city of Antibes-Juan-les-Pins (pop. 70,000), Antibes and Juan-les-Pins are 2km apart and use separate train stations and tourist offices.

ANTIBES. More serene than Nice, **Antibes** is clean and pleasant, with sandy beaches and fascinating museums. Lately, Antibes has been inundated with young, globetrotting "yachtees" looking for lucrative work—a phenomenon that has helped turn the city into an increasingly popular beach town. After lounging in the sun, visitors can retreat to the charming *vieille ville*. The **Musée Picasso**, in the Château Grimaldi on pl. Mariejol, displays works by the master and his contemporaries. (Open June-Sept. Tu-Th and Sa-Su 10am-6pm, F 10am-10pm; Oct.-May daily 10am-noon and 2-6pm. 30F/€4.60, students 15F/€2.30.) **Trains** leave from av. Robert Soleau for: Cannes (15min., every 30min., 14F/€2.15); Marseilles (2½hr., 15 per day, 139F/€21.20); and Nice (40min., every 20min., 26.50F/€4.05). Exit the station, turn right on av. Robert Soleau, and follow the "Maison du Tourisme" signs to the **tourist office,** 11, pl. de Gaulle. (☎04 92 90 53 00. Open July-Aug. M-Sa 8:45am-7:30pm, Su 9:30am-12:30pm; Sept.-June M-F 9am-12:30pm and 2-6:30pm, Sa 9am-noon and 2-6pm.) To get from the train station to the **Crew House**, 1, av. St-Roch, walk down av. de la Liberation until it turns into av. de Verdun, and then turn right onto av. St-Roch. (☎04 92 90 49 39; fax 04 92 90 49 38. Reception 7:30am-9pm. Dorms June-Sept. 125F/€19.05; Oct.-May 100F/€15.25. AmEx/MC/V.) **Postal code:** 06600.

JUAN-LES-PINS. In Juan-les-Pins, Antibes' younger, hipper, and more hedonistic sibling, boutiques remain open until midnight, cafes until 2am, and nightclubs until past dawn. The streets are packed with those seeking the sea, sun, and sex, and nightclubs pulse with promises of decadence. Pickpockets also abound, so never leave belongings out of your sight. **Cafes** are much cheaper than nightclubs and are almost as lively, so even the most miserly traveler can join in the nightly bash. **Discothèques** are generally open from 11pm to 5am. (Cover around 100F/€15.25; includes 1 drink). **Pam Pam Rhumerie,** at 137, bd. Wilson, has a decidedly tropical feel. (Open daily 3pm-5am.) Or, join the crowds piling onto the patios of hip **Che Café,** 1, bd. de la Pinède, and **La Reserve,** across the street. (Open daily 3pm-5am.) **Trains** depart av. l'Esterel for Cannes (10min., 13F/€2) and Nice (30min., 24F/€3.70). To get from Antibes' pl. du Général de Gaulle to Juan-les-Pins by foot, follow bd. Wilson, which runs into the center of town (about 1½km). Instead of making the post-party trek to Antibes, turn right out of the train station and stay at **Hôtel Trianon,** 14, av. de L'Estérel. (☎/fax 04 93 61 18 11. Breakfast 25F/€3.85. Singles 180F/€27.45; doubles 215-260F/€32.80-39.65; triples 260-280F/€39.65-42.70.)

NICE

Sun-drenched and spicy, Nice (pop. 345,892) sparkles as the Riviera's unofficial capital. The city's pumping nightlife, top-notch museums, and bustling beaches enhance its native *Provençal* charms: flowery, palm-lined boulevards, casual affluence, and sea breezes. With excellent transportation and budget lodgings galore, the fifth largest city in France makes a cheap base for sampling the *Côte d'Azur's* pricier delights. Prepare to have more fun than you'll remember.

▆ TRANSPORTATION

Trains: Gare SNCF Nice-Ville, av. Thiers (☎04 92 14 81 62). To: **Cannes** (35min., every 15-45min., 32F/€4.90); **Marseilles** (2¾hr., every 30-90min., 152F/€23.20); **Monaco** (25min., every 10-30min., 20F/€3.05); **Paris** (7hr., 2-3 per day, 484F/€73.80).

Buses: 5, bd. Jean Jaurès (☎04 93 85 61 81), left at the end of bd. Jean Medecin. Tickets sold M-Sa 8am-6:30pm and on buses. To **Cannes** (1½hr., 3 per hr., 37.50F/€5.75) and **Monaco** (40min., 4 per hr., 20F/€3.05).

Ferries: SNCM (☎04 93 13 66 66) and **Corsica Ferries** (☎04 92 00 43 76), both at the port. Take bus #1 or 2 (dir. Port) from pl. Masséna. Reservations daily 8am-noon and 2-5:45pm. To **Corsica** (p. 377).

Public Transportation: Sunbus, 10, av. Félix Faure (☎04 93 16 52 10), near pl. Leclerc and pl. Masséna. Individual ticket 8.50F/€1.30. Bus passes: day pass 25F/€3.85, 10-ticket *carnet* 55F/€8.40, 7-day pass 110F/€16.80. Ask tourist office for **"Sunplan"** bus map and the **"Guide Infobus"** with schedules and routes.

Bike and Scooter Rental: JML Location, 34, av. Auber (☎04 93 16 07 00), opposite the train station. Bikes 70F/€10.70 per day, 301F/€45.90 per week; scooters 240F/€36.60. Credit card deposit 1500F/€228.65 (bikes) or 6000F/€914.80 (scooters). Open daily June-Sept. 8am-6:30pm; Oct.-May M-F 8am-1pm and 2-6:30pm, Sa 8am-1pm, Su 9am-1pm and 4-6:30pm.

◢✳ 🛈 ORIENTATION AND PRACTICAL INFORMATION

From the train station, **avenue Jean-Médecin,** on the left, and **boulevard Gambetta,** going to the right, both lead to the waterfront. **Place Masséna** is 10min. down av. Jean-Médecin. Along the coast, **Promenade des Anglais** is a people-watching paradise. To the southeast, past av. Jean Médecin and toward the bus station, pulsates **Vieux Nice.** Women should not walk alone after sunset, and everyone should be careful at night near the train station, in *Vieux Nice,* and on Promenade des Anglais.

Tourist Office: Av. Thiers (☎04 93 87 07 07; fax 04 93 16 85 16; www.nice-coteazur.org), next to the train station. Go in the morning to make same-day hotel reservations. Open June-Sept. M-Sa 8am-8pm, Su 9am-7pm; Oct.-May M-Sa 8am-7pm.

Currency Exchange: Cambio, 17, av. Thiers (☎04 93 88 56 80), opposite the train station. No commission. Open daily 7am-10pm.

American Express: 11, promenade des Anglais (☎04 93 16 53 53; fax 04 93 16 51 67), at r. des Congrès. Open daily 9am-8:30pm.

Luggage Storage: At the train station. Lockers 15-30F/€2.30-4.60. Open daily 7am-10:30pm.

Laundromat: Laverie Niçoise, 7, r. d'Italie, next to Basilique Notre-Dame. Open M-Sa 8:30am-12:30pm and 2:30-7:30pm.

Emergency: ☎17. **Medical emergency:** ☎15.

Police: ☎04 93 17 22 22. At the opposite end of bd. M. Foch from bd. Jean-Médecin.

Hospital: St-Roch, 5, r. Pierre Devoluy (☎04 92 03 33 75.)

Internet Access: Organic CyberCafé, 16, r. Paganini. Mention *Let's Go* and pay 16F/€2.45 per 30min., 34F/€5.20 per hr. Open daily 9am-10pm. **3.W.O.,** 32, r. Assalit, has American keyboards. 20F/€3.05 per 30min., 30F/€4.60 per hr. Open M-Sa 9am-9pm, Su 9am-6pm.

Post Office: 21, av. Thiers (☎04 93 82 65 22), near the train station. Open M-F 8am-7pm, Sa 8am-noon. 24hr. **ATM.** Address mail to be held: SURNAME, First Name *Poste Restante*, Recette Principale, Nice **06000**, France.

Postal code: 06033 Nice Cedex 1.

▟ ACCOMMODATIONS

To sleep easy, come to Nice with reservations (at least 2-3 weeks ahead in the summer). Affordable places surround the train station, but without reservations, you'll be forced to risk a night on the beach or outside the station.

▨ Hôtel Baccarat, 39, r. d'Angleterre (☎04 93 88 35 73; fax 04 93 16 14 25; www.hotel-baccarat.com). Large, well-kept rooms with showers. Breakfast 10-12F/€1.55-1.85. Reception 24hr. Remember your reservation code! Dorms 95F/€14.50; singles 187F/€28.55; doubles 230F/€35.10; triples 284F/€43.30. AmEx/MC/V.

Relais International de la Jeunesse "Clairvallon," 26, av. Scudéri (☎04 93 81 27 63; fax 04 93 53 35 88), in Cimiez, 4km out of town. Take bus #15 (dir. Rimiez; 20min., every 10min.) from the station or pl. Masséna to Scudéri; then head uphill to the right and take the 1st left. In a luxurious villa with tennis courts and swimming pool. Breakfast included. Check-in 5pm. Lockout 9:30am-5pm. Curfew 11pm. Dorms 82F/€12.50.

Auberge de Jeunesse (HI) (☎04 93 89 23 64; fax 04 92 04 03 10). On rte. Forestière du Mont-Alban, 4km out of town. From the bus station, take bus #14 (dir. Mont Baron) to l'Auberge (M-F every 15min., Sa-Su every 30min.; both until 7:30pm). From the train station, take bus #17 and say you need to switch to the #14. It's a 50min. walk from the train station: turn left, turn right on av. Jean-Médecin, left on bd. Jaurès, right on r. Barla, and follow the signs. Breakfast included. Curfew 12:30am. Dorms 71F/€10.85.

Hôtel des Flandres, 6, r. de Belgique (☎04 93 88 78 94; fax 04 93 88 74 90). Large rooms and bathrooms. Breakfast 30F/€4.60. 5- to 6-bed dorms 110F/€16.80; singles 230F/€35.10; doubles 290-310F/€44.25-47.30; triples 370F/€56.45; quads 390-410F/€59.50-62.50. Extra bed 70F/€10.70. MC/V.

Hôtel Little Masséna, 22, r. Masséna (☎04 93 87 72 34). Small but clean rooms with TV and kitchenette. Singles and doubles 170F/€25.95, with bath 220-270F/€33.55-41.20. Extra person 30F/€4.60. Oct.-May prices 10-30F/€1.50-4.60 less. MC/V.

Hôtel Notre Dame, 22, r. de la Russie (☎04 93 88 70 44; fax 04 93 81 20 38), at the corner of r. d'Italie. Spotless, pleasantly quiet rooms. Singles 200F/€30.50; doubles 250F/€38.15; triples 350F/€53.40; quads 400F/€61. Extra bed 60F/€9.15.

Hôtel Belle Meunière, 21, av. Durante (☎04 93 88 66 15; fax 04 93 82 51 75), on a street facing the train station. A converted mansion with courtyard and gardens. Breakfast included. Dorms 80-115F/€12.20-17.55; doubles 290F/€44.25; triples 255F/€38.90, with shower 345F/€52.60.

Hôtel Les Orangiers, 10bis, av. Durante (☎04 93 87 51 41; fax 04 93 82 57 82). Bright rooms, most with showers. English spoken. Free luggage storage. Breakfast 20F/€4.60. Closed Nov. Dorms 85F/€13; singles 95-100F/€14.50-15.20; doubles 210-230F/€32.05-35.10; triples 270-300F/€41.20-45.70; quads 360F/€54.90. MC/V.

FRANCE

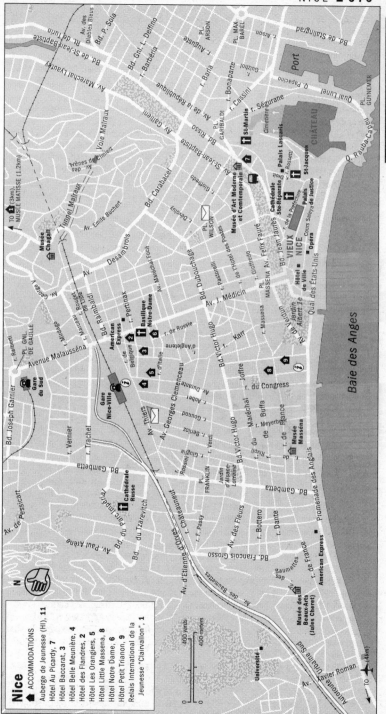

Nice

▲ ACCOMMODATIONS

Auberge de Jeunesse (HI), **11**
Hôtel Au Picardy, **7**
Hôtel Baccarat, **3**
Hôtel Belle Meunière, **4**
Hôtel des Flandres, **2**
Hôtel Les Orangiers, **5**
Hôtel Little Massena, **8**
Hôtel Notre Dame, **6**
Hôtel Petit Trianon, **9**
Relais International de la
Jeunesse "Clairvallon", **1**

Hôtel Petit Trianon, 11, r. Paradis (☎04 93 87 50 46), off r. Masséna. Humble rooms close to the beach and *Vieux Nice*. Showers 10F/€1.55. Breakfast 25F/€3.85. Singles 100F/€15.25; doubles 200F/€30.50; triples 300F/€45.75. Extra bed 50F/€7.65.

Hôtel Au Picardy, 10, bd. Jean-Jaurès (☎04 93 85 75 51), across from the bus station. Excellent proximity to *Vieux Nice*. Singles 125-135F/€19.05-20.60, with shower 179F/€27.30; doubles 179F/€27.30, 209F/€31.90; triples 220-260F/€33.55-39.65; quads 260-299F/€33.65-45.60. Extra bed 45F/€6.90. Cash only.

🍴 FOOD

Nice is above all a city of restaurants, seafood, North African cuisine, and Italian delights. *Vieux Nice* is crowded and touristy, but good eats are easy to find. Stock up at the **Prisunic supermarket,** 42, av. Jean-Médecin. (Open M-Sa 8:30am-8:30pm.)

🍽 **Lou Pilha Leva,** 13, r. du Collet. A wonderful, cheap way to try a lot of *niçois* food. Pizza slices, *socca* (an olive-oil-flavored chickpea bread), and *pissaladière* (anchovy and olive pizza) all 10-12F/€1.50-1.85. Open daily 8am-11pm.

Acchiardo, 38, r. Droite, in *Vieux Nice*. Pastas from 36F/€5.50 are immensely popular with a loyal local clientele. Open M-F noon-1:30pm and 7-9:30pm, Sa noon-1:30am.

👁 SIGHTS

Despite the dreams you've had about Nice's beach, the hard reality is an endless stretch of pebbles. Stroll down the fantastic **Promenade des Anglais,** named after the English expatriates who had it built. Follow the Promenade east of bd. Jean Jaurès to visit **Vieux Nice**'s labyrinthine streets, crowded with tiny flowered balconies and exceptional churches. Continue to **Le Château,** a flowery hillside park crowned by the remains of an 11th-century cathedral. (Open daily 7am-8pm.)

Even burn-hard sunbathers will have a hard time passing up Nice's first-class museums. Walk 15min. north from the train station, and off bd. Cimiez you'll find the moving **Musée National Message Biblique Marc Chagall,** av. du Dr. Ménard, the largest public collection of his works. Take bus #15 (dir. Rimiez) to Musée Chagall. (Open July-Sept. W-M 10am-6pm; Oct.-June W-M 10am-5pm. 36F/€5.50, under 26 26F/€4.) Farther up the hill, an impressive collection of Matisse's Riviera work is housed in the **Musée Matisse,** 164, av. des Arènes de Cimiez. The bronze reliefs and cut-and-paste tableaux are dazzling. Take bus #15, 17, 20, or 22 to Arènes. (Open Apr.-Sept. W-M 10am-6pm; Oct.-Mar. 10am-5pm. 25F/€3.85, students 20F/€3.05.) Matisse, along with Raoul Duffy, is buried nearby in a cemetery beside the **Monastère Cimiez,** which contains a museum devoted to Franciscan art. (Museum open M-Sa 10am-noon and 3-6pm. Cemetery open daily 8am-6pm.) Far to the northwest, the onion-domed **Cathédrale Orthodoxe Russe St-Nicolas,** west of bd. Gambetta near the train station, is a reminder of the days when the Côte d'Azur was a favorite retreat for Russian nobility. (Open daily June-Aug. 9am-noon and 2:30-6pm; Sept.-May 9:30am-noon and 2:30-5pm. 15F/€2.30, students 12F/€1.85.) Closer to *Vieux Nice*, the **Musée d'Art Moderne et d'Art Contemporain,** on Promenade des Arts, at the intersection of av. St-Jean Baptiste and Traverse Garibaldi, features avant-garde works by French and American provocateurs. Take bus #5 (dir. St-Charles) from the station to Garibaldi. (Open W-M 10am-6pm. 20F/€3.05, students 10F/€1.55.) The **Musée des Beaux-Arts,** 33, av. Baumettes, off bd. François Grosso, north of the Promenade des Anglais, has works by Fragonard, Monet, Sisley, and Degas, and sculptures by Rodin and Carpeaux. Take bus #38 from the train station to Chéret or bus #12 to Grosso. (Open Tu-Su 10am-noon and 2-6pm. 25F/€3.85, students 15F/€2.30.)

🎵 🎭 ENTERTAINMENT AND NIGHTLIFE

FNAC, 24, av. Jean-Médecin, in the Nice Etoile shopping center, sells tickets to all musical and cultural events. Nice's **Jazz Festival,** in mid-July at the Parc et Arènes de

Cimiez near the Musée Matisse, attracts world-famous jazz and non-jazz musicians. (☎04 93 21 68 12; fax 04 93 18 07 92. 50-250F/€7.60-38.10.)

Nice guys do finish last—here the party crowd swings long after the folks in St-Tropez and Antibes are asleep. The bars and nightclubs around r. Masséna and *Vieux Nice* jump to jazz and rock. However, the areas around *Vieux Nice* and the Promenade des Anglais are dangerous at night. The dress code is simple: look good. Most will turn you away if wearing shorts, sandals, a T-shirt, or a baseball cap.

De Klomp, 6, r. Mascoinat. A friendly Dutch pub with a mixed crowd. Try one of their 40 whiskeys (from 40F/€6.10) or 18 beers on tap (pint 45F/€6.90). Live music nightly from salsa to jazz. Open M-Sa 5:30pm-2:30am, Su 8:30pm-2:30am.

Le Bar des Deux Frères, 1, r. du Moulin. Hip, local favorite guarantees a good time. A young, funky crowd throws back tequila (20F/€3.05) and beer (15F/€2.30). Open daily 9pm-3:30am; in winter closed M.

La Suite, 2, r. Brea. A well-dressed crowd packs Nice's most chic club. Cover 80F/€12.20. W free. Open W-Su 11:30pm-2:30am.

Le Klub, 6, r. Halévy. A popular gay club for a well-tanned crowd. Cover 70F/€10.70 on Sa. Open July-Aug. daily 11:30pm-6am; Sept.-June closed M.

THE CORNICHES

Rocky shores, pebble beaches, and luxurious villas glow along the coast between hectic Nice and high-rolling Monaco. More relaxing than their glamorous neighbors, these towns glisten with fascinating museums, ancient finds, and breathtaking countryside. The train offers a glimpse of the coast up close, while bus rides on the high roads provide a bird's-eye view of the steep cliffs and crashing sea below.

▐ TRANSPORTATION. Trains run between Nice and Monaco hourly and stop at: Beaulieu-sur-Mer (10min., 16F/€2.45); Cap D'Ail (20min., 21F/€3.20); Eze-sur-Mer (16min., 18F/€2.75); and Villefranche-sur-Mer (7min., 13F/€2). RCA **buses** (☎04 93 85 64 44), which depart from Nice's *gare routière*, run the route more frequently. Bus **#111** leaves Nice and stops in Villefranche-sur-Mer (10 per day). Two buses continue on to St-Jean-Cap-Ferrat (M-Sa): Bus **#117** runs between Nice and Villefranche-sur-Mer (11 per day); and bus **#112** runs between Nice and Monte-Carlo, stopping in Èze-le-Village (7 per day). RCA and Broch (☎04 93 31 10 52) buses run every hour between Nice and: Beaulieu-sur-Mer (20min., 14F/€2.15); Cap d'Ail (30min., 17F/€2.60); Èze-le-Village (25min., 15F/€2.30); Monaco-Ville (40min., 20F/€3.05); Monte-Carlo (45min., 20F/€3.05); and Villefranche-sur-Mer (10min., 9F/€1.40). Most tickets include free same-day return; inquire.

VILLEFRANCHE-SUR-MER. Narrow streets and pastel houses have enchanted Aldous Huxley, Katherine Mansfield, and a bevy of other writers. Strolling from the train station along quai Ponchardier, a sign to the *vieille ville* points toward the spooky 13th-century **r. Obscure,** the oldest street in Villefranche. The **tourist office,** on Jardin François Binon, gives out free maps and information on sights. (☎04 93 01 73 68; fax 04 93 76 63 65; www.villefranche-sur-mer.com. Open daily July-Aug. 9am-noon and 2-6:30pm; mid-Sept. to June M-Sa 9am-noon and 2-6pm.)

ST-JEAN-CAP-FERRAT. A lovely town with an even lovelier beach, St-Jean-Cap-Ferrat is the trump card of the Riviera. **Bus #111** serves the town, but nothing compares to the 25min. ◪**seaside walk,** which winds past lavish villas and secluded rocky beaches. The **Fondation Ephrussi di Rothschild,** just off av. D. Semeria, is a stunning Italianate villa with an impressive, eclectic collection of artwork. (Open July-Aug. daily 10am-7pm; Sept.-Oct. and mid-Feb. to June daily 10am-6pm; Nov. to mid-Feb. M-F 2-6pm, Sa-Su 10am-6pm. 50F/€7.65, students 38F/€5.80.) The town's **beaches** merit the area's nickname *"presqu'île des rêves"* ("Peninsula of Dreams").

ÈZE-LE-VILLAGE. This imposing medieval town (the center of the larger Èze-sur-Mer) features the **Porte des Maures,** which served as a portal for a fatally successful attack by the Moors, and the newly renovated Baroque **Eglise Paroissial,**

decorated with sleek Phoenician crosses and Catholic gilt. (Open daily 9am-noon and 2-6pm.) Climb 40min. up the **Sentier Friedrich Nietzsche,** a windy trail whose namesake found inspiration here for the third part of *Thus Spake Zarathustra.* The trail begins in Èze-Bord-du-Mer, 100m east of the train station and tourist office, and ends near the base of the medieval city, by the Fragonard *parfumerie.*

CAP D'AIL. With 3km of cliff-framed seashore, **Les Pissarelles** draws dozens of **nudists,** while **plage Mala** is frequented by more modest folk. Free maps and lists of daytrips are available from the **tourist office,** 87bis, av. de 3 Septembre. From the train station, walk uphill to the left, turn right at the village, continue on av. de la Gare, and turn right on r. du 4 Septembre. (☎04 93 78 02 33; fax 04 92 10 74 36. Open M-Sa 9am-12:30pm and 2-6pm.) The **Relais International de la Jeunesse "Thalassa,"** on bd. F. de May, can be reached by following signs from the station. (☎04 93 78 18 58; fax 04 93 53 35 88. Breakfast included. Lockout 9:30am-5pm. Curfew midnight. Open Apr.-Oct. Dorms 80F/€12.20.)

MONACO AND MONTE-CARLO

Monaco (pop. 5000) has money, and we're talking about lots of it—invested in ubiquitous surveillance cameras, high-speed luxury cars, and sleek yachts. At Monaco's spiritual heart is its famous casino in Monte-Carlo, a magnet for the wealthy and dissolute since 1885. The sheer spectacle of it all is worth a daytrip from Nice.

PHONE CODE	**Country code:** 377. **International dialing prefix:** 00.

▐ TRANSPORTATION. Trains (☎08 36 35 35 35) run to: Antibes (1hr., every 30min., 38F/€5.80); Cannes (1¼hr., every 30min., 46F/€7.05); and Nice (25min., every 30min., 20F/€3.05). **Buses** (☎04 93 85 61 81) leave pl. d'Armes or pl. du Casino for Nice (45min., every 15min., 20F/€3.05).

▐ PRACTICAL INFORMATION. Follow the signs in the new train station for Le Rocher and Fontvieille to the **avenue Prince Pierre** exit; it's close to the **La Condamine** quarter, Monaco's port and nightlife hub. To the right of La Condamine rises the *vieille ville,* **Monaco-Ville.** Leaving the train station onto bd. Princess Charlotte or pl. St-Devote leads to **Monte-Carlo** and the casino. Five public transportation routes (☎97 70 22 22) connect the entire hilly town every 11 minutes; **bus #4** links the train station to the casino in Monte-Carlo. Buy tickets on board (8.50F/€1.30, 21.50F/€3.30 for a *carte* of 4). The **tourist office,** 2a, bd. des Moulins, near the casino, makes reservations and gives out maps. (☎92 16 61 16; fax 92 16 60 00. Open M-Sa 9am-7pm, Su 10am-noon.) Stop by the lively **fruit and flower market** on pl. d'Armes, at the end of av. Prince Pierre (open daily 6am-1pm) or the huge **Carrefour supermarket** in Fontvieille's shopping plaza (open M-Sa 8:30am-10pm). Access the **Internet** at **Stars 'N' Bars,** 6, quai Antoine 1*er.* (Open daily 10am-midnight. 40F/€6.10 per 30min.) **Postal code:** 06500.

▐▐ ACCOMMODATIONS AND FOOD. There's no need to stay in Monaco since it is easily accessible from nearby coastal towns. Travelers between the ages of 16 and 31 can try the **Centre de Jeunesse Princesse Stéphanie,** 24, av. Prince Pierre, 100m uphill from the station. The hostel is strict and a bit sterile. (☎93 50 83 20. Breakfast included. Laundry 30F/€4.60. July-Aug 5-day max. stay; Sept.-June 7-day max. stay. Check-out 9:30am. Closed mid-Nov. to mid-Dec. Beds 100F/€15.25; July-Aug. 10- and 12-bed dorms 90F/€13.75. Cash only.) **L'Escale,** 17, bd. Albert 1*er,* serves pizzas and pastas from 50F/€7.65. (Open daily noon-3pm and 6-11pm.)

▐▐ SIGHTS AND ENTERTAINMENT. The extravagant **Monte-Carlo Casino,** at pl. de Casino, is where Richard Burton wooed Elizabeth Taylor and Mata Hari shot a Russian spy. The slot machines open at 2pm, while blackjack, craps, and roulette open at noon (50F/€7.65 to enter). Next door, the more relaxed **Café de Paris** opens at 10am and has no cover. The exclusive *salons privés*, where such French games as *chemin de fer* and *trente et quarante* begin at noon, will cost you an extra 50F/€7.65 cover. All casinos have **dress codes** (no shorts, sneakers, sandals, or jeans), and the *salons privés* requires coat and ties. Guards are strict about the 21 age minimum; bring a passport as proof. High above the casino is the **Palais Prin-cier,** the occasional home of Prince Rainier and his tabloid-darling family. When the flag is down, the prince is away and visitors can tour the small but lavish pal-ace, which includes Princess Grace's official state portrait and the chamber where England's King George III died. (Open June-Sept. 9:30am-6pm; Oct. 10am-5pm. 30F/ €4.60, students 15F/€2.30 before 5pm.) Next door, the **Cathédrale de Monaco,** at pl. St-Martin, is the burial site of the Grimaldi family and the site of Prince Rainer and Princess Grace's 1956 wedding; Princess Grace lies behind the altar in a tomb marked simply with her Latinized name, "Patritia Gracia." (Open daily Mar.-Oct. 7am-7pm; Nov.-Feb. 7am-6pm. Free.) The **Private Collection of Antique Cars of H.S.H. Prince Rainier III,** on les Terraces de Fontvielle, showcases 105 of the most glamor-ous cars ever made. (Open Dec.-Oct. daily 10am-6pm. 30F/€4.60, students 15F/ €2.30.) Head to av. St-Martin to see the **Musée Océanographique,** once directed by Jacques Cousteau. It holds the most exotic and bizarre oceanic species. (Open daily July-Aug. 9am-8pm; Apr.-June and Sept. 9am-7pm; Oct. and Mar. 9:30am-7pm; Nov.-Feb. 10am-6pm. 70F/€10.70, students and ages 6-18 35F/€5.35.) Monaco's nightlife centers in **La Condamine,** near the port. **Café Grand Prix,** at 1, quai Antoine 1*er*, serves up live music to a mixed crowd. (Open daily 10am-5am. No cover.)

CORSICA (LA CORSE)

Corsica's time bomb of a populace began the Corsican War of Independence, also known as the Forty Years War, with a series of rebellions in 1729. By 1755, the island had declared itself an autonomous state with its own constitution and uni-versity. Today, the *Front de Libération National de la Corse* (FLNC) continues to try bombing its way to independence. However, these politics have little effect on tourists, who are warmly received throughout the beautiful island.

⌅ TRANSPORTATION. Air France and its subsidary **Compagnie Corse Méditerranée (CCM)** fly to Ajaccio and Bastia from: Lyon (from 1114F/€170, students 924F/€141); Marseilles (912F/€139, students 839F/€128); Paris (1395F/€213, students 1094F/ €167). There is also a direct link from Lille to Bastia (from 1485F/€226.45, students 1360F/€207.35). All fares listed here are one way and without tax. **Ferries** to Cor-sica can be rough and aren't much cheaper than flights. The **Société National Mari-time Corse Méditerranée (SNCM)** sails to Ajaccio, Bastia, and Calvi from Marseilles (265-300F/€40.40-45.70, under 25 230-265F/€35.10-40.40) and Nice (225-255F/ €34.30-38.90, under 25 195-225F/€29.75-34.30). **Corsica Ferries,** at 5bis, r. Chanoine Leschi (☎08 03 09 50 95; www.corsicaferries.com), travels to Livorno and Savona in Italy to Bastia (119-180F/€18.15-27.45). Ferries also cross from Bonifacio, at the southern tip of the island, to Santa Teresa in Sardinia, Italy (4-10 per day, 50-75F/ €7.65-11.45 per person and 140-280F/€21.35-42.70 per car). All tickets must be **reserved** four days in advance. **Train** service in Corsica is slow and limited to the half of the island north of Ajaccio; **railpasses** are not valid. **Eurocorse Voyages buses** (☎04 95 21 06 30) are not much better, but provide more comprehensive service.

Hiking is the best way to explore the island's mountainous interior. The **Mare e Monti** (10 days) and **Da Mare a Mare Sud** (4-6 days) are shorter and easier routes. The **Parc Naturel Régional de la Corse,** 2, Sargent Casalonga, in Ajaccio (☎04 95 51 79 00; www.parc.naturel-corse.com), offers maps and a guide to *gîtes d'étapes*.

AJACCIO (AIACCIU)

Ajaccio (pop. 60,000) swings like nowhere else on the island, with a definite hint of Napoleonic spice. The **Musée National de la Maison Bonaparte,** on r. St-Charles, between r. Bonaparte and r. Roi-de-Rome, is a warehouse of Bonaparte memorabilia, like his smaller-than-average bed. (Open Apr.-Sept. M 2-6pm, Tu-Su 9am-noon and 2-6pm; Oct.-Mar. M 2-4:45pm, Tu-Su 10am-noon and 2-4:45pm. 25F/€3.85, ages 18-25 17F/€2.60.) Inside the **Musée Fesch**, 50-52, r. Cardinal Fesch, is a collection of 14th- to 19th-century Italian paintings, amassed by Napoleon's merchant uncle Fesch before he became a cardinal. Also find the **Chapelle Impériale**, the final resting place of most of the Bonaparte family—although Napoleon himself is buried in a modest Parisian tomb. (Open July-Aug. M 1:30-6pm, Tu-Th 9am-6:30pm, F 9am-6:30pm and 9pm-midnight, Sa-Su 10:30am-6pm; Apr.-June and Sept. M 1-5:15pm, Tu-Su 9:15am-12:15pm and 2:15-5:15pm; Oct.-Mar. Tu-Sa 9:15am-12:15pm and 2:15-5:15pm. Museum 35F/€5.35, students 25F/€3.85; chapel 10F/€1.55, 5F/€0.75.)

TCA bus #8 (☎ 04 95 23 11 03) runs between **Aéroport Campo dell'Oro** and the bus station (26F/€4). **Trains** (☎ 04 95 23 11 03) chug from pl. de la Gare, off bd. Sampiero, to Bastia (4hr., 4 per day, 143F/€21.80) and Calvi (4½hr., 2 per day, 166F/€25.30) via Ponte Leccia. Eurocorse Voyages **buses** (☎ 04 95 21 06 30) go from quai L'Herminier to Bastia (3hr., 110F/€16.80) via Corte (1½hr., 65F/€9.95). **Autocars Les Beux Voyages** (☎ 04 95 65 15 02) runs to Calvi (3½hr., 1 per day, 135F/€20.60). The **tourist office** is at 3, bd. du roi Jérôme. (☎ 04 95 51 53 03; fax 04 95 51 53 01. Open July-Sept. M-Sa 8am-8:30pm, Su 9am-1pm; Nov.-Feb. M-F 8am-6pm, Sa 8am-noon and 2-5pm; Mar.-June M-Sa 8am-7pm, Su 9am-1pm.) **Hôtel Kallisté**, 51, cours Napoléon, is serene. (☎ 04 95 51 34 45; fax 04 95 21 79 00; www.cyrnos.com. July and Sept.-Oct. 290-460F/€44.25-70.15; Aug. 350-560F/€53.40-85.40; Oct.-June 260-380F/€39.65-57.95. AmEx/MC/V.) **Hôtel Marengo**, 2, r. Marengo, is near the beach. (☎ 04 95 21 43 66; fax 04 95 21 51 26. Open Apr.-Oct. Breakfast 35F/€5.35. July-Sept. singles and doubles 370F/€56.45; triples 420F/€64.05; Apr.-June and Oct. singles 275-315F/€41.95-48.05; doubles 295-335F/€45-51.10; triples 340-360F/€51.85-54.90. MC/V.) **Monoprix supermarket** is at 31, cours Napoléon. (Open M-Sa 8:30am-7:30pm.)

BONIFACIO (BONIFAZIU)

The fortified city of Bonifacio (pop. 3000) rises like a majestic sand castle atop jagged limestone cliffs; **Marina Croisères** offers **boat tours** of the hidden coves and grottoes. (☎ 04 95 73 09 77. 70-140F/€10.70-21.35.) All the companies by the port run frequent ferries (30min.) to the pristine sands of **Îles Levezzi**, a natural reserve with beautiful reefs just off its coast perfect for **scuba diving**. To explore the *haute ville*, head up the steep montée Rastello, the wide staircase halfway down the port, where excellent views of the ridged cliffs to the east await. Continue up montée St-Roch to the lookout at **Porte des Gênes**, a drawbridge built by invaders. Then walk to the **place du Marche** to see Bonifacio's famous cliffs and the **Grain de Sable.**

Eurocorse Voyages (☎ 04 95 21 06 30) runs **buses** to Ajaccio (3½hr., 2 per day, 125F/€19.05) as well as Porto Vecchio (30min., 1-4 per day, 40F/€6.10), where connections can be made to Bastia. To reach the **tourist office**, at the corner of av. de Gaulle and r. F. Scamaroni, walk along the port and then up the stairs before the *gare maritime*. (☎ 04 95 73 11 88; fax 04 95 73 14 97. Open May to mid-Oct. daily 9am-8pm; mid-Oct. to Apr. M-F 9am-noon and 2-6pm, Sa 9am-noon.) Finding affordable rooms is difficult in summer; avoid visiting in August, when prices soar. Try **Hôtel des Étrangers**, av. Sylvère Bohn. (☎ 04 95 73 01 09; fax 04 95 73 16 97. June-Sept. singles 290F/€44.25; doubles 360-390F/€54.90-59.50; triples 340-390F/€51.85-59.50; quads 390-490F/€59.50-74.70; Oct.-May singles and doubles 250-290F/€38.10-44.25; triples 340-390F/€51.85-59.50; quads 390-490F/€59.50-74.70. MC/V.) The spacious **Cavallo Morto**, 2km away on N198, offers wooden chalets for four to six people and furnished studios for one to two people. (Open mid-Apr. to mid-Oct. Studios 200-350F/€30.50-53.40; chalets 350-600F/€53.410-91.50. **Camping** 36F/€5.50 per person, 15F/€2.30 per tent or car. Electricity 17F/€2.60. AmEx/MC/V.)

CALVI

Dubbed "Corsica's Côte d'Azur," Calvi offers a cafe- and yacht-lined port as well as gorgeous sandy beaches, warm turquoise waters, and misty mountains. Visit the alluring **citadel** at the end of the day and bask in the setting sun. Gorgeous sand and water stretch as far as the eye can see; 6km of **public beaches** dotted by rocky coves wind around the coast. **Trains** (☎ 04 95 65 00 61) leave pl. de la Gare, on av. de la République near Port de Plaisance, for Bastia (3hr., 2 per day, 108F/€16.50) and Corte (2½hr., 2 per day, 90F/€13.75). Les Beaux Voyages **buses** (☎ 04 95 65 15 02), leave pl. Porteuse d'Eau, by the taxi stand, for Ajaccio (4¾hr., 1 per day, 135F/ €20.60) and Bastia (2¼hr., M-Sa 1 per day, 80F/€12.20). To reach the **tourist office**, at Port de Plaisance, exit from the back of the train station (facing the beach), turn left, and follow the signs. (☎ 04 95 65 16 67; fax 04 95 65 14 09. Open May M-Sa 9am-6:30pm; June to mid-Sept. daily 9am-7pm; mid-Sept. to Apr. M-F 9am-5pm.) To get to the isolated but beautiful **Relais International de la Jeunesse U Carabellu,** exit the station, turn left on av. de la République, turn right at rte. de Pietra-Maggiore, and follow the signs 5km into the hills. Continue past Bella Vista camping, and bear right at the stop sign. (☎ 04 95 65 14 16. Breakfast included. Sheets 20F/€3.05. Open Mar.-Sept. 100F/€15.25.) More central, **BVJ Corsotel** is on av. de la République. (☎ 04 95 65 14 15; fax 04 95 65 33 72. Breakfast 20F/€3.05. Reception 7:30am-1pm and 5-10pm. Open Apr.-Oct. Bunks 115F/€17.55; doubles 115-130F/€17.55-19.85.) For **Camping International,** on RN 197, 1km past town, walk past Super U, Hôtel L'Onda. (☎ 04 95 65 01 75; fax 04 95 65 36 11. Open Apr.-Oct. 22-33F/€3.35-5.05 per person, 15-19F/€2.30-2.90 per tent, 8-10F/€1.25-1.55 per car.)

BASTIA

Corsica's second largest city and a major transport hub, Bastia (pop. 40,000) is a good base from which to explore Cap Corse. The 14th-century **Citadel,** also called Terra Nova, has beautiful views of the sea. The **Oratoire de St-Roch,** on r. Napoleon, is a jewel-box of a church with crystal chandeliers and meticulous *trompe l'oeil* decoration. The neoclassical towers of the **Eglise St-Jean Baptiste,** pl. de l'Hôtel de Ville, cover an immense interior with gilded domes. **Shuttle buses** leave for the **Bastia-Poretta airport** from pl. de la Gare (30min., 50F/€7.65). **Trains** (☎ 04 95 32 80 61) also leave pl. de la Gare for Ajaccio (4hr., 4 per day, 143F/€21.80) and Calvi (3hr., 2 per day, 108F/€16.50). **Eurocorse buses** (☎ 04 95 21 06 30) leave r. Nouveau Port for Ajaccio (3hr., 2 per day, 110F/€16.80). The **tourist office** is on pl. St-Nicholas. (☎ 04 95 54 20 40; fax 04 95 31 81 34. Open July-Sept. daily 8am-8pm; Oct.-June M-Sa 8:30am-6pm.) **SPAR supermarket** is at 14, r. César Campinchini. (Open M-Sa 8:30am-12:30pm and 2:30-7:30pm.) The **Hôtel Univers,** 3, av. Maréchal Sebastiani, has clean and modern rooms. (☎ 04 95 31 03 38; fax 04 95 31 19 91. Breakfast 35F/€5.35. Singles 200-350F/€30.50-53.40; doubles 200-400F/€30.50-61; triples 250-450F/€38.10-68.60; quads 300-600F/€45.70-91.50. Aug. prices 50F/€7.65 higher; Sept.-June 50-100F/€7.60-15.20 lower. AmEx/V.) **Les Orangiers camping** is 4km north in Miomo. (☎ 04 95 33 24 09. Open Apr. to mid-Oct. 25F/€3.85 per person, 13F/€2 per tent, 10F/ €1.55 per car.) Inexpensive cafes crowd **place St-Nicolas.**

⚡ DAYTRIP FROM BASTIA: CAP CORSE. North of Bastia stretches the gorgeous Cap Corse peninsula, a necklace of tiny former fishing villages strung together by a narrow road of perilous curves and breathtaking views. The Cap is a dream for **hikers;** every jungle, forest, and cliff lays claim to some decaying Genoese tower or hilltop chapel. The cheapest and most convenient way to see Cap Corse is to take **bus #4** from pl. St-Nicolas in Bastia, which goes to: Erbalunga (20min., 12F/ €1.85); Macinaggio (50min., 40F/€6.10); and Marina di Siscu (30min., 14F/€2.10). Ask the driver to drop you off wherever you feel the urge to explore. However, most buses serve only the coast; you'll have to hike or hitch to the inland villages.

CORTE

The most dynamic of Corsica's inland towns, Corte combines breathtaking natural scenery with an intellectual flair. Sheer cliffs, snow-capped peaks, and magical gorges create a dramatic backdrop for the island's only university, whose students keep prices surprisingly low. The town's *vieille ville*, with its steep, barely accessible streets and stone **citadel,** has always been a bastion of Corsican patriotism. At the top of r. Scolisca is the engaging **La Musée de la Corse.** The museum also provides entrance to the higher fortifications of the citadel. (Museum open June 20-Sept. 20 daily 10am-8pm; Sept. 21-Nov. Tu-Su 10am-6pm; Dec.-Mar. Tu-Sa 10am-6pm; Apr.-June 19 Tu-Su 10am-6pm. Citadel closes 1hr. earlier than the museum. 35F/€5.35, students 20F/€3.05.) Corte's mountains and valleys feature numerous spectacular trails. Choose from **hiking** (call tourist office for maps and info; call 08 92 68 02 20 for weather), **biking** (see below), and **horseback riding.** Rent **horses** at **Ferme Equestre Albadu,** 1½km from town on N193. (☎04 95 46 24 55. 90F/€13.75 per hr., 200F/€30.50 per half-day, 400F/€61 per day.)

Trains (☎04 95 46 00 97) leave the rotary of av. Jean Nicoli and N193 for: Ajaccio (2hr., 4 per day, 76F/€11.60); Bastia (1½hr., 4 per day, 67F/€10.25); and Calvi (2½hr., 2 per day, 90F/€13.75) via Ponte-Leccia. Eurocorse Voyages (☎04 95 71 24 64) runs **buses** to Ajaccio (1¾hr., M-Sa 2 per day, 65F/€9.95) and Bastia (1¼hr., M-Sa 2 per day, 60F/€9.15). Rent **bikes** from **Corte V.T.T.,** next to the train station. (☎06 12 42 09 45. Open June-Oct. 9am-noon and 2-7pm. 65F/€9.95 half-day, 100F/€15.25 full day.) To reach the center of town from the train station, turn right on the D14 (av. Jean Nicoli), cross two bridges, and follow the road until it ends at **cours Paoli.** Turn left onto **place Paoli,** the town center, and at the top-right corner, climb r. Scolisca to reach the citadel and the **tourist office.** (☎04 95 46 26 70; fax 04 95 46 34 05; www.corte-tourisme.com. Open July-Aug. daily 9am-8pm; May-June and Sept. M-Sa 9am-1pm and 2-7pm; Oct.-Apr. M-F 9am-noon and 2-6pm.) The huge **Casino supermarket** is on allée du 9 Septembre. (Open mid-June to Aug. daily 8:30am-7:30pm; Sept. to mid-June M-F 8:30am-12:30pm and 3-8pm, Sa 8:30am-7:30pm.) In the summer, students can stay in university housing for 100F/€15.25 per night; contact **CROUS,** 7, av. Jean Nicoli, before you arrive. (☎04 95 45 21 00. Open M-F 9am-noon and 2-3:30pm.) **Hôtel-Residence Porette (H-R),** 6, allée du 9 Septembre, is packed with amenities. Bear left from the train station to the stadium and follow it around for 100m. (☎04 95 45 11 11; fax 04 95 61 02 85. Breakfast 34F/€5.20. Reception 24hr. Singles 135F/€21, with bath 199F/€30.35; doubles 145F/€22.15, 279-289F/€42.55; triples 329F/€50.20; quads 350F/€53.36.) **Postal code:** 20250.

THE ALPS (LES ALPES)

Nature's architecture is the real attraction of the Alps. The curves of the Chartreuse Valley rise to rugged crags in the Vercors range and ultimately crescendo into Europe's highest peak, Mont Blanc. Winter **skiers** enjoy some of the world's most challenging slopes and then in the summer, **hikers** take over the mountains for endless vistas and clear air. Skiing arrangements should be made well in advance; Chamonix and Val d'Isère are the easiest bases. TGV **trains** whisk you from Paris to Grenoble or Annecy; scenic trains and slower **buses** service Alpine towns from there. The farther into the mountains you want to go, the harder it is to get there, although service is at least twice as frequent during ski season (Dec.-Apr.).

GRENOBLE

Grenoble (pop. 156,203) has the eccentric cafes and shaggy radicals of any university town, but it also boasts snow-capped peaks and sapphire-blue lakes cherished by athletes and aesthetes alike.

🖪🖪 TRANSPORTATION AND PRACTICAL INFORMATION. Trains arrive in Grenoble at pl. de la Gare from: Annecy (2hr., 9 per day, 91F/€13.90); Lyon (1½hr., 18 per day, 99F/€15.10); Marseilles (2½-4½hr., 15 per day, 196-242F/€29.90-36.95); Nice (5-6½hr., 5 per day, 301F/€45.90); and Paris (3hr., 6 per day, 378-474F/€57.65-72.30). **Buses** leave from the left of the station for Chamonix (3hr., 1 per day, 168F/€25.65) and Geneva (3hr., 1 per day, 158F/€24.10). From the station, turn right into pl. de la Gare, take the third left on av. Alsace-Lorraine, and follow the tram tracks on r. Félix Poulat and r. Blanchard to reach the **tourist office,** 14, r. de la République. (☎04 76 42 41 41; fax 04 76 00 18 98; www.grenoble-isere-tourisme.com. Open M-Sa 9am-6:30pm, Su 10am-1pm and 2-5pm.) **Postal code:** 38000.

⚡🏠 ACCOMMODATIONS AND FOOD. To get from the station to the **Auberge de Jeunesse (HI)**, 10, av. du Grésivaudan, 4km away in Echirolles, follow the tram tracks down av. Alsace-Lorraine, turn right on cours Jean Jaurès, and take bus #1 (dir. Pont Rouge) to La Quinzaine; it's behind the Casino supermarket. (☎04 76 09 33 52; fax 04 76 09 38 99. Breakfast included. Sheets 18F/€2.75. Laundry. Reception M-Sa 7:30am-11pm, Su 7:30-10am and 5:30-11pm. Over 26 102F/€15.60; under 26 4- to 6-bed dorms 72F/€11; singles 110F/€16.80; doubles 170F/€25.95. MC/V.) **Hôtel de la Poste**, 25, r. de la Poste, near the pedestrian zone, has amazing rooms. (☎/fax 04 76 46 67 25. Breakfast 28F/€4.30. Singles 100F/€15.25, with shower 130F/€19.85; doubles 160-170F/€24.40-25.95, 220F/€33.55; triples 190F/€29; quads 220F/€33.55. MC/V.) To reach **Camping Les 3 Pucelles,** 58, r. des Allobroges, in Seyssins, take tram A (dir. Fontaine-La Poya) to Louis Maisonnat, then take bus #51 (dir. Les Nalettes) to Mas des Iles; it's down to the left. (☎04 76 96 45 73; fax 04 76 21 43 73. 48F/€7.35 per person, tent, and car.) **University Restaurants** (URs) sell meal tickets in *carnets* of 10 to those with a student ID. (☎04 76 57 44 00. Open during the school year. Single ticket 15.30F/€2.35.) The two URs in Grenoble *ville* are **Restaurant d'Arsonval,** 5, r. d'Arsonval (Open M-F 11:30am-1:30pm and 6:30-7:45pm) and **Restaurant du Rabot,** r. Maurice Gignoux (Open daily noon-1:15pm and 6:30-7:50pm). **Monoprix,** opposite the tourist office, stocks **groceries.** (Open M-Sa 8:30am-7:30pm.)

📷🏔 SIGHTS AND THE OUTDOORS. *Téléphériques* (lifts) depart from quai Stéphane-Jay every 10min. for the 16th-century **Bastille,** a fort that hovers above town. Enjoy the views from the top, then descend via the **Parc Guy Pape,** which criss-crosses through the fortress and deposits you just across the river from the train station. (Open July-Aug. M 11am-12:15am, Tu-Su 9:15am-12:15am; Nov.-Feb. M 11am-6:30pm, Tu-Su 10:45am-6:30pm; off-season reduced hours.) Cross the Pont St-Laurent and go up Montée Chalemont for the **Musée Dauphinois,** 30, r. Maurice Gignoux, with its futuristic exhibits. (Open W-M June-Sept. 10am-7pm; Oct.-May 10am-6pm. 21F/€3.20, students 10.50F/€1.60.) Grenoble's major attraction is its proximity to the slopes. The biggest and most developed **ski areas** are to the east in **Oisans;** the **Alpe d'Huez** boasts 220km of trails. (Tourist office ☎04 76 11 44 44. 213F/€32.50 per day, 1102F/€168.05 per week.) The **Belledonne** region, northeast of Grenoble, has lower elevation but is cheaper. **Chamrousse,** its biggest and most popular ski area (lift tickets 144F/€22 per day, 564F/€86 per week), has a **youth hostel** (☎04 76 89 91 31; fax 04 76 89 96 96). Only 30min. from Grenoble by **bus** (50F/€7.65), the resort also makes an ideal daytrip in summer.

CHAMONIX

The site of the first winter Olympics in 1924, Chamonix (pop. 10,000) is the ultimate ski town, with soaring mountains and the toughest slopes in the world. The town itself combines the dignity of Mont Blanc, Europe's highest peak (4807m), with the exuberant spirit of the numerous Anglo travelers.

🚆🏛 TRANSPORTATION AND PRACTICAL INFORMATION. Trains leave av. de la Gare (☎04 50 53 12 98) for: Annecy (2½hr., 7 per day, 106F/€16.20); Geneva (2½hr., 6 per day, 135F/€20.60); Lyon (4-5hr., 6 per day, 190F/€29); and Paris (6½hr., 6 per day, 400-504F/€61.76.85). Société Alpes Transports **buses** (☎04 50 53 01 15) leave the train station for: Annecy (2¼hr., 1 per day, 95F/€14.50); Geneva (1½hr., 2 per day, 170-195F/€25.95-29.75); and Grenoble (3hr., 1 per day, 161F/€24.55). **Local buses** connect to ski slopes and hiking trails (7.50F/€1.15). From the station, follow av. Michel Croz, turn left on r. du Dr. Paccard, and take the 1st right to reach pl. de l'Eglise and the **tourist office,** 85, pl. du Triangle de l'Amitié. (☎04 50 53 00 24; fax 04 50 53 58 90. Open daily July-Aug. 8:30am-7:30pm; Dec.-Feb. 8:30am-7pm; Mar.-June and Sept.-Nov. 9am-noon and 2-6pm.) Across from the tourist office, **Compagnie des Guides,** in Maison de la Montagne, leads ski trips and summer hikes. (☎04 50 53 22 88. Open daily Jan.-Mar. and July-Aug. 8:30am-noon and 3:30-7:30pm; Sept.-Dec. and Apr.-June Tu-Sa 10am-noon and 5-7pm.) **Postal code:** 74400.

⚍⚌ ACCOMMODATIONS AND FOOD. Chamonix's *gîtes* (mountain hostels) and dorms are cheap, but they fill up fast; call ahead. The **Auberge de Jeunesse (HI)**, 127, montée Jacques Balmat, in Les Pèlerins at the base of the Glacier de Bossons, offers all-inclusive winter **ski packages** (1550-3650F/€236.35-556.50). Take the bus from the train station or pl. de l'Eglise (dir. Les Houches) to Pèlerins Ecole (4F/€0.60) and follow the signs uphill; by train, get off at Les Pèlerins and follow the signs. (☎ 04 50 53 14 52; fax 04 50 55 92 34; www.aj-chamonix.fr.st. Breakfast included. Reception daily 8am-noon and 5-10pm. Dorms 85F/€12.95; singles and doubles 15F/€2.30 extra per person. MC/V.) **Gîte le Vagabond**, 365, av. Ravanel le Rouge, is a brand-new *gîte* near the center of town. (☎ 04 50 53 15 43; fax 04 50 53 68 21; www.limelab.com/vagabond. Reception daily 8-10:30am and 4:30pm-1am. 4- to 8-bunk dorms 80F/€12.20 with 100F/€15.25 key deposit.) Turn left from the base of the Aiguille du Midi *téléphérique*, continue past the main roundabout, and look right to **camp** at **L'Ile des Barrats**, on rte. des Pélerins. (☎/fax 04 50 53 51 44. Reception daily July-Aug. 8am-10:30pm; May-June and Sept. 8am-noon and 4-7pm. Open May-Sept. 32F/€4.90 per person, 24F/€3.65 per tent, 13F/€2 per car.) Get **groceries** at **Super U**, 117, r. Joseph Vallot. (Open M-Sa 8:15am-7:30pm, Su 8:30am-noon.)

⚍⚌ HIKING AND SKIING. Whether you've come to climb up the mountains or to ski down them, you're in for a challenge. But wherever you go, be cautious—on average, one person a day dies on the mountains. The **l'Aiguille du Midi** *téléphérique* offers a pricey, knuckle-whitening ascent over forests and snowy cliffs to a needlepoint peak at the top. A ride to the top reveals a fantastic panorama from 3842m. (☎ 04 50 53 30 80; 24hr. reservations ☎ 04 50 53 40 00. 210F/€32.05.) Bring your passport to continue by gondola to **Helbronner, Italy** for views of three countries and the **Matterhorn** and **Mont Blanc peaks;** pack a picnic to eat on the glacier (return 315F/€48.05). Hike or take a train to the **ice cave** carved afresh every year by **La Mer de Glace**, a glacier that slides 30m per year. Special trains (☎ 04 50 53 12 54) run from a small station next to the main one (Daily July-Aug. 8am-6pm every 20min.; May-June and early Sept. to mid-Sept. 8:30am-5pm every 30min.; mid-Sept. to Apr. 10am-4pm. Return 82F/€12.50). Sunken in a valley, Chamonix is surrounded by mountains ideal for skiing. To the south, **Le Tour-Col de Balme** (☎ 04 50 54 00 58), above the village of **Le Tour**, is ideal for beginner and intermediate skiers (day pass 153F/€23.35). On the northern side of the valley, **Les Grands Montets** is the *grande dame* of Chamonix ski spots, with all advanced terrain and remodeled **snowboarding** facilities. (☎ 04 50 53 13 18. Lift tickets 230F/€35.10 per day).

ANNECY

With narrow cobblestone streets, winding canals, and a turreted castle, Annecy appears more like a fairy-tale fabrication than a modern city. The **Palais de l'Isle** is a 13th-century fortress that served as a prison for Resistance fighters during World War II. (Open daily June-Sept. 10am-6pm; Oct.-May 10am-noon and 2-6pm. 20F/€3.05, students 5F/€0.80.) The shaded **Jardins de l'Europe** are Annecy's pride and joy. Although it may be hard to tear yourself away from the city's charming **vieille ville**, Annecy's Alpine forests boast excellent **hiking** and **biking trails.** One of the best hikes begins at the **Basilique de la Visitation**, near the hostel. An exquisite 16km scenic *piste cyclable* (bike route) hugs the lake shore along the eastern coast.

Trains (☎ 08 36 35 35 35) arrive at pl. de la Gare from: Chamonix (2½hr., 7 per day, 106F/€16.20); Grenoble (2hr., 12 per day, 91F/€13.90); Lyon (2hr., 7 per day, 117F/€17.85); Nice (6hr., 2 per day, 352F/€53.70); and Paris (4hr., 6 per day, 363F). Autocars Frossard **buses** (☎ 04 50 45 73 90) leave from next to the station for Geneva (1¼hr., 6 per day, 57F/€8.70) and Lyon (3½hr., 2 per day, 102F/€15.55). From the train station, take the underground passage to r. Vaugelas, follow the street left for four blocks, and enter the Bonlieu shopping mall to reach the **tourist office**, 1, r. Jean Jaurès, in pl. de la Libération. (☎ 04 50 45 00 33; fax 04 50 51 87 20; www.lac-annecy.com. Open July-Aug. M-Sa 9am-6:30pm, Su 9am-12:30pm and 1:45-6:30pm; Sept.-June daily 9am-12:30pm and 1:45-6pm.) In summer, you can reach the **Auberge de Jeunesse "La Grande Jeanne" (HI)**, on rte. de Semnoz, via the *ligne d'été* (dir. Semnoz) from the station (6.50F/€1); otherwise, take bus #1 (dir. Marquisats) from the station to Hôtel de Police, turn right on av. du Tresum, and follow signs pointing to Semnoz. (☎ 04 50 45 33 19; fax 04 50 52 77 52. Breakfast included. Sheets 17F/€2.60. Reception daily 8am-10pm. Dorms 74F/€11.30. AmEx/MC/V.) **Camp** at **Camping Bélvèdere** at 8, rte. de Semnoz, near the youth hostel. (☎ 04 50 45 48 30. Reception daily July-Aug. 8am-9pm; mid-Apr. to June and Sept to mid-Oct 8am-8pm. Open mid-Apr. to mid-Oct. 45F/€6.90 per person with tent, 65-85F/€9.95-12.95 per couple with tent; 17F/€2.60 per car.) A **Monoprix supermarket** fills the better part of pl. de Notre-Dame. (Open M-Sa 8:30am-7:30pm.) **Postal code:** 74000.

LYON

France's second largest city is second in little else. Friendlier and more relaxed than Paris, Lyon (pop. 1½ million) boasts a rich history as a prosperous trading center and the headquarters for social movements, such as the Resistance during World War II. Today, the city is a breeding ground for culinary genius and an urban force among major European cities.

⌐ TRANSPORTATION

Trains: Trains passing through Lyon stop only at **Gare de la Part-Dieu,** bd. Marius Vivier-Merle, 3ème (M: Part-Dieu), in the business district on the east bank of the Rhône. Trains terminating at Lyon also stop at **Gare de Perrache,** pl. Carnot, 2ème (M: Perrache). TGV trains to Paris stop at both. **SNCF info and reservation desk** at Perrache open M-F 9am-7pm, Sa 9am-6:30pm; at Part-Dieu open M-F 9am-7pm, Sa 9am-6:30pm. To: **Dijon** (2hr., 13 per day, 137F/€20.90); **Grenoble** (1¼hr., 15 per day, 99F/€15.10); **Marseilles** (3hr., 13 per day, 221F/€33.70); **Nice** (6hr., 15 per day, 299F/€45.60); **Paris** (2hr., 20 TGVs per day, 324-410F/€49.40-62.50).

Buses: On the lowest level of the Gare de Perrache (☎ 04 72 77 63 03), and also at Gare de la Part-Dieu (**Allô Transports,** ☎ 04 72 61 72 61).

Public Transportation: TCL (☎ 04 78 71 70 00), has info offices at both train stations and major métro stops. Tickets are valid for all methods of mass transport, including the **métro, buses, funiculars,** and **trams. Single-fare tickets,** valid for 1hr. in 1 direction, 8.50F/€1.30; **carnet of 10** 68.50F/€10.45, students 58.50F/€8.95. The Ticket Liberté day pass (24F/€3.75), which allows unlimited use of all mass transit for the day, is a great deal. The efficient **métro** runs 5am-midnight. **Buses** run 5am-9pm.

☀7 ORIENTATION AND PRACTICAL INFORMATION

Lyon is divided into nine **arrondissements** (districts). The 1er, 2ème, and 4ème lie on the **presqu'île** (peninsula), which juts south toward the **Saône** (to the west) and the **Rhône** (to the east) rivers. Starting in the south, the 2ème (the centre ville) includes the **Gare de Perrache** and **place Bellecour.** The 1er houses the nocturnal Terraux neighborhood, with its cafes and popular student-packed bars. Farther north is the 4ème and the **Croix-Rousse.** The main pedestrian roads on the presqu'île are **rue de la République** and **rue Victor Hugo.** West of the Saône, **Fourvière Hill** and its basilica overlook **Vieux Lyon** (5ème). East of the Rhône (3ème and 6-8ème) lies the **Part-Dieu** train station (3ème), the commercial complex, and most of the city's population.

Tourist Office: In the Tourist Pavilion, at pl. Bellecour, 2ème (☎ 04 72 77 69 69; fax 04 78 42 04 32). M: Bellecour. Indispensable **"Map and Guide"** (5F/€0.80), hotel reservation office, and SNCF desk. The **Lyon City Card** (90-200F/€13.75-30.50) authorizes unlimited public transport along with admission to 14 museums and various tours. Valid for 1, 2, or 3 days. Open May-Oct. M-Sa 9am-6pm; Nov.-Apr. daily 10am-6pm.

Emergency: ☎ 17. **Medical assistance:** ☎ 15.

Police: 47, r. de la Charité (☎ 04 78 42 26 56).

Hospital: Hôpital Hôtel-Dieu, 1, pl. de l'Hôpital, 2ème (☎ 04 72 41 30 00), near quai du Rhône.

Internet Access: Station-Internet, 4, r. du President Carnot, *2ème.* 40F/€6.10 per hr., students 30F/€4.60. Open M-Sa 10am-7pm.

Post Office: On pl. Antonin Poncet, *2ème* (☎04 72 40 65 22), near pl. Bellecour. **Currency exchange** and *Poste Restante.* Open M-F 8am-5pm, Su 8am-12:30pm. Address mail to be held: SURNAME, First Name *Poste Restante, Recette Principale* pl. Antonin Poncet, **69002** Lyon, France.

Postal Codes: 69001-69009; last digit indicates *arrondissement.*

ACCOMMODATIONS

As a financial center, Lyon's beds are booked during the work week, but there are plenty of vacancies on weekends. It's actually easier and cheaper to find a place in the summer, but making a reservation is still a good idea. Inexpensive hotels cluster east of **place Carnot**, near Perrache, and north of **place des Terreaux.**

■ **Auberge de Jeunesse (HI),** 41/45, Montée du Chemin Neuf, *5ème* (☎04 78 15 05 50; fax 04 78 15 05 51). M: Vieux Lyon. Take the funicular from *Vieux Lyon* to Minimes, walk down the stairs, and go left down the hill for 5min. Bar, laundry, Internet. Breakfast included. Sheets 17F/€2.60. Reception 24hr. Members only. Dorms 75F/€11.45.

■ **Hôtel St-Vincent,** 9, r. Pareille, *1er* (☎04 78 27 22 56; fax 04 78 30 92 87), just off Quai St-Vincent. Simple, elegant rooms close to Lyon's nightlife. Breakfast 30F/€4.60. Reception 24hr. Reserve ahead. English, German, and Italian spoken. Singles 180-230F/€27.45-35.10; doubles 230-270F/€35.10-41.20. MC/V.

Résidence Benjamin Delessert, 145, av. Jean Jaurès, *7ème* (☎04 78 61 41 41; fax 04 78 61 40 24). M: Jean Macé. From Perrache, take buses #11 or 39 to Jean Macé, walk under the tracks, and look left after 3 blocks. College dorm atmosphere. 24hr. reception. Singles 91F/€13.90, with shower 95F/€14.50.

Hôtel d'Ainay, 14, r. des Remparts d'Ainay, *2ème* (☎04 78 42 43 42; fax 04 72 77 51 90). M: Ampère-Victor Hugo. English spoken. Reception 7am-10pm. Singles 145F/€24, with shower 210F/€32.05; doubles 180F/€27.45, 220F/€33.55. MC/V.

Hôtel du Dauphiné, 3, r. Duhamel, *2ème* (☎04 78 37 24 19; fax 04 78 92 81 52), to the right of pl. Carnot near Perrache. Comfortable rooms with showers. Pricier rooms are large. Reception 24hr. Breakfast 27F/€4.15. Singles from 130F/€19.85; doubles from 210F/€32.05; triples from 250F/€38.15; quads 320F/€48.80. MC/V.

FOOD

The galaxy of *Michelin* stars adorning Lyon's restaurants confirm the city's reputation as the culinary capital of the Western world. Cozy **bouchons** serve local cuisine at low prices in the **Terreaux** district (*1er*) and along **rues St-Jean** and **des Marronniers** (both in the *2ème*). Finish off your dinner with *torte tatin* (upside-down apple pie) or *cocons* (chocolates wrapped in marzipan). Ethnic restaurants cluster off **rue de la République** (*2ème*). **Monoprix supermarket** is on r. de la République, in pl. des Cordeliers, *2ème.* (Open M-Sa 8:30am-9:30pm.)

■ **Chez Mounier,** 3, r. des Marronniers, *2ème.* This tiny place satisfies a discriminating local clientele with generous traditional specialties. 4-course *menus* 61-96F/€9.30-14.65. Open Tu-Sa noon-2pm and 7-10:30pm, Su noon-2pm.

Chabert et Fils, 11, r. des Marronniers, *2ème.* One of the better known *bouchons* in Lyon. *Museau de bœuf* (snout of cattle) and *andouillettes* are on the 99F/€15.10 *menu.* Lunch *menus* 50-80F/€7.60-12.20. Open daily noon-2pm and 7-11pm.

Mister Patate, pl. St-Jean, *5ème.* Serves 44 potato dishes. Plates 35-50F/€5.35-7.60. Open M-Sa 11:30am-3pm and 6-11:30pm, Su 11:30-3pm and 6-10pm.

La Crepe d'Or, 2, pl. St-Paul, *5ème* serves enormous crepes. *Menus* 58-85F/€8.85-12.95. Open daily noon-midnight.

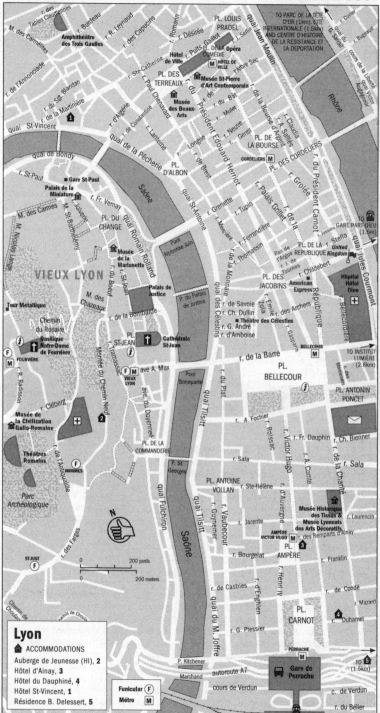

Lyon

🏠 ACCOMMODATIONS

Auberge de Jeunesse (HI), 2
Hôtel d'Ainay, 3
Hôtel du Dauphiné, 4
Hôtel St-Vincent, 1
Résidence B. Delessert, 5

Funicular Ⓕ
Métro Ⓜ

◉ SIGHTS

VIEUX LYON

Nestled along the Saône at the bottom of the Fourvière Hill, the cobblestone streets of *Vieux Lyon* wind between lively cafes and magnificent medieval and Renaissance **townhouses.** (M: Vieux Lyon.) The townhouses are graced with **traboules,** tunnels that lead from the street through a maze of courtyards. (Tours in summer daily 2pm. 60F/€9.15, students 30F/€4.60.) The southern end of *Vieux Lyon* is dominated by the 12th-century **Cathédrale St-Jean,** at pl. St-Jean, and its 14th-century astronomical clock. (Open M-F 8am-noon and 2-7:30pm, Sa-Su 2-5pm. Free.)

FOURVIÈRE AND ROMAN LYON

From the corner of r. du Bœuf and r. de la Bombarde in *Vieux Lyon*, climb the stairs to reach the **Fourvière Hill,** the nucleus of Roman Lyon. (M: Fourvière.) Continue up via the rose-lined **chemin de la Rosarie,** through a garden to the **Esplanade Fourvière,** where a model of the cityscape points out local landmarks. Most prefer to take the funicular *(la ficelle)* from av. A. Max in *Vieux Lyon*, off pl. St-Jean, to the top of the hill. Behind the Esplanade is the **Basilique Notre-Dame de Fourvière,** with multicolored mosaics, gilded pillars, and elaborate carvings. (Open daily 8am-7pm. Free.) Set back into the hillside as you walk down from the church, you'll see signs for the **Musée Gallo-Romain,** 17, r. Cléberg, 5*ème*, and its huge collection of arms, pottery, statues, and jewelry. Check out the bronze tablet inscribed with a speech by Lyon's favorite son, Emperor Claudius. (Open Tu-Su Mar.-Oct. 10am-6pm; Nov.-Feb. 10am-5pm. 25F/€3.85, students 15F/€2.30.)

LE PRESQU'ÎLE AND LES TERREAUX

Monumental squares, statues, and fountains mark the **Presqu'île,** the lively area between the Rhône and the Saône. The heart is **place Bellecour,** a sea of red gravel lined with shops and flower stalls. The pedestrian **rue Victor Hugo** runs south from pl. Bellecour; to the north, the crowded **rue de la République** is the urban artery of Lyon. It terminates at **place Louis Pradel** in the 1*er*, at the tip of the **Terreaux** district. Across the square at pl. Louis Pradel is the spectacular 17th-century **Hôtel de Ville.** In pl. des Terreaux is the huge **Musée des Beaux-Arts,** second only to the Louvre with a comprehensive archaeological wing, works by Spanish and Dutch masters, and a sculpture garden. (Open W-M 10:30am-6pm. 25F/€7.60, students 13F/€2.)

EAST OF THE RHÔNE AND MODERN LYON

Lyon's newest train station and monstrous space-age mall form the core of the ultra-modern Part-Dieu district. The **Centre d'Histoire de la Résistance et de la Déportation,** 14, av. Bertholet, 7*ème*, has documents, photos, and films of the Lyon-based resistance to the Nazis. (M: Jean Mace. Open W-Su 9am-5:15pm. 25F/€3.85, students 13F/€2.) In the futuristic **Cité Internationale de Lyon,** a commercial complex housing offices, shops, theaters, and Interpol's world headquarters, is the **Musée d'Art Contemporain,** quai Charles de Gaulle, 6*ème*. (M: Masséna or take bus #4 from M: Foch. Open W-Su noon-7pm. 25F/€3.85, students 13F/€2.)

🎵📷 ENTERTAINMENT AND NIGHTLIFE

In summer, Lyon explodes with festivals and special events. The **Fête de la Musique,** on June 21, when performers take over the streets, is a day of frenzied fun. The two-week **Festival du Jazz à Vienne,** in late June, welcomes jazz masters to the nearby medieval town of Vienne. (☎04 74 85 00 05. Tickets 160F/€24.40, students 150F/€22.90.) **Les Nuits de Fourvière** is a two-month summer festival in the ancient Théâtre Romain featuring pop and classical concerts and plays. (☎04 72 32 00 00. Tickets and information at Théâtre Romain and the FNAC shop on r. de la République.)

Nightlife in Lyon is fast and furious. **Ayers Rock Café,** 2, r. Desirée, and **Cosmopolitan,** right next door, are packed with students. (Ayers open M-Sa 6pm-3am. Cosmo-

FRANCE

politan open M-W 8pm-2am, Th-Sa 8pm-3am. No cover.) **Le Voxx**, 1, r. d'Algérie, is packed with stylish French and almost-stylish exchange students. (☎04 78 28 33 87. Open M-Sa 8pm-2am, Su 10pm-2am.) **Le Village Club**, 6, r. Violi, off r. Royale, features fabulous drag queens and attracts a thirty-something male crowd. (Open W-Th 9pm-3am, F-Sa 10pm-4am.) The city's best and most accessible late-night spots are a strip of **riverboat dance clubs** by the east bank of the Rhône.

BERRY-LIMOUSIN

All too often passed over for beaches and bigger cities, Berry-Limousin offers peaceful countryside, tiny villages, and fascinating towns. When Bourges served as the capital of France, the king's financier, Jacques Cœur built a lavish string of châteaux throughout the region, now known as the Route Jacques Cœur. Later on, Berry-Limousin became a artistic and literary breeding ground, home to Georges Sand, Auguste Renoir, and Jean Giraudoux.

BOURGES

Bourges (pop. 80,000) is proud of its Berry culture, with its fine regional wines and medieval *vieille ville*, enhanced by cobblestone streets lined with Gothic turrets. Bourges lies in the shadow of the **Cathédrale St-Étienne**, graced with stunning 13th-century handiwork in the cathedral, tower, and crypt. From the train station, follow av. H. Laudier, which turns into av. Jean Jaurès, bear left onto r. du Commerce and continue straight on r. Moyenne. (Open daily Apr.-Sept. M-Su 8:30am-7:15pm; Oct.-Mar. M-Sa 9am-5:45pm. Crypt and tower open July-Aug. daily 9am-6pm. 36F/€5.50, students 23F/€3.50; 30F/€4.60 *billet jumelé* includes entrance to the Palais Jacques Coeur.) The **Palais Jacques-Coeur**, 10bis, r. Jacques Coeur, former home of Charles VII's financial minister, contains lavish carvings. (Open daily July-Aug. 9am-6pm; Apr.-June and Sept. 9am-noon and 2-6pm; Nov.-Mar. 9am-noon and 2-5pm. Tours offered every hr. 36F/€5.50, ages 18-24 23F/€3.50.) A **pedestrian tour** is available from the **tourist office**, 21, r. Victor Hugo, near the cathedral. (☎02 48 23 02 60. Open M-Sa 9am-7pm, Su 10am-7pm.) The **promenade des Remparts**, between r. Bourbonnoux and r. Molière, winds past Roman ramparts and back gardens.

Trains leave from the pl. Général Leclerc for: Paris (2½hr., 5-8 per day, 156F/ €23.80) and Tours (1½hr., 10 per day, 108F/€16.50). To get to the **Auberge de Jeunesse (HI)**, 22, r. Henri Sellier, from the station, follow av. H. Laudier, which becomes av. Jean Jaurès, bear left onto r. du Commerce, bear right on r. des Arènes, which becomes r. Fernault, cross at the intersection to r. René Ménard and follow it to the right, and turn left at r. Henri Sellier. (☎02 48 24 58 09; fax 02 48 65 51 46. Reception M-F 8am-noon and 2pm-1am, Sa-Su 8am-noon and 5-10pm. Dorms 50F/€7.65.) To reach the **Centre International de Séjour, "La Charmille,"** 17, r. Félix-Chédin, from the station, cross the footbridge over the tracks and head up r. Félix-Chédin. (☎02 48 23 07 40; fax 02 48 69 01 21. Dorms 72F/€11 per person; singles 98F/€15. MC/V.) Outdoor tables pack **place Gordaine** and **rue Borbonnoux** while sandwich shops line **rues Moyenne** and **Mirebeau**. The huge **Leclerc supermarket** is on r. Prado, off bd. Juranville. (Open M-F 9am-7:30pm, Sa 8:30am-7:30pm.) Bars and cafés pepper the *vieille ville*. **Postal code:** 18000 (18012 "Bourges Cedex" for *Poste Restante*).

BURGUNDY (BOURGOGNE)

Encompassing the Côte d'Or, the Plateau de Langres, and wild, forested Morvan, Burgundy is best known for its Romanesque architecture and the 40 million bottles of wine it produces annually. The duchy's history is one of a French powerhouse: from the Middle Ages through 19th century, it was at the heart of the religious fever sweeping Europe, spurring the construction of magnificent cathedrals. Today, Burgundy's superb wines and famed cuisine like *coq au vin* and *bœuf bourguinon* have made this region a capital in the hearts of Epicureans everywhere.

DIJON

Dijon (pop. 160,000) is renowned worldwide for its mustard, but also houses a treasure trove of sights and nightlife. The city is filled with varied architecture and museums, and boasts a marvelous culinary tradition. The diverse **Musée des Beaux-Arts** occupies the east wing of the colossal **Palais des Ducs de Bourgogne,** in pl. de la Libération at the center of the *vieille ville.* (Open W-M 10am-6pm. 22F/€3.35, students free; Su free.) At the **Eglise Notre-Dame,** in pl. Notre-Dame, admire the façade of gargoyles and rub the owl on the left side of the exterior for good luck. The Renaissance façade of the **Eglise St-Michel,** in pl. St-Michel, has been beautifully restored. The **Jardin de l'Arquebuse,** 1, av. Albert 1*er*, provides a welcome retreat with reflecting pools and a lush botanical garden. (Open July-Sept. daily 7:30am-8pm; Oct.-Feb. 7:30am-5:30pm; Mar.-June 7:30am-7pm.) **Maille Boutique,** 32, r. de la Liberté, has been making *moutarde au vin,* or **Grey Poupon,** since 1747.

Trains from Cours de la Gare, at the end of av. Maréchal Foch, go to Lyon (2hr., 11 per day, 137F/€20.90) and Paris (1½hr., 14 TGVs per day, 213F/€32.50). The **tourist office,** on pl. Darcy, is a straight shot down av. Maréchal Foch from the station. (☎03 80 44 11 44. Open July-Aug. daily 9am-8pm; Sept.-June 9am-7pm.) To stay at the huge **Auberge de Jeunesse (HI),** 1, av. Champollion, take bus #5 (or night bus A) from pl. Grangier to Epirey. (☎03 80 72 95 20. Breakfast included. Reception 24hr. Dorms 72-78F/€11-11.90; singles 180F/€27.45; doubles and triples 90-155F/€13.75-23.65. MC/V.) ◙**Hôtel Montchapet,** 26-28, r. Jacques Cellerier, north of av. Première Armée Française off pl. Darcy, has homey rooms and lots of students. (☎03 80 53 95 00. Breakfast 33F/€5.05. Reception 7am-10:30pm. Singles 155-250F/€23.65-38.10; doubles 230-296F/€35.10-45.15; triples and quads 347-378F/€52.90-57.65.) **Rues Berbisey** and **Monge** host a variety of low- to mid-priced restaurants. Eat cheap at the **supermarket** downstairs in the **Galeries Lafayette,** 41, r. de la Liberté. (Open M-Sa 9am-7:15pm.) **Postal code:** 21000 (21031 for *Poste Restante).*

▶ DAYTRIP FROM DIJON: BEAUNE. The viticulture hotspot of **Beaune,** 40km south of Dijon (25min., 28 per day, 38F/€5.80), has poured out wine for centuries. Surrounded by the famous Côte de Beaune vineyards, the town itself is packed with wineries offering free tastings. The largest *cave* (wine cellar) in Beaune is the **Patriarche Père et Fils,** 5-7, r. du Collège. Stairs descend from the altar of an 18th-century chapel to a labyrinth of corridors packed with four million bottles. (☎03 80 24 53 78. Open daily 9:30-11:30am and 2-5:30pm. 50F/€7.65.) The **tourist office,** 1, r. de l'Hôtel-Dieu, has free maps and lists of *caves* in the region. (☎03 80 26 21 30. Open mid-June to mid-Sept. M-Sa 9:30am-8pm, Su 9:30am-6pm; mid-Sept. to mid-June closes 1hr. earlier. **Wine Festival,** Nov. 16-18 daily 9am-8pm.)

ALSACE-LORRAINE AND FRANCHE-COMTÉ

As first prize in the endless Franco-German border wars, France's northeastern frontier has had a long and bloody history. Heavily influenced by its tumultuous past, the entire region now maintains a fascinating blend of French and German in the local dialects, cuisine, and architecture. Alsace's well-preserved towns offer half-timbered Bavarian houses flanking tiny crooked streets and canals, while Lorraine's elegant cities spread to the west among wheat fields. In Franche-Comté, the Jura mountains have some of France's finest cross-country skiing.

STRASBOURG

Only a few kilometers from the Franco-German border, Strasbourg (pop. 260,000) has spent much of its history being annexed by one side or another. Today, German is often heard on its streets, and *winstubs* sit next door to *pâtisseries.* Strasbourg is also the joint center, along with Brussels, of the European Union. With half-timbered houses and flower-lined canals, the city makes a fantastic stopover.

📞📱 TRANSPORTATION AND PRACTICAL INFORMATION. Strasbourg is a major rail hub. **Trains** (☎ 03 88 22 50 50) go to: Luxembourg (2½hr., 14 per day, 165F/€25.15); Frankfurt, Germany (3hr., 18 per day, 240F/€36.60); Paris (4hr., 16 per day, 226F/€34.45); and Zürich, Switzerland (3hr., 18 per day, 255F/€38.90). The **tourist office,** 17, pl. de la Cathédrale, makes hotel reservations for 10F/€1.55 plus deposit. (☎ 03 88 52 28 28. Open June-Sept. M-Sa 9am-7pm, Su 9am-6pm; Oct.-May. daily 9am-6pm.) Rent **bikes** at **Vélocation,** at 4, r. du Maire Kuss, near the train station. (30F/€4.60 per day. 300F/€45.75 deposit and copy of ID.) Get on the **Internet** at **Cybermaniak,** on r. du Fosse des Treize. (30F/€4.60 per hr. Open Tu and Th-Sa 2pm-midnight, W 9am-noon, Su 2-8pm.)

🍴🛏 ACCOMMODATIONS AND FOOD. Make reservations or arrive early to find reasonable accommodations. **◙CIARUS (Centre International d'Accueil de Strasbourg),** 7, r. Finkmatt, has large, spotless facilities with an international atmosphere. From the train station, take r. du Maire-Kuss to the canal, turn left, and follow quais St-Jean, Kléber, and Finkmatt; turn left on r. Finkmatt, and it's on the left. (☎ 03 88 15 27 88; fax 03 88 15 29 89; www.ciarus.com. Breakfast included. Reception 24hr. Check-in 3:30pm. Check-out 9am. Curfew 1am. Dorms 94-126F/€14.35-19.25; singles 211F/€32.20. MC/V.) **Hôtel de Bruxelles,** 13, r. Kuhn, is up the street from the train station. Ask to see your room in advance. (☎ 03 88 32 45 31; fax 03 88 32 22 01. Breakfast 35F/€5.35. Singles and doubles 170-285F/€25.95-43.45; triples and quads 285-345F/€43.45-52.60. MC/V.) **Auberge de Jeunesse, Centre International de Rencontres du parc du Rhin (HI),** r. des Cavaliers, is 7km from the station, and 1km from Germany. From the station, take bus #2 (dir. Pond du Rhin) to Parc du Rhin. Facing the tourist office, go to the left and r. des Cavaliers is the street with flashing red lights. (☎ 03 88 45 54 20; fax 03 88 45 54 21. Breakfast included. Reception daily 7am-12:30pm, 2-7:30pm, and 8:30pm-1am. Curfew 1am. Dorms 114F/€17.40; singles 226F/€34.45; doubles 170F/€25.95; nonmembers 19F/€2.90 extra. MC/V.)

Winstubs are informal places that serve Alsatian specialties such as *choucroute garnie* (spiced sauerkraut served with meats)—try the **La Petite France** neighborhood, especially along r. des Dentelles and petite r. des Dentelles. Explore **place de la Cathédrale, rue Mercière,** or **rue du Vieil Hôpital** for restaurants, and **place Marché Gayot,** hidden off r. des Frères, for lively cafes. For **groceries,** swing by the **ATAC Supermarket,** 47, r. des Grandes Arcades, off pl. Kléber. (Open M-Sa 8:30am-8pm.)

📷🎭 SIGHTS AND ENTERTAINMENT. The ornate Gothic **Cathédrale de Strasbourg** sends its tower 142m skyward. Inside, the **Horloge Astronomique** demonstrates the wizardry of 16th-century Swiss clockmakers. While you wait for the clock to strut its stuff—daily at 12:30pm, apostles troop out of the clockface while a cock crows to greet Saint Peter—check out the **Pilier des Anges** (Angels' Pillar), a masterpiece of Gothic sculpture. You can climb the **tower** in front of the clock like the young Goethe, who scaled its 330 steps regularly to cure his fear of heights. (Cathedral open M-Sa 7-11:40am and 12:45-7pm, Su 12:45-6pm. Tickets for the clock on sale 8:30am in cathedral and 11:45am at south entrance; 5F/€0.75. Tower open daily 9am-6:30pm; 20F/€3.05, children 10F/€1.55.) **Palais Rohan,** 2, pl. du Château, houses three small but excellent museums: the **Musée des Beaux-Arts, Musée des Arts Décoratifs,** and **Musée Archéologique.** (Open M and W-Sa 10am-noon and 1:30-6pm, Su 10am-5pm. 20F/€3.05 each; combined ticket 40F/€6.10, students 20F/€3.05.) Take bus #23, 30, or 72 to L'Orangerie for **L'Orangerie,** Strasbourg's most spectacular park; free concerts play in the summer at the Pavilion Joséphine (Th-Tu 8:30pm).

LA ROUTE DU VIN

Since the High Middle Ages, the wines of Alsace have been highly prized—and highly priced—across Europe. The vineyards of Alsace flourish along a corridor of 170km known as La Route du Vin (Wine Route) that begins at **Strasbourg** (p. 388) and stretches south along the foothills of the Vosges, passing through 100 towns along the way to **Mulhouse.** Hordes of tourists are drawn each year to explore the beautifully preserved medieval villages along the route—and, of course, for the free *dégustations* (tastings) along the way.

Colmar (p. 390) and **Sélestat** (p. 390) offer excellent bases and fascinating sights of their own; but don't miss out on smaller, less-touristed villages. The most accessible towns from Strasbourg are **Molsheim**, a medieval university center, and **Barr**, with an intricate old town and a vineyard trail that leads up through the hills. The more famous towns lie to the south: the most visited sight in Alsace, the **Château de Haut Koenigsbourg**, towers over **Kintzheim**; and the 16th-century walled hamlet of **Riquewihr**, the Route's most popular village, houses many of Alsace's best-known wine firms. If you're in Strasbourg and are contemplating a detour along the Wine Route, pick up the ☒*Alsace Wine Route* brochure from a tourist office.

⊟ TRANSPORTATION. Strasbourg, the northern terminus of the Wine Route, is a major rail hub, easily accessible from France, Germany, and Luxembourg. **Trains** from Strasbourg hit many of the towns along the northern half of the Route, including: **Barr** (50min., 35F/€5.35); **Molsheim** (30min., 22F/€3.35); and **Sélestat** (30min., 42F/€6.40). You can also go directly from Strasbourg to **Colmar** (40min., 58F/€8.85), although wine lovers are more likely to get there via train from **Sélestat** (15min., 24F/€3.65). **Bus** lines pepper the southern half of the Route, running from Colmar to **Kaysersberg** (20min., 12.60F/€1.95); **Riquewihr** (30min., 15-20F/€2.30-3.05); and many other small towns on the Route. From Mulhouse, leap into Switzerland from nearby **Basel** (20min., 36F/€5.50); go into **Paris** (4½hr., 9 per day, 280F/€42.70); or return to **Strasbourg** (1hr., 87F/€13.30).

SÉLESTAT. Sélestat (pop. 17,200), between Colmar and Strasbourg, is a charming town often overlooked by tourists on their way to larger Route cities. The **Bibliothèque Humaniste**, 1, r. de la Bibliothèque, founded in 1452, contains a fascinating collection of ancient documents produced during Sélestat's 15th-century humanistic boom. (Open July-Aug. M and W-F 9am-noon and 2-6pm, Sa 9am-noon and 2-5pm, Su 2-5pm; Sept.-June closed Su. 20F/€3.05.) The **tourist office,** 10, bd. Gén. Leclerc, in the Commanderie St-Jean, rents **bikes.** (☎ 03 88 58 87 20; fax 03 88 92 88 63; www.selestat-tourisme.com. 80F/€12.20 per day. Open May-Sept. M-F 9am-12:30pm and 1:30-7pm, Sa 9am-noon and 2-5pm, Su 9am-3pm; Oct.-Apr. M-F 8:30am-noon and 1:30-6pm, Sa 9am-noon and 2-5pm.) The ☒**Hôtel de l'Ill,** 13, r. des Bateliers, off bd. des Thiers, has bright rooms. (☎ 03 88 92 91 09. Breakfast 30F/€4.60. Reception daily 7am-3pm and 5-11pm. Singles 140-165F/€21.35-25.15; doubles 180-240F/€27.45-36.60; triples 400F/€70. MC/V.) **Camping Les Cigognes** is on the south edge of the *vieille ville.* (☎ 03 88 92 03 98. Reception July-Aug. 8am-noon and 3-10pm; May-June and Sept.-Oct 8am-noon and 3-7pm. Open May-Oct. July-Aug. 60F/€9.15 per person, 80F/€12.20 per 2 or 3 people; May-June and Sept.-Oct. 50F/€7.65, 70F/€10.70.) You'll find food on **rue des Chevaliers** and **rue de l'Hôpital. Postal code:** 67600.

COLMAR. Colmar's (pop. 65,000) bubbling fountains, crooked lanes, and pastel houses evoke an intimate charm despite packs of tourists. The collection of **Musée Unterlinden**, 1, r. d'Unterlinden, ranges from Romanesque to Renaissance, with Grünewald's *Issenheim Altarpiece.* (Open daily Apr.-Oct. 9am-6pm; Nov.-Mar. W-M 10am-5pm. 35F/€5.35, students 25F/€3.85.) The **Eglise des Dominicains,** on pl. des Dominicains, has Colmar's other major masterpiece, Schongauer's *Virgin in the Rose Bower.* (Open Apr.-Dec. 10am-1pm and 3-6pm. 8F/€1.25, students 6F/€0.95.)

To get to the **tourist office,** 4, r. d'Unterlinden, from the train station, turn left on av. de la République (which becomes r. Kléber) and follow it to the right to pl. Unterlinden. (☎ 03 89 20 68 92; fax 03 89 20 69 14. Open July-Aug. M-Sa 9am-7pm, Su 9:30am-2pm; Apr.-June and Sept.-Oct. M-Sa 9am-6pm, Su 10am-2pm; Nov.-Mar. M-Sa 9am-noon and 2-6pm, Su 10am-2pm.) To reach the **Auberge de Jeunesse (HI),** 2, r. Pasteur, take bus #4 (dir. Logelbach) to Pont Rouge. (☎ 03 89 80 57 39. Breakfast included. Sheets 20F/€3.05. Reception daily July-Aug. 7-10am and 5pm-midnight; Sept.-June 5-11pm. Lockout 10am-5pm. Curfew midnight. No reservations. Open mid-Jan. to mid-Dec. Dorms 71F/€10.85; singles 172F/€26.25; doubles 101F/€15.40. MC/V.) Take bus #1 (dir. Horbourg-Wihr) to Plage d'Ill for **Camping de l'Ill,** on rte. Horbourg-Wihr. (☎ 03 89 41 15 94. Reception daily July-Aug. 8am-10pm; Feb.-June and Sept.-Nov. 8am-8pm.

Open Feb.-Nov. 18F/€2.75 per person, 10F/€1.55 per child, 10F/€1.55 per tent, 20F/
€3.05 per site. Electricity 15F/€2.30.) Stock up at **Monoprix supermarket,** on pl. Unterlinden. (Open M-F 8am-8pm, Sa 8am-7:55pm.) *Brasseries* are in **La Petite Venise** and
the **Quartier des Tanneurs. Postal code:** 68000.

BESANÇON

Besançon (pop. 120,000) has intrigued military strategists throughout history with
its geographically protected location. Now home to a major university and international language center, Besançon boasts a smart, sexy student population and an
impressive number of museums and discos.

■? TRANSPORTATION AND PRACTICAL INFORMATION. Trains chug from
the station, on av. de la Paix, to: Dijon (1hr., 6 per day, 75F/€11.45); Paris (2hr., 7
per day, 269F/€41.05); and Strasbourg (3hr., 10 per day, 165F/€25.20). From the
train station, cross the parking lot, head downstairs, and walk downhill on av. de
la Paix, which becomes av. Maréchal Foch; continue to the right, and then to the
left as it becomes av. de l'Helvétie, until you reach pl. de la Première Armée
Française (10min.). The *vieille ville* is across the pont de la République; the **tourist office,** 2, pl. de la Première Armée Française, is in the park to the right. (☎03 81
80 92 55; fax 03 81 80 58 30; www.besancon.com. Open M 10am-7pm, Tu-Sa 9am-
7pm; mid-June to mid-Sept. also open Su 10am-noon and 3-5pm; Oct.-Mar. M
10am-6pm, Tu-Sa 9am-6pm.) Surf the **internet** at **Centre Information Jeunesse (CIJ),**
27, r. de la République. (Open M and Sa 1:30-6pm, Tu-F 10am-noon and 1:30-6pm.
Free.) **Postal code:** 25000 (25031 "Besançon-Cedex" for *Poste Restante*).

■■ ACCOMMODATIONS AND FOOD. To get to **Foyer Mixte de Jeunes Travailleurs (HI),** 48, r. des Cras, turn left from the train station's parking lot on av. de la
Paix, which becomes r. de Belfort, and turn left again on r. Marie-Louise, which
turns into r. des Cras; the hostel is uphill on the right. Ask the locals for "Foyer
Mixte Oiseaux." Or take bus #7 (dir. Orchamps, 3 per hr., 6F/€0.95) from pl. Flore,
off r. de Belfort on av. Carnot, to Oiseaux. (☎03 81 40 32 00; fax 03 81 40 32 01.
Breakfast and sheets included. Reception 9am-8pm. Singles 100F/€15.25, 2nd night
90F/€13.75; doubles 80F/€12.20, 140F/€21.35.) Ethnic restaurants line **rue Claude-
Pouillet. ▨ La Boîte à Sandwiches,** 21, r. du Lycée, off r. Pasteur, serves great food
late. (Sandwiches 11-30F/€1.70-4.60. Open M-Sa 11:30am-2:30pm and 6:30pm-mid-
night.) Pick up **groceries** at **Monoprix,** 12, Grande Rue. (Open M-Sa 8:30am-9pm.)

■♪ SIGHTS AND ENTERTAINMENT. The elegant Renaissance buildings gracing the *vieille ville* provide plenty of eye candy during a casual stroll around town,
but the city's true delights lie high above in the **citadel,** at the end of r. des Fusillés
de la Résistance, designed by Louis XIV's architect. It's a grueling trek uphill from
town, but the view and the three museums inside are worth it. Within the citadel,
the **Musée de la Résistance et de la Déportation** chronicles the Nazis' rise to power
and the occupation of France. Other sights inside include a natural history
museum, a zoo, an aquarium, and a folk art museum. Access to the first level, which
includes manicured lawns and a breathtaking panorama, is free. (Grounds open
daily 9am-7pm; Apr.-June and Sept.-Oct. 9am-6pm; Nov.-Mar. 10am-5pm. Museums
open daily 9am-6pm; Nov.-Mar. 10am-5pm. 40F/€6.10, students 30F/€4.60.) The
Cathédrale St-Jean, perched beneath the citadel, mixes architectural styles from the
12th to 18th centuries and is crowned by the intricate **Horloge Astronomique.** (Open
W-M 9am-7pm. Free. Tours 15F/€2.30, children 9F/€1.45.) The **Musée des Beaux-
Arts et d'Archeologie,** on pl. de la Révolution, houses an exceptional collection ranging from ancient Egyptian treasures to artwork by Matisse. (Open W-M 9:30am-
6pm. 21F/€3.20, students free; Su and holidays free for all.) Small bars and *brasseries* line **rues Claude Pouillet** and **Pont Battant.** Every night of the week, local students pack discos, particularly **Le KGB,** 8, av. de Chardonnet. (Cover 50F/€7.65.
Open W-Th 10:30pm-4am, F-Sa 10:30pm-5am.) Shoot pool at the surprisingly hip

Pop Hall, 26, r. Proudhon, across from the post office; check out the amazing bathroom decorations. (Open M-Th 6pm-1am, Sa 3pm-2am, Su 6pm-2am.)

▶ DAYTRIP FROM BESANÇON: PONTARLIER AND THE JURA. The quiet town of **Pontarlier** (840m) is a good base for reaching greater heights in the Haut-Jura Mountains. The Jura mountains, best known for **cross-country skiing,** are covered with over 60km of trails. (Day pass 30F/€4.60, ages 10-16 20F/€3.05.) **Le Larmont** (☎03 81 46 55 20) is the alpine ski area nearest to Pontarlier. **Sport et Neige,** 4, r. de la République, rents ski equipment. (☎03 81 39 04 69. 50F/€7.65 per day, 290F/€44.20 per week. Open 9am-noon and 2-7pm. MC/V.) In summer, **fishing, hiking,** and **mountain biking** are popular. Rent a **bike** from **Cycles Pernet,** 23, r. de la République. (☎03 81 46 48 00. 80F/€12.20 per day plus passport deposit. Open Tu-Sa 9am-noon and 2-7pm.) **Monts Jura buses** (☎03 81 39 88 80) run to Besançon (1hr., 6 per day, 46.50F/€7.10). The **tourist office,** 14bis, r. de la Gare, offers free regional guides and sells maps. (Maps 12-58F/€1.85-8.85. ☎03 81 46 48 33; fax 03 81 46 83 32. Open July-Aug. daily 8:30am-noon and 2-7pm; Sept.-June M-Sa 8:30am-noon and 2-7pm.) **L'Auberge de Pontarlier (HI),** 2, r. Jouffroy, is clean and central. (☎03 81 39 06 57; fax 03 81 39 06 57. Breakfast 19F/€2.90. Sheets 17F/€2.60. Reception 8am-noon and 5:30-10pm. Members only. Dorms 50F/€7.65; doubles 75F/€11.45.) **Postal code:** 25300.

NANCY

Nancy (pop. 100,000) is a model of 18th-century classicism, with broad plazas, wrought-iron grillwork, and cascading fountains. More than just a pretty face, the city reigns as the cultural and intellectual heart of Lorraine. At the **place Stanislas,** Baroque gilded-iron fences wrap around three neoclassical pavilions commissioned in 1737 by former Polish king Stanislas Lesczynski for his nephew Louis XV. Pass through the five-arch **Arc de Triomphe** to the tree-lined **place de la Carrière,** whose northern end segues into the relaxing **Parc de la Pépinière.** The park's aromatic **Roseraie** beckons with colorful blooms from around the world. (Open daily May to mid-Sept. 6:30am-11:30pm; May and Sept. 1-14 closes 10pm; Mar-Apr. and mid-Sept. to Nov. closes 9pm; Dec.-Feb. closes 8pm. Free.) The eye-grabbing **Musée de l'Ecole de Nancy** holds dramatic sculptures, glasswork, and furniture that redefine everyday objects. To get there, take bus #5 (dir. Vandoeuvre Cheminots) to Nancy Thermal. (Open M 2-6pm and W-Su 10:30am-6pm. 30F/€4.60, students 15F/€2.30. W students free, 1st Su of every month everyone free.)

Trains leave pl. Thiers for: Metz (40min., 24 per day, 52F/€7.95); Paris (3hr., 14 per day, 213F/€32.50); and Strasbourg (1hr., 19 per day, 112F/€17.10). Head left from the train station, and turn on r. Raymond Poincaré, which leads straight to the **tourist office,** on pl. Stanislas. Ask for the invaluable *Le Fil d'Ariane* guide. (☎03 83 35 22 41; fax 03 83 35 90 10. Open Apr.-Sept. M-Sa 9am-7pm, Su 10am-5pm; Oct.-May M-Sa 9am-6pm, Su 10am-1pm.) Access the **Internet** at **E-café,** on r. des Quatre Eglises. (35F/€5.35 per hr. Open M-Sa 9am-9pm, Su 2-8pm.) **Centre d'Accueil de Remicourt (HI),** 149, r. de Vandoeuvre, is in Villiers-lès-Nancy, 4km away. From the station, take bus #122 to St-Fiacre (dir. Villiers Clairlieu; 2 per hr., last bus 8pm; confirm direction with the driver); head downhill from the stop, turn right on r. de la Grange des Moines, which turns into r. de Vandoeuvre. Look for signs pointing to Château de Remicourt. (☎03 83 27 73 67; fax 03 83 41 41 35. Breakfast included. Reception daily 9am-9pm. 3- to 4-bed dorms 82F/€12.50; doubles 97F/€14.80. MC/V.) **Hôtel de l'Academie,** 7, r. des Michottes, is convenient with humble yet tidy rooms. (☎03 83 35 52 31; fax 03 83 32 55 78. Breakfast 22F/€3.35. Reception M-Sa 24hr., Su closed noon-4:30pm. Singles and doubles with shower 140-160F/€21.35-24.40, with bath 165-200F/€25.15-30.50. MC/V.) Restaurants cluster around **rue des Maréchaux. Postal code:** 54000 (Nancy-RP 54039 for *Poste Restante*).

CHAMPAGNE AND THE NORTH

Golden vineyards and lush rolling plains fill the small yet strikingly diverse region of Champagne. The word *champagne* is fiercely guarded; the name can be applied only to wines made from regional grapes and produced according to a time-honored method. In Flanders, on the Belgian border, beer is the order of the day, to be quaffed with lots of mussels. Along with the coastal Pas de Calais, this is the final frontier of France: chalk cliffs loom over rugged beaches, while wooden windmills and gabled houses reveal the area's Flemish influence. Don't miss the hidden treasures of the north, including the world-class art collections of Lille.

REIMS

Reims (pop. 185,000) is famous for its cathedral, which has hosted centuries of French monarchs' coronations. The famed **Cathédrale de Notre-Dame,** built with golden limestone quarried in the Champagne *caves,* features a set of sea-blue stained-glass windows by Marc Chagall. (Open daily 7:30am-7:30pm. Tours in English daily 2:30pm; less frequently late Mar. to mid-June and Oct. 35F/€5.35, under 26 20F/€4.60.) Next door is the **Palais du Tau,** pl. du Cardinal Luçon, with dazzling 16th-century tapestries and the 50ft. robes of Charles X. (Open July-Aug. daily 9:30am-6:30pm; Sept. to mid-Nov. and mid-Mar. to June daily 9:30am-12:30pm and 2-6pm; mid-Nov. to mid-Mar. M-F 10am-noon and 2-5pm, Sa-Su 10am-noon and 2-6pm. 26F/€4, students 21F/€3.20.) Four hundred kilometers of *crayères* (Roman chalk quarries) wind under Reims, along with tunnels sheltering the bottled treasures of the great champagne firms. Many houses offer tours by appointment only, so call ahead. The most elegant tour is at **Pommery,** 5, pl. du Général Gouraud. (☎ 03 26 61 62 56. Tours Apr.-Oct. daily 11am-7pm. 46F/€7.05, students 20F/€3.05.) For a spookier look at the fermenting process, explore the ancient tunnels of **Taittinger,** 9, pl. St-Nicaise. (☎ 03 26 85 45 35. Open Apr. to mid-Nov. M-F 9am-1pm and 2-5:30pm, Sa-Su 9-11am and 2-6pm; Dec.-Mar. closed Sa-Su 35F/€5.35.) At night, the cafes and bars along **place Drouet d'Erlon** are packed with people until 1am.

Trains (☎ 03 26 88 11 65) leave from bd. Joffre to Paris (1½hr., 11 per day, 123F/€18.75). To get from the train station to the **tourist office,** 2, r. Guillaume de Machault, follow the right-hand curve of the rotary to pl. Drouet d'Erlon, turn left after Eglise St-Jacques onto r. de Vesle, and turn right on r. du Trésor; it's on the left before the cathedral. (☎ 03 26 77 45 25; fax 03 26 77 45 27. Open mid-Apr. to mid-Oct. M-Sa 9am-7pm, Su 10am-6pm; mid-Oct. to mid-Apr. M-Sa 9am-6pm, Su 10am-5pm.) **Monoprix supermarket** is at the corner of r. de Vesle and r. de Talleyrand. (Open M-Sa 8:30am-9pm.) The spotless **Au Bon Accueil,** 31, r. Thillois, is off pl. d'Erlon. (☎ 03 26 88 55 74; fax 03 26 05 12 38. Breakfast 25F/€3.85. Reception 24hr. Reserve ahead. Singles 100-150F/€15.20-22.90; doubles 140-220F/€21.35-33.55. MC/V.) To get from the train station to the **Auberge de Jeunesse (HI),** on chaussée Bocquaine, cross the park in front of the station, follow the right-hand side of the rotary, turn right on bd. Général Leclerc, follow it to the canal, and cross the first bridge on your left; Bocquaine is the first left. (☎ 03 26 40 52 60; fax 03 26 47 35 70. Breakfast 20F/€3.05. Reception 24hr. Singles 89F/€13.60, with bath 149F/€21.35; doubles 65F/€9.95, 89F/€13.60; triples 59F/€9, 79F/€12.05. Nonmembers 10F/€1.55 fee. MC/V.) Cheap cafes and restaurants pack **place Drouet d'Erlon. Postal code:** 51100.

⚑ **DAYTRIP FROM REIMS: ÉPERNAY.** Unlike the more metropolitan Reims, neighboring Épernay (pop. 30,000) strips away all urban distractions and devotes itself heart and soul to the production of bubbly. **Avenue de Champagne,** one of the richest streets in the world, is distinguished by its palatial mansions, lush gardens, and monumental champagne firms. Swanky **Moët & Chandon,** 20, av. de Champagne, produces the king of all wines: Dom Perignon. (☎ 03 26 51 20 20. Open daily Apr. to mid-Nov. 9:30-11:30am and 2-4:30pm; mid-Nov. to Mar. closed Sa-Su. Tours with one glass 40F/€6.10.) **Mercier,** 70, av. de Champagne, gives fascinating 30min. tours in roller-coaster-like cars. (☎ 03 26 51 22 22. Open Mar.-Nov. M-F 9:30-11:30am and 2-4:30pm, Sa-Su 9:30-11:30am and 2-5pm; Dec. 1-19 and mid-Jan. to Feb. Th-M only.

30min. tours 25F/€3.85.) **Trains** arrive at cour de la Gare from Reims (25min., 16 per day, 34F/€5.20). From the station, walk straight through pl. Mendès France and go one block up r. Gambetta to the central **pl. de la République;** from there, turn left on av. de Champagne to reach the **tourist office,** 7, av. de Champagne.(☎ 03 26 53 33 00; fax 03 26 51 95 22. Open Easter to mid-Oct. M-Sa 9:30am-noon and 1:30-7pm, Su 11am-4pm; mid-Oct. to Easter M-Sa 9:30am-12:30pm and 1:30-5:30pm.)

LILLE

The fourth largest city in France, Lille (pop. 175,000) invites visitors to enjoy its cosmopolitan atmosphere at a leisurely pace. Charles de Gaulle's hometown still retains a Flemish flavor, from its architecture to its residents' rabid consumption of mussels and beer. One of France's most respected museums, the **Musée des Beaux-Arts,** on pl. de la République, boasts an extensive collection of 15th- to 20th-century French and Flemish masters' works. (M: République. Open M 2-6pm, W-Th and Sa-Su 10am-6pm, F 10am-7pm. 30F/€4.60, students 20F/€3.05.) The **Musée d'Art Moderne,** 1, allée du Musée, in the suburb of Villeneuve d'Ascq, showcases Cubist and postmodern art, including works by Braque, Picasso, Léger, Miró, and Modigliani. Take the tram (dir. 4 Cantons) to Pont du Bois. Then take bus #41 (dir. Villeneuve d'Ascq) to Parc Urbain-Musée. (Open W-M 10am-6pm; free first Su of every month 10am-2pm. 43F/€6.55, students 10F/€1.55.) **Vieille Bourse,** on pl. Général de Gaulle, epitomizes the Flemish Renaissance and houses flower and book markets. (Markets open Tu-Su 9:30am-7:30pm.) Pubs line **rues Solférino** and **Masséna.** A college-age crowd frequents **Gino Pub,** 21, r. Massena. (Open daily noon-2am.)

   Trains leave **Gare Lille Flandres,** on pl. de la Gare, near M: Gare Lille Flandres, for Brussels, Belgium (1½hr., 20 per day, 135F/€20.60) and Paris (1hr., 21 per day, 212-287F/€32.35-43.75). **Gare Lille Europe** (☎ 03 36 35 35 35), on r. Le Corbusier, near M: Gare Lille Europe, sends **Eurostar** trains to London, Brussels, and Paris and all **TGVs** to the south of France and Paris. From Gare Lille Flandres, walk straight down r. Faidherbe and turn left through pl. du Théâtre and pl. de Gaulle; behind the huge war monument is the **tourist office,** pl. Rihour, which offers free maps and currency exchange. (☎ 03 20 21 94 21; fax 03 20 21 94 20. M: Rihour. Open M-Sa 9:30am-6:30pm, Su 10am-noon and 2-5pm.) The enormous **Marché de Wazemmes,** pl. de la Nouvelle Aventure, has markets both indoors (M-Th 7am-1pm, F-Sa 7am-8pm, Su 7am-3pm) and outdoors (Su, Tu, and Th 7am-3pm). To reach the **Auberge de Jeunesse (HI),** 12, r. Malpart, from Gare Lille Flandres, head left around the station, turn right onto r. du Molinel, take the second left on r. de Paris, and take your third right onto r. Malpart. (☎ 03 20 57 08 94; fax 03 20 63 98 93. M: Mairie de Lille. Breakfast included. Sheets 18F/€2.75. Reception 7am-noon and 2pm-1am. Check-out 10:30am. Curfew 2am. Open Feb.-Dec. 17. 3- to 6-bed dorms 75F/€11.45; ID or 50F/€7.65 deposit required.) Restaurants cluster around **rue de Béthune** while **rue Léon Gambetta** is a paradise for picnic-seekers. **Postal Code:** 59000.

GERMANY
(DEUTSCHLAND)

GERMAN DEUTSCHMARK

US$1 = DM2.18	1DM = US$0.46
CDN$1 = DM1.47	1DM = CDN$0.68
UK£1 = DM3.23	1DM = UK£0.31
IR£1 = DM2.48F	1DM = IR£0.40
AUS$1 = DM1.27	1DM = AUS$0.79
NZ$1 = DM0.97	1DM = NZ$1.04
ZAR1 = DM0.31	1DM = ZAR3.20
EUR€1 = DM1.96	1DM = EUR€0.51

PHONE CODE	Country code: 49. International dialing prefix: 00. From outside Germany, dial int'l dialing prefix (see inside back cover) + 49 + city code + local number.

Germany is a nation saddled with an incredibly fractured past. Steeped deeply in Beethoven's fiery orchestration and Goethe's Faustian whirlwind, modern Germany must also contend with the legacy of xenophobia and genocide left by Hitler and the Nazi Third Reich. Brahms, Wagner, and Liszt have since given way to Kraftwerk, Rammstein, and Hasselhof. But even now, more than a decade after the fall of the Berlin Wall, Germans are still fashioning a new identity for themselves. After centuries of war and fragmentation, Germany finds itself a wealthy nation at the forefront of both European and global politics. Its medieval castles, snow-covered mountains, and funky metropolises make Germany well worth a visit.

For more comprehensive coverage, treat yourself to *Let's Go: Germany 2002*.

FACTS AND FIGURES

Official Name: Federal Republic of Germany *(Bundesrepublik Deutschland)*.

Capital: Berlin.

Major Cities: Hamburg, Munich, Cologne, Frankfurt.

Population: 82.1 million.

Land Area: 357,021 sq. km.

Climate: Temperate and marine; cool, cloudy, wet winters and summers.

Language: German.

Religions: Lutheran (41%), Catholic (34%), Muslim (3%).

DISCOVER GERMANY

The myriad cultural and historical treasures of **Berlin** (p. 400), not to mention its chaotic nightlife, sprawl over an area eight times the size of Paris. **Dresden** (p. 419) is nearly as intense, with a jumping nightlife and exquisite palaces and museums. **Weimar** (p. 424) rests solidly on the cultural heritage of Goethe, the Bauhaus movement, and Germany's first liberal constitution. To the north, reckless **Hamburg** (p. 427), Germany's second-largest city, fuses the burliness of a port town with cosmopolitan flair, while **Cologne** (p. 434), near the Belgian and Dutch borders, is home to Germany's largest, most poignant cathedral and pounding nightlife. To the south, **Koblenz** (p. 444) is the gateway to the castles and wine towns of the **Rhine Valley.** Farther south, Germany's oldest, most prestigious, and most scenic university sits below the ruins of a castle in **Heidelberg** (p. 446). From there, live out your favorite Grimms' fairy tales in the **Black Forest** (p. 450) or conquer the so-called **Romantic Road** (p. 462), which snakes along the western edge of Bavaria. At the southern end of the trail lie the Mad King Ludwig's **Royal Castles** (p. 464). And no trip to Germany would be complete without visiting the Bavarian capital of **Munich** (p. 453), which takes bucolic merriment to a frothy head with its excellent museums and jovial beer halls.

ESSENTIALS

WHEN TO GO

Germany's climate is temperate, with rain year-round (especially in summer). The cloudy, temperate months of May, June, and September are the best time to go, as there are fewer tourists and the weather is pleasant. Germans head to vacation spots en masse in early July with the onset of school vacations. Winter sports gear up November to April; skiing high season is mid-December to March.

DOCUMENTS AND FORMALITIES

VISAS. Germany requires visas of South Africans, but not of nationals of Australia, Canada, the EU, New Zealand, or the US for stays of less than 90 days.

EMBASSIES. All foreign embassies are in **Berlin** (p. 400). German embassies at home: **Australia,** 119 Empire Circuit, Yarralumla, Canberra, ACT 2600 (☎(02) 62 70 19 11; fax 62 70 19 51); **Canada,** 1 Waverly St., Ottawa, ON K2P OT8 (☎613-232-1101; fax 613-594-9330); **Ireland,** 31 Trimleston Ave., Booterstown, Blackrock, Co. Dublin (☎(01) 269 30 11; fax 269 39 46); **New Zealand,** 90-92 Hobson St., Thorndon, Wellington (☎(04) 473 60 63; fax 473 60 69); **South Africa,** 180 Blackwood St., Arcadia, Pretoria, 0083 (☎(012) 427 89 00; fax 343 94 01); **UK,** 23 Belgrave Sq., London SW1X 8PZ (☎(020) 78 24 13 00; fax 78 24 14 35); and **US,** 4645 Reservoir Rd. NW, Washington, D.C. 20007 (☎202-298-4393; fax 471-5558; www.germany-info.org).

TRANSPORTATION

BY PLANE. Most flights land in Frankfurt; Berlin, Munich, and Hamburg also have international airports. **Lufthansa,** the national airline, has the most flights in and out of the country, but they're not always the cheapest option. Flying within Germany is usually more expensive and less convenient than taking the train.

BY TRAIN. The **Deutsche Bahn (DB)** network (in Germany ☎(0180) 599 66 33; www.bahn.de) is Europe's best but also one of the most expensive. **RE** (Regional-Express) and the slightly slower **RB** (RegionalBahn) trains include a number of rail networks between neighboring cities. **IR** (InterRegio) trains, covering larger networks between cities, are speedy and comfortable. **D** trains are foreign trains that serve international routes. **EC** (EuroCity) and **IC** (InterCity) trains zoom along between major cities every hour from 6am-10pm. The futuristic **ICE** (InterCityExpress) trains approach the luxury and kinetics of an airplane and run at speeds up to 280km per hour. On all trains, second-class compartments are clean and comfortable. You must purchase a **Zuschlag** (supplement) to ride an IC or EC train. (DM7/€3.60 in the station, DM9/€4.60 on the train.)

Designed for tourists, the **German Railpass** allows unlimited travel for four to 10 days within a four-week period. Non-Europeans can purchase German Railpasses in their home countries and—with a passport—in major German train stations (5-day DM418/€214, 10-day DM653/€334). The **German Rail Youth Pass** is for those under 26 (5-day DM333/€170, 9-day DM423/€216). The **Twin Pass** is for two adults traveling together (5-day DM627/€320, 10-day DM978/€500). Travelers ages 12-25 can purchase **TwenTickets,** which knock 20% off fares between DM10-239/€5-123. A **Schönes-Wochenende-Ticket** (DM40/€20.45) gives up to five people unlimited travel on any of the slower trains (*not* ICE, IC, EC, D, or IR) from 12:01am Saturday or Sunday until 3am the next day. The **Guten-Abend-Ticket** is an excellent deal for long-distance night travel and allows travel anywhere (*not* on InterCityNight or City-NightLines) in Germany between 7pm (2pm Saturdays) and 3am (2nd-class DM59/

€30.20; F-Su DM15/€7.70 extra). A great option for those making frequent and extensive use of German trains for more than one month, the **Bahncard** is valid for one year and gives a 50% discount on all trains. Passes are available at major train stations and require a passport-sized photo and mailing address in Germany (2nd-class DM270/€138; ages 18-22, over 60, or students under 27 DM135/€.)

Eurail is valid in Germany and provides free passage on urban S-Bahns and DB buses, but not U-Bahns. **Public transport** is excellent, and comes in four flavors: the **Straßenbahn** (streetcar), **S-Bahn** (surface commuter rail), **U-Bahn** (underground subway), and regular **buses.** Consider buying a day card *(Tageskarte)* or multiple-ride ticket *(Mehrfahrkarte);* they usually pay for themselves quickly.

BY BUS. Bus service between cities and to outlying areas runs from the local **Zentralomnibusbahnhof (ZOB),** which is usually close to the main train station. Buses are often slightly more expensive than trains for comparable distances. Railpasses are not valid on any buses other than a few run by Deutsche Bahn.

BY CAR. German road conditions are generally excellent. It's true, there is no set speed limit on the *Autobahn*, only a recommendation of 130kph (81mph). Germans drive *fast*. Watch for signs indicating right-of-way (usually designated by a yellow triangle). The Autobahn is indicated by an intuitive "A" on signs; secondary highways, where the speed limit is usually 100kph, are accompanied by signs bearing a "B." Germans drive on the right side of the road. In cities and towns, speed limits hover around 30-60kph (31mph). Germans use unleaded gas almost exclusively; prices run around DM8.40/€4.30 per gallon, or about DM2.15/€1.10 per liter.

BY BIKE AND BY THUMB. Germany's wealth of trails make bikes sightseeing power tools. Cities and towns usually have designated bike lanes and biking maps. *Germany by Bike*, by Nadine Slavinski (Mountaineers Books, 1994; US$14.95), details 20 tours throughout the country. *Let's Go* does not recommend hitchhiking. A better option are **Mitfahrzentralen,** agencies that pair up drivers and riders for a small fee; riders then negotiate payment for the trip with the driver.

TOURIST SERVICES AND MONEY

EMERGENCY   **Police:** ☎ 110. **Ambulance** and **Fire:** ☎ 112.

TOURIST OFFICES. Every city in Germany has a tourist office, usually near the main train station *(Hauptbahnhof)* or central square *(Marktplatz)*. All are marked by a thick lowercase "i" sign. The offices often book rooms for a small fee. The tourist information website for Germany is www.germany-tourism.de.

MONEY. The **deutsche Mark** or **Deutschmark** (abbreviated DM) is the unit of currency in Germany. It is one of the most stable and respected currencies in the world. One *Deutschmark* equals 100 *Pfennig* (Pf). Coins come in 1, 2, 5, 10, and 50Pf, and DM1, 2, and 5 amounts. Bills come in DM5, 10, 20, 50, 100, 200, 500, and 1000 denominations, though DM5 bills are now rare. Germany has accepted the **Euro (€)** as legal tender, and Deutschmarks will be phased out by July 1, 2002. For more information, see p. 21. If you stay in hostels and prepare your own food, expect to spend anywhere from DM40-80/US$19-38 per person per day. Tipping is not as common in Germany as elsewhere—most Germans just round up DM1-2/€0.50-1 in restaurants and bars, or when they are the beneficiary of a service, such as a taxi ride. Note that tips in Germany are not left lying on the table, but handed directly to the server when you pay. If you don't want any change, say *Das stimmt so* (das SHTIMMT zo). Germans rarely bargain except at flea markets. Most goods and services bought in Germany will automatically include a VAT of 15%. In German, this is called the *Mehrwertsteuer* (MwSt). Non-EU citizens can get the VAT refunded for large purchases of goods. At the point of purchase, ask for a Tax-Free Shopping Cheque, then have it stamped at customs upon leaving the country or at a customs authority. The goods must remain unused until you leave the country.

COMMUNICATION

MAIL. Mail can be sent through Poste Restante *(Postlagernde Briefe)* to almost any German city or town with a post office. The mail will go to the main post office unless you specify a post office by street address or postal code. Air mail usually takes 3-7 days to North America, Europe, and Australia; 6-12 days to New Zealand.

TELEPHONES. Most public phones only accept telephone cards. You can pick up a Telefonkarte (phone card) in post offices, at a *Kiosk* (newsstand), or at selected Deutsche Bahn counters in major train stations. The cards come in DM12, DM24, and DM50 denominations. There is no standard length for telephone numbers. The smaller the city, the more digits in the city code, while telephone numbers tend to have three to ten digits. International direct dial numbers include: **AT&T,** ☎ (800) 22 55 288; **British Telecom,** ☎ (800) 89 00 49; **Canada Direct,** ☎ (800) 888 00 14; **Ireland Direct,** ☎ (08000) 800 353; **MCI,** ☎ (800) 88 88 000; **Sprint,** ☎ (800) 888 00 13; **Telecom**

New Zealand, ☎(800) 080 00 64; **Telkom South Africa**, (800) 180 00 27; **Telstra Australia**, ☎(800) 08 00 061.

INTERNET ACCESS. Most German cities (as well as a surprising number of smaller towns) have at least one Internet cafe with web access for about DM3-7/€1.50-3.50 per 30min. Some German universities have banks of computers hooked up to the Internet in their libraries, although ostensibly for student use.

LANGUAGE. Many people in Western Germany speak English, but this is less common in the East. The letter **ß** is equivalent to a double *s*. For German tips, see p. 984.

> **!** Germany is no more dangerous than the rest of Western Europe, but violent crime does exist, particularly in big cities and economically depressed regions of the East. Many of Germany's neo-Nazis wear flight jackets over white short-sleeve shirts and tight jeans rolled to reveal high-cut combat boots. Skinheads tend to subscribe to a shoelace code, with white supremacists and neo-Nazis wearing white laces and anti-gay skinheads wearing pink laces. Left-wing anti-Nazi "S.H.A.R.P.s" (Skinheads Against Racial Prejudice) favor red laces.

ACCOMMODATIONS AND CAMPING

Germany currently has about 600 **hostels**—more than any other nation on Earth. Hostelling in Germany is overseen by **Deutsches Jugendherbergswerk (DJH)**, Bismarckstr. 8, D-32756 Detmold, Germany (☎(05231) 740 10; fax 74 01 74; www.djh.de). DJH has recently initiated a growing number of **Jugendgästehäuser**, youth guest-houses that have more facilities, and attract slightly older guests. DJH publishes *Jugendherbergen in Deutschland* (DM14.80/€7.50), a guide to all federated German hostels. Never leave your belongings unattended; crime can occur in even the most demure-looking hostel or hotel. The cheapest **hotel-style** accommodations are places with Pension, Gasthof, Gästehaus, or Hotel-Garni in the name. Hotel rooms start at DM30/€15.35 for singles and DM40/€20.45 for doubles; in large cities, expect to pay nearly twice as much. Breakfast *(Frühstück)* is almost always available and often included. The best bet for a cheap bed is often a **Privatzimmer** (a room in a family home). This option works best if you have a rudimentary knowledge of German. Prices generally run DM20-50/€10-25 per person. Travelers over 26 who would otherwise pay higher prices at youth hostels will find these rooms within budget range. Reservations are made through the local tourist office or through a private Zimmervermittlung (room-booking office) for free or a DM2-8 fee. Germans love **camping;** over 2600 campsites dot the outskirts of even the most major cities. Facilities are well maintained and usually provide showers, bathrooms, and a restaurant or store. Camping costs DM3-10/€1.50-5 per person, with additional charges for tents and vehicles. Blue signs with a black tent on a white background indicate official sites. **Deutscher Camping-Club (DCC)**, Mandlstr. 28, 80802 München (☎(089) 380 14 20), has more information, and the National Tourist Office distributes a free map, *Camping in Germany*.

FOOD AND DRINK

The typical German *Frühstück* (breakfast) consists of coffee or tea with rolls, bread, cold sausage, and cheese. The main meal of the day, *Mittagessen* (lunch), includes soup, broiled sausage or roasted meat, potatoes or dumplings, and a salad or vegetable side dish. *Abendessen* or *Abendbrot* (dinner) is a reprise of breakfast, only beer replaces coffee and the selection of meats and cheese is wider. Many older Germans indulge in a daily ritual of *Kaffee und Kuchen* (coffee and cakes) at 3 or 4pm. Seat yourself at restaurants. To eat on the cheap, stick to the daily *Tagesmenü*, buy food in supermarkets, or, if you have a student ID, head to a university *Mensa* (cafeteria). Fast-food *Imbiß* stands also provide cheap fare; try the delicious Turkish *Döner*, something like a gyro. The average German beer is maltier and more "bread-like" than Czech, Dutch, or American beers; an affectionate German slang term for beer is *Flüßige Brot* ("liquid bread").

HOLIDAYS AND FESTIVALS

Holidays: Epiphany (Jan. 6); Ash Wednesday (Mar. 8); Good Friday (Apr. 21); Easter Sunday and Monday (Apr. 23-24); Labor Day (May 1); Ascension Day (June 1); Whit Sunday (June 11); Whit Monday (June 12); Corpus Christi (June 22); Assumption Day (Aug. 15); Day of German Unity (Oct. 3); Reformation Day (Nov. 1); All Saint's Day (Nov. 1); Christmas (Dec. 25-26).

Festivals: Check out **Fasching** in Munich (Jan. 7-Feb. 12), the **Berlinale Film Festival** (Feb. 6-17), **Karneval** in Cologne (Feb. 7-11), **Christopher St. Day** in Berlin and other major cities (late June to early July), the **Love Parade** in Berlin (early July), the yeasty **Oktoberfest** in Munich (Sept. 21-Oct. 16), and the **Christmas Market** in Nuremberg.

BERLIN   ☎ 030

Don't wait any longer to see Berlin. The city is nearing the end of a massive transitional phase, developing from a newly reunited metropolis reeling in the aftermath of the Cold War to an epicenter of the European Union—and the Berlin of five or even two years into the future will be radically different from the Berlin of today. Berlin's atmosphere is the most diverse and tolerant of any of Germany's cities, with a world-famous gay and lesbian scene, but the real reason to visit is the city's exquisite tension between past and future, conservation and modernization. An old German song goes, "*Es gibt nur einmal/und kommt nicht wieder*" ("it will only happen once, and will never happen again") and it's never been truer than for Berlin today. As with every moment in its past, Berlin will never again be the same—and change is already in the wind.

✈ INTERCITY TRANSPORTATION

Berlin, in the northeastern corner of Germany, is rapidly becoming the hub of the national rail network, with rail and air connections to most other European capitals. Almost all European airlines have service to one of Berlin's three airports.

Flights: For information on all 3 airports, call ☎(0180) 500 01 86. Currently, the city is making the transition from 3 airports to 1 (Flughafen Schönefeld), but for now, **Flughafen Tegel** will remain Western Berlin's main airport. Take express bus #X9 from Bahnhof Zoo, bus #109 from Jakob-Kaiser-Pl. on U7, or bus #128 from Kurt-Schumacher-Pl. on U6. **Flughafen Tempelhof,** Berlin's smallest airport, has flights within Germany and Europe. U6 to Pl. der Luftbrücke. **Flughafen Schönefeld,** southeast of Berlin, has intercontinental flights. S45 or S9 to Flughafen Berlin Schönefeld.

Train Stations: Trains to and from Berlin are serviced by **Zoologischer Garten** (almost always called **Bahnhof Zoo**) in the West and **Ostbahnhof** (formerly the Hauptbahnhof) in the East. Most trains go to both stations, but some connections to cities in the former GDR only stop at Ostbahnhof. For **info,** call ☎(0180) 599 66 33 or visit www.bahn.de. Trains run to: **Dresden** (2¼hr., every 2hr., DM42/€22); **Frankfurt** (4hr., every hr., DM207/€106); **Hamburg** (2½hr., every hr., DM88/€45); **Cologne** (4¼hr., every hr., DM190/€98); **Leipzig** (2-2¾hr., every hr., DM51-65/€26-34); **Munich** (6½-7hr., every hr., DM199/€102). **International connections** to most major European cities. Times and prices change frequently—check at the computers in the train stations.

Buses: ZOB, the central bus station (☎302 53 61), is by the *Funkturm* near Kaiserdamm. U2 to Kaiserdamm or S4, S45, or S46 to Witzleben. Check *Zitty* and *Tip* for deals on long-distance buses, or call **Gulliver's** travel agency, Hardenbergpl. 14 (☎311 02 11), at the opposite end of the bus parking lot from Bahnhof Zoo. Open daily 8am-8pm. To **Paris** (14hr., DM109/€56) and **Vienna** (10½hr., DM89/€46).

Mitfahrzentralen (Ride Sharing): City Netz, Joachimstaler Str. 17 (☎194 44; fax 882 44 20) has a computerized ride-share database. U9 or U15 to Kurfürstendamm. To: **Frankfurt** (DM35/€18); **Hamburg** (DM30/€16); **Hannover** (DM30/€16); **Munich** (DM35/€18). Open M-F 9am-8pm, Sa-Su 9am-7pm. **Mitfahr2000,** Yorckstr. 52 (☎194 20 00;

www.mitfahr.de) was formerly the *Mitfahrtelefon für Schwule und Lesben* (Ride Sharing for Gays and Lesbians). Open daily 8am-8pm.

Hitchhiking: *Let's Go* does not recommend hitchhiking as a safe mode of transportation. It is illegal to hitch at rest stops or anywhere along the highway.

✷ ORIENTATION

Berlin is an *immense* conglomeration of what were once two separate and unique cities. The former East contains most of Berlin's landmarks and historic sites, as well as an unfortunate number of pre-fab concrete socialist architectural experiments. The former West functioned for decades as a small, isolated, Allied-occupied state and is still the commercial heart of united Berlin. The situation is rapidly changing, however, as businesses and embassies move their headquarters to Potsdamer Pl. and Mitte in the East.

The vast **Tiergarten**, Berlin's beloved park, lies in the center of the city; the grand, tree-lined **Straße des 17. Juni** runs through it from west to east and becomes **Unter den Linden** at the **Brandenburg Gate**. North of the Gate is the **Reichstag**, while south of the Gate **Ebertstraße** winds to glitzy **Potsdamer Platz**. Unter den Linden continues east through **Mitte**, location of countless historical sites. The street changes names once again, to **Karl-Liebknecht-Straße**, before emptying into **Alexanderplatz**, home to Berlin's most visible landmark, the **Fernsehturm** (TV tower). At the east end of Mitte is the **Museumsinsel** ("Museum Island"). Cafe- and shop-lined **Oranienburger-straße** cuts through the area of northeastern Mitte known as **Scheunenviertel**, historically Berlin's center of Jewish life.

The commercial district of West Berlin lies at the southwest end of the Tiergarten, centered around **Bahnhof Zoo** and the **Kurfürstendamm** (**Ku'damm** for short). To the east is **Breitscheidplatz**, marked by the bombed-out **Kaiser-Wilhelm-Gedächtniskirche**, and **Savignyplatz**, one of many pleasant squares in **Charlottenburg**, which is home to cafes, restaurants, and *Pensionen*. Southeast of the Ku'damm, **Schöneberg** is a pleasant residential neighborhood and the traditional nexus of the city's gay and lesbian community. At the southeast periphery of Berlin lies **Kreuzberg**, a district home to an exciting mix of radical leftists and punks as well as a large Turkish population. Northeast of the city is **Prenzlauer Berg**, a former working-class area, and east of Mitte is **Friedrichshain**, the center of Berlin's counterculture and nightlife.

If you're planning to stay more than a few days, the **Falk Plan** (available at most kiosks and bookstores) is an indispensable city map that includes a street index and unfolds like a book (DM11/€6). Dozens of streets and subway stations in Eastern Berlin were named after Communist figures. Many, but not all, have been renamed in a process only recently completed; be sure that your map is up-to-date.

▐ LOCAL TRANSPORTATION

Public Transportation: It is impossible to tour Berlin on foot—fortunately, the extensive **U-Bahn** (subway) and **S-Bahn** (surface rail) systems will take you anywhere. The city is divided into 3 transit zones. **Zone A** encompasses central Berlin, including Tempelhof airport. Almost everything else falls into **Zone B**, while **Zone C** contains the outlying areas, including Potsdam and Oranienburg. An **AB ticket** is the best deal, as you can buy regional Bahn tickets for the outlying areas. A single ticket for the combined network (*Langstrecke* AB or BC, DM4.20/€2.30; or *Ganzstrecke* ABC, DM4.80/€2.45) is good for 2hr. after validation and may be used on any S-Bahn, U-Bahn, bus or streetcar. However, it almost always makes sense to buy a pass. A **Tageskarte** (AB DM12.00/€6, ABC DM12.80/€6.50) is valid from validation until 3am the next day. The **Welcome-Card** (DM32/€17) is valid on all lines for 72hr., and the **7-Tage-Karte** (AB DM44/€23, ABC DM55/€28) is good for 7 days. For longer stays, an **Umweltkarte Standard** (AB DM105/€54, ABC DM130/€67) is valid for one calendar month. Buy tickets from *Automaten* (machines) or ticket windows in the U- and S-Bahn stations. Validate your ticket in the box marked "Hier entwerfen" before boarding or risk a DM60/€30 fine.

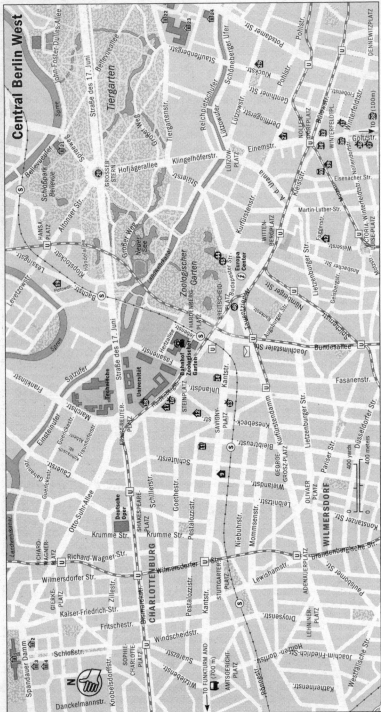

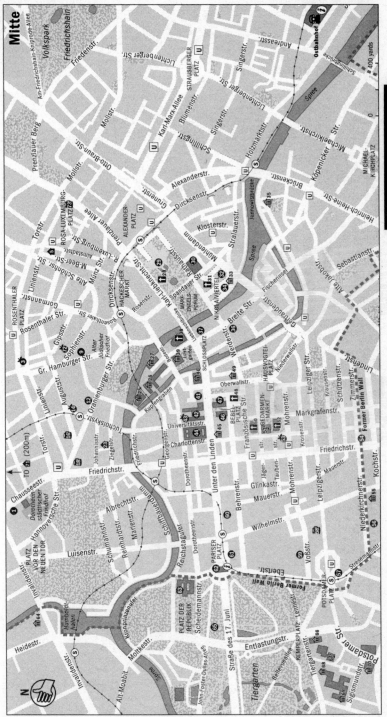

Mitte

GERMANY

GERMANY

Central Berlin West

🏠 ACCOMMODATIONS
Art Hotel Connection, 42
CVJM-Haus, 27
Hotel-Pension Cortina, 9
Hotel Sachsenhof, 39
Hotel-Pension Hansablick, 19
Jugendgästehaus (HI), 25
Jugendgästehaus am Zoo, 17
Pension Knesebeck, 12

 FOOD
Baharat Falafel, 31
Café Hardenberg, 16
Fish and Vegetables, 37
Mensa TU, 18
Schwarzes Café, 13
Sushi am Winterfeldtplatz, 36

🌙 NIGHTLIFE
A-Trane, 11
Café Berio, 33
Metropol, 34
Mister Hu, 28
Omnes, 40
Quasimodo, 14
Slumberland, 35

● SIGHTS
Aquarium, 44
Elefantentor, 45
Kaiser-Wilhelm-Gedächtiskirche, 46
Siegessäule, 20

🏛 MUSEUMS
Ägyptisches Museum, 2
Bröhanmuseum, 4
Gemäldegalerie, 23
Kunstgewerbemuseum, 22
Neue Nationalgalerie, 24
Sammlung Berggruen, 3
Schloß Bellevue, 21
Schloß Charlottenburg, 1

Mitte

🏠 ACCOMMODATIONS
Circus, 5
Clubhouse Hostel, 23
Mitte's Backpacker, 71

 FOOD
Barcomi's Deli, 72
Beth Café, 14
Cafeteria Charlottenstr., 53
Mensa der Humboldt-U, 43
Village Voice, 3

🌙 NIGHTLIFE
Grüner Salon, 73
Tacheles, 18
Tresor/Globus, 58
VEB-OZ, 16

✝ CHURCHES
Berliner Dom, 38
Deutscher Dom, 52
Französischer Dom, 50
Marienkirche, 28
Nikolaikirche, 31
St.-Hedwigs-Kathedrale, 48

🏛 MUSEUMS
Alte Nationalgalerie, 27
Altes Museum, 39
Bodemuseum, 25
Deutsche Guggenheim Berlin, 45
Deutsches Hist. Museum, 40
Gemäldegalerie, 69
Hamburger Bahnhof, 64
Hanfmuseum, 33
Kunstgewerbemuseum, 68
Märkisches Museum, 35
Musikinstrumenten-Museum, 66
Neue Nationalgalerie, 70
Pergamon-Museum, 26
Schinkelmuseum, 49
Topographie des Terrors, 55

● SIGHTS
Alte Bibliothek, 46
Bertolt-Brecht-Haus, 1
Brandenburger Tor, 62
Deutsche Staatsbibliothek, 44
Deutsche Staatsoper, 47
Ephraim-Palais, 34
Fernsehturm, 29
Führerbunker, 59
Haus am Checkpoint Charlie, 54
Hotel Adlon, 61
Humboldt-Universität, 42
Infobox, 57
Jüdische Knabenschule, 9
Knoblauchhaus, 32
Martin-Gropius-Bau, 56
Neue Wache, 41
Neue Synagogue, 12
Palast der Republik, 37
Reichstag, 63
Rathaus, 30
Russian Embassy, 60
Sowjetisches Ehrenmal, 65
Staatsrat, 36

Night Transport: U- and S-Bahn lines generally don't run from 1-4am, although most S-Bahn lines run every hr. on weekend nights. The **U12** runs all night F and Sa, and the **U9** runs 24hr. all week. A system of **night buses** (preceded by the letter N) centered on Bahnhof Zoo runs every 20-30min.; pick up the free *Nachtliniennetz* map at a *Fahrscheine und Mehr* office for more information.

Taxis: ☎26 10 26, 21 02 02; or 690 22. Call at least 15min. in advance.

Car Rental: The **Mietwagenservice**, counter 21 in Bahnhof Zoo's *Reisezentrum*, represents Avis, Europacar (both open 7am-6:30pm), Hertz (open 7am-8pm), and Sixt (open 24 hr.). Most companies also have offices in the Tegel Airport.

Bike Rental: The government's **bikecity** program rents bikes at Bahnhof Zoo (☎07 60 98 21 35 49), at the far end of Hardenbergpl. DM8/€4 per 3hr., students DM5/€3; DM15/€8 per 24hr., students DM8/€4. Open daily 10am-6pm.

🛈 PRACTICAL INFORMATION

TOURIST AND FINANCIAL SERVICES

Tourist Offices: ◼ **EurAide** (www.euraide.de), in Bahnhof Zoo, has comprehensive travel information and makes train and hotel reservations for a DM7/€4 fee. Facing the Reisezentrum, go left and down the corridor on your right; it's on the left. Arrive early—the office can get packed. Open daily 8am-noon and 1-6pm. **Europa-Center,** on Budapester Str., has city maps (DM1/€0.51) and free transit maps. From Bahnhof Zoo, walk along Budapester Str. past the Kaiser-Wilhelm-Gedächtniskirche; the office is on the right after about 2 blocks. Open M-Sa 8:30am-8:30pm, Su 10am-6:30pm.

Tours: Insider Tour (☎692 31 49) has enthusiastic guides. Tours leave from the McDonald's by Bahnhof Zoo. (3½hr., late Mar.-Nov. daily 10am and 2:30pm, DM15/€8.) **Berlin Walks** (☎301 91 94; www.berlinwalks.com) offers a range of English-language walking tours, including Infamous Third Reich Sites, Jewish Life in Berlin, and Discover Potsdam. Their Discover Berlin Walk is one of the best ways to get acquainted with the city. Tours (2½-6hr.) start daily 10am at the taxi stand in front of Bahnhof Zoo (Discover Potsdam meets 9am); in summer, Discover Berlin also meets 2:30pm. All tours DM18/€9, under 26 DM15/€8. Tickets available at EurAide.

Budget Travel: STA, Goethestr. 73 (☎311 09 50). S3, S5, S7, S9, or S75 to Savignypl. Open M-W and F 10am-6pm, Th 10am-8pm.

Embassies and Consulates: The locations of the embassies and consulates remain in a state of flux; for the latest information, call the **Auswärtiges Amt Dienststelle Berlin** (☎20 18 60). **Australia,** Friedrichstr. 200 (☎880 08 80). U2 or U6 to Stadtmitte. Open M-Th 8am-1pm and 2-5pm, F 8am-1pm and 2-4:15pm. Also Uhlandstr. 181-183 (☎880 08 80). U15 to Uhlandstr. Open M-F 8:30am-1pm. **Canada,** Friedrichstr. 95 (☎20 31 20), on 12th fl. of the International Trade Center. S1, S2, S3, S5, S7, S9, S25 or S75 or U6 to Friedrichstr. Open M-F 9am-noon; appointments 2pm. **Ireland,** Friedrichstr. 200 (☎22 07 20). Open M-F 9:30am-noon and 2:30-4:45pm. **New Zealand,** Friedrichstr. 60 (☎20 62 10; fax 20 62 11 14). Open M-F 9am-1pm and 2-5:30pm; closes F 4:30pm. **South Africa,** Friedrichstr. 60 (☎22 07 30). Consulate: Douglasstr. 9 (☎82 50 11 or 825 27 11). S7 to Grunewald. Open M-F 9am-noon. **UK,** Wilhelmstr. 70-71 (☎20 18 40). S1, S2, S3, S5, S7, S9, S25 or S75 or U6 to Friedrichstr. Open M-F 9am-4pm. **US,** Citizens Service/Consulate, Clayallee 170 (☎832 92 33). U1 to Oskar-Helene-Heim. Open M-F 8:30am-noon. After hours, call ☎830 50.

Currency Exchange: Geldwechsel, Joachimstaler Str. 7-9 (☎882 63 71), has decent rates and no commission. **ReiseBank,** at Bahnhof Zoo (☎881 71 17; open daily 7am-10pm) and Ostbahnhof (☎296 43 93; open M-F 7am-10pm, Sa 8am-8pm, Su 8am-12pm and 12:30-4pm), is conveniently located but has worse rates.

American Express: Main Office, Bayreuther Str. 37 (☎21 49 83 63). U1, U2, or U15 to Wittenbergpl. Holds mail and cashes AmEx Traveler's Cheques with no commission. Long lines F-Sa. Open M-F 9am-6pm, Sa 10am-1pm. **Branch office,** Friedrichstr. 172 (☎20 17 40 12). U6 to Französische Str. Open M-F 9am-7pm, Sa 10am-1pm.

LOCAL SERVICES

Luggage Storage: In **Bahnhof Zoo.** Lockers DM2-6/€1-3 per day, depending on size. 72hr. max. M-F 7am-6pm, Sa-Su 9am-6pm. If all lockers are full, try **Gepäckaufbewahrung,** the next window over (DM4/€2 per piece per day). Open daily 6:15am-10:30pm. 24hr. lockers available at **Ostbahnhof** and **Alexanderpl.**

Bi-Gay-Lesbian Organizations: Lesbenberatung, Kulmer Str. 20a (☎215 20 00), offers counseling on lesbian issues. U7 to Kleistpark. Open M-Tu and Th 4-7pm, F 2-5pm. **Mann-o-Meter,** Motzstr. 5 (☎216 80 08), off Nollendorfpl., gives out info on gay night-life and living arrangements. Open M-F 5-10pm, Sa-Su 4-10pm.

Laundromat: Waschcenter Schnell und Sauber, Leibnizstr. 72 in **Charlottenburg** (S3, S5, S7, S9, or S75 to Savignypl.); Wexstr. 34 in **Schöneberg** (U9 to Bundespl.); Mehringdamm 32 in **Kreuzberg** (U6 or U7 to Mehringdamm); Torstr. 115 in **Mitte** (U8 to Rosenthaler Pl.). Wash DM4-7/€2-4; dry DM1/€0.51. Open daily 6am-11pm.

EMERGENCY AND COMMUNICATIONS

Police: ☎110. **Ambulance and Fire:** ☎112.

Handicapped access: Berliner Behindertenverband, ☎20 43 847. Info and advice for the handicapped. Open M-F 8am-4pm.

Pharmacies: Europa-Apotheke, Tauentzienstr. 9-12 (☎261 41 42), near the Europa Center and Bahnhof Zoo. Open M-F 9am-8pm, Sa 9am-4pm. Closed pharmacies post signs directing you to the nearest open one.

Medical Assistance: American and British embassies have lists of English-speaking doctors. **Emergency Doctor,** ☎31 00 31; **Emergency Dentist,** ☎011 41. Both open 24hr.

Internet Access: Easy Everything, on the corner of Kurfürstendamm and Meineckestr. A DM5/€3 card gives 1¼hr. of Internet access. Open 24hr. **Webtimes,** Chausseestr. 8 (☎280 49 890), in Mitte. U6 to Oranienburger Tor. Open M-F 9am-midnight, Sa and Su 10am-midnight. DM7/€4 per hr.

Post Offices: Joachimstaler Str. 7, down the street from Bahnhof Zoo, near the corner of Joachimstaler Str. and Kantstr. **Poste Restante:** Postlagernde briefe für First Name SURNAME, Postamt in der Joachimstaler Str. 7, **10706** Berlin. Open M-Sa 8am-midnight, Su 10am-midnight. Branch office at **Tegel Airport** open daily 6:30am-9pm; branch office at **Ostbahnhof Postamt** open M-Sa 8am-8pm, Su 7am-6pm.

▐ ACCOMMODATIONS AND CAMPING

Hostels in Berlin are either HI-affiliated and state-owned (*Jugendherbergen* and *Jugendgästehäuser*) or privately-owned. **HI hostels** can be a great, cheap sleep, but they fill quickly, often impose a curfew, and are usually for **members only.** There are also over 4000 **private rooms** available in the city; ask at the tourist office for details and be sure to tell them your language abilities (if any), since some host families may not speak English. For visits over four days, the various **Mitwohnzentralen** can arrange for you to housesit or sublet an apartment; for more information, contact **Home Company Mitwohnzentrale,** Joachimstaler Str. 17. (☎194 45; www.HomeCompany.de. U9 or U15 to Kurfürstendamm. Open M-F 9am-6pm, Sa 11am-2pm.) For long stays or on weekends, reservations are essential. During the **Love Parade** (p. 417), call at least two months ahead for a choice of rooms and at least two weeks ahead for any bed at all. Some hostels increase prices that weekend by up to DM20/€10 per night.

MITTE

▓ **Mitte's Backpacker Hostel,** Chausseestr. 102 (☎262 51 40). U6 to Zinnowitzer Str. Friendly English-speaking staff, themed rooms, and a relaxed atmosphere. Bikes DM10/€5 per day. Internet access. Kitchen available. Sheets DM4/€2. Laundry DM5/€3. Reception 24hr. No curfew. Dorms DM25-29/€13-15; doubles DM76/€40; triples DM99/€51; quads DM124/€64.

Circus, Rosa-Luxemburg-Str. 39-41 (☎28 39 14 33). U2 to Rosa-Luxemburg-Pl. Bike rental DM12/€6 per day. Sheets DM4/€2. Reception 24hr. No curfew. Reservations a must in summer; reconfirm 1 day before arrival. 5-6 bed dorms DM25/€13; singles

DM45/€23; doubles DM80/€42; triples DM105/€54; quads DM120/€64. Apartment for 4 with kitchen and bath DM180/€92.

Clubhouse Hostel, Kalkscheunestr. 2 (☎28 09 79 79). S1, S2, or S25 to Oranienburger Str. or U6 to Oranienburger Tor. Enter from Johannisstr. 2 or Kalkscheunestr. Internet access DM1/€0.51 per 5min. Breakfast DM7/€4. Reception 24hr. No curfew. Call at least 2-3 days ahead. 8-10 bed dorms DM25-27/€13-14; 5-7 bed dorms DM30-32/ €16-17; singles DM50-60/€26-31; doubles DM80-88/€42-46.

TIERGARTEN

Jugendgästehaus (HI), Kluckstr. 3 (☎261 10 97 or 261 10 98). From Bahnhof Zoo, take bus #129 (dir. Hermannpl.) to Gedenkstätte or U1 to Kurfürstenstr., then walk up Potsdamer Str., turn left on Pohlstr., and right on Kluckstr. Bike rental DM15/€8 per day, students DM10/€5. Breakfast and sheets included. Key deposit DM10/€5. Reception 24hr. Lockout 9am-1pm. Curfew midnight; stragglers admitted every 30min. 12:30-6am. Reservations strongly recommended. 4-10 bed dorms DM34/€18, over 26 DM43/€22.

Hotel-Pension Hansablick, Flotowstr. 6 (☎390 48 00; reserv@hotel-hansablick.de). S3, S5, S7, S9, or S75 to Tiergarten. All rooms have bath, hair dryer, phone, and cable TV. Reception 24hr. Reserve ahead. Singles DM160/€82; doubles DM195-235/€99-121. In July-Aug. and mid-Nov. to Feb., discount rates available. 5% *Let's Go* discount.

CHARLOTTENBURG

Jugendgästehaus am Zoo, Hardenbergstr. 9a (☎312 94 10), opposite the Technical University Mensa. Take bus #145 to Steinpl., or walk from the back exit of Bahnhof Zoo straight down Hardenbergstr. Push hard on the front door; it's not locked. Reception 9am-midnight. Check-in 10am. Check-out 9am. Lockout 10am-2pm. No curfew. 4-8 bed dorms DM40/€21, under 26 DM35/€18; singles DM52/€27, DM47/€24; doubles DM95/€49, DM85/€44.

Hotel-Pension Cortina, Kantstr. 140 (☎313 90 59). S3, S5, S7, S9, or S75 to Savignypl. High-ceilinged, bright rooms, and a great location. Breakfast included. Reception 24hr. Reservations recommended. Dorms DM38-60/€19-31 depending on group size and season; singles DM60-90/€30-47; doubles DM90-150/€46-77.

Pension Knesebeck, Knesebeckstr. 86 (☎312 72 55; fax 313 95 07). S3, S5, S7, S9, or S75 to Savignypl. Follow Knesebeckstr. to Kantstr., where it becomes Savignypl.; continue forward around the park semicircle. Breakfast included. Laundry DM8/€4. Reception 24hr. Phone reservations must be confirmed by fax, letter or with credit card. Singles DM75/€39, with shower DM85/€44; doubles DM120/€63, DM140/€72.

SCHÖNEBERG AND WILMERSDORF

Studentenhotel Meininger 10, Meininger Str. 10 (☎78 71 74 14). U4, bus #146 or N46 to Rathaus Schöneberg. Walk toward the Rathaus on Freiherr-vom-Stein-Str., turn left onto Martin-Luther-Str. and then right on Meininger Str. Run by students, for students. Breakfast and sheets included. Lockers DM10/€5 deposit. Reception 24hr. Co-ed dorms DM25/€13; 3- to 6-bed rooms DM40/€21; singles DM66/€34; doubles DM88/€46; 5% *Let's Go* discount.

CVJM-Haus, Einemstr. 10 (☎264 91 00). U1, U2, U4, or U15 to Nollendorfpl. Unlike most accommodations at this price, you will not sleep in a room with strangers. One block from the gay nightlife of Nollendorfpl. Breakfast included. Sheets DM3/€1.50. Reception 8-11am and 4-9pm. Quiet time 10pm-7am and 1-3pm. Key available. Book in advance. DM40/€21 per person for singles, doubles, and dorms.

Jugendgästehaus Feurigstraße, Feurigstr. 63 (☎781 52 11). U7 to Kleistpark, or bus #204 or 348 to Kaiser-Wilhelm-Pl. Walk down Hauptstr., take the 2nd left onto Kollonenstr., then a right onto Feurigstr. Relatively close to the Schöneberg bars. Breakfast included. Sheets DM5/€3 if staying fewer than 3 nights, otherwise free. Reception 24hr. Call ahead. Dorms DM40/€21; singles DM55/€29; doubles DM100/€26.

Hotel Sachsenhof, Motzstr. 7 (☎216 20 74). U1, U2, U4, or U15 to Nollendorfpl. Small, well-furnished rooms with phone and TV. Surrounded by the myriad cafes and gay nightlife of Nollendorfpl. Breakfast DM10/€5. Reception 24hr. Call for reservations 7am-11pm.

Singles DM57/€29, with shower DM65/€34; doubles DM99/€51, DM126/€65; new double with shower DM 146/€75, with full bath DM156/€80.

Art Hotel Connection, Fuggerstr. 33 (☎ 217 70 28; fax 217 70 30; info@arthotel-connection.de). U1, U2, or U15 to Wittenbergpl., on a side street off Martin-Luther-Str. For gay and lesbian guests only (though mostly men stay here). Breakfast included. Reservations for weekends required at least 1 month in advance. Singles DM110-160/€56-82; doubles 150-210/€76-108; cheaper in winter.

KREUZBERG

Bax Pax, Skalitzer Str. 104 (☎ 69 51 83 22). U1 or U15 to Görlitzer Bahnhof. Great location at the mouth of mighty Oranienstr. Kitchen open 24hr. Sheets DM4/€2. Reception 7am-10pm. No curfew. DM25-30/€12-16.

Die Fabrik, Schlesische Str. 18 (☎ 611 71 16). U1 or U15 to Schlesisches Tor or bus #N65 to Taborstr. Provides easy access to Kreuzberg nightlife. Breakfast DM5-15/€2-8. Reception 24hr. Reserve or call ahead. No curfew. 16-bed dorm DM30/€16; singles DM66/€34; doubles DM94/€48; triples DM120/€63; quads DM144/€76.

Hotel Transit, Hagelberger Str. 53-54 (☎ 789 04 70). U6 or U7 or bus #N19 to Mehringdamm. Sleek, modern rooms, with big-screen lounge and well-stocked bar. Breakfast included. Reception 24hr. Singles DM100/€52; doubles DM115/€60; triples DM150/€77; quads DM200/€103.

CAMPING

Deutscher Camping-Club runs the following campgrounds. Reservations are recommended; write to Deutscher Camping-Club Berlin, Geisbergstr. 11, 10777 Berlin, or call ☎218 60 71 or 218 60 72. All are DM9.90/€5 per person, DM7.40/€3.80 per tent.

Kohlhasenbrück, Neue Kreisstr. 36 (☎ 805 17 37). S7 to Griebnitzsee, then turn right out of the station and follow Rudolf-Breitscheid-Str., which becomes Neue Kreisstr. One of Berlin's more nature-intensive campgrounds, next to the Griebnitzsee and a protected wildlife area. Relatively easy access to the city. Open Mar.-Oct.

Kladow, Krampnitzer Weg 111-117 (☎ 365 27 97). U7 to Rathaus Spandau, then bus #135 (dir. Alt-Kladow) to the end and bus #234 to Krampnitzer Weg/Selbitzerstr. Swimmable lake, store, and restaurant on premises. Open year-round.

🔲 FOOD

Berlin defies all expectations with both tasty home-grown options and terrific ethnic food from its Turkish, Indian, Italian, and Thai immigrants. Typical Berlin street food is Turkish; most *Imbiße* (fast-food snack stands) are open late. The *Döner Kebap*, a sandwich of lamb or chicken and salad, has cornered the fast-food market, with *Falafel* running a close second; either makes a small meal for DM3-5/€1.50-3. Berlin's numerous relaxed cafes, restaurants, and *Kneipen* are budget friendly and usually offer meals of many sizes.

Aldi, Plus, Edeka, and **Penny Markt** are the cheapest supermarket chains. Supermarkets are usually open Monday to Friday 9am-6pm and Saturday 9am-4pm. At Bahnhof Zoo, **Nimm's Mit** near the Reisezentrum is open at all hours. The best **open-air market** fires up Saturday mornings on Winterfeldtpl.

MITTE

Mensa der Humboldt-Universität, Unter den Linden 6, behind the university's main building. Meals DM2.50-6/€1.30-4. Student ID required. Open M-F 11:30am-2:30pm.

Cafeteria Charlottenstraße, Charlottenstr. 55, at the Hochschule für Musik, near the Gendarmenmarkt. U6 to Französische Str. or U2 or U6 to Stadtmitte. The entrance is in a corridor accessible from Taubenstr. or Charlottenstr. Meals DM4.50/€2.30, students DM2.55/€1.30. Open M-F 8:30am-3pm.

Barcomi's Deli, Sophienstr. 21. A deli haven tucked away in the Sophie-Gips-Höfe. Sandwiches DM7-11/€3-6. Open M-Sa 9am-10pm, Su 10am-10pm.

GERMANY

Beth Café, Tucholskystr. 40, just off Auguststr. S1, S2, or S25 to Oranienburger Str. Kosher restaurant in the heart of the Scheunenviertel. Open M-Th and Su 11am-10pm, F 11am-5pm; in winter closes F 3pm.

Village Voice, Ackerstr. 1a. U8 to Rosenthaler Pl. Tex-Mex cafe/bar/bookstore. Cafe and bar open M-F 11am-2am, Sa-Su noon-2am. Store open M-F 11am-8pm, Sa noon-4pm.

CHARLOTTENBURG

Mensa TU, Hardenbergstr. 34. Bus #145 to Steinpl., or walk 10min. from Bahnhof Zoo. Meals (including good vegetarian dishes) DM4-8/€2-4, students DM4-5/€2-3. Cafeteria downstairs has longer hours and slightly higher prices. *Mensa* open M-F 11:15am-2:30pm. Cafeteria open M-F 8am-7:45pm.

Café Hardenberg, Hardenbergstr. 10. Opposite the TU's *Mensa,* but with a lot more atmosphere. Breakfast (DM6-10/€3-6) served day or night; salads and pasta dishes DM5-13/€2-7. Open M-F 9am-1am, Sa-Su 9am-2am.

Schwarzes Café, Kantstr. 148. S3, S5, S7, S9, or S75 to Savignypl. This cafe is always open, except for Tu 3-11am.

SCHONEBERG

Baharat Falafel, Winterfeldtstr. 37. U1, U2, U4, or U15 to Nollendorfpl. Open daily 11am-2am; closed last week in July.

Fish and Vegetables, Goltzstr. 32. U1, U2, U4, or U15 to Nollendorfpl. A no-nonsense do-it-yourself Thai restaurant. Dishes from DM6/€3. Open daily noon-midnight. Next door, **Rani** serves tasty Indian food in a similar fashion. Open daily 10am-1am.

Sushi am Winterfeldtplatz, Goltzstr. 24. U1, U2, U4, or U15 to Nollendorfpl. Standing-room only Japanese cuisine in the heart of Schöneberg. Open M-Sa noon-midnight, Su 3pm-midnight. Delivery until 1hr. before closing.

KREUZBERG

Hannibal, at the corner of Wienerstr. and Skalitzerstr. U1, U12 or U15, or bus N29 to Görlitzer Bahnhof. Massive "Hannibal-burgers" DM11.50/€6. Open Su-Th 8am-4am, F-Sa 8am-5am.

Amrit, Oranienstr. 202-203. U1 or U15 to Görlitzer Bahnhof. Serves possibly the best Indian food in Berlin. Open Su-Th noon-1am, F-Sa noon-2am.

Abendmahl, Muskauer Str. 9. U1 or U15 to Görlitzer Bahnhof. Delicious vegetarian entrees, fish, and desserts; a favorite of gay Berliners. Open daily after 6pm.

PRENZLAUER BERG

Osswald, Göhrener Str. 5. U2 to Eberswalder Str. Popular with locals, this restaurant/bar caters to locals with simple but tasty German dishes. Open daily 9am-4am.

Ostwind, Husemannstr. 13. U2 to Senefelderpl. Beautifully prepared Chinese specialties. Open M-Sa 6pm-1am, Su 10am-1am.

◉ SIGHTS

Berlin's sights cover an area eight times the size of Paris. For a guide to the city's major neighborhoods, see **Orientation,** p. 401. Below, the sights are organized by *Bezirk* (district), beginning with Mitte and spiralling outward. Many of central Berlin's major sights lie along the route of **bus #100,** from Bahnhof Zoo to Prenzlauer Berg; consider a day pass (DM7.80/€4) or a 7-day pass (DM40/€20.50).

MITTE

Formerly the heart of Imperial Berlin, Mitte contains some of Berlin's most magnificent sights and museums. Unter den Linden, the area between the Brandenburg Gate and Alexanderpl., is best reached by taking S1, S2, or S25 to Unter den Linden; alternatively, bus #100 runs the length of the boulevard every 4-6 min. The sights listed below lie around Unter den Linden, between the Gate in the west and Alexanderpl. in the east.

■ **BRANDENBURGER TOR AND PARISER PLATZ.** For decades a barricaded gateway to nowhere, the **Brandenburg Gate** is the most powerful emblem of reunited Germany and Berlin. Standing right in the center of the city, it was in no-man's land during the time of the wall; today it opens east onto **Pariser Platz** and Unter den Linden and west onto the Tiergarten and Str. des 17. Juni. All but a few of the venerable buildings near the gate have been destroyed, but a massive reconstruction effort has already revived such pre-war staples as the **Hotel Adlon,** once the premier address for all visiting dignitaries and celebrities.

NEUE WACHE. The "New Guardhouse" was designed in unrepentant Neoclassical style. During the GDR era, it was known as the "Monument to the Victims of Fascism and Militarism." After reunification, the building was reopened as a war memorial. The remains of an unknown soldier and an unknown concentration camp victim are buried inside with earth from battlefields and Nazi concentration camps. (Unter den Linden 4. Open daily 10am-6pm.)

BEBELPLATZ. On May 10, 1933, Nazi students burned nearly 20,000 books here by "subversive" authors such as Heinrich Heine and Sigmund Freud. The building with the curved façade is the **Alte Bibliothek,** once the royal library. On the other side of the square is the **Deutsche Staatsoper** (opera house), fully rebuilt after the war from original sketches. The distinctive blue dome at the end of the square belongs to the **St.-Hedwigs-Kathedrale.** Built in 1773 as the first Catholic church in Berlin after the Reformation, it was burnt to a crisp by American bombers in 1943 and was rebuilt in the 1950s. (Cathedral open M-Sa 10am-5pm, Su 1-5pm. Free.)

POTSDAMER PLATZ AND FÜHRERBUNKER. Built under Friedrich Wilhelm I with the primary purpose of moving troops quickly, **Potsdamer Platz** was chosen to become the new commercial center of Berlin after reunification. Completion is now in sight, and many of the cutting-edge, wildly ambitious architectural designs make for some spectacular sight-seeing. (S1, S2, S25 or U2 to Potsdamer Pl.) Near Potsdamer Pl., unmarked and inconspicuous, lies the site of the **Führerbunker** where Hitler married Eva Braun and then ended his life. Tourists looking for it often mistakenly head for the visible bunker at the southern edge of Potsdamer Pl.; it's actually on In den Ministergärten off Eberstr., behind a playground.

GENDARMENMARKT. Several blocks south of Bebelpl., **Gendarmenmarkt** is home to some of Berlin's most impressive 19th-century buildings. During the last week of June and the first week of July, the square transforms into an outdoor stage for classical concerts. At either end are the **Deutscher Dom** (German Cathedral) and the **Französischer Dom** (French Cathedral).

BERLINER DOM. This multiple-domed cathedral, one of Berlin's most recognizable landmarks, was built during the reign of Kaiser Wilhelm II and recently emerged from 20 years of restoration. (Open daily 9am-7:30pm. Dom and crypt DM8/€4, students DM4/€2. Free organ recitals W-F at 3pm.)

ALEXANDERPLATZ AND FERNSEHTURM. Formerly the heart of Weimar Berlin, the plaza was transformed in East German times into an urban wasteland of fountains and pre-fab office buildings. The **Fernsehturm** (TV tower), the tallest structure in Berlin at 368m, is a bizarre building originally intended as proof of East Germany's technological capabilities. When the sun is out, the windows have a crucifix-shaped glint pattern known as the *Papsts Rache* (pope's revenge). (Open daily Mar.-Oct. 9am-1am; Nov.-Feb. 10am-midnight. DM12/€6, under 16 DM5/€3.)

NEUE SYNAGOGE. This huge building survived *Kristallnacht* when a local police chief, realizing that the building was a historic monument, ordered it spared. Its restoration, largely financed by international Jewish organizations, was completed in 1995. The interior now houses an exhibit chronicling the synagogue's history and temporary exhibits on the history of Berlin's Jews. (Oranienburger Str. 30. Open May-Aug. Su-M 10am-8pm, Tu-Th 10am-6pm, F 10am-2pm. Museum DM9/€5, students DM6/€3. Entry to the dome DM3/€1.50, students DM2/€1.)

TIERGARTEN. Once a hunting ground for Prussian monarchs, the lush **Tiergarten** is now a vast landscaped park in the center of Berlin, stretching from Bahnhof Zoo to the Brandenburg Gate. Straße des 17. Juni bisects the park from west to east.

SIEGESSÄULE. In the heart of the Tiergarten, the slender 70m "victory column" commemorates Prussia's humiliating defeat of France in 1870. The gilded statue on top—Victoria, the goddess of victory—is made of melted-down French cannons. The 285 steps lead to a panoramic view of the city. (*Bus #100, 187, to Großer Stern. Open Apr.-Nov. M 1-6pm, Tu-Su 9am-6pm. DM2/€1, students DM1/€0.51.*)

■ **THE REICHSTAG.** Just north of the gate is the current home of Germany's governing body, the *Bundestag*. The glass dome on top is built around an upside-down solar cone that powers the building. A walkway spirals up the inside of the dome, leading visitors around a panoramic view to the top of the cone. (*Open daily 8am-midnight; last entrance 10pm. Free.*)

BERTOLT-BRECHT-HAUS. If any single man personifies the maelstrom of political and aesthetic contradictions that is Berlin, it is **Bertolt Brecht,** who lived and worked in this house from 1953 to 1956. (*Chausseestr. 125, near Schlegelstr. U6 to Zinnowitzer Str. Mandatory German tours every 30min. Tu-F 10-11:30am, Th also 5-6:30pm, and Sa 9:30am-1:30pm; every hr. Su 11am-6pm. DM6/€3, students DM3/€1.50.*) Brecht is buried in the attached **Dorotheenstädtischer Friedhof.** (*Open daily Dec.-Jan. 8am-4pm, Feb. and Nov. 8am-5pm, Mar. and Oct. 8am-6pm, Apr. and Sept. 8am-7pm, May-Aug. 8am-8pm.*)

CHARLOTTENBURG

Charlottenburg, one of the wealthiest areas in Berlin, includes the area between the Ku'damm and the Spree river.

ZOOLOGISCHER GARTEN AND AQUARIUM. Across Bahnhof Zoo and through the maze of bus depots, the renowned **zoo** is one of the best in the world, with many animals displayed in open-air habitats instead of cages. The second entrance across from Europa-Center is the famous **Elefantentor**, Budapester Str. 34, a delightfully decorated pagoda of pachyderms. (*Open daily May-Sept. 9am-6:30pm; Oct.-Feb. 9am-5pm; Mar.-Apr. 9am-5:30pm. DM15/€8, students DM12/€6.*) Within the walls of the Zoo, but independently accessible, is the excellent **aquarium,** which houses broad collections of insects and reptiles as well as endless tanks of wide-eyed, rainbow-colored fish. Its pride and joy is the 450kg Komodo dragon, the world's largest reptile, a gift to Germany from Indonesia. (*Budapester Str. 32. Open daily 9am-6pm. Aquarium DM15/€8, students DM12/€6. Combination ticket to zoo and aquarium DM24/€13, students DM19/€10, children DM12/€6.*)

KAISER-WILHELM-GEDÄCHTNISKIRCHE. Nicknamed "the rotten tooth" by Berliners, the jagged edges of this shattered church stand as a reminder of the destruction caused during World War II. Built in 1852 in a Romanesque-Byzantine style, the church has a striking interior, with colorful mosaics covering the ceiling, floors, and walls. The ruins house an exhibit of shocking photos of the entire city in ruins just after the war. (*Exhibit open M-Sa 10am-4pm. Church open daily 9am-7pm.*)

SCHLOß CHARLOTTENBURG. The broad Baroque palace commissioned by Friedrich I for his second wife, Sophie-Charlotte, sprawls over a park on the northern edge of Charlottenburg. The Schloß's many buildings include the **Neringbau** (or **Altes Schloß**), the palace proper; the **Schinkel-Pavillon,** a museum dedicated to Prussian architect Karl Friedrich Schinkel; **Belvedere,** a small building housing the royal family's porcelain collection; and the **Mausoleum,** the final resting spot for most of the family. The **Schloßgarten** behind the main buildings is a paradise of small lakes, fountains, and carefully planted rows of trees. (*Bus #145 from Bahnhof Zoo to Luisenpl./ Schloß Charlottenburg or U7 to Richard-Wagner-Pl. and walk 15min. down Otto-Suhr-Allee. Altes Schloß open Tu-F 9am-5pm, Sa-Su 10am-5pm; DM10/€5, students DM8/€4. Schinkel-Pavillon open Tu-Su 10am-5pm; DM4/€2, students DM3/€1.50. Belvedere open Apr.-Oct. Tu-Su 10am-5pm, Nov.-Mar. Tu-F noon-4pm and Sa-Su noon-5pm; DM4/€2, students DM3/€1.50. Mausoleum open Apr.-Oct. Tu-Su 10am-noon and 1-5pm; DM3/€1.50, students DM2/€1. Schloßgarten open Tu-Su 6am-9pm; free. Entire complex DM14/€7, students DM10/€5.*)

OLYMPIA-STADION. At the western edge of Charlottenburg, the Olympic Stadium was erected for the 1936 Olympic Games, in which Jesse Owens, an African-American, triumphed over Nazi racial theories by winning four gold medals. Hitler refused to congratulate Owens because of his skin color, but there's now a Jesse-Owens-Allee to the south of the stadium. *(U2 to Olympia-Stadion (Ost) or S5 or S75 to Olympiastadion. DM2/€1. Open daily in summer 8am-8pm; in winter 8am-3pm.)*

FUNKTURM. Erected in 1926 to herald the radio age, the Funkturm offers a stunning view of the city from its 125m observation deck. The world's first television transmission was made here in 1931. *(S45 or S46 to Witzleben or U2 to Kaiserdamm. Panorama deck open daily 10am-11pm. DM6/€3.)*

GEDENKSTÄTTE PLÖTZENSEE. Housed in the terrifyingly well-preserved former execution chambers of the Third Reich, the memorial exhibits document death sentences of "enemies of the people," including the officers who attempted to assassinate Hitler in 1944. More than 2500 people were murdered within this small, stark red brick complex. Still visible are the hooks from which victims were hanged. English literature is available. *(Hüttigpfad, off the main road where the bus stops, down Emmy-Zehden-Weg on Hüttigpfad. Take U9 to Turmstr., then bus #123 (dir. Saatwinkler Damm) to Gedenkstätte Plötzensee. Open daily Mar.-Oct. 9am-5pm; Nov.-Feb. 9am-4pm. Free.)*

SCHÖNEBERG AND KREUZBERG

South of the Ku'damm, Schöneberg is a pleasant, middle-class residential district noted for its shopping, lively cafes, and good restaurants. Schöneberg is also home to the more affluent segments of Berlin's gay and lesbian community (see Gay and Lesbian Berlin, p. 418). Kreuzberg, southeast of Mitte, is filled with diverse ethnic groups, revolutionary graffiti, punks galore, and a large, self-confident gay and lesbian community. It's also the site of the annual May 1st parades.

RATHAUS SCHÖNEBERG. On June 26, 1963, exactly 15 years after the beginning of the Berlin Airlift, 1.5 million Berliners swarmed the streets beneath the windowless tower to hear John F. Kennedy reassure them of the Allies' commitment to the city with the now-famous words "*Ich bin ein Berliner.*" Today, the fortress with the little Berlin bear on top is home to Schöneberg's municipal government. *(John-F.-Kennedy-Pl. U4 to Rathaus Schöneberg. Rathaus open daily 9am-6pm.)*

⊠ HAUS AM CHECKPOINT CHARLIE. A strange, fascinating exhibition on the site of the famous border-crossing point characterized by Eastern sincerity and glossy Western salesmanship, the Haus am Checkpoint Charlie is one of Berlin's most popular tourist attractions. The museum contains all types of devices used to get over, under, or through the wall; artwork; newspaper clippings; and photographs. *(Friedrichstr. 44. U6 to Kochstr. Open daily 9am-10pm. DM12/€6, students DM6/€3.)*

ORANIENSTRAßE. The area was the site of frequent riots in the 1980s, and the May Day parades always start on Oranienpl. The rest of the year, revolution-minded radicals rub shoulders with tradition-oriented Turkish families, while an anarchist punk faction and a boisterous gay and lesbian population make things interesting after hours. Restaurants, clubs, and shops of all possible flavors make it a great place to wander. *(U1 or U15 to Kottbusser Tor or Görlitzer Bahnhof.)*

FRIEDRICHSHAIN AND LICHTENBERG

⊠ EAST SIDE GALLERY. The longest remaining portion of the Wall, the 1.3km stretch of cement and asbestos slabs also serves as the world's largest open-air art gallery. The murals are the efforts of an international group of artists who gathered here in 1989 to celebrate the end of the city's division. In 1999, the same artists came together to repaint their work and cover the scrawlings of later tourists; however, would-be artists are rapidly defacing the wall once again. *(Along Mühlenstr. S3, S5, S6, S7, S9, or S75 or U1 or U15 to Warschauer Str. and walk back toward the river.)*

FORSCHUNGS- UND GEDENKSTÄTTE NORMANNENSTRAßE. In the suburb of Lichtenberg stands perhaps the most hated and feared building of the GDR regime—the headquarters of the East German secret police, the **Staatssicherheit**

GERMANY

or **Stasi.** Since a 1991 law returned the Stasi's dossiers to their subjects, the "Horror-Files" have rocked Germany, exposing informants—and wrecking careers, marriages, and friendships—at all levels of society. Today, it displays tiny microphones and hidden cameras used for surveillance, a GDR shrine full of Lenin busts, and countless other bits of bizarre memorabilia. Recall that this building is part of the history of many still-living people; please be appropriately respectful. *(Ruschestr. 103, Haus 1. U5 to Magdalenenstr. From Ruschestr. exit, walk up Ruschestr. and turn right on Normannenstr. Open Tu-F 11am-6pm, Sa-Su 2-6pm. DM5/€3, students DM3/€1.50.)*

🏛 MUSEUMS

Berlin is one of the world's great museum cities, with collections of art and artifacts encompassing all subjects and eras. The **Staatliche Museen zu Berlin (SMB)** runs over 20 museums located in several major regions—**Museumsinsel, Kulturforum, Mitte/ Tiergarten, Charlottenburg,** and **Dahlem.** A single admission to any of these museums is DM4/€2, students DM2/€1; admission is free the first Sunday of every month. A *Tageskarte* (DM8/€4, students DM4/€2) is valid for all SMB museums on the day of purchase; the *Drei-Tage-Karte* (DM16/€8, students DM8/€4) is valid for three consecutive days. Either can be bought at any SMB museum. Non-SMB-affiliated museums tend to be smaller and quirkier.

MUSEUMSINSEL (MUSEUM ISLAND)
Museumsinsel contains five separate museums, although several are undergoing extensive renovation. Take S3, S5, S7, S9 or S75 to Hackescher Markt or bus #100 to Lustgarten. All museums offer free audio tours in English.

🎨 **Pergamonmuseum,** Kupfergraben. One of the world's great ancient history museums, it's named for Pergamon, the Turkish city from which the enormous Altar of Zeus (180 BC) in the main exhibit hall was taken. The museum features pieces of ancient Mediterranean history as big as they come. Open Tu-Su 10am-6pm. SMB prices.

Alte Nationalgalerie, Am Lustgarten. After extensive renovations, this renowned museum is once more open to the public. Caspar David Friedrich and Karl Friedrich Schinkel are but two names in an all-star cast. Open Tu-Su 10am-6pm. SMB prices.

Altes Museum, Am Lustgarten. The museum contains the *Antikensammlung,* an excellent permanent collection of Greco-Roman art. Open Tu-Su 10am-6pm. SMB prices.

TIERGARTEN-KULTURFORUM
The **Tiergarten-Kulturforum** is a complex of museums at the eastern end of the Tiergarten, near Potsdamer Pl. Take S1, S2, S25 or U2 to Potsdamer Pl. and walk down Potsdamer Str.; the museums will be on your right. All museums are open Tu-F 10am-6pm, Sa-Su 11am-6pm.

🎨 **Gemäldegalerie.** One of Germany's most famous museums, and rightly so. It houses a stunning and enormous collection by Italian, German, Dutch, and Flemish masters. Open Tu-F 10am-6pm, Th until 10pm, Sa-Su 11am-6pm. SMB prices.

🎨 **Hamburger Bahnhof/Museum für Gegenwartkunst,** Invalidenstr. 50-51. Berlin's foremost collection of contemporary art, housed in a converted train station, features works by Warhol, Beuys and Kiefer as well as in-your-face temporary exhibits. S3, S5, S7, S9, or S75 to Lehrter Stadtbahnhof or U6 to Zinnowitzer Str. Open Tu-F 10am-6pm, Th until 10pm, Sa-Su 11am-6pm. DM10/€6, students DM5/€3. Tours Su at 4pm.

Neue Nationalgalerie, Potsdamer Str. 50. This sleek building contains both interesting temporary exhibits and a formidable permanent collection, including works by Warhol, Munch, Kirchner, Pechstein, Beckmann, and Ernst. Open Tu-F 10am-6pm, Th until 10pm, and Sa-Su 11am-6pm. SMB prices for permanent collection; DM12/€6, students DM6/€3 for the whole museum.

CHARLOTTENBURG AND DAHLEM
🎨 **Ägyptisches Museum,** Schloßstr. 70. This stern Neoclassical building contains a famous collection of ancient Egyptian art—animal mummies, elaborately painted coffins, a magnificent

stone arch, original papyrus scrolls, and the famous bust of Queen Nefertiti. Take bus #145 to Luisenpl./Schloß Charlottenburg or U7 to Richard-Wagner-Pl. and walk down Otto-Suhr-Allee. Open Tu-Su 10am-6pm. DM8/€4, students DM4/€2.

Ethnologisches Museum. The Ethnological Museum alone makes the trek to Dahlem worthwhile. The exhibits range from beautiful ancient Central American stonework to ivory African statuettes to enormous boats from the South Pacific. The **Museum für Indisches Kunst** (Museum for Indian Art), and the **Museum für Ostasiatisches Kunst** (Museum for East Asian Art), housed in the same building, are smaller but no less fascinating. Take U1 to Dahlem-Dorf and follow the Museen signs. Open Tu-F 10am-6pm, Sa-Su 11am-6pm. SMB prices.

INDEPENDENT (NON-SMB) MUSEUMS

Deutsche Guggenheim Berlin, Unter den Linden 13-15. Located in a newly renovated building across the street from the Deutsche Staatsbibliothek, the museum features changing exhibits of contemporary avant-garde art. Open daily 11am-8pm, Th until 10pm. DM8/€4, students DM5/€3; M free.

Filmmuseum Berlin, Potsdamer Str. 2, 3rd and 4th fl. of the Sony Center. This brand-spanking-new museum show the development of German film through history. The exhibits (with good captions in English) are fascinating, and the ultra-futuristic entrance is not to be missed. S1, S2, S25 or U#2 to Potsdamer Pl. Open Tu-Su 10am-6pm, Th until 8pm. DM12/€6, students DM8/€4.

Deutsches Historisches Museum, Unter den Linden 1, in the Kronprinzenpalais. Exhibits trace German history until the Nazis, while rotating exhibitions examine the last 50 years. S3, S5, S7, S9, or S75 to Hackescher Markt. Open Th-Tu 3-6pm. Free.

Hanfmuseum, Mühlendamm 5. Learn everything you wanted to know about marijuana, and maybe some things you didn't—did you know that hemp can serve as insulation? U2 to Klosterstr. Open Tu-F 10am-8pm, Sa-Su noon-8pm. DM5/€3.

Topographie des Terrors, behind the Martin-Gropius-Bau, at the corner of Niederkirchnerstr. and Wilhelmstr. This area was the site of the notorious Gestapo's headquarters. The comprehensive exhibit of photographs, documents, and German texts details the Nazi party's rise to power and the atrocities that occurred during the war. The main exhibit hadn't been unveiled by press time but should be available by the time you read this. S1, S2, or U2 to Potsdamer Pl. Open Tu-Su 10am-6pm. Free.

♪ ENTERTAINMENT

CONCERTS AND MUSIC. Berlin reaches its musical zenith during the **Berliner Festwochen,** which lasts almost all of September and draws the world's best orchestras and soloists. The **Berliner Jazztage** in November features top-notch jazz musicians. For more information and tickets, call or write in advance to Berliner Festspiele (☎25 48 92 50; www.berliner festspiele.de). In mid-July, the **Bachtage** offer an intense week of classical music, while every Saturday night in August, the **Sommer Festspiele** turns the Ku'damm into a multi-faceted concert hall with punk, steel-drum, and folk groups competing for attention. Look for concert listings in the monthly pamphlets *Konzerte und Theater in Berlin und Brandenburg* (free) and *Berlin Programm* (DM2.80/€1.40), as well as in the biweekly *Zitty* and *Tip*. The acoustically designed **Berliner Philharmonisches Orchester,** Matthäikirchstr. 1, is one of the world's finest, but it's almost impossible to get tickets. (☎25 48 81 32. S1, S2, S25 or U2 to Potsdamer Pl., then walk up Potsdamer Str.) **Deutsche Oper Berlin,** Bismarckstr. 35, is Berlin's best and youngest opera. (Info ☎341 02 49; tickets ☎343 84 01; toll free ☎0 800 248 98 42. U2 to Deutsche Oper. Closed mid-July to August. Student discounts available one week before performance. Tickets DM20-220/€10-110. Evening tickets available 1hr. before performance. Box office open M-Sa 11am until 1hr. before performance, Su 10am-2pm.)

THEATER AND FILM. Berlin has the best German-language theater in the world as well as a lively English-theater scene; look for listings in *Zitty* or *Tip* that say *in englischer Sprache* (in English) next to them. The **Deutsches Theater,** Schumannstr. 13a, has innovative productions of both classics and newer works. (☎28 44 12 25. Box office open M-Sa 11am-6:30pm, Su 3-6:30pm. Tickets DM12-60/€6-31, students DM16/€8.) **Hebbel-Theater,** Stresemannstr. 29, is the most avant of the avant-garde theaters in Berlin. (☎25 90 04 27. Order tickets at the box office on Stresemannstr., by phone daily 4-7pm, or show up 1hr. before performance.) Berlin is also a movie-loving town; it hosts the international **Berlinale** film festival (Feb. 6-17, 2002), and on any night in Berlin you can choose from over 150 different films, many in the original languages. *O.F.* next to a movie listing means original version (i.e., not dubbed); *O.m.U.* means original version with German subtitles. Check *Tip*, *Zitty*, or the ubiquitous blue *Kinoprogramm* posters plastered throughout the city. Mondays, Tuesdays, or Wednesdays are *Kinotage* at most movie theaters, with reduced prices. Bring a student ID for discounts. **Freiluftkino Hasenheide,** at the Sputnik in Hasenheide park, has open-air screenings of everything from silent films to last year's blockbusters. (☎62 70 58 85. U7 or U8 to Hermannpl. Tickets DM10/€5.) **Freiluftkino Friedrichshain,** in Volkspark Friedrichshain, shows contemporary offerings from Hollywood and German studios. (U5 to Straußberger Pl. DM10/€5.)

■ NIGHTLIFE

Berlin's nightlife is absolute madness. Bars typically open around 6pm and pack in around 10pm, just as the clubs are opening their doors. As bar scenes wind down between midnight and 6am, club dance floors fill up around 1am and groove until dawn, when a variety of after-parties and 24hr. cafes keep up this seemingly perpetual motion. It's completely possible (if you can live without sleep) to party nonstop Friday night through Monday morning. The best sources of information about bands and dance venues are the biweekly magazines *Tip* and the superior *Zitty*, available at all newsstands, or the free and highly comprehensive *030*, distributed in several hostels, cafes, and bars.

In west Berlin, **Savignyplatz,** near Zoologischer Garten, has refined, laid-back cafes and jazz clubs. Gay life in Berlin centers around **Nollendorfplatz,** where the crowds are usually mixed and establishments range from the friendly to the cruisey. **Gneisenaustraße,** on the western edge of Kreuzberg, offers a variety of ethnic restaurants and some good bars. Closer to the former Wall, a dizzying array of clubs and bars on and around **Oranienstraße** rage all night, every night with a superbly mixed crowd of partygoers both gay and straight.

In East Berlin, Kreuzberg's reputation as dance capital of Germany is challenged as clubs sprout up in **Mitte, Prenzlauer Berg,** and near **Potsdamer Platz.** Berlin's largest bar scene sprawls down **Oranienburgerstraße** in Mitte; it's pricey, but never boring. **Prenzlauer Berg,** originally the edgy alternative to Mitte's trendier repertoire, has become a bit more classy and established, especially around **Kollwitzplatz.** South of it all, **Friedrichshain** has developed a reputation for lively, quirky nightlife, with a terrific group of bars along Simon-Dach-Str. and more on Gabriel-Max-Str.

If at all possible, try to hit (or, if you're prone to claustrophobia, avoid) Berlin during the **Love Parade,** usually held in the third weekend of July, when all of Berlin goes wild (see below). Prices tend to hit astronomical heights during this weekend. It's also worth mentioning that Berlin has **de-criminalized marijuana possession** of up to eight grams, although police can arrest you for any amount if they feel the need, so exercise some discretion. Smoking in public is not yet accepted but is becoming common in some clubs—you'll know which ones.

MITTE

▨ **Tresor,** Leipziger Str. 126a. U2, S1, S2, or S25 or bus #N5, N29 or N52 to Potsdamer Pl. One of the most rocking techno venues in Berlin. Open W and F-Sa 11pm-6am. Cover W DM5/€3, F DM10/€5, Sa DM15-20/€7-11.

THE LOVE PARADE Every year during the third weekend in July, the Love Parade brings Berlin to its knees—its trains run late, its streets fill with litter, and its otherwise patriotic populace scrambles to the countryside in the wake of a wave of German teenagers dying their hair, dropping ecstasy, and getting down *en masse*. What started in 1988 as a DJ's birthday party has mutated into the world's only 1.5 million-man rave, dubbed *Die Größte Partei der Welt*, "the biggest party in the world." The city-wide party turns the Str. des 17. Juni into a riotous dance floor and the Tiergarten into a garden of iniquity. The BVG offers a "No-Limit-Ticket," useful for getting around from venue to venue during the weekend's **54 hours of nonstop partying** (DM10/€5, condom included). Club prices skyrocket for the event as the best DJs from Europe are imported for a frantic weekend of beat-thumping madness. It's an experience that you won't forget, unless, of course, if you party *too* hard. Then again, as far as the Love Parade goes, there's no such thing.

VEB-OZ, Auguststr. 92 at the corner of Oranienburgerstr. S1, S2, or S25 to Oranienburger Str. Open until at least 2 or 3am every night, so it's a good weekday watering hole; most other area bars close by 1. Open daily from 6pm.

Tacheles, Oranienburger Str. 53-56. U6 to Oranienburger Tor; S1, S2, or S25 to Oranienburger Str.; or night bus #N6 or N84. A playground for artists, punks, and curious tourists housed in a bombed-out department store and adjacent courtyard.

CHARLOTTENBURG (SAVIGNYPLATZ)

Quasimodo, Kantstr. 12a. U2, U12, S3, S5, S7, S9, or S75 to Zoologischer Garten. The wide variety of artists who play this smoky basement jazz venue attracts a lively crowd. Cover Tu-W DM5/€3; on weekends, cover up to DM45/€24 depending on performance. Open Tu-W and F-Sa from 9pm.

A-Trane, Bleibtreustr. 1. S3, S5, S7, S9, or S75 to Savignypl. Romantic, cozy atmosphere, with a crowd of jazz-loving locals and a complete lack of pretense. Cover DM10-40/€5-21 (about DM20/€10 on weekends). Open M-F 10pm-2am, later on weekends.

SCHÖNEBERG

Slumberland, Winterfeldtpl. U1, U2, U4, U12, or U15 to Nollendorfpl. A cafe/bar with an African motif, R&B, and Bob Marley. Open Su-Th 6pm-2am, F 6pm-5am, Sa 11am-5am.

Mister Hu, Goltzstr. 39. U1, U2, U4 or U15 to Nollendorfpl. Happy hour 5-8pm, Su all cocktails DM9.99/€5. Open daily 5pm-late, Sa 11am-late.

KREUZBERG

SO36, Oranienstr. 190. U1, U12, or U15 to Görlitzer Bahnhof or bus #N29 to Heinrichpl. Berlin's only *truly* mixed club, with a clientele of hip heteros, gays, and lesbians grooving to a mish-mash of wild genres. Open 11pm-late. Cover for parties DM8-15/€4-8, concerts DM15-35/€7-18.

Junction Bar, Gneisenaustr. 18. U7 to Gneisenaustr. or bus #N4 or N19 to Zossener Str. Live rock, funk, jazz, or blues from 5pm Su-Th, from 10pm F-Sa; DJs start 10pm Su-Th, 12:30am F-Sa. Cover DM10/€5 for both; for DJs only Su-Th DM6/€3, F-Sa DM8/€4.

FRIEDRICHSHAIN

Euphoria, Grünbergerstr. 60, on the corner of Simon-Dach Str. Serves what could well be the best mixed drinks in Berlin. Happy hour 6-8pm, all drinks half price. Wide selection of Italian entrees also served. Open Su-Th 10am-midnight, F-Sa 10am-1am.

Maria am Ostbahnhof, Str. der Pariser Kommune 8-10. S3, S5, S7, S9, or S75 to Ostbahnhof. Concert nights bring musicians that vary with the band. Concerts W and Th, DJs F and Sa. Cover DM5-20/€2-11. Open W-Th 10pm-late, F-Sa 11pm-late.

Zehn Vorne, Simon-Dach Str. 9. A jam-packed little bar based mainly on Star Trek. Don't let the theme scare you off—this place is weird and fun. Open daily 3pm-late.

PRENZLAUER BERG

KulturBrauerei, Knaackstr. 97 (☎ 441 92 69). U2 to Eberswalder Str. In a former brewery; houses everything from the highly popular clubs *Soda* and *Kesselhaus* to a Russian theater to an art school. Venues include everything from disco to techno and reggae; cover and opening times vary, so it's best to call ahead.

Pfefferberg, Schönhauser Allee 176. U2 to Senefelderpl. or bus #N58. Features a slightly younger crowd and a rooftop garden. Techno and world music rotate weekly. Cover DM10-20/€5-11. Garden open in summer M-F from 3pm, Sa-Su from 12pm.

▼ GAY AND LESBIAN NIGHTLIFE

Berlin is one of the most gay-friendly cities on the continent. All of **Nollendorfpl.** is a gay-friendly environment. The main streets, including **Goltzstraße, Akazienstraße,** and **Winterfeldtstraße,** tend to contain mixed bars and cafes. The **"Bermuda Triangle"** of Motzstr., Fuggerstr., and Eisenacherstr. is more exclusively gay. For up-to-date events listings, pick up a copy of the amazingly comprehensive *Siegessäule* (free).

SCHÖNEBERG

Metropol, Nollendorfpl. 5. U1, U2, U4, or U15 to Nollendorfpl., or bus #N5, N19, N26, N48, N52, or N75. Houses three dance venues: **Tanz Tempel, West-Side Club** and **Love Lounge.** Every other F the Tanz Tempel and Love Lounge host the heterosexual *Fisch Sucht Fahrrad* party. West-Side Club holds the infamous "Fuck Naked Sex Party," as well as numerous other naked parties. The Love Lounge varies from mixed to completely gay, while Tanz Tempel is nearly always gay and open only on Sa. Hours vary—check *Siegessäule* or *Sergej* for details.

Omnes, Motzstr. 8. U1, U2, U4, or U15 to Nollendorfpl. A mainly male gay bar, it accommodates revelers after a full night of partying. Open M-F from 8am, Sa-Su from 5am.

Café Berio, Maaßenstr. 7. U1, U2, U4, or U15 to Nollendorfpl. Bright, charming cafe caters to a mixed, easy-going crowd. Outdoor seating in summer. Open daily 8am-1am.

KREUZBERG

Rose's, Oranienstr. 187. A mixed gay and lesbian clientele packs this intense and claustrophobic party spot, marked only by "Bar" over the door. Open daily 10pm-6am.

SO36, while usually a mixed club (p. 417), sponsors three predominantly gay events: **Hungrige Herzen** (W after 10pm), a jam-packed gay and (somewhat) lesbian trance and drum 'n bass party; **Café Fatal** (Su after 5pm) with ballroom dancing; and **Gayhane** (last Sa of the month), a self-described "HomOrientaldancefloor" for a mixed crowd of Turks and Germans.

FRIEDRICHSHAIN

Die Busche, Mühlenstr. 12. U1, U12, U15, S3, S5, S6, S7, S9, or S75 to Warschauer Str. East Berlin's largest gay disco, with an incongruous rotation of techno, top 40, and *Schlager.* Open W and F-Su from 9:30pm. The party gets going around midnight. It *really* gets going around 3am. Cover DM6-10/€3-6.

▶ DAYTRIPS FROM BERLIN

POTSDAM. Visitors disappointed by Berlin's unroyal demeanor can get their Kaiserly fix in nearby Potsdam, the glittering city of Friedrich II (the Great). The huge **Park Sanssouci** is Friedrich's testament to his wealth and the diversity of his aesthetic tastes. For information, stop by the **Visitor's Center** at the windmill. A **day ticket** (DM24/€12.27, students DM20/€10.25) gives access to all of the park's castles. ◆**Schloß Sanssouci,** the park's main attraction, was built in 1747 to allow Friedrich to escape his wife. German tours are limited to 40 people and leave every 20min. (Open Tu-Su Apr.-Oct. 9am-5pm; Nov.-Mar. 9am-4pm. DM16/€8.20, students DM10/€5.15.) Don't miss the exotic gold-plated **Chinesisches Teehaus** (DM2/€1.05) and the **Sizilianischer Garten,** perhaps the park's most stunningly beautiful garden.

At the opposite end of the park is the largest of the castles, the 200-room **Neues Palais**. (Open Sa-Th Apr.-Oct. 9am-5pm; Nov.-Mar. 9am-4pm. DM10/€5.10, students DM8/€4.10; DM2/€1.05 extra in summer.) To reach Potsdam's second park, **Neuer Garten,** take bus #692 to **Schloß Cecilienhof,** which was built in the style of an English Tudor manor inside; inside, exhibits document the **Potsdam Treaty,** which was signed here in 1945. It was supposed to be the "Berlin Treaty," but the capital was too bombed out to house the Allies' head honchos. (Open Tu-Su 9am-noon and 12:30-5pm. DM6/€3.10, with tour DM8/€4.10; student discount DM2/€1.05.) Berlin's **S7** runs from Bahnhof Zoo to Potsdam (30min., DM4.70/€2.40).☎**0331.**

DRESDEN. Check out the magnificent art collection in the **Zwinger** and other world-class attractions in **Dresden,** only 2hr. from Berlin by train (p. 419).

LEIPZIG. Once the stomping grounds of Goethe, Nietzsche, and Leibnitz, **Leipzig** (2-3hr. from Berlin by train) now blazes with a student-oriented scene (p. 423).

EASTERN GERMANY

Saxony *(Sachsen)* is known primarily for Dresden and Leipzig, the largest cities in Eastern Germany after Berlin. However, the entire region offers a fascinating historical and cultural diversity. The castles around Dresden testify to the decadence of Saxony's Electors, while the boxy socialist monuments depict the former world of the GDR. Sachsen is also home to the Sorbs, Germany's only national minority, which lends a Slavic feel to many of the region's eastern towns.

DRESDEN ☎0351

The stunning buildings of Dresden's Altstadt look ancient, but most are newly reconstructed—the Allied bombings of February 1945, which claimed over 50,000 lives, destroyed 75% of the city center. Today, Dresden pulses with a historical intensity yet feels fresh and vibrant, engaging visitors with world-class museums and partially reconstructed palaces and churches (reconstruction is scheduled for completion by 2006, the city's 800-year anniversary). However, Dresden is not all nostalgic appeals to the past; the city enters the new millennium as a young, dynamic metropolis propelled by a history of cultural turbulence.

▐ TRANSPORTATION

Trains: From the **Dresden Hauptbahnhof,** in the Altstadt, and **Bahnhof Dresden Neustadt,** across the Elbe, travelers zoom to: **Berlin** (2hr., every 2hr., DM52/€26.60); **Budapest** (10hr., 4 per day, DM125/€64); **Frankfurt** (7hr., 14 per day, DM136/€69.60); **Leipzig** (1½hr., 1-2 per hr., DM33/€16.90); **Munich** (7hr., 24 per day, DM148/€75.70); **Prague** (2½hr., 12 per day, DM38/€19.50); **Warsaw** (8hr., 8 per day, DM53/€27). Buy tickets from the automated machines in the main halls of both stations, or from the staff at the Reisezentrum desk.

Public Transportation: Dresden's **streetcars** are efficient and cover the whole city. **Single-ride** DM2.90/€1.50; 4 or fewer stops DM1.80/€0.95. **Day pass** DM8/€4.10; **weekly pass** DM25/€12.80. Most major lines run every hr. after midnight. Tickets are available from Fahrkarten dispensers at major stops, on the streetcars themselves, and from **Verkehrs-Info** stands in front of the Hauptbahnhof (M-F 7am-7pm). As you board, punch your ticket in the red contraptions at the bottom of the stairwells to each track.

◼▐ ORIENTATION AND PRACTICAL INFORMATION

Dresden is bisected by the Elbe. The **Altstadt** lies on the same side as the Hauptbahnhof; **Neustadt,** to the north, escaped most of the bombing, paradoxically making it one of the oldest parts of the city. Many of Dresden's main attractions are centered between the **Altmarkt** and the **Elbe,** 5min. from the Neustadt.

Tourist Office: Two locations: **Prager Str. 3,** near the Hauptbahnhof (☎49 19 20; open M-F 9am-7pm, Sa 9am-4pm); **Theaterpl.** in the Schinkelwache, in front of the Semper-Oper (open M-F 10am-6pm, Sa 10am-4pm, Su 10am-1pm). Sells city maps (DM3/€1.55) and the **Dresden Card,** which includes 48hr. of public transit, free or reduced entry at many museums, and city tours (DM27/€13.80).

Currency Exchange: ReiseBank, in the Hauptbahnhof. 2.5-4.5% commission, depending on amount; 1-1.5% for traveler's checks. Open M-F 7:30am-7:30pm, Sa 8am-noon and 12:30-4pm, Su 9am-1pm. A self-service machine is available after hours, but the rates are poor.

Luggage Storage: At both train stations. Lockers DM2-4/€1.05-2.05 for 24hr. storage.

Gay and Lesbian Organizations: Gerede-Dresdner Lesben, Schwule und alle Anderen, Prießnitzstr. 18 (☎802 22 51; 24hr. hotline ☎802 22 70). From Albertpl., walk up Bautzner Str. and turn left onto Prießnitzstr. Open Tu 10am-noon and 3-5pm, Th 3-5pm.

Laundromat: Groove Station, Katharinenstr. 11-13. Wash, dry, and cup of coffee DM8/€4.10. Meanwhile, browse tattoos or piercings. Open M-Sa noon-late, Su 2pm-late.

Emergency: Police: ☎110. **Ambulance and Fire:** ☎112.

Pharmacy: Apotheke Prager Straße, Prager Str. 3 (☎490 30 14). Open M-F 8:30am-7pm, Sa 8:30am-4pm. After hours, a sign indicates the nearest open pharmacies.

Internet Access: Mediacenter Internet Cafe, Schandauerstr. 64 (☎311 63 31). DM6/€3.10 per hr. Open M-W 2-9pm, Th 9-midnight, F noon-midnight.

Post Office: Hauptpostamt, Königsbrücker Str. 21/29 (☎819 13 70), in Neustadt. Open M-F 8am-7pm, Sa 9am-1pm. Address mail to be held: *Postlagernde Briefe für* First name SURNAME, Hauptpostamt, D-01099 Dresden, Germany.

ACCOMMODATIONS AND CAMPING

New hotels and hostels are constantly being opened, but on weekends it's hard to get a spot in anything with a good location—so *call ahead.* The tourist office can arrange stays in private rooms and provide information on other options.

Mondpalast Backpacker, Katharinenstr. 11-13 (☎804 60 61). From Bahnhof Neustadt, walk down Antonstr. toward Albertpl., turn left onto Königsbrücker Str., and turn right on Katharinenstr. to reach the hippest place in town. Internet DM6-10/€3.10-5.15 per hr. Breakfast DM8/€4.10. Sheets DM5/€2.60. Key deposit DM10/€5.15. Reception 24hr. 8-bed rooms DM25/€12.80; 3- to 7-bed rooms DM28/€14.35; singles DM40/€20.50; doubles DM32/€16.40.

Hostel Die Boofe, Louisenstr. 20 (☎801 33 61). Immaculate rooms and cushy beds. Rents bikes (DM10/€5.15 per day) and scooters (DM15/€7.70 per day). Internet DM10/€5.15 per hr. Breakfast DM8/€4.10. Sheets DM5/€2.60. Reception 24hr. Dorms DM26/€13.30; doubles DM79/€40.40 with sheets and breakfast.

Jugendherberge Dresden Rudi Arndt (HI), Hübnerstr. 11 (☎471 06 67). Take S8 (dir. Südvorstadt) or S3 (dir. Coschütz) to Nürnberger Platz, follow Nürnberger Str., and turn right onto Hübnerstr. The friendly atmosphere makes up for the size of the rooms. Breakfast included. Sheets DM5/€2.60 (required). Check-in 3pm-1am. Curfew 1am. Dorms DM31/€15.85, under 26 DM26/€15.30. HI members only.

Pension Raskolnikoff, Böhmische Str. 34 (☎804 57 06), in the middle of the Neustadt. This 6-room pension is the perfect way to escape the hostel scene. Singles DM70/€35.80; doubles DM75/€38.35. Call ahead.

Campingplatz Mockritz, Boderitzerstr. 30 (☎47 15 250). Take bus #76 (dir. Mockritz) to Campingplatz Mockritz. This family-run camping spot lets you get away from the hustle and bustle of Dresden. Reception daily 8-11am and 4-9pm. DM8/€4.10 per person; DM4-6/€2.05-3.10 per tent.

FOOD

Unfortunately, the surge in Dresden tourism has raised food prices, particularly in the *Altstadt.* The cheapest eats in the Altstadt are at **supermarkets** or **Imbiß stands** along **Pragerstr.** The **Neustadt,** between Albertpl. and Alaunpl., spawns a new bar every few weeks and is *the* place to go for quirky ethnic and student-friendly restaurants. The free monthly *Spot,* available at the tourist office, details culinary options. **Blumenau,** Louisenstr. 67, is one of the cheapest and most popular restaurants in town. (Most dishes run DM6-10/€3.10-5.15. Open daily 10am-3am.)

👁 SIGHTS

ZWINGER AND SEMPER-OPER. The extravagant art collection of Friedrich August I (the Strong), Prince Elector of Saxony and King of Poland, is housed in the magnificent **Zwinger palace,** a building championed as a triumph of Baroque design. The palace narrowly escaped destruction in the 1945 bombings; workers are busy restoring it to aesthetic perfection. In the Semper wing is the **Gemäldegalerie Alte Meister,** a world-class collection of paintings from 1400-1800. Across from the gallery is the

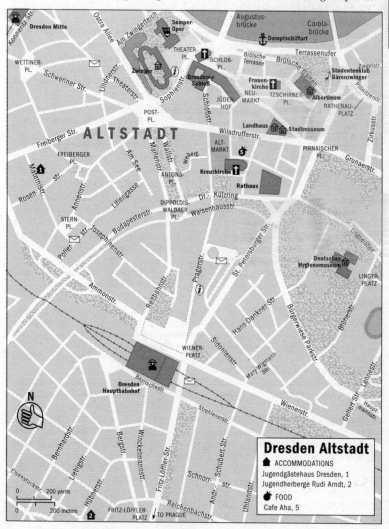

Dresden Altstadt

🏠 ACCOMMODATIONS
Jugendgästehaus Dresden, 1
Jugendherberge Rudi Arndt, 2

🍴 FOOD
Cafe Aha, 5

Rüstkammer, a collection of courtly toys including silver- and gold-plated suits for both man and horse, and a set of toddler-sized armor. *(Both open Tu-Su 10am-6pm. Joint admission DM7/€3.60, students DM4/€2.10. Tours F and Su at 4pm. DM1/€0.55.)* A painstaking restoration has made the nearby **Semper-Oper** (opera house) one of Dresden's major attractions. *(Theaterplatz 2. Check the main entrance for tour times, usually midday. DM9/€4.60, students DM6/€3.10.)*

DRESDENER SCHLOß. Once the proud home of August the Strong, this palace was ruined in the Allied firebombing of 1945, but a good deal of its restoration is nearly complete. The 100m tall ◪**Hausmannsturm** hosts fascinating but sobering photographs and texts on the Allied bombings, and the top floor offers a 360° view of the city. *(Across from the Zwinger on Schloßpl. Open Apr.-Oct. Tu-Su 10am-6pm. DM5/ €2.60, students and seniors DM3/€1.55.)* If you've been mistaking Friedrich the Earnest for Friedrich the Pugnacious, stop by the **Fürstenzug** (Procession of Electors) along Augustusstr., a 102m mural made of 24,000 tiles of Meißen china depicting the rulers of Saxony from 1123-1904.

KREUZKIRCHE. After being leveled four times (in 1669 by fire, in 1760 by the Seven Years War, in 1897 by fire again, and finally in February 1945 by Allied bombing), the interior remains in a damaged state as a powerful reminder of the war's destruction. Climb the tower for a bird's eye view of downtown Dresden. *(An der Kreuzkirche 6. Open in summer M-Tu and Th-F 10am-5:30pm, W and Sa 10am-4:30pm, Su noon-4:30pm; in winter M-Sa 10am-3:30pm, Su noon-4:30pm. Free. Tower closes 30min. before the church. DM2/€1.05, children DM1/€0.55.)*

NEUSTADT. Across the magnificent **Augustusbrücke,** Hauptstr. is home to the **Gold-ener Reiter,** a gold-plated statue of August the Strong. August's nickname was reputedly a homage to his remarkable virility; legend has it he fathered 365 kids, although the official tally is 15. At the other end of Hauptstr., **Albertplatz** is the gateway to the Neustadt scene.

SCHLACHTHOFRINGE. The **Schlachthofringe** (Slaughterhouse Circle) is a 1910 housing complex in a more dismal part of Dresden, used during World War II as a P.O.W. camp. The buildings have been left to waste away. Novelist Kurt Vonnegut was imprisoned here during the bombing of Dresden, inspiring his masterpiece *Slaughterhouse Five.* *(Take bus #82 to Ostragehege.)*

ALBERTINUM. The Albertinum holds the ◪**Gemäldegalerie der Neuen Meister,** which combines an ensemble of German and French Impressionists with a collection of Expressionists and Neue Sachlichkeit modernist works, including Otto Dix's renowned "War" triptych. *(Open F-W 10am-6pm. DM8/€4.10, students and seniors DM4.50/€2.30; includes admission to Grünes Gewölbe, a collection of Saxon figurines.)*

STADTMUSEUM. In the 18th-century Landhaus, the museum tells the story of Dresden since the 13th century. A colorful collection of 20th-century memorabilia completes the tale, from 1945 bomb shells to a collection of protest signs from the 1989 demonstrations. *(Wilsdrufferstr. 2, near Pirnaischer Platz. Open Sa-Th 10am-6pm; May-Sept. also open W 10am-8pm. DM4/€2.05, students DM2/€1.05.)*

▨ **NIGHTLIFE**

Over 50 bars pack the **Neustadt,** roughly bounded by Königsbrückerstr., Bischofsweg, Kamenzerstr., and Albertpl.; *Kneipen Surfer* lists all of them. **Down-Town,** Katharinenstr. 11-13, below the Mondpalast hostel, keeps the beat going fast and furious. (Cover DM7/€3.60, students DM5/€2.60. Open daily 10pm-5am.) **Sche-une,** Alaunstr. 36-40, specializes in world music. (Cover varies. Club opens at 8pm. Bar open M-F 11am-2am, Sa-Su 10am-2am.) **Queens,** Görlitzer Str. 3, is a popular gay bar with plenty of sparkle to go around. (Drinks DM4-12/€2.05-6.15. F '70s/'80s night. Occasional special entertainment. Open daily from 8pm.)

⚡ DAYTRIPS FROM DRESDEN

MEIßEN. Meißen, 30km from Dresden, is another testament to the frivolity of August the Strong. In 1710, the Saxon Elector contracted severe *Porzellankrankheit* (the porcelain "bug," still afflicting tourists today) and turned the city's defunct castle into a porcelain-manufacturing base. The factory was once more tightly guarded than KGB headquarters to prevent competitors from learning its techniques; today anyone can tour the **Staatliche Porzellan-Manufaktur,** Talstr. 9. You can peruse finished products in the **Schauhalle** (DM9/€4.60, students DM7/€3.60), but the real fun lies in the high-tech tour of the **Schauwerkstatt** (show workshop), which demonstrates the manufacturing process. (Open daily 9am-6pm. DM5/€2.60. English headsets available.) The **Albrechtsburg** castle and cathedral overlook the city. (Open Mar.-Oct. daily 10am-6pm; Nov.-Feb. 10am-5pm. Last entry 30min. before closing. DM7/€3.60, students DM5/€2.60.) From the train station, walk straight onto Bahnhofstr. and follow it over the Elbbrücke. Cross the bridge, continue straight to the Markt, and turn right onto Burgstr. At the end of Burgstr., on Hohlweg, take the Schloßstufen on your right, stairs that lead up to Albrechtsburg. Next door looms the **Meißener Dom,** a Gothic cathedral which satisfies visitors with four 13th-century statues by the Naumburg Master, a triptych by Cranach the Elder, and the metal grave coverings of the Wettins. (Open Apr.-Oct. daily 9am-6pm; Nov.-Mar. 10am-4pm. Last entry 30min. before closing. DM4/€2.05, students DM3/€1.50.) Reach Meißen from Dresden by **train** (40min., DM8.70/€4.45). The **tourist office,** Markt 3, is across from the church, and finds private rooms (DM30-50/€15.35-25.60) for a DM4/€2.05 fee. (☎(03521) 419 40. Open Apr.-Oct. M-F 9am-6:30pm, Sa-Su 10am-3pm; Nov.-Mar. M-F 10am-5pm, Sa 10am-3pm.)

SAXON SWITZERLAND. The *Sächsische Schweiz*—so dubbed because of its stunning, Swiss-like landscape—is one of Germany's most popular national parks. Dresden's S1 runs (from west to east) through Wehlen, Rathen, Königstein, and Bad Schandau, but the breathtaking **hikes** that connect the towns are a much more beautiful route. From **Wehlen,** two trails run to **Rathen;** the more impressive (but harder) one climbs the famous **Bastei cliffs.** While in Rathen, stop by the **Felsenbühne,** a beautiful open-air theater with 2000 seats carved into a cliff. (Open 8am, but closed 2hr. before and 1hr. after event.) Tickets and schedules are available from the **Theaterkasse,** on the way to the theater. (☎(035024) 77 70.) Two hikes through one of the park's most stunning valleys link Rathen to the small village of **Hohnstein;** be sure to stop at the **Hockstein,** an outcropping with a spectacular view of the valley below. Above the town of **Königstein** looms a **fortress,** which has huge walls built into stone spires. (Open daily Easter-Sept. 9am-8pm; Oct. 9am-6pm; Nov.-Apr. 9am-5pm. DM7/€3.60, students and seniors DM5/€2.55.)

If you're not into hiking, all of the towns are accessible by Dresden's S-Bahn: at Wehlen, Rathen, Königstein, and Bad Schandau, the S1 stops just across the river from each town; take a ferry (DM1.30/€0.70) to get to the sights. To get to Hohnstein, hop off the S-Bahn at Pirna and take bus #236 or 237. From **Bad Schandau** at the end of the line, ride the S-Bahn back to **Dresden** (50min., every 30min., DM8.70/€4.45), or continue by train to **Prague** (2hr., every 2hr., DM30.80€15.75). Each town has its own **tourist office.**

LEIPZIG   ☎0341

Leipzig may be small, but it's bursting with energy and style in its museums and monuments, cafes, and university culture. As in much of former East Germany, unemployment still poses a problem, but Leipzig's fascinating historical role overshadows any current difficulties.

⚡ TRANSPORTATION AND PRACTICAL INFORMATION. Leipzig lies on the Berlin-Munich line. **Trains** run to: Berlin (2-3hr., 3 per hr., DM51/€26.10); Dresden (1½hr., every hr., DM33/€16.90); Frankfurt (5hr., 2 every 2hr., DM120/€61.40); and

Munich (6hr., every hr., DM133/€68). Leipzig's sights and nightlife lie within a 1km ring. Cross Willy-Brandt-Pl. in front of the station and turn left at Richard-Wagner-Str. to reach the **tourist office**, Richard-Wagner-Str. 1. (Open M-F 9am-7pm, Sa 9am-4pm, Su 9am-2pm.) **Postal Code:** 04109.

⚏⚏ ACCOMMODATIONS AND FOOD. To reach **Hostel Sleepy Lion,** Käthe-Kollwitz-Str. 3, cross both rings from the station and turn right onto Richard-Wagner-Str.; when it ends, cut left through the parking lot and the park, cross the ring, and bear right onto Käthe-Kollwitz-Str. All rooms have shower and bathroom. (☎ 993 94 80. Internet DM4/€2 per hr. Breakfast DM6/€3. Sheets DM4/€2. Reception 24hr. 6-8 bed dorms DM28/€14; singles DM46/€23; doubles DM72/€36; quads DM120/€60.) For **Jugendherberge Leipzig Centrum (HI),** Volksgartenstr. 24, take streetcar #1 to Löbauer Str., head right on Löbauer Str. and turn right onto Volksgartenstr. (☎ 245 70 11. Breakfast included. Sheets DM6/€3.10. Reception 2:30-11pm. Curfew 1am. Dorms DM31/€15.85, under 26 DM26/€13.30.)

The *Innenstadt*, especially **Grimmaischestr.**, has *Imbiß* stands, bistros, and bakeries. Just outside the city center, **Karl-Liebknecht-Str.** (streetcar #1 or 10 to Kochstr.) is packed with cheap *Döner* stands and cafes that double as bars come nighttime. **🍴Avocado,** Karl-Liebknecht-Str. 79, has vegetarian and vegan options. (Open M-F 11:30am-1am, Sa 4pm-2am, Su 11am-1am.) **Zur Pleißenburg,** Schulstr. 2, just down Burgstr. from the Thomaskirche, is popular with locals and serves hearty fare. (Open daily 9am-5am.) There's a **Plus supermarket** on the Brühl, near Sachsenpl. (Open M-F 8am-8pm, Sa 8am-4pm.)

🎭🎵 SIGHTS AND NIGHTLIFE. The heart of Leipzig is the **Marktplatz,** a cobblestoned square guarded by the slanted 16th-century **Altes Rathaus.** Head down Grimmaischestr. to the **Nikolaikirche,** where massive weekly demonstrations led to the fall of the GDR. (Open M-Sa 10am-6pm, Su after services. Free.) Backtrack to the *Rathaus* and follow Thomasg. to the **Thomaskirche;** Bach's grave lies beneath the floor in front of the altar. (Open daily 9am-6pm. Free.) Just behind the church is the **Johann-Sebastian-Bach-Museum,** Thomaskirchhof 16. (Open daily 10am-5pm. DM6/€3.10, students DM4/€2.05. Free English cassette tours.) Head back to Thomasg., turn left, then turn right on Dittrichring to reach Leipzig's most fascinating museum, the **🏛Museum in der "Runden Ecke,"** Dittrichring 24, which displays stunningly blunt exhibits on the history, doctrine, and tools of the *Stasi* (secret police). Ask for an English handout in the office. (Open daily 10am-6pm. Free.) Outside the city ring, the **Völkerschlachtdenkmal** memorializes the 1813 Battle of Nations against Napoleon. Climb the 500 steps for a fabulous view. (Streetcar #15 from the train station to Völkerschlachtdenkmal. Open daily Apr.-Oct. 10am-6pm; Nov.-Mar. 10am-5pm. Free. To ascend DM6/€3.10, students DM4/€2.05.)

Free magazines *Fritz* and *Blitz* and the superior *Kreuzer* (DM3 at newsstands) fill you in on nightlife. **Barfußgäschen,** a street just off the Markt, serves as the see-and-be-seen bar venue for everyone from students to *Schicki-mickis* (yuppies). Just across Dittrichring on **Gottschedstraße** and **Bosestraße** is a similar scene with a slightly younger crowd and slightly louder music. Leipzig university students spent eight years excavating a series of medieval tunnels so they could get their groove on in the **🏛Moritzbastei,** Universitätsstr. 9, which has multi-level dance floors and chill bars in fantastic cavernous rooms with vaulted brick ceilings. (Cover DM4-7/€2.05-3.60 for discos. Open M-F after 10am, Sa after 2pm.)

WEIMAR   ☎ 03643

While countless German towns leap at any excuse to build memorials to Goethe (Goethe slept here, Goethe once asked for directions here, etc.), Weimar features the real thing: the **Goethehaus and Goethe-Nationalmuseum,** Frauenplan 1, present the poet's preserved private chambers. Pick up "Goethe's House on the Frauenplan at Weimar" (DM3/€1.55) at the desk. (Open mid-Mar. to mid-Oct. Tu-Su 9am-6pm; mid-Oct. to mid-Mar. Tu-Su 10am-4pm. Expect a wait of up to 2hr. in summer. DM10/€5.15, students and seniors DM8/€4.10.) Weimar's *other* pride and joy is the Bauhaus architectural movement, which began here; the **Bauhaus-Museum,** Theaterpl., show-cases its history. (Open Apr.-Oct. Tu-Su 10am-6pm; Nov.-Mar. Tu-Su 10am-4:30pm. DM6/€3.10, students and seniors DM4/€2.05.) The **Neuesmuseum,** which opened in 2000, hosts fascinating rotating exhibits of modern art, including an interactive "Ter-rororchestra," composed of knives, nails, and a hammer and sickle. (Weimarpl. 4. Open Tu-Su 10am-6pm. DM6/€3.10, students and children DM4/€2.10.) The sprawl-ing **Park an der Ilm** was landscaped by Goethe. South of the town center in the **His-torischer Friedhof,** Goethe and Schiller rest together in the basement of the **Fürstengruft** (Ducal Vault). Schiller, who died in an epidemic, was originally buried in a mass grave, but Goethe combed through the remains until he identified Schiller and had him interred in a tomb. Skeptics argued that Goethe was mistaken, so a couple of "Schillers" were placed side by side. In the 1960s, a team of Russian scientists deter-mined that Goethe was right after all. (Cemetery open Mar.-Sept. 8am-9pm; Oct.-Feb. 8am-6pm. Tomb open mid-Mar. to mid-Oct. W-M 9am-1pm and 2-6pm; mid-Oct. to mid-Mar. W-M 10am-1pm and 2-4pm. DM4/€2.10, students and seniors DM3/€1.55.) Get a glimpse into Schiller's existence *before* death at **Schillers Wohnhaus,** his home during the last three years of his life. (Schillerstr. 12. Open mid-Mar. to mid-Oct. W-M 9am-6pm; mid-Oct. to mid-Mar. W-M 9am-4pm. DM6/€3.10, students DM4/€2.05.)

Trains run to: Dresden (3hr., 2 per hr., DM58/€29.65); Frankfurt (3hr., 1 per hr., DM78/€39.90); Leipzig (1½hr., 2 per hr., DM25.60/€13.10). To reach **Goetheplatz** (the center of the Altstadt) from the station, follow Carl-August-Allee downhill to Karl-Liebknecht-Str. which leads into Goethepl. (15min.) The **tourist office,** Markt-str. 10, across from the *Rathaus,* hands out free maps, books rooms (DM5/€2.60 fee), and offers **walking tours.** The "Weimarer Wald" desk has lots of info on **outdoor activities** in the area. (☎240 00. Open Apr.-Oct. M-F 9:30am-6pm, Sa 9:30am-4pm, Su 9:30am-3pm; Nov.-Mar. M-F 10am-6pm, Sa and Su 10am-2pm. Tours daily 11am and 2pm. DM12/€7.70, students DM8/€4.10.) To get to the student-run ◼**Hababusch Hos-tel,** Geleitstr. 4, follow Geleitstr. from Goethepl.; after it takes a sharp right, you'll come to a statue on your left. The entrance to the Hababusch is tucked in the ivied corner behind the statue. Smack in the middle of the sights, the hostel has a laid-back, communal atmosphere. (☎85 07 37. No breakfast, but kitchen access. DM20/ €10.25 key deposit. Reception 24hr. DM15/€7.70; doubles DM40/€20.45.) The **Jugendherberge Germania (HI),** Carl-August-Allee 13, is 2min. downhill from the sta-tion. (☎85 04 90. Sheets DM7.50/€3.85. Reception 24hr. Dorms DM27/€13.80, over 26 DM32/16.40.) A combination cafe and gallery, **ACC,** Burgpl. 1-2, is popular with students. (Open daily noon-1am.) For groceries, try the daily **produce market** at Marktpl. (M-Sa 7am-5pm) or the **Rewe grocery store,** in the basement of the *Han-delshaus zu Weimar* on Theaterpl. (Open M-F 7am-8pm, Sa 7am-4pm).

◗ **DAYTRIP FROM WEIMAR: BUCHENWALD.** During World War II, 250,000 Jews, Gypsies, homosexuals, communists, and political prisoners were impris-oned at the labor camp of Buchenwald. Although it was not intended as an exter-mination camp, over 50,000 died here due to the harsh treatment of the SS. The **Nationale Mahnmal und Gedenkstätte Buchenwald** ("National Monument and Memo-rial") has two principal sights. The **K-Z Lager** refers to the remnants of the camps itself ("Konzentration-Lager" means "concentration camp" in German); the large storehouse building documents both the history of Buchenwald (1937-1945) and the general history of Nazism, including German anti-Semitism. The East-German-designed **Mahnmal** (monument) is on the other side of the hill; go straight up the main road which bisects the two large parking lots, or take the footpath uphill from the old Buchenwald Bahnhof and then continue on the main road. Many sim-ple memorials for different groups are scattered around the camp, and the camp **archives** are open to anyone searching for records of family and friends between 1937 and 1945. Call ahead to schedule an appointment with the curator (archives ☎(03643) 43 01 54, library (03643) 43 01 60). Ironically, suffering in Buchenwald did not end with liberation—Soviet authorities used the site as an internment camp, **"Special Camp. No. 2,"** where more than 28,000 Germans, mostly Nazi war criminals and opponents of the Communist regime, were held until 1950; an exhibit detailing this period opened in 1997.

The best way to reach the camp is by bus #6 from Weimar's train station or Goethepl. Check the schedule carefully; some #6 buses go to Ettersburg rather than Gedenkstätte Buchenwald. (M-F 1 per hr., Sa-Su every 2hr.) Buses to Weimar stop at the *KZ-Lager* parking lot and at the road by the *Glockenturm* (bell-tower). There is an **information center** (☎ (03643) 43 00; open Tu-Su May-Sept. 9am-6pm; Oct.-Apr. 8:30am-4:30pm) near the bus stop at Buchenwald, which has brochures (DM0.50/€0.30), offers a walking tour (DM3.50/€1.80), and shows an excellent video with English subtitles on the hour. (Exhibits open Tu-Su May-Sept. 9:45am-5:15pm; Oct.-Apr. 8:45am-4:15pm; camp area open daily until sundown.)

EISENACH   ☎ 03691

Birthplace of Johann Sebastian Bach, Eisenach is also home to one of Germany's most treasured national symbols, **Wartburg castle.** In 1521, the castle sheltered Martin Luther (disguised as a bearded noble named Junker Jörg) after his excommunication. Much of the castle's interior is unfortunately not authentically medieval, but the Wartburg is still enchanting, and the view from the south tower is spectacular. (Open Mar.-Oct. daily 8:30am-5pm; Nov.-Feb. 9am-3:30pm. Mandatory German tour DM11/€5.65, students and children DM6/€3.10.) According to local tradition, Johann Sebastian stormed into the world in 1685 at the **Bachhaus,** Frauenplan 21. Every 40min. a guide gives a presentation on Bach's life in German and English, complete with musical interludes. (Open Apr.-Sept. M noon-5:45pm, Tu-Su 9am-5:45pm.; Oct.-Mar. M 1-4:45pm, Tu-Su 9am-4:45pm. DM5/€2.60, students DM4/€2.05.) Bach was baptized at the 800-year-old **Georgenkirche,** just off the Markt, where members of his family were organists for 132 years. (Open M-Sa 10am-12:30pm and 2-5pm, Su after services.) Just up the street sits the latticed **Lutherhaus,** Lutherpl. 8, young Martin's home in his school days. (Open Apr.-Oct. daily 9am-5pm; Nov.-Mar. 10am-5pm. DM5/€2.60, students DM2/€1.05.)

Trains run frequently to Weimar (1hr., 2 per hr., DM20.20/€10.35). The **tourist office,** Markt 2, sells maps (DM2/€1.05), offers daily city tours (2pm, DM5/€2.60), and books rooms for free. From the train station, follow Bahnhofstr. through the tunnel and angle left until you turn right onto the pedestrian Karlstr. (☎ 67 02 60. Open M 10am-6pm, Tu-F 9am-6pm, Sa-Su 10am-2pm.) To reach the recently renovated **Jugendherberge Arthur Becker (HI),** Mariental 24, take Bahnhofstr. from the station to Wartburger Allee, which runs into Mariental. (☎ 74 32 59. Breakfast included. Sheets DM7.50/€3.85. Reception 7am-10pm. Tell the desk if you'll be out past 11pm. Dorms DM31.50/€16.10, under 26 DM26.50/€13.55.) For groceries, head to **Edeka supermarket** on Johannispl. (Open M-F 7am-7pm, Sa 7am-2pm.) Near the train station, **Café Moritz,** Bahnhofstr. 7, serves Thüringer specialities (DM8-15/€4.10-7.70) and sinful ice cream delicacies. (Open May-Oct. M-F 8am-9pm, Sa-Su 10am-9pm; Nov.-Apr. M-F 8am-7pm, Sa-Su 10am-7pm.) **Postal Code:** 99817.

WITTENBERG   ☎ 03491

The Protestant Reformation began here in 1517 when Martin Luther nailed his *95 Theses* to the door of the Schoßkirche, and Wittenberg has been nuts about its heretical son ever since—in 1938, they even renamed the town "Lutherstadt Wittenberg." All the major sights lie around **Collegienstr.** The **Lutherhalle,** Collegienstr. 54, usually holds texts and art chronicling the Reformation, but while it's closed for renovations until October 2002, the exhibits are housed in the **Rathaus,** Markt 26. (Open Apr.-Oct. daily 9am-6pm, Nov.-Mar. Tu-Su 10am-5pm. DM4/€2.05, students DM2/€1.05.) The **Schloßkirche** holds a copy of Luther's *95 Theses* and (allegedly) Luther's body, and the tower offers a sumptuous view of the countryside. (Down Schloßstr. Church open M-Sa 10am-5pm, Su 11:30am-5pm. Free. Tower open M-F 12-3:30pm, Sa-Su 10am-3:30pm. DM2/€1.05, students DM1/€0.55.)

Trains leave the Hauptbahnhof for **Berlin** (1½hr., every 2hr., DM32/€16.40) and **Leipzig** (1hr., every 2hr., DM17/€8.70). From the station, follow the street as it curves right and continue until Collegienstr., the beginning of the **pedestrian zone.**

The **tourist office,** Schloßpl. 2, at the end of the pedestrian zone, provides maps, leads tours (DM10/€5.15), and books rooms. (☎49 86 10. Open Mar.-Oct. M-F 9am-6pm, Sa 10am-3pm, Su 11am-4pm; Nov.-Feb. M-F 10am-4pm, Sa 10am-2pm and 11am-3pm.) The **Jugendherberge (HI)** is in the castle; cross the street from the tourist office and head into the castle's enclosure, then trek up the stairs to the right. (☎40 32 55. Breakfast included. Sheets DM6/€3.10. Key deposit DM10/€5.15. Reception 5-10pm. Lockout 10pm. Reservations recommended. Dorms DM22/€11.30, over 26 DM27/€13.85.) Cheap eats lie along the Collegienstr.-Schloßstr. strip, and there's a **City-Kauf supermarket,** Coswiger Str. 20, near the tourist office. (Open M-F 7am-6:30pm, Sa 8am-12:30pm.) **Postal Code:** 06886.

NORTHERN GERMANY

Once a favored vacation spot for East Germans, Mecklenburg-Vorpommern, the northeasternmost portion of Germany, has suffered economic depression in recent years. To the west, Schleswig-Holstein, which borders Denmark, maintains close ties with Scandinavia. To the west, Bremen is Germany's smallest *Land*.

HAMBURG   ☎040

The largest port city in Germany, Hamburg radiates an inimitable recklessness. Hamburg gained the status of Free Imperial City in 1618 and proudly retains its autonomy and power as one of Germany's 16 *Länder*. Restoration and riots determined the post-World War II landscape, but today Hamburg has become a haven for contemporary artists and intellectuals and reveling party-goers.

▐ TRANSPORTATION

Trains: The **Hauptbahnhof** handles most traffic to: **Amsterdam** (5½hr., 3 per day, DM132/€67.50); **Berlin** (2½hr., every hr., DM88/€45); **Copenhagen** (4½hr., every hr., DM126/€64.50); **Frankfurt** (3¾hr., every hr., DM191/€97.70); **Hanover** (1¼hr., 3 per hr., DM67€34.25); **Munich** (5½hr., every hr., DM260/€133). Two other stations, **Dammtor** (near the university) and **Altona** (in the west) service the city; frequent trains and the S-Bahn connect the 3 stations. **Lockers** available 24hr. for DM2-4/€1.05-2.05 per day; just follow the overhead signs.

Buses: The **ZOB** is on Steintorpl. across from the Hauptbahnhof, between McDonalds and the Museum für Kunst und Gewerbe. To: **Berlin** (3¼hr., 8 per day, DM43/€22); **Copenhagen** (5½hr., 2 per day, DM59/€30.20); **Paris** (12½hr., daily, DM109/€55.75). Open M-F 9am-8pm, Sa 9:30am-1:30pm and 4-8pm, Su 4-8pm.

Public Transportation: HVV operates an efficient U-Bahn, S-Bahn, and bus network. Most single tickets within the downtown area cost DM1.90/€1, but can vary depending on where you go and what transport you take. 1-day ticket DM9.80/€5, 3-day ticket DM24/€12.30. All tickets can be bought at orange *Automaten,* but consider buying a **Hamburg Card** instead (see Tourist Offices, below).

Hitchhiking: *Let's Go* does not recommend hitchhiking as a safe means of transportation. Locals warn that hitchhiking is extremely dangerous in Hamburg.

✱ ▐ ORIENTATION AND PRACTICAL INFORMATION

Hamburg's city center sits between the Elbe and the two city lakes, **Außenalster** and **Binnenalster.** Most major sights lie between the **St. Pauli Landungsbrücken** port area in the west and the Hauptbahnhof in the east. Both the **Nordbahnhof** and **Süd-bahnhof** U-Bahn stations exit onto the Hauptbahnhof. The **Hanseviertel** is crammed with banks, shops, and art galleries. North of the downtown, the **university** dominates the **Dammtor** area and sustains a vibrant community of students and intellectuals. To the west of the university, the **Sternschanze** neighborhood is a politically active community home to artists, squatters, and a sizeable Turkish population.

GERMANY

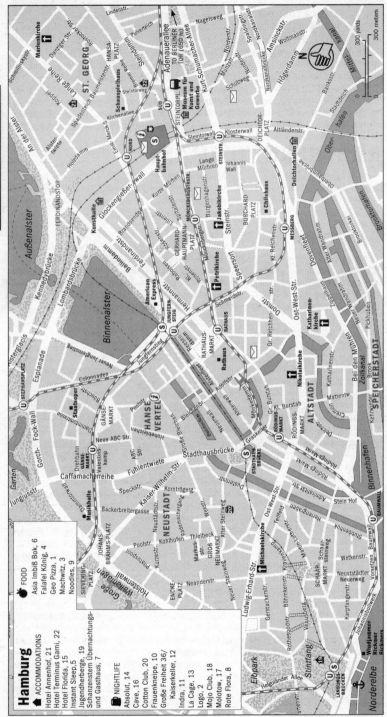

Hamburg

▲ ACCOMMODATIONS
Hotel Annenhof, 21
Hotel Terminus Garni, 22
Hotel Florida, 15
Instant Sleep, 5
Jugendherberge, 19
Schanzenstern Übernachtungs-
   und Gasthaus, 7

■ NIGHTLIFE
Absolut, 14
Cave, 16
Cotton Club, 20
Frauenkneipe, 10
Große Freiheit 36/
   Kaiserkeller, 12
Indra, 11
La Cage, 13
Logo, 2
Mojo Club, 18
Molotow, 17
Rote Flora, 8

● FOOD
Asia Imbiß Bok, 6
Falafel König, 4
Geo Pizza, 1
Machwitz, 3
Noodles, 9

At the south end of town, an entirely different atmosphere reigns in **St. Pauli,** where the raucous **Fischmarkt** (fish market) is juxtaposed by the equally wild (and no less smelly) **Reeperbahn,** home to Hamburg's infamous sex trade.

Tourist Offices: The **Hauptbahnhof office,** in the Wandelhalle near the Kirchenallee exit (☎ 30 05 12 01; info@hamburg-tourism.de; www.hamburg-tourism.de), gives free maps, books rooms for DM6/€3.10, and sells the **Hamburg Card** (DM12.80/€6.55 per day; DM26.50/€13.55 per week), which provides unlimited access to public transportation, reduced admission to most museums, and discounts on bus and boat tours. Open daily 7am-11pm. Other offices: below the **Rathaus** (take the U-bahn to Rathaus; open M-F 8am-7pm, Sa 10am-4pm) and at the **airport** (take bus #110 or the Airport Express; open daily 6am-11pm).

Currency Exchange: ReiseBank, on the 2nd floor of the Hauptbahnhof near the Kirchenallee exit, offers Western Union, cashes traveler's checks, and exchanges money for DM5/€2.60. Open daily 7:30am-10pm.

American Express: Ballindamm 39, 20095 Hamburg (☎ 30 39 38 11 12; fax 30 39 38 12). Take the U-Bahn to Jungfernstieg. Letters held for cardmembers up to 5 weeks; all banking services. Open M-F 9am-6pm, Sa 10am-1pm.

Gay and Lesbian Resources: Hein und Fiete, Pulverteich 21 (☎ 24 03 33). Walk down Steindammstr. away from the Hauptbahnhof and turn right on Pulverteich; it's in the rainbow-striped building. Open M-F 4-9pm, Sa 4-7pm. **Magnus-Hirschfeld-Centrum,** Borgweg 8 (☎ 279 00 69), offers daily counseling sessions. U-Bahn #3 or bus #108 to Borgweg. Center open M and F 2-6pm, Tu-W 7-10pm.

Laundromat: Schnell und Sauber, Grindelallee 158, in the university district. Take S21 or S31 to Dammtor. Wash DM7/€3.60. Open daily 7am-10pm.

Emergency: Police, ☎ 110. **Fire** and **Ambulance,** ☎ 112.

Internet Access: Cyberb@r is on the 3rd floor of the gigantic **Karstadt** department store on Mönckebergstr. DM2/€1.05 per 15min., DM3/€1.55 per 30min.

Post Office: McPaper & Co. AG, at the Kirchenallee exit of the Hauptbahnhof, 20097 Hamburg. Open M-F 8am-10pm, Sa 9am-6pm, Su 10am-6pm. **Poste Restante:** Address mail to be held: Postlagernde Briefe für Johannes GUTENBERG, Post Hamburg-Hauptbahnhof, 20099 Hamburg, Germany.

ACCOMMODATIONS AND CAMPING

A slew of small, relatively cheap *Pensionen* line **Steindamm, Steintorweg, Bremer Weg,** and **Bremer Reihe,** around the Hauptbahnhof. While the area is sketchy, the hotels are for the most part safe. The Sternschanze area has options a bit farther from both the good and the bad aspects of the Hauptbahnhof area. Consult the tourist office's free *Hotelführer* for help in navigating past the filth.

▧ **Schanzenstern Übernachtungs-und Gasthaus,** Bartelsstr. 12 (☎ 439 84 41; fax 439 34 13; info@schanzerstern.de; www.schanzerstern.de). U3 to "Sternschanze," then turn left onto Schanzenstr., right on Susannenstr., and left onto Bartelsstr. In an electrifying neighborhood of students, working-class Turks, and left-wing dissenters, the hostel's rooms are clean, quiet, and bright. Breakfast buffet DM7-11/€3.60-5.65. Wheelchair-accessible. Reception 6:30am-2am. No curfew. Reservations a must in summer and at New Year's. Dorms DM33/€16.90; singles DM65/€33.25; doubles DM95/€48.60; triples DM115/€58.80; quads DM140/€71.60; quints DM175/€89.50.

▧ **Florida the Art Hotel,** Spielbudenpl. 22 (☎ 31 43 93). U3 to St. Pauli, or S1 or S3 to Reeperbahn. Each room of this immaculate hotel reflects the work of a different artist-architect. Breakfast included and available until 5pm. Check-out 4pm. Call ahead. Singles DM110/€56.25; doubles DM165/€84.40.

Jugendherberge auf dem Stintfang (HI), Alfred-Wegener-Weg 5 (☎ 31 34 88). Take S1, S2, S3, or U3 to Landungsbrücke, then uphill on wooded path. Breakfast and sheets included. Laundry DM5/€2.60. Internet access DM5/€2.60 per 25min. Reception 12:30pm-2am. Lockout 9:30-11:30am. Curfew 2am. Call ahead. Dorms DM30.50/€15.60, over 26 DM35.50/€18.15; doubles DM77/€39.40, DM87/€44.50; quads DM134/€68.50, DM154/€78.75. Non-members DM6/€3.10 surcharge.

Instant Sleep, Max-Brauer-Allee 277 (☎ 43 18 23 10; www.instantsleep.de). S3, S21, S31, or U3 to Sternschanze. From the station, go straight on Schanzenstr., turn left on Altonaer Str., and follow it until it becomes Max-Brauer-Allee. This backpacker hostel is a big happy family: rooms are often left open while guests lounge together or cook dinner in the communal kitchen. Sheets DM5/€2.60. Internet access DM2.50/€1.30 per 15min. Reception 9am-2pm. No curfew. Call ahead. Dorms DM29/€14.85; singles DM49/€25.05; doubles DM80/€40.90; triples DM108/€55.25.

Camping: Campingplatz Rosemarie Buchholz, Kieler Str. 374 (☎ 540 45 32; fax 540 25 36; www.camping-buchholz.de). From Altona train station, take bus #182 or 183 to Basselweg, then walk 100m in the same direction as traffic. Breakfast DM7/€3.60; order rolls in advance. Showers DM1.50/€0.80. Reception 8am-noon and 2-10pm. Check-out noon. Quiet hours 10pm-7am. Call ahead. DM7/€3.60 per person, DM12.50/€6.40 per tent per night.

◖ FOOD

The most interesting part of town from a culinary standpoint is **Sternschanze,** where Turkish fruit stands, Asian *Imbiße,* and avant-garde cafes entice hungry passersby with good food and great atmosphere. **Schulterblatt, Susannenstr.,** and **Schanzenstr.** host funky cafes and restaurants, while slightly cheaper establishments abound in the **university** area, especially along **Rentzelstr., Grindelhof,** and **Grindelallee.** The university itself offers tasty food at very low prices as well as a chance to get an inside look at German student life. In **Altona,** the pedestrian zone leading up to the train station is packed with ethnic food stands and produce shops. Check out the market inside Altona's massive **Mercado** mall, which includes everything from sushi bars to Portuguese fast food.

Noodle's, Schanzenstr. 2-4. Along with innovative pasta creations, Noodle's serves up veggie entrees alongside a full bar. Try the broccoli with cheese and ham (DM12/ €6.15). Open M-Th and Su 10am-1am, F-Sa 10am-3am, Su brunch 10am-3pm.

Falafel Factory, Schanzenstr., right across from the S-Bahn station. An excellent option for vegetarians, this tiny Lebanese *Imbiß* makes falafels fresh to order. Basic falafel DM5/€2.60, with one of half a dozen toppings DM6/€3.10. Open daily; hours flexible.

University Mensa, Schlüterstr. 7. S21 or S31 to Dammtor, then turn left on Rothenbaumchaussee, left on Moorweidenstr., and right onto Schlüterstr. This tasty and affordable university cafe offers coffee and a giant piece of cake for DM3.30/€1.70. Meals DM3-6/€1.55-3.10 with student ID, 1DM/€0.50 more for non-students. Open M-Th 10am-7:30pm, F 10am-7pm.

◉ SIGHTS

ALTSTADT. The gargantuan 18th-century **Michaelskirche** is the symbol of Hamburg. Its tower, accessible by foot or elevator, is the only one of the city's six spires that may be climbed. *(Organ music Apr.-Aug. daily noon and 5pm. Tower or church DM5/€2.60, students DM2.50/€1.30. Open M-Sa 9am-6pm, Su 11:30am-5:30pm; Nov.-Apr. M-Sa 10am-4:30pm, Su 11:30am-4:30pm.)* The Rathaus (Town Hall) is a copper-spired Neo-Renaissance monstrosity; inside are displays of the city's history. *(Tours in German every 30min. M-Th 10am-3pm, F-Su 10am-1pm. Tours in English every hr. M-Th 10:15am-3:15pm, F-Su 10:15am-1:15pm. Free.)* The **Nikolaikirche** was devastated by an Allied bomb in 1943 and remains in its hollowed-out state as "a sign for peace." *(Exhibition of its history open M-F 10am-5pm, Sa-Su 11am-4pm. DM3/€1.55.)* The buildings along nearby **Trostbrücke** sport huge copper models of clipper ships on their spires—a testament to Hamburg's sea-trade wealth. *(Just south of the Rathaus, off Ost-West-Str.)*

ST. PAULI LANDUNGSBRÜCKEN. Hamburg's harbor, the largest port in Germany, lights up at night with ships from all over the world. Take the elevator from the building behind Pier 6 to the old **Elbtunnel,** which was built 1907-1911 and runs 1200m under the Elbe—it's still used by commuters. At the **Fischmarkt,**

charismatic vendors haul in and hawk huge amounts of fish, produce, and other goods. Don't shy away if you dislike fish—about 90% of the goods come in another variety. *(U- or S-Bahn to Landungsbrücken or S-Bahn to Königstr. Open Su 6-10am, off-season 7-10am.)*

PLANTEN UND BLOMEN AND ALSTER LAKES. To the west of the Alster lies **Planten und Blomen,** a huge expanse of manicured flower gardens and trees. *(Open 7am-11pm.)* Daily performances ranging from Irish step-dancing to Hamburg's police orchestra shake the outdoor **Musikpavillon** from May to September; there are also nightly **Wasserlichtkonzerte,** in which the fountains are bathed in rainbows of light. *(May-Aug. 10pm, Sept. 9pm.)* North of the city center, the two Alster lakes, bordered by tree-lined paths and parks, provide further refuge from crowded Hamburg.

GEDENKSTÄTTE BULLENHUSER DAMM UND ROSENGARTEN. Surrounded by warehouses, the schoolhouse serves as a memorial to 20 Jewish children brought here from Auschwitz for "testing" and murdered by the S.S. only hours before Allied troops arrived. Visitors are invited to plant a rose for the children in the flower garden behind the school, where plaques with the children's photographs line the fence. *(Bullenhuser Damm 92. S-Bahn #21 to "Rothenburgsort." Follow the signs to Bullenhuser Damm along Ausschlaeger Bildeich and across a bridge; the school is 200m down. Open Su 10am-7pm and Th 2-8pm. Free.)*

MUSEUMS. The dozens of museums in Hamburg range from the erotic to the Victorian. The first-rate **Hamburger Kunsthalle** holds an extensive and dazzling collection spanning medieval to modern art. *(Turn left from the "City" exit of the Hauptbahnhof and cross the street. Open Tu-W and F-Su 10am-6pm, Th 10am-9pm. DM15/€7.70, students DM10/€5.15.)* Hamburg's contemporary art scene resides in the two buildings of the **Deichtorhallen Hamburg,** whose exhibits showcase up-and-coming artists. *(U1 to Steinstr., then follow signs (2 entwined iron circles) from the station. Open Tu-Su 11am-6pm, Th 10am-9pm. Each building DM10/€5.15, students DM8/€4.10.)* Follow the silver sperm painted on the floor through four floors of shocking iniquity at the **Erotic Art Museum.** *(S1 or S3 to Reeperbahn. www.erotic-art-museum.hamburg.de. Open Su-Th 10am-midnight, F-Sa 10am-1am. DM15/€7.70. Under 16 not admitted.)*

🎵 🏴 ENTERTAINMENT AND NIGHTLIFE

MUSIC AND FESTIVALS

The **Staatsoper,** Große Theaterstr. 36, houses one of the best opera companies in Germany, emphasizing classical works; the associated **ballet** company is the acknowledged dance powerhouse of the nation. *(☎356 80. U1 to Stephanspl. Open M-F 10am-6:30pm, Sa 10am-2pm.)* **Orchestras** abound—the Philharmonie, the Norddeutscher Rundfunk Symphony, and Hamburg Symphonia all perform at the **Musikhalle** on Johannes-Brahms-Pl. *(Take U2 to Gänsemarkt or Messehallen. ☎34 69 20; www.musikhalle-hamburg.de.)* Live music prospers in Hamburg, satisfying all tastes. Superb traditional **jazz** swings at the **Cotton Club** and **Indra** (see Nightlife, below). On Sunday mornings, good and bad alike play at the **Fischmarkt.** The **West Port jazz festival,** Germany's largest, runs in mid-July; call the Koncertskasse *(☎32 87 38 54)* for information. The most anticipated festival is the **G-Move** (dubbed the "Love Parade of the North"), which grooves into town early in June. Check www.g-move.com for the dates and performers.

NIGHTLIFE

The infamous **Reeperbahn,** a long boulevard lined with sex shops, strip joints, and peep shows, is the spinal cord of **St. Pauli;** although it's fairly safe, women should not wander into adjacent streets. **Herbertstr.,** Hamburg's only remaining legalized prostitution strip, runs parallel to the Reeperbahn and is open only to men over 18. The prostitutes flaunting their flesh on Herbertstr. are licensed professionals required to undergo health inspections, but others may be venereal roulette wheels. Those trying to avoid the hypersexed Reeperbahn should head north to the trendy streets of **Sternschanze.**

Unlike St. Pauli, these areas are centered around cafes and weekend extravaganzas of an alternative flavor. Much of Hamburg's **gay scene** is in the **St. Georg** area of the city, near Berliner Tor. Gay and straight bars in this area are more welcoming and classier than those in the Reeperbahn. *Szene*, available at newsstands (DM5/€2.60), lists events and parties, while the magazine *hinnerk* (free at tourist offices) lists gay and lesbian events.

    ⬛**Rote Flora**, Schulterblatt 71, is the nucleus of the Sternschanze scene. (Cover DM8/€4.10 or more. Opening times vary.) **Mojo Club**, Reeperbahn 1, is adorned with artsy paper lamps and filled with stylish students. (Cover DM12/€6.15 on weekends. Usually open 11pm-4am.) **Absolut**, Hans-Albers-Pl. 15, hosts the gay scene Saturday nights, spinning until well after the sun is up. (Cover DM10-15/€5.15-€7.70. Open F 11pm-5am, Sa 11pm-6:30am.) **Frauenkneipe**, Stresemannstr. 60, is a club and meeting place for women only, gay or straight. (Open Su-M and W-F from 8pm, Sa from 9pm.) For respite from pounding techno, **Indra**, Große Freiheit 64, offers a haven of calm live jazz. (Cover DM5-10/€2.60-€5.15. Open W-Su from 9pm; music starts 11pm.)

LÜBECK

☎**0451**

Lübeck is easily Schleswig-Holstein's most beautiful city—you'd never guess that the greater part of the city was razed in World War II and reconstructed in the 1950s. In its heyday, it was the capital of the Hanseatic league, controlling trade across Northern Europe. Although no longer a center of political and commercial influence, Lübeck remains home to stunning churches and delicious marzipan.

⛏❼ TRANSPORTATION AND PRACTICAL INFORMATION. Trains depart frequently for Berlin (3¼hr., 1 per hr., DM97/€49.60) and Hamburg (45min., 2 per hr., DM17/€8.70). Avoid the privately owned, expensive tourist office in the train station and head for the **city tourist office** in the Altstadt, Breite Str. 62. (☎122 54 13. Open M-F 9:30am-7pm, Sa-Su 10am-3pm.) **Postal Code:** 23552.

⛏⬚ ACCOMMODATIONS AND FOOD. To reach **Rucksack Hotel**, Kanalstr. 70, walk past the Holstentor from the station, turn left on An der Untertrave, and head right on Beckergrube; the hostel is on the corner of Kanalstr. (☎70 68 92. Breakfast DM5/€2.60. Sheets DM3/€1.55. Reception 9am-1pm and 4-10pm. 6-bed dorms DM26/€13.30, 10-bed dorms DM24/€12.30; double with bath DM80/€40.90; quads DM112/€57.30, with bath DM156/€79.80.) The **Baltic Hotel**, Hansestr. 11, is across the street from the station and 5min. from the Altstadt. (☎855 75. Breakfast included. Reception 8am-10pm. Singles DM50-90/€25-45; doubles DM100-130/€50-65; triples from DM150/€77.) Lübeck's specialty is **marzipan**, a delectable candy made from almonds. Stop by the famous confectionery ⬛**I.G. Niederegger Marzipan Café**, Breitestr. 89, for marzipan in the shape of pigs, jellyfish, and even the town gate. **Tipasa**, Schlumacherstr. 12-14, serves pizza, pasta, and vegetarian dishes, and there's a *Biergarten* in back. (Open M-Th and Su noon-1am, F-Sa noon-2am.)

⬛ SIGHTS. Between the station and the *Altstadt* stands the massive **Holstentor**, one of Lübeck's four 15th-century gates and the symbol of the city; the museum inside displays armor and torture implements. (Open Apr.-Sept. Tu-Su 10am-5pm; Oct.-Mar. 10am-4pm. DM5/€2.60, students DM3/€1.55, under 19 DM1/€0.55.) The city skyline is dominated by the twin brick towers of the **Marienkirche**, a gigantic church housing the largest mechanical organ in the world. Photographs of the destroyed medieval masterpiece **Totentanzbild** ("Dance of the Dead") remind viewers that everything—even paintings—must die. (Open daily in summer 10am-6pm; in winter 10am-4pm. Short organ concerts daily at noon.) The **Dom** (cathedral), on Domkirchhof, shelters a huge crucifix as well as moving paintings and altarpieces. (Open Apr.-Sept. 10am-6pm; Mar. and Oct. 10am-5pm; Nov. 10am-4pm; Dec.-Feb. 10am-3pm. Free.) The floor of the Gothic **Katharinenkirche**, Königstr. 27, is lined with gravestones; formerly a Franciscan monastery, it was used as a stable by Napoleon. (Open Tu-Su 10am-1pm and 2-5pm. DM1/€0.55.) For a sweeping view of the spire-studded *Altstadt*, take the elevator to the 50.5m steeple of the **Petrikirche.** (Church open daily 11am-4pm. Tower open Apr.-Oct. 9am-7pm. DM3.50/€1.80, students DM2/€1.05.) The **Museum Behn- und Drägerhaus,** Königstr. 11, features exquisite paintings and a lovely interior. (Open Apr.-Sept. Tu-Su 10am-5pm; Oct.-Mar. 10am-4pm. DM5/€2.60, students DM3/€1.55. Free first F of every month.) The **Museum für Puppentheater,** Kolk 16, is the largest private puppet collection in the world. (Open daily 10am-6pm. DM6/€3.10, students DM5/€2.60.)

SCHLESWIG
☎ 04621

With a harbor full of sailboats and waterside promenades sprinkled with cafes, Schleswig holds both the air of a seatown and the artistic interest of a big city. Scale the 237 steps of the **St. Petri Dom** (DM2/€1) for a striking birds-eye view of the town. (Open May-Sept. M-Th and Sa 9am-12:30pm and 1:30-5pm, F 9am-12:30pm and 1:30-3pm, Su 1:30-5pm; Oct.-Dec. and Mar.-Apr. M-Th and Sa 10am-12:30pm and 1:30-4pm, F 10am-12:30am and 1:30-3pm, Su 1:30-4pm; Jan.-Feb. M-Th and Sa 10am-noon and 2-4pm, F 10am-noon, Su 2-4pm.) By the harbor, the 16th-century **Schloß Gottorf** houses the **Landesmuseen,** a treasure trove of Dutch, Danish, and Art Deco pieces. On the other side of the *Schloß*, the **Kreuzstall** houses the **Museum des 20. Jahrhunderts,** devoted to artists of the Brücke school. The surrounding park holds an **outdoor sculpture museum.** (All museums open daily Mar.-Oct. 9am-5pm; Nov.-Feb. Tu-Su 9:30am-4pm. DM9/€4.60, students DM5/€2.60.)

Schleswig centers around its **bus terminal (ZOB)** rather than its train station. Single rides on the bus network cost DM1.90. The **train station** is 20min. south of the city center; take bus #1, 2, 4, or 5 from the stop outside the ZOB. Consider buying a **Schleswig Card** (1-day DM15/€7.70, 3-day DM20/€10.25), valid for public transit and admission to most sights. The **tourist office,** Plessenstr. 7, is up the street from the harbor; from the ZOB, walk down Plessenstr. toward the water. The staff books rooms. (☎248 78; room reservations ☎248 32. Open May-Sept. M-F 9:30am-5:30pm, Sa 9:30am-12:30pm; Oct.-Apr. M-Th 10am-4pm, Fri 10am-1pm.) The **Jugendherberge (HI),** Spielkoppel 1, is close to the center of town. Take bus #2 (dir. Hühnhauser Schwimmhalle) from either the train station or the ZOB to Schwimmhalle; the hostel is across the street. (☎238 93. Breakfast included. Sheets DM7/€3.60. Reception 7am-1pm and 5-11pm. Curfew 11pm. Dorms DM23/€11.75, over 26 DM28/€14.35.) Try the fresh and cheap seafood at the **Imbiße** by the Stadthafen.

CENTRAL GERMANY

Lower Saxony (Niedersachsen), which stretches from the North Sea to the hills of central Germany, is mostly agricultural plains, but along the coast fishing boats run along the foggy marshland. Just to the south, North Rhine-Westphalia is the most heavily populated and economically powerful area in Germany. While the region's squalor may have inspired the philosophy of Karl Marx and Friedrich Engels, its natural beauty and intellectual energy also spurred the muses of Goethe, Heine, and Böll. Smack dab in the center of Germany is Hesse, previously a source for mercenary soldiers (many hired by King George III to put down an unruly gang of colonials in 1776); today it's the busiest commercial area in the country.

HANOVER (HANNOVER)
☎ 0511

With economic vigor, a wealth of museums, and a tradition of festivals, Hanover reigns as the political and cultural capital of Lower Saxony. On the outskirts of the **Altstadt** stands the spectacular **Neues Rathaus;** take the elevator (DM3/€1.55, students DM2/€1.05) up the tower for a thrilling view of the city. (Rathaus open May-Sept. M-F 8am-10pm, Sa and Su 10am-10pm.) Right next door, the **Kestner-Museum,** Trammpl. 3, features ancient, medieval, and Renaissance arts. (Open Tu, Th-Su 11am-6pm, W 11am-8pm. DM5/€2.60, students DM3/€1.55; F free.) The nearby **Sprengel Museum,** Kurt-Schwitters-Pl. (at the corner of the Maschsee and Maschpark, near the Neues Rathaus), is a 20th-century art-lover's dream.

(Open Tu 10am-8pm, W-Su 10am-6pm. Permanent collection DM7/€3.60, students DM3.50/€1.80. Special exhibits DM12/€6.15, students DM8/€4.10.) The gems of Hanover are the three paradisiacal **Herrenhausen gardens.** The largest, the geometrically trimmed **Großer Garten,** holds the **Große Fontäne,** Europe's highest fountain, which shoots an astounding 80m. (Fountain spurts M-F 11am-noon and 3-5pm, Sa-Su 11am-noon and 2-5pm. Garden open 8am-8pm; Nov.-Mar. 8am-dusk. DM5/€2.60.)

Trains leave at least every hour to: Amsterdam (4½-5hr., DM80/€41); Berlin (2½hr., DM80/€41); Frankfurt (3hr., DM160/€82); Hamburg (1½hr., DM50/€25.60); Cologne (2hr., DM100/€51.15); and Munich (9hr., DM250/€127.85). To reach the **tourist office,** Ernst-August-Pl. 2, start outside the main entrance of the train station (facing the large rear of the king's splendid steed) and turn right. (☎16 849 700. Open M-F 9am-7pm, Sa 9:30am-3pm.) For the hostel **Naturfreundehaus Stadtheim,** Hermann-Bahlsen-Allee 8, take U3 (dir.: Lahe) or U7 (dir.: Fasanenkrug) to Spannhagengarten, walk 15m back to the intersection, turn left on Hermann-Bahlsen-Allee, and follow the signs. Since it's on the outskirts of town, use caution late at night. (☎69 14 93. Breakfast included. Reception 8am-noon and 3-10pm. No curfew. DM49/€25.05.) To reach **Hotel am Thielenplatz,** Thielenpl. 2, take a left onto Joachimstr. from the station and go one block to Thielenpl. (☎32 76 91 93. Breakfast included. Check-out 11:30am. Singles with shower DM110-150/€56.25-76.70; doubles with shower DM180-220/€93-€112.50; weekdays cheaper.) ▨**Jalda,** Limmerstr. 97, serves Italian, Greek, and Arabic dishes (DM14-17/€7.20-8.70) and has all-you-can-eat schnitzel Friday and Saturday for DM14/€7.20. (Open M-Th and Su 11:30am-midnight, F-Sa noon-1am.) **Uwe's Hannenfaß Hanover,** Knochenhauerstr. 36, in the center of the Altstadt, serves traditional German fare for DM8.90/€4.55 and great brew for DM5.40/€2.80. (Open daily 4pm-2am.) **Spar supermarkets** sit by the Lister Meile and Kröpcke U-Bahn stops. (Open M-F 7am-7pm, Sa 8am-2pm.) From the *Hauptbahnhof,* head to the **Markt-halle,** where a variety of snacks, meals, and booze awaits. (Open M-W 7am-6pm, Th-F 7am-8pm, Sa 7am-4pm.) **The Loft,** Georgstr. 50b, is packed with students on the weekends. (Open M-Th 9pm-2am, F-Sa 9pm-5am, Su 9pm-2am.) **Postal code:** 30159.

COLOGNE (KÖLN)   ☎0221

Founded as a Roman colony (*colonia,* the root of the word "Köln") in AD 48, Cologne gained fame and fortune in the Middle Ages as an elite university town and an important trade hub. While most of the inner city was destroyed in World War II, the magnificent Gothic *Dom* (cathedral) survived no fewer than 14 bombings and remains Cologne's main attraction. Today, tourists come to see this symbol of Cologne's rebirth, participate in bacchanalian celebrations, and immerse themselves in the burgeoning fine arts scene.

▛ TRANSPORTATION

Flights: Flights depart from **Köln-Bonn Flughafen;** a shuttle to **Berlin** leaves 24 times per day. Bus #170 to the airport leaves stop #3 at the train station. (20min; daily 5:30, 6, 6:30am; every 15min. 7am-8pm; every 30min. 8-11pm; DM8.70/€5.)

Trains: To: **Amsterdam** (4hr., every 2hr., DM79/€41); **Berlin** (6½hr., 2 per hr., DM172/€88); **Brussels** (2½hr., every 2hr., DM54/€28); **Düsseldorf** (45min., 5 per hr., DM12.60/€7); **Frankfurt** (2hr., 3 per hr., DM61/€32); **Hamburg** (5hr., 3 per hr., DM123/€63); **Munich** (6hr., 4 per hr., DM173/€89).

▛▟ ORIENTATION AND PRACTICAL INFORMATION

Cologne spans the Rhine via eight bridges, but nearly all sights and the city center can be found on the western side. The train station is in the northern part of the **Innenstadt** (town center).

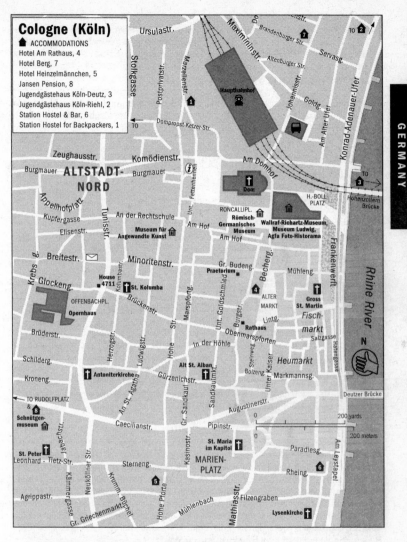

Cologne (Köln)

ACCOMMODATIONS
Hotel Am Rathaus, 4
Hotel Berg, 7
Hotel Heinzelmännchen, 5
Jansen Pension, 8
Jugendgästehaus Köln-Deutz, 3
Jugendgästehaus Köln-Riehl, 2
Station Hostel & Bar, 6
Station Hostel for Backpackers, 1

Tourist Office: Unter Fettenhennen 19 (☎22 12 33 45), across from the main entrance to the *Dom*, provides free city maps and books rooms for DM6/€3. Open May-Oct. M-Sa 8am-10:30pm, Su 9am-10:30pm; Nov.-Apr. M-Sa 8am-9pm, Su 9:30am-7pm.

Currency Exchange: An office at the train station is open daily 7am-9pm, but the service charges are lower at the post office (see below).

Gay and Lesbian Resources: Schulz Schwulen-und Lesbenzentrum, Kartäuserwall 18 (☎93 18 80 80), near Chlodwigpl. Info, advice, and cafe. The tourist office also offers a "Gay City Map" with listings of gay-friendly hotels, bars, and clubs.

Laundry: Eco-Express, at the corner of Richard-Wagner-Str. and Händelstr. Wash DM6/€3; dry DM1/€0.51 per 10min. Soap included. Open M-Sa 6am-11pm.

Police: ☎110. **Fire** and **ambulance:** ☎112.

Pharmacy: Dom-Apotheke, Komödienstr. 5 (☎257 67 54), near the station, posts a list of after-hours pharmacies. English spoken. Open M-F 8am-6:30pm, Sa 9am-1pm.

Internet access: FuturePoint, Richmodstr. 13 (☎206 72 06). Open daily 9am-1am.

Post Office: at the corner of Breite Str. and Tunisstr. in the *WDR-Arkaden* shopping gallery. For **Poste Restante,** address mail: Postlagernde Briefe für First name SURNAME, Hauptpostamt, 50667 Köln, Germany. Open M-F 8am-8pm, Sa 8am-4pm.

♠ ACCOMMODATIONS

Most hotels fill up in spring and fall when conventions come to town, and the two hostels are nearly always booked from June to September, so call ahead.

▒ Station Hostel and Bar, Rheing. 34-36 (☎23 02 47). Clean rooms, a popular bar, and English-speaking staff. Reception 24hr. Reserved rooms held until 6pm. Singles DM50/ €26; doubles DM80/€42; triples DM108/€57; quads DM132/€68.

Jugendgästehaus Köln-Riehl (HI), An der Schanz 14 (☎76 70 81), on the Rhine north of the zoo. U16 (dir. Ebertplatz/Mülheim) to Boltensternstr. Breakfast and sheets included. Reception 24hr. No curfew. Call ahead. 4- to 6-bed dorms DM38.50/€20; singles DM63.50/€33.

Jugendherberge Köln-Deutz (HI), Siegesstr. 5a (☎81 47 11), just over the *Hohenzollernbrücke.* S6, 11, or 12 to Köln-Deutz. Exit the station, walk down Neuhöfferstr., and take the 1st right; the hostel is in a tree-lined courtyard. Small but clean rooms, with free access to washing machines. Breakfast and sheets included. Reception 11am-1am. Curfew 1am. Call ahead. Dorms DM37/€19, under 26 DM33/€17.

Jansen Pension, Richard-Wagner-Str. 18 (☎25 18 75). U1, U6, U7, U15, U17, or U19 to Rudolfpl. Follow Richard-Wagner-Str. Beautiful high-ceilinged rooms in a Victorian house. Breakfast included. Singles DM55-70/€29-36, 2 nights or more DM50-65/ €26-34; doubles DM120/€62, DM110/€57.

Hotel Heinzelmännchen, Hohe Pforte 5-7 (☎21 12 17). Bus #132 (dir. Frankenstr.) to Waidmarkt. This family-run hotel has airy rooms with terraces, TV, and phone. Less for stays over 2 days. Breakfast included. Reception 6am-11pm; call if you're arriving later. Singles DM75/€39; doubles DM115/€59; triples from DM125/€64.

Hotel Am Rathaus, Burgerstr. 6 (☎257 76 24). Standing on the front porch of the *Rathaus,* it's immediately on your right. Reception in the bar below. Breakfast included. Singles DM60/€31; doubles DM110-140/€56-72.

♟ FOOD

Cologne cuisine includes scrumptious *Rievekoochen* (slabs of fried potato dunked in applesauce) and smooth *Kölsch* beer. ▒**Brauhaus Früh am Dom,** Am Hof 12-14, serves some of Cologne's finest Kölsch as well as hearty regional specialties. (Open daily 8am-midnight.) Small cafes and cheap restaurants line **Zülpicherstraße.** (U7 or U9 to Zülpicher Pl.). Mid-priced ethnic restaurants lie around the perimeter of the Altstadt, particularly from **Hohenzollernring** to **Hohenstaufenring;** the city's best cheap eats are on **Weideng** in the Turkish district. **HL,** Hohenzollernring 20, sells **groceries.** (Open M-F 9am-8pm, Sa-Su 8:30am-4pm.)

◉ SIGHTS

▒ **DOM.** Visitors exiting Cologne's train station are immediately treated to the beauty, power, and sorrow that emanate from the colossal High Gothic **Dom,** Germany's greatest cathedral. To the right of the center altar is the **Dombild** triptych, a masterful 15th-century painting. The 976 **Gero crucifix,** in the fenced off area to the left of the center altar, is the oldest intact sculpture of Christus patiens (a crucified Christ with eyes shut). The enormous sculpture behind the altar is the **Shrine of the Magi,** a reliquary of the Three Kings (Cologne's holy patrons) in gold that was brought to the city in 1164. *(Cathedral open daily 6am-7pm. Free. Tours in English M-Sa 10:30am and 2:30pm, Su 2:30pm; DM7/€4, children DM4/€2.)* Fifteen minutes and 509 steps bring you to the top of the **Südturm.** *(Open Nov.-Feb. 9am-4pm; May-Sept. 9am-6pm;*

Mar.-Apr. and Oct. 9am-5pm. DM3/€1.50, students DM1.50/€0.75.) Catch your breath at the **Glockenstube** (a chamber for the tower's nine bells about halfway up).

HOUSE #4711. The magic water **Eau de Cologne,** once prescribed as a drinkable curative, made the town a household name. Today the house, labeled #4711 by a Napoleonic system that abolished street names, is a boutique with a small fountain continually dispensing the famous scented water. *(Glockeng., at the intersection with Tunisstr. From Hohe Str., turn right on Brückenstr., which becomes Glockeng. Open M-F 9:30am-8pm, Sa 9:30am-4pm.)*

RÖMISCHES PRAETORIUM UND KANAL. The excavated ruins of the former Roman military headquarters display remains of Roman gods and a befuddling array of rocks left by early inhabitants. *(From the Rathaus, take a right and then a left onto Kleine Budeng. Open Tu-F 10am-4pm, Sa-Su 11am-4pm. DM3/€1.50, students DM1.50/€0.75.)*

MUSEUMS. ▧**Heinrich-Böll-Platz** houses two complementary collections: the **Museum Ludwig,** which spans Impressionism through Dalí, Lichtenstein, and War-hol; and the **Agfa Foto-Historama,** which chronicles photography of the last 150 years, including a rotating display of Man Ray's works. *(Bischofsgartenstr. 1. Open Tu 10am-8pm, W-F 10am-6pm, Sa-Su 11am-6pm. Tours Tu 6pm, W 4:30pm, Sa 11:30am, Su 11:30am. DM10/€5, students DM5/€3.)* At the **Schokoladen Museum** (Chocolate Museum), you can watch every step of chocolate production from the rainforests to the gold fountain that spurts streams of silky, heavenly, creamy chocolate. Resist the urge to drool and wait for the free samples. *(Rheinauhafen 1a, near the Sev-erinsbrücke. From the train station, head for the river, walk along the Rhine heading right, go under the Deutzer Brücke, and take the 1st footbridge. Open M-F 10am-6pm, Sa-Su 11am-7pm. DM10/€5, students DM5/€3. Tours Sa 2 and 4pm; Su 11:30am, 2, 4pm. DM3/€1.50.)* The **Römisch-Germanisches Museum** (Roman-German Museum) displays a large array of artifacts documenting the daily lives of Romans both rich and poor. *(Roncallipl. 4. Open Tu-Su 10am-5pm, W 10am-7pm. DM10/€5, students DM5/€3.)* **NS-Dokumentations-Zentrum** was once Cologne's Gestapo headquarters; today, it portrays the city as it was during the Nazi regime. *(Am Appellhofpl. 23-25. Open Tu-F 10am-4pm, Sa-Su 11am-4pm. DM5/€3, students DM2/€1.)* The **Käthe-Kollwitz-Museum** houses the world's largest collection of sketches, sculptures, and prints by the brilliant 20th-century artist-activist. *(Neumarkt 18-24. On the top floor in the Neumarkt-Passage. U12, U14, U16, or U18 to Neumarkt. Open Tu-F 10am-6pm, Sa-Su 11am-6pm. DM5/€3, students DM2/€1.)*

🎵🎭 ENTERTAINMENT AND NIGHTLIFE

Cologne explodes in celebration during **Karneval,** a week-long pre-Lent festival that builds up to an out-of-control parade on **Rosenmontag** (Feb. 11, 2002), where every-one's in costume and gets and gives *Bützchen* (kisses on the cheek). For more information, pick up the Karneval booklet at the tourist office.

Many bars and clubs change their music nightly; the best way to know what you'll get is to check the monthly magazine *Kölner* (DM2/€1). The closer to the Rhine or *Dom* you venture, the more quickly your wallet gets emptied. Students congregate in the **Bermuda-Dreieck** ("Bermuda Triangle"), bounded by Zülpicher-str., Zülpicherpl., Roonstr., and Luxemburgstr. The center of **gay nightlife** runs up Matthiasstr. to Mühlenbach, Hohe Pforte, Marienpl., and to the Heumarkt area by the *Deutzer Brücke.* **Alter Wartesaal,** Johannisstr. 11, in the basement of the train station, has an enormous dance floor and an impressively hip crowd. (Open M-Th 10pm-1am, F-Sa 9am-3am.) **M20,** Maastrichterstr. 20, plays some of the best techno and drum 'n bass in town to crowds of locals. (Open M-F 8pm-1am, Sa 8pm-2am.) **Vampire,** Rathenaupl. 5, is a gay and lesbian bar with a chill atmosphere and plenty of delicious "holy water." (Happy Hour 8-9pm. Disco F, Sa. Open Tu-Th and Su 8pm-1am, F-Sa 8pm-3am.)

BONN   ☎ 0228

Once derisively called *Hauptdorf* (capital village) just because it wasn't Berlin, Bonn became capital of West Germany by chance since Konrad Adenauer, the first chancellor, resided in the suburbs. In 1999, the *Bundestag* packed up and moved back to Berlin, allowing Bonn to be itself again. Today, the streets of the *Altstadt* bustle with notable energy. The well-respected university and excellent museums bolster a thriving cultural scene, and Bonn is fast becoming a center for Germany's computer-technology industry.

■🖂 TRANSPORTATION AND PRACTICAL INFORMATION. Trains run to: Cologne (30min., 6 per hr., DM10/€5.15); Frankfurt (1½hr., 1 per hr., DM59/€30.20); and Koblenz (1hr., 3 per hr., DM14.80/€7.60). The **tourist office** is at Windeckstr. 2, near the cathedral on Münsterpl. (☎ 194 33. Open M-F 9am-6:30pm, Sa 9am-4pm, Su 10am-2pm.) Consider buying the **Bonncard** (1-day DM24/€12.30, 3-day DM46/€23.55), which covers transportation (M-F after 9am, Sa-Su 24hr.) and admission to more than 20 museums in Bonn and the surrounding area. The **post office,** Münsterpl. 17, is down Poststr. from the station. (Open M-F 8am-8pm, Sa 8am-4pm.) **Postal code:** 53111.

🖥🍴 ACCOMMODATIONS AND FOOD. Take bus #621 (dir. Ippendorf Altenheim) to Jugendgästehaus for the sparkling, super-modern **Jugendgästehaus Bonn-Venusberg (HI),** Haager Weg 42. (☎ 28 99 70. Wheelchair accessible. Breakfast and sheets included. Laundry DM10/€5.15. Reception 9am-1am. Curfew 1am. Dorm beds DM39/€19.95.) **Hotel Bergmann,** Kasernenstr. 13, is a family-run hotel with cozy, elegant rooms. From the station follow Poststr., turn left at Münsterpl. on Vivatsg., then right on Kasernenstr.; after 10min., the hotel is on the left. (☎ 63 38 91. Reception hours sporadic—call ahead. Singles DM60/€30.70; doubles DM95/€48.60.) To reach **Campingplatz Genienaue,** Im Frankenkeller 49, take U16 or U63 to Rheinallee, then bus #613 (dir. Giselherstr.) to Guntherstr. Turn left on Guntherstr. and right on Frankenkeller. (☎ 34 49 49. Reception 9am-noon and 3-10pm. DM8/€4.10 per person, DM5-8/€2.60-4.10 per tent.)

Carl's Mensa-Bistro, Nassestr. 15, has restaurant-quality meals served cafeteria style. (Open M-Th 10:30am-10pm, F 10:30am-3pm. Hot food served from 11:30am-½hour before closing.) **Cassius-Garten,** Maximilianstr. 28d, at the edge of the Altstadt facing the station, is a scrumptious veggie bar with 50 kinds of salads, noodles, and whole-grain baked goods. (Bistro open M-F 9am-8pm, Sa 9am-4pm. Restaurant open M-Sa from 11:30am.) The **market** on Münsterpl. teems with vendors selling meat, fruit, and vegetables. (Open M-Sa 9am-6pm.) There's a **supermarket** in the basement of the Kaufhof department store on Münsterpl. (Open M-F 9:30am-8pm, Sa 9am-4pm.)

◻🏛 SIGHTS AND NIGHTLIFE. Bonn's lively pedestrian zone is littered with historic niches. **Beethoven Geburtshaus** (Beethoven's birthplace), Bonng. 18-20, hosts a fantastic collection of his personal effects, from his primitive hearing aids to his first violin. *(Open Apr.-Sept. M-Sa 10am-6pm, Su 11am-4pm; Oct.-Mar. M-Sa 10am-5pm, Su 11am-4pm. DM8/€4.10, students DM6/€3.10.)* In its governmental heyday, the transparent walls of the **Bundestag** were meant to symbolize the government's responsibility to the public. *(Take U16, U63, or U66 to Heussallee/Bundeshaus or bus #610 to Bundeshaus.)* Students study within the **Kurfürstliches Schloß,** the huge 18th-century palace now serving as the center of Bonn's **Friedrich-Wilhelms-Universität.** To uncover Bonn's "other" palace, follow Poppelsdorfer Allee to the 18th-century **Poppelsdorfer Schloß,** which boasts beautiful **botanical gardens.** *(Gardens open Apr.-Sept. M-F 9am-6pm, Su 9am-1pm; Oct.-Mar. M-F 9am-4pm. Su 9am-1pm. M-F free, Su DM1/€0.55.)* The **Bonncard** (see Practical Information, above) provides admission to most of Bonn's **"Museum Mile."** To start your museum-crawl, take U16, U63, or U66 to Heussallee or Museum König. **Kunstmuseum Bonn,** Friedrich-Ebert-Allee 2., houses a superb selection of Expressionist and modern German art. *(Open Tu and Th-Su 10am-6pm, W 10am-9pm. DM8/€4.10, students DM4/€2.05.)* One block away, the ◼**Haus der Geschichte** (House of History), Adenauerallee 250/Willy-Brandt 4, examines post-World War II German history through interactive exhibits. *(Open Tu-Su 9am-7pm. Free.)*

For club and concert listings, pick up *Schnüss* (DM2/€1.05). The ◼**Jazz Galerie,** Oxfordstr. 24, hosts jazz and rock concerts as well as a jumping bar and disco.

(Cover DM13/€6.65. Open daily M-Th and Su 9pm-3am, F-Sa 9pm-4am.) **Pantheon,** Bundeskanzlerpl., caters to eclectic tastes with a disco, concerts, and stand-up comedy; follow Adenauerallee out of the city to Bundeskanzlerpl. (Cover DM10/ €5.15. Open M-Sa 8pm-3am.) Bonn has an active gay scene; **Boba's Bar,** Josephstr. 17, is one of Bonn's most popular gay bars. (Open M-Th 6pm-1am, F-Sa 6pm-3am.)

AACHEN
☎ 0241

Charlemagne made this the capital of his Frankish empire in the 8th century, and Aachen still maintains its historical treasures while becoming a thriving forum for up-and-coming European artists. The famous neo-Byzantine **Dom** (cathedral) is in the center of the city; Charlemagne's remains lie in the reliquary behind the altar. (Open M-Sa 11am-7pm, Su 12:30-7pm, except during services. Combination ticket for Dom and Schatzkammer DM15/€8, students DM9/€5.) Just around the corner is the **Schatzkammer,** Klosterpl. 2, a treasury of reliquaries containing John the Baptist's hair and ribs, nails and splinters from the cross, and Christ's scourging robe. A gold-plated silver bust of Charlemagne holds his skull, and a gigantic golden arm statue nearby holds his radius and ulna bones. (Open M 10am-1pm, Tu-W and F-Su 10am-6pm, Th 10am-9pm. DM5/€3, students DM3/€1.50.) The 🖼**Ludwigforum für Internationale Kunst,** Jülicherstr. 97-109, houses a rotating collection of cutting-edge art. (Open Tu and Th 10am-5pm, W and F 10am-8pm, Sa-Su 11am-5pm. Tours Su 11:30am and 3pm. DM6/€3, students DM3/€1.50.)

   Trains run to: Amsterdam (4hr., 1-2 per hr., DM102/€52); Brussels (2hr., 1 per hr., DM51/€26); and Cologne (1hr., 2-3 per hr., DM20/€11). The **tourist office,** on Friedrich-Wilhelm-Pl. in the Atrium Elisenbrunnen, runs tours and finds rooms for free. From the train station, cross the street and head up Bahnhofstr., turn left onto Theaterstr., which becomes Theaterpl., then right onto Kapuzinergraben, which becomes Friedrich-Wilhelm-Pl. (☎ 180 29 60. Open M-F 9am-6pm, Sa 9am-2pm.) The 🖼**Euroregionales Jugendgästehaus (HI),** Maria-Theresia-Allee 260, feels more like a hotel than a hostel. From the station, walk left on Lagerhausstr. until it intersects Karmeliterstr. and Mozartstr., then take bus #2 (dir. Preusswald) to Ronheide or bus #12 (dir. Diepenbendem) to Colynshof. (☎ 71 10 10. Breakfast and sheets included. Curfew 1am. Dorms DM39.50/€21.) **Hotel Marx,** Hubertusstr. 33-35, is a friendly hotel with a great location just outside the *Altstadt.* From the station, take a left on Lagerhausstr., turn right on Stephanstr., and left on Hubertusstr. (☎375 41. Breakfast included. Singles with bath DM85/€44; doubles DM110/€56, with bath DM140/€72.) Aachen's specialities include *Reisfladden* (a rice pudding cake) and *Printen* (spicy gingerbread biscuits). **Van den Daele,** Büchel 18-20, just off the *Markt,* serves these and other Aachen delicacies. (Open M-F 9am-7pm, Sa 9am-9pm, Su 11am-7pm.) For groceries, try **Plus supermarket,** Marienbongard 27, off Pontstr. (Open M-F 8am-8pm, Sa 8am-4pm.) **Postal code:** 52064.

DÜSSELDORF
☎ 0211

As Germany's modish fashion hub and multinational corporation base, the rich city of Düsseldorf crawls with German patricians and wanna-be aristocrats. Set on the majestic Rhine, Düsseldorf's **Altstadt** sponsors the best nightlife along the Rhine in authentic German style.

🚆 **TRANSPORTATION AND PRACTICAL INFORMATION. Trains** run to: Amsterdam (3hr., 1 per hr., DM55/€28); Berlin (4½hr., 1-2 per hr., DM170); Frankfurt (3hr., 3 per hr., DM79/€41); Hamburg (3½hr., 2 per hr., DM116/€59); Munich (6hr., 2-3 per hr., DM184/€94); and Paris (4½hr., 7 per day, DM140/€72). The S-Bahn is the cheapest way to get to Aachen and Cologne. On the **public transportation system,** single tickets cost DM2.10-12/€1-6, depending on distance traveled. The *Tagesticket* (DM11-32/€5-17) lets up to five people travel for 24hr. on any line. Düsseldorf's S-Bahn is integrated into the mammoth regional **VRR** (*Verkehrsverbund Rhein-Ruhr*) system, which connects most surrounding cities. For **schedule information,** call 582 28. To reach the **tourist office,** Konrad-Adenauer-Pl., walk up and to the right from the train station and look for the Immermanhof building. Books **rooms** (M-Sa 8am-8pm, Su 2-8pm) for DM5/€3. (☎17 20 20. Open M-F 8:30am-6pm, Sa 9am-12:30pm.) **Telenet-Center**, Fritz-Vomfelde-Str. 34, near the train station offers **Internet** access. (Open daily 9am-11pm. DM3/€1.50 per 30min.) The **post office**, Konrad-Adenauer-Pl., **40210** Düsseldorf, is a stone's throw to the right of the tourist office. (Open M-F 8am-6pm, Sa 9am-2pm.)

■■ ACCOMMODATIONS AND FOOD. It's not unusual for hotels in Düsseldorf to double their prices during a convention. Call at least a month ahead if possible. **Jugendgästehaus Düsseldorf (HI)**, Düsseldorfer Str. 1, is just over the Rheinkniebrücke from the *Altstadt*. Take U70 or U74-77 to Luegpl., then walk 500m down Kaiser-Wilhelm-Ring. (☎55 73 10. Reception 7am-1am. Curfew 1am, doors open every hr. 2-6am. DM42/€22, under 26 DM39.50/€20.) **Hotel Komet**, Bismarckstr. 93, is straight down Bismarckstr. from the train station and offers bright but snug rooms. (☎17 87 90. Singles with shower DM60/€31; doubles DM80/€41, with shower DM90/€46.) To reach **Hotel Diana**, Jahnstr. 31, head left from the station on Graf-Adolf-Str., left on Hüttenstr., and right on Jahnstr. (☎37 50 71. Breakfast included. Reception 24hr. Singles DM65-90/€34-46; doubles DM90-135/€46-69.) To camp at **Kleiner Torfbruch**, take any S-Bahn to Düsseldorf Geresheim, then bus #735 (dir. Stamesberg) to Seeweg. (☎899 20 38. DM7.50/€4 per person, DM10/€5 per tent.) For a cheap meal, the endless eateries in the *Altstadt* can't be beat; rows of pizzerias, *Döner* stands, and Chinese diners reach from Heinrich-Heine-Allee to the banks of the Rhine. **Otto Mess** is a popular **grocery** chain; the most convenient location is at the eastern corner of Karlspl. in the *Altstadt*. (Open M-F 8am-8pm, Sa 8am-4pm.) There's also a **supermarket** in the basement of **Galeria Kaufhof**, on Bahnhofstr. between Oststr. and Berlinerstr. (Open M-F 9:30am-8pm, Sa 9am-4pm.) **Im Füchschen**, Ratingerstr. 28, is a local favorite for all the local delicacies, including *Blutwurst* (blood sausage), Mainz hand cheese, and delicious *Füchsenbier*. (Open daily 11am-1am, W and Sa until 2am.) **Marché**, Königsallee 60, in the Kö-Galerie mall, is one of the few places to eat on the Kö that won't completely empty your wallet. (Entrees from DM7/€4. Open M-Th and Su 9am-9pm, F-Sa 9am-10pm.)

■ SIGHTS. The glitzy ■**Königsallee** (the **"Kö"**), just outside the *Altstadt*, embodies the vitality and glamour of wealthy Düsseldorf. Midway up is the awesome **Kö-Galerie**, a marble-and-copper highbrow shopping mall where items start at DM200/€102 and even the mannequins have attitude. *(10min. down Graf-Adolf-Str. from the train station.)* The Baroque **Schloß Benrath** in the suburbs of Düsseldorf was originally built as a pleasure palace and hunting grounds for Elector Karl Theodor. Strategically placed mirrors and false exterior windows make the castle appear larger than it is, but the enormous French gardens temper the effect. *(S6 (dir. Köln) to Benrath. Open Tu-Su 10am-5pm. Tours every 30min. DM7/€4, students DM3.50/€1.75.)* At the upper end of the Kö, the **Hofgarten park** is the oldest public park in Germany. At the east end, the 18th-century **Schloß Jägerhof** houses the **Goethemuseum.** *(Jakobistr. 2. Streetcar #707 or bus #752 to Schloß Jägerhof. Open Tu-F and Su 11am-5pm, Sa 1-5pm. DM4/€2, students and children DM2/€1.)* The **Kunstsammlung Nordrhein-Westfalen,** the black glass edifice west of the Hofgarten, houses works by Matisse, Picasso, Surrealists, Expressionists, and hometown boy Paul Klee, as well as changing exhibits of modern art and film. *(Grabbepl. 5. U70, 75, 76, 78, 79 to Heinrich-Heine-Allee. Walk north 2 blocks, or take bus #725 to Grabbepl. Open Tu-Th and Sa-Su 10am-6pm, F 10am-8pm. DM5/€3, students DM3/€1.50. Special exhibits DM12/€6, students DM8/€4.)*

■■ ENTERTAINMENT AND NIGHTLIFE. Folklore says that Düsseldorf's 500 pubs make up *die längste Theke der Welt* (the longest bar in the world). Pubs in the Altstadt are standing-room-only by 6pm, and by nightfall it's nearly impossible to see where one pub ends and the next begins. **Bolkerstraße** is jam-packed nightly with street performers. *Prinz* (DM5/€3) gives tips on happening scenes; it's often given out free at the youth hostel. *Facolte* (DM4/€2), a gay and lesbian nightlife magazine, is available at most newsstands. **Pam-Pam**, Bolkerstr 34, plays house, rock, pop, and plenty of American music. (No cover. Open F-Sa 10pm-dawn.) **La Rocca,** Grünstr. 8, just off the Kö, is a showcase for clothing bought during the day—this is not the place to dress down. (Cover DM8/€4. Open Th-Sa from 10pm-5am.) **Café Rosa,** Oberbilker Allee 310, is the socio-cultural mecca of Düsseldorf's gay community and offers self-defense classes and killer parties. (F women only; Tu men only. Open Tu-Sa 8pm-1am, later on weekends.)

FRANKFURT AM MAIN ☎069

Frankfurt made its first appearance when Charlemagne put the "Ford of the Franks" on the map in 794. Today, its integral economic role as home to the central bank of the European Union lends it a glitzy vitality—international offices, shiny skyscrapers, and expensive cars lie at every intersection. The city government spends more on cultural attractions and tourism than any other German city. If all this isn't enough to make you visit, the likelihood of your passing through Frankfurt's highly trafficked train station or airport probably is.

◩ TRANSPORTATION

Flights: The airport, **Flughafen Rhein-Main** (☎ 69 00), is connected to the Hauptbahnhof by S14 and S15 (every 15min; buy tickets for DM6.10/€3.15 from the green machines marked *Fahrkarten* before boarding).

Trains: Frequent trains leave the **Hauptbahnhof** to: **Amsterdam** (5hr.; every 2hr.; DM120/€61.35, under 26 DM126.50/€64.70); **Berlin** (5-6hr.; 2 per hr.; DM207/€105.85, under 26 DM166/€84.90); **Cologne** (2½hr.; 2 per hr.; DM76/€38.90, under 26 DM61/€31.20); **Hamburg** (6hr.; 2 per hr.; DM191/€97.70, under 26 DM153/€78.25); **Munich** (3½-4½hr.; 2 per hr.; DM212/€108.40, under 26 DM118/€60.35); **Paris** (6-8hr.; every 2 hr.; DM140/€71.60, under 26 DM115/€58.70); **Rome** (15hr.; every hr.; DM279/€142.70, under 26 DM228/€116.60). Call ☎(0180) 599 66 33 for schedules, reservations, and information.

Public Transportation: Runs until about 1am. Refer to the subway **map** in the back of this guide. Single-ride tickets (DM2.10/€1.10, rush hour DM2.90/€1.50) are valid for 1hr. in one direction, transfers permitted. **Eurail** passes valid only on S-Bahn. The **Tageskarte** (day pass, valid until midnight of the day of purchase) provides unlimited transportation on the S-Bahn, U-Bahn, streetcars, and buses; buy from machines in any station (DM8.50/€4.35).

◪◨ ORIENTATION AND PRACTICAL INFORMATION

The train station lies at the end of Frankfurt's red light district; from the station, the **Altstadt** is a 20min. walk down Kaiserstr. or Münchener Str. To the north, the commercial heart of Frankfurt lies along **Zeil**. Cafes, stores, and services cluster in **Bockenheim** (U6 or U7 to Bockenheimer Warte). Across the Main, **Sachsenhausen** draws pub-crawlers and museum-goers (U1, U2, or U3 to Schweizer Pl.).

Tourist Office: (☎ 21 23 88 00; www.frankfurt-tourismus.de), in the Hauptbahnhof. Open M-F 8am-9pm, Sa-Su and holidays 9am-6pm. Sells the **Frankfurt Card** (1-day DM12/€6.15, 2-day DM19/€9.75), which allows unlimited travel on all trains and buses and gives 50% off admission to many museums and attractions .

Laundromat: Schnell & Sauber, Wallstr. 8, near the hostel in Sachsenhausen. Wash DM6/€3.10, dry DM1/€0.55 per 15min. Open daily 6am-11pm.

Emergency: Police, ☎ 110. **Fire** and **ambulance,** ☎ 112.

Disabled travelers: Frankfurt Forum, Römerberg 32 (☎ 21 24 00 00). Publishes a guide to handicapped-accessible locations in Frankfurt. Ask for Mr. Schmidt. Open M and W 10am-4:30pm, Tu 10am-6pm, and Th-F 10am-2pm.

Pharmacy: (☎ 23 30 47), in the Einkaufs passage of the train station. Open M-F 6:30am-9pm, Sa 8am-9pm, Su and holidays 9am-8pm. Emergencies ☎ 192 92.

GERMANY

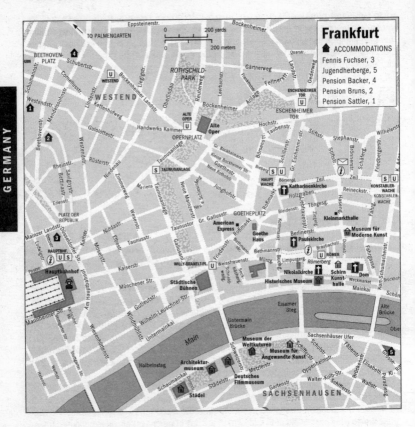

Frankfurt

🏠 ACCOMMODATIONS
Fennis Fuchser, 3
Jugendherberge, 5
Pension Backer, 4
Pension Bruns, 2
Pension Sattler, 1

Internet Access: Sky-Surfer Internet Café, Elisabethstr. 2-4 (☎60 60 55 38), near the hostel. DM2/€1.10 per 15min. Open M-Su 10pm-2am.

Post Office: Main branch, Zeil 90 (☎13 81 26 21; fax 13 81 26 24), inside the *Hertie* department store. U- or S-Bahn: Hauptwache. Open M-F 9:30am-8pm, Sa 9am-4pm. Address mail to be held: Postlagernde Briefe für First Name SURNAME, Hauptpostamt, 60313 Frankfurt, Germany.

🏠 ACCOMMODATIONS

Pension Bruns, Mendelssohnstr. 42, 2nd fl. (☎74 88 96). U6 (dir.: Heerstr.) or U7 (dir.: Hausen) to Westend and take the Siesmayerstr. exit. Once up the escalator, exit left under the sign "Mendelssohn Str.," then walk 1 block and turn left onto Mendelsohnstr. Ring the bell. Breakfast (in bed!) included. Showers DM2/€1.10. Call ahead. Doubles DM90-100/€46-€51.15; triples DM120/€61.40; quads DM160/€81.80.

Jugendherberge (HI), Deutschherrnufer 12 (☎610 01 50). Take bus #46 from the main train station (DM2.40/€1.25, rush hour DM2.90/€1.50) to Frankensteiner Pl. Turn left along the river; the hostel sits at the end of the block. Special day passes for Frankfurt's public transit (DM6.50/€3.35). Unlimited breakfast buffet (7-9am). Reception 24hr. Check-in noon. Check-out 9:30am. No lockout. Curfew 2am. Reservations by phone recommended. Rooms begin at DM33/€16.90, 19 and under DM26/€13.30. Singles (DM55/€28.15) and doubles (DM90/€46) are *rarely* available.

Hotel an der Galluswarte, Hufnagelstr. 4 (☎ 73 39 93). S3 (dir. Hohenmark), S4 (dir. Kronberg), S5 (dir. Friedrichsdorf), or S6 (dir. Galluswarte) to Galluswarte. Exit under the sign marked "Mainzer Landstr.," turn right, walk 1 block, and turn right onto Hufnagelstr. All rooms have TV, shower, and phone. Breakfast included. *Let's Go* discount: singles DM80/€40.90; doubles DM100/€51.15.

🗋 FOOD

Regional specialties include Goethe's favorite, *Handkäse mit Musik* (cheese curd with raw onions); *grüne Sosse* (a green sauce served over boiled eggs or potatoes); and *Ebbelwei* (apple wine, *Äpfelwein* up north). The cheapest meals surround the university in **Bockenheim** and nearby parts of Westend, and many of the pubs in **Sachsenhausen** serve food at a decent price. (For directions, see **Orientation,** above.) Just a few blocks from the youth hostel is a fully stocked **HL Markt,** Dreieichstr. 56 (open M-F 8am-8pm, Sa 8am-4pm) while a **Tengelmann,** Münchener Str. 37, is close to the Hauptbahnhof (open M-F 8:30am-7:30pm, Su 8am-2pm). **Kleinmarkthalle,** on Haseng. between Berliner Str. and Töngesg., is a three-story warehouse with bakeries, butchers, fruit and vegetable stands, and more. Cutthroat competition between the many vendors pushes prices way down. (Open M-F 7:30am-6pm, Sa 7:30am-4pm.)

👁 SIGHTS

Much of Frankfurt's historic splendor lives on only in memories and in reconstructed monuments, since Allied bombing left everything but the cathedral completely destroyed. At the center of the Altstadt is **Römerberg Square** (U-Bahn: Römer), home to half-timbered architecture and a medieval fountain of Justice that once spouted wine. At the west end of the Römerberg, the gables of **Römer** have marked the site of Frankfurt's city hall since 1405; upstairs, the **Kaisersaal,** a former imperial banquet hall, is adorned with portraits of the 52 German emperors from Charlemagne to Franz II. (Open daily 10am-1pm and 2-5pm. DM3/€1.55, students DM1/€0.55.) Next to the Römerberg stands the only building that survived the bombings, the red sandstone **Dom,** which contains several splendidly elaborate altarpieces. A new viewing tower is scheduled to open sometime this year. (Open daily 9am-noon and 2-6pm.) Inside, the **Dom Museum** contains intricate chalices and the venerated robes of the imperial electors. (Open Tu-F 10am-5pm, Sa-Su 11am-5pm. DM3/€1.55, students DM1/€0.55.) A few blocks away is the **Museum für Moderne Kunst,** a triangular building (dubbed "the slice of cake") displaying an array of modern art. (Domstr. 10. ☎21 23 04 47. Open Tu and Th-Su 10am-5pm, W 10am-8pm. DM10/€5.15, students DM5/€2.60; W free.) The ▇**Städel,** Schaumainkai 63, has important paintings from nearly every period in the western tradition. (☎605 09 80. Open Tu and Th-Su 10am-5pm, W 10am-8pm. DM10/€5.15, students DM8/€4.10.) Tired of churches and museums? Take refuge in the **Palmengarten,** in the northwest part of town. (Siesmayerstr. 61-63. ☎21 23 39 39. U6 or U7 to Bockenheimer Warte. Open daily Mar.-Oct. 9am-6pm; Nov.-Jan. 9am-4pm; Feb. 9am-5pm. DM10/€5.15, students DM4.50/€2.30.) For animal lovers, the **Zoo** houses over 650 species; visit at feeding time (around 11) for maximum entertainment value. (Alfred-Brehm-Platz 16. ☎21 23 37 35. U6 or U7 to Zoo. Open mid-Mar. to Sept. M-F 9am-7pm, Sa-Su 8am-7pm; Oct. to mid-Mar. daily 9am-5pm. DM11/€5.65, students DM5/€2.60; show U-Bahn ticket for a discount.)

🎵 🎭 ENTERTAINMENT AND NIGHTLIFE

Frankfurt's ballet, theater, and opera are first-rate. The **Alte Oper,** Opernpl. (☎ 134 04 00; U6 or U7 to Alte Oper), offers a full range of classical music., while the **Städtische Bühne,** Untermainanlage 11 (☎21 23 71 33; U1,U2, U3, or U4 to Willy-Brandt-Pl.), hosts ballets and operas. Shows and schedules are listed in

Fritz and *Strandgut* (free) and the *Journal Frankfurt* (DM3.30/€1.70). For information on tickets at almost any venue, call **Frankfurt Ticket** (☎ 134 04 00).

For a night out drinking, head to the **Alt-Sachsenhausen** district between Brücken-str. and Dreieichstr., home to a huge number of rowdy pubs and taverns. The complex of cobblestoned streets centering on **Grosse** and **Kleine Ritterg.** teems with cafes, bars, restaurants, and Irish pubs. Frankfurt also has a number of thriving discos and prominent techno DJs, mostly in the commercial district between **Zeil** and **Bleichstr.** Wear something dressier than jeans if you plan to get past the picky bouncers. **U60311**, Roßmarkt, on the corner of Goetheplatz, is housed in an old subway station and features the best DJs in Frankfurt. (Cover DM15-30/€7.70-15.35. Open M-F 10pm-10am, Sa-Su 10pm-6am.) **Blue Angel**, Brönnerstr. 17, is a Frankfurt institution and one of the liveliest gay men's clubs around. Ring the bell to be let in. (Cover DM11/€5.65. Open daily 11pm-4am.)

SOUTHWEST GERMANY

The valleys and castles along the Rhine and Mosel valleys feast for the eyes, while a rich agricultural tradition keeps produce in abundance, and dozens of vineyards provide delights for the palate. Just a bit farther south, the bucolic, traditional hinterlands of the Black Forest contrast with the region's modern industrial cities.

RHINE VALLEY (RHEINTAL)

The Rhine River runs from Switzerland to the North Sea, but in the popular imagination it exists only in the 80km Rhine Valley—a region prominent in historical legends, sailors' nightmares, and poets' dreams. The river flows north from **Mainz** (easily accessible from Frankfurt) through **Bacharach** and **Koblenz** to **Bonn.**

⊏ TRANSPORTATION. Two different **train** lines (one on each bank) traverse the Rheintal; the line on the west bank stays closer to the water and provides superior views. If you're willing to put up with lots of tourists, **boats** are probably the best way to see the sights; the **Köln-Düsseldorfer (KD) Line** covers the Mainz-Koblenz stretch three times per day in summer.

MAINZ. The colossal sandstone **Martinsdom** stands as a memorial to former ecclesiastic power; the extravagant tombstones of the archbishops of Mainz line the walls. (Open Apr.-Sept. M-F 9am-6:30pm, Sa 9am-4pm, Su 12:45-3pm and 4-6:30pm; Oct.-Mar. M-F 9am-5pm, Sa 9am-4pm, Su 12:45-3pm and 4-5pm. Free.) Johannes Gutenberg, the father of movable type, is immortalized at the **Gutenberg-Museum,** which contains several Gutenberg Bibles and a replica of his original press. (Liebfrauenpl. 5, across from the Dom. Open Tu-Su, 10am-5pm. DM6/€3.10, students DM3/€1.55.) The Gothic **Stephanskirche**, south of the Dom, hides stunning stained-glass windows created by Russian artist-in-exile Marc Chagall. (From the Dom, take Ludwigstr. until it ends at Schillerpl. and follow Gaustr. up the hill. Open daily 10am-noon and 2-5pm.)

Köln-Düsseldorf ferries (☎23 28 00) depart from the wharves on the other side of the Rathaus. The **tourist office** arranges **tours** (2hr, daily 2pm; Jul.-Aug. also Sa 10am; DM10/€5.15) and gives free maps. (☎28 62 10. Open M-F 9am-6pm, Sa 9am-4pm.) To reach the **Jugendgästehaus (HI)**, Otto-Brunfels-Schneise 4 , take bus #22, 62, 63, or 92 to Jugendherberge/Viktorstift and follow the signs. (☎853 32. Breakfast included. Reception 7am-midnight. Dorms DM30/€15.45; doubles DM40/€20.60. Near the Dom, **Central Café** serves a range of German and American foods. (Open M-Th and Su 10am-1am midnight, F-Sa 10am-1am.) For groceries, try **Supermarkt 2000**, Am Brand 41, under the Sinn-Leffers department store (open M-F 9:30am-8pm, Sa 9am-4pm). ☎**06131.**

BACHARACH. Bacharach lives up to its name ("Altar of Bacchus") with many *Weinkeller* and *Weinstuben* (wine cellars and pubs). **Die Weinstube**, Oberstr. 63, is a family-owned business that makes its own wine on the premises. Nearby is the

14th-century **Wernerkapelle,** the remains of a red sandstone chapel that took 140 years to build but only a few hours to destroy in the Palatinate War of Succession in 1689. The **tourist office,** Oberstr. 45, and the *Rathaus* share a building at one end of the town center. (☎91 93 03. Open Apr.-Oct. M-F 9am-5pm, Sa 10am-4pm; Nov.-Mar. M-F 9am-1pm and 1:30-5pm, Sa 10am-1pm.) Hostels get no better than the unbelievable ⬛**Jugendherberge Stahleck (HI),** a gorgeous 12th-century castle that provides an unbeatable panoramic view of the Rhine Valley. The steep 20min. hike to the hostel is worth every step. Call ahead; they're usually full by 6pm. Make a right out of the station pathway, turn left at the Peterskirche and take any of the marked paths leading up the hill. (☎12 66. Breakfast included. Curfew 10pm. DM25.90/€13.25, doubles DM31.90/€16.35.) At ⬛**Café Restaurant Rusticana,** Oberstr. 40, a lovely German couple serves up three-course meals (DM12-20/€6.15-10.25) and lively conversation. (Open M-F 9am-10pm.) ☎**06743.**

KOBLENZ. Koblenz has long been a strategic hotspot; in the 2000 years since its birth, the city has hosted every empire seeking to conquer Europe. Before reunification, the city served as a large munitions dump, but now the only pyrotechnics are when the **Rhein in Flammen fireworks festival** hits the town in mid-August. The city centers around the **Deutsches Eck** (German Corner), a peninsula at the confluence of the Rhine and Mosel that purportedly witnessed the birth of the German nation in 1216. The **Mahnmal der Deutschen Einheit** (Monument to German Unity) to the right is a tribute to Kaiser Wilhelm I. The ⬛**Museum Ludwig im Deutschherrenhaus,** behind the Mahnmal, features contemporary French art. (Danziger Freiheit 1. ☎30 40 40. Open Tu-Sa 10:30am-5pm, Su 11am-6pm. DM5/€2.60, students DM3/€1.55.) The stained glass windows of the **Baroque Liebfrauenkirche** document the role of women in the Passion and Resurrection of Christ. (Open M-Sa 8am-6pm, Su 9am-12:30pm and 6-8pm; in summer Su 9am-8pm. Free.) Koblenz's most mischievous monument lurks outside the **Jesuitenkirche** on the Marktplatz; the **Schängelbrunnen,** a statue of a boy that spits water on passersby, drives kids into frenzied glee. Head across the river to the **Festung Ehrenbreitstein,** a fortress at the highest point in the city. Today, it's a youth hostel. (Non-hostel guests DM2/€1.05; students DM1/€0.55. Tours DM4/€2.05.)

Trains run to: Bonn (30min., 4 per hr, DM15/€7.70); Frankfurt (2hr., 2 per hr., DM36/€18.45); Cologne (1hr., 3-4 per hr., DM25/€12.80); Mainz (1hr., 3 per hr., DM25/€12.80); and Trier (2hr., 1 per hr., DM30/€15.35). Take a sharp left from the station for the **tourist office,** Löhrstr. 141. (☎313 04; www.koblenz.de. Open M-F 9am-8pm, Sa-Su 10am-8pm.) **Jugendherberge Koblenz (HI),** within the fortress, offers breathtaking views of the Rhine and Mosel. Take bus #9 or 10 from the stop on Löhrstr. (just left of the train station) to Charlottenstr. Then take the chairlift up (operates Mar.-Sept. daily 9am-5:50pm; DM5/€2.60, round-trip DM7/€3.60), or continue along the Rhine side of the mountain on the main road, following the DJH signs, and take the footpath up. (☎737 37. Breakfast included. Reception 7:30am-11:30pm. Curfew 11:30pm. DM28/€14.35; doubles DM80/€40.90.) **Ferries** (DM0.60/€0.35) cross the Mosel to **Campingplatz Rhein-Mosel,** Am Neuendorfer Eck. (☎827 19. Reception 8am-noon and 2-8pm. Open Apr.-Oct. 15. DM6.50/€3.35 per person, DM5/€2.60 per tent.) **Marktstübchen,** Am Markt 220, at the bottom of the hill from the hostel, serves authentic German food at budget prices. (Open M-Tu, Th, and Su 11am-midnight, W 11am-2pm, F 4pm-1am, Sa 11am-1am.) **Plus supermarket** is at Roonstr. 49-51. (Open M-F 8:30am-7pm and Sa 8am-2pm.) ☎**0261.**

TRIER

☎**0651**

The oldest town in Germany, Trier was founded by the Romans and reached its heyday in the 4th century as the capital of the Western Roman Empire and a center for Christianity in Europe. A one-day **combination ticket** provides access to all the city's Roman monuments. (Palm Sunday-Sept. DM9/€4.60, students DM4.50/€2.30; Oct.-Nov. and Jan.-Palm Sunday DM4.50/€2.30; Dec. DM4/€2.05.) The most impressive is the massive 2nd-century **Porta Nigra** (Black Gate), which got its name from the centuries of grime that turned its sandstone face from light yellow to gray. (Open Palm Sunday-Sept. daily 9am-6pm; Oct.-Nov. and Jan.-Palm Sunday 9am-5pm; Dec. 10am-4pm. DM4/€2.05, students DM2/€1.05.) The nearby **Dom** (cathedral) shelters the tombs of archbishops and what is reputedly the Tunica Christi (Holy Robe of Christ). (Open Apr.-Oct daily 6:30am-6pm; Nov.-Mar. 6:30am-5:30pm. Free.) The enormous **Basilika** was originally the location of Emperor Constantine's throne room. (Open M-Sa 9am-6pm, Su 11:30am-6pm. Free.) Near the southeast corner of the city walls, the underground passages of the 4th-century **Kaiserthermen** (Emperor's baths) create a perfect place to play hide-and-seek. (Open Apr.-Sept. 9am-6pm; Oct.-Mar. 9am-5pm. DM4/€2.05, students DM3/€1.55.) A 10min. walk uphill along Olewiger Str. brings you to the **amphitheater;** it's now a peaceful park. (Admission and times same as Porta Nigra but closed Dec.) The **Karl-Marx-Haus,** Brückenstr. 10, where young Karl grew up, is a must-see for indefatigable Marxists. (Open Apr.-Oct. M 1-6pm, Tu-Su 10am-6pm; Nov.-Mar. M 2-5pm, Tu-Su 10am-1pm and 2-5pm. DM3/€1.55, students DM2/€1.05.)

Trains go to Koblenz (1¾hr., 2 per hr., DM30/€15.40) and Luxembourg (45min., 1 per hr., DM15/€7.70). From the station, walk down Theodor-Haus-Allee or Christophstr. to reach the **tourist office,** under the shadow of the Porta Nigra. (☎ 97 80 80; www.trier.de. Open M-Sa 9am-6:30pm, Su 9am-3:30pm. English tours daily 1:30pm, DM10/€5.15.) The staff at nearby **Vinothek,** Margaritengässchen 2a, can give information on **wine tasting** in the region. (☎ 978 08 34. Open daily 10am-7pm.) To reach **Hotel Haus Runne,** Engelstr. 35, follow Theodor-Heuss-Allee from the station and turn right on Engelstr. after the Porta Nigra. (☎ 289 22. Breakfast included. Singles DM45/€23; doubles DM90/€46; quads DM160/€81.80.) ☑**Astarix,** Karl-Marx-Str. 11, serves excellent food at unbelievable prices. It's squeezed into a passageway next to Miss Marple's; if you get to a big white fence on the left, you've gone too far. (Open M-Th 11:30am-1am, F-Sa 11:30am-2am, Su 6pm-1am.) There's a **Plus supermarket** at Brotstr. 54. (Open M-F 8:30am-7pm, Sa 8:30am-4pm.)

HEIDELBERG   ☎ 06221

This sunlight-coated town by the Neckar and its crumbling castle lured writers and artists—including Twain, Goethe, and Hugo—and today, roughly 32,000 tourists are drawn in *each* summer day. However, the incessant buzz of mass tourism is worth enduring to experience beautiful Heidelberg and its lively nightlife.

▐ TRANSPORTATION

Trains run to **Stuttgart** (40min., 1 per hr., DM31/€15.85) and **Frankfurt** (40min., 2 per hr., DM23.40/€12); other trains run regularly to towns in the Neckar Valley. On Heidelberg's **public transportation** system, **single-ride tickets** cost DM3.90/€2; **day passes** (DM10.50/€5.40) are available from the tourist office. *Let's Go* does not recommend **hitchhiking,** but hitchers wait at the western end of Bergheimerstr. The **Mitfahrzentrale,** Bergheimerstr. 125 (☎246 46), matches riders and drivers to: Cologne (DM28/€14.35); Hamburg (DM54/€27.65); and Paris (DM51/€26). (Open M-F 9am-5pm; Apr.-Oct. also Sa 9am-noon.)

▐▐ ORIENTATION AND PRACTICAL INFORMATION

Most of Heidelberg's attractions are in the eastern part of the city, along the south bank of the Neckar. From the train station, take any bus or streetcar to Bismarckpl., then walk east down **Hauptstraße,** the city's spine, to the **Altstadt.** The **tourist office,** in front of the station, offers tours (DM22/€11.25) Th-Su and books rooms for an 8% deposit and a DM5/€2.60 fee. (☎ 13 88 121. Open M-Sa 9am-7pm; Apr.-Oct. also Su 10am-6pm.) They also sell the 2-day **Heidelberg Card,** which includes unlimited public transit and admission to most sights (DM19.80/€10.15). In an **emergency,** call ☎110; for **fire** or an **ambulance,** call ☎ 112. Check your email at **Internet Cafe,** inside Brodl on Hauptstr. 90, near Bismarckpl. (Open M-F 9:30am-7:30pm, Sa 9:30am-4pm. DM6/€3.10 per 30min.) The **post office,** Sofienstr. 8-10, **69155** Heidelberg, is off Bismarckpl. (Open daily 9am-6:30pm.)

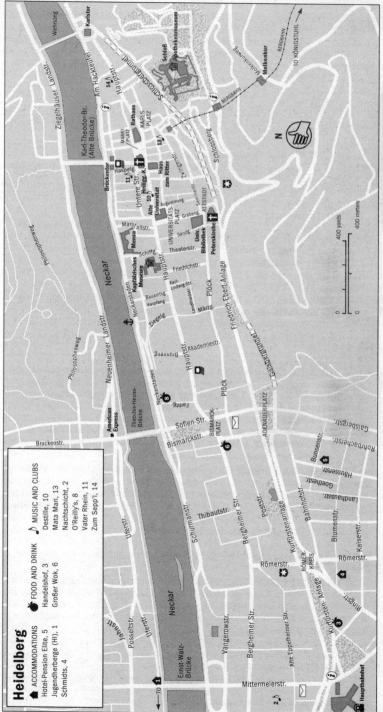

GERMANY

Heidelberg

ACCOMMODATIONS
Hotel-Pension Elite, 5
Jugendherberge (HI), 1
Schmidts, 4

🍴 **FOOD AND DRINK**
Handelshof, 3
Großer Wok, 6

🎵 **MUSIC AND CLUBS**
Destille, 10
Mata Mari, 13
Nachtschicht, 2
O'Reilly's, 8
Vater Rhein, 11
Zum Sepp'l, 14

400 meters
400 yards

TO KÖNIGSTUHL

◪ ◙ ACCOMMODATIONS AND FOOD

In summer, reserve ahead or arrive early in the day to spare yourself a headache. To reach the **Jugendherberge (HI),** Tiergartenstr. 5, take bus #33 (dir. Zoo-Sportzentrum) to Jugendherberge. Crowded and noisy, but its small disco can be fun. Some claim that theft is a common problem at this hostel. (☎41 20 66; fax 40 25 59. Sheets DM5.50/€2.85. Reception until 11:30pm. Lockout 9am-1pm. Curfew 11:30pm; stragglers admitted 1am. Reserve at least a week ahead. **HI members only.** Dorms DM28/ €14.35, under 26 DM24/€12.30.) For **Schmidts,** Blumenstr. 54, follow Kurfürsten Anlage from the station to Romer Kreis, cut back right on Ringstr., and turn left on Blumenstr. (☎272 96. Breakfast included. Singles DM70/€35.80, with shower DM120/€61.40.) At **Hotel-Pension Elite,** Bunsenstr. 15, all rooms have high ceilings, bath, and TV. From Bismarckpl., follow Rohrbacher Str. away from the river and turn right on Bunsenstr; from the train station, take streetcar #1 to Poststr.; the hotel is on the 2nd street behind the Holiday Inn. (☎257 34. Breakfast included. *Let's Go* discounted rates: singles DM75/€38.35; doubles DM100/€51.15.)

Handelshof supermarket, Kurfürsten-Anlage 60, is 200m in front of the station on the right. (Open M-F 7:30am-8pm, Sa 7:30am-4pm). There's also a **fruit market** on Marktpl. on Wednesdays and Saturdays. The **Mensa** (university cafeteria), in the *Marstall* on Marstallstr., serves cheap meals (DM7/€3.60, with student ID DM4/ €2.05; DM3/€1.55 plate deposit). From the Alte Brücke, with your back to the old city, turn left along the river; it's the red fortress on the left. (Lunch M-F 11:30am-2pm, dinner M-Sa 5pm-10pm.) **Großer Wok,** Bergheimer Str. 7, near Bismarckpl., serves Chinese food. (Open M-Sa 11am-10pm, Su 1pm-10pm.) **Thanner,** Bergheimerstr. 71, has an eclectic menu and the only *Biergarten* in Heidelberg allowed to play music. (Open daily 9am-2am, Su until 3am. Garden open until 11pm.)

◉ SIGHTS

▨ **HEIDELBERGER SCHLOß.** Over a period of almost 400 years, the castle's residents commissioned their own distinctive additions, resulting in the conglomeration of styles you see today. The castle **wine cellar** holds the **Großer Faß,** the largest wine barrel ever made, holding 221,726L. *(Grounds open daily 8am-5:30pm. DM3/€1.55, students DM1.50/€0.80. English tours of castle every hr. 11:15am-4:15pm. DM4/€2.05, students DM2/€1.05.)* The *Schloß* is accessible by the **Bergbahn,** the world's oldest cable car. *(Take bus #11 (dir. Köpfel) or 33 (dir. Karlstor). Trams leave the parking lot next to the bus stop every 10min. 9am-7:45pm, return DM5.80/€3.)*

MARKTPLATZ AND UNIVERSITÄT. The Altstadt's center is the cobblestoned **Marktplatz,** where accused witches and heretics were burned at the stake in the 15th century. Heidelberg's oldest structures border the square: the 14th-century **Heiliggeistkirche** (Church of the Holy Spirit) and the 16th-century **Haus Zum Ritter,** opposite the church. *(Church open M-Sa 11am-5pm, Su 1-5pm. Free. Church tower DM0.50.)* Five blocks down Hauptstr. is Germany's oldest and perhaps most prestigious university, established in 1368. More than 20 Nobel laureates have called the university home, and it was here that sociology became a legitimate academic subject under the leadership of Max Weber.

KURPFÄLZISCHES MUSEUM. Artifacts include the jawbone of an unfortunate *homo Heidelbergensis,* one of the earliest humans ever discovered; works of art by Dürer; and an awesome archaeology exhibit. *(Hauptstr. 97. Open Tu and Th-Su 10am-5pm, W 10am-9pm. DM5/€2.60, students DM3/€1.55; Su DM3/€1.55, students DM2/€1.05.)*

PHILOSOPHENWEG. A high path opposite the Neckar from the Altstadt, the Philosophenweg (Philosopher's Way) offers the best views of the city as it traverses the Heiligenberg (Holy Mountain). *(Take streetcar #1 or 3 to Tiefburg, a castle in neighboring Handschuhsheim, to begin the hike upwards, or use the footpath 10m west of the Karl-Theodor-Brücke.)* Along the way are the ruins of the 9th-century **St. Michael Basilika,** the 13th-century **Stefanskloster,** and an **amphitheater** built under Hitler in 1934 on the site of an ancient Celtic gathering place.

⚑ NIGHTLIFE

The **Marktplatz** is the hub of the city's action; most popular nightspots fan out from here. **Unter Straße,** on the Neckar side of the Heiliggeistkirche, boasts the most prolific—and often congested—conglomeration of bars in the city. **Hauptstraße** also harbors a fair number of venues. **VaterRhein,** Untere Neckarstr. 20-22, close to the river and midway between Theodor-Heuss-Brücke and the Alte Brücke, is popular with college students. (Open daily 8pm-3am.) **O'Reilly's,** on the corner of Brückenkopfstr. and Uferstr., was named Guinness's "Best Irish Pub in Germany" in 1999. Cross Theodor-Heuss-Brücke, turn right, and follow the noise. (Open M-Th 5pm-2am, F 5pm-3am, Sa noon-3am, Su noon-2am.) **Mata Hari,** on Zwingerstr. near Oberbadg., is a cramped but mellow gay and lesbian bar. (Tu men only. Beer DM6. Open Tu-Su 9pm-3am.)

STUTTGART ☎ 0711

Forget about *lederhosen*—Porsche, Daimler-Benz, and a host of other corporate thoroughbreds keep Stuttgart speeding along in the fast lane. After almost complete destruction in World War II, Stuttgart was rebuilt in a thoroughly modern, functional, and uninspiring style, but the surrounding forested hills provide welcome tranquility to the busy capital of Baden-Württemberg.

🖪⚐ TRANSPORTATION AND PRACTICAL INFORMATION. Stuttgart has direct **trains** to most major German cities, including: Berlin (5½-12hr., 2 per hr., DM209-256/€107-131); Frankfurt (1½-4½hr., 2 per hr., DM40-88/€20.45-45); and Munich (2½-3½hr., 2-3 per hr., DM40-73/€20.45-37.35). Call 0180 599 66 33 for 24hr. schedule information. Tourist office ⚑**tips 'n' trips,** Lautenschlagerstr. 20, has email access (DM3.50/€1.80 per 30min., students DM2.50/€1.30) and resources on the Stuttgart scene. (☎222 27 30. Open M-F noon-7pm, Sa 10am-2pm.) The **post office** is in the station. (Open M-F 8am-7pm, Sa 8:30am-12:30pm.) **Postal code:** 70173.

🖪⚐ ACCOMMODATIONS AND FOOD. To reach the **Jugendherberge Stuttgart (HI),** Haußmannstr. 27, take streetcar #15 (dir. Heumaden) to Eugenspl. and go downhill on Kernerstr.; the entrance is up the stairs with the red handrail. (☎24 15 83; fax 236 10 41; jh-stuttgart@t-online.de. Breakfast included. Sheets DM6/€3.10. Reception 1pm-1am. Lockout 9:30am-1pm. Curfew 1am, F-Sa 2am. Reserve at least a week ahead by mail, email, or fax. Dorms DM30/€15.35, under 26 DM25/€12.80.) **Hotel Stern,** Neckarstr. 215a, is kept impeccably clean by the attentive staff. Take U1, U14, or streetcar #2 to Metzstr. (☎269 69 41. Breakfast included. Singles DM65/€33.15, with bath DM85/43.55; doubles DM110/€55, DM130/€66.30; triples with bath DM150/€76.50. AmEx/MC/V.) **Iden,** Eberhardstr. 1, serves good vegetarian fare by weight. Take the U-Bahn to Rathaus. (Open M-F 11am-9pm, Sa 10:30am-5pm.) For fruits, vegetables, and other staples, head to **Markthalle,** on Sporerstr. (M-F 7am-6:30pm, Sa 7am-4pm.)

⚐ SIGHTS. The **Schloßgarten,** Stuttgart's principal park, is crammed with fountains and beautiful flower gardens. At the north end is the **Wilhelma,** a large zoological and botanical garden. Take U14 to Wilhelma. (☎540 20. Open daily Mar. and Oct. 8:15am-5pm; Nov.-Feb. 8:15am-4pm; May-Aug. 8:15am-6pm; Apr. and Sept. 8:15am-5:30pm. DM16/€8.20, students DM8/€4.10; after 4pm and Nov.-Feb. DM10/€5.15, DM5/€2.60.) The Schloßgarten runs to Schloßpl., where stodgy bureaucrats gather in the elegant Baroque **Neues Schloß.** The 16th-century **Altes Schloß,** across the street on Schillerpl., contains the ⚑**Württembergisches Landesmuseum,** which details the Swabian region with excellent exhibits on local archaeology. (Open Tu 10am-1pm, W-Su 10am-5pm. DM5/€2.60, students DM3/€1.55.) The superb ⚑**Staatsgallerie Stuttgart,** Konrad-Adenauer-Str. 30-32, houses an excellent collection of modern art in the new wing. (Open Tu-W and F-Su 10am-6pm, Th 10am-9pm. DM9/€4.60, students DM5/€2.60; free W.) The **Mercedes-Benz Museum,** Mercedesstr. 137, displays gleaming historical cars. Take S1 to Daimlerstadion, walk away from the tracks, and follow the signs. (Open Tu-Su 9am-5pm. Free.) Stuttgart harbors amazing **mineral baths** (Mineralbäder)—the perfect remedy for budget traveler exhaustion. **Mineralbad Leuze,** Am Leuzebad 2-6, has indoor, outdoor, and thermal therapy pools. Take U1, U14, or streetcar #2 to Mineralbäder. (☎216 42 10. Open daily 6am-9pm. 2hr. soak DM12/€6.15, students DM9/€4.60.)

BLACK FOREST (SCHWARZWALD)

The Black Forest owes its name to the eerie gloom that prevails under its evergreen canopy. Once inspiration for "Hansel and Gretel" and other Grimms' fairy tales, the region now attracts hikers and skiers with more than just bread crumbs.

⌐ TRANSPORTATION. The main entry point to the Black Forest is **Freiburg,** which is accessible by **train** from Stuttgart and Basel, Switzerland. From Freiburg, it's easy to catch buses or trains to other towns in the area.

FREIBURG IM BREISGAU. Freiburg may be the metropolis of the Black Forest, but it hasn't succumbed to the hectic rhythms of city life. Two medieval gates—the **Schwabentor** and the **Martinstor**—stand within blocks of each other in the southeast corner of the Altstadt, but Freiburg's pride and joy is the majestic **Münster,** a stone cathedral with a 116m spire and a tower with the oldest bell in Germany. (Open M-Sa 10am-6pm, Su 1-6pm. Tower open M-Sa 9:30am-5pm. Su 1-5pm; DM2.50/€1.30, students DM1.50/€0.80.) The **⌂Augustiner Museum,** Salzstr. 32, is set in a 13th-century monastery and contains an impressive medieval sculpture and art collection. (Open Tu-Su 10am-5pm. DM4/€2.05, students DM2/€1.05; free first Su every month.) The surrounding hills brim with fantastic **hiking** trails; maps are available in the tourist office or at most bookstores, and all trails are clearly marked.

Trains run to Basel (40min.-1hr., 1-2 per hr., DM17-30/€8.70-15.35) and Stuttgart (2-3hr., 2 per hr., DM61-68/€31.20-34.80). The **tourist office,** Rotteckring 14, two blocks down Eisenbahnstr. from the station, has maps and books private rooms for DM5/€2.60; these are usually the most affordable accommodations in Freiburg. (Open M-F 9:30am-8pm, Sa 9:30am-5pm, Su 10am-noon; Oct.-May M-F 9:30am-6pm, Sa 9:30am-2pm, Su 10am-noon.) To reach the impeccably clean **Haus Lydia Kalchtaler,** Peterhof 11, take streetcar #1 (dir. Littenweiler) to Lassbergstr., then bus #17 (dir. Kappel) to Kleintalstr. (☎(0761) 671 19. Kitchen available. Sheets DM5/€2.60, included for stays over 3 nights. DM25/€12.80 per person.) The **Freiburger Markthalle,** next to the Martinstor, is home to food-stands serving ethnic specialties for DM5-15/€2.60-7.70. The main entrance is on Grünwälderstr. (☎0761 38 11 11. Open M-F 8am-7pm, Sa 8am-4pm.) **Edeka,** Eisenbahnstr. 39, sells groceries. (Open M-F 7:30am-8pm, Sa 8am-4pm.)

ST. PETER AND ST. MÄRGEN. East of Freiburg, twin villages St. Peter and St. Märgen lie between cow-speckled hills in the High Black Forest. **Bus** #7216 runs from Freiburg to **St. Peter** (25min.); get off at Zähriger Eck to reach St. Peter's **tourist office,** in the Klosterhof, which has a list of affordable **rooms.** (☎07660 91 02 24. Open M-F 9am-noon and 3-5pm; July-Aug. also Sa 10am-noon.) Many hiking paths—most well marked—begin at the tourist office. An easy and very scenic 8km path leads to **St. Märgen;** follow the blue diamonds of the **Panoramaweg.** Alternatively, **bus** #7216 continues on to St. Märgen about half the time; check with the driver. With links to all major Black Forest trails and a number of gorgeous **day hikes,** St. Märgen rightfully calls itself a *Wanderparadies* (hiking paradise). Most of the trails are marked from Hotel Hirschen, uphill from the bus stop. The **tourist office,** in the Rathaus, 100m from the bus stop, provides good hiking (DM5/€2.60) and biking (DM6.80/€3.50) maps and finds rooms for free. (☎07669 91 18 17. Open M-Th 9am-4:30pm, F 9am-2pm; July-Sept. also Sa 10am-noon.)

TRIBERG. The residents of touristy Triberg brag about the **Gutacher Wasserfall**—the highest waterfall in Germany—a series of bright cascades tumbling over moss-covered rocks for 163m. It's more of a mountain stream than a waterfall, but the idyllic hike through the lush park makes up for the unimpressive trickle.

(Park open 9am-7pm. DM2.50/€1.30, students DM2/€1.05.) The area around town offers several beautiful **hikes**—ask at the tourist office for information and maps. **Trains** run to Freiburg (1¾-2½hr., 1-2 per hr., DM32-45/€16.40-23). The **tourist office,** Luisenstr. 10, is on the ground floor of the local Kurhaus; from the station, turn right and follow the signs, or take bus #7265, which runs every hour to Marktpl. The staff sells maps (from DM2/€1.05) and has a mammoth catalog of all hotels, *Pensionen,* and private rooms in the region. (☎07722 95 32 30. Open M-F 9am-5pm; May-Sept. also Sa 10am-noon.) Grab groceries for a picnic at **Plus market,** Schulstr. 5. (Open M-F 8:30am-6:30pm, Sa 8am-2pm.)

CONSTANCE (KONSTANZ)   ☎07531

On the Bodensee (Lake Constance), the charming city of Constance has never been bombed: part of the city extends into Switzerland, and the Allies were leery of accidentally striking neutral territory. Now one of Germany's favorite vacation spots, its narrow streets wind around beautiful Baroque and Renaissance façades, and a palpable jubilation fills the streets. The **Münster** has a 76m Gothic spire and a display of ancient religious objects, but it's being renovated through 2003. (Open M-Sa 10am-6pm, Su noon-6:30pm. Free.) Wander down **Seestraße,** near the yacht harbor on the lake, or down **Rheinsteig,** along the Rhine, for picturesque promenades. Constance boasts a number of **public beaches;** all are free and open May to September; **Strandbad Horn** (bus #5), the largest and most crowded, sports a nude sunbathing section modestly enclosed by hedges.

Trains run from Constance to most cities in Southern Germany. The friendly but tiny **tourist office,** Bahnhofspl. 13, to the right of the train station, provides free walking maps and finds rooms for DM5. (☎13 30 30. Open Apr.-July and Sept.-Oct. M-F 9am-6:30pm, Sa 9am-1pm; Aug. M-F 9am-8pm, Sa 9am-4pm, Su 10am-1pm; Nov.-Mar. M-F 9am-12:30pm and 2-6pm.) Reserve ahead at **Jugendherberge Kreuzlingen (HI),** Promenadenstr. 7, which is actually in Switzerland but closer to Constance than the Constance hostel. From the train station, turn left, cross the bridge over the tracks, turn right, and go through the parking lot to the border checkpoint Klein Venedig. Walk along Seestr. until the sharp right curve, then continue straight ahead on the gravel path through the gate, right through the Seeburg castle parking lot, and right up the hill to the building with a flag on top. (☎+41 (71) 688 26 63. Breakfast and sheets included. Reception 8-10am and 5-9pm. Closed Dec.-Feb. 23SFr or DM29/€15—both currencies accepted. AmEx/MC/V.) Camp by the waterfront at **DKV-Campingplatz Bodensee,** Fohrenbühlweg 45. Take bus #1 to Staad and walk for 10min. with the lake to your left. (☎330 57. Reception closed noon-2:30pm. Warm showers included. DM6/€3.10 per person, DM8/€4.10 per tent.) For **groceries,** head to the basement of the **Karstadt** department store, on Augustinerpl. (Open M-F 9:30am-8pm, Sa 9am-4pm. AmEx/MC/V.)

BAVARIA (BAYERN)

Bavaria is the Germany of Teutonic myth, Wagnerian opera, and the Brothers Grimm's fairy tales. From the Baroque cities along the Danube to Mad King Ludwig's castles high in the Alps, the region draws more tourists than any other part of the country. Most foreigners' notions of Germany are tied to this land of *Biergartens* and *Lederhosen;* mostly rural, Catholic, and conservative, it contrasts sharply with the rest of the country. Local authorities still use Bavaria's proper name, *Freistaat Bayern* (Free State of Bavaria), and its traditions and dialect have been preserved. Residents have always been Bavarians first and Germans second.

REMINDER. HI-affiliated hostels in Bavaria do not admit guests over age 26, although an exception is usually made for those with young children.

GERMANY

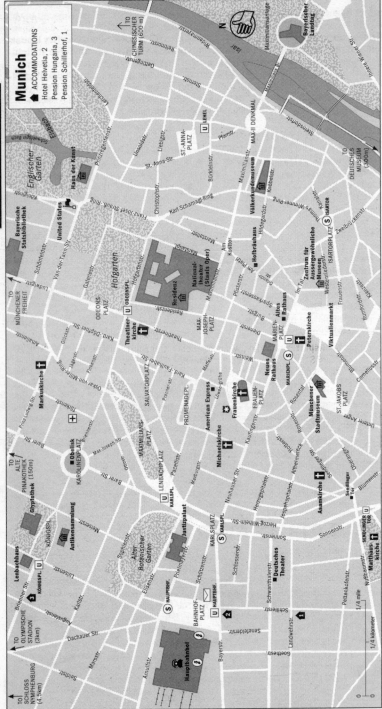

Munich

▲ ACCOMMODATIONS
Hotel Helvetia, 2
Pension Hungaria, 3
Pension Schillerhof, 1

MUNICH (MÜNCHEN) ☎089

The capital and cultural center of Bavaria, Munich is a sprawling, relatively liberal metropolis island in the midst of conservative southern Germany. World-class museums, handsome parks and architecture, a rambunctious arts scene, and an urbane population collide to create a city of astonishing vitality. *Müncheners* party zealously during **Fasching** (Carnival; Jan. 7-Feb. 12, 2002), shop with abandon during the **Christmas Market** (Nov. 30-Dec. 24, 2002), and consume unbelievable quantities of beer during the legendary **Oktoberfest** (Sept. 21-Oct. 6, 2002).

▐▛ TRANSPORTATION

Flights: Flughafen München (☎97 52 13 13). S8 runs between the airport and the Hauptbahnhof (40min., every 20 min., DM15.20/€8 or 8 stripes on the *Streifenkarte*).

Trains: Munich's **Hauptbahnhof** (☎22 33 12 56) is the transportation hub of Southern Germany, with connections to: **Amsterdam** (9hr.; 1 per hr.; DM248/€126, under 26 DM198/€100); **Berlin** (8hr.; 1 per hr.; DM277/€141, under 26 DM222/€113); **Cologne** (6hr.; 2 per hr.; DM173/€88, under 26 DM138/€70); **Frankfurt** (3½hr.; 1 per hr.; DM147/€75, under 26 DM118/€60); **Füssen** (2hr.; 1 per hr.; DM36/€18, under 26 DM29/€15); **Hamburg** (6hr.; 2 per hr.; DM268/€136, under 26 DM214/€109); **Innsbruck** (2hr.; 1 per hr.; DM48/€24, under 26 DM37/€19); **Paris** (10hr.; DM194/€98, under 26 DM156/€79); **Prague** (8½hr.; 3 per day; DM113/€58, under 26 DM85/€43); **Salzburg** (1¾hr.; 1 per hr.; DM41/€20, under 26 DM30/€15); **Vienna** (5hr.; 1 per hr.; DM106/€54, under 26 DM82/€41); **Zurich** (5hr.; every 3 hr.; DM110/€56, under 26 DM85/€43). For 24hr. schedules, fare information, and reservations, call ☎(01805) 99 66 33. **EurAide,** in the station, provides free train information and books train tickets. Information counters open daily 6am-11:30pm.

Public Transportation: MVV, Munich's public transport system, runs Su-Th 5am-12:30am, F-Sa 5am-2am. Eurail, InterRail, and German railpasses are valid on the S-Bahn (S) but *not* on the U-Bahn (U), streetcars, or buses.

Tickets and Schedules: Buy tickets at the blue vending machines and **validate them** in the blue boxes marked with an "E" before entering the platform. Disguised agents check for tickets sporadically; if you jump the fare (known as *schwarzfahren*), you risk a DM60/€30 fine. **Transit maps** and maps of wheelchair accessible stations are available in the tourist office, at EurAide, and at MVV counters in the train station. **Fahrplans** (schedules) cost DM2/€1 at newsstands.

Prices: Single ride tickets (DM4/€2, valid for 3hr.). *Kurzstrecke* (short trip) tickets are good for 2 stops on U or S, or 4 stops on a streetcar or bus (DM2/€1). A **Streifenkarte** (10-strip ticket, DM17.50/€9) can be used by more than 1 person. Cancel 2 strips per person for a normal ride, or 1 strip per person for a *Kurzstrecke*; beyond the city center, cancel 2 strips per additional zone. A **Single-Tageskarte** (single-day ticket) is valid for one day of unlimited travel until 6am the next day (DM9/€5). The **3-Day Pass** (DM22/€11) is also a great deal. The **Munich Welcome Card,** available at the tourist office and in many hotels, is valid for either 1 day (DM12/€6) or 3 days (DM30/€15) of public transportation and includes a 50% discount on many of Munich's museums and 20% on Radius bike rental (see below). Passes can be purchased at the **MVV office** behind tracks 31 and 32 in the Hauptbahnhof, or at any of the *Kartenautomats*.

Taxis: Taxi-Zentrale (☎216 11 or 194 10) has large stands in front of the train station and every 5-10 blocks in the central city. Women can request a female driver.

Bike Rental: Radius Bikes (☎59 61 13), at the far end of the Hauptbahnhof, behind the lockers opposite tracks 30-36. DM5/€3 per hr., DM25/€13 per day, DM75/€38 per week. Deposit DM100/€51, passport, or credit card. 10% student and Eurailpass discount; 20% Munich Welcome Card discount. Open May to mid-Oct. daily 10am-6pm. **Aktiv-Rad,** Hans-Sachs-Str. 7 (☎26 65 06). U1 or U2: Fraunhofer Str. DM20/€10 per day. Open M-F 10am-1pm and 2-6:30pm, Sa 10am-1pm.

✸ ORIENTATION

A map of Munich's center looks like a squashed circle quartered by one horizontal and one vertical line. The circle is the main traffic **Ring,** which changes names frequently around its length. The east-west and north-south thoroughfares cross at Munich's epicenter, the **Marienplatz,** and meet the traffic rings at **Karlsplatz** (called **Stachus** by locals) in the west, **Isatorplatz** in the east, **Odeonsplatz** in the north, and **Sendliger Tor** in the south. In the east beyond the Isartor, the **Isar River** flows by the city center, south to north. The **Hauptbahnhof** (main train station) is just beyond Karlspl. outside the Ring in the west. To get to Marienpl. from the station, use the main exit and head across Bahnhofpl., keep going east through Karlspl., and Marienpl. is straight ahead. Or, take any S-Bahn (dir. Marienpl.) to Marienpl.

The **University** is north of Munich's center, next to the budget restaurants of the **Schwabing** district. East of Schwabing is the **English Garden;** west of Schwabing is the **Olympiapark.** South of town is the **Glockenbachviertel,** filled with all sorts of night hotspots, including many gay bars. The area around the train station, to the west of the city, is rather seedy and is dominated by hotels and sex shops. Oktoberfest is held on the large and open **Theresienwiese,** south-east of the train station on the U4 and U5 lines.

⚡ PRACTICAL INFORMATION

Several publications help visitors navigate Munich. The most comprehensive is the monthly English-language *Munich Found* (DM5.50/€3), available at newsstands and bookshops, which provides a list of services, events, and museums. The bi-weekly *in München* (free at the tourist office) provides detailed movie, theater, and concert schedules. *Prinz* (DM2 at newsstands) is a German-language monthly with endless tips on shopping, art, music, film, concerts, and food.

TOURIST, FINANCIAL, AND LOCAL SERVICES

☒ EurAide in English (☎ 59 38 89), along track 11 (room 3) of the Hauptbahnhof, near the Bayerstr. exit. Books train tickets, explains the public transport, and sells maps (DM1/ €0.51) and tickets for English tours of Munich. Pick up the free brochure *Inside Track*. Open June-Oktoberfest daily 7:45am-noon and 1-5:30pm; Oct.-Apr. M-F 8am-noon and 1-4pm, Sa 8am-noon; May daily 7:45am-noon and 1-4:30pm.

Main Tourist Office: (☎ 233 03 00), on the front (east) side of the train station, next to ABR Travel on Bahnhofpl. They do speak English, but for more in-depth questions, EurAide (see above) will probably better suit your needs. The office **books rooms** for free with a 10-15% deposit, sells English city maps (DM0.50/€0.30), and offers the **München Welcome Card,** which offers free public transportation and reduced prices for 35 different sights and services (1-day DM12/€6, 3-day DM30/€15). Open M-Sa 9am-8pm, Su 10am-6pm. **Branch office** just inside the entrance to the Neues Rathaus on Marienpl. Open M-F 10am-8pm, Sa 10am-4pm.

Consulates: Canada, Tal 29 (☎ 219 95 70). S-Bahn: Isartor. Open M-Th 9am-noon and 2-5pm, F 9am-noon and 2-3:30pm. **Ireland,** Possart 12 (☎ 98 57 23). U4: Prinzregenpl. Open M-F 9am-noon. **South Africa,** Sendlinger-Tor-Pl. 5 (☎ 231 16 30). U1, U2, U3 or U6: Sendlinger Tor. Open M-F 9am-noon. **UK,** Bürkleinstr. 10, 4th fl. (☎ 21 10 90). U4 or U5: Lehel. Open M-Th 8:30am-noon and 1-5pm, F 8:30am-noon and 1-3:30pm; appointments M-F 9-10:30am and M-Tu, Th 1-2:30pm. **US,** Königinstr. 5 (☎ 288 80). Open M-F 8-11am. For visa information, call (0190) 8500 5800; to speak to an official, call ☎ (0190) 850 055 M-F 7am-8pm.

Gay and Lesbian Resources: Gay services information (☎ 260 30 56). **Lesbian information** and **LeTra Lesbentraum** (Angertorstr. 3, ☎ 725 42 72). Telephone times M and W 2:30-5pm, Tu 10:30am-1pm, Th 7-9pm. See also Gay and Lesbian Munich, p. 460.

Disabled Resources: Info Center für Behinderte, Schellingstr. 31 (☎ 21 170; fax 21 17 258; info@vdk.de; www.vdk.bayern.com), has a list of Munich's resources for disabled persons. Open M-Th 9am-noon and 12:30-6pm, F 9am-5pm.

Laundromat: SB Waschcenter, Paul-Heyse-Str. 21, near the train station. Turn right on Bayerstr., then left on Paul-Heyse-Str. Wash DM7/€4; dry DM1/€0.55 per 10min. Open daily 7am-11pm. **Kingsgard Waschsalon,** Amalienstr. 61, near the university. Wash DM6.20/€3; dry DM3/€1.50. Open M-F 8am-6:30pm, Sa 9am-1pm.

EMERGENCY AND COMMUNICATIONS

Police: ☎110. **Ambulance** and **Fire:** ☎112. **Medical service:** ☎192 22.

Pharmacy: Bahnhofpl. 2 (☎59 41 19 or 59 81 19), on the corner outside the train station. Open M-F 8am-6:30pm, Sa 8am-2pm. 24hr. service rotates among the city's pharmacies—check the window of any pharmacy for a list.

Internet Access: EasyEverything (The Internet Shop), on Bahnhofspl. next to the post office. Prices depend on demand (about DM5/€3 per hr., min. DM5/€3). Open 24hr.

Post Office: Bahnhofpl., **80335 Munich.** Walk out of the main train station exit and it's the yellow building across the street. Open M-F 7am-8pm, Sa 9am-4pm, Su 10am-3pm.

☕ ACCOMMODATIONS AND CAMPING

Munich's accommodations usually fall into one of three categories: seedy, expensive, or booked solid. During times like Oktoberfest, only the last category exists. In summer, the best strategy is to start calling before noon or to book a few weeks in advance. At most of Munich's hostels you can check in all day, but try to start your search before 5pm. Don't even think of sleeping in any public area, including the Hauptbahnhof; police patrol frequently all night long.

HOSTELS

▨ **Euro Youth Hotel,** Senefelderstr. 5 (☎59 90 88 11, 599 088 71, or 599 088 72). From the Bahnhofspl. exit of the Hauptbahnhof, make a right on Bayerstr. and a left on Senefelderstr. Outlandishly friendly and well-informed English-speaking staff. All-you-can-eat breakfast buffet DM8.50. Wash DM5.50/€3; dry DM2.50/€1. Reception 24hr. No curfew or lockout. Dorms DM32/€16; doubles DM90/€46, with private shower, telephone, and breakfast DM130/€66; triples DM117/€60; quads DM156/€80. Inquire about their new location on the S6 line, with 1500 beds and shuttle service to and from the airport, scheduled to open soon.

▨ **Jugendlager Kapuzinerhölzl ("The Tent"),** In den Kirschen 30 (☎141 43 00). Streetcar #17 from the Hauptbahnhof (dir. Amalienburgstr.) to Botanischer Garten. Go straight on Franz-Schrank-Str. and left at In den Kirschen. Night streetcars run at least once an hour all night. There's always room for you at The Tent, where you'll sleep with 250 fellow "campers" under a big circus tent on a wooden floor. Internet DM2/€1 per 15min. Free city tours W 9am. Kitchen available. Laundry DM4/€2. Check-in 4:30-10:30pm. Reception 24hr. DM15/€8 gets you a foam pad, multiple wool blankets (you can use your sleeping bag also), bathrooms, shower, rudimentary breakfast, and enthusiastic management. Open July-Aug. Actual beds DM19/€10. Camping DM8/€4 per campsite plus DM8/€4 per person. Passport required as deposit.

Jugendherberge Pullach Burg Schwaneck (HI), Burgweg 4-6 (☎793 06 43), in a castle 12km outside the city center. S7 (dir. Wolfratshausen) to Pullach. Exit the station from the Munich side, walk toward the huge soccer field down Margarethenstr., and follow the signs. Clean rooms are quiet and well-kept. Breakfast and sheets included. Reception 4-11pm. Curfew 11:30pm. Make reservations 9am-1pm. 6- to 8-bed dorms DM26/€13; 12-bed dorm DM25/€13; doubles DM38.50/€20; quads DM29/€15.

Jugendgästehaus Thalkirchen (HI), Miesingstr. 4 (☎723 65 50 or 723 65 60). U1 or U2: Sendlinger Tor, then U3 (dir. Fürstenrieder West) to Thalkirchen. Take the Thalkirchnerpl. exit and follow Schäftlarnstr. toward Innsbruck and bear right around the curve, then follow Frauenbergstr. and head left on Münchner Str.; follow the street as it curves left. Comfortable and newly renovated. TV room and billiards. Sheets and breakfast included. Wash and dry DM5/€3 each. Reception 7am-1am. Check-in 2pm. Curfew 1am. Call in advance. 2- to 15-bed dorms DM35.50/€18; singles DM40-50/€20-25.

Haus International, Elisabethstr. 87 (☎12 00 60). U2 (dir. Feldmoching) to Hohenzollernpl., then streetcar #12 (dir. Romanpl.) or bus #33 (dir. Aidenbachstr.) to Barbarastr. It's the 5-story beige building behind the BP gas station. Pleasantly clean dorms overlook a busy street. Free indoor pool, small beer garden, TV room, and groovy disco with bar. Reception 24hr. Reservations recommended. Singles DM55/€28, with bath DM85/€43; doubles DM49/€25, with shower DM69/€35; triples DM48/€24.

HOTELS AND PENSIONS

While Munich has a surplus of dirt-cheap (and often dirty) accommodations, it's often a better idea to crash in a hostel. A clean room in a safe area costs at least DM55-65 for a single and DM80-100 for a double. Always call ahead. Be forewarned that the rates rise during Oktoberfest.

■ **Hotel Helvetia,** Schillerstr. 6 (☎590 68 50), at the corner of Bahnhofspl., just beyond the Vereinsbank, to the right as you exit the station. The friendliest hotel in all of Munich. Over half of their beautiful rooms were renovated last year. Free Internet. Breakfast included. Laundry DM9.90/€5. Reception 24hr. Singles DM55-69/€28-35; doubles DM75-99/€38-51, with shower DM99-120/€51-61; triples DM105-129/€54-66; quads DM140-172/€72-88. Rates rise 10-15% during Oktoberfest.

Hotel Kurpfalz, Schwanthaler Str. 121 (☎540 98 60). Exit on Bayerstr. from the station, turn right and walk 5-6 blocks down Bayerstr., veer left onto Holzapfelstr., and make a right onto Schwanthaler Str. Or take streetcar #18 or 19 to Holzapfelstr. and walk from there. Satellite TVs, phones, baths, and hardwood furniture in all rooms. Breakfast buffet included. Free email; Internet DM5/€3 per 30min. Reception 24hr. Singles from DM89/€45; doubles from DM109/€56; triples (doubles with cots) DM165/€84.

Pension Schillerhof, Schillerstr. 21 (☎59 42 70). Exit onto Bahnhofpl. from the train station, turn right, and go 2 blocks down Schillerstr. Tidy rooms with TV. Breakfast included. Reception 6am-10pm. Singles DM60-80/€30-40; doubles DM90-120/€45-61; extra bed DM20/€10. Oktoberfest surcharge DM25-40/€13-20 per person.

Pension Hungaria, Briennerstr. 42 (☎52 15 58). From the train station, go left onto Dachauer Str., right on Augustenstr., and across and to the right on Briennerstr.; it's the 2nd building to your left. Or take U1 to Stiglmaierpl., take the Briennerstr./Volkstheater exit, and it's on the next corner at Augustenstr. Oriental rugs, comfortable furnishings, and a small travel library. Breakfast included. Showers DM3/€1.50. Reception 24hr., 2 floors up. Singles DM60-65/€30-33; doubles DM90-95/€45-48; triples DM110/€56; quads DM130/€66. Oktoberfest surcharge DM10/€5 per room.

Pension am Kaiserpl., Kaiserpl. 12 (☎34 91 90). A few blocks from nightlife central—a good location if you doubt your own sense of direction after a couple of beers. U3 or U6: Münchener Freiheit. Take the escalator to Herzogstr., turn left, walk 3 blocks to Viktoriastr., and turn left; it's at the end of the street on the right. Breakfast included. Reception 7am-8pm. 6-bed dorms DM240/€122; singles DM59/€30, with shower DM89/€45; doubles DM95/€48, with shower DM99-109/€50-56.

Hotel-Pension am Markt, Heiliggeiststr. 6 (☎22 50 14), smack dab in the city center, off the Viktualienmarkt. Take any S-bahn to Marienpl., then walk past the Altes Rathaus and turn right down the little alley behind the green Heiliggeist Church. Small but spotless rooms are wheelchair accessible. Breakfast included. Singles DM62-65/€37-38, with shower DM130/€66; doubles DM125-130/€66-68, DM160-180/€87-92; triples DM195/€100, DM240/€123.

CAMPING

Campingplatz Thalkirchen, Zentralländstr. 49 (☎723 17 07). U1 or U2: Sendlinger Tor, then U3: Thalkirchen, and change to bus #57. From the bus stop, cross the busy street on the left and take a right onto the footpath next to the road. The entrance is down the tree-lined path on the left. Well-run, crowded grounds with jogging and bike paths, TV lounge, groceries, and a restaurant. Showers DM2/€1. Wash DM7/€4; dry DM0.50/€0.25 per 6min. Curfew 11pm. Open mid-Mar. to late Oct. DM8.60/€4 per person, DM5.50-7/€3-4 per tent.

◨ FOOD

For an authentic Bavarian lunch, grab a *Brez'n* (pretzel) and spread it with *Leberwurst* (liverwurst) or cheese. **Weißwürste** (white veal sausages) are another native bargain, served in a pot of hot water with sweet mustard and a soft pretzel on the side. Don't eat the skin of the sausage, just slice it open and eat the tender meat. **Leberkäs** is a slice of a pinkish, meatloaf-like compound of ground beef and bacon. **Leberknödel** are liver dumplings, usually served in soup; **Kartoffelknödel** (potato dumplings) and **Semmelknödel** (made from white bread, egg, and parsley) are eaten along with a hearty chunk of German meat.

The vibrant **Viktualienmarkt,** 2min. south of Marienpl., is Munich's gastronomic center, offering both basic and exotic foods and ingredients. It's fun to browse, but don't plan to do any budget grocery shopping here (open M-F 10am-8pm, Sa 8am-4pm). The ubiquitous **beer gardens** serve savory snacks along with booze. The university district off **Ludwigstraße** is Munich's best source of filling meals in a lively, unpretentiously hip scene. Many reasonably priced restaurants and cafes cluster on **Schellingstraße, Amalienstraße,** and **Türkenstraße** (U3 or U6: Universität.)

■ **Marché,** Neuhauser Str., between Karlspl. and Marienpl. The top floor offers cafeteria-style food displays; downstairs are buffet and food stations where chefs prepare every food imaginable, including great vegetarian selections. You'll get a food card that will be stamped for each item you take; pay at the end. Bottom floor open 11am-10pm, top floor open 8am-11pm.

■ **Cafe Hag/Confiserie Retenhäfer,** Residenzstr. 25-26, across from the Residenz. Serves a large variety of cakes and sweets. Breakfast DM8-20/€4-10. Entrees DM9-15/€5-8. Open M-F 8:45am-7pm, Sa 8am-6pm.

Schwimmkrabbe, Ickstattstr. 13. U1 or U2: Fraunhoferstr. Walk 1 block down Baaderstr. and turn right on Ickstattstr. This family-run Turkish restaurant is popular with locals. Filling appetizers DM8-17/€4-9; dishes DM16-29/€8-15. Open daily 5pm-1am.

Gollier, Gollierstr. 83. U4, U5, S7, or S27: Heimeranpl. Walk 2 blocks north on Garmischer Str. and turn left on Gollierstr. Delicious homemade vegetarian fare DM12-22/€6-11. Many summer specials, such as reduced lunch prices and early-bird dinner deals. Open M-F 11:30-3pm and 5pm-midnight, Sa 5pm-midnight, Su 10am-midnight.

Café Ignaz, Georgenstr. 67. U2: Josephspl. Take Adelheidstr. 1 block north and turn right on Georgenstr. Earth-friendly cafe with a nutritious, inexpensive vegetarian menu. Lunch buffet M-F noon-2pm DM13.90/€7, brunch buffet Sa-Su 9am-1pm DM14/€7.20. Open M-F 8am-10pm, Sa-Su 9am-10pm.

◐ SIGHTS

MARIENPLATZ. The **Mariensäule,** an ornate 17th-century monument to the Virgin Mary, was built to commemorate the city's survival during the Thirty Years' War. At the neo-Gothic **Neues Rathaus,** the **Glockenspiel** chimes with a display of jousting knights and dancing coopers. *(Daily 11am and noon; in summer also 5pm.)* At 9pm, a mechanical watchman marches out and the Guardian Angel escorts the *Münchner Kindl* (Munich Child, the town's symbol) to bed. Be careful while ogling the Glockenspiel; of all tourist places in Munich, this is the most likely spot to get pickpocketed. The Rathaus tower offers a sweeping view. *(Tower open M-F 9am-7pm, Sa-Su 10am-7pm. DM3/€1.50.)* On the face of the **Altes Rathaus** tower, to the right of the Neues Rathaus, are all of Munich's coats of arms since its inception as a city but one: when the tower was rebuilt after its destruction in World War II, the local government refused to include the swastika-bearing arms from the Nazi era.

PETERSKIRCHE AND FRAUENKIRCHE. Across from the Neues Rathaus is the 12th-century **Peterskirche,** the city's oldest parish church. More than 300 steps scale the tower (called *der Alter Peter* by locals) to a spectacular view of Munich. *(Open M-Sa 9am-7pm, Su 10am-7pm. DM2.50/€1, students DM1.50/€0.75, children DM0.50/€0.25.)* From the Marienpl., walk one block toward the Hauptbahnhof on Kaufingerstr. to the onion-domed towers of the 15th-century **Frauenkirche**—one of Munich's most notable landmarks and now the symbol of the city. *(Towers open Apr.-Oct. M-Sa 10am-5pm. DM4/€2, students DM2/€1.)*

RESIDENZ. Down the pedestrian zone from Odeonspl., the richly decorated rooms of the **Residenz** (Palace), built from the 14th to 19th centuries, form the material vestiges of the Wittelsbach dynasty. The beautifully landscaped **Hofgarten** behind the Residenz shelters the lovely temple of Diana. The **Schatzkammer** (treasury) contains jeweled baubles, crowns, swords, china, ivory work, and other trinkets. *(Open Apr. to mid-Oct. F-W*

9am-6pm, Th 9am-8pm; in winter daily 10am-4pm. DM8/€4, students DM6/€3.) The **Residen-zmuseum** comprises the former Wittelsbach apartments and State Rooms, a collection of European porcelain, and a 17th-century court chapel. The 120 portraits in the **Ahnen-galerie** trace the royal lineage (perhaps not quite accurately) back to Charlemagne. *(Max-Joseph-pl. 3. Take U3-6 to Odeonspl. Residenz museum open same hours as Schatzkam-mer. DM8/€4, students DM6/€3. Combination ticket DM14/€7, students DM11/€6.)*

ENGLISCHER GARTEN. Extending from the city center is the vast **Englischer Gar-ten** (English Garden), Europe's largest metropolitan public park. On sunny days, all of Munich turns out to bike, fly kites, play badminton, ride horseback, swim in the Eisbach, or sunbathe. The garden includes a Japanese tea house, a Chinese pagoda, a Greek temple, and a few beer gardens. **Nude sunbathing** areas are desig-nated FKK *(Frei-Körper-Kultur)* on signs and park maps. Daring Müncheners surf the rapids of the Eisbach, which flows artificially through the park.

SCHLOß NYMPHENBURG. After 10 years of trying for an heir, Ludwig I cele-brated the birth of his son Maximilian in 1662 by erecting an elaborate summer playground. The Baroque **Schloß Nymphenburg**, in the northwest of town, hides a number of treasures. Check out Ludwig's "Gallery of Beauties"—whenever a woman caught his fancy, he would have her portrait painted (a scandalous as well as ironic hobby, since Ludwig grappled with an affection for men throughout his life). A few lakes and four manors also inhabit the palace grounds: **Amalienburg, Badenburg, Pagodenburg,** and **Magdalen Hermitage.** *(Streetcar #17: Schloß Nymphenburg. All attractions open Apr. to mid-Oct. F-W 9am-6pm, Th 9am-8pm; late Oct. to Mar. daily 10am-4pm. Museum and Schloß open Tu-Su 9am-noon and 1-5pm. Badenburg, Pagodenburg, and Magdalen Hermitage closed in winter. Schloß DM7/€4, students DM5/€3. Each manor DM6/€3, students DM4/€2. Entire complex DM15/€8, students DM12/€6t.)*

OLYMPIAPARK. Built for the 1972 Olympic Games in Munich, the **Olympiapark** con-tains the architecturally daring, tent-like **Olympia-Zentrum** and the **Olympia Turm** (tower), the highest building in Munich at 290m. Two **tours** in English are available: the "Adventure Tour" of the entire park (Apr.-Oct. daily 2pm, DM13/€7) or a tour of just the soccer stadium (Mar.-Oct. daily 11am, DM8/€4). The Olympiapark also hosts **free concerts** in the Theatron every Sunday in July and every day in August. Premium athletic specimens from around the world descend on Munich for the **Rowing World Cup** every July. From Aug. 6-11, 2002, the Olympiapark will host the **European Track & Field Championships.** *(U3: Olympiazentrum. Tower open daily 9am-mid-night. DM5.50/€3. Park open M-F 10am-6pm, Sa 10am-3pm.)*

🏛 MUSEUMS

Munich is a supreme museum city, and many of the city's offerings would require days for exhaustive perusal. The *Münchner Volkshochschule* (☎480 062 29 or 480 062 30; kult_vge@mvhs.de) offers tours of many city museums for DM8/€4. A **day pass** to all of Munich's state-owned museums is sold at the tourist office and many larger museums (DM30/€15). All state owned museums are **free on Su.**

DEUTSCHES MUSEUM. One of the world's largest and best museums of science and technology, with fascinating exhibits, including the first telephone and a min-ing exhibit that winds through a labyrinth of recreated subterranean tunnels. A walk through the museum's 46 departments covers over 17km; grab an English guidebook for DM6/€3. *(Museuminsel 1. S-Bahn: Isartor or street car #18: Deutsches Museum. Open daily 9am-5pm. DM12/€6, students DM5/€3.)*

ALTE PINAKOTHEK AND NEUE PINAKOTHEK. Commissioned in 1826 by King Ludwig I, this world-renowned hall houses Munich's most precious art, including works by Titian, da Vinci, Raphael, Dürer, Rembrandt, and Rubens. *(Barerstr. 27. U2: Königspl. Open Tu-Su 10am-5pm, Th until 8pm. DM9/€5, students DM6/€3; combination ticket for Alte and Neue Pinakotheken DM12/€6, students DM6/€3.)* The **Neue Pinakothek** next door displays paintings and sculptures of the 19th to 20th centuries, including van

Gogh, Klimt, Cézanne, Manet, and more. *(Barerstr. 29. Same prices as the Alte Pina-kothek. Open W-M 10am-5pm, Th until 8pm.)* The **Pinakothek Der Moderne** was under construction at the time of publication; it will eventually house the **Staatsgalerie Moderner Kunst** and is scheduled to open autumn 2002.

BMW-MUSEUM. The ultimate driving museum features a fetching display of past, present, and future BMW products. The English brochure *Horizons in Time* guides you through the spiral path to the top of the museum. *(Petuelring 130. U3: Olympiazentrum. Open daily 9am-5pm. DM5.50/€3, students DM4/€2.)*

ZAM: ZENTRUM FÜR AUSSERGEWÖHNLICHE MUSEEN. Munich's **Center for Unusual Museums** brazenly corrals—under one roof—such treasures as the Padlock Museum, the Museum of Easter Rabbits, the Chamberpot Museum, and the Sisi Musuem (dedicated to Empress Elizabeth of Austria). *(Westenriederstr. 41. Any S-bahn to "Isartor" or streetcar #17 or 18. Open daily 10am-6pm. DM8/€4, students DM5/€3.)*

🎵🎭 ENTERTAINMENT AND NIGHTLIFE

Munich's cultural cachet rivals the world's best. Sixty theaters of various sizes are scattered throughout the city; styles range from dramatic classics at the **Residenztheater** and **Volkstheater** to comic opera at the **Staatstheater am Gärtnerplatz** to experimental works at the **Theater im Marstall** in Nymphenburg. Munich's **opera festival** (in July) is held in the ⬛**Bayerische Staatsoper** (Bavarian National Theater), Max-Joseph-pl. 2. (Tickets ☎21 85 19 30; recorded info ☎21 85 19 19. U3, U4, U5, or U6: Odeonspl. or streetcar #19: Nationaltheater. Standing-room and student tickets DM7-20/€4-10, sold 1hr. before performance at the side entrance on Maximilianstr. Box office open M-F 10am-6pm, Sa 10am-1pm. No performances Aug. to mid-Sept.) *Monatsprogramm* (DM3/€1.50) and *Munich Found* (DM5.50/€3) both list schedules for Munich's stages, museums, and festivals. Munich shows its more bohemian face with scores of small fringe theaters, cabaret stages, art cinemas, and artsy pubs in **Schwabing**.

Munich's nightlife is a curious collision of Bavarian *Gemütlichkeit* and trendy cliquishness. The odyssey begins at one of Munich's beer gardens or beer halls, which generally close before midnight and are most crowded in the early evening. The alcohol keeps flowing at cafes and bars, which, except for Friday and Saturday nights, close their taps at 1am. At 4am discos and dance clubs, sedate before midnight, suddenly spark and throb relentlessly. The trendy bars, cafes, cabarets, and discos along **Leopoldstraße** in **Schwabing** attract tourists from all over Europe. Many of these venues require you to at least attempt the jaded hipster look, and the Munich fashion police generally frown on shorts, sandals, and T-shirts.

BEER GARDENS (BIERGÄRTEN)

The six great Munich labels are *Augustiner, Hacker-Pschorr, Hofbräu, Löwenbräu, Paulaner,* and *Spaten-Franziskaner,* but most restaurants and *Gaststätte* will pick a side by only serving one brewery's beer. There are four main types of beer served in Munich: **Helles** (light), **Dunkles** (dark), **Weißbier** (cloudy blond beer made from wheat instead of barley), and **Radler** (cyclist's brew; half beer and half lemon soda). Saying *"Ein Bier, bitte"* will get you a liter, known as a *Maß* (DM8-12). Specify if you want only a half-*Maß* (DM5-7).

▨ **Augustinerkeller,** Arnulfstr. 52, at Zirkus-Krone-Str. Any S-Bahn: Hackerbrücke. Founded in 1824, *Augustiner* is viewed by most *Müncheners* as the finest beer garden in town. Lush grounds, 100-year-old chestnut trees, and the delicious, sharp *Augustiner* beer (*Maß* DM10.70/€5) support their assertion. Open daily 10:30am-midnight.

Hirschgarten, Hirschgarten 1. U1: Rotkreuzpl., then streetcar #12: Romanpl. Walk south to the end of Guntherstr. to enter the Hirschgarten. The largest beer garden in Europe (seating 9000) is boisterous and pleasant but somewhat remote, near Schloß Nymphenburg. *Maß* DM9.80. Open daily 9am-midnight.

Hofbräuhaus, Platzl 9, 2 blocks from Marienpl. Walk past the Altes Rathaus and take an immediate left onto Sparkassenstr. Turn right immediately onto Lederstr, and then take 1st left on Orlandostr.; Hofbräuhaus is ahead on the right. Although originally reserved for royalty and invited guests, a 19th-century proclamation lowered the price of its beer below normal city prices to "offer the Military and working classes a healthy and good tasting drink." Many tables are reserved for locals, and some *Müncheners* even keep their personal steins in the beer hall's safe. To avoid tourists, go in the early afternoon. *Maß* DM11.40/€6. *Weißwürste* with pretzel DM8.90/€4. Open daily 9am-midnight.

BARS

☒ **Nachtcafe,** Maximianspl. 5. U4 or U5 or any S-bahn to Karlspl. Live jazz, funk, soul, and blues until the wee hours. Very *schicki-micki* (yuppie). Things don't get rolling until midnight. No cover, but outrageous prices, so do your drinking beforehand. Beer DM9 per 0.3L. Easy-going weekdays, very picky on weekends—you'll have to look the part. Open daily 9pm-6am; live music 11pm-4am.

Reitschule, Königinstr. 34. U3 or U6: Giselastr. Above a club, with windows overlooking a horseback-riding school. *Weißbier* DM6.20/€3. Open daily 9am-1am.

Lux, Reichenbachstr. 37. U1, U2, U7, or U8: Frauenhofer. Large pastel asterisks decorate the walls of this popular hang-out. Mostly French cuisine, with many fish dishes. Open M-Th 6pm-1am, F-Sa 6pm-2am.

DISCOS

☒ **Kunstpark Ost,** Grafinger Str. 6. U5 or any S-bahn to Ostbahnhof; follow signs for the Kunstpark Ost exit, turn right onto Friedenstr. and then left onto Grafinger Str. The newest and biggest addition to the Munich nightlife scene, this huge complex has 40 different venues swarming with young people. Try the hip **Milch and Bar** (open M, W-F) with modern hits and old favorites; the psychedelic-trance **Natraj Temple** (open F-Sa); the alternative cocktail and disco joint **K41** (open every night; Th 80s night); or the risque South American rock bar **Titty Twister** (open W-Sa). Hours, cover, and themes vary— check *Kunstpark* for details on specific club nights and specials.

Nachtwerk, Club, and Tanzlokal, Landesberger Str. 185. Streetcar #18 or 19 or bus #83 to Lautensackstr. The older, larger **Nachtwerk** spins mainstream dance tunes for sweaty crowds in a packed warehouse; Sa "Best of the 50s to the 90s" night. Its little sister **Club** offers a 2-level dance floor just as tight and swinging, with mixtures of rock, trip-hop, house, acid jazz, and rare grooves. **Tanzlokal** has hip-hop on F. Beer DM4.50/ €2 all places. Cover DM10/€5. Open daily 10pm-4am.

Ballhaus, Domagkstr. 33, in the Alabamahalle. U6: Alte Heide. Free shuttle from there to the club. On a former military base in Schwabing with 3 other discos. Start out in the beer garden, which opens 8pm. Try **Alabama** for German oldies F (9pm-4am, drinks free until 1am) and hits from the 60s to the 90s Sa (10pm-5am, free drinks all night). **Temple Club** has typical pop music (open Sa 10pm-4am) and **Schwabinger Ballhouse** plays international jams (F-Sa 10pm-5am, cover DM15/€8).

GAY AND LESBIAN MUNICH

Although Bavaria has the reputation of being less welcoming to homosexuality, Munich sustains a respectably vibrant gay nightlife. The center of Munich's homosexual scene is in the **Glockenbachviertel,** stretching from the area south of the Sendlinger Tor through the Viktualienmarkt/Gärtnerpl. area to the Isartor. *Our Munich,* Munich's gay and lesbian leaflet, is available at the tourist office. Pick up the free booklet *Rosa Seiten* at **Max&Milian Bookstore,** Ickstattstr. 2 (open M-F 10:30am-2pm and 3:30-8pm, Sa 11am-4pm), or at any other gay locale, for extensive listings of gay nightlife hotspots and services.

☒ **Bei Carla,** Buttermelcherstr. 9. S1-8: Isartor. Walk 1 block south on Rumfordstr., turn left on Klenzestr. and left onto Buttermelcherstr. This charming and friendly lesbian cafe and bar is one of Munich's best-kept secrets. Open M-Sa 4pm-1am, Su 6pm-1am.

Soul City, Maximilianspl. 5, at the intersection with Max-Joseph-Str. Purportedly the biggest gay disco in Bavaria; music ranges from disco to Latin to techno. Straights always welcome. Cover DM10-25/€5-13. Open W-Sa 10pm-late; Th-Sa in summer.

▌ DAYTRIPS FROM MUNICH

DACHAU. *"Arbeit Macht Frei"* ("work sets one free") was the first thing prisoners saw as they entered Dachau; it's written over the gate of the **Journhaus,** formerly the only entry to the camp. Dachau was primarily a work camp (rather than a death camp, like Auschwitz). Although Dachau has a **gas chamber,** it was actually never used because the prisoners purposely made mistakes and worked slowly in order to delay completion. Once tightly packed **barracks** are now only foundations; however, survivors ensured that at least two barracks would be reconstructed to teach future generations about the 206,000 prisoners who were interned here from 1933 to 1945. The **museum,** located in the former administrative buildings, examines pre-1930s anti-Semitism, the rise of Nazism, the establishment of the concentration camp system, and the lives of prisoners through photographs, documents, and artifacts. The thick **guide** (DM25/€13, available in English) translates the propaganda posters, SS files, documents, and letters. A short **film** (22min.) is screened in English at 11:30am, 2, and 3:30pm. A new display in the **Bunker,** the concentration camp's prison and torture chamber, chronicles the lives and experiences of the camp's special prisoners and the barbarism of SS guards. When you visit, it is important to remember that, while the concentration camp is treated as a tourist attraction by many, it is first and foremost a memorial. *(From Munich, take S2 (dir. Petershausen) to Dachau (20min.; DM7.60/€4, or 4 stripes on the Streifenkarte), then bus #724 (dir. Kraütgarten) or 726 (dir. Kopernikusstr.) to KZ-Gedenkstätte (10min.; DM1.90/€1 or 1 stripe on the Streifenkarte). DM5/€3 donation requested. Call ☎(08131) 17 41 for more info. Camp open Tu-Su 9am-5pm.)*

THE CHIEMSEE. The islands, meadows, forests, and marshland of the **Chiemsee** beckon only one hour from Munich by train (p. 465).

THE BAVARIAN ALPS. The **Bavarian Alps** offer forested slopes and crazy King Ludwig's fabulous castles, only two hours from Munich by train (p. 464).

NUREMBERG (NÜRNBERG)   ☎0911

Nuremberg served as the site of massive annual Nazi rallies; Allies later chose it as the site of the post-war crime trials to foster a sense of justice. Today, the townspeople are working to forge a new image for their city as the "Stadt der Menschenrechte" (City of Human Rights). While physical remnants of Nazi rule remain, Nuremberg's cultural aspects outweigh the bitter memories, and today the city is known for its Christmas market and sausages as much as for its ties to Nazism.

█▌ **TRANSPORTATION AND PRACTICAL INFORMATION. Trains** chug to: Berlin (6hr., every 2hr., DM137/€70); Frankfurt (3½hr., 2 per hr., DM66/€33.75); Munich (2½hr., 2 per hr., DM54/€27.60); and Stuttgart (2¾hr., 6 per day, DM54/€27.60). The **tourist office** is currently in a white booth in the northwest corner of the station but will move to the Kunstlerhaus on Konigsstr. sometime in 2002. (☎233 61 31. Open M-Sa 9am-7pm.) To reach **Internetcafe M@x,** Färberstr. 11, head to the 4th fl. of the complex on the corner of Fraueng. (☎23 23 84. Before 3pm DM5/€2.60 per hr.; after 3pm DM5/€2.60 per 30min., DM9/€4.60 per hr. Open Oct.-May M-Th 1-10pm, F-Sa 1pm-1am, Su 3pm-midnight.) **Postal Code:** 90402.

█▐ **ACCOMMODATIONS AND FOOD.** The **Jugendgästehaus (HI),** Burg 2, is in a castle above the city. From the station, cross Frauentorgraben, turn right, walk along the outside of the city walls, then follow Königstr. through Lorenzerpl. over the bridge to the Hauptmarkt. Head toward the fountain on the left and bear right on Burgstr., then hike up the hill. (☎230 93 60. Reception 7am-1am. Curfew 1am.

Reservations recommended. Dorms DM33/€16.90; singles DM65/€33.25; doubles DM78/€39.90.) For **Hotel Garni Probst,** Luitpoldstr. 9, take the underground passage to Königstor from the station and turn left on Luitpoldstr. It's near seedy sex shops, but the hotel is safe and centrally located. (☎20 34 33. Breakfast included. Singles DM40/20.45, with shower DM78/€39.90, with bath DM90/€46; doubles DM88/€45, with shower or bath DM110-130/€56.25-66.50.) Try Nuremberg's specialty, *Rostbratwurst* (grilled sausage), at the **Bratwursthäusle,** Rathauspl. 1, next to the Sebalduskirche. (Open M-Sa 10am-10:30pm.) **Edeka,** Hauptmarkt 12, near the Frauenkirche, sells **groceries.** (Open M-F 8:30am-7pm, Sa 8am-3pm.)

◙ **SIGHTS.** Since Allied bombing left little of Nuremberg for posterity, almost everything has been reconstructed. The walled-in **Handwerkerhof market** near the station is a tourist trap masquerading as a historical attraction; head up Königstr. for the real sights. To the left are the pillared **Straße der Menschenrechte** ("Avenue of Human Rights") and the **Germanisches Nationalmuseum,** Kartäuserg. 1, which chronicles German art from pre-history to the present. (Museum open Tu and Th-Su 10am-5pm, W 10am-9pm. DM8/€4.10, students DM6/€3.10; free W 6-9pm.) Continue on to the **Lorenzkirche** on Lorenzpl., which features a 20m tabernacle. (Open M-Sa 9am-5pm, Su 1-4pm. Free German tours in summer M-F 11am and 2pm; in winter M-F 2pm.) Across the river are the **Frauenkirche** (open M-Sa 9am-6pm, Su 12:30-6pm) and the **Hauptmarktplatz,** the site of the annual **Christmas market.** There's a seamless gold-colored ring hidden in the fence around the fountain in the northwest corner of the Hauptmarkt; spinning it will supposedly bring good luck. Walk uphill to the **Rathaus;** the dungeons beneath contain medieval torture instruments. (Open Tu-Su 10am-4:30pm. Tours every 30min.; English translation available. DM4/€2.05, students DM2/€1.05.) Across from the Rathaus is the **Sebalduskirche,** which houses the remains of St. Sebaldus for 364 days a year; on the 365th, they're paraded around town. (Open daily Mar.-May and Oct.-Dec. 9:30am-6pm; June-Sept. 9:30am-8pm; Jan.-Feb. 9:30am-4pm.) Atop the hill, the **Kaiserburg** offers the best view of the city. (Open daily Apr.-Sept. 9am-6pm; Oct.-Mar. 10am-4pm. Tours every 30min. DM10/€5.15, students DM8/€4.10.)

The ruins of **Dutzendteich Park,** site of the Nazi Party Congress rallies, remind visitors of Nuremberg's darker history. On the far side of the lake is the **Tribüne,** the marble platform where throngs gathered to hear Hitler. The exhibit "Fascination and Terror," in the **Golden Hall** at the rear of the Tribüne, covers the rise of the Third Reich and the war crimes trials. (Open mid-May to Oct. Tu-Su 10am-6pm. DM5/€2.60, students DM4/2.10.) Take S2 (dir. Freucht/Altdorf) to Dutzendteich, turn left out of the middle exit, take another left after Strandcafe Wanner, and follow the path. Nazi leaders faced Allied judges during the infamous **Nürnberg war crimes trials** in room 600 of the Justizgebäude. (Fürtherstr. 110. U1 to Bärenschanze and continue on Furtherstr. Tours Sa-Su 1, 2, 3, and 4pm. DM4/€2.10.)

ROMANTIC ROAD

The landscape between Würzburg and Füssen is like a mammoth picnic: plates of circular cities, castles in tasty shades of lemon and mint, and dense forests of healthy greenery. The German tourist industry christened the area the Romantic Road (*Romantische Straße*) in 1950; it's now the most visited road in Germany.

▐ **TRANSPORTATION. Europabus** runs daily at 10am from bus platform #13 in Würzburg through Rothenburg ob der Tauber to Füssen. The return bus leaves Füssen at 6:45pm, stops at Würzburg, then continues on to Frankfurt. Students receive a 10% discount, Eurail and German Rail Pass holders 60%. For reservations or additional information, contact **EurAide.** (☎089 59 38 89; fax 089 550 39 65; www.euraide.de/romantic.) A more flexible and economical way to travel the Romantic Road is by the frequent **trains** that connect all the towns.

WÜRZBURG. Surrounded by vineyard slopes and bisected by the Main River, Würzburg is a famous university town. In 1895 Wilhelm Conrad Röntgen discovered X-rays here and was awarded the first Nobel Prize. Inside the striking **Fortress Marienburg** are the 11th-century **Marienkirche,** the 40m **Bergfried watchtower** and the **Hole of Fear** (dungeon), and the **Fürstengarten,** built to resemble a ship. Outside the main fortress is the castle arsenal, which now houses the **Mainfränkisches Museum.** Take bus #9 from the station to Festung, or walk toward the castle on the hill. (Tours depart from the main courtyard Apr.-Oct. Tu-F 11am, 2, 3pm, Sa-Su every hr. 10am-4pm. DM4, students DM3. Museum open Apr.-Oct. Tu-Su 10am-6pm; Nov.-Mar. closes 4pm. DM5, students DM2.50.) The **Residenz,** on Residenzpl., houses the largest ceiling fresco in the world, and the **Residenzhofkirche** inside is a Baroque fantasy of gilding and pink marble. (Open daily Apr. to mid-Oct. 9am-6pm, Th until 8pm; mid-Oct. to Mar. 10am-4pm. DM8, students DM6. English tours Sa-Su 11am and 3pm. Free.) **Trains** head to: Frankfurt (2hr., 2 per hr., DM38); Munich (3hr., 1 per hr., DM76); Nuremberg (1hr., 2 per hr., DM28); and Rothenburg ob der Tauber (1hr., 1 per hr., DM17). The **tourist office,** in the yellow Haus zum Falken on the Marktpl., provides maps and helps find rooms. (☎37 23 98. Open M-F 10am-6pm, Sa 10am-2pm; Apr.-Oct. also Su 10am-2pm.) ☎**0931.**

ROTHENBURG OB DER TAUBER. After being plundered in the Thirty Years' War, Rothenburg had no money to renovate or modernize, so it remained unchanged for 250 years. When it became a tourist destination at the end of the 19th century, new laws were imposed to protect the integrity of the medieval *Altstadt;* today, Rothenburg is probably your only chance to see a walled medieval city without a single modern building. After the war, the conquering general promised to spare the town from destruction if any local could chug a wine keg—3.25L of wine. The mayor successfully met the challenge, then passed out for several days. The **Meistertrunk** is reenacted each year, and the town clock performs a slooow motion version every hour over the Marktpl. For many other fascinating tidbits of Rothenburg history, take the 1hr. English tour led by the ◼**night watchman,** which starts from the Rathaus. (Easter-Christmas daily 8pm. DM6/€3.10.) The 60m tower of the Renaissance **Rathaus,** on Marktpl., provides a panoramic view of the town. (Open Apr.-Oct. daily 9:30am-12:30pm and 1-5pm; Nov.-Mar. M-F 9:30am-12:30pm, Sa-Su noon-3pm. DM2/€1.05.) The ◼**Medieval Crime Museum,** Burgg. 3, exhibits torture instruments and "eye for an eye" jurisprudence. (Open daily Apr.-Oct. 9:30am-6pm; Nov. and Jan.-Feb. 2-4pm; Dec. and Mar. 10am-4pm. DM5/€2.60, students DM4/€2.05.) Head to **Christkindlmarkt** (Christ Child Market), Herrng. 2, and **Weihnachtsdorf** (Christmas Village), Herrng. 1, to explore the town's obsession with Christmas. (Open M-F 9am-6:30pm, Sa 9am-4pm; mid-May to Dec. also Su 11am-6pm.) **Trains** run from Würzburg (40min., 1 per hr., DM15.40/€7.90) and Munich (3hr., 1 per hr., DM60/€30.70) to Steinach, where you can transfer to Rothenburg (15min., 1 per hr., DM3.30/€1.70). The **tourist office,** Marktpl. 2, books rooms for a DM5/€2.60 fee in summer and during Christmas. (☎404 92. Open May-Oct. M-F 9am-noon and 1-6pm, Sa-Su 10am-3pm; Nov.-Apr. M-F 9am-noon and 1-5pm, Sa 10am-1pm.) There are also many **private rooms** not registered with the tourist office; look for Zimmer frei signs and knock on the door to inquire. ☎**09861.**

FÜSSEN. A brightly painted toenail at the tip of the Alpine foothills and the southern end of the Romantic Road, Füssen provides easy access to King Ludwig's famed **Königsschlösser** (royal castles, see p. 464). The inner walls of the **Hohes Schloß** (High Castle) courtyard feature arresting *trompe-l'oeil* windows and towers, and the **Staatsgalerie** in the castle shelters a collection of regional late Gothic and Renaissance art. (Open Tu-Su Apr.-Oct. 11am-4pm; Nov.-Mar. 2-4pm. DM5/€2.60, students DM4/€2.05.) Inside the **Annenkapelle,** macabre paintings depict everyone from the Pope and Emperor to the smallest child engaged in the *Totentanz* (death dance), a public frenzy of despair that overtook Europe during the plague. (Open Tu-Su Apr.-Oct. 11am-4pm, Nov.-Mar. 2-4pm. DM5/€2.50, students DM4/€2.) **Trains** run to **Munich** (2hr., 1 per hr., DM36/€18.40). Füssen is also the last stop on the **Europabus** route; northbound buses leave for Frankfurt daily at 8am, and the southbound bus arrives at 8:15pm. To get from the station to the **tourist office,** Kaiser-Maximilian-Pl. 1, walk the length of Bahnhofstr. and head straight on Luitpoldstr. to the big yellow building. The staff finds **rooms** for free. (☎938 50. Open Apr.-Sept. M-F 8:30am-6:30pm, Sa 9am-12:30pm, Su 10am-noon; Oct.-Mar. M-F 9am-5pm, Sa 10am-noon.) You can also knock on doors bearing Zimmer Frei signs. ☎**08362.**

BAVARIAN ALPS

On a clear day in Munich, you can see the snow-covered peaks and forested slopes of the Bavarian Alps stretching from southeast Germany across Austria and into Italy. It was in this rugged and magical terrain that Ludwig II, the slightly batty king of Bavaria, built his dramatic castles; it's also here that even today people nonchalantly wear *Lederhosen*. The castles and Garmisch-Partenkirchen make good daytrips from Munich or Füssen; Berchtesgaden offers excellent hiking.

KÖNIGSSCHLÖßER (ROYAL CASTLES). King Ludwig II, a zany visionary and fervent Wagner fan, used his cash to create fantastic castles. In 1886, a band of nobles and bureaucrats deposed Ludwig, had him declared insane, and imprisoned him. Three days later, the King and a loyal advisor were mysteriously discovered dead in a nearby lake. The fairytale castles that framed Ludwig's life and the enigma of his death still captivate tourists today. The glitzy ■**Schloß Neuschwanstein** is now Germany's most clichéd tourist attraction and was the inspiration for Disneyland's Cinderella Castle. The completed chambers (63 remain unfinished) include a Byzantine throne room, a small artificial grotto, and an immense *Sängersaal* (singer's hall) built expressly for Wagnerian opera performances. Ludwig grew up in the bright yellow, neo-Gothic **Schloß Hohenschwangau** across the way. (Both open Apr.-Sept. 9am-6pm; Oct.-Mar. 10am-4pm. Mandatory tours DM14/€7.20 per castle, students DM12/€6.15; combination ticket DM26/€13.35, DM22/€11.30.) Tickets can be purchased at the Ticket-Service Center, Alpseestr. 12 (☎08362 930 83 20), about 100m south of the Hohenschwangau bus stop.

From Füssen, hop on **bus** #9713 marked Königsschlösser, which departs from the train station (10min., 2 per hr., DM2.60/€1.35). It will drop you in front of the information booth (open daily 9am-6pm; the Ticket-Service Center is a short walk uphill on Alpseestr. Separate paths lead up to both Hohenschwangau and Neuschwanstein. A *Tagesticket* (DM13/€6.65, from the bus driver) gives castle-hoppers unlimited regional bus use.

GARMISCH-PARTENKIRCHEN. The **Zugspitze** (2964m), Germany's tallest mountain, is the main attraction in town, and there are two ways to conquer it, though they should only be attempted in fair weather. You can take the **cog railway** from the Zugspitzbahnhof (50m behind the Garmisch main station) to the *Zugspitzplatt* outlook (1¼hr., every hr. 7:35am-2:35pm), then continue on the **Gletscherbahn** cable car to the top. (Return with train and cable car DM81/€41.60.) You can also get off the railway at Eibsee and take the **Eibsee Seilbahn,** one of the steepest cable car runs in the world, all the way to the top (1½hr., every hr. 8am-4:15pm, round trip with train and cable car DM81/€41.60). Garmisch-Partenkirchen is accessible by **train** from Innsbruck (1½hr., 1 per hr., DM20.20/€10.50) or Munich (1½hr., 1 per hr., DM27/€14), and by **bus** #1084 from Füssen (2hr., 6-7 per day, DM13/€6.65). To get to the **tourist office,** Richard-Strauss-Pl. 2, turn left on Bahnhofstr. from the train station and turn left onto Von-Brug-Str.; the office faces the fountain on the square. The staff distributes maps and finds rooms for free. (☎18 07 00. Open M-Sa 8am-6pm, Su 10am-noon.) To reach the **Jugendherberge (HI),** Jochstr. 10, cross the street from the train station and take bus #3 (dir. Burgrain) or 4 or 5 (dir. Farchant) to Burgrain. Walk straight down Am Lahner Wiesgraben and turn right after two blocks onto Jochstr. (☎08821 29 80. Ages 18-26 and families only. Reception 7-9am and 5pm-midnight. Lockout 9am-3:30pm. Curfew 11:30pm. Open Jan. to mid-Nov. Dorms DM27.50/€14.30.) **HL Markt,** at the intersection of Bahnhofstr. and Von-Brug-Str., sells groceries. (Open M-F 8am-8pm, Sa 7:30am-4pm.)

BERCHTESGADEN. The area's natural beauty and the sinister attraction of Hitler's mountaintop **Kehlsteinhaus** ("Eagle's Nest") draw world travelers to the town. The stone resort house, now a restaurant, has a spectacular view from the 1834m peak; renovations to add a hotel and golf resort began in July 2001. Take Obersalzburg/Kehlsteinbus #38 (June-Oct. every 45min., round-trip DM6.40/€3.30); hop off at Hintereck and buy a combined ticket for bus #9 to Kehlstein Parkpl./Eagle's Nest and the elevator ride up to the peak (every 30min. 9:30am-4pm, DM23/€11.75). Be sure to reserve your spot for the return bus when you get off. (Open daily May-Oct. except heavy snow days.) **Trains** run hourly to Munich (3hr., DM48/€25.60) and Salzburg (1hr., DM12.60/€6.50). The **tourist office**, Königsseerstr. 2, opposite the station, has tips on **hiking** trails in the Berchtesgaden National Park. (☎96 71 50. Open M-F 8:30am-6pm, Sa 9am-5pm, Su 9am-3pm; Nov. to mid-June M-F 8:30am-5pm, Sa 9am-noon.) To get to the **Jugendherberge (HI)**, Gebirgsjägerstr. 52, turn right from the station, left on Ramsauer Str., right on Gmündbrücke, and left up the steep gravel path. You can also take bus #39 (dir.: Strub Kaserne) to Jugendherberge. (☎943 70. Breakfast and sheets included. Reception 6:30-9am and 5-7pm. Check-in until 10pm. Curfew midnight. Closed Nov.-Dec. 26. 10-bed dorms DM27.50/€14.) **Express-Grill Hendl,** Maximilianstr. 8, serves Bavarian dishes. From the train station, follow the signs marked "Zum Markt" and bear right on Maximillianstr. (Open Tu-Su 11am-8pm.) For groceries, stop by the **Edeka Markt,** Königsseer Str. 22. (Open M-F 7:30am-6pm, Sa 7:30am-noon.) **Postal Code:** 83471. ☎**08652.**

■ **HIKING NEAR BERCHTESGADEN.** From Berchtesgaden, the 5½km path to the Königssee—which winds through fields of flowers, across bubbling brooks, and past several beer gardens—affords a heart-stopping view of the Alps. From the train station, cross the street, turn right, and take a quick left over the bridge. Walk to the right of and past the green-roofed building (but not up the hill) and take a left onto the gravel path near the stone wall, then follow the "Königssee" signs. Alternatively, take bus #41 from the bus station to Königssee (DM6.60/€3.40 return). Once you arrive in Königstein, walk down Seestr. and look for the Nationalpark Informationstelle to your left, which has hiking information. To explore the Berchtesgaden National Park, take bus #46 from Berchtesgaden (15min., every hr. 6am-7:15pm, DM3.80/€1.95 one-way, DM6.50/€3.35 round-trip) to Ramsau, then visit the Ramsau tourist office, Im Tal 2, for trail maps and hiking information. (☎(08657) 98 89 20. Open M-Sa 8am-noon and 1:15-5pm., Su 9am-noon and 2-5pm; Oct-June M-F 8am-noon and 1:15-5pm.)

THE CHIEMSEE ☎08051

The Chiemsee's picturesque islands and dramatic crescent of mountains have long inspired artistic masterpieces. **Ferries** run from Prien to Herreninsel and Fraueninsel (40min., every hr. 6:40am-7:30pm, DM10.80-12.80/€5.50-6.60). To get to the ferry port, turn right from the main entrance of the Prien train station and follow Seestr. for 20min., or hop on the green *Chiemseebahn* steam train from the station (9:40am-6:15pm, round-trip including ship passage DM16.50/€8.50).

PRIEN AM CHIEMSEE. On the southwestern corner of the Chiemsee, Prien is a good base for exploring the islands. **Trains** depart from the station, a few blocks from the city center, for Munich (1hr., every hr., DM23.40/€12) and Salzburg (50min., every hr., DM17/€8.70); call ☎28 74 for information. The **tourist office,** Alte Rathausstr. 11, dispenses maps and books private rooms (Privatzimmer) for free. (☎690 50. Open M-F 8:30am-6pm, Sa 8:30am-noon.) The **Jugendherberge (HI),** Carl-Braun-Str. 66, is a 15min. walk from the station: go right on Seestr. and turn left on Staudenstr., which becomes Carl-Braun-Str. (☎687 70. Showers, lockers, and breakfast included. Reception 8-9am, 5-7pm, and 9:30-10pm. Lockout 9am-1pm. Curfew 10pm. Open early Feb. to Nov. 6-bed rooms DM28.80/€14.75.) For **Campingpl. Hofbauer,** Bernauer Str. 110, turn left on Seestr. from the station, turn left at the next intersection, and walk 25min. along Bernauerstr. heading out of town. (☎41 36. Showers included. Reception 7:30-11am and 2-8pm. Open Apr.-Oct.

DM11/€5.65 per person, DM10/€5.15 per tent and car.) Grab a cheap meal at **Bäck-erei/Cafe Müller,** Marktpl. 8. (M-F 6:30am-6pm, Sa 6:30am-12:30pm.)

HERRENINSEL AND FRAUENINSEL. Ludwig's palace on **Herreninsel** (Gentlemen's Island), **Königsschloß Herrenchiemsee,** is a shameless attempt to be larger, better, and more extravagant than Louis XIV's Versailles. Ludwig bankrupted Bavaria building this place—a few unfinished rooms (abandoned after funds ran out) contrast greatly with the completed portion of the castle. (Open Apr.-Sept. daily 9am-6pm; Oct. 9:40am-5pm; Nov.-Mar. 9:40am-4pm. DM11/€5.65, students DM9/€4.60; obligatory tour.) **Fraueninsel** (Ladies' Island), is home to the **Klosterkirche** (Island Cloister), the nunnery that complemented the former monastery on Herreninsel. The nuns make their own marzipan, beeswax candles, and five kinds of liqueur, for sale in the convent shop (0.2L Klosterlikör DM8.50/€4.40). The 8th-century **Cross of Bischofhofen** and other religious artifacts are displayed in the Michaelskapelle above the **Torhalle** (gate), the oldest surviving part of the cloister. (Open June-Sept. 11am-5pm. DM4/€2.05, students DM3/€1.55.)

REGENSBURG   ☎ 0941

The first capital of Bavaria and eventually the site of the first German parliament, Regensburg is packed with history. The **Dom St. Peter** dazzles with richly colored stained glass. Inside, the **Domschatz** (Cathedral Treasury) displays gold and jewels purchased by the bishops as well as the preserved hand of Bishop Chrysostomus, who died in AD 407. (Cathedral open Apr.-Oct. daily 6:30am-6pm; Nov.-Mar. 6:30am-5pm. Free. Wheelchair accessible. Domschatzmuseum open Apr.-Oct. Tu-Sa 10am-5pm, Su noon-5pm; Nov.-Mar. Tu-Sa 10am-4pm, Su noon-4pm. DM3/€1.55, students DM1.50/€0.80.) A few blocks away, the **Rathaus** (town hall) served as capital of the Holy Roman Empire until 1803; the four long iron rods fastened to its side were the official measurement standards used by merchants in the Middle Ages. The Rathaus also houses the **Reichstagsmuseum.** (English tours May-Sept. M-Sa at 3:15pm. DM5/€2.55, students and seniors DM2.50/€1.30.)

    Trains head to: Munich (1½hr., 1 per hr., DM38/€19.45); Nuremberg (1-1½hr., 1-2 per hr., DM27/€13.80); and Passau (1-1½hr., 1 per hr., DM32/€16.40). To get from the station to the **tourist office,** in the Altes Rathaus on Rathauspl., walk down Maximilianstr., turn left on Grasg., turn right at the end onto Obere Bachg., and follow it for five blocks. (☎507 44 10. Open M-F 8:30am-6pm, Sa 9am-4pm, Su 9:30am-2:30pm; Apr.-Oct. also open Su until 4pm.) To get from the station to the **Jugendherberge (HI),** Wöhrdstr. 60, walk to the end of Maximilianstr., turn right at the *Apotheke* onto Pflugg., turn left immediately at the *Optik* sign onto tiny Erhardig., walk left over the bridge, and veer right onto Wöhrdstr. The hostel is on the right. Or, take bus #3, 8, or 9 (DM2.80/€1.45) from the station to Eisstadion. (☎574 02. Breakfast and sheets included. Reception 6am-1am. Check-in until 1am. Curfew 1am, but access code available. Reservations encouraged. Dorms DM31/€15.85.) **Hinterhaus,** Rote-Hahnen-Gasse 2, serves both vegetarian (from DM5/€2.60) and meat (from DM8.80/€4.50) dishes. (Open daily 6pm-1am.) There's a **supermarket** in the basement of Galeria Kaufhof, on Neupfarrpl. (open M-F 9am-8pm, Sa 9am-4pm). **Postal Code:** 93047.

PASSAU   ☎ 0851

This beautiful 2000-year-old city embodies the ideal Old World European city. Passau's Baroque architecture peaks at the sublime **Stephansdom,** Domplatz, where cherubs sprawl across the ceiling and the world's largest church organ looms above the choir. (Open daily in summer 6:30am-7pm; in winter 6:30am-6pm. Free. Organ concerts May-Oct. M-Sa noon, Th 7:30pm. DM4/€2.10, students DM2/€1.05; Th DM10/€5.15, students DM5/€2.60.) Behind the cathedral is the **Residenz,** home to the **Domschatz** (cathedral treasury), an extravagant collection of gold and tapestries. (Enter through the inside back of the Stephansdom, to the right of the altar. Open Easter-Oct. M-Sa 10am-4pm. DM2/€1.05, students DM1/€0.55.) The heights of the river during various floods are marked on the outside wall of the 13th-century Gothic **Rathaus.** (Open Apr.-Oct. daily 10am-4pm. DM3/€1.55, students DM1/€0.55.) Over the Luitpoldbrücke bridge is the former palace of the bishopric, now home to the **Cultural History Museum.** (Open early Apr. to Oct. M-F 9am-5pm, Sa-Su 10am-6pm; Nov.-Mar. Tu-Su 9am-5pm. DM8/€4.10, students DM3/€1.55.)

Trains depart the **Hauptbahnhof** (☎350 43 47) to: Frankfurt (4½hr., every 2hr., DM125/€64); Munich (2hr., every 2 hr., DM52/€26.60); Nuremberg (2hr., every 2hr., DM60/€30.70); and Vienna (3½hr., 1-2 per hr., DM60/€30.70). To get to the **tourist office,** Rathauspl. 3, follow Bahnhofstr. from the train station to Ludwigspl., bear left downhill across Ludwigspl. to Ludwigstr., which becomes Rindermarkt, Steinweg, and finally Große Messerg.; continue straight on Schusterg. and turn left on Schrottg. (☎95 59 80. Open Easter to mid-Oct. M-F 8:30am-6pm, Sa-Su 9:30am-3pm; Nov.-Easter M-Th 8:30am-5pm, F 8:30am-4pm.) The **Jugendherberge (HI),** Veste Oberhaus 125, is perched high above the Danube. Cross the suspension bridge downstream from the Rathaus, then ignore the misplaced sign pointing up the steps; instead, turn right and proceed through the left hand tunnel. Head up the cobblestone driveway on your left, through the yellow house, and the hostel's on the right. (☎41 35 19. Breakfast included. Reception 7-11:30am and 3:30pm-midnight. New arrivals after 3:30pm. Curfew midnight; door access code available. Reservations recommended. Dorm beds DM26/€13.30.) **Innstr.,** which runs parallel to the Inn River, is lined with good, cheap places to eat. Pick up groceries at **Edeka supermarket,** on Ludwigstr. 2, at the intersection with Grabengasse. (Open M-F 8am-8pm, Sa 7:30am-4pm.) Get fruit, meat, baked goods, sandwiches (DM3.50/€1.80), and salad by weight (DM1.59/€0.85 per 100g) at **Schmankerl Passage,** Ludwigstr. 6. (Open M-F 7:30am-6pm, Sa 7:30am-2pm.) **Postal Code:** 94032.

GREECE (Ελλας)

GREEK DRACHMA

US$1 = 371DR	100DR = US$0.27
CDN$1 = 240DR	100DR = CDN$0.42
AUS$1 = 199DR	100DR = AUS$0.50
UK£1 = 537DR	100DR = UK£0.19
IR£1 = 433DR	100DR = IR£0.23
NZ$1 = 163DR	100DR = NZ$0.61
ZAR1 = 45DR	100DR = ZAR2.23
EUR€1 = 341DR	100DR = EUR€0.29

PHONE CODE	**Country code: 30. International dialing prefix: 00.** From outside Greece, dial int'l dialing prefix (see inside back cover) + 30 + city code + local number.

Over the centuries, Greece has occupied a unique position at the crossroads of Europe and Asia. The relics of Crete's Minoan civilization betray the influence of flowering contemporary cultures in Egypt and Babylon. Greece emerged independent in 1821 under the dual veneer of Classical Athens and Imperial Byzantium, but its Ottoman Empire heritage still persists. Four centuries under the Turks left a certain spice in its food, an Oriental flair in the strains of its *bouzouki* music, and minaret tips in its skylines. The memory of Dionysus, god of the vine, fuels the island circuit—a blur of sun, sand, and sex. In Greece's austere hills, monks and hermits lurk in structures that have weathered well two millennia. As the country embraces the Euro and overhauls its infrastructure for the 2004 Summer Olympics in Athens, development has accelerated at a blistering pace; as Euripides's Medea quipped, "let the world's great order be reversed" and renewed. Still, when you climb above the concrete resorts and whirring tour buses—when you hear the wind's lonely, persistent whistle—you'll know that Greece remains oracles' realm.

For coverage of Greece rivaling that of Pausanias, see *Let's Go: Greece 2002*.

FACTS AND FIGURES

Official Name: Hellenic Republic.
Capital: Athens.
Major cities: Thessaloniki.
Population: 10.6 million.
Land Area: 131,940 sq. km.

Climate: Sunny, hot, and dry summers; cool, rainy winters (50°F). October to March is the rainy season.
Language: Greek.
Religion: Eastern Orthodox (98%).

DISCOVER GREECE

Launch your Greek adventure in the urban sprawl of **Athens** (p. 472), with visits to the Acropolis and the National Museum, a daytrip to Cape Sounion, a sunset atop Lycavittos, and a night out clubbing in Glyfada. Then swing into the Peloponnese: whisper tragic secrets at the theater of **Epidavros** (p. 484) before a sunset stroll among the mansions of **Nafplion** (p. 483). Dash west to **Olympia** (p. 481) for your own Olympic footrace beside the ruins, then ferry from Patras to **Corfu** (p. 490), an isle lovingly immortalized by cultural luminaries (Edward Lear, Oscar Wilde) and wild partyers. Back on the mainland, soak up Greece's second city, **Thessaloniki** (p. 486), where trendy shops neighbor some of Byzantium's most precious ruins. Climb the cliffside **Monasteries of Meteora** (p. 485), then commune with the ancient gods at **Mt. Olympus** (p. 485) and at the fortune-telling Oracle of **Delphi** (p. 479). Hop a ferry from Athens to **Crete,** where the mythical Minotaur munched men (**Knossos,** p. 498); Europe's longest gorge, **Samaria** (p. 499), and unparalleled Mediterranean beaches await to the west.

Greece

Recharge on the white cliffside buildings and black sand beaches of **Santorini** (p. 497), then party for days and nights on **Mykonos** (p. 494); repent with a visit to the Temple of Apollo on the sacred isle of **Delos** (p. 494).

ESSENTIALS

WHEN TO GO

June through August is high season in Greece; consider visiting during May or September, when the weather is beautiful and the crowds thinner. The off season, from mid-September through May, offers cheaper airfares and lodging, but many sights and accommodations have shorter hours or close altogether. Facilities and sights close and ferries run considerably less frequently in winter, although ski areas at Mt. Parnassos, Mt. Pelion, and Metsovo beckon winter visitors.

DOCUMENTS AND FORMALITIES

VISAS. South Africans need a visa to enter Greece; citizens of Australia, New Zealand, Canada, the UK, Ireland, and the US can visit for up to three months without a visa.

EMBASSIES. Foreign embassies for Greece are in Athens (p. 472). For Greek embassies at home: **Australia,** 9 Turrana St., Yarralumla, Canberra, ACT 26000 (☎(02) 6273 3011); **Canada,** 80 MacLaren St., Ottawa, ON K2P 0K6 (☎613-238-6271); **Ireland,** 1 Upper Pembroke St., Dublin 2 (☎(01) 6767 2545); **South Africa,**

1003 Church St. Athlone, Hatfield, 0028, Pretoria (☎ (012) 437 35 13); **UK,** 1a Holland Park, London W113TP (☎ (0171) 229 3850); and **US,** 2221 Massachusetts Ave., N.W., Washington, D.C. 20008 (☎ 202-939-5800).

TRANSPORTATION

BY PLANE. Flying from northern European cities is a popular way of getting to Greece. From North America, an indirect flight through Brussels or Luxembourg may cost less than a flight going directly to Athens. Over the past few years, the domestic *(esoteriko)* service of **Olympic Airways,** Syngrou 96-100, 11741 Athens (☎ (01) 926 91 11), has increased. Even in low season, more remote areas are serviced several times weekly, while developed regions have several flights per day.

BY TRAIN. A number of relatively cheap (and slow) international train routes connect Athens, Thessaloniki, and Larisa to most European cities. For example, a journey from Vienna to Athens takes at least three days. Train service in Greece is limited and sometimes uncomfortable, and no lines go to the western coast. The more extensive and reliable bus system is a better way to get around the country; if you must travel by rail, the new express intercity trains are well worth the price. **Eurail** passes are valid. **Hellenic Railways Organization (OSE)** connects Athens to other major Greek cities. In Greece, call ☎ 145 or 147 for schedules and prices.

BY BUS. Fast, extensive, and reasonably priced, buses are the best alternative for travel within Greece; most are run through **KTEL** (www.ktel.org). **Busabout,** 258 Vauxhall Bridge Rd., London SW1V 1BS, is one of the very few European bus lines that also runs to Greece (☎ (0171) 950 1661), but there are almost no buses running directly from any European city to Greece. Smaller towns may use cafes as bus stops—ask for a schedule. **Confirm your destination** with the driver; signs may be wrong. Along the road, little blue signs marked with white buses or the word "ΣΤΑΣΗ" indicate stops. Drivers usually stop anywhere if you flag them down; let him know in advance where you want to get off; if your stop is passed, yell "Stasi!" (STASH). Intercity buses are usually **blue.**

BY FERRY. Ferry travel is a popular way to get to and travel within Greece and Cyprus; their ports can be reached from a seemingly unlimited number of points, and finding a boat agency to facilitate your trip should not be difficult. Be warned that **ferries run on irregular schedules.** A few websites, like www.gptnet.com and www.ferries.gr, have tried to keep updated schedules online and are worth a try. You should try to take a look at a schedule as close to your departure as possible; you can usually find one at a tourist office or posted at the dock. That said, you should also make reservations, and check in at *least* 2hr. in advance; late boarders may find their seats gone. If you sleep on deck, bring warm clothes and a sleeping bag. Bicycles travel free, but motorcycles will have an additional charge. Don't forget motion sickness medication, toilet paper, and a hand towel. Bring food and drink to avoid high prices on board. The major ports of departure from Italy to Greece are Ancona and Brindisi, on the southeast coast of Italy. Bari, Otranto, and Venice also have a few connections.

BY CAR AND MOPED. Cars are a luxury in Greece, where public transportation is nonexistent after 7pm; mopeds are vastly more popular, especially among young people. Ferries carry cars if you pay a transport fee. Drivers must be comfortable with a stick shift transmission (for cars), hairpin turns on winding mountain roads, reckless drivers (especially in Athens), and the Greek alphabet—signs in Greek appear roughly 100m before the transliterated versions. The **Automobile and Touring Club of Greece (ELPA),** Messogion 395, Athens 11527 (☎ 60 68 800), provides assistance, reciprocal membership to foreign auto club members, 24-hr. emergency road assistance (☎ 104), and an information line. (☎ 174 in Athens, ☎ 01 60 68 838 elsewhere in Greece. Open M-F 7am-3pm.) **Moped** and car rental places proliferate in almost every town. **Taxis** are available in larger towns and cities to take you anywhere for several hundred drachmas; most gather near the central *plateia* or along the waterfront. Expect to pay much higher rates at night.

TOURIST SERVICES AND MONEY

EMERGENCY	Police: ☎ 100. Ambulance: ☎ 166. Hospital: ☎ 106.

TOURIST OFFICES. Tourism is overseen by two national organizations: the **Greek National Tourist Organization (GNTO)** and the **tourist police** *(touristiki astinomia)*. The GNTO main office is at 2 Amerikis St., Athens (☎ (01) 327 1300). The GNTO is known as **EOT** in Greek. The **tourist police** (☎ 171; 24hr.) deal with more local and immediate problems: where to find a room, what the bus schedule is, or what to do when you've lost your passport.

MONEY. Greek **drachmas** (abbreviated "dr") are issued in both paper notes (100, 200, 500, 1000, 5000, and 10,000dr) and coins (5, 10, 20, 50, and 100dr). Greece has adopted the **Euro (€)** as legal tender, and Greek drachmas will be phased out by July 1, 2002. For more information, see p. 24.

A bare-bones day in Greece costs about US$35. Camping can save about US$10-15 per day. A day with more creature comforts runs US$50. With tipping, the more informal the venue, the more flexible the price. Don't tip taxis. At all but the ritziest restaurants, service is included in the bill; instead of adding a tip, round your bill up—a few hundred *drachmas* at most. Feel free to bargain for *domatia* prices and at street markets; for more formal stores or hotels, it is less acceptable to bargain.

BUSINESS HOURS. Businesses generally open in the early morning and close in the hot afternoon hours, to reopen in the evening. On Sundays and holidays most businesses are closed; opening hours aren't strict, but are at the owner's whim.

COMMUNICATION

MAIL. Letters can be sent general delivery to almost any Greek city or town with a post office. Address **Poste Restante** letters to: First name SURNAME, Poste Restante, Vathy, Ithaka, Greece. Mail goes to a special desk in the central post office, unless you specify differently. Letters from Europe generally take at least three days to arrive; airmail from the US, South Africa, and Australia takes 5-10 days.

TELEPHONES. To make calls in Greece, you'll need a **prepaid phone card,** available at street side kiosks and *peripteros*. Time is measured in minutes or talk units (e.g. 100 units=30min. domestic calling). The card usually has a toll-free access telephone number and a **personal identification number (PIN).** Phone rates are highest in the morning, lower in the evening, and lowest on Sunday and late. National phone service long-distance rates can be high—use a calling card to call home. Contact your service provider's Greek operator: **AT&T,** ☎ 00 800 13 11; **BT,** ☎ 00 800 44 11; **Canada,** ☎ 00 800 16 11; **Ireland,** ☎ 155 11 74; **MCI,** ☎ 00 800 12 11; **Sprint,** ☎ 00 900 14 11.

INTERNET. The availability of the Internet in Greece is rapidly expanding. In all big cities, in most small cities and large towns, and on many islands, you can find Internet access. Expect to pay around 1500dr/€4.40 per hour. **Cybercaffe Guide** (www.cyberiacafe.net/cyberia/guide/ccafe.htm) lists cybercafes in Greece.

LANGUAGE. Although many Greeks in Athens and other heavily touristed areas—particularly young people—speak English, rural Greeks rarely do. For the basics, see p. 981. Transliterating from Greek to English can cause some confusion: for instance, Φ and φ can be spelled *ph* or *f*. Greek body language will help you avoid misunderstandings. To say no, Greeks lift their heads back abruptly while raising their eyebrows; they emphatically nod once to say yes. A hand waving up and down that seems to say "stay there" actually means "come."

ACCOMMODATIONS AND CAMPING

Lodging in Greece is a bargain. Only one **hostel** in Greece is HI; the non-HI hostels are in most cases still safe and reputable. Hostel curfews are strict, and may leave you on the street. **Domatia** (rooms to let in Greeks' homes) are an attractive, perfectly dependable option; they're cheap and offer you a truly local experience. Often you'll be approached by locals as you enter town or disembark from your boat, and tourist offices list all *domatia* in town. Have the proprietors point out their establishment on a map before trekking there, and agree on a price before taking a room. **Hotel** prices are regulated, though the owners may push you to take the most expensive room. Check your bill carefully, and threaten to contact the tourist police if you think you are being cheated. **GNTO** offices usually have a list of inexpensive accommodations. Greece hosts plenty of **campgrounds,** which rent tents or even cabins for extremely low prices. Bring a sleeping bag if you plan to camp.

FOOD AND DRINK

Medical studies have highlighted the Greek diet as a model for healthy eating because of its reliance on unsaturated olive oil and vegetables. Penny-pinching carnivores will thank Zeus for lamb, chicken, or beef *souvlaki* and hot-off-the-spit *gyros* stuffed into a pita. Vegetarians can also eat their fill for cheap: try the feta-piled *horiatiki* (Greek salad), savory pastries like *spanakopita* (cheese pie, a pastry full of feta) and *tiropita* (spinach pie), and the fresh fruits and vegetables found at markets and vendor stands in most cities. Greek-style liquid relaxation typically involves a few basic options: the old standbys are *ouzo* (a Greek spirit that will earn your respect) and grainy Greek coffee. A Greek restaurant is known as a *taverna* or *estiatorio;* a grill is a *psistaria.* Don't be suspicious of restaurants without menus; this is common. Waiters will ask you if you want salad, appetizers, or the works, so be careful not to wind up with mountains of food, since Greek portions tend to be large. Service is always included in the check, but it is customary to leave a few *drachmas* as an extra tip.

HOLIDAYS AND FESTIVALS

Holidays: Feast of St. Basil/New Year's Day (Jan. 1); Epiphany (Jan. 6); First Sunday in Lent (Mar. 18); Greek Independence Day (Mar. 25); Good Friday (Apr. 13); St. George's Day (Apr. 23); Labor Day (May 1); Easter (May 5); Ascension (June 13); Pentecost (June 23); Feast of the Assumption (Aug. 15); Virgin Mary's Birthday (Sept. 8); Feast of St. Demetrius (Oct. 26); National Anniversary of Greek Independence (Oct. 28); Commemoration of a Greek university students' uprising (Nov. 17); Christmas (Dec. 25).

Festivals: Starting on Feb. 25 of this year, 3 weeks of feasting and dancing at **Carnival** will precede the Lenten fast.

ATHENS (Αθηνα)   ☎01

One minute of dodging the packs of mopeds in Pl. Syndagma will prove that Athens—the sprawling work of centuries—refuses to become a museum. Ancient ruins sit quietly in glowing white marble amid the hectic modern streets as testaments to the city's rich history. The Acropolis looms larger than life over the city, a perpetual reminder of ancient glory, and Byzantine churches recall an era of foreign invaders. The reborn democracy of the past two centuries has revived the city in a wave of madcap construction: the conflicted, oddly adolescent metropolis gutted its crumbling medieval mansions to become a dense concrete jungle. Crowded, noisy, polluted, and totally alive, Athens will maroon you in traffic at 2am on a Tuesday, but a new subway system should be ready for the 2004 Olympic Summer Games. Still, civil engineers refuse to "destroy everything in the name of the underground," and pick their way among subterranean antiquities, cisterns, and the springs of lost, ancient rivers that sleep beneath the city.

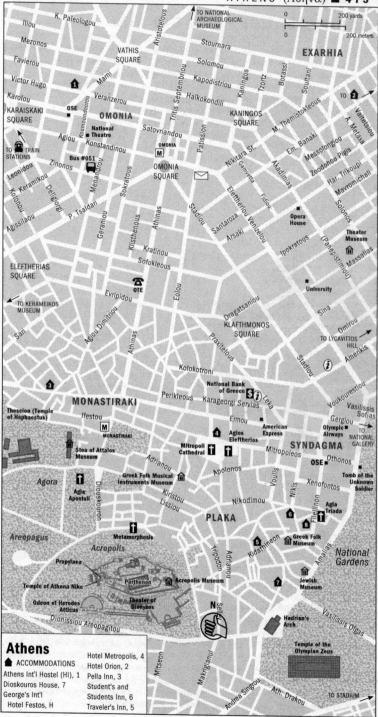

GREECE

Athens

ACCOMMODATIONS

Athens Int'l Hostel (HI), 1
Dioskouros House, 7
George's Int'l
  Hotel Festos, H

Hotel Metropolis, 4
Hotel Orion, 2
Pella Inn, 3
Student's and
  Students Inn, 6
Traveler's Inn, 5

⊏ TRANSPORTATION

Flights: El. Venizelou (☎35 30 000), Greece's new international airport, operates as one massive, yet easily navigable terminal. Arrivals are on the ground floor, departures are on the 2nd floor. Four bus lines run to Athens, Piraeus, and Rafina.

Trains: Larissis Train Station (☎52 98 837) serves northern Greece and the rest of Europe. To: **Thessaloniki** (7hr., 4 per day, 4800dr/€14.25.); **Prague,** Czech Republic (35,000dr/€102.72); **Bucharest, Romania** and **Budapest,** Hungary (40,000dr/€117.39); and **Bratislava,** Slovakia (30,000dr/€88.04). Take trolley #1 from El. Venizelou (Panepistimiou) in Pl. Syndagma (every 10min., 150dr/€0.45), or take the subway to Sepolia. **Peloponnese Train Station** (☎51 31 601) serves Serves Patras (4¼hr., 1800dr/€5.30) as well as major towns in the Peloponnese. Open 24hr. From Larissis, exit to your right and go over the footbridge.

Buses: Terminal A: Kifissou 100 (☎51 24 910). Take blue bus #051 from the corner of Zinonos and Menandrou near Pl. Omonia (every 15min., 150dr/€0.45). Buses depart for **Patras** (3hr., 30 per day, 4000dr/€11.75) and **Thessaloniki** (6hr., 11 per day, 9000dr/€26.45). **Terminal B:** Liossion 260 (☎83 17 153, except Sa-Su). Take blue bus #024 from Amalias outside the National Gardens. (45min., every 20min., 120dr/€0.35). Buses depart for **Delphi** (3hr., 6 per day, 3300dr/€9.70).

Ferries: Check schedules at the tourist office, in the Athens News, or with the Port Authority of Piraeus (☎42 26 000). Most ferries dock at **Piraeus;** some at nearby **Rafina.** See **Piraeus,** p. 479. For information on other ferries, see **By Ferry,** p. 470.

Public Transportation: Purchase tickets for the blue **buses** (designated by 3-digit numbers) or yellow **trolleys** (1-2 digits) from any street kiosk (150dr/€0.45), and validate them on board. The **metro** is under construction; its 3 lines connect northern Kifissia to Piraeus **(M1),** Sepolia to Dafni **(M2),** and Ethniki Amyna to Pl. Syndagma **(M3)** in central Athens. Trains depart from either end of the line every (5min. 5am-midnight). Buy metro **tickets** (250dr/€0.75) in any station.

Taxis: Meter **rates** start at 250dr/€0.75, with an additional 80dr/€0.25 per km within city limits, 150dr/€0.45 per km in the suburbs, 40dr/€0.15 per stationary min. Everything beyond the start price is 150dr/€0.44 between midnight and 5am. 400dr/€1.20 surcharge from the airport; 200dr/€0.60 surcharge for trips from port, bus, and railway terminals; 100dr/€0.30 per piece of luggage over 10kg.

⚡ 🛈 ORIENTATION AND PRACTICAL INFORMATION

Plaka Syndagma is the center of modern Athens. Budget travel offices, eateries, and hostels line **Nikis** and **Filellinon,** which run south from Pl. Syndagma into the eastern part of **Plaka** (bounded by the Acropolis to the southwest and the Temple of Olympian Zeus to the southeast), the center of the old city and temporary home to most tourists. **Monastiraki,** mostly known for its hodge-podge flea market, lies west of Pl. Syndagma. Northwest of Pl. Syndagma, **Plaka Omonia** (which has become increasingly unsafe) is the site of the city's main subway station. North of Pl. Syndagma and east of Omonia, hip **Exarhia** brims with students, while east of Pl. Sydagma lies the glitzy area of **Kolonaki.** Southeast of Pl. Syndagma is large, quiet **Pangrati.** A 30min. ride to the south is **Glyfada,** a seaside suburb where the bacchanalians party. Be aware that Athenian streets often have multiple spellings or names.

Tourist Office: The **central office** and **information booth** are at Amerikis 2 (☎33 10 561; www.areianet.gr/infoxenios/GNTO), off Stadiou near Pl. Syndagma. City maps and transportation information. Open M-F 9am-9pm, Sa-Su 10am-9pm.

Banks: National Bank of Greece, Karageorgi Servias 2 (☎33 40 015), in Pl. Syndagma. Open M-Th 8am-2pm, F 8am-1:30pm; currency exchange only M-Th 3:30-6:30pm, F 3-6:30pm, Sa 9am-3pm, Su 9am-1pm. Currency exchange available 24hr. at the airport, but exchange rates and commissions may be exorbitantly high.

American Express: Ermou 2, P.O. Box 3325 (☎32 44 975 or 32 44 979), above McDonald's in Pl. Syndagma. Cashes traveler's checks commission-free. Open M-F 8:30am-4pm, Sa 8:30am-1:30pm (only travel and mail services Sa).

Bookstores: Eleftheroudakis Book Store, Panepistimiou 17 (☎33 14 180) and Nikis 20 (☎32 29 388). A browser's delight, with Greek, English, French, and German books, classical and recent literature. Open M-F 9am-9pm, Sa 9am-3pm.

Laundromats: Most *plinitirios* have signs reading "Laundry." Wash, dry, and fold for 2500dr/€7.27 at **Angelou Geront 10** in *Plaka*. (Open M-Sa 8am-7pm, Su 9am-2pm.)

Emergency: Police: ☎100. **Ambulance:** ☎166. **Fire:** ☎199. **Doctors:** ☎105 from Athens, ☎101 elsewhere; line open 2pm-7am. **AIDS Help Line:** ☎72 22 222. *Athens News* lists emergency hospitals. Free emergency health care for tourists.

Pharmacies: Check the daily *Athens News* (300dr) for the night pharmacy schedule.

Hospitals: On duty ☎106. **Geniko Kratiko Nosokomio** (Public State Hospital), Mesogion 154 (☎77 78 901). A **public hospital,** Evangelismou 45-47 (☎72 20 101) is near Kolonaki. "Hospital" is *nosokomio* in Greek; call operator at ☎131.

Telephones: OTE, Patission 85 (☎82 14 449 or 82 37 040) or Athinas 50 (☎32 16 699). Open M-F 7am-9pm, Sa 8am-3pm, Su 9am-2pm. Most phone booths in the city operate by **telephone cards** (1000dr/€2.93, 7000dr/€20.54, or 11,500dr/€33.45 at OTE offices, kiosks, and tourist shops). Push the "i" button on the phones for English instructions. For a domestic English-speaking operator, call ☎151.

Internet Access: Carousel Cybercafe, Eftixidou 32 (☎75 64 305), near Pl. Plastira in Pangrati. 1500dr/€4.40 per hr. 750dr/€2.20 minimum. Open daily 11am-midnight.

Post Office: Syndagma (☎32 26 253), on the corner of Mitropoleos. Address mail to be held: First Name SURNAME, Pl. Syndagma Post Office, Athens, Greece **10300.** Open M-F 7:30am-2:30pm, Sa-Su 9am-2pm.

⛺ ACCOMMODATIONS

Greek Youth Hostel Association, Dragatsaniou 4, 7th fl., lists hostels in Greece. Go up Stadiou and then left on Dragatsaniou, then take the elevators on the right as you enter the arcade. (☎32 34 107; fax 32 37 590. Open M-F 9am-3pm.) The **Hellenic Chamber of Hotels,** Karageorgi Servias 2, provides information and reservations for hotels of all classes throughout Greece. Reservations require a cash deposit, length of stay and number of people; you must contact them at least one month in advance. (☎32 37 193; fax 32 25 449; www.users.otenet.gr/~grhotels/index.htm. Open May-Nov. M-Th 8:30am-2pm, F 8:30am-1:30pm, Sa 9am-12:30pm.)

⊠ Hotel Dryades, Dryadon 4 (☎38 27 116). Elegant Dryades offers some of Athens's nicest budget-conscious accommodations, with large rooms and private baths. Full kitchen and TV lounge. Singles 10,000-12,000dr/€29.40-35.25; doubles 13,000-15,000dr/€38.15-45; triples 16,000-18,000dr/€47-52.85.

⊠ Student's and Traveler's Inn, Kidathineon 16 (☎32 44 808). Unrivaled location and lively atmosphere make up for early closing. Bring your own sheets, towel, and ask for toilet paper at the desk. Lockout midnight. Co-ed dorms 4500-5000dr/€13.25-14.70; doubles 12,000-15,000dr/€35.25-44; triples 15,000-18,000dr/€44-52.82; quads 16,000-24,000dr/€46.96-70.43. Call for a reservation and arrive on time.

Hotel Metropolis, Mitropoleos 46 (☎32 17 871), opposite Mitropoli Cathedral. Newly renovated, this hotel is a roomy step up at a good price. Balconies with views of the Acropolis. Laundry 2000dr/€5.90. Singles 10,000-14,000dr/€29.35-41.10; doubles 12,000-16,000dr/€35.25-47; triples 15,000-18,000dr/€44-52.82.

Pella Inn, Karaiskaki 1 (☎32 50 598). Walk 10min. down Ermou from Pl. Syndagma; it's 2 blocks from the Monastiraki subway station. Dorms 3000-4000dr/€8.80-11.74; doubles 10,000-12,000dr/€29.35-35.22; triples 12,000-15,000dr/€35.22-44.

YWCA (XEN), Amerikis 11 (☎36 24 291), up the street from the tourist office. For women only. Spacious building has hand-wash laundry facilities and fridges on each floor. 1000dr/€2.95 membership fee or valid YWCA membership required. Safe and central location make up for strict regulations. Singles 6000dr/€17.61, with bath 7500dr/€22; doubles 9000-9500dr/€26.41-27.88.

Thisseos Inn, Thisseos 10 (☎32 45 960). Take Karageorgi Servias, which becomes Perikleous, and Thisseos is on the right. This home-turned-hostel is close to Syndagma's sights but far from its noise. TV in reception area, full kitchen, fans, and common baths.

Dorms 3500-4500dr/€10.27-13.21; singles 5000-8000dr/€14.67-23.48; doubles 7500-10,000dr/€22-29.35; triples 13,500dr/€39.62.

Dioskouros House, Pitakou 6 (☎32 48 165), on the southwest corner of the National Gardens by the Temple of Olympian Zeus. Dorms 5000dr/€14.67; doubles 13,000dr/€38.15; triples 19,500dr/€57.23; quads 24,000dr/€70.43.

FOOD

Athens offers a melange of stands, open-air cafes, side-street *tavernas*, and intriguing restaurants. Cheap fast food abounds in Syndagma and Omonia—try *souvlaki* (250-400dr/€0.75-1.20), served either on a *kalamaki* (skewer) or wrapped in *pita*; *tost* (a grilled sandwich of variable ingredients, usually ham and cheese; 300-600dr/€0.90-1.80); *tiropita* (hot cheese pie, 300dr/€0.90); or *spanakopita* (hot spinach pie 300dr/€0.90). A *koulouri* (doughnut-shaped, sesame-coated roll; 50-100dr/€0.20-0.30) makes for a quick breakfast. Pick up **groceries** at the market on **Nikis.**

■ **Eden Vegetarian Restaurant,** Lysiou 12 (☎324 8858). Take Kidathineon to Tripidon, then turn left on to Lysiou. Fantastic dishes like *boureki pie* (zucchini with feta cheese. 1600dr/€4.70), and flavorful mushrooms *stifado* with onions and peppers (2900dr/€8.50). Open M and W-Su noon-midnight.

■ **Savvas,** Mitropoleos 86, tucked in a corner off Ermou. For takeout, this grill is a budget eater's dream, with heavenly, cheap gyros (400dr/€1.20). Don't sit down—prices skyrocket by 1500dr/€4.40. Open daily 7:30am-3am.

Jungle Juice, Aiolou 21, under the Acropolis. A fresh-squeezed smoothie and sandwich stand. Snag a turkey sandwich (500dr/€1.50) a "Leone Melone," a drink blend of cantaloupe, mango, and pineapple (900dr/€2.70). Open daily 8am-9pm.

O Barba Giannis, Em. Benaki 94. From Syndagma, walk up Stadiou and make a right on Em. Benaki. Athenian students, execs, and artists all agree that "Uncle John's" is the place for cheap, delicious food and outstanding service. Open daily 1pm-1am; closed Su in summer. Bring a Greek phrasebook; no English is spoken here.

Nikis Cafe, Nikis 3, near Ermou. More of a cafe than an eatery, Nikis does serve fresh baguette sandwiches (900dr/€2.70) and quiche. Strawberry and banana frozen margaritas 2000dr/€5.90. Open M-Sa 8am-1am.

Healthy Food Vegetarian Restaurant, Panepistimiou 57. Wholesomeness to make a *souvlaki* stand blush—everything's made fresh. Try the *muesli* (1050dr/€3.10) or carrot apple-juice (500dr/€1.50). Open daily 8am-9:30pm.

Attalos Restaurant, Adrianou 9, near the Thisseon area. This traditional Greek taverna serves skewered *souvlaki* (1900dr/€5.60), as well as a variety of handmade *croquettes* (a vegetarian plate for 2-4 people 2600dr/€7.65). *Bouzouki* photos adorn the wall. Open daily 9am-2am.

SIGHTS

THE ACROPOLIS

Reach the entrance on the west side of the Acropolis either from Areopagitou to the south by following the signs from Plaka, or by exiting the Agora to the south, following the path uphill, and turning right. Open daily 8am-6:30pm; in winter 8am-2:30pm. Site and Acropolis Museum 2000dr/€5.90, students and EU seniors 1000dr/€2.95, under 18 free.

Perched on a rocky plateau above the city, the Acropolis has crowned Athens since the 5th century BC. At the center, the Parthenon towers over the Aegean and Attic Plains, the ultimate achievement of Athens's classical glory. Although each Greek *polis* had an *acropolis* ("high city"), Athens's magnificent example has effectively monopolized the name. In the last 20 years, acid rain has unfortunately forced works formerly displayed outside to take cover in the on-site museum.

BEULÉ GATE AND PROPYLAEA. The ramp that led to the Acropolis in classical times no longer exists; today's visitors make the 5min. climb to the ticket window, enter through the crumbling Roman **Beulé Gate** (added in the 3rd century AD), and continue through **Propylaea,** which formed the towering entrance in ancient times. The middle gate of the Propylaea opened onto the **Panathenaic Way,** an east-west route cutting across the middle of the Acropolis that was once traveled by Panathenaic processions venerating the goddess Athena.

TEMPLE OF ATHENA NIKE. On the right after leaving the Propylaea, the tiny Temple of Athena Nike, at the cliff's edge, was built during a respite from the Peloponnesian War, the Peace of Nikias (421-415 BC). It once housed a winged statue of the goddess; allegedly, frenzied Athenians who feared that their deity (and peace) would flee the city one day clipped the statue's wings.

ERECHTHEION. The Erechtheion, to the left down the Panathenaic Way, was finished in 406 BC, just prior to Athens' defeat by Sparta. The unique two-level structure was dedicated to Athena, Poseidon, and Erechtheus. Its southern portico, facing the Parthenon, is supported by six much-photographed casts of **caryatids,** sculpted column-women—see the originals in the Acropolis Museum.

PARTHENON. Looming over the hillside, **Temple of Athena Parthenos** (Athena the virgin) keeps vigil over the city, commonly known as the Parthenon. The crowning glory of Pericles' project to beautify Athens, it was designed by the architect Aktinos, who added two extra columns to the usual six in a Doric-style temple. The Parthenon also features other subtle irregularities: the upward bowing of the temple's *stylobate* (pedestal) and the slight swelling of its columns compensated for the optical illusion by which, from a distance, straight lines appear to bend. Its elegant lines reflect the ancient Greek obsession with proportion: everything from its layout to its sculpted details follow a four-to-nine ratio.

ACROPOLIS MUSEUM. Footsteps away from the Parthenon, the museum contains a superb collection of sculptures, including five of the original Erechtheion Caryatids (the sixth accompanies the original entablature in the British Museum, p. 163). Most treasures date from the period of transition between Archaic and Classical Greek art (550-400 BC): compare the stylized, entranced faces and frozen poses of Archaic sculptures such as the famous **Moschophoros** (calf-bearer) to the more human, idealized Classical pieces, like the perfectly balanced, curvaceous **Kritias** boy. Unfortunately, only a few pieces from the Parthenon are here—former British ambassador Lord Elgin helped himself to the rest. *(Open M 11am-6:30pm, Tu-Su 8am-6:30pm; in winter M 11am-2pm, Tu-Su 8am-2pm.)*

SOUTHERN SLOPE. The southwest corner of the Acropolis, you can look over the reconstructed **Odeon of Herodes Atticus,** a still-functioning theater dating from the Roman Period (AD 160). Admire the ruins of the classical Greek **Asclepion** and **Stoa of Eumenes II** as you continue east to the **Theater of Dionysus,** which dates from the 4th century BC and once hosted dramas by Aeschylus and Sophocles and comedies by Aristophanes for audiences of up to 17,000. *(Enter on Dionissiou Areopagitou street. ☎32 21 459. Closed for general admission, but performances go on throughout the summer.)*

OTHER SIGHTS

ANCIENT AGORA. The **Athenian Agora,** at the foot of the Acropolis, was the administrative center and marketplace of Athens from the 6th century BC to the late Roman Period (5th-6th centuries AD). The ▧**Hephaesteion,** on a hill in the northwest corner, is one of the best-preserved Classical temples in Greece, especially notable for its friezes depicting the tales of Hercules and Theseus. To the south, the elongated **Stoa of Attalos,** a multi-purpose building for shops, shelter, and gatherings, was rebuilt between 1953 and 1956 and now houses the **Agora Museum,** which contains a number of relics from the site. *(Enter the Agora in one of three ways: off Pl. Thission, off Adrianou, or as you descend from the Acropolis. Open Tu-Su 8:30am-3pm. 1200dr/€3.55, students and EU seniors 600dr/€1.80, EU students and under 18 free.)*

MOUNT LYCAVITTOS. Don't miss the view from the top of **Mt. Lycavittos,** the biggest of Athens' seven hills. Ascend at sunset to catch a last glimpse of Athens's continuous rooftops and watch the city light up at night. Using the Acropolis as your point of reference, you'll see Monastiraki, Omonia, and Exarhia to your right, then continue spinning clockwise to delight in the flashy lights and music of Lycavittos Theater, several parks, the Panathenaic Olympic Stadium, the National Gardens, and the Temple of Olympian Zeus. *(Hike 15min. to the top, or take the funicular (every 10-15min., return 1000dr/€2.95) from near the end of Ploutarchou in Kolonaki.)*

MUSEUMS. One of the world's finest collections of classical sculpture, ceramics, and bronzework lies in the ■**National Archaeological Museum.** The *Mask of Agamemnon* from Heinrich Schliemann's Mycenae digs and the huge bronze statue of Poseidon are must-sees. *(Patission 44. Walk from Pl. Syndagma down Stadiou to Aiolou and right onto Patission. Open Apr.-Oct. M 12:30-7pm, Tu-Su 8am-7pm; Nov.-Mar. daily 8am-5pm; holidays daily 8:30am-3pm. 2000dr/€5.90, students 1000dr/€2.95; free Su and holidays Nov-Mar.)* The **National Gallery** (Alexander Soutzos Museum) exhibits works by Greek artists, including El Greco. *(Vas. Konstandinou 50. Open M and W-Sa 9am-3pm, Su 10am-2pm. 1500dr/€4.40, students 500dr/€1.50.)*

NEAR PLATEIA SYNDAGMA. Walk along the tranquil paths of the pleasant **National Gardens,** adjacent to Pl. Syndagma. *(Open daily dawn-dusk. Women should avoid coming here alone.)* Don't miss the changing of the guard in front of the **Parliament** building. Unlike their British equivalents, *evzones* occasionally wink, smile, or even say "I love you" to tourists. *(2 sets of guards perform every hour on the hour. Catch a more pomp-filled version—with a complete troop of guards and a band—Su 10:45am.)*

HADRIAN'S ARCH AND TEMPLE OF OLYMPIAN ZEUS. Hadrian's Arch marked the 2nd-century boundary between the ancient city of Theseus and the new city built by Hadrian. Next to the arch, fifteen majestic columns are all that remain of the Temple of Olympian Zeus, the largest temple ever built in Greece. *(Vas. Olgas at Amalias, next to the National Garden. Open Tu-Su 8:30am-3pm. Temple 500dr/€1.50, Arch free.)*

🎵🎭 ENTERTAINMENT AND NIGHTLIFE

FESTIVALS. The **Athens Festival** runs annually from June until September, featuring classical theater groups at the Odeon of Herodes Atticus, at the Lycavittos Theater, and in Epidavros. The Greek Orchestra regularly plays during this festival, and visiting artists have ranged from the Bolshoi Ballet to the Talking Heads. The **Festival Office,** Stadiou 4 sells student tickets for 3000-5000dr/€8.80-14.70. (☎32 21 459. Open M-F 9:30am-4pm, Sa-Su 9:30am-2pm.)

MARKETS. The **Athens Flea Market,** adjacent to Pl. Monastiraki, is a jumble of second-hand junk, high-rent antiques and everything in between. Sunday is the best day. (Open daily 8am-3pm; Tu, Th-F until 8pm.) On Sunday, a sprawling **food market** takes over Athinas between Evripidou and Sofokleous. Not for the faint of heart, the **meat market** overwhelms with sights and smells of liver, kidney, and skinned rabbit. Jostle early with restauranteurs for choice produce. (Open M-Sa 8am-2pm.)

CAFES, BARS AND FILM. ■**Bee,** at Miaoli and Themidos, off Ermou in **Monastiraki,** is a hub of the artistic scene. (Open daily noon-3am.) Millioni St. by **Jackson Hall** is just the right spot for a subdued evening, but for a livelier night head to **Kolonaki** and its cafe-by-day-bar-by-night establishments. **Jazz in Jazz,** Deinokratous 4, Dinokratous 4, draws faithfuls with old jazz records on the box and swing dancing lessons. (1500dr/€4.40 cover includes 1 drink. Open Nov.-May noon-3am.) Enjoy your own *cinema paradiso* at the open-air movie theater **Cine Paris,** Kidatheneon 22 (☎322 2071). Check *Athens News* for showtimes. Tickets 2000dr/€5.90. For something entirely unconventional **Metal Cafe Dionysos,** Em. Benaki 96A & Valtetsiou in Exharia. There, superficial conflict (backgammon vs. heavy-metal decor and music), leads to ultimate fun. (Open daily 1:30pm-3am.) In **Plaka,** colorful **Bretto's,** Kidatheneon 41, distills its own liquor. (Open daily 10am-midnight.)

CLUBS. In summer, hip Athenians head to the seaside clubs in **Glyfada** past the airport. Go for glam; shorts *don't* pass through these doors. Cover is usually 3000dr/€8.80 and drinks vary from 1200-3000dr/€3.52-8.80. Most of the clubs are spread out along Poseidonos Street, each a few kilometers apart. **Privilege, Venue, Prime,**

THE IRONY OF ORACLES The Delphic Oracle was famed for giving obscure, deceptive, and metaphorical answers. Many a suppliant went home more confused than he came, having failed to draw meaning from the answer—or, worse still, having drawn the wrong meaning. In the 6th century BC, King Croesus of Sardis, ruler of most of Asia Minor, came to the Oracle to ask about the threat the Persians posed to his kingdom. The Oracle's answer: "A great empire will be destroyed." Croesus returned to Sardis thinking that he would conquer the Persian Empire; it was not until he watched his own kingdom and capital fall that he realized the fallen empire was his own. Similar stories show that the Oracle's nature was not simply to answer questions, but, as was once inscribed on the Temple of Apollo, to "know thyself."

and **Envy** are worth the trip out. Hoards of serious-looking bouncers with earpieces guard the doorways to swanky open-air bars beneath discoballs and strobe lights. Look also for **+Soda, King Size,** and **Bedside.** Along Pergamon Street look for **Camel Club.** Top 40, funk, or house plays until around 2am, at which point Greek music (live or recorded) takes over. Dance, drink, and eye the beautiful crowd against the backdrop of the ocean, only a few feet away.

DAYTRIPS FROM ATHENS

TEMPLE OF POSEIDON. The **Temple of Poseidon** has for centuries been a dazzling white landmark for sailors at sea, and also offers fantastic views of the blue, blue Aegean. The original temple was constructed around 600 BC, destroyed by the Persians in 480 BC, and rebuilt by Pericles in 440 BC. The 16 remaining Doric columns sit on a promontory at **Cape Sounion,** 65km from Athens. (Open daily 10am-sunset. 1000dr/€2.95, students 500dr/€1.50, EU students free.) Two **bus** routes run to Cape Sounion from Athens; the shorter and more scenic route begins at the Mavromateon 14 stop near Areos Park (2hr., every hr., 1350dr/€4).

DELPHI. Troubled denizens of the ancient world journeyed to the **Oracle of Apollo** at Delphi (Δελφοι), where the Pythia (a priestess of Apollo) gave them profound, if cryptic, advice. Today, tourists flock to modern Delphi (pop. 2500) for its fascinating ruins. Visit early in the morning. **Buses** leave Athens for Delphi from Terminal B at Liossion 260 (3½hr., 6 per day, 3100dr/€9.10). From the bus station at the western end of Delphi, walk east on Pavlou toward Athens (with the mountain edge on your right) to reach the **tourist office,** 12 Friderikis, in the town hall. (Open M-F 7:30am-2:30pm.) Continue east down Pavlou to reach the oracle site.

MARATHON. Gasping out two words—*Νικη ημιν,* "Victory to us"—messenger Phidippides announced the Athenian victory over the Persians in the bloody 490 BC battle of Marathon (Μαραθωνας); he collapsed and died immediately after. His 42km sprint to Athens remains legendary, and today runners trace his Marathon route twice annually, beginning at a commemorative plaque. Others reach Marathon by **bus** from Mavromateon 29 by Areos Park in Athens (1½hr., every hr. 5:30am-10:30pm, 800dr/€2.35). The town itself doesn't inspire, but the five-room **Archaeological Museum** is packed with exciting finds. Ask the driver to let you off at the sign ("Mouseion and Marathonas"), then follow the signs 2km through farmlands (bear right at the one unlabeled fork in the road) to the end of the paved road, 114 Plateion. (☎55 155. Open Tu-Su 8:30am-3pm. 500dr/€1.50, students 300dr/€0.90, EU students, student classicists, and archaeologists free.)

FERRIES FROM ATHENS: PIRAEUS

A far cry from the charm of Plato's *Republic*—set in Piraeus (Πειραιας, "Port") at the height of Athenian power—modern Piraeus is best appreciated only as a point of departure to the Greek isles. **Ferries** sail to nearly all Greek islands (except the Sporades and Ionian Islands). Among them are: **Iraklion,** Crete (8hr., 2 per day, 6900dr/€20.25); **Hania,** Crete (8hr., 2 per day, 5700dr/€16.75); and **Rethymno,** Crete (8hr., 1 per day, 6900dr/€20.25). Travel is sporadic to: **Aegina** (1hr., 1500dr/€4.40), **Naxos** (6hr., 5 per day, 5000dr/€14.70); and **Paros** (6hr., 5 per day, 5200dr/€15.30). Boats leave every evening for **Chios** (9hr., 5800dr/€17.05) and **Lesvos** (12hr., 7200dr/€21.15). More regular departures go to: **Ios** (7½hr., 3 per day, 5400dr/€15.85); **Rhodes** (15hr., 2 per day, 9200dr/€27); and **Santorini** (9hr., 3 per day, 6000dr/€17.65). International ferries run Th at 7pm to **Limassol, Cyprus** (36hr., 25,000dr/€73.37). Twice as fast and twice as expensive, **catamarans** run twice per day to Mykonos, Paros, Naxos, Syros (8800dr/€25.90), and Tinos (9400dr/€27.60); and once per day to Kythnos, Serifos, Sifnos, Milos, and Santorini.

To get to Piraeus, take the **subway** west from Athens to the last stop (20min., 250dr/€0.75). The subway station is a big building adjacent to a busy square on Akti Posidonos (500m from Akti Tzelepi). Most ticket agencies can be found on Akti Tzelepi and along Akti Posidonos; if truly lost, ask there for directions or try the Piraeus **port police** (☎42 26 000) at Akti Zelopi.

THE PELOPONNESE (Πελοποννεσος)

Connected to the mainland by the narrow isthmus of Corinth, the Peloponnese contains the majority of Greece's most stunning and well-preserved archaeological sites, including Olympia, Mycenae, Messene, Ancient Corinth, Mystra, and Epidavros. It has some of the country's most incredible landscapes, ranging from the barren crags of the Mani to the forested peaks of Arcadia. With raw beauty and sparse population, the Peloponnese remain a bastion of Greek village life and culture.

⚒ FERRIES TO ITALY AND CRETE

Boats go from **Patras** to **Brindisi** (20hr., 8000-10,000dr/€23.55-29.45), **Trieste, Bari, Ancona,** and **Venice, Italy.** Ferries also sail from **Gythion** to **Crete** (7hr., 4900dr/€14.40). Eurail holders should check with Tsimaras travel agency (☎622 602) or HML lines to see if they can use their passes for trips to Brindisi. Check the travel offices on Iroon Polytechniou and Othonas Amalias in Patras for tickets and ask about discounts for those under 25.

PATRAS (Πατρας)   ☎061

Sprawling Patras, Greece's third-largest city, serves primarily as a transport hub, but at **Carnival** (mid-Jan. to Ash Wednesday) the port becomes one gigantic dance floor consumed by pre-Lenten madness. During the rest of the year, spend your layover heading inland from town on Ag. Nikolaou and climbing the steps to the 13th-century Venetian **castle.** (Open Tu-Su 8am-7pm. Free.) Then continue to the **Ancient Odeum,** a restored Roman theater. (Open Tu-Su 8:30am-3pm. Free.) Follow the water to the west end of town to reach **Agios Andreas,** the largest Orthodox cathedral in Greece, which holds magnificent frescoes and an unusual relic—St. Andrew's holy head. (Open daily 9am-dusk. Dress modestly.) Sweet black grapes are transformed into *Mavrodaphne* wine at the **Achaïa Clauss winery,** where tourists can enjoy free samples of the country's most famous vineyard. Check with the tourist office for a schedule of daily tours, then take bus #7 from the intersection of Kolokotroni and Kanakari, or in front of Europa Center, next to the bus station on Othonos Amalias (waterfront).

Trains (☎639 110) are found on Othonos Amalias, and run to: Athens (3½-5hr., 8 per day, 1800-3400dr/€5.30-10); Kalamata (5½hr., 2 per day, 1700dr/€5); and Olympia (1½hr., 8 per day, 1000-2000dr/€2.95-6) via Pyrgos. **KTEL buses** (☎623 886, 623 887, or 623 888) go from Othonos Amalias, between Aratou and Zaïmi, to: Athens (3hr., 33 per day, 4000dr/€11.75); Ioannina (4hr., 4 per day, 4750dr/€14); Kalamata (4hr., 2 per day, 4550dr/€13.40); Thessaloniki (8hr., 3 per day, 9200dr/€27.10); and Tripoli (4hr., 2 per day, 3400dr/€10). **Ferries** go to Corfu daily (night ferry 7hr., 6100dr/€17.95) and Ithaka via Kephalonia.

To reach the center of town from the port, turn right after leaving customs and follow Iroon Polytechniou, which becomes Othonos Amalias, then turn left at Pl. Trion Simahon and head inland. The **tourist police** are available on the waterfront in the Customs entrance. (☎451 833. Open M-F 7am-midnight.) Hotels are scattered on **Ag. Andreou,** one block up from the waterfront. The **Youth Hostel,** Iroon Polytechniou 68, occupies a creaky turn-of-the-century mansion. (☎427 278. Dorms 2000dr/€5.90.) Patras's myriad pubs and cafes are generally overpriced; you can self-cater from various **supermarkets** throughout downtown. (Most open Tu-Sa 9am-5pm.) Otherwise, chatty Nikolas will cheerfully explain the menu to you in English at **Taverna O Nikolas,** Ag. Andreou 73, just past Ag. Nikolaou. A bargain meal, if a little reminiscent of fast-food. (Open daily 7am until early morning. All entrees 800-2000dr/€2.35-5.90.) **Postal Code:** 26001.

OLYMPIA (Ολυμπια)   ☎0624

Set among meadows and shaded by cypress and olive trees, modern Olympia is a friendly and comely town that draws tourists with its mega-attraction—the ancient **Olympic arena.** Today, the remains of a gymnasium, palaestra, stadium, and several temples and treasures are scattered around **Ancient Olympia,** although they are not labeled or particularly well preserved. Buy a map to navigate maximally. Follow the main road 5min. out of town with the tourist office on your right and Pirgos behind you to reach the ruins and museum. Dominating the site is the gigantic **Temple of Zeus,** although the 7th-century BC **Temple of Hera** is better preserved. The Temple of Hera is also proximate to the altar where the **Olympic Flame** is lit every four years. Also intact are the remains of a church that was built on top of the workshop of Phidias which once held a statue of Zeus so beautiful that it was considered one of the seven wonders of the ancient world. Across from the site, the **New Museum** houses an array of sculpture that includes the **Nike of Paionios** and the **Hermes of Praxiteles.** (Site open daily 8am-7pm. Museum open M noon-7pm, Tu-Su 8am-7pm. Site or musuem 1200dr/€3.55 each, students 600dr/€1.80; joint ticket 2000dr/€5.90; EU students and children under 18 free.)

In New Olympia, **buses** run from opposite the tourist information booth to Tripoli (4hr., 3 per day, 2600dr/€7.65) and Pirgos (40min., 16 per day, 450dr/€1.35). The **tourist office,** on Kondili, is on the east side of town toward the ruins. (☎231 00. Open M-F 8am-3pm, Sa 9am-3pm, closed Su.) For lodgings, try **Zounis Rooms to Rent,** one block downhill from the Museum of Olympic Games; ask for them at the Anesi Cafe-Tavern. (☎22 644. Singles 5000dr/€14.75; doubles 7000dr/€20.55; triples 8500dr/€25.) **Camping Diana** is further uphill on Kondili from Pension Poseidon. (☎22 314. 1700dr/€5 per person, 1100dr/€3.25 per child, 1100dr/€3.25 per car, 1300-1800dr/€3.85-530 per tent, 2000dr/€5.90 adult with sleeping bag.) **Minimarkets** along Kondili or the road to the train station sell picnic fixings. Most eateries on Kondili are cramped and overpriced, but a walk toward the railroad station or uphill reveals charming, inexpensive tavernas. **Postal Code:** 27065.

TRIPOLI (Τριπολη)   ☎071

Tripoli itself is a transport hub, and offers little more. **Trains** go to: Athens (4hr., 4 per day, 1500dr/€4.40); Corinth (2½hr., 3 per day, 1000dr/€2.95); and Kalamata (2½hr., 4 per day, 900dr/€2.65). **Buses** from Pl. Kolokotronis, east of the center of town, go to Athens (3hr., 14 per day, 3400dr/€10); Kalamata (2hr., 12 per day, 1700dr/€5.00); and Sparta (1hr., 10 per day, 1100dr/€3.25). Crash at **Hotel Alex,** Vas. Georgiou 26, between Pl. Kolokotronis and Pl. Agios Vasiliou. (☎223 465. All rooms with bath. Singles 10,000dr/€29.35; doubles 13,000-15,000dr/€38.25-44.15.) **Postal code:** 22100.

▓ DAYTRIPS FROM TRIPOLI: DIMITSANA AND STEMNITSA. West of Tripoli, the enticing villages of Dimitsana (Δημητσανα) and Stemnitsa (Στεμνιτσα) are good bases for **hiking** in the idyllic, rugged countryside. The quintessentially Arcadian village of **Dimitsana,** clinging to a steep, rocky mountainside covered with pines, is nearly untouched by modern life or tourists. **Buses** run to Dimitsana from Tripoli (1½hr., 1-3 per day, 1400dr/€4.15). Buses to Tripoli and Olympia make frequent stops in **Karkalou,** a 20min. taxi ride away (1000dr/€2.95). **Private rooms** are basically the only option, and, most establishments are beautifully furnished. Try above the grocery store, which lets **rooms.** (☎31 084. Singles 6000dr/€17.65; doubles 12,000dr/€35.30.) A lengthy, but beautiful 11km stroll (or a 1000dr/€2.95 taxi -ride) along the road from Dimitsana will bring you to **Stemnitsa,** with narrow, irregular cobblestone streets that betray its medieval roots. Many consider it the most beautiful town in Greece. The splendid ▇**Hotel Triokolonion,** the only one in town, is on the left side of the main road from Dimitsana. (☎81 297. Breakfast included. Reserve ahead. Singles 8800dr/€25.90; doubles 11,900dr/€35.) ☎**0795.**

KALAMATA AND MESSENE (Καλαματα, Μεσσηνια) ☎**0721**

Kalamata, like Tripoli, is more important as a transport hub to the southern Peloponnese than a place to visit. The well-preserved, massive-walled ruins of **Ancient Messene** in nearby **Mavromati** are some of Greece's most impressive archaeological finds. (Open M-Su all day. Free.) **Trains** run from Sideromikou Stathmou to: Athens (7hr., 4 per day, 2400dr/€7.10) via Tripoli (2½hr., 950dr/€2.80); Corinth (5¼hr., 1900dr/€5.60); Olympia (3hr., 1000dr/€2.95); and Patras (5½hr., 1700dr/€5). **Buses** leave from Kalamata to: Athens (4hr., 11 per day, 4650dr/€13.70); Patras (4 hr., 2 per day, 4500dr/€13.25); Sparta (2hr., 2 per day, 1000dr/€2.95); and Tripoli (2hr., 1500dr/€4.45). Turn right on Frantzi at the end of Pl. Georgiou and walk a few blocks to reach the train station, Internet access, and **Hotel George.** It's not the cheapest option, but your best for cleanliness and taste. (☎27 225. Singles 7000dr/€20.60; doubles 8000dr/€23.55.) Tourist information is available at **D.E.T.A.K.,** Polivou 6, just off Aristomenous near the Old Town, and at the **tourist police** on the waterfront. Before leaving town, sample the famous Kalamata olives and figs. The immense **New Market,** across the bridge from the bus station, has an assortment of meat, cheese, and fruit shops, as well as a daily farmer's market. **Postal code:** 24100.

▶ DAYTRIPS FROM KALAMATA: PYLOS AND METHONI. Unspoiled **Pylos** (Πυλος) offers up its beaches, palace, and two fortresses. **Nestor's Palace,** where Nestor met Telemachus in Homer's *Odyssey*, was built in the 13th century BC. To see the site, still under excavation, take the bus to Kyparissia and get off at the palace (30min., 450dr/€1.35). **Buses** arrive in Pylos from Kalamata (1½hr., 9 per day, 1000dr/€2.95). Look for **Rooms to Let** signs as the bus goes into town (4000-singles 6000dr/€11.75-17.65; doubles 6000-10,000dr/€17.65-29.35; and triples 8000-12,000dr/€23.50-35.25). Buses go on to nearby **Methoni** (Μεθωνη; 15min., 7 per day, 260dr/€0.80), where hibiscus-lined streets wind around the 13th-century **Venetian fortress,** a mini city. (Open M-Sa 8:30am-8pm, Su 9am-8pm. Free.) Try **Ioannis Psiharis** (☎31 406. Singles 8000-9000dr/€23.50-26.50; doubles 9000dr/€26.50) ☎**0723.**

SPARTA AND MYSTRAS (Σπαρτη, Μυστρας) ☎**0731**

While **Ancient Sparta** has been immortalized in the annals of military history, the modern version is noted mostly for its olive oil and orange trees, and as a base for visits to **Mystras,** 4km away. **Buses** arrive from Sparta go to: Areopolis (1½hr., 2 per day, 1400dr/€4.15); Athens (3½hr., 9 per day, 4100dr/€12.10) via Corinth (2½hr., 2550dr/€7.50) and Tripoli (1hr., 1100dr/€3.25); Gythion (1hr., 5 per day, 850dr/€2.50); and Monemvassia (2hr., 3 per day, 2000dr/€5.88). To reach the town center from the bus station, walk 10 blocks west, on Lykourgou; the **tourist office** is to the left of the town hall in the *plateia*. (☎24 852. Open daily 8am-2pm.) **Hotel Cecil** is five blocks north of Lykourgou the corner of Paleologou and Thermopilion. (☎24 980. Singles 8000dr/€23.55; doubles 12000dr/€35.30.)

Once the religious center of Byzantium and the locus of Constantinople's rule over the Peloponnese, **Mystras** and its extraordinary hillside ruins reveal a city of Byzantine churches, chapels, and monasteries. At the extreme left of the lower tier as you face the hillside, is the ▇**Church of Peribleptos** whose exquisite religious paintings remain Mystra's most stunning relics; despite Ottoman vandalization, the church is still Mystras' most stunning relic. (Open in summer daily 8am-7pm; in winter daily 8:30am-3pm. 1200dr/€3.55, students600dr/€1.80.)

Buses from Sparta to Mystra leave from the station, in front of the OTE on Lykourgou, and at the corner of Lykourgou and Kythonigou (20min., 9 per day, 260dr/€0.80).

GYTHION AND AREOPOLIS (Γυθειο, Αρεοπολη) ☎0733

Once plagued by violent family feuds and savage piracy, the sparsely settled **Mani** (Μανη) province derives its name from *manis*, Greek for wrath or fury; history has affirmed its etymological roots many times. Today, fiery Maniot rage is cooled by a coastal breeze. **Gythion,** the "Gateway to the Mani," is the liveliest town in the region, near lovely sand and stone beaches. A tiny causeway connects to the island of **Marathonisi,** where Paris and Helen consummated their ill-fated love. **Buses** arrive at the north end of the waterfront from: Athens (4hr., 6 per day, 4900dr/€14.45) via Tripoli (2hr., 1850dr/€5.45); Corinth (3hr., 3550dr/€10.45); Kalamata (4 per day, 2050dr/€6.05); and Sparta (1hr., 6 per day, 850dr/€2.50). To explore the hard-to-reach parts of Mani, rent a **moped** at **Moto Makis Rent-A-Moped,** on the waterfront near the causeway. (☎25 111. 6500dr/€19.15 per day. Open daily 8:30am-7pm.) ⬛**Xenia Karlaftis Rooms,** on the water 20m from the causeway, rent spacious rooms with gracious service. (☎22 719. Singles 5000dr/€14.75; doubles 7000dr/€20.60; triples 10,000dr/€29.45.) **Meltemi Camping,** is 4km toward Areopolis, is right off the beach and has a pool. (☎22 833. 1500dr/€4.41 per person, 1200-1300dr/€3.55-3.85 per tent, 850dr/€2.50 per car.) **Postal code:** 23200.

From **Areopolis,** along the western coast of Mani, you can visit the spectacular **Vlihada Cave,** 4km from town. The 30min. **boat ride** down the cave's subterranean river passes a forest of stalagmites; the cave is believed to extend all the way to Sparta. (Open daily June-Sept. 8:30am-5:30pm; Oct.-May 8:30am 3pm. 3700dr/€10.90.) A 260dr/€0.80 bus to the caves leaves Areopolis at 11am and returns at 12:45pm. **Buses** stop in Areopolis' main *plateia* and go to: Athens (6hr., 4 per day, 5450dr/€16.05) and Sparta (2hr., 4 per day, 1400dr/€4.15) via Gythion (30min., 4 per day, 550dr/€1.65). To stay at **Tsimova,** turn left at the end of Kapetan Matapan, the road leading from the plateia to the Old Town, toward the ocean. (☎51 301. Singles 5-10,000dr/€17.45-29.45; doubles 10-15,000dr/€29.45-44.15.)

MONEMVASIA AND GEFYRA (Μονεμβασια, Γεφυρα) ☎0732

The city of Monemvasia, a major Peloponnesian tourist sight, has an other-worldly quality. No cars or bikes pass through the city's only gate; pack horses bear groceries into the city, where narrow streets hide stairways, child-sized doors, and flowered courtyards. From the Monemvasia gate, a cobblestone main street winds past tourist shops and restaurants to the town square. At the edge of the cliffs perches the oft-photographed 12th-century **Agia Sofia;** navigate the maze of streets to the edge of town farthest from the sea, where a path climbs the side of the cliff to the church. Stay in the more modern and cheaper **Gefyra;** from there, it's a 20min. walk down 23 Iouliou along the waterfront to the causeway, where an orange **bus** runs to Monemvasia (every 15min. 100dr/€0.30). **Buses** leave Gefyra from 23 Iouliou for: Athens (6hr., 6050dr/€17.80); Corinth (5hr., 5400dr/€15.90); Sparta (2½hr., 2000dr/€5.90); and Tripoli (4hr., 3150dr/€9.30). The *domatia* along the waterfront are your best bet (doubles 5000-8000dr). **Hotel Akrogiali,** across from Malvasia Travel, has clean, white rooms with private baths (☎61 360. Singles 6000-7000dr/€17.65-20.60; doubles 7000-10,000dr/20.60-29.45.) **Camping Paradise,** is 3½km along the water. (☎61 123. 1450dr/€4.30 per person, 1300dr/€3.85 per tent, 850dr/€2.50 per car.) ⬛**To Limanaki,** beside the harbor on the mainland, serves tasty Greek favorites.

NAFPLION (Ναυπλιο) ☎0752

Nafplion is the perfect base from which to play archaeologist, although the Venetian fortresses, *plateias*, Old Town, and pebble beach may tempt you away from the ruins. The town's crown jewel is the 18th-century **Palamidi Fortress,** with spectacular views of the town. To get there, walk the 3km road, or take 999 grueling steps up from Arvanitias, across the park from the bus station. (Open daily 8am-6:45pm; off season daily 8:30am-5:45pm. 800dr/€2.35, students 400dr/€1.20, EU students free.)

Buses arrive on Singrou, near the base of the Palamidi fortress, from Athens (3hr., every hr. 2800dr/€8.25) via Corinth (2hr., 1500dr/€4.45). To reach **Bouboulinas,** the waterfront, walk left from the station as you exit and follow Singrou to the harbor—the **Old Town** is on your left. The **tourist office** is on 25 Martiou across from the OTE. (☎24 444. Open daily 9am-1pm and 4-8pm.) To enjoy the rooftop views of **Dimitris Bekas' Domatia** in the old town, turn up the stairs on Kokinou and follow the sign for rooms off Staikopoulou; climb to the top, turn left, and go up another 50 steps. (☎24 594. Singles 4500-5200dr/€13.25-15.30; doubles 6000-6800dr/€17.65-20.) ◪**Taverna O Vasiles,** on Staikopoulou, serves rabbit (1800dr/€5.30) that will delight even the most avid Beatrix Potter fans. **Postal Code:** 21100.

◪ **DAYTRIPS FROM NAFPLION: MYCENAE AND EPIDAVROS.** The supreme city of Greece from 1600 to 1100 BC, Mycenae (Μυκηνες) was once ruled by Agamemnon, leader of the attacking forces in the Trojan War, gorily detailed in Homer's Iliad. Most of the site's treasures are in Athens, but the remaining Lion's Gate and the Treasury of Atreus are among the most celebrated archaeological finds. (Open daily Apr.-Sept. 8am-7pm; Oct.-Mar. 8am-5pm. 1500dr/€4.45, students 800dr/€2.35, EU students free. Keep your ticket or pay again at Agamemnon's tomb.) Join the illustrious ranks of Heinrich Schliemann, Woolf, Debussy, Faulkner, and Ginsberg, who have all stayed at **Hotel Belle Helene;** it also serves as a bus stop on the main road. (☎76 225. Singles 5500-7000dr/€16.20-20.60; doubles 10,000-13,000dr/€29.45-38.25.) The only direct **bus** to Mycenae comes from Naf-plion (30min., 4 per day, 650dr/1.95) via Argos (20min., 300dr/€0.90). **Trains** run from **Athens** to Fihtia; take the Corinth-Argos road and follow the sign to Mycenae.

The grand **Theater of Epidavros** (Επιδαυρος), built in the early 2nd century BC, is the highlight of the ancient site, and held 14,000 folks at its height. Henry Miller wrote that he heard "the great heart of the world" beat here; the incredible acous-tics allow you to stand at the top row of seats and hear a match lit on stage. (Open daily 7:30am-7pm, F-Sa 7:30am-9pm during theater season. 1500dr/€4.45, students 800dr/€2.35, EU students free.) From late June to mid-August, the **Epidavros Theater Festival** brings performances of classical Greek plays on Friday and Saturday nights. Shows are at 9pm; purchase tickets at the site, in advance in Athens, at the Athens Festival Box Office (☎(01) 322 1459), or at Nafplion's bus station (☎(01) 322 1459; tickets 4000dr/€11.80, students 2000dr/€5.90). **Buses** arrive in Epidavros from Nafplion (1hr., 4 per day, 650dr/€1.95). ☎**0751.**

CORINTH (Κορινθος) ☎0741

Most visitors to the Peloponnese make their first stop at New Corinth and travel to gaze on the ruins of **Ancient Corinth,** at the base of the **Acrocorinth.** Columns, metopes, and pediments lie around the courtyard of the excellent **archaelogical museum** in untouched chaos. As you exit the museum, the 6th-century BC **Temple of Apollo** is downstairs to the left. The **fortress** at the top of Acrocorinth is a tough 2-3hr. hike, but taxis also run to the summit (2000dr/€5.90) and back down (3000dr/€8.80). At the top, explore the surprisingly intact remains of the **Temple to Aphrodite,** where disciples were initiated into the "mysteries of love." (Open in summer 8am-7pm; in winter 8am-5pm. Museum and site 1200dr/€3.55, students 600dr/€1.80.)

In New Corinth, **buses** leave from three different stations; for assistance, you should go to the tourist police. Buses leave station A (☎24 481), behind the train station, for Athens (1½ hr., 30 per day, 1800dr/€5.30). Buses leave station C, **Argolis Station,** (☎24 403 or 25 645) inland from the park on Eth. Antistasis, for: Argos (1000dr/€2.95); Mycenae (800dr/€2.35); and Nafplion (1250dr/€3.70) every hr. **Trains** go from the station on Demokratias to: Athens via Isthmia, (2hr., 14 per day, 900dr/€2.65) and Patras (2½hr., 8 per day, 1000dr/€2.95). The **Tourist Police,** Ermou 51, housed in the same building as the actual police, are located along the city's park, and will provide tourists with maps, brochures, and other general assistance. (☎23 282. Open daily 8am-2pm.) In New Corinth, **Hotel Akti,** Eth. Anti-stasis 3, is the best bet for accommodations, with simple, utilitarian bedrooms and a convenient location. (☎23 337. Singles 5000dr/€14.70; doubles 8000dr/€23.50.)

When mealtime comes, **AXINOS**, Damaskinou 41, offers cheery *al fresco* dining by the waterfront. (☎ 28 889. Pastitsio 1500dr/€4.40; Greek salad 1300dr/€3.85.)

CENTRAL AND NORTHERN GREECE

Under 19th-century Ottoman rule, the provinces of Sterea Ellada, Thessaly, Epirus, Macedonia, and Thrace acquired a Byzantine flavor; forgotten mountain-goat paths lead to these Byzantine treasures. Along the way, you'll encounter glorious mountain-top vistas over silvery olive groves, fruit trees, and patchwork farmland.

OSIOS LOUKAS (Οσιος Λουκας)   ☎ 0267

Osios Loukas delights the eye with its mountain vistas and stunning Byzantine architecture. The exquisite monastery, built in the 10th and 11th centuries and still in use today, overlooks Boeotia and Phokis from the green slopes of Mt. Elikon more than 1700m above sea level. Gold-laden mosaics, vibrant frescoes, and intricate brick- and stonework adorn Osios Loukas, the most famous and perhaps the most gorgeous monastery in Greece. Dress modestly (long skirts for women, long pants for men, no bare shoulders). Two churches are at the site: the **Katholikon,** on the right after the museum, built in AD 1011 and dedicated to the monastery's founding saint, Osios Loukas, is more impressive; the smaller **Church of the Panagia** (Church of the Virgin Mary) holds the dried body of the saint himself in a glass coffin. A **crypt,** accessible from an entrance on the south of the Katholikon, has stunning frescoes and is not to be missed. (Open early May to mid-Sept. daily 8am-2pm and 4-7pm; mid-Sept. to early May 8am-5pm. 800dr/€2.35, seniors 400dr/€1.20, under 18 and students free.) Take a car, moped, or **taxi** (☎ 22 322; 7000dr/€20.55) or walk 9km on the hilly, narrow road from the town of Distomo.

METEORA (Μετεωρα)   ☎ 0432

Southwest of Olympus lie the majestic, iron-gray pinnacles of the Meteora rock formations, bedecked by 24 exquisite, gravity-defying Byzantine monasteries. (500dr/€1.50 per monastery. Dress modestly: women in long skirts; men in long pants; no bare shoulders. No photography.) The **Grand Meteoron Monastery** is the oldest, largest, and most important of the monasteries, with gruesome frescoes of the Roman persecution of Christians. The monastery also houses a **folk museum.** The library of **Varlaam Monastery** contains 290 manuscripts, some housed in the museum, including a miniature Bible from 960. The most popular base for exploring Meteora is the town of **Kalambaka** (Καλαμπακα). **Trains** leave for Athens (4hr., 3 per day 7:08am-5:25pm, 6500dr/€19.10) and Thessaloniki (3hr., daily 9:38am, 4200dr/€12.35). **Buses** depart for: Athens (5hr., 8 per day 7am-8:30pm, 5900dr/€17.35); Patras (6hr., Tu and Th 9am, 5950dr/€14.50); and Thessaloniki (3hr., 6 per day 7:30am-8pm, 3950dr/€11.60). Local buses go from Kalambaka to Meteora (20min.; M-F 9am and 1:20pm, Sa-Su 8:30am and 1:20pm; 260dr/€0.80); a **taxi** costs about 1500dr/€4.40. Most people walk the 6km downhill back to town, visiting the monasteries along the way. The rooms in ▨**Koka Roka** offer an awe-inspiring view of Meteora; from the central square, follow Vlachara until it ends, then bear left and follow the signs to Kanari for 15 minutes. (☎ 24 554. Internet access. Singles 4000dr/€11.75, with bath 6000dr/€17.60; doubles 8000dr/€29.50; triples 10,000dr/€23.50). **Camping** is also a popular option; campsites line the roads in all directions out of town. **Postal code:** 42200.

▨ MOUNT OLYMPUS (Ολυμπος Ορος)   ☎ 0352

Erupting out of the Thermaic Gulf, the height (nearly 3000m) and formidable slopes of Mt. Olympus once so awed the ancients that they envisioned it as the gods' home. A network of well-maintained **hiking** trails now makes the summit accessible to just about anyone with sturdy legs and a taste for adventure, although you may yearn for a pair of Hermes' winged sandals. From **Litohoro,** one route is to hike up via **Prionia,** stay at a refuge, and climb to the summit the next day. You could stay another night and walk down the next day to **Diastavrosi** (about 3-4hr.), or pass by the refuges and arrive at Diastavrosi in late afternoon. There is no bus to the trailheads from **Litohoro,** so you'll have to walk or drive. *Let's Go* does not recommend hitch-hiking. A **taxi** costs about 7000dr/€20.54 to Prionia. Make your ascent between May and October. **Mytikas,** the tallest peak, is inaccessible without special equipment before June. There are three **refuges** near the summits. **Trains** (☎22 522) run from **Athens** (7hr., 3 per day, 3800dr/€11.15) and **Thessaloniki** (1½hr., 5 per day, 1000dr/€2.95) to the Litohoro station; a **taxi** from the train station costs around 2000dr/€5.90. Direct KTEL **buses** (☎81 271) run from **Athens** (6hr., 3 per day, 8000dr/€24.50) and **Thessaloniki** (1½hr., 16 per day, 1900dr/€55.80); they arrive at the station opposite the church in Litohoro's main *plateia*. Down Ag. Nikolaou from the bus stop is the town's **tourist office.** (☎83 100. Mountain maps 1000dr/€2.95. Open daily 9am-midnight.) The most affordable hotel is the **Hotel Park,** Ag. Nikolaou 23, down from the *plateia*. (☎81 252. Singles 6000dr/€17.65; doubles 8000dr/€23.50; triples 9000dr/€26.45.) **Camp** at **Olympus Zeus** (☎22 115 or 22 116) or **Olympus Beach** (☎22 112 or 22 113), on the beach 5km from town; expect to pay at least 3000dr/€8.80.

THE ZAGOROHORIA (Τα Ζαγοροχωια)   ☎0653

The Zagorohoria is a cluster of 46 villages 36km north of Ioannina that surround the famed **Vikos Gorge.** Remarkable for their natural beauty and traditional architecture, the villages offer unparalleled hiking opportunities through the gorge and the surrounding Vikos-Aoös National Park. The complete absence of banks, post offices, and souvenir shops make them a welcome respite from more touristed areas. **Monodendri** can be reached by bus from Ioannina (45min.; 2 per day 7am and 5pm; 800dr/€2.35) and is the best starting point for hiking the Gorge—just follow the signs from the *plateia* below the main road. **Buses** run regularly to Zossimadon 4 in Ioannina from **Athens** (7hr., 9 per day, 8100dr/€23.80) and **Thessaloniki** (7hr., 6 per day, 6650dr/€19.55). **Pension Monodendri,** up the road from the bus stop, has comfortable, traditional Zagori rooms over a *taverna* serving delicious food. The owners can arrange a pick-up from the end of the hike for 8000-10,000dr/€23.50-29.35. (☎71 300. Singles 5000dr/€14.70; doubles 8000dr/€23.50.) At the other end of the 6hr. hike lies the village of **Megalo Papingo,** the most developed Zagorian village, accessible by **bus** from **Ioannina** (1hr., 4 per week, 1200dr/€3.55). Hotel prices are a bit stiffer in Megalo Papingo. **Kalliopi** has consistently priced, beautifully furnished rooms around a vine-canopied patio; follow the road uphill to the right while facing the bell tower. (☎41 081. Singles 10,000dr/€29.35; doubles 14,000dr/€41.10.)

According to the *Guinness Book of World Records*, the **Vikos Gorge,** with 900m deep walls only 1100m apart, is the steepest canyon on earth. Rusted iron deposits in the gorge's rock give the walls an orange-pink sunset tint, even at high noon. The long hike through the gorge is impressive; the nearly vertical canyon sides, to which throngs of trees cling stubbornly, tower hundreds of meters over your head.

THESSALONIKI (Θεσσαλονικη)   ☎031

Thessaloniki is an elusive jumble of ancient, Byzantine, European, Turkish, Balkan, and contemporary Greek cultural and historical debris—pragmatic utility, frilly beauty, and tasteless chintz all mingle. A Byzantine-Turkish fortress oversees the old town, while modern mayhem encircles Byzantine churches, masking interiors of glimmering gold mosaics, masterful frescoes, and floating domes.

▐▅ TRANSPORTATION

Trains: Main Terminal (☎517 517), on Monastiriou in the western part of the city. Take any bus down Egnatia (100dr/€0.30). To: **Athens** (6-8hr., 10 per day, 4800dr/€14.10); **Istanbul, Turkey** (13hr., 1 per day, 12,000dr/€35.25); **Skopje, FYROM** (5hr., 1 per day, 4650dr/€13.65); **Sofia, Bulgaria** (10½hr., 1 per day, 6150dr/€18.05). **OSE** (☎598 112), at Aristotelous and Ermou, has tickets and schedules. Open M-Sa 8am-2:30pm.

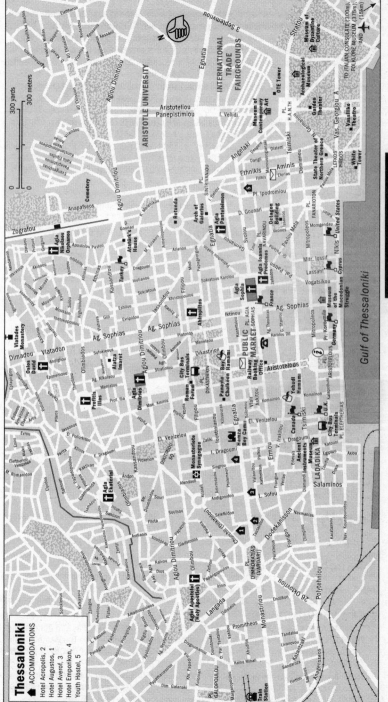

Thessaloniki
ACCOMMODATIONS

Hotel Acropolis, 2
Hotel Augustos, 1
Hotel Averof, 3
Hotel Emporikon, 4
Youth Hostel, 5

Buses: Most **KTEL** buses depart from between the port and railway station or from north of the railway. To: **Athens** (6hr., 20 per day, 9000dr/€26.45) and **Corinth** (7½hr., 1 per day, 9200dr/€27), from Monastiriou 69 (☎527 265); and **Patras** (8hr., 2 per day, 8250dr/€24.25) from Monastiriou 87 (☎525 253). **International buses** (☎599 100) leave from the train station for **Istanbul** (12hr., 2:30am, 24,300dr/€71.35); and **Sofia** (6hr., 4 per day 7am-10pm, 5600dr/€16.45).

Ferries and Hydrofoils: Buy tickets at **Karacharisis Travel and Shipping Agency,** Koundouriotou 8 (☎524 544), on the corner. Open M-F 8:30am-8pm, Sa 8:30am-2:30pm. To: **Chios** (21hr., 3 per week, 8900dr/€26.15); **Lesvos** (9hr., 2 per week, 8300dr/€24.35); **Limnos** (7hr., Tu 6pm, Su 1:30am, 5700dr/€16.75); **Mykonos** (16hr., 3 per week, 9900dr/€29.05); and **Samos** (14hr., 1 per week, 9500dr/€27.90). Buy tickets at **Crete Air Travel,** Dragoumi 1 (☎547 407), across from the main port. Open M-F 8:30am-9pm, Sa 8:30am-3pm, Su 9am-3pm. Dolphin hydrofoils leave June-Sept. Su-Fr 1:45pm, Sa 8am for: **Alonnisos** (5hr., 8900dr/€26.15); **Skiathos** (3¾hr., 8500dr); **Skopelos** (4½hr., 8900dr/€26.15).

Public Transportation: Many **buses** (100dr) traverse the city. Buses #8, 10, 11, and 31 run up and down Egnatia. Buy tickets at kiosks or ticket booths at major stations.

✹ 🛈 ORIENTATION AND PRACTICAL INFORMATION

Egnatia, an old Roman highway, runs down the middle of town and is home to the cheapest hotels. Running parallel to the water, the main streets are **Ermou, Tsimiski, Mitropoleos,** and **Nikis,** which runs along the waterfront. Inland from Egnatia is **Ag. Dimitriou** and the **Old Town** beyond. Intersecting these and leading into town are I. Dragoumi, El. Venizelou, Aristotelous, Ag. Sophias, and Eth. Aminis.

Tourist Office: EOT, Pl. Aristotelous (☎271 888). Open M-Sa 7:30am-3pm.

Consulates: Bulgaria, N. Manou 12 (☎829 210). Open M-F 10am-noon. **Canada,** Tsimiski 17 (☎256 350). Open M-F 9am-12pm. **Cyprus,** L. Nikis 37 (☎260 611). Open M-F 9am-1pm. **Turkey,** Ag. Dimitriou 151 (☎248 452). Open M-F 9am-noon. **UK,** Venizelou 8 (☎278 006). Open M-F 8am-1pm. **US,** Tsimiski 43 (☎242 900). Open M, W, and F 9am-noon.

Currency Exchange: Banks and **24hr. ATMs** line Tsimiski.

American Express: Memphis Travel, Aristotelous 3 (☎282 351). Cashes traveler's checks and exchanges currency. Open M-F 9:30am-3:30pm and Sa 9am-2pm.

Tourist Police: Dodekanissou 4, 5th fl. (☎554 870 or 871). Free maps and brochures. English spoken. Open 24hr. For the **local police,** call (☎553 800 or ☎100).

Telephones: OTE, Karolou Diehl 27 (☎221 899), at the corner of Ermou, one block east of Aristotelous. Open M-F 7:10am-2pm.

Internet Access: Pl@net, 53 Alex. Svolou (☎250 199), one block away from the hostel. The best in town, with 14 fast terminals and jazzy tunes. 600dr/€1.76 per hr. 9am-6pm; 6pm-3am 800dr/€2.35 per hr. 300dr/€0.88 minimum charge.

Post Office: On Aristotelous, just below Egnatia. Open M-F 7:30am-8pm, Sa 7:30am-2pm, Su 9am-1:30pm. A **branch** office (☎227 640), on Eth. Aminis near the White Tower, is open M-F 7am-8pm. Both offer *Poste Restante.* **Postal code:** 54101.

🛏 ACCOMMODATIONS

Most budget hotels cluster along the western end of Egnatia, between Pl. Dimokratias (500m east of the train station) and Pl. Dikastiriou. Egnatia can be noisy and gritty, but you'll have to pay more elsewehere.

🏣 **Hotel Augustos,** Elenis Svoronou 4 (☎522 955). Walking down Egnatia, turn north at the Argo Hotel, and Augustos is straight ahead. The best budget deal in Thessaloniki. Singles 6000dr/€17.65, with bath 8000dr/€23.50; doubles 7000dr/€20.55, 11,000dr/€32.30; triples with bath 13,000dr/€38.15.

Hotel Acropolis, Tantalidou 4 (☎536 170). Tantalidou is the 2nd right off Egnatia after Dodekanissou, coming from Pl. Dimokratias. Very quiet hotel with shared baths. Singles 5500dr/€16.15; doubles 7000dr/€20.55; triples 8000dr/€23.50.

Youth Hostel, Alex. Svolou 44 (☎225 946). Take bus #8, 10, 11, or 31 west down Egnatia and get off at the Arch of Galerius (the Kamara stop); or walk toward the water and turn left after 2 blocks. Reception 9am-11am and 7-11pm. Reception open 9-11am and 7-11pm. Open Mar. 1-Nov. 30. Dorms 2500dr/€7.35.

Hotel Averof, L. Sofou 24 (☎538 840), at Egnatia. Rooms a bit bare and stuffy, but boasts friendly staff and communal TV rooms. Singles 6000dr/€17.65, with bath 9000dr/€26.45; doubles 8000dr/€23.50, 12,000dr/€35.25.

◖ FOOD

Most food can be found in tiny streets on both sides of Aristotelous; the innovative places a block down from Egnatia between Dragoumi and El. Venizelou cater to a younger clientele. **Open-air markets** are on Vati Kioutou, off Aristotelous between Irakliou and Egnatia. **Ouzeri Melathron,** in an alleyway at El. Venizelou 23 has a humorous menu and delicious food. (Entrees 1150-3600dr/€3.40-10.60.) **Ta Adelphi,** in Pl. Navarino, serves great meat dishes at good prices in a bustling atmosphere. (Entrees 1250-1900dr/€3.70-5.60 Open daily noon-midnight.)

◖ ♫ SIGHTS AND ENTERTAINMENT

Salonica (Thessaloniki's former name) was vital to the Byzantines and Ottomans; its modern streets are littered with remnants from both. **Agios Dimitrios,** on Ag. Dimitriou north of Aristotelous, is the city's oldest and most famous church. Although most of its interior was gutted in the 1917 fire, the remaining mosaics are stunning. (Open daily 8am-8pm.) South of Egnatia on the square that bears its name, the **Agia Sophia Rotunda** became a church under the Byzantines. It was built to honor a Roman emperor but was later converted to a mosque; its walls, now under renovation, had some of the city's best mosaics; very few remain. (Open daily 7am-2:30pm.) Head south to the **Arch of Galerius,** built in the 4th century AD, on the eastern end of Egnatia. Back west down Egnatia, don't miss the labyrinthine, perfectly preserved 15th-century **Bey Hamamı,** where the Ottoman governor bathed.

Thessaloniki's **Archaeological Museum** is full of artifacts from Neolithic tombs, mosaics from Roman houses, and dazzling Macedonian gold. Take bus #10 down Egnatia to Pl. Hanth. (Open M 12:30-7pm, Tu-Su 8am-7pm; winter reduced hours. 1500dr/€4.40, students and seniors 800dr/€2.35.) Just across the street on 3 Septembriou, the **Museum of Byzantine Culture** has three huge rooms about Thessalonian daily life. (Open M 12:30-8pm, Tu-Su 8am-7pm; winter reduced hours. 1000dr/€2.95, students and seniors 500dr/€1.50.) All that remains of a 15th-century Venetian seawall, the **White Tower** presides over the eastern edge of the waterfront. (Open Tu-Su 8am-3pm. Free.) In the middle of the marketplace west of Aristoteliou, on Agia Mina, the **Museum of the Jewish Presence** details the long history of Thessaloniki's Sephardic Jews. (Ring bell. Open M-F 10am-1:30pm. Free.)

There are three main hubs for late-night fun: the bars and cafes of the **Ladadika** district, the waterfront, and the open-air discos that throb near the airport exit (2000dr/€5.90 by taxi). **Podon 2000,** 11km east of the city along the main highway, is very Greek, slick, and sophisticated. (Cover 3000dr/€8.80, includes one drink.) **Deka Dance** and **Mousis,** farther down the highway from Teatro, are other popular discos. (Cover 2500dr/€7.35 and 2000dr/€5.90, includes one drink.)

◖ DAYTRIP FROM THESSALONIKI: VERGINA

The tombs of Vergina, final home to ancient Macedonian royalty, lie only 30km from Thessaloniki. The principal site is the **museum,** with the tombs themselves under the **Great Tumulus,** a huge, man-made mount 12m tall and 110m wide. Check out the intricate gold work, brilliant frescoes, and the bones of **Alexander IV,** son of Alexander the Great, as well as the magnificent **Tomb of Philip II,** Alexander's father. (Open M noon-7pm, Tu-Su 8am-7pm; in winter Tu-Su 8:30am-3pm. 1200dr/€3.55,

GREECE

students 600dr/€1.80.) **Buses** run from Thessaloniki (2hr., every 30min., 1450dr/€4.30) to Veria. From Veria take the bus to Vergina (20min., 9 per day, 320dr/€1). You will be dropped off in the Vergina *plateia*; follow the signs to the sights.

IONIAN ISLANDS (Νησια Του Ιονιου)

Just off the western coast of Greece, the Ionian Islands are renowned for their medley of rugged mountains, farmland, shimmering olive groves, and pristine beaches, all surrounded by a seemingly endless expanse of clear, blue water with a sheer beauty that will stun even the most world-weary of world travelers.

▓ FERRIES TO ITALY

To catch a ferry to Italy, buy your ticket at least a day ahead in high season; be sure to find out if the port tax (1500-2200dr) is included. Ferries go from **Corfu** to: **Ancona** (20hr.; 1 per day; 19,000dr/€55.90); **Bari** (9hr.; 1 every other day; 12,400dr/€36.50); **Brindisi** (6-7hr.; 3 per day; 9400-32,000dr/€27.65-94.15); **Trieste** (24hr.; 5 per week; from 12,500dr/€36.77); and **Venice** (24hr.; 1 per day; 14,600-20,900dr/€42.95-61.50). Catamarans also go to **Brindisi** from **Corfu** (3¾hr., 9am, under 26 30% discount). In summer, ferries connect **Kephalonia** to **Brindisi, Venice,** and **Ancona.**

CORFU (KERKYRA; Κερκυρα)   ☎0661

Since Odysseus washed ashore and praised its lush beauty, the seas have brought crusaders, conquerors, and colonists to verdant Corfu. Unfortunately, many others have discovered Corfu's charms and the island swarms with tourists in the summer.

CORFU TOWN. The largest city, **Corfu Town,** exudes a Venetian charm, and offers many sights of its own, such as its two Fortresses, various museums, and the winding streets of its Old Town. However, as with many places in Greece, excursions off the beaten path are richly rewarded. **Paleokastritsa beach** (phone code ☎0663), where Odysseus supposedly landed, lies west of Corfu Town; take a green KTEL **bus** to Paleokastritsa (45min., 7 per day, 500dr/€1.50). A 90min. walk from there will bring you to the white mountaintop monastery **Panagia Theotokos** and the fort of **Angelokastro** (Castle of the Holy Angels), which jut out over the sea.

Ferries run from Corfu Town to Italy as well as Patras (9hr., 1-2 per day, 5800dr/€17.05), and **hydrofoils** run to Kephalonia (2¾hr., W and Sa 9am, 20,000dr/€58.85 return). KTEL runs bus/ferry combos daily to Athens (9hr., 1 per day, 11,000dr/€32.35) and Thessaloniki (9hr., 1 per day, 8750dr/€23.75). KTEL inter-city green buses depart from between I. Theotaki and the New Fortress; **blue buses** (municipal buses) leave from Pl. Sanrocco. From the customs house at the new port, cross the intersection and walk uphill on Avramiou, which becomes I. Theotoki, to reach Pl. Sanrocco (1km). The **EOT Tourist Office** is at the corner of Rizospaston Voulefton and Iak. Polila. (☎37 520 or 37 638. Open M-F 8am-2pm.) **The Association of Owners of Private Rooms and Apartments in Corfu,** Polila 24 (☎26 133), has a complete list of rooms for all of Corfu and can give you numbers to call for your price range. To get to **Hotel Europa,** Giantsilio 10, from the customs house, cross the main street and make a right; Giantsilio is a tiny road on your left just after the road turns and becomes Napoleonta. (☎39 304. Singles 5000-6000dr/€14.75-17.65; doubles 7000-8000dr/€20.60-23.55; triples 9000dr/€26.50.) **Hotel Ionian,** Xen. Sratigou 46, is at the new port. (☎39 915. Singles 7000-8000dr/€14.75-17.65; doubles 9000-11,000dr/€26.50-32.35; triples 12,000-16,000dr/35.30.) A daily open-air **market** sells inexpensive food, including blissfully fresh fruit, on Dessila, off G. Theotoki below the new fortress. (Open 6am-2pm.) **Postal Code:** 49100.

PELEKAS TOWN AND ENVIRONS. South of Paleokastritsa is the hidden jewel, **Pelekas Town** (blue bus #11 from Corfu Town, 30min., 7 per day, 240dr/€0.80); walk 30min. downhill to reach **Pelekas beach.** ▓**Glyfada beach,** is 5km from Pelekas Town. Free shuttles run between Glyfada and Pelekas (10min., 4 per day) and Glyfada is also is accessible by green KTEL **buses** from Corfu Town (30min, 6 per day,

400dr/€1.20). Glyfada is one of Corfu's most popular beaches, and offers, among other water sports, parasailing and waterskiing. North of Glyfada, accessible by a dirt path off the main Pelekas road, lie the isolated beaches of **Moni Myrtidion** and **Myrtiotissa** (the unofficial nude beach). Lodging is available in Paleokastritsa, Pelekas, and Glyfada. Pelekas is your best bet for a cheap night's stay—try **Pension-Tellis and Brigitte.** (☎(0661) 94 326; singles 5000dr/€14.75; doubles 6000-8000dr/€17.65-23.55). **Agios Gordios,** 10km south of Pelekas, offers impressive rock formations, a beach, and the **Pink Palace,** a huge hotel/resort that is immensely popular with young, primarily English-speaking backpackers. On weekends, toga-wearing partygoers have been known to down shots of ouzo as they break plates on each other's heads, all in a spirit of revelry that would make Dionysus proud. The Palace has an impressive list of amenities that helps keep it a self-contained party resort, including clothing-optional cliff-diving (4000dr/€11.80) and other watersports. The Palace also runs express buses to Athens, which bypass Patras. (☎53 024. Breakfast, dinner, ferry pick-up, and drop-off included. A-class rooms 9000dr/€26.50; B-class dorms 7500dr/€22.10). Green KTEL buses run to Agios Gordios from Corfu Town (45min., 7 per day, 300dr/€0.90).**Postal Code:** 49100.

KEPHALONIA (Κεφαλονια)   ☎0671

Kephalonia's diverse natural landscape, endless beaches, and towering peaks have lent it world renown. **Argostoli** (Αργοστολι), the capital and transport hub of Kephalonia and Ithaka, is a hectic and ugly city with palm-lined, traffic-filled streets. Take a **bus** (☎22 281) to the countryside from the station at the southern end of the waterfront. The **tourist office** is beside the port authority. (☎22 248. Open July-Aug. M-Sa 8am-2:30pm and 5:30-9:30pm; in winter M-F 8am-2pm.) To get from the waterfront to the main *plateia*, follow 21 Maiou (to the right of the station as you face inland) up two blocks. Private rooms are the cheapest option, although waterfront hotels are much nicer. **Hotel Tourist,** on the waterfront before the port authority, has great rooms for low prices. (☎22 510. Singles 8000-12,000dr/€23.55-32.25; doubles 14,000-18,000dr/€41.20-52.95.)

A small, picturesque town on a harbor surrounded by steep, lush hills, **Sami** (Σαμη), 24km from Argostoli, offers white-pebble beaches, proximity to **Melissani Lake** as well as underground **Drograti Cave,** and a break from the bustle of Argostoli. **Ferries** sail to Ithaka (40min., 3 per day, 1500dr/€4.45) and Patras (2½hr., 1 per day, 3400dr/€10). **Buses** arrive from Argostoli (3-4 per day, 700dr/€2.05). Hotel Kyma, at the end of the *plateia* away from the water, offers spectacular views. (☎(0674) 22 064. Singles 6000-8000dr/€17.65-23.55; doubles 10,000-15,000dr/€29.45-44.15.)

ITHAKA (Ιθακη)   ☎0674

The least-touristed and perhaps most beautiful of the Ionian Islands, Ithaka (Ithah-KEE) is all too often passed over for the tourist havens of Corfu and Kephalonia. Those who discover Ithaka find pebbled, rocky hillsides and terraced olive groves. Ithaka was the kingdom that **Odysseus** left behind to fight the Trojan War (and star in *The Odyssey*) while his wife **Penelope** faithfully waited 20 years for his return. Ithaka's largest town and capital, **Vathy,** wraps around a circular bay skirted by steep, green hills. Those of poetic bent and sturdy footwear can climb to the **Cave of the Nymphs,** where Odysseus hid the treasure the Phoenicians gave him; bring a flashlight. **Ferries** connect Ithaka to Sami in Kephalonia (1hr., 1500dr/€4.41) to Vasiliki in Lefkada (2½hr., 1000dr/€2.95), and Patras in the Peloponnese (6hr., 3900dr/€11.50). Boats depart from Vathy, Piso Aetos (10min. taxi ride), and Frikes (30min. taxi ride). Due to ever-changing schedules, check with **Delas Tours** (☎32 104; open daily 9am-2pm and 4-10pm) or **Polyctor Tours** (☎33 120; open daily 9am-1:30pm and 3:30-9pm), both in the main square right off the water; both offer help in finding rooms. The island's one **bus** runs north from Vathy, passing through the villages of Lefki, Stavros, Platrithiai, Frikes, and Kioni. Schedules are erratic; check in town, but in the high season, the bus usually runs 1-2 times per day (1hr., 350dr/€1.05 to Frikes). Private *domatia* (6-8000dr/€17.65-23.50 in summer) are your best option for affordable accommodations.

GREECE

Try **Andriana Domatia** on the far right of the waterfront facing inland. (☎32 387. Singles 8000-9000dr/€23.55-26.50; doubles 13,000-14,000dr/€38.25-41.20.) **Taverna To Trexantiri** is the favorite eatery among locals. (Salads 600-1200dr/€1.80-3.55; main dishes under 1800dr/€5.30.) **Postal Code:** 28300.

THE SPORADES (Σποραδες)

Viewed from the chaos of modern Athens, the Sporades and Evia islands circle like a family of enchanted sea-maidens. The matriarch is Evia, Greece's largest island after Crete. The Northern Sporades are her three daughters: quietly sophisticated Skopelos is the eldest, home to moonlit jazz-filled harbors and a population of artists. Restless Skiathos is the middle child, eager to grow up, flaunting her beach-ringed shores and raging with the region's best party scene. Innocent Alonnisos, the youngest, is a pristine wilderness crossed by hiking trails; Skyros, in the east, is the austere grandmother, a purple-hilled keeper of the old ways.

▐ TRANSPORTATION

To get to most of the Sporades from **Athens,** take the daily bus from the station at Liossion 260 to **Ag. Konstantinos** (2½hr., 16 per day, 2650dr/€7.80), where **Hellas Lines ferries** (☎22 209) operates on the corner of Papadiamantis across from the ferry landing. Prices are slightly higher in July and August. Ferries run to: Agios Konstantinos (3½hr., 1-2 per day, 3400dr/€10); Alonnisos (2hr., 1-22-3 per day, 1900dr/€5.60); Glossa (30min., 1-2 per day, 900dr/€2.65); Skopelos (1½hr., 1-3per day, 1500dr/€4.40); and Volos (2½hr., 1-2per day, 2900dr/€8.55). **Flying Dolphins hydrofoils** follow the same routes, at twice the cost and double the speed. Ferries and hydrofoils also connect the various islands.

SKIATHOS (Σκιαθος)   ☎0427

Tourism is a recent phenomenon here, as little Skiathos has grown up almost overnight into a glamorous dancing queen—welcome to the party hub of the Sporades. Package tourists pack the streets of **Skiathos Town,** while budding writers populate the beaches and nature preserves. Buses leave the port in Skiathos Town for the southern **beaches** (3 per hr., 320dr/€0.95), including Megali Ammos, Nostros, Vromolimnos, Kolios, and Trovlos. The road and bus route end in **Koukounaries,** where the more secluded beaches begin, including the lovely, pine-wooded **Biotrope of Koukounaries,** the yellow, curved, nude **Banana Beach,** and nude **Little Banana Beach.** *Domatia* abound, particularly on Evangelista, but in a pinch head to the **Rooms to Let Office,** in the wooden kiosk by the port. (☎22 990. Open daily 8:30am-midnight.) **Pension Danaos,** in an alley off Papadiamantis opposite the OTE, attracts a young backpacker crowd. (☎22 834. Open May 1-Sept. 30. Singles 10,000dr/€29.35; doubles 8,000-15,000dr/€23.48-44.02.) **Camping Koukounaries** is on the bus route to Koukouniares between stops 20 and 21. (☎49 250. 1800dr/€5.30 per person, 1000dr/€2.95 per tent.) Eat at ▓**Chris, Jan & Deborah's Daskalio Pub** with an English crowd; follow Papadiamantis to the kiosk and head right. (Entrees 2500-4000dr/€7.35-11.75. Open May-Sept. Bar open 7pm-3am. Food until 11pm.) Indulge at the countless bars in **Pl. Papadiamantis** or along **Polytechniou** or **Evangelista,** then dance all night long at the clubs on the far right side of the coast.

SKOPELOS (Σκοπελος)   ☎0424

Relaxed Skopelos sits between the glitzy revelry of Skiathos and the pristine wilderness of Alonnisos. The pious head to the wooded hills, where the island's monasteries and shrines hide, and the fading sounds of *rembetika* (folk songs) still echo. By night, the labyrinthine streets of Skopelos Town are filled with murmuring voices, and light drips down from cafes and onto the Aegean. Twelve **buses** per day leave from the stop left of the waterfront, facing inland, for **beaches** near Stafilos, Agnondas, Milia, and Loutraki. **Hiking trails** wind toward monasteries and beaches.

The **Thalpo Travel Agency,** 5m to the right of Galanatsiou along the waterfront, is up on everything from Flying Dolphins tickets to catching octopi. (☎22 947. Open May-Oct. daily 10am-9pm.) Take a *domatia* offer from the dock, or try the **Rooms and Apartments Association of Skopelos,** in the small wooden building near the dock. (☎24 567. Open daily 10am-2pm and 6-10pm.) ▓**Pension Sotos,** 10m left of Thalpos Travel, is a well-located gem. (☎22 549. Singles 5500-10,000/€16.15-29.35 Doubles 6500-12,000dr/€19.10-35.25.) *Gyros* for 350dr/€1.05 abound on **Pl. Platanos. Postal code:** 37003.

ALONNISOS (Αλοννησος) ☎0424

Of the islands comprising Greece's new **National Marine Park,** only Alonnisos is inhabited. Most of the small, remaining islets are strictly regulated—they harbor the undeterred Mediterranean monk seal—and visited only by organized tour boats in summer; trips are sold along the harbor. Alonnisos' unexplored northern coast sends white sands into the sea, and **hiking trails** lace the high heartland; pick up *Alonnisos on Foot* (2800dr/€8.25) in Patitiri. **Alonnisos Travel,** in the center of the waterfront, exchanges currency, books excursions, and sells ferry tickets. (☎65 188. Open daily 9am-10pm.) The **Rooms to Let Office,** next to Ikos Travel, helps find *domatia*. (☎66 188. Open daily 10am-2pm and 6-10pm.) **Panorama,** down the first alley on the left from Ikion Dolophon, rentsbright rooms with private baths. (☎65 240. Doubles 6000-14,000dr/€17.65-41.10.) Locals adore the little *ouzeri* **To Kamaki.** Try the delectable, warm octopus salad for 1700dr/€5. (☎65 245. Open daily noon-2:30pm, and 7pm-late.) Hikers and beachgoers may find the beautiful **Old Town** (Hora; Χωρα) ideal. Many **beaches** are accessible from the island's main road that runs along the spine of the island from Patitiri. A 1½hr. walk leads to **Votsi,** the island's other major settlement. Beyond Votsi, the road passes the pine-girded beaches of **Milia** and **Chrisi Milia.**

SKYROS (Σκυρος) ☎0222

Skyros's hilly terrain once protected the island against pirates and now fights off modern culture. The islands remain traditional and separate, the last stand of ghosts and poets. Stark white, cubist **Skyros Town,** the capital, is a relic of pre-war Greek life; old men sew sandals late into the evening as women embroider intricate patterns. Above Skyros Town, the 1000-year-old **Monastery of Ag. George** and the **Castle of Licomidus** command magnificent views of Skyrian sunsets. (Open daily Mar.-Aug. 7am-10pm; Sept.-Feb. 7:30am-6pm.) The superb ▓**Faltaits Museum,** up the stairs from Pl. Rupert Brooke in Skyros Town, boasts an incredible folk art collection. (Open daily 10am-1pm and 6-9pm. 500dr/€1.50.) **Ferries** arrive in the tiny western port of **Linaria** (2 per day), and are met by **buses** to Skyros Town (20min., 3 per day, 260dr/€0.80); tell the driver where you're going. **Skyros Travel,** past the central *plateia* on Agoras, organizes boat and bus excursions and helps with accommodations. (☎91 123. Open daily 9am-2:30pm and 6:30-11pm.) For a local experience, **bargain** to stay in a traditional Skyrian house; the thick-walled treasure troves are brimming with Delft ceramics and Italian linens, purchased from pirates who conveniently looted much of the known world. The incredible ▓**O Pappou Kai Ego** ("Grandpa and me"), toward the top of Agoras on the right, serves brilliant Skyrian specialties. (Main dishes 1600-2500dr/€4.70-7.35.) **Postal code:** 34007.

THE CYCLADES (Κυκλαδες)

When people wax rhapsodic about the Greek islands, chances are they're talking about the Cyclades. Whatever your idea of Greece—peaceful cobblestone streets and whitewashed houses, breathtaking sunsets, scenic hikes, all-night revelry—you'll find it here. Although each island has quiet villages and untouched spots, in summer most are mobbed by backpackers convening for a post-Eurail party.

▢ TRANSPORTATION

Ferries leave **Athens** for: Ios (7½hr., 3 per day, 5400dr/€15.85); Mykonos (6hr., 2 per day, 5200dr/€15.30); Naxos (6hr., 5 per day, 5000dr/€14.70); and Santorini (9hr., 3 per day, 6000dr/€17.65). Ferries from Crete connect to: Mykonos (8½hr., 5 per week, 6000dr/€17.60); Naxos (7hr., 3 per week, 5200dr/€15.25); Paros (9hr., 7 per week, 5200dr/€15.25); and Santorini (4hr., 2 per day, 3700dr/€10.80). Faster, but more expensive Flying Dolphin **hydrofoils** ply the same routes.

MYKONOS (Μυκονος)   ☎ 0289

Coveted by 18th-century pirates, chic Mykonos is still an object of lust for those seeking revelry, bacchanalian excess, and blond beaches amid rich history. Social life, both gay and straight, abounds, but it's not cheap. You can mingle with the *kosmopolitikos* and then savor the beaches near **Mykonos Town;** losing yourself in its labyrinthine colorful alleyways at dawn or dusk is one of the cheapest and most exhilarating ways to experience the island. On every corner you'll stumble upon a tiny church or quiet corner glowing in ethereal Cycladic light. All Mykonos' beaches are nude, but the degree of bareness varies; the most daring are **Plati Yialos, Paradise Beach, Super Paradise Beach,** and **Elia. Buses** run from South Station to Plati Yialos (every 30min., 250dr/€0.75), where you can catch *caïques* (little boats) to others (around 400dr/€1.20); buses also go to Paradise from South Station (every 30min., 250dr/€0.75) and to Elia from North Station (30min., 8 per day, 350dr/€1.05).

Ferries run to: Naxos (3hr., 1-2 per day, 2100dr/€6.10); Athens (6hr., 2-3 per day, 5600dr/€16.40); Santorini (6hr., 3 per week, 3500dr/€10.30); and Tinos (45min., 3 per day, 1300dr/€6.10). The helpful **tourist police** await at the ferry landing. (☎22 482. Open daily 8am-11pm.) Most budget travelers go to one of Mykonos's several festive campsites. There are information offices for camping (☎23 567), hotels (☎24 540), and domatia (☎24 860). **Paradise Beach Camping** is the liveliest place to stay in town. Take the free shuttle from the port to the campground 6km away. (☎22 852. 1600-2400dr/€4.70-7 per person, 900-1600dr/€2.65-4.70 per tent. Two-person beach cabin 6000-14,000dr/€17.60-41.10.) **Mykonos Camping,** on nearby Paraga Beach, is smaller, quieter, and cleaner. (☎25 915. 1600-2400dr/€4.60-7 per person, 900-1200dr/€2.65-3.55 per tent. Two-person bungalow 6000-12,000dr/€17.60-35.20.) **Hotel Apollon,** on the waterfront, is an antique-laden house with a view of the harbour. (☎22 223. Singles 9,000-15,000dr/€26.40-43.95; doubles 11,500-18,000dr/€33.70-52.70). You'll have to wait for a table at the ▨**Dynasty Thai Chinese Restaurant,** on Pl. Lymni, by the cinema on Meletopoulou, but it's worth it. (Main dishes 1650-2500dr/€4.85-7.35. Open daily 6:30pm-12:45am.) **Caprice Bar,** on the water in Little Venice, is popular, crowded, and breathtaking at sunset. (Open Su-Th 6:30pm-3:30am, F-Sa until 4:30am.) Step into a Toulouse-Lautrec painting at the groovy and mostly gay **Montparnasse Piano Bar,** Agion Anargyron 24, in Little Venice. (Open daily 7pm-3am.) On Matogianni, **Pierro's,** with wild dancing and irresistible hedonism, was the first gay bar in Greece. (Beer 1500dr/€4.40.) **Postal code:** 84600.

▨ DAYTRIP FROM MYKONOS: DELOS.

Delos (Δηλος), the sacred belly button at the center of the whirling Cyclades, is not to be missed. Delos holds the most famous sanctuary in the Cyclades, *the* **Temple of Apollo,** built to commemorate the birthplace of the god and his twin sister, Artemis. After several centuries of inhabitation, Delos was abandoned at the end of the 2nd century AD, taken over by legions of leaping lizards, huge spiderwebs, and members of the French School of Archaeology (the last since 1873). The archaeological site occupies much of the small island and takes several days to explore completely, but highlights gobble up only three hours. From the dock, head straight to the **Agora of the Competaliasts;** continue in the same direction and turn left onto the wide **Sacred Road** to reach the **Sanctuary of Apollo,** a collection of temples built in the god's honor from Mycenaean times to the 4th century BC. The **Great Temple of Apollo,** or **Temple of the Delians,** was completed at the end of the 4th century BC. Continue 50m straight past the end of the Sacred Road to the lovely **Terrace of the Lions.** The **museum,** next to the cafeteria, holds an assortment of finds. (Open Tu-Su 8:30am-3pm. 1200dr/€3.55, students and EU seniors 600dr/€1.76, EU students free.) A path leads to the summit of **Mt. Kythnos,** where Zeus watched Apollo's birth. **Boats** leave from the dock near **Mykonos Town,** not the large ferry dock (35min., Tu-Su every 30-45min., return 1900dr/€5.60).

TINOS (Τηνος)   ☎0283

In southern Tinos, tree-dotted hills gently cascade into the clear sea under the summit of hulking Mt. Exobourgo, wildflowers line the road with brilliant color, and a bit of searching rewards the careful explorer with quiet, secluded beaches. The island is a popular destination for Greek travelers but remains virtually undiscovered by others. Ancient Greeks believed Tinos to be the home of the wind god Aeolus; today the cool sea breeze whispers his legacy. In **Tinos Town (Hora),** the most visited part of the island, the **Panayia Evangelistira Church** houses the miraculous **Icon of the Annunciation,** one of the most sacred relics of the Greek Orthodox Church. (Open daily 7am-8pm. Free. Modest dress required.) **Beaches** surround Tinos Town; **Kardiani** and **Agios Petros,** situated at the base of the mountains, are among the islands' most spectacular, while **Stavros** beach, a 2km walk left out of town, and the nearby **Agios Fokas** (to the right out of town) are more touristy. For the best of the best, head east to the spectacular **Agios Sostis** and **Porto.** Take the KTEL **bus** (3-5 per day, 230dr/€0.70). Many hikes lead up **Mt. Exobourgo,** 14km north of Tinos Town, the site of the Venetian fortress **Xombourgo.**

Ferries run to: Andros (2hr., 2 per day, 1800dr/€5.30); Mykonos (30min., 4-5 per day, 1200dr/€3.55); and Syros (40min., 1-4 per day 10:15am-3:15pm, 1100dr/€3.25). **Catamarans** are twice as fast and twice as expensive as ferries. **Buses** (☎22 440) depart across the street from the National Bank for Porto (260dr/€0.80) and Pyrgos (800dr/€2.35). Check the schedule in the KTEL ticket agency opposite the bus depot. **Vidalis,** Zanaki Alavanou 16 (☎23 400), on the road running inland from the right of the waterfront facing inland, rents **mopeds** 3000dr/€8.80 and up; **cars** start at 8000dr/€23.50. **Dimitris-Maria Thodosis Rooms,** Evangelistrias 33, is midway up the road to the left, on the second floor. The traditional home features flower-laced balconies, a central kitchen and common bathrooms. (☎24 809. Mar.1-Oct. 31. Doubles/triples 10,000dr/€29.35; 4000dr/€11.75 extra for each additional person. **Tinos Camping** is 10min. from the waterfront to the right; follow the signs. (☎22 344. 1200dr/€3.52 per person. 1300dr/€3.81 per tent.) An abundance of *tavernas* tempt tourists to stop for a bite to eat. **Caffé Italia,** Akti Nazou 10 , is one of Tinos's best-kept culinary secrets. (☎25 756. Open daily 9am-12:30am.) For simpler fare, there's a **supermarket** near the post office. (Open daily 9am-12:30am.) **Postal Code:** 84200.

PAROS (Παρος)   ☎0284

Paros, famed throughout antiquity for its pure white marble (sculpted into the Venus de Milo), today retains golden beaches and tangled whitewashed villages. Past the commercial surface of **Paroikia,** Paros' port and largest city, flower-filled streets wind through archways, and past one of the most treasured basilicas of the Orthodox faith. Byzantine buffs will coo over **Panagia Ekatontapiliani** (Church of Our Lady of 100 Gates), which looms over Paroikia's *plateia* and houses three churches, cloisters, and a peaceful courtyard. Tradition holds that only 99 of the church's 100 doors can be counted—when the 100th appears, Constantinople will once again belong to Greece. (Dress modestly. Open daily 8am-8:30pm.) Ten kilometers south of town is the cool, spring-fed **Valley of the Butterflies** *(Petaloudes)*, home to an enormous congregation of rare (and tongue-twisting) *Panaxiaquadripunctaria* moths from June to late-September; please don't disturb by shaking the bushes. Take the bus from Paroikia to Aliki (10min., 8 per day, 300dr/€0.90) and ask to be let off at Petaloudes. Follow the signs 2km up the steep and winding road to the entrance. (Open M-Sa 9am-8pm. 400dr/€1.20.)

Ferries sail to Ios (2½hr., 7-9 per day, 2650dr/€7.80) and Santorini (3½hr., 7-9 per day, 3350dr/€9.85). The **tourist police** are behind the OTE, across the *plateia*. (☎21 673. Open daily 9am-3:30pm.) Turn left at the dock and take a right after the ancient cemetery ruins to reach **Rena Rooms**. (☎22 220. Doubles 6000-13,000dr/€17.60-38.10; triples 9000-15,000dr/€26.40-43.95.) Shuttles run from the port to **Parasporos Camping**, 1½km south of town. (☎22 268. 1300dr/€3.85 per person; 700dr/€2 per tent) The Psychedelic **Happy Green Cow**, just a block off the *plateia* behind the National Bank, serves tasty veggie fare. (Open daily 7pm-midnight.) **Postal code:** 84400.

NAXOS (Ναξος)   ☎0285

The large, gleaming marble arch of a former temple of Apollo forms a worthy portal to the splendid, diverse island of Naxos. The largest of the Cyclades, its vast interior sprawls with olive groves, charming villages, and ruins. Old **Naxos Town** snoozes behind the waterfront shops, on the hill leading up to the **Castro** an old **Venetian Castle**. Architecturally impressive, the new **☒Mitropolis Museum** surrounds the excavated 13th-century BC city. (Open Tu-Su 8:30am-2pm. Free.) The 6th-century BC **Portara** archway, visible from the waterfront, is one of the few archaeological sites in Greece that you can climb all over; it's perfect for late night stargazing. **Buses** run from the port (every 30min., 300dr/€0.90) to beaches **Agios Georgios**, **Ag. Prokopios**, **Ag. Anna**, and **Plaka**—the hands-down favorite for nude frolicking. Climb upstairs, and then stumble back down after a night of boozin' and groovin' under palm trees overlooking the sea at **Caesar's Club** on the inland street to the right of Naxos Tours. **Buses** run from Naxos Town to the small fishing village of **Apollonas**, on the northern tip, via a gorgeous coastal road (2hr., 3 per day, 1100dr/€3.25). The exhilarating gems of the interior, like the vast, Arcadian olive grove of the **Tragea**, aren't serviced by buses; ask for **hiking** information at the tourist office.

Ferries go to: Ios (1½hr., 1 per day, 2350dr/€6.90); Mykonos (1½hr., 2 per week, 2050dr/€6.05); Paros (1hr., 1 per day, 1550dr/€4.55); and Santorini (3hr., 1 per day, 3150dr/€9.25). The **tourist office** is 300m up from the waterfront by the bus station. (☎24 358. Open daily 8am-11pm.) **Hotel Anixis**, in Old Naxos serves breakfast (1200dr/€3.52) in a fabulous rooftop garden overlooking the Temple of Apollo. (☎22 112 Singles 8,000-13,000dr/€23.48-38.15; doubles 10,000-15,000dr/€29.35-44; triples 13,000-18,000dr/€38.15-52.85.) **Dionysus**, in Old Naxos (follow the red hand signs), is spartan, but cheap. (Open July-Aug. Dorms 2000dr/€5.87; singles 4000-5000dr/€11.74-14.67; doubles 6000dr/€17.61.) **Plaka Camping**, by Plaka beach, has studio/apartment options and a bevy of amenities. (☎42 700. Doubles 6000dr/€17.61; tents 500dr/€1.47.) **Postal Code:** 84300.

IOS (Ιος)   ☎0286

Ios can be summed up in three words: frat party run amok. Alright, that was four—after a week on Ios, you won't be able to count either. It has everything your mother warned you about: people swimming less than 30min. after they've eaten, wine being swilled from the bottle at 3pm, drinking games all day long, men and women dancing madly in the streets, and oh so much more. The **port** (Yialos) is at one end; the **village** (Hora) sits above it on a hill. Frenzied **Mylopotas beach** awaits 3km farther. **Buses** shuttle between the port, village, and beach (every 10-20min. 7am-midnight, 260dr/€0.80). **The Jungle**, near the basketball courts, is a good place to start. Thursday nights, 8000dr/€23.50 buys you pizza, cover immunity, a drink, and the right to **get drunk** at games held at the five bars comprising the ultimate pub crawl. Head up from the *plateia* to reach the **Slammer Bar**, where you can **get hammered** on "tequila slammers" 1000dr/€2.95, then migrate with the masses to **Red Bull**, to **get sloshed** on the Red Bull and vodka "energy special" (1500dr/€4.40). Afterwards find techno a go-go at **Scorpion Disco**, on the way to the beach. (Cover 1000dr/€2.95 after 1am.) Wind up your evening at **Sweet Irish Dream**, near the "donkey steps," and for a change of pace, **get smashed** and dance on tables after 2am. Take some aspirin in the morning and head down to the beach, where three **Mylopotas Water Sports Center** shacks along the beach offer **windsurfing**, **water-skiing**, and **snorkelling lessons** rental (2000-6000dr/€5.90-17.65 per hour Open daily Apr.-Oct.).

Ferries go to: Mykonos (4hr., 1 per week, 3375dr/€9.90); Naxos (1¾hr., at least 3 per day, 2350dr/€6.90); and Santorini (1¼hr., 3 per day, 1850dr/€5.45). The **tourist office** is next to the bus stop. (☎91 343. Open daily 8am-midnight.) In the village, take the uphill steps to the left in the *plateia* and take the first left to reach ◪**Francesco's** for spectacular harbor views and a terrace bar. (☎91 706. Dorms 2500dr/€7.35; doubles 3000-8000dr/€8.80-23.50.) **Hotel Sunrise** is at the end of the village, uphill to the right from the bus stop. (☎91 074 Doubles 24,000dr/€70.45; off-season 10,000dr/€29.35.) On the end of Mylopotas Beach, ◪**Far Out Camping** has a pool, plenty of tents, parties, and parties. Did we say parties? ☎92 301. Open Apr.-Sept. 1500dr/€4.40 per person; 500dr/€1.50 per tent; small cabins 1800dr/€5.30; bungalows 2000dr/€5.90.) ◪Ali Baba's is at the right end of the bar strip; ask around—it's tough to find but worth the trip. Try the chicken satay. (Entrees 1300-3000dr/€3.85-8.80.) A **supermarket** is in the *plateia*. **Postal code:** 84001.

SANTORINI (Σαντορινη)   ☎0286

Santorini's landscape is as dramatic as the volcanic eruption that laid it to waste 4500 years ago. Its eruptions—and startlingly beautiful black-sand beaches and mineral-rich fields—suggest it may be Plato's lost island of Atlantis. The center of activity on the island is the capital city **Fira**. Some visitors are shocked to step off the bus from the port and encounter the congested mess of glitzy shops, whizzing mopeds, and scads of tourists, but nothing can destroy the pleasure of the island's narrow streets and stunning sunsets. On the southwestern part of the island, the fascinating excavations at **Akrotiri**, a late Minoan city, are preserved virtually intact under layers of volcanic rock. (Open Tu-Su 8am-7pm. 1200dr/€3.55, students 600dr/€1.80.) **Buses** run to Akrotiri from Fira (30min., 16 per day, 400dr/€1.20). Frequent buses also run from Fira to the **beaches** of **Perissa** (15min., 30 per day, 400dr/€1.20) and **Kamari** (20min., 62 per day, 260/€0.80) in the southeast. The former route stops along the way in **Pyrgos;** from there, you can hike to the **Profitias Ilias Monastery** (45min.) and continue to the ruins of the island's old capital, **ancient Thira** (an additional 1½hr.), near Kamari. The theater, church, and forum of ancient Thira remain visible. (Open Tu-Su 8am-2pm.)

Ferries run to: Ios (1½hr., 3-5 per day, 1800dr/€5.50); Iraklion, Crete (4hr., 1 per day, 4100dr/€12.05); Mykonos (7hr., 2 per week, 3700dr/€10.90); Naxos (4hr., 4-8 per day, 3100dr/€9.10); and Paros (4½hr., 3-5 per day, 3300dr/€9.80). Most land at **Athinios** harbor; frequent buses (30min., 400dr/€1.20) connect to Fira. Share homemade wine with Petros at the ◪**Pension Petros;** from the bus station, go one block up 25 Martiou, make a right, a left at the bottom of the hill, and the first right. (☎22 573. Doubles 7000-17,000dr/€20.55-49.85; triples 9000-20,000dr/€26.40-58.60.) Head 300m north from the *plateia* for the **Thira Youth Hostel**. (☎22 387. Open Apr.-Oct. Dorms 2000-4000dr/€5.90-11.75; doubles 5000-10,000dr/€14.65-29.30.) Or, follow the blue signs east from the *plateia* for **Santorini Camping** (☎22 944. Open Apr.-Oct. 600dr/€4.70 per person, 900dr/€2.65 per tent, 800dr/€2.55 per car.) To bake on the sizzling black sand, stay at the **Youth Hostel Perissa-Anna,** between the first and second bus stops from Fira to Perissa. (☎82 182. Dorms 1000-3000dr/€2.95-8.80; private rooms 3000-4000dr/€8.80-11.75.) Back in Fira, the menu at **Nikolas Taverna** may be all Greek to you, but you can't go wrong; head uphill from the corner of the *plateia* and turn right at Hotel Tataki. (Open M-Sa noon-4pm and 6-11pm, Su 6-11pm.) The **Kira Thira Jazz Club** is across the street. (Open daily 9pm-late.) **Postal code:** 84700.

CRETE (Κρητη)

Greece's largest island embraces an infinite store of mosques, monasteries, mountain villages, gorges, grottoes, and beaches. Since 3000 BC, when the Minoans created their own language, script, and architecture, Crete has been a powerhouse. While Eastern Crete's resort towns seem to spring from the brains of British booking agents, the mountain-gripping highway winding from Malia to Agios Nikolaos and Sitia is absolutely spectacular. The vacation spots of Western Crete have grown around towns with rich histories and distinctive characters.

▣ TRANSPORTATION

Olympic Airways and **Air Greece** go between Athens and: Hania (4 per day, 19,400dr/ €56.85) in the west; Iraklion (45min., 13-15 per day, 27,400dr/€80.30) in the center; and Sitia (2-3 per week, 24,600dr/€72.10) in the east. **Ferries** arrive in Iraklion from thens/Piraeus (14hr., 3 per day, 7000dr/€20.51); Mykonos (8½hr., 5 per week, 6000dr/€17.5); Naxos (7hr., 3 per week, 5200dr/€15.25); Paros (9hr., 7 per week, 5200dr/€15.25); A and Santorini (4hr., 2 per day, 3700dr/€10.85). **Hydrofoils** service most destinations in half the time, but at double the price.

Crete is divided into four prefectures: Hania, Rethymno, Iraklion, and Lasithi. **Bus** networks are based on this division. Buses from Iraklion run west along the northern coast to Rethymno (1½hr., 18 per day, 1550dr/€4.55) en route to Hania (from Iraklion 17 per day, 2900dr/€8.50; from Rethymno 1600dr/€4.70). Buses run from Rethymno, Hania, and Iraklion south to the Samaria Gorge (from Hania 4 per day, return 2800dr/€8.20). Buses also run east from Iraklion to: Heronissos (45min.); Malia (from Iraklion 1hr., 800dr/€2.55; from Heronissos 20min., 240dr/€0.70); and Agios Nikolaos (from Iraklion 1½hr., 20 per day, 1450dr/€4.24; from Malia 1½hr., 2 per hr., 800dr/€2.55). Buses head to Sitia from Agios Nikolaos (1½hr., 4-6 per day, 1550dr/€4.55) and from Iraklion (3¼hr., 4 per day, 2950dr/€8.65).

IRAKLION (Ηρακλιο)   ☎081

Crete's capital and the fifth-largest city in Greece, Iraklion sports a chic native population, a more diverse nightlife than nearby resorts, and an ideal location as a base to tour Crete. Off Pl. Eleftherias, the phenomenal **Archaeological Museum** contains major finds from all over the island and presents a comprehensive island history from the Neolithic period to Roman times. (Open M 12:30-7pm, Tu-Su 8am-7pm. 1500dr/€4.40, students 800dr/€2.35, EU students free.) **Travel Hall Travel Agency,** Hatzimihali Yiannari 13, has information on flights to Athens and elsewhere. (☎341 862. Open M-Tu and Th-F 9am-4pm and 5:30-9pm, W 9am-5pm, Sa 9am-2pm.) **Boat** offices line 25 Augustou. There are several **bus** terminals in Iraklion. KTEL **Terminal A,** between the old city walls and the harbor near the waterfront, sends buses to Agios Nikolaos and Malia; the **Hania-Rethymno** terminal, which serves Hania, Rethymno, and other destinations, is opposite Terminal A, beside the ferry landing. The **tourist office,** Xanthoudidou 1, is opposite the Archaeological Museum in Pl. Eleftherias. (☎228 203. Open M-F 8am-2:30pm; July-Aug. also open evenings and Sa.) The **tourist police** are at 10 Dikeosinis. (☎283 190. Open daily 7am-11pm.)

Rent a Room Hellas, Handakos 24, is two blocks from El Greco Park. (☎288 851. Dorms 2200dr/€6.45; doubles 5000-7500dr/€14.65-21.50; triples 6000-10,000dr/ €17.60-29.35.) To get from Pl. Venizelou to **Hotel Rea,** Kalimeraki, walk down Handakos and turn right. (☎223 638. Singles 5000-7000dr/€14.70-20.55; doubles 7500-8500dr/€17.60-23.45; triples 9000-1050dr/€26.40-30.80.) To get to the **Youth Hostel,** Vyronos 5, from the bus station, take a left on 25 Augustou (with the water on the right) and go right on Vyronos. (☎286 281. Curfew midnight. Dorms 2500dr/€7.35; singles 3000-4000dr/€8.80-11.75; doubles 5500-6000dr/€14.65-17.65; triples 7000-8000dr/€20.55-23.50.) The best show in town is the **open-air market** on 1866, starting near Pl. Venizelon. Walk down D. Beaufort for dancing into the wee hours at **Privilege Club** and **Yacht. Postal code:** 71001.

▣ DAYTRIP FROM IRAKLION: KNOSSOS.

The excavations at Knossos, the most famous archaeological site in Crete, reveal the remains of a Minoan city that thrived here 3500 years ago. Sir Arthur Evans financed and supervised the excavations, and restored large parts of the **palace.** His work often crossed the line from preservation to artistic interpretation, but the site is impressive nonetheless. (From Iraklion, take **bus** #2 from 25 Augustou or Pl. Eleftherias (every 20min., 300dr/ €0.90) and look for the signs. (Open in summer daily 8am-7pm; in winter daily 8am-5pm. 1500dr/€4.40, students 800dr/€2.53, EU students free.)

RETHYMNO (Ρεθυμνο)   ☎0831

Nowhere do reminders of the island's turbulent occupations mingle as magically as in Rethymno's old city, near the cave famed as Zeus' birthplace. Arabic inscriptions lace the walls of the narrow streets, minarets highlight the skyline, and the 16th-century **Venetian fortress** guards the scenic harbor. (Open Tu-Su 8am-7pm. 1000dr/€2.95.) The Rethymno-Hania **bus station** (☎22 212) is south of the fortress on the water, with service to Hania (1hr., 17 per day, 1600dr/€4.70) and Iraklion (1½hr., 18 per day, 1550dr/€4.40). Climb the stairs behind the bus station and go left on Igoumenou Gavriil, which becomes Kountouriotou, and turn left on Varda Kallergi to reach the waterfront and the **tourist office**, on El. Venizelou. (☎29 148. Open M-F 8am-5pm.) To get from the station to the cheerful ▇**Youth Hostel,** Tombazi 41, walk down Igoumenou Gavriil, turn left at the park traffic light, go through the gate, and take the first right. (☎22 848. Breakfast 400-500dr/€1.20-1.50. Sheets 150dr/€0.45. Reception open 8am-noon and 5-9pm. Dorms 1800dr/€5.30.) ▇ **Olga's Pension,** Souliou 57, is off Antistassios. (☎53 206. Singles 6000-7000dr/€17.60-20.55; doubles 7000-10,000dr/20.55-29.35; triples 10,000-11,000dr/€29.30-32.25.) **Postal code:** 74100.

▇ **HIKING NEAR RETHYMNO: SAMARIA GORGE.** The most popular excursion from Hania, Rethymno, and Iraklion is the 5-6hr hike down Samaria Gorge, a spectacular 16km long ravine extending through the White Mountains. Sculpted by the tender ministrations of rainwater over 14 million years, the gorge—the longest in Europe—retains its allure despite having been trampled by thousands of visitors. Rare native plants peek out from sheer rock walls, wild *agrimi* goats clamber about the hills, and endangered griffin vultures as well as golden eagles circle overhead. (Open May to mid-Oct. daily 6am-4pm. 1200dr/€3.55, children under 15 and organized student groups free.) For more information about your friendly, neighborhood gorge, call **Hania Forest Service** (☎92 287). The trail starts at **Xyloskalo;** take the 6:15am or 8:30am **bus** from Hania to Xyloskalo (1½hr., 1300-1400dr/€3.85-4.15 one-way) for a day's worth of hiking. The 1:45pm bus from Hania will put you in **Omalos,** ready for the next morning. If you spend the night, rest up at **Gigilos Hotel** on the main road. (☎67 181. Singles 4000-5000dr/€11.72-14.65; doubles 6000dr/€17.65.) The trail ends in **Agia Roumeli,** on the southern coast, where you can hop on a **boat** to Hora Sfakion (1¼hr.; 4 per day, last ferry 6pm; 1500dr/€4.40) or take a return bus to Hania (1600dr/€4.70). ☎0821

SITIA (Σητεια)   ☎0843

A winding drive east from **Agios Nikolaos** brings you to the fishing and port town of Sitia, where the wave of tourism slows to a trickle and pelicans walk the streets at dawn. The town's **beach** extends 3km to the east, while the hilltop **fortress** (open Tu-Su 8:30am-2:30pm; free) provides views of the town and bay. **Ferries** leave Sitia for: Athens/Piraeus (16-17hr., 5 per week, 7600dr/€22.35) via Agios Nikolaos (1½hr., 1600dr/€4.70); Karpathos (5hr., 3 per week, 3400dr/€10); and Rhodes (12hr., 3 per week, 6000dr/€17.65). With your back to the **bus station** (☎22 272), walk right, take your first right, then take your first left and follow Venizelou to the waterfront. From Polytechiou Sq., head right along the water to reach the **tourist office.** (☎28 300. Open M-F 9am-9pm, Sa-Su 10am-9pm.) To get to the **Youth Hostel,** Therissou 4, walk right from the bus station, go inland, follow signs for the major road to Iraklion and Agios Nikolaos, and bear left; or, call for a ride from the station. (☎22 693. Sheets 100dr/€0.30. Dorms 1700dr/€5 per person; singles 2500dr/€7.35; doubles 4000dr/€11.75; triples 5000dr/€14.70.) **Venus Rooms to Let** is at Kondilaki 60; walk up Kapetan Sifi from the main square and make your first right after the telephone office. (☎24 307. Doubles 7000dr/€20.55.) ▇**Cretan House,** K. Karamanli 10, off the *plateia* and facing the water, serves Cretan entrees for around 1400dr/€4.10. (Open daily 9am-1:30am.) Head to **Hot Summer,** way down the road to Palaikastro by the beach, after midnight. (Cover 1000dr/€2.95.) **Postal code:** 72300

■ **DAYTRIP FROM SITIA: VAI BEACH.** The beaches at **Vai,** to the east, used to be a secret refuge from Sitia's crowds. Today, busloads of tourists roll in every day to swim at a smooth, blue-flag beach and rest in the shade of Europe's only indigenous palm tree forest. For more secluded bathing and a better beach, face the water and head right, up and over the craggy hill. **Buses** arrive from Sitia (1hr., 4-6 per day, 650dr/€1.95) via Palaikastro (300dr/€0.90).

EASTERN AEGEAN ISLANDS

The intricate, rocky coastlines and unassuming port towns of the **Northeastern Aegean Islands** enclose thickly wooded mountains that give way to unspoiled villages and beaches. The islands dispense a sampling of undiluted Greek culture. The landscapes of the **Dodecanese** (Twelve Islands), southeast of the Northeastern Aegean Islands, reflect Greek history from the rise of Christianity to Mussolini's architectural style. In summer, tourists flock to Rhodes and Kos for raucous nightlife, while other islands are best for peaceful relaxation.

✖ FERRIES TO TURKEY

Ferries run to: **Kuşadası** from **Samos** (1¼hr., 5 per week 10,000-14,000dr/€41.10-29.35); and **Bodrum** from **Kos** (1 per day, 10,000-13,000dr/€29.35-38.15 return). As of August 2001, citizens of Australia, Canada, Ireland, the UK, and the US require a visa to enter Turkey. **Port taxes** are typically 3000dr/€8.80.

SAMOS (Σαμος)   ☎0273

Samos is perhaps the most beautiful, and certainly the most touristed, island in the Northeast Aegean. Many stop only briefly en route to **Kuşadası** and the ruins of **Ephesus** on the Turkish coast (see p. 960), but those who return stay longer discover the quiet inland streets, palm trees, and red roof-covered hillside of **Samos Town (Vathy),** one of the Aegean's most attractive port cities. The phenomenal ▨**Archaeological Museum** is behind the municipal gardens. (Open Tu-Su 8:30am-3pm. 800dr/€2.35, students 400dr/€1.20, EU students free.) The beach town of **Pythagorion,** the island's ancient capital, is 14km south of Samos Town. Near the town are the magnificent remains of Polykrates' 6th-century BC engineering projects: the **Tunnel of Eupalinos,** which diverted water from a natural spring to the city, a 40-meter-deep **harbor mole,** and the **Temple of Hera.** (Tunnel open Tu-Su 8:45am-2:45pm. 500dr/€1.50, students 300dr/€0.90, EU students free. Temple open Tu-Su 8:30am-3pm. 800dr/€2.35, students 400dr/€1.20.) Hourly **buses** arrive in Pythagorion from Samos Town (20min., 300dr/€0.90). The temple is in Heraion, a 10min. **bus** ride from Pythagorion.

Ferries arrive in Samos Town from: Athens/Piraeus (12hr., 1 per day, 7100dr/€20.85); Chios (5hr., 4 per week, 3000dr/€8.80); Mykonos (6hr., 6 per week, 5400dr/€15.85); and Naxos (6hr., 3 per week, 5300dr/€15.55) via Paros (4500dr/€13.25). The **tourist office** is on a side street one block before Pl. Pythagoras. (☎28 530. Open July-Aug. M-Sa 8:30am-2pm.) Turn right at the end of the ferry dock onto E. Stamatiadou before the Hotel Aiolis, take the second left, and head uphill for the **Pension Trova,** Kalomiris 26, featuring traditionally furnished rooms, some with bath and balcony. (☎27 759. Singles 6000dr/€17.65; doubles 7000dr/€20.55.) **Postal Code:** 83100.

CHIOS (Χιος)   ☎0271

Chios is where the wild things *were:* Orion hunted every last beast down, leaving the island's mountainsides to pine, cypress, and mastic trees. With increasing accessibility to its striking volcanic beaches and medieval villages, Chios attracts vacationers and package tourists hopping to Çeşme, Turkey. **Pyrgi,** high in the hills 25km from Chios Town, is one of Greece's most striking villages, with black-and-white geometric designs covering its buildings. Farther south lies **Emborio beach,** where beige volcanic cliffs contrast with the black stones and deep-blue water below. **Green buses** in Chios Town make trips to Pyrgi and Emborio. **Ferries** go from

Chios Town to: Athens/Piraeus (8hr., 1-2 per day, 6300dr/€18.50); Lesvos (3hr., 1 per week, 3500dr/€10.30); Rhodes (1 per week, 7100dr/€20.85); and Samos (4hr., 1 per week, 3300dr/€9.70). For the **tourist office,** Kanari 18, turn off the waterfront onto Kanari, walk toward the plateia; look for the "i" sign. (**☎**44 344. Open May-Oct. daily 7am-10pm.) In a yellow building at the far right end of the waterfront, the hospitable owners of **Chios Rooms,** Leofores 114, rent bright and breezy rooms, most with sea views and some with baths. (**☎**20 198. Doubles 8000dr/€23.48; triples 10,000dr/€29.35, with bath 12,000dr/€35.25. **Postal Code:** 82100.

LESVOS (Λεσβος)   ☎ 0251

Once home to the sensual poet Sappho, Lesvos is something of a girl-power pilgrimmage for lesbians paying homage to their legendary etymological roots. Several artist colonies call the island home, as does Nobel Prize-winning poet Odysseus Elytis, taken by island's hot springs, petrified forests, and fabulous beaches. Most travelers pass through the modern **Mytilini,** the capital and central port city. The new ▧**Archaeological Museum,** Argiri Eftalioti 7, houses an impressive collection of the island's archaeological finds. (Open daily 8am-7pm. 500dr/€1.50.)

Ferries go to: Athens/Piraeus (12hr., 1-3 per day, 7700dr/€22.60); Chios (3hr., 1-3 per day, 3600dr/€10.60); Limnos (5hr., 6 per week, 4800dr/€14.10); and Thessaloniki (12hr., 1 per week, 9000dr/€26.45). Book ferries at **NEL Lines,** Pavlou Koudoutrioti 67 (**☎**22 220), along the waterfront. The **tourist police,** in the passport control building at the ferry dock, offer maps and advice. (**☎**22 776. Open daily 7:15am-2:15pm and 5-8pm.) Mytilini has its fair share of enterprising residents, so *domatia* are plentiful and well-advertised. You may also be met at the ferry. Be sure to negotiate; doubles cost 7000-9000dr/€20.55-26.45. Take an intercity **bus** from the station behind Agios Irinis Park, southwest of the harbor, to the north coast artist havens **Petras** and **Molyvos** (2hr., 4-5 per day, 1450dr/€4.30). The **Molyvos tourist office,** just up from the bus stop, helps find rooms. (**☎**71 347. Open Apr.-Oct. daily 7:30am-4pm.) Unhurried **Skala Eressou,** on the opposite end of the island, is the birthplace of Sappho. Its seemingly endless beaches attract archeologists, lesbians, poets, and families. **Sappho Travel,** one block from the bus stop, can help with accommodations and transportation. (**☎**52 140; www.lesvos.co.uk. Open daily May-Oct. 9am-11pm; Nov.-April 9am-2pm and 5-9pm.) **Postal code:** 81100.

RHODES (Ροδος)   ☎ 0241

Although Rhodes is the tourism capital of the Dodecanese, the sandy beaches along its east coast, jagged cliffs skirting its west coast, and green mountains freckled with villages in the interior still retain serenity. The island's most famous sight is one that no longer exists: the **Colossus of Rhodes,** a 35m bronze statue of Helios and one of the seven wonders of the ancient world, straddled the island's harbor and was destroyed by a 237 BC earthquake. The beautiful **City of Rhodes** has been the island's capital for over 20 centuries. The **Old Town,** surrounded by remnants of the 14th-century occupation by the Knights of St. John, lends the city a medieval flair. At the top of the hill looms the **Palace of the Grand Master,** with 300 rooms, moats, drawbridges, huge watchtowers, and colossal battlements. (Open Tu-Su 8.30am-9pm, M 2:30-9pm. 1200dr/€3.55, students 600dr/€1.80.) Down the hill, the former Hospital of the Knights is now the **Archaeological Museum** in nearby Pl. Argykastrou. (Open Tu-F 8am-7pm, Sa-Su 8am-3.30pm. 800dr/€2.35, students and seniors 400dr/€1.20.) The New Town is a mecca for nightlife; **Orfanidou** is popularly known as **Bar Street.** Daytrips to **Faliraki,** which is south of the City of Rhodes and known for its rowdy drinkers and beach bunnies, leave on **excursion boats.** They stop along the way in the town **Lindos,** which is perhaps the island's most picturesque town, with vine-lined streets, courtyards covered in pebble mosaics, and whitewashed houses beneath a castle-capped acropolis. See schedules and prices on the dock along the lower end of the Mandraki (from 3500dr/€10.30). **Buses** also run to Faliraki (17 per day, 500dr/€1.50) and Lindos (14 per day, 1050dr/€3.10).

GREECE

Ferries arrive in: Athens/Piraeus (1-4 per day, 11,300dr/€33.20); Karpathos (3 per week, 4400dr/€12.91); Kos (1-2 per day, 4000dr/€11.75); Patmos (1-2 per day, 5400dr/€15.85); Samos (1 per week, 6500dr/€19.10); and Sitia, Crete (3 per week, 6400/€18.78). The **Greek National Tourist Office (EOT)** is up Papgou, a few blocks from Pl. Rimini, at Makariou. (☎23 255. Open M-F 7:30am-3pm.) ▓**Rhodes Youth Hostel,** Ergiou 12, is packed with interesting young travelers from around the world. Turn off Sokratous onto the tiny side street next to the run down building that looks like a mosque. Keep on walking and at the sign 'youth hostel' take a right: the hostel will be on your left-hand side. (☎30 491. Dorms 2000-2500dr/€5.90-7.35.) Snooze in the New Town at the **New Village Inn,** Konstantopedos 10. (☎34 937. Singles 6000dr/€17.65; doubles 10,000-12,000dr/€29.35-35.25.) Sensuous aromas of traditional Hellenic dishes waft from ▓**Chalki,** Kathopouli 30. Entrees cost around 1800dr/€5.30, including their fabulous moussaka. (Open daily noon-3pm and 6pm-midnight.)

KOS (Κως)   ☎0242

Rivalling Rhodes in the sheer number of its visitors, Kos draws a younger, louder, more intoxicated crowd. Don't be dismayed by the raucous bars and mammoth hotels; perseverance rewards you with quiet nooks and undiscovered golden beaches. In **Kos Town,** minarets of Ottoman mosques rise among massive walls of a Crusader fortress and scattered ruins from the Archaic, Classical, Hellenistic, and Roman eras. The ancient sanctuary of ▓**Asclepion,** 4km west of Kos Town, is dedicated to the god of healing. In the 5th century BC, Hippocrates opened the world's first medical school here; today, doctors still take his oath. From the lowest level (*andiron*), steps lead to the 2nd-century AD **Temple of Apollo** and 4th-century BC **Minor Temple of Asclepios.** Sixty steps lead to the third *andiron*, with the forested remains of the **Main Temple of Asclepios** and a view of the ruins, Kos Town, and the Turkish coast. (Open Tu-Su 8am-6:30pm. 800dr/€2.35, students 400dr/€1.20.) The site is easily reached by **bus** (15min., 16 per day). The best **beaches** stretch along Southern Kos up to Kardamene; the **bus** stops at any of them.

Ferries run to: Athens/Priaeus (11-15hr., 2-3 per day, 5200dr/15.29€); Patmos (4hr., 1-2 per day, 3200dr/€9.45); and Rhodes (4hr., 2 per day, 4200dr/€12.35). A **Greek National Tourist Office,** on Akti Miaouli, provides visitors with maps, brochures, and schedules. (Open M-F 8am-8pm, Sa 8am-3pm.) It's best to find your own room, but if your boat docks in the middle of the night, you might have to go with Kos's notorious dock hawks. Take the first right off Megalou Alexandrou, on the back left corner of the first intersection, to get to ▓**Pension Alexis,** Herodotou 9. (☎28 798. Doubles 5500-8500dr/€16.20-25; triples 9000-10,000dr/€26.50-29.45.) **Hotel Afendoulis,** Evrilpilou 1, is right down Vas. Georgiou near the beach. (☎/fax 25 321. Doubles 7500-12,000dr/€22.10-35.30.) **Kos Camping,** 3km southeast of the center, is accessible by bus from the city center every 30min. (☎23 910. 1100dr/€3.25 per tent. Tent rental 1300dr/€3.85.) Most bars are either in **Exarhia,** also known as **bar street** between Akti Koundouriotou and the ancient *agora,* or the more subdued **Porfiriou,** in the north near the beach. **Fashion Club,** Kanari 2 is huge and jumpin'. (Cover 3000dr/€8.80, includes 1 drink.) **Hamam Club,** near the *agora* and next to the taxi station in Diagoras Square, was once a bathhouse. **Postal code:** 85300.

PATMOS (Πατμος)   ☎0247

The holy island of Patmos balances a weighty religious past with excellent beaches and traces of an artistic community. The white houses of **Hora** and the majestic walls of the **Monastery of St. John the Theologian** above are visible from all over the island. (Monastery and treasure museum open daily 8am-1pm; also Tu, Th, Su 4-6pm. Treasury 1200dr/€3.55. Monastery free.) Hora is 4km from the colorful port town of **Skala.** Take a bus (10min., 11 per day, 400dr/€1.20) or taxi (1000dr/€2.95) from Skala, or tackle the steep hike. Halfway between the two is the **Apocalypsis Monastery** and the **Sacred Grotto of the Revelation,** where St. John dictated the Book of Revelation. (Open daily 8am-1pm; also Tu, Th, Su 4-6pm. Free. Dress modestly.)

Ferries arrive in Skala from: Kos (4hr., 3000dr/€8.85) and Rhodes (9hr., 5800dr/€17.10). The **tourist office** is opposite the dock. (☎316 66. Open daily 7am-2:30pm and 4-9pm.) A battalion of locals greets the plethora of early morning boats each day, offering *domatia* (singles 5000-7000dr/€14.75-20.60; doubles 7000-10,000dr/€20.60-29.45). To get to **Flower Stefanos Camping at Meloi,** 2km northeast of Skala, 10ft. behind Meloi Beach, follow the waterfront road past Apollon Travel as it wraps along the port and up the hill. Camping is on the left at the bottom—look for signs. (☎31 821. 1400dr/€4.15 per person, 800dr/€2.35 per tent.)

HUNGARY
(MAGYARORSZÁG)

HUNGARIAN FORINT

US$1 = 280 FORINTS	100FT = US$0.36
CDN$1 = 180FT	100FT =CDN$0.55
UK£1 = 405FT	100FT = UK£0.25
IR£1 = 325FT	100FT = IR£0.31
AUS$1 = 150FT	100FT = AUS$0.67
NZ$1 = 125FT	100FT = NZ$0.82
ZAR1 = 35FT	100FT = ZAR2.96
DM1 = 130FT	100FT = DM0.76
EUR€1 = 255FT	100FT = EUR€0.39

PHONE CODE	**Country code: 36. International dialing prefix: 00.** From outside Hungary, dial int'l dialing prefix (see inside back cover) + 36 + city code + local number.

Communism was a blip in Hungary's 1100-year history of repression and renewal. Today, the nation appears at ease with its new-found capitalist identity. Although Budapest is Hungary's social and economic keystone, it by no means has a monopoly on cultural attractions; provincial capitals are within reach by train. With wine valleys nestled in the northern hills, a rough and tumble cowboy plain in the south, and a beach resort in the east, don't miss the countryside for a whirlwind tour of the capital.

Hungary for more? Bite down on *Let's Go: Eastern Europe 2002.*

FACTS AND FIGURES

Official Name: Republic of Hungary.

Capital: Budapest.

Major Cities: Eger, Szombathely, Debrecen, Pécs.

Population: 10 million. 90% Magyar, 4% Roma, 3% German, 2% Serb.

Land Area: 92,340 km.

Climate: Temperate; cold, cloudy, humid winters and warm summers.

Language: Hungarian (Magyar).

Religions: Roman Catholic (68%), Calvinist (20%), Lutheran (5%), other (7%).

DISCOVER HUNGARY

Quickly being discovered as Central Europe's most cosmopolitan city, **Budapest** (p. 508) is at the heart of Hungary. When you're ready, head over to the relaxed villages of the **Danube Bend** (p. 518). **Eger** (p. 520) is home to one of Hungary's most important castles, and the wine cellars of the nearby Valley of the Beautiful Women attract the most discriminating drunks. Don't miss charming **Győr**, and the nearby **Archabbey of Pannonhalma** (p. 521). **Lake Balaton** (p. 522), capital of the Hungarian summer, hosts a kitschy beach scene. An escape from the thonged throngs of Siófok's Strand, **Keszthely** (p. 523), on the lake's western end, has a stunning palace and the world's largest radioactive thermal bath.

Hungary

ESSENTIALS

WHEN TO GO

The temperatures are most pleasant May to September. Budapest never feels crowded even in the high season, so time your visit to coincide with some of the summer festivals. Fall and spring can be a bit chillier, though with a sweater, it's quite nice. Winter tends to be very cold, and worth avoiding.

DOCUMENTS AND FORMALITIES

VISAS. Citizens of Canada, Ireland, South Africa, the UK, and the US can visit Hungary without visas for 90 days, provided their passport does not expire within six months of their journey's end. Australians and New Zealanders must obtain 90-day tourist visas from a Hungarian embassy or consulate. For US residents, visas cost: single-entry US$40, double-entry US$75, multiple-entry US$180, and 48hr. transit US$38. Non-US residents pay US$65, US$100, US$200, and US$50. Visa processing takes a few days. Visa extensions are rare; apply at the Hungarian police.

EMBASSIES. All foreign embassies in Hungary are in **Budapest** (see p. 508). For **Hungarian embassies at home: Australia (consulate),** Suite 405, Edgecliff Centre 203-233, New South Head Rd., Edgecliff, NSW 2027 (☎(02) 9328 7859; fax 9327 1829); **Canada,** 299 Waverley St., Ottawa, ON K2P 0V9 (☎613-230-2717; fax 613-230-7560; h2embott@docuweb.ca; www.docuweb.ca/hungary); **Ireland,** 2 Fitzwilliam Pl., Dublin 2 (☎(01) 661 2903; fax 661 2880); **South Africa,** 959 Arcadia St., Hatfield, Arcadia; P.O. Box 27077, Sunnyside 0132 (☎(012) 430 3020; fax 430 3029; hunem@cis.co.za); **New Zealand,** 151 Orangi Kaupapa Rd., Wellington, 6005 (☎644 938 0427; fax 938 0428; sztmay@attglobal.net; www.geocities.com/hu-consul-nz); **UK,** 35 Eaton Pl., London SW1X 8BY (☎(020) 7235 5218; fax 7823 1348; www.huemblon.org.uk); and **US,** 3910 Shoemaker St. NW, Washington, D.C. 20008 (☎202-362-6730; fax 202-966-8135; office@huembwas.org; www.hungaryemb.org).

HUNGARY

TRANSPORTATION

BY PLANE. Hungary's national airline, **Malév,** has daily direct flights from New York to Budapest and from London (both Gatwick and Heathrow) to Budapest. Several other international airlines also fly into Budapest.

BY TRAIN. Most trains *(vonat)* pass through Budapest and tend to be reliable and cheap, although you should be cautious of theft on the Vienna-Budapest line. **Eurail** and **EastRail** are valid in Hungary. Students and those under 26 can be eligible for a 30% discount on train fares; ask ahead and be persistent. An **ISIC** gives discounts at IBUSZ, Express, and station ticket counters. Flash your card and repeat "student," or in Hungarian, *"diák"* (DEE-ahk). Book international tickets in advance. *Személyvonat* trains are slow; *gyorsvonat* (listed on schedules in red) cost the same and are twice as fast. Large towns are accessible by the blue *expressz* lines. Air-conditioned *InterCity* trains are fastest. A seat reservation *(potegy)* is required on trains labeled "R." While you can board an *InterCity* train without a reservation, the fine for doing so is 1000Ft; purchasing the reservation on board will double the price of the ticket. Some basic vocabulary words are: *érkezés* (arrival), *indulás* (departure), *vágány* (track), *állomás* or *pályaudvar* (station, abbreviated *pu.*), and *peron* (platform). Consult www.elvira.hu for schedules and fares.

BY BUS. The cheap, clean, and crowded bus system links many towns that have rail connections only to Budapest. The **Erzsébet tér** bus station in Budapest posts schedules and fares. *InterCity* bus tickets are purchased on board (arrive early if you want a seat). In larger cities, tickets for local transportation must be bought in advance from a newsstand and punched when you get on; there's a fine if you're caught without a ticket. In smaller cities, you pay when you board.

BY FERRY. The Danube **hydrofoil** goes from Budapest to Vienna via Bratislava; contact **Interticket Hungary** in the US (☎781-275-5724; www.interticket.com) or **MAHART Tours International** in Hungary (☎(01) 318 17 43).

BY CAR. International Driving Permits are required of all non-Hungarian drivers. The national motorists' club is **Magyar Autóklub (MAK),** II, Rómer Flóris u. 4/a, 1024 Budapest (☎(1) 345 17 77; www.autoklub.hu). For 24hr. MAK breakdown service, call ☎188.

BY BIKE AND BY THUMB. IBUSZ and Tourinform can provide brochures about cycling in Hungary that include maps, suggested tours, sights, accommodations, bike rental locations, repair shops, and border crossings. Always check the district as well as the kind of street: **út** is a major thoroughfare, **utca (u.)** a street, **körút (krt.)** a circular artery, and **tér** a square. *Let's Go* does not recommend hitchhiking.

TOURIST SERVICES AND MONEY

EMERGENCY	Police: ☎104. Ambulance: ☎105. Fire: ☎107.

TOURIST OFFICES. Tourinform (www.tourinform.hu) has branches in every county, and is generally the most useful tourist service in Hungary; they should be your first stop in any town. They can't make reservations, but they'll check on vacancies, usually in university dorms and private *panzió*. **IBUSZ** offices throughout the country book private rooms, exchange money, sell train tickets, and charter tours, and are generally best at helping with travel plans. Snare the pamphlet *Tourist Information: Hungary* and the monthly entertainment guides *Programme in Hungary* and *Budapest Panorama* (all free and in English). **Express,** the former national student travel bureau, handles hostels and changes money. Regional agencies are most helpful in the outlying areas. **Tourist bureaus** are generally open in summer M-Sa 8am-8pm.

MONEY. The national currency is the **forint**, divided into 100 **fillérs,** which are quickly disappearing from circulation. Keep US dollars or Deutschmarks for visas, international train tickets, and (less often) private accommodations. New Zealand and Australian dollars, as well as South African rand and Irish pounds, are not exchangeable. The maximum permissible commission for cash-to-cash exchange is 1%. Never change money on the street. Convert **traveler's checks** at **OTP Bank** and **Postabank** offices. Currency exchange machines are popping up all over and have excellent rates, although they are slow. **Credit cards** are accepted at expensive hotels and shops. A basic day in Hungary runs about US$25. Rounding up the bill as a **tip** is standard for a job well done. In restaurants, hand the tip to the server when you pay; it's rude to leave it on the table. Foreigners are expected to tip 15%; locals never give more than 10%. Bathroom attendants get 30Ft. You can be refunded up to 16% of the **Value-Added Tax (AFA)** upon leaving Hungary for purchases exceeding 50,000Ft on a single invoice, bought within 90 days of leaving the country, and are unused. You must have a copy of your credit card receipt or documentation from when you exchanged currency.

COMMUNICATION

MAIL. The Hungarian mail system is somewhat reliable; airmail *(légiposta)* takes 5-10 days to the US and the rest of Europe, and two weeks to South Africa, New Zealand, and Australia. If you're mailing to a Hungarian citizen, the family name precedes the given name. Mail can be received through *Poste Restante.*

TELEPHONES. For intercity calls, wait for the tone and dial slowly; "06" goes before the phone code. International calls require red phones or new, digital-display blue ones. Blue phones tend to cut you off after three to nine minutes. Phones often require phone cards *(telefonkártya)*, available at kiosks, train stations, and post offices (800Ft or 1600Ft). Direct calls can also be made from Budapest's phone office. To call collect, dial ☎190 for the international operator. To reach international carriers, put in a 10Ft and a 20Ft coin (which you get back), dial ☎00, wait for the second tone, then dial the international direct dialing number: **AT&T,** ☎06 800 01111; **British Telecom,** ☎06 (wait for dial tone) 800 04411; **Canada Direct,** ☎06 800 01 211; **MCI,** ☎00 800 01411; and **Sprint,** ☎00 800 01 877.

INTERNET. Internet is available throughout the country, and is everywhere in Budapest and major provincial centers. The Hungarian keyboard differs significantly from English-language keyboards. When you first log on, go to the bottom right-hand corner of the screen and look for the *"Hu"* icon; click here to switch the keyboard setting to *"Angol."*

LANGUAGES. Hungarian belongs to the Finno-Ugric branch of the Ugric language family, and is related distantly to Turkish and even more distantly to Estonian and Finnish. It is also spoken by minorities in Slovakia, Romania, and Yugoslavia. After Hungarian and German, English is Hungary's third language. For Hungarian basics, see p. 985.

ACCOMMODATIONS AND CAMPING

Many travelers stay in **private homes** booked through a tourist agency. Singles are scarce—it's worth finding a roommate, as solo travelers often pay for a double room. Agencies may try to foist their most expensive rooms on you. Outside Budapest, the best offices are region-specific (e.g. EgerTourist in Eger). After staying a few nights, you can make arrangements directly with the owner, thus saving yourself the agencies' 20-30% commission. **Panzió,** run out of private homes, are the next most common option, although not always the cheapest. **Hotels** exist in some towns, but most have disappeared. **Hosteling** is becoming more attractive, although it is rare outside Budapest; HI cards are increasingly useful. Sheets are rarely required. Many hostels can be booked through Express, the student travel agency, or the regional tourist office. From June-August, university **dorms** become hostels;

inquire at Tourinform. There are more than 300 **campgrounds** are throughout Hungary open May-September. Tourist offices offer the annual free booklet *Camping Hungary.* For more information and maps, contact Tourinform in Budapest.

HEALTH AND SAFETY

Medical assistance is most easily obtained in Budapest, where embassies carry a list of Anglophone doctors; most hospitals in the capital have English-speaking doctors on staff. Outside Budapest, try to bring a Hungarian speaker with you. Tourist insurance is valid—and often necessary—for many medical services. Tap water is usually clean and drinkable. Public bathrooms vary in cleanliness: pack toilet paper, soap, and a towel, and be prepared to pay the attendant 30Ft. Gentlemen should look for *Férfi,* and ladies for *Női* signs. *Gyógyszertar* (pharmacies) are well-stocked with Western brands and always carry tampons and condoms. In bigger towns, there are usually 24hr. pharmacies. Violent crime in Hungary is low, but in larger cities, especially Budapest, foreign tourists are favorite targets of petty thieves and pickpockets. Homosexuality, although legal, is still not fully accepted in Hungarian society; discretion is wise.

FOOD AND DRINK

Hungarian food is more flavorful and varied than standard Eastern European fare. Paprika, Hungary's chief agricultural export, colors most dishes red. In Hungarian restaurants (*vendéglő* or *étterem*), begin with *halászlé,* a deliciously spicy fish stew. Alternately, try *gyümölcsleves,* a cold fruit soup topped with whipped cream. The Hungarian national dish is *bográcsgulyás* (goulash), a stew of beef, onions, green pepper, tomatoes, potatoes, dumplings, and plenty of paprika. *Borjúpaprikás* is veal with paprika and potato-dumpling pasta. Vegetarians can find recourse in the tasty *rántott sajt* (fried cheese) and *gombapörkölt* (mushroom stew) on most menus. In general, Hungarian food is fried, and fresh vegetables other than peppers and cabbage are a rarity. In a *cukrászda* (confectionery), you can satisfy your sweet tooth cheaply. *Túrós rétes* is a chewy pastry pocket filled with sweetened cottage cheese. *Somlói galuska* is a fantastically rich sponge cake of chocolate, nuts, and cream, all soaked in rum. *Kávé* is espresso, served in thimble-sized cups and so strong your veins will be popping before you finish the first sip. *Unicum,* advertised as the national drink of Hungary, is a very fine herbal liqueur that Habsburg kings used to cure digestive ailments.

HOLIDAYS AND FESTIVALS

Holidays: New Year's Day (Jan. 1); National Day (Mar. 15); Catholic Easter (Apr. 23-24); Labor Day (May 1); Whit Sunday (June 11); Whit Monday (June 12); Constitution Day (St. Stephen's Day; Aug. 20); Republic Day (1956; Aug. 23); Christmas (Dec. 25-26).

Festivals: The best of all worlds come together in the last two weeks of March for the **Budapest Spring Festival,** a showcase of Hungary's premier musicians and actors. Óbudai island in Budapest hosts the week-long **Sziget Festival** (mid-Aug.), Europe's biggest open-air rock festival. An international folk-dance festival, **Eger Vintage Days,** is held daily in the beginning of September.

BUDAPEST   ☎ 1

While the rest of the country lingers, Budapest jets. Ten times larger than any other Hungarian city, cosmopolitan and confident, this Magyar metropolis is reassuming its place as a major European capital. Originally two separate cities, Budapest was created in 1872 with the joining of Buda and Pest, and immediately went on to become the Habsburg Empire's number-two city. World War II punished Budapest severely, but the Hungarians rebuilt it from the rubble with the same pride with which they weathered the Soviet occupation. Neon lights and legions of tourists may draw attention away from the cobblestone streets, wide boulevards, bridges and parks—but beneath it all beats a real Hungarian heart.

☐ TRANSPORTATION

Flights: Ferihegy Airport (☎296 96 96). Malév (Hungarian airlines) flight reservations ☎296 72 11 and 296 78 31. **Centrum buses** go to Erzsébet tér (30min., every 30min. 5:30am-9pm; 800Ft, payable on the bus), but the Ferihegy/red **bus #93**, followed by the M3 at Köbanya-Kispest, is cheapest.

Trains: ☎461 55 00. Most international trains arrive at **Keleti pu.**; some from Prague end at Nyugati pu. or Déli pu. Each station has schedules for the others. To: **Berlin** (12hr., 1 per day, 22,850Ft; night train 15hr., 1 per day, 36,000Ft, 1500Ft reservation fee); **Bucharest** (14hr., 7 per day, 17,000Ft); **Prague** (EuroCity 8hr., 4 per day, 14,000Ft; night train 9hr., 1 per day, 14,000Ft, 1600Ft reservation fee); **Vienna** (3hr.; 17 per day; 7000Ft, 700Ft reservation fee); **Warsaw** (11hr.; 2 per day; 13,950Ft, 2000Ft reservation fee). The daily **Orient Express** stops on its way from Paris to Istanbul. Prices vary widely. 33% student and under-26 discount on international tickets; indicate *diák* (DEE-ak; student). **International Ticket Office**, Keleti pu. Open daily 8am-6pm. **MÁV Hungarian Railways**, VI, Andrássy út 35 (☎/fax 322 84 05), and at all stations. Open M-F 9am-5pm.

Buses: ☎117 29 66. Most buses to Western Europe leave from **Volánbusz main station**, V, Erzsébet tér (international ticket office ☎485 21 00, ext. 211). M1, 2, or 3: Deák tér. Open M-F 6am-6pm, Sa 6:30am-4pm. Buses to much of Eastern Europe depart from **Népstadion**, Hungária körút 48/52 (☎252 18 96). M2: Népstadion. To: **Berlin** (14½hr., 5 per week, 20,000Ft); **Prague** (8hr., 4 per week, 8400Ft); **Vienna** (3-3½hr., 5 per day, 6400Ft). **Domestic buses** are cheap but slower than trains.

Public Transportation: Subways, buses, and **trams** are cheap, convenient, and easy to navigate. The **Metro** has three lines: yellow (M1), red (M2), and blue (M3). Pick up free **route maps** from hostels, tourist offices, and train stations. Night transit ("É") runs midnight-5am along major routes; buses 7É and 78É follow the M2 route, 6É follows the 4/6 tram line, and 14É and 50É follow M3. Blue **single-fare tickets** for all public transport (one-way on one line 100Ft) are sold in Metro stations, in Trafik shops, and by some sidewalk vendors; punch them in the orange boxes at the gate of the Metro or on buses and trams; punch a new ticket when you change lines, or face a 1500- 3000Ft fine. **Day pass** 800Ft; **3-day** 1600Ft; **1-week** 1950Ft.

Taxis: As always, beware of scams. Check that the meter is on. **Budataxi** (☎233 33 33) charges 135Ft per km if you call. **Fötaxi** (☎222 22 22), **6x6 Taxi** (☎266 66 66), and **Tele 5 Taxi** (☎355 55 55) are also reliable.

☀ ORIENTATION

Originally Buda and Pest, two cities separated by the Danube **(Duna)** River, modern Budapest preserves the distinctive character of each. On the west bank, **Buda** has winding streets, breathtaking vistas, a hilltop citadel, and the cobblestone Castle District. On the east bank, bustling **Pest**, the city's commercial center, is home to wide shopping boulevards, theaters, Parliament, and the Opera House. Three bridges join the two halves: **Széchenyi-Lánchíd**, slender **Erzsébet híd**, and green **Szabadság híd**. Just down the north slope of Várhegy, **Moszkva tér** is Budapest's tram and local bus hub. **Batthyány tér**, opposite the Parliament (Országház), is one metro stop past the Danube in Buda, and is the starting point of the **HÉV commuter railway**, which heads north through Óbuda to Szentendre. (Buy HÉV tickets at the station for transport beyond Budapest city limits.) Budapest's three **Metro** lines (M1, M2, and M3) converge at **Deák tér**, at the center of Pest's loosely concentric boulevards, next to the main international bus terminal at **Erzsébet tér**. Two blocks west toward the river lies **Vörösmarty tér**, and the main pedestrian shopping zone, **Váci utca**.

Addresses in Budapest begin with a Roman numeral representing one of the city's 23 **districts**. Central Buda is I; central Pest is V. To navigate Budapest's often-confusing streets, an up-to-date map is essential. The American Express and Tourinform offices have good free tourist maps, as do most hostels and hotels.

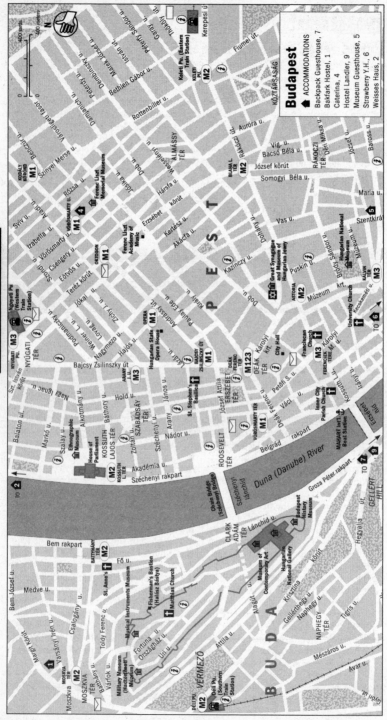

Budapest

▲ ACCOMMODATIONS
Backpack Guesthouse, 7
Bakfark Hostel, 1
Caterina, 4
Hostel Landler, 9
Museum Guesthouse, 5
Strawberry Y.H., 6
Weisses Haus, 2

🛈 PRACTICAL INFORMATION

TOURIST AND FINANCIAL SERVICES

Tourist Offices: All sell the Budapest Card (Budapest Kártya), which provides unlimited public transport, museum admission, and discounts at shops and restaurants (2-day 3400Ft, 3-day 4000Ft). Your first stop should be **Tourinform,** V, Sütő u. 2 (☎317 98 00; hungary@tourinform.hu; www.hungarytourism.hu), off Deák tér behind McDonald's. M1, 2, 3: Deák tér. Open daily 8am-8pm. **Vista Travel Center,** Pauley Ede 7 (☎267 86 03; incoming@vista.hu). M1-3: Deák tér; exit on Bajcsy-Zsilinszky út. The multilingual staff arranges lodgings and books train, plane, and bus tickets. Open M-F 9am-8pm, Sa-Su 10am-6pm. ▧*Budapest in Your Pocket* (www.inyourpocket.com; 300Ft) is a great source of maps, reviews, and practical information.

Embassies: Australia, XII, Királyhágo tér 8/9 (☎457 97 77; austembbp@mail.data-net.hu). M2: Déli pu., then bus #21 or tram #59 to Királyhágo tér. Open M-F 8:30am-4:30pm. **Canada,** XII, Budakeszi út 32 (☎392 33 60). Take bus #158 from Moszkva tér to the last stop. Open M-F 9am-noon. **South Africa,** II, Gárdonyi Géza út 17 (☎392 09 99). **UK,** V, Harmincad u. 6 (☎266 28 88), near the intersection with Vörösmarty tér. M1: Vörösmarty tér. Open M-F 9:30am-noon and 2:30-4pm. **US,** V, Szabadság tér 12 (☎475 44 00; 24hr. ☎266 28 8893 31; fax 475 47 64). M2: Kossuth tér. Walk 2 blocks down Akademia and turn on Zoltán. Open M-F 8:15am-5pm. **New Zealand** and **Irish** nationals should contact the UK embassy.

Currency Exchange: Best rates are in banks. **Citibank,** V, Vörösmarty tér 4 (☎374 50 00.) M1: Vörösmarty tér. Cashes traveler's checks for no commission and, if you bring your passport, provides MC/V cash advances.

American Express: V, Deák Ferenc u. 10 (☎235 43 30; fax 235 43 49; travel@amex.hu). M1: Vörösmarty tér. On the corner with Bécsi u. AmEx **ATM** outside. Open M-F 9am-5:30pm, Sa 9am-2pm.

LOCAL SERVICES

Luggage storage: Lockers at all three **train stations** 200Ft.

English-Language Bookstore: Bestsellers KFT, V, Október 6 u. 11 (☎/fax 312 12 95), near the intersection with Arany János u. M1-3: Deák tér or M1: Vörösmarts tér. Open M-F 9am-6:30pm, Sa 10am-5pm, Su 10am-4pm.

Gay Info: GayGuide.net Budapest (☎(0630) 932 33 34; budapest@gayguide.net; www.gayguide.net/europe/hungary/budapest), maintains a comprehensive website and runs a hotline (daily 4-8pm) with information for gay tourists in Budapest.

EMERGENCY AND COMMUNICATIONS

Police: ☎107. **Ambulance:** ☎104. **Fire:** ☎105.

Tourist Police: V, Vigadó u. 6 (☎235 44 79). M1: Vörösmarty tér. Walk toward the river from the metro to reach the station, just inside Tourinform. The police bring in transla-tors if necessary. Open 24hr.

24-Hour Pharmacies: II, Frankel Leó út 22 (☎212 44 06); III, Szentendrei út 2/A (☎388 65 28); IV, Pozsonyi u. 19 (☎389 40 79); VI, Teréz krt. 41 (☎311 44 39); VII, Rákóczi út 39 (☎314 36 95). At night, call number on door or ring the bell.

Medical Assistance: Falck Személyi Olvosi Szolgálat (SOS) KFT, II, Kapy út 49/B (☎200 01 00 and 275 15 35). First aid free for foreigners. Open 24hr. The US embassy lists English-speaking doctors.

Telephones: Most phones use **phone cards,** available at newsstands, post offices, and metro stations. 50-unit card 800Ft, 120-unit card 1800Ft. Use card phones for **interna-tional calls;** they cut you off after 20min., but that's better than coin phones. Domestic operator ☎191; domestic information ☎198; international operator ☎190.

Internet Access: Cybercafes litter the city, but access can get expensive and long waits are common. Try a wired hostel. **Ami Internet Coffee,** V, Váci u. 40 (☎267 16 44; ami@amicoffee.hu). M3: Ferenciek Tere. No wait. 150Ft for 10min., 350Ft for 30min.

HUNGARY

Eckermann, VI, Andrássy út 24 (☎269 25 42). M1: Opera. Free. Call a week ahead during summer. Open M-F 8am-10pm, Sa 9am-10pm.

Post Office: V, Városház u. 18 (☎318 48 11). **Poste Restante** (Postán Mar). Open M-F 8am-8pm, Sa 8am-2pm. Address mail to be held: SURNAME, First name, *Poste Restante*, V, Városház u. 18, **1052** Budapest, Hungary. **Branches** at Nyugati pu., VI, Teréz krt. 105/107 and Keleti pu., VIII, Baross tér 11/C. Open M-F 8am-9pm, Sa 8am-2pm.

⌂ ACCOMMODATIONS AND CAMPING

Call ahead in summer, or stash your pack while you seek out a bed for the night to save yourself blisters. Travelers arriving at Keleti pu. enter a feeding frenzy as hawkers elbow their way to tourists; be cautious and don't believe all promises of free rides or special discounts, but keep an open mind if you need a place to stay.

ACCOMMODATION AGENCIES

Private rooms, slightly more expensive than hostels (2000-5000Ft per person, depending on location and bathroom quality), usually offer what hostels can't: peace, quiet, and private showers. Arrive early, bring cash, and haggle.

Budapest Tourist, I, Deli Pálaudrar (☎/fax 212 46 25). M2: Déli pu. Underground. Well-established. Singles in Central Pest 5000-7000Ft; doubles 6000-10000Ft; triples 6000-12000Ft. Lower off-season prices. Open M-F 9am-5pm.

IBUSZ, V, Ferenciek tere (☎485 27 67; accomodations@ibusz.hu). M3: Ferenciek tere. Doubles 5000Ft; triples 5000-6000Ft. 1500Ft surcharge if staying fewer than 4 nights. Open M-Th 8:15am-4pm, F 8:15am-3pm.

Non-Stop Hotel Service, V, Apáczai Csere J. u. 1 (☎266 80 42; tribunus.hotel.service@mail.datanet.hu). M1: Vörösmarty tér. Singles 6000Ft. Doubles from 7500Ft in summer, from 6000Ft off season. Triples and quads from 8000Ft; off-season 7000Ft. Open 24hr.

YEAR-ROUND HOSTELS

Budapest's hostels are social centers, with no curfews and beer- and music-filled common rooms that often beat the city's bars and clubs. Most are part of the Hungarian Youth Hostel Association; their staff wear HI t-shirts, and will accost you as soon as you get off the train. They're legit, but don't let them scare you away from more convenient independent hostels or guesthouses. Beware of theft in hostels. Unless otherwise noted, all have luggage storage, kitchens, and TV.

▨ Backpacker's Guesthouse, XI, Takács Menyhért u. 33 (☎/fax 385 89 46; backpackguest@hotmail.com; www.backpackbudapest.hu), in Buda, 12min. from central Pest. From Keleti pu., take bus #7 or 7A toward Buda; get off at Tétenyi u. (5 stops past the river), walk back under the railway bridge, turn left, and go down the 3rd street on the right. Busy but clean bathrooms; superb CD and video collections. Internet 20Ft per 1min. Reception 24hr. Reserve 1-2 weeks ahead. Dorms 1600Ft; doubles 4800Ft.

▨ Museum Youth Guesthouse, VIII, Mikszáth Kálmán tér 4, 1st fl. (☎318 95 08 and 266 88 79; museumgh@freemail.c3.hu), in Pest. M3: Kálvin tér. Take the left exit from the stop onto Baross u., take the left branch at the fork, go to the far right corner at the open square, and ring the buzzer at gate #4. Internet. Laundry. Reception 24hr. Check-out 10am. Reserve ahead. 2500Ft per person, 2000Ft after 2nd night.

Station Guest House (HI), XIV, Mexikói út 36/B (☎221 88 64; station@mail.matav.hu; www.stationguesthouse.hu), in Pest. From Keleti pu., take red bus #7 or night bus #78É 4 stops to Hungária Körút, walk under the railway pass, take an immediate right on Mexikói út, walk 2 blocks, and look for the big yellow house. Free billiards and live music. Laundry. Internet. Reserve ahead or end up in the attic. Attic 1500Ft; 6- to 8-bed dorms 2000Ft; 2- to 3-bed rooms 3000Ft. All prices drop 100Ft with each night you stay. Nonmembers add 200Ft.

Best Hostel, VI, Podmaniczky u. 27, 1st fl. (☎332 49 34; bestyh@mail.datanet.hu; www.besthostel.hu). Ring bell 33 in building across from Nyugati pu. Spacious dorms. Common room and kitchen close nightly at 11pm. Breakfast included. Laundry. Internet. Dorms 2500Ft; doubles 7000Ft. 10% HI discount.

SUMMER HOSTELS

Many university dorms, mostly near Móricz Zsigmond Körtér, reinvent themselves as hostels in July and August. They usually have kitchens and a common room TV, and tend to be quieter than year-round hostels.

Hostel Bakfark, I, Bakfark u. 1/3 (☎329 86 44). M2: Moszkva tér. Go along Margit krt. with Burger King to the right and take the 1st right after Mammut. Comfortable dorms with lofts instead of bunks. Sparkling showers. Check-out 10am. Call ahead. Open mid-June to Aug. 6-bed dorms 3200Ft; quads 300Ft. 300Ft HI discount.

Strawberry Youth Hostels (HI), IX, Ráday u. 43/45 (☎218 47 66; www.strawberryhostel.com). M3: Kálvin tér. With Hotel Mercure on the right, walk down Vámház krt. Ráday is toward the river on the left. Laundry. Reception 24hr. Check-out 10am. Open July-Aug. Doubles 3200Ft; triples and quads 2900Ft. 10% off with HI. **2nd location** on Kinizsi u. 2/6 (☎217 30 33) with same prices. Free Keleti pu. pickup for both hostels.

Hostel Martos, XI, Stoczek u. 5/7 (☎/fax 463 36 50; reception@hotel.martos.bme.hu), near the Technical University. From Keleti pu., take red bus #7 to Móricz Zsigmond Körtér and trek back 300m toward the river on Bartók Béla út.; go right onto Bertalan Lajos, and Stoczek u. is the 3rd right. This student-run hostel offers clean rooms and a kitchen on each floor. Free Internet. Laundry. Satellite TV. Check-out 9-10am. Reserve a few days ahead. Singles 3000Ft; doubles 4000-7000Ft; triples 6000Ft.

Hostel Landler, XI, Bartók Béla út 17 (☎463 36 21). Take bus #7 or 7A across the river and get off at Géllert, take Bartók Béla út away from the river. Comfy dorms. Free ride from the bus or train station. Laundry. Check-out 9am. Open July 5-Sept. 5. Singles 5500Ft; doubles 7000Ft; triples and quads 2900Ft per person. 10% HI discount.

GUESTHOUSES

Guesthouses and rooms in private homes lend a personal touch for about the same price as hostels. Owners prowl for guests in Keleti pu.

Caterina, VI, Andrássy út 47, 3rd fl., apt. #18, in Pest; ring bell #11. (☎291 95 38; caterina@mail.inext.hu). M1: Oktogon; or trams #4 and 6. Across from Burger King. Grandmother-style house—no curfew, but quiet after 10pm. Free Internet. Laundry. Reception 24hr. Check-out 9am. Lockout 10am-2pm. Reserve by email. Dorms 2400Ft; double loft 2900Ft; triples 2900Ft; 6-person apartments US$60.

Mrs. Ena Bottka, V, Garibaldi u. 5 (☎/fax 302 34 57; garibaldiguest@hotmail.com). M2: Kossuth tér. Heading away from Parliament on Nádor u., take first right on Garibaldi u. Charming woman lets spacious rooms in her family's apartment, as well as other apartments in the building. Some with kitchenette, TV, showers, and towels. Rooms 3500Ft per person; apartments 6000-10,000Ft. All prices decrease with longer stays.

Weisses Haus, III, Erdőalja út 11 (☎/fax 387 82 36). M3: Árpád híd. Take ut.-bound tram #1 to Floriantér and bus #137 to Iskola. A family-owned villa in a nice neighborhood 30min. from the city center. Breakfast included. Some English spoken. Laundry. No curfew, but bus #137 stops at 11:30pm. Doubles US$20.

CAMPING

For a full listing, pick up the pamphlet *Camping Hungary* at tourist offices.

Zugligeti "Niche" Camping, XII, Zugligeti út 101 (☎/fax 200 83 46; camping.niche@matavnet.hu). Take bus #158 from Moszkva tér to last stop. Communal showers and a safe. 850Ft per person, 500-900Ft per tent, 700Ft per car.

Római Camping, III, Szentendrei út 189 (☎368 62 60). M2: Batthyány tér. Take HÉV to Római fürdő; walk 100m toward river. Huge site with swimming pool (300Ft). Open June-Aug. June tents 1500Ft; bungalow 1300-1900Ft. July tents 1800-2250Ft; bungalow 1560-2850Ft. 3% tourist tax. 10% HI discount.

◘ FOOD

Eating at family joints can be tastier than eating in big restaurants. Seek out the *kifőzés* or *vendéglő* in your neighborhood; the more you eat, the more you get, well, Hungary. **Non-Stop** corner markets are the best for groceries. The king of them all is ▩ **Grand Market Hall,** IX, Fövamtér 1/3, next to Szabadság híd (M3: Kálvin Tér).

RESTAURANTS

▩ **Fatâl Restaurant,** V, Váci u. 67 (☎266 26 07), in Pest. M3: Ferenciek tér. Packs them in for large and hearty Hungarian meals. Giant, carefully garnished main courses 1070-2790Ft. Reservations only. Open daily 11am-2am.

Gandhi, V, Vigyázó Ferenc u. 4, in Pest. New menu every day at the veggie place. Herbal teas, organic wines, and wheat beers. Dishes 980-1670Ft. Open M-Sa noon-10:30pm.

Söröző a Szent Jupáthoz, II, Retek u. 16, in Buda. M2: Moszkva tér. Huge Hungarian menu and huge Hungarian portions. Main dishes 1090-2590Ft. Open 24hr.

Marxim, II, Kisrókus u. 23, in Buda. M2: Moszkva tér. Go on Margit krt., then turn left down the industrial road. Local teens unite at this tongue-in-cheek Communist-themed pizzeria. Pizzas 440-940Ft. Open M-F noon-1am, Sa noon-2am, Su 6pm-1am.

Paksi Halászcsárda, II, Margit Körút 14, in Buda. Tram #4 or 6 to Margit Híd. Hungarian standbys in an upscale setting. Main dishes 950-1400Ft. Open daily noon-midnight.

CAFES

Once the haunts of Budapest's literary, intellectual, and cultural elite, as well as its political dissidents, many cafes now serve cheap and absurdly rich pastries.

▩ **Művész Kávéház,** VI, Andrássy út 29. M1: Opera. Across from the Opera. An mix of mostly artsy people around polished stone tables. Enjoy a *Művész torta* (jam and hazelnut cake; 260Ft) and cappuccino (260Ft) on the terrace. Open daily 9am-midnight.

Gerbeaud, V, Vörösmarty tér 7. M1: Vörösmarty tér. This cafe has been serving its signature layer cakes (520Ft) and homemade ice cream (95Ft) since 1858. Shaded tables dominate the northern end of Vörösmarty tér. Open daily 9am-9pm.

Ruszwurm, I, Szentháromság u. 7, just off the square on Várhegy in the Castle District. This teeny cafe has been making sweets since it started catering to Habsburg tastes in 1827. Pastries and cake 120-180Ft. Open daily 10am-7pm.

◎ SIGHTS

In 1896, Hungary's 1000th birthday bash prompted the construction of what are today Budapest's most prominent sights. Among the works commissioned by the Habsburgs were **Heroes' Square** (Hősök tere), **Liberty Bridge** (Szbadság híd), **Vajdahunyad Castle** (Vajdahunyad vár), and continental Europe's first metro system. The domes of **Parliament** (Országház) and **St. Stephen's Basilica** (Szent István Bazilika) are both 96m high—vertical references to the historic date. Slightly grayer for wear, war, and Communist occupation, these monuments attest to the optimism of a capital on the verge of its Golden Age. **The Absolute Walking & Biking Tours** (☎211 88 61; imad@matavnet.hu) meets on the steps of the yellow church in Déak tér (mid-May to Sept. daily 9:30am and 1:30pm; 3490Ft, under-26 2990Ft) and at Heroes' Square (daily 10am and 2pm) .

BUDA

On the east bank of the Danube, **Buda** sprawls out from the bases of Castle and Gellért hills into Budapest's main residential areas. Buda is older than Pest, with plenty of parks, lush hills, and islands. The Castle District lies atop **Castle Hill.** South of Castle Hill, also on the banks of the Danube, lies **Gellért Hill.**

CASTLE DISTRICT. Towering above the Danube, the **Castle District** has been razed three times in its 800-year history, most recently in 1945. With its winding, statue-filled streets, breathtaking views, and hodge-podge of architectural styles, the UNESCO-protected district now appears much as it did in Habsburg times. Although bullet holes in the **castle** façade still recall the 1956 Uprising, the reconstructed palace today houses a number of fine museums. *(I, Szent György tér 2, on Castle Hill. M2: Moszkva tér. Walk up to the hill on Várfok u. and enter the castle at Vienna Gate (Becsi kapu). Alternatively, take the funicular (sikly) from the Buda side of the Széchenyi Chain Bridge. (Daily*

9:30am-5:30pm; closed 2nd and 4th M of the month; 300Ft.) The upper lift station sits inside the castle walls near the National Gallery.)

MATTHIAS CHURCH AND FISHERMAN'S BASTION. The multicolored roof of the neo-Gothic **Matthias Church** (Mátyás templom), which was converted into a mosque when Ottoman armies seized Buda in 1541, and reconverted 145 years later when the Habsburgs defeated the Turks, is one of the most popular sights in Budapest. Descend the stairway to the right of the altar to enter the **crypt** and **treasury.** *(On Castle Hill. From the Vienna Gate, walk straight down Fortuna u. From the cable car, turn right on Színház and veer left on Tárnok u. High mass with full orchestra and choir Su 7, 8:30, 10am, 6pm.)* Behind St. Matthias Church is the equestrian monument of King Stephen bearing his trademark double cross in front of the **Fisherman's Bastion** (Halászbástya). The view across the Danube from the fairy-tale **tower** is stunning. *(200Ft.)*

GELLÉRT HILL. The Pope sent Bishop Gellért to the coronation of King Stephen, the first Christian Hungarian monarch, to convert the Magyars; those unconvinced by his message gave the hill its name (Gellért-hegy) by hurling the good bishop to his death from the top. The **Liberation Monument** (Szabadság Szobor), created to honor Soviet soldiers who died "liberating" Hungary, looks over Budapest from atop the hill. The view from the top of the adjoining **Citadel,** built as a symbol of Habsburg power after the foiled 1848 revolution, is especially spectacular at night. At the base of the hill sits the **Gellért Hotel and Baths.** Budapest's most famous Turkish Bath. *(To ascend the hill, take tram #18 or 19 to Hotel Gellért; follow Szaby Verjtók u. to Jubileumi Park, continuing on the marked paths to the summit. Or, take bus #27 to the top; get off at Bosuly Juhósz and walk 5min. to the peak.)*

PEST

The winding streets of Pest were constructed in the 19th century and today host stores, cafes and restaurants, corporations and banks, and monuments. The crowded **Inner City** (Belváros) is based in the pedestrian **Váci u.** and **Vörösmarty tér.**

PARLIAMENT. Pest's riverbank sports a string of luxury hotels leading to its magnificent neo-Gothic **Parliament** (Országház), modeled after Britain's. The massive structure has always been too big for Hungary's government; today, the legislature uses only 12%. *(M2: Kossuth Lajos tér. Mandatory tours in English M-F 10am and 2pm, Sa-Su 10am. 1500Ft, students 750Ft. Purchase tickets at gate #10 and enter at gate #12.)*

ST. STEPHEN'S BASILICA. The city's largest church (Sz. István Bazilika) was decimated by Allied bombs in World War II. Its neo-Renaissance façade is under reconstruction, but the ornate interior attracts both tourists and worshippers. The **Panorama Tower** offers a 360° view, but the oddest attraction is St. Stephen's mummified right hand, one of Hungary's most revered religious relics. For the devout, the macabre, and the simply curious, a 100Ft donation dropped in the box will light up the religious relic for two hot minutes. *(M1-3: Deák tér. Basilica and museum open May-Oct. M-Sa 9am-5pm; Nov.-Apr. M-Sa 10am-4pm, Su 1-5pm. Tower open June-Aug. daily 9:30am-6pm; Sept.-Oct. 10am-5:30pm; Apr.-May 10am-4:30pm. Tower 500Ft, students 400Ft.)*

GREAT SYNAGOGUE. Pest's other major religious sight, the Great Synagogue *(Zsinagóga)* is the largest synagogue in Europe and the second largest in the world, after the temple Emmanuel in New York City. The Moorish building was designed to hold 3000 worshippers. The synagogue has been under renovation since 1988, and much of the artwork is likely to be blocked from view. In the garden (to the left and around the corner, facing the synagogue) is a **Holocaust Memorial,** an enormous metal tree that sits above a mass grave for thousands of Jews killed near the end of the war. Each leaf bears the name of a family that perished. Next door, the **Jewish Museum** (Zsidó Múzeum) documents Hungary's rich Jewish past. *(M2: Astoria. At the corner of Dohóny u. and Wesselónyi u. Open May-Oct. M-Th 10am-5pm, F 10am-3pm, Su 10am-2pm; Nov.-Apr. M-F 10am-3pm, Su 10am-1pm. Synagogue and museum 600Ft, students 250Ft. Guided tours every 30min 10:30am-3:30pm.)*

ANDRÁSSY ÚT & HEROES' SQUARE. Hungary's grandest boulevard, Andrássy út extends from **Erzsébet tér** in downtown Pest to **Heroes' Square** (Hősök tere) to the northeast.

Perhaps the most vivid reminder of Budapest's Golden Age is the **Hungarian National Opera House** (Magyar Állami Operaház), whose gilded interior glows on performance nights. If you can't see an opera, take a tour. *(Andrássy út 22. M1: Opera. Daily English tours 3 and 4pm; 1200Ft, students 600Ft. 20% Budapest card discount.)* At the Heroes' Square end of Andrássy út, the **Millenium Monument** (Millenniumi emlékmű) commemorates the nation's most prominent leaders. Right off Heroes' Square is the **Museum of Fine Arts** (see Museums, below).

CITY PARK. The **Városliget** is home to a zoo, a circus, a run-down amusement park, and the lakeside **Vajdahunyad Castle** (Vajdahunyad Vár), whose Disney-esque collage of Romanesque, Gothic, Renaissance, and Baroque styles is intended to chronicle the history of Hungarian architecture. Outside the castle broods the hooded statue of **Anonymous,** the secretive scribe to whom we owe much of our knowledge of medieval Hungary. Rent a **rowboat** or **ice skates** on the lake next to the castle, or a **bike-trolley** to navigate the paths. *(M1: Szchenyi Fürdő. Pedal cars, electric cars, pedal boats, rowboats, and ice skates rented daily.)*

🏛 MUSEUMS

■ **Museum of Fine Arts** (Szépművészeti Múzeum), XIV, Dózsa György út 41. M1: Hősök tere. A spectacular collection; from Raphael to Rembrandt, Gaugin to Goya, these are the paintings you've never seen but shouldn't miss—especially the El Greco room. Open Tu-Su 10am-5:30pm. 500Ft, students 200Ft. Tours for up to 5 people 2000Ft.

■ **Statue Park** (Szoborpark Múzeum; www.szoborpark.hu), XXII, on the corner of Balatoni út and Szabadkai u. Take the #7-173 express bus from M2: Keleti pu. or M3: Ferenciek tere to the end of the line. From there, take the yellow Volán bus from terminal #2 toward Diosd-Erd. An outdoor collection of communist statuary removed after the collapse of Soviet rule. English guidebook 600Ft. Open Mar.-Nov. daily 10am-dusk; Dec.-Feb. weekends and holidays only. 400Ft, students 200Ft.

Museum of Applied Arts (Iparművészeti Múzeum), IX, Üllői út 33-37. M3: Ferenc körút. Handcrafted art objects, such as Tiffany glass, furniture, and excellent temporary exhibits highlighting specific crafts. Open mid-Mar. to Oct. Tu-Su 10am-6pm; Nov. to mid-Mar. 10am-4pm. 500Ft, students 250Ft.

Hungarian National Museum (Nemzeti Múzeum; www.origo.hnm.hu), VIII, Múzeum krt. 14/16. M3: Kálvin tér. Exhibits from the Hungarian Crown Jewels to Soviet propaganda. English translations *and* historical maps. Open Tu-Su mid-Mar. to mid-Oct. 10am-6pm; mid-Oct. to mid-Mar. Tu-Su 10am-5pm. 600Ft, students 300Ft.

Buda Castle, I. Szent György tér 2 (☎375 75 33), on Castle Hill. Wing A houses the **Museum of Contemporary Art** (Kortárs Művészeti Múzeum) and the **Ludwig Museum,** upstairs, devoted to Warhol, Lichtenstein, and other masters. Wings B-D hold the **Hungarian National Gallery** (Magyar Nemzeti Galéria), a hoard of Hungarian paintings and sculptures. Artifacts from the 1242 castle, revealed by WWII bombings, lie in the **Budapest History Museum** (Budapesti Történeti Múzeum) in Wing E. Wings A-D open Tu-Su 10am-6pm. Wing E open daily mid-May to mid-Sept. 10am-6pm; mid-Sept. to Oct. and Mar. to mid-May M and W-Su 10am-6pm; Nov.-Feb. M and W-Su 10am-4pm. Wing A 400Ft, students 200Ft. Wings B-D 500Ft together, students 250Ft. Wing E 500Ft, students 200Ft.

🎵 ENTERTAINMENT

Budapest Program (www.budapestprogram.com), *Budapest Panorama, Pesti Est* and the classic *Budapest in Your Pocket* (300Ft) are the best English-language guides to entertainment, listing everything from festivals to cinemas to art showings. All are available at most tourist offices and hotels. The "Style" section of the *Budapest Sun* (www.budapestsun.com; 300Ft; published every Th), has a comprehensive 10-day calendar, movie reviews, and a list of every film playing in English. (Tickets 550-890Ft; cinema schedules change on Th.)

THEATER, MUSIC, AND DANCE. Ticket Express, VI, Andrássy út 15 and 18, next to the Opera House (☎312 00 00; open M-F 10am-6pm) and throughout the city, sells tickets to nearly any show for no commission, as does the **Vigadó Ticket Service**, V, Vörösmarty tér 1. (☎327 4322. Open M-F 9am-7pm, Sa-Su 10am-3pm.) For 3000-9800Ft you can enjoy an opera in the splendor of the gilded, neo-Renaissance ▨**State Opera House** (Magyar Allami Operahaz), VI, Andrássy út 22. M1: Opera. The box office on the left side of the building sells cheaper, unclaimed tickets 30min. before showtime. (Box office ☎353 01 70. M-Sa 11am-7pm, Su 4-7pm; cashier closes 5pm on days without performances. Daily English tours 1hr.; 3 and 4pm; 1200Ft, students 600Ft.) The **Philharmonic Orchestra** has equally grand music (concerts almost nightly Sept.-June) in a slightly more modest venue. (Buy tickets at V, Mérleg u. 10. (☎318 02 81. Open daily 9am-3pm. Tickets 2000-5000Ft, less on the day of show.) Many of the world's musicians pass through Budapest. Prices are reasonable; check the **Music Mix '33 Ticket Service**, V, Váci u. 33. V, (☎266 70 70. Open M-F 10am-6pm, Sa 10am-1pm.)

THERMAL BATHS. To soak away the city grime, sink into a nice, hot thermal bath. First built in 1565, their services—from mud baths to massage—are quite cheap. Some baths are meeting spots for Budapest's gay community. ▨ **Gellért**, XI, Kelenhegyi út 4/6, has a rooftop sundeck and outdoor wave pool. Take bus #7 or tram #47 or 49 to Hotel Gellért, at the base of Gellért-hegy. (Open May-Sept. M-F 6am-6pm, Sa-Su 6am-4pm; off-season closes 1pm weekends. Bath and swimming pool 1800Ft. Towel, robe, and suit rental 400Ft each with 3000Ft deposit.)**Széchenyi**, XIV, Állatkerti u. 11/14, has nude sun-bathing on the roof. (Open May-Sept. daily 6am-7pm; Oct.-Apr. M-F 6am-7pm, Sa-Su 6am-5pm. 1000Ft deposit on entry; keep your receipt. 15min. Massage 1200Ft.)

▨ NIGHTLIFE

All-night outdoor parties, elegant after-hours clubs, the nightly thump and grind—Budapest has it all. While pubs and bars bustle until 4am, the streets themselves are surprisingly empty and poorly lit. Cafes and restaurants in **VI, Liszt Ferenc tér** (M1: Oktagon) attract Budapest's youth. In summer, **Peötlfi híd** (Green Park), in Buda, rocks all night every night. Gay life in Budapest is just beginning to make itself visible, so it's safer to be discreet. If you have problems, call the **gay hotline** (see Gay Info, p. 511).

▨**Undergrass,** VI, Liszt Ferenc tér 10. M1: Oktogon. The hottest spot in Pest's trendiest area. A soundproof glass door divides a hip bar from a packed disco. Open daily 8pm-4am; disco Tu-Su 10pm-4am.

Piaf, VI, Nagymező u. 25. A much-loved after-hours place. The beautiful staff is so icy because they can be. Knock on the door to await the approval of the club's matron. Cover 500Ft, includes 1 beer. Open daily 11pm-6am, but don't come before 1am.

Capella, V, Belgrád rakpart 23 (www.extra.hu/capellacafe). With glow-in-the-dark graffiti and an underground atmosphere, this spot draws a mixed gay and straight crowd. Shows at midnight. Women welcome. Cover 1000-1500Ft. Open Tu-Su 9pm-5am.

Fél 10 Jazz Club, VIII, Baross u. 30. M3: Kálvin tér. covers 2 floors with an Escher-like layout. Potent drinks. Cover 400Ft. Open M-F noon-dawn, Sa-Su 6pm-dawn.

Club Seven, Akácfa u. 7. M2: Blaha Lajos tér. Upscale underground music club. M-F no cover; Sa-Su 1000Ft, women free. Coffeehouse open daily 9pm-4am, restaurant 6pm-midnight, dance floor 10pm-5am.

Jazz Garden, V, Veres Páiné u. 44a. The "garden" is actually a vaulted cellar with Christmas lights. Live jazz nightly at 10:30pm. Open Su-F noon-1am, Sa noon-2am.

Angel Bar, VII, Szövetség u. 33. The 1st gay bar in Budapest. Until a few years ago, the club moved weekly; now this huge 3-level disco, cafe, and bar is packed. F and Su night drag shows. Sa men only. Cover around 600Ft; Th free. Open Th-Su 10pm-dawn.

> ▌ **NIGHTLIFE SCAM.** There have been reports of a mafia-organized scam involving
> English-speaking Hungarian women who meet a foreigner in a local bar, suggest
> a new location, asks for a drink, then leave once the drink is bought. The bill,
> accompanied by imposing men, can be up to US$1000 for a single drink. The
> US Embassy has advised against patronizing a number of establishments in the
> Váci u. area, including City Center Club, Mephisto Cafe, Nirvana, The Black &
> White Club, Fontana, La Dolce Vita, Flashdance, and Piccolo. If you are taken in,
> call the police—you'll probably still have to pay, though. Be sure to get a receipt
> so that you can formally issue a complaint at the Consumer Bureau.

THE DANUBE BEND

North of Budapest, the Danube sweeps in a dramatic arc called the Danube Bend
(Dunakanyar), deservedly one of the greatest tourist attractions in Hungary.

SZENTENDRE   ☎ 26

By far the most touristed of the Danube Bend towns, Szentendre delights with narrow cobblestone streets, upscale art galleries, and pricey restaurants. Head up
Church Hill (Templomdomb), above the town center in Fő tér, to a 13th-century
Roman Catholic church. Just across Alkotmány u., the museum at the Baroque **Serbian Orthodox Church** (Szerb Ortodox Templom) displays religious art. The church's
ornate interior, an Orthodox take on Baroque, is also worth a look. (Museum and
church 200Ft, church alone 100Ft. Open Tu-Su 10am-6pm.) The popular **Margit
Kovács Museum,** Vastagh György u. 1, off Görög u., which is off Fő tér, shows whimsical ceramic sculptures and tiles by the 20th-century Hungarian artist Margit
Kovács. (Open Mar.-Oct. daily 10am-6pm; Nov. daily 9am-5pm; Dec.-Feb. Tu-Su
10am-5pm. 400Ft, students 200Ft.) The real thriller at the **Szabó Marzipan Museum
and Confectionary,** Dumtsa Jenő u. 12, is the 80kg. white chocolate statue of Michael
Jackson. (Open daily 10am-6pm. 200Ft.) Take the Skazer bus (20-40min., 1 per hr.)
from terminal #7 to the **Open-Air Village Museum,** which has reconstructed settlements complete with basket-weaving and butter-making. (Open Apr.-Oct. Tu-Su
9am-5pm. 500Ft, students 250Ft.)

   HÉV **trains** travel to Szentendred from Budapest's Batthyány tér (45min., every
10-15min., 278Ft). **Buses** run to Budapest's Árpád híd station (30min., every 20-
40min., 182Ft) and to Esztergom (1½hr., 462Ft). The HÉV commuter train and bus
station are 10min. from Fő tér; descend the stairs past the end of the HÉV tracks, go
through the underpass, and head up Kossuth u. At the fork in the road, bear right
onto Dumsta Jenő u., which leads to the 1763 Plague Cross in the town center.
MAHART **boats** leave from a pier 20min. north of the town center; with the river on
the right, walk along the water to the sign. Late May to Aug. boats run to: Budapest
(3 per day, 760Ft) and Esztergom (1 per day, 800Ft). **Tourinform,** Dumsta Jenő u. 22,
between the town center and the station, has free maps. (☎/fax 317 965; www.szen-
tendre.hu. Open mid-Mar. to Oct. M-F 9-4:30pm, Sa-Su 10am-2pm.) **Ilona Panzió,**
Rákóczi Ferenc u. 11, is in the center of town. (☎313 599. 5000Ft. Breakfast
included.) **Centrum Panzió,** Bem u. and Dunakorzó, on the river north of Fő tér, has
big rooms. (☎/fax 302 500. Doubles 5000Ft.) **Pap-szigeti Camping** sits 2km north of
town on its own island in the Danube. (☎310 697. Open May to mid-Oct. 1900Ft per
tent, 2300Ft per large tent, 900Ft per extra person, 400Ft per child. Hostel singles,
doubles, triples, and quads US$4-6; doubles with shower US$15.) **Kedvac Kifőzde,**
Bükköspart 21, is a tiny lunch spot with incredible food. (Meals 300-460Ft. Open M-
F noon-5pm; Sa noon-3pm.) There's also a **Kaiser Supermarket** near the rail station.
(Open M-W 7am-7pm, Th-F 7am-8pm, Sa-Su 7am-3pm.)

ESZTERGOM   ☎ 33

One thousand years of religious history revolve around a solemn hilltop cathedral in
Esztergom (ESS-ter-gom), nicknamed "the Hungarian Rome." Charming streets and

riverbank location now draw more than just religious pilgrims. Wind up the spiral staircase to the ▨ **cupola** (100Ft) for the best view of the bend, then dive into the **crypt** to honor the remains of archbishops. The **Cathedral Treasury** (Kincstáv) to the right of the main altar has Hungary's most extensive ecclesiastical collection. On a smaller scale, the red marble **Bakócz Chapel,** to the left of the altar, is a masterwork of Renaissance Tuscan craftsmanship. (Open Mar.-Oct. daily 9am-4pm; Nov.-Dec. M-F 11am-3:30pm, Sa-Su 10am-3:30pm. 250Ft, students 150Ft. English-language guide to treasury 80Ft.) Beside the cathedral stands the 12th-century **Esztergom Palace** and its museum. (Open Tu-Su 9am-4pm; in winter Tu-Su 10am-3:30pm. 300Ft, students 150Ft.) At the foot of the cathedral's hill, the **Christian Museum** (Keresztény Múzeum), Berenyi Zsigmond u. 2, houses some quite exceptional religious art. (Open Tu-Su 10am-5:30pm. 300Ft.)

Trains go to Budapest (1½hr., 22 per day, 1206Ft). Facing away from the station, turn left on the main street, Baross Gábor út. Make a right onto Kiss János Altábornagy út, which becomes Kossuth Lajos u., to reach the square. Catch **buses** three blocks away from Rákóczi tér, on Simor János u., to Budapest (2hr., 15 per day, 622Ft) and Szentendre (1½hr., every hr., 462Ft); the bus from Budapest departs from Budapest's M3: Árpád híd. From the bus station in Esztergom, walk up Simor János u. toward the street market to reach Rákóczi tér. **Grantours,** Széchenyi tér 25, at the edge of Rákóczi tér, provides maps (200Ft and 500Ft) and helps locate panzió doubles for 8500Ft or cheaper, less central **private rooms** for 3500Ft, and doubles for 5000Ft. (☎417 052; grantour@mail.holop.hu. Open July-Aug. M-F 8am-6pm, Sa 9am-noon; Sept.-June M-F 8am-4pm, Sa 9am-noon.) **Platán Panzió,** Kis-Duna Sétány 11, to the left down Kis-Duna Sétány coming from Rákóczi tér, is between Rákóczi tér and Primas Sziget. (☎411 355. Reception 24hr. Check-out 10am. Singles 2500Ft; doubles 4000Ft.) **Alabardos Panzió,** Bajcsy-Zsilinszky u.49, has tidy doubles with clean showers and TV for 5400Ft. (☎/fax 312 640. Reception 24hr.) **Gran Camping,** Nagy-Duna Sétány, is on the island of Primas Sziget; turn left on Nagy-Duna Sétány if you're coming from the city. (☎402 513. 900Ft per person; 800Ft per tent or 1150Ft per room.) **Csülök Csárda,** Battyány u. 9, adds some creative variations to the usual menu of roasts and stews. (Main dishes 680-1650Ft. Open daily noon-midnight.) There's also a **Match supermarket** just off of Rákóczi tér. (Open M-F 6:30am-6:30pm, Sa 6:30am-1pm.)

SOUTHERN TRANSDANUBIA

Framed by the Danube to the west, the Dráva to the south, and Lake Balaton to the north, Southern Transdanubia is known for its rolling hills, sunflower fields, mild climate, and good wine. Once the southernmost section of the Roman province of Pannonia, the region's fine churches and architecture give it a Baroque feel.

PÉCS
☎72

At the foot of the Mecsek mountains, Pécs's (PAYCH) climate, vistas, and architecture slow the pace of any walk through the city. University students fuel an intense nightlife, making Pécs one of Hungary's most worthwhile weekend spots. The ▨ **Csontváry Museum,** Janus Pannonius u. 11, displays the works of Tivadar Csontváry Kosztka, known as the Hungarian van Gogh. (Open Tu-Su 10am-6pm. 200Ft, students 150Ft.) In nearby Széchenyi tér, the **Mosque of Ghazi Kassim** (Gázi Kaszim Pasa dzsámija) was once a Turkish mosque built on the site of an earlier church. This fusion of Christian and Muslim traditions has become an emblem of the city. (Open daily 10am-4pm; mid-Oct. to mid-Apr. 10am-noon.) Walk downhill from Széchenyi tér on Irgalmasok u. to Kossuth tér to find another house of worship—Pécs's stunning 1869 **synagogue,** which serves the city's 300 remaining Jews. (Open Su-F 10-11:30am and noon-4pm. 100Ft, students 50Ft.)

The train station is just south of the historic district. Take bus #30, 32, or 33 from the town center. **Trains** arrive from Budapest (3½hr., 3 per day, 1722Ft). **Buses,** at Nagy Lajos Király út and Alsómalom u., go to Budapest (4½hr., 7 per day, 1970Ft). **Tourinform,** Széchenyi tér 9, sells maps and phone cards. (☎211 134. Open M-Sa 9am-5:30pm, Su 9am-2pm; Oct.-May limited hours.) Change money or traveler's checks at

OTP Bank, Rákóczi út 44. (☎502 900. No commission. 24hr ATM outside.) For central accommodations, **private rooms** are the best budget option. **Motel Diana,** Timár u. 4/a, is right off Kossuth tér in the center. (☎328 59; fax 333 373. Singles 3100-6100Ft; doubles 9500Ft.) A bit farther away, **Szent Mór Kollégium,** 48-as tér 4, has spiffy triples in a university. Take bus #21 two stops from the main bus terminal. (☎503 610. Open July-Aug. 1000Ft.) **Caflisch Cukrászda Café,** Király u. 32, is the best cafe in town. (Pastries from 75Ft. Open daily 8am-10pm.) At night, chill with Hungarian youth at ▧ **Cafe Dante,** Janus Pannonis u. 11, in the same building as the Csontváry Museum. (Open daily 10am-1am, later on weekends.) **Postal code:** 7621.

EGER   ☎36

When an Ottoman army once tried to seize Eger Castle, locals fended off the attackers by fortifying themselves with their special "bull's blood" wine. This legend figures prominently in Hungarian lore and lives today in the vibrant wine cellars of the Valley of Beautiful Women and the historical monuments throughout the city.

▣▨ TRANSPORTATION AND PRACTICAL INFORMATION. Trains bound for Budapest-Keleti (2hr., 7 per day, 1182Ft) split in Hatvan; make sure you're in the right car. From the train station, turn right on Deák u., continue right on Kossuth Lajos u., left on Széchenyi u., and right on Érsek u. to get to **Dobó tér** (main square; 20min.). **Tourinform,** Dobó tér 2, has maps and lodgings information. (☎517 715; fax 51 81 15; tourinformagria.hu; www.tourinform.hu. Open M-F 9am-6:30pm, Sa-Su 9:30am-1pm.) **OTP Bank,** Széchenyi u. 2, grants AmEx/MC/V advances, cashes AmEx traveler's checks without commission, and has a **24hr. ATM.** (☎310 866. Exchange open M-F 7:45am-5pm, W open until 6pm.) **Postal code:** 3300.

▮▢ ACCOMMODATIONS AND FOOD. The best accommodations are **private rooms;** look for *Zimmer Frei* signs outside the city center, particularly on Almagyar u. and Mekcsey u. near the castle. **Eger Tourist,** Bajcsy-Zsilinszky u. 9, arranges private rooms for around 3000Ft per person. (☎41 17 24. Open M-F 9am-5pm.) Take bus #5, 11, or 12 north for 20 minutes to get to **Autós Caravan Camping,** Rákóczi u. 79; get off at the Shell station and look for signs. (Open mid-Apr. to mid-Oct. 320Ft per person, 250Ft per tent.) In the Valley of the Beautiful Women, **Kulacs Csárda Borozó's** vine-draped courtyard draws crowds. (☎/fax 311 375. Meals 720-1100Ft. Open Tu-Su noon-10pm.) An **ABC supermarket** is directly off Széchenyi u. between Sandor u. and Szt. Janos u. (Open M-F 6am-6:30pm, Sa 6am-1pm.)

▨▣ SIGHTS AND ENTERTAINMENT. Hungarians revere the medieval **Eger Castle,** where Dobó István and his 2000 men repelled the attacking Ottoman army. The castle includes subterranean barracks, catacombs, a crypt, and a wine cellar. One ticket covers a picture gallery, the **Dobó István Castle Museum,** which displays artifacts and a good array of weapons, and the **Dungeon Exhibition,** a lovely collection of torture equipment. (Castle open daily 8am-8pm. Museums open Tu-Su 9am-5pm; Nov.-Feb. 9am-3pm. Castle 120Ft, students 60Ft. Museums 400Ft, students 200Ft; M reduced admission. Wine cellars 100Ft. English tour 400Ft.) The **Lyceum,** at the corner of Kossuth Lajos u. and Széchenyi u., houses a *camera obscura* that projects a live picture of the surrounding town onto a table. (Open Tu-Su 9:30am-3:30pm; Oct.-Dec. and Mar.-Apr. closes 1pm. 200Ft, students 100Ft. Museum 200Ft.)

RED BULL In 1552, Egri Vár was besieged by 100,000 Ottoman soldiers. To prepare for the attack, Dobó István and his 2000 men downed barrels of the region's wine, which stained their beards red. When the Hungarians didn't succumb to the overwhelming Turkish force, it was rumored among the Turks, who did not drink themselves because of Muslim law, that the fierce Hungarians were quaffing the blood of bulls for strength. The rumor gave the wine a name—*bikáver*, or Bull's Blood.

After a morning exploring Eger's historical sights, spend the early evening in the wine cellars of the ■**Valley of Beautiful Women** (Szépasszonyvölgy). Samples are free, 0.1L cups run 50-80Ft, and 1L of wine costs about 350Ft. To reach the wine cellars, start on Széchenyi u. with Eger Cathedral to your right. Turn right on Kossuth Lajos u., left on Deák Ferenc út. (ignore the sign directing you otherwise), and right on Telekessy u. (which becomes Király u.); continue for about 10min., then bear left onto Szépasszonyvölgy. Sample delicious "bull's-blood" wine (*bikaver*) with the friendly proprietor of **Cellar #2**. For a calmer scene, try **Cellar #17**. Taste all you want, then buy a bottle of your favorite so the cellars can continue to give free tastings. Bring your own container for a discount at some cellars.

In summer, the city's cool **open-air baths** (a.k.a. swimming pools) offer a break from the sweltering city. (Open M-F 6am-7:30pm, Sa-Su 8am-7pm; Oct.-Apr. daily 9am-7pm. 400Ft, students and seniors 250Ft.) Eger celebrates its heritage for two weeks in late July and early August at the **Baroque Festival.** Nightly performances of opera and early court music are held around the city.

▶ DAYTRIP FROM EGER: SZILVÁSVÁRAD. A perfect outing from Eger, Szilvásvárad (SEAL-vash-vah-rod) attracts horse and nature lovers alike. **Horse shows** (800Ft) kick into action on most weekends in the arena on Szalajka u. **Lipicai Stables** is the stud farm for the town's famed Lipizzaner breed. Walk away from the park entrance on Egri út, turn left on Enyves u., and follow signs to the farm. (☎ 35 51 55. Open daily 8:30am-noon and 2-4pm. 80Ft.) Many farms offer **horseback riding**, especially in July and August. **Péter Kovács**, Egri út 62 (☎ 35 53 43), rents horses (1500Ft per hr.) and two-horse carriages (4500Ft per hr.). **Hikers** should head to the nearby **Bükk mountains** and **Szalajka valley.** A 45min. walk along the green trail will lead you to the park's most popular attraction, the **Fátyol waterfall;** a further 30min. hike from the falls leads to the **Istálósk cave,** the Stone Age home to a bear-worshipping cult. **Trains** (1hr., 8 per day, 244Ft) and **buses** (45min., every hr., 278Ft) run to Szilvásvárad from Eger. From the train station (Szilvásvárad-Szalajkavölgy), follow Egri út to Szalajka u. directly to the national park. There is no actual bus station in town; just get off at the second stop in Szilvásvárad (it's the next town after passing the concrete factories of Bükkszentmárton), on Egri út near Szalajka u. Stop by Eger's **Tourinform** (see above) before heading out, as there is no tourist office.

GYŐR
☎ 96

In the far western region of Őrség, Győr's (DYUR) cobblestone streets wind peacefully around a wealth of religious monuments, well-kept museums, and prime examples of 17th- and 18th-century architecture, while the city's lively population keeps the old town hopping. Most sights lie near the center of town. From the train station, go right until you come to the bridge. Turn left just before the underpass, then cross the big street to pedestrian **Baross Gabor u.** Turn left on Kazinczy u. to reach Bécsi Kapu tér, the site of the yellow, 18th-century **Carmelite church** and a **lapidarium**, Bécsi kapu tér 5, filled with fragments of Roman ruins. (Open Apr.-Oct. Tu-Su 10am-6pm. 200Ft, students 140Ft.) Walking uphill on Czuczor Gergely u., (when coming from the station, one street to the right of Baross Gabor u.) will lead you to the striking **Ark of the Covenant statue** (Frigylada szobov) and **Chapter Hill** (Káptalandomb). At the top of the hill is the **Episcopal Cathedral** (Székesegyház). Coming from the Ark of the Covenant Statue, the entrance to the cathedral is on its right side. Legend has it that the **Weeping Madonna of Győr** within wept blood for persecuted Irish Catholics on St. Patrick's Day in 1697. For more religious art, the **Diocesan Library and Treasury** (Egyházmegyei Kincstáv), Káptalandomb 26, hides at the end of an alley off the cathedral's square. (Open Tu-Su 10am-4pm. 300Ft, students 150Ft. English captions.) For contemporary art, head to the **Imre Parkó collection** at Széchenyi tér 4, down Czuczor Gergely u from the statue; enter at Stelczer u. (Open Tu-Su 10am-6pm. 200Ft, students 100Ft.) Across the river from the town center is the huge and popular **water park,** Czirákytér 1. From Bécsi kapu tér, take the bridge over the small island and make the first right on the other side. Make another right onto Cziráky tér, and the park is to the left. (Open daily 8am-7pm. 450Ft, students 350Ft.)

Frequent **trains** go to Budapest (2½hr., 26 per day, 1032Ft) and Vienna (2hr., 13 per day, 3565Ft). **Buses** go to Budapest (2½hr., every hr., 1120Ft). The train station is 3min. from the inner city; the underpass that links the rail platforms leads to the bus station. The **Tourinform kiosk,** Árpád u. 32, is at the corner of Baross Gabór u.; English-speaking staff provides handy free maps and will arrange accommodations. (☎/fax 311 771. Open June-Aug. M-F 8am-8pm, Sa-Su 9am-6pm; Sept.-May M-Sa 9am-4pm.) **Katalin's Yard,** Sarkantyú köz 3, off Bécsi Kapu tér, is a *panzió* with huge rooms that include a couch, TV, towels and shower. (☎/fax 542 088; mobile (30) 277 55 92. Breakfast included. Singles 5800Ft; doubles 7500Ft.) **Hotel Szárn-yaskerék,** Révai u. 5, opposite the train station. Huge hotel with spartan rooms. (☎ 314 629. Doubles 4450Ft, with bath 6700Ft.) ▧ **Matróz Restaurant,** Dunakapu tér 3, off Jedlik Ányos u. facing the river, fries up the most succulent of fish. (Entrees 500-900Ft. Open daily 9am-10pm.) For a Guinness (340Ft), head to **Dublin Gate Irish Pub,** Bécsi kapu tér 8, across from the Carmelite Church. (Open M-Sa noon-midnight, Su noon-11pm.) **Kaiser's Supermarket** is at the corner of Arany János u. and Aradi vér-tanúk. (Open M 7:30am-7pm, Tu-F 6:30am-7pm, Sa 6:30am-2pm.) **Postal code:** 9021.

▣ DAYTRIP FROM GYŐR: ARCHABBEY OF PANNONHALMA. Visible at a distance from Győr, the hilltop **Archabbey of Pannonhalma** (Pannonhalmi Főapátság), a UNESCO World Heritage site, featuring an opulent, treasure-filled library, has seen ten centuries of destruction and rebuilding since it was established by the Benedictine order in 996. Classical music concerts also take place frequently in the acoustic halls of the abbey; inquire at **Pax Tourist** (☎ 570 191; pax@osb.hu). To see the abbey, join a tour group at the Pax Tourist office to the left of the entrance. In summer, when a 1hr. tour is mandatory, English-speaking guides are available at 11am and 1pm. (Purchase tickets at Pax Tourist. Hungarian tour with English text 1000Ft, students 300Ft; English tour 2000Ft, students 1000Ft. English text available in the office to the left inside the big gates.) **Pannonhalma** is an easy daytrip from Győr; take the bus that leaves from stand #11 (45min., 4-5 per day, 75Ft). Ask for Pannonhalma vár and look for the huge gates, as some buses only go as far as the town; the abbey is 1km from there (15min.).

LAKE BALATON

A retreat since Roman times, the warm and shallow Lake Balaton drew Central European elites in the late 19th century. Now, it's a budget paradise for German and Austrian students, who also enjoy museums, hikes, and wine. Be aware that storms roll in quickly. Yellow lights on tall buildings give warnings: one revolution per second means swimmers must get out of the water.

SIÓFOK. Tourist offices are more densely packed in Siófok than any other Hungarian city, reflecting the influx of lake-bound vacationers who come down every summer. Most attractions in Siófok pale in comparison with the **Strand,** a series of park-like lawns running to an extremely un-sandy concrete shoreline. There are public and private (150Ft per person) sections. Bars and **nightclubs** of varying seediness line the lakefront, and **disco boats** push off at 9pm. ▧ **Renegade Pub,** Petőfi Sétány 3, is a casual bar and dance club right in the Strand, with a video arcade and outdoor deck. (No cover. Open daily 10pm-5am.)

Off Fő u., the town's main drag, **trains** go to Budapest (2½hr., every hr., 882Ft); **express buses** *(gyorsjárat)* also head to Budapest (1½hr., 17 per day, 1048Ft) and Pécs (3hr., 4 per day, 1240Ft). **Tourinform,** Fő u. at Szabadsásag tér, in the base of the concrete water tower down Fő u. to the right, helps find rooms and has free maps. (☎ 31 53 55; www.siofok.com. Open July-Aug. M-Sa 8am-8pm, Su 10am-noon; Sept.-June M-F 9am-4pm.) To get to small **Balaton Haus,** Szent László u. 16, turn left as you leave the train station, cross the tracks as soon as you can, turn right onto Ady Endre u., left on Tátra u., and right on Szent László. (☎ 310 571. 4000Ft per person.)

Open July-Aug.) Or try **Hotel Viola,** Bethlen Gabor u. 1, which has an English-speaking staff. From the bus or train station, walk along Fő u. with the tracks on your right, and cross at Bethlen G. u. (☎312 845; violahot@matavnet.hu. Reception 24hr. May-June and Sept.-Oct. 3200Ft. July-Aug. 4600Ft; book well in advance.) ☎**84.**

TIHANY. With its scenic hikes, charming cottages, and panoramic views, the Tihany peninsula is the pearl of Lake Balaton. The **Benedictine Abbey** (Bencés Apátság) draws over a million visitors annually, with luminous frescoes and gold-leaf Baroque altars, and a crypt housing one of Hungary's earliest kings. (Open Mar.-Oct. M-Sa 9am-5:30pm, Su 11am-5:30pm. 220Ft, students 110Ft; Su free.) Continue along the panoramic walkway to **Echo Hill.** You can also **hike** across the Peninsula on one of the many well-marked trails; most hikes are only an hour or two. The green-line trail runs past the **Hermit's Place** (Barátlakások), where the cells and chapel hollowed out by medieval Greek Orthodox hermits are still visible. MAHART **ferries** are the fastest way to reach Tihany from Siófok (1hr., every hr., 640Ft). To reach the town from the ferry pier and neighboring Strand, walk underneath the elevated road and follow the "Apátság" signs up the steep hill to the abbey. ☎**87.**

KESZTHELY. At the lake's west tip, Keszthely (KESS-tay) is a resort town with depth. Once the toy-town of the powerful Austro-Hungarian Festetics family, it now hosts an agricultural college and year-round thermal spring visitors, as well as the usual summer rush. The ◪**Helikon Palace Museum** (Helikon Kastélymúzeum) in the **Festetics Palace** (Kastély) is a storybook Baroque palace with the 90,000-volume **Helikon Library,** an exotic arms collection, and a porcelain exhibit. Visitors must don slippers to preserve the floors. Follow Kossuth Lajos u. from Fő tér toward Tourinform until it becomes Kastély u. (Open Tu-Su 9am-5pm; ticket office closes at 4:30pm. 1400Ft, students 700Ft.) The rocky and swampy **Strand,** on the coast to the right as you exit the train station, attracts crowds in spite of the terrain. From the center, walk down Erzsébet u. as it curves right into Vörösmarty u.; go through the park on the left after the train tracks to the beach. (Open 8:30am-7pm. 250Ft.).

Intercity trains (express) run between Keszthely and Budapest (3hr., 13 per day, 1482Ft). To reach the main square from the train station, walk straight up Mártirok u., which ends in Kossuth Lajos u., turn right, and walk 5min. to Fő tér. **Tourinform,** Kossuth Lajos u. 28, sits on the palace side of Fő tér. (☎314 144. Open Oct.-June M-F 9am-5pm, Sa 9am-1pm; July-Aug. M-F 9am-8pm, Sa-Su 9am-4pm.) **Private rooms** are available through Tourinform (from 2500Ft). Pitch a tent at **Castrum Camping,** Móra Ferene u. 48. (☎312 120. July-Aug. 680Ft per person, 540-680Ft per tent. Sept.-June 410-680Ft per tent. Tax 250Ft.) **Postal code:** 8360. ☎**83.**

HUNGARY

ICELAND (ÍSLAND)

ICELANDIC KRÓNUR

US$1 = 97.44IKR	100IKR = US$1.03
CDN$1 = 63.36IKR	100IKR = CDN$1.58
UK£1 = 140.73IKR	100IKR = UK£0.71
IR£1 = 113.08IKR	100IKR = IR£0.88
AUS$1 = 52.01IKR	100IKR = AUS$1.92
NZ$1 = 42.66IKR	100IKR = NZ$2.34
ZAR1 = 11.81IKR	100IKR = ZAR8.47
EUR€1 = 89.04IKR	100IKR = EUR€1.12

PHONE CODE	**Country code:** 354. **International dialing prefix:** 00. There are no city codes in Iceland. From outside Iceland, dial int'l dialing prefix (see inside back cover) + 354 + local number.

Forged by the power of still-active volcanoes, and raked by the slow advance and retreat of glaciers, Iceland's landscape is uniquely warped and contorted. Nature is the country's greatest attraction; few places allow visitors to walk across moonscapes created by lava rocks, dodge warm water shooting up from geysers, and sail across a glacial lagoon filled with icebergs. Civilization has made a powerful mark on Iceland; the geothermal energy that causes numerous earthquakes now also provides hot water and electricity to Iceland's settlements, and a network of roads carved through seemingly inhospitable terrain connects even the smallest villages to larger cities. A booming tourist industry attests to the fact that physical isolation has not set the country behind the rest of Europe. However, Iceland's island status has allowed it to achieve a high standard of living without losing its deeply rooted sense of community and pristine natural surroundings.

FACTS AND FIGURES

Official Name: Republic of Iceland.

Capital: Reykjavík.

Major Cities: Hafnarfjörðhur, Höfn, Ísafjörðhur, Vík.

Population: 275,000.

Land Area: 103,000 sq. km.

Climate: Cool summers and mild winters.

LANGUAGE: Icelandic; Danish, English, and German are also widely spoken.

Religions: Evangelical Lutheran (96%), other Protestant and Roman Catholic (4%).

DISCOVER ICELAND

Spend a day exploring the heart of **Reykjavík** (p. 528)—feed the birds at Tjörnin and stroll along Laugavegur to appreciate the city's unique blend of natural beauty and modern convenience. To see the water wonders of **Gullfoss, Geysir** (p. 533), and the **Blue Lagoon** (p. 533), take the bus from the capital. Return to the city for coffee—or cocktails—when the sun sets in a cozy cafe. The power of Iceland's volcanoes and great hikes among jagged black cliffs are available at the **Westman Islands** (p. 533).

ESSENTIALS

WHEN TO GO

Tourist season starts in mid-June, but it really isn't high-season until July, when the interior opens up, snow almost disappears, and all the bus lines are running. In summer, the sun dips below the horizon for a few hours each night, but it never gets truly

Iceland

dark, and it's warm enough to camp and hike. With warm clothing you could travel as late as October, but in winter there is very little sun. It rarely gets hotter than 60°F (16°C) in summer or dips below 20°F (-6°C) in winter.

DOCUMENTS AND FORMALITIES

VISAS. South Africans need a visa for stays of any length. Citizens of Australia, New Zealand, Canada, the UK, Ireland, and the US can visit for up to 90 days without one, but this three-month period begins upon entry into any Scandinavian country; for a stay of more than 90 days in any combination of Finland, Iceland, Norway, and Sweden, you will need a visa.

EMBASSIES. Foreign embassies in Iceland are in Reykjavík (p. 450). For Icelandic embassies at home: **Canada,** 360 Albert St., Suite 710, Ottawa, ON KIR 7X7 (☎613-482-1944; fax 613-482-1945); **UK,** 2A Hans St., London SW1X 0JE (☎020 7259 3999; fax 7245 9649; www.iceland.org.uk); and **US,** 1156 15th St. NW Suite 1200, Washington, D.C. 20005 (☎202-265-6653; fax 202-265-6656; www.iceland.org).

TRANSPORTATION

BY PLANE. Icelandair (US ☎800-223-5500) flies to Reykjavík year-round from the US and Europe. Icelandair charges no extra airfare for transatlantic travelers who stop over up to three days in the country in the Awesome Iceland Stopover Package—also ask about their "Take-A-Break" special offers. Domestic-service **Flugfélag Islands** (☎750 30 30) fly between Reykjavík and Iceland's other major towns; tickets can be issued at BSÍ Travel. Another option is the **Air/Bus Rover** (fly one way, bus the other), offered jointly by the domestic air carriers and BSÍ Travel (June-Sept.; Reykjavík to Akureyri 16,475Ikr; Reykjavík to Isafjörður 18,830Ikr; Reykjavík to Höfn 19,750Ikr). Icelandair has some student discounts, including half-price on standby flights. Weather can ground flights; leave yourself time for delays.

BY BUS. Iceland has no trains, and although flying is faster and more comfortable, buses are usually cheaper and provide a close-up look at the terrain. Within Iceland, one tour company, **BSÍ Travel** (☎562 33 20; fax 552 99 73), with offices in the Reykjavík bus terminal, coordinates all schedules and prices. Schedules are available at hostels and tourist offices. BSÍ's main catalog/brochure lists all bus schedules and is a must for anyone traveling the **Ring Road,** a loop that circles Iceland. Buses run daily on each segment from mid-June through August, but frequency drops dramatically off season. The going is slow since some roads are unpaved. The circle can be completed in three days, but to adequately explore, plan for a 10-day journey.

The **Full Circle Passport** (17,700Ikr) lets travelers circle the island at their own pace on the Ring Road (available mid-May to Sept.). It only allows for continuous directional travel, so a traveler must continue either clockwise or counter-clockwise around the country. For an extra 8500Ikr, the pass (which has no time limitation) provides access to the Westfjords in the island's extreme northwest. The **Omnibus Passport** (available all year) gives a period of unlimited travel on all scheduled bus routes including non-Ring roads (1 week 19,400Ikr; 2 weeks 28,200Ikr; 3 weeks 36,100Ikr; 4 weeks 40,100Ikr); prices drop in the off season. Both passes give 5% discounts on many ferries, campgrounds, farms, *Hótel Edda* sleeping-bag dorms, and guided bus tours.

BY FERRY. The best way to see Iceland's rugged shores is on the car and passenger ferry, **Norröna**, Laugavegur 3 in Reykjavík (☎562 63 62; fax 552 94 50), which circles the North Atlantic via Seyðisfjörður, East Iceland; Tórshavn in the Faroe Islands; and from there goes to Hanstholm, Denmark. The ferry returns to Tórshavn before going to Bergen. Those journeying to Bergen and to Seyðisfjörður from Hanstholm have a three-day layover in the Faroe Islands. Students get a 25% discount on all trips (7 days, runs mid-May to Aug., students 42500Ikr). **Eimskip** (reservations ☎585 4070) offers more expensive ferry rides on cargo ships from Reykjavík to Immingham, Rotterdam, and Hamburg.

BY CAR. In Iceland, travelers using cars (preferably 4-wheel-drive) have the most freedom. The country is overflowing with car rental *(bílaleiga)* companies. Prices average about 4900Ikr per day and 39Ikr per km after the first 100km for smaller cars, but are substantially higher for 4-wheel-drive vehicles (ask about special package deals). Some companies also require the purchase of insurance that can cost from 750-2000Ikr. **Ragnar Bjarnason**, Staðarbakka 2, offers the lowest rates. (☎557 42 66; fax 557 42 33. 3700 per day, 27Ikr per km after 100km, insurance included; 6500Ikr unlimited mileage per day.) You are required to keep your headlights on at all times, wear a seatbelt, and drive only on marked roads. A Green Card or other proof of insurance is mandatory.

BY BIKE AND BY THUMB. Cycling is gaining popularity, but ferocious winds, driving rain, and nonexistent road shoulders make it difficult. Buses will carry bikes for a 500-1000Ikr fee, depending on the distance covered. Trekking is extremely arduous; well-marked trails are rare, but several suitable areas await the truly ambitious (ask the tourist office in Reykjavík for maps and more info). Determined hitchers try the roads in summer, but sparse traffic and harsh weather exacerbate the inherent risks of hitching. Nevertheless, for those who last, the ride usually does come (easily between Reykjavík and Akureyri; harder in the east and the south). *Let's Go* does not recommend hitchhiking as a safe mode of transportation.

TOURIST SERVICES AND MONEY

EMERGENCY Police: ☎112. Ambulance: ☎112. Fire: ☎112.

TOURIST OFFICES. Tourist offices in large towns have schedules, maps, and brochures; check at hotel reception desks in smaller towns for local information. Musthaves are the free brochures *Around Iceland* (accommodation, restaurant, and museum listings for every town), *The Complete Iceland Map*, and the BSÍ bus schedule. The **main tourist office** in Reykjavík is at Bankastraeti 2, Rejkjavík (☎562 30 45; fax 562 30 57; www.tourist.reykjavik.is). The US tourist board maintains a helpful website (www.goiceland.org).

MONEY. Iceland's monetary unit is the **króna**, which is divided into 100 aurar. There are 100Ikr, 50Ikr, 10Ikr, 5Ikr, and 1Ikr coins; notes are in denominations of 5000Ikr,

2000Ikr, 1000Ikr, and 500Ikr. Costs are high: on average, a night in a hostel might cost you US$20; a budget hotel US$70-95; a budget restaurant meal US$10; and a day's worth of supermarket food US$25. Tipping is not customary in Iceland. Value-added tax (VAT) is included in all posted prices. VAT refunds (up to 15% of the retail price) are given if departing Iceland within 30 days after purchase. Minimum purchase price is 4000Ikr (VAT included) per receipt; goods must be unopened.

BUSINESS HOURS. Hours generally are Monday to Friday 9am-5pm (6pm in summer) and Saturday mornings.

COMMUNICATION

MAIL. Mailing a postcard/letter from Iceland costs 80IIkr to Australia, Canada, New Zealand, the US, or South Africa; to Europe it costs 55Ikr. Post offices *(póstur)* are generally open M-F 9am-4:30pm. Post offices and hostels hold mail for up to 45 days.

TELEPHONES. Telephone *(sími)* offices are often in the same building as post offices. Pay phones take phone cards or 10, 50, or 100Ikr pieces; local calls are 20Ikr. For the best prices, make calls from telephone offices; next best is a prepaid phone card. To make an international call, insert a phone card or dial direct (see numbers below). To reach the operator, call ☎118 (50Ikr per minute). International direct dial numbers include: **AT&T,** ☎800 90 01; **British Telecom,** ☎800 90 44; **Canada Direct,** ☎800 90 10; **Ireland Direct,** ☎800 93 53; **MCI,** ☎800 90 02; **Sprint,** ☎800 90 03; **Telecom New Zealand Direct,** ☎800 90 64.

INTERNET ACCESS. Internet access is widespread in Iceland, although in small towns it may only be available in public libraries. In Reykjavík there are Internet cafes and public libraries, which are either allow use free of charge or charge 250Ikr per 30min.

ACCOMMODATIONS AND CAMPING

Iceland's 27 **HI youth hostels,** invariably clean and always with kitchens, are uniformly priced at 1400Ikr for members, 1700Ikr for nonmembers. Pick up the free *Hostelling in Iceland* brochure at tourist offices. **Sleeping-bag accommodations** *(svefnpokapláss)*—available on farms, at summer hotels, and in guesthouses *(gistiheimili)*—are relatively cheap (and generally you get at least a mattress). In early June, many schoolhouses become *Hótel Eddas,* which have sleeping-bag accommodations (no kitchens; 950-1500Ikr, 5% bus pass discount). Most also offer breakfast and beds (both quite expensive). Staying in a tiny farm or hostel can be the highlight of a trip, but the nearest bus may be 20km away and run once a week. Many remote lodgings will pick up tourists in the nearest town for a small fee. In cities and nature reserves, **camping** is permitted only at designated campsites. Outside of official sites, camping is free but discouraged; watch out for *Tjaldstæði bönnuð* (No Camping) signs, and always ask at the nearest farm before you pitch a tent. Use gas burners; Iceland has no firewood, and it is illegal to burn the sparse vegetation. Official campsites (summer only) range from rocky fields with cold water taps to the sumptuous facilities in Reykjavík (750-600Ikr). Many offer discounts for students and bus pass holders.

FOOD AND DRINK

Traditional foods include *lundi* (puffin) on the Westman Islands, *rjúpa* (ptarmigan) around Christmas, and *selshreifar* (seal flippers) during the Thorri Feast (Mid-Winter Feast). Fish, lamb, and chicken are the most common components of authentic dishes, although more adventurous diners can try *svið* (singed and boiled sheep's head), *hrútspungur* (ram's testicles), or *hákarl* (rotten shark meat that has been buried underground), all of which are traditional dishes consumed during the Thorri Feast. International cuisine also has a strong presence in Iceland, and Italian, American, and Chinese food are usually found even in smaller towns. Food

ICELAND

is very expensive in Iceland; a *cheap* restaurant meal will cost at least 700Ikr. **Grocery stores** are the way to go; virtually every town has a couple of them. Gas stations usually run a grill and sell snacks. Bonus and Netto are cheaper alternatives to the more ubiquitous Hagkaup and 10-11. Iceland has some of the purest water in Europe. **Beer** costs 500-600Ikr at most pubs, cafes, and restaurants. The national drink is *Brennivín*, a type of schnapps known as "the Black Death," typically consumed during the Thorri Feast as well. The rarely enforced drinking age is 20.

HOLIDAYS

Holidays: New Year's (Jan. 1); Good Friday (Mar. 29); Easter (Mar. 31-Apr. 1); Labor Day (May 1); Ascension Day (May 9); National Day (June 17); Whit Sunday and Monday (May 19-20); Commerce Day (Aug. 5); Christmas Eve and Day (Dec. 24-25); Boxing Day (Dec. 26); New Year's Eve (Dec. 31).

REYKJAVÍK

Reykjavík's character more than makes up for its modest size. Bold, modern architecture complements the backdrop of snow-dusted purple mountains, and the city's refreshingly clear air is matched by its sparkling streets and gardens. Although quiet during the week, the world's northernmost capital comes alive on weekends and its cellular phone-toting inhabitants pride themselves on their modernity. Inviting and virtually crime-free, Reykjavík's only weaknesses are its often blustery weather and its high cost of living.

▐ TRANSPORTATION

Flights: All international flights arrive at **Keflavík Airport,** 55km from Reykjavík. **Flybuses** (☎562 10 11; 850Ikr) depart 45min. after each arrival for the domestic **Reykjavík Airport** and the adjacent Hótel Loftleiðir, just south of town. Once there, smaller Flybus minivans take passengers to other hotels and hostels around the city at no extra charge. Or take city **bus #7** (every 30min., 150Ikr) to Lækjartorg Square downtown. Flybuses pick up passengers from the Hótel Loftleiðir (2hr. before each flight departure) and the Grand Hotel Reykjavík (2½hr. before), as well as from the youth hostel (June-Aug. 4:45am and 1:15pm). Most hostels and guesthouses will arrange for guests to be picked up by the Flybus at no extra charge. The **Omnibus Pass** (but not Full Circle Passport) covers the Flybus; get a refund for your ride into town at BSÍ Travel (see below) or Reykjavík Excursions (in the Hotel Loftleiðir; open 24hr.).

Buses: Umferðarmiðstöð (also known as **BSÍ Station**), Vatnsmýrarvegur 10 (☎552 23 00), off Hringbraut near Reykjavík Airport. Walk 15-20min. south along the pond from city center, or take bus #7 or 8 (every 20-30min., 150Ikr). Open daily 7am-11:30pm; tickets sold 7:30am-10pm. **BSÍ Travel** (☎562 33 20; fax 552 99 73; www.bsi.is), inside the bus terminal, sells bus passes and tour packages. Open June-Aug. M-F 7:30am-7pm, Sa-Su 7:30am-5pm; Sept.-May M-F 9am-5pm.

Public Transportation: Strætisvagnar Reykjavíkur (SVR; ☎551 27 00) operates yellow city buses (150Ikr). Pick up SVR's helpful city map/bus schedule at its terminals to figure out bus routes. Tickets are sold at 5 terminals; the two major terminals are Lækjartorg in the center of town (open M-F 7am-11:30pm, Sa 8am-11:30pm, Su 10am-11:30pm) and Hlemmur (open daily 8am-11:30pm). Buy packages of 8 adult fares (1000Ikr) or 20 senior fares (1200Ikr) beforehand or buy tickets on the bus (exact change only). Ask the driver for a free transfer ticket (*skiptimiði;* valid for 1hr.). Buses run M-Sa 7am-midnight, Su and holidays 10am-midnight. Some night buses with limited routes run until 4:30am on weekends but after midnight you're better off walking or taking a taxi.

Taxis: BSR, Skolatröð 18 (☎561 00 00). 24hr. service. Tipping not customary. City center to BSÍ bus terminal 500-600Ikr, to domestic airport 600-700Ikr.

Bike Rental: At the **youth hostel campground** (see below). 800Ikr per 6hr.

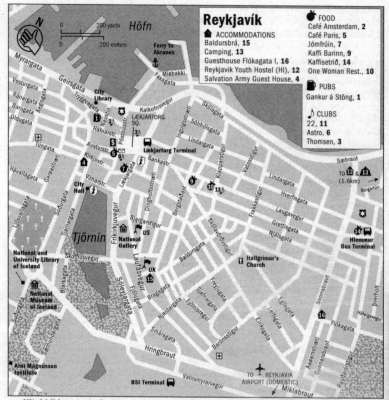

Reykjavík

▲ ACCOMMODATIONS
Baldursbrá, **15**
Camping, **13**
Guesthouse Flókagata I, **16**
Reykjavík Youth Hostel (HI) **12**
Salvation Army Guest House, **4**

🍎 FOOD
Café Amsterdam, **2**
Café Paris, **5**
Jómfrúin, **7**
Kaffi Barinn, **9**
Kaffisetrið, **14**
One Woman Rest., **10**

🍺 PUBS
Gankur á Stöng, **1**

♪ CLUBS
22, **11**
Astro, **6**
Thomsen, **3**

Hitchhiking: *Let's Go* does not recommend hitchhiking. Those hitching take buses #15 or 10 from the Hlemmur station, or bus #110 from the Lækjartorg station to the east edge of town, then stand on Vesturlandsvegur to go north or Suðurlandsvegur to go southeast.

🔳🔟 ORIENTATION AND PRACTICAL INFORMATION

Lækjartorg is Reykjavík's main square. South of Lækjartorg are **Tjörnin** (the pond), the bus station (BSÍ terminal), and the Reykjavík Airport. Extending east and west from Lækjartorg square is the main thoroughfare, which becomes (from west to east) **Austurstræti, Bankastræti,** and **Laugavegur.** City maps are available at the tourist office or around town, and the monthlies *What's On in Reykjavík* and *Reykjavík This Month* provide information about exploring the city (all free).

TOURIST, FINANCIAL, AND LOCAL SERVICES

Tourist Office: Upplýsingamiðstöð Ferðamála í Íslandi, Bankastr. 2 (☎562 30 45), at Lækjartorg and Bankastr. **Branches** at the airport and City Hall. Open mid-May to mid-Sept. daily 8am-7pm; mid-Sept. to mid-May daily 9am-5pm.

Budget Travel: Ferðaskrifstofa Stúdenta (☎570 08 00; www.ist.is), Saetun 1, by Hlemmur bus station. Books international flights and sells ISIC cards and some railpasses. Open M-F 9am-5pm.

Embassies: Canada, Suðurlandsbraut 10, 3rd fl. (☎568 08 20; fax 568 08 99). Open M-F 8am-4pm. **Ireland,** Kringlan 7 (☎588 66 66; fax 588 65 64). Open M-F 8am-4pm. **South Africa,** Kringlan 7 (☎520 33 00; fax 520 33 99). Open M-F 9am-3pm. **UK,** Laufásvegur 31 (☎550 51 00; fax 550 51 05). Open M-F 9am-noon. **US,** Laufásvegur 21 (☎562 91 00; fax 562 91 23). Open M-F 8am-12:30pm and 1:30-5pm. For inquiries regarding visa extensions, open M-F 8-11:30am and 1:30-4pm.

Luggage Storage: At the BSÍ terminal next to ticket window. 150lkr per day. Open daily 7:30am-7pm.

Laundromat: Þvottahusið Emla, Barónsstíg. 3 (☎552 74 99), just south of Hverfisg. Full service. 1400lkr per load. Open M-F 8am-6pm. Many **hostels** also do laundry.

EMERGENCY AND COMMUNICATIONS

Emergency: ☎112.

Police: Headquarters at Hverfisg. 113 (☎569 90 20). Downtown office at Tryggvag. 19 (☎56 90 25).

Pharmacies: Haaleitis Apótek, Haaleitisbraut 68 (☎581 21 01). Open daily 8am-2am. **Lyfja Apótek,** Laugavegur 16 (☎552 40 45). Carries contact lens supplies and beauty products. Open M-F 9am-7pm, Sa 10am-4pm.

Medical Assistance: National Hospital at Fossvogur (☎525 17 00), on Slettuvegur, has a 24hr. emergency ward. From the center of town, take bus #3.

Telephones: Public telephones are available at the tourist office, City Hall, the post office, and in many hotels and hostels. All phones require coins or a phone card (available at the tourist office and most convenience stores; 500 or 1000lkr). For a local call, insert at least 20lkr. Phones accept coins of 10, 50, or 100lkr.

Internet Access: Topshop, Lækjarg. 2a, 2nd fl. (20min. slots, free). Open M-W 10am-7pm, Th-F 10am-8pm, Sa 10am-6pm. **City Hall** cafe, north end of the pond (20min. slots, free). Open M-F 10:30am-6pm, Sa-Su noon-6pm.

Post Office: Íslandspóstur, Pósthússtr. 5, at Austurstr. (☎550 70 10). Address mail to be held: First name SURNAME, Poste Restante, ÍSLANDSPÓSTUR, Pósthússtr. 5, 101 Reykjavík, ICELAND. Mail is held for 45 days. Open M-F 9am-4:30pm.

▗ ACCOMMODATIONS AND CAMPING

Many guesthouses offer "sleeping-bag accommodations" (a shared room and a nice bed with neither sheets nor blanket). A cheap hotel will cost at least 5000lkr. Breakfast costs an extra 700-800lkr; take advantage of Iceland's cheap cereal and yogurt instead. From mid-June to August, call ahead for reservations.

Hjálpræðisherinn Gisti-og Sjómannaheimili (Salvation Army Guest and Seamen's Home), Kirkjustr. 2 (☎561 32 03), in a pale yellow house 1 block north of the pond, at the corner of Kirkjustr. and Tjarnarg. Bustling with backpackers enjoying the fantastic location and friendly staff. May-Sept. sleeping-bag accommodations 1800lkr; singles 3700lkr; doubles 5000lkr. Oct.-Apr. prices drop.

Guesthouse Flókagata 1, Flókag. 1 (☎552 11 55; fax 562 03 55; guesthouse@eyjar.is). Entrance on Snorrabraut. Take bus #1 from BSÍ terminal. Pristine rooms, all with TV and refrigerator. Reception 24hr. May-Sept. sleeping-bag accommodations 2500lkr; singles 5900lkr; doubles 8500lkr. Oct.-Apr. prices drop 10%.

Reykjavík Youth Hostel (HI), Sundlaugavegur 34 (☎553 81 10; fax 588 92 01; info@hostel.is). Take bus #5 from Lækjarg. to Sundlaugavegur. Far from the center of town, but next to Laugardalslaug, the biggest geothermal swimming pool in the city. Sleeping bags allowed. Reception 8am-midnight daily; ring bell after hours. Dorms 1400-1800lkr; singles 1700lkr; doubles 2050-2500lkr. Non-members add 300lkr.

Baldursbrá, Laufásvegur 41 (☎552 66 46; fax 562 66 47; heijfis@centrum.is), 20min. north of BSÍ terminal, 5-10min. south of city center on foot. Cozy family-run guest house in a quiet residential neighborhood. Shared bathroom. Reserve ahead. Kitchen and TVs. Jacuzzi and sauna (300lkr). May-Sept. singles 6320lkr; doubles 8320lkr. Oct.-Apr. singles 4500lkr; doubles 5500lkr. 10% cash discount.

Reykjavík Youth Hostel Campsite (☎568 69 44), next to youth hostel. Take bus #5 from city center. Campsite in a huge field by the geothermal pool (200lkr). Friendly staff. Free transfer from campsite to BSÍ bus terminal at 7:15am daily. Laundry 300lkr. Open mid-May to mid-Sept. 600lkr per person, including shower; 2-bed cabins 3500lkr.

☐ FOOD

An authentic Icelandic meal featuring seafood, lamb, or puffin will cost at least 1000Ikr. If you want to eat well and you're on a budget, head to a market. **10-11,** on Austurstr., is next to the post office. (Open daily 10am-11pm.) There are also several clustered in the city center along **Austurstræti, Hverfisgata,** and **Laugavegur.** Refer to Nightlife (p. 532) for cafes, which provide evening fun as well as daytime meals.

▨ **One Woman Restaurant,** Laugavegur 20B, at the intersection with Klapparstígur. Delicious vegetarian fare and soothing environment appeal to travelers and locals alike. Daily special 850Ikr. Open M-Sa 11:30am-2pm and 6-10pm, Su 6-10pm.

Jómfrúin, Lækjarg. 4. Casual Danish restaurant serves delectable sandwiches (550-1300Ikr). Beer 500-600Ikr. Open daily Apr.-Sept. 11am-10pm; Oct.-Mar. 11am-6pm.

Kebab Húsið, on the corner of Lækjarg. and Austurstr. Serves hearty vegetable, beef, or chicken kebabs on pita bread (450-650Ikr) in a fast food-style atmosphere. Open M-Th and Su 11:30am-midnight, F-Sa 11:30am-7am.

Kaffisetrið, Langaveg. 103, boasts both Thai and Icelandic menus. Locals come for the lunch special (789Ikr). June-Aug. open 7am-11:30pm; Sept.-May 10am-11:30pm.

◉ SIGHTS

The **Reykjavík Card,** available at the tourist office, allows unlimited public transportation, entry to the geothermal pools around Reykjavík, and admission to many sights, including the museums below. (1 day 900Ikr, 2 day 1500Ikr, 3 day 2000Ikr).

SIGHTS. Start your tour of Reykjavík with a trip to the top of **Hallgrímskirkja** (Hallgrímur's Church). The soaring steeple is the highest point in the city and the view provides a good sense of Reykjavík's layout. Turn off Laugavegur to Skólavörðustígur and you can't miss the church. (Open daily 9am-6pm. Services Su 11am. 200Ikr for the elevator ride to the top.) The **Ásmundur Sveinsson Sculpture Museum,** on Sigtún, houses Sveinsson's sculptures and concrete monuments to the working man within a stunning domed gallery. (Take bus #5 from city center. Open daily May-Sept. 10am-4pm; Sept.-May 1-4pm. 400Ikr.) The **Listasafn Íslands** (National Gallery of Iceland), Fríkirkjuvegur 7, on the east shore of Tjörnin displays small, rotating exhibits from the gallery's collection of both traditional and contemporary Icelandic art. It's close to the city center and worth a quick visit. (Enter on Skálholtsstígur. Open Tu-Su 11am-5pm. 400Ikr, seniors 250. W free.) The **Árbaer Open-Air Folk Museum** on Ártúnsholt has exhibits chronicling Icelandic history, along with actors reenacting Icelandic life during different time periods. (Take bus #10 or 110. Open June-Aug. Tu-F 9am-5pm, Sa-Su 10am-6pm; Sept.-May M and F 1-2pm for guided tours. 300Ikr, students free.)

A walk from the city center east along the waterfront or around the Tjörnin pond, leads to the **City Hall.** Inside the hall, on the north end of the pond there's a giant raised relief map of Iceland. (Open M-F 8am-7pm, Sa-Su 10am-6pm.) The **Laugardalslaug** is the largest of Reykjavík's geothermally heated pools. It boasts a giant slide and a series of jacuzzis, each one hotter than the last. (On Sundlaugavegur next to the youth hostel campground. Take bus #5 from city center. Open M-F 6:50am-9pm, Sa-Su 8am-8pm. 200Ikr.) Behind the pool to the south lies the **Heiðmörk Reserve,** a large park and sports complex. Well-marked trails ideal for hiking and picnicking wind through the area.

Ferries run regularly to **Viðey Island** (schedules available at tourist office and BSÍ bus terminal), which provides opportunities for hiking and picnicking. The island has been inhabited since the 10th century and boasts Iceland's second-oldest church. Across the bay from Reykjavík looms **Mt. Esja,** which you can ascend via a well-kept trail in 2-3 hr. While the trail is not difficult, hikers are often assaulted by rain, hail, and snow, even in summer. (Take bus #10 or 110 to Artún and transfer to bus #20, exiting at Mógilsá. Bus #20 runs less frequently; consult SVR city bus schedule before departing.)

NIGHTLIFE

Reykjavík has earned a reputation as a wild party town, and if you're willing to pay for the fun, you won't be disappointed. There's a plethora of cafes, pubs, and clubs, as well as smartly dressed, super-hip Icelandic revelers. In the summer, it never gets truly dark and it's a unique experience to cruise the streets at 3am and feel like you've stepped out for an early dinner. Cafes transform from quiet breakfast places to boisterous bars on weekend nights and Reykjavík's hottest nightspots are mainly located in the city center around **Austurstræti, Tryggvagata,** and **Laugavegur.**

CAFES

Cafe Paris, Austurstr. 14. Packed from morning to night with people enjoying the steaming pots of coffee and intimate atmosphere. Coffee 250Ikr. Beer 500-600Ikr. Open M-Th 8am-midnight, F 8am-1am, Sa 10am-1am, Su 10am-midnight.

Kaffi Barinn, on Bergstaðastr. near Laugavegur. Intimate, largely local crowd. Packed on weekend nights, especially after the DJ shows up on F and Sa. Coffee 200-250Ikr, beer 500-600Ikr. Open M-Th 11am-1am, F 11am-3am, Sa noon-3am, Su 3pm-1am. Kitchen closed Sa-Su.

Cafe Amsterdam, on corner of Tryggvag. and Naustin, across from Gaukur á Stöng. The major attraction is the live music on weekends. You can peer through the floor-to-ceiling windows from the street and decide for yourself whether to head inside. Beer 550Ikr. Cover 1000Ikr after 2am F-Sa. Open M-Th 6pm-1am, F-Sa 6pm-6am.

PUBS AND CLUBS

Thomsen, on Hafnarstr., just down from the SVR Lækjartorg bus station. When many other places close down for the night, the party at this nightclub is just getting started. Cover 500Ikr before 3am, 1000Ikr afterwards. Open F-Sa 11pm to 7 or 9am.

Gaukur á Stöng, Tryggvag. 22. Iceland's first pub and still one of its most popular nightspots. Live music after 11pm. Open Su-Th 6pm-1am, F-Sa 6pm-6am.

Astro, Austurstr. 22, next to McDonald's. Draws a younger, magnificently dressed crowd just as hip as the green and purple color scheme. Expect to wait unless you're tight with the bouncers. Cover 500Ikr after midnight. Open F-Sa 11pm-5am.

22, Laugavegur 22. An artsy hangout that attracts large crowds of students on weekends to its upstairs disco. Cover 500Ikr after 3am. Open M-Th noon-1am, F noon-3am, Sa 6pm-3am, Su 6pm-1am. Upstairs open F-Sa midnight-6am.

DAYTRIPS FROM REYKJAVÍK

Buses traverse the terrain from Reykjavík to various surrounding sights (mostly within an hour or two of downtown), but many opt for comprehensive scheduled tours instead. **Reykjavík Excursions** runs the popular 8hr. **Golden Circle** guided bus tour that departs from Hotel Loftleiðir in Reykjavík daily at 9am and covers Hveragerði, Kerið, Skálholt, Geysir, Gullfoss, and Þingvellir National Park (5400Ikr).

ICELAND WAS THERE FIRST The year 2000 finally put to rest debate about who really discovered North America. While Columbus has traditionally gotten most of the credit, Icelander Leif Eriksson is now acknowledged as the first European ever to set foot in the new world, a millennium ago at L'Anse aux Meadows in eastern Canada. Disputes over the authenticity of the evidence for early Viking settlements in North America have been settled, and international magazines such as *Newsweek* and *National Geographic* have featured 'Leif the Lucky' and his Viking cohorts on their covers. The ruins of the farm built by his parents, Erik the Red and Thjóðhildur, have been turned into a living museum commemorating his birthplace near the village of Dalir in western Iceland. A Viking ship replica set sail in June from the west coast to retrace the Viking's route to Greenland and North America.

ICELAND

Book ahead at their desk in the tourist office or over the phone (☎562 10 11). Free pickup for customers at a number of other hotels and hostels around Reykjavík is available. Another option is to rent a car and embark on your own tour.

BLUE LAGOON. Southwest of Reykjavík lies paradise: a vast pool of geothermally heated water in the middle of a lava field. The lagoon is alongside a natural power plant that provides Reykjavík with electricity and heat by harnessing geothermal steam. The lagoon's unique concentrations of silica, minerals, and algae are thought to soothe skin diseases, and mud sits in buckets for bathers to slather on as they relax in the water. Heavily promoted and very popular with tourists, the Blue Lagoon offers relaxation for the weary traveler. **Buses** run from the BSÍ terminal in Reykjavík to the Blue Lagoon. (Daily 10am, 1:30, 5:15, 6pm; return 12:40, 4:10, 6, 8pm. 1400Ikr.) Three-hour admission to the lagoon is 800Ikr; bathing suits (250Ikr) and towels (300Ikr) are available for rent.)

ÞINGVELLIR NATIONAL PARK. Straddling the divide between the European and North American tectonic plates, Þingvellir National Park features impressive scenery and is only 50km east of its capital. The **Öxará River,** slicing through lumpy lava fields and jagged fissures, leads to the **Drekkingarhylur** (Drowning Pool), where adulterous women were once drowned, and to **Lake Þingvallavatn,** the largest lake in Iceland. Not far from the Drekkingarhylur lies the site of the ancient parliament, the **Alþing,** which marked the beginning of Icelandic parliamentary democracy in the year 930. For almost nine centuries, Icelanders gathered once a year in the shadow of the Lögberg (Law Rock) to discuss matters of blood, money, and justice. A **bus** runs from Reykjavík to Þingvellir (daily May 20-Sept. 10 1:30pm, return 4:50pm; 1400Ikr return), dropping visitors off at an **information center** (☎482 26 60; open May-Sept. 8:30am-8pm). Ask there for directions for the 30-45min. walk along the road to reach the lake or the main historical sites. There is a **campground** by the information center (500Ikr per person).

GULLFOSS & GEYSIR. A glacial river plunging over 30m creates Gullfoss, the "Golden Falls." Perhaps the greatest attraction of Gullfoss, besides the falls themselves, is the stunning view of the surrounding mountains, plains, and glaciers from atop the hill adjacent to the falls. If you take the stairs to the top of the hill overlooking Gullfoss, go right to the observation deck or straight to see a small exhibit detailing the geology of the falls. Only 9km away is the **Geysir** area, a rocky, rugged tundra with steaming pools of hot water every few meters. The energetic **Strokkur** erupts every 5-10min. and reaches heights of up to 25-35m. BSÍ runs **buses** to both sites, stopping at Gullfoss for 30-60min. and Geysir for 1-2hr. The ride is lengthy and roundabout, but the beautiful destinations are worth it. (Departs from Reykjavík daily June-Aug. 9:30am and 12:30pm, return 2:25pm and 4:45pm from Geysir; Sept.-May M-Sa 9:30am and return 2:30pm, Su 12:30pm and return 4:40pm. 3480Ikr)

WESTMAN ISLANDS (VESTMANNAEYJAR)

Vaulting boldly from the depths of the North Atlantic, the black cliffs off the Westman Islands are the most recent products of the volcanic fury that created Iceland. **Heimaey** is the only inhabited island. A town of the same name spreads outward from the island's harbor; it is one of the most important fishing ports in the country. An eruption of another sort, the three-day Þjóðhátíð **(People's Feast),** held the first weekend in August, draws a hefty percentage of Reykjavík's livelier citizens to the island's shores for an annual festival of drinking and dancing. The rest of the year, Heimaey is quiet and subdued.

■⁊ TRANSPORTATION AND PRACTICAL INFORMATION. Getting to and from the Westman Islands is relatively easy. Flugfélag Islands (Air Iceland) has daily flights from Reykjavík (☎570 30 30; one-way from 4765Ikr). A slower but much cheaper option is the Herjólfur ferry (☎481 28 00), which departs from Þorlákshöfn. (3hr; daily noon, Th-F, and Su also 7pm; 1500Ikr. Return daily 8:15am;

ICELAND

Th-F, and Su also 3:30pm.) Buses from Reykjavík go to the dock from the BSÍ terminal 1hr. before departure (750Ikr). The **tourist office** is at Vestmannabraut 38, in the
Samvinnuferðir-Landsyn travel agency. (☎481 12 71. Open June-Sept. M-F 9am-
5pm, Sa-Su 1-5pm; Oct.-May M-F 9am-5pm.) Ask there about island **bus tours** (daily
8am and noon, 1800Ikr) and **boat tours** (daily 10:30am and 3:30pm, 2000Ikr), both of
which run May 20-Sept. 15.

⚏ ACCOMMODATIONS AND FOOD. The **Guesthouse Hreiðreið and Bolið,** Fax-
astigur 33, just past the Volcanic Show cinema on Heiðarvegur, has two locations in
town. (☎481 10 45; fax 481 14 14. Sleeping bag accommodations 1400Ikr; singles
2800Ikr; doubles 4800Ikr.) **Guesthouse Sunnoholl,** Vestmannabraut 28, houses visitors in both sleeping bags and made-up beds in a white house behind Hotel
Þorshamar. (☎481 29 00. Sleeping bags 2700Ikr; 1600Ikr per extra person; dorms
2500Ikr; singles 3200Ikr.) The **campground,** 10min. west of town on Dalvegur near
the golf course, has showers and cooking facilities. (☎692 69 52. 500Ikr per person.)
K.A. supermarket, with a blue and white façade, is on Strandavegur (open M-Th 9am-
7:30pm, F 9am-7pm, Sa 10am-6pm), and **Voruval supermarket** is in the igloo-shaped
building on Vesturvegur (open M-F 7:30am-7pm, Sa 9am-7pm, Su 10am-7pm).

◪ SIGHTS. In 1973, the fiery **Eldfell** volcano tore through the northern sector of
Heimaey island, spewing glowing lava and hot ash in a surprise eruption that forced
the population to flee in a dramatic overnight evacuation. When the eruption finally
ceased five months later, a third of the town's houses had been destroyed while the
island itself grew by the same amount. Nearly all of its former inhabitants returned,
and the town underwent modernization. Today, visitors can feel the heat of the still-
cooling lava, hike among the black and green mountains that shelter its harbor, and
observe the chilling remnants of buildings half-crushed by the lava.

Hiking in the area is encouraged; the tourist office distributes a free map outlining
hiking trails. Spectacular spots include the cliff's edge at **Há** and the puffin colony at
Stórhöfði. From Há, the view of the town below, the twin volcanic peaks across, and
the snow-covered mainland afar is stunning. Both volcanic peaks also await
intrepid hikers, but strong winds often make for rough going over the summits.
Head to one of the country's two **aquariums** on Heiðarvegur (near the gas station on
the 2nd fl.) to see some of the island's strange and wonderful sea creatures. (Open
May-Sept. daily 11am-5pm; Sept.-Apr. Sa-Su 3-5pm. 300Ikr.)

REPUBLIC OF IRELAND

AND NORTHERN IRELAND

IRISH PUNT OR POUND

US$1 = IR£0.86	IR£1 = US$1.16
CDN$1 = IR£0.56	IR£1 = CDN$1.79
UK£1 = IR£1.25	IR£1 = UK£0.80
AUS$1 = IR£0.46	IR£1 = AUS$2.17
NZ$1 = IR£0.38	IR£1 = NZ$2.65
ZAR1 = IR£0.10	IR£1 = ZAR9.62
EUR€1 = IR£0.79	IR£1 = EUR€1.27

PHONE CODES

Country code: 353. International dialing prefix: 00. From outside the Republic of Ireland, dial int'l dialing prefix (see inside back cover) + 353 + city code + local number.

Although the Republic of Ireland and Northern Ireland are grouped together in this chapter for geographical reasons, no political statement is intended. Prices listed in this chapter refer to Irish Pounds unless specifically denoted as British Pounds (UK£). For information on Northern Ireland's currency exchange rates and the like, see **Britain**, p. 136.

This largely agricultural island has retained its natural charm for thousands of centuries. Windswept scenery curls around the coast, and mountains punctuate interior expanses of bogland. The Irish language lives on national papers, literary works and in secluded areas known as *gaeltacht*. Dublin and Belfast meanwhile have flowered into cosmopolitan cities, suffused with sophistication. But, like its natural beauty, centuries-old disputes refuse to die. The English suppressed the Catholic population after the Reformation and fighting eventually degenerated into civil war. The island split into the Irish Free State and Northern Ireland, which remained part of the UK. In 1949, the Free State proclaimed itself the independent Republic of Ireland (Éire), while the British kept control of Northern Ireland. In the 1960s, tensions in Northern Ireland between Catholic Nationalists and Protestant Unionists again erupted into violence. In 1998, the countries adopted a peace accord. 1999 and 2000 have seen the accord's fate fall into uncertainty, but negotiations continue in hopes of peace. For more learned writings on the "Land of Saints and Scholars," leaf through *Let's Go: Ireland 2002*.

FACTS AND FIGURES: REPUBLIC OF IRELAND

Official Name: Éire.

Capital: Dublin.

Major Cities: Cork, Limerick.

Population: 3.8million (58% urban).

Land Area: 70,280 sq. km.

Climate: Warmest and driest in the southeast, wettest in the West.

Languages: English, Irish.

Religions: Roman Catholic (91.6%), Protestant (2.5%), other (5.9%).

DISCOVER IRELAND

Ireland is well-stocked with activities to suit the whims of hikers, bikers, aesthetes, poets, birdwatchers, musicians, and drinkers. Land in **Dublin** (p. 540) and explore this thousand-year-old city, a bastion of literary history and the stomping-ground of international hipsters. Take the train up to **Belfast** (p. 561) and contemplate its complex past, then catch the bus to **Giant's Causeway** (p. 566), a unique formation of rocks called the earth's 8th natural wonder. Ride the bus to **Donegal Town** (p. 560), spend a night at a pub loving *trad*, before climbing **Slieve League** (p. 560), Europe's tallest seacliffs. Next up is **Sligo** (p. 559), once the home of W.B. Yeats. From there, head to **Galway** (p. 557), an artsy student town that draws the island's best musicians. Relax in the picture-perfect **Ring of Kerry** (p. 554) and the **Killarney National Park** (p. 553), with its exquisite mountains, lakes, and wildlife. On the way back to Dublin, take a detour to **Kilkenny** (p. 550) and visit Ireland's oldest brewery.

ESSENTIALS

WHEN TO GO

Traveling during the off season (mid-Sept. to May) has benefits: airfares are cheaper, and you won't have to fend off flocks of fellow tourists. A thriving music scene fills pubs year-round. The acclaimed theater productions of Dublin and Belfast occur mostly during fall and winter. Countless music, film, arts, and, above all, region-specific festivals spring up practically every week. The flip side is that many attractions, hostels, bed and breakfasts (B&Bs), and tourist offices close in winter, and in some rural areas of western Ireland, local transportation drops off significantly or shuts down, and the sun goes down at around 5pm. Also, it's best to avoid traveling in Northern Ireland during Marching Season (July 4-12).

DOCUMENTS AND FORMALITIES

VISAS. Citizens of Australia, Canada, EU countries, New Zealand, South Africa, the UK, and the US do not need visas to visit Ireland for stays shorter than three months.

EMBASSIES. All embassies for the Republic of Ireland are in **Dublin** (p. 487). For Irish embassies at home: **Australia,** 20 Arkana St., Yarralumla, Canberra ACT 2600 (☎(02)6273 3022); **Canada,** 130 Albert St., Ottawa, K1P 5G4 (☎613-233-6281; emb.ireland@sympatico.ca); **New Zealand** (Consulate General), Dingwall Bldg., 6th Fl., 18 Shortland St. 1001, Auckland 1 (☎(09) 302 2867) **South Africa,** TTubach Centre, 1234 Church St., 0083 Colbyn, Pret. (☎(012) 342 5062); **UK,** 17 Grosvenor Pl., London SW1X 7HR (☎(020) 7235 2171; ir.embassy@lineone.net); and **US,** Irish Embassy, 2234 Massachusetts Ave. NW, Washington, D.C. 20008 (☎202-462-3939).

TRANSPORTATION

BY PLANE. Flying to London and connecting to Ireland is often easier and cheaper. **Aer Lingus, British Airways, British Midlands,** and **Ryanair** have flights from

Ireland:
Republic of Ireland
and Northern Ireland

Britain (including Gatwick, Heathrow, Manchester, Birmingham, Liverpool, and Glasgow) and other cites to Dublin, Shannon, Cork, Galway, Sligo, Belfast, and Derry. For information on cheap flights to Britain and the continent, see p. 54.

BY TRAIN. Iarnród Éireann (Irish Rail) is useful only for travel to urban areas. While the **Eurailpass** is not accepted in Northern Ireland, it is accepted on trains (but not buses) in The Republic. The BritRail pass does not cover travel in Northern Ireland, but the month-long **BritRail+Ireland** works in both the North and the Republic with rail options and return ferry service between Britain and Ireland (US$399-569). **Northern Ireland Railways** (☎ (028) 9033 3000; www.nirailways.co.uk) is not extensive but covers the northeastern coastal region well. The major line connects Dublin to Belfast. A valid **Northern Ireland Travelsave** stamp (UK£7, affixed to back of ISIC) will save you up to 33% off all trains and 15% discounts on bus fares over UK£1.45 within Northern Ireland. The **Freedom of Northern Ireland** ticket allows unlimited travel by train and Ulsterbus and can be purchased for 7 consecutive days (UK£40), 3 out of 8 days ($27.50/€35), or a single day ($11/€14).

BY BUS. **Bus Éireann** (the Irish national bus company) reaches Britain and even the continent by working in conjunction with ferry services and the bus company **Eurolines** (UK ☎ (0990) 143 219; www.eurolines.com). Return tickets are always a great value, as is the Éireann **Travel Save Stamp** (£8/€10.20) if you are a student. A combined **Irish Explorer Rail/Bus** ticket allows unlimited travel on bus and rail for 8 of 15 consecutive days (£124/€157.50; child £62/€78.75). Purchase Bus Éireann tickets at their main bus stations in transportation hubs (☎ (0990) 808 080).

Ulsterbus (☎ (028) 9033 3000, Belfast office ☎ (028) 9032 0011; www.ulster-bus.co.uk), runs extensive and reliable routes throughout Northern Ireland. A **Freedom of Northern Ireland** bus and rail pass provides extended travel, see **By Train**, above. The **Irish Rover** pass covers both Bus Éireann and Ulsterbus services (unlimited travel for 3 of 8 days £42/€53.35, child £21/€26.70; for 8 of 15 days £93/€118.10, child £47/€59.70; for 15 of 30 £145/€184.10, child £73/€92.70). The **Emerald Card** offers unlimited travel on Ulsterbus; Northern Ireland Railways; Bus Éireann Expressway, Local, and City services in Dublin, Cork, Limerick, Galway, and Waterford; and intercity, DART, and suburban rail Iarnród Éireann services. The card works for 8 out of 15 consecutive days (£124/€157.50, child £62/€78.75) or 15 out of 30 consecutive days (£214/€271.70, child £107/€135.85).

BY FERRY. Ferries journey between Britain and Ireland several times per day; tickets usually range £18-£35/€23-45. Traveling mid-week at night promises the cheapest fares. **An Óige (HI) members** receive up to a 20% discount on fares from Irish Ferries and Stena Sealink. **ISIC cardholders** with the **Travel Stamp** (see above) receive a 15% discount from Irish Ferries and an average 17% discount (variable among four routes) on StenaLine ferries. Bus tickets that include ferry connections between Britain and Ireland are available. Contact Bus Éireann for info. For more detailed ferry information on companies, routes, and prices, see p. 72.

BY CAR. Drivers in Ireland use the **left side of the road,** and place their steering-wheel on the right side of the car. Petrol prices are high. Be particularly cautious at roundabouts (rotary interchanges)—give way to traffic from the right. Irish law requires drivers and passengers to wear seat belts. People under 21 cannot rent cars, and those under 23 (or even 25) often encounter difficulties. Prices range from £100-300/€127-381 (plus VAT) per week with insurance and unlimited mileage. If you plan to drive a car while in Ireland for longer than a three-month period, you must have an International Driving Permit (IDP). If you rent, lease, or borrow a car, you will need a **green card,** or **International Insurance Certificate,** to certify that you have liability insurance and that it applies abroad.

BY BIKE, BY FOOT, AND BY THUMB. *Let's Go* does not recommend hitchhiking. Those who do hitch say that much of Ireland's countryside is well-suited for cycling. Single-digit N roads in the Republic, are more busily trafficked; try to avoid them. Hitching on M roads in the North is illegal. Locals in Northern Ireland do not recommend hitching there. Ireland's mountains, fields, and heather-covered hills make walking and hiking an arduous joy. The **Wicklow Way** has hostels designed for hikers within a day's walk of each other. The **Ulster Way** encircles Northern Ireland with 900km of marked trails.

TOURIST SERVICES AND MONEY

EMERGENCY	Police, Ambulance, and Fire: ☎999.

TOURIST OFFICES. **Bord Fáilte** (the **Irish Tourist Board**) operates a nationwide network of offices. Most tourist offices book rooms for a small fee (£1-3/€.30-3.85) and a 10% deposit, but many fine hostels and B&Bs are not "approved," so the tourist office can't tell you about them. Bord Fáilte's central office is at Baggot St. Bridge, Dublin 2, in Ireland (☎ (01850) 230 330; www.ireland.travel.ie.)

The **Northern Ireland Tourist Board** offers similar services at locations all over the North. The head office is at 59 North St., Belfast, BT1 1NB, Northern Ireland (☎ (028) 9023 1221; www.discovernorthernireland.com). The Dublin office is at 16 Nassau St., Dublin 2 (☎ (01) 679 1977; CallSave ☎ (1850) 230 230).

MONEY. The currency of the Irish Republic is the **Irish pound** (or **"punt"**), denoted ₤. It comes in the same denominations as the **British pound** (which is called **"sterling"** in Ireland) but has been worth a bit less recently. Prices listed in this chapter refer to Irish Pounds unless specifically denoted as British Pounds (UK₤). Legal tender in Northern Ireland is the British pound. Northern Ireland has its own bank notes, which are identical in value to English and Scottish notes of the same denominations. Although these notes are accepted in Northern Ireland, Northern Ireland bank notes are not accepted across the water. UK coins come in denominations of 1p, 2p, 5p, 10p, 20p, 50p, and ₤1. Residents of both nations refer to pounds as **"quid,"** never "quids." For exchange, only go to banks or bureaux de change that have less than a 5% margin between their buy and sell prices. ATMs and credit cards will often get you the best rates. The majority of towns have 24-hour **ATMs.**

If you stay in **hostels** and prepare your own food, expect to spend about US$18-30 per person per day. Accommodations start at ₤8-10/€10.20-12.70 per night while the a basic sit-down meal begins around ₤6/€7.65. Some restaurants figure a **service charge** into the bill; some even calculate it into the cost of the dishes. The menu often indicates whether or not service is included (ask if you're unsure). If the tip is not included, customers should leave 10-15%. Porters, parking-lot attendants, waitstaff, and hairdressers are usually tipped. Cab drivers are usually tipped 10%. Barmen at older or rural pubs may be offended if you leave them a gratuity, while in cities or at bars with a younger clientele a tip may be expected—the trick is to watch and learn from other customers. Ireland and Northern Ireland charge **Value Added Tax (VAT)** on most goods and some services. The VAT ranges from 0% on food and children's clothing to 17% in restaurants to 21% on other items, such as jewelry and clothing; VAT is usually included in listed prices. The British rate, applicable to Northern Ireland, is 17.5% on many services (such as hairdressers, hotels, restaurants, and car rental agencies) and on all goods (except books, medicine, and food). *Let's Go* prices include VAT. Refunds are available for non-EU citizens and for goods taken out of the country, but not for services.

ACCOMMODATIONS AND CAMPING

Hostel dorms usually cost between ₤7.50-12/€9.50-15.25 and breakfast is often included or can be tacked on for ₤1-3/€1.30-3.80. **An Óige,** the Irish Hostelling International affiliate, runs 32 spartan, out-of-the-way hostels. The North's HI affiliate is **HINI** (Hostelling International Northern Ireland; formerly **YHANI**), which operates eight nicer hostels. The *An Óige Handbook* details all An Óige and HINI hostels. Some hostels belong to **Independent Holiday Hostels (IHH);** they have no lockout or curfew (with a few exceptions), accept all ages, don't require membership, and are approved by Bord Fáilte. Copious **B&Bs** provide a luxurious break; expect to pay ₤15-25/€19-31.75 for singles and ₤20-36/€30.50-50.80 for doubles. "Full Irish breakfasts" are often filling enough to get you through to dinner. **Camping** in Irish State Forests and National Parks is not allowed; camping on public land is permissible only if there is no official campsite nearby. Most caravan and camping parks are open April through October. Pick up the *Caravan and Camping Ireland* guide from any Bord Fáilte office for information on camping in the Republic.

FOOD AND DRINK

Food is expensive, but the basics are simple and filling. "Take-away" (takeout) fish and chips shops are quick, greasy, and very popular. Many pubs serve food as well as drink; typical pub grub includes Irish stew, burgers, soup, and sandwiches. Soda bread is delicious and keeps well, and dairy products are addictive. Pubs are the forum for banter, singing, and *craic* (a good time). In the evenings, many pubs play impromptu or organized traditional music (trad). Guinness, a rich, dark stout, is Ireland's most revered brew. Irish whiskey, which Queen Elizabeth once claimed was her only true Irish friend, is sweeter than its Scotch counterpart. Irish monks invented whiskey, calling it *uisce beatha*, meaning "water of life." Pubs are usually open Monday to Saturday 10:30am to 11 or 11:30pm, Sunday 12:30 to 2pm and 4 to 11pm (in the North Sunday 12:30-2:30pm and 7-10pm).

COMMUNICATION

MAIL. Postcards and letters up to 25g cost £0.30/€0.40 domestically and to the UK, £0.32/€0.45 to the continent; to any other international destination, £0.45/€0.60. Address mail to be held: First name SURNAME, *Poste Restante*, Enniscorthy, Co. Wexford, IRELAND. Airmail letters take about 6-9 days between Ireland and North America.

TELEPHONES. Both the Irish Republic and Northern Ireland have public phones that accept coins (20p for about 4min.) and pre-paid phone-cards. For an international operator, dial ☎114 in the Republic or ☎155 in Northern Ireland; operator, 10 and 100; directory, ☎11850 and ☎192. International direct dial numbers include: **AT&T,** ☎(1800) 550000 in the Republic and ☎(0800) 013 0011 in Northern Ireland; **British Telecom,** ☎(1800) 550 144 Republic Only; **Canada Direct,** ☎(1800) 555 001 and ☎(0800) 890 016; **MCI,** ☎(1800) 551 001 (Both); **Telecom New Zealand,** ☎(1800) 550 064 and ☎(0800) 890 064; **Telekom South Africa,** ☎(1800) 550 027 and ☎(0800) 890 027; and **Telstra Australia,** ☎(1800) 550 061 and ☎(0800) 856 6161;

INTERNET ACCESS. Internet access is available in Irish cities in cafes, hostels, and usually in libraries. One hour of webtime costs about £3-5/€3.80-6.35 (an ISIC card may win you a discount). Look into a county library membership in the Republic (£2/€2.55), which will give you unlimited access to participating libraries, and their internet.

HOLIDAYS AND FESTIVALS

Holidays: Much of Southern Ireland closes for holidays on January 1, St. Patrick's Day (Mar. 17), Good Friday, Easter Monday (Mar. 20-Apr. 1), and Christmas (Dec. 25-26). There are Bank Holidays in the Republic and Northern Ireland during the summer months; check at tourist offices for dates because almost everything shuts down. Northern Ireland adds a holiday on Orange Day (July 12),

Festivals: All of Ireland goes green for **St. Patrick's Day** (Mar. 17th). On **Bloomsday,** (June 16) Dublin traipses about revering James Joyce and *Ulysses* (p. 547).

DUBLIN ☎01

In a country known for its relaxed pace and rural sanctity, Dublin stands out for its international flair and boundless energy. Although the Irish worry that it has taken on the negative characteristics of a big city, it's still as friendly a metropolis as you'll find. The city and suburbs, home to one-third of Ireland's population, are at the vanguard of rapid social change. It's no cultural wallflower either: the ghosts of Swift, Joyce, Beckett, Behan, and others pepper Dublin's neighborhoods with literary attractions. The best trips to Dublin combine its duality and soak up as many of the sights, sips and sounds that the banks of the Liffey can offer.

◪ TRANSPORTATION

Flights: Dublin Airport (☎844 4900). **Dublin buses** #41, 41B, and 41C run to Eden Quay in the city center with stops along the way (every 20min., £1.20/€1.55). The **Airlink shuttle** (☎844 4265) runs non-stop directly to Busáras Central Bus Station and O'Connell St. (30-40min., every 10-15min., £3/€3.85) and onto Heuston Station (50min., £3.50/€4.45). A **taxi** to the city center costs roughly £10-12/€12.70-15.25. **Trains: Irish Rail, Iarnród Éireann** (EER-ann-road AIR-ann) has a travel center at 35 Lower Abbey St. (☎836 6222). Open M-F 9am-5pm, Sa 9am-1pm. **Connolly Station,**

Amiens St. (☎ 702 2358), is north of the Liffey and close to Busáras Bus Station. To: **Belfast** (2¼hr., 5-8 per day, £21/€26.30); **Sligo** (3½hr., 3-4 per day, £14.50/€18.45); and **Wexford** (3hr., 3 per day, £11/€14) via Rosslare. **Heuston Station** (☎ 703 2132) is south of Victoria Quay, well west of the city center, a 25min. walk from Trinity College. Buses #26, 51, and 79 go from Heuston to the city center. Trains to: **Cork** (3½hr., 6-11 per day, £33.50/€42.50); **Galway** (2½hr., 4-5 per day, £16-22/€20.35); **Limerick** (2½hr., 9 per day, £26.50/€33.65); **Tralee** (4½hr., 4-7 per day, £34/€43.20); and **Waterford** (2½hr., 3-4 per day, £13/€16.55).

Buses: Busáras Central Bus Station, Store St. (☎ 836 6111), directly behind the Customs House and next to Connolly Station. Bus Éireann runs to: **Belfast** (3hr., 6-7 per day, £10.50/€13.35); **Derry** (4¼hr., 4-5 per day, £11/€14); **Galway** (3½hr., 13 per day, £9/€11.45); **Limerick** (3½hr., 7-13 per day, £10.50/€13.35); **Rosslare Harbour** (3hr., 7-10 per day, £10/€12.70); **Sligo** (4hr., 4-5 per day, £9.60/€12.20); **Waterford** (2¾hr., 5-7 per day, £7/€8.90); and **Wexford** (2¾hr., 7-10 per day, £8/€10.20).

Ferries: Irish Ferries (☎ 855 2222) has an office off St. Stephen's Green on Merrion Row. Open M-F 9am-5pm, Sa 9:15am-12:45pm. **Stena Line** ferries arrive from **Holyhead, UK** at the **Dún Laoghaire** ferry terminal (☎ 204 7777). **Irish Ferries** (www.irish-ferries.ie) arrive from Holyhead at the **Dublin Port** (☎ 607 5665), where buses #53 and 53A run every hr. to Busáras (£0.80/€1); to get to the ferryport, **Dublin Bus** also runs connection buses timed to fit the ferry schedule (£2-2.50/€2.55-3.20). **Merchant Ferries** also docks at the Dublin ferryport and runs a route to **Liverpool, UK** (7½hr.; 1-2 per day; £50/€63.50 and up, car £170/€215.90); booking for Merchant is only available from **Gerry Feeney,** 19 Eden Quay (☎ 819 2999).

Public Transportation: Dublin Bus, 59 O'Connell St. (☎ 873 4222). Open M 8:30am-5:30pm, Tu-F 9am-5:30pm, Sa 9am-1pm. County Dublin buses run fairly regularly within the city, especially the smaller **City Imp** buses (every 8-15min.). Dublin Bus runs the **NiteLink** service to the suburbs (Th-Sa night 12:30, 1:30, 2:30, 3:30am; £3/€3.85). **Travel Wide** passes offer unlimited rides for a day or a week. (Day £3.50; week £13/€16.55, students with TravelSave stamp £10/€12.70.) **DART** trains run along the coast and serve the suburbs (every 10-15min. 6:30am-11:30pm, £0.55-1.10/€0.70-1.40).

Taxis: National Radio Cabs, 40 James St. (☎ 677 2222). All 24hr. £2.20/€2.80 plus £0.90/€1.15 per mi.; £0.80/€1 call-in charge.

Car Rental: Budget, 151 Lower Drumcondra Rd. (☎ 837 9611), and at the airport. In summer from £35/€44.45 per day, £165/€209.55 per week; in winter £30/€38.10, £140/€177.80. Minimum age 23.

Bike Rental: Dublin Bike Tours (☎ 679 0899), behind the Kinlay House hostel on Lord Edward St., rents and provides advice on route planning. £10/€12.70 per day, £40/€50.80 per week; students £8/€10.20, £35/€44.45; ID deposit.

■✴ ❼ ORIENTATION AND PRACTICAL INFORMATION

The **River Liffey** is the natural divide between Dublin's North and South Sides. The more famous sights, posh stores, excellent restaurants, and Heuston Station are on the **South Side.** The majority of hostels, the bus station, and Connolly Station sprout up on the **North Side.** The streets running alongside the Liffey are called **quays;** their names change every block. Each bridge over the river also has its own name, and streets change names as they cross. If a street is split into "Upper" and "Lower," then the "Lower" is always the part of the street closer to the mouth of the Liffey. **O'Connell Street,** three blocks west of the Busáras Central Bus Station, is the primary link between north and south Dublin. One block south of the Liffey, **Fleet Street** becomes Temple Bar. **Dame Street** runs parallel to Temple Bar with Trinity College as its terminus, and defines the southern edge of the district. **Trinity College** functions as the nerve center of Dublin's cultural activity, drawing legions of bookshops and student-oriented pubs into its orbit. The North Side bustles with urban grit and hawks merchandise generally cheaper than in the more touristed South Side. **Henry Street** and **Mary Street** comprise a pedestrian shopping zone.

TOURIST, FINANCIAL, AND LOCAL SERVICES

Tourist Information: Main Office, Dublin Tourist Centre, Suffolk St. (☎(1850) 230 330; www.visitdublin.com). Exit Connolly Train Station, walk left down Amiens St., take a right onto Lower Abbey St., and continue until O'Connell St. Turn left, cross the bridge, and go past Trinity College; Suffolk St. is on your right. Open Jan.-June and Aug.-Jan. M-Sa 9am-5:30pm; July-Aug. M-F 8:30am-6:30pm, Sa 9am-5:30pm.

Northern Ireland Tourist Board: 16 Nassau St. (☎679 1977 or (1850) 230 230). Books accommodations in the North. Open M-F 9am-5:30pm, Sa 10am-5pm.

Embassies: Australia, Fitzwilton House, 2nd fl., Wilton Terr. (☎676 1517; fax 678 5185). Open M-Th 8:30am-12:30pm and 1:30-4:30pm, F 9am-noon. **Canada,** 65 St. Stephen's Green South (☎417 4100). Open M-F 9am-1pm and 2-4:30pm. **New Zealand** embassy, London. **South Africa,** Alexandra House, 2nd fl., Earlsfort Centre (☎661 5553). Open M-F 8:30am-5pm. **UK,** 29 Merrion Rd. (☎205 3700). Open M-F 9am-5pm. **US,** 42 Elgin Rd., Ballsbridge (☎668 8777). Open M-F 8:30am-4pm.

Banks: Bank of Ireland, AIB, and **TSB** branches with bureaux de change and **24hr. ATMs** cluster on Lower O'Connell St., Grafton St., and in the Suffolk and Dame St. areas. Most bank branches are open M-F 10am-4pm.

American Express: 43 Nassau St. (☎679 9000). Traveler's check refunds. Currency exchange; no commission for AmEx Traveler's Checks. Mail held. Open M-F 9am-5pm.

Luggage Storage: Connolly Station. £2/€2.55 per item per day. Open M-Sa 7:40am-9:20pm, Su 9:10am-9:45pm. **Heuston Station.** £1.50-3.50/€1.90-4.45 per item. Open daily 6:30am-10:30pm.

Laundry: The Laundry Shop, 191 Parnell St. (☎872 3541). Closest to Busáras and the North Side hostels. Wash and dry £6-8/€7.65-10.20. Open M-F 8am-7pm, Sa 9am-6pm, Su 11am-5pm.

EMERGENCY AND COMMUNICATIONS

Emergency: ☎999 or 112; no coins required.

Police (Garda): Dublin Metro Headquarters, Harcourt Terrace (☎666 9500); Store St. Station (☎666 8000); Fitzgibbon St. Station (☎666 8400).

Pharmacy: O'Connell's, 55 Lower O'Connell St. (☎873 0427). Convenient to city bus routes. Open M-Sa 7:30am-10pm, Su 10am-10pm. Other branches are scattered around the city center, including 2 on Grafton St.

Hospital: St. James's Hospital, James St. (☎453 7941). Served by bus #123. **Mater Misericordiae Hospital,** Eccles St. (☎830 1122), off Lower Dorset St. Served by buses #10, 11, 13, 16, 121, and 122.

Internet Access: Several chains abound, the best being **The Internet Exchange,** with branches at 146 Parnell St. in Temple Bar. (Open daily 9am-10:30pm.)

Post Office: General Post Office (GPO), O'Connell St. (☎705 7000). Dublin is the only city in Ireland with postal codes. Even-numbered postal codes are for areas south of the Liffey, odd-numbered for north. *Poste Restante* pick-up at the bureau de change window. Open M-Sa 8am-8pm, Su 10am-6:30pm. **Postal code:** Dublin 1.

⌂ ACCOMMODATIONS

Dublin's accommodations overflow with visitors, especially during Easter, holidays (including Bank holidays in Ireland *and* England), and summer. Reserve ahead. Dorms range from £7-15/€8.90-19.05 per night. Quality **B&Bs** blanket Dublin and the surrounding suburbs, although prices have risen with housing costs (most charge £16-30/€20.35-38.10 per person); many cluster along **Upper and Lower Gardiner Street,** on **Sherriff Street,** and near **Parnell Square.**

HOSTELS

To deal with the large crowds, Dublin's hostels lean toward the institutional, especially in comparison to their more personable country cousins. The beds south of the river fill up fastest, as they are closest to the city's sights and nightlife.

The Brewery Hostel, 22-23 Thomas St. (☎453 8600). Follow Dame St. past Christ Church through name changes, or take bus #123. Next to the Guinness brewery and a 20min. walk from Temple Bar. Continental breakfast included. Laundry across the street. All rooms with bath. 8-bed dorms £12-13.50/€15.25-17; 4-bed £15-16.50/€19-21; doubles £44-46/€56-58.50.

Globetrotter's Tourist Hostel (IHH), 46-7 Lower Gardiner St. (☎873 5893). A dose of luxury for the weary. Spacious dining area, many lounges, friendly staff, huge and very hip painting of U2. Internet access. Hearty, healthy breakfast included. Towels £0.50/€0.65. Dorms £13-17/€16.50-21.60; singles £47.50-52.50/€60.30-66.70; doubles £70-80/€89-100.

Litton Lane Hostel, 2-4 Litton Ln. (☎872 8389), off Bachelor's Quay. A former recording studio for U2 and Van Morrison. Colorful common areas and spacious dorms offset the brand new industrial kitchen. Continental breakfast included. Towel for nominal fee. Key deposit £2/€2.50. Dorms £10.50-16/€13.50-20.30; doubles £44-52/€56-66.

Abraham House, 82-3 Lower Gardiner St. (☎855 0600). Respectable, tidy rooms. Light breakfast and towels included. 12-bed dorms £10-11/€12.70-14; 4-bed £12.50-16/€16-20.50, with bath £14-18/€18-23.

Barnacle's Temple Bar House, 19 Temple Ln. (☎671 6277). A well-kept hostel in the hopping heart of Dublin—expect noise. Continental breakfast included. 10-bed dorms £12-15/€15.50-19; 4-bed £17-18/€20.50-23; singles £44-58/€56-74; twins and doubles £50-58/€62-74.

Kinlay House (IHH), 2-12 Lord Edward St. (☎679 6644). View Christ Church Cathedral from soft couches in the TV room. Breakfast and hand-towel included. Lockers £0.50/€0.65. Dorms £11-15.50/€14; singles £25/€31.75; doubles £38/€48. Nov.-May prices £1-2.50/€1.30-3.20 less.

Avalon House (IHH), 55 Aungier St. (☎475 0001). Turn off Dame St. onto Great Georges St.; the hostel is a 10min. walk down on your right. A stumble away from Temple Bar. Small breakfast included. Towels £1/€1.30 with £5/€6.35 deposit. Dorms £13.50-15.75/€17-19.50; singles £25-30/€31.75-38; twins £24-27.50/€30.50-35.

Abbey Court Hostel, 29 Bachelor's Walk, O'Connell Bridge (☎878 0700). From O'Connell Bridge, turn left for this emphatic blue and orange addition to the hostel scene. A little pricey, but comfy. Continental breakfast included. 12-bed dorms £13.50-16/€17-20; 6-bed £17.50-19.50/€22-25; 4-bed £20-22/€25-28; doubles £60-70/€76-88.

Jacobs Inn, 21-28 Talbot Pl. (☎855 5660). 2 blocks north of the Customs House, Talbot Pl. stretches from the back of the bus station up to Talbot St. Rooms are spacious, clean, and cheery. Towels £1/€1.30. Laundry £5/€6.35. Lockout 11am-3pm. Dorms £10-13/€12.70-16.50; doubles £44-48/€56-61. Weekend £1/€1.30 more.

Ashfield House, 19-20 D'Olier St. (☎679 7734). Smack dab in the center of Dublin. Light breakfast included. Laundry £4/€5. Mar.-Oct. dorms £11.50-18/€14-23; private rooms £13-14/€16.50-18 per person. Weekend prices £1-2/€1.30-2.50 higher.

Dublin International Youth Hostel (An Óige/HI), 61 Mountjoy St. (☎830 4555). O'Connell St. changes names 3 times before the left turn onto Mountjoy St. This convent-turned-hostel has made giant improvements. A keycard system and lockers beef up security. Breakfast included. Towels £1/€1.30. Laundry £4/€5.10. High season dorms £7.50/€9.55, under 18 £10/€13.50.

BED AND BREAKFASTS

B&Bs with a green shamrock sign out front are registered, occasionally checked, and approved by Bord Fáilte. On the North Side, B&Bs cluster along **Upper** and **Lower Gardiner Street,** on **Sheriff Street,** and near **Parnell Square.**

▨ **Rita and Jim Casey,** Villa Jude, 2 Church Ave. (☎668 4982), off Beach Rd. Bus #3 to the first stop on Tritonville Rd.; Church Ave. is back a few yards. Call for directions from the Lansdowne Rd. DART stop. The best B&B value in Dublin. Clean rooms and big breakfasts. Singles £17.50/€22; doubles £35/€44.44.

Parkway Guest House, 5 Gardiner Pl. (☎874 0469). Rooms are plain but high-ceilinged and tidy, and the location (just off Gardiner St.) is excellent. Singles £25/€30.50; doubles £36-40/€46-51, with shower £44-50/€56-63.50.

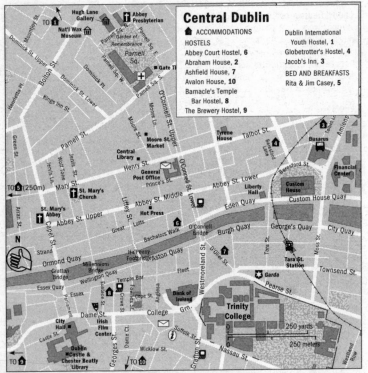

Central Dublin

♠ ACCOMMODATIONS

HOSTELS
Abbey Court Hostel, **6**
Abraham House, **2**
Ashfield House, **7**
Avalon House, **10**
Barnacle's Temple
  Bar Hostel, **8**
The Brewery Hostel, **9**

Dublin International
  Youth Hostel, **1**
Globetrotter's Hostel, **4**
Jacob's Inn, **3**

BED AND BREAKFASTS
Rita & Jim Casey, **5**

The White House, 125 Clontarf Rd. (☎833 3196). Sink into bed and gaze out at rose gardens. Singles £24-25/€30.50-31.75; doubles £44/€56.50, with bath £48/€61.

Mona's B&B, 148 Clonliffe Rd. (☎837 6723). Firm beds in rooms kept tidy by a lovely proprietress who offers homemade bread with her full Irish breakfast. Open May-Oct. Singles £20/€25.40; doubles £40/€50.80.

St. Aidan's B&B, 150 Clonliffe Rd. (☎837 6750). The neighborhood's 1st B&B. Good beds, non-smoking rooms, and friendly owner create a relaxing atmosphere. Breakfast included. Open Apr.-Sept. Singles £20/€25.40; doubles with bath £40/€50.80.

Mrs. Dolores Abbot-Murphy, 14 Castle Park (☎269 8413). Ask the #3 bus driver to drop you off at Sandymount Green. Continue past Browne's Deli and take the 1st left; at the end of the road look right. A 5min. walk from Sandymount DART stop. Singles £25/€31.75; doubles £44/€56.50, with bath £46/€59.

Bayview, 98 Clontarf Rd. (☎833 3950). The Barry family provides fresh, airy rooms and a friendly spot of tea on arrival. Breakfast included. Singles £25-28/€31.75-35.55; doubles with bath £50/€63.50.

Mrs. Geary, 69 Hampton Ct. (☎833 1199). Take bus #130 from Lower Abbey St., and up Vernon Ave. in Clontarf. Ask the bus driver to drop you at Hampton Court, a walled cul-de-sac. Spacious and relaxing. Open Apr.-Sept. Singles £25-27/€31.75-34.30; doubles £38-40/€48-50.80, with bath £43/€54.60.

🍴 FOOD

Dublin's **open-air markets** sell fresh and cheap fixings. On Saturdays, a gourmet open-air market takes place in **Temple Bar** in Meeting House Square. The cheapest **supermarkets** around Dublin are the **Dunnes Stores** chain, with branches at St. Stephen's Green (☎478 0188; open M-W and F-Sa 8:30am-7pm, Th 8:30am-9pm,

Su noon-6pm), the ILAC Centre off Henry St., and on North Earl St. **Temple Bar** is ready to implode from the proliferation of creative eateries catering to all budgets.

⊠ **Cafe Irie,** 11 Fownes St. above the clothing store Sé Sí Progressive. A small eatery with an impressive selection of lip-smackingly good sandwiches under £3/€3.80. Great coffee. A little crunchy, a little jazzy, a whole lotta good. Vegan-friendly. Open M-Sa 9am-8pm, Su noon-5:30pm.

⊠ **Cornucopia,** 19 Wicklow St. This vegetarian horn o' plenty spills huge portions onto your plate. Servers are more than happy to translate organic ingredients. If you can find the space, sit down for a rich meal (about £5/€6.35) or snack (£1.50/€1.90). Open M-W and F-Sa 9am-8pm, Th 9am-9pm.

La Mezza Luna, 1 Temple Ln., on the corner of Dame St. Refined but not pretentious. Celestial food. Try the wok-fried chicken for £7.95/€10. Daily lunch specials around £5/€6.35. Delicious desserts £4/€5. Open M-Th 12:30pm-11pm, F-Sa 12:30-11:30pm, Su 4-10:30pm.

Zaytoons, 14-15 Parliament St. (☎677 3595). Persian food served on big platters of warm bread. A good lunch or a healthy way to satisfy the munchies. Excellent chicken kebab £4.50/€5.70. Open M-Sa noon-4am, Su 1pm-4am.

Yamamori Noodles, 71-72 S. Great Georges St. Exceptional Japanese cuisine, reasonably priced. Entrees for under £10/€12.70; tofu steak £6/€7.60. Open M-W and Su 12:30-11pm, Th-Sa 12:30-11:30pm.

⊙ SIGHTS

Dublin is a walkable city; most of the sights lie less than a mile from O'Connell Bridge. The **Historical Walking Tour** provides a 2hr. crash course in Dublin's history and Irish history, stopping at a variety of Dublin sights. (Meet at Trinity's front gate. ☎878 0227; www.historicalinsights.ie. May-Sept. M-F 11am and 3pm, Sa-Su 11am, noon, and 3pm; Oct.-Apr. F-Su noon. £6/€7.65, students £5/€6.35.)

TRINITY COLLEGE TO ST. STEPHEN'S GREEN. Sprawling at the center of Dublin, **Trinity College** is the *alma mater* of Jonathan Swift, Thomas Moore, Samuel Beckett and Oscar Wilde. The **Old Library,** built in 1712, houses the ⊠**Book of Kells** (c.AD 800), an illuminated four-volume edition of the Gospels; each page holds a dizzingly intricate lattice of Celtic designs interwoven with Latin text. (*Open June-Sept. M-Sa 9:30am-5pm, Su noon-4:30pm; Oct.-May M-Sa 9:30am-5pm, Su noon-4:30pm. £4.50/€5.70, students £4/€5.10.*) The **Trinity College Walking Tour** is run by students and concentrates on University lore. (*☎608 1000. 30min. June-Sept. roughly every 45min. from the information booth inside the front gate. Mar.-May weekends only. £6/€7.60, students £5/€6.35; includes admission to the Old Library and the Book of Kells.*) South of the college, on the block between Kildare St. and Upper Merion Rd., Irish history and culture reign. The **National Museum of Archaeology and History,** on Kildare St., protects the Ardagh Hoard, the Tara Brooch, and other artifacts from the last two millenia. Within the museum, the ⊠**Natural History Museum** in Merion Square West presents a creepy collection, including a skeleton of the ancient Irish Elk, amoeba replicas, and jars of Irish tapeworms. The **National Museum of Decorative Arts and History,** Collins Barracks, Benburb St., explores Irish economic, social, and political history in Europe's oldest military barracks. The **National Gallery,** in Merion Square West has a collection of over 2400 canvases, including paintings by Brueghel, Goya, Caravaggio, Vermeer, Rembrandt, and El Greco. (*The **Museum Link** bus runs from the adjacent Natural History and Archaeology museums to Collins Barracks roughly once an hour. An all-day pass costs £2/€2.50; while one way is £0.85/€1. All open Tu-Sa 10am-5pm, Su 2-5pm. All free.*) Kildare, Dawson and Grafton St. all lead from Trinity to **St. Stephen's Green.** Bequeathed to the city by the Guinness clan, this 9 hectare park boasts arched bridges, a lake, gazebos and a waterfall. On summer days, enjoy outdoor performances near the bandstand. (*Open M-Sa 8am-dusk, Su 10am-dusk.*)

IRELAND

TEMPLE BAR, DUBLIN CASTLE AND THE CATHEDRALS. Between Dame St. and the Liffey, west of Trinity the **Temple Bar** area positively bustles. Narrow neo-cobblestone streets link cheap cafes, hole-in-the-wall theaters, rock venues, as well used clothing and record stores. Next to this hipster scene is **Dublin Castle,** built built in 1204 by King John on top of the first Viking settlement of Dubh Linn; it was the seat of British rule in Ireland for 700 years. (Dame St., at the intersection of Parliament and Castle St. £3/€3.80, students and seniors £2/€2.50. Grounds free.) The body of **St. Patrick's Cathedral** dates to the 12th century, although Sir Benjamin Guinness remodeled greatly in 1864. St. Patrick allegedly baptized converts in the park next door. Jonathan Swift spent his last years as Dean of St. Patrick's; his crypt rises above the south nave. (From Christ Church, Nicholas St. runs south and downhill, eventually becoming Patrick St. Take bus #49, 49A, 50, 54A, 56A, 65, 65B, 77, or 77A from Eden Quay. Open Mar.-Oct. daily 9am-6pm; Nov.-Feb. Sa 9am-5pm and Su 9am-3pm. £2.70/€3.50; students, seniors, and children free.) **Christ Church Cathedral,** like St. Patrick's, is owned by the Church of Ireland, not the Catholic Church. Since the Anglo-Irish aristocracy no longer exists both are considered as works of art rather than places of worship. In the Church's present incarnation, fragments of pillars lie about like bleached bones, and a mummified cat chases a mummified mouse. (At the end of Dame St., uphill and across from the Castle. Take bus #50 from Eden Quay or 78A from Aston Quay. Open daily 9:45am-5:30pm except during services. Donation £2/€2.50. Students £1/€1.30.)

■ **GUINNESS HOPSTORE.** Guinness brews its black magic on Crane St. off James St., and perpetuates the legend of the world's best stout at its Hopstore. Farsighted Arthur Guinness signed a 9000-year lease at the original 1759 brewery nearby. Appreciate the exhibit on Guinness's infamously clever advertising, and then drink, silly tourist, drink. (St. James's Gate. From Christ Church Cathedral, follow High St. west through its name changes—Cornmarket, Thomas, and James. Take bus #51B or 78A from Aston Quay or #123 from O'Connell St. Open Oct.-Mar. 9:30am-5pm; Apr.-Sept. 9:30am-7pm. £9/€11.50, students £6/€7.60, seniors and children £4/€5.10.)

KILMAINHAM GAOL. Almost all of the rebels who fought in Ireland's struggle for independence from 1792 to 1921 spent time here. "The cause for which I die has been rebaptized during this past week by the blood of as good men as ever trod God's earth," wrote Sean MacDiarmada while awaiting execution for participation in the 1916 Easter Rising. Tours wind through the chilly limestone corridors of the prison and end in the haunting atmosphere of Kilmainham's execution yard. (Inchicore Rd. Take bus #51 from Aston Quay, #51A from Lower Abbey St., or #79 from Aston Quay. Open daily Apr.-Sept. 9:30am-4:45pm; Oct.-Mar. M-F 9:30am-4pm and Su 10am-4:45pm. Tours every 35min. £3.50/€4.44, students and children £1.50/€1.90.)

O'CONNELL ST. AND PARNELL SQUARE. This new **James Joyce Cultural Centre** prides itself on Joyceana—feel free to mull over Joyce's works in the library or the tearoom. Call for information on lectures, walking tours, and Bloomsday events. (35 North Great Georges St. Up Marlborough St. and past Parnell St. ☎ 878 8547; joycecen@iol.ie. Open M-Sa 9:30am-5pm, Su 12:30-5pm; July-Aug. extra Su hours 11am-5pm.

DUBLINESE Mastering the Dublin dialect has been a persistent challenge to writers and thespians of the 20th century. The following is a short introduction to Dubliners' favorite phrases. **In Times of Difficulty:** Dublinese is expeditious in keeping others in line. Idiots are rebuked as "eejits;" in dire situations, they are called "head-the-ball." Total exasperation calls for "shite and onions." When all is restored to order, it's said that "the job's oxo and the ship's name is murphy." **Affectionate Nicknames for Civic Landmarks:** Over the past couple decades, the government has graced the city with several public art works that personify the Irish spirit in the female form. Dubliners have responded with poetic rhetoric. Off Grafton St., the statue of the fetching fishmongress Molly Malone is referred to as "the tart with the cart." The goddess of the River Liffey sits in a fountain on O'Connell St. and is popularly heralded as the "floozy in the jacuzzi" and even "the whore in the sewer" (pronounced WHEW-er).

£3/€3.80, students and seniors £2/€2.50.) For a less mentally taxing outing, head over to the ◧**Old Jameson Distillery.** Learn how science, grain, and tradition come together to create the golden fluid called **whiskey.** The experience ends with a glass of the Irish whiskey of your choice; be quick to volunteer in the beginning and you'll get to sample a whole tray of different whiskeys. Feel the burn. *(Bow St. From O'Connell St., turn onto Henry St. and continue straight as the street dwindles to Mary St., then Mary Ln., then May Ln.; the warehouse is on a cobblestone street on the left. ☎807 2355. Tours daily 9:30am-5:30pm. £4.95/€6.30, students and seniors £3/€3.85.)*

🎵🎭 ENTERTAINMENT AND NIGHTLIFE

Be it poetry or punk you fancy, Dublin is equipped to entertain you. The *Event Guide* (free) is available at the tourist office, Temple Bar restaurants, and the Temple Bar information center. Traditional music *(trad)* is an important element of the Irish culture and the Dublin music scene—some pubs in the city center have sessions nightly, others almost every night. **Whelan's** (see Publin, below) is one of the hottest spots in Dublin. Big bands frequent the **Baggot Inn,** 143 Baggot St. (☎676 1430). Part of the National Theater, the **Abbey Theatre,** 26 Lower Abbey St., was founded in 1904 by Yeats and Lady Gregory to promote Irish culture and modernist theater. (☎878 7222. Box office open M-Sa 10:30am-7pm. Tickets £10-17.50/€12.70-22.25, student rate M-Th and Sa matinee £8/€10.20.) Dublin pretty much owns two days of the year. **St. Patrick's Day** (Mar. 17) and the half-week leading up to it host a carnival of concerts, fireworks, street theater, and intoxicated madness. The city returns to 1904 on **Bloomsday** (June 16), the day on which the action of Joyce's *Ulysses* takes place. The **James Joyce Cultural Center** sponsors a reenactment of the funeral and wake, a lunch at Davy Byrne's, and a breakfast with Guinness.

PUBLIN

The Long Stone, 10-11 Townend St. Handcarved banisters and old books give a rustic medieval feel. Lots of interesting rooms, the largest of which has an enormous carving of a bearded man whose mouth serves as a fireplace. Carvery lunches 12:30-2:30pm. Open M-W noon-11:30pm, Th-F 10am-12:30am, Sa 3pm-12:30am, Su 4-11pm.

The Stag's Head, 1 Dame Ct. The beautiful Victorian pub has stained glass, mirrors, and yes, you guessed it, evidence of deer decapitation. The largely student crowd dons everything from T-shirts to tuxes and spills out into the alleys. Excellent grub. Entrees £7/€9. Food served M-F 12:30-3:30pm and 5-7pm, Sa 12:30-2:30pm. Late bar Th-F open until 12:30am. Closed Su.

Whelan's, 25 Wexford St. continue down South Great Georges St. People in the know, know Whelan's. The stage venue in back hosts big-name *trad* and rock, with live music every night from 9:30pm (doors open 8:30pm). Cover £5-8/€6.35-10.20. Open daily 12:30-3:30pm for lunch, open W-Sa late.

The Odeon, Old Harcourt Train Station. The Odeon has a columned façade, and Ireland's second-longest bar (after the one at the Galway races). Everything here is gargantuan. The upstairs is cozier (i.e. still huge). Open Su-W until 12:30am, Th-F 2:30am, Sa 3am.

The Porter House, 16-18 Parliament St. The largest selection of world beers in the country and 8 self-brewed kinds of porter, stout, and ale. An excellent sampler tray includes a sip of stout made with oysters and other oddities (£6/€7.60). Occasional *trad*, blues, and rock. Open F-Sa late.

The Palace, 21 Fleet St. behind Aston Quay. This classic, neighborly pub has old-fashioned wood paneling and close quarters; head for the comfy seats in the skylit back room. The favorite of many a Dubliner.

CLUBLIN

◧**The Kitchen,** The Clarence Hotel, Wellington Quay (☎677 6635), in Temple Bar, through an understated entrance behind the hotel on Essex St. With 2 bars and a dance floor, this U2-owned club is exceptionally well-designed and the hottest spot in town. Impossible to get into on many nights. Dress as a rocker or a model. Cover £5-10/€6.35-12.70, students £1/€1.30 less on W-Th. Cookin' until 2:45am Th-Sa.

Rí-Rá, 1 Exchequer St. Generally good music that steers clear of pop and house extremes. Two floors, several bars, more nooks and crannies than a crumpet, and quite womb-like downstairs. Open daily 11pm-2:30am. Cover £6-7/€7.60-8.90.

PoD, 35 Harcourt St. Spanish-style decor meets hard-core dance music. As trendy as The Kitchen. The truly brave venture upstairs to **The Red Box** (☎478 0225), a separate, more intense club with a warehouse atmosphere. Often hosts big-name DJs—cover charges skyrocket. Cover £8-10/€10.20-12.70; Th ladies free before midnight; Th and Sa £5/€6.35 with ISIC card. Open until 3am. Start the evening at the Chocolate Bar or the Odeon, which share the building (see Publin).

🖎 **The George,** 89 South Great Georges St. This throbbing, purple man o' war is Dublin's 1st and most prominent gay bar. A mixed-age crowd gathers throughout the day to chat and sip. The attached nightclub opens W-Su until 2am. Frequent theme nights. Su night Bingo is accompanied by so much entertainment that sometimes the bingo never happens. Look spiffy—no effort, no entry. Cover £6-8 after 10pm.

The Front Lounge, Parliament St. The velvet seats of this gay-friendly bar are popular with a very mixed, very trendy crowd. Open M and W noon-11:30pm, Tu and Sa noon-12:30am, F noon-1:30am, Su 4pm-11:30pm.

▶ DAYTRIPS FROM DUBLIN

HOWTH. The peninsula of Howth (rhymes with "both") dangles from the mainland in Edenic isolation, less than 15km from Dublin. A three-hour **cliff walk** rings the peninsula, passing heather and thousands of seabird nests. The best section is a hike (1hr.) between the harbor and the lighthouse. To get to the trailhead from town, turn left at the DART station and follow Harbour Rd. around the coast (20min.), or hike from the lighthouse. To reach the private **Howth Castle,** an awkwardly charming patchwork of architectural styles, turn right as you exit the DART station and then left after a quarter-mile, at the entrance to the Deer Park Hotel. Farther up the hill, a path goes around the right side of the hotel to the fabulous **Rhododendron Gardens.** (Open 24hr. Free.) **Ireland's Eye island** once provided monks with religious sanctuary; now it's a bird haven. **Ireland's Eye Boat Trips** (☎831 4200, mobile (087) 267 8211) jets passengers across the water from the east pier (15min.; every 30min. weather permitting; return £5/€6.35, students £3/€3.80, children £2.50/€3.15). To get to Howth, take a northbound DART **train** to the end of the line (30min., 6 per hr., £1.15/€1.25). Turn left out of the station to get to the **tourist office,** in the Old Courthouse on Harbour Rd. (☎832 0405. Open May-Aug. M 11am-1pm, Tu-F 11am-1pm, 1:30-5pm.) Snooze at **Gleann na Smól,** on the left at the end of Nashville Rd., off Thormanby Rd. (☎832 2936. Singles £30/€38.10; doubles £42/€53.35.) Thormanby Rd. houses the main concentration of Howth's **B&Bs.** Bus #31B runs to **Hazelwood** and its comfy beds at the end of the cul-de-sac in the Thormanby Woods estate, 1½km up Thormanby Rd. (☎839 1391. Doubles £60/€76.20.)

BOYNE VALLEY. Along the curves of the river between Slane and Drogheda lie 40 cryptic passage-tombs constructed by Neolithic people around the 4th millenium BC. The tombs, including **Newgrange, Dowth,** and **Knowth,** are archaeological mysteries, although recent excavations are providing clues as to who exactly was interred within their 80-ton rocks. Entrance to Knowth and Newgrange is granted only by paying admission at the 🖎**Brú na Bóinne Visitor Centre,** near Donore on the south side of the River Boyne, across from the tombs. Prepare to wait. (☎(041) 988 0300. Open daily Mar.-Apr. 9:30am-5:30pm; May 9am-6:30pm; June to mid-Sept. 9am-7pm; late Sept. 9am-6:30pm; Oct. 9:30am-5:30pm; Nov.-Feb. 9:30am-5pm. Center and Newgrange tour £4/€5.10, students £3/€3.80; center only £3/€3.80, students £2/€2.55.) **Bus Éireann** shuttles to the Visitor Centre from Dublin (1½hr.; M-Sa every 15 min., Su every hour; £10/€12.70 return). The **Hill of Tara** was Ireland's spiritual and political center until the arrival of Christianity in the 4th century BC. Take any local bus to Navan and ask the driver to let you off at the road 1km from the site (45min., 37 per day, £5.50/€7). Mel Gibson filmed scenes for *Braveheart* in the town of Trim at **Trim Castle,** built in 1172. You may take the tour, but you'll never take his freedom. (Open daily May-Oct. 10am-6pm. Keep tours limited to 15 people. Every 45min, 40min. No tour required to wander the grounds. Tour and grounds £2.50/€3.20, students £1/€1.30; grounds only £1/€1.30.) **Bus Éireann** stops in front of the castle en route to **Dublin** (1hr.; M-Sa roughly 1 per hr., Su 3 per day; £8/€10.15). The **tourist office** is on Mill St. (☎(046) 37111. Open daily 10am-1pm and 1:30-5:30pm.)

SOUTHEAST IRELAND

Historically the power base of the Vikings and then the Normans, the influence of the Celts is felt most faintly in southeast Ireland. While the nightlife rages south from Dublin through Kilkenny and Waterford, the daylight hours are most enjoyably spent exploring the beaches between Rosslare Harbour and Waterford, or traversing the scenic paths through Glendalough and the Wicklow Mountains.

⚓ FERRIES TO FRANCE AND BRITAIN

Irish Ferries sails from Rosslare Harbour to: Pembroke, Wales (4hr.); Roscoff, France (18hr.); and Cherbourg, France (19hr.). Ferries depart daily for Wales and every other day to France. For information, call the Irish Ferries after-hours line at ☎(08705) 171 717 or the desk at Rosslare Harbour (☎(053) 33158. www.irishferries.com. Foot passenger fares to Britain £18-22/€22.90-27.95. "Low" fares to France roughly £35-45/€45-57. **Eurail passes** grant passage on ferries to France). **Stena Line** (☎(053) 331150) runs from Rosslare to Fishguard (3½hr., 2 per day, £18-22/€22.90-27.95; with current ISIC £13-18/€16.55-22.90).

THE WICKLOW MOUNTAINS. Over 600m high, carpeted in fragrant heather and pleated by sparkling rivers, the Wicklow summits are home to grazing sheep and scattered villagers. Smooth glacial valleys embrace the two lakes and the monastic ruins. Public transportation is severely limited, so driving is the easiest way to connect the sights and towns. The lush valley of **Glendalough** draws a steady summertime stream of coach tours filled with hikers and ruin-seekers. **St. Kevin's Bus Service** (☎(01) 281 8119) runs from St. Stephen's Green West in Dublin (2 per day; £6/€7.65, return £10/€12.70) and leaves in the evening (2-3 per day). The **tourist office** is across from the Glendalough Hotel. (☎(0404) 45688. Open mid-June to Sept. M-Sa 10am-6pm; closed 1-2pm for lunch.) The **National Park Information Office,** between the two lakes, is the best source for hiking advice. (☎(0404) 45425. Open May-Aug. daily 10am-6pm; Apr. and Sept. Sa-Su 10am-6pm.) The **Glendaloch Hostel (An Óige/HI)** is 5 min. past the Glendalough tourist office. (☎(0404) 45342. **Internet.** Bike rental £10/€12.70 per day. Laundry £4/€5.10. Dorms £13/€16.55; doubles £32/€40.65; offseason £1-2/€1.30-2.55 less.) For affordable food and B&Bs, head to **Laragh** (LAR-a), 1½km up the road (10min. from the Wicklow Way). ☎**0404.**

ROSSLARE HARBOUR. Rosslare Harbour is a decidedly pragmatic seaside village that mainly functions as an important transportation link to Wales, France, and the Irish coast. **Trains** run from the ferry port to Dublin (3hr., 3 per day, £11/€14) and Limerick (2½hr., 1-2 per day, £12.50/€15.90), via Waterford (1¼hr., £6/€7.65). **Buses** run to Dublin (3hr., 10-12 per day, £10/€12.70); Cork (3-5 per day, £13.50/€17.15) and Galway (4 per day, £17/€21.60), both via Waterford (3-5 per day, £9.20/€11.70); Limerick (3-5 per day, £13.50/€17.15); and Tralee (2-4 per day, £17//€21.60). The Rosslare-Kilrane **tourist information centre** is 1½km from the harbor on Wexford Rd in Kilrane. (☎33622. Open daily 10:30am-8pm.) If you must stay overnight before catching a ferry, try ◪**Mrs. O'Leary's Farmhouse,** Killilane (☎33134), off N25 in Kilrane, a 15min. drive from town on farm, right by the sea. Call for pickup from town. Single £18.15/€23, with bath £20.10/€25.50. ☎**053**

KILKENNY. Ireland's best-preserved medieval town, Kilkenny evokes a bygone era with its 80 pubs and nine churches. Thirteenth-century **Kilkenny Castle,** restored to its former opulence, housed the Earls of Ormonde from the 1300s until 1935. (Open June-Sept. daily 10am-7pm; Oct.-Mar. Tu-Sa 10:30am-12:45pm and 2-5pm, Su 11am-12:45pm and 2-5pm; Apr.-May daily 10:30am-5pm. Mandatory guided tour. £3.50/€4.45, students £1.50/€1.90.) **Tynan Walking Tours** provides the down-and-dirty on Kilkenny's folkloric tradition in an hour. (☎65929. £3.50/€4.45, students and seniors £3/€3.80.) Climb the thin, 30m tower of **St. Canice's Cathedral,** up the hill off Dean St., for a panoramic view of the town. (Open Easter-Sept. M-Sa 9am-1pm and 2-6pm, Su 2-6pm; Oct.-Easter M-Sa 10am-1pm and 2-4pm, Su 2-4pm. £1.50/€1.90.) **Trains** (☎220 24) and **buses** (☎649 33) stop at Kilkenny MacDonagh Station on Dublin Rd.; buses also stop on Patrick St. in the city center. Trains go to Dublin (2hr., £12.50/€15.90) and Waterford (45min., £5.50/€7). Buses go to Cork (3hr., 2-3 per day, £10/€12.70); Dublin (2hr., 5-6 per day, £7/€8.90); Galway (5hr., 3-5 per day, £17/€21.60); Rosslare Harbour (2hr., 3-6 per day, £10.50/€13.35); and Waterford (1½hr., 1-2 per day, £5/€6.35). From MacDonagh Station, turn left on John St. to reach The Parade, dominated by the castle on the left. The **tourist office,** Rose Inn St., has information on **B&Bs.** (☎51500. Open July-Aug. M-Sa 9am-7pm, Su 11am-1pm and 2-5pm; Apr.-June and Sept. M-Sa 9am-6pm, Su 11am-1pm and 2-5pm; Oct.-Mar. M-Sa 9am-5pm.) **Kilkenny Tourist Hostel (IHH),** 35 Parliament St., is always buzzing with activity. (☎63541. Laundry £3/€3.80. Check-out 10am. Dorms £10-11.50/€14.50-12.70. Doubles £13/€16.50.) **Dunnes Supermarket,** Kieran St., has groceries. (Open M-Tu Sa 8:30am-7pm, W-F 8:30am-10pm, Su 10am-6pm.) **The Pump House,** 26 Parliament St. is a favorite among locals and hostelers. ☎**056.**

WATERFORD. Behind an industrial façade of metal silos and cranes lie winding, narrow streets with pubs and shops. The town highlight is the ◙**Waterford Crystal Factory,** 1½km away on the N25 (Cork Rd.). Tours (1hr, every 15min.) show the transformation of molten goo into polished crystal. Catch bus #1 (dir. Kilbarry-Ballybeg; 2 per hr., £0.85/€1.10) across from the Clock Tower. (☎373 311. Gallery open Mar-Dec. daily 8:30am-6pm; Jan. M-F 9-5pm; Feb. daily 9am-5pm. Tours Jan.-Feb. M-F 9am-3:15pm, Mar.-Oct. daily 8:30am-4pm, Nov.-Dec. M-F 9am-5:15pm. Tours £4.50/€5.75.) **Reginald's Tower,** at the end of the Quay, has guarded city's entrance since the 12th century. (☎873 501. Open daily June-Sept. 9:30am-6:30pm; Oct.-May daily 10am-5pm. £1.50/€1.90, students £0.60/€0.80.)

Trains (☎876 243) leave from across the bridge from the Quay; the bus station (☎879 000) is on the Quay by the bridge. Trains run to: Dublin (2½hr., 5-6 per day, £13.50-17/€17.15-21.60); Kilkenny (40min., 3-5 per day, £5.50/€7); Limerick (2¼hr., M-Sa 2 per day, £10.50/€13.35); and Rosslare Harbour (1hr., M-Sa 2 per day, £6.50/€8.25). **Buses** depart for: Cork (2½hr., 10-13 per day, £10/€12.70); Dublin (2¾hr., 6-12 per day, £7/€8.90); Galway (4¾hr., 5-6 per day, £13.50/€17.15); Kilkenny (1hr., M-Su 1 per day, £5/€6.35); Limerick (2½hr., 6 -7 per day, £10.50/€13.35); and Rosslare Harbour (1¼hr., 3-5 per day, £9.20/€11.70). The **tourist office** is in the Granary at the intersection of the Quay and Hanover St. (☎875 788. Open July-Aug. M-Sa 9am-6pm, Su 11am-5pm; Sept.-Oct. M-Sa 9am-6pm; Nov.-Mar. M-Sa 9am-5pm; Apr.-June M-Sa 9am-6pm.) All of Waterford's hostels have gone the way of the dodo, but Mrs. Ryan, the owner of **Beechwood,** 7 Cathedral Sq. will invite you into her charming home. On a silent pedestrian street, her B&B is up Henrietta St. from the quay. (☎876 677. Doubles £32/€40.60.) Get **groceries** at **Treacy's,** on the Quay near the Granville Hotel. (Open daily 8am-11pm.) Pubs cluster on the Quays, John St. and Parnell St. ☎**051.**

CASHEL. Cashel sprawls at the foot of the commanding 90m ◙**Rock of Cashel** (a.k.a. **St. Patrick's Rock**), a huge limestone outcropping topped by medieval buildings. (Open mid-June to mid-Sept. daily 9am-7:30pm; mid-Sept. to mid-Mar. daily 9:30am-4:30pm; mid-Mar. to mid-June 9:30am-5:30pm. £3.50/€4.45, students £1.80/€2.30.) The two-towered **Cormac's Chapel,** consecrated in 1134, holds semi-restored Romanesque paintings. Down the cow path from the Rock lie the ruins of **Hore Abbey,** built by Cistercian monks who were fond of arches; the abbey is presently inhabited by nonchalant sheep. **Bus Éireann** (☎62121) leaves from Bianconi's Bistro, on Main St., for: Cork (1½hr., 6 per day, £9.60/€12.20); Dublin (3hr., 6 per day, £12/€15.25); and Limerick (1hr., 5 per day, £9.20/€11.75). The **tourist office** is in the City Hall on Main St. (☎61333. Open July-Aug. M-Sa 9:15am-6pm, Su 11am-5pm; Apr.-June and Sept. M-Sa 9:15am-6pm.) Just down Dundrum Rd. from town lies the stunning **O'Brien's Farmhouse Hostel.** (☎61003. Laundry £6/€7.60. Dorms £9-10/€11.50-12.70; doubles £30/€38.10. **Camping** £4.50-5/€5.70-6.35.) Just steps from the Rock on Dominic St., the quaint **Rockville House** is a bargain (☎61760. Singles £25/€31.75; doubles £38/€48.25; triples £57/€72.40.) **Centra Supermarket** is on Friar St. (Open daily 7am-11pm.) *Craic* goes nightly at **Feehan's,** Main St. ☎**062.**

SOUTHWEST IRELAND

An astonishing landscape, from ocean-battered cliffs to mystic stretches of lakes and mountains, is matched by a momentous history. Outlaws and rebels once lurked in the Southwest's hidden coves and glens. To escape the West's tourist mayhem, retreat to quieter stretches along the Dingle Peninsula and Cork's southern coast.

☷ FERRIES TO FRANCE AND BRITAIN

Cork-Swansea Ferries (☎(021) 271 166; www.swansea-cork.ie) go between Cork and Swansea, South Wales (10hr., 1 per day, £24-34/€30.50-43); car and driver £89-159/€113-200). **Brittany Ferries** sail from **Cork** to **Roscoff, France** (13½hr.).

CORK CITY   ☎021

Cork (pop. 150,000), Ireland's second-largest city, serves as the center of the southwest's sport, music, and arts scenes. Despite a tumultuous, razed-and-rebuilt history, Cork has regularly refashioned itself. Today a stroll along its pub-lined streets reveals grand architecture juxtaposed with many new commercial and industrial developments. Use Cork as a place to eat, drink, shop, and sleep while exploring the exquisite scenery of the surrounding countryside.

▐▞ TRANSPORTATION AND PRACTICAL INFORMATION. Trains (☎450 6766) leave from Kent Station, Lower Glanmire Rd. across the river for: Dublin (3hr., £33.50/€43.55); Killarney (2hr., £14/€17.80); and Limerick (1½hr., £14/€17.80). **Buses** (☎450 8188) depart from Parnell Pl., along Merchants' Quay, to: Dublin (4½hr., £13/€16.55); Belfast (7½hr., £20/€25.40); and Rosslare Harbor (4hr., £13.50/€17.15). **Brittany Ferries** (☎427 7801) arranges ferry service to Roscoff, France from Ringaskiddy Terminal (☎427 5061), eight miles south of the city (bus available every 30min., £3/€3.85). **Cork-Swansea Ferries** (☎427 1166; UK ☎(0044) 1254 692899) connects to England. Pick up a map and sights guide (£1.50/€1.90) at **Tourist House,** Grand Parade. (☎427 3251. Open July-Aug. M-Sa 9:15am-5:30pm.) Get thirty minutes online for £1 **The Cork City Library,** across from the tourist office on the Grand Parade. (☎427 7110. Open Tu-Sa 10am-1pm and 2-5:30pm. Computers off at 5pm.)

▐▐ ACCOMMODATIONS AND FOOD. Sheila's Budget Accommodation Centre (IHH), 4 Belgrave Pl., by the intersection of Wellington Rd. and York St., lures visitors with a huge kitchen and a sauna. (☎450 5562. Breakfast £1.50. Internet £2 per 20min. Reception 24hr. Dorms £9-10/€11.45-12.70; doubles £24/€30.50.) **Cork City International Hostel, An Oige (HI)** is in a stately Victorian house at 1-2 Redclyffe, Western Rd. Take bus #8, which stops across the street, or walk 15 minutes from Grand Parade. (☎454 3289. Breakfast £2/€2.55. Reception 8am-midnight. Dorms £8-11.50/€10.20-14.60; doubles £28/€35.55.) Prepare to be pampered at the B&B **Riverbank House,** Washington St. Ask for the yellow room. (☎427 8458. Singles from £25/€31.75; doubles from £40/€50.80.) Restaurants and cafes cluster near the city center, especially between **Patrick Street, Paul Street,** and **Oliver Plunkett Street.** The biggest grocery store in town is **Tesco Supermarket** on Paul St. (Open M-W and Sa

IRELAND

8:30am-8pm, Th-F 8:30am-10pm.) The burgers, pizza, and grilled chicken at ◨**Scoozi,** in the alley just off Winthrop Ave., will drive you wild. (Open M-Sa 9am-11pm, Su noon-10pm.) Scrumptious vegetarian delights await at the **Quay Co-op,** 24 Sullivan's Quay. (Restaurant open M-Sa 9am-9pm; store open 9am-6:15pm.)

◙ **SIGHTS.** Downtown Cork is located on the tip of an arrow-shaped island in the River Lee; bridges link the island to Cork's residential south side and less affluent north side. Across the river to the north, walk up Shandon St. and take a right down unmarked Church St. to reach Cork's most famous landmark, **St. Ann's Church.** Climb claustrophobic stairs for a panoramic view or stay below to ring out your favorite melody on the bells (☎ 450 5906. Open M-Sa 9:30am-5:30pm. ₤5/€6.35, students and seniors ₤4/€5.10.) Do not pass go before heading to the **Cork City Gaol,** where multimedia tours of the former prison and a walk through Cork's social history await; cross the bridge at the western end of Fitzgerald Park, turn right on Sunday's Well Rd., and follow the signs. (☎ 430 5022. Open daily Mar.-Oct. 9:30am-6pm; Nov.-Feb. 10am-5pm. ₤4.50/€5.75, students ₤3/€3.85; includes audio-tape tour.) After visiting the jail, taste liberty by wandering the grounds of the nearby **University College Cork,** on the riverbank along Western Rd.

◨◨ **ENTERTAINMENT AND NIGHTLIFE.** Three festivals come to Cork every October. The **Guiness Cork Jazz Festival** brings three days of free performances by big-name musicians in October (☎ 427 8979). Book well ahead at hostels. Also popular are the week-long **International Film Festival** and **The Irish Gay and Lesbian Film Festival.** Cork proudly produces both Murphy's and Beamish, which are stocked in the myriad pubs along **Oliver Plunkett Street, Union Quay,** and **South Main Street.** A traditional pub is **An Spailpín Fánac,** at 28 South Main St. **The Lobby,** 1 Union Quay, arguably Cork's most famous venue, gave some of Ireland's biggest folk acts their big breaks; it features live music nightly. (Occasional cover ₤2-5/€2.55-6.35.) **The Western Star,** Western Rd. (a 25min. walk from the town center), lures a huge student crowd with its outdoor patio and free Friday and Saturday barbecues. **Gallaghers,** MacCurtain St., holds backpacker nights on Mondays and Tuesdays (3-pint pitchers ₤6/€7.65). **Loafer's,** 26 Douglas St., is Cork's sole gay and lesbian pub. When the pubs close, the spotlight shifts to Cork's nightclubs. **Gorbys,** Oliver Plunkett St., features young groovers grinding. (Open W-Sa. Cover ₤2-5/€2.55-6.35.) **Sir Henry's,** South Main St., packs three floors with sweaty bodies. (Open W-Sa. Cover ₤2-11/ €2.55-14.)

◪ **DAYTRIP FROM CORK CITY: BLARNEY.** Busloads of tourists eager for quintessential Irish scenery and a cold kiss head northwest of Cork to see **Blarney Castle** and its legendary **Blarney Stone,** which confers the gift of gab upon those who smooch it while leaning over backwards. While crowds awaiting this opportunity clog the dank passageways, the top of the castle provides an airy and stunning view of the countryside. Try to come early in the morning. (☎ 438 5252. Open June-Aug. 9am-7pm, Su 9:30am-5:30pm; Sept. M-Sa 9am-6:30pm, Su 9:30am-dusk; Oct.-Apr. M-Sa 9am-6pm or dusk, Su 9:30am-5pm or dusk; May M-Sa 9am-6:30pm, Su 9:30am-5:30pm. ₤3.50/€4.45, seniors and students ₤2.50/€3.20, children ₤1/€1.30.)

KINSALE. Affluent tourists come to swim, fish, and eat at Kinsale's famed and pricey 12 restaurants known as the "Good Food Circle." The attractions are cheaper. The star-shaped, 17th-century **Charles Fort** overlooks the town; follow the coastal (ministry of) **Scilly Walk** (30min.) from the end of Pearse St. (Open mid-Mar. to Oct., M-F 10am-6pm; Nov. to mid-Mar. Sa-Su 10am-5pm, weekdays by appointment; ₤2.50/€3.20, students ₤1/€1.30.) Across the harbor, the grass-covered ruins of **James Fort** delight with panoramic views of Kinsale. (Open 24hr. Free.) August's **Kinsale Regatta** and the **Kinsale Gourmet Festival** are pleasant outdoor diversions. **Buses** arrive from **Cork** at the Esso station on the pier (40min., 5 per day, ₤6/€7.65 return). The **tourist office,** Emmet Pl., is on the waterfront. (☎ 477 2234. Open daily Mar.-Nov. M-Sa 9am-6pm.) To reach the **Castlepark Marina Centre (IHH),** walk along the pier away from town (10min.) turn left across Duggan Bridge, take a left past the bridge, and follow the road toward the harbor. (☎477 4959. Open mid-Mar. to Dec. Dorms £10/€12/70; doubles £24/€30.50.) **Dempsey's Hostel (IHH)** is on Cork Rd. (☎772124. Dorms £7/€8.90; doubles £18/€22.90.)

SCHULL AND THE MIZEN HEAD PENINSULA ☎028

The seaside hamlet of **Schull** is an ideal base for exploring the craggy, windswept, and beach-laden southwest tip of Ireland. A calm harbor and numerous shipwrecks make a **diving** paradise; the **Watersports Centre** rents gear. (☎28554. Open M-Sa 9:30am-8:30pm.) Pick up the lengthy *Schull Guide* (£1.50/€1.90) from any store in town. The Mizen becomes more scenic and less populated the farther west you go from Schull. **Betty Johnson's Bus Hire** offers tours of the Mizen via the scenic coast road. (☎28410. Departs June-Aug. Tu and Th 11am. £6/€7.65.) In summer, Schull is also a jumping-off point to ferry to the striking island of **Cape Clear**. (☎28278. Jun.-Sept. 1-3 ferries per day, return £9/€11.45.) **Buses** arrive in Schull from Cork (1-3 per day, £13/€16.55) and Killarney (June-Sept. 1 per day). Once you've reached Schull, there's no further public transportation on the peninsula besides a Bus Éireann bus to Goleen (2 per day). Those who choose to accept the risks of **hitching** often avoid poor public transportation by waiting at the crossroads on Goleen Rd. outside of town. *Let's Go* does not recommend hitchhiking. Confident **cyclists** can daytrip to Mizen Head (29km from Schull). The immaculate **Schull Backpackers' Lodge (IHH)**, Colla Rd., has **hiking** and **biking** maps. (☎28681. Dorms £8/€10.20; doubles £24-26/€30.50-33.05.) **Spar Market** is on Main St. (Open July-Sept. daily 7am-9pm; Oct.-June M-Sa 7am-8pm, Su 8am-8pm.)

KILLARNEY AND KILLARNEY NATIONAL PARK ☎064

The town of Killarney is just minutes from some of Ireland's most glorious natural scenery. The 95 sq. km **national park** outside town blends forested mountains with the famous Lakes of Killarney. **Muckross House,** 5km south of Killarney on Kenmare Rd., is a massive 19th-century manor with a garden that blooms brilliantly each year. (House open July-Aug. daily 9am-7pm; Sept.-Oct. and mid-Mar. to June daily 9am-6pm. £3.80/€4.85, students £1.60/€2.05.) A path leads to the 20m high **Torc Waterfall.** Walk or drive to the 14th-century **Ross Castle** by taking a right on Ross Rd. off Muckross Rd., 3km from Killarney; the numerous footpaths from Knockreer (out of town on New St.) are more scenic. (Open daily June-Aug. 9am-6:30pm; May-Sept. 10am-6pm; mid-Mar. to Apr. and Oct. 10am-5pm. Obligatory tour £3/€3.85, students £1.25/€1.60.) Bike around the **Gap of Dunloe,** which borders **Macgillycuddy's Reeks,** Ireland's highest mountain range. Hop on a **boat** from Ross Castle to the head of the Gap (£8/€10.20; book at the tourist office). From Lord Brandon's Cottage, on the Gap, head left over the stone bridge from continue 3km to the church, follow the hairpin turn, and huff the 2km to the top; your reward is an 11km coast downhill through the park's most breathtaking scenery. The 13km ride to Killarney (bear right after Kate Kearney's Cottage, turn left on the road to Fossa, and turn right on Killorglin Rd.) passes the ruins of **Dunloe Castle,** demolished by Cromwell's armies.

Trains arrive at Killarney station (☎31067) off East Avenue Rd., near Park Rd., from: Cork (2hr., 5 per day, return £14/€17.80); Dublin (3½hr., 4 per day, £35.50/€45.10); and Limerick (3hr., 3-4 per day, £15.50/€19.70). **Buses** (☎30011) rumble from Park Rd. to Cork (2hr., 10-14 per day, £9.40/€11.95) and Dublin (6hr, 5-6 per day, £15/€19.05). **Bike rental** places abound; expect to pay around £7/€8.90. The **tourist office** is on Beech St., off New St. (☎31633. Open July-Aug. M-Sa 9am-8pm, Su 10am-1pm and 2:15-6pm; June and Sept. M-Sa 9am-6pm, Su 10am-1pm and 2:15-6pm; Oct.-May M-Sa 9:15am-5:30pm.) From either station, turn left on College St. and turn right past the courthouse to reach **The Súgán (IHH),** Lewis Rd., where exuberant management compensates for cramped quarters. (☎33104. Dorms £9/€11.45.) The immense **Neptune's (IHH),** Bishop's Ln., is up the first walkway off New St. on the right. (☎35255. Dorms £7.50-10/€9.55-12.70; doubles £26/€33.05.) Call for a ride from the either station to ■**Peacock Farms Hostel (IHH),** 11km from town. (☎33577. Dorms £10-12/€12.70-15.25; doubles £28/€35.55.) Pick up **groceries** at

Tesco, in an arcade off New St. (Open M-W and Sa 8:30am-7pm, Th-F 8:30am-9pm.)
O'Conner's Traditional Pub, 7 High St., mixes locals and tourists. (*Trad* M and Th.)

RING OF KERRY

The Southwest's most beloved peninsula holds wee villages, ancient forts, and rugged mountains. Rewards await those who explore the landscape on foot or by bike.

▐ TRANSPORTATION. The term "Ring of Kerry" usually describes the entire **Iveragh Peninsula,** although it more technically refers to the ring of roads circumnavigating it. Hop on the no-frills circuit run by **Bus Éireann,** which stops at the Ring's major towns (June-Sept. 2 per day): Cahersiveen (from Killorglin 50min., £5/€6.35); Caherdaniel (from Cahersiveen 1hr., £3.10/€3.90); and Killarney (from Caherdaniel 1½hr., £7.30/€9.30; from Cahersiveen 2½hr., £9/€11.50).

CAHERSIVEEN. Cahersiveen (CARS-veen) is known as the birthplace of patriot Daniel "The Liberator" O'Connell, who won Catholic representation in Parliament in 1829. Two miles northwest of town are the ruins of the **Ballycarbery Castle,** once held by O'Connell's ancestors. Past the castle turnoff, you can walk along the 3m-thick walls of **Cahergall Fort** or visit the small stone dwellings of **Leacanabuaile Fort.** The **Celtic Music Weekend** features free concerts in early August. The **tourist office** is directly across from the bus stop next to the post office. (☎(066) 947 2589. Open June to mid-Sept. M-Sa 9:15am-1pm and 2:15-5:30pm.) The welcoming **Sive Hostel (IHH)** is at 15 East End, Main St. (☎(066) 947 2717. Dorms £8/€01.20; doubles £20-25/€25.40-31.75. **Camping** £4/€5.10 per person.) Next to the post office, **O'Shea's B&B** boasts comfortable rooms. (☎(066) 947 2402. Singles £23/€29.20.) The town's 30 pubs may seem excessive, but residents remember when there were 52.

Take a daytrip to quiet **Valentia Island,** where shady country roads link a handful of beehive huts, *ogham* stones, and small ruins. The views over Dingle Bay are reason enough to come to Ireland. Bridges on either end connect to the mainland for an easy **bike** ride; alternatively, a comically short **ferry** runs to the island (3min., every 10min. Apr.-Sept. 8:15am-7:30pm; pedestrians £3/€3.85, cyclists £1.50/€1.90) from **Reenard Point,** 5km west of Cahersiveen. A taxi to the ferry dock from Cahersiveen runs £4/€5.10. Don't miss the **Skellig Rocks,** a stunning mass of natural rubble about 13km off the shore of the Iveragh Peninsula. From your boat, **Little Skellig** will appear snow-capped, but it's actually covered with 24,000 crooning birds. Climb the 650 steps past puffins, kittiwakes, gannets, and petrels to reach a **monastery** built by 6th-century monks, whose beehive-like dwellings are still intact. The hostel and campground in Cahersiveen will arrange the **ferry** ride (45-90min.) for £25/€31.75, including a ride to the dock. ☎**066.**

CAHERDANIEL. There's little in the village of **Caherdaniel** to attract the Ring's droves of buses, but nearby **Derrynane Strand,** 2½km away in Derrynane National Park, delights with 3km of gorgeous beach ringed by picture-perfect dunes. **Derrynane House,** signposted just up from the beach, was the residence of Irish patriot Daniel O'Connell. (Open May-Sept. M-Sa 9am-6pm, Su 11am-7pm; Apr. and Oct. Tu-Su 1-5pm; Nov.-Mar. Sa-Su 1-5pm. £2/€2.55, students £1/€1.30.) Guests have the run of the house at **The Travellers' Rest Hostel.** (☎(066) 947 5175. Breakfast £3/€3.85. Dorms £8.50/€10.80; singles £10.50-13/€13.35-16.55; doubles £21-26.70.)

DINGLE PENINSULA   ☎**066**

For decades the Ring of Kerry's undertouristed counterpart, the gorgeous Dingle Peninsula, with spectacular cliffs and sweeping beaches, has remained more congested with ancient sites than tour buses. A *gaeltacht* to the west of Dingle Town preserves centuries-old Irish heritage preserved by generations of storytellers.

▐ TRANSPORTATION. The best base for exploring the peninsula is Dingle Town, most easily reached by **Bus Éirann** from Tralee (1¼hr., 3-6 per day, £6.20/€7.90).

Other routes run to: Ballydavid (Tu and F 3 per day, £3.15/€4 return); Ballyferriter (M and Th 3 per day, £2.50/€3.20); and Dunquin (1-5 per day, £2.45/€3.15). In summer, additional buses also run along the south of the peninsula from Dingle (June-Sept. M-Sa 2 per day).

DINGLE TOWN. Lively Dingle Town, adopted home of **Fungi the Dolphin** (now a major focus of the tourist industry), serves as a good regional base. **Sciúird Archaeology tours** take you from the pier on a 3hr. whirlwind bus tour of the area's ancient spots. (☎ (066) 915 1606. 2 per day, £9/€11.45. Book ahead.) **Moran's Tours** runs great trips to Slea Head that stop by historical sites, film sets and majestic views. (☎ (066) 915 1155. 2 per day, £8/€10.20. Book ahead) The **tourist office** is on Strand St. (☎ (066) 915 1188. Open July-Aug. M-Sa 9am-7pm, Su 10am-5pm; Sept.-Oct. and mid-Mar. to June M-Sa 9am-6pm, Su 10am-5pm.) **◪Ballintaggart Hostel (IHH),** 25min. east on Tralee Rd. in a stone mansion, is supposedly haunted by the Earl of Cork's wife, whom he strangled here. (☎ (066) 915 1454. Free shuttle to town. Dorms £9-11; doubles £30/€38.10. **Camping** £8/€10.20.) The laid-back **Grapevine Hostel** is on Dykegate St., off Main St. (☎ (066) 915 1434. Dorms £8.50-10.50/€10.80-13.35.) From Dingle Town, a winding cliff-side road runs north by the 450m **Connor Pass.** As the road twists downhill, a waterfall marks the base of **Pedlars Lake.**

SLEA HEAD AND DUNQUIN. Glorious Slea Head impresses with its jagged cliffs and crashing waves. Green hills, interrupted by rough stone walls and occasional sheep, suddenly break off into the foam-flecked sea. The best way to see the area in a day or less is to bike along **Slea Head Drive.** Past Dingle Town toward Slea Head sits the village of **Ventry** (Ceann Trá), home to a sandy beach and the huge beds of the **◪Ballybeag Hostel;** a regular shuttle runs to Dingle Town. (☎ 915 9876; balybeag@iol.ie. Bike rental. Laundry. Dorms £11/€14.) The **◪Celtic and Prehistoric Museum,** down the road, houses an astounding, eclectic collection. (☎ 915 9941. Open Apr.-Oct. daily 10am-5pm, other times call ahead. £3/€3.85.) North of Slea Head, the scattered settlement of **Dunquin** (Dún Chaoin) boasts **Kruger's,** purportedly Europe's westernmost pub. Entrees around £6-8/€7.65-10.20.) On the road to Ballyferriter, the **Blasket Centre** has outstanding exhibits about the isolated Blasket Islands. (Open daily July-Aug. 10am-7pm; Easter-June and Sept.-Nov. 10am-6pm. £2.50, students £1.) **An Óige Hostel (HI)** is across from the turnoff to the Blasket Centre. (☎ 915 6121. Dorms £7.50-9/€9.55-11.45; doubles £20/€25.40.)

TRALEE. Residents proudly identify Tralee (pop. 20,000) as County Kerry's economic center and home to famed gardens. Ireland's second-largest museum, **◪Kerry the Kingdom,** Ashe Memorial Hall, Denny St., covers Irish history from 8000 BC to the present. (Open daily Mar.-Oct. 10am-6pm; Nov.-Dec. noon-4:30pm. £6/€7.65, students £4.75/€6.05.) In late August, the renowned **Rose of Tralee Festival** brings a maelstrom of entertainment to town as lovely lasses compete for the title "Rose of Tralee." **Trains** go from the Oakpark Rd. station to: Cork (2½hr., 3-4 per day, £18/ €22.90); Galway (5-6hr., 3 per day, £35.50/€45.10); and Killarney (40min., 4 per day, £5.50/€7). **Buses** rumble from Oakpark Rd. to: Cork (2½hr., 10-14 per day, £10/ €12.70); Galway (5-6hr., 9-11 per day, £13/€16.55); Killarney (40min., 5-14 per day, £4.60/€5.85); and Limerick (2¼hr., 7-8 per day, £9.60/€12.20). To get from the station to the **tourist office,** Ashe Memorial Hall, head into town on Edward St., turn right on Castle St., and go left on Denny St. (☎ 712 1288. Open July-Aug. M-Sa 9am-7pm, Su 9am-6pm; May-June and Oct. M-Sa 9am-6pm; Oct.-Apr. M-F 9am-5pm.) The centrally located **Courthouse Lodge (IHH),** is nestled at quiet 5 Church St. (☎ 712 7199. Dorms £9/€14.45; singles £17/€21.60; doubles £24/€30.50.) Call for pick-up to the magnificent **◪Collis-Sandes House (IHH).** (☎ 712 8658. Dorms £9-12/€11.50-15; singles £17/€25; doubles £30/€38. **Camping** £5/€6.50.) ☎ **066.**

WESTERN IRELAND

Even Dubliners will admit that the west is the "most Irish" part of Ireland. Hit hardest by the 19th-century potato famine, this land is miserable for farming, but it's a boon for hikers and bikers who enjoy the isolation of mountainous landscapes.

LIMERICK CITY. Despite a thriving trade in off-color poems, hard times in the 20th century spawned poverty. Industrial developments gave the city, with its 18th-century Georgian streets and parks, a dull and urban feel. To reach the castle featured in *Monty Python and the Holy Grail*, **King John's Castle**, on Nicholas St., cross the Abbey River and turn left after St. Mary's Cathedral. (Open Mar.-Dec. daily 9:30am-5:30pm. £5/€6.35, students £3.75/€4.75.) **Trains** (☎315 555) leave Parnell St. for: Cork (2½hr., 5-6 per day, £14/€17.80); Dublin (2hr., 9-10 per day, £27/€34.30); and Waterford (2hr., M-Sa 1-2 per day, £13.50/€17.15). **Buses** (☎313 333) leave the train station for: Cork (2hr., 14 per day, £9.60/€12.20); Dublin (3½hr., 13 per day, £10.50/€13.35); Galway (2hr., 14 per day, £9.60/€12.20); Tralee (2hr., 7 per day, £9.60/€12.20); and Waterford (2½hr.; M-Th, Sa-Su 6 per day, F 7 per day; £10.50/€13.35). The **tourist office** is on Arthurs Quay, in the space-age glass building. From the station, walk straight down Davis St., right on O'Connell St., then left at Arthurs Quay Mall. (☎317 522. Open July-Aug. M-F 9am-6:30pm, Sa-Su 9am-6pm; May-June and Sept.-Oct. M-Sa 9:30am-5:30pm; Nov.-Apr. M-F 9:30am-5:30pm, Sa 9:30am-1pm.) Snooze at **An Óige Hostel (HI)**, 1 Pery Sq., a pleasant Georgian house with park views. (☎314 672. Lockout 10am-2pm. 14-bed dorms June-Sept. £9.50/€12; Oct.-May £8.50/€10.80; £1/€1.30 less for HI members.) Get **groceries** at **Tesco** in Arthurs Quay Mall. (Open M-W, Sa 8:30am-8pm, Th-F 8:30am-10pm, Su noon-6pm.) Limerick's immense student population adds spice to the pub scene. **Dolan's**, on Dock Rd., hosts nightly *trad* and rambunctious local patrons. ☎**065.**

ENNIS. Growing fast but slow to lose its charm, **Ennis** combines city-caliber nightlife with the familiarity of a small town. Ennis's proximity to Shannon Airport and the Burren make it a common stopover for tourists, who come for a day of shopping followed by a night of pub crawling. Not quite so holy as the **Ennis Friary** (once one of Ireland's most important theological schools), but still revered are the 60 pubs that line the streets of Ennis. Most hold *trad* sessions that uphold Clare's reputation of musical excellence. **The Boardwalk**, O'Connell Sq. is a hotspot for *trad*, world, and indie music. (Cover £5/€6.35. Open F-Sa.) **Trains** leave for from the station, a 10min. walk from the town center on Station Rd., for Dublin via Limerick (1-2 per day, £21/€26.70). **Buses** trundle to: Doolin (1hr., 1-3 per day, £5.80/€7.40); Galway (1 hr., 5 per day, £7.70/€9.80); and Shannon Airport (40min., 9-13 per day, £3.70/€6.10). The new **tourist office** is at O'Connell Sq. (☎28366. Open June-Sept. M-F 9:30am-6:30pm, Sa-Su 9:30am-1pm and 2-6:30pm; Mar.-May and Oct.-Nov. M-F 9:30am-1pm and 2-5:30pm.) Crash for the night at **Abbey Tourist Hostel**, Harmony Row. (☎682 2620. Breakfast included. Dorms £10.) ☎**065.**

DOOLIN. Something of a national shrine to Irish traditional music, the little village of **Doolin** draws thousands of visitors every year to its three pubs for nights of *craic* that will go straight from your tappin' toes to your Guinness-soaked head. The names and sociological role of the town's dominant triumvirate are best remembered by the mnemonic **MOM: McDermott's** (Upper Village), **O'Connor's** (Lower), **McGann's** (Upper). All have music sessions nightly at 9:30pm, and the latter two have both won awards for the best *trad* in Ireland. Between the upper and lower villages, ◪**Aille River Hostel (IHH)** feels like its own peaceful hamlet. (☎707 4260. Dorms £8.50/€10.80; doubles £16/€20.35. Camping £4/€5.) **Westwind B&B** sits behind McGann's with sunny and immaculate rooms. The owners give helpful advice to spelunkers and other Burren explorers. (☎707 4227. £13-15/€16.50-19 per person.) Either provide excellent respite to explore the ◪**Cliffs of Moher** 5km to the south. The stunning view from the edge plunges 200m straight down to the open sea; these cliffs are so high you'll be able to see gulls whirling below you. **Bus** #50 runs 15min. to the cliffs; #15 goes to Dublin via Ennis (1-2 per day). ☎**065.**

THE BURREN. If there were wild orchids, cantankerous cows, and B&Bs on the moon, it would probably look a lot like the Burren. Its land comprises nearly 260 sq. km and almost one-third of Co. Clare's coastline. Mediterranean, Alpine, and Arctic wildflowers announce their neon bright, microcosmic contours form cracks in mile-long rock planes, while 28 of Ireland's 33 species of butterfly flutter by. Coming here is like is like entering a skewed fairyland, replete with ruined castles, and ancient megaliths. The best way to see the Burren is to walk or cycle, but it's notoriously difficult to get around. Yellow arrows mark **The Burren Way,** a 40km hiking trail from Liscannor to Ballyvaughan. All of the surrounding tourist offices (at Kilfenora, Ennis, Corofin, and the Cliffs of Moher) have detailed maps of the region. **Bus Éireann** (☎682 41 77) connects Galway to towns in and near the Burren a few times a day during summer but infrequently during winter. The ever expanding **Kinvara,** on Galway Bay, provides welcome rest and **Dunguaire Castle** and an active pub scene. Hit up **Fallon's B&B,** above Kinvara's Spar market (☎637 483. £25/€31.75 per person sharing, all with bath.) or **Cois Cuain B&B,** on the Quay (☎637 119. Open Apr.-Nov. £19/€24 per person sharing) before venturing out into the landscape.

GALWAY CITY ☎091

In the past few years, Galway (pop. 60,000) has earned a reputation as Ireland's cultural capital. With a mix of over 13,000 students at Galway's two major universities, a transient population of twenty-something Europeans, and waves of international backpackers, Galway has developed into one happening college town on *craic.*

◨⊡ TRANSPORTATION AND PRACTICAL INFORMATION. Direct **trains** (☎561 444) run to Dublin (3hr., 3-5 per day, £21/€26.75); transfer at Athlone (£7.50-13.50/€9.50-17.15) for all other cities. **Bus Éireann** (☎562 000) leaves for: Belfast (1-3 per day, £17/€21.60); Cork (5 per day, £12/€15.25); and Dublin (7-9 per day, £8/€10.15). The **tourist office,** Forster St. is a block south of Eyre Sq. (☎563 081. Open July-Aug. daily 9am-7:45pm; May-June and Sept. daily 9am-5:45pm; Oct.-Apr. M-F and Su 9am-5:45pm, Sa 9am-12:45pm.) Check email at **Fun World,** Eyre Sq. (☎561 415. Open M-Sa 10am-11pm, Su 11am-11pm. £3/€3.80 per 30min.)

◸⊡ ACCOMMODATIONS AND FOOD. ⊠**Barnacle's Quay Street Hostel (IHH),** Quay St., is bright and spacious with a peerless location. (☎568 644. All rooms with bath. Laundry £5/€6.35. Dorms £8.50-15/€10.80-19.05; doubles £32-36/€40.65-45.75.) ⊠ **Sleepzone,** Bóthar na mBán, northwest of Eyre Sq. takes the "s" out of "hostel." (☎566 999. All rooms with bath. Laundry £5/€6.35. Dorms £11-13/€14-16.55; doubles £29/€36.85.) **Salmon Weir Hostel,** 3 St. Vincent's Ave. is extremely homey with a down-to-earth vibe. (☎561 133. Laundry £5/€6.35. Dorms £11/€14; doubles £28/€35.50.) For cheap food, head to the east bank; try Abbeygate St. and the blocks around **Quay, High,** and **Shop Streets.** On Saturday mornings, an **open market** sets up in front of St. Nicholas Church on Market St. with seafood, pastries, and fresh fruit. (Open daily 8am-1pm.) Pick up groceries at **Supervalu,** in the Eyre Sq. mall. (Open M-W and Sa 9am-6:30pm, Th-F 9am-9pm.)

◙⊡ SIGHTS AND NIGHTLIFE. Galway's main attractions are its nightlife and setting as a starting point for trips to the Clare Coast or the Connemara. Rent a **rowboat** from **Frank Dolan's,** 13 Riverside, Woodquay, and row/drift down the Corrib for great views of the city, countryside, and nearby castles (£3/€3.85 per hr.). In mid-July, the **Galway Arts Festival** (☎583 800), Ireland's largest arts festival, brings *trad* musicians, rock groups, theater troupes, and filmmakers. Otherwise, rest up for the long nights ahead. Choosing from the endless list of fantastic pubs is a challenge even for residents (nightclubs lag far behind in quality). The beautiful pubs along **Quay Street** generally cater to tourists and students. Try **The King's Head,** High St., which features three floors and a huge stage devoted to nightly rock, and **Seaghan Ua Neachtain** (a.k.a. **Knockton's**), Quay St., the oldest pub in Galway. Afternoon pint-sippers perch outside at streetcorner tables and study streams of pedestrians. Pubs along **Dominick Street** (across the river from the Quay) are local faves; **Roisín Dubh,**

IRELAND

Dominick St., with an intimate bookshelved front, hides one of Galway's hottest live music scenes in the back. (Cover £6-13/€7.60-16.55.) **The Crane,** 2 Sea Rd., a bit beyond the Blue Note, which is well known as *the* place to hear *trad* in Galway. Enter through the side door and hop up to the 2nd floor loft. The huge **Skeffington Arms,** across from Kennedy Park, is a hotel with six bars—a pub crawl unto itself.

ARAN ISLANDS (OILEÁIN ÁRANN)

On the westernmost edge of Co. Galway, isolated from the mainland by 24km of chaotic Atlantic, the Aran Islands feel more like the edge of the world. Their green fields are hatched with a maze of limestone—the result of centuries of farmers piling acres of stones into thousands of feet of walls—and awesome Iron Age forts sit atop stark cliffs. Of the dozens of ruins, forts, churches, and holy wells that rise from the stony terrain of **Inishmore** (Inis Mór; pop. 900), the most amazing is the **Dún Aengus** ring fort, where a small semicircular wall surrounds a sheer 100m drop.

Island Ferries (☎ (091) 568 903) go from **Rossaveal,** west of Galway, to: Inishmore (1-3 per day, 30min.); Inisheer (2 per day); and Inishmaan (1 per day). All routes are £15/€19 return for students. A **bus** to Rossaveal leaves the Galway tourist office 1½hr. before the ferry departure time (£4/€5). **Queen of Aran II,** Inishmore (☎566 535), is based in the islands and leaves for Inishmore (4 per day; £15/€19, students £10/€12.70; bus from Galway included). Both have offices in the Galway tourist office. Ferries land at **Kilronan,** where the **tourist office** holds bags for £0.75/€0.95. (☎(099) 61263. Open July-Sept. daily 10am-6:45pm; Oct. daily 10am-5pm; Nov.-Mar. daily 10am-4pm.) The **Kilronan Hostel** is bright, spotless, and centrally located. (☎(099) 61255. Dorms £10/€12.70, all with bath.) Windswept **Inishmaan** (Inis Meáin; pop. 300) elevates solitude to an art form. **Inisheer** (Inis Oírr; pop. 300), the smallest island, strikes a balance between Inishmaan's absolute loneliness and Inishmore's occasional din. The **Brú Hostel (IHH),** visible from the pier, has great views. (☎75024. Call ahead. Breakfast £2-5/€2.50-5. Dorms £8.50/€10.80.)

CONNEMARA

A largely Gaelic-speaking region comprised of a lacy net of inlets and islands, a rough gang of mountains, and stretches of bog, this region harbors some of Ireland's most breathtaking scenery. The jagged southern coastline teems with sinuous estuaries, safe beaches, and tidal causeways connecting to rocky islands.

CLIFDEN (AN CLOCHÁN). Busy, English-speaking Clifden has more amenities and modernities than its old-world, Irish-speaking neighbors. Clifden's proximity to the scenic bogs and mountains of the region attracts crowds of tourists, who enjoy the frenzied pub scene, shop in its ubiquitous arts and crafts studios, and use it as a base for exploring the region. The **Connemara Walking Centre,** on Market St., runs tours of the bogs. (☎21379 Open Mar.-Oct. M-Sa 10am-6pm. Easter-Oct. 1-2 tours per day. £15-25/€19.05-31.75.) **Bus Éireann** goes from the library on Market St. to Galway via Oughterard (2hr., 1-5 per day, £6.50/€8.25) and Westport via Leenane (1½hr., late June to Aug. 3-4 per day). Michael Nee runs a bus from the courthouse to Galway (June-Sept. 3 per day, £6/€7.65). Rent a **bike** at Mannion's, Bridge St. (☎21160. £7/€8.90 per day, £40/€50.80 per week. Deposit £10/€12.70. Open M-Sa 9:30am-6:30pm, Su 10am-1pm and 5-7pm.) The **tourist office** is on Market St. (☎21163. Open July-Aug. M-Sa 9:45am-5:45pm and Su noon-4pm; May-June and Sept. M-Sa 9:30am-5:30pm.) Check **email** at **Two Dog Cafe,** Church Hill. (☎22186. Open M-Sa 10:30am-5pm.) **B&Bs** litter the streets (£18-20/€22.90-25.40). The excellent **Clifden Town Hostel (IHH)** is on Market St. (☎21076. Dorms £8/€10.20; doubles £24/€30.50; triples £30/€38.10; quads £36/€45.75.) Head straight past the bottom of Market St. to find **Brookside Hostel,** Hulk St. (☎21812. Dorms £8/€10.20; private rooms £8-9/€10.20-11.45; doubles £18/€22.90.) Tranquil **Shanaheever Campsite** is a little over 1½km outside Clifden on Westport Rd. (☎22150. £8/€10.20 per 2 people and tent; £3/€3.85 per additional person.) The **O'Connor's SuperValu supermarket** is on Market St. (Open M-F 8:30am-8pm, Su 9am-7pm.) Shake your booty and down a few pints along **Market Street** in **The Square** and on **Church Hill.** ☎095.

CONNEMARA NATIONAL PARK. Connemara National Park occupies 12½ sq. km of mountainous countryside that thousands of birds call home. The far-from-solid terrain of the park comprises bogs thinly covered by a deceptive screen of grass and flowers—be prepared to get muddy. The **Snuffaunboy Nature Trail** and the **Ellis Wood Trail** are easy 20min. hikes. For the slightly more adventurous, trails lead from the back of the Ellis Wood Trail and 10min. along the Bog Road onto **Diamond Hill,** a 2hr. hike rewarding climbers with views of bog, harbor, and forest. More experienced hikers head for the **Twelve Bens** (Na Benna Beola, a.k.a. the Twelve Pins), a rugged range that reaches 730m heights (not recommended for single or beginning hikers). A guidebook mapping out 30min. walks (£0.50/€0.65) is available at the visitor's center, where the staff helps plan longer hikes. A tour of all 12 Bens takes experienced walkers about 10hr. Biking the 65km circle through Clifden, Letterfrack, and the Inagh Valley is truly captivating, but only appropriate for fit bikers.

Tiny **Letterfrack** is the gateway to the park. The Galway-Clifden **bus** (M-Sa mid-June to Aug. 11 per week, Sept. to mid-June 4 per week) and the summertime Clifden-Westport bus (1-2 per day) stops at Letterfrack. The **Visitors Centre** explains the subtle (and not so subtle) differences between blanket bogs, raised bogs, turf, and heathland. Guides lead free 2hr. **walks** over the hills and through the bogs. (☎41054. Open July-Aug. daily 9:30am-6:30pm; June 10am-6:30pm; May and Sept. 10am-5:30pm. Park £2/€2.55, students £1/€1.30. Tours July-Aug. M, W, and F 10:30am.) Uphill from the intersection in Letterfrack, the ■Old Monastery Hostel is legendary—one of Ireland's finest hostels. (☎41132. Bike £7/€8.90 per day. Internet. Dorms £8-10/€10.20-12.70.) The turnoff to the **Ben Lettery Hostel (An Óige/HI),** Ballinafad, is 13km east of Clifden. (☎51136. £8-9/€10.20-11.45.) ☎095.

WESTPORT. One of the country's few planned towns, Westport (pop. 4300) still looks marvelous in its Georgian-period costume. Tourists savor beer at thriving pubs, drink tea at dapper cafes, and shop for hand-woven scarves. **Trains** arrive at the Altamont St. Station (☎25253), 5min. up North Mall, from Dublin via Athlone (2-3 per day, £15/€19.05). **Buses** leave from the Octagon on Mill St. for Galway (2hr., M-F 6 per day, £8.80/€11.20). The **tourist office** is on James St. (☎25711. Open July-Aug. M-Sa 9am-6:45pm, Su 10am-6pm; Apr.-June and Sept.-Oct. M-Sa 9am-5:45pm.) **B&Bs** are on the Castlebar and Altamont Rd. off North Mall. ■Granary Hostel is a 25min. walk from town, just at the bend in Quay Rd. (☎25903. Open Apr.-Oct. Dorms £7.50/€9.55.) **Old Mill Holiday Hostel (IHH),** James St., is between the Octagon and the tourist office. (☎27045. Bike rental £7/€8.90 per day. Laundry £3/€3.80. Common room lockout 11pm-8am. Dorms £9/€11.45.) The **SuperValu** supermarket on Shop St. (Open M-Sa 8:30am-9pm, Su 10am-6pm) keeps you from the crowds at **McCormack's** on Bridge St. (open M-Tu and Th-Sa 10am-6pm).

Conical **Croagh Patrick** rises 650m over Clew Bay. The summit has been revered since St. Patrick fasted for 40 days and nights in AD 441, arguing with angels and banishing snakes from Ireland. Climbers start at the 15th-century **Murrisk Abbey,** west of Westport on R395 toward Louisburgh (4hr. return). **Buses** go to Murrisk (2-3 per day), but for a group, **cabs** (☎27171) are cheaper. ☎098.

NORTHWEST IRELAND

The farmland of the upper Shannon region spans northward into County Sligo's mountains, lakes, and ancient monuments. A sliver of land connects County Sligo to County Donegal, a storehouse of genuine Irish tradition.

SLIGO. Since the turn of the century, Sligo has been a literary pilgrimage site for William Butler Yeats devotees. The poet summered in town as a child, settled here as an adult, and set many of his poems around the area. The county remains as beautiful today as it was then. **Sligo Town,** the county's commercial center, explodes at night with one of Ireland's most colorful pub scenes, and is an excellent base for exploring Yeat's haunts, most of which are at least a mile from the town center. In town, the well-preserved 13th-century **Sligo Abbey,** Abbey St., is Yeats-free. (Open Apr.-Oct. daily 10am-6pm; Nov.-Mar. call for hours. £1.50/€1.90, students £0.60/ €0.75.) **The Niland Gallery,** Stephen St., houses an excellent modern Irish art collection along with some first editions of Yeats works. (Open Tu-Sa 10am-5:30pm. Free.) Yeats is buried in **Drumcliff churchyard,** on the N15, 6½km northwest of Sligo; his grave is to the left of the church door. **Buses** from Sligo to Derry stop at Drumcliff (10min., 3-4 per day, £2.60/€3.30 return).

Trains (☎698 88) go from Lord Edward St. to Dublin via Carrick-on-Shannon and Mullingar (3 per day, £13.50/€17.15). From the same station, **buses** (☎60066) fan out to: Belfast (4hr., 1-3 per day, £12.40/€15.75); Derry (3hr., 3-6 per day, £10/€12.70); Dublin (4hr., 4 per day, £18/€22.90); Galway (2½hr., 3-4 per day, £11/€14); and Westport (2½hr., 1-3 per day, £9.70/€12.30). Turn left on Lord Edward St., then follow the signs right on Adelaid St. and around the corner to Temple St. to find the **tourist office,** at Charles St. (☎61201. Open M-Tu 10am-7pm, W-F 10am-9pm, Sa 10am-6pm.) **B&Bs** cluster on **Pearse Road,** on the south side of town. ■**Harbour House,** Finisklin Rd., is 10min. from the station. (☎71547. Dorms £11/€14; singles £17/€21.60.) Follow signs from the station to **Railway Hostel,** 1 Union St. (☎44530. Dorms £7.50/€9.55; doubles £9/€11.45 per person.) "Faery vats/Full of berries/And reddest stolen cherries" are not to be found in Sligo today; but **Tesco Supermarket,** O'Connell St., has aisles-worth of cheap food. (Open M-Tu and Sa 8:30am-7pm, W-F 8:30am-9pm, Su 10am-6pm.) ☎**071.**

COUNTY DONEGAL AND SLIEVE LEAGUE. Tourists are a rarity in Co. Donegal. Its geographic isolation in the Northwest has spared it from the widespread deforestation of Ireland; vast wooded areas engulf many of Donegal's mountain chains, while the coastline alternates beaches and cliffs. Travelers use **Donegal Town** as the gateway to the county. **Bus Éireann** (☎21101) runs to Dublin (4hr., 4-6 per day, £10.50/€13.35) and Galway (4hr., 3-5 per day, £10.50/€13.35). Buses stop outside the Abbey Hotel on the Diamond; turn right with your back to the hotel to reach the **tourist office,** on Quay St. (☎21148. Open July-Aug. M-Sa 9am-8pm, Su 10am-4pm; Sept.-Nov. and Easter-June M-F 9am-5pm, Sa 10am-2pm.) **Donegal Independent Town Hostel (IHH)** is on Killybegs Rd. (☎22805. Call ahead. Dorms £7.50/€9.55; doubles £18/€22.90. **Camping** £4/€5.10 per person.)

To the west of Donegal Town, the **Slieve League Peninsula**'s rocky cliffs (Europe's highest) jut out into the Atlantic. The sheer face of its 600m drop into the Atlantic is spectacular, and its rugged, wild appearance shows little evidence of human habitation. **Bus Éireann** runs from Donegal Town to Glencolmcille and Dungloe, stopping in tiny **Kilcar** (1-3 per day), the gateway to Donegal's *gaeltacht* and a commercial base for many Donegal tweed weavers. Most Slieve League hikers stay in Kilcar, from where they can comfortably drive, bike, or walk (about 6hr. return) to the mountain. Over 3km out on the coast road from Kilcar to Carrick is the fabulous ■**Derrylahan Hostel (IHH);** call for pick-up. (☎380 79. Laundry £5/€6.35. Dorms £7/€8.90; private rooms £10/€12.70. **Camping** £4/€5.10). Bus Éireann has services to Donegal Town via Kilcar (3 per day). On the western top of the Slieve League peninsula, **Glencolmcille** (glen-kaul-um-KEEL), a collection of several tiny villages wedged between two monstrous sea cliffs, is renowned for its handmade products, particularly sweaters. On sunny days, trips to the **Silver Strand** reward with stunning views of the gorgeous beach and rocky cliffs; from here, the trek along the Slieve League coastline begins. McGeehan's **buses** leave from Biddy's Bar for Kilcar and Letterkenny (1-2 per day). Snooze at the just peachy ■**Dooey Hostel (IHO).** (☎301 30. Dorms £7/€8.90; doubles £14/€17.80. **Camping** £4/€5.10.) ☎**073.**

DERRYVEAGH MOUNTAINS. Sandy beaches are isolated by the boglands and eerie stillness of the **Derryveagh Mountains.** On the eastern side of the mountains, **Glenveagh National Park** is 60km^2 of forest glens, bogs, and herds of red deer. (☎(074) 37090. £2/€2.55, students £1.50/€1.95. Open daily 10am-5pm.) The coastal road

N56 twists and bends along the jagged edges where Donegal meets the sea, leading through spectacular scenery to **Crolly,** gateway to Mount Errigal and the legendary Poison Glen. From Crolly, Feda O'Donnell (☎48114) has a daily **bus** to Galway and Donegal Town via Letterkenny; Swilly (☎21380) passes Crolly on its Dungloe-Derry route; John McGinley Coaches (☎(074) 35201) goes to Dublin; and O'Donnell Trans-Ulster Express (☎48356) goes to Belfast. **Dunlewy,** in the shadow of Errigal Mountain, rivals Crolly as a base for exploring the Derryveagh Mountains. **Errigal Youth Hostel (An Óige/HI),** along R251, is clean and convenient. (☎31180. Call ahead to see if renovations are complete. Lockout 10am-5pm. Dorms June-Sept. £7.50/€9.55, bunk-bed private rooms £9.50/€12.10; dorms Oct.-May £6.50/€8.25; private rooms £7.50/€9.55.) ☎**075.**

LETTERKENNY. Letterkenny is a traffic-clogged mess; most tourists arrive just to make bus connections to the rest of Donegal, the Republic, and Northern Ireland. **Buses** leave from the roundabout at the junction of Port (Derry) and Pearse Rd. in front of the Letterkenny Shopping Center. **Bus** Éireann (☎21309) runs to: Derry (30min, 3-6 per day, £5/€6.35); Donegal Town (50min., £5/€6.35) on the way to Galway (4¾hr., 4 per day, £12/€15.25); Dublin (4½hr., 5-6 per day, £10/€12.70); and Sligo (2hr., 4-5 per day, £9/€11.45). Lough Swilly Buses (☎22863) head north to Derry (M-Sa 10 per day, £4.40/€5.60) and the Fanad Peninsula (M-Sa 2 per day, £7/€8.90). Northwest Busways (☎(077) 82619) sends buses around the Inishowen Peninsula (3-4 per day). The **Chamber of Commerce Visitors Information Centre** is at 40 Port Rd. (☎248 66. Open M-F 9am-5pm.) ☎**074.**

INISHOWEN PENINSULA AND MALIN HEAD. The Inishowen Peninsula is a mosaic of pristine mountains, forests, meadows, and white-sand beaches that reaches farther north than "the North." The **Inish Eoghain 100** road navigates the peninsula's perimeter, exactly 100 mi. The peninsula's most popular attraction is **Malin Head,** with its rocky coast and sky-high sand dunes, reputedly Europe's highest (over 30m). The scattered town of Malin Head includes **Bamba's Crown,** the northernmost tip of Ireland, a tooth of dark rock rising up from the waves. The nearby beaches are covered with semi-precious stones. Lough Swilly **buses** (☎61340; 1½hr.; M, W, and F 2 per day, Sa 3 per day) and Northwest Buses (☎82619; M-Sa 2 per day) run from Derry, the nearest city to Inishowen, to points on the peninsula including Malin Head. To reach the ▧**Sandrock Holiday Hostel (IHO),** Port Ronan Pier, take the left fork off the Inish Eoghin 100, at the Crossroads Inn. (☎70289. Sheets £1/€1.27. Dorms £7/€8.90.) ☎**077.**

NORTHERN IRELAND

PHONE CODE	The regional code for all of Northern Ireland is 028. From outside Northern Ireland, dial int'l dialing prefix (see inside back cover) + 44 (from the Republic, 048) + 28 + local number.

The predominantly calm tenor of life in the North has been overshadowed overseas by concerns about politics and bombs. Northern Ireland's natural beauty includes the Glens of Antrim's pockets of green and gotta-see-it-to-believe-it geology at the Giant's Causeway. The ceasefires of recent years have allowed Belfast and Derry to develop into hip, pub-loving cities. Pub culture, urban neighborhoods, and tiny villages show everyday life in a divided but mostly peaceful society.

BELFAST

Belfast (pop. 330,000) is the center of the North's cultural, commercial, and political activity. West Belfast's famous sectarian murals are perhaps the most informative source on the effects of the Troubles (sectarian strife). The bar scene—a mix of

Irish and British pub culture, with an international influence—entertains locals, foreigners, and students. Despite its reputation as a terrorist-riddled metropolis, the city feels more neighborly than most foreign (and even Irish) visitors expect.

▟ TRANSPORTATION

Flights: Belfast International Airport (☎9442 2888) in Aldergrove. **Airbus** (☎9033 3000) goes to the Europa (Glengall St.) bus station (M-Sa every 30min., Su every hr.; UK£5). From **Belfast City Airport, trains** go to Central Station (UK£1).

Trains: Central Station, East Bridge St. (☎9089 9400). To **Derry** (2½hr., 3-7 per day, UK£6.70) and **Dublin** (2hr., 5-8 per day, UK£17). The **Centrelink** buses run to the city center, free with rail tickets.

Buses: Europa Station, Glengall St. (☎9032 0011) serves the west, north coast, and the Republic. To: **Derry** (1¾hr., 6-19 per day, UK£6.50) and **Dublin** (3hr., 4-7 per day, UK£10.50). **Laganside Station** (☎9033 3000) Donegall Quay, serves Northern Ireland's east coast. The **Centrelink** bus connects both stations with the city center.

Ferries: SeaCat (☎08705 523 523; www.seacat.co.uk), leaves for: **Heysham, England** (4hr., Apr.-Nov., 1-2 per day); the **Isle of Man** (2¾hr., Apr.-Nov. 1-2 per day); and **Troon, Scotland** (2½hr., 2-3 per day). Fares UK£10-30 without car.

Local Transportation: The red **Citybus Network** (☎9024 6485), is supplemented by **Ulsterbus's** suburban "blue buses". Travel within the city center UK£0.60, students UK£0.30. The **Centrelink** bus traverses the city (every 12min.; M-F 7:25am-9:15pm, Sa 8:36am-9:15pm; UK£0.60, free with bus or rail ticket). Late **Nightlink** buses shuttle to various small towns outside of Belfast 1am and 2am F-Sa (UK£3, payable on board).

Taxis: Value Cabs (☎9023 0000). Residents of West and North Belfast use the huge **black cabs;** some are metered, and some follow set routes (under UK£1 charge).

✦❷ ORIENTATION AND PRACTICAL INFORMATION

Buses arrive at the Europa bus station on Great Victoria St. To the northeast is the **City Hall** in **Donegall Square.** The stretch of Great Victoria St. south of the bus station to where it meets Dublin Rd. at Shaftesbury Sq. is known as the **Golden Mile. Botanic Avenue** and **Bradbury Place** (which becomes University Rd.) extend south from Shaftesbury Sq. into the student-friendly **Queen's University area.** The city center, Golden Mile, and the university area are relatively safe. **West Belfast** is more politically volatile. The Protestant neighborhood lies along **Shankill Road,** just north of the Catholic neighborhood, centered around **Falls Road.** The **River Lagan** divides industrial **East Belfast** from the rest of the city. Use taxis after dark, particularly near the clubs and pubs of the northeast area.

Tourist Office: The Belfast Welcome Centre, 47 Donegall Pl. (☎9024 6609). Has a great booklet on Belfast and info on surrounding areas. The staff likes specific questions. Open June-Sept. M-Sa 9am-7pm, Su noon-5pm; Oct.-May M-Sa 9am-5:30pm.

Banks: Banks and **ATMs** are virtually on every corner. **Bank of Ireland** is at 54 Donegal Pl. (☎9023 4334). Open 9am-4:30pm.

Luggage Storage: For security reasons there is no luggage storage at airports or stations. Hostels will often store bags for guests.

Bisexual, Gay, and Lesbian Information: Rainbow Project N.I., 33 Church Ln. (☎9031 9030). Open M-F 10am-5:30pm.

Laundry: The Laundry Room (Duds n' Suds), Botanic Ave. (☎9024 3956). TV for the wait. About UK£3-4 per load. Open M-F 8am-9pm, Sa 8am-6pm, Su noon-6pm.

Emergency: ☎999; no coins required. **Police,** 65 Knock Rd. (☎9065 0222).

Pharmacy: Boot's, 35-47 Donegall Pl. (☎9024 2332). Open M-W and F-Sa 8:30am-6pm, Th 8:30am-9pm, Su 1-5pm. Also on Great Victoria St.

Hospitals: Belfast City Hospital, 9 Lisburn Rd. (☎9032 9241). From Shaftesbury Sq. follow Bradbury Pl. and take a right at the fork.

Internet Access: The **Belfast Central Library,** 122 Royal Ave. (☎9050 9150). 30min. free email per day; UK£2 per hr. for web access. Open M and Th 9:30am-8pm, Tu-W and F 9:30am-5:30pm, Sa 9:30am-1pm.

Post Office: Central Post Office, 25 Castle Pl. (☎9032 3740). Open M-Sa 9am-5:30pm. *Poste Restante* mail comes here. **Postal code:** BT1 1NB.

ACCOMMODATIONS AND FOOD

Most budget accommodations are by **Queen's University,** south of the city center. You can catch a Centrelink bus to Shaftesbury Sq., or Citybus #59, 69-71, 84, or 85 from Donegall Sq. East to areas to the south. B&Bs occupy every other house on **Eglantine Avenue,** off University Rd. just south of Queen's University.

■ **Arnie's Backpackers (IHH),** 63 Fitzwilliam St. (☎9024 2867). A 10min. walk from Europa Bus Station on Great Victoria St. Take a right and head away from the Europa Hotel; at Shaftesbury Sq., take the right fork on Bradbury Pl. then fork left onto University Rd;

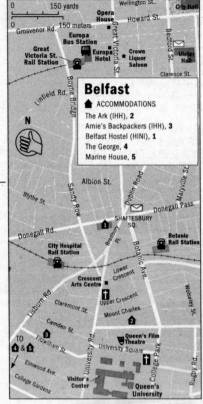

Belfast

▲ ACCOMMODATIONS

The Ark (IHH), **2**
Arnie's Backpackers (IHH), **3**
Belfast Hostel (HINI), **1**
The George, **4**
Marine House, **5**

Fitzwilliam St. is on your right across from the University. Key deposit UK£2 or ID. Luggage storage during the day. 8-bed dorms UK£7; 4-bed UK£8.50.

■ **The Ark (IHH),** 18 University St. (☎9032 9626). From Arnie's Backpackers (see above) it's on the right off University Rd. Weekend luggage storage. Internet access UK£2 per 30min. Laundry UK£4. Curfew 2am. 4- to 6-bed dorms UK£6.50-7.50; doubles UK£28.

Belfast Hostel (HINI), 22 Donegall Rd. (☎9031 5435), off Shaftesbury Sq. Clean and inviting interior despite concrete façade. Also **books tours** of Belfast and Giant's Causeway. Breakfast UK£2. Laundry UK£3. Reception 24hr. Dorms UK£8-10.

■ **Marine House,** 30 Eglantine Ave. (☎9066 2828). B&B with Housekeeping standards as high as the ceilings. Singles UK£22; doubles UK£40, with bath UK£45; triples UK£57.

The George, 9 Eglantine Ave. (☎9068 3212). Renowned for its spotlessness. All rooms in this stained-glass saturated B&B en suite. Singles UK£22; doubles UK£44.

Dublin Road, Botanic Avenue, and the **Golden Mile** have the highest concentration of restaurants. Mismatched dishes mingle with counter-culture paraphernalia at ■**Bookfinders,** 47 University Rd. (Open M-Sa 10am-5:30pm.) The menu ranges from Thai to Cajun at **The Other Place,** 79 Botanic Ave., 133 Stranmillis Rd., and 537 Lisburn Rd. (All open M-Sa 8am-11pm.) **Feasts,** 39 Dublin Rd. is a pleasant streetside cafe, serving Irish and international farmhouse cheeses in sandwiches for UK£3.50. (Open M-F 9am-6:30pm, Sa 10am-6pm.) **Spar** on Botanic Ave. has **groceries.** (Open 24hr.)

◎ SIGHTS

DONEGALL SQUARE. The **Belfast City Hall** is the administrative and geographic center of Belfast. Its green copper dome is visible from any point in the city. Check out the somber statues in the exterior garden. *(1hr. tour June-Sept. M-F 10:30am, 11:30am, 2:30pm; Sa 2:30pm. Oct.-May M-Sa 2:30pm. Free.)* The **Linen Hall Library** contains a comprehensive collection of Christmas cards, posters, hand bills, and newspaper articles related to the Troubles in Northern Ireland. *(17 Donegall Sq. North. Open M-F 9:30am-5:30pm, Sa 9:30am-4:30pm.)*

CORNMARKET AND ST. ANNE'S CATHEDRAL. North of the city center, this shopping district envelops eight blocks around Castle St. and Royal Ave and the area has been a marketplace since Belfast's early days. Relics of old Belfast remain in the **entries**, or tiny alleys. **St. Anne's Cathedral**, also known as the **Belfast Cathedral**, was begun in 1899. Each of its interior pillars name Belfast's 10 professions: Science, Industry, Healing, Agriculture, Music, Theology, Shipbuilding, Freemasonry, Art, and, um, "Womanhood." *(Donegall St., near tourist office. Open M-Sa 9am-5pm, Su services.)*

THE GOLDEN MILE. This strip along Great Victoria St. contains many of Belfast's jewels, including the city's pride and joy, the **Grand Opera House**, which was cyclically bombed by the IRA, restored to its original splendor at enormous cost, and then bombed again. *(Tours Sa 11am; UK£3, seniors and children UK£2. Office open M-W 8:30am-8pm, Th 8:30am-9pm, F 8:30am-6:30pm, Sa 8:30am-5:30pm.)* The National Trust has restored the popular **Crown Liquor Saloon**, 46 Great Victoria St., to a showcase of carved wood, gilded ceilings, and stained glass. Damaged by 32 bombs, the **Europa Hotel** has the dubious distinction of being "Europe's most bombed hotel."

QUEEN'S UNIVERSITY AREA. Designed in 1849, the University was modeled after Oxford's Magdalen College. *(University Road Visitors Centre. ☎ 9033 5252. Open May-Sept. M-Sa 10am-4pm; Oct-Mar. M-F 10am-4pm.)* Bask in Belfast's occasional sun at the meticulously groomed **Botanic Gardens**. *(Open daily 8am-dusk. Free.)* The **Ulster Museum**, within the gardens, contains a hodgepodge of historical exhibits, antiquities, and artwork. *(Off Stranmillis Rd. ☎ 9038 3000. Open M-F 10am-5pm, Sa 1-5pm, Su 2-5pm. Free.)*

WEST BELFAST AND THE MURALS. Separated from the rest of the city by the Westlink motorway, West Belfast has been historically rife with political tension. The Catholic and Protestant neighborhoods are grimly divided by the **peace line**, a gray, seemingly impenetrable wall. The streets display political murals. The Protestant Orangemen's marching season (in early July) is a risky time to visit, since the parades are underscored by mutual antagonism. Michael Johnston of **Black Taxi Tours** has made a name for himself with witty, objective presentations. *(☎ 9064 2264; www.belfasttours.com. £7.50 per person.)*

♫ ▣ ENTERTAINMENT AND NIGHTLIFE

Belfast's cultural events and performances are covered in the monthly *Arts Council Artslink* (free at the tourist office). Belfast's **theater** season runs from September to June. The **Grand Opera House**, on Great Victoria St., resounds with classical vocal music. Buy tickets at the box office, 2-4 Great Victoria St. (☎ 9024 1919, Tickets from UK£8. 50% student rush tickets available M-Th after noon.) The **Queen's University Festival** (☎ 9066 7687) in November draws artists in opera, film, and more.

Pubs close early; start crawling while the sun's still up. In Cornmarket, begin with an afternoon pint at Belfast's oldest pub, **White's Tavern**, Winecellar Entry, off High and Rosemary St. Stumble along Dublin Rd. and the Golden Mile, where some of the best pubs lie. Victorian town landmark **Crown Liquor Saloon**, 46 Great Victoria St., has been faithfully restored. **Robinson's**, 38 Great Victoria St., hosts nightly trad sessions. ◪**Lavery's**, 12 Bradbury Pl. offers three floors of unpretentious socializing. The bars near the university stay open the latest. **The Botanic Inn (the "Bot")**, 23 Malone Rd., and **The Eglantine Inn (the "Egg")**, 32 Malone Rd., are almost official extracurriculars.

Explore the club scene at **The Manhattan,** 23-31 Bradbury Pl., which explodes with gyrating twenty-somethings. Socialites head to **The Fly,** 5-6 Lower Crescent, a cool lounge. **The Kremlin,** 96 Donegall St., is the newest gay hotspot. For more, consult *The List,* available in the tourist office and hostels.

◤ DAYTRIP FROM BELFAST: ULSTER FOLK MUSEUM

In **Holywood,** the **Ulster Folk Museum** and **Transport Museum** stretch over 176 acres. Established by Act of Parliament in the 1950s, the ◪ **Ulster Folk Museum,** which aims to preserve the way of life of Ulster's farmers, weavers, and craftspeople, contains over 30 buildings from the past three centuries. The **Transport Museum** and the **Railway Museum** are across the road. (☎9042 8428. Open Mar.-June M-F 10am-5pm, Sa 10am-6pm, Su 11am-6pm; July-Sept. M-Sa 10am-6pm, Su 11am-6pm; Oct.-Feb. M-F 10am-4pm, Sa 10am-5pm, Su 11am-5pm. Folk Museum UK£4; students UK£2.50. Transport Museum UK£4, UK£2.50. Combined ticket UK£5, UK£3.) **Buses** and **trains** stop here on the way to Bangor.

DERRY (LONDONDERRY)

Although the Derry landscape was once razed by years of bombings, and violence still erupts occasionally during the Marching Season (July 4-12), the rebuilt city looks sparklingly new. Derry's **city walls,** 5.5m high and 6m thick, erected between 1614 and 1619, have never been breached—hence Derry's nickname "the Maiden City." The stone tower along the southeast wall past New Gate was built to protect **St. Columb's Cathedral,** off Bishop St., the symbolic focus of the city's Protestant defenders. (Open M-Sa Easter-Oct. 9am-5pm; Nov.-Mar. 9am-1pm and 2-4pm. Suggested donation UK£1.) At Union Hall Place, just inside Magazine Gate, the **Tower Museum's** engaging exhibits relay Derry's long history. (Open July-Aug. M-Sa 10am-5pm, Su 2-5pm; Sept.-June Tu-Sa 10am-5pm. UK£4.20, students UK£1.60.) Derry's residential neighborhoods, the Catholic **Bogside** and **Fountain Estate** (west of the city walls) and the Protestant **Waterside** (on the Foyle River's east bank) display brilliant murals. Bogside's **Free Derry Corner** and the **Bloody Sunday Memorial** commemorate the 1972 murder of 14 peaceful protestors by British soldiers.

Trains (☎7134 2228) arrive on Duke St., Waterside, on the east bank, from Belfast (2hr., 3-9 per day, UK£7.90). A free **Rail-Link bus** connects the train station and the **bus station,** on Foyle St., between the walled city and the river. Ulsterbus (☎7126 2261) goes to Belfast (1¾hr., 6-15 per day, UK£8) and Dublin (4¼hr., 4-6 per day, UK£11). The **tourist office** is at 44 Foyle St. (☎7126 7284. Open July-Sept. M-F 9am-7pm, Sa 10am-6pm, Su 10am-5pm; Oct.-Feb. M-F 9am-5pm; Mar.-June M-F 9am-6pm, Sa 10am-5pm.) Go down Strand Rd. and turn left on Asylum Rd. just before the RUC station to reach the ◪**Derry City Independent Hostel (Steve's Backpackers),** 4 Asylum Rd. (☎7137 7989. Dorms UK£7.50.) **Derry City Youth Hostel (YHANI/HI),** is on Magazine St. inside the city walls. (☎7128 4100. Laundry £3.50. Check-out 10am. Dorms UK£7-9.50. Double with breakfast and bath UK£26.) **Boston Tea Party,** 13-15 Derry Craft Village, delights with delicious cakes. (Open M-Sa 9:30am-5:30pm.) For nightly trad, head to **Peadar O'Donnell's,** 53 Waterloo St. **Postal code:** BT48 6AA.

GLENS OF ANTRIM

Nine lush green valleys, or "glens," slither from the hills and high moors of Co. Antrim down to the seashore. **Ulsterbus** (Belfast ☎9032 0011) #162 runs from Belfast through Waterfoot, Cushendall, and Cushendun (2-4 per day). The #252 **Antrim Coaster** stops at every coastal town from Belfast to Coleraine (2 per day).

GLENARIFF. Antrim's broadest (and arguably loveliest) glen, Glenariff, lies 6½km south of Waterfoot along Glenariff Rd. in the large **Glenariff Forest Park. Bus** #150 between Ballymena and Glenariff stops at the official park entrance, but if walking from Waterfoot, you can enter the park 2½km downhill from the official entrance by taking the road that branches left toward the Manor Lodge Restau-

I'M TOO SEXY The opulent homes of the local statesmen and merchants were once located within Derry's city walls. When the wealthy wives bought fancy dresses from London, they donned their new garb and strolled about on the city walls. The poverty-stricken residents of the Bogside looked at the ladies on the wall and were enraged at the decadent lifestyle on display, so a few of them wrote a letter to the London papers about the parading "cats." The London press were so amused by the nickname that it stuck, and the phrase "cat walk" fell into common usage.

rant. The stunning ■**Waterfall Trail** follows the cascading, fern-lined Glenariff River from the park entrance to the Manor Lodge. (Open daily 10am-dusk. UK£3 per car; UK£1.50 per adult pedestrian, UK£0.50 per child.)

CUSHENDALL. Cushendall is the "capital" of the Glens, with a variety of services unavailable in the rest of the region. Unfortunately, the closing of its hostel may mean that Cushendall's days as a budget travel mecca are over. **Antrim Coaster** bus #252 runs through Cushendall toward Portrush and Belfast (2 per day). The **tourist office,** 25 Mill St., is near the bus stop at the Cushendun end of town. (☎2177 1180. Open July-Sept. M-F 10am-1pm and 2-5:30pm, Sa 10am-1pm; Oct. to mid-Dec. and Feb.-June Tu-Sa 10am-1pm.) It's hard to imagine a warmer welcome than at **Glendale,** 46 Coast Rd., south of town overlooking the sea. (☎2177 1495. UK£17.)

CAUSEWAY COAST

The northern coast shifts from lyrical into dramatic mode as sea-battered, 182m cliffs tower over white, wave-lapped beaches and give way to **Giant's Causeway. Bushmills Bus** (☎(01265) 7043 3334) outlines the coast between Coleraine, 8km south of Portrush, and Giant's Causeway (July-Aug. 7 per day). In the summer, the Antrim Coaster bus #252 runs up the coast from Belfast to Portstewart via towns listed here (2 per day; UK£13.30 from Belfast, UK£8.80 from Larne).

BALLYCASTLE AND ENVIRONS. The Causeway Coast leaves the sleepy glens behind when it hits this bubbly seaside town that shelters Giant's Causeway-bound tourists. **Ulsterbus** #162A vrooms to Cushendall via Cushendun (50min., M-F 1 per day, UK£3) and #131 goes to Belfast (3hr., 5-6 per day, £6.10). The **tourist office** is in Sheskburn House, 7 Mary St. (☎2076 2024. Open July-Aug. M-F 9:30am-7pm, Sa 10am-6pm, Su 2-6pm; Sept.-June M-F 9:30am-5pm.) Snooze at **Castle Hostel (IHH),** 62 Quay Rd. (☎2076 2337. Dorms UK£8.50), or **Ballycastle Backpackers Hostel,** 4 North St. (☎2076 3612. Dorms UK£7.50).

Off the coast at Ballycastle, **Rathlin Island** ("Fort of the Sea") is home to 20,000 puffins, the odd golden eagle, and 100 humans. Caledonian MacBrayne **ferries** (☎2076 9299) run to the island from the pier at Ballycastle, up the hill from Quay Rd. on North St. (45min., 2-4 per day, return UK£8.20). A **minibus** service (☎2076 3909) drives to the **Kebble Bird Sanctuary** at the western tip of the island, 7km from the harbor. (20min., every 45min., UK£2.50).

Five miles west of Ballycastle, the modest village of **Ballintoy** attracts the crowds on their way to itsy-bitsy teeny-weeny **Carrick-a-rede Island.** Cross the shaky, 10cm wide, 20m long fishermen's rope bridge over the dizzying 30m drop to rocks and sea below; be extremely careful in windy weather. A sign marks the turnoff from the coastal road east of Ballintoy. The aptly titled **Sheep Island View Hostel (IHH),** 42A Main St., has beds and camping facilities. (☎2076 9391. Dorms with bath UK£10.)

GIANT'S CAUSEWAY. Touted as the 8th natural wonder of the world, Giant's Causeway is Northern Ireland's most famous sight. A spillage of 40,000 hexagonal columns of basalt form a 60-million-year-old honeycomb path from the foot of the cliffs far into the sea. The **Giant's Causeway Visitors Centre,** which sits at the entrance to the Causeway from the car park, runs a bus (every 15min.; return UK£1) to the columns. (☎2073 1855. Open June daily 10am-6pm; July-Aug. daily 10am-7pm; Mar.-May and Sept. 10am-5pm; Nov.-Feb. 10am-4:30pm.)

ITALY (ITALIA)

ITALIAN LIRE

PHONE CODE

Country code: 39. International dialing prefix: 00.
The city code always must be dialed, even when calling from
within the city. From outside Italy, dial int'l dialing prefix + 39
+ local number (drop the leading zero).

At the crossroads of the Mediterranean, Italy has served as the home of powerful
empires, eccentric leaders, and great food. The country burst on stage as the base
for the ambitious Roman empire; then it was persecutor and popularizer of an
upstart religion called Christianity; next, Italy became the center of the artistic and
philosophical Renaissance; and finally it emerged as a world power that has
changed governments more than 50 times since World War II. Countless invasions
have left the land rich with examples of nearly every artistic era: Egyptian obelisks,
Etruscan huts, Greek temples, Augustan arches, Byzantine mosaics, Renaissance
palazzi, Baroque fountains, and post-modern superstructures sprawl across the 20
regions. From perfect pasta to the creation of pizza, Italy knows that the quickest
way to a country's happiness is through its stomach. Italy is also the champion of
romance—passionate lovers proclaim their *amore* from the rooftops of southern
Italy and Venice. Somewhere between the leisurely gondola rides and the frenetic
nightclubs, you too will proclaim your love to Italy.

Consume a heaping plate of tasty tips from *Let's Go: Italy 2002* or *Let's Go:
Rome 2002*.

FACTS AND FIGURES

Official Name: Italian Republic.

Capital: Rome.

Major Cities: Florence, Venice, Milan,
Naples.

Population: 56,830,508. Urban 67%,
rural 33%.

Land Area: 301,230 sq. km.

Climate: Mediterranean; Alpine in the far
north, hot and dry in the south.

Language: Italian; some German, French
and Slovenian.

Religions: Roman Catholic (98%).

DISCOVER ITALY

The inevitable place to begin an Italian voyage is in **Rome** (p. 572), where you can
view the rubble of the toga-clad empire, the cathedrals of high Christianity, and the
art of the Renaissance. Shoot north to Umbria and shun worldly wealth à la Saint
Francis in **Assisi** (p. 633), before checking out the black-and-white *duomo* of stunning **Siena** (p. 630) and the medieval towers of **San Gimignano** (p. 631). Continue the
northward jaunt to be enchanted by **Florence** (p. 620), where burnt-orange roofs
shelter incredible works by Renaissance masters. The not-so-Leaning Tower is in
nearby **Pisa** (p. 631). Gritty **Genoa** (p. 613) is no postcard darling, but has personality and palaces. Gawk at the mysterious shroud at **Turin** (p. 603) before exploring
the five bright fishing villages of **Cinque Terre** (p. 616) on the Italian Riviera. Away

ITALY

from the coast, the nightlife in **Milan** (p. 606) is unrivaled, as is the beauty of **Lake Como** (p. 604). Dreamy **Verona** (p. 601) makes it easy to indulge your romantic, star-crossed side while nearby **Trent,** (p. 605) in the Dolomites, offers year-round skiing. In **Venice** (p. 592), misty mornings give way to mystical *palazzi*. For a change of pace, head to fresco-filled **Padua** (p. 600) and glittering **Ravenna** (p. 619), a Byzantine treasure chest on the east coast. Move inland to sample the culinary delights of **Bologna** (p. 617), and then satisfy pizza cravings in **Naples** (p. 634). A daytrip to **Pompeii** (p. 638) reveals Roman remains buried in AD 79. Sail to captivating **Capri** (p. 640) and the **Amalfi Coast** (p. 639), framed by crystal-blue waters. Take the ferry from Naples to vibrant **Palermo** (p. 641), the perfect start to an exploration of Sicily. Round out your tour of Italy at the spectacular **Aeolian Islands** (p. 642), with Stromboli's simmering volcano and beaches of ebony sand.

ESSENTIALS

WHEN TO GO

Traveling to Italy in late May or early September, when the temperature drops to a comfortable 77°F (25°C), will assure a calmer and cooler vacation. Also keep weather patterns, festival schedules, and tourist congestion in mind. Tourism enters overdrive in June, July, and August: hotels are booked solid, with prices limited only by the stratosphere. During *Ferragosto*, a national holiday in August, all Italians take their vacations and flock to the coast like well-dressed lemmings. Northern cities become ghost towns or tourist-infested infernos. Though many visitors find the larger cities enjoyable even during the holiday, most agree that June and July are better months for a trip to Italy.

DOCUMENTS AND FORMALITIES

VISAS. EU citizens may stay in Italy for as long as they like. Citizens of Australia, Canada, New Zealand, South Africa, and the US do not need visas for up to three months. Those wishing to stay in Italy for more than three months must apply for a *permesso di soggiorno* (residence permit) at a police station *(questura)*.

EMBASSIES. Foreign embassies are all in Rome (p. 573). For Italian embassies at home: **Australia,** 12 Grey St., Deakin, Canberra ACT 2600 (☎02 6273 3333; fax 6273 4223; www.ambitalia.org.au); **Canada,** 275 Slater St., 21st fl., Ottawa, ON K1P 5H9 (☎613-232-2401; fax 613-233-1484; www.italyincanada.com); **Ireland,** 63 Northumberland Rd., Dublin (☎(01) 660 1744; fax 668 2759; http://homepage.eircom.net/~italianembassy); **New Zealand,** 34 Grant Rd., Wellington (☎(006) 4473 5339; fax 472 7255; www.italy-embassy.org.nz); **South Africa,** 796 George Ave., Arcadia 0083, Pretoria (☎(012) 43 55 41; fax 43 55 47; www.ambital.org.za); **UK,** 14 Three Kings Yard, London W1Y 2EH (☎(020) 73 12 22 00; fax 74 99 22 83; www.embitaly.org.uk); and **US,** 1601 Fuller St. NW, Washington, D.C. 20009 (☎202-328-5500; fax 202-462-3605; www.italyemb.org).

TRANSPORTATION

BY PLANE. Rome's international airport, known as both Fiumicino and Leonardo da Vinci, is served by most major airlines. You can also fly into Milan's Malpensa or Linate airports or Florence's Amerigo Vespucci airport. **Alitalia** (US ☎800-223-5730; UK (870) 544 8259; www.alitalia.it/eng) is Italy's national airline and may offer off-season youth fares.

BY TRAIN. The Italian State Railway **Ferrovie dello Stato,** or **FS** (National information line ☎147 88 80 88; www.fs-on-line.com), offers inexpensive and efficient service. There are several types of trains: the *locale* stops at every station on a particular line; the *diretto* makes fewer stops than the *locale;* and the *espresso* stops only at major stations. The air-conditioned *rapido*, an **InterCity (IC)** train,

Italy

zips along but costs a bit more. Tickets for the fast, pricey **Eurostar** trains require reservations. If you are under 26 and plan to travel extensively in Italy, the **Cartaverde** should be your *first* purchase. The card (L40,000/€20.65) is valid for one year and gives a 20% discount on state train fare. **Eurail** passes are valid without a supplement on all trains except Eurostar. For a couple or a family, an **Italian Kilometric Ticket** (L200,000-338,000/€103.30-174.45; good for 20 trips or 3000km), can pay off. Otherwise, railpasses are seldom cost effective since regular fares are cheap. For more information, contact the **Italian State Railways** in the US (☎212-730-2121).

BY BUS. Intercity buses serve countryside points inaccessible by train and occasionally arrive in more convenient places in large towns. For city buses, buy tickets in *tabacchi* or kiosks, and validate them on board to avoid a fine.

BY FERRY. Ferry services at the ports of Bari, Brindisi, and Ancona (p. 634) connect Italy to Greece. Boats from Trieste (p. 602) serve the Istrian Peninsula down to

Croatia's Dalmatian Coast. Ferries also connect Italy's islands to the mainland. For Sardinia, boats go from Genoa (p. 613), La Spezia (p. 617), and Naples (p. 634). Travelers to Sicily (p. 641) take the ferry from Naples (p. 634) or Reggio di Calabria.

BY CAR. There are four kinds of roads: *Autostrada* (Superhighway; most of which charge tolls); *strade statali* (state roads); *strade provinciali* (provincial); and *strade communali* (local). Italian driving is frightening; congested traffic is common in large cities and in the north. On three-lane roads, be aware that the center lane is for passing. **Mopeds** (L40,000-60,000/€20.65-31 per day) can be a great way to see the islands and the more scenic areas of Italy, but can be disastrous in the rain and on rough roads. Call the **Automobile Club Italiano (ACI)** at ☎ 116 if you have an emergency breakdown.

BY BIKE AND BY THUMB. Bicycling is a popular national sport, but bike trails are rare, drivers often reckless, and, except in the Po Valley, the terrain challenging. *Let's Go* strongly urges you to consider the risks before choosing to hitchhike. Hitchhiking in Italy, especially in areas south of Rome or Naples, can be unsafe.

TOURIST SERVICES AND MONEY

EMERGENCY	Police: ☎112. Ambulance: ☎113. Fire: ☎115.

TOURIST OFFICES. In provincial capitals, look for the **Ente Provinciale per il Turismo (EPT)** or **Azienda di Promozione Turistica (APT)** for information on the entire province and the town. Local tourist offices, **Informazione e Assistenza ai Turisti (IAT)** and **Azienda Autonoma di Soggiorno e Turismo (AAST)**, are generally the most useful. **Italian Government Tourist Board (ENIT)** includes: **Australia**, Level 26, 44 Market St., Sydney NSW 2000 (☎(02) 9262 1666; fax 9262 5745); **Canada**, 175 E. Bloor St., #907 South Tower, Toronto, ON M4W 3R9 (☎416-925-4887; fax 416-925-4799; initaly@ican.net); **UK**, 1 Princes St., London WIR 9AY (☎(020) 7355 1439; fax 7493 6695; www.enit.it); **US**, 630 5th Ave., #1565, New York, NY 10111 (☎212-245-5618; fax 212-586-9249; www.italiantourism.com).

MONEY. The currency in Italy is the **lira** (plural: *lire*). When changing money in Italy, try to use only banks or *cambii* that have at most a 5% margin between their buy and sell prices. Italy has accepted the **Euro (€)** as legal tender, and *lire* will be phased out by July 1, 2002. For more information, see p. 24. The best rates are available through one of the many ATMs in Italy, where you can access your home bank account. A traveler staying in a hostel and preparing their own food can expect to spend L60,000-140,000/€31-72.30 per day, in addition to transportation costs. At many Italian restaurants, a service charge *(servizo)* or cover *(coperto)* is included in the bill. Taxi drivers expect a 10% tip. The value added tax in Italy (known as IVA) ranges from 12-35%. Upon departure from the EU, non-EU citizens can get a refund of the IVA for purchases over L650,000/€335.

BUSINESS HOURS. Nearly everything closes from around 1 to 3 or 4pm for siesta. Most museums are open 9am-1pm and 3-6pm; some are open through lunch, however. Monday is often their *giorno di chiusura* (day of closure).

COMMUNICATION

MAIL. Airmail letters sent from North America, United Kingdom, or Australia to Italy take anywhere from three to seven days. Since Italian mail is notoriously unreliable, it is usually safer and quicker to send mail express *(espresso)* or registered *(raccomandata)*. *Fermo Posta* is Italian for *Poste Restante*.

TELEPHONES. Pre-paid phone cards, available from *tabacchi*, vending machines, and phone card vendors, carry a certain amount of time depending on the card's denomination (L5000/€2.60; L10,000/€5.20; or L15,000/€7.75). International calls start at L1000/€1.05, and vary depending on where you are calling. A collect call is a *contassa a carico del destinatario* or *chiamata collect*. International direct dial numbers: **AT&T,** ☎172 10 11; **British Telecom,** ☎172 00 44; **Canada Direct,** ☎172 10 01; **Ireland Direct,** ☎172 03 53; **MCI,** ☎172 10 22; **Sprint,** ☎172 18 77; **Telecom New Zealand,** ☎172 10 64; **Telkom South Africa,** ☎172 10 27; **Telstra Australia,** ☎172 10 61.

INTERNET ACCESS. Internet cafes are constantly popping up in Italian cities and larger towns. Universities and libraries may offer free Internet access. For a list of Italian cyberspots, check www.ecs.net/cafe/#list and www.cybercaptive.com.

LANGUAGE. Any knowledge of Spanish, French, Portuguese, or Latin will help you understand Italian. The tourist office staff usually speaks some English. For a traveler's survival kit of basic Italian, see p. 981.

ACCOMMODATIONS AND CAMPING

Associazione Italiana Alberghi per la Gioventù (AIG), the Italian hostel federation is a Hosteling International (HI) affiliate, though not all Italian hostels *(ostelli per la gioventù)* are part of AIG. A full list is available from most **EPT** and **CTS** offices and from many hostels. Prices start at about L24,000/€12.40 per night for dorms. Hostels are the best option for solo travelers (single rooms are relatively scarce in hotels), but curfews, lockouts, distant locations, and less-than-perfect security detract from their appeal. For more information, contact the **AIG office** in Rome, V. Cavour, 44 (☎06 487 11 52; www.hostels-aig.org). Italian **hotel** rates are set by the state; hotel owners will need your passport to register you, don't be afraid to hand it over for a while (usually overnight), but ask for it as soon as you think you will need it. Hotel singles *(camera singola)* usually start at around L50,000-60,000/ €25.85-31 per night, and doubles *(camera doppia* or *camera matrimonale)* start at L70,000-80,000/€36.15-41.35. A room with a private bath *(con bagno)* usually costs 30-50% more. Smaller **pensioni** are often cheaper than hotels. Be sure to confirm the charges before checking in; Italian hotels are notorious for tacking on additional costs at check-out time. The **Azienda di Promozione Turismo (APT),** provides lists of hotels that have paid to be listed; some of the hotels we recommend may not be on the list. **Affittacamere** (rooms for rent in private houses) are another inexpensive option. For more information, inquire at local tourist offices. There are over 1700 **campsites** in Italy; the **Touring Club Italiano,** Corso Italia, 10-20122 Milano (☎02 852 61; fax 53 59 95 40) publishes numerous books and pamphlets on the outdoors. Rates average L8000/€4.15 per person or tent, and L7000/€3.65 per car.

FOOD AND DRINK

Breakfast in Italy often goes unnoticed; lunch is the main feast of the day. A *pranzo* (full meal) is a true event, consisting of an *antipasto* (appetizer), a *primo* (first course of pasta or soup), a *secondo* (meat or fish), a *contorno* (vegetable side dish), and then finally *dolce* (dessert or fruit), a *caffè*, and often an after-dinner liqueur. If you don't have a big appetite, you can buy authentic snacks for a picnic at *salumeria* or *alimentari* (meat and grocery shops). A bar is an excellent place to grab coffee or a quick snack. They usually offer *panini* (hot and cold sandwiches), drinks with or without alcohol, and *gelato*. Grab a lighter lunch at an inexpensive *tavola calda* (hot table), *Rosticceria* (grill), or *gastronomia* (serving hot prepared dishes). *Osterie, trattorie,* and *ristoranti* are, in ascending order, fancier and more expensive. Many restaurants offer a fixed-price tourist menu *(menù turistico)* that includes *primo, secondo,* bread, water, and wine. Italian dinner is a lighter meal, often a snack. In the north, butter and cream sauces dominate, while Rome and central Italy are notoriously spicy regions. Farther south, tomatoes play a significant role. Coffee is another rich and varied focus of Italian life; for a standard cup of *espresso*, request a *caffè; cappuccino* is the breakfast beverage. *Caffè macchiato* (spotted coffee) has a touch of milk, while *latte macchiato* is heavier on the milk and lighter on the coffee. Wines from the north of Italy, such as the Piedmont's *Asti Spumante* or Verona's *Soave*, tend to be heavy and full-bodied;

ITALY

stronger, fruitier wines come from southern Italy and the islands. Almost every Italian shop sells Italy's greatest contribution to civilization: *gelato* (ice cream).

HOLIDAYS AND FESTIVALS

Holidays: New Year's Day (Jan. 1); Epiphany (Jan. 6); Easter Sunday and Monday (Mar. 31 and Apr. 1); Liberation Day (Apr. 25); Labor Day (May 1); Assumption of the Virgin (Aug. 15); All Saints' Day (Nov. 1); Immaculate Conception (Dec. 8); Christmas Day (Dec. 25); and Santo Stefano (Dec. 26).

Festivals: The most common excuse for a local festival is the celebration of a religious event—a patron saint's day or the commemoration of a miracle. Most include parades, music, wine, obscene amounts of food, and boisterousness. **Carnevale,** held in February during the 10 days before Lent, energizes Italian towns; in Venice, costumed Carnevale revelers fill the streets and canals (p. 600). During **Scoppio del Carro,** held in Florence's P. del Duomo on Easter Sunday, Florentines set off a cart of explosives, following a tradition dating back to medieval times. On July 2 and Aug. 16, the **Palio** hits Siena (p. 630) with a bareback horse race around the central *piazza*.

ROME (ROMA)

Italy's massive capital city is an eruption of marble domes, noseless statues, and motorcycle dust. Rome is sensory overload, rushing down the hills of Lazio to knock you flat on your back, leaving you dying for more. The city and those it controlled were responsible for the development of over 2000 years of world history, art, architecture, politics, and literature. From this city, the Roman Empire defined the Western world and the Catholic Church spread its influence worldwide. For the traveler, there is so much to see, hear, and absorb that the city is both exhilarating and overwhelming. Never fear, however, because in *bella Roma*, everything is beautiful and everything tastes good. Liberate your senses from the pollution eroding the monuments and from the maniacal rush of motorcyclists, and enjoy the dizzying paradox that is the *Caput Mundi*, Rome. For more dazzling details about the Eternal City, curl up with *Let's Go: Rome 2002*.

■ INTERCITY TRANSPORTATION

Flights: Da Vinci International Airport (☎06 65951), known as **Fiumicino,** handles most flights. The **Termini line** runs nonstop to Rome's main station, **Termini Station** (30min.; every 35min. 7:37am-10:40pm; L16,000/€8.30, L40,000/€20.70 on board). After hours, take the blue **COTRAL bus** to Tiburtina from the ground floor outside the main exit doors after customs (1:15, 2:15, 3:30, 5am; L8000/€4.15, pay on board). From Tiburtina, take bus #40N to Termini. Most charter flights arrive at **Ciampino** (☎06 79 49 41). To get to Rome, take the COTRAL bus (every 30min. 6:10am-11pm, L2000/€1.05) to Anagnina station on Metro Line A.

Trains: From Termini Station to: **Bologna** (2¾-4¼hr.; L35,600/€18.40); **Florence** (2-3hr.; L40,900/€21.15); **Milan** (4½-8hr.; L50,500/€26.10); **Naples** (2-2½hr., L18,600/€9.60); **Venice** (5hr.; L66,000/€34.10). Trains arriving in Rome between midnight and 5am usually arrive at **Stazione Tiburtina** or **Stazione Ostiense,** which are connected to Termini by the #40N and 20N-21N buses, respectively.

■ ORIENTATION

From the **Termini** train station, **via Nazionale** is the central artery connecting **Piazza della Repubblica** with **Piazza Venezia,** home to the immense wedding-cake-like **Vittorio Emanuele II monument.** West of P. Venezia, **Largo Argentina** marks the start of C.V. Emanuele, which leads to Centro Storico, the medieval and Renaissance tangle of sights around the **Pantheon, Piazza Navona, Campo dei Fiori,** and **Piazza Farnese.** From P. Venezia, V. dei Fori Imperiale leads southeast to the **Forum** and **Colosseum,** south of which are the ruins of the **Baths of Caracalla** and the **Appian Way,** and the neighborhoods of southern Rome, the Aventine, Testaccio, Ostiense, and EUR. **Via del Corso** stretches from P. Venezia north to **Piazza del Popolo.** East of the Corso, fashionable streets border the **Piazza di Spagna** and, to the northeast, the **Villa Borghese.** South and east are the **Fontana di Trevi, Piazza Barberini,** and the **Quirinal Hill.** Across the Tiber to the north are **Vatican City,** and, to the south, **Trastevere,** the best neighborhood for wandering. It's impossible to navigate Rome without a map; pick up a free map from a tourist office. The invaluable **Roma Metro-Bus map** (L8000/€4.13) is available at newsstands.

⌨ LOCAL TRANSPORTATION

Public Transportation: The 2 **Metropolitana** subway lines (A and B) meet at Termini and run 5:30am-11:30pm. **Buses** run 6am-midnight (with limited late night routes); board at the front or back and validate your ticket in the machine. Buy **tickets** (L1500/€0.80) at *tabacchi,* newsstands, and station machines; they're valid for 1 Metro ride or unlimited bus travel within 1¼hr. of validation. **B.I.G. daily tickets** (L8000/€4.15) and **C.I.S. weekly tickets** (L32,000/€16.55) allow unlimited public transport, including Ostia but not Fiumicino. Pickpockets are rampant on buses and trains.

Taxis: Easily located at stands, or flag them down in the street. Ride only in yellow or white taxis, and make sure your taxi has a meter (if not, settle on a price before you get in the car). **Surcharges** at night (L5000/€2.60), on Sundays (L2000/€1.05), and when heading to or from Fiumicino (L14,000/€7.25) or Ciampino (L10,000/€5.20). Fares run about L15,000/€7.75 from Termini to the Vatican; between city center and Fiumicino around L70,000/€36.15.

Bike and Moped Rental: Bikes generally cost L5000/€2.58 per hr. or L15,000/€7.75 per day, but the length of a "day" varies according to the shop's closing time. In summer, try the stands on V.d. Corso, P.d. San Lorenzo, and V. di Pontifici. Open daily 10am-7pm. 16+.

◢ PRACTICAL INFORMATION

TOURIST, FINANCIAL, AND LOCAL SERVICES

▨**Tourist Agency: Enjoy Rome,** V. Marghera, 8a (☎06 445 18 43 or 06 445 68 90; www.enjoyrome.com). From middle concourse of Termini (between trains and ticket booths), exit right, with the trains behind you; cross V. Marsala and follow V. Marghera 3 blocks. Arranges hotel accommodations, walking and bicycle tours, and bus service to Pompeii. Full-service travel agency, booking transportation worldwide and lodgings throughout Italy. Branch office at V. Varese, 39 (walk 1 block down V. Marghera and go right). Open M-F 8:30am-7pm, Sa 8:30am-2pm.

Embassies: Australia, V. Alessandria, 215 (☎06 85 27 21, emergency 800 87 77 90). Open M-Th 9am-5pm, F 9am-12:30pm. **Canada,** V.G.B. de Rossi, 27 (☎06 44 59 81). **Ireland,** P. Campitelli, 3 (☎06 697 91 21). Open M-F 10am-12:30pm and 3-4:30pm. **New Zealand,** V. Zara, 28 (☎06 441 71 71). Passport and consular services M-F 9:30am-noon. Embassy services M-F 8:30am-12:45pm and 1:45-5pm. **South Africa,** V. Tanaro, 14 (☎06 85 25 41). Bus #86 from Termini to P. Buenos Aires. Open M-F 9am-noon. **UK,** V. XX Settembre, 80/A (☎06 482 54 41), near the corner of V. Palestro. Open M-F 9:15am-1:30pm. **US,** V. Veneto, 119/A (☎06 467 41). Passport and consular services M-F 8:30-noon and 1:30-3:30pm. Visas M-F 8:30-10:30am.

American Express: P. di Spagna, 38 (☎06 676 41; lost or stolen cards and checks 722 81). Open Sept.-July M-F 9am-7:30pm, Sa 9am-3pm; Aug. M-F 9am-6pm, Sa 9am-12:30pm. **Holds Mail:** P. di Spagna, 38; 00187 Roma.

Thomas Cook: P. Barberini, 21a (☎06 482 80 82). Open M-Sa 9am-8pm, Su 9:30am-5pm. **Branches:** V. d. Conciliazione, 23-25 (☎06 6830 0435; open M-Sa 8:30am-6pm, Su 9am-5pm); V. del Corso, 23 (☎06 323 00 67; open M-Sa 9am-8pm, Su 9am-1:30pm); P. della Republica, 65 (☎06 48 64 95; open M-F 9am-5pm with 1hr. lunch break, Sa 9am-1pm).

ITALY

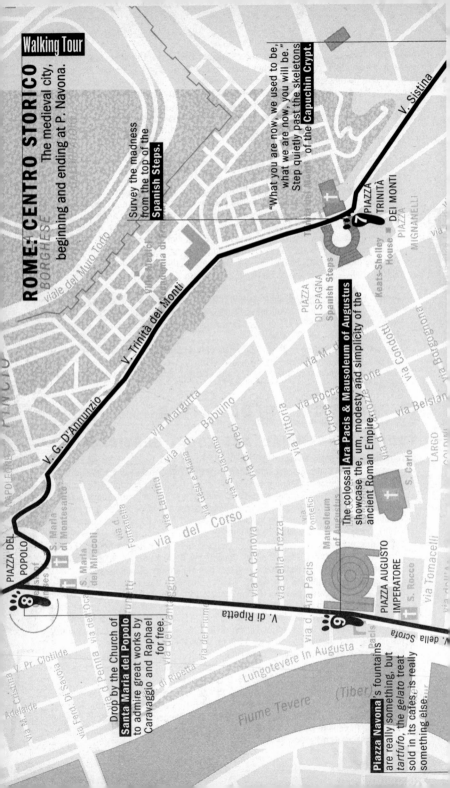

Walking Tour

ROME: CENTRO STORICO

BORGHESE The medieval city, beginning and ending at P. Navona.

Survey the madness from the top of the **Spanish Steps.**

"What you are now, we used to be, what we are now, you will be." Step quietly past the skeletons of the **Capuchin Crypt.**

The colossal **Ara Pacis & Mausoleum of Augustus** showcase the, um, modesty and simplicity of the ancient Roman Empire.

Drop by the Church of **Santa Maria del Popolo** to admire great works by Caravaggio and Raphael for free.

Piazza Navona's fountains are really something, but *tartufo*, the gelato treat sold in its cafés, is really something else.

7 PIAZZA TRINITÀ DEI MONTI

8 PIAZZA DEL POPOLO

9 PIAZZA AUGUSTO IMPERATORE

PINCIO

V. Sistina

PIAZZA TRINITÀ DEI MONTI

PIAZZA MIGNANELLI

Keats-Shelley House

PIAZZA DI SPAGNA — Spanish Steps

via Condotti

via Borgognona

LARGO

S. Carlo

via Belsiana

via della Croce

via Bocca di Leone

via M. de' Fiori

via Mario de' Fiori

via Vittoria

via S. Giacomo

via d. Greci

via d. Babuino

via Margutta

via Gesù e Maria

via Laurina

via d. Fontanella

via della Frezza

via A. Canova

via del Corso

via del Vantaggio

via di Ripetta

V. di Ripetta

Mausoleum of Augustus

Ara Pacis

S. Rocco

S. Carlo

S. Tomacelli

N. della Scrofa

Lungotevere In Augusta

Flume Tevere (Tiber)

V. G. D'Annunzio

V. Trinità dei Monti

viale del Muro Torto

Accademia di

Villa Medici

S. Maria di Montesanto

S. Maria dei Miracoli

via di Gesù

via Ferd. Di Savoia

via V. M. Cristina

V. Pr. Clotilde

Adelaide

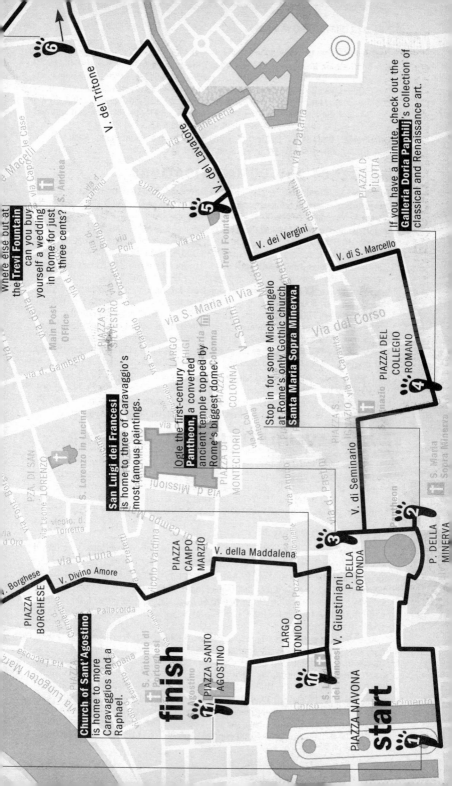

start

PIAZZA NAVONA

finish

Church of Sant'Agostino is home to more Caravaggios and a Raphael.

San Luigi dei Francesi is home to three of Caravaggio's most famous paintings.

Ogle the first-century **Pantheon**, a converted ancient temple topped by Rome's biggest dome.

Stop in for some Michelangelo at Rome's only Gothic church, **Santa Maria Sopra Minerva.**

Where else but at the **Trevi Fountain** can you buy yourself a wedding in Rome for just three cents?

If you have a minute, check out the **Galleria Doria Pamphilj**'s collection of classical and Renaissance art.

PIAZZA BORGHESE

V. Borghese

V. Divino Amore

PIAZZA SANTO AGOSTINO

PIAZZA CAMPO MARZIO

V. della Maddalena

LARGO TONIOLO

V. Giustiniani

P. DELLA ROTONDA

P. DELLA MINERVA

P. MINERVA

S. Maria Sopra Minerva

V. di Seminario

V. di Pastini

PIAZZA DEL COLLEGIO ROMANO

Via del Corso

V. di S. Marcello

V. dei Vergini

V. dei Vergini

Trevi Fountain

V. del Lavatore

V. del Tritone

V. del Tritone

V. Macelli

via Capelle Case

S. Andrea

Main Post Office

via d. Gambero

PZA. DI SAN LORENZO

S. Lorenzo in Lucina

via d. Luna

PIAZZA MONTECITORIO

COLONNA

via S. Maria in Via

Luggage Storage: In train station Termini, by track #1.

Gay and Lesbian Resources: **ARCI-GAY** and **ARCI-Lesbica** share offices at V. Orvinio, 2 (☎06 86 38 51 12) and V. Lariana, 8 (☎06 855 55 22). ARCI-GAY membership (L20,000/€10.33 per yr.) gives admission to all Italian gay clubs. **Circolo di Cultura Omosessuale Mario Mieli,** V. Corinto, 5 (☎06 541 39 85), provides info about gay life in Rome. M: B-San Paolo, walk 1 block to Largo Beato Placido Riccardi, turn left, and walk 1½ blocks to V. Corinto. Open Sept.-July M-F 9am-1pm and 2-6pm.

Laundromat: **OndaBlu,** V. La Mora, 7. Many locations throughout Rome. Wash L6000/€3.10; dry L6000/€3.10 per 6½kg. Soap L1500/€0.80. Open daily 8am-10pm.

EMERGENCY AND COMMUNICATIONS

Police: ☎113. **Carabinieri:** ☎112. **Medical Emergency:** ☎118. **Fire:** ☎115.

Pharmacies: **Farmacia Internazionale,** P. Barberini, 49 (☎06 487 11 95). **Farmacia Piram,** V. Nazionale, 228 (☎06 488 07 54). Both open 24hr.

Hospitals: **International Medical Center,** V.G. Amendola, 7 (☎06 488 23 71; nights and Su 488 40 51). Call first. Prescriptions filled, paramedic crew on call, referral service to English-speaking doctors. General visit L130,000/€67.15. Open M-Sa 8:30am-8pm. On-call 24hr. **Rome-American Hospital,** V.E. Longoni, 69 (☎06 225 51). Private emergency and laboratory services; HIV and pregnancy tests. On-call 24hr.

Internet Service: ■**Trevi Tourist Service: Trevi Internet,** V. dei Lucchesi, 31-32, 1 block from Trevi Fountain (toward P. Venezia on the road that becomes V.d. Pilotta). Central location. L5000/€2.60 per 30min., L10,000/€5.20 per 1½hr. Western Union money transfers, currency exchange, cheap international calls. Open daily 9am-10pm. **Splashnet,** V. Varese, 33, 3 blocks north of Termini. A laundromat with Internet access. Wash and dry L6000/€3.10 each, plus 15min. free Internet time. Internet L5000/€2.60 per hr.; ask for *Let's Go* discount. Open daily 8:30am-10:30pm.

Post Office: Main office, P. San Silvestro, 19, south of P. di Spagna. Come with large packages or to insure mail. Stamps and currency exchange (booths #23-25 and 19). Open M-F 9am-6pm, Sa 9am-2pm. **Large branch,** V. delle Terme di Diocleziano, 30, near Termini. Same hours as San Silvestro branch. **Postal Codes:** 00100-00200.

⛺ ACCOMMODATIONS AND CAMPING

Rome swells with tourists around Easter, from May to July, and in September. Prices vary widely with the time of year, and a proprietor's willingness to negotiate increases in proportion to length of stay, number of vacancies, and group size. Termini swarms with hotel scouts trying to bring you to their establishments. Watch out for sneaky imposters with fake badges, especially late at night.

CENTRO STORICO

If being a bit closer to the sights is worth it to you, then choosing Rome's medieval center over the area near Termini may be worth the higher prices.

Albergo Pomezia, V.d. Chiavari, 12 (☎06 686 13 71), off Corso Vittorio Emanuele II behind Sant'Andrea della Valle. Clean, quiet rooms with phone, fan, and heat in winter. Breakfast included. Singles L90,000/€46.50, with bath L110,000/€56.85; doubles L150,000/€77.40, L200,000/€103.30; triples L210,000/€108.45, L255,000/€131.70. AmEx/MC/V.

Albergo della Lunetta, P. del Paradiso, 68 (☎06 686 10 80), 1st right off V. Chiavari from C.V. Emanuele II behind Sant'Andrea della Valle. Good value in great location (between Campo dei Fiori and P. Navona). Singles L90,000/€46.50, with bath L110,000/€56.85; doubles L150,000/€77.50, L200,000/€103.30; triples L210,000/€108.45, L255,000/€131.70. Reserve with credit card or check. MC/V.

Hotel Piccolo, V.d. Chiavari, 32 (☎06 689 23 30), off Corso Vittorio Emanuele II behind Sant'Andrea della Valle. Recently renovated, family-run establishment next to a bustling grocery store. All rooms have fans and telephones. English spoken. Breakfast L7000/€3.65. Check-out noon. Curfew 1am. Singles L100,000/€51.65, with bath L120,000/

€62; doubles L120,000/€62, L160,000/€82.65; triples with bath L170,000/€87.80; quads with bath L180,000/€93. AmEx/MC/V.

Albergo del Sole, V.d. Biscione, 76 (☎06 68 80 68 73), off Campo dei Fiori. Allegedly the oldest *pensione* in Rome. Comfortable rooms with phone, fan, TV, and fantastic antique furniture. Singles L120,000/€62, with bath 140,000-170,000/€72.30-87.80; doubles L160,000-180,000/€82-93, L200,000-240,000/€103.30-124.

NEAR PIAZZA DI SPAGNA

These accommodations might cost a few thousand *lire* more, but can you really put a price tag on living just a few steps from Prada? John Keats couldn't.

◪ **Pensione Panda,** V.d. Croce, 35 (☎06 678 01 79), between P. di Spagna and V.d. Corso. Newly renovated. Check-out 11am. Reservations recommended. Singles L70,000/€36.15, with bath L100,000-120,000/€51.60-62; doubles L120,000-180,000/€62-93; triples with bath L210,000/€108.45; quads with bath L320,000/€165.30. Ask for *Let's Go* discount.

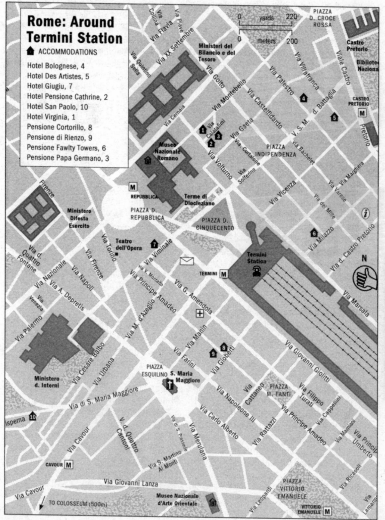

Rome: Around Termini Station

⌂ ACCOMMODATIONS

Hotel Bolognese, 4
Hotel Des Artistes, 5
Hotel Giugiu, 7
Hotel Pensione Cathrine, 2
Hotel San Paolo, 10
Hotel Virginia, 1
Pensione Cortorillo, 8
Pensione di Rienzo, 9
Pensione Fawlty Towers, 6
Pensione Papa Germano, 3

ITALY

Pensione Jonella, V.d. Croce, 41, 4th fl. (☎06 6797966), between P. di Spagna and V.d. Corso. 4 beautiful rooms. Quiet, roomy, and cool in summer. No reception: call ahead to be let in. No private bathrooms. Singles L100,000/€51.60; doubles L120,000/€62. Cash only.

Hotel Boccaccio, V.d. Boccaccio, 25 (☎06 488 59 62). M: A-Barberini. Off V.d. Tritone, near many sights. Singles L80,000/€41.35; doubles L120,000/€62, with bath L160,000/€83.65; triples L162,000-216,000/€84.20-111.55. AmEx/D/MC/V.

BORGO AND PRATI (NEAR VATICAN CITY)

Home to lots of priests and nuns, the Vatican and environs are pretty quiet at night.

▨ **Colors,** V. Boezio, 31 (☎06 687 40 30). M: A-Ottaviano. Or, bus to P. Risorgimento. Take V. Cola di Rienzo to V. Terenzio. Lots of amenities and English-speaking staff. Internet L5000/€2.60 per hr. Laundry L8000/€4.15 per load. Dorms L35,000/€18.10; doubles L120,000-150,000/€62-77.50; triples L140,000-180,000/€72.30-93. Credit card needed for reservations; cash only.

▨ **Pensione Ottaviano,** V. Ottaviano, 6 (☎06 39 73 72 53 or 39 73 72 53), just north of P. del Risorgimento, a few blocks from Metro stop of same name and near St. Peter's. Satellite TV, lockers, fridges, microwave, hot showers, free linens, and Internet access included. Friendly Aussie and British staff. Smoking allowed. Lockout 11:30am-2pm. No curfew. 3- to 6-bed dorms L30,000/€15.50, in winter L25,000/€13; doubles L70,000-90,000/€36.15-46.50; triples L120,000/€62. Cash only.

Hotel Pensione Joli, V. Cola di Rienzo, 243, 6th fl. (☎06 324 18 54), at V. Tibullo, scala A. Nice beds, ceiling fans, and views of the Vatican. Breakfast included. Singles L95,000/€49.10, with bath L120,000/€62; doubles L170,000/€87.80; triples L243,000/€125.50; quads L318,000/€164.25. MC/V.

TRASTEVERE

Hotels here are usually too pricey for budget travelers, but the area does offer great nightlife and a location near the Vatican.

Hotel Carmel, V.G. Mameli, 11 (☎06 580 99 21). Take a right on V. E. Morosini (V.G. Mameli) off V.d. Trastevere. Though a good walk from the heart of Trastevere, this simple hotel offers 9 no-frills, smallish rooms with bath for reasonable prices. Breakfast included. Singles L100,000/€51.60; doubles L150,000/€77.50; triples L190,000/€98.15; quads L220,000/€113.65. AmEx/MC/V.

Hotel Trastevere, V. Luciano Manara, 25 (☎06 581 47 13), right off V.d. Trastevere onto V.d. Fratte di Trastevere. 9 simple, airy rooms with bath, TV, and phone. English spoken. Breakfast included. Singles L130,000/€67.15; doubles 160,000/€82.65; triples L170,000/€87.80; quads L240,000/€1245. AmEx/D/MC/V.

TERMINI AND SAN LORENZO

This is budget traveler central, but the area south of Termini is sketchy at night.

▨ **Pensione Fawlty Towers,** V. Magenta, 39 (☎06 445 03 74). Exit Termini to the right from the middle concourse, cross V. Marsala onto V. Marghera, and turn right onto V. Magenta. Extremely popular 15-room hotel/hostel. Common room has satellite TV, library, refrigerator, microwave, and cheap Internet access. Check-out 9am for dorms, 10am for private rooms. Reservations strongly recommended. Native English-speaking staff. Dorms L30,000-35,000/€15.50-18.10; singles L75,000/€38.75, with shower L90,000/€46.50; doubles L110,000/€56.80, with shower L140,000/€72.30, with bath L150,000/€77.50; triples with bath L165,000/€85.25.

▨ **Hotel Des Artistes,** V. Villafranca, 20 (☎06 445 43 65). From middle concourse of Termini, exit right, turn left onto V. Marsala, right onto V. Vicenza, then left onto 5th cross-street. All rooms have bathroom, refrigerator, and TV. Reception 24hr. Check-out 11am. Dorms L35,000/€18.10; singles L70,000/€36.15; doubles L110,000-170,000/€56.85-87.80; triples L130,000-210,000/€67.15-108.45; in winter 20-30% less.

▨ **Hotel Papa Germano,** V. Calatafimi, 14a (☎06 48 69 19 or 47 82 52 02). From middle concourse of Termini, exit right and go left onto V. Marsala, which becomes V. Volturno;

V. Calatafimi is 4th cross-street on right. Clean rooms all have TV and phone. Check-out 11am. Dorms L30,000-40,000/€15.50-20.70; singles L45,000-70,000/€23.25-36.15; doubles L70,000-130,000/€36.15-67.15, with bath L100,000-160,000/€51.60-82.65; triples L105,000-150,000/€54.25-77.50, with bath L135,000-200,000/€69.75-103.30. AmEx/MC/V.

▧ **Pensione di Rienzo,** V. Principe Amedeo, 79a (☎06 446 71 31). A tranquil, family-run retreat with spacious renovated rooms, some with balcony, TV, and bath. Breakfast L20,000/€10.35. Check-out 10am. Singles L40,000-80,000/€20.70-41.35; doubles L60,000-120,000/€33.57-62. MC/V.

▧ **Pensione Cortorillo,** V. Principe Amedeo, 79a, 5th fl. (☎06 446 69 34). A small and friendly family-run *pensione* with TV in all rooms. English spoken. Breakfast included. Check-out 10am. Singles L80,000-120,000/€41.35-62; doubles L70,000-130,000/€36.15-67.15. Extra bed L30,000/€15.50. AmEx/D/MC/V.

▧ **Hotel San Paolo,** V. Panisperna, 95 (☎06 474 52 13). Exiting from front of train station, turn left onto V. Cavour. After you pass Santa Maria Maggiore (on left), bear right onto V.d. Santa Maria Maggiore (V. Panisperna). 10min. from Termini. Clean, with private hall baths. Breakfast L10,000/€5.20. Check-out 10:30am. Singles L75,000/€38.75; doubles L110,000/€56.80, with bath L150,000/€77.50; triples L150,000/€77.50. 6-10 person suite L50,000-65,000/€25.80-33.60 per person. AmEx/MC/V.

Hotel Pensione Cathrine, V. Volturno, 27 (☎06 48 36 34). From middle concourse of Termini, exit right, turn left onto V. Marsala (V. Volturno). Comfortable *pensione* with spacious rooms and clean common bathrooms. More rooms at V. XX Settembre, 58a. Breakfast L13,000/€6.75. Singles L90,000/€46.50; doubles L130,000-140,000/€67.15-72.30; triples with bath L170,000/€87.80. *Let's Go* discount L10,000/€5.20.

Hotel Bolognese, V. Palestro, 15 (☎06 49 00 45). Some of the 14 bedrooms have attached sitting rooms, bathtubs, and terraces. Check-out 11am. Curfew 2am. Singles L50,000/€25.85, with bath L70,000-80,000/€36.15-41.35; doubles L80,000-120,000/€41.35-65; triples L120,000-150,000/€62-77.50.

Hotel Giu' Giu', V.d. Viminale, 8 (☎06 482 77 34), 2 blocks south of Termini, in an elegant *palazzo.* 12 large, quiet rooms. Breakfast L15,000/€7.75. Check-out 10am. Singles L65,000/€33.60; doubles L105,000/€54.25, with bath L115,000/€59.40; triples with bath L155,000/€80; quads with bath L195,000/€100.75.

CAMPING

Camping on beaches, roads, and inconspicuous plots is illegal and dangerous.

Seven Hills Village, V. Cassia, 1216 (☎06 303 31 08 26), 8km north of Rome. Take bus #907 from M: A-Cipro-Musei Vaticani, or bus #201 from P. Mancini. The bus driver knows when to stop, just 3-4km past the GRA (the big highway that circles the city). Daily shuttles to Rome (L6000/€3.10) or train station near campgrounds (L2000/€1). From stop, follow the country road about 1km until you see the sign. Bar, market, restaurant, and *pizzeria* on premises. Buy a Seven Hills card for use in the campground. Check-in 24hr. Check-out noon. Open late Mar. to late Oct. L14,000/€7.25 per person, L1500/€0.80 per tent. Cash only.

🗅 FOOD

Ancient Roman dinners were lavish, festive affairs lasting as long as 10 hours. Peacocks and flamingos were served with their full plumage, while acrobats and fire-eaters distracted guests between their courses of camels' feet and goats' ears. Meals in Rome are still lengthy affairs, although they have slightly less fanfare. Restaurants tend to close between 3 and 7pm, so plan accordingly.

RESTAURANTS

ANCIENT CITY

Despite its past glory, this area has yet to discover the noble concept of "affordable food." But along **V. dei Fori Imperiali,** several restaurants offer decent prices.

◪ **Taverna dei Quaranta,** V. Claudia, 24, off P. del Colosseo. Not at all touristy. Menu changes weekly, and in summer features sinfully good *oliva ascolane* (olives stuffed with meat and fried; L7500/€3.90) and *ravioli all'Amalfitana* (L11,000/€5.70). ½L of house wine L5000/€2.60. Cover L2500/€1.30. Open daily noon-3:30pm and 7:45pm-midnight. AmEx/D/MC/V.

I Buoni Amici, V. Aleardo Aleardi, 4. From the Colosseum, take V. Labicana to V. Merulana. Turn right, then left on V. A. Aleardi. A long walk, but the cheap, excellent food is worth it. Choices include the *linguine all'astice* (linguine with lobster sauce; L12,000/€6.20) and *penne alla vodka* (L10,000/€5.20). Cover L2500/€1.30. Open M-Sa noon-3pm and 7-11:30pm. AmEx/D/MC/V.

CENTRO STORICO

The twisting streets of Rome's historic center offer many hidden gems, especially just off the main *piazzas*. No matter where you eat, you can expect to be subjected to numerous street performances, especially near P. Navona.

◪ **Pizzeria Baffetto,** V.d. Governo Vecchio, 114, at V. Sora. Be prepared to wait a while for a table outdoors. Pizza L8000-14,000/€4.15-7.25. Open M-F noon-3pm and 7:30pm-1am, Sa-Su noon-3pm and 7:30pm-2am. Cash only.

Pizzeria Corallo, V.d. Corallo, 10-11. Off V.d. Governo Vecchio near P. del Fico. This *pizzeria* is a great place to grab a cheap, late dinner before hitting the bars nearby. Pizza L7000-14,000/€3.65-7.25. Open daily noon-3pm and 7pm-1am. MC/V.

Trattoria dal Cav. Gino, V. Rosini, 4. Off V.d. Campo Marzio across from P. del Parlamente. *Primi* L8000-10,000/€4.15-5.20; *secondi* L15,000-17,000/€7.75-8.80. Open M-Sa 1-3:45pm and 8-10:30pm. Cash only.

CAMPO DEI FIORI AND THE JEWISH GHETTO

◪ **Trattoria da Sergio,** V.d. Grotte, 27. Take V.d. Giubbonari and take the 1st right. Offers honest-to-God Roman ambience (the waiters don't bother with menus) and hearty portions of great food. Try the *spaghetti all'Amatriciana* (with bacon and spicy tomato sauce; L10,000/€5.16). Open M-Sa 12:30-3pm and 7pm-12:30am. MC/V.

◪ **Hostaria Grappolo d'Oro,** P. della Cancelleria, 80-81, between Corso Vittorio Emanuele II and the Campo. This increasingly upscale *hostaria* is running out of space in their front window to plaster all the awards they've won over the years. Small menu changes daily. Offers dishes like *fregnacce al Casaro* (homemade pasta with ricotta and tomato; L19,000/€9.85) and innovative creations such as *controfiletto di manzo* (steak with herbs and goat-cheese; L24,000/€12.40). Cover L2000/€1.05. Open M-Sa noon-2:30pm and 7:30-11pm; closed M lunch. AmEx/MC/V.

◪ **Trattoria Da Luigi,** P.S. Cesarini, 24, near Chiesa Nuova, 4 blocks down Corso Vittorio Emanuele II from Campo dei Fiore. Enjoy inventive cuisine including *tagliolini* with shrimp, asparagus, and tomato (L13,000/€6.75), as well as simple dishes like *vitello con funghi* (veal with mushrooms; L15,000/€7.75). Open Tu-Su 7pm-midnight.

Ristorante da Giggetto, V.d. Portico d'Ottavio, 21-22. Rightfully famous but increasingly pricey, Giggetto serves up some of the finest Roman cooking known to man. Cover L3000/€1.55. Open Tu-Su 12:30-3pm and 7:30-11pm. AmEx/MC/V.

PIAZZA DI SPAGNA

◪ **Trattoria da Settimio all'Arancio,** V.d. Arancio, 50-52. Take V.d. Condotti from P. di Spagna; take the 1st right after V.d. Corso, then the 1st left. Arrive early to avoid the throngs of natives who come for the great service and tasty seafood. Excellent grilled *calamari* (L18,000/€9.30). *Primi* L12,000-15,000/€6.20-7.75; *secondi* L16,000-26,000/€8.30-13.45. Cover L2000/€1.05. Open M-Sa 12:30-3pm and 7:30-11:30pm. AmEx/D/MC/V.

◪ **Vini e Buffet,** P. Torretta, 60. From V.d. Corso, turn onto P.S. Lorenzo in Lucina. Take a left on V. Campo Marzio and a quick right onto V. Toretta. A favorite spot for chic Romans. Don't leave without getting one of their signature yogurt and fruit bowls for dessert; the yogurt, almond, and cassis combination is out of this world. Open M-Sa 12:30-3pm and 7:30-11pm. Cash only.

Il Brillo Parlante, V. Fontanella, 12, near P. del Popolo. The wood-burning pizza oven, fresh ingredients, and excellent wine attract many lunching Italians. Pizza L10,000-15,000/€5.20-7.75. Restaurant open Tu-Su noon-3pm and 7:30pm-1am. MC/V.

BORGO AND PRATI (NEAR VATICAN CITY)

Establishments near the Vatican serve mediocre sandwiches at hiked-up prices, but just a few blocks northeast is better and much cheaper food.

☒ **Franchi,** V. Cola di Rienzo, 200-204. Benedeto Franchi ("Frankie") has been serving superb *tavola calda,* prepared sandwiches, and luxurious picnic supplies for nearly 50 years without an unsatisfied customer. Open M-Sa 8:15am-9pm. AmEx/MC/V.

Pizza Re, V. Oslavia, 39. Some of the best pizza in Rome, this chain serves Neopolitan (thick crust) pizzas with every topping imaginable in cheerful yellow surroundings. Lunch specials (pizza and drink) L13,000/€6.70. Dinner L7000-18,000/€3.60-9.30. Pizzas L3000-5500/€1.55-2.85 less if you take them out. Long lines at dinnertime, so get there early. Open M-Sa noon-3:30pm and 7:30pm-12:30am; closed Su lunch.

TRASTEVERE

☒ **Pizzeria San Calisto,** P.S. Calisto, 9a, right off P.S. Maria in Trastevere. Quite simply the best damn pizza in Rome. Gorgeous thin crust pizzas so large they hang off the plates. Open Tu-Su 7pm-midnight. MC/V.

Augusto, P. de' Rienzi, 15, north of P.S. Maria in Trastevere. Daily lunch pasta specials around L8500/€4.40. The desserts are out of this world, but you may have to be pushy to get service. Open M-F 12:30-3pm and 8-11pm, Sa 12:30-3pm; closed Aug.

TERMINI

☒ **Africa,** V. Gaeta, 26-28, near P. Independenza. A 20-year tradition of serving excellent Eritrean/Ethiopian food. Cover L1500/€0.77. Open M-Sa 8pm-midnight. MC/V.

Trattoria da Bruno, V. Varese, 29, from V. Marsala, next to the train station, walk 3 blocks down V. Milazzo and turn right onto V. Varese. A neighborhood favorite with daily specials. Try the tasty homemade *gnocchi* (L10,000/€5.16). Open daily noon-3:30pm and 7-10:15pm. Closed Aug. AmEx/V.

Ristorante Due Colonne, V.d. Serpenti, 91. Turn right off V. Nazionale before the Palazzo delle Esposizioni. Excellent pizzas L8000-14,000/€4.15-7.25. *Menù* L18,000-26,000/€9.30-13.45. Open M-Sa 9am-3:30pm and 6:30pm-12:30am. AmEx/D/MC/V.

SAN LORENZO

Rome's funky university district offers many good, cheap eateries. From Termini, walk south on V. Pretoriano to P. Tiburtino, or take bus #492. Women may find the walk uncomfortable at night.

☒ **Il Pulcino Ballerino,** V.d. Equi, 66-68, off V. Tiburtina. An artsy atmosphere with cuisine to match. The cook stirs up imaginative dishes and excellent vegetarian dishes. You can prepare your own meal on a warm stone at the table. Cover L1000/€0.55. Open M-Sa 1-3:30pm and 8pm-midnight; closed 2nd and 3rd weeks of Aug. AmEx/MC/V.

Arancia Blu, V.d. Latini, 65, off V. Tiburtina. Elaborate dishes like *tonnarelli con pecorino romano e tartufo* (pasta with sheep cheese and truffles; L12,000/€6.20). Extensive wine list. Open daily 8:30pm-midnight.

La Pantera Rosa, P. Verano, 84-85. At the eastern end of V. Tiburtina. The house specialty is the delicious pink salmon and caviar pizza (L11,000/€5.70). Open Th-Tu noon-3pm and 6:30pm-12:30am. MC/V.

TESTACCIO

This working-class southern neighborhood is the center of Roman nightlife, and eateries here offer food made of just about every animal part imaginable.

Trattoria da Bucatino, V. Luca della Robbia, 84-86. Take V. Luigi Vanvitelli off V. Marmorata, then the 1st left. All the animal entrails you know and love, and plenty of gut-less dishes as well. Cover L2000/€1.05. Open Tu-Su 12:30-3:30pm and 6:30-11:30pm; closed Aug. D/MC/V.

DESSERTS AND WINE BARS

Cheap *gelato* is as plentiful on Roman streets as leather pants. Look for *gelato* with very muted (hence natural) colors, or try some of our favorite places:

☒ **San Crispino,** V.d. Panetteria, 42, near the Trevi Fountain. Facing the fountain, turn right onto V. Lavatore and take the 2nd left; the *gelato* temple is on the right. Positively the best *gelato* in the world. L3000-10,000/€1.55-5.20. Open M and W-Th noon-12:30am, F-Sa noon-1:30am, Su noon-midnight.

☒ **Portico d'Ottavia,** 1. A tiny, take-out only pastry bakery deep in the Jewish Ghetto. Little fanfare, just long lines of locals seeking fabulous blueberry pies, buttery cookies, and chocolate and pudding concoctions, sold by weight at excellent prices (L2000/€1.05 for a wedge of pie). Open Su-Th 8am-8pm, F 8am-5:30pm; closed Jewish holidays.

Tre Scalini, P. Navona, 30. Famous for its *tartufo*, truffled chocolate ice cream rolled in chocolate shavings (L5000/€2.60 at the bar; L11,000/€5.60 sit-down). Bar open Th-Tu 9am-1:30am; restaurant open Th-Tu 12:30-3:30pm and 7:30-9pm.

Trimani Wine Bar, V. Cernaia, 37b, near Termini, perpendicular to V. Volturno (V. Marsala). Filling quiches and desserts worth writing home about—try the heavenly ricotta, amaretto, and raspberry tart (L9000/€4.65). Wines from L3500/€1.80 per glass; L18,000/€9.30 per bottle. Open M-Sa 11am-3:30pm and 6pm-12:30am.

Cul de Sac, P. Pasquino, 73, off P. Navona. Rome's first wine bar, Cul de Sac keeps the customers coming back for a huge selection of great, decently priced wines, and excellent food. House specialty paté (such as pheasant and mushroom; L9500/€4.90) is exquisite. Open M 7pm-12:30am, Tu-Sa 12:30-4pm and 6pm-12:30am. MC/V.

◎ SIGHTS

Rome wasn't built in a day, and you can't see it all in one, either. Ancient temples and forums, Renaissance basilicas, 280 fountains, and 981 churches cluster together in a city bursting with masterpieces from every era of Western civilization. From Etruscan busts to modern canvases, there's more than enough in Rome to captivate visitors for years on end.

ANCIENT CITY

ROMAN FORUM

M: B-Colosseo, or bus to P. Venezia. Main entrance on V.d. Fori Imperiali (at Largo C. Ricci, between P. Venezia and the Colosseum). Open in summer M-Sa 9am-6:30pm, Su 9am-1pm; in winter daily 9am-1hr. before sunset; sometimes closes M-F 3pm, Su and holidays noon. Free. Tour L6000/€3.2. Audioguide L7000/€3.65 in English, French, German, Italian, Japanese, or Spanish available at main entrance.

Here the pre-Romans founded a thatched-hut shantytown in 753 BC. The entrance ramp leads to **Via Sacra,** Rome's oldest street, near the **Basilica Aemilia,** built in 179 BC, and the area once known as the **Civic Forum.** Next to the Basilica stands the **Curia** (Senate House); it was converted to a church in 630 and restored by Mussolini. The broad space in front of the Curia was the **Comitium,** where male citizens came to vote and representatives of the people gathered for public discussion. Bordering the Comitium is the large brick **Rostrum** (speaker's platform) erected by Julius Caesar just before his death. The hefty **Arch of Septimius Severus,** to the right of the Rostrum, was dedicated in 203 to celebrate Caesar's victories in the Middle East. The **market square** holds a number of shrines and sacred precincts, including the **Lapis Niger** (Black Stone), where Romulus was supposedly murdered by Republican senators. Below the Lapis Niger are the underground ruins of a 6th-century BC altar and the oldest known Latin inscription in Rome. In the square the **Three Sacred Trees** of Rome—olive, fig, and grape—have been replanted by the Italian state. The newest part of the Forum is the **Column of Phocas,** erected in 608.

The three great temples of the **Lower Forum** have been closed off for excavations and restoration; however, the eight columns of the 5th-century BC **Temple of Saturn,** next to the Rostrum, have been restored. Around the corner, rows of column bases are all that remain of the **Basilica Julia,** a courthouse built by Julius Caesar in 54 BC. At the far end, three white marble columns mark the massive podium of the recently restored **Temple of Castor and Pollux,** built to celebrate the Roman defeat of the Etruscans. The circular building next to it is the **Temple of Vesta,** where the Vestal Virgins tended the city's sacred fire for more than 1000 years.

In the **Upper Forum** lies the **House of the Vestal Virgins.** For 30 years, the six virgins who officiated over Vesta's rites lived in seclusion here from the ripe old age of seven. As long as they kept their vows of chastity, they remained among the most respected people in ancient Rome. Near here, V. Sacra runs over the **Cloaca Maxima,** the ancient sewer that still drains water from the otherwise marsh-like valley. V. Sacra continues out of the Forum proper to the **Velia** and the gargantuan **Basilica of Maxentius** (also known as the Basilica of Constantine). The middle apse of the basilica once contained a gigantic statue of Constantine with a bronze body and marble head, legs, and arms. The uncovered remains, including a 2m foot, are displayed at the **Palazzo dei Conservatori** on the Capitoline Hill (p. 584). V. Sacra leads to an exit on the other side of the hill to the Colosseum; the path that crosses before the **Arch of Titus** heads to the Palatine Hill.

THE PALATINE HILL

The Palatine rises to the south of the Forum. Open in summer daily 9am-6:30pm; in winter M-Sa 9:30am-1hr. before sunset, Su 9am-1pm; sometimes closes M-F 3pm, Su and holidays noon. L12,000/€6.20; EU citizens ages 18-24 L6000/€3.20; EU citizens under 18 and over 60 free. 5-day ticket book good for the 3 Musei Nazionali Romani (p. 589), the Colosseum, and Palatine Hill L30,000/€15.50; available at the Forum's main entrance.

The best way to attack the Palatine is from the stairs near the Forum's **Arch of Titus.** The hill, actually a plateau between the Tiber and the Forum, was home to the she-wolf that suckled Romulus and Remus. Throughout the garden complex, terraces provide breathtaking views. Lower down, excavations continue on the 9th-century BC village, the **Casa di Romulo.** To the right of the village is the podium of the 191 BC **Temple of Cybele.** The stairs to the left lead to the **House of Livia,** which is connected to the **House of Augustus** next door. Around the corner, the long, spooky **Cryptoporticus** connected Tiberius's palace with the buildings nearby. The short end of the tunnel, the path around the House of Augustus, leads to the vast ruins of a giant palace and is divided into two wings. The solemn **Domus Augustana** was the private space for the emperors; the adjacent wing, the sprawling **Domus Flavia,** once held a gigantic octagonal fountain. Between the Domus Augustana and the Domus Flavia stands the **Palatine Antiquarium,** the museum that houses the artifacts found during the excavations of the Palatine Hill. *(30 people admitted every 20min. from 9:10am. Free.)* Outside on the right, the palace's east wing contains the curious **Stadium of Domitian,** or *Hippodrome,* a sunken oval space once surrounded by a colonnade but now decorated with fragments of porticoes, statues, and fountains.

FORI IMPERIALI. Across the street from the Ancient Forum are the **Fori Imperiali,** a conglomeration of temples, basilicas, and public squares constructed in the 1st and 2nd centuries. Excavations will proceed through 2002, so the area is closed off, but you can still get free views by peering over the railing from V.d. Fori Imperiali or V. Alessandrina. Built between 107 and 113, the **Forum of Trajan** included a colossal equestrian statue of Trajan and an immense triumphal arch. At one end of the now-decimated forum, 2500 legionnaires march their way up the almost perfectly preserved ▇**Trajan's Column,** one of the greatest extant specimens of Roman relief-sculpture. The crowing statue is St. Peter, who replaced Trajan in 1588. Across V. dei Fori Imperiali, in the shade of the Vittorio Emanuele II monument, lie the paltry remains of the **Forum of Caesar,** including the ruins of Julius Caesar's **Temple to Venus Genetrix.** Nearby, the gray tufa wall of the **Forum of Augustus** commemorates Augustus's victory over Caesar's murderers in 42 BC. The aptly named **Forum Transitorium** (also called the **Forum of Nerva**) was a narrow, rectangular space connecting the

Forum of Augustus with the Republican Roman Forum. The only remnant of **Vespatian's Forum** is the mosaic-filled **Church of Santi Cosma e Damiano** across V. Cavour, near the Roman Forum. *(Open daily 9am-1pm and 3-7pm.)*

■ **THE COLOSSEUM.** This enduring symbol of the Eternal City—a hollowed-out ghost of marble that dwarfs every other ruin in Rome—once held as many as 50,000 spectators. Within 100 days of its opening in AD 80, some 5000 wild beasts perished in the arena (from the Latin word for sand, *harena*, which was put on the floor to absorb blood). The floor (now partially restored) covers a labyrinth of brick cells, ramps, and elevators used to transport wild animals from cages up to arena level. *(M: B-Colosseo. Open daily in summer 9am-6:30pm; in winter 9am-1hr. before sunset. L10,000/€5.20; EU citizens ages 18-24 L5000/€2.60; EU citizens under 18 and over 60 free. 5-day ticket book good for the 3 Musei Nazionali Romani (p. 589), the Colosseum, and the Palatine Hill (L30,000/€15.50). Guided tour L6000/€3.20.)*

ARCH OF CONSTANTINE. Between the Colosseum and the Palatine lies the **Arch of Constantine,** one of the latest and best-preserved imperial monuments in the area. Constantine built it in 312 using fragments from earlier monuments of Trajan, Hadrian, and Marcus Aurelius to create the harmonious triple arch.

THE DOMUS AUREA. This park houses just a portion of Nero's "Golden House," which once covered a huge chunk of Rome. After deciding that he was a god, Nero had architects build a house worthy of his divinity. The Forum was reduced to a vestibule of the palace; Nero crowned it with the 35m Colossus, a huge statue of himself as the sun. Nero committed suicide only five years after building his gargantuan pleasure garden, and later emperors tore down his house and replaced all traces of the palace with monuments built for the public good. *(On the Oppian Hill, below Trajan's baths. From the Colosseum, walk through the gates up V.d. Domus Aurea and take 1st right. Open Tu-Su 9am-6:45pm. Groups of 30 admitted every 20min. L10,000/€5.20.)*

THE VELABRUM. The **Velabrum** is a flat flood plain south of the Jewish Ghetto. At the bend of V. del Portico d'Ottavia, a shattered pediment and a few ivy-covered columns are all that remain of the once magnificent **Portico d'Ottavia.** The stocky, gray **Teatro di Marcello** next door is named for Augustus's nephew, whose early and sudden death remains a mystery. Farther down V. di Teatro di Marcello, **Chiesa di San Nicola in Carcere** incorporates three Roman temples originally dedicated to Juno, Janus, and Spes. *(☎06 686 99 72; call to visit the interior. Open Sept.-July M-Sa 7:30am-noon and 4-7pm.)* Across the street, the **Chiesa di Santa Maria in Cosmedin** harbors some of Rome's most beautiful medieval decoration. The Audrey Hepburn film *Roman Holiday* made the portico's relief, the ■**Bocca della Verità,** famous; according to legend, the hoary face will chomp on the hand of a liar. *(Church open daily 10am-1pm and 3-7pm. Portico open daily 9am-7pm.)*

THE CAPITOLINE HILL. Home to the original capitol, the **Monte Capitolino** still serves as the seat of the city government. Michelangelo designed its crowning **Piazza di Campidoglio,** now home to the **Capitoline Museums** (p. 589). Stairs lead up to the rear of the 7th-century **Chiesa di Santa Maria in Aracoeli.** The gloomy **Mamertine Prison,** consecrated the **Church of San Pietro in Carcere,** lies down the hill from the back stairs of the Aracoeli. Saint Peter, imprisoned here, baptized his captors with the waters that flooded his cell. *(Open daily 9am-noon and 2:30-6pm. Donation requested.)* At the far end of the *piazza*, opposite the stairs, lies the turreted **Palazzo dei Senatori,** which houses Rome's mayor. *(To get to the Campidoglio, take any bus that goes to P. Venezia. From P. Venezia, face the Vittorio Emanuele II monument, walk around to the right to P. d'Aracoeli, and take the stairs up the hill.)*

CIRCUS MAXIMUS AND BATHS OF CARACALLA. Boxed in the valley between the Palatine and Aventine Hills, today's **Circus Maximus** is just a grassy shadow of its former glory. After its construction in 600 BC, the circus drew more than 300,000 Romans, who gathered here to watch chariots careen around the quarter-mile track. The remains of the **Baths of Caracalla** are the largest and best-preserved baths in the city. *(Walk down V.d. San Gregorio from the Colosseum to the Circus. Open 24hr.*

To get to baths from the eastern end of Circus Maximus walk up V.d. Terme di Caracalla. Open daily in summer 9am-6pm; in winter 9am-1hr. before sunset. L8000/€4.15.)

CENTRO STORICO

PIAZZA VENEZIA AND VIA DEL CORSO. The **Via del Corso** takes its name from its days as Rome's premier racecourse, running between P. del Popolo and the rumbling P. Venezia. **Palazzo Venezia** was one of the first Renaissance *palazzi* built in the city; Mussolini used it as an office and delivered his famous orations from its balcony, but today it's little more than a glorified traffic circle dominated by the **Vittorio Emanuele II monument.** Off V. del Corso, the picturesque **Piazza Colonna** was named for the colossal **Colonna di Marco Aurelio,** designed in imitation of Trajan's column. Off the northwest corner of the *piazza* is the **Piazza di Montecitorio,** dominated by Bernini's **Palazzo Montecitorio,** now the seat of the Chamber of Deputies.

■ **THE PANTHEON.** This famous temple has remained almost unchanged since the day it was built nearly 2000 years ago. Architects still wonder how it was erected; its dome—a perfect half-sphere made of poured concrete without the support of vaults, arches, or ribs—is the largest of its kind. The light that enters the roof was used as a sundial to indicate the passing of the hours and the dates of equinoxes and solstices. In 606, it was consecrated as the **Church of Santa Maria ad Martyres,** its official name to this day. *(In P. della Rotonda. Open June M-Sa 9am-7pm; Su 9am-1pm; July-Aug. M-Sa 9am-7:30pm, Su 9am-1pm; Oct.-May M-Sa 9am-4pm, Su 9am-1pm. Free.)*

PIAZZA NAVONA. Originally a stadium built in AD 86, the *piazza* once hosted wrestling matches, track and field events, and mock naval battles (in which the stadium was flooded and filled with fleets skippered by convicts). Each of the river god statues in Bernini's **Fountain of the Four Rivers** represents one of the four continents of the globe (as known then): the Ganges for Asia, the Danube for Europe, the Nile for Africa (veiled, since the source of the river was unknown), and the Rio de la Plata for the Americas. At the ends of the *piazza* are the **Fontana del Moro** and the **Fontana di Nettuno,** designed by Giacomo della Porta in the 16th century and renovated by Bernini in 1653. The **Church of Sant'Agnese in Agone** dominates the *piazza*'s western side. *(Open Tu-Sa 4:30-7pm, Su 10am-1pm.)*

OTHER SIGHTS. In front of the temple, the *piazza* centers on Giacomo della Porta's late-Renaissance fountain and an Egyptian obelisk added in the 18th century. Around the left side of the Pantheon, another obelisk marks the center of tiny **Piazza Minerva.** Behind the obelisk, the **Chiesa di Santa Maria Sopra Minerva** hides some Renaissance masterpieces, including Michelangelo's *Christ Bearing the Cross, Annunciation* by Antoniazzo Romano, and a statue of St. Sebastian recently attributed to Michelangelo. The south transept houses the famous **Carafa Chapel,** home to a brilliant fresco cycle by Filippino Lippi. *(Open M-Sa 7am-7pm, Su 7am-1pm and 3:30-7pm.)* From the upper left-hand corner of P. della Rotonda, V. Giustiniani goes north to intersect V. della Scrofa and V. della Dogana Vecchia at the **Church of San Luigi dei Francesi,** home to three of Caravaggio's most famous paintings: *The Calling of St. Matthew, St. Matthew and the Angel,* and *Crucifixion. (Open F-W 7:30am-12:30pm and 3:30-7pm, Th 7:30am-12:30pm.)*

CAMPO DEI FIORI

Campo dei Fiori lies across Corso Vittorio Emanuele II from P. Navona. During papal rule, the area was the site of countless executions; now the only carcasses that litter the *piazza* are the fish in the colorful produce **market** (M-Sa 6am to 2pm). South of the Campo lie P. Farnese and the stately **Palazzo Farnese,** the greatest of Rome's Renaissance *palazzi*. To the east of the *palazzo* is the Baroque façade of the **Palazzo Spada** and the collection of the **Galleria Spada** (p. 591).

THE JEWISH GHETTO. The Jewish community in Rome is the oldest in Europe—Israelites came in 161 BC as ambassadors from Judas Maccabei, asking for Imperial help against invaders. The Ghetto, the tiny area to which Pope Paul IV confined the Jews in 1555, was closed in 1870, but is still the center of Rome's vibrant

Jewish population. In the center of the ghetto are **Piazza Mattei** and the 16th-century **Fontana delle Tartarughe.** Nearby is the **Church of Sant'Angelo in Pescheria;** Jews were forced to attend mass here every Sunday and quietly resisted by stuffing their ears with wax. *(Toward the eastern end of V.d. Portico d'Ottavia. Prayer meetings W 5:30pm and Sa 5pm.)* The **Sinagoga Ashkenazita,** on the Tiber near the Theater of Marcellus, was bombed in 1982; guards now search and question all visitors. *(Open for services only.)*

PIAZZA DI SPAGNA AND ENVIRONS

■ **THE SPANISH STEPS.** Designed by an Italian, funded by the French, named for the Spaniards, occupied by the British, and under the sway of American ambassador-at-large Ronald McDonald, the **Scalinata di Spagna** exude an international air. The pink house to the right of the Steps was the site of John Keats's 1821 death; it's now the **Keats-Shelley Memorial Museum.** *(Open May-Sept. M-F 9am-1pm and 3-6pm; Oct.-Apr. M-F 9am-1pm and 2:30-5:30pm; closed mid-July to mid-Aug. L5000.)*

■ **FONTANA DI TREVI.** The extravagant **Fontana di Trevi** emerges from the back wall of **Palazzo Poli.** Legend says that a traveler who throws a coin into the fountain is ensured a speedy return to Rome; a traveler who tosses two will fall in love in Rome. The reality is that these coins damage the marble: go figure. Opposite the fountain is the Baroque **Chiesa dei Santi Vincenzo e Anastasio,** rebuilt in 1630. The crypt preserves the hearts and lungs of popes from 1590-1903.

MAUSOLEUM OF AUGUSTUS AND ARA PACIS. The circular brick mound of the **Masoleo d'Agosto** once housed the funerary urns of the Imperial family. West of the mausoleum, the glass-encased **Ara Pacis** (Altar of Augustan Peace), is propaganda completed in 9 BC to celebrate Augustus's success. *(In P. Augusto Imperatore. From P. del Popolo, take V. di Ripetta toward the Tiber. Mausoleum tours Tu and F 10pm in English; L10,000/€5.20, students L8000/€4.15. Ara Pacis is closed for renovation until an undisclosed time; it is typically open Tu-Sa 9am-7pm, Su 9am-1pm. L3750/€1.95, students L2500/€1.30.)*

PIAZZA DEL POPOLO. P. del Popolo, once a favorite venue for public executions of heretics, is now the lively "people's square." In the center is the 3200-year-old **Obelisk of Pharaoh Ramses II,** which Augustus brought back as a souvenir from Egypt in the 1st century BC. Behind a simple early Renaissance shell, the **Church of Santa Maria del Popolo** contains several Renaissance and Baroque masterpieces. *(Open M-Sa 7am-noon and 4-7pm, Su and holidays 8am-1:30pm and 4:30-7:30pm.)* The **Cappella della Rovere** holds two exquisite Caravaggios, *The Conversion of St. Paul* and *Crucifixion of St. Peter,* in the **Cappella Cerasi.** Raphael designed the **Cappella Chigi.** At the southern end of the *piazza* are the 17th-century **twin churches** of Santa Maria di Montesano, on the left, and Santa Maria dei Miracoli.

VILLA BORGHESE. To celebrate becoming a cardinal, Scipione Borghese built the **Villa Borghese** north of P. di Spagna and V. V. Veneto. Its huge park is home to three notable art museums: the world-renowned **Galleria Borghese** (p. 589), the stark **Galleria Nazionale d'Arte Moderna** (p. 589), and the intriguing **Museo Nazionale Etrusco di Villa Giulia** (p. 589). North of the Borghese are the **Santa Priscilla catacombs.** *(M: A-Spagna and follow the signs. L14,000/€7.25.)*

TRASTEVERE

Right off the **Ponte Garibaldi** stands the statue of the famous dialect poet G. G. Bellie. On V. di S.Cecilia—behind the cars, through the gate, and beyond the courtyard full of roses—is the **Basilica di Santa Cecilia in Trastevere;** Stefano Maderno's famous statue of Santa Cecilia lies under the altar. *(Open daily 8am-12:30pm and 2:30-7pm.)* From P. Sonnino, V. della Lungaretta leads west to P. di S. Maria in Trastevere, home to numerous stray dogs, ex-pats, and the 4th-century **Chiesa di Santa Maria in Trastevere.** *(Open daily 7:30am-8:30pm.)* North of the *piazza* are the Rococo **Galleria Corsini,** V. della Lungara, 10 (see **Museo Nazionale dell'Arte Antica,** p. 590) and, across the street, the **Villa Farnesina,** the jewel of Trastevere. Atop the Gianicolo hill is the **Chiesa di San Pietro in Montorio,** built on the spot once believed to be the site of St.

ITALY

Peter's upside-down crucifixion. Next door in a small courtyard is Bramante's tiny ▨**Tempietto,** constructed to commemorate the site of Peter's martyrdom. *(Church and Tempietto open daily 9:30am-12:30pm and 4-6:30pm.)*

NEAR TERMINI

The sights in this urban part of town are concentrated northwest of the station and to the south, near P. Vittorio Emanuele II.

BATHS OF DIOCLETIAN. These public baths, which could serve 3000 people at once, contained a heated marble public toilet with seats for 30, pools of various temperatures, gymnasiums, art galleries, gardens, libraries, and concert halls. In 1561, Michelangelo undertook his last architectural work and converted the ruins into the **Chiesa di Santa Maria degli Angeli.** In the floor leading from the east transept to the altar, a sundial has provided the standard time for Roman clocks for hundreds of years. *(Baths open M-F 9am-2pm, Sa-Su 9am-1pm. Free. Church open daily M-Sa 7am-6:30pm, Su 8am-7:30pm.)*

BASILICA OF SANTA MARIA MAGGIORE. As one of the five churches in Rome granted extraterritoriality, this basilica, crowning the Esquiline Hill, is officially part of Vatican City. To the right of the altar is the **tomb of Bernini.** The 14th-century mosaics in the **loggia** recount the story of the August snowfall that showed the pope where to build the church. *(Open daily 7am-7pm. Loggia open daily 9:30am-noon and 2-5:30pm. Tickets in souvenir shop; L5000/€2.60. Dress code enforced.)*

CHURCH OF SANTA MARIA DELLA VITTORIA. This church has one of Bernini's most stunning works, The Ecstacyof St. Theresa, in the Cornaro Chapel (the last one on the left). A Baroque masterpiece, the sculpture shows an angel piercing the saint with a golden arrow. Bernini combined light from a hidden window and golden rays to show divine splendor. *(On the south side of P.S. Bernardo, heading from P. Repubblica. Open daily 7:30am-12:30pm and 4-6:30pm.)*

CHURCH OF SAN PIETRO IN VINCOLO. Michelangelo's imposing ▨**statue of Moses** presides over this 4th-century church. *(M: B-Cavour. Walk southwest on V. Cavour, down toward the Forum, and take the stairs on the left. Open daily 7am-12:30pm and 3:30-7pm.)*

SOUTHERN ROME

The area south of the center is a great mix of wealthy and working class neighborhoods, and is home to the city's best nightlife and some of its grandest churches.

CAELIAN HILL. Southeast of the Colosseum, the Caelian, along with the Esquiline, is the biggest of Rome's seven hills and home to some of the city's greatest chaos. Split into three levels, each from a different era, the **Church of San Clemente** is one of Rome's most intriguing churches. A fresco cycle by Masolino dating from the 1420s graces the **Chapel of Santa Caterina.** *(M: B-Colosseo. Turn left out of the station and walk east on V. Fori Imperiali. Open M-Sa 9am-12:30pm and 3-6pm, Su and holidays 10am-12:30pm and 3-6pm. L5000/€2.60.)* The immense **Chiesa di San Giovanni in Laterano** was the seat of the pope until the 14th century; founded by Constantine in 314, it's Rome's oldest Christian basilica. The two golden reliquaries over the altar contain the heads of **St. Peter and St. Paul.** Across the street is the **Scala Santa,** which houses the *acheropite* image—a depiction of Christ supposedly not created by human hand—and what are believed to be the 28 marble steps used by Jesus outside Pontius Pilate's house in Jerusalem. *(M: A-San Giovanni or bus #16 from Termini. Open M-Sa 6:15am-noon and 3-6:15pm, Su 6:15am-noon and 3:30-6:45pm. L4000/€2.10. Dress code enforced.)*

APPIAN WAY. Since burial inside the city walls was forbidden during ancient times, fashionable Romans made their final resting places along the **Appian Way.** At the same time, early Christians secretly dug maze-like catacombs under the ashes of their persecutors. *(M: A-San Giovanni. Take bus #218 from P. di S. Giovanni to the intersection of V. Ardeatina and V. delle Sette Chiese. L8000/€4.15.)* **San Callisto,** v. Appia Antica, 110, is the largest catacomb in Rome, with nearly 22km of subterranean paths. Its four levels once held 16 popes, seven bishops, St. Cecilia, and 500,000 other Christians.

(Take the private road that runs northeast to the entrance to the catacombs. Open in summer M-Tu and Th-Su 8:30am-5:30pm; in winter Th-Su 8:30am-noon and 2:30-5pm; closed Feb.) **Santa Domitilla** houses an intact 3rd-century portrait of Christ and the Apostles. *(Facing V. Ardeatina from the exit of S. Callisto, cross the street and walk up V. delle Sette Chiese. Open in summer W-M 8:30am-5:30pm; in winter W-M 8:30am-5pm; closed Jan.)* **San Sebastiano,** V. Appia Antica, 136, once housed the bodies of Peter and Paul. *(Open Tu-Su 9am-7pm. L5000/€2.60; EU residents 18-24 L3000/€1.55.)*

EUR. EUR (AY-oor) is an Italian acronym for the 1942 Universal Exposition of Rome that Mussolini intended as a showcase of Fascist achievement. The achievement was apparently Rome's ability to build lots of identical square buildings. The center of the area is **Piazza Guglielmo Marconi** and its 1959 modernist **obelisk.** According to legend, when St. Paul was beheaded at the **Abbazia delle Tre Fontane (Abbey of the Three Fountains),** his head bounced three times, creating a fountain at each bounce. *(M: B-Laurentina. Walk north on V. Laurentina and turn right on V. di Acque Salve; the abbey is at the bottom of the hill. Alternatively, take bus #761 north from the Laurentina stop; ask to get at V. di Acque Salve. Open daily 9am-noon and 3-6pm.)*

VATICAN CITY

M: A-Ottaviano, A-Cipro/Musei Vaticani, bus #64 (beware of pickpockets), #492 from Termini or Largo Argentina, #62 from P. Barberini, or #23 from Testaccio. Papal Audiences every W, usually at 10am behind the colonnade left of the basilica; for free tickets, stop by the Prefettura della Casa Pontificia the day before. Open M-Sa 9am-1pm.

Occupying 108½ independent acres entirely within the boundaries of Rome, Vatican City was once the mightiest power in Europe. The nation preserves its independence by minting coins (in Italian *lire* but with the Pope's face), running a separate postal system, and maintaining an army of Swiss Guards.

BASILICA DI SAN PIETRO (ST. PETER'S). A colonnade by Bernini leads from **Piazza San Pietro** to the church. The **obelisk** in the center is framed by two fountains; stand on the round disks set in the pavement and the quadruple rows of the colonnade will visually resolve into one perfectly aligned row. Above the colonnade are 140 statues; those on the basilica represent Christ, John the Baptist, and the Apostles (except for Peter). The Pope opens the **Porta Sancta** (Holy Door) every 25 years by knocking in the bricks with a silver hammer; the last opening was in 2000. The basilica itself rests on the reputed site of St. Peter's tomb. To the right, Michelangelo's *Pietà* has been protected by bullet-proof glass since 1972, when an axe-wielding fiend smashed Christ's nose and broke Mary's hand. Inside the basilica are four niches with statues of saints—Bernini's **San Longinus** is at the northeast. In the center of the crossing, Bernini's bronze **baldacchino** rises on spiral columns over the marble altar. Below the statue of St. Longinus, steps lead down to the **Vatican Grottoes,** the final resting place of innumerable popes and saints. *(Open daily Apr.-Sept. 7am-7pm, Oct.-Mar. 7am-6pm. Mass M-Sa 9, 10, 11am, noon, 5pm; Su 9, 10:30, 11:30am, 12:10, 1, 4, and 5:45pm. Dress modestly; cover your knees and shoulders.)*

VATICAN MUSEUMS. The Vatican Museums constitute one of the world's greatest collections of art. A good place to start is the stellar **Museo Pio-Clementino,** the world's greatest collection of antique sculpture. Two slobbering Molossian hounds guard the entrance to the **Stanza degli Animali,** a marble menagerie; among other gems, it features the ◪**Apollo Belvedere.** The Simonetti Stairway climbs to the **Museo Etrusco,** filled with artifacts from Tuscany and northern Lazio. From the Room of the Immaculate Conception, a door leads into the first of the four ◪**Stanze di Rafaele,** the apartments built for Pope Julius II in the 1510s. Raphael painted the astonishing **School of Athens** as a trial piece for Julius, who was so impressed that he fired his other painters, had their frescoes destroyed, and commissioned Raphael to decorate the entire suite. The **Stanza della Segnatura** features the *School of Athens,* considered Raphael's masterpiece. From here, a staircase leads to the brilliantly frescoed **Borgia Apartments** and the **Museum of Modern Religious Art,** while another route goes to the Sistine Chapel. *(About 10 blocks north of the right-hand side of*

P. San Pietro along the Vatican wall. All open Oct. 31-Mar. 15 M-Sa 8:45am-1:45pm; Mar. 16-Oct. 30 M-F 8:45am-4:45pm, Sa 8:45am-1:45pm; closed major religious holidays. L18,000/€9.30; with ISIC card L12,000/€6.20; free last Su each month 8:45am-1:45pm.)

■ **SISTINE CHAPEL.** Ever since its completion in the 16th century, the **Sistine Chapel** (named for its founder, Pope Sixtus IV) has served as the chamber in which the College of Cardinals elects new popes. The frescoes on the side walls predate Michelangelo's ceiling; on the right, scenes from the life of Moses complement parallel scenes of Christ's life on the left. The simple compositions and vibrant colors of Michelangelo's unquestioned masterpiece hover above, each section depicting a story from Genesis. The ceiling appears vaulted but is actually flat; contrary to legend, Michelangelo painted not flat on his back but standing up and craning backwards, and he never recovered from the strain to his neck and eyes. In his *Last Judgement*, on the altar wall, the figure of Christ as judge hovers in the upper center, surrounded by his saintly entourage and the supplicant Mary.

CASTEL SANT'ANGELO. Built by **Hadrian** (AD 117-138) as a mausoleum for himself, this hulking mass of brick and stone has served as a fortress, prison, and palace. When the city was wracked with the plague in 590, Pope Gregory saw an angel sheathing his sword at the top of the complex; the plague abated soon after, and the edifice was rededicated to the angel. It now contains a **Museum of Arms and Artillery** and offers an incomparable view of Rome and the Vatican. *(Walk along the river with St. Peter's behind you and the towering castle to the left; follow the signs to the entrance. Open in summer Tu-Su 9am-7pm; in winter daily 9am-7pm. L10,000/€5.20. Audio guide L7000/€3.62.)*

▥ MUSEUMS

Etruscans, emperors, popes, and *condottiere* have been busily stuffing Rome's belly full of artwork for several millennia, leaving behind a city teeming with galleries. Museums are generally closed holidays, Sunday afternoons, and all day Monday.

■ **Capitoline Museums,** atop the Capitoline Hill (behind the Vittorio Emanuele II monument). The collections of ancient sculpture are among the largest in the world, and the frescoes are breathtaking. The Palazzo Nuovo contains the original statue of **Marcus Aurelius** that once stood in the center of the *piazza*, fragments of the **Colossus of Constantine,** and the famous **Capitoline Wolf,** an Etruscan statue that has symbolized the city of Rome since ancient times. Open Tu-Su 10am-8pm, holidays 9am-1:30pm. L15,000/€7.75; with ISIC L11,000/€5.70.

Galleria Borghese, P. Scipione Borghese, 5. M: A-Spagna. Alternatively, take bus #910 from Termini to V. Pinciana. Holds Bernini's most magnificent works, including his *David* and *Apollo and Daphne,* and paintings by Caravaggio, Raphael, Rubens, and Titian. Open Tu-F, Su and holidays 8:30am-7:30pm, Sa 9am-11pm, Su 9am-8pm. Entrance only on the hour, visits limited to 2hr. L8000/€4.15.

Villa Farnesina, V. della Lungara, 230. Just across from Palazzo Corsini off Lungotevere Farnesina. Bus #23. Thought to be the wealthiest man in Europe, Agostino "il Magnifico" Chigi lived here sumptuously and eccentrically. To the right of the entrance lies the breathtaking **Sala of Galatea,** containing Raphael's *Triumph of Galatea.* Open M-Sa 9am-1pm. L8000/€4.15.

Galleria Nazionale d'Arte Moderna, V. delle Belle Arti, 131. M: A-Flaminio. Enter the park and walk up V. George Washington, following the signs. Skip to the 20th-century wing to see pieces by Klimt, Modigliani, Giacometti, Mondrian, Braque, Duchamp, and de Chirico. Open Tu-Su 8:30am-7:30pm. L12,000/€6.20.

Galleria Spada, P. Capo di Ferro, 13, in the elaborate Palazzo Spada. South of Campo dei Fiori. Bus #64. 17th-century Cardinal Bernardino Spada bought a grandiose assortment of art, including works by Tintoretto and Titian and a frieze by Vaga originally intended for the Sistine Chapel. Open Tu-Sa 8:30am-1:30pm, Su 8:30am-12:30pm. L10,000/€5.20.

Museo Nazionale Etrusco di Villa Giulia, P. Villa Giulia, 9, in Villa Borghese. M:A-Flaminio or bus #19 from P. Risorgimento or #52 from P. San Silvestro. Check out the

Etruscan chariot, and the petrified skeletons of 2 horses found beside it, in Room 18. Open Tu-F, Su, and holidays 8:30am-7:30pm, Sa 9am-8pm; extended hours June-Sept. Sa 9am-11pm. L8000/€4.15.

Museo Nazionale d'Arte Antica, V. delle Quattro Fontane, 13, near P. Barberini. **Palazzo Barberini** has paintings from the Middle Ages to the Baroque. Open Tu-Sa 9am-7pm, Su 9am-8pm. L12,000/€6.20; EU citizens 18-25 L7000/€3.65. **Galleria Corsini,** V. della Lungara, 10, opposite Villa Farnesina in Trastevere, holds 17th- and 18th-century works. Open Tu-Su 9am-6pm. L8000/€4.15; EU students L4000/€2.10.

Museo Nazionale Romano Palazzo Massimo, Largo di Via Peretti, 1, in the left-hand corner of P. dei Cinquecento as you stand with your back to Termini. Devoted to the history of Roman art during the Empire, it includes the Lancellotti Discus Thrower, one of Nero's rare mosaics, and ancient coins and jewelry. Open Tu-Su 9am-7:45pm. L12,000/€6.20; EU citizens 18-24 L6000/€3.20.

Museo Nazionale Romano Palazzo Altemps, P.S. Apollinaire, 44, just north of P. Navona. Lots of ancient Roman sculpture, including the 5th-century *Ludovisi Throne*. Open Tu-Su 9am-7pm. L10,000/€5.16.

Museo Preistorico ed Etnografico Luigi Pigorini, P. G. Marconi, 14. An impressive collection of ethnographic artifacts, including the skull of the famous Neanderthal Guattari Man discovered near Circeo. Open daily 9am-8pm. L8000/€4.15.

▧ NIGHTLIFE

PUBS

For organized, indoor drunkenness, stop into any of Rome's countless pubs, many of which have an Irish theme. Drink prices often increase after 9pm.

▧ **Jonathan's Angels,** V.d. Fossa, 14-16, west of P. Navona. Take V.d. Governo Vecchio from Campo dei Fiori, turn left at the Abbey Theatre onto V. Parione, and then left toward the lights. Michelangelo's accomplishments pale before the bathroom at Jonathan's Angels, the finest ▧ bathroom in Rome, nay, Italy. Medium beer on tap L10,000/€5.20. Mercifully free of pub-crawlers. Open daily 4pm-2am.

▧ **Trinity College,** V.d. Collegio Romano, 6, off V.d. Corso near P. Venezia. Offers degrees in such diverse curricula as Guinness, Harp, and Heineken. Tuition L6000-9000/€3.20-4.50. Happy Hour noon-8pm. Classes held daily noon-3am.

Il Simposio, V.d. Latini, 11. The symposium's walls are cluttered with Jackson-Pollock-esque works of local artists, and on any given night a painter may be beautifying a discarded refrigerator. With cocktails from L6000/€3.20 and a glass of *fragolino* for L5000/€2.60, even starving artists can afford to come. Open daily 9pm-2am.

Pub Hallo'Ween, P. Tiburtino, 31, at the corner of V. Tiburtina and V. Marsala. Plastic skulls, fake spiders, and spiderwebs. Draft beer L6-8000/€3.10-4.15. Sandwiches L10,000/€5.16. Open daily 8:30pm-2:30am; closed Aug.

The Drunken Ship, Campo dei Fiori, 20-21. Because you're tired of meeting Italians. Because you have a burning desire to commune with the hosteling set. Beer L8000/€4.13. Happy hour daily 5-9pm. Su Ladies' night, Tu half-price Tequila, W 9-10pm all the beer you can drink (L10,000/€5.20). Open daily 5pm-2am. AmEx/MC/V.

The Nag's Head, V. IV Novembre, 138b, off P. Venezia. Pier the bartender, who is straight out of *Cocktail* (and advertises himself as a master of *"flair estremo"*), makes this place worth a visit. After the bottle-twirling and other excesses, you almost don't mind the L1000/€0.55 he tacks on to your bill as a "tip." Dance floor inside. Guinness L10,000/€5.20; cocktails L14,000/€7.20. Cover L10,000/€5.20; F and Sa men L15,000/€7.75; Su free. Open daily in summer 4pm-3am; in winter noon-3am. MC/V.

CLUBS

Although Italian discos can be a flashy, sweaty good time, the scene changes as often as Roman phone numbers; check *Roma C'è* or *Time Out*. Rome has fewer gay establishments than most cities its size, but those it has are solid and keep late hours.

Many gay establishments require an **ARCI-GAY pass** (L10,000 yearly), available from **Circolo di Cultura Omosessuale Mario Mieli** (☎06 541 39 85).

Charro Cafe, V. di Monte Testaccio, 73. So you wanted to go to Tijuana, but got stuck in Rome. Weep no more: here, Italians guzzle strong Mexican-themed mixed drinks (L10,000/€5.20) and dance themselves silly to pop and house. Cover L10,000/€5.20, includes 1 drink. Open daily 11:30pm-3:30am.

Aquarela, V. di Monte Testaccio, 64, next door to Radio Londra. Built out of ancient trash, then used for years as a vegetable market, the club consists in part of two underground tunnels that remain cool even when the party's heatin' up. Cover L20,000/€10.30, includes 1 drink. Open Tu-Su 8:30pm-3am.

Caruso, V. di Monte Testaccio, 36. No opera here: Caruso is a reliable venue for live salsa, DJed hip-hop, and "music black" (rap and R&B). Five rooms of tropical decor, packed with writhing Latino wannabes Sa nights. Live music F. Monthly *tessera* (pass) L15,000-20,000/€7.75-10.30. Open Tu and Th-Su 11:30pm-3am.

Radio Londra Caffè, V. di Monte Testaccio, 65b. Italian bands cover rock classics badly. Energetic, young crowd. Pizza, *panini*, and hamburgers (L8000-12,000/€4.13-6.20). Monthly *tessera* (pass) L10,000/€5.20. Open Su-F 9pm-3am, Sa 9pm-4am.

C.S.I.O.A. Villaggio Globale, Lungotevere Testaccio (☎06 57 30 03 29). Take bus #27 from Termini, get off before it crosses the river, and head left down the river. Women probably shouldn't travel alone on the Lungotevere at night. One of the best-known *centri sociali* in Rome—your one-stop shop for all things countercultural. Housed in a huge Testaccio slaughterhouse, it hosts live music, films, art exhibits, poetry readings, African cuisine tastings, and more. Hours and cover vary, F nights are usually hopping.

GAY NIGHTLIFE

◪Qube, V. Portonaccio, 212. From P. di Porta Maggiore, take V. Prenestina east; turn left on V. Portonaccio. Seedy neighborhood; plan to take a cab home. A huge warehouse-style disco with 3 packed dance floors. "Transmania" on Su is one of Rome's most popular gay nights. Cover L10,000-20,000/€5.16-10.30. Open Th-Su 11pm-4am.

Piper, V. Tagliamento, 9. From V. XX Settembre, follow V. Piave (V. Salaria) and take a right on V. Po (V. Tagliamento). Or, take bus #319 from Termini to Tagliamento. A popular club that occasionally hosts gay nights. 70s, rock, disco, as well as the standard house and underground. Very gay friendly all the time. Cover L15,000-35,000/€7.75-17.60, includes 1 drink. Open in summer Su 11pm-3am; in winter Sa-Su 11pm-3am.

▸ DAYTRIPS FROM ROME

TIVOLI. From P. Garibaldi, a gauntlet of souvenir stands leads through P. Trento to the ◪**Villa d'Este**, the castle-garden property on the left, which was laid out by Cardinal Ercole d'Este (the son of Lucrezia Borgia) in 1550 to recreate the feel of the ancient Roman nymphaea and pleasure palaces. (Open daily May-Aug. 8:30am-6:30pm; Sept.-Apr. 9am-1hr. before sunset; Su villa closes 1½hr. earlier. L8000/€4.15.) V. di Sibilla runs across town to the beautiful **Villa Gregoriana**, but it's been closed indefinitely for restoration; check at the tourist office for more information. From Tivoli, take the orange #4x **bus** (L1400/€0.70; tickets at the news kiosk) from the P. Garibaldi newsstand to the vast remains of **Hadrian's Villa** (Villa Adriana), the largest and most expensive villa ever built in the Roman Empire. (Open daily 9am-1½hr. before sunset. L12,000/€6.20; EU students L6000/€3.20.) To reach Tivoli, take Rome's Metropolitana to B-Rebibbia, exit the station, and follow signs for Tivoli through the underpass to the other side of V. Tiburtina. Then take the blue **ACOTRAL bus** to Tivoli (25min., L3000/€1.55 in the bar next door or in the subway station), get off past the green P. Garibaldi at **P. delle Nazioni Unite**, and follow the street to the **tourist office**. (☎07 74 31 12 49. Open M-Sa 9:45am-3pm.) The bus back to Rome leaves from **P. Garibaldi**.

TARQUINIA. When Rome was only a few mud huts on the Palatine, Tarquin kings commanded this fledgling metropolis. In P. Cavour stands the majestic **Museo Nazionale**,

ITALY

one of the best collections of Etruscan art outside Rome. (Open Tu-Su 9am-7pm. L12,000/€6.20.) A subterranean **necropolis** lined with vibrant frescoes illustrates Tarquinia's history. (Open 9am-1hr. before sunset. Entrance with ticket to museum.) Take the **bus** marked Cimitero from Barriera S. Giusto or, from the museum, head up Corso Vittorio Emanuele from P. Cavour and turn right on V. Porta Tarquinia (15min.). **Trains** connect Rome's Termini to Tarquinia (1hr.; 11 per day, last train leaves Tarquinia at 10:12pm; L10,200/€5.30). **Buses** run from the train station to the beach (L1100/€0.60) and to the city center (L1500/€0.80) every 30min. until 9:30pm. For bus schedules, stop by the **tourist office** in P. Cavour, near the medieval walls. (☎07 66 85 63 84. Open daily 8am-2pm and 4-7pm.)

THE VENETO

From the rocky foothills of the Dolomites to the fertile valleys of the Po River, the Veneto region has a geography as diverse as its historical influences. Once loosely linked under the Venetian Empire, these towns retained their cultural independence; visitors are more likely to hear regional dialects than standard Italian when neighbors gossip across their geranium-bedecked windows. The sense of local culture and custom that remains strong within each town may surprise visitors lured to the area by Venice, the *bella* of the north.

VENICE (VENEZIA)

Venice's labyrinthine streets lead to a treasury of Renaissance art, housed in scores of palaces, churches, and museums that are themselves an architectural delight. Yet the same streets that once earned the name *La Serenissima* (Most Serene) are now saturated with visitors for half the year. Still, Venice persists beyond the summer crowds and polluted waters, united by intertwining canals and the memory of a glorious past.

▐ TRANSPORTATION

The **train station** is on the northwest edge of the city; be sure to get off at **Santa Lucia,** *not* at Mestre (on the mainland). **Buses** and **boats** arrive at **Piazzale Roma,** across the Canal Grande from the train station. To get from either station to **Piazza San Marco** or the **Ponte di Rialto,** take *vaporetto* #82 or walk, following the signs (40min., exit left from the station onto Lista di Spagna).

Flights: Aeroporto Marco Polo (☎041 260 61 11; www.veniceairport.it), 8km north of the city. Take the **ATVO shuttle bus** (☎041 520 55 30) to Piazzale Roma (30min., 2 per hr., 5:15am-8:30pm, L5000/€2.60).

Trains: Stazione Venezia Santa Lucia, open daily 3:45am-12:30am. To: **Bologna** (2hr., 2 per hr., L20,000/€10.35); **Florence** (3hr., every 2hr., L40,000/€20.65); **Milan** (3hr., 1-2 per hr., L42,000/€21.70); **Padua** (30min., 1-3 per hr., L4100/€2.15); and **Rome** (4½hr., 5 per day, L68,000/€35.15).

Buses: ACTV, Piazzale Roma (☎041 528 78 86). Ticket office open daily 6:30am-midnight. Runs local buses and boats. **ACTV long distance carrier** buses run to nearby cities. ACTV offers a **3-day** discount *vaporetto* pass (L25,000/€5.20) to **Rolling Venice** cardholders (p. 593).

Public Transportation: The **Canal Grande** can be crossed on foot only at the Scalzi, Rialto, and Accademia *ponti* (bridges). Most **vaporetti** (water buses) run 24hr. (less frequently after 11pm). Single ride L6000/€3.10; **24hr. biglietto turistico** pass L18,000/€9.30; **3-day** L35,000/€18.10 (L25,000/€12.95 with **Rolling Venice** card; see p. 593); **7-day** L60,000/€31. Buy tickets from booths in front of *vaporetto* stops, automated machines at the ACTV offices in Piazzale Roma and the Rialto stop, or the conductor. Pick up extra *non timbrati* (non-validated) tickets for when the booths aren't open and validate them yourself before boarding. There is a fine for riding without a valid ticket. **Lines #82** (faster) and **1** (slower) run from the station down the Grande and della Giudecca canals; **line N** goes from the Lido to the station, down the Canale della Giudecca back to S. Marco; **line #52** runs from the station through the Canale della Giudecca to Lido and along the city's northern edge; and **line #12** goes from Fond. Nuove to Murano, Burano, and Torcello.

✴ ORIENTATION

Venice, spanning 118 bodies of land in a lagoon, connects to the mainland city of Mestre by a thin causeway. Venice is notoriously hard to navigate; the best approach is to relax, peel your eyes from the map, and discover unexpected surprises along the way. Start by locating the following landmarks: the **Ponte di Rialto** (in the center); **Piazza San Marco** (central south); the **Ponte Accademia** (southwest), **Ferrovia** (or Stazione Santa Lucia, the train station, in the northwest); and **Piazzale Roma** (directly south of the train station). The Canal Grande snakes through the city's six **sestieri**, or sections: **Cannaregio** includes the train station, Jewish Ghetto, and Cà d'Oro; **Castello** continues east toward the Arsenale; **San Marco,** bounded to the west by P.S. Marco, fills in the remaining area below Cannaregio; **Dorsoduro,** across the Ponte Accademia, stretches the length of the Canale della Giudecca and up to Campo S. Pantalon; **Giudecca** lies just across the Canale della Giudecca, south of Dorsoduro; **San Polo** runs north from Chiesa S. Maria dei Frari to the Ponte di Rialto; and **Santa Croce** lies west of S. Polo, directly across the Canale Grande from the train station. There are no individual street numbers within each *sestiere*— door numbers form one long, haphazard set. If *sestiere* boundaries are confusing, Venice's **parrochie** (parishes) provide a more defined idea of where you are, and *parrochia* signs, like *sestiere* signs, are painted on the sides of buildings.

🛈 PRACTICAL INFORMATION

TOURIST AND FINANCIAL SERVICES

Tourist Offices and Tours: APT, Calle della Ascensione, P.S. Marco, 71/F (☎/fax 041 529 87 40; www.tourismovenezia.it). Opposite the basilica. Open M-Sa 9:30am-3:30pm. **Branches** at the nearby Venice Pavilion, Giardini Ex Reali, S. Marco, 2 (☎041 522 51 50), and the train station (☎/fax 041 71 90 78).

Rolling Venice, Corte Contarina, S. Marco, 1529 (☎041 274 76 50). Exit P.S. Marco opposite the basilica, turn right, follow the road left, continue through the building, look for the yellow "Comune di Venezia" signs, take a left, turn right, and go into the courtyard. Sells the **Rolling Venice youth discount card** (L5000/€2.60), which earns discounts at hotels, restaurants, and museums. Open M, W, and F 9:30am-1pm; Tu and Th 9am-1pm and 3-5pm. Rolling Venice is also available at **ACTV VeLa kiosks** next to the **Ferrovia** and **Rialto** *vaporetto* stops. Open daily 9am-3:30pm.

Budget Travel: CTS, Fond. Tagliapietra, Dorsoduro, 3252 (☎041 520 56 60; www.cts.it). From Campo S. Barnaba, cross the bridge nearest the church, then turn right at the end, left through the *piazza*, and left at the foot of the large bridge. Open M-F 9:30am-1:30pm and 2:30-6:30pm.

Currency Exchange: Banks and 24hr. **ATMs** line **Calle Larga XXII Marzo** (between P.S. Marco and Ponte Accademia) and **Campo S. Bartolomeo** (near Ponte di Rialto).

American Express: Salle S. Moise, S. Marco, 1471 (☎800 87 20 00). Exit P.S. Marco away from the basilica, to the left. No commission; mediocre rates. Mail held for AmEx members and traveler's check customers. Open M-F 9am-8pm, Sa 9am-6pm.

Luggage Storage: Stazione Venezia Santa Lucia, by platform #1. L3000-4000/€1.55-2.10 for 6hr.

English-Language bookstore: Libreria Al Ponte, Calle della Mandola, S. Marco, 3717/D (☎041 522 40 30). Just off Campo Manin near the Ponte di Rialto. Open M-Sa 9:30am-7:15pm, Su 1-6:15pm.

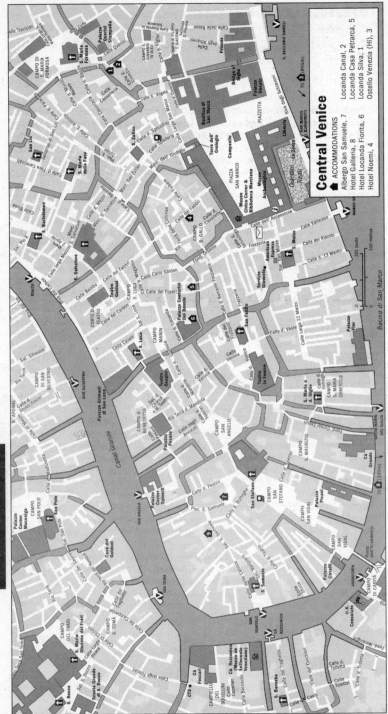

Central Venice

▲ ACCOMMODATIONS

Albergo San Samuele, 7
Hotel Galleria, 8
Hotel Locanda Fiorita, 6
Hotel Noemi, 4

Locanda Canal, 2
Locanda Casa Petrarca, 5
Locanda Silva, 1
Ostello Venezia (HI), 3

ITALY

EMERGENCY AND COMMUNICATIONS

Emergency: ☎113. **First Aid:** ☎118.

Police: Carabinieri, Campo S. Zaccaria, **Castello,** 4693/A (☎041 520 47 77).

Pharmacy: Farmacia Italo Inglese, Calle della Mandola, **S. Marco,** 3717 (☎041 522 48 37), off Campo Manin near Ponte di Rialto. Open M-F 9am-12:30pm and 3:45-7:30pm, Sa 9am-12:30pm. Late-night pharmacies rotate; check the list posted in the window of any pharmacy.

Hospital: Ospedale Civile, Campo S.S. Giovanni e Paolo, **Castello** (☎041 529 41 11).

Internet Access: Horus Explorer, Fond. Tolentini, **S. Croce,** 220 (☎041 71 04 70). Short walk from train station or Piazzale Roma, behind the Giardini Papadopoli. Offers fast Internet connection as well as fax and photocopy services. L10,000/€5.20, 10% discount with Rolling Venice card. Open M-F 8:30am-12:30pm and 3-7:30pm. Get cheap calling cards at **Planet Internet,** Rio Terra S. Leonardo, **Cannaregio,** 1519 (☎041 524 41 88). Open 9am-midnight.

Post Office: Poste Venezia Centrale, Salizzada Fontego dei Tedeschi, **S. Marco,** 5554 (☎041 271 71 11). Off Campo S. Bartolomeo, east of Ponte di Rialto. The palatial building is worth a visit. *Fermo Posta (Poste Restante)* at window #40. Address mail to be held: First name SURNAME, *In Fermo Posta,* Fontego dei Tedeschi, S. Marco 5554, **30124** Venezia, Italia. Open M-Sa 8:10am-6pm.

Postal Codes: S. Marco 30124; Castello 30122; S. Polo, S. Croce, and Cannareggio 30121; Dorsoduro 30123.

◤ ACCOMMODATIONS AND CAMPING

Rooms in Venice cost slightly more than elsewhere in Italy. Dorms are sometimes available without reservations, even in high season, but single rooms vanish quickly. Make reservations up to a month in advance. In *pensioni,* watch out for L10,000/€5.20 breakfasts and other rip-offs. Always agree on the price before taking a room. **AVA,** in the train station, to the right of the tourist office, makes same-day reservations for L1000/€0.55. (☎041 171 52 88; 041 522 22 64 for advance reservations. Open daily 9am-10pm.) However, proprietors are more willing to bargain in person. If you get desperate, ask the tourist office for information about the campgrounds at Mestre, or head to the hostel in nearby Padua (p. 600) or Verona (p. 601).

   Cannaregio offers budget accommodations and a festive atmosphere, although the area is a 20- to 30-minute ride from most major sights. Accommodations in **San Marco,** surrounded by luxury hotels and Venice's main sights, are prime choices if you can get a reservation. **Dorsoduro** is a lively, less-touristed area between the Accademia and the Frari church. **Castello** provides lodging near the Rialto and the city center, a bit removed from the tourist hordes.

HOSTELS AND INSTITUTIONAL ACCOMMODATIONS

Religious institutions around the city offer both dorms (L30,000-50,000/€15.50-25.85) and private rooms (L60,000-130,000/€31-67.15). Options include: **Casa Murialdo,** Fond. Madonna dell'Orto, **Cannaregio,** 3512 (☎041 71 99 33); **Patronato Salesiano Leone XII,** Calle S. Domenico, **Castello,** 1281 (☎041 240 36 11); and **Domus Cavanis, Dorsoduro,** 896 (☎041 528 73 74), near Ponte Accademia.

▨ **Foresteria Valdesi, Castello,** 5170 (☎041 528 67 97; fax 241 62 38; www.chiesavaldese.org/venezia). From the Ponte di Rialto, enter Campo S. Bartolomeo; follow Salizzada S. Lio, and turn left on Calle Mondo Novo; go over the bridge, cross Campo S. Maria Formosa to Calle Lunga S. Maria Formosa. It's in the Palazzo Cavagnis, immediately over the 1st bridge. Clean rooms with dazzling frescoed ceilings. Breakfast included. Reception 9am-1pm and 6-8pm, Su 9am-1pm. Lockout 10am-1pm. Closed 2 weeks in Nov. Dorms L35,000-36,000/€18.10-18.60; doubles L100,000-130,000/€51.65-67.15; quads L180,000/€93. L2000/€1.05 discount per day with Rolling Venice card.

Ostello Venezia (HI), Fond. Zitelle, **Giudecca,** 87 (☎041 523 82 11; fax 523 56 89). Take *vaporetto* #82 or 52 to Zitelle. Institutional but friendly. Breakfast and sheets included. Reception 7-9:30am and 1:30-11:30pm. Lockout 9:30am-1:30pm. Curfew 11:30pm. Reserve through IBN from other HI hostels, online at www.hostelbooking.com, or by phone. Members only; HI cards sold. Dorms L30,000/€15.50. MC/V.

Domus Civica (ACISJF), Campiello Chiovere Friari, **S. Polo,** 3082 (☎041 72 11 03; fax 522 71 39). Between the Basilica dei Frari and Piazzale Roma. From the station, cross the Scalzi bridge, turn right, hang a left on Fond. dei Tolentini, head left through the courtyard on Corso Amai, and it's a few blocks down on the right. Church-affiliated student housing. Open from mid-June to Sept. Ping-pong, TV, and piano. Check-in 7:30am-11:30pm. Curfew 11:30pm. Singles L50,000/€25.85; doubles L90,000/€46.50.

Suore Cannosiano, Fond. del Ponte Piccolo, **Giudecca,** 428 (☎/fax 041 522 21 57). From *vaporetto* #82: Giudecca/Palanca, walk left over the bridge to this nunnery, managed by non-English-speaking nuns. Women only. Check-out 7:30-8:30am. Lockout noon-3pm. Strict curfew 10:30pm. Dorms L23,000/€11.90.

HOTELS

🏨 **Alloggi Gerotto Calderan,** Campo S. Geremia, **Cannaregio,** 283 (☎041 71 55 62; fax 71 53 61). Turn left from the station (3min.) for a backpacker's haven. Huge, bright rooms, some with TV. Check-out 10am. Curfew 12:30-1am. Reserve ahead. Dorms L35,000/€18.10; singles L60,000-70,000/€31-36.15; doubles L90,000-120,000/€46.50-62; triples L120,000-160,000/€62-82.65, with bath L180,000-220,000/€93-113.65.

🏨 **Locanda Cà Foscari,** Calle della Frescada, **Dorsoduro,** 3887b (☎041 71 04 01; fax 71 08 17). From the *vaporetto* #1 or 82: S. Tomà stop, turn left at the dead end, cross the bridge, turn right, and take a left into the alleyway. Homey rooms. Curfew 1am. Rooms held until 2pm. Open Feb.-Nov. Singles L100,000/€51.65; doubles L120,000/€62, with bath L160,000/82.65; triples L156,000/€80.60, L201,000/€103.80, quads L192,000/€99.20, L240,000/€123.95. MC/V.

Hotel Bernardi-Semenzato, Calle de l'Oca, **Cannaregio,** 4366 (☎041 522 72 57; fax 522 24 24). From *vaporetto* #1: Cà d'Oro, turn right on Strada Nuova, left onto Calle del Duca, and right on Calle di Loca. Lovely rooms with Venetian antiques. Breakfast L6000/€3.10. Check-out 10:30am. Flexible curfew 1am. Singles L70,000/€36.15; doubles L100,000/€51.65, with bath L140,000/€72.30; triples L130,000/€67.15, L170,000/€87.80; quads L160,000/€82.65, L190,000/€98.15. AmEx/MC/V.

Hotel Rossi, Calle delle Procuratie, **Cannaregio,** 262 (☎041 71 51 64; fax 71 77 84), off Lista di Spagna. Upon exiting the train station, turn right and then left under the arch on Calle della Procuratie. 14 institutional rooms near loud Lista di Spagna. Breakfast included. Reserve ahead. Singles L90,000/€46.50, with bath L110,000/€56.85; doubles L135,000/€69.75, L165,000/€85.25; triples L200,000/€103.30; quads L235,000/€121.40. 10% Rolling Venice discount. MC/V.

Albergo San Samuele, S. Marco, 3358 (☎/fax 522 80 45). Follow Calle delle Botteghe from Campo S. Stefano (near Ponte Accademia) and turn left on Salizzada S. Samuele. Colorful rooms. Reserve ahead. Singles L80,000/€41.35; doubles L130,000/€67.15, with bath L190,000/€98.15. Triples available with advance notice.

Hotel Locanda Fiorita, Campiello Novo, **S. Marco,** 3457 (☎041 523 47 54). From Campo S. Stefano, take Calle de Pestrin and then climb onto the raised *piazza*. All rooms with phones and A/C. Singles L140,000/€72.30; doubles L190,000/€98.15, with bath L230,000/€118.80. Annex singles L170,000/€87.80; doubles L240,000/€123.95, with bath L250,000/€129.15. Extra bed 30% more. AmEx/MC/V.

Locanda Casa Petrarca, Calle Schiavine, **S. Marco,** 4386 (☎520 04 30). From Rialto, take Calle Larga Mazzini and turn right at the church onto Calle dell'Ovo. Turn left onto Calle dei Fabbri, then right for Campo S. Luca, cross the Campo to Calle dei Fuseri, take the 2nd left, and turn right on Calle Schiavine. 7 clean but tiny rooms. English spoken. Singles L80,000/€41.35; doubles L160,000/€82.65, with bath 200,000/€103.30.

Hotel Galleria, Rio Terra A. Foscarini, **Dorsoduro,** 878/A (☎041 523 24 89; fax 520 41 72). On the left as you face the Accademia museum. Outstanding views, oriental rugs, and tasteful prints lend the Galleria a certain elegance. Breakfast included.

Singles L120,000/€62; doubles L170,000-180,000/€87.80-93, with bath L200,000-250,000/€103.30-129.15. Extra bed 30% more. AmEx/MC/V.

Antica Locanda Montin, Fond. di Borgo, **Dorsoduro,** 1147 (☎041 522 71 51; fax 520 02 55). From *vaporetto*: Cà Rezzonico, head straight to Campo S. Barnaba, then turn left under the *sottoportego,* turn right at the iron sign, and turn left at the canal. 10 simple rooms overlook picturesque canal. Singles 130,000/€67.15; doubles L200,000/€103.30, with bath 250,000/€129.15. AmEx/MC/V.

Locanda Canal, Fond. del Remedio, **Castello,** 4422c (☎041 523 45 38; fax 241 91 38). From S. Marco, head under the clock tower, turn right on Calle Larga S. Marco, go left on Ramo dell'Anzolo, over the bridge, and head left on Fond. del Remedio. 7 large rooms in a converted *palazzo.* Breakfast included. Reserve with 1 night deposit. Doubles L155,000-205,000/€80.05-105.90; triples L185,000-250,000/€95.55-129.15; quads L220,000-300,000/€113.65-154.95.

Locanda Silva, Fond. del Remedio, **Castello,** 4423 (☎041 522 76 43; fax 528 68 17), next to the Locanda Canal (see directions above). 24 clean rooms painted in bright colors. Breakfast included. Open Feb. to mid-Nov. Singles L85,000/€43.90, with bath L120,000/€62; doubles L140,000-190,000/€72.30-98.15; triples L250,000/€129.15; quads L300,000/€155.

Locanda Corona, Calle della Corona, **Castello,** 4464 (☎522 91 74). From *vaporetto:* S. Zaccharia, take Calle degli Albanese to Campo S.S. Fillipo e Giacomo, continue on Rimpetto la Sacrestia, take the 1st right, and turn left on Calle della Corona. Wheelchair-accessible. Closed Jan. Singles L85,000/€43.90; doubles L105,000/€54.25; triples L130,000/€67.15.

CAMPING

Camping Miramare, (☎041 96 61 50; fax 530 11 50), Punta Sabbioni. Take *vaporetto* #14 from P.S. Marco to Punta Sabbioni (40min.). 3-night min. stay. Open Apr. to mid-Nov. L9800/€5.10 per person, L24,000/€12.40 per tent. 4-person bungalows L62,000/€32.05, 5-person 98,000/€50.65. 15% discount with Rolling Venice card.

Camping Fusina, V. Moranzani, 79 (☎041 547 00 55), in Malcontenta. From Mestre, take bus #1. L11,000/€5.70 per person, L7000/€3.65 per tent, L25,000/€12.95 per tent and car, L21,000/€10.85 to sleep in car.

⬤ FOOD

In Venice, dining well on a budget requires exploration. Visit side streets or any *osteria* or *bacaro,* and create a meal from the vast display of *cicchetti* (chee-KET-ee; snacks), including meat- and cheese-filled pastries, seafood, rice, meat, and *tramezzini* (white bread with filling). Venetian cuisine comes from the sea; a plate of *pesce fritta mista* (mixed fried seafood), which may include *calamari* (squid), *polpo* (octopus), or shrimp, costs at least L14,000/€7.35. The internationally renowned **Rialto markets** fill the area between the Canale Grande and the S. Polo side of the Ponte di Rialto every morning except Sunday. Smaller **fruit and vegetable markets** set up in Cannaregio, on **Rio Terra S. Leonardo** by the Ponte di Guglie, and in many *campi* throughout the city. **STANDA supermarket,** Strada Nuova, Cannaregio, 3650, is near Campo S. Felice. (Open M-Sa 8:30am-7:20pm, Su 9am-7:20pm.)

🍴 **Taverna San Trovaso,** Fond. Nani, **Dorsoduro,** 1016. Young, enthusiastic staff serves great pastas and pizzas. *Primi* L10,000-15,000/€5.20-7.75, *secondi* L15,000-27,000/€7.75-13.95, pizzas L8000-14,000/€4.15-7.25. Cover L3000/€1.55. Open Tu-Su noon-2:50pm and 7-9:50pm.

🍴 **Vino, Vino,** Ponte delle Veste, **S. Marco,** 2007a. From Calle Larga XXII Marzo, turn onto Calle delle Veste. Wine bar with delicious, aromatic food. *Primi* L8000/€4.15, *secondi* L15,000/€7.75. Cover L1000/€0.55. 10% discount with Rolling Venice card. Open W-M 10:30am-11pm.

🍴 **Pizzeria La Perla,** Rio Terra dei Franceschi, **Cannaregio,** 4615. From Strada Nuova, turn left onto Salizzade di Pistor in Campo S.S. Apostoli, then turn right. Affordable menu offers 90 types of pizza (L9000-14,000/€4.65-7.25) and pasta (L9000-11,000/€4.65-5.70). Cover L2000/€1.05. Service 10%. Wheelchair-accessible. Closed Aug. Open M-Sa noon-2pm and 7-9:45pm.

Oasi, Calle degli Albanese, **S. Marco,** 4263/a. Between the prisons and the Danieli Hotel. Enormous salads, delectable *frulatti,* and juices. Salads L8000-17,000/€4.15-8.80, *panini* L4000-6000/€2.10-3.10. Open Feb. to mid-Dec. M-Sa noon-3pm.

Rosticceria San Bartomoleo, Calle della Bissa, **S. Marco,** 5424/a. From Campo S. Bartolomeo, follow the neon sign under the last *sottoportego* on the left. Enjoy a large selection of sandwiches and *cichetti. Prosciutto* L2500/€1.30, *secondi* L12,000-23,000/€6.20-11.90. Cover L2500/€2.30. Open Tu-Su 9:30am-9:30pm.

Due Colonne, Campo S. Agostin, **S. Polo,** 2343. Cross the bridge away from the Frari, turn left, cross into Campo S. Stin, turn right on Calle Danà, and cross the bridge. Pizza L6000-13,000/€3.10-6.75. Cover L1500/€0.80. Service 10%. Closed Aug. Open M-Sa 8am-3pm and 6-11pm. Kitchen closes 10pm.

GELATERIE

■ **La Boutique del Gelato,** Salizzada S. Lio, **Castello,** 5727. Go. Go NOW. Enormous cones from L1500/€0.80. Open daily Feb.-Nov. M-Sa 10am-8:30pm.

Gelati Nico, Fond. Zattere, **Dorsoduro,** 922. Try *gianduiotto al passaggetto* (hazelnut ice cream dunked in whipped cream) for L4000/€2.10. Open F-W 6:45am-10:30pm.

👁 SIGHTS

Many churches enforce a strict dress code: shoulders and knees must be covered.

PIAZZA SAN MARCO TO THE RIALTO BRIDGE

■ **BASILICA SAN MARCO.** The crown jewel of Venice is a truly spectacular fusion of gold and marble that glorifies the city center, the **Piazza San Marco,** with its intricate symmetry and lavish frescoes. The basilica's main treasure is the **Pala d'Oro** that rests behind the altar—a Veneto-Byzantine gold bas-relief encrusted with over 3000 precious gems. Try to time your visit for the shortest wait, in the early morning, or best natural illumination of the interior mosaics and exterior frescoes at dusk. *(Basilica open M-Sa 9am-5pm, Su 1-5pm, illuminated 11:30am-12:30pm. Dress code enforced. Free. Pala d'Oro open M-Sa 9:45am-5pm, Su 2-4:30pm. L3000/€1.55.)*

■ **PIAZZA SAN MARCO.** In contrast to the narrow, labyrinthine streets that wind through most of Venice, P.S. Marco (Venice's only official *piazza)* is a magnificent expanse of light and space. Enclosing the *piazza* are the unadorned 16th-century Renaissance **Procuratie Vecchie (Old Treasury Offices),** the more ornate 17th-century Baroque **Procuratie Nuove (New Treasury Offices),** and the smaller neoclassical **Ala Napoleonica,** sometimes called the *Procuratie Nuovissime* (Really New Treasury Offices), which Napoleon constructed when he took the city in 1797. The brick **campanile** (bell tower; 96m) across the *piazza* stands on Roman foundations. *(Campanile open daily 9am-7pm. L10,000/€5.20.)*

PALAZZO DUCALE. To the right of the Basilica stands the **Palazzo Ducale** (Doge's Palace), once home to Venice's mayor and today the site of one of Venice's finest museums. When the city enlarged the palace in the 15th century, it kept the original 14th-century building's graceful design. *(Wheelchair-accessible. Open daily 9am-7pm. Ticket office closes 1½hr. earlier. L18,000/€9.30, students L10,000/€5.20, ages 6-14 L6000/€2.75. Includes entrance to Museo Correr, Biblioteca Nazionale Marciana, Museo Archeologico, Museo di Palazzo Mocenigo, Museo del Vetro di Murano, and Museo del Merletto di Burano.)*

CHIESA DI SAN ZACCARIA. The Gothic church holds one of the masterpieces of the Venetian Renaissance, Giovanni Bellini's *Virgin and Child Enthroned with Four Saints* (1505)—it's the second altar on the left. *(Vaporetto: S. Zaccaria. Or, from P.S. Marco, turn left along the water, cross the bridge, and turn left under the sotoportego. Open daily 10am-noon and 4-6pm. Free.)*

PONTE DI RIALTO. Constructed from 1588-91, the bridge arches over the Canal Grande, whose lacy, delicate *palazzi* testify to the city's wealthy history. To survey the main facades, ride *vaporetto* #82 from the station to P.S. Marco. The view at night, with dazzling reflections of light, is particularly impressive.

CANAL GRANDE. The Canal Grande loops through Venice, and the splendid facades of the *palazzi* that crown its banks testify to the city's history of immense wealth. Although their external decorations vary, the palaces share the same basic structure. A nighttime tour reveals the startling beauty of the *palazzi*. *(Ride vaporetto #82 or the slower #1 from the train station to P.S. Marco.)*

SAN POLO

BASILICA DI SANTA MARIA GLORIOSA DEI FRARI (I FRARI). The Gothic basilica, begun in 1330, houses a moving wooden sculpture of Saint John by Donatello, Bellini's *Madonna and Saints*, and Titian's famous *Assumption*—as well as the remains of Titian himself. *(Vaporetto: S. Tomà. Follow signs to Corso dei Frari. Open M-Sa 9am-6pm, Su 1-6pm. L3000/€1.55.)*

SCUOLA GRANDE DI SAN ROCCO. Venice's most illustrious *scuola*, or guildhall, Jacopo Tintoretto completed all of the paintings in the building in 23 years. The *Crucifixion* in the last room upstairs is the building's crowning glory. *(Behind the Basilica dei Frari in Campo S. Rocco. Open daily 9am-5:30pm. Ticket office closes 30min. earlier. L10,000/€5.20, students L7000/€3.65. Audioguides free.)*

DORSODURO

■**GALLERIE DELL'ACCADEMIA.** The Accademia is a must-see for art lovers; its world-class collection includes the superb Bellini *Pala di San Giobbe*, Giorgione's enigmatic *Tempesta*, and Titian's last work, a brooding *Pietà*. *(Vaporetto: Accademia. Open M 8:15am-2pm, Tu-Su 9:15am-7:15pm. Ticket office closes ½hr. earlier. L12,000/€6.20. Guided tours L10,000/€5.20.)*

■**COLLEZIONE PEGGY GUGGENHEIM.** The collection, in Guggenheim's former Palazzo Venier dei Leoni, includes works by Brancusi, Kandinsky, Picasso, Magritte, Rothko, Ernst, Pollock, and Dalí. *(Calle S. Cristoforo, Dorsoduro, 701. Vaporetto: Accademia. Turn left and then follow the yellow signs. Open M and W-F 10am-6pm, Sa 10am-10pm. L10,000/€5.20, students with ISIC or Rolling Venice L8000/€4.15, under 10 free. Audioguides L8000/€4.15.)*

CHIESA DI SANTA MARIA DELLA SALUTE. The theatrical *chiesa,* poised at the tip of Dorsoduro facing S. Marco, is a prime example of the Venetian Baroque. Next door is the **Dogana,** the old customs house where ships sailing into Venice stopped to pay duties. From its **doors** (walk along the *fondamenta* to the tip of Dorsoduro) there is a marvelous view of the city. *(Vaporetto: Salute. Open daily 9am-noon and 3-5:30pm. Free.)*

NORTHERN VENICE

CHIESA DI SANTISSIMI GIOVANNI E PÁOLO (SAN ZANIPOLO). The final rest place of 25 doges, the *chiesa* was built by the Dominican order from the mid-13th-to mid-15th centuries. Outside stands the bronze equestrian **statue of Bartolomeo Colleoni,** designed in 1479 by Verrochio, da Vinci's teacher. *(Vaporetto: Fond. Nuove. Turn left and then right onto Fond. dei Mendicanti. Open M-Sa 7:30am-12:30pm and 3:30-7pm, Su 3-6pm. Free.)*

JEWISH GHETTO. In 1516, the Doge forced Venice's Jewish population into the old cannon-foundry area, coining the modern term "ghetto" (Venetian for "foundry"). Several synagogues are open for tours; one shares a building with the **Museo Ebraica di Venezia (Hebrew Museum of Venice).** *(Cannaregio 2899/B. Vaporetto: S. Marcuola. Follow the signs straight ahead and then left into Campo del Ghetto Nuovo. Open Su-F June-Sept. 10am-7pm; Oct.-May 10am-4:30pm. Ticket office closes ½hr. earlier. L5000/€2.60, students L3000/€1.55. Entrance to synagogues by guided tour only (40min.). Museum and tour L12,000/€6.20, students L9000/€4.65.)*

ITALY

GIUDECCA, SAN GIORGIO MAGGIORE, AND THE LAGOON. Many of Venice's most beautiful churches are a boat ride away from S. Marco. The **Basilica di San Giorgio Maggiore,** an austere church of simple dignity, is across the lagoon on the island of the same name. *(Vaporetto #52 or 82: S. Giorgio Maggiore. Open M-Sa 10am-12:30pm and 2:30-4:30pm.)* On the adjoining island of Giudecca is the famous **Tempio del S.S. Redentore,** a church the Venetian Senate built to appease God and end the plague. *(Vaporetto #82 from S. Zaccaria: Redentore. Ask to enter the sacristy. Open M-Sa 10am-5pm, Su 1-5pm. L3000/€1.55.)*

North of Venice stretches the **lagoon. San Michele** is Venice's cemetery island and the resting place of Ezra Pound, Igor Stravinsky, and Sergei Diaghilev. *(Vaporetto: Cimitero from Fond. Nuove.)* **Murano** has been famed for its glass-blowing since 1292; ◪**Burano** remains a traditional fishing village with colored facades; and rural **Torcello** boasts a Byzantine cathedral with magnificent medieval mosaics. *(Take vaporetto #12 or 52 from S. Zaccaria or Fond. Nuove to Faro (for Murano), Burano, or Torcello.)* The **Lido** is Venice's beach island as well as the setting for Mann's *Death in Venice. (Vaporetto: Lido.)*

🎵 🎭 ENTERTAINMENT AND NIGHTLIFE

You won't have a true sense of Venice until you quietly slide down its canals and pass its houses and *palazzi.* **Gondola** rides are expensive; the minimum authorized rate starts at L120,000/€62 for one-hour and increases after sunset. Rates are negotiable, but if you still can't afford it, try one of the city's **traghetti,** ferry gondolas that cross the Canal Grande at six points, for a mere L700/€0.40.

The weekly *A Guest in Venice,* free at hotels and tourist offices or online at www.unospitedivenezia.it, lists current festivals, concerts, and gallery exhibits. **Vivaldi** concerts occur fairly regularly; for more info, talk to any of the costumed people scattered throughout town. During the 10 days before Ash Wednesday, Venice's famous **Carnevale** brings masked figures, camera-happy tourists, and outdoor concerts to the city. The famed **Biennle di Venezia** (☎041 521 18 98; www.biennale.org) floods the *Giardini Publici* and the Arsenale every other year with contemporary art.

Venetian nightlife is fairly quiet; even the liveliest places close around 1:30am. Students congregate in **Corso San Margherita** in Dorsoduro and around **Fondamenta della Misericordia** in Cannaregio. ◪**Paradiso Perduto,** Fond. della Misericordia, 2540, is a well-known bar, jazz club, and restaurant; from Strada Nuova, cross Campo S. Fosca and head straight over three bridges. (Open Th-Su 7pm-2am.) **Inishark Irish Pub,** Calle Mondo Novo, **Castello,** 5787, is creatively decorated. (Open Tu-Su 6pm-2am.) Relax to the soulful sounds of jazz while eating huge plates of *cicchetti* (L10,000/€5.20) at **Bacaro Jazz,** Campo S. Bartolomeo, **San Marco,** 5546, across from the post office. (Open Tu-Th 11am-2am.)

🔋 DAYTRIPS FROM VENICE

VERONA. One of the most beautiful cities in northern Italy, Verona is under two hours by train from Venice (p. 601).

TRIESTE. Once occupied by Austria, Trieste beckons with an intriguing Slavic flavor, just two hours by train from Venice (p. 602).

PADUA (PADOVA)   ☎049

Brimming with activity, Padua is a treasury of strident frescoes, sculpture-lined *piazze,* and ethereal nighttime festivals. Art escapes the canvas, covering churches floor to ceiling, while high culture blends with a lively university scene.

🔋 **TRANSPORTATION AND PRACTICAL INFORMATION. Trains** depart from P. Stazione for: Bologna (1½hr., 1-2 per hr., L21,000/€10.85); Milan (2½hr., 1-2 per hr.,

L20,000-31,500/€10.35-16.30); Venice (30min., 3-4 per hr., L4100/€2.15); and Verona (1hr., 1-2 per hr., L7900/€4.10). **Buses** leave P. Boschetti (☎049 820 68 11) for Venice (45min., 2 per hr., L5300/€2.75). The **tourist office** is in the train station. (☎049 875 20 77. Open M-Sa 9:15am-7pm, Su 9:30am-12:15pm.) **Postal code:** 35100.

⌐⌐ ACCOMMODATIONS AND FOOD. The **Ostello Città di Padova (HI)**, V. Aleardi, 30, near Prato della Valle, has an English-speaking staff. Take bus #18 from the station to the stop after Prato della Valle; walk two blocks, go right on V. Marin, left on V. Toresino, right on V. Aleardi, and it's on the left. (☎049 875 22 19. Breakfast included. 5-night max. stay. Reception 7-9:30am and 2:30-11pm. Curfew 11pm. Reserve a week ahead. Dorms L22,000-27,000/€11.40-13.95.) **Hotel Mignon**, V. Bellini, 22, off Prato della Valle, has large, basic rooms. (☎049 66 17 22. Doubles L110,000/€56.85; triples L130,000/€67.15; quads L155,000/€80.05. MC/V.) **Alexander Birreria Paninoteca**, V.S. Francesco, 38, serves sandwiches. (Open M-Sa 8:30am-2am.)

◎⌐ SIGHTS AND ENTERTAINMENT. The one-year **Biglietto Unico**, sold at the tourist office and participating sights, is valid at most of Padua's museums (L15,000/€7.75, students L10,000/€5.20). The **◾Cappella degli Scrovegni** (Arena Chapel), P. Eremitani, 8, contains Giotto's breathtaking floor-to-ceiling fresco cycle, illustrating the lives of Mary, Jesus, and Mary's parents. Buy tickets at the adjoining **Musei Civici Eremitani**, which itself features a restored Giotto crucifix. (Open Feb.-Oct. Tu-Su 9am-7pm; Nov.-Jan. Tu-Su 9am-6pm. Chapel open Feb.-Dec. daily 9am-7pm. L10,000/€5.20, students L7000/€3.65.) Thousands of pilgrims are drawn to Saint Anthony's jawbone and well-preserved tongue at the **Basilica di Sant'Antonio**, in P. del Santo, a medieval conglomeration of eight domes filled with devastatingly beautiful frescoes. (Dress code enforced. Open daily Apr.-Sept. 6:30am-8pm; Nov.-Mar. 6:30am-7pm. L3000/€1.55.) In the center of P. del Santo stands Donatello's bronze equestrian **Gattamelata statue** of Erasmo da Narni (a.k.a. Gattamelata or Calico Cat), a general remembered for his agility and ferocity. Next door to the **duomo**, in P. Duomo, lies the 12th-century **Battistero**, perhaps the most beautiful of Padua's buildings. (Open M-Sa 7:30am-noon and 3:45-7:45pm, Su 7:45am-1pm and 3:45-8:30pm. L3000/€1.55, students L2000/€1.05.) The **Palazzo della Ragione** (Law Court), built in 1218, retains most of its original shape. Astrological signs line the walls, and to the right of the entrance sits the **Stone of Shame**, upon which partially clad debtors were forced to sit. (Open Jan.-Oct. Tu-Su 9am-7pm; Nov.-Dec. Tu-Su 9am-6pm. L10,000/€5.20, students L6000/€3.10.) Buildings of the ancient **university** are centered in **Palazzo Bó**.

VERONA   ☎045

A glorious combination of majestic Roman ruins, colorful Venetian facades, and orange rooftops, Verona is one of the most beautiful cities in Northern Italy. Gazing at the town from one of its many bridges at sunset sets the tone for romantic evenings befitting the home of *Romeo and Juliet*. Meanwhile, its artistic and historical treasures fill days with rewarding sightseeing.

⌐⍰ TRANSPORTATION AND PRACTICAL INFORMATION. Trains (☎045 800 08 61) go from P. XXV Aprile to: Bologna (2hr., every 2hr., L10,500/€5.45); Milan (2hr., every hr., L12,500/€6.45); Venice (1¾hr., every hr., L10,800-17,000/€5.60-8.80). The **tourist office**, in P. Brà, is on the left side the *piazza*, with the Arena on the right. (☎045 806 86 80. Open daily 10am-7pm.)

⌐⌐ ACCOMMODATIONS AND FOOD. Reserve lodgings ahead, especially in opera season (June 26-Sept. 3). The **◾Ostello della Gioventù (HI)**, Villa Francescatti, Salita Fontana del Ferro, 15, in a renovated 16th-century villa with gorgeous gardens; from the station, take bus #73 or night bus #90 to P. Isolo, turn right, and follow the yellow signs uphill. (☎045 59 03 60. Breakfast included. 5-night max. stay. Check-in 5pm. Check-out 7-9am. Lockout 9am-5pm. Curfew 11pm; flexible for opera-goers.

No reservations. Dorms L23,000/€11.90.) Women can also try the beautiful **Casa della Giovane (ACISJF)**, V. Pigna, 7, 3rd fl., in the historic center of town. (☎ 045 59 68 80. Reception 9am-11pm. Curfew 11pm; flexible for opera-goers. Dorms L22,000/€11.40; singles L32,000/€16.55; doubles L25,000-30,000/€12.95-15.50.) To get to **Locanda Catullo**, Vco. Catullo, 1, walk to V. Mazzini, turn onto V. Catullo, and turn left on Vco. Catullo. (☎ 045 800 27 86. July-Sept. 3-night min. stay. Singles L70,000/€36.15; doubles L100,000-120,000/€51.65-62; triples L150,000-180,000/€77.50-93; quads L190,000-230,000/€98.15-118.80.) Verona is famous for its wines, such as the dry white *soave* and red *valpolicella*. Prices in **Piazza Isolo** are cheaper than those in P. delle Erbe. **Brek**, P. Brà, 20, has cheap, delicious food. Pizzas range from L7500-8000/€3.90-4.15. (Open M-Sa 11:30am-3pm and 6:30-10pm.) **METÁ supermarket**, V. XX Settembre, 81, can be reached by taking buses #11-14 or 51. (Open M-Tu and Th-Sa 8:30am-12:45pm and 3:45-7:30pm, W 8:30am-12:45pm.) **Postal code:** 37122.

🔆 **SIGHTS.** The physical and emotional heart of Verona is the majestic, pink-marble, first century **Arena**, in P. Brà. (Open Tu-Su 9am-7pm; in opera season 9am-3pm. L6000/€3.10, students L4000/€2.10.) From P. Brà, V. Mazzini leads to the markets and stunning medieval architecture of **Piazza delle Erbe,** the former Roman forum. The 83m 🔳**Torre dei Lambertini**, in P. dei Signori, offers a stunning view of Verona. (Open Tu-Su 9:30am-6pm. Elevator L4000/€2.10, students L3000/€1.55. Stairs L3000/€1.55, students L2000/€1.05.) The **Giardino Giusti**, V. Giardino Giusti, 2, is a magnificent 16th-century garden with a labyrinth of mythological statues. (Open Apr.-Sept. daily 9am-8pm; Oct.-Mar. 9am-dusk. L7000/€3.65, students L3000/€1.55.) The della Scala fortress, the **Castelvecchio**, down V. Roma from P. Brà, is filled with walkways, parapets, and an extensive art collection including Pisanello's *Madonna and Child*. (Open Tu-Su 9am-7pm. L6000/€3.10, students L4000/€2.10; first Su of each month free.) Thousands of tourists have immortalized **Casa di Giulietta** (Juliet's House), V. Cappello, 23, where the Capulet family never really lived. Avoid wasting money to stand on the balcony. (Open Tu-Su 9am-7pm. L6000/€3.10, students L4000/€2.10.) Down the hill from the hostel is **Locos Café**, V.S. Giovanni in Valle, 28. (Open W-M 9:30am-2pm and 7pm-1am.)

FRIULI-VENEZIA GIULIA

Friuli-Venezia Giulia traditionally receives less than its fair share of recognition. James Joyce lived in Trieste for 12 years, during which he wrote most of *Ulysses;* Ernest Hemingway drew part the plot for *A Farewell to Arms* from the region's role in World War I; and Freud and Rilke both worked and wrote here. Trieste attracts tourists with the cheapest beach resorts on the Adriatic.

TRIESTE (TRIEST)   ☎ 040

In the post-Napoleonic real estate grab, the Austrians snatched up Trieste (pop. 230,000), a city that once rivaled Venice; after a little more ping-pong, the city became part of Italy in 1954, but still remains divided between its Slavic and Italian origins. Trieste's past lingers in its neoclassical architecture, the Slavic nuances of its local cuisine, and the Slovenian still spoken in its streets. The grid-like 19th-century **Città Nuova**, between the waterfront and the Castello di S. Giusto, centers on the **Canale Grande**. Facing the canal from the south is the striking Serbian Orthodox **Chiesa di San Spiridione**. (Dress modestly. Open Tu-Sa 9am-noon and 5-8pm.) The ornate **Municipio** complements the **Piazza dell'Unità d'Italia**, the largest *piazza* in Italy. Trieste's Neoclassical architecture contrasts with its narrow, twisting alleys, reminiscent of its medieval and Roman history. Take bus #24 to the last stop (L1400/€0.75), where the 15th-century Venetian **Castello di San Giusto**, which presides over **Capitoline Hill**, the city's historic center. From P. Goldoni, you can ascend the hill up the daunting 265 steps of **Scala dei Giganti**, or Steps of the Giants. (Castle open daily 9am-dusk.) The **Piazza della Cattedrale** overlooks the sea and downtown Trieste. The archaeological **Museo di Storia e d'Arte**, V. Cattedrale, 15, is on the other side of the hill past the *duomo*. (Open Tu and Th-Su 9am-1pm. L3000/€1.55.)

Trains (☎040 379 47 37) go from P. della Libertà, 8, down Corso Cavour from the quays, to: Budapest (12hr., 2 per day, L130,000/€67.15); Ljubljana (3hr., 3 per day, L40,000/€20.65); and Venice (2hr., 2 per hr., L15,300/€7.90). The **tourist office** is on Riva III Novembre, 9, along the quays near P. della Unita. (☎040 347 83 12; fax 347 83 20. Open M-Sa 7:30am-8:30pm.) **Hotel Alabarda,** V. Valdirivo, 22, has bright, spotless rooms. From P. Oberdan, go down V. XXX Ottobre, and turn right onto V. Valdirivo. (☎040 63 02 69; fax 63 92 84. Singles L50,000-75,000/€25.85-38.75; doubles L80,000-115,000/€41.35-59.39; triples L108,000-155,000/€55.80-80.05; quads L136,000-195,000/€70.25-100.70. AmEx/MC/V.) To get from the station to **Ostello Tegeste (HI)**, V. Miramare, 331, on the seaside, take bus #36 (L1400/€0.75) from across V. Miramare, the street on the left of the station as you exit, and ask the driver for the Ostello stop. Then walk along the Barcola, following the seaside road toward the castle. (☎040 22 41 02. Breakfast and shower included. Reception daily 8am-11:30pm. Check-out 10-11am. Lockout 10am-1pm. Curfew 11:30pm. Dorms L22,000/€11.40.) Stock up at **STANDA**, V. Battisti, 15. (Open M 3:30-7:30pm, Tu-F 9am-1pm and 3:30-7:30pm, Sa 9am-7:30pm.) Savor 50 flavors of *gelato* at **Gelateria Zampolli**, V. Ghega, 10. (Open F-Tu 9am-1am, Th 9am-midnight.) **Postal code:** 34100.

PIEDMONT (PIEMONTE)

Piedmont has been a politically influential region for centuries, as well as a fountainhead of fine food, wine, and nobility. After native-born Vittorio Emanuele II and Camillo Cavour united Italy, Turin served as its capital from 1861 to 1865.

TURIN (TORINO)

☎011

Turin vibrates with economic energy of the new millenium, housing the headquarters of the Fiat Auto Company and preparing to host the 2006 Winter Olympics. It also contains one of the more enigmatic relics of Christianity: the **Holy Shroud of Turin,** housed in the **Cattedrale di San Giovanni,** behind the Palazzo Reale. When the chapel is closed, a life-size canvas copy of the shroud is on display. (Open daily 7am-12:30pm and 3-7pm. Free.) The **Museo Egizio,** in the **Palazzo dell'Accademia delle Scienze,** V. dell'Accademia delle Scienze, 6, has a collection of Egyptian artifacts second only to the British Museum. (Open Tu-F and Su 8:30am-7:30pm, Sa 8:30am-11pm. L12,000/€6.20, ages 18-25 L6000/€3.10.) One of Guarini's great Baroque palaces, the **Palazzo Carignano,** V. dell'Accademia delle Scienze, 5, housed the first Italian parliament. The **Museo Nazionale del Risorgimento Italiano,** in the Palazzo, details Italy's unification from 1706 to 1946. (Open Tu-Su 9am-7pm. L8000/€4.15, students L5000/€2.60. Free tour Su 10-11:30am.)

Trains (☎011 53 13 27) leave Corso Vittorio Emanuele for: Genoa (2hr., every hr., L14,500/€7.50); Milan (2hr., every hr., L21,600/€11.20); and Venice (4½hr., 2 per day, L51,500/€26.60). The **tourist office**, P. Castello, 165, has free maps. (☎011 53 51 81; www.turismotorino.org. Open M-Sa 9:30am-7pm, Su 9:30am-3pm.) To get to the clean and comfortable **Ostello Torino (HI)**, V. Alby, 1, take bus #52 (bus #64 on Su) from Stazione Porto Nuova to the 2nd stop after crossing the river. Turn right onto Corso Lanza to find the Ostello sign on the corner. Follow the signs to V. Gatti and then climb up the road. (☎011 660 29 39; fax 660 44 45. Breakfast and sheets included. Laundry L10,000/€5.20. Reception 7-10am and 3:30-11pm. Curfew 11:30pm; ask for a key if going out. Closed Dec. 20-Jan. 1. Dorms L22,000/€11.40; doubles L48,000/€24.80.) To **camp** at **Campeggio Villa Rey**, Strada Superiore Val S. Martino, 27, take bus #61 north from the right side of the Porta Nuova until P. Vittorio, then take bus #54, and follow signs after the last stop. (☎/fax 011 819 01 17. L7000/€3.65 per person; L4000 for 1 tent, L7000/€3.65 for 2 tents, L9000/€4.65 for up to 5. Electricity L2500/€1.30. Showers L1000/€0.55.) **Spacca Napoli**, V. Mazzini, 19, serves up great pasta and pizza. (Cover L3500/€1.80. Open W-M 6pm-1am.) **Postal code:** 10100.

I FOUND JESUS IN TURIN The Holy Shroud of Turin has been called a hoax by some and a miracle by others. This 1m by 4.5m piece of linen was supposedly wrapped around Jesus's body in preparation for burial after his crucifixion. Although radiocarbon dating places the piece in the 12th century AD, uncanny evidence prevents the shroud's immediate dismissal. Visible on the cloth are outflows of blood: around the head (perhaps from the Crown of Thorns), all over the body (from scourging), and most importantly, on the wrists and feet (where the body was nailed to the cross). Scientists agree that the shroud was wrapped around the body of a 5'7" man who died by crucifixion, but whether it was Jesus remains a mystery. For Christian believers, the importance of the relic is captured by Pope Paul VI's words: "The Shroud is a document of Christ's love written in characters of blood."

THE LAKE COUNTRY

When Italy's monuments and museums start to blur together, escape to the natural beauty of the northern Lake Country, where clear water laps at the foot of the encircling mountains. A youthful crowd descends upon Lake Garda, with its watersports by day and thriving club scene at night; palatial hotels line Lake Maggiore's sleepy shores, while Lake Como's urbane shore hosts three excellent hostels.

LAKE COMO (LAGO DI COMO)

An otherworldly magnificence lingers over the northern reaches of Europe's deepest lake (410m), but peaceful Lake Como is not a figment of your imagination. Bougainvillea and lavish villas adorn the lake's craggy backdrop, warmed by the sun and cooled by lakeside breezes.

Como, the largest city on the lake, on the southwestern tip, is the transportation hub. **Trains** roll into Stazione S. Giovanni from Milan (1hr., every 30min., L9400/€4.85), while **buses** arrive in P. Matteotti from Bergamo (2hr., every 2hr., L8300/€4.30). From Como, take the **C-10** bus near Ferrovia Nord to Domaso or Menaggio (1hr., L4900/€2.55). Hourly **C-30** buses also run to Bellaggio (1hr., L5200/€2.70), on the southern shore of the Centro Lago. **Bellagio** is the favorite lake town of upper crust Milanese society; steep streets lead to sidewalk cafes, silk shops, and the villas of Lombard aristocrats. **Varenna,** on the eastern shore, is more peaceful and scenic. After finding a place to stay, you can spend the day zipping between the gardens, villas, and wineries of the remaining lake towns by ferry.

COMO. For excellent hiking and stunning views, take the **funicular** (☎031 30 36 08) from the far end of Lungo Lario Trieste (every 15-30min.; return L7500/€3.90, through the hostel L5000/€2.60) up to Brunate. To get from the station to the **tourist office,** P. Cavour, 16, walk down the steps to V. Fratelli Ricchi, and turn right on viale Fratelli Rosselli, which leads to P. Cavour via Lungo Lario Trento. (☎031 26 97 12; fax 24 01 11. Open M-Sa 9am-1pm and 2:30-6pm.) **Ostello Villa Olmo (HI),** V. Bellinzona, 2, behind Villa Olmo, offers clean rooms and discounts on various sights in Como. From the train station, walk 20min. down V. Borgo Vico, which becomes V. Bellinzona. (☎/fax 031 57 38 00. Breakfast included. Reception 7-10am and 4-11:30pm. Lockout after 10am. Strict curfew 11:30pm. Open Mar.-Nov. Dorms L21,000/€10.85.) Picnickers will love **G.S. supermarket,** at V. Fratelli Recchi and V. Fratelli Roselli. (Open M 9:30am-9:30pm, Tu-F 8am-9pm, Su 8am-8pm.)

LAKE MAGGIORE (LAGO MAGGIORE)

Lacking the frenzy of its eastern neighbors, Lake Maggiore cradles similar temperate mountain waters and idyllic shores. The romantic resort town **Stresa** is only an hour from Milan by **train** (every hr.; L8400/€4.35, intercity supplement L6000/€3.10). To get from the Stresa train station to the **tourist office,** V. Principe Tommaso, 70/72, turn right and walk down the hill on V. Carducci, which becomes V. Gignous; V.P. Tommaso is on the left. (☎0323 304 16; fax 93 43 35. Open M-F 8:30am-1pm and 2-7pm.) To get to comfy beds at **Hotel Mon Toc,** in Stresa at V. Duchessa di Genova, 67/69, turn right from the station and then right again at the intersection under the tracks. (☎0323 302 82; fax 93 38 60. Breakfast L15,000/€7.75. Singles L70,000/€36.15; doubles L110,000/€56.85. AmEx/D/MC/V.)

◢ **DAYTRIP FROM LAKE MAGGIORE: BORROMEAN ISLANDS.** Stresa is a perfect stepping-stone to the gorgeous Borromean Islands. Daily excursion tickets (L16,000/€8.30) allow you to hop back and forth between Stresa and the three islands—**Isola Bella, Isola Superiore dei Pescatori,** and **Isola Madre.** The islands boast lush, manicured botanical gardens, elegant villas, and an opulent Baroque palace.

LAKE GARDA (LAGO DI GARDA)

Garda, the ultimate resort destination for many Germans, has staggering mountains and breezy summers. **Desenzano,** the lake's southern transport hub, lies on the Milan-Venice line, 30min. from Verona, 1hr. from Milan, and 2hr. from Venice. From Desenzano, the other lake towns are accessible by bus and boat.

SIRMIONE. The crowded neon-lit streets of flashy Sirmione eventually give way farther north to calm walks, Roman ruins, and stellar lake views. The 13th-century **Castello Scaligero** sits in the center of town. (Open Tu-Su 9am-noon. L8000/€4.15.) **Buses** run every hour from Desenzano (20min., L2500/€1.30) to Verona (1hr., L5000/€2.60). **Battelli** (water steamers) run to: Desenzano (20min., L5000/€2.60); Gardone (1¼hr., L10,000/€5.20); and Riva (4hr., L13,900/€7.20). The **Albergo Grifone,** V. Bisse, 5, has prime location near the castle. (☎030 91 60 14; fax 91 65 48. Reserve ahead. Singles L55,000/€28.40; doubles L100,000/€51.65. Extra bed L27,000/€13.95.)

RIVA DEL GARDA. Riva has few sights, but the town is livelier, the crowd younger, and the prices lower than other places on the lake. Travelers **swim, wind-surf, hike,** and **climb** in the most stunning portion of the lake, where Alpine cliffs crash into the water. Riva is accessible by **bus** (☎0464 55 23 23) from Trent (2hr., 6 per day, L6200/€3.20) and Verona (2hr., 11 per day, L9500/€4.90). **Ferries** (☎030 914 95 11), on P. Matteoti, head to Gardone (L12,200/€6.30) and Sirmione (L13,900/€7.20). The **tourist office,** Giardini di Porta Orientale, 8, is near the water. (☎0464 55 44 44; fax 52 03 08. Open M-Sa 9am-noon and 3-6pm, Su 10am-noon and 4-6:30pm.) Snooze at the centrally located **Ostello Benacus (HI),** P. Cavour, 9. From the bus station, walk down V. Trento, take V. Roma, turn left then under the arch, and follow signs. (☎0464 55 49 11; fax 55 65 54. Breakfast, sheets, and shower included. Reception daily 7-9am and 3pm-midnight. Reserve ahead. Dorms L24,000/€12.40.)

THE DOLOMITES (DOLOMITI)

With their sunny skies and powdery, light snow, the Dolomites offer immensely popular downhill skiing. These amazing peaks, which start west of Trent and extend north and east to Austria, are also fantastic for hiking and rock climbing.

TRENT. Between the Dolomites and the Veneto, Trent offers an affordable sampling of northern Italian life with superb restaurants and hikes against dramatic scenery. The **Piazza del Duomo,** Trent's center and social heart, contains the city's best sights. The **Fontana del Nettuno** stands, trident in hand, in the center of the *piazza.* Nearby is the **Cattedrale di San Vigilio,** named for the patron saint of Trent. (Open daily 6:40am-12:15pm and 2:30-7:30pm.) Walk down V. Belenzani and head right on V. Roma to reach the well-preserved **Castello del Buonconsiglio.** (Open daily 10am-6pm. L10,000/€5.20, students and seniors L6000/€3.10.) **Monte Bondone** rises majestically over Trent, making a pleasant daytrip or overnight excursion. Catch the **cable car** (☎0461 38 10 00; every 30min., L4000/€2.10) to **Sardagna** on Mt. Bondone from V. Lung'Adige Monte Grappa, between the train tracks and the river.

ITALY

Trains (☎ 0461 98 36 27) leave V. Dogana for: Bologna (3hr., 13 per day, L19,600/€10.15); Bolzano (45min., 2 per hr., L5600/€2.90); Venice (3hr., 5 per day, L19,300/€10); and Verona (1hr., every hr., L9000/€4.65). Atesina **buses** (☎ 0461 82 10 00) go from V. Pozzo, next to the train station, to Riva del Garda (1hr., every hr., L5500/€2.85). The **tourist office,** V. Alferi, 4, offers advice on biking, skiing, and hiking. (☎ 0461 98 38 80; fax 23 24 26; www.apt.trento.it. Open daily 9am-7pm.) The central **Hotel Venezia** is at P. Duomo, 45. (☎/fax 0461 23 41 14. Breakfast L10,000/€5.20. Singles L52,000/€26.85, with bath 67,000/€34.60; doubles L72,000/€37.20, L92,000/€47.55; triples L92,000/€47.55, L118,000/€60.95; quads L135,000/€69.75. MC/V.) From the station, turn right on V. Pozzo and left on V. Torre Vanga to get to **Ostello Giovane Europa (HI),** V. Torre Vanga, 9. (☎ 0461 26 34 84; fax 22 25 17. Breakfast and sheets included. Reception 3:30-11pm. Check-out 9:30am. Curfew 11:30pm. Reserve ahead. Dorms L22,000/€11.40; singles L42,000/€21.70.) Try delicious pasta at **Patelli,** V. Deitro Le Mura A, 1/5. (Open M noon-2:30pm, Tu-Sa 7-10:30pm.)

BOLZANO. Bolzano's blend of Austrian and Italian influences and its prime location make it a splendid stopover or base for exploring the Dolomites. The Gothic **duomo,** in P. Walther, is filled with frescoes and artwork, while the simple exterior of the **Chiesa dei Francescani,** near P. Erbe, belies the dazzling stained glass within. (Both open M-F 9:45am-noon and 2-5pm, Sa 9:45am-noon. Free.) The intriguing **South Tyrol Museum of Archaeology,** V. Museo, 43, near Ponte Talvera, houses the well-preserved, 5000-year-old body of the **Ice Man.** (Open Tu-Su 10am-6pm, Th 10am-8pm. L13,000/€6.75, students L7000/€3.65.) Take the fresco-covered shuttle bus from P. Walther for the **Castel Roncolo,** up V. Weggerstein to V.S. Antonio, a medieval fortress and eclectic museum. (Open Apr.-Oct. Tu-Su 10am-6pm; frescoes close 5pm. L5000/€2.60.) **Trains** leave P. Stazione for: Milan (3½hr., 3 per day, L25,600/€13.25); Trent (45min., 2 per hr., L5600/€2.90); Verona (2hr., 1-2 per hr., L13,200/€6.85). Walk up V. Stazione from the train station, or V. Alto Adige from the bus stop, to reach the **tourist office,** P. Walther, 8. (☎ 0471 30 70 00; fax 98 01 28; www.bolzano-bozen.it. Open M-F 9am-6:30pm, Sa 9am-12:30pm.) The homey **Croce Bianca,** P. del Grano, 3, is down from P. Walther. (☎ 0471 97 75 52. Singles L52,000/€26.85; doubles L86,000/€44.45, with bath L100,000/€51.65; triples L120,000/€62.)

LOMBARDY (LOMBARDIA)

Over the centuries, Roman generals, German emperors, and French kings have vied for control of Lombardy's rich agricultural wealth and fertile soil. Lombardy has recently become an even sturdier cornerstone of Italy's economy with huge increases in employment and business. While Milan may bask in the cosmopolitan spotlight of glamour and wealth, don't neglect the rich culture and beauty of Bergamo, Mantua, or the nearby foothills of the Alps.

MILAN (MILANO)   ☎ 02

Although it was the capital of the western Roman Empire from 286 to 402, Milan has embraced modern life more forcefully than any other major Italian city. The pace of life is quick, and *il dolce di far niente* (the sweetness of doing nothing) is an unfamiliar taste. Yet football (soccer) unites all Milanese as the city's modern religion, and the bi-annual game between AC Milan and Inter Milan is more important than Christmas. Although Milan's growth has brought petty crime and drugs, the city remains vibrant and on the cutting edge of finance, fashion, and fun.

▗ TRANSPORTATION

Flights: Malpensa Airport (☎ 02 74 85 22 00), 45km from town. Handles intercontinental flights. **Malpensa Express** leaves Cadorna metro station for the airport (45min., L15,000/€7.75). **Linate Airport** (☎ 02 74 85 22 00), 7km away. Covers Europe. Take bus #73 from MM1: P.S. Babila (L1500/€0.80).

Trains: Stazione Centrale, P. Duca d'Aosta (☎02 01 47 88 80 88), on MM2. Office open daily 7am-9:30pm. To: **Florence** (2½hr., every hr., L40,000/€20.70); **Genoa** (1½hr., every hr., L24,000/€12.40); **Rome** (4½hr., every hr., L71,000/€36.70); **Turin** (2hr., every hr., L24,500/€12.70); and **Venice** (3hr., 21 per day, L36,000/€18.60).

Buses: Stazione Centrale. Intercity buses tend to be less convenient and more expensive than trains. **SAL, SIA, Autostradale,** and other carriers leave from P. Castello and nearby (MM1: Cairoli) for Turin, the Lake Country, and Bergamo.

Public Transportation: The **Metropolitana Milanese (MM)** runs 6am-midnight. **Line #1** (red) stretches east to west; **Line #2** (green) links the 3 train stations; **Line #3** (yellow) runs north to south. **ATM buses** (toll free ☎800 01 68 57) handle local transportation. Info and ticket booths open M-Sa 7:15am-7:15pm. Single-fare tickets (L1500/€0.80) are good for 75min. of surface transportation; day passes L5000/€2.60; book of 10 L14,000/€7.25. Buy extra tickets since *tabacchi* close around 8pm.

✦ 🔃 ORIENTATION AND PRACTICAL INFORMATION

Milan's layout resembles a giant target, encircled by a series of ancient concentric city walls, with the **duomo** and **Galleria Vittorio Emanuele II** comprising the bull's-eye. From the train station, a scenic ride on bus #60 or a quick commute on MM3 will take you downtown.

TOURIST, FINANCIAL, AND LOCAL SERVICES

Tourist Office: APT, V. Marconi, 1 (☎02 72 52 43 00; fax 72 52 43 50), in the Palazzo di Turismo, in P. del Duomo. Useful museum guide and map (in Italian). No room reservations, but will check for vacancies. Pick up ▨ *Milano: Where, When, How* and *Milano Mese* for info on activities and clubs. Open M-F 8:30am-8pm, Sa 9am-1pm and 2-7pm, Su 9am-1pm and 2-5pm. **Branch** at Stazione Centrale (☎02 72 52 43 70). Open M-Sa 9am-6pm, Su 9am-12:30pm and 1:30-6pm.

Budget Travel: CIT (☎02 86 37 01), in Galleria Vittorio Emanuele II. Open M-F 9am-7pm, Sa 9am-1pm and 2-6pm. **CTS,** V.S. Antonio, 2 (☎02 58 30 41 21). Open M-F 9:30am-12:45pm and 2-6pm, Sa 9:30am-12:45pm. **Transalpino Tickets** (☎02 67 16 82 28; www.transalpino.com), next to the train office in Stazione Centrale. Discounts for age 26 and under. Open daily 7am-7:45pm.

Currency Exchange: All **Banca d'America e d'Italia** and **Banca Nazionale del Lavoro** branches eagerly await your Visa card. Bank hours in Milan are usually M-F 8:30am-1:30pm and 2:30-4:30pm. **ATMs** abound.

American Express: V. Brera, 3 (☎02 72 00 36 93), on the corner of V. dell'Orso. Holds mail free for AmEx members and receives wired money (L2500/€1.30 fee if over L150,000/€77.50). **Exchanges currency.** Open M-Th 9am-5:30pm, F 9am-5pm.

Luggage storage: Malpensa airport, L4000/€2.10 per 12hr.

Laundromat: Vicolo Lavandai, Viale Monte Grappa, 2 (☎02 498 39 02). MM2: Garibaldi. Wash 7kg L6000/€3.10, dry for L6000/€3.10. Open daily 8am-9pm.

EMERGENCY AND COMMUNICATIONS

Emergency: ☎118.

Police: ☎113 or 02 772 71. **Carabineri:** ☎112.

24-Hour Pharmacy: In Stazione Centrale (☎02 669 07 35).

Hospital: Ospedale Maggiore di Milano, V. Francesco Sforza, 35 (☎02 550 31).

Internet Access: Boomerang, V.F. Filzi, 41 (☎02 669 40 65). To the right of Stazione Centrale behind the park. Fax, printing, and money wiring. L15,000/€7.75 per hr. Open 8:30am-6:30pm. **El Pampero,** V. Gasparotto, 1 (☎02 66 92 21), is across from Boomerang. L10,000/€5.20 per hr. Open M-F 7am-2pm, Sa 9-2pm, Su 5pm-1am.

Post Office: V. Cordusio, 4 (☎02 72 48 22 23), near P. del Duomo. Stamps, *Fermo Posta,* and currency exchange. Address mail to be held: First Name SURNAME, *In Fermo Posta,* Ufficio Postale Centrale di Piazza Cordusio 4, Milano **20100,** Italia. Open M-F 8:30am-7:30pm, Sa 8:30am-1pm. **Postal Code:** 20100.

ITALY

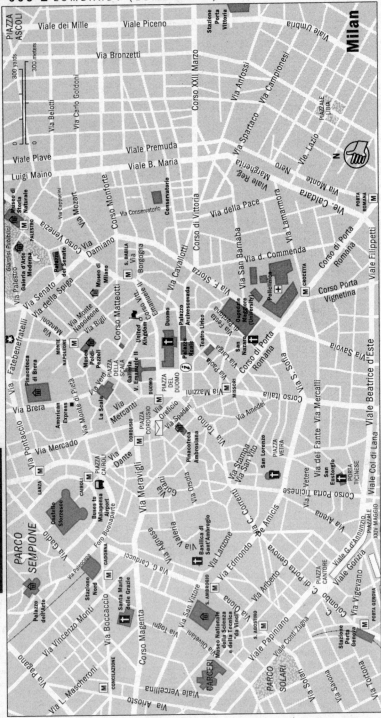

Milan

🏠 ACCOMMODATIONS AND CAMPING

It's always high season in Milan, except in August, when mosquitoes outnumber humans. A decent single under L65,000/€33.60 is a real find. Try east of the train station or the southern periphery of the city for the best deals.

Hotel Ambra, V. Caccianino, 10 (☎02 266 54 65; fax 70 60 62 45.). MM1/2: Loreto. Walk 10 blocks down V. Porpora and turn right on V. Caccianino. 19 spotless rooms. Breakfast L5000/€2.60. Ask for key if going out at night. Reserve ahead. Singles L80,000/€41.35; doubles L110,000/€56.85; triples L140,000/€72.30.

Ostello Piero Rotta (HI), V. Salmoiraghi, 1 (☎02 39 26 70 95). MM1: QT8. Walk to the right from the metro so that the round church is across the street and to your back; it will be on your right. Breakfast included. 3-night max. stay. Reception 7-9:30am and 3:30pm-midnight. Daytime lockout. Curfew 11:30pm. Members only; HI cards available for L30,000/€15.50. Closed Dec.20-Jan.10. 6-bed dorms L30,000/€15.50.

Hotel Rallye, V.B. Marcello, 59 (☎/fax 02 29 53 12 09). MM1: Lima. Take V. Vitruvio for 2 blocks and turn left on V. Marcello. New, simple rooms with telephone and TV. Singles L70,000/€36.15; doubles L110,000/€58.85. AmEx/D/MC/V.

Hotel Due Giardini, V.B. Marcello, 47 (☎02 295 21 093 or 02 29 51 23; fax 29 51 69 33). MM1: Lima. Walk 2 blocks along V. Vitruvio to V. Marcello, and take a left on the far side of the street. 11 minty-green rooms. Some English spoken. Breakfast L7000/€3.65. Doubles L150,000/€77.50; triples L180,000/€93. MC/V.

Hotel Aurora, Corso Buenos Aires, 18 (☎02 204 79 60; fax 204 92 85; www.hotelit-aly.com/hotels/aurora/index.htm). MM1: Porta Venezia. Exit the station onto Corso Buenos Aires, walk straight head for 5min. and it's on the right. Courtyard and sound-proof windows block street noise. Reception 24hr. Reserve ahead. Singles L80,000/€41.35, with bath L90,000-95,000/€46.50-49.10; doubles L120,000/€62, L145,000/€75; 1 triple L190,000/€98.15. AmEx/MC/V.

Pensione Cantore, Calle Porta Genova, 25 (☎/fax 02 835 75 65). Southwest of the *duomo* down V.C. Correnti, near Navigli locks. MM2: Porta Genova. Recently renovated rooms all with showers and a TV. Breakfast included. Reception 24hr. Singles L70,000/€36.15; doubles L100,000/€51.65; triples L150,000/€77.50.

Camping di Monza (☎02 039 38 77 71), in the park of the Villa Reale in Monza. Take a train or bus from Stazione Centrale to Monza, then a city bus. Call ahead. Open Apr.-Aug. L8000/€4.15 per person, L8000/€4.15 per tent, L15,000/€7.75 per caravan (4 people). Hot showers L500/€0.30.

🍴 FOOD

Like its fine *couture*, Milan's cuisine is sophisticated and overpriced. Specialties include *risotto giallo* (rice with saffron), *cotoletta alla milanese* (breaded veal cutlet with lemon), and *cazzouela* (a mixture of pork and cabbage). The largest **markets** are around **Via Fauché** and **Via Papiniano** on Saturdays and Tuesdays, and along P. Mirabello on Mondays and Thursdays. The **Fiera di Sinigallia,** a 400-year-old market extravaganza, occurs on Saturdays on the banks of the Darsena, a canal in the Navigli district (V. d'Annunzio). Splurge on a local pastry at **Sant'Ambroeus,** a Milanese culinary shrine, under the arcades at Corso Matteotti, 7. (Open daily 8am-8pm.) Pick up groceries near Corso Buenos Aires at **Supermarket Regina Giovanna,** V. Regina Giovanna, 34. (Open M-F 8am-9pm, Sa 8am-8pm.)

Brek, V. Lepetit, 20, near Stazione Centrale; others at P. Cavour and Porta Giordano. Elegant self-serve restaurant. Tasty dishes cooked before your eyes. *Primi* around L5000/€2.60, *secondi* around L7500/€3.90. Open M-Sa 11:30am-3pm and 6:30-10:30pm.

Tarantella, Viale Abruzzi, 35, just north of V. Plinio. MM1: Lima. Lively, elegant sidewalk dining. Try the *pasta fresca* (L12,000/€6.20) or the *pizze* (L10,000/€5.20). *Secondi* from L125,000/€64.55. Open Sept.-July M-Su noon-2:30pm and 7-11:30pm.

Ristorante El Recreo, V. Scarlatti, 7. MM1: Lima, then walk north on Corso Bueno Aires and turn left on V. Scarlatti; it's on the 2nd block on the left. Romantic and hip atmosphere with merengue beats in background. Simple homemade Italian cuisine. *Pizze* L7500-13,000/ €3.90-6.75. Open Tu-Su noon-2:30pm and 7pm-11:30pm.

La Crêperie, V.C. Correnti, 21, on the lower continuation of V. Torino. MM2: S. Amborogio. Serves crepes filled with a wide array of ingredients, from *prosciutto* and eggs to banana and Nutella. Crepes L4000-6000/€2.10-3.10. Open daily noon-1am.

Pizzeria Grand'Italia, V. Palermo, 5. MM2: Moscova. Walk down V. Statuto and turn right on V. Palermo. Pizza is sold in huge wedges for L7000-10,000/€3.65-5.20. Open W-M 12:15-2:45pm and 7pm-1:15am; Aug. open daily.

Il Fondaco dei Mori, V. Solferino, 33. MM2: Moscova, then walk north to P. XXV Aprile, turn right onto Porta Nuova, and take your 2nd right onto V. Solferino. No sign; ring the bell. First Middle Eastern restaurant in Italy. Vegetarian lunch menu L14,000/€7.25. Delicious dinner buffet L20,000/€10.35. Try the mango or guava juice, or the excellent ginger coffee. Cover L3000/€1.55. Open Tu-Su 12:30-3pm and 7:30pm-midnight.

◎ SIGHTS

AROUND THE DUOMO

▩ **DUOMO.** The Gothic duomo, on P. del Duomo, is the geographical and spiritual center of Milan. More than 3400 statues, 135 spires, and 96 gargoyles grace this third-largest church in the world. *(MM1: Duomo. Open daily Mar.-Oct. 9am-5:45pm; Nov.-Feb. 9am-4:15pm. Modest dress strictly enforced. Free. Roof access L6000/€3.10, with elevator L9000/€4.65.)* To the right of the *duomo* in Palazzo Reale, the **Museo d'Arte Contemporanea,** holds a fine permanent collection of 20th-century Italian art and a few Picassos. *(Open Tu-Su 9:30am-5:30pm. Free.)*

▩ **TEATRO ALLA SCALA.** Known simply as La Scala, this is the world's most renowned opera house. Singer Maria Callas became a legend in this 18th-century Neoclassical building. Enter through the **Museo Teatrale alla Scala,** which includes such memorabilia as Verdi's famous top hat. *(P. della Scala, at the opposite end of galleria from the duomo. Open daily 9am-noon and 2-5:30pm. L6000/€3.10.)*

PINACOTECA DI BRERA. The Brera Art Gallery presents one of Italy's most impressive collection of paintings, with works by Caravaggio, Bellini, and Raphael. *(V. Brera, 28, immediately after V.G. Verdi coming from La Scala. MM2: Lanza. Open Tu-Sa 9am-7pm, Su 8:30am-11pm. L8000/€4.15.)*

GALLERIA VITTORIO EMANUELE II. On the left as you face the *duomo*, a glass barrel vault covers a five-story arcade of cafes and shops with mosaic floors and walls. *(Open M-Sa 10am-11pm, Su 10am-8pm.)*

NEAR CASTELLO SFORZESCO

▩ **CASTELLO SFORZESCO.** Restored after heavy bomb damage in 1943, the enormous Castello Sforzesco is one of Milan's best-known monuments and a great place for a picnic. It houses the **Musei Civici,** which features Michelangelo's unfinished last work, *Pietà Rondanini. (MM1: Cairoli. Open Tu-Su 9:30am-5:30pm. Free.)*

▩ **CHIESA DI SANTA MARIA DELLE GRAZIE.** An 15th-century convent, the church's Gothic nave is elaborately patterned with frescoes. Next to the church entrance, the **Cenacolo Vinciano** (Vinciano Refectory) displays Leonardo da Vinci's infamous *Last Supper,* which captures the apostles' reaction to Jesus' prophecy: "One of you will betray me." *(P. di S. Maria delle Grazie, 2, on Corso Magenta, off V. Carducci below MM1: Cadorna Cairoli. MM1: Cadorna Cairoli. Open Tu-Su 8am-7:30pm. L12,000/€6.20, under 18 and over 65 free. Arrive early or late to avoid a wait.)*

BASILICA DI SANT'AMBROGIO. A prototype for Lombard-Romanesque churches throughout Italy, Sant'Ambrogio is the most influential medieval building in Milan. The 4th-century **Cappella di San Vittore in Ciel D'Oro,** with exquisite 5th-century mosaics adorning its cupola, lies through the 7th chapel on the right; enter, walk a few paces, and then turn left. *(MM1: Sant'Ambrogio. Open M-Sa 7:30am-noon and 2:30-7pm, Su 3-7pm. Free.)*

CORSO PORTA TICINESE AND THE NAVIGLI

■ NAVIGLI DISTRICT. The "Venice of Lombardy," the Navigli district comes alive at night. Complete with canals, footbridges, open-air markets, and cafes, this area once constituted part of a medieval canal system used to transport tons of marble for the *duomo* and linked Milan to various northern cities and lakes. *(Outside the MM2: Porta Genova station, through the Arco di Porta Ticinese.)*

BASILICA DI SANT'EUSTORGIO. Founded in the 4th century to house the bones of the Magi, the church lost its original function when the dead wise men were spirited off to Cologne in 1164. The triumph of the church is the **Portinari Chapel,** one of the great masterpieces of early Renaissance art. *(P.S. Eustorigio, 3, farther down Corso Ticinese from S. Lorenzo Maggiore. Tram #3. Open W-M 9:30am-noon and 3:30-6pm. Free.)*

CHIESA DI SAN LORENZO MAGGIORE. The oldest church in Milan, San Lorenzo Maggiore testifies to the city's 4th-century greatness. To its right lies the **Cappella di Sant'Aquilino,** which contains a 5th-century mosaic of a beardless Christ among his apostles. *(On Corso Ticinese. MM2: Porta Genova, then tram #3 from V. Torino. Open daily 7:30am-6:45pm. Cappella L2000/€1.05.)*

SOUTH AND EAST OF THE DUOMO

■ PINACOTECA AMBROSIANA. Tiny but lovely, the 23 rooms of the Ambrosiana house 15th- to 17th-century art, including works by Botticelli, Leonardo, Raphael, Bruegel, and Caravaggio. *(P. Pio XI, 2. From V. Torino, turn right on V. Spadari, and make a left on V. Cantù. Open Tu-Su 10am-5:30pm. L12,000/€6.20, children and seniors L6000/€3.10.)*

OSPEDALE MAGGIORE. Built in 1456, this is one of the largest early Renaissance constructions. Now the **University of Milan,** it contains nine courtyards, including a grand 17th-century court and one credited to Bramante. *(On V. Festa del Perdono near P. Santo Stefano.)*

GALLERIA D'ARTE MODERNA. Napoleon lived here with Josephine when Milan was capital of the Napoleonic Kingdom of Italy (1805-1814). The gallery now displays important modern Lombard art and Impressionist works. *(V. Palestro, 16, next to the Giardini Pubblici in the Villa Comunale. MM2: Palestro. Open Tu-Su 9am-5:45pm. Free.)*

◪ NIGHTLIFE

The **Teatri d'Italia di Porta Romana,** Corso di Porta Romana, 124, is building a reputation for experimental productions and first-run mainstream plays. Take bus #13 from V. Marconi off P. del Duomo. (☎ 02 58 31 58 96. Tickets from L28,000/€12.25). If you've come to Milan to (window) **shop,** the city's most elegant boutiques are between the **Corso Vittorio Emanuele** near the *duomo* and **Via Monte Napoleone** off P.S. Babila. More affordable clothing can be found in *blochisti* (wholesale clothing outlets), especially on **Corso Buenos Aires;** check the tourist office brochure *Milano: Where, When, How* for bargain store listings.

The nocturnal scene varies with the hour and the locale. A safe, chic, and tourist-filled district lies by **Via Brera,** northwest of the *duomo* and east of MM1: Cairoli, where you'll find art galleries, small clubs, restaurants, and an upscale thirtysome-thing crowd. Younger Milanese migrate to the areas around **Corso Porta Ticinese** and **Piazza Vetra** (near Chiesa S. Lorenzo) to sip beer at one of the many *birrerie* (pubs). The highest concentration of bars and youth can be found in the wee hours of the morning in the **Navigli district.** Check any paper on Wednesday or Thursday for information on club and weekend events.

■ **Le Trottoir,** near V. Brera. From MM2: Lanza, take V. Tivoli to the Corso Garibaldi intersection. A lively atmosphere with live bands nightly. Open daily 7pm-2:30am.

■ **Scimmie,** V. Sforza, 49. A legendary, energetic bar. Different theme every night and frequent concerts; fusion, jazz, soul, and reggae dominate. Open daily 8pm-1:30am.

Bar Magenta, V. Carducci, 13. A traditional Guinness bar with an overflowing crowd. Open Tu-Su 9am-3am, sometimes until 5am.

Artdecothe, V. Lombro, 7. MM1: Porta Venezia. Walk 3 blocks up Corso Buenos Aires, turn right on V. Melzi, and walk 3 blocks on the left. This discobar defines Milan's elegance. Dancing after midnight. Open daily 7am-2am.

Lollapaloosa, Corso Como, 15. A wild crowd will have you dancing on the tables. L15,000/€7.75 cover includes a drink. Open Su-Th 7pm-2am, F-Sa 7pm-5:30am.

Grand Café Fashion, Corso Porta Ticinese, near V. Vetere. A bar/restaurant/dance club with a stunningly beautiful crowd and velour leopard print couches. Mandatory 1st drink L15,000/€7.75. Happy hour 8pm-2:30am. Open daily noon-3pm, 8pm-3:30am.

Old Fashion, V. Camoens in Parco Sempione. Walk from P. Cadorna on the right in V. Paleocapa, which turns into V.E. Alemagna; the club is in the Palazzo dell'Arte. Frequented by hard-core clubbers and (relatively) normal fashion types. L25,000/€12.95 cover includes one drink. Open F-Sa 11pm-4am.

Le Lephante, V. Melzo, 22. MM2: Porta Venezia; then walk up Corso Buenos Aires and turn right on V. Melzo. A mixed gay/straight crowd. Open Tu-Su 6:30pm-2am.

◪ DAYTRIPS FROM MILAN

BERGAMO. Bergamo's medieval palaces, fabulous art museum, and 12th-century basilica are only a one-hour train ride from Milan (p. 613).

LAKE COUNTRY. The magnificence of Lakes Como, Maggiore, and Garda awaits one hour from Milan by train (p. 604).

MANTUA (MANTOVA) ☎ 0376

Mantua owes its literary fame to its most famous son, the poet Virgil. But the driving force that built the city's *centro storico* was actually the Gonzaga family, who revamped Mantua's small-town image by importing well-known artists and cultivating local talent. Mantua also provides easy passage to the surrounding lakes. Once the largest palace in Europe, the ▣**Palazzo Ducale** towers over the cobblestone **Piazza Sordello.** Over time it absorbed the Gothic **Magna Domus** *(duomo)* and **Palazzo del Capitano** into its complex. Inside, check out frescoes, tapestries, and gardens. Outside, signs point to the **Castello di San Giorgio,** once a formidable fortress. (*Palazzo* open Tu-Su 8:45am-6:30pm. L12,000/€6.20, seniors and children free.) At the south end of the city, down V.P. Amedeo, through P. Veneto, and down Largo Parri, the opulent **Palazzo del Te,** built in 1534 as a suburban retreat for Federico II Gonzaga, is widely considered the finest example of the Mannerist style. (Open M 1-6pm, Tu-Su 9am-6pm. L12,000/€6.20, students and children ages 12-18 L8000/€4.15.) Just south of P. Sordello is the 11th-century Romanesque **Piazza delle Erbe;** opposite the *piazza* is Leon Alberti's **Chiesa di Sant'Andrea,** Mantua's greatest contribution to the Italian Renaissance. (*Piazza* open 10am-12:30pm and 2:30-6:30pm; *chiesa* open daily 8am-noon and 3-6:30pm. Both free.) Walk from P. delle Erbe to P. Broletto and take V. Accademia until the end to reach the fairy tale-like **Teatro Scientifico (Bibiena),** with amazing acoustics.

　Trains (☎ 0376 147 88 80 88) go from P. Don Leoni to Milan (2hr., 9 per day, L16,000/€8.30) and Verona (40min., every hr., L4100/€2.15). From the train station, head left on V. Solferino, through P.S. Francesco d'Assisi to V. Fratelli Bandiera, and turn right on V. Verdi to find the **tourist office,** P. Mantegna, 6, next to Chiesa di Sant'Andrea. (☎ 0376 36 32 53; fax 36 32 92. Open M-Sa 8:30am-12:30pm and 3-6pm.) **Albergo Maragò,** V. Villanova De Bellis, 2, at the Locanda Virgiliana, 2km from the town center, is a bargain with quiet, clean rooms. (☎ 0376 37 03 13. Singles L38,000/€19.65; doubles L55,000/€28.40. AmEx/DC/MC/V.) **Pizzeria/Ristorante Piedigrotta 2,** Corso Liberta, 15, offers great deals on pizza and delicious seafood dishes. (*Pizza margherita* L8000/€4.15; *primi* from L8000/€4.15; *secondi* from L11,000/€5.70. Open Tu-Su noon-3pm and 6:30-12:30am.) **Postal code:** 46100.

BERGAMO
☎035

Originating as a Venetian outpost, Bergamo is now a thriving city that successfully blends the old and new. **Via Pignolo,** in the bustling *città bassa* (lower city), winds past a succession of handsome 16th- to 18th-century palaces. Turn left onto V.S. Tomaso and then right to visit one of Italy's most important galleries, the **Galleria dell'Accademia Carrara,** with works by Titian, Rubens, Breugel, and van Dyck. (Open W-M 9:30am-12:30pm and 2:30-5:30pm. L10,000/€5.20, Su free.) From the Galleria, the terraced **Via Noca** ascends to the *città alta* (upper city) through Porta Sant'Agostino. Stroll down V. Porta Dipinta to V. Gambito, which ends in **Piazza Vecchia,** a majestic ensemble of medieval and Renaissance buildings flanked by restaurants and cafes at the heart of the *città alta.* Head through the archway flanking P. Vecchia to P. del Duomo to reach the **Cappella Colleoni.** (Open Tu-Su Mar.-Oct. 9am-12:30pm and 2-6:30pm; Nov.-Feb. 9am-12:30pm and 2:30-4:30pm. Free.) On the Cappella's left, the 12th century ◪**Basilica di Santa Maria Maggiore** has an ornate Baroque interior and tapestries depicting biblical scenes. (Open May-Sept. M-F 9am-noon and 3-6pm, Sa-Su 8-10:30am and 3-6pm; Oct.-Apr. M-F 9am-noon and 3-4:30pm, Sa-Su 8-10:30am and 3-6pm. Free.) Climb the **Torre Civica** (Civic Tower; L2000/€1.05) for a marvelous view of Bergamo and the hills.

The train and bus stations as well as budget hotels are in the *città bassa.* **Trains** (1hr., L7200/€3.75) and **buses** (L7500/€3.90) pull into P. Marconi from Milan. To get to the **tourist office,** V. Aquila Nera, 2, in the *città alta,* take buses #1 or 1a to the funicular, then follow V. Gambito to P. Vecchia and turn right. (☎035 23 27 30. Open daily 9am-12:30pm and 2-5:30pm.) Take bus #14 from Porto Nuova to "Leonardo da Vinci" and walk uphill to reach the **Ostello della Gioventù di Bergamo (HI),** V. G. Ferraris, 1. (☎035 34 30 38. Breakfast included. Internet. HI members only. Dorms L26,000/€13.45; singles L35,000/€18.10; doubles L60,000/€31.) Take bus #5 or 7 from V. Angelo Maj., or walk for 20min., to reach **Locanda Caironi,** V. Torretta, 6B, off V. Gorgo Palazzo. (☎035 24 30 83. Singles L30,000/€15.50, doubles L55,000/€28.40.) In the *città bassa,* **Capolinea,** V. Giacomo Quarenghi 29, right off V. Zambonate, offers full meals from L15,000/€7.75. (Open Tu-Sa 6:30pm-3am, Su 7pm-3am. Kitchen closes at midnight.) In the *città alta,* play billiards at the airy garden cafe **Circolino Cooperativa Città Alta,** V.S. Agata, 19, while enjoying delicious cheap food. (Sandwiches, pizza, and salads for under L8000/€4.15. Cover L1000/€0.55. Open Th-Tu 8:30am-3am, W 11:30am-3am.) **Postal code:** 24122.

ITALIAN RIVIERA (LIGURIA)

The sun blazes down upon Liguria, the 350km stretch of Italian Riviera that graces the Mediterranean between France and Tuscany, forming the most famous and touristed area of the Italian coastline. Genoa divides the strip into the **Riviera di Levante** ("rising sun") to the east and the **Riviera di Ponente** ("setting sun") to the west. The **Cinque Terre** area, just to the west of La Spezia, is especially enchanting.

All the coastal towns are linked by the main **rail** line, which runs west from Genoa to Ventimiglia (near the French border) and east to La Spezia (near Tuscany), but slow local trains take hours to travel short distances. Frequent intercity **buses** pass through all major towns, and local buses run to inland hill-towns. **Boats** connect most resort towns. **Ferries** go from Genoa to Olbia, Sardinia, and Palermo, Sicily.

GENOA (GENOVA)
☎010

Urban, gritty Genoa has little in common with its picture-perfect resort neighbors. Yet what the city lacks in small-town resort friendliness it makes up in rich history, which includes stars like Chistopher Columbus and Giuseppe Mazzini. Since falling into decline in the 18th century, modern Genoa has turned its attention from industry to the restoration of its bygone grandeur.

ITALY

⚠️ TRANSPORTATION AND PRACTICAL INFORMATION. Most visitors arrive at either **Stazione Principe**, in P. Acquaverde, or **Stazione Brignole**, in P. Verdi. **Trains** go to Rome (5hr., 14 per day, L44,500/€23) and Turin (2hr., 19 per day, L15,900/€8.25). **Ferries** depart from the Ponte Assereto arm of the port; buy tickets at the **Stazione Marittima.** From Stazione Principe, take bus #18, 19, 20, 30, 32, 35, or 41, and from Stazione Brignole, take buses #19 or 40 to reach **Piazza de Ferrari,** the city center. If walking, take V. Balbi to V. Cairoli, which becomes V. Garibaldi, and at P. delle Fontane Marose turn right on V. XXV Aprile. From Stazione Brignole, turn right onto V. Fiume, and take another right onto V. XX Settembre. The **APT tourist office** is on Porto Antico, in Palazzina S. Maria. From the aquarium, walk toward the complex of buildings to the left. (☎010 248 711. Open daily 9:30am-1pm and 3:30-6pm.) Log on at **A.P.C.A.,** V. Colombo, 35r. (L3000/€1.55 for 15min., L10,000/€5.20 per hr. Open M-F 9am-noon and 3-7pm.) **Postal code:** 16121.

🍴 ACCOMMODATIONS AND FOOD. Ostello per la Gioventù (HI), V. Costanzi, 120, has a cafeteria, TV, and a view of the city far below. From Stazione Principe, take bus #35 and tell the driver you want to transfer to bus #40 at V. Napoli; take #40 to the hostel. From Stazione Brignole, take bus #40 (every 15min.) and ask to be let off at the *ostello.* (☎/fax 010 242 24 57. Breakfast included. Laundry L12,000/€6.20 per 5kg. Reception 7-9am and 3:30pm-12:30am. Curfew midnight. HI members only; HI card available. Dorms L25,000/€12.95.) **Albergo Carola,** V. Gropallo, 4/12, is 2 flights up from Albergo Argentina. From Stazione Brignole, turn right on V. de Amicis, turn right when facing Albergo Astoria, and walk 15m. (☎010 839 13 40. Singles L45,000/€23.25; doubles L65,000/€34, with shower L75,000/€38.75.) **Hotel Balbi,** V. Balbi, 21/3, offers large, ornate rooms. (☎/fax 010 25 23 62. Breakfast L7000/€3.65. With *Let's Go:* Singles L40,000/€20.65; doubles L80,000/€41.35, with bath L100,000/€51.65; triples and quads add 30% per person. AmEx/MC/V.) **Camping** is popular; turn to the tourist office for information, as many campgrounds are booked solid. To reach **Villa Doria,** V. al Campeggio Villa Doria, 15, take the train or bus #1-3 from P. Caricamento to Pegli, then walk or transfer to bus #93 up V. Vespucci. (☎010 696 96 00. L10,000/€5.20 per person, L10,000-13,000/€5.20-6.75 per tent. Electricity and showers free.) Genoa is famous for its *pesto* and *focaccia;* try **Trattoria da Maria,** V. Testa d'Oro, 14r, off V. XXV Aprile, which has a new menu every day with dishes for L13,000/€6.75. (Open Su-F noon-2:30pm and 7-9:30pm.)

☀️ SIGHTS. Genoa boasts a multitude of *palazzi,* along with its fine 16th- and 17th-century Flemish and Italian art acquired in its days of commercial power. **V. Balbi,** in the heart of the university quarter, contains some of the most lavish *palazzi* in Genoa. The 18th-century **Palazzo Reale,** V. Balbi, 10, west of V. Garibaldi, is filled with Rococo rooms bathed in gold and upholstered in red velvet. (Open M-Tu 8:15am-1:45pm, W-Su 8:15am-7:15pm. L8000/€4.15, students L4000/€2.10, children and seniors free.) Follow V. Balbi through P. della Nunziata and continue to L. Zecca, where V. Cairoli leads to **V. Garibaldi,** the most impressive street in Genoa, bedecked with elegant *palazzi* that once earned it the names "Golden Street" and "Street of Kings." The **Galleria di Palazzo Bianco,** V. Garibaldi, 11, exhibits Ligurian, Dutch, and Flemish paintings. Across the street, the 17th-century **Galleria Palazzo Rosso,** V. Garibaldi, 18, has magnificent furnishings in a lavishly frescoed interior. (Both open Tu and Th-F 9am-1pm, W and Sa 9am-7pm, Su 10am-6pm. L6000/€3.10 each; L10,000/€5.20 combined; Su free.) The **Villetta Di Negro,** on the hill farther down V. Garibaldi, features waterfalls, grottoes, and terraced gardens. From P. de Ferrari, take V. Boetto to P. Matteotti for the ornate **Chiesa di Gesù.** (Open daily 7:30am-noon and 4-6:30pm. Free.) Head past the *chiesa* down V. di Porta Soprana to reach the medieval twin-towered **Porta Soprana,** the supposed boyhood home of Christopher Columbus. Then walk toward the port on V. Ravecca to reach the **Museo dell'Architettura e Scultura Ligure,** which features surviving art pieces from Genoa's history. (Open Tu-Sa 9am-7pm, Su 9am-12:30pm. L6000/€3.10.) Off V.S. Lorenzo, which emerges from O. Matteotti, is the lopsided **Duomo (San Lorenzo),** P.S. Lorenzo. (Open M-Sa 8am-7pm, Su 7am-7pm. Free.) The *duomo* lies on the southern edge of the **centro storico,** the historical center of town and a dangerous web of alleys bordered by the port, V. Garibaldi, and P. Ferrari. The neighborhood also contains some of Genoa's most notable monuments. Back on P.G. Matteotti, head up V.S. Lorenzo toward the water, turn left on V. Chiabrera, and left on V. di Mascherona to reach the **Chiesa Santa Maria di Castello,** P. Caricamento, a labyrinth of courtyards, cloisters, and crucifixes. (Open daily 9am-noon and 3:30-6:30pm.)

▶ **DAYTRIP FROM GENOA: THE RIVIERA.** Several idyllic Riviera towns are accessible from Genoa by train, including **Finale Ligure** (1hr.; p. 615), **Santa Margherita Ligure** (40min.; p. 616), and **Cinque Terre** (1½hr.; p. 616).

RIVIERA DI PONENTE

FINALE LIGURE   ☎ 019

A plaque along the beachfront promenade announces Finale as the place for *Il riposo del popolo* (the people's rest). A prime spot to vacation from your vacation, Finale Ligure welcomes weary backpackers with soft sands, turquoise sea, and plenty of *gelato*. The city is divided into three sections: **Finalpia** to the east, **Finalmarina** in the center, and the old city **Finalborgo** farther inland to the northwest. You can hike the worthwhile climb to the ruined 13th-century **Castel Govone,** which offers a spectacular view of Finale. Walk east along V. Aurelia through the 1st tunnel for a less crowded **free beach. Trains** leave P. Vittorio Veneto for Genoa (1 hr., every hr., L6900/€3.60). Across from the train station, **SAR buses** run to tiny **Borgo Verezzi** (10min., every 15min., L1800/€0.95), with its tranquil streets and caves, and other nearby towns. Get free maps at the **IAT tourist office,** V.S. Pietro, 14. (☎019 68 10 19; fax 68 18 04. Open M-Sa 9am-12:30pm and 3:30-7pm, Su 9am-noon.) **Simpatia Crai supermarket** is at V. Bruneghi, 2a. (Open M-Sa 8am-12:30pm and 4-6:30pm.)

▓**Castello Wuillerman (HI),** on V. Generale Caviglia, is well worth the tough hike. From the station, take a left onto V. Mazzini, which becomes V. Torino, turn left on V. degli Ulivi, and trudge up the daunting steps. (☎/fax 019 69 05 15. Breakfast and sheets included. Reception 7-10am and 5-10pm. Curfew 11:30pm. No phone reservations. Open mid-Mar. to mid-Oct. HI members only; HI cards are sold there. Dorms L20,000/€10.35.) **Pensione Enzo** at Gradinata delle Rose, 3, provides double rooms at seasonal rates. (☎019 69 13 83. Open Easter-Sept. Doubles L70,000-90,000/€36.15-46.50.) To reach the spotless **Albergo San Marco,** V. della Concezione, 22, walk straight down V. Saccone from the station and turn left on V. della Concezione. (☎019 69 25 33; fax 68 16 187. Breakfast included. Reservations recommended. Open Easter to mid-Oct. Singles L60,000/€31; doubles L80,000/€41.35. AmEx/MC/V.) **Camping Del Mulino** has a bar, restaurant, mini-market and laundry facilities. Take the Calvisio bus to the Boncardo Hotel, and follow the brown and yellow signs to the campsite entrance 300m from the shore. (☎019 60 16 69. Laundry L10,000/€5.20. Reception Apr.-Sept. 8am-8pm. L8000/€4.15 per person, L8000/€4.15 per tent.) Cheap restaurants lie inland along **Via Rossi** and **Via Roma.**

RIVIERA DI LEVANTE

CAMOGLI. Postcard-perfect Camogli shimmers with color. Sun-faded peach houses crowd the hilltop, red and turquoise boats bob in the water, piles of fishing nets cover the docks, and bright umbrellas dot the dark stone beaches. **Trains** run on the Genoa-La Spezia line to: Genoa (20min., 32 per day, L2700/€1.40); La Spezia (1½hr., 21 per day, L6400/€3.30); and Santa Margherita (10min., 24 per day, L1900/€1). Golfo Paradiso **ferries,** V. Scalo, 3 (☎0185 77 20 91; www.golfoparadiso.it), near P. Colombo, go to Portofino (L14,000/€7.25, return L20,000/€10.35) and Cinque Terre (L20,000/€10.35, return L33,000/€17.05). Buy tickets on the dock. Head right from the station to find the **tourist office,** V. XX Settembre, 33, which can help find rooms. (☎0185 77 10 66. Open M-Sa 9am-12:30pm and 3:30-7pm, Su 9am-1pm.) Exit the train station, walk down the stairway to the right, and look for the large blue sign for the 🔲**Albergo La Camogliese,** V. Garibaldi, 55. (☎0185 77 14 02; fax 77 40 24. Reserve ahead. Singles L70,000-110,000/€36.15-56.85; doubles L120,000-140,000/€62-72.30. 10% *Let's Go* discount with cash. AmEx/D/MC/V.)

SANTA MARGHERITA LIGURE. Santa Margherita Ligure led a calm existence as a fishing village until the early 20th century, when it fell into favor with Hollywood stars. Today, grace and glitz paint the shore, but the serenity of the town's early days still lingers. If ocean waves don't invigorate your spirit, try the holy water in seashell basins at the **Basilica di Santa Margherita,** at P. Caprera. **Trains** along the Pisa-Genoa line go from P. Federico Raoul Nobili, at the top of V. Roma, to Genoa (40min., 2-3 per hr., L3600/€1.90) and La Spezia (2 per hr., L6900/€3.60) via Cinque Terre (1½hr., L6000/€3.10). Tigullio **buses** (☎0185 28 88 34) go from P.V. Veneto to Camogli (30min., every hr., L2000/€1.05) and Portofino (20min., 3 per hr., L1700/€0.90). Tigullio **ferries,** V. Palestro, 8/1b (☎0185 28 15 98 or 28 46 70), have tours to Cinque Terre (July-Sept. W and Sa-Su 1 per day; L25,000-30,000/€12.95-15.50, return L35,000-40,000/€18.10-20.65) and Portofino (every hr.; L6000/€3.10, return L10,000/€5.20). Turn right from the train station on V. Roma, left on Corso Rainusso, turn left and take a hard right onto V. XXV Aprile from Largo Giusti to find the **tourist office,** V. XXV Aprile, 2b, which arranges lodging. (☎0185 28 74 85; fax 28 30 34. Open M-Sa 9am-12:30pm and 3-6pm, Su 9:30am-12:30pm.) 🔲**Hotel Nuova Riviera,** V. Belvedere, 10, has spacious rooms. (☎/fax 0185 28 74 03. Breakfast included. Singles L100,000/€51.65; doubles L170,000/€87.80; triples L220,000/€113.65. MC/V.) 🔲**La Piadineria and Creperia,** V. Giuncheto, 5, off P. Martiri della Libertà, serves large portions. (Sandwiches L9000-10,000/€4.60-5.20. Open daily 6pm-midnight.)

PORTOFINO. As long as you don't buy anything, princes and paupers alike can enjoy the curved shores and tiny bay of Portofino. A one-hour walk along the ocean road offers the chance to scout out small rocky **beaches. Njasca** offers boat rental in the summer months (L10,000-25,000/€5.20-12.95 per hr.); **Paraggi** (where the bus stops) is the area's only sandy beach, but only a small strip is free. In town, follow the signs uphill from the bay to escape to the cool interior of the **Chiesa di San Giorgio.** A few minutes up the road toward the **castle** is a serene garden with sea views. (Open daily in summer 10am-6pm; in winter 10am-5pm. L3000/€1.55.) To get to town, take the bus to Portofino Mare (*not* Portofino Vetta). From P. Martiri della Libertà, Tigullio **buses** go to Santa Margherita (3 per hr., L1700/€0.90); buy tickets at the green kiosk. **Ferries** also go to Camogli (2 per day, L13,000/€6.75) and Santa Margherita (every hr. 9am-7pm, L6000/€3.10). The **tourist office,** V. Roma, 35, is on the way to the waterfront from the bus stop. (☎0185 26 90 24. Open daily 9:30am-1:30pm and 2-7pm; in winter 9:30am-12:30pm and 2:30-5:30pm.)

CINQUE TERRE. The five bright fishing villages of Cinque Terre cling to a stretch of terraced hillsides and steep crumbling cliffs, with the dazzling turquoise sea lapping against their shores. You can hike through all five—Monterosso, Vernazza, Corniglia, Manarola, and Riomaggiore—in a few hours. **Monterosso** is the most developed, with sandy beaches and exciting nightlife; **Vernazza** has a seaside *piazza* with colorful buildings and a busy harbor; **Corniglia** hovers high above the sea in peaceful solitude; **Manarola** has quiet streets and a spectacular swimming cove; and **Riomaggiore** has a tiny harbor and lots of rooms for rent. The best views are from the narrow goat paths that link the towns, winding through vineyards, streams, and dense foliage. The best hike lies between Monterosso and Vernazza (1½hr.); the trail between Vernazza and Corniglia (2hr.) also winds through spectacular scenery. The largest **free beach** lies directly below the train station; get there early to reserve a space. Alternatively, follow V. Fegina through the tunnel to get to another free beach near the old town. **Guvano Beach,** a pebbly strip frequented by nudists, is through the tunnel at the base of the steps leading up to Corniglia (L5000/€2.60). Tiny trails off the road to Vernazza lead to popular hidden coves.

The Genoa-La Spezia rail line connects the five towns; Monterosso is the most accessible. From V. Fegina, at the north end of town, **trains** run to: Florence (3½hr., every hr., L14,500/€7.50) via Pisa (2½hr., every hr., L8500/€4.40); Genoa (1½hr., every hr., L7000/€3.65); La Spezia (20min., every 30min., L2300/€1.20); and Rome (7hr., every 2hr., L51,500/€26.60). Trains also connect the five towns (5-20min., every 50min., L1700-2300/€0.90-1.20). Reserve rooms several weeks in advance. Private rooms *(affittacamere)* are the most plentiful and economical options. To find Manarola's hostel, the ▓Albergo Della Gioventù-Ostello "Cinque Terre," V.B. Riccobaldi, 21, turn right from the train station and go uphill 300m to discover more fabulous amenities than can be believed. (☎0187 92 02 15; fax 92 02 18; www.cinqueterre.net. Breakfast L5000/€2.60. Reception daily 7-10am and 5pm-1am. Reserve 1 month ahead. Dorms L30,000/€15.50; quads L120,000/€62. AmEx/MC/V.) In Vernazza, ask in Trattoria Capitano about Albergo Barbara, P. Marconi, 30, top floor, at the port. (☎/fax 0187 81 23 98. 2-night min. stay for a reservation. Doubles L80,000-100,000/€41.35-51.65, triples L120,000/€62; quads L140,000/€72.30.) In Monterosso, try the **tourist office** (☎0187 81 75 06) or Hotel Souvenir, V. Gioberti, 24, the best deal in town. (☎0187 81 75 95. Breakfast L10,000/€5.20. L70,000/€36.15, students L60,000/€31.) For private rooms in Riomaggiore, call Robert Fazioli, V. Colombo, 94. (☎0187 92 09 04. Doubles with bath L80,000/€41.35.) Get supplies for a romantic picnic at Cantina di Sciacchetrà, V. Roma, 7, in Monterosso. (Open Mar.-Oct. daily 9am-11pm; Dec-Feb. open only on weekends; closed Nov.)

LA SPEZIA. A departure point for Corsica and an unavoidable transport hub for Cinque Terre, La Spezia is among Italy's most beautiful ports, with regal palms lining the promenade and citrus trees growing throughout the parks. La Spezia lies on the Genoa-Pisa **train** line. Happy Lines, with a ticket kiosk on V. Italia, sends **ferries** to Corsica (return L124,000/€64.05; low-season L84,000/€43.38). Navigazione Golfo dei Poeti, V. Mazzini, 21, run ferries to: each village in Cinque Terre and Portovenereo (Easter to Nov. 4; L20,000/€10.35, return L33,000/€17.05); Capraia (5hr., return L70,000-80,000/€36.15-41.35); and Elba (3½hr., return L80,000/€41.35.) The **tourist office,** V. Mazzini, 45, is at the port. (☎0187 77 09 00. Open daily 9am-1pm and 3-6pm.) To reach Albergo Terminus, V. Paleocapa, 21, turn left out of the train station. (☎0187 70 34 36; fax 70 00 79. Singles L40,000/€20.65, with bath L55,000/€28.45; doubles L65,000/€33.60, L90,000/€46.50; triples L70,000/€36.15.)

EMILIA-ROMAGNA

Go to Florence, Venice, and Rome to sightsee, but come to Emilia-Romagna to eat. Italy's wealthiest wheat- and dairy-producing region covers the fertile plains of the Po River Valley, fostering the finest culinary traditions on the Italian Peninsula. A stronghold of the left since the 19th-century rise of the Italian Socialist movement, Emilia-Romagna has a distinctly unique look and feel from the rest of Italy.

BOLOGNA
☎051

Bright façades adorn 700-year-old porticoes and cobblestone roads twist by churches, but Bologna's appeal extends far beyond aesthetics. Blessed with prosperity and Europe's oldest university, which counts Dante, Petrarch, and Copernicus among its graduates, Bologna has an open-minded atmosphere with strong political activism. The city also boasts a great culinary heritage, earning the nickname *La Grassa*, or The Fat One.

▐▊ **TRANSPORTATION AND PRACTICAL INFORMATION.** Bologna is a rail hub for all major Italian cities and the Adriatic coast. **Trains** go to: Florence (1½hr., every 2hr., L8200-13,500/€4.25-7); Milan (3hr., 2-3 per hr., L18,000/€9.30); Rome (4hr., 1-2 per hr., L35,000/€18.10); and Venice (2hr., every hr., L14,000/€7.25). Arrive during the day, as the area near the station is not the safest. **Buses** #25 and 30 run between the station and the historic center at Piazza Maggiore (L1800/€0.95). The **tourist office,** P. Maggiore, 6, is next to the Palazzo Comunale. (☎051 23 96 60; fax 23 14 54; www.comune.bologna.it. Open M-Sa 9am-1pm and 2:30-7pm.) Check **email** at Crazy Bull Café, V. Montegrappa, 11/e, off V. dell'Indipendenza near P. Maggiore. (L9000/€4.65 per hr. Open Tu-Sa 10am-2am, Su 7:30pm-2am. Closed Aug.)

LINGUINE LINGO For Italians, the desecration of pasta is a mortal sin. Pasta must be chosen correctly and cooked *al dente* (firm, literally "to the tooth"). The *spaghetti* family includes all variations that require twirling, from hollow cousins *bucatini* and *maccheroni* to the more delicate *capellini*. Flat *spaghetti* include *fettuccini*, *taglierini*, and *tagliatelle*. Short pasta tubes can be *penne*, cut diagonally and occasionally *rigate*, or ribbed, *sedani* (curved), *rigatoni* (wider), or *cannelloni* (usually stuffed). *Fusilli* (corkscrews), *farfalle* (butterflies or bow-ties), and *ruote* (wheels) are fun and functional. Don't be alarmed if you see pastry displays labeled "pasta"; the Italian word refers to anything made of dough.

⌂⊞ ACCOMMODATIONS AND FOOD. To get to **Ostello due Torre San Sisto (HI)**, V. Viadagola, 5, off V.S. Donato in the Località di San Sisto, 6km from the city center, walk down V. dell'Indipendenza from the station, turn right on V. della Mille, catch bus #93 (every 30min.) on the left side of the road, ask the driver for San Sisto, cross the street, and it's on the right. On Sunday, take bus #301 from the station. (☎/fax 051 50 18 10. Breakfast included. Reception 7am-midnight. Lockout 10am-3:30pm. Curfew midnight. L21,000/€10.85; nonmembers L26,000/€13.45.) Walk down V. Rizzoli and turn right into the gallery just before the towers for **Garisenda**, Galleria Leone, 1, 3rd fl. (☎051 22 43 69; fax 22 10 07. Singles L80,000/€41.35; doubles L120,000/€62; triples L160,000/€82.65. AmEx/MC/V.) Bologna's namesake dish, *spaghetti alla bolognese*, has a hearty meat and tomato sauce. Scout **via Augusto Righi, via Piella,** and **via Saragozza** for traditional *trattorie*. ◪**Nuova Pizzeria Gianna**, V.S. Stefano, 76/a, serves pizza from L5000/€2.60. (Open M-Sa for lunch and dinner; closed Aug.) **Il Gelatauro**, V.S. Vitale, 82/b, scoops out cones from L3000/€1.55. (Open June-Aug. Tu-Sa 11am-11pm.) A **PAM supermarket**, V. Marconi, 26, is near V. Riva di Reno. (Open M-W and F-Sa 7:45am-7:45pm, Th 7:45am-1pm.)

◪▣ SIGHTS AND NIGHTLIFE. Forty kilometers of porticoed buildings line the streets of Bologna. Tranquil **Piazza Maggiore** flaunts both Bologna's historical and modern-day wealth. **Basilica di San Petronio**, the city's *duomo*, was built to impress, but its pomp and pageantry allegedly drove a disgusted Martin Luther to reform religion in Germany. (Open M-Sa 7:15am-1pm and 2-6pm, Su 7:30am-1pm and 2-6:30pm.) ◪**Palazzo Archiginnasio**, behind the church, was once a university building; the upstairs theater was built in 1637 to teach anatomy to students. (*Palazzo* open M-F 9am-7pm, Sa 9am-2pm. Theater open M-Sa 9am-1pm. Both closed 2 weeks in Aug. Free.) On the northern side of P. Maggiore is **Palazzo de Podestà**, remodeled by Fioravanti's son Aristotle, who later designed Moscow's Kremlin. Next to P. Maggiore, **Piazza del Nettuno** contains Giambologna's famous 16th-century fountain *Neptune and Attendants*. From P. Nettuno, go down V. Rizzoli to **Piazza Porta Ravegana**, where streets converge to form the medieval quarter. Two towers, the city's emblem, rise from the *piazza;* you can climb the **Torre degli Asinelli**. (Open daily May-Aug. 9am-6pm; Sept.-Apr. 9am-5pm. L5000/€2.60.) Follow V.S. Stefano from V. Rizzoli to P. Santo Stefano, where four of the original seven churches of the Romanesque **Piazza Santo Stefano Church Complex** remain. The **Pinacoteca Nazionale**, V. delle Belle Arti, 56, off V. Zamboni, traces the progress of Bolognese artists. (Open Tu-Sa 9am-1:50pm, Su 9am-12:50pm. L8000/€4.15.) **Cluricaune**, V. Zamboni, 18/b, is an Irish bar packed with students who flock to its pool table and dart boards. (Pints L8000/€4.15. Happy Hour 5-8:30pm, drinks L3000/€1.55. Open M-Th 4pm-2am, F-Sa 4pm-2:30am, Su 11:30pm-2am.)

PARMA
☎0521

Parma's loyalties lie with its excellent food: silky-smooth *prosciutto crudo*, sharp *parmigiano* cheese, and sweet, sparkling white Malvasia wine. Parma's artistic excellence goes beyond the kitchen—Giuseppe Verdi composed some of his greatest works here. From P. Garibaldi, follow Strada Cavour toward the train station and take the third right onto Strada al Duomo to reach the 11th-century

Romanesque ▪**duomo,** one of the country's most vibrant cathedrals. Most spectacular is the **dome,** where Correggio's *Virgin* ascends to a golden heaven in a spiral of white robes, pink *putti,* and blue sky. The pink-and-white marble **baptistery** was built between the Romanesque and Gothic periods. (*Duomo* open daily 9am-12:30pm and 3-7pm. Baptistery open daily 9am-12:30pm and 3-7pm. L5000/€2.60, students L3000/€1.55.) Behind the *duomo* is the frescoed dome of the **Chiesa di San Giovanni Evangelista,** designed by Correggio. (Open daily 9am-noon and 3-7pm.) From P. del Duomo, follow Strada al Duomo across Strada Cavour, continue one block down Strada Piscane, and cross P. della Pace to reach the monolithic **Palazzo della Pilotta,** Parma's artistic treasure chest built in 1602, which today houses the excellent **Galleria Nazionale.** (Open daily 9am-2pm. L8000/€4.15.)

Parma is on the Bologna-Milan rail line. **Trains** go from P. Carlo Alberto della Chiesa to: Bologna (1hr., 2 per hr., L7700/€4); Florence (3hr., 7 per day, L26,300/€13.60); Milan (1½hr., every hr., L11,600/€6). Walk left from the station, turn right on V. Garibaldi, and go left on V. Melloni to reach the **tourist office,** V. Melloni, 1b. (☎/fax 0521 23 47 35. Open M-Sa 9am-7pm, Su 9am-1pm.) From the station, take bus #9 (L1300/€0.70) and get off when the bus turns left on V. Martiri della Libertà to get to the modern **Ostello Cittadella (HI),** on V. Passo Buole, in a corner of a 15th-century fortress. (☎0521 96 14 34. 3-night max. stay. Lockout 9:30am-5pm. Curfew 11pm. Open Apr.-Oct. HI members only. Dorms L16,000/€8.30. **Camping** open Apr.-Oct. L11,150/€5.75 per person, L21,000/€10.85 per site.) **Locanda Lazzaro,** Borgo XX Marzo, 14, is off V. della Repubblica, upstairs from the restaurant of the same name. (☎0521 20 89 44. Reserve ahead. Singles L65,000/€33.60, with bath 75,000/€38.75; doubles L100,000/€51.65.) **Supermarket 2B** is at V. XXII Luglio, 27c. (Open M-W and F-Sa 8:30am-1pm and 4:30-8pm, Th 8:30am-1pm.) **Postal code:** 43100.

RAVENNA
☎0544

Enter a world of wildly colored mosaics in Ravenna, the one-time seat of the Byzantine Empire. Take V. Argentario from V. Cavour to reach the 6th-century ▪**Basilica di San Vitale,** V.S. Vitale, 17. An open courtyard leads to the glowing mosaics inside; those of the Emperor and Empress adorn the lower left and right panels of the apse. Behind San Vitale, the city's oldest and most interesting mosaics cover the glittering interior of the **Mausoleo di Galla Placidia.** (Both open daily Apr.-Sept. 9am-7pm; Oct.-Mar. 9:30am-4:30pm. Joint ticket L6000/€3.10.) Take buses #4 or 44 from opposite the train station (L1300/€0.70) to Classe, south of the city, to see the astounding mosaics at the ▪**Chiesa di Sant'Apollinare in Classe.** (Open M-Sa 8:30am-7:30pm, Su 9am-1pm. L4000/€2.10, Su free.) Much to Florence's dismay, Ravenna also houses the **Tomb of Dante Alighieri,** its most popular sight. In the adjoining **Dante Museum,** his heaven and hell come alive in etchings, paintings, and sculptures. From P. del Popolo, cut through P. Garibaldi to V. Alighieri. (Tomb open daily 9am-7pm; free. Museum open Tu-Su Apr.-Sept. 9am-noon and 3:30-6pm; Oct.-Mar. 9am-noon; L3000/€1.55.) A **comprehensive ticket** (L10,000/€5.20, students L8000/€4.15) is valid at several sights, including the Basilica S. Vitale, Chiesa S. Appollinare, and the Mausoleo. Create your own mosaics at **Colori-Belle Arti,** P. Mameli, 16, off Viale Farini. (Open M-W and F 9am-12:30pm and 4-7:30pm.)

Trains (☎0544 21 78 84) leave P. Farini, at the east end of town, for Bologna (1hr., every 1-2hr., L7400/€3.85) with connections to Ferrara, Florence, and Venice (1hr., every 2hr., L6700/€3.50). Follow Viale Farini from the station to V. Diaz, which runs to the central P. del Popolo and the **tourist office,** V. Salara, 8. (☎0544 354 04; fax 48 26 70. Open M-Sa 8:30am-7pm, Su 10am-4pm; in winter M-Sa 8:30am-6pm, Su 10am-4pm.) Take buses #1 or 70 from V. Pallavicini at the station (every 15min.-1hr., L1300/€0.70) for **Ostello Dante (HI),** V. Nicolodi, 12. (☎/fax 0544 42 11 64. Breakfast included. Reception 7-10am and 5-11:30pm. 4- to 6-bed dorms L24,000/€12.40.) Walk down V. Farini, and go right at P. Mameli for **Albergo Al Giaciglio,** V. Rocca Brancaleone, 42. (☎0544 394 03. Breakfast L7000/€3.65. Closed 2 weeks in Dec. or Jan. Singles L50,000-60,000/€25.85-31; doubles L70,000-90,000/€36.15-46.50; triples L100,000-110,000/€51.65-56.85. MC/V.)

FERRARA ☎0532

Rome has its mopeds, Venice its boats, and Ferrara its bicycles. Young and old whirl through Ferrara's jumble of twisting medieval roads. Bike the tranquil wooded concourse along the city's well-preserved, 9km **medieval wall,** which begins at the far end of Corso Giovecca. Towered, turreted, and moated, **Castello Estense** stands precisely at the center of town. Corso della Giovecca lies along the former route of the moat's feeder canal, separating the medieval section from the part planned by the architect, Biagio Rosetti. Climb the **Torre Leoni** for an unobstructed view of the city. (Open Tu-Su 9:30am-5:30pm. L8000/€4.15, students L6000/€3.10.) From the *castello*, take Calle Martiri della Libertà to P. Cattedrale and the **duomo,** which contains the **Museo della Cattedrale.** (Cathedral open M-Sa 7:30am-noon and 3-6:30pm, Su 7:30am-12:30pm and 4-7:30pm. Museum open Tu-Sa 10am-noon and 3-5pm, Su and holidays 10am-noon and 4-6pm.) From the *castello*, cross Largo Castello to Corso Ercole I d'Este and walk to the corner of Corso Rossetti to reach the aptly named **Palazzo Diamanti,** built in 1493, which outshines all other ducal residences. Inside, the **Pinacoteca Nazionale** contains many of the best Ferrarese works. (Open Tu-W and F-Sa 9am-2pm, Th 9am-7pm, Su and holidays 9am-1pm. L8000/€4.15, EU students L4000/€2.10.) Follow Corso Ercole I d'Este behind the *castello* and turn right on Corso Porta Mare to find the **Palazzo Massari,** Corso Porta Mare, 9, which now houses both the **Museo d'Arte Moderna e Contemporanea "Filippo de Pisis"** and, upstairs, the spectacular **Museo Ferrarese dell'Ottocentro/Museo Giovanni Boldini.** (Both open daily 9am-1pm and 3-6pm. Joint ticket L10,000/€5.20.)

Ferrara **trains,** which run along the Bologna-Venice line, go to: Bologna (30min., 1-2 per hr., L4900/€2.55); Padua (1hr., every hr., L7600/€3.95); Rome (3-4hr., 7 per day, L57,200/€29.55); and Venice (2hr., 1-2 per hr., L10,800/€5.60). ACFT (☎05 32 59 94 92) and GGFP **buses** go from V. Rampari S. Paolo or the train station to Ferrara's beaches (1hr., 12 per day, L7600-8400/€3.95-4.35) and Bologna (1½hr., 3-15 per day, L6000/€3.10). Turn left out of the train station and then right on **Vle. Costituzione,** which becomes **Viale Cavour** and runs to the central Castello Estense (1km). The **tourist office** is in Castello Estense. (☎0532 20 93 70; www.comune.fe.it. Open daily 9am-1pm and 2-6pm.) To reach the convenient **Ostella della Gioventù Estense (HI),** Corso B. Rossetti, 24, go down Corso Ercole d'Este from the *castello*, or take bus #4c from the station and ask for the *castello* stop. (☎/fax 0532 20 42 27. Reception 7-10am and 5-11:30pm. Lockout 10am-3:30pm. Curfew 11:40pm. L23,000/€11.90.) From the *duomo*, head down Corso Porta Reno, left on V. Ragno, and left on V. Vittoria to get to **Casa degli Artisti,** V. Vittoria, 66, in the historic town center near P. Lampronti. (☎0532 76 10 38. Singles L36,000/€18.60; doubles L64,000-90,000/€33.05-46.50.) Get **groceries** at the **Mercato Comunale,** on V. Mercato, off V. Garibaldi next to the *duomo*. (Open M-W 7am-1:30pm and 4:30-7:30pm, Th and Sa 7am-1:30pm, F 4:30-7:30pm.) In July and August, a free **Discobus** (☎0532 59 94 11) runs every Saturday night between Ferrara and the hottest clubs; pick up flyers in the train station. **Postal code:** 44100.

TUSCANY (TOSCANA)

Tuscany is the stuff of Italian dreams (and more than one Brits-in-Italy movie). With rolling hills blanketed in olive groves and grapevines, bright yellow fields of sunflowers, and inviting cobblestone streets, it's hard not to wax poetic. Tuscany's Renaissance culture became Italy's heritage, while its regional dialect, the language of Dante, Petrarch, and Machiavelli, has developed into modern textbook Italian.

FLORENCE (FIRENZE) ☎055

The rays of the setting sun shimmer over a sea of burnt-orange roofs and towering domes to reveal the breathtaking concentration of beauty in Florence. Once a busy 13th-century wool- and silk-trading town, Florence took a decidedly different path under Medici rule. By the mid-15th century, the city was the undisputed European capital of art, architecture, commerce, and political thought. Present-day Florence is a vibrant mix of the young and old: street graffiti quotes Marx and Malcolm X, businessmen whiz by on Vespas, and children play soccer against the *duomo*.

▛ TRANSPORTATION

Flights: Amerigo Vespucci Airport (☎055 306 17 00), in Peretola. Mostly domestic and charter flights. Orange ATAF **bus** #62 runs to the train station (L1500/€0.80). **Galileo Galilei Airport** (☎055 50 07 07), in Pisa, has an info booth at platform #5 in the Florence train station. The **airport express** connects the Florence train station to Pisa (1hr., L9100/€4.70).

Trains: Santa Maria Novella Station (☎055 147 880 88), across from S. Maria Novella. Office open daily 7am-9pm. After hours go to ticket window #20. Trains depart hourly to: **Bologna** (1hr., L14,200/€7.35); **Milan** (3½hr., L39,700/€20.50); **Rome** (2½hr., L35,000-40,000/€18.10-20.65); **Venice** (3hr., L35,100/€18.20).

Buses: LAZZI, P. Adua, 1-4r (☎055 21 51 55). To **Pisa** (L11,200/€5.80). **SITA,** V.S. Caterina da Siena, 15r (☎055 28 46 61). To **Siena** (1¼-2hr., L11,000/€5.70).

Public Transportation: ATAF (☎055 565 02 22), outside the train station, runs orange city buses 6am-1am. **1hr. tickets** L1500/€0.80, packet of 4 L5800/€3; **3hr.** L2500/€1.30; **24hr.** L6000/€3.10; **3-day** L11,000/€5.70. Buy tickets at any newsstand, *tabacchi*, or automated ticket dispenser before boarding. Validate your ticket using the orange machine on board or risk a L75,000/€38.75 fine. 1hr. tickets are sold on the bus from 9pm-6am for L3000/€1.55.

Taxis: (☎055 43 90, 055 47 98, or 055 42 42). Outside the train station.

Bike/Moped Rental: Alinari Noleggi, V. Guelfa, 85r (☎055 28 05 00). Bikes L20,000-40,000/€10.35-20.65 per day, mopeds L35,000-45,000/€18.10-23.25 per day.

Hitchhiking: *Let's Go* does not recommend hitchhiking. Hitchers take the A-1 north to Bologna and Milan or the A-11 northwest to the Riviera and Genoa. Buses #29, 30, or 35 run from the station to the feeder near Peretola. For the A-1 south to Rome and to Siena, they take buses #31 or 32 from the station to Exit 23: Firenze Sud.

▛▟ ORIENTATION AND PRACTICAL INFORMATION

From the train station, a short walk down V. de' Panzani and a left on V. de' Cerretani leads to the **duomo**, the city center. Major arteries connect the instantly recognizable dome with the two major *piazze*. **Via dei Calzaiuoli** runs south from the *duomo* to **Piazza della Signoria,** home of Palazzo Vecchio and the Uffizi Gallery. V. Roma leads to the vast **Piazza della Repubblica,** which has major streets running north to the *duomo* and south to the **Ponte Vecchio.** The Ponte Vecchio is one of five bridges that cross from Florence to the **Oltrarno** district, south of the Arno river. When navigating Florence, note that most streets change names unpredictably, often every few blocks. Grab a **free map** at the tourist office (see below).

Florence's streets are numbered in red and black sequences. Red numbers indicate commercial establishments and black (or blue) numbers denote residential addresses (including most sights and hotels). Black addresses appear in *Let's Go* as a numeral only, while red addresses are indicated with a subsequent "r." If you reach an address and it's not what you're looking for, you probably have the wrong color—just step back and look for the other sequence.

TOURIST, FINANCIAL, AND LOCAL SERVICES

Tourist Office: Informazione Turistica, P. della Stazione, 4 (☎055 21 22 45), across the *piazza* from the main exit. Info on entertainment and cultural events. Be sure to ask for a **free map** with a street index. Open daily 8:30am-7:30pm.

Tours: ▨ **Enjoy Florence** (☎167 27 48 19; www.enjoyflorence.com). Gives fast-paced, informative walking tours of the old city center. Tours meet daily in summer at 10am in front of the Thomas Cook office at the Ponte Vecchio; reduced hours in winter. L30,000/€15.50, under 26 L25,000/€12.95.

Consulates: UK, Lungarno Corsini, 2 (☎055 28 41 33). Open M-F 9:30am-12:30pm and 2:30-4:30pm. **US,** Lungarno Vespucci, 38 (☎055 239 82 76), at V. Palestro, near the station. Open M-F 9am-12:30pm and 2-3:30pm. **Canadians, Australians,** and **New Zealanders** should contact consulates in Rome or Milan.

Currency Exchange: Local banks offer the best rates. Most are open M-F 8:20am-1:20pm and 2:45-3:45pm, some also Sa morning. 24hr. **ATMs** abound.

American Express: V. Dante Alighieri, 20-22r (☎055 509 81). From the *duomo,* walk down V. dei Calzaiuoli and turn left on V. dei Tavolini. Mail held free for AmEx members and check customers, otherwise L3000/€1.55 per inquiry. Open M-F 9am-5:30pm, Sa 9am-12:30pm.

Library: Biblioteca Marucelliana, V. Cavour, 43 (☎055 272 21 or 260 62). 2min. from the *duomo.* Open M-F 8:30am-7pm, Sa 8:30am-1:45pm.

Laundromat: Launderette, V. Guelfa, 55r. Wash and dry L12,000/€6.20. Open daily 8am-10pm.

EMERGENCY AND COMMUNICATIONS

Emergency: ☎113. **Fire:** ☎115. **Police:** V. Zara, 2 (☎055 497 71).

24-Hour Pharmacies: Farmacia Comunale (☎055 28 94 35), in the train station by track 16. **Molteni,** V. dei Calzaiuoli, 7r (☎055 28 94 90).

Medical Emergency: ☎118.

Internet Access: Walk down almost any busy street and you'll find an Internet cafe. Try **Netgate,** V.S. Egidio, 10/20r (☎055 234 79 67). In summer, they set up an evening tent station on the 2nd terrace at P.G. Poggi. L10,000/€5.20 per hr. Open M-Sa 10:30am-10pm; in winter daily 10:40am-8:30pm.

Post Office: V. Pellicceria (☎055 21 61 22), off P. della Repubblica. Send packages from V. dei Sassetti, 4. Address mail to be held: First Name SURNAME, *In Fermo Posta,* L'Ufficio Postale, V. Pellicceria, Firenze, **50100** ITALY. Open M-F 8:15am-7pm, Sa 8:15am-12:30pm. 24hr. telegram office.

Postal Code: 50100.

ACCOMMODATIONS AND CAMPING

Florence abounds with one-star *pensioni* and private *affitta camere.* If you arrive late in the day, consult **Consorzio ITA,** in the train station by track 16. Suggest a price range, and they will find a room for a L4500-15,000/€2.35-7.75 commission. (☎055 28 28 93. Open daily 8:45am-8pm.) Make reservations (*prenotazioni*) at least 10 days in advance during Easter or summer. Immediately cancel any reservations you decide not to keep; hotel owners are disgruntled with no-shows, and many no longer accept reservations for this reason. Expect prices higher than those listed here; rates uniformly increase by 10% or so every year.

The budget accommodations around the **Piazza Santa Maria Novella,** near the train station, are conveniently located near the *duomo.* Although tourists flood the central **Old City,** budget accommodations often provide great views of Florence's monuments or are in Renaissance *palazzi.* From P. della Stazione, **Via Nazionale** leads to budget hotels that are near the *duomo* and the train station. The area near **Piazza Santa Marco** is considerably calm and tourist-free given its proximity to the city center; exit left from the train tracks, turn left on V. Nazionale, and then turn right on V. Guelfa, which intersects V.S. Gallo and V. Cavour. **Oltrarno,** a 10min. walk across the Arno River from the *duomo,* offers a break from Florence's hustle and bustle.

HOSTELS

▧ **Ostello Archi Rossi,** V. Faenza, 94r (☎055 29 08 04). Exit left from the station on V. Nazionale and take the 2nd left on V. Faenza. A patio brimming with young travelers. Wheelchair accessible. Breakfast L3000-4500/€1.55-2.35. Laundry L10,000/€5.20. Lockout 9:30am, from hostel 11am. Curfew 12:30am. No reservations; in summer, arrive before 8am. 4- to 9-bed dorms L35,000-40,000/€18.10-20.65; rooms for handicapped L50,000/€25.85.

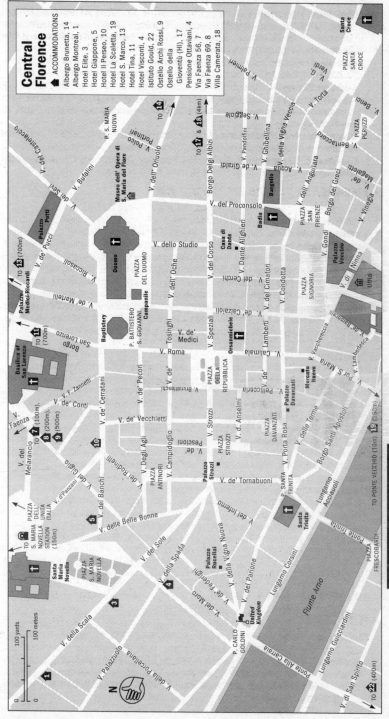

Central Florence

▲ ACCOMMODATIONS

Albergo Brunetta, 14
Albergo Montreal, 1
Hotel Elite, 3
Hotel Giappone, 5
Hotel Il Perseo, 10
Hotel La Scaletta, 19
Hotel S. Marco, 13
Hotel Tina, 11
Hotel Visconti, 4
Istituto Gould, 22
Ostello Archi Rossi, 9
Ostello della
   Gioventù (HI), 17
Pensione Ottaviani, 4
Via Faenza 56, 7
Via Faenza 69, 8
Villa Camerata, 18

ITALY

▓ **Istituto Gould,** V. dei Serragli, 49 (☎055 21 25 76), in the **Oltrarno.** Exit the station by track 16, head right to P. della Stazione, walk to the left of the church, and continue through the P.S. Maria Novella and down V. dei Fossi, which becomes V. dei Serragli after the bridge (15min.). Spotless rooms. Reception M-F 9am-1pm and 3-7pm, Sa 9am-1pm. No check-in or check-out Sa afternoons or Su. Singles L48,000-55,000/€24.80-28.40; doubles L72,000-78,000/€37.20-40.30; triples L78,000-105,000/€40.30-54.25, quads L132,000/€68.20; quints L142,000/€73.35.

Ostello della Gioventù Europa Villa Camerata (HI), V. Augusto Righi, 2-4 (☎055 60 14 51). Take bus #17 from outside the train station, near track #5, or from P. dell'Unità, across from the train station, and get off at Salviatino. In a distant gorgeous villa with *loggia* and gardens. Breakfast and sheets included. Laundry L10,000/€5.20. Reception daily 7am-12:30pm and 1pm-midnight. Curfew midnight. Reserve in writing. Dorms L28,000/€14.50; non-HI members L5000/€2.60 extra per night. If full, sleep on a cot (L20,000/€10.35) in an outdoor tent with wood floors and electricity.

HOTELS

OLD CITY (NEAR THE DUOMO)

▓ **Albergo Brunetta,** Borgo Pinti, 5 (☎055 247 81 34). Exit P. del Duomo on V. dell' Oriuolo behind the *duomo.* After 2 long blocks, turn left on Borgo Pinti. Central location and rooftop terrace with superb view. Excellent value in the center of the city. Singles L80,000/€41.35; doubles L130,000/€67.15; triples L170,000/€87.80. Cash only.

Hotel Il Perseo, V. de Cerretani, 1 (☎055 21 25 04), en route to the *duomo* from the station, opposite the Feltrinelli bookstore. Enthusiastic owners and immaculate rooms with fans. Bar and TV lounge. Breakfast included. Singles L90,000/€46.50; doubles L135,000-160,000/€69.75-82.65; triples L180,000-215,000/€93-111.05. MC/V.

AROUND PIAZZA SANTA MARIA NOVELLA

▓ **Hotel Visconti,** P. Ottaviani, 1 (☎/fax 055 21 38 77). Exit the train station from the left and cross behind S. Maria church into P.S. Maria Novella, and walk to the left until you reach tiny P. Ottaviani. Look for huge Grecian nudes. Breakfast included. Singles L68,000/€35.15, with bath L100,000/€51.65; doubles L104,000/€53.75, L145,000/€74.90; triples L150,000/€77.50, L180,000/€93; quads 168,000/€86.80, L220,000/€113.65.

Hotel Elite, V. della Scala, 12 (☎055 21 53 95). Exit to the right from the train station onto V. degli orti Oricellari, and turn left on V. della Scala. Brass glows in this 2-star hotel's lovely rooms. Breakfast L10,000/€5.20. Singles L100,000-130,000/€51.65-67.15; doubles L130,000-160,000/€67.15-82.65; triples L200,000/€103.30.

Albergo Montreal, V. della Scala, 43 (☎0552 38 23 31), near Hotel Elite (see above). Clean, modern rooms. Curfew 1:30am. Singles L90,000/€46.50; doubles L95,000-110,000/€49.10-56.85; triples L150,000/€77.50; quads L185,000/€95.55.

Albergo Bellavista, Largo F. Alinari, 15, 5th fl. (☎055 28 45 28; fax 28 48 74), just steps from the train station, in an old *palazzo.* Exit from the train station and cross the *piazza* diagonally to the left. Simple, comfortable rooms. Singles L90,000/€46.50, with bath L100,000/€51.65; doubles L170,000/€87.80.

Tourist House, V. della Scala, 1 (☎055 26 86 75). All rooms with bath. Singles L130,000/€67.15; doubles 160,000/€82.65; quads L240,000/€123.95. MC/V.

AROUND PIAZZA SAN MARCO

▓ **Hotel Tina,** V.S. Gallo, 31 (☎055 48 35 19). From P.S. Marco, follow V. XXII Aprile and turn right on V.S. Gallo. *Pensione* with high ceilings, new furniture, and amicable owners. Singles L85,000/€43.90; doubles L120,000-150,000/€62-77.50; triples L160,000/€82.65; quads L200,000/€103.30.

Hotel San Marco, V. Cavour, 50 (☎055 28 42 35), off P.S. Marco. Modern, airy rooms. Breakfast included. Curfew 1:30am; ask for a key. Singles (available Sept.-Mar. only) L80,000-150,000/€41.35-77.50; doubles L120,000-150,000/€62-77.50; triples L200,000/€103.30; quads L260,000/€134.30. MC/V.

ITALY

AROUND VIA NAZIONALE

Via Faenza, 56 houses six separate *pensioni,* among the best deals in the city. From the train station, exit left onto V. Nazionale, walk 1 block, and turn left on V. Faenza. The **prices** and amenities for the **Azzi, Anna,** and **Paola** are listed under the Azzi.

Pensione Azzi (☎055 21 38 06) has large rooms and a terrace. Breakfast included. Singles L80,000/€41.35, doubles L110,000-140,000/€56.85-72.30. AmEx/MC/V.

Albergo Anna (☎055 239 83 22) has lovely singles and doubles with frescoes and fans.

Locanda Paola (☎055 21 36 82) has spartan doubles, some with views of Fiesole and the surrounding hills. Curfew 2am.

Albergo Merlini (☎055 21 28 48; fax 055 28 39 39) has some rooms with views of the *duomo.* Curfew 1am. Singles L85,000/€43.90; doubles L125,000/€64.60. AmEx/MC/V.

Albergo Marini (☎055 28 48 24) boasts spotless rooms. Breakfast L8000/€4.15. Doubles L110,000-130,000/€56.85-67.15; triples L145,000-165,000/€74.90-85.25; quads L180,000-200,000/€93-103.30; quints 215,000-235,000/€111.05-121.40. Cash only.

Albergo Armonia (☎055 21 11 46) decorates its rooms with film posters. Singles L80,000/€41.35; doubles L120,000/€62; triples L145,000/€74.90; quads L170,000/€87.80.

Via Faenza, 69 houses several accommodations. **Locanda Giovanna,** 4th fl., has basic, well-kept rooms with garden views. (☎055 238 13 53. Singles L60,000/€31; doubles L100,000-110,000/€51.65-56.85.) **Hotel Soggiorno d'Errico** has 7 clean rooms. (☎055 21 55 31. Singles L50,000/€25.85; doubles L100,000/€51.65. AmEx/MC/V.) **Hotel Nella/Pina,** 1st and 2nd fl., has 14 basic rooms and Internet. (☎055 265 43 46. Singles L80,000/€41.35; doubles L110,000/€56.85. AmEx/MC/V.)

Ausonia and Kursaal, V. Nazionale, 24 (☎055 49 65 47). Exit train station to the left and turn left on V. Nazionale. Lots of amenities. Wheelchair-accessible. Breakfast included. No curfew. Doubles L155,000-220,000/€80.05-113.65; triples L205,000-270,000/€108.87-139.45; quads L260,000-320,000/€134.30-165.30. MC/V.

Hotel Aline, V. XXVII Aprile, 14 (☎055 48 58 77). Exit train station, turn left onto V. Nazionale. Proceed to P. Indipendenza, then turn right on V. XXVII Aprile (10min.). 6 quiet, basic doubles. Doubles L110,000/€56.85, with toilet L140,000/€72.30.

OLTRARNO

▧ **Hotel La Scaletta,** V. Guicciardini, 13b (☎055 28 30 28). Turn right onto V. Roma from the *duomo,* cross Ponte Vecchio and walk on V. Guicciardini. Has views of Boboli gardens. Breakfast included. Reception open until midnight. Singles L90,000-170,000/€46.50-87.80; doubles L190,000-240,000/€98.15-123.95; triples L200,000-280,000/€103.30-144.60; quads L220,000-300,000/€113.65-154.95. MC/V.

CAMPING

Campeggio Michelangelo, V. Michelangelo, 80 (☎055 681 19 77), beneath Piazzale Michelangelo. Take bus #13 from the bus station (15min.; last bus 11:25pm). Crowded, but has a great view of Florence. Open Apr.-Nov. L11,000/€5.70 per person, L9000/€4.65 per tent, L6000/€3.10 per car, L4000/€2.10 per motorcycle.

Villa Camerata, V. A. Righi 2-4 (☎055 60 03 15), same entrance as the HI hostel on the #17 bus route (p. 622). Breakfast L2500/€1.30. Reception daily 1pm-midnight. Check-out 7-10am. L10,000/€5.20 per person, L8000/€4.15 with camping card; L8000-16,000/€4.15-8.30 per tent, L20,000/€10.35 per car.

◪ FOOD

Florence's hearty cuisine originated from the peasant fare of the surrounding countryside. Specialties include *bruschetta* (grilled bread soaked with olive oil and garlic and topped with tomatoes and basil, anchovy, or liver paste) and *bistecca alla Fiorentina* (thick sirloin steak). Wine is a Florentine staple, and genuine *chianti classico* commands a premium price; a liter costs L7000-10,000/€3.65-5.20 in Florence's *trattorie,* while stores sell bottles for as little as L5000/€2.60. The local dessert is *cantuccini di prato* (almond cookies made with egg yolks) dipped in *vinsanto* (a rich dessert wine made from raisins). Florence's own

Buontalenti family supposedly invented *gelato* centuries ago; true or not, you must sample it. For lunch, visit a *rosticceria gastronomia*, peruse the city's pushcarts, or pick up fresh produce or meat at the **Mercato Centrale**, between V. Nazionale and S. Lorenzo. (Open June-Sept. M-Sa 7am-2pm; Oct.-May M-F 7am-2pm, Sa 7am-2pm and 4-8pm.) To get to **STANDA supermarket**, V. Pietrapiana, 1r, turn right on V. del Proconsolo, take the 1st left on Borgo degli Albizi, continue straight through P.G. Salvemini, and it's on the left. (Open M 2-9pm, Tu-Su 8:30am-9pm.)

OLD CITY (THE CENTER)

☒ **Acqua al Due**, V. Vigna Vecchia, 40r, behind the Bargello. Popular with young Italians. Serves Florentine specialties, including an excellent *assaggio* (L14,500/€7.50). *Primi* L11,500-13,000/€5.95-6.75, *secondi* from L18,000/€9.30. Cover L2000/€1.05. Reserve ahead. Open June-Sept. daily 7:30pm-1am; Oct.-May Tu-Su 8pm-1am.

☒ **Le Colonnine**, V. dei Benci, 6r, north of the Ponte alle Grazie. Delicious traditional fare. Pizza L8500/€4.40; pasta *secondi* from L13,000/€6.75. Famous *paella* could feed a small army (L30,000/€15.50). Open Tu-Su noon-2pm and 7pm-1am.

Trattoria da Benvenuto, V. della Mosca, 16r, on the corner of V. de' Neri. Wonderfully fresh *spaghetti alle vongole* (with clams) for L10,000/€5.20. Cover L3000/€1.55. 10% service charge. Open M-Sa 11am-3pm and 7pm-midnight.

PIAZZE SANTA MARIA NOVELLA AND DEL MERCATO CENTRALE

☒ **Trattoria da Giorgio**, V. Palazzuolo, 100r. Generous portions. *Menù* L16,000-17,000/€8.30-8.80. Expect a wait. Open M-Sa noon-3:30pm and 7-12:30am.

☒ **Trattoria Mario**, V. Rosina, 2r, around the corner from P. del Mercato Centrale. Incredible pasta and cheap meat dishes. *Primi* L5000-8000/€2.60-4.15; *secondi* 7000-17,000/€3.65-8.80. Open M-Sa noon-3:30pm.

Ristorante Il Vegetariano, V. delle Ruote, 30, off V.S. Gallo. No address number posted—look closely for the tiny menu next to the door. Fresh, inventive meat-free dishes. Smoke-free. *Primi* from L9000/€4.65; *secondi* from L11,000/€5.80. Open Tu-F 12:30-3pm and 7:30pm-midnight, Sa-Su 8pm-midnight.

OLTRARNO

☒ **Oltrarno Trattoria Casalinga**, V. Michelozzi, 9r, near P.S. Spirito. Delicious Tuscan specialties. *Primi* L6000-10,500/€3.10-5.45; *secondi* L8000-18,000/€4.15-9.30. Cover L3000/€1.55. Open M-Sa noon-2:30pm and 7-10pm.

Café Cabiria, P.S. Spirito, 5r. Try the *pasta al fiesolana* (meat and cheese; L9000/€4.65). *Primi* L7000/€3.65; *secondi* L12,000/€6.20. Open W-Su 8am-1:30am.

GELATERIE

☒ **Vivoli**, V. della Stinche, 7, behind the Bargello. A renowned Florentine *gelateria* with a huge selection of the self-proclaimed "best ice cream in the world." Cups from L3000/€1.55. Open daily 8am-1am.

☒ **Gelateria Triangolo delle Bermuda**, V. Nazionale, 61r. Blissful *crema venusiana* has hazelnut, caramel, and meringue. Cones L3000/€1.55. Open daily 10am-midnight.

🅖 SIGHTS

Florence's museums have recently doubled their prices (now L6000-12,000/€3.10-6.20 per venue) and no longer offer student discounts. In summer, watch for **Sere al Museo**, evenings when certain museums are free from 8:30-11pm. Also, many of Florence's churches are free treasuries of great art.

PIAZZA DEL DUOMO

DUOMO. The red brick of Florence's *duomo*, the **Cattedrale di Santa Maria del Fiore**, at the center of P. del Duomo, is visible from virtually every part of the city. Filippo Brunelleschi drew from long-neglected classical methods to come up with his revolutionary double-shelled construction that utilized self-supporting interlocking bricks.

Today the *duomo* claims the world's third longest nave. *(Open M-Sa 10am-5pm, Su 1:30-5pm; first Sa of every month 10am-3:30pm. Masses daily 7am-12:30pm and 5-7pm.)* Climb the 463 steps inside the dome to **Michelangelo's lantern,** or cupola, which offers an unparalleled view of the city. *(Open M-F 8:30am-7pm, Sa 8:30am-5:40pm. L10,000/ €5.20.)* The top of the 82m high ■**campanile** next to the *duomo* also has beautiful views. *(Open daily Apr.-Sept. 8:30am-7:30pm. L10,000/€5.20.)*

BATTISTERO. The *battistero* (baptistery) next to the *duomo*, built between the 5th and 9th centuries, was the site of Dante's christening; its Byzantine-style mosaics inspired the details of his *Inferno*. The famous **bronze doors** were a product of intense competition among Florentine artists; Ghiberti was commissioned to forge the last set of doors. The products, reportedly dubbed the ■**Gates of Paradise** by Michelangelo, exchanged his earlier 28-panel design for 10 large, gilded squares, each of which employs mathematical perspective to create the illusion of deep space. Under restoration since a 1966 flood, they will soon be housed in the Museo dell'Opera del Duomo. *(Open M-Sa 10am-5pm, Su 1:30-5pm; first Sa of every month 10am-3:30pm. Masses daily 7am-12:30pm and 5-7pm.)*

MUSEO DELL'OPERA DEL DUOMO. Most of the *duomo*'s art resides behind the cathedral in the Museo dell'Opera del Duomo. Up the first flight of stairs is a late *Pietà* by Michelangelo, who, according to legend, destroyed Christ's left arm with a hammer in a fit of frustration; soon after, a diligent pupil touched up the work, leaving visible scars on parts of Mary Magdalene's head. The museum also houses four frames from the baptistery's *Gates of Paradise*. *(P. del Duomo, 9. Open M-Sa 9am-6:30pm, Su 9am-2pm. Tours in English in summer W-Th 4pm. L10,000/€5.20.)*

PIAZZA DELLA SIGNORIA AND ENVIRONS

From P. del Duomo, the bustling **Via dei Calzaiuoli,** one of the city's oldest streets, runs south through crowds and chic shops to P. della Signoria.

PIAZZA DELLA SIGNORIA. The destruction of powerful Florentine families' homes in the 13th century created a empty space that cried out *"piazza!"*. With the construction of the Palazzo Vecchio in 1299, the square became Florence's civic and political center. In 1497, religious leader and social critic Savonarola convinced Florentines to light the **Bonfire of the Vanities,** a grand roast in the square that consumed some of Florence's best art. A year later, disillusioned citizens sent Savonarola up in smoke on the same spot, marked today by a granite disc. Monumental sculptures cluster in front of the *palazzo*, including a copy of Michelangelo's *David*. The awkward *Neptune* to the left of the Palazzo Vecchio so revolted Michelangelo that he insulted the artist: "Oh Ammannato, Ammannato, what lovely marble you have ruined!" The graceful 14th-century **Loggia dei Lanzi,** built as a stage for civic orators, contains world-class sculpture free of charge.

PALAZZO VECCHIO. Arnolfo del Cambio designed this fortress-like *palazzo* in the late-13th century as the governmental seat. It later became the Medici family home, and in 1470 Michelozzo decorated the ■**courtyard** in Renaissance style. Inside are works by Michelangelo, da Vinci, and Bronzino. *(Open June-Aug. M and F 9am-11pm, Tu-W and Sa 9am-7pm, Th and Su 9am-2pm; Sept.-May M-W and F-Sa 9am-7pm, Th 9am-2pm, Su 9am-2pm. L10,000/€5.20.)*

■**THE UFFIZI.** Vasari designed this palace in 1554 for the offices *(uffizi)* of Duke Cosimo's administration; today, it houses more first-class art per square inch than any other museum in the world. Botticelli, da Vinci, Michelangelo, Raphael, Titian, Giotto, Fra Angelico, Caravaggio, Bronzino, Cimabue, della Francesca, Bellini, even Dürer, Rubens, and Rembrandt—you name it, they have it. *(Extends from P. della Signoria to the Arno River.* ☎ *055 21 83 41. Open Tu-Sa 8:30am-6:50pm, Su 8:30am-1:50pm. L12,000/€6.20. For an extra L2000/€1.05, save yourself hours of waiting by purchasing advance tickets—call 055 29 48 83. Credit card required.)*

PONTE VECCHIO. From the Uffizi, follow V. Georgofili left and turn right along the river to reach the nearby **Ponte Vecchio** (Old Bridge). The oldest bridge in Florence, it replaced an older Roman version in 1345. In the 1500s, the Medici kicked out the butcheries and tanneries that lined the bridge and installed goldsmiths and diamond-carvers instead. The view of the bridge from the neighboring Ponte alle Grazie at sunset is breathtaking, and the bridge itself buzzes with pedestrians and street performers, particularly at night.

BARGELLO. The heart of medieval Florence lies in this 13th-century fortress between the *duomo* and P. della Signoria. Once the residence of the chief magistrate and later a brutal prison with public executions in the courtyard, it was restored in the 19th century and now houses the sculpture-filled **Museo Nazionale.** Donatello's bronze *David*, the first freestanding nude since antiquity, stands opposite the two bronze panels of the *Sacrifice of Isaac*, submitted by Ghiberti and Brunelleschi in the baptistery door competition. Michelangelo's early works, including *Bacchus*, *Brutus*, and *Apollo*, are on the ground floor. (*V. del Proconsolo, 4. Open daily 8:30am-1:50pm; closed on the 1st, 3rd, and 5th Su and the 2nd and 4th M of each month. L8000/€4.15.*)

SAN LORENZO AND FARTHER NORTH

BASILICA DI SAN LORENZO. The Medici, who lent the city the funds to build the church (designed in 1419 by Brunelleschi), retained artistic control over its construction. The family cunningly placed Cosimo Medici's grave in front of the high altar, making the entire church his personal mausoleum. Michelangelo designed the exterior but, disgusted by Florentine politics, he abandoned the project to study architecture in Rome. (☎ 055 21 66 34. *Open daily M-Sa 10am-5pm. L5000/€2.60.*)

To reach the ◪**Cappelle dei Medici** (Medici Chapels), walk around to the back entrance on P. Madonna degli Aldobrandini. The **Cappella dei Principi** (Princes' Chapel) is a rare Baroque moment in Florence, while the **Sacrestia Nuova** (New Sacristy) shows Michelangelo's work and holds two Medici tombs. (*Open daily 8:15am-5pm; closed the 2nd and 4th Su and the 1st, 3rd, and 5th M of each month. L11,000/€5.80.*)

◪**ACCADEMIA.** Michelangelo's triumphant *David* stands in self-assured perfection in a rotunda designed specifically for it. In the hallway stand Michelangelo's four *Prisoners;* the master left these intriguing statues intentionally unfinished, chipping away just enough to liberate the "living stone." (*V. Ricasoli, 60, between churches of S. Marco and S.S. Annunziata. Wheelchair accessible. Open mid-June to mid-Sept. Tu-F 8:30am-6:50pm, Sa 8:30am-10pm; mid-Sept. to mid-June Tu-Su 8:30am-6:50pm. L12,000/€6.20.*)

PIAZZA SANTA CROCE AND ENVIRONS

◪**CHIESA DI SANTA CROCE.** The thrifty Franciscans ironically built the city's most splendid church. Among the luminaries buried here are Machiavelli, Galileo, Michelangelo, who rests at the front of the right aisle in a tomb designed by Vasari, and humanist Leonardo Bruni, shown holding his precious *History of Florence*. Note also Donatello's gilded *Annunciation*. (*Open M-Sa 9:30am-5:30pm, Su and holidays 3-5:30pm.*) Intricate *pietra serena* pilasters and statues of the evangelists by Donatello grace Brunelleschi's small **Cappella Pazzi**, at the end of the cloister next to the church. (*Enter through the Museo dell' Opera. Open Th-Tu 10am-7pm. L5000/€2.60.*)

THE OLTRARNO

Historically disdained by downtown Florentines, the far side of the Arno remains a lively and unpretentious quarter, even in high season.

PALAZZO PITTI. Luca Pitti, a nouveau-riche banker of the 15th century, built his *palazzo* east of Santo Spirito against the Boboli hill. The Medici acquired the *palazzo* and the hill in 1550 and enlarged everything possible. Today, it houses six museums, including the ◪**Galleria Palatina.** The Galleria was one of only a few public galleries when it opened in 1833, and today houses Florence's most important art collection after the Uffizi. Works by Raphael, Titian, Andrea del Sarto, Caravaggio, and Rubens line the walls. Other museums display Medici family treasures, costumes, porcelain, carriages, and *Apartamenti Reale* (royal apartments)—lavish reminders of the time when the *palazzo* was the royal House of Savoy's living quarters. (*Galleria open Su-F 8:30am-9pm, Sa 8:30am-midnight; all other museums open*

8:30am-1:50pm, closed 1st, 3rd, and 5th M, and 2nd and 4th Su of each month. Galleria L12,000/€6.20, other museums L4000/€2.10 each. Inquire at the ticket office for a ticket covering the Galleria, the 4 other museums and the Boboli Gardens for L20,000/€10.35.)

BOBOLI GARDENS. With geometrically sculpted hedges, contrasting groves of holly and cypress trees, and bubbling fountains, the elaborate gardens are an exquisite example of stylized Renaissance landscaping. A large oval lawn is just up the hill from the back of the palace, with an Egyptian obelisk in the middle and marble statues in freestanding niches dotting the hedge-lined perimeter. *(Pass through the courtyard of Palazzo Pitti to the ticket office and entrance. Open daily 8:15am-6:30pm. Closed 1st and last M of each month. L4000/€2.10, EU citizens L2000/€1.05.)*

CHIESA DI SANTA MARIA DEL CARMINE. Inside, the **Brancacci Chapel** holds Masaccio's 15th-century frescoes, declared masterpieces even in their time. With such monumental works as the *Tribute Money*, this chapel drew many artists, including Michelangelo. *(Open M and W-Sa 10am-5pm, Su 1-5pm. L6000/€3.10.)*

🎵 ENTERTAINMENT

In June, the *quartieri* of Florence turn out in costume to play their own medieval version of soccer, known as **calcio storico**, in which two teams of 27 players face off over a wooden ball in one of the city's *piazze*. These games often blur between athletic contest and riot. Tickets (from L24,000/€12.40) are sold at the box office. The **Festival of San Giovanni Battista**, on June 24, features a tremendous fireworks display in P.le Michelangelo (easily visible from the Arno) starting around 10pm. May starts the summer music festivals with the classical **Maggio Musicale.** The **Estate Fiesolana** (June-Aug.) fills the Roman theater in nearby Fiesole with concerts, opera, theater, ballet, and film. September brings the **Festa dell'Unità**, a concert series at Campi Bisenzia (take bus #30). On the first Sunday after Ascension Day is the **Festa del Grillo** (Festival of the Cricket), when crickets in tiny wooden cages are sold in the Cascine park and then released into the grass.

🗲 NIGHTLIFE

For information on what's hot in the nightlife scene, consult the monthly *Firenze Spettacolo* (L3500/€1.80). Begin your nighttime *passeggiata* along V. dei Calzaiuoli and end it with coffee or *gelato* in a ritzy cafe on P. della Repubblica, where singers prance about the stage in front of **Bar Concerto.** In the Oltrarno, **Piazza San Spirito** has plenty of bars and restaurants, and live music in summer.

Monte Carla, V. dei Bardi, 2, in the Oltrarno, off P. de' Mozzi. A 3-tiered wonderland of cougar-print upholstery. This plush club is laidback in the summer and packed in the winter. Mixed drinks L10,000/€5.20. Open daily 11pm-3am.

BeBop, V. dei Servi, 76r. A club with jazz and assorted rock and roll. Bottled beer L8000/€4.15, mixed drinks L10,000/€5.20. Open daily 9pm-1am.

The Red Garter, V. dei Benci, 33r. A raucous mix of international students and the Italian youth who pursue them. Live music and dancing every night. Open daily 8:30pm-1am.

The Lion's Fountain, on P.G. Salvemini. Friendly American crowd. Pints L8000/€4.15, mixed drinks L10,000/€5.20. Open M-Th 6pm-2am, F-Sa 6pm-2:30am, Su 3pm-2am.

Meccanò, V. degli Olmi, 1, by Parco delle Cascinè. Popular with everyone. Cover (L25,000/€12.95) includes 1 drink. Drinks L10,000/€5.20. Open Tu-Sa 11pm-4am.

Central Park, in Parco della Cascinè. Open-air dance floor pulses with hip-hop, jungle, reggae, and "dance rock." Mixed drinks L10,000/€5.20. Open daily 9pm-late.

Blob, V. Vinegia, 21r, behind the Palazzo Vecchio. DJs, movies, foosball, and an evening bar buffet. Mixed drinks L10,000/€5.20. Open 6pm-late.

Andromeda, V. Cimatori, 13. Centrally located, this disco is packed with Italians and tourists anytime after midnight, while the dance floor thumps with British, American, and Italian pop. Cover L10,000/€5.20. Open M-Sa 10:30pm-4am.

🗿 DAYTRIP FROM FLORENCE

SIENA. You can't go wrong with any of the Tuscan towns surrounding Florence; Siena (see below), an 1½-hour train ride from Florence, boasts glorious medieval architecture and the intoxicating pageantry of the wild Palio horse race.

SIENA   ☎ 0577

Many travelers rush directly from Rome to Florence, ignoring gorgeous, medieval Siena. But the city proudly celebrates a rich history in the arts, politics, and commerce. One of Italy's largest celebrations is the biannual **Il Palio**, a wild horse race among Siena's 17 *contrade* (districts).

🖸🔽 TRANSPORTATION AND PRACTICAL INFORMATION. From P. Rosselli, **trains** leave every hour for Florence (1½hr., L8800/€4.55) and Rome (2½hr., L31,400/€16.25). Express **TRA-IN/SITA buses** (☎0577 20 42 45) leave P. Gramsci or the train station every hour for Florence (L12,000/€6.20). The departure display can be confusing, so be sure to ask when you buy a ticket. From the train station, cross the street to take buses #3, 4, 7-10, 14, 17, or 77 to the center of town; buy bus tickets from vending machines (L1500/€0.80). The central **tourist office** is at Il Campo, 56. (☎0577 28 05 51; fax 27 06 76. Open mid-Mar to mid-Nov. M-Sa 8:30am-7:30pm, Su 8:30am-2pm; mid-Nov. to mid-Mar. M-Sa 8:30am-1pm and 3-7pm, Su 9am-1pm.) **Prenotazioni Alberghiere,** in P.S. Domenico, finds rooms for L3000/€1.55. (☎0577 28 80 84; fax 28 02 90. Open M-Sa Apr.-Oct. 9am-8pm; Nov.-Mar. 9am-7pm.) Check **email** at **Engineering Systems,** V. Stalloreggi, 8. (☎0577 27 47 52. L8000/€4.15 per hr., students L7000/€3.65. Open daily 10am-8pm.)

🖪🔂 ACCOMMODATIONS AND FOOD. The **Piccolo Hotel Etruria,** V. Donzelle, 3, has immaculate, modern rooms. (☎0577 28 80 88 or 28 36 85; fax 28 84 61. Curfew 11:30pm. Singles L70,000/€36.15, with bath L80,000/€41.35; doubles L130,000/€67.15; triples L168,000/€86.80; quads L206,000/€106.40. AmEx/MC/V.) For the **Ostello della Gioventù "Guidoriccio" (HI),** V. Fiorentina, 89, in Località Lo Stellino, take bus #15 from P. Gramsci to the front door of the hostel. (☎0577 522 12. Breakfast included. Curfew 11:30pm. Dorms L24,000.) **Albergo Cannon d'Oro,** V. Montanini, 28, has luxurious rooms with lovely views. (☎0577 443 21. Breakfast L10,000/€5.20. Singles L90,000/€46.50; doubles L150,000/€77.50; triples L180,000/€93; quads L205,000/€105.90. AmEx/MC/V.) To **camp** at **Colleverde,** Strada di Scacciapensieri, 47, take bus #3 or 8 from P. del Sale; ask to be sure you are on the right route. (☎0577 28 00 44. Open mid-Mar. to mid-Nov. L15,000/€7.75 per person and tent.) Siena specializes in pastries such as *panforte,* a concoction of honey, almonds, and citron; indulge at **Bar/Pasticceria Nannini,** V. Banchi di Sopra, 22-24. On the far side on Palazzo Pubblico from Il Campo is **Trattoria Papei,** P. del Mercato, 6, a delicious local *trattoria* filled with lively locals. (*Secondi* L11,000-15,000/€8.70-7.75. Cover L2000/€1.05. Open Tu-Su 12:30-3pm and 7-10:30pm.) **Consortio Agrario supermarket,** V. Pianigiani, 5, is off P. Salimberi. (Open M-F 8am-7:30pm.) **Postal code:** 53100.

🖸🔂 SIGHTS AND ENTERTAINMENT. Siena offers two **biglietto cumulativi**—a 5-day pass (L14,000/€7.25) that includes the sights within the *duomo,* and a 7-day pass (L30,000/€15.50) that covers five more sights, including the Museo Civico. Siena radiates from the shell-shaped ▓**Piazza del Campo (Il Campo);** the **Fonte Gaia** is fed by the same aqueduct that Siena used in the 14th century. At the bottom, the **Torre del Mangia** clock tower looms over the graceful Gothic **Palazzo Pubblico.** Inside, the **Museo Civico** contains excellent Gothic and early Renaissance painting; the **Sala del Mappamondo** and the **Sala della Pace** contain stellar works. (*Palazzo,* museum, and tower open daily Mar.-Oct. 10am-7pm; Nov.-Feb. 10am-4pm. Tower L10,000/€5.20; museum L12,000/€6.20, students L6000/€3.10; combined ticket with tower L18,000/€9.30.) From the *palazzo,* take the stairs nearest to the *palazzo* on the right, cross V. di Città, and continue on the same twisting street for Siena's Gothic

⬛duomo, built on the edge of a hill; the apse would have been left hanging in mid-air if not for the construction of the lavishly decorated **baptistery** below. (Open daily mid-Mar. to Oct. 9am-7:30pm; Nov. to mid-Mar. 10am-1pm and 2:30-5pm. Free except when floor is uncovered in Sept. L8000-10,000/€4.15-5.20. Baptistery open daily mid-Mar. to Oct. 9am-7:30pm; Nov. to mid-Mar. 10am-1pm and 2:30-5pm. L4000/€2.10.) The **Libreria Piccolomini,** off the left aisle, holds frescoes and 15th-century scores. (Same hours as *duomo*. L3000/€1.55.) The **Museo dell'Opera della Metropolitana,** to the right of the *duomo*, houses its overflow art. (Open daily mid-Mar. to Oct. 9am-7:30pm; Nov. to mid-Mar. 9am-1:30pm. L6000/€3.05.)

Twice a year Siena's **Il Palio** (July 2 and Aug. 16) throws P. del Campo into utter chaos with a traditional bare-back horse race around the square. Arrive three days early to watch the five trial races and to pick a *contrada* to cheer for. Book rooms at least four months ahead—contact the tourist office for a list of rented rooms.

⬛ DAYTRIP FROM SIENA: SAN GIMIGNANO. The hilltop village of San Gimignano looks like an illumination from a medieval manuscript. Its famous towers earned its nickname as the *Città delle Belle Torri* (City of Beautiful Towers). Inside the **Palazzo del Popolo,** the **Museo Civico** houses an amazing collection of Sienese and Florentine works. Climb the 218 steps of the **Torre Grossa,** the tallest remaining tower, for a panorama of Tuscany. (Palazzo open Tu-Su 9am-7:30pm. Museum and tower open daily Mar.-Oct. 9:30am-7:20pm; Nov.-Feb. Sa-Th 10:30am-4:20pm. Museum L7000/€3.65, students L5000/€2.60; tower L8000/€4.15, L6000/€3.10. Combined ticket L12,000/€6.20, L9000/€4.65.) From the bus station, go through the *porta*, climb the hill, and follow V.S. Giovanni to the central P. della Cisterna, which leads to P. del Duomo and the **tourist office,** P. del Duomo, 1. (☎0577 94 00 08; fax 94 09 03. Open daily Mar.-Oct. 9am-1pm and 3-7pm; Nov.-Feb. 9am-1pm and 2-6pm.) The **Associazione Strutture Extralberghiere,** P. della Cisterna, 6, finds *affitte camere* (private rooms), a cheaper alternative at L75,000/€38.75. (☎0577 94 31 90. Open daily Mar.-Nov. 9:30am-7:30pm.) The reception for **Albero/Ristorante Il Pino** is at V.S. Matteo, 102, and the hotel itself is outside the city walls. (☎/fax 0577 94 04 15. Reserve ahead. Singles L70,000/€36.15; doubles L100,000/€51.65. AmEx/MC/V.) **Camp** at **Il Boschetto,** at S. Lucia, 2½km downhill from Porta S. Giovanni. Buses (L1500/€0.80) run from P. Martiri. (☎0577 94 03 52. Reception daily 8am-1pm, 3-8pm, and 9-11pm. Open Apr. to mid-Oct. L8500/€4.40 per person, L8500/€4.40 per tent. Showers included.) A **market** sells sandwiches at V.S. Matteo, 19. (Open daily Mar.-Oct. 9am-9pm; Nov.-Feb. F-W 9am-8pm, Th 9am-1pm.)

PISA   ☎0583

During the Middle Ages, Pisa was a major port with an empire extending to Corsica, Sardinia, and the Balearics. But when the Arno River silted up and the tower started leaning, the city's power and wealth declined accordingly. Today, the city welcomes tourists and vendors to the **Piazza del Duomo,** also known as the **Campo dei Miracoli** (Field of Miracles), a grassy expanse enclosing the tower, *duomo*, baptistery, and Camposanto. An **all-inclusive ticket** to the Campo's sights costs L19,000/€9.85. To reach the Campo from the train station, take bus #1 (L1500/€0.80), or walk straight up V. Gramsci, go through P. Vittorio Emanuele, walk down Corso Italia as it becomes V. Borgo Stretto, turn left on V.U. Dini, and go through P. dei Cavalieri. Begun in 1173, the famous ⬛**Leaning Tower** had reached a height of 10m when the soil beneath it suddenly shifted; the tower continues to slip 1-2mm every year. In June 2001, a multi-year stabilization effort on it was completed, but visitors are still not allowed to enter. The dazzling **duomo,** also on the Campo, is a treasury of fine art. (Open daily 10am-7:40pm. L3000/€1.55. Su mass free, but piety is a must.) Next door is the **baptistery,** whose acoustics allow a non-amplified choir to be heard 2km away. (Open daily late Apr. to late Sept. 8am-8pm; Oct.-Mar. 9am-5pm. L12,000/€6.20 includes another sight.) The adjoining **Camposanto,** a cloistered cemetery, has a series of haunting frescoes by an unidentified 14th-century artist known only as the "Master of the Triumph of Death." (Open daily late Apr. to late Sept. 8am-7:45pm; Mar. and Oct. 9am-5:40pm; Nov.-Feb. 9am-4:40pm. L12,000/€6.20

ITALY

includes another sight.) The **Museo delle Sinopie,** across the *piazza* from the Camposanto, displays preliminary fresco sketches by Traini, Veneziano, and Gaddi found during post-World War II restoration. Behind the tower is the **Museo dell'Opera del Duomo.** (Both open daily Apr. to late Sept. 8am-7:20pm; Mar.-Oct. 9am-5:20pm; Nov.-Feb. 9am-4:20pm. Each L12,000/€6.20; includes one other sight.) From the Campo, walk down V.S. Maria and over the bridge to the **Chiesa di Santa Maria della Spina,** whose bell tower supposedly holds a thorn from Christ's crown.

Trains (☎147 808 88) go from P. della Stazione, in the southern part of town, to: Florence (1hr., every hr., L9400/€4.85); Genoa (2½hr., L25,300/€13.10) and Rome (3hr., L45,500/€23.50). The **tourist office** is to the left as you exit the station. (☎050 422 91; www.turismo.toscana.it. Open daily M-Sa 9am-7pm, Su 9:30am-3:30pm.) The **Albergo Gronchi,** P. Archivescovado, 1, just off P. del Duomo, has frescoed ceilings. (☎050 56 18 23. Curfew midnight. Singles L36,000/€18.60; doubles L62,000/€32.05.) The **Centro Turistico Madonna dell'Acqua Hostel,** V. Pietrasantina, 15, is 2km from the tower. Take bus #3 from the station (4 per hr.) and ask for the *ostello*. (☎050 89 06 22. Sheets L3000/€1.55. Reception 6-11pm. Check-out 9am. Dorms L23,000; doubles L82,000/€42.35; triples L102,000/€52.70; quads L120,000/€62.) ▓**Il Paiolo,** V. Curtatone e Montanara, 9, near the university, serves a meal for L15,000/€7.75. (Open M-F noon-3pm and 7pm-1am, Sa 7pm-1am.) Get **groceries** at **Superal,** V. Pascoli, 6, off Corso Italia. (Open M-Sa 8am-8pm.) **Postal code:** 56100.

UMBRIA

Umbria is known as the "Green Heart of Italy," a land rich in natural beauty, encompassing wild woods, fertile plains, craggy gorges, and tiny villages. Christianity transformed Umbria's architecture and regional identity, turning it into a breeding ground for saints and religious movements; it was here that St. Francis of Assisi shamed the extravagant church with his humility.

PERUGIA   ☎075

Between Perugia's art and architecture and its big-city vitality and gorgeous countryside, there's no reason not to visit this gem of a city. The city's most popular sights frame **Piazza IV Novembre.** In the center of the *piazza*, the **Fontana Maggiore** is adorned with sculptures and bas-reliefs by Nicolà and Giovanni Pisano. At the end of the *piazza*, the imposing Gothic **duomo** houses the Virgin Mary's purported wedding ring. (Open daily 8am-noon and 4pm-dusk.) The 13th-century **Palazzo dei Priori** presides over the *piazza* and houses the impressive ▓**Galleria Nazionale dell'Umbria,** Corso Vannucci, 19. (Open daily 8:30am-7:30pm; mid-June to mid-Sept. Sa until 11pm; closed Jan. 1, Dec. 25, and 1st M each month. L12,000/€6.20.) At the end of town past the Porta S. Pietro, the **Basilica di San Pietro,** on Corso Cavour, has a beautiful garden. (Open daily 8am-noon and 3:30pm-dusk.)

Trains leave P.V. Veneto, Fontiveggio, for: Assisi (25min., every hr., L3000/€1.55); Florence (2½hr., every hr., from L15,300/€€7.90); and Rome (direct 2½hr., from L28,900/€14.95; via Terontola or Foligno 3hr., from L20,600/€10.65). From the station, take bus #6, 7, 9, 13d, or 15 to the central P. Italia (L1200/€0.65), then walk down Corso Vannucci to P. IV Novembre and the **tourist office,** P. IV Novembre, 3. (☎075 572 33 27; fax 573 93 86. Open M-F 8:30am-1:30pm and 3:30-6:30pm, Sa 8:30am-1:30pm, Su 9am-1pm.) To get from the tourist office to ▓**Ostello della Gioventù/Centro Internazionale di Accoglienza per la Gioventù,** V. Bontempi, 13, walk down Corso Vannucci past the *duomo* and P. Danti, take the farthest street right through P. Piccinino, and turn right on V. Bontempi. (☎/fax 075 572 28 80; www.perugia.it. Sheets L2000/€1.05. Lockout 9:30am-4pm. Curfew midnight. Open mid-Jan. to mid-Dec. Dorms L19,000/€9.85.) **Albergo Anna,** V. dei Priori, 48, off Corso Vannucci, has cozy 17th-century rooms with great views. (☎/fax 075 573 63 04. Singles L60,000/€31, with bath L70,000/€36.15; doubles L80,000/€41.35, L100,000/€51.65; triples L120,000/€62, L140,000/€72.30. AmEx/D/MC/V.) **Ristorante da Gianocarlo,** V. dei Priori, 36, two blocks off Corso Vannucci, is full of locals dining on delicious food.

(*Primi* L11,000-20,000/€5.70-10.35; *secondi* from L15,000/€7.75. Cover L3000/€1.55. Open Sa-Th noon-3pm and 6-10pm.) The **COOP**, P. Matteotti, 15, has **groceries.** (Open M-Sa 9am-8pm.) **Postal code:** 06100.

ASSISI   ☎079

The undeniable jewel of Assisi, and even of Umbria, is the 13th-century ☒**Basilica di San Francesco.** Giotto's renowned *Life of St. Francis* fresco cycle decorates the walls of the upper church, paying tribute to his sainthood and consecration. From P. del Commune, take V. Portica. (Dress code strictly enforced. Lower basilica open daily 6:30am-7pm. Upper basilica open daily 8:30am-7pm.) The dramatic fortress **Rocca Maggiore** towers above town, offering panoramic views. (Open daily Sept.-June 10am-dusk, July-Aug. 9am-dusk. L3000/€1.55, students L2000/€1.05.) The pink and white **Basilica of Santa Chiara** houses St. Francis's tunic, sandals, and crucifix. (Open M-F daily 7am-noon and 2-7pm.)

From the station near the Basilica Santa Maria degli Angeli, **trains** go to: Ancona (from L20,200/€10.45); Florence (2 per day, L17,000/€8.80); and Rome (1 per day, from L25,500/€13.20); more frequent trains go to Rome via Foligno and to Florence via Ternotola. **ASP buses** run from P. Matteotti to Florence (2½hr., 1 per day, L12,400/€6.40) and Perugia (1½hr., 7 per day, L5200/€2.70). From P. Matteotti, follow V. del Torrione, bear left in P.S. Rufino, and take V.S. Rufino to **Piazza del Comune,** the town center, and the **tourist office,** in P. del Comune. (☎075 81 25 34; fax 81 37 27; www.umbria2000.it. Open M-F 8am-2pm and 3:30-6:30pm, Sa 9am-1pm and 3:30-6:30pm, Su 9am-1pm.) For **Ostello della Pace (HI),** V. di Valecchi, 177, turn right out of the station, then left at the intersection on V. di Valecchi. (☎/fax 075 81 67 67. Breakfast included. Reception daily 7-9:15am and 3:30-11:30pm. Check-out 9:30am. Reserve ahead. L23,000/€11.90, with bath L28,000/€14.50. MC/V.) For the brand-new **Ostello Fontemaggio,** V. per l'Eremo delle Carceri, 8, follow V. Eremo from P. Matteotti through Porta Cappuccini 1km up the road and veer right at the sign. A **market** is next door. (☎075 81 36 36; fax 81 37 49. Breakfast L8000/€4.15. No lockout. Curfew 11pm. Dorms L30,000/€15.50. **Camping** L9000/€4.65 per person, L8000/€4.15 per tent, L4000/€2.10 per car. Cash only.) **Postal code:** 06081.

THE MARCHES (LE MARCHE)

In the Marches, green foothills separate the gray shores of the Adriatic from the Apennine peaks and the traditional hill towns from the umbrella-laden beaches. Inland towns, easily accessible by train, rely on agriculture and preserve the region's historical legacy in the architectural remains of Gauls and Romans.

URBINO   ☎0722

Urbino's fairy-tale skyline, scattered with humble stone dwellings and an immense turreted palace, has changed little over the past 500 years. The city's most remarkable monument is the imposing Renaissance **Palazzo Ducale** (Ducal Palace), in P. Rinascimento, though its façade is more thrilling than its interior. The central courtyard is the essence of Renaissance balance and proportion; to the left, stairs lead to the former private apartments of the Duke, which now house the **National Gallery of the Marches.** (Open M 8:30am-2pm, Tu-F 8:30am-7:15pm, Sa 8:30am-10:30pm, Su 8:30am-7:15pm. L8000/€4.15.) Walk back across P. della Repubblica and continue onto V. Raffaello to Raphael's birthplace, the **Casa di Rafaele,** V. Raffaello, 57, now a museum that contains a reproduction of his earliest work, *Madonna e Bambino.* (Open M-Sa 9am-1pm and 3-7pm, Su 10am-1pm. L5000/€2.60.)

Bucci **buses** (☎0722 13 24 01) go from Borgo Mercatale to Rome (5hr., 1 per day 4pm, L32,000/€16.55). Blue SOBET **buses** (☎0722 223 33) run to P. Matteotti and the train station in Pesaro (1hr., 4-10 per day, L3700/€1.95; buy tickets on the bus). From there, a short walk uphill on V.G. Mazzini leads to **P. della Repubblica,** the city center. The **tourist office,** P. Rinascimento, 1, is opposite the palace. (☎0722 26 13; fax 0722 24 41. Open mid-June to mid-Sept. M-Sa 9am-1pm and 3-7pm, Su 9am-1pm;

ITALY

in winter 9am-1pm and 3-6pm.) **Hotel San Giovanni,** V. Barocci, 13, has simple, clean rooms. (☎0722 28 27. Open Aug.-June. Singles L40,000/€20.65, with bath L50,000/€25.85; doubles L70,000/€36.15, L90,000/€46.50; triples L105,000/€54.25.) **Camping Pineta,** on V.S. Donato, is 2km away in Cesane; take bus #4 or 7 from Borgo Mercatale and ask to get off at camping. (☎0722 47 10. Reception daily 9-11am and 3-10pm. Open Apr. to mid-Sept. L10,000/€5.20 per person, L21,000/€10.85 per tent.) **Margherita supermarket** is at V. Raffaello, 37. (Open M-Sa 8am-2pm and 4:30-8pm.)

ANCONA ☎071

Ancona is the epicenter of Italy's Adriatic Coast—a major port in a small, whimsical, largely unexplored city. **Piazza Roma** is dotted with yellow and pink buildings, and **Piazza Cavour** is the heart of the town. Anacona has **ferry service** to Greece, Croatia, and northern Italy. **Adriatica** (☎071 20 49 15; www.adriatica.it), **Jadrolinija** (☎071 20 43 05; www.jadrolinija.tel.hr/jadrolinija), and **SEM Maritime Co.** (☎071 20 40 90; www.sem.hr) run to Croatia (from L70,000-140,000/€36.15-72.30). **ANEK** (☎071 207 23 46; www.anek.gr) and **Blue Star (Strintzis)** (☎071 207 10 68; www.strinzis.gr) ferries go to Greece (from L93,000-120,000/€48.05-62). Schedules and tickets are available at the Stazione Marittima; **reserve ahead** in July or August. **Trains** arrive at P. Rosselli from: Bologna (2½hr., 1-2 per hr., from L19,600/€10.15); Milan (5hr., 24 per day, from L37,500/€19.40); Rome (3-4hr., 9 per day, from L25,000/€12.95); and Venice (5hr., 3 per day, from L26,300/€13.60). Take bus #1, 1/3, or 1/4 (L1400/€0.80) along the port past **Stazione Marittima** and up Corso Stamira to reach P. Cavour. A branch of the **tourist office** is located in Stazione Marittima and provides ferry information. (☎071 20 11 83. Open June-Sept. Tu-Sa 8am-8pm, Su-M 8am-2pm.) From the train station, cross the *piazza*, turn left, then take the 1st right, and make a sharp right behind the newsstand to reach the new **Ostella della Gioventù,** V. Lamaticci, 7. (☎/fax 071 422 57. Reception 6:30-11am and 4:30pm-midnight. Dorms L23,000/€11.90. Cash only.) **CONAD supermarket** is at V. Matteotti, 115. (Open M-F 8:15am-2pm and 5-7:35pm, Sa 8:15am-12:45pm and 5-7:40pm.)

SOUTHERN ITALY

South of Rome, the sun gets brighter, the meals longer, and the passion more intense. The introduction to the *mezzogiorno* (Italian South) begins in Campania, the fertile crescent that cradles the Bay of Naples and the Gulf of Salerno. In the shadow of Mount Vesuvius lie the famous Roman ruins of Pompeii, frozen in time in a bed of molten lava. In the Bay of Naples, Capri is Italy's answer to Fantasy Island, while the Amalfi Coast cuts a dramatic course down the lush Tyrrhenian shore. The region remains justly proud of its open-hearted populace, strong traditions, classical ruins, and relatively untouristed beaches.

NAPLES (NAPOLI) ☎081

Italy's third-largest city is also its most chaotic: shouting merchants flood markets, stoplights are merely suggestions, and summer traffic jams clog the broiling city. The city's color and vitality, evident in the street markets and the world's best pizza, have gradually overcome its traditional rough-edged image. In recent years, aggressive restoration has opened monuments and art treasures to the public for the first time to reveal exquisite architectural works of art.

▐ TRANSPORTATION

Flights: Aeroporto Capodichino, V. Umberto Maddalena (☎081 789 61 11), northwest of the city. Connects to all major Italian and European cities. A CLP **bus** (☎081 531 16 46) leaves from P. Municipio (20min., 6am-10:30pm, L3000/€1.55).

Trains: Ferrovie dello Stato goes from Stazione Centrale to: **Rome** (2hr., 34 per day, L18,600/€9.60); **Brindisi** (5hr., 5 per day, L35,600/€18.40); **Milan** (8hr., 13 per day;

XXXTRA, XXXTRA! Newspapers cover scandalous events, but in Southern Italy this phrase has literal meaning. The old newspapers that cover the windshields of parked cars often serve not to keep out the sun's heat but to conceal the torrid heat coming from within. Beware, virgin eyes—it is the age-old art of *l'amore*.

L96,000/€49.60). **Circumvesuviana** (☎081 772 24 44), also in the station, heads for **Pompeii** (L3200/€1.65) and **Herculaneum** (L2300/€1.20).

Ferries: Depart from **Molo Angioino** and **Molo Beverello,** at the base of P. Municipio. From P. Garibaldi, take tram #1; from P. Municipio, take the R2 bus. **Caremar,** Molo Beverello (☎081 551 38 82), goes frequently to **Capri** and **Ischia** (both 1½hr., L9800/€5.10). **Tirrenia Lines,** Molo Angioino (☎081 720 11 11), goes to **Palermo, Sicily** (11hr., 1 per day, L90,300/€46.65) and **Cagliari, Sardinia** (15hr.; 2 per week, winter 1 per week; L83,900/€43.35). L10,000/€5.20 port tax. Schedules and prices change; check *Qui Napoli.*

Public Transportation: Giranapoli tickets (1½hr.; L1500/€0.80, full-day L4500/€2.35) are valid on **buses, Metro** (subway), **trams,** and **funiculars.**

Taxis: Cotana (☎081 570 70 70) or **Napoli** (☎081 556 44 44). Take metered taxis.

✴🛈 ORIENTATION AND PRACTICAL INFORMATION

The main train and bus terminals are in the immense **Piazza Garibaldi** on the east side of Naples. From P. Garibaldi, broad **Corso Umberto I** leads southwest to Piazza Bovi, from which V. Depretis leads left to **Piazza Municipio,** the city center, and **Piazza Trieste e Trento** and **Piazza Plebiscito.** Below P. Municipio lie the **Stazione Marittima** ferry ports. From P. Trieste e Trento, **Via Toledo** (a.k.a. **Via Roma**) leads through the Spanish quarter to **Piazza Dante.** Make a right into the historic **Spaccanapoli** neighborhood, which follows **Via dei Tribunali** through the middle of town. While violence is rare in Naples, petty theft is relatively common. Always be careful.

Tourist Offices: EPT (☎081 26 87 79), at Stazione Centrale. Helps with hotels and ferries. Grab a map and ▧*Qui Napoli.* Open M-Sa 9am-7pm. **Branches** at P. dei Martiri, 58 and Stazione Mergellina.

Consulates: Canada, V. Carducci, 29 (☎081 40 13 38). **South Africa,** Corso Umberto I (☎081 551 75 19). **UK,** V. Crispi, 122 (☎081 66 35 11). M: P. Amedeo. Open July-Aug. M-F 8am-1:30pm; Sept.-June M-F 9am-12:30pm and 2:30-4pm. **US,** P. della Repubblica (☎081 583 81 11, emergency ☎081 03 37 94 50 83), at the west end of Villa Comunale. Open M-F 8am-5pm.

Currency Exchange: Thomas Cook, at the airport (☎081 551 83 99). Open M-F 9:30am-1pm and 3-6:30pm.

Emergency: ☎113. **Police:** ☎113 or 081 794 11 11. **Carabinieri (civil corps):** ☎112. English spoken.

Hospital: Cardarelli (☎081 747 11 11), north of town on the R4 bus line. **Medical Assistance:** ☎081 752 06 96.

Internet Access: Internetbar, P. Bellini, 74. L5000/€2.60 per 30min. Open M-Sa 9am-2am, Su 8am-2am. **Internet Multimedia,** V. Sapienza, 43. L3000/€1.55 per hr. Scanning and printing available. Open daily 9:30am-9:30pm.

Post Office: P. Matteotti (☎081 552 42 33), at V. Diaz (R2 line). Address mail to be held: First name, SURNAME, *In Fermo Posta,* P. Matteotti, Naples **80100,** ITALY. Open M-F 8:15am-6pm, Sa 8:15am-noon.

🏠 ACCOMMODATIONS

Although Naples has some fantastic bargain lodgings, especially near **Piazza Garibaldi,** be wary and wise about choosing a room. Avoid hotels that solicit customers at the station, never give your passport until you've seen the room, agree on the price *before* unpacking, be alert for unexpected costs, and gauge how secure a lodging seems.The **ACISJF/Centro D'Ascolto,** at Stazione Centrale, helps women find safe rooms. (☎ 081 28 19 93. Open M, Tu and Th 3:30-6:30pm.) Rooms are scarce in the historic district between P. Dante and the *duomo*.

▨ **Casanova Hotel,** V. Venezia, 2 (☎ 081 26 82 87). From P. Garibaldi, follow V. Milano and turn left at the end. Clean, airy rooms, and a rooftop terrace. Breakfast L8000/€4.15. Reserve ahead. Singles L40,000/€20.65, with bath 50,000/€25.85; doubles L70,000/€41.35, L85,000/€43.90; triples L110,000/€56.85; quads L140,000/€72.30. 10% *Let's Go* discount. AmEx/MC/V.

Hotel Eden, Corso Novara, 9 (☎ 081 28 53 44). From the station, turn right on Corso Novara and it's on the left. Prices with *Let's Go:* singles L45,000/€23.25; doubles L70,000/€36.15; triples L100,000/€51.65; quads L120,000/€62. AmEx/MC/V.

Soggiorno Imperia, P. Miraglia, 386 (☎ 081 45 93 47). Take the R2 from the train station, walk up V. Mezzocannone through P.S. Domenico Maggiore, and enter the 1st set of green doors to the left on P. Miraglia. Clean rooms in a 16th-century *palazzo*. Call ahead. Dorms L30,000/€15.50; singles L40,000/€20.65; doubles L70,000-100,000/€36.15-51.65; triples L100,000/€51.65. AmEx/MC/V.

6 Small Rooms, V. Diodato Lioy, 18 (☎ 081 790 13 78), up from P. Monteolovieto. Big rooms in a friendly atmosphere. Singles L45,000/€23.25; doubles L75,000/€38.75.

▣ FOOD

Pizza-making is an art born in Naples; you can't go wrong. ▨ **Pizzeria Brandi,** Salita S. Anna di Palazzo, 1, counts Luciano Pavarotti and Isabella Rossellini among its patrons. (Cover L3000/€4.15. 12% tip. Open M-Su noon-3pm and 7pm-midnight.) To get to **Antica Pizzeria da Michele,** V. Cesare Sersale 1-3, walk up Corso Umberto I from P. Garibaldi and take the first right. Get a slice of *marinara* (tomato, garlic, oregano, and oil) or *margherita* (tomato, mozzarella, and basil) and a beer for L8000/€4.15. (Open M-Sa 8am-11pm.) Some of best pizza in Naples is at **Pizzeria Trianon da Ciro,** V. Pietro Colletta 42/44/46, a block off Corso Umberto I. (Pizza L6000-13,000/€3.10-6.75. 15% service. Open daily 10am-3:30pm and 5:30-11pm.) For a change of culinary pace, take the C25 bus to P. Amedeo for excellent seafood.

◉ SIGHTS

▨ **MUSEO ARCHEOLOGICO NAZIONALE.** This world-class collection houses exquisite treasures from Pompeii and Herculaneum, including the outstanding "Alexander Mosaic." The sculpture collection is also impressive. *(From M: P. Cavour, turn right and walk 2 blocks. Open M and W-Su 9am-7:30pm. L12,000/€6.20.)*

SPACCANAPOLI. This east-west neighborhood overflows with gorgeous architecture, meriting at least a 30min. stroll. From P. Dante, walk through Porta Alba and P. Bellini before turning on V. dei Tribunali, where the churches of **San Lorenzo Maggiore** and **San Paolo Maggiore** lie. Turn right on V. Duomo and turn right again on V.S. Biago to stroll past the **University of Naples** and the **Chiesa di San Domenico Maggiore,** where according to legend, a painting once spoke to Saint Thomas Aquinas. *(In P.S. Domenico Maggiore. Open daily 7:15am-12:15pm and 4:15-7:15pm. Free.)*

DUOMO. The main attraction of the 14th-century *duomo* is the **Cappella del Tesoro di San Gennaro.** A beautiful 17th-century bronze grille protects the high altar, which holds a gruesome display of relics with the saint's head and two vials of his coagulated blood. Supposedly, disaster will strike if the blood does not liquefy on the celebration of his *festa* (three times a year); miraculously, it always does. *(3 blocks up V. Duomo from Corso Umberto I. Open M-F 9am-noon and 4:30-7pm, Sa-Su 9am-noon. Free.)*

MUSEO AND GALLERIE DI CAPODIMONTE. This museum, in a royal *palazzo*, is surrounded by a pastoral park and sprawling lawns. The true gem is the amazing **Farnese Collection,** with works by Bellini and Caravaggio. *(Take bus #110 from P. Garibaldi to Parco Capodimonte; enter by Portas Piccola or Grande. Open Tu-F 10am-7pm, Sa-Su 8:30am-7:30pm. L14,000/€7.25, after 2pm L12,000/€6.20.)*

Naples

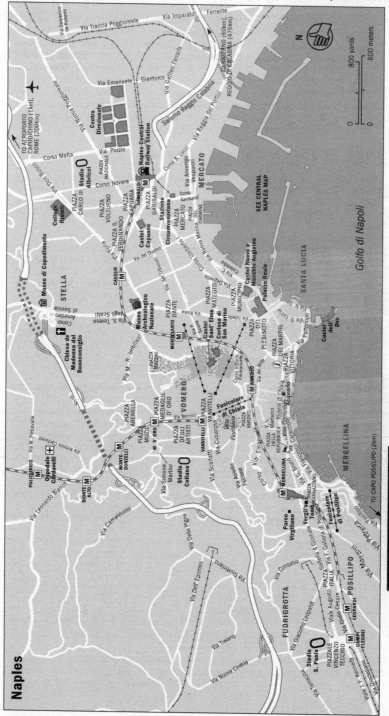

PALAZZO REALE AND CASTEL NUOVO. The 17th-century **Palazzo Reale** contains the **Museo di Palazzo Reale**, opulent royal apartments, and a fantastic view from the terrace of the **Royal Chapel**. The **Biblioteca Nazionale** stores 1½ million volumes, including the scrolls from the **Villa dei Papiri** in Herculaneum. The **Teatro San Carlo** is reputed to top the acoustics in Milan's La Scala. *(Take the R2 bus from P. Garibaldi to P. Trieste e Trento and go around to the P. Plebiscito entrance. Open M-Tu and Th-F 9am-8pm. L8000/€4.15.)* From P. Trieste e Trento, walk up V. Vittorio Emanuele III to P. Municipio for the five-turreted **Castel Nuovo**, built in 1286 by Charles II of Anjou. The double-arched entrance commemorates the arrival of Alphonse I of Aragon in Naples. Inside, admire the **Museo Civico**. *(Open M-Sa 9am-7pm. L10,000/€5.20.)*

🎵🎭 ENTERTAINMENT AND NIGHTLIFE

Piazza Vanvitelli in Vomero is where the cool kids go to relax and socialize. Take the funicular from V. Toledo or the C28 bus from P. Vittoria. Outdoor bars and cafes are a popular choice in **Piazza Bellini**, near P. Dante. Pub-goers flock to **Green Stage**, P.S. Pasquale, 15. From P. Amedeo, take V. Vittorio Colonna to V.S. Pasquale. (Heineken L5000/€2.60. Open Tu-Th 7:30pm-3am, F-Su 7:30pm-4am.) **Itaca**, P. Bellini, 71, mixes eerie trance music with dark decor. (Cocktails from L1000/€0.55. Open daily 10am-3am.) **Camelot**, V.S. Pietro A Majella, 8, just off P. Bellini in the historic district, is mostly pop and house. (Open Sept.-June Tu-Su 10:30pm-4am.) **Tongue**, V. Manzoni, 207, in Posillipo, features visiting DJs. Take nightbus #404d from P. Garibaldi. (Cover L25,000/€12.95. Open Oct.-May F-Sa 11pm-4am.) **ARCI-Gay/Lesbica** (☎081 551 82 93) has information on gay and lesbian nights at local clubs.

🏛 DAYTRIPS FROM NAPLES

Mount Vesuvius, the only active volcano on the European continent, looms over the area east of Naples. Its infamous eruption in AD 79 buried the nearby Roman city of **Ercolano** (Herculaneum) in mud, and neighboring **Pompei** (Pompeii) in ashes.

POMPEII. Since 1748, excavations have unearthed a stunningly well-preserved picture of Roman daily life. The site hasn't changed much since then, and neither have the victims, whose ghastly remains were partially preserved by plaster casts in the hardened ash. Walk down V.D. Marina to reach the ◪**Forum,** which was once the commercial, civic, and religious center of the city, surrounded by a colonnade. Exit the Forum through the upper end by the cafeteria, and head right on V. della Fortuna to reach the ◪**House of the Faun,** where a bronze dancing faun and the spectacular Alexander Mosaic (today in the Museo Archeologico Nazionale) were found. Continue on V. della Fortuna and turn left on V. dei Vettii to reach the **House of the Vettii**, on the left, and the most vivid frescoes in Pompeii. Back down V. dei Vettii, cross V. della Fortuna to V. Storto, turn left on V. degli Augustali, and take a quick right to reach a small **brothel** (the Lupenar). After 2000 years, it's still the most popular place in town. V. dei Teatri, across the street, leads to the oldest standing **amphitheater** in the world (80 BC), which once held up to 12,000 spectators. To get to the ◪**Villa of the Mysteries,** the complex's best-preserved villa, head west on V. della Fortuna, right on V. Consolare, and all the way up Porta Ercolano. (Pompeii open daily 9am-6pm; in winter 9am-3:30pm. L16,000/€8.30.) Take the Circumvesuviana **train** (☎081 772 21 11) from Naples' Stazione Centrale to Pompeii (dir. Sorrento; 2 per hr., L3200/€1.65). To reach the site, head downhill and take your first left to the west (Porta Marina) entrance. To get to the **tourist office**, V. Sacra, 1, walk right from the station and continue to the bottom of the hill. (Open M-F 8am-3:30pm, Sa 8am-2pm.) Food at the on-site cafeteria is expensive, so bring lunch.

HERCULANEUM. Herculaneum is 500m downhill from the "Ercolano" stop on the Circumvesuviana train from Naples (dir. Sorrento; 20min., L3200/€1.65). Stop at the **tourist office**, V. IV Novembre, 84 (☎081 788 12 43), to pick up a free **map**. The city is less excavated than Pompeii, but highlights include the **House of Deer**. (Open daily 9am-1hr. before dusk. L16,000/€8.30.)

MT. VESUVIUS. You can peer into the only active volcano on mainland Europe at Mt. Vesuvius. Trasporti Vesuviani **buses** (buy ticket on board; return L6000/€3.10) run from the Ercolano Circumvesuviana station to the crater. Although Vesuvius hasn't erupted since March 31, 1944—scientists say volcanoes should erupt every 30 years—experts deem the trip safe.

AMALFI COAST. The dramatic scenery and pulsing nightlife of the towns on the Amalfi Coast are easily accessible from Naples by train, ferry, and bus (p. 639).

BAY OF NAPLES. Only an hour away from Naples by ferry, the isles of Capri and Ischia tempt travelers with luscious beaches and enchanting grottos. (p. 640).

AMALFI COAST

The beauty of the Amalfi coast is one of extremes and contrasts. Immense rugged cliffs plunge downward into calm azure waters, while coastal towns climb the sides of narrow ravines. The picturesque villages provide stunning natural panoramas, delicious food, and throbbing nightlife.

▟ TRANSPORTATION. The coast is accessible from Naples, Sorrento, Salerno, and the islands by **ferry** and blue SITA **buses. Trains** run directly to Salerno from Florence (5½-6½hr., 7 per day, L49,000-79,000/€25.35-41.10); Naples (45min., 32 per day, L5100-17,100/€2.65-8.85); Rome (2½-3hr., 18 per day, L22,000-45,000/€11.40-23.25); and Venice (9hr., 1 per day, L64,000/€33.05). **Buses** also link Paestrum and Salerno (1hr., every hr. 7am-7pm, L4700/€2.45). From Salerno, Travelmar (☎089 87 31 90) runs **ferries** to Amalfi (1hr., 3 per day, L9000/€4.65) via Positano (40min., L7000/€3.65). From Sorrento, Linee Marittime Partenopee **ferries** (☎081 878 14 30) run to Amalfi (45min., L16,000/€8.30) via Positano (30min., L15,000/€7.75); and Capri (50min., L8000/€4.15). From Amalfi they go to Salerno (30min., 9 per day, L16,000/€8.30).

AMALFI AND ATRANI. Breathtaking natural beauty surrounds the narrow streets and historic monuments of **Amalfi.** Visitors crowd the P. del Duomo to admire the elegant 9th-century **Duomo di Sant'Andrea** and the nearby **Fontana di Sant'Andrea,** a marble female nude with water spouting from her breasts. **A'Scalinatella,** P. Umberto, 12, has hostel beds and regular rooms all over Amalfi and Atrani. (☎089 87 19 30. Dorms L20,000-35,000/€10.35-18.10; doubles L50,000-120,000/€25.85-62. **Camping** L15,000/€7.75 per person.) The tiny beachside village of **Atrani** is a 10min. walk around the bend from Amalfi. A spectacular **hiking trail** is the 3hr. **Path of the Gods,** which runs along the coast from Bomerano to Positano.

RAVELLO. Perched 330m atop cliffs, Ravello has provided a haven for many celebrity artists over the years. The Moorish cloister and gardens of **Villa Rufolo,** off P. Duomo, inspired Boccaccio's *Decameron* and Wagner's *Parsifal.* (Open daily 9am-dusk. L6000/€3.10.) The small road to the right leads to the impressive **Villa Cimbrone,** whose floral walkways and gardens hide temples and statue-filled grottoes. (Open daily 9am-7:30pm. L8000/€4.15.) **Classical music concerts** are performed in the gardens of the Villa Rufolo; call the *Società di Concerti di Ravello* for more info. (☎089 85 81 49.) All 10 rooms at the **Albergo Garden,** V.G. Boccaccio, 4, have a great view of the cliffs. (☎089 85 72 26; fax 85 81 10. Breakfast included. Reserve ahead. Doubles L145,000/€74.90; off season L125,000/€64.60. AmEx/MC/V.)

POSITANO. Today, Positano's most frequent visitors are the wealthy few who can afford pricey *Positanese* culture. Yet the town has its picturesque charms; as Steinbeck rightly observed, "Positano bites deep." To see the large *pertusione* (hole) in **Montepertuso,** one of three perforated mountains in the world, hike 45 minutes uphill or take the bus from P. dei Mulini. Positano's **beaches** are also popular, and although boutiques may be a bit pricey, no one charges for window-shopping. The **tourist office,** V. del Saraceno, 4 (☎089 87 50 67), is below the *duomo.*

ITALY

Ostello Brikette, V.G. Marconi, 358, 100m up the main coastal road to Sorrento from Viale Pasitea, has incredible views from two large terraces. (☎089 87 58 57. Breakfast and sheets included. Dorms L35,000/€18.10; doubles L100,000/€51.65.) **Casa Guadagno,** V. Fornillo, 22, has 15 spotless rooms. (☎089 87 50 42; fax 81 14 07. Breakfast included. Reserve ahead. With *Let's Go:* Doubles L110,000-120,000/€56.85-62; triples L180,000/€93. MC/V.) Prices in the town's restaurants reflect the high quality of the food. For a sit-down dinner, thrifty travelers head toward **Fornillo.**

SORRENTO. The most heavily touristed town on the peninsula, lively Sorrento makes a convenient base for daytrips around the Bay of Naples. Caremar **ferries** (☎081 807 30 77) go to Capri (50min., 3 per day, L9000/€4.60). The **tourist office,** V. de Maio, 35, is off P. Tasso. (☎08 18 07 40 33. Open Apr.-Sept. M-F 8:45am-7:45pm, Sa 8:45am-7:15pm; Oct.-Mar. M-Sa 8:30am-2pm and 4-6:15pm.) Halfway to the **free beach** at **Punta del Capo** (on bus A), ⬛**Hotel Elios,** V. Capo, 33, has comfy rooms. (☎081 878 18 12. Singles L45,000/€23.25; doubles L80,000/€41.35.) For extensive amenities, stay at **Hotel City,** Corso Italia, 221; turn left on Corso Italia from the station. (☎081 877 22 10. Singles L75,000/€38.75; doubles L125,000/€64.60.) It's easy to find good, affordable food in Sorrento. ⬛**Davide,** V. Giuliani, 39, off Corso Italia, two blocks from P. Tasso, has divine *gelato* and masterful *mousse* (55-80 flavors daily. Open daily 10am-2am.) After 10:30pm, a crowd gathers upstairs in the rooftop lemon grove above **The English Inn,** Corso Italia, 56. (Open daily 9am-1am.)

SALERNO AND PAESTUM. Industrial **Salerno** is best used as a base for daytrips to nearby **Paestum,** the site of three spectacularly preserved ⬛**Doric buildings,** including the **Temple of Ceres,** the **Temple of Poseidon,** and the **basilica.** (Temples open daily 9am-1hr. before dusk. Closed 1st and 3rd M each month. L8000/€4.15.) To sleep at **Ostello della Gioventù "Irno" (HI),** in Salerno at V. Luigi Guercio, 112, go left from the station on V. Torrione, then left under the bridge on V. Mobilio. (☎089 79 02 51. Breakfast included. Curfew 2am. Dorms L17,500/€9.05.)

BAY OF NAPLES ISLANDS

CAPRI. The sheer bluffs, divine landscapes, and azure waters of Capri have beckoned wayfarers from the mainland since Roman times. **Capri proper** is above the ports, while **Anacapri** sits higher up the mountain. From P. Umberto in Capri proper, V. Roma leads to Anacapri. **Buses** also make the trip until 1:40am; a taxi ride will cost about L20,000/€10.35. The ⬛**Grotta Azzurra** (Blue Grotto) is a must-see—light enters the cavern through a hole in the rock under the water, causing the whole grotto to glow neon-blue. (Open daily 9am-6pm. Boat tour L19,000/€9.85.) Take the bus from Capri to Anacapri and a second bus to the Grotto, or go by boat from Marina Grande (L9000/€4.60). Upstairs from P. Vittoria in Anacapri, **Villa San Michele** has lush gardens, ancient sculptures, and a remarkable view of the island. (Open daily 9:30am-1hr. before dusk. L8000/€4.15.) To appreciate Capri's Mediterranean beauty from higher ground, take the **chairlift** up **Monte Solaro** from P. Vittoria. (Open Mar.-Oct. daily 9:30am-1hr. before dusk. Round-trip L7000/€3.65.) From P. Umberto in Capri take V. Longano, which becomes V. Tiberio, to **Villa Jovis** (1hr.), the most magnificent of the 12 villas that the emperor Tiberius built throughout Capri. (Open daily 9am-1hr. before dusk. L4000/€2.10.)

Caremar **ferries** run from Marina Grande to Naples (1¼hr., 6 per day, L12,000/€6.20) and Sorrento (45min., 3 per day, L16,000/ €8.30). Linee Lauro sends **hydrofoils** to Ischia (40min., 1 per day, L20,000/€10.35) and Sorrento (20min., 12 per day, L16,000/€8.30); LineaJet hydrofoils go to Naples (40min., 11 per day, L16,000/€8.30). The Capri **tourist office** (☎081 837 06 34) is at the end of Marina Grande; in Anacapri, it's at V. Orlandi, 59 (☎081 837 15 24), to the right from the P. Vittoria bus stop. (Both open June-Sept. M-Sa 8:30am-8:30pm; Oct.-May 9am-1:30pm and 3:30-6:45pm.) Call the friendly **Alla Bussola di Hermes,** V. Traversa La Vigna, 14, to be picked up from Marina Grande. (☎081 838 20 10. Dorms and doubles L40,000/€20.65 per person.) The comfortable **Hotel Loreley,** V. G. Orlandi, 16, is 20m toward Capri from P. Vittoria on your left. (☎081 837 14 40; fax 081

837 13 99. Open Apr.-Oct. *Let's Go* discount: Doubles L180,000/€93; triples L220,000/€113.65. AmEx/MC/V.) In Capri, **Pensione Stella Maris,** V. Roma, 27, is opposite the bus stop. (☎081 837 04 52; fax 837 86 62. Doubles L120,000-180,000/€62-93. AmEx/MC/V.) Get **groceries** at **STANDA** in Capri. Head right at the fork at the end of V. Roma. (Open M-Sa 8:30am-1:30pm and 5-9pm, Su 9am-noon.) At night, dressed-to-kill Italians come out for Capri's *passegiatta;* bars around **Piazza Umberto** keep the music pumping late. Anacapri is cheaper and more fun. **Postal code:** Capri: 80073; Anacapri: 80021.

ISCHIA. Across the bay from crowded Capri, Eden-like Ischia offers sandy beaches, natural hot springs, ruins, forests, vineyards, and lemon groves. SEPSA **buses** #1, CD, and CS (every 20min., L1700/€0.90, day pass L5200/€2.70) follow the coast in a circular route, stopping at: **Ischia Porto,** a port formed by the crater of an extinct volcano; **Casamicciola Terme,** with a crowded beach and legendary thermal waters; **Lacco Ameno,** the oldest Greek settlement in the western Mediterranean; and finally, popular **Forio,** with its lively bars. Caremar **ferries** (☎081 98 48 18) arrive from Naples (1½hr., 14 per day, L9800/€5.10). **Linee Marittime Partenopee** (☎081 99 18 88) runs hydrofoils from Sorrento (L18,000/€9.30). Stay in Ischia Porto only if you want to be close to the ferries and nightlife—most *pensioni* are in Forio. **Pensione Di Lustro,** V. Filippo di Lustro, 9, is near the beach. (☎081 99 71 63; . Breakfast included. Doubles L90,000-120,000/€46.50-62.) The **Ostello "Il Gabbiano" (HI),** Strada Statale Forio-Panza, 162, between Forio and Panza, is accessible by buses #1, CS, or CD, and near the beach. (☎081 90 94 22. Breakfast included. Lockout 10am-1pm. Curfew 12:30am. Open Apr.-Sept. Dorms L30,000/€15.50; doubles L60,000/€31.) **Camping Internazionale** is at V. Foschini, 22, 15 minutes from the port. Take V. Alfredo de Luca from V. del Porto; bear right on V. Michele Mazzella at P. degi Eroi. (☎081 99 14 49; fax 99 14 72. Open mid-Apr. to mid-Oct. L16,000/€8.30 per person, L10,000/€5.20 per tent. 2-person bungalows L80,000/€41.35.)

SICILY (SICILIA)

With a history so steeped in chaos, catastrophe, and conquest, it's no wonder that the island of Sicily possesses such passionate volatility. The tempestuousness of Sicilian history and political life is matched only by the island's dramatic landscapes, dominated by craggy slopes. Entire cities have been destroyed in seismic and volcanic catastrophes, but those that have survived have lived up to the cliché and grown stronger; Sicilian pride is a testament to resilience during centuries of occupation and destruction.

▐ TRANSPORTATION

Tirrenia ferries (☎(091) 33 33 00) offers extensive service. From southern Italy, take a **train** to **Reggio di Calabria,** then a NGI or Meridiano **ferry** (40min.; NGI 10-12 per day, L1000/€0.55, Meridiano 11-15 per day, L3000/€1.55) or Ferrovie Statale **hydrofoil** (☎096 586 35 40) to **Messina,** Sicily's transport hub (25min., 12 per day, L5000/€2.60). Ferries also go to **Palermo** from: Cagliari, Sardinia (14hr., L60,500-78,000/€31.25-40.30); Genoa (20hr., 6 per week, L123,000-181,000/€63.55-93.50); Naples (11hr., 2 per day, L68,000-77,000/€35.15-39.80). **SAIS Trasporti** (☎091 617 11 41) and **SAIS** buses (☎091 616 60 28) serve destinations throughout the island, including **Corleone,** hometown of the Godfather. **Trains** head to **Messina** directly from Naples (4½hr., 7 per day, L41,800/€21.60) and Rome (9hr., 7 per day, L57,000/€29.45). Trains continue west to **Palermo** (3½hr., 15 per day, L19,500/€10.10) via **Milazzo** (45min., L4500/€2.35) and south to **Syracuse** (3hr., 14 per day, L17,000/€6.75) via **Taormina** (1hr., L5500/€2.85)

PALERMO   ☎091

From twisting streets lined by ancient ruins to the symbolic marionette strings of Italian organized crime, gritty urban Palermo is a city tied both to the past and present. To get to the magnificent **Teatro Massimo,** where the climactic opera scene of *The Godfather: Part III* was filmed, walk up V. Maqueda past the intersection of Quattro Canti and Corso Vittorio Emanuele. (Open Tu-Su 10am-3:30pm for

LA FAMIGLIA Pin-striped suits, machine guns, and *The Godfather* are a far cry from the reality of the **Sicilian Mafia.** The system has its roots in the *latifondi* (agricultural estates) of rural Sicily, where land managers and salaried militiamen (a.k.a. landlords and bouncers) protected their turf and people. Powerful because people owed them favors, strong because they supported one another, and feared because they did not hesitate to kill offenders, they founded a tradition that has dominated Sicilian life since the late 19th century. Since the mid-1980s, the Italian government has worked to curtail Mafia influence. Today Sicilians shy away from any Mafia discussion, referring to the system as *Cosa Nostra* (our thing).

20min. tours.) Up Corso Vittorio Emanuele, the **Palazzo dei Normanni** contains the ⬛**Cappella Palatina,** with gold, glass, and woodcarvings, and incredible golden mosaics. (Open M-Sa 9am-noon and 3-4:45pm, Su 9-10am and noon-1pm.) The morbid **Cappuchin Catacombs,** in P. Cappuccini, are only for the strong of stomach. Eight thousand corpses and twisted skeletons line the underground labyrinth. To get there, take buses #109 or 318 from Stazione Centrale to P. Indipendenza and then transfer to bus #327. (Open M-Su 9am-noon and 3-5pm. L2500/€1.30.)

Trains leave Stazione Centrale, in P. Giulio Cesare, at V. Roma and V. Maqueda, for Milan (19½hr., 2 per day, L95,000/€49.10) and Rome (11hr., 7 per day, L75,000/€38.75). All four **bus** lines run from V. Balsamo, next to the train station. After purchasing tickets, ask exactly where your bus will arrive and its logo. Ask an **AMAT** or **Metro** information booth for a combined metro and bus map. The **tourist office,** P. Castelnuovo, 34, is opposite Teatro Politeama; from the train station, take a bus to P. Politeama, at the end of V. Maqueda. (☎091 605 83 51; fax 58 63 38. Open daily 8am-5pm.) Homey **Hotel Regina,** Corso Vittorio Emanuele, 316, is off V. Maqueda. (☎091 611 42 16; fax 612 21 69. Kitchen. Singles L30,000/€15.50; doubles L70,000-80,000/€36.15-41.35.) To reach the **Hotel Cortese,** V. Scarparelli, 16, from the station, walk 10min. down V. Marqueda to V. dell'Università; look for the yellow sign to your left. (☎/fax 091 33 17 22. Breakfast L8000/€4.15. Singles L45,000-55,000/€23.25-28.40; doubles L70,000-85,000/€36.15-43.90. AmEx/D/MC/V.) Grab a bite to eat at **Pizzeria Bellini,** P. Bellini, 6. (Pizza from L7000/€3.65; cover L2000/€1.05. Open W-M 6am-1am.) **Postal code:** 90100.

AEOLIAN ISLANDS (ISOLE EOLIE)

Residents refer to this archipelago as *Le Perle di Mare* (The Pearls of the Sea), and Homer thought the **Aeolian** (or **Lipari**) **Islands** to be the second home of the gods. Sparkling seas, incomparable beaches, and fi3ery volcanoes all contribute to the area's stunning beauty.

▌ TRANSPORTATION. The archipelago lies near Sicily, north of **Milazzo,** the principal embarkation point. Hop off a **train** from Messina (40min., L4500/€2.35) or Palermo (3hr., L15,500/€8) and onto an orange **AST bus** for the port (10min., every hr., L1200/€0.65). Navigazione Generale Italiana (☎09 09 28 40 91) and Siremar (☎09 09 28 32 42) **ferries** depart for: Lipari (2hr., L10,500-11,500/€5.45-5.95); Stromboli (5hr., L16,500-19,000/€8.55-9.85); Vulcano (1½hr., L10,000-11,000/€5.20-5.70). Siremar and SNAV (☎09 09 28 45 09) **hydrofoils** *(aliscafi)* make the trip in half the time but cost almost twice as much. All three have ticket offices on V. Dei Mille facing the port in Milazzo. Ferries leave for the islands less frequently from **Naples'** Molo Beverello port. Ferries between Lipari and Vulcano cost L4500/€2.35; between Lipari and Stromboli, L25,500/€13.20.

LIPARI. With cheap hostels, great beaches, and hopping nightlife, Lipari, the largest and most developed island, is an ideal launching point for daytrips to the six other islands. Lipari's best sights, aside from its beaches, are in the medieval **castello,** the site of an ancient Greek acropolis. The fortress shares its hill with an **archaeological park,** the **San Bartolo church,** and the superb ⬛**Museo Archeologico Eoliano,** which houses galleries of 4th- and 5th-century Greek and Sicilian pottery.

(Open May-Oct. M-Su 9am-1:30pm and 4-7pm; Nov.-Apr. M-Su 9am-1:30pm and 3-6pm. L8000/€4.15.) The popular **Spiaggia Bianca** and **Spiaggia Porticello** beaches are *the* spot for semi-nude sunbathing; to get there, take the Lipari-Cavedi **bus** to Canneto. Rent a raft, canoe, or kayak (L6000-8000/€3.10-4.15 per hr., L25,000-35,000/€12.95-18.10 per day) to explore the nearby **coves** or **pumice mines.** Take the Lipari-Quattropani bus to the Pianoconte stop for a great view of the island from **Monte S. Angelo;** ask for directions to the path.

The **AAST delle Isole Eolie tourist office,** Corso Vittorio Emanuele, 202, is up the street from the ferry dock. (☎ 090 988 00 95. Open July-Aug. M-Sa 8am-2pm and 4-10pm, Su 8am-2pm; Sept.-June M-F 8am-2pm and 4:30-7:30pm, Sa 8am-2pm.) Down a quiet street in the center of town, **Casa Vittorio,** Vico Sparviero, 15, offers a variety of rooms. If the door is locked, continue to the end of the street and turn right; the owner lives at the red iron gate. (☎ 090 981 15 23. May-July singles L30,000-40,000/€15.50-20.65; doubles L60,000-80,000/€31-41.35.) **Tivoli (Quatropani),** has the best views on the island. Take the bus to Quatropani and follow signs to the hotel. (☎ 090 988 60 31. June L60,000/€31; July-Aug. L80,000/€41.35; half-*pension* L80,000/€41.35. Child discounts.) **Camp** at **Baia Unci,** V. Marina Garibaldi, 2, 2km from Lipari at the entrance to the hamlet of Canneto. (☎ 09 09 81 19 09. Reserve Aug. Open mid-Mar. to mid-Oct. June-Aug. L15,000-27,000/€7.75-13.95 per person; Mar.-May L11,000-14,000/€5.70-7.25 per person.) **Il Galeone,** Corso Vittorio Emanuele, 220, close to the ferry dock, serves excellent food on an outdoor shaded terrace. (Pizza, *primi*, and *menù* from L7000/€3.65. Open June-Sept. daily 8am-midnight; Oct.-May Th-Tu 8pm-midnight.) Stock up at **UPIM supermarket,** Corso Vittorio Emanuele, 212. (Open M-Sa 8am-3:20pm and 4-11pm.) **Postal code:** 98055. ☎ 090.

STROMBOLI. Stromboli's active **volcano** spews orange cascades of lava and molten rock roughly every 10min. each night. **Hiking** the *vulcano* on your own, particularly the descent, is **illegal** and **dangerous,** but **Guide Alpine Autorizzate** offers tours. (☎ 090 98 62 11. Tours depart P. Vincenzo M, W, and Sa-Su 5:30pm; return midnight. L35,000/€18.10.) Bring sturdy shoes, a flashlight, snacks, water, and warm clothes. From July to September, forget finding a room unless you have a reservation; your best bet may be one of the non-reservable *affittacamere.* Expect to pay between L30,000/€15.50 and L50,000/€25.85 for a room.

LATVIA (LATVIJA)

LATVIAN LAT

US$1 = 0.62LVL	1LVL = US$1.61
CDN$1 = 0.40LVL	1LVL = CDN$2.49
UK£1 = 0.90LVL	1LVL = UK£1.11
IR£1 = 0.72LVL	1LVL = IR£1.39
AUS$1 = 0.33LVL	1LVL = AUS$3.02
NZ$1 = 0.27LVL	1LVL = NZ$3.67
ZAR1 = 0.075LVL	1LVL = ZAR13.38
DM1 = 0.29LVL	1LVL = DM3.45
EUR€1 = 0.57LVL	1LVL = EUR€1.76

PHONE CODE	**Country code:** 371. **International dialing prefix:** 00. From outside Latvia, dial int'l dialing prefix (see inside back cover) + 371 + city code + local number.

With the smallest majority of natives of the three Baltic States, Latvia remains the least developed. Except for a brief period of independence that ended with World War II, Latvia was ruled by Germans, Swedes, and Russians from the 13th century until 1991. A half-century of Soviet occupation resulted in a mass exodus of Latvians and a huge influx of Russians. Attitudes toward the many Russians who still live in the country are softening, but evidence of national pride abounds, from patriotically renamed streets filled with crimson-and-white flags to a rediscovery of native holidays predating Christian invasions. Although the rest of the country is mostly a provincial expanse of green hills covered by tall birches and pines, Rīga is a westernizing capital attracting more and more international attention.

Latvia is best enjoyed with a chilled glass of *Let's Go: Eastern Europe 2002*.

FACTS AND FIGURES

Official Name: Republic of Latvia.
Capital: Rīga.
Population: 2.4 million.
Land Area: 64,589 sq. km.

Climate: Maritime; wet, moderate winters, and temperate, pleasant summers.
Languages: Lettish, Lithuanian, Russian.
Religions: Lutheran, Roman Catholic, Russian Orthodox.

ESSENTIALS

DOCUMENTS AND FORMALITIES

VISAS. Irish, UK, and US citizens can visit Latvia for up to 90 days without a visa. Citizens of Australia, Canada, New Zealand, and South Africa require 90-day visas, obtainable at a Latvian consulate. Travelers may obtain 10-day visas at the airport in Rīga. Single-entry visas cost US$15; multiple-entry cost US$30 to US$75. For extensions, apply in Rīga to the Department of Immigration and Citizenship, Raiņa bulv. 5 (☎ 721 91 81).

EMBASSIES. All foreign embassies are in **Rīga** (see p. 646). For Latvian embassies at home: **Australia** (consulate), P.O. Box 457, Strathfield NSW 2135 (☎ (61) 3 949 969 20); **Canada,** 280 Albert St. Ste. 300, Ottawa, ON K1P 5G8 (☎613-238-6014; www.magmacom.com/~latemb); **South Africa** (consulate), 4 Lafayette, 3a Harrow Road, Sandhurst, Sandton 2196 (☎ (27) 11 783 9442); **UK,** 45 Nottingham Pl., London W1M 3FE (☎ (0171) 312 00 40; and **US,** 4325 17th St. NW, Washington, D.C. 20011 (☎202-726-8213; www.latvia-usa.org).

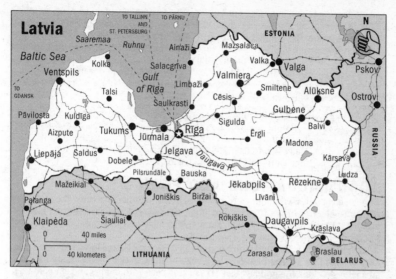

TRANSPORTATION

Air Baltic, SAS, Finnair, Lufthansa, and others fly into Rīga's airport. **Trains** link Latvia to Berlin, Moscow, St. Petersburg, Tallinn, Lviv, Odessa, and Vilnius. Trains are cheap and efficient, but stations aren't well marked, so always have a map. The **suburban rail** system renders the entire country a suburb of Rīga. For daytrips from Rīga, you're best off taking the **electric train. Eurail** is not valid. Latvia's quicker **bus** network reaches Prague, Tallinn, Vilnius, and Warsaw. **Ferries** run to Rīga from Stockholm, Sweden and Kiel, Germany. **Hitchhiking** is common, but hitchers may be expected to pay. *Let's Go* does not recommend hitchhiking.

TOURIST SERVICES AND MONEY

EMERGENCY   Police: ☎ 02. Ambulance: ☎ 03. Fire: ☎ 01.

Look for the green "i" marking some **tourist offices,** which are rather scarce. Private tourist offices such as **Patricia** are much more helpful. The Latvian currency is the **Lat,** divided into 100 *santims*. Inflation averages around 3%. There are many ATMs in Rīga linked to Cirrus, MC, and Visa, and at least one or two in larger towns. Larger businesses, restaurants, and hotels accept MC and Visa. Traveler's checks are harder to use; both AmEx and Thomas Cook can be converted in Rīga, but Thomas Cook is a safer bet elsewhere. It's often hard to exchange currencies other than US dollars. If a tip is expected, it will most often be included in the bill. Expect to be bought a drink if you talk with someone awhile; repay the favor in kind.

COMMUNICATION

MAIL. Ask for *gaisa pastu* to send something by airmail. Letters abroad cost 0.40Ls, postcards 0.30Ls. Mail can be received through *Poste Restante*. Address envelope as follows: First Name SURNAME, *Poste Restante*, Stacijas laukums 1, Rīga LV-1050, LATVIA.

TELEPHONES. Latvia is by far the most difficult of the Baltic states from which to call the US; there's no way to make a free call on a Latvian phone to an international operator. Most telephones take cards (available in 2, 3, 5, or 10Ls denominations) from post offices, telephone offices, and large state stores. International calls can

LATVIA

be made from telephone offices or booths. Access numbers include: **AT&T,** ☎ 700 70 07 in Rīga, ☎ 8 2 700 70 07 everywhere else in Latvia; **British Telecom** ☎ 800 1044; and **MCI,** ☎ 800 88 88. If a number is only six digits long, you must dial a ☎ 2 before the number; if it's seven digits, you don't need to dial anything extra before the number. To call abroad from an analog phone, dial ☎ 1, then 00, then the country code. From a digital phone, simply dial ☎ 00, then the country code. The phone system has been undergoing changes; phone offices and *Riga in Your Pocket* have the latest information. **Email** is only available in Rīga.

LANGUAGES. Heavily influenced by German, Russian, Estonian, and Swedish, Latvian is one of two languages (the other is Lithuanian) in the Baltic language group. Russian is in disfavor in the countryside but is more acceptable and widespread in Rīga. Many young Latvians study English, but don't rely upon it. Older Latvians know some German. For Latvian basics, see p. 985.

ACCOMMODATIONS AND FOOD

College **dormitories,** which open to travelers in the summer, are often the cheapest places to sleep. In Rīga, Patricia arranges **homestays** and apartment **rentals** for around 10Lt per night (see p. 647). Many towns have only one hotel (if any) in the budget range; expect to pay 3-15Ls per night.

Latvian food is heavy and starchy, but tasty. Big cities offer foreign cuisine, and Rīga is one of the easiest places to be a vegetarian in all the Baltics. Tasty national specialties include the holiday dish *zirņi* (gray peas with onions and smoked fat), *maizes zupa* (bread soup usually made from corn bread, and full of currants, cream, and other goodies), and the warming *Rīgas* (or *Melnais*) *balzams* (a black liquor great with ice cream, Coke, or coffee). Dark rye bread is a staple. Try *speķa rauši*, a warm pastry, or *biezpienmaize*, bread with sweet curds. Dark-colored *kaņepju sviests* (hemp butter) is good but too diluted for "medicinal" purposes. Latvian beer, primarily from the Aldaris brewery, is stellar, particularly *Porteris*.

HOLIDAYS

New Year's Day (Jan. 1); Good Friday (Mar. 29); Catholic Easter (Mar. 29); Labor Day (May 1); Ligo (Midsummer Festival; June 23); Independence Day (1918; Nov. 18); Ziemsvetki (Christmas; Dec. 25-26); New Year's Eve (Dec. 31).

RĪGA   ☎ 02

The self-proclaimed capital of the Baltics, sprawling Rīga feels strangely out of proportion as the capital of small, struggling Latvia. Rīga envisions itself as the "Paris of the East," but 24hr. casinos and tinted windows make it feel more like Las Vegas. Since the fall of the USSR, Rīga has been rebuilding, trying new political and economic systems, and at long last testing out what it means to be Latvian. While the city has a long way to go to becoming a major European capital, it has established a new identity as the cultural and social center of the Baltics.

▐ TRANSPORTATION

Flights: Lidosta Rīga (☎ 720 70 09), 8km southwest. Take bus #22 from Gogol iela.

Trains: Centrālā Stacija (Central Station) Stacijas laukums (☎ 583 30 95), down the street from the bus station, behind the giant digital clock tower, with long-distance trains in the larger building to the left. To: **Moscow** (15½hr., 2 per day, 32Ls); **St. Petersburg** (13hr., 1 per day, 26Ls); **Vilnius** (8hr., 1 per day, 14Ls).

Buses: Bus station (Autoosta), Prāgas 1 (☎ 721 36 11), 200m closer to the Daugava River than the train station, across the canal from the central market. To: **Minsk** (10hr., 2 per day, 7Ls); **Tallinn** (5-6hr., 7 per day, 6-7Ls); **Vilnius** (6hr., 3 per day, 6Ls). **Eurolines** (☎ 721 40 80; fax 750 31 34), at the bus station right of the ticket windows, goes to **Prague** (30hr., 1 per week, 38Ls) and **Warsaw** (14hr., 1 per day, 15Ls). Open M-F 8am-7pm, Sa 9am-6pm.

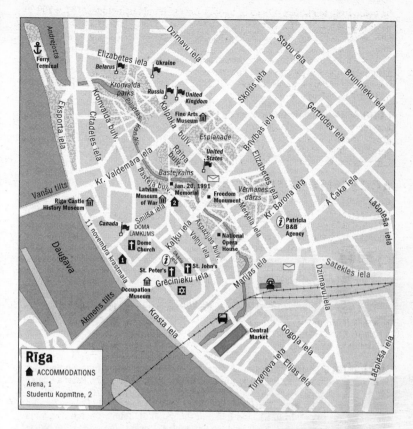

Rīga
▲ ACCOMMODATIONS
Arena, 1
Studentu Kopmītne, 2

🔋 ORIENTATION AND PRACTICAL INFORMATION

The city is neatly divided in half by **Brīvības bulvāris,** which leads from the outskirts to the **Freedom Monument** in the center, continuing through **Vecrīga** (Old Rīga) as **Kaļķu iela.** WIth your back to the trains, turn left on the busy Marijas iela and right on any of the small streets beyond the canal to reach Vecrīga. For good maps and tons of information, pick up *Riga in Your Pocket* (0.60Ls) at kiosks, hotels, or travel agencies.

Tourist Office: Patricia, Elizabetes iela 22-26, 3rd fl. (☎728 48 68; www.baltic-travel.net), 2 blocks from the train station. Arranges home stays (US$20) and can help with Russian visas (6-day US$80). Open M-F 9:15am-8pm, Sa-Su 10:15am-1pm.

Embassies: Canada, Doma laukums 4, 3rd and 4th fl. (☎722 63 15; fax 783 01 40). Open M-F 9am-3pm. **Russia,** Antonijas iela 2 (☎721 25 79). Open M-F 9am-5:30pm. **UK,** Alunāna iela 5 (☎733 81 26; fax 733 81 32). Open M-F 9am-1pm and 2-5pm. **US,** Raiņa bulv. 7 (☎721 00 05; fax 782 00 47). Open M-F 9am-noon and 2-4pm.

Currency Exchange: At any of the *Valutos Maiņa* kiosks or shops in the city. **Unibanka,** Kaļķu iela 13, with long hours, gives cash advances (4% commission) and cashes AmEx and Thomas Cook traveler's checks (3% commission). **ATMs** are common.

Pharmacies: Mēness aptieka, Brīrības 121 (☎737 78 89). Open 24hr.

Internet Access: Latnet, Raiņa 29 (☎721 12 41). 0.50Ls per hr. Open M-Th 9am-6pm, F 9am-5pm.

Telephones: Brīvības bulv. 19 (☎701 87 38). Open 24hr.

Post Offices: Stacijas laukums 1 (☎ 701 88 04; www.riga.post.lv), near the train station. *Poste Restante* at window #2. Open M-F 8am-7pm, Sa 8am-4pm, Su 10am-4pm. Address mail to be held: First name SURNAME, *Poste Restante*, Stacijas laukums 1, Riga, **LV-1050** LATVIA.

ACCOMMODATIONS

Rīga's prices for decent rooms are generally the highest in the Baltics. If you are interested in a **private room,** try your luck with **Patricia** (see Tourist Office, above).

■ **Arena,** Palasta iela 5 (☎ 722 85 83), unmarked, by Dome Cathedral. The cheapest place in town. Beautiful views of Vecrīga. Call ahead. Open Apr.-Oct. 3- and 4-bed dorms 4Ls.

Studentu Kopmītne (Student Dormitories), Basteja bul. 10 (☎ 721 62 21). From the bus station, cross under the tracks, take the foot tunnel under the highway, and bear right on Aspazijei bul. Call ahead. Curfew midnight. Doubles 4-5Ls per person.

Turība, Graudu iela 68 (☎ 761 75 43; hotel@tmc.lv). From Latviešu Strēlnika Laukums (statue of the riflemen), take trolleybus #8 to the Grauda stop. Backtrack to the corner and turn left onto Graudu iela; reception in the far campus building next to the minigolf. Student dorms. Buses rare after 11:30pm. Triples and quads 2.50-8Ls per person.

FOOD

Look for 24-hour food and liquor stores along **Elizabetes, Marijas,** and **Gertrūdes iela.** The **Centrālais Tirgus** (Central Market) is one of the largest in Europe. (Open M-Sa 8am-5pm, Su 8am-3pm.) Descend from the entrance on Arsenāla to **Alus Arsenāls,** Pils Laukums 4, for cheap, excellent Latvian cuisine. (Open daily 11am-midnight.)

SIGHTS

VECRĪGA (OLD RĪGA). Take time to peruse Vecrīga's winding streets and ponder its unusual architecture. From the top of the dark 123m spire of **St. Peter's Church** (Sv. Pētera baznīca), you can see the entire city and the Baltic. *(On Kungu iela, off Kaļķu iela. Open Tu-Su 10am-7pm. Church free. Tower 1.50Ls, students 1Ls.)* Follow Skārņu iela, opposite the church, to Jāņa iela and the small **St. John's Church** (Sv. Jāņa baznīca); an alleyway on the left leads to **St. John's Courtyard** (Jāņa sēta), the oldest populated site in Rīga, where the city's first castle stood. *(Church open Tu-Su 11am-6pm.)* Follow Kungu iela across Kaļķu iela and take a right on Jauniela into cobblestone **Dome Square,** home of the **Dome Cathedral** (Doma baznīca), begun in 1226. *(Open Tu-F 1-5pm, Sa 10am-2pm. 0.50Ls. Concerts W and F 7pm.)* Follow Jēkaba iela to Smilšu iela to eight floors of fun and eight centuries of destruction at the ■**Latvian Museum of War** (Latvijas kara muzejs), Smilšu iela 20, inside the cannon-ball studded walls of the **Powder Tower,** Rīga's most interesting military site. *(Open Tu-Su 10am-6pm. 0.50Ls, students 0.25Ls. Foreign-language tours 3Ls.)*

FREEDOM MONUMENT AND ENVIRONS. In the center of the city stands the beloved **Freedom Monument** (Brivibas Piemineklis; affectionately known as "Milda"). *(At the corner of Raiņa bul. and Brīvības iela.)* Continuing along Kaļķu iela from the Freedom Monument toward the river, you'll see the **Latvian Riflemen Monument,** in honor of Lenin's famous bodyguards, one of the few Soviet monuments not torn down. Rising behind the statues are the black walls of the ■**Occupation Museum** (Okupācijas muzejs), Strēlnieku laukums 1, perhaps the finest museum in the Baltics. The initial Soviet occupation is depicted so vividly that you can almost hear the Red Army marching through the streets of Rīga. *(Open daily 11am-5pm. Free.)* Just beyond the museums stands the unusual and magnificent **Blackheads House,** Ratslavkums 7. Built in 1344 and completely destroyed between the Nazis and the Soviets, it was reconstructed in 2001 in honor of Rīga's 800th birthday.

BASTEJKALNS. A central park near the old city moat **Pīlsētas kanāls,** Bastejkalns houses ruins of the old city walls. Across and around the canal, five red stone slabs

THE BOY WHO CRIED "NAPOLEON!" In 1812,

Rīga was devastated by a single herd of cattle. Traveling happily through the countryside, the nefarious bovines raised a cloud of dust that was clearly visible to the city's residents. Believing the herd to be Napoleon's army, the people set fire to the city, razing 740 buildings and hundreds of acres of farmland. The citizens later realized that the fearsome marauders were really only looking for grass and a good human to milk them. Meanwhile, Napoleon entered via a different route, wreaking his own havoc.

stand as memorials to the dead of January 20, 1991, when Soviet special forces stormed the Interior Ministry on Raiņa bul. At the north end of Bastejkalns, on Kr. Valdemāra iela, sits the **National Theater,** where Latvia first declared its independence on November 18, 1918. *(Open daily 10am-7pm.)*

ENTERTAINMENT AND NIGHTLIFE

Summer is the off season for ballet, opera, and theater; the rest of the year, purchase tickets at Teātra 10/12. (☎722 57 47. Open daily 10am-7pm.) The **Rīga Ballet** carries on the proud dancing tradition of native star Mikhail Baryshnikov. **Paddy Whelan's,** Grēcineku iela 4, is Rīga's first Irish pub. (Guinness 1.50Ls. Open Su-Th 10am-midnight, F-Sa 10am-2am.) **Groks Stacija,** Kaļķu iela 22, near the Freedom Monument, is just like a Metro stop, except it's a disco. (Aldaris 0.70Ls. Open daily noon-6am.) For a queer spot, try **XXL,** A Kalina 4, off K. Barona iela; buzz door to be let in. (www.gay.lv/xxl. Open 4pm-6am.)

DAYTRIPS FROM RĪGA

DĀRZIŅI. The **Salaspils Memorial** marks the remains of the Kurtenhof concentration camp, which claimed 100,000 victims in the name of the Third Reich. The inscription over the entrance reads "Beyond this gate the earth moans." Four clusters of massive sculptures watch over the Way of Suffering, the circular path that connects barracks foundations. A black box covered in wreaths emits a low ticking sound, like the pulse of a beating heart. Green electric **trains** travel frequently from Rīga to Dārziņi (*not* "Salaspils" on the Krustpils line; 20-30min., 14 per day, 0.30Ls). Make sure the train will be stopping at Dārziņi before leaving Rīga.

JŪRMALA. Sun-bleached, powder-fine sand, warm waters, and boardwalks have drawn visitors to this narrow spit since the 19th century. Jūrmala (YOUR-ma-la) became a popular summer resort with the Soviet elite, and as a result, Latvian independence proved disastrous to the area. Nonetheless, Jūrmala is swiftly recovering, as crowds of tourists again discover its beaches and shops. Any of the coastal towns between **Bulduri** and **Dubulti** are popular for sunning and swimming, but if you're looking for Jūrmala's social center, go to **Majori.** Trainloads of people file to the beach or wander along **Jomas iela,** Majori's pedestrian street, lined with cafes, restaurants, and shops. From the train station, cross the road, walk through the cluster of trees in the small park, turn right, and you're there. The **tourist office** is at Jomas iela 42. (☎642 76; jurmalainfo@mail.bkc.lv; www.jurmala.lv. Open M-F 9am-5pm.) Dining and drinking options abound along **Jomas iela.**

Lielupe, the town with beach access closest to Rīga, offers dramatic sand dunes. At the other end of Jūrmala, **Ķemeri** was once the Russian Empire's prime health resort. Therapeutic mud baths, sulfur water, and other cures have operated here since the mid-18th century. A handful of towns dot the coast; from Rīga, beachless **Priedaine** is the first train stop in Jūrmala; the tracks then pass over the Lielupe River and quickly run through Lielupe, Bulduri, Dzintari, Majori, Dubulti, Jaundubulti, Pumpuri, Melluži, Asari, and Vaivari before heading back inland to Sloka, Kudra, and Ķemeri. The **commuter rail** runs trains in both directions (every 30min., from 5am-11:30pm), and to **Majori** (30min., 0.40Ls). **Public buses** (0.18Ls) and **microbuses** (0.20-0.30Ls) also string together Jūrmala's towns.

LIECHTENSTEIN

PHONE CODE **Country code: 0423. International dialing prefix: 00.**

A tourist brochure for Liechtenstein (pop. 31,000) amusingly mislabeled the already tiny 160 sq. km country as an even tinier 160 sq. m; that's just about how much most tourists see of the world's only German-speaking monarchy. To enter Liechtenstein, catch a **bus** from **Sargans** or **Buchs** in Switzerland, or from **Feldkirch,** Austria (20min., 3.60SFr). A cheap, efficient **Post Bus** system links all 11 villages (short trips 2.40SFr; long trips 3.60SFr; students half-price; SwissPass valid). Remember to carry your passport when traveling. The **official language** is German; the **currency** is the Swiss franc (SFr). **Police:** ☎ 117. **Medical emergencies:** ☎ 144. **Postal code:** FL-9490.

VADUZ AND LOWER LIECHTENSTEIN. More a hamlet than a national capital, Vaduz is not a budget-friendly place. Above town, the 12th-century **Schloß Vaduz** is home to Hans-Adam II, Prince of Liechtenstein. It's not open to tourists, but every year the prince invites everyone in the country to celebrate Liechtenstein's national day (Aug. 15). Stamp collectors will enjoy the one-room **Briefmarkenmuseum** (Stamp Museum), Städtle 37. (Open daily Apr.-Oct. 10am-noon and 1:30-5:30pm; Nov.-Mar. 10am-noon and 1:30-5pm. Free.) Liechtenstein's **national tourist office,** Städtle 37, one block up the hill from the Vaduz Post Bus stop, stamps passports (2SFr or 20AS), sells **hiking maps** (15.50SFr), locates rooms, and has free maps and hiking advice. (☎ 232 14 43. Open July-Sept. M-F 8am-5:30pm, Sa-Su 9am-noon and 1:30-5pm; Oct.-June M-F 8am-noon and 1:30-5:30pm; Apr. and Oct. also Sa 9am-noon and 1:30-5pm; May also Sa-Su 9am-noon and 1:30-5pm.) Take bus #1 to Mühleholz to reach **Jugendherberge (HI),** Untere Rüttig. 6, in nearby Schaan. (☎ 232 50 22. Breakfast and showers included. Laundry 8SFr. Reception 7-10am and 5-10pm. No lockout. Curfew 10pm; key code for the door available. Open Feb.-Oct. Dorms 27.60SFr; doubles 36.60SFr; quads 126.4SFr. HI members only.) Your best bet for a cheap meal is **Migros supermarket,** Aulestr. 20, across from the tour bus parking lot in Vaduz. (Open M-F 8am-1pm and 1:30-6:30pm, Sa 8am-4pm.)

Liechtenstein

UPPER LIECHTENSTEIN. The villages in the upper country have gorgeous views and great hiking. **Triesenberg** (take bus #10), the principal town, was founded in the by the Walsers, who fled Switzerland in the 13th century. The **tourist office** (☎262 19 26) shares a building with the **Walser Heimatmuseum.** (Both open Sept.-May Tu-F 1:30-5:30pm, Sa 1:30-5pm; June-Aug. also Su 2-5pm. Museum 2SFr.) Signs at the post office point to a variety of walks and **hikes. Malbun** offers great **hiking** and affordable **skiing** on the other side of the mountain (ski day pass 33SFr; 6-day pass 136SFr, off season 129SFr). Contact the **tourist office** for more information. (☎263 65 77. Open June-Oct. and mid-Dec. to mid-Apr. M-Sa 9am-noon and 1:30-5pm.) The best place to stay for hiking and skiing access is **Hotel Alpen,** which is close to the bus stop and tourist office. (☎263 11 81. Reception 8am-10pm. Open mid-May to Oct. and mid-Dec. to Apr. In summer 45-55SFr per person, with amenities 70-85SFr; in winter add 20SFr.)

LITHUANIA
(LIETUVA)

LITUANIAN LITAI

US$1 = 4.00LT	1LT = US$0.25
CDN$1 = 2.59LT	1LT = CDN$0.39
UK£1 = 5.78LT	1LT = UK£0.17
IR£1 = 4.64LT	1LT = IR£0.22
AUS$1 = 2.13LT	1LT = AUS$0.47
NZ$1 = 1.75LT	1LT = NZ$0.57
ZAR1 = 0.48LT	1LT = ZAR2.08
DM1 = 1.87LT	1LT = DM0.53
EUR€1 = 3,66LT	1LT = EUR€0.287

PHONE CODES	**Country code:** 370. **International dialing prefix:** 810. From outside Lithuania, dial int'l dialing prefix (see inside back cover) + 370 + city code + local number.

Once the largest country in Europe, stretching into modern-day Ukraine, Belarus, and Poland, Lithuania has since faced oppression from tsarist Russia, Nazi Germany, and Soviet Russia. The first Baltic nation to declare its independence from the USSR in 1990, Lithuania has become more Western with every passing year. Its spectacular capital city of Vilnius welcomes droves of tourists into the largest old town in Europe, recently covered in a bright new coat of paint from city-wide renovations. In the other corner of the country, the mighty Baltic Sea washes up against Palanga and Kuršių Nerija, also called the Curonian Spit.

For the pith of Lithuania, *Let's Go: Eastern Europe 2002* is all the mania.

FACTS AND FIGURES

Official Name: Republic of Lithuania.
Capital: Vilnius.
Major cities: Šiauliai, Klaipėda.
Population: 3.6 million.
Land Area: 65,200 sq. km.

Climate: Rain, especially in winter; cold winters and moderate summers.
Languages: Lithuanian, Polish, Russian.
Religions: Roman Catholic (80%), Lutherans largest minority.

DISCOVER LITHUANIA

Vilnius is touted as the "New Prague" for its thriving art scene and sprawling Old Town (p. 654); don't miss the nearby fairy-tale **Trakai Castle.** Sun, fun, and sea lions welcome visitors to **Klaipėda** (p. 658), the Curonian Spit's premier beach town.

ESSENTIALS

DOCUMENTS AND FORMALITIES

VISAS. Citizens of Australia, Canada, Ireland, New Zealand, the UK, and the US do not need a visa for visits up to 90 days. Citizens of South Africa who have visas from Estonia or Latvia can use those to enter Lithuania; otherwise, regular 90-day visas are required. Obtain visas from the nearest embassy or consulate: single-entry visas cost US$10; multiple-entry visas US$20; transit visas (good for 48hr.) US$5. Obtaining a visa extension is tricky; try the **Immigration Service** in Vilnius, Virkių g. 3 #6 (☎75 64 53) or at the **Immigration Department,** Saltoniškių 19 (☎72 58 64).

EMBASSIES. Foreign embassies in Lithuania are in Vilnius (see p. 654). For Lithuanian embassies at home: **Australia** (consulate), 47 Somers St., Burwood Victoria 3125 (☎(03) 98 08 83 00; fax 98 08 83 00); **Canada** (consulate), 1573 Bloor W., Toronto, ON (☎416-538-2992); **South Africa** (consulate), Killarney Mall, 1st fl., Riviera Rd., Killarney Johannesburg; P.O. Box 1737, Houghton, 2041 (☎(011) 486 36 60; fax 486 36 50); **UK**, 84 Gloucester Pl., London W1H 3HN (☎(20) 74 86 64 01; fax 74 86 64 03; www.users.globalnet.co.uk/~lralon/); and **US**, 2622 16th St. NW, Washington, D.C. 20009-4202 (☎202-234-5860; fax 202-328-0466; www.ltembassyus.org).

TRANSPORTATION

Planes land in Vilnius from: Berlin (2hr.); Moscow (2hr.); and Stockholm (2hr.); and Warsaw (1¼hr.). Ferries connect Klaipėda with German cities Kiel (34hr.) and Muhkran (18hr.). Vilnius, Kaunas, and Klaipėda are easily reached by train or bus from Belarus, Estonia, Latvia, Poland, and Russia. Domestically, **buses** are faster, more common, and only a bit more expensive than the often crowded **trains.** If you do ride the rails, two major lines cross Lithuania: one runs north-south from Latvia through Šiauliai and Kaunas to Poland, and the other runs east-west from Belarus through Vilnius and Kaunas to Kaliningrad.

TOURIST SERVICES AND MONEY

EMERGENCY	Police: ☎02. Ambulance: ☎03. Fire: ☎01.

Tourist offices are generally knowledgeable. **Litinterp** is the most helpful; they will reserve accommodations, usually without a surcharge. Vilnius, Kaunas, and Klaipėda each have an edition of the *In Your Pocket* series.The unit of currency is the Litas (1Lt=100 centų), plural Litai. Since 1994, it has been fixed to the US dollar at US$1 = 4Lt. It's difficult to exchange currencies other than US dollars and Deutschmarks. Traveler's checks, especially AmEx and Thomas Cook, can be cashed at most banks (usually for a 2-3% commission). Cash advances are available on Visa cards. Vilniaus Bankas accepts major credit cards and traveler's checks for a small commission. ATMs, especially Cirrus, are readily available in most cities. Hostel beds run US$6-8, hotels US$15-20, and meals US$4-6. Tipping is not expected, but some Lithuanians leave 10% for excellent service.

COMMUNICATION

MAIL AND TELEPHONES. Airmail *(oro paštu)* letters abroad cost 1.70Lt, postcards 1.20Lt, and usually take about 7 days to reach the US. EMS international mail takes 3-5 days. There are two kinds of public phones: rectangular ones accept magnetic strip cards and rounded ones accept chip cards. Both are sold at phone offices and many kiosks in denominations of 3.54Lt, 7.08Lt, and 28.32Lt. Calls to Estonia and Latvia cost 1.65Lt per minute; Europe 5.80Lt; and the US 7.32Lt. Most countries can be dialed directly. Dial ☎8, wait for the 2nd

tone, dial ☎10, then enter the country code and number. International direct dialing numbers include: **AT&T,** ☎(8) 80 09 28 00; **British Telecom,** ☎(8) 80 09 00 44; **Canada Direct,** ☎(8) 80 09 10 04; and **Sprint,** ☎(8) 80 09 10 04. For countries to which direct dialing is unavailable, dial ☎8, wait for the 2nd tone, and dial ☎194 or 195 for English-speaking operators.

LANGUAGES. Lithuanian is one of only two Baltic languages (Latvian is the other). Polish is helpful in the south, German on the coast, and Russian most places. For phrases, see p. 986.

ACCOMMODATIONS

Lithuania has several **youth hostels,** with plans for more to open. HI membership is nominally required, but a LJNN guest card (US$3 at any of the hostels) will suffice. The head office in Vilnius has *Hostel Guide*, a handy booklet with info on bike and car rentals, reservations, and maps showing how to reach various hostels.

HEALTH AND SAFETY

A triangle pointing downward indicates men's bathrooms; an upward-facing triangle indicates women's bathrooms. Many restrooms are nothing but a hole in the ground. Well-stocked pharmacies are everywhere. Drink bottled water, and boil tap water for 10 minutes first if you must drink it.

FOOD AND DRINK

Lithuanian cuisine tends to be heavy and very greasy. Keeping a vegetarian or kosher diet will prove difficult, if not impossible. Restaurants serve various types of *blynai* (pancakes) with *mėsa* (meat) or *varške* (cheese). *Cepelinai* are heavy, potato-dough missiles of meat, cheese, and mushrooms, launched from street stands throughout Western Lithuania. *Šaltibarščiai* is a beet and cucumber soup prevalent in the east. *Karbonadas* is breaded pork fillet, and *koldunai* are meat dumplings. Lithuanian beer is very good. *Kalnapis* is popular in Vilnius and most of Lithuania, *Baltijos* reigns supreme around Klaipėda, and the award-winning *Utenos* is widely available. Lithuanian vodka *(degtinė)* is also very popular.

HOLIDAYS

Holidays: New Year's Day (Jan. 1); Independence Day (1918; Feb. 16); Restoration of Lithuanian Statehood (Mar. 11); Catholic Easter (Apr. 15-16); Labor Day (May 1); Midsummer Night (June 23); Day of Statehood (July 6); All Saints' Day (Nov. 1); All Souls' Day (Nov. 2); Christmas (Dec. 24-25).

VILNIUS ☎822

Deluged by new businesses and foreign investment, Vilnius remains self-aware, proud, and staunchly Lithuanian. Founded in 1321 after a prophetic dream by Grand Duke Gediminas, Vilnius was among the chief cities of the Polish-Lithuanian Commonwealth, the largest empire in Europe, within 60 years. After World War II, the city fell into the grip of the USSR but managed to resist the mass Sovietization that befell other provincial capitals. Today Vilnius's narrow, cobblestoned streets are the cleanest and safest in the Baltics.

▌ TRANSPORTATION

Flights: The airport *(oro uostas),* Rodūnės Kelias 2 (☎30 66 66), is 5km south. Take bus #1 from the station or #2 from the Sparta stop of trolley bus #16 on Kauno g.

Trains: Geležinkelio Stotis, Geležinkelio g. 16 (☎33 00 86). Tickets for all trains are sold in the yellow addition left of the main station; windows #3 and 4 are specifically for trains to western Europe. All international trains (except those heading north) pass through Belarus; for visa info, see p. 111. To: **Berlin** (22hr., 1 per day, 317Lt); **Moscow**

(17hr., daily, *coupé* 128Lt); **Rīga** (7½hr., 5 per day, *coupé* 72Lt); **St. Petersburg** (18hr., 3 per day, *coupé* 110Lt); **Warsaw** (8hr., 4 per day, *coupé* 115Lt).

Buses: Autobusų Stotis, Sodų g. 22 (☎26 24 82; reservations ☎26 29 77), opposite the train station. **Tarpmiestinė Salė** covers long-distance buses; windows #13-15 serve destinations outside the former Soviet Union. Open daily 7am-8pm. To: **Minsk** (5hr., 5:50am and 9am, 22Lt); **Rīga** (6hr., 5 per day, 30-40L); **Tallinn** (10hr., 7am and 9:45pm, 90Lt); **Warsaw** (9½hr., 4 per day, 60-80Lt).

Public Transportation: Buses and **trolleys** run daily 6am-midnight. Buy tickets at any kiosk (0.80Lt) or from the driver (1Lt); punch them on board to avoid the hefty fine. Monthly passes available (students 5Lt).

Taxis: State Taxis (☎22 88 88). 1.30Lt per km. **Private taxis** show a green light in the windshield; agree on the fare before getting in.

⚎ 🛈 ORIENTATION AND PRACTICAL INFORMATION

The **train** and **bus stations** are directly across from each other. Geležinkelio g. running right from the train station, leads to Aušros Vartų g., which leads downhill through the **Aušros Vartai** (Gates of Dawn) and into **Senamiestis** (Old Town). Aušros Vartų g. changes its name first to Didžioji g. and then Pilies g., before reaching the base of Gediminas Hill. Here, the **Gediminas Tower** of the Higer Castle presides over **Arkikatedros aikštė** (Cathedral Sq.) and the banks of the river Neris. **Gedimino pr.,** the commercial artery, leads west from the square in front of the cathedral's doors.

Tourist Offices: Tourist Information Centre, Pilies str. 42 (☎/fax 62 07 62). Sells *Vilnius in Your Pocket* (4Lt). Open M-F 9am-7pm, Sa-Su 10am-4pm.

Budget Travel: Lithuanian Student and Youth Travel, V. Basanavičiaus g. 30, #13 (☎22 13 73). Great deals for those under 27. Open M-F 8:30am-6pm, Sa 10am-2pm.

Embassies: Australia (consulate), Gaono 6 (☎/fax 22 33 69). **Canada,** Gedimino pr. 64 (☎22 08 98). Open M and W 9am-noon. **Russia,** Latvių g. 53/54 (☎72 17 63; visas ☎72 38 93). Open M-F 8:30am-12:30pm and 2:30-5pm. **UK,** Antakalnio g. 2 (☎22 20 70; www.britain.lt). Open M-F 9-11am. **US,** Akmenų g. 6 (☎22 30 31; www.usembassy.lt). Open M-Th 8:30am-5:30pm.

Currency Exchange: Geležinkelio 6, left of the stations. Open 24hr. **Vilniaus Bankas,** Gedimino pr. 12, gives MC/V cash advances and cashes traveler's checks.

Pharmacy: Gedimino Vaistinė, Gedimino pr. 27 (☎61 06 08). Open 24hr.

Medical Assistance: Baltic-American Medical & Surgical Clinic, Antakalnio g. 124 (☎34 20 20), at Vilnius University Hospital. Open 24hr.

Internet Access: V002, Ašmenos 8 (☎79 18 66). 8Lt per hr. Open daily 8am-midnight.

Post Office: Centrinis Paštas, Gedimino pr. 7 (☎61 67 59), west of Arkikatedros aikštė. Address mail to be held: First name SURNAME, Centrinis Paštas, Gedimino pr. 7, Vilnius **LT-2000,** LIETUVA. Open M-F 7am-7pm, Sa 9am-4pm.

🏠 ACCOMMODATIONS

Old Town Hostel (HI), Aušros vartų g. 20-15a (☎62 53 57; livijus@pub.osf.lt), 100m south of the "Gates of Dawn" in the Old Town. Internet free. Laundry. Dorms 32Lt, nonmembers 34Lt; singles and doubles 40-60Lt.

Filaretai Youth Hostel (HI), Filaretų g. 17 (☎25 46 27; filareta@post.omnitel.lt). Take bus #34 from the right of the station (across from McDonald's) to 7th stop (10min.). Reception 7am-midnight. Curfew midnight-1am. Reserve ahead. Dorms 29-42Lt.

Litinterp, Bernardinų 7, #2 (☎22 38 50; vilnius@litinterp.lt; www.litinterp.lt). Quiet, clean rooms with shared bath. Breakfast included. Reception M-F 8:30am-5:30pm, Sa 8:30am-3:30pm. Reserve ahead. Singles 80-100Lt; doubles 120-140Lt. 5% ISIC off.

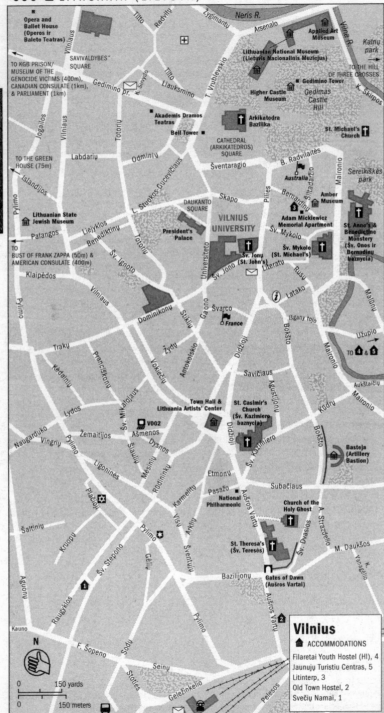

Vilnius

LITHUANIA

Neris R.

Opera and Ballet House (Operos ir Baleto Teatras)

TO KGB PRISON/ MUSEUM OF THE GENOCIDE VICTIMS (400m), CANADIAN CONSULATE (1km), & PARLIAMENT (1km)

SAVIVALDYBĖS SQUARE

Arsenalo

Applied Art Museum

Lithuanian National Museum (Lietuvis Nacionalinis Muziejus)

Kaïnų park

TO THE HILL OF THREE CROSSES

Gedimino Tower

Higher Castle Museum

Gediminas Castle Hill

TO THE GREEN HOUSE (75m)

Akademis Dramos Teatras

Bell Tower

CATHEDRAL (ARKIKATEDROS) SQUARE

Arkikatedra Bazilika

St. Michael's Church

Šventaragio

B. Radvilaitės

Australia

Sereikiškės park

Lithuanian State Jewish Museum

DAUKANTO SQUARE

Skapo

Amber Museum

TO BUST OF FRANK ZAPPA (50m) & AMERICAN CONSULATE (400m)

President's Palace

VILNIUS UNIVERSITY

Adam Mickiewicz Memorial Apartment

St. Anne's & Benedictine Monstery (Šv. Onos ir Bernardinu baznyčia)

Šv. Mykolo (St. Michael's)

Klaipėdos

Šv. Jonų (St. John's)

Latako

Išgany tojo

Užupio

TO ❹ & ❺

France

Savičiaus

Basteja (Artillery Bastion)

Town Hall & Lithuania Artists' Center

V002

Ašmenos

St. Casimir's Church (Šv. Kazimiero baznyčia)

National Philharmonic

Pasalo

Church of the Holy Ghost

St. Theresa's (Šv. Teresės)

Bazilijonų

Gates of Dawn (Aušros Vartai)

Kauno

N

0   150 yards
0   150 meters

Vilnius

⌂ ACCOMMODATIONS

Filaretai Youth Hostel (HI), 4
Jaunųjų Turistiu Centras, 5
Litinterp, 3
Old Town Hostel, 2
Svečių Namai, 1

■ FOOD

Iki supermarkets, which stock foreign brands, are all over Vilnius. The Iki at the bus station is the closest branch to the old station. (Open daily 8am-10pm.) ▨ **Ritos Smuklė** (Rita's Tavern), Žirmūnų g. 68, aims to capture the "spirit of Lithuania's past as it really was" with traditional music and costumes. Take trolleybus #12, 13, or 17. (Main dishes 15-30Lt. Live folk music W-Sa. Open daily 11am-midnight.) **Baku-Tiblisi,** Traku 15, serves Georgian and Azerbajiani specialities. Try *dolma* (meat-stuffed grape leaves) with garlic sauce. (Georgian wines 6-8Lt. Open daily 11am-midnight.) Once a bomb shelter, **Ritos Slėptuvė,** A. Goštaulto g. 8 is now *the* place to go. After 4pm, it becomes a bar. (Meals 10Lt. Live music Su. Open M-Th 7am-2am, F 7am-6am, Sa 8am-6am, Su 8pm-2am.)

◉ SIGHTS

With the largest Old Town in Eastern Europe, Vilnius has no shortage of architectural wonders and historic spots. The moment you reach the end of Geležinkelio g. and turn left, the 16th-century **Gates of Dawn** (Aušros Vartai), the only surviving portal of the old city walls, welcome you in.

OLD TOWN (SENAMIESTIS). Through the gates, enter the first door on the right to ascend the 17th-century **Chapel of the Gates of Dawn** (Aušros Vartų Koplyčia), packed with locals praying to the icon and selling holy paraphernalia. Head back to the street and through the doorway at the building's end to reach **St. Theresa's Church** (Šv. Teresės bažnyčia), known for its Baroque sculptures, multicolored arches, and frescoed ceiling. A few steps farther down, a gateway leads to the bright 17th-century **Church of the Holy Ghost** (Šv. Dvasios bažnyčia), seat of Lithuania's Russian Orthodox Archbishop. The street merges with the pedestrian Pilies g. and leads to the main entrance of **Vilnius University** (Vilniaus Universitetas), at Pilies g. and Šv. Jono g., founded in 1579. Follow Bernardinų g. off Pilies g., at the end stands **St. Anne's Church.** Continue north on Pilies g. to **Cathedral Square** (Arkikatedros aikštė), depicted on the 50Lt bill. Built on a pagan worship site, the Cathedral resembles a Greek temple. Behind the cathedral, walk up the Castle Hill path to **Gedimino tower** for a great view of Vilnius's spires. Behind the tower lies the **Lithuanian National Museum,** Arsenalo g. 1., which chronicles the history of the Lithuanian people through 1940. *(Open W-Su 10am-5pm. 4Lt, students 2Lt.)* Off Pylimo, between Kalinausko 1 and 3, shoots up the most random monument on the continent, a 4-meter steel shaft capped with a bust of the late freak-rock legend **Frank Zappa.**

THE OLD JEWISH QUARTER AND GENOCIDE MEMORIAL. Vilnius was once a center of Jewish life comparable to Warsaw and New York, with a Jewish population of 100,000 (in a city of 230,000) at the start of World War II. Nazi persecution left only 6000 survivors and only one of pre-war Vilnius's 105 **synagogues,** at Pylimo g. 39. The **Lithuanian State Jewish Museum,** housed in two buildings at Pylimo g. 4, offers a variety of exhibits about the vitality of Yiddish culture in Lithuania and the tragedy of the Holocaust. *(Open M-Th 9am-5pm, F 9am-4pm. Donation requested.)* The **Genocide Memorial,** Agrastų g. 15, is 10-15min. away by train in **Paneriai** (1.30Lt). With your back to the train tracks, head right and follow Agrastų g. straight to the memorial. Between 1941 and 1944, 100,000 people, including 70,000 Jews, were shot, burned, and buried here. Paved paths connect the pits that served as mass graves. *(Open M and W-Sa 11am-6pm.)* For information on the Jewish Quarter or locating ancestors, visit the **Jewish Cultural Centre.** (Šaltinių g. 12. ☎ 41 88 09.)

▨ **MUSEUM OF GENOCIDE VICTIMS.** Don't miss the Museum of Genocide Victims (Genocido Aukų Muziejus), in the old **KGB prison.** Built in 1899, the Nazis turned it into a Gestapo headquarters during World War II. When the Soviets came to town, the building became Vilnius' KGB headquarters. One of the guides, G. Radžius, was once a prisoner in its cells; it's worth it to find a translator. *(Gedimino pr. 40. Enter around the corner at Aukv g. 4. Open mid-May to mid-Sept. Tu-Su 10am-6pm; off-season Tu-Su 10am-4pm. Tours in Lithuanian and Russian, captions in English.)*

🎵🎭 ENTERTAINMENT AND NIGHTLIFE

In summer, festivals and pop concerts come to town; check *Vilnius in Your Pocket* or the Lithuanian morning paper *Lietuvos Rytas* for performances. New discos, bars, and clubs spring up daily to entertain the influx of foreigners and the city's younger crowd. Check out posters in the Old Town or wander down Gedimino prosp. toward the thumping music. Lithuanian hipsters Eduardas and Vladimiras organize a **gay disco** every Saturday night at a different venue; call for information. (☎(8) 287 25 879. Cover 15Lt. Usually open F-Sa 10pm-6am.) **The PUB (Prie Universiteto),** Dominikonų g. 9, in the heart of the Old Town and near the university, is a traditional English pub with a heavy wooden interior and a cozy 19th-century dungeon. (W night jazz, Su night disco. Cover 8Lt. Open daily 11am-2am.) **Savas Kampas** (Your Corner), Vokiečių g. 4, is a laid-back option for a more mature set listening to 60s, 70s, and 80s tunes. (Local bands F-Sa. Open daily midnight-3am.) Mingle with the locals at **Amatininskv Užeiga,** Didžiogi g. 19, #2. (Open M-F 8am-5am, Sa-Su 11am-5am.) **Naktinis Vilkas** (Night Wolf), Lukišų g. 3., features a local student crowd. (21+. Cover M-Sa 5-10Lt. Open daily 10pm-6am.)

🏰 DAYTRIP FROM VILNIUS: TRAKAI CASTLE

Trakai's fairy-tale castle has been the stuff of legend since its construction in the 15th century. In 1665, the Tsar of Russia accomplished what the Germans could not—the Imperial Army plundered the town and razed the castle. Following a lengthy process of restoration from 1952 to 1980, five stories of red bricks now tower over some of the most beautiful lakes and woods in Lithuania. Climb the spiral staircase in the **watchtower** to the third floor for a magnificent view of the medieval courtyard below. Across from the tower, the **City and Castle History Museum** features furniture, clocks, and an immense collection of tobacco and opium pipes. With your back to the footbridge leading to the Insular Castle, walk left and explore the ruins of the Peninsular Castle and Dominican monastery. (Tower and museum open daily 10am-7pm. 7Lt, students 3.5Lt. Tours 40Lt, students 15Lt.) The easiest way to navigate Trakai is by boat; boat owners line the shore by the footbridge to the castle. East of Vilnius, Trakai is accessible by **bus** (45min., over 25 per day, 2.80Lt; buy tickets on the bus). The last return is usually at 9pm.

TAKING HEADS Legend has it that the serene, rippling waters surrounding Trakai Castle are more sinister than they seem. Lake Galvė derives its name from the Lithuanian word for "head." It seems Grand Duke Vytautas got a little carried away in his victory dance after defeating the Germanic crusaders of the Teutonic Order and spiked the head of a decapitated crusader into the lake's sparkling waters. The lake fell head over heels for this mortal morsel and now will not freeze before it takes its "head," usually a drowned drunkard or lost tourist.

KLAIPĖDA   ☎826

Guarding the Curonian Lagoon with its fortress on the tip of the Neringa peninsula, Klaipėda, Lithuania's third-largest city, may be a little too strategically located for its own good. Briefly the Prussian capital in the 19th century, the town was handed to France in the 1919 Treaty of Versailles and served as a German U-boat base in World War II before being industrialized by the Soviets after the war. On mainland Klaipėda, the **Clock Museum** (Laikrodživ Muziejus), Liepv g. 12, is a little overwhelming for the perennially late. From S. Daukanto g., turn right on H. Manto and left on Liepv g. (Open Tu-Su 9am-5:30pm. 4Lt, students 2Lt. English tour 40Lt.) **Klaipėda Drama Theater** (Klaipėdos Dramos Teatras), Teatro aikštė, on the other side of Manto g., dominates the Old Town center. The theater was one of Wagner's favorite haunts. (Tickets ☎31 44 53. Open Tu-Su 11am-7pm.) **Smiltynė,** across the lagoon, houses the 🏛**Maritime Museum, Aquarium, and Dolphinarium** (Jurv muziejus ir Akvariumas),

Tomo g. 10, in an 1860s fortress. (www.juru.muziejus.lt. Open June-Aug. Tu-Su 11am-7pm; May and Sept. W-Su 11am-6pm; Oct.-Apr. Sa-Su 11am-5pm. 5Lt, students 3Lt.) Aquatic attractions are in **Kopgalis,** at the head of the Spit, 1½km from the ferry landing. Forest paths lead west 500m to the **beaches.** The permanently moored ▨**Meridianas,** Daués Krautiné (river bank), serves booze. (Cover 20-30Lt. Open daily 3pm-5am.) Follow Naujoji Uosto g. over the bridge to get drunk at **Indigo,** J. Janonio 27. (Open Su-W 8pm-2am, Th 8pm-4am, F-Sa 8pm-6am.)

    Trains (☎31 36 76) go from Priestoties 1 to Vilnius (5hr., 5 per day, 40Lt). **Ferries** (☎31 42 57; info ☎31 11 57) run from Old Castle Port, Žveju 8, and connect with microbuses to Nida (1hr., 7Lt). The **tourist office,** Tomo g. 2, sells maps, arranges tours, and provides tons of useful information. (☎41 21 86; kltic@takas.lt. Open M-F 8:30am-5pm; May-Oct. also open Sa 9am-3pm.) **Litinterp,** S. Šimkaus g. 21/8, arranges **rooms.** (☎31 14 90. Singles 70Lt; doubles 120Lt. Open M-F 8:30am-5:30pm, Sa 10am-3pm.) To reach the central **Hotel Viktorija,** S. Šimkaus g. 2, head down H. manto from the stations, turn right onto Vytautog, and the hotel is on the corner to the left at the end of the block. (☎40 00 55. Singles 40-45Lt; doubles 60-120Lt.) To get to **Klaipėda Traveller's Guesthouse (HI),** Turgaus 3/4, in the Old Town, walk left from the train station (right from the bus station) down Trilapio, turn right on Liepu, and left on H. Manto, which crosses the river; Turgaus is the 2nd left after the bridge. (☎21 49 35; oldtown@takas.lt. Free beer and bike rental with email reservation. 32Lt; nonmembers 34Lt.) **BonTon,** Turgaus 4/2, serves local dishes (2-8Lt) in a courtyard complete with mini-waterfall. (Open M-F 8am-8pm, Sa-Su 10am-7pm.) **IKI supermarket** is at M. Mažvyado 7. (Open daily 8am-10pm.) **Postal code:** LT-5800.

▨ **DAYTRIP FROM KLAIPĖDA: NIDA AND PALANGA.** The magical rise of wind-swept white sand dunes has long drawn summer vacationers to **Nida,** only 3km north of the Kaliningrad region on the Curonian Spit. From the remains of the immense **sundial**—the highest point on the Spit—you can look down on a glorious vista: the dunes, the Curonian Lagoon, the Baltic, and even Russia. Walk along the **beach** or through forest paths to reach steps leading to surreal mountains and sheets of white sand blowing gracefully into the sea from 100m above. From the center of town, walk along the promenade by the water and bear right on Skruzdynės g. to reach the **Thomas Mann House** (Thomo Manno Namelis) at #17. Mann built the cottage in 1930 and wrote *Joseph and His Brothers* here, but had to give up the house when Hitler invaded. From Naglių 18, **microbuses** (☎524 72) run to Smiltynė (1hr., 8Lt; buy tickets on board). The last one should get you there to catch the 11:15pm ferry back to mainland Klaipėda. The **Tourist Info Center,** Taikos g. 4, opposite the bus station, arranges homestays for a 5Lt fee. (☎523 45. Open June-Aug. M-Sa 8am-8pm, Su 8am-3pm; Sept.-May M-F 8am-noon and 1-5pm.) ☎8259.

    Palanga is the hottest summer spot in Lithuania, with over 20km of shoreline, the largest park in the country, and tight nightlife. And the sunsets are gorgeous. Palanga's main streets are **Vytauto gatrė,** which runs parallel to the beach and passes the bus station, and **J. Basanavičiaus,** which runs perpendicular to Vytauto g. and finishes in a boardwalk. **Buses** from Klaipeda (20min., every 30min., 2.50Lt) arrive at Kretinjos 1. **Litinterp** in Klaipėda (see above) arranges private rooms in Palanga (singles 100-120Lt; doubles 140Lt). J. Basanavičiaus g. is lined with cafes and restaurants with outdoor seating.

LUXEMBOURG

LUXEMBOURG FRANCS

US$1 = 44.03LF	10LF = US$0.23
CDN$1 = 28.57LF	10LF = CDN$0.35
UK£1 = 63.52LF	10LF = UK£0.16
IR£1 = 51.22LF	10LF = IR£0.20
AUS$1 = 23.60LF	10LF = AUS$0.42
NZ$1 = 19.36LF	10LF = NZ$0.52
ZAR1 =5.32LF	10LF = ZAR1.88
EUR€ = 40.34LF	10LF = EUR€0.25

PHONE CODE	**Country code: 352. International dialing prefix:** 00. Luxembourg has no city codes. From outside Luxembourg, dial int'l dialing prefix (see inside back cover) + 352 + local number.

Too often overlooked by budget travelers, Luxembourg boasts beautiful hiking and impressive fortresses, remnants of successive waves of Burgundians, Spaniards, French, Austrians, and Germans. Only after the last French soldier returned home in 1867 and the Treaty of London restored its neutrality did Luxembourg begin to cultivate its current image of peacefulness. Today the wealthy nation is an independent constitutional monarchy, part of the European Union, and a tax haven for investors worldwide. From the wooded and hilly Ardennes in the north to the fertile vineyards of the Moselle Valley in the south, the country's unspoiled rural landscapes are a sharp contrast to the high-powered banking in the small capital city.

FACTS AND FIGURES

Official Name: Grand Duchy of Luxembourg.

Capital: Luxembourg City.

Population: 415,870.

Land Area: 2586 sq. km.

Climate: Mild, with considerable precipitation.

Languages: French, German, Luxembourgian.

Religions: Roman Catholic (90%).

DISCOVER LUXEMBOURG

Luxembourg is a charming stopover between France or Belgium and Germany. **Luxembourg City** (p. 662) is arguably one of Europe's most beautiful capitals. Your next stop should be **Vianden** (p. 666), whose gorgeous château and outdoor opportunities make it well worth an overnight stay . If you have extra time, consider daytripping to **Diekirch** (p. 666), or hiking and biking around **Echternach** (p. 667).

ESSENTIALS

DOCUMENTS AND FORMALITIES

VISAS. Visas are generally not required for tourist stays under three months; South African citizens are the exception.

EMBASSIES. All foreign embassies are in **Luxembourg City** (p. 662). Foreign embassies in Brussels also have jurisdiction over Luxembourg. For Luxembourg embassies at home: **Australia** (consulate), Level 18, Royal Exchange Building, 56 Pitt St., Sydney NSW 2000 (☎(02) 92 41 43 22; fax 92 51 11 13); **Canada** (consulate), 3877 Draper Ave, Montreal, PQ H4A 2N9 (☎514-849-2101); **South Africa** (consulate), P.O. Box 782922, Sandton 2146 (☎(011) 463 17 44; 463 32 69); **UK,** 27 Wilton Crescent,

London SW1X 8SD (☎(020) 7235 6961; fax 7235 9734); and **US,** 2200 Massachusetts Ave. NW, Washington, D.C. 20008 (☎202-265-4171; fax 202-328-8270).

TRANSPORTATION

The Luxembourg City airport is serviced by **Luxair** (☎479 81, reservations ☎4798 42 42) and with flights from the UK and throughout the continent. Cheap last-minute flights on Luxair are available at www.luxair.lu. A **Benelux Tourrail Pass** allows five days of unlimited **train** travel in a one-month period in Belgium, The Netherlands, and Luxembourg (6400LF/€158.65, under 26 4400LF/€109.10). The **Billet Réseau** (180LF/€4.50), a network ticket, is good for one day of unlimited bus and train travel; even better is the **Luxembourg Card** (350LF/€8.70; see below), which covers unlimited transportation and most entrance fees. **Bikes** aren't permitted on buses, but are allowed on many trains for 45LF/€1.15.

TOURIST SERVICES AND MONEY

EMERGENCY	**Police:** ☎112. **Ambulance:** ☎112. **Fire:** ☎112.

TOURIST OFFICES. Luxembourg National Tourist Office, P.O. Box 1001, L-1010 Luxembourg (☎(352) 42 82 82 10; fax 42 82 82 38; tourism@ont.smtp.etat.lu; www.etat.lu/ tourism). The **Luxembourg Card,** available from Easter to October at tourist offices, hostels, and many hotels and public transportation offices, provides unlimited transportation on national trains and buses and includes admission to 32 tourist sites (1-day 350LF/€8.70, 2-day 600LF/€14.90, 3-day 850LF/ €27).

MONEY. The currency is the Luxembourg **franc.** Luxembourg *francs* are worth the same as Belgian *francs;* you can use Belgian money in Luxembourg, but not vice versa. Luxembourg has accepted the **Euro (€)** as legal tender, and francs will be phased out by July 1, 2002. For more information, see p. 21. Expect to pay 1200-1500LF/€29.75-37.20 for a hotel room, 435-650LF/€10.80-16.15 for a hostel bed, and 280-400LF/€6.95-9.95 for a restaurant meal. Service (15-20%) is included in the price; tip taxi drivers 10%. The value-added tax is already included in most prices. Luxembourg's VAT refund threshold (US$85) is lower than most other EU countries; refunds are usually 13% of the purchase price.

Luxembourg

TO LIÈGE

BELGIUM

Troisvierges

Clervaux

Our R.

THE ARDENNES

Clerf R.

GERMANY

Esch-sur-Sûre

Vianden

Sûre R.

Sûre R.

Ettelbrück

Diekirch

Echternach

Alzette R.

TO TRIER

Hollenfels

Bourglinster

Wasserbillig

Arlon

Moselle R.

Luxembourg City

Remich

Longwy

FRANCE

0 ——— 10 miles

0 ——— 10 kilometers

TO METZ & PARIS

COMMUNICATION

MAIL. Mailing a postcard or a letter (up to 20g) from Luxembourg costs 21LF/ €0.55 to the UK and Europe and 30LF/€0.75 anywhere else.

TELEPHONES. There are no city codes; just dial ☎352 plus the local number. International direct dial numbers include: **AT&T,** ☎0800 01 11; **British Telecom,** ☎0800 89 0352; **Canada Direct,** 800 20 119; **Ireland Direct,** ☎0800 89 35 30; **MCI,** ☎800 01 12; **Sprint,** 0800 01 15; **Telecom New Zealand,** ☎0800 57 84; and **Telstra Australia,** ☎0800 00 61.

LANGUAGES. French, German, and, since a referendum in 1984, *Letzebuergesch*, a mixture of the other two that sounds a bit like Dutch. French is most common in the city, where most people also speak German. For basic phrases, see p. 984.

ACCOMMODATIONS AND CAMPING

Luxembourg's 12 **HI youth hostels** *(Auberges de Jeunesse)* are often filled with school groups. Check the sign posted in any hostel to find out which hostels are full or closed each day. Prices range from 435-650LF/€10.80-16.15, under 27 355-650LF/ €8.80-16.15; nonmembers pay about 110LF/€2.75 extra. Breakfast is included, a packed lunch costs 125LF/€3.10, and dinner 260LF/€6.45. Sheets are 125LF/€3.10. Half of the hostels close from mid-November to mid-December, and the other half close from mid-January to mid-February. Contact **Centrale des Auberges de Jeunesse Luxembourgeoises** (☎22 55 88; fax 46 39 87; information@youthhostels.lu) for information. **Hotels** advertise 900-1500LF/€22.35-37.20 per night but may try to persuade tourists to take more expensive rooms. Luxembourg is a **camping** paradise. Two people with a tent will typically pay 200-360LF/€5-8.95 per night.

HOLIDAYS

Holidays: New Year's Day (Jan. 1); Carnival (Feb. 11); Easter (Mar. 31); Easter Monday (Apr. 1); May Day (May 1); Ascension Day (May 9); Whit Sunday and Monday (May 19-20); National Holiday (June 23); Assumption Day (Aug. 15); All Saints Holiday (Nov. 1); Christmas (Dec. 25); Boxing Day (Dec. 26).

LUXEMBOURG CITY (VILLE DE LUXEMBOURG)

With a medieval fortress perched on a cliff that overlooks lush green river valleys, Luxembourg City (pop. 80,000) is one of Europe's most attractive and dramatic capitals. As an international banking capital, it's home to thousands of frenzied foreign business executives, but most visitors find it surprisingly relaxed and idyllic.

▉ TRANSPORTATION

Flights: Findel International Airport, 6km from the city. **Bus #9** (40LF/€1) is cheaper than the Luxair bus (150LF/€3.75) and runs the same route every 20min.

Trains: ☎49 90 49 90; www.cfl.lu. **Gare CFL,** av. de la Gare, near the foot of av. de la Liberté, 10min. south of the city center. To: **Amsterdam** (5¾hr.; 1680LF/€41.65, under 26 1360LF/€33.75); **Brussels** (2¾hr.; 940LF/€23.30, under 26 520LF/ €12.90); **Frankfurt** (5hr.; 1720LF/€42.65, under 26 1530 LF/€37.95); **Paris** (3½-4hr., 1560LF/€38.70).

Buses: Buy a **billet courte distance** (short-distance ticket) from the driver (single-fare 45LF/€1.15, full-day 180LF/€4.50), or pick up a package of 10 (320LF/€7.95) at the train station. These tickets are also valid on **local trains.**

Taxis: ☎48 22 33. 32LF/€0.80 per km. 10% premium 10pm-6am; 25% premium on Su. 700-800LF/€17.35-19.85 from the city center to the airport.

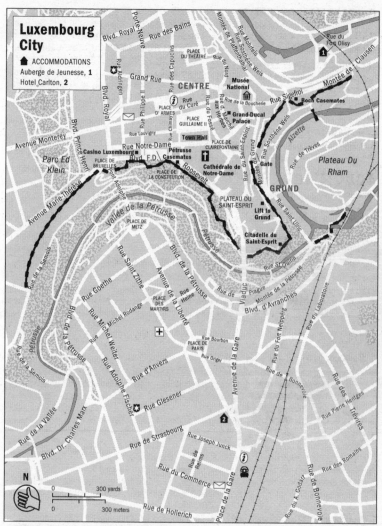

Luxembourg City

⌂ ACCOMMODATIONS
Auberge de Jeunesse, 1
Hotel Carlton, 2

Bikes: Biking is the ideal way to see Luxembourg. **Velo en Ville,** 8, r. Bisserwé (☎47 96 23). Open M-F 1-8pm, Sa-Su 9am-noon and 1-8pm. 250LF/€6.20 per half-day, 400LF/€9.95 per day. 20% discount if under 26.

■⚡ ORIENTATION AND PRACTICAL INFORMATION

Five minutes by bus and 15min. by foot from the train station, Luxembourg City's historic center revolves around the **place d'Armes.** Facing the tourist office, in the commemorative Town Hall, turn right down r. Chimay to reach **boulevard Roosevelt.** To reach the museums, Grand Ducal Palace and Bock Casemates, from the information office, walk straight ahead and onto **rue Sigeroi.**

Tourist Offices: Grand Duchy National Tourist Office, in the train station, avoids the long lines of the office in town. (☎42 82 82 20; fax 42 82 82 30; www.etat.lu/ tourism.) Open July-Sept. 9am-7pm; Oct.-June 9:15am-12:30pm and 1:45-6pm.

Municipal Tourist Office, pl. d'Armes (☎22 28 09; fax 46 70 70; touristinfo@lux-embourg-city.lu; www.luxembourg-city.lu/touristinfo). Open Apr.-Sept. M-Sa 9am-7pm, Su 10am-6pm; Oct.-Mar. M-F 9am-6pm, Su 10am-6pm.

Embassies: Ireland, 28, r. d'Arlon (☎45 06 10; fax 45 88 20). Open M-F 10am-12:30pm and 2:30-5pm. **UK,** 14 bd. Roosevelt (☎22 98 64; fax 22 98 67). Open M-F 9am-12:30pm. **US,** 22 bd. E. Servais (☎46 01 23; fax 46 14 01). Open M-F 8:30am-12:30pm; visas M-Tu and Th-F 3:30-4:30pm. Australians, Canadians, New Zealanders, and South Africans should contact embassies in France or Belgium.

Laundromat: Quick Wash, 31, r. de Strasbourg, near the station. Wash and dry 390LF/€9.70. Open M-Sa 8:30am-6:30pm. Doing your laundry is cheaper at the HI hostel (350LF/€8.70).

Emergency: Police: ☎113. **Ambulance:** ☎112.

Pharmacy: Pharmacie Goedert, 5 pl. d'Armes (☎22 39 91). Open M 1-6:15pm, Tu-F 8am-6:15pm, Sa 8am-12:30pm. Check any pharmacy window for night information.

Telephones: Outside post offices and at the train station. Coin-operated phones are rare; buy a 50-unit **phone card** at either place (each good for 50 local calls; 250LF/€6.20).

Internet Access: Sparky's, 11a Ave Monterey (☎26 20 12 23), at the pl. d'Armes. 5LF/€0.15 per min. The only Internet cafe in town. Open M-Sa 8am-8pm, Su 2-8pm.

Post Office: 25, r. Aldringen, near the pl. D'Armes (open M-F 7am-7pm, Sa 7am-5pm), and 38 pl. de la Gare, across the street, left of the train station (for *Poste Restante;* open M-F 6am-7pm, Sa 6am-noon). Address mail to be held: First name SURNAME, *Poste Restante,* Recette Principale, **L-1009** Luxembourg City, LUXEMBOURG.

■ ACCOMMODATIONS AND CAMPING

Budget travelers have two basic options in Luxembourg City: the city's hostel, often booked solid by school and tour groups in the summer, and the relatively inexpensive accommodations near the train station.

Auberge de Jeunesse (HI), 2, r. du Fort Olisy (☎22 19 20 or 22 68 89; luxembourg@youth.hostels.lu). Take bus #9 and ask to get off at the hostel stop; head under the bridge and turn right down the steep path. Breakfast included. Sheets 125LF/€3.10. Laundry 300LF/€7.45. Reception 7am-2am. Curfew 2am. Max 5-night stay in high season. Dorms 520-580LF/€12.90-14.40, under 26 435-485LF/€10.80-12.05; doubles 1340LF/€33.25, under 26 1140LF/€28.30. Nonmembers add 110LF/€2.75.

Hotel Carlton, 9, r. de Strasbourg (☎29 96 60; carlton@pt.lu). Clean rooms in a marble building. Singles 900-1200LF/€22.35-29.75, with bath 1500-2500LF/€37.20-62; doubles 1400-1600LF/€34.75-39.70, 1700-3000LF/€42.15-74.40.

Hotel Pax, 121, rte. de Thionville (☎48 25 63). Prime location near the train station. Reception 11:45am-10:30pm. Singles 1500LF/€37.20, with bath 1700LF/€42.15; doubles 2000LF/€49.60, 2600LF/€64.45.

Camping: Kockelscheuer (☎47 18 15), outside Luxembourg City. Take bus #2 to Cloche d'Or/Kockelscheuer from the station. Showers included. Open Easter-Oct. 120LF/€3 per person, 140LF/€3.50 per tent.

■ FOOD

The area around **place d'Armes** teems with touristy fast-food options and pricey restaurants. **Restaurant Bacchus,** 32, r. Marché-aux-Herbes, down the street from the Grand Ducal palace, serves excellent pizza and pasta for 290-440LF/€7.20-10.90. (Open Tu-Su noon-10pm.) **Caffe-Veneziano,** 16, r. Philippe II, dishes out crepes piled high with fruit and scoops of ice cream for 80-350LF/€2-8.70. (Open daily 7am-11pm.) Stock up at **Alima supermarket** on r. Bourbon near the train station. (Open M-Sa 8am-6:30pm, Su 8am-6pm.)

👁 SIGHTS

Luxembourg City is compact enough that you'll bump into the major sights by just wandering around. Signs point out the **Wenzel Walk,** which leads visitors through 1000 years of history, winding around the old city and down into the casemates.

FORTRESSES AND THE OLD CITY. The 10th-century **Bock Casemates** fortress, part of Luxembourg's original castle, looms over the Alzette River Valley and offers a fantastic view of the Grund and the Clausen. The strategic stronghold was closed in 1867, but was used during World War II to shelter 35,000 people while the rest of the city was ravaged. *(Entrance on r. Sigefroi just past the bridge leading to the hostel. Open Mar.-Oct. daily 10am-5pm. 70LF/€1.75.)* The **Pétrusse Casemates** were built by the Spanish in the 1600s and later improved by the Austrians. *(Pl. de la Constitution. Open July-Sept. 70LF/€1.75, children 40LF/€1. Tours every hr. 11am-4pm.)* The view from the nearby **Place de la Constitution** is incredible. From there, stroll down into the lush valley or catch one of the green tourist trains. *(Trains ☎ 65 11 65 1. Apr.-Oct. every 30min. 10am-6pm except 1pm. 250LF/€6.20.)*

MUSEUMS. The **Luxembourg Card** (p. 661) covers entrance to all museums in the city. The **All-in-One Ticket** covers five museums in two days (350LF/€8.70 at the Municipal Tourist Office). The eclectic collection at the **Musée National d'Histoire et d'Art** chronicles the influences of the various European empires that controlled Luxembourg. *(Marché-aux-Poissons, at rues Boucherie and Sigefroi. ☎ 47 93 30 1. Open Tu-Su 10am-5pm. 100LF/€2.50.)* The **Musée d'Histoire de la Ville de Luxembourg** features quirky exhibits that allow you to view the history of the city through photographs, films, and music clips. *(14, r. du St-Esprit. ☎ 22 90 50 1. Open Tu-Su 10am-6pm, Th until 8pm. 200LF/€5, students 150LF/€3.75.)*

OTHER SIGHTS. Built as the city hall in 1574, the Renaissance **Grand Ducal Palace** became the official city residence of the Grand Duke in 1890. *(Mandatory tours mid-July to Sept. 2 M-F afternoons and Sa mornings; tickets sold at the Municipal Tourist Office. Reservations ☎ 22 28 09; specify if you want an English language tour. 220LF/€5.45.)* Nearby, the 7th-century **Cathedral of Notre Dame,** which incorporates features of the Dutch Renaissance and early Baroque styles, houses the tombs of John the Blind, the 14th-century King of Bohemia and Count of Luxembourg. *(Entrance at bd. Roosevelt. Open daily 10am-noon and 2-5:30pm. Free.)*

🎵🎭 ENTERTAINMENT AND NIGHTLIFE

At night, the **place d'Armes** comes to life with free concerts and stand-up comedy. Pick up *La Semaine à Luxembourg* at the tourist office. On the Grand Duke's birthday (June 23), the city shuts down to host a military and religious procession. Nightlife centers on the valley in the **Grund** (by the elevator lift on pl. du St-Esprit). Check *Nightlife.lu*, available at most cafes and newsstands. Warm up in the Grund at the candlelit piano bar **🎵Café des Artistes,** 22 montée du Grund, with beer for 100LF/€2.50. (Piano W-Sa 10:30pm-2am. Open daily 2:30pm-2am.)

THE ARDENNES

Almost six decades ago, the Battle of the Bulge mashed Luxembourg into slime and mud. Today, the forest is verdant again, and the quiet towns, looming castles, and pleasant hiking trails are powerful draws.

ETTELBRÜCK. Ettelbrück's position on the main railway line between Luxembourg City and Liège, Belgium makes it a transportation hub for the Ardennes region. To get to the city center from the train station, go left on r. du Prince Henri, continue right on the same street, then turn left on the Grand Rue, and follow it to the pl. de l'Église. The **General Patton Memorial Museum,** 5, r. Dr. Klein, commemorates the liberation of Luxembourg during World War II. Walk along the Grand Rue, away from the pl. de l'Église, until it becomes av. JFK,

LUXEMBOURG

and then go left onto r. Dr. Klein (☎81 03 22. Open July to mid-Sept. daily 10am-5pm; mid-Sept. to June Su 2-5pm. 100LF/€2.50.) The **tourist office** at the train station has information about excursions to the surrounding Ardennes towns. (☎81 20 68; site@pt.lu. Open M-F 9am-noon and 1:30-5pm, Sa-Su 10am-noon and 2-4pm.) To get to the **Ettelbrück Hostel (HI)**, r. G. D. Josephine-Charlotte, follow signs from the station. (☎81 22 69; ettelbruck@youthhostels.lu. Breakfast included. 505LF/€12.55, under 26 445LF/€11.) **Camping Kalkesdelt** is at 22, r. du Camping. (☎81 21 85. Reception 7:30am-noon and 2-10pm. 120LF/€3 per person, 130LF/€3.25 per tent.)

VIANDEN. Hidden in the dense Ardennes woods, the village of Vianden is not to be missed. Backpackers **hike** and **kayak** along the Sûre River, or **bike** to Diekirch (15-20min.) and Echternach (30min.). The **château,** one of Europe's most impressive, is filled with medieval armor, 16th-century furniture, and 17th-century tapestries. From April to September, and March through October, the château hosts classical weekend concerts. (☎83 41 08. Open Apr.-Sept. daily 10am-6pm.; Mar. and Oct. 10am-5pm; Nov.-Feb. 10am-4pm. 180LF/€4.50, students 130LF/€3.25. Concerts 300-500LF/€7.45-12.40.) For a stellar view of the château, ride the **télésiège** (chairlift), 39 r. de Sanatorium. (Information ☎83 43 23.) From the tourist office, cross the river, go left on r. Victor Hugo, then left again on r. de Sanitorium. (Open Easter-Oct. daily 10am-5pm; July and Aug. until 6pm. 110LF/€2.75; return 160LF/€4.)

  Buses arrive from Ettelbrück (90LF/€2.25) via Diekirch twice every hour. The **tourist office,** 1, r. du Vieux Marché, next to the main bus stop, sells trail maps and gives information on kayaking and private rooms. (☎83 42 57; fax 84 90 81. Open Sa 10am-2pm, M-F 8am-noon and 1-6pm, Su 2-4pm.) To reach the **HI youth hostel,** 3 montée du Château, from the bus stop or tourist office, follow the Grande Rue away from the river and head up the hill; branch off onto montée du Château and follow the signs. (☎83 41 77; vianden@youthhostels.lu. Sheets 125LF/€3.10. Reception 8-10am and 5-9pm. Lockout 10am-5pm. Curfew 11pm. Open mid-Mar. to mid-Nov. Dorms 455LF/€11.30, under 26 395LF/€9.80.) **Camp op dem Deich,** r. Neugarten, 5min. downstream from the tourist office, is in the shadow of the château. (☎83 43 75. Open Easter-Oct. 150LF/€37.20 per person, 150LF/€37.20 per tent.)

DIEKIRCH. The **National Museum of Military History,** 10 Bamertal, presents a comprehensive exhibition of relics from World War II's Battle of the Bulge. (Open daily Apr.-Nov. 10am-6pm; Dec.-Mar. 2-6pm. 200LF/€5, students 120LF/€3.) Downhill from the museum, turn right onto Esplanade and then onto the *Zone Pietone* (pedestrian area) to find the **Église Saint-Laurent,** built upon Roman ruins. (Open Easter-Oct. Tu-Su 10am-noon and 2-6pm.)

  Trains arrive hourly from Ettelbrück; **buses** roll in from Echternach hourly. To get to the **tourist office,** 3 pl. de la Liberation, take the underground stairs to r. St. Antione, walk to the end, and it's directly across the Place. (☎80 30 23. Open daily 9am-noon and 2-5pm. Free guided tours daily 3pm.) Stay across from the bus stop, at **Au Beau-Sejour,** 12 Esplanade. (☎80 34 03; hotelbeausejour@hotmail.com. Reception 8am-midnight. Singles 1500LF/€37.20; doubles 2500LF/€62.)

CLERVAUX. In little Clervaux, the **château** houses the striking **Family of Man** exhibition, a collection of over 500 pictures depicting human emotion. (Open Mar.-Dec. Tu-Su 10am-noon and 1-6pm. 150LF/€3.75, students 80LF/€2.) To get to the château and the **Benedictine Abbey,** turn left from the train station and walk straight. (Abbey open daily 9am-7pm. Free.) Clervaux lies right on the main **railway** line between that connects Luxembourg City, Ettelbrück, and Liège, Belgium. The **tourist office,** in the château, books private rooms at Clervaux's B&Bs. (☎92 00 72. Open Apr.-June daily 2-5pm; July-Oct. 9:45am-11:45am and 2-6pm; Sept. and Oct. closed Su.)

LITTLE SWITZERLAND (LE MULLERTHAL)

ECHTERNACH. A favorite vacation spot of European families, the Lower-Sûre village of **Echternach** is famous for its millennial rock formations and 7th-century monastic center. In the Middle Ages, the monastic center was known for its ▨**illuminated manuscripts;** several are at the 18th-century Benedictine **Abbaye.** From the bus station, go left at the marketplace on r. de la Gare, take the last left, and walk past the basilica. (Open July-Aug. daily 10am-6pm; June and Sept. 10am-noon and 2-6pm; Oct.-May 10am-noon and 2-5pm. 80LF/€2.) Echternach is accessible by **bus** from Ettelbrück and Luxembourg City. The **tourist office** is on Porte St-Willibrord next to the abbey. (☎72 02 30. Open M-F 9am-noon and 2-5pm; in high season open weekends.) To get from the bus station to the **youth hostel (HI),** 9, r. André Drechscher, turn left on av. de la Gare, and take the last right. (☎72 01 58; echternach@youthhostels.lu. Breakfast included. Sheets 125LF. Reception 5-11pm. Lockout 10am-5pm. Closes one month in winter. 455LF/€11.30, under 26 395LF/€9.80.)

LUXEMBOURG

MOROCCO المغرب

MOROCCAN DIRHAM

US$1 = 2.20DH	1DH = US$0.09
CDN$1 = 1.50DH	1DH = CDN$0.14
UK£1 = 3.20DH	1DH = UK£0.06
IR£1 = 2.50DH	1DH = IR£0.08
AUS$1 = 1.30DH	1DH = AUS$0.17
NZ$1 = 0.94DH	1DH = NZ$0.20
ZAR1 = 0.32DH	1DH = ZAR0.74
EUR€1 = 1.96DH	1DH = EUR€0.10

PHONE CODE

Country code: 212. International dialing prefix: 00. From outside Morocco, dial int'l dialing prefix (see inside back cover) + 212 + city code + local number.

Morocco has carved its identity out of a host of influences. At the crossroads of Africa, Europe, and the Middle East, it boasts Arab culture and religion, African history and landscape, European influences and ties, and languages of all three. At the same time, the country teeters between the past and present as both an ancient civilization descended from nomadic tribes and as a modern nation that has struggled against imperial powers for its sovereignty. For travelers weary of another visit to a Spanish cathedral, a short excursion into Morocco can unexpectedly become the highlight of their trip. Excitement and adventure do not need to be planned or paid for lavishly: just step outside your hotel door and wander down an ancient medina street for an introduction to the Islamic and African world. While Morocco is only a few hours from Europe, it's an entirely different place—and that's exactly why you've come.

For more Moroccan enlightenment, peruse *Let's Go: Spain and Portugal 2002*.

FACTS AND FIGURES

Official Name: Kingdom of Morocco.
Capital: Rabat.
Major Cities: Fez, Marrakesh, Meknes.
Population: 30,122,350.
Land Area: 446,500 sq. km.

Climate: Mediterranean, becoming more extreme in the interior.
Languages: Arabic. The dialect *Darija* is by far the most commonly used language.
Religion: Muslim (99%).

DISCOVER MOROCCO

The draw of Morocco often pulls tourists south through Andalucia. Give in to the exotic allure Morocco and skim across the Straight. Spend as little time as possible in Tangier and instead discover the charm of the brilliant white medina and beaches of **Asilah** (p. 672) or the majesty of **Chefchaouen** (p. 673), high in the Rif Mountains. Of Morocco's three imperial cities (Fez, Meknes, and Marrakesh), **Fez** (p. 673) is the most easily accessible. Marvel at the city's bustling medina, which epitomizes traditional Morocco.

Morocco

100 miles
100 kilometers

N

SPAIN · Gibraltar
Tangier · Ceuta · Mediterranean Sea
· Tetouan · Oran
Chefchaouen · Al Hoceima · Melilla
· Ouazzane · Ketama · Nador · Berkane
· Taounate · Taourirt · Oujda · Tlemcen
Kénitra · Sidi-Kacem · Oued S. · Guercif · Za
Salé · Volubilis · Taza · Aïn-Benimathar
Rabat · Fès
Casablanca · Moulay · Meknes · Sefrou
· Idriss · Azrou · Ifrane
Al-Jadida
Oualidia · Khouribga · Midelt · Talsinnt · Bouâfra
Safi · Oum er R. · O. el Abid · Boudnib · Figuig
Essaouira · Marrakesh · Azilal · Al-Rachidia
Chichaoua · Boumalne · Tinerhir · Erfoud
· Asni · Merzouga · Erg
Ouarzazate · O. Dadès · Alnif · Chebbi
Agadir · Oued Sous · Agdz · O. Drâa
Taroudannt · Zagora
Tiznit · Tata · M'Hamid
· Tafraoute · Oued Drâa
Sidi Ifni
TO CANARY ISLANDS · Goulimine
ALGERIA

ATLANTIC OCEAN

ESSENTIALS

DOCUMENTS AND FORMALITIES

VISAS. Citizens of Canada, Ireland, Australia, New Zealand, South Africa, the UK, and the US may enter Morocco for a maximum of 90 days with a valid passport.

EMBASSIES. Foreign embassies in Morocco are all in Rabat. Moroccan embassies at home: **Australia,** 11 West St., Suite #2, North Sydney, NSW 2060 (☎(2) 99 22 49 99; fax 99 23 10 53; maroc@magna.com.au); **Canada,** 38 Range Rd., Ottawa, ON K1N 8J4 (☎613-236-7391 or 613-236-7392; fax 613-236-6164); **South Africa,** 799 Shoeman St., Pretoria (☎(12) 343 0230; fax 343 0613); **UK,** 49 Queens Gate Gardens, London SW7 5NE (☎(20) 7581 5001; fax 7225 3862); and **US,** 1601 21st St. NW, Washington, D.C. 20009 (☎202-462-7979; fax 202-265-0161).

TRANSPORTATION

BY PLANE. Royal Air Maroc (☎2 31 41 41 in Casablanca or ☎2 33 90 00 at airport; in US ☎800-344-6726; in UK ☎171 439 43 61), Morocco's national airline, flies between most major cities in Europe, including Madrid and Lisbon.

BY FERRY. For travel from Spain to Morocco, the most budget-minded mode is by sea. Spanish-based **Trasmediterranea** (☎+34 902 45 46 45; www.trasmediterranea.es/homei.htm) runs ferries on a shuttle schedule from Algeciras (☎+34 956 65 62 44, Recinto del Puerto) to Cuenta (☎+34 956 50 94 11; Muelle Cañonero Dato, 6) and Tangier. Trasmediterranea is represented in Tangier by **Limadet** (☎212 39/93 50 76; 3, r. IBN Rochd., Tangier). "Fast" Ferries run from Algeciras to Ceuta (45min., every hr. 8am-10pm; 3000-4000ptas/€18-24). Algeciras to Tangier (2½hrs., every hr., 8am-10pm, 5000ptas/€30.05). Comarit (☎956 66 84 62; www.comarit.com. Avda. Virgen della Carmen, 3-1°Cial.) runs from Algeciras to Tangier. (3-4 per day, Class "B" 3740ptas/€22.50).

BY TRAIN. Where possible, trains are the best way to travel. Second-class train tickets are slightly more expensive than corresponding CTM bus fares; first-class tickets cost around 20% more than those second-class. The main line runs from Tangier via Rabat and Casablanca to Marrakesh. A spur connects Fez, Meknes, and points east with the main line at Sidi Kasem, near Meknes. There is one nightly *couchette* train between Fez and Marrakesh. **InterRail** is valid in Morocco, but **Eurail** is not. Fares are so low, however, that InterRail is not worth using in Morocco.

BY BUS. Plan well ahead if you are thinking of using buses as your method of transport. They're not all that fast and they're not very comfortable, but they're extremely cheap and travel to nearly every corner of the country. **Compagnie de Transports du Maroc** (CTM), the state-owned line, has the best buses. In many cities, CTM has a station separate from other lines; reservations are usually not necessary.

BY CAR AND BY TAXI. Taxis are dirt cheap by European standards. Make sure the driver turns the meter on. There is a 50% surcharge after 8pm. Don't be surprised if the driver stops for other passengers or picks you up with other passengers in the car, but if you are picked up after the meter has been started, note the initial price. *Grand taxis*, typically beige or dark-blue Mercedes sedans congregate at a central area in town and won't go until it is filled with passengers going in the same direction. Only rent a car in Morocco for large group travel, or travel to areas not reached by Morocco's public transportation system.

BY THUMB. Almost no one in Morocco hitches. If Moroccans do pick up a foreigner, they will expect payment for the ride. Hitching is more frequent in the south and in the mountains, where transportation is irregular. *Let's Go* does not recommend hitchhiking.

TOURIST SERVICES AND MONEY

EMERGENCY | **Police:** 19. **Highway services:** 177.

TOURIST OFFICES. Tourist offices in Morocco tend to be few and far between. However, existing offices are often offer lists of available accommodations and a an official tour-guide service, like the Syndicat d'Initiative office in Fez (p. 673).

MONEY. In Morocco, banking hours are Monday through Friday 8:30 to 11:30am and 2:30 to 4:30pm, during Ramadan from 9:30am to 2pm. In the summer, certain banks close at 1pm and do not reopen in the afternoon. Beware of converting large sums of money into dirhams, as you may only convert back to another currency half of the original amount converted to dirhams. Do not try the black market for currency exchange—you'll probably be swindled. Taxes are generally included in the price of purchases, though in malls and *grandes surfaces* (supermarkets and larger superstores) you will find a 7% Value-Added Tax on food and a 22% tax on luxury goods. **Bargaining** (see below) is definitely a legitimate part of the Moroccan shopping experience—it is most commonly accepted in outdoor markets. Do not try to bargain in supermarkets or established stores.

BARGAINING 101 You'll have to do it for everything from taxi rides to camel treks, carpets to ice cream cones, so you might as well do it right. You'll get the best deals if you bargain in Arabic; key phrases include *sh-HAL ta-MAN* (how much does it cost) and *GHEH-lee bez-ZAF* (too expensive). You'll have to make a counter-offer to the initial asking price. Decide what you want to ultimately pay (probably half to one-third of the initial price) then offer one-third to half of *that*. The shopkeeper may respond harshly, at which point you may choose to politely but firmly walk out. Invariably, you will be dragged back in. You can gauge the seller's willingness to negotiate by how quickly (and by how much) he drops his price. If you're at a standstill, tell the shopkeeper that you have made your final offer: *A-khir TA-man d-YA-li HU-wa HA-da.*

COMMUNICATION

Pay phones accept either coins (2dh will cover most local calls) or Moroccan phone cards. The rates for the two types of phones are the same. The best way to make international calls is with a calling card. To call home with a calling card, contact the operator for your service provider in Morocco by dialing the appropriate toll-free access number. Sending something **air mail** (*par avion*) can take a week to a month to reach the US or Canada (about 10dh for a slim letter, postcards 4-7dh). Less reliable surface mail (*par terre*) takes up to two months. Express mail (*recommandé* or *exprès postaux*), slightly faster than regular air mail, is also more reliable. Post offices, shops, and some *tabacs* sell postcards and stamps. For very fast service (two days to the US), your best bet is DHL (www.dhl.com), which has drop-off locations in most major cities. **Cybercafes** aren't everywhere, but they can be found at least in most major cities, as well as in the more-touristed towns.

ACCOMMODATIONS AND CAMPING

The **Federation Royale des Auberges de Jeunesse (FRMAJ)** is the Moroccan Hosteling International (HI) affiliate. Beds cost 20-40dh per night, and there is a surcharge for non-members. **Camping** is popular and cheap (about 10dh per person), especially in the desert, mountains, and beaches. Like hotels, conditions vary widely. You can usually expect to find restrooms, but electricity is not as readily available. Use caution if camping unofficially, especially on beaches, as theft is a problem.

SAFETY AND SECURITY

Visitors should be suspicious of people offering free food, drinks, or cigarettes, as they have been known to be drugged. Avoid fake tour guides in large cities like Tangier and Fez. Women should dress conservatively and never travel alone. Travelers should drink only bottled or boiled water, and should avoid tap water, fountain drinks, and ice cubes. It's also advisable to only eat fruit and vegetables that are cooked and that you have peeled yourself. Stay away from food sold by street vendors, and check to make sure that dairy products have been pasteurized.

HOLIDAYS

Holidays: New Year's (Jan. 1); Independence Manifesto (Jan. 11); National Day (Mar. 3); Islamic New Year (Mar. 26); Labor Day (May 1); National Day (May 23); Ras al-Sana (July 30); Reunification Day (Aug. 14); Anniversary of the King's and the People's Revolution (Aug. 20); Young People's Day (Aug. 21); Anniversary of the Green March (Nov. 6); Independence Day (Nov. 18); Ramadan (Nov. 17-Dec. 16); 'Eid al-Fitr (Dec. 16).

TANGIER طنجة ☎039

For travelers venturing out of Europe for the first time, disembarking in Tangier (pop. 500,000), Morocco's main port of entry, can be a distressing experience. Many traveler's stories make the city out to be a living nightmare, but in reality there is little about the city to warrant such a reputation. If you have a few extra hours, learn about Tangier's international past at the ■**Old American Legation,** 8 r. d'America. (Open M-F 10am-1pm and 3-5pm. Free; donations appreciated.) Or visit the opulent palace-turned-museum **Dar al-Makhzen** (open W-M 9am-12:30pm and 3-5:30pm; 10dh) and the hectic **markets** in the **Grand Socco.** In the evening sip mint tea in front of the **Café de Paris,** 1 pl. de France, which hosted countless rendezvous between secret agents during World War II. Coming from the Grand Socco, look to the left. (Open daily 7am-11:30pm.)

Flights arrive at the **Royal Air Maroc** (☎039 37 95 08) from Barcelona, Madrid, Marrakesh, London, and New York. **Trains** leave from Mghagha Station (☎95 25 55), 6km from the port to Asilah (1hr., 3 per day 7am-10:30pm, 13dh). **Buses** leave from Av. Yacoub al-Mansour, 2km from the port entrance at pl. Jamia al-Arabia, for Fez (6hr., 10 per day 8:40am-9:30pm, 63dh) and Marrakesh (10hr., 5 per day 6:45am-8:30pm, 115dh).

MOROCCO

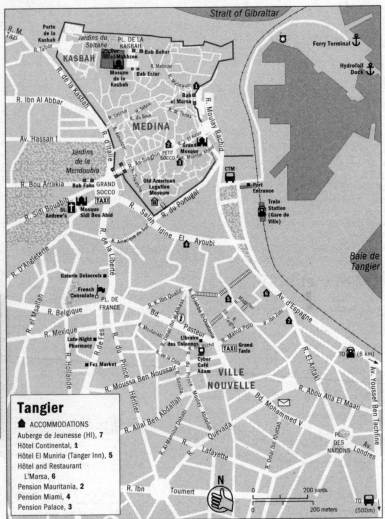

Tangier

⌂ ACCOMMODATIONS

Auberge de Jeunesse (HI), **7**
Hôtel Continental, **1**
Hôtel El Muniria (Tanger Inn), **5**
Hôtel and Restaurant
  L'Marsa, **6**
Pension Mauritania, **2**
Pension Miami, **4**
Pension Palace, **3**

The CTM Station (☎93 11 72) near the port entrance offers posher (and pricier) bus service to the same destinations. **Ferries,** 46, av. d'Espagne (☎94 26 12) head to Algeciras (2½hr., every hr. 7am-9pm, Class B 2960ptas or 210dh) and Tarifa (35min., 3-5 per day, 200dh). You'll need a boarding pass, available at any ticket desk, and a customs form (ask uniformed agents). The **tourist office,** 29, bd. Pasteur, has a list of accommodations available. (☎94 80 50. Open M-F 8:30am-7:30pm.) Expect to pay around 50-60dh for a single and 80-100dh for a double. The most convenient hostels cluster near **rue Mokhtar Ahardan** (formerly r. des Postes), off the Petit Socco; from the Grand Socco, take the first right down rue al-Siaghin. **Pension Mauritania,** r. des Almohades, at the Petit Socco, is a backpacker's mecca. (☎93 46 77. 45dh per person.)

ASILAH أصيلة ☎039

Just a short trip from Tangier, Asilah offers sandy shores, a laid-back atmosphere, and a brilliant white medina. Except for the first two weeks in August when an international art festival is held, Asilah remains a peaceful spot for kicking back and soaking up the sun on Atlantic beaches. The stunning ▨**medina** is bound by heavily fortified 15th-century Portuguese walls. Bab Kasaba, the gate off r. Zallakah, leads past the **Grand Mosque.** Right across from the mosque is the modern and spacious **Centre Hassan II des Rencontres Internationales,** which houses a collection of excellent art created during the great International Festival. (Open daily 9am-12:30pm and 3:30-7:30pm. Free.) There are two popular coastal stretches of beach: the closest is toward the train station along the Tangier-Asilah highway (about 15min. from the medina), but the nicest is the enclosed ▨**Paradise Beach,** an hour's walk from the medina in the opposite direction. Those with extra cash can take a horse-drawn wagon (150-200dh return).

Trains (☎41 73 27) run to Marrakesh (9hr., 11pm, 132-173dh) and Tangier (40min., 4 per day 5:15am-9:20pm, 14dh). The train station is a 25min. walk from town on the Asilah-Tangier highway, past a strip of campgrounds; a taxi to or from town costs about 10dh. **Buses** (☎41 80 91) go to: Fez (3½hr., 3 per day 10:45am-11pm, 55dh); Marrakesh (9hr., 7:30am and 5pm, 130dh); and Tangier (1hr., every 30min. 7:45am-5:15pm, 10dh). Many buses arrive full, so get to the station early, especially during the summer; from pl. Mohammed V, head away from the medina, take a right on av. de la Liberté, go one block up, and turn left. Grand taxis cluster in pl. Mohammed V, by the bus station, and head to Tangier (12dh). The main strip of restaurants, accommodations, and cafes are on **rue Zallakah,** which radiates from pl. Mohammed V, and the adjoining av. Hassan II which borders the medina. Av. Hassan II hold the town **market.**

CHEFCHAOUEN شفشاون ☎039

High in the Rif Mountains, but easily accessible from Tangier or Fez, Chefchaouen (Chaouen; pop. 30,000) refreshes with its cool mountain air. Its steep ▨**medina** is one of Morocco's best. Enter through Bab al-Ain and walk uphill toward pl. Uta al-Hammam, the center of the medina. In the *place* stands the 16th-century **Grand Mosque** with its red-and-gold minaret, and a *kasbah* built in the 17th century. (Open daily 9am-1pm and 3-6:30pm. 10dh.) Chefchaouen's **souq** operates Mondays and Thursdays outside the medina, and below both av. Hassan II and av. Allal ben Abdalallah. The town makes a spectacular base for **hiking;** follow the Ras al-Ma river upstream into the hills for a few kilometers. For a quick view of the city from the hills, hike toward the Hotel Asmaq (follow signs for the *ville nouvelle*). Highlights of the trail include the **Spanish mosque** and the rocky arch **Pont de Dieu.**

Buses (☎98 95 73) arrive from Fez (5hr., 1:15 and 3pm, 45-55dh) and Tangier (via Tetouan, 28-33dh). From the bus station, head up the steep hill and turn right after several blocks onto the large road, which leads to the circular pl. Mohammed V; it's about a 20min. walk to the center of town. Cross the *place* and continue east on **avenue Hassan II,** the main road of the *ville nouvelle.* Chefchaouen has no tourist office. A slew of budget hotels are on Bab al-Ain and pl. Uta al-Hammam, uphill in the medina. The best of the lot is ▨**Hotel Andalus,** 1, r. Sidi Salem, directly behind Credit Agricola on pl. Uta al-Hammam. (☎98 60 34. Singles 30dh; doubles 60dh; triples 90dh; quads 120dh.)

FEZ فاس ☎055

Fez's bustling, colorful medina epitomizes Morocco—no visit to the country is complete without seeing it. Artisans bang out sheets of brass, donkeys strain under crates of Coca-Cola, children balance trays of dough on their heads, and tourists struggle to stay together. Founded in the 8th century, Fez rose to prominence with the construction of the Qairaouine, a university-mosque complex. Today, post-independence Fez has been somewhat eclipsed by Rabat (the political capital), Casablanca (the economic capital), and Marrakesh (the tourist capital), yet it remains at the artistic, intellectual, and spiritual helm of the country.

MOROCCO

▐ TRANSPORTATION

Flights arrive at **Aérodrome de Fès-Saïs** (☎62 47 12), 12km out of town on the road to Immouzzèr. **Royal Air Maroc** (RAM), 54, av. Hassan II (☎62 55 16), flies daily to Casablanca. RAM also services Marseilles, Paris, Marrakesh, and Tangier. **Trains** (☎93 03 33), at the intersection of av. Almohades and r. Chenguit, travel to: Marrakesh (9hr., 5 per day 7:15am-2:40am, 130dh); Meknes (1hr., 9 per day 7:15am-2:40am, 16.50dh); and Tangier (5hr., 4 per day 7:15am-1:20am, 72dh). **CTM Buses** (☎73 29 92) run to: Chefchaouen (4hr., 3 per day 8am-11:45pm, 50dh); Marrakesh (8hr., 2 per day, 130dh); Meknes (1hr., 6 per day 9:30am-1am, 18dh); and Tangier (6hr., 3 per day 11am-1am, 85dh). Buses stop near pl. d'Atlas, at the far end of the *ville nouvelle*. From pl. Florence, walk 15min. down bd. Mohammed V, turn left onto av. Youssef ben Tachfine, and take the first right at pl. d'Atlas.

▐◪ ORIENTATION AND PRACTICAL INFORMATION

Fez is large and spread out but still manageable. Essentially three cities in one, the main areas of Fez are: fashionable **ville nouvelle**, a couple kilometers from the medina; Arab **Fez al-Jdid** (New Fez), which sits next to the medina and contains both the Jewish cemetery and the palace of Hassan II; and the enormous medina area of **Fez al-Bali** (Old Fez). Hire an official local guide at the **Syndicat d'Initiative tourist office**, pl. Mohammed V. (☎62 34 60. 3hr. guide 120-150dh, 5hr. 150-200dh. Open M-F 8:30am-noon and 2:30-6:30pm, Sa 8:30am-noon.) Access the **Internet** at **Soprocon**, off pl. Florence, upstairs from a teleboutique. (10dh per hr. Open daily 9am-11pm.)

▐◪ ACCOMMODATIONS AND FOOD

Rooms in the *ville nouvelle* are convenient to local services and more comfortable than those in the medina, which is only a quick cab ride away. The cheapest lodgings and food joints surround **boulevard Mohammed V**, between av. Mohammed al-Slaoui near the bus station and av. Hassan II near the post office. ◪**Hôtel Central,** 50, r. Brahim Roudani, off pl. Mohammed V, is the best deal. (☎62 23 33. Singles 59dh, with shower 89dh; doubles 89dh/119dh; triples 150dh/180dh.) **Hotel du Commerce,** pl. Alaouites, by the Royal Palace in Fez al-Jdid, is close to the medina without the annoyance of hustlers. (☎62 22 31. Singles 50dh; doubles 90dh.) Budget rooms fill the **Bab Boujeloud** area. **Hôtel Cascade**, 26, Serrajine Boujeloud, is a popular place with backpackers and families. (☎63 84 42. 40dh per person.)

For local eats, poke through stalls of fresh food at the **central market** on bd. Mohammed V, two blocks up from pl. Mohammed V. (Open daily 7am-1pm.) For some of the cheapest eateries in Morocco, go left from Tala'a Kebira at Madrasa al-Atarrine, and head deeper in the medina toward pl. Achabine. **Restaurant des Jeunes,** 16, r. Serrajine, next to Hotel Cascade by Bab Boujeloud, serves inexpensive Moroccan specialties. (Open daily 6am-midnight.)

◉▮ SIGHTS AND ENTERTAINMENT

Hiring an official guide at the Syndicat d'Iniative (see tourist office, above) will save you time, discourage hustlers, and provide detailed explanations; make sure to nail down an itinerary and price beforehand.

FEZ AL-BALI. Fez's **medina** is the handicraft capital of the country and exports goods around the world. With over 9000 streets and nearly 500,000 residents, the crowded medina is also possibly the most difficult to navigate in all Morocco. Its frenzied narrow streets contain fabulous mosques, *madrassas*, and *souqs*. At the head of the main thoroughfare, Tala'a Kebira, is the spectacular ◪**Bou Inania Madrasa,** a school built in 1326 for teaching the Qur'an and other Islamic sciences. *(Undergoing renovation; reopening date uncertain. Normally open daily 9am-5:30pm. 10dh.)*

Down Tala'a Kebira, the otherwise-mundane **Nejjarine Museum of Art** holds a tranquil rooftop **salon de thé** (tea room) and Morocco's finest bathrooms. *(Open daily 10am-5pm. 10dh.)* Back on the Tala'a Kebira, the **Attarine ("Spice") Souq,** perhaps the most exotic market, awaits. Walking through the market leads to **Zaouia Moulay Idriss II,** the resting place of the Islamic saint credited with founding Fez. Non-Muslims are not allowed to enter but can peer through the doors. Exiting the *madrasa,* turn left, and then left again; a few meters down is a little opening into the **Qairaouine mosque,** which can hold up to 20,000 worshippers (second only to Hassan II in Casablanca). Non-Muslims may not enter through the portal. Keeping the mosque on the right, you'll eventually come to pl. Seffarine, known for its fascinating **metal souq,** which deafens travelers with incessant cauldron-pounding. To exit the medina or reach **Bab al-Rcif,** a major bus and cab hub, follow the street heading away from the mosque to its end, turn left, and then right.

FEZ AL-JDID. In Fez al-Jdid, the gaudy **Dar al-Makhzen,** former palace of Hassan II, borders pl. Alaouites. Tourists may enter the grounds but not the palace. Nearby is the *mellah* or Jewish ghetto. The **jewelers' souq** glitters at the top of Grande Rue des Merinides. Cackling chickens, salty fish, and dried okra vie for attention in the **covered market,** inside Bab Smarine at the entrance to Fez al-Jdid proper.

SEEING RED You may see the hands, feet, and hair of Moroccan women decorated with the original temporary tattoo, *henna.* Stemming from the Arabic words for "tenderness" and "good luck," *henna* is made from the leaf of the *tafilat* plant, ground into a powder, and mixed with warm water or tea to make a paste. The dye comes in different colors, including red, black, and green, and is used for ceremonies such as weddings and the "Festival of the Girls" during Ramadan. Its application to the skin can take hours, and is both an art and a ceremony unto itself. The intricate motifs are painted on freehand or using a pattern, and are left to sit from a few hours to overnight before being rubbed off. The resulting decorations on the skin can last for weeks.

MOROCCO

THE NETHERLANDS (NEDERLAND)

GUILDERS

US$1 = F2.46	F1 = US$0.41
CDN$1 = F1.61	F1 = CDN$0.62
UK£1 = F3.50	F1 = UK£0.29
IR£1 = F2.80	F1 = IR£0.36
AUS$1 = F1.27	F1 = AUS$0.79
NZ$1 = F1.05	F1 = NZ$0.95
ZAR1 = F0.29	F1 = ZAR3.40
EUR€1 = F2.20	F1 = EUR€0.45

PHONE CODE	Country code: 31. International dialing prefix: 00. From outside the Netherlands, dial int'l dialing prefix (see inside back cover) + 31 + city code + local number.

The Dutch say that although God created the rest of the world, they created The Netherlands (pop. 15.9 million; 41,532 sq. km). The country is a masterful feat of engineering; since most of it is below sea level, vigorous pumping and many dikes were used to create dry land. What was once the domain of seaweed is now packed with windmills, bicycles, tulips, and wooden shoes. The Netherlands' wealth of art, its canal-lined towns, and the, ahem, uniqueness of Amsterdam's hedonism and indulgent perpetual party draw hordes of travelers.

For a more in-depth look at The Netherlands' favorite playground, pick up *Let's Go: Amsterdam 2002*.

FACTS AND FIGURES

Official Name: The Kingdom of The Netherlands.

Capital: Amsterdam. The Hague.

Major Cities: Rotterdam, Utrecht, Maastricht.

Population: 15,691,000.

Land Area: 13,255 sq. km.

Climate: Temperate, but with rainfall year-round.

Language: Dutch.

Religions: Catholic (32%), Protestant (23%), Muslim (4%).

DISCOVER THE NETHERLANDS

Roll it, light it, then smoke it in **Amsterdam** (p. 680), a hedonist's dream, with chill coffeeshops and breathtaking museums. Clear your head in the rustic Dutch countryside; the amazing **Hoge Veluwe National Park** (p. 699), southeast of Amsterdam, shelters within its 30,000 wooded acres one of the finest modern art museums in Europe. Beautifully preserved **Leiden** (p. 695) and **Utrecht** (p. 698), less than 30 minutes away, delight with picturesque canals. Dutch politics and museums abound in **The Hague** (p. 696); for more innovative art and architecture, step into futuristic **Rotterdam** (p. 697). An afternoon in **Delft** (p. 697) provides a dose of small-town Dutch charm. Visit the sand dunes and isolated beaches of the tiny **Wadden Islands** (p. 700), a biker's paradise.

ESSENTIALS

WHEN TO GO

Mid-May to early October is the ideal time to visit, when day temperatures are generally 20-31°C (70-80°F), with nights around 10-20°C (50-60°F). However, it can be quite rainy; bring an umbrella. The tulip season runs from April to mid-May.

DOCUMENTS AND FORMALITIES

VISAS. Visas are generally not required for tourist stays under three months; South African citizens are the exception.

EMBASSIES. All foreign embassies and most consulates are in The Hague (p. 696). The US has a consulate in Amsterdam (p. 680). For Dutch embassies at home: **Australia,** 120 Empire Circuit, Yarralumla Canberra, ACT 2600 (☎(02) 62 73 31 11; fax 62 73 32 06); **Canada,** 350 Albert St., Ste. 2020, Ottawa ON K1R 1A4 (☎613-237-5030; fax 613-237-6471); **Ireland,** 160 Merrion Rd., Dublin 4 (☎(012) 69 34 44; fax 283 96 90); **New Zealand,** P.O. Box 840, Cnr. Ballonce and Featherston St., Wellington (☎(04) 471 63 90; fax 471 29 23); **South Africa,** P.O. Box 346, Cape Town 8000 (☎(021) 421 56 60; fax 418 26 90); **UK,** 38 Hyde Park Gate, London SW7 5DP (☎(020) 75 90 32 00; fax 75 81 34 58); and **US,** 4200 Linnean Ave., NW, Washington, D.C. 20008 (☎202-244-5300; fax 202-362-3430; www.netherlands-embassy.org).

TRANSPORTATION

BY PLANE. KLM Royal Dutch Airlines, Martinair, Continental, Delta, Northwest, United, and **Singapore Airlines** serve Amsterdam's Schiphol Airport. Amsterdam is a major hub for cheap transatlantic flights (p. 54).

BY TRAIN. The national rail company is the efficient **Nederlandse Spoorwegen** (NS; Netherlands Railways; www.ns.nl). Train service tends to be faster than bus service. *Sneltreins* are the fastest; *stoptreins* make the most stops. One-way tickets are called *enkele reis;* normal return tickets, *retour;* and day return tickets (valid only on day of purchase, but cheaper than normal round-trip tickets), *dagretour.* **Day Trip (Rail Idee)** programs, available at train stations, have reduced-price combination transportation/entrance fees. **Eurail** and **InterRail** are valid in The Netherlands. The **Holland Railpass** (US$52-98) is good for three or five travel days in any one-month period. Although available in the US, the Holland Railpass is cheaper in the Netherlands at DER Travel Service or RailEurope. (See www.ns.nl/reisplan2.asp.) The **Euro Domino Holland** card similarly allows three (ƒ130/€59, under 26 ƒ100/€45.40), five (ƒ200/€90.80, ƒ150/€68.10), or 10 days (ƒ350/€158.85, ƒ275/€124.80) of unlimited rail travel in any one-month period, but is only available to those who have lived in Europe for at least six months and cannot be bought in the Netherlands. **One-day train passes** cost ƒ45.25-75.50/€20.55-34.30. The **Meerman's Kaart** grants a day of unlimited travel for two to six people (ƒ114-192/€51.75-87.15).

BY BUS. A nationalized fare system covers city buses, trams, and long-distance buses. The country is divided into zones; the number of strips on a **strippenkaart** (strip card) required depends on the number of zones through which you travel. A trip between destinations in the same zone costs one strip; a trip that traverses two zones requires two strips. On buses, tell the driver your destination and he or she will cancel the correct number of strips; on trams and subways, stamp your own *strippenkaart* in either a yellow box at the back of the tram or in the subway station. Bus and tram drivers sell two- (ƒ3.50/€2) and three-strip tickets (ƒ4.75/€2.20), but they're *much* cheaper in bulk, available at public transit counters, tourist offices, post offices, and some tobacco shops and newsstands (8-strip ƒ12/€5.45; 15-strip ƒ12.50/5.70, children and seniors ƒ7.75/€3.55; 45-strip ƒ36.75/€16.70). Day passes *(dagkarten)* are valid for unlimited use in any zone (ƒ11/€5, children and seniors ƒ7.50/€3.40). Unlimited-use passes are valid for one week in the same zone (ƒ18.75/8.55; requires a passport photo and picture ID). Riding without a ticket can result in a ƒ60/€27.25 fine plus the original cost of the ticket.

BY FERRY. Ferries cross the North Sea, connecting England to The Netherlands. Boats arrive in Hook of Holland, near Delft (p. 697), from Harwich, northeast of London (5hr.); in Rotterdam from Hull (13½hr.), near York (p. 191); and in Amsterdam from Newcastle-upon-Tyne (14hr.; p. 193). For more information, see p. 62.

BY CAR. The Netherlands has well-maintained roadways. North Americans and Australians need an International Driver's License; if your insurance doesn't cover you abroad, you'll also need a green insurance card. Fuel comes in two types; some cars use benzene (ƒ2.70/€1.25 per liter), while others use gasoline (ƒ1/€0.45 per liter). The **Royal Dutch Touring Association** (ANWB) offers roadside assistance to members. (☎0800 08 88.) For more information, contact the ANWB at Wassenaarseweg 220, 2596 EC The Hague (☎070 314 71 47), or Museumsplein 5, 1071 DJ Amsterdam (☎0800 05 03).

BY BIKE AND BY THUMB. Cycling is the way to go in The Netherlands—distances between cities are short, the countryside is absolutely flat, and most streets have separate bike lanes. Bikes run about ƒ10/€4.55 per day or ƒ35/€15.90 per week plus a ƒ50-200/€22.70-90.80 deposit (railpasses will often earn you a discount). Bikes are sometimes available at train stations and hostels, and *Let's Go* also lists bike rental shops in many towns. For more information try www.visitholland.com. Hitchhiking is somewhat effective, but on the roads out of Amsterdam there is cutthroat competition. For more information on hitching, visit www.hitchhikers.org. *Let's Go* does not recommend hitchhiking.

TOURIST SERVICES AND MONEY

EMERGENCY Police, Ambulance, and **Fire: ☎** 112.

TOURIST OFFICES. VVV (vay-vay-vay) tourist offices are marked by triangular blue signs. The website www.goholland.com is also a useful resource.

MONEY. The Dutch currency is the **guilder** (abbreviated ƒ, ƒl, or hƒl as it was formerly called the florin), made up of 100 cents. Coins include the *stuiver* (5¢), *dubbeltje* (10¢), *kwartje* (25¢), *rijksdaalder* (ƒ2.50), and a five-*guilder* piece. The Netherlands has accepted the **Euro (€)** as legal tender, and *guilders* will be phased out by July 1, 2002. For more information, see p. 24. Post offices and major banks both offer reasonable currency exchange rates. GWKs (*grenswisselkantoorbureaux;* open 24hr.) often have the best rates and offer ISIC holders a reduced commission. Otherwise, expect a flat fee of about ƒ5/€2.30 and a 2.25% commission. A bare-bones day traveling in The Netherlands will cost US$20-25; a slightly more comfortable day will run US$30-40. The value added tax and service charges are always included in bills for hotels, shopping, taxi fares, and restaurants. Tips for services are accepted and appreciated but not necessary. Taxi drivers are generally tipped 10% of the fare. VAT (BTW in The Netherlands) refunds are usually 13.5%, and are available on purchases of more than ƒ300/€136.20 made during a single visit to a store.

BUSINESS HOURS. Most stores are open Monday to Friday 9am-6pm, and generally open late at night on the weekends. During holidays and the tourist season, hours are extended into the night and stores open their doors on Sundays. Banks are typically open the same hours as shops but remain closed on Sundays. Post offices close at noon on Saturdays and remain closed on Sundays.

COMMUNICATION

MAIL. Post offices are generally open Monday to Friday 9am-6pm, and some are also open Saturday 10am-1:30pm; larger branches may stay open later. Mailing a postcard or letter to anywhere in the EU costs ƒ1/€0.45; to destinations outside Europe, postcards cost ƒ1/€0.45, letters (up to 20g) ƒ1.60/€0.75. Mail takes 2-3 days to the UK, 4-6 to North America, 6-8 to Australia and New Zealand, and 8-10 to South Africa.

TELEPHONES. When making international calls from pay phones, phone cards (in denominations of ƒ10/€4.55 and ƒ25/€11.35; available at post offices and train stations) are the most economical option. The cards include a computer chip preprogrammed with a set amount of minutes; just slide it into the slots on the payphones and make your call. International calls are cheapest at night (8pm-8am). For directory assistance, dial ☎09 00 80 08; for collect calls, dial ☎06 04 10. International dial direct numbers include: **AT&T,** ☎0800 022 91 11; **British Telecom,** ☎0800 022 00 44; **Canada Direct,** ☎0800 022 91 16; **Ireland Direct,** ☎0800 02 20 353; **MCI,** ☎0800 022 91 22; **Telecom New Zealand,** ☎0800 022 44 64; **Sprint,** ☎0800 022 91 19; **Telkom South Africa,** ☎0800 022 02 27; and **Telstra Australia,** ☎0800 022 20 61.

INTERNET ACCESS. Email is easily accessible within The Netherlands. Cybercafes are listed in most towns and all cities. In small towns, if Internet access is not listed, try the library or even your hostel. Internet access generally runs ƒ10/€4.55 per hour, except in libraries where it's often free.

LANGUAGE. Dutch is the official language of The Netherlands, however most natives speak English fluently. Knowing a few words of Dutch can't hurt though. Fill up on *dagschotel* (dinner special), *broodje* (bread or sandwich), *bier* (beer), and *kaas* (cheese). Dutch uses a gutteral "g" sound for both "g" and "ch." "J" is usually pronounced as "y"; e.g., *hofje* is "hof-YUH." "Ui" is pronounced "ow," and the dipthong "ij" is best approximated in English as "ah" followed by a long "e." For Dutch lingo, see p. 983.

THE NETHERLANDS

ACCOMMODATIONS AND CAMPING

VVV offices supply accommodation lists and can nearly always reserve rooms in both local and other areas (fee around ƒ4/€1.85). **Private rooms** cost about two-thirds as much as hotels, but they are hard to find; check with the VVV. During July and August, many cities add ƒ2.50/€1.15 tourist tax to the price of all rooms. The country's best values are the 34 **HI youth hostels**, run by the **NJHC (Dutch Youth Hostel Federation)**. Hostels are divided into four price categories based on quality. Most are exceedingly clean and modern and cost ƒ28-34/€12.75-15.45 for bed and breakfast, plus high-season or prime-location supplements (ƒ1-3/€0.45-1.40). The VVV has a hostel list, and the useful *Jeugdherbergen* brochure describes each one (both free). For more information, contact the NJHC at P. O. Box 9191, 1006 AD, Amsterdam (☎(010) 264 60 64; www.njhc.org). Pick up a membership card at hostels (ƒ30/€13.65); nonmembers are charged an additional ƒ5/€2.30. **Camping** is available across the country, but many sites are crowded and trailer-ridden in summer. An international camping card is not required.

FOOD AND DRINK

Dutch food is hearty and simple. Pancakes, salted herring, and pea soup are national specialties. Dutch cheeses transcend Gouda and Edam; try spicy Leiden, mild Belegen, and creamy Kernhem. A typical breakfast consists of meat and cheese on bread and a soft-boiled egg. For a hearty brunch, sample *uitsmijter*, which packs in salad, ham, cheese, and fried eggs. The traditional Dutch lunch is *pannenkoeken* (buttery, sugary, golden-brown pancakes) topped with everything from ham and cheese to strawberries and whipped cream. At dinner, reap the benefits of Dutch imperialism: *rijsttafel* is an Indonesian specialty comprising up to 25 different dishes, including curried chicken or lamb with pineapple. Wash it all down with a small, foamy glass of domestic beer: Heineken or Amstel.

HOLIDAYS AND FESTIVALS

Holidays: New Year's Day (Jan. 1); Good Friday (Mar. 29); Easter Monday (Mar. 31); Liberation Day (May 5); Ascension Day (May 9), Whit Sunday and Whit Monday (June 3-4); Christmas Day (Dec. 25); Boxing Day (Dec. 26; also called Second Christmas Day).

Festivals: Koninginnedag (Queen's Day; Apr. 30) turns the country into a huge carnival. The **Holland Festival** (in June) features more than 30 productions in a massive celebration of the arts. **Bloemen Corso** (Flower Parade; first Sa in Sept.) runs from Aalsmeer to Amsterdam. Many historical canal houses and windmills are open to the public for **National Monument Day** (2nd Sa in Sept.). The **Cannabis Cup** (November) celebrates the magical mystery weed that brings millions of visitors to Amsterdam every year.

AMSTERDAM ☎ 020

Some people say the best vacation to Amsterdam is one you can't remember. The city lives up to its reputation as a never-never land of bacchanalian excess: the aroma of cannabis wafts from coffeeshops, and the city's infamous sex scene swathes itself in red lights. Amsterdam will give you the choice of exactly how you want to trip, turn, or twist through reality. But one need not be naughty to enjoy Amsterdam. Art enthusiasts will delight in the troves of Rembrandts, Vermeers, and van Goghs, and romantics can stroll along endless sparkling canals.

▐ TRANSPORTATION

Flights: Schiphol Airport (SKIP-pull; ☎0800-SCHIPHOL). **Trains** connect the airport to Centraal Station (20min., every 10min., ƒ10/€4.55).

Trains: Centraal Station, Stationspl. 1, at the end of the Damrak (international info ☎09 00 92 96; domestic info ☎09 00 92 92, ƒ0.50/€0.25 per min.; www.ns.nl). To: **Berlin** (8hr.); **Brussels** (3-4hr.); **Frankfurt** (5¼-6hr.); **Hamburg** (5hr.); **Paris** (8hr.). For international info and reservations, take a number and wait (up to 1hr. in summer). Info desk open 24hr. International reservations made daily 6:30am-11:30pm. **Lockers** ƒ6-8/€2.75-3.65 per hr.

Buses: Trains are quicker, but the **GVB** (public transportation authority) will direct you to a bus stop for destinations not on a rail line. **Muiderpoort** (2 blocks east of Oosterpark) sends buses east; **Marnixstation** (at the corner of Marnixstr. and Kinkerstr.) west; and the **Stationsplein depot** north and south.

Public Transportation: GVB (☎09 00 92 92), Stationspl.; in front of Centraal Station. Open M-F 7am-9pm, Sa-Su 8am-9pm. Tram, metro, and bus lines radiate from Centraal Station. Trams are most convenient for inner-city travel; the metro leads to farther-out neighborhoods. The last trams leave Centraal Station M-F at midnight; Sa-Su 12:25am. Pick up a *nachtbussen* (night bus) schedule from the GVB office. The 45-strip *strippen-kaart* (ƒ36.75/€16.70) is the best deal; it can be used on trams and buses throughout The Netherlands and is available at the VVV, the GVB, and many hostels.

Bike Rental: Bikes run about ƒ10-15/€4.55-6.85 per day plus a ƒ50-200/€22.70-90.80 deposit. Try **Frederic Rent a Bike,** Brouwersgracht 78 (☎62 45 509; www.frederic.nl), in the Shipping Quarter. From Centraal Station, head down Damrak, turn right at Nieuwendijk, left after you cross the Harlemmersluis bridge, and follow along the Brouwersgracht for about 7 blocks. ƒ10/€4.55 per day. Reserve online. Theft/damage insurance ƒ5/€2.30 per day. No charge for deposit. AmEx/MC/V.

✴ ORIENTATION

A series of roughly concentric canals ripple out around the **Centrum** (city center), resembling a giant horseshoe with its opening to the northeast. Emerging from Centraal Station, at the top of the horseshoe, you'll hit **Damrak,** a key thoroughfare leading to the **Dam,** the main square. Just east of Damrak in the Centrum is Amsterdam's famed **Red Light District,** bounded by Warmoestr., Zeedijk, Damstr., and Kloven-niersburgwal. Don't head into the area until you've locked up your bags, either at the train station or at a hostel or hotel. South of the Red Light District but still within the horseshoe lies the **Rembrandtplein.** The canals radiating around the Centrum (lined by streets of the same names) are **Singel, Herengracht, Keizergracht,** and **Prinsengracht.** West of the Centrum, beyond Prinsengracht, lies the **Jordaan,** an attractive residential neighborhood. Moving counterclockwise around Prinsengracht you'll hit the **Leidseplein,** which lies just across the canal from the **Museum District** and **Vondelpark.**

🛈 PRACTICAL INFORMATION

TOURIST, FINANCIAL, AND LOCAL SERVICES

Tourist Office: VVV Stationspl. 10 (☎(0900) 400 40 40), to the left and in front of Centraal Station. Hefty ƒ6/€2.75 fee for room booking. **Branches** at Centraal Station, platform 2, Leidsepl. 1, and the airport open daily.

Budget Travel: NBBS, Rokin 66 (☎0900 235 62 27; reservations ƒ0.75/€0.34 per min.). Open Tu-W and F 9:30am-6pm, Th 9:30am-9pm, Sa 10am-5pm. Special student and youth fares. Also at Haarlemmerstr. 115, and Utrechtstr. 48. Call ☎0900 235 62 27. **Eurolines,** Rokin 10 (☎560 87 88). Open M-F 9:30am-5:30pm, Sa 10am-4pm.

Consulates: All foreign embassies are in **The Hague** (p. 696). **US** consulate, Museumpl. 19 (☎575 53 09). Open M-F 8:30am-noon.

Currency Exchange: Best rates at **American Express** (see below). **GWK** in Centraal Station, with **Change** locations at Damrak 86, Leidsestr. 106, and Kalverstr. 150, charges ƒ7.50/€3.40 plus 2.25% commission. 25% ISIC discount. 3% commission for traveler's checks. Open M-W and F-Sa 8:30am-7pm, Th 8:30am-9pm, Su 10:30am-6pm. Location at Schiphol open 24hr. **Change Express,** Kalverstr. 150 (☎627 80 87; open M-Sa 8:30am-8pm, Su 10:30am-6pm), or Leidestr. 106 (☎622 14 25; open daily 8am-11pm), has good rates and 2.25% commission plus ƒ7.50/€3.40 fee.

American Express: Damrak 66 (☎504 87 70). Excellent rates and no commission on traveler's checks. Mail held. Open M-F 9am-5pm, Sa 9am-noon.

English-Language Bookstores: Spui, near the Amsterdam University, is lined with bookstores. **Oudemanhuispoort,** in the Oude Zijd, is a book market. Open daily; times vary.

Gay and Lesbian Services: COC, Rozenstr. 14 (☎626 30 87), is the main source of info. Open M-Tu, Th-F 10am-5pm, W 10am-8pm. **Gay and Lesbian Switchboard** (☎623 65 65) takes calls daily 10am-10pm.

Laundry: Look for a *Wasserette* sign. **Wasserette-Stomerij 'De Eland',** Elandsgr. 59 (☎625 07 31), has self-service. ƒ8.75/€4 per 4kg, ƒ11.25/€5.10 per 6kg. Open M-Tu and Th-F 8am-8pm, W 8am-6pm, Sa 9am-5pm.

Condoms: Condomerie, Warmoesstr. 141 (☎627 41 74), next to the Red Light district. Open M-Sa 11am-6pm.

EMERGENCY AND COMMUNICATIONS

Emergency: ☎112 (Police, Ambulance, and Fire Brigade).

Police: Headquarters, Elandsgracht 117 (☎559 91 11).

Crisis Lines: General counseling at **Telephone Helpline** (☎675 75 75). Open 24hr. **Rape crisis hotline** (☎613 02 45). Staffed M-F 10:30am-11pm, Sa-Su 3:30pm-11pm. **Drug counseling,** Jellinek clinic (☎570 23 55). Open M-F 9am-5pm.

Medical Assistance: Tourist Medical Service (☎592 33 55). Open 24hr. For hospital care, call **Academisch Medisch Centrum,** Meibergdreef 9 (☎566 91 11), near the Holendrecht Metro stop. For free emergency medical care, visit the **Kruispost,** Oudezijds Voorburgwal 129 (☎624 90 31). Open M-F 7-9:30pm. **STD Line** (☎555 58 22). Hotline and free clinic at Groenburgwal 44. Open M-F 8-10:30am and 1:30-3:30pm.

Pharmacy: Most open M-F 8:30am-5pm. When closed, each *apotheek* (pharmacy) posts a sign directing you to the nearest one open.

Internet Access: easyEverything, Reguliersbreestr. 22 near Rembrandtpl. and Damrak 34. Base price ƒ5/€2.30 buys differing amounts of time depending on computer availability. Open 24hr. **La Bastille,** Lijnbaansgracht 246 (info@labastille.nl; www.labastille.nl), 2 blocks east of the Leidsepl. ƒ5/€2.30 per 30min. (15min. minimum). Open daily 10am-midnight. **Cyber Cafe Amsterdam,** Nieuwendijk 17, has the same deal as the Internet Cafe. Open Su-Th 10am-1am, F-Sa 10am-2am.

Post Office: Singel 250 (☎556 33 11), at Raadhuisstr. behind the Dam. Address mail to be held: First name SURNAME, *Poste Restante,* Singel 250, Amsterdam **1016 AB,** THE NETHERLANDS. Open M-W and F 9am-6pm, Th 9am-9pm, Sa 10am-1:30pm.

ACCOMMODATIONS

Accommodations closer to **Centraal Station** often take good security measures in face of the chaos of the nearby Red Light District. Hostels and hotels in **Vondelpark** and the **Jordaan** are quieter (by Amsterdam's standards) and safer. They are also close to bars, coffeeshops, large museums, and the busy Leidsepl., and are only 15min. by foot or 2min. by train from the city center. The hotels and hostels in the **Red Light District** (in the Oude Zijd) are often bars with beds over them. Consider just how much pot, noise, and music you want to inhale before booking a bed there. Accommodations are listed by neighborhoods.

OUDE ZIJD, NIEUWE ZIJD, AND REMBRANDTPLEIN

Hotel Groenendael, Nieuwendijk 15 (☎624 48 22; www.hotelgroenendael.com). Friendly hotel right by Centraal Station. Well-lit, cheerful rooms and clean bathrooms. Breakfast included. Free lockers. Key deposit ƒ10/€4.55. Singles ƒ70/€31.80; doubles ƒ110/€49.95, with shower ƒ120/€54.45; triples ƒ165/€74.90. AmEx.

Durty Nelly's Hostel, Warmoesstr. 115/117 (☎638 01 25; nellys@xs4all.nl; http://xs4all.nl/~nellys). From Centraal Station, go south on Damrak, turn right on Brugsteeg, and then right on Warmoesstr.; Nelly's is 2 blocks on the left. Cozy hostel above an Irish pub. Breakfast included. Towel deposit ƒ5/€2.30. Reception 24hr. No reservations. Dorms ƒ45/€20.45.

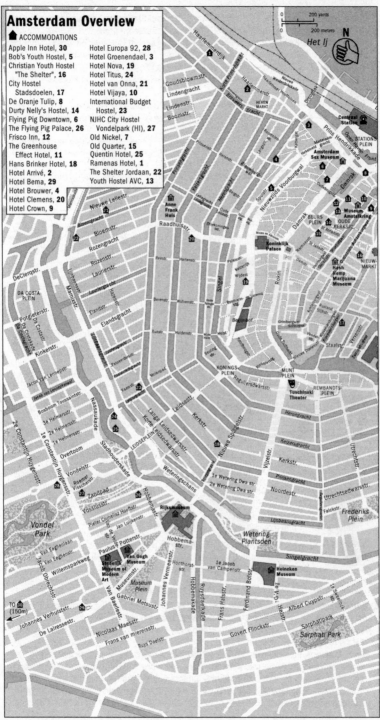

Frisco Inn, Beursstr. 5 (☎620 16 10). From Centraal Station, go south on Damrak, then left at Brugsteeg, and take the next right onto Beursstr.; it's the 2nd building on your left. Centrally located hotel behind the Beurs van Berlage has 28 beds. Smoking allowed. Reception 24hr. No curfew. Rooms from ƒ60/€27.25 per person.

Youth Hostel AVC, Warmoesstr. 87 (☎625 59 74; fax 422 0885). Low-key, basic budget digs in a youthful environment. No smoking in rooms. Dorms ƒ30-44/€13.65; doubles ƒ100/€45.40; triples ƒ125/€56.75; quads ƒ175/€79.45.

Christian Youth Hostel "The Shelter," Barndesteeg 21-25 (☎625 32 30; reservations.city@shelter.nl; www.shelter.nl), off the Nieuwmarkt. Finding virtue amid the red lights, travelers get incredibly clean rooms and a friendly staff at this hostel. Breakfast included. No drugs; cigarette-smoking only in hallways. Key deposit ƒ10/€4.55. Single-sex dorms. Locker deposit ƒ10/€4.55. Linens included. Reception 24hr. Curfew Su-Th midnight, F-Sa 1am. Dorms Oct.-Mar. ƒ25-30/€11.35-13.60.

Hotel Crown, Oudezijds Voorburgwal 21 (☎626 96 64; www.web2day.com). This British-owned hotel provides clean, handsome digs located in the picturesque end of the Red Light District. Singles ƒ100/€45.40; doubles ƒ200/€90.75, with shower ƒ220/€99.85); triples ƒ300/€136.13, with shower ƒ330/€149.75); quads ƒ400/€181.50, with shower ƒ440/€199.60; 6-person room with shower ƒ660/€299.50.

Hotel Vijaya, Oudezijds Voorburgwal 44 (☎626 94 06 or 638 01 02; fax 620 52 77). Very clean rooms on the fringe of the pulsing Red Light District. Breakfast included. ƒ120-275/€54.45-124.80; off-season ƒ85-250/€38.60-113.45.

The Greenhouse Effect Hotel, Warmoesstr. 55 (☎624 49 74; fax 427 79 06; www.the-greenhouse-effect.com). Reasonably priced theme rooms (including Arabian Nights) await you. 5min. from Centraal Station. Hotel guests are treated to an all-day Happy Hour at the bar. 1- to 5-person rooms ƒ60-250/€27.25-113.45.

Old Quarter, Warmoesstr. 20-22. (☎626 64 29) Turn right onto Warmoesstr from Old Nickel. Very clean accommodations ranging from basic to luxury (canal view, TV, private shower, toilet). *Bruine cafe* downstairs. Live jazz Th-Sa. Reception 24hr. Doubles from ƒ125/€56.75.

Old Nickel, Nieuwebrugsteeg 11 (☎624 19 12). Quiet hotel 2min. from the train station; turn onto Warmoesstr. at the end nearest Centraal Station, and the Old Nickel is diagonal to the Hotel International. Breakfast included. Reception 8am-midnight. Singles ƒ65/€29.50; doubles ƒ90-125/€40.85-56.75; quads ƒ160-200/€72.60-90.80.

De Oranje Tulp, Damrak 32 (☎428 16 18; fax 428 60 44; reservations@oranje-tulphotel.a2000.nl; http://people.a2000.nl/oranje00). Great location and super value for slick, well-appointed rooms. Singles ƒ100/€45.40; doubles ƒ160/€72.60; triples ƒ180/€81.70; quads ƒ200/€90.75; quints ƒ275/€124.80. Prices higher July-Aug.

Bob's Youth Hostel, Nieuwezijds Voorburgwal 92 (☎623 00 63). Well-known by European backpackers everywhere, Bob's provides the bare necessities. Young clientele. Liberal drug policy. Breakfast included. Lockers and luggage storage available. Linens provided, but bring a towel. Laundry facilities nearby. Key deposit ƒ10/€4.55. 2-night min. stay on weekends, 7-day max. stay. Reception 8am-3am. No lockout or curfew. No reservations, so arrive before 10am to get a room. Dorms ƒ33/€15.

SHIPPING QUARTER, CANAL RING WEST, AND THE JORDAAN

Ramenas Hotel, Haarlemerdijk 61 (☎624 69 60 30; fax 420 22 61; www.amsterdam-hotels.com). Walk from Centraal Station along Nieuwendijk as it turns into Haarlemerstr. and then Haarlemerdijk. Ordinary rooms above a friendly cafe. Breakfast included. ƒ60/€27.25 per person, with bath ƒ75/€34.05. Cash only.

Hotel Arrivé, Haarlemmerstr. 65-67 (☎622 14 39; fax 622 19 83). Close to the action of Nieuwendijk, Arrivé has plain rooms with bare lightbulbs. Breakfast included. All rooms have shared bath. Singles ƒ70/€31.85; doubles ƒ120/€54.55; triples ƒ160/€72.75. Add 20% for weekend rates.

Hotel Clemens, Raadhuisstr. 39 (☎624 60 89; fax 626 96 58; info@clemenshotel.nl; www.clemenshotel.nl). A true gem with elegant deluxe and budget rooms, all of which will be renovated by Jan. 2002. Phone, fridge, TV, and hairdryer in all rooms. Breakfast ƒ15.45/€7. Key deposit ƒ50/€22.69. 3-night min. stay during weekends. Internet. Budget singles ƒ88-125/€40-56; doubles ƒ154/€70. Cash only for budget rooms.

Hotel Brouwer, Singel 83 (☎624 63 58; fax 520 62 64; akita@hotelbrouwer.nl; www.hotelbrouwer.nl). From Centraal Station, cross the water, turn right onto Prins Hendrikkade and left onto Singel. Gorgeously restored rooms, each with private bathroom and canal view. Breakfast included. No smoking in the rooms. Singles ƒ88/€40; doubles ƒ165/€75. Cash only.

The Shelter Jordaan, Bloemstr. 179 (☎624 47 17; fax 627 61 37; jordan@shelter.nl; www.shelter.nl). Tram #13 or 17 to Marnixstr.; it's on the corner of Lijnbaansgr. and Bloemstr. Clean, comfortable hostel in quiet Jordaan. Breakfast and sheets included. Single-sex dorms. No smoking, no alcohol. Internet free. Age limit 35. Curfew 2am. Dorms July-Aug. ƒ30/€13.65; Apr.-June and Sept. ƒ28/€12.75; Oct.-Mar. ƒ25/€11.35. Cash only.

Hotel van Onna, Bloemgr. 104 (☎626 58 01; www.netcentrum.com/onna). Tram #13 or 17 from Centraal Station to Westermarkt, also close to the Bloemgr. stop on tram #10. Quiet rooms all have private bathrooms. No smoking. Breakfast included. Reception 8am-11pm. Rooms for 1-4 people ƒ80/€40 per person. Cash only.

LEIDSEPLEIN AND MUSEUMPLEIN

⊠ **NJHC City Hostel Vondelpark (HI),** Zandpad 5 (☎589 89 93; www.njhc.org/vondelpark), bordering Vondelpark. Take tram #1, 2, or 5 from the station to Leidsepl., cross the canal and the street (Stadhouderskade), turn left, then take 2nd right before the park entrance onto Zandpad. This palatial hostel offers clean rooms all with bath. Bike rental and Internet access. Breakfast and sheets included. Lockers ƒ3/€1.35, bring a padlock. Reception 7:30am-midnight. 10- to 20-person dorm ƒ39/€17.70; 6- to 8- person dorm ƒ43/€19.50; doubles ƒ145/€65.80; quads ƒ208/€94.38 per room, ƒ52/€19.50 per person. MC/V (4% surcharge).

⊠ **The Flying Pig Palace,** Vossiusstr. 46-47 (☎400 41 87; palace@flyingpig.nl; www.flypig.nl). Take tram #1, 2, or 5 from Centraal Station to Leidsepl., cross the canal and the street, look for the entrance to the Vondelpark on the left, take 1st right after the entrance. This vibrant hostel maintains a fun atmosphere in a beautiful location. Internet free. Breakfast included. Key deposit ƒ10/€4.55. Sheets included. Reception 8am-9pm. Ages 16-35 only. Stop by at 8am or call at 8:30am to reserve a room for the same night; make reservations via Internet and pay 10% deposit ahead of time. 6- to 10-bed dorms ƒ35.50-47.50/€16.15-21.55; doubles ƒ130/€59; triples ƒ154.50/€70.10; quads ƒ194/€88.05.

International Budget Hostel, Leidsegr. 76-1 (☎624 27 84; fax 626 18 39; info@internationalbudgethostel.com; www.internationalbudgethostel.com). Take tram #1, 2, or 5 to Prinsengr., turn right and walk along Prinsengr. to Leidsegr. Like sleepover camp from the 70s. Breakfast ƒ7/€3.20. 2-night min. stay in summer. Dorms ƒ7.71-10.43/€17-23; rooms from ƒ22.69/€50. 5% credit card surcharge.

Quentin Hotel, Leidsekade 89 (☎626 21 87; fax 622 01 21). Quentin proves that budget accommodations can have style. Basic singles from ƒ100/€45.45; basic doubles from ƒ145/€65.90; single with phone and bath from ƒ135/€61.35; doubles from ƒ275/€125; triples from ƒ275/€125. AmEx/MC/V (5% surcharge).

Hans Brinker Hotel, Kerkstr. 136 (☎622 06 87; www.hansbrinker.com). Take tram #1, 2, or 5 from Centraal Station, get off at Kerkstr., and it's 1 block down on the left. Large budget hotel offers clean, safe, spartan digs, all with baths. No visitors. All-you-can-eat breakfast buffet included. Key deposit ƒ10/€4.55. Reception 24hr. Dorms (single-sex and mixed) ƒ42.50/€19.35; singles ƒ114/€51.85; doubles ƒ152/€69.10; triples ƒ198/€90; quads ƒ220/€100; quints ƒ262.50/€119.10.

Hotel Titus, Leidsekade 74 (☎626 57 58; info@hoteltitus.nl; www.hoteltitus.nl). Fancier than most budget hotels, these sparkling rooms come equipped with TV and phones. Singles from ƒ75/€34.10, with bath from ƒ125/€56.85; quints from ƒ400/€181.85.

Hotel Bema, Concertgebouw 19b (☎679 13 96; postbus@hotel-bema.demon.nl), across from the Concertgebouw. Tram #16 to Museumpl.; it's 1 block up on the left. Free breakfast delivered to the room. 3-night min. stay on weekends in summer. Reception 8am-midnight. Singles from ƒ95/€43.15; doubles ƒ110/€49.95; triples ƒ165/€74.90; quads with shower ƒ225/€102.10. Credit cards accepted (5% surcharge).

Hotel Europa 92, 1e Constantijn Huygensstr. 103-105 (☎618 88 08; fax 683 64 05; info@europa92.nl; www.europa92.nl). Tram #1, 6 to 1e Constantijn Huygensstr. Converted from 2 adjacent houses into 1 labyrinthine hotel. Clean rooms and a nice garden terrace. Apr.-Aug. singles ƒ190/€86.25; doubles ƒ250/€113.45; triples ƒ335/€152.05; quads ƒ350/€158.85. Oct.-Mar. singles ƒ155/€70.35; doubles ƒ200/€90.80; triples ƒ300/€136.15; quads ƒ280/€127.05. Credit cards accepted.

Apple Inn Hotel, Koninginneweg 93 (☎662 78 94). Take tram #2 to Emmastr. and walk 200m away from Centraal Station. Removed from the bustle of the city's center. Breakfast included. Apr.-Sept. singles ƒ185/€83.95; doubles ƒ245/€111.20; triples ƒ295/€133.90; quads ƒ345/€156.55. Nov.-Mar. singles ƒ115/€52; doubles ƒ135/€61.35; triples ƒ165/€74.90; quads ƒ185/€83.95. Credit cards accepted.

NIEUWMARKT

🏅 **Flying Pig Downtown,** Nieuwendijk 100 (☎420 68 22; downtown@flyingpig.nl; www.flyingpig.nl). From the main entrance of Centraal Station, walk toward Damrak. Pass the Victoria Hotel and take the 1st alley on your right. At the end of that alley you'll find Nieuwendijk. Helpful staff as well as a knockout location make the Flying Pig Downtown a perennial favorite. Spacious dorms. Internet. Kitchen. Ages 18-35 only. Breakfast included. Sheets provided; towels ƒ1.50/€0.70. Key deposit ƒ30/€13.60. 7-day max. stay. Dorms ƒ35.50/€16.60; doubles ƒ75/€34.05. Credit cards accepted.

City Hostel Stadsdoelen, Kloveniersburgwal 97 (☎624 68 32; www.hostelbooking.com; www.njhc.org). Take tram #4, 9, 16, 20, 24, or 25 to Muntpl. Proceed down Nieuwe Doelenstr. (which is just off of Muntpl.); Kloveniersburgwal will be on your right over the bridge. Clean, drug-free, and secure lodgings for very reasonable prices. Breakfast, lockers, and linens included. Internet. Reception 7am-1am. Dorms ƒ42/€19.10; ISIC ƒ37/€16.90. Credit cards accepted.

Hotel Nova, Nieuwezijds Voorburgwal 276 (☎623 00 66). An excellent value. Clean, complete rooms with bath, color TV, phone, and mini-fridge. Breakfast included. Singles ƒ165-195/€74.90-88.50; doubles ƒ205-270/€93.05-122.55; triples from ƒ255-325/€115.70-147.50; quads ƒ305-375/€138.40-170.20.

⬛ FOOD

Many cheap restaurants cluster around **Leidseplein, Rembrandtplein,** and the **Spui.** Cafes, especially in the Jordaan, serve inexpensive sandwiches (ƒ4-9/€1.85-4.10) and good meat-and-potatoes fare (ƒ12-20/€5.45-9.10). Bakeries line **Utrechtsestraat,** south of Prinsengr. Fruit, cheese, flowers, and even live chickens fill the **markets** on **Albert Cuypstraat,** behind the Heineken brewery. (Open M-Sa 9am-6pm.)

NIEUWE ZIJD, SHIPPING QUARTER, CANAL RING WEST, AND THE JORDAAN

Ristorante Caprese, Spuistr. 259-261. Truly excellent Italian food in a stylish but casual atmosphere for reasonable prices. Try the amazing *carbonara* for a paltry ƒ16/€7.25. Open daily 5-10:45pm.

Keuken Van 1870, Spuistr. 4. Legendary. Serves traditional Dutch food for cheap. *Prix fixe* ƒ12.50/€5.70. Open M-F 12:30-8pm, Sa-Su 4-9pm.

Pannenkoekenhuis Upstairs, Grimburgwal 2. From the Muntpl. tram stop, cross the bridge, walk along the Singel and turn right on Lange Brugsteeg, which connects to Grimburgwal. A tiny nook with some of the best pancakes in the city. Pancakes ƒ7.50-17.50/€3.40-7.95. Open M-F noon-7pm, Sa noon-6pm, Su noon-5pm.

Padi, Harlemmerdijk 50. Locals rave about this Thai *eethuis*. Cheap food, lots of veggie options. *Rendang* or *ikan rica* will fire you up, while *lontong opor* (coconut-simmered chicken; ƒ15.50/€7.05) will cool you down. Open daily 5-10pm.

Het Molenpad, Prinsengr. 653. *Gezelligheid* at its best—locals fill up the canalside seats in summer and the narrow, inviting bar in winter at this traditional *bruine cafe*. Usual *eetcafe* offerings (soup ƒ9.50/€4.30; main dishes ƒ17.50/€13.60) go perfectly with a beer (ƒ3.75/€1.70). Open Su-Th noon-1am, F-Sa noon-2am.

Lunchcafe Neilsen, Berenstr. 19. An extra-bright ray of light in an already shining neighborhood. Breakfast and lunch served all day. *Tostis* from ƒ5.50/€2.50 and clubs run to ƒ13.50/€6.15. Salads from ƒ16/€7.40. Vegetarian-friendly. Open Tu-F 8am-5pm, Sa 8am-6pm, Su 9am-5pm.

Wolvenstraat 23, Wolvenstr. 23. Lunch here means sandwiches (ƒ4-12/€1.82-5.45), salads (ƒ12.50-15/€5.70-6.85), and omelettes (ƒ6.50-9/€2.95-4.10). Dinner is strictly Chinese cuisine (ƒ19.50-28.50/€8.85-12.95). Lunch menu 8am-3:30pm; dinner 6-10:30pm. Open M-Th 8am-1am, F 8am-late, Sa 9am-late, Su 10am-1am.

De Vliegende Schotel, Nieuwe Leliestr. 162-168 (☎ 625 20 41). Order at the counter of this vegetarian establishment and then enjoy your meal in one of the easygoing dining rooms. Some vegan options and a few fish dishes available. Entrees and salads ƒ15-28/€6.85-12.75.

LEIDSEPLEIN

🏠 **Bojo,** Lange Leidsedwarsstr. 51. Shaggy palm fronds and sassy waitstaff predominate at this popular Indonesian joint. You can't go wrong with the tender, savory lamb or chicken satay (ƒ20/€9.10) or the multicourse *dagschotel* (around ƒ25/€11.35). Open M-Th 4pm-2am, F 4pm-4am, Sa noon-4am, Su noon-2am.

🏠 **Santa Lucia,** Leidsekruisstr. 20-22. Damn fine pizza in a city where a decent slice is hard to come by. Corner location puts you in the middle of the action just off Leidsepl. Vivacious waitstaff. Hot pies bubbling with cheese (tomato and cheese ƒ9/€4.05) and all types of toppings (mushroom ƒ11/€5; pepperoni ƒ15/€6.80). Lasagna ƒ17/€7.70. Open daily noon-11pm.

🏠 **Wagamama,** Max Euwepl. 10. Loud, crowded Japanese noodle joint devoted to "the way of the noodle." *Yaki Udon* features shiitake mushrooms, egg, leeks, prawns, chicken, red peppers, and Japanese fishcake sauce (ƒ22/€10). Big glass of Heineken ƒ5/€2.75. Open daily noon-11pm.

MUSEUMPLEIN, VONDELPARK, AND DE PIJP

Bistoom, 1e Constantijn Huygensstr. 115. Trams #1 or 6 to Constantijn Huygensstr. stop. Persian fare relies heavily on lamb and rice. Appetizers ƒ6-9/€2.72-4.10; kebab and stewed dishes ƒ24-30/€10.90-15.90. Open daily 5pm-midnight.

Frans and Daantje Cafe, Daniel Stalpertstr. 36. Guest chefs take over the kitchen every night to prepare creative, fusion-oriented dishes (3-course meal ƒ30-40/€13.60-18.15). Nice wine selection (glasses ƒ6/€2.75, bottles from ƒ25/€11.35) and delectable sandwiches (ƒ6-9/€2.75-4.10). Open daily 9am-midnight.

De Soepwinkel, 1e Sweelinckstr. 19F, just off the Albert Cuypmarkt. Soup-making brought to a fine art form. Vegetarian options available. Small soups ƒ7.50/€3.40; large ƒ19.50/€8.85. Open M-Sa 11am-9pm.

👁 🏛 SIGHTS AND MUSEUMS

Amsterdam is fairly compact, so tourists can easily explore the area from the Rijksmuseum to the Red Light District on foot. **Circle Tram 20,** geared toward tourists, stops at 30 attractions throughout the city (every 10min. 9am-7pm; one-day pass ƒ11/€5; buy on the tram or at VVV offices). The more peaceful **Museumboot Canal Cruise** allows you to hop on and hop off along its loop from the VVV to the Anne Frank Huis, the Rijksmuseum, the Bloemenmarkt, Waterloopl., and the old shipyard—buy tickets at any stop. (☎530 10 90. Departs every 30min. 10am-5pm; ƒ27.50/€12.50; pass also yields 20% off at all museums.) Rent a canal bike to power your own way through the canals. (☎626 55 74. Required deposit ƒ100/€45.40. 1-2 people ƒ15/€6.80 per hr.; 3 or more people ƒ12.50/€5.70; pick up and drop-off points at Rijksmuseum, Leidsepl., Keizergr. at Leidsestr., and Anne Frank Huis. Open daily 10am-10pm.) **Mike's Bike Tours** provide an entertaining introduction to the city's sites and the surrounding countryside. (☎622 79 70. Reserve by phone. Tours start from the entrance of the Rijksmuseum. ƒ44/€20.)

The economical **Museumkaart** (MJK) grants year-long discounts or admission to museums and transportation throughout the country (*f*70/€31.80; under 25 *f*30/€13.60; buy at museums throughout The Netherlands).

MUSEUMPLEIN

■**VAN GOGH MUSEUM.** This architecturally breathtaking museum houses the largest collection of van Goghs in the world and a variety of 19th-century paintings by artists who influenced or were contemporaries of the master. The Japanese impact on Van Gogh is demonstrated by a sushi bar in the middle of the museum. *(Paulus Potterstr. 7. Tram #2, 5, or 20 from the station. Open daily 10am-6pm. f15.50/€7.05.)*

■**STEDELIJK MUSEUM OF MODERN ART.** Impressionist painters Picasso, Pollock, de Kooning, Newman, Stella, and Ryman are all members of the Stedelijk's outstanding permanent collection. So too is Piet Mondrian; despite the modern master's later move to New York City, the Stedelijk chronicles his Dutch days. Exciting up-and-coming contemporary work also often exhibited. *(Paulus Potterstr. 13, next to the Van Gogh Museum. Open daily 11am-5pm. f11/€5.)*

RIJKSMUSEUM (NATIONAL MUSEUM). If you've made it to Amsterdam, it would be sinful to leave without seeing the Rijksmuseum's impressive collection of works by Rembrandt, Vermeer, Hals, and Steen. With thousands of Dutch Old Master paintings, it can be an overwhelming place—a good approach is to follow the crowds to Rembrandt's famed militia portrait *The Night Watch*, in the Gallery of Honor, and then proceed into **Aria**, the interactive computer room, which can create a personalized map of the museum. *(On Stadhouderskade. Take tram #2 or 5 from the station. Open daily 10am-5pm. f17.50/€8.)*

HEINEKEN EXPERIENCE. Busloads of tourists haul in daily to discover that no beer is made in the Heineken Brewery. Plenty is served, however. Your visit includes three beers and a souvenir glass, all of which is in itself well worth the price of admission. The brewery itself has been transformed and renamed the "Heineken Experience," an alcohol-themed amusement park. Highlights include the "bottle ride," which replicates the experience of becoming a Heineken beer. *(Stadhouderskade 78, a red brick edifice looming at the corner of Ferdinand Bolstr. Open Tu-Su 10am-6pm. f11/€5. 18+.)*

REMBRANDTPLEIN AND ENVIRONS

VERSETZMUSEUM. In the heart of a historically Jewish neighborhood, the Dutch Resistance Museum brings the struggles and strategies of the movement down to the local level. Notes thrown to loved ones on trains to Aushwitz convey the extensive effort to keep networks alive, and a neighborhood tour tells how 150 Jewish people were successfully hidden in the lion cage in the Artis Zoo, across the street. *(Plantage Kerklaan 61. Tram #9 or 20 to Plantage Kerklaan; #6 or 14 to Plantage Middenlaan/Kerklaan. Open Tu-F 10am-5pm, Sa-M noon-5pm; public holidays reduced hours; closed Jan. 1, Apr. 30, Dec. 25. f9/€4.10, ages 7-15 f5/€2.75, under 7 free.)*

TUSCHINSKI THEATER. This fabulously ornate movie theater is one of Europe's first experiments in Art Deco. Although a group of drunk Nazis once got out of hand and started a fire in its cabaret, the theater miraculously survived World War II and has remained in operation for over 75 years. *(Reguliersbreesstr., between Rembrandtspl. and Muntpl. ☎ 0900 202 53 50. Tours in summer Su-M 10:30am; f10/€4.55.)*

JOODS-PORTUGUESE SYNAGOGUE AND JOODS HISTORISCH MUSEUM. After being expelled from their countries in the 15th century, a sizable number of Spanish and Portuguese Jews established a community in Amsterdam and in 1675 built the handsome **Joods-Portuguese Synagogue.** The Dutch government protected the building from the Nazis' torches by declaring it a national historic site. Across the street, the **Joods Historisch Museum (Jewish Historical Museum),** housed in three connected former synagogues, traces the history of Dutch Jews. *(Jonas Daniel Meijerpl., at Water-*

loopl. Take tram #9 14, or 20. Synagogue open daily 10am-4pm. ƒ10/€4.55. Museum open daily 11am-5pm; closed Yom Kippur. ƒ10/€4.55, seniors 65+ and ISIC holders ƒ5.50/€2.50, ages 6-13 ƒ2.50/€1.15, ages 13-18 ƒ4.50/€2.05, 6 and under free.)

OTHER SIGHTS. Thanks to the Dutch East India company, the **Museum of the Tropics (Tropenmuseum)** multimedia presentation of artifacts from Asia, Africa, and Latin America has especially fine Indonesian art in addition to an engaging children's wing. *(Linnaeusstr. 2. Both tram #9 and bus #22 stop right outside the museum; trams #3, 7, 10, and 14 also go to the museum, though not directly from Centraal Station. Open daily 10am-5pm; Dec. 5, 24, and 31 open 10am-3pm. ƒ15/€6.85, ages 6-17 ƒ7.50/€3.40, students and seniors 65+ ƒ10/€4.55, under 6 free; family ticket for 1-2 adults and max. 4 children ƒ40/€18.15.)* Stroll along the stately Herengr. on your way to the **Museum Willet-Holthuysen,** a 18th-century canal house with 19th-century furnishings and a peaceful garden. *(Herengr. 605, between Reguliersgr. and Vijzelstr., 3min. from Rembrandtpl. Open M-F 10am-5pm, Sa-Su 11am-5pm. ƒ7.50/€3.40.)* Recently restored in 17th-century fashion, the **Museum het Rembrandt** was the home of the master Rembrandt until the city confiscated the house for taxes. It holds 250 of Rembrandt's etchings and dry points, as well as many of his tools and plates. *(Jodenbreestr. 4-6, at the corner of the Oudeschans Canal. Take tram #9, 14, 20. Open M-Sa 10am-5pm, Su 1-5pm. ƒ15/€6.80, ISIC ƒ10/€4.55, ages 6-15 ƒ2.50/€1.15, under 6 free.)*

RED-LIGHT DISTRICT

The Red Light District is surprisingly liveable. For every thrill to be bought, no matter how extreme, there is an equal number of folks there who have nothing to do with the debauchery. **Sex shows** (ƒ10-50/€4.55-22.70) consist of costumed, disaffected couples repeatedly acting out your "wildest" dreams. Red neon marks houses of legalized ill repute, where prostitutes display themselves in windows. During the day, the red-light district is comparatively flaccid, with tourists milling about and consulting their maps. As the sun goes down, people get braver, and the area pulses. Cops from the police station on Warmoestr. patrol the district until midnight. Women may feel uncomfortable walking through this area, and all tourists are prime targets for pickpockets.

OUR LORD IN THE ATTIC. An oasis of virtue hides in the **Museum Amstelkring, Ons' Lieve Heer op Solder** ("Our Lord in the Attic"), where a Catholic priest, forbidden to practice his faith in public during the Reformation, established a surprisingly grand chapel in the attic. *(Oudezijds Voorburgwal 40, at the corner of Oudezijds Armstr., 5min. from the station. Open M-Sa 10am-5pm, Su and holidays 1-5pm. ƒ10/€4.55, students ƒ6/€2.75.)*

THE VICES. For a historical, chemical, and agricultural breakdown of all the wacky tobacky you've been smelling, drop by the informative **Hash Hemp Marijuana Museum.** Though the museum collection is roughly 50% pro-pot pamphlets, posters, and propaganda for cannabis reform in the United States, the growroom in back reminds you that you are still in Amsterdam. *(Odezijds Achterburwal 130. Open daily 11am-10pm. ƒ12.50/€5.70. Seeds ƒ20-275/€9.10-124.80.)* See sex in every way you dreamed possible (and many you didn't) at the **Amsterdam Sex Museum,** which showcases an "only in Amsterdam" collection of erotic art and hard-core porn through the ages. *(Damrak 18, near the station. Open daily 10am-11:30pm. 18+. ƒ4.95/€2.25.)*

OTHER SIGHTS. The area in and around the Red Light District (the oldest part of the city) contains some of Amsterdam's most interesting buildings. Amsterdam's former town hall, **Koninklijk Palace** *(Dam 1. ☎620 40 60, call for exact opening hours),* may be a symbol of 17th-century commercialism, but its majesty is topped by the stunning **Magna Plaza Mall** next door, the 20th-century monument to commercialism. *(Open Su-M 11am-7pm, Tu-Sa 9:30am-9pm.)*

THE JORDAAN

Lose the hordes in the narrow streets of the Jordaan, built as an artisan district in the Golden Age. Bounded roughly by Prinsengr., Brouwersgr., Marnixstr., and Lauriersgr., and teeming with small cafes, galleries, and chocolate shops, the area is

THE NETHERLANDS

possibly the prettiest and most peaceful in the city. You can also take refuge from Amsterdam's mobbed sights and seamy streets in **Begijnhof,** a beautifully maintained grassy courtyard surrounded by 18th-century buildings between Kalverstr. and the Spui. *(Open daily 10am-5pm. Free.)* For a bigger dose of nature, birdwatching, pick-up soccer, and llama-grazing, relax in the sprawling **Vondelpark.**

ANNE FRANK HUIS. The museum chronicles the two years that the Frank family and four other Jews spent hiding in the *achterhuis*, or annex, of Otto Frank's warehouse on the Prinsengr. The rooms are no longer furnished, but personal objects in display cases and text panels with excerpts from the diary bring the story of the eight inhabitants to life. *(Prinsengr. 267. Trams #13, 14, 17, or 20 to Westermarkt. Open daily Apr.-Aug. 9am-9pm; Sept.-Mar. 9am-7pm. Last admission 30min. before closing. Closed on Yom Kippur. ƒ12.50/€5.70, ages 10-17 ƒ5/€2.30.)* While you're there, check out the **Homomonument,** in front of the Westerkerk at the banks of the canal, a memorial to those persecuted for their sexual orientation.

ELSEWHERE IN AMSTERDAM

MARKETS. An open-air art market takes place every Sunday in the **Spui**, where local and international artists regularly present their oils, etchings, sculptures, and jewelry; a book market occasionally yields rare editions and 17th-century Dutch romances. *(Art market open Mar.-Dec. daily 10am-6pm. Book market open F 10am-6pm.)* Pick up bulbs at the flower market, **Bloemenmarkt.** *(Open daily 8am-8pm.)* Mill with the masses at the famous flea market on **Waterlooplein,** where you can try your hand at bargaining for antiques, birds, or farm tools. *(Open M-Sa 9am-5pm.)*

🎵 ENTERTAINMENT

Amsterdam in the summertime is like a new love affair: often alluring, sometimes confusing, but always deliciously entertaining. The **Amsterdams Uit Buro (AUB),** Leidsepl. 26, is stuffed with fliers, pamphlets, and guides to help you sift through what's being offered at any given time. Pick up the free monthly *UITKRANT* at any AUB office to see what's on. (☎09 00 01 91, ƒ0.75/€0.35 per min.; www.uitlijn.nl. Open F-W 10am-6pm, Th 10am-9pm.) The **VVV's** theater desk, Stationspl. 10, can also make reservations for cultural events. (Open M-Sa 10am-5pm.) The monthly *Day by Day* (ƒ2.50/€1.35), available from the tourist office, also provides comprehensive cultural listings.

CONCERTS

In the summer, the Vondelpark Openluchttheater hosts free performances of all sorts every Wednesday through Sunday. (☎673 14 99; www.openluchttheater.nl.) From September through May, the Concertgebouw, **Stadhuis-Muziektheater,** and IJsbreker all hold lunchtime concerts for thrifty music lovers. Call the venues for complete listings, details, and times. The **Royal Concertgebouw Orchestra** at the Concertgebouw on Van Baerlestr. is one of the world's finest. Take tram #316 to "Museumplein." (☎671 83 45. Tickets from ƒ14/€6.35. Guided tours Su 9:30am; ƒ7.75/€3.55. Ticket office open daily 10am-7pm.)

FILM AND THEATER

Check out the free www.movieguide.nl in pure pulp or on the web for movie listings. When you're in the Vondelpark, head left from the main entrance on Stadhouderskade to see what's on at the stately **Filmmuseum** independent movie theater. (☎589 14 00; info@filmmuseum.nl; www.filmmuseum.nl. Info center open M-F from 10am; Sa-Su box office opens 1hr. prior to first showing. ƒ12.50/€5.70, students ƒ10/€4.55.) Also check out **The Movies,** Harlemmerstr. 159, is the city's oldest movie theater, and has been restored to its original classic art deco style. (☎624 57 90. Open M-Tu and Th 4:15-10:15pm, W 2-10:15pm, F 4:15pm-12:30am, Sa 2pm-12:30am, Su 11:30am-10:15pm.)

COFFEESHOPS AND SMART SHOPS

COFFEESHOPS

Yes, the rumors are true: marijuana and hashish have been decriminalized in The Netherlands. Places calling themselves coffeeshops sell pot or hash or will let you buy a drink and smoke your own stuff. Look for the green and white "Coffeeshop BCD" sticker that certifies a coffeeshop's credibility and means that the shop is reputable. Although Amsterdam is known as the hash capital of the world, **marijuana** is increasingly popular. You can legally possess up to 5g of marijuana or hash (the previous 30g limit was reduced in response to foreign criticism). Pick up a free copy of the *BCD Official Coffeeshop Guide* for the pot-smoker's map of Amsterdam. For information on the legal ins and outs, call the **Jellinek clinic** at ☎ 570 23 55. Never buy drugs from street dealers. Remember that any experimentation with drugs can be dangerous. Never smoke pot on the street; it's offensive to the Dutch.

Spacecakes and **spaceshakes** are made with hash or weed. The butter used in the cake is hash- or weed-based. Because they need to go to your blood, and be digested, they take longer to affect you and longer to rinse out. **Hash** comes in two varieties, black (like Afghani and Nepali; ƒ10-24/€4.55-10.90 per g.) and blonde (like Moroccan); black tends to be heavier and hits harder. Any **weed** with white in its name, such as white widow, white butterfly, or white ice, is guaranteed to be strong. Pot in The Netherlands is incredibly strong. As with alcohol, take it easy so you don't pass out. The Dutch tend to mix tobacco with their pot as well, so joints are harsher on your lungs. Ask the dealer at coffeeshops if pre-rolled joints are rolled with tobacco or are pure cannabis. Dutch marijuana is the most common and costs ƒ12-20/€5.45-9.10 per gram, ƒ25-30/€11.35-13.65 per bag. The smaller the quantity, the smoother and more potent. Staff at coffeeshops are used to explaining the different kinds of pot on the menu to tourists. It is recommended that you buy one gram at a time.

SMART SHOPS

Also legal are **smart shops,** which peddle a variety of **"herbal enhancers"** and **hallucinogens** that walk the line between soft and hard drugs. Some shops are alcohol-free and all have a strict no-hard-drugs policy. **All hard drugs are illegal** and possession is treated as a serious crime. **Mushrooms** start to work after 30min-1hr. and act on your system for 4-8hr. A bad trip will most likely come about if you mix 'shrooms with alcohol; drinking a Coke may help because of the sugar. If a friend is tripping, it's important to never leave his or her side. **Call** ☎ **122** to go to the hospital. If you are having a bad trip, don't be ashamed to tell someone, because you won't be arrested in Amsterdam. It's not a crime, and they've seen it all before.

SHOPS BY NEIGHBORHOOD

🌿 **Abraxas,** J. Roelensteeg 12-14 (www.coffeeshop-abraxas.com). One of the swankiest coffeeshops in Amsterdam. Full palette of hash and weed in a casual, no-pressure atmosphere. Open daily 10am-1am.

🌿 **Siberie,** Brouwersgr. 11 (www.siberie.net), close to Centraal Station. This quality coffeeshop still brings in regulars and locals. Wide selection of weed and hash from around the world, including ice-o-lator hash for ƒ35/€15.90 per g. and cheaper stuff from ƒ5/€2.30. Open Su-Th 11am-11pm, F-Sa 11am-midnight.

🌿 **The Rookies,** Korte Leidsedwarsstr. 145-147. A rustling crowd packs into this lively coffeehouse even on weeknights. All bags, such as the potent house specialty "Rookie Skunk," sold in ƒ25/€11.40 increments. Open Su-Th 10am-1am, F-Sa 10am-3am.

Hill Street Blues, Warmoesstr. 52. From Centraal Station, go south on Damrak, then turn right on Brugsteeg, then left on Warmoesstr.; it'll be about a block down on the left. Plenty of good deals on quality pot (such as the Hill Street Special; ƒ16/€7.25 per g.) and a party-intensive atmosphere. Open Su-Th 9am-1am, F-Sa 9am-3am.

Freeland, Lange Niezel 27. Perhaps the most bizarrely decorated cafe in a city dedicated to embracing the bizarre. Heavy-hitting "Bubble Gum" weed ƒ25/€11.35 for 1g. Space cakes ƒ8/€3.65, space fruitshakes ƒ10/€4.55. Open daily 9:30am-1am.

The Bold Man Smoke Supplies, Oude Hoogstr. 35-37. A headshop fully stocked with bongs, pipes, and any other hardware you might need to fly sky-high. Open M-Sa 10am-10pm; Su reduced hours.

The Bulldog, Oudezijds Voorburgwal 90 (www.bulldog.nl). The most famous of Amsterdam's coffeeshop chains set up its 1st shop here in the Red Light District in 1975. Grass and hash min. purchase ƒ25/€11.35. Open daily 9am-1am.

Elements of Nature, Warmoesstr. 54, Warmoesstr. 97, Kolksteeg 4, Amstelstr. 17, and Haringpakkerssteeg 11-13. A large smart shop chain in Amsterdam that sells a wide range of products from 'shrooms to sex stimulants and everything in between. Open daily 11am-10pm.

Kadinsky, Rosmarijnsteeg 9, near the intersection of Spui and Nieuwezijds Voorburgwal. Stylish place hidden off an alley near Spui. Weekly deals on weed and hashish (from ƒ20/€9.10 per gram). Joints ƒ5/€2.30. Open daily 10am-1am.

Blue Velvet, Haarlemmerstr. 64. White and ice-blue environs feel as cool as they look. Beer ƒ3-4/€1.40-1.85; mixed drinks ƒ8-13/€3.65-5.90. Pre-rolled joints ƒ6-8/€2.75-3.65. Open Su-Th 10-1am, F-Sa 10-2am.

La Tertulia, Prinsengr. 312. Defies coffeeshop preconceptions with its big tropical plants, flowers, and shelves full of board games around an indoor waterfall. Rolled joints ƒ5/€2.25. Brownies ƒ8.50/€3.90. Open Tu-Su 11am-7pm.

Paradox, 1e Bloemdwarsstr. 2. The owners match the feel of this place: fun, free, and ready to have a good time. Weed and hash from ƒ10-50/€4.55-22.75. Open daily 10am-8pm; kitchen closes 5pm.

Stix, Utrechtestr. 21, a block south of Rembrandtpl. Locals chill to cool jazz in this stylish, sophisticated coffeeshop. House blends of weed, Royal Stix, and Edelweiss pack the strongest kick. ƒ10-28/€4.55-12.70 per g. Pre-rolled joints ƒ6-9/€2.75-4.10. Open daily 11am-1am.

■ NIGHTLIFE

CAFES AND BARS

Amsterdam's finest cafes are the old, dark, wood-paneled *bruine cafes* (brown cafes) of the **Jordaan,** many of which have outdoor seating lining the canal on **Prinsengracht. Leidseplein** is the liveliest nightspot, with loud coffeeshops, loud bars, and tacky clubs galore. Dutch soap stars frequent Palladium and Raffles, also in Leidesplein, where many a beautiful person comes to be seen and to drink up for surprisingly reasonable prices. **Rembrandtsplein** is the place to watch soccer and sing with drunk revelers. Gay bars line **Reguliersdwarsstraat,** which connects Muntpl. and Rembrandtspl., and **Kerkstraat,** five blocks north of Leidsepl.

Durty Nelly's Pub, Warmoesstr. 115-117. From Centraal Station, go south on Damrak, turn right on Brugsteeg, and then right on Warmoesstr.; Nelly's is 2 blocks on the left. Down-home Irish pub on the edge of the Red Light District. Open Su-Th 9am-1am, F-Sa 9am-3am; kitchen open Tu-Th noon-midnight, F-M 9am-10pm.

Cafe Heffer, Oudebrugsteeg 7, at Beursstr. Pop music prevails throughout, but booze fans need not fear; the menu is packed with excellent Dutch and Belgian brews (ƒ5-8/€2.30-3.65). Divine *appeltaart* ƒ7/€3.20. Open daily 9am-3am.

The Tara, Rokin 85-89. Vast Irish-themed watering hole with a maze-like interior featuring plenty of cozy, candlelit corners. Slightly older crowd gets raucous on weekend nights. Beer ƒ5/€2.30; pints ƒ8/€3.65. Open Su-Th 11-1am, F-Sa 11-3am.

Belgique, Gravenstr. 2, between Niewendijk and Nieuwezijds Voorburgwal. If you're ready to graduate from keg swill to the real stuff, this bar specializes in 50 high-quality (and high-alcohol) Belgian brew. Open Su-Th 3pm-midnight, F-Sa noon-3am.

De Blauwe Druife (The Blue Grape), Harlemmerstr. 91, at Binnen Bowers Straat. Walk into old-school Amsterdam at this brown cafe, popular with locals since its inception in 1733. Beers on tap include Heineken (f3.50/€2), de Koninck (f4.50/€2.05), and WiecckseWitte (f4.50/€2.05). Open daily noon-1am.

Café 't Smalle, Egelantiersgr. 12, at the corner of Prinsengr. and Egelantiersgr. Intimate, tiny bar founded in 1780. Open Su-Th noon-12:15am, F-Sa noon-2am.

Lux, Marnixstr. 403. Bench seats and coffee tables give the place a 70's rec-room feel, hipped up for today's trendsetters. Beer runs f4/€1.85; vodka f7.50/€3.40. Open Su-Th 8pm-3am, F-Sa 8pm-4am.

Cafe de Koe, Marnixstr. 381. A relaxed crowd, rock music, and slightly haphazard decor. Beer from f3.75/€1.70; liquor from f7.50/€3.40. Cafe open M-Th 4pm-1am, F-Sa 3pm-3am, Su 3pm-1am.

Mr. Coco's, Thorbeckepl. 8-12. Same hideously ugly clown mascot as the Nieuwendijk location, but with more local students and fewer tourists. Happy Hour daily 5-6pm; F also noon-3pm. Open W 5pm-1am, Th noon-1am, F-Sa noon-3am.

Montmartre, Halvemaarsteg 17. Houses the wildest parties in Amsterdam for men and the men they love. Happy Hour M-Th 6-10pm. Voted Amsterdam's best gay bar by gay mag *Gay Krant* 5 years running. Open Su 4pm-1am, M-Th 5pm-1am, F-Sa 4pm-3am.

LIVE MUSIC

Bourbon Street Jazz & Blues Club, Leidsekruisstr. 6-8 (☎623 34 40). Head north on Leidsestr., then go east on Lange Leidsedwarsstr., and turn north on Leidsekruisstr. Blues, soul, funk, and rock bands keep the crowds heavy. The Stones have played here; so have BB King and Sting. Beer f6/€2.75. Cover Su-Th f3/€1.35, F-Sa f5/€2.30. Open Su-Th 10pm-4am, F-Sa 10pm-5am.

Paradiso, Weteringschans 6-8 (☎626 45 21; www.paradiso.nl). When big-name punk, new-wave, and reggae bands come to Amsterdam, they almost invariably play here in this former church that has been converted into a temple to rock 'n' roll. See where Lenny Kravitz got his big break and the Stones taped their latest live album. Tickets range from f10-50/€4.55-22.70.

Melkweg, Lijnbaasgr. 234a (☎624 17 77), in a warehouse off Leidsepl. Legendary nightspot where live bands, theater, films, dance shows, and an art gallery (free W-Su 2-8pm) make for sensory overload. Concert tickets from f5-50/€2.30-22.70. Club nights F-Sa 1-5am (cover f10/€4.55). Membership fee f5/€2.27 (good for 1 month). Box office open M-F 1-5pm, Sa-Su 4-6pm; until 7:30pm on show days.

Casablanca, Zeedijk 24-26 (☎625 56 85; www.casablanca-amsterdam.nl), between Oudezijds Kolk and Vredenburgersteeg. Though its heyday as *the* jazz bar in Amsterdam has faded, it's still one of the best spots to hear live jazz. Jazz only Su-W; DJ-hosted dance parties Th-Sa. No cover. Open Su-Th 8pm-3am, F-Sa 8pm-4am.

Vive La Vie, Amstelstr. 7 (☎624 01 14), just east of Rembrandtpl. Fun, friendly lesbian bar where the emphasis is on good times, good folks, and good drinking, all without a shred of attitude. No dance floor, but that doesn't stop the ladies—and a few select male friends—from grooving to feel-good pop anthems. Open Su-Th 3pm-1am, F-Sa 3pm-3am.

CLUBS AND DISCOS

Many clubs charge a membership fee in addition to normal cover, so the tab can be harsh. Be prepared for cocky doormen who love to turn away tourists; show up early or hope the bouncer thinks you're cute. A promised tip of f10-20/€4.55-9.10 (left on your way out) may help you. There are pricey discos aplenty on **Prinsengracht,** near **Leidsestraat,** and on **Lange Leidsedwarsstraat.** Gay discos line **Amstelstraat** and **Reguliersdwarsstraat** and cater almost exclusively to men. Pick up a wallet-sized *Clu* guide, free at cafes and coffeeshops, for a club map of the city, and *Gay and Night,* a free monthly magazine, for information on gay parties.

Cockring, Warmoestr. 90. From Centraal Station, head down Damrak, then left on Brugsteeg and right on Warmoesstr. The club will be 2 blocks down on the right; just look for the giant cockring. Something between a sex club and a disco; you can dance or get lucky. DJs spin nightly for a youngish crowd of men who strip as things heat up. Dark room in the back where anything goes. Open Su-Th 9pm-4am, F-Sa 9pm-5am.

THE NETHERLANDS

Item, Nieuwezijds Voorburgwal 163-165. Young, trendy, and tourist-oriented. Standard dance floor topped by an upstairs lounge. Cool bar with waterfall behind it. Cover ƒ20-28/€9.10-12.75. Open Su-Th 11pm-4am, F-Sa 11pm-5am.

Bep, Nieuwezijds Voorburgwal 260. Created in the image of the space-age bachelor pad, with fake stone walls and a glittery disco ball. Tiny, but very popular with the pre-club crowd, it gets very crowded on weekend nights—the crowd of sharply done-up hipsters spills out onto the front patio. Open Su-Th noon-1am, F-Sa noon-3am.

West Pacific, Polonceaukade 3, at the Westergasfabriekterrein. Out past the Wester-park, this is where "real" Amsterdammers head to party. Though DJ-driven house music dominates, it's not so hardcore that you can't shake that thang. Membership may be required on the most popular nights; apply beforehand at the restaurant. Cover ƒ5/€2.30. Music starts 11pm, goes 1am Su-Th, 3am F-Sa.

Mazzo, Rozengr. 114 (www.mazzo.nl). Even the bouncers are nice here. The usual black walls, colored spotlights, and pumping music are complemented by a large bar in the back with lots of room to rest up until the next wave of energy hits you. Beer ƒ4/€1.80; mixed drinks ƒ11/€5. Cover ƒ10-20/€4.55-9.10; Sa ƒ20/€9.10. Open W-Th and Su 11pm-4am, F-Sa 11pm-5am.

Escape, Rembrandtpl. 11. Massive venue where differently themed clubs host Amster-dam's most popular nightclubs. 2 floors with 4 bars (including a champagne bar staffed by particularly beautiful girls), a chillout space upstairs, and a huge, sensually charged dance floor downstairs, where scenesters groove to house, trance, disco, and dance classics. Be sober, well-dressed, and female to increase your chances of entry. Beer ƒ5/€2.30; mixed drinks ƒ14/€6.35. Open Th-Su 11pm-4am, F-Sa 11pm-5am.

The Ministry, Reguliersdwarsstr. 12 (www.ministry.nl). The very popular Ministry is upscale enough to be classy and hip, but without any attitude or exclusivity; it's all about getting your groove on to some seriously good tunes. Cover ƒ12.50-25/€5.70-11.35; F-Sa tends to be more expensive. Open Su-Th 11pm-4am, F-Sa 11pm-5am.

▶ DAYTRIPS FROM AMSTERDAM

EDAM. Right outside free-living Amsterdam, Edam offers cottages, parks, and a whole lot of cheese. Farmers still bring their famed cheese to **market** by horse and boat. (July-Aug. W 10am-12:30pm.) From the left of the market, walk straight on Eilandsgracht and turn left on Nieuw Vaartje to reach the 15th-century **Grote of St. Nicholaaskerk,** which has exquisite stained-glass windows. (Open May-Sept. daily 2-5:30pm. Free.) At **Alida Hoeve,** Zeddewed 1, Edam cheese is still made by hand. (Open daily 9am-6pm. Free samples.) Rent a bike at **Ronald Schot,** Grote Kerk-straat. 7/9, (☎37 21 55; www.ronaldschot.nl. ƒ12 per day; ƒ8.50 per half-day), and head there by following the bike path in the direction of Volendam and Amster-dam. Farther down the path from Alida Hoeve stands a towering **windmill** that you can climb for ƒ1. (Open Apr.-Oct. daily 9:30am-4:30pm.)

Buses #110, 112, and 114 run from Amsterdam's Centraal Station to Edam (30min., 7 strips). The VVV **tourist office,** Damplein 1, in the old town hall, helps find rooms. To get there from the bus stop, walk down Schepenmakersdijk to the white Kwakelbrug bridge, and follow Lingerzijde to the center of town. (☎31 51 25; fax 37 42 36; info@vvv-edam.nl. Open M-Sa Mar.-Nov. 10am-5pm; Nov.-Mar. 10am-3pm; July-Aug. also open Su 1-4:30pm.) ☎**0299.**

UTRECHT. Just 25 minutes from Amsterdam by train, Utrecht is a popular daytrip; Its canals and prestigious university may coerce you into a longer stay (p. 698).

HAARLEM   ☎ 023

Surrounded by fields of tulips and daffodils, it's clear why Haarlem inspired native Frans Hals and other Golden Age Dutch artists. The **Grote Markt** (city center) pulsates with cafes, and the narrow streets are filled with boutiques. To reach Grote Markt from the train station, head down Kruisweg; at the Nieuwe Gracht, Kruisweg turns into Kruisstr., which then becomes Barteljorisstr. Along Kruisweg in the Grote Markt is the glorious **Stadhuis** (Town Hall), originally the hunting lodge of the Count of Holland. The **Grote Kerk,** at the opposite end of the Markt, houses the mammoth Müller organ once played by an 11-year-old Mozart. (Open M-Sa 10am-4pm. ƒ2.75/€1.25.) From the church, turn left onto Damstr. and follow it until Spaarne, where you will find the **Teyler's Museum,** Spaarne 16. The Netherlands' oldest museum, it contains an eclectic assortment of scientific instruments, fossils, paintings, and drawings, including works by Raphael, Michelangelo, and Rembrandt. (Open Tu-Sa 10am-5pm, Su noon-5pm. ƒ10/€4.55, students ƒ5/€2.30.) The **Frans Hals Museum,** Groot Heiligland 62, is a former almshouse; from the Teyler's, turn right, walk along the Zuider Buitenspaarne canal, turn right onto Kampverst., then left onto Groot Heiligland. The museum contains work by the portraitist and a collection of modern art. (Open M-Sa 11am-5pm, Su noon-5pm. ƒ10/€4.55, seniors ƒ7.50/€3.40, under 19 free.)

Reach Haarlem from Amsterdam by **train** (15min., ƒ6.50/€2.95) from Centraal Station or by **bus** #80 from Marnixstr., near Leidsepl. (2 per hr., 2 strips). The VVV **tourist office,** Stationspl. 1, finds private rooms (from ƒ38/€17.25) for a ƒ10/€4.55 fee. (☎(0900) 616 16 00; info@vvvzk.nl; www.vvvzk.nl. Open M-F 9:30am-5:30pm, Sa 10am-2pm; summer also open Sa 2-4pm.) The lively **NJHC-herberg Jan Gijzen (HI),** Jan Gijzenpad 3, is 3km from the station on the banks of a canal. Take bus #2 (dir. Haarlem-Nord) and get off at Jeugdeherberg or tell the driver your destination. (☎537 37 93; www.njhc.org/haarlem. Breakfast included. Key deposit ƒ25/€11.35 or passport. Non-member surcharge ƒ3-8/€1.40-3.65.) **Hotel Carillon,** Grote Markt 27, is ideally located. (☎531 05 91. Breakfast included. Reception and bar 7:30am-1am. Singles ƒ60-110/€27.25-49.95; doubles ƒ110-142/€49.95-64.45.) To **camp** at **De Liede,** Lie Over 68, take bus #2 (dir. Zuiderpolder) and walk 10min. from the bus stop. (☎535 86 66. ƒ6/€2.75 per person; ƒ6/€2.75 per tent. In summer add ƒ2.50/€1.15 tax.) Try cafes in the **Grote Markt** for cheap meals.

🖪 DAYTRIPS FROM HAARLEM. The seaside town of **Zandvoort** boasts several **nude beaches** south of town, along with more modest sands. From the train station, follow signs to the Raadhuis and head down Kerkstr. to reach the shore. A 30min. walk in the opposite direction brings you to the hip **Blomendaal** beach, with the popular clubs The NL Republic, Zomers, Solaris, and Woodstock. **Trains** arrive in Zandvoort from Haarlem (10min., return ƒ6/€2.75). The VVV **tourist office,** Schoolpl. 1, in the town center, sells a lodgings guide (ƒ2/€0.95). Follow signs from the station. (☎(023) 571 79 47; fax 571 70 03. Generally open M-Sa 9am-5pm.) The **Hotel-Pension Noordzee,** Hogeweg 15, is 100m from the beach. (☎(023) 571 31 27. Breakfast included. Singles ƒ55/€25; doubles ƒ90/€40.85.)

In nearby **Aalsmeer,** 90 million flowers are auctioned every day at the world's largest flower auction. Self-guided tours cover the auction's gargantuan warehouse and auction rooms. (☎297 39 21 85; info@vba.net; www.vba-aalsmeer.nl. Open M-F 7:30-11am.) From Haarlem's train station, take **bus** #140 (45min., every 30min.). The auction is also accessible from Amsterdam's Centraal Station; buses #77 and 172 (dir. Naar Kudelstaart) stop at the warehouse every 30min.

For even more flowers, check out the town of **Lisse** in late spring. The **Keukenhof** gardens become a kaleidoscope as over 5 million bulbs come to life. (Open daily late Mar. to mid-May 8am-7:30pm; Aug. to mid-Sept. 9am-6pm; last entry 6pm. ƒ4-6/€1.85-2.75.) Look for petals in motion at the **April flower parade** (Apr. 20, 2002). Take **bus** #50 or 51 from the Haarlem train station; combo bus/museum tickets are available at the station (ƒ21/€9.55). The VVV **tourist office** is at Grachtweg 53. (☎(0252) 41 42 62. Open M noon-5pm, Tu-F 9am-5pm, Sa 9am-4pm.)

LEIDEN

☎071

Home to one of the oldest and most prestigious universities in Europe, Leiden brims with bookstores, bicycles, windmills, gated gardens, and hidden walkways. Rembrandt's birthplace and the site of the first **tulips,** the Netherlands' third-largest city offers visitors a gateway to flower country. Sharing a main gate with the Academy building is the university's 400-year-old garden, the **Hortus Botanicus,** Rapenburg 73, where the first Dutch tulips were grown. Its grassy knolls alongside the **Witte Singel** canal make it an ideal picnic spot. (Open Mar.-Nov. daily 10am-6pm; Nov.-Feb. Su-F 10am-4pm. ƒ8/€3.65.) Across the footbridge from the main gate to the Hortus Botanicus, the **Rijksmuseum van Oudheden** (National Antiquities Museum), Rapenburg 28, holds the restored Egyptian Temple of Taffeh, a gift removed from the reservoir basin of the Aswan Dam. (www.rmo.nl. Open Tu-F 10am-5pm, Sa-Su noon-5pm. ƒ13.20/€6, ages 16-18 ƒ12.10/€5.50; included in Museumkaart.) The ◼**Rijksmuseum voor Volkenkunde** (National Museum of Ethnology), Steenstr. 1, is one of the world's oldest anthropological museums, with a fantastic collection from the Dutch East Indies. (www.rmv.nl. Open Tu-Su 10am-5pm. ƒ13.50/€6.15, students ƒ7.50/€3.40; included in Museumkaart.) Scale steep staircases to inspect the inside of a functioning windmill at the **Molenmuseum ("De Valk"),** 2e Binnenvestgracht 1. (Open Tu-Sa 10am-5pm, Su 1pm-5pm. ƒ5/€2.30; included in Museumkaart.) The **Museum De Lakenhal,** Oude Singel 32, exhibits works by Rembrandt and Jan Steen. (Open Tu-Sa 10am-5pm, Su noon-5pm. ƒ8/€3.65; included in Museumkaart.)

Leiden is easily reached by **train** from the Hague (20min., ƒ10/€4.55) or Amsterdam (30min., ƒ24/€10.90). The VVV **tourist office,** Stationsweg 2d, sells maps (ƒ2.50/€1.15) and walking tour brochures (ƒ1-4/€0.45-1.85), and finds **private rooms** (fee ƒ4.50/€2.50 for one person, ƒ3.50/€2 for each additional person). Head straight from the main entrance to the station; it's on the right after about three blocks; look for blue and white signs. (☎(0900) 222 23 33; fax (071) 516 12 27; www.leiden.nl. Open M-F 10am-6:30pm, Sa 10am-4:30pm; Apr.-May and July-Aug. also open Su 11am-3pm.) The **Hotel Pension Witte Singel,** Witte Singel 80, 5min. from Hortus Botanicus, has immaculate rooms. Take bus #43 to Merenwijk and tell the driver your destination. (☎512 45 92; fax 514 78 90; wvanvriel@pensionews.demon.nl. Singles ƒ60/€27.25; doubles ƒ93-120/€42.20-54.45.) Especially on weekend nights, locals and students pack into the popular **de Oude Harmonie,** Breestr. 16, just off Rapenburg. (Beer ƒ3-7/€1.40-3.20. Open Su-Th noon-1am, F-Sa 3pm-3am.) The **Super de Boer supermarket** is opposite the train station at Stationsweg 40. (Open M-F 7am-9pm, Sa 9am-8pm, Su noon-7pm.)

THE HAGUE (DEN HAAG)   ☎070

William II moved the royal residence to the Hague in 1248, prompting the creation of Parliament buildings, museums, and sprawling parks. During the **North Sea Jazz Festival** (www.northseajazz.nl) in mid-July, the city draws world-class musicians and 50,000 fans. The rest of the year, museum-gazing and embassy-sleuthing are the main attractions. For snippets of Dutch politics, visit the **Binnenhof,** the Hague's Parliament complex. Guided tours leave from Binnenhof 8a and visit the 13th-century **Ridderzaal** (Hall of Knights) as well as the chambers of the States General. (Open M-Sa 10:15am-4pm. ƒ10/€4.55.) Just outside the north entrance of the Binnenhof, the 17th-century **Mauritshuis,** Korte Vijverberg 8, features an impressive collection of Dutch paintings, including works by Rembrandt and Vermeer. (www.mauritshuis.nl. Open Tu-Sa 10am-5pm, Su 11am-5pm. ƒ15/€6.85, children ƒ7.50/€3.40.) The impressive modern art collection at the **Gemeentemuseum,** Stadhouderslaan 41, displays Piet Mondrian's *Victory Boogie Woogie.* Take tram #7 from Holland Spoor or bus #4 from Centraal Station. (www.gemeentemuseum.nl. Open Tu-Su 11am-5pm. ƒ15/€6.85.) Andrew Carnegie donated the **Peace Palace,** the home of the International Court of Justice at Carnegiepl., 3min. on tram #7 or 8 north from the Binnenhof. (www. vredespaleis.nl. Tours M-F 10, 11am, 2, 3, 4pm. Book through the tourist office. ƒ7.50/€3.40, children ƒ5/€2.30.)

Trains roll in from Amsterdam (50min., ƒ31/€14.10) and Rotterdam (25min., ƒ15/€6.85) to both of the Hague's major stations, Centraal Station and Holland Spoor. Trams #1, 9, and 12 connect the two stations. The VVV **tourist office,** Kon. Julianapl. 30, just outside the north entrance to Centraal Station and right next to the Hotel Sofitel, books rooms for a ƒ4/€1.85 fee and sells detailed city maps. (☎(0900) 340 35 05; www.denhaag.com. Open M and Sa 10am-5pm, Tu-F 9am-5:30pm, Su 11am-5pm. Hotel booking computer available 24hr.) Most foreign **embassies** are in The Hague: **Australia,** Carnegielaan 4, 2517 KH (☎310 82 00; open M-F 8:30am-4:55pm); **Canada,** Sophialaan 7, 2514 JP (☎311 16 00; open M-F 9am-12:45pm and 1:45-5:30pm); **Ireland,** 9 Dr. Kuyperstr., 2514 BA (☎363 09 93; call for hours); **New Zealand,** Carnegielaan 10, 2517 KH (☎346 93 24; open M-F 9am-12:30pm and 1:30-5:30pm); **South Africa,** Wassenaarseweg 40, 2596 CJ (☎392 45 01; open daily 9am-noon); **UK,** Lange Voorhout 10, 2514 ED (☎427 04 27; call for hours); **US,** Lange Voorhout 102, 2514 EJ (☎310 92 09; open M-F 8:15am-5pm). The **NJHC City Hostel,** Scheepmakerstr. 27, is near Holland Spoor; turn right from the station, follow the tram tracks, turn right at the big intersection, and Scheepmakerstr. is 3min. down on your right. From Centraal Station, take tram #1 (dir. Delft), 9 (dir. Vrederust), or 12 (dir. Duindrop) to Rijswijkseplein (2 strips); cross to the left in front of the tram, cross the big intersection, and Scheepmakerstr. is straight ahead. (☎315 78 78; denhaag@njhc.org. In-house restaurant-bar. Breakfast included. Lockers ƒ3/€1.40 per day. Dorms ƒ42/€19.10; doubles ƒ80/€36.30. Nonmembers add ƒ5/€2.30.) Budget takeaway places line **Lage Poten** and **Korte Poten** near the Binnenhof. For vibrant nightlife, prowl the Strandweg in nearby **Scheveningen.**

DELFT ☎015

Delft's lilied canals and stone footbridges offer the same images that native Johannes Vermeer immortalized in paint over 300 years ago. It's best to visit on Thursdays and Saturdays, when townspeople flood the marketplace. The town is renowned for **Delftware,** blue-on-white china developed in the 16th century. Samples of the precious platters and hourly demonstrations await at **De Porceleyne Fles,** Rotterdamseweg 196. Take bus #63, 121, or 129 from the station to Jaffalaan. Walk to the end of Jaffalaan, bear left, and cross the intersection. (www. royaldelft.com. Open Apr.-Oct. M-Sa 9am-5pm, Su 9:30am-5pm; Nov.-Apr. closed Su. ƒ5/€2.30.) In town, the **Nieuwe Kerk** in the central Markt holds the restored mausoleum of Dutch liberator William of Orange. Climb the tower, which holds a 48-bell carillon, for a view of old Delft. (Church open Apr.-Oct. M-Sa 9am-6pm; Nov.-Mar. M-F 11am-4pm, Sa 11am-5pm. ƒ4.50/€2.05. Tower closes 1hr. earlier. ƒ3.50/€1.60.) Built as a 15th-century nun's cloister, **Het Prinsenhof,** Sint Agathapl. 1, off Oude Singel, was William's abode until an assassin hired by Spain's Phillip II slew him in 1584. Today it houses paintings, tapestries, and pottery. (Open Tu-Sa 10am-5pm, Su 1-5pm. ƒ7.50/€3.40.) **Rondvaart Delft,** Koormarkt 113, offers canal rides and rents water bikes. (☎212 63 85. Open mid-Mar. to Oct. daily 9:30am-6pm.)

Trains arrive from: Amsterdam (1hr.); The Hague (15min., ƒ4/€1.85); and Leiden (30min., ƒ6.50/€2.95). For **train** or **bus** info, call ☎(0900) 92 92. The VVV **tourist office** has hiking, cycling, and walking route maps, and also books rooms (ƒ3.50/€1.60 fee plus 10% deposit). From the station, cross the bridge, turn left, go right at the first light, and follow signs to the Markt. (☎213 01 00; www.vvvdelft.nl. Open Apr.-Sept. M-Sa 9am-5:30pm, Su 11am-3pm; Oct.-May closed Su.) To reach the unmarked **Van Leeuwen,** Achterom 143, exit straight from the station, cross four canals, and turn right on Achterom. (☎212 37 16. Singles ƒ35/€15.90; doubles ƒ70/€31.80.) More affordable hotels are near the Markt. To **camp** on **Korftlaan** in the Delftse Hout area, take bus #64 to Aan't Korft. (☎213 00 40; info-delftsehout@tours.nl. Laundry. Reception May to mid-Sept. 9am-10pm; mid-Sept. to Apr. 9am-6pm. ƒ30/€13.65 per tent.) Restaurants line **Volderstraat** and **Oude Delft.**

ROTTERDAM ☎010

After Rotterdam was bombed in 1940, experimental architects replaced the rubble with striking (some say strikingly ugly) buildings, creating an urban, industrial conglomerate. For a dramatic example of Rotterdam's eccentric designs, check out the **Kijk-Kubus** (cube houses) by Piet Blom. Take tram #1 or the metro to Blaak, turn left, and look up. (Open Mar.-Dec. daily 11am-5pm; Jan.-Feb. F-Su 11am-5pm. ƒ3.50/€1.60.) Try to decipher the architectural madness at the **Netherlands Architecture Institute**, Museumpark 25. (Open Tu 10am-9pm, W-Sa 10am-5pm, Su 11am-5pm. ƒ7.50/€3.40). Then, refresh yourself with Rubens, van Gogh, Rembrandt, Rubinstein, Lichtenstein, Rothko, and Magritte across the street at the **Museum Boijmans van Beuningen,** Museumpark 18-20. (Metro: Eendractspl., or tram #5. Open Tu-F 10am-5pm, Su 11am-5pm. ƒ12.50/€5.70.) The stately **Schielandshuis** (Historical Museum), Korte Hoogstr. 31, recounts the history of the city. (Open Tu-F 10am-5pm, Sa-Su 11am-5pm. ƒ6/€2.75.) Opposite the plaza lies the powerful Zadkine, or the **Monument for the Destroyed City,** a statue of an anguished man with a hole in his heart that memorializes the 1940 bombing raid. **Museumpark** features sculptures, mosaics, and monuments designed by some of the world's foremost artists and architects; take tram #5 to reach this outdoor exhibit (free).

Trains run to: Amsterdam (1½hr., ƒ23/€10.45); the Hague (20min., ƒ7.50/€3.40); and Utrecht (45min., ƒ15/€6.85). For information on **ferries** to Hull, England, see p. 678. The VVV **tourist office,** Coolsingel 67, opposite the *Stadhuis*, books rooms for a ƒ3.50/€2 fee. (☎ 403 40 65. ƒ0.50/€0.25 per min. Open M-Th 9:30am-6pm, F 9:30am-9pm, Sa 9:30am-5pm, Su noon-5pm.) To reach the **NJHC City-Hostel Rotterdam (HI),** Rochussenstr. 107-109, take the metro to Dijkzigt; at the top of the metro escalator, exit onto Rochussentr and turn left. (☎ 436 57 63. Breakfast included. Sheets ƒ7/€3.20. Reception 7am-midnight. Dorms ƒ35-45/€15.90-20.45 per person; doubles ƒ90-110/€40.90-49.95. Nonmembers add ƒ5/€2.30.) To get from the station to the **Hotel Bienvenue,** Spoorsingel 24, exit through the back, walk straight along the canal for 5min., and it's on the right. Bienvenue offers clean rooms with TV in a safe area. (☎ 466 93 94. Reception M-F 7:30am-9pm, Sa-Su 8am-9pm. Singles ƒ90/€40.85; doubles ƒ150/€68.10; triples ƒ185/€83.95; quads ƒ20/€9.10.) The **Oude Haven** and **Oostplein** brim with cafes. Buy **groceries** at **Albert Heyn,** Lijnbaanplein. From the tourist office, take two lefts; it's toward the end of the Lijnbaan shopping plaza. (Open M-Th 8am-8pm, F 8am-9pm, Sa 8am-7pm, Su 1-6pm.) Cafes line **Oude Binnenweg** and **Nieuwe Binnenweg.** Dance the night away at **Night Town,** West Kruiskade 28. (Cover ƒ10-25/€4.55-11.35 plus ƒ5/€2.30 membership fee. Open F-Sa 11pm-5am.) **Postal code:** 3016 CM.

UTRECHT   ☎ 030

With pretty canals, a Gothic cathedral, and a prestigious university, Utrecht (pop. 233,000) pulses with a dynamic student scene. Get information on churches and museums at **RonDom,** Domplein 9, the Utrecht visitor's center for cultural history. At the heart of the old city stands the awe-inspiring **Domkerk,** begun in 1254 and finished 250 years later. Initially a Roman-Catholic cathedral, the Domkerk has held Protestant services since 1580. (Open M-Sa 10am-5pm, Su 2-4pm. Free.) The **Domtoren,** blown off the cathedral during a medieval tornado, is the highest tower in the Netherlands. (Open M-Sa 10am-5pm, Su noon-5pm. Tour tickets sold at RonDom; ƒ9.95/€4.55, children ƒ5.95/€2.70.)

Trains from Amsterdam (25min., 3-6 per hr., day return ƒ19.75/€9) arrive in the Hoog Catharijne mall. To get to the VVV **tourist office,** Vinkenbrgstr. 19, follow the signs to Vredenberg, which heads to the town center. (☎ (090) 04 14 14 14; info@vvvutrecht.nl. Open M-F 9am-6pm, Sa 9am-5pm.) ◪**Hostel Strowis,** Boothstr. 8, is 15min. from the train station; take bus #3, 4, 8, or 11 to Janskerkhof. (☎ 238 02 80; fax 241 54 51; strowis@xs4all.nl; www.strowis.nl. Internet free. Breakfast ƒ8.50/€3.90. Lockers ƒ25/€11.35. Sheets ƒ2.50/€1.15. Reception 24hr. Curfew Su-W 2am. Dorms ƒ25/€11.35; doubles ƒ80/€36.30; triples ƒ100/€45.40.) **NJHC Ridderhofstad Rhijnauwen (HI),** Rhijnauwenselaan 14, is in nearby Bunnik. Take bus #41 from Centraal Station (12min., every 30min., 3 strips) and tell the driver your destination; from the stop, cross the street, backtrack, turn right on Rhijnauwenselaan, and it's ½km down the road. (☎ 656 12 77; fax 657 10 65; bunnik@njhc.org; www.njhc.org. Breakfast included. Dorms

July-Aug. ƒ39.25/€17.85, off season ƒ34.95/€15.95; singles ƒ46/€20.90; doubles ƒ92/€49.75; triples ƒ138/€62.65; quads ƒ167.75/€76.15. Nonmembers add ƒ5/€2.30.) Look for cheap meals along **Nobelstraat.** Pick up a copy of *UiLoper* at bars or restaurants to scout the bar and cultural scene. Students party at **Woolloo Moollo** on Janskerkhof 14 (open W-Sa 11pm-late; cover varies; student ID required), and **De Beurs,** Neude 35-37, right next to the post office (open daily 10am-late; Th-Sa disco with pop and top 40).

HOGE VELUWE NATIONAL PARK

Don't miss the impressive **Hoge Veluwe National Park** (HO-geh VEY-loo-wuh), a 13,000-acre preserve of woods, heath, dunes, red deer, and wild boars. (www.hogeveluwe.nl. Park open daily Nov.-Mar. 9am-5:30pm; Apr. 8am-8pm; May and Aug. 8am-9pm; June-July 8am-10pm; Sept. 9am-8pm; Oct. 9am-7pm. ƒ10/€4.55, children 6-12 ƒ5/€2.30; 50% discount May-Sept. after 5pm.) Deep in the park, the **Rijksmuseum Kröller-Müller** has troves of van Goghs from the Kroller-Muller family's outstanding collection, as well as key works by Seurat, Mondrian, Picasso, and Brancusi. The museum's striking **sculpture garden,** one of the largest in Europe, has exceptional works by Rodin, Bourdelle, and Hepworth. (Museum open Tu-Su 10am-5pm. Sculpture garden open Tu-Su 10am-4:30pm. ƒ10/€4.55, children ƒ5/€2.30.) Take one of the free **bikes** in the park and get a map at the **visitor's center** to explore over 33km of paths. (☎ 055 378 81 19. Visitor center open daily 10am-5pm.)

Arnhem and **Apeldoorn** (both 15km from the park) are good bases for exploration. **Bus** #12 runs from Arnhem to the park entrance and the museum, while bus #110 runs from Apeldoorn (20min.). Contact the park or either **tourist office** (Arnhem ☎ (090) 02 02 40 75; www.vvvarnhem.nl. Apeldoorn ☎ (0900) 168 16 36) for more information. In Arnhem, stay at the **NJHC Herberg (HI),** Diepenbrocklaan 27. Take bus #3 from the station (dir. Alteveer) to Rijnstate Hospital; turn right facing the hospital, turn left on Cattepoelseweg across the street, turn right up the brick path, and turn right at the stop of the steps. (☎ (026) 351 48 92; arnhem@njhc.org. Breakfast included. Reception 8am-11pm. Curfew 12:30am. Dorms ƒ43-45/€19.55-20.45; singles ƒ60-63/€27.25-28.60; doubles ƒ105-110/€47.65-49.95; triples ƒ142-145/€64.45-65.80; quads ƒ180-190/€81.70-86.25. Nonmembers add ƒ5/€2.30.) To get to Apeldoorn's lively **De Grote Beer (HI),** Asselsestr. 330, take bus #4 or 7 (dir. Orden) from the station, get off at Chamavenlaan, cross the intersection and go right. (☎ (055) 355 31 18; fax 355 38 11; apeldoorn@njhc.org. Breakfast and sheets included. Reception 8am-10pm. Curfew midnight. Dorms ƒ37.50-ƒ46/€17-20.90; nonmembers add ƒ5/€2.30.)

MAASTRICHT   ☎ 043

On a narrow strip of land between Belgium and Germany, Maastricht (pop. 120,000) is one of the oldest cities in The Netherlands. Home of the prestigious **Jan van Eyck Academie of Art,** Maastricht is also known for its abundance of art galleries and antique stores. The striking **Bonnefantenmuseum,** av. Ceramique 250, contrasts Maastricht's traditional Dutch brickwork with its futuristic rocketship design. The museum houses permanent collections of archaeological artifacts, medieval sculpture, Northern Renaissance painting, and contemporary art. (Open Tu-Su 11am-5pm. Free; special exhibits ƒ8/€3.65.) The **Mount Saint Peter Caves,** with a maze-like 20,000 underground passages, were used as a siege shelter as late as World War II and contain inscriptions and artwork by generations of inhabitants. Access to the caves is possible only with a tour guide at two locations: the **Northern System (Grotten Noord),** Luikerweg 71 (tours in Dutch only; ƒ6.50/€2.95, ages 12 and under ƒ4.25/€1.95); and the **Zonneberg Caves,** Slavante 1 (tours in English July-Aug. daily 2:45pm; ƒ6.50/€2.95, ages 12 and under ƒ4.25/€1.95).

The train station is on the eastern side of town, but buses run frequently to the Markt. **Trains** arrive from: Amsterdam (2½hr., ƒ52.50/€23.85); Liège, Belgium (1hr., ƒ44/€20); and Cologne, Germany (2½hr., ƒ63/€28.60). The VVV

tourist office, Kleine Staat 1, is a block from the Markt at Het Dinghuis. From the Markt bus stop, walk toward the river and turn right on Muntstr. (☎325 21 21; www.vvvmaastricht.nl. Open May-Oct. M-Sa 9am-6pm, Su 11am-3pm; Nov.-Apr. M-F 9am-6pm, Sa 9am-5pm.) To get from the station to **City-Hostel de Dousberg (HI),** Dousbergweg 4, take bus #11 on weekdays, bus #28 on weeknights after 6pm, and bus #8 or 18 on weekends. (☎346 67 77; fax 346 67 55. Breakfast included. Dorms ƒ45/€20.45, non-members ƒ5/€2.30 extra; triples ƒ150/€68.10; quads ƒ185/€83.95; quints ƒ220/€99.85.) Cheap food can be found around the central **Vrijthof** area. **Night Live,** Kesselkade 43, is a church converted to a disco. (Cover from ƒ7.50/€3.40. Open Th-Sa 11pm-6am.)

GRONINGEN   ☎050

With 35,000 students and the nightlife to prove it, the small city of Groningen (pop. 175,000) supports eccentric museums and galleries, and trendy cafes. The town's spectacular ⚑**Groninger Museum,** a unique pastel assemblage of squares, cylinders, and metal, forms a bridge between the station and the city center. The multicolored galleries create a futuristic laboratory atmosphere for their contemporary art exhibits. (www.groninger-museum.nl. Open Tu-Su 10am-5pm; July and Aug. also open M 1-5pm. ƒ10/€4.55, seniors ƒ7.50/€3.40, children ƒ5/€2.30.) Admire the city from atop the Grote Markt's **Martinitoren Tower,** which weathered the German attacks during World War II. (Open Apr.-Oct. daily 1-5pm; Nov.-Mar. noon-4pm. ƒ3/€1.40.) Relax in the serene 16th-century **Prinsenhoftuin** (Princes' Court Gardens); the entrance is on the canal 10min. away from the Martinitorin. (Open Apr. to mid-Oct. 10am-dusk.) The tiny **Theeschenkerij Tea Hut** has 130 kinds of tea amidst ivy-covered trellises and towering rose bushes. (Cup ƒ1.75/€0.80.) Or, cool off in the **Noorderplantsoen Park,** host space to the huge **Noorderzon** (Northern Sun Festival), Groningen's annual cultural climax in late August.

Trains roll in from Amsterdam (3hr., every 30min., ƒ52.50/€23.85). To reach the VVV **tourist office,** Grote Markt 25, turn right as you exit the station, walk along the canal, turn left at the first bridge, head straight through the Hereplein on Herestr, cross Gedempte Zuiderdiep, and keep on Herestr. until it hits the Grote Markt. (☎(0900) 202 30 50; info@vvvgroningen.nl; www.vvvgroningen.nl. Open M-F 9am-6pm, Sa 10am-5pm.) Hang out with a fun crowd at **Simplon Youth Hotel,** Boterdiep 72-73. Take bus #1 from the station (dir. Korrewegwijk) to Boterdiep and the hostel is through the yellow- and white-striped entranceway. (☎313 52 21; fax 360 31 39; simplon-jongerenhotel@xs4all.nl; www.xs4all.nl/~simplon. Breakfast ƒ7.50/€3.40. Free lockers. Linens ƒ5.50/€2.50, included in private rooms. Lockout noon-3pm. All-female dorm available. Dorms ƒ24/€10.90; singles ƒ52.50/€23.85; doubles ƒ82.50/€37.45; triples ƒ120/€54.45; quads ƒ155/€70.35.) Pick up a free copy of *UILoper* from the tourist office to find out what's going on each night. The intimate, candlelit **de Spieghel Jazz Café,** Peperstr. 11, has two floors of live jazz, funk, or blues every night. (Wine ƒ4/€1.85 per glass. Open daily 8pm-4am.) **Postal code:** 9725 BM.

WADDEN ISLANDS (WADDENEILANDEN)

Wadden means "mudflat" in Dutch, but sand is the defining characteristic of these islands: isolated beaches hide behind dune ridges with windblown manes of golden grass. Dutch vacationers are secretive about these gems; deserted, tulip-lined bike trails carve through vast, flat stretches of grazing land to the sea.

▣ **TRANSPORTATION.** The islands arch clockwise around the northwestern coast of Holland: Texel (closest to Amsterdam), Vlieland, Terschelling, Ameland, and Schiermonnikoog. To reach **Texel,** take the train from Amsterdam to **Den Helder** (70min., ƒ40/€18.15), bus #3 (2 strips or ƒ3/€1.40), and a ferry to 't Hoorntje, the southernmost town on Texel (20min., every hr. 6:30am-9:30pm, return ƒ9/€4.10).

TEXEL. The largest of the Wadden Islands, Texel boasts stunning beaches and museums. **Beaches** lie near De Koog, on the western side of the island; **nude**

beaches await 2km south of Den Hoorn near paal 9 and 5km west of De Cocks-dorp near paal 28. You can only visit the **nature reserves** on a guided tour; book in advance at **Ecomare Museum and Aquarium,** Ruyslaan 92, in De Koog, and specify English-speaking tours. (www.ecomare.nl. ƒ15/€6.85, children under 13 ƒ7.50/€3.40.) A **Texel Ticket** allows unlimited one-day travel on the island's bus system (runs mid-June to mid-Sept.; ƒ7/€3.20). The VVV **tourist office,** Emmaln 66, lies just outside Den Burg; follow the blue signs about 300km west of the main bus stop. (☎31 28 47; vvv@texel.net; www.vvv-wadden.nl. Open M-Th 9am-6pm, F 9am-9pm, Sa 9am-5pm; July-Aug. also Su 10am-1:30pm.) Rent a **bike** from **Verhuurbedrijf Heijne,** opposite the 't Horntje ferry dock in Texel. (From ƒ9/ €4.10 per day. Open daily Apr.-Oct. 9am-8pm; Nov.-Mar. 9am-6pm.) Take bus #29 and tell the driver your destination to reach **Panorama (HI),** Schansweg 7, snuggled amid sheep pastures, 7km from the dock at 't Horntje and 3km from Den Burg's center. (☎31 54 41. Bikes ƒ8/€3.65 per day. Sheets included; towels ƒ8/€3.65. Reception 8:30am-10:30pm. Dorms ƒ14.70-17.75/€6.70-8.05.) **Camp-grounds** cluster south of De Koog and near De Cocksdorp (ƒ4-7/€1.85-3.20 per person, ƒ15/€6.85 per tent); ask at the tourist office. ☎**0222.**

NORWAY (NORGE)

NORWEGIAN KRONER

US$1 = 8.90KR	1KR = US$0.11
CDN$1 = 5.79KR	1KR = CDN$0.17
UK£1 = 12.85KR	1KR = UK£0.08
IR£1 = 10.33KR	1KR = IR£0.09
AUS$1 = 4.75KR	1KR = AUS$0.21
NZ$1 = 3.90KR	1KR = NZ$0.26
ZAR1 = 1.08KR	1KR = ZAR0.93
EUR€1 = 8.13KR	1KR = EUR€0.12

PHONE CODE: **Country code: 47. International dialing prefix: 095.** There are no city codes in Norway. From outside Norway, dial int'l dialing prefix (see inside back cover) + 47 + local number.

Norway is blessed with an abundance of natural beauty, from the renowned fjords to turquoise rivers and glacier-capped mountain ranges. Its long history manifests itself in its intimate relationship with the sea. The country's original seafarers were Norse Vikings, who dominated a realm that spanned from the British Isles to southern Europe. The late-19th century saw Norway's artistic rise with luminaries like Edvard Munch and Henrik Ibsen. In the years since World War II, Norway has developed into a modern welfare state. Although prices and taxes are among the world's highest, they translate into unparalleled social services, little class stratification, and a high standard of living. As a result of Norway's low crime rate and burgeoning prosperity, visitors encounter a safe and easy place to travel and can focus their attention on the country's main attraction—the breathtaking scenery.

FACTS AND FIGURES

Official Name: Kingdom of Norway.

Capital: Oslo.

Major Cities: Bergen, Stavanger, Trondheim.

Population: 4,439,000.

Land Area: 103,000 sq. km.

Climate: Cool summers and mild winters.

Language: Icelandic; Danish, English, and German are also widely spoken.

Religions: Evangelical Lutheran (96%), other Protestant and Roman Catholic (4%).

DISCOVER NORWAY

Cosmopolitan **Oslo** (p. 707), the first stop on most travelers' itineraries, swarms with lively cafes and museums. After you've exhausted the capital, hop on the gorgeous **Oslo-Bergen rail line** (p. 713) to fjord country. At the other end lies cultural **Bergen,** a former Hanseatic stronghold with pointed gables lining the wharf (p. 714). If you only have one day to see the fjords, spend it exploring the **Sognefjord** (p. 720); the popular **"Norway in a Nutshell"** (p. 717) tour, a daytrip from Bergen, gives a glorious glimpse of fjord country's scenery. With more time for the fjords, check out the **Jostedalsbreen Glacier** and nearby towns (p. 721) or head to **Hardangerfjord** (p. 718). **Trondheim** (p. 723), at the northern end of fjord country, feels more authentic than tourist-oriented Bergen or Oslo (p. 723). If you have substantially more time in Norway, go north to the isolated **Lofoten Islands** (p. 726); or head to the southern coast and explore the lively cities of **Kristiansand** (p. 724) and **Stavanger** (p. 725).

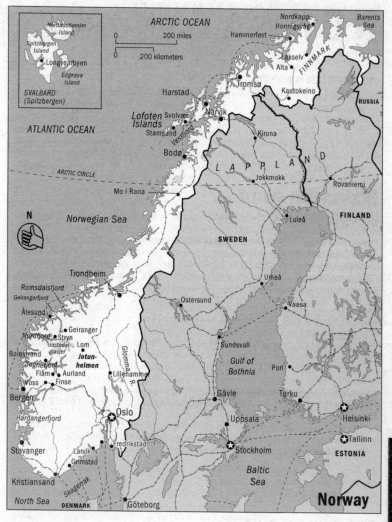

ESSENTIALS

WHEN TO GO

The majority of hostels are crowded with tourists in July and August; June or September may be a better time to go. Climate can also serve as a good guide for when to travel. Oslo averages 18°C (63°F) in July and -4°C (24°F) in January. In the north, average temperatures drop, and it is also wetter than the south and east. For a few weeks around the summer solstice (June 21), the area north of Bodø basks in the midnight sun. You stand the best chance of seeing the Northern Lights (Nov.-Feb.) from above the Arctic Circle. Skiing is best just before Easter.

DOCUMENTS AND FORMALITIES

VISAS. Visas are not required for citizens of Australia, Canada, the EU, New Zealand, or the US for stays shorter than three months. These three months begin upon entry into any Nordic country; more than 90 days in any combination of Finland, Iceland, Norway, or Sweden requires a visa. South Africans need a visa for stays of any length.

EMBASSIES. Foreign embassies are in **Oslo** (see p. 707). Norwegian embassies at home: **Australia,** 17 Hunter St., Yarralumla, Canberra ACT 2600 (☎(26) 273 34 44; fax 273 36 69); **Canada,** 90 Sparks St., Ottawa, ON K1P 5B4 (☎613-238-6571; fax 613-238-2765); **Ireland,** 34 Molesworth St., Dublin 2 (☎(01) 662 18 00; fax 662 18 90); **New Zealand,** 61 Molesworth St., Wellington (☎(04) 471 25 03); **South Africa,** 1166 Park St., Pretoria, 0083 (☎(012) 342 61 00; fax 342 60 99); **UK,** 25 Belgrave Sq., London SW1X 8QD (☎(171) 591 55 00; fax 245 69 93); and **US:** 2720 34th St. NW, Washington D.C. 20008 (☎202-333-6000; fax 202-337-0870; www.norway.org).

TRANSPORTATION

BY PLANE. The main international airport is in Oslo, though a few flights land at Trondheim and Bergen. **SAS** (US ☎800-221-2350) flies to Norway, as does **Finnair** (US ☎800-950-5000) and **Icelandair** (US ☎800-223-5500). Those under 25 or students under 32 qualify for special youth fares that make flying an option for domestic travel. **SAS** (☎81 00 33 00) offers domestic standby tickets *(sjanse billetter)*. Any trip ending either north or south of Trondheim is around 450kr one-way (both zones approx. 800kr).

BY TRAIN. Norway's train system includes an extensive commuter train network around Oslo and long distance lines running from Oslo to Bergen, to Stavanger via Kristiansand, and to Trondheim. From Trondheim, the northern lines run only as far north as Bodø, where buses take over. Trains farther north move along the Swedish line through Kiruna, ending at Narvik on the Norwegian coast. All stations have an information desk; regional schedules are available at the stations. Seat reservations (30kr) are compulsory on many trains, including the high-speed Signatur trains, which cover some departures on the long-distance lines.

Eurail is valid on all trains. The **Norway Railpass** and *buy-in-Scandinavia* **Scanrail Pass** both allow five days within 15 (1620kr, 25% under-26 discount) or 21 consecutive days (2510kr, 25% under-26 discount) of unlimited rail travel through Norway, as well as discounted fares on many ferries and buses. These offers differ from the *buy-outside-Scandinavia* **Scanrail Pass** (p. 68).

BY BUS. Buses are quite expensive, but are the only land option north of Bodø and in the fjords. **Norway Bussekspress** (☎23 00 24 40) operates 75% of the domestic bus routes and publishes a free timetable *(Rutehefte)* containing schedules and prices that's available at bus stations and on buses. Scanrail and InterRail pass holders are entitled to a 50% discount on most bus routes, and students are entitled to a 35% discount on most routes—be insistent and follow the rules listed in the Norway Bussekspress booklet. Bus passes, valid for one (1375kr) or two (2200kr) weeks, are good deals for those exploring the fjords or the north.

BY FERRY. Car ferries *(ferjer)* are usually much cheaper (and slower) than the many passenger express boats *(hurtigbat or ekspressbat)* cruising the coasts and fjords; both often have student, Scanrail, and InterRail discounts. The **Hurtigruten** (the famed Coastal Steamer; see p. 715) takes six days for the fantastic voyage from Bergen to Kirkenes on the Russian border; there is one northbound and one southbound departure from each of its 34 stops per day. There are no railpass discounts, but students get 50% off. Generally buses and trains will be more affordable, but there are exceptions. For **boats** from Kristiansand to Hirtshals, Denmark, see p. 724. For **ships** connecting Stavanger and Newcastle, see p. 725. For **ferries** from Bergen to Hanstholm, Denmark; Newcastle; the Faroe Islands; the Shetland Islands; and Iceland see p. 714.

BY CAR. Roads in Norway are in good condition, although they can be frighteningly narrow in some places and blind curves are common. Drivers should remember to be cautious, especially on mountain roads and tunnels. Driving around the fjords can be frustrating, as only Nordfjord has a road that completely circumnavigates them; there are numerous car ferries, but check a timetable in advance to connect with boat departures. RVs are common. Rental cars are expensive, but for groups they can be more affordable than buying separate railpasses. Gas is prohibitively expensive at about 10-11kr per liter; plan carefully since distances between stations can be substantial. Vehicles are required to keep headlights on at all times. For maps, ask at local tourist offices or contact the **Sons of Norway** in the US and Canada at ☎800-945-8851.

BY BIKE AND BY THUMB. Biking is becoming increasingly common. The beautiful scenery is rewarding for cyclists, although the hilly terrain can be rough on bikes. Contact **Syklistenes Landsforening** (Oslo ☎22 41 50 80) for maps, suggested routes, and other information. Hitching is notoriously difficult in Norway and not recommended by *Let's Go*. Some Norwegians hitch beyond the rail lines in northern Norway and the fjord areas of the west, but many others try for six hours and end up exactly where they started. Hitchers should bring several layers of clothing, rain gear, and a warm sleeping bag.

TOURIST SERVICES AND MONEY

EMERGENCY	**Police:** ☎110. **Ambulance:** ☎113. **Fire:** ☎112.

TOURIST OFFICES. Virtually every town and village has a **Turistinformasjon** office; look for a white lower-case "i" on a square green sign. In July and the first half of August, all tourist offices are open daily; most have reduced hours the rest of the year. For more information, contact the **Norwegian Tourist Board,** P.O. Box 2893 Solli, N-0230 Oslo (☎(47) 22 92 52 00; fax 22 56 05 05; norway@ntr.no; www.ntr.no).

MONEY. The Norwegian **kroner** (kr) is divided into 100 *øre*. Banks and large post offices change money, usually for a commission but at good rates. Prices are sky-high throughout all of Norway. As a general rule, more isolated areas have even higher prices. The Lofoten Islands are especially pricey. A 15% service charge is often included in hotel bills, but it is customary to tip 5-10% for restaurant service. Value-added tax refunds (10-17% of the price) are available for single-item purchases of more than 300kr in a single store in a single visit. Ask for a refund form when you make your purchase and then hand it in at the tax refund desk at the airport or ferry terminal when you leave the country.

BUSINESS HOURS. Business hours are short in summer, especially on Friday and in August, when Norwegians vacation. Shop hours are Monday to Friday 10am-5pm, Saturday 10am-1pm; hours may be extended on Thursday. Banks are generally open Monday to Wednesday and Friday 8:15am-3pm, Thursday 8:15am-5pm.

COMMUNICATION

MAIL. Mailing a postcard/letter from Norway costs 10kr to regions outside of Europe. Sending mail within Europe costs 9kr.

TELEPHONES. Phone calls are expensive. There are three types of public phones; the black and gray phones accept 1, 5, 10, and 20kr coins; green phones accept only phone cards; and red phones accept coins, phone cards, and major credit cards. All calls, including international direct dial calls, usually require at least 5kr. Buying a phone card (*telekort;* 40, 90, or 140kr at Narvesen Kiosks and post offices) is more economical. Pay phones cost twice as much as calls from private lines; between 5pm and 8am prices drop. To make domestic collect calls, dial ☎117; international collect calls, ☎115. **International direct dial** numbers include: **AT&T,** ☎800 190 11; **British Telecom,** ☎800 199 44; **Canada Direct,** ☎800 191 11; **Ireland Direct,** ☎800 19 353; **MCI,** ☎800 199 12; **Sprint,** ☎800 198 77; **Telecom New Zealand,** ☎800 14058; **Telkom South Africa Direct,** ☎800 199 27; **Telstra Australia** ☎800 199 61.

NORWAY

INTERNET ACCESS. There are a good number of Internet cafes in Oslo and Bergen. Smaller cities might have one or two Internet cafes, but most have a public library open on weekdays that offers free Internet access in 15-30min. time slots.

LANGUAGE. Norway is officially bilingual: the Danish-influenced *bokmal* Norwegian used in Oslo and the standardized *nynorsk* Norwegian based on the dialects of western Norway are both taught in schools. Sami is spoken by the indigenous people of the same name who live in northern Norway. Most Norwegians speak good to fluent English. For Norwegian basics, see p. 986.

ACCOMMODATIONS AND CAMPING

HI youth hostels *(vandrerhjem)* are run by **Norske Vandrerhjem,** Dronninggensgt. 26, in Oslo (☎23 13 93 00; fax 23 13 93 50). Beds run 85-180kr; another 40-60kr usually covers breakfast. Sheets typically cost 40-60kr per stay. Usually only rural or smaller hostels have curfews, and only a few are open year-round. Most open in mid- to late June and close after the third week in August. Most tourist offices book **private rooms** and last-minute hotel rooms for a fee (25-35kr). When in Norway, **camp.** Norwegian law allows free camping anywhere on public land for up to two nights, provided that you keep 150m from all buildings and fences and leave no trace behind. **Den Norske Turistforening** (DNT; Norwegian Mountain Touring Association) sells excellent maps (60-70kr), offers guided hiking trips, and maintains about 350 **mountain huts** *(hytter)* throughout the country. (☎22 82 28 00; www.turistforeningen.no. Membership cards available at DNT offices, huts, and tourist offices; 365kr, under 25 175kr. 65-170kr per night; nonmembers add 50kr.) Staffed huts, open around Easter and from late June to early September, serve meals. Unstaffed huts are open from late February until mid-October; if you're a member, you can pick up entrance keys (100kr deposit) from DNT and tourist offices. Official campgrounds charge about 110-125kr for one or two people in a tent. Some also have cabins (450-800kr). Hot showers almost always cost extra.

FOOD AND DRINK

Eating in Norway is pricey; markets and bakeries are the way to go. The supermarket chain Rema 1000 generally has the best prices (usually open M-F 9am-8pm, Sa 9am-6pm). You can also join Norwegians at outdoor markets for cheap seafood and fruit. Many restaurants have cheap *dagens ret* (dish of the day) specials (full meal 70-80kr); otherwise, you'll rarely spend less than 100kr. All-you-can-eat buffets and self-service *kafeterias* are other less expensive options. Fish in Norway—cod, salmon, and herring—is fresh, good, and (relatively) inexpensive. National specialties include *ost* (cheese); *kjøttkaker* (pork and veal meatballs) with boiled potatoes; and, for full-fledged carnivores, the more exotic reindeer, *ptarmigan* (a type of bird), and *hval* (whale meat). Norway grows divine berries. Around Christmas, you can also delight in a special meal consisting of *lutefisk* (dried fish soaked in water). Beer is very expensive (45-50kr for ½L in a bar). Beer is cheapest in supermarkets, and alcohol is almost exclusively available in bars and government-operated liquor stores. You must be 18 to buy beer and 20 to buy wine and alcohol.

HOLIDAYS AND FESTIVALS

Holidays: New Year's Day (Jan. 1); Easter Sunday and Monday (Mar. 31-Apr. 1); May Day (May 1); National Independence Day (May 17); Ascension Day (May 9); Christmas Eve and Day (Dec. 24-25); Boxing Day (Dec. 26); New Year's Eve (Dec. 31).

Festivals: For information about Norway's festivals, check out the website www.norway-festivals.com. The **Bergen Festival** in May offers world-class performances in music, dance, and theater. The **Norwegian Wood** (www.norwegianwood.no) rock festival in early June in Oslo features big-name rock bands, while Kristiansand's week-long **Quart** (www.quart.no) music festival in early July attracts acts from Moby to Beck to Ben Harper. **Midsummer Night** (St. Hansaften), June 23, the longest day of the year, is celebrated with bonfires and huge parties.

OSLO

As far as European capitals go, Oslo's small size (pop. 500,000) sets it apart. Its tree-lined streets and compact city center make it an easy place for travelers to explore for a day or two before heading east to Stockholm or west to Bergen and the fjords. Bordered by pine-covered hills to the north and the waters of the Oslofjord to the south, Oslo boasts several inviting public parks and avoids the sprawl that plagues many cities. Its urban edge is typified by classy cafes, cool boutiques, and beautiful Norwegians in tight, trendy clothes. In winter, the short days and blue light may remind you of the gloomier works of native artists Edvard Munch and Henrik Ibsen, but in summer the midnight sun comes out and seems to never set.

▐ TRANSPORTATION

Flights: White "Flybussen" buses run every 15-20min. between **Gardermoen Airport** and the city (1hr.; 90kr, students 45kr), with pick-up and drop-off at the bus and train stations, and the Radisson SAS Scandinavia Hotel. To airport daily 4:15am-10pm; from airport daily 5:15am-midnight.

Trains: Oslo Sentralstasjon (Oslo S; ☎81 50 08 88). Trains run by NSB (www.nsb.no). Reduced fares *(minipriser)* available M-Th and Sa to major cities if you book 5 days ahead (40% discount). Trains run to: **Bergen** (6-7hr., 600kr); **Copenhagen** (8hr.; 2 per day, 1 per night; 614kr, under 26 454kr, night train 514kr); **Stockholm** (6hr.; 2 per day; 511kr, under 26 358kr); **Trondheim** (6-7hr., 680kr). Mandatory reservations (30kr) for regular trains and for 2nd class on *Signatur* trains running on the Oslo-Kristiansand and Oslo-Trondheim lines; 200-250kr for 1st class.

Buses: Norway Bussekspress, Schweigårdsgate 8 (☎23 00 24 40). Follow the signs from the train station through the Oslo Galleri Mall to the Bussterminalen Galleriet. Schedules at the terminal's information office. Students usually receive a 35% discount on fares; InterRail and Scanrail pass holders usually receive a 50% reduction.

Ferries: Color Line (☎22 94 44 44; fax 22 83 20 96). To **Hirtshals, Denmark** (8hr., 7:30pm, 690kr) and **Kiel, Germany** (19½hr., 1:30pm, 1300-1400kr). InterRail 50% discount; 50% student discount mid-Aug. to mid-June. **DFDS Seaways** (☎22 41 90 90; fax 22 41 38 38) go to **Helsingborg, Sweden** (14hr.), and **Copenhagen** (16hr.) daily at 5pm (in summer 960kr shared cabin, single 1750kr); 25% student discount shared cabin. Color Line departs west of train station (20min); DFDS from 10min. south.

Public Transportation: Trafikanten (☎177), in front of train station, with information. Tourist office also has comprehensive schedules. Bus, tram, subway, and ferry 20kr per ride; 750-1500kr fine for traveling without valid ticket. **Dagskort** (day pass) 50kr; **7-day Card** 150kr; **Flexicard** (8 trips) 125kr. The **Oslo Card** (see below) grants unlimited public transport. Late-night service midnight-5am, double price of normal ticket.

Bike Rental: For information on cycling, contact **Syklistenes Landsforening** (☎22 41 50 80). They have maps and can suggest routes.

Hitchhiking: *Let's Go* does not recommend hitchhiking. Persistent hitchers go to gas stations and ask everyone who stops. Those heading southwest (E-18 to **Kristiansand** and **Stavanger**) take bus #31 or 32 to Maritim. Hitchers to **Bergen** take bus #161 Skui to the last stop; to **Trondheim**, bus #32 or 321, or Metro #5 to Grorud; to **Sweden**, bus #81, 83, or 85 to "Bekkelaget" or local train (dir.: Ski) to Nordstrand.

▐▌▐ ORIENTATION AND PRACTICAL INFORMATION

Karl Johans gate is Oslo's main street and runs from the train station, **Oslo S,** to the **Royal Palace.** Most sights are in the city center within walking distance from Karl Johans gate. Sights a little farther away can be reached via an excellent network of public trams, buses, and subways that pass by Oslo S and the **National Theater,** which sits near the Royal Palace between Karl Johans gate and Stortingsgata. Don't be confused by the word gate, which simply means "street" in Norwegian.

TOURIST, FINANCIAL, AND LOCAL SERVICES

Tourist Offices: Main Tourist Office, Brynjulf Bullsplass 1 (☎23 11 78 80; fax 22 83 81 50; www.oslopro.no), in a big yellow building between the City Hall and Aker Brygge by the waterfront. Sells the **Oslo Card,** which covers public transit and admission to nearly all sights (1-day 180kr; 2-day 290kr; 3-day 390kr). Open daily June-Aug. 9am-7pm; Sept. and April-May M-Sa 9am-5pm; Oct.-Mar. M-F 9am-4pm. Branch at **Oslo S** train station that books hotel rooms (35kr fee) and sells Oslo Card. Open May-Aug. daily 8am-11pm; Sept. M-Sa 8am-11pm; Oct.-Apr. M-Sa 8am-5pm.

Embassies: Australia (consulate), Jermbanetorget 2 (☎22 47 91 70; fax 22 42 26 83). Open M-F 9am-noon and 2-4pm. **Canada,** Wergelandsveien 7 (☎22 99 53 00; fax 22 99 53 01). Open M-F 8:30am-12:30pm. **Ireland,** P.O. Box 5683, Briskeby, N-0209 (☎22 36 11 57; fax 22 12 20 71). **New Zealand** (consulate), Billingstadsletta 19b (Aug.-June ☎66 77 53 30; July 41 43 29 15). Open M-F 10am-3pm. **South Africa,** Drammensveien 88c (☎23 27 32 20; fax 22 44 39 75). Open M-F 9am-noon. **UK,** Thomas Heftyesgt. 8 (☎23 13 27 00; fax 23 13 27 38). Open M-F 9am-12:30pm. **US,** Drammensveien 18 (☎22 44 85 50; fax 22 44 04 36; www.usembassy.no). Open M-F 9am-noon.

Currency Exchange: Available at AmEx office, the main post office, and the banks along Karl Johans gt. On weekends, try the branch of K Bank in the Oslo S train station. Open M-F 7am-7pm, Sa-Su 8am-5pm.

American Express: Fridtjof Nansens Plass 6 (☎22 98 37 35), across from City Hall. Open M-F 9am-4:30pm, Sa 10am-3pm. July to mid-Aug. also Su 11am-3pm.

Luggage Storage: Lockers at the train station. 15-25kr per 24hr. 7-day max. Some hostels offer luggage storage and bags can be left in the Use It office (see **Accommodations** below) for an afternoon or night.

Laundromat: Look for the word *Myntvaskeri.* **Selvbetjent Vask,** Ullevålsveien 15. Wash 30-60kr (soap included); dry 30kr. Open daily 8am-9pm. The *Streetwise Budget Guide to Oslo* (available at Use It, see **Accommodations** below) lists other laundromats.

Gay and Lesbian Services: The Landsforeningen for Lesbisk og Homofil fri gjøring (LLH), St. Olavs plass 2 (☎22 11 05 09; fax 22 20 24 05). Pick up *Blick* (30kr), a monthly newspaper with attractions and nightlife listings. Open M-F 9am-4pm.

EMERGENCY AND COMMUNICATIONS

Emergency: Police: ☎112. **Ambulance:** ☎113. **Fire:** ☎110.

Pharmacy: Jernbanetorvets Apotek (☎22 41 24 82), opposite train station. Open 24hr.

Medical Assistance: Oslo Kommunale Legevakt, Storgata 40 (☎22 11 80 80). On-call 24hr.

Internet Access: Deichmanske Library, Henrik Ibsensgate 1. Sign up for free 30min. slots. Open June-Aug. M-F 10am-6pm, Sa 9am-2pm. Sept.-May 10am-8pm, Sa 9am-3pm. **National Library** (Nasjonal Biblioteket), corner of Drammensveien and Frognerveien. Take tram #10, 12, 13, or 15 or bus #30, 31, or 32 to Solli. Free 15min. slots. **Studenten,** corner of Karl Johans gt. and Universitetsgata. Open Tu-Sa noon-8pm, Su-M noon-10pm. 20kr per 15min., 30kr per 30min., 55kr per hr.

Post Office: Main post office at Dronningens gt. 15 (☎23 14 78 02); enter at Prinsens gt. Mail for travelers should be addressed: First name, SURNAME, *Poste Restante,* Dronningens Gate 15, N-0101 Oslo 1, NORWAY. Open M-F 9am-5pm. Other post office branches around the city center.

▐ ACCOMMODATIONS

Hostels in Oslo fill up quickly in the summer—make reservations, especially if traveling in a group. The **private rooms** arranged by **Use It,** Møllergata 3, are a good deal for 125kr, with sleeping bag 100kr. (☎22 41 51 32; www.unginfo.oslo.no. Open July-Aug. daily 7:30am-5pm, Sept.-June M-W and F 11am-5pm, Th 11am-6pm.) **Pensions** *(pensjonater)* are usually cheaper than hotels. Some **hotels** offer cheaper last-

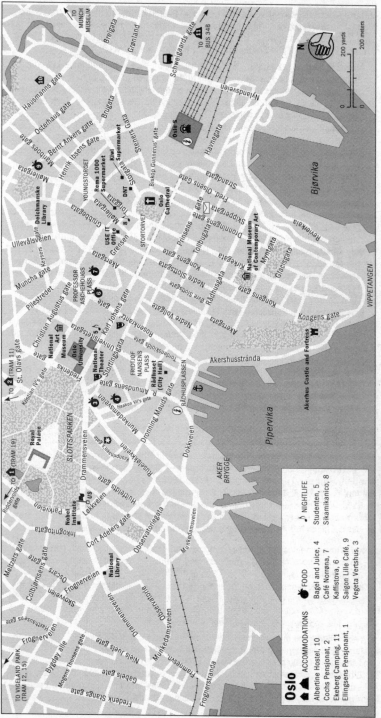

Oslo

♠▲ ACCOMMODATIONS
Albertine Hostel, 10
Cochs Pensjonat, 2
Ekeberg Camping, 11
Elingsens Pensjonat, 1

● FOOD
Bagel and Juice, 4
Café Norrøna, 7
Kaffistova, 6
Saigon Lille Café, 9
Vegeta Vertshus, 3

♪ NIGHTLIFE
Studenten, 5
Sikamikanico, 8

minute prices on vacant rooms through the tourist office. In principle, the Norwegian *allmansrett* gives you the right to **free camp,** but no one really camps on private lawns. Free camping is in the forest north of town as long as you avoid public areas; try the end of the Sognsvann line. Fires are not allowed.

Albertine Hostel, Storgata 55 (☎/fas 22 99 72 00). Walk along Karl Johans gt. from the train station, around the cathedral, and up Storgata. Or take tram #11, 12, 15, or 17 to Hausmanns gate; it's 100m up Storgata on the left, behind the Anker Hotel. Closest hostel to the city center. Breakfast 55kr. Sheets 40kr. Reception 24hr. Open June-Aug. Dorms 125kr; singles and doubles 370kr; quads 600kr.

Ellingsens Pensjonat, Holtegata 25 (☎22 60 03 59; fax 22 60 99 21). Take tram #19 to Briskeby. From the intersection of Holtegata and Uranienborgveien, walk away from the church and it's an unmarked grey house on the right. Popular with backpackers due to its central location, pleasant surroundings, and friendly mother-daughter management. Reception M-F 7:30am-10:30pm, Sa-Su 8am-10:30pm. Singles 300kr; doubles 490kr, with bath 430kr; doubles with bath 560kr.

Cochs Pensjonat, Parkveien 25 (☎23 33 24 00; fax 23 33 24 10), at Hegdehaugsveien. From the train station, walk 25min. along Karl Johans gt. through Slottsparken; or take tram #11 or 19 to the end of the park. Quiet rooms on the upper floors of a building next to the royal park. Reception on 3rd fl. Singles 350kr; doubles 500kr.

Oslo Vandrerhjem Haraldsheim (HI), Haraldsheimveien 4 (☎22 15 50 43 or 22 22 29 65; fax 22 22 10 25). Take tram #15 or 17, or the Flybus from the airport, to Sinsenkrysset; follow the dirt path across the field and up the hill. The hostel is on the far, righthand side of the field. Internet 10kr per 15min. Reception 24hr. Lockout 10am-3pm. Dorms 160kr, with bath 180kr; singles 280kr/350kr; doubles 380kr/460kr.

Oslo Vandrerhjem Holtekilen (HI), Michelets vei 55 (☎67 51 80 40; fax 67 59 12 30). Take bus #151/161, 251/252, or 261 to Kveldsroveien (20min), or take the local commuter train to Stabekk. Popular, although far from central Oslo. Dorms 165kr; singles 265kr; doubles 430kr. Nonmembers add 25kr.

Ekeberg Camping, Ekebergveien 65 (☎22 19 85 68), 3km from town. Take bus 34B from the train station (10min.). Marvelous view from a bluff overlooking the city. Cooking facilities, grocery store (open daily 8am-10pm), and laundry. Showers included. Reception daily 7:30am-11pm. Open May 25-Aug. Tent 120kr per 2 people, with car 160kr. Extra person 40kr. 20% Inter- or Scanrail discount.

▣ FOOD

Visitors should have no trouble finding authentic Norwegian meals or dishes from any part of the globe. Prices are high, however, and **grocery stores** may be the best option for those on a tight budget: try **Rema 1000,** Torggata 2-6 (open M-F 9am-8pm, Sa 9am-6pm), or **Kiwi** supermarket, Storgata 11 (open M-F 7am-9pm, Sa 9am-6pm). You can eat out without hurting your wallet in the **Grønland** district east of the train station, in the international food court in the **Paléet** shopping mall on Karl Johans gt., and at **lunch buffets** offered by most restaurants in the city center.

▨ **Kaffistova,** intersection of Rosenkrantz gt. and Kristian IV gt. Beautiful, cafeteria-style eatery with traditional Norwegian meat and fish dishes, porridges, and desserts. Vegetarian options. Entrees 80-100kr. Open M-F 9:30am-8pm, Sa-Su 10:30am-5pm.

Café Norrøna, Grensen 19, on Professor Aschehougs plass. Relatively upscale cafe with Norwegian specialties and great all-you-can-eat deals on soup and salad (69kr) and dessert (55kr). Open June to mid-Aug. M-F 7am-8pm, Sa-Su noon-6pm; mid-Aug. to May M-F 6:30am-9pm, Sa 11am-6pm, Su noon-6pm.

Vegeta Vertshus, Munkedamsveien 3b, off Stortings gt. near the National Theater. Cafeteria-style vegetarian buffet and salad bar. All-you-can-eat 125kr; single serving 90kr. Open daily 11am-11pm; buffet closes 10pm.

Sult, Thorvald Meyersgt. 26, in the trendy Grüner Løkka neighborhood north of the Albertine Hostel. Tasty and artfully presented food. Dinner 100-170kr. Beer 44kr. Open Tu-F 4pm-12:30am, Sa-Su 1pm-12:30am. Kitchen closes daily 10pm.

PAINT THE TOWN GREEN Oslo may be expensive, but some of its greatest resources, its parks and tree-lined streets, are free. You can admire over 200 captivating sculptures in Vigeland Park, toss a frisbee in the beautiful royal park (*Slottsparken*), enjoy a picnic by the scenic pond on the grounds of the Akershus Fortress, or relax with a novel in the quiet park just to the west of the Munch Museum. Nearly all visitors to Oslo will stroll beneath the stately trees along Karl Johans gate and there are also plenty of quiet, shady streets worth exploring in the Uranienborg and Briskeby neighborhoods between the Royal Palace and Vigeland Park. Small parks dot the city, and if you wander away from the center of town and off the beaten path, you're bound to discover a place to relax and take a break from traditional sightseeing.

Bagel and Juice, Haakon VII gt. 5, between the City Hall and Slottsparken. Bagels 28kr with cream cheese. A popular bar after hours, especially F-Sa when there's a DJ. Open M-Th 10am-12:30am, F-Sa 10am-2:30am, Su 11am-12:30am.

Saigon Lille Cafe, Møllergaten 32C/Bernt Ankers gate. No English makes this place an adventure. Most entrees 59-80kr. Open daily 11am-11pm.

👁 SIGHTS

▧ VIGELAND PARK. Also known as **Vigelandsparken** and located within the larger **Frognerparken**. The 80-acre park is home to over 200 of Gustav Vigeland's creative sculptures depicting each stage of the human life cycle. More than one million visitors come annually, making the park Norway's most visited attraction. Highlights include a towering monolith created using a single piece of granite. (*Entrance on Kirkeveien. Take bus #20 or tram #12 or 15 to Vigelandsparken. Open 24hr. Free.*)

EDVARD MUNCH. The **Munch Museum** (Munch-museet) displays rotating exhibitions of the more than 20,000 paintings, prints, drawings, and watercolors that Munch bequeathed to the city of Oslo before his death in 1944. (*Tøyengata 53. Take bus #20 to Munch-museet, the subway to Tøyen, or walk 10min. northeast from the train station. Open June to mid-Sept. daily 10am-6pm; mid-Sept. to May Tu-W and F-Sa 10am-4pm, Th and Su 10am-6pm. 60kr, students 30kr, free with Oslo Card.*) The **National Art Museum** (Nasjonal-galleriet) houses a large collection of Scandinavian artwork and also has several rooms dedicated to the works of Impressionists. (*Universitetsgaten 13. Take tram #12, 13, or 19, or the subway to Nationaltheatret. Open M, W, and F 10am-6pm, Th 10am-8pm, Sa 10am-4pm, Su 11am-4pm. Free.*) Next door at **Oslo University,** several gigantic murals by Munch grace the walls of a concert hall. (*Enter through door by columns off Karl Johans gt. Open mid-June to mid-Aug. M-F 10am-2:45pm. Free.*)

RÅDHUS (CITY HALL). The annual Nobel Peace Prize ceremony takes place here Dec. 10. in the huge main room, which features towering murals on all sides. Upstairs there are several exhibits, including an evocative Per Krohg mural that covers every inch of wall and ceiling in a long, narrow room. (*South of the National Theater and Karl Johans gt. on Fridtjof Nansens plass, near the harbor. Open daily 9am-5pm. 25kr, students, seniors, and children 15kr, free with Oslo Card. Tours daily 10am, noon, and 2pm.*)

AKERSHUS CASTLE AND FORTRESS. Built in 1299, this waterfront complex was transformed into a Renaissance palace by Christian IV between 1637 and 1648. Explore dungeons, underground passages, and vast halls. (*Take bus #60 to Bankplassen or tram #10 or 15 to Christianiatorv. Fortress complex open daily 6am-9pm. Free. Castle open May to mid-Sept. M-Sa 10am-4pm, Su 12:30-4pm; mid to late Apr. and mid-Sept. to Oct. Su 12:30-4pm. 30kr, students, seniors, and children 10kr. Tours of the castle M-Sa 11am, 1, 3pm; Su 1 and 3pm.*) Down the hill, the powerful **Hjemmefrontmuseet** (Resistance Museum) in the fortress documents Norway's efforts to subvert Nazi occupation. (*Open mid-June to Aug. M-Sa 10am-5pm, Su 11am-5pm; Sept. to mid-June closes 1-2hr. earlier. 25kr, students, seniors, and children 10kr, free with Oslo Card.*)

NORWAY

BYGDØY. The peninsula of Bygdøy is right across the inlet from downtown Oslo; although mainly residential, it boasts some of the city's best museums and even has a few beaches. You can reach the peninsula by ferry in the summer from in front of the City Hall or by city bus year-round. The ferry stops first at Dronningen, at the Norsk Folkemuseum and Viking Ship Museum, and then travels to Bygdøynes, where you can find the Kon-Tiki Museum and the Fram Museum. Your best bet may be to get off at the first stop, see the museums there, and then catch bus #30b to the other museums at Bygdøynes before getting back on the ferry to downtown Oslo. All of the museums on Bygdøy are free with the Oslo Card. *(To reach Bygdøy, take the public ferry from pier 3 in front of the City Hall. 10min.; May-Sept. every 40min. M-F 7:45am-9:05pm, Sa-Su 9:05am-9:05pm; 20kr, seniors and children 10kr. Ferry information ☎ 23 35 68 90. Or take bus #30 from the National Theater or Oslo S to Folkemuseet or Bygdøynes.)* The **Norsk Folkemuseum** is one of Europe's largest open-air museums and features buildings from various eras and parts of the country. The highlight is a beautifully crafted 13th-century **stave church,** one of the last of its kind in existence. *(Museumsveien 10. Walk up the hill leading away from the dock and follow signs to the right (10min.); or take bus #30 to Folkemuseet. Open mid-May to mid-Sept. daily 10am-6pm; mid-Sept. to mid-May M-F 11am-3pm, Sa-Su 11am-4pm. 70kr, students and seniors 40kr.)* Less than a 5min. walk from the Norsk Folkemuseum is the **Viking Ship Museum,** which houses three wooden vessels promoted as being the best preserved of their kind. *(Walk straight up the hill from the Dronningen ferry stop (10min.) or take bus #30 to Vikingskipshuset. Open daily May-Sept. 9am-6pm; Oct.-Apr. 11am-4pm. 40kr, students and children 20kr.)* At the ferry's second stop, Bygdøynes, the **Fram Museum** contains the enormous polar ship "Fram," which was used by three of Norway's most famous explorers for arctic expeditions in the late 19th and early 20th centuries. *(Open daily mid-June to Aug. 9am-6:45pm; reduced hours rest of year. 25kr, students and children 15kr.)* Across the street from the Fram Museum is the **Kon-Tiki Museum,** which highlights Norwegian Thor Heyerdahl's daring 1947 ocean crossing from South America to Polynesia. *(Open daily June-Aug. 9:30am-5:45pm; Apr., May, Sept. 10:30am-5pm; Oct.-Mar. 10:30am-4pm. 30kr, students 20kr.)* On the southwestern side of Bygdøy, there are two popular beaches, **Huk** and **Paradisbukta.** Huk appeals to a younger crowd while Paradisbukta is more family oriented. The stretch of shore between them is a nude beach. *(Take bus #30 or walk south for 25min. from the Bygdøynes ferry stop.)*

OTHER SIGHTS. The subdued **National Museum of Contemporary Art** (Museet for samtidskunst) is near Akershus Fortress. *(Bankplassen 4. Open Tu-W, and F 10am-5pm, Th 10am-8pm, Sa 11am-4pm, Su 11am-5pm. 40kr, students and seniors 20kr; free with Oslo Card and on Th.)* The **Royal Palace,** on a hill at the western end of Karl Johans gt., is open to the public via guided tours, but tickets sell out well in advance. *(Purchase tickets from any post office. 65kr.)* You can watch the changing of the guard for free daily at 1:30pm in front of the palace. *(Take tram #12, 15, or 19, or bus #30-32 or 45 to Slottsparken.)* For a great panorama of **Oslofjord** and the city, head to the mighty ski jump Holmenkollen at the world's oldest **Ski Museum.** A simulator recreates the adrenaline rush of a leap off a ski jump and a 4min., 130km-per-hour downhill ski run. *(Take subway #1 on the Frognerseteren line to Holmenkollen. It's a 10min. walk uphill from the subway stop. Open daily June-Aug. 9am-8pm; May and Sept. 10am-5pm; Oct.-Apr. 10am-4pm. Museum 60kr, students 50kr, children 30kr; free with Oslo Card. Simulator 45kr.)*

🎵🎭 **ENTERTAINMENT AND NIGHTLIFE**

The monthly *What's On in Oslo* (free at tourist offices) details Oslo's opera, symphony, and theater. **Filmenshus,** Dronningsgt. 16 (☎22 47 45 00), is the center of Oslo's art film scene, while Hollywood flicks are screened at **Saga Cinema,** Stortingsgata 28 (M-Th 60kr, F-Su 75kr). In addition to the countless bars along **Karl Johans gate** and in the **Aker Brygge** harbor complex, Oslo boasts a number of nightclubs and cafes with busy DJs and live music. **So What!,** Grensen 9, is popular with a young, alternative crowd. (Beer 42kr. 2-3 concerts per week. Cover 60-150kr. Open daily 1pm-3am. Dance floor opens daily 11pm, or 9pm if there's a concert.)

Sikamikanico, Møllergata 2, is one of Oslo's hipper coffee bars and DJs spin techno every night. (Cover 30-50kr. Open June-Aug. M-Sa 3pm-3am; Sept.-May daily 3pm-3am.) If you're in the mood for Top 40-type hits, try **Studenten,** on the corner of Karl Johans gt. and Universitetsgata. A piano player performs downstairs Tu-Sa. (Cover F-Sa after 9pm 40kr. Open M-Sa 11am-3am, Su noon-3am.)

⬛ DAYTRIPS FROM OSLO

The nearby islands of inner **Oslofjord** offer cheap, delightful daytrips. The ruins of a **Cistercian Abbey** lie on the landscaped island of **Hovedøya,** while **Langøyene** has Oslo's best **beach.** Take bus #60 (20kr) from the City Hall to **Vippetangen** to catch a ferry to either island. About an hour from Oslo by ferry, **Drøbak** has traditional wooden houses. The **ferry** (☎22 08 40 00) to Drøbak leaves from in front of the Rådhus. To bask in Norway's natural grandeur, take the Sognsvann subway from the National Theater or Oslo S to the end of the line. Ask the tourist office about cross-country ski rental. **The Wilderness Centre** (*Villmarkssenteret*), Christian Krohgs gt. 16 (☎22 05 05 25), rents canoes and kayaks on the Akerselva river.

ALONG THE OSLO-BERGEN RAIL LINE

The 7hr. rail journey from Oslo to Bergen is one of the most famous scenic rides in the world. From Oslo, there are stops at **Finse, Myrdal** (the transfer point for the **Flåm railway**), and **Voss,** before the train finally pulls into Bergen.

FINSE. Outdoor enthusiasts hop off at Finse and hike north for several beautiful days down the Aurlandsdal Valley to **Aurland,** 10km from Flåm. Be sure to ask about trail conditions before you set off at either the Finse station or the DNT in Oslo or Bergen. You can sleep in DNT *hytte,* all spaced a day's walk apart along the trail to Aurland. For maps, prices, and reservations, inquire at DNT in Oslo (☎22 82 28 22) or Bergen (☎55 32 22 30).

VOSS. Stretched along a glassy lake that reflects surrounding snow-capped mountains, Voss is an adventurer's dream. In winter, skiing is plentiful; in summer there's kayaking, paragliding, horseback riding, and whitewater rafting. Book through the **Voss Adventure Center** (☎56 51 36 30), in a mini-golf hut behind the Park Hotel, or head across the parking lot behind the hotel to the recommended sea kayaking outfit **Nordic Ventures** (☎56 51 00 17; www.nordicventures.com), or the **Voss Rafting Center** (☎56 51 05 25; www.bbb.no). **Trains** leave for Oslo (5½-6hr., 5 per day, 510kr) and Bergen (1¼hr., 16 per day, 130kr). **Buses** also run from Voss to Gudvangen (50-70min.; M-F 10 per day, Sa-Su 4 per day; 67kr) on the Sognefjord, and it is possible to make bus connections to Bergen, Oslo, and Lillehammer (ask at the station for more details). Trains and buses arrive at a central station near the downtown area; to get to the **tourist office,** Hestavangen 10, turn left as you exit the station and bear right at the fork by the church. (☎56 52 08 00. Open June-Aug. M-Sa 9am-7pm, Su 2-7pm; Sept.-May M-F 9am-4pm.) Turn right as you exit the station and walk along the lakeside road to reach Voss's modern, well-equipped **HI youth hostel,** where you can admire the terrific view or relax in the sauna. (☎56 51 20 17. Canoe, rowboat, bike, and kayak rental. Reception 24hr. Dorms 220kr; 10% off for members.) To reach **Voss Camping,** head left from the station, stick to the lake shore, and follow the road until you hit the campground pool. (☎56 51 15 97. Tent and 4 people 80kr.) Pick up groceries at **Kiwi** supermarket, on the main street just past the post office. (Open M-F 9am-9pm, Sa 9am-6pm.)

⬛ FLÅM AND THE FLÅM RAILWAY. The spectacular railway connecting **Myrdal** (a stop on the Oslo-Bergen line) to the tiny fjord town of Flåm is one of Norway's most famous attractions. Descending almost 864m in 55min., the railway is an incredible feat of engineering, winding through tunnels past rushing waterfalls to the valley below. Be sure to see the magnificent **Kjosfossen falls** when the train makes its stop there (and be prepared for the most unusual juxtaposition of nature and entertainment that you'll see in Norway). Alternatively, a 20km **hike** (4-5hr.) on well-tended paths from Myrdal to Flåm allows for extended lingering and free camping amid the rainbow-capped waterfalls and snowy mountain vistas. Flåm sits at the edge of the **Aurlandsfjord,** an inlet off the Sognefjord. During the day, the tiny town is heavily touristed; in the off season, the stunning surroundings make Flåm a terrific, soothing place to spend a night or two. The **tourist office** is in the large building beside the train station. (☎57 63 21 06. Open daily mid-June to mid-Aug. 8:30am-3:30pm and 4-8pm, reduced hours in the off season.) From Flåm, there are daily express boats to Aurland, Sogndal, Balestrand and Bergen, and ferries to Gudvangen (inquire at the tourist office for up-to-date schedules).

THE FJORDS AND WEST COUNTRY

Spectacular views and summer's long days make fjord country irresistible to all types of travelers. Buses and ferries wind through this unique and scenic coastal region, and although transportation can be complicated, the scenery through the window is half the fun. **Bergen** is the major port for boats serving the region; **HSD express boats** (☎55 23 87 80; ticket office at Strandkaiterminalen) run to the Hardangerfjord, Stavanger, and points south of the city, while **Fylkesbaatane** (☎55 90 70 71; tickets also at Strandkaiterminalen) takes care of boat transport north into the Sognefjord and surrounding areas. Main **bus** departure points in the region are Bergen (see below), Sogndal (see p. 722), and Førde (a large town north of the Sognefjord); bus connections to almost all fjord towns can be reached through them. Call ☎177 for regional **transportation information;** tourist offices, boat terminals, and bus stations can help plan routes through the fjords.

BERGEN

Tucked in a scenic spot between steep, forested mountains and the waters of the Puddefjorden, Bergen bills itself the "Gateway to the Fjords." Despite being Norway's second biggest city, Bergen has a compact downtown and most attractions can be reached on foot. Yet despite the city's small size, it has long been an intellectual and commercial center.

TRANSPORTATION

Trains: ☎81 50 08 88. Daily to: **Myrdal** (2½hr., 8 per day, 185kr); **Oslo** (6½hr., 4 per day, 600kr); **Voss** (1¼hr., 16 per day, 130kr).

Buses: Busstasjon, Strømgaten 8, enter through building with "Bergen Storsenter" sign (☎177, outside Bergen 55 55 90 70). Serves neighboring areas, the **Hardangerfjord** area, **Ålesund** (514kr, 25% student discount, 50% Inter- and Scanrail discount), **Oslo** (610kr; 25% student discount), and **Trondheim** (755kr, 25% student discount, 50% Inter- and Scanrail discount). Ticket office open M-F 7am-6pm, Sa 7am-2pm.

Ferries: The **Hurtigruten** (☎81 03 00 00; www.hurtigruten.com) begins its journey along the coast to **Kirkenes** from **Bergen** (Apr.-Sept. daily 8pm, 4466kr; Oct.-Apr. daily 10:30pm, 4058kr; 50% student discount).

Fjord Line, on Skoltegrunnskaien (☎55 54 88 00), goes to **Hanstholm, Denmark** (26hr., M, W, and F 4:30pm, from 1210kr; off season from 710kr; return 10% off) and **Newcastle, England** (23hr.; Tu, F and Su, in winter M and Th; from 1610kr, in winter 1130kr). **Smyril Line,** Slottsgaten 1, 5th fl. (☎55 32 09 70; fax 55 96 02 72), has one ship that departs for: the **Faroe Islands** (24hr., from 610-840kr); **Iceland** (45hr., from 1290-1840kr); and the **Shetland Islands** (12hr.; June-Aug. Tu 3pm; from 480-690kr, 25% student discount). All international ferries, except the Hurtigruten, depart from **Skoltegrunnskaien,** a 10-15min. walk past Bryggen along the right side of the harbor.

Public Transportation: Yellow and red buses chauffeur you around the city. 20kr per ride in city center. Bus #100 is free from the bus station to the Galleriet shopping mall on Torgalmenningen by the harbor.

CRUISING THE WEST COAST Known as the "Hurtigruten," the coastal steamer's route begins in Bergen and ends at Kirkenes, on the Norwegian-Russian border. Although now primarily used as passenger cruise ships, the 11 vessels serving the route still carry out their historical function delivering supplies to its 34 ports of call along the western coast. Most passengers purchase a cabin and stay on board for the return journey from Bergen; but with a north- and southbound ship stopping at all ports every day, the Hurtigruten is the swankiest way for those traveling shorter distances to get from one place to the next.

ORIENTATION AND PRACTICAL INFORMATION

The **train station** lies at the opposite end of the city center, 10min. from the harbor. As you face the harbor, **Bryggen** (the extension of Kong Oscars gt.) and the town's most imposing mountains are to your right; most of the main buildings are to the left. The **Torget,** Bergen's famous outdoor market, is at the harbor's tip.

Tourist Office: Vågsalmenningen 1 (☎55 32 14 80; fax 55 32 14 64), just past the Torget. Books private rooms (25kr fee) and has free copies of the useful *Bergen Guide*. A special section in the office helps visitors plan travel through the fjords. The **Bergen Card** covers museum admissions, public transportation, and offers other discounts (1-day 150kr, 2-day 230kr). Open June-Aug. daily 8:30am-10pm; May and Sept. 9am-8pm; Oct.-Apr. M-Sa 9am-4pm. **DNT,** Tverrgt. 4-6 (☎55 32 22 30), off Marken, sells detailed topological maps for all of Norway and provides comprehensive hiking information. Open M-W and F 10am-4pm, Th 10am-6pm.

Currency Exchange: At banks near the harbor (generally open M-W and F 9am-3pm, Th 9am-5:30pm) and the post office. After hours the tourist office will change currency at a rate less favorable than the bank rate, but no commission.

Luggage storage: At the train and bus stations. 20kr per day. Open daily 7am-10:50pm.

Emergency: Police: ☎112. **Ambulance:** ☎113. **Fire:** ☎110.

Pharmacy: Apoteket Nordstjernen (☎55 21 83 84), on 2nd fl. of the bus station. Open M-Sa 8am-midnight, Su 9:30am-midnight.

Medical Assistance: 24-hour Accident Clinic, Vestre Strømkai 19 (☎55 32 11 20).

Internet Access: Bibliotek (public library), Stromgata Vestre Strømkaien. Free, but limited to 15min. **CyberHouse,** Vetrlidsalm 13, near the funicular. 20kr per 30min. Open June-Aug. 24hr; Sept.-May M-Th 10am-midnight, F-Sa 10am-8pm, Su noon-midnight.

Post Office: Småstrandgt. (☎55 54 15 00). Open M-F 8am-6pm, Sa 9am-3pm. Address to be held: First name SURNAME, *Poste Restante*, Postkontor, Olav Kyrres gate, N-5002, Bergen, NORWAY. *Poste Restante* office open M-F 8am-3pm, Sa 9am-3pm.

ACCOMMODATIONS AND CAMPING

In the summer, it's best to reserve ahead. The tourist office books rooms in private homes for a 25kr fee (singles 185-210kr; doubles 295-430kr).

Intermission, Kalfarveien 8 (☎55 30 04 00). Head right from the train or bus station and right down Kong Oscars gt., which becomes Kalfarveien, and look for the white house on the left (5min.). Friendly staff and communal atmosphere. Reception 7-11am and 5pm-midnight, F-Sa until 1am. Lockout 11am-5pm. Curfew M-Th and Su midnight, F-Sa 1am. Open mid-June to mid-Aug. 100kr. Camping in backyard 100kr.

Marken Gjestehus, Kong Oscars gt. 45 (☎55 31 44 04; fax 55 31 60 22; markengjestehus@smisi.no). Entrance around corner on Tverrgaten. Reception on 4th fl. Small, centrally located guesthouse. Simple, clean rooms, some with nice views of the nearby mountains. Reception May-Sept. 9am-10:30pm; Oct.-Apr. 9am-7pm. Dorms 160kr; singles 310kr; doubles 410kr.

YMCA InterRail Center, Nedre Korskirkealmenningen 4 (☎55 31 72 52; fax 55 31 35 77). Exit the train or bus station and turn right, and head up the hill; then turn left onto Kong Oscars gt. and left again when you reach Nedre Korskirk (7-10min.). Often crowded with backpackers, thanks to low prices and an excellent location. Reception 7am-midnight. Lockout noon-4pm. Dorms 110kr; 4-6 person room 160kr per person.

Montana Youth Hostel (HI), Johan Blyttsvei 30 (☎55 20 80 70; fax 55 20 80 75), 5km from the city center. Take bus #31 (dir. Lægdene; 20kr) from the post office to "Montana" (10min.). Don't miss the commanding views from the lookout point. Breakfast included. Kitchen. Sheets 50kr. Laundry 40kr. Reception 24hr. Lockout 10am-3pm. Dorms 120kr; doubles with bath 500kr. Nonmembers add 25kr.

Camping: Bergen Camping Park, Haukås i Åsane (☎55 24 88 08). Take bus #285 from the bus station to Breistein (30min.). 125kr for 1 or 2 people with tent. Cabins 440-750kr. Or **free camp** on the far side of the hills above town.

🍴 FOOD

Bergen's culinary centerpiece is the **fish market** that springs up on the Torget; it's unclear, however, whether fish or tourists are the main haul. (Open in summer M-F 7am-4pm, Th 7am-7pm, Sa 7am-3pm; opens later in off season.) **Fellini,** Tverrgt., just off Marken, serves up Italian specialties and great pizza from 49kr. (Open M-Sa 2pm-midnight, Su 2-11pm.) Enjoy Norwegian cuisine with the older set at **Kaffistova til Ervingen,** Strandkaien 2B, on the 2nd floor next to the harbor, a cafeteria-style joint with *dagens tilbur* (daily offer) including coffee for 83kr, soup with homemade bread for 35kr, and main dishes from 48kr. (Open M-F 8am-7pm, Sa 8am-5pm, Su noon-7pm.) Grab **groceries** at **Rimi,** Marken 3 (open M-F 7am-9pm, Sa 7am-6pm), or at several other markets by the harbor.

👁 🏞 SIGHTS AND THE OUTDOORS

BRYGGEN AND BERGENHUS. From the Torget, gazing down the right side of the harbor yields a view of **Bryggen's** pointed gables. This row of medieval buildings has survived half-a-dozen fires and the explosion of a Nazi munitions ship. Today, it's listed by UNESCO as one of the world's most significant examples of the history and culture of the Middle Ages. Guided walking tours of Bryggen in English run from the Bryggens Museum (1½hr., June-Aug. daily 11am and 1pm, 70kr). The **Hanseatic Museum** displays secret compartments, mummified hanging fish, and other relics from the life of 18th-century Hanseatic merchants in one of Bergen's oldest wooden buildings. *(At the end of Bryggen, near the Torget. Open daily June-Aug. 9am-5pm; Sept.-May 11am-2pm. May-Sept. 40kr; Oct.-Apr. 25kr.)* The **Bryggens Museum** displays old costumes, runic inscriptions, and scenes from life in medieval Norway. *(Dreggsalm. 3, behind a small park at the end of the Bryggen houses. Open May-Aug. daily 10am-5pm; Sept.-Apr. M-F 11am-3pm, Sa noon-3pm, Su noon-4pm. 30kr, students 15kr.)* The former city fortress, **Bergenhus,** teeters at the end of the quay. On its grounds lie the **Rosenkrantz Tower,** in late medieval splendor, and the cavernous 13th-century hall **Håkonshallen,** which is all that remains of the royal residence. *(At the far end of Bryggen; walk along the harbor away from the Torget. Hall and tower open mid-May to Aug. daily 10am-4pm; Sept. to mid-May tower open Su noon-3pm; hall open M-W and F-Su noon-3pm, Th 3-6pm. Guided tours every hr. in summer. 20kr for each building, students and children 10kr.)*

ART MUSEUMS AND GALLERIES. There are three branches of the **Bergen Art Museum** lining the west side of the Lille Lungegårdsvann pond near the city center. The **Stenersen Collection** features works by Picasso, Miró, and Munch while the **Rasmus Meyer Collection** provides an overview of Norwegian Naturalists, Impressionists, and Expressionists. The **City Art Collection** focuses primarily on Norwegian art. *(Rasmus Meyers allé 3 and 7, and Lars Hilles gt. 10, respectively. All 3 open mid-May to mid-Sept. daily 11am-5pm; mid-Sept. to mid-May Tu-Su 11am-5pm. 35kr for all 3 museums, temporary exhibits additional 15kr.)*

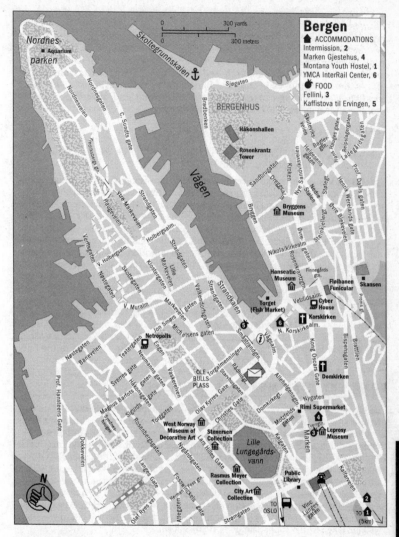

Bergen

🏠 ACCOMMODATIONS
Intermission, 2
Marken Gjestehus, 4
Montana Youth Hostel, 1
YMCA InterRail Center, 6
🍴 FOOD
Fellini, 3
Kaffistova til Ervingen, 5

OTHER SIGHTS. The University of Bergen has tastefully documented the history of one disease in a 19th-century hospital at the **Leprosy Museum.** (Kong Oscars gt. 59. Open late May to Aug. daily 11am-3pm. 30kr, students 15kr.) For an authentic taste of the city, explore the steep streets between the **Korskirken** church and the **Skansen** tower. You can also check out the **Sydneskleiben** and **Dragefjellsbarker** neighborhoods near the university campus; to get there, walk west from the city center along Christies gt. to where the street begins to slope steeply upward.

NORWAY IN A NUTSHELL. An immensely popular tour, "Norway in a Nutshell" combines a ride along the stunning rail line between **Myrdal** and **Flåm** (55min.; 8-10 per day; 120kr, with railpass 85kr), a cruise through the narrowest branches of the **Sognefjord** between Gudvangen and Flåm (2hr.; 2 per day; 160kr, 50% student and InterRail discount), and a twisting bus ride over the mountains from **Gudvangen** to **Voss** (1¼hr., 4-8 per day, 60kr). The tour is unguided and extremely flexible, allowing "nutshellers" to complete the trip in one day or take stopovers at transfer points. From **Bergen,** most people take the train to Myrdal and begin the tour there, heading to Flåm, Gudvangen, and finally catching a train back to Bergen. Since Myrdal lies on the Oslo-Bergen rail line, the tour can also be done return from **Oslo,** or while en route to another city. **Tickets** can be bought separately for each leg of the journey while traveling, or purchased in advance as a package from tourist offices and train stations in Oslo and Bergen *(580kr return from Bergen, 1140kr return from Oslo, 840kr from Bergen to Oslo).* Railpass holders and students can get a better deal by purchasing individual tickets along the way.

FJORDS. Bergen is considered the capital of Norway's famous fjords, and many visitors use it as a launchpad for daytrips to the individual fjords (see below). **Bergen Fjord Sightseeing** offers tours of the fjords. *(☎55 25 90 00. 290kr for 4hr. Tickets available at the tourist office.)*

HIKING. A vast archipelago spreads westward from Bergen, and towering mountains encroach from all other directions. Trails surrounding the city are well kept and easily accessible. The **Fløibanen funicular** runs up **Mt. Fløyen** to a spectacular lookout point. *(From the Torget, follow Vetrlidsalm. east and up a small hill to the funicular. Runs Sept.-May M-Th 7:30am-11pm, F 7:30am-11:30pm, Sa 8am-11:30pm, Su 9am-11pm; June-Aug. until midnight. Return 50kr, children 25kr.)* At the summit, you can enjoy the terrific views with the camera-clutching clan or join up with one of the many intersecting **hiking** trails that meander through a striking landscape dotted by mammoth boulders, springy moss, pristine waterfalls, and quiet ponds. Free classical music concerts are held indoors at the top of Mt. Fløyen weekdays from mid-June to mid-August at 8pm. A 4hr. trail from Fløyen leads to the top of **Mt. Ulriken,** the highest peak above Bergen, and a panoramic view over the city, fjords, mountains, and nearby islands. A **cable car** also runs to the top of Mt. Ulriken, and many choose to first ride to the top and then follow the hiking trails downward. *(Car runs daily every 7min. May-Sept. 9am-10pm; Oct.-Apr. 10am-5pm. Return 70kr.)* Pick up **maps** of the hills above Bergen at the DNT office (simple maps free; more detailed ones 70-85kr).

🎵 🎭 ENTERTAINMENT AND NIGHTLIFE

The city pulls out all the stops for the annual **Bergen International Festival,** a 12-day program of music, ballet, folklore, and drama, and the simultaneous **Night Jazz Festival** in late May. The **Garage Bar,** at the corner of Nygårdsgaten and Christies gt., is Bergen's most popular rock club, with two pubs and a disco downstairs. (Cover 10kr Su-Th after 1am, 30kr F-Sa after 12:30am. Open M-Th 1pm-3am, F-Sa 1pm-3:30am, Su 3pm-3am.) The milder scene is on at **Café Opera,** Engen 18, a mellow cafe-restaurant that serves light meals and drinks. Things heat up with dance music after 11pm on weekends. (No cover. Open Su-M noon-1:30am, Tu-Th noon-3am, F-Sa noon-3:30am.) **Rick's,** Veiten 3, with a main entrance around the corner on Ole Bulls pass, has three bars, a disco, and an upscale nightclub. (Cover 50kr F-Sa after 10:30pm. Open Su-Th 10pm-3am, F-Sa 10pm-3:30am.)

HARDANGERFJORD

Slicing through one of Norway's fruit-growing regions, the steep banks of the Hardangerfjord, south of Bergen, are lined with orchards and waterfalls. Local tourist offices distribute the free *Hardanger Guide,* which provides detailed information about transportation and accommodations. At Bergen's tourist office, find more information on **Hardanger Sunnhordlandske Dampskipsselskap (HSD;** ☎55 23 87 80), which offers day cruises through the Hardangerfjord, with stops at larger towns. Most tours depart from platforms #4 or 21 at Bergen's bus station.

ROSENDAL. Perched at the mouth of the fjord, Rosendal is a good base for exploring nearby glaciers and waterfalls. The town itself is home to Norway's only **baronial manor** (10-15min. walk from tourist office) and its beautiful rose garden. Walking trails around the town will lead you to **Hattbergfossen** (30min. walk), the towering

The Western Fjords

Trondheim

Norsekehavet

Hareyfjord

NORDMØRE
Molde

Moldefjord

Ålesund

Åndalsnes   MØRE OG

SUNNMORE

ROMSDAL

Hellesylt   Geiranger
Stryn   GEIRANGERFJORD   Dombås

NORDFJORD

Lom

Otta

Fjærland   JOTUNHEIMEN
NATIONAL PARK

SUNNFJORD   SOGN OG
Førde   FJORDANE
Balestrand   Søgndal

Søgnefjord

Lillehammer

Aurland
Flåm   HEMSEDALSFJELLA
Voss   Myrdal

Bergen   HORDALAND

Hardangerfjord

Eidfjord

HARDANGERVIDDA   BUSKERUD

Rosendal

Hønefose

Oslo

Drammen

Haugesund

RYFYLKE   TELEMARK

Nedstrandsfjord

Boknfjord   ROGALAND   VESTFOLD

Oslofjord

Stavanger
Sandness

VESTAGDER

Egersund   AUSTAGDER

Arendal

N

Kristiansand

Skagerrak

0 _____ 50 miles
0 _____ 50 kilometers

NORWAY

waterfall behind Rosendal. **Buses** from Bergen connect directly with **ferry** departures to Rosendal (2½hr., 1 per day 8:10am, one way 160kr, 35% student discount; return 4:25pm, 167kr). The **tourist office,** next to the harbor, can help you find a place to stay. (☎53 48 42 80. Open May-Sept. daily 10am-5pm.)

EIDFJORD. Stampeding hikers can be heard in beautiful Eidfjord, 45km southeast of Voss on RV13, as they pass through this gateway to **Hardangervidda,** Norway's largest national park. Walk 1km from the town to see the **Viking Burial Place** in Hereid, or take the bus 20km to **Vøringstossen,** one of Norway's most famous waterfalls. A **bus/ferry** combo will get you to Eidfjord from Bergen (4½hr.; 1 per day; return 440kr, students 240kr; change from bus to ferry at Norheimsund). Duck into the **tourist office** for an information refill. (☎53 67 34 00. Open July to mid-Aug. M-F 9am-8pm, Sa 9am-6pm, Su 11am-8pm; late June and late Aug. M-Sa 9am-6pm; Sept. to mid-June M-F 8:30am-4pm.) Ask the tourist office to find you a bed (huts from 200kr), or try **Saebø Camping.** (☎53 66 59 27. 55kr per person and tent, 70kr per 2 people; 95kr per person, tent, and car, 110kr per 2 people; 220-600kr per cabin.)

SOGNEFJORD

The slender fingers of Sognefjord, the longest and deepest fjord in Europe, reach all the way to the foot of the Jotunheimen Mountains in central Norway. Sognefjord is just a short, stunning ride north of the rail line running west from Oslo, or a quick boat trip from Bergen. **Fylkesbaatane** (☎55 90 70 70) sends boats on daytrips to towns on the Sognefjord and back to Bergen, and offers day tours of the Sognefjord and Flåm valley. The boats depart from Strandkaiterminalen; buy tickets here or at Bergen's tourist office. Transportation on the northern coast of the Sognefjord and up to the Geirangerfjord can be confusing and frustrating due to the limited number of bus routes (especially on weekends). Planning ahead and consulting tourist offices will help in navigating the area.

BALESTRAND. On the north side of Sognefjord between Bergen and Flåm, Balestrand is a quiet town in a beautiful setting and is also an ideal base for fjord and glacier excursions. Enjoy the views of the fjord from the front of historic Kvikne's Hotel near the quay, or take a stroll down the road heading west past the brown church. **Ferries** run from Balestrand up the Fjærlandsfjord to Fjærland (1¼hr.; 8:20am and noon; 130kr, 50% student and railpass discount), allowing for daytrips to the Jostedal glacier. **Hiking** in the area immediately around Balestrand is also excellent. Follow the blue-marked trail above the town to **Balastølen,** a mountain meadow with a great view of the fjord. Get maps and information at the **tourist office,** near the quay. (☎57 69 12 55. Open late June to Aug. M-F 7:30am-9pm, Sa 7:30am-6:30pm, Su 8am-6pm.) **Express boats** connect Bergen and Balestrand (4hr.; 2 per day; 355kr, 50% student and railpass discount). The **Kringsjå Hotel and Youth Hostel (HI)** is 100m up the hill behind town. (☎57 69 13 03. Breakfast included. Kitchen. Laundry. Open mid-June to mid-Aug. Dorms 180kr, nonmembers 200kr; doubles 520kr/560kr.) **Sjøtun Camping,** 1km past the brown church on the coastal road, has tent sites and huts. (☎57 69 12 23. Reception 9-9:30am, 6-7pm, and 9-9:30pm. Open June to mid-Sept. 15kr per person, 40kr per tent, 220-300kr per cabin.)

▶ DAYTRIP FROM SOGNEFJORD: FJÆRLANDSFJORD. With Balestrand perched at its mouth, Fjærlandsfjord branches off from Sognefjord in a thin northward line to the tiny town of **Fjærland,** which is tucked in a gorgeous spot at the end of the fjord and beneath the looming Jostedalsbreen, the Jostedal glacier. The town is home to a number of fine hikes and an incongruous "book town"—a small village of 13 multilingual used book stores. The ◨**Glacier Museum,** 3km outside town, shows a beautiful panoramic film about Jostedalsbreen and the surrounding national park. (Open daily June-Aug. 9am-7pm; Apr.-May and Sept.-Oct. 10am-4pm. 70kr, students 35kr.) **Express boats** from Balestrand make the run to Fjærland. **Buses** connect with boat arrival times and shuttle passengers to the Glacier Museum and, after a stopover, whisk them to view two offshoots of the Jostedal

SEA KAYAKING THE FJORDS If you want to avoid ferries jammed with camera-toting tourists but would still like to see the fjords, your best bet may be to take to the water in a sea kayak. You can rent a kayak or sign up for guided daytrips in Hardangerfjord or Sognefjord (see Voss, **Nordic Ventures**, p. 713). Sea kayaking through the fjords has become an increasingly popular activity in recent years, and for good reason: the views of towering cliffs and scenic waterfalls are only enhanced by the peace and quiet that comes with gliding through the water. A daytrip through the **Nærøyfjord,** the world's narrowest fjord, is highly recommended. Sea kayaking is easy for beginners to pick up, and though a daytrip may stretch your budget, it's an experience that's well worth the money.

glacier, then return them to Fjærland's harbor in time to catch the boat back to Balestrand. Tickets (90-110kr) can be purchased on the boat or at the Balestrand tourist office. **Buses** run from Fjærland to: Ålesund (6hr., 1 per day, 304kr); Førde (1¼hr.; 2-3 per day; 114kr, 25% student discount); and Sogndal (30min.; 7 per day; 78kr, 25% student discount). and other destinations in the fjord region. Buses leave 200m up the road from the Glacier Museum on Route 5. Travelers just passing through Fjaerland should take the bus to the Glacier Museum one-way (20kr) to reach the stops; ask bus drivers for assistance in navigating bus connections. The **tourist office** helps solve transportation woes and provides hiking maps. (☎57 69 32 33. Open late May to mid-Sept. daily 9:30am-5:30pm.)

NORDFJORD AND JOSTEDAL GLACIER

Enveloping 800km of the area around **Nordfjord** in an icy cocoon, **Jostedalsbreen**, the Jostedal glacier, is difficult to miss as it winds its way through mountain passes in frozen cascades of luminous blue. Nordfjord itself is less impressive than Geirangerfjord and Sognefjord, to the north and south, respectively. Jostedalsbreen, in contrast, is an increasingly popular destination, and a there are a number of companies leading glacier walks. Without a car, it's difficult to take advantage of the more substantial tours in the space of one day, as bus arrivals and departures are not often conveniently timed. However, shorter tours are convenient and make glacier-walking trips possible for backpackers. It is dangerous to venture onto glaciers without a guide, as all glaciers have hidden soft spots and crevices.

STRYN (BØDALSBREEN AND BRIKSDAL). Stryn is wedged between the mountains near the inner end of Nordfjord, just northwest of the glacier. It's not an attraction in and of itself but you can embark on glacier walks from Stryn or connect to other towns in the fjords. **Briksdal Breføring** (☎57 87 68 00) and **Olden Aktiv** (☎57 87 38 88) run a variety of tours for different fitness and skill levels (230-400kr) on the nearby Briksdalsbreen arm of Jostedalsbreen. **Stryn Fjell-og Breførarlag** (☎57 87 68 00) runs longer, more intense hikes on **Bødalsbreen** (3hr. on ice, 350kr), a different limb of the glacier. A bus (daily 10am, 100kr) leaves Stryn for **Briksdal,** dropping passengers off at a mountain lodge where tickets and tour information are available; the meeting point for glacier walks is a mild half-hour walk from there. However, time is limited for carless travelers: the return bus leaves Briksdal at 2pm, meaning that anyone relying on the bus for transport back can only spend an hour actually on the ice. The more determined can camp in Briksdal's campgrounds or dish out the dough for a room at **Melkevoll Bretun,** the mountain lodge. (☎57 87 38 64; fax 57 87 38 90. Cabins for 4 people 200-370kr.) The town has excellent walking paths and is home to a popular summer **ski center.** (☎57 87 40 40. Open May-June and Aug.-Sept. daily 10am-4pm. Tickets 240kr. 1-day rental 220kr. Bus from Stryn leaves 9am and returns 4:15pm. 65kr.)

Buses connect Stryn to **Otta** (240kr), which lies along the rail line, allowing connections to Åndalsnes, Trondheim, Lillehammer, and Oslo by train. Buses also come and go from Hellesylt on the Geirangerfjord (76kr), Ålesund (203kr), and Førde (165kr), where buses leaves for Bergen and all western fjord destinations; 25% student discount, 50% railpass discount. To get to the **tourist office,** Perhusveien

19, walk past the Esso station, and follow the signs. (☎57 87 40 40. Open daily June and Aug. 8:30am-6pm; July 8:30am-8pm; Sept.-May M-F 8:30am-3:30pm.) The **youth hostel (HI)** is a hike up the hill behind town. (☎57 87 11 06. Breakfast included. Laundry 30kr. Reception 8-11am and 4-11pm. Open June-Aug. Dorms 170kr; singles 250kr; doubles 400kr. Nonmembers add 25kr.) **Stryn Camping** is in the center of town. (☎57 87 11 36. Reception 8am-10:30pm. 80kr per person and tent.)

SOGNDAL (NIGARDSBREEN). Although not as picturesque as Balestrand, Sogndal is another town on the northern coast of the Sognefjord that makes a good base for exploring the area. In particular, it offers access to glacier walking routes on the icy expanse of the nearby **Nigardsbreen** arm of Jostedalsbreen. **Breheimsenteret Jostedal** (☎57 68 32 50) runs everything from 1hr. outings to full-day jaunts (100-500kr). Buses (8:25am, return 5pm; 100kr) leave Sogndal for the glacier. Fylkesbaatane **express boats** run between: Balestrand (105kr); Bergen (430kr); and Flåm (145kr). Get ticket information at the tourist office and harbor; 50% student discount. Local **buses** head to Lom (3½hr.; mid-June to late Aug. 2 per day; 185kr, students 139kr), where a connection can be made to Otta and the train lines. Norway Bussekspress buses leave for Fjaerland (30min., 8 per day, 78kr) and Førde (2hr., 8 per day, 171kr), which lead to all major bus routes (25% student discount, 50% railpass). The **campground** at Nigardsbreen also has huts. (☎57 68 31 35. 60kr per person with tent, 380kr per 4-person cabin.) Contact the **tourist office,** in the Sogndal Kulturhus at the corner of Gravensteingata and Hovevegen, for more information. (☎57 67 30 83. Open June 18-Aug. 20 M-F 9am-8pm, Sa 9am-5pm, Su 3-8pm.) The Sogndal **youth hostel (HI)** has a fjord-side spot and clean rooms east of the town center. From the bus station, turn left on Dalavegen, then left on Gravensteinsgata, follow it past the roundabout until it becomes Helgheimsvegen, and follow the signs. (☎57 67 20 33. Open mid-June to mid-Aug. Dorms 100kr; singles 165kr; doubles 230kr. Nonmembers add 25kr.)

GEIRANGERFJORD

Only 16km long, the narrow Geirangerfjord's cliffs and waterfalls make it one of the prettiest places in Norway. While cruising through the green-blue water, watch for the **Seven Sisters** waterfalls and the **Suitor** geyser opposite them. The Geirangerfjord can be reached from the north via the famous Tollstigen road from Åndalsnes, or by the bus from Ålesund that stops in Hellesylt. From the south, Stryn (see p. 721) has a direct bus connection to Hellesylt, but those departing from other fjord towns can easily reach this route by transferring buses in Førde. Hellesylt and Geiranger are connected by a stunning 1hr. ferry ride. During the summer months, the **Hurtigruten** coastal steamer sails into the fjord, connecting Geiranger to Ålesund (April-Sept.; 1:30pm; 328kr, 50% student and senior discount).

GEIRANGER. Geiranger is dramatically surrounded by the glorious Geirangerfjord's eastern end. An endpoint of the famous **Tollstigen** road with spectacular views and sheer inclines, the town is one of Norway's most visited destinations. Even the tourists don't overwhelm the area, which is truly picture perfect. **Hiking** abounds in this charmed country; consider the hike to the path below the **Storseter Waterfall, Flydalsjuvet Cliff, Skageflå Farm,** or **Dalsnibba Mountain** (which you can also reach on the daily 9:40am and 2:20pm buses from the church next to the hostel; return 12:40pm and 6:10pm; 100kr). The **tourist office,** up from the ferry landing, helps find private rooms. (☎70 26 30 99. Open late May to Aug. daily 9:15am-8pm.) **Geiranger Camping** is by the water, 500m past the ferry dock. (☎70 26 31 20. Open-late May to early Sept. 10kr per person, 60kr per tent.) For the fantastic view of the fjord at **Vinjebakken Hostel,** follow the main road up the hill behind town to the church and look for the sign. (☎70 26 32 05. Reception 8-11am and 3pm-midnight. Open mid-June to mid-Aug. 130kr.) **Geiranger Fjordservice** runs sightseeing tours on the fjord's chilly waters. (☎70 26 57 86. Cruises 1½hr. return. June-Aug. 5-6 per day 10am-7:30pm; 75kr.) **Buses** run to Åndalsnes (3.5hr.; 1pm and 6:10pm; 137kr, 50% railpass discount), allowing connections to Trondheim, Oslo, and Lillehammer.

ÅLESUND

The largest city between Bergen and Trondheim, Ålesund (OH-les-oond) is renowned for its art nouveau architecture and beautiful oceanside location. For a view of the splendid city and the distant mountains, gasp up the 418 steps to the ◪Aksla viewpoint in the park near the city center; look for the stairs leading up to the park from the main pedestrian street, **Kongens gate.** Immerse yourself in Ålesund's marine life at the **Atlantic Sea Park;** the innovative tanks are actually submerged in the ocean. Take bus #18 (6-7 per day, 20kr) from St. Olavs Pass to Atlanterhavsparken. (Open mid-June to mid-Aug. Su-F 10am-7pm, Sa 10am-4pm; mid-Aug. to mid-June M-Sa 11am-4pm, Su noon-5pm. 85kr, students and seniors 70kr.) Take bus #13, 14, 18, or 24 (10min., every 15min., 18kr.) to get to the **Sunnmøre Museum,** Borgundgavlen, which displays old local fishing boats and a reconstructed Viking ship from AD 800. (Open late June-Aug. M-Sa 11am-5pm, Su noon-5pm; off season reduced hr. 50kr, students 40kr.) To learn more about Ålesund's architecture, take a guided walking tour of the city beginning at the tourist office (mid-June to mid-Aug.; 1½hr., 1pm, 60kr.) There's an old Viking site and 12th-century marble church on the nearby island of **Giske.** Bus #64 travels through the tunnel connecting Ålesund and Giske (20min.; M-F 8 per day, Sa 3 per day; 43kr).

Buses run to and from Åndalsnes and connect with trains there (2½hr.; 3-4 per day; 162kr, 50% railpass discount). **Buses** run to Åndalsnes and connect with trains there (2½hr.; 3-4 per day; 162kr, 50% railpass discount). Buses also travel to Stryn (3½hr.; 2-3 per day; 203kr, 50% railpass discount) via Hellesylt (2½hr., 138kr), and to Trondheim (8hr., 2 per day, 458kr). The **Hurtigruten** also docks here twice daily. The **tourist office,** on Keiser Wilhelms gt., is opposite the bus station in the city hall. From St. Olavs pass, head away from the pedestrian walkway along Notenesgata, then take a left on Korsegata and a right on Keiser Wilhelms gt. (☎70 15 76 00. Open June-Aug. M-F 8:30am-7pm, Sa 9am-5pm, Su 11am-5pm; Sept.-May M-F 8:30am-4pm.) It's a 5min. walk from the bus station to **Ålesund Vandrerhjem,** Parkgata 14, across from the city park. (☎70 11 58 30. Open May-Sept. Reception 8:30-11am and 3pm-midnight. Dorms 180k, nonmembers 205kr.) **Volsdalen Camping** is 2km out along the main highway next to a beach. Take bus #13, 14, 18, or 24 (15kr), to Hellandbakken, turn right off the highway, follow the road downhill, turn left across the overpass, turn right, and it's 200m down on the left. (☎70 12 58 90. Reception daily 9am-9pm. Open May to mid-Sept. 100kr per tent; 270-370kr per cabin.)

TRONDHEIM

A thousand years ago, Viking kings turned Trondheim (then "Nidaros") into Norway's seat of power. Today, the city's wide boulevards, low-key style, and university town status make it an enjoyable place to stop for a day or two when heading north to the Arctic Circle and Lofoten Islands or south to the fjords.

🚆🚌 **TRANSPORTATION AND PRACTICAL INFORMATION. Trains** head to: Bodø (11hr., 2-3 per day, 770kr); Oslo (6½hr., 4-5 per day, 680kr); and Stockholm (11hr., 2 per day, 564-755kr). **Long-distance buses** leave from the train station. **City buses** go from Munkeg., Dronningensg., and Olav Tryggvasong, and along Dronningensg. between Prinsensg. and Munkeg. (15kr within city center, 22kr to outlying regions). To get from the train station to the **tourist office,** Munkegt. 19, cross the bridge, walk six blocks down Søndreg., go right on Kongensg., and look to your left as you approach the roundabout. (☎73 80 76 60. Open July M-F 8:30am-10pm, Sa-Su 10am-8pm; June and early Aug. M-F 8:30am-8pm, Sa 10am-4pm, Su 10am-5pm; late May and late Aug. M-F 8:30am-4pm, Sa-Su 10am-4pm; Sept. to early May M-F 9am-4pm.) **DNT,** Sandgata 30, has information on huts and trails. (☎73 92 42 00. Open M-W and F 8am-4pm, Th 8am-6pm.)

🏠🍴 **ACCOMMODATIONS AND FOOD.** To get from the station to the lively **InterRail Centre,** Elgeseter. 1, in the Studentersamfundet, take bus #41, 44, 46, 48, 49, 52, or 63 (15kr) to Samfundet. (☎73 89 95 38; tirc@stud.ntnu.no. Breakfast included. Free Internet. Sheets 25kr. Open late June to mid-Aug. Sleeping-bag dorms 115kr.) For more peaceful lodging, walk up Lillegårdsbakken, off Øvre Bakklandet near the Old Town Bridge, to the student-run **Singsaker Sommerhotell,** Rogertsg. 1, near the Kristiansten Fortress. (☎73 89 31 00. Open June to mid-Aug. Sleeping-bag dorms 125kr; singles 255kr; doubles 400kr; triples 570kr.) To reach the institutional but comfortable **Trondheim Vandrerhjem (HI),** Weidemannsvei 41, from the station, cross the bridge, head left on Olav Tryggvasonsg. across the bridge, bear left onto Innherredsvein, turn right on Nonneg., and left onto Weidemannsvei. (☎73 87 44 50. Breakfast included. Sheets 50kr. 175-185kr; nonmembers 200-210kr.) For cheap Italian food, try **Ristorantino Italiano,** Nordre gt. 4, a block from Kongens gt. (Open daily noon-11pm.) You can also check out the cluster of smart cafes on the far end of the Old Town Bridge or pick up groceries at **Rema 1000** on the main square. (Open M-F 9am-9pm, Sa 9am-6pm.)

◙ **SIGHTS.** Most of the sights are concentrated in the south end of town around the gigantic **Nidaros Cathedral,** easily the main attraction. The cathedral is the site of all Norwegian coronations and the repository of the crown jewels, which are on display in summer. (Open June 20-Aug. 20 M-F 9am-3pm, Sa 9am-2pm, Su 1-4pm; May-June 20 and Aug. 20 to mid-Sept. M-F 10am-3pm, Sa 10am-2pm, Su 1-4pm; off season reduced hr. 35kr. Crown jewels on display June 20-Aug. 20 M-Sa 9am-12:30pm, Su 1-4pm.) In the complex next door to cathedral are the **Archbishop's Palace** (open June 20-Aug. 20 M-F 10am-5pm, Sa 10am-3pm, Su noon-5pm) and the **Rustkammeret** (Army Museum) with the **Hjemmefrontmuseet** (Resistance Museum) on the 3rd floor. (Open June-Aug. M-F 9am-3pm, Sa-Su 11am-4pm; May and Sept.-Oct. Sa-Su 11am-4pm. Free.) Just down Bispegata from the cathedral is the **Trondheim Kunstmuseum,** Bispegata 7B, which has a hallway devoted to Edvard Munch. (Open June-Aug. daily 10am-5pm; Sept.-May Tu-W and F-Sa 10am-3pm, Th 10am-5pm, Su noon-4pm. 30kr, students 20kr.) The image of Olav Tryggvason, who founded Trondheim in 997, perches on a pillar over the main market square, **Torget.** Across the **Gamle Bybro** (Old Town Bridge), you'll find the **old district,** where former fishing houses have been transformed into galleries and cafes. To reach the bridge from the Torget, head toward the spires of Nidaros Cathedral, then turn left when you reach Bispegata and follow it around to the bridge. On the hill above the old district the **Kristiansten Fortress** yields a splendid view. Trondheim is a bike-friendly city and you can borrow one of the 270 **city bicycles** parked at stations in town (deposit 20kr) and ride up the unique **bike lift** (by placing your right foot on a small pedal that pushes you up the hill) toward the fortress from the base of the Old Town Bridge (pick up key-card at tourist office or adjacent cafes; 100kr deposit).

SOUTHERN NORWAY

Norway's southern coast substitutes serenity for drama, and is the premier Norwegian summer holiday destination. *Skjærgard*, archipelagos of water-worn rock, hug the shore and stretch smoothly southward from Oslo to pleasant beaches past Kristiansand. Fishing, hiking, rafting, and canoeing are popular in summer, while cross-country skiing reigns in winter.

KRISTIANSAND

Kristiansand attracts glacier- and winter-weary Norwegian tourists with its summer weather and **beaches.** The city center's grid layout is easy to navigate: the harbor and train station sit at the bottom of the grid; **Markensgata,** the main street, is a block from the water; **Posebyen,** a well-preserved, old town begins two blocks farther away at Festningsgata.

◪▞ **TRANSPORTATION AND PRACTICAL INFORMATION.** Daily **trains** chug to Oslo (4½-5½hr., 5 per day, 480kr). Color Line **ferries** (☎81 00 08 11) run from Kristiansand to Hirsthals, Denmark (2½-4½hr., in summer from370-410kr). Ferries also run from Kristiansand to the scenic Skerries (tiny islands and fjords; 1½hr. 90kr;

2½-3hr. 160kr); for more information, ask at the **tourist office,** at Henrik Wegerland-sgt. and Vestre Strandsgt., opposite the train station. They can also arrange elk safa-ris in local forests. (☎ 38 12 13 14. Open mid-June to Aug. M-F 8:30am-6pm, Sa 10am-6pm, Su noon-6pm; Sept. to mid-June M-F 8:30am-3:30pm.)

▐▍▐▌ ACCOMMODATIONS AND FOOD. The **Kristiansand Youth Hostel (HI),** Skansen 8, is 25min. from the harbor and train station. Walk away from the water until you reach Elvegata, turn right, and then left onto Skansen following the signs. (☎ 38 02 83 10. Breakfast included. Kitchen. Laundry. Lockers. Reception mid-June to mid-Aug. 24hr.; mid-Aug. to mid-June 5-11pm. Dorms 180kr; singles 340kr. Non-members add 25kr.) The noisy **Roligheden campground** is 35min. from town, or take bus #15 or 16 from the city center; ask the driver to let you off at the campground turnoff. (☎ 38 09 67 22. Showers 10kr per 5min. Laundry 60kr. Open June-Aug. Reception 7am-midnight. 25kr per person, 60kr per tent.) The area around Kristian-sand's main street, **Markensgata,** one block north of the harbor and train station, is full of affordable bars, cafes, and restaurants. **Husholdnings,** on Gyldenløves gt. in the old town, serves authentic Norwegian cuisine. (June 20-Aug. 20 open M-F 9am-4pm; rest of year closes 5pm.) The pub **Munch,** Kristian IV gt. 1, opposite the train station, attracts local drinkers and travelers waiting for the next train.

◎▐▊ SIGHTS AND ENTERTAINMENT. The city's best-known attraction is ▐Dyreparken, "the living park," which contains a zoo, an amusement park, and a cir-cus. The zoo is one of Europe's best, and its animals roam freely. Take bus #1 toward Sørlandsparken from the stop on Henrik Wergelands gt. in front of the tour-ist office to Dyreparken. (Open July to mid-Aug. daily 10am-7pm; 200kr, seniors 110kr, children 170kr. May 18-June 21 and mid-Aug. to Sept. daily 10am-7pm; 120kr, seniors 75kr, children 100kr. Sept.-May M-F 10am-3:30pm, Sa-Su 10am-5pm; 80kr, seniors and children 65kr.) The open-air **Vest-Agder Fylkesmuseum,** Vigeveien 22b, showcases 17th-century southern Norwegian farmhouses and traditional folk danc-ing. Take bus #2, 4, or 6 from H. Wergelandsgt. and ask the driver to let you off at the museum. (Open mid-June to mid-Aug. M-Sa 10am-6pm, Su noon-6pm; mid-Aug. to mid-June Su noon-5pm. 30kr, students 20kr, seniors and children 10kr.) The remains of a Nazi bunker and the world's second-largest cannon are on display at the **Kristiansand Kanonenmuseum.** Take bus #1 from H. Wergelandsgt. (Open early June to Aug. daily 11am-6pm; May to early June and Sept. Th-Su 11am-6pm. 50kr, seniors 30kr, children 20kr.) Scramble up the walls of the 17th-century circular stone **Christiansholm Fortress** for a great view of the beach and islands near the city. (Open mid-May to Sept. daily 9am-9pm.) **Posebyen,** the pleasant old town just two blocks from Markensgate, is worth a visit. Meander by simple houses lined up side-by-side that all look alike but for their many different colors. In early July, Kristian-sand hosts the **Quart Festival** (www.quart.yahoo.no), which draws major hip-hop, rock, and pop acts. Headliners in 2001 included Beck, Wyclef Jean, and P.J. Harvey.

STAVANGER

Stavanger is a delightful port town with colorful wooden fishing houses along its pier and a daily fish market. On the eastern side of the harbor is **Gamle Stavanger,** a neighborhood of winding cobblestone streets restored to its prosperous 19th-cen-tury state. The Gothic **Stavanger Domkirke** (cathedral) broods in medieval solem-nity in the modern town center. (Open mid-May to mid-Sept. M-Tu 11am-6pm, W-Sa 10am-6pm, Su 1-6pm; mid-Sept. to mid-May W-Sa 10am-3pm. Free.) Discover the driving force behind Norway's powerful oil industry at the **Norsk Oljemuseum** (Norwegian Petroleum Museum). Walk along Kirkegata from the cathedral; the museum lies on Havneringen by the water. (Open June-Aug. daily 10am-7pm; Sept.-May M-F 10am-4pm, Su 10am-6pm. 75kr, students, seniors and children 35kr.) Feel like a Norse god, but don't tumble over the edge of **Pulpit Rock** (Preikes-tolen) in nearby **Lysefjord,** one of Norway's postcard darlings. To get there, take the ferry to Tau (40min.; June 21-Sept. 7, 8:20 and 9:05am, return 2:35 and 4:15pm; 29kr), catch the waiting bus (45kr), and hike on up (2hr.)

Trains pull in from Oslo (9hr., 3 per day, 700kr) and via Kristiansand (3hr., 8 per day, 320kr). Trains and buses arrive at Stavanger's central station; from the front entrance, walk around the pond and down the stairs to reach the harbor. Flaggruten (☎51 86 87 80) **boats** speed to Bergen (4hr.; 2-3 per day; 590kr, students 325kr; 50% railpass discount), arriving upon return to Stavanger at a terminal on the eastern side of the city; exit the terminal through the main door and walk straight ahead along Kirkegata to reach the cathedral and town center. Three Fjordline **ferries** per week go to Newcastle, England (☎81 53 35 00; booking@fjordline.com. 18hr., July-Aug. from 980kr, Sept.-June around 400kr; prices vary), departing and arriving at a terminal on the western side of the harbor; walk along the water to reach the city center. (Ferry terminal open Tu 9pm-midnight, F 2:30-5:30pm, Su 8-11pm.) The **tourist office**, Roskildetorget 1, is on the harbor across from the fish market. (☎51 85 92 00. Open June-Aug. daily 9am-8pm; Sept.-May M-F 9am-4pm, Sa 9am-2pm.) **Rogalandsheimen Guesthouse**, Musegata 18, provides spacious accommodations in a centrally located manor house. Walk around the pond, bearing right past the train station on Olva V's gate; from the Rica Park Hotel, continue straight on Musegata past the Stavanger Museum and the guest house is on the next block on the left. (☎/fax 51 52 01 88. Singles from 400kr; doubles from 550kr.) The **Mosvangen Vandrerhjem (HI)**, Ibsensgt. 21, is Stavanger's youth hostel. (☎51 87 29 00. Open mid-May to mid-Sept. Reception daily 8-11am and 3-10pm. 145kr; nonmembers 170kr.) Take buses #25, 78-79, or 97 from in front of the cathedral. The **market** opposite the cathedral will satisfy culinary needs; look for fresh Norwegian strawberries. (Open M-F 9am-5pm, Sa closes earlier.) **Postal code:** 4000.

EASTERN NORWAY

The faster of the two train lines that shoot north from Oslo to Trondheim heads through the **Gudbrandsdalen** valley via Lillehammer. Farther up the valley, the **Rondane** and **Dovrefjell** mountain ranges offer hiking opportunities, while the truly breathtaking scenery is in the **Jotunheimen** mountains to the west.

LILLEHAMMER

Lillehammer, site of the 1994 Winter Olympic Games, is a small city set in a valley at the edge of a lake. The **museum** traces the history of the modern Olympic Games, which date back to 1896. From the train station, it's a 15-20min. walk; head two blocks uphill, turn left on Storgata, turn right on Tomtegata, go up the stairs, and follow the road uphill to the left. (Open mid-May to mid-Sept. daily 10am-6pm; mid-Sept. to mid-May Tu-Su 11am-4pm. 60kr, students 50kr.) You can climb up the infinite steps of an Olympic **ski jump** in sight of the museum spire (open daily mid-June to mid-Aug. 9am-8pm; early June and late Aug. 9am-5pm; Sept.-Oct. and Feb.-May 11am-4pm; 15kr) or give your spine a jolt on a **bobsled simulator** (40kr) at the bottom of the ski-jumping hills.

Daily **trains** run to Oslo (2hr., over 20 per day, 255kr) and Trondheim (4½hr., 6 per day, 460kr). Most restaurants and fast-food kiosks are around the pedestrian section of **Storgata**, two blocks uphill from the bus/train station. The **tourist office**, Elvegata 19, one block uphill from Storgata, has good information on hiking and attractions. (☎61 25 92 99. Open mid-June to mid-Aug. M-Sa 9am-9pm, Su 11am-6pm; mid-Aug. to mid-June M-F 9am-4pm, Sa 10am-2pm.) The comfy **Lillehammer Youth Hostel (HI)** is on the top floor of the bus/train station. (☎61 24 87 00. Sheets 50kr. Dorms 175kr.) Try the popular lunch (59kr; 11am-3pm) or dinner (89kr; 3-11pm) specials at **Nikkers** cafe/pub, just before the tourist office on Elvegata.

LOFOTEN ISLANDS

Emerald and slate colored mountains and rustic fishing villages are the main attractions of the Lofoten Islands. Keep an eye out for bird colonies, grazing sheep, and panoramic ocean views, and enjoy the peaceful atmosphere that makes the Lofotens a magical place to visit. As late as the 1950s, fishermen lived in small *rorbuer*, yellow and red wooden shacks along the coast. Today, tourists book the *rorbuer* solid (125-350kr per person in groups of 4 or more).

⌐ TRANSPORTATION. The two best mainland springboards to the islands are **Bodø,** accessible by train from Trondheim (11hr., 2-3 per day, 770kr; mandatory seat reservations) and **Narvik,** reached by bus from Bodø (6½hr.; 2 per day; 379kr, 50% student and railpass discount). From Bodø, the Lofotens are most easily reached by either **car ferry** (to Moskenes; 3-4hr., 4-5 per day, 116kr), **express boat** (to Svolvær; 3½hr.; Su-F 1 per day; 246kr, 50% student discount), or the **Hurtigruten** (to Stamsund; 4½hr., 306kr; and Svolvær; 6hr., 328kr), though you can also take the **bus** (to Svolvær; 7-8hr., daily 7:40am and 4:25pm; 352kr, 50% student and railpass discount). Within the islands, **buses** are the main form of transport; pick up the *Lofoten Trafikklag* bus timetable at tourist offices in Bodø, Narvik, or larger towns in the Lofotens. Dial 177 to reach a regional **transport information** desk. An **InterRail** pass allows you to pay children's prices on all routes within the islands; **Scanrail** discounts are available only if your destination is on a rail line.

MOSKENES AND FLAKSTAD. Travelers are drawn to Moskenes and Flakstad by their jagged mountains and quaint fishing communities. Most of the **ferries** running to the islands from Bodø dock in **Moskenes,** the southernmost of the large Lofotens. The **tourist office,** by the ferry landing, has tours of the **Maelstrom,** one of the most dangerous currents in the world, and information on the **Refsuika caves** and their 3000-year-old drawings. (☎76 09 15 99. Open early June M-F 9am-5pm; mid-June to mid-Aug. daily 10am-9pm.) **Adventure Rafting Lofoten** (☎76 09 20 00) runs similar tours (350-690kr). Incoming ferry passengers usually head 5km south to **Å** (OH), a tiny fishing village at the end of E10 highway, via a bus that departs 5-15min. after boat landings. Six of Å's buildings comprise the **Norsk Fiskeværsmuseum,** which depicts life in an old-fashioned fishing village. (Open mid-June to mid-Aug. daily 10am-6pm; mid-Aug. to mid-June M-F 10am-3:30pm. 40kr, students 30kr.) The **Å Vandrerhjem and Rorbuer** has bunks in 19th-century buildings. (☎76 09 11 21. Laundry. Rowboats and bikes 150kr per day. Reserve ahead. 125kr, nonmembers 150kr, *rorbuer* 550-1000kr.) To get to **Moskenes-Straumen Camping,** follow E10 until it stops at the southern edge of Å. (☎76 09 11 48. 70kr per person with tent, 20kr additional person. Showers 10kr.) Or, **camp** for free on the shores of the lake behind town.

To the north, the next large island is **Flakstad,** centered on the hamlet of **Ramberg.** Flakstad offers some excellent **hiking** trails and hardy souls can brave the arctic waters that lap Ramberg's **white sand beach.** The **tourist office** books rooms from 100kr per person; call ahead to secure accommodations. (☎76 09 34 50. Open mid-June to mid-Aug. daily 10am-7pm.)

VESTVÅGØY AND AUSTVÅGØY. Farther north is **Vestvågøy,** an island that some travelers visit just so they can stay at the sea-side ⊠**Justad youth hostel (HI).** A 15min. walk from the ferry dock in the hamlet of **Stamsund,** the cozy hostel is a great place to meet backpackers, take it easy for a few days, and engage in lively conversation with the charismatic owner. (☎76 08 93 34. Laundry 50kr. Showers 5kr per 5min. Fishing gear 100kr deposit; rowboats free. Bikes 80kr per day. Open mid-Dec. to mid.-Oct. Dorms 90kr; doubles 250kr; *rorbuer* 400-600kr.) The nocturnal **tourist office** sits at the coastal steamer and ferry dock. (☎76 08 97 92. Open mid-June to mid-Aug. daily 6-9:30pm.) North of Stamsund, on the road between Leknes and Svolvær, **Borg** is the site of the largest Viking building ever found; the longhouse holds the **Lofotr viking museum** staffed by costumed Norse folk who do full-scale reenactments. (Open late May to early Sept. daily 10am-7pm. 80kr; students 65kr. Reached by bus from Leknes: 15min.; M-F 7 per day, Sa-Su 3 per day; 26kr.)

NORWAY

FARTHER NORTH

TROMSØ. Tromsø is a compact city in a mountainous setting that serves as the capital for northern Norway. It's a pleasant place from which to launch trips even farther north and offers a few attractions of its own. **Polaria** boasts an aquarium, a simulated arctic environment, and plenty of information about polar regions. From the tourist office, walk down Storgata away from the yellow church, and it's the next left after Mack's Brewery. (Open daily mid-May to Aug. 10am-7pm; Sept. to mid-May noon-5pm. 70kr, students and seniors 55kr.) The hard-to-miss **Arctic Cathedral,** across the bridge, contains one of the largest stained glass windows in Europe. Take bus #26 (20kr) from in front of Peppes Pizza or walk across the bridge. (Open June to mid-Aug. M-Sa 10am-8pm, Su 1-8pm. 20kr.) The **Polar Museum** has displays on polar explorers and hunters and is located in an historic building built in 1830. The museum is housed in a red building on the harbor just before the bridge.

Accessible from the Lofoten Islands, Tromsø can be reached by **bus** from Narvik (4½hr.; M-F 3 per day, Sa-Su 1-2 per day; 305kr, 50% student and railpass discount). Buses head farther north to **Alta** (6½hr.; 1-2 per day; 345kr, 50% student and railpass discount), where local buses connect to Hammerfest and Nordkapp. The **tourist office,** Storgata 63, books rooms in private homes. (☎77 64 73 70. Open June to mid-Aug. M-F 8:30am-6pm, Sa 10am-5pm, Su 10:30am-5pm; mid-Aug. to mid-Sept. and mid- to late May M-F 8:30am-4pm, Sa-Su 10:30am-4pm; mid-Sept. to mid-May M-F 8:30am-4pm.) Spend the night at the hilltop **Tromsø Vandrerhjem (HI),** which is reached by taking bus #26 from in front of the yellow church downtown or by walking uphill (20-25min.) along Kirkegårdsvegen, then taking the gravel road Prost Schieldrupsgate and following it to the end. (☎77 68 53 19. Open mid-June to mid-Aug. Reception daily 8-11am and 5-11pm. Dorms 125kr; singles 225kr; doubles 300kr; nonmembers add 25kr.) You can pick up groceries at **Coop Mega,** on the main plaza across from Peppes Pizza. (Open M-F 9am-8pm, Sa 10am-6pm.)

POLAND
(POLSKA)

ZŁOTY, OR PLZ

US$1 = 4.30ZŁ	1ZŁ = US$0.36
CDN$1 = 2.80ZŁ	1ZŁ = CDN$0.16
UK£1 = 6.20ZŁ	1ZŁ = UK£0.20
IR£1 = 5ZŁ	1ZŁ = IR£0.44
AUS$1 = 2.30ZŁ	1ZŁ = AUS$0.53
NZ$1 = 1.90ZŁ	1ZŁ = NZ$1.52
ZAR1 = 2ZŁ	1ZŁ = ZAR0.50
EUR€1 = 3.95ZŁ	1ZŁ = EUR€0.26

Poland has always been caught at the threshold of East and West, and its moments of freedom have been brief. From 1795 to 1918, Poland simply did not exist on any map of Europe, and its short spell of independence thereafter was brutally dissolved. Ravaged by World War II and suppressed by Stalin and the USSR, Poland has at long last been given room to breathe, and its residents are not letting the opportunity slip by. The most prosperous of the "Baltic tigers," Poland now has a rapidly expanding GDP, a new membership in NATO, and a likely future membership in the EU. With new wealth, the Poles have been returning to their cultural roots and repairing buildings destroyed in the wars. Capitalism, however, has brought with it Western problems, like rising crime and unemployment, issues politicians have begun to recognize as serious. But there are few Poles complaining about the events of the past ten years.

Even the Pope kicks back with a copy of *Let's Go: Eastern Europe 2002*.

FACTS AND FIGURES

Official Name: Republic of Poland.

Capital: Warsaw.

Major Cities: Łódź, Kraków, Lublin, Poznań, Katowice, Gdańsk, Wrocław.

Population: 39 million.

Land Area: 312,683 sq. km.

Climate: Temperate; cold, cloudy, winters with frequent precipitation; mild summers.

Language: Polish.

Religions: Roman Catholic (95%).

DISCOVER POLAND

Over 19 million visitors flock annually to Poland's spectacular castles, Old Towns, and museums, as well as villages, forests, and beaches. **Warsaw** (p. 733), a wild, vibrant capital, gives living testimony to its recent past. Much-adored **Kraków** (p. 742), the only Polish city to make it through the 20th century unscathed by natural disaster or war, offers a magnificent castle and perfectly preserved Old Town. In the south, in the heart of the High Tatras, **Zakopane** (p. 747) has ear-popping hikes, music festivals, and a plenty of Tatran folk culture. **Gdańsk** (p. 749) is the site of the start of World War II and of Poland's anti-Communist Solidarity movement in the 1980s. On the Baltic Coast, **Sopot** (p. 752) shelters Poland's best beaches, while **Malbork** is home to the biggest brick castle in the world.

Poland

ESSENTIALS

WHEN TO GO

Winters are dreary unless you're heading to the Tatras: anytime between November and February is ideal for skiing, and August is the perfect hiking month. Otherwise, summer and autumn are the best times to visit.

DOCUMENTS AND FORMALITIES

VISAS. Citizens of Ireland and the US can travel to Poland without a visa for up to 90 days and UK citizens for up to 180 days. Australians, Canadians, New Zealanders, and South Africans need visas. Single-entry visas (valid for 180 days) cost US$60 (children and students under 26 pay US$45); multiple-entry visas cost US$100 (students US$75); and 48-hour transit visas cost US$20 (students US$15). Visas can only be obtained through an embassy or a consulate; no visas are available at the border. To extend your stay, apply at the local province office *(urząd wojewódzki)*, or in Warsaw to the Ministry of Internal Affairs at ul. Kruzca 5/11 (☎ (022) 625 59 04).

EMBASSIES. All foreign embassies are in Warsaw (see p. 733); there are US and UK consulates in Kraków (see p. 742). Polish embassies at home: **Australia,** 7 Turrana St., Yarralumla ACT 2600 Canberra (☎(06) 273 1208 or 273 1211; fax 273 3184; ambpol@clover.com.au); **Canada,** 443 Daly St., Ottawa, ON, K1N 6H3 (☎613-789-0468;

fax 613-789-1218; polamb@hookup.com); **Ireland,** 5 Ailesbury Rd., Ballsbridge, Dublin 4 (☎(01) 283 0855; fax 269 8309 or 283 7562); **New Zealand,** 17 Upland Rd., Kelburn, Wellington (☎(04) 712 456; fax 712 455; polishembassy@xtra.co.nz); **South Africa,** 14 Amos St., Colbyn, Pretoria 0083 (☎(012) 432 631; fax 432 608; amb.pol@pixie.co.za). **UK:** 47 Portland Pl., London W1N 4JH (☎(020) 7580 4324; fax 7323 4018); and **US:** 2640 16th St. NW, Washington, D.C. 20009 (☎202-234-3800; fax 202-328-6271; embpol@dgs.dgsys.com; www.polandembassy.org).

TRANSPORTATION

BY PLANE. LOT, British Airways, and **Delta** fly into Warsaw's Okęcie Airport from London, New York, Chicago, and Toronto (among other cities).

BY TRAIN. Eurail passes are not valid in Poland. **Almatur** offers ISIC holders a discount of 192zł. **BIJ-Wasteels** tickets and **Eurotrain** passes, sold at Almatur, Orbis, and major train stations, get under-26 travelers 40% off international train fares. For all but daytrips, **PKP trains** are preferable to and, for long hauls, usually cheaper than buses. Train stations have boards that list towns alphabetically, and posters that list trains chronologically. *Odjazdy* (departures) are in yellow; *przyjazdy* (arrivals) are in white. **InterCity** and *Ekspresowy* (express) trains are listed in red with an "IC" or "Ex" in front of the train number. *Pośpieszny* (direct; also in red) are almost as fast. *Osobowy* (in black) are the slowest but are 35% cheaper than *pośpieszny*. All InterCity, *ekspresowy*, and some *pośpieszny* trains require seat reservations; if you see a boxed R on the schedule, ask the clerk for a *miejscówka* (myay-SOOV-ka; reservation). Buy surcharged tickets on board from the *konduktor* before he or she finds (and fines) you. Most people purchase *normalny* tickets, while students and seniors buy *ulgowy* (half-price) tickets. Foreign travelers are not eligible for discounts; you risk a hefty fine by traveling with an *ulgowy* ticket without Polish ID. On Sundays, tickets cost 20% less. Train tickets are good only for the day they're issued. Allot time for long, slow lines or buy your ticket in advance at the station or an Orbis office. Stations are not announced and can be poorly marked.

BY BUS AND BY FERRY. PKS buses are cheapest and fastest for short trips. Like trains, there are *pośpieszny* (direct; marked in red) and *osobowy* (slow; in black). Purchase advance tickets at the bus station, and expect long lines. However, many tickets can only be bought from the driver. In the countryside, PKS markers (steering wheels that look like upside-down, yellow Mercedes-Benz symbols) indicate bus stops, but drivers will often stop if you flag them down. Traveling with a backpack can be a problem if the bus is full, since there are no storage compartments. **Ferries** run from Sweden and Denmark to Gdańsk (see p. 271).

BY CAR. Road conditions are generally safe, except at night and harvest season, when horse-drawn wagons carrying agricultural products pack the roads. For roadside assistance, contact **Polski Związek Motorowy (PZM),** ul. Solec 85, 00950 Warsaw (☎(022) 849 93 61; www.pzm.com.pl). For 24-hour PZM roadside assistance, dial ☎981. All PZM services are free for AAA members.

BY BIKE, BY TAXI, AND BY THUMB. Biking is relatively common; bicycle rentals are available through most tourist offices. Taxi drivers generally try to rip off foreigners; arrange the price before getting in or be sure the meter's on. The going rate is 1.50-2zł per km. Arrange cabs by phone rather than hailing one on the street. Though legal, hitchhiking is rare and more dangerous for foreigners. Hand-waving is the accepted sign. *Let's Go* does not recommend hitchhiking.

TOURIST SERVICES AND MONEY

EMERGENCY **Police:** ☎997. **Ambulance:** ☎999. **Fire:** ☎998.

TOURIST OFFICES. City-specific offices are generally more helpful than the bigger chains. You can count on all offices to provide free information in English and to be of some help with accommodations for a nominal fee. **Orbis,** the state-sponsored

POLAND

travel bureau staffed by English speakers, operates luxury hotels and sells transportation tickets. **Almatur,** the Polish student travel organization, sells ISICs, helps find dorm rooms in summer, and sells student tickets. Both provide maps and brochures, as do **PTTK** and **IT** *(Informacji Turystycznej)* bureaus.

MONEY. The Polish **złoty**—plural *złote*—is fully convertible (1 *złoty* = 100 *grosze*). For cash, private kantor offices (except for those at the airport and train stations) offer better exchange rates than banks. Bank PKO S.A. also has fairly good exchange rates; they cash traveler's checks and give Visa and Mastercard cash advances. ATMs *(Bankomat)* are everywhere except the smallest villages. Mastercard and Visa are the most widely accepted ATM networks. Budget accommodations rarely, if ever, accept credit cards, although some restaurants and pricier shops will. In restaurants, leave a 10% tip by telling the server how much change you want back. If you're paying with a credit card, give the tip in cash.

BUSINESS HOURS. Business hours tend to be Monday to Friday 10am-6pm and Saturday 9am-2pm. Saturday hours vary, as some shops in Poland distinguish "working" *(pracująca)* Saturdays, when they work longer hours, from "free" *(wolna)* ones, when hours are shorter. Very few stores or businesses are open on Sunday. Museums are generally open Tuesday to Sunday 10am-4pm. Banks are open Monday to Friday 9am to 3 or 6pm.

COMMUNICATION

MAIL. Mail is becoming increasingly efficient, although there are still incidents of theft. Airmail *(lotnicza)* usually takes a week to reach the US. For *Poste Restante*, put a "1" after the city name to ensure that it goes to the main post office. Letters abroad cost 1.60zł (air mail 1.80-2.20zł) for up to 20g. When picking up *Poste Restante*, you may have to pay a small fee (0.70-1zł) or show your passport.

TELEPHONES. Card telephones have become the public phone standard. Cards, which come in several denominations, are sold at post offices, *Telokomunikacja Polska* offices, and most kiosks. To make a collect call, write the name of the city or country and the number plus "*Rozmowa 'R'*" on a slip of paper, hand it to a post office clerk, and be patient. International direct dial numbers include: **AT&T,** ☎00 800 111 1111; **British Telecom,** ☎00 800 441 11 44; **Canada Direct,** ☎00 800 111 41 18; **MCI,** ☎00 800 111 21 22; and **Sprint,** ☎00 80 01 11 31 15.

INTERNET. Most mid-sized towns have at least one Internet club/cafe and any larger city has several.

LANGUAGES. Polish varies little across the country; the exceptions are Kaszuby, with a Germanized dialect, and Karpaty, where the highlanders' accent is extraordinarily thick. In western Poland and Mazury, German is the most commonly known foreign language, although many Poles in big cities, especially students, will speak English. Try English and German before Russian, which many Poles show an aversion to speaking. Most Poles can understand Czech or Slovak. Students may also know French. For basic phrases in all these languages and more, see p. 986.

POLSKI PHONE HOME?
After making a call from one of Warsaw's spiffy new magnetic card telephones, you may find yourself accosted by any number of locals—from young girls to elderly gentlemen—staring at your card longingly and bargaining at you in Polish like a used-car salesman. Before you write these poor souls off as free-loaders who couldn't bother to buy their own phone card, know that the opposite is more likely true: they probably have plenty of cards and are looking to add yours to their collection. If you need confirmation of this bizarre factoid, most collectors will whip out their collection with great pride if asked. The cards with pictures on the back are the most coveted; if you find you're holding the Honus Wagner of phone cards—a 1999 Pope John Paul II—you'll have to fend off an ugly mob to escape.

HEALTH AND SAFETY

Public restrooms are marked with an upward-pointing triangle for men and a circle for women, and can cost up to 0.70zł. Pharmacies are well-stocked, and at least one in each large city stays open 24hr. There are usually clinics in major cities with private, Anglophone doctors. Expect to pay 50zł per visit. Avoid state hospitals if you can help it. Tap water is theoretically drinkable, but bottled mineral water, available carbonated *(gazowana)* or flat *(nie gazowana)*, will spare you from some unpleasant metals and chemicals. Always be on your guard against pickpockets when at big train stations, while finding a train compartment, and when aboard crowded public buses and trams.

ACCOMMODATIONS AND CAMPING

Grandmotherly **private room** owners drum up business at the train station or outside the tourist office. Private rooms are usually safe, clean, and convenient, but can be far from city centers. Expect to pay about US$10 per person. **Youth hostels** (schroniska młodzieżowe) abound and average 9-25zł per night. They are often booked solid, however, by school or tour groups; call at least a week in advance. **PTSM** is the national hostel organization. **University dorms** transform into spartan budget housing in July and August; these are an especially good option in Kraków. The Warsaw office of **Almatur** can arrange stays in all major cities. **PTTK** runs a number of hotels called **Dom Turysty,** which have multi-bed rooms as well as budget singles and doubles. Hotels generally cost 30-50zł per night. Many towns have a **Biuro Zakwaterowań,** which arranges stays in private homes. Rooms come in three categories based on location and availability of hot water (one is the best). **Campsites** average US$2 per person; with a car, US$4. **Bungalows** are often available; a bed costs about US$5. *Polska Mapa Campingów* lists all campsites.

FOOD AND DRINK

Polish food favors meat, potatoes, cabbage, and butter. A Polish meal always starts with soup, usually *barszcz* (clear broth), *chłodnik* (a cold beet soup with buttermilk and hard-boiled eggs), *kapuśniak* (cabbage soup), or *żurek* (barley-flour soup loaded with eggs and sausage). Filling main courses include *gołąbki* (cabbage rolls stuffed with meat and rice), *kotlet schabowy* (pork cutlet), *naleśniki* (cream-topped crepes filled with cottage cheese or jam), and *pierogi* (dumplings with various fillings—meat, potato, cheese, blueberry). Poland bathes in beer, vodka, and spiced liquor. *Żywiec* is the most popular strong beer; *EB* is its excellent, gentler brother. Other available beers include *Okocim* and *Piast*. *Wódka* (vodka) ranges from wheat to potato. *Wyborowa, Żytnia,* and *Polonez* usually decorate private bars, while *Belweder* is Poland's proudest alcoholic export.

HOLIDAYS AND FESTIVALS

Holidays: New Year's Day (Jan. 1); Catholic Easter (Apr. 15-16); Labor Day (May 1); Constitution Day (May 3); Corpus Christi (June 14); Assumption Day (Aug. 15); Independence Day (1918; Nov. 11); Christmas (Dec. 25); Boxing Day (Dec. 26).

Festivals: Kraków is Poland's festival capital, especially in summer. Some of the most notable are the **International Short Film Festival** (late-May), the **Festival of Jewish Culture** (early June), and the **Jazz Festival** (Oct.-Nov.).

WARSAW (WARSZAWA) ☎022

According to legend, Warsaw was created when a fisherman netted and released a mermaid *(syrena)* who promised that if he founded a city, she would protect it forever. In World War II alone, however, two-thirds of the population was killed and 83% of the city destroyed. Today, Warsaw is once again the world's largest Polish city (a title long held by Chicago) and is quickly throwing off its Soviet legacy to emerge as an important international business center. Skyscrapers are popping up all over, and the university infuses Warsaw with energetic youth.

◤ TRANSPORTATION

Flights: Port Lotniczy Warszawa-Okęcie (Terminal 1; airport info ☎650 41 00, reservations 0800 300 952), ul. Żwirki i Wigury. Take **bus #175** (bus #611 after 11pm) to the city center; buy tickets at the Ruch kiosk in the departure hall or at the *kantor* outside. 2.40zł, students 1.20zł; extra tickets required for luggage. Open M-F 7:30am-8pm.

Trains: Warszawa Centralna, al. Jerozolimskie 54 (☎94 36). English is rare; write down where and when you want to go, then ask *Który peron?* ("Which platform?"). The IT office inside can help with schedules and translations. Yellow signs list departures *(odjazdy)*, white signs list arrivals *(przyjazdy)*. To: **Berlin** (6hr., 6 per day, 110zł); **Bratislava** (8-11hr., 2 per day, 136zł); **Budapest** (10½hr., 2 per day, 190zł); **Gdańsk** (3½-4½hr., 5-16 per day, 35-65zł); **Kiev** (21hr., 3 per day, 147zł); **Kraków** (2½hr., 14-18 per day, 33-63zł); **Minsk** (12hr., 1 per day, 105zł); **Moscow** (22hr., 2 per day, 250zł); **Prague** (12-14hr., 3 per day, 153zł); **St. Petersburg** (28hr., 2per day, 160zł); **Vilnius** (10hr., 1 per day, 136zł).

Buses: PKS Warszawa Zachodnia, al. Jerozolimskie 144 (☎822 48 11; international ☎823 55 70; domestic ☎94 33), in same building as Warszawa Zachodnia train station. For info on international bus tickets, check the **Centrum Podróży AURA** at the Zachodnia station. (☎823 68 58. Open M-F 9am-6pm, Sa 9am-2pm.) Buses depart for: **Copenhagen** (330zł); **London** (450zł); **Minsk** (84zł); **Paris** (399zł); **Prague** (94zł); **Venice** (340zł). **PKS Warszawa Stadion**, on the other side of the river, sends buses east and south. **Polski Express**, al. Jana Pawła II (☎630 03 20), in a kiosk near Warsawa Centralna train station, offers fast, comfortable bus service to: **Gdańsk** (6hr., 2 per day, 37zł); **Kraków** (6hr., 2 per day, 33zł); **Lublin** (3hr., 7 per day, 17zł).

Public Transportation: (☎94 84; www.ztm.waw.pl) **Trams, buses,** and **Metro** run 5am-11pm. One ride 2.40zł, ISIC 1.20zł; night bus 7.20zł; extra ticket required for large baggage. **Day pass** 7.20zł, students 3.60zł. Buy tickets at kiosks or from the driver at night. Punch the end marked by the arrow and *tu kasować* in the machines on board. Bus #175 runs from the airport to Stare Miasto via the central train station, the town center, and ul. Nowy Świat. Buses #127, 508, and 517 connect Warszawa Zachodnia with Centralna. Warsaw's single **Metro** line runs north-south through the center. Two new **sightseeing bus routes** have been added to please tourists: #100 and #180.

Taxis: MPT Radio Taxi (☎919), **Euro Taxi** (☎96 62), or **Halo Taxi** (☎96 23). Call for pickup to avoid overcharging. State-run cabs with a mermaid sign tend to be safe. Fares from 4zł, plus 1.60zł per km. Legal daytime max. 2zł per km, night 2.40zł.

✷ ORIENTATION

The main part of Warsaw lies west of the **Vistula River.** Though the city is huge, its grid-like layout and efficient public transportation system make it easy to navigate. The main east-west thoroughfare, **Aleje Jerozolimskie,** is intersected by several north-south avenues. **Ul. Marszałkowska** is a major tram route in the heart of the city *(centrum).* At the intersection of the two, the enormous **Pałac Kultury i Nauki** (Palace of Culture and Science) hulks over **pl. Defilad** (Parade Square); its clock tower, visible from most places near the city center, is useful to get your bearings. A stone's throw to the west, **Warszawa Centralna,** the main train station, lies at the intersection of Al. Jerozolimskie with **Al. Jana Pawła II.** To the east lies **Rondo Charles de Gaulle,** the traffic circle where **ul. Nowy Świat** (New World Street) intersects al. Jerozolimskie. Al. Jerozolimskie then becomes **ul. Krakowskie Przedmiescie** as it leads into **Stare Miasto** (Old Town). Going south the road becomes **Al. Ujazdowskie** as it runs past embassy row to palaces and gardens.

▤ PRACTICAL INFORMATION

TOURIST AND FINANCIAL SERVICES

Tourist Offices: Informacji Turystyczna (IT), al. Jerozolimskie 54 (☎94 31; info@warsawtour.pl; www.warsawtour.pl), in the main train station. Very helpful staff provides maps, currency exchange, and hotel reservations. Open daily May-Sept. 8am-8pm, Oct.-Apr. 8am-6pm. **Branch** at ul. Krakowskie Przedmiescie 89, across from Plac Zamkowy.

Same hours. English-language *Warsaw Insider* (7zł) on sale in kiosks just outside the office. **City Information System,** Plac Defilad 1 (☎656 68 54; fax 656 71 36; msitur@msiwarszawa.com.pl; www.msiwarszawa.com.pl), in Pałac Kultury, also provides travel and cultural events information.

Budget Travel: Almatur, ul. Kopernika 23 (☎826 35 12; fax 826 45 92), off ul. Nowy Świat. International bus and plane tickets at student discounts. English spoken. Open M-F 9am-7pm, Sa 10am-3pm. **Orbis,** ul. Bracka 16 (☎827 07 30; fax 827 76 05). Entrance is on al. Jerozolimskie near ul. Nowy Świat. Sells plane, train, ferry, and international bus tickets. Open M-F 8am-6pm, Sa 9am-3pm.

Embassies: Most are near ul. Ujazdowskie. **Australia,** ul. Nowogrodska 11 (☎617 60 81). Open M-F 9am-1pm and 2-4pm. **Canada,** al. Jerozolimskie 123, 5th fl. (☎629 80 51). Open M-F 8am-4:30pm. **South Africa,** ul. Koszykowa 54 (☎625 62 28). Open M-F 9am-noon. **UK,** ul. Róż 1 (☎628 10 01). Open M-F 9am-noon and 2-4pm. **US,** al. Ujazdowskie 29/31 (☎628 30 41). Open M-F 8:30am-5pm.

Currency Exchange: Private *kantory* have the best rates. **24hr. exchange** is available at Warszawa Centralna and the airport. **Bank PKO S.A.,** pl. Bankowy 2 (☎637 10 61); and ul. Grójecka 1/3 (☎658 82 17), in Hotel Sobieski. AmEx/Visa **traveler's checks** are cashed into US dollars or *złoty.*

American Express: ul. Krakowskie Przedmieście 11 (☎551 51 52). Cash and traveler's check exchange at no commission. Open M-F 9am-6pm.

LOCAL SERVICES

Luggage Storage: At Warszawa Centralna train station, below the main hall. 4zł per day per item, plus 2.25zł per 50zł of declared value. Open 24hr. In Zachodnia Station, 4zł for a big pack. Open daily 7am-7pm.

English-Language Bookstore: American Bookstore, ul. Koszykowa 55 (☎660 56 37). Open M-Sa 11am-7pm, Su 11am-6pm. Also at ul. Nowy Świat 61.

Gay and Lesbian Information: The Rainbow Helpline (☎628 52 22) speaks English and Polish. Tu Gay Catholic support, W lesbian support, F gay. 6-9pm, F 4-10pm.

Laundromat: ul. Karmelicka 17 (☎831 73 17). Take bus #180 or 516 from ul. Marszałkowska toward Żoliborz, get off at ul. Anielewicza, and go back one block. Wash and dry 26.60zł. Detergent 3zł. Open M-F 9am-5pm, Sa 9am-1pm. Call ahead.

EMERGENCY AND COMMUNICATIONS

Emergency: Ambulance: ☎999. **Police:** ☎997. **Fire:** ☎998.

Pharmacy: Apteka Grabowskiego (☎825 13 72), at the main train station. Open 24hr.

Medical Assistance: American Medical Center, ul. Wilcza 23 m. 29 (☎622 04 89; 24hr. emergency ☎0 602 24 30 24). Provides English-language referrals. General practice clinic open M-Sa 8am-6pm.

Telephones: At the post office; sells tokens and cards. **Directory assistance:** ☎913.

Internet Access: e-cafe, ul. Marszałkowska off the sidewalk across Galeria Centrum from the street, inside the Kino Relax complex. Open daily 10am-9pm. **Empik Zaprasza,** ul. Marszałkowska 116, inside the Junior Empik megastore on each level. Open M-Sa 9am-10pm, Su 11am-7pm.

Post Office: ul. Świętokrzyska 31/33 (☎827 00 52; info ☎826 75 11). Take a ticket at the entrance and wait in line. For stamps and letters, push "D"; for packages, push "F"; for *Poste Restante,* turn left into the other room, push "C" at the computer, and pick it up at window #12. **Photocopy** and **fax** bureau (fax 30 00 21) open 7am-10pm. Address mail to be held: First name SURNAME, *Poste Restante,* ul. Świętokrzyska 31/33, Warsaw 1, **00-001** POLAND.

▛ ACCOMMODATIONS AND CAMPING

Prices rise and rooms become scarce in summer; call ahead, particularly for hostels. For help finding **private rooms,** check in with the **Biuro Kwater Prywatnych** (Office of Private Quarters), ul. Krucza 17, off al. Jerozolimskie, near Hotel Syrena. (☎628 75 40. Open M-Sa 9am-7pm, Su 9am-5pm. Singles from 72zł; doubles from 96zł.) **Almatur** and **IT** can arrange stays in **university dorms** in July and August.

▨ **Dom Przy Rynku,** Rynek Nowego Miasta 4 (☎/fax 831 50 33). Take bus #175 from the center to Franciszkańska; walk straight, turn right on Franciszkańska, right on Rynek, and it's on your left. Cozy rooms with clean baths. TV room, ping pong, and kitchenette. Open July-Aug. only. Reception 24hr. Lockout 10am-5pm. Flexible curfew 11pm. 2-5 bed rooms 45zł per person.

Schronisko Młodzieżowe (HI), ul. Smolna 30, top fl. (☎827 89 52), across from the National Museum. From the train station, take any eastbound tram to the 3rd stop, Muzeum Narodowe. Great location. Sheets 4zł. Lockout 10am-4pm. Curfew 11pm. 3-day max. stay. Call 2 weeks ahead in summer, 2 days before otherwise. Dorms 30-33zł; singles 60zł; doubles 110zł; triples 150zł .

Schronisko Młodzieżowe #6 (HI), ul. Karolkowa 53a (☎632 88 29). Take tram #12, 22 or 24 west from al. Jerozolimskie or the train station to "D. T. Wola" and turn right at the underpass; follow the green IYH signs. English spoken. Sheets 4zł. Reception 6-10am and 5-11pm. Lockout 10am-5pm. Curfew 11pm. 7- to 14-bed dorms 31.50zł, non-members 35zł; member students 14.50zł, non-member students 16zł. Singles with bath 160zł; doubles with bath 260zł; triples and quads 50zł per person.

Schronisko Młodzieżowe "Agrykola," ul. Myśliwiecka 9 (☎622 91 10; fax 622 91 05). Near Łazienki Park. From Marszałkowska, take bus #107, 420 or 520 to Rozbrat, continue as it turns into Myśliwiecka, then turn right at the path that leads to Ujazdowski Castle. The future of youth hostels. Curfew midnight. Dorms 40zł per person; singles 249zł; doubles 299zł; triples and quads 60zł per person.

Hotel Metalowcy, ul. Długa 29 (☎831 40 21, ext. 29). Take any tram north along ul. Marszałkowska to Plac Bankowy, walk in the direction of the tram, and turn right on Długa; it's on the right. Great location. Clean but aging rooms. Singles 56zł; roomier doubles 88zł; quads with bath 155zł.

Hotel Mazowiecki, ul. Mazowiecka 10 (☎/fax 827 23 65). A bit more than a block from ul. Krakowskie Przedmieście off ul. Świętokrzyska. One of the poshest budget hotels downtown. Check-in 2pm. Check-out noon. Singles 139zł; doubles 198zł; triples 252zł.

Atos/Portos/Aramis, ul. Mangalia 1/3a/3b (☎/fax 841 43 95, 842 68 52, and 842 09 74). From ul. Marszałkowska, take bus #110 or 414, toward "Wilanów" to "Mangalia." Turn right on ul. Mangalia; they're on the right. Rooms with bath in three side-by-side hotels. Singles 104zł; doubles 118zł; triples 128zł.

Hotel Belfer, ul. Wybrzeże Kościuszkowskie 31/33 (☎/fax 625 51 85). From the train station, take any tram east to Most Poniatowskiego, then walk along ul. Wybrzeże Kościuszkowskie with the river on your right. English spoken. Check-in 2pm. Check-out noon. Singles 132zł, with bath 176zł; doubles 178zł/230zł; triples with bath 270zł.

Camping "123," ul. Bitwy Warszawskiej 1920r. 15/17 (☎822 91 21), by the main bus station, across from the hotel Vera. Take bus #127, 130, or 517 to Zachodnia, cross the street at the traffic circle and turn left to Bitwy Warszawskiej. Open May-Sept. Guarded 24hr. English spoken. 10zł per person, 10zł per tent. Electricity 10zł.

🖪 FOOD

Food stands are all over the city center. **Milk bars** (*bar mleczny*), which are like cafeterias, are inexpensive and decent. There are 24hr. **supermarkets** at the central train station, as well as several late-night **delikatesy**, including those on ul. Nowy Świat 53 and al. Solidarnosci 82a. (☎826 03 22. Open daily 7am-5am.) The **upscale** restaurants tend to be along along ul. Foksal.

RESTAURANTS

▨ **Gospoda Pod Kogutem,** ul. Freta 48 in Old Town. Scarf down the tasty grub in the barn-themed interior or, during the summer, outside in the relaxed garden. Beer 5zł. Main dishes 10-20zł. Open daily 11am-midnight.

▨ **Pod Samsonem,** ul. Freta 3/5, between Stare Miasto and Nowe Miasto. Hearty Polish-Jewish cuisine to make you big and strong like Samson. Decorated with photos of pre-war life. Meals 8-30zł. Open daily 10am-11pm.

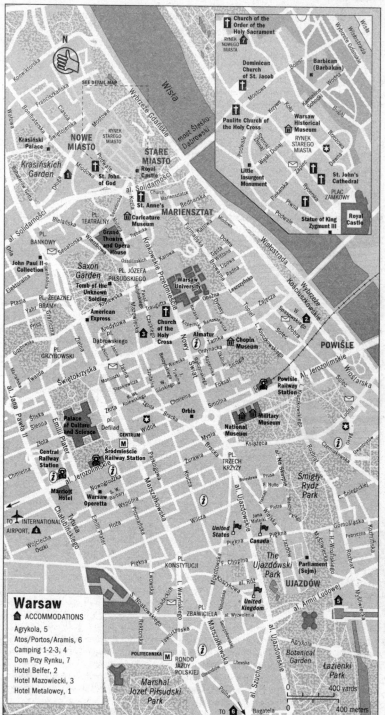

Warsaw

🏠 ACCOMMODATIONS

Agrykola, 5
Atos/Portos/Aramis, 6
Camping 1-2-3, 4
Dom Przy Rynku, 7
Hotel Belfer, 2
Hotel Mazowiecki, 3
Hotel Metalowcy, 1

POLAND

Barek Smaczny Kącik ("Tasty Nook"), ul. Smolna 40, in the courtyard. This local favorite is one of the few places in the city where you can get a sit-down dinner for 12-19zł. Open M-F 10am-7pm.

Mata Hari, ul. Nowy Świat 52. This tiny hole-in-the-wall serves incredibly cheap veggie dishes, including a variety of samosas, soups, and calzones (2.50-5zł). It'll come on a paper plate, but it'll be really good. Open M-F 11am-7pm, Sa noon-6 pm.

Bar Mleczny Familijny, ul. Nowy Świat 39. No-nonsense, and lines at the counter, but with grandma's-kitchen style food at these prices, who can complain? Soups 1zł. Meals 2-6zł. Open M-F 7am-8pm, Sa-Su 9am-5pm.

Pod Gołebiami, ul. Piwna 4a. The real reason to visit this Old Town spot is for the best *naleśniki* (Polish crepes) in town, made before your eyes and served folded into an ice-cream cone (4-8zł). Main dishes 9-30zł.

CAFES

▨ **Antykwariat Cafe,** ul. Żurawia 45, 2 blocks south of Rondo de Gaulle'a. Comfy; students linger for hours. Coffee 5-10zł. Open M-F 11am-11pm, Sa-Su 1pm-11pm.

Pożegnanie z Afryka, ul. Freta 4/6. Best coffee in town. Worth the wait for 1 of 6 tables. Coffee 7-8zł. Open daily 11am-9pm.

Same Fusy Herbaciarnia, ul. Nowomiejska 10. Head down the steps to this fragrant, candle-lit refuge in Old Town. 150 varieties of tea (10-30zł per pot, iced teas 6-11zł per glass). Open 1-11pm, and later on weekends.

◆ SIGHTS

Razed beyond recognition during World War II, Warsaw was almost entirely rebuilt from the rubble. Thanks to the wonders of Soviet upkeep, most of the buildings look older than their 50 years. As sights are spread out and distant from the center, the new tourist buses are much needed: **Route #100** begins at Plac Zamkowy and runs along Plac Teatralny, ul. Marszalkowska, al. Ujazdowskie, Łazienki Park, and back up the Royal Route, then loops through Praga before returning to Plac Zamkowy. **Route #180** runs in the south from Wilanów past Łazienki and up the Royal Route, before turning west to pass the Jewish Cemetery, and doubling back.

STARE MIASTO AND NOWE MIASTO. Warsaw's postwar reconstruction shows its best face in the cobblestone streets and colorful façades of the **Old Town** (Stare Miasto), at the very end of ul. Krakowskie Przedmieście in pl. Zamkowy. *(Take bus #175 or E3 from the city center to Miodowa.)* The landmark **Statue of King Zygmunt III Waza,** constructed in 1644 to honor the king who transferred the capital from Kraków to Warsaw, towers over the entrance to Stare Miasto. To the right stands the impressive **Royal Castle** (Zamek Królewski). In the late-16th century it replaced Kraków's Wawel as the official royal residence. When it was plundered and burned down by the Nazis in September 1939, many Varsovians risked their lives hiding priceless works in the hope they might one day be returned. Today the castle houses the ▨**Royal Castle Museum,** which has paintings, artifacts, and the stunning Royal Apartments. *(Pl. Zamkowy 4. Open M 11am-4pm, Tu-Sa 10am-4pm, Su 11am-6pm; last entry 1hr. before closing. Tickets to Royal Apartments (Route 2) 14zł, students 6zł; Su free. Tours M-Sa 70zł.)* Across ul. Świętojańska sits Warsaw's oldest church, the **Cathedral of St. John** (Anrchi-Katedra św. Jana), decimated in the 1944 Uprising but rebuilt after the war. (Cathedral open daily 10am-1pm and 3-5:30pm. Crypts open 10am-1pm. Crypts 2zł, students 1zł.) Ul. Świętojańska leads to the restored Renaissance and Baroque **Old Town Square** (Rynek Starego Miasta). A stone plaque at the entrance commemorates its reconstruction, finished in 1953-54, and recalls the square's prewar history. **Crooked Wheel** (Ul. Krzywe Kozło) starts in the northeast corner of the *rynek* and leads to the restored **barbakan,** a rare example of 16th-century Polish fortification and a popular spot for locals and tourists alike to relax. The *barbakan* opens onto ul. Freta, the edge of **Nowe Miasto,** whose 18th- and 19th-century buildings have been repaired from wartime destruction.

OUT OF LINE If you're in any reasonably touristed spot you'll likely encounter "Kwierunek Zwiedzania" arrows that point out the proper sightseeing route. Note that these aren't mere suggestions; should you decide to peruse the paintings (or costumes, or ice fishing equipment) in your own order, you'll be accosted by flustered museum employees. So be an individual—stick to the road more traveled.

TRAKT KRÓLEWSKI (ROYAL WAY). The most attractive thoroughfare in Warsaw (named the Royal Way because it leads south toward Kraków, Poland's former capital) starts at **pl. Zamkowy**, at the entrance to Stare Miasto, and stretches 4km south, changing its name from **ul. Krakowskie Przedmieście** to **ul. Nowy Świat** to **al. Ujazdowskie**. On the left as you leave pl. Zamkowy, the 15th-century **St. Anne's Church** (Kościół św. Anny) looms. Rebuilt in Baroque style, its most striking feature is its gilded altar. *(Open daily dawn-dusk.)* Fryderyk Chopin, who spent his childhood in the neighborhood near ul. Krakowskie Przedmieście, gave his first public concert in **Pałac Radziwiłłów** (a.k.a. Pałac Namiestnikowski) 46/48, the building guarded by four stone lions; today, an armed guard stands watch alongside his feline counterparts outside the now-Polish presidential mansion. **Pałac Czapskich** was Chopin's last home before he left for France in 1830; today the palace houses Chopin's Drawing Room (Salonik Chopinów) and the Academy of Fine Arts. *(Ul. Krakowskie Przedmieście 5. Open M-F 10am-2pm. 3zł, students 2zł.)* Chopin died abroad at the age of 39 and was buried in Paris, but his heart belongs to Poland; it now rests in an urn in the **Holy Cross Church** (Kościół św. Krzyża), next to the Academy. If you haven't gotten enough of the mop-topped composer, waltz on over to the **Fryderyk Chopin Museum** (Muzeum Fryderyka Chopina), which has a small collection of original letters, scores, paintings, and keepsakes, including the great composer's last piano and a section of his first polonaise, penned when he was seven years old. *(Ul. Okólnik 1; enter from ul. Tamka. Open May-Sept. M, W, F 10am-5pm, Th noon-6pm, Sa-Su 10am-2pm; Oct.-Apr. M-W and F-Sa 10am-2pm, Th noon-6pm. 8zł, students 4zł. Audio guides 4zł.)*

The Royal Way continues down **ul. Nowy Świat**, the city's most fashionable street. Turn left just after rondo Charles de Gaulle to reach Poland's largest museum, the **National Museum** (Muzeum Narodowe). *(Al. Jerozolimskie 3. Open Tu-W and F 10am-4pm, Th noon-5pm, Sa-Su 10am-5pm. 13zł, students 7zł; Sa free.)* Further down, the Royal Way turns into al. Ujazdowskie and runs alongside **Łazienki Park** (on your left). Farther into the park is the striking Neoclassical **Palace on Water** (Pałac na Wodzie), also called Pałac Łazienkowski, which houses galleries of 17th- and 18th-century art. *(Take bus #116, 180 or 195 from ul. Nowy Świat or #119 from the city center south to Bagatela. Park open daily dawn-dusk. Palace open Tu-Su 9:30am-4pm. 11zł, students 8zł. Tours in English 66zł.)* Just north of the park, off ul. Agrykola, the exhibitions in the **Center of Contemporary Art** (Centrum Sztuki Współczesnej), al. Ujazdowskie 6, break all aesthetic barriers. *(Open Sa-Th 11am-5pm, F 11am-9pm. 10zł, students 5zł.)*

THE FORMER WARSAW GHETTO AND SYNAGOGUE. Still referred to as the Ghetto, the modern **Muranów** ("walled") neighborhood northwest of the city center holds few traces of the nearly 400,000 Jews who made up one-third of the city's population prior to World War II. The **Umschlagplatz**, at the corner of ul. Dzika and ul. Stawki was the railway platform where the Nazis gathered 300,000 Jews for transport to death camps. *(Take tram #35 from ul. Marszałkowska to Dzika.)* With the monument that stands in its place to your left, continue down Stawki and turn right on ul. DuBois, which becomes ul. Zamenhofa; you will pass a stone monument marking the location of the command bunker of the 1943 ghetto uprising. Farther on, in a large park to your right, note the large **Monument of the Ghetto Heroes** (Pomnik Bohaterów). Continue along ul. Zamenhofa for two blocks and then take a right on Dzielna. On the corner of Dzielna and Al. Jana Pawall, the **Museum of Pawiak Prison** (Muzeum Więzienia Pawiak) exhibits photographs and artifacts, including the artwork and poetry of many former prisoners. Over 100,000 Poles were imprisoned here from 1939-1944; 37,000 were executed and 60,000 were transferred to concentration camps. *(Ul. Dzielna 24/26. ☎831 13 17. Open M 10am-5pm, Tu 9am-5pm, Th and Sa 9am-4pm, Su 10am-4pm. English captions. Free; donation requested.)* Follow Al. Jana Pawall up to a left on ul. Anielewicza, and continue for five blocks to reach the **Jewish Cemetery** (Cmentarz Żydowski), in the western corner of Muranów. Thickly wooded and several kilometers long, the cemetery is the final resting place of 200,000 of Warsaw's Jews. *(You can also take tram #22 from the city center to Cm. Żydowski. Open Su-Th Mar.-Sept. 9am-4pm, Oct.-Feb. 9am-3pm. 4zł.)* The beautifully reconstructed **Nożyk Synagogue** (Synagoga Nożyka), is a living remnant of Warsaw's Jewish life. The only synagogue to survive the war, today it serves as the spiritual home for the few hundred observant Jews who remain in Warsaw. *(Ul. Twarda 6, north of the Palace of Culture and Science (Pałac Kultury). From the central train station, take any tram north along ul. Jana Pawla II to Rondo ONZ. Turn right on Twarda and left at the Jewish Theater (Teatr Żydowski). Or, from the tourist office, walk west down Świętokrzyska, turn right on Emilii Plater, and cross Twarda. ☎620 43 24 for a schedule of daily services. Open Su-F 7am-8pm. 5zł.)*

WILANÓW. After his coronation in 1677, King Jan III Sobieski bought the sleepy village of Milanowo, had its existing mansion rebuilt into a Baroque palace, and named the new residence Villa Nova *(Wilanów)*. Since 1805, **Pałac Wilanowski** has functioned both as a museum and as a residence for the highest-ranking guests of the Polish state. Inside are lovely frescoed rooms, countless 17th- to 19th-century portraits, and extravagant royal apartments. You can break off from the slow-moving Polish-language tour to explore on your own with the multilingual signs along the way. *(☎842 81 01. Take bus #180, 410, or 414 from ul. Marszałkowska, or bus #519 from the train station south to "Wilanów"; cross the street and the road to the palace will be to your right. Palace open mid-June to mid-Sept. M, W-Sa 9:30am-3:30pm; Su 10:15am-5:30pm; mid-Sept. to mid-June 9:30am-2:30pm. 15zł, students 8zł. English tours 100zł; groups of 6-35 20zł each. Garden open M and W-F 9:30am-dusk. 3zł, students 2zł.)* On the way out, take a left to see ads, art, and everything in between at the **Poster Museum.** *(Open Tu-F 10am-4pm, Sa-Su 10am-5pm. 7zł, students 5zł; W free.)*

ELSEWHERE IN CENTRAL WARSAW. The center of Warsaw's commercial district, southwest of Stare Miasto near the main train station, is dominated by the 70-story Stalinist **Palace of Culture and Science** (Pałac Kultury), ul. Marszałkowska. Locals claim the view from the top is the best in Warsaw—because it's the only place from which you can't see the building, which is reviled more as a symbol of Soviet domination than as an eyesore. Below, **Parade Square** (pl. Defilad), Europe's largest square (even bigger than Moscow's Red Square) swarms with freelance capitalists. Adjacent to **Saxon Garden** (Ogród Saski) is the **John Paul II Collection,** with over 400 works by artists including Dalí, Titian, Rembrandt, van Gogh, Goya, Renoir, and others. *(Pl. Bankowy 3/5. Open Tu-Su 10am-5pm; last entry 4pm. 8zł, students 4zł.)*

🎵🍸 ENTERTAINMENT AND NIGHTLIFE

After you've digested your dinner *pierogi* and *kiełbasa*, Warsaw is full of excitement. To get the latest schedule of events, call the tourist information line (☎94 31). A large variety of pubs attract big crowds with live music, and cafes *(kawiarnie)* around Stare Miasto and ul. Nowy Świat serve late. In summer, large outdoor beer gardens complement the pub scene.

CONCERTS, OPERA, AND THEATER. Classical concerts fill Pałac na Wodzie in Łazienki on summer Saturdays. (June-Sept. 4pm. 15zł, students 10zł.) Inquire about concerts at the **Warsaw Music Society** (Warszawskie Towarzystwo Muzyczne), ul. Morskie Oko 2. (☎849 68 56. Take tram #4, 18, 19, 35, or 36 to Morskie Oko from ul. Marszałkowska. Concerts frequent, but none in summer.) The **Warsaw Chamber Opera** (Warszawska Opera Kameralna), al. Solidarności 76B (☎831 22 40), hosts a Mozart festival each year in early summer, with performances throughout the city. The **Chopin Monument** (Pomnik Chopina), nearby in Łazienki Park, hosts free Sunday performances. (May-Oct. noon and 4pm.) **Teatr Wielki,** pl. Teatralny 1 (☎692 07 58), Warsaw's main opera and ballet hall, offers performances almost daily. **Sala Kongresowa** (☎620 49 80), in the Palace of Culture and Science on the train station side with the casino, hosts serious jazz and rock concerts with famous international bands; enter from ul. Emilii Plater. **Warsaw Summer Jazz Days** is in June. **Empik Megastore** sells rock concert tickets (☎625 12 19).

BARS AND NIGHTCLUBS. Drinks are pricey, but many pubs have live music. The nightclub and dance scene shifts frequently; check posters around town. Gay life is a bit underground; call ☎628 52 22 for information. (Open Tu-W 6-9pm, F 4-10pm.) *Inaczej* and *Filo* list gay establishments. **Piwnica Pod Harendą,** ul. Krakowskie Przedmiescie 4/6, at Hotel Harenda, has an outdoor beer garden. just off the street. (Beer 10zł. Live music Tu, Th. Cover 10-15zł. Disco F 10pm, Sa 9pm. Open daily 8am-3am.) **Empik Pub,** ul. Nowy Swiat 15/17, in the basement of the Empike Megastore, is the place for blues in Warsaw. (No cover. Live music M-Sa 9pm, Su 8pm.) *The* nightclub is ▓**Piekarnia,** ul. Mlocinska 11. The packed dance floor, sparse clothing, and expert DJs are so hip it hurts. (Cover 20-25zł. Open F-Sa 10am-late.)

▶ DAYTRIP FROM WARSAW

ŻELAZOWA WOLA. The birthplace of Fryderyk Chopin, Żelazowa Wola is a must see. The pianist's cottage and gardens reveal his origin. (10zł, students 5zł; park only 4zł, students 2zł.) The **museum** in the house (☎(46) 863 33 00) recreates early 19th century living, with rooms devoted to each of Chopin's parents and the era in which they lived. The best reason to make the trip, however, is to catch a **concert** of the composer's works. From May to September, music fans gather to listen to Polish musicians perform. (Concerts Su at 11am and 3pm.) The schedule of music and performers, posted throughout Warsaw, is available at the Chopin museum (see p. 739). Concerts are free if you're content to listen from the park benches outside the music parlor. Seats in the parlor itself cost 30zł.

Two **buses** daily pass through Żelazowa Wola (53km west of Warsaw) but they aren't clearly marked; take the Wyszogrod bus. Żelazowa Wola is just a stop on the route (1hr.,8.50zł). Only the 9:45am bus arrives in time.

ŁÓDŹ   ☎042

Poland's second-largest city, Łódź (WOODGE) once held the largest Jewish ghetto in Europe, which doubled as a Nazi textile factory during World War II. Of its 70,000 residents, many deported to death camps as late as 1944 because of the ghetto's strategic value as a source of forced labor, 20,000 survived—the Red Army saved another 800 Łódź Jews from mass execution. The **Jewish cemetery** (Cmentarz Żydowski) is the largest in Europe, with over 200,000 graves. Near the entrance is a memorial to the Jews killed in the ghetto; signs lead the way to the **Ghetto Fields** (Pole Ghettowe), lined with their faintly marked graves. (Take tram #1 from ul. Kilinskiego, north to "Strykowska" Inflancka at the end of the line. Continue up the street and take a left on ul. Zmienna, and enter by the small gate in the wall on your right. Open May-Sept. M-F and Su 9am-5pm; Oct.-Apr. M-F and Su 10am-3pm. 4zl; free for those visiting relatives' graves.) Back in the center of town, the **Jewish Community Center** (Gmina Wyznaniowa Żydowska), Ul. Pomorska 18, has information on those buried in the cemetery. (Open M-F 10am-3pm. Services daily.) **Ul. Piotrkowska,** the main thoroughfare, is bustling by day and raucous by night.

Trains run to Kraków (3hr., 3 per day, 33.12zł); Toruń (2½hr., 6 per day, 26.88zł); and Warsaw (2hr., 17 per day, 35.30zł). Polski Express **buses** go from the front of the PKS station to Kraków (5hr., 3 per day, 37zł) and Warsaw (2½hr., 7 per day, 25 zł). **IT,** ul. Piotrkowska 153, has tourist and lodgings info. (☎/fax 633 71 69; www.lodzonline.com. Open M-F 8:30am-4:30pm, Sa 10am-2pm.)

KRAKÓW ☎ 012

Kraków (KRAH-koof) only recently emerged as a trendy international hot spot, but it has always figured prominently in Polish history. The city protected centuries of central European kings and astounding architectural achievements, many of which still stand in the colorful Old Town. Between the notorious Nowa Huta steelworks from the Stalinist era to the east and the Auschwitz-Birkenau death camp 70km to the west, Kraków has endured the darkness of the 20th century to earn UNESCO's protection as one of the world's 12 most important cultural monuments.

▮ TRANSPORTATION

Flights: Balice airport (☎411 19 55; tickets 411 67 00; airport@lotnisko-balice.pl), 15km west of the center. Connected to the main train station by northbound bus #192 or 208 (40min.) or express bus #502 (30min.). A taxi to the center costs 30-50zł.

Trains: Kraków Główny, pl. Kolejowy 1 (☎624 54 39; info 624 14 36). To: **Berlin** (11hr., 2 per day, 110zł); **Budapest** (11hr., 1 per day, 145zł); **Bratislava** (8hr., 1 per day, 112zł); **Gdańsk** (destination "Gdynia"; 6½hr., 11 per day, 60.86zł); **Kiev** (22hr., 1 per day, 180zł); **Prague** (9hr., 1 per day, 145zł); **Lviv** (12½hr., 1 per day, 85zł); **Vienna** (8½hr., 2 per day, 149zł); **Warsaw** (3hr., 34 per day, 50.69zł); **Zakopane** (5hr., 19 per day, 37.44zł). Some trains to southeast Poland leave from **Kraków Płaszów,** pl. Dudzinskich 1 (☎933). Take the train from Kraków Główny or tram #3 or 13 from the center south to ul. Wielicka.

Buses: ☎9316. On ul. Worcella, directly across from Kraków Główny. **Sindbad** (☎421 02 40), in the main hall, sells international tickets. Open M-Sa 8am-5:30pm, Su 9am-2pm. To: **Berlin** (12hr., 3 per week, 142zł); **Budapest** (11hr., 2 per week, 116zł); **Lviv** (10hr., 1 per day, 50zł); **Prague** (11hr., 3 per week, 139zł); **Warsaw** (5hr., 4 per day, 40zł); **Zakopane** (2hr., 26 per day, 10zł). Comfortable **Polski Express** (☎022 620 03 30) buses depart from outside the main bus station to **Warsaw** (8hr., 2 per day, 45zł).

Public Transportation: Buy tickets at kiosks near **bus** and **tram** stops (2.20zł, after 11pm 4zł); punch them on board or face a fine. Large backpacks need their own tickets. **Day pass** 9zł. 50% student discount does not apply to foreigners.

Taxis: Barbakan Taxi (☎96 61, toll-free 0800 400 400); **Euro Taxi** (☎96 64); **Wawel Taxi** (☎96 66); **Radio Taxi** (☎919).

☀ ORIENTATION

The true heart of the city is the huge **Main Market** (Rynek Główny), in the center of **Old Town** (Stare Miasto). Circling Stare Miasto are the **Planty** gardens and a ring of roads including Basztowa, Dunajewskiego, Podwale, and Westerplatte. South of the *rynek,* the gigantic **Wawel Castle** looms. The **Wista** river snakes past the castle and borders the old Jewish village of **Kazimierz,** which is accessible from the market by ul. Starowiślna (called ul. Sienna by the *rynek*). The **bus** and **train** stations are conveniently located just to the northeast of the Planty ring. To reach the *rynek* from either, follow the "do centrum" signs through the underpass to Planty garden. A number of paths and streets cut from there to the square (10min.).

▮ PRACTICAL INFORMATION

Tourist Offices: MCI, Rynek Główny 1/3 (☎428 36 00; info@mcit.pl; www.mcit.pl). Sells the handy *Kraków in Your Pocket* guide (5zł). Open May-Sept. M-F 9am-8pm, Sa 9am-3pm; Oct.-Apr. M-F 9am-6pm.

Budget Travel: Orbis, Rynek Główny 41 (☎422 40 35; fax 422 28 85; incoming@orbis.travel.krakow.pl). Arranges trips to Wieliczka and Auschwitz, among others. English spoken. Open M-F 9am-6pm, Sa 9am-2pm, Su 10am-2pm.

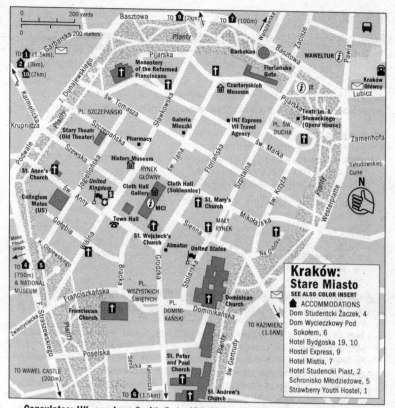

Kraków: Stare Miasto

SEE ALSO COLOR INSERT

♠ ACCOMMODATIONS
Dom Studentcki Żaczek, 4
Dom Wycieczkowy Pod Sokołem, 6
Hotel Bydgoska 19, 10
Hostel Express, 9
Hotel Mistia, 7
Hotel Studencki Piast, 2
Schronisko Młodzieżowe, 5
Strawberry Youth Hostel, 1

Consulates: UK, sw. Anny 9, 4th fl. (☎421 70 30; fax 422 42 64; ukconsul@bci.krakow.pl). Open M-F 9am-2pm. **US,** ul. Stolarska 9 (☎429 66 55; fax 421 8292; emergency ☎429 66 58; www.usconsulate.krakow.pl). Open M-F 8:30am-4:30pm.

Currency Exchange: At *kantory*, Orbis, and hotels. Best rates far from train station. 24hr. exchange at the **Forum Hotel,** ul. M. Konopnickiej 28.

American Express: Rynek Główny 41 (☎422 91 80), in the Orbis office (see above).

Luggage Storage: Kraków Główny. 1% of luggage value plus 3.90zł per day. Open 24hr.

English-Language Bookstore: Szawal, ul. Długa 1. Open daily 10am-6pm, Sa 10am-2pm.

Laundromat: Ul. Piastowska 47, in the basement of the Piast hotel. Wash and dry 8zł each. Open Tu, Th, Sa noon-6pm.

Pharmacy: Apteka Pod Złotym Tygrysem, Szczepańska 1 (☎422 92 93). Open M-F and Su 8am-8pm, Sa 8am-2pm. Lists weekly 24hr. pharmacies in window.

Medical Assistance: Medicover, ul. Krótka 1 (☎422 76 33; emergency ☎430 00 34; fax 429 43 05; poland@medicover.com; www.medicover.com). English spoken. Open M-F 8am-8pm, Sa 9am-2pm.

Telephones: At the post office and opposite the train station, ul. Lubicz 4. Open 24hr. **Fax at Telekomunikacja Polska,** Rynek Główny 19 (☎429 17 11; fax 423 00 19).

Internet Access: Cafe Internet, ul. Sienna 14 (☎431 23 94. 5zł per hr. Open Su-Th 9am-2am, F-Sa 24hr.).

Post Office: Ul. Westerplatte 20 (422 86 48). *Poste Restante* at counter #1. Open M-F 7:30am-8:30pm, Sa 8am-2pm, Su 9-11am. Address mail to be held: First name SURNAME, Poste Restante, Kraków 1, **31-045,** Poland.

⎡ ACCOMMODATIONS

Call ahead in summer. **Waweltur,** ul. Pawia 8, arranges **private rooms.** (☎422 16 40. Open M-F 8am-8pm, Sa 8am-2pm. Singles 75zł; doubles 118zł). Żaczek, Bydgoska and Piast are student dorms with several rooms open year-round. **Strawberry Youth Hostel,** ul. Racławicka 9, is a dorm open only July-Aug. (☎636 15 00; www.strawberryhostel.com.)

▓ **Dom Wycieczkowy Pod Sokołem,** ul Sokolska 17 (☎292 01 99). Take tram #8 or 10 from the train station toward Łagiewniki and get off at the 1st stop after the bridge. Backtrack toward the river, then turn left on ul. Sokolska, using the stairs just before the bridge. No curfew. Dorms 40zł.

Hostel Express, ul. Wrocławska 91 (☎/fax 633 88 62; express91@rodan.net). From the train station, take bus #130 5 stops, then it's just uphill. Bungalows with baths, TV, kitchens. No curfew. Dorms 29zł; doubles 70zł; triples 99zł.

Schronisko Młodzieżowe (HI), ul. Oleandry 4 (☎633 88 22). Take tram #15 from the train station toward Cichy Kącik; get off just after the National Museum, at Cracovia. Take the right fork up 3-go Maja, then turn right on Oleandry. Spartan, but close to the center. Flexible lock-out 10am-5pm. Curfew midnight. Dorms 20-30zł.

Dom Studentcki Żaczek, ul. 3-go Maja 5 (☎633 54 77; www.zaczek.com.pl), just on the *rynek* side of Młodzieżowe hostel (above). Good location, but the basement disco may keep you up. Singles 70-90zł; doubles 80-140zł; triples 105-150zł; quads 130zł.

Hotel Studentcki Piast, ul. Piastowska 47 (☎637 49 33; piast.bratniak.krakow.pl). Take bus #501 or 511 from the train station to Nawojki, walk to the corner, and it's on the right. Singles 65-125zł; doubles 88-120zł; triples with bath 168zł.

Hotel Bydgoska 19, ul. Bydgoska 19 (☎636 80 00). Take tram #4, 8, or 14 from the train station toward Os. Bronowice Nowe and get off at Biprostal. Take the 1st left on al. Kijowska, the 1st right on ul. Lea, then a left on ul. Skarbińskiego, which ends in ul. Bydgoska. Dorms 22-29zł; singles 45-90zł; doubles 58-112zł; triples 78-132zł.

Hotel Mistia, ul. Szlak 73a (☎ 633 29 26), on the corner of ul. Warszawska, north of ul. Basztowa. Close to the city center. Breakfast included. Singles 143zł; doubles 116-166zł; triples with bath 179zł.

⎡ FOOD

Many restaurants and cafes are on and around the *rynek*. Grocery stores surround the bus and train stations; more can be found near the *rynek*.

▓ **Chimera,** ul. św. Anny 3. Cellar and romantic ivy garden. The oldest and most famous salad joint in town. Salad 7-10zł. Open M-Sa 9am-11pm, Su 9am-10pm.

▓ **Camelot,** ul. św. Tomasza 17. An Old Town legend. Cafe/gallery serves sandwiches (3-6zł), salads (18-20zł). Music or cabaret on W and F 8pm. Open daily 9am-midnight.

Jadłodajnia u Stasi, ul. Mikołajska 16. A one-man operation serving old-fashioned budget dinners. *Pierogi* 2-4zł. Open M-F 12:30pm until the food runs out, around 3 or 4pm.

Cafe Zakątek, ul. Grodzka 2. Fresh sandwiches, salads, and a stack of sentimental albums in this tiny *zakątek* (niche). Breakfast 6zł. Open M-Sa 8:30am-8pm.

Jadłodajnia "Anna Kwaśniewska," ul. Sienna 11, serves traditional main dishes 4.50-9zł. Open M-F 9am-5pm, Sa 10am-3pm.

Różowy Słoń (Pink Elephant), ul. Szpitalna 38, Sienna 1, and Straszewskiego 24. Fast and hearty, from Polish to pizza for under 5zł. Open M-Sa 9am-9pm, Su 10am-9pm.

Restauracja Ariel, ul. Szeroka 18, in Kazimierz, south of the *rynek*. Non-kosher Polish-Jewish cuisine. Music nightly 8pm; cover 20zł. Open daily 9am-midnight.

👁 SIGHTS

OLD TOWN. At the center of the Old Town (Stare Miasto) spreads Europe's biggest square, **Rynek Główny**, a sea of cafes and bars, not to mention tourists and Poles. A trumpet call blares from the towers of **St. Mary's Church** (Kościół Mariacki) once in each direction every hour; its abrupt ending recalls the destruction of Kraków in 1241, when the invading Tartars are said to have shot down the trumpeter in the middle of his song. The interior of the church, with stunning blues and golds, encases the world's largest Gothic altarpiece, a 500-year-old treasure once dismantled by the Nazis. *(At the corner of the rynek closest to the train station. Open M-Sa 11:30-6pm, Su 2pm-6pm. Altar 3zł, students 2zł.)* In the middle of the *rynek*, the yellow Italianate **Cloth Hall** (Sukiennice) houses vendors hawking souvenirs downstairs. Upstairs, in a gallery of the **National Museum** (Muzeum Narodowe), the art is a lot better. *(Open Tu-W and F-Su 10am-3:30pm, Th 10am-6pm. 6zł, students 2.50zł.)* Ul. Floriańska runs from the corner of the *rynek* closest to the train station to the **Barbakan,** the only remnant of the city's medieval fortifications. At the top of the street, **Floriańska Gate** (Brama Floriańska), the old entrance to the city, is the centerpiece of the only surviving remnant of the city wall. Walking down Grodzka from the corner of the *rynek* closest to **Wojciech's Church,** turn right one block to the **Franciscan Church** (Kościół Franciszkański), which houses Stanisław Wyspiański's famed stained-glass window, *God the Father: Let it Be.*

AROUND WAWEL CASTLE. 🔲**Wawel Castle** (Zamek Wawelski) is one of the finest pieces of architecture in Poland. Begun in the 10th century but remodeled during the 1500s, the castle contains 71 chambers, including a magnificent sequence of 16th-century tapestries commissioned by the royal family. *(Open Tu and F 9:30am-4:30pm, W-Th 9:30am-3pm, Sa 9:30am-3pm, Su 10am-3pm. Royal chambers 12zł, students 7zł; armory and treasury 10zł, students 6zł. W free.)* Next door, in the **Wawel Cathedral** (Katedra Wawelska), the native Krokovian Karol Wojtyła was archbishop before he became Pope. Earlier ages saw Poland's monarchs crowned and buried here. Climb the steep wooden stairs from the church to reach **Sigismund's Bell** (Dzwon Zygmunta). It sounds on major holidays and its tones echo for miles. *(Open May-Sept. M-Sa 9am-5:15pm, Su 12:15-5:15pm; Oct.-Apr. M-Sa 9am-3:15pm, Su 12:15-3:15pm. Cathedral free; tombs and bell 6zł, students 3zł.)* The entrance to **Dragon's Cave** (Smocza Jama) is in the complex's southwest corner. Legend has it that a shepherd left a poison sheep outside the cave; the dragon took the bait and got so thirsty it drank itself to death from the Wisła river. *(Open May-Sept. daily 10am-5pm. 2zł.)*

KAZIMIERZ. South of the Stare Miasto lies Kazimierz, for 600 years Kraków's **old Jewish quarter.** On the eve of World War II, 64,000 Jews lived in the Kraków area, many of them in Kazimierz, but Nazi policies forced most out. All were deported by March 1943, many to the nearby Płaszów (where parts of *Schindler's List* were filmed) and Auschwitz-Birkenau concentration camps. Kazimierz today is a focal point for the 5000 Jews living in Poland and serves as a starting place for those seeking their roots. *(The walk from the rynek leads down ul. Sienna by St. Mary's Church and opposite the statue of Adam Mickiewicz; ul. Sienna turns into Starowiślna. After 1km, turn right on Miodowa, then take 1st left onto Szeroka. Or, take tram #3, 13 or 24 toward Bieżandw Nowy from the train station.)* The tiny **Remuh Synagogue** is surrounded by **Remuh's Cemetery,** one of Poland's oldest Jewish cemeteries, with graves dating back to the plague of 1551-52 and a wall partially constructed from tombstones recovered after Nazi destruction. *(Szeroka 40. Open M-F 9am-4pm. 5zł, students 2zł. Services F dusk and Sa morning.)* Back on Szeroka is **Old Synagogue** (Stara Synagoga), Poland's oldest synagogue. It now houses a museum of sacred art. *(Szeroka 24. Open Mar.-Oct. W-Th and Sa-Su 9am-3pm, F 11am-6pm; Nov.-Feb. W-Th 9am-3pm, F 11am-5pm, Sa-Su 9am-4pm. Closed 1st weekend of every month; open 1st M of every month. 6zł, students 4zł. W free.)* **The Center for Jewish Culture,** in the former Bene Emenu prayer house, operates a library, supports restoration efforts, and arranges heritage tours. *(Rabina Meiselsa 17, just off Mały Rynek.)*

POLAND

♬♪ ENTERTAINMENT AND NIGHTLIFE

The **Cultural Information Center,** ul. św. Jana 2, sells the comprehensive monthly guide *Karnet* (3zł) and tickets for upcoming events. (☎ 421 77 87; www.krakow2001.pl. Open M-F 10am-7pm, Sa 11am-7pm.) Festivals abound in Kraków, particularly in summer. Note the **International Short Film Festival** (late May), the **Festival of Jewish Culture** (early June), the **Street Theater Festival** (early July), and the **Jazz Festival** (Oct.-Nov.). The opera performs at the **J. Słowacki Theater,** Plac Św. Ducha 1. (☎ 422 40 22; www.slowacki.krakow.pl. Box office open M-Sa 11am-2pm and 3-7pm, Su 2hr. before performance.) The **Stary Teatr** has several stages in the city. (Tickets: plac Szczepański 1. ☎ 422 40 40. Open M-F 8am-4pm, Sa 8am-1pm.)

At night, cozy pubs in the brick basements of 14th-century buildings line the streets of the *Rynek.* **Klub Kulturalny,** ul. Szewska 25, unmarked and hidden below ground, offers plenty of nooks to schmooze over. (Beer 5zł. Open M-F noon-2am.) **Bastylia,** ul. Stolarska 3, has four floors of friendly pub; peep into any of the faux doors in the walls for a surprise. (Open Su-Th 1pm-1am, F-Sa 1pm-2am.) **Pod Papugami** (Under the Parrots), ul. Mikołajska 2, is a laid-back disco with plenty of alcoves for chilling out. (Open daily 7pm-3am. 21+. Cover F 8zł, Sa 12zł.) Good jazz sessions go on at **Indigo,** ul. Floriańska 26 (☎/fax 429 17 43), **U Muniaka,** ul. Floriańska 3 (☎ 432 12 05), and **Piec Art,** ul. Szewska 12 (☎ 429 64 25).

☑ DAYTRIPS FROM KRAKÓW

AUSCHWITZ-BIRKENAU. An estimated 1½ million people, mostly Jews, were murdered—and thousands more suffered unthinkable horrors—in the Nazi concentration camps at **Auschwitz** (in Oświęcim) and **Birkenau** (in Brzezinka). The smaller **Konzentrationslager Auschwitz I** is located within the limits of the town of Oświęcim; the gates over the camp are inscribed with the ironic dictum *Arbeit Macht Frei* (Work Makes You Free). Tours begin at the **museum** at Auschwitz; as you walk past the remnants of thousands of lives—suitcases, shoes, glasses, and more than 100,000 pounds of women's hair—the sheer enormity of the evil committed starts to dawn on you. There's an English-language **film** shown at 11am and 1pm, shot by the Soviet Army that liberated the camp on January 27, 1945. (Open June-Aug. daily 8am-7pm; May and Sept. 8am-6pm; Apr. and Oct. 8am-5pm; Mar. and Nov. to mid-Dec. 8am-4pm; mid-Dec. to Feb. 8am-3pm. 3½hr. tour in English daily at 11:30am. 20zł.)

If you can help it, don't leave without visiting the starker and larger **Konzentrationslager Auschwitz II-Birkenau,** in the countryside 3km from the original camp. A 30min. walk along a well-marked route or a quick **shuttle** ride from the parking lot of the Auschwitz museum (mid-Apr. to Oct., every hr. 11:30am-5:30pm, 1zł) will get you there. Birkenau was built later in the war, when the Nazis developed a more brutally efficient means of exterminating the massive numbers of Jews, Roma, Slavs, homosexuals, communists, disabled people, and others flooding Auschwitz. The site today is only a small section of the original camp; the remainder was destroyed by retreating Nazis trying to conceal their genocide. The train tracks, reconstructed after the liberation, lead to the ruins of the crematoria and gas chambers, where a memorial pays tribute to all those who died in the Auschwitz system. Near the monument lies a pond, still gray from the ashes deposited there half a century ago.

The **Auschwitz Jewish Center and Synagogue** helps people of Jewish descent connect to their past, featuring exhibits on pre-war Jewish life in the town of Oświęcim, films based on survivors' testimonies, genealogy resources, and a reading room. Tours of Auschwitz are available. (*Plac Ks. Jana Skarbka 5. ☎ 33 844 70 02; www.ajcf.org. Take bus #1, 3, 4, 5, 6, or 8 from the train station to the town center, get off at the 1st stop after the bridge, and backtrack to Plac Ks. Jana Skarbka. Or take a taxi (approx. 15zł). Open Su-Th 8:30am-5pm; Nov.-Feb. F 8:30am-2pm, Mar.-Oct F 8:30-5pm.)*

Buses from Kraków's central bus station go to **Oświęcim** (1½hr., 10 per day, 7zł). The bus back to Kraków leaves from the stop on the other side of the parking lot— go right out of the museum to reach it. Less convenient **trains** leave from Kraków

KEEPING THE FAITH It's difficult to visit the camps at Auschwitz and Birkenau without hearing the name of Maksymilian Kolbe, the priest who sacrificed his own life while a prisoner in Auschwitz. When another man was sentenced to death by starvation, Kolbe willingly took the man's place, submitting himself to even more ghastly torture than he was already enduring. He was able to keep up his strength and stave off death for two weeks, but then his efforts proved to be in vain—frustrated by how long it was taking to kill Kolbe, the Nazis shot him. After his death, Kolbe became a strong symbol within the Catholic Church of faith in the face of persecution: in 1971 he became the first Nazi victim to be proclaimed blessed by the Catholic Church and then, in 1982, he was canonized by Pope John Paul II. The man whom Kolbe replaced survived, living to see not only the liberation of the camp, but also old age. He died four years ago. Kolbe's starvation cell (#18), located in barrack II of Auschwitz I, can be seen by visitors. A tribute to the priest has been set up inside.

Główny (1¾hr., 3 per day, 8.70zł) and from Kraków Plaszów, south of the town center. Buses #2-5 from the Oświęcim train station then connect to *"Muzeum Oświęcim"*; or, walk right as you exit the station, walk a block, turn left onto ul. Więźniów Oświęcimia, and walk 1.6km to Auschwitz, on the right.

WIELICZKA. A 1000-year-old ■**salt mine** sits at ul. Daniłowicza 10 in the tiny town of Wieliczka, 13km southeast of Kraków. Pious Poles carved the immense 20-room underground complex out of salt; in 1978, UNESCO declared the mine one of the 12 most priceless monuments in the world. The most spectacular cavern is the 60m by 11m **St. Kinga's Chapel,** complete with salt chandeliers, an altar, and relief works. (☎278 73 66; www.kopalnia.pl. Open Apr.-Oct. daily 7:30am-7:30pm; Nov.-Mar. 8am-4pm. Tours 33zł, students 22zł.) Most travel companies, including **Orbis** (p. 735), organize daily trips to the mines, but the easiest and cheapest way to go is one of the private **minibuses** which depart from between the train and bus stations (every 15min., 2zł). Look for minibuses with *"Wieliczka"* on the door. In Wieliczka, follow the path of the former tracks, then the *"do kopalni"* signs.

ZAKOPANE   ☎018

Set in a valley surrounded by jagged Tatran peaks and alpine meadows, Zakopane, Poland's premier year-round resort, swells with hikers and skiers during peak seasons (Jan.-Feb. and July-Sept.). Visitors come for the magnificent **Tatran National Park** (Tatrzański Park Narodowy), a terrific venue for outdoor adventure. Entrances to the park lie at the trailheads. (2zł, students 1zł; high season 3zł. Keep your ticket.) The bus station is on the corner of ul. Kościuszki and ul. Jagiellońska, across from the train station. **Buses** (☎201 46 03) go to: Kraków (2hr., 22 per day, 11zł); Warsaw (8½hr., 3 per day, 63zł); and Poprad, Slovakia (2¼hr., 2 per day, 15zł). A private express line runs between Zakopane and Kraków (2-3hr., 7 per day, 10zł); buses leave from a stop on ul. Kosciuszki, 50m toward the center from the station. **Trains** (☎201 45 04) go to Warsaw (8hr., 3 per day, 63zł). Walk down ul. Kościuszki to reach the central ul. Krupówki (15min.). **Tourist Agency Redykołka,** ul. Kościeliska 1, runs English language tours and gives information on private rooms (30-40zł). (☎/fax 201 32 53; info@tatratours.pl; www.tatratours.pl. Open M-Sa 9am-5pm, Su 10am-5pm.) When it's time to crash, look for *pokój, noclegi,* or *Zimmer* signs (25-30zł). **Schronisko Morskie Oko,** by the Morskie Oko lake, is a gorgeous hostel in an ideal hiking location. Take the bus from the station to Palenice Bialczanska or a direct minibus from opposite the bus station. (☎207 76 09. Reserve weeks ahead in July-Sept. Dorms 35zł, 28zł if you bring your own sleeping bag.) **PTTK Dom Turysty,** ul. Zaruskiego 5, is a large chalet in the center of town. Walk down ul. Kościuszki from the bus station; it turns into ul. Zaruskiego. (☎206 32 07; informacja@domturysty.zakopane.pl. Curfew 11pm. Dorms 16-55zł.) Most restaurants are expensive; **Delikatesy grocery,** ul. Krupówki 41, is cheap. (Open M-Sa 7am-10pm, Su 8am-10pm.) **Postal code:** 34-500.

▨ HIKING NEAR ZAKOPANE. To start hiking, catch a bus or minibus to **Kuźnice** (every 20min.), south of central Zakopane. Or, walk from the train station along ul. Jagiellonska, which becomes ul. Chałubińskiego, then continue down ul. Przewodników Tatrzańskich to catch the 1987m Kasprowy Wierch **cable car.** (July-Aug. daily 7:30am-6:30pm; June and Sept. 7:30am-5pm; Oct. 7:30am-3pm. 27zł, students 18zł.) Before hiking, pick up the tourist map *Tatrzański Park Narodowy.*

Mt. Giewont (1894m; 6½hr.) has a silhouette that looks like a man lying down. It's crowded and the final ascent is steep, so be careful. From Kuźnice, take the blue trail to the peak for a view of Zakopane, the Tatras, and Slovakia.

Valley of the Five Polish Lakes (Dolina Pięciu Stawów Polskich) is a beautiful full-day hike. It starts at Kuźnice and follows the blue trail to Hala Gąsienicowa. After several steep ups and downs, the blue trail ends at Morskie Oko. From here, it's 2km farther down to a parking lot in Palenica Bialczanska, then a bus to Zakopane.

Sea Eye Lake (Morskie Oko; 1406m; 5-6hr.) dazzles tourists each summer. Take a bus from the Zakopane station (45min., 11 per day, 4zł), or a private minibus (6-10zł) from opposite the station to Palenica Białczańska. Take the 18km round-trip hike on a paved road, or take a horse and carriage (return 2½hr.; 30zł up, 15zł down).

Dolina Kościeliska (full day) offers an easy and lovely hike crossing the valley of Potok Kościeliski. A bus shuttles from Zakopane to Kiry (every 30min., 2zł) and the trailhead.

WROCŁAW ☎ 071

Since Wrocław's elaborate post-war and post-communist reconstructions, only photographs recall its destruction in World War II. Now, the city charms visitors with the antique grace of its many 19th-century buildings and lush parks. The heart of the city, **Stare Miasto** (Old Town) centers around **Main Market Square** (Rynek Główny), towered over by the gothic **ratusz** (town hall). **Ul. Świdnicka,** a central street by the *rynek,* is so beautiful that the Germans tried to have its cobblestones moved to their soil. Entering the **Racławice Panorama,** ul. Purkyniego 11, which depicts the 18th-century peasant insurrection led by Tadeusz Kosiuśzko against the Russian occupation, is like stepping right onto a battlefield. With your back to the town hall, bear left onto Kuźnicza, and turn right onto Kotlarska, which becomes ul. Purkyniego, to find the rotunda housing the exhibit. (Open Tu-Su 9am-4pm. 16zł, students 10zł.) Just across the street, you can wander the halls of the massive **National Museum,** Plac Powstancow Warszawy 5. (Open Tu, W, F 10am-2pm, Th 9am-4pm, Sa-Su 10am-4pm. 6zł, students 5zł; Th free.) The center of Wrocław's cultural life, the **University** (Uniwersytet Wrocławski), pl. Uniwersytecki 1, houses many architectural gems, including the **Aula Leopoldina,** an 18th-century lecture hall with magnificent frescoes, and the adjacent **cathedral.** (Open Th-Tu 10am-3:30pm. 3zł, students 1.5zł.) After a day in the lively city center, discover the peace of the **Cathedral Square** (Plac Katedralny), flanked by the Oder river. With your back to the town hall, take any street forward until you hit ul. Piaskowy; take a left over Piakowsky bridge to **Cathedral Island,** then a right onto Tumski bridge to pl. Katedralny, where you'll see the stately **Cathedral of St. John the Baptist** (Katedra św. Jana Chrzciciela). Bearing right down Kapitalna brings you to the **Botanical Gardens** (Ogród Botaniczny), ul. Sienkiewicza 23. (Open daily 8am-6pm. 4zł, students 3zł.)

Trains, ul. Piłsudskiego 105 (☎368 83 33), go from Wrocław Głowny to: Berlin (6hr., 3 per day, 84zł); Budapest (6.5hr., 1 per day, 164zł); Dresden (5½hr., 4 per day, 82zł); Kraków (4½hr., 7 per day, 35zł); Moscow (36hr., 1 per day, 270zł); Poznań (2hr., 21 per day, 29zł); Prague (7hr., 3 per day, 86zł); and Warsaw (5hr., 11 per day, 40zł). **Buses** leave from behind the train station; they are generally slower and more expensive. With your back to the train station, turn left on ul. Piłsudskiego, take your third right on ul. Świdnicka, and go past Kosciuszki pl. over the Podwale river to reach the main market square. **IT,** ul. Rynek 14, can help with rooms. (☎344 31 11; fax 44 29 62. Open M-F 9am-5pm, Sa 10am-3pm.) Surf the **Internet** at **Cyber-Herbaciarnia,** ul. Kuźnicza 29a, entrance from ul. Nozownicza. (6zł first hr.; 3zł next hr. Open daily 10am-10pm.) The clean and spacious **HI youth hostel,** ul. Kołłątaja 20, is directly opposite the train station on the road perpendicular to ul. Piłsudskiego. (☎343 88 56. Lockout 10am-5pm. Curfew 10pm. Call ahead. Dorms and doubles 18zł per person.) **Postal code:** 50-900.

TORUŃ
☎ 056

Toruń bills itself as the birthplace and childhood home of **Copernicus**, the man who "stopped the sun and moved the earth." After wandering its medieval cobblestone streets, you might wonder why he ever left. The **Old Town** (Stare Miasto), on the right bank of the Wisła River, was constructed by the Teutonic Knights in the 13th century. Copernicus' birthplace, **Dom Kopernika**, ul. Kopernika 15/17, has been meticulously restored and features a "traditional" sound and light show. (Open Tu-Su 10am-4pm. 6zł, students 4zł.) The **Regional Museum** (Muzeum Okręgowe) is housed in the 14th-century **Town Hall** (Ratusz), Rynek Staromiejski 1, in the center of the tourist district. (Open Tu-Su 10am-4pm. 6zł, students 4zł. Su free.) A city-wide burghers' revolt in 1454 led to the destruction of the **Teutonic Knights' Castle**, but the ruins on ul. Przedzamcze are still impressive. (Open daily 10am-6pm. 0.50zł.) The 50-foot **Leaning Tower**, Ul. Krzywą Wieżą 17, was built in 1271 by a Teutonic knight as punishment for falling in love with a peasant girl. The **Cathedral of St. John the Baptist and St. John the Evangelist** (Bazylika Katedralna pw. Św. Janów), at the corner of ul. Zeglarska and Sw. Jana, is the most impressive of the tall Gothic churches poking up from the low skyline. From there, it's a short walk across the *rynek* to ul. Panny Marii and the stained glass of the **Church of the Virgin Mary** (Kościół Św. Marii). After sunset, stroll along **Bulwar Filadelfijski** (named for Toruń's sister city, Philadelphia), where fishermen and couples line the stone steps.

The **train station,** across the Wisła River from the city center at Ul. Kujawska 1, serves: Gdańsk (3hr., 6 per day, 32.30zł); Kraków (8 hr., 3 per day, 40.50zł); and Warsaw (3hr., 5 per day, 33.20zł). **Polski Express buses** leave from pl. Teatralny for Szczecin (5½hr., 2 per day, 36zł) and Warsaw (3½hr., 13 per day, 20-37zł). **Dworzec PKS buses,** ul. Dąbrowskiego 26, leave for **Gdańsk** (3½hr., 2 per day, 28zł) and Warsaw (4hr., 4 per day, 32zł). The **IT tourist office,** Rynek Staromiejski 1, offers helpful advice in English and helps find lodgings. From the station, take city bus #22 or 27 to pl. Rapackiego (the first stop across the river), head through the little park area, and it's on your left. (☎621 09 31; fax 621 09 30; www.it.torun.pl. Open M and Sa 9am-4pm, Tu-F 9am-6pm, Su 9am-3pm; Sept.-Apr. closed Su.) Check email at **Internet Club Jeremi,** Rynek Staromiejski 33. (5zł per hr. Open 24hr.) **Postal code:** 87-100.

Hotel Trzy Korony, Rynek Staromiejski 21 (☎/fax 622 60 31) is centrally located. (Singles 80zł; doubles 90zł, with bath 190zł; triples 110/230zł, apartments 230zł.) To reach **PTTK Dom, Turystycyny,** ul. Legionów 24, from the old town *rynek*, follow ul. Chelmińska past pl. Teatralny to the second right after the park and turn left onto ul Legionów; after three blocks, it's on the right. (☎/fax 622 38 55. Check-in 2pm; check-out noon. 4-bed dorms 30zł.) ▓**U Soltysa,** ul. Mostowa 17, serves up hearty Polish food (*pierogi* 7.5-13 zł). There's a 24-hr. **grocery store** at ul. Chelmińska 22.

GDAŃSK
☎ 058

The strategic location of Gdańsk on the Baltic Coast and at the mouth of the Wisła has put it at the forefront of Polish history for more than a millennium. As the free city of Danzig, it was treasured by Poles as the "gateway to the sea" during long years of occupation in the 18th and 19th centuries. During World War II, it was the site of the first deaths of the war and of the Germans' last stand, and by the early 1980s, it was back in the spotlight as the birthplace of Lech Wałęsa's Solidarity trade union. The recent millennium celebration restored Gdańsk to much of its former splendor; it's the perfect starting point to explore Malbork and Sopot.

▐ TRANSPORTATION

Trains: Gdańsk Główny, ul. Podwale Grodzkie 1 (☎94 36). To: **Berlin** (8hr., 1 per day, 124.50zł); **Kraków** (7hr., 11 per day, 42.90zł); **Prague** (14hr., 1 per day, 166zł); **Warsaw** (5hr., 18 per day, 59zł). **Commuter trains (SKM)** run to Sopot (20min.; every 20min.; 2.80zł, students 1.40zł).

POLAND

Buses: ul. 3 Maja 12 (☎302 15 32), behind the train station via the underground passageway. To **Berlin** (8½hr., 2 per week, 153zł) and **Warsaw** (4½hr., 6 per day, 45zł).

Local Transportation: Buses and **trams** cost 1.10-3.30zł; day pass 5.50zł. Students pay half-price. Prices rise at night. Baggage needs a ticket.

Taxis: Super Hallo Taxi: ☎301 91 91. **Hallo Taxi:** ☎91 97. Both 1.80zł per km.

✸⚡ ORIENTATION AND PRACTICAL INFORMATION

From the **Gdańsk Główny** train station, the city center lies a few blocks southeast, bordered on the west by **Wały Jagiellońskie** and on the east by the **Motława**. Take the underpass in front of the train station, go right, exit the shopping center, then turn left on ul. Heweliusza. Turn right on ul. Rajska and follow the signs to **Główne Miasto** (Main Town), turning left on ul. Długa. Długa becomes **Długi Targ** as it widens near Motława. Gdańsk has a number of suburbs, all north of Główne Miasto.

Tourist Offices: IT Gdańsk, Ul. Długa 45 (☎301 91 51; www.pttk-gdansk.com.pl), in Główne Miasto. Open daily June-Aug. 10am-8pm, Sept.-May 10am-6pm.

Budget Travel: Adamar (☎/fax 301 68 99; adamar@gd.onet.pl) sells international train tickets in the basement of the train station. Open M-F 9am-5pm, Sa 10am-1pm. **Orbis,** ul. Podwale Staromiejskie 96/97 (☎/fax 301 84 12; orbis.gdanskpod@pop.com.pl). Ferry, train, and plane tickets. Open M-F 9am-6pm, Sa 10am-3pm.

Currency Exchange: The train station has a 24hr. *bureau de change* and an **ATM. Bank Gdański,** Wały Jagiellońskie 14/16 (☎307 92 12), cashes traveler's checks for 1% commission and provides cash advances for no commission. Open M-F 9am-6pm.

Internet Access: Rudy Kot Internet Music Café, ul. Garncarska 18/20 (☎301 86 49). Off Podwale Staromiejskie. 2.50zł per 30min. Open daily 10am-midnight.

Post Office: Ul. Długa 22/28 (☎301 88 53). *Poste Restante* is around the back through a separate entrance. Open M-F 8am-8pm, Sa 9am-3pm. Address mail to be held: First name SURNAME, *Poste Restante*, Gdańsk 1, **80-801**, POLAND.

⌂ ACCOMMODATIONS

Try to book ahead in summer or get a private room through **Gdańsk-Tourist** (Biuro Zakwaterowania), ul. Podwale Grodzkie 8, downstairs in the City Forum shopping mall, connected underground to the train station. (☎301 26 34. Open July-Aug. daily 8am-7:30pm; Sept.-June M-Sa 9am-6pm. Singles 40-50zł; doubles 70-80zł.)

Schronisko Młodzieżowe (HI), ul. Wałowa 21 (☎301 23 13). Cross the street in front of the train station, head up ul. Heweliusza, turn left at ul. Łagiewniki, then right after the church onto Wałowa; the hostel is on the left. Sheets 3.21zł. Lockout 10am-5pm. Curfew midnight. Dorms 16zł; singles and doubles 27-30zł.

Dom Studnck Angielski, ul. Chlebnicka 13/16 (☎301 28 16), 1 block off Długi Targ. Amazing location. Funky murals. Open July-Aug. 26.75zł per person.

Schronisko Młodzieżowe, ul. Grunwaldzka 244 (☎341 41 08). From the train station, take tram #6 or 12 north (to your left facing away from the station) and get off at Abrahama, 14 stops later; you will see a complex of tram garages on the left (20-25min.). Turn right on ul. Abrahama, then right again on Grunwaldzka; the hostel is just ahead by the sports complex. Lockout 10am-5pm. Curfew midnight. Dorms 14.40zł, nonmembers 16zł; singles and doubles 27zł per person, 30zł.

Hotel Zaułek, ul. Ogarna 107/108 (☎301 41 69). Ogarna runs parallel to Długi Targ, 1 block farther when coming from the train station. Check-in and check-out noon. Singles 60zł; doubles 80zł; triples 100zł; quads 115zł; quints 120zł; 6-bed rooms 140zł.

Hotel Dom Nauczyciela, ul. Uphagena 28 (☎/fax 341 91 16), in Gdańsk-Wrzeszcz. Take tram #6 or 12 north from the train station to Miszewskiego (7 stops). Turn right on ul. Miszewskiego and take the next right onto Uphagena; the hotel will be ahead on the left, across from the tennis courts. Check-in and check-out 10am. Singles 50-125zł; doubles 70-180zł; triples 100-105zł; quads 140zł.

POLAND

FOOD

For fresh produce, try **Hala Targowa** on ul. Pańska, in the shadows of Kościół św. Katarzyny just off Podwale Staromiejskie. (Open M-F 9am-6pm, 1st and last Sa of every month 9am-3pm.) ▧**Green Way Vegetarian Bar,** ul. Garncarska 4/6, creates stellar soups, samosas, stuffed pitas, and fruit juices. (Entrees 4-9zł. Open M-F 10am-8pm, Sa-Su noon-8pm.) Or, eat hearty Polish food at **Bar Mleczny,** ul. Długa 33/34. (Full meals 5-10zł. Open M-F 7am-6pm, Sa-Su 9am-5pm.) **Cafe Kamienica,** ul. Mariacka 37/39, in the shadow of St. Mary's church on ul. Mariacka, serves *szarlotka* (apple pie) for 5zł, and coffee for 5zł.

SIGHTS

GŁÓWNE MIASTO. The handsome market square, **Długi Targ,** forms the heart of Główne Miasto, where the 16th-century façade of Arthur's Court (Dwór Artusa) faces out onto Neptune Fountain (Fontanna Neptuna). The court now houses a branch of the **Gdańsk History Museum** (Muzeum Historii Gdańska) that's only worth seeing for the indoor architecture of the Court itself. Next to the fountain, where ul. Długa and Długi Targ meet, the 14th-century **town hall** (ratusz) houses another branch of the **Gdańsk History Museum**, where you can admire both the grand hall rooms and an amazing collection of amber. Pay an extra 2zł to climb the **tower** for a city view. *(Both museums open Tu and Th 11am-6pm, W 10am-4pm, F-Sa 10am-5pm, Su 11am-5pm. 5zł, students 2.50zł; W free.)* A block toward the train station is the world's largest brick cathedral, the 14th-century **Church of the Blessed Virgin Mary** (Kościół Najświętszej Marii Panny). Climb the 405 steps to the top of the steeple for another fantastic vista. *(Open M-Sa 9am-5:30pm. 3zł.)* The cobblestone ul. Mariacka, with Gdansk's famous stone porch steps and gaping dragon's-head gutterspouts, leads to riverside ul. Długie Pobrzeże. The Gothic **Harbor Crane,** part of **Central Maritime Museum** (Centralne Muzeum Morskie), is along the left. The other two branches lie across the river; one on land, the other on board the ship *Sołdek.* *(All branches open June-Aug. daily 10am-6pm, Sept.-May. Tu-Su 9:30am-4pm. Museums and ferry 12zł, students 7zł.)* The flags of Lech Wałęsa's trade union *Solidarność* fly high once again at the **Gdańsk Shipyard** (Stocznia Gdańska) and at the **Solidarity monument,** on pl. Solidarności, north of the city center at the end of ul. Wały Piastowskie.

GDAŃSK-OLIWA. The most beautiful of Gdańsk's many suburbs, Oliwa provides a respite from the big city. From the city center take the commuter rail (15min.; 2.50zł, students 1.25zł). Trams #6 and 12 get you there more slowly (30-35min.). From the Oliwa train station, go up ul. Poczty Gdańskiej, turn right on ul. Grundwaldzka, then left at the signs for the cathedral on ul. Rybińskiego. To the right you'll find the lush green shade and ponds of **Park Oliwski.** *(Open daily May-Sept. 5am-11pm; Mar.-Apr. and Oct. 5am-8pm.)* Within the park's gates is the oldest church in the Gdańsk area, the 13th-century **Oliwska Cathedral** (Katedra), which houses a magnificent 18th-century Rococo organ. *(Consult "Informator Turystyczney," at the tourist office for a complete schedule of daily concerts.)*

WESTERPLATTE. When Germany attacked on September 1, 1939, the little island **fort** guarding Gdańsk's harbor gained the unfortunate distinction of being the target of the first shots of World War II. Its defenders held out bravely for a week, until a lack of food and munitions forced them out. **Guardhouse #1** has been converted into a museum about the fateful day. *(Take bus #106 or 158 south from the train station to the last stop (20min.). Open May-Sept. 9am-dusk. 2zł, students 1.50zł.)* The path beyond the museum passes the ruins of a command building and, farther up, the massive **Memorial to the Heroes of the Coast** (Pomnik Obrońców Wybrzeża), with views of the bay. Giant letters below spell out "Nigdy Więcej Wojny" (No More War).

BRZEZNO. For some fun at the beach, Brzezno—though it may not be as trendy as Sopot—is perfect. What it does have over Sopot is Park Brzeznienski, a wondrous escape full of tall pine trees. *(Take tram #13, 15, or 63 north from the train station to the last stop, Brzezno. Follow the footpath in the wooded area ahead to reach the beach.)*

◢ NIGHTLIFE

Dlugi Targ hums at night as crowds of all ages pack the pubs, clubs, and beer gardens late into the evening. Near the intersection of ul. Podwale Staromiejskie and ul. Podmlynska, ◢**Latający Holender Pub,** ul. Waly Jagiellonskie 2/4, near the end of ul. Dluga in the basement of the LOT building, doubles as a coffeehouse. (Beer 6zł. Coffee 4zł. Open daily noon-midnight.) The new **Blue Cafe,** ul. Chmielna 103/104, just across the first bridge at the end of Dlugi Targ, is already known for its jazz and blues. (M-Th live music 8pm. F-Sa dance. Beer 7zł. Open daily 11am-late.)

◢ DAYTRIPS FROM GDAŃSK: MALBORK AND SOPOT

MALBORK. Malbork is home to the largest brick castle in the world, which is composed of three parts: the high, middle and low **castles.** The best point from which to see the entire castle is across the river, on the other side of the complex from the train and bus stations. **Trains** (40-60min., 37 per day, 8.50zł) run from Gdansk to Malbork. Facing away from the station, walk right on ul. Dworcowa, left at the fork, around the corner to the roundabout and cross to ul. Kosciuszki, until you can veer right on ul. Piaslowska, where signs for the castle appear. (Entire castle open Tu-Su May-Sept. 9am-5pm; Oct.-Apr. 9am-3pm. 19.50zł, students 11.50zł. Mandatory 3hr. tour in Polish. Reservations ☎272 26 77; www.zamek.malbork.com.pl.) Buy the red English booklet sold in the kiosks for 7zł or call ahead to be sure to get a 126zł English guide. Courtyards, terraces, and moats. (Open daily May-Sept. 9am-6pm; Oct.-Apr. 9am-4pm. 6zł, students 4zł.) ☎**055.**

SOPOT. Sopot is a beach resort: white, sandy, big, and recreational. The most popular sands are at the end of ul. Monte Cassino, where the 512m pier (molo) begins. (M-F 2.10zł, Sa-Su 2.80zł.) The **commuter rail** (SKM) connects Sopot to Gdańsk (20min.; 2.50zł, students 1.25zł). Ul. Dworcowa begins at the train station and leads to the pedestrian ul. Monte Cassino, which runs along the sea to the pier. **Ferries** (☎551 12 93) go from the end of the pier to Gdańsk (1hr.; 2 per day; return 42zł, students 30zł). IT, ul. Dworcowa 4, by the train station, arranges rooms. (☎550 37 83. Singles 39zł; doubles 68zł; triples 90zł; quads 110zł. Accommodations bureau open M-F 8:30am-5pm, Sa-Su 9am-2pm.) Sopot has realized that the fun doesn't have to end when the tide comes in, as seen by the generous number of street-side cafes, pubs, and discos along the tree-lined ul. Monte Cassino. ☎**058.**

PORTUGAL

ESCUDOS

US$1 = 219$	100$ = US$0.55
CDN$1 = 142$	100$ = CDN$0.85
UK£1 = 317$	100$ = UK£0.38
IR£1 = 255$	100$ = IR£0.47
AUS$1 = 116$	100$ = AUS$1.03
NZ$1 = 96$	100$ = NZ$1.25
ZAR1 = 26$	100$ = ZAR4.56
EUR€1 = 200$	100$ = EUR€0.60

PHONE CODE	**Country code: 351. International dialing prefix:** 00. There are no city codes in Portugal. From outside Portugal, dial int'l dialing prefix (see inside back cover) + 351 + local number.

In the era of Christopher Columbus, Vasco da Gama, and Magellan, Portugal was one of the world's most powerful nations, ruling a wealthy empire that stretched from America to Asia. Today, it is often overshadowed by its larger neighbor Spain. But while it shares the beaches, nightlife, and strong architectural heritage of the Iberian Peninsula, Portugal is culturally and geographically quite unique. It contains the most pristine wilderness areas in all of Europe and some villages in the northeast have not changed in over 800 years. Despite ongoing modernization in Lisbon and beyond, some of Portugal's age-old and rich traditions seem destined never to change—Porto's wines are as fine as ever, immaculate beaches still line the Atlantic seaboard, and the country's loyal people continue to stand proud. *Let's Go: Spain & Portugal 2002* has more information on fabulous, vibrant Portugal.

FACTS AND FIGURES

Official Name: República Portuguesa.

Capital: Lisbon.

Major Cities: Porto.

Population: 9,998,000.

Land Area: 92,389 sq. km.

Climate: Hot and dry May to Oct.; cooler and rainy Nov. to Apr.

Language: Portuguese.

Religion: Christian (95%).

DISCOVER PORTUGAL

Most grand tours start at vibrant **Porto** (p. 770), home of port, the strong dessert wine. Continue on to the thriving university town **Coimbra** (p. 769). Next, hit the sights, sounds, and cafes of fascinating **Lisbon** (p. 756). Climb to the castles of nearby **Sintra** (p. 763), then head south to the **Algarve** for wild nightlife, spectacular beaches, and luscious **Lagos** (p. 766). Nearby are **Sagres** (p. 768) and the glorious beach **Praia da Rocha** (p. 768).

ESSENTIALS

WHEN TO GO

Summer is high season, but the southern coast draws tourists March through November. In the off season, many hostels cut their prices by 50% or more, and reservations are seldom necessary. But while Lisbon and some of the larger towns (especially Coimbra, with its university) burst with vitality year-round, many smaller towns virtually shut down, and sights cut their hours nearly everywhere.

DOCUMENTS AND FORMALITIES

VISAS. Citizens of the US, Canada, the UK, and New Zealand can travel without visas for up to 90 days. Australian and South African citizens need visas.

EMBASSIES. Most foreign embassies are in Lisbon (p. 757). Australians can use their embassy in France (p. 321); Canada's consulate is in Faro and the UK's is in Porto. For Portuguese embassies at home: **Australia,** 23 Culgoa Circuit, O'Malley, ACT 2603. Mailing address P.O. Box 9092, Deakin, ACT 2600 (☎02 62 90 17 33); **Canada,** 645 Island Park Dr., Ottawa, ON K1Y OB8 (☎613-729-0883); **South Africa,** 599 Leyds St., Mucklenuk, Pretoria (☎012 341 2340); **UK,** 11 Belgrave Sq., London SW1X 8PP (☎020 72 35 53 31); and **US,** 2125 Kalorama Rd. NW, Washington, D.C. 20008 (☎202-328-8610). **New Zealanders** should refer to embassy in Australia.

TRANSPORTATION

BY PLANE. Most international airlines serve Lisbon; some go to Porto, Faro, and the Madeiras. Portugal's national airline **TAP Air Portugal** (in US and Canada ☎800-221-7370; in UK ☎207 630 07 46; in Lisbon ☎218 43 11 11; www.tap.pt) also serves international cities. The smaller **Portugália** (www.pga.pt) flies to Porto, Faro, Lisbon, major Spanish cities, and other Western European destinations. It has offices in Lisbon (☎218 42 55 00) and Manchester (☎161 489 50 40).

BY TRAIN. Caminhos de Ferro Portugueses is the national railway, but for travel outside of the Braga-Porto-Coimbra-Lisbon line, buses are much better. Around Lisbon, though, local trains and commuter rails are fast and efficient. When you arrive in town, go to the ticket booth to check the departure schedule; trains often run at irregular hours, and posted schedules *(horarios)* are not always accurate. Unless you have a Eurailpass, the trip back on return tickets must be used before 3am the following day. Anyone riding without a ticket can be fined over 3500$/€21. The **Portugal Flexipass** is not worth purchasing. **Eurail** is valid in Portugal.

BY BUS. Buses are cheap, frequent, and go to just about every town. **Rodoviária** (☎21 354 57 75), the national bus company, has recently been privatized. Each company name corresponds to a particular region, such as Rodoviária Alentejo or Minho e Douro, with notable exceptions such as EVA in the Algarve. There are other private companies, including Cabanelas, AVIC, and Mafrense. Be wary of stop-happy non-express buses. *Expressos* (express coach service) between major cities is very good; cheap city buses often run to nearby towns. Schedules are usually posted, but check with the ticket vendor to make sure they're accurate.

BY CAR. Portugal has a particularly high rate of automobile accidents. The new highway system (IP) is quite good, but off the main arteries, the narrow, twisting roads prove difficult to negotiate. The locals' testy reputation is well deserved. Speed limits are effectively ignored, recklessness common, and lighting and road surfaces often inadequate. Buses and trucks are safer options. Moreover, parking space in cities is almost nonexistent. Gas comes in super (97 octane), normal (92 octane), and unleaded and unusually runs 130-200$/€0.70-1.20 per liter. Portugal's national automobile association, the **Automóvel Clube de Portugal (ACP),** R. Rosa Araújo, 42, 1250 Lisbon (☎21 318 01 00), provides breakdown and towing service (M-F 9am-5pm) and 24hr. first-aid.

BY THUMB. In Portugal, hitchers are rare. Rides are easiest to come by at gas stations near highways and rest stops. *Let's Go* does not recommend hitchhiking.

TOURIST SERVICES AND MONEY

TOURIST OFFICES. The official tourism website is www.portugalinsite.pt. When in Portugal, stop by municipal and provincial tourist offices for maps and advice. Offices abroad include: **Canada,** Portuguese Trade and Tourism Commission, 60

Bloor St. West, Suite 1005, Toronto, ON M4W 3B8 (☎416-921-7376; fax 416-921-1353; iceptor@idirect.com). **UK,** Portuguese Trade and Tourism Office, 22-25A Sackville St., 2nd-4th fl., London W1X 2LY (☎20 7474 1441; fax 20 7494 1441; iceplond@aol.com). **US,** Portuguese National Tourist Office, 590 Fifth Ave., 4th fl., New York, NY 10036 (☎212-354-4403; fax 212-764-6137; www.portugal.org). Additional office in Washington D.C. (☎202-331-8222).

MONEY. Money in Portugal comes in the form of the **escudo,** available in coins of 1, 2, 5, 10, 20, 50, 100, 200 and notes of 500, 1000, 2000, 5000, and 10,000. Portugal has accepted the **Euro (€)** as legal tender, and *escudos* will be phased out by July 1, 2002. For more information, see p. 24. Tips are customary only in fancy restaurants or hotels. Some restaurants include a 10% service charge. Taxi drivers only expect a tip after a long trip. Bargaining is uncommon, but try it at markets or when room hunting. Taxes are included in all prices and are not redeemable upon departure. Official **banking hours** are Monday through Friday 8:30am to 3pm.

COMMUNICATION

EMERGENCY	**Police:** ☎112. **Ambulance:** ☎112. **Fire:** ☎112.

MAIL. Air mail *(via aerea)* takes one week within Europe, at least 10 days to reach the US or Canada, and over two weeks to reach Australia, New Zealand, and South Africa. Registered or blue mail and EMS (Express Mail) arrive more quickly but cost more. Stamps are available at post offices *(correios)* and stamp machines.

TELEPHONES. Phones accept phone cards. For the Credifone and Telecom Portugal systems, local calls cost 18$/€0.10. Use a calling card for international calls. International direct dial numbers include: **AT&T,** ☎0800 80 01 28; **British Telecom,** ☎800 800 440; **Canada Direct,** ☎800 800 122; **Ireland Direct,** ☎800 800 353; **MCI,** ☎800 800 123; **Sprint,** ☎800 800 187; **Telecom New Zealand,** ☎800 800 640; **Telkom South Africa,** ☎800 800 270; and **Telstra Australia,** ☎800 800 610.

LANGUAGE. Portuguese is a Romance language similar to Spanish. English, Spanish, and French are fairly widely spoken. To snuggle up to Portuguese and get Romantic with other members of the family, see p. 987.

ACCOMMODATIONS AND CAMPING

Movijovem, Av. Duque de Ávila, 137, 1050 Lisbon (☎21 359 60 00; fax 21 359 60 01), is the Portuguese Hosteling International affiliate. A bed in a *pousada da juventude* (not to be confused with plush *pousadas*) costs 2000-3000$/€10-15. An **HI card**

(3000$/€18) is usually mandatory for HI hostels. To reserve a high-season bed, get an **International Booking Voucher** from Movijovem (or your HI affiliate) and send it to the desired hostel at least a month in advance. **Pensões** (or *residencias*), are cheaper than hotels and only slightly more expensive than youth hostels. During the high season, many *pensões* do not take reservations, but for those that do, book a week ahead. **Hotels** tend to be pricey. When business is weak, try bargaining down in advance. **Quartos** are rooms in private residences, similar to Spain's *casas particulares*. These rooms may be the only option in smaller towns (particularly in the south) or the cheapest one in bigger cities; tourist offices can usually help you. Prices can drop as much as 500-1000$/€3-6 with bargaining. There are over 150 official **campgrounds** (parques de campismo) with lots of amenities. Police are strict about illegal camping, so don't try it—especially by official campgrounds. Tourist offices stock the free Portugal: *Camping and Caravan Sites*, an official campgrounds guide. Or, write the **Federação Portuguesa de Campismo e Caravanismo**, Av. Coronal Eduardo Gallardo, 24D, 1170 Lisbon (☎21 812 68 90).

FOOD AND DRINK

Dishes are seasoned with olive oil, garlic, herbs, and sea salt, but few spices. The fish selection includes *chocos grelhados* (grilled cuttlefish), *linguado grelhado* (grilled sole), and *peixe espada* (swordfish). S*andes* (cheese sandwiches) come on delectable bread. For dessert, try *pudim* or *flan* (caramel custard). The hearty *almoço* (lunch) is eaten between noon and 2pm and *jantar* (dinner) between 8pm and midnight. *Meia dose* (half-portions) are often adequate; full portions may satisfy two. The *prato do dia* (special of the day) or *ementa* (menu) of appetizer, bread, entree, and dessert are filling. *Vinho do porto* (port) is a dessert in itself. *Madeira* wines have a unique "cooked" flavor. Coffees are *bica* (black espresso), *galão* (with milk, served in a glass), and *café com leite* (with milk, served in a cup).

HOLIDAYS AND FESTIVALS

Holidays: New Year's Day (Jan. 1); Good Friday (Mar. 29); Easter (Mar. 31); Liberty Day (Apr. 25); Labor Day (May 1); Assumption Day (Aug. 15); Republic Day (Oct. 5); All Saints' Day (Nov. 1); Restoration of the Independence (Dec. 1); Feast of the Immaculate Conception (Dec. 8); Christmas Eve (Dec. 24); Christmas (Dec. 25).

Festivals: All of Portugal will celebrate **Carnival** Feb. 7-17 and the **Holy Week** March 24-31. Coimbra holds the **Burning of the Ribbons** festival in early May, and Lisbon hosts the **Feira Internacional de Lisboa** in June. Coimbra's **Feira Popular** takes place the 2nd week of July. For more information on Portuguese festivals, see www.portugal.org.

LISBON (LISBOA)   ☎21

Lisbon, once the center of the world's richest and farthest-reaching empire, has overcome its social and political problems to reclaim its place as one of Europe's grandest cities. It has preserved tradition by renovating historic monuments and meticulously maintaining its black-and-white mosaic sidewalks, pastel facades, and medieval alleys. The 1998 World Expo sparked massive construction and a city-wide face-lift, while helping to boost Lisbon to the forefront of European culture.

▰ TRANSPORTATION

Flights: Aeroporto de Lisboa (☎21 841 37 00), on the city's northern edge. **Buses** #44 and 45 (20-40min., 175$/€0.90) or the express **AeroBus** #91 (15min., every 20min., 460$/€2.30) go to Pr. Restauradores from outside the terminal. A **taxi** to downtown costs about 2000$/€10, plus a 300$/€1.50 luggage fee.

Trains: Caminhos de Ferro Portuguêses (☎(800) 20 09 04; www.cp.pt). Four main stations, each serving different destinations. Portuguese trains are usually quite slow; buses are often a better choice.

Estação Santa Apolónia, on Av. Infante D. Henrique, east of the Alfama on the Rio Tejo, runs the international, northern, and eastern lines. Take bus #9, 39, or 46 to Pr. Restauradores and Estação Rossio. To: **Coimbra** (2½hr., 7 per day 8am-8pm, 1510-2700$/€7.55-13.50); **Madrid** (10hr., 10:05 pm, 8200$/€41); **Paris** (21hr., 6:05pm, 29,000$/€144.65); **Porto** (4½hr., 12 per day 8am-8pm, 2080-3700$/€10.40-18.50).

Estação Barreiro, across the Rio Tejo, goes south. Station accessible by ferry (included in train ticket) from the Terreiro do Paço dock off Pr. Comércio (30min., every 30min.). Trains to **Évora** (2½hr., 7 per day 6:50am-11:50pm, 1200$/€6) and **Lagos** (5½hr., 5 per day 7:35am-7:45pm, 2800$/€14).

Estação Rossio, serves points west. M: Rossio or Restauradores. To **Sintra** (45min., every 15-30min. 6am-2am, 210$/€1.05) via **Queluz** (140$/€0.70).

Estação Cais do Sodré, to the right of Pr. Comércio when walking from Baixa. M: Cais do Sodré. To **Estoril** and **Cascais** (30min., every 20min., 210$/€1.05).

Buses: Arco do Cego, Av. João Crisóstomo, around the block from the M: Saldanha. All "Saldanha" buses (#36, 44, 45) stop in the *praça* (175$/€0.90). This is the terminal for virtually all buses. The terminal has fast **Rede Expressos** (☎21 354 54 39 or 310 31 11; www.rede-expressos.pt) to many destinations. To: **Coimbra** (2½hr., 16 per day 7am-12:15am, 1500$/€7.50); **Évora** (2hr., 13 per day 7am-9:30pm, 1500$/€7.50); **Lagos** (5hr., 9 per day 5am-1am, 2500$/€12.50); and **Porto** (4hr., 7per day 7am-12:15am, 2300$/€11.50), via **Leiria.**

Public Transportation: CARRIS (☎21 361 30 00; www.carris.pt) operates **buses, trams,** and **funiculars** (each 175$/€0.90); *passe turistico* (tourist pass) good for unlimited CARRIS travel. 1-, 3-, 4-, and 7-day passes (460$/€2.30, 1100$/€5.50, 1810$/€9, 2560$/€12.80). **Metro** (☎21 355 84 57; www.metrolisboa.pt) covers downtown and the modern business district. Individual tickets 100$/€0.50; book of 10 tickets 900$/€4.50. Trains run daily 6:30am-1am; some stations close earlier.

Taxis: Rádio Táxis de Lisboa (☎21 811 90 00), **Autocoope** (☎21 793 27 56), and **Teletáxi** (☎811 11 00) cluster along Av. Liberdade and Av. Rossio.

✳ 🛈 ORIENTATION AND PRACTICAL INFORMATION

The center is the **Baixa,** the old business area, between the **Bairro Alto** and the **Alfama.** The Baixa's grid of mostly pedestrian streets is bordered to the north by Rossio (a.k.a. Praça Dom Pedro IV), adjacent to Praça da Figueira and Praça dos Restauradores (at the tourist office and airport buses stop); Av. da Liberdade runs north, uphill from Pr. Restauradores. At the Baixa's southern end is the **Praça do Comércio,** on the **Rio Tejo** (River Tagus). Along the river are the Expo '98 grounds, now called the **Parque das Nações** (Park of Nations), and the fast-growing **Alcantara** and **Docas** (docks) regions. **Alfama,** a labyrinth of narrow alleys and stairways beneath the Castelo de São Jorge, is the city's oldest district. Across the Baixa from Alfama is **Bairro Alto,** and its upscale shopping district, the **Chiado,** which is traversed by R. do Carmo and R. Garrett, near much of the city's nightlife.

TOURIST, FINANCIAL, AND LOCAL SERVICES

Tourist Offices: Palácio da Foz, Pr. Restauradores (☎21 346 33 14), M: Restauradores. This is the mother of all Portugal tourist offices. Open daily 9am-8pm. The **Welcome Center,** Pr. Comércio (☎21 031 28 10), is the office for the city of Lisbon. Open daily 9am-8pm. Office at the **Aeroporto de Lisboa** (☎21 849 43 23), just outside the baggage claim area. Open daily 6am-2am. Look for kiosks with signs that read "Ask me about Lisboa" at Santa Apolónia and other parts of the city.

Embassies: Australia, refer to the Australian Embassy in Paris (☎01 40 59 33 00; fax 01 40 59 35 38); an embassy in Lisbon is scheduled to open soon, but the embassy in Paris will still offer information and can redirect calls. **Canada,** Av. Liberdade, 144/56, 4th fl. (☎316 46 00; fax 316 46 91); **Ireland,** R. Imprensa à Estrela, 4th fl. (☎392 94 40; fax 397 73 63); **New Zealand,** Av. Antonio Agusto Aguiar, 122, 9th fl. (☎350 96 90; fax 347 20 04); **South Africa,** Av. Luis Bivar, 10 (☎353 50 41; fax 353 57 13); **UK,** R. São Bernardo, 33 (☎392 40 00; fax 392 41 83); **US,** Av. das Forças Armadas (☎726 91 09; fax 727 91 09).

American Express: Top Tours, Av. Duque de Loulé, 108 (☎21 319 42 90). M: Marquês de Pombal; walk up Av. Liberdade toward Marquês de Pombal statue and turn right; the office is 2 blocks up on the left side of the street. The often-crowded Top Tours office handles all AmEx functions. English spoken. Open M-F 9:30am-1pm and 2:30-6:30pm.

Luggage Storage: Estação Rossio, between Pr. Restauradores and Pr. Dom Pedro IV (Rossio). M: Rossio. Lockers 550$/€2.75 per 48hr. Open daily 8:30am-11:30pm.

English-Language Bookstore: Livraria Británica, R. Luis Fernandes 14-16 (☎21 342 84 72), in the Bairro Alto. Walk up R. São Pedro de Alcântara and go straight as it becomes R. Dom Pedro V and then R. Escola Politécnica. Turn left on R. São Marcal, then right after 2 blocks onto R. Luis Fernandes. Open M-F 9:30am-7pm.

Laundromat: Lavatax, R. Francisco Sanches 65A (☎21 812 33 92). M: Arroios. Wash, dry, and fold 1100$/€5.50 per 5kg. Open M-F 8:30am-1pm and 3-7pm, Sa 8:30am-1pm.

EMERGENCY AND COMMUNICATIONS

Emergency: ☎112. **Ambulance** ☎21 942 11 11.

Police: R. Capelo, 3 (☎21 346 61 41). English spoken.

24-Hour Pharmacy: ☎118 (directory assistance). The name and address of the next night's open location is posted on the door of each pharmacy in town.

Medical Services: British Hospital, R. Saraiva de Carvalho, 49 (☎21 395 50 67). **Cruz Vermelha Portuguesa,** R. Duarte Galvão, 54 (☎21 771 40 00).

Internet Access: Web C@fé, R. Diário de Notícias, 126 (☎21 342 11 81). 300$/€1.50 for 15min., 500$/€2.50 per 30min., 800$/€4 per hr. Open daily 4pm-2am.

Post Office: Marked by red *Correios* signs. **Main office** (☎21 323 89 71), Pr. Restauradores. Telephone, fax, *Posta Restante,* and international express mail (EMS). Open M-F 8:00am-10pm, Sa-Su 9am-6pm. **Postal Code:** 1100 for central Lisbon.

▮ ACCOMMODATIONS

Most hotels are in the town center on **Avenida Liberdade,** while in the **Baixa** budget *pensões* line the **Rossio** and **Rua Prata, Rua Correeiros,** and **Rua Ouro.** Lodgings in the steep streets of **Alfama** or nightlife hot-spot **Bairro Alto** are closer to sights. If more central accommodations are full, head east along **Avenida Almirante Reis.** Youth hostels are inconveniently located but super cheap. At night, be careful in the Bairro Alto, the Alfama, and the Baixa; many streets are empty and poorly lit.

▨ **Hospedagem Estrela da Serra,** R. dos Fanqueiros, 122, 4th fl. (☎21 887 42 51), at the end of R. São Nicolau, on the edge of the Baixa toward the Alfama. Singles 2000-2500$/€10-12.50; doubles 3000-4000$/€15-20.

▨ **Residencial Duas Nações,** R. Vitória, 41 (☎21 346 07 10), on the corner of R. Augusta, 3 blocks up from M: Baixa-Chiado. Breakfast included. Reserve ahead during the summer. May-Sept. singles 3500$/€17.50, with bath 6500$/€32.50; doubles 4500$/€22.50, 8500$/€42.40; triples with bath 10,500$/€52.40. Oct.-Apr. singles 3000$/€15, with bath 6000$/€30; doubles 4000$/€20, 7500$/€37.40.

Residencial Florescente, R. Portas de Santo Antão, 99 (☎21 342 66 09; fax 21 342 77 33), 1 block from Pr. Restauradores. M: Restauradores. Reserve 2-3 weeks ahead during summer. June-Sept. singles 5000$/€25, with bath 8000$/€40; doubles 6000$/€30, 9000$/€45; triples 9000$/€45, 12,000$/€60. Oct.-May 1000$/€5 less.

Pensão Ibérica, Praça da Figueira, 10, 2nd fl. (☎21 886 70 26; fax 21 886 74 12). Newly renovated and repainted, with some rooms overlooking the plaza. Reserve a month ahead in summer. July-Sept. singles 4000$/€20, with bath 5000$/€25; doubles 7000$/€35, 8000$; triples 8500$/€42.50. Oct.-June 1000$/€5 less.

Pensão Estação Central, Calçada da Carmo, 17, 2nd-3rd fl. (☎21 342 33 08; fax 21 316 94 97), open block from the central station, across the Largo Duque Cadaval. M: Rossio. Rooms without full bath have shower. June-Sept. singles 3000$/€15, with bath 4000$/€20; doubles 5500$/€27.50, 6500$/€32.50. Oct.-May 500$/€2.50 less.

Casa de Hóspedes Globo, R. Teixeira, 37 (☎/fax 21 346 22 79), on a small street across from the Parque São Pedro de Alcântara at the top of the funicular. From the park entrance, cross the street and go one block on Trav. da Cara, then turn right onto R.

PORTUGAL

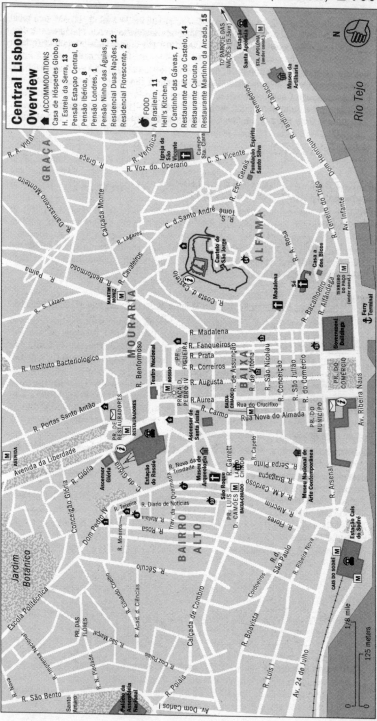

Central Lisbon Overview

▲ ACCOMMODATIONS
Casa de Hóspedes Globo, 3
H. Estrela da Serra, 13
Pensão Estação Central, 6
Pensão Ibérica, 8
Pensão Londres, 1
Pensão Ninho das Águias, 5
Residencial Duas Nações, 12
Residencial Florescente, 2

◆ FOOD
A Brasileira, 11
Hell's Kitchen, 4
O Cantinho das Gáveas, 7
Restaurante Arco do Castelo, 14
Restaurante Calcuta, 9
Restaurante Martinho da Arcada, 15

Teixeira. All rooms with phones, most with TV, and all but two with bath. Ask for a room with a veranda. Laundry 2000$/€10 per load. Reserve 3 weeks ahead in summer. June-Sept. singles 3000-4000$/€15-20, with bath 5000$/€25; double with bath 6000$/€30; triple with bath 8000$/€40. Oct.-May ask for lower rates.

Pensão Londres, R. Dom Pedro V, 53, 2nd fl. (☎21 346 22 03; fax 21 346 56 82; www.desenvolve.com/plondres). Take the Ascensor Glória from Pr. Restauradores to the top. Turn right and walk up R. S. Pedro to R. Dom Pedro V. Spacious, well-lit rooms (all with phones, some with TV) overlook the old town. Breakfast included. Reserve a month ahead in summer. Singles 5500-9000$/€27.50-45; doubles 7700-12,200$/€38.40-60.85; triples 15,200$/€75.80; quads 17,200$/€85.80.

Pensão Ninho das Águias, R. Costa do Castelo, 74 (☎21 885 40 70), right behind the Castelo. From Pr. Figueira take R. Madalena to Largo Adelino Costa, then head uphill to R. Costa do Castelo. Canary-filled garden looks out over the old city. Reserve a month ahead or more during the summer. Singles 5000$/€25; doubles 7500$/€37.50, with bath 8000$/€40; triples 10,000$/€50.

Pousada da Juventude de Lisboa (HI), R. Andrade Corvo, 46 (☎21 353 26 96). M: Picoas. Exit the metro station, turn right, and walk 1 block; the hostel is on your left. Huge, ultra-clean youth haven in an inconvenient location. English spoken. Breakfast included. Lockers 300$ per day. Reception 8am-midnight. Check out 10:30am. HI card required. June-Sept. dorms 2900$/€14.50; doubles with bath 6500$/€32.50. Oct.-May dorms 2000$/€10; doubles 5000$/€25.

▶ FOOD

Lisbon has some of the least expensive restaurants and some of the best wine of any European capital. A full dinner costs about 1800-2200$/€9-11 per person; the *prato do dia* (daily special) is often a great deal. Head to the **Calçada de Santa Ana** to find small, authentic restaurants that cater to locals. Snack on a surprisingly filling, incredibly cheap, and sinfully delicious Portuguese pastry; *pastelarias* (pastry shops) are everywhere. Specialties include *amêjoas à bulhão pato* (steamed clams), *creme de mariscos* (seafood chowder with tomatoes), and *bacalhau cozido com grão e batatas* (cod with chickpeas and boiled potatoes doused in olive oil). The **Mercado Ribeira,** Av. 24 de Julho, is a cheap, conveniently located **supermarket.** (Open M-Sa 6am-2pm.)

▨ Martinho da Arcada, Pr. do Comércio, 3, at the back left corner of the Baixa plaza when facing the river. Founded in 1782, Lisbon's oldest restaurant is predictably and justifiably expensive (entrees 1900-2950$/€9.50-14.75). The **cafe** next door makes excellent pastéis de nata (150$/€0.75) and offers the best lunch deal in the Baixa, with excellent daily specials served from noon-3pm (entrees 800-900$/€4-4.50). Open M-Sa 7am-10pm.

Pastelaria Anunciada, Largo da Anunciada, 1-2, on the corner of R. de S. José. Like many of the Baixa's pastelarias, Anunciada has good, inexpensive lunches and is a haven for locals on a street lined with touristy places. Open daily 6:30am-10pm; meals served noon-10pm.

O Cantinho das Gáveas, R. das Gáveas, 82-84, at the corner of Trav. Poço Cidade. Popular restaurant in the Bairro Alto serves typical Portuguese dishes at surprisingly reasonable prices. Open daily noon-3pm and 7pm-midnight.

Hell's Kitchen, R. Atalaia, 176. From the top of C. Glória (the steep hill from Pr. Restauradores), walk a few blocks into Bairro Alto and turn right on R. Atalaia. Small, but with an extensive selection of delicious main dishes (1100-1600$/€5.50-8), including vegetarian options. Open Tu-Su 8pm-12:30am.

Restaurante Calcuta, R. do Norte, 17, near Lg. Camões in the Bairro Alto. Fancy yet inexpensive Indian restaurant with a wide selection of vegetarian meals (900-1000$/€4.50-5). Meat dishes 1200-1700$/€6-8.50. Open M-F noon-3pm and 6:30-11pm, Sa-Su 6:30-11pm.

A Brasileira, R. Garrett, 120-122, in the Chiado neighborhood, is considered by many to be "the best cafe in Portugal." Coffee 80-250$/€0.40-1.25. Mixed drinks 1000$/€5. Open daily 8am-2am.

Restaurante Arco do Castelo, R. Chão de Feira, 25, in the Alfama across from the gate to the Castelo de São Jorge. A Portuguese-Indian mix, including specialties from Goa, Portugal's former colony in India. Entrees 1400-2100$/€7-10.50. Open M-Sa 12:30pm-midnight.

⊙ SIGHTS

THE BAIXA. Start at Lisbon's heart—the **Rossio** (also known as the **Praça Dom Pedro IV**). Once a cattle market, the site of public executions, a bullfighting arena, and a carnival ground, the *praça* is now the domain of drink-sipping tourists and heart-stopping traffic whizzing around a statue of Dom Pedro IV. Past the train station, an obelisk and a sculpture of the "Spirit of Independence" in the **Praça dos Restauradores** commemorate Portugal's independence from Spain in 1640. The *praça* is the start of **Avenida da Liberdade,** Lisbon's most imposing, elegant promenade. Modeled after the wide boulevards of 19th-century Paris, this shady mile-long thoroughfare ends at **Praça do Marquês do Pombal.** On the other side of the Rossio from Pr. Restauradores, the **Baixa**'s grid of pedestrian streets with wide mosaic sidewalks invites wandering. From the Baixa, all roads lead to **Praça do Comércio,** on the banks of the Rio Tejo, where several government ministries are housed.

BAIRRO ALTO. From the Baixa, walk uphill to the *bairro* or view the neighborhood from on high in the historic **Ascensor de Santa Justa,** a 1902 elevator in a Gothic wrought-iron tower. *(Elevator runs M-F 7am-11pm, Sa-Su 9am-11pm. 175$/€0.90 one way.)* At the center of the **Chiado,** Biarro Alto's chic shopping neighborhood, Praça Camões joins Largo Chiado at the top of R. Garrett. To reach R. Garrett, turn left from the elevator, walk one block, and it's on the right. Half-mad Maria I, desiring a male heir, made fervent religious vows promising God anything if she were granted a son. When she bore a baby boy, she built the exquisitely ornate ⊠**Basílica da Estrêla.** *(On Pr. Estrêla. Take tram #28 from Pr. Comércio 175$/€0.90. Open daily 8am-12:30pm and 3-7:30pm. Free.)* For a perfect picnic, walk up R. Misericórdia to the shady **Parque de São Pedro de Alcântara.** The European paintings at the ⊠**Museu Nacional de Arte Antiga** date to the 12th century. *(☎21 391 28 00. R. das Janelas Verdes, Jardim 9 Abril. 30min. down Av. Infante Santo from the Ascensor de Santa Justa. Buses #40 and 60 stop to the right of the museum exit and head back to the Baixa. Open Tu 2-6pm, W-Su 10am-6pm. 600$/€3, students 300$/€1.50. Su before 2pm free.)*

ALFAMA. Lisbon's medieval quarter slopes in tiers from the **Castelo de São Jorge,** facing the Rio Tejo. Between the Alfama and the Baixa is the **Mouraria** (Moorish quarter), established after the Crusaders expelled the Moors in 1147. Walking is the best way to explore the neighborhood: from Pr. Comércio, follow R. Alfandega two blocks, climb up R. Madalena, turn right after the church on Largo Madalena, follow R. Santo António da Sé, and follow the tram tracks to the richly ornamented 1812 **Igreja de Santo António da Sé.** *(Open daily 8am-7pm. Mass daily 11am, 5, 7pm.)* Follow yellow signs to the 5th-century ⊠**Castelo de São Jorge,** a Visigoth castle expanded by the Moors which offers a spectacular ocean view. *(Open daily Apr.-Sept. 9am-9pm; Oct.-Mar. 9am-6pm. Free.)*

SALDANHA. Lisbon's business center, this modern district has two excellent museums, both owned by the Fundação Gulbenkian. The ⊠**Museu Calouste Gulbenkian** houses oil tycoon Calouste Gulbenkian's collection, including an extensive array of ancient art as well as more modern European pieces. *(Av. Berna 45. M: Palhavã or S. Sebastião. Bus #16, 31, or 46. Open Tu-Su 10am-5pm. 500$/€2.50, students and seniors Su morning free.)* The adjacent **Museu do Centro de Arte Moderna** has a sizeable modern art collection, as well as beautiful gardens. *(On R. Dr. Nicolau Bettencourt. Open Tu-Su 10am-5pm. 500$/€2.50, students and seniors Su morning free.)*

BELÉM. A pseudo-suburb of Lisbon, Belém showcases the opulence and extravagance of the Portuguese empire with well-maintained museums and historical sites. King Dom Manuel I established the monastery in 1502 to give thanks for Vasco da Gama's successful Indian voyage. *(Take tram #15 from Pr. Comércio (15min., 175$/ €0.90), bus #28 or 43 from Pr. Figueira (15min., 175$/€0.90), or the train from Estação Cais do Sodré (10min., every 15min., 140$/€0.70). From the train station, cross the tracks and the street, then go left. The Mosteiro dos Jerónimos, on the banks of the Tejo, is to the right walking from the train station, through the public gardens. Open Tu-Su 10am-5pm. 600$/€3, students 300$/€1.50. Cloisters open Tu-Su 10am-5pm. Free.)* Take the underpass beneath the highway to the ✪**Torre de Belém** (10min.), with views of Belém, the Tejo, and the Atlantic beyond. Surrounded by the ocean due to the receding shoreline, it's only accessible by bridge. *(Open Tu-Su 10am-6pm. 600$/€3, students and seniors 300$/€1.50.)*

PARQUE DAS NAÇÕES (PARK OF NATIONS). The government took a chance on the former Expo '98 grounds, spending millions to convert it into the ✪Parque das Nações. The gamble paid off—the futuristic park is constantly packed. Take M: Oriente and enter through the Centro Vasco de Gama shopping mall to the center of the grounds. The biggest attraction is the Pavilhão dos Oceanos, the largest oceanarium in Europe. The 145m Torre Vasco de Gama offers spectacular views of the city. *(**Shopping mall** open daily 10am-midnight. **Oceanarium** open daily Apr.-Sept. 10am-7pm; Oct.-Mar. 10am-6pm. 1700$/€8.50, under 18 or over 65 900$/€4.50. **Torre** open daily 10am-8pm. 500$/€2.50, under 18 or over 65 250$/€1.25.)*

🎵 ENTERTAINMENT

Agenda Cultural and *Follow Me Lisboa*, free at kiosks in the Rossio, on R. Portas de Santo Antão, and at the tourist office, have information on arts events and bullfights. Lisbon's trademark is *fado*, an art combining singing and narrative poetry that expresses sorrowful *saudade* (nostalgia and yearning). The Bairro Alto has many *fado* joints off R. Misericórdia and on streets by the Museu de São Roque; but the prices are sky high. Various bars offer free performances. **Adega Machado,** R. Norte, 91, is one of the larger *fado* restaurants. (Minimum consumption 3100$/€1550. Open Tu-Su 8pm-3am.)

🎿 NIGHTLIFE

The **Bairro Alto** is the first place to go for nightlife, where a plethora of small bars and clubs invites exploring the side streets. In particular, **Rua Norte, Rua Diário Notícias,** and **Rua Atalaia** have many small clubs packed into three short blocks, making club-hopping as easy as crossing the street. Most gay and lesbian clubs are found between Pr. Camões and Trav. da Queimada, as well as in the **Rato** area near the edge of Bairro Alto. **Avenida 24 de Julho** and the **Rua das Janelas Verdes** in the **Santos** area above have some of the most popular bars and clubs. Newer expansions include the area along the river across from the **Santa Apolo'nia** train station. There's no reason to arrive before midnight; crowds flow in around 2am.

✪ **Lux/Fra'gil,** Av. Infante D. Henrique, A. In a class and location of its own, Lux is the newest big thing in Lisbon; take a taxi to the area across from the Sta. Apolo'nia train station to get to this imaginative mix of lights and boxes. Minimum consumption 2000$/ €10 (can be up to 30,000$/€150 if the bouncer's not a fan). Beer 300-500$/€1.50-2.50. Open Tu-Sa 6pm-6am; arrive after 2am if you desire company.

✪ **Litro e Meio (1,5 Lt.),** R. das Janelas Verdes, 27, in the Santos area above the clubs on Av. 24 de Julho. This friendly new bar attracts a mostly young crowd and plays house and Latin music. Most popular from 1-2:30am before clubbing on the street below. Minimum consumption usually 1000$/€5. Open M-Sa 10pm-4am.

Resto*, R. Costa do Castelo, 7, in the Alfama. Known as Chapito*, as identified by the large white sign at the entrance, this bar is at a circus school. Huge outdoor patio has one of the best views of the city. Filled with a young crowd, especially 10pm-midnight. Live Portuguese guitar F-Su. Open M-F 7:30pm-2am, Sa-Su 11pm-2am.

Kapital, Av. 24 de Julho, 68. The classiest club in Lisbon, with a ruthless door policy that makes admission a competitive sport. Don't expect to get in; for your best chance, go with Portuguese regulars and keep your mouth shut. If you're still there at the 6am closing time, take the back tunnel directly into neighboring Kremlin to continue partying. Open M-Sa 11pm-6am.

Kremlin, Escandinhas da Praia, 5, off Av. 24 de Julho next to Kapital. Caters to a mixed crowd. Set in an old convent, Kremlin has giant fake statues and 3 rooms with throbbing house and dance music. Cover usually 1000$/€5; 2000$/€10 for men; includes one drink. Open F-Sa midnight-9:30am, Th midnight-8am, Tu-W midnight-6am.

Trumps, R. Imprensa Nacional, 104B, in the Bairro Alto. Lisbon's biggest gay club features several bars in addition to a massive dance floor. Minimum consumption 1000$/€5. Open Tu-Th and Su 11:30pm-4:30am, F-Sa 11:30pm-6:30am.

▶ DAYTRIPS FROM LISBON

ESTORIL AND CASCAIS. Glorious beaches draw sun-loving tourists and locals alike to Estoril and neighboring Cascais. For the beach-weary, the marvelous (and air-conditioned) gaming palace, Casino Estoril, Europe's largest casino, is a welcome relief. (☎214 66 77 00. No swimwear, jeans, or shorts. Slots and game room 18+. Bring passport. Open daily 3pm-3am.)

Trains from Lisbon's Estação do Sodré (M: Cais do Sodré) stop in Cascais via Estoril (30min., every 20min. 5:30am-2:30am, 210$/€1.10). Estoril and Cascais are only a 20min. stroll along the coast or Av. Marginal from each other. **Bus** #418 to Sintra departs from Av. Marginal, down the street from the train station (40min., every hr. 6:10am-11:40pm, 460$/€2.30). From the station, cross Av. Marginal and head to the Estoril **tourist office,** which is left of the Casino on Arcadas do Parque, for a free map of both towns. (☎214 66 38 13. Open M-Sa 9am-7pm, Su 10am-6pm.) Ask for help finding a room (from 5000$/€25) at the Cascais **tourist office,** Av. dos Combatantes da Grande Guerra, 25. From the Cascais train station, cross the square and take a right onto Av. Valbom. Look for a small sign at Av. Combatantes. (☎214 86 82 04. Open M-Sa 9am-8pm, Su 10am-6pm; mid-Sept. to June M-Sa 9am-7pm, Su 10am-6pm.)

SINTRA. With fairy-tale castles, enchanting gardens, and spectacular mountain vistas, Sintra (pop. 20,000) is a favorite among tour groups and backpackers alike. A mix of Moorish, Gothic, and Manueline styles, the Palácio Nacional de Sintra, in Pr. República, was once the summer residence of Moorish sultans and their harems. (☎219 10 68 40. Open Th-Tu 10am-5:30pm; closed bank holidays. Buy tickets by 5pm. 600$/€3, students 300$/€1.50.) Perched on the mountain overlooking the old town, the **Castelo dos Mouros** provides stunning views of the mountains and coast. Follow the blue signs 3km up the mountain or take bus #434 (15min., every 30min., day-pass 600$/€3), which runs to the top from the tourist office. (Open daily 9am-8pm; Oct.-May 9am-7pm. Free.) Farther uphill is the **Palácio Nacional da Pena,** which looks like it belongs in Disney World with its Arabic minarets and Russian onion domes. (Open Tu-Su 10am-6:30pm; Oct.-June 2-5pm. 600$/€3, students 400$/€2; Oct.-Apr. 200$/€1.)

Trains (☎219 23 26 05) arrive on Av. Dr. Miguel Bombarda from Lisbon's Estação Rossio (45min., every 15min. 6am-2am, 210$/€1.05). Stagecoach **buses** leave from outside the train station for Cascais (#417, 40min., every hr. 6:35am-7pm, 520$/€2.60) and Estoril (#418, 40min., every hr. 6am-9:40pm, 460$/€2.30). Down the street, Mafrense buses go to Ericeira (50min., every hr. 6:25am-7:25pm, 410$/€2.05) with connections to points north. To get to the **tourist office,** Pr. República, 23, in Sintra-Vila from the bus station, turn left on Av. Bombarda, which becomes the winding Volta do Duche. Continue straight into the Praça da República; the Palácio Nacional de Sintra is ahead, and the tourist office is to the left. (☎21 923 11 57; fax 21 23 51 76.) To reach the **Pousada da Juventude de Sintra (HI),** on Sta. Eufémia, take bus #434 from the train station to the Palácio da Pena. Walk through the palace garden to the hostel (look for signs). Or, hike 2km uphill to São Pedro, but beware of the confusing *escadinha* (stair-alley) shortcut. (☎/fax 21 924 12 10. Reception daily 8am-midnight. Reservations recommended. Dorms 1900$/€9.50; doubles 4200-4600$/€20.95-22.95.)

ERICEIRA. Primarily a fishing village, Ericeira has become known for its spectacular beaches and surf-ready waves. The main beaches, **Praia do Sol** and **Praia do Norte,** crowd quickly; for something more secluded, stroll down the Largo da Feira toward Ribamar until you reach the stunning sand dunes of **Praia da Ribeira d'Ilhas.** If you stay, ask about rooms at the tourist office. Mafrense **buses** run from Lisbon's Campo Grande to Ericeira (1¼-1½hr., every hr. 6:30am-11:20pm, 720$/€3.75); get off at the Centro Rodoviario Municipal (Ericeira's bus station). Buses from Ericeira run to Mafra (20min., every hr., 240$/€1.20). The **tourist office** is at R. Eduardo Burnay, 46. (☎261 86 31 22. Open Su-Th 9:30am-8pm, F-Sa 9:30am-midnight.)

MAFRA. The **Palácio Nacional de Mafra,** one of Portugal's most impressive sights, is in this sleepy town. The massive 2000-room castle, including a cathedral-sized church, a monastery, a library, and a palace, took 50,000 workers 13 years to complete. (Open W-M 10am-5pm; closed national holidays. Free tours in English 11am and 2:30pm. 600$/€3, students 300$/€1.50.) Mafrense **buses,** which also serve Lisbon's Campo Grande (1-1½hr., every hr., 550$/€2.75) and Ericeira (20min., every hr., 7:30am-midnight, 240$/€1.20), stop in front of the palace. Don't take the **train** from Lisbon's Estação Sta. Apolónia unless you want a two-hour walk to town.

CENTRAL PORTUGAL

Jagged cliffs and whitewashed fishing villages line the Costa de Prata (Silver Coast) of **Estremadura,** with beaches that rival even those in the Algarve. In the fertile region of the **Ribatejo** (Banks of the Tejo), lush greenery surrounds historic sights.

LEIRIA   ☎244

Capital of the surrounding district and an important transport hub, prosperous and industrial Leiria fans out from a fertile valley, 22km from the coast. Chosen to host the Euro 2002 soccer finals, Leiria is busy preparing itself for the crowds that will flood the city. Leiria's most notable sight is the **Castelo de Leiria,** a granite fort built by Dom Afonso Henriques after he snatched the town from the Moors atop the crest of a volcanic hill. The terrace opens onto a panoramic view of the town and river. (Castle open Apr.-Sept. M-F 9am-6:30pm, Sa-Su 10am-6:30pm; Oct.-Mar. M-F 9am-5:30pm, Sa-Su 10am-5:30pm. 155$/€0.75.) Nearby **beaches,** including **Vieira, Pedrógão,** and **São Pedro de Muel,** are all easily accessible via buses from the station.

Leiria makes a practical base for exploring the nearby region. **Trains** (☎244 88 20 27) run from the station 3km outside town to Coimbra (1½hr., 7 per day 6:55am-8:50pm, 770$/€3.85) and Lisbon, via Caldas da Rainha (3½hr., 8 per day 8am-8:30pm, 1220$/€6.10). **Buses** (☎244 81 15 07), just off Pr. Paulo VI, next to the main park and close to the tourist office, run to: Batalha (20min., 9 per day 7:15am-7:10pm, 210$/€1); Coimbra (1hr., 11 per day 7:15am-2am, 1150$/€5.75); Lisbon (2hr., 11 per day 7:15am-11pm, 1400$/€7); Porto (3½hr., 10 per day 7:15am-2am, 1800$/€9) Santarém (2hr., 5 per day 7:15am-7:05pm, 900-1550$/€4.50-7.75); and Tomar (1½hr.; M-F 2 per day 7:15am and 5:45pm, Sa 6:15pm; 570-1200$/€2.90-6). Buses also run between the train station and the **tourist office** (15min., every hr. 7am-7:20pm, 150$/€0.75), in the Jardim Luís de Camões. (☎244 82 37 73. Open May-Sept. daily 10am-1pm and 3-7pm; Oct.-Apr. 10am-1pm and 2-6pm.) If you're going to spend the night, go to **Pousada da Juventude de Leiria (HI),** on Largo Cândido dos Reis, 9. (☎244 83 18 68. Mid-June to mid-Sept. dorms 1900$/€9.50; doubles 4200$/€21. Mid-Sept. to mid-June dorms 1500$/€7.50; doubles 3500$/€17.50.) Largo Cândido dos Reis is lined with bars like **Anubis, Estrebaria, Sebentas,** and **Os Filipes. Xannax Dance Club,** R. C. Mouzinho de Albuquerque, 168, turns from bar to disco around 3am.

TOMAR   ☎249

The arcane Knights Templar—made up of monks and warriors—plotted crusades from a convent-fortress high above this small town. The ■**Convento de Cristo** complex was the Knights' powerful and mysterious headquarters. The first structure was built in 1160, but some cloisters, convents, and buildings were added later. The **Claustro dos Felipes** is a masterpiece of Renaissance architecture. (☎249 31 34 81. Complex open June-Sept. daily 9am-6pm; Oct.-May 9am-5pm. 600$/€3, students 300$/€1.50.) The **Museu dos Fósforos** (match museum), in the Convento de São Francisco, opposite the train and bus stations, exhibits Europe's largest matchbox collection. (Open daily 10-noon and 3-5pm. Free.) **Trains** (☎249 31 28 15) go from Av. Combatentes da Grande Guerra, at the southern edge of town, to: Coimbra (2½hr., 6 per day 6am-6pm, 960-1200$/€4.80-6); Lisbon (2hr., 18 per day 5am-10pm, 1010-2040$/€5-10); Porto (4½hr., 7 per day 8am-8pm, 1510-2210$/€7.60-11); and Santarém (1hr., 12 per day 5am-10pm, 520-840$/€2.60-4.20). Rodoviaria Tejo **buses** (☎249 31 27 38) leave from Av. Combatentes Grande Guerra, by the train station, for: Coimbra (2½hr., 7am, 1650$/€8.25); Lisbon (2hr., 4 per day 9:15am-6pm, 1200$/€6); Porto (4hr., 7am, 2100$/€10.50); and Santarém (1hr., 9:15am and 6pm, 1200$/€6). From the bus or train station, take a right onto Av. Combatentes de Grande Guerra and then a left onto Av. Torres Pinheiro and continue straight past the traffic circle on R. Everaro; the **tourist office** is on the left just past the bridge. (☎249 32 24 27. Open July-Sept. daily 10am-8pm; Oct.-June 10am-6pm.) **Postal code:** 2300.

BATALHA
☎244

The only reason to visit Batalha is the gigantic, flamboyant ▨**Mosteiro de Santa Maria da Vitória.** Built by Dom João I in 1385 to commemorate his victory over the Spanish, the complex of cloisters and chapels remains one of Portugal's greatest monuments. To get to the monastery, enter through the church. (Open Apr.-Sept. daily 9am-6pm; Oct.-Mar. 9am-5pm. Monastery 600$/€3, under 25 with student ID 360$/€1.80, seniors 300$/€1.50, under 14 free. Church free.) Buses run from across the monastery to: Leiria (20min., 10 per day 7:50am-8:25pm, 210$/€1.05); Lisbon (2hr., 6 per day 7:25am-6:55pm, 1200$/€6); and Tomar (1½hr.; 8am, noon, 6pm; 520$/€2.60). The **tourist office**, on Pr. Mouzinho de Albuquerque along R. Nossa Senhora do Caminho, stands opposite the monastery. (☎244 76 51 80. Open May-Sept. daily 10am-1pm and 3-7pm; Oct.-Apr. 10am-1pm and 2-6pm.)

ÉVORA
☎266

Évora (pop. 54,000), considered Portugal's foremost showpiece of medieval architecture, is justly known as the "Museum City." Its picture-perfect streets wind past a Roman temple, an impressive cathedral, and a 16th-century university.

⊫ TRANSPORTATION. Trains (☎266 70 21 25) run from the end of R. Dr. Baronha to Lisbon (3hr., 5 per day, 1380$/€6.90) and Porto (6½hr., 3 per day, 2650$/€13.30). **Buses** (☎266 76 94 10) run from the continuation of R. Raimundo, 15min. downhill from Pr. Giraldo, past the gas station, to Lisbon (2-2½hr., every 1-1½hr., 1550$/€7.75) and Faro (5hr., 4 per day, 1900$/€9.50).

⛊ PRACTICAL INFORMATION. The **tourist office** is at Pr. Giraldo, 73. (☎266 70 26 71. Open Apr.-Sept. M-F 9am-7pm, Sa-Su 9am-12:30pm and 2-5:30pm; Oct.-Mar. daily 9am-12:30pm and 2-5:30pm.) Check email at ▨**Oficin@**, R. Moeda, 27, off Pr. Giraldo. (500$/€2.50 per hr. Open Tu-F 8pm-3am, Sa 9pm-3am; Oct.-Mar. Tu-F 8pm-2am, Sa 9pm-2am.) **Postal code:** 7000.

⛊▢ ACCOMMODATIONS AND FOOD. *Pensões* cluster around **Pr. Giraldo.** Take a right from the tourist office and then the first right onto R. Bernardo Mato to **Casa Palma,** R. Bernardo Mato 29-A. (☎266 70 35 60. Singles 4000-75,000$/€20-37.40; doubles 6000-9000$/€30-45.) **Orbitur's Parque de Campismo de Évora,** on Estrada das Alcáçovas, branches off the bottom of R. Raimundo. (☎266 70 51 90. Laundry. Reception 8am-10pm. 400-680$/€2-3.40 per person; 310-960$/€1.55-4.80 per tent; 340-600$/€1.70-3 per car.) Many budget restaurants are near Pr. Giraldo, particularly along **Rua Mercadores.** Grab **groceries** at **Maxigrula,** R. João de Deus, 130. (Open M-Sa 9am-7pm.)

🞕🎵 **SIGHTS AND ENTERTAINMENT.** The city's most famous monument is the second-century **Roman temple**, on Largo do Vila Flor. Facing the temple is the **Igreja de São João Evangelista**, whose interior is covered with dazzling tiles; ask to see the hidden chambers. (Open Tu-Su 10am-12:30pm and 2-6pm. Church 500$/€250.) From Pr. Giraldo, head up R. 5 de Outubro to the colossal 12th-century **cathedral;** the 12 apostles on the doorway are masterpieces of medieval Portuguese sculpture. The **Museu de Arte Sacra**, above the nave, has religious artifacts. (Open daily 9am-12:30pm and 2-5pm. Cloisters and museum 500$/€2.50. Cathedral free.) Attached to the pleasant **Igreja Real de São Francisco,** the bizarre 🞕**Capela dos Ossos** (Chapel of Bones) was built out of the bones of 5000 people by three Franciscan monks. From Pr. Giraldo, follow R. República; the church is on the right and the chapel around back to the right of the main entrance. (Open M-Sa 9am-1pm and 2:30-6pm, Su 10am-1pm; May and Oct.-Mar. M-Sa 9am-1pm and 2:30-5:30pm, Su 10am-1pm. 100$/€0.50, students 50$/€0.25.) After sunset head to 🞕**Jonas,** R. Serpa Pinta, 67, a bar that provides a dual atmosphere—warm and busy downstairs, and blue and mellow upstairs. (☎964 82 16 47. Open M-Sa 10:30am-3am.) A Portuguese-style country fair accompanies the **Feira de São João** festival the last week of June.

ALGARVE

Nearly 3000 hours of sunshine per year have transformed the Algarve, a desert on the sea, into a vacation spot. In July and August, sun-seeking tourists mob the resorts, packing the bars and discos from sunset until way past sunrise. In the off season, the resorts become pleasantly de-populated, and the sun eases.

LAGOS   ☎282

As the town's countless international expats will attest, Lagos is a black hole: come for two days and you'll never leave. Though not much more than beaches and bars, Lagos will keep you busy soaking in the view from the cliffs, the sun on the beach, and the drinks at the bars.

▛ TRANSPORTATION

Trains: ☎282 76 29 87. Across the river (over the metal drawbridge) from the city center. To **Évora** (6hr., 2 per day 8:50am-5pm, 1930$/€9.65) and **Lisbon** (5hr., 6 per day 6:55am-10:30pm, 2110-2800$/€10.55-14).

Buses: EVA bus station (76 29 44), off Av. Descobrimentos, just past the train station bridge as you leave town. To: **Lisbon** (5hr., 12 per day 7:40am-1:30am, 2500-2600$/€12.50-13); **Sagres** (1hr., 17 per day 7:15am-8:30pm, 480$/€2.40); **Sevilla, Spain** via Albufeira (5hr., 7:30am and 2pm, 3000$/€15).

▞🔢 ORIENTATION AND PRACTICAL INFORMATION

Avenida dos Descobrimentos, the main road, runs along the river. From the train station, exit left, go around the pink building, cross the river, and turn left on Av. Descobrimentos. From the **train station,** walk through the pastel pink marina and cross the channel over the pedestrian suspension bridge. Turn left onto Av. Descobrimentos. Exiting the bus station, walk straight until you hit Av. Descobrimentos and turn right. After 15m, take another right on R. Porta de Portugal to reach **Praça Gil Eanes,** the center of the old town. Most everything hovers near this *praça*, the adjoining **Rua 25 de Abril,** and the parallel **Rua Cândido dos Reis.** Farther down Av. Descobrimentos, on the right, closer to the fortaleza, is **Praça República.**

Tourist Office: (☎282 76 30 31), R. Vasco de Gama, an inconvenient 25min. walk from the bus station. Follow R. Vasco da Gama until it crosses Av. da República; from there it's another 150m on the right. Open daily 9:30am-12:30pm and 2-5:30pm.

Emergency: ☎112. **Police:** (☎282 76 29 30), R. General Alberto Silva.

Medical Services: Hospital (☎282 76 30 34), R. Castelo dos Governadores.

Internet Access: Irish Rover, R. de Ferrador, 9 (☎282 76 80 33). 300$/€1.50 per 15min., 500$/2.50 per 30min., 900$/€4.50 per hr. Open July-Sept. daily 2pm-2am; Oct.-June 6pm-2am.

Post Office: (☎282 77 02 50), R. Portas de Portugal, between Pr. Gil Eanes and the river. Open M-F 9am-6pm. For *Poste Restante*, label all letters "Estação Portas de Portugal" or they may arrive at the branch office. **Postal Code**: 8600.

▸ ACCOMMODATIONS AND CAMPING

In the summertime, *pensões* (and the youth hostel) fill up quickly and cost a bundle. Reserve rooms over a week in advance. Rooms in *casas particulares* run around 2000-3000$/€10-15 per person in summer; haggle with owners.

▨ Pousada da Juventude de Lagos (HI), R. Lançarote de Freitas, 50 (☎282 76 19 70). From the train and bus stations, head into town on Av. Descubrimentos, turn right at Pr. Infante Don Henrique, pass the old (and thankfully, defunct) slave market and follow Tr. Do Mar to R. Lançarote de Freitas. Reception daily 9am-1am. In summer, book through the central **Movijovem** office (☎282 359 60 00; movijovem@mail.telepac.pt). July-Sept. dorms 2500$/€12.50; doubles with bath 4300$/€21.50. Oct.-June dorms 1700$/€8.50; doubles with bath 3800$/€19. AmEX/MC/V.

Residencial Rubi Mar, R. Barroca 70 (☎282 76 31 65; rubimar01@hotmail.com), off Pr. Gil Eanes toward Pr. Infante Dom Henrique. Reserve 2 weeks ahead in summer. July-Oct. doubles 7000$/€35, with bath 8500$/€42.50; quads 15,000$/€75. Nov.-June doubles 5500$/€27.50, with bath 6500$/€32.50; quads 10,000$/€50.

Residencial Gil Vicente, R. Gil Vicente, 26, 2nd fl. (☎/fax 282 76 29 82; ggh@clix.pt), behind the youth hostel. Business card says it's a "gay guest house," but it's open to anyone. Reception Oct.-June 8am-9pm; July-Aug. 24hr. Reserve a month ahead in the summer. Apr.-Oct. singles 5000$/€25; doubles 6000-7000$/€30-35. Nov.-Mar. singles 3000$/€15; doubles 5000$/€25. AmEx/MC/V.

Residencial Caravela, R. 25 de Abril, 8 (☎282 76 33 61), just up the street from Pr. Gil Eanes. Reception 9am-11:30pm. Singles 4300$/€21.50; doubles 6000$/€30, with bath 6500$/€32.50; triples 9000$/€45.

Camping: The way most Europeans experience the Algarve; sites are crowded and expensive. **Camping Trindade** (☎282 76 38 93), just outside of town. Follow Av. Descubrimentos toward Sagres. 580$/€2.85 per person, 630-735$/€3.15-3.70 per tent, 620$/€3.10 per car. **Camping Valverde** (☎282 78 92 11), on a beach 5km outside Lagos. 790$/€3.95 per person, 650-790$/€3.25-3.95 per tent, 680$/€3.40 per car.

▸ FOOD

Peruse multilingual menus around **Praça Gil Eanes** and **Rua 25 de Abril.** For authentic Portuguese seafood, try **Praça Luis Camoes.** The morning **market** is cheap, on Av. Descobrimentos, 5min. from the town center. **Supermercado São Toque**, R. Portas de Portugal, 61, is opposite the post office. (☎282 76 28 55. Open July-Sept. M-F 9am-8pm, Sa 9am-7pm; Oct.-June M-F 9am-7:30pm, Sa 9am-7pm). Hordes of backpackers enjoy 700$/€3.50 meals at ▨**Casa Rosa**, R. Ferrador, 22. (Open daily 7pm-2am.)

▸ ▧ BEACHES AND NIGHTLIFE

Flat, smooth, sunbathing sands can be found at **Meia Praia**, across the river from town. Hop on the 30-second ferry near Pr. República (70$/€0.35). For beautiful cliffs with less-crowded beaches and caves, follow Av. Descobrimentos toward Sagres to the **Praia de Pinhão** (20min.). A bit farther, **Praia Dona Ana** features the sculpted cliffs and grottos that grace most Algarve postcards.

You're tan, you're glam, now go find yourself a (wo)man. The streets of Lagos pick up as soon as the sun dips down, and by midnight the city's walls are shaking. The area between **Pr. Gil Eanes** and **Pr. Luis de Camões** is filled with cafes. For late-night bars and clubs, try: R. Cândido dos Reis, R. do Ferrador, and the intersection of R. 25 de Abril, R. Silva Lopes, and R. Soeiro da Costa. Staggered happy hours make drinking easy, even on the tightest of budgets. ■The Red Eye, R. Candido dos Reis, 63, is the hottest new place in town. (Beer 300$/€1.50. Mixed drinks 500-700$/€2.50-3.50. Open daily 3pm-2am.)

▣ DAYTRIPS FROM LAGOS

SAGRES. Marooned atop a bleak desert plateau in Europe's southwestern-most corner, desolate Sagres and its cape were once considered the edge of the world. Near the town lurks the ■Fortaleza de Sagres, the fortress where Prince Henry stroked his beard, decided to map the world, and founded his famous **school of navigation.** (Open May-Sept. daily 10am-8:30pm; Oct.-Apr. 10am-6:30pm. 600$/€3.) Six kilometers west lies the dramatic **Cabo de São Vicente,** where the second most powerful lighthouse in Europe shines over 100km out to sea. To get there on weekdays, take the bus from the bus station on R. Comandante Matos near the tourist office (10min.; 11:15am, 12:30, 4:15pm; 180$/€0.90). Alternatively, hike 1hr. or bike past the several fortresses perched atop the cliffs. The most notable **beach** in the area is **Mareta,** at the bottom of the road from the town center. Just west of town, **Praia de Martinhal** and **Praia da Baleeira** have great windsurfing. The nearby coves of **Salema** and **Luz** are intimate and picturesque. At night, the young crowd fills the lively bar **Rosa dos Ventos** in Pr. República. (Open daily 10am-2am.)

EVA **buses** (☎282 76 29 44) run from Lagos (1hr., 17 per day 7am-8:30pm, 480$/€2.40). The **tourist office,** on R. Comandante Matoso, is up the street from the bus stop. (☎282 62 48 73. Open Tu-Sa 9:30am-12:30pm and 2-5:30pm.)

PRAIA DA ROCHA. A short jaunt from Lagos, this grand **beach** is perhaps the very best the Algarve has to offer. With vast expanses of sand, surfable waves, rocky red cliffs, and plenty of secluded coves, Praia da Rocha has a well-deserved reputation and the crowds to match. From Lagos, take a bus to Portimão (40min., 14 per day 7:15am-8:15pm, 360-450$/€1.55-2.25), then switch to the Praia da Rocha bus (10min., every 30min. 7:30am-8:30pm, 230$/€1.15). The **tourist office** is at the end of R. Tomás Cabreina. (☎282 41 91 32. Open May-Sept. daily 9:30am-7pm; Oct.-Apr. M-F 9:30am-12:30pm and 2-5:30pm, Sa-Su 9:30am-12:30pm.)

TAVIRA   ☎281

Farmers teasing police by riding their motor scooters over the Roman pedestrian bridge may be about as crazy as Tavira gets. But for most visitors to this relaxing haven—speckled with white houses, palm trees, and Baroque churches—that's just fine. Steps from the central Pr. República lead up to the 16th-century **Igreja da Misericórdia.** (Open daily 9:30am-noon and 2:30-5:30pm. Free.) Just beyond the church, the remains of the city's **Castelo Mouro** (Moorish Castle) sit next to the **Santa Maria do Castelo.** (Castle and church open daily 9am-5pm. Free.) Local beaches, including **Araial do Barril,** are accessible year-round by the bus to Pedras D'el Rei (10min., 8 per day 8:25am-6:10pm, 170$/€0.85). To reach the golden shores of **Ilha da Tavira,** an island 2km away, take the ferry from the end of Estrada das 4 Aguas downstream (every 15min. 8:30am-midnight, return 250$/€1.20).

Trains (☎281 32 23 54) leave Tavira for Vila Real de Santo António (30min., 14 per day 6:55am-1:10am, 260$/€1.10) and Faro (40min., 6 per day 6:24am-10:14pm, 300$/€1.44). EVA **buses** (☎281 32 25 46) leave from the station upriver from Pr. República for Faro (1hr., 11 per day 6:50am-7:10pm, 435$/€2.09). From the **train station** you can catch the local TUT bus to the town center (10min., every 30min. 8am-8pm, 150$/€0.72) or call a taxi (☎281 32 15 44 or 32 67 88; about 650$/€3.25). **Postal code:** 8800.

NORTHERN PORTUGAL

In the north, trellised vineyards for *porto* and *vinho verde* wines beckon connoisseurs, and *azulejo*-lined houses draw visitors to charming streets. The Three Beiras region offers a sample of the best of Portugal: the unspoiled Costa da Prata (Silver Coast), the plush greenery of the interior, and the rugged peaks of the Serra Estrela.

COIMBRA   ☎239

The country's only university city from the mid-16th to the early-20th century, charming and vibrant Coimbra is a mecca for the country's youth.

🖃🔁 TRANSPORTATION AND PRACTICAL INFORMATION. Trains (☎239 83 49 98) from other regions stop only at **Estação Coimbra-B (Velha)**, 3km northwest of town, while regional trains stop at both Coimbra-B and **Estação Coimbra-A (Nova)**, two blocks from the lower town center. A train connects the two stations (4min., runs immediately after trains arrive, 140$/€0.70). Trains run to Lisbon (3hr., 23 per day 5:30am-2:20am, 2700$/€13.50) and Porto (2hr., 21 per day 5:10am-3:10am, 1050-1900$/€5.25-9.50). **Buses** (☎239 82 70 81) go from Av. Fernão Magalhães, on the university side of the river 10min. from town, past Coimbra-A, to: Lisbon (2½hr., 17per day 7:30am-2:15am, 1550$/€7.75); Luso (45min., M-F 7 per day, Sa-Su 2 per day; 480$/€2.45); and Porto (1½hr., 10 per day, 1400$). From the bus station, go right on Av. Fernão Magalhães to Coimbra-A, then walk upstream to Largo Portagem to the **tourist office.** (☎239 85 59 50. Open M-F 9am-6pm, Sa-Su 10am-1pm and 2:30-5:30pm.) Use the **Internet** at **Museu Sandwich Bar,** R. da Matemática, 46, near the university. (600$/€3 per hr. Open M-F 4-7pm and 10:30pm-3am, Sa 10:30pm-3am.)

🔃🗎 ACCOMMODATIONS AND FOOD.   To get from Coimbra-A or Largo Portagem to the welcoming ▨Pousada de Juventude de Coimbra (HI), R. Henrique Seco, 14, walk uphill on R. Olímpio Nicolau Rui Fernandes to Pr. República, go up R. Lourenço Azevedo (left of the park), take the second right, and it's on the right. Or, take bus #7, 8, 29, or 46 to Pr. República and walk. (☎239 82 29 55. Breakfast included. Reception 8am-noon and 6pm-midnight. Dorms 1700-1900$/€8.50-9.50; doubles 4300-4600$/€21.50-23.) Follow R. Ferreira Borges as it becomes R. Visconde da Luz and leads to Pensão Santa Cruz, Pr. 8 de Maio, 21, 3rd floor. (☎/fax 239 82 61 97. Singles or doubles 4000$/€20; triples 5000$/€25.) The best cuisine lies around R. Direita, off Pr. 8 de Maio, on the side streets between the river and Largo Portagem, and around Pr. República in the university district. Supermercado Minipreço, R. António Granjo, 6C, is in the lower town center; turn left as you exit Coimbra-A and take another left. (Open M-Sa 8:30am-8pm, Su 9am-1pm and 3-7pm.) Postal code: 3000.

🖸🎴 SIGHTS AND ENTERTAINMENT. Take in the old town sights by climbing from the river up the narrow stone steps to the university. Begin your ascent at the **Arco de Almedina,** a remnant of the Moorish town wall, one block uphill from Largo Portagem. At the top is the looming 12th-century Romanesque **Sé Velha** (Old Cathedral), complete with tombs, Gregorian chants, and a cloister. (Open M-Th 10am-noon and 2-7:30pm, F-Su 10am-1pm. Cloister 150$/€0.75, students 100$/€0.50.) Follow signs to the late-16th-century **Sé Nova** (New Cathedral), built for the Jesuits (open Tu-Sa 9am-noon and 2-6:30pm; free), just a few blocks from the 16th-century **University of Coimbra.** The **Porta Férrea** (Iron Gate), off R. São Pedro, opens onto the old university, whose buildings were Portugal's de facto royal palace when Coimbra was the kingdom's capital. (Open May-Sept. daily 9am-7:30pm; Oct.-Apr. 9:30am-12:30pm and 2-5:30pm.) The stairs to the right lead to the **Sala dos Capelos,** which houses portraits of Portugal's kings, six of them Coimbra-born. (Open daily 9:30am-12:30pm and 2-5:30pm. 500$/€2.50.) The **university chapel** and the mind-boggling, entirely gilded 18th-century **Biblioteca Joanina** (the university library) lie past the Baroque clock tower. Press the buzzer by the library door to enter three golden halls with 300,000 works from the 12th through 19th centuries. (Open May-Sept. daily 9am-7:30pm; Oct.-Apr. 9:30am-noon and 2-5:30pm. 500$/€2.50, students free. All university sights 800$/€4; buy tickets from the office in the main quad.) The 12th-century **Igreja de Santa Cruz**, Pr. 8 de Maio, at the far end of R. Ferreira Borges in the lower town, sits in somber, 12th-century beauty. (Open M-Sa 9am-noon and 2-5:45pm. Cloisters and sacristy 200$/€1.) Cross the bridge in front of Largo Portagem to find the 14th-century **Convento de Santa Clara-a-Velha** and the 17th-century **Convento de Santa Clara-a-Nova**.

Nightlife in Coimbra gets highest honors. **Café Tropical**, R. Nova, 30, is a great place to start the night. (Open M-Sa 9am-2am.) For clubs try **Via Latina**, R. Almeida Garrett, 1, around the corner and uphill from Pr. República, which is hot in all senses of the word (open M-Sa 11pm-7am); or **Hups!**, R. Castro Matoso, 11, one of the newest dance clubs in town (open Tu-Su 10pm-5am). Dance *and* use the **Internet** at **@caffé**, Lg. da Sé Velha, 4-8. (Open June to mid-Sept. M-Sa 11am-4am, mid-Sept. to May M-Sa 9pm-4am.) **The English Bar**, R. Lourenço de Almeida Azevedo, 24, is new and hip. (Open M-Sa 10pm-4am.) **Diligência Bar**, R. Nova 30, off R. Sofia, is known for its *fado*. (Open daily 10pm-2am.) In early May, graduates burn narrow ribbons they got as first-years and get wide ones in return during Coimbra's week-long festival, the **Queima das Fitas** (Burning of the Ribbons).

PORTO (OPORTO)   ☎22

Porto is famous for its namesake—sugary-strong port wine. Developed by English merchants in the early 18th century, the port industry is at the root of the city's successful economy. But there's more to Porto than just port (no, really). Situated on a gorge cut by the Douro River, Portugal's second-largest city is punctuated with granite church towers, orange-tiled houses, and graceful bridges.

█▓ TRANSPORTATION AND PRACTICAL INFORMATION. All trains pass through Porto's main station, **Estação Campanhã** (☎22 536 41 41), on R. da Estação. Trains run to: Coimbra (2hr., every hr. 5:05am-12:05am, 1050$/€5.25); Lisbon (4-4½hr., 14 per day 6am-8:05pm, 2150-3700$/€10.75-18.50); and Madrid (13-14hr., 6:10pm, 9030-9655$/€45-48.50). **Estação São Bento** (☎22 200 27 22), Pr. Almeida Garrett, centrally located one block off Pr. Liberdade, is the terminus for trains with local and regional routes. Rede Expresso **buses**, R. Alexandre Herculano, 366 (☎22 205 24 59), in the Garagem Atlântico, has buses to Coimbra (1½hr., 11 per day 7:15am-12:45am, 1410$/€7) and Lisbon (4hr., 12 per day 7:15am-12:45am, 2300$/€11.50). REDM (☎22 200 31 52), R. Dr. Alfredo Magalhães, 94, two blocks from Pr. República, sends buses to Braga (1hr.; M-F 26 per day 6:45am-8pm, Sa-Su 9-12 per day 7:15am-8pm; 680$/€3.40). Buy tickets for the **intracity buses** and **trams** from small kiosks around the city, or at the **STCP office**, Pr. Almeida Garrett, 27, downhill and across the street from Estação de São Bento (pre-purchased single ticket 85$/€0.45; 1-day unlimited ticket 500$/€2.50). Get a map at the **tourist office**, R. Clube dos Fenianos, 25, off Pr. Liberdade. (Open July-Sept. daily 9am-7pm; Oct.-June M-F 9am-5:30pm, Sa-Su 9:30am-4:30pm.) Check **email** at **Portweb**, Pr. Gen. Humberto Delgado 291, by Pr. Liberdade. (100-240$/€0.50-1.20 per hr. Open M-Sa 10am-2am, Su 3pm-2am.) The **post office** is on Pr. Gen. Humberto Delgado. (☎22 340 02 00. Open M-F 8:30am-9pm, Sa-Su 9am-6pm.) **Postal code:** 4000.

█▐ ACCOMMODATIONS AND FOOD. For good deals, look west of Av. Aliados or on R. Fernandes Tomás and R. Formosa, perpendicular to **Aliados Square**. **Pensão Duas Nações**, Pr. Guilherme Gomes Fernandes, 59, offers a variety of rooms at corresponding prices. (☎22 208 96 21. Curfew 2am. Singles 2200-2500$/€11-12.50; doubles 3800$/€19.) A few blocks away from the noisy city center, **Pensão Portuguesa**, Tr. Coronel Pacheco, 11, is one of the cheapest options in the city. (☎22 200 41 74. July-Aug. singles 2500$/€12.50, with bath 3000$/€15; doubles 3000$/€15, 4000$/€20. Sept.-June singles 2000$/€10; doubles 2500/€12.50.) Take bus #35 from Estação Campanha or #37 from Pr. Liberdade to **Pousada de Juventude do Porto (HI)**, R. Paulo da Gama, 551. (☎22 617 72 47. Reception daily 8am-

THAT TOOK GUTS When native son Henry the Navigator geared up to conquer Cueta in the early 15th century, Porto's residents slaughtered their cattle, gave the meat to Prince Henry's fleet, and kept only the entrails. This dramatic generosity came in the wake of the Plague, when food supplies were crucial. The dish *tripàs a moda do Porto* commemorates their culinary sacrifice; to this day, the people of Porto are known as *tripeiros* (tripe-eaters). If you're feeling adventurous, try some of the tripe dishes, which locals—and few others—consider quite a delicacy.

midnight. June-Sept. dorms 2500$/€12.50; doubles with bath 6000$/€30. Oct.-May dorms 2000$/€10; doubles 5000$/€25.) Take bus #6, 50, 54, or 87 from Pr. Liberdade (only buses #50 and 54 run at night) to **camp at Prelada,** on R. Monte dos Burgos, in Quinta da Prelada, 3km from the town center. (☎22 831 26 16. Reception 8am-11pm. 620$/€3.10 per person, 520-590$/€2.60-3 per tent, and 520$/€2.60 per car.) Look near the river in the **Ribeira** district on C. Ribeira, R. Reboleira, and R. Cima do Muro for great restaurants. The ■**Majestic Café**, R. de Santa Catarina, 112, is the oldest, most famous cafe in Porto. (Open M-Sa 9:30am-midnight.) Across the street, **Confeitaria Império**, R. de Santa Catarina, 149-151, serves excellent pastries and inexpensive lunch specials. (Open M-Sa 7:30am-8:30pm.)

■🎵 **SIGHTS AND ENTERTAINMENT.** Your first brush with Porto's rich stock of fine artwork may be the celebrated collection of *azulejos* (tiles) in the **São Bento train station.** Walk past the station and uphill on Av. Afonso Henriques to reach Porto's pride and joy, the 12th- to 13th-century Romanesque **cathedral.** (Open M-Sa 9am-12:30pm and 2:30-6pm, Su 2:30-6pm. Cloister 250$/€1.25.) From the station, follow signs downhill on R. Mouzinho da Silveira to R. Ferreira Borges and the ■ **Palácio da Bolsa** (Stock Exchange), the epitome of 19th-century elegance. The ornate **Sala Árabe** (Arabic Hall) took 18 years to decorate. (Open M-F 9am-6:40pm, Sa-Su 9am-12:30pm and 2-6:30pm. Tours every 30min, 800$/€4.) Next door, the Gothic **Igreja de São Francisco** glitters with an elaborately gilded wooden interior. Thousands of human bones are stored under the floor. (Open daily 9am-6pm. 500$/€2.50, students 250$/€1.25.) From Pr. Liberdade up R. dos Clérigos rises the **Torre dos Clérigos** (Tower of Clerics), adjacent to the **Igreja dos Clérigos.** (Tower open daily June-July 10am-7pm; Aug. 10am-10pm; Sept.-May 10am-noon and 2-5pm. 200$/€1. Church open M-Th 10am-noon and 2-5pm, Sa 10am-noon and 2-8pm, Su 10am-1pm. Church free.) From there, head up R. Restauração, turn right on R. Alberto Gouveia, and go left on R. Dom Manuel II to reach the **Museu Nacional Soares dos Reis**, R. Dom Manuel II, 44. This former royal residence now houses an exhaustive collection of 19th-century Portuguese painting and sculpture. (Open Tu 2-6pm, W-Su 10am-6pm. 600$/€3, students and seniors 300$/€1.50.) To get to Porto's rocky and polluted (but popular) **beach,** in the ritzy Foz district, take bus #1 from the São Bento train station or tram #1 from Igreja de São Francisco.

But we digress—back to your main focus of interest. Fine and bounteous port wines are available for tasting at 20-odd **port wine lodges,** usually *gratuito* (free). The lodges are all across the river in **Vila Nova da Gaia**—from the Ribeira district, cross the lower level of the large bridge. **Sandeman,** with its costumed guides (500$/€2.50), is a good start. **Ferreira,** one block up from the end of Av. Ramos Pinto, creates a memorable atmosphere. ■**Taylor's**, R. do Choupelo, 250, has a terrace with views of the city. (Most open daily 10am-6pm.)

BRAGA
☎253

Braga (pop. 160,000) originally served as the capital of a district founded by Celtic tribes in 300 BC. Today's residents still consider their city's beautiful gardens, plazas, museums, and markets worthy of the nickname "Portuguese Rome." In Portugal's oldest **cathedral,** the treasury showcases the archdiocese's most precious paintings and relics, including a collection of *cofres cranianos* (brain boxes). (Cathedral and treasury open daily June-Aug. 8:30am-6:30pm; Sept.-May 8:30am-5:30pm. Cathedral free. Treasury 300$/€1.50.) Braga's most famous landmark, **Igreja**

do Bom Jesús, is actually 5km outside of town. To visit Bom Jesús, either take the 285m ride on the antique funicular (8am-8pm; 120$/€0.60), or walk 25-30min. up the granite-paved pathway that forks into two zig-zagging 565-step stairways.

Buses (☎253 61 60 80) leave Central de Camionagem for: Coimbra (3hr.; M-F 6-9 per day, Sa-Su 7 per day 6am-11:30pm; 1600$/€8); Guimarães (1hr., every 30min. 7am-8pm, 385$/€2); Lisbon (5¼hr., 8-9 per day 9:30am-11:30pm, 2300$/€11.50); and Porto (1½hr., every 45min. 6:45am-8pm, 680$/€3.40). The **tourist office,** Av. Central, 1, is on the corner of Pr. República. (☎253 26 25 50. Open July-Sept. M-F 9am-7pm, Sa-Su 9am-12:30pm and 2-5:30pm; Oct.-June M-F 9am-7pm, Sa 9am-12:30pm and 2-5:30pm.)

⚄ DAYTRIP FROM BRAGA: GUIMARÃES. Ask any Portugal native about the city of Guimarães (pop. 60,000), and they will tell you that it was the birthplace of the nation. It is here that one of Portugal's most gorgeous palatial estates resides. The ⚄Paço dos Duques de Bragança (Ducal Palace) is modeled after the manor houses of northern Europe. Overlooking the city is the Monte da Pena, home to an excellent campsite as well as picnic areas, mini-golf, and cafes. To get there, take the teleférico (skyride), that runs in summer from Lg. das Hortas. (☎253 51 50 85. Open June-July and Sept. M-F 11am-7pm, Sa-Su 10am-8pm; Aug. daily 10am-8pm. 300$/€1.50, 500$/€2.50 return.) The **tourist office** is on Alameda de São Dámaso, 83, facing Pr. Toural. (☎253 41 24 50. Open M-Sa June-Sept. 9:30am-7pm; Oct.-May 9:30am-6pm.) Guimarães is best reached by **bus** from Braga. REDM buses (☎253 51 62 29) run frequently between the cities until 8:30pm (40min., 400$/€2).

VIANA DO CASTELO   ☎258

Situated in the northwestern corner of the country, Viana do Castelo (pop. 20,000), is one of the loveliest coastal cities in all of Portugal. Even in a country famed for its impressive squares, Viana do Castelo's ⚄**Praça da República** is remarkable. Diagonally across the plaza, granite columns support the flowery façade of the **Igreja da Misericórdia.** Known for its *azulejo* interior, the ⚄**Monte de Santa Luzia,** overlooking the city, is crowned by magnificent Celtic ruins and the **Templo de Santa Luzia,** an early 20th-century neo-Byzantine church. The view of Viana from the hill is fantastic. For more views of the harbor and ocean, visit the **Castelo de São Tiago da Barra,** built by Felipe I of Spain. Viana do Castelo and the surrounding coast feature excellent beaches. Most convenient are **Praia Norte,** at the end of Av. do Atlántico at the west end of town, and **Praia da Argaçosa,** on Rio Lima.

Trains (☎258 82 13 15), at the top of Av. Combatentes da Grande Guerra, run to Porto (2hr., 13-14 per day 5am-9:27pm, 800$/€4.00). **Buses** run to: Braga (1½hr.; M-Sa 6-8 per day 7am-6:35pm, Su 4 per day 8:15am-6:35pm; 700$/€3.50); Porto (2hr.; M-F 9 per day 6:45am-6:30pm, Sa-Su 4-6 per day 8:20am-6:30pm; 750-1050$/€3.50-5.25); and Lisbon (5½hr.; Su-F 3 per day 8am-11:45pm, Sa 7am and 12:30pm; 2500$/€17.50). The **tourist office,** R. do Hospital Velho, at the corner of Pr. Erva. has a helpful English-speaking staff and offers maps and accommodations lists. (☎258 82 26 20. Open May-July and Sept. M-Sa 9am-1pm and 2:30-6pm, Su 9:30am-1pm; Aug. daily 9am-7pm; Oct.-Apr. M-Sa 9am-12:30pm and 2:30-5:30pm.) The ⚄**Pousada de Juventude de Viana do Castelo (HI),** R. da Argaçosa (Azenhas D. Prior), is right on the marina, off Pr. de Galiza. (☎258 80 02 60; fax 258 82 08 70. Reception 8am-midnight. Checkout 10am. Reservations recommended. Mid-Sept.to mid-June dorms 2000$/€10.00; doubles with bath 5000$/€25.00. Mid-June to mid-Sept. dorms 2500$/€17.50.)

ROMANIA
(ROMÂNIA)

PHONE CODES | **Country code:** 40. **International dialing prefix:** 00. From outside Romania, dial int'l dialing prefix (see inside back cover) + 40 + city code + local number.

Devastated by the lengthy reign of Nicolae Ceauşescu, Romania today suffers under the effects of a sluggish economy and a government that seems to care little for ordinary people. Some Romanians are eager to move the country to Western European standards, while others are eager to simply move to Western Europe. The resulting state of flux, combined with a largely undeserved reputation for poverty and crime, has discouraged many foreigners from visiting. But travelers who dismiss Romania do themselves an injustice—whatever else may be, it is a country rich in history, rustic beauty, and hospitality. The general absence of tourists is bad for Romania, but good for visitors as prices remain low and sights remain untainted by the hand of commercialism. But things are changing. A recent change in visa regulations has made it easier for EU citizens to enter the country—more and more Europeans are including Bucharest on their itineraries. These visitors are discovering a land of cosmopolitan cities, lovely medieval villages and endless stretches of pristine countryside. So go find out for yourself, before the tourists beat you to it.

For more on Romania, check out *Let's Go: Eastern Europe 2002*.

FACTS AND FIGURES

Official Name: Romania.

Capital: Bucharest (pop. 2,100,000).

Major Cities: Bucharest, Cluj-Napoca, Braşov.

Population: 22,400,000.

Land Area: 230,340 sq. km.

Climate: Temperate and continental.

Languages: Romanian (official), Hungarian, German.

Religions: Romanian Orthodox (70%), Roman Catholic (6%), Protestant (6%).

DISCOVER ROMANIA

Romania is blessed with snowy peaks, a superb chunk of Black Sea coast, and culturally rich cities—all at half the price of similar attractions in Western Europe. Vast and hectic **Bucharest** (p. 777), the capital, surprises with good museums, expanses of green parks, myriad historical monuments, and an *über*-hip, *über*-Euro night scene. For a hefty dose of Transylvanian vampire mythology, visit **Bran** (p. 781), home to the legendary castle of Count Dracula. Nearby **Braşov** (p. 781) provides access to the trails and slopes of the Transylvanian Alps.

Culture is centered in **Cluj-Napoca** (p. 781), Romania's student capital and the most diverse city in the country. For a holier take on Romania, visit the secluded **Bukovina Monasteries** (p. 783) near Gura Humorului.

ESSENTIALS

WHEN TO GO

As Romania suffers fairly hot summers and cold winters, spring and fall are the best times to visit. Winters can be very cold and the mountains are always colder than the lowlands; there is often a lot of precipitation. The coasts are more moderate.

DOCUMENTS AND FORMALITIES

VISAS. Citizens of Australia, Canada, Ireland, New Zealand, South Africa, and the UK all need visas to enter Romania. Americans do not need visas for stays of up to 30 days; Americans can obtain a visa extension at police headquarters in large cities or at Bucharest's passport office, Str. Luigi Cazzavillan 11. Apply early to allow the bureaucratic process to run its slow, frustrating course. The best way to cross the border is to take a direct train from Bucharest to the capital city of the neighboring country; the next best options are planes and buses.

EMBASSIES. Foreign embassies in Romania are in **Bucharest** (p. 777). For Romanian embassies at home: **Canada,** 655 Rideau St., Ottawa, ON K1N 6A3 (☎613-789-5345; fax 613-789-4365; romania@cyberus.ca); **Ireland,** 47 Ailesbury Rd. Ballsbridge, Dublin 4 (☎(353) 269 2852 or 269 2142; fax 269 2122); **South Africa,** 117 Charles St., Brooklyn, Pretoria; P.O. Box 11295, Brooklyn, 0181 (☎(012) 466 940; fax 466 947); **UK,** 4 Palace Green, Kensington, London W8 4QD (☎(020) 7937 9666; fax 7937 8069); and **US,** 1607 23rd St. NW, Washington, D.C. 20008 (☎202-332-4848; fax 232-4748; consular@roembus.org; www.roembus.org).

TRANSPORTATION

BY PLANE. Numerous airlines fly into Bucharest. **TAROM** (Romanian Airlines) is in the process of updating its aging fleet; it flies direct from Bucharest to New York, Chicago, and major European cities. The renovation of Bucharest's Otopeni International Airport has improved it, but the airport is still far from ideal.

BY TRAIN. Trains, a better option than buses, head daily to Western Europe via Budapest. To buy **international tickets** in Romania, go to the **CFR** (Che-Fe-Re) office in larger towns. While students discounts are technically for Romanians only, an ISIC might get you a 50% discount. **CFR** sells domestic **train** tickets up to 24hr. before the train's departure. After that, only train stations sell tickets. The English timetable *Mersul Trenurilor* is useful (L12,000). Schedule information is available at ☎221 in most cities. **Interrail** is accepted; **Eurail** is not. There are four types of trains: *InterCity* ("IC" on timetables and at train stations), *rapid* (in green), *accelerat* (red), and *personal* (black). International trains (often blue) are usually indicated by "i" on timetables. *InterCity* trains stop only at major cities. *Rapid* trains (also 3 digits) are the next fastest; *accelerat* trains have four digits starting with "1" and are slower. Take the fastest train you can, most often *accelerat*. There's not a big difference between **first class** (*clasa una;* wagons marked with a "1" on the side; 6 people per compartment) and **2nd class** (*clasa dova;* 8 people), except on **personal trains,** when it's well worth it. On an **overnight train,** shell out for first class in a *vagon de dormit* (sleeping carriage).

BY BUS. Buses connect major cities in Romania to Athens, Istanbul, Prague, and various cities in Western Europe. Since plane and train tickets to Romania are often expensive, buses are a good—if slow—option. It is best to take a domestic train to the border and catch an international bus from there. Buying tickets straight from the carrier saves you from paying commission. Only use

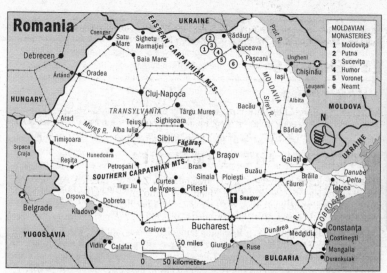

Romania

MOLDAVIAN MONASTERIES
1 Moldovița
2 Putna
3 Sucevița
4 Humor
5 Voroneț
6 Neamt

the local bus system if there is no other option; look for signs for the *autogară* (bus station) in each town.

BY BIKE AND BY THUMB. Biking is neither common nor very safe. *Let's Go* does not recommend **hitchhiking**. If you do go, know that drivers expect a payment similar to the price of a train ticket for the distance traveled, although some kind souls will take you for free or accept what you can afford. Never hitchhike at night.

TOURIST SERVICES AND MONEY

EMERGENCY   Police: ☎ 955. Ambulance: ☎ 961. Fire: ☎ 981.

MONEY. The Romanian unit of currency is the *leu*, plural *lei* (abbreviated L). The banknotes are L500, 1000, 5000, 10,000, 50,000, and 100,000. While many establishments accept US dollars or DM, you should pay for everything in *lei* to avoid rip-offs and to save your hard currency for bribes and emergencies. Private exchange bureaus litter the country; not many take credit cards or traveler's checks. Shop around for good rates. Dollars and Deutchmarks are preferred, although other Western currencies can usually be exchanged somewhere. ATMs, which generally accept Cirrus, Plus, MC, and Visa and give *lei* at reasonable rates, are rare outside major cities. It is customary to give inexact change for purchases, generally rounding to the nearest L500; this suffices as a tip in restaurants.

BUSINESS HOURS. Posted hours are not definite, and many banks and businesses may be closed on Friday afternoons.

COMMUNICATION

MAIL. Request *par avion* for airmail, which takes 2-3 weeks to reach international destinations. Mail can be received general delivery through *Poste Restante*.

TELEPHONES. Almost all public phones are orange and accept **phone cards**, although a few archaic blue phones take L500 coins. Buy L50,000, 100,000, and 200,000 phone cards at telephone offices, major Bucharest Metro stops, and some post offices. Rates run L10,000 per min. to neighboring countries, L14,000 per min. to most of Europe, and L18,000 per min. to the US. International direct

ROMANIA

> **BILLS, BILLS, BILLS** Romanian currency may seem a bit like
> play currency. The following is a handy guide to some of the finer aspects of Romanian
> bank notes. The L1000 bills feature a portrait of Mihai Eminescu, Romania's national
> poet, along with the linden flower, one of his favorite subjects. The L2000 note com-
> memorates the solar eclipse that was seen over the country in 1999. This bill, like the
> L10,000 note, is made of plastic. Try to tear it. Go ahead try. You can't. The L10,000
> bill has a portrait of statesman Nicolae Iorga (1871-1940) as well as a description of
> the monastery at Curtea de Arges, with its four domes and beautiful, twisted spires.

dial numbers include: **AT&T,** ☎01 800 4288; **British Telecom,** ☎01 800 4444; **Canada
Direct,** ☎01 800 5000; and **Sprint,** ☎01 800 0877. Make calls from orange phones in
major cities, and press "i" to operate in English. Local calls cost L595 per min.
and can be made from any phone; a busy signal may just indicate a connection
problem. To make a phone call *prin comandă* (with the help of the operator)
at the telephone office, write down the destination, duration, and phone number
for your call. Pay up front, and ask for the rate per minute.

LANGUAGES. Romanian is a Romance language; those familiar with French, Italian, Spanish, or Portuguese should be able to read signs. German and Hungarian
are widely spoken in Transylvania. German and French are 2nd languages for the
older generation, English for the younger. Get just enough Romanian on p. 987.

ACCOMMODATIONS AND CAMPING

While some **hotels** charge foreigners 50-100% more than locals, lodging is still
relatively cheap (US$6-20). One-star hotels are on par with mediocre European
youth hostels, two-star places are decent, and those with three are good but
expensive. **Private accommodations** are generally the way to go; be aware that
renting a room "together" means sharing a bed. Rooms run US$5-15 per per-
son, sometimes with breakfast and other amenities. See the room and fix a
price before accepting. Many towns allow foreign students to stay in **university
dorms** at low prices, but may be hard to find if you don't speak Romanian.
Campgrounds are crowded and often have frightening bathrooms. Relatively
cheap **bungalows** are often full in summer.

HEALTH AND SAFETY

Most public restrooms lack soap, towels, and toilet paper; carry a roll with you.
Beware the manic drivers in congested Bucharest, unlit carriages and carts, as well
as sheep and cows. *Farmacies* (drugstores) are a crapshoot and may not have
what you need. *Antinevralgic* is for headaches (though many pharmacists refer to
this painkiller as "tylenol"), *aspirină* or *piramidon* for colds and the flu, and *sap-
rosan* for diarrhea. *Prezervatives* (condoms) are available at all drugstores and at
many kiosks. There are some American medical clinics in Bucharest that have
some English-speaking doctors.

FOOD AND DRINK

Romanian food is fairly typical of Central Europe, with a bit of Balkan and
French influence thrown in. Bucharest is the only place to find non-Romanian
cuisine. Lunch usually starts with a soup, called *supă* or *ciorbă* followed by a
main dish (typically grilled meat) and dessert. Soups can be very tasty; try
ciorbă de perişoare (with vegetables and ground meatballs) or *supă cu găluşte*
(with fluffy dumplings). Pork comes in several varieties, of which *muşchi* and
cotlet are the best quality. For dessert, *clătite* (crepes), *papanaşi* (doughnuts
with jam and sour cream), and *tort* (creamy cakes) can all be fantastic if they're
fresh. Some restaurants charge by weight (usually 100g) rather than by portion.
Garnituri, the extras that come standard with a meal, are usually charged sep-

arately, down to that dollop of mustard. As a rule, you're paying for everything the waiters put in front of you. "Fast food" in Romania means pre-cooked and microwaved. Check expiration dates on everything you buy.

HOLIDAYS

Holidays: New Year's (Jan. 1-2); Epiphany (Jan. 6); Easter (Apr. 15-16); Labor Day (May 1); National Day (Dec. 1); Christmas (Dec. 25-26).

BUCHAREST   ☎01

Once a fabled beauty on the Orient Express, Bucharest is fabled today mostly for its infamous makeover under communist dictator Nicolae Ceauşescu; during his 25 years in power, grand boulevards and Ottoman remnants were replaced with wide highways and concrete blocks. Bucharest may not be beautiful, but it's never boring. Explore its historic neighborhoods, secluded parks, and serious club scene—before the tourist hordes realize what they've been missing.

▛ TRANSPORTATION

Flights: Otopeni Airport (☎230 00 22), 18km from the city. M2: Piaţa Universităţii. Buses from the airport go to Centru near Hotel Intercontinental Piaţa Universităţii. Bus #783 to Otopeni leaves from Piaţa Unirii every 20min. Buy **international tickets** at the **CFR/TAROM office,** Str. Brezoianu 10 (☎313 42 95). M2: Piaţa Universităţii; with the National Theater on your left, go right onto B-dul Regina Elisabeta, left after McDonald's, and left after 1 block onto Brezoianu.

Trains: Gara de Nord (☎228 08 80). M3: Gara de Nord. The main station. L3000 to enter the station if you're not catching a train. To: **Budapest** (14-17hr., 5 per day, L830,000); **Cluj-Napoca** (8hr., 3 per day, L237,000); **Iaşi** (7hr., 3 per day, L237,000); **İstanbul** (20hr., 1 per day, L700,000); **Sofia** (10-12hr., 3 per day, L580,000).

Buses: Filaret, Cuţitul de Argint 2 (☎335 11 40). M2: Tineretului. South of the Center. To Athens, your best bet is **Fotopoulos Express** (☎335 82 49). To Istanbul, catch a **Toros** or a **Murat** bus from outside Gara de Nord. **Double T,** Str. Ankara 12 (☎313 36 42), affiliated with Eurail, or **Eurolines Touring,** str. Ankara 6 (☎230 03 70) can get you to Western Europe. All international bus companies are near Piaţa Dorobanţilor.

Public Transportation: Buses, trolleys, and **trams** cost L5000. Buy tickets from a kiosk; you can't get them on board. Validate on board or face a fine. All **express buses** except #783 take only magnetic cards (L20,000 return). Beware pickpockets during peak hrs. The **Metro** offers reliable, less-crowded service to major points (5am-11:30pm). Magnetic cards L10,000 for 2 trips; L37,000 for 10 trips; L15,000 for a day pass.

Taxis: Cobălcescu (☎94 51), **Cristaxi** (☎94 61), **Perozzi** (☎96 31). Ask the drivers to use the meter. Expect to pay L4000-5000 per km.

✴▮ ORIENTATION AND PRACTICAL INFORMATION

Bucharest's six sectors circle clockwise around the city. In the northern portion are **Piaţa Victoriei** and **Piaţa Romană,** as well as the train station, **Gara de Nord.** In the southeast corner are what remains of Bucharest's **Old Town** and **Piaţa Unirii, Piaţa Universităţii,** and **Piaţa Revolutiei.** Gara de Nord lies along the M3 Metro line just west of Centru. Take a train (dir. Dristor II) one stop to Piaţa Victoriei, change to the M2 line to Depoul; take this train one stop to Piaţa Romana, two stops to Piaţa Universităţii, or three stops to Piaţa Unirii. For a great guide to the city, get *Bucharest in Your Pocket* (L20,000) at many museums, bookstores, and some hotels.

Police: ☎955. **Ambulance:** ☎961. **Fire:** ☎981.

Tourist Information: Several private tourist offices on Gara de Nord. Hotels and hostels are another good source of information.

Embassies: Australia, Bd. Unirii 74, Et. 5 (☎320 98 02). M2: Piaţa Unirii. Open M-Th 9:30am-12:30pm. **Canada,** Str. Nicolae Iorga 36 (☎307 50 00). M2: Piaţa Romană. Open M-Th 8:30am-5pm, F 8:30am-2pm. **Irish Consulate,** Str. V. Lascăr 42-44 (☎211 39 67). M2: Piaţa Romană. Open M-F 10am-noon and phone inquires 2-4pm. **UK,** Str. Jules Michelet 24 (☎312 03 03). M2: Piaţa Romană. Open M-Th 8:30am-1pm and 2-5pm, F 8:30am-1:30pm. **US,** Str. Tudor Arghezi 7/9 (☎210 40 42; after hours ☎210 01 49). M2: Piaţa Universităţii. Citizens of **New Zealand** should contact UK embassy. Citizens of **South Africa** should contact their embassy in Budapest (p. 511).

Currency Exchange: Exchange houses are everywhere; **ATMs,** at major banks, always give the best rates. Don't change money on the street; it's almost always a scam.

American Express: Marshall Tourism, Bd. Magheru 43, 1st fl., #1 (☎223 12 04). M2: Piaţa Romană. Cannot cash traveler's checks. Open M-F 9am-5pm, Sa 9am-1pm.

Luggage Storage: At Gara de Nord. Foreigners pay L13,000 or L26,000. Open 24hr.

Pharmacy: Farmadex, Calea Moşilor 280 (☎211 95 60).

Internet Access: D&D Internet Cafe, Bd. Carol I 25, (☎313 10 48). M2: Piaţa Universităţii. Head east on Bd. Carol I past Piaţa Rosetti. L40,000 per hr. Open 24hr.

Telephones: Telephone office, Calea Victoriei 37. Open M-F 8am-8pm, Sa 8am-2pm. Phone cards L50,000, L100,000, or L200,000.

Post Office: Str. Matei Millo 10 (☎315 90 30). M2: Piaţa Universităţii. Open M-F 7:30am-7:30pm, Sa 7:30am-2pm. *Poste Restante* nearby, next to Hotel Carpati. Address mail to be held: First name SURNAME, *Poste Restante,* Str. Matei Millo 10, Bucharest **70000** ROMANIA.

ACCOMMODATIONS

Renting private rooms is not common. However, you can't can't go wrong with either of Bucharest's two youth hostels.

■ **Villa Helga Youth Hostel,** Str. Salcâmilor 2 (☎610 22 14). M2: Piaţa Romană. Take bus #86, 79, or 133 from Gara de Nord to Piaţa Gemeni. Continue 1 block on Bd. Dacia and turn right on Str. Viitorului. Romania's original hostel. Call ahead in summer. Breakfast. Kitchen. US$12 per day; US$72 per week; US$196 per month.

■ **Elvis's Villa,** Str. Avram Iancu 5 (☎(01) 315 5273; www.elvisvilla.ro). M2: Piaţa Universităţii. From Gara de Nord, take trolley bus #85 to the Calea Moşilor stop. Continue along Bd. Carol I into Piaţa Protopescu, turn right onto Str. Sfantul Ştefan and left onto Str. Avram Iancu. Brand-new hostel run by Australians. A/C and fat mattresses. TV, laundry-service, Internet, drinks and breakfast included. US$12 per day; $72 per week.

Hotel Cerna, Str. Golescu 29 (☎311 05 35). M3: Gara de Nord. One-star hotel next to train station. Singles L315,000, with bath L450,000; doubles L450-600,000.

FOOD

Open-air markets offer veggies, fruits, meat, and cheese in Bucharest—a good one is at **Piaţa Gemeni,** near the corner of Bd. Dacia and Str. Lascăr. Eat at **La Mama,** Str. Barbu Văcărescu 3 at M3: Ştefan cel Mare. (☎212 40 86. Traditional Romanian dishes L50-80,000. Reservations recommended. Open daily 10am-2am.) From Villa Helga, turn right out of the hostel and take the first right to get to **Nicoreşti,** Str. Maria Rosetti 40, if you're still in the mood for Romanian. (M2: Piaţa Romană or trolley #79, 86, or 226. Main dishes L40-60,000. Open M-Sa 11am-11pm, Su 1-11pm.)

SIGHTS

Wide streets with villas, green parks, Communist apartments, and fledgling businesses leave a confusing impression of the past. Bucharest is on the brink of something, but nobody seems to know what it is.

CIVIC CENTER. In order to create the long dreamed-of Socialist capital, Ceauşescu destroyed 5 sq. km of Bucharest's historic center, demolishing over 9000 19th-century houses and displacing more than 40,000 Romanians. The

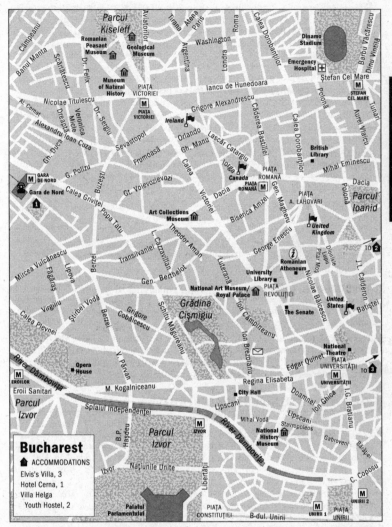

Bucharest

⌂ ACCOMMODATIONS

Elvis's Villa, 3
Hotel Cerna, 1
Villa Helga
Youth Hostel, 2

unfinished **Civic Center** lies at the end of the 6km. B-dul Unirii, intentionally built slightly larger than the Champs-Elysées, after which it was modeled. Its centerpiece, the **Parliamentary Palace** (Palatul Parlamentului), is the world's second-largest building (after the Pentagon in Washington, D.C.) and was built by 70,000 workers using wood and marble exclusively from Romania. *(M1, 3: Izvor. Entrance off Calea 13 Septembrie, on the left side of building from Bd. Unirii. Open daily 10am-4pm. Tours L60,000, students L25,000.)*

SIGHTS OF THE REVOLUTION. Bucharest is slowly putting the memory of its 1989 revolution behind it. Demonstrators were killed fighting Ceauşescu's forces here December 21, 1989, the day before his fall. After Ceauşescu was deposed, students gathered in the small Piaţa 22 Decembrie 1989, opposite Hotel Intercontinental, to protest the neo-Communist government that succeeded him. In June, the government bused in 10,000 Romanian miners to quash the protestors, killing 21 students. White crosses and plaques remind visitors of those who died during the revolution of 1989. **Piața Universității** houses memorials to victims of both the 1989 and June 1990 revolutions. *(M2: Piața Universității; behind the fountain.)* With Hotel Intercontinental on your left, make a right onto Bd. Regina Elisabeta and then a right onto Calea Victoriei to reach **Piața Revoluției,** where the first shots of the revolution were fired.

PARKS. Bucharest's extensive park system is a nice break from the urban grime. The **botanical gardens,** surrounding a pristine lake, were the site of demonstrations during the 1848 revolution. *(M1: Politehnica. Buses #62, 71, 93, 61, 306, and 336 stop at entrance, Şos. Cotroceni 32. Open in summer M-Sa 8am-8pm, Su 9am-1pm. L10,000, students L5000.)* Sprawling **Herăstrău Park** is just north of downtown. Within the park lies Bucharest's largest lake, wandering peacocks, and the small Island of Roses. *(M2: Aviatorilor.)* One of Bucharest's oldest parks, the **Cişmigiu Gardens,** is filled with elegant paths and another little lake with paddle boats. *(M2: Piața Universității. With Hotel Intercontinental on your left, make a right on Bd. Regina Elisabeta. Open daily 8am-8pm.)*

MUSEUMS. The **National Art Museum** (Muzeul National de Artă), Calea Victorei 49-53, in Piata Revolutiei., has just reopened, with works by Rembrandt, Monet, and Romania's own impressionist Nicolae Grigorescu. *(M2: Piața Universitatii. Open W-Sa 11am-7pm. L30,000, students L15,000.)* The **Museum of the Romanian Peasant** (Muzeul Tbranului Român), 7os. Kiseleff 3, is worth a visit. *(M2, 3: Piata Victoriei. Open Tu-Su 10am-6pm. L25,000, students L5000.)*

OTHER SIGHTS. If you're in the mood for something truly Romanian, visit the huge **market** at the Obor Metro stop. Among other things, you're likely to find eggs, raw wool, rusty nails, Bulgarian cigarettes, Turkish Levis, shower heads, ceramic plates, and ducks. *(M3: Obor.)* Several of modern Bucharest's most fashionable streets are sights in and of themselves; be sure to stroll along **Calea Victoriei, Şos. Kiseleff, B-dul. Aviatorilor,** and **B-dul. Magheru.** The sidestreets just off Piața Victoriei and Calea Dorobanților, with names like Paris, Washington, and Londra, brim with villas and houses typical of beautiful 19th-century Bucharest.

🎵 🎭 ENTERTAINMENT AND NIGHTLIFE

MUSIC, THEATER AND OPERA. Bucharest hosts some of the biggest rock festivals this side of Berlin (Michael Jackson once greeted screaming fans here with "Hello, Budapest!") **Theater** and **opera** are cheap in Bucharest (L6,000-55,000), but there are no shows June-Sept. Tickets go on sale at each theater's box office the Saturday before the performance. Try the **Teatrul Național,** Bd. N. Bălcescu 2 (M2: Piața Universității), for drama shows. **Atheneul Român** (☎315 89 98; M2: Piața Universități) holds classical music concerts. **Opera Romănă,** Bd. M.L. Kogălniceanu 70 (☎313 18 57; M1, 3: Eroilor), stages top-notch opera for very low prices.

Pack a map and cab fare—streets are poorly lit and public transportation stops at 11:30pm. **Swing House,** Str. Gabroveni 20, has live blues and jazz on weekends. (M2: Piața Unirii. Open daily 6pm-late.) **Club A,** Str. Blanari 14, is always crowded. (M2: Piața Universității. Cover F-Sa. Open M-Th 11pm-5am, F 11pm-7am, Sa 9pm-7am, Su 9pm-5am.) **Twice,** Str. Sfânta Vineri 4, is a massive complex of bars, lounges, and dance floors. (M2: Piata Universitbtii. Open daily 9pm-late.)

TRANSYLVANIA

Although the name evokes images of a dark land of black magic and vampires, Transylvania *(Ardeal)* is a region of green hills and mountains descending gently from the Carpathians to the Hungarian Plain. The vampire legends, have their roots in the architecture: Transylvanian buildings are tilted, jagged, and more sternly Gothic than anywhere else in Eastern Europe.

CLUJ-NAPOCA
☎064

Cluj-Napoca is Transylvania's unofficial capital and student center. Colorful, relaxed, and relatively Western (with a sizable Hungarian minority), Cluj is a good starting point for a journey farther into Transylvania or north to Maramureş. The 80m Gothic steeple of the Catholic **Church of St. Michael** (Biserica Sf. Mihail) pierces the skyline in **Piaţa Unirii.** Standing in Piaţa Unirii and looking up Str. Regele Ferdinand toward the train station, turn right onto B-dul 21 Dicembrie 1989 to arrive at Piaţa Avram Iancu and its centerpiece, the Byzantine-Roman **Orthodox Cathedral** (Catedrala Arhiepiscopală). To reach **Cetătuie Hill,** where a dazzling view of the city awaits, walk back to Piaţa Unirii and take a right on Bd. Ferdinand. After you cross the river, take a left on Str. Dragalina and climb the stairs to your right. To visit the serene **Botanical Gardens** (Grădină Botanica), go back to Piaţa Unirii, take a right (with your back to the statue) on Str. Napoca, and take a left on Str. Coh. Bilaşcu. (Open daily 9am-6pm. L5000.)

Trains (☎42 30 01) run from Piaţa Mihai Viteazul to: Bucharest (7hr.; 6 per day; *accelerat* L120,000); Iaşi (9hr.; 3 per day; *accelerat* L138,000); and Budapest (10hr.; 2 per day; return L440,000). **Buses** (☎43 52 78) leave from Str. Giordano Bruno 3, near the train station. **Local buses** and **trams** run 5am-midnight; buy tickets (return L8500) at **RATUC** kiosks. **Taxis** line up at the bus and train stations. (☎953, 946, or 948. About L5000 per km.) **ATMs** are along Bd. Ferdinand and surround Piaţa Unirii. Check email at the **Kiro Internet Cafe,** Bd. Ferdinand 6, 3rd fl. (L7-9000 per hr. Open 24hr.) **Hotel Vladeasa,** Str. Regele Ferdinand 20, has clean, simple rooms around small courtyard. (☎19 44 29. Breakfast included. Singles L315,000, with shower L360,000; doubles L510-570,000.) **Postal code:** 3400.

BRAŞOV
☎068

Braşov is an ideal starting point for trips into the mountains. Its exquisite city center is also a worthwhile stop in itself. Beyond the square along Str. Gh. Bariţiu looms the Lutheran **Black Church** (Biserica Neagră), Romania's most celebrated Gothic church, so named because it was charred by fire in 1689. (Open M-Sa 10am-5pm. L8100, students L4000.) **Piaţa Sfatului** and **Str. Republicii** are perfect for a stroll. To see the mountains without breaking a sweat, ride a **cable car** *(telecabina)* up Muntele Tâmpa from Aleea T. Brediceanu. Walk up Str. Republicii from Piaţa Sfatului and turn right onto Str. M. Weiss, then right on Str. Brediceanu, left onto steep Str. Suişul Castalului, and right on a paved road to climb two flights of stairs. (Runs M-F 9:30am-7pm, Sa-Su 9:30am-8pm. L30,000 return). To climb a road less traveled, trails on Aleea T. Brediceanu lead to the **Weaver's Bastion** and other medieval ruins.

Trains go to: Bucharest (3-4hr.; 19 per day; L64,000); Cluj-Napoca (5-6hr.; 6 per day; L70,000); and Iaşi (7hr.; 1 per day; L135,000). Get train information at **CFR,** str. Republicii 53. (Open M-F 8am-7pm, Sa 9am-1pm.) To get from the station to town, take bus #10 to the main **Piaţa Sfatului** (10min.); get off in front of Black Church. Good maps are at kiosks on Str. Republicii. Expect to pay US$8-12 for a private room. **Casa Beke,** Str. Cerbului 32, rents rooms just a few blocks from the main square. Follow Str. Republicii to Piaţa Sfatului, turn left onto Str. Apollonia Hirscher, then take the second right on Str. Cerbului. (L250,000 per person.) **Hotel Aro Sport,** Str. Sfântul Ioan 3, has pleasant rooms. Walk up Str. Mureşenilor from Piaţa Sfatului and turn right on Str. Sfântul Ioan. (☎47 88 00. Reception 24hr. Singles L272,000; doubles L340,000.) For Romanian and Mexican food and free shots of *palinka*, head to **Bella Musica,** Str. G. Baritu nr. 2. (Main dishes L50-70,000. Open daily 1pm-midnight.) **Postal code:** 2200.

⚑ DAYTRIPS FROM BRAŞOV: BRAN AND SIGHIŞOARA. It's a dark and stormy night—the perfect setting for **Bran,** once the home of Vlad Ţepeş Dracula (literally Vlad the Impaler, son of Dracul), the supposed villain-hero of Bram Stoker's famed novel *Dracula.* As Prince of Wallachia, Vlad Ţepeş was charged with protecting the Bran pass and had to impale some Turks as part of his job; no

I VANT TO... While Bran castle may be underwhelming, the gruesome exploits of its temporary tenant make the horror novel pale in comparison. Born in Sighişoara in 1431, Vlad Ţepeş' father (also Vlad) was a member of the Order of the Dragon, a society charged with defending Catholicism from infidels. Hence the name by which he ruled: Vlad Dracul ("Dragon"), and his son's moniker Dracula, "son of the dragon," which was corrupted to "son of the devil" as word of his atrocities spread. In 1444, Vlad's father shipped his two sons off to a Turkish prison to placate an Ottoman ruler. There Vlad learned the tortures for which he would become infamous, including a method that can only be described as horse-powered anal impalement. When the Turks invaded Wallachia in 1462, they were met by some 20,000 of their kinsmen impaled this way outside Dracula's territory. Horrified, the Turks retreated. Dracula also practiced such terror tactics on his own people. In order to alleviate poverty in his realm, for example, the he invited the destitute and disabled to his palace for a banquet ... and then had them burned to death.

blood-drinking or biting is on the record. Vampires aside, the **castle** is worth a visit. (Open Tu-Su 9am-5pm. L50,000, students L15,000.) To get to Bran from Braşov, take a **trolleybus** to Autogară 2 (officially Gară Bartolomeu), where **buses** go to Bran (45min., every hr., L16000). To reach the castle, get off at the main stop by the "Cabana Bran Castle—500m" sign. Then take the main road back toward Braşov and take the first right. (Open daily 8am-6pm.)

Sighişoara (see-ghee-SHWAH-rah) is perhaps Transylvania's most pristine and enchanting medieval town. Surrounded by mountains and crowning a green hill, the citadel's gilded steeples and old clock tower have survived centuries of attacks, fires, and dozens of floods. The **Citadel** (Cetate), built by the Saxons in 1191, is now a tiny medieval city-within-a-city. For a walking tour of the Citadel, follow the white and red arrows that start next to Vlad Dracul's house. (Open Tu-F 9am-6pm, Sa-M 9am-4pm.) Once a year, in July or August, the town hosts a huge free **medieval festival.** To reach the center from the train station, take a right on **Str. Libertăţii,** and your first left onto **Str. Gării,** veer left at the Russian cemetery, turn right, cross the footbridge over river **Târnava Mare,** and walk down Str. Morii. **Trains** run to Bucharest (5hr.; 9 per day; L83,000) and Brasov (2hr.; L80,000). ☎065

SINAIA   ☎044

The Romanian royal family chose to live in Sinaia when they were away from Cotroceni in Bucharest. Although the construction of ◪**Peleş Castle** (Castelul Peleş) began in 1873, it has central heating, electric lights, and an elevator. (Open Tu 12:15-5pm, W-Su 9am-5pm. L60,000; students L25,000.) While Peleş was built by King Carol I, the equally striking ◪**Pelişor Castle,** built in the early-20th century, was designed by his wife Queen Maria, who wanted it to fit progressive modern tastes. (Open Th 12:15am-5pm, W-Su 9am-5pm. L40,000; students L15,000.) The cable car *(telecabina)* to **Cota 1400** (L20,000; return L35,000) leads to alpine hikes. Along the Bucegi range, the yellow stripe trail leads intense hikers on a strenuous 4hr. climb from **Cota 2000,** past **Babele** (2200m, accessible by cable car from the nearby town of Buşteni) to **Omu** (2500m), the highest peak of Bucegi. **Trains** go to Braşov (2½hr.; 3 per day; L65,000) and Bucharest (6hr.; 7 per day; L107,000). From the station, cross the street, climb two flights of stairs, take a left onto a cobblestone ramp at the first landing, climb the first steps, and take two left turns onto Bd. Carol I, the main street. From Str. Magheru, walk to the far side of Pţa. Mare and head right. past the museum and down the stairs on the right, then left to get to the hostel-like ◪**Hotel Pensiune Leu,** Str. Moş Ion Roată 6. (☎21 83 92. Reception 24hr. L150,000 per bed.) If a real hotel is more your bag, try **Hotel Bulevard,** Pţa. Unirii 10. (☎21 60 60. Singles L530,000; doubles L920,000.) To reach an **outdoor market,** follow the directions to Hotel Pensiune Leu, but walk straight instead of turning left at the bottom of the stairs. (Open dawn-dusk.) **Postal code:** 2180.

MOLDAVIA AND BUKOVINA

Eastern Romania, known as Moldavia, extends from the Carpathians to the Prut River. Starker than Transylvania and more developed than Maramureş, Moldavia is home to the beautifully painted monasteries of Bukovina.

IAŞI ☎ 032

Iaşi (YASH) rose to prominence in the 19th century as the home of a famous literary society, and still retains much of its original Neoclassical architecture. From the main square, **Piaţa Unirii**, Str. Ştefan cel Mare leads south past the gorgeous 1637 Trei **Ierarchi church**, whose walls display Moldavian and Turkish patterns in raised relief, to the massive, neo-Gothic **Place of Culture** (Palatul Culturi), which contains historical, ethnographic, polytechnic, and art museums. (Open Tu-Su 10am-5pm. Each museum L10,000). North of the main square, Bd. Copou leads north from Piata Eminescu past some of the most beautiful buildings in Iaşi to **Park Copou**. **Libraria Junimea**, Piaţa Unirii 4, offers maps.

The **train station**, Str. Silvestru, connects to: Bucharest (6hr., 6 per day, *accelerat* L133,000); Constanta (7hr., 1 per day); and Oradea (14hr., 1 per day, *accelerat* L140,000). **CFR**, Piaţa Unirii 9/11, sells train tickets. (☎14 76 73. Open M-F 8am-8pm). **Buses**, Str. Arcu (☎14 65 87), connect to Braşov (7hr., 1 per day, L140,000). **Hotel Continental**, Str. Cuza Vodă 4, is offers decent rooms with TVs, phones, and private baths. Follow Str. Garii away from the train station parking lot and turn right with the tram tracks onto Str. Arcu, which becomes Str. Cuza Vodă. (☎21 18 46. Breakfast included. Singles L330,000; doubles L517,000.) Established in 1786, **Bolta Rece**, Str. Rece 10, serves some of Iaşi's best dishes; check out the cold vault downstairs. Follow Str. Cuza Vodă past Hotel Continental and turn left on Str. Bratianu; at B-dul. Independentei, make a right and an immediate left onto M. Eminescu; a few streets up, turn left onto Str. Rece. **Postal code:** 6600.

GURA HUMORULUI ☎ 033

Within walking distance of the Humor and Voroneţ monasteries, the small town of Gura Humorului is ideal for exploring the area. Car tours of the region's **monasteries** and an underground salt mine featuring two chapels and a tennis court are available at the **Dispecerat de Cazare**, Str. Câmpului nr. 30; take a left off Ştefan cel Mare from the train station. (☎23 88 63. Open 24hr. Tours US$20-30 per car.) **Trains** come from: Bucharest (8hr.; 1 per day; L131,100); Cluj-Napoca (6hr.; 5 per day; L82,900); and Suceava (1hr.; 5 per day; L25,000). To reach the town center from the station, make a right onto Ştefan cel Mare and continue over the bridge. The **Dispecerat de Cazare** (see above) provides rooms in villas in the hills. (Doubles US$8-10. Sept.-June 20-30% discount.) Get **groceries** from the markets lining Ştefan cel Mare.

■ **DAYTRIP FROM GURA HUMORULUI: BUKOVINA MONASTERIES.** Bukovina's painted monasteries hide among green hills and farming villages. Built 500 years ago by Ştefan cel Mare and his successors, the serene structures mix Moldavian architecture, Romanian soul, and Christian dogma. Reaching them on public transport can be a trial of faith; instead, go on a tour organized by the tourist office in Gura Humorului. Dress modestly.

Voroneţ has not been restored since conservationists have not been able to reproduce the distinctive pigment, Voroneţ Blue (Albastru de Voroneţ). The frescoes on the monastery's porch are a panorama representing the Eastern Orthodox ecclesiastical calendar. Jesse's Tree, on the south wall, displays the genealogy of Jesus, while the north wall depicts scenes from Genesis and Adam's pact with the Devil. To reach Voronet from Gura Humorului, catch a bus from the bus station (10min.; M-F 3 per day; L10,000); or, on foot, take a left from the train station and another left onto Cartierul Voronet; the monastery is at the end of a 5km walk. (Open daily 8am-8pm. L10,000, students L5000. Cameras L20,000.)

Humor, displaying the oldest frescoes in Bukovina, is known for the depiction of the Virgin Mary's life on the south wall. Based on a poem by the patriarch of Constantinople, it shows her saving Constantinople from a Persian attack in 626. The Siege is part of a larger Hymn and Prayer to the Saints. The Final Judgment is on the porch. To get to Humor from Gura Humorului, walk right on Ştefan cel Mare from the train or bus station to the center of town. At the fork near a park on the right, take Str. M. Humorulu to the left and continue 6km to the monastery. (Open daily 8am-8pm. L10,000, students L5000. Cameras L20,000.)

Moldoviţa, known for its yellow, is the largest of the painted monasteries, and its frescoes are among the best preserved. Painted in 1537, it has a Last Judgment, Jesse's Tree, and a monumental Siege of Constantinople. The Siege of 626, painted on the exterior wall to the right of the entrance, depicts the ancient fortress in an uncanny 16th-century light. (Open daily 7am-8pm.) **Buses** run from the bus station in Gura Humorului to Vatra Dornei (45min.; 3 per day; L30,000).

The pure-white **Putna** complex includes the tomb of Ştefan cel Mare and a museum. (Monastery open daily 8am-8pm; free. Museum open daily 9am-5pm; L5000, students L1500. Church open daily 9am-5pm; free.) Built between 1466 and 1469, Putna was the first of 38 monasteries founded by Ştefan cel Mare, who built one church for each battle he won. He left Putna's location up to God: climbing a nearby hill to the left of the monastery (marked by a cross), he shot an arrow into the air. A piece of the oak it struck is on display at the museum, along with manuscripts and religious garb. For the scenic ride to Putna, catch direct **trains** from Suceava, 75km southeast (2hr.; 5 per day; L26,000). Exiting the platform, take a right, then a left at the first intersection and keep walking.

RUSSIA (РОССИЯ)

RUBLES

US$1 = 29.4R	1R = US$0.03
CDN$1 = 19.1R	1R = CDN$0.05
UK£1 = 42.5R	1R = UK£0.02
IR£1 = 34.2R	1R = IR£0.03
AUS$1 = 15.8R	1R = AUS$0.06
NZ$1 = 12.9R	1R = NZ$0.08
ZAR1 = 3.5R	1R= ZAR0.28
DM1 =13.8R1R = DM0.07	
EUR€1 = 26.9R	1R = EUR€0.04

PHONE CODES

Country code: 7. **International dialing prefix:** 810. From outside Russia, dial int'l dialing prefix (see inside back cover) + 7 + city code + local number.

Over a decade after the fall of the Soviet Union, we still don't understand Russia, and it still doesn't understand us. Former Communists run the state, while impoverished pensioners long for a rosy-tinted Soviet past. Heedless of the failing provinces, Moscow chugs down hyper-capitalism, while St. Petersburg steadily rebuilds its reputation as one of Europe's cultural centers. No one has much affection left for the West, by whom most Russians feel profoundly betrayed. Though it can be a bureaucratic nightmare, Russia is in many ways the ideal destination for a budget traveler—inexpensive and well served by public transportation, with hundreds of monasteries, kremlins, and churches.

How can you just sit there without *Let's Go: Eastern Europe 2002?*

FACTS AND FIGURES

Official Name: Russian Federation.
Capital: Moscow.
Population: 146 million.
Land Area: 17,075,200 sq. km.

Climate: Humid continental to sub-arctic.
Languages: Russian.
Religions: None (74%), Russian Orthodox (16%), Muslim (10%).

DISCOVER RUSSIA

Moscow (p. 790) is more than memories of revolution: the spires of St. Basil's are more brilliant in real life than in photos, and the collections of the Kremlin are mind-boggling. Rivaling other cultural capitals, **St. Petersburg** (p. 800) flaunts Europe's largest art collection at the Hermitage, the opulence of the Summer and Winter Palaces, and one of the world's best ballet companies.

ESSENTIALS

WHEN TO GO

The best time to visit is May through September. Spring and fall can be unpredictable with periodic snow flurries; it is also very slushy. Winter in Moscow and St. Petersburg can be very picturesque, uncrowded, and romantic. Dress warmly.

DOCUMENTS AND FORMALITIES

VISAS. Citizens of Australia, Canada, Ireland, New Zealand, South Africa, the UK, and the US all require a visa to enter Russia; you need an **invitation** stating your itinerary and dates of travel to get a visa. Travel agencies that advertise discounted tickets to Russia often can provide visas. **Info Travel,** 387 Harvard St., Brookline, MA 02146 (☎617-566-2197; infostudy@aol.com), and **Academic Travel,** 1302 Commonwealth Ave., Boston, MA 02134 (☎617-566-5272; actravel@gis.com), both provide invitations and visas to Russia starting at US$150. Visa assistance (US$30-45) is also available at www.visatorussia.com. A larger but more expensive operation (US$225) is **Russia House.** In the US, they are at 1800 Connecticut Ave. NW, Washington, D.C. 20009 (☎202-986-6010; lozansky@aol.com). In Russia, contact them at 44 Bolshaya Nikitskaya, Moscow 125040 (☎(095) 290 34 59; rushouse@clep.ru). The following can also give invitations and/or visas for tourists: **Host Families Association (HOFA),** 5-25 Tavricheskaya, 193015 St. Petersburg, Russia (☎/fax (812) 275 19 92; hofa@usa.net); **Red Bear Tours/Russian Passport,** Suite 11, 401 St. Kilda Rd., Melbourne 3004, Australia (☎(613) 98 67 38 88; www.travelcentre.com.au); **Traveler's Guest House,** Bolshaya Pereyaslavskaya 50, 10th Fl., Moscow, Russia 129401 (☎(095) 971 40 59; tgh@startravel.ru). Many hotels will register your visa for you on arrival, as should the organizations listed above. Some travel agencies in Moscow and St. Petersburg will also register your visa for approximately US$30. As a last resort, you'll have to climb into the 7th circle of bureaucratic hell known as the central **OVIR** (ОВИР) office (in Moscow called UVIR—УВИР) to register.

EMBASSIES. All foreign embassies are in Moscow (p. 790); many consulates are also in St. Petersburg (p. 800). For Russian embassies at home: **Australia,** 78 Canberra Ave., Griffith ACT 2603 Canberra (☎(06) 295 90 33, visa information ☎295 1847; fax 295 9474); **Canada,** 285 Charlotte St., Ottawa, ON K1N 8L5(☎613-235-4341, visa information ☎613-236-0920; fax 613-236-6342); **Ireland,** 186 Orwell Rd., Rathgar, Dublin 14 (☎/fax (01) 492 35 25, visa information ☎492 34 92; russiane@indigo.ie); **New Zealand,** 57 Messines Rd., Karori, Wellington (☎(04) 476 61 13, visa information ☎476 67 42; fax 476 38 43; eor@netlink.co.nz); **South Africa,** Butano Building, 316 Brooks St., Menlo Park 0081, Pretoria; P.O. Box 6743, Pretoria 0001 (☎(012) 362 13 37, visa information ☎344 48 12; www.icon.co.za/~rusco); **UK,** 13 Kensington Palace Gardens, London W8 4QX (☎(020) 72 29 36 28, visa information ☎72 29 80 27; fax 77 27 86 25; www.russialink.org.uk/embassy); and **US,** 2650 Wisconsin Ave. N.W., Washington, D.C. 20007 (☎202-298-5700; fax 202-298-5735; www.russianembassy.org).

TRANSPORTATION

Upon entrance to the country, you'll be given a **Customs Declaration Form** to declare all your valuables and foreign currency; don't lose it. Everything listed on the customs form must be on you when you leave the country. Anything that might be regarded by the customs officials as a work of art or any "old" books—that is, those published before 1975—must be assessed by the Ministry of Culture (located at 17 Malaya Morskaya in St. Petersburg and at Neglinnaya 8/10, office 29 in Moscow). These kind folks will look over your find and usually assess a 100% tax; be sure to have your receipt to establish the value of your item. You will not be permitted to take these items out of the country without a receipt proving you have paid the tax. Keep receipts for any expensive or antique-looking souvenirs. You cannot legally bring rubles into or out of the country. In August 1999, the US State Department issued a travel advisory regarding bringing Global Positioning Systems (G.P.S.), cellular phones, and other radio transmission devices into Russia. Failure to register such devices can (and does) result in search, seizure, and arrest.

BY PLANE. Flying into Moscow or St. Petersburg is the easiest way to enter Russia, which boasts a not-so-reliable air system almost monopolized by **Aeroflot.** Budding alternative **Transair** serves only select cities.

BY TRAIN. If you find yourself passing through Belarus by train, you will need a US$20-30 **transit visa.** Trains are generally the best way to move about the country; buy your ticket well ahead of time if you have an important connection to make or your visa is about to expire. If you plan ahead, you'll have your choice of four classes. The best is *lyuks* (люкс), or *2-myagky* (2-person soft; мягкий)—a place in

Russia

a two-bunk cabin in the same car as second-class *kupeyny* (купейный), which has four bunks. On hot nights, air-conditioned *lyuks*, available on major lines, may be worth the cost. The next class is *platskartny* (плацкартный), a car with 52 shorter, harder bunks. Aim for places 1-33; places 34-37 are next to the foul bathrooms, and places 38-52 get horribly hot in the summer. Women traveling alone can try to buy out a *lyuks* compartment for security, or can travel *platskartny* with the regular folk and depend on the crowds to shame would-be harassers. *Platskartny* is also a good idea on the theft-ridden St. Petersburg-Moscow line. *Elektrichka* (commuter rail; marked on signs as пригородные поезда; *prigorodnye poezda*) has its own platforms; buy tickets at the *kassa*.

BY BUS. Buses, cheaper than trains, are your best bet for shorter distances. They are often crowded and overbooked, however; don't be shy about ejecting people who try to sit in your seat. On the Hungarian **Ikarus** buses, you'll get seated in a fairly comfy reclining chair, and should be able to store luggage for free.

BY TAXI AND BY THUMB. In Russia, hailing a taxi is a lot like hitchhiking, and should be treated with equal caution. Most drivers who stop will be private citizens trying to make a little extra cash (despite the recent restriction on this technically illegal activity). Those seeking a ride should stand off the curb and hold out a hand into the street, palm down; when a car stops, riders tell the driver the destination before getting in; he will either refuse the destination altogether or ask *Skolko?* (How much?), leading to protracted negotiations. Non-Russian speakers will get ripped off unless they manage a firm agreement on the price—if the driver agrees without asking for a price, you must ask *skolko* ("How much?") yourself (sign language works too). Never get into a car that has more than one person in it.

TOURIST SERVICES AND MONEY

EMERGENCY	Police: ☎02. Ambulance: ☎03. Fire: ☎01.

TOURIST OFFICES. There are two types of Russian tourist office—those that only arrange tours and those that offer general travel services. Offices of the former type are often unhelpful or even rude, but those of the latter are often eager to assist, particularly with visa registration. Big hotels are often a better bet for maps.

MONEY. The **ruble** was revalued in 1998, losing three zeros; the old currency is gradually being phased out. You must show your passport when you exchange money. Find an *Obmen Valyuty* (Обмен Валюты; currency exchange), hand over your currency—most will exchange US dollars and *Deutschmarks*, and some also accept French francs and British pounds—and receive your rubles. Do not exchange money on the street. Banks offer the best combination of good rates and security. You'll have no problem changing rubles back at the end of your trip (just keep exchange receipts), but don't exchange large sums at once, as the rate is unstable. ATMs (банкомат; *bankomat*) linked to all major networks and credit cards can be found all over most cities. Major credit cards, especially Visa, are often accepted. Main branches of banks will usually accept traveler's checks and give cash advances on credit cards, most often Visa. Although you'll have to pay in rubles, it's wise to keep US$20 on hand. Be aware that most establishments do not accept crumpled, torn, or written-on bills. A budget day will run you between US$30-40. In St. Petersburg and Moscow, a 5-10% tip is becoming customary.

BUSINESS HOURS. Most establishments, even train ticket offices and "24-hour stores," close for a lunch break sometime between noon and 3pm. Places tend to close at least 30 minutes earlier than they should, if they choose to open at all.

COMMUNICATION

MAIL. Mail service is much more reliable leaving the country than coming in. Letters to the US will arrive as soon as a week after mailing, although letters to other destinations take 2-3 weeks. Airmail, if you want to risk it, is *avia* (авиа). Send your mail certified (заказное; 16R) to reduce the chance of it being lost. If you're sending anything other than paper goods into the abyss that is the Russian mail system, you'll need to fill out a customs form at the post office. Regular letters to the US cost 7R; postcards cost 5R. DHL operates in most large cities. *Poste Restante* is "Письмо До Востребования" (Pismo Do Vostrebovania).

TELEPHONES. Direct international calls can be made from telephone offices and hotel rooms: dial ☎8, wait for the tone, then dial ☎10 and the country code. Calls to Europe run US$1-1.50 per min.; to the US and Australia about US$1.50-2.00. You cannot call collect, unless using AT&T service (same access number as listed below), which will cost your party dearly (US$8 first min.; US$2.78 each additional min. to the US). Prices for calls to the US range from 9R-25R per minute, depending on where you're calling from. To make inter-city calls from a telephone office, you can buy tokens or phone cards, or simply prepay your calls (depending on the city) and use the *mezhdugorodnye* telephones; be sure to press the ответ (reply; *otvet*) button when your party answers. For international calls, see p. 792. If there are no automatic phones, pay for your call at the counter and have it dialed for you by the operator. Several hotels in Moscow now have direct-dial booths operated by a special card or credit card. The cost is astronomical (at least US$6 per min. to the US). Direct dial numbers include: **AT&T,** ☎755 5042 in Moscow, ☎325 5042 in St. Petersburg; **British Telecom,** ☎810 800 110 10 44; **Canada Direct,** ☎810 800 110 1012; **MCI,** ☎960 2222 in Moscow, ☎346 8022 in St. Petersburg; **Sprint,** ☎747 33 24; **Telecom New Zealand,** ☎810 800 110 1064; **Telkom South Africa,** ☎810 800 120 1027; and **Telstra Australia,** ☎810. When calling from another city, dial ☎8-095 or 8-812 before these codes; you pay for the call to Moscow or St. Petersburg in addition to the international connection. Calling into the country is less frustrating. Most countries have direct dial to Moscow and St. Petersburg; for other cities, go through the international operator. As the phone system charges very high rates, **email** is your best bet for keeping in touch.

LANGUAGE. Take some time with the Cyrillic alphabet; it will make getting around and getting by immeasurably easier. For more information on Cyrillic and some Russian phrases, see p. 987.

ACCOMMODATIONS AND CAMPING

The only **hostels** in Russia are in St. Petersburg and Moscow, and even those average US$18 per night. Reserve well in advance, especially in summer. **Hotels** offer several classes of rooms. "Lux," usually two-room doubles with TV, phone, fridge, and bath, are the most expensive. "Polu-lux" rooms are singles or doubles with TV, phone, and bath. The lowest-priced rooms are bez udobstv (без удобств), which means one room with a sink. Expect to pay 300-450R for a single in a budget hotel. Usually only cash is accepted as payment. In many hotels, hot water (and sometimes all water) is only on a few hours per day. Reservations may help you get on the good side of management, which is often inexplicably suspicious of backpackers. **University dorms** offer cheap rooms; some accept foreign students for about US$5-10 per night. Don't expect sparkling bathrooms or reliable hot water. Make arrangements with an institute from home. **Homestays,** arranged through a tourist office, are often the cheapest (50-100R per night) and best option in the country.

HEALTH AND SAFETY

Russian bottled water is often mineral water; water in much of Russia is drinkable in small doses, but not in Moscow and St. Petersburg; boil it to be safe. A gamma globulin shot will lower your risk of hepatitis A. For medical emergencies, either leave the country or go to the American Medical Centers at St. Petersburg or Moscow; these clinics have American-born and trained doctors and speak English (p. 792 and p. 802). Reports of **crime** against foreigners are on the rise, particularly in Moscow and St. Petersburg. Although it is hard to look Russian (especially with a huge pack on your back), try not to flaunt your true nationality. Your trip will be that much more pleasant if you never have to file a crime report with the local *militsia*, who will not speak English and will probably not help you. Reports of mafia warfare are scaring off tourists, but unless you bring a shop for them to blow up, you are unlikely to be a target. After the recent eruption of violence in the Northern Caucasus, the Dagestan and Chechnya regions of Russia are to be avoided.

FOOD AND DRINK

Cuisine is a medley of dishes both delectable and disgusting; tasty borscht can come in the same meal as *salo* (pig fat). Food is generally better in the south. The largest meal of the day, *obed* (lunch; обед), includes: *salat* (salad; салат), usually cucumbers and tomatoes or beets and potatoes with mayonnaise or sour cream; *sup* (soup; суп); and *kuritsa* (chicken; курица) or *myaso* (meat; мясо), often called *kotlyety* (cutlets; котлеты) or *beefshteaks* (beefsteaks; бифштекс). Ordering a few *zakuski* (small appetizers; закуски) instead of a main dish can save money. A cafe (кафе) or *stolovaya* (cafeteria; столовая) is cheaper than a restaurant, but the latter may be unsanitary. The *rynok* (market; рынок) sells fruits and vegetables, meat, fresh milk, butter, honey, and cheese. Wash and dry everything before you eat it. On the streets, you'll see *blini* (stuffed crepes), *shashlyki* (barbecued meat on a stick; шашлыки) and *kvas* (квас), an alcoholic dark-brown drink.

HOLIDAYS AND FESTIVALS

Holidays: New Year's (Jan. 1-2); Orthodox Christmas (Jan. 7); Defenders of the Motherland Day (Feb. 23); Orthodox Easter (Apr. 15); Labor Day (May 1-2); Victory Day (May 9); Independence Day (June 12); Day of Accord and Reconciliation (Nov. 7); Constitution Day (Dec. 12).

Festivals: In June, when the sun barely touches the horizon, St. Petersburg holds a series of evening concerts as part of the **White Nights Festival.**

MOSCOW (МОСКВА)　　　☎(8)095

Like few other cities on Earth, Moscow has an audacity about it, a sense of itself as the focus of world history. If you keep to the 16th-century side streets, it's still possible to glimpse a few of the same quiet, golden domes which Napoleon saw after conquering the city in 1812. Of course, when Communism swept through, it leveled most of the domes and left behind massive buildings, crumbling outskirts, and countless statues of Lenin. But now that residents are once again opening up, speaking up, and building up, Moscow is recreating itself as a beautiful capital, using the same resourcefulness that helped it engineer (and then survive) the most ambitious social experiment in history.

▣ TRANSPORTATION

Flights: International flights arrive at **Sheremetyevo-2** (Шереметьево-2; ☎956 46 66 and 578 75 18). Take the van under the "автолайн" sign in front of the station to M2: Rechnoy Vokzal (Речной Вокзал; 20min., every 10min. 7am-10pm, 15R). Or, take bus #851 or 551 to M2: Rechnoy Vokzal or bus #517 to M8: Planyornaya (Планёрная; 10R). Buses run 24hr., but the Metro doesn't. Most domestic flights and many flights within the former USSR originate at: **Bikovo** (Биково; ☎558 47 38); **Domodedovo** (Домодедово; ☎323 81 60); **Sheremetyevo-1** (☎578 23 72); **Vnukovo** (Внуково; ☎436 28 13). Tickets can be bought at the kassa (касса) at the **Tsentralny Aerovokzal** (Центральный Аэровокзал; Central Airport Station), Leningradsky pr. 37 corpus 6 (☎941 99 99), 2 stops on almost any tram or trolley from M2: Aeroport (sign on front of bus should say Центральный Аэровокзал). **Taxis** to the center charge up to US$60; make sure to bargain (prices as low as US$25 were possible in June 2001). Agree on a price before getting into the cab.

Trains: Buying tickets in Russia can be enormously frustrating. If you don't speak Russian, you may want to buy through **Intourist** or your hotel; you'll pay more, but you'll be spared the hassle of the *vokzal* (station; вокзал) experience. Buy tickets for the *elektrichka* (local trains) at the *prigorodniye kassa* (local ticket booths; пригородная касса) in each station. Tickets for longer trips can be purchased at the **Central Train Agency** (Tsentralnoe Zheleznodorozhnoe Agenstvo; Центральное Железнодорожное Агенство), to the right of Yaroslavsky Vokzal (see below). Schedules are posted on both sides of the hall. (*Kassa* open M-F 1am-9pm, Sa 7am-7pm, Su 7am-6pm.) There is 24hr. service at the stations themselves. Tickets to Helsinki are sold on the 2nd fl. of Leningradsky Vokzal, at windows #19 and 20. (Open daily 10am-1pm and 2-10pm.) Moscow's 9 train stations are on the metro's circle line (M5).

Belorussky Vokzal (Белорусский), Tverskaya Zastavy pl. 7. To: Berlin (27hr., 1 per day, 3780R); Minsk (10hr., 3-4 per day, 304R); Prague (35hr., 1 per day, 3360R); Vilnius (16hr., 1-2 per day, 720R); and Warsaw (21hr., 2 per day, 2520R).

Kazansky Vokzal (Казанский), Komsomolskaya pl. 2, opposite Leningradsky Vokzal, serves the east and southeast.

Kievsky Vokzal (Киевский), Kievskovo Vokzala pl., sends trains to Kiev (14hr., 3 per day, 374R).

Kursky Vokzal (Курский), ul. Zemlyanoi Val 29/1 serves Sevastopol (26hr., 1 per day, 573R) and the Caucasus.

Leningradsky Vokzal (Ленинградский), Komsomolskaya pl. 3. M1, 5: Komsomolskaya. To: Helsinki (13hr. 1 per day, 2800R); St. Petersburg (5-9hr., 13 per day, 188R); and Tallinn (14hr., 1 per day, 1297R).

Paveletsky Vokzal (Павлецкий), Paveletskaya pl. 1, serves the Crimea and eastern Ukraine.

Rizhsky Vokzal (Рижский) Rizhkaya pl. 79/3. To Rīga (16hr., 2 per day, 514R) and Estonia.

Yaroslavsky Vokzal (Ярославский), Komsomolskaya pl. 5, is the starting point for the Trans-Siberian Railroad. To Novosibirsk (48hr., 1-3 per day, 385R).

Public Transportation: The **Metro** is large and efficient—a masterpiece of Stalinist urban planning. The 9 Metro lines run daily 6am-1am. Passages between lines or stations are indicated by signs of a man walking up stairs; individual exit signs indicate street names. A station serving more than 1 line may have more than 1 name. Buy token-cards (4R) from the *kassa* inside stations. Consult the color **metro maps** at the end of this book. Buy **bus** and **trolley** tickets from gray kiosks labeled "проездные билеты" or from the driver (4R). Punch your ticket when you get on, or risk a 10R fine.

Taxis: Taxi stands have a round sign with a green T. If you don't speak Russian, you'll get ripped off, particularly if you don't know Moscow. Ask around for the going rate and agree on a price before you get in. Be sure the meter is turned on.

ORIENTATION AND PRACTICAL INFORMATION

A series of concentric rings radiates outward from the **Kremlin** (Kreml; Кремль) and **Red Square** (Krasnaya ploshchad; Красная Площадь). The outermost **Moscow Ring Road** marks the city limits, but most sights lie within the **Garden Ring** (Sadovoe Koltso; Садовое Кольцо). Main streets include **Ulitsa Tverskaya** (Тверская), which extends north along the green line, and **Arbat** (Арбат) and **Novy Arbat** (Новый Арбат), which run west parallel to the metro's blue lines. Familiarize yourself with the Cyrillic alphabet and orient yourself by the Metro (which stops within 15min. of anywhere in the city). Cyrillic maps are at kiosks all over the city. Also refer to the **color maps** in the back of this book, in both English and Cyrillic. Be careful when crossing streets—drivers are notoriously oblivious to pedestrians.

> **PAYING IN RUSSIA.** Due to the fluctuating value of the Russian ruble, some establishments list their prices in US dollars. For this reason, some prices in this book may also appear in US$, but be prepared to pay in rubles.

TOURIST, FINANCIAL, AND LOCAL SERVICES

Tourist Offices: Intourist, ul. Mokhovaya 16 (Моховая; ☎292 52 30 and 203 69 62). General information. Branch at Stoleshnikov per. 11 (Столешников; ☎923 57 63; fax 928 48 13). Museum tours and translation services.

Budget Travel: Student Travel Agency Russia (STAR), ul. Baltyskaya 9, 3rd fl. (чл. Ьелтийская; ☎797 95 55; www.startravel.ru). M2: Sokol. Open M-F 10am-6pm, Sa 11am-4pm.

Embassies: Australia, Kropotkinsky per. 13 (Кропоткинский; ☎956 60 70). M3: Smolenskaya. Open M-F 9am-noon. **Canada,** Starokonyushenny per. 23 (Староконюшенный; ☎956 66 66). M1: Kropotkinskaya. Open M-Tu and Th-F 8:30am-1pm and 2-5pm. **Ireland,** Grokholsky per. 5 (Грохольский; ☎937 59 11). M5, 6: Prospekt Mira. Open M-F 9:30am-1pm and 2:30pm-5:30pm. **New Zealand,** ul. Povarskaya 44 (Поварская; ☎956 35 79). M5,7: Krasnopresnenskaya. Open daily 9am-5:30pm. **South Africa,** Bolshoy Strochinovsky per. 22/25 (Большой Строченовский; ☎230 68 69). **UK,** Smolenskaya nab 10 (Смоленская; ☎956 72 00). M3: Smolenskaya. Open M-F 9am-1pm and 2-5pm. **US,** Novinsky 19/23 (Новинский; ☎728 50 00; fax 728 50 90; usembassy.state.gov/moscow). Consular ☎728 55 88. American Citizen Services (ACS) ☎728 55 77; after-hours emergency ☎728 51 07. M7: Krasnopresnenskaya. Flash a US passport to cut long lines. Embassy open M-F 9am-6pm. Consular open M-F 9am-noon.

Currency Exchange: *Moscow Express Directory,* free in most luxury hotels, lists places to buy and cash traveler's checks. Usually only main branches of large banks will change traveler's checks or issue cash advances. Nearly every bank and hotel has an **ATM.**

American Express: ul. Usacheva 33 (Усачева; ☎933 84 00). M1: Sportivnaya. Exit at the front of the train, turn right, and turn right again after the Global USA shop onto Usacheva. One of the only places in Moscow that cashes **traveler's checks.** Open M-Th 9am-6pm, F 9am-5pm.

English Bookstore: Angliyskaya Kniga (Английская Книга), ul. Kuznetsky most 18. M7: Kuznetsky most. Open M-F 10am-2pm and 3-7pm, Sa 10am-2pm and 3-6pm.

Laundromat: California Cleaners, Pokhodny 24 (Походный; ☎493 53 11). 20 locations around Moscow. Free pick-up and delivery. 105R per kg.

RUSSIA

EMERGENCY AND COMMUNICATIONS

Emergency: Police: ☎02. **Ambulance:** ☎03. **Fire:** ☎01.

24-Hour Pharmacies: Look for "круглосуточно" (kruglosutochno; always open) signs. Leningradsky pr. 74 (Ленинградский; ☎151 45 70). M2: Sokol. Ul. Tverskaya 25 (Тверская; ☎299 24 59 and 299 79 69). M2: Tverskaya. Ul. Zemlyanoi Val 25 (Земляной Вал; ☎917 12 85). M5: Kurskaya.

Medical Assistance: American Medical Center, Prospekt Mira 26 (☎933 77 00; fax 933 77 01). M5: Prospekt Mira. Walk left out of the metro. Entrance on Grokholsky per. (Грохольский). Walk-in medical care for hard currency. US$175 per visit. Membership US$50 per year, students $40; price doubles if you want bills sent to your insurance company. Open 24hr. **Mediclub Moscow,** Michurinsky pr. 56 (Мичуринский; ☎931 50 18 and 931 53 18). M1: Prospekt Vernadskovo. Private Canadian clinic offering full-scale emergency service. Medical consultations 550R. Payment in rubles or MC/V only. Open M-F 9am-8pm.

Internet Access: Timeonline, on the lower level of the Okhotny Ryad mall (☎363 00 60). M1: Okhotny Ryad. A large, English-friendly, 24hr. Internet cafe with over 200 computers in the very center of the city. 30-60R per hr. depending on time of day. At night, enter through the metro underpass. **Image.ru** (Имидж.ру), ul. Novoslobodskaya 16 (Новослободская; ☎737 37 00, ext. 146). M9: Mendeleevskaya. Drinks available. 40R per hr. Open daily 9am-9pm. Also at Traveler's Guest House for 3R per min., G&R Hostel Asia for 2R per min., and hall 3 of Moscow Central Telegraph for 13R per 15min.

Telephones: Moscow Central Telegraph (see Post Offices below). To **call abroad,** go to the 2nd hall with phones. No collect or calling card calls. Prepay at counter. Use the *mezhdunarodnye telefony* (international telephones; международные телефоны). To Europe 20.5R per min.; to the 25.2R per min; to Australia 37.2R per min. Open 24hr. **Local calls** require new phone cards; buy from Metro stops and kiosks.

Post Offices: Moscow Central Telegraph, ul. Tverskaya 7, uphill from the Kremlin. M1: Okhotny Ryad. **International mail** at window #13; **faxes** at windows #11-12. Open M-F 8am-2pm and 3-9pm, Sa 8am-2pm and 3-7pm, Su 9am-2pm and 3-7pm. Address mail to be held: RUSSIA, Москва **103 009,** До востребования (Poste Restante), First name SURNAME. Pick up mail at window #24, although they might send you to Myasnitskaya 26 (Мясницкая) if they don't have it. **Postal code:** 103 009.

⚑ ACCOMMODATIONS

The lack of backpacking culture in Moscow results in slim pickings and overpriced rooms. Women standing outside major rail stations rent **private rooms** (*sdayu komnatu;* сдаю комнату) or **apartments** (*sdayu kvartiru;* сдаю квартиру). US-based **Moscow Bed and Breakfast** rents apartments in the city center. (US☎603-585-3347; fax 603-585-6534; jkates@top.monad.net. Contact before you arrive. Singles US$35; doubles US$52.) The places below are as cheap as it gets.

▨ **G&R Hostel Asia,** ul. Zelenodolskaya 3/2 (Зеленодольская; ☎/fax 378 28 66; hostel-asia@mtu-net.ru; www.hostels.ru). M7: Ryazansky Prospekt (Рязанский Проспект). In the tall gray building with "Гостиница" in large letters on top, visible from either Metro exit. Clean rooms and helpful staff. TV, fridge in each room. Far from the center, but close to the Metro. Transport to or from the airport US$25. Dorms US$16; singles US$20-25; doubles US$35-40. MC/V.

Traveller's Guest House, ul. Bolshaya Pereyaslavskaya 50, 10th fl. (Большая Переяслаская; ☎971 40 59; tgh@startravel.ru; www.infinity.ru/tgh). M5, 6: Prospekt Mira (Проспект Мира). From the Metro, walk 10min. north along pr. Mira, take the 3rd right on Banny per. (Банный), and turn left at the end of the street. It's in the white, 12-story building across the street. TGH's greatest virtue is its clientele; almost every budget traveler stays there, and the bulletin board serves as an open forum for travel advice. Clean, comfortable, no-frill rooms. Laundry US$2. Check-out 11am. Airport pick-up and drop-off US$40. Russian visa invitations US$40. Dorms US$18; singles US$36; doubles US$48-54. MC/V.

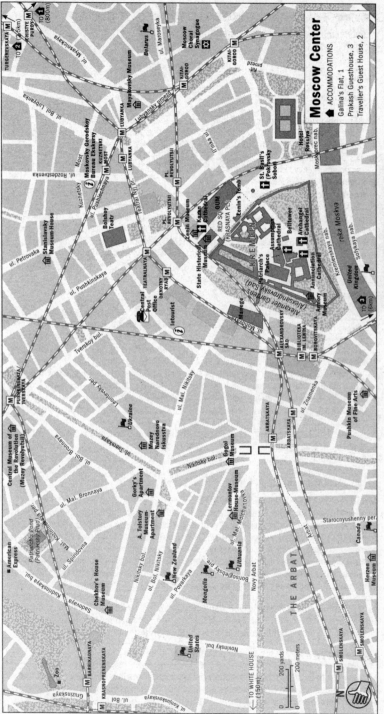

Moscow Center

▲ ACCOMMODATIONS
Galina's Flat, 1
Prakash Guesthouse, 3
Traveller's Guest House, 2

RUSSIA

Galina's Flat, ul. Chaplygina 8, #35 (Чаплыгина; ☎921 60 38; galinas.flat@mtu-net.ru). M1: Chistye Prudy. Take bul. Chistoprudny (Чистопрудный) past the statue of Griboedov, then take the 1st left onto Kharitonevsky per. (Харитоньевский), and the 2nd right on Chaplygina. Go through the courtyard, turn right, and enter by the "Уникум" sign; it's upstairs on the right. Homey apartment with cats. Hot showers. Kitchen facilities. Only 7 beds, so call ahead. Dorms US$8; doubles US$20.

Gostinitsa Kievskaya (Гостиница Киевская), ul. Kievskaya 2 (☎240 14 44). M3, 5: Kievskaya. Just outside the train station. Spacious old rooms and soft beds in a great location. Singles with bath 460R; doubles with bath 630R; luxury suite 805-930R.

Don (Дон), ul. Yaroslavskaya 8, #4 (Ярославская; ☎217 67 86). M6: VDNKh. Walk down ul. Kosmonavtov (Космонавтов) and take a right on Yaroslavskaya; enter on Kibalchicha (Кибальчича). A budget hotel with clean, cheap rooms in an out-of-the-way location. Singles with bath 490-520R; doubles with bath 630-650R; suite 800-1200R.

🍴 FOOD

Eating out ranges from expensive to insanely expensive. Many restaurants list prices in US dollars to avoid changing their menus to keep up with inflation. The ubiquitous and varied kiosk fare are a cheap alternative. Local cuisine is often affordable, and many of the higher-priced places have begun to offer lunch specials (бизнес ланч; typically available noon-4pm; US$4-6). **Russkoe Bistro** (Русское Бистро) is like a Russian McDonald's—traditional food, fast—with locations all over town. (Open daily 9am-11pm.)

RUSSIAN

🌑 **Vremya Yest** (Время Есть), ul. Lesnaya 1/2 (Лесная). M5: Belorusskaya. In the complex across the street from the station. Tavern-like restaurant serving Russian food with a creative, European twist. Friendly service and one of Moscow's largest selections of beer. English menu. Main dishes 195-295R. Happy hour M-F 3-7pm. Open daily noon-5am.

Moo Moo (My My), Arbat 45/24 (☎241 13 64). M3: Smolenskaya. A good, cheap, buffet-style restaurant with a large array of tasty dishes, including many vegetarian options. Life-size fake cow for the kids, people-watching on the patio for the grown-ups. English menu. Soups 40-55R; main dishes 30-55R. Open daily 10am-11pm.

Ulitsa O.G.I. (Улица О.Г.И.), Petrovka 26, str. 8. M7: Kuznetsky Most. Walk through the arch under the small blue 26 sign on Petrovka, to the right of the bank. The entrance is on the right, past the playground. Delicious Russian and European food. Full meal 250-500R. Open daily 8am-midnight.

Guria's, Komsomolsky pr. 7/3 (Комсомольский). M1, 5: Park Kultury; on the corner of ul. Frunze opposite St. Nicholas of the Weavers. Tasty Georgian fare. Most main dishes 40-90R. Open daily 11am-10pm.

MARKETS AND SUPERMARKETS

Vendors bring everything from a handful of cherries to an entire produce section to sell at Moscow's many markets. A visit is worthwhile just for the sights: sides of beef, piles of peaches, jars of glowing honey, and huge pots of flowers. Impromptu markets, where produce is sold by the kilogram (bring your own bag), spring up around metro stations (usually 10am-8pm); try Turgenevskaya, Kuznetsky Most, Kievskayana, Aeroport, Baumanskaya, and between Novoslobodskaya and Mendeleevskaya. **Eliseevsky Gastronom** (Елисеевский), ul. Tverskaya 14 (M2: Tverskaya), is Moscow's most famous grocery store and is as much a feast for your eyes as it is a place to buy food. (Open M-F 8am-9pm, Sa 10am-7pm.) There are other supermarkets all over the place; look for "продукты" (prodookty; food products) signs. Wash fruit and vegetables with bottled or boiled water.

🏛 SIGHTS

Moscow's sights reflect the city's strange history: visitors can choose between 16th-century churches and Soviet-era museums, but there's little in between. Moscow suffers from the 200 years when St. Petersburg was the tsar's seat—there are no grand palaces, and the city's art museums, lacking the Hermitage's financial resources for purchases of foreign art, only contain the very best Russian works. Despite the fact that the Soviet regime destroyed 80% of the city's pre-revolutionary splendor, the capital still packs in enough sights to occupy visitors for over a week.

RED SQUARE (KRASNAYA PLOSHCHAD)

Red Square, a 700m-long lesson in history and culture, has been the site of everything from a giant farmer's market to public hangings, from Communist parades to a renegade Cessna landing. Not everything here is red; *krasnaya* meant "beautiful" long before the Communists co-opted it. On one side, the **Kremlin,** home of the early tsars and the seat of the Communist Party for 70-odd years, is the historical and religious heart of Russia; on the other, **GUM,** once a market and the world's largest purveyor of Soviet 'consumer goods,' is now an upscale shopping mall. Also flanking the square are **St. Basil's Cathedral,** the **State Historical Museum,** and the **Lenin Mausoleum,** and the pink-and-green **Kazan Cathedral.**

ST. BASIL'S CATHEDRAL. There is perhaps no more familiar symbol of Moscow than St. Basil's Cathedral (Sobor Vasiliya Blazhennovo; Собор Василия Блаженного), with its onion domes. Completed in 1561, it was commissioned by Ivan the Terrible to celebrate his 1552 victory over the Tatars in Kazan. The cathedral bears the name of a holy fool, Vasily (Basil in English), who predicted that Ivan would murder his own son. The labyrinthine interior—unusual for Orthodox churches—is filled with both religious and decorative frescoes. *(M3: Ploshchad Revolutsii; Площадь Революции. Open M, W-Su 11am-6pm. 90R, students 45R. Buy tickets from kassa to left of entrance, then proceed upstairs.)*

LENIN'S TOMB. You've seen his likeness in bronze all over the city; now see him in the eerily luminescent flesh. In the glory days, this squat red structure (Mavzoley V.I. Lenina; Мавзолей В.И. Ленина) was guarded by fierce guards, and the line to get in was three hours long. The line is still long, and the guards are still stone-faced, but on the whole, amused curiosity characterizes the atmosphere. Entrance to the mausoleum also gives access to the **Kremlin wall,** where Stalin, Brezhnev, Andropov, Gagarin, and John Reed (author of *Ten Days That Shook the World*) are buried. *(Open Tu-Th and Sa-Su 10am-1pm.)*

THE KREMLIN

Complex open F-W 10am-5pm. Armory open F-W 10-11:30am, noon-1:30pm, 2:30-4pm, and 4:30-6pm. Diamond Fund open F-W 10am-1pm and 2am-5pm. All cathedrals 200R, students 110R; after 4pm 150R. Armory 290R, students 145R. Diamond Fund 350R, students 250R. Camera use and mandatory bag check 30R each. Buy tickets and enter at the midpoint of Alexander Gardens, on the west side of the Kremlin. English-speaking guides offer tours at outrageous prices; haggle away.

The Kremlin (Kreml; Кремль) sits geographically and historically in the center of Moscow. Here, Ivan the Terrible reigned with his iron fist and Stalin ruled the lands behind the Iron Curtain. Napoleon simmered here while Moscow burned, and the USSR was dissolved here in 1991. The glory and the riches of the Russian Empire are all on display in the Kremlin's **Armory** and in the magnificent churches. Besides the sights listed below, the only other place in the complex you can actually enter is the **Kremlin Palace of Congresses,** the square white monster built by Khrushchev in 1961 for Communist Party Congresses; today it's a theater.

▨ ARMORY MUSEUM AND DIAMOND FUND. The Armory Museum and Diamond Fund (Oruzheynaya i Vystavka Almaznovo Fonda; Оружейная и Выставка Алмазного Фонда), at the southwest corner of the Kremlin complex, contain all of the riches of the Russian Church and state not currently in St. Petersburg's Hermitage. Among all the imperial thrones, coaches, crowns, and other royal necessities are the legendary **Fabergé eggs** in room 2, each revealing an intricate jewelled miniature. The Diamond Fund, in an annex of the Armory, has still more glitter, including a 190-carat diamond given to Catherine the Great by Gregory Orlov, a "special friend." The display is a must-see to comprehend the opulence of the Russian court.

CATHEDRAL SQUARE. Follow the eager masses to Cathedral Square, home to the most famous gold domes in Russia. The church closest to the Armory is the **Annunciation Cathedral** (Blagoveshchensky Sobor; Благовещеискии Собор), which guards luminous icons by Andrei Rublev and Theophanes the Greek. The square **Archangel Cathedral** (Arkhangelsky Sobor; Архангельский Собор), gleaming with vivid icons and metallic coffins, is the final resting place for many of the tsars who ruled before Peter the Great, including Ivans III (the Great) and IV (the Terrible) and Mikhail Romanov. **Assumption Cathedral** (Uspensky Sobor; Успенский Собор), at the center of the square, dates from the 15th century and was used as a stable by Napoleon in 1812. Next to it is the small **Patriarch's Palace** (Patriarshy Dvorets; Патриарший Дворец), which now houses the **Museum of 17th-Century Russian Applied Art and Life,** and the even smaller **Church of the Deposition of the Robe.** To the right of the Assumption Cathedral is the **Ivan the Great Belltower** (Kolokolnya Ivana Velikovo; Колокольня Ивана Великого), now a display space for temporary exhibits. Directly behind the belltower is the **Tsar Bell** (Tsarkolokol; Царь-колокол), the world's largest. It has never rung and probably never will—a 1737 fire caused an 11½-ton piece to break off.

NORTH OF RED SQUARE

The area just north of Red Square is a major cultural, government, and shopping center. Bordering Red Square are two other squares: on the West side is **Manezh Square** (Manezhnaya Ploschad; Манежная площадь), a favorite spot for teenagers, tourists, and street performers. The famous **Moscow Hotel** (the big white "Baltica" sign on the roof is a beer ad) overlooks the square and separates it from the older, smaller **Revolution Square** (Ploschad Revolutsii; Площадь Революции). Both squares are bounded on the North by **Okhotny Ryad** (Hunters' Row; Охотный Ряд), once a market for game. Across Okhotny Ryad from the Moscow Hotel is the **Duma,** or lower house of Parliament, and across from Revolution Square is **Theatre Square** (Teatralnaya Ploschad; Театральная площадь), home of the **Bolshoi and Maly Theatres** (see Entertainment, p. 799). The glass domes on Manezh Square provide sunlight to the ritzy **Okhotny Ryad underground mall,** overflowing with new trends and New Russians. (Open daily 11am-11pm. Enter directly from the square or through the metro underpass.) More posh hotels, chic stores, and government buildings line **Tverskaya Street** (Тверская), the closest Moscow gets to a main thoroughfare. Tverskaya starts at Manezh Square and runs northwest through **Pushkin Square,** where missionaries, amateur politicians, and the headquarters of Russian newspapers make use of their newfound freedom of speech.

CHURCHES, MONASTERIES, AND SYNAGOGUES

CATHEDRAL OF CHRIST THE SAVIOR. The city's most controversial landmark is the enormous, gold-domed Cathedral of Christ the Savior (Khram Khrista Spositelya; Храм Христа Спасителя). Stalin demolished a similar cathedral on this site to make way for a gigantic Palace of the Soviets, but Khruschev abandoned the project and built an outdoor pool instead. In 1995, after the pool's water vapors had damaged paintings in the nearby Pushkin Museum, the Orthodox Church and mayor Yury Luzhkov won the battle for the site and reconstructed the cathedral in a mere two years. As for where they got the money—well, let's just say it was a miracle. *(M1: Kropotkinskaya; between ul. Volkhonka (Волхонка) and the Moscow River. Free, but donations welcome. Service schedule varies.)*

NOVODEVICHY CONVENT AND CEMETERY. You can't miss this most famous of Moscow's monasteries (Новодевичий Монастырь), thanks to its high brick walls, golden domes, and tourist buses. Tsars and nobles kept the coffers filled by exiling their well-dowried wives and daughters here when they grew tired of them. The **Smolensk Cathedral** (Smolensky Sobor; Смоленский Собор), in the center of the convent, shows off Russian icons and frescoes. As you exit the convent gates, turn right and follow the exterior wall back around to the **cemetery** (kladbishche; кладбище)—a pilgrimage site that holds the graves of famous artists, politicians, and military men, including Gogol, Chekhov, Stanislavsky, Bulgakov, Shostakovich,

PETER THE VERY VERY GREAT He towers over the Moscow River. He almost blocks out the sun. And he's really, really ugly. He's a giant, kitschy statue of Peter the Great, built in 1997 to commemorate Moscow's 850th birthday. Peter stands 100m tall at the mast of a ship, riding a gigantic column of water out of which other ships and flags stick out in every direction, forming a barely intelligible mass of bronze, lead, and steel. His creator, Zurab Tsereteli, has had other monumental sculptures built in Europe, the Americas, and his native Georgia and is a favorite of Mayor Yuri Luzhkov. Most Muscovites have disliked the statue from the start. Unfortunately, attempts to blow up the statue during construction failed, and now we can only marvel at the, ahem, greatness of the Russian state.

and Mayakovsky. *(M1: Sportivnaya. Take the exit out of the Metro that doesn't go to the stadium, take a right, and it's several blocks down on the left. Open W-M 10am-5:30pm. Closed first M of every month. 30R, students 15R. Smolensk Cathedral special exhibits 73R, students 43R. Cemetery open daily 9am-7pm; in winter 9am-6pm; 20R. Helpful English maps of cemetery 5R. Buy tickets at the small kiosk outside the entrance.)*

DANILOVSKY MONASTERY. This monastery (Даниловский) is home to the Patriarch, head of the Russian Orthodox Church—hence the men in uniform overrunning the place. The well-preserved and recently restored white exterior is complemented by stunning grounds and long-robed monks; unfortunately, visitors can enter only the church and the small museum, both to the left of the main entrance. The Patriarch's office is hard to miss, marked by an enormous mosaic of a stern-looking man watching over the visitors to his domain. *(M9: Tulskaya. From the square, follow the trolley tracks down Danilovsky val., away from the gray buildings. The monastery is a few blocks down on the right. Open daily 6am-8pm. Services M-F 6am, 7am, 5pm, Sa-Su 6:30am, 9am, 5pm. Museum open W and Sa-Su 11am-1pm and 1:30-4pm.)*

MOSCOW CHORAL SYNAGOGUE. First constructed in the 1870s, the Synagogue is a break from the city's ubiquitous onion domes. Though it functioned during Soviet rule, all but the bravest Jews were deterred by KGB agents who photographed anyone who entered. Today more than 200,000 Jews officially live in Moscow, and services are increasingly well attended. The graffiti occasionally sprayed on the building serves as a sad reminder that anti-Semitism in Russia is not dead. *(Bolshoy Spasoglinishchevsky per. 10 (Большой Спасоглинищевский). M5,6: Kitai-Gorod. Go north on Solyansky Proezd (Солянский Проезд) and take the 1st left. Open daily 9:30am-8pm; Shabbat services Sa 9am.)*

AREAS FOR WALKING

THE ARBAT. Now a pedestrian shopping arcade featuring McDonald's and Benetton, the Arbat was once a showpiece of *glasnost* and a haven for political radicals, Hare Krishnas, street poets, and *metallisty* (heavy metal rockers). The many outdoor cafes are good for people-watching. Intersecting but nearly parallel to the Arbat runs the bigger, newer, uglier **Novy Arbat,** a thoroughfare lined with gray highrises, foreign businesses, and massive Russian stores. *(M3: Arbatskaya.)*

MOSCOW METRO. The Metro (Московское Метро), one of the most beautiful in the world, is worth a tour of its own. All of the stations are unique, and those inside the Circle Line are elaborate, with mosaics, sculptures, stained glass, and crazy chandeliers. It's only 5R and you can stay as long you as like. Stations Kievskaya, Mayakovskaya, and Ploshchad Revolutsii are noteworthy, as are Komsomolskaya, Novoslobodskaya, Rimskaya, and Mendeleevskaya. *(Open daily 6am-1am.)*

VICTORY PARK. On the left past the **Triumphal Arch,** which celebrates the victories of 1812, Victory Park (Park Pobedy; Парк Победы) was built as a lasting monument to World War II. It includes the gold-domed **Church of St. George the Victorious** (Храм Георгия Победоносного; Khram Georgiya Pobedanosnova) and the impressive **Museum of the Great Patriotic War** (Музей Отечественной Войны; Muzey Otechestvennoy Voyny). In the park behind the museum is the **Exposition of War**

Technology (Експозиция Военной Техники; Expozitsiya Voyennoy Tekhniki), a large outdoor display of aircraft, tanks, and weaponry. *(M3: Kutuzovskaya. Museum open Tu-Su 10am-6pm. 80R, students 40R. Exposition open Tu-Su 10am-5pm. Free.)*

KOLOMENSKOYE SUMMER RESIDENCE. Another respite from Moscow's chaos is the tsars' summer residence, set on a wooded slope above the Moskva River. The cone-shaped, 16th-century **Assumption Cathedral** (Uspenskaya Sobor) and the nearby Church of Our Lady of Kazan, with its seven blue-and-gold cupolas, are the centerpieces of the grounds. Peter the Great's 1702 log cabin is the most notable of the park's several small museums. *(M2: Kolomenskaya; follow the exit signs to "к музею Коломенское." Turn right out of the Metro and walk down the tree-shaded path, through the small black gate, and down the leftmost path up the hill to the main entrance gate (12min). Grounds open daily 7am-10pm, Sept.-Mar. 9am-7pm. Free. Museums open Tu-Su 11am-5:30pm. Each museum 60-70R, students 30-35R.)*

🏛 MUSEUMS

Moscow's museum scene is the part of the city which remains the most patriotic and untouched by the West. Large government museums and small galleries alike proudly display Russian art, and dozens of historical and literary museums are devoted to the nation's impressive past and its major figures. Each is guarded by a team of loyal *babushki*. Come prepared for inconvenience; most museums stop selling tickets up to an hour before closing time, many have Russian-only captions, and prices can get astronomically high. Most major art and literary museums are concentrated in the southern and western parts of central Moscow.

▨ **Tretyakov Gallery** (Tretyakovskaya Galereya; Третьяковская Галерея), Lavrushinsky per. 10 (Лаврушинский). M7: Tretyakovskaya. Turn left and then left again, take an immediate right onto Bolshoy Tolmachevsky per. (Большой Толмачевский пер.), and turn right after 2 blocks on Lavrushinsky per. A veritable treasure chest of 18th- to early 20th-century Russian art, the museum also plays host to a magnificent collection of icons, including works by Andrei Rublyov and Theophanes the Greek. 210R, students 120R. Open Tu-Su 10am-7:30pm.

▨ **New Tretyakov Gallery** (Tretyakovskaya Galereya; Государственная Третьяковская Галерея), ul. Krymsky Val 10 (Крымский Вал). M1, 4: Park Kultury. Shares a building with the **Central House of Artists** gallery, across the river from the metro; enter the Tretyakov on the right, through the sculpture garden. Picks up chronologically where the first Tretyakov leaves off, displaying the greatest Russian art of the 20th century. Open Tu-Su 10am-7:30pm; *kassa* closes at 6:30pm. 210R, students 120R.

Pushkin Museum of Fine Arts (Muzey Izobrazitelnykh Iskusstv im. A.S. Pushkina; Музей Изобразительных Искусств им. А.С. Пушкина), ul. Volkhonka 12. M1: Kropotkinskaya. Moscow's most important collection of non-Russian art, with major Renaissance, Egyptian, and classical works, a superb showing of modern French painting, and rotating exhibits. To the left of the main building is the blue **Museum of Private Collections,** with foreign and Russian art from the 19th and 20th centuries. Pushkin open Tu-Su 10am-7pm; *kassa* closes at 6pm. 160R, students 60R. Private Collections open W-Su noon-7pm; *kassa* closes at 6pm. 40R, students 20R.

Museum of Contemporary Art (Muzey Sovremennovo Iskusstva; Музей Современного Искусства), Petrovka 25 (Петровка). M9: Chekhovskaya. Walk down Strasnoy bul. and take a right on Petrovka. A large collection of works by foreigners (like Dalí and Miro) and locals (like Zurab Tsereteli). Open M and W-Su noon-8pm. 90R, students 45R.

Museum of Contemporary Russian History (Tsentralny Muzei Sovremennoi Istorii Rossii; Централный Музей Современной Истории России), ul. Tverskaya 21. One block uphill from M6: Pushkinskaya, on the left. Covers Russian history from the late 19th century to present day in exhaustive if somewhat disorganized detail. All signs in Russian. Open Tu-Sa 10am-6pm, Su 10am-5pm. 20R.

Central Museum of the Armed Forces of the USSR (Tsentralny Muzey Vooruzhennykh Sil SSSR; Центральный Музей Вооруженных Сил СССР), ul. Sovetskoy Armii 2 (Советской Армии). M4: Novoslobodskaya. Walk down ul. Seleznevskaya

(Селезневская) to the rotary (10min.), turn left just after the huge theater, and bear right at the fork. One of the more interesting military museums. Open W-Su 10am-5pm. Closed 2nd Tu and last week of every month. 15R, students 10R.

HOMES OF THE LITERARY AND FAMOUS

Pushkin Literary Museum (Literaturny Muzey Pushkina; Литературный Музей Пушкина), ul. Prechisterka 12/2 (Пречистерка). Entrance on Khrushchevsky per. (Хрущевский). M1: Kropotkinskaya. If you haven't seen Pushkin-worship first-hand, this will either convert or frighten you. Open Tu-Su 11am-7pm. 15R, students 8R.

Tolstoy Museum (Muzey Tolstovo; Музей Толстого), ul. Prechistenka 11 (Пречистенка). M1: Kropotkinskaya. From the Metro, walk 3 blocks down Prechistenka; the museum is on the left. Displays original texts, paintings, and letters related to Tolstoy's works. Open Tu-Su 11am-5pm. 70R, students 30R. Camera 50R.

Mayakovsky Museum (Muzey im B.B. Mayakovskovo; Музей им. В. В. Маяковского), Lubyansky pr. 3/6 (Лубянский). M1, 8: Lubyanka. Behind a bust of Mayakovsky on ul Myasnitskaya (Мясницкая). More a walk-through work of futurist art than a museum. Mayakovsky's papers and work are arranged in a four-story assemblage of skewed chairs, spilled paint, and chicken wire. Open M-Tu and F-Su 10am-6pm, Th 1-9pm. 50R. Call ahead for an English tour (600R).

Gorky Museum-House, ul. Malaya Nikitskaya 6/2 (Малая Никитская). M3: Arbatskaya; cross Novy Arbat, turn right on Merelyakovsky per. (Мерзляковский пер.), cross the small park, and it's directly across from you. Entrance is on ul. Spiridonovka to the left. A pilgrimage site as much for its art nouveau architecture as for its collection of Maxim Gorky's stuff. Open W and F noon-7pm, Th and Sa-Su 10am-5pm. Closed last Th of each month. Free; 5-10R donation requested.

♫ ENTERTAINMENT

Moscow is a large, fast-paced city with the entertainment options to prove it. From September to June, it boasts some of the world's best theater, ballet, and opera, along with excellent orchestras. Advance tickets can be very cheap (US$2-5).

Bolshoy Teatr (Big Theater; Большой Театр), Teatralnaya pl. 1 (☎292 00 50). M2: Teatralnaya pl. Home to both the opera and the world-renowned ballet companies, with consistently excellent performances. Champagne and caviar at intermission. *Kassa* open noon-7pm. Daily performances Sept.-June at noon and 7pm. Tickets 10-1750R.

Maly Teatr (Small Theater; Малый Театр), Teatralnaya pl. 1/6 (☎923 26 21). M2: Teatralnaya. Just right of the Bolshoy. Affiliate at Bolshaya Ordynka 69 (☎237 31 81). Shows different productions nightly, mostly Russian classics of the 19th and 20th centuries, like Tolstoy or Chekhov. *Kassa* open Tu-Su noon-3pm and 4-7pm. Daily performances at 7pm. All performances in Russian. Tickets from 10-300R.

Musical Operetta Theater, ul. Bolshaya Dmitrovka 6 (☎292 12 37; www.operetta.com.ru). M2: Teatralnaya. Shows M-Th 7pm, F-Su 6pm. Tickets 30-300R.

Stanislavsky Theater, ul. Tverskaya 23 (Тверская; ☎299 72 24). M2: Tverskaya. Avant-garde productions. *Kassa* open Sept.-June 30 daily noon-3pm and 4-7pm. From 80R.

◙ NIGHTCLUBS AND BARS

Moscow's nightlife is the feistiest this side of the Volga, and certainly the most varied, expensive, and dangerous in Eastern Europe. Many of the more interesting clubs enjoy flaunting their high cover charges and strict face control policies. Check the weekend editions of *The Moscow Times* or *The Moscow Tribune* for club reviews and music festival listings. *The Moscow Times's* Friday pull-out section, *The Beat*, and *The Exile's* nightlife section (www.exile.ru) give good summaries of the week's events, as well as up-to-date restaurant, bar, and club reviews.

■ **Propaganda,** Bolshoy Zlatoustinsky per. 7 (Большой Златоустинский). M6, 7: Kitai-Gorod. Walk down ul. Maroseika and take the 1st left on Bolshoy Zlatoustinsky per. Unpretentious student crowd bounces in the black-light. Beer 50-110R. Cover F-Sa 70R. Open M-W and Su noon-12:30am, Th noon-3am, F 10pm-6am, Sa 3pm-6am.

■ **Projekt OGI,** 8/12 Potapovsky per., bldg. 2 (Потаповский; proekt.ogi.ru). M1: Chistye Prudy. Head down bul. Chistoprudny, take the 1st right, then the 1st left onto Potapovsky per. Exceptional food and wine, cheap. Live folk music F-Su 10pm. Cover 50R. Open daily 8am-6am.

Central Station, 16/2 Bolshaya Tartarskaya ul., bldg. 2 (www.gaycentral.ru). M5: Tretyakov. Turn right and then left on Bolshaya Tartarskaya ul., the 2nd street after the first light. Mayor Luzhkov's continued rejection of petitions for a gay pride parade haven't kept the patrons of this post-gender hotspot from coming out in full regalia. Live shows Th-Su 1:30-3am. Cover before 1am 160R, women 500R; students half-price.

Doug and Marty's Boar House, Zemlyanoi val 26. M3: Kurskaya, opposite the train station. About as American as you can get in Moscow, prices included. Packed on weekends. Beer 50-110R. Cover for men 100R, women 75R. Open 24hr.

Hungry Duck, Pushechnaya ul. 9 (Пушечная). M1: Kuznetsky Most. Enter the courtyard beyond the iron gate and follow the red neon arrows in. Lively crowd dances on the table, the bar, and everywhere in between. A bizarre variety of theme nights. Beers 60-90R. Cover for men 100-200R, women free-50R. Open daily 8pm-6am.

Crazy Milk, ul. Bolshaya Polyanka 54 (Большая Полянка). M5: Dobryninskaya. Cross ul. Zhitnaya to your left and make another left on Bolshaya Polyanka. Buffalo wings US$1 Tu and Th 6pm-midnight. 2-for-1 M-Th and Su midnight-6am. Cuban cigars 200-350R. Ask for the patio menu; it's the cheapest. Beer US$3-5. Open daily noon-6am.

◪ DAYTRIP FROM MOSCOW: SERGIEV POSAD

Possibly Russia's most famous pilgrimage point, Sergiev Posad (Сергиев Посад) attracts wandering Orthodox believers with a mass of churches huddled at its main sight—**St. Sergius's Trinity Monastery** (Свято-Троицкая Сергиева Лавра; Svyato-Troitskaya Sergieva Lavra). After decades of state-propagated atheism, the stunning monastery, founded around 1340, is again a religious center; the paths between the churches are dotted with monks in flowing robes. **Assumption Cathedral** (Успенский Собор; Uspensky Sobor), modeled after its namesake cathedral in Moscow's Kremlin, is the centerpiece of the complex, but the magnificent frescoes of the **Refectory** (Трапезная; Trapeznaya) and the Andrei Rublyov icons of **Trinity Cathedral** (Троицкий Собор; Troitsky Sabor) are just as captivating. *Elektrichki* (commuter trains) run to Sergiev Posad from Moscow's Yaroslavsky Vokzal (1½hr., every 30-40min., return 32R). To get to the monastery from the station, turn right, cross the street, and walk straight down the road until you see the domes. (10-15min; open daily 9am-6pm.)

ST. PETERSBURG (САНКТ-ПЕТЕРБУРГ) ☎812

In St. Petersburg, Russia suddenly becomes wide boulevards, bright façades, glorious palaces, and artistic revelry. This splendor is exactly what Peter the Great intended when he founded the city in 1703 on a Finnish swamp; the land was strategically chosen to drag Russia away from Byzantium and toward the West. But St. Petersburg was also the birthplace of the 1917 revolution, which would turn Russia decisively away from the western world. The city has been an inspiration for Dostoevsky, Gogol, Tchaikovsky, and Stravinsky, while its cafes fostered the revolutionary dreams of Lenin and Trotsky. Moscow may be the home of Mother Russia's post-apocalyptic youth, but St. Petersburg remains the majestic and mysterious symbol of Peter's great Russian dream.

NOT IN MY BACKYARD With so many sights clumped at the end of Nevsky Prospekt and just across the Neva, you may find yourself nursing blisters and wondering if the 20min. walk from the Hermitage to the nearest Metro station is Stalin's revenge on Western tourists, or just Soviet planning in all its glory. It's actually neither–a station, Admiralteystvo (Адмалтейство), does exist in the area and some maps even show it. The problem? After construction was completed, local residents refused to allow the authorities to build an entrance or exit connecting the station to the surface. Wave at the empty station as the train flies by.

▐▛ TRANSPORTATION

Flights: The main airport, **Pulkovo** (Пулково), has two terminals: Pulkovo-1 for domestic and Pulkovo-2 for international flights. M2: Moskovskaya. From the Metro, take bus #39 for Pulkovo-1 (20-25min.), or bus #13 for Pulkovo-2 (25-30min.). Hostels can usually arrange for a taxi (usually US$30-40).

Trains: Tsentralnye Zheleznodorozhnye Kassy (Центральные Железнодорожные Кассы; Central Ticket Offices), Canal Griboedova 24. International tickets at windows #4-6. Expect long lines and few English-speaking tellers. Prices vary; go to the **Intourist** office at each of the stations to purchase tickets on the day of departure. Check your ticket to see from which station your train leaves. Open M-Sa 8am-8pm, Su 8am-4pm.

Finlyandsky Vokzal (Финляндский Вокзал). M1: Pl. Lenina. To **Helsinki** (6hr., 2 per day, 1500R).

Moskovsky Vokzal (Московский Вокзал). M1: Pl. Vosstaniya. To **Moscow** (5-9hr., 12-15 per day, 170-400R). Anna Karenina threw herself under a train here.

Vitebsky Vokzal (Витебский Вокзал). M1: Pushkinskaya. To: **Kiev** (25hr., 2 every 2 days, 506-637R); **Odessa** (36hr., 1 per day, 654R); **Rīga** (13hr., 1 per day, 887R); **Tallinn** (9hr., 1 per day, 350R); **Warsaw** (27hr., 1 per day, 1090-1340R).

Buses: Nab. Obvodnovo Kanala 36 (Обводного Канала; ☎166 57 77). M4: Ligovsky pr. Take tram #19, 25, 44, or 49 or trolley #42 from the M1 stop across the canal. Facing the canal, turn right and walk 2 long blocks. The station is on your right. For the Baltics, the **Eurolines Agency** (Агенство Евролайнс; Agenstro Eurolains; ☎168 27 40), ul. Shkapina 10 (Щкапина), M1: Baltiiskaya, sends buses to Tallinn, Riga, and Vilnius.

Local Transportation: The efficient, safe **Metro** (Метро) has 4 lines running from the outskirts through the center. A Metro **token** (жетон; *zheton*) costs 5R. For **buses, trams,** and **trolleys,** buy tickets (4R) from the driver. All open 6am-midnight.

Taxis: Marked cabs are 10R per km. Haggle over flat fares for unofficial cabs. They are generally safe, but never get into a car with more than one person already in it.

▚▐ ORIENTATION AND PRACTICAL INFORMATION

The city center lies on mainland St. Petersburg between the south bank of the **Neva River** and the **Fontanka River. Nevsky prospekt** (Невский Проспект) runs through this downtown area, holding most of St. Petersburg's major sights, including the Winter and Summer Palaces and the Hermitage. **Moscow Train Station** (Московский Вокзал; Moskovsky Vokzal), is near the midway point of Nevsky pr. East of downtown and across the Neva sprawls **Vasilevsky Island,** the city's largest island; most of its sights lie on the eastern edge in the **Strelka** neighborhood. On the north side of the Neva and across from the Winter Palace is a small archipelago housing the **Peter and Paul Fortress,** the **Petrograd Side** residential neighborhood, and the wealthy **Kirov Island;** this is the historic heart of the city. The easiest way to get around is the **Metro.** In the center, **trolleys** #1, 5, and 22 go up and down Nevsky pr.

TOURIST, FINANCIAL AND LOCAL SERVICES

Tourist Office: Ost-West Contact Service, ul. Mayakovskovo 7 (Маяковского; ☎327 34 16; www.ostwest.com). Visa service. Open M-F 10am-6pm, Sa noon-6pm.

Budget Travel: Sindbad Travel (FIYTO), 3-ya Sovetskaya ul. 28 (3-я Советская; ☎327 83 84; sindbad@sindbad.ru; www.sindbad.ru). In the International Hostel. Arranges tickets, tours, and adventure trips. 10-80% discounts on plane tickets. English spoken. Open M-F 9:30am-8pm, Sa-Su 10am-5pm.

Adventure Travel: Wild Russia, ul. Mokhovaya 28-10 (Моховая; ☎273 65 14; www.wildrussia.spb.ru). Outdoor trips around St. Petersburg (weekends US$40-100).

Consulates: Canada, Malodetskoselsky pr. 32 (Малодетскосельский; ☎325 84 48). M1: Tekhnologichesky Institut. Open M-F 9am-5pm. **UK,** pl. Proletarskoi Diktatury 5 (Пролетарской Диктатуры; ☎320 32 00; www.britain.spb.ru). M1: Chernyshevskaya. Open M-F 9:30am-1pm and 2-5:30pm. **US,** ul. Furshtatskaya 15 (Фурштатская; ☎275 17 01; 24hr. emergency ☎274 86 92; acs_stpete@state.gov). M1: Chernyshevskaya. Open M-F 9:30am-5:30pm. Services for US citizens 9:30am-1:30pm. Citizens of **Australia** and **New Zealand** should contact their embassies in Moscow (p. 791), or the UK consulate in an emergency.

Currency Exchange: Look for "Обмен валюты" *(obmen valyuty)* signs everywhere. Avoid the black market. **Menatep Bank** (Менатеп; ☎326 39 01), Nevsky pr. 1, at the corner of Admiralteysky pr. M2: Nevsky Prospekt. Also cashes traveler's checks and offers Western Union services. Open daily 10:30am-1:30pm and 2:30-9pm.

English-Language Bookstore: Anglia British Bookshop (Англия), nab. Reki Fontanki 40 (Реки Фонтанки; ☎279 82 84; www.anglophile.ru). Open daily 10am-9pm.

EMERGENCY AND COMMUNICATIONS

Emergency: Police: ☎02. Multilingual police office for crimes against foreigners at ul. Zakharevskaya 19 (Захаревская; ☎278 30 14). Get consular help to report crime.

Pharmacy: Nevsky pr. 22. Open M-F 8am-10pm, Sa 10am-9pm, Su 11am-7pm.

Medical Assistance: American Medical Center, ul. Serpukhovskaya 10 (Серпуховская; ☎326 17 30). M1: Tekhnologichesky Institut (Технологический Институт). 24hr.

Internet Access: In back of the Central Telephone and Telegraph (see below) for 40-80R per hr. (30min. minimum). Prepay at *kassa* #6. Open daily 9am-9pm. Both **Hostel Holiday** and **International Youth Hostel (HI)** have free email.

Telephones: Central Telephone and Telegraph, Bolshaya Morskaya ul. 3/5 (Большая Морская). Facing the Admiralty, it's right off Nevsky pr. near Dvortsovaya pl. Prepay phone calls in the *kassa* in the 2nd (intercity) or 3rd (international) hall. When your party answers, push the round button with an arrow for a few seconds. Open 24hr. **Intercity calls** can also be made from any pay phone that takes phone cards (25 units cost 61R, 400 units 368R. 1 unit per min. for local calls; 48 per min. to the US). Cards can be purchased from the Central Telephone Office, metro stations, and news kiosks.

Post Office: ul. Pochtamtskaya 9 (Почтамтская). From Nevsky pr., go west on ul. Malaya Morskaya (Малая Морская), which becomes ul. Pochtamtskaya. It's about two blocks past Isaakievsky Sobor on the right. Open M-Sa 9am-8pm, Su 10am-6pm. Address mail to be held: First name, SURNAME, До Востребования, **190 000** Санкт-Петербург, Главпочтамт, RUSSIA.

▐ ACCOMMODATIONS

☒ International Youth Hostel (HI), 3-ya Sovetskaya ul. 28 (3-я Советская; ☎329 80 18; fax 329 80 19; ryh@ryh.ru). M1: Pl. Vosstaniya. Walk along Suvorovsky pr. (Суворовский) for 3 blocks, then turn right on 3-ya Sovetskaya ul. A cheery, tidy hostel in a pleasant neighborhood. Breakfast included. Minimal kitchen. Laundry. Internet. Check-out 11am. Curfew 1am. Dorms US$19; US$1 off with ISIC; US$2 off with HI.

Puppet Hostel (HI), ul. Nekrasova 12 (Некрасова; ☎272 54 01; puppet@ryh.ru; www.hostelling-russia.ru). M3: Mayakovskaya. Take the 2nd left on Nekrasova, and the hostel is next to the Bolshoy Puppet Theater, on the 4th floor. Friendly, English-speaking staff and clean, simple rooms. Breakfast included. Reception 8am-midnight. Check-out noon. No curfew. Call ahead. Dorms US$16; doubles US$19 per person. US$1 HI/ISIC discount. Groups over 10 US$15 per person.

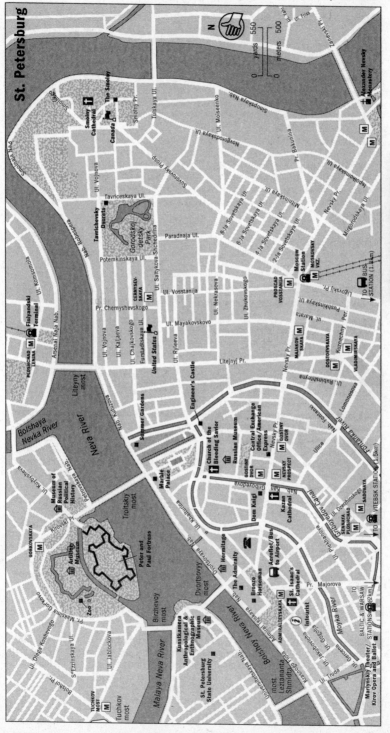

St. Petersburg

Hostel "Holiday" (HI), Nab. Arsenalnaya 9 (Арсенальная; ☎327 10 70; info@hostel.spb.ru). M1: Pl. Lenina. Exit at Finlyandsky Vokzal, turn left on ul. Komsomola (Комсомола), right on ul. Mikhailova. At the end of the street turn left on Arsenalnay; it's on the left. Visa support (single-entry US$30). Breakfast. Internet. Call ahead. Dorms US$14; doubles US$76. US$1 HI/ISIC discount; US$2 after five days.

Petrovsky Hostel, ul. Baltyskaya 26 (Балтийская; ☎/fax 252 75 63). M1: Narvskaya. From the Metro, turn left on pr. Stachek (Стачек). Don't cross the street into the park with the change; turn left on ul. Baltyskaya. Although far from the center, it's clean and comfy. Call 2-3mos. ahead for summer. Kitchen. Check-in by midnight. Dorms 200R; luxury rooms 350-600R.

Hotel Olgino (Отель Ольгино), Primorskoye Shosse 18 (Приморское Шоссе; ☎238 36 71; fax 238 37 63). M4: Staraya Derevnya. From the Metro, take bus #110. Outside city limits, but quiet. Horseback riding, bowling, billiards, and bath. Restaurant and disco. Check-in 24hr. Check-out noon. Call ahead. English spoken. Camping 232R per person; parking 116R. Singles 975R; doubles 1065R; luxury rooms 1500-1700R.

🗋 FOOD

St. Petersburg's menus vary little, but many places harbor top-secret methods of preparing tasty old Russian classics. Unfortunately, menus are often only in Cyrillic. Fast food venues dot the city. Today's cafes are mostly mainstream, with only vague echoes of Dostoevsky and Lenin. Markets stock tons of stuff; bargain and play hard to get. The **covered market,** at Kuznechny per. 3 (Кузнечный), just around the corner from M1: Vladimirskaya, and the **Maltsevsky Rynok** (Мальцевский Рынок), ul. Nekrasova 52 (Некрасова), at the top of Ligovsky pr. (Лиговский; M1: Pl. Vosstaniya), are the biggest and most exciting. For **groceries,** head to **Magazin #11** (Магазин; M1, 3: Pl. Vosstaniya), Nevsky pr. 105. (Open daily 10am-10pm.)

> ❗ Note that there is no effective water purification system in St. Petersburg, making exposure to **giardia** very likely. Boil tap water or drink bottled water.

▓ **The Idiot** (Идиоть), nab. Moyky 82 (Мойки). M4: Sadovaya. 5min. down the Moyka from Isaakievskaya pl. Expat hangout with vegetarian cuisine. Homemade meals 150-300R. Happy Hour 6:30-7:30pm. Open daily 11am-1am.

Tbilisi (Тбилиси), ul. Sytninskaya 10 (Сытнинская). M2: Gorkovskaya. Follow the wrought-iron fence around Park Lenina away from the fortress until the Sytny (Сытный) market; Tbilisi is behind it. Georgian cuisine is some of the best in Russia; good food for a good atmosphere. Entrees 40-150R. Open daily noon-11pm.

Kafe Hutorok (Хуторок), 3-ya Sovetskaya ul. 24. M1: Pl. Vosstaniya. Very Russian: good food and lots of alcohol. Entrees 75-140R. Alcohol 10-90R. Open daily 10am-11pm.

Tandoor (Тандур), Voznesensky pr. 2. M2: Nevsky Prospekt. On the corner of Admiralteysky pr., 2 blocks to the left after the end of Nevsky pr. Quality Indian food worth the price. Dinner 420-700R; lunch special noon-4pm 290R. Open daily noon-11pm.

Tyoshi na Blinakh (Тещи на Блинах; Mother-in-law's Bliny), Zagorodny pr. 18 (Загородый), M1: Vladimirskaya. Cheap, homestyle *bliny* stuffed with your choice of savory or sweet fillers. Open 24hr.

🗋 SIGHTS

▓ **THE HERMITAGE.** Originally a collection of 225 paintings bought by Catherine the Great in 1764, the State Hermitage Museum (Эрмитаж), the world's largest art collection, rivals the Louvre and the Prado in architectural, historical, and artistic significance. The **Winter Palace** (Зимний Дворец; Zimny Dvorets), commissioned in 1762, reflects the extravagant tastes of the Empress Elizabeth, Peter the Great's daughter. The collection grew too large for the Winter Palace by the end of the

1760s, and Catherine appointed Vallin de la Mothe to build the **Small Hermitage** (Малый Эрмитаж; Maly Hermitage), where she could retreat by herself or with one of her lovers. The **Great Hermitage** (Великий Эрмитаж; Veliky Hermitage) and the **Hermitage Theater** (Эрмитажный Театр; Hermitazhny Teatr) were completed in the 1780s. Stasov, a famous imperial Russian architect, built the fifth building, the **New Hermitage** (Новый Эрмитаж; Novy Hermitage), in 1851. The tsars lived with their collection here until 1917, after which the museum complex was nationalized. It is impossible to absorb the whole museum in a day or even a week—only 5% of the three million-piece collection is on display at any one time. Ask for an English floor plan at the information desk near the *kassa*.

Palace Square (Дворцовая Площадь; Dvortsovaya Ploshchad), the huge windswept expanse in front of the Winter Palace, has witnessed many turning points in Russia's history. Catherine took the crown here after overthrowing Tsar Peter III, her husband; Nicholas II's guards fired into a crowd of peaceful demonstrators on "Bloody Sunday" in 1905, leading to the 1905 revolution; and Lenin's Bolsheviks seized power from the provisional government during the storming of the Winter Palace in October 1917. The 700-ton **Alexander Column,** held in place by its massive weight alone, commemorates Russia's defeat of Napoleon in 1812. On the other side of the Hermitage, across the river, **Vasilevsky Island** splits the Neva in two. The area closest to the Hermitage, depicted on the 50R note, was a center for sea trade and now houses many of the city's best and strangest museums. *(Dvortsovaya nab. 34 (Дворцовая). M2: Nevsky Prospekt. Exiting the Metro, turn left and walk down Nevsky pr. to Admiralty. The Hermitage is to the right; enter on river side. Open Tu-Su 10:30am-6pm; cashier and upper floors close 1hr. earlier. 300R, students free. Cameras 100R. Long lines; come early.)*

■ **ST. ISAAC'S CATHEDRAL.** Glittering, intricately carved masterpieces of iconography await beneath the dome of **St. Isaac's Cathedral** (Исаакиевский Собор; Isaakievsky Sobor), a massive example of 19th-century architecture. On a sunny day, the 100kg of pure gold that coat the dome shine for miles. The 360-degree view atop the **colonnade** is stunning. *(M2: Nevsky Prospekt. Exiting the Metro, turn toward the Admiralty and walk almost to the end of Nevsky pr. Turn left onto Malaya Morskaya. Open M-Tu and Th-Su 11am-7pm. 230R, students 100R. Colonnade open M-Tu and Th-Su 11am-6pm. 80R, students 40R. Last entry 1hr. before closing. The kassa is to the right of the main entrance, on the south side. Foreigners buy tickets inside.)*

FORTRESS OF PETER AND PAUL. Across the river from the Hermitage stand the walls and golden spire of the **Fortress of Peter and Paul** (Петропавловская Крепость; Petropavlovskaya Krepost). Construction of the fortress began on May 27, 1703, which is considered the birthday of St. Petersburg. Intended as a defense against the Swedes, it never saw battle; Peter I defeated the northern invaders before the bulwarks were finished. Inside, the **Peter and Paul Cathedral** (Петропавловский Собор; Petropavlovsky Sobor) glows with rosy marble walls and a breathtaking Baroque iconostasis—a partition with intricate iconography. The cathedral holds the remains of Peter the Great and all but two of the other Romanov tsars. Before entering the main vault you pass through the **Chapel of St. Catherine the Martyr.** The bodies of the last Romanovs—Tsar Nicholas II and his family, along with their faithful servants—were entombed here on July 17, 1998, the 80th anniversary of their murders at the hands of the Bolsheviks. After the fortress ceased to function as a defense against the Swedes, Peter turned it into a prison for dissidents; the condemned were held at **Trubetskoy Bastion** (Трубецкой Бастион). The fortress's southwest corner is a reconstruction of the prison where Peter the Great held and tortured his first son, Aleksei. Dostoevsky, Gorky, Trotsky, and Lenin's older brother also spent time here. *(M2: Gorkovskaya. Exiting the Metro, turn right on Kamennoostrovsky pr. (Каменноостровский), the street in front of you (there is no sign). Follow the street to the river and cross the wooden bridge to the island fortress. Open M and Th-Su 11am-6pm, Tu 11am-5pm; closed last Tu of each month. Purchase a single ticket for most sites sights (80R, students 20R) at the kassa in the "boathouse" in the middle of the complex.)*

ALEKSANDR NEVSKY MONASTERY. A major pilgrimage spot and peaceful strolling place, **Aleksandr Nevsky Monastery** (Александро-невская Лавра; Aleksandro-Nevskaya Lavra) became one of four Orthodox monasteries to have received the highest monastic title of "lavra" in 1797. The 1716 **18th-Century Necropolis,** the city's oldest burial ground, houses Pushkin's wife and several famous architects. The nearby **Artists' Necropolis** (Некрополь Мастеров Искусств; Nekropol Masterov Uskusstv) is the permanent resting place of Fyodor Dostoevsky and composers Tchaikovsky, Rimsky-Korsakov, and Mussorgsky. The **Church of the Annunciation** (Благовещенская Церковь; Blagoveshchenskaya Tserkov), farther along the central stone path on the left, holds the remains of war heroes **Alexander Suvorov** and **Mikhail Kutuzov,** and is the original burial place of the Romanovs, who were moved to Peter and Paul Cathedral in 1998. The **Trinity Cathedral** (Свято-Троицкий Собор; Svyato-Troitsky Sobor) is at the end of the path, teeming with *babushki* energetically crossing themselves. *(M3, 4: Pl. Aleksandra Nevskovo. The 18th-century Necropolis lies to the left of the entrance; the Artists' Necropolis is to the right. Cemeteries open M-W and F-Su 10am-5pm. Cemeteries 40R, students 20R. Dress modestly.)*

ALONG NEVSKY PROSPEKT. Most of St. Petersburg's biggest sights cluster around the western end of vibrant Nevsky pr., the city's 4½km main thoroughfare. The Prospekt runs to Nevsky Monastery from the **Admiralty** (Адмиралтий; Admiralteystvo), the former naval headquarters whose golden spire—painted black during World War II to disguise it from German artillery bombers—towers over the surrounding gardens and most of Nevsky pr. In the park to the left of the Admiralty as you face it from the Nevsky side, the **Bronze Horseman** (Peter the Great) is one of the most widely recognized symbols of the city; copies are all over Russia. *(M2: Nevsky. Exit the Metro and walk to the end of Nevsky pr. toward the golden spire.)* Walking back east on Nevsky pr., the enormous, Roman-style **Kazan Cathedral** (Казанский Собор; Kazansky Sobor) looms to the right. *(M2: Nevsky. Open daily 8:30am-7:30pm. Free.)* Half a block down, looking up Canal Griboedova to the left, you can see the brilliantly colored **Church of the Bleeding Savior** (Спас На Крови; Spas Na Krovi), which sits on the site of the 1881 assassination of Tsar Aleksandr II. *(Open M-Tu and Th-Su 11am-7pm; kassa closes at 6pm. 250R, students 100R.)* To the right is the yellow 220-year-old Gostiny Dvor mall (Гостиный Двор; Merchants' Yard). *(M3: Gostiny Dvor. Open M-Sa 10am-10pm, Su 11am-9pm.)* Also to the right is **Ostrovskovo Square** (пл. Островского; Pl. Ostrovskovo), which houses the historic Alexandrinsky Theater and an impressive monument to Catherine the Great. Much farther down Nevsky, **Uprising Square** (Площадь Восстания; Ploshchad Vosstaniya) is where the bloodiest confrontations of the February Revolution of 1917 took place in. *(M1: Ploshchad Vosstaniya.)*

SUMMER GARDENS AND PALACE. (Летний Сад и Дворец; Letny Sad i Dvorets). The long, shady paths of the Summer Gardens are a lovely place to rest and cool off. In the northeast corner sits Peter the Great's **Summer Palace;** the decor reflects Peter's European tastes, with everything from Spanish and Portuguese chairs to Dutch tile and German clocks. **Mars Field** (Марсово Поле; Marsovo Polye), so named because of military parades held here in the 19th century, extends next to the Summer Gardens and is now a memorial to the victims of the Revolution and the Civil War (1917-19). Don't walk on the grass; you'd be treading on a massive common grave. *(M2: Nevsky. Turn right at the Griboyedov Canal, pass the Church of the Bleeding Savior, cross the Moyka, and turn right onto ul. Pestelya (Пестеля). The palace and gardens are on your left, just after the next small canal. Garden open May-Oct. daily 10am-10pm; 6R, students 4R, children 2R. Nov.-Apr. open 10am-8pm; free. Palace open May-Oct. M and W-Su 11am-6pm; closed last M of the month. 60R, students 30R.)*

PISKARYOV MEMORIAL CEMETERY. (Пискарёвское Мемориальное Кладбище; Piskaryovskoye Memorialnoye Kladbishche). To understand St. Petersburg's obsession with World War II, come to the remote and hauntingly tranquil Piskaryov Memorial Cemetery. Close to a million people died during the 900-day German siege of the city; 490,000 of them are buried here. An eternal flame and grassy

JUBILEE All of St. Petersburg is gearing up for its year-long 300th anniversary celebration in 2003. Billions of roubles have gone into restoring major sights and planning glorious displays. In an effort to outshine Moscow's 850th anniversary in 1997, annual city festivals will be bigger than ever. If you plan on being here in 2003, book accomodations well in advance. Check the *St. Petersburg Times* or the jubilee's official website (www.300.spb.ru) to get the scoop on the latest shows and exhibits.

mounds are all that mark the dead. The monument says: "No one is forgotten; nothing is forgotten." *(M2: Ozerki (Озерки). Go right out of the exit to bus #123. Ride 20 stops; the cemetery's on the left, marked by a low granite wall and 2 gate buildings. Open 24hr. Free.)*

OTHER MUSEUMS. The ◼ **Russian Museum** (Русский Музей; Russky Muzey) boasts the world's second largest collection of Russian art. *(M3: Gostiny Dvor. Down ul. Mikhailovskaya past the Grand Hotel Europe. Open M 10am-5pm, W-Su 10am-6pm; kassa closes 1hr. earlier. 240R, students 120R.)* At the **Kunstkamera Anthropological and Ethnographic Museum** (Кунсткамера), "lives and habits" of the world's indigenous peoples join Peter the Great's anatomical collection, featuring severed heads and deformed fetuses. Don't miss the two-headed calf. *(Open Tu-Su 11am-6pm; kassa closes at 4:45pm. 100R, students 20R.)* Find Soviet propaganda and artifacts from the "Great Patriotic War" at the **Museum of Russian Political History** (Музей Политической Истории России; Muzey Politicheskoy Istorii Rossii), ul. Kuybysheva 2/4. *(M2: Gorkovskaya. Go down Kamennoostrovsky toward the mosque and turn left on Kuybysheva. Open F-W 10am-6pm. 60R, students 30R.)*

🎵 🎭 ENTERTAINMENT AND NIGHTLIFE

St. Petersburg's famed White Nights lend the night sky a pale glow from mid-June to early July. In summer, loners stroll under the illuminated night sky and watch the bridges over the Neva go up at 1:30am. Walk on the same side of the river as your hotel—the bridges don't go back down until 4-5am, although some close briefly between 3 and 3:20am.

It is fairly easy to get tickets to world-class performances for as little as 20-30R, although many of the renowned theaters are known to overcharge foreigners; buying Russian tickets from scalpers will save you money but you'll have to dress up and play Russian at the show. The **Mariinsky Teatr** (Мариийнский), a.k.a. the "Kirov," Teatralnaya pl. 1 (Театральная), M4: Sadovaya, where Tchaikovsky's *Nutcracker* and *Sleeping Beauty* premiered, is one of the most famous ballet halls in the world. Pavlova, Nureyev, Nizhinsky, and Baryshnikov all started here. In June, the theater hosts the **White Nights Festival.** Tickets go on sale 10 days in advance. (☎114 43 44. 20-300R for foreigners. *Kassa* open W-Su 11am-3pm and 4-7pm.) **Maly Teatr** (Малый Театр; Small Theater), a.k.a. "Mussorgsky," pl. Iskusstv 1 (Искусств), is open July to August, when Mariinsky is closed. (☎219 19 49. Shows noon and 7pm. Tickets 5-30R for Russians, up to 200R for foreigners. *Kassa* open daily 11am-3pm and 4-7:15pm. Bring your passport.) **Shostakovich Philharmonic Hall,** Mikhailovskaya ul. 2, opposite the Grand Hotel Europe, has both classical and modern concerts. (☎110 42 57. M3: Gostiny Dvor. Performances at 4 and 7pm. Tickets from 20R.) **Aleksandrinsky Teatr** (Александринский Театр), pl. Ostrovskovo 2, attracts famous Russian actors and companies. (☎110 41 03. M3: Gostiny Dvor. Tickets 10-80R. *Kassa* open M-F 11am-3pm and 4-7:15pm, Sa-Su 11am-3pm and 4-6:15pm.)

During the pre-Gorbachev era, St. Petersburg was the heart of the Russian underground music scene; today, the city still hosts a large number of interesting clubs. Be careful when going home; cabs are usually a safe bet, but make sure your bridge isn't up. Check the Friday issue of *St. Petersburg Times* and *Pulse* for current events, special promotions, and up-to-the-minute club reviews. **Griboyedov** (Грибоедов), ul. Voronezhskaya 2A (Воронежная), once a bomb shelter, is now one of the hottest clubs in the city. (M4: Ligovsky Prospekt. Cover 60-100R. Open daily 6pm-6am.) **Moloko** (Молоко; Milk), Perekupnoy per. 12 (Перекупной), is a

---

THOSE PUSHY BABUSHKI They shove harder than anyone on the buses and metro. They bundle up to the ears on even the hottest days in scarves and winter coats, then strip down to teeny-weeny bikinis and sunbathe on the banks of the Neva. They are *babushki,* and they mean business. Technically, *babushka* means grandma, but under the Soviet system, Russians began using it as a generic term for elderly women. In any case, be warned: if a *babushka* gets on the bus or metro, no matter how hardy she looks, and how weak and tired you feel, surrender your seat, or prepare for the verbal pummeling of a lifetime.

---

rock club. (M3, 4: Pl. Aleksandra Nevskovo. Cover 40-80R.) **JFC Jazz Club** is at Shpalernaya ul. 33 (Шпалерная). (M1: Chernyshevskaya. Cover 50-100R. Open daily 7-11pm.) **Greshniki** (•••• ••••; Sinners), nab. Canala Griboyedova 28/1 (Канала Грибоедова), is a down-to-earth gay club with four floors of dance rooms and chill-out space. Walk two blocks off Nevsky pr., past the Kazan Cathedral. (M2: Nevsky Prospekt. Drag shows W-Su 1 and 2am. 18+. Open daily 8pm-6am.)

◪ DAYTRIP FROM ST. PETERSBURG: PETERHOF

Peterhof (Петергоф) is the largest and the best-restored of the Russian palaces. It was burned to the ground during the Nazi retreat, but Soviet authorities provided the staggering sums needed to rebuild it. The entire complex is 300 years old, although many tsars have added their own touches since then. To get through the gates you must pay an admission fee that grants access to the **Lower Gardens,** a perfect place for a picnic along the shores of the Gulf of Finland. (Open daily 9am-9pm. 120R, students 60R.) To work up an appetite, tour through the **Grand Palace** (Большой Дворец; Bolshoy Dvorets). Wanting to create his own Versailles, Peter started building the first residence here in 1714, but his daughter Empress Elizabeth (and later, Catherine the Great) greatly expanded and remodeled it. (Open Tu-Su 10:30am-6pm; closed last Tu of the month. English tours 120R. 240R, students 120R.) From the palace, the gravity-powered fountains of the Grand Cascade send their waters into the Grand Canal. To enter the cozy but impressive stone grotto underneath the fountains, buy tickets just outside the palace. (Grotto open Tu-Su 11am-4:30pm. 90R, students 45R.) See **Monplaisir,** where Peter actually lived; the big palace was only for special occasions. (Open M-Tu and Th-Su 10:30am-6pm. 170R, students 85R.) Next door is the **Catherine Building** (Екатерининский Корпус; Ekaterininsky Korpus), where Catherine the Great lay low while her husband was being overthrown on her orders. (Open M-Tu and Th-Su 10:30am-5pm. 180R, students 90R.) Take the **train** from the Baltyskaya Vokzal (Балтийская; M1: Baltiyskaya; 40min., every 15min., 8R). Buy tickets from the office (Пригородные касса; *prigorodnye kassa*) in the courtyard. Get off at Novy Peterho. Or, in summer, take the **hydrofoil** from the quay on Dvortsovaya nab. (Дворцовая) in front of the Hermitage (30min., every 20-40min. 9:30am-6pm, 300R).

SLOVAKIA

(SLOVENSKO)

SLOVAK KORUNA

US$1 = 49SK	10SK = US$0.21
CDN$1 = 31SK	10SK = CDN$0.33
UK£1 = 68SK	10SK = UK£0.15
IR£1 = 55SK	10SK = IR£0.18
AUS$1 = 25SK	10SK = AUS$0.40
NZ$1 = 21SK	10SK = NZ$0.48
ZAR1 =5.7SK	10SK = ZAR1.75
DM1 =22SK	10SK = DM0.45
EUR€ = 43SK	10SK = EUR€0.23

PHONE CODE	**Country code: 421. International dialing prefix:** 00. From outside Slovakia, dial int'l dialing prefix (see inside back cover) + 421 + city code + local number.

After a centuries of nomadic invasions and Hungarian domination, and 40 years of Soviet rule, Slovakia has finally emerged as an independent country. After rejecting communism while still part of Czechoslovakia in the 1989 Velvet Revolution, Slovakia split from its Czech neighbor in 1993. Many rural Slovaks still stick to their peasant traditions, while their offspring flock to the city. Castle ruins, spectacular outdoor terrain, and low prices keep Slovakia a haven for budget travelers.

For more on Slovakia, why not try a little *Let's Go: Eastern Europe 2002?*

FACTS AND FIGURES

Official Name: Slovak Republic.
Capital: Bratislava.
Population: 5,400,000.
Land Area: 48,800 sq. km.

Climate: Temperate.
Languages: Slovak, Hungarian.
Religions: Roman Catholic (60%), atheist (10%), Protestant (8%), other (22%).

DISCOVER SLOVAKIA

Slovakia is an outdoor-lover's paradise. In the west, the **Low Tatras** near **Liptovský Mikuláš** (p. 816) are a relatively deserted mountain range with everything from day hikes in the wooded foothills to overnight treks above the tree line. You'll have to battle with German and Slovak tourists to tackle the trails and slopes of the **High Tatras** near **Starý Smokovec** (p. 816), but it'll be worth it to witness the snow-capped peaks of this range, one of the best—and cheapest—mountain playlands in Europe. Farther south, **Slovenský Raj National Park** (p. 817) offers miles of ravine-crossing, cliff-climbing, heart-stopping treks and ice caves ripe for spelunking. And don't forget **Bratislava,** the often-overlooked capital, whose ruined castle towers over the Danube.

ESSENTIALS

WHEN TO GO

The weather is best May through September. Rain is not uncommon any time of the year—winters are very cold, damp, and snowy. No matter what time of year, take warm clothing if you plan to travel into the mountains. November through February is the best time for skiing, and August is the best time for hiking.

DOCUMENTS AND FORMALITIES

VISAS. Citizens of South Africa and the US can visit Slovakia without a **visa** for up to 30 days; Australia, Canada, Ireland, New Zealand, and the UK 90 days. To apply for a visa, contact an embassy or consulate in person or by mail; processing takes two business days (single-entry US$20; double-entry US$22; 90-day multiple-entry US$40; 180-day multiple-entry US$62; transit—good for 30 days—US$20). Visa prices vary with exchange rate. Travelers must also register their visa within three days of entering Slovakia; hotels will do this automatically. If you intend to stay longer or get a visa extension, notify the Office of Border and Alien Police.

EMBASSIES. All foreign embassies are in Bratislava (see p. 813). For Slovakian embassies at home: **Australia**, 47 Culgoa Circuit, O'Malley, Canberra ACT 2606 (☎(06) 290 1516; fax 290 1755); **Canada**, 50 Rideau Terrace, Ottawa, ON K1M 2A1 (☎613-749-4442; fax 613-749-4989; slovakemb@sprint.ca); **Ireland**, 20 Clyde Rd. Ballsbridge, Dublin 4 (☎660 0012 or 660 0008); **South Africa**, 930 Arcadia St., Arcadia, Pretoria; P.O. Box 12736, Hatfield, 0028 (☎(012) 342 2051; fax 342 3688); **UK**, 25 Kensington Palace Gardens, London W8 4QY (☎(020) 7243 0803; fax 7313 6481; mail@slovakembassy.co.uk; www.slovakembassy.co.uk); and **US**, 2201 Wisconsin Ave. NW, Suite 250, Washington, D.C. 20007 (☎202-965-5160; fax 202-965-5166; svkem@concentric.net; www.slovakemb.com).

TRANSPORTATION

BY PLANE. Bratislava does have an international airport, but entering the country by air may be inconvenient and expensive. Flying to nearby Vienna, Austria, and taking a bus or train from there is much cheaper and takes about the same time.

BY TRAIN. International rail links connect Slovakia to its neighbors. **EastRail** is valid in Slovakia; **Eurail** is not. You'll pay extra for an *InterCity* or *EuroCity* fast train, and if there's a boxed R on the timetable, a *miestenka* (reservation; 7Sk) is required. If you board the train without a reservation, expect to pay an extra 150Sk fine. Larger towns on the railway have many *stanice* (train stations); the *hlavná stanica* is the main one. Tickets must be bought before boarding the train, except in the tiniest towns. **ŽSR** is the national train company. **Cestovný poriadok** (58Sk), the master schedule, is also printed on a large, round board in stations. In western Slovakia, *odchody* (departures) and *príchody* (arrivals) are posted on yellow and white signs, respectively—double check the display board for the *nástupište* (gate). In eastern Slovakia, ask *"Je to správne nástupište do...?"* ("Is this the right platform for...?") Reservations are recommended for *expresný* trains and first-class seats, but are not necessary for *rychlík* (fast), *spešný* (semi-fast), or *osobný* (local) trains. First and second class are relatively comfortable.

BY BUS. In many hilly regions, ČSAD or SAD **buses** are the best and sometimes the only option. Except for long trips, buy tickets on the bus. Schedule symbols include: **X**, weekdays only; **a**, Saturdays and Sundays only; **r** and **k**, excluding holidays. Numbers refer to the days of the week on which the bus runs—1 is Monday, 2 is Tuesday, and so forth. *"Premava"* means including and *"nepremava"* is except; following those words are often lists of dates (day, then month).

BY CAR, BIKE, AND THUMB. Car rentals are rare. **Taxis** are fairly safe and convenient, but expensive; be sure to check the price of the trip before getting in. The Slovaks love to ride **bikes**, especially in the Tatras, the foothills of West Slovakia, and Šariš. VKÚ publishes color maps of most regions (70-80Sk). *Let's Go* does not recommend **hitchhiking**, which is neither successful nor common; if you do, use a sign.

TOURIST SERVICES AND MONEY

> **EMERGENCY**   **Police:** ☎ 158. **Ambulance:** ☎ 155. **Fire:** ☎ 150.

TOURIST OFFICES. The main tourist offices form a loose conglomeration called **Asociácia Informačných Centier Slovenska (AICS)**; look for the green logo. The offices are invariably on or near the town's main square; the nearest one can often be found by dialing ☎ 186. English is often spoken here. **SATUR**, the Slovak branch of the old Czechoslovakian Čedok, seems more interested in flying Slovaks abroad on package tours, but may be of some help.

MONEY. One hundred *halér* make up one **Slovak koruna (Sk)**. The currency rates above are those for September, 2001; with inflation around 8%, expect both rates and prices quoted in *koruny* to change significantly over the next year. Post offices tend to have better exchange rates than banks. **Všeobecná Úverová Banka (VÚB)** has offices in even the smallest towns and cashes AmEx/Eurocheque traveler's checks for a 1% commission; most offices give MC cash advances. Many Slovenská Sporiteľňa bureaus handle Visa cash advances. MC/Visa ATMs can be found in all but the smallest towns. Leave your AmEx at home—it's useless in Slovakia. Tipping is common in restaurants. Most people round up; an 8-10% tip is generous.

BUSINESS HOURS. Many banks close at 3:30pm, whiles shops are usually open 9am-6pm during the week and close at noon on Saturdays.

COMMUNICATION

MAIL. Slovakia has an efficient mail service, taking two to three weeks depending on the destination. Almost every post office *(pošta)* provides **Express Mail Services**, but to send a package abroad, a trip to a *colnice* (customs office) is in order. *Poste Restante* mail with a "1" after the city name will arrive at the main post office.

TELEPHONE AND INTERNET. Card phones are common, and although they sometimes refuse your card (150Sk), they're much better than the coin-operated variety. Purchase cards at kiosks and telecommunications offices near some post offices. International direct dial numbers include: **AT&T**, ☎ 00 42 100 101; **British Telecom**, ☎ 0800 04 401; **Canada Direct**, ☎ 08 00 00 01 51; **MCI**, ☎ 08000 00 112; **Sprint**, ☎ 0042 187 187. **Internet** access is available in large cities and some mid-sized ones.

LANGUAGES. Slovak, closely related to Czech, is a tricky Slavic language, but any attempt to speak it will be appreciated. English is not uncommon among Bratislava youth, but people outside the capital are more likely to speak German, and those near the border, Polish. You can find English-speakers in tourist offices and cities. Russian is understood, but not always welcome. For Slovak basics, see p. 988.

ACCOMMODATIONS AND CAMPING

Foreigners will often pay up to twice as much as Slovaks for the same room. Finding cheap accommodations in Bratislava before the student dorms open in July is impossible, and without reservations, the outlook in Slovenský Raj and the Tatras can be bleak. Otherwise, it's not difficult to find a bed as long as you call ahead. The tourist office, SATUR, or Slovakotourist can usually help. **Juniorhotels (HI),** though uncommon, are a step above the usual hostel. In the mountains, **chaty** (mountain huts/cottages) range from plush quarters for 400Sk per night to a friendly bunk and outhouse for 200Sk. **Hotel** prices fall dramatically outside Bratislava and the High Tatras, and hotels are rarely full. **Pensions** *(penzióny)* are less expensive than hotels and often more fun. **Campgrounds** lurk on the outskirts of most towns, and many offer bungalows. Camping in national parks is illegal.

HEALTH AND SAFETY

Tap water varies in quality and appearance but is generally safe. A reciprocal agreement between Slovakia and the UK entitles Brits to free medical care here. *Drogerie* (drugstore) shelves heave with Western brand names: bandages are *obväz*, aspirin *aspirena*, tampons *tampony*, and condoms *kondómy*. Slovakia is friendly toward **lone women travelers,** though they may encounter stares. Although homosexuality is legal, it is not always tolerated. There are virtually no minorities in Slovakia except for the Roma, who face discrimination.

FOOD AND DRINK

Slovakia emerged from its 1000-year Hungarian captivity with a taste for paprika, spicy *guláš*, and fine wines. The national dish, *bryndžové halušky*, is a plate of dumpling-esque pasta smothered in a thick sauce of sheep or goat cheese that sometimes comes flecked with bacon. Slovakia's second-favorite dish is *pirogy*, a pasta-pocket filled with potato or *bryndža* cheese, topped with bacon bits. *Pstruh* (trout), often served whole, is also popular. *Kolačky* (pastry) is baked with cheese, jam or poppy seeds, and honey. Enjoy flavorful wines at a *vináreň* (wine hall). *Pivo* (beer) is served at a *pivnica* or *piváreň* (tavern). The favorite Slovak beer is *Zlatý Bažant*, a light, slightly bitter Tatran brew. Slovakia produces several brandies: *slivovica* (plum), *marhulovica* (apricot), and *borovička* (juniper-berry).

HOLIDAYS

Holidays: Independence Day (Jan. 1); Epiphany (Jan. 6); Good Friday (Apr. 21); Easter (Apr. 24); Labor Day (May 1); Sts. Cyril and Methodius Day (July 5); Anniversary of Slovak National Uprising (Aug. 29); Constitution Day (Sept. 1); Our Lady of the Seven Sorrows (Sept. 15); All Saint's Day (Nov. 1); Christmas (Dec. 24-26).

BRATISLAVA   ☎07

Directly between Vienna and Budapest, Bratislava is experienced most often as a pit stop on the way to bigger cities. For hundreds of years it has been abused by foreign rulers, but in the last five years major renovations have improved the city's outlook. The Old Town is all cobblestones, baroque buildings and cafes, while the outskirts are laced with vineyards and ruins. Bratislava Castle, a symbol of Slovak pride, looms alongside the New Bridge (Nový Most), a symbol of Soviet excess. Resist the temptation to pass over Bratislava for Prague: it will surprise you.

⌐ TRANSPORTATION

Trains: Bratislava **Hlavná stanica** (☎52 49 82 75), north of the city center. From the center, head up Štefánikova, turn right onto Šancová, and then head left up the road that goes past the waiting buses. International tickets at counters #5-13. **Wasteels** (☎52 49 93 57; www.wasteels.host.sk), with an office in front, sells discounted tickets to those under 26. Open M-F 8:30am-4:30pm. To: **Vienna** (1½hr.; 3 per day; 561Sk, Wasteels 490Sk); **Budapest** (2½-3hr., 7 per day, 499/446Sk); **Prague** (5hr., 7 per day, 415Sk); **Warsaw** (8hr., 1 per day, 1707Sk/1121Sk); **Kraków** (8hr., 1 per day, 1460/1121Sk); and **Berlin** (10hr., 2 per day, 3136/2470Sk).

Buses: Mlynské nivy 31 (☎55 42 16 67), east of the city center. From Nám SNP, take a left onto Suché mýto, then a left on Dunajska. Bear right onto Mlynské nivy (2km). To: **Vienna** (1½hr., 7 per day, 350Sk); **Budapest** (4hr., 2 per day, 480Sk); and **Prague** (5hr., 7 per day, 320Sk); **Warsaw** (13hr., F 9:20pm, 670sk); and **Berlin** (12hr., 9pm on F, 1800Sk). More reliable than trains for domestic transport. Check ticket for bus number (*č. aut.*) since several different buses may depart from the same stand.

Public Transportation: Tickets for daytime **trams** and **buses** (4am-11pm) are sold at kiosks and orange *automats* in bus stations (10Sk for 10min., 14Sk for 30min., 20Sk for 60min.). **Night buses** marked with black and orange numbers in the 500s require 2 tickets; they run at midnight and 3am. Most trams pass by Nám. SNP, while most buses stop at the north base of Nový Most. 1000Sk fine for no ticket. **Tourist passes** sold at some kiosks: 1-day 70Sk, 2-day 130Sk, 3-day 160Sk, 7-day 240Sk.

Taxis: Bratislava **Profi** (☎53 41 96 96; 24hr. service), **Profit Taxi** (☎45 24 67 16). Expect to pay 300Sk from center to bus station, 700Sk from center to airport.

Hitchhiking: Hitchers to **Vienna** tend to cross most SNP and walk down Viedenská cesta; this road also goes to **Hungary** via Győr, but fewer cars head in that direction. Hitchers to **Prague** will take bus #121 or 122 from the city center to the Patronka stop. Hitching is legal (except on major highways) and common, but not recommended by *Let's Go.*

◢? ORIENTATION AND PRACTICAL INFORMATION

Bratislava is a stone's throw from the borders of Austria and Hungary. Avoid getting off at the **Nové Mesto** train station; it's much farther from the center than **Hlavná stanica** (Main Station). To get downtown from Hlavná stanica, head straight past the waiting buses, turn right on Šancová and left on Štefánikova; or take tram #1 to "Poštová" at Nám. SNP (the city center lies between Nám. SNP and the river). From there, Uršulínska leads to the tourist office. Take trolleybus #215 from the bus station to the center; or turn right on Mlynské nivy, walk 10min. to Dunajska, then follow it to Kamenné nám. (a block from the tourist office).

Tourist Office: Bratislavská Informačná Služba **(BIS)**, Klobučnicka 2 (☎54 43 27 70 and 54 43 37 15; bis@isnet.sk; www.bratislava.sk/bis). **Maps** (50Sk). Gives tours, and books rooms (singles 600-2500Sk) for a 50Sk fee. Open M-F 8am-5pm, Sa 8am-5pm.

Embassies: Canada (consulate), Mišíkova 28 (☎52 41 21 75; fax 52 41 21 76). Open M-F 8:30am-noon and 1:30pm-4pm. **UK**, Panská 16 (☎54 41 96 32; fax 54 41 00 02; bebra@internet.sk). Open M-F 8:30am-12:30pm and 1:30-5pm. **US**, Hviezdoslavovo nám. 4 (☎54 43 08 61; emergency ☎(0903) 70 36 66; fax 54 41 51 48; embassy@sae.sk). Open M-F 8am-4:30pm. **South Africa,** Jančova 8 (☎53 11 582; fax 53 12 581). Open M-F 8:30am-5pm. Citizens of **Australia, Ireland,** and **New Zealand** should contact the UK embassy.

Currency Exchange: VÚB, Gorkého 7 (☎59 55 11 11). 1% commission on traveller's checks. **Cash advances** on V, MC. Open M-W and F 8am-5pm, Th 8am-noon. A **24hr. currency exchange** machine is outside Československá Obchodná Banka. Changes US$, DM, UK£ into Sk for no commission. **ATMs** are all over the center.

Emergency: Fire: ☎150. **Medical:** ☎155. **Police:** ☎158.

Pharmacy: Lekáreň Novaform, Nám. SNP 20 (☎54 43 29 52), at Gorkého and Laurinská. Open M-F 7:30am-7pm, Sa 8am-5pm, Su 9am-5pm. 24hr. emergency service.

SLOVAKIA

YOU WANT FRIES WITH THAT? Just when you thought the hardest challenge in ordering food was comprehending Slovak, you come to a Bratislava burger stand. A *syrový burger* (cheeseburger) costs less than a *hamburger so syrom* (hamburger with cheese) because, as the stand owner will explain with humiliatingly clear logic, a cheeseburger is made of cheese—*only* cheese. A *pressburger*, named after Bratislava's former moniker Pressburg, consists of bologna on a bun, and hamburgers are actually ham. Everything comes boiled except, of course, the cheese.

Internet Access: Internet Centrum, Michaelská 2 (☎ 090 595 72 07). 1Sk per min.
Post Office: Nám. SNP 34 (☎ 54 43 51 80). *Poste Restante* at counter #5, closed weekends. Open M-F 7am-8pm, Sa 7am-6pm, Su 9am-2pm. Address mail to be held: First name SURNAME, Poste Restante, Nám. SNP 35, **81000** Bratislava 1, SLOVAKIA.

▐ ACCOMMODATIONS

In July and August, several dorms open as hostels. Good off-season deals are hard to find. Most cheap beds are near the station on the northeast side of town, a 20min. walk or 5min. tram ride from the city center. Pensions or private rooms (see Tourist Office, above) are a cheap and comfortable alternative.

Výskumný ústav zváračský, Pionierska 17 (☎ 49 24 67 61). Take tram #3 from the train station to "Pionierska." The entrance is 150m up the street on the right. Dozens of modest doubles with the best off-season prices in town. Limited English. Check-out 9am. Curfew midnight. 600Sk. Mid-June to Aug. and weekends 400Sk, students 330Sk.

Youth Hostel Bernolak, Bernolákova 1 (☎ 52 49 77 21). From the train station, take bus #23, 74, or 218 or tram #3 to "Račianské Mýto." From the bus station, take bus #121 or 122. Head toward the center on Račinska two blocks, then turn left on Benolákova. A friendly hostel with purple and orange shutters. Check-out 9am. Open July to mid-Sept. 300Sk per person. Euro26, HI, or ISIC 10% off.

Youth Hostel, Wilsonova 6 (☎ 52 49 77 35). See directions for YH Bernolak—Wilsonova runs parallel to Bernolákova. Remarkable only for the price. Check-out 9am. Open July-Aug. Shared bath. 2- to 4-bed dorms 130Sk per person. Euro26, HI, or ISIC 30% off.

Pension Gremium, Gorkého 11 (☎ 54 13 10 26). Just off Hviezdoslavovo námestí. Sparkling private showers. Check-out noon. Only 5 rooms, so call several weeks in advance. Single 890Sk; doubles 1290Sk; larger double 1600Sk.

▐ FOOD

West Slovakia produces a celebrated full-bodied *Modra* wine. A few restaurants serve the region's spicy meat mixtures. If all else fails, you can chow at one of the city's ever-present burger stands. For **groceries,** try **Tesco Potraviny,** Kamenné nám. 1. (Open M-W 8am-7pm, Th 8am-8pm, F 8am-9pm, Sa 8am-6pm, Su 9am-6pm.)

▨ Diétna Reštarácia, Laurinská 8. Cafeteria-style lunch spot popular with young Slovak herbivores and business types. Quick, tasty meals 50-100Sk. Open M-F 11am-3pm.

Prašná Bašta, Zámočnícka 11. Slovak dishes 100-185Sk. Open daily 11am-11pm.

Cafe London, Panská 17, in the British Council's courtyard. Sandwiches and light meals 85-118Sk. Cappuccino 60-119Sk. Open M-F 9am-9pm.

◉ SIGHTS

NÁMESTI SNP AND ENVIRONS. With the exception of Devín Castle, almost all of the sights worth seeing are in **Old Bratislava** (Stará Bratislava). From Nám. SNP, which commemorates the bloody Slovak National Uprising (SNP) against fascism, walk down Uršulínska to Primaciálné nám. and the neoclassical **Primate's Palace** (Primaciálný Palác), Primaciálné nám. 1. Napoleon and Austrian Emperor Franz I signed the Peace of Pressburg here in 1805. *(Open Tu-Su 10am-5pm. 30Sk.)* A walk to the left as you exit the palace down Kostolná leads to **Hlavné**

Bratislava

🔺 ACCOMMODATIONS

Pension Gremium, 1
Výskunný Ústav Zváračský, 4
Youth Hostel Bernolak, 2
Youth Hostel, 3

námesti. On your left as you enter the square is the **Town History Museum** (Muzeum Histórie Mesta) with a wonderful 1:500 model of 1945-55 Bratislava. *(Open Tu-F 10am-5pm, Sa-Su 11am-6pm. Model free. 25Sk, students 10Sk.)* Continue to the opposite side of the square and take a left onto Rybárska Brána to reach the eastern side of **Hviezdoslavovo námesti.** Continue straight down Mostová (the continuation of Rybárska Brána on the other side of the square) and turn left at the Danube to reach the **Slovak National Gallery,** Rázusovo nábr., which displays artwork from the Gothic and Baroque periods as well as some modern works. *(Open Tu-Su 10am-6pm. 25Sk, students 20Sk.)* Continue with the Danube on your left to take a look at the **New Bridge** (Nový Most), then turn right on Rigoleho. Continue straight onto Strakova (which becomes Ventúrska, then Michalská) and pass through **St. Michael's Tower,** Bratislava's last remaining medieval gateway. Keep going as Michalská becomes Župnénám, and take a left onto Kapucinska. Cross the highway using the pedestrian overpass to the **Museum of Jewish Culture** (Múzeum Židovskej Kultúry), Židovská 17. *(Open M-F and Su 11am-5pm. Last entry 4:30pm. 60Sk, students 40Sk.)*

CASTLES. Visible from much of the city, the four-towered **Bratislava Castle** (Bratislavský hrad) is the city's defining landmark. If you continue on Židovská, bearing right until it becomes Zámocké schody, you'll be winding uphill toward the castle. The castle burned in 1811 and was bombed during World War II; what's left today is a communist-era restoration. Its towers provide fantastic views of the Danube.

The ruins of **Devín Castle** sit above the Danube and Morava rivers. Take bus #29 from below Nový Most to 9km west of Bratislava (Štrbská stop). The site has been one of strategic importance since 5000 BC, and recovered artifacts from its history are displayed inside.

THE TATRA MOUNTAINS (TATRY)

The mesmerizing High Tatras span the border between Slovakia and Poland, and are home to hundreds of hiking and skiing trails along the Carpathians' highest peaks (2650m). One of the most compact ranges in the world, they feature sky-scraping hikes, glacial lakes, and super-deep snows. Cheap mountain railways and accommodations add to the allure for the budget hiker.

> ❗ The Tatras are a great place for a hike, but in winter a guide is almost always nec-essary; many of the hikes are extremely demanding and require experience, even in summer. For current conditions, check www.tanap.sk.

STARÝ SMOKOVEC. Starý Smokovec is the High Tatras's most central resort. Cheap beds down the road in **Horný Smokovec** make it accessible to the budget trav-eler. The trails from town are spectacular. The funicular to **Hrebienok** (1285m) leads to hiking country; to hike it, start at the funicular station behind Hotel Grand (behind the train station) and head 35min. up the green trail. Another 20min. from Hrebienok, the green trail leads north to the foaming **Cold Waterfall** (Studeného Potoka). The eastward blue trail descends from the waterfall to **Tatranská Lomnica** (1¾hr.). The hike to **Malá Studená Dolina** (Little Cold Valley) is also fairly relaxed; take the red trail from Hrebienok to the hut **Zamkovského chata** (☎442 26 36; 290Sk per person) and onto the green trail which climbs above the tree-line to a high lake and **Téryho chata** (☎442 52 45; 2hr.; 280Sk per person).

TEŽ **trains** arrive from Poprad (40min., every hr., 16Sk) at the town's lowest point, below the central road. **Buses** to many Tatra resorts stop in a parking lot to the right of the train station. Facing uphill, head up the road that runs just left of the train station, then cross the main road veering left. The **Tatranská Informačná Kancelária,** in Dom Služieb, has weather information and sells hiking maps, including the crucial **VKÚ sheet 113.** (Open M-F 8am-5:30pm, Sa 8am-1pm.) Turn right on the main road from the stations and walk 10min. to **Hotel Šport,** which offers a cafe, sauna, pool, and massage parlor. (☎442 23 61; fax 442 27 19. Break-fast 70Sk. Singles 405Sk; doubles 710Sk; triples 1005Sk.) **Grocers** clutter Starý Smokovec; five are on the main road. ☎**0969.**

ŠTRBSKÉ PLESO. Placid Štrbské Pleso (Lake Štrbské) is the Tatras's most-beloved ski resort. Many beautiful **hikes** begin from the town, but just one lift runs in summer, hoisting visitors to **Chata pod Soliskom** (1840m), overlooking the lake and the plains behind Štrbské Pleso. (June 25-Sept. 9 8:30am-4pm; July-Aug. 115Sk, return 160Sk; June and Sept. 80Sk/100Sk.) The yellow route heads from the east side of the lake (follow the signs to Hotel Patria) out along **Mlynická dolina** to moun-tain lakes and **Vodopády Skok** (waterfall). It then crosses **Bystré Sedlo** (saddle; 2314m) and circles **Štrbské Solisko** (2302m) before returning to Štrbské Pleso (8-9hr.). TEŽ **trains** arrive hourly from Starý Smokovec (30min., every 30min., 20Sk).

LIPTOVSKÝ MIKULÁŠ. Liptovský Mikuláš (LIP-tov-skee mee-koo-LASH) is fairly drab, but it's a good springboard for hiking in the **Low Tatras** (Nízke Tatry). To scale **Mt. Ďumbier,** the region's tallest peak (2043m), catch an early bus (25min., every hr., 13Sk) from platform #11 at the bus station to Liptovský Ján and follow the blue trail up the Štiavnica River to the **Ďumbierske sedlo** (saddle) by Chata (hut) generála M.R. Štefanika (5hr.). Then take the red trail to the ridge, which leads to the summit (1½hr.). Descend the ridge and follow the red sign to neighboring peak **Chopok** (2024m), the second-highest in the range. Stay overnight at the hut there, **Kammená chata** (80Sk), or just have a beer (30Sk). From Chopok, it's a pleasant and winding walk down the blue trail to the **bus** stop behind the Hotel Grand at Orupné (1¾hr.). **Trains** from Bratislava to Liptovský Mikuláš (4hr., 9 per day, 280Sk) are cheaper and more frequent than buses. Get to the town center by following Štefánikova toward the gas station at the far end of the bus station, then turn right onto Hodžu. The **tour-ist office,** Nám. Mieru 1, in the Dom Služieb complex on the north side of town, books private rooms (180-400Sk; 20% deposit) and sells local hiking maps; ask for VKÚ sheets #122 and 123 (89Sk each). (☎ 552 24 18; infolm@trynet.sk; www.lmiku-las.sk. Open M-F 8am-7pm, Sa 8am-2pm, Su noon-6pm; reduced hrs. off season) **Hotel Kriváň**, Štúrova 5, is across the square from the tourist office. (☎ 552 24 14. Singles 300, with bath 420Sk; doubles 470-620Sk.) ☎ **0849.**

SLOVENSKÝ RAJ. The Slovenský Raj (Slovak Paradise) National Park lies southeast of the Nizke Tatry. Instead of heavily touristed peaks, there are forested hills and deep ravines with terrific waterfalls. Life moves at a slightly slower pace in the tiny villages and grassy meadows. **Dedinky** (pop. 400) is the largest town on Slovenský Raj's southern border. Get a copy of **VKÚ sheet #4** (99-119Sk) before entering the region. The **Dobšinská Ice Caves** (Dobšinská ľadová jaskyňa), a 23km stretch of ice, holds 110,000 cubic meters of water still frozen from the last Ice Age. The 30min. tour covers 475m of the cave, with hall after hall of frozen columns, gigantic ice wells, and hardened waterfalls. To get here from Dedinky, take the **train** for two stops (15min., 12:37pm and 2:37pm, 10Sk). The one road from the cave train station leads 100m out to the main road. Turn left, and the cave parking lot is 250m ahead. From the parking lot, the blue trail leads up a steep incline to the cave. (Open July-Aug. 9am-4pm; mid-May to June and Sept. Tu-Su 9:30am-2pm. English tours every hr. 140Sk, students 110Sk. 20-person min.) No one said getting to paradise was easy, but the best way is to catch the **bus** from **Poprad** (dir. Rožňava; 1hr., 6 per day, 38Sk), which stops at a junction 2km south of Dedinky. Watch for the huge blue road sign at the intersection, just before the bus stop. From the intersection, walk down the road that the bus didn't take, turn right at the intersection after the basin, cross the dam after the train station, turn left, and walk 10min. to Dedinky. **Hotel Priehrada** rents comfortable rooms. (☎ 798 12 12. Reduced rates Sept. to mid-Dec. and Apr.-June. 250Sk per person. **Camping** 25Sk per person. Tents 25Sk.) ☎ **0942.**

SLOVENIA
(SLOVENIJA)

SLOVENIAN TOLARS

US$1 = 240SIT	100SIT = US$0.45
CDN$1 = 155SIT	100SIT = CDN$0.65
UK£1 = 345SIT	100SIT = UK£0.30
IR£1 = 280SIT	100SIT = IR£0.40
AUS$1 = 130SIT	100SIT = AUS$0.80
NZ$1 = 105SIT	100SIT = NZ$0.95
ZAR1 = 30SIT	100SIT = ZAR3.45
DM1 = 120SIT	100SIT = DM0.90
EUR€ = 220SIT	10LF = EUR€0.45

PHONE CODES	**Country code:** 386. **International dialing prefix:** 00. From outside Slovenia, dial int'l dialing prefix (see inside back cover) + 386 + city code + local number

Slovenia, the most prosperous of Yugoslavia's breakaway republics, revels in its newfound independence, modernizing rapidly while turning a hungry eye toward the West. It has quickly separated itself from its neighbors, using liberal politics and a high GDP to gain entrance into highly sought-after trade and security alliances. For a country half Switzerland's size, Slovenia, on the "sunny side of the Alps," is also extraordinarily diverse: in a day, you can breakfast on an Alpine peak, lunch under the Mediterranean sun, and dine in a vineyard on the Pannonian plains.

For more coverage of Slovenia, check out *Let's Go: Eastern Europe 2002*.

FACTS AND FIGURES

Official Name: Republic of Slovenia.

Capital: Ljubljana (pop. 276,000).

Population: 2,000,000.

Land Area: 20,256 sq. km.

Climate: Mediterranean, Alpine, continental.

Languages: Slovenian.

Religions: Roman Catholic (82%), atheist (4%), other (14%).

DISCOVER SLOVENIA

Any visit should start in youthful **Ljubljana** (p. 821), which has the majesty of the Habsburg cities and a cafe scene on par with Paris or Vienna. In the **Julian Alps, Lake Bled** (p. 823) and **Lake Bohinj** (p. 824) are traversed by miles of hikes—ranging from relaxed to treacherous—in summer. In winter, they host very snowy, steep, and relatively cheap skiing.

ESSENTIALS

WHEN TO GO

April through October is a a great time to visit; it's warm and dry, perfect beach weather. It can be chilly in the mountains, even in summer. Tourists show up in July and August, so earlier or later is best. Winter is cold and snowy, perfect for skiing.

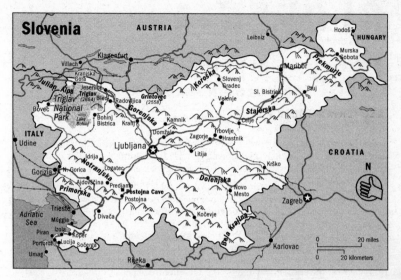

DOCUMENTS AND FORMALITIES

VISAS. Australian, Canadian, Irish, New Zealand, UK, and US citizens can visit without visas for up to 90 days. South Africans need visas (3-month single-entry or 5-day transit US$26; 3-month multiple entry US$52). Apply in your home country.

EMBASSIES. Foreign embassies are in **Ljubljana** (p. 821). For Slovenian embassies at home: **Australia,** Level 6, Advance Bank Center, 60 Marcus Clarke St. 2608, Canberra ACT 2601 (☎(06) 243 4830; fax 243 4827); **Canada,** 150 Metcalfe St., #2101, Ottawa, ON K2P 1P1 (☎613-565-5781; fax 613-565-5783); **New Zealand Honorary Consul,** Eastern Hutt Rd., Pomare, Lower Hutt, Wellington (☎(04) 567 27; fax 567 24); **UK,** Cavendish Ct. 11-15, Wigmore St., London W1H 9LA (☎(020) 7495 7775; fax 7495 7776; www.embassy-slovenia.org.uk); **US,** 1525 New Hampshire Ave. NW, Washington, D.C. 20036 (☎202-667-5363; fax 202-667-4563; www.embassy.org/slovenia).

TRANSPORTATION

BY PLANE. Commercial flights arrive at the Ljubljana Airport, which has regular bus service to the city 23km away. The national carrier **Adria Airways** (☎(386) 1 43 13 000 99 or toll-free within Slovenia ☎080 13 00; www.adria.si/eng) flies to European capitals. Flying into the country is the best option if you're traveling a long distance; otherwise, trains are better. Flying to Vienna and taking the train from there to Ljubljana is most cost-efficient but more time-consuming.

BY TRAIN. Trains are cheap, clean, and reliable. It's best to avoid peak commuting hours near Ljubljana. Return tickets are 20% cheaper than two one-way tickets. For most international destinations, travelers under 26 can get a 20% discount; check at the Ljubljana station (look for the BIJ-Wasteels logo). First and second class do not differ much; save your money and opt for the latter. Domestic tickets are 30% off for ISIC holders. Ask for a *"popust"* (discount). *"Vlak"* means train, *"prihodi vlakov"* means arrivals, and *"odhodi vlakov"* means departures. Schedules usually list trains by direction; look for trains that run *dnevno* (daily).

BY BUS. Buses are roughly 25% more expensive than trains, but run to some otherwise inaccessible places in the mountains. Tickets are sold at the station or on board; put your luggage in the passenger compartment if it's not too crowded.

BY BOAT, CAR, BIKE, OR THUMB. A regular hydrofoil service runs between Venice and Portorož. For those traveling by car, the Automobile Association of Slovenia's emergency telephone number is ☎987. If not traveling by bus or train, most Slovenes transport themselves by bike; most towns have a bike rental office. *Let's Go* does not recommend hitchhiking, which is uncommon in Slovenia.

TOURIST SERVICES AND MONEY

EMERGENCY	Police: ☎ 112. Ambulance: ☎ 112. Fire: ☎ 113.

TOURIST OFFICES. Tourist offices are located in most major cities and tourist spots. The English- and German-speaking staff are helpful, and assist in finding accommodations. The main tourist organization in Slovenia is **Kompas.**

MONEY. The national currency is the Slovenian tolar (Sit). Currency prices tend to be stable and are measured in Deutschmarks (DM) rather than dollars (US$). Rates vary, but tend to be better in major cities; post offices have the worst of all. Most exchange offices are quicker, easier, and offer fair rates. It's unpredictable where major credit cards are taken, but AmEx traveler's checks and Eurocheques are often accepted. ATMs are common. Tipping is not expected, but rounding up is appreciated. There's a 20% value-added tax, but for purchases over 9000Sit, it is refundable at the border (ask in the store for a tax-free check).

BUSINESS HOURS. Hours are generally Monday to Friday 8am-5pm and Saturday 8am-noon.

COMMUNICATION

MAIL. Mail is cheap and reliable. Air mail takes 1-2 weeks to reach North America, Australia, New Zealand, and South Africa. To send letters via airmail, ask for *letalsko*. To the US, letters cost 105Sit and postcards cost 95Sit; to the UK, 100Sit for letters, 90Sit for postcards; to Australia and New Zealand, 110Sit and 100Sit. Mail can be received general delivery through *Poste Restante.*

TELEPHONES. All phones now take phone cards, which are sold at post offices, kiosks, and gas stations (750Sit per 50 impulses, which yields ½min. to the US). Most international telecommunications companies **do not have international direct dialing** numbers in Slovenia and **MCI Worldphone,** whose access number is supposedly ☎080 8808, is not reliable here. Dial ☎115 for English-speaking operator-assisted collect calls. Calling the US is over US$6 per minute. If you must, try the phones at the post office and pay when you're finished. Slovenia is changing all of its numbers. Many will change through 2002, so some of the numbers we list will be wrong; however, changed numbers should direct you to the new number in English and Slovenian.

LANGUAGES. Slovene, a Slavic language, employs the Latin alphabet. Most young people speak at least some English, but the older generation (especially in the Alps) is more likely to understand German (in the north) or Italian (along the Adriatic). You also might find some Hungarian in the East. For Slovene basics, see p. 988.

ACCOMMODATIONS AND CAMPING

At the height of tourist season, prices are steep, services slow, and rooms scarce. Call at least a month ahead in peak season; otherwise, reserve at least days in advance. The seaside, packed as early as June, is claustrophobic in July and August. Tourists also tend to swarm to the mountains during these months. **Youth hostels** and **student dormitories** are cheap, but are generally open only in summer (June 25-Aug. 30). While **hostels** are often the cheapest (2500-3000Sit) and most fun option, **private rooms** are the only cheap option on the coast and at Lake Bohinj; prices rarely exceed US$30. Inquire at the tourist office or look for *Zimmer frei* or *Sobe* signs on the street. **Pensions** are common, and often have inexpensive triples and dorms. **Campgrounds** can be crowded, but are in excellent condition.

FOOD AND DRINK

For homestyle cooking, try a *gostilna* or *gostišče* (interchangeable words for a restaurant with a country flavor). Start with *jota*, a soup with potatoes, beans and sauerkraut. *Svinjska pečenka* (roast pork) is tasty, but vegetarians should look for *štruklji*—large, slightly sweet dumplings eaten as a main dish. Pizzerias area also a safe bet for meatless dishes. A favorite dessert is *potica*, a sheet of pastry spread with a rich filling (usually walnut) and rolled up. The country's wine making tradition dates from antiquity. *Renski Rizling* and *Šipon* are popular whites. while *Cviček* and *Teran* are well-known reds. Good beers include *Laško* and *Union*. For something stronger, try *žganje*, a strong fruit brandy. The most enchanting alcoholic concoction is *Viljamovka*, distilled by monks who get a full pear inside the bottle. Tap water is drinkable everywhere.

HOLIDAYS AND FESTIVALS

Holidays: New Year's Day (Jan. 1); Culture Day (Prešeren Day; Feb. 8); Easter (Mar. 31); National Resistance Day (WWII; Apr. 27); Labor Day (May 1-2); Pentecost (May 19); National Day (June 25); Assumption (Aug. 15); Reformation Day (Oct. 31); Remembrance Day (Nov. 1); Christmas (Dec. 25); Independence Day (Dec. 26).

Festivals: The International Summer Festival in Ljubljana is a two-month (July-Aug.) extravaganza of opera, theater, and classical music.

LJUBLJANA   ☎061

With the cosmopolitan feel of a capital city, Ljubljana can still be traversed in half an hour by foot. The city's architecture is relatively new for Europe, having been rebuilt since an 1895 earthquake. A massive student population ensures that bars and clubs can be found on virtually every corner, but the scene thrives more on cafes and arts festivals.

▣ TRANSPORTATION

Trains: Trg. O.F. 6 (☎291 33 32). To: **Budapest** (9hr., 2 per day, 9400Sit); **Trieste** (3hr., 2 per day, 4171Sit); **Venice** (6hr., 3 per day, 6191Sit); **Vienna** (5-6hr., 2 per day, 10,945Sit); **Zagreb** (2½hr., 5 per day, 2452Sit).

Buses: Trg. O.F. 4 (☎090 42 30), by train station. **Zagreb** (3hr., 3 per day, 2740Sit).

Public Transportation: Buses run until 11pm. Drop 210Sit in change in the box beside the driver or buy 150Sit tokens at post offices and kiosks. Daily passes (600Sit) sold at **Ljubljanski potniški promet**, Trdinova 3.

✳❼ ORIENTATION AND PRACTICAL INFORMATION

The **train** and **bus stations** are on **Trg Osvobodilne Fronte** (**Trg O.F.** or **O.F. Square**). Turn right as you exit the train station. Turn left on **Miklošiceva cesta**, and follow it to **Prešernov Trg**, the main square. After crossing the **Tromostovje** (Triple Bridge), you'll find **Stare Miasto** (Old Town) at the castle hill's base.

Tourist Office: Tourist Info Center (TIC), Stritarjeva 1, on the left at the corner of Stritarjeva and Adamič-Lundrovo nabr. English brochures and free maps. (☎306 12 15; pcl.tic-lj@ljubljana.si; www.ljubljana.si. Open M-F 8am-8pm, Sa-Su 10am-6pm; Oct.-May M-F 8am-6pm, Sa-Su 10am-6pm. Also see www.ljubjanalife.com.)

Embassies and Consulates: Australia, Trg Republike 3 (☎425 42 52). Open M-F 9am-1pm. **UK,** Trg Republike 3 (☎200 39 10; fax 425 01 74). Open M-F 9am-noon. **US,** Prešernova cesta (☎200 55 00; fax 200 55 55). Open M-F 8am-5pm. **Canada,** Miklošiceva 19 (☎430 35 70; fax 430 35 75). Open M-F 9am-1pm.

Currency Exchange: Finicky **ATMs** all over the city, but accepted cards vary.

Luggage storage: At train station; look for *garderoba*. 250Sit per day. Open 24hr.

24hr. Pharmacy: Miklošičeva 24 (☎231 45 58).

Internet: Free access upstairs of **Pizzeria Bar** (see Accommodations and Food, below).

Post Office: Slovenska 32. *Poste Restante* (☎426 46 68) held for 1 month at counter labeled "*poštno ležeče pošiljke.*" Open M-F 7am-8pm, Sa 7am-1pm. Address mail to be held: First name SURNAME, *Poste Restante*, Slovenska 32, **1101** Ljubljana, SLOVENIA.

ACCOMMODATIONS AND FOOD

Ljubljana is not heavily touristed by backpackers, so it lacks true budget accommodations. There is a nightly **tourist tax** (160Sit). The tourist office (see above) finds private singles (2200-3500Sit) and doubles (4000-5500Sit). The **Slovene National Hostel Association** (PZS; ☎231 21 56) provides information about youth hostels in both the area of Ljubljana and throughout Slovenia.

Dijaški Dom Tabor (HI), Vidovdanska 7 (☎234 88 40; fax 234 88 55). Go left from the train station, right on Resljeva, left on Komenskega, and left on Vidovdanska. Clean and popular with backpackers. Breakfast included. Laundry 1000Sit. Free Internet 6am-10pm. Open June 25-Aug. 28. 2750-3850Sit per person with student ID.

Dijaški Dom Bežigrad, Kardeljeva pl. 28 (☎534 28 67; fax 534 28 64). From the train station, cross the street, turn right and walk to the intersection with Slovenska. Take bus #6 (Črnuče) or #8 (Ježica), get off at "Stadion" (5min.), then walk 1 block to the crossroads. Negotiable check-out 8am. Open mid-June to Aug. Singles 3000Sit, with shower 3500Sit; doubles and triples 2000/3000Sit.

Hotel Park, Tabor 6 (☎433 13 06; fax 433 05 46). The cheapest option for the off-season backpacker, aside from private rooms. Clean, with knowledgeable staff. Singles 7900Sit; doubles 9900Sit; triples 11,900Sit. Students 10% discount.

The cheapest eateries are **cafeterias.** In the basement of **Maximarket** on Trg Republike is a **grocery store** (open M-Th 9am-8pm, F 9am-10pm, Sa 8am-3pm). Try a traditional Slovenian meal at **Gostilna Pri Pavli,** Stari Trg 21. Or, watch your pizza cooked at **Cerin Pizzeria Bar,** Trubarjeva 52, which has free Internet access upstairs.

SIGHTS AND ENTERTAINMENT

The best way to see the city is to meet in front of the *rotovž* (city hall), Mestni trg. 1, for the two-hour **walking tour** in English and Slovene. (Daily 5pm; Oct.-May Su 11am. 700Sit, students 500Sit.) A short walk from the *rotovž* down Stritarjeva across the **Triple Bridge** (Tromostovje), which majestically guards the **Old Town,** leads to the main square, **Prešernov Trg,** with its 17th-century **Franciscan Church** (Frančiškanska cerkev). Cross the bridge back to the Old Town and take a left along the water. Continuing along the river, you'll see a big **outdoor fruit market** on the right (M-Sa 9am-6pm, Su 9am-2pm), and a few minutes later, you will reach Vodnikov Trg., where the **Dragon Bridge** (Zmajski most) stretches back across the Ljubljanica. On the far side of Vodnikov Trg, the narrow path Studentovska leads uphill to **Ljubljana Castle** (Ljubljanski Grad). This castle dates from at least 1144, although what you see is 400-500 years younger. (Open 10am-dark, Oct.-May 10am-5pm. Tower 200Sit, students 150Sit.) Back across the river at Prešernov trg., take a left onto Wolfova, which becomes Gosposka, then take a right onto Zoisova cesta and a left onto Emonska ul. Across the bridge and behind the church is the **Plečnik Collection** (Plečnikova zbirka), Karunova 4, which shows the works of Ljubljana's most famous architect. (Open Tu and Th 10am-2pm. 600Sit, students 300Sit.) Walking back, take a left onto Zoistova and a right onto Slovenska. After the **Ursuline Church,** take a left to find **Trg Republike,** home to the national Parliament, the large Maximarket, and *Cankarjev Dom*, the city's cultural center.

The **Ljubljana International Summer Festival** (July-Aug.) has opera, theater, and music performances. Named after Hemingway, ■ **Casa del Papa,** Celovška 54a,

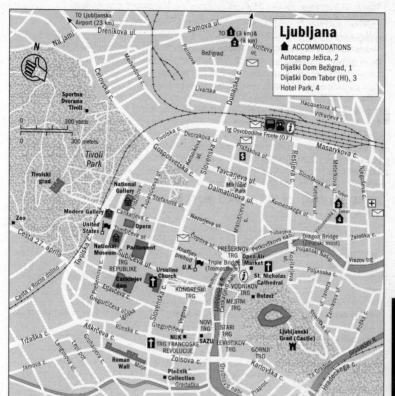

Ljubljana

⌂ ACCOMMODATIONS
Autocamp Ježica, 2
Dijaški Dom Bežigrad, 1
Dijaški Dom Tabor (HI), 3
Hotel Park, 4

draws an older crowd but stays lively into the wee hours. (Open Th-Sa 9pm-5am.) The younger crowd drinks up at **Joe Peñas Cantina Y Bar,** Cankarjeva 6, right across from the Komuna cinema. (M-Th 4pm-midnight, F-Sa 4pm-1am.)

🔁 DAYTRIP FROM LJUBLJANA: ŠKOCJANSKE CAVES

Škocjanske is an amazing system of **caverns** said to have inspired literary greats like Dante Alighieri, with limestone formations and a 120m gorge created by the Reca River. Follow signs out of town (40min.). Be prepared, it's an adventure. (☎63 28 40; www.gov.si/parkskj. Tours June-Sept. daily 10am-5pm every hr.; Oct.-May 10am, 1, and 3pm. 1500Sit, students 700Sit.) **Trains** run from Ljubljana to Divača (1½hr., 10 per day, 1370Sit).

BLED
☎04

Alpine hills, snow-covered peaks, an opaque lake, and a stately castle make Bled one of Slovenia's most striking destinations. On the island in the middle of the lake, the **Church of the Assumption,** largely rebuilt in the 17th century, retains a unique pre-Romanesque apse. Get there by renting a boat (1500Sit per hr.), hopping on a gondola-style boat (return 1500Sit), or even swimming. High above the water perches the picture-perfect 16th-century **Bled Castle** (Blejski grad), which houses a museum detailing the history of the Bled region; the path to the castle is on Grajska cesta. (Open daily 8am-8pm. 600Sit, students 500Sit.) ■ **Blejski Vintgar,** a 1.6km gorge traced by the waterfalls and rapids of the Radovna River, carves through the rocks of the **Triglav National Park** (Triglavski Narodni). To see the 16m **Sum Waterfall,** go over the hill on Grajska cesta and turn right at the bottom. After 100m, turn left and follow the signs for Vintgar.

Trains (☎74 11 13) arrive in Lesce, 5km from Bled on the Ljubljana-Salzburg-Munich line (from Ljubljana 1hr., 500 Sit). Frequent **buses** (10min., 260Sit) shuttle to **Ljubljanska** (the main street) and then the **bus station** (☎74 11 14), cesta Svobode 4, closer to the hostel and castle. **Buses** also run directly from Ljubljana (1½hr., 1 per hr., 1100Sit). **Turističko društvo**, Cesta Svobode 15, has maps and the *Bled Tourist News*. (☎574 15 55; td-bled@g-kabel.si. Open M-Sa 8am-7pm, Su and holidays 11am-5pm.) To find **private rooms**, look for *sobe* signs on Prešernova and Ljubljanska. The ▓**Bledec Youth Hostel**, Grajska cesta 17, was just renovated. From the bus station, turn left and follow the street to the top, bearing left at the fork. (☎574 52 50; mlino@siol.net; www.mlino.si. Reserve ahead July-Aug. Reception 24hr. 4000Sit, HI 3600Sit.) To get to **Camping Bled**, Kidričeva 10c, from the bus station, walk downhill on cesta Svobode, turn left, and walk along the lake for 25min. with the water to the right. (☎575 20 00; campingbled@s5.net. Reception 24hr. Check-out 3pm. Open Apr.-Oct. 1100-1725Sit.) Grab **groceries** at **Mercator** in the shopping complex on Ljubljanska cesta 13. (Open M-Sa 7am-7pm, Su 8am-noon.) **Postal code:** 4260.

LAKE BOHINJ (BOHINJSKO JEZERO)   ☎04

Although only 30km southwest of Bled, Bohinjsko Jezero is worlds away. Surrounded by the **Triglav National Park**, the glacial lake is Slovenia's center for alpine tourism. Three villages border the lake: **Ribcez Laz, Stara Fuzina and Ukanc.** Hikes from the lake's shores range from casual to nearly impossible. Trails throughout Slovenia are marked with a white circle inside a red circle; look for the blaze on trees and rocks. Pick up maps at the tourist office (see below). **Triglav,** the highest point in Slovenia, is a challenging two-day journey from town. The most popular and accessible destination is ▓**Savica Waterfall** (Slap Savica). Take a bus from Ribčev Laz to Bohinj-Zlatorog, get off at Hotel Zlatorog, and follow signs uphill (1hr. to trailhead at Koča pri Savici, then 20min. to waterfall).

The nearest town is **Bohinjska Bistrica**, 6km to the east. **Trains** from Ljubljana (2½hr., 8 per day, 1200Sit) pass through Jesenice. **Buses** from Ljubljana (2hr., every hr., 1400Sit) pass through Bled (40min., 600Sit) and Bohinjska Bistrica (10min., 250Sit) on their way to the lake; they stop at Hotel Jezero in Ribčev Laz before continuing on to Hotel Zlatorog in Ukanc, on the other side of the lake. The **tourist office**, Ribčev Laz 48, arranges accommodations and changes money. (☎574 60 10; tdbohinj@bohinj.sn; www.bohinj.com. Open July-Aug. M-Sa 8am-6pm, Su 9am-3pm.) To get to **AvtoCamp Zlatorog**, Ukanc 2, take the bus to Hotel Zlatorog and backtrack a bit. (☎572 34 82; fax 572 34 46. Check-out noon. July-Aug. 1600Sit. May-June and Sept. 1000Sit. Tourist tax 154Sit per night.) A **Mercator supermarket** is next to the tourist office. (Open M-F 7am-7pm, Sa 7am-5pm.) **Postal code:** 4265.

SPAIN (ESPAÑA)

PESETAS

US$1 = 181PTAS	100PTAS = US$0.55
CDN$1 = 118PTAS	100PTAS = CDN$0.85
UK£1 = 263PTAS	100PTAS = UK£0.38
IR£1 = 211PTAS	100PTAS = IR£0.47
AUS$1 = 97PTAS	100PTAS = AUS$1.03
NZ$1 = 80PTAS	100PTAS = NZ$1.25
ZAR1 = 22PTAS	100PTAS = ZAR4.56
EUR€1 = 166PTAS	100PTAS = EUR€0.60

PHONE CODES

Country code: 34. **International dialing prefix:** 00. Spain has no city codes. From outside Spain, dial int'l dialing prefix (see inside back cover) + 34 + local number.

Spain is a budget traveler's dream. The landscape is a microcosm of all that Europe has to offer, with lush wilderness reserves, long sunny coastlines, snowy mountain peaks and the dry, and golden plains wandered by Don Quijote. Art lovers flock to the northeast, home to the likes of Chagall, Dalí and Gaudí. Adventure-seekers trek through the northern Pyrenees, and architecture buffs are drawn to the country's stunning Baroque, Mudejar and Mozarabic cathedrals and palaces. From the south come flamenco, bullfighting and *tapas*, the passionate cultural expressions that set Spain apart from the rest of Europe. The raging nightlife of Madrid, Barcelona and the Balearic Islands continues well after sunrise. You can do Spain in one week, one month, or one year. But you must do it at least once.

For more detailed coverage of the glories of Spain, grab the scintillating and delicious *Let's Go: Spain and Portugal 2002*.

FACTS AND FIGURES

Official Name: Kingdom of Spain.

Capital: Madrid.

Major Cities: Barcelona, Valencia, Sevilla, Granada.

Population: 39,371,000; urban 78%, rural 22%.

Land Area: 504,784 sq. km.

Climate: Hot and relatively dry during summer months (Apr.-Oct.) and wetter during winter months.

Language: Spanish (Castilian); Catalan, Valencian, Basque, Galician dialects.

Religions: Roman Catholicism (though no longer the official religion).

DISCOVER SPAIN

Begin in **Madrid** (p. 830), soaking in its unique blend of art, architecture, and cosmopolitan life; after days of ogling at art and nights of the dance 'til dawn regime; take your bleary-eyed self to the austere palace of **El Escorial** (p. 841) outside the city and the twisting streets of **Toledo** (p. 842), once home to El Greco and a thriving Jewish community. Head off into Central Spain, Don Quixote territory, to the famed university town of **Salamanca** (p. 844) and then down to beautiful and intriguing **Sevilla** (p. 852), the center of Andalucía, Spain's southernmost region. Delve deeper into Arab-influenced Andalucía at the stunning mosque in **Córdoba** (p. 847) and the world-famous Alhambra in **Granada** (p. 860). The tanning fields of the **Costa del Sol** stretch along the Mediterranean; join in at posh **Marbella** (p. 859). Move up along the east coast to **Valencia** (p. 866) to indulge in native *paella* and oranges. The northeast's gem is **Barcelona** (p. 867) one of Europe's most vibrant cities. After a tour of bizarre Modernista architecture and raging nightlife, discover the beaches of the **Costa Brava** and enchanting seaside resort of **Tossa de Mar** (p. 880). The nearby town of **Figueres** (p. 880) is home to Salvador Dalí's engaging museum/monument to himself, while **Girona** boasts a perfectly preserved medieval center (p. 879). Farther north is the natural haven of the **Pyrenees** (p. 881), where adventure tourism reigns. Moving westward, in the heart of the Basque Country, **San Sebastián** (p. 884) entertains with beaches and fabulous tapas bars; **Bilbao** (p. 887), home of the incredible Guggenheim museum, is only a daytrip away. The pilgrimage of the **Camino de Santiago** (p. 892) winds along the northern coast to the cathedral of **Santiago de Compostela** (p. 891), the unrivaled monarch of Spanish religious monuments. Spain also offers some of the world's craziest nightlife, the most famous being the 24-hour party that is **Ibiza** (p. 889) on the Balearic Islands.

ESSENTIALS

WHEN TO GO

Summer is **high season** (*temporada alta*) for the coastal and interior regions; winter is high season for ski resorts. In many parts of the country, high season includes **Semana Santa** (Holy Week; mid-April) and festival days. Tourism reaches its height in August; the coastal regions overflow while inland cities empty out, leaving behind closed offices, restaurants and lodgings. Traveling in the **off season** (*temporada baja*) has the advantage of noticeably lighter crowds and lower prices, but smaller towns virtually shut down, and tourist offices and sights cut their hours nearly everywhere.

DOCUMENTS AND FORMALITIES

VISAS. A passport allows Australian, Canadian, British, New Zealand, and US citizens to remain for 90 days. South African citizens need a visa to enter.

EMBASSIES. Foreign embassies are in Madrid (p. 834); all countries have consulates in Barcelona (p. 870). Australia, UK, and US also have consulates in Sevilla (p. 852). Another Canadian consulate is in Málaga; a South African consulate is in Bilbao; UK consulates are also in Bilbao, Palma de Mallorca, Ibiza, Alicante, and Málaga; more US consulates are in Málaga, Valencia, La Coruña, and Palma de Mallorca. For Spanish embassies at home: **Australia,** 15 Arkana St., Yarralumla, ACT 2600. Mailing address: P.O. Box 9076, Deakin, ACT 2600. (☎(02) 62 73 35 55); **Canada,** 74 Stanley Ave., Ottawa, ON K1M 1P4 (☎613-747-2252); **Ireland,** 17A Merlyn Park, Ballsbridge, Dublin 4 (☎(01) 269 1640); **South Africa,** 169 Pine St., Arcadia, P.O. Box 1633, Pretoria 0083 (☎(012) 344 3875); **UK,** 39 Chesham Pl., London SW1X 8SB (☎(020) 72 35 55 55); and **US,** 2375 Pennsylvania Ave. NW, Washington, D.C. 20037 (☎202-452-0100).

TRANSPORTATION

BY PLANE. Airports in Madrid and Barcelona handle most international flights; Sevilla also has a major international airport. **Iberia** serves all domestic locations and all major international cities. **Air Europa** (US☎888-238-7672 or 718-244-6016; Spain ☎902 30 06 00; www.air-europa.es) flies out of New York City and most European cities to Spain and has discounts available for those under 22.

BY TRAIN. RENFE (www.renfe.es), the Spanish centralized national rail system, has clean, punctual, reasonably priced trains with various levels of service. Its network radiates from Madrid; many small towns are not served. *Alta Velocidad Española* (AVE) trains are the fastest between Madrid-Córdoba-Sevilla. *Talgos* are almost as fast; *Talgo 200s* run on *AVE* rails—there are four lines from Madrid to Málaga, Algeciras, Cádiz, and Huelva. *Intercity* is cheaper, but still fairly fast. *Estrellas* are slow night trains with bunks. *Cercanías* (commuter trains) go from cities to suburbs and nearby towns. *Tranvía*, *semidirecto*, and *correo* trains are slower-than-slow. Trains connect with most major European cities via France. The

Spain

FRANCE

PYRENEES

ANDORRA

GALICIA
La Coruña
Oviedo
Santander
San Sebastián
ASTURIAS
Picos de Europa
CANTABRIA
Hondarribia
Guernica
Bilbao
PAIS
VASCO
NAVARRA
Pamplona
Jaca
Vielha
Núria
Empúries
Figueres
Astorga
León
Burgos
LA RIOJA
CATALUÑA
Girona
Palafrugell
Orense
CASTILLA
Y LEON
Valladolid
Duero
Zaragoza
Montserrat
Tossa de Mar
Barcelona
Sitges
Zamora
Salamanca
Béjar
Segovia
Sigüenza
ARAGON
Ávila
Madrid
Escorial
Tajo
Balearic
Sea
TO MENORCA
PORTUGAL
MADRID
Toledo
Cuenca
Golfo de
Valencia
Mallorca
Palma
Cáceres
Trujillo
Aranjuez
VALENCIA
Valencia
ISLAS BALEARES
EXTREMADURA
Mérida
Guadiana
CASTILLA-
LA MANCHA
Cullera
Gandía
Denia
Ibiza
Ibiza
Formentera
Badajoz
Zafra
Calpe
Menorca
Ciudadela
Mahón
Córdoba
Guadalquivir
MURCIA
Alicante
Sevilla
ANDALUCIA
Granada
Mediterranean Sea
ATLANTIC
OCEAN
Golfo de Cádiz
Arcos de la
Frontera
Jerez de
la Frontera
Ronda
Sierra Nevada
Cádiz
Algeciras
Málaga
Marbella
ALGERIA
Tarifa
Gibraltar
Ceuta
Strait of Gibraltar
MOROCCO

N

0   100 mi
0   150 km

other train company in Spain is **FEVE,** which sluggishly but dependably runs between many northern towns not served by RENFE.

There are several **RailEurope** passes that cover travel within Spain. You must purchase railpasses at least 15 days before departure. Call ☎1-800-4EURAIL in the US or go to www.raileurope.com. **Spain Flexipass** offers three days of unlimited travel in a two-month period (First class US$200/€232; 2nd class US$155/€180). **Iberic Railpass** is good for three days of unlimited first-class travel in Spain and Portugal for US$205/€240. **Spain Rail 'n' Drive Pass** is good for three days of unlimited first-class train travel and two days of unlimited mileage in a rental car.

BY BUS. In Spain, ignore romanticized versions of European train travel—buses are cheaper, run more frequently, and are sometimes faster than trains. Bus routes, far more comprehensive than the rail network, provide the only public transportation to many isolated areas and almost always cost less than trains. Spain has numerous private companies; the lack of a centralized bus company may make itinerary planning an ordeal. **ALSA** (☎902 42 22 42), serves Madrid, Galicia, Asturias, and Castilla y León, as well as international destinations in Portugal, Morocco, France, Italy, and Poland. **Auto-Res/Cunisa, S.A.** (☎902 02 09 99), serves Madrid, Castilla y León, Extremadura, Galicia, and Valencia.

BY CAR. Spain has an extensive road grid covering close to 340,000km; of this total, 7,000km are highways (toll motorways, freeways, and dual-carriageways). Gas prices average 130-140ptas/€0.75-0.85 per liter. Speeders beware: police can "photograph" the speed and license plate of your car, and issue a ticket without pulling you over. **Renting a car** in Spain is considerably cheaper than in many other

Western European countries. International rental companies offer services throughout the country, but you may want to check with **Atesa** (www.atesa.es), Spain's largest national rental agency. The Spanish automobile association is **Real Automóbil Club de España (RACE)**, C. Jose Abascal, 10, Madrid (☎91 594 74 75). Taxis are readily available in almost every Spanish city, and they are a much wiser form of transportation than a personal car in Madrid and Barcelona.

BY BIKE AND BY THUMB. With hilly terrain and extremely hot summer weather, biking is difficult but can be done. Renting a bike should be easy, especially in the flatter southern region. Hitchers report that Castilla, Andalucía, and Madrid offer little more than a long, hot wait. The Mediterranean Coast and the islands are much more promising. *Let's Go* does not recommend hitchhiking.

TOURIST SERVICES AND MONEY

EMERGENCY	**Emergency:** ☎112. **Local Police:** ☎092. **National Police:** ☎091. **Ambulance:** ☎124.

TOURIST OFFICES. The Spanish Tourist Office operates an extensive official website (www.tourspain.es) and has 29 offices abroad. Municipal tourist offices, called *oficinas de turismo*, are a good stop to make upon arrival in a town; they usually have free maps and region-specific advice for travelers.

MONEY. Money in Spain comes in the form of the **peseta** (ptas), available in coins of 1, 5, 10, 25, 50, 100, 200 and 500ptas and notes of 1000, 2000, 50000, and 10,0000ptas. Spain has accepted the **Euro (€)** as legal tender, and *pesetas* will be phased out by July 1, 2002. For more information, see p. 24. Travelers checks are widely accepted and used in Spain; ATM cards are probably an even easier way to exchange money and will earn you a better rate. If you are using travelers' checks, Banco Central Hispano often provides good rates. **Tipping** is not very common. In restaurants, all prices include service charge. Satisfied customers occasionally toss in some spare change—usually no more than 5%—but this is purely optional. Many people give train, airport and hotel porters 100ptas/€0.60 per bag, while taxi drivers sometimes get 5-10%. Bargaining is common at flea markets and with street vendors. Travelers can try bargaining for hostel prices in the off season, especially in less-touristed areas. Spain has a 7% Value Added Tax, known as IVA, on all restaurant and accommodations. The prices listed in *Let's Go* include IVA unless otherwise mentioned. Retail goods bear a much higher 16% IVA, although listed prices are usually inclusive. Non-EU citizens who have stayed in the EU fewer than 180 days can claim back the tax paid on purchases at the airport. Ask the shop for a tax return form.

BUSINESS HOURS. Banking hours in Spain from June through September are generally Monday through Friday 9am to 2pm; from October to May, banks are also open Saturday 9am to 1pm. Some banks are open in the afternoon as well.

COMMUNICATION

MAIL. Air mail *(por avión)* takes around six business days to reach the US and Canada, approximately three days to the UK and Ireland and up to 10 days to Australia and New Zealand. Standard postage is 115ptas/€0.70 to North America. Surface mail *(por barco)*, while considerably less expensive than air mail, can take over a month, and packages will take two to three months. Registered or express mail *(registrado* or *certificado)*, is the most reliable way to send a letter or parcel home, and takes four to seven business days (letter postage 237ptas). Stamps are sold at post offices and tobacconists *(estancos* or *tabacos)*. To send mail *Poste Restante* to Spain, address the letter as follows: SURNAME, First name; Lista de Correos; City Name; Postal Code; SPAIN; AIR MAIL.

TELEPHONES. The central Spanish phone company is Telefónica. Local calls cost 20ptas. The best way to make local calls is with a phone card, issued in denominations of 1000 and 2000ptas (€6-12) and available at tobacconists (*estancos* or *tabacos*) and most post offices. International calls can be made using phone cards, but are very expensive; the best way to call home is with an international calling card issued by your phone company. To call home with your calling card, contact the operator for your service provider in Spain by dialing the appropriate international direct dial: **AT&T,** ☎900 99 00 11; **British Telecom,** ☎900 99 00 44; **Canada Direct,** ☎900 99 00 15; **Ireland Direct,** ☎900 99 03 53; **MCI,** ☎900 99 00 14; **Sprint,** ☎900 99 00 13; **Telecom New Zealand,** ☎900 99 00 64; **Telkom South Africa,** ☎900 99 00 27; and **Telstra Australia,** ☎900 99 00 61.

INTERNET ACCESS. An increasing number of bars offer Internet access for 600-1000ptas per hour. Sometimes libraries or tourist offices offer access for a small fee. The website www.tangaworld.com also lists 200 cybercafes across Spain.

LANGUAGE. Catalán is spoken in Catalunya, Valencian in Valencia. The Basque (Euskera) language is common in north-central Spain, and Galician (Gallego, related to Portuguese) is in the once-Celtic northwest. Spanish (Castilian, or *castellano*) is spoken everywhere. For Spanish phrases, see p. 989.

ACCOMMODATIONS AND CAMPING

The cheapest and barest options are **casas de huéspedes** and **hospedajes,** while **pensiones** and **fondas** tend to be a bit nicer. All are basically just boarding houses. Higher up the ladder, **hostales** generally have sinks in bedrooms and provide sheets and lockers, while **hostal-residencias** are similar to hotels in overall quality. The government rates *hostales* on a two-star system; even establishments receiving one star are typically quite comfortable. The system also fixes each *hostal*'s prices, posted in the lounge or main entrance. If you have any trouble with rates or service, ask for the *libro de reclamaciones* (complaint book), which by law must be produced on demand. The argument will usually end immediately, since all complaints must be forwarded to the authorities within 48 hours. **Red Española de Albergues Juveniles (REAJ),** C. José Ortega y Gasset, 71, Madrid 28006 (☎91 347 77 00; fax 91 401 81 60), the Spanish Hostelling International (HI) affiliate, runs 165 youth hostels year-round. Prices depend on location (typically some distance away from town center) and services offered, but are generally 1500-2500ptas (9-15.0£) for guests under 26 and higher for those 26 and over. Breakfast is usually included; lunch and dinner are occasionally offered at an additional charge. Hostels usually lockout around 11:30am, and have curfews between midnight and 3am. As a rule, don't expect much privacy—rooms typically have from four to 20 beds in them. To reserve a bed in high season (July-Aug. and during fiestas), call well in advance. A national **Youth Hostel Card** is usually required (see **Hostels,** p. 37). **Campgrounds** are generally the cheapest choice for two or more people. Most charge separate fees per person, per tent, and per car; others charge for a *parcela*—a small plot of land—plus per-person fees. Tourist offices provide information, including the *Guía de campings*. Reservations are necessary in the summer.

FOOD AND DRINK

Breakfast consists of coffee or hot chocolate and *bollos* (rolls) or *churros* (lightly fried fritters). Lunch, served between 2 and 3pm, is several courses. Supper, a light meal, begins at around 10pm. Some restaurants are "open" from 8am until 1 or 2am, but most only serve meals from 1 to 4pm and from 8pm until midnight. Prices for a full meal start at about 800ptas in the cheapest *bare-restaurantes*. Many places offer a *plato combinado* (main course, side dishes, bread, and sometimes a beverage) for about 500-1200ptas/€3-7.20 or a *menú del día* (two or three set dishes, bread, beverage, and dessert) for roughly 800-1500ptas/€4.80-9. If you ask for a *menu*, this is what you may receive; the word for menu is *carta*. Tapas (small nibbles of savory meats and vegetables cooked according to local recipes) are truly tasty. *Raciones* are large tapas served as entrees. Bocadillos are sandwiches on hunks of bread. Specialties include *tortilla de patata* (potato omelette), *jamón serrano* (smoked ham), *calamares fritos* (fried squid), *arroz* (rice), *chorizo* (spicy sausage), *gambas* (shrimp), *lomo* (pork), *paella* (steamed saffron rice with seafood, chicken, and vegetables), and *gazpacho* (cold tomato-based soup). Vegetarians should learn the phrase *"yo soy vegetariano"* (I am a vegetarian) and specify that means no *jamón* (ham) or *atún* (tuna). *Vino blanco* is white wine and *tinto* is red. Beer is *cerveza;* Mahou and Cruzcampo are the most common brands. *Sangría* is red wine, sugar, brandy, and fruit.

HOLIDAYS AND FESTIVALS

Holidays: New Year's Day (Jan. 1); Epiphany (Jan. 6); Maundy Thursday (Mar. 28); Good Friday (Mar. 29); Easter (Mar. 31); Labor Day (May 1); La Asunción (Aug. 15); National Day (Oct. 12); All Saints' Day (Nov. 1); Constitution Day (Dec. 6); Feast of the Immaculate Conception (Dec. 8); Christmas (Dec. 25).

Festivals: Just about everything closes down during festivals. Almost every town has several, and in total there are more than 3000. All of Spain will celebrate **Carnaval** from Feb. 7 to 17; the biggest parties are in Catalunya and Cádiz. Valencia will host the annual **Las Fallas** in mid-Mar. From Mar. 24-31, the entire country will honor the Holy Week, or **Semana Santa.** Sevilla's **Feria de Abril** takes place in late Apr. Pamplona's infamous **San Fermines** (Running of the Bulls) will break out from July 6 to 14. For more fiesta info, see www.tourspain.es, www.SiSpain.org, or www.cyberspain.es.

MADRID ☎91

After decades of Franco's totalitarian repression, Madrid's youth burst out during the 1980s, an era known as *la Movida* (the "Movement"). The newest generation, too young to recall the Franco years, seems neither cognizant of the city's historic landmarks nor preoccupied with the future—youths have taken over the streets, shed their parents' decorous reserve, and captured the present. Bright lights and a perpetual stream of cars and people blur the distinction between 4pm and 4am, and infinitely energized *madrileños* crowd bars and discos until dawn. Madrid's sights and culture equal its rival European capitals, and have twice the intensity.

⬛ TRANSPORTATION

Flights: All flights land at **Aeropuerto Internacional de Barajas,** 20min. northeast of Madrid. The **Barajas metro line** connects the airport to all of Madrid (145ptas/€0.90). From the airport, follow signs to the metro. Another option is the green **Bus-Aeropuerto #89** (look for EMT signs just outside the doors), which leaves from the national and international terminals and runs to the city center (every 25min. 4:45-6:17am, every 15min. 6:17am-10pm, every hr. 10pm-1:45am; 400ptas/€2.40). The bus stops underground beneath the Jardines del Descubrimiento in **Plaza de Colón** (M: Colón). Serving national and international destinations, **Iberia** is at Santa Cruz de Marcenado, 2 (☎91 587 81 56). M: San Bernardo. Open M-F 9:30am-2pm and 4-7pm. 24 hr. reservations and info (☎(902) 40 05 00).

Trains: Two *Largo Recorrido* (long distance) **RENFE** stations, **Madrid-Chamartín** and **Madrid-Atocha,** connect Madrid to the rest of the world. Call RENFE (☎91 328 90 20; www.renfe.es) for reservations and info. **RENFE Main Office,** C. Alcalá, 44, at Gran Vía (M: Banco de España) sells tickets.

Estación Chamartín (24hr. info for international destinations ☎934 90 11 22; domestic destinations ☎(902) 24 02 02, Spanish only), Agustín de Foxá. M: Chamartín. Bus #5 runs to and from Sol (45min.). Ticket windows open 8:30am-10:30pm. Chamartín services both international and domestic destinations in the Northeast and South. Most *cercanías* (local) trains leave from Chamartín; many stop at Atocha. To: **Barcelona** (7hr., 10 per day 7am-12:50am, 6785ptas/ €40.80); **Lisbon** (10hr., 10:45pm, 6900ptas/€41.50); **Nice** (22hr., 10am, 21,500ptas/ €129.20); and **Paris** (13hr., 7pm, 19,500ptas/€117.20).

Estación Atocha (☎91 328 90 20). M: Atocha. Ticket windows open 6:30am-11:30pm. Trains to: Andalucía, Castilla-La Mancha, Extremadura, Valencia, Castilla y León, Sierra de Guadarrama, and El Escorial. AVE service (☎91 534 05 05) to **Córdoba** (1¾hr., 16 per day 7am-10pm, 5100-7200ptas/€30.65-43.30) and **Sevilla** (2½hr., 20 per day 7am-9pm, 8600-10,000ptas/€51.70-60.10). Luggage storage (400-600ptas/€2.40-3.60).

Intercity Buses: Numerous private companies, each with its own station and set of destinations, serve Madrid; many buses pass through the **Estación Sur de Autobuses.**

Estación Sur de Autobuses, C. Méndez Alvaro (☎91 468 42 00). M: Méndez Álvaro. Info booth open daily 7am-11pm. **Empressa Galiano Continental** (☎91 527 29 61) to **Toledo** (1hr., M-Sa every 30min. 8:30am-midnight, 605ptas/€3.60). **Empressa Larrea** (☎91 539 00 05) to **Avila** (2hr.; M-F 8 per day 7am-8pm, Sa-Su 3 per day 10am-8pm; 950ptas/€5.70).

Estación Auto Res, Pl. Conde de Casal, 6 (☎91 551 72 00). M: Conde de Casal. To: **Cuenca** (3hr.; M-F 8-10 per day 6:45am-10pm, Sa-Su 5-6 per day 8am-8pm; 1325ptas/€8); **Salamanca** (3-3¼hr., 7 per day 8:30am-6pm, 1505ptas/€9); **Trujillo** (3¼hr., 11-12 per day 8am-1am, 2035ptas/€12.25); and **Valencia** (5hr., 4 per day 1am-2pm, 2875ptas/€17.30). Express trains also available.

Estación La Sepulvedana, Po. Florida, 11 (☎91 530 48 00). M: Príncipe Pío (via extension from M: Ópera). To **Segovia** (1½hr., every 30 min. 6:30am-10:15pm, 840ptas/€5).

Intracity Buses: For general info, call **Empresa Municipal de Transportes** (☎91 406 88 10, Spanish only). 6am-11:30pm, 145ptas/€0.90. *Buho* (owl), the night bus service, runs from Pl. Cibeles to the outskirts (every 20min. midnight-3am, every hr. 3-6am; N1-20) and is the cheapest form of transportation for late-night revelers.

Public Transportation: Metro: Madrid's metro puts most major subway systems to shame. Green timers hanging above most platforms show the amount of time since the last train departed. Individual metro tickets cost 145ptas/€0.90, but savvy riders opt for **bonotransporte** (ticket of 10 rides for metro or bus system) at 760ptas/€5. Buy both at machines in any metro stop, *estanco* (tobacco shop), or newsstand. For more details, call **Metro info** (☎91 580 59 09) or ask at any ticket booth.

Taxis: Call ☎91 445 90 08 or 91 447 32 32. A *libre* sign in the window or a green light indicates availability. Base fare 190ptas/€1.15, plus 50-75ptas/€0.30-0.45 per km.

Hitchhiking: Hitchhiking, neither popular nor safe, is rarely legal; the Guardia Civil de Tráfico deposits highway hitchers at nearby towns or on a bus. Hitchers try message boards at HI hostels for ride-share offers. *Let's Go* does not recommend hitchhiking.

■🛈 ORIENTATION AND PRACTICAL INFORMATION

Marking the epicenter of both Madrid and Spain, **"Kilometro 0"** in **Puerta del Sol** ("Sol" for short) is within walking distance of most sights. To the west is the **Plaza Mayor,** the **Palacio Real,** and the **Ópera** district. East of Sol lies **Huertas**—centered around Pl. Santa Ana, bordered by C. Alcalá to the north, Po. Prado to the east, and C. Atocha to the south—the pulse of cafe, theater, and museum life. The area north of Sol is bordered by the **Gran Vía,** which runs northwest to **Plaza de España.** North of Gran Vía are three club and bar-hopping districts, linked by **Calle de Fuencarral: Malasaña, Bilbao,** and **Chueca.** Modern Madrid is beyond Gran Vía and east of Malasaña and Chueca. East of Sol, the tree-lined thoroughfare **Paseo de la Castellana-Paseo de Recoletos-Paseo de Prado** splits Madrid in two, running from **Atocha** in the south to **Plaza Castilla** in the north, passing the Prado, the fountains of **Plaza Cibeles,** and **Plaza Colon.** Northwest of Sol lies **Argüelles,** an energetic neighborhood of families and students from **Moncloa,** the student district centered on C. Isaac Peral. Get a map from the tourist office and use the **color map** of Madrid's metro in the back of this book. Madrid is safer than its European counterparts, but Gran Vía, Pl. Dos de Mayo in Malasaña, Pl. de Chueca, and Pl. de España are intimidating late at night.

TOURIST, FINANCIAL, AND LOCAL SERVICES

🔲**Tourist Offices: Municipal,** Pl. Mayor, 3 (☎91 366 54 77; fax 91 366 54 77). M: Sol. Open M-Sa 10am-8pm, Su 10am-2pm. **Regional/Provincial Office of the Comunidad de Madrid,** main office, Duque de Medinaceli, 2 (☎91 429 49 51). Brochures, transport info, and maps for towns in Comunidad. Offices at Estación Chamartín and airport.

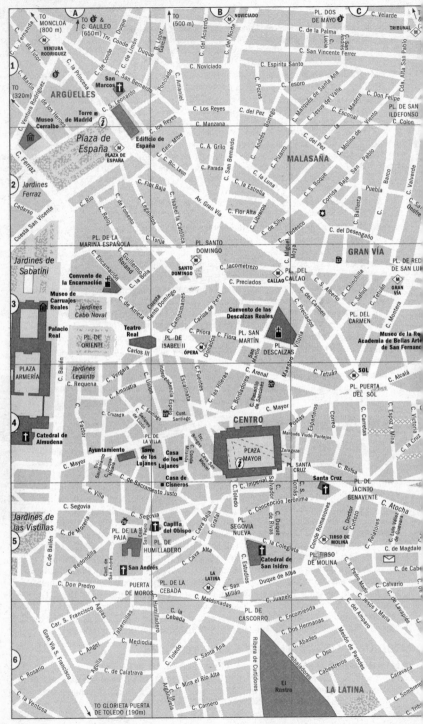

Central Madrid

🏠 ACCOMMODATIONS

Albergue Juvenil Santa Cruz de Marcenado (HI), 2	B1
Hostal Esparteros, 21	C4
Hostal Gonzalo, 24	E5
Hostal Lorenzo, 15	D3
Hostal Margarita, 12	B2
Hostal Paz, 16	B3
Hostal Palacios, 9	C2
Hostal-Residencia Domínguez, 7	D1
Hostal-Residencia Luz, 18	B4
Hostal-Residencia Rober, 17	B3
Hostal-Residencia Sud-Americana, 25	E5
Hostal Ribadavia, 9	C2
Hostal Triana, 14	C3
Hostal Villar, 22	D4

🍴 FOOD

Ananias, 1	A1
Arepas con Todo, 4	D1
Café Gijón, 11	E2
Casa Alberto, 23	D5
Cáscaras, 5	A1
Champagneria Gala, 27	E5
El 26 de Libertad, 10	D2
El Estragón, 28	A5
La Granja Restaurante Vegetariano, 3	C1

♦ NIGHTLIFE

Acuarela, 8	D2
El Barbu, 19	B4
El Café de Sheherezade, 26	D5
Kapital, 29	E6
Palacio de Gaviria, 20	B4
Sugar Hill, 13	C3
Valvén, 6	D1

Budget Travel: Viajes TIVE, C. Fernando el Católico, 88 (☎91 543 74 12; fax 91 544 00 62). M: Moncloa. Exit the metro at C. Isaac Peral, walk straight down C. Arcipreste de Hita, and turn left on C. Fernando el Católico; it's on your left. ISIC 700ptas/€4.20, HI card 1800ptas/€10.80. Open M-F 9am-2pm, Sa 9am-noon.

Embassies: Australia, Pl. Descubridor Diego de Ordás, 3 (☎91 441 60 25; fax 91 441 93 00; information@embaustralia.es; www.embaustralia.es). **Canada,** C. Núñez de Balboa, 35 (☎91 423 32 50; fax 91 423 32 51; www.canada-es.org). **Ireland,** Po. Castellana, 46, 4th fl. (☎91 576 35 00; fax 91 435 16 77). **New Zealand,** Pl. Lealtad, 2, 3rd fl. (☎91 523 02 26; fax 91 523 01 71). **South Africa,** Claudio Coello, 91, 6th fl. (☎91 436 37 80; fax 91 577 74 14). **UK,** C. Fernando el Santo, 16 (☎91 700 82 00; fax 91 700 83 11). **US,** C. Serrano, 75 (☎91 587 22 00; fax 91 587 23 03).

Currency Exchange: Banco Central Hispano charges no commission on cash or traveler's checks. **Main branch,** Pl. Canalejas, 1 (☎91 558 11 11). M: Sol. From Sol, follow C. San Jeronimo to Pl. Canalejas. Open Apr.-Sept. M-F 8:30am-2:30pm, Sa 8:30am-1pm; Oct.-Mar. M-Th 8:30am-4:30pm, F 8:30am-2pm, Sa 8:30am-1pm.

American Express: Pl. Cortés, 2 (☎91 527 03 03; info ☎91 322 54 00). M: Sevilla. From the metro stop, take a right on C. Alcala, another right down C. Cedacero and a left on C. San Jerónimo; office is on the left. Open M-F 9am-5:30pm, Sa 9am-noon.

Luggage Storage: Barajas Airport. Follow the signs to *consigna.* One day 425ptas/€2.55, 2-15 days 530-740ptas/€3.20-4.45 per day, after 15 days 105-210ptas/€0.60-1.25 per day. **Estación Chamartín** and **Estación Atocha.** Lockers 400-600ptas/€2.40-3.60 per day. Open daily 6:30am-12:30am.

Gay and Lesbian Services: Colectivo de Gais y Lesbianas de Madrid (COGAM), C. Fuencarral, 37 (☎/fax 91 523 00 70). M: Gran Vía. Provides a wide range of services and activities and HIV support group (☎91 522 45 17; M-F 6-10pm). Reception daily M-Sa 5:30-9pm. Free counseling M-Th 7-9pm.

Laundromat: Lavandería, C. Cervantes, 1. M: Puerta del Sol or Banco de España. From Pl. Santa Ana follow C. Prado, turn right on C. Leon, and then go left onto C. Cervantes. Wash 500ptas/€3, dry 100ptas/€0.60 per 9min. Open M-Sa 9am-8pm.

EMERGENCY AND COMMUNICATIONS

Emergency: General: ☎112. Medical: ☎061. Police: ☎091, 092. **General Info Line:** ☎010. 20ptas/€0.10 per min. Outside Madrid ☎90 130 06 00. **Police:** C. de los Madrazo, 9 (☎91 541 71 60). M: Sevilla. From C Arenal make a right onto C. Cedacneros and a left onto C. los Madrazo. English forms available. To report crimes committed in the **metro,** go to the office in the Sol station (☎91 521 09 11). Open daily 8am-11pm.

Crisis Lines: Rape Hotline (☎91 574 01 10). Open M-F 10am-2pm and 4-7pm.

Medical Services: Equipo Quirúrgico Municipal No. 1, C. Montesa, 22 (☎91 588 51 00). M: Manuel Becerra. **Hospital Ramón y Cajal** (☎91 336 80 00), Ctra. Colmenar Viejo. Bus #135 from Pl. Castilla.

Internet Access: Oficina13, C. Mayor, 1, 4th fl. M: Sol. Take the elevator up and buzz the office. Absolutely unbeatable 200ptas/€1.20 per hr., 150ptas/€0.90 per 30min. Open daily 10am-11pm. **Interpublic,** C. San Jeronimo 18, 1st fl. M: Sol. 300ptas/€1.80 per hr. Open daily 9am-midnight.

Post Office: Palacio de Comunicaciones, C. Alcala, 51, on Pl. Cibeles (☎(902) 19 71 97). M: Banco de España. Windows open M-Sa 8:30am-9:30pm, Su 9am-2pm for stamp purchases, certified mail, telex, and fax service. **Postal Code:** 28080.

ACCOMMODATIONS AND CAMPING

Make reservations for summer visits. Expect to pay 2800ptas/€16.80 in a basic hostel, less for a *pensión,* and more in a two-star *hostal.* Tourist offices provide information about the 13 or so **campsites** within 50km of Madrid. **Centro,** the triangle between Puerta del Sol, Opera, and Plaza Mayor, is full of *hostales.* You'll pay for the prime location. The cultural hotbed of **Huertas,** framed by C. San Jeronimo, C. las Huertas and C. Atocha, is almost as central and more fun. Festive **Malasaña** and

Chueca, bisected by C. Fuencarral, host cheap rooms in the heart of the action, but the party won't stop for sleep. *Hostales*, like temptations, are everywhere among **Gran Vía's** sex shops and scam artists.

EL CENTRO: SOL, ÓPERA, AND PLAZA MAYOR

■ **Hostal Paz,** C. Flora, 4, 1st and 4th fl. (☎91 547 30 47). M: Ópera. Don't be deterred by the dark street, parallel to C. Arenal, off C. Donados or C. Hileras. Peaceful rooms with large windows are sheltered from street noise and lavished with comfort-enhancers. Reservations advised. Singles 2500ptas/€15; doubles 4100-4800ptas/€24.70-28.80; triples 6000ptas/€36. MC/V.

■ **Hostal-Residencia Luz,** C. Fuentes, 10, 3rd fl. (☎91 542 07 59 or 91 559 74 18; fax 91 542 07 59), off C. Arenal. M: Ópera. Neck in neck with Hostel Paz for the best digs in Madrid, the 12 sunny, newly redecorated rooms ooze with comfort. Singles 2500ptas/€15; doubles 3700ptas/€22.20; triples 5500ptas/€33.

Hostal Esparteros, C. Esparteros, 12, 4th fl. (☎/fax 91 521 09 03). M: Sol. The best owner in Madrid speaks English and ensures a terrific stay. Singles 2000-2200ptas/€12-13.20, with bath 2700ptas/€16.20; doubles 3200ptas/€19.20, 3700ptas/€22.20. Discounts for longer stays.

Hostal-Residencia Rober, C. Arenal, 26, 5th fl. (☎91 541 91 75). M: Ópera. Brilliant balcony views down Arenal. Singles with double bed and shower 3800ptas/€22.80, with bath 4800ptas/€28.80; doubles with bath 6000ptas/€36; triples with bath 7800ptas/€46.80.

HUERTAS

■ **Hostal Villar,** C. Príncipe, 18, 1st-4th fl. (☎91 531 66 00; fax 91 521 50 73; www.arrakis.es/~h-villar). M: Sol. From the metro, walk down C. San Jerónimo and turn right on C. Príncipe. Lounge for the young crowd. Singles 3000ptas/€18, with bath 3500ptas/€21; doubles 4000ptas/€24, 5300ptas/€31.80; triples 5600ptas/€33.60, 7400ptas/€44.40. AmEx/MC/V.

Hostal Gonzalo, C. Cervantes, 34, 3rd fl. (☎91 429 27 14; fax 91 420 20 07). M: Antón Martín. Off C. León, which is off C. Atocha. Run by a friendly family. In all, a budget traveler's dream. Leather-plush lounge. Singles 5500ptas/€33; doubles 6500ptas/€39; triples 8500ptas/€51. AmEx/MC/V.

Hostal-Residencia Sud-Americana, Po. Prado, 12, 6th fl. (☎91 429 25 64), across from the Prado. M: Antón Martín or Atocha. Airy doubles facing the Prado with incredible views of the Paseo are the reason to stay. Singles 2800ptas/€16.80; doubles 5500ptas/€33; triples 7000ptas/€42.

GRAN VÍA

Hostal Margarita, Gran Vía, 50, 5th fl. (☎/fax 91 547 35 49). M: Callao. Stucco walls, light wood shutters, and baby-blue beds make for an airy feel. Reservations wise. Singles 3500ptas/€21; doubles 5400ptas/€32.40, with bath 5800ptas/€34.80; triples with bath 7500ptas/€45. MC/V.

Hostal Triana, C. de la Salud, 13, 1st fl. (☎91 532 68 12; fax 91 522 97 29; www.hostaltriana.com). M: Callao or Gran Vía. From Gran Vía, turn onto C. Salud, the sign is quite visible. Catering to those seeking a little more comfort than the standard hostal. Reserve 2 weeks ahead. Singles 4900ptas/€29.30; doubles 6200ptas/€37.20.

MALASAÑA AND CHUECA

■ **Hostal Palacios** and **Hostal Ribadavia,** C. Fuencarral, 25, 1st-3rd fl. (☎91 531 10 58 or 91 531 48 47). M: Gran Vía. Run by the same cheerful family. Singles 2500ptas/€15, with bath 4000ptas/€24; doubles 4000ptas/€24, 5500ptas/€33; triples 6600ptas/€39.60, 7500ptas/€45. AmEx/MC/V.

Hostal Lorenzo, C. las Infantas, 26, 3rd fl. (☎91 521 30 57; fax 91 532 79 78). M: Gran Vía. From the metro, walk up C. Del Clavel. It's on the corner of the plaza. Slightly upscale from the standard *hostal*. Reservations recommended. Singles 5950ptas/€30; doubles 8500ptas/€51; triples 9700ptas/€59.20 (IVA not included). AmEx/MC/V.

Hostal-Residencia Domínguez, C. Santa Brígida, 1, 1st fl. (☎/fax 91 532 15 47). M: Tribunal. Go down C. Fuencarral toward Gran Vía, turn left on C. Santa Brígida, and climb up a flight. Hospitable young owner ready with tips on local nightlife. English spoken. Singles 3000ptas/€18, with bath 4500ptas/€27; doubles with bath and A/C 6000ptas/€36.

ELSEWHERE IN MADRID

Albergue Juvenil Santa Cruz de Marcenado (HI), C. Santa Cruz de Marcenado, 28 (☎91 547 45 32; fax 91 548 11 96). M: Argüelles. From the metro, walk 1 block down C. Alberto Aguilera away from C. Princesa, turn right on C. Serrano Jóve, then left on C. Santa Cruz de Marcenado. Modern, recently renovated facilities near the student district mostly house traveling college students. 3-night max. stay. Curfew 1:30am. Reception daily 9am-1:30pm. Reserve space (by mail, fax, or in person) in advance, or arrive early and pray. HI (YHA) card required; purchase for 1800ptas/€10.80. Dorms 1820ptas/€11; under 26 yrs. 1200ptas/€7.20.

Camping Alpha (☎91 695 80 69; fax 91 683 1659), on a tree-lined site 12.4km down the Ctra. de Andalucía in Getafe. M: Legazpi. From metro station, take bus #447, which stops next to Nissan dealership (10min., every 30min. until 10pm, 190ptas/€1.15). Ask driver to stop at the pedestrian overpass for the campsite. Cross the bridge and walk 1½km back toward Madrid along a busy highway; camping signs lead the way. Cars, trailers, and tents crowd the lots. Alpha has a pool, showers, laundry, and other amenities. 715ptas/€4.25 per person, per tent, and per car. (IVA not included.)

◖ FOOD

In Madrid, it's not hard to fork it down without forking over too much. Most restaurants offer a *menú del día*, which includes bread, one drink, and one choice from each of the day's selections for appetizers, main courses, and desserts (1100-1500ptas/€6.60-9). Many small eateries line **Calles Echegaray, Bentura de la Vega,** and **Manuel Fernández González** in Huertas. **Calle Agurrosa** at Lavapiés has some funky outdoor cafes and there are good restaurants up the hill toward Huertas. **Calle Fuencarral** in Gran Vía is lined with cheap eats. Bilbao, the area north of Glorieta de Bilbao, in the "v" formed by C. Fuencarral and C. Luchana and including Pl. Olavide, is the ethnic food center of Madrid; also, a stroll alone **Calle Hartzenbusch and Calle Cisneros** offers endless food options that serve cheap *tapas* to a youthful crowd. Keep in mind the following essential buzz words for quicker, cheaper *madrileño* fare: *bocadillo* (a sandwich on a long, hard roll, 350-450ptas/€2.10-2.70); *sandwich* (a sandwich on sliced bread, ask for it *a la plancha* if you want it grilled, 300ptas/€1.80); *ración* (a large *tapa*, served with bread 300-600ptas/€1.80-3.60); and *empanada* (a puff pastry with meat fillings, 200-300ptas/€1.20-1.80). Vegetarians should check out the *Guía del Ocio*, which has a complete listing of Madrid's vegetarian havens under the section "Otras Cocinas." For **groceries, %Dia** and **Simago** are the cheapest supermarket chains. More expensive are **Mantequerías Leonesas, Expreso,** and **Jumbo.**

▨ **Champagneria Gala,** C. Moratín, 22. Down the hill on Moratín from C. Atocha. The *paella* buck stops here, with decor as colorful and varied as its specialty. *Menú* 1750ptas/€10.50. Make reservations for weekends. Open daily 1:30-5pm and 9pm-12:30am.

▨ **El Estragón,** Pl. de la Paja, 10. M: La Latina. From the metro, follow C. Duque de Alba, turn right through to Pl. Puerta de Moros, and leave the church on your right; it's on the far side of Pl. de la Paja. Perhaps the best mid-priced restaurant in Madrid, with vegetarian food that could turn die-hard carnivores into switch-hitters. *Menú* M-F 1500ptas/€9; Sa-Su and evenings 2975ptas/€17.75. Open daily 1:30-4:30pm and 8pm-1am.

El 26 de Libertad, C. Libertad, 26, off C. las Infantas. M: Chueca. Innovative and exotic Spanish cuisine. Fantastic lunchtime *menú* (1400ptas). Dinner served in a yellow room whose cheeriness helps you swallow the price (3000ptas/€18 before tax). Open M-Th 1-4pm and 8pm-midnight, F-Sa 1-4pm and 9pm-midnight, Su 1-4pm.

Arepas con Todo, C. Hartzenbusch, 19, off C. Cardenal Cisneros, which is off C. Luchana. Hanging gourds and waitresses in festive dress garnish this classic Colombian restaurant which really does have *todo:* with a different *menú* (1600-2000ptas/€9.60-12) every night of the month, and 60 fixed dishes (1800-2400ptas/€10.80-14.40), only the live music repeats itself. For dinner, make reservations. Open M-W 2pm-1am.

Casa Alberto, C. Huertas, 18. M: Antón Martín. Patrons spill out into the night air to wait for a spot at the bar. Interior dining room decorated with bullfighting and Cervantine relics; Cervantes wrote the second part of "El Quijote" here. The *tapas* are all original house recipes. Sit-down dinner is pricey. Open Tu-Sa noon-1:30am, Su noon-4pm.

La Granja Restaurante Vegetariano, C. San Andrés, 11, off Pl. 2 de Mayo. M: Tribunal and Bilbao. Youthful crowd as light as the well-portioned nourishment. Lunchtime *menú* 1100ptas/€6.60. Open W-M 1:30-4:30pm and 9pm-midnight.

Cáscaras, C. Ventura Rodríguez, 7. M: Ventura Rodríguez. Facing the green outside the metro, take your first right off C. Princesa. Exotic vegetarian entrees 800-985ptas/€4.80-5.90. Non-vegetarian fare as well. Open M-F 7am-1am, Sa-Su 10am-1am.

Ananias, C. Galileo, 9. M: Argüelles. From C. Alberto Aguilera, take a left onto C. Galileo. Packed on Su. Entrees 1500-2500ptas/€9-15. Open Su-Tu, Th-F 1-4pm, 9-11:30pm, Sa 9-11:30pm.

Pizzeria Cervantes, C. Leon, 8, off C. del Prado. Offering much more than pizza, this place is hands down the best cheap lunch in Huertas. Most entrees 950ptas/€5.70. Open M, W-F 11am-12:30am, Tu 7pm-12:30am, Sa noon-1:30am, Su noon-12:30am.

Museo del Jamón, C. San Jerónimo, 6. M: Sol. Five other much-loved locations throughout the city, including one at C. Mayor, 7. Generous combo plates 650-950ptas/€3.90-5.70. Open M-Th 9am-12:30pm, F-Sa 9am-1am, Su 10am-12:30pm.

El Cuchi, C. Cuchilleros, 3. Just outside Plaza Mayor, this is better and cheaper than the restaurants inside it. Entrees 900-2900ptas/€5.40-17.40. Open M-Sa 1pm-1am, Su 1pm-midnight.

⊙ SIGHTS

Madrid, as large as it may seem, is a walker's city. The word *paseo* refers to a major avenue, but literally means "a stroll." From Sol to Cibeles and from the Plaza Mayor to the Palacio Real, sights will kindly introduce themselves. The shade of the **Retiro** or a sidewalk cafe allows a break from Madrid heat and a chance to take in the best sight—its people. The municipal tourist office's *Plano de Transportes* map, which marks monuments as well as bus and metro lines, is indispensable.

EL CENTRO: SOL, ÓPERA, AND PLAZA MAYOR

PUERTA DEL SOL. Kilómetro 0—the origin of six national highways—marks the center of the city (and of the country) in the most chaotic of Madrid's plazas. Puerta del Sol (Gate of Sun) blazes with taxis, bars, and street performers. The statue **El Oso y el Madroño,** a bear and strawberry tree, is a popular meeting place. *(M: Sol.)*

PLAZA MAYOR. Juan de Herrera, architect of El Escorial, also designed this plaza. Its elegant arcades, spindly towers, and verandas, erected for Felipe III in 1620, came to define "Madrid-style" architecture and inspired every peering *balcón* thereafter. Toward evening, Pl. Mayor awakens as *madrileños* resurface, tourists multiply, and cafe tables fill with lively patrons. Live performances of flamenco and music are a common treat. On Sunday mornings, the plaza marks the starting point of **El Rastro** (see p. 839). *(M: Sol. From Pta. Sol, walk down C. Mayor. The plaza is on the left.)*

CATEDRAL DE SAN ISIDRO. Designed in the Jesuit Baroque style at the beginning of the 17th century, the cathedral received San Isidro's remains in 1769. During the Civil War rioting workers burned the exterior and damaged much of the cathedral—only the primary nave and a few Baroque decorations remain from the original. *(M: Latina. From Pta. Sol, take C. Mayor to Pl. Mayor, cross the plaza, and exit onto C. Toledo. Open for mass only. Mass daily 9, 10, 11am, noon.)*

PLAZA DE LA VILLA. Pl. Villa marks the heart of what was once old Madrid. Though only a handful of medieval buildings remain, the plaza still features a stunning courtyard (surrounding the statue of Don Alvara de Bazón), beautiful tilework, and eclectic architecture. Across the plaza is the 17th-century **Ayuntamiento (Casa de la Villa),** designed in 1640 by Juan Gomez de Mora as both the mayor's home and the city jail. *(M: Sol. From Pta. Sol, go down C. Mayor, past Pl. Mayor.)*

AROUND THE PALACIO REAL. This amazingly luxurious palace was built for the first Bourbon King, Felipe V, to replace the Alcázar after it burned down. It took 40 years to build, and the decoration of its 2000 rooms with 20km of tapestry dragged on for a century. *(M: Sol. From Pta. Sol, take C. Mayor and turn right on C. Bailen. Open Apr.-Sept. M-Sa 9am-6pm, Su 9am-3pm; Oct.-Mar. M-Sa 9:30am-5pm, Su 9am-2pm. 1000ptas/€6, students 500ptas/€3. Tour 1150ptas/€6.90. W free for EU citizens.)* The palace faces Plaza de Oriente, a sculpture garden. *(From Pta. Sol, take C. Arenal to the plaza. Free.)* Next door to the palace is the Cathedral de la Almudena, begun in 1879 and finished a century later. The cathedral's interior is a modern contrast to the gilded Palacio Real. The stained-glass windows and frescoes are an almost psychedelic mix of the traditional and the abstract. *(M: Sol. From Pta. Sol, go down C. Mayor and it's just across C. Bailén. Open M-Sa 1-7pm. Closed during mass. Free.)*

HUERTAS, GRAN VÍA, MALASAÑA, CHUECA, AND ARGÜELLES

East of Pta. del Sol, the **Huertas** reflects its literary ilk, from famed authors' houses to legendary cafes. Home to Cervantes, Góngora, Calderón, and Moratín, the neighborhood enjoyed a fleeting return to literary prominence when Hemingway hung out here. *(M: Sol.)* **Gran Vía,** which stretches from Pl. de Callao to Pl. de España and is lined with massive skyscrapers, fast-food joints, and bustling stores, is the busiest street in Madrid. *(M: Callao and Pl. España.)* ▓**Malasaña** and **Chueca** represent Madrid's alternative scene; the area between C. de Fuencarral and C. de San Bernardo, north of Gran Vía, boasts avant-garde architecture, chic eateries, and the city's hippest fashion. Out of the way in **Argüelles,** Goya's frescoed dome in the beautiful **Ermita de San Antonio de la Florida** arches above his own buried corpse. *(M: Principe Pio. From the metro, go left on C. de Buen Altamirano, walk through the park, and turn left on Po. Florida; the Ermita is at the end of the street. Open Tu-F 10am-2pm and 4-8pm, Sa-Su 10am-2pm. Free.)* **Temple de Debod,** Spain's only Egyptian temple, was built by Pharaoh Zakheramon in the 4th century BC. *(M: Ventura Rodríguez. From the metro, walk down C. Ventura Rodriguez into the Parque de la Montaña; the temple is on the left. Open in summer Tu-Su 10am-1:45pm and 6–7:45pm; off-season Tu-F 10am-1:45pm and 4-6pm, Sa-Su 10am-2pm. 300ptas/€1.80, students 150ptas/€0.90. W and Su free.)* The **Faro de Moncloa,** a 92m metal tower, offers spectacular views of the city. *(Open M-Su. 10am-1:45pm, 5-8:45pm. 200ptas/€1.20. to ascend the Faro de Moncloa.)*

▓ RETIRO

Join an array of vendors, palm-readers, soccer players, and sunbathers in what Felipe IV once intended to be a hunting ground, a "buen retiro" (nice retreat). This finely landscaped 300-acre Parque del Buen Retiro is centered around the rectangular lake and magnificent monument to King Alfonso XII. Dubbed **Estanque Grande,** this central location is popular among casual rowers—the perfect way to cool off— especially on Sundays. *(Boat rentals daily 10am-8:30pm. Paddle boats 575ptas/€3.50 for 4 people, motorboats 165ptas/€1 per person.)* Built by Ricardo Velázquez to exhibit Filippino flowers, the exquisite steel-and-glass **Palacio de Cristal** hosts a variety of art shows. *(Open Tu-Sa 11am-2pm and 5-8pm, Su 10am-2pm. Admission varies, but mostly free.)* All artists should dream of having their art displayed in the **Palacio de Velázquez,** with its billowing ceilings, marble floors, and ideal lighting. Avoid venturing alone into the park after dark. *(Past the Estanque, turn left on Paseo del Venezuela. Open M-Sa 11am-8pm, Su 11am-6pm. Free.)*

EL PARDO

Built as a hunting lodge for Carlos I in 1547, El Pardo was enlarged by generations of Habsburgs and Bourbons. El Pardo gained attention in 1940 when Franco made it his home; he resided here until his death in 1975. Renowned for its collection of tapestries—several of which were designed by Goya—the palace also holds paintings by Velázquez and Ribera. *(Take bus #601 (15min., 150ptas/€0.90) from the stop in front of the Ejército del Aire building. M: Moncloa. Palace open Apr.-Sept. M-F 10:30am-6pm, Su 9:25am-1:40pm; Oct.-Mar. M-F 10:30am-5pm, Su 9:55am-1:40pm. Compulsory 45min. guided tour in Spanish. 800ptas/€4.80, students 250ptas/€1.50. W free for EU citizens.)*

🏛 MUSEUMS

The worthwhile **Paseo del Arte** ticket grants admission to the Museo del Prado, Colección Thyssen-Bornemisza, and Centro de Arte Reina Sofía (1275ptas/€7.65).

■ **Museo Thyssen-Bornemisza** (www.museothyssen.org), on the corner of Po. Prado and C. San Jerónimo. M: Banco de España. Bus #6, 14, 27, 37, or 45. This 18th-century palace houses a fabulous art collection accumulated by generations of the Austro-Hungarian magnates. The museum surveys it all, parading canvases and sculptures by many of the greats, including El Greco, Titian, Caravaggio, Picasso, Rothko, Hopper, Renoir, Klee, Chagall, and Dalí. To view the collection in chronological order, observing the evolution of styles and themes, begin on the top floor and work your way down. Open Tu-Su 10am-7pm. 700ptas/€4.20, students 400ptas/€2.40, under 12 free.

■ **Museo Nacional Centro de Arte Reina Sofía,** C. Santa Isabel, 52, opposite Estación Atocha at the southern end of Po. Prado. M: Atocha. The centerpiece of the 20th-century collection is Picasso's masterwork *Guernica,* displaying the agony of the Nazi bombing of the Basque town of Guernica for the Fascists during the Spanish Civil War. Works by Miró, Julio González, Juan Gris, Picasso, and Dalí also illustrate the essential role of Spanish artists in Cubism and Surrealism. Open M, W-F 10am-9pm, Su 10am-2:30pm. 500ptas/€3, students 250ptas/€1.50; Sa after 2:30pm and Su free.

■ **Museo del Prado,** on Po. Prado at Pl. Cánovas del Castillo. M: Banco de España. One of Europe's finest museums, it has walls graced by Goya's "black paintings," Velázquez's *Las Meninas,* a strong Flemish collection with works by Van Dyck, van der Weyden, Albrecht Dürer, Pieter Brueghel the Elder, and Rubens (a result of the Spanish Hapsburgs' long reign over the Netherlands), and other works by Titian, Raphael, Tintoretto, Botticelli, Bosch, and El Greco. Open Tu-Sa 9am-7pm, Su 9am-2pm. 500ptas/€3, students 250ptas/€1.50; Sa 2:30-7pm and Su free.

Museo de América, Av. Reyes Católicos, 6, next to the Faro de Moncloa. M: Moncloa. This under-appreciated museum documents the cultures of America's pre-Columbian civilizations and the effects of the Spanish conquest. Open Tu-Sa 10am-3pm, Su 10am-2:30pm. 500ptas/€3, students 250ptas/€1.50; Su free.

Museo de la Real Academia de Bellas Artes de San Fernando, C. Alcalá, 13. M: Sol or Sevilla. An excellent collection of the Old Masters, surpassed only by the Prado. Open Tu-F 9am-7pm, Sa-M 9am-2:30pm. 400ptas/€2.40, students 200ptas/€1.20; W and Oct. 12, May 18, and Dec. 16 free.

🎵 ENTERTAINMENT

■ **EL RASTRO (FLEA MARKET).** For hundreds of years, El Rastro has been a Sunday morning tradition in Madrid. From Pl. Mayor and its Sunday stamp and coin market, walk down C. Toledo to Pl. Cascorro (M: La Latina), where the market begins, and follow the crowds to the end, at the bottom of C. Ribera de Curtidores.

CLASSIC CAFES. Spend an afternoon lingering over a *café con leche* and soak up Madrid's culture in historic cafes. ■**Café Gijón,** Po. Recoletos, 21 (M: Colón), a 113-year-old literati hangout, hopes its historical significance will divert attention from its high prices. (Open daily 9am-1:30am.) Or, gaze at the Palacio Real from the ritzy **Café de Oriente,** Pl. Oriente, 2. (M: Ópera. Open daily 8:30am-1:30am.)

MUSIC AND FLAMENCO. Anyone interested in live entertainment should stop by the **Circulo de Bellas Artes,** C. Marquez de Casa Riera, 2 (M: Sevilla or Banco de España. ☎91 360 54 00; fax 91 523 13 06; presa@c-bellasartes.es) at C. Alcala, 47.

Their monthly magazine, *Minerva*, is indispensable. Check the *Guía del Ocio* (125ptas/€0.75) and the entertainment supplements of Friday's newspapers for information on the city-sponsored movies, plays, and concerts. **Flamenco** in Madrid is tourist-oriented and expensive. A few nightlife spots are authentic, but pricey. **Casa Patas,** C. Cañizares, 10 is good quality, for less than usual. (☎91 369 04 96.) At **Corral de la Morería,** C. Morería, 17, by the Viaducto on C. Bailén, shows start at 9:45pm and last until 2am. (☎91 521 99 98. M: Sol. Tickets 700-2000ptas/€4.20-12.)

SPORTS. Spanish sports fans go ballistic for **fútbol** (soccer to North Americans). Every Sunday and some Saturdays from September to June, one of two local teams plays at home. **Real Madrid** plays at Estadio Santiago Bernabeu, Po. Castellana, 104. (☎91 457 11 12; M: Lima). **Atlético de Madrid** plays at Estadio Vicente Calderón, C. Virgen del Puerto 67. (☎366 47 07. M: Pirámides or Marqués de Vadillos. Tickets 3000-7000ptas/€18-42.) **Corridas** (bullfights) are held during the Festival of San Isidro and every Sunday from March to October; they are less frequent the rest of the year. **Plaza de las Ventas,** C. Alcalá, 237, east of Madrid, is the world's largest bullfighting ring. (☎91 356 22 00. M: Ventas. Tickets 450-15,200ptas/€2.70-90.)

◖ NIGHTLIFE

Spaniards average one hour less sleep each night than other Europeans, and *madrileños* claim to need even less than that. Proud of their nocturnal offerings (they'll say with a straight face that Paris or New York bored them), they don't retire until they've "killed the night"—and a good part of the next morning. As the sun sets, *terrazas* and *chiringuitos* (outdoor cafes/bars) spill across sidewalks. *Madrileños* start in the *tapas* bars of **Huertas,** move to the youthful scene in **Malasaña,** and end at the crazed parties of the **Chueca** or late-night clubs of Gran Vía. **Bilbao** and **Moncloa** are student-filled. Madrid's gay scene, centered on **Plaza Chueca,** is fantastic. Most clubs don't heat up until around 2am; don't be surprised by a line still waiting outside at 5:30am. The *entrada* (cover) can be as high as 2000ptas/€12, but usually includes a drink. Bouncers on power trips love to make examples; dress well and avoid being overcharged or denied. Women may not be charged at all.

■ **Palacio de Gaviria,** C. Arenal, 9, M: Sol or Opera. Pick a country to represent on International Thursdays when Palacio is at its best. A grand red carpet leads to two huge ballrooms turned club spaces with dancers and blazing light shows; Madrid's most exceptional of the grandiose discotecas. Open M-Sa 10:30pm-late, Su 8pm-late.

■ **El Barbu,** C. Santiago, 3, across C. Mayor from the Ayuntamiento. M: Sol or Ópera. Chill to lounge music in a brick, three-room interior. Open Tu-Su 8pm-3am. Sundays transform the bar into **"8th,"** a rave-like setting with popular local DJs. Cover 1000ptas/€6. Open 7pm-5:30am.

El Café de Sheherezade, C. Santa María, 18, a block from C. Huertas. M: Antón Martín. Surrounded by Middle Eastern music and decor, groups cluster around *pipas* (pipes; 1100-1600ptas/€6.60-9.60) that filter sweet smoke through whiskey or water. Open daily 7pm-5am.

Acuarela, C. Gravina, 8, off C. Hortaleza. M: Chueca. A welcome alternative to the club scene. Buddhas and candles surround antique furniture grouped into enclaves. Spend hours just chilling. Coffees and liquers 500-700ptas/€3-4.20. Open M-Su 3pm-3am.

Sugar Hill, C. Fundadores, 7. M: Manuel Becerra or O'Donell. Named after the original, this is the only real hip-hop club in town. Cover 1500ptas/€9, includes 1 drink. Drinks 1000ptas/€6. Open Sa 12:45-5:30am.

Café Central, Pl. Angel, 10, off Pl. Santa Ana. M: Antón Martín or Sol. Art Deco meets old-world cafe in one of Europe's top-10 jazz venues. An older audience. Beer 300-500ptas/€1.80-3. Cover 1200-2500ptas/€7.20-15. Shows nightly. Open daily 1:30pm-3:30am.

Vaivén, Travesía de San Mateo, 1. M: Tribunal. Swivel hips with the best at this exclusive salsa club, crawling with well-dressed locals. Mid-week concerts. Beer 600ptas/€3.60. Mixed drinks 1000ptas/€6. Open daily 9pm-4am.

Barnon, C. Santa Engracia, 17. www.barnon.visualdisco.com. M: Alonso Martínez. Barnon actually bars many from its funky hip-hop scene. International crowd riles the wire railings as serious grinding ensues. Tu salsa night. Mixed drinks 1600ptas/€9.60. Open Su-Th 11pm-4am, F-Sa midnight-5am.

Black & White, C. Libertad, 34. M: Chueca. A lively disco/bar with room to chat, mingle, and groove on packed dance floors. 2 floors of male fun for a gay crowd. W international exchange night. Beer 500ptas/€3. Mixed drinks 1000ptas/€6. Open Su-Th 9pm-5am, F-Sa 9pm-6am.

Kapital, C. Atocha, 125, a block off Po. Prado. M: Atocha. To be safe, take the metro. One of the most extreme results of *la Movida,* this *macro-discoteca* tries even harder than its glittered 20-something clientele. From hip-hop to house, open *terraza* to cinema, 7 floors of over-stimulation necessitate a ground-floor directory. Cover 2000ptas/€12, includes 1 drink. Open Th 12:30-6am, F-Sa 6-10:30pm and midnight-6am.

▶ DAYTRIPS FROM MADRID

EL ESCORIAL. The **Monasterio de San Lorenzo del Escorial** was a gift from Felipe II to God, the people, and himself, commemorating his victory over the French at the battle of San Quintín in 1557. Near the town of **San Lorenzo,** El Escorial is filled with artistic treasures, two palaces, two pantheons, a church, and a magnificent library. *Don't* come on Monday, when the complex and most of the town shut down. To avoid crowds, enter via the gate on the west side on C. Florida Blanca into a collection of Flemish tapestries and paintings. The adjacent **Museos de Arquitectura** and **Pintura** chronicle the construction of El Escorial and include masterpieces by Bosch, El Greco, Titian, Tintoretto, Velázquez, Zurbarán, and Van Dyck. The **Palacio Real,** lined with 16th-century *azulejos* (tiles), includes the majestic **Salón del Trono** (Throne Room), Felipe II's spartan 16th-century apartments, and the luxurious 18th-century rooms of Carlos III and Carlos IV. The macabre **Panteón Real** is filled with tombs of monarchs and glitters with gold-and-marble designs. (Complex ☎91 890 59 03. Open Apr.-Sept. Tu-Su 10am-6pm; Oct.-Mar. 10am-5pm. Last admission 1hr. before closing. Monastery 1000ptas/€6, students and seniors 500ptas/€3. Guided tour 1150ptas/€6.90.) **Autocares Herranz buses** leave from **Madrid's** Moncloa **Metro station** (50min.; every 15min. M-F 7am-11:30pm, Sa 9am-10:15pm, Su 9am-11pm; 445ptas/€2.70) and return to Madrid (every 15min. M-F 6:15am-10:30pm, Sa 7:45am-9pm, Su 9am-10pm).

EL VALLE DE LOS CAÍDOS. In a valley of the Sierra de Guadarrama, Franco built the overpowering **Santa Cruz del Valle de los Caídos** (Valley of the Fallen) as a memorial to those who died in the Civil War. The massive granite cross was meant to honor only those who died "serving *Dios* and *España*," i.e., the fascist Nationalists. Thousands of non-fascists forced to build the monument died during its construction. Franco is buried beneath the high altar, but there is no mention of his tomb in tourist literature—testimony to the dictator's legacy. It is accessible only via El Escorial. (Mass M-Sa 11am, Su 11am, 12:30, 1, 5:30pm. Entrance gate open Tu-Su 10am-6pm; basilica open 10am-6:30pm. 800ptas/€4.80, seniors and students 400ptas/€2.40. W free EU citizens. Funicular to the cross 400ptas/€2.40.) Autocares Herranz runs one **bus** to the monument (15min.; leave El Escorial Tu-Su 3:15pm, returns 5:30pm; round-trip plus admission 1150ptas/€6.90.)

CENTRAL SPAIN

Castilla La Mancha, surrounding Madrid to the west and south, is one of Spain's least-developed regions; medieval cities and olive groves sprinkle the land. On the other sides of Madrid are **Castilla y León's** dramatic cathedrals. Despite glorious historical architecture and history, the region has not been as economically successful as its more high-tech neighbors. Farther west, bordering Portugal, stark **Extremadura's** arid plains bake under intense summer sun, relieved by scattered patches of glowing sunflowers and refreshingly few tourists.

CASTILLA LA MANCHA

Cervantes chose to set Don Quixote's adventures in La Mancha (*manxa* is Arabic for parched earth) in an effort to evoke a cultural and material backwater. No fantasy of the Knight of the Sad Countenance is needed to transform the austere beauty of this battered, windswept plateau. Its tumultuous history, gloomy medieval fortresses, and awesome crags provide enough food for the imagination.

TOLEDO ☎925

Cossío called Toledo "the most brilliant and evocative summary of Spain's history." Toledo (pop. 65,000) may today be marred by armies of tourists and caravans of kitsch, but this former capital of the Holy Roman, Visigoth, and Muslim empires remains a treasure trove of Spanish culture. The city's numerous churches, synagogues, and mosques share twisting alleyways, emblematic of a time when Spain's three religions coexisted peacefully.

TRANSPORTATION AND PRACTICAL INFORMATION. Trains, Po. Rosa, 2 (☎925 22 30 99), arrive from Madrid's Estación Atocha (1½hr., 9-10 per day, 780ptas/€4.70). **Buses** (☎925 21 58 50), 5min. from the city gate, go to Valencia (5½hr.; M-F 3pm, 2600ptas/€16; buy ticket on the bus). Take bus #5 or 6 from the right of the station to Pl. Zocodóver (120ptas/€0.75), follow C. Armas downhill as it changes names and leads through the gates (Puerta Nueva de Bisagra), and cross the intersection to reach the **tourist office.** (☎925 22 08 43. Open July-Sept. M-Sa 9am-7pm, Su 9am-3pm; Oct.-June M-F 9am-6pm, Sa 9am-7pm, Su 9am-3pm.) Surf the **Internet** at **Punto Com,** C. Armas, 4, 2nd fl., in Pl. Zocodóver. (150ptas/€0.90 per 15min., 250ptas/€1.50 per 30min. Open M-Sa 11:30am-10pm, Su 4-10pm.) **Postal code:** 45070.

ACCOMMODATIONS AND FOOD. The **Residencia Juvenil San Servando (HI),** on Castillo San Servando (10min.), uphill from the train station, has a gorgeous pool in the summer. (☎925 22 45 54. Reception 7-9:40am, 10am-7:40pm, and 8-11:50pm. Dorms 1800ptas/€10.85, under 27 1400ptas/€8.40.) From Pl. Zocodóver, take C. Armas downhill, then the first left up C. Recoletos to get to **Pensión Castilla,** C. Recoletos, 6. (☎925 25 63 18. Singles 2200ptas/€14; doubles with bath 3900ptas/€24.) At the edge of the old city and downhill from Po. San Cristobal you'll find the high-class **Pensión Descalzos,** C. Descalzos, 30. (☎925 22 28 88. Apr.-Oct. singles 4000ptas/€24; doubles 6420-7250ptas/€39-44. Oct.-Mar. singles 3750ptas/€23; doubles 5600-6500ptas/€34-39.) Try Toledo's marzipan delights at the *pastelerías,* or have a square meal at **La Abadía,** Pl. San Nicolás, 3. (*Menú* 1375ptas/€8.30. Open M-Th 8am-midnight, F 8am-1:30am, Sa noon-2:30am, Su noon-midnight.)

SIGHTS AND NIGHTLIFE. The vast collection of museums, churches, synagogues, and mosques (many closed on Mondays) lie within the city walls; despite well-marked streets, you'll probably get lost. Southwest of Pl. Zocodóver, Toledo's grandiose **cathedral** at the Arco de Palacioz, boasts five naves, delicate stained glass, and unapologetic ostentatiousness. (Open June-Aug. 10am-noon and 4-7pm; Sept.-May 10am-noon and 4-6pm.) Toledo's most formidable landmark, the **Alcázar,** Cuesta Carlos V, 2, uphill from Pl. Zocodóver, has been a stronghold of Romans, Visigoths, Moors, and Fascists. Today, it houses a national military museum. (Open Tu-Su 9:30am-2:30pm. 200ptas/€1.20; free W.) El Greco spent most of his life in Toledo. Many of his works are displayed throughout town; on the west side of town, the **Iglesia de Santo Tomé,** on Pl. Conde, houses his famous *El entierro del Conde de Orgaz (Burial of Count Orgaz).* (Open daily 10am-7pm. 200ptas/€1.20.) Downhill and to the left lies the **Casa Museo de El Greco,** C. Samuel Levi 3, with 19 works by the master. (Open daily Mar.-Oct.15 10am-6:45pm; Oct.16-Feb. 10am-5:45pm. 200ptas/€1.20, under 18, students and seniors 150ptas/€0.90.) The simple exterior of the 14th-century **Sinagoga del Tránsito,** on C. Samuel Levi, hides ornate Mudéjar plasterwork, an intricate wooden ceiling, and Hebrew inscriptions.

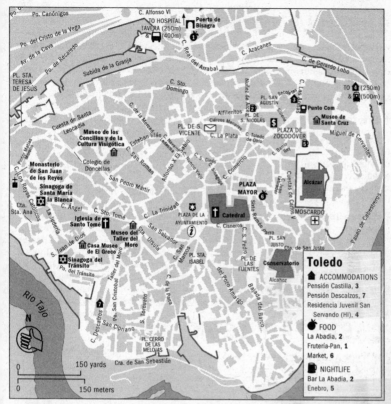

(Open Tu-Sa 10am-1:45pm and 4-5:45pm, Su 10am-2pm. 400ptas/€2.40, students and under 18 200ptas/€1.20, Sa after 4pm and Su free.) The 12th-century **Sinagoga de Santa María la Blanca,** down the street to the right, was built as a mosque and then used as the city's main synagogue until converted to a church in 1492. (Open daily June-Aug. 10am-1:45pm and 3:30-6:45pm; Sept.-May 10am-1:45pm and 3:30-5:45pm. 200ptas/€1.20; students, children under 16, and seniors 150ptas/€0.90.) At the western edge of the city resides the Franciscan **Monasterio de San Juan de los Reyes,** commissioned by Isabel and Fernando. (Open daily Apr.-Sept. 10am-1:45pm and 3:30-6:45pm; Oct.-Mar. 10am-1:45pm and 3:30-6pm. 200ptas/€1.20.)

For nightlife, try **Calle Santa Fe,** east of and through the arch from Pl. Zocodóver, which brims with beer and local youths. **Trébol,** C. Sante Fe, 1, has excellent *tapas.* (Open M-Sa 10am-3:30pm and 7pm-midnight, Su 1-3:30pm and 7pm-midnight.) Look for **Enebro,** tucked away on small Pl. Santiago balleros off C. Cervantes whose claim to fame is free *tapas* in the evenings. (No cover. Open daily 11am-4pm and 7pm-2:30am.) **Calle Sillería** and **Calle Alfileritos,** west of Pl. Zocodóver, are home to more upscale bars and clubs, including **Bar La Abadía,** Pl. San Nicolás, 5. (Open M-Th 8am-midnight, F 8am-1:30am, Sa noon-2:30am, Su noon-midnight.)

CUENCA ☎ 969

Cuenca (pop. 47,000) is a vertical hilltop city surrounded by two rivers and stunning rock formations. The enchanting ■old city safeguards most of Cuenca's unique charm, including the famed *casas colgadas* (hanging houses) that dangle high above the Río Huécar, on C. Obispo Vaero off Pl. Mayor. Cross the San Pablo bridge to **Hoz del Huécar** for a spectacular view of the *casas* and cliffs. Many of the *casas* now house museums; on Pl. Ciudad de Ronda is the excellent **Museo de Arte Abstracto Español.** (Open Tu-F and holidays 11am-2pm and 4-6pm, Sa 11am-2pm and 4-8pm, Su 11am-2:30pm. 500ptas, students and seniors 250ptas.) In the Pl. Mayor, the perfectly square **cathedral** is the only Anglo-Norman Gothic cathedral in Spain. (Open Tu-Sa 9am-2pm and 4-6pm, Su 9am-2pm. Mass daily 9:20am; Su also noon and 1pm. Museum open same hours as cathedral. 200ptas/€1.20.)

   Trains (☎ (902) 24 02 02) leave from Po. Ferrocarril, in the new city to Madrid (2½-3hr., 5-6 per day 7:05am-6:55pm, 1430ptas/€8.60) and Valencia (3-4hr.; 3-4 per day, M-F 7:40am-6:40pm, Sa-Su 11:19am-6:40pm; 1575ptas/€9.50). **Buses** (☎ 969 22 70 87) depart from C. Fermín Caballero for: Barcelona (3½hr.; M-Sa 9:30am, July-Aug. extra bus Su 2pm; 4550ptas/€27); Madrid (2½hr.; 8-9 per day M-Sa 7:30am-8pm, Su 8am-10pm; 1370-1695ptas/€8.20-10.15); and Toledo (3hr., M-F 5:30am, 1620ptas/€9.75). From either station, go left to the first bus shelter and take bus 1 (every 20min., 85ptas/€0.50) to the last stop in the old city. The **tourist office** is in Plaza Mayor. (☎ 969 23 21 19. Open July-Sept. M-Sa 9am-9pm, Su 9am-2pm; Oct.-June M-Sa 9am-2pm and 4-6pm, Su 9am-2pm.) **Hostal-Residencia Posada de San José,** C. Julián Romero, 4, a block up from the left side of the cathedral, is worth cashing the extra traveler's check. History echoes through this 17th-century convent with gorgeous views. (☎ 969 21 13 00. F-Sa and July-Aug. daily singles 3000ptas/€18, with full bath 6400ptas/€39; doubles 4900ptas/€29, 9500ptas/€57.) To reach **Pensión Tabanqueta,** C. Trabuco 13, in the old city, head up C. San Pedro from the cathedral, which turns into C. Trabuco after Pl. Trabuco. (☎ 969 21 12 90. Doubles 4000ptas/€24; triples 6000ptas/€36.) Budget eateries line **Calle Cervantes** and **Calle República Argentina.** Grab **groceries** at **%Día,** on Av. Castilla La Mancha. (Open M-Th 9:30am-2pm and 5:30-8:30pm, F-Sa 9am-2:30pm and 5:30-9pm.) **Postal Code:** 16004.

CASTILLA Y LEÓN

Castilla y León's cities emerge like islands from a sea of burnt sienna. The majestic Gothic cathedrals, slender Romanesque belfries along the Camino de Santiago, and Salamanca's intricate sandstone have emblazoned themselves as national images.

SALAMANCA   ☎ 923

For centuries, the gates of Salamanca have welcomed scholars, saints, rogues, and royals. The bustling city is famed for its golden sandstone architecture as well as for its university—the oldest in Spain, and once one of the "four leading lights of the world," along with the universities of Bologna, Paris, and Oxford.

◪◪ TRANSPORTATION AND PRACTICAL INFORMATION. Trains chug from Po. Estación Ferrocarril (☎ 923 12 02 02) to Lisbon (6hr., 4:38am, 5460ptas/€32.75) and Madrid (2½hr., 4 per day 7:45am-7:40pm, 2175ptas/€16.70). **Buses** run from Av. Filiberto Villalobos 71-85 (☎ 923 23 67 17) to: León (2½hr.; M-F 3 per day 11am-6:30pm, Sa 11am, Su 10pm; 1200ptas/€7.20); Madrid (3hr., express 2½hr.; M-Sa 15 per day 6am-9:30pm, Su 15 per day 8am-11pm; 1530ptas/€9.20, express 2600ptas/€15.60); and Segovia (3hr.; M-F 7:30am and 1:30pm, Sa 7:30am and 9:30am, Su 1:30pm and 8:45pm; 3140ptas/€19). The **tourist office** is at Pl. Mayor, 14. (☎ 923 21 83 42. Open M-Sa 9am-2pm and 4:30-6:30pm, Su 10am-2pm and 4:30-6:30pm.) Access the **Internet** at **Informática Abaco Bar,** C. Zamora, 7. (Open M-F 9:30am-2am. 150ptas/€0.90 per 15min.)

◪◘ ACCOMMODATIONS AND FOOD. Reasonably priced *hostales* and *pensiones* cater to the floods of student visitors, especially off Pl. Mayor and C. Meléndez. **Pensión Las Vegas,** C. Meléndez, 13, 1st fl., has friendly owners. (☎ 923 21 87 49. Singles 2000ptas/€12; doubles 3500ptas/€21, with bath 4000ptas/€24; triples with bath 6000ptas/€36. MC/V.) **Pensión Bárez,** C. Meléndez, 19, 1st fl., has several large, simple rooms. (☎ 923 21 74 95. Showers 150ptas. Singles 1500ptas/€9; doubles 3000ptas/€18; triples 4500ptas/€27.) Albetur buses shuttle **campers** from Gran Vía (every 30min.) to the first-class **Regio,** 4km toward Madrid on the Ctra. Salamanca. (☎923 13 88 88. 450ptas/€2.70 per person, 850ptas/€5.10 per tent, 450ptas/€2.70 per car.) **Champion,** C. Toro 64, has a downstairs supermarket. (Open M-Sa 9:15am-9:15pm.) Cafes and restaurants surround **Plaza Mayor;** full meals in cheaper back alley spots run around 1000ptas/€6. ◪**Restaurante El Bardo,** C. Compañía 8, between the Casa de Conchas and the Clerecía, is a traditional Spanish restaurant with veggie options and a lively bar downstairs. (*Menú* 1400ptas/€8.40. Open daily 1:30-4:30pm and 9:30-11:30pm, bar until 1am.) **Postal code:** 37080.

◨ SIGHTS. The ◪**Plaza Mayor,** designed by Alberto Churriguera, has been called one of the most beautiful squares in Spain. Between its nearly 100 sandstone arches hang medallions with bas-reliefs of famous Spaniards, from El Cid to Franco. Walk down C. Rua Mayor to Pl. San Isidro to reach the 15th-century **Casa de las Conchas** (House of Shells), one of Salamanca's most famous landmarks, adorned with over 300 rows of scallop shells chiseled in sandstone. Go down Patio de las Escuelas, off C. Libreros (which leads south from Pl. San Isidro), to enter the ◪**Universidad,** founded in 1218. The university's 16th-century **entry façade** is one of the best examples of Spanish Plateresque, named for the delicate filigree work of *plateros* (silversmiths). Hidden in the sculptural work lies a tiny hidden frog; according to legend, those who can spot the frog without assistance will be blessed with good luck and even marriage. Inside the Patio de Escuelas Menores, the University Museum contains the **Cielo de Salamanca,** a 15th-century fresco of the zodiac. (Open M-F 9:30am-1:30pm and 4-7:30pm, Sa 9:30am-1:30pm and 4-7pm, Su 10am-1:30pm. 300ptas/€1.80, students 150ptas/€0.90.) Continue down R. Mayor to Pl. Anaya to reach the *vieja* (old) and *nueva* (new) cathedrals. Begun in 1513 to accommodate the growing tide of Catholics, the spindly spired late-Gothic **Catedral Nueva** wasn't finished until 1733. The Romanesque **Catedral Vieja** (1140) has a striking cupola with depictions of apocalyptic angels separating the sinners from the saved. The **museum** in the latter houses a Mudéjar Salinas organ, one of the oldest organs in Europe. (*Nueva* open daily Apr.-Sept. 9am-2pm and 4-8pm; Oct.-Mar. 9am-1pm and 4-6pm. Free. *Vieja,* cloister, and museum open Apt.-Sept. daily 10am-1:30pm and 4-7:30pm. 300ptas/€1.80.) If religious zeal intrigues you, inquire at the tourist office about Salamanca's impressive **convents.** Resembling a Tiffany jewelry box, **Casa Lis Museo Art Nouveau Y Art Deco,** C. Gibraltar, 14, behind the cathedrals, houses the oddities of Miguel de Lis's art nouveau and art deco collection. (Open Apr. to mid-Oct. Tu-F 11am-2pm and 5pm-9pm, Sa-Su 11am-9pm; mid-Oct. to Mar. Tu-F 11am-2pm and 4-7pm, Sa-Su 11am-8pm. 300ptas/€1.80.)

♪▣ ENTERTAINMENT AND NIGHTLIFE. Nightlife centers on **Plaza Mayor.** Student nightlife spreads out to **Gran Vía, Calle Bordadores,** and side streets. Discos/bars, or *pafs,* blast music into the wee hours of the morning. **Calle Prior** and **Calle Rua Mayor** are full of bars; locals gather in the terrazas on **Plaza de la Fuente,** off Av. Alemania. Intense partying occurs off **Calle Varillas,** where chupiterías (bars that mostly serve shots) take precedence over pafs. Drink to modern funk jazz at ◪**Birdland,** C. Azafranal, 57. **Camelot,** C. Bordadores 3, a monastery-turned-club. Swing to Top 40 songs at the popular **Café Moderno,** Gran Vía, 75. A mixed clientele grooves under black lights at **Submarino,** C. San Justo 27.

▣ DAYTRIP FROM SALAMANCA: ZAMORA. Perched atop a rocky cliff over the Rio Duero, Zamora (pop. 65,000) is an intriguing mix of the modern and medieval: 11th-century churches rub shoulders with Mango and Zara, and 15th-century palaces harbor Internet cafes and luxury hotels. Zamora's foremost monument is its Romanesque **cathedral,** built from the 12th to 15th centuries. Highlights are its intricately carved choir stalls (complete with seated apostles laughing and singing) and the main altar, an ornate structure of marble, gold, and silver. Inside the cloister, the **Museo de la Catedral** features the priceless 15th-century Black Tapestries. (Cathedral and museum open Tu-F 10am-2pm and 4-8pm, Sa-Su 10am-8pm. Mass daily at 10am, also Sa 6pm and Su 1pm. Cathedral free.) All in all, twelve handsome Romanesque churches remain within the walls of the old city, gleaming in the wake of recent restoration. Most visitors follow the **Romanesque Route,** a self-guided tour of all of the churches available from the tourist office. The ▨**Museo de Semana Santa,** in sleepy Pl. Santa Maria La Nueva, 9, is a rare find. Hooded mannequins stand guard over elaborately sculpted floats, dating back to the early-17th century. (Open M-Sa 10am-2pm and 5-8pm, Su 10am-2pm. 300-450ptas/€1.80-2.70.) **Buses** depart from C. Alfonso Peña, 3 (☎980 52 12 81), to Salamanca on Zamora/Salamanca (1hr.; M-F 25 per day 6:40am-9:35pm, Sa 10 per day 7:45am-8:30pm, Su 8 per day 10am-9pm; 565ptas/€3.40).

LEÓN ☎987

Formerly the center of Christian Spain, today León is best known for its 13th-century Gothic ▨**cathedral** on La Pulchra Leonina, arguably the most beautiful cathedral in Spain. Its spectacular blue stained-glass windows have earned the city the nickname *La Ciudad Azul* (The Blue City) and alone warrant a trip to León. The cathedral's **museum** displays gruesome wonders, including a sculpture depicting the skinning of a saint. (Cathedral open daily in summer 8:30am-1:30pm and 4-8pm; in winter 8:30am-1:30pm and 4-7pm. Free. Museum open in summer daily 9:30am-1:30pm and 4-6:30pm; in winter M-Sa 9:30am-1pm and 4-6pm. 500ptas/€3.) The **Basílica de San Isidoro,** dedicated in the 11th century to San Isidoro de Sevilla, houses the bodies of countless royals in the impressive *Panteón Real.* From Pl. Santo Domingo, walk up C. Ramon y Cajal; the basilica is up the flight of stairs on the right just before C. La Torre. (Open M-Sa 9am-8pm, Su 9am-2pm. 400ptas/€2.40.) For nearby bars, discos, and techno music, head to the *barrio húmedo* (drinker's neighborhood) around **Plaza de San Martín** and **Plaza Mayor.** Unfortunately, most of the city's best clubs are only accessible by cab. Try **Oh León!** or **La Tropicana. Fiestas** commemorating St. John and St. Peter take place June 21-30, as does a *corrida de toros* (bullfight).

Trains (☎ (902) 24 02 02) run from Av. Astorga, 2, to Madrid (4½hr., M-Sa 7 per day 1:12am-6:12pm, 3420ptas/€20.55). **Buses** (☎987 21 10 00) leave from Po. Ingeniero Saenz de Miera for Madrid (4½hr.; M-F 12 per day 2:30am-10:30pm, Sa-Su 8 per day 2:30am-7:30pm; 2680ptas/€16). Av. Palencia (a left out of the main entrance of the bus station or right out of the main entrance of the train station) leads across the river to **Plaza Glorieta Guzmán el Bueno,** where, after the rotary, it becomes **Avenida de Ordoño II** and leads to León's cathedral and the adjacent **tourist office,** Pl. Regla, 3. (☎987 23 70 82; fax 987 27 33 91. Open M-F 9am-2pm and 5-7pm, Sa-Su 10am-2pm and 5-8pm.) Many accommodations cluster on **Avenida de Roma, Av. Ordoño II,** and **Avenida República Argentina,** which lead into the old town from Pl. Glorieta Guzmán el Bueno. **Hostal Orejas,** C. Villafranca, 6, 2nd fl., is just down Av. República Argentina from Pl. Glorieta Guzmán el Bueno. Large windows illuminate each brand-new room, complete with bath, shower, and cable TV. (☎987 25 29 09. Free Internet. Singles 4500ptas/€27; doubles 5500ptas/€33.) Inexpensive eateries fill the area near the cathedral and on the small streets off C. Ancha; also check **Plaza San Martín,** near Pl. Mayor. **Postal Code:** 24004.

▨ **DAYTRIP FROM LEÓN: ASTORGA.** Astorga's fanciful ▨**Palacio Episcopal,** designed by Antoni Gaudí in the late-19th century, now houses the **Museo de los Caminos.** (☎987 61 88 82. Open M-Sa 10am-1:30pm and 4-7:30pm, Su 10am-1:30pm. 500ptas/€3.) Opposite the *palacio* is Astorga's cathedral and museum. (Cathedral and museum open daily 10am-2pm and 4-8pm. Cathedral free; museum 250ptas/€1.50.) Astorga is most easily reached by **bus** from León (45min.; M-F 16 per day 6:15am-9:30pm, Sa-Su 6-7 per day 8:30am-8:30pm; 430ptas/€2.60).

EXTREMADURA

In a land of harsh beauty and cruel extremes, arid plains bake under an intense summer sun, relieved only by scattered patches of glowing sunflowers. These lands hardened New World conquistadors such as Hernán Cortés and Francisco Pizarro.

TRUJILLO
☎927

The gem of Extremadura, hill-perched Trujillo (pop. 10,000), is an unspoiled joy, often called the "Cradle of Conquistadors." Over 600 explorers and plunderers of the New World, including Peru's conqueror Francisco Pizarro and the Amazon's explorer, Francisco de Orellana, hailed from here. Scattered with medieval palaces, Roman ruins, Arabic fortresses, and churches of all eras, Trujillo is a glorious hodgepodge of histories and cultures. Its most impressive monument is its highest, the 10th-century **Moorish castle** which commands a stunning panoramic view of surrounding plains. The **Plaza Mayor** was the inspiration for the Plaza de Armas in Cuzco, Perú, which was constructed after Francisco Pizarro defeated the Incas. Festooned with stork nests, **Iglesia de San Martín** dominates the northeastern corner of the plaza. (All churches open daily June-Sept. 10am-2pm and 5-8:30pm; Oct.-May 9:30am-2pm and 4:30-7:30pm. Each 200ptas/€1.20; all 700ptas/€4.20.)

Buses run from Madrid (2½hr., 12-14 per day, 2100ptas/€12.60). To get to the Plaza Mayor, turn left as you exit the station (up C. de las Cruces), right on C. de la Encarnación, following signs to the tourist office, then left on C. Chica; turn left on C. Virgen de la Guia and right on C. Burgos, continuing onto the Plaza (15min.). The **tourist office** is across the plaza and posts information in its windows when closed. (☎927 32 26 77. Open June-Sept. 9:30am-2pm and 4:30-7:30pm; Oct.-May 9:30am-2pm and 4-8pm.) **Pensión Boni**, C. Mingo de Ramos, 117, is off Pl. Mayor to the right of the church. (☎927 32 16 04. Singles 2000ptas/€12; doubles 3500ptas/€21, with bath 5000ptas/€30.) The Plaza Mayor teems with tourist eateries. **Meson Alberca**, C. Victoria, 8, has a shaded interior garden and an excellent *menú* for 1850ptas/€11. (Open Su-T and Th-Sa 11am-1am.)

SOUTHERN SPAIN (ANDALUCÍA)

Andalucía is all that you expect Spain to be—white-washed villages and streets lined with orange trees, olive groves, flamenco shows, bullfighting, and tall pitchers of *sangria*. The Moors arrived in AD 711 and bequeathed the region with far more than the flamenco music and gypsy ballads proverbially associated with southern Spain by sparking the European Renaissance and reintroducing the wisdom of Classical Greece and the Near East. Under their rule, Sevilla and Granada reached the pinnacle of Islamic arts, and Córdoba matured into the most culturally influential Islamic city. Despite (or perhaps because of) the poverty and high unemployment in their homeland, Andalucians have always maintained a passionate, unshakable dedication to living the good life. The never-ending *festivales*, *ferias*, and *carnavales* of Andalucía are world-famous for their extravagance.

CÓRDOBA
☎957

Nowhere else do the remnants of Spain's ancient Islamic, Jewish, and Catholic heritage so visibly intermingle, a legacy reflected in Córdoba's unique art and architecture. Today, springtime festivals, flower-filled patios, and a busy nightlife still make Córdoba (pop. 315,000) one of Spain's most beloved cities.

▪ TRANSPORTATION

Trains: Plaza de las Tres Culturas, Av. América. (☎957 40 02 02). To: **Madrid** (AVE 2hr., 18 per day 7:15am-10:45pm, 5100-6100ptas/€30.6-36.60; regular 2-6hr., 14 per day 2am-11:15pm, 3700-6000ptas/€22.20-36); **Barcelona** (10-11hr., 3 per day 9:45am-10:20pm, 6100-8400ptas/€36.60-50.40); **Cádiz** (AVE 2¾hr., 2 per day, 3700ptas/€22.20; regular 3-4hr., 5 per day, 2370-3700ptas/€14.25-22.20); **Málaga** (AVE 2¼hr., 5 per day, 2000-2200ptas/€12-13.20; regular 3hr., 9 per day 6:40am-

10:10pm, 1650-3000ptas/€9.90-18); and **Sevilla** (AVE 45min., 18 per day 8:40am-11:40pm, 2300ptas/€13.80). For international tickets, contact **RENFE,** Ronda de los Tejares, 10 (☎957 49 02 02).

Buses: Estación de Autobuses, Glorieta de las Tres Culturas (☎957 40 40 40) across from the train station. **Alsina Graells Sur** (☎957 27 81 00) covers most of Andalucía. To: **Algeciras** (5hr., 2 per day 2805ptas/€16.85); **Cádiz** via Los Amarillos or Comes Sur (4-5hr., 1 per day 7am, 2120ptas/€12.75); **Granada** (3hr., 8-11 per day 5:20am-8:30pm, 1605-1710ptas/€9.65-10.30); **Málaga** (3-3½hr., 5 per day 8am-7pm, 1630ptas/€9.80); **Marbella** (4hr., 8am and 3:15pm, 2310ptas/€13.88); and **Sevilla** (2hr., 10-13 per day 7am-10pm, 1330ptas/€8). **Bacoma** (☎957 45 65 14) runs to **Barcelona** (10hr., 1 per day 6:25pm, 8475ptas/€51). **Secorbus** (☎(902) 22 92 92) sends exceptionally cheap buses to **Madrid** (4½hr., 7 per day 1pm-8pm, 1675ptas/€10.10) and departs from C. de los Sastres in front of Hotel Meliá. **Empresa Rafael Ramírez** (☎957 42 21 77) runs buses to nearby towns and camping sites.

ORIENTATION AND PRACTICAL INFORMATION

Córdoba is split into two parts: the **old city** and the **new city.** The modern and commercial northern half extends from the train station on **Avenida América** down to **Plaza de las Tendillas,** the center of the city. The old section in the south is a medieval maze known as the **Judería** (Jewish quarter). The easiest way to reach the old city from the train station and the bus station (which are right next to each other) is to take city bus #3 to **Campo Santo de los Mártires** (125ptas/€0.75.) Alternatively, the walk is about 20 minutes. From the train station, with your back to the platforms, exit left, cross the parking plaza and make a right onto Av. de los Mozarabes. When you reach the Roman columns, turn left and cross Gta. Sargentos Provisionales. Make a right on Paseo de la Victoria and continue until you reach Puerto Almodovar and the old city.

Tourist Offices: Oficina Municipal de Turismo y Congresos (☎957 20 05 22; fax 957 20 02 77), Pl. Judá Leví, next to the youth hostel, has maps and many free brochures about festivals and events in the Cordoba region. Open M-F 8:30am-2:30pm. **Tourist Office of Andalucía,** C. Torrijos, 10 (☎957 47 12 35; fax 957 49 17 78), in the Junta de Andalucía, across from the Mezquita. From the train station, take bus #3 (bus stops on Av. América between the train and bus stations) along the river until the stone arch is on the right. Office is 1 block up C. Torrijos. Open May-Sept. M-F 9:30am-8pm, Sa 10am-7pm, Su 10am-2pm; Oct.-Apr. M-Sa 9:30am-6pm, Su 10am-2pm.

Currency Exchange: Banco Central Hispano (☎957 47 42 67), Pl. Tendillas. No commission. Open June-Aug. M-F 8:30am-2:30pm; Sept.-May M-F 8:30am-2:30pm, Sa 9am-1pm. Banks and **ATMs** dot Pl. Tendillas.

Emergency: ☎092. **Police** (☎957 47 75 00), Av. Medina Azahara.

Medical Assistance: Red Cross Hospital (☎957 42 06 66; emergency ☎957 22 22 22), Po. Victoria. English spoken. **Ambulance,** ☎957 29 55 70.

24-Hour Pharmacy: On a rotating basis. Refer to the list posted outside the pharmacy in Pl. Tendillas or the local newspaper.

Internet Access: El Burladero Café Internet, C. Llanos del Pretorio, 1 (☎957 49 75 36), at the intersection of Av. América and Paso del Brillante. 300ptas/€1.80 per 30min., 500ptas/€3 per hr. Open daily 8am-4pm and 5pm-3am.

Post Office: C. Cruz Conde, 15 (☎(902) 19 71 97), 2 blocks up from Pl. Tendillas. Lista de Correos. Open M-F 8:30am-8:30pm, Sa 9:30am-2pm. **Postal Code:** 14070.

ACCOMMODATIONS AND CAMPING

Most accommodations cluster around the whitewashed walls of the Judería, and in old Córdoba between Mezquita and C. San Fernando, a quieter and more residential area. Call up to several months ahead during *Semana Santa* and summer.

■ **Residencia Juvenil Córdoba (HI)** (☎957 29 01 66; fax 957 29 05 00), Pl. Juda Leví, next to the municipal tourist office and a 2min. walk from the Mezquita. A backpacker's utopia. Internet 100ptas/€0.60 per 15min. Reservations recommended. 24hr. reception. 2050ptas/€12.30 per person; ages 26 and up 2675ptas/€16.

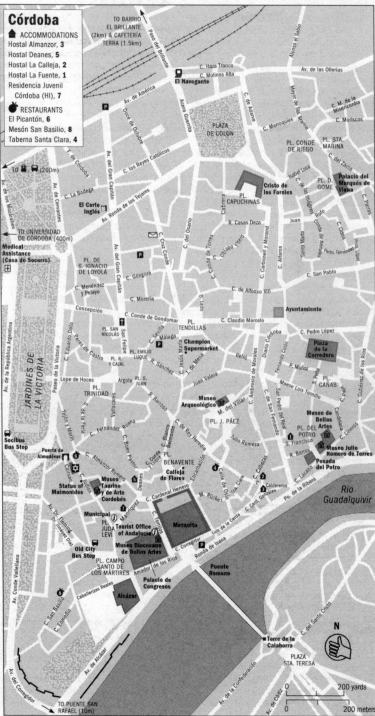

Córdoba

ACCOMMODATIONS
Hostal Almanzor, **3**
Hostal Deanes, **5**
Hostal La Calleja, **2**
Hostal La Fuente, **1**
Residencia Juvenil
  Córdoba (HI), **7**

RESTAURANTS
El Picantón, **6**
Mesón San Basilio, **8**
Taberna Santa Clara, **4**

SPAIN

Hostal La Fuente, C. San Fernando, 51 (☎957 48 78 27 or 48 14 78; fax 957 48 78 27), between C. San Francisco and C. Julio Romero. Relax amidst the tiled splendor of La Fuente's traditional Andalucian courtyard. All rooms with bath. Singles 4000 ptas/€24; doubles 6500ptas/€39; large groups 1800ptas/€10.85 per person.

Hostal La Calleja, Calleja de Rufino Blanco y Sánchez, 6 (☎/fax 957 48 66 06), at the intersection of C. Calereros and C. Cardenal Gonzalez. Reception 24hr. Singles 2800ptas/€16.85; doubles 4200ptas/€25.20, with bath 4800ptas/€28.85.

Hostal Deanes, C. Deanes, 6 (☎957 29 37 44). From the top left corner of the Mezquita take C. Cardenal, then take a sharp right onto C. Romero which becomes C. Deanes. Situated in a 16th-century home with an elegant *cordobés* patio, this intimate hostel has only 5 rooms and requires reservations 1-2 months in advance. Reception 24hr. Doubles 5000ptas/€30; triples 6500ptas/€39; quad 8000ptas/€48.

Hostal Almanzor, C. Cardenal González, 10 (☎/fax 957 48 54 00), 3 blocks from the Mezquita at the end of C. Rey Heredia closest to the river. Reception 24hr. Singles 1500-2000ptas/€9-12; doubles with bath 3000-5000ptas/€18-30.

Camping Municipal, Av. Brillante, 50 (☎957 28 21 65). From the train station, turn left on Av. América, left on Av. Brillante, and walk uphill for about 20min; or take bus #10 or 11 from Av. Cervantes near the station. Pool, currency exchange, supermarket, restaurant, and laundry service. Camping equipment for rent. Wheelchair accessible. Individual tents 400ptas/€2.40, family tents 560ptas/€2.15.

🍴 FOOD

The Mezquita area attracts nearly as many high-priced eateries as tourists to eat in them, but a five-minute walk in any direction yields local specialties at reasonable prices. In the evenings, locals converge at the outdoor *terrazas* between **Calle Severo Ochoa** and **Calle Dr. Jimenez Diaz** for drinks and tapas before dinner. Cheap eateries cluster farther away from the Judería in **Barrio Cruz Conde,** around **Av. Menéndez Pidal and Pl. Tendillas.** Regional specialties include *salmorejo* (a gazpacho-like cream soup topped with hard-boiled eggs and pieces of ham) and *rabo de toro* (bull's tail simmered in tomato sauce). **Supermarket Champion,** C. Jesús María, lies half a block from Pl. Tendillas. (Open M-Sa 9:15am-9:15pm.)

Taberna Santa Clara, C. Osio, 2. From the right side of the Mezquita, take C. Martinez Rucker and turn left. Women of Córdoba stop by in the early evening to have a glass of their very own white wine, La Peresosa. *Menú* 1300ptas/€7.80, main dishes 800-1800ptas/€4.80-10.80, salads 650ptas/€3.90. Open Th-Tu noon-4pm and 7-11pm.

Mesón San Basilio, C. San Basilio, 19, to the left of the Alcázar, past Campo Santo de los Martires. The locals love it, and so will you. *Menú del día* 1000ptas/€6, *raciones* 450-2000ptas/€2.70-12, meat and fish dishes 800-1750ptas/€4.80-10.50. Open daily 1-4pm and 8pm-midnight.

El Picantón, C. F. Ruano, 19, 1 block from the Puerta de Almodovar. From the top right corner of the Mezquita, walk up Romero and turn left. Take ordinary tapas, pour on some *salsa picante,* stick it in a roll, and voilà, you've got lunch (150-300ptas/€0.90-1.80). Nothing else as cheap or as filling. Open daily 10am-3pm and 8pm-midnight.

👁 SIGHTS

Considered the most important Islamic monument in the Western world, Córdoba's famous ▓**Mezquita** was built in AD 784 to surpass all other mosques in grandeur. Visitors enter through the **Patio de los Naranjos,** an arcaded courtyard featuring carefully spaced orange trees and fountains; inside, 850 pink and blue marble, alabaster, and stone columns support hundreds of two-tiered, red-and-white striped arches. At the far end of the Mezquita lies the **Capilla Villaviciosa,** which had a strong influence on Spanish architecture. In the center, intricate marble Byzantine mosaics—a gift from Emperor Constantine VII—shimmer across the arches of the **Mihrab,** the dome where the Muslims guarded the Quran. Although the town rallied violently against the proposed erection of a **cathedral** in the center of the mosque after the

Christians conquered Córdoba in 1236, the towering **Crucero** (transept) and **Coro** (choir dome) were soon built. (Open Apr.-June daily 10am-7:30pm; July-Oct. 10am-7pm; Nov.-Mar. 10am-6pm. 1000ptas/€6, ages 8-13 500ptas/€3.) The same ticket valid for the **Museo Diocesano de Bellas Artes.** (Open M-Sa 8:30am for mass which starts at 9:30am; Su mass 11am, noon, and 1pm.)

The **Judería** (Jewish quarter) is the historic area northwest of the Mezquita. Downhill from the Moorish arch, the small **Sinagoga,** on C. Judíos, is one of Spain's few remaining synagogues, a solemn reminder of the 1492 expulsion of the Jews. (Open Tu-Sa 10am-2pm and 3:30-5:30pm, Su 10am-1:30pm. Free.) Just to the south along the river is the 🖼**Alcázar,** constructed for Catholic monarchs in 1328 during the conquest of Granada. Ferdinand and Isabella bade Columbus adios here, and the building served as Inquisition headquarters. (Open May-Sept. Tu-Sa 10am-2pm and 6-8pm, Su 9:30am-3pm; Oct.-Apr. Tu-Sa 10am-2pm and 4:30-6:30pm, Su 9:30am-3pm. Gardens open July-Aug. 8pm-midnight. 300ptas/€1.80, students 150ptas/€0.90; F free.) The **Museo Taurino y de Arte Cordobés,** on Pl. Maimonides, highlights the history of the bullfight. (Open May-Sept. Tu-Sa 10am-2pm and 5:30-7:30pm, Su 9:30am-3pm; Oct.-Apr. M-Sa 10am-2pm and 5-7pm, Su 9:30am-2:30pm. 450ptas/€2.70, students 225ptas/€1.35; F free.) There is a **combined ticket** for the Alcázar, Museo Taurino y de Arte Cordobés, and the **Museo Julio Romero,** which displays Romero's sensual portraits of Córdoban women. (450ptas/€2.70, students 225ptas/€1.35.)

🎵 🍸 ENTERTAINMENT AND NIGHTLIFE

Hordes of tourists flock to see the flamenco dancers at the **Tablao Cardenal,** C. Torrijos 10, facing the Mezquita. (2800ptas includes 1 drink. Shows Tu-Sa 10:30pm.) The price is high, but a bargain compared to Sevilla and Madrid standards. Or check out **La Bulería,** C. Pedro López 3. (1500ptas includes 1 drink. Shows daily at 10:30pm.) Starting the first weekend in June, the **Barrio Brillante,** uphill from Av. de América, is the place to be. Well-dressed young Córdobeses walk the streets, hopping from one packed outdoor bar to another until reaching a dance club. Take bus #10 from RENFE until 11pm; a cab should cost 500-900ptas/€3-4.70. Or walk up Av. Brillante to where C. Poeta Emilia Prados meets C. Poeta Juan Ramon Jiménez. Go through **Cafetería Terra** to discover a massive open-air patio where a myriad of **bars** converge. Proceed down Av. Brillante toward the city center, passing the popular nightclub **El Cachao,** as well as **Pub La Mondoa, Club Pon Luis, Club Kachomba,** and **Bar Chicote.** During the cooler winter months, nightlife shifts to the pubs surrounding the Universidad de Córdoba, mostly on C. Antonio Maura and C. Camino de los Sastres. Of Córdoba's festivals, floats, and parades, **Semana Santa** in early April is the most extravagant. During the **Festival de los Patios** in the first two weeks of May, the city erupts with classical music concerts, flamenco dances, and a city-wide decorated patio contest. Late May brings the **Feria de Nuestra Señora de la Salud** (*La Feria*), a week of colorful garb, live dancing, and nonstop drinking.

🔲 DAYTRIP FROM CÓRDOBA: MADINAT AL-ZAHRA

Built in the **Sierra Morena** mountain range by Abderramán III for his favorite wife, Azahara, this 10th-century medina was considered one of the greatest palaces of its time. The site, long thought to be mythical, was discovered in the mid-19th century, excavated in the early 20th-century, and today is one of Spain's most impressive archaeological finds. (Open May-Sept. Tu-Sa 10am-2pm and 6-8:30pm, Su 10am-2pm; Oct.-Apr. Tu-Sa 10am-2pm and 4-6:30pm, Su 10am-2pm. 250ptas/€1.50, EU citizens free.) **Córdoba Vision** offers a 2½-hour guided visit to the site in English. (☎957 23 17 34. 2500ptas/€15.) Reaching Madinat Al-Zahra takes some effort if you don't go with an organized tour. The **0-1 bus** leaves ten after every hour from Av. República Argentina in Córdoba for Cruce Medina Azahara; from there walk 45 minutes to the palace. (☎957 25 57 00. 125ptas/€0.75.)

SEVILLE (SEVILLA)   ☎954

Site of a Roman acropolis, capital of the Moorish empire, focal point of the Spanish Renaissance, and guardian angel of traditional Andalusian culture, Sevilla has yet to disappoint visitors. Flamenco, *tapas*, and bullfighting are at their best here, and the city's cathedral is among the most impressive in Spain. But it is the infectious spirit of the city that really draws visitors: Sevilla's yearly *Semana Santa* and *Feria de Abril* celebrations are among the most extravagant in all of Europe.

▄ TRANSPORTATION

Flights: All flights depart and land at **Aeropuerto San Pablo** (☎954 44 90 00), 12km out of town on Ctra. Madrid. **Los Amarillos** (☎954 98 91 84) runs a bus from outside the Hotel Alfonso XIII at the Pta. Jerez (M-F every 30-45min., Sa-Su every hr. 6:15am-11pm; 350ptas/€2.10).

Trains: All train services are centralized in the modern **Estación Santa Justa** (☎954 41 41 11), on Av. Kansas City. Buses C1 and C2 link Santa Justa and the Prado de San Sebastián bus station. In town, the **RENFE** office, C. Zaragoza, 29 (☎954 54 02 02), is near Pl. Nueva. Open M-F 9am-1:15pm and 4-7pm. **AVE** trains run to **Córdoba** (45min., 17 per day 6:30am-9pm, 2400-2800ptas/€14.40-16.80) and **Madrid** (2½hr., 20 per day 6:30am-9pm, 8400-9900ptas/€50.40-59.40). **Talgo** trains run to: **Barcelona** (12hr.; M-F 8, 9am, 9:30pm; 8500ptas/€51); **Granada** (3hr., 5 per day 7am-6pm, 2660ptas/€15.60); **Valencia** (8½hr., 4 per day 8:11am-9:50pm, 5600ptas/€33.60).

Buses: The old bus station at Prado de San Sebastián (☎954 41 71 11), C. Manuel Vazquez Sagastizabal, mainly serves Andalucía:

Transportes Alsina Graells (☎954 41 88 11). To: **Córdoba** (2hr., 10-13 per day 8am-9pm, 1350ptas/€8.10); **Granada** (3hr., 9 per day 8am-11pm, 2500ptas/€15); **Málaga** (2½hr., 10-12 per day 7am-midnight, 2100ptas/€12.60).

Transportes Comes (☎954 41 68 58). To **Cádiz** (1½hr., 12 per day 7am-8:45pm, 1445ptas/€8.67) and; **Jerez de la Frontera** (2hr., 6 per day 11:30am-8:30pm, 935ptas/€5.61).

Los Amarillos (☎954 98 91 84). To **Arcos de la Frontera** (2hr., 8am and 4:30pm, 980ptas/€5.88) and **Marbella** (3hr., 1-2 per day 8am-8pm, 1050ptas/€6.30).

Enatcar-Bacoma (☎(902) 42 22 42). To **Barcelona** (16hr.; 4:30pm; 10,200ptas/€61.20) and **Valencia** (10hr., 2 per day 9am and 4:30pm, 6700ptas/€40.20).

Plaza de Armas (☎954 90 77 37), the newer bus station on the river bank at the Puente del Cachorro. Serves destinations beyond Andalucía, including Portugal and other European countries. Open daily 5:30am-1:30am. Buses C1, C2, C3, and C4 stop nearby.

Socibus (☎954 90 11 60). To **Lagos** (6hr.; Jan.-May Th-Su, June-Oct. Tu-Su 7:30am and 4:30pm; from 2460ptas/€14.76) and **Madrid** (6hr., 15 per day 1pm-midnight, 2745ptas/€16.47).

Public Transportation: TUSSAM (☎(900) 71 01 71), the city bus network, is extensive and useful. Most lines converge on Pl. Nueva, Pl. Encarnación, or in front of the cathedral on Av. Constitución (every 10min. 6am-11:15pm). Limited night service departs from Pl. Nueva (every hr. midnight-2am; 125ptas/€0.75, *bonobús* (10 rides) 650ptas/€3.90). Particularly useful are buses C3 and C4, which circle the center, and #34, which hits the youth hostel, university, cathedral, and Pl. Nueva.

▟ ORIENTATION AND PRACTICAL INFORMATION

Most of the city, including the old **Barrio de Santa Cruz**, lies on the east bank of the **Río Guadalquivir**. The historic **Barrio de Triana**, the **Barrio de Santa Cecilia**, and the **fairgrounds** occupy the west bank. The **cathedral**, next to Barrio de Santa Cruz, is Sevilla's centerpiece; **Avenida de la Constitución** runs alongside it. **El Centro** (downtown), a busy commercial pedestrian zone, lies north of the cathedral starting where Av. Constitución hits **Plaza Nueva**. To reach El Centro from the **train station**, catch bus #32 to Plaza de la Encarnacíon, north of the cathedral. Walk from the **Prado de San Sebastián bus station**; cross the main road, and head to the right one block past the Jardines de Murillo. C. Santa María La Blanca will be on the left. From Barrio Santa Cruz it's a 10min. walk along C. Ximénez de Enciso and C. Rod-

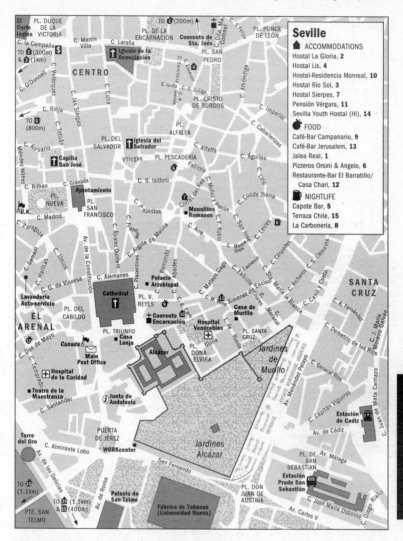

Seville

🏠 ACCOMMODATIONS
Hostal La Gloria, 2
Hostal Lis, 4
Hostal-Residencia Monreal, 10
Hostal Río Sol, 3
Hostal Sierpes, 7
Pensión Vérgara, 11
Sevilla Youth Hostal (HI), 14

🍎 FOOD
Café-Bar Campanario, 9
Café-Bar Jerusalem, 13
Jalea Real, 1
Pizzeros Orsini & Angelo, 6
Restaurante-Bar El Barratillo/
   Casa Chari, 12

🍷 NIGHTLIFE
Capote Bar, 5
Terraza Chile, 15
La Carbonería, 8

rigo Caro to the cathedral. Bus C4 connects Plaza de Armas to Pr. San Sebastián. To walk to El Centro from the **Plaza Armas bus station** (10min.), walk along the river on the left three blocks and make a right onto C. Alfonso XII.

Tourist Offices: Centro de Información de Sevilla, Av. Constitución, 21B (☎954 22 14 04; fax 954 22 97 53), 1 block from the cathedral. Regional and city maps and info. English spoken. Always swamped, but most crowded before and after siesta. Open M-F 9am-7pm, Sa 10am-2pm and 3-7pm, Su 10am-2pm. **Info booths** in Est. Santa Justa and Pl. Nueva carry maps and bus guides.

Currency Exchange: Banco Central Hispano, C. Sierpes, 55 (☎954 56 26 84). Open M-F 8:30am-2:30pm, Sa 8:30am-1pm.

American Express: Pl. Nueva, 7 (☎954 21 16 17). Changes cash and traveler's checks without commission, holds mail, and offers emergency services for cardholders. Open M-F 9:30am-1:30pm and 4:30-7:30pm, Sa 10am-1pm.

Luggage Storage: At Pr. San Sebastián bus station (250ptas/€1.50 per day; open 6:30am-10pm), Pl. Armas bus station (300ptas/€1.80 per day), and Santa Justa train station (300-500ptas/€1.80-3 per day).

Gay and Lesbian Services: COLEGA (Colectiva de Lesbianas y Gays de Andalucía), Cuesta del Rosario, 8 (☎954 18 65 10). Open M-F 10am-2pm.

Laundromat: Lavandería Auto-servicio, C. Castelar, 2 (☎954 21 05 35). From the cathedral, walk 2 blocks down C. Vinuesa and turn left. Wash and dry 1000ptas/€9. Open M-F 9:30am-1:30pm and 3-8:30pm, Sa-Su 9am-2pm.

Emergency: ☎112. **Police,** Po. Delicias, 15 (☎954 61 54 50).

24-hour Pharmacy: Check list posted at any pharmacy.

Medical Assistance: Ambulatorio Esperanza Macarena (☎954 42 01 05). Hospital Universitario Virgen Macarena (☎954 24 81 81), Av. Dr. Fedriani. English spoken.

Internet Access: WORKcenter, C. San Fernando, 1 (☎954 21 20 74), at the Puerta de Jerez. 100ptas/€0.60 per 10min. Fax services. Open 24hr.

Post Office: Av. Constitución, 32 (☎954 21 64 76), opposite the cathedral. Lista de Correos and fax. Open M-F 10am-8:30pm, Sa 9:30am-2pm. **Postal Code:** 41080.

ACCOMMODATIONS AND CAMPING

Rooms vanish and prices soar during *Semana Santa* and the *Feria de Abril;* reserve ahead. The narrow streets east of the cathedral around **Calle Santa María la Blanca** are full of cheap, central hostels. Hostels by the **Plaza de Armas** bus station, mostly on C. Gravina, are most convenient to **El Centro** and the lively C. Betis on the west bank of the river. The disorienting array of narrow streets by Pl. de la Encarnación in El Centro hosts fewer hostels.

▓ **Pensión Vergara,** C. Ximénez de Enciso, 11, 2nd fl. (☎954 21 56 68), in Santa Cruz at C. Mesón del Moro. Steep wooden stairs lead past a giftshop to this newly renovated medieval home. Up to 4 people in each room. All rooms have fans. Reception 24hr. Towels on request. 2500ptas/€15 per person.

▓ **Hostal-Residencia Monreal,** C. Rodrigo Caro, 8 (☎954 21 41 66), in Santa Cruz. From the cathedral, walk up C. Mateos Gago and take the 1st right. Enterprising owner has opened a bustling restaurant on the ground level. A/C rooms, many with verandas overlooking a nearby plaza. Singles 3000ptas/€18; doubles 6000ptas/€36, with bath 8000ptas/€48; triples 11,000-12,000ptas/€66-72. MC/V.

▓ **Hostal Lis,** C. Escarpín, 10 (☎954 21 30 88; hostal_lis@terra.es), in El Centro on an alley near Pl. Encarnación. Each room decorated with a unique pattern of blue, and yellow Sevillian tiles. Glistening bathrooms. All rooms have fans. Singles 3000ptas/€18; doubles 6000ptas/€36, with bath 7000ptas/€42; triples with bath 9000ptas/€54.

Hostal Río Sol, C. Márquez de Parada, 25 (☎954 22 90 38), extremely convenient location 1 block from Plaza de Armas bus station. Small rooms with newly renovated bathrooms and blustery A/C. Singles with sink 2000ptas/€12, with bath 3000-4000ptas/€18-24; doubles with bath 6500ptas/€39; triples with bath 9000ptas/€54. MC/V.

Hostal La Gloria, C. San Eloy, 58, 2nd fl. (☎954 22 26 73), in El Centro at the end of a lively shopping street. Singles 2500ptas/€15; doubles 4000ptas/€24, with bath 4500ptas/€27; triples 6000ptas/€36.

Hostal Sierpes, C. Corral del Rey, 22 (☎954 22 49 48; fax 954 21 21 07), in Santa Cruz on the continuation of C. Argote de Molina. Lavender and Andalusian tile adorn the elegant lobby. Singles 4500-9000ptas/€27-54; doubles 6000-11,000ptas/€36-66; triples 7500-15,000ptas/€45-90; quads 9000-19,000ptas/€54-114. MC/V.

Sevilla Youth Hostel (HI), C. Isaac Peral, 2 (☎954 61 31 50; fax 954 61 31 58). Take bus #34 across from the tourist office near the cathedral; the stop is behind the hostel, just after Po. Delicias. Up to 4 per room. A/C. Many private baths. Breakfast included. Dorms 2675ptas/€16.05, under 26 2050ptas/€12.30. Nonmembers pay additional 500ptas/€3 per night for 6 nights to become members.

Camping Sevilla, Ctra. Madrid-Cádiz, (☎954 51 43 79), near airport. From Pr. San Sebastián, take bus #70. Hot showers, supermarket, and pool. 475ptas/€2.85 per person, per car, and per tent; children 375ptas/€2.25.

◯ FOOD

Sevilla, which claims to be the birthplace of *tapas*, keeps its cuisine light. *Tapas* bars cluster around **Plaza San Martín** and along **Calle San Jacinto**. Popular venues for *el tapeo* (*tapas*-barhopping) are **Triana, Barrio Santa Cruz**, and **El Arenal**. Locals imbibe Sevilla's own Cruzcampo beer, a light, smooth pilsner. **Mercado del Arenal**, near the bullring on C. Pastor y Leandro, has fresh meat and produce. (Open M-Sa 9am-2pm.) For a supermarket, try **%Día**, C. San Juan de Ávila, near El Corte Inglés. (Open M-F 9:30am-2pm and 6:30-9pm, Sa 9am-1pm.)

■ **Restaurante-Bar El Baratillo/Casa Chari,** C. Pavía, 12, on a tiny street off C. Dos de Mayo. A local favorite. Call or ask at least an hour in advance for the tour-de-force: homemade *paella* with a jar of wine, beer, or *sangría* (2500ptas/€15 for 2). *Menú* 650ptas/€3.90. Open M-F 9am-11pm, Sa noon-5pm.

■ **Pizzeros Orsini & Angelo,** C. Luchana, 2, 2 blocks from Pl. del Salvador. Crisp and filling pizza served straight from the oven. Romantic outdoor seating in front of a Baroque church. Pizzas 400-950ptas/€2.40-5.70. Open daily 1-4pm and 8pm-1am.

  Jalea Real, Sor Ángela de la Cruz, 37. From Pl. Encarnación, walk 150m on C. Laraña, then turn left at Iglesia de San Pedro. Fabulous vegetarian cuisine. *Menú* 1400ptas/ €8.40. Open M-F 1:30-5pm and 8:30-11:30pm, Sa 8:30-11:30pm; closed Aug.

  Café-Bar Campanario, C. Mateos Gago, 8, half a block from the cathedral. Mixes the best (and strongest) jugs of *sangría* around (1200-1500ptas/€7.20-9). *Tapas* 275-350ptas/€1.65-2.10; *raciones* 650-1000ptas/€3.90-6. Open daily noon-midnight.

  Café-Bar Jerusalem, C. Salado, 6, at C. Virgen de las Huertas. Chicken, lamb, or pork and cheese *shwarmas* called a *bocadillo hebreo*—it's not kosher, but it's tasty (500-700ptas/€3-4.20). Open daily 8pm-3am.

◉ SIGHTS

■ **THE CATHEDRAL.** To clear space for Sevilla's most impressive sight, Christians razed an Almohad mosque in 1401, leaving only the **Patio de Los Naranjos** (orange trees) and the famed **La Giralda** minaret. That tower and its siblings in Marrakesh and Rabat are the oldest and largest surviving Almohad minarets. The **cathedral**— the third-largest in the world—took over 100 years to complete and is the largest Gothic edifice ever constructed. The ■**retablo mayor** (altarpiece) is a golden wall of intricately wrought disciples and saints. Circle the choir to view the **Sepulcro de Cristóbal Colón** (Columbus' tomb). His coffin-bearers represent the grateful kings of Castilla, León, Aragón, and Navarra. The cathedral's **Sacristía Mayor** museum holds Riberas, Murillos, and a glittering Corpus Christi icon. The neighboring **Sacristía de los Cálices** (or **de los Pintores**) displays canvases by Zurbarán and Goya. In the corner of the cathedral are the perfectly oval **cabildo** (chapter house) and **Sala de Las Columnas.** *(Open M-Sa 10am-5pm, Su 2-7pm. Tickets sold until 1hr. before closing. 800ptas/ €4.80, seniors and students 200ptas/€1.20, under 12 free. Su free. Mass in Capilla Real M-F 8:30, 9, 10am; Sa 8:30, 10am, 8pm; Su 8:30, 10, 11am, noon, and 1pm.)*

■ **ALCÁZAR.** The imposing 9th-century walls of the Alcázar, which faces the cathedral next to Pl. Triunfo, date from the Moorish era—as does the exquisitely carved **Patio de las Muñecas** (Patio of the Dolls). Of the later Christian additions to the palace, the most exceptional is the **Patio de las Doncellas** (Maid's Court), with ornate archways and complex tilework. The astonishing golden-domed **Salón de los Embajadores** is where Fernando and Isabel supposedly welcomed Columbus back from America. *(Pl. Triunfo, 7. Open Tu-Sa 9:30am-7pm, Su 9:30am-6pm. 700ptas/€4.20; students, seniors, and under 16 free. Audio guides 400ptas/€2.40.)*

■ **MUSEO PROVINCIAL DE BELLAS ARTES.** This museum contains Spain's finest collection of works by painters of the Sevilla school, notably Murillo, Valdés Leal, and Zurbarán, as well as El Greco and Dutch master Jan Breughel. The building itself is a work of art—take time to sit in its shady gardens. *(Pl. Museo, 9, off C. Alfonso XII. Open Tu 3-8pm, W-Sa 9am-8pm, Su 9am-2:30pm. 250ptas/€1.50.)*

PLAZA DE TOROS DE LA REAL MAESTRANZA. The tiled boardwalk leads to Pl. de Toros de la Real Maestranza, a temple of bullfighting. Home to one of the two great bullfighting schools (the other is in Ronda), the plaza fills to capacity for the 13 *corridas* of the *Feria de Abril* as well as weekly fights. The museum inside has costumes, paintings, and antique posters. *(Open non-bullfight days 9:30am-2pm and 3-7pm, bullfight days 9:30am-3pm. Tours every 30min., 500ptas/€3.)*

BARRIO DE SANTA CRUZ. King Fernando III forced Jews fleeing Toledo to live in the Barrio de Santa Cruz, now a neighborhood of weaving alleys and courtyards. Beyond C. Lope de Rueda, off C. Ximénez de Enciso, is the **Plaza de Santa Cruz.** South of the plaza are the **Jardines de Murillo,** a shady expanse of shrubbery. Pl. Santa Cruz's church houses the grave of the artist Murillo, who died after falling from a scaffold while painting ceiling frescoes in a Cádiz church. Nearby, **Iglesia de Santa María la Blanca,** built in 1391, features Murillo's *Last Supper.* *(Open M-Sa 10-11am and 6:30-8pm, Su 9:30am-2pm and 6:30-8pm.)*

LA MACARENA. This area northwest of El Centro is named for the Virgin of Sevilla, not the popular mid-90's dance. A stretch of 12th-century **murallas** (walls) runs between the Pta. Macarena and the Pta. Córdoba on the Ronda de Capuchinos road. At the west end is the **Basílica Macarena,** whose venerated image of *La Virgen de la Macarena* is paraded through town during *Semana Santa.* A **treasury** within glitters with the virgin's jewels and other finery. *(Basilica open daily 9:30am-1pm and 5-9pm; free. Treasury open daily 9:30am-1pm and 5-8pm; 400ptas/€2.40.)* Toward the river is **Iglesia de San Lorenzo y Jesús del Gran Poder,** with Montañés's remarkably lifelike sculpture *El cristo del gran poder.* Worshipers kiss Jesus' ankle through an opening in the bulletproof glass for luck. Semana Santa culminates in a procession honoring his statue. *(Open Sa-Th 8am-1:45pm and 6-9pm, F 7:30-10pm. Free.)*

OTHER SIGHTS. Lovely tropical gardens and innumerable courtyards abound in the monstrous ◪**Parque de María Luisa,** southeast of the city center. *(Open daily 8am-10pm.)* Bordering the park, the neighboring **Plaza de España** showcases mosaics. In the Aristocratic Quarter, the 15th-century **Casa de Pilatos** displays medieval and Renaissance influences. *(Pl. Pilatos. Open daily 9am-7pm. 1000ptas/€6.)* **Triana,** the neighborhood west of the cathedral and across the river, was Sevilla's chaotic 16th- and 17th-century mariners' quarters. North of Triana, visit the **Museo de Arte Contemporáneo.** *(Open Tu-Sa 10am-8pm, Su 10am-3pm. 300ptas/€1.80. Tours 11am, noon, 5, 6pm.)*

🎵 🎭 ENTERTAINMENT AND NIGHTLIFE

Get your flamenco fix at **Los Gallos,** Pl. Santa Cruz, 11, on the west edge of Barrio Santa Cruz. (Cover 3500ptas/€21, includes 1 drink. Shows nightly 9pm and 11:30pm.) If you're going to see a bullfight somewhere in Spain, Sevilla is probably the best place to do it; the bullring here is generally considered to be the most beautiful in the country. The cheapest place to buy **bullfight** tickets is at the ring on Po. Marqués de Contadero; or try the booths on C. Sierpes, C. Velázquez, or Pl. Toros (3000-13,000ptas/€18-78). Sevilla's world-famous ◪**Semana Santa** (Holy Week) festival, during which penitents in hoods guide candle-lit floats, lasts from Palm Sunday to Good Friday. The last week of April, the city rewards itself for its Lenten piety with the **Feria de Abril.**

Sevilla's reputation for gaiety is tried and true—most clubs don't get going until well after midnight, and the real fun often starts after 3am. Popular bars can be found around **C. Mateos Gago** near the cathedral, **C. Adriano** by the bullring, and **C. Betis** across the river in Triana. ◪**Terraza Chile,** Paseo de las Delicias, at the intersection of Av. Uruguay and Av. Chile. Salsa and Spanish pop keep this breezy dance club packed and pounding through the early morning hours. (Open in summer M-Sa 9pm-6am.) ◪**La Carbonería,** C. Levies 18, off C. Santa María La Blanca, in Santa Cruz, has a huge patio and free nightly flamenco. (Open M-Sa 8pm-3:30am, Su 8pm-2:30am.) Throngs of young people start the night at ◪**Capote Bar,** next to Pte. Isabel II, in El Centro. Live music, from pop-rock to Latin, plays all summer. (Open daily 11pm-3am.) **Palenque,** Av. Blas Pascal, on the grounds of Cartuja '93 is the largest dance club in Sevilla. (Mainly Sevillano university crowd. Beer 400ptas/€2.40. Mixed drinks 700ptas/€4.20. Cover 1000ptas/€6. Open in summer Th, F, Sa 11pm-7am.) The tourist office and stores distribute *El Giraldillo*, a free monthly magazine with complete listings on music, art exhibits, theater, dance, fairs, and film.

🔋 DAYTRIPS FROM SEVILLA

CÁDIZ. Founded by the Phoenicians in 1100 BC, Cádiz (pop. 155,000) is considered the oldest inhabited city in Europe. **Carnaval** is perhaps Spain's most dazzling party (Feb. 7-17 in 2002), but year-round the city offers golden sand **beaches** that put its pebble-strewn eastern neighbors to shame. **Playa de la Caleta** is the most convenient, but better sand awaits in the new city; take bus #1 from Pl. España (120ptas/€0.72) and get off at Pl. Glorieta Ingeniero (in front of Hotel Victoria) to roast at the squeaky clean ◼**Playa Victoria**. Back in town, the gold-domed, 18th-century **cathedral** is considered the last great cathedral built by colonial riches. From Pl. San Juan de Dios, follow C. Pelota. (Museum open Tu-F 10am-12:45pm and 4:30-6:45pm, Sa 10am-12:45pm. 500ptas/€3, children 200ptas/€1.20. Cathedral open M-F 5:30-8pm. Free.) From the train station, walk two blocks past the fountain, with the port on your right, and look left for **Plaza San Juan de Dios** (the old town center). Transportes Generales Comes **buses** (☎956 22 78 11) arrive at Pl. Hispanidad, 1, from Sevilla (1½hr., 12 per day 7am-8:45pm, 1445ptas/€8.67). From the bus station, walk 5min. down Av. Puerto with the port on your left and Pl. de San Juan de Dios will be after the park on your right, with the **tourist office** at #11. (☎956 24 10 01. Open M-F 9am-1pm and 5-8pm.) Most *hostales* huddle around the harbor, in Pl. San Juan de Dios, and just behind it on C. Marqués de Cádiz. **Quo Qádis**, C. Diego Arias, 1, one block from Pl. Falla, offers flamenco classes, planned excursions, and vegetarian dinners. (☎/fax 956 22 19 39. Dorms 1000ptas/€6; singles 2100ptas/€12.60; doubles 4000ptas/€24.)

ARCOS DE LA FRONTERA. With Roman ruins and castles at every turn, Arcos (pop. 33,000) is in essence a historic monument. Wander the winding white alleys, ruins, and hanging flowers of the **old quarter,** and marvel at the stunning view from **Plaza Cabildo.** In the square is the **Iglesia de Santa María,** a mix of Baroque, Renaissance, and Gothic styles. To reach the old quarter from the bus station, exit left, turn left, and continue 20min. uphill on C. Muñoz Vásquez as it changes names. **Buses** (☎956 70 20 15), C. Corregidores, come from Cádiz (1½hr., 6 per day 7am-6pm, 710ptas/€4.27) and Sevilla (2hr.; 8am and 4:30pm; 980ptas/€5.88). Buses return to Sevilla (2hr., 7am and 5pm, 905ptas/€5.43). The **tourist office** is on Pl. Cabildo. (☎956 70 22 64. Open June-Aug. M-Sa 10am-3pm and 4-8:30pm, Su 10:30am-3pm; Sept.-May M-F 9am-2pm and 5-7pm, Sa 10am-2pm and 5-6:30pm.) **Hostal San Marcos,** C. Marqués de Torresoto, 6, past C. Dean Espinosa and Pl. Cabildo is run by a friendly, young family and crowned by a scenic rooftop terrace. (☎956 70 07 21. Singles 2500-3000ptas/€15-18; doubles 4000-5000ptas/€24-30.)

RONDA. Most people's strongest impression of Ronda (pop. 38,000), the birthplace of bullfighting, is the stomach-churning ascent to get there. A precipitous gorge, carved by the Río Guadalevín, dips below the **Puente Nuevo,** opposite Pl. España. Bullfighting aficionados charge over to Ronda's **Plaza de Toros,** Spain's oldest bullring (est. 1785) and cradle of the modern *corrida.* For a less conventional experience, visit the **Museo del Bandolero,** C. Armiñán, 59, dedicated to presenting "pillage, theft, and rebellion in Spain since Roman times." (☎952 87 77 85. Open daily summer 10am-9pm; in winter 10am-6pm. 400ptas/€2.40.) **Buses** (☎952 18 70 61) go from Pl. Concepción García Redondo, 2, near Av. Andalucía, to Málaga (2½hr., 5 per day 6:30am-7:30pm, 1275ptas/€7.65); Marbella (1½hr., 5 per day 6:30am-8:30pm, 670ptas/€4.02); and Sevilla (2½hr., 5 per day 7am-7pm, 1395ptas/€8.37). The **tourist office** is at Pl. España 1. (☎952 87 12 72. Open M-F 9am-2pm and 4-7pm, Sa-Su 10am-3pm.) **Hostal Ronda Sol** is at C. Almendra, 11. (☎952 87 44 97. Singles 1700ptas/€10.20; doubles 2800ptas/€16.80.) **Postal code:** 29400.

GIBRALTAR

PHONE CODE	☎350 from the UK; ☎350 from the US; ☎9567 from Spain. For **USA Direct,** ☎88 00; for **BT Direct,** ☎84 00.

Emerging from the morning mist, the Rock of Gibraltar towers like a primordial sentinel over those who approach its shores. Bastion of empire, Jerusalem of Anglophilia, this rocky peninsula is among history's most contested plots of land. Ancient seafarers called the Rock of Gibraltar one of the Pillars of Hercules, believing that it marked the end of the world. After numerous squabbles between Moors, Spaniards, and Turks, the English successfully stormed Gibraltar in 1704 and have remained ever since. About halfway up the Rock is the infamous **Apes' Den,** where barbary monkeys cavort on the sides of rocks, the tops of taxis, and tourists' heads. At the northern tip of the Rock facing Spain are the **Great Siege Tunnels.** Originally used to fend off a combined Franco-Spanish siege at the end of the American Revolution, the tunnels were later expanded during World War II to span 33 miles underground. The eerie chambers of **St. Michael's Cave,** located ½km opposite the siege tunnels, were cut into the rock by thousands of years of water erosion. (Cable car M-Su every 10min. 9:30am-5:15pm. Combined admittance ticket, including one-way cable car ride £6/€9.80, children £5/€8.15.)

Buses arrive in the bordering Spanish town of **La Línea** from: Algeciras (45min., every 30min. 7am-9:30pm, 245ptas/€1.50); Cádiz (3hr., 4 per day 8am-8:30pm, 1565ptas/€9.40); and Granada (4½hr., 8am and 3pm, 2580ptas/€15.50). From the bus station, walk directly toward the Rock; the border is 5min. away. After bypassing the line of motorists, Spanish customs, and Gibraltar's passport control, catch bus #9 or 10 or walk across the airport tarmac and along the highway into town (20min.). Stay left on Av. Winston Churchill when the road forks with Corral Lane. Gibraltar's **Main Street,** a commercial strip lined with most services, begins at the far end of a square, past the Burger King on the left. The **tourist office,** in Duke of Kent House, Cathedral Sq., is across the park from the Gibraltar Museum. (☎450 00; fax 749 43. Open M-F 9am-5:30pm.) **Emile Youth Hostel Gibraltar,** Montague Boston, off Line Wall Rd., across from the square at the beginning of Main St., offers cramped bunkbeds but clean communal bathrooms. (☎511 06. Lock-out 10:30am-4:30pm. Dorms UK£12/€19.56; singles UK£15/€24.45; doubles £26/€42.38.)

✠ FERRIES TO MOROCCO

Ferries hop the Straits of Gibraltar from **Gibraltar** and **Algeciras.** Spanish-based **Trasmediterránea** (☎+34 902 45 46 45; www.trasmediterranea.es/homei.htm) runs ferries on a shuttle schedule from Algeciras (☎+34 956 65 62 44; Recinto del Puerto) to Cueta (☎+34 956 50 94 11; Muelle Cañonero Dato, 6) and Tangier. Trasmediterránea is represented in Tangier by **Limadet** (☎212 39/93 50 76; 3, Rue IBN Rochd., Tangier) which journeys from Algeciras to Tangier (2½hr., every hr. 8am-10pm, 5000ptas/€30.05).

ALGECIRAS   ☎956

Algeciras has some pleasant older areas, but most tourists see only the dingy port, which offers easy access to Gibraltar and Morocco. **RENFE trains** (☎(902) 24 02 02) run from Ctra. Cádiz, way down C. Juan de la Cierva, to Granada (4hr., 3 per day 7am-4:25pm, 2465-2715ptas/€16.29) and Ronda (1½hr., 4 per day 7am-6:25pm, 1020ptas/€6.12). **Empresa Portillo buses** (☎956 65 10 55) leave from Av. Virgen del Carmen, 15 for: Córdoba (6hr., 3-4 per day 8am-3:15pm, 3030ptas/€18.18); Granada (5hr., 4 per day 10:30am-5pm, 2655ptas/€15.93); Málaga (1¾-3hr., 8-9 per day 8am-8pm, 1450ptas/€8.70); and Marbella (1hr., 8-9 per day 8am-9pm, 805ptas/€4.83). **Transportes Generales Comes** (☎956 65 34 56) goes from C. San Bernardo 1 to Cádiz (2½hr., 10 per day 7am-10:30pm, 1315ptas/€7.89). **La Línea** runs to: Gibraltar (45min., every 30min. 7am-9:30pm,

245ptas/€1.47); Madrid (8hr., 5 per day 8:10-9:45pm, 3530ptas/€21.18); and Sevilla (4hr., 4 per day 7:30am-4:45pm, 2195ptas/€13.17). To get to the **ferries** from the bus and train stations, follow C. San Bernardo to C. Juan de la Cierva and turn left at the end of the street; the port entrance will be on your right. Buy tickets at the travel agency in town or at the port. In summer ferries head to: Cueta (35min.; 18 per day 6:30am-10pm; 3400ptas/€20.40, under 12 1700ptas/€10.20, car 9800ptas/€58.80, motorcycle 3175ptas/€19.05) and Tangier (2½hr.; 12 per day 6am-10pm; 3740ptas/€22.44, under 12 1870ptas/€11.22, car 11,540ptas/€69.24, motorcycle 3560ptas/€21.36; at Trasmediterránea, adult fare 2992ptas/€17.95 with Eurail pass.) Service is limited in winter and is not offered during bad weather. The **tourist office,** is on C. Juan de la Cierva. (☎956 57 26 36. Open M-F 9am-2pm.) Hostels cluster around **Calle José Santacana,** parallel to Av. Marina one block inland. To get to **Hostal Rif,** C. Rafael de Muro, 11, follow C. Santacana into the market square, bear left around the kiosk, and continue one block up C. Rafael del Muro. (☎956 65 49 53. Singles 1300ptas/€7.80; doubles 2600-2800ptas/€15.60-16.80.) **Postal code:** 11203.

COSTA DEL SOL

The coast sold its soul to the Devil, and now he's collecting; artifice covers once-natural charms, as chic promenades and swank hotels line its shore. To the northeast, rocky beaches have preserved some natural beauty. Summer brings swarms of tourists (reserve ahead), but nothing detracts from the coast's eight months of spring and four months of summer.

MARBELLA. International jet-setters choose five-star Marbella (pop. 100,000) for their yachts and glam life, but it's possible to have a budgeted good time. The beaches beckon with 320 days of sunshine per year, but no visit would be complete without a stroll through the **casco antiguo** (old town), a maze of streets and whitewashed façades. City buses along Av. Richard Soriano (dir. San Pedro; 135ptas/€0.80) bring you to chic and trendy **Puerto Banús.** Buffered by imposing white yachts, this is where it's at. With 22km of **beach,** Marbella offers a variety of sizzling settings, from below its chic promenade to **Playa de las Chapas,** 10km east via the Fuengirola bus. The **Museo del Grabado Español Contemporáneo,** on C. Hospital Bazán, is a treasure trove of engravings by Miró, Picasso, Dalí, and Goya. (Open M-F 10:15am-2pm and 5:30-8:30pm. 300ptas/€1.80.) Mellow bars abound in the *casco antiguo.* Between the beach and the old town, C. Puerta del Mar is home to several gay bars. Later in the evening, the city's young 'uns head to the **Puerto Deportivo** ("The Port"), a world of disco-bars. Nightlife in Marbella begins and ends late. The rowdiest corner of the *casco antiguo* is where C. Mesoncillo meets C. Peral. Loud music and cheery Spaniards spill out from **El Güerto,** C. Peral, 9, and **The Tavern,** C. Peral, 7. (Both open daily at 10pm.)

Accessible only by bus, the new station atop Av. Trapiche (☎95 276 44 00) sends **buses** to: Algeciras (1½hr., 9 per day 6:10am-8:30pm, 825ptas/€4.95); Barcelona (16hr.; 11:30am, 5:40, 8:30, 10:25pm; 10,135ptas/€60.81); Cádiz (4hr., 6 per day, 7:30am-8:45pm, 2140ptas/€12.84); Granada (4hr., 7 per day 8:30am-6:55pm, 1895ptas/€11.37); Madrid (7½hr., 10 per day 7:30am-11:30pm, 3060ptas/€18.36); Málaga (1½hr., every 30min. 7am-8:45pm, 670ptas/€4.02); and Sevilla (4hr., 3 per day, 2065ptas/€12.39). The **tourist office** is on Pl. Naranjos. (☎95 282 35 50. Open June-Aug. M-F 9:30am-9pm; Sept.-May M-F 9:30am-8pm, Sa 10am-2pm.) The area in the *casco antiguo* around Pl. Naranjos is packed with quick-filling hostels. **Hostal del Pilar,** C. Mesoncillo, 4, is off either C. Peral, an extension of C. Huerta Chica; or from the bus station it is off C. San Francisco. (☎95 282 99 36. 2000-3000ptas/€12-18 per person.) The excellent **Albergue Juvenil (HI),** Av. Trapiche, 2, downhill from the bus station, is just like a proper hotel, only affordable. (☎95 277 14 91. Call ahead. 2050ptas/€12.30 per person, over 26 2675ptas/€16.05.) A **24hr. minimarket** beckons from the corner of C. Pablo Casals and Av. Fontanilla. **Postal Code:** 29600.

GRANADA
☎958

When, in 1492, Moorish ruler Boabdil fled Granada, the last Muslim stronghold in Spain, his mother berated him for casting a longing look back at the Alhambra, saying, "You do well to weep as a woman for what you could not defend as a man." A spectacular palace celebrated by poets and artists throughout the ages, the Alhambra continues to inspire melancholy in those who depart from its timeless beauty. The Albaicín, an enchanting maze of Moorish houses and twisting alleys, is Spain's best-preserved Arab quarter and the only part of the Muslim city to survive the *Reconquista* intact.

▐▀ TRANSPORTATION

Trains: RENFE Station (☎(902) 24 02 02), Av. Andaluces. To: **Algeciras** (5-7hr., 3 per day 7:15am-5:50pm, 2715ptas/€16.29); **Madrid** (5-6hr., 7:55am and 4:40pm, 4300-5300ptas/€25.80-31.80); **Sevilla** (4-5hr., 4 per day 8:18am-8:15pm, 2715ptas/€16.29).

Buses: Ctra. Madrid, near C. Arzobispo Pedro de Castro. To: **Córdoba** (3hr., 10 per day 7:30am-8pm, 1605ptas/€9.63); **Málaga** (2hr., 16 per day 7am-9pm, 1255ptas/€7.53); **Sevilla** (3hr., 9 per day 8am-3am, 2480ptas/€14.88). **La Línea** runs to **Algeciras** (5hr., 6 per day 9am-8pm, 2705ptas/€16.23) and **Madrid** (5hr., 14 per day 7am-1:30am, 2075ptas/€12.45). **Bacoma** (☎958 15 75 57) goes to: **Alicante** (6hr., 5 per day, 3510ptas/€21.06); **Barcelona** (14hr., 3 per day, 8300ptas/€49.80); **Valencia** (8hr., 4 per day, 5145ptas/€30.87). All buses run 10:15am-1:45am.

Public Transportation: Take bus #10 from the bus station to the youth hostel, C. de Ronda, C. Recogidas, or C. Acera de Darro; or bus #3 from the bus station to Av. Constitución, Gran Vía, or Pl. Isabel la Católica. Bus Alhambra leaves from Pl. Nueva. All buses 130ptas/€0.78, bonobus (10 tickets) 1000ptas/€6. Free map at tourist office.

▄✳▌ ORIENTATION AND PRACTICAL INFORMATION

The geographic center is the small **Plaza de Isabel la Católica,** at the intersection of the city's two main arteries, **Calle de los Reyes Católicos** and **Gran Vía de Colón.** To reach Gran Vía and the **cathedral** from the train station, walk three blocks up Av. Andaluces to take bus #3-6, 9, or 11 from Av. Constitución; from the bus station, take bus #3. Two blocks uphill on C. Reyes Católicos sits **Plaza Nueva.** Downhill on C. Reyes Católicos lies Pl. Carmen, site of the **Ayuntamiento** and Puerta Real. The **Alhambra** commands the steep hill up from Pl. Nueva.

Tourist Office: Oficina Provincial, Pl. Mariana Pineda, 10 (☎958 24 71 28; www.dipgra.es). From Pta. Real, turn right onto C. Angel Ganivet, then take a right 2 blocks later to reach the plaza. Open M-F 9:30am-7pm, Sa 10am-2pm.

American Express: C. Reyes Católicos, 31 (☎958 22 45 12), between Pl. Isabel la Católica and Pta. Real. Exchanges money, cashes checks, and holds mail for members. Open M-F 9am-1:30pm and 2-9pm, Sa 10am-2pm and 3-7pm.

Luggage Storage: At the train and bus stations. 400ptas/€2.40. Open daily 4-9pm.

Laundromat: C. La Paz, 19. From Pl. Trinidad, take C. Alhóndiga, turn right on C. La Paz, and walk 2 blocks. Wash 500ptas/€3, dry 150ptas/€0.90 per 15min. Open M-F 9:30am-2pm and 4:30-8:30pm, Sa 9am-2pm.

Emergency: ☎112. **Police:** C. Duquesa, 21 (☎958 24 81 00). English spoken.

Medical Assistance: Clínica de San Cecilio, C. Dr. Oloriz, 16 (☎958 28 02 00 or 27 20 00), on the road to Jaén. **Ambulance:** ☎958 28 44 50.

Internet Access: Net (☎958 22 69 19) has 3 locations: C. Santa Escolástica, 13, up C. Pavaneras from Pl. Isabel la Católica; Pl. de los Girones, 3; C. Buensucesco, 22, 1 block from Pl. Trinidad. 200ptas/€1.20 per hr. All open M-Sa 9am-1am, Su 3pm-1am.

Post Office: (☎958 22 48 35; fax 958 22 36 41), Pta. Real, on the corner of C. Acera de Darro and C. Angel Ganinet. **Lista de Correos** and **fax** service. Open M-F 8am-9pm, Sa 9:30am-2pm. Wires money M-F 8:30am-2:30pm. **Postal Code:** 18009.

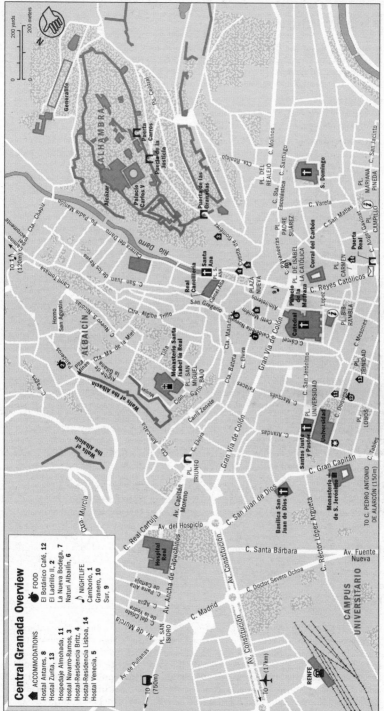

Central Granada Overview

▲ ACCOMMODATIONS
Hostal Antares, **8**
Hostal Zurita, **13**
Hospedaje Almohada, **11**
Hostal Navarro-Ramos, **3**
Hostal-Residencia Britz, **4**
Hostal-Residencia Lisboa, **14**
Hostal Venecia, **5**

● FOOD
El Botánico Café, **12**
El Ladrillo II, **2**
La Nueva Bodega, **7**
Naturi Albaílín, **6**

♪ NIGHTLIFE
Camborio, **1**
Granero, **10**
Sur, **9**

ACCOMMODATIONS

Hostels line **Cuesta de Gomérez,** near Pl. Nueva leading uphill to the Alhambra. The area around C. Mesones and C. Alhóndiga is close to the cathedral; hostels cluster around **Plaza Trinidad,** at the end of C. Mesones as you approach from Pta. Real. Hostels are sprinkled along **Gran Vía.** Call ahead during *Semana Santa.*

☒ **Hostal Venecia,** Cuesta de Gomérez, 2, 3rd fl. (☎958 22 39 87). Wake up to a soothing cup of tea, candles, and a hint of incense. Singles 2000ptas/€6; doubles 4000ptas/€24; triples and quads 1800ptas/€10.80 per person.

Hostal Residencia Britz, Cuesta de Gomérez, 1 (☎/fax 958 22 36 52), on the corner of Pl. Nueva. Large rooms with luxurious beds. Singles 2500ptas/€15, with bath 4000ptas/€24; doubles 4100ptas/€24.60, 5700ptas/€34.20.

Hostal Navarro-Ramos, Cuesta de Gomérez, 21 (☎958 25 05 55), near the outer walls of the Alhambra. Singles 1700ptas/€10.20; doubles 2700ptas/€16.20, with bath 4500ptas/€27; triples with bath 6000ptas/€36.

Hospedaje Almohada, C. Postigo de Zarate, 4 (☎958 20 74 46). From Pl. Trinidad, follow C. Duquesa to C. Málaga and take a right; it's the red door with the small sign on your right. A successful experiment in communal living: guests cook for each other with produce from a local market. Dorms 1800ptas/€10.80; singles 2200ptas/€13.20; doubles 3900ptas/€23.40. Longer stays 37,000ptas/€222 per month.

Hostal Antares, C. Cetti Meriém, 10 (☎958 22 83 13), on the corner of C. Elvira, 1 block from Gran Vía and the cathedral. Singles 2500ptas/€15; doubles 4000ptas/€24, with bath 5500ptas/€33; triples 5250ptas/€31.50. Rooms with A/C and TVs available upstairs: doubles 6000ptas/€36; triples 10,500ptas/€63.

Hostal-Residencia Lisboa, Pl. Carmen, 29 (☎958 22 14 13 or 22 14 14; fax 958 22 14 87). Take C. Reyes Católicos from Pl. Isabel la Católica; Pl. Carmen is on the left. Singles 2700ptas/€16.20, with bath 4000ptas/€24; doubles 4000ptas/€24, 5800ptas/€34.80; triples 5400ptas/€32.40, 7800ptas/€46.80. MC/V.

Hostal Zurita, Pl. Trinidad, 7 (☎958 27 50 20). Beautiful rooms, high-quality beds. Singles 2500ptas/€15; doubles 4500ptas/€27, with bath 5500ptas/€33; triples 6500ptas/€39, with bath 7500ptas/€45.

FOOD

Cheap North African cuisine abounds near the **Albaicín,** while near Pl. Nueva and Pl. Trinidad, the usual *menú* fare awaits. The adventurous eat well in Granada—try *tortilla sacromonte* (omelette with calf's brains, bull testicles, ham, shrimp, and veggies). Feast on sumptuous seafood at **El Ladrillo II,** C. Panaderos 13. (Entrees 1100-2000ptas/€6.60-12. Open daily 12:30pm-1:30am.) **Naturi Albaicín,** C. Calderería Nueva, 10, serves excellent vegetarian cuisine in a serene Moroccan ambiance. (Alcohol not served. *Menús* 950-1150ptas/€5.70-6.90. Open Sa-Th 1-4pm and 7-11pm, F 7-11pm.) **La Nueva Bodega,** C. Cetti Meriém, 9, off C. Elvira, serves *menús* for 1000-1100ptas/€6-6.60. (Open daily noon-midnight.) Students hang out at **Botánico Cafe,** C. Málaga, 3, two blocks from Pl. Trinidad. (800-1500ptas/€4.80-9. Open M-Th 10am-3am, Su noon-1am.)

SIGHTS

☒ **THE ALHAMBRA.** The age-old saying holds true: "If you have died without seeing the Alhambra, you have not lived." From the streets of Granada, the Alhambra appears simple, blocky, faded—but up close the fortress-palace reveals its astoundingly elaborate detail. The first Nazarite King Alhamar built the fortress **Alcazaba,** the section of the complex with the oldest recorded history. A dark, spiraling staircase leads up to a 360° view of Granada and the mountains. Follow signs to the *Palacio Nazaries* to see the stunningly ornate

Alcázar, a royal palace built for the Moorish rulers Yusuf I (1333-1354) and Mohammed V (1354-1391), where tourists gape at dripping stalactite archways, multicolored tiles, and sculpted fountains. Fernando and Isabel restored the Alcázar after they drove the Moors from Spain, but two generations later, Emperor Carlos V demolished part of it to make way for his **Palacio de Carlos V;** although glaringly incongruous when juxtaposed with such Moorish splendor, many consider it one of the most beautiful Renaissance buildings in Spain. Over a bridge are the vibrant blossoms, towering cypresses, and streaming waterways of ⬛**El Generalife,** the sultan's vacation retreat. *(Take C. Cuesta de Gomérez off Pl. Nueva (20min.; no unauthorized cars 9am-9pm). Or take the cheap, quick Alhambra-Neptuno microbus (every 5min., 130ptas/€0.80) from Pl. Nueva. Open Apr.-Sept. daily 8:30am-8pm; Oct.-Mar. M-Sa 9am-5:45pm. Nighttime visits June-Sept. Tu, Th, and Sa 10-11:30pm; Oct.-May Sa 8-10pm. All visits 1000ptas/€6. Limited visitors each day; get there early and stand in line. Enter the Palace of the Nazarites (Alcázar) during the time specified on your ticket, but stay as long as desired. It is possible to reserve tickets a few days in advance at banks for a 125ptas/€0.75 service charge.)*

THE ALBAICÍN. A labyrinth of steep streets and narrow alleys, the Albaicín was the only Moorish neighborhood to escape the torches of the *Reconquista* and remains a quintessential part of Granada. After the fall of the Alhambra, a small Muslim population remained here until being expelled in the 17th century. Today, with its abundance of North African cuisine and the recent construction of a mosque near Pl. San Nicolás, the Albaicín attests to the persistence of Islamic influence in Andalucía. Spectacular sunsets over the surrounding mountains can be seen from C. Cruz de Quirós, above C. Elvira. Although generally safe, the Albaicín is disorienting and should be approached with caution at night. *(Bus #12 runs from beside the cathedral to C. Pagés at the top of the Albaicín. There is another bus that departs from Pl. Nueva and weaves its way to the top. From here, walk down C. Agua through Pta. Arabe.)*

OTHER SIGHTS. Downhill from the Alhambra's Arab splendor, the Capilla Real (Royal Chapel), Fernando and Isabel's private chapel, exemplifies Christian Granada. In the **sacristy** resides Isabel's private **art collection,** the first Christian banner to flutter in triumph over the Alhambra, and the glittering **royal jewels.** *(Capilla Real and Sacristy both open daily M-Sa 10:30am-1pm and 4-7pm, Su 11am-1pm and 4-7pm. 350ptas/ €2.10.)* The adjacent **cathedral** was built from 1523 to 1704 by Fernando and Isabel upon the foundation of an Arab mosque. The first purely Renaissance cathedral in Spain, its Corinthian pillars support an astonishingly high (45m) vaulted nave. *(Open M-Sa 10:45am-1:30pm and 4-7pm, Su 4-7pm; Oct.-Mar. M-Sa 10:30am-1:30pm and 3:30-6:30pm, Su 11am-1:30pm; closed Su morning. 350ptas/€2.10.)*

🎵🍸 ENTERTAINMENT AND NIGHTLIFE

The *Guía del Ocio,* sold at newsstands (100ptas/€0.60), lists clubs, pubs, and cafes. The tourist office also distributes a monthly guide, *Cultura en Granada.* Perhaps the most boisterous nightspots belong to **Calle Pedro Antonio de Alarcón,** running from Pl. Albert Einstein to Ancha de Gràcia, while hip new bars and clubs line **Calle Elvira** from Cárcel to C. Cedrán. **Gay bars** cluster around Carrera del Darro; a complete list of gay clubs and bars is available at the tourist office. Tourists and locals alike flock to **Los Jardines Neptuno,** C. Arabial, near the Neptuno shopping center. (Cover 3800ptas/€22.80, includes 1 drink and a bus ride to Albaicín.) A smoky, intimate setting awaits at **Eshavira,** C. Postigo de la Cuna, in an alley off C. Azacayes, between C. Elvira and Gran Vía, is *the* place to go for flamenco, jazz, or a fusion of the two. Gypsies and highwaymen once roamed the caves of Sacromonte, now scantily-clad clubbers can also at **Camborio,** Camino del Sacromonte, 48. (Open Tu-Sa 11pm-dawn.) **Granero,** Pl. Luis Rosales, near Pl. Isabel Católica, is a New Age barn loft bulging with grooving young Spanish professionals. (Open daily 10pm-dawn.) **Sur,** C. Reyes Católicos, 55, is the hottest bar near Pl. Nueva. (Open daily 10pm-6am.)

⚑ HIKING AND SKIING NEAR GRANADA: SIERRA NEVADA

The peaks of **Mulhacén** (3481m) and **Veleta** (3470m), Spain's highest, sparkle with snow and buzz with tourists for most of the year. **Ski** season runs from December to April. The rest of the year, tourists **hike, parasail,** and take **jeep tours.** Call **Cetursa** (☎958 24 91 11) for information on outdoor activities. The Autocares Bonal bus (☎958 27 31 00) between the bus station in Granada and Veleta, is a bargain (9am, returns 5pm from Albergue; return 900ptas/€5.40).

EASTERN SPAIN (VALENCIA)

Valencia's rich soil and famous orange groves, nourished by Moor-designed irriga-
tion systems, have earned its nickname, *Huerta de España* (Spain's Orchard).
Dunes, sandbars, jagged promontories, and lagoons mark the grand coastline, and
lovely fountains and pools grace carefully landscaped public gardens in Valencian
cities. The famed Spanish rice dish *paella* was created somewhere in Valencia.

ALICANTE (ALACANT)   ☎965

Sun-drenched Alicante (pop. 285,000) is dutifully entertaining, yet quietly charming.
While nightlife energizes the city, Alicante's mosaic-lined waterside Explanada
relaxes it at sunset. High above the rows of bronzed bodies, the ancient *castillo*,
spared by Franco, guards the tangle of streets in the cobblestone *casco antiguo*.

🖬🖷 TRANSPORTATION AND PRACTICAL INFORMATION. RENFE **trains**
(☎(902) 24 02 02) run from Estación Término on Av. Salamanca, at the end of Av.
Estación, to: Barcelona (4½-6hr., 9 per day 6:55am-6:30pm, 6000-10400ptas/€36-
62.40); Madrid (4hr., 9 per day 7am-8pm, 5600-8600ptas/€33.60-51.60); Valencia
(1½hr., 10 per day 6:55am-10:20pm, 1430-5300ptas/€8.60-31.80). Trains from Ferro-
carriles de la Generalitat Valenciana, Estació Marina, Av. Villajoyosa, 2, on Explanada d'Espanya (☎965 26 27 31), serve the Costa Blanca. **Buses,** C. Portugal, 17
(☎965 13 07 00), run to: Barcelona (7hr., 11 per day 1am-10:30pm, 4790ptas/€28.25);
Granada (6hr., 7 per day 1:15am-10:45pm, 3510ptas/€21.10); Madrid (5hr., 9 per day
8am-midnight, 3465-5000ptas/€20.80-30). The **tourist office** is on Rbla. de Méndez
Núñez, 23. (☎965 20 00 00. Open June-Aug. M-F 10am-8pm; Sept.-May M-F 10am-
7pm, Sa 10am-2pm and 3-7pm.) Log on to the **Internet** at **Yazzgo,** Explanada, 3. (Open
M-Sa 8am-11pm, Su 9am-11pm. 8am-4pm 250ptas/€1.5 per hr.; 4-11pm 250ptas/€1.5
per 30min.) **Postal code:** 03070.

🖬🖫 ACCOMMODATIONS AND FOOD. The ⬛**Hostal Les Monges Palace,** C. San
Augustín, 4, behind the Ayuntamiento, is in the center of the historic district and
one of the most luxurious hostels in Spain. (☎965 21 50 46. Singles 3000ptas/€18,
with shower 2600ptas/€15.60; doubles with shower 5500ptas/€33.) **Habitaciones Méx-
ico,** C. General Primo de Rivera 10, off the end of Av. Alfonso X El Sabio, wins the
award for friendliest atmosphere. (☎965 20 93 07. Free Internet. Singles 2200ptas/
€13.20; doubles 4000ptas/€24; triples 1800ptas/€10.80.) Take bus #21 to **camp** at
Playa Mutxavista. (☎965 65 45 26. June-Sept. 1845ptas/€11.10 per tent, 570ptas/€3.45
per person; Oct.-May 1250ptas/€7.50, 350ptas/€2.10 per person.)

Try the family-run *bar-restaurantes* in the *casco antiguo*, between the cathe-
dral and the castle steps. ⬛**Kebap,** C. Italia, 2, serves heaping entrees of Middle
Eastern cuisine. (Open daily 1-4pm and 8pm-midnight.) Buy basics at **Supermarket
Mercadona,** C. Alvarez Sereix 5, off Av. Federico Soto. (Open M-Sa 9am-9pm.)

⊙⊞ SIGHTS AND ENTERTAINMENT. The ancient Carthaginian **Castell de Santa Bárbara,** complete with drawbridges, dark passageways, and hidden tunnels, keeps silent guard over Alicante's beach. A paved road from the old section of Alicante leads to the top, but most people take the **elevator** from a hidden entrance at the end of the tunnel that begins on Av. Jovellanos, across the street from Playa Postiguet. (Castle open daily Apr.-Sept. 10am-7:30pm; Oct.-Mar. 9am-6:30pm. Free. Elevator 400ptas/€2.40.) A crowd of Valencian modernist art pieces reside along with works by Miró, Picasso, Kandinsky, and Calder in the **Museu de Arte del Siglo XX La Asegurada,** Pl. Santa María 3, at the east end of C. Mayor. (Open mid-May to mid-Sept. M-F 10am-2pm and 5-9pm, Sa-Su 10:30am-2:30pm; mid-Sept. to mid-May M-F 10am-2pm and 4-8pm, Sa-Su 10:30am-2:30pm. Free.) Alicante's own **Playa del Postiguet** attracts sun worshipers, as do nearby **Playa de San Juan** (take TAM bus #21, 22, or 31) and **Playa del Mutxavista** (take TAM bus #21; all buses depart every 15min., 125ptas/€0.75). Most everyone begins the night bar-hopping in the *casco antiguo;* the complex of bars that overlook the water in Alicante's **main port** tend to fill up a little later. For an even crazier night-life, the **Tresnochador** night train (July-Aug. F-Sa every hr. 9pm-5am, Su-Th 4 per night 9pm-5am; return 150-700ptas/€0.90-4.20) runs from Estació Marina to Discotecas and other stops along the beach, where discos are packed until dawn. Try **Pachá, KU, KM,** and **Space** (open nightly until 9am) at the Disco Benidorm stop (return 650ptas). During the hedonistic **Festival de Sant Joan** (June 20-29), *fogueres* (symbolic or satiric effigies) are erected around the city and then burned in the streets on the 24th.

VALENCIA
☎963

Stylish, cosmopolitan, and business-oriented, Valencia is a striking contrast to the surrounding orchards and mountain ranges. Parks and gardens soothe the city's congested environment, and nearby beaches complement the frenetic pace.

▐▞ TRANSPORTATION AND PRACTICAL INFORMATION. Trains arrive at C. Xàtiva, 24 (☎963 52 02 02). RENFE (24hr. ☎(902) 24 02 02) runs to: Alicante (2-3hr., 9 per day 10am-9pm,1430-4100ptas/€8.60-24.60); Barcelona (3hr., 12 per day 6:35am-8:05pm, 5200ptas/€31.20); and Madrid (3½hr., 9 per day 6:45am-8:15pm, 4700ptas/€28.20). **Buses** (☎963 49 72 22) go from Av. Menéndez Pidal, 13 to: Alicante via the Costa Blanca (4½hr., 13 per day 6:30am-6pm, 2000ptas/€12); Barcelona (4½hr., 15 per day 1am-10pm, 3135ptas/€18.85); Madrid (4hr., 13 per day 7am-3am, 3470ptas/€20.85); and Sevilla (11hr., 4 per day 2:45-10:30pm, 6725ptas/€40.35). Bus #8 (130ptas/€0.80) connects to Pl. Ayuntamiento and the train station. Trasmediterránea **ferries** (☎(902) 45 46 45) sail to the Balearic Islands (see p. 888).

The main **tourist office,** C. Paz, 46-48, has branches at the train station and on Pl. Ayuntamiento. (☎963 98 64 22. Open M-F 10am-6pm, Sa 10am-2pm.) **Email** your mom at **Powernet,** C. Quart, 112. (100ptas/€0.60 per 15min. Open M-Th 11am-10pm, F-Sa 11am-2am, Su 4-10pm.) The **post office** is at Pl. Ayuntamiento, 24. (Open M-F 8:30am-8:30pm, Sa 9:30am-2pm.) **Postal Code:** 46080.

▐▐ ACCOMMODATIONS AND FOOD. The best lodgings are around **Plaza Ayuntamiento** and **Plaza Mercado.** To get from the train station to the **Pilgrim's Youth Hostel,** Pl. Hombres del Mar 25, take the metro to Benimaclet, switch to L4 toward Av. Dr. Lluch, and get off at Las Arenals; the entrance is on the other side of the building. (☎963 56 42 88; albergue@ran.es. Internet. Reception 24hr. Reserve ahead. 1500-2000ptas/€9, under 27 1000ptas/€6.) To get from the train station to the spotless **Hostal-Residencia El Cid,** C. Cerrajeros, 13, pass Pl. Ayuntamiento and take the second left off C. Vicente Mártir. (☎963 92 23 23. Singles 1800ptas/€10.80; doubles 3400ptas/€26.40.) **Hostal El Rincón,** C. Carda, 11, is near Plaza del Mercado. Brightly lit hallways lead to clean rooms. (☎963 91 79 98. Singles 1660ptas/€10; doubles 3000ptas/€18.) *Paella* is the most famous of Valencia's 200 rice dishes; try as many as you can before leaving. Buckets of fresh fish, meat, and fruit are sold at the **Mercado Central,** on Pl. Mercado. (Open M-F 7am-3pm.) For **groceries,** stop by the basement of **El Corte Inglés,** C. Colon, or the fifth floor of the C. Pintor Sorilla building. (Open M-Sa 10am-10pm.)

◧ **SIGHTS.** Most of the sights line the **Río Turia** or cluster near **Plaza Reina,** which is linked to Pl. Ayuntamiento by C. San Vicente Mártir. EMT bus #5, dubbed the Bus Turistic (☎963 52 83 99), makes a loop around the old town sights (130/€0.80ptas; 1-day pass 500ptas/€3). The 13th-century ◪**cathedral,** on Pl. Reina, was built on the site of an Arab mosque. The **Museo de la Catedral** squeezes many treasures into very little space. (Cathedral open daily 8am-2pm and 5-8pm; in winter closes earlier. Free. Tower open daily 10am-1pm and 4:30-7pm. 200ptas/€1.20. Museum open Mar.-May and Oct.-Nov. M-F 10am-1pm and 4:30-6pm; June-Sept. 10am-1pm and 4:30-7pm, Dec.-Feb. 10am-1pm. Open year-round Sa-Su 10am-1pm.) Across the river, the **Museu Provincial de Belles Artes,** on C. Sant Pius V, next to the **Jardines del Reial,** displays superb 14th- to 16th-century Valencian art. (Open Tu-Sa 10am-2:15pm and 4-7:30pm, Su 10am-7:30pm. Free.) West across the old river, the **Instituto Valéncia de Arte Moderno (IVAM),** C. Guillem de Castro, 118, has works by 20th-century sculptor Julio González. (Open Tu-Su 10am-7pm. 350ptas/€2.10, students 175ptas/€1.05; Su free.) Modern, airy, and thoroughly fascinating, Valencia's ◪**Ciudad de las artes y las ciencias** has created quite a stir. This mini-city has become the fourth biggest tourist destination in Spain. The complex is divided into four large attractions: **L'Hemisfèric** wows the eyes with its IMAX theater and planetarium; **L'Oceanografic** is an underground water-world and recreation of diverse aquatic environments; the beautiful **Palau de les Arts** houses stages for opera, theater and dance; and the ◪**Museu de Les Ciencias Principe Felipe** is an interactive playground for science and technology fiends. (South along the riverbed off the highway to Salér. Bus #35 runs from Pl. Ayuntamiento. www.cac.es. IMAX shows 1100ptas/€6.60, weekdays children and students 800ptas/€4.80. Museum and aquarium open M-Th 10am-8pm, F-Su 10am-9pm. 1000ptas/€6 each.) The most popular **beaches** are **Las Arenas** and **Malvarrosa,** connected by a boardwalk—buses #20, 21, 22, and 23 all pass through. To get to the more attractive **Salér,** 14km from the center of town, take an Autobuses Buñol **bus** (☎963 49 14 25) from Gran Vía Germanias and C. Sueca (25min., every 30min. 7am-10pm, 150ptas/€0.90).

◪◪ **ENTERTAINMENT AND NIGHTLIFE.** Bars and pubs abound in the El Carme district. Follow Pl. Mercado and C. Bolsería (bear right at the fork) to Pl. Tossal to guzzle *agua de Valencia* (orange juice, champagne, and vodka) with the masses, then head to Av. Blasco Ibañez with your dancing shoes. In summer, however, the only places to be seen are the outdoor discos at Playa de Malvarrosa. Caballito de Mar, C. Eugenia Viñes, 22, is the most popular and heats up with a psychedelic tunnel and huge outdoor deck. For more information, consult the *Qué y Dónde* weekly magazine, available at newsstands, or the weekly entertainment supplement, *La Cartelera* (125ptas/€0.75) The most famed festival in Valencia is Las Fallas (Mar. 12-19), which culminates with a burning of gigantic (up to 30m) satirical papier-maché effigies.

COSTA BLANCA

This "white coast," extending from Denía through Calpe, Alicante, and Elche derives its name from its fine white sands. ALSA **buses** (☎90 242 22 42) run from Valencia to: Alicante (4½hr., 13 per day 6:30am-6pm, 2000ptas/€12); Calpe and Altea (3-3½hr., 12 per day 6:30am-6pm, 1315-1420ptas/€7.90-8.50); and Gandía (1hr., 13 per day 6:30am-9:15pm, 735ptas/€4.40). From Alicante buses run to Altea (1¼hr., 18 per day 6:30am-9pm, 560ptas/€3.36) and Calpe (1½hr., 18 per day 6:30am-9pm, 675ptas/€4.05). Going to **Calpe** (Calp) is like stepping into a Dalí landscape. The town cowers beneath the **Peñó d'Ifach** (327m), which face drops straight to the sea in one of the most picturesque coastal settings in Spain. **Gandía** attracts with fine sand beaches. The **tourist office,** Marqués de Campo, is opposite the train station. (☎96 287 77 88. Open June-Aug. M-F 9:30am-1:30pm and 4:30-7:30pm, Sa 10am-1:30pm; Sept.-May 9:30am-1:30pm and 4-7pm, Sa 10am-1pm.) La Amistad **buses** (M-Sa, 4-5 per day 8:45am-8:30pm, 125ptas/€0.75) go from outside the train station in Gandía to **Platja de Piles,**

10km south, where you'll find many beaches. To sleep at the fantastic **Alberg Mar i Vent (HI)** in Platja, follow the signs down C. Dr. Fleming. (☎96 283 17 48. Washing machine and library. 3-day max. stay, flexible if uncrowded. Sheets 300ptas/€1.80. Curfew Su-F 2am, Sa 4am. Open mid-Feb. to mid-Dec. Dorms 800ptas/€4.60, over 26 1100ptas/€6.60 extra.)

NORTHEAST SPAIN

Northeastern Spain encompasses the country's most avidly regionalistic areas as well as some of its best cuisine. **Catalán** are justly proud of their treasures, from mountains to beaches to hip Barcelona. The glorious **Pyrenees** line the French border, presenting a prickly face to the rest of the continent. Little-known **Navarra** basks in the limelight once a year when bulls race through the streets of Pamplona. Industrious **Aragón** packs in busy cities and the most dramatic parts of the Pyrenees. The **Basques** are fiercely regionalistic, but happily share their beautiful coasts and rich history. The **Balearic Islands** are always ready for the next party.

CATALUÑA

From rocky Costa Brava to the lush Pyrenees and chic Barcelona, Catalunya is a vacation in itself. Graced with the nation's richest resources, it is one of Spain's most prosperous regions. Catalán is the region's official language (though most everyone is bilingual), and local cuisine is lauded throughout Spain.

BARCELONA

If you make it until 6am, you'll see the quiet side of Barcelona. While the city is dark, the occasional worker battles Catalán separatist graffiti, the empty streets are scrubbed by hulking machines, and pigeons and parrots share the same branch, cooing with their heads under their wings. Enjoy the calm—it won't last. With sunrise, you'll see a different city. Cash boxes ring with the sounds of commerce and style; tourists marvel at monsters that residents call buildings; museums fill with avant-garde; pedestrians salivate at exotic delicacies; beaches overflow with bronzed nudity; a white gorilla terrifies and delights children of all ages. On this side of 6am, Barcelona is sensory overload. After you spend twenty-four hours with Barcelona's schizophrenic personalities, Barcelona will have exhausted herself—and you. When 6am rolls around again, you'll be glad for the quiet.

Barcelona is a gateway city: the gateway to Catalunya, to Spain, to the Mediterranean, to the Pyrenees. Pack your swimsuit and your skis, your art book and your clubbing shoes, an extra bag to fill with souvenirs, and don't worry that you don't speak Spanish: neither does Barcelona.

▐▀ TRANSPORTATION

Flights: El Prat de Llobregat airport (☎93 298 38 38; www.aena.es/ae/bcn/homepage), 12km southwest of Barcelona. To get to the central Pl. Catalunya, take the **Aerobus** (40min., every 15min., 525ptas/€3) or a RENFE **train** (20min., every 30min., 350ptas/€2.10).

Trains: Estació Barcelona-Sants (☎902 24 02 02), on Pl. Països Catalans. M: Sants-Estació. Main domestic and international terminal. RENFE train line has service almost anywhere in Spain and Europe (☎902 24 02 02; www.renfe.es). To: **Madrid** (7-8hr., 7 per day, 5100-6900ptas/€36-41); **San Sebastián** (8-9hr., 3 per day, 5000ptas/€30); **Sevilla** (11-12hr., 3per day, 6400-10200ptas/€39-61); **Valencia** (3-5hr., 16 per day 7am-9pm, 3120-5200ptas/€20-33). Also serves **Milan** (through Nice) and Montpellier with connections to Geneva and Paris. **Estació França,** on Av. Marquès de l'Argentera. M: Barceloneta. Services regional destinations and some international arrivals.

Buses: Most buses arrive at the **Barcelona Nord Estació d'Autobuses,** C. Ali-bei, 80 (☎93 265 61 32). M: Arc de Triomf. **Enatcar** (www.enatcar.es) runs to **Madrid** (8hr., 18 per day, 2690ptas/€16) and **Valencia** (4hr., 16 per day, 2690ptas/€16). **Sarfa** (☎90 230 20 25; www.sarfa.com) runs to **Cadaqués** (2½hr., 10:45am and 7:45pm, 2250ptas/€13.50) and **Tossa de Mar** (1½hr., 9 per day 8:15am-8:15pm, 1070ptas/ €6.50). **Linebús:** (☎93 265 07 00) runs to **London** (25hr.; 3 per week; 14,650ptas/ €88) and **Paris** (15hr.; M-Sa 8pm, 1280-23,600ptas/€77-142).

Ferries: Trasmediterránea (☎902 45 46 45), Estació Marítima-Moll Barcelona, Moll de Sant Bertran. M: Drassanes. Follow Las Ramblas to the Columbus monument, which points the way. In summer, boats go almost daily to the Balearic Islands (see p. 888).

Public Transportation: ☎010. Pick up a *Guia d'Autobusos Urbans de Barcelona* for metro and bus routes. **Buses** run 5am-10pm and cost 150ptas/€0.90 per ride. The **metro** runs M-Th 5am-11pm, F-Sa 5am-2am, Su 6am-midnight; buy tickets from vending machines or stations (160ptas/€1). A **T1 Pass** (885ptas/€5) is valid for 10 rides on the bus, metro, and commuter rail. A **T-DIA Card** (1600ptas/€9) gives 3 days of unlimited bus or metro travel. **Nitbus** (160ptas/€1) runs 10:30pm-4:30am.

Taxis: ☎93 330 03 00.

Car Rental: Docar, C. Montnegre 18 (☎93 439 81 19). From 2300ptas/€14 per day, plus insurance. Open M-F 8:30am-2pm and 3:30-8pm, Sa 9am-2pm.

✦ ORIENTATION

Barcelona's layout is simple. Imagine yourself perched on Columbus' head at the **Monument a Colom** (on **Passeig de Colom,** along the shore), viewing the city with the sea at your back. From the harbor, the city slopes upward to the mountains. From the Columbus monument, **Las Ramblas** (see p. 873), the main thoroughfare, runs from the harbor up to **Plaça de Catalunya** (M: Catalunya), the city's center. The **Ciutat Vella** (Old City) is the heavily touristed historical neighborhood, which centers around Las Ramblas and includes the Barri Gòtic, La Ribera, and El Raval. The **Barri Gòtic** is east of Las Ramblas (to the right, with your back to the sea), enclosed on the other side by **Via Laietana.** East of Via Laietana lies the maze-like neighborhood of **La Ribera,** which borders Parc de la Ciutadella and the Estació França train station. To the west of Las Ramblas (to the left, with your back to the sea) is **El Raval.** Beyond La Ribera, (farther east, outside the Ciutat Vella) is the **Poble Nou** neighborhood and the **Vila Olímpica,** with its twin towers (the tallest buildings in Barcelona) and an assortment of discos and restaurants. Beyond El Raval (to the west) rises **Montjuïc,** crammed with gardens, museums, the 1992 Olympic grounds, Montjuïc castle, and other attractions. Directly behind the Monument a Colom is the **Port Vell** (Old Port) development, where a wavy bridge leads across to the ultramodern shopping and entertainment complexes **Moll d'Espanya** and **Maremagnum.** Beyond the Ciutat Vella, is **l'Eixample,** the gridded neighborhood created during the expansion of the 1860s, which runs from Pl. Catalunya toward the mountains. **Gran Via de les Corts Catalanes** defines its lower edge and **Passeig de Gràcia,** l'Eixample's main street, bisects the neighborhood. **Avinguda Diagonal** marks the border between l'Eixample and the **Zona Alta** ("Uptown"), which includes Pedralbes, Gràcia, and other older neighborhoods in the foothills. The peak of Tibidabo, the northwest border of the city, offers the most comprehensive view of the city.

🗗 PRACTICAL INFORMATION

TOURIST AND FINANCIAL SERVICES

Tourist Info: (☎010, 906 30 12 82, 93 304 34 21; www.barcelonaturisme.com). Barcelona has 4 main tourist offices and numerous mobile information stalls.

Informacio Turistica at Plaça Cataluña, Pl. Cataluña, 17S. M: Cataluña. The biggest, best, and busiest tourist office. Open daily 9am-9pm.

Informacio Turista at Plaça Sant Jaume, Pl. Sant Jaume, 1, off of C. Ciutat. M: Jaume I. Open M-Sa 10am-8pm, Su 10am-2pm.

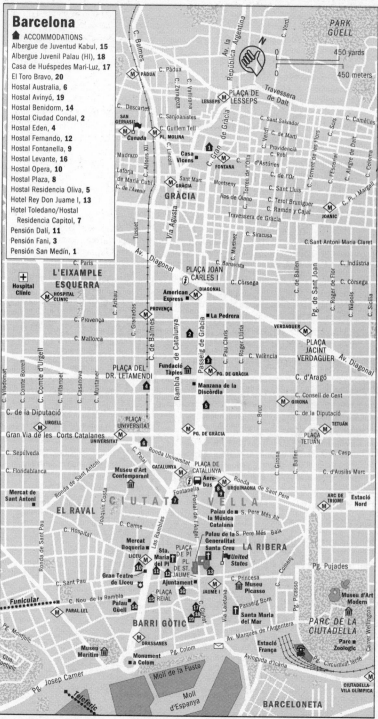

Barcelona

🏠 ACCOMMODATIONS

Albergue de Juventud Kabul, **15**
Albergue Juvenil Palau (HI), **18**
Casa de Huéspedes Mari-Luz, **17**
El Toro Bravo, **20**
Hostal Australia, **6**
Hostal Avinyó, **19**
Hostal Benidorm, **14**
Hostal Ciudad Condal, **2**
Hostal Eden, **4**
Hostal Fernando, **12**
Hostal Fontanella, **9**
Hostal Levante, **16**
Hostal Opera, **10**
Hostal Plaza, **8**
Hostal Residencia Oliva, **5**
Hotel Rey Don Juame I, **13**
Hotel Toledano/Hostal
　Residencia Capitol, **7**
Pensión Dalí, **11**
Pensión Fani, **3**
Pensión San Medín, **1**

Oficina de Turisme de Catalunya, Pg. de Gràcia, 107 (☎93 238 40 00; fax 93 292 12 70; www.gencat.es/probert). M: Diagonal. Open M-Sa 10am-7pm, Su 10am-2pm.

Estació Central de Barcelon-Sants, Pl. Països Cataláns, in the Barcelona-Sants train station. M: Sants-Estació. Open M-F 4:30am-midnight, Sa-Su 5am-midnight.

Aeroport El Prat de Llobregat (☎93 478 05 65), in the international terminal. Open daily 9am-9pm. English-speaking agents available.

Budget Travel: usit UNLIMITED, Ronda Universitat, 16 (☎934 12 01 04; fax 934 12 39 84; www.unlimted.es). Open M-F 10am-8:30pm and Sa 10am-1:30pm.

Consulates: Australia, Gran Vía Carlos III, 98, 9th fl. (☎93 330 94 96); **Canada,** Elisenda de Pinos, 8 (☎93 204 27 00); **New Zealand,** Traversa de Gràcia, 64, 4th fl. (☎93 209 03 99); **South Africa,** Teodora Lamadrid 7-11 (☎93 418 64 45); **US,** Pg. Reina Elisenda, 23 (☎932 80 22 27).

Currency Exchange: General banking hours M-F 8:30am-2pm. **Banco de Espanya,** Pl. Cataluña, 17 (☎93 482 47 00) and the Am Ex office. No commission.

American Express: Pg. Gràcia, 101 (24hr. traveler's check info ☎90 099 44 26). M: Diagonal. Entrance on C. Rosselló. Open M-F 9:30am-6pm, Sa 10am-noon. Also at Las Ramblas, 74 (☎93 301 11 66). Open daily 9am-8pm.

Luggage Storage: Estació Barcelona-Sants. M: Sants-Estació (see **Transportation;** open daily 5:30am-11pm). **Estació França** (see **Transportation;** open daily 7am-10pm). **Estació del Nord,** M: Arc de Triomf. Large lockers 700ptas/€4.20 for 24hr., small 500ptas/€3. Open 24hr.

El Corte Inglés: Pl. Catalunya, 14 (☎933 06 38 00). M: Catalunya. Free **map** of Barcelona; also has English books. Open M-Sa and 1st Su every month 10am-10pm.

English-Language Bookstore: Llibreria del Raval, C. Elisabets, 6 (☎933 17 02 93). M: Catalunya, in El Raval. Open M-F 10am-8:30pm, Sa 10am-2:30pm and 5-8pm.

Laundromat: Tintorería Ferran, C. Ferran, 11. M: Liceu. Full service 1500ptas/€9. Open daily 8:30am-2pm and 4:30-7:30pm.

EMERGENCY AND COMMUNICATIONS

Emergency: ☎112. **Local police:** ☎092. **National police:** ☎091. **Medical:** ☎061.

Police: Las Ramblas, 43 (☎93 344 13 00), across from Pl. Reial and next to C. Nou de La Rambla. M: Liceu. Multilingual officers. Open 24hr.

Late-Night Pharmacy: Pharmacies open 24hr. on a rotating basis.

Hospital: Hospital Clinic, Villarroel, 170 (☎932 27 54 00). M: Hospital Clinic. Main entrance at the intersection of C. Roselló and C. Casanova.

Internet Access: Easy Everything, Las Ramblas, 31. M: Liceu. 200ptas/€1.20 for 40min. Open 24hr. Also on Ronda Universitat, 35, next to Pl. Catalunya. **bcnet (Internet Gallery Café),** Barra de Ferro, 3 (☎932 68 15 07), down the street from the Picasso museum. M: Jaume I. 600ptas/€4 per hr. Open daily 10am-1am.

Post Office: Lista de Correos, Pl. de Antoni López (info ☎902 197 197). M: Jaume I or Barceloneta. Fax and *lista de correos.* Open M-F 8:30am-9:30pm. **Postal Code:** 08003.

█ ACCOMMODATIONS AND CAMPING

The area between Pl. Catalunya and the water—the Barri Gòtic, El Raval, and La Ribera—offers budget beds, but reservations are a must. Last-minute travelers can crash in Gràcia or l'Eixample, outer boroughs with more vacancies that are easily accessible to the rest of Barcelona.

LOWER BARRI GÒTIC

■ **Hostal Fernando,** C. Ferran, 31 (☎/fax 93 301 79 93). M: Liceu. So clean it shines; fills from walk-ins. Dorms with lockers 2500ptas/€15; doubles 5000-6000ptas/€30-36, with bath 7000-8000ptas/€42-48; triples 8500-9500ptas/€51-57. MC/V.

■ **Casa de Huéspedes Mari-Luz,** C. Palau, 4 (☎/fax93 317 34 63). M: Liceu. The owners make their hostel feel like home. Doubles June 21-Aug. 15 6000ptas/€36, Aug.16-June 20 4800ptas/€29. MC/V.

Albergue Juvenil Palau (HI), C. Palau, 6 (☎93 412 50 80). M: Liceu. A budget refuge. Kitchen open daily 7-10pm. Dining room. 45 clean dorms, 3-8 people each. Reception 7am-3am. Curfew 3am. No reservations. Dorms 1900ptas/€12. Cash only.

Hostal Avinyó, C. Avinyó, 42 (☎93 318 79 45; www.hostalavinyo.com). M: Drassanes. The most modern spot in the Barri Gòtic. Singles 2500ptas/€15; doubles 4000-4600ptas/€12-14, with bath 5000-6000ptas/€15-18. Cash only.

Hostal Levante, Baixada de San Miguel, 2 (☎93 317 95 65; www.hostallevante.com). M: Liceu. Large, tastefully decorated rooms. Singles 4000ptas/€24; doubles 6500ptas/€39; 4-8 person suite 4000ptas/€24 per person. MC/V.

Hotel Rey Don Jaume I, C. Jaume I, 11 (☎/fax 93 310 62 08; r.d.jaume@atriumhotels.com). M: Jaume I. Stark rooms have balconies, phones, and bath. Safes available. Reservations recommended 1-2 months ahead. Singles 6000ptas/€36; doubles 9000ptas/€54; triples 12,000ptas/€72. AmEx/MC/V.

Albergue de Juventud Kabul, Pl. Reial, 17 (☎93 318 51 90). M: Liceu. Legendary co-ed dorm rooms can pack 200 frat boys. Internet. Dorms June-Sept. 2900ptas/€17.50; Oct.-May 1900ptas/€11.50. Cash only.

UPPER BARRI GÒTIC

Between C. Fontanella and C. Ferran, accommodations are pricier, but more serene, than the lower Barri Gòtic. Early reservations are obligatory in summer. The nearest Metro stop is Catalunya, unless otherwise specified.

▨ **Hotel Toledano/Hostal Residencia Capitol,** Las Ramblas, 138 (☎93 301 08 72; www.hoteltoledano.com). Bordering on luxurious. 4th-fl. Hotel Toledano: singles 4600ptas/€28; doubles 7900ptas/€48; triples 9900ptas/€60; 5th-fl. Hostal Residencia Capitol: singles 3400ptas/€21; doubles 5400ptas/€33; triples 6900ptas/€41.50; quads 7900ptas/€48. Reserve early over website. AmEx/MC/V.

▨ **Hostal Benidorm,** Las Ramblas, 37 (☎93 302 20 54; www.barcelona-on-line.es/benidorm). M: Drassanes. With phones and baths in every neat room, this could be the best value on Las Ramblas. Singles 4000ptas/€24; doubles 5500ptas/€33; triples 7000ptas/€42; quads 9000ptas/€54; quints 10,500ptas/€63.

Hostal Plaza, C. Fontanella, 18 (☎/fax 93 301 01 39; www.plazahostal.com). Savvy Texan owners and quirky rooms. Singles 7000ptas/€42, with bath 9000ptas/€54; doubles 9000ptas/€54, 10,000ptas/€60; triples 12,000ptas/€72, 13,000ptas/€78. Discount Nov. and Feb. AmEx/MC/V.

Pensión Dalí, C. Boqueria, 12 (☎93 318 55 90; pensiondali@wanadoo.es). M: Liceu. Designed by Moderinist Domènech i Montaner. Internet. Singles 4400ptas/€27, with bath 6000ptas/€36; doubles 6500ptas/€39, 7500ptas/€45; triples 10,200ptas/€62; quads 12,800ptas/€77. AmEx/MC/V.

Hostal Fontanella, Via Laietana, 71 (☎/fax 93 317 59 43). M: Urquinaona. Singles 3300ptas/€20, with bath 4300/€26; doubles 5500ptas/€23, 7500ptas/€45; triples 7700ptas/€46, 9100ptas/€55. AmEx/MC/V.

EL RAVEL

Hostal Australia, Ronda Universitat, 11 (☎933 17 41 77). M: Universitat. Guests are family here. Be prepared for the family-style quiet time starting at 10pm. Curfew 4am. Singles 3300ptas/€19.80; doubles 5400ptas/€32.40, with bath 7000ptas/€42.

Hostal Opera, C. Sant Pau, 20 (☎933 18 82 01). M: Liceu, off Las Ramblas. Like the opera house next door, the hostel has been recently renovated. Singles 5000ptas/€30.10; doubles 8000ptas/€48.20; triples 10,000ptas/€60.30. MC/V.

L'EIXAMPLE AND GRÀCIA

▨ **Hostal Ciudad Condal,** C. Mallorca, 255 (☎932 15 10 40). M: Diagonal, just off Pg. de Gràcia. Rooms with bath and phones. Reception 24hr. Singles 8500ptas/€51; doubles 13,000-14,000ptas/€78-84. Prices drop in winter. MC/V.

▨ **Pensión Fani,** C. València, 278 (☎932 15 36 45). M: Catalunya. Oozes character. Bring a towel. 3000ptas/€18 per person.

▨ **Hostal Residencia Oliva,** Pg. de Gràcia, 32 (☎934 88 01 62). M: Pg. de Gràcia. Reservations a must. Laundry 2000ptas/€12. Singles 3500ptas/€21; doubles 6500ptas/€39, with bath 7500ptas/€45; triple with bath 10,500ptas/€63. Cash only.

▨ **Hostal Eden,** C. Balmes, 55 (☎934 52 66 20; www.eden.iberica.com). M: Pg. de Gràcia. Stained-glass and floral tiles. May-Oct. singles 4815ptas/€29, with bath 6420ptas/€38; doubles 5885ptas/€35, 8560ptas/€50. Nov.-Apr. singles 3815ptas/€23, with bath 5350ptas/€32; doubles 4815ptas/€29, 7500ptas/€45. AmEx/MC/V.

Pensión San Medín, C. Gran de Gràcia, 125 (☎932 17 30 68; fax 934 15 44 10; www.sanmedin.com). M: Fontana. Curtains and tiling abound. Singles 4000ptas/€24, with bath 5000ptas/€30; doubles 7000ptas/€42, 8000ptas/€48. MC/V.

CAMPING

El Toro Bravo (☎936 37 34 62), 11km south of Barcelona. Take intercity bus L95 (200ptas/€1.20) from Pl. Catalunya or Pl. Espanya.

🍴 FOOD

Drawing from both Spanish and Catalán culinary traditions, Barcelona's restaurants are a mix of authentic neighborhood haunts and stylish cosmopolitan cuisine. The *Guia del Ocio* is an invaluable source of culinary suggestions. Port Vell and Port Olímpic are known for seafood. The restaurants on C. Aragó by Pg. de Gràcia have great lunchtime *menús*, and the Pg. de Gràcia has beautiful outdoor dining. Gràcia's Pl. Sol and La Ribera's Santa Maria del Mar are the best places to head for *tapas*. If you want to live cheap and do as Barceloneses do, buy your food fresh at a *mercat* (marketplace). For wholesale fruit, cheese, and wine, head to **La Boqueria** (Mercat de Sant Josep), outside M: Liceu. For groceries, head to **Champion Supermarket,** Las Ramblas, 11. (M: Liceu. Open M-Sa 9am-9pm.)

BARRI GÒTIC

▨ **Els Quatre Gats,** C. Montsió, 3. M: Catalunya. The 2nd left off Portal de l'Angel. Picasso's old Modernist hangout; he designed a personalized menu. Entrees around 2000ptas/€12; *tapas* 200-600ptas/€1.50-3.60. Live piano and violin 9pm-1am. Open M-Sa 9am-2am, Su 5pm-2am. Closed Aug.

▨ **Betawi,** C. Montsió, 6. M: Catalunya. A peaceful Indonesian restaurant; food verges on gourmet in taste and size. *Menú* 1275ptas/€8. Entrees 1200-1500ptas/€7-9. Open M-Sa 1-4pm, Tu-Th 8-11pm, and F-Sa 8-11:30pm.

Los Caracoles, C. Escudellers, 14. M: Drassanes. What started as a snail shop in 1835 is now a Catalán restaurant. Expect a wait. Open daily 1pm-midnight.

Restaurante Bidasoa, C. Serra, 21. M: Drassanes. Follow C. Clavé to the 3rd left. Fresh Catalán food is good, cheap, and plentiful. Most dishes 500ptas/€3. Open Tu-Su 1:30-4pm and 8pm-midnight, closed Aug. Cash only.

Juicy Jones, Cardenal Casañas, 7. M. Liceu. Vegan *menú* (1175ptas/€7). Open daily Oct.-Apr. 10am-11:15pm; May-Sept. 8am-11:15pm. Cash only.

Il Mercante Di Venezia, C. Jose Anselmo Clavé, 11 (☎933 17 18 28). M: Drassanes. Dim lighting and Italian food—perfect for a romantic meal. Pasta 1000ptas/€6. Reservations recommended. Open Tu-Su 1:30-3:30pm and 8:30pm-midnight.

Govinda, Pl. Vila de Madrid, 4. M: Catalunya. Vegetarian Indian food served a few feet from a row of Roman tombs nearly 2000 years old. Entrees around 1200ptas/€7. Open daily 1-4pm; also Tu-Th 8-11pm and F-Sa 8-11:45pm.

ELSEWHERE IN BARCELONA

▨ **Bar Ra,** Pl. Garduña (☎933 01 41 63). M: Liceu. In El Raval behind Las Ramblas' Boqueria market. A mixture of traditional Spanish and trendy California cuisine. *Menú* 1300ptas/€8. Open M-Sa 1:30-4pm and 9:30pm-2am. Dinner by reservation.

▩ **Buenas Migas,** Pl. Bonsuccés, 6. M: Catalunya. Off Las Ramblas. Enjoy coffee (120-160ptas/€1) at a shaded table. Open Su-W 10am-10pm, Th-Sa 10am-midnight.

▩ **La Habana Vieja,** C. Banys Vells, 2. M: Jaume I. In La Ribera. Cuban music sets the mood. Large portions perfect for sharing. Open daily 10am-4:30pm and 8:30pm-1am.

▩ **Xampanyet,** C. Montcado, 22. M: Jaume I. In La Ribera near the Museu Picasso. The house *cava* is served at a colorful bar. Glasses 120ptas/€1. Bottles 900ptas/€5. Open Tu-Sa noon-4pm and 7-11:30pm, Su 7-11:30pm. Closed Aug.

Laie Llibreria Café, C. Pau Claris, 85. M: Urquinaona. An ultra-cool lunchspot in L'Eixample. Cheap, fresh buffet lunch (1250ptas/€8) in an open, bamboo-draped lunch room. Open M-F 9am-1am, Sa 10am-1am.

La Gavina, C. Ros de Olano, 17, in Grácia. Funky pizzeria complete with life-size patron saint. Pizzas 750-1450ptas/€5-9. Open Tu-Su 2pm-1am, F-Sa 2pm-2am.

La Buena Tierra, C. Encarnació, 56. M: Joanic. Follow C. Escorial for 2 blocks and turn left on C. Encarnació. Vegetarian delicacies 650-1050ptas/€4-6.50. Open M-Sa noon-4pm and 8pm-1am.

👁 SIGHTS

Architecturally, Barcelona is defined by its unique Modernist treasures. Las Ramblas—a bustling avenue smack in the city center—and the Barri Gòtic, Barcelona's "old city," are the traditional tourist areas. But don't neglect vibrant La Ribera and El Raval, the upscale avenues of l'Eixample, the panoramic city views from Montjuïc and Tibidabo, Gaudí's Park Güell, and the harbor-side Port Olímpic. The **Ruta del Modernisme** pass is the cheapest and most flexible option for those with a few days and an interest in seeing all the biggest sights. Passes (600ptas/€4, students and over 65 400ptas/€2, groups over 10 500ptas/€3 per person) are good for a month and give holders a 50% discount on entrance to Palau Güell, La Sagrada Família, Casa Milà, Palau de la Música Catalana, Casa-Museu Gaudí, Fundació Antoni Tàpies, the Museu d'Art Modern, the Museu de Zoologia, a tour of El Hospital de la Santa Creu i Sant Pau, tours of the façades of La Manzana de la Discòrdia (Casas Amatller, Lleó Morera, and Batlló), and other attractions. Purchase passes at **Casa Amatller,** Pg. Gràcia, 41 (☎934 88 01 39. M: Pg. de Gràcia.)

LAS RAMBLAS

Las Ramblas's pedestrian-only median strip is a veritable urban carnival, where street performers dance, fortune-tellers tell, human statues shift poses, and vendors sell birds—all, of course, for a small fee. The sights below are arranged beginning with Pl. Cataluña in the north, continuing to the port in the south.

UPPER LAS RAMBLAS. A port-ward journey begins at the **Font de Canaletes** (more a pump than a fountain), where visitors who wish to eventually return to Barcelona are supposed to sample the water. The upper part of Las Ramblas has been dubbed "Rambla de las Flores" for the numerous flower vendors that inhabit it. Halfway down Las Ramblas, **Joan Miró's** pavement mosaic brightens up the street.

GRAN TEATRE DEL LICEU. Once one of Europe's leading stages, the Liceu has been ravaged by anarchists, bombs, and fires. It is adorned with palatial ornamentation, gold façades, sculptures, and grand side rooms—including a Spanish hall of mirrors. *(Las Ramblas, 51-59, by C. Sant Pau. Office open M-F 2-8:30pm and 1hr. before performances. ☎934 85 99 13. Guided tours 9:30-11am, reservation only (☎934 85 99 00). 800ptas/€4.80, students 600ptas/€3.60.)*

MONUMENT A COLOM. Ruis i Taulet's Monument a Colom towers at the port end of Las Ramblas. Ninteenth-century Renaixença enthusiasts convinced themselves that Columbus was Catalán, from a town near Girona. The fact that Columbus points proudly toward Libya, not the Americas, doesn't help the claim; historians agree that Columbus was from Italy. Take the elevator to the top and get a stunning view. *(Portal de la Pau. M: Drassanes. Elevator open daily June-Sept. 9am-8:30pm; Oct.-Mar. M-F 10am-1:30pm and 3:30-6:30pm, Sa-Su 10am-6:30pm; Apr.-May M-F 10am-1:30pm and 3:30-7:30pm, Sa-Su 10am-7:30pm. 300ptas/€1.80, children and over 65 200ptas/€1.20.)*

BARRI GÒTIC

While the weathered, narrow streets of the Barri Gòtic, including **Carrer de la Pietat** and **Carrer del Paradis,** have preserved their medieval charm, the ever-growing tourist economy has infused a new, multilingual liveliness into the area.

ESGLÉSIA CATEDRAL DE LA SANTA CREU. This is one of Barcelona's most popular monuments. Beyond the **choir** are the altar with the bronze **cross** designed by Frederic Marès in 1976, and the sunken **Crypt of Santa Eulalia,** one of Barcelona's patron saints. The **cathedral museum** holds Bartolomé Bermejo's *pietà,* the image of Christ dying in the arms of his mother. The front of the cathedral is the place to catch a performance of the **sardana,** the traditional Catalán dance. Performances occur Sunday after mass from noon to 6:30pm. *(M: Jaume I, in Pl. Seu, up C. Bisbe from Pl. St. Jaume. Cathedral open daily 8am-1:30pm and 4-7:30pm. Cloister open daily 9am-1:15pm and 4-7pm; 225ptas/€1.50. Elevator to roof open M-F 10:30am-12:30pm and 4:30-6pm, Sa-Su 10:30am-12:30pm; 150ptas/€1.)*

PLAÇA DE SANT JAUME. Plaça de Sant Jaume has been Barcelona's political center since Roman times. Two of Catalunya's most important buildings have dominated the square since 1823: the **Palau de la Generalitat,** the headquarters of Catalunya's autonomous government, and the **Ajuntament,** the city hall. *(Palau de la Generalitat open the 2nd and 4th Su of each month 10am-2pm. 30min. mandatory tours in English, French, Spanish, and Catalán. Ajuntament open Sa-Su 10am-1:45pm. Free.)*

LA RIBERA

As the stomping ground of fishermen and merchants, La Ribera has always had a plebian feel. Recently, the neighborhood has evolved into Barcelona's bohemian nucleus, with art galleries, chic eateries, and exclusive bars.

■ **PALAU DE LA MÚSICA CATALANA.** In 1891, the Orfeó Catalán choir society commissioned Modernist Luis Domènech i Montaner to design this must-see concert venue. The music hall glows with tall, stained-glass windows, an ornate chandelier, marble reliefs, intricate woodwork, and ceramic mosaics. Concerts given at the Palau include all varieties of symphonic and choral music in addition to more modern forms of pop, rock, and jazz. *(C. Sant Francesc de Paula, 2. www.palaumusica.org. M: Jaume I. Entrance only with tour. Reserve ahead. Buy tickets at gift shop next door. Palau open daily 10am-3:30pm, Aug. 10am-6pm. Box office open M-Sa 10am-9pm, Su 1hr. before concert. Check the Guía del Ocio for listings. 800ptas/€5, students and seniors 600ptas/€3.60. Concert tickets 1300-26,000ptas/€8-125. MC/V.)*

■ **MUSEU PICASSO.** This incredible museum traces the development of Picasso as an artist, with a collection of his early works that weaves through five connected mansions once occupied by nobility. *(C. Montcada, 15-19. ☎ 933 19 63 10. M: Jaume I. Walk down C. Princesa from the Metro, and turn right on C. Montcada. Open Tu-Sa 10am-8pm, Su 10am-3pm. 800ptas/€5, students and seniors 400ptas/€2.50. Free 1st Su each month.)*

SANTA MARIA DEL MAR. This architectural wonder was built in the 14th century in a quick 55 years. At a distance of 13m apart, the supporting columns span a width greater than any other medieval building in the world. A fascinating example of the limits of Gothic architecture—were it 2ft. higher, it would collapse from structural instability. *(Open M-Sa 9am-1:30pm and 4:30-8pm, Su 9am-2pm and 5-8:30pm.)*

PARC DE LA CUITADELLA. Host of the 1888 Universal Exposition, the park harbors several museums, well-labeled horticulture, the wacky Cascada fountains, a pond, and a zoo. Buildings of note include Domènech i Montaner's Modernista **Castell dels Tres Dragons** (now Museu de Zoología), the geological museum (a few buildings down P. Picasso from M. Zoología), and Josep Amergós's Hivernacle. ■ **Floquet de Neu** (a.k.a. *Copito de Nieve* and Little Snowflake), the world's only white gorilla behind bars, lounges in the Parc Zoològic, on the end of the park closer to the sea.

MATING GAME Some call him Snowflake, but in his native Catalán he's Floquet de Neu, the world's only white gorilla. Taken from the forest in west Africa in the 60s, Floquet has been the toast of Barcelona ever since. With gorillas and other apes in endangered species status, zoos are making concerted efforts to aid breeding. Because of Floquet's dashing good looks, special measures are taken in his case. In an effort to breed another white gorilla, he has been encouraged to mate with his daughters. With over a dozen offspring to date, there's still no Floquet Jr.; Floquet de Neu may be the last of his kind, all the more reason for a pilgrimage to Barcelona.

(Open Nov.-Feb. 10am-5pm, Mar. and Oct. 10am-6pm, Apr. and Sept. 10am-7pm, May-Aug. 9:30am-7:30pm. 850ptas/€4.80.) In the center of the park the **Museu d'Art Modern,** houses a potpourri of works by 19th-century Catalán artists. *(M: Barceloneta or Arc de Triomf. Open Tu-Sa 10am-7pm, Su 10am-2:30pm. 500ptas/€3, students 350ptas/€2.10.)*

EL RAVAL

■ **PALAU GÜELL.** Gaudí's Palau Güell (1886)—the Modernist residence built for patron Eusebi Güell (of Park Güell fame)—has one of Barcelona's most spectacular interiors. Güell and Gaudí spared no expense. *(C. Nou de La Rambla, 3-5. ☎933 17 39 74. M: Liceu. Open M-Sa 10am-1pm and 4:15-7pm. 400ptas/€2.40, students 200ptas/€1.20. Mandatory tour every 15min.)*

MUSEU D'ART CONTEMPORANI (MACBA). This monstrosity of a building was constructed with the idea that sparse decor would allow the art to speak for itself. The MACBA has received world-wide acclaim for its focus on avant-guard art between the two world wars, as well as surrealist and contemporary art. *(Pl. dels Angels, 1. M: Catalunya. Open July-Sept. M, W, F 11am-8pm; Th 11am-9:30pm; Sa 10am-8pm, Su 10am-3pm. Oct.-June M-F 11am-7:30pm, Sa 10am-8pm, Su 10am-3pm. Closed Tu. 800ptas/€5, students 550ptas/€3.50.)*

WATERFRONT

■ **L'AQUÀRIUM DE BARCELONA.** Barcelona's aquarium—the largest in Europe—is an aquatic wonder, featuring copious amounts of octopi and a plethora of penguins. The highlight is an 80m long glass tunnel through a tank of sharks and sting rays. *(Moll d'Espanya, next to Maremagnum. M: Drassanes. Open daily July-Aug. 9:30am-11pm; Sept.-June 9:30am-9pm. 1550ptas/€9, children under 12 and seniors 950ptas/€6, 10% student discount. Last entrance 1hr. before closing.)*

VILA OLÍMPICA. The Vila Olímpica, beyond the east side of the zoo, was built (on top of what was once a working-class neighborhood) to house 15,000 athletes and entertain millions of tourists for the 1992 Summer Olympics. These days, it's home to several public parks, a shopping center, and business offices. In the area called **Barceloneta,** mediocre beaches stretch out from the port. *(From M: Ciutadella/Vila Olímpica. Walk along the waterfront on Ronda Litoral toward the two towers.)*

L'EIXAMPLE

The Catalán Renaissance and the growth of Barcelona during the 19th century pushed the city past its medieval walls and into modernity. Ildefons Cerdà drew up a plan for a new neighborhood where people of all social classes could live side by side. However, l'Eixample (pronounced luh-SHOMP-luh) did not thrive as a utopian community but rather as a playground for the bourgeois.

■ **LA SAGRADA FAMÍLIA.** Only Antoni Gaudí could draw thousands of tourists to an unfinished church. He gave 43 years of his life to the task, living in the basement before his death in 1926. Of the three proposed façades, only the first (a smaller one), the Nativity Façade, was finished under Gaudí. A furor has arisen over recent additions, especially sculptor Josep Subirach's Cubist Passion Façade on C. Sardenya, which is criticized for being inconsistent with the Gaudí-endorsed Nativity Façade. The **museum** displays artifacts relating to the building's construc-

SPAIN

tion. *(C. Mallorca, 401. M: Sagrada Família. Open Nov.-Feb. 9am-6pm, elevator 9:30am-5:45pm; Mar., Sept., and Oct. 9am-7pm, elevator 9:30am-6:45pm; Apr.-Aug. 9am-8pm, elevator 9:30am-7:45pm. Guided tours Apr.-Oct. daily 11:30am, 1, 4, 5:30pm; Nov.-Mar. F-M 11:30am and 1pm; 500ptas/€3. Tickets 850ptas/€5, students 650ptas/€4.50.)*

■ **LA MANZANA DE LA DISCÒRDIA.** A short walk from Pl. Catalunya, the odd-numbered side of Pg. Gràcia between C. Aragó and Consell de Cent is popularly known as *la manzana de la discòrdia* (block of discord), referring to the stylistic clashing of the three buildings. Regrettably, the bottom two floors of **Casa Lleó i Morera,** by Domènech i Montaner, were destroyed to make room for a fancy store, but you can buy the **Ruta del Modernisme pass** (p. 873) there and take a tour of the upstairs, where sprouting flowers, stained glass, and legendary doorway sculptures adorn the interior. Puig i Cadafalch opted for a geometric, Moorish-influenced pattern on the façade of **Casa Amatller** at #41. Gaudí's balconies ripple like skulls, and tiles sparkle in blue-purple glory on **Casa Batlló,** #43. The most popular interpretation of Casa Batlló is that the building represents Catalunya's patron Sant Jordi (St. George) slaying a dragon; the chimney plays the lance, the scaly roof is the dragon's back, and the bony balconies are the remains of his victims.

■ **CASA MILÀ (LA PEDRERA).** Modernism buffs argue that the spectacular Casa Milà apartment building, an undulating mass of granite popularly known as *La Pedrera* (the Stone Quarry), is Gaudí's most refined work. Note the intricate ironwork around the balconies and the irregularity of the front gate's egg-shaped window panes. The roof sprouts chimneys that resemble armored soldiers, one of which is decorated with broken champagne bottles. Rooftop tours provide a closer look at the "Prussian helmets". The winding brick attic has been transformed into the **Espai Gaudí,** a multimedia presentation of Gaudí's life and works. *(Pg. Gràcia, 92. Open daily 10am-8pm. 1000ptas/€6; students and over 65 500ptas/€3. Free guided tours M-F 5:30pm (English and Catalán) and 6pm (Spanish), Sa-Su 11am (English and Catalán) and 11:30pm (Spanish).*

MONTJUÏC

Throughout Barcelona's history, whoever controlled Montjuïc (Hill of the Jews) controlled the city. Dozens of rulers have modified the **fortress,** built atop an ancient Jewish cemetery; Franco made it one of his "interrogation" headquarters. The fort was not available for recreational use until Franco rededicated it to the city in 1960—a huge stone monument expresses Barcelona's (forced) gratitude for its return. The three statues in the monument symbolize the three seas surrounding Spain. *(To get to Parc de Montjuïc, take the metro to Pl. Espanya (M: Espanya) and catch bus #50 (every 10min.) at Av. Reina María Cristina.)*

FONTS LUMINOSES. The Illuminated Fountains, dominated by the huge central **Font Mágica** (Magic Fountain), are visible from Pl. Espanya up Av. Reina María Cristina. During the summer, they're used in a weekend music and laser show that illuminates the mountainside and the **Palau Nacional,** behind the fountains. *(Shows June-Sept. Th-Su every 30min. 9:30pm-12:30am; Oct.-May F-Sa 7-8:30pm. Free.)* The palace now houses the **Museu Nacional d'Art de Cataluña.** *(M: Espanya. Walk up Av. Reina María Cristina, away from the twin brick towers, and take the escalators. www.mnac.es. Open Tu–Sa 10am-7pm, Su 10am-2:30pm. 800ptas/€4.80, with temporary exhibits 1000ptas/€6; students and seniors 550ptas/€3.40; 700ptas/€4.20. Museum entrance free 1st Th every month.)*

OLYMPIC RING. In 1929, Barcelona inaugurated the **Estadi Olímpic de Montjuïc** in its bid for the 1932 Olympic games. Over 50 years later, Catalán architects Federic Correa and Alfons Milà, who were also responsible for the overall design of the **Anella Olímpica** (Olympic Ring) esplanade, renovated the shell with the help of Italian architect Vittorio Gregotti. *(Open daily 10am-8pm. Free.)* Designed by Japanese architect Arata Isozaki, the **Palau d'Esports Sant Jordi** is the most technologically sophisticated of the structures. Test your swimming mettle in the **Olympic pools** or

FAR-OUT FAÇADE Gaudí was religious, and his plans for La Sagrada Família called for elaborate symbolism in almost every element of the church. On the left of the **Passion Façade**, a snake lurks behind Judas, symbolizing the disciple's betrayal of Jesus. The 4x4 box of numbers next to Him contains 310 combinations of four numbers, each of which adds up to 33, Christ's age at death. The faceless woman in the center of the façade, **Veronica**, represents the Biblical woman with the same name and the miraculous appearance of Christ's face on the cloth she wiped Him with. The cypress tree on the **Nativity Façade** has been interpreted as a stairway to heaven (cypress trees do not put down deeper roots with time but still grow taller); the tree is crowned with the word "Tau," Greek for the name of God. The top of the eight finished towers carries the first letter of one of the names of the apostles (and the words "Hosanna" and "Excelsis" are written in a spiral up the sides of the towers). Inside, on the **Portal of the Rosary**, overt references to modern life lurk amongst more traditional religious imagery: the Temptation of Man is represented in one carving by the devil handing a bomb to a terrorist and in another by his waving a purse at a prostitute.

visit the **Galeria Olímpica.** (*Galeria open Oct.-Mar. M-F 10am-1pm and 4-6pm; Apr.-May M-F 10am-2pm and 4-7pm; June M-Sa 10am-2pm and 4-7pm, Su 10am-2pm; July-Sept. M-Sa 10am-2pm and 4-8pm, Su 10am-2pm. 400ptas/€2.40, students 350ptas/€2, seniors 170ptas/€1. Combined visit with Poble Espanyol (see below) 1200ptas/€7.*)

■ **FUNDACIÓ MIRÓ.** Designed by Miró's friend Josep Luís Sert and tucked into the side of Montjuïc, the Fundació links interior and exterior spaces with massive windows and outdoor patios. Sky lights illuminate an extensive collection of statues, and paintings from Miró's career. His best-known pieces in the museum include *El Carnival de Arlequin*, *La Masia*, and *L'or de L'azuz*. Room 13 displays experimental work by young artists. The Fundació also sponsors music and film festivals. (*Av. Miramar, 71-75. Open July-Sept. Tu-W and F-Sa 10am-8pm, Th 10am-9:30pm, Su 10am-2:30pm; Oct.-June Tu-W and F-Sa 10am-7pm, Th 10am-9:30pm, Su 10am-2:30pm. 1200ptas/€7, students and seniors 650ptas/€4.*)

■ **CASTELL DE MONTJUÏC.** A visit to this historic fortress and its ■**Museum Militar** is a great way to get an overview of the city—both of its layout and its history. (*M: Paral.lel. Take the funicular to Av. Miramar and then the Teleféric de Montjuïc. The funicular runs from inside M: Paral.lel at Av. Paral.lel and Nou de la Rambla. Teleféric open M-Sa 11:15am-9pm. Alternatively, walk up the steep slope on C. Foc, next to the funicular station. Open mid-Mar. to mid-Nov. Tu-Su 9:30am-8pm; mid-Nov. to mid-Mar. Tu-Su 9:30am-5pm. Museum 400ptas/€2.50. Mirador 100ptas/€1.*)

GRÀCIA

Just beyond L'Eixample, this neighborhood charms and confuses with its narrow alleys and numerous plazas. In August, Gràcia hosts one of Barcelona's best festivals, **Fiesta Mejor.**

PARK GÜELL. The park was designed entirely by Gaudí, and—in typical Gaudí fashion—was not completed until after his death. Gaudí intended Park Güell to be a garden city, and its multicolored dwarfish buildings and sparkling ceramic-mosaic stairways to house the city's elite. The longest park bench in the world, a multicolored serpentine wonder made of tile shards, decorates the top of the pavilion. In the midst of the park is the **Casa-Museu Gaudí.** (*Bus #24 from Pg. Catalunya stops at the upper park entrance. Open daily May-Sept. 10am-9pm; Mar.-Apr. and Oct. 10am-7pm; Nov.-Feb. 10am-6pm. Free.*)

CASA VICENS. One of Gaudí's earliest projects, Casa Vicens is decorated with cheerful ceramic tiles. The *casa* shows the influence of Arabic architecture and a rigidness that is uncharacteristic of Gaudí's later works. The hard lines contrast with Gaudí's trademark fluid ironwork on the balconies and façade. (*C. Carolines, 24-26. M: Fontana. Walk Gran de Gràcia and turn left onto C. Carolines.*)

🎵 ENTERTAINMENT

For entertainment tips, pick up the *Guía del Ocio* (www.guiadelociobcn.es) at any newsstand. Most of Barcelona's galleries are in **La Ribera** around C. Montcada. Grab face paint to join F.C. Barcelona at the Nou Camp stadium for **fútbol.** (☎93 496 36 00. Box office C. Aristedes Maillol 12-18.) The **sardana,** Catalunya's regional dance, is a popular Barcelona amusement; join the dance circle in front of the cathedral after mass on Sundays. Bullfights are held at the **Plaça de Toros Monumental,** on C. Castillejos, 248. (☎93 245 58 04. 2600-15,000ptas/€15.60-90.) The **Festa de Sant Jordi** (St. George; Apr. 23) celebrates Catalunya's patron saint with a feast. Men give women roses, and women give men books. On August 15-21, city folk jam at Gràcia's **Fiesta Mayor.** Lights blaze in the plazas and rock bands play all night. On September 11, the **Fiesta Nacional de Cataluña** brings traditional costumes, dancing, and Catalán flags hanging from balconies.

🎭 NIGHTLIFE

The Barcelona evening begins at *bares-restaurantes* or *cervecerías*, moves to the *bares-musicales*, and ends after sunrise in discotecas. The trendiest *bares-musicales* are scattered around **Gràcia.** Consult the *Guía del Ocio* for information on movies, live concerts, bars and discos, and cultural events.

■ **El Bosq de les Fades,** just off Las Ramblas near the wax museum. M: Drassanes. A fairy-tale world with gnarled trees and a bridge. Open M-Th until 1:30am, F-Sa until 2:30am.

■ **Molly's Fair City,** C. Ferran, 7. M: Liceu. Molly's has become *the* meeting place for English-speaking backpackers in the Barri Gòtic, although plenty of Spaniards squeeze in as well. Guinness on tap 800ptas/€5. Open M-F 8pm-2:30am and Sa-Su 7pm-3am.

La Oveja Negra, C. Sitges 5. M: Catalunya. The most touristed tavern in town. Pitchers of beer 1000ptas/€6. Open M-Th 9am-2:30am, F 9am-3:30am, Sa-Su 5pm-3am.

Gasteare, C. Verdi 39. M: Fontana. Yellow walls cast a warm glow in this table-less bar. Open Su-Tu and Th 7:30pm-1am, F-Sa 7:30pm-2am.

Jamboree, Pl. Reial, 17. M: Liceu. In the corner immediately to your right coming from Las Ramblas. What was once a convent now serves as one of the city's most popular live music venues. Jazz or blues performances daily 11pm-1am (1000-2000ptas/€6-12). At 1:30am, the basement area turns into a packed hip-hop dance club, open until 5am. Upstairs, the attached club **Tarantos** plays pop and salsa for an older crowd.

Luna Mora, C. Ramón Trias Fargas. The best place for late-night dancing on the beach. Cover F-Sa 2000ptas/€12. "House couture session" F-Sa after 3:30am. Open Th-Sa 11:30pm-6am; the mostly local crowd doesn't arrive until 3am.

Baja Beach Club, Pg. Marítim 34. If Baywatch were a club, this would be it. Indoor/outdoor restaurant. Food served until 1am; entrees 1200-1700ptas/€7.20-10.25. Cover 2000ptas/€12; Su free for ladies. Open June-Sept. M-W 1pm-1am, Th and Su 1pm-5am, F-Sa 1pm-6am; Oct.-May M-W 1-5pm, Th-Sa 1pm-1am.

I COULD HAVE DANCED ALL NIGHT

Barcelona's clubs don't heat up until 2am, and most don't wind down until morning. If you are planning on clubbing, make sure to look your finest—many of the most popular *discotecas* expect a certain level of formality. Club bouncers can be finicky, and what's hip varies daily. Guys should beware of ridiculously high covers. Expect to pay 600ptas/€3.60 for a beer and at least 900ptas/€5.40 for drinks, more still at Maremagnum and Port Olímpic. Lower Montjuïc houses the "disco theme park" **Poble Espanyol,** Av. Marqués de Comillas, Barcelona's craziest disco experience. Clubs include the outdoor **La Terrazza, Torres de Avila,** and **Sixty Nine.** (M: Pl. Espanya. Open nightly July-Aug., Sept.-June Th-Sa.) Clubs get going after 1:30am; dancing lasts until 9am. *Discotecas* blare music all over **Olympic Village.** Walk down Las Ramblas and cross the wavy bridge to **Maremagnum** for a three-level maze of clubs. Some of the biggest and best *discotecas* are outside the Ramblas area. Try **Otto Zutz,** C. Lincoln, 15, (M: FFCC Muntaner; open Tu-Sa midnight-6:30am).

⚡ DAYTRIPS FROM BARCELONA

MONTSERRAT

An hour northwest of Barcelona, the mountain of Montserrat is where a wandering 9th-century mountaineer had a blinding vision of the Virgin Mary. In the 11th century, a monastery was founded to worship the Virgin, and the site has since evolved into a major pilgrimage center. The **monastery's** ornate **basilica** is above Pl. Creu. Right of the main chapel is a route through the **side chapels** that leads to the 12th-century Romanesque **La Moreneta** (the black Virgin Mary), Montserrat's venerated icon. (Open daily in summer 8-10:30am, noon-6:30pm, and 7:30-8:30pm.) In Pl. Santa María, the **Museo de Montserrat** exhibits a sweeping range of art, from an Egyptian mummy to several Picassos. (Open daily in summer 9am-6pm; off-season 9:30am-6:30pm. 500ptas/€3, students 300ptas/€1.80.) The **Santa Cova funicular** descends from Pl. Creu to paths that wind along to ancient hermitages. (In summer daily every 20min. 10am-1pm and 2-6pm, off-season Sa-Su only; return 360ptas/€2.15.) Take the **St. Joan funicular** up for more inspirational views. (Spring through fall every 20min. 10am-7pm; return 975ptas/€6.) The dilapidated **St. Joan monastery** and **shrine** are only 20min. from the highest station. The real prize is **St. Jerónim** (1235m), about 2hr. from Pl. Creu (1hr. from the terminus of the St. Joan funicular); take the sharp left after 45min. at the little old chapel.

FFCC **trains** (☎93 205 15 15) to Montserrat leave from M: Espanya in Barcelona (1hr., every hr., return including cable car 1875ptas/€11.30); get off at Aeri de Montserrat, not Olesa de Montserrat. From the base of the mountain at the other end, the Aeri cable car runs up to the monastery (every 15min. daily 9:25am-1:45pm and 2:20-6:35pm; return 950ptas/€5.90, included in train fare). From the upper cable car station, turn left and walk to Pl. Creu, where there's an information booth. (☎93 877 72 01. Open July-Sept. daily 10am-7pm; Oct.-June M-F 9am-6pm, Sa-Su 10am-7pm.)

SITGES

Forty kilometers south of Barcelona, the resort town of Sitges is famed for its prime tanning grounds, lively cultural festivals, international gay community, and wired nightlife. Long considered a watered-down Ibiza, Sitges has better beaches than the notorious Balearic hotspot, and on mainland Spain, you won't find much crazier beach-oriented nightlife. The beach is 10min. from the train station via any street. In town, Calle Parellades is the main tourist drag. Late-night foolhardiness clusters around Calle Primer de Maig, which runs directly from the beach, and its continuation, Calle Marques Montroig. The wild things are at the "disco-beach" **Atlántida,** in Sector Terramar. Shuffle your feet at **Pachá,** on Pg. Sant Didac, in nearby Vallpineda. Buses run from midnight to 4am to the two discos from C. Primer de Maig. During Carnaval, February 7-17 in 2002, Spaniards crash the town for a frenzy of dancing, costumes, and alcohol. The **tourist office,** on Pg. Vilafranca, is near the **train station.** From the station, turn right on C. Artur Carbonell and go downhill. (☎938 94 42 51; fax 938 94 43 05. Open in summer daily 9am-9pm; in winter W-M 9am-2pm and 4-6:30pm.) If you plan to stay the night, reserve early. **Hostal Internacional** is at Sant Francesc, 52. (☎93 894 26 90. Doubles 5500ptas/€3.30.) Cercanías **trains** (☎934 90 02 02) link Sitges to Barcelona-Sants Station and M: Gràcia (40min., every 15min., 350ptas/€2.10; last train back 11pm).

GIRONA (GERONA)   ☎972

A world-class city patiently waiting for the world to notice, Girona (pop. 70,500) is really two cities in one: a hushed medieval masterpiece on one riverbank, and a thriving, modern metropolis on the other. Though founded by the Romans, the city owes more to the renowned *cabalistas de Girona*, who for centuries spread the teachings of Kabbalah (mystical Judaism) in the West. Still a cultural center and university town, Girona is a magnet for artists, intellectuals, and activists. Most sights are in the old city, across the river from the train station. The **Riu Onyar** separates the new city from the old. The **Pont de Pedra** bridge connects the two banks and leads into the old quarter by way of C. Ciutadans, C. Peralta, and C. Força, which lead to the cathedral and ■El Call, the medieval Jewish neighborhood. A thriving community in the Middle Ages, El Call was virtually wiped out by the 1492 expulsion, mass emigration, conversion, and the Inquisition. The entrance to **Centre Bonastruc Ça Porta,** the site of the last synagogue in Girona (today a museum), is off C. Força, about halfway up the hill. (Open June-Oct. M-Sa 10am-8pm, Su 10am-2pm; Nov.-May M-Sa 10am-6pm, Su 10am-3pm. Museum 300ptas/€1.80, students and seniors 150ptas/€0.90. The tourist office also offers guided tours of El Call in July and Aug.) Uphill on C. Força and around the corner to the right, the Gothic **cathedral** rises a record-breaking 90 Rococo steps from the plaza below. The **Tesoro Capitular** within contains some of Girona's most precious possessions, including the *Tapis de la Creació*, a 15th-century tapestry depicting the creation story. (Both open Tu-Sa July-Sept. 10am-2pm and 4-7pm; Oct.-Mar. 10am-2pm and 4-6pm; Mar.-June 10am-2pm and 4-7pm; open year-round Su-M and holidays 10am-2pm. Tesoro and cloister 500ptas/€3.) **La Rambla** and **Plaza de Independència** are the places to see and be seen in Girona. The expansive, impeccably designed Parc de la Devesa explodes with *carpas*, temporary outdoor bars. Bars in the old quarter draw crowds in the early evening. Café la Llibreria, C. Ciutadans 15, has live music on W and F after 11pm. (Open M-Sa 8:30am-1am, Su 8:30am-midnight.)

RENFE **trains** (☎972 24 02 02) depart from Pl. de Espanya to: Barcelona (1¼hr., 21 per day 6:12am-9:29pm, 930ptas/€5.60); Figueres (30-40min., 24 per day 6:15am-10:44pm, 390ptas/€2.30); and Madrid (10½hr., 8:21pm, 6800ptas/€41). **Buses** (☎972 21 23 19) depart from just around the corner. The **tourist office,** Rambla de la Libertat 1, is directly on the other side. (☎972 22 65 75; fax 972 22 66 12. Open M-F 8am-8pm, Sa 8am-2pm and 4-8pm, Su 9am-2pm.) Most budget accommodations are in the old quarter and are well kept and reasonably priced. The **Pensió Viladomat,** C. Ciutadans 5, next to the hostel, has light, open, well-furnished rooms. (☎972 20 31 76. Singles 2500ptas/€15; doubles 5000ptas/€30, with bath 7500ptas/€45.) Girona abounds with innovative Cataluñan cuisine; by far the best place to find good, cheap food is on **Calle Cort Reial. Restaurante La Poma,** C. Cort Reial 16, offers internationally influenced cuisine at unbelievable prices. (Open W-M 7:30pm-midnight.) Pick up **groceries** at **Caprabo,** C. Sequia 10, a block from C. Nou off the Gran Via. (Open M-Sa 9am-9pm.) **Postal Code:** 17070.

▐ DAYTRIPS FROM GIRONA: THE COSTA BRAVA

TOSSA DE MAR. Falling in love in (and with) Tossa is easy. The pretty town (pop. 3800), 40km north of Barcelona, is packed with tourists every summer. But Tossa draws on its legacy as a 12th-century village, its cliff-studded landscape, its *calas* (small coves), and its small-town charm to resist becoming an average resort. Inside the walled **Vila Vella** (Old Town), spiraling alleys lead to a tiny plaza, where the **Museu Municipal** displays 20s and 30s art. (Open early June M-F 11am-1pm and 3-5pm, Sa-Su 11am-6pm; late June to early Sept. 10am-8pm; late Sept. M-F 11am-1pm and 3-5pm, Sa-Su 11am-6pm; Oct. M-F 11am-1pm and 3-5pm, Sa-Su 11am-5pm. 500ptas/€3, students and seniors 300ptas/€1.80.) Sarfa **buses** run to Pl. de les Nacions Sense Estat, at Av. de Pelegrí from Barcelona (1½hr., 15 per day, 1150ptas/€6.90) and Girona (1hr., 1-2 per day, 580ptas/€3.50). The **tourist office** shares the same building. (☎972 34 01 08. Open mid-June to mid-Sept. M-Sa 9am-9pm, Su 10am-2pm and 4-8pm; Apr.-May and Oct. M-Sa 10am-2pm and 4-8pm, Su 10:30am-1:30pm; Mar. and Nov. M-Sa 10am-1pm and 4-7pm; Dec.-Feb. M-F 10am-1pm and 4-7pm, Sa 10am-1pm.) To get to ■**Fonda/Can Lluna,** C. Roqueta 20, turn right off Pg. Mar onto C. Peixeteras, walk through C. Estalt, turn left at the end, and head straight. (☎972 34 03 65. 2500ptas/€15 per person.) The old quarter has the best cuisine and ambiance in Tossa. **Postal Code:** 17320.

FIGUERES. In 1974, Salvador Dalí chose his native, beachless **Figueres** (pop. 35,000), 36km north of Girona, as the site to build a museum to house his works, catapulting the city to instant fame. Despite his reputation as a self-promoting fascist, his self-monument is undeniably a masterpiece—and Spain's second most popular museum. The ▩**Teatre-Museu Dalí**, in Pl. Gala i S. Dalí, parades the artist's erotically nightmarish drawings, extraterrestrial landscapes, and bizarre installations. From the Rambla, take C. Girona, which becomes C. Jonquera, and climb the steps. (Open Tu-Su Oct.-May 10:30am-5:45pm; June 10:30am-5:45pm; July-Sept. 9am-7:45pm. 1200ptas/€7, students and seniors 800ptas/€4.80.) **Trains** (☎ (902) 24 02 02) run to Barcelona (1½hr., 21 per day 6:11am-8:58pm, 1200ptas/€7) and Girona (30min., 21 per day 6:11am-8:58pm, 390ptas/€2,30). **Buses** (☎972 67 33 54), in Pl. Estació, go to: Barcelona (2¼hr., 4-6 per day, 1885ptas/€11); Cadaqués (1hr.; July-Aug. 5 per day, Sept.-June 2-3 per day; 540ptas/€3.50); and Girona (1hr., 4-6 per day, 540ptas/€3.50). The **tourist office** is in Pl. Sol. (☎972 50 31 55. Open July-Aug. M-Sa 9am-9pm and Su 9am-3pm; Apr.-June and Oct. M-Sa 9am-2pm and 4:30-8pm; Sept. and Nov.-Apr. M-F 9am-3pm.) **Hostal La Barretina**, C. Lasauca 13, is luxurious. (☎972 67 64 12. Singles 3500ptas/€21; doubles 6000ptas/€36.) **Postal Code:** 17600.

CADAQUÉS. The whitewashed houses and rocky beaches of Cadaqués (pop. 1800) have attracted artists, writers, and musicians—not to mention tourists—ever since Dalí built his summer home here in the 30s. ▩**Casa-Museu Salvador Dalí**, Port Lligat, Dalí's home until 1982, is complete with a pop-art miniature Alhambra and lip-shaped sofa. Follow the signs to Port Lligat (bear right with your back to the statue of liberty) and then to the Casa de Dalí. (Open mid-June to mid-Sept. daily 10:30am-9pm; mid-Mar. to mid-June and mid-Sept. to Nov. Tu-Su 10:30am-6pm. Make reservations for a tour 1-2 days in advance. 1300ptas/€7.80; students, seniors, and children 800ptas/€4.80.) **Buses** arrive from: Barcelona (2½hr., 4-6 per day, 2365ptas/€14.20); Figueres (1hr., 5-7 per day, 540ptas/€3.30); and Girona (2hr., 1-2 per day, 1040ptas/€6.10). With your back to the Sarfa office at the bus stop, walk right along Av. Caritat Serinyana; the **tourist office**, C. Cotxe 2, is off Pl. Frederic Rahola opposite the *passeig*. (☎972 25 83 15. Open July-Aug. M-Sa 9am-2pm and 4-9pm, Su 10:30am-1pm; Sept.-June M-Sa 9am-2pm and 4-7pm.) **Hostal Cristina**, C. Riera, has newly renovated waterfront rooms. (☎972 25 81 38. Singles 4000ptas/€24; doubles 6000ptas/€36.) Pack a picnic from **Super Auvi**, C. Riera. (Open mid-July to Aug. M-Sa 8am-2pm and 4:30-9pm, Su 8am-2pm; Sept. to mid-July M-Sa 8:30am-1:30pm and 4:30-9pm, Su 8am-2pm.) **Postal Code:** 17488.

THE PYRENEES ☎973

The jagged green mountains, Romanesque churches, and tranquil towns of the Pyrenees draw hikers and high-brow skiers in search of outdoor adventures. Spectacular views make simply driving through the countryside an incredible experience. *Ski España* lists vital statistics of all ski stations in Spain. Without a car, transport is tricky but feasible.

VAL D'ARAN. Some of the Catalán Pyrenees' most dazzling peaks cluster around Val d'Aran, in the northwest corner of Cataluña. Val d'Aran is best known for its chic ski resorts—the Spanish royal family's favorite slopes are those of Baquiera-Beret. Ladies, it's probably as good a place as any to have a chance encounter with the eligible Prince Felipe. For skiing information, contact **Oficeria de Baquiera-Beret** (☎973 63 90 10) or the **tourist office** in Vielha (☎973 64 01 10). Albergue Era Garona (HI), a few kilometers away in the lovely town of Salardú, is accessible by shuttle bus in high-season from Vielha. (☎973 64 52 71; eragarona@aran.org. HI members only. HI cards sold. Breakfast included. Sheets 350ptas/€2.10. Jan.-Apr. dorms 2350ptas/€14.20, over 25 3000ptas/€18; May-Nov. dorms 1775ptas/€10.70, 2400ptas/€14.50; Dec. dorms 2000ptas/€12, 2700ptas/€16.25.) While in town do not miss Salardú's impressive 12th-century church. A colorful mural and one of the valley's most coveted paintings—the image of Santo Christo with the mountains of Salardú in the background—grace the walls.

The biggest town in the valley, **Vielha** (pop. 3500) welcomes hikers and skiers to its lively streets. Shuttle **buses** connect Vielha and Bacquiera-Beret in July and August (schedules at tourist office). **Alsina Graells buses** (☎973 27 14 70) also run to Barcelona (5½hr., 5:30am and 1:30pm; 3725ptas/€22.40). The **tourist office,** C. Sarriulèra, 6, is one block upstream from the *plaça*. (☎973 64 01 10; fax 973 64 03 72. Open Sept.-July M-Sa 10am-1pm and 4:30-7:30pm, Aug. daily 9am-9pm.) Several inexpensive *pensiones* cluster at the end of C. Reiau, off Pg. Libertat (which intersects Av. Casteiro at Pl. Sant Antoni). Try **Casa Vicenta** at C. Reiau 3. (☎973 64 08 19. mid-July to mid-Sept. and Dec.-May singles 3600ptas/€21.70; doubles 6300ptas/€37.90. Rest of the year singles 2500ptas/€15; doubles 5000ptas/€30.) **Postal code:** 25530.

PARQUE NACIONAL DE ORDESA. Ordesa's Aragonese Pyrenees will reduce even the most seasoned travelers to stupefaction. Well-maintained trails cut across idyllic forests, jagged rock faces, canyons, snow-covered peaks, rushing rivers, and magnificent waterfalls. The **visitors center** "El Parador" is beyond the Ordesa park entrance. (Open Apr. daily 9am-1:30pm and 3-6pm; May-Oct. 9am-2pm and 4:30-7pm.) The **Soaso Circle** is the most practical hike; frequent signposts mark the five-hour journey, which can be cut to a 2hr. loop. Enter the park through the village of **Torla,** where you can buy the indispensable *Editorial Alpina* guide (775ptas/€4.70). **La Oscense** (☎974 35 50 60) sends a bus from Jaca to Sabiñánigo (20min.; M-Sa 8 and 10:15am, daily 3 and 5:15pm). Sabiñánigo is also easily accessible by train; all trains on the Zaragoza-Huesca-Jaca line stop here. From there **Compañía Hude-bus** (☎974 21 32 77) runs to Torla (55min.; July-Aug. 11am and 6pm; Sept.-June 11am; 355ptas). A bus shuttles between Torla and Ordesa (every 15min. June 30-Aug. 6am-10pm, Sept. 6am-9pm; 275ptas/€1.65, 400ptas/€2.40 round-trip.) Off-season, you'll have to hike the 8km to the entrance or cab it. (☎974 48 62 43. 2000ptas/€12.) To leave the area, catch the bus as it passes through Torla at 3:30pm on its way back to Sabiñánigo. In the park, many refugios (mountain huts) allow overnight stays. The 120-bed **Refugio Góriz** is a 4hr. hike from the parking lot. (☎974 34 12 01. 1500ptas/€9 per person.) In Torla, ascend C. Francia one block to reach **Refugio L'Atalaya,** C. a Ruata, 45 (☎974 48 60 22), and **Refugio Briet** (☎974 48 62 21), across the street. (Both 1000ptas per person.) Outside Torla are **Camping Río Ara** (☎974 48 62 48) and **Camping San Anton** (☎974 48 60 63). (Open Apr.-Oct. Both 550ptas per person, per tent, and per car.) Stock up at **Supermercado Torla,** on C. a Ruata. (Open May-Oct. daily 9am-2pm and 5-8pm; Nov.-Apr. closed Su.)

JACA. For centuries, pilgrims bound for Santiago would cross the Pyrenees into Spain, spend the night in Jaca (pop. 14,000), and be off by dawn. They had the right idea; use it as launching pad for the Pyrenees. RENFE **trains** (☎974 36 13 32) run from C. Estación to Madrid (7hr., 1 per day, 4400ptas/€26.40) and Zaragoza (3hr., daily 7:36am and 6:11pm, 1400ptas/€8.40). La Oscense **buses** (☎974 35 50 60) run to Pamplona (2hr., 1-3 per day, 900ptas/€5.40) and Zaragoza (2hr., 2-5 per day, 1540ptas/€9.40). The **tourist office,** Av. Regimiento de Galicia 2, is off C. Mayor. (☎974 36 00 98. Open July-Aug. M-F 9am-2pm and 4:30-8pm, Sa 9am-1:30pm and 5-8pm, Su 10am-1:30pm; Sept.-June M-F 9am-1:30pm and 4:30-7pm, Sa 10am-1pm and 5-7pm.) From the bus station cross the park and head right following the church completely around to the next plaza to find **Hostal Paris,** one of the best deals in town. (☎974 36 10 20. Mid-July to mid-Sept. singles 2675ptas/€9.25; doubles 4280ptas/€25.75. Mid-Sept. to mid-July 2460ptas/€14.80; doubles 3850ptas/€23.14.) Or check out the decidedly hip *casa rural* **El Arco,** C. San Nicolas, 4, where each room has its own distinctive flavor. (☎974 36 44 48. 2000ptas/€12 per person.)

NAVARRA

The spirit of the Navarrese emanates from the rustic Pyrenean *pueblos* on the French border to bustling Pamplona to the dusty villages in the south. Bordered by Basque Country and Aragón, these tiny villages welcome tourists.

PAMPLONA (IRUÑA)   ☎948

Long, long ago, Pamplona's fiesta in honor of its patron saint, San Fermín, was just
another religious holiday. But ever since Ernest Hemingway wrote *The Sun Also
Rises*, hordes of visitors from around the world have come the week of July 6-14 to
witness and experience *San Fermines*, the legendary "Running of the Bulls."

⬛🔢 TRANSPORTATION AND PRACTICAL INFORMATION. RENFE trains
(☎(902) 24 02 02) run from off Av. San Jorge to Barcelona (6-8hr.; daily 12:55am,
12:20 5:10pm; 4400ptas/€26.40) and Madrid (5hr., 7:05am and 6:10pm, 4400ptas/
€26.40). **Buses** go from C. Conde Oliveto, at C. Yanguas y Miranda, to: Barcelona
(5½hr.; 8:30am, 4:30pm and 1am; 2855ptas/€17.40); Bilbao (2hr., 3-7 per day 7am-
7pm, 1685ptas/€10); Madrid (5hr., 4-7 per day 7am-6:30pm, 3430ptas/€20.60); San
Sebastián (1hr., 7-9 per day 7am-9pm, 845ptas/€5); and Zaragoza (2-3hr., 6-8 per
day 7:15am-8:30pm, 1600-1760ptas/€9.60-10.55). From Pl. Castillo, take C. San
Nicolas, turn right on C. San Miguel, and go through Pl. San Francisco to get to
the **tourist office**, C. Eslava, 1. (☎948 20 65 40. Open during *San Fermines* daily
9am-8pm; July-Aug. M-Sa 10am-2pm and 4-7pm, Su 10am-2pm; Sept.-June M-F
10am-2pm and 4-7pm, Sa 10am-2pm.) During *San Fermines*, **store luggage** at the
Escuelas de San Francisco, the big stone building at one end of Pl. San Francisco.
(300ptas/€1.80. Open 24hr.) **Email** from the **iturNet cibercafé**, C. Iturrama, 1, at C. Abe-
jeras. (500ptas/€3 per hr. Open M-Th 9am-10pm, F 9am-midnight, Sa-Su 10am-mid-
night; during *San Fermines* daily 9am-5pm.) **Postal code:** 31001.

🔢⬛ ACCOMMODATIONS AND FOOD. And now, a lesson in supply and
demand: smart *san ferministas* book their rooms up to a year (at least two
months) in advance, and avoid paying rates up to four times higher than those
listed here. Beware of hawkers at the train and bus stations—quality and prices
vary tremendously. Check the newspaper *Diario de Navarra* for **casas particulares.** Many roomless folks are forced to sleep on the lawns of the Ciudadela or on
Pl. Fueros, Pl. Castillo, or the banks of the river. Be careful—if you can't store your
backpack (storage fills fast), sleep on top of it. To reach the impressive **Pensión
Santa Cecilia**, C. Navarrería, 17, follow C. Chapitela, take the first right on C. Merca-
deres, and make a sharp left. (☎948 22 22 30. *San Fermines* dorms 7000ptas/€35.
Otherwise singles 2500ptas/€15; doubles 4000-5000ptas/€24-30; triples 6000ptas/
€36.) **Pensión Otaño**, C. San Nicolás, 5, is a great place to eat and sleep, but is booked
for the next five years during *San Fermines*. (☎948 22 70 36. Singles 2000ptas/€12;
doubles 5000-6000ptas/€30-36.) Clean doubles await at **Fonda La Aragonesa**, at C. San
Nicolás, 22. (☎948 22 34 28. *San Fermines* 12,000ptas/€72; otherwise 3745/
€19ptas.) Show up early during the fiesta to get a room at **Fonda La Montañesa**, C.
San Gregorio, 2. (☎948 22 43 80. *San Fermines* singles 6000ptas/€36; doubles
12,000ptas/€72. Otherwise 2000ptas/€12; 4000ptas/€24. No reservations.) To get to
Camping Ezcaba, in Eusa, take the La Montañesa **bus** from Pl. Toros to Eusa (4 per
day) to the end. (☎948 33 03 15. *San Fermines* 1370ptas/€8.20 per person, per tent,
and per car. Otherwise 575ptas/€3.45 per person, 565ptas/€3.40 per tent and per
car.) Look for food near Pensión Santa Cecilia, above **Plaza San Francisco**, and
around **Paseo Ronda**. **Calles Navarrería** and **Paseo Sarasate** host *bocadillo* bars. **Vendi,**
at C. Hilarión Eslava and C. Mayor, has **groceries.** (Open during *San Fermines* M-Sa
9am-2pm; otherwise M-F 9am-2pm and 5:30-7:30pm, Sa 9am-2pm.)

⬛🔢 SIGHTS AND NIGHTLIFE. Pamplona's rich architectural legacy is reason
enough to visit during the 51 other weeks of the year. The restored late-14th-cen-
tury Gothic **cathedral** is at the end of C. Navarrería. (Open M-F 10am-1:30pm and 4-
7pm, Sa 10am-1:30pm. Ask about guided tours. 550ptas/€3.30.) The impressive
walls of the pentagonal **Ciudadela** once humbled even Napoleon; today the
Ciudadela hosts free exhibits and concerts in summer. From the old quarter, pick
up C. Redín at the far end of the cathedral plaza, head left along the walls past the
Portal de Zumalacárregui and along the Río Arga, and bear left through the **Parque de
la Taconera**. (Open daily 7am-10pm; closed for *San Fermines*. Free.) Throughout the

year, **Plaza de Castillo** is the social heart of the city. Hemingway's favorite haunt was the **Café-Bar Iruña,** immortalized in *The Sun Also Rises.* (Open M-Th 1:15-4pm and 8:15-11pm, F-Sa 1:15-4pm and 9-11pm. Open *San Fermines* daily 1:15-4pm, F-Sa evening.) The young and the restless booze up at bars in the *casco antiguo,* around **Calles de Jarauta, San Nicolás,** and **San Gregorio.**

> Although Pamplona is usually very safe, crime skyrockets during *San Fermines.* Beware of assaults and muggings, do not roam alone at night, and take care in the *casco antiguo.*

🎇 **LOS SAN FERMINES (JULY 6-14).** Visitors overcrowd Pamplona for one week in search of Europe's greatest party. Pamplona delivers an eight-day frenzy of parades, bullfights, parties, dancing, fireworks, concerts, and wine. Pamplonese, clad in white with red sashes and bandanas, literally throw themselves into the merry-making, displaying obscene levels of both physical stamina and alcohol tolerance. The "Running of the Bulls," called the *encierro,* is the focal point of *San Fermines;* the first *encierro* of the festival takes place on July 7 at 8am and is repeated at 8am every day for the next seven days. Hundreds of bleary-eyed, hungover, hyper-adrenalized runners flee from large bulls as bystanders cheer from barricades, windows, balconies, and doorways. Both the bulls and the mob are dangerous; terrified runners flee for dear life, and react without concern for those around them. Hemingway had the right idea: don't run. Watch the *encierro* from the bullring; arrive around 6:45am. Tickets for the Grada section of the ring are available before 7am. (M-F 450ptas/€2.70, Sa-Su 600ptas/€3.60.) You can watch for free, but the free section is overcrowded, making it hard to see and breathe. If you want to participate in the bullring excitement, line up by the Pl. Toros well before 7:30am and run in *before* the bulls are in sight. **Be very careful; follow the tourist office's guidelines for running.** To watch a bullfight, wait in the line that forms at the bullring around 8pm (from 2000ptas). As one fight ends, tickets go on sale for the next day. Once the running ends, insanity spills into the streets and gathers steam until nightfall, when it explodes with singing in bars, dancing in alleyways, spontaneous parades, and a no-holds-barred party in Pl. de Castillo, Europe's biggest open-air dance floor.

BASQUE COUNTRY (PAÍS VASCO)

Basque Country's varied landscape resembles a nation complete unto itself, combining cosmopolitan cities, verdant hills, industrial wastelands, and quaint fishing villages. Many believe that the strongly nationalistic Basques are the native people of Iberia, as their culture and language date back several millennia.

SAN SEBASTIÁN (DONOSTIA)   ☎943

Glittering on the shores of the Cantabrian Sea, coolly elegant San Sebastián (pop. 180,000) welcomes visitors. Locals and tourists down *pintxos* (tapas) and drinks in the *parte vieja* (old city), which claims the world's most bars per square meter.

▙ TRANSPORTATION

Trains: RENFE, Estación del Norte (☎(902) 24 02 02), on Po. Francia, on the east side of Puente María Cristina. Info office open daily 7am-11pm. To: **Barcelona** (9hr., daily 10:30am and Su-F 10:59pm, 5000ptas/€30); **Madrid** (8hr., Su-F 8:30am and daily 10:30pm, 4900-6300ptas/€30-38); **Zaragoza** (4hr., daily 10:30am and Su-F 10:59pm, 3100ptas/€18.60).

Buses: Several private companies run from different points in the city but most set up shop at the tiny "station," right around the corner from the main concourse at Po. Vizcaya, 16. Buses drop off on Pl. Pío XII, a block from the river and about 13 blocks south of Av. Libertad on Av. Sancho el Sabio. Public bus #28 goes to the city center from the bus station. To: **Barcelona** (7hr.; 7:30am, 3:30, 11:20pm; 3430ptas/€20.60); **Bilbao** (1¼hr.; M-F every 30min., Sa-Su every hr. 6am-10:30pm; 1200ptas/€7.20); **Madrid** (6hr., 7-9 per day 7:15am-12:30am, 3990ptas/€24); **Pamplona** (1hr.; 9 per day 7am-9pm, Su 9am-9pm; 845ptas/€5.10)

✴❷ ORIENTATION AND PRACTICAL INFORMATION

The city center and most monuments and beaches lie on a peninsula on the west side of the **Río Urumea;** at the tip, the **Monte Urgulla** juts out into the bay. Inland, nightlife rages and budget accommodations and restaurants cluster in the **parte vieja.** At the south end of the peninsula is the commercial area. From the bus station, head right (north) up Av. Sancho el Sabio toward the cathedral, ocean, and *parte vieja.* East of the river are the **RENFE station, Barrio de Gros,** and the **Playa de la Zurriola.** Head straight from the train station, cross the Puente María Cristina (bridge), head right at the fountain for four blocks, then turn left on Av. Libertad to the port; the *parte vieja* will lie to your right and the **Playa de la Concha** to your left.

Tourist Office: Centro de Atracción y Turismo, C. Reina Regente, 3 (☎943 48 11 66), next to the theater and in front of the Puente Zurriola. From the train station, turn right immediately after crossing Puente María Cristina. Continue until reaching Puente Zurriola; office will be on the left. From the bus station, go down Av. Sancho el Sabio. At Pl. Centenario, bear right on C. Prim and follow the river. At the 3rd bridge, Puente Zurriola, look to the plaza at your left and the office is on the corner. (Open June-Sept. M-Sa 8am-8pm, Su 10am-2pm; Oct.-May M-Sa 9am-1:30pm and 3:30-7pm, Su 10am-2pm.)

Luggage Storage: Lockers at **RENFE station.** 500ptas/€3 per day. Open daily 7am-11pm. Buy tokens at ticket counter.

Laundromat: Lavomatique, C. Iñigo, 13 (☎943 42 38 71), off C. San Juan in the parte vieja. Self-service. 600ptas/€3.60. Open M-F 9:30-2pm and 4-7pm, Sa-Su 10am-2pm.

Hiking Info: Izadi, C. Usandizaga, 18 (☎943 29 35 20). Sells hiking guides and maps, some in English. Organizes tours and rents skis, wet-suits, and hiking equipment. Open M-F 10am-1pm and 4-8pm, Sa 10am-1:30pm and 4:30-8pm.

Emergency: ☎091 or 092. **Police,** Municipal (☎943 45 00 00), C. Easo, 41.

Medical Services: Casa de Socorro, Bengoetxea, 4 (☎943 44 06 33).

Internet Access: Zarr@net, C. San Lorenzo, 6 (☎943 43 33 81). 550ptas/€3.30 per hr. Open daily 10am-10pm. **Netline,** C. Urdaneta, 8 (☎943 44 50 76). 250ptas/€1.50 per 30min. Open M-Sa 10am-10pm.

Post Office: Po. De Francia, 13 (☎943 44 68 26), near the RENFE station. Cross the Santa Catalina bridge, turn right, and the office is on the left. Open M-F 8:30am-8:30pm, Sa 9:30am-2pm. Address mail to be held: First name SURNAME; Lista de Correos; Oficina Principal de Correos, Po. de Francia, 13, San Sebastián, **20006.**

▌ ACCOMMODATIONS AND CAMPING

Desperate backpackers will scrounge for rooms in July and August, particularly during *San Fermines* (July 6-14) and *Semana Grande* (starts Su of the week of Aug. 15); September's film festival is not much better. Budget options center in the *parte vieja* and by the cathedral. The tourist office has lists of accommodations and most hostel owners know of **casas particulares**—feel free to ask for help.

PARTE VIEJA

Pensión Amaiur, C. 31 de Agosto, 44, 2nd fl. (☎943 42 96 54). From Alameda del Boulevard, go up C. San Jerónimo to the end and turn left. *Semana Santa*-Oct. 2500-3500ptas/€15-21 per person; Nov.-*Semana Santa* 1900-2500ptas/€12-15. MC/V.

Pensión San Lorenzo, C. San Lorenzo, 2 (☎943 42 55 16), off C. San Juan. Cheerful doubles all have TV, radio and small fridge. Immaculate modern bathrooms. July-Sept. doubles 8000ptas/€48; Oct.-June 4000ptas/€24.

Pensión Larrea, C. Narrica, 21, 2nd fl. (☎943 42 26 94). Adorable and adoring owners have a reputation as the "best mom and pop in town." July-Aug. singles 3500ptas/€21; doubles 5000ptas/€30; triples 6500/€39. Sept.-June about 1000ptas/€6 less. .

Pensión Loinaz, C. San Lorenzo, 17 (☎943 42 67 14), off C. San Juan. July-Aug. doubles 6500ptas/€39; Apr.-June 5000ptas/€30; Sept.-Mar. 4000ptas/€24.

Pension Urgull, Esterlines, 10, 3rd fl. (☎943 43 00 47). Attractive old rooms with tall windows, small balconies, and convenient location. July-Aug. doubles 6000-7000ptas/ €36-42. Sept.-June singles 2500ptas/€15; doubles 4000ptas/€24.

Pensión Boulevard, Alameda del Boulevard, 24 (☎943 42 94 05). Beautiful, modern rooms, all with radios, some with balconies. July-Aug. doubles 8000ptas; Sept.-June 4000-7000ptas/€24-42.

Pensión Puerto, C. Puerto, 19, 2nd fl. (☎943 43 21 40), off C. Mayor. Clean rooms with big closets, good beds, and some balconies. 2500-5000ptas/€15-30 per person.

OUTSIDE PARTE VIEJA

Most of these hostels lie in the heart of the commercial zone, around the cathedral. They tend to be quieter than those elsewhere in the city, yet are still close to the port, beach, bus, and train stations, and all of the action in the *parte vieja.*

Albergue Juvenil la Sirena (HI), Po. Igueldo, 25 (☎943 31 02 68). A big, light-pink building 3min. from the beach at the far west end of the city. Buses #24 and 27 run from the train and bus stations to Av. Zumalacárregui. HI members and ISIC-carriers only. Lockout 10am-3pm. May-Sept. 1885-2070ptas/€11.30-12, over 25 2205-2335ptas/€13.20-14. Oct.-Apr. 1700ptas/€10, over 25 2070ptas/€12.50.

Pensión Urkia, C. Urbieta, 12, 3rd fl. (☎943 42 44 36), on C. Urbieta between C. Marcial and C. Arrasate. Borders the Mercado de San Martín. Rooms with full bathrooms and TV. July-Sept. doubles 6500ptas/€33; triples 9000ptas/€54. Oct.-June singles 3500-4000ptas/€21-24; doubles 4500ptas/€27; triples 6000ptas/€36.

Pensión La Perla, C. Loiola, 10, 2nd fl. (☎943 42 81 23), on the street directly ahead of the cathedral. Grand stairway leads to attractive rooms with polished floors. July-Sept. singles 4000ptas/€24; doubles 6000ptas/€36. Oct.-June singles 3500ptas/€21; doubles 4500ptas/€27.

Camping: Camping Igueldo (☎943 21 45 02), 5km west of town. Bus #16 (Barrio de Igueldo-Camping) runs between the site and Alameda del Boulevard (every 30min., 125ptas/€0.75). Reception June-Aug. 8am-midnight; Sept.-May 9am-1pm and 5-9pm. *Parcela* (including tent and up to 2 people) June-Aug. and *Semana Santa* 1725ptas/ €10.37, extra person 525ptas/€3.16. Sept.-May 1475ptas/€8.85.

🗒 FOOD

🍢*Pintxos* (tapas; rarely more than 200ptas/€1.20 each), chased down with the fizzy regional white wine txacoli, are a religion here; bars in the old city spread an array of enticing tidbits on toothpicks or bread. The entire *parte vieja* seems to exist for no other purpose than to feed. The chef at 🍢**Kursaal,** Zurriola, 1, is a legend among the locals. (Menú 1650-2300ptas/€10-14.) Sample the to-die-for delicacies at **Bar La Cepa,** C. 31 de Agosto, 7-9. (*Pintxos* 160-325ptas. *Bocadillos* 475ptas/€2.90. Open daily 1pm-midnight.) **Mercado de la Bretxa,** on Alameda del Boulevard at C. San Juan, sells fresh produce. (Open M-Sa 9am-9pm.) **Super Todo Todo,** on Alameda del Boulevard around the corner from the tourist office, also sells **groceries.** (Open M-Sa 8:30am-9pm, Su 10am-2pm.)

👁 🎵 SIGHTS AND ENTERTAINMENT

San Sebastián's most attractive sight is the city itself—green walks, grandiose buildings, and the placid bay. The views from 🏔**Monte Igueldo,** west of the center, are the best in town: by day, the countryside meets the ocean in a line of white and blue, and by night the flood-lit **Isla Santa Clara** (island) seems to float on a ring of light. The walk up the mountain is not too strenuous, but the weary can take a funicular. A mini amusement park also awaits those who scale the peak (170ptas). Across the bay from Monte Igueldo, **Monte Urgull**, at the northern tip of the *parte vieja* jutting out into the bay, is crowned by the overgrown **Castillo de Santa Cruz de la Mota,** in turn topped by the statue of the **Sagrado Corazón de Jesús.** (Open daily June-Aug. 8am-8pm; Sept.-May 8am-6pm.) Directly below the hill, on Po. Nuevo in the *parte vieja*, the serene **Museo de San Telmo** resides in a Dominican monastery strewn with Basque funerary relics, a montage of artifacts, El Grecos, and dinosaur skeletons. (Open Tu-Sa 10:30am-1:30pm and 4-8pm, Su 10:30am-2pm. Free.) The gorgeous **Playa de la Concha** curves along the city's western shore, which turns into the smaller and steeper **Playa de Ondarreta** beyond the **Palacio de Miramar.** Across the river from Mr. Urguel, surfers crowd ▨**Playa de la Zurridia.**

Tickets sell out for the five-day **Festival de Jazz** (☎943 48 11 79; www.jazzaldia.com), in mid- to late July. **Semana Grande** (Big Week; week of Aug. 15) explodes with concerts, a fireworks festival, and more. All year, the *parte vieja* lets loose after dark. **Calle Fermín Calbetón,** three blocks in from Alameda del Boulevard, sweats bars. Along the beach, music starts thumping at midnight. A favorite among expats and young travelers, **The World's End,** Po. de Salamanca, 14, is a block from the *parte vieja* toward the beach. (Open Su-Th 2pm-2:30am, F-Sa 2pm-3:30am.) **Bar Tas-Tas,** C. Fermín Calbetón, 35, attracts backpackers. (Open daily 3pm-4am.) **Zibbibo,** Plaza Sarriegi, 8, is a hip club with a dance floor and a blend of hits and techno. (Open daily 2pm-4am.) **Molly Malone,** C. San Martin, 55, off the Paseo de la Concha, outside the *parte vieja*, is an Irish pub popular with locals. (Open July-Aug. Su-Th 3pm-3am, F-Sa 3pm-4:30am; rest of year 11am-3am.)

BILBAO (BILBO)   ☎944

Graced with the marvelous new Guggenheim Museum, Bilbao (pop. 358,000) is finally overcoming its reputation as a bourgeois, business-minded industrial center. Its medieval *casco viejo*, wide 19th-century boulevards lined by grand buildings, and stunning new subway and riverwalk make Bilbao well worth a stop.

▉☎ TRANSPORTATION AND PRACTIAL INFORMATION. RENFE **trains** (☎944 23 86 23) arrive at the **Estación de Abando,** Pl. Circular 2, from Barcelona (9½-11hr., 10am and 10:45pm, 5200ptas/€31.20); Madrid (5¾-9hr.; Su-F 4:30pm and 11:05pm, Sa 9:50am; 4600ptas-5800ptas/€27.60-34.80); and Salamanca (5½-6½hr., 9:25am and 2:05pm, 3700ptas/€22.20). From Pl. Circular, head right around the station and cross the Puente del Arenal (bridge) to reach Pl. Arriaga, the entrance to the *casco viejo*. Most **bus companies** leave from the **Termibús terminal,** C. Gurtubay 1 (☎944 39 50 77; M: San Mamés), on the west side of town, for: Barcelona (7¼hr. 3-4 per day M-F 6:30am-11pm; 5375ptas/€32.25); Madrid (4-5hr.; M-F 10-17 per day 7am-1:30am, Sa-Su 8am-1:30am; 3480ptas/€20.90); Pamplona (2hr., 4-6 per day 7:30am-8pm, 1580ptas/€9.50); and San Sebastián (1¼hr.; M-F every 30min.-1hr. 6am-10:30pm, Sa every hr. 7:30am-10:30pm, Su every hr. 9am-10:30pm; 1200ptas/€7.20.) The **tourist office** is on Pl. Arenal, to the left of the **Plaza de Arriaga,** the entrance to the *casco viejo*. (☎944 79 57 60; www.bilbao.net. Open M-F 9am-2pm and 4-7:30pm, Sa 9am-2pm, Su 10am-2pm.) Surf the Internet at **L@Ser,** C. Sendaja, 5. Standing with your back to the tourist office, take a left away from the park, and walk about a block up on the right (250ptas/€1.50 per 30min).

▉▉ACCOMMODATIONS AND FOOD. Pl. Arriaga and C. Arenal have tons of budget accommodations. **Pensión Méndez,** C. Santa María, 13, 4th fl., is insulated from the raging nightlife below. From the Puente del Arenal, take C. Bidebbarrieta (to the right of Café Boulevard); after two blocks take a right onto C. Perro, turn right when you reach C. Santa María, *pensión* is on the right. (☎944 16 03 64. Singles 3000-4000ptas/€18-24; doubles 5000ptas/€30.) To get to **Pensión Ladero,** C. Lotería, 1, 4th fl., from the Puente del Arenal, take C. Correo (to the left of Café Boulevard), take a right after three blocks onto C. Lotería, across from Hostal Roquefer. (☎944 15 09 32. Singles 3000ptas/€18; doubles 4500ptas/€27.) **Mercado de la Ribera,** on the bank of the river at the bottom of the old city, is the biggest indoor **market** in Spain. (Open M-Sa 8am-2:30pm, also F 4:30-7:30pm.) Get **groceries** at the huge **Champión,** Pl. Santos Juanes. (Open M-Sa 9:15am-9:15pm.) **Postal code:** 48008.

■ ■ **SIGHTS AND ENTERTAINMENT.** Frank O. Gehry's ■**Guggenheim Museum Bilbao** can only be described as breathtaking. Lauded by the international press, it has catapulted Bilbao into cultural stardom. The building's undulating curves of glistening titanium, limestone, and glass resemble an iridescent scaly fish. The museum currently hosts rotating exhibits culled from the Guggenheim Foundation's collection. From Pl. Circular, head down Gran Vía, right across Pl. de Frederico Moyúo, and down Alameda de Recalde. *(Av. Abandoibarra, 2. www.guggenheim.bilbao.es. Open July-Aug. daily 9am-9pm; Sept.-June Tu-Su 10am-8pm. 1200ptas/€7.20, students and seniors 600ptas/€3.60, under 12 free. Guided tours in English Tu-F 11am, 12:30, 4:30, 6:30pm, Sa-Su 1 and 4pm; sign up 30min. before tour at info desk.)* The often overshadowed **Museo de Bellas Artes** hordes an impressive collection of 12th- to 20th-century art. *(Pl. Museo, 2. From the Guggenheim, follow the Alameda de Mazarredo. Open Tu-Sa 10am-8pm, Su 10am-2pm. 600ptas/€3.60, seniors and students 300ptas/€1.80; free W.)* Revelers in the *casco viejo* spill into the streets, especially on **Calle Barrencalle** (Barrenkale). A young crowd jams at **Calle Licenciado Poza** on the west side of town. For a mellower scene, people-watch at the elegant 19th-century **Café Boulevard,** C. Arenal, 3. **The Cotton Club,** C. Gregorio de la Revilla, 25, decorated with over 30,000 beer caps, draws a huge crowd on Friday and Saturday nights. (Open M-Th 4:30pm-3am, F 4:30pm-6am, Sa 6:30pm-6am, and Su 6:30pm-3am. Cash only.) The massive blowout fiesta in honor of *Nuestra Señora de Begoña* takes place during **Semana Grande,** a nine-day party beginning the Saturday after Aug. 15.

■ **DAYTRIP FROM BILBAO: GUERNICA (GERNIKA).** On April 26, 1937, the Nazi "Condor Legion" released an estimated 29,000kg of explosives on Guernica, obliterating 70% of a city in three hours. The nearly 2000 people who were killed in the bombings were immortalized in Pablo Picasso's stark masterpiece *Guernica,* now in Madrid's Reina Sofía gallery (see p. 839). The rebuilt city offers little aside from the **Gernika Museoa,** Foru Plaza 1, which features an exhibition chronicling the bombardment. (Open mid-June to Aug. M-Sa 10am-7pm, Su 10am-2pm; Sept. to mid-June M-Sa 10am-2pm and 4-7pm, Su 10am-2pm. 600ptas/€3.60.) **Trains** (☎902 543 210; www.euskotren.es) roll in from Bilbao (45min.; every 30min. M-F 6:15am-10:15pm, Sa-Su every 30min. 8:15am-10:15pm; 325ptas/€2).

BALEARIC ISLANDS

Perhaps dreaming of the fortunes to be made in today's tourist industry, nearly every culture with boats tried to conquer the *Islas Baleares*. The foreign invasion continues as two million visitors flood the islands' discos and beaches each year. Culture-philiacs and shopaholics will fall for the high-class act and stunning natural beauty of **Mallorca.** A counterculture haven since the 1960s, **Ibiza** offers some of the best nightlife in all of Europe. The smaller islands **Formentera** and **Menorca** rest upon unspoiled sands, hidden coves, and mysterious Bronze Age megaliths.

▐ TRANSPORTATION

Flights to the islands are the easiest way to get there. Those under 26 often get discounts from **Iberia/Aviaco Airlines** (☎902 40 05 00; www.iberia.com), which flies to Palma de Mallorca and Ibiza from: Barcelona (40min., 10,000-20,000ptas/ €60-120); Madrid (1hr., 25,000-30,000ptas/€150-180); and Valencia. **Air Europa**

(☎902 24 00 42) and **SpanAir** (☎902 13 14 15; www.spanair.com) offer budget flights to and between the islands. Most cheap return **charters** include a week's stay in a hotel; some companies called *mayoristas* sell leftover spots as "seat-only" deals. **Ferries** to the islands are less popular. **Trasmediterránea** (☎902 45 46 45; www.trasmediterranea.com) departs from Barcelona's Estació Marítima Moll and Valencia's Estació Marítima for Mallorca and Ibiza. **Buquebus** (☎902 41 42 42 or 934 81 73 60.) goes from Barcelona to Palma (4hr., 2 per day, 8150ptas/€49). Book airplane or ferry tickets through a travel agency in Barcelona, Valencia, or on the islands.

Within the islands, **ferries** are the most cost-efficient. A day's **car** rental costs around 6000ptas/€36, **mopeds** 3000ptas/€18 per day, and **bikes** 1000ptas/€6 per day.

MALLORCA

Since Roman times, Mallorca has been a popular member of the in-crowd. Lemon groves and olive trees adorn the jagged cliffs of the north coast, and lazy bays and caves scoop into the rest of the coast. The capital of the Balearics, **Palma** (pop. 323,000) embraces conspicuous consumption but still pleases with its well-preserved old quarter, colonial architecture, and local flavor. The tourist office distributes a list of over 40 nearby **beaches**, many a mere bus ride from Palma; one popular choice is **El Arenal** (Platja de Palma; bus #15), 11km southeast toward the airport. When the sun sets, **La Bodeguita del Medio,** C. Vallseca, 18, keeps its crowd dancing to Cuban rhythms. (Open Th-Sa 8pm-3am, Su-W 8pm-1am.) Follow the Aussie voices down C. Apuntadores to the popular **Bar Latitude 39,** C. Felip Bauza, 8, a self-proclaimed "yachtie" bar. (Open M-Sa 7pm-3am.) Palma's clubbers start their night in the *bares-musicales* lining the **Paseo Marítimo** strip like salsa-happy **Made in Brasil,** Po. Marítimo, 27 (open daily 8pm-4am) and dance-crazy **Salero,** Po. Marítimo, 31 (open daily 8pm-6am). Other party-goers head to the beaches and the nightclubs near **El Terreno.** When the bar scene starts to fade around 3am, partiers migrate to Palma's *discotecas.* **Tito's Palace,** Po. Marítimo, is Palma's hippest disco. (Cover 2500-3000ptas/€15-18. Open daily 11pm-6am.)

To get from the airport to the center, take bus #17 to **Plaza d'Espanya** (15min., every 20min., 295ptas/€1.80). To continue to the **tourist office,** C. Sant Dominic, 11, take Pg. Marítim (a.k.a. Av. Juan Roca) to Av. Antoni Maura, follow C. Conquistador out of Pl. de la Reina, and continue on C. Sant Dominic. (☎971 71 15 27. Open M-F 9am-8pm, Sa 9am-1:30pm.) **Branches** are in Pl. Reina and the airport. **Hostal Apuntadores,** C. Apuntadores, 8, is in the middle of the action, less than a block from Pl. Reina. (☎971 71 34 91. Dorms 2000ptas/€12; singles 3000ptas/€18; doubles 5000ptas/€30.) **Hostal Brondo,** C. Can Brondo, 1, off Pl. Rei Joan Carles I, is an old, converted house with character. (☎971 71 90 43. Reception M-Sa 9am-2pm and 6-8pm, Su 10am-1:30pm. Singles 3500ptas/€21; doubles 5500ptas/€33.) **Hostal Cuba,** C. San Magí, 1, is at C. Argentina, on the edge of the town; from Pl. Joan Carles I, turn left and walk down Av. Jaume III, cross the river, and turn left on C. Argentina. (☎971 73 81 59. Singles 2500-3000ptas/€15-18; doubles 5000-5500ptas/€30-33.) Truly budget eaters tend to head to the side streets off **Passeig Born,** to the plethora of cheap digs along **Avenida Joan Miró,** or to the carbon-copy pizzerias along **Paseo Marítimo. Servicio y Precios,** on C. Felip Bauzà, near Pl. Reina, has **groceries.** (Open M-F 8:30am-8:30pm, Sa 9am-2pm.)

IBIZA

A 1960's hippie enclave, Ibiza (pop. 84,000) has long forgotten its roots in favor of new-age decadence, as style warriors arrive in droves to debauch themselves in a sex- and substance-driven summer culture. Ibiza's thriving gay community lends credence to its image as a center of tolerance, but the island's high price tags preclude true diversity. None of Ibiza's beaches is within quick walking distance of **Eivissa (Ibiza City),** but **Platja de Talamanca, Platja des Duros, Platja d'en Bossa,** and **Platja Figueredes** are at most 20min. away by bike; buses also leave from Av. Isidor Macabich 20 for Platja d'en Bossa (every 30min., 125ptas/€0.75).

The most beautiful beach near Eivissa is **Playa de Las Salinas,** where the nude sunbathers are almost as perfect as the crystal-blue water and silky sand. The crowds return from the beaches by nightfall, when the largest party on earth begins. The bar scene centers around **Calle Barcelona. Calle Virgen** is the center of gay nightlife. The island's ▓**discos** (most of which have a mixed gay/straight crowd) are world-famous. Refer to *Ministry in Ibiza* or *DJ*, free at many hostels, bars, and restaurants. The **Discobus** runs to and from all the major hotspots (leaves Eivissa every hr. 12:30am-6:30am, schedule for other stops available at tourist office and hotels, 250ptas/€1.5). Wild, wild ▓**Privilege** is the world's largest club and best known for Monday night "manumission" parties featuring kinky live sex. (Open daily June-Sept. midnight-7am.) At **Amnesia,** on the road to San Antonio, you can forget who you are, where you're from, and who you came with, at what may just be the craziest disco scene ever. (Cream parties Th; foam parties W and Su. Open daily midnight-7am.) Both lie on the discobus route to San Antonio. Playful **Pachá,** on Pg. Perimitral, is 20min. from the port. (Open daily midnight-7:30am.) Cap off your night in **Space,** which starts hopping around 8am, peaks mid-afternoon, and doesn't wind down until 5pm.

The local paper *Diario de Ibiza* (www.diariodeibiza.es; 125ptas/€0.75) features an *Agenda* page with everything you need to know about Ibiza. The **tourist office,** C. Antoni Riquer, 2, is on the water. (☎971 30 19 00; www.ibizaonline.com. Open M-F 9:30am-1:30pm and 5-8pm, Sa 10:30am-1pm.) Get cleaned up for the night out and check email at **Wash and Dry,** Av. España, 53. (☎971 39 48 22. 700ptas/€4.20 each. Internet 900ptas/€5.40 per hr. Open M-F 10am-3pm and 5-10pm, Sa 10am-5pm.)

The letters "CH" *(casa de huespedes)* mark many doorways; call the owners at the phone number on the door. **Hostal Residencia Ripoll** is at C. Vicente Cuervo, 14. (☎971 31 42 75. July-Sept. singles 4500ptas/€27; doubles 6500ptas/€39; 3-person apartments with TV, patio, and kitchen 12,000ptas/€72.) **Hostal Juanito and Hostal Las Nieves,** C. Juan de Austria, 17-18, are run by the same owner. (☎971 19 03 19. Singles 3000ptas/€18; doubles 6000ptas/€36.) **Hostal La Marina,** Puerto de Ibiza, C. Barcelona, 7, is across from Estació Marítima but right in the middle of the raucous bar scene. (☎971 31 01 72. Singles 4500-8000ptas/€27-48; doubles 7000-16,000ptas/€42-96.) For a supermarket, try **Hiper Centro,** C. Ignasi Wallis, near C. Juan de Austria. (☎971 19 20 41. Open M-Sa 9am-2pm and 5-9pm.) Cheap accommodations in town are rare. Consider staying in San Antonio, a town 14km away.

MENORCA

Menorca's 200km coastline of raw beaches, rustic landscape, and well-preserved ancient monuments draw ecologists, sun worshippers, and photographers alike. Unfortunately, the island's unique qualities have resulted in elevated prices. Perched atop a steep bluff, **Mahón** (pop. 23,300) is the main gateway to the island. The **tourist office,** is at Sa Rovellada de Dalt, 24. (☎971 36 37 90; fax 971 36 74 15. Open M-F 9am-1:30pm and 5-7pm, Sa 9am-1pm.) To get to **Hostal La Isla,** C. Santa Catalina 4, take C. Concepció from Pl. Miranda. (☎971 36 64 92. Singles 2500ptas/€15; doubles 5000ptas/€30.) To reach the **Hostal Orsi,** C. Infanta, 19, from Pl. s'Esplanada, take C. Ses Moreres, which becomes C. Hannover, turn right at Pl. Constitució, and follow C. Nou through Pl. Reial. (☎971 36 47 51. Breakfast included. Singles 3500ptas/€21; doubles 5800/€35.)

The more popular **beaches** outside Mahón are accessible by bus (30min., 50-250ptas). Transportes Menorca buses (7 per day) leave from C. Josep Quadrado for ▓**Platges de Son Bou,** which offers 4km of gorgeous beaches on the southern shore. Autocares Fornells **buses** (7 per day) leave C. Vasallo in Mahón for sandy **Arenal d'en Castell,** while TMSA buses (6 per day) go to touristy **Calean Porter** and its white-washed houses, orange stucco roofs, and red sidewalks. A 10min. walk away, the ▓ **Covas d'en Xoroi** are caves perched on cliffs high above the sea.

NORTHWESTERN SPAIN

Northwestern Spain is the country's best-kept secret; its seclusion is half its charm. Rainy **Galicia** hides mysterious Celtic ruins, left when the Celts made a pit stop on its quiet beaches along the west coast. Tiny **Asturias** is tucked on the northern coast, allowing access to its dramatic Picos de Europa.

GALICIA (GALIZA)

If, as the Galician saying goes, "rain is art," then there is no gallery more beautiful than the Northwest's misty skies. Often veiled in silvery drizzle, it is a province of fern-laden eucalyptus woods, slate-roofed fishing villages, and endless white beaches. Locals speak *gallego*, a linguistic link between Castilian and Portuguese.

SANTIAGO DE COMPOSTELA   ☎981

Santiago has long drawn pilgrims eager to gaze at one of Christianity's holiest cities. The cathedral marks the end of the *Camino de Santiago*, a pilgrimage believed to halve one's time in purgatory. Today, sunburnt pilgrims, street musicians, and hordes of tourists fill the streets.

█▐ TRANSPORTATION AND PRACTICAL INFORMATION. Trains (☎981 52 02 02) go from C. De Hórreo, in the southern end of the city, to Madrid (8hr.; M-F 1:47 and 10:25pm, Sa 10:30pm, Su 9:52am, 1:47 and 10:30pm; 5900ptas/€35); complete schedule printed daily in *El Correo Gallego*. To reach the city, take bus #6 to Pr. Galicia or walk up the stairs across the parking lot from the main entrance, cross the street, and bear right onto R. do Hórreo, which leads to Pr. Galicia. **Buses** (☎981 58 77 00) run from C. San Cayetano (20min. from downtown) to: Bilbao (11¼hr., 9am and 9:30pm, 6500ptas/€39); Madrid (8-9hr., 4 per day 8am-9:30pm, 5160ptas/€31); and San Sebastián (13½hr., 8am and 4:30pm, 7275ptas/€44). From the station, take bus #10 or bus C Circular to Pr. Galicia (every 15-20min. 6:30am-10pm, 105ptas/€0.65). The **tourist office** is at R. Vilar, 43. (☎981 58 40 81. Open M-F 10am-2pm and 4-7pm, Sa 11am-2pm and 5-7pm, Su 11am-2pm.) Check **email** at **Nova 50**, R. Nova, 50. (200ptas/€1.20 per hr. Open daily 9am-1am.) **Postal code:** 15701.

▐▙ ACCOMMODATIONS AND FOOD. Nearly every street in the old city houses at least one or two *pensiones*. The liveliest and most popular streets, however, are **Rúa Vilar** and **Rúa Raíña**. ◪**Hospedaje Ramos,** C. Raíña, 18, 2nd fl., above O Papa Una restaurant, is in the center of the *ciudad viaje*. (☎58 18 59. Singles 1900ptas/€11.40; doubles 3450ptas/€21.) **Hospedaje Santa Cruz** is at C. Vilar 42, 2nd fl. (☎981 58 28 15. June-Sept. singles 1500ptas/€9; doubles 4000ptas/€24, with bath 5000ptas/€30.) **Hospedaje Sofía**, C. Cardenal Paya, 16, off Pl. Mazarelos, offers spacious, serene rooms. (☎981 58 51 50. Singles 2500-3000ptas/€15-18; doubles 4500-5000ptas/€27-30.) Take bus #6 or 9 to get to **Camping As Cancelas,** C. 25 de Xullo, 35, 2km from the cathedral on the northern edge of town. (☎981 58 02 66. 600ptas/€3.60 per person, 650ptas/€3.90 per car and per tent.) Bars and cafeterias line the old town streets, offering a variety of remarkably inexpensive *menús*; most restaurants are on R. Vilar, R. Franco, R. Nova, and R. Raíña. Santiago's **market,** between Pl. San Felix and Convento de San Augustín, is a sight in its own right. (Open M-Sa 7:30am-2pm.) **Supermercado Lorenzo Froiz,** Pl. Toural, is one block into the old city from Pr. Galicia. (Open M-Sa 9am-3pm and 4:30-9pm, Sa 9am-3pm and 5-9pm.)

◪▐ SIGHTS AND NIGHTLIFE. Offering a cool, quiet sanctuary to priest, pilgrim, and tourist alike, Santiago's **cathedral** rises above the lively old city center. Each of its four façades is a masterpiece from a different era, and entrances open up onto four

THESE BOOTS WERE MADE FOR WALKING

One night in AD 813, a hermit trudged through the hills on the way to his hermitage. Suddenly, bright visions revealed the long-forgotten tomb of the Apostle James ("Santiago" in Spanish). Around this *campus stellae* (field of stars) the cathedral of Santiago de Compostela was built, and around this cathedral a world-famous pilgrimage was born. Since the 9th century, thousands of pilgrims have traveled the 750-870km of the Camino de Santiago. Clever Benedictine monks built monasteries to host *peregrinos* (pilgrims) along the *camino*, helping to make Santiago's cathedral the world's most frequented Christian shrine. Shelters along the way offer free lodging to pilgrims and stamp "pilgrims' passports." At 30km per day, walking the entire *camino* takes about a month. For inspiration along the way, keep in mind that you are joining the ranks of such illustrious pilgrims as Fernando and Isabel, Francis of Assisi, Pope John Paul II, and Shirley MacLaine. For more information, contact the Officinal de Acogida del Peregrino, C. Vilar 1 (☎981 56 24 19).

plazas: Platerías, Quintana, Obradoiro, and Azabaxería. The southern **Praza de Platerías** is the oldest of the façades; the Baroque **Obradoiro** façade encases the Maestro Mateo's **Pórtico de la Gloria,** considered the crowning achievement of Spanish Romanesque sculpture. The remains of **St. James** lie beneath the high altar in a silver coffer. Inside the **museum** are gorgeous 16th-century tapestries and two poignant statues of the pregnant Virgin Mary. (Cathedral open daily 7am-7pm. Museum open June-Sept. M-Sa 10am-1:30pm and 4-7:30pm, Su and holidays 10am-1:30pm; Oct.-Feb. M-Sa 11am-1pm and 4-6pm, Su and holidays 11am-1pm; Mar.-June M-Sa 10:30am-1:30pm and 4-6:30pm, Su 10:30-1:30pm. Museum and cloisters 500ptas/€3.) Those curious about the Camino de Santiago can head to the ■**Museo das Peregrinacións,** Pl. San Miguel. (Open Tu-F 10am-10pm, Sa 10:30am-1:30pm and 5-8pm, Su 10:30am-1:30pm. 400ptas/€2.40, children and seniors 200ptas/€1.20; free during the Apostolo.) At night, crowds looking for post-pilgrimage consumption flood cellars throughout the city. To boogie with local students, hit the bars and clubs off **Praza Roxa** (take C. Montero Ríos). ■**Casa das Crechas,** Vía Sacra 3, just off Pl. Quintana, is a smoky pub with a witchcraft theme. (Open M-F noon-2am, Sa-Su noon-4am.) **cafedelmercado,** R. Cardenal Playa, 3, is Santiago's trendiest night spot. (Open daily 9am-2am.) If you want to dance the night away to Spanish pop, head to **Septimo Cielo,** R. da Rama, 20. Don't arrive too early. (Open daily 8pm-6am.)

▶ DAYTRIP FROM SANTIAGO: O CASTRO DE BAROÑA. Nineteen kilometers south of the town of **Noya** is a little-known treasure of historical intrigue and mesmerizing natural beauty: the seaside remains of the 5th-century Celtic fortress ■**O Castro de Baroña.** Its foundations dot the isthmus, ascending to a rocky promontory above the sea and then descending to a crescent **beach,** where clothing is notoriously optional. Castromil **buses** from Santiago to Muros stop in Noya (1hr.; M-F 15 per day 6:15am-8pm, Sa 10 per day 7am-8pm, Su 8 per day 8am-8:30pm; 420ptas/€2.50) and Hefsel **buses** from Noya to Riveira stop at O Castro—tell the driver your destination (30min.; M-F 14 per day 6:50am-9:30pm, Sa 7 per day 8am-9pm, Su 11 per day 8am-10pm; 210ptas/€1.25).

ASTURIAS

Sky-scraping cliffs and hell-reaching ravines lend an epic scope to the tiny land of Asturias, tucked between the Basque Country and Galicia.

PICOS DE EUROPA

A mere flapping of Mother Nature's limestone bedsheet erected the Picos de Europa, a mountain range of curious variation and chaotic beauty. Most of the area has environmental protection as the **Picos de Europa National Park.** Near the **Cares**

Gorge (Garganta del Cares) lie the most popular trails and peaks. For a list of mountain **refugios** (cabins with bunks but not blankets) and general park info, contact the **Picos de Europa National Park Visitors Center** in Cangas de Onís. (☎ 985 84 86 14. Open daily 10am-2pm and 4-6:30pm.)

CANGAS DE ONÍS. During the summer months Cangas's streets are packed with mountaineers and vacationing families looking to spelunk and hanglide in the Picos de Europa National Park. Cangas itself is, if not particularly thrilling, a relaxing town rich in history. The **tourist office,** Jardines del Ayuntamiento, 2, is just off Av. Covadonga across from the bus stop. (☎ 985 84 80 05. Open daily May-Sept. 10am-10pm; Oct.-Apr. 10am-2pm and 4-7pm.) **ALSA,** Av. Covadonga, 18 (☎ 985 84 81 33), in the Picaro Inmobiliario building across from the tourist office, runs **buses** to Madrid (7hr., 2:35pm, 3920ptas/€23.55) via Valladolid (5hr., 2350ptas/€14.10).

SPAIN

SWEDEN (SVERIGE)

SWEDISH KRONOR

US$1 = 10.20KR	1KR = US$0.10
CDN$1 = 6.65KR	1KR = CDN$0.15
UK£1 = 14.75KR	1KR = UK£0.07
IR£1 = 11.90KR	1KR = IR£0.09
AUS$1 = 5.50KR	1KR = AUS$0.18
NZ$1 = 4.50KR	1KR = NZ$0.22
ZAR1 = 1.25KR	1KR = ZAR0.81
EUR€1 = 9.40KR	1KR = EUR€0.12

PHONE CODE	**Country code:** 46. **International dialing prefix:** 009. From outside Sweden, dial int'l dialing prefix (see inside back cover) + city code + local number.

The Swedish concept of *lagom* (moderation) implies that life should be lived somewhere between wealth and poverty, ecstasy and depression. Yet Sweden defies the *lagom* stereotype with definite extremes, stretching from the mountainous Arctic reaches of northern Kiruna to the flat farmland and white sand beaches of Skåne and Småland in the south. Dalarna, Värmland, and Norrland evoke images of quiet woods, folk music, and rustic country Midsummer celebrations, while the capital city of Stockholm shines as a thoroughly cosmopolitan center. Sweden's mythic early history of violent Viking conflict and conquest has given way to a successful experiment with egalitarian socialism and a role as an international peacekeeper.

FACTS AND FIGURES

Official Name: Kingdom of Sweden.

Capital: Stockholm.

Major Cities: Gothenburg, Malmö, Uppsala.

Population: 8,900,000.

Land Area: 410,930 sq. km.

Climate: Cold winter, cool summers.

Language: Swedish.

Religions: Lutheran (87%), Roman Catholic (1.5%).

DISCOVER SWEDEN

The natural starting point for any tour of Sweden is vibrant **Stockholm** (p. 898), arguably one of the most attractive capitals in Europe. Daytrip to the similarly awe-inspiring **Drottningholm Palace** (p. 905), home to the Swedish royal family, and the university town of **Uppsala** (p. 906). If you want to go north, consider a student flight or a night train to **Kiruna** (p. 913), where you can explore Sami culture, underground mines, and vast stretches of true Arctic wilderness. On the western coast, Sweden's second-largest city, **Gothenburg** (p. 909), counterbalances Stockholm's frenetic atmosphere with a laid-back attitude and elegant cafe culture. Off the eastern coast in the Baltic Sea, the island of **Gotland** (p. 907), rife with medieval churches, white-sand beaches, and prehistoric sites, invites travelers to bike, camp, and enjoy many of its attractions for free.

ESSENTIALS

WHEN TO GO

The best time to visit Sweden is in the summer, when daytime temperatures average 20°C (68°F) in the south and 16°C (61°F) in the north; nights can get chilly. Bring an umbrella for frequent light rains. If you go in winter, bring heavy cold-weather gear; temperatures are frequently below -5°C (23°F). The midnight sun is best seen early June to mid-July.

Sweden

DOCUMENTS AND FORMALITIES

VISAS. South Africans need a visa for stays of any length. Citizens of Australia, Canada, Ireland, New Zealand, the UK, and the US can visit for up to 90 days without one, but this three-month period begins upon entry into any Scandinavian country; for more than 90 days in any combination of Finland, Iceland, Norway, and/or Sweden, you will need a visa.

EMBASSIES. Foreign embassies in Sweden are in Stockholm (p. 778). For Swedish embassies at home: **Australia,** 5 Turrana St., Yarralumla, Canberra, ACT 2600 (☎(62) 73 30 33; fax 73 32 98); **Canada,** 377 Dalhousie St., Ottawa ON K1N 9N8 (☎613-241-8553; fax 613-241-2277); **South Africa,** P.O. Box 3982, Cape Town 8000 (☎(021) 25 39 88; fax 25 10 16); **UK,** 11 Montagu Pl., London W1H 2AL (☎(020) 79 17 64 00; fax 79 17 64 75); and **US,** 1501 M St. NW, Washington, D.C. 20005 (☎202-467-2600; fax 202-467-2656).

TRANSPORTATION

BY PLANE. Most international flights land in Stockholm, although domestic flights also connect to northern Sweden. **Transwede** (☎ (020) 22 52 25) and **SAS**, in Australia (☎ (02) 92 99 98 00); South Africa (☎ (021) 419 86 86 or ☎ (011) 884 56 00); Sweden (☎ (020) 72 77 27); UK (☎ (0845) 60 72 77 27); US (☎ 800-221-2350); www.scandinavian.net/travel/start/se/index.asp), offer youth fares on flights within Scandinavia. SAS also offers domestic and international "Air Passes".

BY TRAIN. Statens Järnvägar (SJ), the state railway company, runs reliable and frequent trains throughout the southern half of Sweden. Seat reservations (15-40kr) are required on some trains (indicated by a R, IN, or IC on the schedule), and are recommended on all other routes. Reservations are also mandatory on the new high-speed **X2000** trains (to Stockholm, Gothenburg, Malmö, and Mora); they are included in the normal ticket price, but not for railpass holders (reservations ☎ (020) 75 75 75; toll-free in Sweden). In southern Skåne, private **pågatågen** trains service Helsingborg, Lund, Malmö, and Ystad; **InterRail** and **Scanrail** passes are valid. Northern Sweden is served by two main rail routes: the coastal **Malmbanan** runs north from Stockholm through Boden, Umeå, and Kiruna to Narvik, Norway; from Midsummer (June 21-23, 2002) to early August, the privately run **Inlandsbanan** also travels farther inland from Mora to Gällivare. **Eurailpass** is valid in Sweden. The *buy-in-Scandinavia* **Scanrail Pass** allows five days within 15 (1575kr, under 26 1190kr) or 21 consecutive days (2510kr, 1815kr) of unlimited rail travel through Scandinavia, and free or discounted ferry rides. This differs from the *buy-outside-Scandinavia* **Scanrail Pass** (p. 68). A rail link over the new **Øresund bridge** connects Copenhagen, Denmark to Malmö in a breezy 35 minutes, certainly the fastest way to enter Sweden from Continental Europe.

BY BUS. In the north, buses may be a better option than trains. **Swebus** (☎ (08) 655 90 00) is the main company, offering service all over Sweden, Norway, and Denmark. **Swebus Express** (☎ (020) 64 06 40; toll-free in Sweden) serves southern Sweden only. **Bus Stop** (☎ (08) 440 85 70) reserves tickets for buses from Stockholm. Bus tickets are treated as an extension of the rail network, and can be bought from state railways. You can also buy tickets on the bus. Express buses offer discounts for children, seniors, students, and youth. Bicycles are not allowed on buses.

BY FERRY. If you don't want to take the new Øresund bridge, you can ferry from Copenhagen to Malmö (p. 908). Ystad (p. 909) sends boats to Bornholm and Poland. Ferries from Gothenburg (p. 909) serve Frederikshavn, Denmark; Kiel, Germany; and Newcastle and Harwich, England. From Stockholm (p. 898), ferries run to the Åland Islands, Gotland, Turku, and Helsinki. North of Stockholm, **Silja Line ferries** (☎ (090) 71 44 00) connect Umeå and Vaasa, Finland.

BY CAR. Swedish roads are good, and remarkably uncrowded. Unleaded gas costs an average of US$1 per liter. When gas stations are closed, look for pumps marked "*sedel automat*," which operate after hours. To get on the *strak* (highway), look for the *entre* (entrance); getting off, look for an *aufart* (exit), and then for *parkering* (parking). Renting a car within Sweden averages US$30-50 per day, including VAT. Special discounts abound, particularly if you opt for a fly/drive package or if you rent for an extended period.

BY BIKE. Sweden is a biker's heaven; paths cover most of the country, particularly in the south, and you can complete a trip of Sweden on the hostel-spotted **Sverigeleden bike route.** Contact STF (see below) for information.

TOURIST SERVICES AND MONEY

TOURIST OFFICES. Towns and nearly every village has a tourist office. For more information before arriving in Sweden, contact the **Swedish Tourist Board: UK,** 11 Montagu Pl., London W1H 2AL (☎ (020) 77 24 58 68; fax 77 24 58 72); **US,** 655 Third Ave., New York, NY 10017 (☎ 212-885-9700; fax 212-885-9710; www.gosweden.org).

MONEY. The unit of Swedish currency is the krona, divided into 100 *öre*. Bills come in denominations of 20, 50, 100, and 500kr; coins come in 1 and 5kr, and 10 and 50 *öre*. Many post offices are also banks. Tipping is not common, as gratuities are usually added to the bill; however, tipping a few coins is appropriate at restaurants in cities. Add 10% for taxis. The VAT in Sweden is a shocking 25%. Luckily, for purchases of more than $13 in a single store during a single visit, you can receive a VAT refund of 20%.

BUSINESS HOURS. Banks are usually open Monday to Friday 9:30am-3pm (6pm in some large cities). Stores stay open Monday to Friday 10am-6pm, Saturday 10am-1pm. Museums open Tuesday to Sunday, anywhere from 10am-noon, and close 4-6pm. Some are open until 9pm on Tuesday or Wednesday.

COMMUNICATION

EMERGENCY	Police, Ambulance, and Fire: ☎ 112.

MAIL. Mailing a postcard or letter from Sweden to Australia, Canada, New Zealand, the US, and South Africa costs 8kr.

TELEPHONES. Most payphones only accept phone cards *(Telefonkort)*; buy them at newsstands and post offices in 30, 60, or 120 units (35kr, 60kr, and 100kr). International direct dial numbers include: **AT&T,** ☎ 020 79 56 11; **British Telecom,** ☎ 020 79 91 44; **Canada Direct,** ☎ 020 79 90 15; **Ireland Direct,** ☎ 020 79 93 53; **MCI,** ☎ 020 79 59 22; **Sprint,** ☎ 020 79 90 11; **Telecom New Zealand,** ☎ 020 79 84 31; **Telkom South Africa,** ☎ 020 79 90 27; and **Telstra Australia,** ☎ 020 79 90 61.

LANGUAGE. Swedish. Almost all Swedes speak some English; most under 50 are fluent. Impress that special Swedish someone with a few phrases from p. 989.

ACCOMMODATIONS AND CAMPING

Youth hostels *(vandrarhem)* in Sweden cost about 112-200kr per night. The 300 HI-affiliated hostels run by the **Svenska Turistföreningen (STF)** are invariably top-notch (nonmembers pay 40kr extra per night). Most hostels have kitchens, laundry, and common areas. To reserve ahead, call the hostel directly or contact the STF headquarters in Stockholm (☎ (08) 463 22 70); all sell **Hostelling International (HI)** membership cards (250kr) or offer guest cards. Tourist offices often book beds in hostels for no fee, and can help find **private rooms** (200-350kr). **Private hotels** are very good as well. More economical hotels are beginning to offer reduced-service rooms at prices competitive with hostels, especially for groups of three or more. STF also manages **mountain huts** in the northern wilds with 10-80 beds that cost 155-195kr in high season (nonmembers 195-245kr). Huts are popular; plan ahead. Many **campgrounds** (80-110kr per site) also offer *stugor* (cottages) for around 85-175kr per person. **International Camping Cards** are not valid in Sweden; **Swedish Camping Cards** are virtually mandatory. Year-long memberships (60kr per family) are available through **Sveriges Campingvärdars Riksförbund (SCR),** Box 255, 451 17 Uddevalla (ck@camping.se), or at any SCR campground. You may camp for free for one or two nights anywhere as long as you respect the flora, fauna, and the owner's privacy, and pick up all garbage. Pick up the *Right (and Wrongs) of Public Access in Sweden* brochure from STF or from tourist offices, or call the **Swedish Environmental Protection Agency** (☎ (08) 698 10 00).

FOOD AND DRINK

Food is very expensive in restaurants and not much cheaper in grocery stores. Rely on supermarkets and outdoor fruit and vegetable markets. Ubiquitous stands provide the most kebabs for your *krona* (45-65kr for meat, rice, and veggies). Potatoes are the national staple; these and other dishes are invariably smothered with dill. Try tasty dairy products like *messmör* (spreadable cheese) and *filmjölk*, a fluid

MIDSUMMER MADNESS For Midsummer (June 21-23, 2002), Swedes celebrate the sun after a long, dark winter. Villagers dance around the Midsommarstång, a cross-shaped pole with two rings dangling from the ends always erected on the Friday of the festival. Its phallic construction symbolizes the fertilization of the soil it is staked in; going along with the fertilization theme, girls sometimes place flowers under their pillows to induce dreams of their future spouses. The largest celebrations are in Dalarna, where alcohol and pickled herring flow freely and people flood the city. Note that during Midsummer most transportation lines run on holiday schedules and most establishments are closed.

yogurt. When you tire of groceries, seek out restaurants offering an affordable *dagens rätt* (55-70kr), a daily lunch special including an entree, salad, bread, and drink. A real beer *(starköl)* costs 10-15kr in stores and 30-50kr per pint in city pubs. The cheaper, weaker *lättöl* (alcohol up to 3.5%) can be purchased at supermarkets and convenience stores for 8-12kr per 0.5L; you must be 20 to buy alcohol. Although the drinking age is 18, bars and many nightclubs have age restrictions as high as 25.

HOLIDAYS AND FESTIVALS

Holidays: New Year's Day (Jan. 1); Epiphany (Jan. 5-6); Easter Sunday and Monday (Apr. 23-24); Valborg's Eve (Apr. 30); May Day (May 1); Ascension Day (June 2); National Day (June 6); Whit Sunday and Monday (June 11-12); Midsummer's Eve and Midsummer (June 21-23); All Saints' Eve and Day (Nov. 2-3); Christmas Eve and Day (Dec. 24-25); Boxing Day (Dec. 26); New Year's Eve (Dec. 31).

Festivals: Midsummer (June 21-23) incites family frolicking and bacchanalian dancing around Midsummer poles. July and Aug. bring two special festivals, the *surströmming* (rotten herring) and crayfish parties.

STOCKHOLM ☎08

Stockholm may be the best-kept secret in Europe. Neutrality in the past century's wars has preserved Stockholm's history in the cobblestoned Old Town and in the elegant North Island. But the city pushes ahead on the cutting edge of Internet technology, interior and industrial design, architecture, and pop music. Stockholm's cosmopolitan streets teem with world-class museums, chic nightspots, and friendly locals who make any stay a pleasant experience.

▐▘ TRANSPORTATION

Flights: Arlanda Airport (☎797 60 00), 45km north of the city. **Flygbussar** shuttles (☎686 37 87) run between the airport and the bus station (40min., every 10min. 4am-10pm, 70kr; public transport passes not valid). **Bus #583** runs from the airport to "J" railway stop Märsta (10min., 35kr or 5 coupons; SL pass valid); Centralen is 40min. farther by train (140kr). Without a Stockholm card or SL pass, buses are better deals.

Trains: Centralstation (info and reservations ☎(020) 75 75 75). T-bana: T-Centralen. To: **Oslo** (6hr.; 2 per day; 505kr, under 25 353kr); **Copenhagen** (7-8hr.; 5-6 per day; 527kr, 371kr); **Berlin** (18hr.; 2 per day; 1100kr, 900kr). See p. 896 for info on **reservations. Lockers** 15-35kr per 24hr. **Showers** 25kr.

Buses: Cityterminalen, above Centralstation. **Terminal Service** (☎762 59 97) to the airport (70kr) and to Gotland ferries (65kr). **Bus Stop** (☎440 85 70) handles longer routes. To: **Copenhagen** (10hr., 1 per day, 390kr); **Gothenburg** (7hr.; 7 per day; 220-315kr, under 25 175-250kr); **Malmö** (10hr., 2 per day, 280-395kr, 225-315kr).

Ferries: Most ferries discounted 50% with Scanrail and free with Eurail. **Silja Line,** Kungsg. 2 (☎22 21 40), sails overnight to Finland: **Helsinki** (16hr., 1 per day, 585kr; book ahead); **Mariehamn** (5hr., 1 per day, 99kr); **Turku (Åbo)** (10-11hr., 2 per day, 275-385kr). To get to the terminal, take T-bana to Gärdet and follow "Värtahamnen" signs, or take the Silja bus (20kr) from Cityterminalen. **Viking Line** sails to: **Helsinki**

(15hr., 1 per day, 321kr); **Mariehamn** (5½hr., 1 per day, return 99kr); and **Turku (Åbo)** (12hr.; 2 per day; 222-321kr, with Scanrail 111kr). Viking Line terminal is at Stadsgården on Södermalm. T-bana: Slussen. **Destination Gotland** (☎20 10 20) sails to **Visby, Gotland** from Nynäshamn, 1hr. south of the city (p. 907).

Public Transportation: SL office (☎600 10 00), Sergels Torg. T-bana: T-Centralen. Open M-F 7am-9pm, Sa-Su 8am-9pm. **Walk-in office** in Centralstation basement open M-Sa 6:30am-11:15pm, Su 7am-11:15pm. Most destinations cost 2 coupons (14kr, 1hr. unlimited bus/subway transfer). **Rabattkuponger** (110kr), books of 20 coupons, are at Pressbyrån news agents. The **SL Turistkort** (Tourist Card) is valid on buses, subways, commuter trains, trams, and ferries to Djurgården (24hr. 70kr; 72hr. 135kr). The **Stockholm Card** is valid. **Tunnelbana** (subway) runs 5am-12:30am. From 12:30-5:30am, it's replaced by night buses. Check schedules at bus stops.

Taxis: High fares. Many cabs have fixed prices; try to agree on a price beforehand. 435kr from airport to Centralstation. **Taxi Stockholm** (☎15 00 00); **Taxicard** (☎97 00 00).

Bike Rental: Skepp & Hoj (☎660 57 57), on Djurgårdsbron. Bikes and rollerblades 150kr per day, 500kr per week. Open daily 9am-9pm.

Hitchhiking: Waiting on highways is illegal in Sweden, and hitching is uncommon among travelers. Hitchers going south take the T-bana to the gas station on Kungens Kurva in Skärholmen; those going north take bus #52 to Sveaplan and stand on Sveav. at Nortull. *Let's Go* does not recommend hitchhiking.

ORIENTATION

The compact city spans seven small islands (linked by bridges and the T-bana) at the junction of **Lake Mälaren** to the west and the **Baltic Sea** to the east. The northern island is divided into two sections: **Norrmalm,** home to Centralstation and the shopping district on Drottningg., and **Östermalm,** which boasts the elegant waterfront **Strandvägen** and much of the nightlife fanning out from **Stureplan Square.** The mainly residential western island, **Kungsholmen,** has the Stadshuset (City Hall) and grassy beaches. The southern island of **Södermalm,** formerly a slum, is known as Stockholm's SoHo and hosts cafes, artists, and an extensive gay scene. Södermalm's little sister, **Långholmen,** is a nature preserve, while **Djurgården** holds the Nordiska and Vasa Museums. At the center of these five islands is **Gamla Stan** (Old Town) island. Gamla Stan's neighbor **Skeppsholmen** (via Norrmalm) harbors mostly museums. The city's streets are easy to navigate for even the hapless tourist: each one begins with the number one at the end closest to the city palace (in Gamla Stan)—the lower the numbers, the closer you are to Gamla Stan.

PRACTICAL INFORMATION

Tourist Offices: Sweden House, Hamng. 27 (☎789 24 90; fax 789 24 91; info@stoinfo.se; www.stoinfo.se), in the northeast corner of Kungsträdgården. From Centralstation, walk up Klarabergsg. to Sergels Torg (the plaza with the 50ft. glass tower) and bear right on Hamng. A vital resource for travelers staffed by friendly, multilingual agents. Sells the **Stockholm Card** and the **Touristcard.** Arranges and sells tickets for excursions, theater, opera, and concerts. Open June-Aug. M-F 8am-7pm, Sa-Su 9am-5pm; Sept.-May M-F 9am-6pm, Sa-Su 10am-3pm. The **Hotel Centralen,** at the train station (☎789 24 25; fax 791 86 66; hotels@stoinfo.se), books rooms (20-50kr). Color map 15kr. Open daily June-Aug. 8am-8pm; Sept.-May 9am-6pm.

Embassies: Australia, Sergels Torg 12, 11th fl. (☎613 29 00; emergency 020 79 84 80; fax 24 74 14). **Canada,** Tegelbacken 4 (☎453 30 00; fax 24 24 91). **Ireland,** Ostermalmsg. 97 (☎661 80 05; fax 660 13 53). **South Africa,** Linnég. 76 (☎24 39 50; emergency 07 08 56 75 35; fax 660 71 36). **UK,** Skarpög. 6-8 (☎671 90 00; emergency 07 04 28 49 97; fax 662 99 89). **US,** Strandvagen 101 (☎783 53 00; fax 661 19 64).

Currency Exchange: Forex in Centralstation (☎411 67 34; open daily 7am-9pm), in Cityterminalen (☎21 42 80; open M-F 7am-10pm, Sa 8am-5pm), and at Sweden House

SWEDEN

(☎20 03 89; open M-F 8am-7pm, Sa-Su 9am-5pm). 15kr commission per traveler's check, 20kr for cash.

American Express: Norrlandsg. 21 (☎411 05 40). T-bana: Östermalmstorg. No fee to cash AmEx traveler's checks, 20kr for cash. Open M-F 9am-5pm, Sa 9am-1pm.

Gay and Lesbian Services: RFSL (Swedish Federation for Sexual Equality), Sveav. 57 (☎736 02 13; www.rfsl.se). T-bana: Rådmansg. Distributes *Queer Xtra (QX)*, with bar, club, and events listings. Open M-Th noon-8pm, F noon-6pm, Sa-Su 1-4pm. **Sweden House** distributes *QX* as well as the **QueerMap**, which maps Stockholm's gay hotspots.

Emergency: Ambulance, fire, and **police:** ☎112.

Pharmacy: Look for the green and white "Apotek" signs. **Apotek C. W. Scheele,** Klarabergsg. 64, at the overpass over Vasag. T-bana: T-Centralen. Open 24hr.

Medical Assistance: ☎32 01 00.

Internet Access: ICE, Stora Nyg. 31, 2 blocks opposite the water from T-bana: Gamla Stan. 60kr per hr.; inquire about low membership fees. Open Su-Th 10am-midnight, F-Sa 11am-3am. **Stadsbibliotek,** Odeng. 59, in the annex. T-bana: Odenplan. 10min. free. Open M-Th 11am-7pm.

Telephones: Buy phone cards at **Pressbyrån** stores for 30 (35kr), 60 (60kr), or 120 (100kr) units. **National directory assistance:** ☎079 75. 15kr per min.

Post Office: Drottningg. 53 (☎781 46 82). Open M-F 8am-7pm, Sa 10am-3pm. Address mail to be held: First name SURNAME, *Poste Restante,* Drottningg. 53, **10110** Stockholm 1, Sweden. Also in Centralstation (☎020 232 21). Open daily 10am-7pm.

▌ ACCOMMODATIONS AND CAMPING

Summer demands reservations, and many HI hostels limit stays to five nights. If you haven't booked ahead, arrive around 7am. Stockholm's several **boat-hostels (botels)** are a novel solution to space issues, but they can be cramped and noisy—request a room on the water side of the boat. Note that many independent (non-HI) hostels are hotel/hostels; specify if you want to stay in a dorm-style hostel, or risk paying hotel rates. **Campers** should bring insect repellent to ward off the infamous Swedish mosquitoes. If you don't have a (mandatory) **Swedish Camping Card,** either site below will sell you one for 49kr. Using an SL bus pass (or Stockholm Card) is the cheapest way to get to the more remote campsites.

▨ **City Backpackers' Vandrarhem,** Upplandsg. 2A (☎20 69 20; www.svif.se). From Centralstation, go left on Vasag. and bear right on Upplandsg. (10min.). Airy hostel close to the station with great amenities. Kitchen. Breakfast buffet 40kr. Laundry 30kr. Reception June-Sept. 7:30am-noon and 1:30-7pm; Oct.-May 8:30am-noon and 2-7pm. Dorms 160-190kr; doubles 470kr.

Hostel af Chapman/Skeppsholmens Vandrarhem (HI/STF) (☎463 22 66; www.stfchapman.com; info@chapman.stfturist.se), on Skeppsholmen. From T-Centralen, take bus #65 to the base of the parking lot or walk 20min. along the waterfront over the Skeppsh. Olmsbron bridge. A modern on-shore hostel and a 19th-century sailing ship with a great view of the Old Town. Some non-reservable beds available daily at 7:15am. Kitchen. Breakfast 55kr. Laundry 35kr. Reception 24hr. Lockout 11am-3pm. Boat curfew 3am. Dorms 115-160kr; doubles 300kr. Nonmembers add 40kr.

Långholmens Vandrarhem (HI), Langhoms Muren 20 (☎668 05 10; vandrarhem@langholmen.com), on Långholmen. T-bana: Hornstull. Walk north on Långholmsg., turn left onto Högalidsg., hang a right on Långholmsbron over the bridge, turn left and follow the peach gate to the end; reception on the right. Clean converted prison cells in a quiet lakeside hostel and hotel. Kitchen, cafe/pub, and laundry. Breakfast 65kr. Sheets 40kr. Reception 24hr. Check-out 10am. Hostel rooms 165-190kr; nonmembers add 45kr.

Hostel MITT/CITY, Västmannag. 13 (☎21 76 30; stores@hostal.com). T: Centralen; then turn left up Vasag. and bear left on Vastmannag. for 2 blocks to reach the neat hostel. Breakfast included. Sheets 50kr. Reception 24hr on 5th fl. Dorms 175kr; doubles 285kr; quads 225kr.

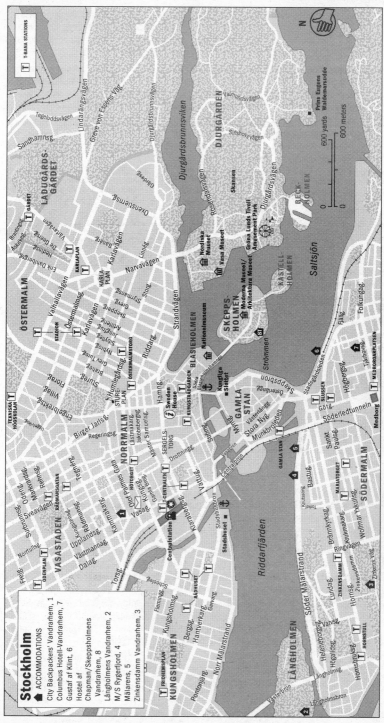

Stockholm

⚑ ACCOMMODATIONS

City Backpackers' Vandrarhem, 1
Columbus Hotell-Vandrarhem, 7
Gustaf af Klint, 6
Hostel af
Chapman/Skeppsholmens
Vandrarhem, 8
Långholmens Vandrarhem, 2
M/S Rygerfjord, 4
Mälarens, 5
Zinkensdamm Vandrarhem, 3

T T-BANA STATIONS

SWEDEN

Columbus Hotell-Vandrarhem, Tjärhovsg. 11 (☎644 17 17; columbus@columbus.se), in Södermalm. T-bana: Medborgarplatsen. Walk 3 blocks down Tjarhovsg. and it's on the left. This former brewery, prison, and plague hospital is clean and spacious. Kitchen and bar. Breakfast 55kr. Reception 24hr. Dorms 500-990kr.

Mälarens, Södermälarstrand, Kajplats 6 (☎644 43 85; www.rodabatan.nu). T-bana: Gamla Stan. Cross Central bridge, and walk 100m along the shore down Södermälar-strand. Small rooms with red velvet. Breakfast 55kr. Reception in cafe 8-11pm. Check-out 9am. Dorms 185kr; singles 400kr; doubles 225kr; quads 215kr.

Zinkensdamm Vandrarhem (HI), Zinkens Väg 20 (☎616 81 00; info@zinkens-damm.swedenhotels.se), in Södermalm. T-bana: Zinkensdamm. Head south on Ringv. 3 blocks, then turn right and head down Zinkens Väg. Kitchen, TV, laundry, and bike rental. Reception 24hr. 145kr, nonmembers 190kr.

M/S Rygerfjord, Södermälarstrand Kajplats 12 (☎84 08 30; www.rygerfjord.se). T-bana: Mariatorget. Exit toward Mariatorget, follow Torkel Knutssonsg. down to the water, and look for the botel's sign. Breakfast 55kr. Reception 24hr. Check-out 11am. Dorms 185kr; quads 195kr.

Gustaf af Klint, Stadsgårdsleden 153 (☎640 40 77; www.gustafafklint.com), in Söder-malm. T-bana: Slussen. From the lower exit, turn right on Stadsgårdsleden and walk 200m. A former Navy ship with small rooms. Breakfast 45kr. Laundry. Reception 24hr. in summer. Dorms 120kr; cabins 150kr; doubles 170kr.

Ängby Camping, Blackebergsv. 24 (☎37 04 20; reservation@angbycamping.se), on Lake Mälaren. T-bana: Ängbyplan. Go downstairs, turn left on Färjestadsvägen, bear left at the fork, and it's at the bottom of the road. Reception in summer 7am-11pm; off sea-son 8am-10pm. 115kr per family with tent, 300-674kr per family in cabin.

◖ FOOD

Your best budget bet is to gorge on all-you-can-eat breakfasts offered by most hos-tels, then track down lunch specials (*dagens rätt,* 45-80kr, usually 11:30am-3pm). Cafes line **Götgatan,** in Södermalm (T-bana: Slussen or Medborgarplatsen), and many cheap eateries are on **Odengatan** (T-bana: Odengatan or Tekniska Hogskolan). Groceries are easy to find around any T-bana station. You can also try **Hempköp City,** on Sergels Torg (walk left out of the train station and turn right on Klarabergsg.; open M-F 8am-9pm, Sa-Su 10am-9pm); **Wasahalla,** Upplandsg. 28 (T-bana: Cen-tralen, then turn left on Vasag. and bear right on Upplandsg.; open daily 9am-8pm); or the **open-air fruit market,** at Hötorget Sq. (M-Sa 7am-6pm).

Café Birger, Birger Jarlsg. 11. T-bana: Östermalmstorg. Walk down Birger Jarlsg. toward the water. The only thing that beats the king-sized sandwiches is the people-watching on chic Birger Jarlsg. Sandwiches 30-50kr. Open Su-Th 8am-11pm, F-Sa usually 24hr.

Old Town Cafe, Vastalangg. 34. T-bana: Gamla Stan. Walsk 3 blocks away from the water. Relaxed cafe on top of Stockholm's oldest city wall. Lunch special 55kr. Open daily 10am-6pm.

Sandy's, Kungsg. 57 and Klarabergsg. 31. Coffee, fresh-squeezed OJ, yogurt, fruit, and sandwiches (39-44kr). Open M-F 7:30am-7pm, Sa 11am-5pm.

Herman's, Fjällg. 23A, in Södermalm. T-bana: Slussen. Take the steps or the lift up to Katarinavägen, walk away from Gamla Stan (8min.), and bear left on Fjällg. Vegetarian buffet and one of Stockholm's best views. Lunch 65kr; dinner 95kr. Open in summer daily 11am-11pm; in winter M-F 11am-9pm, Sa-Su noon-10pm.

Pauli's Café, Dramaten 2 trappen, 2nd fl., in Nybroplan. T-bana: Östermalmstorg. Walk down Birger Jarlsg. toward the water. Upstairs in the National Theater, with views of trendy Birger Jarlsg. and the sea. Seafood salad 85kr. Open daily 11:30am-midnight.

👁 SIGHTS

Stockholm's long history and rich cultural tradition even trickles down to the subway—the decorated stops are called the longest art exhibit in the world. The **Stockholmskortet** (Stockholm Card; 24hr. 220kr; 48hr. 380kr; 72hr. 540kr), available at tourist offices in Sweden House and Central Station, covers most museums and allows unlimited transportation on the subways and buses.

KUNGSHOLMEN AND STADSHUSET (CITY HALL). On the tip of Kungsholmen closest to Gamla Stan towers the regal **Stadshuset.** Jutting 106m into the skyline, the **Stadshustornet** (city hall tower) offers a stunning aerial view of downtown. The interior contains municipal chambers in the shape of Viking Ships; the **Blå Hallen** (Blue Hall, although it is *not* blue), where the Nobel Prize dinner is held; and the mosaic-tiled **Gyllene Hallen** (Gold Hall), where Nobels, nobles, and other notables dance the rest of the night away. *(Hantverkarg. 1. T-bana: Rådhuset. Walk east on Hantverkarg. Compulsory tours daily June-Aug. 10, 11am, noon, 2, 3pm; Sept.-May 10am, noon. 40kr. Tower open daily May-Sept. 10am-4:30pm. 15kr.)*

GAMLA STAN (OLD TOWN). Across the water from Stadshuset and at the center of Stockholm's islands is the city's medieval core. The main pedestrian street, **Västerlånggatan,** is packed with cafes, shops, and cheesy tourist paraphernalia. *(T-bana: Gamla Stan. Or take bus #46 or 55.)* On nearby **Stora Nygatan** and **Österlånggatan,** the commercial onslaught is a little less severe, and quiets down at night. *(Tours of the Old Town depart June-Aug. daily 11:30am and 2:30pm. Meet at the Royal Opera House. 85kr.)* At the top of Gamla Stan's winding streets is the **Stortorget** (town square), where the annual **Julmarknad** (Christmas Fair) serves hot *glögg* (spiced wine) and sells handicrafts. Behind the square is the impressive **Storkyrkan** (Royal Chapel), site of royal weddings and the dramatic medieval sculpture of Stockholm's patron Saint Göran (George) slaying the dragon. *(Open daily May-Aug. 9am-6pm; Sept.-Apr. 9am-4pm. 15kr.)* The jewel of Gamla Stan is the stunning **Kungliga Slottet** (Royal Palace), winter home of the Swedish royal family and site of the daily Changing of the Guard. The **State Apartments** are the most worthwhile attraction, although you can also swing by the **Skattkammaren** (Royal Treasury) to drool over royal regalia and the crown jewels or visit the **armory** and **Gustav III's Antikmuseum** (Museum of Antiquities). *(www.royalcourt.se. All 4 open May-Aug. daily 10am-4pm; Sept.-Apr. Tu-Su noon-3pm. State apartments 60kr; treasury 60kr; armory 65kr; Museum of Antiquities 60kr; ticket for all 4 100kr, students 70kr. English-language tours included. Changing of the Guard (30 min.) in summer M-Sa noon, Su 1pm; rest of year W and Sa at noon and Su 1pm.)*

SKEPPSHOLMEN AND BLASIEHOLMEN. On Skeppsholmen, the island east of Gamla Stan, the **Moderna Museet** (Modern Museum) and **Arkitektur Museet** (Architecture Museum) are housed in adjacent buildings recently designed by Rafael Moneo. The unappealing exterior belies the fine collection of art inside, which includes Dalis and Picassos. *(T-bana: Kungsträdgården. Walk toward the water on Södra Blasieholmshamner, cross the bridge to Skeppsholmen, and follow the signs. Both open Tu-Th 11am-10pm, F-Sa 11am-6pm. Moderna Museet 75kr, students 50kr; Arkitekturmuseet 60kr, 30kr; joint ticket 95kr, 75kr.)* On Södra Blasieholmshamnen before the bridge to Skeppsholmen, the **National Museet** (National Museum) has works by Rembrandt, Renoir, and Rodin, but also honors national artists such as Carl Larsson, Anders Zorn, and Eugen Jansson. *(www.nationalmuseum.se. T-bana: Kungsträdgården. Walking toward the water, the museum is on the left before Skeppsh Olmsbron bridge. Open Tu and Th 11am-8pm, W and F-Su 11am-5pm; in summer closes Th 5pm. 75kr, under 16 free, W reduced fee.)*

DJURGÅRDEN. The extraordinary 🔲**Vasa Museet** houses a mammoth wooden warship that sank on her maiden voyage in 1628, before even leaving the harbor; it was discovered, raised, and salvaged in the 60s and 70s. *(Galärvarvsv. 14. Take bus #44, 47, or 69. Open June 10-Aug. 20 daily 9:30am-7pm; Aug. 21-June 9 M-Tu and Th-Su 10am-5pm, W 10am-8pm. 70kr.)* Next door, the **Nordiska Museet** (Nordic Museum) presents an innovative exhibit on Swedish history and culture from the Viking age to the modern era of Volvo, ABBA, and Electrolux. *(Djurgårdsvägen 6-16. Bus #44 or 47. Open daily 10am-9pm. 70kr.)* On the far side of the island, **Prins Eugens Waldemarsudde,** home of the full-time prince and part-time painter, contains his major works and personal collection. The seaside grounds also boast a spectacular sculpture garden. *(Prins Eugen Väg 6. Bus #47. Open Tu-Su May-Aug. 11am-5pm, Sept.-Apr. 11am-4pm. 60kr.)* A national park in the heart of the city occupies most of Djurgården. ■**Skansen,** Stockholm's most popular attraction, is an open-air museum featuring 150 historical buildings, handicrafts, and a zoo. The homes—extracted from different periods of Swedish history—are inhabited by costumed actors. *(Bus #44 or 47 from Drottningg. and Klarabergsg. in Sergels Torg, opposite T-Centralen. Park and zoo open daily May 10am-8pm; June-Aug. 10am-10pm; Sept.-Apr. 10am-4pm. Historical buildings open daily May-Aug. 11am-5pm; Sept.-Apr. 11am-3pm. 60kr, 30kr in winter.)*

🎵 ENTERTAINMENT

The six stages of the national theater, **Dramaten,** Nybroplan (☎667 06 80), feature Swedish- and English-language performances of August Strindberg and other playwrights (120-260kr). The **Operan** (☎24 82 40) offers opera and ballet (135-450kr). Student, obstructed view, and rush tickets (1hr. before show) are often available for 35-50% less. The **Konserthuset** at Hötorget (☎10 21 10) features classical music by the Stockholm Philharmonic; concerts are also held at the **Globen** arena (☎600 34 00; 50-300kr). Pop music venues include **Skansen** (☎57 89 00 05) and the stage at **Gröna Lund** (☎670 76 00), Djurgården's huge outdoor Tivoli amusement park. (Open late Apr. to early Sept. M-Th noon-11pm, F-Sa noon-midnight, Su noon-9pm. Tickets 150-495kr.) Check theater and concert listings in *Stockholm this Week,* and visit Sweden House or call BiljettDirekt (☎077 170 70 70) for tickets to events and performances. In summer, **Kungsträdgården** (a large park bordered by Kungsträdgårdsg. and Vastra Trädgårdsg.) hosts several free outdoor concerts. For events information, check out *What's On,* available at the tourist office.

Stockholm's festivals include the world-class **Jazz and Blues Festival** in July at Skansen (☎747 92 36; www.stockholmjazz.com); **Strindberg Festival** (late Aug. or early Sept.; ☎34 14 01; www.strindberg.stockholm.se/festivalen); and **Stockholm Pride** (late July or early Aug.; ☎33 59 55; www.stockholmpride.org).

🔈 NIGHTLIFE

Stockholm's beautiful people try to prove that blondes have more fun, partying until 5am at the many nightclubs and bars around Stureplan in **Östermalm** (T-bana: Östermalmtorg). Be prepared for steep cover and long lines. **Södermalm** ("Söder"), across the river, is the core of Stockholm's gay scene; pick up *QX (Queer Extra)* or the QueerMap for entertainment and nightlife information. Most establishments close between 1 and 3am. Bars and cafes line **Götgatan** (T-bana: Slussen, Medborgplatsen, or Skanstull); new cafes and bars are also blossoming in **Vasastaden** (T-bana: Sankt Eriksplan) and **Kungsholmen** (T-bana: Rådhuset). Stockholm's size and the excellent **night bus** service allow revelers to partake of any or all of these scenes in a single night. Alcohol is expensive at bars (35-55kr) but cheap (10-15kr per ½L) at **Systembolaget** state liquor stores. (Most open M-F 9am-5pm.)

■ **Daily News Cafe,** Kungsträgården, next to Sweden House. T-bana: T-Centralen. Walk down Klarabergsg. as it turns into Hamng. and turn right at Sweden House. The "Daily," as regulars call it, delivers great live and house music to a slick but friendly clientele. Different music and cover each night; call for a schedule. Cover 60-90kr; occasionally includes drinks. Open Su-Th 9pm-3am, F-Sa 9pm-5am.

Fasching, Kungsg. 63. T-bana: T-Centralen. Sweden's best spot for live jazz, latin, blues, funk, fusion, and world music in a funky loft-like space. Cover around 150kr. Open daily 8pm-midnight. Used as a regular disco F-Sa midnight-3am.

Pelikan, Blekingeg. 40, in Söder. T-bana: Skanstull. Walk up Götg. away from the Globe Arena and right on Blekingeg. Unpretentious crowds fill this smoky, well-lit beer hall adjoining the darker and artsier **Kristaller** for food and drinks. Beer 40-45kr, mixed drinks 55-65kr. 23+. Open daily noon-1am.

Tip Top, Sveav. 57. T-bana: Rådmansg.. Walk one block left of the station. This trendy gay club draws a mixed crowd on the weekends with its large dance floor. Beer 39kr, mixed drinks 49kr. Cover 70kr F-Sa after 9pm. Open M-Sa 4pm-3am.

La Cucaracha, Bondeg. 2, in Söder. T-bana: Skanstull. Walk up Götg. away from the Globe Arena (giant golf ball) and turn right on Bondeg. Latin rhythms heat the dance floor after 11pm. Beer 39kr, mixed drinks 60-70kr. 23+. Open daily 5pm-1am.

Bröderna Olssons Garlic and Shots, Folkungag. 84 in Söder, across from the Columbus Hostel. T-bana: Medborgarplatsen. Walk 3 blocks up Fulkungag. Funky vodka bar with an electric atmosphere. Trademark garlic-flavored beer 39kr. 101 unique shots (35kr each). Open daily 5pm-1am.

Snaps, Medborgarplatsen. T: Medborgarplatsen. Across the street from the station exit in the free-standing yellow house. Popular bar and bistro with a basement dance floor (jungle, reggae, and dance music). Beer 38kr, mixed drinks 70-80kr. Women 23+, men 25+. Open M-Sa 4pm-3am.

🢒 DAYTRIPS FROM STOCKHOLM

Stockholm is situated in the center of an archipelago, where the mainland gradually crumbles into the Baltic. The islands in either direction—east toward the Baltic or west toward Lake Mälaren—are well worth exploration. Visit the **Excursion Shop** in Sweden House (p. 899). **Ferries** to the archipelago leave from the **Stromkajen** docks between Gamla Stan and Skeppsholmen in front of the Grand Hotel (T-Bana: Jakobskyrka) or the **Nybrohamnen** docks (T-Bana: Ostermalmstorg.; walk down Birger Jarlsg. toward the water).

LAKE MÄLAREN. The island of **Björkö** on Lake Mälaren is home to **Birka,** where the Vikings established the country's first city. It was also the site of Sweden's first encounter with Christianity in AD 829. Today you can visit the fabulously interesting excavation sites, burial mounds, and Viking museum. A **ferry** departs Stockholm from the **Stadshusbron** docks next to the Stadshuset at 10am (1¾hr.). Go to T-Centralen, then walk toward the water. The boat leaves Björkö at 3:45pm. (1hr. guided tour, museum admission, and round-trip ferry 200kr; available May-Sept.)

The Swedish royal family's home, **Drottningholm Palace,** is only 45 minutes away by ferry. The ghost of Drottning (Queen) Larisa Ulrika, for whom the palace was a wedding gift, presides over the lush Baroque gardens and extravagant Rococo interiors. Catch the English tour of the palace's **theater.** (2 per hr.; 40kr, students 10kr). **Kina Slott,** Drottningholm's Chinese pavilion, was an 18th-century royal summer cottage. (Palace open daily May-Aug. 10am-4:30pm; Sept. noon-3:30pm. 50kr, students 25kr. Pavilion open daily May-Aug. 11am-4:30pm; Sept. noon-3:30pm; Apr. and Oct. 1-3:30pm. 50kr, 25kr.) Strömma Kanalbolaget **ferries** depart from Stadshusbron mid-June to mid-August (every 30min. 9:30am-4pm; return every hr. 10:30am-5:30pm; 90kr). Or, take the **subway** to T-bana: Brommaplan, then take **bus** #301-323.

Gripsholm Castle, adorned with original Renaissance wall paintings and furniture, looms over the bucolic hamlet of **Mariefred.** (Open May-Aug. daily 11am-4pm; Sept. Tu-Su 10am-3pm; Oct.-Dec. Sa-Su 10am-3pm; Jan.-Apr. Sa-Su noon-3pm. 50kr, students 25kr.) A short walk from the castle is **Grafikens Hus,** once the royal barn and now an international center of graphic art. (Open May-Aug. daily 11am-5pm; Sept.-Apr. Sa-Su 11am-5pm. 40kr.) To get to Mariefred, take the **train** to Läggesta, then catch **bus** #303 (15kr) and ask the driver to drop you off at the castle (1hr. total).

THE ARCHIPELAGO (SKÄRGÅRD). The wooded islands of the Stockholm archipelago grow increasingly rocky and dramatic closer to the Baltic. The archipelago is perfect for picnicking and hiking, as well as swimming if you can brave the cold waters. The **Waxholmsbolaget ferry company** (☎679 58 30) serves even the tiniest islands and offers the 16-day **Båtluffarkortet card** (300kr), good for unlimited boat travel. The excursions shop at Sweden House in Stockholm (p. 899) sells the ferry pass and has information on hostels and camping, as well as kayak and canoe rentals. Overnight stays in the area's 20 **hostels** must be booked months ahead, but the odd night may be available on short notice. There are hostels on **Möja** in the outer archipelago (☎ 571 647 20) and **Vaxholm**, near Stockholm (☎ 679 58 30). Consult Sweden House for complete listings. Or, enjoy **free camping** courtesy of the law of public access (p. 897) on almost any island except Sandhamn. (Some islands are also in military protection zones and are not open to foreigners.)

To fish or investigate the waterways by canoe or kayak, rent **boats** on Vaxholm (☎ 541 377 90) or on Üto (☎ 501 576 68). **Vaxholm,** a fortress town founded in 1647, is small enough to explore by foot and accessible by boat. (A ferry departs from Nybroplar in Stockholm at noon, returns 4:30pm.) **Utö** has great bike paths; **bike rental** and ferry packages are available from Sweden House. **Sandhamn,** three hours from Stockholm, is ideal for swimming and **sailing**. On **Öja,** puzzle your way through the labyrinth north of Landsort, reputed to bring luck to fishermen. Take the *pendeltag* (commuter train) from Stockholm to Nynashamn, then ride bus #852 from there to Ankarudden, and hop the ferry to Landsort (2½hr.).

UPPSALA. In a beautiful urban setting with grand churches and footbridges, Uppsala is *the* Nordic Oxford and Cambridge, sheltering the 20,000 students of Sweden's oldest university. Scandinavia's largest cathedral, the magnificent Gothic **Domkyrka,** where Swedish monarchs were once crowned, looms just over the river. (Open daily 8am-6pm. Tours in English June-Aug. M-Sa 1pm.) The university museum, **Gustavianum,** across from the Domkyrka, houses scientific curiosities and the **Anatomical Theater,** the site of 18th-century public human dissections. (Open May-Sept. daily 11am-4pm; Sept.-May W and F-Su 11am-4pm, Th 11am-9pm.) Some claim that **Gamla Uppsala** (Old Uppsala), 4km north of the town center, was the site of a pagan temple. Today, little remains except huge burial mounds of monarchs and the **Gamla Uppsala Kyrka,** one of Sweden's oldest churches. (Open daily May-Aug. 9am-6pm; Sept.-Apr. 9am-4pm. Free.) Near the mounds, a new museum, the **Gamla Uppsala Historiskt Centrum,** outlines the history of the mounds and the archaeological excavations there. (Open daily May 20-Aug. 20 10am-5pm; Aug. 21-Sept. 30 10am-4pm. 50kr, students 40kr, under 16 free.) Take bus #2, 20, 24, or 54 (16kr) north from Dragarbrunnsg. After exhausting Uppsala, hop the boat to **Skokloster,** a dazzling Baroque palace. (Open May-Aug. daily 11am-4pm. Entrance and tour 65kr, students 50kr. Boat departs in summer Tu-Su 11:30am from Islandsbron on Östra Åg. and Munkg.; returns 5:15pm. Return 115kr.)

Trains pull in from **Stockholm** (40min.; every 30min.; 70kr, under 25 55kr) after a stop at Arlanda Airport. To get from the station to the **tourist office,** Fyristorg 8, walk right on Kungsg., left on St. Persg., and cross the bridge. (☎ 27 48 00. Open in summer M-F 10am-6pm, Sa 10am-3pm, Su noon-4pm; in winter closed Su.) You can check email right around the corner from the tourist office at **Internet Horna,** Drottning. 3, on the first floor of the city newspaper office. (20kr per 30min. Open M-F 9:30am-5:30pm, Sa 10:30am-2:30pm.) For renovated rooms in a lovely pastoral setting, try **Sunnersta Herrgård (HI),** Sunnerstav. 24, 6km south of town. Take bus #20, 25, 50, or 802 (16kr) from Dragarbrunnsg. to Herrgårdsv., cross the street, walk two blocks down the path behind the kiosk, and walk 50m left. (☎ 32 42 20. Breakfast 60kr. Reception 8-11am and 5-9pm. Open May-Aug. Dorms 175kr, nonmembers 220kr; singles 325kr, 370kr.) **Fyrishov Camping,** Idrottsg. 2, off Svartbäcksg., is 2km from the city center. Take bus #4 or 6 (bus #50 or 54 at night; 10min.) to Fyrishov. (☎ 27 49 60. Reception 7am-10pm. Tents 85kr; 4- to 5-bed huts 695-795kr. Swedish Camping Card required. 60kr.) Uppsala offers a hot night scene. Choose from over 100 types of whiskey and beer (42-52kr) at ■O'Connors, Stortorget 1, which also offers Swedish and Irish food. (Live music M-Sa 9:30pm-1:30am. Cover 20kr after 9pm. 22+. Open in summer M-Th 5pm-1am, F-Sa 5pm-2am, Su 5pm-midnight; in winter Su-Th 4pm-1am, F 2pm-2am, Sa noon-2am.) **Postal code:** 75101. ☎ **018.**

GOTLAND

Gotland, 300km south of Stockholm, is Sweden's biggest island. Famed for its green meadows, white sand beaches, and its capital, **Visby**, whose wall is the oldest medieval monument in Scandinavia, Gotland is an ideal mix of leisure and excitement.

⚡ TRANSPORTATION. Destination Gotland ferries (☎(0498) 20 10 20) sail to Visby from **Nynäshamn**, south of Stockholm (3-5hr.), and **Oskarshamn**, north of Kalmar (2½-4hr.). Fares are highest on weekends and from mid-June to Aug. (145-465kr) and cheapest for early-morning and late-night departures (June-Aug. 2-5 per day, Oct.-May 1 per day; 130-205kr, students 80-145kr; 40% Scanrail discount). To get to Nynäshamn from **Stockholm**, take the *Flygbussar* bus from Cityterminalen (1hr., 70kr) or the *pendeltag* from Centralstation (45min., 40kr; *rabattkuponger* and SL passes valid). To get to Oskarshamn, hop on a bus (2hr., 75kr) or train from **Kalmar.** If you're planning your trip from Stockholm, **Gotland City**, Kungsg. 57A, books ferries and has tourist information. (☎(08) 406 15 00. Open June-Aug. M-F 9:30am-6pm, Sa 10am-2pm; Sept.-May M-F 9:30am-5pm.)

To explore the island, pick up a bus timetable at the ferry terminal or at the Visby **bus station**, outside the wall north of the city at Kung Magnusväg 1 (☎(0498) 21 41 12). Bus rides cost 12-43kr (bikes 20kr extra). **Cycling** along Gotland's extensive paths and bike-friendly motorways is the best way to explore its flat terrain; bike rental shops are all over the island, especially in Visby and Klintehamn.

VISBY. This sleepy village looks straight out of a fairy tale with its medieval wall and twisting cobblestone streets. Visby comes to life in August (between the 31st and 32nd Sundays of the year) during **Medeltidsveckan**, a recreation of Visby's medieval past complete with costumes and tournaments. Once you reach Gotland, walk 10min. to the left as you exit the ferry terminal to get to the **tourist office**, Hamng. 4. (☎20 17 00. Open mid-June to mid-Aug. M-F 7am-7pm, Sa-Su 8am-6pm; May to mid-June and late Aug. M-F 8am-5pm, Sa-Su 10am-4pm; Sept. M-F 8am-5pm, Sa-Su 11am-2pm; Oct.-Apr. M-F 10am-noon and 1-3pm.) Dozens of **bike rental** shops surround the ferry terminal. Stay at **Visby Fängelse Vandrarhem**, Skeppsbron 1, 300m to the left as you exit the ferry terminal. You'll recognize it by the barbed wire atop the walls—the yellow building housed a 19th-century prison. (☎20 60 50. Reception M-F summer 11am-2pm and 5-6:30pm; off season 11am-2pm; call ahead to arrive at another time. Reserve ahead. Dorms 150-200kr; bed in a double cell 200-300kr.) Otherwise, **Gotlandsresor**, Färjeleden 3, 75m right of the ferry terminal, will help you book ferries, rent a bicycle, and find a room. (☎20 12 60. Open daily June-Aug. 6am-10pm, 11:30pm when a late ferry comes in; Sept.-May 8am-6pm.) **Private rooms** cost 420-590kr for singles and 600-750kr for doubles (outside the city walls 240kr and 380kr). **Postal code:** 62101. ☎**0498.**

ELSEWHERE ON GOTLAND. Great daytrips from Visby during the high season include visits to the mystical monoliths on **Fårö**, off the northern tip of the island (bus #23, 2hr.); the blazing beaches of **Tofta**, 15km south (bus #31, 30min.); and the calcified cliffs of **Hoburgen**, at the island's southernmost tip (bus #11, 3hr.). At **Gotlandsresor** (see above) can get you information on the more than 30 hostels, campgrounds, and bike rentals elsewhere on the island. You can also take advantage of the right of public access (p. 897).

SOUTHERN SWEDEN

Swedes love their summer houses in this mild region, graced with wide fields of waving grasses and flat beaches. The **Halland** coast and southwest **Småland** coastline, between Västervik and Kalmar, are especially popular.

KALMAR   ☎ 0480

Journey from downtown Kalmar to the 16th century as you step across the footbridge of the Renaissance **Kalmar Slott.** (Open daily June-Aug. 10am-6pm; Sept.-May 10am-5pm. 70kr, students 40kr.) The castle hosts an annual **Renaissance Festival** in late June and early July (☎45 06 62 for information and tickets). Down the street from the castle to the left of the park, the **Kalmar Konstmuseum,** Slottsvagan ID, is a center for modern Swedish art and design. (Open M-F 10am-5pm and 7-9pm; Sa-Su 11am-5pm. 40kr, students 30kr.) The Baroque **Kalmar Domkyrka,** on Stortorget, has the splendor of a major cathedral. (Open M-F 8am-7pm, Sa-Su 9am-7pm.) The **Kalmar Läns Museum,** Skeppsbrog. 49, has relics from the wreckage of the 17th-century warship Kronan, which sank in a battle against the Danes. (Open daily mid-June to mid-Aug. 10am-6pm; mid-Aug. to mid-June 10am-4pm. 50kr, students 25kr.)

Trains and **buses** arrive south of town, across the bay from the castle. To get from the train station to the **tourist office,** Larmg. 6, go right on Stationsg., turn left on Ölandsg., and look left. (☎153 50. Open June and Aug. M-F 9am-7pm, Sa 10am-3pm; Su 1-6pm; July M-F 9am-8pm, Sa 10am-5pm; Oct.-Apr. M-F 9am-5pm; May and Sept. M-F 9am-5pm, Sa 10am-1pm.) To hike from the tourist office to the **Kalmar Vandrarhem (HI),** Rappeg. 1, on the island of Ängö, go north on Larmg., turn right on Södra Kanalg., cross the bridge, and turn left on Angöleden; it will be on the right. (☎129 28. Breakfast 55kr. Reception June-Aug. 8-10am and 4-10pm; Sept.-May 8-10am and 4-9pm. 150kr, nonmembers 195kr.) **Stensö Camping** is 2km south of Kalmar; take bus #3. (☎888 03. Call ahead. June-Aug. 125kr; Apr. and Sept.-Oct. 100kr.) Restaurants cluster around **Larmtorget. Postal code:** 39101.

■ **DAYTRIPS FROM KALMAR: ÖLAND AND GLASRIKET.** Visible from Kalmar's coast, the island of **Öland** stretches over 100km of green fields and white sand beaches. The royal family roosts here on holiday, and Crown Princess Victoria's birthday, Victoriadagen (July 14), is celebrated island-wide. Commoners flock to the **beaches** of Löttorp and Böda in the north and Grönhögen and Ottenby in the south. **Buses** #101 and 106 go from Kalmar's train station to Öland (30-40kr). Öland's **tourist office** (☎56 06 00) is outside Färjestaden; take the bus to the first stop after the bridge and follow signs. Sleep at **Vandrarhem Borgholm,** Södra Vägan 7, Rosenfors (☎107 56), or **Vandrarhem Böda** (☎220 38), on Melböda in Löttorp. ☎ **0485.**

In nearby towns, collectively dubbed **Glasriket** (Kingdom of Crystal), artisans craft exquisite hand-blown crystal. To visit workshops at **Orrefors** (☎(0481) 341 95) and **Kosta Boda** (☎(0478) 345 00), take bus #138 (1hr., 60kr) from the train station. (Both open M-F 9am-6pm, Sa 10am-4pm, Su noon-4pm.)

MALMÖ   ☎ 040

As the Swedish endpoint of the new bridge to Copenhagen, Malmö is a town to watch. To reach **Stortorget** square from the train station, walk straight out onto Malarbron Hamng. Continue through the square and look left for another square, **Lilla Torg.** The **Form Design Center,** Lilla Torg 9, presents the cutting edge of Swedish design. (☎664 51 50. Open Tu-F 11am-5pm, Th 11am-6pm, Sa 11am-4pm, Su noon-4pm. Free.) In the west end, **Malmöhus Castle** houses the **Malmös Museer,** which documents the city's history. (☎34 44 37. Open daily June-Aug. 10am-4pm; Sept.-May noon-4pm. 40kr, students 20kr.) The **Malmö Konsthall,** St. Johannesg. 7, exhibits modern art. (☎34 12 93. Open daily 11am-5pm, W 11am-11pm. Free.)

The **train station** and **harbor** lie north of the Old Town. Pilen **ferries** (☎23 44 11) run to Copenhagen (45min., 59kr). **Trains** arrive from Copenhagen (35min.; 200kr, under 25 145kr), Gothenburg (3½hr., 415kr, 295kr) and Stockholm (4½-6hr., 585kr, 415kr). The **tourist office** is in the train station. (Open June-Aug. M-F 9am-7pm, Sa-Su 10am-5pm; Sept.-May M-F 9am-6pm, Sa 10am-3pm, Su 10am-3pm.) Log on at the stylish **Cyberspace C@fé,** Engelbrektsg. 13, off Lilla Torg. (44kr per hr. Open M-F 10am-midnight, Sa noon-midnight, Su noon-10pm.) From the train station or harbor, cross the canal and Norra Vallg. and take bus #21 to Vandrarhemmet and the **Vandrarhem Malmö (HI),** Backav. 18. (☎822 20. Breakfast 45kr. Reception 8-10am and 4-10pm. 130kr, nonmembers 175kr.) To reach **Bosses Gast-Och Foretags Vaningar,** Södra Förstadsg. 110B, which has hostel prices with hotel amenities, take bus #15 to Södervärn and cross the street. (☎32 62 50. Breakfast 45kr. Sheets 45kr. Singles 250kr.) **Camp** in the giant Malmöhus Park for free. **Postal code:** 20110.

LUND   ☎046

What Oxford and Cambridge are to England, Uppsala and Lund are to Sweden. Lund University's antagonism with its scholarly northern neighbors in Uppsala has inspired countless pranks, drag shows, and drinkfests in Lund's bright streets. The town's ancient Romanesque **cathedral**, St. Laurentius, is an impressive 900-year-old reminder of the time when Lund was the religious center of Scandinavia; note the 14th-century astronomical clock. To find the cathedral from the train station, walk straight across Bang. and Knut den Storestorg, then turn left on Kyrkog. (Open M-Sa 8am-6pm, Su 9am-6pm.) Head through the park behind the cathedral to the University campus, where you'll find events information at **Student Info,** Sang. 2, in the student union. (☎38 49 49; http://af.lu.se. Open Sept.-May M-F 10am-4pm.) **Kulturen,** at the end of Sankt Anneg. on Tegnerplastén, is an engrossing open-air museum with 17th- and 18th-century homes, churches, and history displays. (Open May-Sept. daily 11am-5pm; Oct.-Apr. Tu-Su noon-4pm. 50kr.) **Stortorget,** Storotorget 1, is a bar, nightclub, and restaurant. (Bar open Su-W 11:30am-midnight, Th 11:30am-2am, F-Sa 11:30am-3am. Nightclub open Th-Sa 10pm-3am. 22+ after 9pm Th-Sa; 20+ with student ID.)

Lund is easily accessible from Malmö on most **SJ trains** and by local **pågatågen** (10min., every hr., 34kr; railpasses valid). The **tourist office,** Kyrkog. 11, opposite the cathedral, books 200kr rooms for a 50kr fee. (☎35 50 40. Open June-Aug. M-F 10am-6pm, Sa-Su 10am-2pm; Sept.-May M-F 10am-5pm.) Rest at the delightful but cramped **HI Hostel Tåget** (The Train), Vävareg. 22, housed in a 1940s train. Take the overpass to the park side of the station. (☎14 28 20. Reception daily Apr.-Oct. 8-10am and 5-8pm; Nov.-Mar. 5-7pm. Call ahead. 110kr, nonmembers 155kr.) To get to **Källby Camping,** take bus #1 (dir. Klostergården) and get off at the campground. (☎35 51 88. Open mid-June to Aug. 40kr per tent.) Mårtenstorget features a fruit and vegetable **market.** (Open M-Sa 7am-2:30pm.) **Mejeriet,** Stora Söderg. 64, packs a bar, movie theater, and summer events into a former dairy. Hours vary with shows; call ☎12 38 11 for information. **Postal code:** 22101.

YSTAD   ☎0411

Travelers passing through Ystad en route to Bornholm, Denmark (p. 279) often miss out on this quiet town's charms. The pedestrian **Stora Östergatan** leads to **Stortorget,** the market square; south of the square lies the ancient monastery **Gråbrödraklostret.** (Open M-F noon-5pm, Sa-Su noon-4pm. 20kr.) **Ales Stenar** (Ale's Stones), a mysterious circular stone formation outside the city dating from the late Iron Age, is accessible in summer via bus #322 (30min., 23kr; bus rarely runs Sa-Su). Trafikken (☎130 13) and Scandlines (☎(042) 18 63 00) **ferries** leave from behind the train station for Bornholm (2½hr., 3 per day in summer, 150kr) and Świnoujście, Poland. **Trains** pull in from Malmö (1hr., 5-6 per day, 70kr). The **tourist office** is across from the station. (☎57 76 81. Open mid-June to mid-Aug. M-F 9am-7pm, Sa 10am-7pm, Su 11am-6pm; mid-Aug. to mid-June M-F 9am-5pm.) The train station houses the new hostel **Vandrarhemmet Stationer.** (☎(070) 857 79 95. Breakfast 45kr. Reception June-Aug. 9-10am and 5-7pm; Oct.-May 5-6pm. 170kr.) To get to the beachfront **Vandrarhem Kantarellen** or **Sandskogens Camping,** turn right from the station and walk about 2km on Österleden, then turn right on Fritidsvägen (30min.). Or, take bus #572 (5min., 10kr) from the station. (Hostel ☎665 66. Kitchen. Reception 9-10am and 4-8pm. Call ahead. 120kr, nonmembers 160kr. Camping ☎192 70. 125kr.) Get **groceries** at **Saluhallen,** off the main square at the corner of Theatergrand and St. Västerg. (Open daily 8am-9pm.) **Postal code:** 27101.

GOTHENBURG (GÖTEBORG)   ☎031

The hub of Swedish industry and home to a once-bustling industrial port, Gothenburg now moves at a slow, leisurely pace. Passenger ferries line up under the mostly silent harbor-side cranes, and locals and travelers alike find themselves with plenty of time to enjoy the thriving cafe culture of this luxurious, tasteful city.

TRANSPORTATION AND PRACTICAL INFORMATION. Trains go from Nordstaden to: Malmö (3½hr.; 12 per day; 390kr, under 25 165kr); Oslo (4½hr.; 2 per day; 447kr, 208kr); and Stockholm (3½-6hr.; 10 per day; 545kr, 195kr). Stena Line **ferries** (☎704 00 00) sail to Frederikshavn, Denmark (3hr., 15 per day, 95kr) and Kiel, Germany (14hr., 300-750kr depending upon the season). DFDS Seaways (☎65 06 50) sends **ferries** to Newcastle, England (22hr., 525-1095kr depending upon the season). The **tourist office,** Kungsportsplatsen 2, sells **Göteborg Cards,** which grant public transit and admission to various attractions (95kr). From the station, cross Drottningtorget and follow Östra Larmag. from the right of the Radisson (☎61 25 00. Open May daily M-F 9am-6pm; late June to early Aug. daily 9am-8pm; early June and late Aug. M-F 9am-6pm, Sa-Su 10am-2pm; Sept.-Apr. M-F 9am-5pm, Sa 10am-2pm.) The stylish **stadsbibliotek** (city library), on Götaplatsen, has free **Internet.** (Open M-Th 10am-8pm, F 10am-6pm, Sa 11am-4pm.) **Postal code:** 40401.

ACCOMMODATIONS AND FOOD. To reach the modern, spacious **Slottsko-gens Hostel (STF/HI),** Vegag. 21, take tram #1 or 2 (dir. Frölunda) to Olivedalsg. and walk uphill to Vegag. (☎42 65 20; fax 14 21 02; www.slottsskogenvh.se. Kitchen, sauna, and **bike rental.** Reception 3pm-noon. Check-in 3-6pm. Dorms 100kr; singles 215kr; nonmembers add 40kr.) **Masthuggsterrassen (SVIF),** Masthuggsterrassen 8, has rooms with fantastic views of the harbor. Take tram #3, 4, or 9 to Masthuggstor-get, cross the square diagonally, go down Angra Långg away from the center, walk up the stairs, and follow the signs along the terrace. (☎42 48 20; fax 42 48 21. Reception 8-10am and 5-8pm. Dorms 130kr; doubles 350kr; quads 480kr.) To reach the **Stigbergsliden Hostel (STF/HI),** Stigbergsliden 10, take tram #3, 4, or 9 to Stigberg-storget and walk east down the hill. (☎24 16 20; fax 24 65 20; www.hostel_gothenburg.com. Reception 8am-noon and 4-10pm. Check-in 4-6pm. Dorms 110kr; singles 205kr; doubles 260kr; nonmembers add 40kr.) Pitch your tent at **Kärralund Camping,** Olbersg. Catch tram #5 to Welanderg., then go east on Olbersg., crossing the highway. (☎84 02 00; fax 84 05 00. Reception 7am-11pm. 120kr per tent; rooms 595-995kr.) ▪**Eva's Paley,** Kungportsavenyn 39, offers a salad lunch buffet with any sandwich (60kr), and has outdoor dining on Gothenburg's coolest street. (Open M-Th 8am-11pm, F 8am-1am, Sa 10am-1am, Su 10am-11pm.) **Pasta, etc.,** at the corner of Nordhamsg. and Plantageg. in Linnéstan, serves up amazing pasta for 70kr.

SIGHTS AND NIGHTLIFE. To the south of Nordstaden, just across Drott-ningtorget (main square) and the Hamn canal, is the bustling shopping district of **Inom Vallgraven. Kungsport Avenyn,** the city's main drag, stretches from Kungsports-platsen next to the tourist office all the way to **Götaplatsen,** site of Carl Milles' famous **sculpture fountain** of Poseidon. The size of Poseidon's manhood caused an uproar when the design was unveiled; it was later modified. On the same square, the regal **Konstmuseet** houses a thoroughly engrossing collection of Nordic art as well as the **Hasselblad Center,** an excellent photo exhibition. (Open May-Aug. M-F 11am-4pm, Sa-Su 11am-5pm; Sept.-Apr. Tu and Th-F 11am-4pm, W 11am-9pm, Sa-Su 11am-5pm. 40kr.) The **Göteborgs Operan,** Lilla Bommen (☎13 13 00), an architectural marvel that mimics a ship at full mast, is en route to the **Göteborg Maritime Centrum,** which features a large number of docked ships and sailing vessels that you can board and tour. (Opera in session during winter; inquire about tickets at the tourist office. Maritime center open daily Mar.-May and Sept.-Nov. 10am-4pm; June and Aug. 10am-6pm; July 10am-7pm. 40kr.) The **Stadsmuseet,** Norra Hamng. 12, houses exhibits on city history, from Vikings to the city's post-industrial rebirth. (Open daily June-Aug. 11am-5pm; Sept.-May 11am-5pm. 40kr, students 10kr.) One canal farther to the west lies **Linnéstan,** easily the most charming neighborhood in the city. This picturesque and relatively untouristed quarter branches off in winding streets from Linnég and Järntorget. **Göteborgs Skärgård** (archipelago) is a summer paradise for beach-goers and sailors. The islands range from 7min. to 1hr. away from the mainland. The secluded beach on **Vrångö** island in the archipelago makes a good daytrip; take tram #4 to Saltholmen, then catch a **ferry** (☎69 64 00).

Gothenburg has a thriving theater and classical music scene—pick up *What's on in Göteborg* at the tourist office. At night, a chic crowd struts down **Kungports-avenyn**. A more relaxed bar culture can be found in **Linnéstan**; get warmed up at the pub **Bryggeriet**, Kungportsavenyn 19 (open F-Sa until 3am, Su-Th until 2am). **Saray**, Kungportsavenyn 15, spins a mix of salsa, house, and ethnic music. (Cover 60kr; women 25+, men 27+. Open daily around midnight.)

⧖ DAYTRIP FROM GOTHENBURG: VARBERG. Between Gothenburg and Malmö, coastal Varberg beckons with expansive beaches and the spectacular **Varberg Fortress** overlooking the waters of the Kattegatt. (Tours mid-June to mid-Aug. every hr. 11am-4pm. 40kr.) South of town, the shallow bay of **Apelviken** offers some of the best windsurfing and surfing in northern Europe. Follow the *Strand-promenaden* along the beach 2km south of town. **Surfer's Paradise**, Söderg. 22, rents gear and gives tips. From the tourist office, walk away from the train station on Västra Vallg., then turn left on Söderg. (☎67 70 55. Call ahead.) To explore the gorgeous beaches (some nude), **rent bikes** at BF Cykel, Östra Langg. 47. From the tourist office, walk away from the water on Kyrkog. until you reach Östra Langg. (85kr per day. Open M-F 10am-6pm, Sa 10am-2pm.) **Trains** arrive from Gothenborg (1hr., 105-195kr) and Malmö (2½hr., 290-505kr). To get from the station to the **tourist office**, in Brunnsparken, walk four blocks right on Västra Vallg. (☎887 70. Open mid-June to mid-Aug. M-Sa 9am-7pm, Su 3-7pm; mid-Aug. to mid-June M-F 9am-6pm.) Sleep at **Varbergs Fästning Vandrarhem**, inside the fortress, which was used as the Crown Jail from 1852 to 1931. Being locked up has never been this popular; book ahead. (☎887 88. Reception June-Aug. 8-10am and 5-9pm; Sept.-May call ahead. Dorms 145kr; singles 165kr.) **Apelvikens Camping** is on the beach. (☎141 78. Open late Mar. to Oct. 115-185kr.) **Postal code:** 43201. ☎ **0340.**

GULF OF BOTHNIA

Sweden's Gulf of Bothnia can be gentle and dramatic, rural and sophisticated, lively and peacefully remote. The beautiful, unblemished stretch of coastline south of Örnsköldsvik contrasts with the lively university town of Umeå.

ÖRNSKÖLDSVIK. Off the beaten track and main train route is Örnsköldsvik (Urn-SHULDS-vik; Ö-vik to locals), surrounded by hills and a harbor of tiny islands waiting to be explored. Most visitors use the town as a base for superb **hiking**. The 130km **Höga Kusten Leden (High Coast Trail)** links Ö-vik with Veda in the south and winds along the most beautiful, dramatic section of Sweden's Baltic coast. Pick up a trail guide (80kr) at the tourist office for information on transport links and huts along the way. Several **day hikes** are also nearby—the **Yellow Trail** loops an easy 6km. You'll find the trailhead on Hantverkareg; from the tourist office, walk uphill on Nyg. and turn right on Hantverkareg. Throughout the island of **North Ulvön** are scenic hiking trails, the most rewarding of which leads to the peak of **Lotsberget Mountain.** The **M/S Otilia** sails from Örnsköldsvik at 9:30am, arrives at Ulvön at noon, and departs for Ö-vik at 3pm (110kr round-trip), stopping en route at the island of **Trysunda**, which also has beautiful hiking trails and a beach (arrives 11am, departs for Ö-vik 4pm; 70kr round-trip). **Gene Fornby**, a 2000-year-old settlement 6km from Ö-vik, has been rebuilt to look as it did in AD 500; to reach it, take bus #1 to the Nybyggarevagen stop. (Open late June to early Aug. daily 11am-5pm; tours every hr. 1-4pm. 50kr, children 20kr.)

Buses run to Örnsköldsvik from Umeå (2hr., 95kr) and Östersund (4½hr., 220kr) in the north, and Sundsvall in the south (2hr., 6-7 per day, 129kr). To get from the train to the bus station in Sundsvall, take a left out of the train station, walk through the tunnel, turn right into another tunnel, look for Kyrkog., and turn left. You will run into the main esplanade; turn right and the bus terminal is at the end. The **tourist office**, Nyg. 18, books rooms and cottages for 40kr. (☎125 37; fax 881 23. Open mid-June to mid-Aug. M-F 9am-7pm, Sa 9am-3pm, Su 10am-3pm; Oct.-May M-F 10am-5pm; Sept. M-F 10am-5pm, Sa-Su

10am-3pm.) To get there, walk up the steps behind the bus station, follow Fabriksg., and turn left on Nyg. **Strand City Hotel,** Nyg. 2, is downhill from the tourist office and offers no-frills rooms. (☎106 10. Singles 450kr, in winter 650kr; doubles 550kr, 900kr.) **STF Vandrarhem Örnsköldsvik (HI),** Högsnäsgården pl. 1980, is a 15min. ride on bus #42 (19kr; M-F last bus 9pm) into the isolated countryside. (☎702 44. Reception in summer 9-10am and 5-7pm; off season 9-10am. 120kr, nonmembers 155kr.) **Postal code:** 89101. ☎ **0660.**

UMEÅ. Umeå (OOM-eh-oh), the largest city in northern Sweden, is a lively and fast-growing university town. Adventurous souls head for the 30km **Umeleden bike and car trail,** which snakes past old hydropower stations, gardens, restaurants, and **Baggböle Herrgård,** a delightful cafe in a 19th-century mansion. (Open Tu-Su noon-8pm.) A bridge upriver allows for a more manageable 15km loop. **Cykel och Mopedhandlaren,** Kungsg. 101, rents and repairs **bikes.** (☎14 01 70. 70kr per day, 195kr per week. Open summer M-F 8am-5:30pm, Sa 10am-1pm; in winter M-F 9:30am-5:30pm, Sa 10am-1pm.) Regular trains do not run out of Umeå, but the private **Sweden Train Company** goes from Umeå north to Kiruna and Narvik, Norway. The company honors some Sweden Rail passes; for information, call the **Avanda travel office** in Umeå (☎14 28 90). **Trains** run from Umeå to Luleå (4-5hr., 250kr) and Gothenburg (13hr., 350kr). **Buses** operated by Norrlands Kusten (toll-free ☎(020) 51 15 13) and Ybuss (toll-free ☎(0200) 33 44 44) run down the coast to Stockholm (10hr., 300kr) and north to Luleå and on to Kiruna and Narvik. The train station is across from the bus terminal. **Ferries** (☎18 52 20) to Vasa, Finland are available daily in summer for 360kr. To get to the **tourist office,** Renmarkstorget 15, which lists private rooms from 150kr, walk straight down Rådhusesplanaden from the train station and turn right on Skolg. (☎16 16 16; www.umea.se. Open mid-June to late Aug. M-F 8am-7pm, Sa 10am-5pm, Su 11am-5pm; late Aug. to Sept. M-F 10am-6pm, Sa 10am-2pm; Oct.-Apr. M-F 10am-5pm; May to mid-June M-F 10am-6pm, Sa 10am-2pm.) To get to the **Youth Hostel (HI),** V. Esplanaden 10, from the train station, go straight up Rådhusesplanaden, turn right on Skolg., and head left on V. Esplanaden. (☎77 16 50. Laundry 10kr. Reception 8-10am and 5-9pm. 110-130kr, nonmembers 150-170kr.) Take Holmsund bus #124 from Vasaplan to **Ljumvikens Camping;** tell the bus driver your destination. (☎417 10. 75kr per tent.) **Postal code:** 90101. ☎ **090.**

LULEÅ. At the mouth of the **Lule Älv** lies Luleå (LOOL-eh-oh), a perky town with lively cafes, parks, and life-sized chess games in its streets. The nearby 15th-century church town **Gammelstad** is a UNESCO World Heritage site. Going to church used to require a day's travel in winter, so local farmers built hundreds of tiny cottages near the church to house their families on Sunday night. Take bus #8, 9, or 32 for 20kr. (Church open in summer M-F 8am-5pm, Sa 8am-2pm, Su 8am-5pm; off season call 43 51 12 to arrange a visit.) The mostly uninhabited **Luleå archipelago** awaits exploration by ferry, canoe, or kayak; the **M/S Favourite** (book through the tourist office day tours, 200kr) and the **M/S Laponia** (☎29 35 00, day tours 220kr) both run daily ferries to different islands. **Storgatan,** the main drag, is full of cafes and bars that convert the laidback daytime atmosphere into an energetic night scene. For highly regarded drinks, food, and dancing, **Magneto's,** Storg. 40, is the place to be. (Beer 36kr, mixed drinks 59kr. No cover. Open M-F 11am-1am, Sa noon-1am.) The **tourist office,** Storg. 43b, books rooms (120-450kr) for free. From the train station, cross Prästg. and follow it to the right, walk diagonally across the park, cross Hermalingsg., and tromp up Storg. (☎29 35 00. Open in summer M-F 9am-7pm, Sa-Su 10am-4pm; off season M-F 10am-6pm, Sa 10am-2pm.) The only hostel in town is the **Luleå Vandrarhem & Mini-Hotel,** Sandsvikg. 26. From the tourist office, follow Storg., take a left on Radstug., and turn right on Sandsvik. (☎22 26 60. Call before 6pm. Dorms 150kr; singles 190kr.) **EFS Sundet** is the closest **campground;** take bus #6. (☎25 20 74. Reception 8am-9pm. Open June-Aug. 75kr per tent; 2-bed cabins 300kr.) **Postal code:** 97101. ☎ **0920.**

SWEDEN

It's Your World...

www.mci.com/worldphone

WorldPhone. Worldwide.

MCI^{SM} gives you the freedom of worldwide communications whenever you're away from home. It's easy to call to and from over 70 countries with your MCI Calling Card:

1. Dial the WorldPhone® access number of the country you're calling from.
2. Dial or give the operator your MCI Calling Card number.
3. Dial or give the number you're calling.

• Austria	0800-200-235	• Netherlands	0800-022-91-22
• Belgium	0800-10012	• Poland	00-800-111-21-22
• Denmark	8001-0022	• Romania	01-800-1800
• France	0-800-99-0019	• Spain	900-99-0014
• Germany	0800-888-8000	• Switzerland	0800-89-0222
• Ireland	1-800-55-1001	• United Kingdom	0800-89-0222 BT
• Italy	172-1022		0500-89-0222 CWC

Sign up today!

Ask your local operator to place a collect call
(reverse charge) to MCI in the U.S. at:

1-712-943-6839

For additional access codes or to sign up, visit us at www.mci.com/worldphone.

www.mci.com/worldphone

LAPLAND (SÁPMI)

Lapland is where Sweden's ancestral past lives in the present, among the vast, isolated natural beauty of the Arctic Circle. The wildlife is exactly that—wild, with roaming reindeer, moose, and bears. Lapland's lure is nature, from the swampy forests in the vast lowlands to the mountains that meet the Norwegian border. It is a region rich in the culture of the **Sami,** descendants of prehistoric Scandinavians, who now use helicopters and snowmobiles to attend their herds of reindeer.

■ TRANSPORTATION

There are two **rail** routes to Lapland. The **coastal route** runs from Stockholm through Boden, Umeå, and Kiruna to Narvik, Norway, along the **Malmbanan.** From Midsummer (June 21-23 in 2002) to early August, the privately run **Inlandsbanan** travels from Mora to Gällivare. A train leaves daily at 7:30am from the Morastrand train station in **Mora** and arrives at **Östersund** at 1:55pm (160kr); another train leaves Östersund daily at 7:05am and arrives at **Gällivare** at 10pm (320kr, from Mora 480kr). Another private company, **Tågkompaniet,** often provides the only train link between towns; unfortunately, its schedules are not observed very strictly. For information, contact any Avanda travel agency in Umeå (☎ (090) 14 28 90). **Buses,** most of which do not accept railpasses, are the only way to smaller towns and are generally the best way to travel in the north. Call (020) 47 00 47 for schedules.

■ TRAINS AND BUSES TO NORWAY AND FINLAND

Two **trains** go daily from **Luleå** to **Narvik, Norway** (6½hr.), stopping in **Gällivare, Kiruna,** and **Abisko.** The route from Kiruna to Narvik is gorgeous. **Buses** link Kiruna to **Karesuando** on the Finnish border (2½hr., 1-2 per day, 125kr), then continue to **Skibotn, Norway,** or **Kilpisjärvi** and **Muonio.** Finland is also accessible by bus from **Boden.** Railpasses are valid on all **buses** from Boden to **Haparanda,** on the Finnish border.

KIRUNA. The only large town in Swedish Lapland, Kiruna (pop. 90,000) is a wilderness oasis. The world's largest underground **mine** (Malmberget) put Kiruna on the map and is still the main draw. (Mandatory tours depart from the tourist office June-Aug. every hr. 10am-5pm. 140kr.) Nearby **Jukkasjärvi** is home to the spectacular **Ice Hotel.** For obvious reasons, the hotel exists only in the winter and is rebuilt every fall, although part of it is preserved in a warehouse year-round. (Tours depart from the tourist office 4-5 times per day. 100kr.) **ESRANGE,** a space center with a mapping control center and rocket/balloon launch facility, lies 40km outside Kiruna. Astronomers come here to study the *aurora borealis* and the ozone layer. (Tours depart from the tourist office June-Aug. M-F noon. 190kr.) **Buses** run regularly to Kiruna from Luleå (200kr) and Jokkmokk (100kr). Tågkompaniet **trains** run from Luleå and north to Abisko and Riksgränsen, Sweden, and Narvik, Norway. Regular **flights** (☎ 680 00) go to and from Stockholm for the **Kiruna Flygplats.** (2-3 per day; 500kr, students 300kr, standby 250kr.) The **Kiruna-Lapland tourist office** is in the **Folkshuset** in the town center. Walk straight from the train station, follow the footpath through the tunnel, and then walk uphill to the top. The agents book rooms, schedule tours, and arrange dog-sled adventures in winter. (☎ 188 80; www.lappland.se. Open June-Aug. M-F 9am-9pm, Sa-Su 9am-7pm; Sept.-May M-F 9am-5pm.) The **Yellow House Hostel,** Hantverkorg. 25, has spacious rooms with TVs and kitchenettes. (☎ 137 50. Dorms 120kr; singles 300kr; doubles 200kr.) From the tourist office, go up Hjalmer Lundbohmsv., turn right on Adolf Hedinsv., and turn left on Hantverkareg.; the hostel is 75m on the left. **Postal code:** 98135. ☎ **0980.**

GÄVLE. One of Sweden's most vibrant small cities, friendly Gävle has a thriving city center and beautiful parks. Although a fire burned down most of Gävle in 1869, colorful wooden houses still stand in **Gamla Gefle,** the old town. The **City Fest festival** brings artists and music during the second week of August (www.cityfesten.se).

Nearby **Limön** offers nature walks, bike trails, and a beach; **boats** leave from Södra Skeppsbron daily in summer (45min., 3 per day). South of Gävle, a **zoo** and **amusement park** are accessible by bus #838 (2 per hr.). **Trains** run to Stockholm (1½hr.; 15 per day; adults 250kr, under 25 175kr) with a stop at the Arlanda Airport. For **bus** information, call Express Bus (☎(0200) 21 82 18). To reach the **tourist office,** Drottningg. 37, from the train station, cross the street and follow Drottningg for 50m. (☎14 74 30. Open in summer M-F 9am-6pm, Sa 9am-2pm, Su 11am-4pm; in winter M-F 9am-5pm.) To reach **STF Youth Hostel,** S. Radmansg. 1, walk down Store Esplanadg. over the bridge, take a right on Brunnsgatan, and turn right again on S. Radmansg. (☎62 17 45; stf.vandrarhem@telia.com. Breakfast 45kr. Sheets 50kr. Reception in summer 8-10am and 5-8pm; in winter 7-10am and 5-7pm. Dorms 120kr; singles 210kr; doubles 280kr; nonmembers add 40kr.) **Postal code:** 80135. ☎**026.**

ÖSTERSUND. Östersund is a natural stopover from Trondheim for travelers heading to or from Norway and a required one for those riding the length of the **Inlandsbanan.** The hilly lakeside town welcomes visitors with boating and swimming in summer and skiing in winter. **Lake Storsjön** is home to a cousin of the Loch Ness monster, which is "spotted" every year by lucky eyewitnesses. Check out the harpoons of the whalers who tried unsuccessfully to capture the monster at the **Jamtli museum,** north of the city center on Kyrkg., which also features Sami photography, crafts, Viking paintings, and costumed actors in an open-air museum. Take bus #2 from the city center. (Open mid-June to Aug. daily 11am-5pm, 90kr; Sept. to mid-June Tu-Su 11am-5pm, 60kr.) The **Storsjö monster** mania persists today—there is a 10,000kr prize for the best summer sighting and the city is sponsoring a name contest. Rent a **bike** at **Cykelogen,** Kyrkg. 45. (☎12 20 80; open M-F 10am-1pm and 2-6pm, Sa 10am-2pm; 100kr per day), and pedal over the footbridge to **Frösön Island,** once thought to be the home of Viking gods. **Trains** run to Trondheim (5½hr., 300kr) and Stockholm (6hr., 500kr), and into Lapland (1 per day to Gällivare, 320kr). The **tourist office,** Rådhusg. 44, books rooms for free. From the train station, walk up the hill on your left and continue down Prästg.; hang a right up Postgränd one block. (☎14 40 01. Open June-Aug. M-Sa 9am-9pm, Su 10am-7pm; Sept.-May M-F 9am-5pm.) Wild strawberries grow on the thatched roof of **Frösötornets Härbärge hostel,** overlooking the city. Take bus #5 from the city center (last bus 10:20pm) to avoid most of the hellish climb. (☎51 57 67. Reception 9am-9pm. Call ahead; check-in anytime. Open May-Oct. 125kr.) Take bus #2, 6, or 9 to **Östersunds Camping** at Fritidsbyn. (☎14 46 15. Tents 90kr.) Stock up at the **supermarket Hemköp** at Kyrkg. 56. (Open M-F 9am-7pm, Sa 9am-4pm, Su noon-5pm.) **Postal code:** 83101. ☎**063.**

DALARNA

Three hours west of Stockholm, Dalarna is the seat of Sweden's folk culture and the birthplace of the national symbol, the Dala horse. This is the place to be for spirited Midsummer celebrations, or for those seeking serene green fields. Scores of Swedes spend their summer holidays here in the woods to commune with nature, themselves, and their significant others.

MORA. An excellent base for exploring Dalarna, bright and compact Mora skirts the western shore of Lake Siljan and inspired Swedish painter Anders Zorn, whose collection and house are at the **Zornmuseet,** Vasag. 36. (Open May-Sept. M-Sa 9am-5pm, Su 11am-5pm; Oct.-Apr. M-Sa noon-5pm, Su 1-4pm. 35kr, students 30kr. Guided tours 40kr, 35kr.) The legendary red wooden **dalahäst** (Dala horses) are hand-made in **Nusnäs,** 10km east of Mora (bus #108, 15min., 15kr). Brothers Nils and Grannas Olsson now run competing factories. (Open mid-June to mid-Aug. M-F 9am-6pm, Sa-Su 9am-5pm; mid-Aug. to mid-June M-F 8am-5pm, Sa 10am-2pm. Free.) The **Inlandsbanan** train route begins in Mora (p. 913) and runs to Östersund and Gällivare. The **tourist office,** which books 135-155kr rooms for 25kr, is in Mora's Central train station. (☎59 20 20. Open mid-June to mid-Aug. M-F 9am-6pm, Sa-Su 10am-5pm; mid-Aug. to mid-June M-F 9am-5pm, Sa 10am-1pm.)

The Morastrand stop is closer to the sites in town. The **Youth Hostel (HI),** Fredsg. 6, is 500m from Morastrand; turn right on the main road and cross the street when you see Målkull Ann's Cafe, which is the hostel office after hours. (☎381 96. Reception 8-10am and 5-7pm. 160kr, nonmembers 206kr.) Browse the bakeries on **Kyrkogatan.** Load up at the **ICA supermarket,** also on Kyrkog. (Open M-Sa 9am-8pm, Su 11am-8pm.) **Postal code:** 79201. ☎**0250.**

LEKSAND. Over 20,000 people flock to this town above Lake Siljan for Midsummer festivities, featuring a maypole, folk music, and the **Siljansrodden,** a series of churchboat competitions that revives the tradition of rowing to church. The annual **Musik vid Siljan** festival in Leksand and Rättvik (the first week of July) has classical and folk music from around the world. (☎(0248) 102 90; www.siljan.se. Tickets 60-320kr.) The **tourist office,** Stationsg. 14, inside the Leksand train station, has more details. (☎803 00; www.siljan-dalarna.com. Open mid-June to mid-Aug. M-F 9am-8pm, Sa-Su 10am-5pm; mid-Aug. to mid-June M-F 10am-5pm.) From Leksand's quay you can take breezy summer **cruises** on the *M/S Gustaf Wasa* a few times a day to Rättvik and Mora (☎(070) 542 10 25; 2-4hr., 80-235kr).

Accommodations are often hard to come by (packed during Midsummer), but the tourist office can find you a private room for a 25kr fee (doubles from 275kr). **Camping** options abound; check out www.leksand.se/turism/turism/html. The **STF hostel (HI)** is 2½km from the train station; take bus #58 from the bus station before 7pm. (☎152 50. Reception 8-10am and 5-8pm. 100kr; nonmembers add 45kr.) A 20min. walk along the road toward Tällberg brings you to **Leksands Camping Stugby.** (☎/fax 803 13. 100kr per tent.) Pick up the essentials at **ICA Supermarket,** Leksandsv. 5. (Open M-Sa 9am-8pm, Su 10am-8pm.) **Postal code:** 79301. ☎**0247.**

SWITZERLAND

(SCHWEIZ, SVIZZERA, SUISSE)

SWISS FRANCS

US$1 = 1.66SFR	1SFR = US$0.60
CDN$1 = 1.09SFR	1SFR = CDN$0.92
UK£1 = 2.40SFR	1SFR = UK£0.42
IR£1 = 1.93SFR	1SFR = IR£0.52
AUS$1 = 0.88SFR	1SFR = AUS$1.14
NZ$1 = 0.72SFR	1SFR = NZ$1.38
ZAR1 = 0.20SFR	1SFR = ZAR4.94
EUR€1 = 1.52SFR	1SFR = EUR€0.66

PHONE CODE	**Country code:** 41. **International dialing prefix:** 00. From outside Switzerland, dial int'l dialing prefix (see inside back cover) + 41 + city code + local number.

The unparalleled natural beauty of Switzerland entices hikers, skiers, bikers, and scenery gazers from all over the globe to romp in its Alpine playground. Three-fifths of the country is dominated by mountains: the Jura cover the northwest region bordering France, while the Alps stretch gracefully across the entire lower half of Switzerland, colliding with Austria in the eastern Rhaetian Alps. While the stereotypes of Switzerland as a "Big Money" banking and watch-making mecca are to some extent true, its energetic youth culture belies its staid reputation. Although the country is not known for being cheap, the best things—warm Swiss hospitality and sublime vistas—are priceless.

Want to know more? Check out *Let's Go: Austria and Switzerland 2002*.

FACTS AND FIGURES

Official Name: Confederation Helvetica.

Capital: Bern.

Major Cities: Geneva, Basel, Zurich, Lucerne, Lugano.

Population: 7,500,000.

Land Area: 41,290 sq. km.

Climate: Varies with altitude; cold, rainy or snowy winters; cool to warm summers.

Languages: Swiss German, French, Italian, Romansch.

Religions: Roman Catholic (46%), Protestant (40%).

DISCOVER SWITZERLAND

Head directly for **Interlaken** (p. 936), a backpacker town brimming with paragliding, bungee jumping, canyoning, river rafting, kayaking, and other adventure opportunities. Most importantly, Interlaken provides easy access to the other wonders of the **Jungfrau Region.** Continue on to the **Valais,** with hiking and year-round skiing in **Zermatt** (p. 937). While many come to Switzerland to commune with nature, others come to commune with other backpackers: popular hotspots include **Montreux** (especially during the Jazz Festival; p. 925), cosmopolitan **Geneva** (p. 920), and cutting-edge, consumer-culture **Zurich** (p. 928). Finally, taste the *dolce vita* in Italian Switzerland with stops at **Lugano** (p. 939) and **Locarno** (p. 938).

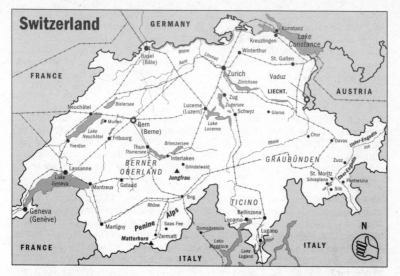

ESSENTIALS

WHEN TO GO

November to March is ski season; prices in eastern Switzerland double and travelers need reservations months in advance. The situation is reversed in the summer, when the flatter, western half of Switzerland fills up. Sights and accommodations are cheaper and less crowded in the shoulder season (May-June and Sept.-Oct.); call ahead to check if the Alpine resort areas will be open then.

DOCUMENTS AND FORMALITIES

VISAS. Switzerland does not require visas for nationals of Australia, Canada, the EU, New Zealand, South Africa, or the US for stays shorter than three months.

EMBASSIES. Most foreign embassies are in **Bern** (p. 934). For Swiss embassies at home: **Australia,** 7 Melbourne Ave., Forrest, Canberra, ACT 2603 (☎(02) 62 73 39 77; fax 62 73 34 28); **Canada,** 5 Marlborough Ave., Ottawa, Ontario KIN 8E6 (☎613-235-1837; fax 613-563-1394); **Ireland,** 6 Ailesbury Rd., Ballsbridge, Dublin 4 (☎(01) 218 63 82 or 218 63 83; fax 283 03 44); **New Zealand,** 22 Panama St., Wellington (☎(04) 472 15 93 or 472 15 94; fax 499 63 0; **South Africa,** 818 George Ave., Arcadia 0083, P.O. Box 2289, 0001 Pretoria (☎(012) 430 67 07; fax 430 67 71); **UK,** 16-18 Montague Pl., London W1H 2BQ (☎(020) 76 16 60 00; fax 77 24 70 01); and **US,** 2900 Cathedral Ave. NW, Washington D.C. 20008-3499 (☎202-745-7900; fax 202-387-2564).

TRANSPORTATION

BY PLANE. Major international airports for oversees connections are in Bern, Geneva, and Zurich. From the UK, **easyJet** (☎(0870) 600 00 00; www.easyjet.com) has flights from London to Geneva, and Zurich (UK£47-136). From Ireland **Aer Lingus** (☎(01) 886 88 88; www.aerlingus.ie) has return tickets from Dublin, Cork, Galway, Kerry, and Shannon to Munich, and Zürich for IR£102-240.

BY TRAIN. Federal **(SBB, CFF)** and private railways connect most towns, with trains running frequently. **Eurail, Europass,** and **Interrail** passes are all valid on Switzerland's trains. The **SwissPass,** which is sold worldwide, offers five options for unlimited rail travel: 4, 8, 15, or 21 consecutive days, or 1 month. In addition to rail travel, it entitles you to unlimited urban transportation in 36 cities and unlimited travel on certain private railways and lake steamers (2nd-class 4-day pass US$160, 8-day US$220, 15-day US$265, 21-day US$305, 1-month US$345). The **Swiss Flexipass** entitles you to any 3-9 days of unlimited rail travel within a 1-month period, with the same benefits as the Swiss Pass (2nd-class 3-day pass US$132, 4-day US$156, 5-day US$180, 6-day US$204, 7-day US$222, 8-day US$240, 9-day US$258.)

BY BUS. PTT Post Buses, a barrage of government-run banana-colored coaches, connect rural villages and towns where trains don't run. SwissPasses are valid on many buses; Eurailpasses are not. Even with the SwissPass, you might have to pay a bit extra (5-10SFr) if you're riding one of the direct, faster buses. *Tageskarten*, valid for 24hr. of free travel, run around 7.50SFr, but most Swiss cities are small enough to cover on foot.

BY CAR. With armies of mechanized road crews ready to remove snow at a moment's notice, roads at altitudes of up to 1500m generally remain open throughout winter. The speed limit is 50kph in cities, 80kph on open roads, and 120kph on highways in Switzerland. Many small Swiss towns forbid cars to enter; some forbid only visitors' cars, require special permits, or restrict driving hours. The **Swiss Touring Club,** 4, chemin de Blandonnet, 1214 Vernier, Case Postale 820 (☎ (022) 417 27 27) operates road patrols. Call ☎ 140 for roadside assistance.

BY BIKE AND BY THUMB. Cycling, though strenuous, is a splendid way to see the country; most train stations rent bikes and allow you to return them at another station. The **Touring Club Suisse,** chemin de Blandonnet 4, Case Postale 820, 1214 Vernier (☎ (022) 417 27 27; fax 417 20 20), is a good source of information, maps, brochures, and route descriptions. *Let's Go* does not recommend hitchhiking.

TOURIST SERVICES AND MONEY

EMERGENCY   Police: ☎ 117. **Ambulance:** ☎ 144. **Fire:** ☎ 118.

TOURIST OFFICES. The **Swiss National Tourist Office,** marked by a standard blue "i" sign, is represented in nearly every town in Switzerland; most speak English. The tourist information website for Switzerland is www.myswitzerland.ch.

MONEY. The Swiss monetary unit is the **Swiss Franc (SFr),** divided into 100 *centimes* (called *Rappen* in German Switzerland). Coins come in 5, 10, 20, and 50 *centimes* and 1, 2, and 5SFr; bills come in 10, 20, 50, 100, 500, and 1000SFr. Switzerland is not the cheapest destination; if you stay in hostels and prepare your own food, expect to spend 45-100SFr (US$30-65), per day. There is no VAT, although there are frequently tourist taxes of a few SFr for a night at hostel. Gratuities are automatically factored into prices. However, it is considered polite to round up your bill 1-2SFr as a nod of approval for good service.

COMMUNICATION

MAIL. Airmail from Switzerland averages 7-20 days to North America, although times are more unpredictable from smaller towns. Domestic letters take 1-3 days.

TELEPHONES. Wherever possible, use a calling card for international phone calls, as the long-distance rates for national phone services are often exorbitant. Most pay phones in Switzerland accept only prepaid phone cards. Phone cards are available at kiosks, post offices, or train stations. Direct dial access numbers include: **AT&T,** ☎ (0800) 89 00 11; **British Telecom,** ☎ (0800) 55 25 44; **Canada Direct,** ☎ (0800) 55 83 30); **Ireland Direct,** ☎ 0800 55 11 74; **MCI,** ☎ (0800) 89 02 22; **Sprint,** ☎ (0800) 89 97 77; **Telecom New Zealand,** ☎ (0800) 55 64 11; **Telkom South Africa,** ☎ 0800 55 85 35.

INTERNET ACCESS. Most towns have Internet cafes (access about 12SFr per hr).

LANGUAGES. German, French, Italian, and Romansch are the national languages. Most urban Swiss speak English fluently, but outside of cities and among older residents you may need our language charts (p. 982).

ACCOMMODATIONS AND CAMPING

There are **hostels** (*Jugendherbergen* in German, *Auberges de Jeunesse* in French, *Ostelli* in Italian) in all big cities and in most small towns. *Schweizer Jugendherbergen* (SJH, or Swiss Youth Hostels) runs HI hostels in Switzerland and has a website with contact information for member hostels (www.youthhostel.ch). Hostel beds are usually 20-34SFr. Non-HI members can stay in all of these hostels but are usually charged a surcharge. The smaller, more informal **Swiss Backpackers (SB)** organization (www.backpacker.ch) has 28 hostels for the young, foreign traveler interested in socializing. Most Swiss **camping sites** are not isolated areas but large plots with many camper vans and cars; camping in Switzerland is less about getting out into nature and more about having a cheap place to sleep. Most sites are open in the summer only. Prices average 6-9SFr per person and 4-10SFr per tent site. **Hotels** and **pensions** tend to charge at least 50-75SFr for a single room, 80-150SFr for a double. The cheapest have Gasthof, Gästehaus, or Hotel-Garni in the name. **Privatzimmer** (rooms in a family home) run about 25-60SFr per person. Breakfast is included at most hotels, pensions, and Privatzimmer.

FOOD AND DRINK

Switzerland's hearty cooking will keep you warm through those frigid alpine winters but will make your cholesterol skyrocket. Bernese *Rösti*, a plateful of hash-brown potatoes (sometimes flavored with bacon or cheese), is prevalent in the German regions; cheese- or meat-*fondue* is popular in the French. Try Valaisian *raclette*, made by melting cheese over a fire, then scraping it onto a baked potato and garnishing it with meat or vegetables. Supermarkets Migros and Co-op double as self-serve cafeterias; stop in for a cheap meal as well as groceries. The world-famous Swiss culinary delight, milk chocolate (*Lindt*, *Toblerone*, and *Nestlé* are native favorites) is cheap and abundant. Each canton has its own local beer—it's relatively cheap, often less expensive than Coca-Cola.

HIKING AND SKIING. Nearly every town has **hiking trails;** consult the local tourist office. Lucerne, Interlaken, Grindelwald, and Zermatt offer particularly good hiking opportunities. Trails are usually marked with either red-white-red markers (only sturdy boots and hiking poles needed) or blue-white-blue markers (mountaineering equipment needed). **Skiing** in Switzerland is often less expensive than in North America if you avoid pricey resorts. **Ski passes** run 30-50SFr per day, 100-300SFr per week; a week of lift tickets, equipment rental, lessons, lodging, and *demi-pension* (half-board—breakfast plus one other meal) averages 475SFr. **Summer skiing** is less common than it once was but is still available in a few towns, such as Zermatt and Saas Fee.

HOLIDAYS AND FESTIVALS

Holidays: New Year's Day (Jan. 1-2); Good Friday (Mar. 29); Easter Monday (Apr. 1); Labor Day (May 1); Ascension Day (May 9); Whit Monday (May 20); Swiss National Day (Aug. 1); Christmas (Dec. 25-26).

Festivals: Two raucous festivals are the **Fasnacht** (Carnival, Mar.) in Basel and the **Escalade** (early Dec.) in Geneva. **"Open-Air"** music festivals occur throughout the summer, including the **Montreux JazzFest** (July) and the **Open-Air St. Gallen** (late June).

FRENCH SWITZERLAND

GENEVA (GENÈVE, GENF)   ☎022

There is no typical resident of this small but feisty city; Geneva's long tradition of battling for its political and religious independence is perhaps the one theme uniting the city's wildly diverse group of citizens. In 1536, Geneva welcomed a young, unknown John Calvin to its cathedral; later, aesthetes and free thinkers, including Voltaire and Rousseau, lived here. Today, multinational organizations (including the Red Cross and the United Nations) continue to lend the city an international feel that contrasts strongly with the homogeneity of most Swiss towns. Many say the only thing Geneva shares with the rest of Switzerland is its neutral foreign policy and the state religion, banking.

◪ INTERCITY TRANSPORTATION

Flights: Cointrin Airport (☎717 71 11, flight info ☎799 31 11) is a hub for **Swissair** (☎(0848) 80 07 00) and also serves **Air France** (☎827 87 87) and **British Airways** (☎(0848) 80 10 10). Several direct flights per day to Amsterdam, London, New York, Paris, and Rome. To reach the city, go up a level from the arrivals hall and catch bus #10 outside (15min., every 6min., 2.20SFr; exact change required) or the train (6min., every 10min., 4.80SFr) to Gare Cornavin.

Trains: Trains run approximately 4:30am-1am. **Gare Cornavin,** pl. Cornavin, is the main station. To: **Basel** (3hr., every hr., 72SFr); **Bern** (2hr., every hr., 40SFr); **Interlaken** (3hr., every hr., 65SFr); **Lausanne** (40min., every 20-30min., 20SFr); **Montreux** (1hr., 2 per hr., 29SFr); **Zurich** (3½hr., every hr., 77SFr). Ticket counter open M-F 8:30am-6:30pm, Sa 9am-5pm. **Gare des Eaux-Vives** (☎736 16 20), on av. de la Gare des Eaux-Vives (tram #12, "Amandoliers SNCF"), connects to France's regional rail through **Annecy** (1½hr., 6 per day, 14SFr) or **Chamonix** (2½hr., 4 per day, 24SFr). Ticket office open M-F 9am-6pm, Sa 11am-5:45pm.

▣ LOCAL TRANSPORTATION

Carry your passport with you at all times; the French border is never more than a few minutes away and buses frequently cross it. Ticket purchasing is largely on the honor system, but you may be fined 60SFr for evading fares. Much of the city can be walked in good weather.

Public Transportation: Geneva has an efficient bus and tram network. **Transport Publics Genevois** (☎308 34 34), next to the tourist office in Gare Cornavin, provides *Le Réseau* (a free map of bus routes) and inexpensive timetables. Open M-Sa 7am-7pm, Su 10am-6pm. **Day passes** 6.30SFr-12SFr. Stamp multi-use tickets before boarding. Buses run roughly 5:30am-midnight; **Noctambus** (3SFr, 1:30-4:30am) runs when the others don't. SwissPass valid on all buses; Eurail not valid.

Taxis: Taxi-Phone (☎331 41 33). 6.30SFr plus 2.70SFr per km. Taxi from airport to city 25-30SFr., max. 4 passengers (15-20min.).

Bike Rental: Geneva has well-marked bike paths and special traffic lights for spoked traffic. For routes, get *Itineraires cyclables* or *Tours de ville avec les vélos de location* from the tourist office. Behind the station, **Genève Roule,** pl. Montbrillant 17 (☎740 13 43), has 25 free bikes available (50SFr deposit; hefty fine if bike is lost or stolen). Slightly nicer neon bikes from 5SFr per day. Open daily 7:30am-9:30pm.

Hitchhiking: *Let's Go* does not recommend hitchhiking; however, hitchers say that Switzerland is one of the safer countries in Europe in which to hail a ride. Those headed to Germany or northern Switzerland take bus #4 to Jardin Botanique. Those headed to France take bus #4 to Palettes, then line D to St. Julien.

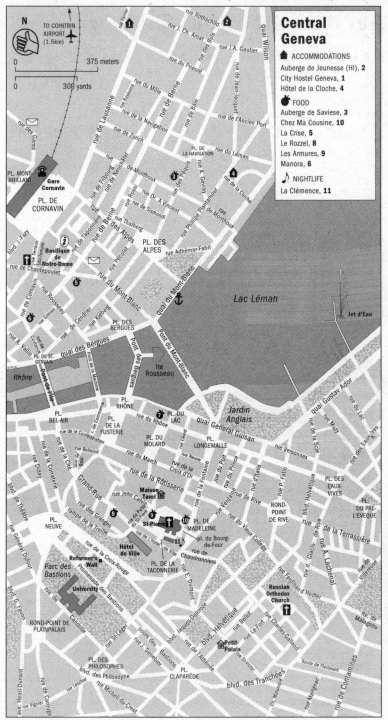

Central Geneva

🏠 **ACCOMMODATIONS**
Auberge de Jeunesse (HI), **2**
City Hostel Geneva, **1**
Hôtel de la Cloche, **4**

🍎 **FOOD**
Auberge de Saviese, **3**
Chez Ma Cousine, **10**
La Crise, **5**
Le Rozzel, **8**
Les Armures, **9**
Manora, **6**

♪ **NIGHTLIFE**
La Clémence, **11**

SWITZERLAND

✦ ❼ ORIENTATION AND PRACTICAL INFORMATION

The labyrinthine cobbled streets and quiet squares of the historic *vieille ville*, around **Cathédrale de St-Pierre,** are the heart of Geneva. Across the **Rhône River** to the north, banks and five-star hotels gradually give way to lakeside promenades, **International Hill,** and rolling parks. Across the **Arve River** to the south lies the village of **Carouge,** home to student bars and clubs (take tram #12 or 13 to pl. du Marché).

TOURIST, FINANCIAL, AND LOCAL SERVICES

Tourist Offices: The **main office,** r. du Mont-Blanc 18 (☎909 70 00), lies 5min. away from Cornavin toward the pont du Mont-Blanc in the Central Post Office Building. Staff books hotel rooms for 5SFr, leads walking tours, and offers free city maps. Open July-Aug. daily 9am-6pm; Sept.-June M-Sa 9am-6pm. During the summer, head for **Centre d'Accueil et de Renseignements** (CAR; ☎731 46 47), an office-in-a-bus parked in pl. Mont-Blanc, by the Metro Shopping entrance to Cornavin Station. Lists free performances and makes hotel reservations. Open mid-June to mid-Sept. daily 9am-11pm.

Consulates: Australia, chemin des Fins 2 (☎799 91 00). **Canada,** av. de l'Ariana 5 (☎919 92 00). **New Zealand,** chemin des Fins 2 (☎929 03 50). **South Africa,** r. de Rhône 65 (☎849 54 54). **UK,** r. de Vermont 37 (☎918 24 26). **US,** World Trade Center Bldg. #2 (☎798 16 05; recorded info ☎798 16 15).

Currency Exchange: ATMs offer the best rates. **Gare Cornavin** has good rates and no commission on traveler's checks, advances cash on credit cards (min. 200SFr), and arranges Western Union transfers. Open daily Nov.-Mar. 6:45am-8pm, Apr.-Oct. 6:45am-9:30pm. Western Union desk open daily 7am-7pm.

Bi-Gay-Lesbian Organizations: Dialogai, r. de la Navigation 11-13 (☎906 40 40). From Gare Cornavin, turn left, walk 5min. down r. de Lausanne, and turn right onto r. de la Navigation. Resource group with programs from support groups to outdoor activities. Mostly male, but women welcome.

EMERGENCY AND COMMUNICATIONS

Emergency: Police: ☎117. **Ambulance:** ☎144. **Fire:** ☎118.

Medical Assistance: Hôpital Cantonal, r. Micheli-du-Crest 24 (☎372 33 11). Bus #1 or 5 or tram #12. Door #2 is for emergency care, door #3 for consultations. For information on walk-in clinics call the **Association des Médecins** (☎320 84 20).

Internet Access: Point 6, r. de Vieux-Billard 7a, off r. des Bains (☎800 26 00). 4SFr per 30min., 6SFr per hr. Open M-Tu and Th noon-midnight, W 10am-midnight, F noon-2am, Sa 10am-2am, Su 10am-10pm.

Post Office: Poste Centrale, r. de Mont-Blanc 18, a block from Gare Cornavin in the stately Hôtel des Postes. Open M-F 7:30am-6pm, Sa 8:30-noon. Address mail to be held: *Poste Restante,* First Name SURNAME, Genève 1 Mont-Blanc, **CH-1211,** Geneva.

⌂ ACCOMMODATIONS

The indispensable *Info Jeunes,* free at the tourist office, lists about 50 options; the highlights are below. Even for short stays, reservations are a must.

City Hostel Geneva, r. Ferrier 2 (☎901 15 00). From the station, turn left on r. de Lausanne, left onto r. de Prieuré, and right onto r. Ferrier. TV room, kitchen, and book exchange. Internet 8SFr per hr. Heinekens sold at the desk. Linens 3SFr. Reception 8am-12:15pm and 1-10pm. Checkout 10am. No curfew or lockout. Single-sex, 4-bed dorms 25SFr; singles 55SFr; doubles 80SFr. MC/V.

Auberge de Jeunesse (HI), r. Rothschild 28-30 (☎732 62 60). Walk 10min. left from the station down r. de Lausanne, then turn right on r. Rothschild. Restaurant, kitchen facilities (1SFr per 30min.), TV room, library, and 3 Internet stations (7SFr per hr.) Breakfast, hall showers, lockers, and sheets included. Laundry 6SFr. Special facilities for disabled guests. 6-night max. stay. Reception June-Sept. 6:30-10am and 2pm-1am;

Oct.-May 6:30-10am and 4pm-midnight. Lockout 10am-2pm; in winter 10am-4pm. Curfew 1am; in winter midnight. Dorms 25SFr; doubles with toilet 70SFr, with toilet and shower 80SFr; quads 110SFr. MC/V.

Cité Universitaire, av. Miremont 46 (☎839 22 11). Take bus #3 (dir. Crets-de-Champel) from the station to the last stop. TV rooms, restaurant, disco (Th and Sa, free to residents), and a small grocery shop. Hall showers included. Reception M-F 8am-noon and 2-10pm, Sa 8am-noon and 6-10pm, Su 9-11am and 6-10pm. Checkout 10am. Dorm lockout 11am-6pm. Dorm curfew 11pm. Dorms (July-Sept. only) 19SFr; singles 41SFr; doubles 57SFr; studios with kitchenette and bathroom 74SFr.

Hôtel de la Cloche, r. de la Cloche 6 (☎732 94 81), off quai du Mont-Blanc across from the Noga Hilton. Breakfast and showers included. Reception 8am-10pm. Singles 65SFr in summer, 55SFr in winter; doubles 85SFr/95SFr; triples 95SFr/105SFr, with bath 120SFr; quads with toilet and shower 140SFr. AmEx/D/MC/V.

Camping Pointe-à-la-Bise, Chemin de la Bise (☎752 12 96). Take bus #8 to Rive, then bus E (north) to Bise and walk 10min. to the lake. Reception 8am-noon and 4-8pm. Open Apr.-Sept. 6SFr per person, 9SFr per tent space. No tents provided. Beds 18SFr. 4-person bungalows 85SFr.

🍴 FOOD

You can find anything from sushi to *paella* in Geneva, but you may need a banker's salary to foot the bill. Do-it-yourselfers can pick up basics at *boulangeries, pâtisseries,* or at the ubiquitous supermarkets. Many supermarkets also have attached cafeterias; try the **Co-op** on the corner of r. du Commerce and r. du Rhône, in the Centre Rhône Fusterie. (Open M 9am-6:45pm; Tu-W and F 8:30am-6:45pm; Th 8:30am-8pm; Sa 8:30am-5pm.) There are cheap restaurants in the *vieille ville* near the cathedral. To the south, the village of Carouge is known for its cozy pizzerias and funky, chic brasseries. Around pl. du Cirque and plaine de Plainpalais, cheap, student-oriented "tea rooms" offer traditional fare at reasonable prices.

Le Rozzel, Grand-Rue 18. Take bus #5 to pl. Neuve, then walk up the hill past the cathedral on r. Jean-Calvin to Grand-Rue. Large dinner crêpes (7-17SFr), dessert crêpes (5-19SFr), menü 19SFr. Open M 7am-4pm, Tu-F 7am-10pm, Sa 9am-10pm.

Restaurant Manora, r. de Cornavin 4, to the right of the station in the Placette department store. This huge self-serve restaurant has a fresh, varied, high-quality selection and free water (rare in Switzerland). Open M-Sa 7am-9pm, Su 9am-9pm.

Globus, 48 r. de Rhône, on the pl. du Molard. Inexpensive gourmet delights, including fresh seafood. Open M-W and F 7:30am-6:45pm, Th 7:30am-8pm, Sa 8am-5:45pm.

Chez Ma Cousine, rue de Bourg-Four 6, in the *vieille ville.* Their specialty is chicken (13.90SFr). Open M-F 7am-midnight, Sa 11am-midnight, Su 11am-11pm.

La Crise, r. de Chantepoulet 13. From the station, turn right on r. de Cornavin and left on r. de Chantepoulet. This tiny, veggie-friendly restaurant has healthy portions and slender prices. Open M-F 6am-8pm, Sa 6am-3pm.

👁 SIGHTS

The city's most interesting historical sites are in a dense, easily walkable space. The tourist office offers 2hr. **walking tours.** (June 14-Oct. 2 M-F 10am; Sa 10am year-round. 12SFr, students and seniors 8SFr.)

VIEILLE VILLE. From 1536 to 1564, Calvin preached at the **Cathédrale de St-Pierre.** The **north tower** provides a commanding view of the old town. (*Open June-Sept. M-Sa 9am-7pm, Su noon-7pm; Oct.-May M-Sa 10am-noon and 2-5pm, Su 1:30-5pm. Tower closes 30min. earlier. July-Aug. 3SFr.*) Ruins, including a Roman sanctuary and a 4th-century basilica, rest in an **archaeological site** below the cathedral. (*Open June-Sept. Tu-Sa 11am-5pm, Su 10am-5pm; Oct.-May Tu-Sa 2-5pm, Su 10am-noon and 2-5pm. 5SFr, students 3SFr.*) At the west end of the *vieille ville* sits the 14th-century **Maison Tavel,** which now houses a history **museum.** (*Open Tu-Su 10am-5pm. Free.*) Across the street is the

Hôtel de Ville (town hall), where world leaders met on August 22, 1864, to sign the Geneva Convention that still governs war conduct today. The **Grand-Rue,** which begins at the Hôtel de Ville, is crammed with clustered medieval workshops and 18th-century mansions; plaques commemorate famous residents, including **Jean-Jacques Rousseau,** born at #40. Below the cathedral, along r. de la Croix-Rouge, the **Parc des Bastions** stretches from pl. Neuve to pl. des Philosophes and includes **Le Mur des Réformateurs (Reformers' Wall),** a sprawling collection of bas-relief figures of the Reformers themselves. The park's center walkway leads to the ⚡**Petit-Palais,** Terrasse St-Victor 2, a beautiful mansion containing art by Picasso, Renoir, Gauguin, and Chagall, as well as themed exhibitions. *(Bus #17 to Petit Palais or #1, 3, or 5 to Claparède. Open M-F 10am-6pm, Sa-Su 10am-5pm. 10SFr, students 5SFr.)*

WATERFRONT. As you descend from the cathedral to the lake, medieval lanes give way to wide quays and chic boutiques. Down quai Gustave Ardor, the **Jet d'Eau,** the world's highest fountain, spews a spectacular 7-ton plume of water 140m into the air. The **floral clock** in the nearby **Jardin Anglais** pays homage to Geneva's watch industry. It's probably Geneva's most overrated attraction and was also the most hazardous: the clock had to be cut back almost 1m because tourists, intent on taking the perfect photograph, continually backed into oncoming traffic. On the north shore, the beach **Pâquis Plage,** quai du Mont-Blanc 30, is popular with locals. *(Open 9am-8:30pm. 2SFr.)*

INTERNATIONAL HILL. The International Red Cross building contains the ⚡**International Red Cross and Red Crescent Museum,** Av. de la Paix 17. *(Bus #8, F, V or Z to Appia or Ariana. Open W-M 10am-5pm. 10SFr, students 5SFr.)* The nearby European headquarters of the **United Nations** is in the same building that sheltered the now-defunct League of Nations. The constant traffic of international diplomats (often in handsome non-Western dress) provides more excitement than the dull guided tour. *(Open July 10am-5pm; Apr.-June and Aug.-Oct. 10am-noon and 2-4pm; Nov.-Mar. M-F 10am-noon and 2-4pm. 8.50SFr, seniors and students 6.50SFr.)*

🎵 🎭 ENTERTAINMENT AND NIGHTLIFE

Genève Agenda, available at the tourist office, is your guide to fun, with event listings ranging from major festivals to movies (be warned—a movie runs about 16SFr). In July and August, the **Cinelac** turns Genève Plage into an open-air cinema screening mostly American films. Geneva hosts the biggest celebration of the **American Independence Day** outside the US (July 4), and the **Fêtes de Genève** in early August is filled with international music and fireworks. The best party in Geneva is **L'Escalade** in early December, which lasts a full weekend and commemorates the dramatic repulsion of invading Savoyard troops.

Place Bourg-de-Four, in the *vieille ville* below the cathedral, attracts students and professionals to its charming terraces and old-world atmosphere. **Place du Molard,** on the right bank by the pont du Mont-Blanc, offers terrace cafes and big, loud bars and clubs. **Les Paquis,** near Gare Cornavin and pl. de la Navigation, is the city's red-light district, but it also has a wide array of rowdy, low-lit bars, many ethnically themed. **Carouge,** across the river Arve, is a student-friendly locus of nightlife activity. Generations of students have eaten at the famous ⚡**La Clémence,** pl. du Bourg-de-Four 20. (Open M-Th 7am-12:30am, F-Sa 7am-1:30am.)

LAUSANNE ☎ 021

Lausanne has a split personality: the medieval town center, or *vieille ville,* is cosmopolitan and businesslike, while the lakefront at Ouchy is lazy and decadent. In the *vieille ville,* two flights of medieval stairs lead to the Gothic **Cathédrale.** (Open July to mid-Sept. M-F 7am-7pm, Sa-Su 8am-7pm; mid-Sept. to June closes 5:30pm.) Below the cathedral, the **Hôtel de Ville** (city hall), on pl. de la Palud, is the meeting point for guided tours of the town. (Tours M-Sa 10am and 3pm. 10SFr, students free. English available.) The ⚡**Collection de l'Art Brut,** av. Bergières 11, is filled with disturbing and beautiful sculptures, drawings, and paintings by artists on the fringe—including institutionalized schizophrenics, poor and uneducated peasants, and convicted criminals. Take bus #2 or 3 to Jomini. (Open Sept.-June M 11am-1pm and 2-6pm, Tu-F 11am-1pm and 2-6pm; July-Aug Sa-Su 11am-6pm. 6SFr, students 4SFr.) The **Musée Olympique,** Quai d'Ouchy 1, is a high-tech temple to modern Olympians with a smaller exhibit dedicated to the ancient games and an extensive video collection, allowing visitors to relive almost any Olympic moment. Take bus #2 to Ouchy. (Open May-Sept. M-W and F-Su 9am-6pm, Th 9am-8pm; Oct.-Apr. Tu-W and F-Su 9am-6pm, Th 9am-8pm. 14SFr, students 9SFr.) In Ouchy, several booths along quai de Belgique and pl. de la Navigation rent **pedal boats** (10SFr per 30min.) and offer water skiing or wake boarding on **Lake Léman** (30SFr per 15min.).

Trains leave from pl. de la Gare 9 to: Basel (2½hr., 2 per hr. 5:20am-9:10pm, 62SFr); Geneva (50min., every 20min. 4:20am-12:45am, 20SFr); Montreux (20min., every 30min. 5:45am-2:25am, 9.40SFr); Paris (4hr., 4 per day 7:35am-5:50pm, 93SFr); and Zurich (2½hr., 3 per hr. 5:25am-9:25pm, 67SFr). Take **bus** #1, 3, or 5 from the station to reach downtown. The **tourist office,** in the train station, reserves rooms. (☎613 73 73. Open daily 9am-7pm.) To reach the large and gleaming **Jeunotel (HI),** Chemin du Bois-de-vaux 36, take bus #2 (dir. Bourdonnette) to Bois-de-Vaux, cross the street, and follow the signs. Courtyards with ping pong tables, a bowling alley next door, an in-house bar and restaurant, and a mostly young backpacker crowd enliven its concrete sterility. (☎626 02 22. Breakfast and linens included. Call ahead in summer. Reception 24hr. Dorms 25SFr; singles 53SFr, with shower 77SFr; doubles 78SFr/94SFr; triples 90SFr; quads 120SFr. AmEx/MC/V.) **Camping de Vidy,** chemin du Camping 3, has a restaurant (open May-Sept. 8am-midnight), supermarket, and pool. Take bus #2 (dir. Bourdonnette) to Bois-de-Vaux, cross the street, follow chemin du Bois-de-Vaux past Jeunotel and under the overpass, and it's straight ahead across rte. de Vidy. (☎622 50 00. Showers included. Electricity 4SFr. Reception Sept.-June 8am-12:30pm and 5-8pm; July-Aug. 8am-9pm. Open year-round. 6.50SFr per person, students 6SFr. 8-12SFr per tent; 1- to 2-person bungalow 54SFr; 3- to 4-person bungalow 86SFr. Cash only.) Restaurants, cafes, and bars cluster around **place St.-François** and the *vieille ville,* while *boulangeries* sell cheap sandwiches on every street and grocery stores abound. **Manora,** pl. St-François 17, beneath the Zürich Bank sign, offers fresh food and "the longest buffet in Lausanne." (Hot food 11am-10pm. Buffet 10:45am-10:30pm. Open daily 7am-10:30pm.)

MONTREUX
☎021

Montreux is postcard Switzerland at its swanky, genteel best. The crystal-blue water of Lac Léman (Lake Geneva) and the snow-capped Alps are a photographer's dream. The gloomy medieval fortress, the **Château de Chillon,** on a nearby island, is one of the most visited attractions in Switzerland. It features all the comforts of home—including prison cells, a torture chamber, and a weapons room. The priest François de Bonivard spent four years chained to a pillar in the dungeon for aiding the Reformation and inspired Lord Byron's *The Prisoner of Chillon* as well as works by Rousseau, Hugo, and Dumas. Take the CGN **ferry** (13SFr, under 26 5.50SFr) or bus #1 (2.60SFr) to Chillon. (Open daily Apr.-Sept. 9am-6pm; Mar. and Oct. 9:30am-5pm; Nov.-Feb. 10am-4pm. 7.50SFr, students 6SFr.) The **Montreux Jazz Festival,** world-famous for exceptional musical talent and one of the biggest parties in Europe, pushes everything aside for 15 days starting the first Friday in July. Check out www.montreuxjazz.com for information and tickets (39-69SFr). If you can't get tickets, come anyway for the **Jazz Off,** 500hr. of free, open-air concerts by new bands and established musicians.

Trains leave the station, on av. des Alpes, to: Bern (1½hr., every hr. 5:35am-10:35pm, 40SFr); Geneva (1hr., every 30min. 5:35am-11:35pm, 29SFr); and Lausanne (20min., 3-5 per hr. 5:25am-noon, 9.40SFr). Descend the stairs opposite the station, head left on Grand Rue, and look to the right for the **tourist office,** on pl. du Débarcadère. (☎962 84 84. Open mid-June to mid-Sept. daily 8:30am-7pm; late Sept. to early June M-F 8:30am-5pm, Sa-Su 10am-3pm.) Cheap rooms are scarce in Montreux and almost non-existent during the jazz festival; book ahead. To get to **Auberge de Jeunesse Montreux (HI),** passage de l'Auberge 8, walk 20min. along the lake past the Montreux Tennis Club. Clean, spacious, and family-owned, this hostel offers many conveniences, including a waterfront location and dining room, but be aware that trains run nearby. (☎963 49 34. Breakfast and linens included. Lockers 2SFr deposit. Reception 7:30-10am and 5-10pm. Check-out 10am. Dorms 30SFr; doubles 38SFr, with shower and bathroom 42SFr. Nonmembers add 6SFr per night. AmEx/MC/V.) To camp, take bus #1 to Villeneuve and follow the lake to the left to **Les Horizons Bleus.** (☎960 15 47. Showers included. Electricity 4SFr. Discount in winter. Reception 7am-11:30pm and 2-9pm. 7SFr per person, 7-14SFr per tent.) Markets with reasonable prices lie on Grand Rue and av. de Casino. **Marché de Montreux,** pl. du Marché, is an outdoor food market (F 7am-1pm), and there's a **Co-op supermarket** at Grand Rue 80. (Open M-F 8am-12:15pm and 2-6:30pm, Sa 8am-5pm.)

NEUCHÂTEL   ☎032

Neuchâtel is famous for the rich treats in its *pâtisseries*, but it also glows with a remarkable medieval beauty. The heart of town (the *vieille ville*) is a block to the right of **place Plury,** centered around **place des Halles;** r. de Château leads to up to the **Collégiale** church (open Oct.-Mar. 9am-6:30pm, Apr.-Sept. 9am-8pm) and the **château** that gives the town its name. The nearby **Prison Tower (Tour des Prisons),** on r. Jehanne-de-Hochberg, has a magnificent view. (Open Apr.-Sept. daily 8am-6pm. 1SFr.) The **Museum of Art and History (Musée d'Art et d'Histoire),** Esplanade Léopold-Robert 1, houses an eclectic collection; most descriptions are in French only. (Open Tu-Su 10am-6pm. Open M Easter-Pentecost. 7SFr, students 4SFr; W free.) The **Museum of Natural History (Musée d'Histoire Naturelle),** off r. de l'Hôpital, displays Swiss animals mounted in surprisingly entertaining dioramas. (Turn right from pl. des Halles onto Croix du Marché, which becomes r. de l'Hôpital. Open Tu-Su 10am-5pm. 6SFr, students 3SFr; W free.)

Trains run to: Basel (1¾hr., every hr. 8am-9pm, 37SFr); Bern (45min., every hr. 5:15am-11:20am, 17.20SFr); and Geneva (1½hr., 2 per hr. 5:55am-9:50pm, 42SFr). A tram runs from the station to the shore area, where you can catch bus #1 to pl. Plury. From there, face the lake and walk left two blocks to the **tourist office,** in the same building as the post office. (☎889 68 90. Open mid-June to mid-Sept. M-F 9am-6:30pm, Sa 9am-5pm, Su 2-5pm; late Sept. to early June M-F 9am-noon and 1:30-5:30pm, Sa 9am-noon.) To reach **Oasis Neuchâtel,** r. du Suchiez 35, take bus #1 to Vauseyon and walk in the same direction around the bend; the hostel will be on the left side. (☎731 31 90. Breakfast 6.50SFr. Shower and sheets included. Reception 8-10am and 5-10pm. No curfew. Reservations recommended. 4-6-bed dorms 25SFr; doubles 60SFr; 2-person garden teepee in summer 40SFr.) If Oasis is full, check the *Hôtel Restaurant* guide for cheap options in nearby towns. **Migros,** r. de l'Hôpital 12, has groceries. (Open M 1:15-6:30pm, Tu-W 8am-6:30pm, Th 8am-8pm, F 7:30am-6:30pm, Sa 7:30am-5pm.)

GERMAN SWITZERLAND

BASEL (BÂLE)   ☎061

Situated on the Rhine near France and Germany, Switzerland's third largest city is home to a large medieval quarter as well as one of the oldest universities in Switzerland—graduates include Erasmus, Bernoulli, and Nietzsche. In Basel (rhymes with "nozzle"), you'll encounter art from Roman times to the 20th century and be serenaded by musicians on every street corner year-round.

■☑ TRANSPORTATION AND PRACTICAL INFORMATION. Basel has three **train stations:** the French SNCF (☎157 22 22) and Swiss SBB stations (☎157 22 22; 1.19SFr per min.) on Centralbahnpl., near the Altstadt, and the German DB station (☎690 11 11) across the Rhine down Greifeng. **Trains** leave from the SBB to: Bern (1¼hr., every hr. 5:50am-10am, 37SFr); Geneva (3hr., every hr. 6:20am-6:20pm, 72SFr); Lausanne (2½hr., every hr. 9am-9:50pm, 62SFr); Zurich (1hr., every 15-

30min. 4:40am-midnight, 31SFr). Make international connections at the French (SNCF) or German (DB) stations. Ages 16-25 receive 25% discount on international trips. To reach the **tourist office,** Schifflände 5, from the SBB station, take tram #1 to Schifflände; the office is on the river, near the Mittlere Rheinbrücke. (☎268 68 68; www.baseltourismus.ch. Open M-F 8:30am-6pm.) For information on **bi-gay-lesbian** establishments, stop by **Arcados,** Rheing. 69, at Clarapl. (☎681 31 32. Open Tu-F 12-7pm, Sa 11am-4pm.) For **Internet access,** head to **Domino,** Steinenvorstadt 54. (10SFr per hr., 12SFr per hr. after 6pm. 18+. Open M-Th 9:30am-midnight, F-Sa 9am-1am, Su 1pm-midnight.) Take tram #1 or 8 to Marktpl. and walk one block back (away from the river) to reach the **post office,** Rüdeng 1. (Open M-W and F 7:30am-6:30pm, Th 7:30am-8pm, Sa 8am-noon.) **Poste Restante:** Postlagernde Briefe für Firstname SURNAME, Rüdengasse, CH-4001 Basel, Switzerland.

🛏🍴 ACCOMMODATIONS AND FOOD. Basel's shortcoming is its lack of cheap lodgings. Call ahead to ensure a spot in the town's only hostel, the **Jugendherberge (HI),** St. Alban-Kirchrain 10. Walk 10-15min. from the SBB station down Aeschen-graben to St. Alban Anlage and follow the signs. (☎272 05 72. Breakfast, showers, and sheets included. Internet 10SFr per hr. Laundry 7SFr. Reception Mar.-Oct. 7-10am and 2-11:30pm; Nov.-Feb. 2-11pm. Check-out 7-10am. Dorms 29-31SFr; singles 79SFr; doubles 98SFr. Jan. 1-Feb. 19 and Nov.-Dec. 2.50SFr less. Non-members add 6SFr. AmEx/D/MC/V.) For **Hotel Steinenschanze,** Steinengraben 69, turn left on Cen-tralbahnstr. from the SBB and follow signs for Heuwaage; go up the ramp under the bridge to Steinengraben and turn left. (☎272 53 53. Breakfast included. Reception 24hr. Singles 110-180SFr, under 25 with ISIC 60SFr for up to 3 nights; doubles with shower 160-250SFr, 100SFr. AmEx/D/MC/V.) **Camp Waldhort,** Heideweg 16, is in a quiet location far from Basel. Take tram #11 to Landhof, backtrack 200m toward Basel, cross the main street, and follow the signs; takes 10min. (☎71 64 29. Recep-tion 7am-noon and 2-10pm. Open Mar.-Oct. 7SFr per person, 10SFr per tent.)

Because of the high student population, there are tons of cheap eateries. **Bar-füsserpl., Marktpl.,** and the streets connecting them are especially full of restaurants. **Zum Schnabel,** Trillengässlein 2, serves tasty German fare. (Open M-Th, Sa 8am-mid-night, F 8am-1am. AmEx/D/MC/V.) Vegetarians can dine at **Café Gleich,** Steinen-vorstadt 23. (Open M-F 9am-9:30pm.) Migrate to **Migros supermarket,** in the SBB station, for groceries. (Open M-F 6am-10pm, Sa-Su 7:30am-10pm.)

◧ SIGHTS. Groß-Basel (Greater Basel), near most sights and the train station, lies on the left bank of the Rhine; **Klein-Basel (Lesser Basel)** occupies the right bank. The very red **Rathaus** brightens Marktpl. with its blinding façade and gold and green statues. Behind the Marktpl. is the 775-year-old **Mittlere Rheinbrücke** (Middle Rhine Bridge) which connects the two halves of Basel. At the other end of Mark-tpl. is a spectacular **Jean Tinguely Fountain,** also known as the **Fasnachtsbrunnen.** Behind Marktpl. stands the red sandstone **Münster,** where you can visit the tombs of Erasmus and Bernoulli or climb the tower for a spectacular view of the city. (Open Easter-Oct.15 M-F 10am-5pm, Sa 10am-4pm, Su 1-5pm; Oct. 16-Easter M-Sa 11am-4pm, Su 2-4pm. Free. Tower closes 30min. before the church. 3SFr.) The **Zoologischer Garten,** Binningerstr. 40, is one of the best zoos in Europe; take tram #1 or 8 to Zoo Bachletten. (Open May-Aug. daily 8am-6:30pm; Sept.-Oct. and Mar.-Apr. 8am-6pm; Nov.-Feb. 8am-5:30pm. 14SFr, students and seniors 12SFr.)

🏛🎭 MUSEUMS AND ENTERTAINMENT. Basel has over 30 museums; pick up the comprehensive museum guide at the tourist office. The **Basel Card,** available at the tourist office, provides admission to all museums as well as discounts around town. (24hr. card 25SFr, 48hr. card 33SFr, 72hr. card 45SFr.) The ◧**Kunstmuseum** (Museum of Fine Arts), St. Alban-Graben 16, houses outstanding collections of old and new masters; admission also gives access to the **Museum für Gegenwartskunst** (Modern Art), St. Alban-Rheinweg 60. (Tram #2. Kunstmuseum open Tu and Th-Su 10am-5pm, W 10am-7pm. Gegenwartskunst open Tu-Su 11am-5pm. Combined ticket 10SFr, students 8SFr, first Su of every month free.) At ◧**Museum Jean**

Tinguely, Grenzacherstr. 214a, everything rattles and shakes in homage to the Swiss sculptor's vision of metal and movement. Take tram #2 or 15 to Wettsteinpl. and bus #31 to Museum Tinguely. (Open W-Su 11am-7pm. 7SFr, students 5SFr.) The **Fondation Beyeler,** Baselstr. 101, is one of Europe's finest private art collections, housing works by nearly every major artist. Take tram #6 to Riehendorf, then walk straight for 3min. (Open daily 10am-6pm, W until 8pm. 15SFr, students 5SFr.)

In a year-round party town, Basel's carnival, or **Fasnacht,** still manages to distinguish itself. The festivities commence the Monday before Lent with the *Morgestraich,* a not-to-be-missed, 600-year-old, 72hr. parade beginning at 4am (Feb. 18-20 in 2002). The goal is to scare away winter (it rarely succeeds). During the rest of the year, head to **Barfüsserplatz** for an evening of bar-hopping. ■**Atlantis,** Klosterberg 10, is a multi-level, sophisticated bar with reggae, jazz, and funk. (Open M-Th 11am-2am, F 11am-4am, Sa 5pm-4am.) **Brauerei Fischerstube,** Rheing. 45, brews the delectably sharp ■*Hell Spezial* ("light special") beer. (Open M-Th 10am-midnight, F-Sa 10am-1am, Su 5pm-midnight. Full dinner menu from 6pm. MC/V.)

ZURICH (ZÜRICH) ☎01

Zurich contains a disproportionate number of Switzerland's many banks, but there's more to Zurich than money. The city was once the focal point of the Reformation in German Switzerland, led by Ulrich Zwingli. In the 20th century, Zurich's Protestant asceticism succumbed to avant-garde artistic and philosophical radicalism: James Joyce toiled away at *Ulysses,* the quintessential modernist novel, in one corner of the city, while Russian exile Vladimir Lenin read Marx and dreamt of revolution in another; meanwhile, a group of raucous young artists calling themselves the Dadaists founded the Cabaret Voltaire. A walk through Zurich's *Altstadt* and student quarter will immerse you in the energetic youth counter-culture that spawned these subversive thinkers, only footsteps away from the rabid capitalism of the famous Bahnhofstraße shopping district.

■ TRANSPORTATION

Flights: Kloten Airport (☎816 2500) is the main hub for **Swissair** (☎084 880 07 00) with daily connections to Frankfurt, Paris, London, and New York. Trains leave every 10-20 min. for the *Hauptbahnhof* (main train station).

Trains: From the **Hauptbahnhof** at Bahnhofpl. to: **Basel** (1hr., 2-4 per hr. 5:55am-1am, 31SFr); **Bern** (1¼hr., 1-2 per hr. 4:45am-midnight, 48SFr); **Geneva via Bern** (3hr., every hr. 5:25am-8:30pm, 77SFr); **Lucerne** (1hr., every hr. 6am-12:15am, 22SFr); **Lugano** (3hr., every hr. 6:30am-10pm, 62SFr); **Milan** (4½hr., every hr. 6:30am-11pm, 76SFr); **Munich** (4hr., 4 per day 7:30am-5:30pm, 91SFr); **Paris** (6-8hr., 3-4 per day 7:10am-10:50pm, 137SFr); **Salzburg** (6hr., 3 per day 7:10am-10:30pm, 102SFr); **Vienna** (9hr., 3 per day 7:10am-10:30pm, 131SFr). Reduction for under age 26 on international trains.

Public Transportation: Public buses, trams, and trolleys run 5:30am-midnight. **Short rides** (under 5 stops) 2.10SFr (yellow button on ticket machine); **long rides** 3.60SFr (blue button). Buy tickets before boarding and validate in machine or face a fine (from 50SFr). A **Tageskarte** (7.20SFr) is valid for 24hr. of unlimited public transport. **Nightbuses** run from the center of the city to outlying areas F-Sa 1-3am.

Bike Rental: Bike loans free at **Globus** (☎(079) 336 36 10); **Enge** (☎(079) 336 36 12); **Hauptbahnhof** (☎210 13 88), at the very end of track 18. Passport and 20SFr deposit required. Open daily 7:30am-9:30pm.

✳ ⓘ ORIENTATION AND PRACTICAL INFORMATION

The **Limmat River** splits the city down the middle on its way to the **Zürichsee.** On the west side of the river is the **Hauptbahnhof** and **Bahnhofstraße,** which begins just outside the *Hauptbahnhof* and runs parallel to the Limmat. Halfway down Bahnhof-

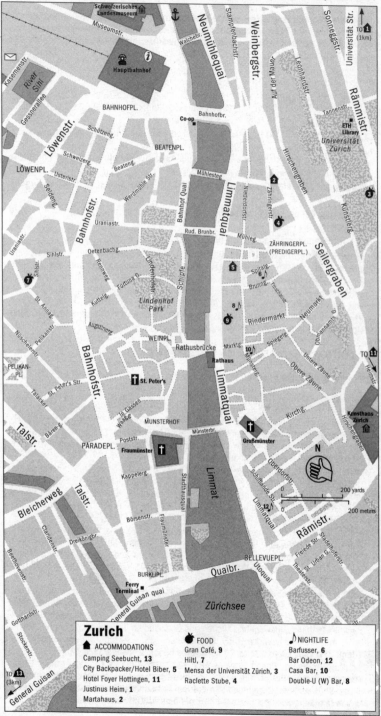

Zurich

🏠 **ACCOMMODATIONS**
Camping Seebucht, **13**
City Backpacker/Hotel Biber, **5**
Hotel Foyer Hottingen, **11**
Justinus Heim, **1**
Martahaus, **2**

🍅 **FOOD**
Gran Café, **9**
Hiltl, **7**
Mensa der Universität Zürich, **3**
Raclette Stube, **4**

♪ **NIGHTLIFE**
Barfusser, **6**
Bar Odeon, **12**
Casa Bar, **10**
Double-U (W) Bar, **8**

SWITZERLAND

str. lies **Paradeplatz**, the town center; **Bürkliplatz** is at the far end of Bahnhofstr. On the east side of the river is the University district, which stretches above the narrow **Niederdorfstr.** and pulses with bars, restaurants, and hostels.

Tourist Offices: Main office (☎215 4000; www.zurichtourism.ch; hotel reservation service ☎215 4040), in the main station. Open Apr.-Oct. M-F 8:30am-8:30pm, Sa-Su 8:30am-6:30pm; Nov.-Mar. M-F 8:30am-7pm, Sa-Su 8:30am-6:30pm.

Currency Exchange: At the main train station. Cash advances with D/MC/V and photo ID. Open daily 6:30am-10pm. **Credit Suisse,** Bahnhofstr. 53, 2.50SFr commission. Open M-F 9am-6pm, Th 9am-7pm, Sa 9am-4pm.

Luggage Storage: At the Hauptbahnhof. Lockers 5SFr and 8SFr per day. Luggage watch 5SFr at the *Gepäck* counter. Open daily 6am-10:50pm.

Bi-Gay-Lesbian Organizations: Ask the tourist office for **Zürich Gay Guide,** which lists support groups, discos, saunas, bars, and restaurants.

Laundromat: Selbstbedienung-Wäscherei (☎242 9914), Müllerstr. 55. Wash and dry 10.20SFr per 5kg. Open daily 6am-11pm.

Emergency: Police: ☎117. **Ambulance:** ☎144. **Fire:** ☎118.

Rape Crisis Line: ☎291 46 46.

24-Hour Pharmacy: Theaterstr. 14 (☎252 5600), on Bellevuepl.

Internet Access: The **ETH Library,** Ramistr. 101, in the Hauptgebäude, has 3 free computers. Take tram #6, 9, or 10 to ETH, enter the main building, and take elevator to fl. H. Open M-F 8:30am-9pm, Sa 9am-2pm. **Telefon Corner,** downstairs in the station next to Marché Mövenpick. 5SFr per hr. (10SFr deposit). Open daily 9am-10:30pm.

Post Office: Main office, Sihlpost, Kasernestr. 97, just behind the station. Open M-F 7:30am-8pm, Sa 8am-4pm. Address *Poste Restante* to: First name SURNAME, Sihlpost, Postlagernde Briefe, **CH-8021** Zürich, SWITZERLAND.

⌂ ACCOMMODATIONS AND CAMPING

Reserve at least a day in advance, especially during the summer.

Martahaus, Zähringerstr. 36 (☎251 45 50). From the station, cross Bahnhofbrücke, and take the 2nd (sharp) right after Limmatquai at the Seilgraben sign. Breakfast and Internet access included. Reception 24hr. Partitioned dorms 37SFr; singles 75-80SFr; street-side doubles 98SFr; quiet-side doubles 110SFr; triples 110SFr. AmEx/D/MC/V. The owners also run the nearby **Luther Pension,** a women-only residence that shares reception facilities with Martahaus.

Hotel Foyer Hottingen, Hottingenstr. 31 (☎256 19 19). Take tram #3 (dir. Kluspl.) to Hottingerpl. Only women are allowed in the partitioned dorms during summer, but both men and women can rent other rooms. Breakfast and kitchen access included. Laundry 5SFr. Reception 7am-11pm. Dorms 35SFr; singles 70SFr, with shower and toilet 105SFr; doubles 110SFr/150SFr; triples 140SFr; quads 180SFr. MC/V.

Justinus Heim Zürich, Freudenbergstr. 146 (☎361 38 06). Take tram #9 or 10 to Seilbahn Rigiblick, then take the hillside tram (by the Migros) uphill to the end. Breakfast and kitchen access included. Reception daily 8am-noon and 5-9pm. Checkout 10am. Singles 40SFr, with shower 70SFr; doubles 90SFr/120SFr; triples 135SFr, with shower 165SFr; all rates reduced for multiple week stays. V.

The City Backpacker-Hotel Biber, Niederdorfstr. 5 (☎251 90 15). From the station, cross Bahnhofbrücke; turn right on Niederdorfstr. Tightly packed rooms are balanced by the hostel's fun location and atmosphere. Pick up a free copy of the very helpful *Swiss Backpacker News.* Showers and kitchen access included. Internet 12SFr per hr. Sheets 3SFr, towels 3SFr. Laundry 10SFr. Key deposit 20SFr. Reception 8am-noon and 3-10pm. Checkout 10am. Dorms 29SFr; singles 65SFr; doubles 88SFr. MC/V.

Camping Seebucht, Seestr. 559 (☎482 1612; fax 482 1660). Take tram #11 to Bürklipl. where you catch bus #161 or 165 to Stadtgrenze. Market and cafe on premises. Showers 2SFr. Reception M-Sa 7:30am-noon and 3-10pm, Su 8am-noon. Open May to late Sept. 8SFr per person, 12SFr per tent. 1.50SFr tax.

◧ FOOD

Zurich's specialty is *Geschnetzeltes mit Rösti*, slivered veal in cream sauce with hash-brown potatoes. The cheapest meals (around 6SFr) are along **Niederdorf-straße.** Try the **farmer's market,** Burklipl. (Tu and F 6-11am), or stop by the **Co-op Super-Center,** next to the train station, for groceries (open M-F 7am-8pm, Sa 7am-4pm). There's also a **Migros supermarket** with adjoining restaurant, Mutschellenstr. 191, near the hostel. (Supermarket open M-F 8am-6:30pm, Sa 8am-4pm. Restaurant open M-F 7am-7pm, Sa 7am-6pm.) Check out *Swiss Backpacker News* (at the tourist office and Hotel Biber) for more information on budget meals in Zurich.

▧ **Gran-Café,** Limmatquai 66. Sit right by the Limmat and enjoy some of the cheapest (yet tastiest) meals around. Daily *Menü* around 11.80SFr. Open M-F 6:15am-11:30pm, Sa 7am-11:30pm, Su 7:30am-11:30pm. AmEx/MC/V.

Hiltl, Sihlstr. 28. The lack of meat makes things surprisingly cheap at this swank vegetarian restaurant (all-day salad or Indian buffet 4.60SFr per 100g). Open M-Sa 7am-11pm, Su 11am-11pm.

Raclette Stube, Zähringerstr. 16 (☎251 4130). Serves high-quality, classic Swiss fare in an authentic Swiss atmosphere. Open daily from 6pm.

Mensa der Universität Zürich (University of Zurich cafeteria), Rämistr. 71 (☎632 6211). Take streetcar #6 to ETH Zentrum from Bahnhofpl. Hot dishes 7.50SFr with ISIC card, salad buffet 6SFr. Open July 15-Oct. 21 M-F 11am-2pm; Oct. 22-July 14 M-F 11am-2:30pm and 5-7:30pm.

◉ SIGHTS

ALTSTADT. Right off Paradepl. stands the 13th-century **Fraumünster;** although it's a Protestant church, Jewish artist Marc Chagall agreed to design the beautiful stained-glass windows in the late 1960s. Outside the church, a mural in the courtyard depicts Felix and Regula, the decapitated patron saints of Zurich, with their heads in their hands. *(Open May-Sept. 9am-6pm; Oct., Mar.-Apr. 10am-5pm; Nov.-Feb. 10-4pm.)* Next door, **St. Peter's Church** has the largest clock face in Europe. The twin towers of the nearby **Großmünster** have become a symbol of Zurich. Zwingli spearheaded the Reformation here, and one of his bibles lies in a case near the pulpit from which he preached. A column tells the legend of the church: while chasing a stag from Aachen, Charlemagne supposedly stumbled over the graves of Felix and Regula, prompting him to build *Großmünster*. Venture downstairs to the 12th-century crypt to see Charlemagne's statue and 2m-long sword, then climb to the top of the towers for a panoramic view of Zurich. *(Church open Mar.-Oct. 9am-6pm; Nov.-Feb. 10am-5pm. Tower open daily Mar.-Oct. 1:30-5pm, Oct.-Mar. Sa-Su 9:15am-5pm. Tower 2SFr.)*

MUSEUMS. The incredible ▧**Kunsthaus Zürich,** Heimpl. 1, covers Western art from the 15th century on. *(Take tram #3, 5, 8, or 9 to Kunsthaus. Audio tours in English, French and German. Open Tu-Th 10am-9pm, F-Su 10am-5pm. 10SFr, students 6SFr; W free.)* ▧**Museum Rietberg,** Gablerstr. 15, presents an exquisite collection of Asian, African, and other non-European art. *(Take tram #7 to Museum Rietberg. Open Tu and Th-Su 10am-5pm, W 10am-8pm. 5SFr, students 6SFr.)* The **Schweizerisches Landesmuseum,** Museumstr. 2, next to the main train station, encapsulates Swiss history; exhibits include 16th-century astrological instruments, Ulrich Zwingli's weapons from the Battle of Kappel in which he died (1531), and a tiny bejeweled clock with a golden skeleton morbidly pointing to the hour. *(Open Tu-Su 10:30am-5pm. Students 3SFr.)* The **Museum Bellerive,** Höschg. 3, features rotating "out-of-the-ordinary" themes. Past exhibitions include "Made in Japan" (a room full of plastic Japanese meals); "The 70s and 80s" starts in January 2002. *(☎383 4376. Take tram #4 or 2 to Höschg. Open Tu-Th 10am-8pm, F 10am-5pm, Sa-Su 11am-5pm. 6SFr, students and children 3SFr. Closed between exhibits, so call ahead.)* The museum at the **Lindt and Sprüngli Chocolate Factory,** Seestr. 204, has exhibits in German only, but the free chocolates transcend language barriers. *(☎716 2233. Bus #165 to Schooren. Open W-F 10am-noon and 1-4pm. Free.)*

CHOCOHOLICS The Swiss have long had a love affair with chocolate–milk chocolate was first concocted in here in 1876, and Nestlé, Lindt, and Toblerone all call Switzerland home. But has this seemingly innocuous romance turned into an obsession? In May 2001, the Swiss government introduced postage stamps that look and smell like squares of chocolate. (The original design called for chocolate-*flavored* stamps, but the idea was dropped for hygienic reasons.) The stamps are even packaged on paper designed to look like foil wrappers. Officially, they commemorate the centennial of Chocosuisse, the association of chocolate makers and importers, but it might just be evidence that the Swiss truly are addicted.

◤ NIGHTLIFE

Niederdorfstraße rocks as the epicenter of Zurich's nightlife (although women may not want to walk alone in this area at night), and **Münsterg.** and **Limmatquai** are lined with cafes and bars. Pick up *ZüriTip* for more information. On Friday and Saturday nights in summer, **Hirschenpl.** (on Niederdorfstr.) hosts sword-swallowers and other daredevil street performers. Locals and students guzzle beer (from 10SFr) on the terrace at **Double-U (W) Bar,** Niederdorfstr. 21. (Open M-Th from 2pm, F-Su from 4pm. **Casa Bar,** Münsterg. 30, has pricey beer (from 13.50SFr) but great live jazz and no cover. (Open daily 11am-2am.) Thornton Wilder and Vladimir Lenin used to get sloshed at the posh, artsy **Bar Odeon,** Limmatquai 2. (Open Su-Th 7am-2am, F-Sa 7am-4am.) **Barfusser,** Spitalg. 14, is Europe's oldest gay bar. (Open daily until 2am.)

ST. GALLEN   ☎071

St. Gallen's main draw is the **Stiftsbibliothek** (Abbey Library), a baroque library designated a World Heritage Treasure by UNESCO. Visitors ooh and aah over the lavishly carved and polished shelves, rows of gilt-spined books, and ancient manuscripts. (☎227 34 16. Open Apr.-Oct. M-Sa 9am-noon and 1:30-5pm, Su 10am-noon and 1:30-4pm; Nov.-Mar. M-Sa 9am-noon and 1:30-4pm. 7SFr, students 5SFr.) Often overshadowed by the library, but no less beautiful, is the **Kathedrale St. Gallen,** which has enormous stained glass windows, intricately carved confessionals, and impressive murals. (☎227 33 88. Open daily 7am-6pm except during mass.) Follow Marktpl. away from the train station to reach **Museumstr.,** home to St. Gallen's four museums. The best are the small but fascinating **Natural History Museum** (☎242 06 70) and the **Historisches Museum** (☎242 06 42). (All open Tu-F 10am-noon and 2-5pm, Sa-Su 10am-5pm. All four museums 6SFr, students 2SFr.) In late June, the **Open Air St. Gallen Music Festival** features over 20 live bands; past headliners have included the Red Hot Chili Peppers, B.B. King, and James Brown. (☎(087) 887 79 94; www.openairsg.ch. 144SFr.)

 Trains roll to: Bern (2½hr., 5am-10:40pm, 65SFr); Geneva (4½hr., 5am-8:40pm, 95SFr); Munich (3hr., 4 per day 8:30am-6:30pm, 63SFr, under 26 49SFr); and Zurich (1hr., 5am-10:40pm, 29SFr). To get to the **tourist office,** Bahnhofpl. 1a, from the train station, head through the bus stop and past the fountain on the left; it's on the right. (☎227 37 37. Open Oct.-May M-F 9am-noon and 1-6pm, Sa 9am-noon; June-Sept. 9am-6pm, Sa 9am-noon. City tours June 12-Sept. M, W, and F 2pm. 15SFr.) Get on the Internet at **Media Lounge,** Katherineng. 10. (☎244 30 90. 2SFr per 10min., 1 SFr per additional 5min., 12 SFr per hr. Open M-F 9am-9pm, Sa 10am-5pm.) Perched on a hill above town, the ◼**Jugendherberge St. Gallen (HI),** Jüchstr. 25, has a TV room, library, and Internet access (1SFr per 4min.). From the Appenzeller/Trogener station next to the main station, take the orange train to Schülerhaus; walk uphill, turn left across the tracks, and head downhill. (☎245 47 77. Reception daily 7-10am and 5-10:30pm. Check-out 10am. Closed Dec. 1 to late Feb. Dorms 26SFr; singles 46SFr; doubles 72SFr; non-members add 6SFr. AmEx/DC/MC/V.) **Restaurant Scheitlinsbüchel,** Scheitlinsbüchelweg 10, offers a sublime view from its outdoor patio. (Open Tu-Su 9am-late.) The **Migros supermarket** and adjoining buffet restaurant, St. Leonhardstr., are one block behind the train station. (Open M-W and F 8am-6:30pm, Th 8am-9pm, Sa 8am-5pm.) **Postal code:** CH-9000.

LUCERNE (LUZERN)   ☎ 041

Lucerne is the Swiss traveler's dream come true. The city is small but cosmopolitan, satisfying sophisticated culture lovers and also providing outdoor opportunities for the adventurous. Sunrise over the famous **Mt. Pilatus** has hypnotized hikers and artists—including Twain, Wagner, and Goethe—for centuries.

⬛🔢 TRANSPORTATION AND PRACTICAL INFORMATION. Trains leave Bahnhofpl. (☎ 157 22 22) to: Basel (1¼hr., 1-2 per hr. 4:40am-11:50pm, 31SFr); Bern (1½hr., 1-2 per hr. 4:40am-11:50pm, 32SFr); Geneva (3½hr., every hr. 4:40am-9:55pm, 70SFr); Interlaken (2hr., every hr. 6:30am-7:30pm, 26SFr); Lausanne (2½hr., every hr. 5:55am-9:55pm, 58SFr); Lugano (2¾hr., every hr. 5:50am-10:15pm, 58SFr); and Zurich (1hr., 2 per hr. 4:55am-11:10pm). **VBL buses** depart from in front of the station and provide extensive coverage of Lucerne (1 zone 1.70SFr, 2 zones 2.20SFr; day pass 10SFr; Swiss Pass valid); **route maps** are available at the tourist office. The **tourist office,** in the station, has free city guides, makes hotel reservations for free, and sells the **Visitor's Card,** which, with a hotel or hostel stamp, gives discounts at museums, stores, bars, and more. (☎ 227 17 17. Open May-Oct. M-F 8:30am-7:30pm, Sa-Su 9am-7:30pm; Nov.-May M-F 8:30am-6pm, Sa-Su 9am-6pm.) **C+A Clothing,** on Hertensteinstr. at the top of the Altstadt, has two free but busy **Internet** terminals. (Open M-W 9am-6:30pm, Th-F 9am-9pm, Sa 8:30am-4pm.) The **post office** is on the corner of Bahnhofstr. and Bahnhofpl. Address mail to be held: Postlagernde Briefe für First Name SURNAME, Hauptpost, **CH-60000** Luzern 1. (Open M-F 7:30am-6:30pm, Sa 8am-noon.)

🔢🔳 ACCOMMODATIONS AND FOOD. Relatively inexpensive beds are limited in Lucerne, so call ahead to ensure a roof over your head. Until 1998, **Hotel Löwengraben,** Löwengraben 18, was a prison, but it was converted into a trendy, clean hostel with a bar, restaurant, Internet (15SFr per hr.), and all-night dance parties for guests every summer Saturday. (☎ 417 1212. Breakfast 9SFr. Sheets included. 4-bed dorms 25SFr; 3-bed dorms 30-35SFr; double with shower 80-99SFr.) **Tourist Hotel Luzern,** St. Karliquai 12, on the *Altstadt* side of Spreuerbrücke, is very close to the center of the *Altstadt.* (☎ 410 2474. Internet 10SFr per hr. Bike rental 15SFr per day. Breakfast included. Laundry 10SFr. Reception 7am-10:30pm. Dorms 30-33SFr; quads 172SFr, students 156SFr. Dec.-May rooms 40-60SFr less. Add 10SFr per person for private shower. AmEx/MC/V.) **Kam Tong Chinese Take Away,** Inseliquai 8, serves large portions of cheap, tasty Asian fare for 10-15SFr. (Open M-W 9am-6:30pm, Th-F 9am-9pm, Sa 9am-4pm.) There's a **Migros supermarket** at the station. (Open M-W and Sa 6:30am-8pm, Th-F 6:30am-9pm, Sa-Su 8am-8pm.)

🔳🔢 SIGHTS AND NIGHTLIFE. The *Altstadt,* across the river over Spreuerbrücke from the station, is famous for its frescoed houses, especially those on Hirschenpl. The 660-year-old **Kapellbrücke,** a wooden-roofed bridge, runs from left of the train station to the Altstadt and is ornately decorated with Swiss historical scenes; further down the river, the **Spreuerbrücke,** which is decorated by Kaspar Meglinger's eerie *Totentanz* (Dance of Death) paintings. On the hills above the river, the **Museggmauer** and its towers are all that remain of the medieval city's ramparts. Three of the towers are accessible to visitors, and the **Zeitturm** (clock tower) provides a particularly pleasing panorama of the city; walk along St. Karliquai, turn right (uphill), and follow the brown castle signs. (Open daily 8am-7pm.) To the east is the magnificent **Löwendenkmal** (Lion Monument), the dying lion of Lucerne, which is carved into a cliff on Denkmalstr. The **Picasso Museum,** Am Rhyn Haus, Furreng. 21, displays 200 intimate photographs of Picasso as well as a large collection of unpublished Picasso works. From Schwanenpl., take Rathausquai to Furreng. (Open daily Apr.-Oct. 10am-6pm; Nov.-Mar. 11am-1pm and 2-4pm. 6SFr, with guest card 5SFr, students 3SFr.) The **▨Verkehrshaus der Schweiz** (Swiss Transport Museum), Lidostr. 5, has interactive displays on all kinds of vehicles, but the real highlight is the trains. Take bus #6, 8, or 24 to Verkehrshaus. (Open daily Apr.-Oct. 9am-6pm; Nov.-Mar. 10am-5pm. 18SFr, students 16SFr; 33% Eurail or guest

S W I T Z E R L A N D

card discount.) The **Richard Wagner Museum**, Wagnerweg 27, was once the composer's lakeside home and now exhibits original letters, scores, and instruments. Take bus #6, 7 or 8 to Wartegg. (Open mid-Mar. to Nov. Tu-Su 10am-noon and 2-5pm. 5SFr, students and guest card holders 4SFr.)

Lucerne's nightlife is more about lingering than club-hopping. **The Loft**, Haldenstr. 21, is a trendy club with hip-hop and house in a cloud of smoke. (Open W-Th 9pm-3am and F-Su 9pm-4am. No cover W and Su; Th 10SFr; F 12SFr; Sa 15SFr.) Lucerne attracts big names for its **Blue Balls Festival** (3rd week in July) and **Blues Festival** (2nd week in Nov.).

▶ DAYTRIPS FROM LUCERNE: MT. PILATUS AND RIGI KULM. The view of the Alps from the top of **Mt. Pilatus** (2132m) is absolutely phenomenal. For the most memorable trip, catch a boat from Lucerne to Alpnachstad (90min.), ascend by the world's steepest **cogwheel train** (48° gradient), then descend by cable car to Krienz and take the bus back to Lucerne (entire trip 77.60SFr; Eurail or Swisspass 41SFr). For less money and more exercise, take a train or boat to Hegiswil and hike up to Fräkmüntegg (3hr.), a half-way point on the cable car (22SFr, 25% Eurail or Swisspass discount). Across the sea from Pilatus soars the **Rigi Kilm**, which has a magnificent view of the lake and its neighbor. Ferries run from Lucerne to Vitznau, where you can catch a cogwheel train to the summit. You can also conquer Rigi on foot; it's 5hr. from Vitznau to the top, and anyone who tires out halfway can pick up the train at Rigi Kaltbad (3hr. up the hill) and ride the rest of the way. Return by train, take the cable car from Rigi Kaltbad to Weggis, and return to Lucerne by boat (return 87SFr; Eurail or Swisspass 42SFr).

BERN ☎ 031

The city has been Switzerland's capital since 1848, but don't expect fast tracks and power politics—Bern prefers to focus on the lighter things in life, such as local Toblerone chocolate and sumptuous flower gardens.

▤ TRANSPORTATION. The **airport** (☎960 21 11) is 20min. from the city; a bus runs from the train station 50min. before each flight (10min., 14SFr). **Trains** depart the station at Bahnhofpl., in front of the tourist office, to: Basel (1¼hr., every hr. 5:45am-9:45pm, 37SFr); Geneva (2hr., every 30min. 5:40am-11:20pm, 50SFr); Interlaken (50min., every hr. 7:25am-11:25pm, 25SFr); Lausanne (1¼hr., every 20min. 5am-11:20pm, 32SFr); Lucerne (1½hr., every hr. 6:40am-10:40pm, 32SFr); and Zurich (1¼hr., every 30min. 5:50am-11:50pm, 48SFr). International fares are reduced 25% for ages 26 and under. **Bike Rental** is available from the **SwissCom Kiosk** outside the train station. (Free, but 20SFr deposit plus ID required. Same-day return. Open May-Oct. 7:30am-9:30pm.)

⚐ PRACTICAL INFORMATION. Most of medieval Bern lies in front of the train station and along the Aare River. In the **train station**, check-in, information, buses, and a pharmacy are upstairs; tickets, lockers, police, showers, toilets, and currency exchange are downstairs. The **tourist office**, on the street level of the station, offers daily **city tours** (8-24SFr) in the summer by bus, on foot, or by raft. (Open June-Sept. daily 9am-8:30pm; Oct.-May M-Sa 9am-6:30pm, Su 10am-5pm.) Get online at **Soundwerk Café**, Wasserwerkg. 5, at the Aare River near the bottom of Nydeggbrücke. (Open M-F 11am-7pm, Sa 11am-4pm. Free.) The **post office**, Schanzenpost 1, is next to the train station. (Open M-F 7:30am-6:30pm, Sa 8am-noon.) For **Poste Restante**, address mail to be held: Postlagernde Briefe für First name SURNAME, Schanzenpost **3000**, Bern 1, SWITZERLAND.

▤▢ ACCOMMODATIONS AND FOOD. From the train station, turn left on Spitalg., left on Kornhauspl., and right on Rathausg. to reach **Backpackers Bern/Hotel Glocke**, Rathausg. 75. (☎311 37 71. Internet and kitchen access. Laundry 3.80SFr. Reception June-Aug. 8-11am and 3-10pm; Sept.-May 8-11am and 3-8pm. Dorms 32SFr 1st night, 27SFr subsequent nights; singles 75SFr; doubles 120SFr, with bath

GRIN AND BEAR IT Legend has it that Duke Berchtold V of Zähringen, founder of Bern, wanted to name the city after the first animal he caught when hunting on the site. The animal was a you-know-what, and Bern (derived from *Bären*, or "bears") was born. The *Bärengraben* themselves weren't built until the Bernese victory at the Battle of Nouana in 1513, when they dragged home a live bear as part of the war booty. A hut was erected for the beast in what is now Bärenplatz (Bear Square) and his descendants have been Bern's collective pets ever since.

160SFr. Apr.-May and Sept.-Oct. dorms 2SFr less, other rooms 5SFr less; Nov.-Mar. 4SFr, 10SFr less.) Take bus #20 (dir. Wyler) to Gewerbeschule, then the 1st right for Pension Marthahaus, Wyttenbachstr. 22a, which offers free bikes and Internet access. (☎ 332 4135; martahaus@bluewin.ch. Breakfast included. Laundry 8SFr. Reception 7am-9pm. Check-out 11am. Reservations recommended. Singles 60SFr, with shower 90SFr; doubles 95SFr/120SFr; triples 120SFr/150SFr. Prices drop 5-10SFr in winter. MC/V.) The tourist office also has a list of private rooms.

Almost every "-platz" overflows with cafes and restaurants, though the bigger ones tend to be pricier and more touristy. **Fruit and vegetable markets** sell fresh produce on Bärenpl. (May-Oct. daily 8am-6pm) and on Bundespl. (every Tu and Sa). **Manora,** Bubenbergpl. 5A, over the tramlines from the station, is a self-service chain with nutritious, cheap food. (Open M-Sa 6:30am-11pm, Su 8:30am-11:15pm.) The **Migros supermarket,** Marktg. 46, also has a restaurant and take-away counters. (Open M 9am-6:30pm, Tu-W and F 8am-6:30pm, Th 8am-9pm, Sa 7am-4pm.)

⑤ SIGHTS. The massive **Bundeshaus,** the seat of the Swiss national government, dominates the Aare. *(Tour every hr. M-Sa 9-11am and 2-4pm, Su 10-11am and 2-3pm; free.)* From the Bundeshaus, turn left off Kocherg. at Theaterpl. to reach the 13th-century **Zytglogge** (clock tower). At 4min. before the hour, figures on the tower creak to life, but it's more entertaining to watch the tourists ooh and aah. Continue down Kocherg. to the **Protestant Münster** (cathedral); for a fantastic view, climb the Münster's 100m spire. *(Open Easter-Oct. Tu-Sa 10am-5pm, Su 11:30am-5pm; Nov.-Easter Tu-F 10am-noon and 2-4pm, Sa 10am-noon and 2-5pm, Su 11am-2pm. Tower closes 30min. earlier. 3SFr.)* Several steep walkways lead from the Bundeshaus to the **Aare River;** on hotter days, locals dive lemming-style from the bridges, but only experienced swimmers should join in due to swift currents. Across the Nydeggbrücke lie the **Bärengraben** (bear pits), which were recently renovated—perhaps in an attempt to make up for the indignity of being on display for gawking crowds. *(Open June-Sept. daily 9am-6pm; Oct.-May 9am-4pm. 3SFr to feed bears.)* The path up the hill to the left leads to the ❀**Rosengarten** (Rose Garden), which has one of the best views of the *Altstadt.*

🏛 MUSEUMS. The **Kunstmuseum** (art museum), Hodlerstr. 8-12, near the Lorrainebrücke, houses the world's largest Paul Klee collection and a smattering of other 20th-century artists. *(Open Tu 10am-9pm, W-Su 10am-5pm. Mandatory lockers 2SFr. 7SFr, students and seniors 5SFr, under 16 free.)* The **Bernisches Historische Museum,** Helvetiapl. 5, is jam-packed with anything and everything from Bern's lengthy history. *(Open Tu-Su 10am-5pm. 7SFr, students 5SFr, under 16 free; Sa free.)* **Albert Einstein's House,** Kramg. 49, where he conceived the theory of general relativity, is now filled with his photos and letters. *(Open Feb.-Nov. Tu-F 10am-5pm, Sa 10am-4pm. 3SFr, students 2SFr.)*

🎭🎵 ENTERTAINMENT AND NIGHTLIFE. Luminaries such as Bob Dylan and Björk have played at the **Gurten Festival** in July (www.gurtenfestival.ch), while jazz-lovers flock to the **International Jazz Festival** (www.jazzfestivalbern.ch) in early May. The orange grove at Stadgärtnerei Elfnau (tram #19 to Elfnau) has free Sunday **concerts** in summer, and from mid-July to mid-August **OrangeCinema** (www.orangecinema.ch) screens recently released films in the open air; tickets are available from the tourist office in the train station.

At night, the fashionable folk linger in the bars and cafes of the *Altstadt* while a seedier crowd gathers under the gargoyles of the Lorrainebrücke. **Le Pery Bar,**

Schmiedenpl. 3, is a popular nightspot. (Open M-W 5pm-1:30am, Th 5pm-2:30am, F-Sa 5pm-3:30am.) **Sous le Pont** is a den of alternative culture with an unnaturally relaxed, predominantly male clientele; from Bollwerk, head left before Lorraine-brücke through the cement park. (Open M and Sa after 5pm, Tu-F 11pm-1am.) **Warning:** Like many cities, Bern has a drug community; it tends to congregate around the Parliament park and terraces.

INTERLAKEN
☎033

Interlaken, whose name means "between lakes," lies between the Thunersee and the Brienzersee at the foot of the largest mountains in Switzerland. With easy access to these natural playgrounds, Interlaken has earned its rightful place as one of Switzerland's prime tourist attractions and as its top outdoor adventure spot.

🖪🖪 **TRANSPORTATION AND PRACTICAL INFORMATION.** The Westbahnhof (☎826 47 50) and Ostbahnhof (☎828 73 19) have **trains** to: Basel (6:30am-11:30pm, 56SFr); Bern (6:30am-11:30pm, 8.60SFr); Geneva (5:30am-9:40pm, 65SFr); Lucerne (5:30am-7:15pm, 27SFr); Lugano/Locarno (5:30am-5:15pm, 72SFr); and Zurich (6:30am-11:30pm, 62SFr). The Ostbahnhof also sends trains to Grindelwald (June-Sept. every 30min., Sept.-May every hr. 6:35am-11:35pm; 9.40SFr).

The **tourist office**, Höheweg 37, in the Hotel Metropole, offers free maps. (☎826 53 00. Open July-Aug. M-F 8am-6pm, Sa 9am-noon, Su 5-7pm; Sept.-June M-F 8am-noon and 2-6pm, Sa 9am-noon.) Rent **bikes** at either train station. (27SFr per day. Open daily 6am-10pm.) For **snow and weather information,** call ☎855 10 22. In case of emergency, call the **police** (☎117) or the **hospital** (☎826 26 26). **The Wave,** Rosenstr. 13, right at the main circle between the station and the tourist office, provides late-night Internet access. (14SFr per hr., students 11SFr. Open M-F 11am-11pm, Sa-Su 2-11pm.) **Postal Code:** CH-3800.

🖪🖪 **ACCOMMODATIONS AND FOOD.** 🖪**Backpackers Villa Sonnenhof,** Alpenstr. 16, diagonally across the Höhenmatte from the tourist office, is quiet. Call or arrive early in the morning. (☎826 71 71. Internet 10SFr per hr. Mountain bikes 18SFr per half day. Full-service laundry 12SFr. Breakfast, towels, sheets and lockers included. Reception 7:30-11am and 4-10pm. No curfew. 4-6 bed dorms 29SFr; doubles 74SFr; triples 99SFr. 5SFr extra for balcony or bathroom. AmEx/MC/V.) To reach party-happy **Balmers Herberge,** Hauptstr. 23-25, walk diagonally across the Höhenmatte from the tourist office and follow signs down Parkstr. No reservations—just sign in, drop off your pack, and return at 5pm when beds are assigned. (☎822 19 61. Free sleds and 20% discount on ski and snowboard rental in winter. Mountain bikes 30SFr per day. Internet 10SFr per hr. Kitchen 1SFr per 20min. Breakfast included. Laundry 8SFr. Reception in summer 6:30am-11pm; in winter 6:30-9am and 4:30-11pm. Check-out 9am. Lockout 9:30am-4:30pm. No curfew. Mattress 15SFr; dorms 22-24SFr; doubles 68SFr; triples 90SFr; quads 112SFr. AmEx/MC/V.) Most hostels serve cheap food, but you can also swing by **Migros supermarket,** across from the Westbahnhof, which houses a restaurant. (Open M-Th 8am-6:30pm, F 8am-9pm, Sa 7:30am-4pm). **Restaurant Goldener Anker,** Marktg. 57, serves traditional specialties alongside low-fat and vegetarian dishes. (Open M-W and F-Su 10am-12:30am.).

🖪🖪 **OUTDOORS AND HIKING.** Interlaken offers a wide range of adrenaline-pumping activities. **Alpin Raft** (☎823 41 00), the most established company in Interlaken, has qualified, personable guides and offers: paragliding (140SFr); canyoning (95SFr); river rafting (95SFr); skydiving (380SFr); bungee jumping (155SFr); and hang gliding (155SFr); and sea-kayaking on the Brienzersee (30SFr). All prices include transportation to and from any hostel in Interlaken. A number of horse and hiking tours, as well as rock-lessons, are also available upon request. The owner of **Skydiving Xdream,** Stefan Heuser, has been on the Swiss skydiving team for 17 years. (Skydiving 380SFr. ☎079 759 3484. Open Apr.-Oct.)

Interlaken's most traversed trail climbs to the **Harder Kulm** (1310m). From the Ostbahnhof, head toward town, take the 1st road bridge right across the river, and

Interlaken's adventure sports industry is thrilling, but accidents do happen. On July 27, 1999, 19 tourists were killed by a sudden flash flood while canyoning. Be aware that you participate in all adventure sports at your own risk.

follow the yellow signs that later give way to white-red-white markings on the rocks. From the top, signs lead back down to the Westbahnhof. A funicular runs from the trailhead near the Ostbahnhof to the top from May-October. (2hr. up, 1½hr. down. 12.80SFr, return 20SFr; 25% Eurailpass and SwissPass discount.) For flatter **trails**, turn left from the train station and left before the bridge, then follow the canal over to the nature reserve on the shore of the Thunersee. The trail winds up the Lombach river and through pastures at the base of the Harder Kulm back toward town (2hr.).

JUNGFRAU REGION

The Jungfrau area has attracted tourists for hundreds of years with glorious hiking trails and permanently snow-capped peaks. The three most famous mountains are the Jungfrau (Maiden), the Eiger (Ogre), and the Mönch (Monk). Locals say that the monk protects the maiden by standing between her and the ogre, but at 4158m, she could probably beat up the puny Eiger (3970m). From Interlaken, the valley splits at the foot of the Jungfrau: the eastern valley contains Grindelwald and the western valley holds many smaller towns. The two valleys are divided by an easily hikeable ridge. Pick up the *Lauterbrunnen/Jungfrau Region Wanderkarte* (15SFr at any tourist office) for an overview of the hikes.

GRINDELWALD ☎036

Grindelwald is the launching point to the only glaciers accessible by foot in the Bernese Oberland. The town has all kinds of hikes, from easy valley walks to challenging climbs. The **Bergführerbüro** (Mountain Guides Office), 200m past the tourist office, sells hiking maps and arranges glacier walks and mountaineering. (☎853 52 00. Open June-Oct. M-Sa 9am-noon and 3-6pm, Su 4-6pm.) The 4hr. **Lower Glacier** *(Untere Grindelwaldgletscher)* hike is moderately steep and can be done in tennis shoes; to reach the trailhead, walk up the main street away from the station and follow the signs downhill to Pfinstegg. For the **Upper Glacier** *(Obere Grindelwaldgletscher)* hike, take the postal bus from Grindelwald (dir. Grosse Scheidegg) to Oberslaubkule and follow the signs uphill for Glecksteinhütte.

The Jungfraubahn runs from the Interlaken Ostbahnhof (9.40SFr). The **tourist office** is in the Sport-Zentrum to the right of the station. (☎854 121. Open July-Aug. M-F 8am-7pm, Sa 8am-5pm, Su 9-11am and 3-5pm; Sept.-June M-F 8am-noon and 2-6pm, Sa 8am-noon and 2-5pm). Access the **Internet** (15SFr per hr.) at **Ernst Schudel's**, opposite the tourist office. (Open daily 9am-noon and 2-6:30pm.) To reach the **Jugendherberge (HI)**, head left out of the train station for 400m, then cut uphill to the right just before Chalet Alpenblume and follow the steep trail (400m) all the way up the hill. (☎853 10 09. Mountain bikes 15SFr per day. Breakfast, sheets, and lockers included. Laundry 5SFr. Reception daily 7-10am and 3-11pm. No lockout. Dorms 29.80SFr; doubles with toilet and shower 51.30SFr. Apr.-Oct. prices 3.50SFr lower. Non-members add 5SFr. AmEx/D/MC.) **Gepsi Bar**, just past the tourist office on the left, serves cheap food. (Open daily 8:30-11:30pm.) There's **Co-op supermarket** across from the tourist office. (Open M-F 8am-6:30pm, Sa 8am-4pm.)

ZERMATT AND THE MATTERHORN ☎027

The valley blocks out the great Alpine summits that ring Zermatt, allowing the **Matterhorn** (4478m) to rise alone above the town. Miles of spectacular, well-marked ski paths are accessible to all visitors, including **Europe's longest run**, the 13km trail from Klein Matterhorn to Zermatt. A one-day **ski pass** for any of the area's regions runs 62-77SFr. The **Zermatt Alpin Center**, which houses both the **Bergführerbüro** (Guide's Office; ☎966 2460) and the **Skischulbüro** (Ski School Office; ☎967 2466), is past the post office from the station; here you can pick up detailed 4-day weather forecasts, ski passes, and information on guided climbing expeditions. (Both offices open July-Sept. M-F 8:30am-noon and 4-7pm, Sa 4-7pm, Su 10am-noon and 4-7pm.) Rental prices for **skis** and **boots** are set throughout Zermatt (winter 38SFr per day, summer 28SFr per day, cheaper for longer periods). Try **Slalom Sport,** on Kirchstr. (☎966 2366; open M-Sa 8am-noon and 2-7pm, Su 8am-noon and 4-6:30pm) or **Bayard Sports** (☎966 4960; open M-Sa 8am-noon and 2-7pm) directly across from the station. **Freeride Film Factory** (☎213 3807) offers custom **hiking** and **climbing** expeditions (160SFr-250SFr) and will even give you a videotape of your trek.

Cars and buses are illegal in Zermatt to preserve the Alpine air—the only way in is the hourly **BVZ** (Brig-Visp-Zermatt) rail line. Connect from Visp (from Lausanne; 35SFr, return 58SFr) or Stalden-Saas (from Saas Fee; 1hr.; 23.60SFr, return 31SFr). The **tourist office,** on Bahnhofpl. in the station complex, sells the **Wanderkarte** (hiking map) for 24.90SFr. (☎967 0181. Open mid-June to mid-Oct. M-F 8:30am-6pm, Sa 8:30am-7pm, Su 9:30am-noon and 4-7pm; mid-Oct. to mid-June M-Sa 8:30am-noon and 1:30-6pm.) **Hotel Bahnhof,** on Bahnhofstr. to the left of the station, provides hotel housing at hostel rates. (☎967 24 06. Reception 8am-8pm. Open mid-Dec. to mid-Oct. Dorms 30SFr; 4-bed rooms with private showers 40SFr; singles with shower 48-62SFr; doubles 70-86SFr, with shower 80-96SFr. MC/V.) **Walliserkanne,** on Bahnhofstr. next to the post office, offers filling Swiss fare at reasonable prices. (Open 11:30am-2pm and 6-10pm. Pizzeria downstairs open 7pm-2am. AmEx/D/MC/V.) **Café du Pont,** on Bahnhofstr., is Zermatt's oldest restaurant and has multilingual menus burnt into slabs of wood hanging on the wall. (Open June-Oct. and Dec.-Apr. daily 9am-11pm; food served 11am-10pm.) Pick up groceries at the **Co-op Center** opposite the station. (Open M-Sa 8:30am-12:15pm and 1:45-6:30pm.) **Postal code:** CH-3920.

ITALIAN SWITZERLAND (TICINO)

Ever since Switzerland won the Italian-speaking canton of Ticino (Tessin in German and French) from Italy in 1512, the region has been renowned for its mix of Swiss efficiency and Italian *dolce vita*—no wonder the rest of Switzerland vacations here among jasmine-laced villas painted the bright colors of Italian *gelato*.

LOCARNO   ☎091

For centuries, visitors have journeyed to Locarno solely to see the orange-yellow **Church of Madonna del Sasso** (Madonna of the Rock), founded in 1487. A 20min. walk up Via al Sasso leads to the top. Hundreds of silver medallions on the church walls commemorate Mary's interventions in the lives of pilgrims, and the **museum** next door houses ancient reliquaries, pilgrims' souvenirs, and a collection of disaster paintings commissioned by survivors to thank the Madonna. (Grounds open 6:30am-7pm. Museum open Apr.-Oct. M-F 2-5pm, Su 10am-noon and 2-5pm. 2.50SFr, students 1.50SFr.) Each August, Locarno swells with pilgrims of a different sort: its world-famous **film festival** draws visitors from all over the globe.

Trains run frequently from P. Stazione (☎743 65 64) to: Lucerne (3hr., every 30min. 6am-12:30am, 56SFr); Lugano (45min., every 30min. 5:50am-11:50pm, 16.40SFr); Milan (2½hr., several per day 6:30am-8:30pm, 63SFr); and Zurich (2¾hr., every hr. 6:25am-9pm, 60SFr). The **tourist office** is on P. Grande in the *Kursaal* (casino). (☎791 00 91. Open M-F 9am-6pm, Sa 9am-5pm, Su 10am-noon and 1-3pm.) To reach **Pensione Città Vecchia,** 13 Via Toretta, turn right onto Via Toretta from P. Grande. (☎751 45 54. Breakfast and sheets included for doubles, otherwise 4.50SFr each. Bike rental 15SFr per day. Check-in 1-6pm; reservations 1-9pm; call ahead if arriving after 6pm. Dorms 22-33SFr; doubles 64-74SFr; triples 31-34SFr; quads 29-33SFr.) **Ristorante Manor,** 1 Via della Stazione, left of the station, provides quality food cafeteria style. Open M-Sa 7:30am-9pm, Su 8am-9pm; Mar.-Oct. open until 10pm.) For **groceries,** there's an **Aperto** at the station (open 6am-10pm) and a **Migros supermarket** on P. Grande (open M-Sa 9am-7pm). **Postal code:** CH-6900.

LUGANO
☎ 091

Set in a valley between two mountains, Lugano draws plenty of visitors with its seamless blend of religious beauty, artistic flair, and natural spectacle. The frescoes of the 16th-century **Cattedrale San Lorenzo,** just below the train station, are still magnificently vivid. The most spectacular fresco in town, however, is the gargantuan *Crucifixion* in the **Chiesa Santa Maria degli Angiuli,** on the waterfront to the right of the tourist office. Armed with topographic maps and trail guides (sold at the tourist office), hikers can tackle the nearby mountains, **Monte Bré** (933m) and **Monte San Salvatore** (912m). Alpine guides at the **ASBEST Adventure Company,** V. Basilea 28 (☎966 11 14), offer everything from snowshoeing and skiing (full-day 90SFr) to paragliding (165SFr) and canyoning (from 90SFr).

   Trains leave P. della Stazione to: Locarno (1hr., every 30min. 5:30am-midnight, 16.40SFr); Milan (1½hr., every hr. 5:30am-10:45pm, 14SFr); and Zurich (3½hr., every hr. 5:55am-8:35pm, 62SFr). To reach the **tourist office,** cross the footbridge labeled "Centro" from the station and head down Via Cattedrale; turn left on Via dei Pesci and left on Riva Via Vela, which becomes Riva Giocondo Albertolli. The office is just past the fountain on the left, across the street from the ferry launch. (Open Apr.-Oct. M-F 9am-6:30pm, Sa 9am-12:30pm and 1:30-5pm, Su 10am-2pm; Nov.-Mar. M-F 9am-12:30pm and 1:30-5:30pm.) **Hotel Montarina,** 1 Via Montarina, is a palm-tree-enveloped hostel with a swimming pool, kitchen, and terrace. (☎966 72 72. Buffet breakfast 12SFr. Sheets 4SFr. Laundry 4SFr, soap 1.50SF. Reception 8am-9pm. Open Mar.-Oct. Call 2 weeks in advance for reservations July-Aug. Dorms 25SFr; singles 50-65SFr; doubles 100SFr, with bath 120SFr.) **Migros super-market,** 15 Via Pretoria, two blocks left from the post office down Via Pretorio, has a food court on the ground floor. (Open M-F 8am-6:30pm, Sa 7:30am-5pm.)

TURKEY (TÜRKİYE)

TURKISH LIRA

US$1 = 1,480,000TL	1,000,000TL = US$0.68
CDN$1 = 969,350TL	1,000,000 TL = CDN$1.04
UK£1 = 2,132,300TL	1,000,000 TL = UK£0.47
IR£1 = 1,716,000TL	1,000,000 TL = IR£0.59
AUS$1 = 782,950TL	1,000,000 TL = AUS$1.29
NZ$1 = 642,350TL	1,000,000 TL = NZ$1.57
ZAR1= 179,950TL	1,000,000 TL = ZAR1.07
EUR€1 = 1,351,000TL	1,000,000 TL = EUR€0.75

PHONE CODE

Country code: 90. **International dialing prefix:** 00. From outside Turkey, dial int'l dialing prefix (see inside back cover) + 90 + city code + local number.

Merely 77 years old, Turkey has inherited the combined riches of Ancient Greeks and Romans, Byzantines, and Ottomans. Asia Minor has seen more than 10,000 years of cultural traffic, and each civilization has left a layer of debris for the traveler to unearth. Pristine meadows, sun-soaked beaches, cliffside monasteries, medieval churches, archaeological treasures, and countless cups of *çay* (tea) all await the explorer. Following the creation of the East Roman Empire, Constantinople (İstanbul) became the center of Greek Orthodox culture. The Selçuk Turks encroached upon the Byzantine Empire from the 11th to 14th centuries, and the Ottomans conquered İstanbul in 1453. The Ottoman Empire lasted from the early 1400s to the end of World War I. Early 20th-century leader Mustafa Kemal (Atatürk), equating modernization with Westernization, abolished the Ottoman Caliphate, romanized the alphabet, and set up a democratic government. Recent history is dominated by the military, which occupied Northern Cyprus in 1974, organized three coups, and spearheaded conflicts with Kurdish rebels in the southeast. In December 1999, after a long struggle, partially due to a questionable human rights record, Turkey was nominated for EU membership.

You'll thank us when you get your own copy of *Let's Go: Turkey 2002*.

FACTS AND FIGURES

Official Name: Turkey.
Capital: Ankara (3.5 million).
Major Cities: İstanbul, İzmir.
Population: 65,000,000.
Land Area: 770,760 sq. km.

Climate: Temperate; hot, dry summers with mild, wet winters; harsher in interior.
Languages: Turkish (official), Kurdish, Arabic.
Religions: Sunni Muslim (98.8%), Shiite Muslim (1%), Christian and Jewish (0.2%).

DISCOVER TURKEY

Bargain at bazaars and marvel at Ottoman palaces in **İstanbul** (p. 944). Swing northeast to **Edirne** (p. 954), the former Ottoman capital and home to the finest mosque in all of Turkey, before trekking down the sparkling **Aegean Coast.** From **Çanakkale** (p. 957), make daytrips to the famed battlefield of **Gallipoli** and the ruins of **Troy**, then head south to the unparalleled ruins of **Ephesus** (p. 960). Get sweet in the morning in **Bodrum** (p. 961), the "Bedroom of the Mediterranean," then head inland to **Aphrodisias**, near **Pamukkale** (p. 960), to visit some of antiquity's best temples. From there it's just a bit farther south to the **Mediterranean Coast,** where **Ölüdeniz**, near **Fethiye** (p. 963), shelters a secluded blue lagoon. Pass through **Kaş** to reach the eternal flame of **Olimpos** (p. 964). Then hit the central **Cappadocia** region, known for its surreal rock formations and backpacker scene, and the underground cities of **Göreme** (p. 966).

ESSENTIALS

WHEN TO GO

Summer (especially July-Aug.) is high tourist season. Late-spring and early-fall temperatures are far milder and prices may be 10% lower, but some facilities and sights close in the off-season. During Ramadan, the Islamic holy month, public eating, drinking, and smoking are generally taboo during daylight hours.

DOCUMENTS AND FORMALITIES

VISAS. As of August 2001, citizens of Australia, Canada, Ireland, the UK, and the US require a visa to enter Turkey. New Zealanders may stay for up to three months with a valid passport, South Africans for up to one month. Though visas can be obtained from a Turkish embassy or consulate in your home country, it is most convenient to get them upon arrival in Turkey, at the airport or border. A three-month visa costs AUS$30 for Australians, UK£10 for British citizens, IR£13 for Irish citizens, and US$45 for US citizens.

EMBASSIES. Foreign embassies are all in **Ankara** (p. 965); consulates are in İstanbul (p. 945). For Turkish embassies at home: **Australia,** 60 Mugga Way, Red Hill, Canberra ACT 2603 (☎(02) 62 95 02 27; fax 62 39 65 92; turkembs@ozemail.com.au); **Canada,** 3 Crescent Rd. Rockcliffe, **Ontario** KIM ON1 (☎613-748-3737; fax 613-789-3442; turkish@magma.ca); **Ireland,** 11 Clyde Rd., Ballsbridge, Dublin 4 (☎(01) 668 52 40; fax 668 5014; turk@embiol.ie); **New Zealand,** 15-17 Murphy St., Level 8, Wellington (☎(04) 472 12 90; fax 472 12 77; turkem@xtra.co.nz); **South Africa,** 1067 Church St., Hatfield, Pretoria 0028 (☎(012) 342 60 53; fax 342 60 52; www.turkishembassy.co.za); **UK,** 43 Belgrave Sq., London SWIX 8PA (☎(020) 73 93 02 02; fax 73 93 00 66; www.turkishembassy-london.com); and **US,** 2525 Massachusetts Ave. NW, Washington, DC 20008 (☎202-612-6700; fax 202-612-6744; info@turkey.org; www.turkey.org).

TRANSPORTATION

BY PLANE. Turkish Airlines (THY), Delta, and major European airlines fly into İstanbul, with some flights to Ankara and Antalya. **THY** (www.thy.com), with offices in New York (☎212-339-9602), Sydney (☎(02) 92 99 84 00), and London (☎(020)766 93 00), connects over 30 Turkish cities.

BY TRAIN. Trains link Turkey to Athens and Bucharest, but some lines may be suspended due to political crises in the Balkans. Trains are cheap, but they follow circuitous routes painfully slowly. **Eurail** is not valid; **InterRail** passes are. With a Eurail pass, take the train to Alexandroupolis, Greece, and ride the bus from there.

BY BUS. Frequent, modern, and cheap, buses connect all Turkish cities and are the best way to get around. In large cities, bus companies run free shuttles called *servis* from their town offices to the *otogar* (bus station), which is often quite a distance away. Buy tickets from local offices or purchase them directly at the station. Many lines grant students a 10% discount. **Fez Travel**, 15 Akbıyık Cad., Sultanahmet, İstanbul (☎(212) 516 90 24; www.feztravel.com) offers a hop-on, hop-off "backpacker bus" loop (June-Oct. US$175, under 26 US$168).

 Road travel in Turkey is considered dangerous by European and US standards. Whether taking a bus or driving, travelers should educate themselves about road conditions. Travel only on reputable bus companies such as **Ulusoy, Varan,** and **Kamil Koç,** and avoid travel at night and in inclement weather.

BY FERRY. Multiple ferry routes connect **Greece** and Turkey's **Aegean Coast:** boats run from Lesvos and Hios to Çeşme; Samos to Kuşadası; Kos to Bodrum; and Rhodes to Bodrum. Boats also arrive from Italy: ferries go from Venice to İzmir and Antalya, and from Brindisi to Çeşme. For more on ferries connecting to and from the Aegean Coast, see p. 956. Boats also connect Greece to Turkey's Mediterranean Coast, for example, from Rhodes to Marmaris; see p. 962. Domestic **Turkish Maritime Lines** (TML) ferries sail from İstanbul to İzmir and to destinations on the Black Sea Coast. Most ferries are comfortable and well equipped. Fares jump sharply in July and August, but student discounts are often available. Reserve ahead, and check in at least two hours in advance. If you arrive in Turkey by boat, expect to pay a US$11 Turkish port tax. Most countries also charge a port tax for exit.

BY DOLMUŞ AND BY CAR. Shared taxis known as *dolmuş* (usually minibuses) let passengers off at any point along a fixed route; they post their destination on the windshield and leave whenever they fill up. Sit first and pay later. The speed limit is 50kph. (31mph) in cities, 90kph. (55mph) on highways, and 130kph. (80mph) on *oto yolu* (toll roads). You must have an International Driving Permit (IDP) to drive; *Let's Go* does not encourage driving. If you get in an accident, file a report with the traffic police (☎118). Contact the **Turkish Touring and Automobile Association** in the U.S. (TTOK; ☎212-282 81 40) for more information.

BY MOPED AND BY THUMB. Mopeds are an easy, cheap way to tour coastal areas and the countryside. Expect to pay US$20-35 per day; remember to bargain. Be sure to ask if the quoted price includes tax and insurance. *Let's Go* does not recommend hitchhiking in Turkey. Lone women should never hitchhike. However, those who choose to accept the risks of hitchhiking generally pay half what the trip would cost by bus. The hitching signal is a waving hand or the standard thumb.

TOURIST SERVICES AND MONEY

EMERGENCY   Police: ☎110. Ambulance: ☎112. Fire: ☎155.

TOURIST OFFICES. Virtually every town has a tourist office. The website for Turkish tourism is www.turkey.org.

MONEY. Turkey's currency, the **lira** (TL), comes in denominations of 100,000; 250,000; 500,000; 1,000,000; 5,000,000; and 10,000,000TL. Coins are in values of 5000; 10,000; 25,000; 100,000; and 25,000TL. Because the *lira* suffers from sky-high inflation, *Let's Go* quotes prices in US dollars. Tip taxi drivers, hotel porters, and waiters (leave it on the table) about US$1 for good service. 15-20% tips are required only in ritzy restaurants, where service may be included (*servis dahil*). Bargaining is common at markets, bazaars, and carpet shops. Allow the seller to name a price, counter with a lower price (less than what you intend to pay, but not less than half the seller's price), and let the fun begin! A 10-20% value-added tax (*katma değer vergisi;* KDV) is included in the prices of most goods. Theoretically, it can be reclaimed upon departure.

COMMUNICATION

MAIL. PTTs (Post, Telegraph, and Telephone offices) are well marked by yellow signs. Some PTTs may charge a small sum for *Poste Restante.* Airmail from Turkey takes 1-2 weeks; mark cards and envelopes "uçak ile" and tell the vendor the letter's destination: *Avustralya, Kanada, Büyük Bretanya* (Great Britain), *İrlanda, Yeni Zelanda* (New Zealand), *Güney Afrika* (South Africa), or *Amerika.*

TELEPHONES. Make international calls at post offices. New phones accept phone cards *(telekart)*, available at the PTT, while old ones require tokens *(jeton)*. Card phones have English directions. For directory assistance, dial ☎118; for an international operator, dial ☎115. International direct dial numbers include: **AT&T,** ☎00 800 122 77; **British Telecom,** ☎00 800 89 0900; **Canada Direct,** ☎00 800 166 77; **Ireland Direct,** ☎00 800 353 11 77; **MCI,** ☎00 800 111 77; **Sprint,** ☎00 800 144 77; and **Telkom South Africa,** ☎00 800 27 11 77.

LANGUAGE AND CUSTOMS. When a Turk raises his chin and clicks his tongue, he means *hayır* (no); this gesture is sometimes accompanied by a shutting of the eyes or the raising of eyebrows. *Evet* (yes) may be signalled by a sharp downward nod. It is considered rude to point your finger or the sole of your shoe toward someone. Although public displays of affection are considered inappropriate, Turks often greet one another with a kiss on both cheeks. For Turkish basics, see p. 989.

ACCOMMODATIONS AND CAMPING

Clean, cheap accommodations are available nearly everywhere. Basic rooms cost US$6-8 for a single and US$12-16 for a double. **Pensions** *(pansiyon)*, by far the most common accommodations, are often private homes with rooms for travelers; don't expect toilet paper or towels. Most towns have a **hamam**, or bathhouse, where you can get a steam bath for US$4; they schedule different times for men and women. **Camping** is popular, and cheap campgrounds abound (around US$2-4 per person). Official government campsites are open from April or May to October.

HEALTH AND SAFETY

The most significant health concerns are parasites and other gastrointestinal ailments. Never drink unbottled or unpurified water, and be wary of food from street vendors. Eat fruits with thick peels that can be removed. Always carry toilet paper; expect to encounter pit toilets. Signs in pharmacy windows indicate night-duty pharmacies *(nöbetçi)*. If you're caught doing **drugs** in Turkey (or are caught in the company of someone who is), you're screwed. Stories of dealer-informers and lengthy prison sentences are true; embassies are utterly helpless in all cases. Exporting antiques is punishable by imprisonment. Foreign **women,** especially those traveling alone, attract significant attention. Catcalls and other forms of verbal harassment are common; physical harassment is rare. One way of deflecting unwanted attention is showing displeasure by making a scene; try the expressions *"ayıp!"* ("shame!") or *"haydi git"* ("go away"). Holler *"eem-DAHT"* ("help") if the situation gets out of hand. Touristed areas may be more comfortable for women. Dress modestly, especially farther east. While Kurdish guerillas are no longer active in the southeast, political tensions remain in that region. Recent terrorist acts by Chechen sympathizers have targeted tourists. While neither of these circumstances is reason to curtail a visit, travelers should stay away from large crowds and all political demonstrations, and should stay abreast of recent developments. The US State Department issues travel warnings (www.state.gov).

FOOD AND DRINK

Staples like *çorban salatası* (shepherd's salad), *mercimek çorbası* (lentil soup), rice pilaf, and *yoğurt* are not listed on *lokanta* (restaurant) menus; their availability is understood. *Et* is the word for meat: lamb is *kuzu*, veal is *dana eti*. Chicken, usually called *tavuk*, becomes *piliç* when roasted. *Kebap*, the most famous Turkish meat dish, ranges from skewer *(şiş)* or spit *(döner)* broiling to oven roasting. *Köfte* are medallion-sized, spiced meatballs. Turks eat a lot of seafood; *kalamar* (squid), *midye* (mussels), and *balık* (fish). Vegetarians often enjoy *meze* (appetizers). *Dolma* are peppers, grape leaves, or eggplant stuffed with rice and served with or without meat. Turks drink *çay* (tea) hot, with sugar. *Kahve* (coffee) comes *sade* (unsweetened), *orta* (medium-sweet), and *şekerli* (sweet). Ice-cold *rakı*, an anise seed liquor, is the national drink. *Baklava*, a flaky pastry with nuts and soaked in honey, and *lokum* (Turkish delight) are the most famous Turkish sweets.

HOLIDAYS

Holidays: New Year's Day (Jan. 1); National Sovereignty and Children's Day (Apr. 23); Ataturk Commemoration and Youth and Sports Day (May 1); Victory Day (Aug. 30); and Republic Day (Oct. 29). During **Ramadan** (roughly Nov. 6-Dec. 5), pious Muslims abstain from eating, drinking, smoking, and sex between dawn and dusk; businesses may have shorter hours, and public eating is inappropriate. **Eid al-Fitr** breaks the Ramadan fast. During the 3-day **Şeker Bayramı** (Sugar Holiday), which marks the end of Ramadan, bus and train tickets and hotel rooms may be scarce. **Kurban Bayramı** (Sacrifice Holiday), when animals are slaughtered and distributed to the poor, occurs a few months after Ramadan.

İSTANBUL

CITY CODES	☎212 (European side) and ☎216 (Asian side)

Straddling two continents and three millennia of history, İstanbul exists on an incomprehensible scale, set against a dense landscape of Ottoman mosques, Byzantine mosaics, and Roman masonry. The Bosphorus Straits have proven both a blessing and a curse, providing a strategic location that has attracted countless sieges. Having survived wars, natural disasters, and foreign occupations, İstanbul comprises a unique mix of civilizations which also shows through in religious practices and everyday customs. Conservative black-veiled women merge in the swelling crowds with younger women in Western dress, and major religious and historical sights double as the backdrops for Turkish pop videos. Explore the İstanbul beyond carpet salesmen and backpacker bars, and venture out into neighborhood produce markets and back-alley tea shops.

▌ TRANSPORTATION

Flights: Atatürk Havaalanı, 30km from the city. The domestic and international terminals are connected by **bus** (every 20min. 6am-11pm). To reach **Sultanahmet,** take a Havaş **shuttle bus** from either terminal to Aksaray (every 30min., US$7), then walk 1 block south to Millet Cad. and take an Eminönü-bound **tram** to the Sultanahmet stop. Or take a **taxi** (US$4) to the Yeşilköy train station and take the commuter rail *(tren)* to the end of the line in Sirkeci. A direct taxi to Sultanahmet costs US$9. To reach **Taksim,** take the Havaş shuttle to the end of the line (every 30min., 6am-9pm, US$5). To reach the airport, have a private service such as **Karasu** (☎638 66 01) or **Zorlu** (☎638 04 35) pick you up from your hostel (US$5.50) or take the Havaş shuttle from the McDonald's in Taksim (45min., every 30min., US$6.75).

Buses: Esenler Otobüs Terminal (☎658 00 36), in Esenler, 3km from central İstanbul. Serves intercity buses. To get there, take the tram to Yusufpaşa (1 stop past Aksaray; US$0.50), walk 1min. to the Aksaray Metro station on broad Adnan Menderes Bul., and take the Metro to the *otogar* (15min., US$0.40). Most companies have **courtesy buses** *(servis)* that run to the *otogar* from Eminönü, Taksim, and elsewhere in the city (free with bus ticket purchase). Various companies serve additional international destinations. The following have good reputations; be careful when choosing a company. Many find it easier to use a travel agency (see p. 946).

Kamil Koç (☎658 20 03). To **Ankara** (6hr.; every hr.; US$22, students US$20) and **Bursa** (4hr.; every 30min.; US$9, students US$8.25).

Pamukkale (☎/fax 658 22 22). To **Pamukkale** (10hr.; 7 per day; US$21, students US$19).

Parlak Tur (☎658 17 55). To **Prague** (2 days; Sa 4pm; US$100, students US$95).

Ulusoy (☎658 30 00; fax 658 30 10). To: **Athens** (21hr.; Th and Şa 1 per day; US$60, students US$51); **Bodrum** (13hr.; 3 per day; US$31, students US$27); **İzmir** (9hr.; 4 per day; US$28, students US$24).

Varan (☎658 02 74). To **Ankara** (6hr.; 7 per day; US$25, students US$23) and **Bodrum** (14hr.; 2 per day; US$31, students US$28.50).

Trains: In virtually every case, it's faster and cheaper to take intercity buses. All trains to Anatolia leave from **Haydarpaşa Garı** (☎(216) 336 04 75), on the Asian side. Take the ferry (every 20min., US$0.65) from Karaköy pier #7, halfway between Galata Bridge and the Karaköy tourist office. Rail tickets for Anatolia can be bought in advance at the **TCDD** office upstairs. To Ankara (6½-9½hr., 6 per day, US$6-12). Europe-bound trains via Athens or Bucharest leave from **Sirkeci Garı** (☎(212) 527 00 50), in Eminönü, downhill from Sultanahmet toward the Golden Horn. Some lines may be suspended due to political crises in the Balkans. Call ahead for info and student fares. To: **Athens** (24hr., 1 per day, US$60); **Bucharest** (17hr., 1 per day, US$30); and **Budapest** (40hr., 1 per day, US$90).

Ferries: Turkish Maritime Lines (☎249 92 22), near Karaköy pier #7, just left of the **Haydarpaşa** ferry terminal. Look for the building with the blue awning marked *Denizcilik İşletmeleri*. Ferries leave for **Bandırma**, with train connections to **İzmir** (combination ticket US$10-25). Points on the Bosphorus are served by less frequent and more expensive day cruises. Local ferries run between Europe and Asia. Pick up a timetable *(feribot tarifesi;* US$0.60) at any pier. Fast **seabus** catamarans also run along the ferry routes. Address any questions to **Seabus Information** (☎(216) 362 04 44).

Public Transportation: Buses serve most stops every 10min. 5am-10:30pm, less frequently 10:30pm-midnight. Signs on the front indicate destination; on the right side, major stops. **Dolmuş** run during daylight hours and early evening and are found near most major bus hubs, including Aksaray and Eminönü. In neighborhoods far from the bustle of Taksim and Sultanahmet they serve as local group taxis, it's best to hail them on their way back into the center of İstanbul. A **tramvay** (tram) runs from Eminönü to Zeytinburnu (US$0.50); follow the tracks back to Sultanahmet even if you don't actually take it. **AKBİL** is an **electronic ticket system** that works on municipal ferries, buses, trams, seabuses, and the subway (but not *dolmuş*). A deposit of US$5 will get you a plastic tab to which you can add money in 1,000,000TL increments and which will save you 15-50% on fares. Add credit at any white IETT public bus booth with the "AKBİL *satılır*" sign (at bigger bus and tram stops); press your tab into the reader, remove it, insert a 1,000,000TL note, and press again. **Regular tickets** are not interchangeable. Tickets for trams and buses without ticket sellers are available from little white booths, while ferries and seabuses take *jeton* (tokens), available at ferry stops.

Taxis: Little yellow speed-demons. Taxi drivers are even more reckless than other İstanbul drivers. Scams are widespread. Be alert when catching a cab in Sultanahmet or Taksim. One light on the meter means day rate while 2 mean night rate. Check change carefully. Rides within the city center shouldn't be more than US$5.

◀⚫❷ ORIENTATION AND PRACTICAL INFORMATION

The **Bosphorus Strait** (Boğaz) separates Asia from Europe. Turks call the western, European side of İstanbul **Avrupa** and the eastern, Asian side **Asya**. The **Golden Horn**, a river originating outside the city, splits Avrupa into northern and southern parts. Directions are usually specified by district (i.e. Kadıköy, Taksim, or Fatih). Most of the sights and tourist facilities are in **Sultanahmet,** south of the Golden Horn, toward the eastern end of the peninsula. The other half of "Europe" is focused on **Taksim Square,** the commercial and social center of the northern European bank. Two main arteries radiate from the square: **İstiklâl Caddesi,** the main downtown shopping street, and the hotel-lined **Cumhuriyet Caddesi.** The Asian side of İstanbul is mostly residential but offers wandering at a relaxed pace, including the Kadıköy district.

TOURIST, FINANCIAL, AND LOCAL SERVICES

Tourist Office: 3 Divan Yolu (☎/fax 518 87 54), in Sultanahmet, in the white metal kiosk at the north end of the Hippodrome. Open daily 9am-5pm. **Branches** in the Sirkeci train station (☎511 58 11; open daily 8:30am-5:30pm) and in the Atatürk Airport (☎573 41 36; open 24hr). In Taksim the main office (☎233 05 92; open daily 9am-5pm) is in the **Hilton Hotel Arcade** on Cumhuriyet Cad.

Travel Agencies: Tourist agencies line the beginning of Divan Yolu Cad. and Akbıyık Cad., the main backpacker drag in Sultanahmet. **7-Tur,** 37 Gümüşsuyu Cad., 2nd fl., is İstanbul's STA Travel equivalent, and does all STA ticket changes. ISICs available ($15). From Taksim Sq., walk downhill to the right of Atatürk Cultural Center. **Tur-Ista,** 16 Divan Yolu (☎527 70 85; fax 519 37 92), convenient for Sultanahmet, will arrange a free transport to the bus or train station if you buy a ticket through them.

Consulates: Area code ☎212. **Australia,** 58 Tepecik Yolu, Etiler (☎257 70 50; fax 257 70 54). **Canada,** 107/3 Büyükdere Cad., Bengün Han, Gayrettepe (☎272 51 74; fax 272 34 27). **Ireland** (honorary), 25/A Cumhuriyet Cad., Mobil Altı, Elmadağ (☎246 60 25). **New Zealand,** Level 24, 100-102 Maya Akar Center, Büyükdere Cad., Esentepe (☎275 28 89; fax 275 50 08). **South Africa,** Serbetci iş Merkezi, 106/15 Büyükdere Cad., Esentepe (☎288 04 28; fax 275 76 42). **UK,** 34 Meşrutiyet Cad., PK33, Beyoğlu/Tepebaşı (☎293 75 40; fax 245 49 89). **US,** 104-108 Meşrutiyet Cad., Tepebaşı (☎251 36 02; fax 251 32 18).

Currency Exchange: Exchange shops open M-F 8:30am-noon and 1:30-5pm; most charge no commission. Banks exchange traveler's checks.

American Express: Türk Express, 47/1 Cumhuriyet Cad., 3rd fl. (☎235 95 00), uphill from Taksim Sq. Open M-F 9am-6pm. Their office in the Hilton Hotel lobby (☎230 15 15), Cumhuriyet Cad., helps when Türk Express is closed. Neither grants cash advances or accepts wired money. Open daily 8:30am-8:30pm. AmEx's agent is **Akbank,** with branches across the city. To get a cash advance on your card, you must have a personal check or know the account number and address of your bank. Attempt this service only after visiting an AmEx branch office.

Laundromats: Star Laundry, 18 Akbıyık Cad. (☎638 23 02), below Star Pension in Sultanahmet. Wash and dry US$1.50 per kg (2kg min.). Open daily 8am-8pm.

EMERGENCY AND COMMUNICATIONS

Emergency: ☎155. **Tourist Police:** at the beginning of Yerebatan Cad. in Sultanahmet (24hr. ☎527 45 03 or ☎528 53 69; fax 512 76 76).

Medical Assistance: American Hospital, Admiral Bristol Hastanesi, 20 Güzelbahçe Sok., Nişantaşı (☎231 40 50). The **German Hospital,** 119 Sıraselviler Cad., Taksim (☎251 71 00) is more conveniently located for Sultanahmet hostelers.

Pharmacy: The Turkish word for pharmacy (or chemist) is *eczanesi*. **Çemberlitaş Eczanesi,** No. 46 Vezirhan Cad. (☎522 69 69), off Divan Yolu by the Çemberlitaş tram stop, is among the most helpful. Open M-Sa 7:30am-8pm.

Internet Access: The **Antique Internet Café,** 51 Kutlungun Sok., offers a fast connection—despite its name. US$1.50 per hr. Open 24hr.

Post Office: The **PTT** (Post, Telegraph, and Telephone) office nearest Sultanahmet is the yellow booth opposite the entrance to Aya Sofia. **Main branch,** 25 Büyük Postane Sok, in Sirkeci. Stamp and **currency exchange** services open 8:30am-midnight. Phones open 24hr. Address mail to be held: First name SURNAME, *Poste Restante,* Merkez 3 Postane, PTT, Sirkeci, 25 Büyük Postane Sok., **5270050** İstanbul, TURKEY.

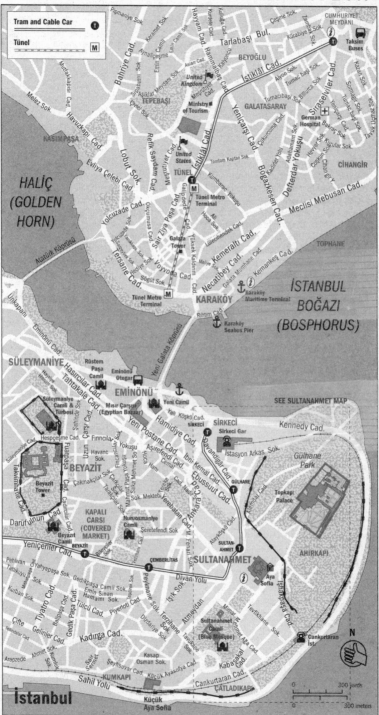

TURKEY

İstanbul

TURKEY

▐ ACCOMMODATIONS

Budget accommodations are mainly in **Sultanahmet,** bounded by Aya Sofia, the Blue Mosque, and Topkapı Palace. The **Taksim** district, home to many five-star hotels and a few budget lodgings, is less touristy. The sidestreets around **Sirkeci** train station and **Aksaray** offer tons of dirt-cheap hotels, but may not be the most pleasant places to stay. **Lâleli** is the center of prostitution in İstanbul and should be avoided. Rates can rise by 20% in July and August.

▨ **İstanbul Hostel,** 35 Kutlugün Sok. (☎516 93 80). From the path between the Aya Sofia and the Blue Mosque, walk south down Tevkifane Sok. to Kutlugün Sok; it's on the right. Spotless. Internet. Happy hour 6:30-9:30pm. Dorms US$7; doubles US$16.

▨ **Moonlight Pension,** 87 Akbıyık Cad. (☎517 54 29; moonlight@superonline.com). Clean rooms, a kind staff, and clear rooftop views away from the noisy backpacker scene. Laundry. Kitchen. Internet. Dorms US$5; doubles US$16; triples US$21.

▨ **Side Pension/Hotel Side,** 20 Utangaç Sok. (☎517 65 90; www.sidehotel.com), near the entrance of the Four Seasons Hotel. Occupies the 2 wooden buildings by the corner of Tevkifane Sok. and Utangaç Sok. *Pension* singles US$20; doubles US$25; triples US$35. Add US$10 for bath. Hotel singles US$40; doubles US$50; triples US$60.

Seagull Pension, Küçük Ayasofya Cad., Aksakal Sok. 22 (☎517 11 42; seagullpension@hotmail.com). From Aya Sofya, head down the hill on Küçük Ayasofya Cad toward the Marmara. A block before Kennedy Cad and the sea; close to the train. Internet. Dorms US$5; singles US$10; doubles US$20-25.

Alp Guesthouse, Akbıyık Cad., 4 Adliye Sok. (☎517 95 70; www.alpguesthouse.com). Head down Tevkifane Sok., turn left after the Four Seasons, and take the 1st right. Family-run hotel with spacious, spotless rooms and a Mediterranean feel. Free airport transport with 3-day stay. Free Internet. Singles US$30; doubles US$50; triples US$60.

Hotel Plaza, 19-21 Aslanyatağı Sok. (☎245 32 73). In Taksim. Down Arslanyata Sok., the small side street off Siraselviler. Bear left when Arslanyata turns right, and look for the big building in a courtyard. Quiet, classy rooms with Bosphorus views, sitting rooms, fridges, glass tables, and large windows. Breakfast included. Singles $20; doubles $40; "student rooms" around $7 per night.

Nayla Palace Pension, 22 Kutlugün Sok. (☎516 35 67; nayla@superonline.com). A homey atmosphere, quiet garden courtyard, and rooftop lounge. Breakfast included. Internet. Dorms US$5; singles US$15; doubles US$25-30; triples US$35.

Yücelt Hostel/Interyouth Hostel, 6/1 Caferiye Cad. (☎513 61 50; www.yucelthostel.com). Massive 3-building complex has billiards, table tennis, Internet, travel library, book exchange, safes, luggage storage, and videos in the rooftop lounge. Laundry. Dorms US$4-7; doubles US$16-20; dorms US$6-8 per person.

Bahaus Guesthouse, Akbıyık Cad., 11 Bayram Fırını Sok. (☎517 66 97). From the front of the Blue Mosque, strut down Mimar Mehmet Ağa Cad. 2 blocks, and turn left on Akbıyık Cad. Spare, standard rooms. Terrace has various musical instruments available. Breakfast included. Singles US$20; doubles US$30-35; triples US$40.

Hotel As, 26 Bekar Sok in Taksim. (☎252 65 25; fax 245 00 99), off upper İstiklâl Cad. Unbeatable price and location. Tiny balconies overlook busy cafe alleys. All rooms with bath and phone. Singles $10; doubles $17; triples $21. Parties of 10 or more: singles $8; doubles $14; triples $18.

▐ FOOD

Sultanahmet's heavily advertised "Turkish" restaurants are easy to find, but much better meals can be found on **İstiklâl Caddesi** and around **Taksim.** Small Bosphorus towns such as **Arnavutköy** and **Sarıyer** (on the European side) and **Çengelköy** (on the Asian side) are the best places for fresh fish. **Kanlıca,** on the Asian side, reputedly has the best **yogurt.** Covered boats in **Eminönü** and **Karaköy** fry up **fish sandwiches** on board (US$1.50). Good *kebap* shops are everywhere, but quality tends to be better in more residential areas. **Ortaköy** is the place for baked potatoes stuffed with all

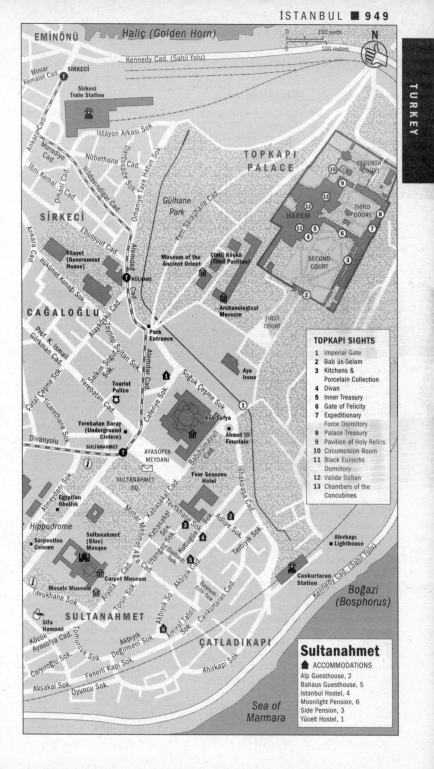

EMİNÖNÜ

Haliç (Golden Horn)

0   100 yards
0   100 meters

N

Kennedy Cad. (Sahil Yolu)

Mimar
Kemalet Cad.   SİRKECİ

Sirkeci
Train Station

Istayon Arkası Sok.

Ankaracad.
Muradiye
Cad.
İbni Kemal
Cad.
Orhani Cad.
Nöbethane Cad.
Hüdavindigar Cad.
Darüssade Sok.
Ohanım Taya Hatun Sok.
Alemdağ Cad.

SİRKECİ

Ebussuut Cad.

Gülhane
Park

TOPKAPI
PALACE

FOURTH
COURT

10

9

13

THIRD
COURT

8

12

HAREM

11

4 5

7

Yeni Saraçhane Cad.

Museum of the
Ancient Orient

Çinili Köşkü
(Tiled Pavilion)

6

SECOND
COURT

3

Vilayet
(Government
House)

Ankara Cad.
Hükümet Konağı Sok.

GÜLHANE

CAĞALOĞLU

Prof. K. İsmail
Gürkman Cad.
Alayköşkü Cad.
Salkım Soğut Sok.
Yerebatan Cad.
Çatal Çeşme Sok.
Ticaretnane Sok.
Divanyolu Sok.

Archaeological
Museum

FIRST
COURT

Aya
Irene

2

Park
Entrance

Cafenye Sok.

Tourist
Police

1

Soğuk Çeşme Sok.

1

Yerebatan Saray
(Underground
Cistern)

Divanyolu

SULTANAHMET

Aya Sofya

Babıhümayün Cad.

Ahmet III
Fountain

AYASOFYA
MEYDANI

İshakpaşa Cad.

TOPKAPI SIGHTS
1 Imperial Gate
2 Bab üs-Selam
3 Kitchens &
   Porcelain Collection
4 Divan
5 Inner Treasury
6 Gate of Felicity
7 Expeditionary
   Force Dormitory
8 Palace Treasury
9 Pavilion of Holy Relics
10 Circumcision Room
11 Black Eunuchs
   Dormitory
12 Valide Sultan
13 Chambers of the
   Concubines

SULTANAHMET
SQ.

Four Seasons
Hotel

Atmeydan Sok.

Egyptian
Obelisk

Hippodrome

Serpentine
Column

Sultanahmet
(Blue)
Mosque

Mimar Mehmet Ağa Cad.
Kabasakal Cad.
Tevfikhane Sok.
Kabasakal
Sok.
Utangaç Sok.
Dalbastı Sok.
Kutlugün Sok.
Adliye Sok.
Akbıyık Sok.
Terbıyık Sok.
Bayram-
fırın Sok.
Cankurtaran Cad.
Amiral Tafdil
Sok.

2

3

4

5

Carpet Museum

Arasta Sok.

Mosaic Museum

Tavukhane Sok.

Şifa
Hamamı

Küçük
Ayasofya Cad.
Cariyınoğlu Sok.
Aksakal Sok.
Tomurcuk Sok.
Oyuncu Sok.
Değirmeni Sok.
Fenerli Kapı Sok.
Akbıyık
Sok.

6

Ahırkapı Sok.

 Torun Sok.

Ahırkapı
Lighthouse

Cankurtaran
Station

Kennedy Cad. (Sahil Yolu)

Boğazi
(Bosphorus)

ÇATLADIKAPI

Sea of
Marmara

Sultanahmet

⌂ ACCOMMODATIONS
Alp Guesthouse, 2
Bahaus Guesthouse, 5
Istanbul Hostel, 4
Moonlight Pension, 6
Side Pension, 3
Yücelt Hostel, 1

kinds of fillings. Because of space considerations and cultural differences, there are very few supermarkets. Luckily, **markets** all over the city sell cheese, bread, produce, and more—all at rock-bottom prices. Browse the fresh selection of produce in the city's **open-air markets;** the best is the daily one in **Beşiktaş,** near Barbaros Cad.

SULTANAHMET AND DİVAN YOLU

◼ **Doy-Doy,** 13 Şifa Hamamı Sok. From the south end of the Hippodrome, walk down the hill around the Blue Mosque and look for the blue and yellow signs. Best of Sultanahmet's cheap eats. Tasty *kebap* and salads (US$3.50 and under). Open daily 8:30am-late.

Can Restaurant, 10 Divan Yolu. Across the street from the tourist information office at the north end of the Hippodrome. A no-nonsense, dirt-cheap cafeteria. Veggie combination plates from US$1.75; meat dishes US$2.50-5. Open daily 8am-9pm.

Pudding Shop, 6 Divan Yolu. A pitstop on the Hippie Trail to the Far and Middle East during the 70s, it was the setting for the drug deal scene in *Midnight Express.* It is now a self-serve restaurant (dishes US$1.50-2.50) and super dessert stop whose walls are lined with newspaper clippings and notes about its storied past. Continental breakfast US$2.

İSTİKLÂL CADDESİ AND TAKSİM

◼ **Hacı Abdullah,** 17 Sakizağacı Cad., down the street from Ag'a Camii. This family style restaurant has been serving it up since 1888. Main dishes US$3-6, delicious soups US$1. Open daily noon-11pm.

◼ **Naregatsi Cafe,** upstairs at the mouth of Sakizağacı Cad., across from the Ağa Camii. Gourmet cafe fare in a kitschy setting. Inflatable superheroes, live accordion, and cappuccino (US$3.50). Open daily noon-11:30pm.

Hacı Baba, 49 İstiklâl Cad., has perfected a wide range of Turkish standards in its nearly 80 years. The menu is extensive; pick something from the deli case in front or try the huge vegetarian *meze* selection. Main dishes US$3.50-6.50. Open daily 10am-10pm.

Şampiyon, Balık Pazarı (*Sahne Sok.*). Next to Çiçek Pasajı. Famous across Turkey for *kokoreç* (grilled tripe cooked with spices and tomatoes). For something quick, visit the stand out front for fresh mussels (US$0.25 each). Open daily 8:30am-midnight.

GOLDEN HORN

Cibalikapi Balikçisi Fish Restaurant, right along the Golden Horn in Fatih, serves fresh fish starting at US$2.60 and veggies starting at US$1.30.

Tarihi Haliç Işkembecisi, along the Golden Horn. Their specialty is the *Işkembe Çorbası,* a bizarre but appetizing soup of butter, garlic, and shredded fish meat (US$1.30).

◉ SIGHTS

İstanbul hosts an incomparable array of world-famous churches, mosques, palaces, and museums. Most budget travelers spend a lot of time in **Sultanahmet,** the area around the **Aya Sophia,** south of and uphill from Sirkeci. Merchants crowd the district between the **Grand Bazaar,** east of the university, and the **Egyptian Bazaar,** just southeast of Eminönü.

AYA SOFİA (HAGIA SOPHIA)

Aya Sofia, built in just five years, opened in December of AD 537. Covering 7570 sq. meters and rising 55.6m, it was then the biggest building in the world. Twenty years later, an earthquake brought the dome crashing to the ground. The new dome went up in AD 563. After falling to the Ottomans in 1453, Aya Sofia was converted into a mosque and remained one until Atatürk established it as a museum in 1932. Aya Sofia's austere interior just makes it seem bigger. The nave is overshadowed by the massive, gold-leaf mosaic dome. The **mihrab,** the calligraphy-adorned portal pointing toward Mecca, stands in the **apse,** which housed the altar during the mosque's Orthodox incarnation. The elaborate marble square in the floor marks the spot where Byzantine emperors were once crowned. The **minber,** the platform used to address the crowd during prayer, is atop the stairway to the right of the *mihrab.* At the back end of the **narthex,** a quiet hallway with lace-like column capitals at the north side of the building, is the famed **sweating pillar,** sheathed in bronze. The pillar has a hole where you can insert your finger to collect the odd drop of water, believed to possess healing powers. Be prepared to wait a while. The **gallery** contains Byzantine mosaics uncovered from beneath a thick layer of Ottoman plaster. *(Museum open Tu-Su 9:30am-4:30pm. Gallery open Tu-Su 9:30-4pm. US$6.50.)*

BLUE MOSQUE (SULTANAHMET CAMii)

Between the Hippodrome and Aya Sofia, the Blue Mosque, Sultan Ahmet's response to Aya Sofia in 1617, is named for its beautiful blue İznik tiles. Not as large as Aya Sofia, but still massive, the mosque's internal framework of iron bars enables the entire structure to bend in earthquakes (so far, it has withstood 20). Enter from the east side through the **courtyard.** The mosque's **six minarets** are the primary source of its fame; at the time, only the mosque at Mecca had six minarets, and the thought of equaling that sacred edifice was considered heretical. Sultan Ahmet circumvented this difficulty by financing the construction of a seventh minaret at Mecca. A small stone from the **Ka'aba** at Mecca is almost invisible from the tourists' area. *(Open Tu-Sa 8:30am-12:30pm, 2-4:45pm, and 5:45-6:30pm. Donation requested. Dress modestly—no shorts or tank tops, and women must wear head coverings. Speak quietly.)* The small, square, single-domed structure in front of the Blue Mosque, **Sultan Ahmet's Tomb** (Sultanahmet'in Türbesi), contains the sultan's remains as well as those of his wife and sons, Osman II and Murat IV. The holy relics include strands of Muhammed's beard. *(Open Tu-Su 9:30am-4:30pm. US$1, students free.)*

THE HIPPODROME (AT MEYDANI)

Behind the Blue Mosque, the remains of this ancient Roman circus form a pleasant park whose tranquility defies its turbulent history. Built by the Roman Emperor Septimus Severus in AD 200, the Hippodrome was the site of chariot races and public executions. Constantine, the first Byzantine Emperor, enlarged the racetrack to 500m on each side. The tall, northernmost column with hieroglyphics is the **Egyptian Obelisk** (Dikili Taş), erected by the Pharaoh Thutmosis III in 1500 BC and brought from Egypt to Constantinople in the 4th century by Emperor Theodosius I. Farther south, the subterranean bronze stump is all that remains of the **Serpentine Column,** originally placed at the Oracle of Delphi. The southernmost column is the **Column of Constantine,** whose original gold-plated bronze tiling was looted by members of the Fourth Crusade during the sack of Constantinople. On the east side of the Hippodrome along Atmeydanı Sok. is the superb **Museum of Turkish and Islamic Art** (İbrahim Paşa Sarayı). The Ottoman calligraphy is particularly impressive. *(Museum open Tu-Su 9:30am-4:30pm. US$2, students US$1.20.)*

TOPKAPI PALACE (TOPKAPI SARAYI)

Main entrance on Babıhümayun Cad., the cobblestone street off Aya Sofia square. Open Tu-Su 9am-4:30pm. US$6.50. Harem open Tu-Su 9am-4pm; mandatory tours every 30min. 9:30am-3:30pm. US$4.

Towering from the high ground at the tip of the old city, hidden behind walls up to 12m high, Topkapı Palace was the nerve center of the Ottoman Empire from the 15th to the 19th centuries. Topkapı offers unparalleled insight into the wealth, excess, cruelty, and artistic vitality that characterized the Ottoman Empire at its peak. Built by Mehmet the Conqueror between AD 1458 and 1465, the palace became an imperial residence under Süleyman the Magnificent. The palace is divided into a series of courts surrounded by palace walls.

FIRST AND SECOND COURTYARDS. The general public was permitted entrance via the **Imperial Gate** to the first courtyard, where they watched executions, traded, and viewed the nexus of the Empire's glory. At the end of the first courtyard, the capped conical towers of the **Gate of Greeting** (Bab-üs-Selam) mark the entrance to the second courtyard. To the right beyond the colonnade, the **Imperial kitchens** feature distinctive vaulted chimneys and house three collections of porcelain and silver. The last set of doors on the left of the narrow alley leads to the palace's world-famous **Chinese and Japanese porcelain collections.** Across the courtyard, where ostriches and eunuchs once roamed, lie the **Privy Chambers** *(Kubbealtı),* whose window grilles, awnings, walls, and ceilings are bathed in gold leaf. The **Council Chamber,** the room closest to the Harem, retains its original classical Ottoman calligraphic decor. Abutting the Council Chamber is the plush Rococo room in which the **Grand Vizier** received foreign dignitaries. Next door and to the right is the **Inner Treasury,** which holds various cutting and bludgeoning instruments.

THIRD COURTYARD. The third courtyard, officially known as **Enderun** (inside), is accessible through the **Gate of Felicity.** The **School of Expeditionary Pages** holds a costume collection that traces the evolution of imperial costumes. Move along down the colonnade to the incredible **Palace Treasury,** where ornate gold objects, the legendary **Topkapı dagger** (essentially three giant emeralds with a knife sprouting out of them), the 86-carat **Spoonmaker's Diamond,** and much more await your ogling. Just on the other side of the courtyard is the **Pavilion of Holy Relics,** which houses the booty taken by Selim the Grim after the Ottoman capture of Egypt, as well as gifts sent by the governor of Mecca and Medina upon Selim's victory.

FOURTH COURTYARD. Three passages lead into the fourth courtyard. If Topkapı can be thought of as the brain of the Ottoman Empire, then the fourth courtyard certainly qualifies as the pleasure center, as it was amongst these pavilions, gardens, and fountains that the infamous merriments and sordid garden parties occurred. From the broad marble terrace at the west end, you can take in the uninterrupted vistas of the Sea of Marmara and the Bosphorus. The **Revan Pavilion,** the building farthest from the edge of the terrace, was built in 1635 to commemorate Sultan Murat IV's Revan campaign; at the other end of the portico is the **Circumcision Room,** an octagonal chamber that overhangs the edge of the pavilion, built by Ibrahim the Mad. At the other end of the terrace stands the **Bağdat Köşku,** Murat I's monument to his capture of Baghdad in 1638. An octagonal/cruciform base supports the dome; the interior sports an amazing radial symmetry.

HAREM. These 400-plus rooms housed the sultan, his immediate family, and a small army of servants, eunuchs, and general assistants. Because it was forbidden for men other than the sultan and his sons to live here, the Harem became a source of intrigue and the subject of endless gossip. The mandatory tour proceeds to the **Black Eunuchs' Dormitory** on the left, then into the women's section of the harem, beginning with the chambers of the **Valide Sultan,** the sultan's mother. If a concubine attracted the sultan's affections or if the sultan spent a night with her, she would be promoted to nicer quarters with the chance for further advancement; if she bore the sultan a son, she could become his wife (one of eight).

OTHER SIGHTS

THE ARCHAEOLOGICAL MUSEUM COMPLEX. Mehmet the Conqueror built the **tiled pavilion** to view athletic competitions below; the display covers the spectrum of Ottoman tile-making, including some rare early İznik tiles. The smaller building adjacent to the tiled pavilion, the ◪**Museum of the Ancient Orient,** is rarely open; hidden inside is an excellent collection of stone artifacts from Anatolia, Mesopotamia, and Egypt dating from the first and 2nd millennia BC. The **Archaeology Museum** contains one of the world's great collections of Classical and Hellenistic art. *(About 100m downhill from the 1st courtyard of Topkapı Palace. When the palace is closed, enter the museums through Gülhane Park; a separate road next to the park ticket booths leads to the complex. Complex open Tu-Su 9:30am-5pm. US$5.)*

GRAND BAZAAR (KAPALI ÇARŞISI). With over 4000 shops, several banks, mosques, police stations, and restaurants, this enormous "covered bazaar" could be a city in itself. It began in 1461 as a modest affair during the reign of Mehmet the Conqueror, but today forms the entrance to the massive galleria that starts at Çemberlitaş and covers the hill down to Eminönü, ending at the **Egyptian Spice Bazaar** (Mısır Çarşısı) and the Golden Horn waterfront. You'll get lost, so enjoy it. *(From Sultanahmet, follow the tram tracks toward Aksaray for 5min. until you see the Nuruosmaniye Camii on the right. Walk one block down Vezirhanı Cad., keeping the mosque on your left. Follow the crowds left into the bazaar. Open M-Sa 9am-7pm.)*

▓ YEREBATAN SARAYI (UNDERGROUND CISTERN). This subterranean "palace" is actually a vast underground cavern whose shallow water eerily reflects the images of its 336 supporting columns, all illuminated by colored ambient lighting. Echoing sounds of dripping water and muted classical tunes accompany strolls across the elevated wooden walkways. Underground walkways linking it to Topkapı Palace were blocked to curb rampant trafficking in stolen goods and abducted women. *(With your back to Aya Sofia, the entrance is 175m away on the left side of Yerebatan Cad. Open daily 9:30am-5:30pm. US$4, students US$3.25.)*

SÜLEYMANİYE COMPLEX (SÜLEYMANİYE KÜLLİYESİ). To the north of İstanbul University sits the massive and elegant **Süleymaniye Camii,** one of architect Sinan's great masterpieces, part of a larger complex that includes tombs, an *imaret* (soup kitchen), and several *medreses* (Islamic schools). Walk along the Süleymaniye Camii's southwest side to the large arch just below the dome and enter the mosque's central courtyard through the smaller tourist entrance to the left of the main door. After removing your shoes (women should also put on a headscarf), proceed inside the vast and perfectly proportioned mosque. The stained-glass windows are the work of the master Sarhoş İbrahim (İbrahim the Drunkard). *(From the university, head out the northwest gate to Süleymaniye Cad. From Sultanahmet, either walk along the tramvay (15min.) or take it to the Üniversite stop, walk across the square, and take Besim Ömer Paşa Cad. past the walls of the university to Süleymaniye Cad. Mosque open Tu-Su 9:30am-4:30pm, except during prayers.)* Prof. Sıddık Sami Onar Sok. runs between the university and the mosque. Passing through the graveyard brings you to the superbly decorated **royal tombs** of Süleyman I and his wife, Haseki Hürrem. *(Open Tu-Su 9:30am-4:30pm. Donation requested.)*

PRINCE'S ISLANDS (ADALAR). The craggy Prince's Islands are known simply as the *Adalar* (islands). **Büyükada** is the largest and most enjoyable island, with pine forests, swimming spots, and peaceful walks. **Yörük Ali** is the main beach and picnicking spot; you can also take the buggy to **Luna Park**, the local amusement park on the far side of the island (10-15min.; no more than US$7.50). The main forms of transportation on the islands are walking, biking, and horse-and-buggy rides. The lovely ▓ **Ideal Aile Pansiyon,** 14 Kadıyoran Cad., is a big old house with huge rooms. (☎382 68 57. US$13 per person.) **Ferries** depart from the north side of Eminönü or Kabataş; look for "Sirkeci Adalar" signs. (3-4 per day, return US$2.)

HAMAMS (TURKISH BATHS)

Women should request female washers. Self service is always an option; signal your preference by showing the attendants your bar of soap and wash cloth.

▓ **Çemberlitaş Hamamı,** 8 Verzirhan Cad. Near Çemberlitaş tram stop. Built by Sinan in 1584, this place has beautiful and clean marble interiors and good service. Vigorous "towel service" after bath requires a tip of US$1.50-3. Bath with your own towel and soap $9; with a sudsy rubdown, massage and wash US$15 (tip included, but after you change the washers wait around for another US$1-3). Open daily 6am-midnight.

Mihrimah Hamamı is next to Mihrimah Mosque on Fevzi Paşa Cad., about 50m from Edirnekapı. One of the better local baths: large, quiet, clean, cheap, and hot. Women's facilities are good, though smaller. Bath $3; massage $2.50. Men's section open 7am-midnight; women's section 8am-7pm.

Galatasaray Hamamı is at the end of Turanacıbaşı Sok., off İstiklâl Cad., on a side street across from the Galatasaray high school on İstiklâl; just uphill from Galatasaray. Bath and massage $15.50. Men's section open daily 7am-11pm; women's 8am-8pm.

▓ NIGHTLIFE

İstanbul's best clubs and bars are poorly advertised, so unplanned club hopping usually proves fruitless, but options abound. Small, relaxed **cafe-bars** serve tea in the afternoon and alcohol in the evening, often with a jazz soundtrack. Cavernous **rock bars** range from dark heavy metal halls to mellow classic rock hangouts.

HAIL, TARKAN! Turkey's king of pop can be seen not only on hundreds of billboards (including one in Taksim square that is at least 30m high) but also on every Pepsi can and bottle. His voice booms out of every storefront and passing car, and graces the dance floors of every nightclub, from the classiest to the seediest. Born in the early '70s in a village in the Kocaeli district, Tarkan got his start singing at weddings around İzmir before skyrocketing to international superstardom. Famous everywhere from Germany to North Africa to India, he is loved nowhere as much as in his native Turkey.

Convenient and cheap backpacker bars are concentrated in the **Sultanahmet** area. The hippest clubs and discos often move from unlisted locations in Taksim in the winter to unlisted summer locations throughout the city. The Beşiktaş end of **Ortaköy** is a maze of upscale hangouts; along the coastal road toward **Arnavutköy** are a string of open-air clubs (cover US$18-45). Bouncers are highly selective, but wander between Ortaköy and **Bebek** and try your luck. Men heading out without female companions will have a tough time getting into some of the more upscale clubs and bars, which require every man to be accompanied by at least one woman in order to keep the dance floors co-ed. İstanbul night action is centered around **Taksim** and **İstiklâl Cad.** Sultanahmet's bars all lie within 100m of one another; beer is standardized at US$1-1.25. Male-only *çay* houses, backgammon parlors, and dancing shows tend to be dingy and dangerous. *Let's Go* does not recommend these establishments. Team up with others and take cabs when out late, even in nicer areas. Cafe-bars and backpacker bars tend to be less threatening than rock bars or clubs.

Jazz Stop, at the end of Büyük Parmakkapı Sok in Taksim. Live music nightly 11pm. Beer US$3. No cover June-Aug.; Sept.-May F-Sa US$10. Open 11am-4am.

Riddim, 6 Büyük Parmakkapı Sok., in Taksim, spins reggae, island, and African music all night long. Unaccompanied men turned away on weekends. Beer US$2.50. Open F-Sa 8pm-4am, Su-Th 9pm-1:30am.

Cheers, Akbıyık Cad. Best music on backpacker alley, with comfortable outdoor benches. Delicious fresh fruit soaking in bottled water and a friendly scene make this one of the best places to grab a beer in the area.

Traveler's Cafe and Bar, Akbıyık, is a good place to trade adventures with the super-friendly staff. Also offers a *nargile* (water pipe) and a standard bar menu. Beer $1.80.

Madrid Bar, İpek Sok., off Küçük Parmakkapı Sok., which is off İstiklâl Cad. Surrealist Spanish paintings decorate this small, mellow spot, popular with Turkish students and young foreigners looking for the cheapest pints in Taksim (US$1.25). Open 2pm-2am.

NIGHTLIFE SCAMS. Though most tourists have no problem when out on the town, scams do exist. One involves Turkish men who befriend a male tourist, lead him to a bar where they are joined by women who order drinks and then leave, and stick the tourist with a big bill. Buying drinks for women can be a front for prostitution; that $50 "drink" might get you more than you bargained for. There have also been reports of tourists being given drugged drinks and then robbed. While a drink invitation is usually simply a gesture of hospitality, use your best judgement when accepting drinks from strangers.

EDİRNE ☎ 284

In almost 2000 years of historical prominence, Edirne has experienced a mixed and fickle fate, ranging from imperial splendor to hostile occupation. It has been a Roman outpost, an Ottoman capital, and a modern Greek military possession. An easy *dolmuş* ride from the Greek (7km away) or Bulgarian (20km) border, Edirne once nourished the genius of Sinan, the quintessential Ottoman architect. His masterpiece, the ■**Selimiye Camii,** considered by many to be Turkey's finest mosque, presides over the city with 71m-tall minarets, a 32m-wide dome, and 999 windows.

Its vast, ornately-decorated interior is even more impressive. Another Edirne must-see is the **Beyazıt Complex,** built in the late 1480s by the court architect of Beyazıt II. The centerpiece is the **Beyazıt Camii,** a beautiful, single-domed mosque surrounded by multi-domed buildings designed to be schools, storehouses, and asylums. For a long but pleasant walk to the complex, follow Horozlu Bayir Cad. from its origin near the Sokollu Hamamı across two bends of the river. Unfortunately, only the wing once used for medical purposes is open; it now houses Trakya University's Museum of Health. (Open Tu-Su 8:30am-5:30pm. US$1.50.) Back in town, Sinan's 16th-century **Sokollu Hamamı,** (Sokollu Bath) beside the Üç Şerefeli Camii, has superior service and inspiring architecture. (☎225 21 93. US$2.50, with massage US$6.25. Open daily 7am-11pm for men; 9am-6pm for women.) Those less interested in cleanliness can get down and dirty with the competitors who don giant leather breeches, slather themselves in oil, and hit the mats for the **Kırkpınar Grease Wrestling Festival,** which comes to town in early July; call tourist office for details.

Numerous companies send **buses** from the *otogar,* 2km from the city center, to: Ankara (9hr., US$20); Bursa (7hr., US$16.50); İstanbul (2-3½hr., US$5-8.25); and İzmir (9hr., US$15.50). Before you buy a ticket, especially to İstanbul, be sure to shop around. Upon arrival, walk across the four-lane road opposite the *otogar* and hail one of the frequent *dolmuş* heading to town. The **tourist office,** 17 Talat Paşa Cad., 300m from the town center, has free maps. (☎213 92 08. Open June-Aug. M-F 8:30am-5:30pm and occasional weekend hours; Sept.-May M-F 8:30am-5:30pm.) Luxurious █**Efe Hotel,** 13 Maarif Cad, offers modern bathrooms, phones, and TV. (☎213 61 66; www.efehotel.com. Breakfast included. Singles US$16.50; doubles US$23; triples US$27; suites US$35.) The basic **Hotel Aksaray** is at the intersection of Maarif Cad. and Ali Paşa Ortakapı Cad. (☎225 39 01. Singles US$5.50-12.50; doubles $11-16; triples $13.50-19.) Sip *çay* (US$0.25-0.40) at **Şera Park Café,** on Selimiye Meydanı, in the park between Selimiye Camii and Eski Camii. **Postal code:** 22100.

BURSA   ☎224

In the shadow of the slopes of Mt. Uludağ, Bursa is both one of Turkey's holiest cities and a major industrial center. Surrounded by fertile plains and filled with vast gardens and parks, the city has been dubbed "Green Bursa." Its fantastic early Islamic architecture is also some of the most stunning in all of Turkey. Most of Bursa's sights lie roughly in a long row along Atatürk Cad. and its continuations. The immense **Ulu Cami** stands in the center of town on Atatürk Cad. The domes, arranged in four rows of five with a glass center, hover above a large fountain, one of the more unique features of the mosque. From the statue of Atatürk, head east along Atatürk Cad., bear right, and continue along Yeşil Cad. following the "Yeşil" signs to reach the blue-green hilltop **Yeşil Türbe** (Green Tomb; open daily 8:30am-noon and 1-5:30pm) and the onion-shaped minaret caps of the 15th-century **Yeşil Camii** across the street. *Şehade* (royal sons) are buried in tombs surrounding the **Muradiye Camii,** a testament to the early Ottoman practice of fratricide (the eldest son made a practice of killing his younger brothers to ensure a smooth succession). To reach the complex, catch a "Muradiye" *dolmuş* or bus from the Atatürk Cad.-Heykel area. (Open daily 8:30am-noon and 1-5:30pm. US$0.60.) Bursa's fabled **mineral baths** are in the **Çekirge** ("Grasshopper") area west of the city. On Çekirge Cad. is the shiny █**Eski Kaplıca** ("old bath"), one of the finest baths in the country, with a hot pool, a hotter pool, and a great massage room. Take bus #40 or a Çekirge *dolmuş* and ask for Eski Kaplıca. (☎233 93 00. Men US$4; women US$3.30; scrub or massage US$3.) On the road to Çekirge is the **Karagöz Sanat Evi** with exhibitions on shadow theater from around the world. (Open M-Sa 11am-4pm. US$1.50, students US$0.80.) The master **puppeteer** R. Sinasi Çelikkol gives performances every Wednesday and Saturday at 11am. A short trip away, **Mt. Uludağ** is a popular ski area during the winter and a picturesque picnic area, with bright flowers and carpets of evergreen trees, in summer. From Bursa, take bus 3-C, 3-İ, or any with a "Teleferik" sign from Peron 1 on Atatürk Cad. (every 5-10min., US$0.40). Alternately, catch the *dolmuş* from behind Adliye and Heykel (US$0.60).

In Bursa, Kamil Koç **buses** go from the terminal, 20km outside the city center, to: Ankara (5½hr., every hr., US$6); Çeşme (8hr., 2 per day, US$6.70); İstanbul (3½hr., very frequent, US$5); İzmir (5hr., every hr., US$5); and Kuşadası (7½hr, 4 per day, US$6.60). Local bus #90/A goes downtown (US$0.45). **Seabuses** (☎(226) 812 04 99) go between İstanbul and Yalova (30-40min., 14 per day, US$2), from which buses connect to Bursa (1hr., every 30min., US$2.50). To get to the **tourist office,** head to the Ulu Cami side of Atatürk Cad., walk past the fountain toward the Atatürk statue, and go down the stairs on the left. (☎220 18 48. Open M-Sa 8:30am-6pm; Oct.-Apr. M-Sa 8am-5pm.) **Elite Internet Cafe** is at 37 Yeşil Cad. before the overpass leading to the Emir Sultan Cami. (US$1.30 per hr. Open daily 10am-1am.) Find the basic but friendly **Otel Güneş** at 75 İnebey Cad. (☎222 14 04. Singles US$5; doubles US$7.50; triples US$14.50; quads US$20.) Walk along Atatürk Cad. with the mosque on your right and turn left after the Sümerbank, then right onto Veziri Cad. to reach **Otel Deniz,** 19 Tahtakale Veziri Cad. (☎222 92 38. Shared bath and free laundry. Singles $4; doubles $8.) ▧**Kebapçı İskender** claims to have invented the unbeatable dish *İskender kebap* (lamb with tomato sauce, bread, and yogurt; US$2.50); one branch is at 7 Ünlü Cad. and another by the Cultural Center on Atatürk Bul. (Open daily 11am-9pm.) **Postal code:** 16300.

▨ BORDER CROSSINGS: BULGARIA AND GREECE

By far the easiest way to cross into **Bulgaria** from Turkey is to take a direct bus from İstanbul. Or, for a more adventurous route, take a local bus (US$1) to **Kapıkale,** the Turkish border town, 18km west of Edirne, where a *dolmuş* will drop you directly at the entrance (both $1). Although going on foot is possible (if the guards on duty allow it), the several (hot) kilometers between the two border towns makes walking impractical. On the other side, you have to catch a taxi from Andreevo to **Plovdiv,** the closest town with direct transport to Sofia.

The easiest way to cross into **Greece** is also a direct bus from İstanbul; the border crossing between **Pazarkule** and the Greek border (open 9am-noon) is inconvenient, but feasible. From Edirne, you can either take a taxi all the way to Pazarkule (15min., US$6.25), or catch the local bus to **Karaağiç** (US$0.50) and then walk the remaining 2km to Pazarkule. Although the 1km between the Turkish and Greek borders is a no-man's land (no one may walk through without a military escort), Greek taxis usually wait at the border to ferry travelers across the stretch to **Kastanies,** from which you can make bus and train connections to elsewhere in Greece.

AEGEAN COAST

With classical ruins and hidden beaches, Turkey's winding Aegean coastline has become popular with tourists. In Pergamon, Ephesus, and Pamukkale, ruins lie where they fell when earthquakes leveled them centuries ago—this area's 5000-year legacy isn't going anywhere.

▨ FERRIES TO GREECE AND ITALY

From **Çeşme,** ferries run to **Chios, Greece** (1hr.; June Tu, Th-Sa; July-Aug. Tu-Su; Sept. 21-Oct. and May Tu and Th; Nov.-Apr. Th; US$30, return US$40; US$10 Greek port tax for stays longer than one day). From June to September, **Turkish Maritime Lines** (☎(232) 712 10 91) runs ferries from **Çeşme** to **Brindisi, Italy** (34hr.; Tu 11am, US$90; F 11pm, US$100). From **Kuşadası,** ferries head to **Samos, Greece** (1½hr.; daily 8:30am and 4:30pm, in winter 2 per week; US$30 including port tax). From Bodrum, **Bodrum Express Lines** (☎(252) 316 40 67) runs ferries to **Kos** (1½hr., May-Oct. 1 per day) as well as hydrofoils to **Kos** (20min.; 1 per day; US$18, return US$28) and **Rhodes** (2¼hr.; 6 per week; US$46, return US$57).

UNCANNY CARTOGRAPHY Statues all over Gelibolu celebrate the achievements of the town's local hero Piri Reis, a seaman and cartographer born in Gelibolu in 1470. As an admiral in the Ottoman Navy, he collected new charts and maps from the bazaars of his many ports-of-call. In 1513, he used his extensive library of charts to draw a map of the world. Reis's map resurfaced in 1929, when a group of historians discovered it while poking around in İstanbul's Topkapı Palace. They were astonished to discover that the 1513 map showed the coastal outlines of South and North America and included precise data on Antarctica, supposedly not discovered until 1818. Further studies of Reis's map have suggested that his reference charts may have been drawn from aerial pictures; the rivers, mountain ranges, islands, deserts, and plateaus are drawn with unusual accuracy.

GALLIPOLI (GELİBOLU) AND ECEABAT ☎ 286

The strategic position of the Gallipoli Peninsula on the Dardanelles made it the backdrop of a major World War I Allied offensive to take Constantinople and create a Balkan front. Eighty thousand Ottomans and more than 200,000 soldiers of the British Empire—Englishmen, Australians, New Zealanders, and Indians—lost their lives in the blood-soaked stalemate. This battle launched its hero **Atatürk** into his status as Turkey's founding father. It's best to visit the battlefields from nearby Eceabat or Çanakkale. **TJ's Tours** (☎814 31 21; tjs_tours@excite.com) offers tours through TJ's Hostel in Eceabat and the Yellow Rose Pension in Çanakkale. **Hassle Free Travel Agency** (☎213 59 69; hasslefree@anzachouse.com), runs tours through Anzac House, in Çanakkale.

Eceabat is cheaper and more convenient than Gallipoli Town as a base for exploring the Gallipoli battlefields. **Minibuses** run there (30min., every hour, US$1). **TJ's Hostel,** Cumhuriyet Sok., to the right of the main square, has clean rooms. (☎814 10 65; fax 814 29 41. Dorms US$4.50; singles US$6; doubles US$9.)

ÇANAKKALE ☎ 286

With cheap accommodations and good bus connections, Çanakkale (pop. 60,000) is a great base for exploring Gallipoli and Troy. The **Çimenlik Kalesi** (Grassy Castle), 200m from the harbor, combines a park and naval museum. (Open Tu-W and F-Su 9am-noon and 1:30-5pm. US$0.50, students US$0.20.) **Buses** arrive frequently from: Bursa (4½hr., US$6.50); İstanbul (5hr., US$10); and İzmir (5hr., US$7). To get to the **tourist office,** 67 İskele Meydanı, go left from the bus station, take a right on Demircioğlu Cad, and follow the signs marked *Feribot* to the docks; it's on the left. (☎/fax 217 11 87.) **Yellow Rose Pension** arranges tours of Gallipoli through TJ's Tours (above). Turn right at the clock tower, then take the second right. (☎217 33 43. Dorms US$3; singles US$6; doubles US$11.) **Anzac House,** 61 Cumhuriyet Meydanı, arranges tours of Gallipoli and Troy through the Hassle Free Tour Agency (above). Facing Cumhuriyet Meydani with your back to the ferry docks, it's immediately on your right. (☎213 59 69. Dorms US$3; singles US$7; doubles US$11.50.)

■ **DAYTRIP FROM ÇANAKKALE: TROY (TRUVA).** Troy, made famous by Homer, remained under a blanket of mythology until archaeologist Heinrich Schliemann uncovered the ancient city 32km south of Çanakkale—proving that the stories about Helen and the wooden horse are more than myth. The ruins as they appear today, however, are a little underwhelming. Nine layers of Bronze Age fortifications are explained in the **Excavation House.** (Site and house open daily in summer 8am-7pm; off-season 8am-5pm. US$3, students US$1.50.) **TJ's Tours,** based in Eceabat (see Gallipoli), has excellent tours (US$14). **Anzac House** (see above) leads tours from Çanakkale at 8:30am (US$14); bring water. Or, visit the site by taking a **dolmuş** from the lot in Çanakkale (every hr., US$0.75).

BERGAMA (PERGAMON)   ☎232

Ancient Pergamon, capital of the Roman province of Asia, once had the second-largest library in the world. Oh well—it's all ruins now. From the river (near the Pension Athena), cross the bridge, head diagonally to the right and uphill through the old town, and follow the paved road until you come to a gate and a cluster of concrete buildings. Pass between the road's chain-like fence and the perimeter fence of the compound, following the path through the gymnasium and the Temple of Demeter, which gets you to the main ruins of the **Acropolis** at the top of the hill. As you exit the lower city, the Hellenistic **theater,** which once seated 10,000, comes into view. Farther up, you can try to land three coins on top of the column inside the **wishing well** for good luck, or marvel at the newly restored **Temple of Trajan.** Follow the yellow signs from Atatürk Meydanı on the west side of town to reach the famed **Asclepion,** a healing center where a very important ancient doctor, Galen, once worked. A marble colonnade, theater, and healing rooms remain today. (Open daily 8am-6:30pm. US$3, ISIC free.) Near the river and the old part of Pergamon stand the remnants of **Kızıl Avlu** (Red Basilica), a pagan temple that became one of the Seven Churches of the Apocalypse mentioned in the Book of Revelations. The ruins of ancient Pergamon are scattered about the modern town of Bergama, which sends **buses** to: Ankara (10hr., 9pm, US$11.50); İstanbul (10hr., 10am and 9:15pm, US$13); and İzmir (2hr., every 45min., US$2.25). From the bus station, walk 1km right on İzmir Cad. and turn left on Cumhuriyet Meydanı to reach the **tourist office.** (☎631 28 51. Open daily M-F 8:30am-noon and 1-5:30pm.) **Pension Athena,** on the road beyond İstiklâl Meydanı, boasts, "Not the best, but we're trying to get there." Charming honesty, but a bit of an undersell. (☎633 34 20. Laundry. Internet. US$4.50-5.75 per person; 10% *Let's Go* discount.) **Postal code:** 35700.

İZMİR   ☎232

İzmir (pop. 3 million), formerly **Smyrna** (reputed to be the birthplace of Homer), rose from the rubble of the 1922 Turkish War of Independence to become Turkey's third-largest city. Wide boulevards, plazas, and plenty of greenery line the waterfront; but inland, İzmir is a factory-bleak wasteland. *Çay salonular* (teahouses), street vendors, and a full-fledged **bazaar** (open M-Sa 9am-8pm) line the streets of Anafartalar Cad. İzmir's **Archaeological Museum,** near Konak Sq., houses finds from Ephesus and other local sites. (Open Tu-Su 9am-5pm. US$1.75, students US$1.) Uphill from the archaeological museum, the **Ethnographical Museum** displays traditional folk art and Ottoman weaponry. (Open Tu-Su 9am-noon and 1-5pm. US$0.75, students US$0.40.) From mid-June to early August, the **International İzmir Festival** brings Turkish and international acts to İzmir, Çeşme, and Ephesus. (For tickets and info, call the numbers listed in the İzmir Festival brochure distributed at the tourist office, or visit www.izmirfestival.org. Tickets US$7.50-38.) Budget hotels, cheap restaurants, bus company offices, and the **Basmane train station** are around **9 Eylül Meydanı,** a rotary at the center of the Basmane district. **Buses** run from **Yeni Garaj,** İzmir's new intercity bus station, to: Ankara (8hr., every hr., US$9.25); Bodrum (4hr., every hr., US$6); Bursa (5hr., 10 per day, US$6.50); İstanbul (9hr., every hr., US$13); Kuşadası (1hr., every hr., US$2.25); and Marmaris (5hr., every hr., US$6.50). Take city bus #50, 51, 53, 54, 60, 601, or 605 from the station (US$0.50; buy tickets from the kiosk before boarding) and tell the driver you want "Basmane Meydanı," which is the same as 9 Eylül Meydanı. From there, walk down Gazi Bul. to the first main intersection, then turn right onto Gazi Osmanpaşa Bul. The **tourist office** is on the right at 1/1D Gazi Osman Paşa Bul., 30m past the Hilton Hotel toward the sea. (☎445 73 90. Open daily 8:30am-5:30pm.) **Lâleli Otel,** 1368 Sok. #5-6, one block from 9 Eylül Meydani off 1369 Sok., has spacious rooms with private baths. (☎484 09 01. US$5.75 per person.) **Hotel Oba,** 1369 Sok. #27, four blocks down 1369 Sok from 9 Eylül Meydanı, is pricier, but more comfortable. (☎441 96 05. Breakfast included. Singles US$11.50.) **Postal code:** 35000.

DAYTRIP FROM IZMIR: SART (SARDIS). While small, Sart stands out as Turkey's best-restored archaeological site. The **old city** boasts a magnificent two-story **gymnasium,** a long-deserted **swimming pool,** a ruined **Palaestra,** and a gorgeous **synagogue.** The patterns of the synagogue's 3rd-century mosaic floors are strangely juxtaposed with Corinthian and Doric columns. (Open daily 8am-6pm. US$1, students US$0.50.) The amazing 4th-century BC **Temple of Artemis** was one of the largest temples of the ancient world. (Open daily 8am-5pm. US$1, students US$0.50.) Take a **bus** bound for Salihli from the upper floor of İzmir's Yeni Garaj (1½hr., every 30min., US$1) and ask to be let off at Sart; you will be dropped near a yellow "Temple of Artemis" sign, by the shops scattered along the highway. The gymnasium, synagogue, and baths are about 50m ahead on the left. To catch a return bus to İzmir, follow the road across from the sign to the right as it splits, until you reach another highway. Flag a bus down at the pull-off on the far side (US$1).

ÇEŞME   ☎223

A breezy seaside village an hour west of İzmir, Çeşme has gained popularity for its cool climate, crystal-clear waters, and proximity to the Greek island of Chios. With a long ribbon of clean white sand flanked by rolling dunes, **Altınkum Beach** is one of Turkey's finest. **Dolmuş** run to Altınkum from the lot in Çeşme, by the tourist office (15min., June-Sept. every 20min., US$1). Çeşme's most impressive site is the **castle,** which houses a sparse **Archaeological Museum.** (Open Tu-Su 8am-noon and 1-6pm. US$2.50.) **Buses** (☎712 64 99) run from the *otogar,* at the corner of A. Menderes Cad. and Çevre Yolu Cad., to: Ankara (10hr., 9:30pm, US$12); İstanbul (11hr., 2 per day, US$13); and İzmir (1½hr., every 20min., US$2.50). Buy **ferry** tickets from **Ertürk Tourism and Travel Agency,** 6/7 Beyazıt Cad., next to the *kervansaray.* (☎712 67 68. Open daily 8am-9pm; in winter 8am-6pm.) From the main gate of the *otogar,* follow Turgutozal Cad. down to the sea, turn right, and walk 300m to the main square in front of the castle. The **tourist office,** 8 İskele Meydanı, is across from the castle and *kervansaray,* by numerous budget accommodations. (☎/fax 712 66 53. Open M-F 8:30am-5:30pm, Sa-Su 9am-5pm; in winter M-F 8:30am-5:30pm.) **Alim Pension,** Tarini Turk Hamami Yani, is on the corner past the *kervansaray* and hamam as you walk with the sea on your right on Alpaslan Cad. (☎712 83 19. US$4 per person.) Walking away from the sea, turn onto Mektep Sok off İnkılap Cad. and then right again onto Dellal Sok.; the refreshingly clean **Filiz Pension** is at #16. (☎712 67 94. Doubles US$8.) **Postal code:** 35930.

SELÇUK   ☎232

Selçuk is a convenient base from which to explore Ephesus, and offers its own archaeological sites as well. The colossal **Basilica of Saint John** lies off Atatürk Cad. on the supposed site of St. John's grave. (Open daily 8am-7pm. US$1.75.) The stunning 14th-century **İsa Bey Camii** is at the foot of the hill on which the Basilica of St. John and the Ayasoluk castle stand. (Open 10min. before and after prayer times.) A few hundred meters down Dr. Sabri Yayla Bulvarı, walking away from town with the tourist office on your right, are the sad remains of the **Temple of Artemis,** one of the seven wonders of the ancient world. (Open daily 8:30am-5:30pm. Free.) The **Ephesus Museum** (Efes Müzesi), directly across from the tourist office, houses a world-class collection of recent finds from Ephesus. (Open daily 8:30am-noon and 1-7pm. US$5.) **Trains** go to İzmir (1½hr., 7 per day, US$1). **Buses** run from the *otogar,* at the corner of Şabahattın Dede Cad. and Atatürk Cad., to: Ankara (9hr., 3 per day, US$11.25); Bodrum (3hr., every hr., US$5); Fethiye (6hr., every 2hr., US$7.25); İstanbul (10hr., 5 per day, US$11.25); İzmir (1hr., every 30min., US$1.50); and Marmaris (4hr., every hr., US$5.75). **Minibuses** run to Kuşadası (20min., every 20min., US$1). The **tourist office,** 35 Agora Çarşısı, Atatürk Mah., is on the southwest corner of Sabahattındede and Atatürk Cad. (☎892 63 28. Open Apr.-Dec. M-F 8am-noon and 1-5pm, Sa-Su 9am-5pm.) Guests at the ▨**Artemis Guest House,** Atatürk Mah., 1012 Sok. 2, will find clean rooms and an attentive staff. (☎892 19 82; enquiries@artemisguesthouse.com. US$5.) The **All Blacks Hotel and Pension,** has some of the nicest rooms in the budget circuit. (☎892 36 57; abnomads@egenet.com.tr. Singles US$6.50; doubles US$9.75.)

▶ **DAYTRIP FROM SELÇUK: EPHESUS (EFES).** Ephesus has a concentration of Classical art and architecture surpassed only by Rome and Athens; the ruins rank first among Turkey's ancient sites in terms of sheer size and state of preservation. Guided tours are not necessary. (Site open 8am-6pm. US$6.50 entrance fee.) On the left of the road to the lower entrance is the **Vedius Gymnasium,** built in AD 150; beyond the vegetation are the horseshoe-shaped remains of the city's **stadium.** Just inside the lower entrance, a dirt path leads to the right to the ruins of the **Church of the Seven Councils.** After the Ecumenical Council met here to question the Virgin Mary's divinity, the church became known as the **Church of the Virgin Mary.** A tree-lined path leads from the main entrance to the **Arcadiane,** Ephesus's main drag. **The Grand Theater** is a stunning, restored beast carved into the side of Mt. Pion. From the theater, walk along **Marble Way,** which has a metal inscription thought to be the world's first advertisement—it's for a brothel. The slight incline signals the beginning of the **Street of Curetes,** which leads to the **Library of Celsus,** the brothel, the 5th-century **Baths of Scholastica,** and the ruins of the **Temple of Hadrian.** Across from the temple are the newly excavated **Terrace Houses,** whose mosaics, frescoes, and peristyle architecture are believed to date back to the 6th century. (Open daily 8am-6:30pm. US$5.75.) Farther up the hill on the left are the ruins of the exquisite **Fountain of Trajan.** The building on the left as you walk up the ramp is the **Prytaneion,** which was dedicated to the worship of Vesta and contained an eternal flame tended by the Vestal Virgins. The road that runs by the top entrance leads to the **House of the Virgin Mary** (8km, US$15 taxi ride), where Mary lived after leaving Jerusalem. The easiest way to get to Ephesus from **Selçuk** is to take hotels' free shuttle service. Or, from the Kuşadası *otogar,* take a **dolmuş** to Selçuk and ask to stop at Ephesus (30min., US$1). From the Selçuk *otogar,* take a Pamucak-bound *dolmuş* (5min., every 15-20min., US$0.75). **Taxis** run from Selçuk to the site (US$4). It's also an easy **walk** from Selçuk (25min.).

PAMUKKALE   ☎258

Pamukkale ("Cotton Castle"), formerly ancient Hierapolis (Holy City), has been drawing the weary and the curious to its thermal springs for more than 23 centuries. A favorite getaway spot for vacationing Romans almost two millennia ago, the warm **baths** at Pamukkale still bubble away. (Open 24hr. US$3.20, students US$.80.) Don't leave town without a dip in the sacred fountain at the **Pamukkale Motel,** (☎272 20 24. Pool open daily 8am-8pm. US$4 per 2hr.) Behind the Motel, the enormous and well-preserved **Grand Theater** dominates the **ruins of Hierapolis.** The former city bath has been converted into an **Hierapolis Museum** housing finds unearthed by Italian archaeologists. (Open daily 9am-6pm. US$1.20, students US$0.40.) **Buses** to Pamukkale stop in the center of Pamukkale Köyü; some direct buses arrive from Kuşadası and pass through Selçuk (3½hr.; daily 9am, return 5pm; US$6.50), but the usual route is through **Denizli,** where buses arrive from: Bodrum (5hr., 5 per day, US$5.60); İstanbul (10hr., 6 per day, US$14.40); İzmir (4hr., 30 per day, US$4.80); Kuşadası (4hr., take any İzmir bus and get off at Selçuk for a *dolmuş,* US$4); and Marmaris (4hr., 8 per day, US$4.80). *Dolmuş* go between Denizli and Pamukkale (30min., every 15min., US$0.40). Many accommodations, including those listed here, offer free pick-up from Denizli. The **tourist office** is at the top of the hill, within the site gates. (☎272 20 77. Open daily 8am-noon and 1:30-6:30pm; in winter M-F 8am-noon and 1-5:30pm.) Just outside Cumhuriyet Meydanı, the backpacker-friendly ■**Meltem Motel** is at 9 Kuzey Sok. (☎272 24 13; meltenmotel@superonline.com.tr. Dorms US$3.20; singles US$4.) The **Koray Hotel,** 27 Fevzi Çakmak Cad., has a beautiful courtyard adorned with grapevines. (☎272 23 00. Singles US$16; doubles US$24.) Both hotels have swimming pools with local thermal water.

⚡ DAYTRIP FROM PAMUKKALE: APHRODISIAS. Still under excavation, the ruins of Aphrodisias are expected to eclipse Ephesus in grandeur. The highlights include the soaring Ionic columns of the **Temple of Aphrodite,** an ancient 30,000-seat **stadium,** one of the best-preserved stadiums ever excavated, and a new and well-funded **museum** near the site entrance that features a fabulous collection of Roman-era sculpture. (Site open daily 8am-8pm; in winter 8am-5pm. Museum open daily 9am-6:30pm; in winter 9am-5pm. US$3.20 each, students US$1.20.) **Buses** leave Pamukkale daily at 9:30am and depart Aphrodisias at 2:30pm (2hr., return US$10). Many hotels make additional trips if they have enough interested guests.

BODRUM ☎ 252

Bodrum is known for nightlife, impressive ruins, and some of the best beaches in Turkey. Before it became the "Bedroom of the Mediterranean," the ancient city of **Halicarnassus** was known for **Herodotus,** the "father of history," and for the 4th-century BC funerary monument to King Mausolus, so magnificent that its **mausoleum** (from which we get the word) was declared one of the seven wonders of the ancient world. Unfortunately, most of the remains were destroyed, buried beneath modern Bodrum, incorporated into the Bodrum castle, or shipped to London's British Museum. Take Kulucii Sok from behind the *otogar* and the mausoleum will be on your right. (Open Tu-Su 8am-noon and 1-5pm, students US$1.) Bodrum's formidable **castle,** built over the ruins of an ancient acropolis by crusaders from the Knights of St. John, now features a flock of peacocks, exhibits, the remains of a 4th-century BC Carian Princess, and the **Glass Hall,** home of the oldest shipwreck ever discovered. (Open Tu-F 10am-noon and 1-5pm. US$5, students US$2.50.) The opulent **◪Halikarnas Disco,** on Z. Müren Cad., at the far end of Cumhuriyet Cad. from the marina, flashes strobes 1km from the center of town. (Cover US$12. Beer US$3.) The club **Hadi Gari,** Cumhuriyet Cad., by the castle, fuses elegance and funk. (Open midnight-4am.) Nightlife abounds on **Cumhuriyet Cad.,** the road that runs along the beach beyond the marina.

From the *otogar* on Cevat Şakir Cad., Pamukkale **buses** (☎316 663 26) go to: Bursa (10hr., 3 per day, US$13); Fethiye (5hr., 4 per day, US$7); İstanbul (12hr., 3 per day, US$18); İzmir (4hr., every hr., US$7.50); Kuşadası (2½hr., every hr., US$6); Marmaris (3hr., every hr., US$5); and Pamukkale (5hr., 3 per day, US$7). **Dolmuş** go from the *otogar* to Marmaris (3hr., every hr., US$5). **Turkish Airlines** (☎313 12 03) flies to İstanbul and Ankara (1hr., 5 per day, US$98). **Bodrum Express Lines** (☎316 40 67; fax 313 00 77) has offices in the *otogar* and past the castle on the left toward the sea. For information on **ferries** to Greece, see p. 956. The **tourist office,** 48 Barış Meydanı, at the foot of the castle, has room listings. (☎316 10 91; fax 316 76 94. Open Apr.-Oct. daily 8:30am-5:00pm; Nov.-Mar. M-F 8am-noon and 1-5pm.) To get from the *otogar* to the peaceful **Emiko Pansiyon,** Atatürk Cad., 11 Uslu Sok., follow Cevat Şakir Cad. toward the castle, turn left on Atatürk Cad., and turn right after 50m down the sign-covered alley, including one for Emiko Pansiyon. (☎/fax 316 55 60. Breakfast US$2. Kitchen. Singles US$10; doubles US$16.) **Otel Kilavuz,** 50 Atatürk Cad., boasts a pool and bar. (☎316 38 92; fax 316 28 52. Singles US$12; doubles US$16.) On your right before the mosque lies **Zetas Saray Restaurant,** whose fine Turkish cuisine is savored by locals and tourists alike. (Meals $3-10. Open 9am-3am.) **Postal code:** 48400.

⚡ DAYTRIP FROM BODRUM: BODRUM PENINSULA. Bodrum's popularity among Turks stems largely from its location at the head of the **Bodrum Peninsula,** where traditional villages mingle with coastal vistas and dramatic crags. Explore the peninsula's greener northern coast or its drier, sandier southern coastline. Tour **boats** bound for **beaches** on the peninsula's southern coast skirt the front of the castle (daily 9am-noon, return 5-6pm; US$10-12 including lunch). Check the tour schedule at the dock. Popular destinations include **Kara Ada** (Black Island), where orange clay from deep within a cave is said to restore youthful beauty, and **Deveplajı** (Camel Beach), where you can get a camel ride (US$4 per 10min.). The peninsula's northern end, calmer than the southern coast, has rocky beaches and deep water.

Dolmuş depart frequently from Bodrum's *otogar* for the quiet shores, swimming docks, and clear water of **Gölköy** and **Türkbükü** (30min., US$1); the sand paradise of **Yahşi,** Bodrum's longest beach (30min., every 10min., US$0.80); the peaceful shore of **Bağla** (30min., every 30min., US$1); and the sunken ruins of **Mindos,** near **Gümüşlük's** beach (40min., US$1.40).

MEDITERRANEAN COAST

At turns chic, garish, and remote, the Mediterranean coast stretches along lush national parks, sun-soaked beaches, and shady pine forests. By day, travelers take peaceful boat trips, hike among waterfalls, and explore submerged ruins; by night, they visit Ephesus, dance under the stars, and sleep in treehouses.

⚓ FERRIES TO GREECE

From **Marmaris: catamarans** (1hr., May-Oct. 1 per day, return US$40); **hydrofoils** (1hr., May-Oct. 2 per day, US$40-60); and **ferries** (2hr., when there are enough cars, return US$40 plus taxes) all go to **Rhodes.** Make reservations the day before at a travel agency; try **Yeşil Marmaris** (☎(252) 412 64 86).

MARMARİS ☎ 252

Marmaris contains all the beach town necessities: eclectic tourist shops, seaside restaurants, beautiful wooden yachts, a boisterous beachfront, and decadent night-time festivities. Boats set off from the natural harbor for spectacular nearby coves, where pine-blanketed cliffs reach down into the clear water and toward the Greek island of Rhodes (ask at the Interyouth Hostel about excursions). To get from the tourist office to the 16th-century **castle,** take the street to the right, turn left into the bazaar, go right down the alley after the Sultan Restaurant, and climb to the top of the stairs. A lush garden complete with peacocks and turtles fills the inner court-yard, while the paths along the ramparts offer panoramic views of the Marmaris harbor. (Open Tu-Su 8:30am-noon and 2-5:30pm. US$1.20, students US$0.60.) It's hard to tell which is hotter in Marmaris: the burning sun or the blazing nightlife. Head to bars behind the tourist office on **Barlar Sok.** (a.k.a. Bar St.). **Buses** (☎412 30 37) go from Mustafa Münir Elgin Bul. to: Ankara (10hr., 10am and 9pm, US$14); Bodrum (3¾hr., every hr., US$6); Göreme (14hr., 3pm, US$18); İstanbul (12½hr., 7 per day, US$18); İzmir (4½hr., every hr., US$10); Kuşadası (5hr., 10:45am and 6pm, US$9); and Pamukkale (4½hr., every hr., US$7). From the bus station, out of town on Mustafa Münir Elgin Bul., take a *dolmuş* (US$0.40) or taxi (US$3) to the central Ulusal Egemenlik Bul., which hosts the Tansaş Shopping Center and the *dolmuş* hub. The **tourist office** is 250m along Kordon Cad. (☎412 10 35. Open daily 8:30am-7:30pm; in winter M-F 8am-5pm.) The ⬛**Interyouth Hostel,** Tepe Mah., 42 Sok. #45, is deep in the bazaar; from the Atatürk statue, take the first left. Turn right inside the bazaar and the youth hostel is on the right. (☎412 36 87; interyouth@turk.net. Laundry. Internet. Breakfast and dinner included. Dorms US$5; rooms US$12; ISIC, HI, or IYTC US$1 discount.) **Postal code:** 48700.

HOW TO DRINK RAKI
The art of drinking *rakı,* Turkey's most famous and potent local drink, is a skill deeply ingrained for most Turks and pitifully elusive to most foreigners. Made with aniseed and white grapes, *rakı* contains 40% alcohol and smells strongly of licorice. The best *rakı,* coming from **Tekirdağ,** near İstanbul, is best complemented by white cheese, watermelon, or fish, which bring out the flavor while soothing the stomach from the fiery impact of the liquor. Though most commonly drunk mixed with cold water (which turns it a cloudy white), *rakı* is occasionally mixed with orange juice or *salgam,* a spicy turnip juice. However you take it, *rakı* is best drunk slowly—you'll learn to respect its kick—and in the company of good friends. Try drinking a spoonful of olive oil beforehand if you want to stay sober.

DALYAN AND KAUNOS (CAUNOS) ☎252

The placid village of Dalyan seems to have grown out of the nearby breezy river. Carian **rock tombs** built into cliffs are visible from the harbor, and thick reed beds teem with wildlife just a few minutes away. Dalyan's sites are best seen on **boat tours** that visit the ruins of ancient **Kaunos** (open daily 8am-7pm; Nov.-May daily 9am-5pm. US$1.50); **İztuzu Beach,** where endangered loggerhead turtles lay their eggs by night (open 8am-8pm; beach chair rental US$4); and local **mud baths** and **thermal springs** (open 7am-7:30pm; US$0.90). Boat tour offices are behind the turtle statue in town on Maraş Sok. (Tours US$10 including lunch). The *dolmuş* from Ortaca stops in front of the mosque. Facing the PTT (post office), turn left and follow the road right, then go straight. City **buses** go to Ortaca (20min., every 15min., US$0.40), where you can get a bus headed to Fethiye (1¼hr., US$2.40) and Marmaris (1½hr., US$2.40). A new *dolmus* line runs directly to Marmaris and Fethiye (3 per day, US$1.80). With your back to the turtle statue, head into the passageway across from the statue to reach the **tourist office**. (☎284 42 35. Open daily in summer 8:30am-noon and 1-6pm; in winter 8:30am-noon and 1-5:30pm.) From the turtle statue, walk 75m down Maraş Sok., make the 2nd left on 10 Sok., and walk a block to find **Gül Motel Pension.** (☎284 24 67. Singles US$7; doubles US$12.) You'll find plenty of *pansiyons*, restaurants, and some bars on Maraş Sok. **Postal code:** 48840.

FETHIYE ☎252

Fethiye, on a harbor ringed by pine forests and mountains, is a peaceful base on the backpacker circuit because of its unique hiking opportunities. Daytrips to **Saklikeut Gorge** allow you to wade in a river and scale waterfalls. (Entrance US$0.60, students US$0.30). The ghost town of **Kayaköy** offers many hikes; call the nearby Kayaköy Motel and Restaurant (☎(258) 618 00 69) for trekking advice. The marvelous pebble beach and **Blue Lagoon** in **Ölüdeniz**—a peninsula of beach cradled in wooded hills and lapped by clear water—are an easy trip. Enter from Tabiat Park, on the right of the road. From the *dolmuş* station, it's a 20min. walk or a US$3.50 taxi ride to the tip. (Park and lagoon open 8am-7pm. US$0.75.) To reach Saklikeut, Kayaköy, or Ölüdeniz from Fethiye, take a *dolmuş* from the stop near the intersection of Hastane and Atatürk Cad, near the mosque. (25-45min., every 10min., return US$2-3). Take a boat from the beach in Ölüdeniz (45min., 3 per day, US$3) to reach the tiny, beautiful bay of **Butterfly Valley,** home to waterfalls and the nocturnal orange-and-black Jersey Tiger butterfly. Paths marked by blue dots wind their way up to two waterfalls (US$1). **Fetur,** 50m past the tourist office on Fevzi Çakmak Cad., arranges daily tours. (☎614 20 34. Open daily 9am-5:30pm.)

Buses run frequently from Fethiye's *otogar* on Ölüdeniz Cad. Coastal road buses can drop off passengers anywhere, so there's no need to wait for a specific bus into town. If there are no shuttles to the center, take a *dolmuş* to the PTT in town (every 5min., US $0.40). From there, walk down Atatürk Cad. through the harbor to the **tourist office.** (☎/fax 612 19 75. Open daily 8:30am-5pm; in winter M-F 8:30am-5pm.) Call for free pickup from the *otogar* to ▣**Ideal Pansiyon,** Karagözler Zafer Cad. #1 (☎/fax 614 19 81. Breakfast included. Delicious dinner US$3.50. Laundry. Dorms US$6.50 per room.) **Postal code:** 48300.

KAŞ ☎242

Sandwiched between sea and mountains, cosmopolitan Kaş is hassle-free. Its pleasant streets are lined with cheap, hospitable lodgings, excellent restaurants, and laid-back bars. A peninsula curving around one side of the town's harbor creates a calm, rock-lined lagoon ideal for swimming in the cool turquoise water. The city also serves as a gateway to the backpacker haven of Olimpos (see below). The *otogar*, uphill on Atatürk Cad., sends buses to: Ankara (12hr., 8:30pm, US$19); Antalya (3hr., every 30min., US$5.40); Fethiye (2hr., 5 per day, US$2.50); İstanbul (15hr., 6:30pm, US$21); and İzmir (9hr., 2 per day, US$12.50). The **tourist office,** 5 Cumhuriyet Meydanı, is to the left as you face the back of the Atatürk statue. (☎836 12 38. Open daily 8am-noon and 1-7pm; in winter M-F 8am-5pm.) Budget **pansiyons** line the sidestreets to the right of Atatürk Bul. (as you head from the *otogar* to the waterfront). A breezy rooftop terrace awaits at **Ateş Pension,** Yeni Cami Cad. No. 3. (☎836 13 93; atespension@superonline.com. Breakfast included. Free Internet. Singles US$7; doubles US$14.) **Postal code:** 07580.

OLIMPOS ☎242

Olimpos awes visitors with its scenery. Tall cliffs streaked mauve, red, and gray tower above acres of pine forest and orange orchards. **Roman and Byzantine ruins** lie hidden among the vines of a marshy jungle. Wander through to discover ancient temples and the crumbling walls of medieval castles. A pebble beach awaits at the end of the road. (Ruins and beach US$5, students US$2. Hold on to your ticket stub.) The town's other main attraction is **Chimæra,** the perpetual flame springing from the mountainside 7km away. Mythology explains the flame as the breath of a mythical beast; geologists suggest natural methane gas. **Bus tours** leave Olimpos at 9pm (3hr., US$3); ask at any hostel for details. To get to Olimpos from Kaş, take an Antalya-bound **bus.** Buses stop at a rest station on the main road. From there, *dolmuş* (15min., every hr., US$1.25) run to the tree-house-*pansiyons*, dropping passengers off at the place of their choice. As Olimpos is classified as an archaeological site, the use of concrete is banned, so resourceful locals have constructed **treehouse pansiyons,** which line the dirt road to the beach and ruins. **Bayram's Treehouse Pension** (☎892 12 43; bayrams1@turk.net) is the ultimate black hole of chill, with colorful bungalows and a friendly staff. (Internet access. Arranges travel. Close to beach and ruins.) **Postal code:** 07350.

ANTALYA ☎242

Antalya's concrete block buildings encircle *Kaleiçi* ("inside the fortress"), the crescent-shaped old city that brims with Ottoman houses, pensions, and restaurants. **The Antalya Museum,** 2 Konyaatı Bul., 2½km from town, won the 1988 European Museum of the Year Award for its exhibits ranging from prehistoric times to the founding of the Turkish Republic. *Dolmuş* labeled "Konyaaltı/Liman" head along Cumhuriyet Bul., which changes its name to Konyaaltı Bul., stopping at the large "D" signs (US$0.30). Get off at the yellow museum signs before heading downhill to the beach. The tram (US$0.25) also runs from Kaleiçi to the museum. (Open Tu-Su 9am-6pm; in winter 8am-5pm. US$6, students US$4.50.) **Lara** and **Konyaaltı** beach are both accessible by *dolmuş* (to Lara from the Doğu Garaj, to Konyaaltı from Konyaaltı Bul.; US$0.30). Every fall, the huge **Antalya Altın Portakal** ("Golden Orange") Film Festival features international and Turkish cinema.

Flights from Antalya International Airport (domestic flights ☎330 30 30, international flights ☎330 36 00), 15km outside of town, leave for İstanbul (US$61, students US$51) and various foreign cities. Buses run between the Turkish Airlines THY office, next to the tourist office, and Antalya Airport in summer (10 per day, US$3). **Buses** leave from the orange *otogar*, 4km out of town at Anadolu Kavşağı, for: Bodrum (8hr., US$15); Göreme (10hr., 2 per day, US$16); İstanbul (12hr., US$17); Kaş (3hr., every 30min., US$4); and Olimpos (1¼hr., every 20min., US$1.50). Gray buses (US$0.40) run from outside the *otogar* to the city center, near Kaleiçi. The **tourist office,** on Cumhuriyet Cad., is to the left of the red minaret and past the military complex. (☎241 17 47. Open M-F 8am-7pm, Sa-Su 9am-7pm; in winter M-F 8am-5pm, Sa-Su 10am-5pm.) Almost all the 200 pensions and hotels within the ancient walls of Kaleiçi include private shower and breakfast in prices. **La Paloma Pansiyon,** Kılıçarslan Mah., 60 Hesapçı Sok., offers gorgeous rooms. (☎244 79 24. Singles US$20; doubles US$35.) Backpackers hang out at **Sabah Pansiyon,** Kaleiçi Kılıçarslan Mah., 60 Hesapçı Sok. (☎247 53 45. Singles US$6; doubles US$8-18; roof, couch, or floor US$3. Camping US$2.50-3.) **Postal code:** 07000.

ANTAKYA ☎326

East of Cyprus, the Mediterranean coast hooks southward and the cities take on a more Syrian feel. This is the Hatay, territory that was contested between Rome and Persia, and more recently, between Turkey and Syria. **Antakya,** the region's largest city, offers sprawling markets, manicured tea gardens, and the ■**Hatay Museum,** housing the world's finest collection of Roman mosaics. (Open Tu-Su 8:30am-noon and 1:30-6pm. US$3.50, students US$1.50.) The crumbling walls along the surrounding mountain ridge are evidence of the city's former glory. The side of Mt. Stauros is riddled with caves and tunnels where an underground sect practiced 2 millennia ago. The **Grotto of Saint Peter** is where the group first named their new religion "Christianity." To reach the church, walk 2km north on Kurunus Cad. and take the erratic city bus #6, or a taxi. (Open Tu-Su 8am-noon and 1:30-4:30pm. US$3, students US$1.)

Buses leave from the **otogar,** on the eastern side of the Asi River, to: Ankara (10hr., 6 per day, US$13); Antalya (14hr., 10 per day, US$13); and İstanbul (16hr., 8 per day, US$19). Get a visa at home or in Ankara if you want to take a bus to Aleppo, Syria (3-4hr., 4 per day, US$8) or Damamscus (9hr., 9:30am and noon; US$15). From the otogar, the center of town is 700m along **İstiklâl Cad.** The **tourist office** is in the Valiliki building at the end of İstiklâl Cad., just past the Antik Beyazıt Hotel. (☎216 06 10. Open M-F 8am-noon and 1:30-5:30pm.) ■**Jasmin Hotel,** 14 İstiklâl Cad., has a rooftop patio and shared bathrooms. (☎212 71 71. Singles US$5; doubles US$8; triples US$10.) The best of the middle range choices is **Hotel Saray,** 3 Hürriyet Cad. (☎/fax 214 90 01. Breakfast included. Singles US$10; doubles US$16; triples US$25.) In the third week of July, Antakya hosts a **music festival** with marching bands, DJ carts, and traditional singers. **Postal code:** 31000.

CENTRAL TURKEY

Central Turkey is less heavily touristed than the Aegean and Mediterranean coasts. It offers cooler weather, a wealth of ancient ruins, and some of the country's most hospitable towns—from sophisticated Ankara to the surreal cities of Cappadocia.

ANKARA   ☎312

Ankara is a new city with an ancient history. In 1923, after the Turkish War of Independence, Atatürk transformed the small town into an administrative metropolis. The city has vibrant nightlife, being the nation's premier college town.

█� **TRANSPORTATION AND PRACTICAL INFORMATION. Trains** arrive from the *otogar,* 1.5km southwest of Ulus Square on the end of Cumhuriyet Bul., from İstanbul (6½-9½hr., 7 per day, US$4-35) and İzmir (15hr., 3 per day, US$9). To get to the city center, follow the covered tunnel past the last platform into the "Maltepe" station of the east-west **Ankaray subway,** which stops in Kızılay and Ulus (5-ride pass US$2.50, students US$1.50). The **tourist office,** 121 Gazi Mustafa Kemal Bul., is directly outside the "Maltepe" Ankaray station. (☎231 55 72. Open daily 9am-5pm.) **Embassies** in Ankara include: **Australia,** 83 Nenehatun Cad., Gaziomanpaşa (☎446 11 80); **Canada,** 75 Nenehatun Cad. (☎436 12 75); **New Zealand,** 13/4 İran Cad., Kavaklıdere (☎467 90 56); **Northern Cyprus,** 20 Rabat Sok., Gaziosmanpaşa (☎446 29 20); **South Africa,** 27 Filistin Sok., Gaziomanpaşa (☎446 40 56); **UK,** 46A Şehit Ersan Cad., Çankaya (☎468 62 30); and **US,** 110 Atatürk Bul. (☎468 61 10). Check **email** at the ■**Internet Center Café,** 107 Atatürk Bul. (US$1.25 per hr. Open daily 9am-11pm.)

█▝ **ACCOMMODATIONS AND FOOD.** Of the two main accommodations centers, **Ulus** is cheaper and closer to sights, but student-oriented **Kızılay** is cleaner. In Ulus, the safest bet for quality and price is at **Otel Zümrüt,** 16 Şehit Teğmen Kalmaz Cad. From the equestrian statue, go south on Atatürk Bul. and take the second left. (☎311 33 93. Singles US$5-8; doubles US$12-17; triples US$17-21.) **Otel Hisar,** Hisarparkı Cad., #6, is east of the statue, toward the citadel. (☎311 98 89. Singles US$6.50; doubles US$11.) In Kızılay, to reach peaceful **Otel Ertan,** 70 Selânik Cad., head south on Atatürk Bul., take the fourth left after the McDonald's on Meşrutiyet Cad., and take the third right on Selânik Cad. (☎418 40 84. Singles US$15.50; doubles US$24.50.) The main culinary neighborhoods are **Gençlik Park** (cheap), **Kızılay** (mid-range), **Hisar** (formal), and **Kavaklıdere** (upscale). In Kızılay, ■**Göksu Restaurant,**

22A Bayındur Sok., has classy Turkish and European food at the right price. (Open daily noon-midnight.) Many other places dot Karanfil Sok. and Selânik Sok. Gima **supermarkets** are on Anafartalar Cad. in Ulus and Atatürk Bul. in Kızılay. Cheaper markets abound in Ulus. **Postal code:** 06443.

◉◈ SIGHTS AND NIGHTLIFE. The award-winning **Museum of Anatolian Civilizations** (Anadolu Medeniyetleri Müzesi) lies at the foot of the citadel looming over the old town. The museum is in a restored 15th-century Ottoman covered bazaar and features a tightly organized collection of world-class artifacts. From the equestrian statue in Ulus, walk to the top of Hisarparkı Cad., turn right at the bottom of the Citadel steps, and follow the Citadel boundaries. (Open Tu-Su 8:30am-5:30pm. US$3, students US$2.) Don't miss **Atatürk's mausoleum, Anıt Kabir;** nearly 1km long, it houses Atatürk's sarcophagus and personal effects. Take the subway to Tandoğan and follow the signs; when you reach the unmarked entrance guarded by two soldiers, head 10min. uphill. (Open M 1:30-5pm, Tu-Su 9am-5pm. Free.) The immense **Kocatepe Mosque** looms east of Kızılay on Mithat Paşa Cad. Take the subway to Kızılay then walk along Ziya Gökalp Cad. until you hit Mithat Paşa Cad (10min.). Completed in 1987, it's billed as a 16th-century mosque utilizing 20th-century technology, like glowing digital clocks that indicate prayer times. At night, enjoy live music in the bars of **Kızılay;** pub life centers on **İnkilâp Sok.** and the livelier **Bayındır Sok.,** to the left of Kızılay. **S.S.K. İşhanı,** on the corner of Ziya Gökalp Cad. and Selânik Cad., is packed with live music bars.

CAPPADOCIA

Cappadocia's unique landscape began to take shape 10 million years ago, when volcanic lava and ash hardened into a layer of soft rock called tufa. Rain, wind, and flooding from the Kızılırmak River shaped the tufa into cone-shaped monoliths called *peribaca* ("fairy chimneys"), grouped in cave-riddled valleys and along gorge ridges. Throughout Cappadocia, stairs, windows, and sentry holes have been carved into the already eroded rock.

GÖREME   ☎384

Göreme is the capital of Cappadocia's backpacker scene. The city goes all out with its cave theme—most bars and discos are subterranean, and pensions often have "cave" rooms. Visitors have been known to extend their stays: a local saying goes, "Once you've tasted Göreme's water, you're bound to come back."

▐▊ TRANSPORTATION AND PRACTICAL INFORMATION. Buses via Nevşehir to: Ankara (4hr., 9 per day, US$8); Bodrum (14hr., 3 per day, US$20); Bursa (10hr., 2 per day, US$16); İstanbul (11hr., 7 per day, US$16); İzmir (12hr., 6per day, US$16); Marmaris (14hr., 5 per day, US$20); Olimpos (12hr., 8 per day, US$19); and Pamukkale (10hr., 4 per day, US$14). The *otogar* **(bus station),** in the center of town, contains the town's only official **tourist office** (☎271 25 58), which has information on most of Göreme's 64 plus lodgings. As you exit the station, the main road is directly in front of you. The **Post Office (PTT),** which has the best exchange rate in town, is on the main road just after the turnoff for the Open-Air Museum. Open daily 8:30am-12:30pm and 1:30-5:30pm. **Postal code:** 50180.

▐▊ ACCOMMODATIONS AND FOOD. The city government has set prices for non-dorm rooms in the town's **hostels:** US$5 per person, with bath US$7, and up to US$10 for a single. Starred **hotels** can charge higher rates. Most lodgings will pick you up at the *otogar* if you call ahead.

▦ **Kelebek Hotel** (☎271 25 31; ali@kelebekhotel.com; www.kelebekhotel.com). Just uphill from Tuna Caves. Clean and well-run with spectacular views of surrounding valleys. Dorms US$4; fairy chimney rooms US$12, with shower US$18; deluxe suites US$50.

Tuna Caves Pension (☎271 26 81; tunacaves@hotmail.com). From the *otogar*, take the first right after the ATM and follow signs. Recently refurbished. Terrace views and stone courtyard with shaded lounge. Dorms US$4; singles US$6; deluxe suites $23.

Special Cave Pension (☎271 23 47; cheilker@yahoo.com). Coziest caves in town with with clean private showers in every room. Plush cave bar. US$7 per person.

Kookabura Pansiyon (☎271 25 49). Stunning views and cave bar with old Turkish flair. Breakfast $3. Dorms US$4; singles US$5, with shower US$7.

For meals, ▨**Sedef Restaurant**, on the left as you head out of Göreme on Bilal Eroglu Cad, serves a bulging stuffed eggplant (US$1.50) to live music. **Orient Restaurant** makes a great *sac tava* (US$4).

■▨ **SIGHTS AND HIKING.** One of Cappadocia's biggest draws is its **Open-Air Museum,** 2km out of Göreme on the Ürgüp road, which contains seven Byzantine churches, a convent, and a kitchen. In the 4th century, St. Basil founded one of the first Christian monasteries here, setting down religious tenets that influenced the entire Western monastic movement. The churches are full of frescoes; spectacular scenes from Jesus' life lie within the **Karanlık Kilise** (Dark Church). Follow the canal downhill from the bus station. With the canal on your left, take a left at the first major intersection. (Open 8am-5pm. Museum US$3. Dark Church US$7.)

Cappadocia's breathtaking landscape is a **hiking** heaven. On the way, you can descend into **Kirmizi Vadi** (Rose Valley), where bizarre, multi-colored rock formations make for one of the area's better hikes. Although rewarding, the 10km valley can be confusing. There are exits at 3km and 7km for those who wish to arrange return transportation. You'll end up in Çavuşin, where you can take the Avanos-Nevşehir **bus** or the Avanos-Zelve-Göreme-Ürgüp **dolmuş** back to Göreme (M-F every 30min. until 6pm, Sa-Su every hr.); or, take a **taxi** (US$5). Other notable hikes include more challenging **Pigeon Valley,** and smoldering **Love Valley** (a.k.a "Penis Valley"), named after its massive yet gentle, shaft-like rock formations. Although most area hikes are moderate and safe, hiking with friends or guides are your best bets to stay safe, navigate trickier areas, and see all sights. **Women traveling alone** might especially want to consider this option. Competing guided tour companies offer similar deals (US$30-150). **Alpino Tours** (☎271 27 27; www.alpino.com.tr), can even get you behind the wheel of a jeep.

▶ **DAYTRIPS FROM GÖREME: UNDERGROUND CITIES AND ÇAVUŞIN.** Cappadocia contains almost 200 **underground cities; Kaymaklı** and **Derinkuyu** are the largest. Carved from tufa, the cities were designed with mind-boggling ingenuity. Beware of uncharted tunnels. All explorable areas are marked and lit (flashlights still handy)—red arrows lead down, blue arrows lead up. (Cities open daily 8am-5pm; closed winter. US$3.75.) From Göreme, **dolmuş** run to Nevşehir (US$0.50) and go on to Kaymaklı (30min., US$0.60) and Derinkuyu (45min., US$0.80).

Escape to the nearby provincial village of **Çavuşin** (2km from Göreme) to visit Cappadocia's oldest church, the 5th-century **St. John the Baptist.** Or head over to Zelve's **Open Air Museum** (open daily 8am-5:30pm; US$4), where ruins of tufa villages make for hours of exploring, climbing, and burrowing (but mind gaps and holes underfoot). Both the Ürgüp-Avanos **dolmuş** and the Göreme-Avanos **bus** pass through Çavuşin. On foot, follow the main road past Çavuşin, take a right up the dirt road behind the pottery shop, and continue to climb for a magnificent ridge walk.

ÜRGÜP
☎384

Ürgüp emerges from a collage of odd rock formations, early Christian dwellings, and old Greek mansions. The city offers fewer pensions and neo-hippies than Göreme, but tourists will appreciate Ürgüp's organized information network, central *otogar*, and proximity to points of interest. **Kayseri Cad,** the main road, and **Güllüce Cad.,** which leads the 20m from the *otogar*, intersect at the town square, marked by an Atatürk statue. Bring a friend to the co-ed **Tarihi Şehir Hamamı,** in the main square. (Massage, scrub, and sauna US$8 per person. Open daily 7am-11pm.) Cappadocia is one of Turkey's major winemaking regions, with its center in Ürgüp.

Uphill to the right behind the Atatürk statue is the renowned **Turasan Winery,** supplier of 60% of Cappadocia's wines, which offers free tours and tastings in its rock-carved wine cellar. (Open 8am-8pm; tours until 5pm.) Several wine shops around the main square also offer free tastings. **Han Çırağan,** across the street from the Atatürk statue, serves a special of cheese, mushrooms, carrots, and peppers (US$4). At night, the dance floor is packed at **Prokopi Pub Bar,** in the town square, until around 3am.

Buses head to a range of cities, but schedules are highly spontaneous. English-speaking **Aydın Altan** of **Nevtur** (☎341 43 02) will answer bus-related questions. The **tourist office** is in the garden on Kayseri Cad.; follow the signs from anywhere in the city. (☎341 40 59. Open daily 8am-7pm; Nov.-Mar. 8am-5pm.) **Hotel Kemer** (☎341 21 68; hotelkemer@hotmail.com) offers clean, basic rooms with shower for US$9 near the center. Or, fork right at the *hamam* and head uphill to **Hotel Surban.** (☎341 47 61; hotelsurban.com.tr. Singles US$20, doubles US$30, triples US$40.)

🔁 DAYTRIP FROM ÜRGÜP: SOĞANLI VALLEY. About 40km south of Ürgüp, the **Soğanlı Valley** is one of the few places in Cappadocia where beauty remains untarnished by tourism. About 150 stone churches sit in the valley; although most have been destroyed, some have partly intact frescoes. Getting to the valley on your own isn't easy: a taxi may cost up to $50, while tour companies and public transit only go to Mustafapaşa. The cheapest way is to rent a scooter in Ürgüp ($20, gas $2.50) and brave the Turkish roads armed with nothing but a crash helmet. (Valley open daily 8:30am-5:30pm. US$1.)

UKRAINE (УКРАЇНА)

UKRANIAN HRYVNY

US$1 = 5.30HV	1HV = US$0.19
CDN$1 = 3.45HV	1HV = CDN$0.29
UK£1 = 7.75HV	1HV = UK£0.13
IR£1 = 6.20HV	1HV = IR£0.16
AUS$1 = 2.85HV	1HV = AUS$0.35
NZ$1 = 2.35HV	1HV = NZ$0.43
ZAR1 = 0.65HV	1HV = ZAR1.57
DM1 = 2.50HV	1HV = DM0.40
EUR€1 = 4.90HV	1HV = EUR€0.20

PHONE CODE	**Country code:** 380. **International dialing prefix:** 00. From outside Ukraine, dial int'l dialing prefix (see inside back cover) + 380 + city code + local number.

Vast and fertile, perpetually tempting to invaders, newly independent Ukraine is caught between overbearing Russia on one side and a bloc of *nouveau riche* on the other. Ukraine offers fascinating but uncrowded museums and theaters, wonderful castles, and the magnificent Black Sea coast, spirited and lively even after years of Soviet order and post-Soviet chaos. With no beaten path from which to stray, Ukraine will rewards travelers for their trouble.

Do Ukraine in style with post-tourist *Let's Go: Eastern Europe 2002*.

FACTS AND FIGURES

Official Name: Ukraine.

Capital: Kyiv.

Major cities: Kyiv, Lviv, Odessa.

Population: 49 million.

Land Area: 603,700 sq. km.

Climate: Temperate continental.

Languages: Ukrainian, Russian, Romanian, Polish, Hungarian.

Religions: Ukrainian Orthodox (29%), Uniate (7%), Protestant (4%).

DISCOVER UKRAINE

Getting to Ukraine is worth the hassle: the country has impressive cities, miles of Black Sea beaches, and expanses of countryside sprawling in between. Start any trip to Ukraine in **Kyiv** (p. 973); once the seat of the Kyivan Rus dynasty, the modern city's park-covered environs and riverside vistas are a breathtaking backdrop to an incomparable mix of urban rush and provincial charm. **Lviv** (p. 976), in Western Ukraine, is an undiscovered jewel. Khrushchev gave **Crimea** (p. 978) to Ukraine, and the Russians didn't object—unfortunately for them, they didn't realize how much sun and fun they were losing. Farther west, **Odessa** (p. 978), the former-USSR party town, has an international feel.

ESSENTIALS

WHEN TO GO

The best time to visit is between May and September, when it's warmer. Spring and early fall can be unpredictable; snow flurries are almost always possible. Winter is bitter cold. Along the Black Sea, summers are hot and winters are mild.

DOCUMENTS AND FORMALITIES

VISAS. Travelers from Australia, Canada, Ireland, New Zealand, the UK and the US arriving in Ukraine must have a **visa**, which requires an **invitation** from a citizen or official organization, or a tourist voucher from a travel agency. Regular single-entry visa processing for Americans at a Ukrainian embassy or consulate ordinarily takes up to nine days, not including mailing time (enclose pre-paid FedEx envelope to speed the return). Single-entry visas cost US$30, double-entry US$60, multiple-entry US$120, and transit US$15, not including the US$45 processing fee. Visa fees are waived for children and American students with proper documents. For transit visas no invitation is required. See Russia (p. 785) for organizations that arrange invitations and visas. **Diane Sadovnikov** also arranges invitations; fax her a month in advance (US ☎ 757-463-6906; fax 463-5526; UKR ☎/fax 044 516 2433; travel-ims@attglobal.net; www.travel-ims.com). When proceeding through **customs** you will be required to declare all valuables and foreign currency above US$1000 (including traveler's checks). It is illegal to bring Ukrainian currency to Ukraine. Foreigners arriving at Kyiv's Borispol airport must buy a US$23 health insurance policy; it is essentially an entry tax and doesn't provide health care.

As of June 15, 2001, it is no longer mandatory to register with the regional offices of the Ministry of Internal Affairs. The **Office of Visas and Registration** (UVIR; ОВИР), in Kyiv at blv. Tarasa Shevchenka 34 (Тараса Шевченка), and police stations in smaller cities extend visas. Do not lose the paper given to you when entering the country to supplement your visa; it is required to leave the country. If you have a double-entry visa, you'll be given a re-entry slip (*vyezd;* въезд) when you arrive.

EMBASSIES. All **foreign embassies** are in Kyiv (see p. 974). For **Ukrainian Embassies at home: Australia Honorary Consul,** #3, ground fl., 902-912 Mt. Alexander Rd., Essendon, Victoria 3040; **Canada,** 331 Metcalf St., Ottawa, ON K2P 0J9 (☎ 613-230-2961; fax 613-230-2400); **Ireland,** 78 Kensington Park Rd., London W11 2PL (☎ 727 6312; fax 792 1708); **South Africa,** 398 Marais Brooklyn, Pretoria; P.O. Box 57291 Arcadia, 0181 (☎ (012) 461 946; fax 461 944); **UK,** 60 Holand Park Rd., London W11 3SJ (☎ (020) 7727 6312; 7792 1708); **US,** 3350 M St. NW, Washington, D.C. 20007 (☎ 202-333-0606; fax 202-333-0817; www.ukremb.com).

TRANSPORTATION

BY PLANE. Ukraine International Airlines (US ☎800-876-0114; in Kyiv ☎ (44) 461 5656 or 234 4528; fax 216 7994; www.ukraine-international.com/eng) flies to Kyiv, Lviv, and Odessa from a number of European capitals. **Air France, ČSA, Lufthansa, LOT, Malév, SAS,** and **Swissair** also fly to Kyiv, generally once or twice per week.

BY TRAIN. Trains run frequently from all of Ukraine's neighbors, and are the most popular way of entering the country and traveling long distances. When coming from a non-ex-Soviet country, expect a two-hour stop at the border. On most trains within Ukraine there are two classes: *platzkart*, where you'll be crammed in with *babushki* and their baskets of strawberries, and *coupé*, a more private 4-person compartment, but still with disgusting bathrooms. Unless you are determined to live local, pay the extra two dollars for *coupé*; it can make the trip tolerable. Arrive well before the train departs so you can show your ticket to cashiers or fellow passengers, look helpless, and say "платформа?" (plaht-FORM-ah).

BY BUS. Buses are cheaper and more frequent than trains and provide the best means to travel around the country. Bus schedules are generally reliable, but low demand can cause cancellations. Buy tickets at the *kassa* (box office); if they're sold out, go directly to the driver, who might just magically find a seat.

BY FERRY, TAXI, AND THUMB. Ferries across the Black Sea are limited to a few routes from Odessa, Sevastopol, and Yalta to **Istanbul.** In cities, private minibuses called *marshrutke* run along the same routes as public transport; they are slightly more expensive but faster. **Taxi** drivers may try to gouge foreigners, so negotiate the price beforehand. **Hitchhikers** are common on Ukrainian roads, holding signs with the desired destination. *Let's Go* does not recommend hitchhiking.

TOURIST SERVICES AND MONEY

EMERGENCY	Fire: ☎01. Police: ☎02. Emergency: ☎03.

TOURIST OFFICES. There is no state-run tourist office. Remnants of Soviet **Intourist** have offices in hotels and provide tourist-related information, although usually not in English. They're used to dealing with groups, to whom they sell "excursion" packages to nearby sights.

MONEY. In September 1996, Ukraine decided to wipe the extraneous zeros off most prices by replacing the **karbovanets** (Krb; a.k.a. kupon) with a new currency, the hryvnia (гривна; hv; plural hryvny); each hryvnia is worth 100,000 karbovantsi. Exchanging US dollars and Deutschmarks is simple, but other currencies pose difficulties. *Obmin Valyut* (Обмін Валют) kiosks in the center of most cities offer the best rates. Traveler's checks can be changed into dollars for small commissions. Western Union is everywhere. Most banks will give Visa and Mastercard cash advances for a high commission. The lobbies of fancier hotels usually exchange US dollars at poor rates. Private money changers lurk near legitimate kiosks, ready with brilliant schemes for ripping you off. Do not exchange money with them; it's illegal. ATMs abound in cities. Although locals don't usually leave tips, most expats give 10%. Accommodations in Ukraine average US$10-12; meals run US$5-7.

COMMUNICATION

MAIL. Mail is cheap and quite reliable (about 10 days to the US). The easiest way to mail letters is to buy pre-stamped envelopes at the post office. Poste Restante (До Востребования in Russian, До Запитание in Ukrainian) is available.

TELEPHONES. Telephones are stumbling toward modernity. The easiest way to make international calls with a calling card or collect is with Utel (Ukraine telephone). Buy a Utel phonecard (sold at most Utel phone locations) and dial the international direct dial number (counted as a local call): **AT&T,** ☎(8) 100 11—wait for another tone after the 8; **British Telecom,** ☎ (8) 10 04 41; **Canada Direct,** ☎(8) 100 17; **MCI,** ☎(8) 100 13; and **Sprint,** ☎(8) 100 15. Or, call at the central telephone office—guess how long your call will take, pay at the counter, and they'll direct you to a booth. Dial 810, followed by country code, city code, and number. Calling is expensive: per minute charges are, to Eastern Europe US$0.06; Western Europe US$1.50; and North America US$2.50 per minute. There's no need to dial a country code when calling Moldova. For intercity calls inside Ukraine, dial ☎8, then the city code and number. Local calls from gray pay phones generally cost 10-30hv. For an English-language operator, dial ☎8 192.

LANGUAGES. It's extremely difficult to travel without knowing some Ukrainian or Russian. In Kyiv, Odessa, and Crimea, Russian is more common than Ukrainian (although all official signs are in Ukrainian). In Transcarpathia, Ukrainian is preferred—people will speak Russian with you only if they know you are not Russian. *Let's Go* uses Ukrainian names in Kyiv and Western Ukraine, and Russian in Crimea and Odessa. For basic phrases, see p. 981.

ACCOMMODATIONS AND CAMPING

Not all **hotels** accept foreigners, and those that do often charge them many times more than what a Ukrainian would pay. Although room prices in Kyiv are astronomical, singles run anywhere from 5hv to 90hv in the rest of the country. The phrase *samoe deshovoe miesto* (самое дешёвое место) means "the cheapest place." More expensive hotels aren't necessarily nicer, and in some hotels, women lodging alone may be mistaken for prostitutes. Most cities have cheap hotels above the train stations—these tend to be seedy and unsafe. Standard hotel rooms include a TV, phone, and a refrigerator. You will be given a *vizitka* (визитка; hotel card) to show to the hall monitor (дежурная; dezhurnaya) to get a key; surrender it on leaving the building. Valuables should never be left unattended; ask at the desk if there's a safe. Hot water is a rarity—ask before checking in. **Private rooms** can be arranged through overseas agencies or bargained for at the train station. Most cities have a **campground,** which is a remote hotel with trailers for buildings. The old Soviet complexes can be quite posh (and quite expensive), with saunas and restaurants. Free camping is illegal, and enforcement is merciless.

FOOD AND DRINK

There are few choices between new, fancy restaurants catering to tourists and the *stolovayas* (cafeterias), dying bastions of cheap, hot food. Non-fresh *stolovaya* food can knock you out of commission for hours, while a good *stolovaya* meal is a triumph of the human spirit. Vegetarians will have to create their own meals from potatoes, mushrooms, and cabbage. Produce is sold at markets; bring your own bag. State food stores are classified by content: *hastronom* (гастроном) sell packaged goods; *moloko* (молоко) milk products; *ovochi-frukty* (овочі-фрукты) fruits and vegetables; *myaso* (мясо) meat; *hlib* (хліб) bread; *kolbasy* (колбаси) sausage; and *ryba* (риба) fish. Drinking tea is a national ritual.

HEALTH AND SAFETY

While Ukraine is neither violent nor politically volatile, it is poor. Keep a low profile, watch your belongings, and don't make easy acquaintances, especially on the street. Don't be afraid to initiate contact; people who don't go out of their way to approach you can generally be trusted. The risk of crime, although made much of, isn't much greater than in the rest of Eastern Europe. It's a wise idea to register with your embassy once you get to Ukraine.

Water is bad and hard to find in bottled form; it's best to boil it or learn to love brushing your teeth with soda. Fruits and vegetables from open markets are generally safe, although storage conditions and pesticides make thorough washing imperative. Meat purchased at public markets should be checked very carefully and cooked thoroughly.

THE ARTIFICIAL FAMINE In 1930, the first of the USSR's five-year plans collectivized agriculture and set state quotas for agricultural production. In Ukraine the policies were met with fierce opposition and farmers destroyed their livestock in protest. Stalin, in order to break the resistance, raised grain quotas for the Crimea, the Caucasus, the lower Volga, and part of Belarus to impossible levels. Exit visas for the region were prohibited and taking from the harvest before the state had had its "share" was punishable by death. The effects were devastating: the most conservative estimates put the death toll from starvation from winter 1932 to summer 1933 at 4.8 million, not including the atrocities committed by the thousands of troops sent to enforce collectivization. Stalin himself confessed to "ten of millions" of deaths in a conversation with Winston Churchill in August 1942. Historians, pouring over what Soviet records they could find, put the official number at 6-8 million.

Embassy officials say that Chernobyl-related radiation poses minimal risk to short-term travelers, but the region should be given a wide berth. Public toilets range from yucky to scary; pay toilets are cleaner and (gasp!) might provide toilet paper, but bring your own anyway.

HOLIDAYS AND FESTIVALS

Holidays: New Year's (Jan. 1); Orthodox Christmas (Jan. 7); International Women's Day (Mar. 8); Good Friday (Apr. 13); Orthodox Easter (Apr. 15); Labor Day (May 1-2); Victory Day (1945; May 9); Holy Trinity (June 18-19); Constitution Day (June 28); Independence Day (1991; Aug. 24).

Festivals: Every Mar., Kyiv hosts international troupes for a 2-week theater festival.

KYIV (КИЇВ)   ☎044

Straddling the wide Dnieper River and layered with hills, Kyiv surprises visitors with golden-domed churches, a sprawling old town, and winding streets. The cradle of Slavic Orthodox culture, and once the USSR's third-largest city, Kyiv hasn't quite figured out how to attract foreign tourists, who often pass it by for Moscow. Extensive reconstruction projects, however, are in progress.

▐▀ TRANSPORTATION

Flights: International **Kyiv-Borospil Airport** (Київ-Бороспіль; ☎296 72 43), 30min. southeast of the city. The city **bus** or a *marshrutne taksi* (маршрутне таксі) runs to MR: Livoberezhna (Лівобережна) every 20min. or when they fill up (10-20hv).

Trains: Kyiv-Passazhyrsky (Київ-Пассажирський), Vokzalna pl. (☎005). MR: Vokzalna. In the main ticketing room on the 1st fl., arrivals are listed on the left, departures on the right. **Tickets** can be purchased on the 1st fl. in hall 4 or at **Intourist**, 2nd fl. Open daily 8am-1pm, 2-7pm, and 8pm-7am. **Passports** are required to purchase all tickets. If Intourist or the *kassa* claims not to have tickets, try again 6hr. and 2hr. before departure. Scalpers add 4-6hv to the price, but may have unavailable tickets. To: **Bratislava** (18hr., 1 per day, 500hv); **Budapest** (25hr., 1 per day, 440hv); **Minsk** (12-13hr., 1 per day, 70hv); **Moscow** (15-17hr., 15 per day, 60-95hv); **Prague** (34hr., 1 per day, 650hv); **Warsaw** (15hr., 2 per day, 190hv).

Buses: Tsentralny Avtovokzal (Центральний Автовокзал), Moskovska pl. 3 (Московьска; ☎265 04 30), is 10min. past Libidska, the last stop on the MG line. Go right and then left out of the Metro; take bus #4 or walk 100m down the big highway and follow it to the right for 300m. To: **Moscow** (21hr., 2 per day, 75hv); **Odessa** (10hr., 6 per day, 55hv); **Prague** (30hr., 2 per day, 330hv).

Public Transportation: The 3 intersecting lines of the **Metro** are efficient but limited: blue (MB), green (MG), and red (MR). Purchase blue tokens, good on all public transport, at the "каса" *(kasa)*. "Перехід" *(perekhid)* indicates a walkway to another station, "вихід у місто" *(vykhid u misto)* an exit onto the street, and "вхід" *(vkhid)* an entrance to the metro. **Trolleys, buses,** and **marshrutne taksi** (private vans numbered with bus routes) go where the Metro doesn't. Bus tickets (0.50hv) are sold at kiosks; *marshrutke taksi* tickets (0.75hv) are sold on board.

⚜ ✈ ORIENTATION AND PRACTICAL INFORMATION

Almost all attractions and services lie in western Kyiv, on the right bank of the Dnipro. Two Metro stops away from the train station, the busy boulevard **Khreshchatik** (Хрещатик; on the red line) satisfies most tourist needs, except housing. The center of Kyiv is vul. Khreshchatik's fountained **Maydan Nezalezhnosti** (Майдан Незалежності; on the blue line).

Tourist Office: Kyiv still lacks decent tourist offices. **Tourist Office** (Туристичне бюро; Turistichne byuro), vul. Khmelnytskoho 26. (Хмельницького; ☎ 229 82 46; uit@uit.kiev.ua; www.uit.com.ua). Open M-F 9am-5pm. **Yana** (Яна), vul. Saksahanskoho 42 (Саксаганського; ☎ 443 84 39). Open M-F 9am-5pm.

Embassies: Australia, vul. Kominternu 18/137 (Комінтерну; ☎ 235 75 86). Open 10am-1pm. **Canada,** vul. Yaroslaviv Val 31 (Ярославів Вал; ☎ 464 11 44). Open M-Th 8:30am-noon. **Russia,** visa section at vul. Kotuzova 8v (Котузова; ☎ 296 45 04). Open M, W, F 9am-1pm and 3-6pm. **UK,** vul. Desyatynna 6 (☎ 462 00 11). **US,** vul. Pimonenka 6 (Пімоненка; ☎ 216 44 22, emergency ☎ 216 38 05; www.usinfo.usemb.kiev.ua). Open M-F 9-6pm. Call ahead to make an appointment.

Medical Assistance: Check with the **US Embassy** (see above) for a list of safe hospitals. **Emergency Care Center,** vul. Mechnikova 1 (☎ 227 92 30). **American Medical Center,** vul. Berdicherska 1 (☎/fax 490 7600; patientservices@amc.com.ua) is expensive.

Internet Access: Cyber Cafe (Кібер Кафе), Proriznaya 21 (☎ 228 05 48; www.cyber-cafe.com). 8hv per hr. Open daily 9am-11pm.

Telephones: Myzhmisky Perehovorny Punkt (Мижміський Переговорний Пункт), at the post office. **Telefon-Telefaks** (Телефон-Телефакс), around the corner (enter on Khreshchatyk). Both open 24hr. Dial AT&T or MCI operators from **Utel** phones. Calls within Kyiv require phone cards. Buy Utel **phone cards** (10hv, 20hv, 40hv) at post offices or hotels. For more info, see p. 971.

Post Office: vul. Khreshchatyk 22, next to Maydan Nezalezhnosti. Address mail to be held: First name SURNAME, *Poste Restante,* 01001 Київ-1, Почтамт до Воетребовании, UKRAINE. Open M-Sa 8am-9pm, Su 9am-7pm.

⌂ ☕ ACCOMMODATIONS AND FOOD

It can be hard to find a decent room in Kyiv at a reasonable price. The best values in town are the private rooms offered at the train station. **Hotel Express** (Експрес), blv. Shevchenka 38/40, is straight up vul. Kominternu from the train station. It has clean, renovated rooms and communal showers. (☎ 223 54 55. Breakfast included. Singles US$21; doubles US$33.) **Grazhdanski Aviatski Institut Student Hotel**

KYIV 3, NAZIS 0 After the Nazis invaded Kyiv and took thousands of Ukrainians as prisoners in September 1941, a German soldier supposedly discovered that one of his prisoners was a member of the city's *Dynamo Kyiv* soccer team. Apparently, his discovery was enough to prompt soccer frenzy: the Nazi officers quickly rounded up the other players and arranged a "death match" between them and the German army team. Despite the Dynamo's players weakened condition and a referee dressed in a Gestapo uniform, Ukraine won, 3-0. Shortly thereafter the entire team was thrown into a concentration camp, where most of them perished in front of a firing squad. Their memory—and Kyiv's pride—lives on in a monument overlooking Khreshchaty Park. Some recent scholarship suggests, however, that such a match never took place and was, in fact, fiction created by Soviet propagandists.

(Гражданский Авіатский), vul. Nizhinska 29E (Ніжінська), is a good deal if you don't mind the schlep. From behind MR: Vokzalna, turn right into the passageway leading to the trams. Ride 6 or 7 stops on tram #1K or 1 to Harmatna (Гарматна); get off at Industrialna (Індустріальна). Backtrack 1½ blocks, turn right onto vul. Nizhinska, cross at the first intersection with a trolleybus, then follow the stairs up into the complex. Keep the first building on your right as you walk diagonally to block "Ä." After passing Ä on the right, look for the Hotel NAU (Готел НАУ) sign above. (☎ 484 90 59. Check-out noon. Singles 37hv; doubles 24-28hv; dorms 16hv.)

For those on a tight budget, the best food option is a trip to one of Kyiv's *rynki* (markets); **Bessarabsky Rynok** (Бессарабский Ринок), at vul. Khreshchatyk and bul. Shevchenka (Шевченка), has the best meat and produce. **Supermarket 7/24**, vul. Baseyna 1/2 (Басеїна), behind Bessarabsky Rynok, is open, well, 24/7. **Domashnaya Kukhnya** (Домашная Кухня), vul. Bohdan Khmelnitsky 166, diagonally across from the Opera Theater (MR: Teatralna), serves a homestyle Ukrainian buffet. (Entrees 2-8hv. Coffee 1.50hv. Open daily 8am-11pm.) **Kaffa** (Каффа), pr. Shevchenko 3 (MB: Maidan Nezalezhnasti), Kyiv's newest coffeehouse, and plenty of outdoor seating. (Iced coffee 8hv. Chocolate 1-7hv. Open daily.)

👁 SIGHTS

VULITSYA KHRESHCHATYK AND ENVIRONS. Broad and commercial **vul. Khreshchatyk** (Хрещатик) begins at the intersection with Boulevard Taras Shevchenko and goes up to **Independence Plaza** (Maydan Nezalezhnosti) filled with fountains and street performers. *(MR: Khreschatyk or MB: Maydan Nezalezhnosti.)* Historical monuments celebrating Prince Volodymyr (who converted Kyivan Rus to Christianity) and the brave soccer players who (according to legend) resisted the Nazis are found in **Khreshchaty Park**, under the silver **Arch of the Brotherhood**.

VOLODYMYRSKA VULITSYA: ST. SOPHIA TO GOLDEN GATE. The **St. Sophia Monastery** complex, with its splendid icons, was the religious center of Kyivan Rus and is currently a focal point of Ukrainian nationalism. Its golden domes, separated from those of the St. Mikhail monastery by the austere statue of Bohdan Khmelnytsky, are what tourists come to to see in Kyiv. *(One stop on tram #16, from next to the McDonald's on Maydan Nezalezhnosti, or a short walk up the hill from the tram stop. Volodymyrska vul. 24. Open F-Tu 10am-5:30pm, W 10am-4:30pm. 6hv. 1hr. tour 10hv. Architectural museum and exhibits each 2hv extra. Cameras 10hv.)* The **Golden Gate** (Золоти Ворота; Zoloty Vorota), once the entrance to the city, houses a small museum; next to it is a statue of Yaroslav the Wise. *(MR, MG: Zoloty Vorota.)* Several other small churches are scattered throughout the area.

ANDRIYIVSKY UZVIZ AND THE PODIL DISTRICT. **Andriyivsky Uzviz** (path) can be reached by funicular from the subway. *(Funicular departs across from MB: Poshtova Ploscha. From St. Mikhailivska Square, walk past the heavily columned government building directly across from the church, keeping it to your right. Runs daily every 5min. 6:30am-11pm; 0.30hv.)* Climb the gray steps at the corner of Desatynia and Volodymyrska to see the ruins of the oldest stone church of Kyivan Rus and the **National History Museum**. *(Open M-Sa 9am-5pm.)* Nearby is the impressive **St. Andrew's Cathedral**. Down twisting streets are a collection of local art displays. The path spills out into the **Podil** district, the church-filled center of Kyiv in the 10th and 11th centuries. Just east of the *ploscha*, the 🏛**Chernobyl Museum**, Provulok Zhorevii 1, details the legacy of the nuclear disaster; ask to see the video of the explosion. *(Open M-Sa 10am-6pm; closed last M each month. Free.)*

KYIV-PECHERY MONASTERY. Kyiv's oldest and holiest religious site, the mysterious **Kyiv-Pechery Monastery** (Kievo-Pecherska Lavra; Києво-Печерська Лавра) deserves a full day of exploration. Apart from the many museums, the complex houses the **Holy Trinity Church**, the **Refractory Church**, and the fascinating 🏛**caves** where saints and the monastery's monks lie mummified and entombed. Buy a candle (0.50hv) before you enter to help you navigate the caves. Turning left from the

GOD OR VODKA? Since the end of the Communist ban on religious practices, Orthodoxy, with all its sacramental bells and whistles, has flourished in Kyiv. It has every reason to—as the capital of Kyivan Rus, the first great civilization of the Eastern Slavs, Kyiv was the birthplace of Slavic Orthodoxy. While Princess Olga had been privately baptized in the mid-900s, it wasn't until her grandson Volodymyr ascended to the throne that Christianity caught on among the Slavs. After an unpromising beginning that included paganism and promiscuity, Volodymyr decided that an up-and-coming empire needed an advanced religion. He first considered Islam, but the ban on alcohol was too much for the prince to handle. "Drinking is the joy of the Russes," he said, "and we cannot exist without that pleasure." Among the remaining options, Volodymyr and his Kyivan entourage chose Eastern Orthodoxy, after a visit to Byzantium's Constantinople convinced them that nothing can beat well-spaced golden domes. Orthodoxy was officially proclaimed the imperial religion, and the residents of Kyiv were herded into the Dnieper for baptism in 988.

monastery exit and continuing down the street brings you to a series of patriotic monuments, culminating with the huge silver **motherland statue** overlooking the eternal flame with gorgeous views of the river. *(MR: Arsenalna. Turn left as you exit; walk 20min. down vul. Sichnevoho Povstanyiya. Monastery open daily 9:30am-7pm. Ticket for churches and exhibitions 8hv, students 4hv. Caves open W-M 9-11:30am and 1-4pm. Dress modestly.)*

BABYN YAR AND ST. CYRIL'S. The **monument at Babyn Yar** is a moving tribute to the first victims of the Nazis in Ukraine. The statue, a group of interlocking figures falling to their deaths from an incline above the grass that now covers the pit, is accompanied by a plaque stating that 100,000 Kyivans died there, though current estimates count the victims' numbers—mostly Jews—at twice that figure. *(From Maydan Nezalezhnosti, 10 stops on trolley #16.)* **St. Cyril's Church,** the multi-domed shelter of Kyiv's frescoes, is nearby. *(From Babyn Yar, 6 stops on trolley #27 toward MB: Petrivka.)*

MUSEUM OF FOLK ARCHITECTURE AND RURAL LIFE. Over 70 huts from around the country are spread over the grounds of this open-air museum. Men dressed in Cossak uniforms ride bareback around the complex, musicians play traditional folk tunes, and cafes serve Ukrainian specialities. *(Outside Kyiv in the Pirohiv village. From MB: Libidska, take trolleybus #11 to park entrance. Walk 10min. to museum entrance. Open daily 10am-5pm. English-language tour 1hr. 60hv, 2hr. 80hv. Map 1hv. Ticket 3hv.)*

■ NIGHTLIFE

Check out *Kyiv Post* and *What's On* (www.whatson-kyiv.com) for listings. **Eric's Bierstube,** Velika Vasylkivska 20 (Василькивска) directly across from the Kyiv movie theater packs in the ex-pats. (M: Lva Tolstoho. Live music Tu, Th 8pm-1am. Beer 5-10hv. Open daily 8am-2am.) **Club 111,** Peremohy pl. 1, is a hot club with a revolving bar. It's across from the circus, in the Hotel Lybid. (Cover F, Sa 20hv. Open daily 7am-2am.).

LVIV (ЛЬВIВ)   ☎(8)0

After 600 years as part of Poland, and over 40 years of Soviet occupation, Lviv is now a center of Ukrainian industry and culture. Though often overlooked, its steeple-filled center, castle, museums, and theater make Lviv worth a visit.

◫⊡ TRANSPORTATION AND PRACTICAL INFORMATION. Trains (☎748 20 68) go from pl. Vokzalna (Вокзальна) to: Bratislava (18hr., 1 per day, 203hv); Budapest (14hr., 1 per day, 234hv); Kyiv (12hr., 9 per day, 32-50hv); Kraków (8hr., 1 per day, 95hv); Moscow (29hr., 2 per day, 88-136hv); Odessa (14hr., 2 per day, 33-50hv); and Prague (21hr., 1 per day, 317hv). **Tickets** are available at Intourist window #17 on the second floor. The main **bus station,** on vul. Stryska (Стрийська;

☎63 24 73), on the outskirts of town, sends buses to Kraków (8hr., 1 per day, 73hv) and Warsaw (10hr., 5 per day, 82hv). From the bus station, bus #18 goes to the train station, from which trams go into town. **Lviv Tourist Info Center**, pl. Rynek 1, in the city hall *(ratusha)*, sells brochures and maps. (☎97 57 67; ltb@city-adm.lviv.ua; www.about.lviv.ua. Open M-F 9am-6pm.) Check email at **Internet Klub**, vul. Dudaeva. (www.internetclub.lviv.ua. 4hv per hr.) **Postal code:** 79000.

🏠🍴 ACCOMMODATIONS AND FOOD. Afew blocks north of pr. Svobody lies **Hotel Lviv**, vul. Chornovola 7 (Чорновола). Take tram #6 from the train station to the Opera House; the hotel is seven blocks behind it on the left. (☎79 22 70. Singles 35hv, with bath 50hv; doubles 23hv, 50hv.) **Hotel George,** pl. Mitskevycha 1, is pretty but pricey; take tram #1 to Doroshenka (Дорошенка). (☎72 59 52. Breakfast included. Singles 111hv, with bath 361hv; doubles 157/381hv.) Pl. Rynok is the restaurant and cafe center of Lviv; the most convenient market is **Halytsky Rynok** (Галицький Ринок), behind the flower stands across from St. Andrew's Church. **U Pani Steftsi** (У Пані Стефи), pr. Svobody 8, serves traditional Ukrainian food. (Main dishes 10-15hv. Open daily 10am-10pm.)

🎭🎨 SIGHTS AND ENTERTAINMENT. Before you venture into the heart of the city, introduce yourself to Lviv by climbing up to **High Castle Hill** (Vysoky Zamok; Высокий Замок), the former site of the Galician King's Palace. Now a Ukrainian flag and a television tower hover above the panoramic view. Follow vul. Krivonoca (Кривоноса) from its intersection with Hotny and Halytskono, go until you pass #39, then take a left down the long dirt road to wind your way up around the hill counter-clockwise. Begin a walking tour of the city on Pr. Svobody, dominated by the dazzling exterior of the ◼**Theater of Opera and Ballet** (Teatr Opery ta Baletu; Театра Опери та Балету; ☎72 88 60. Tickets from 10hv.) The ◼**Open-Air Museum of Folk Architecture and Rural Life** (Muzey Narodnoi Architektury ta Pobutu u Lvovi; Музей Народної Архітектури та Побуту у Львові) at Shevchenkivsky Hay (Шевченківський Гай), can be reached on tram #2 or 7 to Mechnikova; head all the way up the hill, bearing right at the top. (☎71 23 60. Open Apr.-Oct. Tu-Su 11am-7pm; Nov.-Mar. 10am-6pm. 1.50hv. English tour 10hv; call ahead.) The heart of the city is **ploschad Rynok,** the historic market square, surrounded by countless churches and richly decorated merchant homes dating from the 16th to 18th centuries. Just beyond the gaze of the trident-wielding Neptune statue atop the 19th-century **town hall** is pl. Katedralna (Катедральна), where the grand Polish **Catholic Cathedral** (Katolitsky Sobor; Католицкий собор) stands.

Cheap tickets for shows from opera to experimental drama are available at each theater's *kasa* or at the *teatralny kasy* (ticket windows; театральни каси), pr. Svobody 37. (Open M-Sa 10am-1pm and 2-5pm.) Before the show, stop at a club-cafe, such as ◼**Club-Cafe Lyalka** (Клуб-Кафе Лялька), vul. Halytskoho 1 (Галицького), below the Puppet Theater (Teatr Lyalok). (Wine 3hv. Cover 7-10hv. Live music M-W. Open M-Th 11am-midnight, F-Su 11am-2am.)

SIMFEROPOL (СІМФЕРОПОЛЬ)   ☎0652

God made all of Crimea, and all Simferopol got was an unavoidable train station. **Trains** run from ul. Gagarina (Гагарина; ☎005) to: Kyiv (19hr., 5 per day, 73hv); Lviv (32hr., 2 per day, 73hv); Minsk (35hr., 1 per day, 210hv); Moscow (28hr., 4 per day, 153hv); and Odessa (14hr., 1 per day, 38hv). **Buses** for Yalta leave from the train station (2hr., 3 per hr., 4hv), but most other buses leave from the bus station, ul. Kievskaya 4, accessible from the train station by bus #2 and 6 and by bus #4 from the city center. The best place to sleep is on the train out of town, but if you have a layover, you can stay at **Gostinitsa Ukraina** (Украина), ul. Rozy Lyuksemburg 7-9. Ride bus #5 three stops to the hotel. (☎51 05 83. Singles 37.50-90hv; doubles 57-127hv; triples 75hv.) To get to the ancient Tartar town of **Bakhchisarai,** in the dry cliffs of the Central Crimean steppe, take the **electrichka** from the train station (1hr., 8 per day, 2.5hv). A challenging hike will take you past the Khan's Palace, the Saint Assumption Monastery and the excavated Jews' Fortress. *Moloko,* the local specialty of cannabis boiled in goat's milk, is regrettably illegal; discretion is the word.

YALTA (ЯЛТА) ☎ 0654

The gaudy Yalta waterfront, with its hot dog vendors and computerized astrology stands, dashes any illusion that this is still the city of Chekhov, Rachmaninov, and Tolstoy. Enjoy Yalta for what it is: a lovely, historic city weathering the storm of capitalism as best it can. If you're an Anton Chekhov fan, head to ul. Kirova 112, where you can explore **White Dacha,** the house he built, the garden he planted, and the museum about him. Take trolleybus #1 to Pioneerskaya (Пионерская), cross the street, and walk up the hill. (Open Tù-Su 10am-5pm. 10hv, students 5hv.)

Buses (☎34 20 92) leave from Moskovskaya ul. 57 for Simferopol (2hr., every 10-30min., 7.5hv). Across the way, the **trolleybus station** sends more comfortable trolleys to the Simferopol train station (2½hr., every 20min., 6hv). From either station, take trolleybus #1 uphill to Sovetskaya pl. (Советская), then walk two blocks toward the sea. City maps are available at kiosks (5-6hv). **Eugenia Travel,** Ul. Roosvelta 5, is at the Sea Terminal (Morskoy Vokzal; ☎32 81 40). Internet access is available at **Internet Center,** ul. Ekatepinskaya 3, a block from nab. Lenina. (6hv per hr. Open 24hr.) Bus station *babushki* often offer great deals on private rooms (30-60hv is good; more as you approach the waterfront). **Gostinitsa Krym** (Крым), Moskovskaya ul. 1/6, three stops from the station on bus #1, is a central hotel. (☎27 24 01. Call ahead. Singles 45hv; doubles 60hv; triples 72hv.) To get to **Motel-Camping Polyana Skazok** (Поляна Сказок), ul. Kirova 167 (Кірова), take bus #11, 26, or 27 from the bus station or bus #8 from city center to Polyana Skazok (Поляна Сказок) then walk 20min. uphill. (☎39 52 19. No tents. Motel doubles 120hv.) **Yalos** (Ялос), nab. Lenina, serves Ukrainian, American, and Italian cuisine. (Live music nightly. Main dishes 5-39hv. Open daily 10am-late.)

■ **DAYTRIP FROM YALTA: LIVADIA.** Only an hour **hike** or a 15min. **boat** ride from Yalta, **Livadia** hosted the imprecisely named **Yalta Conference,** when Churchill, Roosevelt, and Stalin met in February 1945 at Tsar Nicholas II's summer palace to hash out postwar territorial claims. History aside, the **Great Palace** (Великий Дворец; Veliky Dvorets) is worth the visit. (Open in summer daily 10am-5:30pm; off-season Th-Tu 10am-4pm. 6hv.) **Buses** #5, 26 and 27 run to Livadia from Yalta (25min., every 30-40min., 0.65hv).

ODESSA (ОДЕССА) ☎ 0482

When Catherine the Great decided to build up Odessa with limestone mined from below, she left behind the longest network of catacombs in the world. Odessa became an crucial port, home to merchants and vagabonds from across Europe and Central Asia; luck and geography allowed it to prosper to the point of decadence. A haven for intellectuals, *mafiosi*, and the summer flood of Black Sea cruise groups, Odessa is pricey—but often worth it.

■ **TRANSPORTATION AND PRACTICAL INFORMATION. Trains** go from pl. Privokzalnaya (Привокзальная), at the north end of ul. Pushkinskaya, to: Kyiv (12hr., 2 per day, 55hv); Lviv (12hr., 2 per day, 55hv); Moscow (26hr., 3 per day, 155hv); and St. Petersburg (35hr., 1 per day, 170hv). Trams #2, 3, and 12 run along ul. Preobrazhenskaya to ul. Deribasovskaya. **Buses** go from ul. Dzerzhinskovo 58 (Дзержинского) to Kyiv (12hr., 4 per day, 39hv) and Simferopol (8hr., 2 per day, 26hv); take tram #5 from the train station or #15 from downtown. Both stop four blocks from the station. Buy tickets at least the night before. Morskoy Vokzal (Морской Вокзал; Sea Terminal), ul. Suvorov 12 (Суворов) sends **ferries** to Istanbul (1-2 days, 2 per week, US$100-185). **FGT Travel** (also known as Fagot) ul. Rishelievskaya 4, in the wax museum, offers tours and lodging information. (☎22 34 36; museum@mail.od.ua. Open daily 8:30am-10pm.)

■ **ACCOMMODATIONS AND FOOD. Private rooms** are cheap (from US$5 per person). Take tram #3 or 12 from the train station to the downtown hotels, all near noisy pl. Grecheskaya (Греческая) and ul. Deribasovskaya (Дерибасовская).

A TASTE OF KVAS When the sun is high and the steppe is hotter than a Saharan parking lot, Aussies thirst for a *Fosters*, Czechs a *Pilsner*, and Yankees a *Bud*, but a true Ukrainian won't have anything other than a ladle of **kvas** (квас). In Kyiv you'll see it served from siphons, in the provinces from rusty cisterns. The taste—kind of like beer without the hops—varies depending on the container, but it all comes down to acidic bread bubbles; the drink is based on a sourdough solution that rushes tingling into your bloodstream. It's so addictive that Kyiv drinks *kvas* all summer, even in the rain, when groups of young tots, middle-aged shoppers, and love-struck teenagers huddle around toothless tap-masters, all under one leaky umbrella.

Charming **Passazh** (Пассаж), ul. Preobrazhenskaya 34, is next to the real Passazh. (☎20 48 49. Singles 65-119hv; doubles 112-157hv.) **Spartak** (Партак), ul. Deribasovskaya 25, offers basic, clean rooms in a great location. Too bad there's no water in the summer. (Dorms 29hv; singles 60hv; doubles 92hv.) **Odessa State University Dormitory #8**, ul. Dovzhenko 9B (Довженко), lets spartan rooms July-Aug. (☎21 87 60; reservations ☎63 08 95. Dorms 10hv.) **Klarabara** (Кларабара), ul. Preobrazhenskaya 28, is in the Gorsad. (Dishes 26-39hv. Live music F-Su 8-11pm. Open Su-Th 10am-midnight, F-Sa 10am-1am.) The Privoz **mega-market** (Привоз), Privoznaya ul., is across from the train station; watch for pickpockets. (Open daily 8am-6pm.)

◙🚶 SIGHTS AND ENTERTAINMENT. Street culture centers on **ul. Deribasovskaya,** inhabited by jazz musicians, mimes, and young hipsters. Turn right on Preobrazhenska, left on Sofiivska, and walk up two blocks to the **Odessa Art Museum** (Одеський художественый музей), ul. Sofiyevskaya 5a (Софиевская) where you can explore the cool grotto below. (Grotto tour with guide only. Museum 2hv; grotto 2hv, plus guide fee. Open W-M 10:30am-6pm; closed last F oevery month.) Left off ul. Deribasovskaya onto ul. Yekaterinskaya, the statue of the **Duc de Richelieu,** the city's first governor, stares down the **Potemkin Stairs** (Potomkinski skhody; Потемкинскан схогп) toward the shiny port, **Morskoy Vokzal.** The **Literature Museum** (Литературный Музей; Literaturny muzey), Lanzheronovskaya 2, takes a look at the city's intellectual and cultural heritage. (Open Tu-Su 10am-5pm. 6hv.) Odessa's main quarry lies directly underneath the city and over time became the world's longest series of ■**catacombs.** During the Nazi occupation, the resistance was based here, and the city has set up a superb subterranean **museum** in its honor. FGI (see above) gives tours in English (US$75 per group; times and prices negotiable). The farther from the center you go, the cleaner the **beaches;** most are reachable either by public transport or walking. Trolley #5 goes to: **Arkadiya** (Аркадия); **Lanzheron** (Ланжерон), the beach closest to central Odessa; and **Otrada** (Отрада). Trams #17 and 18 go to **Golden Shore** (Золотой Берег; Zolotoy Bereg). **Chayka** (Чайка), and **Kurortny** (Курортный) beaches. **Vidrada** (Видрада) is a pleasant walk from Odessa through Park Shevchenko.

The **Opera and Ballet Theater** (Театр Оперы и Балета; Teatr Opery i Baleta), at the end of ul. Rishelevskaya, has Sunday shows at noon. Buy tickets in advance from the ticket office to the right of the theater. (Open Tu-Su 10am-6pm. 15-30hv, major acts 100-600hv.) Odessa truly never sleeps. The restaurants, cafes, and bars on **ul. Deribasovskaya** go all night with beer, vodka, and music ranging from Euro-techno to Slavic folk. ■**Gambrinus** (Гамбринус), at #31, at the intersection with ul. Zhukova (Жукова), was ground zero of the cultural scene before the Revolution. (Open daily 10am-11pm.) The open-air discos in **Arkadiya** (trolley #7 from the train station, #5 from pl. Grechskaya) is *the* place to dance. So dance.

LANGUAGE BASICS

GLOSSARY

addition (F): check
aérogare (F): air terminal
affitacamere (I): room for rent
agora (Gr): city square; market-place
albergo (I): hotel
albergue (S): youth hostel
alcázar (S): Muslim fortress-palace
állomás (H): station
Altstadt (G): old city
apse: nook beyond church altar
arrondissement (F): city district
auberge de jeunesse (F): youth hostel
autoroute (F): motorway
ayuntamiento (S): city hall
azulejo (P, S): glazed tile
Bahnhof (G): train station
barrio viejo (S): old city
billet (F): ticket
boulangerie (F): bakery
Brücke (G): bridge
brug (Du): bridge
calle (I, S): street
campanile (I): bell tower
campo (I): square
carabinieri (I): civil police
carrer (S): street
casco antiguo (S): old city
casco viejo (S): old city
cave (F): (wine) cellar
çay (T): tea
centre commercial (F): shopping plaza
centre ville (F): city center
centro (S): city center
cerveza (S): beer
chambres d'hôtes (F): bed and breakfasts
charcuterie (F): butcher
château (F): castle
chiesa (I): church
ciudad nueva (S): new city
cloître (F): cloister
compline: last church service of the day
confiserie (F): candy store
correspondance (F): connection, transfer (subway)
corso (I): principal street or avenue
craic (Ir): a good (pub) time
dégustation (F): tasting (i.e., wine tasting)
domatia (Gr): room in private home
Dom (G): cathedral
duomo (I): cathedral
église (F): church
entrée (F): appetizer
essence (F): gasoline

estación (S): station
evensong: church service just before dusk
fermo posta (I): *Poste Restante*
ferrovia (I): railways
Flughafen: airport
foyer (F): student dorm
gabinetto (I): toilet, WC
gade (D): street
gare (F): train station
Gästehaus: guesthouse
gîte d'étape (F): rural hostel
gracht (D): canal
grilli (Fi): fast-food stand
Hauptbahnhof (G): main train station
hebdomadaire (F): weekly
hospedajes (S): cheap accommodations
hostal (S): hostel
hôtel de ville (F): town hall
iglesia (S): church
igreja (P): church
Innenstadt (G): city center
Jugendherberge (G): youth hostel
Kauppatori (Fi): market square
Kerk (Du): church
Kirche (G): church
Kirke (D): church
laverie (F): laundromat
leoforeo (Gr): bus
mairie (F): mayor's office
marché (F): outdoor market
marché aux puces (F): flea market
Marktplatz (G): marketplace
Mensa (G): university cafeteria
monnaie (F): change
museo (S): museum
nádraží (C): station
náměstí (C): square
nave: central body of a church
navette (F): shuttlebus
Neustadt (G): new city
ostello (I): youth hostel
paella (S): rice dish with seafood, meat, and vegetables
palais (F): palace
palazzo (I): palace
paleohora (Gr): old town
pályaudvar (H): station
panini (I): sandwiches
pansiyon (T): typical accommodation
parque (S): park
paseo (S): promenade (abbreviated *po.*)
passeig (S): promenade (*pg.*)
pâtisserie (F): pastry shop
pensione (I): room in private home

pensao (P): cheap accommodation
pietà (I): scene of the Virgin mourning the dead Christ
plaça (S): square
place (F): square
plage (F): beach
plat (F): main course
plateia (Gr): town square
Platz (G): square
playa (S): beach
plaza (S): square
plein (Du): town square
pleio (Gr): ferry
piazza(le) (I): city square
pont (F): bridge
ponte (I, P): bridge
praça (P): square
praia (P): beach
primi (I): first course (usually pasta)
Privatzimmer (G): room in a private home
puente (S): bridge
quartier (F): neighborhood
Rådhuspladsen (D): main town square
Rathaus: city hall
secondi (I): second course (usually meat or fish)
smørrebrød (D): open-faced sandwich
souvlaki (Gr): skewered meat
spiaggia (I): beach
spotted dick (B): steamed sponge pudding with raisins
stadhuis (Du): town hall
stazione (I): station
straat (Du): street
Straße (G): street
tabac (F): all-purpose newsstand
tabbacchi (I): all-purpose newsstand
Tageskarte (G): day pass
tapas (S): appetizers; snacks
taverna (Gr): restaurant
télécarte (F): phone card
télépherique (F): cable car lift
tér (H): square
TGV (F): super-fast train
torvet (D): main square
trad (Ir): traditional Irish music
traiteur (F): delicatessen
transept: arm of the church that intersects the nave
ulice (C): street
utca (H): street
vendange (F): grape harvest
via(le) (I): street
vicolo (I): alley, lane
vieille ville (F): old city
vino (S): wine
Zug (G): train

USEFUL WORDS AND PHRASES

ENGLISH	BULGARIAN	PRONUNCIATION
hello	Добър ден	DOH-bur den
goodbye	Довиждане	doh-VEEZH-dan-eh
please	Извинете	eez-vi-NEH-teh
thank you	Благодаря	blahg-oh-dahr-YAH
yes / no	Да/Не	dah/neh
sorry / excuse me	съжалявам	suhj-ha-LYA-vahm
Do you speak English?	Говорите ли Английски?	go-VO-rih-te li an-GLEES-keeh
Help!	Помощ!	PO-mosht
Where is...?	Къде е?	kuh-DEH eh
left / right / straight ahead	отляво/отдясно/направо	ot-LYAH-vo/ot-DYAHS-no/na-PRA-vo
What time does the [train / bus / boat] (depart / arrive)?	В колко часа (заминава/пристига) [влакът/автобус/ферибот]?	V kol-ko cha-sah (za-mee-NAH-va/prih-STEE-ga) [VLA-kat/af-toe-BUS/feh-ree-bot]
today / tomorrow / yesterday	Днес/утре/вчера	dness/oo-treh/VCHEH-rah
I'd like a (one-way / return) ticket.	Искам един билет (отиване/отиване и връщане).	EES-kahm eh-DEEN bee-LEHT (oh-TEE-va-neh/oh-TEE va-neh ee VRIH-shta-neh)
How much does it cost?	Колко Струва?	KOHL-ko STROO-va
hostel / hotel	/ хотел	ob-shteh-jeet-yeh / hotel
I'd like a (single / double) room.	Искам (самостоятелна/за двама) стая.	EES-kahm (sa-mo-sto-YA-tel-na/za DVA-ma) STA-ya

ENGLISH	CZECH	PRONUNCIATION
hello	Dobrý den	DO-bree den
goodbye	Na shledanou	nah SLEH-dah-noh-oo
please	Prosím	PROH-seem
thank you	Děkuji	DYEH-koo-yih
yes / no	Ano / ne	AH-no / neh
sorry / excuse me	Promiňte	PROH-mihn-teh
Do you speak English?	Mluvíte anglicky?	MLOO-vit-eh ahng-GLIT-ski
Help!	Pomoc!	POH-mots
Where is...?	Kde...?	k-DEH
left / right / straight ahead	vlevo / vpravo / rovně	LEH-vah / PRAH-vah / ROV-nyeh
What time does the [train / bus / boat] (depart / arrive)?	Kdy (odjíždí / přijíž) [vlak / autobus / loď]?	k-DEE (OT-yeezh-dee / PREE-yeezh) [vlahk / OUT-oh-boos / LOHD-yeh]
today / tomorrow / yesterday	dnes / zítra / včera	dness / ZEE-tra / FCHE-rah
I'd like a (one-way / return) ticket.	Rád (m.) / Ráda bych (f.) (jen tam / zpáteční) jízdenku.	rahd / RAHD-ah bikh (yen tam / SPAH-tech-nyee) YEEZ-denkoo
How much is it?	Kolik stojí?	KOH-lihk STOH-yee
hostel / hotel	mládežnická nocleháma / hotel	MIA-dezh-nit-ska NOTS-le-har-na / ho-TELL
I'd like a (single / double) room.	Máte volné (jednolůžkový / dvolůžkový) pokoj.	MAH-te VOL-nee (YED-no-loosh-ko-vee / DVOH-loosh-ko-vee) PO-koy

ENGLISH	DANISH	PRONUNCIATION
hello	goddag	go-DAY
goodbye	farvel	fah-VEL
please	vær så venlig	vair soh VEN-li
thank you	tak	tack
yes / no	ja / nej	ya / nye
sorry / excuse me	undskyld	UN-scoold
Do you speak English?	Taler du engelsk?	TAY-luh dou ENG-elsk
Help!	Hjælp!	yelp
Where is...?	Hvor er...?	voa aïr
left / right / straight ahead	til venstre / til højre / lige ud	till VEN-struh / till HOY-ruh / lee oothe
What time does the [train / bus / boat] (depart / arrive)?	Hvomår (går / ankommer) [toget / bussen / båden]?	vor-NOR (gore / AN-kom-ma) [TOE-et / BOOSE-en / BOTHE-en]
today / tomorrow / yesterday	i dag / i morgen / i går	ee-DAY / ee-MORN / ee-GORE
I'd like a (one-way / return) ticket.	Eg vil gerne ha en (enkelbillet / tur-retur billet).	YAI vil GAIR-nuh ha een (EHN-kul-bill-ETT / TOOR-re-TOOR bill-ETT)
How much does it cost?	Hvad koster det?	va KOS-tor dey
hostel / hotel	vandrerhjem / hotel	VAN-drar-yem / ho-TELL
I'd like a (single / double) room.	Jeg ønsker et (enkeltværelse / dob-beltværelse).	YAI URN-ska it (EHN-kult-vair-ELL-sih / DOP-ult-vair-ELL-sih)

ENGLISH	DUTCH	PRONUNCIATION
hello	hallo	hallo
goodbye	tot ziens	toht zeens
please	alstublieft	ALST-ew-bleeft
thank you	dank u wel	dahnk ew vel
yes / no	ja / nee	ya / nay
sorry / excuse me	excuseert u mij	ex-kew-ZAYRT ew my
Do you speak English?	Spreekt u engels?	sprayhkt ew ENG-els
Help!	help!	help
Where is...?	Waar iz...?	var iss
left / right / straight ahead	links / rechts / recht door	links / hrechts / hrecht door
What time does the [train / bus / boat] (depart / arrive)?	Hoe laat (vertrekt / komt) de [trein / bus / kom]?	hoo laht (ver-TRECHT / komt) deh [trine / buhs / kom]
today / tomorrow / yesterday	vandaag / morgen /gisteren	fon-DAHG / MOR-ghun / GHIST-er-un
I'd like a (one-way / return) ticket.	Ik wil graag (een enkele reis / een retour).	ik vil khrahk ayn (ENG-kuh-luhrice / ayn ruh-TOOR)
How much is it?	Wat kost dit?	vaht kost dit
hostel / hotel	jeugdherberg / hotel	YOORGH-hayr-bayrgh / ho-TELL
I'd like a (single / double) room.	Ik wil graag een (een- / twee-) persoonska-mer.	ik vil ghrahgh ayn (AYN / TVAY) per-sohns-kah-mer

ENGLISH	ESTONIAN	PRONUNCIATION
hello	tere	TEH-re
goodbye	head aega	hed AEH-gah
please	palun	PA-lun
thank you	tänan	TEH-nan
yes / no	jaa/ei	yah/ay
sorry / excuse me	Vabandage	vah-pan-TAGE-euh
Do you speak English?	Kas te räägite inglise keelt?	Kas te RA-A-gite ING-lise keelt
Help!	Appi!	APP-pi
Where is...?	Kus on...?	kuhs on
left / right / straight ahead	vasakul/paremal/otse edasi	VA-sa-cul/PA-ray-mal/AWT-seh AY-duh-see
What time does the [train / bus / boat] (depart / arrive)?	Mis kell (lähels/saabub) [rong/buss/paat]?	meese kell (LA-helss/SAH-boob) [hrong/bus/paht]?
today / tomorrow / yesterday	täna/eile/homme	TEN-ah/EYHL/OH-may
I'd like a (one-way / return) ticket.	Palun, (üheotsa/edasi-tagasi) piletit	PA-loon (EW-heh-awt-sah/Eh-da-see-TA-ga-see) PEE-let-it
How much does it cost?	Kui palju?	kwee PAL-you
hostel / hotel	ühiselamu / hotell	ew-hee-sel-a-moo / ho-TELL
I'd like a (single / double) room.	Ma sooviksin(ühelist/kahelist).	ma SOO-vik-sin (EW-hel-ist/KA-hel-ist)

ENGLISH	FINNISH	PRONUNCIATION
hello	hei	hey
goodbye	näkemiin	NA-kay-meen
please	pyydän	BU-dan
thank you	kiitos	KEE-tohss
yes / no	kyllä/ei	EW-la/AY
sorry / excuse me	anteeksi	ON-take-see
Do you speak English?	Puhutteko englantia?	POO-hoot-teh-kaw ENG-lan-ti-ah?
Help!	Apua!	AH-poo-ah
Where is...?	Missä on...?	MEESS-ah OWN
left / right / straight ahead	vasen/oikea/suoraan	VAHSS-en/OY-kay-ah/SOOA-rahn
What time does the [train / bus / boat] (depart / arrive)?	Mihin aikaan [juna/bussi/laiva] (lähtee/saapuu)	ME-hin EYE-ka-ahn [yoo-na/BOOSE-ee/LIVE-a] (leh-tee/SAA-poo-oo)?
today / tomorrow / yesterday	tänään/huomenna/eilen	YEH-nehhn/HOOA-main-na/EYE-lane
I'd like a (one-way / return) ticket.	Saisinko (menolipun/menopaluulipun).	SAY-sing-koah (MAY-no-LIP-poon/MAY-no-PAH-looo-LIP-poon)
How much does it cost?	Paljonko tämä maksaa?	PA-lee-onk-o teh-meh MOCK-sah
hostel / hotel	retkeilymaja / hotelli	rett-keh-eel-oo-my-ah / ho-TELL-ee
I'd like a (single / double) room.	Haluaisin (yhden/kahden) hengen huoneen.	HAH-loo-eye-seen (oo-den/kah-den) hen-gen hoo-oh-neen

APPENDIX

ENGLISH	FRENCH	PRONUNCIATION
hello	bonjour	bohn-ZHOOR
goodbye	au revoir	oh ruh-VWAHR
please	s'il vous plaît	seel voo pleh
thank you	merci	mehr-SEE
yes / no	oui / non	wee / nohn
sorry / pardon me	pardon	pahr-DOHN
Do you speak English?	Parlez-vous anglais?	PAR-lay-voo ahn-GLEH
Help!	Au secours!	oh suh-KOOR
Where is...?	Où se trouve...?	oo seh troov
left / right / straight ahead	gauche / droite / tout droit	gohsh / drwaht / too drwah
What time does the [train / bus / boat] (depart / arrive)?	À quelle heure est-que le [train / bus / bateau] (part / arrive)?	ah kel ur ES-keh luh [trah / bews / baht-OH] (pahr / ah-REEV)
today / tomorrow / yesterday	aujourd'hui / demain / hier	oh-zhoor-DWEE / duh-MAH / ee-YEHR
I'd like a (one-way / return) ticket.	Je voudrais un billet (simple / aller-retour).	zhuh voo-DREH uhn bee-YAY (SAH-pluh / ah-LAY ruh-TOOR)
How much does it cost?	Ça coute combien?	sah coot kohn-BYAN
hostel / hotel	auberge de jeunesse / hôtel	oh-BEHRZH duh zhu-NES / oh-TEL
I'd like a (single / double) room.	Je voudrais une chambre pour (une personne / deux personnes).	zhuh voo-DREH ewn SHAH-bruh poor (ewn perh-SUHN / duh pehr-SUHN)

ENGLISH	GERMAN	PRONUNCIATION
hello	hallo	HA-lo
goodbye	Auf Wiedersehen	owf VEE-der-zayn
please	bitte	BI-tuh
thank you	danke	DAHNG-kuh
yes / no	ja / nein	yah / nan
sorry / excuse me	Entschuldigung / Verzeihung	ent-SHOOL-di-gung / fer-TSAI-ung
Do you speak English?	Sprechen Sie Englisch?	SHPRE-khen zee ENG-glish
Help!	Hilfe!	HIL-fuh
Where is...?	Wo ist...?	vo ist
left / right / straight ahead	links / rechts / gerade aus	links / rechts / ge-RAH-duh ows
What time does the [train / bus / boat] (depart / arrive)?	Um wieviel Uhr (fährt / kommt) [der Zug / der Bus / die Fähre] (ab / an)?	oom VEE-feel oor (fayrt/komt) [dare tsoog / dare OW-toh-boos / dee FAY-ruh] (ahb / ahn)
today / tomorrow / yesterday	heute / morgen / gestern	HOY-tuh / MOR-gen / GES-tern
I'd like a (one-way / return) ticket.	Ich möchte eine (Hinfahrkarte / Rückfahrkarte).	ikh MEUKH-tuh Al-nuh HIN-far-kar-tuh / REUKH-far-kar-tuh)
How much is it?	Wieviel kostet...?	vee-feel KOS-tet
hostel / hotel	Jugendherberge / Hotel	YOO-gent-hayr-bayr-guh / ho-TEL
I'd like a (single / double) room.	Ich möchte ein (Einzelzimmer / Doppelzimmer).	ikh MEUKH-tuh ain (AIN-tsel-tsi-muh / DOH-pel-tsi-muh)

ENGLISH	GREEK	PRONUNCIATION
hello	Γεια σου	YAH-soo
goodbye	αντιο	an-DEE-oh
please	Παρακαλω	pah-rah-kah-LO
thank you	Ευχαριστω	ef-hah-ree-STO
yes / no	Ναι / Οχι	neh / OH-hee
sorry / excuse me	Συγνωμη	sig-NO-mee
Do you speak English?	μιλας αγγλικα?	mee-LAHS ahn-glee-KAH
Help!	βοηθεια!	vo-EE-thee-ah
Where is...?	Που ειναι...?	pou EE-neh
left / right / straight ahead	αριστερα / δεξια / ευθεια	ah-rees-teh-RAH / dhek-see-AH / ef-THEE-a
What time does the [train / bus / boat] (depart / arrive)?	Τι ωρα (φευγει / φτανει) το [τρενο / λεωφορειο / καραβι]?	tee OR-ah (FEEV-yee / FTAH-nee) toe [TRAY-no / lee-oh-for-EE-oh / kah-RAH-vee]
today / tomorrow / yesterday	σημερα / αυριο/ χθες	SEE-mer-a / AV-ree-o / kthes
I'd like a (one-way / return) ticket.	Θα ηθελα (μονο εισιτηριο / εισιτηριο με επιστροφη).	tha ETH-eh-la (mo-NO ee-see-TEE-ree-o / ee-see-TEE-ree-o me eh-pee-stro-FEE)
How much does it cost?	ποσο κανει.	PO-so KAH-nee
hostel / hotel	ξεναωαζ νεοτητοζ / ξενοδοχειο	kse-NO-naz nee-OH-tee-toes / kse-no-dho-HEE-o
I'd like a (single / double) room.	Θελω ενα (μονο / διπλο) δωματιο	THEL-oh EH-na (mon-OH / dee-PLO) doh-MA-tee-oh

ENGLISH	HUNGARIAN	PRONUNCIATION
hello	jó napot	YOH-na-pot
goodbye	szia	SEE-ya
please	kérem	KAY-rem
thank you	köszönöm	KUH-sur-num
yes / no	igen / nem	EE-gen / nem
sorry / excuse me	sajnálom	shoy-NA-lawm
Do you speak English?	Beszél angolul?	BESS-ayl AWN-gohl-ul
Help!	Segítség!	SHEH-gheet-shayg
Where is...?	Hol van...?	hawl von
left / right / straight ahead	bal / jobb / elõre	ball / yobe / eh-LEW-ray
What time does the [train / bus / boat] (depart / arrive)?	Mikor (indul / érkesik) [vonat / busz-komp]?	MEE-kawr (EEN-dool / AIR-keh-zik) [VO-nawt / boose / komp]
today / tomorrow / yesterday	ma / holnap / tegnap	ma / OLE-nap / TEG-nap
I'd like a (one-way / return) ticket.	Szeretnék egy (jegyet csak oda / returje-gyet).	SEH-rett-nayk edge (YED-jet chok AW-daw / rih-toor-YED-jet)
How much does it cost?	Mennyibe kerül?	MEN-yee-beh KEH-rewl
hostel / hotel	szálló / szálloda	SA-lo / SA-lo-da
I'd like a (single / double) room.	Szeretnék egy (egyágyas / kétágyas) szobát.	SEH-rett-nayk edge (EDGE-ah-dyosh / KAY-tah-dyosh) SAW-baat

ENGLISH	ITALIAN	PRONUNCIATION
hello	buon giorno	bwon JOR-no
goodbye	arrivederci	a-ree-vuh-DAYR-chee
please	per favore	payr fa-VOR-ay
thank you	grazie	GRA-tsee-ay
yes / no	sì / no	see / no
sorry / excuse me	mi dispiace / scusi	mee dees-spee-ACH-ay / SKOO-zee
Do you speak English?	Parla inglese?	PAR-la ing-GLAY-zay
Help!	Aiuto!	ai-OO-toh
Where is...?	Dov'è...?	DOH-vay
left / right / straight ahead	sinistra / destra / sempre diritto	see-NEES-tra / DES-tra / SEM-pray deer-EE-toh
What time does the [train / bus / boat] (depart / arrive)?	A che ora (parte / arriva) [il treno / l'auto-bus / il traghetto]?	a kay OH-ra (PAR-tay / AH-reev-a) [eel TRAY-noh / LOW-toh-boos / eel tra-GE-toh]
today / tomorrow / yesterday	oggi / domani / ieri	OH-jee / doh-MAH-nee / ee-AYR-ee
I'd like a (one-way / return) ticket.	Vorrei un biglietto (solo andata / andata e ritoma).	vo-RAY oon bee-LYEH-toh (SO-lo an-DAH-ta / an-DAH-ta ay ree-TOR-na)
How much does it cost?	Quanto costa...?	KWAN-to KOHS-sta
hostel	ostello / albergo	oh-STEL-oh / al-BAYR-go
I'd like a (single / double) room.	Vorrei una càmera (síngola / doppia).	vor-AY OO-na KAH-may-rah (SING-go-la / DOH-pyah)

ENGLISH	LATVIAN	PRONUNCIATION
hello	labdien	LAHB-dyen
goodbye	Uz redzēšanos	ooz red-zee-shun-wass
please	lūdzu	LOOD-zuh
thank you	paldies	PAHL-dee-yes
yes / no	jā/nē	yah/ney
sorry / excuse me	atvainojos	AHT-vine-wa-ywoss
Do you speak English?	Vai Jūs runājat angliski	vie yoose ROO-na-yaht AHN-glee-skee
Help!	Palidzājiet!	PAH-leedz-ayee-et
Where is...?	Kur ir...?	kuhr ihr
left / right / straight ahead	kreisi/labi/pa taisno	kray-sih/lah-bih/puh-TICE-nwah
What time does the [train / bus / boat] (depart / arrive)?	Kad (atiet/pienākt) [vilciens/autobuss/prâmis].	cud (uh-tyat/pyah-nahkt) [VILLT-see-anss/OW-to-boose/prah-miss]
today / tomorrow / yesterday	šodien/rīt/vakar	SHWA-dee-ahn/reet/VAH-kahr
I'd like a (one-way / return) ticket.	Es vēlos (vienā virzienāÈturp un atpakal) bileti.	ess VAIH-lywoss (VYA-na VIR-zeea-na/toorp oon AHT-pa-kal) bee-let-ee
How much does it cost?	Cik maksā?	sikh MAHK-sah
hostel	jaunieðu viesnīca / viesnīca	yow-nya-duh vyess-nee-tsah / vyess-nee-tsah
I'd like a (single / double) room.	Es vēlos istabu (vienai/divām) personām.	ess VAIH-lywoss IH-stah-boo (VYA-nye/DIH-vahm) PAIR-swa-nahm

ENGLISH	LITHUANIAN	PRONUNCIATION
hello	Labądien	Lah-bah-DEE-yen
goodbye	viso gero	VYEE-so GYEH-ro
please	Prašau	prah-SHAU
thank you	Ačiu	AH-chyoo
yes / no	Taip/Ne	TAY-p/neh
sorry / excuse me	Atsiprašau	ahts-yi-prah-SHAoo
Do you speak English?	Ar Jūs kalbate angliškai?	ahr yoose KAHL-bah-te AHNG-lish-kigh
Help!	Gelbėkite!	GYEL-beh-kyi-te
Where is...?	Kur yra...?	koor ee-RAH
left / right / straight ahead	į kairę/į dešinę/važiuokite pirmyn	EE kigh-reh/EE deh-shi-neh/vazh-yo-kee-tay PEER-meen
What time does the [train / bus / boat] (depart / arrive)?	Kada (atvyksta/išvyksta) [traukinys/auto-busas/laivas]?	ka-DAH (aht-vyook-sta/EESH-vooksta) [trav-KEEN-oose/OW-toe-bus/LIVE-us]
today / tomorrow / yesterday	šiandien/vakar/rytoj	SHYEN-dien/VAA-car/ree-TOY
I'd like a (one-way / return) ticket.	Aš norėčiau bilieta į vieną/abi puses.	ahsh no-RYEH-chi-aoo
How much does it cost?	Kiek kainuoja?	KEE-yek KYE-new-oh-yah
hostel / hotel	jaunimo viešbutis / viešbutis	YAWN-ee-mo VYESH-boo-teese / VYESH-boo-teese
I'd like a (single / double) room.	Aš norėčiau kambario (vienviečio/dviviečio).	ahsh no-RYEH-chi-aoo KAHM-bah-rio (vyen-VYEA-chyo/dvyee-VYEEA-chyo)

ENGLISH	NORWEGIAN	PRONUNCIATION
hello	hallo	hah-LOH
goodbye	ha det	HAA-deh
please	vær så god	VAIR-seh go
thank you	takk	TAHK
yes / no	Ja/Ikke or Ne	yah/IK-eh, nay
sorry / excuse me	unnskyld	OON-shool
Help!	Hjelpe!	YELP-eh
Where is...?	Hvor er...?	VOR air...?
left / right / straight ahead	til venstre/til høyre/rett frem.	till VEN-struh/till HOY-ruh/reht frem
What time does the [train / bus / boat] (depart / arrive)?	Når (går/kommer) [toget/bussen/båten]?	nor (gore/COMB-air) TOE-geh/BOOSE-en/BOAT-en
today / tomorrow / yesterday	i dag/morgen/i går	ee DAHG/ee MORN/ee GORE
I'd like a (one-way / return) ticket.	Jeg vil gjerne ha (enkeltbillet/tur-retur)	YAI vill YAR-na ha (ENG-kult-bill-LET/TOOR rih-TOOR)
How much does it cost?	Hvor mye koster det?	VOR MEW-eh KOST-er deh?
hostel / hotel	vandrerhjem / hotell	VON-druh-yem / ho-TELL
I'd like a (single / double) room.	Jeg vil gjerne ha et (enkeltrom/dobbel-trom)	YAI vill YAIR-na ha ett (ENG-kult-room/DUB-elt-room)

ENGLISH	POLISH	PRONUNCIATION
hello	cześć	tcheshch
goodbye	do widzenia	doh vee-DZHEN-ya
please	proszę	PROH-sheh
thank you	dziękuję	jeng-KOO-yeh
yes / no	tak/nie	tak/nyeh
sorry / excuse me	Przepraszam	psheh-PRAH-sham
Do you speak English?	Czy Pan(i) mówi po anglicki?	tcheh PAHN (-ee) MOO-vee poh an-GLITS-kee
Help!	Na pomoc!	nah POH-motz
Where is...?	Gdzie jest...?	gdzheh yest
left / right / straight ahead	lewo/prawo/prosto	leh-vo/prah-vo/pross-toh
What time does the [train / bus / boat] (depart / arrive)?	O której godzinie (przychodzi/odchodzi) [pociąg/autobus]?	POHT-shawng/OW-toh-boos
today / tomorrow / yesterday	dzis/jutro/wczoraj	dzeess/yeeoo-tro/VCHORE-eye
I'd like a (one-way / return) ticket.	Poproszę bilet (w jedną stronę/tam i z pow-rotem)	poh-PROH-sheh BEE-leht (VYEHD-nawng STROH-neh/tahm ee spoh-VROH-tehm)
How much does it cost?	Ile to kosztuje?	EE-leh toh kosh-TOO-yeh
hostel	schronisko młodzieżowe / hotel	schrhon-isk-oh mwod-zyeh-zhoh-veh / ho-tell
I'd like a (single / double) room.	Chciał(a) bym pokój (jednoosbowy/dwuo-sobowy)	KHTS-HAHW(a) bihm POH-kooy (yehd-noo-soh-BOH-vih/dvohoo-soh-BOH-vih)

ENGLISH	PORTUGUESE	PRONUNCIATION
hello	olá	oh-LAH
goodbye	adeus	ah-DAY-oosh
please	por favor	pur fah-VOR
thank you	obrigado(-a) *(m./f.)*	oh-bree-GAH-doo / -da
yes / no	sim / não	seeng / now
sorry / excuse me	disculpe	dish-KOOL-peh
Do you speak English?	Fala inglês?	FAH-lah een-GLAYSH
I don't understand.	não compreendo	now kompree-AYN-doo
Help!	Socorro!	so-ko-RO
Where is...?	Onde é que é ...?	OHN-deh eh keh eh
left / right / straight ahead	esquerda / direita / em frente	ish-CARE-da / dee-RAY-ta / ayn FRAIN-teh
What time does the [train / bus / boat] (depart / arrive)?	A que horas (parte / chega) o [combóio / camioneta / barco]?	ah keh AW-rahsh (PAR-teh / cheh-gah) oh [kohn-BOY-oo / kam-yoo-NET-ah / bar-koh]
today / tomorrow / yesterday	hoje / amanhã / ontem	OH-zheh / ah-ming-YAH / OHN-tane
I'd like a (one-way / return) ticket.	Queria um bilhete (simples / de ida e volta)	kay-REE-ah um bee-YEH-teh (SEEM-plays / deh EE-da ee VOL-ta)
How much does it cost?	Quanto custa?	KWAHN-too KOOSH-tah
hostel / hotel	pousada de juventude / hotel	poh-ZA-da deh zhoo-vain-TOO-deh / ot-TEL
camping	campismo	cahm-PEEZ-mo
I'd like a (single / double) room.	Tem um quarto individual / duple?	tem om-KWAR-toe een-DE-vee-DU-ahl / DOO-play

ENGLISH	ROMANIAN	PRONUNCIATION
hello	bună ziua	BOO-nuh zee-wah
goodbye	la revedere	la reh-veh-deh-reh
please	Vă rog	vuh rohg
thank you	Mulțumesc	mool-tsoo-MESK
yes / no	da/nu	dah/noo
sorry / excuse me	Scuzați-mă	skoo-ZAH-tzee muh
Help!	Ajutor!	AH-zhoot-or
Where is...?	Unde...?	OON-deh
left / right / straight ahead	stânga/dreapta/drept înainte	stoong-gah/DRAY-ahp-ta/DREPT oon-EYE-een-tay
What time does the [train / bus / boat] (depart / arrive)?	La ce oră (pleacă/soseşte) [trenul/autobuzul/vaporul]?	la-CHAY orr-uh (PLAYUH-ker/so-SESH-teh) [tray-nool/OW-toe-booze-ool/va-poe-rool]
today / tomorrow / yesterday	astăzi/mâine/ieri	AHSS-teuh-zi/MUH-ee-neh/YAIR-ee
I'd like a (one-way / return) ticket.	Aș dori un bilet (dus/dus întors)	AHSH doe-ree oon bee-LET (doose/doose uhn-torse)
How much does it cost?	Cât costă?	kiht KOH-stuh
hostel / hotel	pensiune / hotel/motel	pen-SYOO-neh / hotel/motel
I'd like a (single / double) room.	Aș dori o cameră cu (un loc/două locuri).	AHSH doe-ree oh cah-meh-ruh koo (oon lok/DOE-uh LOK-oor-ee).

ENGLISH	RUSSIAN	PRONUNCIATION
hello	добрый день	DOH-brih DYEN
goodbye	До свидания	dah svee-DA-nya
please	пожалуйсто	pa-ZHA-loo-sta
thank you	спасибо	spa-SEE-bah
yes / no	да/нет	dah/nyet
sorry / excuse me	извините	eez-vee-NEET-yeh
Do you speak English?	Вы говорите по-английски?	vih go-vo-REE-tyeh po ahn-GLEE-ske?
Help!	Помогите!	pah-mah-GHEE-tyeh
Where is...?	Где...?	g-dye
left / right / straight ahead	налево/направо/прямо	na-LYEV-ah/na-PRA-va/PRYA-moh
What time does the [train / bus / boat] (depart / arrive)?	В котором часу [поезд/автобус/корабль] (приезжает/уезжает)?	V kah-tor-um cha-soo [poy-yezd/af-toe-boose/kah-rah-bil] (pree-yeh-zhy-yet/oo-yeh-zhy-yet)
today / tomorrow / yesterday	сегодня/завтра/вчера	see-VOD-nya/ZAHF-tra/fchee-RAH
I'd like a (one-way / return) ticket.	Можно билет (ь один конец/туда и обратно)	MWOZH-nuh beel-yet (v ah-DEEN kah-NYETS/too-DAH ee ah-BRAHT-na)
How much does it cost?	Сколько стоит?	SKOHL-ka STOH-yet?
hostel / hotel	общежитие / гостиница	ahb-SHAZH-eet-tyeh / gah-STEE-nyit-sa
I'd like a (single / double) room.	Я бы хотел номер на (одного/двоих)	yah kah-TYEL bee NAW-meer na (AHD-na-vo/dvah-EEK)

ENGLISH	SERBO-CROATIAN	PRONUNCIATION
hello	dabardan/*bog*	do-bar-DAHN/*bog*
goodbye	bog	bog
please	molim	MO-leem
thank you	hvala vam	HVAH-la vahm
yes / no	da/ne	da/neh
sorry / excuse me	oprostite	aw-PROSS-tee-tay
Do you speak English?	Govorite li engleski?	GO-vor-i-teh lee eng-LEH-ski
Help!	U pomoć!	OO pomoch
Where is...?	Gdje je?	g-DYEH YEH
left / right / straight ahead	lijevo/desno/pravo	LYEH-vo/DESS-no/PRAH-vo
What time does the [train / bus / boat] (depart / arrive)?	Kada [vlak/autobus/brod] (polazil/dola-zil)?	KAH-da [vlok/ow-TOE-boose/brod] (poh-la-zil/doh-la-zil)
today / tomorrow / yesterday	danas/sutra/jučer	DA-nass/SOO-tra/YOO-chay
I'd like a (one-way / return) ticket.	Htio bih (u jednom smjena/povratna karta) za...	HTEE-o beeh (oo YEH-dnom smee-YEH-roo/POV-rat-na KAR-ta) zah...
How much does it cost?	Koliko to košta?	KO-li-koh toh KOH-shta
hostel / hotel	omladinsko prenoćište / hotel	om-la-din-skoh preh-no-chish-teh / hotel
I'd like a (single / double) room.	Želio bih (jednokrevetnu/dvokrevetnu) sobu.	ZHEL-i-o bih (yed-no-KREH-vet-noo/dvoh-KREH-vet-noo) SO-bu

ENGLISH	SLOVAK	PRONUNCIATION
hello	dobrý deň	DOH-bree dyeny
goodbye	do videnia	doh vee-DEN-yah
please	prosím	PROH-seem
thank you	dakujem	dyak-uh-yem
yes / no	áno/nie	AH-no/nyieh
sorry / excuse me	prepáčte	preh-padch-tyeh
Do you speak English?	Hovoríte po anglicky?	HO-voh-ree-tyeh poh ahn-glits-kih
Help!	Pomoc!	poh-mots
Where is...?	Kde je?	gDYEH yeh
left / right / straight ahead	vlavo/vpravo/rovno	VLYAH-vo/VPRAH-vo/ROHV-no
What time does the [train / bus / boat] (depart / arrive)?	Kedy (odchádza/prichádza) [vlak/auto-bus/loč]?	keh-dee (wode-chahdz-ah/pree-chahdz-ah) [vlahk/ow-toe-bus/loatch]
today / tomorrow / yesterday	dnes/zajtra/včera	dnyes/zai-tra/fcheh-rah
I'd like a (one-way / return) ticket.	Prosím si... (jedniosmemy/spiatočný) lís-tok.	Prosím si... (jednosmerny/spiatočný) lís-tok.
How much does it cost?	Coto stojí?	KOH-to STOH-yee
hostel / hotel	turistická ubytovňa mládeže / hotel	TOO-rist-ih-kah OO-bit-ov-nya MLAH-deh-zhe / HO-tell
I'd like a (single / double) room.	Potrebujem (jednoložkovú izbu/izbu pre dve osoby)	PO-tre-bu-yem (YED-no-loozh-ko-voo iz-buh) (IZ-buh preh DVEH oh-so-bih)

ENGLISH	SLOVENE	PRONUNCIATION
hello	idravo	ee-drah-voh
goodbye	na svidenje	nah SVEE-den-yeh
please	prosim	PROH-seem
thank you	hvala	HVAA-lah
yes / no	ja/ne	yah/neh
sorry / excuse me	oprostite	oh-proh-stee-teh
Do you speak English?	Govorite angleško?	go-vo-REE-te ang-LEH-shko
Help!	Na pomoč!	na poh-MOTCH!
Where is...?	Kje je...?	kyeh yeh...?
left / right / straight ahead	na levi/na desni/naravnost	na leh-wee/na des- nee/nar-ow-nost
What time does the [train / bus / boat] (depart / arrive)?	Ob kateri uri [vlak/avtobus/ladja] (odpelje/pripelge)	op ka-teh-ree oo-ree [wlahk/AW-toe-bus/lad-ya](ot-PEL-yeh/prip-el-geh)
today / tomorrow / yesterday	danes/jutri/včeraj	DAH-ness/YOU-tree/WCHEH-ray
I'd like a (one-way / return) ticket.	Rad bi (enosmerno/povratno) vozovnico.	rat bih za (EH-no-smer-no/po-VRUT-no) voh-ZOW-nih-tso
How much does it cost?	Koliko to stane?	koh-lee-koh toh stah-neh
hostel / hotel	mladinski dom / hotel	mla-dinsk-ih dom / hoh-tel
I'd like a (single / double) room.	Rad/Rada (*m/f*) bi (enoposteljno/dvopos-teljo) sobo	aht/RA-da bee (en-o-POST-el-nyo/dvoh -POST-el-nyo) so-bo.

ENGLISH	SPANISH	PRONUNCIATION
hello	hola	oh-LAH
goodbye	adios	ah-THYOHSS
please	por favor	pohr fah-BOHR
thank you	gracias	GRAH-syahss
yes / no	sí / no	see / noh
sorry / excuse me	perdón	pehr-DOHN
Do you speak English?	¿Habla inglés?	AH-blah een-GLEHSS
Help!	¡Secorro!	soh-KOH-rroh
Where is...?	¿Dónde está...?	DOHN-deh ehss-TAH
left / right / straight ahead	izquierda / derecha / recto	eess-KYEHR-thah / deh-REH-chah / REK-toh
What time does the [train / bus / boat] (depart / arrive)?	¿Cuándo (llega / sale) [el tren / el auto-bús / el barco)?	KWAHN-doh (YEH-gah / SAH-leh) [ehl TREHN / ehl ow-toh-BOOSS / ehl BAHR-koh]
today / tomorrow / yesterday	hoy / mañana / ayer	oy / mah-NYAH-nah / ah-YEHR
I'd like a (one-way / return) ticket.	Quisiera un billete (ida / de ida y vuelta).	kee-SYEH-rah oon bee-YEH-teh (EE-thah / deh EE-thah ee BWEHL-tah)
How much does it cost?	¿Cuánto cuesta?	KWAHN-toh KWEHSS-tah
hostel	albergue de juventud / hotel	ahl-BEHR-gheh de hoo-behn-TOOTH / oh-TEHL
I'd like a (single / double) room.	Quisiera un cuarto simple / un doble	kee-SYEH-rah oon KWAHR-toh SEEM-pleh / oon DOH-bleh

ENGLISH	SWEDISH	PRONUNCIATION
hello	goddag/hej	go-DOG/HEY
goodbye	adjö/hej då	a-DYEUH/HEY-daw
please	var så snålla	VARR so SNELL-uh
thank you	tack	talk
yes / no	ja/nej	yah/ney
sorry / excuse me	förlåt	fer-LOTT
Do you speak English?	pratar du engelska?	PROH-ter doo ENG-ell-skuh?
Help!	Hjälp!	yelp!
Where is...?	Var är... ?	varr air...
left / right / straight ahead	vänster/höger/rakt fram	VENN-ster/HEUR-ger/rakt FRAHM
What time does the [train / bus / boat] (depart / arrive)?	När (avgår/kommer) [tåget/bussen/ båten]?	NAIR (AHV-gore/KOM-mar) [TOE-get/ BOOSE-en/BO-ten]
today / tomorrow / yesterday	idag/imorgon/igår	ee-DOG/ee-MOR-on/ee-GOR
I'd like a (one-way / return) ticket.	Jag vil gärna ha en (enkelbiljett/returbil-jett)	YAW vil-YAIR-nuh-ha en (EN-kul-bill-yet/re-TOOR-bill-yet)
How much does it cost?	Hur mycket kostar det?	hoor-MOOK-eh KOST-ar day?
hostel / hotel	vandrarhem / hotell	VON-dra-hem / ho-TELL
I'd like a (single / double) room.	Jag vil gärna ha ett (enkelrum/dubbel-rum)?	YAW vil-YAIR-nuh-ha et (EHN-kel-room/ DOO-bel-room)

ENGLISH	TURKISH	PRONUNCIATION
hello	merhaba	MEHR-hah-bah
goodbye	alahsmaladžk	eee-YEE gooń-lehr
please	lütfen	LEWT-fen
thank you	teşekkur ederim	tesh-ekur edeh-rim
yes / no	evet/hayır	EH-vet/HI-yuhr
sorry / excuse me	affedersiniz	ahf-feh-DER-see-neez
Do you speak English?	İngilizce biliyor musunuz?	EEN-gee-leez-jeh bee-lee-YOR-moo-su-nooz
Help!	Imdat!	EEEm-Daht!
Where is...?	...nerede?	NEHR-eh-deh
left / right / straight ahead	sol/sağ/doğru	sohl/sa-a/doh-roo
What time does the [train / bus / boat] (depart / arrive)?	[Otobüs/Tren/Vapur] ne zaman (kalkar/ gelir)	[oh-toe-boose/tren/va-POOR] neh za-mahn (kal-kar/geh-leer)
today / tomorrow / yesterday	bugün/yann/dün	boo-goon/yahr-un/doon
I'd like a (one-way / return) ticket.	(sırf gidiş/gidiş-dönüş) bir bilet istiyorum	(serf gi-DEESH/gi-DEESH der-NYOOSH) beer be-LET i-STEE-yo-rum
How much does it cost?	...ne kadar?	neh kah-dar?
hostel / hotel	gençlik yurdu / otel	gench-LIK YOOR-du / oh-tell
I'd like a (single / double) room.	(Tek/çif) kişilik bir oda istiyorum.	(Tehk/cheeft) keesh-ee-leek beer aw-dah ee-STEE-yo-rum.

Europe Time Zones

GMT = Greenwich Mean Time
GMT = UTC (Coordinated Universal Time)

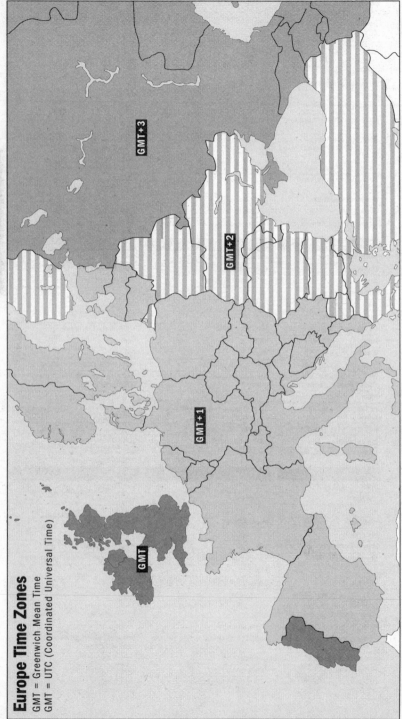

It's not where you are going...
it's how you get there that counts.

Eurail: A European Tradition

Maps

Will you have enough stories to tell your grandchildren?

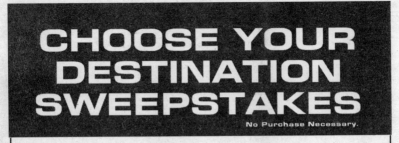

CHOOSE YOUR DESTINATION SWEEPSTAKES

No Purchase Necessary.

Explore the world with Let's Go® and StudentUniverse!
Enter for a chance to win a trip for two to a Let's Go destination!
Separate Drawings! May & October 2002.

GRAND PRIZES:
Roundtrip StudentUniverse Tickets

✓ Select one destination and mail your entry to:

☐ Costa Rica
☐ London
☐ Hong Kong
☐ San Francisco
☐ New York
☐ Amsterdam
☐ Prague
☐ Sydney

* Plus Additional Prizes!!

Choose Your Destination Sweepstakes
St. Martin's Press
Suite 1600, Department MF
175 Fifth Avenue
New York, NY 10010-7848

Restrictions apply; see offical rules for
details by visiting Let'sGo.com or sending SASE
(VT residents may omit return postage) to the address above.

Name: _____

Address: _____

City/State/Zip: _____

Phone: _____

Email: _____

Grand prizes provided by:

 StudentUniverse.com   Real Travel Deals